MAJOR WRITERS OF AMERICA

I

Bradford · Taylor · Franklin · Edwards

Irving · Cooper · Bryant · Poe

Emerson · Thoreau · Hawthorne

Longfellow · Lowell

Melville · Whitman

HARCOURT, BRACE & WORLD, INC.

COPYRIGHTS AND ACKNOWLEDGMENTS

WILLIAM BRADFORD. Selections from *Of Plymouth Plantation*. Text reprinted from *Of Plymouth Plantation* by William Bradford, edited by Samuel Eliot Morison, Alfred A. Knopf, Inc., 1952. Footnote matter reprinted by permission of Alfred A. Knopf, Inc. Copyright 1952 by Alfred A. Knopf, Inc.

EDWARD TAYLOR. "Huswifery," "Christ's Reply," and "The Joy of Church Fellowship rightly attended," from *The New England Quarterly*, X (1937), "Meditations," 1st Series, No. 40, and "Meditations," 2nd Series, No. 114, from *The New England Quarterly*, XVI (1943). Reprinted by permission of *The New England Quarterly*. Selections from *The Poetical Works of Edward Taylor*, edited by Thomas H. Johnson, Rockland Editions, 1939, copyright 1943 by Princeton University Press. Reprinted by permission of the Princeton University Press. Edward Taylor's thirty-second "Meditation," *Yale University Library Gazette*, XXVIII (January, 1954). Reprinted by permission of the *Yale University Library Gazette*. Letter of Edward Taylor to Elizabeth Fitch, Westfield, July 8, 1674 (Z117.203). Reprinted by permission of *The New England Quarterly*, the Yale University Library, and William B. Goodman. Selections from *The Poems of Edward Taylor*, edited by Donald E. Stanford, Yale University Press, 1960. Reprinted by permission of the publisher. Passage from a sermon preached in 1701, from *Christographia* by Edward Taylor, from an edition of the Christographia sermons, Norman Grabo, editor, in preparation. Reprinted by permission of the Yale University Press.

JONATHAN EDWARDS. Selections from *Images or Shadows of Divine Things*, by Jonathan Edwards, edited by Perry Miller, Yale University Press, 1948. Reprinted by permission of the publisher.

NATHANIEL HAWTHORNE. Selections from *The American Notebooks of Nathaniel Hawthorne*. Reprinted by permission of the publishers from Randall Stewart, editor, *The American Notebooks of Nathaniel Hawthorne*, Cambridge, Mass.: Harvard University Press, Copyright, 1932, 1960, by The President and Fellows of Harvard College. Selections from *The English Notebooks*, by Nathaniel Hawthorne, edited by Randall Stewart, Modern Language Association of America, 1941. Reprinted by permission of the publisher.

HERMAN MELVILLE. *Billy Budd*. Reprinted by permission of the publisher from Melville's *Billy Budd* (edited by Frederic Barron Freeman and corrected by Elizabeth Treeman), Cambridge, Mass.: Harvard University Press, Copyright, 1948, 1956, by The President and Fellows of Harvard College.

A NOTE ON THE COVER: The eagle incorporated in the cover design is copyrighted by America House and is used by kind permission.

Library of Congress Catalog Card Number: 62–12181

PRINTED IN THE UNITED STATES OF AMERICA

HERE we find a vast stock of proper materials for the art and ingenuity of man to work on,—treasures of immense worth, concealed from the poor, ignorant, aboriginal natives. . . . As the celestial light of the gospel was directed here by the finger of God, it will doubtless finally drive the long, long night of heathenish darkness from America. . . . So arts and sciences will change the face of nature in their tour from hence over the Appalachian Mountains to the Western Ocean; and as they march through the vast desert, the residence of wild beasts will be broken up, and their obscene howl cease forever. Instead of which, the stones and trees will dance together at the music of Orpheus, the rocks will disclose their hidden gems, and the inestimable treasures of gold and silver be broken up. Huge mountains of iron ore are already discovered; and vast stores are reserved for future generations. This metal, more useful than gold and silver, will employ millions of hands, not only to form the martial sword and peaceful share alternately, but an infinity of utensils improved in the exercise of art and handicraft amongst men. . . . Shall not then these vast quarries that teem with mechanic stone,—those for structure be piled into great cities, and those for sculpture into statues, to perpetuate the honor of renowned heroes—even those who shall now save their country? O ye unborn inhabitants of America! should this page escape its destined conflagration at the year's end, and these alphabetical letters remain legible when your eyes behold the sun after he has rolled the seasons round for two or three centuries more, you will know that in Anno Domini, 1758, we dreamed of your times.

NATHANIEL AMES
from Almanac (1758)

Contents

BENJAMIN FRANKLIN
JONATHAN EDWARDS

EDITED BY
Perry Miller

Franklin

Edwards

WASHINGTON IRVING

EDITED BY

William L. Hedges

JAMES FENIMORE COOPER
WILLIAM CULLEN BRYANT

EDITED BY

Marius Bewley

Bryant

EDGAR ALLAN POE

EDITED BY
Richard Wilbur

RALPH WALDO EMERSON

EDITED BY
Newton Arvin

HENRY DAVID THOREAU

EDITED BY
Kenneth S. Lynn

NATHANIEL HAWTHORNE

EDITED BY
Edward H. Davidson

HENRY WADSWORTH LONGFELLOW
JAMES RUSSELL LOWELL

EDITED BY

William Charvat

Longfellow

Lowell

HERMAN MELVILLE

EDITED BY
Richard Chase

WALT WHITMAN

EDITED BY
R. W. B. Lewis

A Preface

BY THE GENERAL EDITOR

MAJOR WRITERS OF AMERICA is made possible at this point in time not so much because the energies of its editors have been prodigious but because the study of American literature—inside and outside the universities—is now systematic and mature. This happy state of affairs is relatively recent. In fact, like the professional study of English literature, it is only about seventy-five years old. Of the two literatures, however, the American remained largely terra incognita for several decades after its discovery. History repeated itself: the Old World was settled first. Yet the New did not lack for those who could rise to the challenge of its promise. The essential landmarks were discerned. The terrain was mapped. In the perspective of these seventy-five years of discovery and exploration then, the present work acknowledges many profound debts: to the pioneer adventurers, such as Moses Coit Tyler, William Peterfield Trent, and Barrett Wendell; to subsequent masters who are represented herein by entries in the bibliographies as well as by their students; and, further, to a host of scholars contemporary with the editors, often younger than they, who attest the vitality of the vocation.

It was altogether natural that in the initial stages of this American "Great Instauration" claimants to academic dignity should strive to impress their colleagues in departments devoted to the magnificent literatures of England or of the Continent or of antiquity by heaping up as mountainous a bulk of American expression as research could excavate. While it was indisputably evident that American literary history was of painfully short duration—commencing with the seventeenth century and even then for a hundred years or more offering only "colonial" documents—still there were unearthed such permanently significant minorities as Philip Freneau, Joel Barlow, Charles Brockden Brown, and the authors of *The Contrast* and *Modern Chivalry*.

These beginnings made, the advance continued into the wilderness. New recruits expended tremendous energy in "rediscovering" forgotten authors—

or sometimes in actually discovering those who had never been known at all. Among the former the pre-eminent names are Herman Melville and Emily Dickinson; among the latter, Edward Taylor. The great object in view was to establish the canon of American literature on as broad a basis as possible. Nothing canonizes literature more quickly than print. It followed that anthologies of constantly increasing poundage were compiled, and with an ever lengthening array of persons deserving inclusion, if only because they had written in America or about American things. The tacit assumption of almost all these productions was that they had to silence professional rivals who would constantly inquire, with eyebrows raised in elaborately simulated ignorance, "American literature? Oh, is there any?"

Today, after seven or eight decades of skirmishing, the battle for American literature is won. It is established as a reputable and incontestable subdivision of the English department. Courses in it proliferate. Outside the academies it has triumphed even more conclusively: hundreds of "popular" surveys, biographies, interpretations—most of them eschewing the stigmata of scholarship—are sold annually. In fact, among conscientious practitioners a dreadful anxiety now arises for fear the victory has been too overwhelming. No doubt, Philip Freneau—to take him as a test case—is a fascinating figure; but is it really a healthy curriculum which requires that he be read by a student who is utterly ignorant of Racine?

The premise of *Major Writers of America* is by no means intended as a hostile comment on those compilations which exhibit the now vast accumulation of American writings. A serious student of American civilization must come to terms with Philip Freneau, as with a multitude of his stature. Yet, while the canon is at long last becoming established, a realization gradually forces itself upon us that, as the age of discovery and of elementary mapping closes, the era of evaluation opens. Not that any piece of terrain, however minute, should be forgotten once more; nor should any possible open territory be foreclosed. Yet it is incumbent upon us to make clear which are the few peaks and which the many low-lying hills. We must, if we can, suppress an undiscriminating pedantry by distinguishing just wherein the great are truly great. We must set apart those who belong to world literature rather than merely to local (or, to what is worse, regional) patriotism. We must vindicate the study of American literature because primarily the matter is literature, and only secondarily because it is American. For this end *Major Writers of America* has been designed.

The first requirement of the design, therefore, was inevitably that the authors so nominated be represented fully enough to testify to their superiority. This meant that exclusions had to be perpetrated with surgical ruthlessness. There can be no question that Edwards, Emerson, Hawthorne, Melville, Henry James, and Mark Twain belong. When the problem arises of, say Longfellow or Whittier, decision necessarily becomes arbitrary. And, as the list extends into the twentieth century, determinations are bound to appear, even to those who make them, not much more than arbitrary or even capricious indulgences of taste. However, the editors stake their credibility upon the choices they have made; moreover they have endeavored in lengthy Introductions to make plain their particular sense of the writers from whose works they have made coherent selections.

An immediately apparent corollary of this policy was a recognition that for most writers of fiction no portions of long novels could be included. Spacious as these pages be, they are not copious enough to include all of *The Scarlet Letter*, *Moby-Dick*, *The Adventures of Huckleberry Finn*, *The Ambassadors*. Certain set-pieces, separable from the narrative in Cooper's romances, or the chapters reproduced from the novels of Adams and Dreiser that have an independence vigorous enough to sustain the separation, may legitimately be taken out of context. But no segments of more closely knit works of art can be so excised. The editors feel consoled for these omissions because by now inexpensive paperback reprints of all the formidable titles are available. Wherever possible we have exhibited the techniques of master storytellers in long short stories, with what Henry James liked to call the "blest *nouvelle*."

An anthology designed to give a generous sample of the record in all its representative particulars is obliged to include too many writers. The result inevitably distorts the literary stature of the more important writers. For the purposes of a historical survey such even-handed continuity is necessary. When, however, attention is turned from the record itself to the delicate task of evaluation, no one editor, nor partnership of editors, is capable of supplying the essential discrimination. There still remains, of course, the need for respecting continuity, of remembering the historical forces, and above all for reverencing chronology. Also there persists an obligation to relate, in some degree, the works to the authors' biographies, especially when, as with Franklin and Henry Adams, the historical biography is parallel to but far from identical with the literary rendition. Still, fully granting these considerations, the second requirement of our design demanded that each major author, or each grouping of major figures—where two or three writers obviously belong together—be dealt with by an editor solely responsible for the selection, the criticism, the annotations, and the bibliographies. Not only has there been no "party line" to which individual editors were obliged to cleave, there has been no substantive line whatsoever. Certain minor editorial uniformities have been maintained—e.g., minimum standards for what in the texts required footnoting and what did not—but these were kept to a reasonable minimum. There was also an implicit rule that each contributor should be dedicated to the highest standards of excellence and clarity he could conceive, but it never had to be explicitly promulgated.

In matters of spelling, punctuation, and capitalization editors have exercised their discretion. After the early decades of the nineteenth century, the standard printed texts have generally been followed. A date at the end of the selection, when on the right, is that of composition; on the left, that of publication. Omissions within texts, when they constitute more than a paragraph, are indicated by the insertion of ellipses at the end of one paragraph and at the beginning of the next. A note has been appended to the introductory essays whenever there are variations from this practice. Unless otherwise indicated, footnotes are those of the editor of the section. Bibliographies have been kept to an essential minimum for obvious reasons of spatial economy. The reader who wishes to pursue a writer further should turn to the third volume (*Bibliography*) of the Robert E. Spiller *et al. Literary History of the United States* (1948) and to the *Bibliographical Supplement* (1959) of the same work, edited by Richard M. Ludwig.

The General Editor thinks it fair to say that while these volumes have been composed with the student chiefly in mind, yet the editors have striven to make *Major Writers of America* something more than a textbook. The concerted aim of the enterprise has been to construct a book with which anyone might sit down and in which he might read with pleasure. We have thought of students as those who help to constitute the noble company of "general readers," not merely as undergraduates earning course credits. We have, in short, endeavored to pay both the student and the general reader the compliment of treating them as interchangeable designations.

The Publisher and the General Editor take pleasure in thanking the several editors for their patience, their readiness to heed suggestions, to conform their presentations to spatial formats dictated by practical necessities. In one sense, this thanks should also mention their cooperation, for cooperate in myriad ways they did. In a more basic sense, however, the thanks must recognize their healthy lack of cooperation. The finished achievement is in no strict sense a collaboration, the report of a committee of certified experts. Beyond agreement among contributors to cultivate their own gardens intensely and to raid the plots and seedbeds of others solely under the decorous excuse of enriching comparative judgments, no demands were made by Publisher or General Editor. But this is not to say that the American *writers* represented in the pages which follow left their editors alone. Quite the contrary. In fact, *Major Writers of America* may best be taken as a varied testimony to the force that the literature continues to exert over and against time. Such attraction at such a distance is what signalizes a major writer.

PERRY MILLER

Cambridge, Massachusetts
December 15, 1961

MAJOR WRITERS OF AMERICA

SAMUEL ELIOT MORISON
Editor

William Bradford

1590–1657

THE HISTORY *Of Plymouth Plantation* by William Bradford, governor of the Pilgrim Fathers' colony for over thirty years, is not the earliest history of an English colony in America. That palm goes to Captain John Smith's *Generall Historie of Virginia, New England, and the Summer Isles,* printed in London in 1624. Although the full text of Bradford's History was not printed until 1856, the most moving and eloquent parts of Book I were paraphrased by Nathaniel Morton, the Governor's nephew, in *New England's Memoriall,* printed in Cambridge in 1669. The manuscript was used by colonial historians of New England such as Increase and Cotton Mather, William Hubbard, Thomas Prince, and Thomas Hutchinson. Thus, the Pilgrims' story, as related by their own governor, entered very early into the stream of American consciousness; and it has endured, for reasons which the reader will readily grasp.

The manuscript of the History had almost as many adventures as the Pilgrims themselves. The Governor began to write in 1630, finished through Chapter 10 that year, and wrote the rest "in pieces," as he says, until 1646, adding a few items from time to time, down to his death in 1657. The manuscript, although frequently lent to others, remained in the possession of his descendants until 1726, when the Rev. Thomas Prince borrowed it from the Governor's grandson, and, after pasting his own bookplate inside the cover, added it to his "New England Library" in the steeple of the Old South Meeting House, Boston. That building was used as a riding school during the 1775–76 siege of Boston by British soldiers, one of whom carried the manuscript to London as a "souvenir" of his unhappy sojourn in the Bay State capital. Somehow, probably through a second-hand bookstore, it was acquired by a bishop of London for his library in Fulham Palace, where it was "discovered" by an English antiquarian around mid-century. The Massachusetts Historical Society obtained a copy of the manuscript and published the first full edition of the text in 1856; it made a literary sensation. An exact facsimile of the entire manuscript was printed in London in 1896. A very careful, scholarly edition, with copious notes, illustrations, and facsimiles, was prepared by Worthington C. Ford for the Massachusetts Historical Society and published in two volumes in 1912. The original manuscript, after long negotiations, was presented by the Diocese of London to the Commonwealth of Massachusetts, which has faithfully preserved it in a bronze case, in the State Library at the State House, Boston. Unfortunately, in making this gracious return of a priceless manuscript of early American history, the English lawyer who drafted the deed of gift described it as "The Log of the *Mayflower*," which it definitely is not, "narrated by Captain William Bradford," whom the lawyer seems to have supposed to have been the *Mayflower*'s skipper; and that false title has proved difficult to shake off. Bradford's own title to his manuscript is simply "Of Plim̃oth plantation," which, with modern spelling of Plymouth, we use here.

All the editions above-mentioned proved difficult for modern readers to follow, because the editors meticulously preserved Bradford's manuscript abbreviations (such as y^{e}, y^{t}, w^{ch}), his wild spelling and capitalization, and his complete inconsistency in punctuation and paragraphing. Accordingly, your present editor prepared, and Alfred A. Knopf published in 1952, a completely new text from the original manuscript, in which all abbreviations and contractions are expanded, and modern usage is adopted in spelling, capitalization, and punctuation. But Bradford's language is scrupulously respected, and not one word altered.

Bradford's erratic spellings and the like do not indicate that he was illiterate; far from it. By the standards of his day he was a well-read man. Educated largely through his own efforts, he learned how to write good, taut, racy English. Authors in those days were not expected to spell or punctuate. It was the business of the printer to set these things right, and Bradford never had the benefit of being printed during his lifetime.

He was born at Austerfield, Yorkshire, England, in mid-March, 1590, to a substantial farmer and his wife, the daughter of a village shopkeeper. His father died when he was a baby, his mother married again, and he went to live with his uncles, farmers who had no higher ambition for the lad than to make him a rural laborer. A puny boy, he was unhappy doing heavy farm chores; but a new life opened at the age of twelve, when he began to read the Bible and to attend the sermons of a nearby Puritan preacher. Against his uncles' wishes, and braving the jeers of other young fellows in the neighborhood, he joined a small prayer-meeting, which met at the home of a university-educated gentleman named William Brewster in nearby Scrooby. These people organized as a Congregational church, separate from the established Church of England, when Bradford was sixteen years old.

That was a dangerous move; something akin to forming a Communist cell today. But the Scrooby people so firmly believed that they were right that they were willing to suffer, and did suffer, for their faith; and as that faith is the background of Bradford's History, and of the founding of Plymouth Colony, we had better try to describe what it was.

These men could have stayed in England if they had even outwardly conformed to the Church of England; but it never occurred to them to do that. They could later have had security in Holland if that had been what they wanted; but security was not what they were after. Their ambition was to found a community where they would have liberty to worship God in their own way and to follow the way of life that they found in the New Testament.

A Pilgrim Father, William Wright, who died at Plymouth in 1633, made this confession of faith in his will, which is the best expression we know of what the Pilgrims fundamentally believed:

> I give and bequeath my body to the dust, and my soul unto the hands of God that gave it, being persuaded in myself that although my body shall be laid in the earth, there to return to dust from whence it came, yet at the last day when all flesh shall appear before the tribunal bar of God's justice, that then my soul and body shall be reunited, and that both soul and body shall receive recompense of reward. And whereas I am sensible of the wrath of God which I have incurred to myself by reason of my manifold failings and disobedience to my God, whereby He hath just cause to appear to me as an angry judge; yet I do believe that Jesus Christ, perfect God and perfect man, hath fully and sufficiently satisfied to God His Father for all my sins, and that by His blood alone I stand freely justified before God, and not by any desert, merit or worthiness of mine own, for in me dwelleth nothing that is good, and all my righteousness is filthy and abominable, and that this death is but a passage to life eternal. And I do desire my God to give me patience that I may bear His hand, and that all the days of mine appointed time I may wait until my change shall come. For I know my Redeemer liveth, and that I shall shortly see Him

with these eyes, and I am willing to leave this frail and troublesome life and to be with Christ my Saviour, which is best of all.

There was nothing new or queer about this confession of faith; it was and is basic Christian doctrine, to which Catholics and Protestants alike subscribed, and in which they are supposed to believe today. It was not this faith that marked off the Pilgrims from their fellows; it was their idea of how the Christian Church should be organized, and how they should worship. They insisted on reorganizing along New Testament lines, without regard to custom or tradition. This meant no more bishops or deans, no sacraments except baptism and holy communion, no set prayer book, no ritual, no altars, candles, organs, or incense. Each church must be independent, its ministers and other "elders" (officers) elected by the congregation. Services should consist only of Bible readings, a sermon, and extempore prayer; except that the "Our Father" was all right, because Our Lord told us to use it.

Thousands and thousands of people in England, Scotland, and Ireland came to believe as Brewster and Bradford did. In derision they were called Puritans because they were always talking about "purifying" the Church of England. They didn't like the name at first, and Bradford never uses it in his History, but in the course of time they accepted it, just as the Society of Friends accepted being called Quakers.

The greater number of Puritans were willing to bide their time; to attend Anglican services, provided they could hear sermons on the side, and to hope for the best. But the Separatists, such as the Scrooby group, were unwilling to wait. They agreed with the Rev. Robert Browne, who preached sermons on the text: "Come out from among them, and be ye *separate,* saith the Lord, and touch not the unclean thing; and I will receive you." That's what St. Paul said that Our Lord had said, so what else could a good Christian do?

Within a year after its "gathering" the Scrooby congregation obtained as preacher the Rev. John Robinson, a gentleman, scholar, and man of the world, "courteous, affable and sociable in his conversation." A graduate of Cambridge University, he embraced the Separatist idea, renounced his Anglican orders, and chose poverty and hardship in order to minister to the faithful few at Scrooby.

The situation of these Separatists was uncomfortable and even dangerous. What they were doing was illegal. Brewster, to be sure, had powerful friends, but there was no assurance that the whole congregation might not be thrown into jail at any time, and the leaders tried for treason. Moreover, the rest of the community around Scrooby and Austerfield was hostile. Bradford later described the attitude of his neighbors as "ignorant and licentious." He had to endure "the wrath of his uncles" and the "scoff of his neighbors." He and his friends probably had to fight their way to their own meeting-house every Sunday, or dodge brickbats when they came out. Nobody would have anything to do with them. The girls they might have courted were ordered not to speak to them, merchants would not buy their farm products, and shopkeepers refused to sell them supplies.

Their situation became so intolerable that, in 1607, the congregation voted to emigrate to the "Low Countries," the Netherlands. The Dutch, although not very tolerant among themselves, welcomed foreigners and let them worship as they pleased. Two other English Separatist congregations had already gone there and reported that they were not troubled by the authorities, and had found work.

To cross the North Sea to the Low Countries was no easy matter. Leaving England was illegal unless you had a passport from the authorities, and passports were not granted to "traitors." A sea passage cost money, and only Mr. Brewster had money. He sold most of his property and offered to pay the expenses of any members of the congregation who would go along, most of whom did. After two false starts, followed by terms in jail, about 125 members of the Scrooby church, including Brewster and the Rev. Mr. Robinson, "gat over" to Holland in 1608, as Bradford wrote.

After a year's sojourn at Amsterdam the Pilgrims removed to Leyden, which Bradford described as "a fair and beautiful city and of a sweet situation, but made more famous by the university." The main business of Leyden was the spinning and weaving of woolen cloth.

Most of the Pilgrims, being farmers, knew nothing of this occupation. "It was not long before they saw the grim and grisly face of poverty coming upon them like an armed man." However, "at length they came to raise a competent and comfortable living, but with hard and continual labour."

The Dutch were very decent to the Pilgrims. They allowed a number to become naturalized Netherlanders. No effort was made to prevent them from earning their living in a humble occupation, although they could not join the trade gilds (corresponding to our labor unions), which monopolized the best-paying jobs. Some learned to comb or card wool for the spinners of yarn; others spun and wove. Bradford became a weaver of fustian, a coarse woolen cloth. Isaac Allerton, a London tailor who came over to join them, plied his old trade in Leyden. Brewster bought a press on which he printed Puritan books that the censors would not allow in England; Edward Winslow, a well-educated young man from another part of England, came over and helped him. The English Government tried to have Brewster arrested and sent home for trial, but the Dutch protected him.

The Pilgrim congregation, numbering over two hundred by 1615, bought a house for Mr. Robinson and held church services on the ground floor. At the age of twenty-three Bradford married a young girl named Dorothy May who arrived from England with her parents, and he, too, bought a house. Elder Brewster and the Rev. Mr. Robinson were welcomed at the university to take part in Latin debates on theology. Thus, the Pilgrims did not have too hard a time in Leyden: but they were not content to stay there.

We shall leave it to Bradford himself to relate "the Reasons and Causes of Their Removal," the story of their departure from Holland, their "sea of troubles" over getting the ship laden and bound away, and their troubles at sea; the details of the voyage, the Mayflower Compact for self-government, the first landing at the site of Provincetown on November 15, the exploring expeditions of Cape Cod and Plymouth Bay in which Bradford took an active part, the landing of the exploring party in the shallop (traditionally on Plymouth Rock) on December 11, the decision to make Plymouth (so called on Captain John Smith's map of New England) the seat of the settlement, and the frightful hardships of the first winter, when almost half the company died.

In May, 1621, after the death of John Carver, who had been elected the first governor under the Mayflower Compact, the surviving freemen elected William Bradford their governor. From that time forth—as indeed since 1620—his life was inseparable from that of the colony. He was re-elected no fewer than thirty times, for a total term of thirty-three years (two of his terms being for two years each, the others annual). Thus he was governor of Plymouth Colony continuously from 1621 to his death in 1657, except for five years when he begged off but was elected one of the assistants to Governors Winslow or Prence.

At the time of Bradford's first election the great sickness had passed, but the colony's situation was still serious. The survivors numbered only eleven heads of families, four wives, six young men, and a few children. Perhaps the best evidence of the character of these men and women is that not one took the opportunity to return on the *Mayflower* when she sailed for England April 5, 1621. Provisions were running low, and there would be no harvest until the fall. No early colony was so ill-equipped in skills as this; the Pilgrims were almost all farmers and artisans, who knew nothing of fishing or fur trading and had few means to do either. Bradford indicates that in his opinion only the guiding hand of God kept the colony alive. The discovery of a cache of Indian corn, the arrival of Squanto as a sort of scoutmaster, the friendly attitude of Massasoit, the appearance off the coast of a jolly mariner from Virginia (who sold them food and warned them of the Indian massacre), the mysterious voice that told them of the fire in the storehouse, the "sweet and gentle showers" that fell out of a clear sky just in time to save the corn crop—such breaks were so frequent that Bradford, sure of their source, remarks: "Behold now another providence of God."

It is an old proverb that God helps those who help themselves. Bradford, and his loyal supporters such as Brewster, Winslow, Standish, Alden, and Howland, certainly deserved what help they got; for in their small sphere—the colony numbered only three hundred souls after ten years, and only twenty-five hundred at Bradford's death—these men showed qualities of statesmanship. They conducted Indian relations so that the colony had peace for over fifty years; they handled the arrogant Massachusetts Bay Colony so that they obtained a good boundary decision; they dealt with disturbers of their peace and polity, such as the lewd pastor Lyford and "Mad Jack" Oldham, Weston the adventurer and Morton the gay blade of Merrymount, so that all in the end were removed; and they did this without the purges, treason trials, and assassinations which are the common means employed by modern petty governments to assert their authority.

All the extracts from Bradford's History which we have reprinted below, with the exception of the memoir of Elder Brewster, were written in 1630, a year which proved to be a turning point in the history of Plymouth Colony. The Massachusetts Bay Colony, founded by Governor Winthrop that year, attracted thousands of English Puritans, who afforded Plymouth farmers a nearby market for their corn and cattle. Many new immigrants also spilled over into Plymouth territory. This brought about the first expansion of the colony from the original settlement north to Duxbury and Scituate, east into Cape Cod, and south to the estuaries of Narragansett Bay. The Governor did not like this movement, as he wished everyone to live in Plymouth-town like a band of brothers; but he had to accept it.

Another important event of 1630 was the obtaining of a patent from the Council of New England, which for the first time gave Plymouth Colony legal standing and a definite territory, corresponding roughly to the present Plymouth, Barnstable, and Bristol Counties of Massachusetts. Also, an event very gratifying to Bradford was an invitation from the Massachusetts Bay Puritans for advice and help in establishing their Congregational churches. That is mainly why Bradford concludes his chapter on the year 1630 with a touching reflection, and remarkable prophecy:

> Thus out of small beginnings greater things have been produced by His hand that made all things of nothing, and gives being to all things that are; and, as one small candle may light a thousand, so the light here kindled hath shone unto many, yea in some sort to our whole nation; let the glorious name of Jehovah have all the praise.

II

NO WORD or hint has come down to us as to Bradford's appearance, and his History is almost completely bare of references to himself, owing to innate modesty and a feeling that he was but an instrument of Providence. He doubtless wore a beard, as almost all adult Englishmen did in his day. He enjoyed rugged health, and did not hesitate to put off in a small boat in the dead of winter to rescue survivors of a wreck on the back side of Cape Cod. He became a shrewd fur-trader with the Indians.

Bradford was twice married. When he returned to the *Mayflower* after exploring Plymouth Bay in December, 1620, he found that Dorothy, his first wife, had fallen overboard and been drowned. (One wonders whether she did not drown herself deliberately, having gazed for weeks on the barren sand dunes of Cape Cod, such a contrast to the green England she had left.) Alice Southworth, the young widow of a former member of the Leyden congregation, arrived at Plymouth with her two small boys in July, 1623. The Governor lost no time in courting Alice, and they were married on August 14. Fortunately for us, since Bradford does not mention the event, Captain Emmanuel Altham of the *Little James* was present at the wedding, and described it in a letter to his brother. Prominent guests were Massasoit, chief of the Wampanoag, wearing a black wolfskin and a belt of wampum; his number-one wife "the Queen," four subordinate sagamores, and about 120 warriors. They were received upon their arrival at Plymouth with a volley of musketry, and, to prevent accidents, were persuaded to deposit their weapons in the Governor's house. They presented the bridegroom with four fat bucks and a turkey, and staged a dance for his benefit. Altham speaks of the "great cheer we had at the Governor's marriage"—a dozen venison pies, roasted venison "and other such good cheer in such quantity that I could wish you some of our share," including wild grapes, plums, and nuts. We may imagine the rest: home-brewed beer, green corn, fish, clams, and lobsters, of which John Pory of Virginia, a visitor the previous year, recorded that you could buy ten, big enough to feed forty men, for a knife worth three cents. Considering that the colony had already held a special thanksgiving day on July 30 for the "sweet and gentle showers" that saved their corn crop, and that they as yet had no cattle or swine, this was doing pretty well.

Altham described Bradford as "a wise gentleman," and John Pory, too, praised him, and borrowed some of his books to read on the voyage home. Isaack de Rasieres, secretary of the Dutch colony at New Amsterdam, who visited Plymouth in 1627, "accompanied by a noise of trumpeters," also had a high opinion of Governor Bradford. The Rev. Gabriel Druillettes, S. J., who came to Plymouth from Canada in 1651 to discuss Indian relations, was graciously received by the Governor, who had specially prepared a fish dinner for him, because it was Friday.

William and Alice Bradford had a daughter and two sons, one of whom, William, Jr., became a military leader of renown in King Philip's War, and as deputy governor of the colony lived long enough to see it peaceably annexed to Massachusetts in 1691. The inventory of Governor Bradford's possessions made after his death on May 9, 1657, includes a "great beer bowle," six dozen pewter dishes and vessels, two silver wine cups and four Venetian glasses, an extensive library of books in English, French, Latin, Dutch, and Hebrew (a language that the Governor learned in his old age), a red suit of clothes, a violet-colored cloak, and "two hats—a black one and a colored one." This indicates clearly that the Governor enjoyed gay-colored apparel, popular illustrations of black-garbed Pilgrims to the contrary notwithstanding.

Besides the History, Bradford, like most educated Englishmen of his day, wrote a good deal of indifferent verse, which he left in "a little black book." Some of this appeals from its simplicity and sincerity. For instance:

From my years young in days of youth,
God did make known to me his truth,
And call'd me from my native place
For to enjoy the means of grace.

In wilderness he did me guide,
And in strange lands for me provide.
In fears and wants, through weal and woe,
A Pilgrim passed I to and fro.

In addition, Bradford wrote three "Dialogues," the record of conferences between young men born in Plymouth and "sundry ancient men" of the original migration. In these "Dialogues," two of which were printed in the nineteenth century, Bradford elucidates the Pilgrims' faith, tells about Puritan martyrs who were burned or hanged, and defines the differences among Protestant sects.

Governor Bradford wrote his History principally to tell the story of the little enterprise with which he was so intimately connected, and which, as he rightly prophesied, would lead to an extensive settlement of New England. His secondary object, which appears on almost every page of the narrative, was to prove that God favored the Pilgrims. *The Wonder-Working Providence of Sion's Saviour in New England*, the title of a later Puritan history of this region by Edward Johnson, might well have been Bradford's. These Puritans were, above all things, eager to know and to do the will of God; and the modest success of the Plymouth experiment, despite initial hardships, poor soil, fishing failures, and the like, convinced the Governor (as he wished to convince his readers) that they had followed the divinely approved line.

It was a general belief among all Christians in Bradford's era, taking literally Christ's declaration of His Father's interest even in "the fall of a sparrow," that the hand of God was in every event, no matter how trivial. God must, therefore, be keenly interested in this experiment in New Testament living. Bradford ventured to compare the Pilgrims' enterprise with that of the Jewish exodus from Egypt, and was much concerned lest the Pilgrims misbehave in their Promised Land as the Children of Israel frequently did, and call down the wrath of God on their heads. When the Plymouth colonists did wrong, he put everything down, not to titillate his readers, but because he knew that God knew all about what went on, so who was he to try to conceal it?

Bradford first organized his History as a straight narrative, divided into ten chapters, which took the story through the landing of the *Mayflower* at Plymouth. In starting "The Second Book" he decided "for brevity's sake," as he wrote, to handle the rest "by way of annals," beginning the events of each year on March 25, which according to the custom of the time was New Year's Day.[1]

Moses Coit Tyler states in his now classic history of early American literature—*A History of American Literature During the Colonial Period* (1897)—that Bradford should properly be called the father of American history. "His mind was placid, grave, well-poised; he was a student of many books and of many languages, and being thus developed both by letters and by experience, he was able to tell well the truth of history as it had unfolded itself during his own strenuous and benignant career." The "commanding qualities" of his mind, wrote Tyler, are "justice, breadth, vigor, dignity, directness, and an untroubled command of strong and manly speech."

It must be admitted that the first ten chapters are much better composed than "The Second Book," which suffers for lack of revision; for Bradford was writing for posterity—not for publication. His main sources, besides his own and his companions' memoirs, were his own day-by-day journal, which has disappeared, and a letter book into which he copied all letters written by him or to him. Part of this has survived.

Much conscious art, and of the finest kind that conceals its own artistry, is displayed in Bradford's style. At the outset he promises his reader to "truly unfold" the history of his "Plantation," and "endeavor to manifest" it "in a plain style, with singular [i.e., single-minded] regard unto the simple truth in all things," so far as his "slender judgment can attain the same." Note how disarming this statement is: I am not omniscient. I cannot aspire to the "high style" that English readers like; but I shall tell you the truth about our colony. That he was acquainted with the "high," euphuistic style of the seventeenth century is evident from his quoting two monuments of that style: Lord Berners' translation of Guevara's *Libro Aurea*, called *The Golden Book of Marcus Aurelius;* and Richard Eden's translation of Peter Martyr's *De Orbe Novo*, called *Decades of the New World*. The plain style that he chose to follow was that of the Geneva version (1560) of the Bible, from which he always quotes, rather than the King James, or Authorized, Version of 1611 that we still use.

Two devices that Bradford frequently employs he did not get from the Bible, but from contemporary literature. These are alliteration, repetition of the same initial letter; and couplings, using two or more words for the same, or nearly the same, concept or thing. For instance, in the General Confession and Absolution, at the beginning of the Book of Common Prayer, we find:

> godly, righteous and sober life;
> devices and desires of our own heart;
> declare and pronounce to his people;
> things which are requisite and necessary.

Bradford's History is full of such alliterations and couplings, as:

> those that were close and cleaving to themselves;
> a wild and savage hue;
> quaffing and drinking;
> their lands and livings;
> cruel and fierce storms;
> common course and condition;
> the ship was shroudly shaken;
> this resolution of their removal;
> load and burden men's consciences;
> bloody and barbarous persecutions;
> in these hard and difficult beginnings.

Additional evidence of Bradford's having composed his History with considerable care and thought are his figures of speech: similes such as "a sea of troubles" (which he may have picked up from *Hamlet*); the description of Morton's alcoholic filling station at Merry-

[1] Thus, events between January 1 and March 24, 1621, are treated as a part of 1620. Bradford used the Julian calendar, although the Dutch followed the Gregorian; to make his dates correspond to those of the present calendar, add ten days.

mount as "a nest of unclean birds"; personification and metaphors such as:

> the grave mistress of experience;
> the grim and grisly face of poverty coming upon them like an armed man with whom they must buckle and encounter.[1]

And it is amusing to find, in Book II, that, like modern serial writers, he stimulates the reader's continuing interest by breaking off a story at the end of a chapter, promising "more in the next."

The narrative is not without humor, as in the accounts of Lyford and Morton, and the Governor's reply to the Christmas Day bowlers; but Bradford makes a very sparing use of puns, a favorite form of wit in the literature of his day. His style has certain defects, such as the use of "as" for "that," confusion as to the antecedents of "they" and "them," interruption of the narrative by letters which would better have been in appendices.

But the story is the thing. Although this small group of English Puritans, in their basic thinking, are as far removed as early Romans from us of the late twentieth century, although their scene was small and their scope narrow, their story is a vignette of American history. At several points we seem to see afar off, as through binoculars, the great questions of our day—how to deal with want and poverty and dissenters from one's basic polity, provide incentive (which the Pilgrims discovered some three centuries before the Russian Communists did), find a balance between the burdens of military security and the desire to live well, deal with other races. Here is an absorbing story of humble people, impelled by their ardent faith to courage in danger, perseverance through every sort of discomfort and discouragement, and resourcefulness in dealing with new and unexpected problems. Bradford's prophecy reached even further than he anticipated: "The light here kindled" hath indeed "shone unto many; yea, in some sort, to our whole nation."

[1] Suggested doubtless by Prov. 24:34: "So thy poverty cometh as one that travelleth by the way, and thy necessity like an armed man."

READING SUGGESTIONS

SOURCES

The rest of the History *Of Plymouth Plantation*, either in the present editor's edition (Alfred A. Knopf, 1952, 1959), from which the following extracts are quoted, or in the Worthington C. Ford edition (Massachusetts Historical Society, 1912), which follows Bradford's exact spelling, and has copious footnotes.

Mourt's Relation, the exact title of which is *A Relation or Journall of the Beginning and Proceedings of the English Plantation settled at Plimoth in New England* (1622). This consists of extracts from Bradford's and Edward Winslow's diaries (now lost) of the first two years of the colony, put together by an English editor who signed the preface "G. Mourt." It has been reprinted several times, the best edition being H. M. Dexter's (1865).

Alexander Young, editor, *Chronicles of the Pilgrim Fathers* (1844), also reprints *Mourt's Relation*, together with an important tract by Edward Winslow, *Good Newes from New England*.

Two valuable accounts of the colony by outsiders are John Pory, *Description of Plymouth Colony*, ed. by Champlin Burrage (1918), and Isaack de Rasieres' description of his visit to New Plymouth in 1627, trans. by J. F. Jameson in *Narratives of New Netherland* (1919).

SECONDARY AUTHORITIES

Roland G. Usher, *The Pilgrims and Their History* (1918).

Samuel Eliot Morison, *The Story of the "Old Colony" of New Plymouth, 1620–1692* (1956).

Bradford Smith, *Bradford of Plymouth* (1951). The only biography of Bradford since Cotton Mather's in his *Magnalia* (1702), and an excellent one.

Dictionary of American Biography (1928–36). For biographical sketches of Isaac Allerton, William Bradford, William Brewster, John Carver, Massasoit, John Oldham, Squanto, Myles Standish, Thomas Weston, and Edward Winslow.

J. Truslow Adams, *The Founding of New England* (1921). For a carping and critical view of the Pilgrims.

Perry Miller, *New England Mind: The Seventeenth Century* (1939, 1954).

Charles Francis Adams, *Three Episodes of Massachusetts History* (1892). For a diverting account of the Pilgrims' relations with Thomas Morton and Weston's colony.

D. Plooij, *The Pilgrim Fathers from a Dutch Point of View* (1932). For details on their residence in Holland.

Charles E. Banks, *The English Ancestry and Homes of the Pilgrims* (1929), for the English background; and Roland G. Usher, *The Reconstruction of the English Church* (1910), for the religious background.

E. S. Morgan, *The Puritan Family: Essays on Religion*

and Domestic Relations in Seventeenth-Century New England (1944).

KENNETH B. MURDOCK, *Literature and Theology in Colonial New England* (1949).

W. S. NICKERSON, *Land Ho!—1620* (1931). For an old sailor's reconstruction of the *Mayflower*'s voyage.

ERNEST GÉBLER, *The Plymouth Adventure: A Chronicle Novel of the Voyage of the Mayflower* (1950). Best of the fictionalized narratives of the voyage of the *Mayflower*.

A visit to Pilgrim's Hall, Plymouth, and to the nearby Pilgrim Village and Fort reconstructed in the 1950's by Plimoth Plantation, Inc., is most instructive. The same corporation has on sale several good pamphlets; notably, Harold L. Peterson, *Arms and Armor of the Pilgrims*, and Rose T. Briggs, *Plymouth Rock: Its History and Its Significance*.

For a study of the Bradford History as literature, Moses Coit Tyler, *History of American Literature: 1607–1765* (1878, 1949), Vol. I, chap. 6; A. H. Quinn, editor, *The Literature of the American People* (1951), chap. 5 (by Kenneth B. Murdock); E. F. Bradford, "Conscious Art in Bradford's History," *New England Quarterly*, I (1928), 133–57.

For the Pilgrims' place in American history, Edward Channing, *History of the United States* (1905, 1928), Vol. I, chaps. 10, 11, and Samuel Eliot Morison, *By Land and by Sea* (1953), chap. 10.

For other references, see Oscar Handlin *et al.*, *Harvard Guide to American History*, secs. 84, 89, 90.

OF PLYMOUTH PLANTATION

THE FIRST BOOK

[CHAPTERS 1 and 2 give Bradford's views on the Protestant Reformation, and an account of his congregation's trials and tribulations leaving England for Holland in 1608.]

CHAPTER 3

OF THEIR SETTLING IN HOLLAND, AND THEIR MANNER OF LIVING, AND ENTERTAINMENT THERE

BEING now come into the Low Countries, they saw many goodly and fortified cities, strongly walled and guarded with troops of armed men. Also, they heard a strange and uncouth language, and beheld the different manners and customs of the people, with their strange fashions and attires; all so far differing from that of their plain country villages (wherein they were bred and had so long lived) as it seemed they were come into a new world. But these were not the things they much looked on, or long took up their thoughts, for they had other work in hand and another kind of war to wage and maintain. For although they saw fair and beautiful cities, flowing with abundance of all sorts of wealth and riches, yet it was not long before they saw the grim and grisly face of poverty coming upon them like an armed man, with whom they must buckle and encounter, and from whom they could not fly. But they were armed with faith and patience against him and all his encounters; and though they were some times foiled, yet by God's assistance they prevailed and got the victory.

Now when Mr. Robinson, Mr. Brewster and other principal members were come over (for they were of the last and stayed to help the weakest over before them) such things were thought on as were necessary for their settling and best ordering of the church affairs.

And when they had lived at Amsterdam about a year, Mr. Robinson their pastor and some others of best discerning, seeing how Mr. John Smith and his company was already fallen into contention with the church that was there before them, and no means they could use would do any good to cure the same, and also that the flames of contention were like to break out in that ancient church itself (as afterwards lamentably came to pass); which things they prudently foreseeing thought it was best to remove before they were any way engaged with the same, though they well knew it would be much to the prejudice of their outward estates, both at present and in likelihood in the future; as indeed it proved to be.

For these and some other reasons they removed to Leyden, a fair and beautiful city and of a sweet situation, but made more famous by the university wherewith it is adorned, in which of late had been so many learned men. But wanting that traffic by sea which Amsterdam enjoys, it was not so beneficial for their outward means of living and estate. But being now here pitch[ed],[1]

OF PLYMOUTH PLANTATION. Chapter 3. 1. pitched: settled.

they fell to such trades and employments as they best could, valuing peace and their spiritual comfort above any other riches whatsoever. And at length they came to raise a competent and comfortable living, but with hard and continual labor.

Being thus settled (after many difficulties) they continued many years in a comfortable condition, enjoying much sweet and delightful society and spiritual comfort together in the ways of God, under the able ministry and prudent government of Mr. John Robinson and Mr. William Brewster who was an assistant unto him in the place of an Elder,[2] unto which he was now called and chosen by the church. So as they grew in knowledge and other gifts and graces of the Spirit of God, and lived together in peace and love and holiness and many came unto them from divers parts of England, so as they grew a great congregation. And if at any time any differences arose or offenses broke out (as it cannot be but some time there will, even amongst the best of men) they were ever so met with and nipped in the head betimes, or otherwise so well composed as still love, peace, and communion was continued. Or else the church purged off those that were incurable and incorrigible when, after much patience used, no other means would serve, which seldom came to pass.

Yea, such was the mutual love and reciprocal respect that this worthy man had to his flock, and his flock to him, that it might be said of them as it once was of that famous Emperor Marcus Aurelius,[3] and the people of Rome, that it was hard to judge whether he delighted more in having such a people, or they in having such a pastor. His [4] love was great towards them, and his care was always bent for their best good, both for soul and body. For besides his singular abilities in divine things (wherein he excelled) he was also very able to give directions in civil affairs and to foresee dangers and inconveniences, by which means he was very helpful to their outward estates and so was every way as a common father unto them. And none did more offend him than those that were close and cleaving to themselves and retired from the common good; as also such as would be stiff and rigid in matters of outward order and inveigh against the evils of others, and yet be remiss in themselves, and not so careful to express a virtuous conversation. They in like manner had ever a reverent regard unto him and had him in precious estimation, as his worth and wisdom did deserve. And though they esteemed him highly whilst he lived and labored amongst them, yet much more after his death, when they came to feel the want of his help and saw (by woeful experience) what a treasure they had lost, to the grief of their hearts and wounding of their souls. Yea, such a loss as they saw could not be repaired; for it was . . . hard for them to find such another leader and feeder . . . Such was the true piety, the humble zeal and fervent love of this people (whilst they thus lived together) towards God and His ways, and the singleheartedness and sincere affection one towards another, that they came as near the primitive pattern of the first churches as any other church of these later times have done, according to their rank and quality.[5] . . .

. . . And first, though many of them were poor, yet there was none so poor but if they were known to be of that congregation the Dutch (either bakers or others) would trust them in any reasonable matter when they wanted money, because they had found by experience how careful they were to keep their word, and saw them so painful and diligent in their callings. Yea, they would strive to get their custom and to employ them above others in their work, for their honesty and diligence.

Again, the magistrates of the city, about the time of their coming away or a little before, in the public place of justice gave this commendable testimony of them, in the reproof of the Walloons who were of the French church in that city. These English, said they, have lived amongst us now these twelve years, and yet we never had any suit or accusation come against any of them; but your strifes and quarrels are continual, etc. . . .

CHAPTER 4

SHOWING THE REASONS AND CAUSES OF THEIR REMOVAL

AFTER they had lived in this city about some eleven or twelve years (which is the more observable being the whole time of that famous truce

2. **Elder:** Not only the Separatists but all Puritans called the principal officers of their churches Elders. The two clerical ones, ordained by laying on of hands, were the Preaching Elder or Pastor and the Teaching Elder or Teacher; the other two, laymen both, were the Ruling Elders. 3. **Marcus Aurelius:** Golden Book, etc. [Bradford's note]. Lord Berners' translation, *The Golden Book of Marcus Aurelius*, was one of the most popular books of the day. 4. **His:** the Rev. John Robinson's.

5. **Such . . . quality:** Bradford's picture of the Pilgrim church at Leyden (numbering over four hundred in 1620), and of their pastor, is not overdrawn. Unlike the other exiled English churches in the Netherlands, this was free of factions, and Robinson's own writings show him to have been a clergyman of relatively broad views, catholic spirit, and human sympathy.

between that state and the Spaniards) and sundry of them were taken away by death and many others began to be well stricken in years (the grave mistress of Experience having taught them many things), those prudent governors with sundry of the sagest members began both deeply to apprehend their present dangers and wisely to foresee the future and think of timely remedy. In the agitation of their thoughts, and much discourse of things hereabout, at length they began to incline to this conclusion: of removal to some other place. Not out of any newfangledness or other such like giddy humor by which men are oftentimes transported to their great hurt and danger, but for sundry weighty and solid reasons, some of the chief of which I will here briefly touch.

And first, they saw and found by experience the hardness of the place and country to be such as few in comparison would come to them, and fewer that would bide it out and continue with them. For many that came to them, and many more that desired to be with them, could not endure that great labor and hard fare, with other inconveniences which they underwent and were contented with. . . . Yea, some preferred and chose the prisons in England rather than this liberty in Holland with these afflictions. But it was thought that if a better and easier place of living could be had, it would draw many and take away these discouragements. Yea, their pastor would often say that many of those who both wrote and preached now against them, if they were in a place where they might have liberty and live comfortably, they would then practice as they did.

Secondly. They saw that though the people generally bore all these difficulties very cheerfully and with a resolute courage, being in the best and strength of their years, yet old age began to steal on many of them; and their great and continual labours, with other crosses and sorrows, hastened it before the time. So as it was not only probably thought, but apparently seen, that within a few years more they would be in danger to scatter, by necessities pressing them, or sink under their burdens, or both. And therefore according to the divine proverb, that a wise man seeth the plague when it cometh, and hideth himself (Prov. 22:3), so they like skillful and beaten soldiers were fearful either to be entrapped or surrounded by their enemies so as they should neither be able to fight nor fly. And therefore thought it better to dislodge betimes to some place of better advantage and less danger, if any such could be found.

Thirdly. As necessity was a taskmaster over them so they were forced to be such, not only to their servants but in a sort to their dearest children, the which as it did not a little wound the tender hearts of many a loving father and mother, so it produced likewise sundry sad and sorrowful effects. For many of their children that were of best dispositions and gracious inclinations, having learned to bear the yoke in their youth and willing to bear part of their parents' burden, were oftentimes so oppressed with their heavy labors that though their minds were free and willing, yet their bodies bowed under the weight of the same, and became decrepit in their early youth, the vigor of nature being consumed in the very bud as it were. But that which was more lamentable, and of all sorrows most heavy to be borne, was that many of their children, by these occasions and the great licentiousness of youth in that country,[1] and the manifold temptations of the place, were drawn away by evil examples into extravagant and dangerous courses, getting the reins off their necks and departing from their parents. Some became soldiers, others took upon them far voyages by sea, and others some worse courses tending to dissoluteness and the danger of their souls, to the great grief of their parents and dishonor of God. So that they saw their posterity would be in danger to degenerate and be corrupted.

Lastly (and which was not least), a great hope and inward zeal they had of laying some good foundation, or at least to make some way thereunto, for the propagating and advancing the gospel of the kingdom of Christ in those remote parts of the world; yea, though they should be but even as stepping-stones unto others for the performing of so great a work.

These and some other like reasons moved them to undertake this resolution of their removal; the which they afterward prosecuted with so great difficulties, as by the sequel will appear.

The place they had thoughts on was some of those vast and unpeopled countries of America, which are fruitful and fit for habitation, being devoid of all civil inhabitants, where there are only savage and brutish men which range up and down, little otherwise than the wild beasts of the same. This proposition being made public and coming to the scanning of all, it raised many variable opinions amongst men and caused many fears and doubts amongst themselves. Some, from their reasons and hopes conceived, labored to

Chapter 4. 1. licentiousness . . . country: The Dutch did not "keep the Sabbath" in the strict sense that other Calvinists did. Sunday after church was a day of feasting and merrymaking, especially for children.

stir up and encourage the rest to undertake and prosecute the same; others again, out of their fears, objected against it and sought to divert from it; alleging many things, and those neither unreasonable nor unprobable; as that it was a great design and subject to many unconceivable perils and dangers; as, besides the casualties of the sea (which none can be freed from), the length of the voyage was such as the weak bodies of women and other persons worn out with age and travail (as many of them were) could never be able to endure. And yet if they should, the miseries of the land which they should be exposed unto, would be too hard to be borne and likely, some or all of them together, to consume and utterly to ruinate them. For there they should be liable to famine and nakedness and the want, in a manner, of all things. The change of air, diet and drinking of water [2] would infect their bodies with sore sicknesses and grievous diseases. And also those which should escape or overcome these difficulties should yet be in continual danger of the savage people, who are cruel, barbarous and most treacherous, being most furious in their rage and merciless where they overcome; not being content only to kill and take away life, but delight to torment men in the most bloody manner that may be; flaying some alive with the shells of fishes, cutting off the members and joints of others by piecemeal and broiling on the coals, eat the collops of their flesh in their sight whilst they live, with other cruelties horrible to be related. . . .

. . . It was further objected that it would require greater sums of money to furnish such a voyage and to fit them with necessaries, than their consumed estates would amount to; and yet they must as well look to be seconded with supplies as presently to be transported. Also many precedents of ill success and lamentable miseries befallen others in the like designs were easy to be found, and not forgotten to be alleged; besides their own experience, in their former troubles and hardships in their removal into Holland, and how hard a thing it was for them to live in that strange place, though it was a neighbor country and a civil and rich commonwealth.

It was answered, that all great and honorable actions are accompanied with great difficulties and must be both enterprised and overcome with answerable courages. It was granted the dangers were great, but not desperate. The difficulties were many, but not invincible. . . . True it was that such attempts were not to be made and undertaken without good ground and reason, not rashly or lightly as many have done for curiosity or hope of gain, etc. But their condition was not ordinary, their ends were good and honorable, their calling lawful and urgent; and therefore they might expect the blessing of God in their proceeding. Yea, though they should lose their lives in this action, yet might they have comfort in the same and their endeavours would be honorable. They lived here but as men in exile and in a poor condition, and as great miseries might possibly befall them in this place; for the twelve years of truce were now out and there was nothing but beating of drums and preparing for war, the events whereof are always uncertain. The Spaniard might prove as cruel as the savages of America, and the famine and pestilence as sore here as there, and their liberty less to look out for remedy.

After many other particular things answered and alleged on both sides, it was fully concluded by the major part to put this design in execution and to prosecute it by the best means they could.

[IN Chapter 5 Bradford outlines the discussions as to the Pilgrims' overseas destination. Guiana, so gloriously promoted by Sir Walter Raleigh and others, was ruled out as too near the Spaniards and of a climate which "would not so well agree with our English bodies." The Prince of Orange turned down an application for a slice of New Netherland. Virginia was objected to because the long arm of the English church might reach them there. But William Brewster had a connection with Sir Edwin Sandys, treasurer of the Virginia Company, which had adopted a policy of granting self-government and a generous amount of land to "particular plantations," or organized groups, and the company granted the Pilgrims a patent which could be located anywhere within Virginia's then ample borders, extending up into the present New York State. The company apparently was persuaded to do this by a letter from the Rev. John Robinson and Elder Brewster, in which they made this prophetic statement:

> Lastly, it is not with us as with other men, whom small things can discourage, or small discontentments cause to wish themselves at home again. We know our entertainment in England and in Holland. We shall much prejudice both our arts and means by removal; who, if we should be driven to return, we should not hope to recover our present helps and comforts, neither indeed look ever, for ourselves, to attain unto the like in any other place during our lives, which are now drawing towards their periods.

Having obtained a patent, the next problem for these poor people was to raise expenses to pay for ships and supplies. Here there came into the picture Thomas

2. **drinking of water:** It was a general opinion of the time that water was an unwholesome beverage, as indeed it was when drawn from a contaminated well in a city or farmyard. The common table beverages of poor families in England and Holland were beer and cider.

Weston, a London hardware merchant and small-time capitalist of the type nowadays known as a "chiseler." He organized the Company of Adventurers, which made a very good thing out of exploiting the Pilgrims. The Adventurers agreed to pay all expenses of chartering and operating the ships, and of provisions, tools, and supplies to get the colony over and keep it going. In return the emigrants, then called the Planters, must work without wages for the Adventurers for seven years, all profits going into dividends to the investors. At the end of that time all assets would be divided up, each Adventurer to the amount of ten pounds to receive the same as a person who had labored for seven years. These terms were so harsh that a majority of the Leyden congregation refused to leave; so, to Bradford's great chagrin, the Rev. John Robinson had to stay behind. And, as the number who decided to see it through was not enough to fill the *Mayflower*, Weston filled up her complement with strangers, some of whom made trouble at Plymouth.]

CHAPTER 7

OF THEIR DEPARTURE FROM LEYDEN, AND OTHER THINGS THEREABOUT; WITH THEIR ARRIVAL AT SOUTHAMPTON, WHERE THEY ALL MET TOGETHER AND TOOK IN THEIR PROVISIONS

AT LENGTH, after much travel and these debates, all things were got ready and provided. A small ship [1] was bought and fitted in Holland, which was intended as to serve to help to transport them, so to stay in the country and attend upon fishing and such other affairs as might be for the good and benefit of the colony when they came there. Another was hired at London, of burthen about 9 score,[2] and all other things got in readiness. So being ready to depart, they had a day of solemn humiliation, their pastor taking his text from Ezra 8:21: "And there at the river, by Ahava, I proclaimed a fast, that we might humble ourselves before our God, and seek of him a right way for us, and for our children, and for all our substance." Upon which he spent a good part of the day very profitably and suitable to their present occasion; the rest of the time was spent in pouring out prayers to the Lord with great fervency, mixed with abundance of tears. And the time being come that they must depart, they were accompanied with most of their brethren out of the city, unto a town sundry miles off called Delftshaven, where the ship lay ready to receive them. So they left that goodly and pleasant city which had been their resting place near twelve years; but they knew they were pilgrims,[3] and looked not much on those things, but lift up their eyes to the heavens, their dearest country, and quieted their spirits.

When they came to the place they found the ship and all things ready, and such of their friends as could not come with them followed after them, and sundry also came from Amsterdam to see them shipped and to take their leave of them. That night was spent with little sleep by the most, but with friendly entertainment and Christian discourse and other real expressions of true Christian love. The next day (the wind being fair) they went aboard and their friends with them, where truly doleful was the sight of that sad and mournful parting, to see what sighs and sobs and prayers did sound amongst them, what tears did gush from every eye, and pithy speeches pierced each heart; that sundry of the Dutch strangers that stood on the quay as spectators could not refrain from tears. Yet comfortable and sweet it was to see such lively and true expressions of dear and unfeigned love. But the tide, which stays for no man, calling them away that were thus loath to depart, their reverend pastor falling down on his knees (and they all with him) with watery cheeks commended them with most fervent prayers to the Lord and His blessing. And then with mutual embraces and many tears they took their leaves one of another, which proved to be the last leave to many of them.

Thus hoising sail,[4] with a prosperous wind they came in short time to Southampton, where they found the bigger ship come from London, lying ready, with all the rest of their company. After a joyful welcome and mutual congratulations, with other friendly entertainments, they fell to parley about their business, how to dispatch with the best expedition; as also with their agents about the alteration of the conditions. . . .

[After sundry altercations with Weston, who refused to honor some of the bills for ships' stores,] all things being now ready, and every business dispatched, . . . they ordered and distributed their company for either ship, as they conceived for the best; and chose a governor and two or three assistants for each ship, to order the people by the way, and see to the disposing of their

Chapter 7. 1. **A small ship:** "Of some sixty tun" [B]. This was the *Speedwell*. 2. **Another . . . score:** the *Mayflower*, 180 tons. The *Mayflower II*, which crossed the ocean in 1957 under Captain Villiers, was built to this measurement. She was about ninety feet long, with three masts.

3. **So . . . pilgrims:** Heb. 11:13–16 [B]. It was owing to this passage, first printed in 1669, that the *Mayflower*'s company came to be called the Pilgrim Fathers. 4. **Thus . . . sail:** "This was about 22 of July" [B].

provisions and such like affairs. All which was not only with the liking of the masters of the ships but according to their desires. Which being done, they set sail from thence about the 5th of August. But what befell them further upon the coast of England will appear in the next chapter.

CHAPTER 8

OF THE TROUBLES THAT BEFELL THEM ON THE COAST, AND AT SEA, BEING FORCED AFTER MUCH TROUBLE TO LEAVE ONE OF THEIR SHIPS AND SOME OF THEIR COMPANY BEHIND THEM

BEING THUS put to sea, they had not gone far but Mr. Reynolds, the master of the lesser ship, complained that he found his ship so leaky as he durst not put further to sea till she was mended. So the master of the bigger ship (called Mr. Jones) [1] being consulted with, they both resolved to put into Dartmouth and have her there searched and mended, which accordingly was done, to their great charge and loss of time and a fair wind. She was here thoroughly searched from stem to stern, some leaks were found and mended, and now it was conceived by the workmen and all, that she was sufficient, and they might proceed without either fear or danger. So with good hopes from hence, they put to sea again, conceiving they should go comfortably on, not looking for any more lets [2] of this kind; but it fell out otherwise. For after they were gone to sea again above 100 leagues without the Lands End, holding company together all this while, the master of the small ship complained his ship was so leaky as he must bear up or sink at sea, for they could scarce free her with much pumping. So they came to consultation again, and resolved both ships to bear up back again and put into Plymouth, which accordingly was done. But no special leak could be found, but it was judged to be the general weakness of the ship, and that she would not prove sufficient for the voyage. Upon which it was resolved to dismiss her and part of the company, and proceed with the other ship. The which (though it was grievous and caused great discouragement) was put into execution.

So after they had took out such provision as the other ship could well stow, and concluded both what number and what persons to send back, they made another sad parting; the one ship going back for London and the other was to proceed on her voyage. . . . And thus, like Gideon's army, this small number was divided, as if the Lord by this work of His providence thought these few too many for the great work He had to do. . . .

. . . Amongst those that returned was Mr. Cushman and his family, whose heart and courage was gone from them before (as it seems) though his body was with them till now he departed; as may appear by a passionate letter he writ to a friend in London from Dartmouth whilst the ship lay there a-mending. . . . And though it discover some infirmities in him (as who under temptation is free) yet after this he continued to be a special instrument for their good, and to do the offices of a loving friend and faithful brother unto them, and partaker of much comfort with them. The letter is as followeth.

TO HIS LOVING FRIEND EDWARD SOUTHWORTH [3] AT HENEAGE HOUSE IN THE DUKE'S PLACE, THESE, ETC.

Dartmouth, Aug. 17.

LOVING FRIEND,

My most kind remembrance to you and your wife, with loving E. M. etc., whom in this world I never look to see again. For besides the eminent dangers of this voyage, which are no less than deadly, an infirmity of body hath seized me, which will not in all likelihood leave me till death. What to call it I know not, but it is a bundle of lead, as it were, crushing my heart more and more these fourteen days; as that although I do the actions of a living man, yet I am but as dead, but the will of God be done.

Our pinnace [4] will not cease leaking, else I think we had been halfway at Virginia. Our voyage hither hath been as full of crosses as ourselves have been of crookedness. We put in here to trim her; and I think, as others also, if we had stayed at sea but three or four hours more, she would have sunk right down. And though she was twice trimmed at Hampton, yet now she is as open and leaky as a sieve; and there was a board a man might have pulled off with his fingers, two foot long, where the water came in as at a mole hole. We lay at Hampton seven days in fair weather, waiting for her, and now we lie here

Chapter 8. 1. So . . . Jones: Christopher Jones, master of the *Mayflower*. A native of Rotherhithe, he had for several years been a quarter owner of the *Mayflower*, as well as her master.
2. lets: obstructions; a meaning of the word that survives in the game of tennis.

3. Edward Southworth: a member of the Leyden congregation who did not emigrate, died in 1623; his widow became Bradford's second wife. **4. Our pinnace:** the *Speedwell*.

waiting for her in as fair a wind as can blow, and so have done these four days, and are like to lie four more, and by that time the wind will happily turn as it did at Hampton. Our victuals will be half eaten up, I think, before we go from the coast of England, and if our voyage last long, we shall not have a month's victuals when we come in the country. . . .

. . . Friend, if ever we make a plantation, God works a miracle, especially considering how scant we shall be of victuals, and most of all ununited amongst ourselves and devoid of good tutors and regiment.[5] Violence will break all. Where is the meek and humble spirit of Moses? and of Nehemiah who re-edified the walls of Jerusalem, and the state of Israel? Is not the sound of Rehoboam's brags daily here amongst us? [6] Have not the philosophers and all wise men observed that, even in settled commonwealths, violent governors bring either themselves or people or both to ruin? How much more in the raising of commonwealths, when the mortar is yet scarce tempered that should bind the walls! If I should write to you of all things which promiscuously forerun our ruin, I should over-charge my weak head and grieve your tender heart. Only this, I pray you prepare for evil tidings of us every day. But pray for us instantly, it may be the Lord will be yet entreated one way or other to make for us. I see not in reason how we shall escape even the gasping of hunger-starved persons; but God can do much, and His will be done. It is better for me to die than now for me to bear it, which I do daily and expect it hourly, having received the sentence of death both within me and without me. Poor William Ring and myself do strive who shall be meat first for the fishes; but we look for a glorious resurrection, knowing Christ Jesus after the flesh no more, but looking unto the joy that is before us, we will endure all these things and account them light in comparison of that joy we hope for. . .

Dartmouth,

Your loving friend,

Aug. 17. 1620 ROBERT CUSHMAN

These being his conceptions and fears at Dartmouth, they must needs be much stronger now at Plymouth.[7]

5. tutors and regiment: leaders and discipline. **6. Is . . . us?:** "My father . . . chastised you with whips . . . I will chastise you with scorpions" (I Kings 12:14). **7. These . . . Plymouth:** Bradford seems to have taken a sly pleasure in recording this gloomy letter of Cushman's to show how wrong he was. But there was much truth in the letter. The Pilgrims were less prepared for wilderness life than any English emigrating company of the century, and it was indeed a miracle that they survived.

CHAPTER 9

OF THEIR VOYAGE, AND HOW THEY PASSED THE SEA; AND OF THEIR SAFE ARRIVAL AT CAPE COD

September 6. These troubles being blown over, and now all being compact together in one ship, they put to sea again with a prosperous wind, which continued divers days together, which was some encouragement unto them; yet, according to the usual manner, many were afflicted with seasickness. And I may not omit here a special work of God's providence. There was a proud and very profane young man, one of the seamen, of a lusty, able body, which made him the more haughty; he would alway be contemning the poor people in their sickness and cursing them daily with grievous execrations; and did not let to tell them that he hoped to help to cast half of them overboard before they came to their journey's end, and to make merry with what they had; and if he were by any gently reproved, he would curse and swear most bitterly. But it pleased God before they came half seas over, to smite this young man with a grievous disease, of which he died in a desperate manner, and so was himself the first that was thrown overboard. Thus his curses light on his own head, and it was an astonishment to all his fellows for they noted it to be the just hand of God upon him.

After they had enjoyed fair winds and weather for a season, they were encountered many times with cross winds and met with many fierce storms with which the ship was shroudly [1] shaken, and her upper works made very leaky; and one of the main beams in the midships was bowed and cracked, which put them in some fear that the ship could not be able to perform the voyage. So some of the chief of the company, perceiving the mariners to fear the sufficiency of the ship as appeared by their mutterings, they entered into serious consultation with the master and other officers of the ship, to consider in time of the danger, and rather to return than to cast themselves into a desperate and inevitable peril. And truly there was great distraction and difference of opinion amongst the mariners themselves; fain would they do what could be done for their wages' sake (being now near half the seas over) and on the other hand they were loath to hazard their lives too desperately. But in examining of all opinions, the master and others affirmed they knew the ship to be strong and firm under water;

Chapter 9. 1. shroudly: an old form of "shrewdly," in its original meaning "wickedly."

and for the buckling of the main beam, there was a great iron screw the passengers brought out of Holland, which would raise the beam into his place; the which being done, the carpenter and master affirmed that with a post put under it, set firm in the lower deck and otherways bound, he would make it sufficient. And as for the decks and upper works, they would caulk them as well as they could, and though with the working of the ship they would not long keep staunch, yet there would otherwise be no great danger, if they did not overpress her with sails. So they committed themselves to the will of God and resolved to proceed.

In sundry of these storms the winds were so fierce and the seas so high, as they could not bear a knot of sail, but were forced to hull [2] for divers days together. And in one of them, as they thus lay at hull in a mighty storm, a lusty [3] young man called John Howland, coming upon some occasion above the gratings was, with a seele [4] of the ship, thrown into sea; but it pleased God that he caught hold of the topsail halyards which hung overboard and ran out at length. Yet he held his hold (though he was sundry fathoms under water) till he was hauled up by the same rope to the brim of the water, and then with a boat hook and other means got into the ship again and his life saved. And though he was something ill with it, yet he lived many years after and became a profitable member both in church and commonwealth. In all this voyage there died but one of the passengers, which was William Butten, a youth, servant to Samuel Fuller, when they drew near the coast.

But to omit other things (that I may be brief) after long beating at sea they fell with that land which is called Cape Cod; [5] the which being made and certainly known to be it, they were not a little joyful. After some deliberation had amongst themselves and with the master of the ship, they tacked about and resolved to stand for the southward (the wind and weather being fair) to find some place about Hudson's River for their habitation.[6] But after they had sailed that course about half the day, they fell amongst dangerous shoals and roaring breakers, and they were so far entangled therewith as they conceived themselves in great danger; and the wind shrinking upon them withal, they resolved to bear up again for the Cape and thought themselves happy to get out of those dangers before night overtook them, as by God's good providence they did. And the next day [7] they got into the Cape Harbor [8] where they rid in safety. . . .

. . . Being thus arrived in a good harbor, and brought safe to land, they fell upon their knees and blessed the God of Heaven who had brought them over the vast and furious ocean, and delivered them from all the perils and miseries thereof, again to set their feet on the firm and stable earth, their proper element. And no marvel if they were thus joyful, seeing wise Seneca was so affected with sailing a few miles on the coast of his own Italy, as he affirmed, that he had rather remain twenty years on his way by land than pass by sea to any place in a short time, so tedious and dreadful was the same unto him.[9]

But here I cannot but stay and make a pause, and stand half amazed at this poor people's present condition; and so I think will the reader, too, when he well considers the same. Being thus passed the vast ocean, and a sea of troubles before in their preparation (as may be remembered by that which went before), they had now no friends to welcome them nor inns to entertain or refresh their weatherbeaten bodies; no houses or much less towns to repair to, to seek for succour. It is recorded in Scripture [10] as a mercy to the Apostle and his shipwrecked company, that the barbarians showed them no small kindness in refreshing them, but these savage barbarians, when they met with them (as after will appear) were readier to fill their sides full of arrows than otherwise. And for the season it was winter, and they that know the winters of that country know them to be sharp and violent, and subject to cruel and fierce storms, dangerous to travel to known places, much more to search an unknown coast. Besides, what could they see but a hideous and desolate wilderness, full of wild beasts and wild men—and what multitudes there might be of them they knew not. Neither could they, as it were, go up to the top of

2. **to hull:** to lay-to under short sail and drift with the wind. 3. **lusty:** lively, merry; no sexual connotation. Howland, a servant of Governor Carver, rose to be one of the leading men of the Colony. 4. **seele:** roll or pitch. 5. **But . . . Cape Cod:** at daybreak November 9, 1620. 6. **After . . . habitation:** This is the only direct statement as to whither the *Mayflower* was bound. The Virginia Company, which had granted the patent that the Pilgrims brought with them, had a right to colonize up to lat. 41° N, which included Manhattan Island. The Dutch did not settle Manhattan until 1626, although they claimed the region by virtue of Hudson's voyage in 1609; the English never admitted their claim. The theory that Master Jones of the *Mayflower* was bribed by the Dutch to set the Pilgrims ashore at a safe distance from Manhattan has no basis in fact. No seaman who has weathered Cape Cod needs any better explanation than a head wind on unbuoyed Pollock Rip to explain why the *Mayflower* turned back. 7. **the next day:** November 11, 1620. The *Mayflower*'s passage from Plymouth took sixty-five days. 8. **Cape Harbor:** now Provincetown Harbor. 9. **that . . . him:** Epistle 53 [B]. The sentence is in Seneca, *Ad Lucilium Epistulae Morales.* 10. **It . . . Scripture:** Acts 28 [B]; verse 2.

Pisgah to view from this wilderness a more goodly country to feed their hopes; for which way soever they turned their eyes (save upward to the heavens) they could have little solace or content in respect of any outward objects. For summer being done, all things stand upon them with a weather-beaten face, and the whole country, full of woods and thickets, represented a wild and savage hue. If they looked behind them, there was the mighty ocean which they had passed and was now as a main bar and gulf to separate them from all the civil parts of the world. If it be said they had a ship to succour them, it is true; but what heard they daily from the master and company? But that with speed they should look out a place (with their shallop) where they would be, at some near distance; for the season was such as he would not stir from thence till a safe harbor was discovered by them, where they would be, and he might go without danger; and that victuals consumed apace but he must and would keep sufficient for themselves and their return. Yea, it was muttered by some that if they got not a place in time, they would turn them and their goods ashore and leave them. Let it also be considered what weak hopes of supply and succour they left behind them, that might bear up their minds in this sad condition and trials they were under; and they could not but be very small. It is true, indeed, the affections and love of their brethren at Leyden was cordial and entire towards them, but they had little power to help them or themselves; and how the case stood between them and the merchants at their coming away hath already been declared.

What could now sustain them but the Spirit of God and His grace? May not and ought not the children of these fathers rightly say: "Our fathers were Englishmen which came over this great ocean, and were ready to perish in this wilderness; but they cried unto the Lord, and He heard their voice and looked on their adversity," [11] etc. "Let them therefore praise the Lord, because He is good: and His mercies endure forever." "Yea, let them which have been redeemed of the Lord, shew how He hath delivered them from the hand of the oppressor. When they wandered in the desert wilderness out of the way, and found no city to dwell in, both hungry and thirsty, their soul was overwhelmed in them. Let them confess before the Lord His lovingkindness and His wonderful works before the sons of men." [12]

11. **"Our . . . adversity"**: Deut. 26:5, 7 [B]. 12. **"Let . . . men"**: Ps. 107:1–5, 8 [B].

CHAPTER 10

SHOWING HOW THEY SOUGHT OUT A PLACE OF HABITATION; AND WHAT BEFELL THEM THEREABOUT

BEING thus arrived at Cape Cod the 11th of November, and necessity calling them to look out a place for habitation (as well as the master's and mariners' importunity); they having brought a large shallop with them out of England, stowed in quarters in the ship, they now got her out and set their carpenters to work to trim her up; but being much bruised and shattered in the ship with foul weather, they saw she would be long in mending. Whereupon a few of them tendered themselves to go by land and discover those nearest places, whilst the shallop was in mending; and the rather because as they went into that harbor there seemed to be an opening some two or three leagues off, which the master judged to be a river. It was conceived there might be some danger in the attempt, yet seeing them resolute, they were permitted to go, being sixteen of them well armed under the conduct of Captain Standish,[1] having such instructions given them as was thought meet.

They set forth the 15th of November; and when they had marched about the space of a mile by the seaside, they espied five or six persons with a dog coming towards them, who were savages; but they fled from them and ran up into the woods, and the English followed them, partly to see if they could speak with them, and partly to discover if there might not be more of them lying in ambush. But the Indians seeing themselves thus followed, they again forsook the woods and ran away on the sands as hard as they could, so as they could not come near them but followed them by the track of their feet sundry miles and saw that they had come the same way. So, night coming on, they made their rendezvous and set out their sentinels, and rested in quiet that night; and the next morning followed their track till they had headed a great creek and so left the sands, and turned another way into the woods. But they still followed them by guess, hoping to find their dwellings; but they soon lost both them and themselves, falling into such thickets as were ready to tear their clothes and armor in pieces; but were most

Chapter 10. 1. Captain Standish: Myles Standish was about thirty-six years old. A soldier in the wars of the Netherlands, he was engaged to go with the colonists and handle their military affairs. Though a "stranger" to the Leyden Pilgrims, Standish, like John Alden the hired cooper, became one of their staunchest supporters. Bradford himself was in the exploring party.

distressed for want of drink. But at length they found water and refreshed themselves, being the first New England water they drunk of, and was now in great thirst as pleasant unto them as wine or beer had been in foretimes.

Afterwards they directed their course to come to the other shore, for they knew it was a neck of land they were to cross over, and so at length got to the seaside and marched to this supposed river, and by the way found a pond of clear, fresh water, and shortly after a good quantity of clear ground where the Indians had formerly set corn, and some of their graves. And proceeding further they saw new stubble where corn had been set the same year; also they found where lately a house had been, where some planks and a great kettle was remaining, and heaps of sand newly paddled with their hands. Which, they digging up, found in them divers fair Indian baskets filled with corn, and some in ears, fair and good, of divers colors, which seemed to them a very goodly sight (having never seen any such before). This was near the place of that supposed river they came to seek, unto which they went and found it to open itself into two arms with a high cliff of sand in the entrance [2] but more like to be creeks of salt water than any fresh, for aught they saw; and that there was good harborage for their shallop, leaving it further to be discovered by their shallop, when she was ready. So, their time limited them being expired, they returned to the ship lest they should be in fear of their safety; and took with them part of the corn and buried up the rest. And so, like the men from Eshcol, carried with them of the fruits of the land and showed their brethren; [3] of which, and their return, they were marvelously glad and their hearts encouraged.

After this, the shallop being got ready, they set out again for the better discovery of this place, and the master of the ship desired to go himself. So there went some thirty men but found it to be no harbor for ships but only for boats. There was also found two of their houses covered with mats, and sundry of their implements in them, but the people were run away and could not be seen. Also there was found more of their corn and of their beans of various colours; the corn and beans they brought away, purposing to give them full satisfaction when they should meet with any of them as, about some six months afterward they did, to their good content.

And here is to be noted a special providence of God, and a great mercy to this poor people, that here they got seed to plant them corn the next year, or else they might have starved, for they had none nor any likelihood to get any till the season had been past, as the sequel did manifest. Neither is it likely they had had this, if the first voyage had not been made, for the ground was now all covered with snow and hard frozen; but the Lord is never wanting unto His in their greatest needs; let His holy name have all the praise.

The month of November being spent in these affairs, and much foul weather falling in, the 6th of December they sent out their shallop again with ten of their principal men [4] and some seamen, upon further discovery, intending to circulate that deep bay of Cape Cod. The weather was very cold and it froze so hard as the spray of the sea lighting on their coats, they were as if they had been glazed. Yet that night betimes they got down into the bottom of the bay, and as they drew near the shore they saw some ten or twelve Indians very busy about something. They landed about a league or two from them, and had much ado to put ashore anywhere—it lay so full of flats. Being landed, it grew late and they made themselves a barricado with logs and boughs as well as they could in the time, and set out their sentinel and betook them to rest, and saw the smoke of the fire the savages made that night. When morning was come they divided their company, some to coast along the shore in the boat, and the rest marched through the woods to see the land, if any fit place might be for their dwelling. They came also to the place where they saw the Indians the night before, and found they had been cutting up a great fish like a grampus, being some two inches thick of fat like a hog, some pieces whereof they had left by the way. And the shallop found two more of these fishes dead on the sands, a thing usual after storms in that place, by reason of the great flats of sand that lie off.

So they ranged up and down all that day, but found no people, nor any place they liked. When the sun grew low, they hasted out of the woods to meet with their shallop, to whom they made signs to come to them into a creek hard by,[5] the which they did at high water; of which they were very glad, for they had not seen each other all that day since the morning. So they made them a bar-

2. This . . . entrance: Pamet River, a salt creek that almost bisects the Cape in Truro. **3. And . . . brethren:** Num. 13:23–26.

4. With . . . men: including Standish, Carver, Bradford, Winslow, and the *Mayflower* pilots, John Clarke and Robert Coppin, the master gunner, and three sailors. **5. a creek hard by:** the mouth of Herring River, Eastham. The beach north of the river mouth, where the action took place, is still called First Encounter Beach.

ricado as usuallv they did every night, with logs, stakes and thick pine boughs, the height of a man, leaving it open to leeward, partly to shelter them from the cold and wind (making their fire in the middle and lying round about it) and partly to defend them from any sudden assaults of the savages, if they should surround them; so being very weary, they betook them to rest. But about midnight they heard a hideous and great cry, and their sentinel called "Arm! arm!" So they bestirred them and stood to their arms and shot off a couple of muskets, and then the noise ceased. They concluded it was a company of wolves or such like wild beasts, for one of the seamen told them he had often heard such a noise in Newfoundland.

So they rested till about five of the clock in the morning; for the tide, and their purpose to go from thence, made them be stirring betimes. So after prayer they prepared for breakfast, and it being day dawning it was thought best to be carrying things down to the boat. But some said it was not best to carry the arms down, others said they would be the readier, for they had lapped them up in their coats from the dew; but some three or four would not carry theirs till they went themselves. Yet as it fell out, the water being not high enough, they laid them down on the bank side and came up to breakfast.

But presently, all on the sudden, they heard a great and strange cry, which they knew to be the same voices they heard in the night, though they varied their notes; and one of their company being abroad came running in and cried, "Men, Indians! Indians!" And withal, their arrows came flying amongst them. Their men ran with all speed to recover their arms, as by the good providence of God they did. In the meantime, of those that were there ready, two muskets were discharged at them, and two more stood ready in the entrance of their rendezvous but were commanded not to shoot till they could take full aim at them. And the other two charged again with all speed, for there were only four had arms there, and defended the barricado, which was first assaulted. The cry of the Indians was dreadful, especially when they saw their men run out of the rendezvous toward the shallop to recover their arms, the Indians wheeling about upon them. But some running out with coats of mail on, and cutlasses in their hands, they soon got their arms and let fly amongst them and quickly stopped their violence. Yet there was a lusty man, and no less valiant, stood behind a tree within half a musket shot, and let his arrows fly at them; he was seen [to] shoot three arrows, which were all avoided. He stood three shots of musket, till one taking full aim at him and made the bark or splinters of the tree fly about his ears, after which he gave an extraordinary shriek and away they went, all of them. They [6] left some to keep the shallop and followed them about a quarter of a mile and shouted once or twice, and shot off two or three pieces, and so returned. This they did that they might conceive that they were not afraid of them or any way discouraged.

Thus it pleased God to vanquish their enemies and give them deliverance; and by His special providence so to dispose that not any one of them were either hurt or hit, though their arrows came close by them and on every side [of] them; and sundry of their coats, which hung up in the barricado, were shot through and through. Afterwards they gave God solemn thanks and praise for their deliverance, and gathered up a bundle of their arrows and sent them into England afterward by the master of the ship, and called that place the First Encounter.

From hence they departed and coasted all along but discerned no place likely for harbor; and therefore hasted to a place that their pilot (one Mr. Coppin who had been in the country before) did assure them was a good harbor, which he had been in, and they might fetch it before night; of which they were glad for it began to be foul weather.

After some hours' sailing it began to snow and rain, and about the middle of the afternoon the wind increased and the sea became very rough, and they broke their rudder, and it was as much as two men could do to steer her with a couple of oars. But their pilot bade them be of good cheer for he saw the harbor; but the storm increasing, and night drawing on, they bore what sail they could to get in, while they could see. But herewith they broke their mast in three pieces and their sail fell overboard in a very grown sea, so as they had like to have been cast away. Yet by God's mercy they recovered themselves, and having the flood with them, struck into the harbor. But when it came to, the pilot was deceived in the place, and said the Lord be merciful unto them for his eyes never saw that place before; and he and the master's mate would have run her ashore in a cove full of breakers before the wind. But a lusty seaman which steered bade those which rowed, if they were men, about with her or else they were all cast away; the which they did with speed. So he bid them be of good cheer and row lustily, for there was a fair sound before them, and he doubted not but they should find one place or other

6. **They:** the English.

where they might ride in safety. And though it was very dark and rained sore, yet in the end they got under the lee of a small island and remained there all that night in safety.[7] But they knew not this to be an island till morning, but were divided in their minds; some would keep the boat for fear they might be amongst the Indians, others were so wet and cold they could not endure but got ashore, and with much ado got fire (all things being so wet); and the rest were glad to come to them, for after midnight the wind shifted to the northwest and it froze hard.

But though this had been a day and night of much trouble and danger unto them, yet God gave them a morning of comfort and refreshing (as usually He doth to His children) for the next day was a fair, sunshining day, and they found themselves to be on an island secure from the Indians, where they might dry their stuff, fix their pieces and rest themselves; and gave God thanks for His mercies in their manifold deliverances. And this being the last day of the week, they prepared there to keep the Sabbath.

On Monday they sounded the harbor and found it fit for shipping, and marched into the land and found divers cornfields and little running brooks, a place (as they supposed) fit for situation.[8] At least it was the best they could find, and the season and their present necessity made them glad to accept of it. So they returned to their ship again with this news to the rest of their people, which did much comfort their hearts.

On the 15th of December they weighed anchor to go to the place they had discovered, and came within two leagues of it, but were fain to bear up again; but the 16th day, the wind came fair, and they arrived safe in this harbor. And afterwards took better view of the place, and resolved where to pitch their dwelling; and the 25th day began to erect the first house for common use to receive them and their goods.

THE SECOND BOOK

THE REST of this history (if God give me life and opportunity) I shall, for brevity's sake, handle by way of annals, noting only the heads of principal things, and passages as they fell in order of time, and may seem to be profitable to know or to make use of. And this may be as the Second Book.[1]

CHAPTER 11

THE REMAINDER OF ANNO 1620

[THE MAYFLOWER COMPACT]

I SHALL a little return back, and begin with a combination made by them before they came ashore; being the first foundation of their government in this place. Occasioned partly by the discontented and mutinous speeches that some of the strangers amongst them had let fall from them in the ship: That when they came ashore they would use their own liberty, for none had power to command them, the patent they had being for Virginia and not for New England, which belonged to another government, with which the Virginia Company had nothing to do.[1] And partly that such an act by them done, this their condition considered, might be as firm as any patent, and in some respects more sure.

The form was as followeth:

In the Name of God, Amen.

We whose names are underwritten, the loyal subjects of our dread Sovereign Lord King James, by the Grace of God of Great Britain, France, and Ireland King, Defender of the Faith, etc.

Having undertaken, for the Glory of God and advancement of the Christian Faith and Honour of our King and Country, a Voyage to plant the First Colony in the Northern Parts of Virginia, do by these presents solemnly and mutually in the presence of God and one of another, Covenant and Combine ourselves together into a Civil Body Politic, for our better ordering and preservation and furtherance of the ends aforesaid; and by virtue hereof to enact, constitute and frame such just and equal Laws, Ordinances, Acts, Constitutions and Offices, from time to time, as shall be

7. **And . . . safety:** The rowers, encouraged by the "lusty seamen" at the steering oar, managed to weather Saquish Head, Plymouth Bay, behind which they found shelter late in the night of Friday, December 8, 1620. 8. **On . . . situation:** Here is the only contemporary authority for the "Landing of the Pilgrims on Plymouth Rock" on Monday, December 11, 1620. It is clear that the landing took place from the shallop, not the *Mayflower*, which was then moored in Provincetown Harbor; that no women were involved, and no Indians were on the receiving end.

The Second Book. 1. The editor has added chapter numbers for the reader's convenience (Bradford started to do so but crossed out "the 11 chapter") and subheadings in square brackets. Bradford's year begins March 25 and he often extends his narrative into the following summer before starting another chapter. **Chapter 11. 1. That . . . do:** The Pilgrims were now in New England, rendering the patent that they brought with them invalid. With mutiny threatened, something had to be done; and the church covenants, or compacts, with which all Puritans were familiar, suggested this famous "Mayflower Compact." It was signed by forty-one adult males, including some but not all the hired men, known as "servants." These, according to the English custom of the time, were young men or boys who received no wages but were treated as members of a family.

thought most meet and convenient for the general good of the Colony, unto which we promise all due submission and obedience. In witness whereof we have hereunder subscribed our names at Cape Cod, the 11th of November, in the year of the reign of our Sovereign Lord King James, of England, France and Ireland the eighteenth, and of Scotland the fifty-fourth. Anno Domini 1620.

After this they chose, or rather confirmed, Mr. John Carver (a man godly and well approved amongst them) their Governor for that year. And after they had provided a place for their goods, or common store (which were long in unlading for want of boats, foulness of the winter weather and sickness of divers) and begun some small cottages for their habitation; as time would admit, they met and consulted of laws and orders, both for their civil and military government as the necessity of their condition did require, still adding thereunto as urgent occasion in several times, and as cases did require.

In these hard and difficult beginnings they found some discontents and murmurings arise amongst some, and mutinous speeches and carriages in other; but they were soon quelled and overcome by the wisdom, patience, and just and equal carriage of things, by the Governor and better part, which clave faithfully together in the main.

[THE STARVING TIME]

But that which was most sad and lamentable was, that in two or three months' time half of their company died, especially in January and February, being the depth of winter, and wanting houses and other comforts; being infected with the scurvy and other diseases which this long voyage and their inaccommodate condition had brought upon them. So as there died some times two or three of a day in the foresaid time, that of 100 and odd persons, scarce fifty remained.[2] And of these, in the time of most distress, there was but six or seven sound persons who to their great commendations, be it spoken, spared no pains night nor day, but with abundance of toil and hazard of their own health, fetched them wood, made them fires, dressed them meat, made their beds, washed their loathsome clothes, clothed and unclothed them. In a word, did all the homely and necessary offices for them which dainty and queasy stomachs cannot endure to hear named; and all this willingly and cheerfully, without any grudging in the least, showing herein their true love unto their friends and brethren; a rare example and worthy to be remembered. Two of these seven were Mr. William Brewster, their reverend Elder, and Myles Standish, their Captain and military commander, unto whom myself and many others were much beholden in our low and sick condition. And yet the Lord so upheld these persons as in this general calamity they were not at all infected either with sickness or lameness. And what I have said of these I may say of many others who died in this general visitation, and others yet living; that whilst they had health, yea, or any strength continuing, they were not wanting to any that had need of them. And I doubt not but their recompense is with the Lord.

But I may not here pass by another remarkable passage not to be forgotten. As this calamity fell among the passengers that were to be left here to plant, and were hasted ashore and made to drink water that the seamen might have the more beer, and one [3] in his sickness desiring but a small can of beer, it was answered that if he were their own father he should have none. The disease began to fall amongst them also, so as almost half of their company died before they went away, and many of their officers and lustiest men, as the boatswain, gunner, three quartermasters, the cook and others. At which the Master was something strucken and sent to the sick ashore and told the Governor he should send for beer for them that had need of it, though he drunk water homeward bound.

But now amongst his company there was far another kind of carriage in this misery than amongst the passengers. For they that before had been boon companions in drinking and jollity in the time of their health and welfare, began now to desert one another in this calamity, saying they would not hazard their lives for them, they should be infected by coming to help them in their cabins; and so, after they came to lie by it, would do little or nothing for them but, "if they died, let them die." But such of the passengers as were yet aboard showed them what mercy they could, which made some of their hearts relent, as the boatswain (and some others) who was a proud young man and would often curse and scoff at the passengers. But when he grew weak, they had compassion on him and helped him; then he confessed he did not deserve it at their hands, he had abused them in word and deed. "Oh!" (saith he) "you, I now see, show your love like Christians indeed one to another, but we let one another lie and die like dogs." Another lay cursing

2. So . . . remained: Of the 102 *Mayflower* passengers who reached Cape Cod, four died before she made Plymouth; and by the summer of 1621 the total deaths numbered fifty.

3. and one: "Which was this author himself" [B].

his wife, saying if it had not been for her he had never come this unlucky voyage, and anon cursing his fellows, saying he had done this and that for some of them; he had spent so much and so much amongst them, and they were now weary of him and did not help him, having need. Another gave his companion all he had, if he died, to help him in his weakness; he went and got a little spice and made him a mess of meat once or twice. And because he died not so soon as he expected, he went amongst his fellows and swore the rogue would cozen[4] him, he would see him choked before he made him any more meat; and yet the poor fellow died before morning.[5]

[INDIAN RELATIONS]

All this while the Indians came skulking about them, and would sometimes show themselves aloof off, but when any approached near them, they would run away; and once they stole away their tools where they had been at work and were gone to dinner. But about the 16th of March, a certain Indian came boldly amongst them and spoke to them in broken English, which they could well understand but marveled at it. At length they understood by discourse with him, that he was not of these parts, but belonged to the eastern parts where some English ships came to fish, with whom he was acquainted and could name sundry of them by their names, amongst whom he had got his language. He became profitable to them in acquainting them with many things concerning the state of the country in the east parts where he lived, which was afterwards profitable unto them; as also of the people here, of their names, number and strength, of their situation and distance from this place, and who was chief amongst them. His name was Samoset.[6] He told them also of another Indian whose name was Squanto, a native of this place, who had been in England and could speak better English than himself.

Being, after some time of entertainment and gifts dismissed, a while after he came again, and five more with him, and they brought again all the tools that were stolen away before, and made way for the coming of their great Sachem, called Massasoit.[7] Who, about four or five days after, came with the chief of his friends and other attendance, with the aforesaid Squanto. With whom, after friendly entertainment and some gifts given him, they made a peace with him (which hath now continued this 24 years) in these terms:

1. That neither he nor any of his should injure or do hurt to any of their people.

2. That if any of his did hurt to any of theirs, he should send the offender, that they might punish him.

3. That if anything were taken away from any of theirs, he should cause it to be restored; and they should do the like to his.

4. If any did unjustly war against him, they would aid him; if any did war against them, he should aid them.

5. He should send to his neighbors confederates to certify them of this, that they might not wrong them, but might be likewise comprised in the conditions of peace.

6. That when their men came to them, they should leave their bows and arrows behind them.

After these things he returned to his place called Sowams, some 40 miles from this place, but Squanto continued with them and was their interpreter and was a special instrument sent of God for their good beyond their expectation. He directed them how to set their corn, where to take fish, and to procure other commodities, and was also their pilot to bring them to unknown places for their profit, and never left them till he died. He was a native of this place, and scarce any left alive besides himself. He was carried away with divers others by one Hunt, a master of a ship,[8] who thought to sell them for slaves in Spain. But he got away for England and was entertained by a merchant in London, and employed to Newfoundland and other parts, and lastly brought hither into these parts by one Mr. Dermer, a gen-

4. **cozen:** cheat. 5. **And . . . morning:** *Mourt's Relation* adds more details. On every fair day the men worked building houses. On January 8, 1621, Master Jones and some of the men caught three seals and a codfish, and Francis Billington, the *Mayflower's* bad boy, sighted from a treetop "a great sea, as he thought," but found it to be a lake; it is still called Billington's Sea. On the 16th a man out fowling saw twelve Indians. After that some of the ordnance from the *Mayflower* was mounted on the hill. On March 3 the wind turned south and "birds sang in the woods most pleasantly." 6. **Samoset:** an Algonkian sagamore of Pemaquid Point, Me., a region much frequented by English fishermen.

7. **Massasoit:** chief of the Wampanoag, had his principal seat in the present town of Barrington, R.I. On this visit he was accompanied by his brother and sixty warriors. *Mourt's Relation* describes the meeting. The Pilgrims "conducted him to an house then in building, where we placed a green rug and three or four cushions. Then instantly came our Governor, with drum and trumpet after him, and some few musketeers. After salutations. our Governor kissing his hand, the King kissed him; and so they sat down. The Governor called for some strong water [brandy] and drunk to him; and he drunk a great draught, that made him sweat all the while after." 8. **He . . . ship:** Squanto, sole survivor of the Pawtuxet tribe. Kidnapped at Plymouth by Captain Thomas Hunt in 1614, he had the strange career that Bradford relates.

tleman employed by Sir Ferdinando Gorges and others for discovery and other designs in these parts. Of whom I shall say something, because it is mentioned in a book set forth Anno 1622 by the President and Council for New England,[9] that he made the peace between the savages of these parts and the English, of which this plantation, as it is intimated, had the benefit; but what a peace it was may appear by what befell him and his men. . . .

. . . These things [10] were partly the reason why they kept aloof and were so long before they came to the English. Another reason as after themselves made known was how about three years before, a French ship was cast away at Cape Cod, but the men got ashore and saved their lives, and much of their victuals and other goods. But after the Indians heard of it, they gathered together from these parts and never left watching and dogging them till they got advantage and killed them all but three or four which they kept, and sent from one sachem to another to make sport with, and used them worse than slaves. Of which the aforesaid Mr. Dermer redeemed two of them; and they conceived this ship [11] was now come to revenge it.

Also, as after was made known, before they came to the English to make friendship, they got all the Powachs [12] of the country, for three days together in a horrid and devilish manner, to curse and execrate them with their conjurations, which assembly and service they held in a dark and dismal swamp.

But to return. The spring now approaching, it pleased God the mortality began to cease amongst them, and the sick and lame recovered apace, which put as [it] were new life into them, though they had borne their sad affliction with much patience and contentedness as I think any people could do. But it was the Lord which upheld them, and had beforehand prepared them; many having long borne the yoke, yea from their youth. Many other smaller matters I omit, sundry of them having been already published in a journal made by one of the company,[13] and some other passages of journeys and relations already published, to which I refer those that are willing to know them more particularly.

And being now come to the 25th of March, I shall begin the year 1621.

9. book . . . New England: page 17 [B]; a reference to *A Briefe Relation of the Discovery and Plantation of New England* (1622). **10. These things:** The bad usage of the local Indians by Hunt, Thomas Dermer, and other shipmasters who had visited this region before 1620. **11. this ship:** the *Mayflower*. **12. Powachs:** Powwows, medicine men. **13. journal . . . company:** *Mourt's Relation* (see Reading Suggestions).

CHAPTER 12

ANNO 1621

THEY now began to dispatch the ship away which brought them over, which lay till about this time, or the beginning of April.[1] The reason on their part why she stayed so long, was the necessity and danger that lay upon them; for it was well towards the end of December before she could land anything here, or they able to receive anything ashore. Afterwards, the 14th of January, the house which they had made for a general rendezvous by casualty fell afire, and some were fain to retire aboard for shelter; then the sickness began to fall sore amongst them, and the weather so bad as they could not make much sooner any dispatch. Again, the Governor and chief of them, seeing so many die and fall down sick daily, thought it no wisdom to send away the ship, their condition considered and the danger they stood in from the Indians, till they could procure some shelter; and therefore thought it better to draw some more charge upon themselves and friends than hazard all. The master and seamen likewise, though before they hasted the passengers ashore to be gone, now many of their men being dead, and of the ablest of them (as is before noted), and of the rest many lay sick and weak; the master durst not put to sea till he saw his men begin to recover, and the heart of winter over.

Afterwards they (as many as were able) began to plant their corn, in which service Squanto stood them in great stead, showing them both the manner how to set it, and after how to dress [2] and tend it. Also he told them, except they got fish and set with it in these old grounds it would come to nothing. And he showed them that in the middle of April they should have store enough come up the brook by which they began to build, and taught them how to take it, and where to get other provisions necessary for them. All which they found true by trial and experience. Some English seed they sowed, as wheat and pease, but it came not to good, either by the badness of the seed or lateness of the season or both, or some other defect.

In this month of April, whilst they were busy about their seed, their Governor (Mr. John Carver) came out of the field very sick, it being a hot day. He complained greatly of his head and lay down, and within a few hours his senses failed, so as he never spake more till he died, which was

Chapter 12. 1. They . . . April: The *Mayflower* sailed April 5 and arrived in England May 6. **2. dress:** cultivate.

within a few days after. Whose death was much lamented and caused great heaviness amongst them, as there was cause. He was buried in the best manner they could, with some volleys of shot by all that bore arms. And his wife, being a weak woman, died within five or six weeks after him.

Shortly after, William Bradford was chosen Governor in his stead, and being not recovered of his illness, in which he had been near the point of death, Isaac Allerton was chosen to be an assistant unto him who, by renewed election every year, continued sundry years together. Which I here note once for all.

May 12 was the first marriage in this place which, according to the laudable custom of the Low Countries, in which they had lived, was thought most requisite to be performed by the magistrate, as being a civil thing, upon which many questions about inheritances do depend, with other things most proper to their cognizance and most consonant to the Scriptures (Ruth 4) and nowhere found in the Gospel to be laid on the ministers as a part of their office.[3] . . . And this practice hath continued amongst not only them, but hath been followed by all the famous churches of Christ in these parts to this time—Anno 1646.

[INDIAN DIPLOMACY]

Having in some sort ordered their business at home, it was thought meet to send some abroad to see their new friend Massasoit, and to bestow upon him some gratuity to bind him the faster unto them; as also that hereby they might view the country and see in what manner he lived, what strength he had about him, and how the ways were to his place, if at any time they should have occasion. So the second of July they sent Mr. Edward Winslow and Mr. Hopkins, with the foresaid Squanto for their guide; who gave him a suit of clothes and a horseman's coat, with some other small things, which were kindly accepted; but they found but short commons and came both weary and hungry home. For the Indians used then to have nothing[4] so much corn as they have since the English have stored them with their hoes, and seen their industry in breaking up new grounds therewith.

They found his place to be forty miles from hence, the soil good and the people not many, being dead and abundantly wasted in the late great mortality, which fell in all these parts about three years before the coming of the English, wherein thousands of them died. They not being able to bury one another, their skulls and bones were found in many places lying still above the ground where their houses and dwellings had been, a very sad spectacle to behold. But they brought word that the Narragansetts lived but on the other side of that great bay, and were a strong people and many in number, living compact together, and had not been at all touched with this wasting plague.

About the latter end of this month, one John Billington lost himself in the woods, and wandered up and down some five days, living on berries and what he could find. At length he light on an Indian plantation twenty miles south of this place, called Manomet; they conveyed him further off, to Nauset among those people that had before set upon the English when they were coasting whilst the ship lay at the Cape, as is before noted. But the Governor caused him to be inquired for among the Indians, and at length Massasoit sent word where he was, and the Governor sent a shallop for him and had him delivered. Those people also came and made their peace; and they gave full satisfaction to those whose corn they had found and taken when they were at Cape Cod.

Thus their peace and acquaintance was pretty well established with the natives about them. And there was another Indian called Hobomok come to live amongst them, a proper lusty man, and a man of account for his valor and parts amongst the Indians, and continued very faithful and constant to the English till he died. He and Squanto being gone upon business among the Indians, at their return (whether it was out of envy to them or malice to the English) there was a sachem called Corbitant, allied to Massasoit but never any good friend to the English to this day, met with them at an Indian town called Namasket, fourteen miles to the west of this place, and began to quarrel with them and offered to stab Hobomok. But being a lusty man, he cleared himself of him and came running away all sweating, and told the Governor what had befallen him. And he feared they had killed Squanto, for they threatened them both; and for no other cause but because they were friends to the English and serviceable unto them. Upon this the Governor taking counsel, it was conceived not fit to be borne; for if they should suffer their friends and messengers thus to be wronged, they should have none would cleave to them, or give them any intelligence, or do them service afterwards, but next they would fall upon themselves. Whereupon it was resolved to

3. **first . . . office:** The marriage was that of Edward Winslow, whose first wife died in the great sickness, to Susannah, widow of William White, another victim of the first winter. Bradford quotes a French history of Holland as authority for the Dutch insisting on civil marriage.

4. **nothing:** in no respect.

send the Captain [5] and fourteen men well armed, and to go and fall upon them in the night. And if they found that Squanto was killed, to cut off Corbitant's head, but not to hurt any but those that had a hand in it.

Hobomok was asked if he would go and be their guide and bring them there before day. He said he would, and bring them to the house where the man lay, and show them which was he. So they set forth the 14th of August, and beset the house round. The Captain, giving charge to let none pass out, entered the house to search for him. But he was gone away that day, so they missed him, but understood that Squanto was alive, and that he had only threatened to kill him and made an offer to stab him but did not. So they withheld and did no more hurt, and the people came trembling and brought them the best provisions they had, after they were acquainted by Hobomok what was only intended. There was three sore wounded which broke out of the house and assayed to pass through the guard. These they brought home with them, and they had their wounds dressed and cured, and sent home. After this they had many gratulations from divers sachems, and much firmer peace; yea, those of the Isles of Capawack sent to make friendship; and this Corbitant himself used the mediation of Massasoit to make his peace, but was shy to come near them a long while after.

After this, the 18th of September they sent out their shallop to the Massachusetts, with ten men and Squanto for their guide and interpreter, to discover and view that Bay and trade with the natives. The which they performed, and found kind entertainment. The people were much afraid of the Tarentines, a people to the eastward which used to come in harvest time and take away their corn, and many times kill their persons. They returned in safety and brought home a good quantity of beaver, and made report of the place, wishing they had been there seated. But it seems the Lord, who assigns to all men the bounds of their habitations,[6] had appointed it for another use. And thus they found the Lord to be with them in all their ways, and to bless their outgoings and incomings, for which let His holy name have the praise forever, to all posterity.

[THANKSGIVING AND THE FORTUNE]

They began now to gather in the small harvest they had, and to fit up their houses and dwellings against winter, being all well recovered in health and strength and had all things in good plenty. For as some were thus employed in affairs abroad, others were exercised in fishing, about cod and bass and other fish, of which they took good store, of which every family had their portion. All the summer there was no want; and now began to come in store of fowl, as winter approached, of which this place did abound when they came first (but afterward decreased by degrees). And besides waterfowl there was great store of wild turkeys, of which they took many, besides venison, etc. Besides they had about a peck a meal a week to a person, or now since harvest, Indian corn to that proportion. Which made many afterwards write so largely of their plenty here to their friends in England, which were not feigned but true reports.[7]

In November, about that time twelvemonth that themselves came, there came in a small ship to them unexpected or looked for,[8] in which came Mr. Cushman (so much spoken of before) and with him thirty-five persons to remain and live in the plantation; which did not a little rejoice them. And they when they came ashore and found all well and saw plenty of victuals in every house, were no less glad; for most of them were lusty young men, and many of them wild enough, who little considered whither or about what they went till they came into the harbor at Cape Cod and there saw nothing but a naked and barren place. They then began to think what should become of them, if the people here were dead or cut off by the Indians. They began to consult (upon some speeches that some of the seamen had cast out) to take the sails from the yard lest the ship should get away and leave them there. But the master, hearing of it, gave them good words and told them if anything but well should have befallen the people here, he hoped he had victuals enough to carry them to Virginia; and whilst he had a bit they should have their part, which gave them good satisfaction.

5. **the Captain:** Myles Standish. 6. **They . . . habitations:** Deut. 32:8. The fur trade, economic salvation of Plymouth, here began, Squanto acting as buyer.

7. **Which . . . reports:** Edward Winslow's letter of December 11, 1621, to a friend in England describing the "First Thanksgiving" is printed in *Mourt's Relation*, pp. 60–65: "Our harvest being gotten in, our Governor sent four men on fowling, that so we might after a more special manner rejoice together, after we had gathered the fruit of our labours. They four in one day killed as much fowl as, with a little help besides, served the Company almost a week. At which time, amongst other recreations, we exercised our arms, many of the Indians coming amongst us, and amongst the rest their greatest king, Massasoit with some 90 men, whom for three days we entertained and feasted. And they went out and killed five deer which they brought to the plantation and bestowed on our Governor and upon the Captain and others." The actual date of this festival is nowhere stated.
8. **In . . . for:** "She came the 9th to the Cape" [B]. This was the *Fortune*, which the Adventurers had despatched in July.

So they were all landed; but there was not so much as biscuit-cake or any other victuals [9] for them, neither had they any bedding but some sorry things they had in their cabins; nor pot, or pan to dress any meat in; nor overmany clothes, for many of them had brushed away [10] their coats and cloaks at Plymouth as they came. But there was sent over some Birching Lane [11] suits in the ship, out of which they were supplied. The plantation was glad of this addition of strength, but could have wished that many of them had been of better condition, and all of them better furnished with provisions. But that could not now be helped.

In this ship Mr. Weston sent a large letter to Mr. Carver, the late Governor, now deceased; full of complaints and expostulations about former passages at Hampton, and the keeping the ship so long in the country, and returning her without lading, etc., which for brevity I omit. The rest is as followeth:

PART OF MR. WESTON'S LETTER

. . . That you sent no lading in the ship [12] is wonderful, and worthily distasted. I know your weakness was the cause of it, and I believe more weakness of judgment than weakness of hands. A quarter of the time you spent in discoursing, arguing and consulting would have done much more; but that is past, etc. If you mean, bona fide, to perform the conditions agreed upon, do us the favor to copy them out fair and subscribe them with the principal of your names. And likewise give us account as particularly as you can, how our moneys were laid out. And then I shall be able to give them [13] some satisfaction, whom I am now forced with good words to shift off. And consider that the life of the business depends on the lading of this ship, which if you do to any good purpose, that I may be freed from the great sums I have disbursed for the former and must do for the latter, I promise you I will never quit the business, though all the other Adventurers should.

We have procured you a charter, the best we could, which is better than your former, and with less limitation.[14] For anything that is else worth writing Mr. Cushman can inform you. I pray write instantly for Mr. Robinson to come to you. And so praying God to bless you with all graces necessary both for this life and that to come, I rest

Your very loving friend,

London, July 6, 1621 THOMAS WESTON

This ship (called the *Fortune*) was speedily dispatched away, being laden with good clapboard [15] as full as she could stow, and two hogsheads of beaver and otter skins which they got with a few trifling commodities brought with them at first, being altogether unprovided for trade. Neither was there any amongst them that ever saw a beaver skin till they came here and were informed by Squanto. The freight was estimated to be worth near £500. Mr. Cushman returned back also with this ship, for so Mr. Weston and the rest had appointed him, for their better information. And he doubted not, nor themselves neither, but they should have a speedy supply, considering also how by Mr. Cushman's persuasion and letters received from Leyden wherein they willed them so to do, they yielded to the aforesaid conditions and subscribed them with their hands.

But it proved otherwise, for Mr. Weston, who had made that large promise in his letter (as is before noted) that if all the rest should fall off, yet he would never quit the business but stick to them, if they yielded to the conditions, and sent some lading in the ship; and of this Mr. Cushman was confident, and confirmed the same from his mouth, and serious protestations to himself before he came. But all proved but wind, for he was the first and only man that forsook them, and that before he so much as heard of the return of this ship, or knew what was done. So vain is the confidence in man; but of this, more in its place.

A letter in answer to his writ to Mr. Carver, was sent to him from the Governor, of which so much as is pertinent to the thing in hand, I shall here insert:

SIR:

Your large letter, written to Mr. Carver and dated the 6th of July 1621, I have received the 10th of November, wherein after the apology made for yourself you lay many heavy imputations upon him and us all. Touching him, he is departed this life and now is at rest in the Lord from all those troubles and encumbrances with which we are yet to strive. He needs not my apology; for his care and pains was so great for the common good, both ours and yours, as that there-

9. **So . . . victuals:** "Nay, they were fain to spare the ship some to carry her home" [B]. 10. **brushed away:** sold at a loss. 11. **Birching Lane:** a street in London where cheap, ready-made clothes were sold. 12. **the ship:** the *Mayflower*. 13. **them:** the Company of Adventurers. 14. **We . . . limitation:** the patent dated June 1, 1621, from the Council for New England, to take the place of the patent from the Virginia Company. It confirmed the Mayflower Compact and promised that within seven years it would be replaced with definite bounds.

15. **clapboard:** split or sawn cedar boards for wainscoting rooms.

with (it is thought) he oppressed himself and shortened his days; of whose loss we cannot sufficiently complain.

At great charges in this adventure I confess you have been, and many losses may sustain; but the loss of his and many other honest and industrious men's lives cannot be valued at any price. Of the one there may be hope of recovery; but the other no recompense can make good. But I will not insist in generals, but come more particularly to the things themselves.

You greatly blame us for keeping the ship [16] so long in the country, and then to send her away empty. She lay five weeks at Cape Cod whilst with many a weary step (after a long journey) and the endurance of many a hard brunt, we sought out in the foul winter a place of habitation. Then, we went in so tedious a time to make provision to shelter us and our goods; about which labor, many of our arms and legs can tell us to this day, we were not negligent. But it pleased God to visit us then with death daily, and with so general a disease that the living were scarce able to bury the dead, and the well not in any measure sufficient to tend the sick. And now to be so greatly blamed for not freighting the ship doth indeed go near us and much discourage us. But you say you know we will pretend weakness. And do you think we had not cause? Yes, you tell us you believe it, but it was more weakness of judgment than of hands. Our weakness herein is great we confess, therefore we will bear this check patiently amongst the rest, till God send us wiser men. But they which told you we spent so much time in discoursing and consulting, etc., their hearts can tell their tongues they lie. They cared not, so they might salve their own sores, how they wounded others. Indeed, it is our calamity that we are, beyond expectation, yoked with some ill-conditioned people who will never do good, but corrupt and abuse others, etc.

The rest of the letter declared how they had subscribed those conditions according to his desire, and sent him the former accounts very particularly; also how the ship [17] was laden and in what condition their affairs stood; that the coming of these people would bring famine upon them unavoidably if they had not supply in time, as Mr. Cushman could more fully inform him and the rest of the Adventurers. Also that seeing he was now satisfied in all his demands, that offenses would be forgotten and he remember his promise, etc.

16. **the ship:** the *Mayflower*. 17. **the ship:** the *Fortune*.

After the departure of this ship, which stayed not above fourteen days, the Governor and his assistant having disposed these late comers into several families as they best could, took an exact account of all their provisions in store and proportioned the same to the number of persons, and found that it would not hold out above six months at half allowance, and hardly that; and they could not well give less this winter time till fish came in again. So they were presently put to half allowance, one as well as another, which began to be hard, but they bore it patiently under hope of supply.

[NARRAGANSETT CHALLENGE]

Soon after this ship's departure, that great people of the Narragansetts, in a braving manner, sent a messenger unto them with a bundle of arrows tied about with a great snakeskin, which their interpreters told them was a threatening and a challenge. Upon which the Governor, with the advice of others, sent them a round answer that if they had rather have war than peace, they might begin when they would; they had done them no wrong, neither did they fear them or should they find them unprovided. And by another messenger sent the snakeskin back with bullets in it. But they would not receive it, but sent it back again.[18]. . .

But this made them the more carefully to look to themselves, so as they agreed to enclose their dwellings with a good strong pale, and make flankers in convenient places with gates to shut, which were every night locked, and a watch kept; and when need required, there was also warding in the daytime. And the company was by the Captain's and the Governor's advice divided into four squadrons, and everyone had their quarter appointed them unto which they were to repair upon any sudden alarm. And if there should be any cry of fire, a company were appointed for a guard, with muskets, whilst others quenched the same, to prevent Indian treachery. This was accomplished very cheerfully, and the town impaled round by the beginning of March, in which every family had a pretty garden plot secured.

And herewith I shall end this year. Only I shall remember one passage more, rather of mirth than of weight. On the day called Christmas Day, the Governor called them out to work as was used. But the most of this new company excused themselves and said it went against their consciences to work on that day. So the Governor told them that

18. **Soon . . . again:** Canonicus, sachem of the Narragansett, sent the challenge; Squanto did the interpreting. This happened in January, 1622.

if they made it matter of conscience, he would spare them till they were better informed; so he led away the rest and left them. But when they came home at noon from their work, he found them in the street at play, openly; some pitching the bar, and some at stool-ball and such like sports. So he went to them and took away their implements and told them that was against his conscience, that they should play and others work. If they made the keeping of it matter of devotion, let them keep their houses; but there should be no gaming or reveling in the streets. Since which time nothing hath been attempted that way, at least openly.[19]

CHAPTER 13

ANNO 1622

[SQUANTO AND MASSASOIT]

AT THE spring of the year they had appointed the Massachusetts to come again and trade with them, and began now to prepare for that voyage about the latter end of March; but upon some rumors heard, Hobomok, their Indian, told them upon some jealousies[1] he had, he feared they were joined with the Narragansetts and might betray them if they were not careful. He intimated also some jealousy of Squanto, by what he gathered from some private whisperings between him and other Indians. But they resolved to proceed, and sent out their shallop with ten of their chief men about the beginning of April, and both Squanto and Hobomok with them, in regard of the jealousy between them.

But they had not been gone long, but an Indian belonging to Squanto's family came running in seeming great fear and told them that many of the Narragansetts, with Corbitant and he thought also Massasoit, were coming against them, and he got away to tell them, not without danger; and being examined by the Governor, he made as if they were at hand, and would still be looking back as if they were at his heels. At which the Governor caused them to take arms and stand on their guard, and supposing the boat to be still within hearing (by reason it was calm) caused a warning piece or two to be shot off, the which they heard and came in. But no Indians appeared; watch was kept all night, but nothing was seen. Hobomok was confident for Massasoit, and thought all was false; yet the Governor caused him to send his wife privately, to see what she could observe (pretending other occasions), but there was nothing found, but all was quiet. After this they proceeded on their voyage to the Massachusetts, and had good trade, and returned in safety, blessed be God.

But by the former passages, and other things of like nature, they began to see that Squanto sought his own ends and played his own game, by putting the Indians in fear and drawing gifts from them to enrich himself, making them believe he could stir up war against whom he would, and make peace for whom he would. Yea, he made them believe they kept the plague buried in the ground, and could send it amongst whom they would, which did much terrify the Indians and made them depend more on him, and seek more to him, than to Massasoit. Which procured him envy and had like to have cost him his life; for after the discovery of his practices, Massasoit sought it both privately and openly, which caused him to stick close to the English, and never durst go from them till he died. They also made good use of the emulation that grew between Hobomok and him, which made them carry more squarely. And the Governor seemed to countenance the one, and the Captain the other, by which they had better intelligence, and made them both more diligent.

Now in a manner their provisions were wholly spent, and they looked hard for supply but none came. But about the latter end of May, they spied a boat at sea (which at first they thought had been some Frenchman), but it proved a shallop which came from a ship[2] which Mr. Weston and another had set out afishing, at a place called Damariscove, forty leagues to the eastward of them, where were that year many more ships come afishing. This boat brought seven passengers and some letters, but no victuals nor any hope of any.[3] . . .

19. **On . . . openly:** All English and Scots Puritans objected to the celebration of Christmas as a pagan revelry, their theory being that December 25 was not the correct date of the Nativity. **stool-ball:** an old country game something like cricket, in which a ball is batted about from stool to stool. **Chapter 13. 1. jealousies:** apprehensions. Winslow states that they "came to this resolution, so it would not now stand with our safety to mew [i.e., shut] up ourselves in our new-enclosed town; partly because our store was almost empty, and therefore must seek out for our daily food, without which we could not long subsist; but especially for that thereby they would see us dismayed and be encouraged to prosecute their malicious purposes with more eagerness. . . ." The frequency with which the Pilgrims had to meet the same sort of problems that twentieth-century statesmen handle on a world basis is no less amazing than their response to every challenge.

2. **a ship:** the *Sparrow.* 3. **This . . . any:** First of many such incidents which made things more difficult for the Pilgrims. Weston or the Adventurers would send over groups of men "on their Particular," without food or supplies to maintain them. The Pilgrims had to feed these people, who refused to take part in common labors but diverted furs from the common stock to

. . . All this was but cold comfort to fill their hungry bellies; and a slender performance of his former late promise; . . . And as they were now failed of supply by him and others in this their greatest need and wants, which was caused by him and the rest who put so great a company of men upon them as the former company were, without any food, and came at such a time, as they must live almost a whole year before any could be raised, . . .

[DESPERATE STRAITS; SUCCOR FROM VIRGINIA]

All these things they pondered and well considered; yet concluded to give his men friendly entertainment, partly in regard of Mr. Weston himself, considering what he had been unto them and done for them, and to some more especially; and partly in compassion to the people, who were now come into a wilderness (as themselves were) and were by the ship [4] to be presently put ashore (for she was to carry other passengers to Virginia, who lay at great charge); and they were altogether unacquainted and knew not what to do. So as they had received his former company of seven men and victualed them as their own hitherto, so they also received these (being about sixty lusty men) and gave housing for themselves and their goods. And many being sick, they had the best means the place could afford them. They stayed here the most part of the summer till the ship came back again from Virginia. Then, by his direction or those whom he set over them, they removed into the Massachusetts Bay, he having got a patent for some part there (by light of their former discovery in letters sent home). Yet they left all their sick folk here till they were settled and housed; but of their victuals they had not any, though they were in great want, nor anything else in recompense of any courtesy done them; neither did they desire it, for they saw they were an unruly company and had no good government over them, and by disorder would soon fall into wants if Mr. Weston came not the sooner amongst them; and therefore, to prevent all after occasion, would have nothing of them.[5]

Amidst these straits, and the desertion of those from whom they had hoped for supply, and when famine began now to pinch them sore, they not knowing what to do, the Lord (who never fails His) presents them with an occasion beyond all expectation; this boat which came from the eastward brought them a letter from a stranger of whose name they had never heard before,[6] being a captain of a ship come there a-fishing. . . .

. . . By this boat the Governor returned a thankful answer, as was meet, and sent a boat of their own with them, which was piloted by them, in which Mr. Winslow was sent to procure what provisions he could of the ships; who was kindly received by the foresaid gentleman, who not only spared what he could, but writ to others to do the like. By which means he got some good quantity and returned in safety. By which the Plantation had a double benefit; first, a present refreshing by the food brought and, secondly, they knew the way to those parts for their benefit hereafter. But what was got, and this small boat brought, being divided among so many, came but to a little; yet by God's blessing it upheld them till harvest. It arose but to a quarter of a pound of bread a day to each person, and the Governor caused it to be daily given them; otherwise, had it been in their own custody, they would have ate it up and then starved; but thus, with what else they could get, they made pretty shift till corn was ripe.

[THE FORT BUILT; VISITORS FROM VIRGINIA]

This summer they built a fort with good timber, both strong and comely, which was of good defense, made with a flat roof and battlements, on which their ordnance were mounted, and where they kept constant watch, especially in time of danger. It served them also for a meeting house and was fitted accordingly for that use. It was a great work for them in this weakness and time of wants, but the danger of the time required it; and both the continual rumors of the fears from the Indians here, especially the Narragansetts, and also the hearing of that great massacre in Virginia, made all hands willing to dispatch the same.[7]

private purses. And they complained bitterly at being fed on what the colony offered—corn, game, shellfish, and drinking water—instead of the Englishman's favorite wheat bread, beef, and beer. **4. the ship:** the *Charity*, another ship of Weston's which arrived at Plymouth about June 30, 1622. **5. All . . . them:** Weston's "sixty lusty men" sponged on the Pilgrims until September, 1622, when they established a settlement in the present town of Weymouth, called by the Indians Wessagusset, of which we shall hear more.

6. stranger . . . before: Captain John Huddleston, master of the *Bona Nova* of two hundred tons, belonging to the Virginia Company. On a fishing voyage to Maine, he gave the Pilgrims news of the Indian massacre in Virginia. **7. This . . . same:** The fort required ten months to complete. "Amongst us, divers seeing the work prove tedious, would have dissuaded from proceeding, flattering themselves with peace and security, and accounting it rather a work of superfluity and vainglory than of simple necessity," says Winslow. This fort, on Burial Hill, was also used for divine worship. The Sunday procession up the hill, every man armed, is well known from the description of a Dutch visitor in 1627.

Now the welcome time of harvest approached, in which all had their hungry bellies filled. But it arose but to a little, in comparison of a full year's supply; partly because they were not yet well acquainted with the manner of Indian corn (and they had no other), also their many other employments; but chiefly their weakness for want of food, to tend it as they should have done. Also, much was stolen both by night and day before it became scarce eatable, and much more afterward. And though many were well whipped, when they were taken for a few ears of corn; yet hunger made others, whom conscience did not restrain, to venture. So as it well appeared that famine must still ensue, the next year also if not some way prevented, or supply should fail, to which they durst not trust. Markets there was none to go to, but only the Indians, and they [8] had no trading commodities.

Behold, now, another providence of God. A ship comes into the harbor, one Captain Jones being chief therein.[9] They were set out by some merchants to discover all the harbors between this and Virginia, and the shoals of Cape Cod, and to trade along the coast where they could. This ship had store of English beads (which were then good trade) and some knives; but would sell none but at dear rates and also a good quantity together. Yet they were glad of the occasion and fain to buy at any rate; they were fain to give after the rate of cento per cento,[10] if not more; and yet pay away coat-beaver at 3*s* per pound, which in a few years after yielded 20*s*. By this means they were fitted again to trade for beaver and other things, and intended to buy what corn they could.

But I will here take liberty to make a little digression. There was in this ship a gentleman, by name Mr. John Pory.[11] He had been secretary in Virginia and was now going home, passenger in this ship. After his departure he writ a letter to the Governor, in the postscript whereof he hath these lines:

To yourself and Mr. Brewster, I must acknowledge myself in many ways indebted; whose books I would have you think very well bestowed on him, who esteemeth them such jewels. My haste would not suffer me to remember, much less to beg, Mr. Ainsworth's elaborate work upon the five books of Moses. . . .

8. they: the Pilgrims. **9. one . . . therein:** Thomas Jones, now commanding the *Discovery*, belonging to the Virginia Company. **10. cento per cento:** one hundred per cent. **11. John Pory:** a learned and much traveled gentleman. His own account of this visit to Plymouth has been published (see Reading Suggestions). He had nothing but praise for the Pilgrims' hospitality and military preparedness.

These things I here insert for honor sake of the author's memory, which this gentleman doth thus ingeniously acknowledge. And himself, after his return, did this poor Plantation much credit amongst those of no mean rank. But to return.

[VOYAGE IN SEARCH OF CORN]

Shortly after harvest Mr. Weston's people who were now seated at the Massachusetts, and by disorder (as it seems) had made havoc of their provisions, began now to perceive that want would come upon them. And hearing that they here had bought trading commodities and intended to trade for corn, they writ to the Governor and desired they might join with them, and they would employ their small ship [12] in the service; and further requested either to lend or sell them so much of their trading commodities as their part might come to, and they would undertake to make payment when Mr. Weston, or their supply, should come. The Governor condescended upon equal terms of agreement, thinking to go about the Cape to the southward with the ship, where some store of corn might be got.

All things being provided, Captain Standish was appointed to go with them, and Squanto for a guide and interpreter, about the latter end of September; but the winds put them in again, and putting out the second time, he fell sick of a fever, so the Governor went himself. But they could not get about the shoals of Cape Cod for flats and breakers, neither could Squanto direct them better nor the master durst venture any further. So they put into Manamoyick Bay and got what they could there. In this place Squanto fell sick of an Indian fever, bleeding much at the nose (which the Indians take for a symptom of death) and within a few days died there; desiring the Governor to pray for him that he might go to the Englishmen's God in Heaven; and bequeathed sundry of his things to sundry of his English friends as remembrances of his love; of whom they had a great loss.

They got in this voyage, in one place and other, about 26 or 28 hogsheads of corn and beans, which was more than the Indians could well spare in these parts, for they set but a little till they got English hoes. And so were fain to return, being sorry they could not get about the Cape, to have been better laden. Afterward the Governor took a few men and went to the inland places to get what he could, and to fetch it home at the spring, which did help them something.

After these things, in February a messenger

12. small ship: the *Swan*, Weston's vessel.

came from John Sanders, who was left chief over Mr. Weston's men in the Bay of Massachusetts, who brought a letter showing the great wants they were fallen into; and he would have borrowed a hogshead of corn of the Indians, but they would lend him none. He desired advice whether he might not take it from them by force to succor his men till he came from the eastward whither he was going. The Governor and rest dissuaded him by all means from it, for it might so exasperate the Indians as might endanger their safety, and all of us might smart for it; for they had already heard how they had so wronged the Indians by stealing their corn, etc. as they were much incensed against them. Yea, so base were some of their own company as they went and told the Indians that their Governor was purposed to come and take their corn by force. The which, with other things, made them enter into a conspiracy against the English, of which more in the next. Herewith I end this year.

CHAPTER 14

ANNO DOM: 1623

[STRAITS OF WESTON'S MEN; INDIAN CONSPIRACY]

IT MAY be thought strange that these people should fall to these extremities in so short a time; being left competently provided when the ship left them, and had an ambition by that moiety of corn that was got by trade, besides much they got of the Indians where they lived, by one means and other. It must needs be their great disorder, for they spent excessively whilst they had or could get it; and, it may be, wasted part away among the Indians; for he that was their chief was taxed by some amongst them for keeping Indian women, how truly I know not. And after they began to come into wants, many sold away their clothes and bed coverings; others (so base were they) became servants to the Indians, and would cut them wood and fetch them water for a capful of corn; others fell to plain stealing, both night and day, from the Indians, of which they grievously complained. In the end, they came to that misery that some starved and died with cold and hunger. One in gathering shellfish was so weak as he stuck fast in the mud and was found dead in the place. At last most of them left their dwellings and scattered up and down in the woods and by the watersides, where they could find ground nuts [1] and clams, here six and there ten.

By which their carriages [2] they became contemned and scorned of the Indians, and they began greatly to insult over them in a most insolent manner. Insomuch that many times as they lay thus scattered abroad and had set on a pot with ground nuts or shellfish, when it was ready the Indians would come and eat it up; and when night came, whereas some of them had a sorry blanket or such like to lap themselves in, the Indians would take it and let the other lie all night in the cold, so as their condition was very lamentable. Yea, in the end they were fain to hang one of their men whom they could not reclaim from stealing, to give the Indians content.

Whilst things went in this manner with them, the Governor and people here had notice that Massasoit their friend was sick and near unto death. They sent to visit him, and withal sent him such comfortable things as gave him great content and was a means of his recovery. Upon which occasion he discovers the conspiracy of these Indians, how they were resolved to cut off Mr. Weston's people for the continual injuries they did them, and would now take opportunity of their weakness to do it, and for that end had conspired with other Indians their neighbors thereabout; and, thinking the people here would revenge their death, they therefore thought to do the like by them, and had solicited him to join with them. He advised them therefore to prevent it, and that speedily, by taking of some of the chief of them before it was too late, for he assured them of the truth hereof.

This did much trouble them, and they took it into serious deliberation, and found upon examination other evidence to give light hereunto, too long here to relate. In the meantime, came one of them from the Massachusetts with a small pack at his back, and though he knew not a foot of the way, yet he got safe hither but lost his way; which was well for him for he was pursued, and so was missed. He told them here, how all things stood amongst them, and that he durst stay no longer; he apprehended they (by what he observed) would be all knocked in the head shortly.

This made them make the more haste, and dispatched a boat away with Captain Standish and some men, who found them in a miserable condition, out of which he rescued them and helped them to some relief, cut off some few of the chief conspirators, and according to his order, offered to bring them all hither if they thought good, and they should fare no worse than themselves, till Mr. Weston or some supply came to them. Or, if

Chapter 14. 1. ground nut: a low plant with edible tubers on its roots, then common in New England.

2. carriages: conduct.

any other course liked them better, he was to do them any helpfulness he could. They thanked him and the rest, but most of them desired he would help them with some corn, and they would go with their small ship to the eastward, where haply they might hear of Mr. Weston or some supply from him, seeing the time of the year was for fishing ships to be in the land; if not, they would work among the fishermen for their living and get their passage into England, if they heard nothing from Mr. Weston in time. So they shipped what they had of any worth, and he[3] got them all the corn he could (scarce leaving to bring him home), and saw them well out of the bay, under sail at sea, and so came home, not taking the worth of a penny of anything that was theirs. . . .

This was the end of these, that some time boasted of their strength (being all able, lusty men) and what they would do and bring to pass in comparison of the people here, who had many women and children and weak ones amongst them. And said at their first arrival, when they saw the wants here, that they would take another course and not to fall into such a condition as this simple people were come to. But a man's way is not in his own power, God can make the weak to stand. Let him also that standeth take heed lest he fall. . . .

[END OF THE "COMMON COURSE AND CONDITION"]

All this while no supply was heard of, neither knew they when they might expect any. So they began to think how they might raise as much corn as they could, and obtain a better crop than they had done, that they might not still thus languish in misery. At length, after much debate of things, the Governor (with the advice of the chiefest amongst them) gave way that they should set corn every man for his own particular, and in that regard trust to themselves; in all other things to go on in the general way as before. And so assigned to every family a parcel of land, according to the proportion of their number, for that end, only for present use (but made no division for inheritance) and ranged all boys and youth under some family. This had very good success, for it made all hands very industrious, so as much more corn was planted than otherwise would have been by any means the Governor or any other could use, and saved him a great deal of trouble, and gave far better content. The women now went willingly into the field, and took their little ones with them to set corn; which before would allege weakness and inability; whom to have compelled would have been thought great tyranny and oppression.

The experience that was had in this common course and condition, tried sundry years and that amongst godly and sober men, may well evince the vanity of that conceit of Plato's and other ancients applauded by some of later times; that the taking away of property and bringing in community into a commonwealth would make them happy and flourishing; as if they were wiser than God.[4] For this community (so far as it was) was found to breed much confusion and discontent and retard much employment that would have been to their benefit and comfort. For the young men, that were most able and fit for labor and service, did repine that they should spend their time and strength to work for other men's wives and children without any recompense. The strong, or man of parts, had no more in division of victuals and clothes than he that was weak and not able to do a quarter the other could; this was thought injustice. The aged and graver men to be ranked and equalized in labors and victuals, clothes, etc., with the meaner and younger sort, thought it some indignity and disrespect unto them. And for men's wives to be commanded to do service for other men, as dressing their meat, washing their clothes, etc., they deemed it a kind of slavery, neither could many husbands well brook it. Upon the point all being to have alike, and all to do alike, they thought themselves in the like condition, and one as good as another; and so, if it did not cut off those relations that God hath set amongst men, yet it did at least much diminish and take off the mutual respects that should be preserved amongst them. And would have been worse if they had been men of another condition. Let none object this is men's corruption, and nothing to the course itself. I answer, seeing all men have this corruption in them, God in His wisdom saw another course fitter for them.

[SHORT RATIONS AND MORE TO FEED]

But to return. After this course settled, and by that their corn was planted, all their victuals were spent and they were only to rest on God's providence; at night not many times knowing where to have a bit of anything the next day. And so, as one well observed, had need to pray that God

3. **he:** Myles Standish.

4. **The . . . God:** Bradford had read the gibes at Plato's *Republic* in Jean Bodin's *De Republica* (1586), a copy of which he owned. "But he [Plato] understood not that by making all things thus common, a Commonweal must needs perish: for nothing can be public, where nothing is private. . . . Albeit that such a Commonweal should also be against the law of God and Nature."

would give them their daily bread, above all people in the world. Yet they bore these wants with great patience and alacrity of spirit; and that for so long a time as for the most part of two years. . . .

. . . They having but one boat left and she not over-well fitted, they were divided into several companies, six or seven to a gang or company, and so went out, with a net they had bought, to take bass [5] and such like fish by course, every company knowing their turn. No sooner was the boat discharged of what she brought, but the next company took her and went out with her. Neither did they return till they had caught something, though it were five or six days before, for they knew there was nothing at home, and to go home empty would be a great discouragement to the rest. Yea, they strive who should do best. If she stayed long or got little, then all went to seeking of shellfish, which at low water they digged out of the sands. And this was their living in the summer time, till God sent them better; and in winter they were helped with ground nuts and fowl. Also in the summer they got now and then a deer, for one or two of the fittest was appointed to range the woods for that end, and what was got that way was divided amongst them. . . .

. . . These passengers,[6] when they saw their low and poor condition ashore, were much daunted and dismayed, and according to their divers humors were diversely affected. Some wished themselves in England again; others fell a-weeping, fancying their own misery in what they saw now in others; other some pitying the distress they saw their friends had been long in, and still were under. In a word, all were full of sadness. Only some of their old friends rejoiced to see them, and that it was no worse with them, for they could not expect it should be better, and now hoped they should enjoy better days together. And truly it was no marvel they should be thus affected, for they were in a very low condition; many were ragged in apparel and some little better than half naked, though some that were well stored before were well enough in this regard. But for food they were all like, save some that had got a few pease of the ship that was last here. The best dish they could present their friends with was a lobster or a piece of fish without bread or anything else but a cup of fair spring water. And the long continuance of this diet, and their labors abroad, had something abated the freshness of their former complexion; but God gave them health and strength in a good measure, and showed them by experience the truth of that word, (Deut. 8:3) "That man liveth not by bread only, but by every word that proceedeth out of the mouth of the Lord doth a man live."

When I think how sadly the Scripture speaks of the famine in Jacob's time, when he said to his sons, "Go buy us food, that we may live and not die," (Gen. 42:2 and 43:1) that the famine was great or heavy in the land. And yet they had such great herds and store of cattle of sundry kinds, which, besides flesh, must needs produce other food as milk, butter and cheese, etc. And yet it was counted a sore affliction. Theirs here must needs be very great, therefore, who not only wanted the staff of bread but all these things, and had no Egypt to go to. But God fed them out of the sea for the most part, so wonderful is His providence over His in all ages; for His mercy endureth for ever.

I may not here omit how, notwithstand all their great pains and industry, and the great hopes of a large crop, the Lord seemed to blast, and take away the same, and to threaten further and more sore famine unto them. By a great drought which continued from the third week in May, till about the middle of July, without any rain and with great heat for the most part, insomuch as the corn began to wither away though it was set with fish, the moisture whereof helped it much. Yet at length it began to languish sore, and some of the drier grounds were parched like withered hay, part whereof was never recovered. Upon which they set apart a solemn day of humiliation, to seek the Lord by humble and fervent prayer, in this great distress. And He was pleased to give them a gracious and speedy answer, both to their own and the Indians' admiration that lived amongst them. For all the morning, and greatest part of the day, it was clear weather and very hot, and not a cloud or any sign of rain to be seen; yet toward evening it began to overcast, and shortly after to rain with such sweet and gentle showers as gave them cause of rejoicing and blessing God. It came without either wind or thunder or any violence, and by degrees in that abundance as that the earth was thoroughly wet and soaked and therewith. Which did so apparently revive and quicken the decayed corn and other fruits, as was wonderful to see, and made the Indians astonished to behold. And afterwards the Lord sent them such seasonable showers, with interchange of fair warm weather as, through His blessing, caused a fruitful and liberal harvest, to their no small comfort and rejoicing. For which mercy,

5. **bass:** The striped bass, now a favorite game fish along the New England coast, was then the favorite food fish. 6. **These passengers:** in the ship *Anne* and pinnace *Little James.* Some were from the Leyden congregation.

in time convenient, they also set apart a day of thanksgiving.

On the other hand, the Old Planters[7] were afraid that their corn, when it was ripe, should be imparted to the newcomers, whose provisions which they brought with them they feared would fall short before the year went about, as indeed it did. They came to the Governor and besought him that as it was before agreed that they should set corn for their Particular (and accordingly they had taken extraordinary pains thereabout) that they might freely enjoy the same; and they would not have a bit of the victuals now come, but wait till harvest for their own and let the newcomers enjoy what they had brought; they would have none of it except they could purchase any of it of them by bargain or exchange. Their request was granted them, for it gave both sides good content; for the newcomers were as much afraid that the hungry Planters would have ate up the provisions brought, and they should have fallen into the like condition.

This ship was in a short time laden with clapboard by the help of many hands. Also they sent in her all the beaver and other furs they had, and Mr. Winslow was sent over with her to inform of all things and procure such things as were thought needful for their present condition. By this time harvest was come, and instead of famine now God gave them plenty, and the face of things was changed, to the rejoicing of the hearts of many, for which they blessed God. And the effect of their particular planting was well seen, for all had, one way and other, pretty well to bring the year about;[8] and some of the abler sort and more industrious had to spare, and sell to others; so as any general want or famine hath not been amongst them since to this day. . . .

. . . The ship[9] stayed here and fitted herself to go for Virginia, having some passengers there to deliver. And with her returned sundry of those from hence which came over on their Particular, some out of discontent and dislike of the country, others by reason of a fire that broke out and burned the houses they lived in, and all their provisions so as they were necessitated thereunto.

This fire was occasioned by some of the seamen that were roistering in a house where it first began, making a great fire in very cold weather, which broke out of the chimney into the thatch and burned down three or four houses and consumed all the goods and provisions in them. The house in which it began was right against their storehouse, which they had much ado to save, in which were their common store and all their provisions, the which, if it had been lost, the plantation had been overthrown. But through God's mercy it was saved by the great diligence of the people and care of the Governor and some about him. Some would have had the goods thrown out; but if they had there would much have been stolen by the rude company that belonged to these two ships, which were almost all ashore. But a trusty company was placed within, as well as those that with wet cloths and other means kept off the fire without, that if necessity required they might have them out with all speed. For they suspected some malicious dealing, if not plain treachery, and whether it was only suspicion or not, God knows; but this is certain, that when the tumult was greatest, there was a voice heard (but from whom it was not known) that bid them look well about them, for all were not friends that were near them. And shortly after, when the vehemency of the fire was over, smoke was seen to arise within a shed that was joined to the end of the storehouse, which was wattled up with boughs, in the withered leaves whereof the fire was kindled; which some running to quench, found a long firebrand of an ell long, lying under the wale[10] on the inside, which could not possibly come there by casualty but must be laid there by some hand, in the judgment of all that saw it. But God kept them from this danger, whatever was intended. . . .

CHAPTER 15

ANNO DOM: 1624

[WRECKS, CATTLE, AND CORN]

THE TIME of new election of their officers for this year being come, and the number of their people increased, and their troubles and occasions therewith, the Governor desired them to change the persons, as well as renew the election, and also to add more Assistants to the Governor for help and counsel and the better carrying on of affairs. Showing that it was necessary it should be so; if it was any honor or benefit, it was fit others should be made partakers of it; if it was a burthen (as doubtless it was) it was but equal others should help to bear it, and that this was the end[1] of annual elections. The issue was, that as before there was but one Assistant, they now chose five, giving

7. **the Old Planters:** those that came in the *Mayflower*.
8. **pretty . . . about:** about enough to last to the year's end.
9. **The ship:** the *Swan*.
10. **wale:** a horizontal member in the basket-like construction of a shed. **Chapter 15. 1. end:** object. The Pilgrims held annual elections because that was the custom in English trading corporations.

the Governor a double voice; and afterwards they increased them to seven, which course hath continued to this day.

They having with some trouble and charge new-masted and rigged their pinnace, in the beginning of March they sent her well victualed to the eastward on fishing. She arrived safely at a place near Damariscove, and was there well harbored, in a place where ships used to ride, there being also some ships already arrived out of England. But shortly after there arose such a violent and extraordinary storm, as the seas broke over such places in the harbor as was never seen before, and drove her against great rocks, which beat such a hole in her bilge as a horse and cart might have gone in, and after drove her into deep water, where she lay sunk. The master was drowned, the rest of the men, all save one, saved their lives with much ado; all her provision, salt, and what else was in her was lost. And here I must leave her to lie till afterward. . . .

. . . Shortly after, Mr. Winslow came over and brought a pretty good supply, and the ship [2] came on fishing—a thing fatal to this plantation. He brought three heifers and a bull, the first beginning of any cattle of that kind in the land, with some clothing and other necessaries, as will further appear; but withal the report of a strong faction amongst the Adventurers against them, and especially against the coming of the rest from Leyden, and with what difficulty this supply was procured, and how, by their strong and long opposition, business was so retarded as not only they were now fallen too late for the fishing season, but the best men were taken up of the fishermen in the West Country; and he was forced to take such a master and company for that employment as he could procure upon the present. . . .

. . . I must speak a word of their planting this year. They having found the benefit of their last year's harvest, and setting corn for their Particular, having thereby with a great deal of patience overcome hunger and famine. Which makes me remember a saying of Seneca's Epistle 123: "That a great part of liberty is a well governed belly, and to be patient in all wants."

They began now highly to prize corn as more precious than silver, and those that had some to spare began to trade one with another for small things, by the quart, pottle [3] and peck, etc.; for money they had none, and if any had, corn was preferred before it. That they might therefore increase their tillage to better advantage, they made suit to the Governor to have some portion of land given them for continuance, and not by yearly lot. For by that means, that which the more industrious had brought into good culture (by much pains) one year, came to leave it the next, and often another might enjoy it; so as the dressing of their lands were the more slighted over, and to less profit. Which being well considered, their request was granted. And to every person was given only one acre of land, to them and theirs, as near the town as might be; and they had no more till the seven years were expired. The reason was that they might be kept close together, both for more safety and defense, and the better improvement of the general employments.

Which condition of theirs did make me often think of what I had read in Pliny [4] of the Romans' first beginnings in Romulus's time. How every man contented himself with two acres of land, and had no more assigned them. And, Chapter 3, "It was thought a great reward, to receive at the hands of the people of Rome a pint of corn." And long after, the greatest present given to a captain that had got a victory over their enemies, was as much ground as they could till in one day. And he was not counted a good, but a dangerous man, that would not content himself with seven acres of land. As also how they did pound their corn in mortars; as these people were forced to do many years before they could get a mill. . . .

[LYFORD AND OLDHAM]

The third eminent person (which the letters before mention) was the minister which they sent over, by name Mr. John Lyford. Of whom and whose doing I must be more large, though I shall abridge things as much as I can. When this man first came ashore, he saluted them with that reverence and humility as is seldom to be seen, and indeed made them ashamed, he so bowed and cringed unto them, and would have kissed their hands if they would have suffered him; yea, he wept and shed many tears, blessing God that had brought him to see their faces, and admiring the things they had done in their wants, etc., as if he had been made all of love and the humblest person in the world. And all the while (if we may judge by his after carriages) he was but like him mentioned in Psalm 10:10, "That croucheth and boweth, that heaps of poor may fall by his might." Or like to that dissembling Ishmael, who, when he had slain Gedaliah, went out weeping and met them that were coming to offer incense in the

2. **the ship:** the *Charity*, arriving in March, 1624. The lost ship was the *Little James*. 3. **pottle:** two quarts.

4. **I had read in Pliny:** Pliny, *Naturalis Historiae* lib. 18, chap. 2 [B].

house of the Lord, saying "Come to Gedaliah" when he meant to slay them.[5]

They gave him the best entertainment they could, in all simplicity, and a larger allowance of food out of the store than any other had; and as the Governor had used, in all weighty affairs, to consult with their Elder, Mr. Brewster, together with his Assistants, so now he called Mr. Lyford also to counsel with them in their weightiest businesses. After some short time he desired to join himself a member to the church here, and was accordingly received. He made a large confession of his faith, and an acknowledgment of his former disorderly walking and his being entangled with many corruptions, which had been a burthen to his conscience, and blessed God for this opportunity of freedom and liberty to enjoy the ordinances of God in purity among His People; with many more such like expressions.

I must here speak a word also of Mr. John Oldham, who was a copartner with him in his after courses. He had been a chief stickler in the former faction among the Particulars, and an intelligencer to those in England. But now, since the coming of this ship and he saw the supply that came, he took occasion to open his mind to some of the chief amongst them here, and confessed he had done them wrong both by word and deed, and writing into England. But he now saw the eminent hand of God to be with them, and His blessing upon them, which made his heart smite him; neither should those in England ever use him as an instrument any longer against them in anything. He also desired former things might be forgotten, and that they would look upon him as one that desired to close with them in all things, with such like expressions. Now whether this was in hypocrisy, or out of some sudden pang of conviction, which I rather think, God only knows. Upon it they show all readiness to embrace his love, and carry towards him in all friendliness, and called him to counsel with them in all chief affairs, as the other, without any distrust at all.

Thus all things seemed to go very comfortably and smoothly on amongst them, at which they did much rejoice. But this lasted not long, for both Oldham and he[6] grew very perverse, and showed a spirit of great malignancy, drawing as many into faction as they could. Were they never so vile or profane, they did nourish and back them in all their doings, so they would but cleave to them and speak against the church here. So as there was nothing but private meetings and whisperings amongst them; they feeding themselves and others with what they should bring to pass in England by the faction of their friends there, which brought others as well as themselves into a fool's paradise. Yet they could not carry so closely but much of both their doings and sayings were discovered; yet outwardly they still set a fair face of things.

At length when the ship[7] was ready to go, it was observed Lyford was long in writing and sent many letters, and could not forbear to communicate to his intimates such things as made them laugh in their sleeves, and thought he had done their errand sufficiently. The Governor and some other of his friends, knowing how things stood in England and what hurt these things might do, took a shallop and went out with the ship a league or two to sea, and called for all Lyford's and Oldham's letters. Mr. William Peirce being master of the ship (and knew well their evil dealing both in England and here) afforded him all the assistance he could. He found above twenty of Lyford's letters, many of them large and full of slanders and false accusations, tending not only to their prejudice, but to their ruin and utter subversion. Most of the letters they let pass, only took copies of them; but some of the most material they sent true copies of them and kept the originals lest he should deny them, and that they might produce his own hand against him. Amongst his letters they found the copies of two letters which he sent enclosed in a letter of his to Mr. John Pemberton, a minister and a great opposite[8] of theirs. These two letters, of which he took the copies, were one of them writ by a gentleman in England to Mr. Brewster here, the other by Mr. Winslow to Mr. Robinson in Holland, at his coming away, as the ship lay at Gravesend. They lying sealed in the great cabin, whilst Mr. Winslow was busy about the affairs of the ship, this sly merchant takes and opens them, takes these copies and seals them up again; and not only sends the copies of them thus to his friend and their adversary, but adds thereto in the margin many scurrilous and flouting annotations.

This ship went out towards evening, and in the night the Governor returned. They were somewhat blank at it, but after some weeks when they heard nothing, they then were as brisk as ever, thinking nothing had been known but all was gone current, and that the Governor went but to dispatch his own letters. The reason why the Governor and rest concealed these things the longer was to let things ripen that they might better discover their intents and see who were their adherents. And the rather because amongst the rest they

5. **Or . . . them:** Jer. 41:6 [B]. 6. **he:** Lyford.

7. **the ship:** the *Charity*. 8. **opposite:** opponent.

found a letter of one of their confederates, in which was written that Mr. Oldham and Mr. Lyford intended a reformation in church and commonwealth, and as soon as the ship was gone, they intended to join together and have the sacraments, etc.

For Oldham, few of his letters were found (for he was so bad a scribe as his hand was scarce legible) yet he was as deep in the mischief as the other. And thinking they were now strong enough, they began to pick quarrels at everything; Oldham being called to watch (according to order) refused to come, fell out with the Captain,[9] called him rascal and beggarly rascal, and resisted him, drew his knife at him; though he offered him no wrong nor gave him no ill terms, but with all fairness required him to do his duty. The Governor, hearing the tumult, sent to quiet it, but he ramped more like a furious beast than a man, and called them all traitors and rebels and other such foul language as I am ashamed to remember. But after he was clapped up a while, he came to himself and with some slight punishment was let go upon his behavior for further censure.

But to cut things short, at length it grew to this issue, that Lyford with his complices, without ever speaking one word either to the Governor, Church, or Elder, withdrew themselves and set up a public meeting apart on the Lord's Day; with sundry such insolent carriages, too long here to relate, beginning now publicly to act what privately they had been long plotting.

It was now thought high time, to prevent further mischief, to call them to account. So the Governor called a court and summoned the whole company to appear. And then charged Lyford and Oldham with such things as they were guilty of; but they were stiff, and stood resolutely upon the denial of most things, and required proof. They first alleged what was writ to them out of England, compared with their doings and practices here, that it was evident they joined in plotting against them, and disturbing their peace, both in respect of their civil and church state, which was most injurious. For both they and all the world knew they came hither to enjoy the liberty of their conscience and the free use of God's Ordinances, and for that end had ventured their lives and passed through so much hardship hitherto; and they and their friends had borne the charge of these beginnings, which was not small. And that Lyford for his part was sent over on this charge, and that both he and his great family was maintained on the same, and also was joined to the church and a member of them. And for him to plot against them, and seek their ruin, was most unjust and perfidious. And for Oldham or any other that came over at their own charge, and were on their Particular: seeing they were received in courtesy by the Plantation, when they came only to seek shelter and protection under their wings, not being able to stand alone. That they (according to the fable) like the hedgehog whom the cony in a stormy day in pity received into her burrow, would not be content to take part with her, but in the end with her sharp pricks forced the poor cony to forsake her own burrow; so these men, with the like injustice, endeavoured to do the same to those that entertained them.

Lyford denied that he had anything to do with them in England, or knew of their courses, and made other things as strange, that he was charged with. Then his letters were produced and some of them read, at which he was struck mute. But Oldham began to rage furiously because they had intercepted and opened his letters, threatening them in very high language, and in a most audacious and mutinous manner stood up and called upon the people, saying, "My masters, where is your hearts? Now show your courage, you have oft complained to me so and so. Now is the time, if you will do anything, I will stand by you," etc. Thinking that everyone (knowing his humor) that had soothed and flattered him, or otherwise in their discontent uttered anything unto him, would now side with him in open rebellion. But he was deceived, for not a man opened his mouth, but all were silent, being strucken with the injustice of the thing.

Then the Governor turned his speech to Mr. Lyford and asked him if he thought they had done evil to open his letters; but he was silent, and would not say a word, well knowing what they might reply. Then the Governor showed the people he did it as a magistrate, and was bound to it by his place, to prevent the mischief and ruin that this conspiracy and plots of theirs, would bring on this poor Colony. But he, besides his evil dealing here, had dealt treacherously with his friends that trusted him, and stole their letters and opened them, and sent copies of them, with disgraceful annotations, to his friends in England. And then the Governor produced them and his other letters under his own hand (which he could not deny) and caused them to be read before all the people, at which all his friends were blank, and had not a word to say. . . .

. . . In conclusion, he was fully convicted, and burst out into tears, and confessed he "feared he was a reprobate, his sins were so great that he

9. **the Captain:** Myles Standish.

doubted God would not pardon them, he was unsavory salt," etc. And that he had "so wronged them as he could never make them amends," confessing all he had writ against them was "false and nought, both for matter and manner." And all this he did with as much fullness as words and tears could express.

After their trial and conviction, the court censured them to be expelled the place; Oldham presently,[10] though his wife and family had liberty to stay all winter or longer till he could make provision to remove them comfortably. Lyford had liberty to stay six months. It was, indeed, with some eye to his release if he carried himself well in the meantime, and that his repentance proved sound. Lyford acknowledged his censure was far less than he deserved. Afterwards, he confessed his sin publicly in the church, with tears more largely than before. I shall here put it down as I find it recorded by some who took it from his own words, as himself uttered them. Acknowledging "That he had done very evil, and slanderously abused them; and, thinking most of the people would take part with him, he thought to carry all by violence and strong hand against them. And that God might justly lay innocent blood to his charge, for he knew not what hurt might have come of these his writings, and blessed God they were stayed." And that he spared not to take knowledge from any, of any evil that was spoken, but shut his eyes and ears against all the good; and if God should make him a vagabond in the earth, as was Cain, it was but just for he had sinned in envy and malice against his brethren as he did. And he confessed three things to be the ground and causes of these his doings: pride, vainglory, and self-love. Amplifying these heads with many other sad expressions, in the particulars of them. So as they began again to conceive good thoughts of him upon this his repentance, and admitted him to teach amongst them as before; and Samuel Fuller (a deacon amongst them) and some other tenderhearted men amongst them, were so taken with his signs of sorrow and repentance, as they professed they would fall upon their knees to have his censure released.

But that which made them all stand amazed in the end, and may do all others that shall come to hear the same (for a rarer precedent can scarce be shown) was, that after a month or two, notwithstanding all his former confessions, convictions, and public acknowledgments, both in the face of the church and whole company, with so many tears and sad censures of himself before God and men, he should go again to justify what he had done. For secretly he writ a second letter to the Adventurers in England, in which he justified all his former writings (save in some things which tended to their damage) . . .

[SALVAGE OF THE *Little James*]

The pinnace that was left sunk and cast away near Damariscove as is before showed; some of the fishing masters said it was a pity so fine a vessel should be lost and sent them word that if they would be at the cost, they would both direct them how to weigh her and let them have their carpenters to mend her. They thanked them and sent men about it, and beaver to defray the charge, without which all had been in vain. So they got coopers to trim I know not how many tun of cask, and being made tight and fastened to her at low water, they buoyed her up; and then with many hands hauled her on shore in a convenient place where she might be wrought upon. And then hired sundry carpenters to work upon her, and other to saw plank, and at last fitted her and got her home. But she cost a great deal of money in thus recovering her, and buying rigging and sails for her, both now and when before she lost her mast; so as she proved a chargeable vessel to the poor Plantation. So they sent her home, and with her Lyford sent his last letter in great secrecy, but the party entrusted with it gave it the Governor.

The winter was passed over in their ordinary affairs, without any special matter worth noting; saving that many who before stood something off from the church, now seeing Lyford's unrighteous dealing and malignity against the church, now tendered themselves to the church and were joined to the same; professing that it was not out of the dislike of anything that they had stood off so long, but a desire to fit themselves better for such a state, and they saw now the Lord called for their help.

And so these troubles produced a quite contrary effect, in sundry here, than these adversaries hoped for. Which was looked at as a great work of God, to draw on men by unlikely means, and that in reason which might rather have set them further off. And thus I shall end this year.

CHAPTER 16

ANNO DOM: 1625

[OLDHAM AND LYFORD DISPOSED OF]

AT THE spring of the year, about the time of their Election Court, Oldham came again amongst

10. presently: immediately.

them; and though it was a part of his censure for his former mutiny and miscarriage not to return without leave first obtained, yet in his daring spirit he presumed without any leave at all; being also set on and hardened by the ill counsel of others. And not only so, but suffered his unruly passion to run beyond the limits of all reason and modesty, insomuch that some strangers which came with him were ashamed of his outrage and rebuked him. But all reproofs were but as oil to the fire, and made the flame of his choler greater. He called them all to nought in this his mad fury, and a hundred rebels, and traitors and I know not what. But in conclusion they committed him till he was tamer, and then appointed a guard of musketeers which he was to pass through, and every one was ordered to give him a thump on the breech with the butt end of his musket, and then was conveyed to the waterside where a boat was ready to carry him away. Then they bid him go and mend his manners. . . .

. . . But that I may here make an end with him, I shall here once for all relate what befell concerning him in the future, and that briefly. After the removal of his family from hence, he fell into some straits (as some others did) and about a year or more afterwards, towards winter, he intended a voyage for Virginia. But it so pleased God that the bark that carried him and many other passengers was in that danger as they despaired of life; so as many of them, as they fell to prayer, so also did they begin to examine their consciences and confess such sins as did most burthen them. And Mr. Oldham did make a free and large confession of the wrongs and hurt he had done to the people and church here, in many particulars, that as he had sought their ruin, so God had now met with him and might destroy him; yea, he feared they all fared the worse for his sake. He prayed God to forgive him and made vows that if the Lord spared his life he would become otherwise, and the like. This I had from some of good credit, yet living in the Bay, and were themselves partners in the same dangers on the shoals of Cape Cod, and heard it from his own mouth.

It pleased God to spare their lives, though they lost their voyage; and in time afterwards, Oldham carried himself fairly towards them, and acknowledged the hand of God to be with them, and seemed to have an honorable respect of them; and so far made his peace with them as he in after time had liberty to go and come and converse with them at his pleasure. He went after this to Virginia and had there a great sickness, but recovered and came back again to his family in the Bay, and there lived till some store of people came over. At length, going a trading in a small vessel among the Indians, and being weakly manned, upon some quarrel they knocked him in the head with a hatchet, so as he fell down dead and never spake word more. Two little boys that were his kinsmen were saved, but had some hurt, and the vessel was strangely recovered from the Indians by another that belonged to the Bay of Massachusetts; and this his death was one ground of the Pequot War which followed.

I am now come to Mr. Lyford. His time being now expired, his censure was to take place. He was so far from answering their hopes by amendment in the time, as he had doubled his evil as is before noted. But first behold the hand of God concerning him, wherein that of the Psalmist is verified: Psalm 7:15: "He hath made a pit and digged it, and is fallen into the pit he made." He thought to bring shame and disgrace upon them, but instead thereof opens his own to all the world. For when he was dealt withal about his second letter, his wife was so affected with his doings as she could no longer conceal her grief and sorrow of mind, but opens the same to one of their deacons and some other of her friends, and after uttered the same to Mr. Peirce upon his arrival. Which was to this purpose, that she feared some great judgment of God would fall upon them and upon her, for her husband's cause, now that they were to remove. She feared to fall into the Indians' hands and to be defiled by them as he had defiled other women; or some such like judgment, as God had threatened David, II Samuel 12:11: "I will raise up evil against thee and will take thy wives and give them," etc. . . .

. . . From hence Lyford went to Nantasket in the Bay of the Massachusetts, with some other of his friends with him, where Oldham also lived. From thence he removed to Naumkeag, since called Salem. But after there came some people over, whether for hope of greater profit or what ends else I know not, he left his friends that followed him and went from thence to Virginia, where he shortly after died; and so I leave him to the Lord. His wife afterwards returned again to this country. And thus much of this matter. . . .

[LOSSES AND CROSSES AT SEA]

They [1] sent over also two ships on fishing on their own account. The one was the pinnace that was cast away the last year here in the country and recovered by the Planters (as was before related); who, after she came home, was attached by one

Chapter 16. 1. They: the Adventurers.

of the Company for his particular debt, and now sent again on this account. The other was a great ship,[2] who was well fitted with an experienced master and company of fishermen, to make a voyage, and to go to Bilbao or Sebastians with her fish. The lesser, her order was to load with cor-fish [3] and to bring the beaver home for England that should be received for the goods sold to the Plantation. This bigger ship made a great voyage of good dry fish, the which if they had gone to a market with, would have yielded them (as such fish was sold that season) £1800, which would have enriched them. But because there was a bruit of war with France, the master neglected (through timorousness) his order, and put first into Plymouth and after into Portsmouth, and so lost their opportunity and came by the loss. The lesser ship had as ill success, though she was as hopeful as the other for the merchants' profit; for they had filled her with goodly cor-fish taken upon the bank, as full as she could swim, and besides she had some 800 pounds' weight of beaver, besides other furs to a good value from the Plantation.

The master seeing so much goods come, put it aboard the bigger ship for more safety. But Mr. Winslow, their factor in this business, was bound in a bond of £500 to send it to London in the small ship; there was some contending between the master and him about it. But he told the master he would follow his order about it; if he would take it out afterward, it should be at his peril; so it went in the small ship and he sent bills of lading in both. The master was so careful, being both so well laden, as they went joyfully home together, for he towed the lesser ship at his stern all the way over bound, and they had such fair weather as he never cast her off till they were shot deep into the English Channel, almost within the sight of Plymouth. And yet there she was unhaply taken by a Turks' man of war and carried into Sallee,[4] where the master and men were made slaves and many of the beaver skins were sold for 4*d* apiece.

Thus was all their hopes dashed and the joyful news they meant to carry home turned to heavy tidings. Some thought this a hand of God for their too great exaction of the poor Plantation, but God's judgments are unsearchable, neither dare I be bold therewith. But, however, it shows us the uncertainty of all human things and what little cause there is of joying in them or trusting to them. . . .

. . . In the meantime it pleased the Lord to give the Plantation peace and health and contented minds, and so to bless their labors as they had corn sufficient, and some to spare to others, with other food; neither ever had they any supply of food but what they first brought with them. After harvest this year, they send out a boat's load of corn 40 or 50 leagues to the eastward, up a river called Kennebec, it being one of those two shallops which their carpenter had built them the year before, for bigger vessel had they none. They had laid a little deck over her midships to keep the corn dry, but the men were fain to stand it out all weathers without shelter, and that time of the year begins to grow tempestuous. But God preserved them and gave them good success, for they brought home 700 pounds of beaver, besides some other furs, having little or nothing else but this corn which themselves had raised out of the earth. This voyage was made by Mr. Winslow and some of the old standers,[5] for seamen they had none.

[Chapter 17, 1626, omitted]

CHAPTER 18

ANNO DOM: 1627

. . . .

[WRECK OF THE *Sparrowhawk* AND RESCUE OF THE VIRGINIANS]

THERE is one thing that fell out in the beginning of the winter before, which I have referred to this place, that I may handle the whole matter together. There was a ship,[1] with many passengers in her and sundry goods bound for Virginia. They had lost themselves at sea, either by the insufficiency of the master, or his illness, for he was sick and lame of the scurvy, so that he could but lie in the cabin door and give direction, and it should seem was badly assisted either with mate or mariners. Or else, the fear and unruliness of the passengers were such as they made them steer a course between the southwest and the northwest, that they might fall with some land, whatsoever it was they cared not. For they had been six weeks at sea and had no water nor beer nor any wood left, but had burnt up all their empty cask; only one of the company had a hogshead of wine or two which was also almost spent, so as they feared

2. a great ship: the *White Angel*. **3. cor-fish:** cod, etc., cured on the shore a few days after being caught; better esteemed than the hard-dried kind, called poor-john. **4. Sallee:** Salé, on the coast of Morocco, near which American troops landed in November, 1942, was formerly a notorious pirate stronghold.

5. old standers: the *Mayflower* passengers. **Chapter 18. 1. a ship:** the *Sparrowhawk*. Her actual timbers, preserved in the sand, now rest in Pilgrim Hall, Plymouth.

they should be starved at sea or consumed with diseases, which made them run this desperate course.

But it pleased God that though they came so near the shoals of Cape Cod or else ran stumbling over them in the night, they knew not how, they came right before a small blind harbor that lies about the middle of Manamoyick Bay to the southward of Cape Cod, with a small gale of wind, and about high water touched upon a bar of sand that lies before it, but had no hurt, the sea being smooth; so they laid out an anchor. But towards the evening the wind sprung up at sea, and was so rough as broke their cable and beat them over the bar into the harbor, where they saved their lives and goods, though much were hurt with salt water. For with beating they had sprung the butt end of a plank or two, and beat out their oakum; but they were soon over and ran on a dry flat within the harbor close by a beach. So at low water they gat out their goods on dry shore and dried those that were wet and saved most of their things without any great loss; neither was the ship much hurt but she might be mended, and made serviceable again.

But though they were not a little glad that they had thus saved their lives, yet when they had a little refreshed themselves and began to think on their condition, not knowing where they were nor what they should do, they began to be strucken with sadness. But shortly after they saw some Indians come to them in canoes, which made them stand upon their guard; but when they heard some of the Indians speak English unto them, they were not a little revived, especially when they heard them demand if they were the Governor of Plymouth's men or friends; and that they would bring them to the English houses or carry their letters.

They feasted these Indians and gave them many gifts. And sent two men and a letter with them to the Governor and did intreat him to send a boat unto them, with some pitch and oakum and spikes, with divers other necessaries for the mending of their ship, which was recoverable. Also, they besought him to help them with some corn and sundry other things they wanted, to enable them to make their voyage to Virginia. And they should be much bound to him and would make satisfaction for anything they had, in any commodities they had aboard. After the Governor was well informed by the messengers of their condition, he caused a boat to be made ready, and such things to be provided as they writ for; and because others were abroad upon trading and such other affairs, as had been fit to send unto them, he went himself, and also carried some trading commodities to buy them corn of the Indians. It was no season of the year to go without the Cape, but understanding where the ship lay, he went into the bottom of the bay on the inside, and put into a creek called Namskaket where it is not much above two mile over land to the bay where they were, where he had the Indians ready to carry over anything to them. Of his arrival they were very glad, and received the things to mend their ship, and other necessaries. Also he bought them as much corn as they would have; and whereas some of their seamen were run away among the Indians, he procured their return to the ship, and so left them well furnished and contented, being very thankful for the courtesies they received. But after the Governor thus left them, he went into some other harbors thereabout and loaded his boat with corn which he traded and so went home.

But he had not been at home many days but he had notice from them that by the violence of a great storm and the bad mooring of their ship after she was mended, she was put ashore, and so beaten and shaken as she was now wholly unfit to go to sea. And so their request was that they might have leave to repair to them and sojourn with them till they could have means to convey themselves to Virginia, and that they might have means to transport their goods, and they would pay for the same, or anything else wherewith the Plantation should relieve them. Considering their distress, their requests were granted and all helpfulness done unto them; their goods transported, and themselves and goods sheltered in their houses as well as they could.

The chief amongst these people was one Mr. Fells and Mr. Sibsey,[2] which had many servants belonging unto them, many of them being Irish. Some others there were that had a servant or two apiece, but the most were servants, and such as were engaged to the former persons who also had the most goods. After they were hither come and something settled, the masters desired some ground to employ their servants upon. Seeing it was like to be the latter end of the year, before they could have passage for Virginia. And they had now the winter before them, they might clear some ground and plant a crop, seeing they had tools and necessaries for the same, to help to bear their charge and keep their servants in employment; and if they had opportunity to depart before the same was ripe, they would sell it on the ground. So they had ground appointed them in

2. **Mr. Sibsey:** Captain John Sibsey, who settled in Norfolk County, Va., and became a burgess and councilor of the colony.

convenient places and Fells and some other of them raised a great deal of corn, which they sold at their departure. This Fells, amongst his other servants, had a maidservant which kept his house and did his household affairs, and by the intimation of some that belonged unto him he was suspected to keep her as his concubine. And both of them were examined thereupon but nothing could be proved, and they stood upon their justification. So with admonition they were dismissed, but afterward it appeared she was with child, so he got a small boat and ran away with her for fear of punishment. First he went to Cape Ann, and after into the Bay of the Massachusetts, but could get no passage, and had like to have been cast away; and was forced to come again and submit himself. But they packed him away and those that belonged unto him by the first opportunity, and dismissed all the rest as soon as could, being many untoward people amongst them; though there were also some that carried themselves very orderly all the time they stayed.

And the Plantation had some benefit by them in selling them corn and other provisions of food, for clothing; for they had of divers kinds, as cloth, perpetuanes [3] and other stuffs, besides hose and shoes and such like commodities as the Planters stood in need of. So they both did good, and received good one from another. And a couple of barks carried them away at the latter end of summer. And sundry of them have acknowledged their thankfulness since from Virginia.

[TRADING WITH THE DUTCH AT BUZZARDS BAY]

That they might better take all convenient opportunity to follow their trade, both to maintain themselves and to disengage them of those great sums which they stood charged with and bound for, they resolved to build a small pinnace at Manomet, a place 20 miles from the Plantation, standing on the sea to the southward of them, unto which by another creek on this side they carry their goods within four or five miles, and then transport them overland to their vessel.[4] And so avoid the compassing of Cape Cod and those dangerous shoals, and so make any voyage to the southward in much shorter time and with far less danger. Also for the safety of their vessel and goods they built a house there and kept some servants, who also planted corn and reared some swine and were always ready to go out with the bark when there was occasion. All which took good effect and turned to their profit.

They now sent with the return of the ships Mr. Allerton again into England, giving him full power under their hands and seal to conclude the former bargain with the Adventurers, and sent their bonds for the payment of the money. Also they sent what beaver they could spare to pay some of their engagements and to defray his charges, for those deep interests still kept them low. Also he had order to procure a patent for a fit trading place in the river of Kennebec. For being emulated both by the planters at Piscataqua and other places to the eastward of them, and also by the fishing ships which used to draw much profit from the Indians of those parts, they threatened to procure a grant and shut them out from thence, especially after they saw them so well furnished with commodities as to carry the trade from them. They thought it but needful to prevent such a thing, at least that they might not be excluded from free trade there, where themselves had first begun and discovered the same and brought it to so good effect.

This year also they had letters and messengers from the Dutch plantation sent unto them from the Governor there written both in Dutch and French. The Dutch had traded in these southern parts divers years before they came, but they began no plantation here till four or five years after their coming and here beginning.[5] . . .

CHAPTER 19

ANNO DOM: 1628

. . . .

[THOMAS MORTON OF MERRYMOUNT]

ABOUT SOME three or four years before this time, there came over one Captain Wollaston (a man of pretty parts) [1] and with him three or four more of some eminency, who brought with them a great many servants, with provisions and other implements for to begin a plantation. And pitched themselves in a place within the Massachusetts which they called after their Captain's name, Mount Wollaston. Amongst whom was one Mr. Morton, who it should seem had some small ad-

3. **perpetuanes:** a coarse woolen cloth. 4. **That . . . vessel:** Manomet was an Indian village in the present town of Bourne, where Manomet has been corrupted to "Monument." Across this narrow neck of Cape Cod the Cape Cod Canal was dug early in the present century. The Indians had used this carrying place since time immemorial; and both Dutch and French had come there to trade. The site of the trading house that the Pilgrims built near Manomet, at a place called by the Indians Aptucxet, has been excavated and the house faithfully restored.

5. **The . . . beginning:** New Amsterdam on Manhattan, founded 1626. **Chapter 19. 1. pretty parts:** fine qualities.

venture of his own or other men's amongst them, but had little respect amongst them, and was slighted by the meanest servants. Having continued there some time, and not finding things to answer their expectations nor profit to arise as they looked for, Captain Wollaston takes a great part of the servants and transports them to Virginia, where he puts them off at good rates, selling their time to other men; and writes back to one Mr. Rasdall (one of his chief partners and accounted their merchant) to bring another part of them to Virginia likewise, intending to put them off there as he had done the rest. And he, with the consent of the said Rasdall, appointed one Fitcher to be his Lieutenant and govern the remains of the Plantation till he or Rasdall returned to take further order thereabout. But this Morton abovesaid, having more craft than honesty (who had been a kind of pettifogger of Furnival's Inn) in the others' absence watches an opportunity (commons being but hard amongst them) and got some strong drink and other junkets and made them a feast; and after they were merry, he began to tell them he would give them good counsel. "You see," saith he, "that many of your fellows are carried to Virginia, and if you stay till this Rasdall return, you will also be carried away and sold for slaves with the rest. Therefore I would advise you to thrust out this Lieutenant Fitcher, and I, having a part in the Plantation, will receive you as my partners and consociates; so may you be free from service, and we will converse, plant, trade, and live together as equals and support and protect one another," or to like effect. This counsel was easily received, so they took opportunity and thrust Lieutenant Fitcher out o' doors, and would suffer him to come no more amongst them, but forced him to seek bread to eat and other relief from his neighbors till he could get passage for England.

After this they fell to great licentiousness and led a dissolute life, pouring out themselves into all profaneness. And Morton became Lord of Misrule, and maintained (as it were) a School of Atheism. And after they had got some goods into their hands, and got much by trading with the Indians, they spent it as vainly in quaffing and drinking, both wine and strong waters in great excess (and, as some reported) £10 worth in a morning. They also set up a maypole, drinking and dancing about it many days together, inviting the Indian women for their consorts, dancing and frisking together like so many fairies, or furies, rather; and worse practices. As if they had anew revived and celebrated the feasts of the Roman goddess Flora, or the beastly practices of the mad Bacchanalians. Morton likewise, to show his poetry composed sundry rhymes and verses, some tending to lasciviousness, and others to the detraction and scandal of some persons, which he affixed to this idle or idol maypole.[2] They changed also the name of their place, and instead of calling it Mount Wollaston they call it Merry-mount, as if this jollity would have lasted ever. But this continued not long, for after Morton was sent for England (as follows to be declared) shortly after came over that worthy gentleman Mr. John Endecott, who brought over a patent under the broad seal for the government of the Massachusetts. Who, visiting those parts, caused that maypole to be cut down and rebuked them for their profaneness and admonished them to look there should be better walking. So they or others now changed the name of their place again and called it Mount Dagon.[3]

Now to maintain this riotous prodigality and profuse excess, Morton, thinking himself lawless, and hearing what gain the French and fishermen made by trading of pieces, powder and shot to the Indians, he as the head of this consortship began the practice of the same in these parts. And first he taught them how to use them, to charge and discharge, and what proportion of powder to give the piece, according to the size or bigness of the same; and what shot to use for fowl and what for deer. And having thus instructed them, he employed some of them to hunt and fowl for him, so as they became far more active in that employment than any of the English, by reason of their swiftness of foot and nimbleness of body, being also quick-sighted and by continual exercise well knowing the haunts of all sorts of game. So as when they saw the execution that a piece would do, and the benefit that might come by the same, they became mad (as it were) after them and would not stick to give any price they could attain

2. **Morton . . . maypole:** Morton gives some of the verses, which he says "puzzled the Separatists most pitifully to expound," in his *New English Canaan*, the book which he wrote to get even with the Pilgrims, pp. 277–81. The best is a drinking song, of which one verse goes:

> Give to the Nymph that's free from scorn
> No Irish stuff nor Scotch over-worn.
> Lasses in beaver coats, come away,
> Ye shall be welcome to us night and day.
> Then drink and be merry, merry, merry boys,
> Let all your delight be in Hymen's joys;
> Io! to Hymen, now the day is come,
> About the merry Maypole take a room.

It perhaps should be explained that the "Irish stuff" and "Scotch" were not whisky but woolens. Neither whisky nor rum had as yet appeared in New England; the only strong liquors known were aqua vitae and brandy.

3. **Mount Dagon:** after the god of the Philistines—Judg. 16:23.

to for them; accounting their bows and arrows but baubles in comparison of them.

And here I may take occasion to bewail the mischief that this wicked man began in these parts, and which since, base covetousness prevailing in men that should know better, has now at length got the upper hand and made this thing common, notwithstanding any laws to the contrary. So as the Indians are full of pieces all over, both fowling pieces, muskets, pistols, etc. They have also their moulds to make shot of all sorts, as musket bullets, pistol bullets, swan and goose shot, and of smaller sorts. Yea, some have seen them have their screw-plates to make screw-pins themselves when they want them, with sundry other implements, wherewith they are ordinarily better fitted and furnished than the English themselves. Yea, it is well known that they will have powder and shot when the English want it nor cannot get it; and that in a time of war or danger, as experience hath manifested, that when lead hath been scarce and men for their own defense would gladly have given a groat a pound, which is dear enough, yet hath it been bought up and sent to other places and sold to such as trade it with the Indians at 12*d* the pound. And it is like they give 3*s* or 4*s* the pound, for they will have it at any rate. And these things have been done in the same times when some of their neighbors and friends are daily killed by the Indians, or are in danger thereof and live but at the Indians' mercy. Yea some, as they have acquainted them with all other things, have told them how gunpowder is made, and all the materials in it, and that they are to be had in their own land; and I am confident, could they attain to make saltpeter, they would teach them to make powder.

O, the horribleness of this villainy! How many both Dutch and English have been lately slain by those Indians thus furnished, and no remedy provided; nay, the evil more increased, and the blood of their brethren sold for gain (as is to be feared) and in what danger all these colonies are in is too well known. O that princes and parliaments would take some timely order to prevent this mischief and at length to suppress it by some exemplary punishment upon some of these gain-thirsty murderers, for they deserve no better title, before their colonies in these parts be overthrown by these barbarous savages thus armed with their own weapons, by these evil instruments and traitors to their neighbors and country! But I have forgot myself and have been too long in this digression; but now to return.

This Morton having thus taught them the use of pieces, he sold them all he could spare, and he and his consorts determined to send for many out of England and had by some of the ships sent for above a score. The which being known, and his neighbors meeting the Indians in the woods armed with guns in this sort, it was a terror unto them who lived stragglingly and were of no strength in any place. And other places (though more remote) saw this mischief would quickly spread over all, if not prevented. Besides, they saw they should keep no servants, for Morton would entertain any, how vile soever, and all the scum of the country or any discontents would flock to him from all places, if this nest was not broken. And they should stand in more fear of their lives and goods in short time from this wicked and debased crew than from the savages themselves.

So sundry of the chief of the straggling plantations, meeting together, agreed by mutual consent to solicit those of Plymouth (who were then of more strength than them all) to join with them to prevent the further growth of this mischief, and suppress Morton and his consorts before they grew to further head and strength. Those that joined in this action, and after contributed to the charge of sending him for England, were from Piscataqua, Naumkeag, Winnisimmet, Wessagusset, Nantasket and other places where any English were seated. Those of Plymouth being thus sought to by their messengers and letters, and weighing both their reasons and the common danger, were willing to afford them their help though themselves had least cause of fear or hurt. So, to be short, they first resolved jointly to write to him, and in a friendly and neighborly way to admonish him to forbear those courses, and sent a messenger with their letters to bring his answer.

But he was so high as he scorned all advice, and asked who had to do with him, he had and would trade pieces with the Indians, in despite of all, with many other scurrilous terms full of disdain. They sent to him a second time and bade him be better advised and more temperate in his terms, for the country could not bear the injury he did. It was against their common safety and against the King's proclamation. He answered in high terms as before; and that the King's proclamation was no law, demanding what penalty was upon it. It was answered, more than he could bear—His Majesty's displeasure. But insolently he persisted and said the King was dead and his displeasure with him, and many the like things. And threatened withal that if any came to molest him, let them look to themselves for he would prepare for them.

Upon which they saw there was no way but to

take him by force; and having so far proceeded, now to give over would make him far more haughty and insolent. So they mutually resolved to proceed, and obtained of the Governor of Plymouth to send Captain Standish and some other aid with him, to take Morton by force. The which accordingly was done. But they found him to stand stiffly in his defense, having made fast his doors, armed his consorts, set divers dishes of powder and bullets ready on the table; and if they had not been over-armed with drink, more hurt might have been done. They summoned him to yield, but he kept his house and they could get nothing but scoffs and scorns from him. But at length, fearing they would do some violence to the house, he and some of his crew came out, but not to yield but to shoot; but they were so steeled with drink as their pieces were too heavy for them. Himself with a carbine, over-charged and almost half filled with powder and shot, as was after found, had thought to have shot Captain Standish; but he stepped to him and put by his piece and took him. Neither was there any hurt done to any of either side, save that one was so drunk that he ran his own nose upon the point of a sword that one held before him, as he entered the house; but he lost but a little of his hot blood.

Morton they brought away to Plymouth, where he was kept till a ship went from the Isle of Shoals for England, with which he was sent to the Council of New England, and letters written to give them information of his course and carriage. And also one was sent at their common charge to inform their Honors more particularly and to prosecute against him. But he fooled of the messenger, after he was gone from hence, and though he went for England yet nothing was done to him, not so much as rebuked, for aught was heard, but returned the next year. Some of the worst of the company were dispersed and some of the more modest kept the house till he should be heard from. But I have been too long about so unworthy a person, and bad a cause. . . .

[AS WE are offering no extracts from the next thirteen chapters of the History, a brief summary is in order.

In 1629 more of the Leyden congregation came over; among them Thomas Willet, who, thirty-five years later, became the first English mayor of New York City. Plymouth Colony obtained its first ordained minister, the Rev. Ralph Smith, who "proved but a poor help to them, . . . being of very weak parts." Isaac Allerton persuaded the colony to set up a trading post near Castine, Maine, which proved to be unprofitable: the French broke it up in 1631. The first Bay Colony Puritans, at Salem, invited Plymouth to help them form a Congregational Church.

The History of the years immediatedly following is filled with accounts of Allerton's rash business enterprises, and contentions with the English partners about paying off the debt. In the meantime the extension of English emigration to Massachusetts Bay offered a new market for Plymouth corn and cattle, and the colony began to expand: northward to Scituate, southward to Cape Cod and Buzzards Bay. A patent from the Council for New England confirmed this territory to the colony, which now set up a representative assembly; but the freemen re-elected Bradford governor every year but five, when he "by importunity gat off." The colony established a trading post on the Connecticut River at the site of Windsor and did fairly well in the fur trade. It took part in the war against the Pequot Indians and, despite several boundary disputes, remained on friendly terms with the newer colonies of Massachusetts Bay, Rhode Island, and Connecticut.]

CHAPTER 33

ANNO DOM: 1643

[THE LIFE AND DEATH OF ELDER BREWSTER]

I AM to begin this year with that which was a matter of great sadness and mourning unto them all. About the 18th of April died their Reverend Elder and my dear and loving friend Mr. William Brewster, a man that had done and suffered much for the Lord Jesus and the gospel's sake, and had borne his part in weal and woe with this poor persecuted church above 36 years in England, Holland and in this wilderness, and done the Lord and them faithful service in his place and calling. And notwithstanding the many troubles and sorrows he passed through, the Lord upheld him to a great age. He was near fourscore years of age (if not all out) when he died. He had this blessing added by the Lord to all the rest; to die in his bed, in peace, amongst the midst of his friends, who mourned and wept over him and ministered what help and comfort they could unto him, and he again recomforted them whilst he could. His sickness was not long, and till the last day thereof he did not wholly keep his bed. His speech continued till somewhat more than half a day, and then failed him, and about nine or ten a clock that evening he died without any pangs at all. A few hours before, he drew his breath short, and some few minutes before his last, he drew his breath long as a man fallen into a sound sleep without any pangs or gaspings, and so sweetly departed this life unto a better. . . .

. . . I should say something of his life, if to say a little were not worse than to be silent. But I cannot wholly forbear, though happily more may be done hereafter. After he had attained some learning, viz. the knowledge of the Latin tongue and some insight in the Greek, and spent some small time at Cambridge, and then being first seasoned with the seeds of grace and virtue, he went to the Court and served that religious and godly gentleman Mr. Davison, divers years when he was Secretary of State. Who found him so discreet and faithful as he trusted him above all other that were about him, and only employed him in all matters of greatest trust and secrecy; he esteemed him rather as a son than a servant, and for his wisdom and godliness, in private he would converse with him more like a friend and familiar than a master. . . .

. . . After they were joined together in communion, he was a special stay and help unto them. They ordinarily met at his house on the Lord's Day (which was a manor of the bishop's) and with great love he entertained them when they came, making provision for them to his great charge, and continued so to do whilst they could stay in England. And when they were to remove out of the country he was one of the first in all adventures,[1] and forwardest in any charge. He was the chief of those that were taken at Boston, and suffered the greatest loss, and of the seven that were kept longest in prison and after bound over to the assizes. After he came into Holland he suffered much hardship after he had spent the most of his means, having a great charge and many children; and in regard of his former breeding and course of life, not so fit for many employments as others were, especially such as were toilsome and laborious. But yet he ever bore his condition with much cheerfulness and contentation.

Towards the latter part of those twelve years spent in Holland, his outward condition was mended, and he lived well and plentifully; for he fell into a way (by reason he had the Latin tongue) to teach many students who had a desire to learn the English tongue, to teach them English; and by his method they quickly attained it with great facility, for he drew rules to learn it by after the Latin manner. And many gentlemen, both Danes and Germans, resorted to him as they had time from other studies, some of them being great men's sons. He also had means to set up printing by the help of some friends, and so had employment enough, and by reason of many books which would not be allowed to be printed in England, they might have had more than they could do.

But now removing into this country all these things were laid aside again, and a new course of living must be framed unto, in which he was no way unwilling to take his part, and to bear his burthen with the rest, living many times without bread or corn many months together, having many times nothing but fish and often wanting that also; and drunk nothing but water for many years together, yea till within five or six years of his death. And yet he lived by the blessing of God in health till very old age. And besides that, he would labor with his hands in the fields as long as he was able. Yet when the church had no other minister, he taught [2] twice every Sabbath, and that both powerfully and profitably, to the great contentment of the hearers and their comfortable edification; yea, many were brought to God by his ministry. He did more in this behalf in a year than many that have their hundreds a year do in all their lives.

For his personal abilities, he was qualified above many. He was wise and discreet and well spoken, having a grave and deliberate utterance, of a very cheerful spirit, very sociable and pleasant amongst his friends, of an humble and modest mind, of a peaceable disposition, undervaluing himself and his own abilities and sometime overvaluing others. Inoffensive and innocent in his life and conversation, which gained him the love of those without as well as those within; yet he would tell them plainly of their faults and evils, both publicly and privately, but in such a manner as usually was well taken from him. He was tenderhearted and compassionate of such as were in misery, but especially of such as had been of good estate and rank and were fallen unto want and poverty either for goodness and religion's sake or by the injury and oppression of others; he would say of all men these deserved to be pitied most. And none did more offend and displease him than such as would haughtily and proudly carry and lift up themselves, being risen from nothing and having little else in them to commend them but a few fine clothes or a little riches more than others.

In teaching, he was very moving and stirring of affections,[3] also very plain and distinct in what he taught; by which means he became the more profitable to the hearers. He had a singular good gift in prayer, both public and private, in ripping up the heart and conscience before God in the humble confession of sin, and begging the mercies of God in Christ for the pardon of the same. He always thought it were better for ministers to pray oftener and divide their prayers, than be long and

Chapter 33. 1. **adventures:** expenditures.

2. **taught:** preached and expounded Scripture. 3. **affections:** emotions.

tedious in the same, except upon solemn and special occasions as in days of humiliation and the like. His reason was that the heart and spirits of all, especially the weak, could hardly continue and stand bent as it were so long towards God as they ought to do in that duty, without flagging and falling off.

For the government of the church, which was most proper to his office, he was careful to preserve good order in the same, and to preserve purity both in the doctrine and communion of the same, and to suppress any error or contention that might begin to rise up amongst them. And accordingly God gave good succcss to his endeavors herein all his days, and he saw the fruit of his labors in that behalf. But I must break off, having only thus touched a few, as it were, heads of things.

I cannot but here take occasion not only to mention but greatly to admire the marvelous providence of God! That notwithstanding the many changes and hardships that these people went through, and the many enemies they had and difficulties they met withal, that so many of them should live to very old age! It was not only this reverend man's condition (for one swallow makes no summer as they say) but many more of them did the like, some dying about and before this time and many still living, who attained to sixty years of age, and to sixty-five, divers to seventy and above, and some near eighty as he did. It must needs be more than ordinary and above natural reason, that so it should be. For it is found in experience that change of air, famine or unwholesome food, much drinking of water, sorrows and troubles, etc., all of them are enemies to health, causes of many diseases, consumers of natural vigor and the bodies of men, and shorteners of life. And yet of all these things they had a large part and suffered deeply in the same. They went from England to Holland, where they found both worse air and diet than that they came from; from thence, enduring a long imprisonment as it were in the ships at sea, into New England: and how it hath been with them here hath already been shown, and what crosses, troubles, fears, wants and sorrows they had been liable unto is easy to conjecture. So as in some sort they may say with the Apostle, II Corinthians 11:26, 27, they were "in journeyings often, in perils of waters, in perils of robbers, in perils of their own nation, in perils among the heathen, in perils in the wilderness, in perils in the sea, in perils among false brethren; in weariness and painfulness, in watching often, in hunger and thirst, in fasting often, in cold and nakedness."

What was it then that upheld them? It was God's visitation that preserved their spirits. Job 10:12: "Thou hast given me life and grace, and thy visitation hath preserved my spirit." He that upheld the Apostle upheld them. "They were persecuted, but not forsaken, cast down, but perished not." "As unknown, and yet known; as dying, and behold we live; as chastened, and yet not killed"; II Corinthians 6:9.

God, it seems, would have all men to behold and observe such mercies and works of His providence as these are towards His people, that they in like cases might be encouraged to depend upon God in their trials, and also to bless His name when they see His goodness towards others. Man lives not by bread only, Deuteronomy 8:3. It is not by good and dainty fare, by peace and rest and heart's ease in enjoying the contentments and good things of this world only that preserves health and prolongs life; God in such examples would have the world see and behold that He can do it without them; and if the world will shut their eyes and take no notice thereof, yet He would have His people to see and consider it. Daniel could be better liking with pulse than others were with the king's dainties. Jacob, though he went from one nation to another people and passed through famine, fears and many afflictions, yet he lived till old age and died sweetly and rested in the Lord, as infinite others of God's servants have done and still shall do, through God's goodness, notwithstanding all the malice of their enemies, "when the branch of the wicked shall be cut off before his day" (Job 15:32) "and the bloody and deceitful men shall not live [out] half their days"; Psalm 55:23. . . .

AUSTIN WARREN
Editor

Edward Taylor

1642(?)–1729

THE POETRY of Edward Taylor—"the Aged, Venerable, Learned and Pious Pastor of the Church of Christ in this Town," as his tombstone in the old Westfield graveyard describes him—was unpublished during his life, and he forbade his heirs to publish it, for reasons upon which one can only—as in the case of Emily Dickinson's refusal to publish during her life—but speculate. It is highly unlikely that Emily thought her work not worth publishing: pride and a sense that her work would not be properly praised seem far more probable deterrents.

As for Taylor, he is an awkward, often inept, metrist compared not only with George Herbert and with Francis Quarles in England but with Anne Bradstreet and Urian Oakes in New England; yet he can scarcely have regarded his work as inferior to Michael Wigglesworth's *Day of Doom* (1662) or to the *Bay Psalm Book* (1640). It seems more likely that he was aware how much in a dated style, style of the "last age"—Elizabethan and Jacobean and Caroline—his poetry was; but it is most likely of all that he felt it some kind of spiritual profanation to publish the 217 Meditations (written from 1682 to 1725) as his private dialogues with God, his private preparation for receiving the body and blood of Christ in the Lord's Supper. This seems the more probable, since his *Christographia*, a series of fourteen sermons written in 1701 to 1703, was apparently intended, and ready, for publication. Yet this must all be speculation. George Herbert, dying, left the decision whether *The Temple* should be published or no to his devout friend, Nicholas Ferrar of Little Gidding; Edward Taylor, so far as one knows, had no analogous kinsman in the spirit to make the decision.

Taylor was born about 1642 in or near Coventry, a clothmaking center of England. His family were pious dissenters from the Church of England. During the period of the Commonwealth, the Presbyterians and Independents, together with many other varieties of Protestants, had "liberty of prophecying"; but, with the restoration of the Stuart monarchy in 1660, their liberty was lost or at least sharply abridged.

The Great Migration of the Puritans to New England took place when, in the 1630's and forties, Archbishop Laud, Primate of the Anglican Church, silenced and otherwise persecuted the Puritans (a name which, at its vaguest, means all pious persons who judged the English Reformation incomplete, but a half-way Reformation—all Protestants to the left of the Established Church, which still retained the "historic episcopate" and a fixed liturgy, the organ in church, sacerdotal vestments, wedding rings, and the baptismal sign of the cross).

In 1662, two thousand Puritan clergy were

ejected from the parishes and university posts —from which, in their turn, the Puritans had earlier ejected the Anglican clergy of Laudian "churchmanship." This ejection undoubtedly was responsible for Taylor's migration to America. The facts of his early life are obscure: he may have had a year or more at Cambridge University; he may have taught school for a time in Leicestershire. He must have been a young candidate for the ministry held in esteem by prominent Puritans of his native region; for when, in 1668, he sailed for Boston, he carried letters of introduction to Increase Mather, minister of the Second Church, and to John Hull, wealthy merchant and mintmaster, whose guest he was till he entered Harvard. At the college, he was given advanced standing and the responsible post of college butler. The judge and diarist Samuel Sewall was for two years his "chamber fellow and bed-fellow" at Harvard; indeed, according to Sewall's statement, it was Taylor's presence which drew him there.

When one knows of Taylor's connections, life-long, with influential men of the Bay Colony like Judge Sewall and the Mathers (both Increase and his son Cotton), when one finds Sewall writing of his old friend, "I have heard him preach a sermon at the Old South [Church of Boston], upon short warning, which, as the phrase in England is, might have been preached at Paul's Cross [in London]," when, too, one has read his sermons oneself, one is puzzled that, after graduation from Harvard, Taylor was not settled as minister, or junior colleague of some pastor, of a church near Boston. Instead—and for whatever motives, and after some indecision and consultation with Increase Mather and President Chauncy —he accepted, in 1671, the invitation to organize a church in the frontier town of Westfield, Massachusetts.

The journey to Westfield, about a hundred miles, was through snow, over rocks and mountains, the route discernible, "a great part of the way,"—as Taylor wrote in his diary, "by marked trees." A year later, a meetinghouse was built, and the town voted to "settle" Taylor as its minister—I say the "town," because the Congregational Church was in New England, till after the American Revolution, the Established Church. Since King Philip's War soon broke out, and the few inhabitants were in constant danger of assault by the Indians, the Westfield Church was not formally organized till 1679.

In those rigorous days, no one was admitted to Church membership without a "Relation," an accounting to the clergy and the church of his personal religious experience—his awakening, conviction of sin, conversion, and grounds for believing himself of God's "elect." Before his installation, at which were clergy from Windsor, Springfield, Hadley, and Northampton—the last of these towns represented by Solomon Stoddard, Jonathan Edwards' grandfather—Taylor himself made out a seventy-page account of his religious experience and profession of doctrinal faith.

It was the custom in old New England, well into the nineteenth century, for a young man to become settled over a parish and to spend his life there—not to view his village pastorate but as an apprenticeship to a city parish. Taylor was pastor of Westfield for almost fifty years, assisted, during his last, and senile, three or four years (as was the custom when a parish had an elderly clergyman) by a younger man, the Rev. Nehemiah Bull, a Yale graduate, his successor in the pastorate.

Taylor followed the usual pattern of New England clergyman: he was the philosopher-king of his village as well as its priest and pastor: in Taylor's case, as often, he was also the town physician. Thus to be both the physical and spiritual doctor of a village Cotton Mather once termed an "Angelical Conjunction." Marriage was almost as obligatory among the Congregational clergy as celibacy among the Catholic—marriage and children; and Taylor was twice married, first to Elizabeth Fitch of Norwich, Connecticut, and second to Ruth Wyllys of Hartford. The first Mrs. Taylor bore eight children, the second, six. Of the six, five were daughters, all of whom married clergymen, one of them the Rev. Isaac Stiles of New Haven, father of the Rev. Ezra Stiles, one of Yale's famous presidents. It is President Stiles who gives the most vivid impression of his grandfather:

> He was very curious in botany and different branches of natural history: —an incessant stu-

dent, but used no spectacles to his death . . . He concerned himself little about domestic secular affairs; attended to the state of the Provinces [of America] and the Parliament; greatly detested King James [the IInd] and Sir Edmund Andros and Randolph; gloried in King William and the Revolution of 1688 . . . He had a steady correspondence with Judge Sewall of Boston, who duly communicated to him all the transactions in the Assembly and occurrences in the Nation. He was a man of small stature, but firm; of quick passions, yet serious and grave; exemplary in piety and for a very sacred observance of the Lord's day.

For a frontier clergyman, Taylor owned a rich library. According to the itemized inventory of his estate, filed in 1729, it numbered something like two hundred books. It contains school and college texts in Hebrew, Greek, Latin, and rhetoric, and metaphysics. There are eight or ten books on medicine—for example, John Woodall's *The Surgeon's Mate* (1617), Caspar Hoffman's *De medicamentis officinalibus* (1649), Johann Schoeder's *Pharmacopoeia medico-chymica* (1644), and two books by Nicholas Culpeper, the *London Dispensatory* (1649) and *Medicaments for the Poor; or Physick for the Common People* (London, 1670). There are, of course, many theological, ecclesiastical, and exegetical works, chiefly by Continental and English Protestant clergymen, but including a folio volume of St. Augustine, a folio of Origen's homilies (possibly the celebrated homilies on the book of Scripture variously called the Song of Solomon, the Song of Songs, or the Canticles). But there are also what Emerson used to call "fact-books,"—Sir Walter Raleigh's *History of the World*, the *Cosmography* of Peter Heylyn (Laud's biographer), four books by the seventeenth-century Englishman, Nathaniel Crouch —among them the *Admirable Curiosities, Rarities, and Wonders in England, Scotland, and Ireland*.

His library, according to family tradition, included also transcribed and handbound copies of books he had borrowed. Some such books have been identified as gifts to Yale University, the Westfield Athenaeum, and the Redwood Athenaeum at Newport, Rhode Island. One of them includes 142 pages, headed "China's Description," copied from the *Memoirs and Observations* of the French Jesuit, Louis le Compte (London edition, 1697); another, a "Metallographia," includes 115 pages drawn chiefly from John Webster's *Metallographia* (London, 1671); another, the "Dispensatory," is a 500-page book of extracts describing the medicinal properties of earths, waters, minerals, stones, herbs, roots, and gums; another, a copybook in English bound in hogskin, translates, from the Latin of Rufinus, the Greek of Origen's masterpiece of philosophical theology, *De Principiis;* another is a 485-page folio combining a Harmony of the Gospels—that is, an attempt to assemble and reconcile the miracles, sayings, parables, and life of Jesus—with a commentary drawing doctrine and practical application from the Gospels.

Taylor, in short, was one of those extraordinary examples who appear among the New England clergy of the first hundred years—a man who, without the intellectual stimulus of a city or a university and the scholars and literary men who abound in either, pursues his "incessant" studies. The popular notion that the Reformers held the English Bible to be self-interpreting and interpretable by any devout soul is, of course, an illusion. The reforming "fathers" knew that the infallible Scriptures were written in Hebrew and Greek and that the minister of the church must "search the Scriptures" in their original tongues, in order that he might properly "open" them to the laymen. Nor did they despise commentaries—many of which, even when by Protestants, were written in Latin.

Certainly the Puritans, by and large, objected to the pulpit citation both of foreign tongues and of authorities (especially, to be sure, the Fathers of the Pre-Reformation Church and those pagan poets and philosophers whom the seventeenth-century Cambridge Platonists and the seventeenth-century Anglican Bishop Jeremy Taylor quote almost more than the Bible); but it was citation or quotation, not consultation, to which they objected. The clearest statements come from *The Art of Prophecying* (1592), a treatise on homiletics, or sermon-making, by William Perkins, one of the most influential of the English Puritans. "*Human* wisdom must be *concealed*, whether it be in the matter of the sermon or in the setting forth of the words, because the preaching of the Word is the testimony of God." But "the minister may,—yea and must—privately use at his liberty the arts, philosophy, and variety of reading whilst he is framing his sermon . . ."

As Edward Johnson wrote of the clergy in his *Wonder-Working Providence of Sion's Saviour* (1654), the history of the New England plantation, "Let not Satan delude you by persuading their learned skill is unnecessary; soon then will the Word of God be slighted as translated [translated and interpreted] by such, and you shall be left bewildered with strange revelations of every fantastic brain,"—those of Anne Hutchinson, for example, or of the Quakers. The Puritan clergy were scholars. The Rev. John Cotton, as his grandson and namesake Cotton Mather notes in the *Magnalia Christi Americana,* was at his books twelve hours a day. In the next century, Jonathan Edwards, Samuel Hopkins, and Timothy Dwight were at their books yet longer. Protestantism—as the Seekers and Quakers showed the seventeenth century, as the lay exhorters and revivalists showed Edwards and the eighteenth century—was always in danger of what conservative Protestantism never intended—the infallible Book infallibly interpreted by the infallible layman reading it in English.

II

TAYLOR'S fourteen sermons entitled *Christographia, or a Discourse concerning Christ's Person, Natures, the Personal Union of the Natures . . . ,* show that elaborate sermon structure was admissible, even in sermons addressed to a village congregation, in the seventeenth century. In his *Country Parson* (1652), George Herbert tells us that "The Parson exceeds not an hour in preaching, because all ages [i.e., historical periods] have thought that a competency." In our age, a half-hour or even twenty minutes is commonly all that will be tolerated, and often the discourse is fittingly called by the preacher what it is—"a few random thoughts loosely strung together." Herbert's remark—that not of a Puritan but of an orthodox Anglican—implies, surely, that the preacher needs exhortation to confine, rather than to expand, himself to an hour.

The Puritans, who exalted the sermon and its disguised equivalent, the afternoon "lecture," were more generous and more admirative of the preacher who turned the hourglass. Certainly they desired something substantial: the text properly "opened" or explained in its context; then a clearly reasoned statement of the "doctrine" drawn from the text, with counterstatements disposing of those who from the same fount drew alien doctrine; lastly, the "uses" or practical applications which follow from the doctrine—uses which include warning to those not yet converted and consolation to those who are.

The seventeenth century, in France, England, and America was a Golden Age of the pulpit. Theories and styles differed; and Roman Catholics, Anglo-Catholics, Puritans, and Cambridge Platonists had, all of them, their modes. One thing was certain, however, that a master in any of these styles could command a large, an eager, and an attentive audience. There was Court preaching (for which James I and his son Charles had such fondness); there was preaching to the Inns of Court (like that delivered by John Donne at Lincoln's Inn and by the Puritan Richard Sibbes at Gray's Inn); there was preaching to the Universities, like that of the great Puritan theologian, William Perkins, and the great Cambridge Platonist, John Smith; there was preaching to the City, like that of Thomas Adams, incumbent of St. Gregory's, London; there was even, at least during the Commonwealth, preaching before the House of Commons, like the magnificent if diffuse discourse delivered in 1647 by Ralph Cudworth, author of *The True Intellectual System of the Universe.*

Almost all hearers wanted a full and rich discourse—a kind of virtuoso performance. Many came, trained in some system of shorthand and equipped with paper, to take down notes. The young were trained to reproduce, at school or at home, at the least the "heads" of the discourse, its thematic structure. Beyond that came the conflict of principles and methods. Was it permissible to quote pagan philosophers and poets, as Jeremy Taylor and the Cambridge Platonists did? To quote the medieval Schoolmen, as did Donne? To tell illustrative anecdotes not drawn from the Bible or to devise metaphors not of Divine authorship? To be witty and poetic as well as instructive and hortatory? To quote in languages other than the vernacular? Should the preacher speak from notes, or write out his sermon and then memorize it? These issues were all debated and variously answered.

In general, the Puritan answer was that the sermon should be a reasoned discourse, the quotations and citations only from the Bible, the style "plain"—that is, straightforward in structure and in vocabulary not beyond that of academically uneducated people.

One may take as example a sermon from Taylor's *Christographia*, preached in 1701. The text is taken from the Epistle to the Hebrews, 10:5, "A body hast Thou prepared me "—that is, God the Father prepared a special human body for the Incarnation of His Son. It is written, for the most part, in good standard turn-of-the-century English, though its language is sometimes learned and its style sometimes eloquent. In this—as well as in the other sermons—Taylor introduces words and phrases from the two languages in which the Scriptures were composed—Hebrew and Greek; but they are preceded or followed, commonly—as was the case even with Court preachers like Lancelot Andrewes and Donne—by some kind of English paraphrase.

In "opening" the text, he moves, as he frequently does, into the history of theology—especially that of the ancient Christological heresies—ancient but repetitiously reappearing. The reality of the Incarnation, of God taking Flesh, is denied, at one extreme, by such as the Ebionites and the Arians, who assert "our Blessed Lord Christ" to have been "a mere man" and, at the other extreme, by such as the Marcionites, who assert "the Body of Christ to be spectral or phantasmical . . . an imaginary body only, and not a real body." Then follows a reference to the revival of these heresies; and here Taylor seems to be referring to the Quakers (whom he elsewhere attacks by name)—perhaps to the Cambridge Platonists also: in our "last age," he says, "though not in express terms," men have despised that Christ who "was born of the Virgin Mary and suffered at Jerusalem under Pontius Pilate, advancing a Christ within as the only one," a concept which at its best never ascends above the Light of Nature (which is human insight as distinguished from revelation) "but for the most part is the descending . . . upon their hearts."

Of the polar heresies—that which reduces Christ to man, and that which simplifies Him into God—Taylor feared more the doctrine, so variously stated in varying ages, which denies the Divine *Humanity*, which refuses to identify Christ, the Eternal Word and Wisdom, with the historic Jesus. For him and his times, the dangerous heresy was that associated with Quakerism, or more generally with mysticism—the doctrine which places the Incarnation in the spiritual quickening of the soul not in an event at once supernatural *and* historic.

And now Taylor comes to what is expressly defined and treated "Doctrine": "That God the Father hath prepared a body, or an human nature, for Christ." And the "doctrine" is expounded by asking questions, stating objections, and offering the "solutions": thus,

> First. When did God prepare a body for this Son? Solution: 1. *Ab Aeterno*. Before the world was. And this preparation was made in the Eternal Purpose and Decree of God. . . . 2. *In tempore*. When His human nature was conceived by the power of the Holy Ghost in the womb of the Virgin. Lu[ke] 1:35. . . . Secondly. How did God prepare Christ's body or human nature? In what proceedings doth it consist? Solution. In answer to this inquiry, I lay down Negatively/Affirmatively. . . .

The "doctrine" is stated at great length in this "scholastic" fashion; but at last, Taylor says, "I come to make some improvement of this truth"; and he begins his application of doctrine by "Use 1. Of Information" and "Use 2. By way of Conviction," that is by way of direct appeal:

> Is it thus that God hath prepared a Body for Christ? Then how doth this convict all such of great sin that set against this Body and put unsuitable reflections upon it. The Jews did vilify it, and Christ in His Person. Heretics put various contempts upon it, some denying it to be an extraordinary body but that it was by common generation as other persons' bodies are . . . It is impossible for the slighter of the body of Christ ever to be saved. I say not that it's a sin that cannot be repented of and pardoned; but I say

that it is impossible for such a one to be saved that goes on in it.

Use 3. By way of exhortation. Is it thus that God hath prepared a body for Christ? Then this doctrine will call us to several duties of great moment to us in the way of our glorifying God.

This Use has five subdivisions—five duties, of which the first is:

To set an high esteem on that individual body of Christ which is united hypostatically to Him . . . It's the glory of all the creation; it is to the astonishment of reason; it's for the exaltment of man; it's the utter confounding of devils; it is the wonderment of saints, the amazement of angels, and the everlasting astonishment of all things to be found within the circumference of the elaborated labyrinth of created nature.

The third, fourth, and final, the fifth, subdivisions of Use 3 exhort believers to the imitation of Christ. "Other examples are to be attended as they are exemplary." But

our imitation of the saints hath its limitations annexed . . . There is something in the examples of the saints not exemplary as to practice. There is some fault to be found in their best copies. But it is not so with Christ: He is all Example, and exemplary, save on only in such things in which he is above exemplariness—as in all His life taken as Mediator.

And Taylor concludes his sermon with this: "Oh, then let this consideration excite us to follow Christ's example; and so we shall be found amongst them for whom the Spirit of God makes this prayer or apostolical benediction (Galatians 6:16): 'As many as walk according to this rule, peace be upon them and mercy.' For indeed they are the Israel of God."

Taylor rarely uses overt *exempla*, anecdotes, or similitudes. In behalf of doctrines advanced, he cites Scripture copiously—often, indeed, cites without quoting. It seems impossible that even a seventeenth-century congregation could have taken in or taken down all the references and doubtful whether, in preaching, Taylor would have cited these lengthy lists. On the supposition which I think correct, that Taylor meant to publish *Christographia*, this set of sermons on the two natures of Christ, the "hypostatic union" of the human and the Divine, one must suppose that these citations were for the reader, to be printed either directly after the doctrine for which they serve as "proof-texts," or, as was often the seventeenth-century habit, in the margins of the page.

The Use of Exhortation introduces something of Taylor the poet in its apostrophic intensity and in its fascinated play with a key word in its shifting grammatical forms—the figure called, by Quintilian, the master Roman rhetorician, *polyptoton* and, by Puttenham (in his *Art of English Poesie*, 1589) "enallage"—brilliantly exemplified in the passage I have just quoted by his "example" and "exemplary" and "exemplariness." But, in general, the sermons represent a high level of "Protestant scholasticism." Until one comes to the "Uses," one is getting something which, in the Middle Ages and in Catholic countries, would be addressed not to the laity but to scholars and clerics. In Scotland and in New England, the laity were not given what St. Paul terms "milk for babes" but a reason for the faith that was in them. Church-going was an education as well as an edification.

III

TAYLOR'S *Christographia* and his *Meditations* show the "two natures" of Taylor. With one exception, fourteen of the Meditations (Nos. 42–56 of the Second Series) correspond in Bible texts and dates of composition with the fourteen sermons. In his manuscript, "Poetical Works," there are contained 217 poems written from 1682 to 1725, which Taylor described as "Preparatory Meditations before my approach to the Lord's Supper, chiefly upon the doctrine preached upon the day of administration." It thus seems that not merely fourteen but most of what President Stiles, annotating his grandfather's manuscript, called his "Sacramental Meditations" stood in a special relation to the sermons Taylor delivered at the generally bimonthly Sacrament Sunday.

Theologically Taylor was, to be sure, a "Covenant" Calvinist, "sound" on predestination and on Christ's presence in the Sacrament as subjective (or *real* only to the receiver). But in his poems, even his theological epic, *God's Determinations*, he dwells by preference on the "elect," not the damned; Christ's presence in the Sacrament is "real" to him even if he does not hold the Catholic view of how it is present; and Christ is for him the loving "dear, dear" Mediator and Saviour.

The aims of religious "meditation," a Catholic system adopted and adapted by Anglicans and made Puritan by Richard Baxter, in the Fourth Part of his *Saints' Everlasting Rest* (1650), are many. But its final aim is to transfer truth from the memory and intellect to the affections and the heart and the will—subjectively and interiorly and emotionally to appropriate that which one holds to be objectively true. Taylor's sermons represent, especially in their subtle and complex statement of "doctrine," a form of intellectual meditation. And then the "uses" are meditation on how the doctrine applies to all men, the unregenerate and the regenerate: the men whom, following the terminology of St. Paul, the Puritans called the "elect" or the "saints," men now called to apply the doctrine to their hearts.

But Taylor's poetic meditations were, like the *Devotions* of Bishop Andrewes, written for himself. They are private prayers, private psalms. I use the word "psalms" designedly; for, though Taylor does not often take his text from the Psalms, he seems to have the analogy of his poems to them frequently in mind. Rather constantly, the poems begin with some equivalent of the Catholic prayer before receiving the Sacrament, *Non sum dignus*—"Lord, I am not worthy "—this, in Taylor's case, is sometimes ambiguous, combining spiritual unworthiness and incapacity properly to speak, to sing, the praise of the ineffable God; and almost all of them end with some reference to music—and praise. Unlike George Herbert, who was a skillful lutanist and violist, Taylor was not a musician as well as a poet; but the metaphors of making music are always with him. Elizabethan viols needed constant retuning; the strings were ever slipping from pitch and needing to be tightened.

To tune one's instrument is one reliable analogy to the process of spiritual meditation. But there are others. In one Meditation, for example, the initial figure is that of a metal implement—a plowshare or a sword or a chisel: some symbol of the imagination which, dull, needs to be sharpened before it can do the Lord's work.

Dull, Dull, my Lord, my fancy dull I finde.
  Hast thou allowd no Grindlestone at all,
Unto thy Zion Fancies dull to grinde
  And make sharp edged when that thou dost call
  Thy Servants up to carry on thy worke
  That from the Same they may not ever shurk?

And this poem, one on Canticles 6:2 ("To the Beds of Spice to feed in the Garden, and to gather Lillies") ends:

If thou, my Lord, thy Spice bed make my Heart
  My Heart shall welcome thee with spic'de joy.
If I'm thy lilly made by Grace's Art
  I shall adorn thy Palace fragrantly.
  And when thou mee thy spic'de bed interst in
  I'le thee on my Shoshannim Spic'de Songs sing.

The Hebrew word "Shoshannim" occurs in the headings to Psalms 45 and 69 and probably is the name of a stringed instrument; but all of these obscure Hebrew rubrics—especially "michtam," which Taylor interprets as the word for psalm or for a Davidic psalm—seem to him proper for use in an ending line.

Writing of preaching in *The Country Parson*, George Herbert advises, as of first importance, "choosing texts of devotion, not controversy,—moving and ravishing texts, whereof the Scriptures are full." Such are Taylor's texts for his *Meditations*—and, by implication, sermons. They come chiefly from the Gospels, especially those of SS. John and Luke, from St. Paul's Epistles, from the Book of Revelation—more frequently than from any other book from the Canticles (as Taylor always refers to the Song of Solomon).

Taylor loves to linger over his texts—even if not to the extent of St. Bernard of Clairvaux (1091–1153), whose eighty-six sermons on the Canticles do not complete the exegesis of the first and second chapters. There are whole clusters of Meditations on "splintered" or "analyzed" texts. For example, I Corinthians 3:21–23, gives the titles for seven Meditations of the First Series: 31, "All things are yours"; 32, "Whether Paul or Apollos or Cephas"; 33, "Life is yours"; 34, "Death is yours"; 35, "Things present"; 36, "Things to come"; 37, "You are Christ's." In the Second Series, there are three Meditations on Canticles 1:2, the first pair on

"Let him kiss me with the kiss of his mouth," and the third on the second half of the verse, "Thy love is better than wine."

In the Second Series of the Meditations there are included two sequences, one on Old Testament prefigurements or Types of Christ: Isaac, Moses, Samson, David, Solomon, and several sequences on texts from the Canticles—notably Meditations 115–53, all on texts, or parts of texts, from the fifth, sixth, and seventh chapters of the Song of Songs.

Taking over the Hebrew Scriptures, the Church Christianized them, finding Messianic prophecies in the Psalms and in the Prophets. The Gospel of St. Matthew abounds in quotations from the Old Testament which are viewed as "proof-texts," as prophecies of the actions and sufferings of Jesus: e.g., "Now all this was done that it might be fulfilled which was spoken by the Prophet" (Matt. 1:22). The Epistle to the Hebrews, indeed, is chiefly an argument from typology—including a whole chapter on Melchisedek (so briefly mentioned in Genesis) as a type of the Christ-fulfilled King and Priest, and three chapters on Christ as fulfilling and consummating the High Priesthood of the Temple and its ceremonial sacrifices. Writing of Abraham's two sons, one by his bondmaid and one by his wife, St. Paul adds—in a phrase which Taylor used as text for one of his Meditations—"Which things are an allegory" (Gal. 4:24).

The Song of Songs had already been allegorized by the Jews; among Christians, Catholic, Anglican, and Protestant, it was interpreted as expressing the love of Christ either for the individual soul or for the Church, or (by natural overlap) for both. Christ is the Bridegroom; the Church, or the devout soul (mystic or "saint") is the bride. The chapter headings of the Song in the King James Version still offer the reader such an exegesis. Thus Chapter 4, a favorite of Taylor's, is headed "Christ setteth forth the graces of the Church. He showeth His love to her. The Church prayeth to be made fit for this presence."

In addition to the canticles of Scripture, Taylor certainly must have been familiar with English poetry and with more of it than the sole volume which appears in the inventory of his library—the poems of Anne Bradstreet. *The Tenth Muse, lately sprung up in America* (1650) inaccurately was linked by her admirers with the French Protestant poet, Du Bartas, whose *La première semaine* ("the week when the world was created") (1578) had been Englished by Joshua Sylvester in 1605, to the youthful admiration of poets as different as Milton and Dryden. Taylor is far nearer to the style of Du Bartas and Sylvester than Mrs. Bradstreet could ever manage, especially in his Preface to *God's Determinations;* for Du Bartas is extravagantly fond of what the eighteenth century found a form of false wit—the analogizing of natural objects to artifacts. Dryden admired, when a boy, Du Bartas' lines about winter which began to "periwig with snow the bald-pate woods." In his "Nativity Ode," the youthful Milton gave a simile to "the sun in bed/ Curtained with cloudy red."[1] And Taylor's Preface abounds in this kind of comparison.

Presumably he also had read Quarles, the best of the strictly "Puritan" English poets, who in his *Emblems, Divine and Moral* (1635), the last three books of which, accompanied by engravings borrowed from a Jesuit's emblem-book, *Pia Desideria,* had many poems on texts from the Psalms and the Song of Solomon. But Quarles is, by comparison with Taylor, a smooth metrist and an unexploring and unexplosive metaphorist. It is barely possible that he read Crashaw's *Steps to the Temple* (1646); but it may be taken as next to certain that he had read George Herbert's *The Temple* (1633). Herbert, the most catholic of the Anglican poets, was well known by Dr. Increase Mather and precious to many Puritans and later Nonconformists. The venerated Richard Baxter ends his once celebrated *Saints' Everlasting Rest* by quoting in its entirety Herbert's long and touching "Home"; and, in the Preface to his own *Poetical Fragments* (1681), he says, with penetration,

> I must confess, after all, that next to the Scripture poems [doubtless referring to the Psalms and the Song of Songs], there are none so savory to me as Mr. George Herbert's . . . Herbert speaks to God like one that really believeth a God, and whose business in the world is most with God.

[1] "On the Morning of Christ's Nativity," ll. 229–30.

Heart-work and Heaven-work make up his books.

IV

RICHARD BAXTER'S judgment of Herbert's poems, which is a religious and psychological, not a literary, judgment, I find substantially true of Edward Taylor's. The faith, the heart-work, and—I would add—the head-work in Herbert and Taylor make their impression on the reader partly by their persistence. Dear as Herbert's poems always were to me, I think now that I used to underrate *The Temple*—as similarly I underrated *The Well-Tempered Clavichord* of J. S. Bach—judging it in terms of some poems which I had halfway learned. With both Bach and Herbert, I continued to discover pieces at least as good as those I knew, till my belief in the total achievement was accompanied by awareness that I would have to know all the "parts" before I could make comparative judgments.

There is an incongruity in mentioning Bach and Edward Taylor in the same sentence; yet such a mention has its uses, since I believe that the inner, the pious, Bach is contained in the Chorale-Preludes, as the Taylor most worth attention is in the Sacramental *Meditations*, which develop, or hover around, a text from Scripture as the Preludes "open" and ornament one of the great German hymn-tunes. But the point I chiefly intend is that Taylor, the least and humblest of the three artists invoked, is really not apprehended—as Thomas Carew or Edgar Allan Poe can be—through a few anthology pieces.

Bach and Herbert are always schooled, accomplished masters. Taylor, like Whitman and Emily Dickinson, is very uneven,—always trying to work out a mode of his own; and it is the persistence of his literary-spiritual endeavor to discover and celebrate "ultimate reality" which is more impressive than any single poem or selection of poems.

In Taylor's poems there are occasional analogies to phrases in George Herbert's. More patent borrowings from Herbert, even titles, appear in the poems of Herbert's professed disciple, Henry Vaughan. But neither can imitate: they are too obstinate or too original. Their temperaments and spirits are too different. Herbert's poems, as he described them just before his death, are "a picture of the many spiritual conflicts that have past betwixt God and my soul before I could subject mine to the will of Jesus my Master."

There is far less sense of struggle in Taylor. To be sure, there are some few poems in which he accuses himself of all manner of *generalized* sin: "My heart's a swamp, brake, thicket vile of sin./ My head's a bog of filth." Or again, "Was ever heart like mine? So bad? black? vile?/ Is any devil blacker? Or can hell produce its match?" Yet, without doubting Taylor's sincerity, these generalized confessions, these claims to be "the chief of sinners" (the phrase is St. Paul's and Bunyan's), these assertions of man's "original" or congenital sin, are far less impressive, in poetry as well as out of poetry, than specificities.

What seem deepest and most real in Taylor are his sense of wonder at Infinite God's bothering with finite man; his constant sense of inadequacy to apprehend, to take in, with heart, the wonders of the Incarnation and Redemption; his sense of incapacity to "render unto the Lord any service." He prods and pricks himself to awake from the lethargy of taking God's Grace to him (whose election he seems never to have doubted); the anxiety at the beginning of many Meditations is just this desire to feel and say to the full extent of finite capacity the might and glory of God.

Taylor clearly belongs to the English metaphysical school—the school of John Donne, George Herbert, Richard Crashaw—ending, in England, with two such diverse poets as John Cleveland and Samuel Butler. This "school" received a shrewd, if wrong-headed, obituary critique from Dr. Samuel Johnson in the critique following his life and judgment of Cowley (*Lives of the English Poets*, 1779–81), but has come into its own again in our time; so that Taylor. the most belated representative of it, did well—for whatever motives—to let his poetry slumber in manuscript till something like twenty years ago.

The "metaphysicals" had no manifestoes like those of Amy Lowell and Ezra Pound. Their "intent" has to be made out by a few catch-phrases used of them by friend and foe—phrases like "strong lines" (i.e., lines more vigorous than smooth or mellifluous), a taste rather than distaste for obscurity (i.e., the requirement that the poem cannot be apprehended at a single reading), and a shrinking from the traditional apparatus of Greek mythology, a psychologism which is concerned with the analysis of states —especially the fluctuating states—of the psyche rather than with telling stories, whether in the manner of Ovid or Spenser. Like Catullus, they said *Odi et amo* (I hate and I love); but their interest was in making out how two such contrary states could concurrently exist in the same man.

They did not object to complexity in poetry because they recognized it in man, and the object of poetry is not to simplify but to clarify man. It can be objected that their love of complexity, of ingenuity, extended beyond this. Taylor liked, and in his youth practised, the more fantastic varieties of verse form—the anagram, the acrostic, the "shaped verses" (of which George Herbert has left specimens in "The Altar" and "Easter Wings")—poems in which the visual form on the page corresponds to, or prefigures, the subject of the poem.

But these are eccentricities at least as harmless as women's needlework. The chief, stylistic trait of the metaphysical poets rests on ground more solid—that of what was called the "conceit" (Italian, *concetto*). One takes an analogy, or what might now be called a metaphor, preferably not the most obvious or honorific, and sees what can be done with it: "My love is like a red, red rose" is not a conceit (though what follows "like" has no strict relation to a woman's pink cheeks); but, to choose an example I once proposed, "Why (or how) is love like an electric lawn mower?" is.

What seem to us the good and poetically successful conceits of the seventeenth-century poets vary much in the degree of remoteness of the objects compared and in the method by which they are worked out. The most serious theory one could advance for them is that they bear testimony to "coexistence"—or, less politically and more metaphysically—that all objects, persons, and essences we, with varying degrees of knowledge, know, constitute, belong to, one world.

The universe is not a student's notebook in which his courses are segregated: science, philosophy, theology, art, cookery, love of animals, love of other persons all have somehow to be integrated; and a real believer believes they are, and such is the deepest theory behind metaphysical poetry.

Some of our twentieth-century critics were fond of praising Donne's poems because the poem was coterminous with the conceit, i.e., that the *idea* and the *image* developed side by side on terms of parity; and they cited Donne's compass figure in "A Valediction Forbidding Mourning." But one has only to examine the poem to see that it is not so coterminous. In practise, as one can see from Taylor's poems, there is latitude.

"Huswifery" is a poem in which a single conceit—that of weaving—is never relinquished. This kind of conceit makes a particularly neat and thrifty effect. But then there are poems like "My Father, and Your Father" (in which the image of treegrafting dominates, but is dropped for a stanza), and "The Reflection" (dominated by the Rose figure, but not dominated to the exclusion of by-images). I find myself unable to make a dogmatic judgment that "Huswifery" is more "metaphysical" or better poetry than those poems which operate more freely "by association." Perhaps the central thing to say is that in good metaphysical poetry like Taylor's one has a thinking, an intellection, never dissociated from images, a thinking *through* images.

And now something—not too alien—must be said about Taylor's diction. There are periods when poetry means a retrenched vocabulary as well as restriction of themes. In the metaphysical period which formed Taylor's taste, as in the poetry of our own century, there was nothing a poet couldn't turn to account. To use the present tense of both that period and our own: there is nothing a poet can't use. Poetry is not the dropping out of a man's learning or of the shrewd, close scrutiny of things before his senses, or of speculation, or of passion. Its glory lies in juxtaposition, metamorphosis, in proportion and intensity of inclusion. Even "heaven-work" is not—at least for the poet—negation but transformation. The seventeenth century delighted in St. Augustine's saying that "the holy Magdalen changed her object only not her passion." "Heaven-work" is the dedication of all we know, have, and are to God, and the sight of all things as types, shadows, emblems, and (in St. Bonaventure's word) "footprints"—*vestigia*.

As a preacher, Taylor reasoned closely and used "correct" language. But the "Meditations" come out of his religious experience, the beginnings of which antedated—probably long antedated—his transplantation to America. The head goes on learning and revising and correcting; the heart keeps its felt continuity with things past. So the metaphors of his poetry are from things seen and heard in his childhood and youth—the clothmaking of Coventry, the games and sports which the "ungodly" used to indulge themselves in—barley-break, bowling, cudgells, kit-kat, cards, and dice.

And because Taylor was writing for himself, and not to communicate to others, he was free to write in a language as linguistically and literarily exciting and engaging as it is difficult—composed of obsolete and obsolescent words, the provincial words of his native county, coinages, words shifted from one part of speech to another, and words whose *roots* bear all manner of grammatical fruits—now adjective, now verb, now noun—and perhaps two nouns from one. The flexibility of his language is rather Elizabethan than Stuart. The only Colonial "American" writer I can think of who uses as unlicensed and ranging a vocabulary as Taylor in the "Meditations" is Nathaniel Ward in *The Simple Cobbler of Agawam* (1647). But Ward is most savory when he is most satirical; and Taylor's intent is other—to see God in and through everything; to celebrate the neighborliness of God as well as His transcendent Kingship.

I have just put *American* in quotes. It is a nice theoretical question whether Taylor is an "American" poet. To the extent that he is, it is his isolation which makes him so. In his elegies, even that on the death of his first wife, whom he undoubtedly loved, he is systematic, prosaic, commonplace. Such elegies were doubtless passed to others in manuscript if not in broadside; and they had to communicate in something equivalent to the famous "plain style" of Puritan preachers. The "Meditations" were—like Emily Dickinson's poems, which, in their defects and virtues, they most resemble—the fruits of his aloneness.

NOTE

Taylor's poems are reprinted from *The Poems of Edward Taylor*, ed. by Donald E. Stanford (New Haven: Yale University Press, 1960). The letter of proposal to Elizabeth Fitch reproduces the text as given by William B. Goodman, "Edward Taylor Writes His Love," *New England Quarterly*, XXVII (December, 1954), 510–15. The passages from Taylor's sermon quoted in the introductory essay are drawn from Norman Grabo's edition of *Christographia*, a transcript of which Mr. Grabo generously gave me in advance of its publication by the Yale University Press.

READING SUGGESTIONS

EDITIONS

THOMAS H. JOHNSON, editor, *The Poetical Works of Edward Taylor* (1939). This, the first edition of Taylor, prints his long poem, *Gods Determinations*—a kind of "morality play," as Johnson calls it—in its entirety; gives but selections from the "Sacramental Meditations."

DONALD E. STANFORD, editor, *The Poems of Edward Taylor* (1960). This gives, in their entirety, both *Gods Determinations* and the some 200 *Preparatory* [i.e. Sacramental] *Meditations*, together with a selection from the "miscellaneous poems." The glossary—and Taylor, with his archaisms, dialect words, and coinages much needs one—is far fuller than Johnson's.

GENERAL WORKS

HAROLD JANTZ, *The First Century of New England Verse* (1944).

PERRY MILLER, *The New England Mind: The Seventeenth Century* (1939; 1954).

W. FRASER MITCHELL, *English Pulpit Oratory from Andrewes to Tillotson* (1932).

SAMUEL ELIOT MORISON, *The Intellectual Life of Colonial New England* (1956; originally published, 1935, as *The Puritan Pronaos*).

CRITICAL ESSAYS

HERBERT BLAU, "Heaven's Sugar Cake: Theology and Imagery in the Poetry of Edward Taylor," *New England Quarterly*, XXVI (1953).

WALLACE C. BROWN, "Edward Taylor: An American Metaphysical," *American Literature*, XVI (1944).

LOUIS L. MARTZ, Foreword to *The Poems of Taylor, ed. by* Donald E. Stanford (1960). An introductory essay on Taylor, one of the best.

ROY HARVEY PEARCE, "Edward Taylor: The Poet as Puritan," *New England Quarterly*, XXIII (1950).

AUSTIN WARREN, "Edward Taylor," *Rage for Order* (1948). An essay first published in the *Kenyon Review* (1941).

[ANON.], "Poet in a Wilderness," London *Times Literary Supplement* (February 3, 1961). An essay occasioned by Stanford's edition.

[A LETTER METAPHYSICALLY AND SUCCESSFULLY PROPOSING MARRIAGE]

◇

THIS love letter is, as Donald Stanford rightly describes it (*The Poems of Edward Taylor*, p. xlii), "a curious mixture of Christian piety and the tender passion expressed in elaborate artificial rhetoric." The mixture of love for one's wife and love for God is more simply to be seen in Governor John Winthrop's letters to his wife. But the admixture, in some degree, seems proper to all sincere Puritans. How can a marriage be deeply happy which is not founded on shared religious convictions, shared love of two of His creatures for their Creator? And conjugal love must always be "subordinate to God's Glory."

◇

This for my friend and only beloved
MISS ELIZABETH FITCH,
at her father's house in Norwich,
WESTFIELD, MASS., 8th day of the 7th month, 1674.

MY DOVE:—I send you not my Heart, for that I hope is sent to heaven long since, and unless it has awfully deceived me it hath not taken up its lodgings in any one's bosom on this side of the Royal City of the Great King; but yet the most of it that is allowed to be layed out upon any creature doth solely and singly fall to your share. So much my Post Pigeon presents you with here in these lines. Look not (I entreat you) on it as one of Love's hyperboles. If I borrow the beams of Some Sparkling Metaphor to illustrate my Respects unto thyself by, for you having made my breast the cabinet of your affections (as I yours mine), I know not how to offer a fitter Comparison to Set out my Love by, than to Compare it to a Golden Ball of pure Fire rolling up and down my Breast, from which there flies now and then a Spark like a Glorious Beam from the Body of the Flaming Sun. But I, alas! striving to Catch these sparks into a Love Letter unto yourself, and to gild it with them as with a Sun Beam, find that by what time they have fallen through my pen upon my Paper, they have lost their shine, and fall only like a little Smoke thereon instead of gilding them. Therefore, finding myself so much deceived, I am ready to begrudge my Instruments, for thou my love within my breast is So large that my heart is not sufficient to Contain it, yet they can make it no more room to ride into, than to Squeeze it up betwixt my black Ink and White Paper. But know that it is the coarsest part thereof 'tis couchant [1] there. For the purest is too fine to clothe in any Linguas [2] huswifry; or to be expressed by words, and though this letter bears but the coarsest part to you, yet the purest is improved for you. But now, My Dear Love, lest my Letter Should be judged the Layish Language of a lover's pen,[3] I shall endeavor to Show that Conjugal Love ought to exceed all other love. 1. Appears from that which it represents, viz: that respect which is betwixt Christ and his church, Eph. 5:25, although it differs from that in kind; for that is Spiritual and this is human, and in degree, that is boundless and transcendent; this limited and subordinate; yet it holds out that this should be a Cordial and with respect to all other transcendent. 2. Because Conjugal Love is the ground of Conjugal Union, or conjugal sharing the Effects of this Love, is also a ground of this Union. 3 From those Christian Duties which are incumbent on persons in this State as not only serving God together, a Praying together, a Joining in the Ruling and Instructing their family together, which could not be carried on as it Should without a great degree of true love, (and also) a mutual Giving Each other to Each other, and a mutual Succoring each other in all states, Ails, Grievances; And how can this be where there is not a Love exceeding all other Love to any Creature? And hereby, if persons in this state have not love exceeding all other love, it's

A LETTER. 1. **couchant:** latent, lurking, hidden. 2. **Linguas:** language's. 3. The "Layish Language of a lover's pen does not mean layman's: it is one of his coinages (not in the *OED*) which blends like a "lay" or lyric with "lavish." The three numbered points which follow are serious statements of the orthodox Christian doctrine of marriage. If they seem in any way a "mock sermon," it is in the familiar sermonic division into numbered propositions.

with them for the most part as with the strings of an instrument not tuned together, when struck upon makes but a jarring harsh sound. But when equally drawn up, and rightly Struck upon, sound together, make sweet music whose harmony doth enravish the ear; so when the Golden Strings of true affection are Struck up into a right conjugal love, thus sweetly doth this State then Harmonise to the comfort of each other, and to the Glory of God when Sanctified. But yet, though Conjugal Love must exceed all other, yet it must be kept within bounds too. For it must be Subordinate to God's Glory. The wish that mine may be so, it having got you into my Heart, doth offer my heart with you in it as a more rich Sacrifice unto God through Christ, and so it subscribeth myself,

Your True Love till Death,

EDWARD TAYLOR.

FROM

GODS DETERMINATIONS TOUCHING HIS ELECT . . .

◊

Gods Determinations is a kind of survival of the medieval morality plays like *Everyman* and medieval (and later) "debates" between the arts and sciences or—more significantly—between Body and Soul: the characters are not individuated but typical. This "long poem," after a debate between Justice and Mercy, deals—sometimes in dialogue, sometimes in narrative, sometimes in lyric—with the fight between Satan, a shrewd fellow, and God, who, being Almighty, the "I am that I am," does not have to argue or psychologize. Satan would "deceive if possible the very elect" (Mark 13:22). Some men are easily drawn to revolt against God; the subtler argumentation of the Evil One is directed against the reality of religious experience; and subtler yet is the counterargument of the "saint," the experienced Christian, who can resolve the difficulties and doubts which Satan has raised.

The full title of the poem should be noted: unlike *The Day of Doom,* the Puritan best-seller, this poem deals with the "elect," the "chosen," with those who, whatever their difficulties and doubts, have been chosen by God before the foundation of the world as those who are to be saved at the last.

It has been difficult to choose selections from this long poem. I have given the general prologue, which suggests God's questions when He answers Job "out of the whirlwind" (Chaps. 38–41) and which, stylistically, resembles Joshua Sylvester's translation of the Huguenot Du Bartas' *La divine semaine* (a version of the Creation myth much longer than either that in Genesis or in *Paradise Lost,* Book VII); and then I have given an engaging example of what begins as a kind of sacred lullaby, and then the concluding poem (with refrain) on those who at last have the right to go to Heaven not on foot, or on horseback, but by the Church's Coach.

The puzzling passages in this poem all arise from Taylor's desire to show that, whatever skills, handicrafts, and arts man has learned, God has surpassed them. In so arguing, he feels no hesitation in citing human skills and devices like the canopied bed, the lanterns, the rods which fasten the tapestry (predecessor to wallpaper) to the walls, the bowling alley.

◊

THE PREFACE.

Infinity, when all things it beheld
In Nothing, and of Nothing all did build,
Upon what Base was fixt the Lath, wherein
He turn'd this Globe, and riggalld it so trim?
Who blew the Bellows of his Furnace Vast?
Or held the Mould wherein the world was Cast?
Who laid its Corner Stone? Or whose Command?
Where stand the Pillars upon which it stands?
Who Lac'de and Fillitted the earth so fine,
With Rivers like green Ribbons Smaragdine?
Who made the Sea's its Selvedge, and it locks
Like a Quilt Ball within a Silver Box?
Who Spread its Canopy? Or Curtains Spun?
Who in this Bowling Alley bowld the Sun?
Who made it always when it rises set
To go at once both down, and up to get?
Who th'Curtain rods made for this Tapistry?
Who hung the twinckling Lanthorns in the Sky?
Who? who did this? or who is he? Why, know
Its Onely Might Almighty this did doe.
His hand hath made this noble worke which Stands
His Glorious Handywork not made by hands.
Who spake all things from nothing; and with ease
Can speake all things to nothing, if he please.
Whose Little finger at his pleasure Can
Out mete ten thousand worlds with halfe a Span:
Whose Might Almighty can by half a looks

GODS DETERMINATIONS. **3–4. Upon . . . trim?:** The lathe is the potter's lathe, a revolving circular disk. To riggle it is to give the completing touches. **9–10. Who . . . Smaragdine?:** The figures are those of another craft, that of the dressmaker; the "green Ribbons Smaragdine" carries out that of lacing and filleting. "Smaragdine" is an archaic word meaning the jewel which is emerald green. **11. Selvedge:** selvage, or border. A term derived from the weaver's art, the border of a fabric which keeps it from being unraveled. The figure in the next line seems to mean that a ball of cord or wool, however precious, can be unraveled unless—when not in use—enclosed in a Silver Ball (Ball = Rivers).

Root up the rocks and rock the hills by th'roots.
Can take this mighty World up in his hande,
And shake it like a Squitchen or a Wand.
Whose single Frown will make the Heavens shake
Like as an aspen leafe the Winde makes quake.
Oh! what a might is this Whose single frown
Doth shake the world as it would shake it down?
Which All from Nothing fet, from Nothing, All:
Hath All on Nothing set, lets Nothing fall.
Gave All to nothing Man indeed, whereby
Through nothing man all might him Glorify.
In Nothing then imbosst the brightest Gem
More pretious than all pretiousness in them.
But Nothing man did throw down all by Sin:
And darkened that lightsom Gem in him.
  That now his Brightest Diamond is grown
  Darker by far than any Coalpit Stone.

CHRISTS REPLY.

¶ THIS is a reply to Satan's assault on the first rank of converts, those who trusting in God's mercy for their "election" are tormented by doubts both of the "inward man" (doubts concerning their motives and intentions) and of the "outward man" (doubts concerning their life as professed Christians).

Peace, Peace, my Hony, do not Cry,
My Little Darling, wipe thine eye,
  Oh Cheer, Cheer up, come see.
Is anything too deare, my Dove,
Is anything too good, my Love
  To get or give for thee?

If in the severall thou art
This Yelper fierce will at thee bark:
  That thou art mine this shows.
As Spot barks back the sheep again
Before they to the Pound are ta'ne,
  So he and hence 'way goes.

But yet this Cur that bayghs so sore
Is broken tootht, and muzzled sure,
  Fear not, my Pritty Heart.
His barking is to make thee Cling
Close underneath thy Saviours Wing.
  Why did my sweeten start?

And if he run an inch too far,
I'le Check his Chain, and rate the Cur.
  My Chick, keep clost to mee.
The Poles shall sooner kiss, and greet
And Paralells shall sooner meet
  Than thou shalt harmed bee.

He seeks to aggrivate thy sin
And screw them to the highest pin,
  To make thy faith to quaile.
Yet mountain Sins like mites should show
And then these mites for naught should goe
  Could he but once prevaile.

I smote thy sins upon the Head.
They Dead'ned are, though not quite dead:
  And shall not rise again.
I'l put away the Guilt thereof,
And purge its Filthiness cleare off:
  My Blood doth out the stain.

And though thy judgment was remiss
Thy Headstrong Will too Wilfull is.
  I will Renew the same.
And though thou do too frequently
Offend as heretofore hereby
  I'l not severly blaim.

And though thy senses do inveagle
Thy Noble Soul to tend the Beagle,
  That t'hunt her games forth go.
I'le Lure her back to me, and Change
Those fond Affections that do range
  As yelping beagles doe.

Although thy sins increase their race,
And though when thou hast sought for Grace,
  Thou fallst more than before
If thou by true Repentence Rise,
And Faith makes me thy Sacrifice,
  I'l pardon all, though more.

Though Satan strive to block thy way
By all his Stratagems he may:
  Come, come though through the fire.
For Hell that Gulph of fire for sins,
Is not so hot as t'burn thy Shins.
  Then Credit not the Lyar.

Those Cursed Vermin Sins that Crawle
All ore thy Soul, both Greate, and small

30. Squitchen: a branch or twig; very likely "switch" is the closest survivor of this vanished word. CHRISTS REPLY. **7. severall:** one who feels his isolation. **10. Spot:** name for a dog who pursues the wandering sheep before they are impounded. **11. Pound:** must here be used in what the *OED* recognizes as a figurative meaning—a "spiritual fold"—i.e., the Church. **13. But . . . sore:** In the Bible, as one can see by consulting a concordance, *dog* has none of the honorific sense currently accorded the domestic pet. Satan is a "dog," a "cur"; the Christian is a "sheep" or a "bird" (a "chick"), as well as a child—all Biblical parallels. In these opening stanzas, Taylor freely moves between the three. Satan, for all his threats, is limited in his power, not co-equal with God.

26. And . . . pin: musical allusion to tightening up the strings of the lute. Satan both tries so to magnify one's sense of sin that one doubts God's mercy to forgive and, if one surrenders one's faith in that mercy, makes great sins seem not sins at all. **44. Beagle:** small English hound used for hunting hares. **61–72. Those . . . thee:** God will forgive His elect all sins.

Are onely Satans own:
Which he in his Malignity
Unto thy Souls true Sanctity
In at the doors hath thrown.

And though they be Rebellion high,
Ath'ism or Apostacy:
Though blasphemy it bee:
Unto what Quality, or Sise
Excepting one, so e're it rise.
Repent, I'le pardon thee.

Although thy Soule was once a Stall
Rich hung with Satans nicknacks all;
If thou Repent thy Sin,
A Tabernacle in't I'le place
Fild with Gods Spirit, and his Grace.
Oh Comfortable thing!

I dare the World therefore to show
A God like me, to anger slow:
Whose wrath is full of Grace.
Doth hate all Sins both Greate, and small:
Yet when Repented, pardons all.
Frowns with a Smiling Face.

As for thy outward Postures each,
Thy Gestures, Actions, and thy Speech,
I Eye and Eying spare,
If thou repent. My Grace is more
Ten thousand times still tribled ore
Than thou canst want, or ware.

As for the Wicked Charge he makes,
That he of Every Dish first takes
Of all thy holy things.
Its false, deny the same, and say,
That which he had he stool away
Out of thy Offerings.

Though to thy Griefe, poor Heart, thou finde
In Pray're too oft a wandring minde,
In Sermons Spirits dull.
Though faith in firy furnace flags,
And Zeale in Chilly Seasons lags.
Temptations powerfull.

These faults are his, and none of thine
So far as thou dost them decline.
Come then receive my Grace.
And when he buffits thee therefore
If thou my aid, and Grace implore
I'le shew a pleasant face.

But still look for Temptations Deep,
Whilst that thy Noble Sparke doth keep
Within a Mudwald Cote.
These White Frosts and the Showers that fall
Are but to whiten thee withall.
Not rot the Web they smote.

If in the fire where Gold is tride
Thy Soule is put, and purifide
Wilt thou lament thy loss?
If silver-like this fire refine
Thy Soul and make it brighter shine:
Wilt thou bewaile the Dross?

Oh! fight my Field: no Colours fear:
I'l be thy Front, I'l be thy reare.
Fail not: my Battells fight.
Defy the Tempter, and his Mock.
Anchor thy heart on mee thy Rock.
I do in thee Delight.

THE JOY OF CHURCH FELLOWSHIP RIGHTLY ATTENDED.

¶[THE opening lines seem to express a vision, or rather auditory image, which the poet has in his meditation: that of the "saints" (which, to the Puritans as to St. Paul, meant all Church members going to heaven in "togetherness").

The stanza beginning with line 25 allows, as all charitable Christians have, of there being some who, because of *time* or *place,* make their way to heaven individually, finding the Road but not in the Coach of the Church.

In Heaven soaring up, I dropt an Eare
On Earth: and oh! sweet Melody:
And listening, found it was the Saints who were
Encoacht for Heaven that sang for Joy.
For in Christs Coach they sweetly sing;
As they to Glory ride therein.

Oh! joyous hearts! Enfir'de with holy Flame!
Is speech thus tassled with praise?
Will not your inward fire of Joy contain;

Presumably the only unforgivable one is the sin against the Holy Ghost (Matt. 12:31–32), which appears to mean the disbelief that God can forgive sin, a state of total despair. **91. As . . . Charge:** This passage refers to Satan's preceding charge that men always have mixed motives: if they seem religious it is to seem so to men, or at best out of fear of hell, not out of what Jonathan Edwards called "disinterested benevolence," love of God for Himself alone.

111. Mudwald Cote: a cottage the walls of which are mud. ("And the Lord God formed man of the dust of the ground . . ." —Gen. 2:7.) **114. Web:** The reference to the web—rather incongruous or unexpected—reminds us of the Coventry business of cloth-weaving: cf. "Huswifery." THE JOY OF CHURCH FELLOWSHIP. **8. tassled:** bound into adornments (tassels) so as to prevent free movement. Johnson's edition reads "tasseled," which makes the line metrically smooth.

That it in open flames doth blaze?
For in Christ's Coach Saints sweetly sing,
As they to Glory ride therein.

And if a string do slip, by Chance, they soon
Do screw it up again: whereby
They set it in a more melodious Tune
And a Diviner Harmony.
For in Christs Coach they sweetly sing
As they to Glory ride therein.

In all their Acts, publick, and private, nay
And secret too, they praise impart.
But in their Acts Divine and Worship, they
With Hymns do offer up their Heart.
Thus in Christs Coach they sweetly sing
As they to Glory ride therein.

Some few not in; and some whose Time, and Place
Block up this Coaches way do goe
As Travellers afoot, and so do trace
The Road that gives them right thereto
While in this Coach these sweetly sing
As they to Glory ride therein.

HUSWIFERY

◇

THIS, perhaps the most anthologized of Taylor's poems, identifies the duty and art of the housewife entirely with one of her functions, that of making *homespun* clothes. The figure, essentially a single conceit, may have been suggested by the craft of the weaving town of Coventry, not far from Taylor's birthplace; but compare also Proverbs 31:10–31, the Old Testament eulogy of the virtuous housewife.

I italicize "homespun," but the point of the poem is that only God can make one able to perform the series of operations described.

The first stanza describes the making of yarn on the spinning wheel. The second turns to the loom, upon which the fabric is made. The third is the process of clothing the "saint."

◇

Make me, O Lord, thy Spining Wheele compleate.
Thy Holy Worde my Distaff make for mee.
Make mine Affections thy Swift Flyers neate
And make my Soule thy holy Spoole to bee.
My Conversation make to be thy Reele
And reele the yarn thereon spun of thy Wheele.

Make me thy Loome then, knit therein this Twine:
And make thy Holy Spirit, Lord, winde quills:
Then weave the Web thyselfe. The yarn is fine.
Thine Ordinances make my Fulling Mills.
Then dy the same in Heavenly Colours Choice,
All pinkt with Varnisht Flowers of Paradise.

Then cloath therewith mine Understanding, Will,
Affections, Judgment, Conscience, Memory
My Words, and Actions, that their shine may fill
My wayes with glory and thee glorify.
Then mine apparell shall display before yee
That I am Cloathd in Holy robes for glory.

FROM

SACRAMENTAL MEDITATIONS

I AM THE ROSE OF SHARON.

[*Cant. 2:1, Meditation 4, First Series*]

EACH chapter of the Song of Songs bears, in the King James Bible, a gloss on its allegorical meaning; and the second chapter is thus interpreted as "The mutual love of Christ and his church." Taylor takes the Rose of Sharon as being Christ; but, like other devotional commentators on the Song, interprets the Bride as either the church or the soul of the believer (which is, of course, a member, a part, of the church).

The connection between Christ as the Rose and Christ at the Table head (of the Last Supper, the Communion) is supplied by the propinquity to verse 1 ("I am the Rose") of verse 4, obviously spoken by the *anima*, the woman, "He brought me to the banqueting house, and his banner over me was love."

THE REFLEXION.

Lord, art thou at the Table Head above
Meat, Med'cine, sweetness, sparkling Beautys to
Enamour Souls with Flaming Flakes of Love,

HUSWIFERY. 10. **Ordinances:** the sacraments and disciplines of the Church. **Fulling Mills:** places in which the cloth is cleansed with fuller's earth or soap. 12. **pinkt:** adorned. **Varnisht:** polished or more permanent. The word has lost status since Taylor's time. I AM THE ROSE OF SHARON. 2. **Meat:** in Elizabethan English, any kind of solid food. 3. **Flakes:** surviving in the compound, "snowflakes," the word in earlier Eng-

And not my Trencher, nor my Cup o'reflow?
Be n't I a bidden Guest? Oh! sweat mine Eye.
Oreflow with Teares: Oh! draw thy fountains dry.

Shall I not smell thy sweet, oh! Sharons Rose?
Shall not mine Eye salute thy Beauty? Why?
Shall thy sweet leaves their Beautious sweets upclose?
As halfe ashamde my sight should on them ly?
Woe's me! for this my sighs shall be in grain
Offer'd on Sorrows Altar for the same.

Had not my Soule's thy Conduit, Pipes stopt bin
With mud, what Ravishment would'st thou Convay?
Let Graces Golden Spade dig till the Spring
Of tears arise, and cleare this filth away.
Lord, let thy spirit raise my sighings till
These Pipes my soule do with thy sweetness fill.

Earth once was Paradise of Heaven below
Till inkefac'd sin had it with poyson stockt
And Chast this Paradise away into
Heav'ns upmost Loft, and it in Glory Lockt.
But thou, sweet Lord, hast with thy golden Key
Unlockt the Doore, and made, a golden day.

Once at thy Feast, I saw thee Pearle-like stand
'Tween Heaven, and Earth where Heavens Bright glory all
In streams fell on thee, as a floodgate and,
Like Sun Beams through thee on the World to Fall.
Oh! sugar sweet then! my Deare sweet Lord, I see
Saints Heavens-lost Happiness restor'd by thee.

Shall Heaven, and Earth's bright Glory all up lie
Like Sun Beams bundled in the sun, in thee?
Dost thou sit Rose at Table Head, where I
Do sit, and Carv'st no morsell sweet for mee?
So much before, so little now! Sprindge, Lord,
Thy Rosie Leaves, and me their Glee afford.

Shall not thy Rose my Garden fresh perfume?
Shall not thy Beauty my dull Heart assaile?
Shall not thy golden gleams run through this gloom?
Shall my black Velvet Mask thy fair Face Vaile?
Pass o're my Faults: shine forth, bright sun: arise
Enthrone thy Rosy-selfe within mine Eyes.

MY FATHER, AND YOUR FATHER, TO MY GOD, AND YOUR GOD.

[*John 20:17, Meditation 29, First Series*]

¶ A POEM almost entirely developing the conceit of God as a golden tree and man as grafted into the tree. On the figure of man (since the Fall) as grafted, compare Romans 11:17, 19, 23, 24.

My shattred Phancy stole away from mee,
(Wits run a Wooling over Edens Parke)
And in Gods Garden saw a golden Tree,
Whose Heart was All Divine, and gold its barke.
Whose glorious limbs and fruitful branches strong
With Saints, and Angells bright are richly hung.

Thou! thou! my Deare-Deare Lord, art this rich Tree
The Tree of Life Within Gods Paradise.
I am a Withred Twig, dri'de fit to bee
A Chat Cast in thy fire, Writh off by Vice.
Yet if thy Milke white-Gracious Hand will take mee
And grafft mee in this golden stock, thou'lt make mee.

Thou'lt make me then its Fruite, and Branch to spring.
And though a nipping Eastwinde blow, and all
Hells Nymps with spite their Dog's sticks thereat ding

lish was rather associated with fire-flakes ("portions of ignited matter," *OED*). **4. Trencher:** a dish plate (earliest made of wood). **13. Had . . . bin:** Had not the pipes of my soul, Thy conduit (aqueduct, channel of grace) been stopped up. **19. Paradise:** original sense, in Greek, a garden—the Garden of Eden. **21–22. And . . . Loft:** Now Paradise, once on earth, has been transferred to being the highest human state in Heaven. **25. Pearle-like:** Christ as the Pearl. Cf. Matt. 14:45–46. **35. Sprindge:** spread about. **36. Glee:** delight, state of exaltation.

40. my black Velvet Mask: Women used to wear such to shelter their complexions against the sun; but such a mask both symbolizes sin and shuts out the Sun of Righteousness. MY FATHER, AND YOUR FATHER. **2. a Wooling:** wool gathering. **Edens Parke:** the Garden of Eden. **10. Chat:** a small branch used for kindling. **Writh:** used as a past participle—twisted off. **15. Nymps:** here used, as the context shows, not in its classical sense but broadened to mean supernatural spirits, evil and male, as in *imps.* **ding:** hammer, thump (arch. or dial.).

To Dash the Grafft off, and it's fruits to fall,
Yet I shall stand thy Grafft, and Fruits that are
Fruits of the Tree of Life thy Grafft shall beare.

I being grafft in thee there up do stand
In us Relations all that mutuall are.
I am thy Patient, Pupill, Servant, and
Thy Sister, Mother, Doove, Spouse, Son, and Heire.
Thou art my Priest, Physician, Prophet, King,
Lord, Brother, Bridegroom, Father, Ev'ry thing.

I being grafft in thee am graffted here
Into thy Family, and kindred Claim
To all in Heaven, God, Saints, and Angells there.
I thy Relations my Relations name.
Thy Father's mine, thy God my God, and I
With Saints, and Angells draw Affinity.

My Lord, what is it that thou dost bestow?
The Praise on this account fills up, and throngs
Eternity brimfull, doth overflow
The Heavens vast with rich Angelick Songs.
How should I blush? how Tremble at this thing,
Not having yet my Gam-Ut, learnd to sing.

But, Lord, as burnish't Sun Beams forth out fly
Let Angell-Shine forth in my Life out flame,
That I may grace thy gracefull Family
And not to thy Relations be a Shame.
Make mee thy Grafft, be thou my Golden Stock.
Thy Glory then I'le make my fruits and Crop.

HE IS A NEW CREATURE.

[II Cor. 5:17, Meditation 30, First Series]

¶ THE whole fifth chapter of II Corinthians should be read, so wide is its range. Dealing with the "future life," it deals more centrally with "eternal life," something which, by "conversion," can be man's here and now, through the atoning power of Jesus, the "Rod of Davids Root."

The Daintiest Draught thy Pensill ever Drew:
The finest vessell, Lord, thy fingers fram'de:
The statelist Palace Angells e're did view,
Under thy Hatch betwixt Decks here Contain'd
Broke, marred, spoild, undone, Defild doth ly
In Rubbish ruinde by thine Enemy.

What Pittie's this? Oh Sunshine Art! What Fall?
Thou that more Glorious wast than glories Wealth!
More Golden far than Gold! Lord, on whose Wall
Thy scutchons hung, the Image of thyselfe!
Its ruinde, and must rue, though Angells should
To hold it up heave while their Heart Strings hold.

But yet thou stem of Davids stock when dry
And shrivled held, although most green was lopt
Whose sap a sovereign Sodder is, whereby
The breach repared is in which its dropt.
Oh Gracious Twig! thou Cut off? bleed rich juyce
T'Cement the Breach, and Glories shine reduce?

Oh Lovely One! how doth thy Loveliness
Beam through the Chrystall Casements of the Eyes
Of Saints, and Angells sparkling Flakes of Fresh
Heart Ravishing Beauty, filling up their joyes?
And th'Divells too; if Envies Pupills stood
Not peeping there these sparkling Rayes t'exclude?

Thou Rod of Davids Root, Branch of his Bough
My Lord, repare thy Palace, Deck thy Place.
I'm but a Flesh and Blood bag: Oh! do thou
Sill, Plate, Ridge, Rib, and Rafter me with Grace.
Renew my Soule, and guild it all within:
And hang thy saving Grace on ery Pin.

My Soule, Lord, make thy Shining Temple, pave
Its Floore all o're with Orient Grace: thus guild
It o're with Heavens gold: Its Cabbins have

21–24. I . . . thing: These metaphors are Scriptural, arranged after an impassioned loose arrangement, too complicated for brief explanation: Patient-Physician; Pupil-Prophet. The strangest—"I am thy . . . Mother"—is most likely a reference to Matt. 12:47–50. **36. Gam-Ut:** gamut, or a scale in music.

HE IS A NEW CREATURE. **10. scutchons:** escutcheons, shields bearing the coat of arms: man was created in the image and likeness of God (Gen. 1:26). **28. Sill . . . Rafter:** architectural terms, all retained except "plate," which refers to putting a horizontal timber at the top or bottom of a framing. **30. Pin:** probably the architectural figure still: a small piece of wood or metal used to hold together parts of a structure—a peg, a bolt. **33. Cabbins:** cabin, a small room, a cabinet.

Thy Treasuries with Choicest thoughts up filld.
Pourtray thy Glorious Image round about
Upon thy Temple Walls within, and Out.

Garnish thy Hall with Gifts, Lord, from above
With that Rich Coate of Male thy Righteousness,
Truths Belt, the Spirits Sword, the Buckler Love
Hopes Helmet, and the Shield of Faith kept fresh.
The Scutchons of thy Honour make my Sign
As Garland Tuns are badges made of Wine.

New mould, new make me thus, me new Create
Renew in me a spirit right, pure, true.
Lord make me thy New Creature, then new make
All things to thy New Creature here anew,
New Heart, New thoughts, New Words, New wayes likewise.
New Glory then shall to thyselfe arise.

WHETHER PAUL OR APOLLOS, OR CEPHAS.

[*I Cor. 3:22, Meditation 32, First Series*]

THE Bible text, St. Paul's, refers to quarrels at Corinth over spiritual leaders. But all were ministers of Grace: "Whether Paul, Apollos, Cephas [St. Peter], all are thine." The relation of the text to the poem is not clear in the poem: it would appear, however, to be Taylor's attempt to assure himself that he should not desire "this man's art or that man's skill": if not the best preacher, theologian, or poet, God can still use him. He is trying to write a poem on Grace and feels uninspired, inadequate.

Thy Grace, Dear Lord's my golden Wrack, I finde
Screwing my Phancy into ragged Rhimes,
Tuning thy Praises in my feeble minde
Untill I come to strike them on my Chimes.
Were I an Angell bright, and borrow could
King Davids Harp, I would them play on gold.

But plung'd I am, my minde is puzzled,
When I would spin my Phancy thus unspun,
In finest Twine of Praise I'm muzzled.
My tazzled Thoughts twirld into Snick-Snarls run.
Thy Grace, my Lord, is such a glorious thing,
It doth Confound me when I would it sing.

Eternall Love an Object mean did smite
Which by the Prince of Darkness was beguilde,
That from this Love it ran and sweld with spite
And in the way with filth was all defilde
Yet must be reconcild, cleansd, and begrac'te
Or from the fruits of Gods first Love displac'te.

Then Grace, my Lord, wrought in thy Heart a vent,
Thy Soft Soft hand to this hard worke did goe,
And to the Milke White Throne of Justice went
And entred bond that Grace might overflow.
Hence did thy Person to my Nature ty
And bleed through humane Veans to satisfy.

Oh! Grace, Grace, Grace! this Wealthy Grace doth lay
Her Golden Channells from thy Fathers throne,
Into our Earthen Pitchers to Convay
Heavens Aqua Vitae to us for our own.
O! let thy Golden Gutters run into
My Cup this Liquour till it overflow.

Thine Ordinances, Graces Wine-fats where
Thy Spirits Walkes, and Graces runs doe ly
And Angells waiting stand with holy Cheere
From Graces Conduite Head, with all Supply.

38. that Rich Coate of Male: a passage worked out from St. Paul's famous "take unto you the whole armour of God" (Eph. 6:13–17). **42. Garland Tuns:** barrels with garlands bedecking them show that they hold not beer but wine. WHETHER PAUL. **1. Wrack:** in the *OED* there are many approximately suitable meanings. The sense seems to be the torment, the golden torment, of trying to write on Grace, when the poet's imagination (Phancy) and his "feeble mind" are inadequate to so lofty a subject: if only I were King David.

9. In . . . muzzled: My fancy, confused when I try to construct, doesn't help me to "spin": the finest "twine" to weave praise with keeps me from speaking. **10. tazzled:** tangled, fuzzy. **Snick-Snarls:** tangles. Possibly a coinage of Taylor's: the whole line is a strong and vivid metaphor (drawn, presumably, from weaving) of the construction ending in confusion. **11–12. Thy . . . sing:** Characteristic of Taylor is this setting down of the difficulty he has in composing on a great subject and of letting the apologetic prelude stand instead of striking it out. Here, with the third stanza, he is sure of himself. **13. Object mean:** man in his fallen state, seduced by Satan. **smite:** God's necessity of punishing man and expelling him from the Garden. **19. my Lord:** here and elsewhere in the poem is Jesus, not God the Father. **23. Hence . . . ty:** Jesus bound His pre-existent Divine name to "my [human] Nature," the central theme of Taylor's *Christographia;* and He "entred bond"—offered Himself—as bail for man (one theory of the Atonement). **28. Aqua Vitae:** water of life. **29. Gutters:** Gutters had in Taylor's time a more general sense than now—i.e., a conduit or pipe for the outflow of fluid. **31. Wine-fats:** "Fat" is a now obsolete version of "vat." **32. runs:** like "Walkes," a noun. It is a regular track made by certain animals: cf. sheep-run; deer-run.

These Vessells full of Grace are, and the Bowls
In which their Taps do run, are pretious Souls.

Thou to the Cups dost say (that Catch this Wine,)
This Liquour, Golden Pipes, and Wine-fats plain,
Whether Paul, Apollos, Cephas, all are thine.
Oh Golden Word! Lord speakc it ore again.
Lord speake it home to me, say these are mine.
My Bells shall then thy Praises bravely chime.

AN ADVOCATE WITH THE FATHER.

[*I John 2:1, Meditation 38, First Series*]

¶ AT THE end of man's earthly life, his deeds, both good and bad (the "White and Black" of line 8) are weighed for and against him at the "heavenly trial" where God is judge, Christ is "advocate," "attorney," or intercessor for man. The central motif of the poem is thus built upon the theology of the Redemption, illustrated in a court setting and described in legal terminology.

Oh! What a thing is Man? Lord, Who am I?
That thou shouldst give him Law (Oh! golden Line)
To regulate his Thoughts, Words, Life thereby.
And judge him Wilt thereby too in thy time.
A Court of Justice thou in heaven holdst
To try his Case while he's here housd on mould.

How do thy Angells lay before thine eye
My Deeds both White, and Black I dayly doe?
How doth thy Court thou Pannellst there them try?
But flesh complains. What right for this? let's know.
For right, or wrong I can't appeare unto't.
And shall a sentence Pass on such a suite?

Soft; blemish not this golden Bench, or place.
Here is no Bribe, nor Colourings to hide
Nor Pettifogger to befog the Case
But Justice hath her Glory here well tri'de.
Her spotless Law all spotted Cases tends.
Without Respect or Disrespect them ends.

God's Judge himselfe: and Christ Atturny is,
The Holy Ghost Regesterer is founde.
Angells the sergeants are, all Creatures kiss
The booke, and doe as Evidences abounde.
All Cases pass according to pure Law
And in the sentence is no Fret, nor flaw.

What saist, my soule? Here all thy Deeds are tri'de.
Is Christ thy Advocate to pleade thy Cause?
Art thou his Client? Such shall never slide.
He never lost his Case: he pleads such Laws
As Carry do the same, nor doth refuse
The Vilest sinners Case that doth him Choose.

This is his Honour, not Dishonour: nay
No Habeas-Corpus gainst his Clients came
For all their Fines his Purse doth make down pay.
He Non-Suites Satan's Suite or Casts the Same.
He'l plead thy Case, and not accept a Fee.
He'l plead Sub Forma Pauperis for thee.

My Case is bad. Lord, be my Advocate.
My sin is red: I'me under Gods Arrest.
Thou hast the Hint of Pleading; plead my State.
Although it's bad thy Plea will make it best.
If thou wilt plead my Case before the King:
I'le Waggon Loads of Love, and Glory bring.

AN ADVOCATE WITH THE FATHER. **2. Line**: lineage, or heritage. **6. housd on mould**: residing on earth. **9. Pannellst**: impanel, of a jury. **14. Colourings**: good appearances, but hiding evil things. **15. Pettifogger**: a legal practitioner of low status who conducts petty cases and sustains his arguments by quibbling and chicanery.

20. Regesterer: registrar, or recorder of the Court, and keeper of the "booke" in which man's deeds appear. **21. sergeants**: sergeants-at-law, here attendants to the "Regesterer." **22. Evidences**: witnesses. **24. Fret**: ill-humor, vindictiveness. **27. Such . . . slide**: Christ shall never err, or go wrong. **28–30. he . . . Choose**: Christ will act for those who "carry" (i.e., maintain) God's laws, and those who, going astray, seek forgiveness through Him. **32. Habeas-Corpus**: Latin, "Thou shalt have the body [in court]." In common law, no person may be kept under arrest without the charge against him being brought before judge or court: Christ's "clients" need ask for no such writ, for they face their charges at once; and at Christ's own expense—by His precious Passion—they can make atonement for their wrongs. **34. Non-Suites**: a legal term, to stop a suit, i.e., a legal prosecution, when the plaintiff (here Satan) fails to bring sufficient evidence. **Casts**: dismisses. **36. Sub Forma Pauperis**: Latin, "according to the form of poverty." In law, one may be allowed, on account of poverty, to sue or defend in a court of law, without paying costs (*OED*). Taylor pleads to being so poor a creature because of his great sins; he is therefore bound to fall on Christ's mercy.

HE IS THE PROPITIATION FOR OUR SIN.

[*I John 2:2, Meditation 40, First Series*]

¶ THIS poem should not, I think, be read as autobiography. Taylor mentions many rural games which he had witnessed or heard of and of which the Puritans disapproved; but there is no evidence that, even before he left England, where they were practiced, he had indulged in them. They are best taken as figurative. But Christianity teaches that all sins are ultimately one, and that even the Christian of admirable conduct may have evil imaginings or desires—out of which *actual* sins may or may not come.

This poem is unlike the generality of Taylor's in dwelling on sin; but this may have been prompted by the text of the meditation rather than any particular state of religious depression. Certainly he was not any more than Bunyan, who wrote an autobiography, *Grace Abounding* (1666), the "chief of sinners"—to call oneself which is to fall into a perverse kind of spiritual pride.

Still I complain; I am complaining still.
Oh! woe is me! Was ever Heart like mine?
A Sty of Filth, a Trough of Washing-Swill
A Dunghill Pit, a Puddle of mere Slime.
A Nest of Vipers, Hive of Hornets; Stings.
A Bag of Poyson, Civit-Box of Sins.

Was ever Heart like mine? So bad? black? Vile?
Is any Divell blacker? Or can Hell
Produce its match? It is the very Soile
Where Satan reads his Charms, and sets his Spell.
His Bowling Ally, where he sheeres his fleece
At Nine Pins, Nine Holes, Morrice, Fox and Geese.

His Palace Garden where his courtiers walke.
His Jewells Cabbinet. Here his Caball
Do sham it, and truss up their Privie talk
In Fardells of Consults and bundles all.
His shambles, and his Butchers stale's herein.
It is the Fuddling Schoole of every sin.

Was ever Heart like mine? Pride, Passion, fell.
Ath'ism, Blasphemy, pot, pipe it, dance
Play Barlybreaks, and at last Couple in Hell.
At Cudgells, Kit-Cat, Cards and Dice here prance.
At Noddy, Ruff-and-trumpt, Jing, Post-and-Pare,
Put, One-and-thirty, and such other ware.

Grace shuffled is away: Patience oft sticks
Too soon, or draws itselfe out, and's out Put.
Faith's over trumpt, and oft doth lose her tricks.
Repentance's Chalkt up Noddy, and out shut.
They Post, and Pare off Grace thus, and its shine.
Alas! alas! was ever Heart like mine?

Sometimes methinks the serpents head I mall:
Now all is still: my spirits do recreute.
But ere my Harpe can tune sweet praise, they fall
On me afresh, and tare me at my Root.
They bite like Badgers now nay worse, although
I tooke them toothless sculls, rot long agoe.

My Reason now's more than my sense, I feele
I have more Sight than Sense. Which seems to bee
A Rod of Sun beams t'whip mee for my steele.
My Spirits spiritless, and dull in mee
For my dead prayerless Prayers: the Spirits winde
Scarce blows my mill about. I little grinde.

HE IS THE PROPITIATION. **2. Was . . . mine?:** Persisting refrain—conceivably modeled as a reverse or penitential parody of "Was ever Grief like mine?"—the refrain of Herbert's long poem on Christ's Passion, "The Sacrifice." **6. Civit-Box:** civet box. **10. Charms . . . Spell:** magic incantations of the Evil One. **12. At . . . Geese:** Popular games during Taylor's youth in England: nine-pins = skittles, a bowling game; nine holes, a boys' game played with a ball and nine round holes in the ground or in a board; morrice = nine men's Morris, rather like checkers or chess but played in an open field; fox and geese, a boy's game played with marbles or pegs. These sports represent chiefly the sins of childhood. **13. His . . . walke:** We turn from rural pastimes (generally disapproved of by the Puritans) to sins of the Court. **14. His Jewells:** means, I take it, the prized counsellors of Satan's "cabinet." **Caball:** This word was, in the reign of Charles II, applied to a small committee of the Privy Council which was the precursor of the modern King's (or President's) Cabinet (*OED*). **15. truss up:** bundle, stow away closely (hence, in this context, conceal).

16. Fardells: bundles, sometimes wrapped bundles. **Consults:** the results of a meeting, especially of a *cabal* (*OED*). **17. Butchers stale's:** stale = stall. **18. Fuddling Schoole:** the school in which to learn the art of muddling distinctions. **19. fell:** adjective, obsolete or rhetorical in the senses here appropriate: fierce, destructive, etc. **20. pot:** verb, to drink beer, tipple. **21. Barlybreaks:** a game played by three couples: one stands in "hell," as it was called—a plot of ground between the other two plots, and tries to catch other couples as they pass through (Stanford). **22. Kit-Cat:** a game rather like baseball, commonly limited to boys (though not by the context it would seem, for this stanza is concerned with figures drawn from the popular pastimes of adults). **23. Noddy:** a card game like cribbage. **Ruff-and-trumpt, Jing, Post-and-Pare:** all card games. **24. Put, One-and-thirty:** also card games. **25–30. Grace . . . mine:** The figure of card games is continued, most obviously to a modern ear in "Faith's over trumpt, and oft doth lose her tricks." **Chalkt up:** refers to the still surviving rural habit of keeping scores on a slate or blackboard. **31. Sometimes . . . mall:** The "serpent" is Satan. **37. sense:** spiritual sense, which should dominate both reason and the outward senses.

Was ever Heart like mine? My Lord, declare.
I know not what to do: What shall I doe?
I wonder, split I don't upon Despare.
Its grace's wonder that I wrack not so.
I faintly shun't: although I see this Case
Would say, my sin is greater than thy grace.

Hope's Day-peep dawns hence through this chinck. Christs name
Propitiation is for sins. Lord, take
It so for mine. Thus quench thy burning flame
In that clear stream that from his side forth brake.
I can no Comfort take while thus I see
Hells cursed Imps thus jetting strut in mee.

Lord take thy sword: these Anakims destroy:
Then soake my soule in Zions Bucking tub
With Holy Soap, and Nitre, and rich Lye.
From all Defilement me cleanse, wash and rub.
Then wrince, and wring mee out till th' water fall
As pure as in the Well: not foule at all.

And let thy Sun, shine on my Head out cleare.
And bathe my Heart within its radient beams:
Thy Christ make my Propitiation Deare.
Thy Praise shall from my Heart breake forth in streams.
This reeching Vertue of Christs blood will quench
Thy Wrath, slay Sin and in thy Love mee bench.

HE SENT A MAN BEFORE THEM, EVEN JOSEPH, WHO WAS SOLD.

[*Ps. 105:17, Meditation 7, Second Series*]

AN INSTANCE of Taylor's typological poems: Old Testament figures are taken as prefigurements of Christ. This is a method not peculiar to the Puritans. Instances occur in the New Testament (e.g., the treatment of Melchisedec in the Epistle to the Hebrews, 7:1–17).

All Dull, my Lord, my Spirits flat, and dead
All water sockt and sapless to the skin.
Oh! Screw mee up and make my Spirits bed
Thy quickening vertue For my inke is dim,
My pensill blunt. Doth Joseph type out thee?
Haraulds of Angells sing out, Bow the Knee.

Is Josephs glorious shine a Type of thee?
How bright art thou? He Envi'de was as well.
And so was thou. He's stript, and pick't, poore hee,
Into the pit. And so was thou. They shell
Thee of thy Kirnell. He by Judah's sold
For twenty Bits, thirty for thee he'd told.

Joseph was tempted by his Mistress vile.
Thou by the Divell, but both shame the foe.
Joseph was cast into the jayle awhile.
And so was thou. Sweet apples mellow so.
Joseph did from his jayle to glory run.
Thou from Death's pallot rose like morning sun.

Joseph layes in against the Famine, and
Thou dost prepare the Bread of Life for thine.
He bought with Corn for Pharaoh th'men and Land.
Thou with thy Bread mak'st such themselves Consign
Over to thee, that eate it. Joseph makes
His brethren bow before him. Thine too quake.

Joseph constrains his Brethren till their sins
Do gall their Souls. Repentance babbles fresh.
Thou treatest sinners till Repentance springs
Then with him sendst a Benjamin like messe.
Joseph doth Cheare his humble brethren. Thou
Dost stud with Joy the mourning Saints that bow.

Josephs bright shine th'Eleven Tribes must preach.
And thine Apostles now Eleven, thine.
They beare his presents to his Friends: thine reach
Thine unto thine, thus now behold a shine.
How hast thou pensild out, my Lord, most bright
Thy glorious Image here, on Josephs Light.

45. **I . . . Despare:** It's a wonder that (like a ship) I don't split, wreck, on Despair—hopeless. 55. **Anakims:** giants hostile to God's people; cf. Josh. 11:21. 56. **Bucking tub:** the figure comes from the cleansing of yarn and cloth in a lye of wood ashes. HE SENT. 2. **sockt:** soaked. 3. **Screw mee up:** the tightening of lute strings to pitch.

6. **Haraulds:** heralds. 7. **Josephs . . . Type:** Joseph (Gen. 37:23) and Jesus were both stripped of their garments. **shine:** a favorite noun of Taylor's. As a noun, it currently survives only (or chiefly) in compounds like *shoeshine* and *sunshine.* 18. **pallot:** pallet, a small, mean bed: here the grave. 25. **Joseph . . . Brethren:** Cf. Gen. 42: 45. 28. **a Benjamin like messe:** Cf. Gen. 43:34.

This I bewaile in me under this shine
To see so dull a Colour in my Skin.
Lord, lay thy brightsome Colours on me thine.
Scoure thou my pipes then play thy tunes therein.
I will not hang my Harp in Willows by.
While thy sweet praise, my Tunes doth glorify.

THE ALMIGHTY.

[*Rev. 1:8, Meditation 48, Second Series*]

❡ A POEM constructed on a "homophone" (i.e., two words of different origins which are pronounced alike) which is also, in this case, a pair of contraries: power and, comparatively, powerlessness; a poem on a single conceit, only the conceit is not metaphorical but verbal. The first two stanzas admit of three categories: *mite* (something very small and poor); *might* (human strength, with its limits); the Almighty (God, Whose might has no limits).

O! What a thing is Might right mannag'd? 'Twill
That Proverb brain, whose face doth ware this paint.
(Might ore goe's Right) for might doth Right fulfill
Will Right revive when wrong makes Right to faint.
Might hatches Right: Right hatches Might, they are
Each Dam, and Chick, to each: a Lovely paire.

Then Might well mannag'd riseth mighty: yet
Doth never rise up to Almightiness.
Almightiness nere's in a mortall bit.
But, Lord, thou dost Almightiness possess.
Might in it's fulness: all mights Fulness bee
Of ery Sort and Sise stow'd up in thee.

But what am I, poor Mite, all mightless thing!
That cannot rive a rush, that I should e're
Adventure t'dress Almighty up, or bring
Almightiness deckt in its mighty geere?
Then spare my Stutting Stamring, inky Quill,
If it its bowells on thy Power distill.

My Mite (if I such Solicisms might
But use) would spend its mitie Strength for thee
Of Mightless might, of feeble stronge delight.
Its little ALL thy Sacrifice showld bee.
For thee't would mock at all the Might and Power
That Earth, and Hell possess: and on thee shower.

A Fig for Foes, for Divells, Hell, and all
The powres of darkness, thou now on my Side
Their Might's a little mite, Powers powerless fall.
My Mite Almighty will not let down slide.
I will not trust unto this Might of mine:
Nor in my Mite distrust, while I am thine.

Thy Love Almighty is, to Love mee deare,
Thy Grace Almighty mee to save: thy Truth
Almighty to depend on. Justice cleare
Almighty t'justify, and judge. Grace shewth.
Thy Wisdom too's Almighty all to eye,
And Holiness is such to sanctify.

If thy Almightiness, and all my Mite
United be in sacred Marriage knot,
My Mite is thine: Mine thine Almighty Might.
Then thine Almightiness my Mite hath got.
My Quill makes thine Almightiness a String
Of Pearls to grace the tune my Mite doth sing.

WHILE THE KING SITTETH AT HIS TABLE, MY SPICKNARD SENDETH FORTH THE SMELL THEREOF.

[*Cant. 1:12, Meditation 62, Second Series*]

❡ GOD invites the soul to His table; and the soul, conscious of unworthiness, begs to be made ready.

This is a poem full of references to herbs, with which Taylor, the owner of Culpeper's *Dispensatory*, was familiar—the vulneraries (herbs to heal wounds), purges (cathartics), and unguents (salves to soothe inflammations and soreness). Fallen man spiritually needs the psychic equivalents of all three categories.

Oh! thou, my Lord, thou king of Saints, here mak'st
A royal Banquet thine to entertain.
With rich, and royall fare, Celestiall Cates,

41. hang my Harp in Willows: Cf. Ps. 137:2. THE ALMIGHTY. **6. Dam:** as late as Dryden still could be used of any female parent—as *sire* of any male. **Chick:** in dialect, could be used of the young of any bird, and, by transference, as a term of endearment for a child. **14. rive a rush:** rive, tear apart. **16. geere:** gear seems used in its archaic sense of armor.

WHILE THE KING SITTETH AT HIS TABLE. **3. Cates:** choice food, dainties.

And sittest at the Table rich of fame.
Am I bid to this Feast? Sure Angells stare,
Such Rugged looks, and Ragged robes I ware.

I'le surely come, Lord fit mee for this feast:
Purge me with Palma Christi from my Sin.
With Plastrum Gratiae Dei, or at least
Unguent Apostolorum healing bring.
Give me thy Sage, and Savory: me dub
With Golden Rod, and with Saint Johns Wort good.

Root up my Henbain, Fawnbain, Divells bit.
My Dragons, Chokewort, Crosswort, Ragwort, vice,
And set my knot with Honysuckles, stick
Rich Herb-a-Grace, and Grains of Paradise
Angelica, yea Sharons Rose the best
And Herba Trinitatis in my breast.

Then let thy Sweetspike sweat its liquid Dew
Into my Crystall Viall: and there swim.
And as thou at thy Table in Rich Shew
With royal Dainties, sweet discourse as King
Dost Welcome thine. My Spiknard with its Smell
Shall vapour out perfumed Spirits Well.

Whether I at thy Table Guest do sit,
And feed my tast: or Wait, and fat mine Eye
And Eare with Sights and Sounds, Heart Raptures fit,
My Spicknard breaths its sweet perfumes with joy.
My heart thy Viall with this spicknard fill.
Perfumed praise to thee then breath it will.

6. Rugged: rude, uncultivated. **8. Palma Christi:** though in Latin, the popular, not the botanical, name for castor oil, the beans of which come from a tropical tree resembling the palm. **9–10. With . . . bring:** On the other hand, the Latin phrases, *Plastrum Gratiae Dei*, plaster of the Grace of God, *Unguent Apostolorum*, unguent of the Apostles, and *Herba Trinitatis*, herb of the Trinity, are theological-botanical inventions of Taylor's own. **11. Give . . . Savory:** It seems likely that "sage" and "savory," familiar seasoning herbs, are used here for their connotative names. **11–12. me . . . good:** Goldenrod and St. John's Wort are specifics in Culpeper, the latter with many uses and prepared in many ways. "Dub" must (out of the *OED* meanings) mean "smear with oil." **13. Root up:** In this stanza, we turn from herbs applied by an herb doctor to a different figure: a garden from which the weeds (vices) must be rooted out and salutary herbs and flowers planted in their place. **15. set my knot:** seems to mean arrange my garden. **23. Spiknard:** (or spikenard) a fragrant oil or ointment applied to the body. Sometimes within the poem it is called God's, sometimes man's: if man's, it is God's received by Grace.

I HAVE EATE MY HONY COMB WITH MY HONY. I HAVE DRUNK MY WINE WITH MY MILK.

[*Cant. 5:1, Meditation 85, Second Series*]

Oh! Angells, stand agastard at my Song;
The Aire scarce e're sedans such news as this.
The Soule, Christs Spouse his garden Bed's become
Where Christ doth walk in Aromatick bliss.
Sin slaying Grace he gets as Myrrh and Spice.
Grace Nutritive's his Wine, Milk, Hony Choice.

Repentance, Patience, and Humility
And Graces such that mortify our Sin
Thou gatherst up as garden fruits with joy,
Thy bitter Myrrh and Sweet Spice note this thing.
The Exercising of these graces Choice,
Perfume thy Ambient aire with Holy Spice.

Faith, Hope, and Love with Heavenizing Joy.
These graces Nutritive to Souls arise
As Honey in its Comb, deliciously
Unto thy Palate in their Exercise.
Thou in the Garden eats as Hony Good,
And drinkst as wine and milk, sweet Sillibub.

Hast set these Slips, Lord, of the Holy Ghost
In me thy gardens bed? Do they grow there
And bear thee spirituall fruits the which thou dost
Delight thy Palate with, as Choicest Cheere?
Oh! Do these graces that thou sets in mee
Thy Hony, Wine, and Milk Cook up for thee?

Who could believe it, if thou hadst not said
I'm come into my Garden, in its Shine
Have got my myrrh with Spice up. (Oh! sweet trade)
My Hony ate and drunk with milk my Wine?

I HAVE EATE MY HONY COMB. **1. agastard:** aghast, i.e., amazed. **2. sedans:** carries, as in a sedan chair, an aristocratic form of conveyance. **5. Sin . . . Spice:** The first two words should be taken as a compound, Sin-slaying Grace, and Grace as thus negative is contrasted and joined with Nutritive Grace (grace positive). **11–12. The . . . Spice:** Choice and Spice were an accurate rhyme even in the age of Pope. **13. Heavenizing:** a Taylorian coinage (i.e., heaven-making joy). **18. Sillibub:** (or syllabub) a drink made of milk or cream curdled by the admixture of wine and often spiced and sweetened.

Hast Eate and drunk my Holy Fair and Good?
Hony ints Comb, and Winemilk Sillibub?

What thing is this? How sweet? How Good? How brave?
Oh! Leape my Soule for joy: art thou become
A Spice bed in Christ's Garden where each Wave
Of spiced aire brieze all his Walks along:
Oh! dress thy Garden, Lord; it fatten well
That I its bed may with such Fruits excell.

Be thou my Gardener, Lord, make my Soule
Thy Gardens Knot. Thy Grace my plants set there.
And make my fruits, thy Myrrh and Spice out rowle,
My Hope, Faith, Charity, thy Chiefe good cheere.
Then Hony, Wine, and Milk Well Spic'de by mee
Shall disht with Praise, thy entertainment bee.

I GIVE UNTO THEM ETERNAL LIFE.

[*John 10:28, Meditation 90, Second Series*]

ETERNITY as timelessness—"world without end"—cannot be comprehended by a time-bound creature; it "snick-snarls" his brains. As for "eternal damnation"—which Taylor does not doubt and to which he gives the third stanza of this poem—it is not rightly called life but "Living Death."

Eternal Life! What Life is this, I pray?
Eternity snick snarls my Brains, thought on:
Its the Arithimaticians Wrack each way.
It hath begining, yet it end hath none.
He that hath been ten thousand years therein,
'S as far from 'ts end, as when they did begin.

Eternity indeed is Adjunct to
The Life of Man. Of all men Good, and Bad.
As to Deaths Darksom Entery they goe
They e're shall live and joyous be, or sad.
Eternall life, then is dicotamizd
Into a Life of Joy or miseries.

This last is Calld Everlasting Punishment
Or Everlasting sad Distruction,
Or second Death. Not Life. Its Life all shent
Of Good, and filld with Deaths Edition.
This though the Worms alive, is Living Death,
A thousand times worse than to have no breath.

Eternall Life then's in a right Sense this.
That All things blissfull do to it belong
Life Naturall, and Spirituall Life's in bliss
Eternizde in Eternall Joyes that throng.
Though all by Nature Death indeed doth fine.
Yet, Lord, thou giv'st Eternall Life to thine.

Oh! what a Lord is mine? How rich? that he
Gives his, Eternall Life: that doth Contain
All Heaven and its Glory, Bliss, and Glee
Within it; Hee is Rightfull Lord of th'Same.
For none can give that which he never had:
Wheather that gift he gives be good, or bad.

And though he give this Gift so rich to his
His Wealth and Glory's not thereby Diminish:
He hath the Spring of Life, and Life of bliss.
When they their Pilgrimage have fully finisht,
Out of His Spring of life and Bliss that flowth,
Confer Eternall Life on them he doth.

Life Naturall (although Essentiall to
All Living things) and Spirituall Life indeed,
Peculiar to Rationalls also
Containd are in Christs Gift as in a Seed,
Are both Adjuncted with Eternity
In that he gives them them Eternally.

Ripe Grace in all its Orient Blossoms bright
Ripe Glory in its flower of brightest Shine,
Ripe joy upon the highest branch full ripe
Are in this Life Eternall made most fine,
All blanched o're in orient Glory all
Do send their Shining Rayes on them to fall.

Oh! Boundless Sea, and Bottomless of Love,

34. brieze: breeze (used as a verb). **38. Knot:** the center of an intricately laid out flower bed. **39. my fruits:** my good affections. I GIVE UNTO THEM ETERNAL LIFE. **11. dicotamizd:** dichotomized—divided into two sections.

15. shent: deprived of. **21. Life Naturall:** probably a reference to the "Resurrection of the Body": the "spiritual Body," of which St. Paul speaks, has its part in "eternal life." **37–42. Life . . . Eternally:** Both Natural Life (that of the body) and Spiritual Life ("Peculiar to Rationalls"—men with reason) are "Adjuncted"—added—to Eternity. **47. blanched:** whitened.

Confer'd on Saints. Oh! richest gift ere gi'n!
Worth more than thousands Worlds: all Heaven above,
Whole Heavens of Love; and God to boot therein:
God, Bliss, Joy, Glory, Eternal Life enjoy'de
Oh! Happiness! Saints Happy shall abide.

Hence, Lord, I kiss thy Feet, and humbly Cry
Give mee this Gift, Eternall Life I pray.
'Twill gild my Harp O're very gloriously,
And spiritualize my Strings thy tunes to play.
Life Naturall's the Base: the Spirituall is
The Meane: the Tenour is Eternall Bliss.

Lord, make my Person, subject of thy Gift
Eternal Life its Adjunct gi'n by thee.
My Person then, thy Well-Tun'de Harp shall lift
Thy Praises up in Tunes sung forth by mee.
Then on my Spirituall Wiars harmoniously
Thy Sweetest Tunes shall ring Eternall Joy.

LET HIM KISS ME WITH THE KISSES OF HIS MOUTH.

[*Cant. 1:2, Meditation 97, Second Series*]

❡ THE SECOND of two meditations on the same text.

My onely Lord, when with no muddy Sight,
Mine Eyes behold that ardent Flame of Love,
Thy Spouse, when that her day Light seemed night
In passionate affection seemd to move. 4
When thou to her didst onely Cease to show
Thy sweet love token: makes me cry out, Oh!

Although in trying, I through grace can finde
My heart holds such Conclusions in't, that I
Account this World, Silver, and Gold, refinde
Pearles, Pretious Stones, Riches, and Friends a toy.
Methinks I could part with them all for thee
Yet know not what I should if tri'de should bee.

I dare not say, such ardent flames would rise
Of true Loves passion, in its Blinks or Blisses,
As in thy Holy Spouse's heart that cries
Oh! let him kiss mee with his orall kisses.
Should he but stop such acts of love and grace
Making dark Clouds mask up his brightsom face.

If such strong Flame of Love, be made the mark
And Cata Pantos of true Love, then who
Can prove his marriage knot to Christ in's heart
That doth not finde such ardent flames oreflow?
When thy bright Sun-Shine Face doth weare a Cloude
Methinks my Soule in Sorrows thicket shroudes.

Yet pardon, Lord, give me this word again:
I feare to wrong myselfe, or Gracious thee.
This I can say, and can this say mentain,
If thou withdrawst, my heart soon sinks in mee.
Though oftentimes my Spirits dulled, grow,
If so I am, I am not alwayes soe:

When thou dost shine, a Sunshine day I have:
When I am cloudy then I finde not thee:
When thou dost cloud thy face, thy Face I crave.
The Shining of thy face enlivens mee.
I live and dy as Smiles and Frowns take place:
The Life, and Death of Joy Lodge in thy face.

But yet methinks my pipkin is too small.
It holds too little of Loves liquour in't.
All that it holds for thee seems none at all.
Thou art so dear, it is too cheape a Drink.
If I had more thou shouldst have more of mee 41
If Better, better too. I all give thee.

If thou, my Lord, didst not accept a mite
More than a mountain, if the mite doth hold
More than a mountain of the heart Love right
I should be blankt, my heart would grow so cold.
A Quarter of a Farthen halfe a mite
Of Love thou likest well, its heart delight.

52. to boot: a phrase still surviving in rural New England, meaning "in addition." **59–60. Base . . . Tenour**: a three-part harmonization, the bass, the mean (or middle) voice, the tenor. LET HIM KISS ME. **3. Thy Spouse**: the soul. **14. Blinks**: periods of being ignored; glimpses in contrast to steady illuminations and assurances.

20. Cata Pantos: *kata pantos*, first of the three Aristotelian laws of method—this, the *lex de omni*, or law of universal application. Cf. Stanford, p. 256, and W. J. Ong, *Ramus* (1958), pp. 258–59. **27. this say**: noun, followed by "maintain" (verb). **37. pipkin**: small earthen pot or cup. **38. liquor**: liquid. **46. blankt**: nonplussed; frustrated; blenched (turn white). **47. Farthen**: farthing; a coin of small worth.

Then let thy Loveliness, Lord touch my heart.
And let my heart imbrace thy loveliness:
That my small mite of Love might on thee dart,
And thy great selfe might my poor love possess.
My little mite of Love shall musick sweet
Tune forth on thee, its harp, that heaven shall greet.

WHEN THEY HAD SUNG AN HYMN.

[*Matt. 26:30, Meditation 110, Second Series*]

❡ THE Lord's Supper, with its Hymn, re-enacted with memories of the Death to follow, by the Church.

The Angells sung a Carole at thy Birth,
My Lord, and thou thyselfe didst sweetly sing
An Epinicioum at thy Death, on Earth
And order'st thine, in memory of this thing
Thy Holy Supper, closing it at last
Up with an Hymn, and Choakst the foe thou hast.

This Feast thou madst in memory of thy death
Which is disht up most graciously: and towers
Of reeching vapours from thy Grave (Sweet breath)
Aromatize the Skies. That sweetest Showers
Richly perfumed by the Holy Ghost,
Are rained thence upon the Churches Coast.

Thy Grave beares flowers to dress thy Church withall.
In which thou dost thy Table dress for thine.
With Gospell Carpet, Chargers, Festivall
And Spirituall Venison, White Bread and Wine
Being the Fruits thy Grave brings forth and hands
Upon thy Table where thou waiting standst.

Dainties most rich, all spiced o're with Grace,
That grow out of thy Grave do deck thy Table
To entertain thy Guests, thou callst, and place
Allowst, with welcome, (and this is no Fable)
And with these Guests I am invited to't
And this rich banquet makes me thus a Poet.

Thy Cross planted within thy Coffin beares
Sweet Blossoms and rich Fruits, Whose steams do rise
Out of thy Sepulcher and purge the aire
Of all Sins damps and fogs that Choake the Skies.
This Fume perfumes Saints hearts as it out peeps
Ascending up to bury thee in th'reechs.

Joy stands on tiptoes all the while thy Guests
Sit at thy Table, ready forth to sing
Its Hallilujuhs in sweet musicks dress
Waiting for Organs to imploy herein.
Here matter is allowd to all, rich, high,
My Lord, to tune thee Hymns melodiously.

Oh! make my heart thy Pipe: the Holy Ghost
The Breath that fills the same and Spiritually.
Then play on mee thy pipe that is almost
Worn out with piping tunes of Vanity.
Winde musick is the best if thou delight
To play the same thyselfe, upon my pipe.

Hence make me, Lord, thy Golden Trumpet Choice
And trumpet thou thyselfe upon the same
Thy heart enravishing Hymns with Sweetest Voice.
When thou thy Trumpet soundst, thy tunes will flame.
My heart shall then sing forth thy praises sweet
When sounded thus with thy Sepulcher reech.

Make too my Soul thy Cittern, and its wyers
Make my affections: and rub off their rust
With thy bright Grace. And screw my Strings up higher
And tune the same to tune thy praise most Just.
Ile close thy Supper then with Hymns, most sweet
Burr'ing thy Grave in thy Sepulcher's reech.

WHEN THEY HAD SUNG AN HYMN. **3. Epinicioum:** ἐπινίκιον, song of victory. **15. Carpet:** earlier had a wider signification, and here doubtless means a cloth on the communion table. **Chargers:** a large plate or flat dish, doubtless here to hold the communion bread. **16. Venison:** probably in apposition with "White Bread," both (in the Elizabethan sense of the word) being "meat."

34–36. Waiting . . . melodiously: The organ was not used in New England churches in Puritan times. The sense here is the human organs like the larynx—more generally, instrumentalities. **49. Cittern:** cithern, a sort of guitar, strung with wire and struck with a plectrum. **54. Burr'ing:** burying? Taylor seems to intend some distinction between "grave" and "sepulchre," though not merely the usual one of *grave* = place for the burial of one dead body and *sepulchre* = tomb, a building rising above the ground and enclosing more than one grave.

I AM THE ROOT AND OFFSPRING OF DAVID.

[*Rev. 22:16, Meditation 113, Second Series*]

IN THE "mystical" Book of Revelation, Jesus declares himself to be both the root (the origin) of David and also his offspring. This is the central orthodox paradox, that of the God-man, incarnated in time as to His human nature but existing as God before all time.

The identification of the tree with a grape tree is probably a combination of Christ's saying to His disciples, "I am the true vine" (John 15:1) and the use of wine made of grapes in the Lord's Supper. This is the central conceit of the poem; the subordinate figure is the labyrinth or the door which needs a key: both types of the mystery of how One can be at once "root" and "offspring."

Help, oh! my Lord, anoint mine Eyes to see
How thou art Wonderfull thyselfe all ore,
A Common Wealth of Wonders: Rich Vine tree
Whose Boughs are reevd with miracles good Store.
Let thy Sweet Clew lead me thy Servant right
Throughout this Labyrinth of Wonders bright.

Here I attempt thy rich delightfull Vine
Whose bowing boughs buncht with sweet clusters, ripe
Amongst the which I take as Cordiall wine
This Bunch doth bleed into my Cup delight.
It Cramps my thoughts. What Root, and Offspring too
Of David: Oh! how can this thing be true?

What top and bottom, Root and Branch unto
The selfe same tree how can this be? oh-fiddle!
It cannot be. This thing may surely goe
As harder far to read than Sampsons Riddle.
A Father and a Son to th'selfe same man!
This wond'rous is indeed: read it who can.

The Root the tree, the Tree the branch doth beare.
The tree doth run between the branch, and Root.
The root and branch are too distinct a pair
To be the same: Cause and Effect they sute.
How then is Christ the Root, and Offspring bright
Of David, Shew, come, read this riddle right.

Lend me thy key, holy Eliakim,
T'unlock the doore untill thy glory shine.
And by thy Clew me thorow lead and bring
Cleare through this Labyrinth by this rich twine.
Posamnitick's Labyrinth now doth appeare
An Easy thing unto the passage here.

But this doth seem the key unto the Lock.
Thy Deity, my Lord, is Davids root:
It sprang from it: its rooted on this rock.
Thy Humane nature is its Offspring-Sute.
Thy Deity gave David Being, though
Thy Humane Being did from David flow.

Hence thou both Lord, and Son of David art,
Him Being gav'st, and Being tookst of him.
This doth unbolt the Doore, and light impart
To shew the nature of this wondrous thing.
Hence two best natures do appeare to stand
United in thy Person hand in hand.

My blessed Lord, thou art like none indeed.
Godhead, and Manhood harmonize in thee.
Hence thou alone wee mediator read,
'Tween God, and Man, and setst Gods Children free
From all Gods wrath, and wholy them restore
Into that Favour, which they lost before.

Hence give thou me true Faith in thee to have:
Make me thy branch, be thou my root thyselfe,
And let thy Grace root in my heart, I Crave
And let thy purchase be my proper Wealth:
And when this Sweet hath in my heart full Sway
My sweetest musick shall thy praise display.

I AM THE ROOT AND OFFSPRING OF DAVID. **16. Sampsons Riddle**: Cf. Judg. 14:8–14. **25. Eliakim**: Cf. Isa. 22:20–22, with its reference to Eliakim as possessing "the key of the house of David."

THE BRIGHT AND MORNING STAR.

[*Rev. 22:16, Meditation 114, Second Series*]

ON EARTH, Christ is the morning star; in Heaven (in His eternal form), the sun of righteousness, where we shall one day so behold Him.

But by night God has also given a polestar, which guides through the night of man's fallen nature and consequent intellectual darkness to the morning star.

A Star, Bright Morning Star, the shining Sun
Of Righteousness, in Heaven Lord thou art.

29. Posamnitick's Labyrinth: The famous labyrinth built by Psammetichus, Egyptian ruler of the thirteenth dynasty.

Thou pilotst us by night, which being run
Away, thou bidst all darkness to depart.
The Morning Star peeps up an usher gay
'Fore th'Sun of Righteousness to grace the day.

All men benighted are by fall, and Sin:
Thou Graces pole star art to pilote's from it:
The night of Sorrow and Desertion spring,
Thou morning Starr dost rise, and not a Comet.
This night expired now, is dead and gone:
The Day Spring of sweet Comfort cometh on.

The Morning Star doth rise, Dews gracious fall:
And spirituall Herbs, and sweet Celestiall flowers
Sprinkled therewith most fragrantly do call
The Day Star up, with golden Curls, and Towers
Put back the Curtains of the azure skies
And gilde the aire while that the Sun doth rise.

The night of Persecution up arose.
Not Even, but the morning star there to
Soon riseth: vant ill looks: the last Cock Crows
The Morning Star up: out the Sun doth go.
Farewell darke night, Welcome bright gracious day.
As Joy Divine comes on, Griefe goes away.

This world's a night-shade, or a pitchy night,
All Canopi'de with storms and Cloudes all darke.
Sending out thunders, Lightnings and with might,
But thou our Pole star art, which we must marke.
While th'morning Star hands dawning light along:
Let Grace sing now, Birds singing time is come.

Whilst thou, my Pole-star shinst my Lord, on mee
Let my poore pinnace saile thereby aright,
Through this darke night untill its harbor bee
The Daystars bay, the spring of dayly light,
The Usher bidding of the night, good night
And Day, Good morrow lightend with delight.

If I by thee, my Pole star, steere aright
Through this dark night of foule hard weather here
My Vessell safely to the harbour bright
Of thee, my Morning Star, ere shining clear.
I then shall soon Eternal Day possess
Wherever shines the Sun of Righteousness.

Grant me, my Lord, by thee, my Star to steere.
Through this darke vale of tears untill I meet,
Thee here my morning Star outshining cleare,
Shewing my night is past, and day doth peep.
When thou my Sun of Righteousness makst day.
My Harp shall thy Eternall praise then play.

Thou Jacobs Star, in's Horizon didst rise.
And fix't in Heaven, Heavens Steeridge Star.
To steer poor sinners out from Enemies
Coasts unto Graces Realm, (Best State by far).
Thou sentst a star in th'East to lead Wise men
Thence to thyselfe, when born in Bethlehem.

The golden locks of this bright star, I pray,
Make leade us from sins quarters to the Coast
Of Graces tillage: darkness from, to th'Bay
Of Consolation and the Holy Ghost.
And from this Vale of tears to Glory bright
Where our tunde breath shall ne're be Choakt by th'night.

MY DOVE IS ONE THE ONELY ONE OF HER MOTHER THE CHOICE ONE OF HER THAT BARE HER.

[*Cant. 6:9, Meditation 142, Second Series*]

THROUGHOUT this poem, the Spouse is the Church. The soul prays in the last stanza to be made "a member of this Spouse" (cf. St. Paul, Rom. 12:4–8 on the meaning of "member"—literally, part of the body; spiritually, performing its own use). Taylor does not attempt to fix the allegorical meaning of the Spouse's Mother (the Synagogue?) or the other "Queens and Concubines" (the "higher religions"?).

What shall I say, my Deare Deare Lord? most Deare
Of thee! My choisest words when spoke are then
Articulated Breath, soon disappeare.

THE BRIGHT AND MORNING STAR. **16. Curls:** anything spiral. **Towers:** vertical ascent.

49. Jacobs Star: Cf. Num. 24:17: "There shall come a Star out of Jacob," traditionally interpreted as prophecy of the Messiah. **53. a star in th'East:** Cf. Matt. 2:1–12. **60. tunde:** tun'd.

If wrote are but the Drivle of my pen
Beblackt with my inke, soon torn worn out unless
Thy Holy Spirit be their inward Dress.

What, what a Say is this. Thy Spouse doth rise.
Thy Dove all Undefiled doth excell
All though but one the onely in thine Eyes
All Queen and Concubines that bear the bell.
Her excellence all excellency far
Transcends as doth the Sun a pinking Star.

She is the Onely one her mother bore
Jerusalem ever above esteems
Her for her Darling her choice one therefore
Thou holdst her for the best that ere was seen.
The Sweetest Flower in all thy Paradise
And she that bore her Made her hers most Choice.

That power of thine that made the Heavens bow,
And blush with shining glory ever cleare
Hath taken her within his glorious brow
And made her Madam of his Love most Deare
Hath Circled her within his glorious arms
Of Love most rich, her shielding from all harms.

She is thy Dove, thy Undefiled, she shines
In thy rich Righteousness all Lovely, White
The onely Choice one of her Mother, thine
Most beautifull beloved, thy Delight.
The Daughters saw and blessed her, the Queens
And Concubines her praisd and her esteem.

Thy Love that fills the Heavens brimfull throughout
Coms tumbling on her with transcendent bliss
Even as it were in golden pipes that spout
In Streams from heaven, Oh! what love like this?
This comes upon her, hugs her in its Arms
And warms her Spirits. Oh! Celestiall Charms.

Make me a member of this Spouse of thine
I humbly beg deck thus, as Tenis Ball
I shall struck hard on th'ground back bounce with Shine
Of Praise up to the Chamber floor thy Hall,
Possesses. And at that bright Doore I'l sing
Thy sweetest praise untill thou'st take me in.

WHO IS SHE THAT LOOKS FORTH AS THE MORNING. FARE AS THE MOON CLEAR AS THE SUN. TERRIBLE AS AN ARMY WITH BANNERS.

[*Cant. 6:10, Meditation 143, Second Series*]

THROUGH most of the poem, the Church is the Spouse of Christ; as the last stanza makes—perhaps too prosaically—evident, the Soul of the communicant, "the saint," is a "member" of the Spouse, like "a Toe, or Finger." But, at least by metonymy (the use of the part for the whole), Taylor also, like mystical writers, begins his poem with the assurance that his own soul is "espoused" to God.

Wonders amazed! Am I espousd to thee?
My Glorious Lord? What! shall my bit of Clay
Be made more bright than brightest Angells bee,
Looke forth like as the Morning every way?
And shall my lump of Dirts ware such attire?
Rise up in heavenly Ornaments thus, higher?

But still the Wonders stand, shall I looke like
The glorious morning that doth gilde the Skie
With golden beams that make all day grow light
And View the World ore with its golden Eye?
And shall I rise like fair as the fair Moon,
And bright as is the Sun, that lights Each room?

When we behold a piece of China Clay
Formd up into a China Dish compleat
All spiced ore as with gold Sparks display

MY DOVE IS ONE THE ONELY ONE. **10. bear the bell:** a homely English phrase for "take first place"—as does the bell-wether or leading sheep. **12. pinking Star:** pinking = blinking—ultimately, now seen, now not seen—transient, at least to observation. **37–41. Make . . . Possesses:** Syntax and punctuation are obscure. There should be a full stop after "thine," it would seem; and "deck" would seem to mean "place" (noun) rather than "adorn" (verb). The general sense is clear. Let me (let a tennis ball) be struck so hard that I bounce up to the "Chamber floor": "Hall" is, architecturally, the vaguer term; "Chamber" the room of Bridegroom and Spouse (the "Church").

WHO IS SHE THAT LOOKS FORTH. **2. my bit of Clay:** the body. **13–18. When . . . Skill:** Clay transfigured by art (of which Taylor had read in a Jesuit's book on China) is like human nature or the body—which is clay—transfigured by Grace. **15. spiced:** not to be interpreted in terms of odor but of visual variety of touches, traces, dashes.

Their beauty all under a glass robe neate,
We gaze thereat and wonder rise up will
Wondring to see the Chinees art and Skill.

How then should we and Angells but admire
Thy Skill and Vessell thou hast made bright thus
Out for to look like to the Morning tire
That shineth out in all bright Heavenly plush?
Whose golden beams all Varnish ore the Skies
And gild our Canopy in golden wise?

Wonders are nonplust to behold thy Spouse
Look forth like the morning whose sweet rayes
Gild ore our Skies as with transparent boughs
Like Orient gold of a Celestiall blaze.
Fair as the Moon bright as the Sun most cleare
Gilding with spirituall gold graces bright Sphere.

O Blessed! Virgin Spouse shall thy sharp lookes
Gild o're the Objects of thy Shining Eyes
Like fairest Moon, and Brightest Sun do th'Fruits
Even as that make the morning shining rise?
The fairest moon in'ts Socket's Candle light
Unto the Night and th'Sun's days Candle bright.

Thy Spouses Robes all made of Spirituall Silk
Of th'Web wove in the Heavens bright Loom indeed,
By the Holy Spirits hand more white than milk
And fitted to attire thy Soule that needs.
As th'morning bright's made of the Suns bright rayes
So th'Spirits Web thy Souls rich Loom o're layes.

Oh! Spouse adorned like the morning Cleare
Chasing the night out from its Hemesphere.
And like the fair face of the Moon: whose Cheere
Is very brave and like the bright Sun peare,
Thus gloriously fitted in brightest Story
Of Grace espousd to be the king of glory.

16. glass robe: the glaze of the porcelain. **21. tire:** attire. **22. plush:** once, at least, considered grander than velvet. Cf. *OED.* **23. Varnish:** once capable of an honorific meaning: adorn, beautify. **43–48. Oh . . . glory:** The Spouse is like the moon; the Bridegroom (God) like the Sun. **45. Cheere:** expression of face. **46. brave:** once had a wider meaning than now: cf. Herbert: "Sweet rose whose hue, angry and brave" (splendid, handsome). **46. peare:** doubtful: possibly *appears;* possibly *peer* (equal to).

And thus deckt up methinks my Eare attends
Kings, Queens and Ladies Query. Who is this?
Enravisht at her Sight, how she out sends
Her looks like to the morning filld with Bliss,
Fair as the Moon Clear as the Sun in'ts Costs
And terrible as is a bannerd host?

And all in Graces Colours thus bedight
That do transend with glorys Shine, the Sun
And Moon for fairness and for glorious light
As doth the Sun a gloworms Shine out run.
No wonder then and if the Bridesgroom say
Thou art all fair my Love, Yea Everyway.

May I a member be, my Lord, once made
Here of thy Spouse in truest Sence, though it bee
The meanest of all, a Toe, or Finger 'rayde
Ist have enough of bliss, espousd to thee.
Then I in brightest glory ere't belong
Will Honour thee singing that Wedden Song.

RETURN, OH SHULAMITE, RETURN RETURN.

[*Cant. 6:13, Meditation 146, Second Series*]

THE Shulamite is the peasant love of King Solomon—at least in the traditional conception of the poem. (An admirable summary of more recent views will be found in Hugh J. Schonfield's *The Song of Songs,* 1959.) In devotional literature, the theme is recurrent of the appearance and disappearance of "sensible devotion." This—one of Taylor's most moving lyrics—is an appeal to the *Deus absconditus,* the "hidden God," to manifest Himself again.

There are two striking figures—the earlier and briefer, that of the child who has lost sight of his nurse; the second, worked out in something like the manner of Donne, that of usury.

Usury is taking interest on a loan which cannot be repaid. *Rent, use,* and *interest* are all technical terms. Man can never repay God's love; the *principal* can never be restored. So God is the greatest Usurer, yet His usury (however high the rate of interest) is blessed.

My Deare Deare Lord, I know not what to say:
Speech is too Course a web for me to cloath
My Love to thee in or it to array,
Or make a mantle. Wouldst thou not such loath?

53. Costs: course. **63. 'rayde:** arrayed. **65. ere't belong:** before it be long. **66. Wedden Song:** wedding song.

Thy Love to mee's too great, for mee to shape
A Vesture for the Same at any rate.

When as thy Love doth Touch my Heart down tost
It tremblingly runs, seeking thee its all,
And as a Child when it his nurse hath lost
Runs seeking her, and after her doth Call.
So when thou hidst from me, I seek and sigh.
Thou saist return return Oh Shulamite.

Rent out on Use thy Love thy Love I pray.
My Love to thee shall be thy Rent and I
Thee Use on Use, Intrest on intrest pay.
There's none Extortion in such Usury.
I'le pay thee Use on Use for't and therefore
Thou shalt become the greatest Usurer.
But yet the principall I'le neer restore.
The Same is thine and mine. We shall not Jar.
And so this blessed Usury shall be
Most profitable both to thee and mee.

And shouldst thou hide thy shining face most fair
Away from me. And in a sinking wise
My trembling beating heart brought nigh t'dispare
Should cry to thee and in a trembling guise
Lord quicken it. Drop in its Eares delight
Saying Return, Return my Shulamite.

PERRY MILLER
Editor

Benjamin Franklin

1706–1790

Jonathan Edwards

1703–1758

THE INTELLECTUAL history—or, if you will, the spiritual history—of the United States has been dramatized by a series of pairs of personalities, contemporaneous and contrasting, which have become avatars of the contradictory thrusts within our effort to find or to create a national identity.

To begin with, there is in primordial Virginia a swashbuckling adventurer, Captain John Smith, frankly announcing that only the search for wealth will found a commonwealth and that the wilderness will become a theater of gigantic economic exploitation; whereas, on the rock-bound and unfertile coast of New England there is William Bradford directing an energy no less Elizabethan toward the realization of a holy society. After the Revolution emerge the exemplary figures of Jefferson and Hamilton, who form the division between the political convictions that have since contended for mastery. In the Civil War the sectional strife finds its perfect symbolism in the opposition of Robert E. Lee and Abraham Lincoln. But of all these, and of several lesser pairs, the pre-eminently eloquent linked antagonists in American culture will always be Jonathan Edwards and Benjamin Franklin.

This duel is all the more eloquent, not because the two met in open debate, as did Jefferson and Hamilton in the 1790's—they showed little or no awareness of each other's existence—but because they started in their contrary directions from the same parent stock, the Puritanism of New England. Each may be said to realize a potentiality that in the original creed was concealed beneath the supposed unity of this highly systematized version of Protestantism. As they divide the heritage between them, Franklin and Edwards expose the inner tensions which not only the Puritans but all Protestant immigrants—the Dutch and Scotch-Irish Presbyterians, Baptists, Quakers, German Calvinists and Lutherans, and eventually the Methodists—brought to these shores. They make wonderfully clear how this incipient civil war within the piety could be brought into the open only by the conditions of this new world, where there were not the social or institutional complexities which in Europe prevented it from pre-empting the center of the intellectual stage.

Puritans originally got their name from their enemies, because their avowed purpose in England was to "purify" the Church of England from what they considered the remnants of medieval Catholicism that still adhered to it—the hierarchy, vestments, prescribed prayers, and stated forms of traditional ritual. They declared that the Church should be stripped of these "rags and tatters of the Whore of Babylon"—to use their blunt language—until it was reduced to the sparse simplicity of organization and conduct which they believed had been meticulously set forth in the New Testament. Hence the Churchmen called them "Puritans," but also, in still angrier derision, more exactly, "Precisians." Puritans wanted life to be regulated precisely by the rules of the supreme legal code of Christendom, the whole Bible, which in their comprehension provided precepts for all departments of life—for family, economic activity, and political policy as well as for ecclesiastical polity. In theology the Puritans were at one with the other branches of international Calvinism—Swiss, French, German, Dutch, and Scottish. But in this vast communion, the English Puritans were distinguished by the zeal with which they pressed theological considerations into the secular realms of human behavior.

A few of them, generally of the simpler and less prosperous sort, were so impelled by this temper that they became, as Bradford recounts, "Separatists." Wherefore, they were harried out of the land. One band eventually became the Pilgrims of Plymouth in Massachusetts Bay. However, the majority of Puritans refused to "separate" because they wanted to fight within the Church for ultimate conquest. They did not want even toleration, let alone liberty: they intended to rule. In 1630 that hope had become remote; hence a compact company, having somehow secured a charter from Charles I which bestowed legality upon the venture, arrived at the site of Boston. In the next decade some ten thousand followed; these expanded across Massachusetts and into Connecticut; from them comes everything that has been praised or cursed in America under the name of "Puritanism." From their ranks come the two most distinguished intellects and prose artists of the tradition, who in these selections pose for us the paradox of Puritan materialism and immateriality.

The inmost essence of the Puritan spirit is certainly embodied in the cadences of William Bradford. Yet, since he was a Separatist, he is not quite representative of the mass of Puritan immigrants to New England. Edward Taylor, in his isolation at Westfield, was driven to an inward analysis of his spiritual condition which is the heart of the Puritan's demand upon himself—that nervous tic of introspection which survives even today as what has been nicknamed, generally in tones of ridicule, "The New England Conscience." Still, in his secret self-examinations through verses of a "metaphysical" sort, he was also unrepresentative of the dominant literary ethos. In the New England of Taylor's time, and in the youthful decades of both Edwards and Franklin, this rule was deliberately termed the "plaine stile." Both Edwards and Franklin are thus heirs of a once unitary tradition, which they split asunder but of which they are alike legitimate descendants. Franklin in the life of the world and Edwards in the life of the spirit both strove for, and each in his widely differing manner attained, a clarity, simplicity, directness—a suppression of all showy and "literary" embellishments—which is the lasting impress of the Puritan spirit upon American expression. Not, of course, that many writers have not revolted against it, including several lineal descendants of the Puritan founders; but on the whole, one is safe in saying, the literature of America is marked by its concern, often neurotic rather than sanative, that literature be not regarded as an end in itself, but that expression be put to work in the service of a creed, a career, a philosophy, a disgruntlement or a rage.

This rule of efficiency as the governing purpose of the spoken or written word was part and parcel of the conception Puritans brought into the control of all areas of their behavior, most strenuously into that of their pecuniary labor. The whole complex of that code has been summarized by modern sociologists as "the Protestant ethic." Though elements of it may be found in all the emerging business cultures of the time, the English Puritans perfected it more highly than others in Europe, and the New England Puritans brought it to an even higher degree of articulation. Edwards in his pulpit and in his study, Franklin in his printing shop and in the diplomatic chambers of Versailles were both assiduously practicing the ethic of their fathers.

Fundamentally, this mentality was a revulsion against what Protestants held to be the unprofitable monasticism of the Medieval Church, which centered holiness upon withdrawal from the economy of production and distribution, which consigned these crass functions to the inferior orders of peasants or merchants. Instead, the Puritans declared, every "calling"—whether it be ditch-digging, fishing, sailing a vessel, managing a bank, governing a colony or preaching a sermon—was as much a religious exercise as any other. In this view the clergy, though of course commissioned to instruct the yeomen in faith and morals, were no whit superior to their pupils. The great sin in their society was to endeavor to live without a calling, without being industrious at *something*, as did both the Catholic monk and the European nobleman. The Rev. John Cotton, in the classic New England formulation (printed in 1641, but spoken earlier), said, "If thou beest a man that lives without a calling, though thou hast two thousands to spend, yet if thou hast no calling tending to public good, thou art an unclean beast." Yet the ethic was more subtle than merely an injunction to find a job and to work in it as a holy duty: it insisted that energy expended in a calling be regarded as a service for God, and not as a means of profit or of social betterment. Wherefore the Puritan exerts himself the more vigorously in proportion to the more, again in the language of Cotton, "he depends upon God for the quickening and sharpening of his gifts in that calling." That is, he applies himself stoutly, but he attributes success not to his efforts but only to the favor, the complaisance, of God. Likewise, if despite his most energetic performance he encounters disaster—a shipwreck, a plague of locusts, a military defeat—he perceives in the reversal a chastisement of the Lord, rained upon him for his sins. Thereupon he renews with increased vigor his assault upon prosperity.

Therefore, let us be clear that for the Puritan founders the same rationale served in either ditch-digging or manufacturing as in the physical act of putting words on paper: nobody was doing it to amuse himself or others, and not directly with the intention of making money or winning converts. He was doing the job in obedience to the commands of God, or of conscience, or of probity; but he did not, if he was sanctified, bank upon his own talents for success. He cultivated and improved them assiduously, day and night, in order to make an acceptable sacrifice of them to the Puritan Jehovah, who might then be graciously inclined to bestow the desired results, but who might also be inclined, with every right on His side, to reward the desperate effort with complete devastation. Although Franklin blithely put aside the theology out of which this peculiar code arose, he as much as Edwards exemplified it every day of his life. And Edwards, even while refashioning the Jehovah of early Puritanism into a highly impersonalized design of the Newtonian universe, went on offering himself a willing victim to the whims of a Divinity bound by no such rules of justice as were supposed to prevail in human intercourse.

For Edwards, the endeavor resulted in ghastly failure, in the abject humiliation of his dismissal from the Northampton pulpit in 1750, and in his eight years of penurious exile in Stockbridge. For Franklin, the application produced wealth, fame, and the universal approbation of his contemporaries and of posterity. Both of them, in the center of their beings, were indifferent to the consequences, ill or bountiful; both were so caught up, with or without theology, in a vision of ultimate disinterestedness in relation to which either personal triumph or defeat was inconsequential, that the most ethereal writings of Edwards can be easily translated into the most mundane of Franklin's frivolities. Yet the division is not superficial: it is profound, irreconcilable. It also provides a theme, probably the basic and sundering theme, of American literature.

II

COMMENCING his *Autobiography* at the age of sixty-five, in 1771, Franklin recollects that his father's small library contained books on polemic divinity, which he read—always he would read anything that came to hand—and then serenely announces how he subsequently had regretted that "more proper" books had not fallen in his way. The revolutionary violence of Franklin's development is concealed in the casualness of this remark which is, however, like everything he ever wrote, extremely calculated. This child of New England Puritanism simply dumped the whole theological preoccupation overboard; but, not in the slightest ceasing to be a Puritan, he went about his business.

And a very busy business it turned out to be. The mind of Jonathan Edwards is difficult for modern Americans to comprehend because it is so detached from the physical world; the mind of Franklin is equally a mystery because it is so utterly immersed in the world. The life of Edwards can be recounted in a few paragraphs, but the life of Franklin requires volumes. It is possible here to recite only a few of his infinite activities. A journalist of matchless skill, a dabbler in scientific research, where he made important contributions to experimental wisdom (most notably with the kite and key apparatus, which won him the admiration of Europe), founder of a university and of the American Philosophical Society, organizer of the first police department in America and of the first fire department in the modern world, inventor of a stove, of bifocal lenses, and of a harmonica—one runs out of breath trying to enumerate his performances. Postmaster general of the colonies, he developed the most efficient delivery system the world had yet beheld. Starting with nothing, he accumulated a solid fortune before he was fifty. He matched his wits with the best brains of Europe, and never lost a trick. Everything he touched he made a success, gained a profit either for himself or for mankind, and always made the doing a delight.

In between times, he improved his leisure—thus in effect depriving himself of any!—by cultivating the convivial arts, by learning French, Spanish, Latin and Greek, by writing skits and fantasies that rank with the most sophisticated productions of the age, and by producing one indisputable literary classic which, significantly, is about himself.

His birth itself furnishes the first of the myriad differences from Edwards. Where Edwards was born to the clerical elite, Franklin arose out of the yeoman laboring class, out of what Samuel Stone, a pioneer expounder of the New England church polity, had said should be a "silent democracy" in the face of a "speaking aristocracy." His father was a member of the old South Church; this means that he had made a profession of faith and was allowed to participate in the Lord's Supper, but we may be sure he bowed low and yielded the wall to Judge Sewall, also a member, whenever he encountered that worthy. As a worker in a shop Franklin wore the then customary garb, and later, even amid the splendors of Versailles, took care to remind courtiers that he was "a leather aproned man."

The *Autobiography* tells us how he first appeared as an author by working a deception upon his brother. Though he was but sixteen, he already possessed in full the powers of wit, a genial tolerance for all manifestations of humanity, and a resolute will to rise in the world by making fun of whatever stood in his way. So he ridiculed Cotton Mather in the very choice of a *nom de plume*, satirized Harvard College, and looked with a benevolent eye upon the prostitutes of Boston. He tells us that his familiarity with these unfortunates was not academic, that he had intrigues with them and ran the risk of a venereal infection, "though by great good luck I escaped it." Punishment for Edwards was, of course, eternal torment, and Edwards used the plain style to spell out in detail the unceasing agony of the fire which burns the flesh but never consumes it. For Franklin, punishment was the expense and inconvenience which these tawdry affairs cost him. By the time he organized his business in Philadelphia he could exhibit the breadth of his tolerance for the minutiae of existence by vending, in addition to his printing, a staggering variety of items, ranging from soap and ballads to quills, sherry, cheese, lottery tickets, linen rags, plus a salve concocted by his mother-in-law, according to a secret formula, which was guaranteed to cure the itch.

All this was laboring in a calling with a vengeance! We may rest assured that Franklin spent as many hours a day at his occupation as did Edwards. It is important to insist that Franklin's pursuit was as much an abnegation of self as was Edwards'. But Edwards subjected himself to the unremitting discipline in the solitude of his study and let the results appear to his fellow men only in the terrible or serene moments of utterance from his exalted pulpit. Franklin found it not incompatible with a pure devotion to his function to allow his neighbors to behold the process.

There are those who sneer at the *Autobiography* as a vulgar book, brazenly narrating the cheapest piece of social climbing this democracy has ever known. Obviously, it is a success story, and one that often is maddeningly smug. But today we are apt not to notice how it modestly insinuates that Franklin did not proceed only upon an ulterior motive, not even when he pushed his newsprint conspicuously through the streets by wheelbarrow in order to impress the Quaker burghers of Philadelphia. His philosophy and his interest always coincided. We can readily see the splendid coherence of his "Apology for Printers," which is assuredly a brave manifesto for freedom of the press, for the independence of editors, and hence a document of prime importance in the growth of liberty in America. Yet it does include, as being on the same level of respectability with any of the resounding declarations, "I got five shillings by it."

This combination of disinterested devotion to a noble cause, for which Franklin repeatedly held himself as expendable as he did when he risked life and fortune in the Revolution in 1776, with a knack of making it pay in the long run, is his way of perpetuating the Puritan ethic. He is not an exploiter or a gambler; he is not even, in the modern sense of the word, an entrepreneur. He did not so much seek the profit as he let the profit accrue to him because of his virtues.

As soon as he had accumulated what he thought would be a competence, in 1748, he wrote to a friend:

> Thus you see I am in a fair way of having no other tasks than such as I shall like to give myself, and of enjoying what I look upon as a great happiness, leisure to read, study, make experiments, and converse at large with such ingenious and worthy men as are pleased to honour me with their friendship or acquaintance, on such points as may produce something for the common benefit of mankind, uninterrupted by the little cares and fatigues of business.

This is a far remove from the schemes of the normal aspirant for success in the American system, who works in his calling in order eventually to make some sort of splurge, in a mansion, yacht, collection of paintings or of race horses. Franklin put the benefit of mankind in the place of the Puritan's glory of God; thus he could move at ease from Calvinism into the Enlightenment. Hence he could be a bit more candid about counting the fee in shillings as well as in self-congratulation. But he still saw the utility of an occupation as no more than an adjunct to such a calling as was in itself meritorious. It was not as a means for enhancing his material prestige but rather a demonstration of his probity.

This un-puritanized Puritanism is what gives a special quality not only to what Franklin says but to the method in which he says it. His prose works for an effect: to instruct, to persuade or to satirize. The style follows afterwards, so to speak, and surrounds the meaning as an additional dividend; thus in return it renders the meaning twenty times more effective. In his writing as in his business, prosperity pursued virtue, not the other way around. Purity, which was fully content to be merely its own reward, thereupon was bountifully reimbursed for its unselfishness.

Franklin tells how he wrote a pamphlet in favor of paper money; this was a cause of the people against the colony's proprietors and money-men, and here the political issue was the concrete subject of his argument. At the same time, the piece was so well written, and so warmed the hearts of the populace, that they brought all their printing jobs to him: once more he made money. "This," he modestly remarks, "was another advantage gain'd by my being able to write." But a writing which was not manufactured for communication, such as the poetry of Edward Taylor—had he known about it—would have seemed to Franklin no writing at all. "In matters of general concern to the people, and especially where burthens are to be laid upon them, it is of use to consider, as well what they will be apt to think and say, as what they ought to think." His epic of success—as politician and statesman no less than as writer—consists in his never forgetting his audience. What is astounding about his epic is that he found no substantial difference between the audiences of dissolute London or sophisticated Paris, and those of provincial Philadelphia. Or at least, while there may have been wide divergencies, the technique he had perfected in the province proved equally efficacious in the capitals.

Franklin discovered, or rather was born already knowing, that men everywhere, and women even more eagerly, would respond to the same obvious devices for titillating their half-suppressed emotions or their more profane risibilities, for leading them on to the awaited anticlimax, and for preserving their respectability in a humorous explosion. When they were in that mood, assured that while he took them out to sea for a thrill he would land them safely on the shores of morality, they could be maneuvered to ends which Franklin wanted them to reach as though they had conceived of these on their own. Prostitutes on the Boston Common expanded into the heroic sexuality of Polly Baker's speech, then were transformed into the spectacular leap of the whale *up* the Falls of Niagara, and still were inspiring Franklin's aged voice as he amused the grand ladies of France by such elegant nonsense as his dialogue with the gout. When Franklin appears to us most profligate, most immoral in matters of sex or money, most cynical about human motives, he is then the most resolutely—I would even say most cunningly—innocent.

Here he is in truth the adversary of Jonathan Edwards, who in his monogamous love for Sarah Pierrepont never even dreamed of the lures of "loose women," and who yet was infinitely more persuaded of the depravity of the human heart than Franklin would bring himself flatly to confess. Still, in another sense, we may ask ourselves whether both of them, being children of New England, were not acutely conscious of this malediction; we may even allow ourselves to wonder whether, of the two, Franklin, the success-boy and the meliorist, was not really the more pessimistic about the human species than the rigid Calvinist. For it was Franklin, not Edwards, who could write thus to Joseph Priestly in 1782:

> Men I find to be a sort of being very badly constructed, as they are generally more easily provoked than reconciled, more disposed to do mischief to each other than to make reparation, much more easily deceived than undeceived, and having more pride and even pleasure in killing than in begetting one another; for without a blush they assemble in great armies at noonday to destroy, and when they have killed as many as they can, they exaggerate the number to augment the fancied glory; but they creep into corners, or cover themselves with the darkness of night, when they mean to beget, as being ashamed of a virtuous action. A virtuous one it would be, and a vicious one the killing of them, if the species were really worth producing or preserving; but of this I begin to doubt.

Yes, Franklin in 1782 was a tired man, and a certain amount of this must be discounted as the affection of the benevolent eighteenth century to deplore the frailties of mankind in a tone which was not intended really to carry conviction. Still, not even in jest, not even in the most burning sincerity, could Jonathan Edwards, supreme pontiff of human damnation, bring himself to speak so despairingly, contemptuously, of his fellow creatures.

These qualities emerge in the very texture of Franklin's compositions. Probably, because of this seemingly unstable admixture, they can be extravagantly admired, and also, with even more vehemence, denounced as a prostitution of language to the supreme Philistine of the Republic's history, the model of the American who not only has lost his soul but has not enough awareness to realize that he ever had one to lose. Because Franklin has been enshrined, as one historian phrases it, as the "perfect civic leader," the youth of today may understandably find him a bore. We have to exercise a vigorous historical imagination in order to comprehend how brutal was the fight through which Franklin ascended, and how ruthlessly he made his ability to manage words a weapon in that march to victory.

When he started his business in Philadelphia, and saw that he would need an Almanac were he to count on a steady income, he found the small town occupied by a printer named Titan Leeds. Franklin had to get Leeds out of the way. He resorted to a trick which he borrowed from Jonathan Swift, but he never told the Philadelphians where he got it. He predicted the death of Leeds for October 17, 1733. The more Leeds denounced him, the more publicity Franklin received, the affair climaxing in the total destruction of Franklin's victim after the seventeenth when Leeds, foolishly insisting that he still lived, was described by Franklin as an imposter. Even in sober Philadelphia Leeds could not endure the guffaws; he had to migrate to New York. Franklin then had the field to himself, and as he smugly mentions in the *Autobiography* (not relating his discomfiture of Leeds), he made *Poor Richard's Almanack* a highly remunerative enterprise.

In the shop, then, surrounded by the dizzy array of vendible articles, Franklin perfected what he had already displayed to his astonished and envious brother, the art of writing. Simple country boys from Boston to Charleston shouted with self-approving glee once they deciphered the point of such a prognostication as this, for 1734:

> There will be but two eclipses: The first, April 22; the second, October 15. Both of the sun; and both, like Mrs. ——'s modesty, and old neighbor Scrape-all's money, invisible.

His mordant understanding of human nature, which in these years of achievement seldom lapsed—or at least not publicly—into the pessimism of 1782, enabled him to spice the Protestant ethic with enough ribaldry to keep his readers content with their harsh lot. For examples:

> After three days men grow weary of a wench, a guest, and weather rainy.

> A ship under sail and a big-bellied woman are the handsomest things that can be seen common.

> Keep your eyes wide open before marriage, half shut afterwards.

> He who marries for love without money has sorry days and happy nights.

What it means for a literary genius to appear in a congregation of mediocrity—if, that is, the genius elects to devote himself to public relations rather than to court ostracism into Stockbridge—is displayed in the use Franklin made of the truisms of his hapless rival. Leeds had written, "Necessity is a mighty weapon." Franklin, in his always piratical manner, stole this and rephrased it, "Necessity never made a good bargain." Leeds pontificated, "Be careful of the main chance, or it will never take care of you." Franklin brought the idea to earth with "Keep thy shop, and thy shop will keep thee." Where Leeds wrote, "'Tis best to make a good use of another's folly," Franklin drove the moral home with, "Fools make feasts, and wise men eat them." Leeds endeavored to preach that "Bad hours and ill company have ruined many fine young people." Franklin put the message so that the veriest bumpkin could not miss it: "The rotten apple spoils his companions."

Thus he made his *Poor Richard*, as he was delighted to relate, "both entertaining and useful." When he summarized his accumulated sagacity in *The Way to Wealth* (1757), he spoke to the emerging mentality of business enterprise throughout the globe; the declamation was soon translated into all civilized languages, including, once-upon-a-time, the Chinese. In the modern world, the content of *The Way to Wealth* may well be taken either as a pious or a hypocritical profession of the ethic of a nascent capitalism. It may even be dismissed as sanctimonious pretense by the most powerful of capitalists. While the outcome remains to be seen, we are left with the memorial of Franklin's prose style. There are no better words to describe it than his own injunction:

> The words used should be the most expressive that the language affords, provided that they are the most generally understood. Nothing should be expressed in two words that can as well be expressed in one; that is, no synonyms should be used, or very rarely, but the whole should be as short as possible, consistent with clearness; the words should be so placed as to be agreeable to the ear in reading; summarily, it should be

smooth, clear, and short, for the contrary qualities are displeasing.

Indeed, the contrary qualities are displeasing. Franklin sought to ingratiate himself with his listeners, even when they were bound to be his adversaries. Recent investigation [1] has shown that he did not make quite so amicable a conquest of Philadelphia as the *Autobiography* intimates; in the election of 1764, when he was defeated for representative to the Assembly, he was severely traduced in the public press. Franklin could take rebuffs in stride, as Edwards never could. His writings are a constant witness, from the beginning to the end, of his fabulous equanimity. Nothing is to be gained by modern attacks upon his equilibrium, not even when they are launched by so passionate an enemy as D. H. Lawrence. There is not much to learn by attempting to subject him to the terminology of psychoanalysis; he eludes Freud as simply as he eludes the Romantics, and the would-be destroyer ends by wrecking himself, while Franklin remains, as he did in his lifetime, unscathed. He is what he was. Coming out of the Puritan calculation of motives and expenditures, Franklin figured that the arithmetic could be done in this world as well as in relation to the spiritual considerations outside it. Even from his deathbed in 1790 he was able to balance and to close his ledgers, as he did in the blandly heroic letter to Ezra Stiles. In this mode he wrote, and, accordingly, his writings are an imperishable treasure of the race as well as of the nation.

III

JONATHAN EDWARDS, son of the majestic pastor of East Windsor, Connecticut, was born (1703) to command. But, being a child of New England, and of its most cherished class, he was required from the dawn of consciousness to search his soul, to ask of himself interminably the question of whether he was actually qualified to assume the perquisites of the station to which he had been elevated.

By comparison with the living conditions in —shall we say?—an apartment in a modern American city, or indeed any oil-heated house in the present New England countryside, the circumstances of mere physical survival in the parsonage of the Rev. Timothy Edwards during the early years of the eighteenth century presented hazards. Young Jonathan survived these, leaving no reference to such mundane business as stoking the fireplace in the freezing winters—though from his later allusions it is evident that he knew the full horrors of a New England winter and the anguish of its spring. Nor is there any overt recognition of the surely basically formative fact that he was the one boy in a family which otherwise consisted of ten daughters, all of them, as far as we can gather, adoring him. Evidently, he did not have to kindle the fires. Even in Connecticut, the land of steady habits, ministers of the stature of Timothy could employ servants. Jonathan was raised for the life of the mind, as that sort of life was conceived in this virtually frontier community, and to such a life he was dedicated with what proved to be ferocious intensity.

His mother's father was Solomon Stoddard of Northampton. Known as "Pope Stoddard," he dominated the Connecticut Valley from Deerfield to the Sound, an ecclesiastical empire which he defended successfully against the attacks of Boston rivals and of Harvard College. When this principality finally raised up its own college, Edwards inevitably went to Yale, entering at the age of thirteen in 1716. There could never be the slightest question about his "calling": he was predestined to the pulpit. So, after his graduation in 1720, he studied theology in New Haven, served briefly as minister in New York, and then returned for three years as tutor at Yale during an interregnum in the presidency, so that in effect he governed the institution. In 1726 Stoddard was nearing the end of his reign in Northampton (he had come there when it was a frontier outpost, in 1669), and decided that of all his grandsons and his many pupils Jonathan was the one to succeed him. Edwards was ordained early in 1727 and in July married Sarah Pierrepont, then age seventeen, about whom he had written his amazing prose poem before he had ever seen her. Stoddard died in 1729, leaving Edwards seated on the nearest thing to a pontifical throne that New England could devise.

[1] See J. Philip Gleason, "A Scurrilous Colonial Election and Franklin's Reputation," *William and Mary Quarterly*, XVII (January, 1961), 68–84.

Lofty as was that eminence, the mind of Edwards had already climbed intellectual heights far, far above it. While still an undergraduate he read John Locke and Sir Isaac Newton; he saw in a flash of profound insight that these two minds had put mankind into a new and terrifying universe. In their formulation the human organism was irresistibly conditioned by its environment and the physical order would henceforth be a vast impersonal mechanism, following cosmic laws which made no accommodations whatever to the feeble aspirations of the race. Edwards understood at once that in this awful perspective everything that Christian theology supposed it had achieved before the advent of a psychology based upon physical sensation and the mechanistic cosmos was made hopelessly obsolete. If religion was to survive, and especially if the Calvinism of New England was to be retained, then every doctrine would have to be restated in the radically altered philosophical context. He set himself, at that early age, to work out his answer, and thus wrote the "Notes on the Mind"—which he never had the opportunity to systematize into a finished work—and which were printed long after his death. Yet they are the basis, however concealed—and deliberately concealed—of all his thought and extensive expression.

For our purpose it is of primary importance to note that to Edwards the intellectual revolution produced by Locke and Newton not only made imperative a complete restatement of such ideas as predestination, religious emotion, freedom of the will and benevolence, but a still more rigorous reformulation of the plain style. He drew up rules for himself as a writer to which he subjected himself unmercifully and from which his prose derives its distinctive qualities of calmness and lucidity, its unique combination of consuming passion and flawless restraint:

> When I would prove any thing, to take special care that the matter be so stated, that it shall be seen, most clearly and distinctly, by everyone, just how much I would prove, and to extricate all questions from the least confusion or ambiguity of words, so that the ideas shall be left naked.

The founders had insisted upon the plain style as a way of communicating with ordinary congregations; but their aesthetic permitted considerable elocution which, by contrast with that of Edwards, seems a riot of metaphor, exclamation, and rhetorical flourish. By "naked ideas" Edwards intended no less than these, in and of themselves, to communicate. In his more notorious utterances, such as "Sinners in the Hands of an Angry God," or as in the one I give as an example of this vein, "The Future Punishment of the Wicked," posterity has often concluded that he communicated only too well, or rather too disgustingly. He drove his listeners into paroxysms of terror which became so spectacular a legend as to create the popular image of a monster who did nothing but hail down fire and brimstone. Today it requires an extraordinary effort of the scholar to win a hearing for the more prevailing tone of Edward's preaching, such as "A Divine and Supernatural Light," in which the technique of stripping ideas of all extraneous or ambiguous wrappings is quietly and beautifully evident.

Another of his youthful admonitions to himself runs: "To be very moderate in the use of terms of art. Let it not look as if I was much read, or was conversant with books, or with the world." He succeeded in this direction so drastically that the mass of his hearers, and most of those who read him—either in admiration or from enmity—never grasped the elaborate metaphysical depths out of which the sermons or tracts arose. These were to be sounded only when "Notes on the Mind" were revealed; his still unpublished notebooks will someday expose them even more fully to critical analysis. But the palpable deliberateness of Edwards' endeavor to practice concealment further underscores the deceptive simplicity of his writing. His aim was to present vast ideas clean and whole, pure and crystal clear. His paragraphs move slowly, smoothly unfold, are kept under strict control. He uses few metaphors, and when he does employ one, he dwells exclusively on it for as long as possible, extracting bit by bit all the value it can be compelled to provide. He employs few adjectives to distract attention; curiously, they are usually not specific and they blend with the noun to form a bare extraction which is more shattering than the admired concreteness of Franklin: "fine appearances," "rough places," "worldly possessions," "flowery meadows." The result can be called monotonous, but the intentional and studied character of the monotony becomes a strange allurement. Edwards did not depart from it in even the most horrendous of the revival sermons. One of the Northampton townsmen, referring to the physical structure of the crude churches of the time, in which the rope for the bell by which the deacon summoned them to the church hung limply down at the opposite end from the pulpit, recollected: "Mr. Edwards in preaching used no gestures, but looked straight forward; Gideon Clark said 'he looked on the bell rope until he looked it off.' "

The primitive polity of the Puritans had not been what we would call "revivalist" or even "evangelical." The founders came from an England in which there had existed stable communities, centered around a common and a church, in the pulpit of which there was a regular succession of pastors. They never had any intention of going up and down the land, like the Methodists of the eighteenth century, preaching in the fields and arousing the populace to intemperate exhibitions of zeal, or of upsetting the parish structure of the society. The only complaint of the Puritans was that they should control this structure and so purify the parish churches into the Bibilical pattern of worship. When they were defeated, or thought they were, and therefore migrated in companies to the wilderness, they strove in Massachusetts and Connecticut to realize the English ideal. They settled not as individuals on the frontier, but in towns—Boston, Malden, Hartford—each a close community with a common and a church. The essential difference from England was that this church was Congregational instead of Episcopal. That is, the membership consisted only of those who had given evidence of their conversion and so presumably—the founders never said absolutely—of their election. These "visible saints" would choose the minister and govern the "church," while the rest of the town, which constituted the "congregation," would be required by law to attend services and to pay for the support of the minister. Thus the assumption ran that in the ordinary year-to-year conduct of the community a certain number would, in the providence of God, undergo the experience of regeneration, make a public profession of faith, and regularly fill up the ranks of the saints. Preaching and ecclesiastical administration would be a "means" of this recruiting, but only as they were conduits through which the waters of divine grace flowed. Never, it was held, would the words of the preacher be themselves the cause of the saving emotion. Hence, once more, the aesthetic of the plain style, which, like pious labor, depended for its effect not on its own skill but upon divine blessing.

The experience of a century showed, to the bafflement of Puritan theorists, that, once the first blush of excitement wore off, the children and grandchildren of the founders failed to encounter the cataclysm of conversion. They continued earnest and pious, and worked strenuously in their callings, but fewer and fewer of them could honestly make the profession. Several devices were tried, such as the "Half-Way Covenant" (1662) by which the children of members might have their own children baptized even though they themselves could demonstrate no right to the Lord's Supper. It was Solomon Stoddard who roughly decided that the original theory was both impractical and unscriptural. He renounced the entire church covenant and the exclusive membership; he boldly took the entire town into the "church" and to the Lord's Supper. He declared the communion a "converting ordinance," and directed his preaching to the direct stimulation of fear, guilt and emotion among his people. He demonstrated that once the concept of religious government was thus centralized there would come moments in which the ever-smoldering anxiety of the people could be fanned by a powerful preacher into a communal flame. Stoddard called these outbursts his "harvests," and he managed to instigate five of them, in 1679, 1683, 1696, 1712, and 1718, in each of which, as he boasted, "the bigger Part of the Young People in the Town, seemed mainly concerned for their eternal salvation." Increase and Cotton Mather attacked these unseemly measures, they seeking to preserve at least the skeleton of the old Puritan conception. Stoddard stood them off; secure in his effrontery, he lead the Connecticut Valley into the perilous but exhilarating era of the "revival." When Edwards succeeded to his grandfather's office, it was incumbent upon him that he prove his princely descent by producing another "harvest," or engineering one even more spectacular than those of his predecessor's, one so earthshaking that the world would have to acknowledge it a genuine outpouring of God's spirit upon the land.

In 1735 he succeeded, although of course Edwards attributed the efficient provocation to divine agency and took no credit unto himself or his "naked ideas." This flare-up soon died down, but not until Edwards had written an account of it, significantly entitled *A Faithful Narrative of the Surprising Work of God in the Conversion of Many Hundred Souls in Northampton, and the Neighboring Towns and Villages*. This became a guidebook to revivalism, but more importantly it prescribed the model for the truly colossal revival which he led, with some assistance from an English Methodist, George Whitfield, and from other divines both within New England and from the other colonies, in 1740. For several months Edwards was the most powerful mortal on the North American continent; in the full flood of this overwhelming success he delivered the "terror" sermons by which he kept the crowd in a state of religious panic.

While the Great Awakening, as it soon was termed, burned at white heat, nobody in New England dared speak out against him. Still, a number were appalled by its noise, its violence, the convulsions of those stricken with guilt, and by the dissensions erupting inside the churches. When even this mighty upheaval began to subside, as had the "surprising" work of 1735, and as would every subsequent "revival" in American history, the opponents launched a counterattack. These men were, as exemplified by their chief spokesman, Charles Chauncy of the First Church in Boston, men of reason. They were colonial versions of the Enlightenment, and though far from being Deists, they had interpreted Locke and Newton to mean that Christianity could now be presented as a rational religion, demanding no emotional excesses and permitting men a responsible exercise of their own unhindered wills. Officially they and their churches were still loyal to Calvinism, but in their daily practice and even in their Sabbath discourses the *Westminster Confession*, framed by the English Puritans and formally endorsed by New England in 1648, was being silently ignored. The Great Awakening and Edwards' preaching obliged them, much against their inclination, to avow publicly that they no longer adhered to the doctrines of their forefathers.

Edwards lashed all these respectable gentlemen as being cryptic "Arminians." This word descends from one Arminius, a Dutch theologian of the early seventeenth century who proposed a very slight liberalization of the rigid—or "high"—Calvinistic doctrine of the absolute enslavement of the natural will of man until released by a capricious bestowal of divine grace. Arminianism was soundly condemned by the orthodox majority at the Synod of Dort in 1619; since then, in England and in New England, anybody who so much as hinted that the volition of unregenerate man was capable of any good action was smeared as being "Arminian," though the culprit might never have heard of the Dutch heretic. As a matter of fact, however, the founders of New England, while abhorring Arminianism, contrived to formulate their Calvinism through a peculiar idiom, later denominated the "federal" or "covenant" theology, by which, even within a show of Protestant orthodoxy, the freedom of created beings could be asserted. Wherefore, opponents of the tumultuous revival insisted that they really were standing by the creed of the founders, and that Edwards was the actual subversive, that his version of Calvinism was a distortion of the sound faith.

In the initial phases of the debate the fundamental issue, that of the human will, was not brought forward; what the critics principally charged was that the Awakening was an artificial incitation, manufactured by such sensational preaching as these riotously calm sermons of Edwards, and that it was thus an exercise in psychological malpractice. They said it was not an authentic outpouring of the divine spirit but merely an exciting of animal passions by material stimulants. From a religious point of view, they said it was simply a substitute for New England's already redoubtable rum.

As the Awakening subsided, as it turned toward embittered disillusionment, not only among those who had resisted it from the beginning but more nastily among those who had surrendered themselves to it, a rage against Edwards mounted in the Connecticut Valley as well as at Harvard College. Indeed, in the Valley it became a frenzy more intense than the exultation of the revival had been, especially because it was fomented by several blood relatives of Edwards, who resented his succession to the mantle of Stoddard. These, in the now established pattern of New England families, were resolved upon destroying the cousin who had, no matter his merit, arrogantly undertaken to become the dominant member of the tribe.

Edwards had no other course left to him, therefore, but to apply his vast energies and his judicious mind to defending the thesis that the Awakening had been, despite its subsiding, a veritable "work" of God upon New England and the other colonies. And he had to do this within a mentality conditioned by his secret —or rather by his publicly withheld—apprehension of Locke and Newton, and against a benign rationalism which had commenced to interpret these prophets of the eighteenth century in a quite other sense. Consequently he had to attempt a work of what later might be called a "psychology of religion" without openly exposing, or at the most merely hinting at, the metaphysical apparatus he was employing. The culmination of this endeavor to vindicate the reality of the Awakening is *A Treatise Concerning Religious Affections*. It was first delivered as a sequence of sermons during the severe winter of 1742–43, when the Awakening was turning from ecstasy to confusion, and then was published in 1746 when Edwards had abjectly lost. He had no chance to treat a desperate cause with humorous detachment, as Franklin could treat the Revolution. He was obliged to explore, in the starkest sincerity, the depths of the recalcitrant psyche, with all the tools of analysis available to him, in order to demonstrate through his refinements of rationality that man is basically a creature of emotions—the word which in our discourse has replaced, though not too accurately, "affections"—rather than of reason.

The book remains the first, and also the most penetrating, analysis of the religious mentality in American intellectual history—its only rival is possibly William James's *Varieties of Religious Experience*—and in the whole of Western culture is assuredly one of the few enduring classics of such introspection. It is all the more a classic because the premises arrived at introspectively are thereupon examined with the utmost objectivity. Of course, by the insights of a twentieth century, in an age of Freud and Jung, Edwards may seem confined to the distressingly simple mechanics of John Locke's "sensationalism." Yet even within those rudimentary limitations he was working upon a passionate organism existing inside the natural cosmos; so he was confronting a central, indeed *the* central, challenge to what was historically known as the "spirit" in a modern concatenation of behavioristic psychology and materialistic physics.

So far as Northampton was concerned, Edwards failed. At the end of a long and bitter struggle, the details of which are horrifying but need not be related here, he was expelled from his superb pulpit. Upon leaving it, Edwards delivered his "Farewell Sermon," which I print here as though at the end of his career, because it is his farewell—"a long farewell" to all his greatness—though it was spoken in 1750, and though his major writings were yet to follow. We are hard put to conceive how his congregation, most of whom had by then worked day and night to get rid of him, sat through the delivery of this superhuman adjudication, but they held their precarious ground. Edwards and his family marched over the mountains to the then frontier outpost of Stockbridge. There, in conditions of virtual poverty, in an isolation even more stark than that in which Edward Taylor had dwelt and dreamed, Edwards wrote the massive philosophical works that constitute the grounds for his being rated one of the few original intellects of modern Christianity.

Of these, the masterpiece of ratiocination is undoubtedly *A Careful and Strict Enquiry into the Modern Prevailing Notions of That Freedom of Will Which Is Supposed To Be*

Essential to Moral Agency, Virtue and Vice, Reward and Punishment, Praise and Blame. In this work, he went, like a terrier to the jugular of a rat, to the throat of all opponents of the Awakening. It is so closely knit a book that efforts to present extracts from it seem to me self-defeating; hence I make no attempt to use it in this anthology, assuming that students sufficiently interested will read it in its entirety, particularly as there is a fine modern edition prepared by Paul Ramsey. On the lowest level, we may say that the book is an elaborate demonstration—some will venture an irrefutable proof—that while the acts of a man's will are always "caused," he is still responsible for them. On a deeper level, it clusters around an assertion that as a man perceives, so he acts; thus it translates the Calvinist doctrine of predestination into a language acceptable to modern psychology and physics. But on the deepest level, though it does not stoop to name them, it is a gigantic refutation of those rationalizers who condemned the Awakening as being the work of ecclesiastical demagogues, a denunciation of those who drove him out of Northampton as being a traitor to the stupendous achievements of his grandfather.

The hinge of his dispute with the townspeople in Northampton was that, while he did not propose to revive the church covenant within the formal theory of the founders, he did nevertheless endeavor to restrict admission to the "church" only to those who could show the overt signs of a certifiable spiritual encounter. Edwards, thinking of experience in the abstruse terms of Lockean psychology and inside the frame of a Newtonian physics, set a standard of disinterested spirituality to which few countrymen could possibly come up. We may justifiably surmise, therefore, that once he was cast out, once he was exiled into the wilderness, he should in the 1750's devote his last terrible energies to setting forth in two companion pieces the dual aspect of the problem of actual holiness, the psychological and the cosmic. These treatises were not published until after his death, in 1765, but in the parade of American literature (if that may be considered something slightly other than American metaphysics), *The Nature of True Virtue* and *Dissertation Concerning the End for Which God Created the World* are his masterpieces. Though inevitably more elaborate than his anticipation of Sarah Pierrepont, they utter their implacable thoughts with the same poetic serenity; they constitute, quite apart from the theological sense, a music which sounds its own self-sufficing melody.

Both the cadences of the prose and the cleanliness of the argument make these works a triumph of the plain style, which was, we have seen, an ethic not only of ordering words but also of conducting life and earning a living. And in them, at what seems on the surface an extreme divergence from Franklin, Edwards shows himself, upon any critical analysis, Franklin's brother. Carl Becker said, in the most perceptive sentence yet written about Franklin, that it was no wonder he sought for his ultimate satisfaction in natural science, because only in the physical universe could he find a "disinterestedness" equal to his own.[1] For most readers of Franklin this observation requires second thoughts, for at first sight Franklin seems a man excessively occupied in self-seeking and self-advancement. Yet after one has reread him, and read him yet again, one learns to appreciate that the actual charm of his writing is his disengagement from all the multifarious activities of his career. He could never have described them, or written about them when in the midst of the drama, in exactly the quizzical spirit he unfailingly maintains, unless he had somewhere in his intricate constitution an ultimate sense that all these local aims were subordinate to a larger one, in relation to which they were indeed trivial.

In Edwards' two final statements he strove to define this larger, this ultimate aim, in such a manner that nothing particular, selfish, patriotic, or charitable would stand for a moment against the vastness of perfection. In *True Virtue* he defines the subjection of the temporal to the eternal from the standpoint of finite humanity, showing how every "secondary" virtue —love of self, of family, of country, of mankind itself—must be merged into the all-effacing love for "Being in general." In the *Dissertation*, Edwards comes to the same center from the presumptuous starting point of the

[1] See Carl Becker's now classic piece on Franklin in the *Dictionary of American Biography*.

Godhead, who is shown to be, and inescapably to be, the only object of His own adoration, who creates a world not for the benefit of His creatures nor in order to add anything unto Himself, but solely for the ecstasy of His own expression. *True Virtue* makes the sensational psychology the basis of a cosmology; the *Dissertation* is a vision of how, within a coherent cosmology, a created being can live through brute sensation without even in his worst abominations marring the beauty of the supreme design. Franklin gingerly avoided all such speculation; the older he grew, the more he let such considerations alone. Yet the older he grew, the more by his very geniality, in his weary games with the ladies of the French Court, he demonstrated the Edwardsean thesis that the universe is its own excuse for being. Both Edwards and Franklin, the former the archspiritualist of American history and the second its master worldly-wiseman, assert that he who labors in whichever of the callings, if he push either to its extreme, finds himself a negligible finite in the face of a glorious incomprehensibility. To put Edwards' *Farewell Sermon* alongside Franklin's letter to Ezra Stiles is to perceive the vastness of their divergence, yet also to sense the mysterious identity of their underlying mood.

IV

FOR a large part of our national existence, Franklin has figured as a culture hero, while Edwards, if known as anything other than the lurid preacher of hell-fire, has been widely held a fanatical reactionary. In 1926, for instance, the great Vernon Parrington, in his pioneer history of thought in America, dismissed Edwards as an "anachronism." To the nineteenth century Franklin appeared the prophet of technology, the apostle of rationality, and the supreme vindication of the American ideal of the "self-made man."

By the middle of the twentieth century there has arisen a strong dissent from this view. No doubt thousands of practical Americans still find Franklin congenial and Edwards repulsive. Yet several hundreds discover increasingly a fascination in the mind and style of Edwards that surprises them as much as it delights them. To some of these Franklin now appears as the mummified example of the insensitive businessman, deaf to poetry and passion, translating all ideals into dollars and cents. After Sinclair Lewis made the name "Babbitt" stand for everything that many critics considered reprehensible in American civilization, Franklin was widely termed the first Babbitt, and the most contemptible of the lot. To others likewise put off by him, Franklin is the one who started the nation toward a "gadgeteers' paradise," which in their view leads to the supreme gadget, an instrument for mass destruction. Hence there has recently occurred a marked revival of interest in Jonathan Edwards. Those who bring themselves to reject Franklin flee to Edwards, as though he could offer them salvation—or at least peace of mind.

Both approaches will mislead us, give us images that are sadly mangled. Franklin was indeed a self-made triumph, but he was not a Babbitt: he strove to be a *philosophe* in the grand manner of the eighteenth century. As a matter of fact, despite his lightning experiment, he never quite made the stiff grade. He was hailed by a theater crowded with sentimental rationalists when he, in a box, embraced Voltaire. Yet he was no Voltaire, not at all a Diderot; he was an ingenious Yankee who promoted a knack for tinkering and for employing the written word to gain his usually homely ends into a reputation which, actually, he never had sufficient intellect to sustain—though he never allowed the world to realize his deficiency!

Likewise, Jonathan Edwards was by the very nature of his situation in place and in history a provincial, with no acquaintance of the great world, his reading pathetically limited, and his mind incapable of the wide metaphysical ranging of, let us say, a Thomas Aquinas or a Pascal, and not remotely up to the spontaneity of a Kierkegaard.

Even so, it may be that exactly in their limitations, their narrowness, these two figures are most American; herein they may be of greatest value as well as most perplexing to all who would endeavor to comprehend the baffling intellect of this Republic. Again we must be cautious not to insist that their New England consanguinity should be so presented as to minimize the chasm between them. Yet even while we have appreciated how permanently they are irreconcilable, we return to a fresh, and exhilarating, sense of their complementary natures. They are a kind of Shem and Shaun, as in *Finnegan's Wake*. They are sworn enemies, eternal foes, though we as readers cannot dispense with either of them. To us, they are the Gemini who share the same soul, one occupying it while the other sleeps; yet each insists that he never sleeps, and, that being so, the alternation never ends.

In the fatigued mood of his communications to Priestly in 1782, Franklin, still harping on his boredom with humanity, continued thus:

> I should rejoice much, if I could once more recover the leisure to search with you into the works of nature; I mean the inanimate not the animate or moral part of them: the more I discovered of the former the more I admired them; the more I know of the latter the more I am disgusted with them.

In the dread isolation of Stockbridge—which could not conceivably have been more opposite to Passy—Edwards, writing of *True Virtue* and stripping all human pretensions to moral worth from any title to merit, centered his definition of that which is incontestably worthy upon this conception of the Godhead:

> Because God is not only infinitely greater and more excellent than all other being, but he is the head of the universal system of existence; the foundation and fountain of all being and all beauty; from whom all is perfectly derived, and on whom all is most absolutely and perfectly dependent; of whom, and through whom, and to whom is all being and all perfection; and whose being and beauty are, as it were, the sum and comprehension of all existence and excellence: much more than the sun is the fountain and summary comprehension of all the light and brightness of the day.

Franklin's "works of nature" should not be cheaply made into an interchangeable term with Edwards' "sum and comprehension of all existence and excellence." Yet, the phrases have affinities. In relation to finite human experience, they can signify essentially the same disregard of personal convenience. So we come back to our opening reflection, though I hope with a more enlightened concern. While individual predilections are not to be scorned, and each reader may prize the one more than the other, still the serious student of America, seeking accurate knowledge of the intellectual heritage, must learn fully to understand, in their own terms, *both* these massively symbolic characters.

NOTE

Wherever four dots appear in the selections that follow, the first is the author's punctuation, the other three are the editor's ellipses. A full line of space has been inserted within the text in the case of an omission of a paragraph or more.

READING SUGGESTIONS

FRANKLIN

EDITIONS

Since 1905–07, the standard version has been Albert Henry Smyth, *The Writings of Benjamin Franklin*, 10 vols. More recently however, this edition has been displaced increasingly by the immensely definitive, *The Papers of Benjamin Franklin* (1959–), ed. by Leonard W. Labaree, undertaken by Yale University Press in association with the American Philosophical Society.

CARL VAN DOREN, *Benjamin Franklin's Autobiographical Writings* (1945). A wise selection out of Franklin's works of passages which pertain to himself.

FRANK LUTHER MOTT AND CHESTER E. JORGENSON, *Benjamin Franklin*, in American Writers Series (1936). This is the most convenient assembly of Franklin's basic writings, supported by introductions and notes.

BIOGRAPHY AND CRITICISM

CARL VAN DOREN, *Benjamin Franklin* (1938). The classic biography; little has since been added to this account.

CARL BECKER, "Benjamin Franklin," in *Dictionary of American Biography*, VI (1931), 585–98.

V. W. CRANE, *Benjamin Franklin: Englishman and American* (1936).

P. L. FORD, *The Many-Sided Franklin* (1899).

M. R. EISLEN, *Franklin's Political Theories* (1928).

D. H. LAWRENCE, *Studies in Classic American Literature* (1923), chap. 2.

LOIS M. MACLAURIN, *Franklin's Vocabulary* (1928).

PAUL ELMER MORE, "Benjamin Franklin," in *Shelburne Essays*, Fourth Series (1906).

C. A. SAINTE-BEUVE, *Portraits of the Eighteenth Century*, tr. by Katharine P. Wormeley (1905). The two essays here pieced together constitute the standard "Continental" accusation against Franklin.

EDWARDS

EDITIONS

Students have hitherto been obliged to study Edwards in the imperfect editions put out by Samuel Austin, 8 vols. (1808–09), or of Sereno E. Dwight, 10 vols. (1829–30). As of this writing, a project is under way by the Yale University Press for the publication of the complete works, those printed and those hitherto unprinted. Two important volumes have appeared: *Freedom of the Will,* ed. by Paul Ramsey, and *A Treatise Concerning Religous Affections,* ed. by John E. Smith. Both editors, in their introductions and notes, have brought the scholarship up to date. Meanwhile, the most usable collection of Edwards' texts is *Jonathan Edwards,* ed. by Clarence H. Faust and Thomas H. Johnson, American Writers Series (1935).

Also valuable for textual material are:

PERRY MILLER, editor, *Images or Shadows of Divine Things* (1948).

H. G. TOWNSEND, *The Philosophy of Jonathan Edwards from His Private Notebooks* (1955).

BIOGRAPHY

OLA E. WINSLOW, *Jonathan Edwards* (1941). The comprehensive biography.

CRITICISM

F. H. FOSTER, *A History of New England Theology* (1907).

JOSEPH HAROUTINIAN, *Piety Versus Moralism* (1932).

A. C. MCGIFFERT, JR., *Jonathan Edwards* (1932).

PERRY MILLER, *Jonathan Edwards* (1949).

KENNETH B. MURDOCK, *Literature and Theology in Colonial New England* (1949).

H. RICHARD NIEBUHR, *The Kingdom of God in America* (1956).

C. WRIGHT, *The Beginnings of Unitarianism in America* (1955)

DOUGLAS J. ELWOOD, *The Philosophical Theology of Jonathan Edwards* (1960).

Benjamin Franklin

FROM AUTOBIOGRAPHY [to 1723]

◇

FRANKLIN commenced the story of his life, as he took pains to indicate, while staying as a guest for a week in June, 1771, with Bishop Jonathan Shipley at Twyford, near Winchester. In that brief time he wrote, with matchless precision, his report up to the year 1730 of his existence, reading aloud in the evenings to the Shipley family what he had composed during the days. Obliged then to break off, and hindered by a multitude of events from continuing, he was able to resume his tale thirteen years later, 1784, in Passy, outside of Paris. He endeavored to add two more chapters in the last year of his life, 1789, in Philadelphia. The history of the partial and inaccurate publication is a bibliographical nightmare. Not until 1868 was a "first" complete edition of the four sections printed. It is, of course, one of the great "unfinished" masterpieces, since even in his last exertions Franklin was able to bring the narrative up to only his fiftieth year. The most spectacular decades of his career he had no chance to recount.

◇

Twyford, *at the Bishop of St. Asaph's,* 1771.

DEAR SON: [1] I have ever had the pleasure in obtaining any little anecdotes of my ancestors. You may remember the inquiries I made among the remains of my relations when you were with me in England, and the journey I undertook for that purpose. Imagining it may be equally agreeable to you to know the circumstances of my life, many of which you are yet unacquainted with, and expecting the enjoyment of a week's uninterrupted leisure in my present country retirement, I sit down to write them for you. To which I have besides some other inducements. Having emerged from the poverty and obscurity in which I was born and bred, to a state of affluence and some degree of reputation in the world, and having gone so far through life with a considerable share of felicity, the conducing means I made use of, which with the blessing of God so well succeeded, my posterity may like to know, as they may find some of them suitable to their own situations, and therefore fit to be imitated.

That felicity, when I reflected on it, has induced me sometimes to say, that were it offered to my choice, I should have no objection to a repetition of the same life from its beginning, only asking the advantages authors have in a second edition to correct some faults of the first. So I might, besides correcting the faults, change some sinister accidents and events of it for others more favorable. But though this were denied, I should still

AUTOBIOGRAPHY. 1. **Son:** William Franklin (1731–1813), the last royal governor of New Jersey (1763–76) who was arrested and imprisoned during the Revolution for his Tory sympathies.

accept the offer. Since such a repetition is not to be expected, the next thing most like living one's life over again seems to be a recollection of that life, and to make that recollection as durable as possible by putting it down in writing.

Hereby, too, I shall indulge the inclination so natural in old men, to be talking of themselves and their own past actions; and I shall indulge it without being tiresome to others, who, through respect to age, might conceive themselves obliged to give me a hearing, since this may be read or not as one pleases. And, lastly (I may as well confess it, since my denial of it will be believed by nobody), perhaps I shall a good deal gratify my own *vanity*. Indeed, I scarce ever heard or saw the introductory words, *"Without vanity I may say," &c.*, but some vain thing immediately followed. Most people dislike vanity in others, whatever share they have of it themselves; but I give it fair quarter wherever I meet with it, being persuaded that it is often productive of good to the possessor, and to others that are within his sphere of action; and therefore, in many cases, it would not be altogether absurd if a man were to thank God for his vanity among the other comforts of life.

And now I speak of thanking God, I desire with all humility to acknowledge that I owe the mentioned happiness of my past life to His kind providence, which lead me to the means I used and gave them success. My belief of this induces me to *hope*, though I must not *presume*, that the same goodness will still be exercised toward me, in continuing that happiness, or enabling me to bear a fatal reverse, which I may experience as others have done; the complexion of my future fortune being known to Him only in whose power it is to bless to us even our afflictions.

The notes one of my uncles (who had the same kind of curiosity in collecting family anecdotes) once put into my hands, furnished me with several particulars relating to our ancestors. From these notes I learned that the family had lived in the same village, Ecton, in Northamptonshire, for three hundred years, and how much longer he knew not (perhaps from the time when the name of Franklin, that before was the name of an order of people, was assumed by them as a surname when others took surnames all over the kingdom), on a freehold of about thirty acres, aided by the smith's business, which had continued in the family till his time, the eldest son being always bred to that business; a custom which he and my father followed as to their eldest sons. When I searched the registers at Ecton, I found an account of their births, marriages and burials from the year 1555 only, there being no registers kept in that parish at any time preceding. By that register I perceived that I was the youngest son of the youngest son for five generations back. My grandfather Thomas, who was born in 1598, lived at Ecton till he grew too old to follow business longer, when he went to live with his son John, a dyer at Banbury, in Oxfordshire, with whom my father served an apprenticeship. There my grandfather died and lies buried. We saw his gravestone in 1758. His eldest son Thomas lived in the house at Ecton, and left it with the land to his only child, a daughter, who, with her husband, one Fisher, of Wellingborough, sold it to Mr. Isted, now lord of the manor there. My grandfather had four sons that grew up, viz.: Thomas, John, Benjamin and Josiah. I will give you what account I can of them, at this distance from my papers, and if these are not lost in my absence, you will among them find many more particulars.

Thomas was bred a smith under his father; but, being ingenious, and encouraged in learning (as all my brothers were) by an Esquire Palmer, then the principal gentleman in that parish, he qualified himself for the business of scrivener; became a considerable man in the county; was a chief mover of all public-spirited undertakings for the county or town of Northampton, and his own village, of which many instances were related of him; and much taken notice of and patronized by the then Lord Halifax. He died in 1702, January 6, old style, just four years to a day before I was born. The account we received of his life and character from some old people at Ecton, I remember, struck you as something extraordinary, from its similarity to what you knew of mine. "Had he died on the same day," you said, "one might have supposed a transmigration."

John was bred a dyer, I believe of woolens. Benjamin was bred a silk dyer, serving an apprenticeship at London. He was an ingenious man. I remember him well, for when I was a boy he came over to my father in Boston, and lived in the house with us some years. He lived to a great age. His grandson, Samuel Franklin, now lives in Boston. He left behind him two quarto volumes, MS., of his own poetry, consisting of little occasional pieces addressed to his friends and relations, of which the following, sent to me, is a specimen.[2] He had formed a short-hand of his own, which he taught me, but, never practicing it, I have now forgot it. I was named after this uncle, there being a particular affection between him and my fa-

2. **a specimen**: on the margin of the manuscript Franklin wrote, "Here insert it," but he never found time to do so, and his uncle's verse is thus lost to posterity.

ther. He was very pious, a great attender of sermons of the best preachers, which he took down in his short-hand, and had with him many volumes of them. He was also much of a politician; too much, perhaps, for his station. There fell lately into my hands, in London, a collection he had made of all the principal pamphlets relating to public affairs, from 1641 to 1717; many of the volumes are wanting as appears by the numbering, but there still remain eight volumes in folio, and twenty-four in quarto and in octavo. A dealer in old books met with them, and knowing me by sometimes buying of him, he brought them to me. It seems my uncle must have left them here when he went to America, which was above fifty years since. There are many of his notes in the margins.

This obscure family of ours was early in the Reformation, and continued Protestants through the reign of Queen Mary, when they were sometimes in danger of trouble on account of their zeal against popery. They had got an English Bible, and to conceal and secure it, it was fastened open with tapes under and within the cover of a joint-stool. When my great-great grandfather read it to his family, he turned up the joint-stool upon his knees, turning over the leaves then under the tapes. One of the children stood at the door to give notice if he saw the apparitor coming, who was an officer of the spiritual court. In that case the stool was turned down again upon its feet, when the Bible remained concealed under it as before. This anecdote I had from my uncle Benjamin. The family continued all of the Church of England till about the end of Charles the Second's reign, when some of the ministers that had been outed for non-conformity holding conventicles in Northamptonshire, Benjamin and Josiah adhered to them, as so continued all their lives: the rest of the family remained with the Episcopal Church.

Josiah, my father, married young, and carried his wife with three children into New England, about 1682. The conventicles having been forbidden by law, and frequently disturbed, induced some considerable men of his acquaintance to remove to that country, and he was prevailed with to accompany them thither, where they expected to enjoy their mode of religion with freedom. By the same wife he had four children more born there, and by a second wife ten more, in all seventeen; of which I remember thirteen sitting at one time at his table, who all grew up to be men and women, and married; I was the youngest son, and the youngest child but two, and was born in Boston, New England. My mother, the second wife, was Abiah Folger, daughter of Peter Folger, one of the first settlers of New England, of whom honorable mention is made by Cotton Mather, in his church history of that country, entitled Magnalia Christi Americana, as *"a godly, learned Englishman,"* if I remember the words rightly. I have heard that he wrote sundry small occasional pieces, but only one of them was printed, which I saw now many years since. It was written in 1675, in the home-spun verse of that time and people, and addressed to those then concerned in the government there. It was in favor of liberty of conscience, and in behalf of the Baptists, Quakers, and other sectaries that had been under persecution, ascribing the Indian wars, and other distresses that had befallen the country, to that persecution, as so many judgments of God to punish so heinous an offense, and exhorting a repeal of those uncharitable laws. The whole appeared to me as written with a good deal of decent plainness and manly freedom. The six concluding lines I remember, though I have forgotten the two first of the stanza; but the purport of them was, that his censures proceeded from good will, and, therefore he would be known to be the author.

"Because to be a libeller (says he)
I hate it with my heart;
From Sherburne town, where now I dwell
My name I do put here;
Without offense your real friend,
It is Peter Folgier."

My elder brothers were all put apprentices to different trades. I was put to the grammar-school at eight years of age, my father intending to devote me, as the tithe of his sons, to the service of the Church. My early readiness in learning to read (which must have been very early, as I do not remember when I could not read), and the opinion of all his friends, that I should certainly make a good scholar, encouraged him in this purpose of his. My uncle Benjamin, too, approved of it, and proposed to give me all his short-hand volumes of sermons, I suppose as a stock to set up with, if I would learn his character. I continued, however, at the grammar-school not quite one year, though in that time I had risen gradually from the middle of the class of that year to be the head of it, and farther was removed into the next class above it, in order to go with that into the third at the end of the year. But my father, in the mean time, from a view of the expense of a college education, which having so large a family he could not well afford, and the mean living many so educated were afterwards able to obtain —reasons that he gave to his friends in my hearing—altered his first intention, took me from the grammar-school, and sent me to a school for writing and arithmetic, kept by a then famous man, Mr. George Brownell, very successful in his profession, generally, and that by mild, encouraging methods. Under him I acquired fair writing pretty soon, but I failed in the arithmetic, and made no progress in it. At ten years old I was taken home to assist my father in his business, which was that of a tallow-chandler and sopeboiler;[3] a business he was not bred to, but had assumed on his arrival in New England, and on finding his dying trade would not maintain his family, being in little request. Accordingly, I was employed in cutting wick for the candles, filling the dipping mold and the molds for cast candles, attending the shop, going of errands, etc. . . .

I continued thus employed in my father's business for two years, that is, till I was twelve years old; and my brother John, who was bred to that business, having left my father, married, and set up for himself at Rhode Island, there was all appearance that I was destined to supply his place, and become a tallow-chandler. But my dislike to the trade continuing, my father was under apprehensions that if he did not find one for me more agreeable, I should break away and get to sea, as his son Josiah had done, to his great vexation. He therefore sometimes took me to walk with him, and see joiners, bricklayers, turners, braziers, etc., at their work, that he might observe my inclination, and endeavor to fix it on some trade or other on land. It has ever since been a pleasure to me to see good workmen handle their tools; and it has been useful to me, having learnt so much by it as to be able to do little jobs myself in my house when a workman could not readily be got, and to construct little machines for my experiments, while the intention of making the experiment was fresh and warm in my mind. My father at last fixed upon the cutler's trade, and my uncle Benjamin's son Samuel, who was bred to that business in London, being about that time established in Boston, I was sent to be with him on liking. But his expectations of a fee with me displeasing my father, I was taken home again.

From a child I was fond of reading, and all the little money that came into my hands was ever laid out in books. Pleased with the Pilgrim's Progress, my first collection was of John Bunyan's works in separate little volumes. I afterwards sold them to enable me to buy R. Burton's Historical Collections; they were small chapmen's books, and cheap, 40 or 50 in all. My father's little library consisted chiefly of books in polemic divinity, most of which I read, and have since often regretted that, at a time when I had such a thirst for knowledge, more proper books had not fallen in my way, since it was now resolved I should not be a clergyman. Plutarch's Lives there was in which I read abundantly, and I still think that time spent to great advantage. There was also a book of De Foe's, called an Essay on Projects,[4] and another of Dr. Mather's, called Essays to do Good,[5] which perhaps gave me a turn of thinking that had an influence on some of the principal future events of my life.

This bookish inclination at length determined my father to make me a printer, though he had already one son (James) of that profession. In 1717 my brother James returned from England with a press and letters to set up his business in Boston. I liked it much better than that of my father, but still had a hankering for the sea. To prevent the apprehended effect of such an inclination, my father was impatient to have me bound to my brother. I stood out some time, but at last was persuaded, and signed the indentures when I was yet but twelve years old. I was to serve as an apprentice till I was twenty-one years of age, only I was to be allowed journeyman's wages during the last year. In a little time I made great proficiency in the business, and became a useful hand to my brother. I now had access to better books. An acquaintance with the apprentices of booksellers enabled me sometimes to borrow a small one, which I was careful to return soon and

3. **sopeboiler:** soap boiler.

4. **an Essay on Projects:** This, the first complete book by Daniel Defoe (1660–1731) was published in 1697 as *An Essay upon Projects*. It is universally considered as beginning, in a genuinely homely and practical spirit hitherto unprecedented in English literature, the idea of a planned system of governmental benevolence. It proposed simplifications in legal procedure, construction of highways at public expense, insane asylums, an academy for the regularization of the English language, and a collegiate school for women. Considering Franklin's career, we can see how readily his youthful temperament would have jibed with that of Defoe.

5. **Essays to do Good:** Franklin refers to a book by Cotton Mather, published in 1710, the accurate title of which (even when abbreviated) is: *Bonifacius, an Essay upon the Good Which Is to be Devised and Designed by Those Who Desire . . . to Do Good While They Live.* Known by its running title, *Essays to Do Good*, it was widely read in the colonies and even in England, and is a milestone in the development of New England Calvinism from a "theocracy" to a social conscience. By it and other efforts Cotton Mather was striving to mobilize the churches into a program of moral supervision that would replace the political control lost by the abrogation of the original charter and by the defection (as he conceived it) of Solomon Stoddard in the Connecticut Valley. The young Franklin bespoke the irritation of the unelected against Mather's scheme by inventing the name of "Silence Dogood" for his satirical forays, especially because Mather was the least silent of men. The old Franklin, we should note, always spoke reverently of the book—possibly because of this youthful arrogance—and insisted that it guided him into his lifelong devotion to the public welfare.

clean. Often I sat up in my room reading the greatest part of the night, when the book was borrowed in the evening and to be returned early in the morning, lest it should be missed or wanted. . . .

About this time I met with an odd volume of the *Spectator*. It was the third. I had never before seen any of them. I bought it, read it over and over, and was much delighted with it. I thought the writing excellent, and wished, if possible, to imitate it. With this view I took some of the papers, and, making short hints of the sentiment in each sentence, laid them by a few days, and then, without looking at the book, try'd to compleat the papers again, by expressing each hinted sentiment at length, and as fully as it had been expressed before, in any suitable words that should come to hand. Then I compared my *Spectator* with the original, discovered some of my faults, and corrected them. But I found I wanted a stock of words, or a readiness in recollecting and using them, which I thought I should have acquired before that time if I had gone on making verses; since the continual occasion for words of the same import, but of different length, to suit the measure, or of different sound for the rhyme, would have laid me under a constant necessity of searching for variety, and also have tended to fix that variety in my mind, and make me master of it. Therefore I took some of the tales and turned them into verse; and, after a time, when I had pretty well forgotten the prose, turned them back again. I also sometimes jumbled my collections of hints into confusion, and after some weeks endeavored to reduce them into the best order, before I began to form the full sentences and compleat the paper. This was to teach me method in the arrangement of thoughts. By comparing my work afterwards with the original, I discovered many faults and amended them; but I sometimes had the pleasure of fancying that, in certain particulars of small import, I had been lucky enough to improve the method or the language, and this encouraged me to think I might possibly in time come to be a tolerable English writer, of which I was extreamly ambitious. My time for these exercises and for reading was at night, after work or before it began in the morning, or on Sundays, when I contrived to be in the printing-house alone, evading as much as I could the common attendance on public worship which my father used to exact of me when I was under his care, and which indeed I still thought a duty, though I could not, as it seemed to me, afford time to practise it. . . .

My brother had, in 1720 or 1721, begun to print a newspaper. It was the second that appeared in America, and was called the New England Courant.[6] The only one before it was the Boston News-Letter. I remember his being dissuaded by some of his friends from the undertaking, as not likely to succeed, one newspaper being, in their judgment, enough for America. At this time (1771) there are not less than five-and-twenty. He went on, however, with the undertaking, and after having worked in composing the types and printing off the sheets, I was employed to carry the papers thro' the streets to the customers.

He had some ingenious men among his friends, who amus'd themselves by writing little pieces for this paper, which gain'd it credit and made it more in demand, and these gentlemen often visited us. Hearing their conversations, and their accounts of the approbation their papers were received with, I was excited to try my hand among them; but being still a boy, and suspecting that my brother would object to printing anything of mine in his paper if he knew it to be mine, I contrived to disguise my hand, and, writing an anonymous paper, I put it in at night under the door of the printing-house. It was found in the morning, and communicated to his writing friends when they call'd in as usual. They read it, commented on it in my hearing, and I had the exquisite pleasure of finding it met with their approbation, and that, in their different guesses at the author, none were named but men of some character among us for learning and ingenuity. I suppose now that I was rather lucky in my judges, and that perhaps they were not really so very good ones as I then esteem'd them.

Encourag'd, however, by this, I wrote and convey'd in the same way to the press several more papers which were equally approv'd; and I kept my secret till my small fund of sense for such performances was pretty well exhausted, and then I discovered it, when I began to be considered a little more by my brother's acquaintance, and in a manner that did not quite please him, as he thought, probably with reason, that it tended to make me too vain. And, perhaps, this might be one occasion of the differences that we began to have about this time. Though a brother, he considered himself as my master, and me as his ap-

6. **New England Courant:** In point of fact, the *Courant* was the third newspaper in Boston and the fourth in the colonies (following one in Philadelphia), but the predecessors were merely collections of reports from Europe and attempted nothing of the literary character with which James Franklin strove, to his ultimate destruction, to invest his foredoomed venture.

prentice, and, accordingly, expected the same services from me as he would from another, while I thought he demean'd me too much in some he requir'd of me, who from a brother expected more indulgence. Our disputes were often brought before our father, and I fancy I was either generally in the right, or else a better pleader, because the judgment was generally in my favor. But my brother was passionate, and had often beaten me, which I took extreamly amiss; and, thinking my apprenticeship very tedious, I was continually wishing for some opportunity of shortening it, which at length offered in a manner unexpected.[7]

One of the pieces in our newspaper on some political point, which I have now forgotten,[8] gave offense to the Assembly. He was taken up, censur'd, and imprison'd for a month, by the speaker's warrant, I suppose, because he would not discover his author. I too was taken up and examin'd before the council; but, tho' I did not give them any satisfaction, they content'd themselves with admonishing me, and dismissed me, considering me, perhaps, as an apprentice, who was bound to keep his master's secrets.

During my brother's confinement, which I resented a good deal, notwithstanding our private differences, I had management of the paper; and I made bold to give our rulers some rubs in it, which my brother took very kindly, while others began to consider me in an unfavorable light, as a young genius that had a turn for libelling and satyr. My brother's discharge was accompany'd with an order of the House (a very odd one), that *"James Franklin should no longer print the paper called the New England Courant."*

There was a consultation held in our printing-house among his friends, what he should do in this case. Some proposed to evade the order by changing the name of the paper; but my brother, seeing inconveniences in that, it was finally concluded on as a better way, to let it be printed for the future under the name of BENJAMIN FRANKLIN; and to avoid the censure of the Assembly, that might fall on him still printing it by his apprentice, the contrivance was that my old indenture should be return'd to me, with a full discharge on the back of it, to be shown on occasion: but to secure him the benefit of my service, I was to sign new indentures for the remainder of the term, which were to be kept private. A very flimsy scheme it was; however, it was immediately executed, and the paper went on accordingly, under my name for several months.

At length, a fresh difference arising between my brother and me, I took upon me to assert my freedom, presuming that he would not venture to produce the new indentures. It was not fair in me to take this advantage, and this I therefore reckon one of the first errata of my life; but the unfairness of it weighed little with me, when under the impressions of resentment for the blows his passion too often urged him to bestow upon me, though he was otherwise not an ill-natur'd man: perhaps I was too saucy and provoking.

When he found I would leave him, he took care to prevent my getting employment in any other printing-house of the town, by going round and speaking to every master, who accordingly refus'd to give me work. I then thought of going to New York, as the nearest place where there was a printer; and I was rather inclin'd to leave Boston when I reflected that I had already made myself a little obnoxious to the governing party, and, from the arbitrary proceedings of the Assembly in my brother's case, it was likely I might, if I stay'd, soon bring myself into scrapes; and farther, that my indiscrete disputations about religion began to make me pointed at with horror by good people as an infidel or atheist. I determin'd on the point, but my father now siding with my brother, I was sensible that, if I attempted to go openly, means would be used to prevent me. My friend Collins, therefore, undertook to manage a little for me. He agreed with the captain of a New York sloop for my passage, under the notion of my being a young acquaintance of his, that had got a naughty girl with child, whose friends would compel me to marry her, and therefore I could not appear or come away publicly. So I sold some of my books to raise a little money, was taken on board privately, and as we had a fair wind, in three days I found myself in New York, near 300 miles from home, a boy of but 17, without the least recommendation to, or knowledge of any person in the place, and with very little money in my pocket. . . .

7. **manner unexpected:** On the margin of the manuscript Franklin notes, "I fancy his harsh and tyrannical treatment of me might be a means of impressing me with that aversion to arbitrary power that has stuck to me through my whole life."
8. **on . . . forgotten:** Franklin had, either through failure of memory or because of convenience, elected to forget that the offending article was not "political" but a satire upon the clergy, aimed primarily against Cotton Mather.

DOGOOD PAPERS

◇

THESE skits demonstrate how effectively Franklin's system of self-instruction had taught him to handle words. In his worldly way, at sixteen he was as precocious as Edwards in the realm of the mind. Yet it is obviously revealing that the poor son of a soap boiler would commence his literary career by an attack on Harvard College and by openly exulting in the presence of prostitutes upon the streets of the Boston of Cotton Mather.

◇

NO. 4 [1]

An sum etiam nunc vel Graecè loqui vel Latinè docendus? [2] CICERO.

TO THE AUTHOR OF THE *New-England Courant.*
SIR,

Discoursing the other Day at Dinner with my Reverend Boarder, formerly mention'd, (whom for Distinction sake we will call by the Name of Clericus,) concerning the Education of Children, I ask'd his Advice about my young Son William, whether or no I had best bestow upon him Academical Learning, or (as our Phrase is) *bring him up at our College:* He perswaded me to do it by all Means, using many weighty Arguments with me, and answering all the Objections that I could form against it; telling me withal, that he did not doubt but that the Lad would take his Learning very well, and not idle away his Time as too many there now-a-days do. These Words of Clericus gave me a Curiosity to inquire a little more strictly into the present Circumstances of that famous Seminary of Learning; but the Information which he gave me, was neither pleasant, nor such as I expected.

As soon as Dinner was over, I took a solitary Walk into my Orchard, still ruminating on Clericus's Discourse with much Consideration, until I came to my usual Place of Retirement under the *Great Apple-Tree;* where having seated my self, and carelessly laid my Head on a verdant Bank, I fell by Degrees into a soft and undisturbed Slumber. My waking Thoughts remained with me in my Sleep, and before I awak'd again, I dreamt the following DREAM.

DOGOOD PAPERS. No. 4: 1. No. 4 of the *Dogood Papers* was printed in the *New-England Courant* for May 14, 1722. 2. *An . . . docendus:* "Do I have to be taught even now to speak in Latin or Greek?"

I fancy'd I was travelling over pleasant and delightful Fields and Meadows, and thro' many small County Towns and Villages; and as I pass'd along, all Places resounded with the Fame of the Temple of LEARNING: Every Peasant, who had wherewithal, was preparing to send one of his Children at least to this famous Place; and in this Case most of them consulted their own Purses instead of their Childrens Capacities: So that I observed, a great many, yea, the most part of those who were travelling thither, were little better than Dunces and Blockheads. Alas! alas!

At length I entered upon a spacious Plain, in the Midst of which was erected a large and stately Edifice: It was to this that a great Company of Youths from all Parts of the Country were going; so stepping in among the Crowd, I passed on with them, and presently arrived at the Gate.

The Passage was kept by two sturdy Porters named *Riches* and *Poverty,* and the latter obstinately refused to give Entrance to any who had not first gain'd the Favour of the former; so that I observed, many who came even to the very Gate, were obliged to travel back again as ignorant as they came, for want of this necessary Qualification. However, as a Spectator I gain'd Admittance, and with the rest entered directly into the Temple.

In the Middle of the great Hall stood a stately and magnificent Throne, which was ascended to by two high and difficult Steps. On the Top of it sat LEARNING in awful State; she was apparelled wholly in Black, and surrounded almost on every Side with innumerable Volumes in all Languages. She seem'd very busily employ'd in writing something on half a Sheet of Paper, and upon Enquiry, I understood she was preparing a Paper, call'd, *The New-England Courant.* On her Right Hand sat *English,* with a pleasant smiling Countenance, and handsomely attir'd; and on her left were seated several *Antique Figures* with their Faces vail'd. I was considerably puzzl'd to guess who they were, until one informed me, (who stood beside me,) that those Figures on her left Hand were *Latin, Greek, Hebrew,* &c. and that they were very much reserv'd, and seldom or never unvail'd their Faces here, and then to few or none, tho' most of those who have in this Place acquir'd so much Learning as to distinguish them from *English,* pretended to an intimate Acquaintance with them. I then enquir'd of him, what could be the Reason why they continued vail'd, in this Place especially: He pointed to the Foot of the Throne, where I saw *Idleness,* attended with *Ignorance,* and these (he informed me) were they, who first vail'd them, and still kept them so.

Now I observed, that the whole Tribe who entered into the Temple with me, began to climb the Throne; but the Work proving troublesome and difficult to most of them, they withdrew their Hands from the Plow, and contented to sit at the Foot, with Madam *Idleness* and her Maid *Ignorance,* until those who were assisted by Diligence and a docible Temper, had well nigh got up the first Step: But the Time drawing nigh in which they could no way avoid ascending, they were fain to crave the Assistance of those who had got up before them, and who, for the Reward perhaps of a *Pint of Milk,* or a *Piece of Plumb-Cake,*[3] lent the Lubbers a helping Hand, and sat them in the Eye of the World, upon a Level with themselves.

The other Step being in the same Manner ascended, and the usual Ceremonies at an End, every Beetle-Skull seem'd well satisfy'd with his own Portion of Learning, tho' perhaps he was *e'en just* as ignorant as ever. And now the time of their Departure being come, they march'd out of Doors to make Room for another Company, who waited for Entrance: And I, having seen all that was to be seen, quitted the Hall likewise, and went to make my Observations on those who were just gone before me.

Some I perceiv'd took to Merchandizing, others to Travelling, some to one Thing, some to another, and some to Nothing; and many of them from henceforth, for want of Patrimony, liv'd as poor as Church Mice, being unable to dig, and asham'd to beg, and to live by their Wits it was impossible. But the most Part of the Crowd went along a large beaten Path, which led to a Temple at the further End of the Plain, call'd *The Temple of Theology*. The Business of those who were employ'd in this Temple being laborious and painful, I wonder'd exceedingly to see so many go towards it; but while I was pondering this Matter in my Mind, I spy'd *Pecunia* behind a Curtain, beckoning to them with her Hand, which Sight immediately satisfy'd me for whose Sake it was, that a great Part of them (I will not say all) travel'd that Road. In this Temple I saw nothing worth mentioning, except the ambitious and fraudulent Contrivances of Plagius,[4] who (notwithstanding he had been severely reprehended for such Practices before) was diligently transcribing some eloquent Paragraphs out of Tillotson's *Works,*[5] &c. to embellish his own.

Now I bethought my self in my Sleep, that it was Time to be at Home, and as I fancy'd I was travelling back thither, I reflected in my Mind on the extream Folly of those Parents, who, blind to their Childrens Dulness, and insensible of the Solidity of their Skulls, because they think their Purses can afford it, will needs send them to the Temple of Learning, where, for want of a suitable Genius, they learn little more than how to carry themselves handsomely, and enter a Room genteely, (which might as well be acquir'd at a Dancing-School,) and from whence they return, after Abundance of Trouble and Charge, as great Blockheads as ever, only more proud and self-conceited.

While I was in the midst of these unpleasant Reflections, Clericus (who with a Book in his Hand was walking under the Trees) accidentally awak'd me; to him I related my Dream with all its Particulars, and he, without much Study, presently interpreted it, assuring me, *That it was a lively Representation of* HARVARD COLLEGE, *Etcetera.* I remain, Sir, Your Humble Servant,

SILENCE DOGOOD

NO. 13[1]

TO THE AUTHOR OF THE *New-England Courant.*
SIR,

In Persons of a contemplative Disposition, the most indifferent Things provoke the Exercise of the Imagination; and the Satisfactions which often arise to them thereby, are a certain Relief to the Labour of the Mind (when it has been intensely fix'd on more substantial Subjects) as well as to that of the Body.

In one of the late pleasant Moon-light Evenings, I so far indulg'd in my self the Humour of the Town in walking abroad, as to continue from my Lodgings two or three Hours later than usual, and was pleas'd beyond Expectation before my Return. Here I found various Company to observe, and various Discourse to attend to. I met indeed

3. **Piece of Plumb-Cake:** for several decades before this writing, the custom had grown that at Harvard Commencements plum cake was served. In New England eyes, it seemed the ultimate in dissipation. The authorities censured it as an extravagance and in 1722 were exerting vain efforts to prevent the students from this indulgence. 4. **Plagius:** Franklin's no doubt deliberate and mischievous pun on Pelagius, a British theologian of the fifth century who reputedly proclaimed freedom of the will and who therefore had been constantly condemned by Calvinist and Puritan divines.

5. **Tillotson's *Works:*** John Tillotson (1630–94), Archbishop of Canterbury, was a theological moderate, whose writings became, even in Puritan New England, the model of that rational elegance which Franklin admired and Edwards abhorred. Franklin's broad thrust is against the Harvard faculty, which still officially professed the Calvinist creed, but in fact was tending toward the mild "Arminianism" of Tillotson's school (which the Revival of 1740 would accuse of being both "Pelagian" and "Arminian"). **No. 13:** 1. No. 13 of the *Dogood Papers* was printed in the *New-England Courant,* dated September 24, 1722.

with the common Fate of *Listeners,* (who *hear no good of themselves,*) but from a Consciousness of my Innocence, receiv'd it with a Satisfaction beyond what the Love of Flattery and the Daubings of a Parasite could produce. The Company who rally'd me were about Twenty in Number, of both Sexes; and tho' the *Confusion of Tongues* (like that of Babel) which always happens among so many impetuous Talkers, render'd their Discourse not so intelligible as I could wish, I learnt thus much, That one of the Females pretended to know me, from some Discourse she had heard at a certain House before the Publication of one of my Letters; adding, *That I was a Person of an ill Character, and kept a criminal Correspondence with a Gentleman who assisted me in Writing.* One of the Gallants clear'd me of this random Charge, by saying, *That tho' I wrote in the Character of a Woman, he knew me to be a Man;* But, continu'd he, *he has more need of endeavouring a Reformation in himself, than spending his Wit in satyrizing others.*

I had no sooner left this Set of Ramblers, but I met a Crowd of *Tarpolins* and their Doxies, link'd to each other by the Arms, who ran (by their own Account) after the Rate of *Six Knots an Hour,* and bent their Course towards the Common. Their eager and amorous Emotions of Body, occasion'd by taking their Mistresses *in Tow,* they call'd *wild Steerage:* And as a Pair of them happen'd to trip and come to the Ground, the Company were call'd upon to *bring to,* for that Jack and Betty were *founder'd.* But this Fleet were not less comical or irregular in their Progress than a Company of Females I soon after came up with, who, by throwing their Heads to the Right and Left, at every one who pass'd by them, I concluded came out with no other Design than to revive the Spirit of Love in Disappointed Batchelors, and expose themselves to Sale to the first Bidder.

But it would take up too much Room in your Paper to mention all the Occasions of Diversion I met with in this Night's Ramble. As it grew later, I observed, that many pensive Youths with down Looks and a slow Pace, would be ever now and then crying out on the Cruelty of their Mistresses; others with a more rapid Pace and chearful Air, would be swinging their Canes and clapping their Cheeks, and whispering at certain Intervals, *I'm certain I shall have her! This is more than I expected! How charmingly she talks! &c.*

Upon the whole I conclude, That our *Night-Walkers* are a Set of People, who contribute very much to the Health and Satisfaction of those who have been fatigu'd with Business or Study, and occasionally observe their pretty Gestures and Impertinencies.

But among Men of Business, the *Shoemakers,* and other Dealers in Leather, are doubly oblig'd to them, inasmuch as they exceedingly promote the Consumption of their Ware: And I have heard of a *Shoemaker,* who being ask'd by a noted Rambler, *Whether he could tell how long her Shoes would last;* very prettily answer'd *That he knew how many Days she might wear them, but not how many Nights; because they were then put to a more violent and irregular Service than when she employ'd her self in the common Affairs of the House.* I am, Sir, Your Humble Servant,

SILENCE DOGOOD

AUTOBIOGRAPHY
[continued]

◊

¶ HAVING interrupted the narrative to show what Franklin actually contributed to the *New-England Courant,* I now allow him to resume the essentials of his own account.

◊

MY INCLINATIONS for the sea were by this time worne out, or I might now have gratify'd them. But, having a trade, and supposing myself a pretty good workman, I offer'd my service to the printer in the place, old Mr. William Bradford, who had been the first printer in Pennsylvania, but removed from thence upon the quarrel of George Keith. He could give me no employment, having little to do, and help enough already; but says he, "My son at Philadelphia has lately lost his principal hand, Aquila Rose, by death; if you go thither, I believe he may employ you." Philadelphia was a hundred miles further; I set out, however, in a boat for Amboy, leaving my chest and things to follow me round by sea.

In crossing the bay, we met with a squall that tore our rotten sails to pieces, prevented our getting into the Kill, and drove us upon Long Island. In our way, a drunken Dutchman, who was a passenger too, fell overboard; when he was sinking, I reached through the water to his shock pate, and drew him up, so that we got him in again. His ducking sobered him a little, and he went to sleep, taking first out of his pocket a book, which he desir'd I would dry for him. It proved to be my old favorite author, Bunyan's Pilgrim's Progress, in Dutch, finely printed on good paper, with copper cuts, a dress better than I had ever seen it wear in its own language. I have since found that it has been translated into most of the languages of Europe, and suppose it has been more generally read than any other book, except perhaps the Bible. Honest John was the first that I know of who mix'd narration and dialogue; a method of writing very engaging to the reader, who in the most interesting parts finds himself, as it were, brought into the company and present at the discourse. De Foe in his Cruso, his Moll Flanders, Religious Courtship, Family Instructor, and other pieces, has imitated it with success; and Richardson has done the same in his Pamela, etc.[1]

When we drew near the island, we found it was a place where there could be no landing, there being a great surff on the stony beach. So we dropt anchor, and swung round towards the shore. Some people came down to the water edge and hallow'd to us, as we did to them; but the wind was so high, and the surff so loud, that we could not hear so as to understand each other. There were canoes on the shore, and we made signs, and hallow'd that they should fetch us; but they either did not understand us, or thought it impracticable, so they went away, and night coming on, we had no remedy but to wait till the wind should abate; and, in the mean time, the boatman and I concluded to sleep, if we could; and so crowded into the scuttle, with the Dutchman, who was still wet, and the spray beating over the head of our boat, leak'd thro' to us, so that we were soon almost as wet as he. In this manner we lay all night, with very little rest; but, the wind abating the next day, we made a shift to reach Amboy before night, having been thirty hours on the water, without victuals, or any drink but a bottle of filthy rum, the water we sail'd on being salt.

In the evening I found myself very feverish, and went into bed; but, having read somewhere that cold water drank plentifully was good for a fever, I follow'd the prescription, sweat plentifully most of the night, my fever left me, and in the morning, crossing the ferry, I proceeded on my journey on foot, having fifty miles to Burlington, where I was told I should find boats that would carry me the rest of the way to Philadelphia.

It rained very hard all the day; I was thoroughly soak'd, and by noon a good deal tired; so I stopt at a poor inn, where I staid all night, beginning now to wish that I had never left home. I cut so miserable a figure, too, that I found, by the questions ask'd me, I was suspected to be some runaway servant, and in danger of being taken up on that suspicion. However, I proceeded the next day, and got in the evening to an inn, within eight or ten miles of Burlington, kept by one Dr. Brown. He entered into conversation with me while I took some refreshment, and, finding I had read a little, became very sociable and friendly. Our acquaintance continu'd as long as he liv'd. He had been, I imagine, an itinerant doctor, for there was no town in England, or country in Europe, of which he could not give a very particular account. He had some letters, and was ingenious, but much of an unbeliever, and wickedly undertook, some years after, to travestie the Bible in doggrel verse, as Cotton had done Virgil. By this means he set many of the facts in a very ridiculous light, and might have hurt weak minds if his work had been published; but it never was.

At his house I lay that night, and the next morning reach'd Burlington, but had the mortification to find that the regular boats were gone a little before my coming, and no other expected to go before Tuesday, this being Saturday; wherefore I returned to an old woman in the town, of whom I had bought gingerbread to eat on the water, and ask'd her advice. She invited me to lodge at her house till a passage by water should offer; and being tired with my foot travelling, I accepted the invitation. She understanding I was a printer, would have had me stay at that town and follow my business, being ignorant of the stock necessary to begin with. She was very hospitable, gave me a dinner of ox-cheek with great good will, accepting only a pot of ale in return; and I thought myself fixed till Tuesday should come. However, walking in the evening by the side of the river, a boat came by, which I found was going towards Philadelphia, with several people in her. They took me in, and as there was no wind, we row'd all the way; and about midnight, not having yet seen the city, some of the company were confident we must have passed it, and would row no farther; the others knew not where we were; so we put toward the shore, got into a creek, landed

AUTOBIOGRAPHY (CONT.). 1. **in his Pamela, etc.:** Franklin here advertises the range, and the limitations, of his aesthetic sensibility. By "Cruso" he obviously means Defoe's *Robinson Crusoe* (1719). *Moll Flanders*, also by Defoe, was published in 1722, as was his dehumanized *Religious Courtship*. His still more ceremonial *Family Instructor* was first printed in 1715 and was constantly reprinted during the century. There can hardly elsewhere be found a more stuffy monument to the dehydrated manners of the polite era. To this body of ritualistic literature, Franklin joined Samuel Richardson's (1689–1761) *Pamela* (1740), which—oddly enough—was the one work of fiction that Jonathan Edwards would approve.

near an old fence, with the rails of which we made a fire, the night being cold, in October, and there we remained till daylight. Then one of the company knew the place to be Cooper's Creek, a little above Philadelphia, which we saw as soon as we got out of the creek, and arriv'd there about eight or nine o'clock on the Sunday morning, and landed at the Market-street wharf.

I have been the more particular in this description of my journey, and shall be so of my first entry into that city, that you may in your mind compare such unlikely beginnings with the figure I have since made there. I was in my working dress, my best cloaths being to come round by sea. I was dirty from my journey; my pockets were stuff'd out with shirts and stockings, and I knew no soul nor where to look for lodging. I was fatigued with travelling, rowing and want of rest, I was very hungry; and my whole stock of cash consisted of a Dutch dollar, and about a shilling in copper. The latter I gave the people of the boat for my passage, who at first refus'd it, on account of my rowing; but I insisted on their taking it. A man being sometimes more generous when he has but a little money than when he has plenty, perhaps thro' fear of being thought to have but little.

Then I walked up the street, gazing about till near the market-house I met a boy with bread. I had made many a meal on bread, and, inquiring where he got it, I went immediately to the baker's he directed me to, in Second-street, and ask'd for bisket, intending such as we had in Boston; but they, it seems, were not made in Philadelphia. Then I asked for a three-penny loaf, and was told they had none such. So not considering or knowing the difference of money, and the greater cheapness nor the names of the bread, I bad him give me three-penny worth of any sort. He gave me, accordingly, three great puffy rolls. I was surpriz'd at the quantity, but took it, and, having no room in my pockets, walk'd off with a roll under each arm, and eating the other. Thus I went up Market-street as far as Fourth-street, passing by the door of Mr. Read, my future wife's father; when she, standing at the door, saw me, and thought I made, as I certainly did, a most awkward, ridiculous appearance. Then I turned and went down Chestnut-street and part of Walnut-street, eating my roll all the way, and coming round, found myself again at Market-street wharf, near the boat I came in, to which I went for a draught of river water; and, being filled with one of my rolls, gave the other two to a woman and her child that came down the river in the boat with us, and were waiting to go farther.

Thus refreshed, I walked again up the street, which by this time had many clean-dressed people in it, who were all walking the same way. I joined them, and thereby was led into the great meeting-house of the Quakers near the market. I sat down among them, and, after looking round awhile and hearing nothing said, being very drowsy thro' labor and want of rest the preceding night, I fell fast asleep, and continu'd so till the meeting broke up, when one was kind enough to rouse me. This was, therefore, the first house I was in, or slept in, in Philadelphia. . . .

Before I enter upon my public appearance in business, it may be well to let you know the then state of my mind with regard to my principles and morals, that you may see how far those influenc'd the future events of my life. My parents had early given me religious impressions, and brought me through my childhood piously in the Dissenting way. But I was scarce fifteen, when, after doubting by turns of several points, as I found them disputed in the different books I read, I began to doubt of Revelation itself. Some books against Deism fell into my hands; they were said to be the substance of sermons preached at Boyle's Lectures. It happened that they wrought an effect on me quite contrary to what was intended by them; for the arguments of the Deists, which were quoted to be refuted, appeared to me much stronger than the refutations; in short, I soon became a thorough Deist. My arguments perverted some others, particularly Collins and Ralph; [2] but, each of them having afterwards wrong'd me greatly without the least compunction, and recollecting Keith's conduct towards me [3] (who was another freethinker), and my own towards Vernon [4] and Miss Read,[5] which at times gave me great trouble, I began to suspect that this doctrine, tho' it might be true, was not very

2. **Collins and Ralph:** John Collins was a boyhood friend of Franklin's in Boston and later a companion in Philadelphia; he borrowed money from Franklin and disappeared into Barbados without repaying it. James Ralph, a Philadelphia clerk with poetic aspirations, went with Franklin to London and remained there, dying in 1762. 3. **Keith's conduct towards me:** Sir William Keith (1680–1749), governor of Pennsylvania (1717–49), promised to help Franklin to a position of profit in London, but neglected to write the requisite letters and so left the boy destitute in the metropolis. 4. **towards Vernon:** Samuel Vernon, a silversmith in Newport, R.I., commissioned Franklin to recover a debt of thirty-five pounds in Pennsylvania; Franklin secured the money, but lost most of it by lending to Collins. 5. **and Miss Read:** Franklin had "made some courtship" to Deborah ("Debby") before going to England, but gave every appearance of deserting her. She made an unfortunate marriage, which was dissolved by the time he returned. He made amends by marrying her in 1730.

useful. My London pamphlet,[6] which had for its motto these lines of Dryden:

> "Whatever is, is right. Though purblind man
> Sees but a part o' the chain, the nearest link:
> His eyes not carrying to the equal beam,
> That poises all above;"

and from the attributes of God, his infinite wisdom, goodness and power, concluded that nothing could possibly be wrong in the world, and that vice and virtue were empty distinctions, no such things existing, appear'd now not so clever a performance as I once thought it; and I doubted whether some error had not insinuated itself unperceiv'd into my argument, so as to infect all that follow'd, as is common in metaphysical reasonings.

I grew convinc'd that *truth, sincerity* and *integrity* in dealings between man and man were of the utmost importance to the felicity of life; and I form'd written resolutions, which still remain in my journal book, to practice them ever while I lived. Revelation had indeed no weight with me, as such; but I entertain'd an opinion that, though certain actions might not be bad *because* they were forbidden by it, or good *because* it commanded them, yet probably those actions might be forbidden *because* they were bad for us, or commanded *because* they were beneficial to us, in their own natures, all the circumstances of things considered. And this persuasion, with the kind hand of Providence, or some guardian angel, or accidental favourable circumstances and situations, or all together, preserved me, thro' this dangerous time of youth, and the hazardous situations I was sometimes in among strangers, remote from the eye and advice of my father, without any willful gross immorality or injustice, that might have been expected from my want of religion. [Some foolish intrigues with low women excepted, which from the expense were rather more prejudicial to me than to them.] [7] I say willful, because the instances I have mentioned had something of *necessity* in them, from my youth, inexperience, and the knavery of others. I had therefore a tolerable character to begin the world with; I valued it properly, and determin'd to preserve it. . . .

I began now gradually to pay off the debt I was under for the printing-house. In order to secure my credit and character as a tradesman, I took care not only to be in *reality* industrious and frugal, but to avoid all appearances to the contrary, I drest plainly; I was seen at no places of idle diversion. I never went out a fishing or shooting; a book, indeed, sometimes debauch'd me from my work, but that was seldom, snug, and gave no scandal; and, to show that I was not above my business, I sometimes brought home the paper I purchas'd at the stores thro' the streets on a wheelbarrow. Thus being esteem'd an industrious, thriving young man, and paying duly for what I bought, the merchants who imported stationery solicited my custom; others proposed supplying me with books, and I went on swimmingly. In the mean time, Keimer's credit [8] and business declining daily, he was at last forc'd to sell his printing-house to satisfy his creditors. He went to Barbadoes, and there lived some years in very poor circumstances. . . .

I had been religiously educated as a Presbyterian; [9] and tho' some of the dogmas of that persuasion, such as *the eternal decrees of God, election, reprobation, etc.*, appeared to me unintelligible, others doubtful, and I early absented myself from the public assemblies of the sect, Sunday being my studying day, I never was without some religious principles. I never doubted, for instance, the existence of the Deity; that he made the world, and govern'd it by his Providence; that the most acceptable service of God was the doing good to man; that our souls are immortal; and that all crime will be punished, and virtue rewarded, either here or hereafter. These I esteem'd the essentials of every religion; and, being to be found in all the religions we had in our country, I respected them all, tho' with different degrees of respect, as I found them more or less mix'd with other articles, which, without any tendency to inspire, promote, or confirm morality, serv'd principally to divide us, and make us unfriendly to one another. This respect to all, with an opinion that the worst had some good effects, induc'd me to avoid all discourse that might tend to lessen the

6. My London pamphlet: *A Dissertation on Liberty and Necessity, Pleasure and Pain* (1725), printed by himself. He later strove to destroy all copies. **7. Some . . . them:** In the manuscript, the words within brackets are struck out, but are still legible. **8. Keimer's credit:** Samuel Keimer employed Franklin in his printing shop in 1723, rehired him in 1728, and by 1729 was driven out of Philadelphia by Franklin's brilliance and his own inefficiency. **9. Presbyterian:** This selection comes from the portion written at Passy in 1784; though it has the Franklinian consistency of tone, it displays the immense amount of experience he had undergone since 1771. Franklin was brought up as what we call a Congregationalist, but since his father's church, the Third of Boston, formally accepted the Westminster Confession, he was content to call the creed Presbyterian. His nonchalance about the term advertises his indifference to denomination niceties.

good opinion another might have of his own religion; and as our province increas'd in people, and new places of worship were continually wanted, and generally erected by voluntary contribution, my mite for such purpose, whatever might be the sect, was never refused.

Tho' I seldom attended any public worship, I had still an opinion of its propriety, and of its utility when rightly conducted, and I regularly paid my annual subscription for the support of the only Presbyterian minister or meeting we had in Philadelphia. He us'd to visit me sometimes as a friend, and admonish me to attend his administrations, and I was now and then prevail'd on to do so, once for five Sundays successively. Had he been in my opinion a good preacher, perhaps I might have continued, notwithstanding the occasion I had for the Sunday's leisure in my course of study; but his discourses were chiefly either polemic arguments, or explications of the peculiar doctrines of our sect, and were all to me very dry, uninteresting, and unedifying, since not a single moral principle was inculcated or enforc'd, their aim seeming to be rather to make us Presbyterians than good citizens.

At length he took for his text that verse of the fourth chapter of Philippians, *"Finally, brethren, whatsoever things are true, honest, just, pure, lovely, or of good report, if there be any virtue, or any praise, think on these things."* And I imagin'd, in a sermon on such a text, we could not miss of having some morality. But he confin'd himself to five points only, as meant by the apostle, viz.: 1. Keeping holy the Sabbath day. 2. Being diligent in reading the holy Scriptures. 3. Attending duly the publick worship. 4. Partaking of the Sacrament. 5. Paying a due respect to God's ministers. These might be all good things; but, as they were not the kind of good things that I expected from that text, I despaired of ever meeting with them from any other, was disgusted, and attended his preaching no more. I had some years before compos'd a little Liturgy, or form of prayer, for my own private use (viz., in 1728), entitled, *Articles of Belief and Acts of Religion.* I return'd to the use of this, and went no more to the public assemblies. My conduct might be blameable, but I leave it, without attempting further to excuse it; my present purpose being to relate facts, and not to make apologies for them.

It was about this time I conceiv'd the bold and arduous project of arriving at moral perfection. I wish'd to live without committing any fault at any time; I would conquer all that either natural inclination, custom, or company might lead me into. As I knew, or thought I knew, what was right and wrong, I did not see why I might not always do the one and avoid the other. But I soon found I had undertaken a task of more difficulty than I had imagined. While my care was employ'd in guarding against one fault, I was often surprised by another; habit took the advantage of inattention; inclination was sometimes too strong for reason. I concluded, at length, that the mere speculative conviction that it was our interest to be completely virtuous, was not sufficient to prevent our slipping; and that the contrary habits must be broken, and good ones acquired and established, before we can have any dependence on a steady, uniform rectitude of conduct. For this purpose I therefore contrived the following method.

In the various enumerations of the moral virtues I had met with in my reading, I found the catalogue more or less numerous, as different writers included more or fewer ideas under the same name. Temperance, for example, was by some confined to eating and drinking, while by others it was extended to mean the moderating every other pleasure, appetite, inclination, or passion, bodily or mental, even to our avarice and ambition. I propos'd to myself, for the sake of clearness, to use rather more names, with fewer ideas annex'd to each, than a few names with more ideas; and I included under thirteen names of virtues all that at that time occur'd to me as necessary or desirable, and annexed to each a short precept, which fully express'd the extent I gave to its meaning.

These names of virtues, with their precepts were:

1. TEMPERANCE. Eat not to dullness; drink not to elevation.

2. SILENCE. Speak not but what may benefit others or yourself; avoid trifling conversation.

3. ORDER. Let all your things have their places; let each part of your business have its time.

4. RESOLUTION. Resolve to perform what you ought; perform without fail what you resolve.

5. FRUGALITY. Make no expense but to do good to others or yourself; i.e., waste nothing.

6. INDUSTRY. Lose no time; be always employ'd in something useful; cut off all unnecessary actions.

7. SINCERITY. Use no hurtful deceit; think innocently and justly; and, if you speak, speak accordingly.

8. JUSTICE. Wrong none by doing injuries, or omitting the benefits that are your duty.

9. MODERATION. Avoid extreams; forbear resenting injuries so much as you think they deserve.

10. CLEANLINESS. Tolerate no uncleanliness in body, cloaths, or habitation.

11. TRANQUILLITY. Be not disturbed at trifles, or at accidents common or unavoidable.

12. CHASTITY. Rarely use venery but for health or offspring, never to dullness, weakness, or the injury of your own or another's peace or reputation.

13. HUMILITY. Imitate Jesus and Socrates.

My intention being to acquire the *habitude* of all these virtues, I judg'd it would be well not to distract my attention by attempting the whole at once, but to fix it on one of them at a time; and, when I should be master of that, then to proceed to another, and so on, till I should have gone thro' the thirteen; and, as the previous acquisition of some might facilitate the acquisition of certain others, I arrang'd them with that view, as they stand above. Temperance first, as it tends to procure that coolness and clearness of head, which is so necessary where constant vigilance was to be kept up, and guard maintained against the unremitting attraction of ancient habits, and the force of perpetual temptations. This being acquir'd and establish'd, Silence would be more easy; and my desire being to gain knowledge at the same time that I improv'd in virtue, and considering that in conversation it was obtain'd rather by the use of ears than of the tongue, and therefore wishing to break a habit I was getting into of prattling, punning, and joking, which only made me acceptable to a trifling company, I gave *Silence* the second place. This and the next, *Order,* I expected would allow me more time for attending to my project and my studies. *Resolution,* once become habitual, would keep me firm in my endeavours to obtain all the subsequent virtues; *Frugality* and Industry freeing me from my remaining debt, and producing affluence and independence, would make more easy the practice of Sincerity and Justice, etc., etc. Conceiving then, that, agreeably to the advice of Pythagoras in his Golden Verses, daily examination would be necessary, I contrived the following method for conducting that examination.

I made a little book, in which I allotted a page for each of the virtues. I rul'd each page with red ink, so as to have seven columns, one for each day of the week, marking each column with a letter for the day. I cross'd these columns with thirteen red lines, marking the beginning of each line with the first letter of one of the virtues, on which line, and in its proper column, I might mark, by a little black spot, every fault I found upon examination to have been committed respecting that virtue upon that day.

FORM OF THE PAGES.

TEMPERANCE.							
EAT NOT TO DULLNESS; DRINK NOT TO ELEVATION.							
	S.	M.	T.	W.	T.	F.	S.
T.							
S.	*	*		*		*	
O.	* *	*	*		*	*	*
R.			*			*	
F.		*			*		
I.			*				
S.							
J.							
M.							
C.							
T.							
C.							
H.							

I determined to give a week's strict attention to each of the virtues successively. Thus, in the first week, my great guard was to avoid even the least offence against *Temperance,* leaving the other virtues to their ordinary chance, only marking every evening the faults of the day. Thus, if in the first week I could keep my first line, marked T, clear of spots, I suppos'd the habit of that virtue so much strengthen'd, and its opposite weaken'd, that I might venture extending my attention to include the next, and for the following week keep both lines clear of spots. Proceeding thus to the last, I could go thro' a course compleat in thirteen weeks, and four courses in a year. And like him who, having a garden to weed, does not attempt to eradicate all the bad herbs at once, which would exceed his reach and his strength, but works on one of the beds at a time, and, having accomplish'd the first, proceeds to a second, so I should have, I hoped, the encouraging pleasure of seeing on my pages the progress I made in virtue, by clearing sucessively my lines of their spots, till in the end, by a number of courses, I should be happy in viewing a clean book, after a thirteen weeks' daily examination.

This my little book had for its motto these lines from Addison's *Cato:*

"Here will I hold. If there's a power above us
(And that there is, all nature cries aloud
Thro' all her works), He must delight in virtue;
And that which he delights in must be happy."

Another from Cicero,

"O vitae Philosophia dux! O virtutum indagatrix expultrixque vitiorum! Unus dies, bene et ex praeceptis tuis actus, peccanti immortalitati est anteponendus." [10]

Another from the Proverbs of Solomon, speaking of wisdom or virtue:

"Length of days is in her right hand, and in her left hand riches and honour. Her ways are ways of pleasantness, and all her paths are peace." iii.16, 17.

And conceiving God to be the fountain of wisdom, I thought it right and necessary to solicit his assistance for obtaining it; to this end I formed the following little prayer, which was prefix'd to my tables of examination, for daily use.

"O powerful Goodness! bountiful Father! merciful Guide! Increase in me that wisdom which discovers my truest interest. Strengthen my resolutions to perform what that wisdom dictates. Accept my kind offices to thy other children as the only return in my power for thy continual favours to me."

I used also sometimes a little prayer which I took from Thomson's Poems, viz.:

"Father of light and life, thou Good Supreme!
O teach me what is good; teach me Thyself!
Save me from folly, vanity, and vice,
From every low pursuit; and fill my soul
With knowledge, conscious peace, and virtue pure;
Sacred, substantial, never-fading bliss!"

The precept of *Order* requiring that *every part of my business should have its allotted time,* one page of my little book contain'd the following scheme of employment for the twenty-four hours of a natural day.

THE MORNING. *Question.* What good shall I do this day?	5, 6, 7	Rise, wash, and address *Powerful Goodness!* Contrive day's business, and take the resolution of the day; prosecute the present study, and breakfast.
	8, 9, 10, 11	Work.
NOON.	12, 1	Read, or overlook my accounts, and dine.
	2, 3, 4, 5	Work.
EVENING. *Question.* What good have I done to-day?	6, 7, 8, 9	Put things in their places. Supper. Music or diversion, or conversation. Examination of the day.
NIGHT.	10, 11, 12, 1, 2, 3, 4	Sleep.

I enter'd upon the execution of this plan for self-examination, and continu'd it with occasional intermissions for some time. I was surpris'd to find myself so much fuller of faults than I had imagined; but I had the satisfaction of seeing them diminish. To avoid the trouble of renewing now and then my little book, which, by scraping out the marks on the paper of old faults to make room for new ones in a new course, became full of holes, I transferr'd my tables and precepts to the ivory leaves of a memorandum book, on which the lines were drawn with red ink, that made a durable stain, and on those lines I mark'd my faults with a black-lead pencil, which marks I could easily wipe out with a wet sponge. After a while I went thro' one course only in a year, and afterward only one in several years, till at length I omitted them entirely, being employ'd in voyages and business abroad, with a multiplicity of affairs that interfered; but I always carried my little book with me.

My scheme of ORDER gave me the most trouble; and I found that, tho' it might be practicable where a man's business was such as to leave him the disposition of his time, that of a journeyman printer, for instance, it was not possible to be exactly observed by a master, who must mix with

10. ***"O . . . anteponendus":*** "O philosophy, guide of life! O explorer of virtue and expeller of vice! A single day, spent well and in accordance with your precepts, is to be preferred to an eternity of wrong-doing" (Cicero, *Tusculans,* 5.5).

the world, and often receive people of business at their own hours. *Order,* too, with regard to places for things, papers, etc., I found extreamly difficult to acquire. I had not been early accustomed to it, and, having an exceeding good memory, I was not so sensible of the inconvenience attending want of method. This article, therefore, cost me so much painful attention, and my faults in it vexed me so much, and I made so little progress in amendment, and had such frequent relapses, that I was almost ready to give up the attempt, and content myself with a faulty character in that respect, like the man who, in buying an ax of a smith, my neighbor, desired to have the whole of its surface as bright as the edge. The smith consented to grind it bright for him if he would turn the wheel; he turn'd, while the smith press'd the broad face of the ax hard and heavily on the stone, which made the turning of it very fatiguing. The man came every now and then from the wheel to see how the work went on, and at length would take his ax as it was, without farther grinding. "No," said the smith, "turn on, turn on; we shall have it bright by-and-by; as yet it is only speckled." "Yes," says the man, "*but I think I like a speckled ax best.*" And I believe this may have been the case with many, who, having, for want of some such means as I employ'd, found the difficulty of obtaining good and breaking bad habits in other points of vice and virtue, have given up the struggle, and concluded that "*a speckled ax was best;*" for something, that pretended to reason, was every now and then suggesting to me that such extream nicety as I exacted of myself might be a kind of foppery in morals, which, if it were known, would make me ridiculous; that a perfect character might be attended with the inconvenience of being envied and hated; and that a benevolent man should allow a few faults in himself, to keep his friends in countenance.

In truth, I found myself incorrigible with respect to Order; and now I am grown old, and my memory bad, I feel very sensibly the want of it. But, on the whole, tho' I never arrived at the perfection I had been so ambitious of obtaining, but fell far short of it, yet I was, by the endeavour, a better and a happier man than I otherwise should have been if I had not attempted it; as those who aim at perfect writing by imitating the engraved copies, tho' they never reach the wish'd-for excellence of those copies, their hand is mended by the endeavour, and is tolerable while it continues fair and legible.

It may be well my posterity should be informed that to this little artifice, with the blessing of God, their ancestor ow'd the constant felicity of his life, down to his 79th year, in which this is written. What reverses may attend the remainder is in the hand of Providence; but, if they arrive, the reflection on past happiness enjoy'd ought to help his bearing them with more resignation. To Temperance he ascribes his long-continued health, and what is still left to him of a good constitution; to Industry and Frugality, the early easiness of his circumstances and acquisition of his fortune, with all that knowledge that enabled him to be a useful citizen, and obtained for him some degree of reputation among the learned; to Sincerity and Justice, the confidence of his country, and the honourable employs it conferred upon him; and to the joint influence of the whole mass of the virtues, even in the imperfect state he was able to acquire them, all that evenness of temper, and that cheerfulness in conversation, which makes his company still sought for, and agreeable even to his younger acquaintance. I hope, therefore, that some of my descendants may follow the example and reap the benefit.

It will be remark'd that, tho' my scheme was not wholly without religion, there was in it no mark of any of the distinguishing tenets of any particular sect. I had purposely avoided them; for, being fully persuaded of the utility and excellency of my method, and that it might be serviceable to people in all religions, and intending some time or other to publish it, I would not have any thing in it that should prejudice any one of any sect, against it. I purposed writing a little comment on each virtue, in which I would have shown the advantages of possessing it, and the mischiefs attending its opposite vice; and I should have called my book THE ART OF VIRTUE, because it would have shown the means and manner of obtaining virtue, which would have distinguished it from the mere exhortation to be good, that does not instruct and indicate the means, but is like the apostle's man of verbal charity, who only without showing to the naked and hungry how or where they might get clothes or victuals, exhorted them to be fed and clothed.—James ii. 15, 16.

But it so happened that my intention of writing and publishing this comment was never fulfilled. I did, indeed, from time to time, put down short hints of the sentiments, reasonings, etc., to be made use of in it, some of which I have still by me; but the necessary close attention to private business in the earlier part of my life, and public business since, have occasioned my postponing it; for, it being connected in my mind with *a great and extensive project,* that required the whole man to execute, and which an unforeseen succession of employs prevented my attending to, it has hitherto remain'd unfinish'd.

In this piece it was my design to explain and enforce this doctrine, that vicious actions are not hurtful because they are forbidden, but forbidden because they are hurtful, the nature of man alone considered; that it was, therefore, every one's interest to be virtuous who wish'd to be happy even in this world; and I should, from this circumstance (there being always in the world a number of rich merchants, nobility, states, and princes, who have need of honest instruments for the management of their affairs, and such being so rare), have endeavoured to convince young persons that no qualities were so likely to make a poor man's fortune as those of probity and integrity.

My list of virtues contain'd at first but twelve; but a Quaker friend having kindly informed me that I was generally thought proud; that my pride show'd itself frequently in conversation; that I was not content with being in the right when discussing any point, but was overbearing, and rather insolent, of which he convinc'd me by mentioning several instances; I determined endeavouring to cure myself, if I could, of this vice or folly among the rest, and I added *Humility* to my list, giving an extensive meaning to the word.

I cannot boast of much success in acquiring the *reality* of this virtue, but I had a good deal with regard to the *appearance* of it. I made it a rule to forbear all direct contradiction to the sentiments of others, and all positive assertion of my own. I even forbid myself, agreeably to the laws of our Junto, the use of every word or expression in the language that imported a fix'd opinion, such as *certainly, undoubtedly,* etc., and I adopted, instead of them, *I conceive, I apprehend,* or *I imagine* a thing to be so or so; or it *so appears to me at present.* When another asserted something that I thought an error, I deny'd myself the pleasure of contradicting him abruptly, and of showing immediately some absurdity in his proposition; and in answering I began by observing that in certain cases or circumstances his opinion would be right, but in the present case there *appear'd* or *seem'd* to me some differences, etc. I soon found the advantage of this change in my manner; the conversations I engag'd in went on more pleasantly. The modest way in which I propos'd my opinions procur'd them a readier reception and less contradiction; I had less mortification when I was found to be in the wrong, and I more easily prevail'd with others to give up their mistakes and join with me when I happened to be in the right.

And this mode, which I at first put on with some violence to natural inclination, became at length so easy, and so habitual to me, that perhaps for these fifty years past no one has ever heard a dogmatical expression escape me. And to this habit (after my character of integrity) I think it principally owing that I had early so much weight with my fellow citizens when I proposed new institutions, or alterations in the old, and so much influence in public councils when I became a member; for I was but a bad speaker, never eloquent, subject to much hesitation in my choice of words, hardly correct in language, and yet I generally carried my points.

In reality, there is, perhaps, no one of our natural passions so hard to subdue as *pride*. Disguise it, struggle with it, beat it down, stifle it, mortify it as much as one pleases, it is still alive, and will every now and then peep out and show itself; you will see it, perhaps, often in this history; for, even if I could conceive that I had compleatly overcome it, I should probably be proud of my humility.

A WITCH TRIAL AT MOUNT-HOLLY

¶ THIS joke was printed in the *Pennsylvania Gazette* for October 22, 1730. There is no direct evidence that Franklin wrote it, and he seems never to have claimed it, but it has long been assigned to him, is clearly in his literary character, and is too precious to be given to anybody else. In studying it the student must recollect that only thirty-eight years before, not much more than a generation earlier, had occurred the infamous witch hysteria at Salem in Franklin's native Massachusetts.

BURLINGTON, Oct. 12. Saturday last at Mount-Holly, about 8 miles from this Place, near 300 People were gathered together to see an Experiment or two tried on some Persons accused of Witchcraft. It seems the Accused had been charged with making their Neighbors Sheep dance in an uncommon Manner, and with causing Hogs to speak, and sing Psalms, &c. to the great Terror and Amazement of the King's good and peaceful Subjects in this Province; and the Accusers being very positive that if the Accused were weighted in Scales against a Bible, the Bible would prove too heavy for them; or that, if they were bound and put into the River, they would swim; the said Accused desirous to make their Innocence appear, voluntarily offered to undergo the said Trials, if 2 of the most violent of their Accusers would be tried with them. Accordingly the Time and Place was agreed on, and advertised about the Country; The Accusers were 1 Man and 1 Woman; and the Accused the same. The Parties being met, and the People got together, a grand Consultation was held, before they proceeded to Trial; in which it was agreed to use the Scales first; and a Committee of Men were appointed to search the Men, and a Committee of Women to search the Women, to see if they had any Thing of Weight about them, particularly Pins. After the Scrutiny was over, a huge great Bible belonging to the Justice of the Place was provided, and a Lane through the Populace was made from the Justices House to the Scales, which were fixed on a Gallows erected for that Purpose opposite to the House, that the Justice's Wife and the rest of the Ladies might see the Trial, without coming amongst the Mob; and after the Manner of Moorfields, a large Ring was also made. Then came out of the House a grave tall Man carrying the Holy Writ before the supposed Wizard, &c. (as solemnly as the Sword-bearer of London before the Lord Mayor), the Wizard was first put in the Scale, and over him was read a Chapter out of the Books of Moses, and then the Bible was put in the other Scale, (which being kept down before) was immediately let go; but to the great Surprize of the Spectators, Flesh and Bones came down plump, and outweighed that great good Book by abundance. After that same Manner, the others were served, and their Lumps of Mortality severally were too heavy for Moses and all the Prophets and Apostles. This being over, the Accusers and the rest of the Mob, not satisfied with this Experiment, would have the Trial by Water; accordingly a most solemn Procession was made to the Mill-pond; where both Accused and Accusers being stripp'd (saving only to the Women their Shifts) were bound Hand and Foot, and severally placed in the Water, lengthways, from the Side of a Barge or Flat, having for Security only a Rope about the Middle of each, which was held by some in the Flat. The Accuser Man being thin and spare, with some Difficulty began to sink at last; but the rest every one of them swam very light upon the Water. A Sailor in the Flat jump'd out upon the Back of the Man accused, thinking to drive him down to the Bottom, but the Person bound, without any Help came up some time before the other. The Woman Accuser, being told that she did not sink, would be duck'd a second Time; when she swam again as light as before. Upon which she declared, That she believed the Accused had bewitched her to make her so light, and that she would duck the Devil out of her. The accused Man, being surpriz'd at his own Swimming, was not so confident of his Innocence as before, but said, *If I am a Witch, it is more than I know*. The more thinking Part of the Spectators were of Opinion, that any Person so bound and plac'd in the Water (unless they were mere Skin and Bones) would swim till their Breath was gone, and their Lungs fill'd with Water. But it being the general Belief of the Populace, that the Womens Shifts, and the Garters with which they were bound help'd to support them; it is said they are to be tried again the next warm Weather, naked.

APOLOGY FOR PRINTERS

◇

¶ THIS, by now, classic statement was printed casually in the *Pennsylvania Gazette*, for June 10, 1731. Apparently Franklin had accepted and printed a routine announcement of the sailing of a ship, but the skipper was one who believed that the clergy, in their black cloaks, were Jonahs. We assume that Franklin printed a handbill expressing the Captain's prejudice, since there is no text of the full advertisement in the *Gazette*. At any rate, the background is clear: Franklin was attacked in Philadelphia for lending himself as a commercial printer to anticlerical superstition. The chance to vindicate his rooted convictions about freedom of the press was to him irresistible.

◇

BEING frequently censur'd and condemn'd by different Persons for printing Things which they say ought not to be printed, I have sometimes thought it might be necessary to make a standing Apology for my self, and publish it once a Year, to be read upon all Occasions of that Nature. Much Business has hitherto hindered the execution of this Design; but having very lately given extraordinary Offence by printing an Advertisement with a certain N.B. at the End of it, I find an Apology more particularly requisite at this

Juncture, tho' it happens when I have not yet Leisure to write such a thing in the proper Form, and only in a loose manner throw those Considerations together which should have been the Substance of it.

I request all who are angry with me on the Account of printing things they don't like, calmly to consider these following Particulars

1. That the Opinions of Men are almost as various as their Faces; an Observation general enough to become a common Proverb, *So many Men so many Minds.*

2. That the Business of Printing has chiefly to do with Men's Opinions; most things that are printed tending to promote some, or oppose others.

3. That hence arises the peculiar Unhappiness of that Business, which other Callings are no way liable to; they who follow Printing being scarce able to do any thing in their way of getting a Living, which shall not probably give Offence to some, and perhaps to many; whereas the Smith, the Shoemaker, the Carpenter, or the Man of any other Trade, may work indifferently for People of all Persuasions, without offending any of them: and the Merchant may buy and sell with Jews, Turks, Hereticks, and Infidels of all sorts, and get Money by every one of them, without giving Offence to the most orthodox, of any sort; or suffering the least Censure or Ill-will on the Account from any Man whatever.

4. That it is as unreasonable in any one Man or Set of Men to expect to be pleas'd with every thing that is printed, as to think that nobody ought to be pleas'd but themselves.

5. Printers are educated in the Belief, that when Men differ in Opinion, both Sides ought equally to have the Advantage of being heard by the Publick; and that when Truth and Error have fair Play, the former is always an overmatch for the latter: Hence they chearfully serve all contending Writers that pay them well, without regarding on which side they are of the Question in Dispute.

6. Being thus continually employ'd in serving all Parties, Printers naturally acquire a vast Unconcernedness as to the right or wrong Opinions contain'd in what they print; regarding it only as the Matter of their daily labour: They print things full of Spleen and Animosity, with the utmost Calmness and Indifference, and without the least Ill-will to the Persons reflected on; who nevertheless unjustly think the Printer as much their Enemy as the Author, and join both together in their Resentment.

7. That it is unreasonable to imagine Printers approve of every thing they print, and to censure them on any particular thing accordingly; since in the way of their Business they print such great variety of things opposite and contradictory. It is likewise as unreasonable what some assert, *That Printers ought not to print any Thing but what they approve;* since if all of that Business should make such a Resolution, and abide by it, an End would thereby be put to Free Writing, and the World would afterwards have nothing to read but what happen'd to be the Opinions of Printers.

8. That if all Printers were determin'd not to print any thing till they were sure it would offend no body, there would be very little printed.

9. That if they sometimes print vicious or silly things not worth reading, it may not be because they approve such things themselves, but because the People are so viciously and corruptly educated that good things are not encouraged. I have known a very numerous Impression of *Robin Hood's Songs* go off in this Province at 2/ per Book, in less than a Twelvemonth; when a small Quantity of *David's Psalms* (an excellent version) have lain upon my Hands above twice the Time.

10. That notwithstanding what might be urg'd in behalf of a Man's being allow'd to do in the Way of his Business whatever he is paid for, yet Printers do continually discourage the Printing of great Numbers of bad things, and stifle them in the Birth. I my self have constantly refused to print any thing that might countenance Vice, or promote Immorality; tho' by complying in such Cases with the corrupt Taste of the Majority, I might have got much Money. I have also always refus'd to print such things as might do real Injury to any Person, how much soever I have been solicited, and tempted with Offers of great Pay; and how much soever I have by refusing got the Ill-will of those who would have employ'd me. I have heretofore fallen under the Resentment of large Bodies of Men, for refusing absolutely to print any of their Party or Personal Reflections. In this Manner I have made my self many Enemies, and the constant Fatigue of denying is almost insupportable. But the Publick being unacquainted with all this, whenever the poor Printer happens either through Ignorance or much Persuasion, to do any thing that is generally thought worthy of Blame, he meets with no more Friendship or Favour on the above Account, than if there were no Merit in't at all. Thus, as Waller says,

Poets lose half the Praise they would have got
Were it but known what they discreetly blot;

Yet are censur'd for every bad Line found in their Works with the utmost Severity.

I come now to the particular Case of the N.B. above-mention'd, about which there has been more Clamour against me, than ever before on any other Account. In the Hurry of other Business an Advertisement was brought to me to be printed; it signified that such a Ship lying at such a Wharff, would sail for Barbadoes in such a Time, and that Freighters and Passengers might agree with the Captain at such a Place; so far is what's common; But at the Bottom this odd Thing was added, N.B. *No Sea Hens nor Black Gowns will be admitted on any Terms.* I printed it, and receiv'd my Money; and the Advertisement was stuck up around the Town as usual. I had not so much Curiosity at that time as to enquire the Meaning of it, nor did I in the least imagine it would give so much Offence. Several good Men are very angry with me on this Occasion; they are pleas'd to say I have too much Sense to do such things ignorantly; that if they were Printers they would not have done such a thing on any consideration; that it could proceed from nothing but my abundant Malice against Religion and the Clergy: They therefore declare they will not take any more of my Papers, nor have any farther Dealings with me; but will hinder me of all the Custom they can. All this is very hard!

I believe it had been better if I had refused to print the said Advertisement. However, 'tis done and cannot be revok'd. I have only the following few Particulars to offer, some of them in my behalf, by way of Mitigation, and some not much to the Purpose; but I desire none of them may be read when the Reader is not in a very good Humour.

1. That I really did it without the least Malice, and imagin'd the N.B. was plac'd there only to make the Advertisement star'd at, and more generally read.

2. That I never saw the Word *Sea-Hens* before in my Life; nor have I yet ask'd the meaning of it; and tho' I had certainly known that *Black Gowns* in that Place signified the Clergy of the Church of England, yet I have the confidence in the generous good Temper of such of them as I know, as to be well satisfied such a trifling mention of their Habit gives them no Disturbance.

3. That most of the Clergy in this and the neighbouring Provinces, are my Customers, and some of them my very good Friends; and I must be very malicious indeed, or very stupid, to print this thing for a small Profit, if I had thought it would have given them just Cause of Offence.

4. That if I have much Malice against the Clergy, and withal such Sense; 'tis strange I never write or talk against the Clergy my self. Some have observed that 'tis a fruitful Topic, and the easiest to be witty upon of all others. I can print any thing I write at less Charge than others; yet I appeal to the Publick that I am never guilty this way, and to all my Acquaintance as to my Conversation.

5. That if a Man of Sense had Malice enough to desire to injure the Clergy, this is the foolishest Thing he could possibly contrive for that Purpose.

6. That I got Five Shillings by it.

7. That none who are angry with me would have given me so much to let it alone.

8. That if all People of different Opinions in this Province would engage to give me as much for not printing things they don't like, as I can get by printing them, I should probably live a very easy Life; and if all Printers were every where so dealt by, there would be very little printed.

9. That I am oblig'd to all who take my Paper, and am willing to think they do it out of meer Friendship. I only desire they would think the same when I deal with them. I think those who leave off, that they have taken it so long. But I beg they would not endeavour to dissuade others, for that will look like Malice.

10. That 'tis impossible any Man should know what he would do if he was a Printer.

11. That notwithstanding the Rashness and Inexperience of Youth, which is most likely to be prevail'd with to do things that ought not to be done; yet I have avoided printing such Things as usually give Offence either to Church or State, more than any Printer that has followed the Business in this Province before.

12. And lastly, That I have printed above a Thousand Advertisements which made not the least mention of *Sea-Hens* or *Black Gowns;* and this being the first Offence, I have the more Reason to expect Forgiveness.

I take leave to conclude with an old Fable, which some of my Readers have heard before, and some have not.

"A certain well-meaning Man and his Son, were travelling towards a Market Town, with an Ass which they had to sell. The Road was bad; and the old Man therefore rid, but the Son went a-foot. The first Passenger they met, asked the Father if he was not ashamed to ride by himself, and suffer the poor Lad to wade along thro' the Mire; this induced him to take up his Son behind him: He had not travelled far, when he met others, who said, they were two unmerciful Lubbers to get both on the Back of that poor Ass, in such a deep Road. Upon this the old Man gets off, and let his Son ride alone. The next they met called the Lad a graceless, rascally young Jackanapes, to ride in that Manner thro' the Dirt, while his aged Father trudged along on Foot; and they said the old Man was a Fool, for suffering it. He then bid his Son come down, and walk with him, and they travell'd on leading the Ass by the Halter; 'till they met another Company, who called them a Couple of sensless Blockheads, for going both on Foot in such a dirty Way, when they had an empty Ass with them, which they might ride upon. The old Man could bear no longer; My Son, said he, it grieves me much that we cannot please all these People: Let us throw the Ass over the next Bridge, and be no farther troubled with him."

Had the old Man been seen acting this last Resolution, he would probably have been call'd a Fool for troubling himself about the different Opinions of all that were pleas'd to find Fault with him: Therefore, tho' I have a Temper almost as complying as his, I intend not to imitate him in this last Particular. I consider the Variety of Humours among Men, and despair of pleasing every Body; yet I shall not therefore leave off Printing. I shall continue my Business. I shall not burn my Press and melt my Letters.

THE SPEECH OF POLLY BAKER

◊

¶ THERE is still a deep mystery as to where this extravaganza was published. Presumably it was in Philadelphia, but the first authentic version is that of the *Gentleman's Magazine* of London for April, 1747.

◊

THE SPEECH of Miss Polly Baker before a Court of Judicature, at Connecticut near Boston in New England; where she was prosecuted for the fifth time, for having a Bastard Child: Which influenced the Court to dispense with her Punishment and which induced one of the Judges to marry her the next Day—by whom she had fifteen Children.

"May it please the honourable bench to indulge me in a few words: I am a poor, unhappy woman, who have no money to fee lawyers to plead for me, being hard put to it to get a living. I shall not trouble your honours with long speeches; for I have not the presumption to expect that you may, by any means, be prevailed on to deviate in your Sentence from the law, in my favour. All I humbly hope is, that your honours would charitably move the governor's goodness on my behalf, that my fine may be remitted. This is the fifth time, gentlemen, that I have been dragg'd before your court on the same account; twice I have paid heavy fines, and twice have been brought to publick punishment, for want of money to pay those fines. This may have been agreeable to the laws, and I don't dispute it; but since laws are sometimes unreasonable in themselves, and therefore repealed; and others bear too hard on the subject in particular circumstances, and therefore there is left a power somewhere to dispense with the execution of them; I take the liberty to say, that I think this law, by which I am punished, both unreasonable in itself, and particularly severe with regard to me, who have always lived an inoffensive life in the neighbourhood where I was born, and defy my enemies (if I have any) to say I ever wrong'd any man, woman, or child. Abstracted from the law, I cannot conceive (may it please your honours) what the nature of my offense is. I have brought five fine children into the world, at the risque of my life; I have maintain'd them well by my own industry, without burthening the township, and would have done it better, if it had not been for the heavy charges and fines I have paid. Can it be a crime (in the nature of things, I mean) to add to the king's subjects, in a new country, that really wants people? I own it, I should think it rather a praiseworthy than a punishable action. I have debauched no other woman's husband, nor enticed any other youth; these things I never was charg'd with; nor has any one the least cause of complaint against me, unless, perhaps, the ministers of justice, because I have had children without being married, by which they have missed a wedding fee. But can this be a fault of mine? I appeal to your honours. You are pleased to allow I don't want sense; but I must be stupified to the last degree, not to prefer the honourable state of wedlock to the condition I have lived in. I always was, and still am willing to enter into it; and doubt not my behaving well in it, having all the industry, frugality, fertility, and skill in economy appertaining to a good wife's character. I defy any one to say I ever refused an offer of that sort: on the contrary, I readily consented to the only proposal of marriage that ever was made me, which was when I was a virgin, but too easily confiding in the person's sincerity that made it, I unhappily lost my honour by trusting to his; for he got me with child, and then forsook me.

"That very person, you all know, he is now become a magistrate of this country; and I had hopes he would have appeared this day on the bench, and have endeavoured to moderate the Court in my favour; then I should have scorn'd to have mentioned it; but I must now complain of it, as unjust and unequal, that my betrayer and undoer, the first cause of all my faults and miscarriages (if they must be deemed such), should be advanced to honour and power in this government that punishes my misfortunes with stripes and infamy. I should be told, 'tis like, that, were there no act of Assembly in the case, the precepts of religion are violated by my transgressions. If mine is a religious offense, leave it to religious punishments. You have already excluded me from the comforts of your church communion. Is not that sufficient? You believe I have offended heaven, and must suffer eternal fire: Will not that be sufficient? What need is there then of your additional fines and whipping? I own I do not think as you do, for, if I thought what you call a sin was really such, I could not presumptuously commit it. But, how can it be believed that heaven is angry at my having children, when to the little done by me towards it, God has been pleased to add his divine skill and admirable workmanship in the formation of their bodies, and crowned the whole by furnishing them with rational and immortal souls?

"Forgive me, gentleman, if I talk a little extravagantly on these matters; I am no divine, but if you, gentlemen, must be making laws, do not turn natural and useful actions into crimes by your prohibitions. But take into your wise consideration the great and growing number of batchelors in the country, many of whom, from the mean fear of the expenses of a family, have never sincerely and honourably courted a woman in their lives; and by their manner of living leave unproduced (which is little better than murder) hundreds of their posterity to the thousandth generation. Is not this a greater offense against the publick good than mine? Compel them, then, by law, either to marriage, or to pay double the fine of fornication every year. What must poor young women do, whom customs and nature forbid to solicit the men, and who cannot force themselves upon husbands, when the laws take no care to provide them any, and yet severely punish them if they do their duty without them; the duty of the first and great command of nature and nature's God, *encrease and multiply;* a duty, from the steady performance of which nothing has been able to deter me, but for its sake I have hazarded the loss of the publick esteem, and have frequently endured publick disgrace and punishment; and therefore ought, in my humble opinion, instead of a whipping, to have a statue erected to my memory."

THE WAY TO WEALTH

Preface to *Poor Richard Improved*

◇

ON THE long voyage to England during June and July of 1757, Franklin employed his enforced leisure by composing what he at first supposed would be a conventional Preface to his next almanac. He must have had with him a file of the twenty-five numbers he had already issued, though he could possibly have depended on his fabulous memory.

During these twenty-five years he had, as he tells us, been contriving homely aphorisms out of whatever source he could tap and improving most of them with his gift for pungency and imagery. They had become the staple of his successful enterprise. On this voyage he endeavored to assemble all of them he had written, or could remember, and some which he then invented. These he put into the mouth of a no doubt fictional creation, a projection by his middle-aged self into the dream of his old-aged self (which he eventually became), and so wove a tapestry of his adages.

Franklin's nephew, Benjamin Mecom, published the compilation in Boston in 1758 as *Father Abraham's Speech*. Under the more accepted title of *The Way to Wealth* it has been republished more times than bibliographers can count, translated into all Western languages and many Oriental ones, and become, in short, the handbook of creative industry in all countries where wealth is sought.

◇

Courteous Reader,

I have heard that nothing gives an Author so great pleasure, as to find his Works respectfully quoted by other learned Authors. This Pleasure I have seldom enjoyed; for tho' I have been, if I may say it without Vanity, an *eminent Author* of Almanacks annually now a full Quarter of a Century, my Brother Authors in the same Way, for what Reason I know not, have ever been sparing in their Applauses; and no other Author has taken the least Notice of me, so that did not my Writings produce me some solid *Pudding*, the great Deficiency of *Praise* would have quite discouraged me.

I concluded at length, that the People were the best Judges of my Merit; for they buy my Works; and besides, in my Rambles, where I am not personally known, I have frequently heard one or other of my Adages repeated, with, *as Poor Richard says,* at the End on't; this gave me some Satisfaction, as it showed not only that my Instructions were regarded, but discovered likewise some Respect for my Authority; and I own, that to encourage the Practice of remembering and repeating those wise Sentences, I have sometimes *quoted myself* with great Gravity.

Judge then how much I must have been gratified by an Incident I am going to relate to you. I stopt my Horse lately where a great Number of People were collected at a Vendue of Merchant Goods. The Hour of Sale not being come, they were conversing on the Badness of the Times, and one of the Company call'd to a plain clean old Man, with white Locks, *Pray, Father* Abraham, *what think you of the Times? Won't these heavy Taxes quite ruin the Country? How shall we ever be able to pay them? What would you advise us to?*——Father *Abraham* stood up, and reply'd, If you'd have my Advice, I'll give it you in short, for a *Word to the Wise is enough,* and *Many Words won't fill a Bushel,* as *Poor Richard says.* They join'd in desiring him to speak his Mind, and gathering round him, he proceeded as follows;

"Friends, says he, and Neighbours, the Taxes are indeed very heavy, and if those laid on by the Government were the only Ones we had to pay, we might more easily discharge them; but we have many others, and much more grievous to some of us. We are taxed twice as much by our *Idleness,* three times as much by our *Pride,* and four times as much by our *Folly,* and from these Taxes the Commissioners cannot ease or deliver us by allowing an Abatement. However let us hearken to good Advice, and something may be done for us; *God helps them that help themselves,* as *Poor Richard* says, in his Almanack of 1733.

It would be thought a hard Government that should tax its People one tenth Part of their *Time,* to be employed in its Service. But *Idleness* taxes many of us much more, if we reckon all that is spent in absolute *Sloth,* or doing of nothing, with that which is spent in idle Employments or Amusements, that amount to nothing. *Sloth,* by bringing on Diseases, absolutely shortens Life. *Sloth, like Rust, consumes faster than Labour wears, while the used Key is always bright,* as *Poor Richard* says. But *dost thou love Life, then do not squander Time, for that's the Stuff Life is made of,* as *Poor Richard* says.—How much more than is necessary do we spend in *sleep!* forgetting that *The sleeping Fox catches no Poultry,* and that *there will be sleeping enough in the Grave*, as *Poor Richard* says. If Time be of all Things the most precious, *wasting Time* must be, as *Poor Richard* says, *the greatest Prodigality,* since, as he elsewhere tells us, *Lost Time is never found again;* and what we call *Time-enough, always proves little enough:* Let us then up and be doing, and doing to the Purpose; so by Diligence shall we do more with less Perplexity. *Sloth makes all Things difficult, but Industry all easy,* as *Poor Richard* says; and *He that riseth late, must trot all Day, and shall scarce overtake his Business at Night.* While *Laziness travels so slowly, that Poverty soon overtakes him,* as we read in *Poor Richard*, who adds, *Drive thy Business, let not that drive thee;* and *Early to Bed, and early to rise, makes a Man healthy, wealthy and wise.*

So what signifies *wishing* and *hoping* for better Times [?] We may make these Times better if we bestir ourselves. *Industry need not wish,* as *Poor Richard* says, and *He that lives upon Hope will die fasting. There are no Gains, without Pains;* then *Help Hands, for I have no Lands,* or if I have, they are smartly taxed. And as *Poor Richard* likewise observes, *He that hath a Trade hath an Estate*, and *He that hath a Calling, hath an Office of Profit and Honour;* but then the *Trade* must be worked at, and the *Calling* well followed, or neither the *Estate,* nor the *Office,* will enable us to pay our Taxes.—If we are industrious we shall never starve; for, as *Poor Richard* says, *At the working Man's House* Hunger *looks in, but dares not enter.* Nor will the Bailiff or the Constable enter, for *Industry pays Debts, while Despair encreaseth them,* says *Poor Richard.*—What though you have found no Treasure, nor has any rich Relation left you a Legacy, *Diligence is the Mother of Good luck,* as *Poor Richard* says, *and God gives all Things to Industry.* Then *plough deep, while Sluggards sleep, and you shall have Corn to sell and to keep,* says *Poor Dick.* Work while it is called To-day, for you know not how much you may be hindered To-morrow, which makes *Poor Richard* say, *One To-day is worth two To-morrows;* and farther, *Have you somewhat to do To-morrow, do it To-day.* If you were a Servant, would you not be ashamed that a good Master should catch you idle? Are you then your own Master, *be ashamed to catch yourself idle,* as *Poor Dick* says. When there is so much to be done for yourself, your Family, your Country, and your gracious King, be up by Peep of Day; *Let not the Sun look down and say, Inglorious here he lies.* Handle your Tools without Mittens; remember that *the Cat in Gloves catches no Mice*, as *Poor Richard* says. 'Tis true there is much to be done, and perhaps you are weak handed, but stick to it steadily, and you will see great Effects, for *constant Drooping wears away Stones,* and by *Diligence and Patience the Mouse ate in two the Cable;* and *little Strokes fell great Oaks,* as *Poor Richard* says in his Almanack, the Year I cannot just now remember.

Methinks I hear some of you say, *Must a Man afford himself no Leisure?*—I will tell thee, my Friend, what *Poor Richard* says, *Employ thy Time well if thou meanest to gain Leisure;* and *since thou art not sure of a Minute, throw not away an Hour.* Leisure, is Time for doing something useful; this Leisure the diligent Man will obtain, but the lazy Man never; so that, as *Poor Richard* says, *a Life of Leisure and a Life of Laziness are two things.* Do you imagine that Sloth will afford you more Comfort than Labour? No, for as *Poor Richard* says, *Trouble springs from Idleness, and grievous Toil from needless Ease. Many without Labour, would live by their* WITS *only, but they break for want of Stock.* Whereas Industry gives Comfort and Plenty, and Respect: *Fly Pleasures, and they'll follow you. The diligent Spinner has a large Shift;* and *now I have a Sheep and a Cow, every Body bids me Good morrow;* all which is well said by *Poor Richard.*

But with our Industry, we must likewise be *steady, settled* and *careful,* and oversee our own Affairs *with our own Eyes,* and not trust too much to others; for, as *Poor Richard* says,

I never saw an oft removed Tree,
Nor yet an oft removed Family,
That throve so well as those that settled be.

And again, *Three Removes is as bad as a Fire;* and again, *Keep thy Shop, and thy Shop will keep thee;* and again, *If you would have your Business done, go; If not, send.* And again,

He that by the plough would thrive,
Himself must either hold or drive.

And again, *The Eye of a Master will do more Work than both his Hands;* and again, *Want of Care does us more Damage than Want of Knowledge*; and again, *Not to oversee Workmen, is to leave them your Purse open.* Trusting too much to others Care is the Ruin of many; for, as the *Almanack* says, *In the Affairs of this World, Men are saved, not by Faith, but by the Want of it;* but a Man's own Care is profitable; for, saith *Poor Dick, Learning is to the Studious, and Riches to the Careful,* as well as *Power to the Bold,* and *Heaven to the Virtuous.* And farther, *If you would have a faithful Servant, and one that you like, serve yourself.* And again, he adviseth to Circumspection and Care, even in the smallest Matters, because sometimes *a little Neglect may breed great Mischief;* adding, *For want of a Nail the Shoe was lost; for want of a Shoe the Horse was lost; and for want of a Horse the Rider was lost,* being overtaken and slain by the Enemy, all for want of Care about a Horse shoe Nail.

So much for Industry, my Friends, and Attention to one's own Business; but to these we must add *Frugality,* is we would make our *Industry* more certainly successful. A Man may, if he knows not how to save as he gets, *keep his Nose all his Life to the Grindstone,* and die not worth a *Groat* at last. *A fat Kitchen makes a lean Will,* as *Poor Richard* says; and,

Many Estates are spent in the Getting,
Since Women for Tea forsook Spinning and Knitting,
And Men for Punch forsook Hewing and Splitting.

If you would be wealthy, says he, in another Almanack, *think of Saving as well as of Getting: The* Indies *have not made* Spain *rich, because her* Outgoes *are greater than her* Incomes. Away then with your expensive Follies, and you will not have so much Cause to complain of hard Times, heavy Taxes, and chargeable Families; for, as *Poor Dick* says,

Women and Wine, Game and Deceit,
Make the Wealth small, and the Wants great.

And farther, *What maintains one Vice, would bring up two Children.* You may think perhaps, That a *little* Tea, or a *little* Punch now and then, Diet a *little* more costly, Clothes a *little* finer, and a *little* Entertainment now and then, can be no *great* Matter; but remember what *Poor Richard* says, *Many* a Little *makes a Mickle;* and farther, *Beware of* little *Expenses; a small Leak will sink a great Ship;* and again, *Who Dainties love, shall Beggars prove;* and moreover, *Fools make Feasts, and wise Men eat them.*

Here you are all got together at this Vendue of *Fineries* and *Knicknacks.* You call them *Goods*, but if you do not take Care, they will prove *Evils* to some of you. You expect they will be sold *cheap,* and perhaps they may for less than they cost; but if you have no Occasion for them, they must be *dear* to you. Remember what *Poor Richard* says, *Buy what thou hast no Need of, and ere long thou shalt sell thy Necessaries.* And again, *At a great Pennyworth pause a while:* He means, that perhaps the Cheapness is *apparent* only, and not *real;* or the Bargain, by straitning thee in thy Business, may do thee more Harm than Good. For in another Place he says, *Many have been ruined by buying good Pennyworth.* Again, *Poor Richard* says, *'Tis foolish to lay out Money in a Purchase of Repentance;* and yet this Folly is practised every Day at Vendues, for want of minding the Almanack. *Wise Men,* as *Poor Dick* says, *learn by others Harms, Fools scarcely by their own;* but *Felix quem faciunt aliena Pericula cautum.* Many a one, for the Sake of Finery on the Back, have gone with a hungry Belly, and half starved their Families; *Silks and Sattins, Scarlet and Velvets,* as *Poor Richard* says, *put out the Kitchen Fire.* These are not the *Necessaries* of Life; they can scarcely be called the *Conveniences,* and yet only because they look pretty, how many *want* to *have* them. The *artificial* Wants of Mankind thus become more numerous than the *natural;* and, as *Poor Dick* says, *For one* poor *Person, there are an hundred* indigent. By these, and other Extravagancies, the Genteel are reduced and forced to borrow of those whom they formerly despised, but who through *Industry* and *Frugality* have maintained their Standing in which Case it appears plainly, that a *Ploughman on his Legs is higher than a Gentleman on his Knees,* as *Poor Richard* says. Perhaps they have had a small Estate left them which they knew not the Getting of; they think *'tis Day, and will never be Night;* that a little to be spent out of *so much,* is not worth minding; (*a Child and a Fool,* as *Poor Richard* says, *imagine* Twenty Shillings *and Twenty Years can never be spent*) but, *always taking out of, the Meal-tub, and never putting in, soon comes to the Bottom;* then, as *Poor Dick* says, *When the Well's dry, they know the Worth of Water.* But this they might have known before, if they had taken his Advice; *If you would know the Value of Money, go and try to borrow some;* for, *he that goes a borrowing gets a sorrowing;* and indeed so does he that lends to such People, when he goes *to get it in again.—Poor Dick* farther advises, and says,

Fond Pride of Dress *is sure a very Curse;*
E'er Fancy *you consult, consult your Purse.*

And again, *Pride is as loud a Beggar as Want, and a great deal more saucy.* When you have bought one fine Thing you must buy ten more, that your Appearance may be all of a Piece; but *Poor Dick* says, *'Tis easier to* suppress *the first Desire, than to* satisfy all that follow it. And 'tis as truly Folly for the Poor to ape the Rich, as for the Frog to swell, in order to equal the Ox.

Great Estates may venture more,
But little Boats should keep near Shore.

'Tis however a Folly soon punished; for *Pride that dines on Vanity sups on Contempt,* as *Poor Richard* says. And in another Place, *Pride breakfasted with Plenty, dined with Poverty, and supped with Infamy.* And after all, of what Use is this *Pride of Appearance,* for which so much is risked, so much is suffered? It cannot promote Health, or ease Pain; it makes no Increase of Merit in the Person, it creates Envy, it hastens Misfortune.

What is a Butterfly? At best
He's but a Caterpiller drest.
The gaudy Fop's his Picture just,

as *Poor Richard* says.

But what Madness must it be to *run in Debt* for these Superfluities! We are offered by the Terms of this Vendue, *Six Months Credit;* and that perhaps has induced some of us to attend it, because we cannot spare the ready Money, and hope now to be fine without it. But, ah, think what you do when you run in Debt; *You give to another, Power over your Liberty.* If you cannot pay at the Time, you will be ashamed to see your Creditor; you will be in Fear when you speak to him; you will make poor pitiful sneaking Excuses, and by Degrees come to lose your Veracity, and sink into base downright lying; for, as *Poor Richard* says, *The second Vice is Lying, the first is running in Debt.* And again, to the same Purpose, *Lying rides upon Debt's Back.* Whereas a freeborn *Englishman* ought not to be ashamed or afraid to see or speak to any Man living. But Poverty often deprives a Man of all Spirit and Virtue: *'Tis hard for an empty Bag to stand upright,* as *Poor Richard* truly says. What would you think of that Prince, or that Government, who should issue an Edict forbidding you to dress like a Gentleman or a Gentlewoman, on Pain of Imprisonment or Servitude? Would you not say, that you are free, and have a Right to dress as you please, and that such an Edict would be a Breach of your Privileges, and such a Government tyrannical? And yet you are about to put yourself under that Tyranny when you run in Debt for such Dress! Your Creditor has Authority at his pleasure to deprive you of your Liberty, by confining you in Gaol for Life, or to sell you for a Servant, if you should not be able to pay him! When you have got your Bargain, you may, perhaps, think little of Payment; but *Creditors, Poor Richard* tells us, *have better Memories than Debtors;* and in another Place says, *Creditors are a superstitious Sect, great Observers of set Days and Times.* The Day comes round before you are aware, and the Demand is made before you are prepared to satisfy it. Or if you bear your Debt in Mind, the Term which at first seemed so long, will as it lessens, appear extreamly short. *Time* will seem to have added Wings to his Heels as well as Shoulders. *Those have a short Lent,* saith *Poor Richard, who owe Money to be paid at Easter.* Then since, as he says, *The Borrower is a Slave to the Lender, and the Debtor to the Creditor,* disdain the Chain, preserve your Freedom; and maintain your Independency: Be *industrious* and *free;* be *frugal* and *free.* At present, perhaps, you may think yourself in thriving Circumstances, and that you can bear a little Extravagance without Injury; but,

For Age and Want, save while you may;
No Morning Sun lasts a whole Day,

as *Poor Richard* says—Gain may be temporary and uncertain, but ever while you live, Expence is constant and certain; and *'tis easier to build two Chimnies than to keep one in Fuel,* as *Poor Richard* says. So *rather go to Bed supperless than rise in Debt.*

Get what you can, and what you get hold;
'Tis the Stone that will turn all your Lead into Gold,

as *Poor Richard* says. And when you have got the Philosopher's Stone, sure you will no longer complain of bad Times, or the Difficulty of paying Taxes.

This Doctrine, my Friends, is *Reason* and *Wisdom;* but after all, do not depend too much upon your own *Industry,* and *Frugality,* and *Prudence,* though excellent Things, for they may all be blasted without the Blessing of Heaven; and therefore ask that Blessing humbly, and be not uncharitable to those that at the present seem to want it, but comfort and help them. Remember *Job* suffered, and was afterwards prosperous.

And now to conclude, *Experience keeps a dear School, but Fools will learn in no other, and scarce in that;* for it is true, *we may give Advice, but we cannot give Conduct,* as *Poor Richard* says: However, remember this, *They that won't be counselled, can't be helped,* as *Poor Richard* says: And farther, That *if you will not hear Reason, she'll surely rap your Knuckles.*["]

Thus the old Gentleman ended his Harangue. The People heard it, and approved the Doctrine and immediately practised the contrary, just as if it had been a common Sermon; for the Vendue opened, and they began to buy extravagantly, notwithstanding all his Cautions, and their own Fear of Taxes.—I found the good Man had thoroughly studied my Almanacks, and digested all I had dropt on those Topicks during the Course of Five-and-twenty Years. The frequent Mention he made of me must have tired any one else, but my Vanity was wonderfully delighted with it, though I was conscious that not a tenth Part of the Wisdom was my own which he ascribed to me, but rather the *Gleanings* I had made of the Sense of all Ages and Nations. However, I resolved to be the better for the Echo of it; and though I had at first determined to buy Stuff for a new Coat, I went away resolved to wear my old One a little longer. *Reader,* if thou wilt do the same, thy Profit will be as great as mine.

I am, as ever,
Thine to serve thee,
July 7, 1757 RICHARD SAUNDERS.

TO JARED INGERSOLL

◇

JARED INGERSOLL (1722–81), scion of one of the leading families of Connecticut, served as agent for that colony during the first years of Franklin's agency for Pennsylvania; they were good friends. However, as the tone of this epistle shows, they could enjoy mild jokes about the "land of steady habits." Franklin made the tour of Belgium and Holland to which he here refers in August of 1761. When he writes, he has returned to Philadelphia, supposing his career as agent over. Later, after he went back to England, he made one of the few gaffs of his career: assuming that the Stamp Tax of 1765 would excite no opposition in the colonies, he advised Ingersoll to take the agency for Connecticut. The unfortunate man did, and was mobbed. As the controversy widened, Ingersoll became a Tory and, we must assume, plentifully cursed Benjamin Franklin.

◇

Philadelphia, December 11, 1762.

DEAR SIR:—

I thank you for your kind congratulations. It gives me pleasure to hear from an old friend; it will give me much more pleasure to see him. I hope, therefore, nothing will prevent the journey you propose for next summer and the favour you intend me of a visit. I believe I must make a journey early in the spring to Virginia, but purpose being back again before the hot weather. You will be kind enough to let me know beforehand what time you expect to be here, that I may not be out of the way, for that would mortify me exceedingly.

I should be glad to know what it is that distinguishes Connecticut religion from common religion. Communicate, if you please, some of these particulars that you think will amuse me as a virtuoso. When I travelled in Flanders, I thought of your excessively strict observation of Sunday; and that a man could hardly travel on that day among you upon his lawful occasions without hazard of punishment; while, where I was, every one travelled, if he pleased, or diverted himself in any other way; and in the afternoon both high and low went to the play or the opera, where there was plenty of singing, fiddling and dancing. I looked around for God's judgments, but saw no signs of them. The cities were well built and full of inhabitants, the markets filled with plenty, the people well favoured and well clothed, the fields well tilled, the cattle fat and strong, the fences, houses, and windows all in repair, and no Old Tenor [1] anywhere in the country; which would almost make one suspect that the Deity is not so angry at that offence as a New England Justice.

I left our Friend Mr. Jackson [2] well, and I had the great pleasure of finding my little family well when I came home, and my friends as cordial and more numerous than ever. May every prosperity attend you and yours. I am, dear friend, yours affectionately,

B. Franklin.

TO THE EDITOR OF A NEWSPAPER

◇

IN THE spring of 1765 Franklin suffered an attack of gout which confined him to Craven Street for two weeks. He then composed this squib. The manuscript survives, but it is not known for what newspaper it was designed or even whether it was ever printed. In the Parliamentary debates about the Stamp Act, English apprehension about the possibilities of colonial manufactures becoming a threat to British industry was revealed; the disclosure was accompanied by many jibes at American culture and natural resources. Franklin characteristically replied by *not* losing his temper.

◇

Monday, May 20 [1765].

Sir,

In your Paper of Wednesday last, an ingenious Correspondent that calls himself The Spectator, and dates from *Pimlico,* under the Guise of Good Will to the Newswriters, whom he calls an "useful Body of Men in this great City," has, in my Opinion, artfully attempted to turn them & their Works into Ridicule, wherein if he could succeed, great Injury might be done to the Public as well as to those good People.

Supposing, Sir, that the *"We hears"* they give us of this & t'other intended Voyage or Tour of this & t'other great Personage, were mere Inventions, yet they at least offer us an innocent Amusement while we read, and useful Matter of Conversation when we are dispos'd to converse.

Englishmen, Sir, are too apt to be silent when they have nothing to say; too apt to be sullen when they are silent; and when they are sullen, to hang themselves. But, by these *We hears,* we are supplied with abundant funds of Discourse, we discuss the Motives for such Voyages, the Probability of their being undertaken, and the Practicability of their Execution. Here we display our Judgment in Politics, our Knowledge of the Interests of Princes, and our Skill in Geography, and (if we have it) show our Dexterity moreover in Argumentation. In the mean time, the tedious Hour is kill'd, we go home pleas'd with the Applauses we have receiv'd from others, or at least with those we secretly give to ourselves: We sleep soundly, & live on, to the Comfort of our Families. But, Sir, I beg leave to say, that all the Articles of News that seem improbable are not mere Inventions. Some of them, I can assure you on the Faith of a Traveller, are serious Truths. And here, quitting Mr. Spectator of Pimlico, give

TO JARED INGERSOLL. 1. **Old Tenor:** Franklin's jibe refers to the paper money issued in periods of financial distress by both Massachusetts Bay and Connecticut. Generally these emissions were supposed to be based upon real estate or upon yet unsettled lands; they always declined in value, frequently becoming of no commercial worth whatsoever. Franklin never touched a shilling of them, and enjoyed jabbing his New England friends who lost fortunes in a patriotic endeavor to support these worthless notes. 2. **Mr. Jackson:** Richard Jackson (d. 1787), known in London as "Omniscient," was a member of Parliament, and ultimately a Lord of the Admiralty, who throughout his career, even in the London of George III, managed to be a friend to the colonial cause.

me leave to instance the various numberless Accounts the Newspapers have given us, with so much honest Zeal for the welfare of *Poor Old England,* of the establishing Manufactures in the Colonies to the Prejudice of those of this Kingdom. It is objected by superficial Readers, who yet pretend to some Knowledge of those Countries, that such Establishments are not only improbable, but impossible, for that their Sheep have but little Wooll, not in the whole sufficient for a Pair of Stockings a Year to each Inhabitant; and that, from the Universal Dearness of Labour among them, the Working of Iron and other Materials, except in some few coarse Instances, is impracticable to any Advantage.

Dear Sir, do not let us suffer ourselves to be amus'd with such groundless Objections. The very tails of the American Sheep are so laden with Wooll, that each has a little Car or Waggon on four little Wheels, to support & keep it from trailing on the Ground. Would they caulk their Ships, would they fill their Beds, would they even litter their Horses with Wooll, if it were not both plenty and cheap? And what signifies Dearness of Labour, when an English Shilling passes for five and Twenty? Their engaging 300 Silk Throwsters here in one Week, for New York, was treated as a Fable, because, forsooth, they have "no Silk there to throw." Those who made this Objection, perhaps did not know, that at the same time the Agents from the King of Spain were at Quebec to contract for 1000 Pieces of Cannon to be made there for the Fortification of Mexico, and at N York engaging the annual Supply of woven Floor-Carpets for their West India Houses, other Agents from the Emperor of China were at Boston treating about an Exchange of raw Silk for Wooll, to be carried in Chinese Junks through the Straits of Magellan.

And yet all this is as certainly true, as the Account said to be from Quebec, in all the Papers of last Week, that the Inhabitants of Canada are making Preparations for a Cod and Whale Fishery this "Summer in the upper Lakes." Ignorant People may object that the upper Lakes are fresh, and that Cod and Whale are Salt Water Fish: But let them know, Sir, that Cod, like other Fish when attack'd by their Enemies, fly into any Water where they can be safest; that Whales, when they have a mind to eat Cod, pursue them wherever they fly; and that the grand Leap of the Whale in that Chase up the Fall of Niagara is esteemed, by all who have seen it, as one of the finest Spectacles in Nature. Really, Sir, the World is grown too incredulous. It is like the Pendulum ever swinging from one Extream to another. Formerly every thing printed was believed, because it was in print. Now Things seem to be disbelieved for just the very same Reason. Wise Men wonder at the present Growth of Infidelity. They should have consider'd, when they taught People to doubt the Authority of Newspapers and the Truth of Predictions in Almanacks, that the next Step might be a Disbelief in the well vouch'd Accts of Ghosts Witches, and Doubts even of the Truths of the Creed!

Thus much I thought it necessary to say in favour of an honest Set of Writers, whose comfortable Living depends on collecting & supplying the Printers with News at the small Price of Sixpence an Article, and who always show their Regard to Truth, by contradicting in a subsequent Article such as are wrong,—for another Sixpence, —to the great Satisfaction & Improvement of us Coffee-house Students in History & Politics, and the infinite Advantage of all future Livies, Rapins, Robertsons, Humes, and McAulays, who may be sincerely inclin'd to furnish the World with that *rara Avis,* a true History. I am, Sir, your humble Servant,

A TRAVELLER.

AN EDICT BY THE KING OF PRUSSIA

◊

¶ FRANKLIN published this hoax in the *Gentleman's Magazine* for October, 1773. Stories survive of many Englishmen taking it seriously, at least on first reading. It immediately became popular and was widely reprinted. "Such papers may seem to have a tendency to increase our divisions," he wrote in November, "but I intend a contrary effect, and hope that by comprising in a little room and setting in a strong light the grievances of the colonies, more attention will be paid to them by our administration; and that, when their unreasonableness is generally seen, some of them will be removed, to the restoration of harmony between us."

◊

Dantzic, Sept. 5 [1773].

WE HAVE long wondered here at the supineness of the English nation, under the Prussian impositions upon its trade entering our port. We did not, till lately, know the claims, ancient and modern, that hang over that nation; and therefore could not suspect that it might submit to those impositions from a sense of duty or from principles of equity. The following Edict, just made publick, may, if serious, throw some light upon this matter.

"FREDERIC, by the grace of God, King of Prussia, &c. &c. &c., to all present and to come, (*à tous présens et à venir,*) Health. The peace now enjoyed throughout our dominions, having afforded us leisure to apply ourselves to the regulation of commerce, the improvement of our finances, and at the same time the easing our domestic subjects in their taxes: For these causes, and other good considerations us thereunto moving, we hereby make known, that, having deliberated these affairs in our council, present our dear brothers, and other great officers of the state, members of the same, we, of our certain knowledge, full power, and authority royal, have made and issued this present Edict, viz.

"Whereas it is well known to all the world, that the first German settlements made in the Island of Britain, were by colonies of people, subject to our renowned ducal ancestors, and drawn from their dominions, under the conduct of Hengist, Horsa, Hella, Uff, Cerdicus, Ida, and others; and that the said colonies have flourished under the protection of our august house for ages past; have never been emancipated therefrom; and yet have hitherto yielded little profit to the same: And whereas we ourself have in the last war fought for and defended the said colonies, against the power of France, and thereby enabled them to make conquests from the said power in America, for which we have not yet received adequate compensation: And whereas it is just and expedient that a revenue should be raised from the said colonies in Britain, towards our indemnification; and that those who are descendants of our ancient subjects, and thence still owe us due obedience, should contribute to the replenishing of our royal coffers as they must have done, had their ancestors remained in the territories now to us appertaining: We do therefore hereby ordain and command, that, from and after the date of these presents, there shall be levied and paid to our officers of the *customs,* on all goods, wares, and merchandizes, and on all grain and other produce of the earth, exported from the said Island of Britain, and on all goods of whatever kind imported into the same, a duty of four and a half per cent *ad valorem,* for the use of us and our successors. And that the said duty may more effectually be collected, we do hereby ordain, that all ships or vessels bound from Great Britain to any other part of the world to Great Britain, shall in their respective voyages touch at our port of Koningsberg, there to be unladen, searched, and charged with the said duties.

"And whereas there hath been from time to time discovered in the said island of Great Britain, by our colonists there, many mines or beds of iron-stone; and sundry subjects, of our ancient dominion, skilful in converting the said stone into metal, have in time past transported themselves thither, carrying with them and communicating that art; and the inhabitants of the said island, presuming that they had a natural right to make the best use they could of the natural productions of their country for their own benefit, have not only built furnaces for smelting the said stone into iron, but have erected plating-forges, slitting-mills, and steel-furnaces, for the more convenient manufacturing of the same; thereby endangering a diminution of the said manufacture in our ancient dominion;—we do therefore hereby farther ordain, that, from and after the date hereof, no mill or other engine for slitting or rolling of iron, or any plating-forge to work with a tilt-hammer, or any furnace for making steel, shall be erected or continued in the said island of Great Britain: And the Lord Lieutenant of every county in the said island is hereby commanded, on information of any such erection within his county, to order and by force to cause the same to be abated and destroyed; as he shall answer the neglect thereof to us at his peril. But we are nevertheless graciously pleased to permit the inhabitants of the said island to transport their iron into Prussia, there to be manufactured, and to them returned; they paying our Prussian subjects for the workmanship, with all the costs of commission, freight, and risk, coming and returning; any thing herein contained to the contrary notwithstanding.

"We do not, however, think fit to extend this our indulgence to the article of wool; but, meaning to encourage, not only the manufacturing of woollen cloth, but also the raising of wool, in our ancient dominions, and to prevent both, as much as may be, in our said island, we do hereby absolutely forbid the transportation of wool from thence, even to the mother country, Prussia; and that those of islanders may be farther and more effectually restrained in making any advantage of their own wool in the way of manufacture, we command that none shall be carried out of one country into another; nor shall any worsted, bay, or woollen yarn, cloth, says, bays, kerseys, serges, frizes, druggets, cloth-serges, shalloons, or any other drapery stuffs, or woollen manufactures whatsoever, made up or mixed with wool in any of the said counties, be carried into any other county, or be waterborne even across the smallest river or creek, on penalty of forfeiture of the same, together with the boats, carriages, horses, &c., that shall be employed in removing them. Nevertheless, our loving subjects there are hereby permitted (if they think proper) to use all their wool as manure for the improvement of their lands.

"And whereas the art and mystery of making hats hath arrived at great perfection in Prussia, and the making of hats by our remoter subjects ought to be as much as possible restrained: And forasmuch as the islanders before mentioned, being in possession of wool, beaver and other furs, have presumptuously conceived they had a right to make some advantage thereof, by manufacturing the same into hats, to the prejudice of our domestic manufacture; We do therefore hereby strictly command and ordain, that no hats or felts whatsoever, dyed or undyed, finished or unfinished, shall be loaded or put into or upon any vessel, cart, carriage, or horse, to be transported or conveyed out of one county in the said island into another county, or to any other place whatsoever, by any person or persons whatsoever; on pain of forfeiting the same, with a penalty of five hundred pounds sterling for every offence. Nor shall any hat-maker, in any of the said counties, employ more than two apprentices, on penalty of five pounds sterling per month; we intending hereby, that such hatmakers, being so restrained, both in the production and sale of their commodity, may find no advantage in continuing their business. But, lest the said islanders should suffer inconveniency by the want of hats, we are farther graciously pleased to permit them to send their beaver furs to Prussia; and we also permit hats made thereof to be exported from Prussia to Britain; the people thus favoured to pay all costs and charges of manufacturing, interest, commission to our merchants, insurance and freight going and returning, as in the case of iron.

"And, lastly, being willing farther to favour our said colonies in Britain, we do hereby also ordain and command, that all the *thieves,* highway and street robbers, house-breakers, forgerers, murderers, s—d—tes, and villains of every denomination, who have forfeited their lives to the law in Prussia; but whom we, in our great clemency, do not think fit here to hang, shall be emptied out of our gaols into the said island of Great Britain, for the better peopling of that country.

"We flatter ourselves, that these our royal regulations and commands will be thought just and reasonable by our much-favoured colonists in England; the said regulations being copied from their statutes of 10 and 11 William III. c. 10, 5 Geo. II. c. 22, 23, Geo. II. c. 29, 4 Geo. I. c. 11, and from other equitable laws made by their parliaments; or from instructions given by their Princes; or from resolutions of both Houses, entered into for the good government of their *own colonies in Ireland and America.*

"And all persons in the said island are hereby cautioned not to oppose in any wise the execution of this our Edict, or any part thereof, such opposition being high treason; of which all who are suspected shall be transported in fetters from Britain to Prussia, there to be tried and executed according to the Prussian law.

"Such is our pleasure.

"GIVEN AT POSTDAM, *this twenty-fifth day of the month of August, one thousand seven hundred and seventy-three, and in the thirty-third year of our reign.*

"By the King, in his Council.

"RECHTMAESSIG, *Sec.*"

Some take this Edict to be merely one of the King's *Jeux d' Esprit:* others suppose it serious, and that he means a quarrel with England; but all here think the assertion it concludes with, "that these regulations are copied from acts of the English parliament respecting their colonies," a very injurious one; it being impossible to believe, that a people distinguished for their love of liberty, a nation so wise, so liberal in its sentiments, so just and equitable towards its neighbours, should, from mean and injudicious views of petty immediate profit, treat its own children in a manner so arbitrary and tyrannical!

THE SALE OF THE HESSIANS

◊

¶ THIS skit, which barely disguises the fury of Franklin's contempt for Britain's hiring of German mercenaries, was first published in French. Though he gives it a date in February of 1777, Franklin must have written it later, when he had learned, in March, of the capture of the Hessians at Trenton the day after Christmas. There was a real Count Schaumburg who served as agent for George III in purchasing soldiers in Germany; so Franklin pilloried him forever by giving his name to the Hessian ruler.

◊

FROM THE COUNT DE SCHAUMBERGH TO THE BARON HOHENDORF, COMMANDING THE HESSIAN TROOPS IN AMERICA

Rome, February 18, 1777.

MONSIEUR LE BARON:—

On my return from Naples, I received at Rome your letter of the 27th December of last year. I have learned with unspeakable pleasure the courage our troops exhibited at Trenton, and you cannot imagine my joy on being told that of the 1,950 Hessians engaged in the fight, but 345 escaped. There were just 1,605 men killed, and I cannot sufficiently commend your prudence in sending an exact list of the dead to my minister in London. This precaution was the more necessary, as the report sent to the English ministry does not give but 1,455 dead. This would make 483,450 florins instead of 645,500 which I am entitled to demand under our convention. You will comprehend the prejudice which such an error would work in my finances, and I do not doubt you will take the necessary pains to prove that Lord North's list is false and yours correct.

The court of London objects that there were a hundred wounded who ought not to be included in the list, nor paid for as dead; but I trust you will not overlook my instructions to you on quitting Cassel, and that you will not have tried by human succor to recall the life of the unfortunates whose days could not be lengthened but by the loss of a leg or an arm. That would be making them a pernicious present, and I am sure they would rather die than live in a condition no longer fit for my service. I do not mean by this that you should assassinate them; we should be humane, my dear Baron, but you may insinuate to the surgeons with entire propriety that a crippled man is a reproach to their profession, and that there is no wiser course than to let every one of them die when he ceases to be fit to fight.

I am about to send to you some new recruits. Don't economize them. Remember glory before all things. Glory is true wealth. There is nothing degrades the soldier like the love of money. He must care only for honour and reputation, but this reputation must be acquired in the midst of dangers. A battle gained without costing the conqueror any blood is an inglorious success, while the conquered cover themselves with glory by perishing with their arms in their hands. Do you remember that of the 300 Lacedaemonians who defended the defile of Thermopylae, not one returned? How happy should I be could I say the same of my brave Hessians!

It is true that their king, Leonidas, perished with them: but things have changed, and it is no longer the custom for princes of the empire to go and fight in America for a cause with which they have no concern. And besides, to whom should they pay the thirty guineas per man if I did not stay in Europe to receive them? Then, it is necessary also that I be ready to send recruits to replace the men you lose. For this purpose I must return to Hesse. It is true, grown men are becoming scarce there, but I will send you boys. Besides, the scarcer the commodity the higher the price. I am assured that the women and little girls have begun to till our lands, and they get on not badly. You did right to send back to Europe that Dr. Crumerus who was so successful in curing dysentery. Don't bother with a man who is subject to looseness of the bowels. That disease makes bad soldiers. One coward will do more mischief in an engagement than ten brave men will do good. Better that they burst in their barracks than fly in battle, and tarnish the glory of our arms. Besides, you know that they pay me as killed for all who die from disease, and I don't get a farthing for runaways. My trip to Italy, which has cost me enormously, makes it desirable that there should be a great mortality among them. You will therefore promise promotion to all who expose themselves; you will exhort them to seek glory in the midst of dangers; you will say to Major Maundorff that I am not at all content with his saving the 345 men who escaped the massacre of Trenton. Through the whole campaign he has not had ten men killed in consequence of his orders. Finally, let it be your principal object to prolong the war and avoid a decisive engagement on either side, for I have made arrangements for a grand Italian opera, and I do not wish to be obliged to give it up. Meantime I pray God, my dear Baron de Hohendorf, to have you in his holy and gracious keeping.

THE EPHEMERA

◊

¶ FRANKLIN spent a day at the country seat of a friend on the Moulin Joli, an island in the Seine, in, as he said, "the pleasing society of the ingenious, learned and very polite persons who inhabit it." Among these was the charming Madame Brillon ("*Brillante*") with whom he conducted a long flirtation which, along with his other games, embellished the severity of his task as ambassador. At the time all polite Paris was divided into two camps over a dispute about musical style, the one party adhering to the German Gluck and the other to the Italian Piccini. During a promenade, the company noticed hundreds of dead and dying ephemeras (May flies). Franklin suddenly remembered a piece he had published in 1735 in the *Pennsylvania Gazette,* by a writer he could not recollect, on "Human Vanity." In this an insect philosopher had mourned over the brevity of life. Franklin then addressed this compliment to Madame Brillon, in French. The ladies of the court copied it, so that it became widely known. Franklin then had it printed, in French, on the little press he set up in his house at Passy. Indeed, he may have put it into type with his own hands.

◇

AN EMBLEM OF HUMAN LIFE

YOU MAY remember, my dear friend, that when we lately spent that happy day in the delightful garden and sweet society of the Moulin Joly, I stopt a little in one of our walks, and staid some time behind the company. We had been shown numberless skeletons of a kind of little fly, called an ephemera, whose successive generations, we were told, bred and expired within the day. I happened to see a living company of them on a leaf, who appeared to be engaged in conversation. You know I understand all the inferior animal tongues: my too great application to the study of them is the best excuse I can give for the little progress I have made in your charming language. I listened through curiosity to the discourse of these little creatures; but as they, in their natural vivacity, spoke three or four together, I could make but little of their conversation. I found, however, by some broken expressions that I heard now and then, they were disputing warmly on the merit of two foreign musicians, one a *cousin,* the other a *moscheto;* in which dispute they spent their time, seemingly as regardless of the shortness of life as if they had been sure of living a month. Happy people! thought I, you live certainly under a wise, just, and mild government, since you have no public grievances to complain of, nor any subject of contention but the perfections and imperfections of foreign music. I turned my head from them to an old grey-headed one, who was single on another leaf, and talking to himself. Being amused with his soliloquy, I put it down in writing, in hopes it will likewise amuse her to whom I am so much indebted for the most pleasing of all amusements, her delicious company and heavenly harmony.

"It was," said he, "the opinion of learned philosophers of our race, who lived and flourished long before my time, that this vast world, the Moulin Joly, could not itself subsist more than eighteen hours; and I think there was some foundation for that opinion, since, by the apparent motion of the great luminary that gives life to all nature, and which in my time has evidently declined considerably towards the ocean at the end of our earth, it must then finish its course, be extinguished in the waters that surround us, and leave the world in cold and darkness, necessarily producing universal death and destruction. I have lived seven of those hours, a great age, being no less than four hundred and twenty minutes of time. How very few of us continue so long! I have seen generations born, flourish, and expire. My present friends are the children and grandchildren of the friends of my youth, who are now, alas, no more! And I must soon follow them; for, by the course of nature, though still in health, I cannot expect to live above seven or eight minutes longer. What now avails all my toil and labor, in amassing honey-dew on this leaf, which I cannot live to enjoy! What the political struggles I have been engaged in, for the good of my compatriot inhabitants of this bush, or my philosophical studies for the benefit of our race in general! for, in politics, what can laws do without morals? Our present race of ephemerae will in a course of minutes become corrupt, like those of other and older bushes, and consequently as wretched. And in philosophy how small our progress! Alas! art is long, and life is short! My friends would comfort me with the idea of a name, they say, I shall leave behind me; and they tell me I have lived long enough to nature and to glory. But what will fame be to an ephemera who no longer exists? And what will become of all history in the eighteenth hour, when the world itself, even the whole Moulin Joly, shall come to its end, and be buried in universal ruin?"

To me, after all my eager pursuits, no solid pleasures now remain, but the reflection of a long life spent in meaning well, the sensible conversation of a few good lady ephemerae, and now and then a kind smile and a tune from the ever amiable *Brillante*.

B. FRANKLIN.

THE WHISTLE

◇

[MADAME BRILLON evidently had written to Franklin, in that semisolemn vein which Franklin subtly cultivated among his female entourage at Passy, on the joys of paradise and how therefore men and women ought to make the best of this present existence. Presumably, Franklin sent his answer in French. A manuscript draft, in his own handwriting, does exist; it is in many details different from the text here reprinted, which has long stood as the standard. Whether Franklin or some editor translated the French back into this English redaction remains a mystery.

◇

TO MADAME BRILLON

Passy, November 10, 1779.

I RECEIVED my dear friend's two letters, one for Wednesday and one for Saturday. This is again Wednesday. I do not deserve one for to-day, because I have not answered the former. But, indolent as I am, and averse to writing, the fear of having no more of your pleasing epistles, if I do not contribute to the correspondence, obliges me to take up my pen; and as Mr. B has kindly sent me word, that he sets out to-morrow to see you, instead of spending this Wednesday evening as I have done its namesakes, in your delightful company, I sit down to spend it in thinking of you, in writing to you, and in reading over and over again your letters.

I am charmed with your description of Paradise, and with your plan of living there; and I approve much of your conclusion, that, in the meantime, we should draw all the good we can from this world. In my opinion, we might all draw more good from it than we do, and suffer less evil, if we would take care not to give too much for *whistles*. For to me it seems, that most of the unhappy people we meet with, are become so by neglect of that caution.

You ask what I mean? You love stories, and will excuse my telling one of myself.

When I was a child of seven years old, my friends, on a holiday, filled my pocket with coppers. I went directly to a shop where they sold toys for children; and, being charmed with the sound of a *whistle,* that I met by the way in the hands of another boy, I voluntarily offered and gave all my money for one. I then came home, and went whistling all over the house, much pleased with my *whistle,* but disturbing all the family. My brothers, and sisters, and cousins, understanding the bargain I had made, told me I had given four times as much for it as it was worth; put me in mind what good things I might have bought with the rest of the money; and laughed at me so much for my folly, that I cried with vexation; and the reflection gave me more chagrin than the *whistle* gave me pleasure.

This however was afterwards of use to me, the impression continuing on my mind; so that often, when I was tempted to buy some unnecessary thing, I said to myself, *Don't give too much for the whistle;* and I saved my money.

As I grew up, came into the world, and observed the actions of men, I thought I met with many, very many, who *gave too much for the whistle.*

When I saw one too ambitious of court favour, sacrificing his time in attendance on levees, his repose, his liberty, his virtue, and perhaps his friends, to attain it, I have said to myself, *This man gives too much for his whistle.*

When I saw another fond of popularity, constantly employing himself in political bustles, neglecting his own affairs, and ruining them by that neglect, *He pays, indeed,* said I, *too much for his whistle.*

If I knew a miser, who gave up every kind of comfortable living, all the pleasure of doing good to others, all the esteem of his fellow-citizens, and the joys of benevolent friendship, for the sake of accumulating wealth, *Poor man,* said I, *you pay too much for your whistle.*

When I met with a man of pleasure, sacrificing every laudable improvement of the mind, or of his fortune, to mere corporeal sensations, and ruining his health in their pursuit, *Mistaken man,* said I, *you are providing pain for yourself, instead of pleasure; you give too much for your whistle.*

If I see one fond of appearance, or fine clothes, fine houses, fine furniture, fine equipages, all above his fortune, for which he contracts debts, and ends his career in a prison, *Alas!* say I, *he has paid dear, very dear, for his whistle.*

When I see a beautiful, sweet-tempered girl married to an ill-natured brute of a husband, *What a pity,* say I, *that she should pay so much for a whistle!*

In short, I conceive that great part of the miseries of mankind are brought upon them by the false estimates they have made of the value of things, and by their *giving too much for their whistles.*

Yet I ought to have charity for these unhappy people, when I consider, that, with all this wisdom of which I am boasting, there are certain things in the world so tempting, for example, the apples of King John, which happily are not to be bought; for if they were put to sale by auction, I might very easily be led to ruin myself in the purchase, and find that I had once more given too much for my *whistle*.

Adieu, my dear friend, and believe me ever yours very sincerely and with unalterable affection,

B. FRANKLIN.

DIALOGUE BETWEEN FRANKLIN AND THE GOUT

◇

DESPITE all the rules and regulations of his program for achieving perfection, Franklin proved unable to control his diet. He enjoyed his wine. In October, 1780, he was brought down with a spell of gout which kept him in his house for six painful weeks. In the midst of it he wrote this piece of self-accusation.

It, like the two preceding selections, was composed for the delight of his friends, and in French. The manuscript contains marginal notations by Madame Brillon. She had sent him a verse dialogue, *Le Sage et la Goutte*, in which the Sage admits to having mistresses, enjoying wine, and insists he does not always win at chess. This English version first appeared in an edition of Franklin's then known *Works*, in London, 1806.

◇

Midnight, October 22, 1780.

FRANKLIN. Eh! Oh! Eh! What have I done to merit these cruel sufferings?

GOUT. Many things; you have ate and drank too freely, and too much indulged those legs of yours in their indolence.

FRANKLIN. Who is it that accuses me?

GOUT. It is I, even I, the Gout.

FRANKLIN. What! my enemy in person?

GOUT. No, not your enemy.

FRANKLIN. I repeat it; my enemy; for you would not only torment my body to death, but ruin my good name; you reproach me as a glutton and a tippler; now all the world, that knows me, will allow that I am neither the one nor the other.

GOUT. The world may think as it pleases; it is always very complaisant to itself, and sometimes to its friends; but I very well know that the quantity of meat and drink proper for a man, who takes a reasonable degree of exercise, would be too much for another, who never takes any.

FRANKLIN. I take—Eh! Oh!—as much exercise —Eh!—as I can, Madam Gout. You know my sedentary state, and on that account, it would seem, Madam Gout, as if you might spare me a little, seeing it is not altogether my own fault.

GOUT. Not a jot; your rhetoric and your politeness are thrown away; your apology avails nothing. If your situation in life is a sedentary one, your amusements, your recreations, at least, should be active. You ought to walk or ride; or, if the weather prevents that play at billiards. But let us examine your course of life. While the mornings are long, and you have leisure to go abroad, what do you do? Why, instead of gaining an appetite for breakfast, by salutary exercise, you amuse yourself, with books, pamphlets, or newspapers, which commonly are not worth the reading. Yet you eat an inordinate breakfast, four dishes of tea, with cream, and one or two buttered toasts, with slices of hung beef, which I fancy are not things the most easily digested. Immediately afterward you sit down to write at your desk, or converse with persons who apply to you on business. Thus the time passes till one, without any kind of bodily exercise. But all this I could pardon, in regard, as you say, to your sedentary condition. But what is your practice after dinner? Walking in the beautiful gardens of those friends, with whom you have dined, would be the choice of men of sense; yours is to be fixed down to chess, where you are found engaged for two or three hours! This is your perpetual recreation, which is the least eligible of any for a sedentary man, because, instead of accelerating the motion of the fluids, the rigid attention it requires helps to retard the circulation and obstruct internal secretions. Wrapt in the speculations of this wretched game, you destroy your constitution. What can be expected from such a course of living but a body replete with stagnant humours, ready to fall a prey to all kinds of dangerous maladies, if I, the Gout, did not occasionally bring you relief by agitating those humours, and so purifying or dissipating them? If it was in some nook or alley in Paris, deprived of walks, that you played awhile at chess after dinner, this might be excusable; but the same taste prevails with you in Passy, Auteuil, Montmartre, or Sanoy, places where there are the finest gardens and walks, a pure air, beautiful women, and the most agreeable and instructive conversation; all of which you might enjoy by frequenting the walks. But these are rejected for this abominable game of chess. Fie, then Mr. Franklin! But amidst my instructions, I had almost forgot to administer my wholesome corrections; so take that twinge,—and that.

FRANKLIN. Oh! Eh! Oh! Ohhh! As much instruction as you please, Madam Gout, and as many reproaches; but pray, Madam, a truce with your corrections!

GOUT. No, Sir, no,—I will not abate a particle of what is so much for your good,—therefore—

FRANKLIN. Oh! Ehhh!—It is not fair to say I take no exercise, when I do very often, going out to dine and returning in my carriage.

GOUT. That, of all imaginable exercises, is the most slight and insignificant, if you allude to the motion of a carriage suspended on springs. By observing the degree of heat obtained by different kinds of motion, we may form an estimate of the quantity of exercise given by each. Thus, for example, if you turn out to walk in winter with cold feet, in an hour's time you will be in a glow all over; ride on horseback, the same effect will scarcely be perceived by four hours' round trotting; but if you loll in a carriage, such as you have mentioned, you may travel all day, and gladly enter the last inn to warm your feet by a fire. Flatter yourself then no longer, that half an hour's airing in your carriage deserves the name of exercise. Providence has appointed few to roll in carriages, while he has given to all a pair of legs, which are machines infinitely more commodious and serviceable. Be grateful, then, and make a proper use of yours. Would you know how they forward the circulation of your fluids, in the very action of transporting you from place to place; observe when you walk, that all your weight is alternately thrown from one leg to the other; this occasions a great pressure on the vessels of the foot, and repels their contents; when relieved, by the weight being thrown on the other foot, the vessels of the first are allowed to replenish, and, by a return of this weight, this repulsion again succeeds; thus accelerating the circulation of the blood. The heat produced in any given time, depends on the degree of this acceleration; the fluids are shaken, the humours attenuated, the secretions facilitated, and all goes well; the cheeks are ruddy, and health is established. Behold your fair friend at Auteuil; a lady who received from bounteous nature more really useful science, than half a dozen such pretenders to philosophy as you have been able to extract from all your books. When she honours you with a visit, it is on foot. She walks all hours of the day, and leaves indolence, and its concomitant maladies, to be endured by her horses. In this see at once the preservative of her health and personal charms. But when you go to Auteuil, you must have your carriage, though it is no further from Passy to Auteuil than from Auteuil to Passy.

FRANKLIN. Your reasonings grow very tiresome.

GOUT. I stand corrected. I will be silent and continue my office, take that, and that.

FRANKLIN. Oh! Ohh! Talk on, I pray you!

GOUT. No, no; I have a good number of twinges for you to-night, and you may be sure of some more to-morrow.

FRANKLIN. What, with such a fever! I shall go distracted. Oh! Eh! Can no one bear it for me?

GOUT. Ask that of your horses; they have served you faithfully.

FRANKLIN. How can you so cruelly sport with my torments?

GOUT. Sport! I am very serious. I have here a list of offences against your own health distinctly written, and can justify every stroke inflicted on you.

FRANKLIN. Read it then.

GOUT. It is too long a detail; but I will briefly mention some particulars.

FRANKLIN. Proceed. I am all attention.

GOUT. Do you remember how often you have promised yourself, the following morning, a walk in the grove of Boulogne, in the garden de la Muette, or in your own garden, and have violated your promise, alleging, at one time, it was too cold, at another too warm, too windy, too moist, or what else you pleased; when in truth it was too nothing, but your insuperable love of ease?

FRANKLIN. That I confess may have happened occasionally, probably ten times in a year.

GOUT. Your confession is very far short of the truth; the gross amount is one hundred and ninety-nine times.

FRANKLIN. Is it possible?

GOUT. So possible, that it is fact; you may rely on the accuracy of my statement. You know M. Brillon's gardens, and what fine walks they contain; you know the handsome flight of an hundred steps, which lead from the terrace above to the lawn below. You have been in the practice of visiting this amiable family twice a week, after dinner, and it is a maxim of your own, that "a man may take as much exercise in walking a mile, up and down stairs, as in ten on level ground." What an opportunity was here for you to have had exercise in both these ways! Did you embrace it, and how often?

FRANKLIN. I cannot immediately answer that question.

GOUT. I will do it for you; not once.

FRANKLIN. Not once?

GOUT. Even so. During the summer you went there at six o'clock. You found the charming lady, with her lovely children and friends, eager to walk with you, and entertain you with their agreeable conversation; and what has been your choice? Why to sit on the terrace, satisfying yourself with the fine prospect, and passing your eye over the beauties of the garden below, without taking one step to descend and walk about in them. On the contrary, you call for tea and the chessboard; and lo! you are occupied in your seat till nine o'clock, and that besides two hours' play after dinner; and then, instead of walking home, which would have bestirred you a little, you step into your carriage. How absurd to suppose that all this carelessness can be reconcilable with health, without my interposition!

FRANKLIN. I am convinced now of the justness of poor Richard's remark, that "Our debts and our sins are always greater than we think for."

GOUT. So it is. You philosophers are sages in your maxims, and fools in your conduct.

FRANKLIN. But do you charge among my crimes, that I return in a carriage from Mr. Brillon's?

GOUT. Certainly; for, having been seated all the while, you cannot object the fatigue of the day, and cannot want therefore the relief of a carriage.

FRANKLIN. What then would you have me do with my carriage?

GOUT. Burn it if you choose; you would at least get heat out of it once in this way; or, if you dislike that proposal, here's another for you; observe the poor peasants, who work in the vineyards and grounds about the villages of Passy, Auteuil, Chaillot, &c.; you may find every day, among these deserving creatures, four or five old men and women, bent and perhaps crippled by weight of years, and too long and too great labour. After a most fatiguing day, these people have to trudge a mile or two to their smoky huts. Order your coachman to set them down. This is an act that will be good for your soul; and, at the same time, after your visit to the Brillons, if you return on foot, that will be good for your body.

FRANKLIN. Ah! how tiresome you are!

GOUT. Well, then, to my office; it should not be forgotten that I am your physician. There.

FRANKLIN. Ohhh! what a devil of a physician!

GOUT. How ungrateful you are to say so! Is it not I who, in the character of your physician, have saved you from the palsy, dropsy, and apoplexy? one or other of which would have done for you long ago, but for me.

FRANKLIN. I submit, and thank you for the past, but entreat the discontinuance of your visits for the future; for, in my mind, one had better die than be cured so dolefully. Permit me just to hint, that I have also not been unfriendly to *you.* I never feed physician or quack of any kind, to enter the list against you; if then you do not leave me to my repose, it may be said you are ungrateful too.

GOUT. I can scarcely acknowledge that as any objection. As to quacks, I despise them; they may kill you indeed, but cannot injure me. And, as to regular physicians, they are at last convinced that the gout, in such a subject as you are, is no disease, but a remedy; and wherefore cure a remedy?—but to our business,—there.

FRANKLIN. Oh! oh!—for Heaven's sake leave me! and I promise faithfully never more to play at chess, but to take exercise daily, and live temperately.

GOUT. I know you too well. You promise fair; but, after a few months of good health, you will return to your own habits; your fine promises will be forgotten like the forms of last year's clouds. Let us then finish the account, and I will go. But I leave you with an assurance of visiting you again at a proper time and place; for my object is your good, and you are sensible now that I am your *real friend.*

TO SAMUEL MATHER

◇

❡ SAMUEL MATHER (1706–85) was a son of that famous Cotton Mather who had called James Franklin and his band "the Hell-Fire Club" and whom young Benjamin had tried to ridicule in assuming the guise of Silence Dogood. Samuel was ordained as minister in his father's church, the Second, in 1732; after a fracas within the church, he and some ninety-three members seceded, to form a new body, over which he presided until his death, though in his last years it was only a corporal's guard. Trying to imitate his father, he kept publishing up to his last moment; in 1784 he produced *The Dying Legacy*, a copy of which he thoughtfully sent to Franklin in France, from whom he received this acknowledgment.

◇

Passy, May 12, 1784.

REV SIR,

I received your kind letter, with your excellent advice to the people of the United States, which

I read with great pleasure, and hope it will be duly regarded. Such writings, though they may be lightly passed over by many readers, yet, if they make a deep impression on one active mind in a hundred, the effects may be considerable. Permit me to mention one little instance, which, though it relates to myself, will not be quite uninteresting to you. When I was a boy, I met with a book, entitled *"Essays to do Good,"* which I think was written by your father. It had been so little regarded by a former possessor, that several leaves of it were torn out; but the remainder gave me such a turn of thinking, as to have an influence on my conduct through life; for I have always set a greater value on the character of a *doer of good,* than on any other kind of reputation; and if I have been, as you seem to think, a useful citizen, the public owes the advantage of it to that book.

You mention your being in your 78th year; I am in my 79th; we are grown old together. It is now more than 60 years since I left Boston, but I remember well both your father and grandfather, having heard them both in the pulpit, and seen them in their houses. The last time I saw your father was in the beginning of 1724, when I visited him after my first trip to Pennsylvania. He received me in his library, and on my taking leave showed me a shorter way out of the house through a narrow passage, which was crossed by a beam over head. We were still talking as I withdrew, he accompanying me behind, and I turning partly towards him, when he said hastily, *"Stoop, stoop!"* I did not understand him, till I felt my head hit against the beam. He was a man that never missed any occasion of giving instruction, and upon this he said to me, *"You are young, and have the world before you;* STOOP *as you go through it, and you will miss many hard thumps."* This advice, thus beat into my head, has frequently been of use to me; and I often think of it, when I see pride mortified, and misfortunes brought upon people by their carrying their heads too high.

I long much to see again my native place, and to lay my bones there. I left it in 1723; I visited it in 1733, 1743, 1753, and 1763. In 1773 I was in England; in 1775 I had a sight of it, but could not enter, it being in possession of the enemy. I did hope to have been there in 1783, but could not obtain my dismission from this employment here; and now I fear I shall never have that happiness. My best wishes however attend my dear country. *Esto perpetua.* It is now blest with an excellent constitution; may it last for ever!

This powerful monarchy continues its friendship for the United States. It is a friendship of the utmost importance to our security, and should be carefully cultivated. Britain has not yet well digested the loss of its dominion over us, and has still at times some flattering hopes of recovering it. Accidents may increase those hopes, and encourage dangerous attempts. A breach between us and France would infallibly bring the English again upon our backs; and yet we have some wild heads among our countrymen, who are endeavouring to weaken that connexion! Let us preserve our reputation by performing our engagements; our credit by fulfilling our contracts; and friends by gratitude and kindness; for we know not how soon we may again have occasion for all of them. With great and sincere esteem, I have the honour to be, &c.

B. FRANKLIN.

TO EZRA STILES

◇

❡ EZRA STILES (1727–95), president of Yale College since 1778, felt he had a right to demand of America's Sage, even though he knew that Franklin was in the last gasps, "the opinion of my venerable friend concerning Jesus of Nazareth." Stiles had been brought up in the severe Calvinism of Connecticut, and graduated from Yale in 1746. Although licensed by the Consociation to preach, he underwent a long period of doubt, and in despair turned to the study of law, being admitted to the bar in 1753. While in the throes of this crisis, he delivered the complimentary oration upon the visit of Franklin to New Haven in 1755. Thence onward, he and Franklin were fast friends, the tie strengthened by Stiles's great interest in science.

Stiles emerged from his struggle with skepticism to become a firm believer in divine revelation, and to serve for twenty years as minister to the Second Church of Newport, Rhode Island. He continued to correspond with Franklin; his friend persuaded the University of Edinburgh to bestow upon Stiles an honorary Doctorate of Divinity. Stiles was an ardent patriot, supported the Revolution, and carried Yale College through the crisis. In 1790 he knew that Franklin could not live long, and that Franklin would reply, as he did, from his deathbed. Yet he had to ask, and Franklin contrived to answer. This letter was written on March 9, 1790. Franklin expired on April 17.

◇

Philad, March 9, 1790.

REVEREND AND DEAR SIR,

I received your kind Letter of Jan'y 28, and am glad you have at length received the portrait of Gov'r Yale from his Family, and deposited it in the College Library. He was a great and good Man, and had the Merit of doing infinite Service to your Country by his Munificence to that Institution. The Honour you propose doing me by placing mine in the same Room with his, is much too great for my Deserts; but you always had a Partiality for me, and to that it must be ascribed. I am however too much obliged to Yale College, the first learned Society that took Notice of me and adorned me with its Honours, to refuse a Request that comes from it thro' so esteemed a Friend. But I do not think any one of the Portraits you mention, as in my Possession, worthy of the Place and Company you propose to place it in. You have an excellent Artist lately arrived. If he will undertake to make one for you, I shall cheerfully pay the Expense; but he must not delay setting about it, or I may slip thro' his fingers, for I am now in my eighty-fifth year, and very infirm.

I send with this a very learned Work, as it seems to me, on the antient Samaritan Coins, lately printed in Spain, and at least curious for the Beauty of the Impression. Please to accept it for your College Library. I have subscribed for the Encyclopaedia now printing here, with the Intention of presenting it to the College. I shall probably depart before the Work is finished, but shall leave Directions for its Continuance to the End. With this you will receive some of the first numbers.

You desire to know something of my Religion. It is the first time I have been questioned upon it. But I cannot take your Curiosity amiss, and shall endeavour in a few Words to gratify it. Here is my Creed. I believe in one God, Creator of the Universe. That he governs it by his Providence. That he ought to be worshipped. That the most acceptable Service we render to him is doing good to his other Children. That the soul of Man is immortal, and will be treated with Justice in another Life respecting its Conduct in this. These I take to be the fundamental Principles of all sound Religion, and I regard them as you do in whatever Sect I meet with them.

As to Jesus of Nazareth, my Opinion of whom you particularly desire, I think the System of Morals and his Religion, as he left them to us, the best the World ever saw or is likely to see; but I apprehend it has received various corrupting Changes, and I have, with most of the present Dissenters in England, some Doubts as to his Divinity; tho' it is a question I do not dogmatize upon, having never studied it, and think it needless to busy myself with it now, when I expect soon an Opportunity of knowing the Truth with less Trouble. I see no harm, however, in its being believed, if that Belief has the good Consequence, as probably it has, of making his Doctrines more respected and better observed; especially as I do not perceive, that the Supreme takes it amiss, by distinguishing the Unbelievers in his Government of the World with any peculiar Marks of his Displeasure.

I shall only add, respecting myself, that, having experienced the Goodness of that Being in conducting me prosperously thro' a long life, I have no doubt of its Continuance in the next, though without the smallest Conceit of meriting such Goodness. My Sentiments on this Head you will see in the Copy of an old Letter enclosed, which I wrote in answer to one from a zealous Religionist, whom I had relieved in a paralytic case by electricity, and who, being afraid I should grow proud upon it, sent me his serious though rather impertinent Caution. I send you also the Copy of another Letter, which will shew something of my Disposition relating to Religion. With great and sincere Esteem and Affection, I am, Your obliged old Friend and most obedient humble Servant

B. FRANKLIN.

P.S. Had not your College some Present of Books from the King of France? Please to let me know, if you had an Expectation given you of more, and the Nature of the Expectation? I have a Reason for the Enquiry.

I confide, that you will not expose me to Criticism and censure by publishing any part of this Communication to you. I have ever let others enjoy their religious Sentiments, without reflecting on them for those that appeared to me unsupportable and even absurd. All Sects here, and we have a great Variety, have experienced my good will in assisting them with Subscriptions for building their new Places of Worship; and, as I have never opposed any of their Doctrines, I hope to go out of the World in Peace with them all.

Jonathan Edwards

PERSONAL NARRATIVE

◊

THE "Personal Narrative" of Jonathan Edwards was revealed to the world only fifty years after his death, in an edition of his *Works* published in 1808. So far as we now know, the original manuscript does not survive. We remain therefore at the mercy of his transcribers.

Had he ever completed his own story, the result would surely have been a masterpiece of self-exposition which could be the perfect obverse to the reverse of Franklin's *Autobiography*. In one sense, his motives for talking about himself were widely different from Franklin's: he did not yet want to prove any success; he merely wished to leave a factual record of his spiritual (*not* his clerical) experience, so that any surgical examination of his pretensions could be diagnosed. Yet in another sense, and a happily congenial sense, he must have entertained an aspiration to do exactly what Franklin more largely did achieve. He sought to establish the criterion of success within the terms of his standards of authentic experience.

Edwards was never allowed the leisure, once he became his grandfather's heir (cf. "since I lived in this town," p. 141), to find the time for further recounting of himself. Hence he had only the opportunity for a fragment of autobiography—as ultimately Franklin had only a scrap of time. Both of them, ironically, were obliged to leave unfinished statements of themselves to a posterity called to evaluate their comparative merits. The final judgment has not yet been recorded.

◊

I HAD a variety of concerns and exercises about my soul from my childhood; but had two more remarkable seasons of awakening, before I met with that change by which I was brought to those new dispositions, and that new sense of things, that I have since had. The first time was when I was a boy, some years before I went to college, at a time of remarkable awakening in my father's congregation. I was then very much affected for many months, and concerned about the things of religion, and my soul's salvation; and was abundant in duties. I used to pray five times a day in secret, and to spend much time in religious talk with other boys; and used to meet with them to pray together. I experienced I know not what kind of delight in religion. My mind was much engaged in it, and had much selfrighteous pleasure; and it was my delight to abound in religious duties. I with some of my schoolmates joined together, and built a booth in a swamp, in a very retired spot, for a place of prayer. And besides, I had particular secret places of my own in the woods, where I used to retire by myself; and was from time to time much affected. My affections seemed to be lively and easily moved, and I seemed to be in my element when engaged in religious duties. And I am ready to think, many are deceived with such affections, and such a kind of delight as I then had in religion, and mistake it for grace.

But in process of time, my convictions and affections wore off; and I entirely lost all those affections and delights and left off secret prayer, at least as to any constant performance of it; and returned like a dog to his vomit, and went on in the ways of sin. Indeed I was at times very uneasy, especially towards the latter part of my time at college; when it pleased God, to seize me with a pleurisy; in which he brought me nigh to the grave, and shook me over the pit of hell. And yet, it was not long after my recovery, before I fell again into my old ways of sin. But God would not suffer me to go on with any quietness; I had great and violent inward struggles, till, after many conflicts with wicked inclinations, repeated resolutions, and bonds that I laid myself under by a kind of vows to God, I was brought wholly to break off all former wicked ways, and all ways of known outward sin; and to apply myself to seek salvation, and practise many religious duties; but without that kind of affection and delight which I had formerly experienced. My concern now wrought more by inward struggles and conflicts, and selfreflections. I made seeking my salvation the main business of my life. But yet, it seems to me, I sought after a miserable manner; which has made me sometimes since to question, whether ever it issued in that which was saving; being ready to doubt, whether such miserable seeking ever succeeded. I was indeed brought to seek salvation in a manner that I never was before; I felt a spirit to part with all things in the world, for an interest in Christ. My concern continued and prevailed, with many exercising thoughts and inward struggles; but yet it never seemed to be proper to express that concern by the name of terror.

From my childhood up, my mind had been full of objections against the doctrine of God's sovereignty, in choosing whom he would to eternal life, and rejecting whom he pleased; leaving them eternally to perish, and be everlastingly tormented in hell. It used to appear like a horrible doctrine to me. But I remember the time very well, when I seemed to be convinced, and fully satisfied, as to this sovereignty of God, and his justice in thus eternally disposing of men, according to his sovereign pleasure. But never could give an account, how, or by what means, I was thus convinced, not in the least imagining at the time, nor a long time after, that there was any extraordinary influence of God's Spirit in it; but only that now I saw further, and my reason apprehended the justice and reasonableness of it. However, my mind rested in it; and it put an end to all those cavils and objections. And there has been a wonderful alteration in my mind in respect to the doctrine of God's sovereignty, from that day to this; so that I scarce ever have found so much as the rising of an objection against it, in the most absolute sense, in God's shewing mercy to whom he will shew mercy, and hardening whom he will. God's absolute sovereignty and justice, with respect to salvation and damnation, is what my mind seems to rest assured of, as much as of any thing that I see with my eyes; at least it is so at times. But I have often, since that first conviction, had quite another kind of sense of God's sovereignty than I had then. I have often since had not only a conviction, but a delightful conviction. The doctrine has very often appeared exceeding pleasant, bright, and sweet. Absolute sovereignty is what I love to ascribe to God. But my first conviction was not so.

The first instance that I remember of that sort of inward, sweet delight in God and divine things that I have lived much in since, was on reading those words, I Tim. i. 17. *Now unto the King eternal, immortal, invisible, the only wise God, be honour and glory for ever and ever, Amen.* As I read the words, there came into my soul, and was as it were diffused through it, a sense of the glory of the Divine Being; a new sense, quite different from any thing I ever experienced before. Never any words of scripture seemed to me as these words did. I thought with myself, how excellent a Being that was, and how happy I should be, if I might enjoy that God, and be rapt up to him in heaven, and be as it were swallowed up in him for ever! I kept saying, and as it were singing over these words of scripture to myself; and went to pray to God that I might enjoy him, and prayed in a manner quite different from what I used to do; with a new sort of affection. But it never came into my thought, that there was any thing spiritual, or of a saving nature in this.

From about that time, I began to have a new kind of apprehensions and ideas of Christ, and the work of redemption, and the glorious way of salvation by him. An inward, sweet sense of these things, at times, came into my heart; and my soul was led away in pleasant views and contemplations of them. And my mind was greatly engaged to spend my time in reading and meditating on Christ, on the beauty and excellency of person, and the lovely way of salvation by free grace in him. I found no books so delightful to me, as those that treated of these subjects. Those words Cant. ii. I, used to be abundantly with me, *I am the Rose of Sharon, and the Lily of the valleys.* The words seemed to me, sweetly to represent the loveliness and beauty of Jesus Christ. The whole book of Canticles used to be pleasant to me, and I used to be much in reading it, about that time; and found, from time to time, an inward sweetness, that would carry me away, in my comtemplations. This I know not how to express otherwise, than by a calm, sweet abstraction of soul from all the concerns of this world; and sometimes a kind of vision, or fixed ideas and imaginations, of being alone in the mountains, or some solitary wilderness, far from all mankind, sweetly conversing with Christ, and wrapt and swallowed up in God. The sense I had of divine things, would often of a sudden kindle up, as it were, a sweet burning in my heart; an ardor of soul, that I know not how to express.

Not long after I first began to experience these things, I gave an account to my father of some things that had passed in my mind. I was pretty much affected by the discourse we had together; and when the discourse was ended, I walked abroad alone, in a solitary place in my father's pasture, for contemplation. And as I was walking there, and looking up on the sky and clouds, there came into my mind so sweet a sense of the glorious *majesty* and *grace* of God, that I know not how to express. I seemed to see them both in a sweet conjunction; majesty and meekness joined together; it was a sweet, and gentle, and holy majesty; and also a majestic meekness; an awful sweetness; a high, and great, and holy gentleness.

After this my sense of divine things gradually increased, and became more and more lively, and had more of that inward sweetness. The appearance of every thing was altered; there seemed to be, as it were, a calm, sweet cast, or appearance of divine glory, in almost every thing. God's excellency, his wisdom, his purity and love, seemed to appear in every thing: in the sun, moon, and stars; in the clouds, and blue sky; in the grass, flowers, trees; in the water, and all nature; which used greatly to fix my mind. I often used to sit and view the moon for continuance; and in the day, spent much time in viewing the clouds and sky, to behold the sweet glory of God in these things; in the mean time, singing forth, with a low voice my contemplations of the Creator and Redeemer. And scarce any thing, among all the works of nature, was so sweet to me as thunder and lightning; formerly, nothing had been so terrible to me. Before, I used to be uncommonly terrified with thunder, and to be struck with terror when I saw a thunder storm rising; but now, on the contrary, it rejoiced me. I felt God, so to speak, at the first appearance of a thunder storm; and used to take the opportunity, at such times, to fix myself in order to view the clouds, and see the lightnings play, and hear the majestic and awful voice of God's thunder, which oftentimes was exceedingly entertaining, leading me to sweet contemplations of my great and glorious God. While thus engaged, it always seemed natural to me to sing, or chant for my meditations; or, to speak my thoughts in soliloquies with a singing voice.

I felt then great satisfaction, as to my good state; but that did not content me. I had vehement longings of soul after God and Christ, and after more holiness, wherewith my heart seemed to be full, and ready to break; which often brought to my mind the words of the Psalmist, Psal. cxix. 28. *My soul breaketh for the longing it hath.* I often felt a mourning and lamenting in my heart, that I had not turned to God sooner, that I might have had more time to grow in grace. My mind was greatly fixed on divine things; almost perpetually in the contemplation of them. I spent most of my time in thinking of divine things, year after year; often walking alone in the woods, and solitary places, for meditation, soliloquy, and prayer, and converse with God; and it was always my manner, at such times, to sing forth my contemplations. I was almost constantly in ejaculatory prayer, wherever I was. Prayer seemed to be natural to me, as the breath by which the inward burnings of my heart had vent. The delights which I now felt in the things of religion, were of an exceeding different kind from those before mentioned, that I had when a boy; and what I then had no more notion of, than one born blind has of pleasant and beautiful colors. They were of a more inward, pure, soul animating and refreshing nature. Those former delights never reached the heart; and did not arise from any sight of the divine excellency of the things of God; or any taste of the soul satisfying and life-giving good there is in them.

My sense of divine things seemed gradually to increase, until I went to preach at New York,[1] which was about a year and a half after they began; and while I was there, I felt them, very sensibly, in a much higher degree than I had done before. My longings after God and holiness, were much increased. Pure and humble, holy and heavenly Christianity, appeared exceeding amiable to me. I felt a burning desire to be in every thing a complete Christian; and conformed to the blessed image of Christ; and that I might live, in all things, according to the pure, sweet and blessed rules of the gospel. I had an eager thirsting after progress in these things; which put me upon pursuing and pressing after them. It was my continual strife day and night, and constant inquiry, how I should *be* more holy, and *live* more holily, and more becoming a child of God, and a disciple of Christ. I now sought an increase of grace and holiness, and a holy life, with much more earnestness, than ever I sought grace before I had it. I used to be continually examining myself, and studying and contriving for likely ways and means, how I should live holily, with far greater diligence and earnestness, than ever I pursued any thing in my life; but yet with too great a dependence on my own strength; which afterwards proved a great damage to me. My experience had not then taught me, as it has done since, my extreme feebleness and impotence, every manner of way; and the bottomless depths of secret corruption and deceit there was in my heart. However, I went on with my eager pursuit after more holiness, and conformity to Christ.

The heaven I desired was a heaven of holiness; to be with God, and to spend my eternity in divine love, and holy communion with Christ. My mind was very much taken up with contemplations on heaven, and the enjoyments there; and living there in perfect holiness, humility and love: And it used at that time to appear a great part of the happiness of heaven, that there the saints could express their love to Christ. It appeared to me a great clog and burden, that what I felt within, I could not express as I desired. The inward ardour of my soul, seemed to be hindered

PERSONAL NARRATIVE. 1. **New York:** Edwards served as minister to a Scotch-Presbyterian church which met in a building at William Street, between Liberty and Wall, in New York City, from August, 1722, to May, 1723.

and pent up, and could not freely flame out as it would. I used often to think, how in heaven this principle should freely and fully vent and express itself. Heaven appeared exceedingly delightful, as a world of love; and that all happiness consisted in living in pure, humble, heavenly, divine love.

I remember the thoughts I used then to have of holiness; and said sometimes to myself, "I do certainly know that I love holiness, such as the gospel prescribes." It appeared to me, that there was nothing in it but what was ravishingly lovely; the highest beauty and amiableness . . . a *divine* beauty; far purer than any thing here upon earth; and that every thing else was like mire and defilement, in comparison of it.

Holiness, as I then wrote down some of my contemplations on it, appeared to me to be of a sweet, pleasant, charming, serene, calm nature; which brought an inexpressible purity, brightness, peacefulness and ravishment to the soul. In other words, that it made the soul like a field or garden of God, with all manner of pleasant flowers; all pleasant, delightful, and undisturbed; enjoying a sweet calm, and the gently vivifying beams of the sun. The soul of a true Christian, as I then wrote my meditations, appeared like such a little white flower as we see in the spring of the year; low and humble on the ground, opening its bosom to receive the pleasant beams of the sun's glory; rejoicing as it were in a calm rapture; diffusing around a sweet fragrancy; standing peacefully and lovingly, in the midst of other flowers round about; all in like manner opening their bosoms, to drink in the light of the sun. There was no part of creature holiness, that I had so great a sense of its loveliness, as humility, brokenness of heart and poverty of spirit; and there was nothing that I so earnestly longed for. My heart panted after this, to lie low before God, as in the dust; that I might be nothing, and that God might be ALL, that I might become as a little child.

While at New York, I was sometimes much affected with reflections of my past life, considering how late it was before I began to be truly religious; and how wickedly I had lived till then; and once so as to weep abundantly, and for a considerable time together.

On *January* 12, 1723. I made a solemn dedication of myself to God, and wrote it down; giving up myself, and all that I had to God; to be for the future, in no respect, my own; to act as one that had no right to himself, in any respect. And solemnly vowed, to take God for my whole portion and felicity; looking on nothing else, as any part of my happiness, nor acting as if it were; and his law for the constant rule of my obedience: engaging to fight, with all my might, against the world, the flesh, and the devil, to the end of my life. But I have reason to be infinitely humbled, when I consider, how much I have failed, of answering my obligation.

I had, then, abundance of sweet, religious conversation, in the family where I lived, with Mr. John Smith, and his pious mother. My heart was knit in affection, to those, in whom were appearances of true piety; and I could bear the thoughts of no other companions, but such as were holy, and the disciples of the blessed Jesus. I had great longings, for the advancement of Christ's kingdom in the world; and my secret prayer used to be, in great part, taken up in praying for it. If I heard the least hint, of any thing that happened, in any part of the world, that appeared, in some respect or other, to have a favourable aspect, on the interests of Christ's kingdom, my soul eagerly catched at it; and it would much animate and refresh me. I used to be eager to read public news-letters, mainly for that end; to see if I could not find some news, favourable to the interest of religion in the world.

I very frequently used to retire into a solitary place, on the banks of Hudson's River, at some distance from the city, for contemplation on divine things and secret converse with God: and had many sweet hours there. Sometimes Mr. Smith and I walked there together, to converse on the things of God; and our conversation used to turn much on the advancement of Christ's kingdom in the world, and the glorious things that God would accomplish for his church in the latter days. I had then, and at other times, the greatest delight in the holy scriptures, of any book whatsoever. Oftentimes in reading it, every word seemed to touch my heart. I felt a harmony between something in my heart, and those sweet and powerful words. I seemed often to see so much light exhibited by every sentence, and such a refreshing food communicated, that I could not get along in reading; often dwelling long on one sentence, to see the wonders contained in it; and yet almost every sentence seemed to be full of wonders.

I came away from New York in the month of April, 1723, and had a most bitter parting with Madam Smith and her son. My heart seemed to sink within me, at leaving the family and city, where I had enjoyed so many sweet and pleasant days. I went from New York to Wethersfield, by water; and as I sailed away, I kept sight of the city as long as I could. However, that night after this sorrowful parting, I was greatly comforted in God at Westchester, where we went ashore to lodge: and had a pleasant time of it all the voyage to Saybrook. It was sweet to me to think of meeting dear Christians in heaven, where we should never part more. At Saybrook we went ashore to lodge on Saturday, and there kept the Sabbath; where I had a sweet and refreshing season, walking alone in the fields.

After I came home to Windsor, I remained much in a like frame of mind, as when at New York; only sometimes I felt my heart ready to sink, with the thoughts of my friends at New York. My support was in contemplations on the heavenly state; as I find in my Diary of May 1, 1723. It was a comfort to think of that state, where there is fulness of joy; where reigns heavenly, calm, and delightful love, without alloy; where there are continually the dearest expressions of this love; where is the enjoyment of the persons loved, without ever parting; where those persons who appear so lovely in this world, will really be inexpressibly more lovely, and full of love to us. And how sweetly will the mutual lovers join together, to sing the praises of God and the Lamb! How will it fill us with joy to think, that this enjoyment, these sweet exercises, will never cease, but will last to all eternity. . . . I continued much in the same frame, in the general, as when at New York, till I went to New Haven, as Tutor of the College: [2] particularly, once at Bolton, on a journey from Boston, while walking out alone in the fields. After I went to New Haven, I sunk in religion; my mind being diverted from my eager pursuits after holiness, by some affairs, that greatly perplexed and distracted my thoughts.

In September, 1725, I was taken ill at New Haven, and while endeavouring to go home to Windsor, was so ill at the North Village, that I could go no farther; where I lay sick, for about a quarter of a year. In this sickness, God was pleased to visit me again, with the sweet influences of his Spirit. My mind was greatly engaged there, on divine and pleasant contemplations, and longings of soul. I observed, that those who watched with me,[3] would often be looking out wishfully for the morning; which brought to my mind those words of the Psalmist, and which my soul with delight made its own language, *My soul waiteth for the Lord, more than they that watch for the morning; I say, more than they that watch for the morning*; and when the light of day came in at the window, it refreshed my soul, from one morning to another. It seemed to be some image of the light of God's glory.

I remember, about that time, I used greatly to long for the conversion of some, that I was concerned with; I could gladly honour them, and with delight be a servant to them, and lie at their feet, if they were but truly holy. But some time after this, I was again greatly diverted with some temporal concerns, that exceedingly took up my thoughts, greatly to the wounding of my soul; and went on, through various exercises, that it would be tedious to relate, which gave me much more experience of my own heart, than I ever had before.

Since I came to this town, I have often had sweet complacency in God, in views of his glorious perfections and the excellency of Jesus Christ. God has appeared to me a glorious and lovely Being, chiefly on account of his holiness. The holiness of God has always appeared to me the most lovely of all his attributes. The doctrines of God's absolute sovereignty, and free grace, in shewing mercy to whom he would shew mercy; and man's absolute dependence on the operations of God's Holy Spirit, have very often appeared to me as sweet and glorious doctrines. These doctrines have been much my delight. God's sovereignty has ever appeared to me, great part of his glory. It has often been my delight to approach God, and adore him as a sovereign God, and ask sovereign mercy of him.

I have loved the doctrines of the gospel; they have been to my soul like green pastures. The gospel has seemed to me the richest treasure; the treasure that I have most desired, and longed that it might dwell richly in me. The way of salvation by Christ has appeared, in a general way, glorious and excellent, most pleasant and most beautiful. It has often seemed to me, that it would in a great measure spoil heaven, to receive it in any other way. That text has often been affecting and delightful to me, Isa. xxxii. 2. *A man shall be an hiding place from the wind, and a covert from the tempest, &c.*

It has often appeared to me delightful, to be united to Christ; to have him for my head, and to be a member of his body; also to have Christ for my teacher and prophet. I very often think with sweetness, and longings, and pantings of soul, of being a little child, taking hold of Christ, to be led by him through the wilderness of this world. That text, Matth. xviii. 3, has often been sweet to me, *except ye be converted and become as little children, &c.* I love to think of coming

2. **as Tutor of the College:** Edwards was the senior tutor at Yale, 1724–26. There was then no president, so that he was effectively in charge of a student body of sixty youths.

3. **watched with me:** Edwards, thus characteristically reticent, means his mother, who came to North Haven to nurse him through this dangerous illness.

to Christ, to receive salvation of him, poor in spirit, and quite empty of self, humbly exalting him alone; cut off entirely from my own root, in order to grow into, and out of Christ; to have God in Christ to be all in all; and to live by faith on the Son of God, a life of humble, unfeigned confidence in him. That scripture has often been sweet to me, Psal. cxv. 1. *Not unto us, O Lord, not unto us, but unto thy name give glory, for thy mercy, and for thy truth's sake.* And those words of Christ, Luke x. 21. *In that hour Jesus rejoiced in spirit, and said, I thank thee, O Father, Lord of heaven and earth, that thou hast hid these things from the wise and prudent, and hast revealed them unto babes: Even so, Father, for so it seemed good in thy sight.* That sovereignty of God which Christ rejoiced in, seemed to me worthy of such joy; and that rejoicing seemed to shew the excellency of Christ, and of what spirit he was.

Sometimes, only mentioning a single word caused my heart to burn within me; or only seeing the name of Christ, or the name of some attribute of God. And God has appeared glorious to me, on account of the Trinity. It has made me have exalting thoughts of God, that he subsists in three persons; Father, Son and Holy Ghost. The sweetest joys and delights I have experienced, have not been those that have arisen from a hope of my own good estate; but in a direct view of the glorious things of the gospel. When I enjoy this sweetness, it seems to carry me above the thoughts of my own estate; it seems at such times a loss that I cannot bear, to take off my eye from the glorious, pleasant object I behold without me, to turn my eye in upon myself, and my own good estate.

My heart has been much on the advancement of Christ's kingdom in the world. The histories of the past advancement of Christ's kingdom have been sweet to me. When I have read histories of past ages, the pleasantest thing in all my reading has been, to read of the kingdom of Christ being promoted. And when I have expected, in my reading, to come to any such thing, I have rejoiced in the prospect, all the way as I read. And my mind has been much entertained and delighted with the scripture promises and prophecies, which relate to the future glorious advancement of Christ's kingdom upon earth.

I have sometimes had a sense of the excellent fulness of Christ, and his meetness and suitableness as a Saviour; whereby he has appeared to me, far above all, the chief of ten thousands. His blood and atonement have appeared sweet, and his righteousness sweet; which was always accompanied with ardency of spirit; and inward strugglings and breathings, and groanings that cannot be uttered, to be emptied of myself, and swallowed up in Christ.

Once, as I rode out into the woods for my health, in 1737, having alighted from my horse in a retired place, as my manner commonly has been, to walk for divine contemplation and prayer, I had a view that for me was extraordinary, of the glory of the Son of God, as Mediator between God and man, and his wonderful, great, full, pure and sweet grace and love, and meek and gentle condescension. This grace that appeared so calm and sweet, appeared also great above the heavens. The person of Christ appeared ineffably excellent with an excellency great enough to swallow up all thought and conception . . . which continued as near as I can judge, about an hour; which kept me the greater part of the time in a flood of tears, and weeping aloud. I felt an ardency of soul to be, what I know not otherwise how to express, emptied and annihilated; to lie in the dust, and to be full of Christ alone; to love him with a holy and pure love; to trust in him; to live upon him; to serve and follow him; and to be perfectly sanctified and made pure, with a divine and heavenly purity. I have, several other times, had views very much of the same nature, and which have had the same effects.

I have many times had a sense of the glory of the third person in the Trinity, in his office of Sanctifier; in his holy operations, communicating divine light and life to the soul. God, in the communications of his Holy Spirit, has appeared as an infinite fountain of divine glory and sweetness; being full, and sufficient to fill and satisfy the soul; pouring forth itself in sweet communications; like the sun in its glory, sweetly and pleasantly diffusing light and life. And I have sometimes had an affecting sense of the excellency of the word of God, as a word of life; as the light of life; a sweet, excellent lifegiving word; accompanied with a thirsting after that word, that it might dwell richly in my heart.

Often, since I lived in this town, I have had very affecting views of my own sinfulness and vileness; very frequently to such a degree as to hold me in a kind of loud weeping, sometimes for a considerable time together; so that I have often been forced to shut myself up. I have had a vastly greater sense of my own wickedness, and the badness of my heart, than ever I had before my conversion. It has often appeared to me, that if God should mark iniquity against me, I should appear the very worst of all mankind; of all that have been, since the beginning of the world to this time; and that I should have by far the lowest place in hell. When others, that have come to talk with me about their soul concerns, have expressed the sense they have had of their own wickedness, by saying that it seemed to them, that they were as bad as the devil himself; I thought their expressions seemed exceeding faint and feeble, to represent my wickedness.

My wickedness, as I am in myself, has long appeared to me perfectly ineffable, and swallowing up all thought and imagination; like an infinite deluge, or mountain over my head. I know not how to express better what my sins appear to me to be, than by heaping infinite upon infinite, and multiplying infinite by infinite. Very often, for these many years, these expressions are in my mind, and in my mouth, "Infinite upon infinite . . . Infinite upon infinite!" When I look into my heart, and take a view of my wickedness, it looks like an abyss infinitely deeper than hell. And it appears to me, that were it not for free grace, exalted and raised up to the infinite height of all the fulness and glory of the great Jehovah, and the arm of his power and grace stretched forth in all the majesty of his power, and in all the glory of his sovereignty, I should appear sunk down in my sins below hell itself; far beyond the sight of every thing, but the eye of sovereign grace, that can pierce even down to such a depth. And yet it seems to me, that my conviction of sin is exceeding small, and faint; it is enough to amaze me, that I have no more sense of my sin. I know certainly, that I have very little sense of my sinfulness. When I have had turns of weeping and crying for my sins I thought I knew at the time, that my repentance was nothing to my sin.

I have greatly longed of late, for a broken heart, and to lie low before God; and, when I ask for humility, I cannot bear the thoughts of being no more humble than other Christians. It seems to me, that though their degrees of humility may be suitable for them, yet it would be a vile selfexaltation in me, not to be the lowest in humility of all mankind. Others speak of their longing to be "humbled to the dust;" that may be a proper expression for them, but I always think of myself, that I ought, and it is an expression that has long been natural for me to use in prayer, "to lie infinitely low before God." And it is affecting to think, how ignorant I was, when a young Christian, of the bottomless, infinite depths of wickedness, pride, hypocrisy and deceit, left in my heart.

I have a much greater sense of my universal, exceeding dependence on God's grace and strength, and mere good pleasure, of late, than I used formerly to have; and have experienced more of an abhorrence of my own righteousness. The very thought of any joy arising in me, on any consideration of my own amiableness, performances, or experiences, or any goodness of heart or life, is nauseous and detestable to me. And yet I am greatly afflicted with a proud and self-righteous spirit, much more sensibly than I used to be formerly. I see that serpent rising and putting forth its head continually, every where, all around me.

Though it seems to me, that, in some respects, I was a far better Christian, for two or three years after my first conversion, than I am now; and lived in a more constant delight and pleasure; yet, of late years, I have had a more full and constant sense of the absolute sovereignty of God, and a delight in that sovereignty; and have had more of a sense of the glory of Christ, as a Mediator revealed in the gospel. On one Saturday night, in particular, I had such a discovery of the excellency of the gospel above all other doctrines, that I could not but say to myself, "This is my chosen light, my chosen doctrine;" and of Christ, "This is my chosen Prophet." It appeared sweet, beyond all expression, to follow Christ, and to be taught, and enlightened, and instructed by him; to learn of him, and live to him. Another Saturday night, (*January,* 1739) [4] I had such a sense, how sweet and blessed a thing it was to walk in the way of duty; to do that which was right and meet to be done, and agreeable to the holy mind of God; that it caused me to break forth into a kind of loud weeping, which held me some time, so that I was forced to shut myself up, and fasten the doors. I could not but, as it were, cry out, "How happy are they which do that which is right in the sight of God! They are blessed indeed, they are the happy ones!" I had, at the same time, a very affecting sense, how meet and suitable it was that God should govern the world, and order all things according to his own pleasure; and I rejoiced in it, that God reigned, and that his will was done.

4. **Another Saturday night, (*January,* 1739):** The insertion indicates that the "Personal Narrative," in so far as written, was abandoned after the ebbing of the first revival Edwards had supervised at Northampton, at a moment of doubt as to whether another one would be given him. At this hour he was striving with might and main how he might get a second one under way, all the time depending upon the unpredictable assistance of divine mediation. When in 1740, with the mediation of George Whitefield, Edwards had his Great Awakening, he could find no further time for the "Personal Narrative," nor did he ever discover, after the tragic collapse of that endeavor, the heart to finish his own story.

SARAH PIERREPONT

◇

THIS amazing address to the "young lady" in New Haven was written, according to legend, on the blank leaf of a book, evidently when Edwards let his attention wander from the printed page. It is traditionally dated 1723. If that is correct, she was then thirteen and he twenty.

◇

THEY say there is a young lady in [New Haven] who is beloved of that Great Being who made and rules the world, and that there are certain seasons in which this Great Being, in some way or other invisible, comes to her and fills her mind with exceeding sweet delight, and that she hardly cares for any thing, except to meditate on him—that she expects after a while to be received up where he is, to be raised up out of the world and caught up into heaven; being assured that he loves her too well to let her remain at a distance from him always. There she is to dwell with him, and to be ravished with his love and delight forever. Therefore, if you present all the world before her, with the richest of its treasures, she disregards it and cares not for it, and is unmindful of any pain or affliction. She has a strange sweetness in her mind, and singular purity in her affections; is most just and conscientious in all her conduct; and you could not persuade her to do any thing wrong or sinful, if you would give her all the world, lest she should offend this Great Being. She is of a wonderful sweetness, calmness and universal benevolence of mind; especially after this Great God has manifested himself to her mind. She will sometimes go about from place to place, singing sweetly; and seems to be always full of joy and pleasure; and no one knows for what. She loves to be alone, walking in the fields and groves, and seems to have some one invisible always conversing with her.

FROM

NOTES ON THE MIND

◇

EDWARDS evidently commenced the "Notes" while an undergraduate in 1716. Technically he was entered into Yale College, but a fierce dispute was raging about where the college should be located, and he was then studying with Elisha Williams at Wethersfield, where that faction remained until 1719. It was here that he first read, with consuming enthusiasm, Locke's *An Essay Concerning Human Understanding,* and immediately set himself, aged thirteen or fourteen, the task of writing a complete, authoritative, and definitive treatise on the human mind, as though he, in a single sweep of his own mind, had solved the mystery of the centuries. Benjamin Franklin could never have matched such sublime conceit!

Undeterred by any considerations of his youth or lack of acquaintance with the history of philosophy, he proposed to himself the title of this masterpiece-to-be in these formidable terms:

> *The Natural History of the Mental World, and of the Internal World: being a Particular Enquiry into the Nature of the Human Mind, with respect to both its Faculties—the Understanding and the Will—and its various Instincts, and Active and Passive Powers.*

He set down, probably not all at once, a miscellaneous list of subjects to be handled in this treatise, which is even more staggering than the pretentiousness of the title. He proposed to determine the exact difference between pleasure and pain, between natural appetite and rational desire, to define prejudice and liberty, to explain "How some men have Strong Reason, but not Good Judgment," and most significantly—considering what would be his life's work and the central theme of his writing—"Concerning Speculative Understanding, and Sense of Heart."

As the manuscript survives, entries are made under a variety of headings—Space, Substance, Thought, Motion, Memory, Perception, Ideas, etc. Some of these may date from his postgraduate studies in 1720–22, but internal evidence suggests that a few were made later. The outlines of all Edwards' subsequent thinking are found in the "Notes." This one, "Existence," is the very heart of his proposed system.

◇

EXISTENCE

IF WE HAD only the sense of Seeing, we should not be as ready to conclude the visible world to have been an existence independent of perception, as we do; because the ideas we have by the sense of Feeling, are as much mere ideas, as those we have by the sense of Seeing. But we know, that the things that are objects of this sense, all that the mind views by Seeing, are merely mental Existences; because all these things, with all their modes, do exist in a looking-glass, where all will acknowledge, they exist only mentally.

It is now agreed upon by every knowing philosopher,[1] that Colours are not really in the things, no more than Pain is in a needle; but strictly no where else but in the mind. But yet I think that Colour may have an existence out of the mind, with equal reason as any thing in the Body has any existence out of the mind, beside the very substance of the body itself, which is nothing but the Divine power, or rather the Constant Exertion of it. For what idea is that, which we call by the name of Body? I find Colour has the chief share in it. 'Tis nothing but Colour, and Figure, which is the termination of this Colour, together with some powers, such as the power of resisting, and motion, &c. that wholly makes up what we call Body. And if that, which we principally mean by the thing itself, cannot be said to be in the thing itself, I think nothing can be. If Colour exists not out of the mind, then nothing belonging to Body, exists out of the mind but Resistance, which is Solidity, and the termination of this Resistance, with its relations, which is Figure, and the communication of this Resistance, from space to space, which is Motion; though the latter are nothing but modes of the former. Therefore, there is nothing out of the mind but Resistance. And not that neither, when nothing is actually resisted. Then, there is nothing but the Power of Resistance. And as Resistance is nothing else but the actual exertion of God's power, so the Power can be nothing else, but the constant Law or Method of that actual exertion. And how is there any Resistance, except it be in some mind, in idea? What is it that is resisted? It is not Colour. And what else is it? It is ridiculous to say, that Resistance is resisted. That, does not tell us at all what is to be resisted. There must be something resisted before there can be Resistance; but to say Resistance is resisted, is ridiculously to suppose Resistance, before there is any thing to be resisted. Let us suppose two globes only existing, and no mind. There is nothing there, ex confesso, but Resistance. That is, there is such a Law, that the space within the limits of a globular figure shall resist. Therefore, there is nothing there but a power, or an establishment. And if there be any Resistance really out of the mind, one power and establishment must resist another establishment and law of Resistance, which is exceedingly ridiculous. But yet it cannot be otherwise, if any way out of the mind. But now it is easy to conceive of Resistance, as a mode of an idea. It is easy to conceive of such a power, or constant manner of stopping or resisting a colour. The idea may be resisted, it may move, and stop and rebound; but how a mere power, which is nothing real, can move and stop, is inconceivable, and it is impossible to say a word about it without contradiction. The world is therefore an ideal one; and the Law of creating, and the succession, of these ideas is constant and regular.

Coroll. 1. How impossible is it, that the world should exist from Eternity, without a Mind.

Coroll. 2. Since it is so, and that absolute Nothing is such a dreadful contradiction; hence we learn the necessity of the Eternal Existence of an All-comprehending Mind; and that it is the complication of all contradictions to deny such a mind.

When we say that the World, i.e. the material Universe, exists no where but in the mind, we have got to such a degree of strictness and abstraction, that we must be exceedingly careful, that we do not confound and lose ourselves by misapprehension. That is impossible, that it should be meant, that all the world is contained in the narrow compass of a few inches of space, in little ideas in the place of the brain; for that would be a contradiction; for we are to remember that the human body, and the brain itself, exist only mentally, in the same sense that other things do; and so that, which we call *place,* is an idea too. Therefore things are truly in those places; for what we mean, when we say so, is only, that this mode of our idea of place appertains to such an idea. We would not therefore be understood to deny, that things are where they seem to be. For the principles we lay down, if they are narrowly looked into, do not infer that. Nor will it be found, that they at all make void Natural Philosophy, or the science of the Causes or Reasons of corporeal changes; For to find out the reasons of things, in Natural Philosophy, is only to find out the proportion of God's acting. And the case is the same, as to such proportions, whether we suppose the World, only mental, in our sense or no.

Though we suppose, that the existence of the whole material Universe is absolutely dependent on Idea, yet we may speak in the old way, and

NOTES. 1. **every knowing philosopher:** The young Edwards here grandly assumes that any philosopher worth his salt must now agree with Locke (whom he characteristically does not name) that "ideas" are derived through the senses from concrete experiences. Starting from this proposition, he develops the "method of ideas" beyond what Locke would have permitted, asserting that the primary qualities of objects (qualities which are felt) are as purely "mental" as the secondary (those which are seen). On the subject of "Colours" Edwards was here drawing also upon his reading of Sir Isaac Newton's *Opticks* (first edition, 1704).

as properly, and truly as ever. God, in the beginning, created such a certain number of Atoms, of such a determinate bulk and figure, which they yet maintain and always will, and gave them such a motion, of such a direction, and of such a degree of velocity; from whence arise all the Natural changes in the Universe, forever, in a continued series. Yet, perhaps all this does not exist any where perfectly, but in the Divine Mind. But then, if it be enquired, What exists in the Divine Mind; and how these things exist there? I answer, There is his determination, his care, and his design, that Ideas shall be united forever, just so, and in such a manner, as is agreeable to such a series. For instance, all the ideas that ever were, or ever shall be to all eternity, in any created mind, are answerable to the existence of such a peculiar Atom in the beginning of the Creation, of such a determinate figure and size, and have such a motion given it; That is, they are all such, as Infinite Wisdom sees would follow, according to the series of nature, from such an Atom, so moved. That is, all ideal changes of creatures are just so, as if just such a particular Atom had actually all along existed even in some finite mind, and never had been out of that mind, and had, in that mind, caused these effects, which are exactly according to nature, that is, according to the nature of other matter, that is actually perceived by the mind. God supposes its existence; that is, he causes all changes to arise, as if all these things had actually existed in such a series, in some created mind, and as if created minds had comprehended all things perfectly. And, although created minds do not; yet, the Divine Mind doth; and he orders all things according to his mind, and his ideas. And these hidden things do not only exist in the Divine idea, but in a sense in created idea; for that exists in created idea, which necessarily supposes it. If a ball of lead were supposed to be let fall from the clouds, and no eye saw it, 'till it got within ten rods of the ground, and then its motion and celerity was perfectly discerned in its exact proportion; if it were not for the imperfection and slowness of our minds, the perfect idea of the rest of the motion would immediately, and of itself arise in the mind, as well as that which is there. So, were our thoughts comprehensive and perfect enough, our view of the present state of the world, would excite in us a perfect idea of all past changes.

And we need not perplex our minds with a thousand questions and doubts that will seem to arise: as, To what purpose is this way of exciting ideas; and, What advantage is there in observing such a series. I answer, It is just all one, as to any benefit or advantage, any end that we can suppose was proposed by the Creator, as if the Material Universe were existent in the same manner as is vulgarly thought. For the corporeal world is to no advantage but to the spiritual; and it is exactly the same advantage this way as the other, for it is all one, as to any thing excited in the mind.

It is hardly proper to say, that the dependence of ideas of sensation, upon the organs of the body, is only the dependence of some of our ideas upon others. For the organs of our bodies, are not our ideas, in a proper sense, though their existence be only mental. Yet there is no necessity of their existing actually in our minds, but they exist mentally, in the same manner as has been explained. The dependence of our ideas upon the organs, is the dependence of our ideas on our bodies, after the manner there explained, mentally existing. And if it be enquired, To what purpose is this way of exciting ideas? I answer, To exactly the same purpose as can be supposed, if our organs are actually existing, in the manner vulgarly conceived, as to any manner of benefit, or end, that can be mentioned.

It is not proper at all, nor doth it express the thing we would, to say *that bodies do not exist without the mind*. For the scheme will not allow the mind to be supposed determined to any place, in such a manner as to make that proper; for *Place itself* is mental, and *Within* and *Without,* are mere mental conceptions. Therefore, that way of expressing, will lead us into a thousand difficulties and perplexities. But when I say, the Material Universe exists only in the mind, I mean, that it is absolutely dependent on the conception of the mind for its existence, and does not exist as Spirits do, whose existence does not consist in, nor in dependence on, the conception of other minds. We must be exceedingly careful, lest we confound ourselves in these by mere imagination. It is from hence I expect the greatest opposition. It will appear a ridiculous thing, I suppose, that the material world exists no where, but in the soul of man, confined within his skull; but we must again remember what sort of existence the head and brain have.—The soul, in a sense, has its seat in the brain; and so, in a sense, the visible world is existent out of the mind, for it certainly, in the most proper sense, exists out of the brain.

Things, as to God, exist from all Eternity, alike; that is, the idea is always the same, and after the same mode. The existence of things, therefore, that are not actually in created minds, consists only in Power, or in the Determination of God, that such and such ideas shall be raised in created minds, upon such conditions.

Since all material existence is only idea, this question may be asked, In what sense may those things be said to exist, which are supposed, and yet are in no actual idea of any Created minds? I answer, they exist only in Uncreated idea. But how do they exist, otherwise than they did from all Eternity, for they always were in Uncreated idea, as did every thing else, and as they do at present, but not in Created idea. But it may be asked, How do these things exist, which have an actual existence, but of which no created mind is conscious?—For instance, the Furniture of this room, when we are absent, and the room is shut up, and no created mind perceives it; How do these things exist?—I answer, There has been in times past such a course and succession of existences, that these things must be supposed to make the series complete, according to Divine appointment, of the order of things. And there will be innumerable things consequential, which will be out of joint, out of their constituted series, without the supposition of these. For, upon supposition of these things, are infinite numbers of things otherwise than they would be, if these were not by God thus supposed. Yea, the whole Universe would be otherwise; such an influence have these things, by their attraction and otherwise. Yea, there must be an universal attraction, in the whole system of things, from the beginning of the world to the end; and, to speak more strictly and metaphysically, we must say, in the whole system and series of ideas in all Created minds; so that these things must necessarily be put in, to make complete the system of ideal world. That is, they must be supposed, if the train of ideas be, in the order and course, settled by the Supreme mind. So that we may answer in short, That the existence of these things is in God's supposing of them, in order to the rendering complete the series of things, (to speak more strictly, *the series of ideas,*) according to his own settled order, and that harmony of things, which he has appointed. The supposition of God, which we speak of, is nothing else but God's acting, in the course and series of his exciting ideas, as if they, (the things supposed,) were in actual idea.

But you may object, But there are many things so infinitely small, that their influence is altogether insensible; so that, whether they are supposed or not, there will no alteration be made in the series of Ideas. *Answer*, But though the influence is so small, that *we* do not perceive, yet who knows how penetrating other spirits may be, to perceive the minutest alterations. And whether the alterations be sensible, or not, at present, yet the effect of the least influence will be sensible, in time. For instance, Let there be supposed to be a Leaden Globe, of a mile in diameter, to be moving in a right line, with the swiftness of a cannon ball, in the Infinite Void, and let it pass by a very small Atom, supposed to be at rest. This Atom will somewhat retard this Leaden Globe in its motion, though at first, and perhaps for many ages, the difference is altogether insensible. But let it be never so little, in time it will become very sensible. For if the motion is made so much slower, that in a million of years it shall have moved one inch less than it would have done otherwise, in a million million it will have moved a million inches less. So now the least Atom, by its existence or motion, causes an alteration, more or less, in every other Atom in the Universe; so the alteration in time will become very sensible; so the whole Universe, in time, will become all over different from what it would otherwise have been. For if every other Atom is supposed to be either retarded, or accelerated, or diverted; every Atom, however small for the present, will cause great alterations, as we have shown already, or Retardation. The case is the same as to Acceleration; and so as to Diversion, or varying the direction of the motion. For let the course of the body be never so little changed, this course, in time, may carry it to a place immensely distant from what the other would have carried it to, as is evident enough. And the case is the same still, if the motion that was before was never so slow is wholly stopped; the difference, in time, will be immense; for this slow motion would have carried it to an immense distance, if it were continued.

But the Objector will say, I acknowledge it would be thus, if the bodies, in which these insensible alterations are made, were free, and alone, in an Infinite Void, but I do not know but the case may be far otherwise, when an insensible alteration is made in a body, that is among innumerable others, and subject to infinite jumbles among them.—*Answer*. The case is the same, whether the bodies be alone in a Void, or in a System of other bodies; for the influence of this insensible alteration continues as steadily forever, through all its various interchanges and collisions with other bodies, as it would if it were alone in an Infinite Void: so that in time, a particle of matter, that shall be on this side of the Universe, might have been on the other. The existence and motion of every Atom, has influence, more or less, on the motion of all other bodies in the

Universe, great or small, as is most demonstrable from the Laws of Gravity and Motion. An alteration, more or less, as to motion, is made on every Fixed Star, and on all its Planets, Primary and Secondary. Let the alteration made in the Fixed Stars, be never so small, yet in time it will make an infinite alteration, from what otherwise would have been. Let the Fixed Stars be supposed, for instance, before to have been in perfect rest; let them now be all set in motion, and this motion be never so small, yet, continued forever, where will it carry those most immense bodies, with their Systems[?] Let a little alteration be made in the motion of the Planets, either Retardation or Acceleration; this, in time, will make a difference of many millions of Revolutions: and how great a difference will that make in the floating bodies of the Universe.

Coroll. By this we may answer a more difficult question, viz. If material existence be only mental, then our bodies and organs are ideas only; and then in what sense is it true, that the Mind receives ideas by the Organs of Sense; seeing that that the Organs of Sense, themselves, exist no where but in the Mind?—*Answer.* Seeing our Organs, themselves, are ideas; the connection, that our ideas have with such and such a mode of our Organs, is no other than God's constitution, that some of our ideas shall be connected with others, according to such a settled Law and Order, so that some ideas shall follow from others as their cause.—But how can this be, seeing that ideas most commonly arise from Organs, when we have no idea of the mode of our Organs, or the manner of external objects being applied to them? I answer, Our Organs, and the motions in them and to them, exist in the manner explained above.

A DIVINE AND SUPERNATURAL LIGHT

◇

THIS sermon was preached at Northampton in 1734, and published at the willing expense of his then admiring congregation. It was the second of Edwards' works to appear in print. It is his classic in the serene, calm manner in which he preached many more sermons than he ever did in the vein of terror. The doctrine is not properly to be termed a "mysticism," for Edwards does not permit a direct communication to the mind of truths or propositions; it is rather a translation of the old Puritan theology of regeneration into the language of the "new" psychology, in which the experience of regeneration, being received by sensation, works more upon the "heart" than upon the speculative reasoning of theologians. So while he is emphatically not moving in an "Antinomian" direction, he is taking up what his critics would call a dangerous position by inviting the emotions to assume a larger part in the process of conversion than seventeenth-century Puritans would have allowed.

◇

MATTHEW xvi. 17.—And Jesus answered and said unto him, "Blessed art thou, Simon Barjona: for flesh and blood hath not revealed it unto thee, but my Father which is in heaven."

DOCTRINE

THAT there is such a thing as a Spiritual and Divine Light, immediately imparted to the soul by God, of a different nature from any that is obtained by natural means.

In what I say on this subject, at this time, I would,

I. Show what this divine light is.

II. How it is given immediately by God, and not obtained by natural means.

III. Show the truth of the doctrine.

And then conclude with a brief improvement.

I. I would show what this spiritual and divine light is. And in order to it, would show,

First, In a few things what it is not. And here,

1. Those convictions that natural men may have of their sin and misery, is not this spiritual and divine light. Men in a natural condition may have convictions of the guilt that lies upon them, and of the anger of God, and their danger of divine vengeance. Such convictions are from light or sensibleness of truth. That some sinners have a greater conviction of their guilt and misery than others, is because some have more light or more of an apprehension of truth than others. And this light and conviction may be from the Spirit of God; the Spirit convinces men of sin: but yet nature is much more concerned in it than in the communication of that spiritual and divine light that is spoken of in the doctrine; it is from the Spirit of God only as assisting natural principles, and not as infusing any new principles. Common grace differs from special, in that it influences only by assisting of nature; and not by imparting grace, or bestowing any thing above nature. The light that is obtained is wholly natural, or of no supe-

rior kind to what mere nature attains to, though more of that kind be obtained than would be obtained if men were left wholly to themselves: or, in other words, common grace only assists the faculties of the soul to do that more fully which they do by nature, as natural conscience or reason will, by mere nature, make a man sensible of guilt, and will accuse and condemn him when he has done amiss. Conscience is a principle natural to men; and the work that it doth naturally, or of itself, is to give an apprehension of right and wrong, and to suggest to the mind the relation that there is between right and wrong, and a retribution. The Spirit of God, in those convictions which unregenerate men sometimes have, assists conscience to do this work in a further degree than it would do if they were left to themselves: he helps it against those things that tend to stupify it, and obstruct its exercise. But in the renewing and sanctifying work of the Holy Ghost, those things are wrought in the soul that are above nature, and of which there is nothing of the like kind in the soul by nature; and they are caused to exist in the soul habitually, and according to such a stated constitution or law that lays such a foundation for exercises in a continued course, as is called a principle of nature. Not only are remaining principles assisted to do their work more freely and fully, but those principles are restored that were utterly destroyed by the fall; and the mind thenceforward habitually exerts those acts that the dominion of sin had made it as wholly destitute of, as a dead body is of vital acts.

The Spirit of God acts in a very different manner in the one case, from what he doth in the other. He may indeed act upon the mind of a natural man, but he acts in the mind of a saint as an indwelling vital principle. He acts upon the mind of an unregenerate person as an extrinsic, occasional agent; for in acting upon them, he doth not unite himself to them; for notwithstanding all his influences that they may be the subjects of, they are still sensual, having not the Spirit, Jude 19. But he unites himself with the mind of a saint, takes him for his temple, actuates and influences him as a new supernatural principle of life and action. There is this difference, that the Spirit of God, in acting in the soul of a godly man, exerts and communicates himself there in his own proper nature. Holiness is the proper nature of the Spirit of God. The Holy Spirit operates in the minds of the godly, by uniting himself to them, and living in them, and exerting his own nature in the exercise of their faculties. The Spirit of God may act upon a creature, and yet not in acting communicate himself. The Spirit of God may act upon inanimate creatures; as, the *Spirit moved upon the face of the waters,* in the beginning of the creation; so the Spirit of God may act upon the minds of men many ways, and communicate himself no more than when he acts upon an inanimate creature. For instance, he may excite thoughts in them, may assist their natural reason and understanding, or may assist other natural principles, and this without any union with the soul, but may act, as it were, as upon an external object. But as he acts in his holy influences and spiritual operations, he acts in a way of peculiar communication of himself; so that the subject is thence denominated spiritual.

2. This spiritual and divine light does not consist in any impression made upon the imagination. It is no impression upon the mind, as though one saw any thing with the bodily eyes: it is no imagination or idea of an outward light or glory, or any beauty of form or countenance, or a visible lustre or brightness of any object. The imagination may be strongly impressed with such things; but this is not spiritual light. Indeed when the mind has a lively discovery of spiritual things, and is greatly affected by the power of divine light, it may, and probably very commonly doth, much affect the imagination; so that impressions of an outward beauty or brightness may accompany those spiritual discoveries. But spiritual light is not that impression upon the imagination, but an exceeding different thing from it. Natural men may have lively impressions on their imaginations; and we cannot determine but the devil, who transforms himself into an angel of light, may cause imaginations of an outward beauty, or visible glory, and of sounds and speeches, and other such things; but these are things of a vastly inferior nature to spiritual light.

3. This spiritual light is not the suggesting of any new truths or propositions not contained in the word of God. This suggesting of new truths or doctrines to the mind, independent of any antecedent revelation of those propositions, either in word or writing, is inspiration; such as the prophets and apostles had, and such as some enthusiasts pretend to. But this spiritual light that I am speaking of, is quite a different thing from inspiration: it reveals no new doctrine, it suggests no new proposition to the mind, it teaches no new thing of God, or Christ, or another world, not taught in the Bible, but only gives a due apprehension of those things that are taught in the word of God.

4. It is not every affecting view that men have of the things of religion that is this spiritual

and divine light. Men by mere principles of nature are capable of being affected with things that have a special relation to religion as well as other things. A person by mere nature, for instance, may be liable to be affected with the story of Jesus Christ, and the sufferings he underwent, as well as by any other tragical story: he may be the more affected with it from the interest he conceives mankind to have in it: yea, he may be affected with it without believing it; as well as a man may be affected with what he reads in a romance, or sees acted in a stage play. He may be affected with a lively and eloquent description of many pleasant things that attend the state of the blessed in heaven, as well as his imagination be entertained by a romantic description of the pleasantness of fairy land, or the like. And that common belief of the truth of the things of religion, that persons may have from education or otherwise, may help forward their affection. We read in Scripture of many that were greatly affected with things of a religious nature, who yet are there represented as wholly graceless, and many of them very ill men. A person therefore may have affecting views of the things of religion, and yet be very destitute of spiritual light. Flesh and blood may be the author of this: one man may give another an affecting view of divine things with but common assistance: but God alone can give a spiritual discovery of them.

But I proceed to show,

Secondly, Positively what this spiritual and divine light is.

And it may be thus described: a true sense of the divine excellency of the things revealed in the word of God, and a conviction of the truth and reality of them thence arising.

This spiritual light primarily consists in the former of these, viz., a real sense and apprehension of the divine excellency of things revealed in the word of God. A spiritual and saving conviction of the truth and reality of these things, arises from such a sight of their divine excellency and glory; so that this conviction of their truth is an effect and natural consequence of this sight of their divine glory. There is therefore in this spiritual light[:]

1. A true sense of the divine and superlative excellency of the things of religion; a real sense of the excellency of God and Jesus Christ, and of the work of redemption, and the ways and works of God revealed in the gospel. There is a divine and superlative glory in these things; an excellency that is of a vastly higher kind, and more sublime nature than in other things; a glory greatly distinguishing them from all that is earthly and temporal. He that is spiritually enlightened truly apprehends and sees it, or has a sense of it. He does not merely rationally believe that God is glorious, but he has a sense of the gloriousness of God in his heart. There is not only a rational belief that God is holy, and that holiness is a good thing, but there is a sense of the loveliness of God's holiness. There is not only a speculatively judging that God is gracious, but a sense how amiable God is upon that account, or a sense of the beauty of this divine attribute.

There is a twofold understanding or knowledge of good that God has made the mind of man capable of. The first, that which is merely speculative and notional; as when a person only speculatively judges that any thing is, which, by the agreement of mankind, is called good or excellent, viz., that which is most to general advantage, and between which and a reward there is a suitableness, and the like. And the other is, that which consists in the sense of the heart: as when there is a sense of the beauty, amiableness, or sweetness of a thing; so that the heart is sensible of pleasure and delight in the presence of the idea of it. In the former is exercised merely the speculative faculty, or the understanding, strictly so called, or as spoken of in distinction from the will or disposition of the soul. In the latter, the will, or inclination, or heart, is mainly concerned.

Thus there is a difference between having an opinion, that God is holy and gracious, and having a sense of the loveliness and beauty of that holiness and grace. There is a difference between having a rational judgment that honey is sweet, and having a sense of its sweetness. A man may have the former, that knows not how honey tastes; but a man cannot have the latter unless he has an idea of the taste of honey in his mind. So there is a difference between believing that a person is beautiful, and having a sense of his beauty. The former may be obtained by hearsay, but the latter only by seeing the countenance. There is a wide difference between mere speculative rational judging any thing to be excellent, and having a sense of its sweetness and beauty. The former rests only in the head, speculation only is concerned in it; but the heart is concerned in the latter. When the heart is sensible of the beauty and amiableness of a thing, it necessarily feels pleasure in the apprehension. It is implied in a person's being heartily sensible of the loveliness of a thing, that the idea of it is sweet and pleasant to his soul; which is a far different thing from having a rational opinion that it is excellent.

2. There arises from this sense of divine excellency of things contained in the word of

God, a conviction of the truth and reality of them; and that either directly or indirectly.

First, Indirectly, and that two ways.

1. As the prejudices that are in the heart, against the truth of divine things, are hereby removed; so that the mind becomes susceptive of the due force of rational arguments for their truth. The mind of man is naturally full of prejudices against the truth of divine things: it is full of enmity against the doctrines of the gospel; which is a disadvantage to those arguments that prove their truth, and causes them to lose their force upon the mind. But when a person has discovered to him the divine excellency of Christian doctrines, this destroys the enmity, removes those prejudices, and sanctifies the reason, and causes it to lie open to the force of arguments for their truth.

Hence was the different effect that Christ's miracles had to convince the Scribes and Pharisees. Not that they had a stronger reason, or had their reason more improved; but their reason was sanctified, and those blinding prejudices, that the Scribes and Pharisees were under, were removed by the sense they had of the excellency of Christ and his doctrine.

2. It not only removes the hinderances of reason, but positively helps reason. It makes even the speculative notions the more lively. It engages the attention of the mind, with the more fixedness and intenseness to that kind of objects; which causes it to have a clearer view of them, and enables it more clearly to see their mutual relations, and occasions it to take more notice of them. The ideas themselves that otherwise are dim and obscure, are by this means impressed with the greater strength, and have a light cast upon them; so that the mind can better judge of them. As he that beholds the objects on the face of the earth, when the light of the sun is cast upon them, is under greater advantage to discern them in their true forms and mutual relations, than he that sees them in a dim starlight or twilight.

The mind having a sensibleness of the excellency of divine objects, dwells upon them with delight; and the powers of the soul are more awakened and enlivened to employ themselves in the contemplation of them, and exert themselves more fully and much more to the purpose. The beauty and sweetness of the objects draws on the faculties, and draws forth their exercises: so that reason itself is under far greater advantages for its proper and free exercises, and to attain its proper end, free of darkness and delusion.

But,

Secondly. A true sense of the divine excellency of the things of God's word doth more directly and immediately convince of the truth of them; and that because the excellency of these things is so superlative. There is a beauty in them that is so divine and godlike, that is greatly and evidently distinguishing of them from things merely human, or that men are the inventors and authors of; a glory that is so high and great, that when clearly seen, commands assent to their divinity and reality. When there is an actual and lively discovery of this beauty and excellency, it will not allow of any such thought as that it is a human work, or the fruit of men's invention. This evidence that they that are spiritually enlightened have of the truth of the things of religion, is a kind of intuitive and immediate evidence. They believe the doctrines of God's word to be divine, because they see divinity in them; i.e., they see a divine, and transcendent, and most evidently distinguishing glory in them; such a glory as, if clearly seen, does not leave room to doubt of their being of God, and not of men.

Such a conviction of the truth of religion as this, arising, these ways, from a sense of the divine excellency of them, is that true spiritual conviction that there is in saving faith. And this original of it, is that by which it is most essentially distinguished from that common assent, which unregenerate men are capable of.

II. I proceed now to the second thing proposed, viz., to show how this light is immediately given by God, and not obtained by natural means. And here,

1. It is not intended that the natural faculties are not made use of in it. The natural faculties are the subject of this light: and they are the subject in such a manner, that they are not merely passive, but active in it; the acts and exercises of man's understanding are concerned and made use of in it. God, in letting in this light into the soul, deals with man according to his nature, or as a rational creature; and makes use of his human faculties. But yet this light is not the less immediately from God for that; though the faculties are made use of, it is as the subject and not as the cause; and that acting of the faculties in it, is not the cause, but is either implied in the thing itself (in the light that is imparted) or is the consequence of it. As the use that we make of our eyes in beholding various objects, when the sun arises, is not the cause of the light that discovers those objects to us.

2. It is not intended that outward means have no concern in this affair. As I have observed already, it is not in this affair, as it is in inspiration,

where new truths are suggested: for here is by this light only given a due apprehension of the same truths that are revealed in the word of God; and therefore it is not given without the word. The gospel is made use of in this affair: this light is the light of the glorious gospel of Christ, 2 Cor. iv. 4. The gospel is as glass, by which this light is conveyed to us 1 Cor. xiii. 12. Now we see through a glass.—But,

3. When it is said that this light is given immediately by God, and not obtained by natural means, hereby is intended, that it is given by God without making use of any means that operate by their own power, or a natural force. God makes use of means; but it is not as mediate causes to produce this effect. There are not truly any second causes of it; but it is produced by God immediately. The word of God is no proper cause of this effect: it does not operate by any natural force in it. The word of God is only made use of to convey to the mind the subject matter of this saving instruction; and this indeed it doth convey to us by natural force or influence. It conveys to our minds these and those doctrines; it is the cause of the notion of them in our heads, but not of the sense of the divine excellency of them in our hearts. Indeed a person cannot have spiritual light without the word. But that does not argue, that the word properly causes that light. The mind cannot see the excellency of any doctrine, unless that doctrine be first in the mind; but the seeing of the excellency of the doctrine may be immediately from the Spirit of God; though the conveying of the doctrine or proposition itself may be by the word. So that the notions that are the subject matter of this light, are conveyed to the mind by the word of God; but that due sense of the heart, wherein this light formally consists, is immediately by the Spirit of God. As for instance, that notion that there is a Christ, and that Christ is holy and gracious, is conveyed to the mind by the word of God: but the sense of the excellency of Christ by reason of that holiness and grace, is nevertheless immediately the work of the Holy Spirit.

THE FUTURE PUNISHMENT OF THE WICKED UNAVOIDABLE AND INTOLERABLE

◇

¶ THIS "Terror" sermon was delivered in April, 1741, three months before the more famous (or rather, more notorious!) "Sinners in the Hands of an Angry God." Though the latter is indubitably the masterpiece in this sort of literature, and therefore has been widely reprinted, this one is perhaps a better example of the usual devices of rhetoric Edwards employed in order to make language (which according to John Locke was an arbitrary construction and so could bear no organic relation to the objects it described) serve as a "sensational" experience. The carefully constructed paragraph leading the imagination of his trembling audience from fifteen minutes through an hour, a day, a year, into eternity is a fine example of his implacable artistry.

◇

EZEKIEL xxii. 14.—Can thine heart endure, or can thine hands be strong in the days that I shall deal with thee? I the Lord have spoken it, and will do it. . . .

DOCTRINE

SINCE God hath undertaken to deal with impenitent sinners, they shall neither shun the threatened misery, nor deliver themselves out of it, nor can they bear it. . . .

I shall show what is implied in God's undertaking to deal with impenitent sinners. Others are not able to deal with them. They baffle all the means used with them by those that are appointed to teach and to rule over them. They will not yield to parents, or to the counsels, warnings, or reproofs of ministers: they prove obstinate and stiff-hearted. Therefore God undertakes to deal with them. This implies the following things:

1. That God will reckon with them, and take of them satisfaction to his justice. In this world God puts forth his authority to command them; and to require subjection to him. In his commands he is very positive, strictly requiring of them the performance of such and such duties, and as positively forbidding such and such things which were contrary to their duty. But they have no regard to these commands. God continues com-

manding, and they continue rebelling. They make nothing of God's authority. God threatens, but they despise his threatening. They make nothing of dishonoring God; they care not how much their behavior is to the dishonor of God. He offers them mercy, if they will repent and return. Thus they are continually plunging themselves deeper and deeper in debt, and at the same time imagine they shall escape the payment of the debt, and design entirely to rob God of his due.

But God hath undertaken to right himself. He will reckon with them; he hath undertaken to see that the debts due to him are paid. All their sins are written in his book; not one of them is forgotten, and every one must must be paid. . . .

4. God hath undertaken to rectify their judgments. Now they will not be convinced of those things which God tells them in his word. Ministers take much pains to convince them, but all is in vain. Therefore God will undertake to convince them, and he will do it effectually. Now they will not be convinced of the truth of divine things. They have indeed convincing arguments set before them; they hear and see enough to convince them; yet so prone are they to unbelief and atheism, that divine things never seem to them to be real. But God will hereafter make them seem real. . . .

Impenitent sinners, while in this world, hear how dreadful hell is. But they will not believe that it is so dreadful as ministers represent. They cannot think that they shall to all eternity suffer such exquisite and horrible torments. But they shall be taught and convinced to purpose, that the representations ministers give of those torments, agreeable to the word of God, are no bugbears; and that the wrath of God is indeed as dreadful as they declare. Since God hath undertaken to deal with sinners, and to rectify their judgments in these matters, he will do it thoroughly; for his work is perfect; when he undertakes to do things, he doth not do them by halves; therefore before he shall have done with sinners, he will convince them effectually, so that they shall never be in danger of relapsing into their former errors any more. He will convince them of their folly and stupidity in entertaining such notions as they now entertain. . . .

I come now,

To show, that therefore impenitent sinners shall not avoid their due punishment. God hath undertaken to inflict it; he hath engaged to do it; he takes it as his work, as what properly belongs to him, and we may expect it of him. If he hath sworn by his life, that he will do it; and if he hath power sufficient; if he is the living God, doubtless we shall see it done. . . .

No; let no impenitent sinner flatter himself so vainly and foolishly. If it were indeed only a man, a being of like impotency and mutability with themselves, who had undertaken to deal with them, they might perhaps with some reason flatter themselves, that they should find some means to avoid the threatened punishment. But since an omniscient, omnipotent, immutable God hath undertaken, vain are all such hopes.

There is no hope that possibly they may steal away to heaven, though they die unconverted. There is no hope that they can deceive God by any false show of repentance and faith, and so be taken to heaven through mistake; for the eyes of God are as a flame of fire; they perfectly see through every man; the inmost closet of the heart is all open to him.

There is no hope of escaping the threatened punishment by sinking into nothing at death, like brute creatures. Indeed, many wicked men upon their deathbeds wish for this. If it were so, death would be nothing to them in comparison with what it now is. But all such wishes are vain.

There is no hope of their escaping without notice, when they leave the body. There is no hope that God, by reason of the multiplicity of affairs which he hath to mind, will happen to overlook them, and not take notice of them, when they come to die; and so that their souls will slip away privately, and hide themselves in some secret corner, and so escape divine vengeance.

There is no hope that they shall be missed in a crowd at the day of judgment, and that they can have opportunity to hide themselves in some cave or den of the mountains, or in any secret hole of the earth; and that while so doing, they will not be minded, by reason of the many things which will be the objects of attention on that day. Neither is there any hope that they will be able to crowd themselves in among the multitude of the saints at the right hand of the Judge, and so go to heaven undiscovered. Nor is there any hope that God will alter his mind, or that he will repent of what he hath said; for he is not the son of man that he should repent. Hath he said, and shall he not do it? Hath he spoken, and shall he not make it good? When did God ever undertake to do any thing and fail? . . .

I come now,

To show, that neither will they be able to bear it. Neither will their hands be strong to deliver themselves from it, nor will their hearts be able to endure it. It is common with men, when they meet with calamities in this world, in the first place to endeavor to shun them. But if they find, that they cannot shun them, then after they are come, they endeavor to deliver themselves from them as soon as they can; or at least, to order things so, as to deliver themselves in some degree. But if they find that they can by no means deliver themselves, and see that the case is so that they must bear them; then they set themselves to bear them: they fortify their spirits, and take up a resolution, that they will support themselves under them as well as they can. They clothe themselves with all the resolution and courage they are masters of, to keep their spirits from sinking under their calamities.

But it will be utterly in vain for impenitent sinners to think to do thus with respect to the torments of hell. They will not be able to endure them, or at all to support themselves under them: the torment will be immensely beyond their strength. What will it signify for a worm, which is about to be pressed under the weight of some great rock, to be let fall with its whole weight upon it, to collect its strength, to set itself to bear up the weight of the rock, and to preserve itself from being crushed by it? Much more in vain will it be for a poor damned soul, to endeavor to support itself under the weight of the wrath of Almighty God. What is the strength of man, who is but a worm, to support himself against the power of Jehovah, and against the fierceness of his wrath? What is man's strength, when set to bear up against the exertions of infinite power? Matt. xxi. 44: "Whosoever shall fall on this stone shall be broken; but on whomsoever it shall fall, it will grind him to powder." . . .

I come now as was proposed,

To answer an inquiry which may naturally be raised concerning these things.

INQUIRY. Some may be ready to say, "If this be the case, if impenitent sinners can neither shun future punishment, nor deliver themselves from it, nor bear it; then what will become of them?"

ANSWER. They will wholly sink down into eternal death. There will be that sinking of heart, of which we now cannot conceive. We see how it is with the body in extreme pain. The nature of the body will support itself for a considerable time under very great pain, so as to keep from wholly sinking. There will be great struggles, lamentable groans and panting, and it may be convulsions. These are the strugglings of nature to support itself under the extremity of the pain. There is, as it were, a great lothness in nature to yield to it; it cannot bear wholly to sink.

But yet sometimes pain of body is so very extreme and exquisite, that the nature of the body cannot support itself under it; however loth it may be to sink, yet it cannot bear the pain; there are a few struggles, and throes, and pantings, and it may be a shriek or two, and then nature yields to the violence of the torments, sinks down, and the body dies. This is the death of the body. So it will be with the soul in hell; it will have no strength or power to deliver itself; and its torment and horror will be so great, so mighty, so vastly disproportioned to its strength, that having no strength in the least to support itself, although it be infinitely contrary to the nature and inclination of the soul utterly to sink; yet it will sink, it will utterly and totally sink, without the least degree of remaining comfort, or strength, or courage, or hope. And though it will never be annihilated, its being and perception will never be abolished; yet such will be the infinite depth of gloominess that it will sink into, that it will be a state of death, eternal death.

The nature of man desires happiness; it is the nature of the soul to crave and thirst after well-being; and if it be under misery, it eagerly pants after relief; and the greater the misery is, the more eagerly doth it struggle for help. But if all relief be withholden, all strength overborne, all support utterly gone; then it sinks into the darkness of death.

We can conceive but little of the matter; we cannot conceive what that sinking of the soul in such a case is. But to help your conception, imagine yourself to be cast into a fiery oven, all of a glowing heat, or into the midst of a glowing brick-kiln, or of a great furnace, where your pain would be as much greater than that occasioned by accidentally touching a coal of fire, as the heat is greater. Imagine also that your body were to lie there for a quarter of an hour, full of fire, as full within and without as a bright coal of fire, all the while full of quick sense. What horror would you feel at the entrance of such a furnace! And how long would that quarter of an hour seem to you! If it were to be measured by a glass, how long would the glass seem to be running! And after you had endured it for one minute, how overbearing would it be to you to think that you had it to endure the other fourteen!

But what would be the effect on your soul, if you knew you must lie there enduring that torment to the full for twenty-four hours! And how much greater would be the effect, if you knew you must endure it for a whole year; and how vastly greater still, if you knew you must endure it for a thousand years! O then, how would your heart sink, if you thought, if you knew, that you must bear it forever and ever! That there would be no end! That after millions of millions of ages, your torment would be no nearer to an end, than ever it was; and that you never, never should be delivered!

But your torment in hell will be immensely greater than this illustration represents. How then will the heart of a poor creature sink under it! How utterly inexpressible and inconceivable must the sinking of the soul be in such a case!

This is the death threatened in the law. This is dying in the highest sense of the word. This is to die sensibly; to die and know it; to be sensible of the gloom of death. This is to be undone; this is worthy of the name of destruction. This sinking of the soul under an infinite weight, which it cannot bear, is the gloom of hell. We read in Scripture of sinners being lost, and of their losing their souls: this is the thing intended; this is to lose the soul: they that are the subjects of this are truly lost.

APPLICATION.

THIS subject may be applied in a use of *awakening* to impenitent sinners. What hath been said under this doctrine is for thee, O impenitent sinner, O poor wretch, who art in the same miserable state in which thou camest into the world, excepting that thou art loaded with vastly greater guilt by thine actual sins. These dreadful things which thou hast heard are for thee, who art yet unconverted, and still remainest an alien and stranger, without Christ and without God in the world. They are for thee, who to this day remainest an enemy to God, and a child of the devil, even in this remarkable season, when others both here and elsewhere, far and near, are flocking to Christ; for thee who hearest the noise, the fame of these things, but knowest nothing of the power of godliness in thine own heart.

Whoever thou art, whether young or old, little or great, if thou art in a Christless, unconverted state, this is the wrath, this is the death to which thou art condemned. This is the wrath that abideth on thee; this is the hell over which thou hangest, and into which thou art ready to drop every day and every night. . . .

Doth it seem to thee incredible, that God should be so utterly regardless of the sinner's welfare, as so to sink him into an infinite abyss of misery? Is this shocking to thee? And is it not at all shocking to thee, that thou shouldst be so utterly regardless as thou hast been of the honor and glory of the infinite God?

It arises from thy foolish stupidity and senselessness, and is because thou hast a heart of stone, that thou art so senseless of thine own wickedness as to think thou hast not deserved such a punishment, and that it is to thee incredible that it will be inflicted upon thee.—But if, when all is said and done thou be not convinced, wait but a little while, and thou wilt be convinced: God will undertake to do the work which ministers cannot do. Though judgement against thine evil works be not yet executed, and God now let thee alone, yet he will soon come upon thee with his great power, and then thou shalt know what God is, and what thou art.

Flatter not thyself, that if these things shall prove true, and the worst shall come, thou wilt set thyself to bear it as well as thou canst. What will it signify to set thyself to bear, and to collect thy strength to support thyself, when thou shalt fall into the hands of that omnipotent King, Jehovah? He that made thee, can make his sword approach unto thee. His sword is not the sword of man, nor is his wrath the wrath of man. If it were, possibly stoutness might be maintained under it. But it is the fierceness of the wrath of the great God, who is able to baffle and dissipate all thy strength in a moment. He can fill thy poor soul with an ocean of wrath, a deluge of fire and brimstone; or he can make it ten thousand times fuller of torment then ever an oven was full of fire; and at the same time, can fill it with despair of ever seeing any end to its torment, or any rest from its misery: and then where will be thy strength? What will become of thy courage then? What will signify thine attempts to bear? . . .

If the strength of all the wicked men on earth, and of all the devils in hell, were united in one, and thou wert possessed of it all; and if the courage, greatness, and stoutness of all their hearts were united in thy single heart, thou wouldst be nothing in the hands of Jehovah. If it were all collected, and thou shouldst set thyself to bear as well as thou couldst, all would sink under his great wrath in an instant, and would be utterly abolished: thine hands would drop down at once and thine heart would melt as wax.—The great mountains, the firm rocks, cannot stand before the power of God; as fast as they stand, they are tossed hither and thither, and skip like lambs, when God appears in his anger. He can tear the earth in pieces in a moment; yea, he can shatter the whole universe, and dash it to pieces at one blow. How then will thine hands be strong, or thine heart endure? . . .

Some of you have seen buildings on fire; imagine therefore with yourselves, what a poor hand you would make at fighting with the flames, if you were in the midst of so great and fierce a fire. You have often seen a spider, or some other noisome insect, when thrown into the midst of a fierce fire, and have observed how immediately it yields to the force of the flames. There is no long struggle, no fighting against the fire, no strength exerted to oppose the heat, or to fly from it; but it immediately stretches forth itself and yields; and the fire takes possession of it, and at once it becomes full of fire; and is burned into a bright coal.—Here is a little image of what you will be the subjects of in hell, except you repent and fly to Christ. However you may think that you will fortify yourselves, and bear as well as you can; the first moment you shall be cast into hell, all your strength will sink and be utterly abolished. To encourage yourselves, that you will set yourself to bear hell torments as well as you can, is just as if a worm, that is about to be thrown into a glowing furnace, should swell and fortify itself, and prepare itself to fight the flames. . . .

It is probable that here are some, who hear me this day, who at this very moment are unawakened, and are in a great degree careless about their souls. I fear there are some among us who are most fearfully hardened: their hearts are harder than the very rocks. It is easier to make impressions upon an adamant than upon their hearts. I suppose some of you have heard all that I have said with ease and quietness: it appears to you as great big sounding words, but doth not reach your hearts. You have heard such things many times: you are old soldiers, and have been too much used to the roaring of heaven's cannon, to be frighted at it. It will therefore probably be in vain for me to say any thing further to you; I will only put you in mind that erelong God will deal with you. I cannot deal with you, you despise what I say; I have no power to make you sensible of your danger and misery, and of the dreadfulness of the wrath of God. The attempts of men in this way have often proved vain.

However, God hath undertaken to deal with such men as you are. It is his manner commonly first to let men try their utmost strength: particularly to let ministers try, that thus he may show ministers their own weakness and impotency; and when they have done what they can, and all fails, then God takes the matter into his own hands. So it seems by your obstinacy, as if God intended to undertake to deal with you. He will undertake to subdue you; he will see if he cannot cure you of your senselessness and regardlessness of his threatenings. And you will be convinced; you will be subdued effectually; your hearts will be broken with a witness; your strength will be utterly broken, your courage and hope will sink. God will surely break those who will not bow. God having girded himself with his power and wrath, hath heretofore undertaken to deal with many hard, stubborn, senseless, obstinate hearts; and he never failed, he always did his work thoroughly.

It will not be long before you will be wonderfully changed. You who now hear of hell and the wrath of the great God, and sit here in these seats so easy and quiet and go away so careless; by and by will shake, and tremble, and cry out, and shriek, and gnash your teeth, and will be thoroughly convinced of the vast weight and importance of these great things, which you now despise. You will not then need to hear sermons in order to make you sensible; you will be at a sufficient distance from slighting that wrath and power of God, of which you now hear with so much quietness and indifference.

FROM

THOUGHTS ON THE REVIVAL OF RELIGION IN NEW ENGLAND

◇

¶ WHEN the full fury of the Great Awakening broke upon the land, Edwards was supremely confident that he knew the difference between an authentic experience of divine grace and a simulated one. By the second summer of the outburst, 1741, as it was producing more and more extravagant and noisy demonstrations, those who objected to the violent methods (and in 1740 had not dared speak out) gathered courage and commenced to denounce the whole affair as a hysteria cunningly fomented by such preaching as Edwards' use of terror. Edwards delivered his first defense of the Awakening in a long sermon at Yale on September 10, 1741, which was published as *The Distinguishing Marks of A Work of the Spirit of God*. His confidence was not yet even shaken, and he could enumerate the signs and manifestations of a true work of the spirit so readily as to appear almost (for him) glib. By the next year he was beginning to wonder, and the attacks of the opponents were pressing him hard. He undertook a longer and more carefully considered exposition, from which this section, pleading that the division be not allowed to become irrevocable, is taken. The horrible prospect was opening before him: despite his dialectical ingenuity in uniting heart and head, the impact of the Awakening was threatening to sunder New England piety so deeply (into an emotionalism on the one hand and a rationalism on the other) that the solidity of the faith would be forever lost. Charles Chauncy's *Seasonable Thoughts on the State of Religion* was a direct and snarling reply of the rationalists (in Edwards' terminology, the "Arminians") which widened the separation, left Edwards isolated between them and the extreme revivalists, and insured that eventually he should be deserted even by his own people, as came about in 1750.

◇

. . . Upon the whole it appears manifest to me, that things have as yet never been set a going in their right channel; if they had, and means had been blessed in proportion as they have been now, this work would so have prevailed, as before this time to have carried all before it, and have triumphed over New England as its conquest.

The devil, in driving things to these extremes, besides the present hinderance of the work of God, has, I believe, had in view a twofold mischief hereafter, in the issue of things; one with respect to those that are more cold in religion; to carry things to such an extreme, that people in general, at length, having their eyes opened, by the great excesses, and seeing that things must needs be wrong, he might take the advantage to tempt them entirely to reject the whole work, as being all nothing but delusion and distraction. And another is with respect to those that have been very warm and zealous, of God's own children, that have been out of the way, to sink them down in unbelief and darkness. The time is coming, I doubt not, when the bigger part of them will be convinced of their errors; and then probably the devil will take advantage to lead them into a dreadful wilderness, and to puzzle and confound them about their own experiences, and the experiences of others; and to make them to doubt of many things that they ought not to doubt of, and even to tempt them with atheistical thoughts. I believe if all true Christians all over the land, should now at once have their eyes opened, fully to see all their errors, it would seem for the present to damp religion; the dark thoughts, that it would at first be an occasion of, and the inward doubts, difficulties, and conflicts that would rise in their souls, would deaden their lively affections and joys, and would cause an appearance of a present decay of religion. But yet it would do God's saints great good in their latter end; it would fit them for more spiritual joys, and would greatly tend to a more powerful, extensive, and durable prevalence of vital piety.

I do not know but we shall be in danger by and by, after our eyes are fully opened to see our errors, to go to contrary extremes. The devil has driven the pendulum far beyond its proper point of rest; and when he has carried it to the utmost length that he can, and it begins by its own weight to swing back, he probably will set in, and drive it with the utmost fury the other way; and so give us no rest: and if possible prevent our settling in a proper medium. What poor, blind, weak, and miserable creature is man, at his estate! We are like poor helpless sheep; the devil is too subtle for us; what is our strength! What is our wisdom! How ready arc we to go astray! How easily are we drawn aside, into innumerable snares, while we in the meantime are bold and confident, and doubt not that we are right and safe! We are foolish sheep, in the midst of subtle serpents and cruel wolves, and do not know it. Oh! how unfit are we to be left to ourselves! and how much do we stand in need of the wisdom, the power, the condescension, patience, forgiveness, and gentleness of our good Shepherd! . . .

And in order to this, there must be a great deal done at confessing of faults on both sides: for undoubtedly many and great faults that have been committed, in the jangling and confusions, and mixtures of light and darkness, that have been of late. There is hardly any duty more contrary to our corrupt dispositions, and mortifying to the pride of man; but it must be done. . . .

Contrary to this mutual meekness, is each party's stigmatizing one another with odious names; as is done in many parts of New England: which tends greatly to widen and perpetuate the breach. Such distinguishing names of reproach, do as it were divide us into two armies, separated, and drawn up in battle array, ready to fight one with another; which greatly hinders the work of God. . . .

Thus I have (I hope, by the help of God) finished what I proposed. I have taken the more pains in it, because it appears to me, that God is giving us the most happy season to attempt a universal reformation, that ever was given in New England. And it is a thousand pities, that we should fail of that which would be so glorious, for want of being sensible of our opportunity, or being aware of those things that tend to hinder it, or our taking improper courses to obtain it, or not being sensible in what way God expects we should seek it. It should please God to bless any means for the convincing the country of His hand in this work, and bringing them fully and freely to acknowledge His glorious power and grace in it, and engage with one heart and soul, by due methods, to endeavor to promote it, it would be a dispensation of divine providence, that would have a most glorious aspect, happily signifying the approach of great and glorious things to the church of God, and justly causing us to hope that Christ would speedily come, to set up his kingdom of light, holiness, peace and joy on earth, as is foretold in His word. Amen: even so come Lord Jesus!

FROM

A TREATISE CONCERNING RELIGIOUS AFFECTIONS

◊

BY THE autumn of 1742 it was everywhere evident in New England that the Great Awakening was dead. There was no longer any point in Edwards' defending the revival. Either he had to admit defeat and conduct a post-mortem, or else mobilize all his logical power and psychological acumen to make forever clear precisely wherein the difference consists between the one genuine religious insight and all subtle but unredeemably "natural" simulations. Because the opposition had now settled on the line that the revival had been nothing but a riot of emotions and lusts, Edwards resolved to put them right on the heart of the matter, which was the nature of religious emotion. He gave the substance of his argument as a series of sermons during the winter of 1742–43. He worked these into a sustained treatise and had it published in Boston, 1746. It was soon reprinted in England and Scotland, and remains a pioneer analysis of religious psychology, somehow wonderfully meaningful today even though the Lockean psychology on which he depended seems, to modern students of the mind, pathetically crude. The profundity of Edwards' conviction, the depths of his own passionate nature, and the rigor with which he subjected that passion to the control of an almost inhuman orderliness, meant that he could soar with his sensational apparatus to heights no other sensationalist—or we might say "behaviorist"—has ever attained.

◊

I. PETER I: 8: *Whom having not seen, ye love: in whom, though now ye see him not, yet believing, ye rejoice with joy unspeakable, and full of glory. . . .*

THE proposition or doctrine, that I would raise from these words is this,

DOCTRINE. True religion, in great part, consists in holy affections. . . .

It may be inquired, what the affections of the mind are?

I answer, the affections are no other than the vigorous and sensible exercises of the inclination and will of the soul.

God has indued the soul with two faculties: one is that by which it is capable of perception and speculation, or by which it discerns and views and judges of things; which is called the understanding. The other faculty is that by which the soul does not merely perceive and view things, but is some way inclined with respect to the things it views or considers; either is inclined to 'em, or is disinclined, and averse from 'em; or is the faculty by which the soul does not behold things, as an indifferent unaffected spectator, but either as liking or disliking, pleased or displeased, approving or rejecting. This faculty is called by various names: it is sometimes called the *inclination:* and, as it has respect to the actions that are determined and governed by it, is called the *will:* and the *mind,* with regard to the exercise of this faculty, is often called the *heart.*

The exercises of this faculty are of two sorts; either those by which the soul is carried out towards the things that are in view, in approving of them, being pleased with them, and inclined to them; or those in which the soul opposes the things that are in view, in disapproving them, and in being displeased with them, averse from them, and rejecting them.

And as the exercises of the inclination and will of the soul are various in their kinds, so they are much more various in their degrees. There are some exercises of pleasedness or displeasedness, inclination or disinclination, wherein the soul is carried but a little beyond a state of perfect indifference. And there are other degrees above this, wherein the approbation or dislike, pleasedness or aversion, are stronger; wherein we may rise higher and higher, till the soul comes to act vigorously and sensibly, and the actings of the soul are with that strength that (through the laws of the union which the Creator has fixed between soul and body) the motion of the blood and animal spirits begins to be sensibly altered; whence oftentimes arises some bodily sensation, especially about the heart and vitals, that are the fountain of the fluids of the body: from whence it comes to pass, that the mind, with regard to the exercises of this faculty, perhaps in all nations and ages, is called the *heart.* And it is to be noted, that they are these more vigorous and sensible exercises of this faculty, that are called *affections.*

The will, and the affections of the soul, are not

two faculties; the affections are not essentially distinct from the will, nor do they differ from the mere actings of the will and inclination of the soul, but only in the liveliness and sensibleness of exercise.[1] . . .

The Author of the human nature has not only given affections to men, but has made 'em very much the spring of men's actions. As the affections do not only necessarily belong to the human nature, but are a very great part of it; so (inasmuch as by regeneration, persons are renewed in the whole man, and sanctified throughout) holy affections do not only necessarily belong to true religion, but are a very great part of that. And as true religion is of a practical nature, and God has so constituted the human nature, that the affections are very much the spring of men's actions, this also shows, that true religion must consist very much in the affections.

Such is man's nature, that he is very inactive, any otherwise than he is influenced by some affection, either love or hatred, desire, hope, fear or some other. These affections we see to be the springs that set men agoing, in all the affairs, of life, and engage them in all their pursuits: these are the things that put men forward, and carry 'em along, in all their worldly business; and especially are men excited and animated by these, in all affairs, wherein they are earnestly engaged, and which they pursue with vigor. We see the world of mankind to be exceedingly busy and active; and the affections of men are the springs of the motion: take away all love and hatred, all hope and fear, all anger, zeal and affectionate desire, and the world would be, in a great measure, motionless and dead; there would be no such thing as activity amongst mankind, or any earnest pursuit whatsoever. 'Tis affection that engages the covetous man, and him that is greedy of worldly profits, in his pursuits; and it is by the affection, that the ambitious man is put forward in his pursuit of worldly glory; and 'tis the affections also that actuate the voluptuous man, in his pursuit of pleasure and sensual delights: the world continues, from age to age, in a continual commotion and agitation, in a pursuit of these things; but take away all affection, and the spring of all this motion would be gone, and the motion itself cease. And as in worldly things, worldly affections are very much the spring of men's motion and action; so in religious matters, the spring of their actions are very much religious affections: he that has doctrinal knowledge and speculation only, without affection, never is engaged in the business of religion.

Nothing is more manifest in fact, than that the things of religion take hold of men's souls, no further than they affect them. There are multitudes that often hear the Word of God, and therein hear of those things that are infinitely great and important, and that most nearly concern them, and all that is heard seems to be wholly ineffectual upon them, and to make no alteration in their disposition or behavior; and the reason is, they are not affected with what they hear. There are many that often hear of the glorious perfections of God, his almighty power, and boundless wisdom, his infinite majesty, and that holiness of God, by which he is of purer eyes than to behold evil, and cannot look on iniquity, and the heavens are not pure in his sight, and of God's infinite goodness and mercy, and hear of the great works of God's wisdom, power, and Goodness, wherein there appear the admirable manifestations of these perfections; they hear particularly of the unspeakable love of God and Christ, and of the great things that Christ has done and suffered, and of the great things of another world, of eternal misery, in bearing the fierceness and wrath of Almighty God, and of endless blessedness and glory in the presence of God, and the enjoyment of his dear love; they also hear the peremptory commands of God, and his gracious counsels and warnings, and the sweet invitation of the gospel; I say hear these things, and yet remain as they were before, with no sensible alteration on them, either in heart or practice, because they are not affected. I am bold to assert, that there never was any considerable change wrought in the mind or conversation of any one person, by anything of a religious nature, that ever he read, heard or saw, that had not affections moved. Never was a natural man engaged earnestly to seek his salvation: never were any such brought to cry after wisdom, and lift up their voice for understanding, and to wrestle with God in prayer for mercy; and never was one humbled,

A TREATISE CONCERNING RELIGIOUS AFFECTIONS. **1. sensibleness of exercise:** The radical innovation in Edwards' formulation of his psychological premises was this deceptively calm assertion that the affections are not distinct from the will. For centuries Christian thinking had assumed that the affections were responses to things, most of them external, which affected a man; but they were under the rule of his will—or rather should have been under that rule but had escaped its control as a result of the Fall of Adam. Hence the "Arminian" tendency, as Edwards saw it, came in the form of a constant lecturing the people to control, by will power, their lusts. By his identification of the so-called will with the affections, by defining these as actings of the will, Edwards sought to cut the ground from under the feet of his opponents. They refused to be convinced, went on talking of a reason which informs the will which in turn subdues the affections, and so never caught even a glimpse of Edwards' magnificent humanism.

and brought to the foot of God, from anything that ever he heard or imagined of his own unworthiness and deservings of God's displeasure; nor was ever one induced to fly for refuge unto Christ, while his heart remained unaffected. Nor was there ever a saint awakened out of a cold, lifeless frame, or recovered from a declining state in religion, and brought back from a lamentable departure from God, without having his heart affected. And in a word, there never was anything considerable brought to pass in the heart or life of any man living, by the things of religion, that had not his heart deeply affected by those things. . . .

. . . .

I come now to the second thing appertaining to the trial of religious affection, which was proposed, viz. to take notice of some things wherein those affections that are spiritual and gracious, do differ from those that are not so. . . .

I. Affections that are truly spiritual and gracious, do arise from those influences and operations on the heart, which are *spiritual, supernatural* and *divine*.

I will explain what I mean by these terms, whence will appear their use to distinguish between those affections which are spiritual, and those which are not so.

We find that true saints, or persons who are sanctified by the Spirit of God, are in the New Testament called spiritual persons. And their being spiritual is spoken of as their peculiar character, and that wherein they are distinguished from those who are not sanctified. This is evident because those who are spiritual are set in opposition to natural men, and carnal men. Thus the spiritual man, and the natural man, are set in opposition one to another; "The natural man receiveth not the things of the Spirit of God, for they are foolishness unto him; neither can he know them; because they are spiritually discerned. But he that is spiritual judgeth all things" (I Cor. 2:14–15). The Scripture explains itself to mean an ungodly man, or one that has no grace, by a natural man: thus the apostle Jude, speaking of certain ungodly men, that had crept in unawares among the saints, ver. 4 of his Epistle, says, ver. 19: "These are sensual, having not the Spirit." This the Apostle gives as a reason why they behaved themselves in such a wicked manner as he had described. Here the word translated "sensual," in the original is ψυκικοι; which is the very same, which in those verses in I Cor. ch. 2 is translated "natural." In the like manner, in the continuation of the same discourse, in the next verse but one, spiritual men are opposed to carnal men: which the connection plainly shows mean the same, as spiritual men and natural men, in the foregoing verses; "and I, brethren, could not speak unto you, as unto spiritual, but as unto carnal;" i.e. as in a great measure unsanctified. That by carnal the Apostle means corrupt and unsanctified, is abundantly evident, by Rom. 7:25 and 8:1, 4–9, 12, 13; Gal. 5:16 to the end; cf. Col. 2:18. Now therefore, if by natural and carnal, in these texts, he intended "unsanctified;" then doubtless by spiritual, which is opposed thereto, is meant "sanctified" and gracious. . . .

From these things it is evident, that those gracious influences which the saints are subjects of, and the effects of God's Spirit which they experience, are entirely above nature, altogether of a different kind from anything that men find within themselves by nature, or only in the exercise of natural principles; and are things which no improvement of those qualifications, or principles that are natural, no advancing or exalting them to higher degrees, and no kind of composition of them, will ever bring men to; because they not only differ from what is natural, and from everything that natural men experience, in degree and circumstances; but also in kind; and are of a nature vastly more excellent. And this is what I mean by supernatural, when I say, that gracious affections are from those influences that are supernatural.

From hence it follows, that in those gracious exercises and affections which are wrought in the minds of the saints, through the saving influences of the Spirit of God, there is a new inward perception or sensation of their minds, entirely different in its nature and kind, from anything that ever their minds were the subjects of before they were sanctified. For doubtless if God by his mighty power produces something that is new, not only in degree and circumstances, but in its whole nature, and that which could be produced by no exalting, varying or compounding of what was there before, or by adding anything of the like kind; I say, if God produces something thus new in a mind, that is a perceiving, thinking, conscious thing; then doubtless something entirely new is felt, or perceived, or thought; or, which is the same thing, there is some new sensation or perception of the mind, which is entirely of a new sort, and which could be produced by no exalting, varying or compounding of that kind of perceptions or sensations which the mind had before; or there is what some metaphysicians call a new simple idea. If grace be, in the sense above described, an entirely new kind of principle; then the exercises of it are also entirely a new kind of exercises. And if there be in the soul a new sort of exercises which it is conscious of, which the soul knew nothing of before, and which no improvement, composition or management of what it was before conscious or sensible of, could produce, or anything like it; then it follows that the mind has an entirely new kind of perception or sensation; and here is, as it were, a new spiritual sense that the mind has, or a principle of new kind of perception or spiritual sensation, which is in its whole nature different from any former kinds of sensation of the mind, as tasting is diverse from any of the other senses; and something is perceived by a true saint, in the exercise of this new sense of mind, in spiritual and divine things, as entirely diverse from anything that is perceived in them, by natural men, as the sweet taste of honey is diverse from the ideas men get of honey by only looking on it, and feeling of it. So that the spiritual perceptions which a sanctified and spiritual person has, are not only diverse from all that natural men have, after the manner that the ideas or perceptions of the same sense may differ one from another, but rather as the ideas and sensations of different senses do differ. Hence the work of the Spirit of God in regeneration is often in Scripture compared to the giving a new sense, giving eyes to see, and ears to hear, unstopping the ears of the deaf, and opening the eyes of them that were born blind, and turning from darkness unto light. And because this spiritual sense is immensely the most noble and excellent, and that without which all other principles of perception, and all our faculties are useless and vain; therefore the giving this new sense, with the blessed fruits and effects of it in the soul, is compared to a raising the dead, and to a new creation.

This new spiritual sense, and the new dispositions that attend it, are no new faculties, but are new principles of nature. I use the word "principles," for want of a word of a more determinate signification. By a principle of nature in this place, I mean that foundation which is laid in nature, either old or new, for any particular manner or kind of exercise of the faculties of the soul; or a natural habit or foundation for action, giving a person ability and disposition to exert the faculties in exercises of such a certain kind; so that to exert the faculties in that kind of exercises, may be said to be his nature. So this new spiritual sense is not a new faculty of understanding, but it is a new foundation laid in the nature of the soul, for a new kind of exercises of the same faculty of understanding. So that new holy disposition of heart that attends this new sense, is not a new faculty of will, but a foundation laid in the nature of the soul, for a new kind of exercises of the same faculty of will.

The Spirit of God, in all his operations upon the minds of natural men, only moves, impresses, assists, improves, or some way acts upon natural principles; but gives no new spiritual principle. Thus when the Spirit of God gives a natural man visions as he did Balaam, he only impresses a natural principle, viz. the sense of seeing, immediately exciting ideas of that sense; but he gives no new sense; neither is there anything supernatural, spiritual or divine in it. So if the Spirit of God impresses on a man's imagination, either in a dream, or when he is awake, any outward ideas of any of the senses, either voices, or shapes and colors, 'tis only exciting ideas of the same kind that he has by natural principles and senses. So if God reveals to any natural man, any secret fact; as for instance, something that he shall hereafter see or hear; this is not infusing or exercising any new spiritual principle, or giving the ideas of any new spiritual sense; 'tis only impressing, in an extraordinary manner, the ideas that will hereafter be received by sight and hearing. So in the more ordinary influences of the Spirit of God on the hearts of sinners, he only assists natural principles to do the same work to a greater degree, which they do of themselves by nature. Thus the Spirit of God by his common influences may assist men's natural ingeniosity, as he assisted Bezaleel and Aholiab in the curious works of the tabernacle: so he may assist men's natural abilities in political affairs, and improve their courage, and other natural qualifications; as he is said to have put his Spirit on the seventy elders, and on Saul, so as to give him another heart: so God may greatly assist natural men's reason, in their reasoning about secular things, or about the doctrines of religion, and may greatly advance the clearness of their apprehensions and notions of things of religion in many respects, without giving any spiritual sense. So in those awakenings and convictions that natural men may have, God only assists conscience, which is a natural principle, to do that work in a further degree, which it naturally does. Conscience naturally gives men an apprehension of right and wrong, and suggests the relation there is between right and wrong, and a retribution: the Spirit of God assists men's consciences to do this in a greater degree, helps conscience against the stupefying influence of worldly objects and their lusts. And so there are many other ways might be mentioned wherein the Spirit acts upon, assists and moves natural principles; but after all, 'tis no more than nature moved, acted and improved; here is nothing supernatural and divine. But the Spirit of God in his spiritual influences on the hearts of his saints, operates by infusing or exercising new, divine and supernatural principles; principles which are indeed a new and spiritual nature, and principles vastly more noble and excellent than all that is in natural men.

From what has been said it follows, that all spiritual and gracious affections are attended with, and do arise from some apprehension, idea or sensation of mind, which is in its whole nature different, yea exceeding different from all that is or can be in the mind of a natural man; and which the natural man discerns nothing of, and has no manner of idea of (agreeable to I Cor. 2:14), and conceives of no more than a man without the sense of tasting can conceive of the sweet taste of honey, or a man without the sense of hearing can conceive of the melody of a tune, or a man born blind can have a notion of the beauty of the rainbow. . . .

From hence it may be surely inferred, wherein spiritual understanding consists. For if there be in the saints a kind of apprehension or perception, which is in its nature, perfectly diverse from all that natural men have, or that it is possible they should have, till they have a new nature; it must consist in their having a certain kind of ideas or sensations of mind, which are simply diverse from all that is or can be in the minds of natural men. And that is the same thing as to say, that it consists in the sensations of a new spiritual sense, which the souls of natural men have not; as is evident by what has been before, once and again observed. But I have already shown what that new spiritual sense is, which the saints have given them in regeneration, and what is the object of it. I have shown that the immediate object of it is the supreme beauty and excellency of the nature of divine things, as they are in themselves. And this is agreeable to the Scripture: the Apostle very plainly teaches that the great thing discovered by spiritual light, and understood by spiritual knowledge, is the glory of divine things, "But if our gospel be hid, it is hid to them that are lost; in whom the God of this world hath blinded the minds of them that believe not, lest the light of the glorious gospel of Christ, who is the image of God, should shine unto them" (II Cor. 4:3–4), together with: "For God who commanded the light to shine out of darkness, hath shined in our hearts, to give the light of knowledge of the glory of God in the face of Jesus Christ" (ver. 6): and ch. 3:18 preceding: "But we all, with open face, beholding as in a glass, the glory of the Lord, are changed into the same image, from glory to glory, even as by the Spirit of the Lord." And it must needs be so, for as has been before observed, the Scripture often teaches that all true religion summarily consists in the love of divine things. And therefore that kind of understanding or knowledge, which is the proper foundation of true religion, must be the knowledge of the loveliness of divine things. For doubtless, that knowledge which is the proper foundation of love, is the knowledge of loveliness. What that beauty or loveliness of divine things is, which is the proper and immediate object of a spiritual sense of mind, was showed under the last head insisted on, viz. that it is the beauty of their moral perfection. Therefore it is in the view or sense of this, that spiritual understanding does more immediately and primarily consist. And indeed it is plain it can be nothing else for (as has been shown) there is nothing pertaining to divine things besides the beauty of their moral excellency, and those properties and qualities of divine things which this beauty is the foundation of, but what natural men and devils can see and know, and will know fully and clearly to all eternity.

From what has been said, therefore, we come necessarily to this conclusion, concerning that wherein spiritual understanding consists; viz. that it consists in a sense of the heart, of the supreme beauty and sweetness of the holiness or moral perfection of divine things, together with all that discerning and knowledge of things of religion, that depends upon, and flows from such a sense.

Spiritual understanding consists primarily in a sense of heart of that spiritual beauty. I say, a sense of heart; for it is not speculation merely that is concerned in this kind of understanding: nor can there be a clear distinction made between the two faculties of understanding and will, as acting distinctly and separately, in this matter. When the mind is sensible of the sweet beauty and amiableness of a thing, that implies a sensibleness of sweetness and delight in the presence of the idea of it: and this sensibleness of the amiableness or delightfulness of beauty, carries in the very nature of it, the sense of the heart; or an effect and impression the soul is the subject of, as a substance possessed of taste, inclination and will.

There is a distinction to be made between a mere notional understanding, wherein the mind only beholds things in the exercise of a speculative faculty; and the sense of the heart, wherein the mind don't only speculate and behold, but relishes and feels. That sort of knowledge, by which a man has a sensible perception of amiableness and loathsomeness, or of sweetness and nauseousness, is not just the same sort of knowledge with that, by which he knows what a triangle is, and what a square is. The one is mere speculative knowledge; the other sensible knowledge, in which more than the mere intellect is concerned; the heart is the proper subject of it, or the soul as a being that not only beholds, but has inclination, and is pleased or displeased. And yet there is the nature of instruction in it; as he that has perceived the sweet taste of honey, knows much more about it, than he who has only looked upon and felt of it.

The Apostle seems to make a distinction between mere speculative knowledge of the things of religion, and spiritual knowledge, in calling that the form of knowledge, and of the truth; "which has the form of knowledge, and of the truth in the law" (Rom. 2:20). The latter is often represented by relishing, smelling, or tasting; "Now thanks be to God, which always causeth us to triumph in Christ Jesus, and maketh manifest the savor of his knowledge, in every place" (II Cor. 2:14). "Thou savorest not the things that be of God, but those things that be of man" (Matt. 16:23). "As newborn babes, desire the sincere milk of the word, that ye may grow thereby; if so be ye have tasted that the Lord is gracious" (I Pet. 2:2–3). "Because of the savor of thy good ointment, thy name is as ointment poured forth; therefore do the virgins love thee" (Cant. 1:3); compared with: "But ye have an unction from the holy One, and ye know all things" (I John 2:20).

Spiritual understanding primarily consists in this sense, or taste of the moral beauty of divine things; so that no knowledge can be called spiritual, any further than it arises from this, and has this in it. But secondarily, it includes all that discerning and knowledge of things of religion, which depends upon, and flows from such a sense.

When the true beauty and amiableness of the holiness or true moral good that is in divine things, is discovered to the soul, it as it were opens a new world to its view. This shows the glory of all the perfections of God, and of everything appertaining to the divine being: for, as was observed before, the beauty of all arises from God's moral perfection. This shows the glory of all God's works, both of creation and providence: for 'tis the special glory of them, that God's holiness, righteousness, faithfulness and goodness are so manifested in them; and without these moral perfections, there would be no glory in that power and skill with which they are wrought. The glorifying of God's moral perfections is the special end of all the works of God's hands. By this sense of the moral beauty of divine things, is understood the sufficiency of Christ as a mediator: for 'tis only by the discovery of the beauty of the moral perfection of Christ, that the believer is let into the knowledge of the excellency of his person, so as to know anything more of it than the devils do: and 'tis only by the knowledge of the excellency of Christ's person, that any know his sufficiency as a mediator; for the latter depends upon, and arises from the former. 'Tis by seeing the excellency of Christ's person, that the saints are made sensible of the preciousness of his blood, and its sufficiency to atone for sin: for therein consists the preciousness of Christ's blood, that 'tis the blood of so excellent and amiable a person. And on this depends the meritoriousness of his obedience, and sufficiency and prevalence of his intercession. By this sight of the moral beauty of divine things, is seen the beauty of the way of salvation by Christ: for that consists in the beauty of the moral perfections of God, which wonderfully shines forth in every step of this method of salvation, from beginning to end. By this is seen the fitness and suitableness of this way; for this wholly consists in its tendency to deliver us from sin and hell, and to bring us to the happiness which consists in the possession and enjoyment of moral good, in a way sweetly agreeing with God's moral perfections. And in the way's being contrived so as to attain these ends, consists the excellent wisdom of that way. By this is seen the excellency of the Word of God: take away all the moral beauty and sweetness in the Word, and the Bible is left wholly a dead letter, a dry, lifeless, tasteless thing. By this is seen the true foundation of our duty; the worthiness of God to be so esteemed, honored, loved, submitted to, and served, as he requires of us, and the amiableness of the duties themselves that are required of us. And by this is seen the true evil of sin: for he who sees the beauty of holiness, must necessarily see the hatefulness of sin, its contrary. By this men understand the true glory of heaven, which consists in the beauty and happiness that is in holiness. By this is seen the amiableness and happiness of both saints and angels. He that sees the beauty of holiness, or true moral good, sees the greatest and most important thing in the world, which is the fullness of all things, without which all the world is empty, no better than nothing, yea, worse than nothing. Unless this is seen, nothing is seen, that is worth the seeing: for there is no other true excellency or beauty. Unless this be understood, nothing is understood, that is worthy of the exercise of the noble faculty of understanding. This is the beauty of the Godhead, and the divinity of Divinity (if I may so speak), the good of the infinite Fountain of Good; without which God himself (if that were possible to be) would be an infinite evil: without which, we ourselves had better never have been; and without which there had better have been no being. He therefore in effect knows nothing, that knows not this: his knowledge is but the shadow of knowledge, or the form of knowledge, as the Apostle calls it. . . .

FROM

THE NATURE OF TRUE VIRTUE

◊

THIS short but packed treatise was written at Stockbridge, probably in 1755. It was published after the death of Edwards, in 1765, and is remarkable not only for its clear and simple beauty of statement but also for being the only nonpolemical work that Edwards ever found the time to compose.

In the first two chapters Edwards has defined true virtue as "benevolence to being in general," or, he says, to speak more accurately, "it is that consent, propensity and union of heart to being in general, which is immediately exercised in a general good will." In this third chapter, the crucial point in his argument, he defines the conception negatively, by contending that those actions which men naturally think virtuous are not true virtue. Though they partake of the absolute virtue, still they are infinitely below it. Love to Being in general must "radically and essentially" be a supreme love to God, and a finite creature, with interests in his own welfare, cannot attain in this life the self-effacement which this love demands. Its immense value, for Edwards at least, is that it remains in the mind as the unchanging criterion of virtue, and so prevents the person who has it from ever being deceived by facile though attractive imitations.

◊

CHAPTER 3

CONCERNING THE SECONDARY AND INFERIOR KIND OF BEAUTY.

THOUGH this which has been spoken of, alone, is justly esteemed the true beauty of moral agents, or spiritual Beings; this alone being what would appear beautiful in them, upon a clear and comprehensive view of things; and therefore alone is the moral amiableness of Beings that have understanding and will in the eyes of him that perfectly sees all things as they are; yet there are other qualities, other sensations, propensities and affections of mind, and principles of action, that often obtain the epithet of *virtuous,* and by many are supposed to have the nature of true virtue; which are entirely of a distinct nature from this, and have nothing of that kind; and therefore are erroneously confounded with real virtue—as may particularly and fully appear from things which will be observed in this and the following chapters.

That consent, agreement, or union of Being to Being, which has been spoken of, viz., the union or propensity of *minds* to mental or spiritual existence, may be called the highest, and first, or primary beauty that is to be found among things that exist: being the proper and peculiar beauty of spiritual and moral Beings, which are the highest and first part of the universal system, for whose sake all the rest has existence. Yet there is another inferior, secondary beauty, which is some image of this, and which is not peculiar to spiritual Beings, but is found even in inanimate things; which consists in a mutual consent and agreement of different things in form, manner, quantity, and visible end or design; called by the various names of regularity, order, uniformity, symmetry, proportion, harmony, &c. Such is the mutual agreement of the various sides of a square, or equilateral triangle, or of a regular polygon. Such is, as it were, the mutual consent of the different parts of the periphery of a circle, or surface of a sphere, and of the corresponding parts of an ellipsis. Such is the agreement of the colors, figures, dimensions and distances of the different spots on the chess board. Such is the beauty of the figures on a piece of chints, or brocade.—Such is the beautiful proportion of the various parts of a human body, or countenance. And such is the sweet mutual consent and agreement of the various notes of a melodious tune. This is the same that Mr. Hutcheson,[1] in his treatise on beauty, expresses by uniformity in the midst of variety. Which is no other than the consent or agreement of different things, in form, quantity,

THE NATURE OF TRUE VIRTUE. 1. **Mr. Hutcheson:** Francis Hutcheson (1694–1746), author of *An Inquiry into the Original of Our Ideas of Beauty and Virtue* (1725). This work, immensely admired by the sort of eighteenth-century rationalists whom Edwards called "Arminians," argued that just as men have naturally an internal sense by which they are pleased with harmonious forms, so they have a moral sense which is pleased in the presence of moral beauty.

&c. He observes, that the greater the variety is, in equal uniformity, the greater the beauty. Which is no more than to say, the more there are of different mutually agreeing things, the greater is the beauty. And the reason of that is, because it is more considerable to have many things consent one with another, than a few only.

The beauty which consists in the visible fitness of a thing to its use and unity of design, is not a distinct sort of beauty from this. For it is to be observed, that one thing which contributes to the beauty of the agreement and proportion of various things, is their relation one to another; which connects them, and introduces them together into view and consideration, and whereby one suggests the other to the mind, and the mind is led to compare them, and so to expect and desire agreement. Thus the uniformity of two or more pillars, as they may happen to be found in different places, is not an equal degree of beauty, as that uniformity in so many pillars in the corresponding parts of the same building. So means and an intended effect are related one to another. The answerableness of a thing to its use is only the proportion, fitness, and agreeing of a cause or means to a visibly designed effect, and so an effect suggested to the mind by the idea of the means. This kind of beauty is not entirely different from that beauty which there is in fitting a mortise to its tenon. Only when the beauty consists in unity of design, or the adaptedness of a variety of things to promote one intended effect, in which all conspire, as the various parts of an ingenious complicated machine, there is a double beauty, as there is a twofold agreement and conformity. First, there is the agreement of the various parts to the designed end. Secondly, through this, viz., the designed end or effect, all the various particulars agree one with another, as the general medium of their union, whereby they being united in this third, they thereby are all united one to another.

The reason, or at least one reason why God has made this kind of mutual consent and agreement of things beautiful and grateful to those intelligent Beings that perceive it, probably is, that there is in it some image of the true, spiritual, original beauty which has been spoken of; consisting in Being's consent to Being, or the union of minds or spiritual Beings in a mutual propensity and affection of heart. The other is an image of this, because by that uniformity, diverse things become as it were one, as it is in this cordial union. And it pleases God to observe analogy in his works, as is manifest in fact in innumerable instances; and especially to establish inferior things in an analogy to superior. Thus, in how many instances has he formed brutes in analogy to the nature of mankind? And plants in analogy to animals with respect to the manner of their generation, nutrition, &c.? And so he has constituted the external world in an analogy to things in the spiritual world, in numberless instances; as might be shown, if it were necessary, and here were proper place and room for it.—Why such analogy in God's works pleases him, it is not needful now to inquire. It is sufficient that he makes an agreement or consent of different things, in their form, manner, measure, &c., to appear beautiful, because here is some image of a higher kind of agreement and consent of spiritual Beings. It has pleased him to establish a law of nature, by virtue of which the uniformity and mutual correspondence of a beautiful plant, and the respect which the various parts of a regular building seem to have one to another, and their agreement and union, and the consent or concord of the various notes of a melodious tune, should appear beautiful; because therein is some image of the consent of mind, of the different members of a society or system of intelligent Beings, sweetly united in a benevolent agreement of heart.—And here, by the way, I would further observe, probably it is with regard to this image or resemblance, which secondary beauty has of true spiritual beauty, that God has so constituted nature, that the presenting of this inferior beauty, especially in those kinds of it which have the greatest resemblance of the primary beauty, as the harmony of sounds, and the beauties of nature, have a tendency to assist those whose hearts are under the influence of a truly virtuous temper, to dispose them to the exercises of divine love, and enliven in them a sense of spiritual beauty.

From what has been said we may see, that there are two sorts of agreement or consent of one thing to another. (1.) There is a *cordial* agreement; that consists in concord and union of mind and heart; which, if not attended (viewing things in general) with more discord than concord, is true virtue, and the original or primary beauty, which is the only true *moral* beauty. (2.) There is a *natural* union or agreement; which, though some image of the other, is entirely a distinct thing; the will, disposition, or affection of the heart having no concern in it, but consisting only in uniformity and consent of nature, form, quantity, &c. (as before described), wherein lies an inferior secondary sort of beauty, which may, in distinction from the other, be called *natural* beauty.—This may be sufficient to let the reader know how I shall hereafter use the phrases of cordial, and natural agreement; and moral, spiritual, divine, and primary original beauty, and secondary, or natural beauty.

Concerning this latter, inferior kind of beauty, the following things may be observed:

1. The *cause* why secondary beauty is grateful to men, is only a *law of nature,* which God has fixed, or an *instinct* he has given to mankind; and not their perception of the same thing which *God* is pleased to have regard to, as the ground or rule by which he has established such a law of nature. —This appears in two things.

(1.) That which God has respect to, as the rule or ground of this law of nature he has given us, whereby things having a secondary beauty are made grateful to men, is their mutual agreement and proportion, in measure, form, &c. But in many instances persons that are gratified, and have their minds affected, in presenting this beauty, do not reflect on that particular agreement and proportion which, according to the law of nature, is the ground and rule of beauty in the case, yea, are ignorant of it. Thus, a man may be pleased with the harmony of the notes in a tune, and yet know nothing of that proportion or adjustment of the notes which by the law of nature is the ground of the melody. He knows not, that the vibrations in one note regularly coincide with the vibrations in another; that the vibrations of a note coincide in time with two vibrations of its octave; and that two vibrations of a note coincide with three of its fifth, &c. Yea, he may not know, that there are vibrations of the air in the case, or any corresponding motions in the organs of hearing, in the auditory nerve, or animal spirits.—So, a man may be affected and pleased with a beautiful proportion of the features in a face, and yet not know what that proportion is, or what measures, quantities, and distances it consists in.

In this a sensation of secondary beauty differs from a sensation of primary and spiritual beauty, consisting in a spiritual union and agreement. What makes the latter grateful, is perceiving the union itself. It is the immediate view of that wherein the beauty fundamentally lies, that is pleasing to the virtuous mind.

(2.) As was observed before, God, in establishing such a law that mutual natural agreement of different things, in form, quantity, &c., should appear beautiful or grateful to men, seems to have had regard to the image and resemblance there is in such a natural agreement, of that spiritual cordial agreement, wherein original beauty consists, as one reason why he established such a law. But it is not any reflection upon, or perception of, such a resemblance of this to spiritual beauty, that is the reason why such a form or state of objects appears beautiful to men: but their sensation of pleasure, on a view of this secondary beauty, is immediately owing to the law God has established, or the instinct he has given.

2. Another thing observable concerning this kind of beauty, is, that it affects the mind more (other things being equal) when taken notice of in objects which are of considerable importance, than in little trivial matters. Thus the symmetry of the parts of a human body, or countenance, affects the mind more than the beauty of a flower. So, the beauty of the solar system, more than as great and as manifold an order and uniformity in a tree. And the proportions of the parts of a church, or a palace, more than the same proportions in some little slight compositions, made to please children.

3. It may be observed (which was hinted before) that not only uniformity and proportion, &c., of different things is requisite in order to this inferior beauty, but some relation or connection of the things thus agreeing one with another. As, the uniformity or likeness of a number of pillars, scattered hither and thither, does not constitute beauty, or at least by no means in an equal degree as uniformity in pillars connected in the same building, in parts that have relation one to another. So, if we see things unlike, and very disproportioned, in distant places, which have no relation to each other, this excites no such idea of deformity, as disagreement and inequality or disproportion in things related and connected: and the nearer the relation, and the stricter the connection, so much the greater and more disgustful is the deformity, consisting in their disagreement.

4. This secondary kind of beauty, consisting in uniformity and proportion, not only takes place in material and external things, but also in things immaterial; and is, in very many things, plain and sensible in the latter, as well as the former: and when it is so, there is no reason why it should not be grateful to them that behold it, in these as well as the other, by virtue of the same sense, or the same determination of mind to be gratified with uniformity and proportion. If uniformity and proportion be the things that affect, and appear agreeable to, this sense of beauty, then why should not uniformity and proportion affect the same sense in immaterial things as well as material, if there be equal capacity of discerning it in both? And indeed *more* in spiritual things (*caeteris paribus*), as these are more important than things merely external and material.

This is not only reasonable to be supposed, but it is evident in fact, in numberless instances. There is a beauty of order in society, besides what consists in benevolence, or can be referred to it, which is of the secondary kind. As, when the different members of society have all their appointed office, place and station, according to their several capacities and talents, and every one keeps his place, and continues in his proper business. In this there is a beauty, not of a different kind from the regularity of a beautiful building, or piece of skilful architecture, where the strong pillars are set in their proper place, the pilasters in a place fit for them, the square pieces of marble in the pavement, in a place suitable for them, the panels in the walls and partitions in their proper places, the cornices in places proper for them, &c. As the agreement of a variety in one common design, of the parts of a building, or complicated machine, is one instance of that regularity, which belongs to the secondary kind of beauty in immaterial things, in what is called *wisdom,* consisting in the united tendency of thoughts, ideas, and particular volitions, to one general purpose: which is a distinct thing from the goodness of that general purpose, as being useful and benevolent.

So there is a beauty in the virtue called *justice,* which consists in the agreement of different things, that have relation to one another, in nature, manner and measure: and therefore is the very same sort of beauty with that uniformity and proportion, which is observable in those external and material things that are esteemed beautiful. There is a natural agreement and adaptedness of things that have relation one to another, and a harmonious corresponding of one thing to another; that he who from his will *does* evil to others, should *receive* evil from the will of others, or from the will of him or them whose business it is to take care of the injured, and to act in their behalf: and that he should suffer evil in *proportion* to the evil of his doings. Things are in natural regularity and mutual agreement, not in a metaphorical but literal sense, when he whose heart opposes the general system, should have the hearts of that system, or the heart of the head and ruler of the system, against him: and that in consequence, he should receive evil in proportion to the evil tendency of the opposition of his heart. —So, there is a like agreement in nature and measure, when he that loves, has the proper returns of love; when he that from his heart promotes the good of another, has his good promoted by the other; as there is a kind of justice in a becoming gratitude.

Indeed most of the duties incumbent on us, if well considered, will be found to partake of the nature of justice. There is some natural agreement of one thing to another; some adaptedness of the agent to the object; some answerableness of the act to the occasion; some equality and proportion in things of a similar nature, and of a direct relation one to another. So it is in the relative duties; duties of children to parents, and of parents to children; duties of husbands and wives; duties of rulers and subjects; duties of friendship and good neighborhood: and all duties that we owe to God, our Creator, preserver, and benefactor; and all duties whatsoever, considered as required by God, and as branches of our duty to him, and also considered as what are to be performed with a regard to Christ, as acts of obedience to his precepts, and as testimonies of respect to him, and of our regard to what he has done for us, the virtues and temper he has exercised towards us, and the benefits we have or hope for therefrom.

It is this secondary kind of beauty, which belongs to the virtues and duties required of us, that Mr. *Wollaston*[2] seems to have had in his eye, when he resolved all virtue into an agreement of inclinations, volitions and actions with *truth.* He evidently has respect to the justice there is in the virtues and duties that are proper to be in one Being towards another; which consists in one Being's expressing such affections and using such a conduct towards another, as hath a natural agreement and proportion to what is in them, and what we receive from them; which is as much a natural conformity of affection and action with its ground, object and occasion, as that which is between a true proposition and the thing spoken of in it.

But there is another and higher beauty in true virtue, and in all truly virtuous dispositions and exercises, than what consists in any uniformity or similarity of various things, viz., the *union of heart to Being in general,* or to God the Being of Beings, which appears in those virtues; and which those virtues, when true, are the various expressions or effects of.—Benevolence to Being in general, or to Being simply considered, is entirely a distinct thing from uniformity in the midst of variety, and is a superior kind of beauty.

It is true, that benevolence to Being in general, when a person hath it, will naturally incline him to justice, or proportion in the exercises of it. He that loves Being, simply considered, will naturally (as was observed before), other things being equal, love particular Beings, in a proportion to their dignity. For the dignity of any Being consists in those two things. Respect to Being, in this

2. **Mr.** ***Wollaston:*** William Wollaston (1659–1724), *The Religion of Nature Delineated* (1722).

proportion, is the first and most general kind of justice; which will produce all the subordinate kinds. So that, after benevolence to Being in general exists, the proportion which is observed in objects, may be the cause of the proportion of benevolence to those objects: but no proportion is the cause or ground of the existence of such a thing as benevolence to Being. The tendency of objects to excite that degree of benevolence which is proportionable to the degree of Being, &c., is the *consequence* of the existence of benevolence; and not the ground of it. Even as a tendency of bodies, one to another, by mutual attraction, in proportion to the quantity of matter, is the consequence of the Being of such a thing as mutual attraction; and not attraction the effect of proportion.

By this it appears, that *just* affections and acts have a beauty in them, distinct from, and superior to, the uniformity and equality there is in them; for which he that has a truly virtuous temper, relishes and delights in them. And that is the expression and manifestation there is in them of benevolence to Being in general.—And besides this, there is the agreement of *justice* to the will and command of God; and also something in the tendency and consequences of justice, that is agreeable to general benevolence, viz., as in many respects it tends to the glory of God, and the general good. Which tendency also makes it beautiful to a truly virtuous mind. So that the tendency of general benevolence to produce justice, also the tendency of justice to produce effects agreeable to general benevolence, both render justice pleasing to a virtuous mind. And it is on these accounts *chiefly,* that justice is grateful to a virtuous taste, or a truly benevolent heart. But, though it be true, there is that in the uniformity and proportion there is in justice, which is grateful to a benevolent heart, as this uniformity and proportion tends to the general good; yet that is no argument, that there is no other beauty in it but its agreeing with benevolence. For so the external regularity and order of the natural world gratifies benevolence, as it is profitable, and tends to the general good; but that is no argument, that there is no other sort of beauty in external uniformity and proportion, but only its suiting benevolence by tending to the general good.

5. From all that has been observed concerning this secondary kind of beauty, it appears that that disposition or sense of the mind, which consists in determination of mind to approve and be pleased with this beauty, considered simply and by itself, has nothing of the nature of true virtue, and is entirely a different thing from a truly virtuous taste. For it has been shown, that this kind of beauty is entirely diverse from the beauty of true virtue, whether it takes place in material or immaterial things. And therefore it will follow, that a taste of this kind of beauty is entirely a different thing from a taste of true virtue. Who will affirm, that a disposition to approve of the harmony of good music, or the beauty of a square, or equilateral triangle, is the same with true holiness, or a truly virtuous disposition of mind! It is a relish of uniformity and proportion, that determines the mind to approve these things. And if this be all, there is no need of any thing higher, or of any thing in any respect diverse, to determine the mind to approve and be pleased with equal uniformity and proportion among spiritual things which are equally discerned. It is virtuous to love true virtue, as that denotes an agreement of the heart with virtue. But it argues no virtue, for the heart to be pleased with that which is entirely distinct from it.

Though it be true, there is some analogy in it to spiritual and virtuous beauty, as much as material things can have analogy to things spiritual (on which they can have no more than a shadow), yet, as has been observed, men do not approve it because of any such analogy perceived.

And not only reason, but experience plainly shows, that men's approbation of this sort of beauty, does not spring from any virtuous temper, and has no connection with virtue. For, otherwise, men's delight in the beauty of squares, and cubes, and regular polygons, in the regularity of buildings, and the beautiful figures in a piece of embroidery, would increase in proportion to men's virtue; and would be raised to a great height in some eminently virtuous or holy men; but would be almost wholly lost in some others that are very vicious and lewd. It is evident in fact, that a relish of these things does not depend on general benevolence, or any benevolence at all to any Being whatsoever, any more than a man's loving the taste of honey, or his being pleased with the smell of a rose. A taste of this inferior beauty in things immaterial, is one thing which has been mistaken by some moralists, for a true virtuous principle, implanted naturally in the hearts of all mankind.

FROM

DISSERTATION CONCERNING THE END FOR WHICH GOD CREATED THE WORLD

◊

❡ THIS majestic work, like the *True Virtue,* was composed in Edwards' last years at Stockbridge and published along with it under the title *Two Dissertations,* in 1765. It is his last attack upon Arminianism, but the polemical purpose is fortunately subordinated to the assertion of his primary vision of the universe.

◊

SECTION I.

SOME THINGS OBSERVED IN GENERAL, WHICH REASON DICTATES.

1. THAT no notion of God's last end in the creation of the world is agreeable to reason, which would truly imply or infer any indigence, insufficiency and mutability in God; or any dependence of the Creator on the creature, for any part of his perfection or happiness. Because it is evident, by both Scripture and reason, that God is infinitely, eternally, unchangeably, and independently glorious and happy; that he stands in no need of, cannot be profited by, or receive any thing from the creature; or be truly hurt, or be the subject of any sufferings, or *impair* of his glory and felicity from any other being. I need not stand to produce the proofs of God's being such a one, it being so universally allowed and maintained by such as call themselves Christians. The notion of God's creating the world in order to receive any thing properly from the creature, is not only contrary to the nature of God, but inconsistent with the notion of creation; which implies a being's receiving its existence, and all that belongs to its being, out of nothing. And this implies the most perfect, absolute, and universal derivation and dependence. Now, if the creature receives its all from God entirely and perfectly, how is it possible that it should have anything to add to God, to make him in any respect more than he was before, and so the Creator become dependent on the creature?

2. Whatsoever is good and valuable in itself, is worthy that God should value for itself, and on its own account; or which is the same thing, value it with an ultimate value or respect. It is therefore worthy to be ultimately sought by God, or made the last end of his action and operation, if it be a thing of such a nature as to be properly capable of being attained in any divine operation. For it may be supposed that some things, which are valuable and excellent in themselves, are not properly capable of being attained in any divine operation; because they do not remain to be attained; but their existence in all possible respects, must be conceived of prior to any divine operation. Thus God's existence and infinite perfection, though infinitely valuable in themselves, and infinitely valued by God, yet cannot be supposed to be the end of any divine operation. For we cannot conceive of them as in any respect consequent on any works of God: but whatever is in itself valuable, absolutely so, and that is capable of being sought and attained, is worthy to be made a last end of the divine operation. Therefore,

3. Whatever that be which is in itself most valuable, and was so originally, prior to the creation of the world, and which is attainable by the creation, if there be any thing which was superior in value to all others, *that* must be worthy to be God's last end in the creation; and also worthy to be his highest end. In consequence of this, it will follow,

4. That if God himself be in any respect properly capable of being his own end in the creation of the world, then it is reasonable to suppose that he had respect to *himself* as his last and highest end in this work; because he is worthy in himself to be so, being infinitely the greatest and best of beings. All things else, with regard to worthiness, importance and excellence, are perfectly as nothing in comparison of him. And, therefore, if God esteems, values, and has respect to things according to their nature and proportions, he must necessarily have the greatest respect to himself. It would be against the perfection of his nature, his wisdom, holiness, and perfect rectitude, whereby he is disposed to do every thing that is fit to be done, to suppose otherwise. At least a great part of the moral rectitude of the heart of God, whereby he is disposed to every thing that is fit, suitable and amiable in itself, consists in his having infinitely the highest regard to that which is in itself infinitely highest and best: yea, it is in this that it seems chiefly to consist. The moral rectitude of God's heart must consist in a proper and due respect of his heart to things that are objects of moral respect; that is, to intelligent beings capable of moral actions and relations. And there-

fore it must chiefly consist in giving due respect to that Being to whom most is due; yea, infinitely most, and in effect all. For God is infinitely the most worthy of regard. The worthiness of others is as nothing to his: so that to him belongs all possible respect. To him belongs the whole of the respect that any moral agent, either God, or any intelligent being is capable of. To him belongs all the heart. Therefore, if moral rectitude of heart consists in paying the respect or regard of the heart which is due, or which fitness and suitableness requires, fitness requires infinitely the greatest regard to be paid to God; and the denying supreme regard here, would be a conduct infinitely the most unfit. Therefore a proper regard to this Being, is what the fitness of regard does infinitely most consist in. Hence it will follow—That the moral rectitude and fitness of the disposition, inclination or affection of God's heart, does chiefly consist in a respect or regard to himself infinitely above his regard to all other beings: or, in other words, his holiness consists in this.

And if it be thus fit that God should have a supreme regard to himself, then it is fit that this supreme regard should appear, in those things by which he makes himself known, or by his *word* and *works;* i.e., in what he says, and in what he does. If it be an infinitely amiable thing in God, that he should have a supreme regard to himself, then it is an amiable thing that he should act as having a chief regard to himself; or act in such a manner, as to show that he has such a regard; that what is highest in God's heart, may be highest in his actions and conduct. And if it was God's intention, as there is great reason to think it was, that his works should exhibit an image of himself their author, that it might brightly appear by his works what manner of being he is, and afford a proper representation of his divine excellencies, and especially his *moral* excellence, consisting in the *disposition of his heart;* then it is reasonable to suppose that his works are so wrought as to show this supreme respect to himself, wherein his moral excellency does primarily consist. . . .

SECTION II.

SOME FARTHER OBSERVATIONS CONCERNING THOSE THINGS WHICH REASON LEADS US TO SUPPOSE GOD AIMED AT IN THE CREATION OF THE WORLD, SHOWING PARTICULARLY WHAT THINGS THAT ARE ABSOLUTELY GOOD, ARE ACTUALLY THE CONSEQUENCE OF THE CREATION OF THE WORLD.

1. It seems a thing in itself fit, proper and desirable, that the glorious attributes of God, which consist in a sufficiency to certain acts and effects, should be exerted in the production of such effects, as might manifest the infinite power, wisdom, righteousness, goodness, &c., which are in God. If the world had not been created, these attributes never would have had any exercise. The power of God, which is a sufficiency in him to produce great effects, must for ever have been dormant and useless as to any effect. The divine wisdom and prudence would have had no exercise in any wise contrivance, any prudent proceeding or disposal of things; for there would have been no objects of contrivance or disposal. The same might be observed of God's justice, goodness and truth. Indeed God might have known as perfectly that he possessed these attributes, if they had never been exerted or expressed in any effect. But then if the attributes which consist in a sufficiency for correspondent effects, are in themselves excellent, the exercise of them must likewise be excellent. If it be an excellent thing that there should be a sufficiency for a certain kind of action or operation, the excellency of such a sufficiency must consist in its relation to this kind of operation or effect; but that could not be, unless the operation itself were excellent. A sufficiency for any act or work is no farther valuable, than the work or effect is valuable. As God therefore esteems these attributes themselves valuable, and delights in them; so it is natural to suppose that he delights in their proper exercise and expression. From the same reason that he esteems his own sufficiency wisely to contrive and dispose effects, he also will esteem the wise contrivance and disposition itself. And for the same reason, as he delights in his own disposition to do justly, and to dispose of things according to truth and just proportion; so he must delight in such a righteous disposal itself.

2. It seems to be a thing in itself fit and desirable, that the glorious perfections of God should be known, and the operations and expressions of

them seen by other beings besides himself. If it be fit, that God's power and wisdom, &c., should be exercised and expressed in some effects, and not lie eternally dormant, then it seems proper that these exercises should appear, and not be totally hidden and unknown. For if they are, it will be just the same as to the above purpose, as if they were not. God as perfectly knew himself and his perfections, had as perfect an idea of the exercises and effects they were sufficient for, antecedently to any such actual operations of them, as since. If therefore it be nevertheless a thing in itself valuable, and worthy to be desired, that these glorious perfections be actually expressed and exhibited in their correspondent effects; then it seems also, that the knowledge of these perfections, and the expressions and discoveries that are made of them, is a thing valuable in itself absolutely considered; and that it is desirable that this knowledge should exist. As God's perfections are things in themselves excellent, so the expression of them in their proper acts and fruits is excellent; and the knowledge of these excellent perfections, and of these glorious expressions of them, is an excellent thing, the existence of which is in itself valuable and desirable. It is a thing infinitely good in itself that God's glory should be known by a glorious society of created beings. And that there should be in them an increasing knowledge of God to all eternity, is an existence, a reality infinitely worthy to be, and worthy to be valued and regarded by him, to whom it belongs to order that to be, which, of all things possible, is fittest and best. If existence is more worthy than defect and nonentity, and if any created existence is in itself worthy to be, then knowledge or understanding is a thing worthy to be; and if any knowledge, then the most excellent sort of knowledge, viz., that of God and his glory. The existence of the created universe consists as much in it as in any thing: yea, this knowledge is one of the highest, most real and substantial parts of all created existence, most remote from nonentity and defect.

3. As it is a thing valuable and desirable in itself that God's glory should be seen and known, so when known, it seems equally reasonable and fit, it should be valued and esteemed, loved and delighted in, answerably to its dignity. There is no more reason to esteem it a fit and suitable thing that God's glory should be known, or that there should be an idea in the understanding corresponding unto the glorious object, than that there should be a corresponding disposition or affection in the will. If the perfection itself be excellent, the knowledge of it is excellent, and so is the esteem and love of it excellent. And as it is fit that God should love and esteem his own excellence, it is also fit that he should value and esteem the love of his excellency. For if it becomes any being greater to value another, then it becomes him to love to have him valued and esteemed: and if it becomes a being highly to value himself, it is fit that he should love to have himself valued and esteemed. If the idea of God's perfection in the understanding be valuable, then the love of the heart seems to be more especially valuable, as moral beauty especially consists in the disposition and affection of the heart.

4. As there is an infinite fulness of all possible good in God, a fulness of every perfection, of all excellency and beauty, and of infinite happiness; and as this fulness is capable of communication or emanation *ad extra;* so it seems a thing amiable and valuable in itself that it should be communicated or flow forth, that this infinite fountain of good should send forth abundant streams, that this infinite fountain of light should, diffusing its excellent fulness, pour forth light all around—and as this is in itself excellent, so a disposition to this, in the Divine Being, must be looked upon as a perfection or an excellent disposition, such an emanation of good is, in some sense, a multiplication of it; so far as the communication or external stream may be looked upon as any thing besides the fountain, so far it may be looked on as an increase of good. And if the fulness of good that is in the fountain, is in itself excellent and worthy to exist, then the emanation, or that which is as it were an increase, repetition or multiplication of it, is excellent and worthy to exist. Thus it is fit, since there is an infinite fountain of light and knowledge, that this light should shine forth in beams of communicated knowledge and understanding; and as there is an infinite fountain of holiness, moral excellence and beauty, so it should flow out in communicated holiness. And that as there is an infinite fulness of joy and happiness, so these should have an emanation, and become a fountain flowing out in abundant streams, as beams from the sun.

From this view it appears another way to be a thing in itself valuable, that there should be such things as the knowledge of God's glory in other beings, and a high esteem of it, love to it, and delight and complacence in it;—this appears, I say, in another way, viz., as these things are but the emanations of God's own knowledge, holiness and joy.

Thus it appears reasonable to suppose, that it was what God had respect to as an ultimate end of his creating the world, to communicate of his own infinite fulness of good; or rather it was his last end, that there might be a glorious and abundant emanation of his infinite fulness of good *ad extra,* or without himself; and the disposition to communicate himself, or diffuse his own FULNESS, which we must conceive of as being originally in God as a perfection of his nature, was what moved him to create the world. But here, as much as possible to avoid confusion, I observe, that there is some impropriety in saying that a disposition in God to communicate himself *to the creature,* moved him to create the world. For though the diffusive disposition in the nature of God, that moved him to create the world, doubtless inclines him to communicate himself to the creature, when the creature exists; yet this cannot be all: because an inclination in God to communicate himself to an object, seems to presuppose the existence of the object, at least in idea. But the diffusive disposition that excited God to give creatures existence, was rather a communicative disposition in general, or a disposition in the fulness of the divinity to flow out and diffuse itself. Thus the disposition there is in the root and stock of a tree to diffuse and send forth its sap and life, is doubtless the reason of the communication of its sap and life to its buds, leaves and fruits, after these exist. But a disposition to communicate of its life and sap to its fruits, is not so properly the cause of its producing those fruits, as its disposition to communicate itself, or diffuse its sap and life in general. Therefore, to speak more strictly according to truth, we may suppose, *that a disposition in God, as an original property of his nature, to an emanation of his own infinite fulness, was what excited him to create the world; and so that the emanation itself was aimed at by him as a last end of the creation. . . .*

SECTION VII.

SHOWING THAT THE ULTIMATE END OF THE CREATION OF THE WORLD, IS BUT ONE, AND WHAT THAT ONE END IS.

FROM what has been observed in the last section, it appears, that however the last end of creation is spoken of in Scripture under various denominations; yet if the whole of what is said relating to this affair, be duly weighed, and one part compared with another, we shall have reason to think, that the design of the Spirit of God does not seem to be to represent God's ultimate end as manifold, but as one. For though it be signified by various names, yet they appear not to be names of different things, but various names involving each other in their meaning; either different names of the same thing, or names of several parts of one whole, or of the same whole viewed in various lights, or in its different respects and relations. For it appears that all that is ever spoken of in the Scripture as an ultimate end of God's works, is included in that one phrase, *the glory of God;* which is the name by which the last end of God's works is most commonly called in Scripture; and seems to be the name which most aptly signifies the thing.

The thing signified by that name, *the glory of God*, when spoken of as the supreme and ultimate end of the work of creation, and of all God's works, is the emanation and true external expression of God's internal glory and fulness; meaning by his fulness, that has already been explained. Or, in other words, God's internal glory extant, in a true and just exhibition, or external existence of it. It is confessed that there is a degree of obscurity in these definitions; but perhaps an obscurity which is unavoidable, through the imperfection of language, and words being less fitted to express things of so sublime a nature. And therefore the thing may possibly be better understood, by using many words and a variety of expressions, by a particular consideration of it, as it were by parts, than by any short definition.

There is included in this, the exercise of God's perfections to produce a proper effect, in opposition to their lying eternally dormant and ineffectual; as his power being eternally without any act or fruit of that power; his wisdom eternally ineffectual in any wise production, or prudent disposal of any thing, &c. The manifestation of his internal glory to created understandings. The communication of the infinite fulness of God to the creature. The creature's high esteem of God, love to God, and complacence and joy in God, and the proper exercises and expressions of these.

These at first view may appear to be entirely distinct things: but if we more closely consider the matter, they will all appear to be one thing, in a variety of views and relations. They are all but the emanation of God's glory; or the excellent brightness and fulness of the Divinity diffused, overflowing, and as it were, enlarged; or, in one word, existing *ad extra.* God's exercising his perfection to produce a proper effect, is not distinct from the emanation or communication of his fulness; for this effect, viz., his fulness communicated, and the producing this effect is the communication of his fulness; and there is nothing in this effectual exerting of God's perfection, but the emanation of God's internal glory. The emanation or communication is of the internal glory or fulness of God as it is. Now God's internal glory, as it is in God, is either in his understanding or will. The glory or fulness of his understanding, is his knowledge. The internal glory and fulness of God, which we must conceive of as having its special seat in his will, is his holiness and happiness. The whole of God's internal good or glory, is in these three things, viz., his infinite knowledge; his infinite virtue or holiness, and his infinite joy and happiness. Indeed there are a great many attributes in God, according to our way of conceiving or talking of them; but all may be reduced to these, or to the degree, circumstances and relations of these. We have no conception of God's power, different from the degree of these things, with a certain relation of them to effects. God's infinity is not so properly a distinct kind of good in God, but only expresses the *degree* of the good there is in him. So God's eternity is not a distinct good; but is the duration of good. His immutability is still the same good, with a negation of change. So that, as I said, the fulness of the Godhead is the fulness of his understanding, consisting in his knowledge, and the fulness of his will, consisting in his virtue and happiness. And therefore the eternal glory of God consists in the communication of these. The communication of his knowledge is chiefly in giving the knowledge of himself; for this is the knowledge in which the fulness of God's understanding chiefly consists. And thus we see how the manifestation of God's glory to created understandings, and their seeing and knowing it, is not distinct from an emanation or communication of God's fulness, but clearly implied in it. Again, the communication of God's virtue or holiness is principally in communicating the love of himself, (which appears by what has before been observed.) And thus we see how, not only the creature's seeing and knowing God's excellence, but also supremely esteeming and loving him, belongs to the communication of God's fulness. And the communication of God's joy and happiness, consists chiefly in communicating to the creature, that happiness and joy, which consists in rejoicing in God, and in his glorious excellency; for in such joy God's own happiness does principally consist. And in these things, viz., in knowing God's excellency, loving God for it, and rejoicing in it; and in the exercise and expression of these, consists God's honor and praise; so that these are clearly implied in that glory of God, which consists in the emanation of his internal glory. And though we suppose all these things, which seem to be so various, are signified by that *glory,* which the Scripture speaks of as the last end of all God's works; yet it is manifest there is no greater, and no other variety in it, than in the internal and essential glory of God itself. God's internal glory is partly in his understanding, and partly in his will. And this internal glory, as seated in the will of God, implies both his holiness and his happiness; both are evidently God's glory, according to the use of the phrase. So that as God's external glory is only the emanation of his internal glory, this variety necessarily follows. And again, it hence appears that here there is no other variety or distinction, but what necessarily arises from the distinct faculties of the creature, to which the communication is made, as created in the image of God; even as having these two faculties of understanding and will. God communicates himself to the understanding of the creature, in giving him the knowledge of his glory; and to the will of the creature, in giving him holiness, consisting primarily in the love of God; and in giving the creature happiness, chiefly consisting in joy in God. These are the sum of that emanation of divine fulness, called in Scripture *the glory of God.* The first part of this glory is called *truth,* the latter, *grace.* John i. 14, "We beheld his *glory,* the glory as of the only begotten of the Father, full of *grace* and *truth.*"

Thus we see that the great and last end of God's works which is so variously expressed in Scripture, is indeed but *one;* and this *one* end is most properly and comprehensively called, THE GLORY OF GOD; by which name it is most commonly called in Scripture: and is fitly compared to an effulgence or emanation of light from a luminary, by which this glory of God is abundantly represented in Scripture. Light is the external expression, exhibition and manifestation of the excellency of the luminary, of the sun for instance: it is the abundant, extensive emanation and communication of the fulness of the sun to innumerable beings that partake of it. It is by this that the sun itself is seen, and his glory beheld, and all other things are discovered; it is by a participation of this communication from the sun, that surrounding objects receive all their lustre, beauty and brightness. It is by this that all nature is quickened and receives life, comfort and joy. Light is abundantly used in Scripture to represent and signify these three things, knowledge, holiness and happiness. It is used to signify knowledge, or that manifestation and evidence by which knowledge is received, Psalm xix. 8, and cxix. 105, 130. Prov. vi. 23. Isaiah viii. 20, and ix. 2, and xxix. 18. Dan. v. 11. Eph. v. 13, "But all things that are reproved are made manifest by the light; for whatsoever doth make manifest, is light." And in other places of the New Testament innumerable.

It is used to signify virtue or moral good, Job xxv. 5, and other places. And it is abundantly used to signify comfort, joy and happiness, Esth. viii. 16, Job xviii. 18, and many other places.

What has been said may be sufficient to show how those things which are spoken of in Scripture as ultimate ends of God's works, though they may seem at first view to be distinct, are all plainly to be reduced to this one thing, viz., God's internal glory or fulness extant externally, or existing in its emanation. And though God in seeking this end, seeks the creature's good; yet therein appears his supreme regard to himself.

The emanation or communication of the divine fulness, consisting in the knowledge of God, love to God, and joy in God, has relation indeed both to God, and the creature; but it has relation to God as its fountain, as it is an emanation from God; and as the communication itself, or thing communicated, is something divine, something of God, something of his internal fulness, as the water in the stream is something of the fountain, and as the beams of the sun, are something of the sun. And again, they have relation to God, as they have respect to him as their object; for the knowledge communicated is the knowledge of God; and so God is the object of the knowledge, and the love communicated is the love of God; so God is the object of that love, and the happiness communicated is joy in God; and so he is the object of the joy communicated. In the creature's knowing, esteeming, loving, rejoicing in, and praising God, the glory of God is both exhibited and acknowledged; his fulness is received and returned. Here is both an *emanation* and *remanation*. The refulgence shines upon and into the creature, and is reflected back to the luminary. The beams of glory come from God, and are something of God, and are refunded back again to their original. So that the whole is *of* God, and *to* God, and God is the beginning, middle and end in this affair.

And though it be true that God has respect to the creature in these things; yet his respect to himself and to the cretaure in this matter, are not properly to be looked upon, as a double and divided respect of God's heart. What has been said in Chap. I. Sect. 3, 4, may be sufficient to show this. Nevertheless, it may not be amiss here briefly to say a few things; though they are mostly implied in what has been said already.

When God was about to create the world, he had respect to that emanation of his glory, which is actually the consequence of the creation, just as it is with regard to all that belongs to it, both with regard to its relation to himself, and the creature. He had regard to it, as an emanation from himself, and a communication of himself, and as the thing communicated, in its nature returned to himself, as its final term. And he had regard to it also, as the emanation was to the creature, and as the thing communicated was in the creature, as its subject. And God had regard to it in this manner, as he had a supreme regard to himself, and value for his own infinite, internal glory. It was this value for himself that caused him to value and seek that his internal glory should flow forth from himself. It was from his value for his glorious perfections of wisdom and righteousness, &c., that he valued the proper exercise and effect of these perfections, in wise and righteous acts and effects. It was from his infinite value for his internal glory and fulness, that he valued the thing itself, which is communicated, which is something of the same, extant in the creature. Thus, because he infinitely values his own glory, consisting in the knowledge of himself, love to himself, and complacence and joy in himself; he therefore valued the image, communication or participation of these, in the creature. And it is because he values himself, that he delights in the knowledge, and love, and joy of the creature; as being himself the object of this knowledge, love and complacence. For it is the necessary consequence of the true esteem and love of any person or being (suppose a son or friend) that we should approve and value others' esteem of the same object, and disapprove and dislike the contrary. For the same reason is it the consequence of a being's esteem and love of himself, that he should approve of others' esteem and love of himself.

Thus it is easy to conceive, how God should seek the good of the creature, consisting in the creature's knowledge and holiness, and even his happiness, from a supreme regard to himself; as his happiness arises from that which is an image and participation of God's own beauty; and consists in the creature's exercising a supreme regard to God, and complacence in him; in beholding God's glory, in esteeming and loving it, and rejoicing in it, and in his exercising and testifying love and supreme respect to God; which is the same thing with the creature's exalting God as his chief good, and making him his supreme end.

And though the emanation of God's fulness which God intended in the creation, and which actually is the consequence of it, is to the creature as its object, and the creature is the subject of the fulness communicated, and is the creature's good; and was also regarded as such, when God sought it as the end of his works; yet it does not necessarily follow, that even in so doing, he did not make himself his end. It comes to the same thing. God's respect to the creature's good, and his respect to himself, is not a divided respect; but both are united in one, as the happiness of the creature aimed at, is happiness in union with himself. The creature is no further happy with this happiness which God makes his ultimate end, than he becomes one with God. The more happiness the greater the union: when the happiness is perfect, the union is perfect. And as the happiness will be increasing to eternity, the union will become more and more strict and perfect; nearer and more like to that between God the Father, and the Son; who are so united, that their interest is perfectly one. If the happiness of the creature be considered as it will be, in the whole of the creature's eternal duration, with all the infinity of its progress, and infinite increase of nearness and union to God; in this view the creature must be looked upon as united to God in an infinite strictness.

If God has respect to something in the creature, which he views as of everlasting duration, and as rising higher and higher through that infinite duration, and that not with constantly diminishing (but perhaps an increasing) celerity; then he has respect to it, as in the whole, of infinite height, though there never will be any particular time, when it can be said already to have come to such a height.

Let the most perfect union with God be represented by something at an infinite height above us; and the eternally increasing union of the saints with God, by something that is ascending constantly towards that infinite height, moving upwards with a given velocity, and that is to continue thus to move to all eternity. God, who views the whole of this eternally increasing height, views it as an infinite height. And if he has respect to it, and makes it his end, as in the whole of it, he has respect to it as an infinite height, though the time will never come when it can be said it has already arrived at this infinite height.

God aims at that which the motion or progression which he causes, aims at, or tends to. If there be many things supposed to be so made and appointed, that by a constant and eternal motion, they all tend to a certain centre; then it appears that he who made them, and is the cause of their motion, aimed at that centre, the term of their motion, to which they eternally tend, and are eternally, as it were, striving after. And if God be this centre, then God aimed at himself. And herein it appears, that as he is the first author of their being and motion, so he is the last end, the final term, to which is their ultimate tendency and aim.

We may judge of the end that the Creator aimed at, in the being, nature and tendency he gives the creature, by the mark or term which they constantly aim at in their tendency and eternal progress; though the time will never come, when it can be said it is attained to, in the most absolutely perfect manner.

But if the strictness of union to God be viewed as thus infinitely exalted, then the creature must be regarded as infinitely, nearly, and closely united to God. And viewed thus, their interest must be viewed as one with God's interest, and so is not regarded properly with a disjunct and separate, but an undivided respect. And as to any difficulty of reconciling God's not making the creature his ultimate end, with a respect properly distinct from a respect to himself, with his benevolence and free grace, and the creature's obligation to gratitude, the reader must be referred to Chap. I. Sec. 4, Object. 4, where this objection has been considered and answered at large.

If by reason of the strictness of the union of a man and his family, their interest may be looked upon as one, how much more one is the interest of Christ and his church (whose first union in heaven is unspeakably more perfect and exalted than that of an earthly father and his family), if they be considered with regard to their eternal and increasing union! Doubtless it may justly be esteemed as so much one, that it may be supposed to be aimed at and sought, not with a distinct and separate, but an undivided respect.

It is certain that what God aimed at in the creation of the world, was the good that would be the consequence of the creation, in the whole continuance of the thing created.

It is no solid objection against God's aiming at an infinitely perfect union of the creature with himself, that the particular time will never come when it can be said, the union is now infinitely perfect. God aims at satisfying justice in the eternal damnation of sinners; which will be satisfied by their damnation, considered no otherwise than with regard to its eternal duration. But yet there never will come that particular moment, when it can be said, that now justice is satisfied. But if this does not satisfy our modern freethinkers, who do not like the talk about satisfying justice with an infinite punishment; I suppose it will not be denied by any, that God, in glorifying the saints in heaven with eternal felicity, aims to satisfy his infinite grace or benevolence, by the bestowment of a good infinitely valuable, because eternal; and yet there never will come the moment, when it can be said, that now this infinitely valuable good has been actually bestowed.

FAREWELL SERMON

◇

¶ EDWARDS delivered this sermon in Northampton on July 2, 1750, after his people had formally and furiously repudiated him. The text is from II Cor. 1:14: "As also ye have acknowledged us in part, that we are your rejoicing, even as ye also are ours, in the day of the Lord Jesus." It is the most personal expression in all the published works, though at the same time the most thorough example of Edwards' strict obedience to the canons of the selfless plain style. The "doctrine" is that ministers and people must eventually meet before the throne of judgment; at conventional length he argues the proposition abstractly, and then in the "application" comes to this tremendous address to those who were driving him into the wilderness.

◇

BUT NOW I have reason to think, my work is finished which I had to do as your minister: you have publicly rejected me, and my opportunities cease.

How highly therefore does it now become us, to consider of that time when we must meet one another before the chief Shepherd? When I must give an account of my stewardship, of the service I have done *for,* and the reception and treatment I have had *among,* the people he sent me to: and you must give an account of your own conduct towards me, and the improvement you have made of these *three and twenty years* of my ministry. For then both you and I must appear together, and we both must give an account, in order to an infallible, righteous and eternal, sentence to be passed upon us, by him who will judge us, with respect to all that we have said or done in our meetings here, all our conduct one towards another, in the house of God and elsewhere, on sabbath-days and on other days; who will try our hearts, and manifest our thoughts, and the principles and frames of our minds, will judge us with respect to all the controversies: there is nothing covered, that shall not be revealed, nor hid, which shall not be known; all will be examined in the searching, penetrating light of God's omniscience and glory, and by him whose eyes are as a flame of fire; and truth and right shall be made plainly to appear, being stripped of every veil; and all error, falsehood, unrighteousness and injury, shall be laid open, stripped of every disguise; every specious pretence, every cavil, and all false reasoning, shall vanish in a moment, as not being able to bear the light of that day. And then our hearts will be turned inside out, and the secrets of them will be made more plainly to appear than our outward actions do now. Then it shall appear what the ends are, which we have aimed at, what have been the governing principles which we have acted from, and what have been the dispositions, we have exercised in our ecclesiastical disputes and contests. Then it will appear, whether I acted uprightly, and from a truly conscientious, careful regard to my duty to my great Lord and Master, in some former ecclesiastical controversies, which have been attended with exceeding unhappy circumstances, and consequences: it will appear, whether there was any just cause for the resentment which was manifested on those occasions. And then our late grand controversy, concerning the Qualifications necessary for admission to the privileges of members, in complete standing, in the Visible Church of Christ, will be examined and judged, in all its parts and circumstances, and the whole set forth in a clear, certain and perfect light. Then it will appear, whether the doctrine, which I have preached and published, concerning this matter, be Christ's own doctrine, whether he will not own it as one of the precious truths which have proceeded from his own mouth, and vindicate and honour, as such, before the whole universe. Then it will appear, what was meant by *the man that comes without the wedding garment;* for that is the day spoken of, Matt. xxii. 13., wherein such an one *shall be bound hand and foot, and cast into outer darkness, where shall be weeping and gnashing of teeth.* And then it will appear, whether, in declaring this doctrine, and acting agreeably to it, and in my general conduct in this affair, I have been influenced from any regard to my own temporal interest, or honour, or any desire to appear wiser than others; or have acted from any sinister, secular views whatsoever; and whether what I have done has not been from a careful, strict and tender regard to the will of my Lord and Master, and because I dare not offend him, being satisfied what his will was, after a long, diligent, impartial and prayerful, enquiry; having this constantly in view and prospect, to engage me to great solicitude, not rashly to determine truth to be on this side of the question, where I am now persuaded it is, that such a determination would not be for my temporal interest, but every way against it, bringing a long series of extreme difficulties, and plunging me into an abyss of trouble and sorrow. And then it will appear, whether my people have done their duty to their pastor, with respect to this matter; whether they have shown a right temper and spirit on this occasion; whether they have done me justice in hearing, attending to, and considering, what I had to say in evidence of what I believed and taught, as part of the counsel of God; whether I have been treated with that impartiality, candour and regard, which the just Judge esteemed due; and whether, in the many steps which have been taken, and the many things that have been said and done, in the course of this controversy, righteousness and charity and Christian decorum have been maintained: or, if otherwise, to how great a degree these things have been violated. Then every step of the conduct of each of us, in this affair, from first to last, and the spirit we have exercised in all, shall be examined and manifested, and our own consciences will speak plain and loud, and each of us shall be convinced, and the world shall know; and never shall there be any more mistake, misrepresentation or misapprehension of the affair, to eternity. . . .

THE BEAUTY OF THE WORLD

◇

¶ THIS fragment survives among Edwards' papers. To what place in his projected great synthesis of Christian doctrine it was designed to appertain is unknown. The theme is similar to that suggested in some passages of *True Virtue*. The dwelling on visual effects comes from his close study of Newton's *Opticks*. The concluding corollary, that men so love the beauty of this physical world they will prefer to live in it though in pain and anguish, reveals the passion with which Edwards had to contend against his own powerfully sensuous impulses.

◇

THE BEAUTY of the world consists wholly of sweet mutual consents, either within itself or with the supreme being. As to the corporeal world, though there are many other sorts of consents, yet the sweetest and most charming beauty of it is its resemblance of spiritual beauties. The reason is that spiritual beauties are infinitely the greatest, and bodies being but the shadows of beings, they must be so much the more charming as they shadow forth spiritual beauties. This beauty is peculiar to natural things, it surpassing the art of man.

Thus there is the resemblance of a decent trust, dependence and acknowledgment in the planets continually moving round the sun, receiving his influences by which they are made happy, bright and beautiful: a decent attendance in the secondary planets, an image of majesty, power, glory, and beneficence in the sun in the midst of all, and so in terrestrial things, as I have shown in another place.

It is very probable that that wonderful suitableness of green for the grass and plants, the blues of the skie, the white of the clouds, the colours of flowers, consists in a complicated proportion that these colours make one with another, either in their magnitude of the rays, the number of vibrations that are caused in the atmosphere, or some other way. So there is a great suitableness between the objects of different senses, as between sounds, colours, and smells; as between colours of the woods and flowers and the smells and the singing of birds, which it is probable consist in a certain proportion of the vibrations that are made in the different organs. So there are innumerable other agreeablenesses of motions, figures, etc. The gentle motions of waves, of [the] lily, etc., as it is agreeable to other things that represent calmness, gentleness, and benevolence, etc., the fields and woods seem to rejoice, and how joyfull do the birds seem to be in it. How much a resemblance is there of every grace in the field covered with plants and flowers when the sun shines serenely and undisturbedly upon them, how a resemblance, I say, of every grace and beautifull disposition of mind, of an inferiour towards a superiour cause, preserver, benevolent benefactor, and a fountain of happiness.

How great a resemblance of a holy and virtuous soul is a calm, serene day. What an infinite number of such like beauties is there in that one thing, the light, and how complicated an harmony and proportion is it probable belongs to it.

There are beauties that are more palpable and explicable, and there are hidden and secret beauties. The former pleases, and we can tell why; we can explain the particular point for the agreement that renders the thing pleasing. Such are all artificial regularities; we can tell wherein the regularity lies that affects us. [The] latter sort are those beauties that delight us and we cannot tell why. Thus, we find ourselves pleased in beholding the colour of the violets, but we know not what secret regularity or harmony it is that creates that pleasure in our minds. These hidden beauties are commonly by far the greatest, because the more complex a beauty is, the more hidden is it. In this latter fact consists principally the beauty of the world, and very much in light and colours. Thus mere light is pleasing to the mind. If it be to the degree of effulgence, it is very sensible, and mankind have agreed in it: they all represent glory and extraordinary beauty by brightness. The reason of it is either that light or our organ of seeing is so contrived that an harmonious motion is excited in the animal spirits and propagated to the brain. That mixture we call white is a proportionate mixture that is harmonious, as Sir Isaac Newton has shown, to each particular simple colour, and contains in it some harmony or other that is delightfull. And each sort of rays play a distinct tune to the soul, besides those lovely mixtures that are found in nature. Those beauties, how lovely is the green of the face of the earth in all manner of colours, in flowers, the colour of the skies, and lovely tinctures of the morning and evening.

Corollary: Hence the reason why almost all men, and those that seem to be very miserable, love life, because they cannot bear to lose sight of such a beautiful and lovely world. The ideas, that every moment whilst we live have a beauty that we take not distant notice of, brings a pleasure that, when we come to the trial, we had rather live in much pain and misery than lose.

FROM

IMAGES OR SHADOWS OF DIVINE THINGS

◇

¶ EDWARDS kept on his desk a special notebook in which he recorded observations under the wide heading of "images and shadows" observed in the world about him. Obviously he could have filled this with thousands of symbolical readings. Characteristically, he kept himself under severe control; he marked out only those phenomena in which he felt assured that he could discern a divine message. The rigor of his restraint and the delight with which he yielded himself to the rendering of an "image," once he felt it was clear, testify once more to the curiously Puritan passion with which he loved a world of manifestations, to which of course he would never permit himself to yield except by these indirections.

◇

1. DEATH temporal is a shadow of eternal death. The agonies, the pains, the groans and gasps of death, the pale, horrid, ghastly appearance of the corps, its being laid in the dark and silent grave, there putrifying and rotting and become exceeding loathsome and being eaten with worms (Isa. 66.24), is an image of the misery of hell. And the body's continuing in the grave, and never rising more in this world, is to shadow forth the eternity of the misery of hell.

13. THUS I believe the grass and other vegetables growing and flourishing, looking green and pleasant as it were, ripening, blossoming, and bearing fruit from the influences of the heavens, the rain and wind and light and heat of the sun, to be on purpose to represent the dependence of our spiritual wellfare upon God's gracious influences and the effusions of His holy spirit. I am sure there are none of the types of the Old Testament are more lively images of spiritual things. And we find spiritual things very often compared to them in Scripture.

21. THE PURITY, beauty, sublimity, and glory of the visible heavens as one views it in a calm and temperate air, when one is made more sensible of the height of them and of the beauty of their colour, when there are here and [there] interposed little clouds, livelily denotes the exaltedness and purity of the blessedness of the heavenly inhabitants. How different is the idea from that which we have in the consideration of the dark and dire caverns and abyss down in the depths of the earth! This teaches us the vast difference between the state of the departed saints and of damned souls; it shows the ineffable glory of the happiness of the one and the unspeakable dolefullness and terrours of the state of the other.

25. THERE are many things in the constitution of the world that are not properly shadows and images of divine things that yet are significations of them, as children's being born crying is a signification of their being born to sorrow. A man's coming into the world after the same manner as the beasts is a signification of the ignorance and brutishness of man, and his agreement in many things with the beasts.

79. THE WHOLE material universe is preserved by gravity or attraction, or the mutual tendency of all bodies to each other. One part of the universe is hereby made beneficial to another; the beauty, harmony, and order, regular progress, life, and motion, and in short all the well-being of the whole frame depends on it. This is a type of love or charity in the spiritual world.

156. THE BOOK of Scripture is the interpreter of the book of nature two ways, viz., by declaring to us those spiritual mysteries that are indeed signified and typified in the constitution of the natural world; and secondly, in actually making application of the signs and types in the book of nature as representations of those spiritual mysteries in many instances.

200. THOSE machines for the measuring of time are by wheels and wheels within wheels, some lesser, some greater, some of quicker, others of slower revolution, some moving one way, others another, some wheels dependent on others, and all connected together, all adjusted one to another, and all conspiring to bring about the same effect, lively represents the course of things in time from day to day, from year to year, and from age to age, as ordered and gouverned by divine providence.

WILLIAM L. HEDGES
Editor

Washington Irving

1783–1859

THE YOUNGEST child in the large family of a New York tradesman who had emigrated from Scotland a few years before the American Revolution, Washington Irving grew up in the expectation of making a career in law or business. The elder Irving's firm, which gradually expanded and passed into the hands of the several sons, traded in a variety of importations including dry goods, sugar, wine, and hardware. Two of the sons, Peter and John Treat, educated at Columbia College, became respectively doctor and lawyer. Washington was apprenticed to a lawyer at sixteen; three years later he transferred to the office of the prominent Federalist judge, Josiah Ogden Hoffman.

Outwardly, as one peruses it, the biography reads like a version of the American success story: from inconspicuous middle-class beginnings Irving rose to become his nation's first esteemed professional man of letters. His career often reveals a capacity, similar to that observable in the Irvings generally, for adapting to practical situations and making the most of business, social, and political opportunities. But his success was by no means guaranteed in advance. With the winning of political independence Americans had begun demanding a literature expressive of their distinctiveness as a nation. There was now, at least in theory, a place in American society for the creative writer. But the writer who deliberately set out to make a living at his calling faced stiff competition from British authors, whose work, in the absence of international copyright laws, was blithely reprinted in the United States without recompense to them. Many American readers remained hesitant about accepting native books lest the response be taken as a sign of bad taste. And while little patronage was to be looked for in a bourgeois republic, American Grubstreets, in New York, Philadelphia, or Boston, were not likely to provide young writers with the kind of stimulation that would help them finally to escape from hack work or routine journalism.

True, it was the gentlemanly thing for a man in business or one of the professions to take an interest in the arts, and New York in the first decade of the nineteenth century had something of the appearance of a boom town in fashion and culture. Literary societies flourished, and Irving's brothers participated in them. Peter and William Irving became minor writers, the former a newspaper editor as well, and though his New York *Morning Chronicle* served chiefly as a noisy conveyance for the Irvings' political views, which were at the time Burrite Republican, Peter did print Washington's early venture in theatrical criticism, *The Letters of Jonathan Oldstyle* (1802–03). The family thus recognized and encouraged the youngest son's talent. Sent abroad in 1804 on a cure for a mild consumptive tendency, Irving was expected to make his journey a kind of grand tour, improving his time in the galleries and museums. But when he returned in 1806, it was with the prospect of finally taking the bar examination. Literature was to be an avocation. For years he tried to accommodate himself to what his father and brothers considered their better judgment, that he should not altogether abandon the security of the law office or a business connection. And it was only in finally shaking off this affectionate but persistent solicitude at the age of thirty-six, long after he had achieved a minor literary triumph with *Knickerbocker's History of New York* (1809), that he made a career for himself as a writer.

Meanwhile, however, as an amateur, not dependent for his livelihood on selling his wares, Irving had been able to afford the luxury of brashness and irreverence. An element of practical joking, of hiding behind pen names and momentarily hoodwinking an audience, characterizes his youthful performances, culminating in the well-known spurious advertisements in the New York *Evening Post* in 1809 which explained that an eccentric antiquarian named Diedrich Knickerbocker had disappeared from a New York lodging-house leaving behind a manuscript history which was to be published to compensate the landlord for back rent. And in not going to college, Irving, whatever the disadvantage, at least escaped the ponderous indoctrination in religion, ethics, and the classics which American higher education in his day tended to promote. He read haphazardly but voraciously, as the breadth of allusion in *Knickerbocker* attests. He toured Europe in the same informal but enthusiastic way, learning to look at France and Italy through the eyes of Sterne, Addison, Pope, Ann Radcliffe, Claude Lorrain, Poussin, and Salvator Rosa, though he drew his brother William's censure because he passed up both Florence and Venice for the sake of "good company" on the road to Switzerland.

He was always an adept, though not an aggressive, socializer, and while he passed the bar examination in 1806—only, he later claimed, because "the examiners were prepossessed in my favour"—and entered a partnership with his brother John Treat, he preferred attending dances or indulging his taste for champagne, cigars, and good talk. Out of his mild carousing with other young business and professional men came the inspiration for *Salmagundi*, a periodical paper or magazine of burlesque humor and social satire with which Irving, his brother William, and James Kirke Paulding dazzled New York for a season in 1807–08.

Soon afterwards, as he worked with Peter Irving on the project which evolved into *Knickerbocker*, his realization that he had fallen in love with Judge Hoffman's daughter Matilda brought him to a crisis. For if he was to marry, he would have to earn a regular living. His prospects not being very bright, the sympathetic Hoffman offered to take him into his law firm. Irving agreed, though he dreaded the drudgery to which he felt he was condemning himself. Marriage would mean a drastic curtailment of his literary activities. But in February, 1809, Matilda fell ill of consumption and in April she died. There was a grievous irony in this catastrophe. Overwhelmed with sorrow at Matilda's death, he was yet freed from his bargain with Judge Hoffman. The complex shock suffered at this time is undoubtedly reflected in the sometimes frenzied and grotesque humor of *Knickerbocker*; Peter having gone abroad, Irving threw himself with such grim determination into the writing of the book that it was published before the year was out.

The immediate success of *Knickerbocker* established him as the leading practitioner of a school of satire and burlesque in New York which endured under the auspices of minor writers such as Paulding, Fitz-Greene Halleck, and Joseph Rodman Drake long after Irving had outgrown it. But he was left more hesitant than ever, unable to choose between literature and business. The next few years were largely unproductive, and it was to take another crisis to bring him to a final decision.

Going somewhat aimlessly to England in 1815, he found the Liverpool branch of the family enterprise on the verge of failure and Peter, who was in charge there, seriously ill. For more than two years Irving nursed the pair of invalids, until the Liverpool firm expired in bankruptcy. This exhausting and demoralizing experience, daily renewing his loathing for what he had earlier called a "sordid, dusty, soul killing way of life," removed any remaining doubts he had about trying to earn his living as a writer. By 1817 he was at work in his spare time on what was to become *The Sketch Book*, filling his notebooks with rough drafts and ideas for essays and tales, with descriptions of scenes and events encountered during holiday excursions in England, Wales, and Scotland. He made a pilgrimage to Abbotsford to see Sir Walter Scott, an admirer of *Knickerbocker*, and on Scott's advice began reading widely in German romantic literature.

As he wrote, he exercised a more restrained, studied style than that of his early period. He had an eye to immediate sales and could no longer afford to write for a purely local audience. Paying close attention to current literary vogues, he began to experiment with legendary, picturesque, sentimental, and Gothic elements in his work. When he was finally ready to publish, he carefully launched *The Sketch Book* piecemeal, watching the public's reaction to the early installments before risking others; in 1819 and 1820 he sent the material for seven separate booklets back to New York, where one of his brothers saw it through the press.

The Sketch Book had a good initial sale in the United States; even more important for his future reputation, the English edition, appearing almost simultaneously, won the warm approval of English critics, who praised it as the first readable piece of imaginative literature by an American. Furthermore, by retaining control of both the English and American editions, Irving prevented the book's being widely pirated and thus earned royalties in both countries at once, a stratagem which other American writers were quick to adopt.

Success kept him in Europe, following up one literary opportunity or another, for twelve more years. He was a literary celebrity now, praised by Byron, accepted by Francis Jeffrey of the *Edinburgh Review* and by that scourge of American authors, William Gifford of the *Quarterly*, and on friendly terms with a number of British writers, including Scott, Thomas Moore, Thomas Campbell, and Samuel Rogers. Having won his reputation by presenting himself in *The Sketch Book* as "Geoffrey Crayon, Gent.," an American exploring England and the English past, he went on to build *Bracebridge Hall* (1822) around Crayon's extended visit to an old English manor house. His next book, *Tales of a Traveller* (1824), published after an extended stay in Germany and France, was poorly received, but the setback to his reputation was only temporary. Early in 1826 he went to Spain at the behest of Alexander Everett, head of the American legation in Madrid, whose idea it was that Irving should translate Martín Fernández de Navarrete's recently published collection of documents relevant to the voyages of Columbus. Sensing instead the need for a full-scale biography based on unused sources, Irving was soon at work in Spanish libraries and archives. He stayed the better part of four years in Spain, long enough not only to publish both *The Life and Voyages of Christopher Columbus* (1828) and a second history, *A Chronicle of the Conquest of Granada* (1829), but also to find in his visit to Granada in 1828, during which he resided in the old Moorish palace of the Alhambra, inspiration for a Spanish "sketch book."

The Alhambra was published in 1832, the year in which Irving at last returned to the United States, to be greeted as a conquering hero. The year before, he had been given an honorary degree by Oxford. Henceforth he was increasingly to function as a kind of elder statesman of American literature. As early as 1826, while working on *Columbus*, he had been officially a member of the American legation. His legal training and knowledge of documents, his reputation as a writer, his social charm made him diplomatically negotiable. He had returned to London in 1829 as secretary to the legation there. Twelve years later, after having been courted for public office by both political parties, he was to accept appointment under President Tyler and Secretary of State Daniel Webster as minister to Spain.

Irving lived until 1859, enshrined after 1836 (except for the four-year mission to Spain) at Sunnyside, the old Dutch farmhouse at Tarrytown which he had converted into a studiedly picturesque country house, thereby lending his prestige to what soon became the rage for antique frills in American architecture. The last twenty-five years of his life reveal less the writer of fiction than the man of letters deemed capable of handling almost any topic with grace and distinction. John Jacob Astor furnished him with the documentary materials for a history of the noted fur-trading venture at the mouth of the Columbia River; these Irving developed into *Astoria* (1836). *The Crayon Miscellany* (1835) contained an account of his own trans-Mississippi trip in 1832. After a book on James Bonneville's trapping and exploring expedition in the Rocky Mountains, Irving produced biographies of Oliver Goldsmith and Mahomet, and terminated his career with the five-volume tribute to his namesake, *The Life of George Washington* (1855–59).

II

THE ENDURING reputation of Irving throughout the nineteenth century is an important aspect of the history of American taste. He gave the nation its first example of how to succeed at "culture," perhaps its first popular image of what it is to be cultured. He was, at least in his later years, that "dear and good Washington Irving" whom Thackeray knew, "gentle, generous, good-humored, affectionate, self-denying, . . . a delightful example of complete gentlemanhood"—all the more remarkable because, as Thackeray recalled, he was "born in no very high sphere." He had developed a smooth, "correct" prose style, which served as a model for generations of students of English composition. He was a lover of soft, picturesque landscapes. Like countless other American tourists, whose attitudes he had helped to mold, he could go giddy at the sight of a Gothic cathedral or an ivy-mantled tower. He was, as Thackeray said, "the first Ambassador from the New World of Letters . . . to the Old." As one who respected European taste, he tended to identify culture with a benign sense of the past. In short, the later Irving seemed a living demonstration of the primacy in art of the qualities which the Victorian era took for beauty: polish, ornamentation, and prettiness.

Modern criticism has on the whole been too ready to accept this view, with the result that in the revolution in literary taste which this century has undergone, Irving's reputation has steadily declined. Some attention has been called to the merits of his early satire, which is apt to attract the modern reader more than the sentiment. But the legendary Irving, the genial gentleman at Sunnyside, the old-bachelor uncle playing father to a bevy of nieces and encouraging young writers, still gets in the way of a real understanding and appreciation of the more significant and complex Irving of the years before the homecoming. Too often his earlier works are misread through a compulsion to fit him as nearly as possible, from beginning to end, into the mold of the Federalist gentleman of the old school, the softspoken romantic escapist, or the gentle, warm-hearted humorist.

Humor is at the root of almost everything that is important in Irving, but one needs to ask what he was laughing at, why he needed to laugh at all. It is a myth that his humor is always affectionate and well-meaning. Some of the laughter of the early period is closer to indignation than amusement. At nineteen he was using the signature "Jonathan Oldstyle," a curious yoking of conflicting associations, for Jonathan was the name commonly applied to the ordinary American, the Yankee Doodle who had put John Bull in his place. Irving could not with a straight face pretend to be an Oldstyle. The humor implicit in tying Jonathan to such a cognomen reflects the dilemma of a young writer trying to pass as a sophisticate in a culturally provincial community. From the time of Addison, the British, and later the American, essayist had spoken in the authoritative voice of a mature, if not elderly, gentleman of considerable experience, sense, and good taste. But New York in 1800 was not Augustan London. American newspapers, depending heavily on a broad, explosive humor and sarcasm, had vulgarized the periodical-essay tradition. Irving's humor, consciously playing with an empty form, makes a laughingstock of Oldstyle, who begins apologetically, "If the observations of an odd old fellow are not wholly superfluous, I would thank you to shove them into a spare corner of your paper." Irving goes on in the *Oldstyle* letters, and later in *Salmagundi* and *Knickerbocker*, to substitute frequently for the grace, wit, and restrained irony of the *Spectator* a humor of hyperbole, grotesque caricature, flagrant puns, and thunderous invective—the literary equivalent of theatrical slapstick.

With the nonsense rubric, beginning "In hoc est hoax," carried at the top of each number of *Salmagundi*, and the calculated contradictions in the traditional statement of purpose in the first number, the burlesque of the periodical-essay convention becomes explicit. The gesture is to some extent one in the direction of American literary independence. While reference to such obviously native elements as Indians, the wilderness, and the Revolutionary War had given the United States by the turn of the century the semblance of a national literature, American poems, novels, and plays remained essentially English in form and spirit. But in Irving's early work the masquerade, which the reader is intended to see through, of youthfulness posing as senility, exposes—and largely triumphs over—the futility of the American writer's dependence on hackneyed forms and techniques.

Irving belonged to a young society which was as suspicious of England and the Continent as it was eager for Old World approval. While Americans acknowledged their comparative backwardness and barrenness in the arts, the realization was irksome. It is not surprising to find an undercurrent of outright philistinism, of middle-class distrust of genuine cultivation in *Salmagundi*. The satire, however, cuts several ways at once. As a whole the papers give the impression of a society intensely busy with purely local affairs but apprehensive of the existence somewhere of a more cosmopolitan point of view, a society starved for culture but hardly willing to admit it. The foreign travelers lampooned by the magazine may be too quick to criticize American fashions, but New York's dependence on English and French milliners and French dancing masters invites the ridicule of Irving and his collaborators. Parvenuism runs rampant in the city; money is more important than taste, and what culture there is consists largely of lavish display. In *Salmagundi*'s conceit the stylish women at the Ballston spa are literally dressed in tobacco, cotton, and codfish, the produce on which their husbands' fortunes are built. Drama critics are mere pedants, businessmen and legislators slick operators and loud talkers. Aldermen's banquets count for more than decent government. The magazine suggests a society feverishly active but getting nowhere, composed of what are essentially "Little Great Men."

The authors seem alternately horrified and intrigued by the spectacle. The old bachelors who serve Paulding and the Irvings as pseudonyms sometimes seek refuge in rural retreats or recollections of a more placid past, but in so doing risk making even themselves look absurd, as they are at least half aware. Like many of Irving's works, even in the 1820's, *Salmagundi* pits a longing for sentiment against a readiness to ridicule sentimentality. The authors of *Salmagundi* could not be certain of their own superiority to their fellow citizens. One of the old bachelors, Launcelot Langstaff, rails furiously at politicians who abandon ideals and principles in order to seek preferment by doing the dirty-work of the ward boss. But "to stand up solely for the broad interests" of the whole nation, Langstaff admits, is to be "like a body in a *vacuum* between two planets," suspended "forever . . . motionless." This is about what Langstaff and his colleagues are reduced to—inertia.

Expressions of a yearning for a staid gentility, such as those sometimes made by the old bachelors, are usually taken too much at face value in interpretations that read everything in Irving in terms of a longing for a return of the good old days. He had never known good old days; he had known only the political wrangling of a young republic. And he was not above working as a ward politician himself, even at the time of *Salmagundi*, though he professed that "this serving of one's country is a nauseous piece of business." He remained suspicious of the temptation, which he was increasingly to feel, to believe that there had been a happier age which he had not experienced.

The fear that republicanism would degenerate into mob rule had made staunch, articulate conservatives out of many of the most forceful writers who had matured in the era of the Revolutionary War. That Irving picked up some of the attitudes and tricks of the trade of older American satirists—such as Joseph Dennie, Timothy Dwight, and John Trumbull—is shown in *Salmagundi*'s and *Knickerbocker*'s willingness to ridicule Thomas Paine and

Thomas Jefferson and to make scornful references to political factions as mere rabble. But Irving was not impressed by what the Federalists considered the enlightened self-interest of American lawyers, landowners, and businessmen. Conservative doctrine rested on a reverence for education, authority, and tradition, a faith which Irving called into question in the very act of burlesquing the periodical essay, since it was founded on similar assumptions.

Long uncertain as to basic philosophical issues more fundamental than politics, he could never take particular political dogmas as seriously as intellectual historians might wish he had. His father had been a stern and pious Presbyterian deacon, and Irving, recoiling into religious indifference and disgust at the hypocrisy he saw in the spectacle of pompous churchgoing, avoided formal affiliation until late in life. But emotionally he missed religion and found no substitute faith to which he could commit himself intellectually. During his early trip to Europe the artistic side of Catholicism, the beauty of church architecture, music, and liturgy, attracted him, but the doctrine, the hierarchy, and the "superstition," on which, typical of his age, he blamed peasant ignorance and impoverishment, appalled him.

Meanwhile the excesses of the French Revolution and the turmoil of the period of the Napoleonic Wars had somewhat cooled American ardor for the ideas of the Enlightenment. Neoclassical Reason had not, apparently, brought on a moral and social millenium, even in the United States. And the lesson which Irving learned on his first trip to Europe—Italy was the prime illustration—the lesson implied in the contemporary pre-Romantic vogue of ruins, stayed with him: it was that of the inevitable fall of empires, the transience of high civilization and political power.

Eventually he was to modulate his response to the mutability of human achievement into the melancholy key which was partially responsible for the popularity of *The Sketch Book.* His initial response, however, was far less restrained. *Salmagundi* and *Knickerbocker*, appropriating most of the basic devices of eighteenth-century English and American satire, generate an impression of a world turned topsy-turvy. Mock-heroic and mock-epic styles are so used as to make both the present and the past look out of joint. Suggesting Sterne in the tendency to expose every kind of behavior as eccentric, abnormal, *humour*ous, the early Irving lacks Sterne's warm sympathy for the essential human-ness of folly. He sometimes uses the irony of extended reversal in which Swift and Franklin ("An Edict by the King of Prussia," "The Sale of the Hessians") [1] specialized, where the reasonableness of patent absurdities is firmly and unconditionally insisted on. But in Irving an excited, shrill manner replaces the sophisticated patience behind the Swiftian pose.

The key to the *History of New York* is Diedrich Knickerbocker, a narrator so thoroughly confused as to keep the reader guessing whether Irving ever intends anything seriously. Knickerbocker is more than a pedantic antiquarian, more than another device—like the lumber of cryptic footnotes and citations of learned authorities—for satirizing dry-as-dust or overpretentious scholarship. He is a scholar whose wits seem to have been turned by the momentous burden laid upon him by his profession, the responsibility of ascertaining the true facts about the past, interpreting them reliably, and making them seem significant to the reader. On one level the book is a commentary on historiography, skeptical in its implications. Bewildered by conflicting conceptions of proper historiographical procedures, Knickerbocker inadvertently exposes their various limitations in shifting distractedly from one to another. From time to time he even gives way to guilt feelings, blaming himself as an historian for luring men on after enduring fame and greatness, in the pursuit of which they must inevitably inflict suffering on fellow human beings.

A caricature, of course, not a realistic portrayal, the eccentric Knickerbocker in his sad plight is hardly intended to compel the reader's sympathy. He is a metaphor through which the author suggests the failure of the world as he sees it to make complete sense. Knickerbocker's wildest statements are referable not so much to a real state of mind as, in some accidental and yet half-meaningful way, to the general state of human affairs. Irving's skill is in keeping his narrator consistently inconsist-

[1] See pp. 125–27 and 127–28 of this volume.

ent so that the reader can accept flat contradictions, irrelevant garrulity, and abrupt shifts of tone and style as all in keeping with Knickerbocker's character. Plausibly juxtaposing shrewd insight and arrant nonsense, *Knickerbocker* constantly teases the reader into the suspicion that it may be impossible to distinguish between the two.

Knickerbocker's want of discrimination tends to make opposites look surprisingly alike—savage and sophisticate, past and present, Catholic and Puritan, New Amsterdam and New York, North and South, the United States and Europe. Comparisons and contrasts, stated or implied, serve as constant springboards to points of view from which even the highest and mightiest can be looked down on—thus, Knickerbocker suggests, the man in the moon may look down on modern Europeans as savages. Irving's ability to put a finger on human pettiness is almost as striking as Swift's, but he has difficulty measuring degrees of it. *Knickerbocker*, for instance, lacks a scale of values such as that implied in *Gulliver's Travels* in the range from Yahoos to humans to Houyhnhnms. Irving presents no clear image of common sense. William Kieft, the thinly disguised philosopher-president Jefferson, is easily identifiable as an intellectual quack. But Peter Stuyvesant's common sense is hard to separate from his hard-headed anti-intellectualism and from a stubbornness which is sometimes the next thing to stupidity. If Irving, in spite of the irony of Knickerbocker's exorbitant insistence on Stuyvesant's greatness, succeeds in arousing the reader's sympathies for the Dutch governor, it is for qualities of courage, honesty, and loyalty which are constantly threatened with extinction, even by forces within the man himself. Perhaps the alarming thing about *Knickerbocker* is that it asks in effect whether *common* sense isn't simply a myth, whether human beings can in fact ever for very long overcome private prejudices and temperamental distractions so that they see things objectively, in the light of common interests. The total effect of *Knickerbocker* is a combination of sheer delight in a world in which everything has its comic side and occasional anxiety over the possibility that what can so easily be made comic may at bottom be meaningless. It is a distortion to ignore either part of the composite impression.

At a time when the desire for a distinctively national literature was prodding writers into inflating the image of the American past through historical novels and epic poems, such as Joel Barlow's *Columbiad* (1807), Irving's *History* offered the nation, as James Russell Lowell was to say, "dry and unpoetic" facts; and the "clear, prosaic daylight" in which they were presented made "the actors and the deeds they were concerned in seem ludicrously small when contrasted with the semi-mythic grandeur in which we have clothed them." A fat, phlegmatic, comfort-loving race, so encumbered by layer upon layer of protective clothing that strenuous puffing on a leisurely pipe is apt to exhaust them, Irving's Dutchmen, though they are now and then aroused by the beauty of the American landscape, hear no call to heroic action in the settlement of a new world. The voyage of the *Half Moon* under Henry Hudson proves singularly uneventful: "They [ate] hugely, drank profusely, and slept immeasurably." The departure of the Dutch colonists in a vessel "full in the bows, with a pair of enormous cat-heads, a copper bottom, and withal a most prodigious poop," floating "sideways" out of the harbor, like a "majestic goose," bears scant resemblance to the sailing of the *Mayflower*, or of the *Nina*, *Pinta*, and *Santa Maria*.

Irving makes the Dutch the primary symbol of the stolid middle-class materialism which, like ballast, weighs down, and sometimes virtually sinks, American life, in spite of the lofty pull of professed ideals. In *Knickerbocker* self-government sometimes seems no more than the petty wrangling of "meddlesome" burghers in New Amsterdam. The mock-historian compares the intolerance of partisan politicians and editors in contemporary New York with the persecution of Quakers and Anabaptists and the hanging of witches in seventeenth-century Massachusetts. In effect the book denies the newness of the New World, sees Americans through their susceptibility to human weakness and error as belonging to the world that is as old as Adam. Northerner or Southerner, Yankee or New Yorker, they are a nation of farmers and tradesmen, who are apt to drive a hard bargain, take advantage of Indians and Negroes, and show more interest in political banquets, horse races, cocktails, and bundling than in things of the mind or spirit.

III

THE HUMOR of Irving's early work fully exposed the inapplicability to current awarenesses of various eighteenth-century literary conventions and assumptions. This effort ultimately relates him to other writers for whom the older forms were becoming intolerable restraints in the face of growing Romantic demands for a more personalized, a more intensely emotional expression. Meanwhile, however, his inability to locate reliable standards by which he could make judgments without misgivings had brought his sense of the ridiculous to the verge of nonsense. His subsequent advancement as a writer involved efforts to escape this trap.

While it was natural that in the sort of intellectual vacuum he had come to inhabit he should be increasingly responsive to the appeals of Romanticism, there long remained forces within him that balked at the response. He had a personal stake in the forms and attitudes which he was beginning to investigate at the time of *The Sketch Book*—eager as he was also to please an audience—but his original pseudosophistication continued to involve him in a fear of seeming to take anything too seriously. There were limits to his capacity for renewing himself in literature with sentimental or sensational indulgences. And when a limit was reached, the satirical impulse would reassert itself. From *The Sketch Book* through *The Alhambra* the nonhistorical works are often curious compounds of direct demands on readers' emotions and humorous undercuttings of these same effects. Indeed Irving's real strength in this period depends on the resistance he offers to his own weakness for melancholy rumination, rhapsodic flights of fancy, and Gothic titillation.

The uneasiness of his accommodation to the newer fashions shows constantly in *The Sketch Book*. References in "The Author's Account of Himself" to the "gigantic race" in England from which Americans are "degenerated" raise questions as to the seriousness of the preceding passages which invoke with exaggerated eloquence the contrasting beauties of American and English scenes. And "Rip Van Winkle," a story of a shrewish wife and a good-for-nothing husband, mocks by its position the sentimentalism of the narrative which it immediately follows, called "The Wife," a tale of an earnest, hard-working young businessman and his brave, devoted little suburban housewife.

What holds the disparate pieces together and staves off chaos is the ingenious device of the pseudonym; Geoffrey Crayon converts Irving's intellectual and temperamental indecisiveness into a positive asset. Irving was still tentatively hanging on to one of the formalities of the eighteenth-century periodical, trying to give a unity to his somewhat miscellaneous materials by presenting every item as in some way a reflection of the interests and personality of the fictitious author-editor. An inscription on the title page establishes Crayon as a "mere spectator of other men's fortunes and adventures." He is not, however, a spectator of the Addisonian stamp, calm and serene at his vantage point above the moil and toil of daily life. Irving's inscription significantly comes from *The Anatomy of Melancholy* and connects Crayon with Burton's Democritus Junior, an uncertain and somewhat neurotic spectator who would like to be more deeply involved in the world's affairs but is fearful of becoming too involved.

Behind Crayon one senses the actual Irving, almost an old bachelor himself by now, his life still unsettled, drifting into middle age, fearful of failure, the genial exterior often masking an inner anxiety. Through Crayon he makes a fiction of his own situation, dramatizing both his interests in the antique, the picturesque, the sentimental, and his fears that such interests may make him ridiculous. He invites the reader to feel comfortably superior to Crayon if he wants to, to laugh off some of the excesses of sentiment and platitude in *The Sketch Book* as nothing more than the self-indulgence of an avowed believer in broken hearts. It is appropriate, given Crayon's character, for him to be interested in homes, houses, lovers' quarrels, marriages, and mother love. He *knows* he is a bit sentimental and laughs at himself for it. Lacking real attachments, he makes more than he should of casual ones, of remembered ones, searches in old books for the meanings he fails to find in life.

The complexity of tone and feeling in *The Sketch Book* can be seen clearly in its attitude toward the past. In spite of the mockery of history in *Knickerbocker,* Irving was becoming increasingly curious about the past. Less suspicious of Europe now than as a young man, and partly prompted by the Romanticists' interest in folklore and the Middle Ages, he was beginning to formulate what later writers from Cooper to Henry James would develop into a classic contrast between Europe and the United States. As Crayon was to say in *Bracebridge Hall,* "To a man from a young country, all old things are in a manner new. . . ." Sketches of Crayon retracing the footsteps of Falstaff and Prince Hal to the Boar's Head Tavern, of his trying at Stratford-on-Avon to get the feel of Shakespeare's early life, undoubtedly had a peculiar intensity for American readers. For it was the antique finish everywhere visible on the surface of the parent culture that, when one felt the rough edges of earnest practicality protruding from American life, defined Europe.

The Sketch Book gives the first important display in American literature of affection for England, for what Hawthorne was to call "our old home," for English landscape and village life, for English character and the forms and ceremonies that regulate English behavior, for architectural landmarks and monuments crusted over with associations of a memorable past. "The great charm," says Crayon,

> of English scenery is the moral feeling that seems to pervade it. It is associated in the mind with ideas of order, of quiet, of sober well-established principles, of hoary usage and reverend custom. Every thing seems to be the growth of ages of regular and peaceful existence.

Yet there is an ominous note in Crayon's flirtation with history. Often his encounters with old buildings or old books become direct confrontations of a disturbing aspect of the past. A frequently repeated image in *The Sketch Book* is that of Crayon passing through an ancient Gothic portal, as in "Westminster Abbey," into an inner enclosure, where, immured with relics of previous ages, he is temporarily cut off from an actual present. Although at first in the Abbey he seems to experience the escapist's thrill that, availing himself of Romantic jargon, he rather fatuously talks about in "The Author's Account of Himself," there comes a moment when the sculpture and ornament in the chapels and about the tombs suggest a life so remote in time and so different from that of the present as to have no real connection with it. Before the sketch is over the only meaning he can discover in the ruin and decay of history is the mutability of all earthly accomplishment.

Crayon's desire to "lose myself in the shadowy grandeurs of the past" thus often carries him further than he expected, sometimes almost turning his interest in the past into a morbid fear of death. Little old men, images of life over and done with and passed into history, prowl through *The Sketch Book*—"an old verger, in his black gown" in Westminster Abbey, "seeming like a spectre from one of the neighboring tombs"; the bowlers in the ampitheater in "Rip Van Winkle"; the "superannuated" retainers in the nooks and crannies of John Bull's mansion. Such figures seem to haunt Crayon, satirizing an antiquarianism which threatens to make him another Knickerbocker.

Irving was living, perhaps helping to create, an American conflict. At a time when the nation's history seemed peculiarly brief and largely unformulated, the effort to discover or create a past either at home or in Europe became for some American writers a search for identity, an effort of self-understanding. Yet often underneath nagged the notion of the United States as a land so much of the future as to render the past irrelevant. In "English Writers on America" in *The Sketch Book,* while urging patience and tolerance in England of American efforts to achieve cultural maturity, Crayon calls upon Americans to acknowledge that their natural cultural ties are with England:

> We are a young people, necessarily an imitative one, and must take our examples and models, in a great degree, from the existing nations of Europe. There is no country more worthy of our study than England.

This outlook on American literature and culture, which was to be encouraged by later writers, particularly Lowell, is, of course, the logical one to contrast with the view so vigorously proclaimed in Emerson's "The American Scholar." Irving, however, was not always so sanguine about "jolly, old England," or about his own understanding of the problem of culture. Crayon later in *The Sketch Book* regrets having dared to "play" the "preceptor," doubts that "the world" is "to be made wiser by [his] talk." What finally distinguishes *The Sketch Book* is not an act of unabashed, uncritical submission to English supremacy in the arts and literature so much as an impression the book gives through Crayon of an American's now curious, now awe-inspired, now anxious and even fearful investigation of his cultural heritage in England coupled with his occasional longing looks over his shoulder at the country he is leaving behind.

For ironically Irving's best work in *The Sketch Book* is in the American stories, which have absolutely nothing to do with hedgerows, Yorkshire pudding, or Robin Goodfellow. As the introductory descriptions, which avoid the inflated rhetoric of "The Author's Account of Himself," make clear, "Rip Van Winkle" and "The Legend of Sleepy Hollow" are, in spite of being adaptations of German folk tales, tributes to the natural beauty of the American countryside, an opulent, amenable terrain which the author had known in the summers of his boyhood and which remained clear in his mind even as he began to find himself a figure in an ordered, park-like English landscape.

Only gradually, as he learned what his readers would tolerate and to what extent he could square his own interests with those of his public, did Irving's Romanticism jell into the set of stock responses with which his position in American literature finally became associated. In *Bracebridge Hall* his affection for the quainter aspects of the English scene proved harder to sustain, though his audience may not have been aware of the fact. Unable to take his manor-house characters, their attitudes, ideals, and eccentricities as seriously as so extensive a work demanded, he began to make them appear more ridiculous than in his moods of Anglophilia he must originally have intended. Ironically it is a few brawling satirical scenes reminiscent of the subversive humor of his early period, together with one or two interpolated stories, that come close to saving the book today.

In *Tales of a Traveller* he cut down on mere sentiment and worked toward a curious yoking of broad humor and Gothic sensationalism. Poe was later to speak approvingly of the book in his review of Hawthorne's *Twice-Told Tales* (see pp. 465–69), but the failure of Irving's *Tales* with the public helped turn him toward the safer ground of nonfiction. He worked hard at making himself a historian, learning Spanish and taking particular pains in *Columbus* to achieve factual accuracy. He produced a biography which, emphasizing the failures and disappointments of Columbus's previously neglected third and fourth voyages, long remained historically useful. But Irving's effectiveness as a historian was limited by his refusal to concern himself deeply with political, economic, and social problems. Here his successors in Romantic historiography, Prescott, Parkman, and Motley, had the better of him; they were thorough students of history before they began to write it. Irving remained primarily a fictionalist. What finally interested him in Columbus was the mythic quality of the man's life; he worked instinctively to present him as an example of the archetypal romantic, quixotic visionary, by no means consistently practical, doomed to endless searching and long-suffering by the combined brilliance and blindness of his imagination. The symbolic concern, carried to an extreme, begins to turn Irving's biography into fiction.

In the *Conquest of Granada* he showed his fictionalist's hand openly by reverting to the use of a pen name. An account, full of exotic costuming and pageantry, of the final expulsion of the Moors from Spain, the book is essentially true in fact, but Irving, eschewing scholarly objectivity, pretends that his narrative is a translation of a medieval chronicle written by a bigoted old ecclesiastic, Fray Antonio Agapida. If the reader is invited to laugh occasionally at Agapida's superstitiousness he is also invited to view the wars of Granada with him in a framework of Christian mythology. The result is a legendary, romance-like quality, the book symbolically suggesting and reiterating the axiom of the inevitable doom of even the most heroic of man's attempts to re-establish a paradise on earth.

Irving was, of course, still working variations on the theme of mutability. This one had already been to a considerable extent prefigured in *Tales of a Traveller*'s emphasis on the vanity of "golden dreams"—Tom Walker's, for instance. *The Alhambra* intensifies and makes more personal the same quixotic element by unifying various tales, scraps of history, and scenic sketches around Irving's own situation as a temporary occupant of the ancient palace. There is a falling off in the purely fictitious pieces in *The Alhambra*, but the over-all impression is not without force, as the author succeeds in identifying his own restless existence with that of the Moors exiled from the gardens of Granada in the fifteenth century and with that of the Spaniards living sometimes forlornly in the shadow of their Golden Age.

When the American exile returned to his native land, he found a home at last, and conflicts ceased. Unlike Cooper, who, two years later, in 1834, after a stay in Europe, angrily discovered an America menaced by Jacksonian vulgarity and conformism, Irving, for all his love of old things, largely accepted the affluent and expanding, hard working and self-satisfied mid-century America which had so eagerly accepted him. He left to younger writers the job of finding meanings in American life. He was getting old and had scrambled too hard simply to become a writer. Assured of an audience, he did not scruple now to write in the Romantic idiom in which they and he were fully conversant.

Looking at the wild West, he was apt to see knights and squires, noble savages, picturesque groupings around a campfire, landscapes suggesting the "golden tone" of Claude Lorrain, and light filtering through forest trees like "sunshine among the stained windows and clustering columns of a Gothic cathedral." Often, he abandoned such language in favor of a more nearly objective kind of reporting which stressed ludicrous detail. The inconsistencies were less apparent and less important to an age that had not, like ours, been bred to realism. As long as he confined himself, as he usually did, to externals, he was helping Americans to *see* the West.

Inevitably his Oliver Goldsmith turned out rather like the popular image of Washington Irving, both as a man and as a writer. And in the biography of Washington (1855–59) he tried to animate the conventional metaphor of "the father of his country." Increasingly the dry ring of mid-Victorian eloquence sounded in his later prose; he was capable of complaining of the "stupid, commonplace, and often ribald" place names, like "Big River," which the settlers in the West had substituted for more picturesque Indian names. Only occasionally in these years does one come across such satirical outcroppings as when, in the late thirties, the spectacle "of that eagerness for gain, and rage for improvement, which keep our people continually on the move" ("The Creole Village"), prompted him to coin the phrase "the almighty dollar."

IV

IRVING's literary significance begins with his instinctive realization, important in his day in a nation as puritanical in background as the United States, that literature's first function is to engage and entertain the reader. He had a healthy respect for the priority of style, the way a thing is said, to message or moral. His exuberant early style, through the popularity of *Knickerbocker*, helped establish a tradition of verbal extravagance combined with bluntness of tone which still persists at a certain level of American journalistic prose. The youthful style is itself something of a salmagundi, a conglomeration in which elegant phrases and imagery, literary echoes (used either soberly or in mockery), technical jargon, and homely idiom ironically jostle one another. The mixture of attitudes in the early work encourages and often justifies the eclecticism.

Irving's delight in language seems to begin as a response to sounds, to the brazenness, for instance, of colloquial invective—"slang-whangers," Salmagundese for newspaper editors—or to the harsh pedantry of a coinage like "logocracy"—a government by words. He is willing to go out of his way for special effects in making words jingle and clatter against one another, the most obvious instance coming in *Knickerbocker* when at the battle of Fort Christina he marshals the awkward-sounding Dutch names in a long, rhyming, rhythmic list. Above all he likes the solid, unadorned sounds of the words for the objects and activities by which most of the every-day business of the world is transacted—"market-baskets, butchers' blocks, and wheelbarrows"; a "cit" who "rattles away" "in a buggy or tim-whisky." The absence of pretty melody in such concatenations, which are often nonetheless highly alliterative, seems to amuse the Oldstyle in Irving, while the roughness appeals to the Jonathan and curiously relates the prose on one level to early American plainness.

The mature style strives on the whole for smoother, softer sounds, for an over-all sense of grace. It relies heavily on medium to longish sentences, balanced phrasing, and a judicious mixing of latinate abstractions and concrete English nouns, adjectives, and verbs. While derived from the English eighteenth century, from Addison and Goldsmith, this style is a flexible one, on the whole more informal, less bookish than Cooper's, Hawthorne's or Poe's. Under the polished surface there still lurks a fondness for the ordinary. It was only later, as he settled into the role of national celebrity, that his attitude in favor of the picturesque and against the commonplace hardened. In the works of the 1820's much of his concern is with commonplace material. The opening paragraphs of "The Stout Gentleman," for instance, revel in the prosaic language which describes the drab exterior and interior of a small English inn for commercial travelers.

Numerous passages in Irving's stories and sketches seek to give a half humorous impression of the hustle and bustle of daily affairs by invoking a torrent of terms belonging to a particular occupation or locale. Dolph Heyliger in *Bracebridge* "was soon up to his ears in medical studies, being employed, morning, noon, and night, in rolling pills, filtering tinctures, or pounding the pestle and mortar in one corner of the laboratory. . . ." In a similar fashion commonplace diction and metaphor starkly and ludicrously mire Ichabod Crane in his backwater rural neighborhood, for all his "gentlemanlike" pretensions: on horseback "his sharp elbows [stick] out like grasshoppers' " and "the motion of his arms [is] not unlike the flapping of a pair of wings"; on foot, he is like a "scarecrow," has a "spindle neck," a "snipe nose," a head like a "weathercock," and feet like "shovels." Again, connection with proverbial wisdom gives vitality to Rip Van Winkle, who likes to "take the world easy, eat white bread or brown, . . . and would rather starve on a penny than work for a pound"; as for his wife—"a tart temper never mellows with age, and a sharp tongue is the only edged tool that grows keener with constant use."

Elsewhere mundane and erudite connotations clash comically. Rip's dog, threatened with a "broomstick or ladle," makes for the door with "yelping precipitation." "Sleepy Hollow" begins in the mild, perhaps unconscious, whimsy of an extensively latinate diction brought to bear on the homely scene of Tarry Town, and in the euphemistic discussion of Rip's plain, ordinary laziness the exploitation of the incongruity between refined style and commonplace subject becomes quite deliberate: "The great error in Rip's composition was an insuperable aversion to all kinds of profitable labor."

At its best then Irving's mature style, though in a much more restrained way than in *Knickerbocker*, still plays off the elegant and the commonplace, the narrative voice never fully identifying with either. The peculiar sensibility of Geoffrey Crayon, the American as "Gent.," is a product of the tension. Having risen above vulgar origins, Crayon (or Irving) can contemplate the ordinary with amused fondness. At the same time he can see the humorous side of his claim to cultivation and make fun of the tendency toward inflated language which often accompanies a fashionable style.

Beyond style, though not unrelated to it, lies Irving's contribution to the development of the short story. In part this came through the invention of Crayon. For out of Crayon's situation comes Irving's most distinctive type of sketch, not a flat description of scene or character or an unrelieved evocation of mood or atmosphere, but a first-person narrative in which Crayon, as he speaks, inadvertently reveals almost as much about himself as about his surroundings. Often he appears partially alienated from the world at large, able to see it or hear it only imperfectly, at a distance or through a shadow or distraction.

Implicit in the Crayonesque sketch is the irony of the limited viewpoint, which American fiction from Irving through Melville half-consciously utilized before Henry James began to exploit it systematically. Many of Irving's sketches, such as "The Mysterious Chambers," retain some of the atmosphere of suspense which characterizes Gothic fiction: Crayon (or Irving) exploring secluded passageways, for instance, parallels the Gothic protagonist braving the haunted house. But the sketch, like some of Poe's first-person narratives and like Melville's "Bartleby" (see pp. 904–20), begins to throw the emphasis from spectacle back to spectator, to ask what the situation may mean to him, to interpret what he sees as at least partially a function of his character.

Irving was no psychologist, but in finding a place in his sketches for a figure embodying some of the salient features of his own personality, he helped introduce into American fiction a potentially subtle, subjective element. Hawthorne's sketches, reflecting another partially alienated observer, use a narrative voice carrying Crayonesque overtones. It is a voice which, finally projected through Miles Coverdale in *The Blithedale Romance*, becomes insistent enough to divert Hawthorne's attention from the main complication his narrator is supposed to be reporting to the question of the healthiness of Coverdale's motives in wanting to unravel the mystery of other people's lives.

In "The Stout Gentleman" from *Bracebridge Hall* the Crayonesque sketch becomes a self-contained story. Ostensibly about the title character, the narrative proves finally to be a joke on the narrator, not Crayon but another "nervous" gentleman. Irving plays a characteristic trick on the unsophisticated reader overly intent on action, suspense, and sensational disclosure, for "The Stout Gentleman" discloses nothing. It must be accepted on a more mundane level, where Irving's talent for registering prosaic detail on the surface of ordinary existence sustains an illusion of life—life going on too busily for the imaginative spectator, the armchair philosopher or storyteller to comprehend fully in one searching glance or ingenious hypothesis.

In his short stories Irving usually starts with stock characters—the shiftless husband, for instance, and the termagant wife. Yet he manages in his better work to set them in homely situations and surroundings which give them a kind of vitality. And his choice of incidents and descriptive details that offset, echo, or otherwise interact with one another touches off patterns of imagery which symbolically amplify basic themes. "Rip Van Winkle" and "The Legend of Sleepy Hollow" also have a mock-Gothic quality about them. Rip gets lost in an enchanted wood, but the ghosts he encounters prove merely silent and indifferent. And the only ghost in Sleepy Hollow is Brom Bones with his pumpkin. Yet these stories are more than burlesques. "The Legend of Sleepy Hollow" is a fable about American affluence. Lacking all the commonplace American virtues —physical prowess, business sense, a cheery appetite for hard work—Ichabod Crane, who enjoys frightening himself with ghost stories, is a sorry misfit doomed from the start to defeat at the hands of Brom Bones. Though he lusts after the plump Katrina and her father's fat estate from afar, the lean and hungry schoolmaster is too diffident to win his wife and fortune in the ordinary straightforward American way. He is a potential old-bachelor recluse and pedant, the likes of which Irving (or Crayon) may be half-inclined to deny in himself. Not until he has been nearly scared out of his wits does the doleful Ichabod learn to settle down to enjoying the good things of this life, which, the story seems to say, are there for anyone who is not simply afraid to reach for them. Though much of the strength of "Sleepy Hollow" stems from the fact that the author's sympathy for its quixotic mock-hero is maintained almost to the end, Irving now looks more fondly than in *Knickerbocker* on his fat, pipe-smoking Dutchmen and on a land which seems to sprout prosperity as an annual crop, a reward for American good humor.

As for the overly aggressive tendencies, the

blustering and hard-bargaining that had upset Knickerbocker, "Rip Van Winkle" suggests that they may be quietly lived down. "Rip" is a justifiably famous story, though its richness of implication has until recently been largely obscured by its reputation as a children's story and by the memory of the sentimentalized play version, which the actor Joseph Jefferson made into a great nineteenth-century hit. Beneath the obvious humor and pathos signs of decay, sterility, and impotence point to the fact that the story, like Hawthorne's "Wakefield" (see pp. 709–12), deals with the loss or surrender of manhood. An exchange is made of what ought to be the best twenty years of Rip's life, the years of his active maturity, for a peaceful old age. He sleeps, dreaming at first only of the silent little men playing at bowls, then of nothing. Meanwhile, back home men fight a war and establish a new nation. In the end Rip becomes, in effect, a benign old bachelor. Irving does not blink the grave difficulties involved in accommodating to such a fate. They are felt in a few fearful passages, in Rip's first glance into the deep glen, in his bewilderment on waking up, in his re-entry into his deserted house.

But Rip is resilient enough to slough off his misfortune and turn it to advantage. For he has slept out a fate worse than the loss of twenty years; he has, after all, escaped that nagging, insistent spirit of American industry, his wife. And now he makes a big success of failure, as Irving's humor continues to deflate American myths. Rip gets by famously as an idler, a gossip, a dreamer, as someone who helps his neighbors and gets on well with children, not as a man who minds his own business and zealously guards his reputation for keeping his nose to the grindstone.

Part I of *Tales of a Traveller*, after a prefatory note in which a confident, almost cocky, Crayon presents Irving's most determinedly antididactic statement of his theory of literature, gives (as Part III does later) a sort of laboratory demonstration of his conception of the short story. It starts with comic ghost stories, outright burlesques of the haunted-house convention, and works up gradually to a story packed with as much violent action as a Gothicist could want. Significantly, however, ghost and horror are referred back to the mind and character of the protagonist. The "Adventure of the German Student" comes about midway in this development, at the point where the narratives begin to take on seriousness. It can be read either ironically or straight. Symbolically it makes perfect sense as the fantasy of one of Irving's isolated scholarly bachelors with fearfully mixed feelings toward the opposite sex. But the coda makes another joke of the tale, and the hurried, overwrought style, suggesting a parody in advance of Poe, invites reservations.

Irving could not work inside character (except with someone like Crayon) sufficiently well to give his more dramatic stories the psychological authenticity they demand. His best efforts come through the lighter, more relaxed, half-humorous approach. "The Devil and Tom Walker," for instance, spares the reader an obvious moral, yet in its somewhat harum-scarum, folktalish way it begins to bring certain aspects of Puritanism into dramatic focus. Irving uses a comic-Yankee stereotype and a relatively stock conception of Puritanism; as in his satiric broadsides against Puritan bigotry and superstition in *Knickerbocker*, he is still the more or less unsympathetic outsider looking on. It was to take a Hawthorne in "Young Goodman Brown" (see pp. 702–09) to get inside the individual Puritan's dilemma. But the two stories are worth comparing in detail. For Irving, in relating Yankee shrewdness to Puritan respectability, is already developing an imagery of darkness, rottenness, and emptiness to contrast with the seemingly shining solidity of proper and pious professions; he sees the traditional encounter with the devil in forest and swamp as a function of attitudes visible in pulpit and counting-house.

He had not learned, as Hawthorne and, particularly, Poe were to learn, the full value of compactness in the short story. He builds toward the series of tales rather than toward the single story. But the rich profusion of Romantic props manipulated for symbolic effect—mirrors, portraits, masquerades, gardens, fountains, astrologers, buried treasure—conventional though much of it is, and often extended as a not entirely satisfactory substitute for more compact action, makes Irving's work a kind of seedbed of imagery in early American fiction. He points to the possibility of going beyond the contemporary journalistic tale, beyond the *Blackwood's* "intensities," which Poe was to satirize, to a short fiction which, while still using Gothic devices, can begin to suggest real intricacies of character and motive.

READING SUGGESTIONS

EDITIONS

Irving revised most of his work between 1848 and 1850. The standard edition is *The Works of Washington Irving*, 21 vols. (1860–61). Many of the notebooks and journals have been edited. There are modern reprints of the original editions of *Knickerbocker*, Introduction by Stanley T. Williams and Tremaine McDowell (1927), and *The Letters of Jonathan Oldstyle*, Introduction by Stanley T. Williams (1941). John F. McDermott has edited *A Tour on the Prairies* (1956).

BIOGRAPHY

The definitive biography, an invaluable work and a monument to scholarship, is Williams' *The Life of Washington Irving* (1935). A good general introduction to Irving and the background of his work is available through Henry Seidel Canby's *Classic Americans* (1931), Henry A. Pochmann's Introduction to *Washington Irving: Representative Selections* (1934), Williams' chapter on Irving in R. E. Spiller *et al.*, editors, *Literary History of the United States* (1948), and Edward Wagenknecht's *Washington Irving* (1962). Pierre M. Irving's *The Life and Letters of Washington Irving* (1862–64) contains useful source material. A special biographical study is Walter A. Reichart, *Washington Irving and Germany* (1957). Pochmann's "Irving's German Sources in *The Sketch Book*," *Studies in Philology*, XXVII (1930), 477–507, contains important discoveries.

CRITICISM

Detailed interpretation and criticism of individual works exist only in article form:

E. A. Greenlaw, "A Comedy of Politics," *Texas Review*, I (1916), 291–306. On *Knickerbocker*.

William L. Hedges, "Knickerbocker, Bolingbroke, and the Fiction of History," *Journal of the History of Ideas*, XX (1959), 317–28.

Louis Le Fevre, "Paul Bunyan and Rip Van Winkle," *Yale Review*, XXXVI (1946), 66–76.

Marcel Heiman, "Rip Van Winkle: A Psychoanalytic Note on the Story and Its Author," *American Imago*, XVI (1959), 3–47.

Philip Young, "Fallen from Time: The Mythic Rip Van Winkle," *Kenyon Review*, XXII (1960), 547–73.

Terence Martin, "Rip, Ichabod, and the American Imagination," *American Literature*, XXXI (1959), 137–49.

Daniel G. Hoffman, "Irving's Use of American Folklore in 'The Legend of Sleepy Hollow,'" *PMLA*, LXVIII (1953), 425–35.

William L. Hedges, "Irving's *Columbus:* The Problem of Romantic Biography," *The Americas*, XIII (1956), 127–40.

SALMAGUNDI:
or, The Whim-Whams and Opinions of Launcelot Langstaff, Esq., and Others [1]

◇

THE AUTHORSHIP of individual items in *Salmagundi* is often uncertain. Although William Irving was almost solely responsible for the poetry, it seems safe to assume that Paulding and Washington Irving both had a hand in most of the prose, each helping to revise what he did not compose initially. The text used here, with minor corrections, is that prepared in 1860 by Evert A. Duyckinck, who modernized spelling and punctuation and added explanatory notes.

◇

In hoc est hoax, cum quiz et jokesez,
Et smokem, toastem, roastem folksez,
Fee, faw, fum. *Psalmanazar* [2]

With baked and boiled, and stewed and toasted;
And fried and broiled, and smoked and roasted,
We treat the town.

FROM NO. I.—SATURDAY, JANUARY 24, 1807.

As EVERYBODY knows, or ought to know, what a SALMAGUNDI is, we shall spare ourselves the

SALMAGUNDI. 1. **Others:** Will Wizard and Anthony Evergreen were Langstaff's chief associates.

2. *Psalmanazar:* George Psalmanazar (pseudonym), a Frenchman who perpetrated a literary hoax in England early in the eighteenth century by posing as a Formosan.

trouble of an explanation; besides, we despise trouble as we do everything low and mean, and hold the man who would incur it unnecessarily as an object worthy our highest pity and contempt. Neither will we puzzle our heads to give an account of ourselves, for two reasons; first, because it is nobody's business; secondly, because if it were, we do not hold ourselves bound to attend to anybody's business but our own; and even *that* we take the liberty of neglecting when it suits our inclination. To these we might add a third, that very few men *can* give a tolerable account of themselves, let them try ever so hard; but this reason, we candidly avow, would not hold good with ourselves.

There are, however, two or three pieces of information which we bestow gratis on the public, chiefly because it suits our own pleasure and convenience that they should be known, and partly because we do not wish that there should be any ill will between us at the commencement of our acquaintance.

Our intention is simply to instruct the young, reform the old, correct the town, and castigate the age; this is an arduous task, and therefore we undertake it with confidence. We intend for this purpose to present a striking picture of the town; and as everybody is anxious to see his own phiz on canvas, however stupid or ugly it may be, we have no doubt but the whole town will flock to our exhibition. Our picture will necessarily include a vast variety of figures; and should any gentleman or lady be displeased with the inveterate truth of their likenesses, they may ease their spleen by laughing at those of their neighbors—this being what *we* understand by *poetical justice.*

Like all true and able editors, we consider ourselves infallible; and therefore, with the customary diffidence of our brethren of the quill, we shall take the liberty of interfering in all matters either of a public or private nature. We are critics, amateurs, dilettanti and cognoscenti; and as we know "by the pricking of our thumbs," [3] that every opinion which we may advance in either of those characters will be correct, we are determined, though it may be questioned, contradicted, or even controverted, yet it shall never be revoked.

We beg the public particularly to understand that we solicit no patronage. We are determined, on the contrary, that the patronage shall be entirely on our side. We have nothing to do with the pecuniary concerns of the paper; its success will yield us neither pride nor profit—nor will its failure occasion to us either loss or mortification. We advise the public, therefore, to purchase our numbers merely for their own sakes; if they do not, let them settle the affair with their consciences and posterity.

To conclude, we invite all editors of newspapers and literary journals to praise us heartily in advance, as we assure them that we intend to deserve their praises. To our next-door neighbor, *Town,*[4] we hold out a hand of amity, declaring to him that, after ours, his paper will stand the best chance for immortality. We proffer an exchange of civilities: he shall furnish us with notices of epic poems and tobacco; and we, in return, will enrich him with original speculations on all manner of subjects, together with "the rummaging of my grandfather's mahogany chest of drawers," "the life and amours of mine Uncle John," "anecdotes of the Cockloft family," and learned quotations from that unheard of writer of folios, *Linkum Fidelius.*[5]

FROM NO. XVI.—THURSDAY, OCTOBER 15, 1807.

STYLE, AT BALLSTON.

BY WILLIAM WIZARD, ESQ.

NOTWITHSTANDING Evergreen has never been abroad, nor had his understanding enlightened, or his views enlarged by that marvellous sharpener of the wits, a salt water voyage, yet he is tolerably shrewd, and correct, in the limited sphere of his observations; and now and then astounds me with a right pithy remark, which would do no discredit even to a man who had made the grand tour.

In several late conversations at Cockloft Hall, he has amused us exceedingly by detailing sundry particulars concerning that notorious slaughter-house of time, Ballston Springs,[1] where he spent a considerable part of the last summer. The following is a summary of his observations.

Pleasure has passed through a variety of sig-

3. **"by . . . thumbs"**: Cf. *Macbeth*, IV.i.44.

4. ***Town:*** "The title of a newspaper published in New York, the columns of which, among other miscellaneous topics, occasionally contained strictures on the performances at the theatres" [Irving's note added in the Paris edition of his works, 1834].

5. **together . . . *Fidelius***: an elaborate way of saying "with all sorts of nonsense and odds and ends." The phrasing suggests not only Sterne's *Tristram Shandy* but also a comic work by Isaac D'Israeli published in London two years before *Salmagundi, Film-Flams! or, The Life and Errors of My Uncle and the Amours of My Aunt!* The Cocklofts are eccentric friends of the fictional editors. The quotations from *Linkum Fidelius*, another fiction, are more mad than learned. **Style, at Ballston.** 1. **Ballston Springs:** fashionable spa of the period, near Saratoga Springs, N.Y.

nifications at Ballston. It originally meant nothing more than a relief from pain and sickness; and the patient who had journeyed many a weary mile to the Springs, with a heavy heart and emaciated form, called it pleasure when he threw by his crutches, and danced away from them with renovated spirits and limbs jocund with vigor. In process of time, pleasure underwent a refinement, and appeared in the likeness of a sober, unceremonious country-dance, to the flute of an amateur or the three-stringed fiddle of an itinerant country musician. Still everything bespoke that happy holiday which the spirits ever enjoy, when emancipated from the shackles of formality, ceremony, and modern politeness; things went on cheerily, and Ballston was pronounced a charming, humdrum, careless place of resort, where every one was at his ease, and might follow unmolested the bent of his humor—provided his wife was not there; when, lo! all on a sudden, Style made its baneful appearance in the semblance of a gig and tandem, a pair of leather breeches, a liveried footman, and a cockney! Since that fatal era pleasure has taken an entire new signification, and at present means nothing but STYLE.

The worthy, fashionable, dashing, good-for-nothing people of every state, who had rather suffer the martyrdom of a crowd than endure the monotony of their own homes, and the stupid company of their own thoughts, flock to the Springs; not to enjoy the pleasures of society, or benefit by the qualities of the waters, but to exhibit their equipages and wardrobes, and to excite the admiration, or what is much more satisfactory, the envy of their fashionable competitors. This, of course, awakens a spirit of noble emulation between the eastern, middle, and southern States; and every lady hereupon finding herself charged in a manner with the whole weight of her country's dignity and style, dresses and dashes, and sparkles, without mercy, at her competitors from other parts of the Union. This kind of rivalship naturally requires a vast deal of preparation and prodigious quantities of supplies. A sober citizen's wife will break half a dozen milliners' shops, and sometimes starve her family a whole season, to enable herself to make the Springs campaign in style. She repairs to the seat of war with a mighty force of trunks and band-boxes, like so many ammunition chests, filled with caps, hats, gowns, ribands, shawls, and all the various artillery of fashionable warfare. The lady of a southern planter will lay out the whole annual produce of a rice plantation in silver and gold muslins, lace veils, and new liveries; carry a hogshead of tobacco on her head, and trail a bale of sea-island cotton at her heels; while a lady of Boston or Salem will wrap herself up in the net proceeds of a cargo of whale oil, and tie on her hat with a quintal of codfish.

The planters' ladies, however, have generally the advantage in this contest; for, as it is an incontestable fact, that whoever comes from the West or East Indies, or Georgia, or the Carolinas, or in fact any warm climate, is immensely rich, it cannot be expected that a simple cit [2] of the North can cope with them in style. The planter, therefore, who drives four horses abroad, and a thousand negroes at home, and who flourishes up to the Springs, followed by half a score of black-a-moors, in gorgeous liveries, is unquestionably superior to the northern merchant, who plods on in a carriage and pair; which, being nothing more than is quite necessary, has no claim whatever to style. He, however, has his consolation in feeling superior to the honest cit, who dashes about in a simple gig; he, in return, sneers at the country squire, who jogs along with his scrubby, long-eared pony and saddle-bags; and the squire, by way of taking satisfaction, would make no scruple to run over the unobtrusive pedestrian, were it not that the last, being the most independent of the whole, might chance to break his head by way of retort.

The great misfortune is, that this style is supported at such an expense as sometimes to encroach on the rights and privileges of the pocket; and occasions very awkward embarrassments to the tyro of fashion. Among a number of instances, Evergreen mentions the fate of a dashing blade from the South, who made his *entrée* with a tandem and two outriders, by the aid of which he attracted the attention of all the ladies, and caused a coolness between several young couples who, it was thought before his arrival, had a considerable kindness for each other. In the course of a fortnight his tandem disappeared!—the class of good folk who seem to have nothing to do in this world but pry into other people's affairs, began to stare. In a little time longer an outrider was missing!—this increased the alarm, and it was consequently whispered that he had eaten the horses and drank the negro. N. B. Southern gentlemen are very apt to do this on an emergency. Serious apprehensions were entertained about the fate of the remaining servant, which were soon verified by his actually vanishing; and in "one little month" [3] the dashing Carolinian modestly took his departure in the stage-coach!—universally regretted by the friends who had generously released him from his cumbrous load of style.

2. **cit:** short for "citizen," usually applied to an urban resident.
3. **"one . . . month":** Cf. *Hamlet,* I.ii.147.

Evergreen, in the course of his detail, gave very melancholy accounts of an alarming famine which raged with great violence at the Springs. Whether this was owing to the incredible appetities of the company, or the scarcity which prevailed at the inns, he did not seem inclined to say; but he declares, that he was for several days in imminent danger of starvation, owing to his being a little too dilatory in his attendance at the dinner table. He relates a number of "moving accidents," which befell many of the polite company in their zeal to get a good seat at dinner; on which occasion a kind of scrub-race always took place, wherein a vast deal of jockeying and unfair play was shown, and a variety of squabbles and unseemly altercations occurred. But when arrived at the scene of action, it was truly an awful sight to behold the confusion, and to hear the tumultuous uproar of voices crying some for one thing, and some for another, to the tuneful accompaniment of knives and forks—rattling with all the energy of hungry impatience. The feast of the Centaurs and the Lapithæ [4] was nothing when compared with a dinner at the great house. At one time, an old gentleman, whose natural irascibility was a little sharpened by the gout, had scalded his throat, by gobbling down a bowl of hot soup in a vast hurry, in order to secure the first fruits of a roasted partridge before it was snapped up by some hungry rival; when, just as he was whetting his knife and fork, preparatory for a descent on the promised land, he had the mortification to see it transferred, bodily, to the plate of a squeamish little damsel who was taking the waters for debility and loss of appetite. This was too much for the patience of old Crusty; he lodged his fork into the partridge, whipt it into his dish, and cutting off a wing of it,—"There, Miss, there's more than you can eat. Oons! what should such a little chalky-faced puppet as you do with a whole partridge!" At another time a mighty sweet disposed old dowager, who loomed most magnificently at the table, had a sauce-boat launched upon the capacious lap of a silver sprigged muslin gown, by the manœuvring of a little politic Frenchman, who was dextrously attempting to make a lodgment under the covered way of a chicken-pie; human nature could not bear it!—the lady bounced round, and, with one box on the ear, drove the luckless wight to utter annihilation.

But these little cross accidents are amply compensated by the great variety of amusements which abounds at this charming resort of beauty and fashion. In the morning the company, each like a jolly Bacchanalian, with glass in hand, sally forth to the Springs: where the gentlemen, who wish to make themselves agreeable, have an opportunity of dipping themselves into the good opinion of the ladies: and it is truly delectable to see with what grace and adroitness they perform this ingratiating feat. Anthony says that it is peculiarly amazing to behold the quantity of water the ladies drink on this occasion, for the purpose of getting an appetite for breakfast. He assures me he has been present when a young lady, of unparalleled delicacy, tossed off, in the space of a minute or two, one and twenty tumblers and a wine-glass full. On my asking Anthony whether the solicitude of the bystanders was not greatly awakened as to what might be the effects of this debauch, he replied, that the ladies at Ballston had become such great sticklers for the doctrine of evaporation,[5] that no gentleman ever ventured to remonstrate against this excessive drinking for fear of bringing his philosophy into contempt. The most notorious water-drinkers, in particular, were continually holding forth on the surprising aptitude with which the Ballston waters evaporated; and several gentlemen, who had the hardihood to question this female philosophy, were held in high displeasure.

After breakfast, every one chooses his amusement; some take a ride into the pine woods, and enjoy the varied and romantic scenery of burnt trees, post and rail fences, pine flats, potato patches, and log huts; others scramble up the surrounding sandhills, that look like the abodes of a gigantic race of ants;—take a peep at other sandhills beyond them;—and then—come down again. Others who are romantic, and sundry young ladies insist upon being so whenever they visit the Springs, or go anywhere into the country, stroll along the borders of a little swampy brook that drags itself along like an Alexandrine, and that so lazily as not to make a single murmur, watching the little tadpoles as they frolic, right flippantly, in the muddy stream, and listening to the inspiring melody of the harmonious frogs that croak upon its borders. Some play at billiards, some play at the fiddle, and some—play the fool;—the latter being the most prevalent amusement at Ballston.

These, together with abundance of dancing, and a prodigious deal of sleeping of afternoons, make up the variety of pleasures at the Springs—a delicious life of alternate lassitude and fatigue; of laborious dissipation, and listless idleness; of sleep-

4. **feast . . . Lapithæ:** In Greek mythology the Centaurs came to the wedding of Pirithous, king of the Lapiths, got drunk, started a brawl, and were driven out.

5. **doctrine of evaporation:** theory of curing illness by perspiration, discharging noxious humors through the pores of the body.

less nights, and days spent in that dozing insensibility which ever succeeds them. Now and then, indeed, the influenza, the fever-and-ague, or some such pale-faced intruder, may happen to throw a momentary damp on the general felicity; but on the whole, Evergreen declares that Ballston wants only six things, to wit: good air, good wine, good living, good beds, good company, and good humor, to be the most enchanting place in the world ——excepting Botany Bay, Mosquito Cove, Dismal Swamp, and the black hole at Calcutta.

1807

A HISTORY OF NEW YORK

FROM THE BEGINNING OF THE WORLD TO THE END OF THE DUTCH DYNASTY BY DIEDRICH KNICKERBOCKER

◇

IRVING substantially changed *Knickerbocker,* first in 1812, then in 1848. Grown more skilled in narrative, he made structural improvements, sometimes inventing wholly new episodes. At the same time, particularly in 1848, he toned down the style, pruning it of certain awkward excesses but also eliminating some of the youthful vigor (and in spots frenzy) of the original. The 1848 edition, the only one commonly read today, represents the older Irving, more sensitive to Victorian notions of delicacy—though still by no means prudish.

The selections given here are designed to illustrate the change. The first, Book I, Chapter 5, is taken from the 1809 edition, with unorthodox spelling and punctuation, except for obvious errors, retained. The differences between the early and late editions of this chapter are stylistic rather than structural and include certain sizable deletions made after 1809, apparently in the interest of not offending the reader. The second selection, which includes all but the final chapter of Book V, is taken from the 1848 edition. Here important structural changes make the later version more readable. The final selection, Book VI, Chapters 7 and 8 (in 1848 they became 8 and 9), again comes from the 1809 edition. The exuberance of Irving's early style renders the mock-epic account of the Battle of Fort Christina more ludicrous in the original than in the revised version.

Book I of *Knickerbocker* covers the history of the world from its creation through the early explorations of America. The founding of New Amsterdam occurs in Book II. Books III and IV give an account of the governorships of Van Twiller and Kieft, and V to VII of that of Peter Stuyvesant. Following his difficulties with New England in Book V, Stuyvesant becomes involved in a border dispute with the colony of New Sweden, founded by Peter Minuit in the region of the Delaware River in 1638. The dispute culminates in the Battle of Fort Christina, the climax (or grand anticlimax) of the book.

Knickerbocker's learned allusions, partly designed to lampoon pedantry, continue to mock the modern scholar who tries to decipher them. Most appear to have some basis in actuality, but Irving, frequently citing writers and works he has not himself consulted, is often cryptic and ambiguous in his references.[1]

◇

FROM BOOK I [1809]

CHAPTER 5

IN WHICH THE AUTHOR PUTS A MIGHTY QUESTION TO THE ROUT, BY THE ASSISTANCE OF THE MAN IN THE MOON—WHICH NOT ONLY DELIVERS THOUSANDS OF PEOPLE FROM GREAT EMBARRASSMENT, BUT LIKEWISE CONCLUDES THIS INTRODUCTORY BOOK

THE WRITER of a history may, in some respects, be likened unto an adventurous knight, who having undertaken a perilous enterprise by way of establishing his fame, feels bound in honour and chivalry, to turn back for no difficulty nor hardship, and never to shrink or quail whatever enemy he may encounter. Under this impression, I resolutely draw my pen and fall to, with might and main, at those doughty questions and subtle paradoxes, which, like fiery dragons and bloody giants, beset the entrance to my history, and would fain repulse me from the very threshold. And at this moment a gigantic question has started up, which I must take by the beard and utterly subdue, before I can advance another step in my historic undertaking—but I trust this will be the last adversary I shall have to contend with, and that in the next book, I shall be enabled to conduct my readers in triumph into the body of my work.

The question which has thus suddenly arisen, is, what right had the first discoverers of America to

A HISTORY OF NEW YORK. 1. See Williams and McDowell's Introduction to *Knickerbocker* (1927), and H. M. Lydenberg, "Irving's *Knickerbocker* and Some of Its Sources," *Bulletin of the New York Public Library* LVI (1952), pp. 544–53, 596–619.

land, and take possession of a country, without asking the consent of its inhabitants, or yielding them an adequate compensation for their territory?

My readers shall now see with astonishment, how easily I will vanquish this gigantic doubt, which has so long been the terror of adventurous writers; which has withstood so many fierce assaults, and has given such great distress of mind to multitudes of kind-hearted folks. For, until this mighty question is totally put to rest, the worthy people of America can by no means enjoy the soil they inhabit, with clear right and title, and quiet, unsullied consciences.

The first source of right, by which property is acquired in a country, is DISCOVERY. For as all mankind have an equal right to any thing, which has never before been appropriated, so any nation, that discovers an uninhabited country, and takes possession thereof, is considered as enjoying full property, and absolute, unquestionable empire therein.[2]

This proposition being admitted, it follows clearly, that the Europeans who first visited America, were the real discoverers of the same; nothing being necessary to the establishment of this fact, but simply to prove that it was totally uninhabited by man. This would at first appear to be a point of some difficulty, for it is well known, that this quarter of the world abounded with certain animals, that walked erect on two feet, had something of the human countenance, uttered certain unintelligible sounds, very much like language, in short, had a marvellous resemblance to human beings. But the host of zealous and enlightened fathers, who accompanied the discoverers, for the purpose of promoting the kingdom of heaven, by establishing fat monasteries and bishopricks on earth, soon cleared up this point, greatly to the satisfaction of his holiness the pope, and of all Christian voyagers and discoverers.

They plainly proved, and as there were no Indian writers arose on the other side, the fact was considered as fully admitted and established, that the two legged race of animals before mentioned, were mere cannibals, detestable monsters, and many of them giants—a description of vagrants, that since the times of Gog, Magog and Goliath, have been considered as outlaws, and have received no quarter in either history, chivalry or song; indeed, even the philosopher Bacon, declared the Americans to be people proscribed by the laws of nature, inasmuch as they had a barbarous custom of sacrificing men, and feeding upon man's flesh.

Nor are these all the proofs of their utter barbarism: among many other writers of discernment, the celebrated Ulloa [3] tells us "their imbecility is so visible, that one can hardly form an idea of them different from what one has of the brutes. Nothing disturbs the tranquillity of their souls, equally insensible to disasters, and to prosperity. Though half naked, they are as contented as a monarch in his most splendid array. Fear makes no impression on them, and respect as little."—All this is furthermore supported by the authority of M. Bouguer.[4] "It is not easy," says he, "to describe the degree of their indifference for wealth and all its advantages. One does not well know what motives to propose to them when one would persuade them to any service. It is vain to offer them money, they answer that they are not hungry." And Vanegas confirms the whole, assuring us that "ambition, they have none, and are more desirous of being thought strong than valiant. The objects of ambition with us, honour, fame, reputation, riches, posts and distinctions, are unknown among them. So that this powerful spring of action, the cause of so much *seeming* good and *real* evil in the world has no power over them. In a word, these unhappy mortals may be compared to children, in whom the development of reason is not completed."

Now all these peculiarities, though in the unenlightened states of Greece, they would have entitled their possessors to immortal honour, as having reduced to practice those rigid and abstemious maxims, the mere talking about which, acquired certain old Greeks the reputation of sages and philosophers;—yet were they clearly proved in the present instance, to betoken a most abject and brutified nature, totally beneath the human character. But the benevolent fathers, who had undertaken to turn these unhappy savages into dumb beasts, by dint of argument, advanced still stronger proofs; for as certain divines of the sixteenth century, and among the rest Lullus affirm—the Americans go naked, and have no beards!—"They have nothing," says Lullus, "of the reasonable animal, except the mask."—And even that

Book I. 2. **therein:** "Grotius. Pufendorf, b.4. c.4. Vattel, b.I c.18, et alii" [I]. The legal works referred to here are Hugo Grotius (1583–1645), *De Jure Belli et Pacis;* Samuel von Pufendorf (1632–94), *De Jure Naturae et Gentium;* Emmerich von Vattel (1714–67), *Le Droit des Gens.* In "et alii" he refers vaguely to other authorities.

3. **Ulloa:** Most of the material in the quotations in this paragraph closely parallels passages in Antonio de Ulloa and Don George Juan [de Santacillia], *A Voyage to South-America* (London, 1758), Book VI, Chap. 6. 4. **M. Bouguer:** apparently a mistake for M. Bouquer, a geodesist who accompanied Ulloa on a scientific expedition to South America in the 1730's.

mask was allowed to avail them but little, for it was soon found that they were of a hideous copper complexion—and being of a copper complexion, it was all the same as if they were negroes —and negroes are black, "and black" said the pious fathers, devoutly crossing themselves, "is the colour of the Devil!" Therefore so far from being able to own property, they had no right even to personal freedom, for liberty is too radiant a deity, to inhabit such gloomy temples. All which circumstances plainly convinced the righteous followers of Cortes and Pizarro, that these miscreants had no title to the soil that they infested —that they were a perverse, illiterate, dumb, beardless, bare-bottomed *black-seed*—mere wild beasts of the forests, and like them should either be subdued or exterminated.

From the foregoing arguments therefore, and a host of others equally conclusive, which I forbear to enumerate, it was clearly evident, that this fair quarter of the globe when first visited by Europeans, was a howling wilderness, inhabited by nothing but wild beasts; and that the transatlantic visitors acquired an incontrovertible property therein, by the *right of Discovery*.

This right being fully established, we now come to the next, which is the right acquired by *cultivation*. "The cultivation of the soil" we are told "is an obligation imposed by nature on mankind. The whole world is appointed for the nourishment of its inhabitants; but it would be incapable of doing it, was it uncultivated. Every nation is then obliged by the law of nature to cultivate the ground that has fallen to its share. Those people like the ancient Germans and modern Tartars, who having fertile countries, disdain to cultivate the earth, and choose to live by rapine, are wanting to themselves, and *deserve to be exterminated as savage and pernicious beasts*." [5]

Now it is notorious, that the savages knew nothing of agriculture, when first discovered by the Europeans, but lived a most vagabond, disorderly, unrighteous life,—rambling from place to place, and prodigally rioting upon the spontaneous luxuries of nature, without tasking her generosity to yield them any thing more; whereas it has been most unquestionably shewn, that heaven intended the earth should be ploughed and sown, and manured, and laid out into cities and towns and farms, and country seats, and pleasure grounds, and public gardens, all which the Indians knew nothing about—therefore they did not improve the talents providence had bestowed on them—therefore they were careless stewards—therefore they had no right to the soil—therefore they deserved to be exterminated.

It is true the savages might plead that they drew all the benefits from the land which their simple wants required—they found plenty of game to hunt, which together with the roots and uncultivated fruits of the earth, furnished a sufficient variety for their frugal table;—and that as heaven merely designed the earth to form the abode, and satisfy the wants of man; so long as those purposes were answered, the will of heaven was accomplished.—But this only proves how undeserving they were of the blessings around them—they were so much the more savages, for not having more wants; for knowledge is in some degree an increase of desires, and it is this superiority both in the number and magnitude of his desires, that distinguishes the man from the beast. Therefore the Indians, in not having more wants, were very unreasonable animals; and it was but just that they should make way for the Europeans, who had a thousand wants to their one, and therefore would turn the earth to more account, and by cultivating it, more truly fulfil the will of heaven. Besides—Grotius and Lauterbach, and Pufendorf and Titius and a host of wise men besides, who have considered the matter properly, have determined, that the property of a country cannot be acquired by hunting, cutting wood, or drawing water in it —nothing but precise demarcation of limits, and the intention of cultivation, can establish the possession. Now as the savages (probably from never having read the authors above quoted) had never complied with any of these necessary forms, it plainly follows that they had no right to the soil, but that it was completely at the disposal of the first comers, who had more knowledge and more wants than themselves—who would portion out the soil, with churlish boundaries; who would torture nature to pamper a thousand fantastic humours and capricious appetites; and who of course were far more rational animals than themselves.[6] In entering upon a newly discovered, uncultivated country therefore, the new comers were but taking possession of what, according to the aforesaid doctrine, was their own property—therefore in opposing them, the savages were invading their just rights, infringing the immutable laws of nature and counteracting the will of heaven—therefore they were guilty of impiety, burglary and trespass on the case,—therefore they

5. **"The . . . *beasts*":** "Vattel—B. i, ch. 17. See likewise Grotius, Pufendorf, et alii" [I]. The quotation is from the seventh, not the seventeenth, chapter of the first book of Vattel's *Le Droit des Gens*.

6. **portion . . . themselves:** In revising, Irving omitted this passage.

were hardened offenders against God and man ——therefore they ought to be exterminated.

But a more irresistible right than either that I have mentioned, and one which will be the most readily admitted by my reader, provided he is blessed with bowels of charity and philanthropy, is the right acquired by civilization. All the world knows the lamentable state in which these poor savages were found. Not only deficient in the comforts of life, but what is still worse, most piteously and unfortunately blind to the miseries of their situation. But no sooner did the benevolent inhabitants of Europe behold their sad condition than they immediately went to work to ameliorate and improve it. They introduced among them the comforts of life, consisting of rum, gin and brandy —and it is astonishing to read how soon the poor savages learnt to estimate these blessings—they likewise made known to them a thousand remedies by which the most inveterate diseases are alleviated and healed, and that they might comprehend the benefits and enjoy the comforts of these medicines they previously introduced among them the diseases which they were calculated to cure. By these and a variety of other methods was the condition of these poor savages, wonderfully improved; they acquired a thousand wants, of which they had before been ignorant, and as he has most sources of happiness, who has most wants to be gratified, they were doubtlessly rendered a much happier race of beings.

But the most important branch of civilization, and which has most strenuously been extolled, by the zealous and pious fathers of the Roman Church, is the introduction of the Christian faith. It was truly a sight that might well inspire horror, to behold these savages, stumbling among the dark mountains of paganism, and guilty of the most horrible ignorance of religion. It is true, they neither stole nor defrauded, they were sober, frugal, continent, and faithful to their word; but though they acted right habitually, it was all in vain, unless they acted so from precept. The new comers therefore used every method, to induce them to embrace and practice the true religion—except that of setting them the example.

But notwithstanding all these complicated labours for their good, such was the unparalleled obstinacy of these stubborn wretches, that they ungratefully refused, to acknowledge the strangers as their benefactors, and persisted in disbelieving the doctrines they endeavoured to inculcate; most insolently alledging, that from their conduct, the advocates of Christianity did not seem to believe in it themselves. Was not this too much for human patience?—would not one suppose, that the foreign emigrants from Europe, provoked at their incredulity and discouraged by their stiff-necked obstinacy, would forever have abandoned their shores, and consigned them to their original ignorance and misery?—But no——so zealous were they to effect the temporal comfort and eternal salvation of these pagan infidels, that they even proceeded from the milder means of persuasion, to the more painful and troublesome one of persecution——Let loose among them, whole troops of fiery monks and furious bloodhounds—purified them by fire and sword, by stake and faggot; in consequence of which indefatigable measures, the cause of Christian love and charity was so rapidly advanced, that in a very few years, not one fifth of the number of unbelievers existed in South America, that were found there at the time of its discovery.

Nor did the other methods of civilization remain unenforced. The Indians improved daily and wonderfully by their intercourse with the whites. They took to drinking rum, and making bargains. They learned to cheat, to lie, to swear, to gamble, to quarrel, to cut each other's throats, in short, to excel in all the accomplishments that had originally marked the superiority of their Christian visitors. And such a surprising aptitude have they shewn for these acquirements, that there is very little doubt that in a century more, provided they survive so long the irresistible effects of civilization; they will equal in knowledge, refinement, knavery, and debauchery, the most enlightened, civilized and orthodox nations of Europe.[7]

What stronger right need the European settlers advance to the country than this. Have not whole nations of uninformed savages been made acquainted with a thousand imperious wants and indispensible comforts of which they were before wholly ignorant—Have they not been literally hunted and smoked out of the dens and lurking places of ignorance and infidelity, and absolutely scourged into the right path. Have not the temporal things, the vain baubles and filthy lucre of this world, which were too apt to engage their worldly and selfish thoughts, been benevolently taken from them; and have they not, in lieu thereof, been taught to set their affections on things above— And finally, to use the words of a reverend Spanish father, in a letter to his superior in Spain— "Can any one have the presumption to say, that these savage Pagans, have yielded any thing more than an inconsiderable recompense to their benefactors; in surrendering to them a little pitiful tract

7. **Nor . . . Europe:** This entire paragraph was omitted in the revision.

of this dirty sublunary planet, in exchange for a glorious inheritance in the kingdom of Heaven!"

Here then are three complete and undeniable sources of right established, any one of which was more than ample to establish a property in the newly discovered regions of America. Now, so it has happened in certain parts of this delightful quarter of the globe, that the right of discovery has been so strenuously asserted—the influence of cultivation so industriously extended, and the progress of salvation and civilization so zealously prosecuted, that, what with their attendant wars, persecutions, oppressions, diseases, and other partial evils that often hang on the skirts of great benefits—the savage aborigines have, some how or another, been utterly annihilated—and this all at once brings me to a fourth right, which is worth all the others put together—For the original claimants to the soil being all dead and buried, and no one remaining to inherit or dispute the soil, the Spaniards as the next immediate occupants entered upon the possession, as clearly as the hang-man succeeds to the clothes of the malefactor—and as they have Blackstone,[8] and all the learned expounders of the law on their side, they may set all actions of ejectment at defiance—and this last right may be entitled, the RIGHT BY EXTERMINATION, or in other words, the RIGHT BY GUNPOWDER.

But lest any scruples of conscience should remain on this head, and to settle the question of right forever, his holiness Pope Alexander VI, issued one of those mighty bulls, which bear down reason, argument and every thing before them; by which he generously granted the newly discovered quarter of the globe, to the Spaniards and Portuguese; who, thus having law and gospel on their side, and being inflamed with great spiritual zeal, shewed the Pagan savages neither favour nor affection, but prosecuted the work of discovery, colonization, civilization, and extermination, with ten times more fury than ever.

Thus were the European worthies who first discovered America, clearly entitled to the soil; and not only entitled to the soil, but likewise to the eternal thanks of these infidel savages, for having come so far, endured so many perils by sea and land, and taken such unwearied pains, for no other purpose under heaven but to improve their forlorn, uncivilized and heathenish condition—for having made them acquainted with the comforts of life, such as gin, rum, brandy, and the small-pox; for having introduced among them the light of religion, and finally——for having hurried them out of the world, to enjoy its reward!

But as argument is never so well understood by us selfish mortals, as when it comes home to ourselves, and as I am particularly anxious that this question should be put to rest forever, I will suppose a parallel case, by way of arousing the candid attention of my readers.

Let us suppose then, that the inhabitants of the moon, by astonishing advancement in science, and by a profound insight into that ineffable lunar philosophy, the mere flickerings of which, have of late years, dazzled the feeble optics, and addled the shallow brains of the good people of our globe—let us suppose, I say, that the inhabitants of the moon, by these means, had arrived at such a command of their *energies,* such an enviable state of *perfectability,* as to controul the elements, and navigate the boundless regions of space. Let us suppose a roving crew of these soaring philosophers, in the course of an ærial voyage of discovery among the stars, should chance to alight upon this outlandish planet.

And here I beg my readers will not have the impertinence to smile, as is too frequently the fault of volatile readers, when perusing the grave speculations of philosophers. I am far from indulging in any sportive vein at present, nor is the supposition I have been making so wild as many may deem it. It has long been a very serious and anxious question with me, and many a time, and oft, in the course of my overwhelming cares and contrivances for the welfare and protection of this my native planet, have I lain awake whole nights, debating in my mind whether it was most probable we should first discover and civilize the moon, or the moon discover and civilize our globe. Neither would the prodigy of sailing in the air and cruising among the stars be a whit more astonishing and incomprehensible to us, than was the European mystery of navigating floating castles, through the world of waters, to the simple savages. We have already discovered the art of coasting along the ærial shores of our planet, by means of balloons, as the savages had, of venturing along their sea coasts in canoes; and the disparity between the former, and the ærial vehicles of the philosophers from the moon, might not be greater, than that, between the bark canoes of the savages, and the mighty ships of their discoverers. I might here pursue an endless chain of very curious, profound and unprofitable speculations; but as they would be unimportant to my subject, I abandon them to my reader, particularly if he is a philosopher, as matters well worthy his attentive consideration.

8. Blackstone: "Black. *Com.* B II, c.i" [I]: William Blackstone (1723–80), *Commentaries on the Laws of England.*

To return then to my supposition—let us suppose that the ærial visitants I have mentioned, possessed of vastly superior knowledge to ourselves; that is to say, possessed of superior knowledge in the art of extermination—riding on Hypogriffs,[9] defended with impenetrable armour—armed with concentrated sun beams, and provided with vast engines, to hurl enormous moon stones: in short, let us suppose them, if our vanity will permit the supposition, as superior to us in knowledge, and consequently in power, as the Europeans were to the Indians, when they first discovered them. All this is very possible, it is only our self-sufficiency that makes us think otherwise; and I warrant the poor savages, before they had any knowledge of the white men, armed in all the terrors of glittering steel and tremendous gunpowder, were as perfectly convinced that they themselves were the wisest, the most virtuous, powerful and perfect of created beings, as are, at this present moment, the lordly inhabitants of old England, the volatile populace of France, or even the self-satisfied citizens of this most enlightened republick.

Let us suppose, moreover, that the ærial voyagers, finding this planet to be nothing but a howling wilderness, inhabited by us, poor savages and wild beasts, shall take formal possession of it, in the name of his most gracious and philosophic excellency, the man in the moon. Finding however, that their numbers are incompetent to hold it in complete subjection, on account of the ferocious barbarity of its inhabitants; they shall take our worthy President, the King of England, the Emperor of Hayti, the mighty little Bonaparte, and the great King of Bantam, and returning to their native planet, shall carry them to court, as were the Indian chiefs led about as spectacles in the courts of Europe.

Then making such obeisance as the etiquette of the court requires, they shall address the puissant man in the moon, in, as near as I can conjecture, the following terms:

"Most serene and mighty Potentate, whose dominions extend as far as eye can reach, who rideth on the Great Bear, useth the sun as a looking glass and maintaineth unrivalled controul over tides, madmen and sea-crabs. We thy liege subjects have just returned from a voyage of discovery, in the course of which we have landed and taken possession of that obscure little scurvy planet, which thou beholdest rolling at a distance. The five uncouth monsters, which we have brought into this august presence, were once very important chiefs among their fellow savages; for the inhabitants of the newly discovered globe are totally destitute of the common attributes of humanity, inasmuch as they carry their heads upon their shoulders, instead of under their arms—have two eyes instead of one—are utterly destitute of tails, and of a variety of unseemly complexions, particularly of a horrible whiteness—whereas all the inhabitants of the moon are pea green!

"We have moreover found these miserable savages sunk into a state of the utmost ignorance and depravity, every man shamelessly living with his own wife, and rearing his own children, instead of indulging in that community of wives, enjoined by the law of nature, as expounded by the philosophers of the moon. In a word they have scarcely a gleam of true philosophy among them, but are in fact, utter heretics, ignoramuses and barbarians. Taking compassion therefore on the sad condition of these sublunary wretches, we have endeavoured, while we remained on their planet, to introduce among them the light of reason—and the comforts of the moon.—We have treated them to mouthfuls of moonshine and draughts of nitrous oxyde, which they swallowed with incredible voracity, particularly the females; and we have likewise endeavoured to instil into them the precepts of lunar Philosophy. We have insisted upon their renouncing the contemptable shackles of religion and common sense, and adoring the profound, omnipotent, and all perfect energy, and the extatic, immutable, immoveable perfection. But such was the unparalleled obstinacy of these wretched savages, that they persisted in cleaving to their wives and adhering to their religion, and absolutely set at naught the sublime doctrines of the moon—nay, among other abominable heresies, they even went so far as blasphemously to declare, that this ineffable planet was made of nothing more nor less than green cheese!"

At these words, the great man in the moon (being a very profound philosopher) shall fall into a terrible passion, and possessing equal authority over things that do not belong to him, as did whilome his holiness the Pope, shall forthwith issue a formidable bull,——specifying, "That—whereas a certain crew of Lunatics have lately discovered and taken possession of that little dirty planet, called *the earth*—and that whereas it is inhabited by none but a race of two legged animals, that carry their heads on their shoulders instead of under their arms; cannot talk the lunatic language; have two eyes instead of one; are destitute of tails, and of a horrible whiteness, instead of pea green——therefore and for a variety of other ex-

9. **Hypogriffs:** usually "hippogriffs"; fabulous creatures with the head and wings of an eagle and the body of a horse.

cellent reasons—they are considered incapable of possessing any property in the planet they infest, and the right and title to it are confirmed to its original discoverers.—And furthermore, the colonists who are now about to depart to the aforesaid planet, are authorized and commanded to use every means to convert these infidel savages from the darkness of Christianity, and make them thorough and absolute lunatics."

In consequence of this benevolent bull, our philosophic benefactors go to work with hearty zeal. They seize upon our fertile territories, scourge us from our rightful possession, relieve us from our wives, and when we arc unreasonable enough to complain, they will turn upon us and say—miserable barbarians! ungrateful wretches!—have we not come thousands of miles to improve your worthless planet—have we not fed you with moonshine—have we not intoxicated you with nitrous oxyde——does not our moon give you light every night and have you the baseness to murmur, when we claim a pitiful return for all these benefits? But finding that we not only persist in absolute contempt to their reasoning and disbelief in their philosophy, but even go so far as daringly to defend our property, their patience shall be exhausted, and they shall resort to their superior powers of argument—hunt us with hypogriffs, transfix us with concentrated sun-beams, demolish our cities with moonstones; until having by main force, converted us to the true faith, they shall graciously permit us to exist in the torrid deserts of Arabia, or the frozen regions of Lapland, there to enjoy the blessings of civilization and the charms of lunar philosophy—in much the same manner as the reformed and enlightened savages of this country, are kindly suffered to inhabit the inhospitable forests of the north, or the impenetrable wildernesses of South America.

Thus have I clearly proved, and I hope strikingly illustrated, the right of the early colonists to the possession of this country——and thus is this gigantic question, completely knocked in the head—so having manfully surmounted all obstacles, and subdued all opposition, what remains but that I should forthwith conduct my impatient and way-worn readers, into the renowned city, which we have so long been in a manner besieging.—But hold, before I proceed another step I must pause to take breath and recover from the excessive fatigue I have undergone, in preparing to begin this most accurate of histories. And in this I do but imitate the example of the celebrated Hans Von Dunderbottom, who took a start of three miles for the purpose of jumping over a hill, but having been himself out of breath by the time he reached the foot, sat himself quietly down for a few moments to blow, and then walked over it at his leisure.

1809

FROM BOOK V [1848]

CONTAINING THE FIRST PART OF THE REIGN OF PETER STUYVESANT, AND HIS TROUBLES WITH THE AMPHICTYONIC COUNCIL

CHAPTER 1

IN WHICH THE DEATH OF A GREAT MAN IS SHOWN TO BE NO VERY INCONSOLABLE MATTER OF SORROW—AND HOW PETER STUYVESANT ACQUIRED A GREAT NAME FROM THE UNCOMMON STRENGTH OF HIS HEAD

TO A PROFOUND philosopher like myself, who am apt to see clear through a subject, where the penetration of ordinary people extends but halfway, there is no fact more simple and manifest than that the death of a great man is a matter of very little importance. Much as we may think of ourselves, and much as we may excite the empty plaudits of the million, it is certain that the greatest among us do actually fill but an exceeding small space in the world; and it is equally certain, that even that small space is quickly supplied when we leave it vacant. "Of what consequence is it," said Pliny, "that individuals appear, or make their exit? the world is a theatre whose scenes and actors are continually changing." Never did philosopher speak more correctly; and I only wonder that so wise a remark could have existed so many ages, and mankind not have laid it more to heart. Sage follows on in the footsteps of sage; one hero just steps out of his triumphal car, to make way for the hero who comes after him; and of the proudest monarch [1] it is merely said, that "he slept with his fathers, and his successor reigned in his stead."

The world, to tell the private truth, cares but little for their loss, and if left to itself would soon forget to grieve; and though a nation has often been figuratively drowned in tears on the death of a great man, yet it is ten to one if an individual tear has been shed on the occasion, except-

Book V. 1. **proudest monarch:** Solomon. Cf. I Kings 11:43.

ing from the forlorn pen of some hungry author. It is the historian, the biographer, and the poet, who have the whole burden of grief to sustain,—who—kind souls!—like undertakers in England, act the part of chief mourners,—who inflate a nation with sighs it never heaved, and deluge it with tears it never dreamt of shedding. Thus, while the patriotic author is weeping and howling, in prose, in blank verse, and in rhyme, and collecting the drops of public sorrow into his volume, as into a lachrymal vase, it is more than probable his fellow-citizens are eating and drinking, fiddling and dancing, as utterly ignorant of the bitter lamentations made in their name as are those men of straw, John Doe and Richard Roe, of the plaintiffs for whom they are generously pleased to become sureties.

The most glorious hero that ever desolated nations might have mouldered into oblivion among the rubbish of his own monument, did not some historian take him into favor, and benevolently transmit his name to posterity; and much as the valiant William Kieft [2] worried, and bustled, and turmoiled, while he had the destinies of a whole colony in his hand, I question seriously whether he will not be obliged to this authentic history for all his future celebrity.

His exit occasioned no convulsion in the city of New Amsterdam nor its vicinity: the earth trembled not, neither did any stars shoot from their spheres; the heavens were not shrouded in black, as poets would fain persuade us they have been, on the death of a hero; the rocks (hardhearted varlets!) melted not into tears, nor did the trees hang their heads in silent sorrow; and as to the sun, he lay abed the next night just as long, and showed as jolly a face when he rose as he ever did on the same day of the month in any year, either before or since. The good people of New Amsterdam, one and all, declared that he had been a very busy, active, bustling little governor; that he was "the father of his country"; that he was "the noblest work of God," [3] that "he was a man, take him for all in all, they ne'er should look upon his like again"; [4] together with sundry other civil and affectionate speeches regularly said on the death of all great men; after which they smoked their pipes, thought no more about him, and Peter Stuyvesant succeeded to his station.

Peter Stuyvesant was the last, and, like the renowned Wouter Van Twiller, the best of our ancient Dutch governors. Wouter having surpassed all who preceded him, and Peter, or Piet, as he was sociably called by the old Dutch burghers, who were ever prone to familiarize names, having never been equalled by any successor.[5] He was in fact the very man fitted by nature to retrieve the desperate fortunes of her beloved province, had not the fates, those most potent and unrelenting of all ancient spinsters, destined them to inextricable confusion.

To say merely that he was a hero, would be doing him great injustice: he was in truth a combination of heroes; for he was of a sturdy, rawboned make, like Ajax Telamon, with a pair of round shoulders that Hercules would have given his hide for (meaning his lion's hide) when he undertook to ease old Atlas of his load. He was, moreover, as Plutarch describes Coriolanus, not only terrible for the force of his arm, but likewise of his voice, which sounded as though it came out of a barrel; and, like the self-same warrior, he possessed a sovereign contempt for the sovereign people, and an iron aspect, which was enough of itself to make the very bowels of his adversaries quake with terror and dismay. All this martial excellency of appearance was inexpressibly heightened by an accidental advantage, with which I am surprised that neither Homer nor Virgil have graced any of their heroes. This was nothing less than a wooden leg, which was the only prize he had gained in bravely fighting the battles of his country, but of which he was so proud, that he was often heard to declare he valued it more than all his other limbs put together; indeed so highly did he esteem it, that he had it gallantly enchased and relieved with silver devices, which caused it to be related in divers histories and legends that he wore a silver leg.[6]

Like that choleric warrior Achilles, he was somewhat subject to extempore bursts of passion, which were rather unpleasant to his favorites and attendants, whose perceptions he was apt to quicken, after the manner of his illustrious imitator, Peter the Great, by anointing their shoulders with his walking-staff.

Though I cannot find that he had read Plato, or Aristotle, or Hobbes, or Bacon, or Algernon Sydney,[7] or Tom Paine, yet did he sometimes manifest a shrewdness and sagacity in his measures, that one would hardly expect from a man who did

2. **William Kieft:** Stuyvesant's predecessor as governor or director-general of New Netherland; "William the Testy" (d. 1647). 3. **"the . . . God":** Cf. Pope, *Essay on Man*, IV.248. 4. **"he . . . again":** Cf. *Hamlet*, I.ii.187.

5. **Peter . . . successor:** Stuyvesant was the last Dutch governor and (in *Knickerbocker*) Van Twiller ("Wouter the Doubter") the first. 6. **leg:** "See the histories of Masters Josselyn and Blome" [I]. These are John Josselyn, *Chronological Observations of America* (London, 1674); and Richard Blome, *Present State of His Majesty's Isles and Territories* (London, 1687). 7. **Algernon Sydney:** seventeenth-century English political theorist and republican.

not know Greek, and had never studied the ancients.[8] True it is, and I confess it with sorrow, that he had an unreasonable aversion to experiments, and was fond of governing his province after the simplest manner; but then he contrived to keep it in better order than did the erudite Kieft, though he had all the philosophers, ancient and modern, to assist and perplex him. I must likewise own that he made but very few laws; but then, again, he took care that those few were rigidly and impartially enforced; and I do not know but justice, on the whole, was as well administered as if there had been volumes of sage acts and statutes yearly made, and daily neglected and forgotten.

He was, in fact, the very reverse of his predecessors, being neither tranquil and inert, like Walter the Doubter, nor restless and fidgeting, like William the Testy,—but a man, or rather a governor, of such uncommon activity and decision of mind, that he never sought nor accepted the advice of others,—depending bravely upon his single head, as would a hero of yore upon his single arm, to carry him through all difficulties and dangers. To tell the simple truth, he wanted nothing more to complete him as a statesman than to think always right; for no one can say but that he always acted as he thought. He was never a man to flinch when he found himself in a scrape, but to dash forward through thick and thin, trusting, by hook or by crook, to make all things straight in the end. In a word, he possessed, in an eminent degree, that great quality in a statesman, called perseverance by the polite, but nicknamed obstinacy by the vulgar,—a wonderful salve for official blunders, since he who perseveres in error without flinching gets the credit of boldness and consistency, while he who wavers in seeking to do what is right gets stigmatized as a trimmer. This much is certain; and it is a maxim well worthy the attention of all legislators, great and small, who stand shaking in the wind, irresolute which way to steer, that a ruler who follows his own will pleases himself, while he who seeks to satisfy the wishes and whims of others runs great risk of pleasing nobody. There is nothing, too, like putting down one's foot resolutely when in doubt, and letting things take their course. The clock that stands still points right twice in the four-and-twenty hours, while others may keep going continually and be continually going wrong.

Nor did this magnanimous quality escape the discernment of the good people of Nieuw Nederlands; on the contrary, so much were they struck with the independent will and vigorous resolution displayed on all occasions by their new governor, that they universally called him Hard-Koppig Piet, or Peter the Headstrong,—a great compliment to the strength of his understanding.

If, from all that I have said, thou dost not gather, worthy reader, that Peter Stuyvesant was a tough, sturdy, valiant, weather-beaten, mettlesome, obstinate, leathern-sided, lion-hearted, generous-spirited old governor, either I have written to but little purpose, or thou art very dull at drawing conclusions.

This most excellent governor commenced his administration on the 29th of May, 1647,—a remarkably stormy day, distinguished in all the almanacs of the time which have come down to us by the name of *Windy Friday*. As he was very jealous of his personal and official dignity, he was inaugurated into office with great ceremony,—the goodly oaken chair of the renowned Wouter Van Twiller being carefully preserved for such occasions, in like manner as the chair and stone were reverentially preserved at Schone, in Scotland, for the coronation of the Caledonian monarchs.

I must not omit to mention that the tempestuous state of the elements, together with its being that unlucky day of the week termed "hanging-day," did not fail to excite much grave speculation and divers very reasonable apprehensions among the more ancient and enlightened inhabitants; and several of the sager sex, who were reputed to be not a little skilled in the mystery of astrology and fortune-telling, did declare outright that they were omens of a disastrous administration;—an event that came to be lamentably verified, and which proves beyond dispute the wisdom of attending to those preternatural intimations furnished by dreams and visions, the flying of birds, falling of stones, and cackling of geese, on which the sages and rulers of ancient times placed such reliance; or to those shootings of stars, eclipses of the moon, howlings of dogs, and flarings of candles, carefully noted and interpreted by the oracular sibyls of our day,—who, in my humble opinion, are the legitimate inheritors and preservers of the ancient science of divination. This much is certain, that Governor Stuyvesant succeeded to the chair of state at a turbulent period: when foes thronged and threatened from without; when anarchy and stiff-necked opposition reigned rampant within; when the authority of their High

8. **man . . . ancients:** In this paragraph Stuyvesant is consistently contrasted with Kieft; references to Kieft's classical learning, knowledge of philosophy, and fondness for experiments are part of the satire against Thomas Jefferson, whom Kieft is made to resemble. On the political satire, especially in Book IV, see *Knickerbocker* (1927), pp. lxi–lxxiii, and Greenlaw, "A Comedy of Politics."

Mightinesses the Lords States General,[9] though supported by economy and defended by speeches, protests, and proclamations, yet tottered to its very centre; and when the great city of New Amsterdam, though fortified by flag-staffs, trumpeters, and wind-mills,[10] seemed, like some fair lady of easy virtue, to lie open to attack, and ready to yield to the first invader.

CHAPTER 2

SHOWING HOW PETER THE HEADSTRONG BESTIRRED HIMSELF AMONG THE RATS AND COBWEBS ON ENTERING INTO OFFICE—HIS INTERVIEW WITH ANTONY THE TRUMPETER, AND HIS PERILOUS MEDDLING WITH THE CURRENCY

THE VERY first movements of the great Peter, on taking the reins of government, displayed his magnanimity, though they occasioned not a little marvel and uneasiness among the people of the Manhattoes.[11] Finding himself constantly interrupted by the opposition, and annoyed by the advice of his privy council, the members of which had acquired the unreasonable habit of thinking and speaking for themselves during the preceding reign, he determined at once to put a stop to such grievous abominations. Scarcely, therefore, had he entered upon his authority, than he turned out of office all the meddlesome spirits of the factious cabinet of William the Testy; in place of whom he chose unto himself counsellors from those fat, somniferous, respectable burghers who had flourished and slumbered under the easy reign of Walter the Doubter. All these he caused to be furnished with abundance of fair long pipes, and to be regaled with frequent corporation dinners, admonishing them to smoke, and eat, and sleep for the good of the nation, while he took the burden of government upon his own shoulders,—an arrangement to which they all gave hearty acquiescence.

Nor did he stop here, but made a hideous rout among the inventions and expedients of his learned predecessor,—rooting up his patent gallows, where caitiff vagabonds were suspended by the waistband,—demolishing his flag-staffs and wind-mills, which, like mighty giants, guarded the ramparts of New Amsterdam,—pitching to the duyvel whole batteries of quaker guns,—and, in a word, turning topsy-turvy the whole philosophic, economic, and wind-mill system[12] of the immortal sage of Saardam.[13]

The honest folk of New Amsterdam began to quake now for the fate of their matchless champion, Antony the Trumpeter,[14] who had acquired prodigious favor in the eyes of the women, by means of his whiskers and his trumpet. Him did Peter the Headstrong cause to be brought into his presence, and eying him for a moment from head to foot, with a countenance that would have appalled anything else than a sounder of brass,—"Pr'ythee, who and what art thou?" said he. "Sire," replied the other, in no wise dismayed, "for my name, it is Antony Van Corlear; for my parentage, I am the son of my mother; for my profession, I am champion and garrison of this great city of New Amsterdam." "I doubt me much," said Peter Stuyvesant, "that thou art some scurvy costard-monger knave. How didst thou acquire this paramount honor and dignity?" "Marry, sir," replied the other, "like many a great man before me, simply *by sounding my own trumpet.*" "Ay, is it so?" quoth the governor; "why, then let us have a relish of thy art." Whereupon the good Antony put his instrument to his lips, and sounded a charge with such a tremendous outset, such a delectable quaver, and such a triumphant cadence, that it was enough to make one's heart leap out of one's mouth only to be within a mile of it. Like as a war-worn charger, grazing in peaceful plains, starts at a strain of martial music, pricks up his ears, and snorts, and paws, and kindles at the noise, so did the heroic Peter joy to hear the clangor of the trumpet; for of him might truly be said, what was recorded of the renowned St. George of England, "there was nothing in all the world that more rejoiced his heart than to hear the pleasant sound of war, and see the soldiers brandish forth their steeled weapons." Casting his eye more kindly, therefore, upon the sturdy Van Corlear, and finding him to be a jovial varlet, shrewd in his discourse, yet of great discretion and immeasurable wind, he straightway conceived a

9. **Lords States General:** governing body of the United Netherlands. 10. **flag-staffs . . . wind-mills:** See 12 n. and 14 n., f. 11. **the Manhattoes:** the settlement of New Amsterdam on the island of Manna-hata (Manhattan).

12. **Nor . . . system:** This is further satire against Jefferson, who was an amateur scientist and inventor and who, as President, was charged by his opponents with substituting a system of "economy" for national defense. 13. **Saardam:** more properly Zaandam, the city in Holland from which Kieft came. 14. **Antony the Trumpeter:** According to Knickerbocker, Antony's trumpet had been the key to Kieft's scheme of defense. The trumpet is sometimes obviously used as a hyperbolic slang substitute for Antony's Nose, a physical attribute suggested to Irving by the promontory on the Hudson called Antony's Nose. Reminiscent of "Slawkenbergius's Tale" in *Tristram Shandy*, this imagery often carries risqué overtones.

vast kindness for him, and discharging him from the troublesome duty of garrisoning, defending, and alarming the city, ever after retained him about his person, as his chief favorite, confidential envoy, and trusty squire. Instead of disturbing the city with disastrous notes, he was instructed to play so as to delight the governor while at his repasts, as did the minstrels of yore in the days of glorious chivalry,—and on all public occasions to rejoice the ears of the people with warlike melody, —thereby keeping alive a noble and martial spirit.

But the measure of the valiant Peter which produced the greatest agitation in the community, was his laying his hand upon the currency. He had old-fashioned notions in favor of gold and silver, which he considered the true standards of wealth and mediums of commerce; and one of his first edicts was, that all duties to government should be paid in those precious metals, and that seawant, or wampum, should no longer be a legal tender.

Here was a blow at public prosperity! All those who speculated on the rise and fall of this fluctuating currency, found their calling at an end; those, too, who had hoarded Indian money by barrels full, found their capital shrunk in amount; but, above all, the Yankee traders, who were accustomed to flood the market with newly coined oyster-shells, and to abstract Dutch merchandise in exchange, were loud-mouthed in decrying this "tampering with the currency." It was clipping the wings of commerce; it was checking the development of public prosperity; trade would be at an end; goods would moulder on the shelves; grain would rot in the granaries; grass would grow in the market-place. In a word, no one who has not heard the outcries and howlings of a modern Tarshish,[15] at any check upon "paper-money," [16] can have any idea of the clamor against Peter the Headstrong, for checking the circulation of oyster-shells.

In fact, trade did shrink into narrower channels; but then the stream was deep as it was broad; the honest Dutchmen sold less goods; but then they got the worth of them, either in silver and gold, or in codfish, tin ware, apple-brandy, Weathersfield onions, wooden bowls, and other articles of Yankee barter. The ingenious people of the east, however, indemnified themselves another way for having to abandon the coinage of oyster-shells; for about this time we are told that wooden nutmegs made their first appearance in New Amsterdam, to the great annoyance of the Dutch housewives.

15. **Tarshish:** The Bible makes frequent reference to Tarshish as a commercial center. 16. **"paper-money":** government-issued notes or government-authorized bank notes, promises to pay, as opposed, say, to gold-backed certificates. Paper money was a problem in the United States during the period of the Articles of Confederation and again in the 1830's and 1840's after Jackson's veto of the bill for the United States Bank. Irving added this and an earlier section on cheap money (wampum) to the 1848 edition of *Knickerbocker*. His involvement in the ups and downs of the business cycle—some of his own investments turned out badly—had aroused his interest in questions of finance and speculation. See "The Devil and Tom Walker," pp. 265–70.

NOTE

From a manuscript record of the province; Lib. N. Y. Hist. Society.—We have been unable to render your inhabitants wiser and prevent their being further imposed upon than to declare absolutely and preemptorily that henceforward seawant shall be bullion,—not longer admissible in trade, without any value, as it is indeed. So that every one may be upon his guard to barter no longer away his wares and merchandises for these bubbles,—at least not to accept them at a higher rate, or in a larger quantity, than as they may want them in their trade with the savages.

In this way your English [Yankee] neighbors shall no longer be enabled to draw the best wares and merchandises from our country for nothing,—the beavers and furs not excepted. This has indeed long since been insufferable, although it ought chiefly to be imputed to the imprudent penuriousness of our own merchants and inhabitants, who, it is to be hoped, shall through the abolition of this seawant become wiser and more prudent.

27th January, 1662.

Seawant falls into disrepute; duties to be paid in silver coin.

CHAPTER 3

HOW THE YANKEE LEAGUE WAXED MORE AND MORE POTENT; AND HOW IT OUTWITTED THE GOOD PETER IN TREATY-MAKING

Now it came to pass, that, while Peter Stuyvesant was busy regulating the internal affairs of his domain, the great Yankee league,[17] which had caused such tribulation to William the Testy, continued to increase in extent and power. The grand Amphictyonic council of the league was held at Boston, where it spun a web, which threatened to link within it all the mighty principalities and powers of the east. The object proposed by this formidable combination was, mutual protection and defence against their savage neighbors; but all the

17. **Yankee league:** the United Colonies of New England or the New England Confederation founded 1643, comprising Massachusetts Bay, Plymouth, Connecticut, and New Haven.

world knows the real aim was to form a grand crusade against the Nieuw Nederlands, and to get possession of the city of the Manhattoes,—as devout an object of enterprise and ambition to the Yankees as was ever the capture of Jerusalem to ancient crusaders.

In the very year following the inauguration of Governor Stuyvesant, a grand deputation departed from the city of Providence (famous for its dusty streets and beauteous women) in behalf of the plantation of Rhode Island, praying to be admitted into the league.

The following minute of this deputation appears in the ancient records of the council.[18]

"Mr. Will. Cottington and Captain Partridg of Rhoode Island presented this insewing request to the commissioners in wrighting—

"Our request and motion is in behalfe of Rhoode Iland, that wee the Ilanders of Roode-Iland may be rescauied into combination with all the united colonyes of New England in a firme and perpetual league of friendship and amity of ofence and defence, mutuall advice and succor upon all just occasions for our mutuall safety and wellfaire, etc.

"WILL COTTINGTON,
"ALICXSANDER PARTRIDG."

There was certainly something in the very physiognomy of this document that might well inspire apprehension. The name of Alexander, however misspelt, has been warlike in every age; and though its fierceness is in some measure softened by being coupled with the gentle cognomen of Partridge, still, like the color of scarlet, it bears an exceeding great resemblance to the sound of a trumpet. From the style of the letter, moreover, and the soldier-like ignorance of orthography displayed by the noble Captain Alicxsander Partridg in spelling his own name, we may picture to ourselves this mighty man of Rhodes,[19] strong in arms, potent in the field, and as great a scholar as though he had been educated among that learned people of Thrace, who, Aristotle assures us, could not count beyond the number four.

The result of this great Yankee league was augmented audacity on the part of the moss-troopers of Connecticut,—pushing their encroachments farther and farther into the territories of their High Mightinesses, so that even the inhabitants of New Amsterdam began to draw short breath and to find themselves exceedingly cramped for elbow-room.

Peter Stuyvesant was not a man to submit quietly to such intrusions; his first impulse was to march at once to the frontier and kick these squatting Yankees out of the country, but, bethinking himself in time that he was now a governor and legislator, the policy of the statesman for once cooled the fire of the old soldier, and he determined to try his hand at negotiation. A correspondence accordingly ensued between him and the grand council of the league; and it was agreed that commissioners from either side should meet at Hartford, to settle boundaries, adjust grievances, and establish a "perpetual and happy peace."

The commissioners on the part of the Manhattoes were chosen, according to immemorial usage of that venerable metropolis, from among the "wisest and weightiest" men of the community, that is to say, men with the oldest heads and heaviest pockets. Among these sages the veteran navigator, Hans Reinier Oothout, who had made such extensive discoveries during the time of Oloffe the Dreamer,[20] was looked up to as an oracle in all matters of the kind; and he was ready to produce the very spy-glass with which he first spied the mouth of the Connecticut river from his masthead; and all the world knows the discovery of the mouth of a river gives prior right to all the lands drained by its waters.

It was with feelings of pride and exultation that the good people of the Manhattoes saw two of the richest and most ponderous burghers departing on this embassy,—men whose word on 'change was oracular, and in whose presence no poor man ventured to appear without taking off his hat: when it was seen, too, that the veteran Reinier Oothout accompanied them with his spy-glass under his arm, all the old men and old women predicted that men of such weight, with such evidence, would leave the Yankees no alternative but to pack up their tin kettles and wooden wares, put wife and children in a cart, and abandon all the lands of their High Mightinesses, on which they had squatted.

In truth, the commissioners sent to Hartford by the league seemed in no wise calculated to compete with men of such capacity. They were two lean Yankee lawyers, litigious-looking varlets, and evidently men of no substance, since they had no rotundity in the belt, and there was no jingling of money in their pockets; it is true, they had longer

18. "Haz. Col. Stat. Pap." [I]: Ebenezer Hazard, *Historical Collections* (1792–94). **19. mighty . . . Rhodes:** a play on "colossus of Rhodes."

20. Oloffe the Dreamer: Oloffe Van Kortlandt, member of the Dutch council in New Amsterdam, prominent in Book II.

heads than the Dutchmen; but if the heads of the latter were flat at top, they were broad at bottom, and what was wanting in height of forehead was made up by a double chin.

The negotiation turned as usual upon the good old corner-stone of original discovery,—according to the principle that he who first sees a new country has an unquestionable right to it. This being admitted, the veteran Oothout, at a concerted signal, stepped forth in the assembly with the identical tarpauling [21] spy-glass in his hand, with which he had discovered the mouth of the Connecticut, while the worthy Dutch commissioners lolled back in their chairs, secretly chuckling at the idea of having for once got the weather-gage of the Yankees; but what was their dismay when the latter produced a Nantucket whaler with a spy-glass twice as long, with which he discovered the whole coast, quite down to the Manhattoes, and so crooked, that he had spied with it up the whole course of the Connecticut river. This principle pushed home, therefore, the Yankees had a right to the whole country bordering on the Sound; nay, the city of New Amsterdam was a mere Dutch squatting-place on their territories.

I forbear to dwell upon the confusion of the worthy Dutch commissioners at finding their main pillar of proof thus knocked from under them; neither will I pretend to describe the consternation of the wise men at the Manhattoes when they learned how their commissioner had been outtrumped by the Yankees, and how the latter pretended to claim to the very gates of New Amsterdam.

Long was the negotiation protracted, and long was the public mind kept in a state of anxiety. There are two modes of settling boundary questions when the claims of the opposite are irreconcilable. One is by an appeal to arms, in which case the weakest party is apt to lose its right, and get a broken head into the bargain; the other mode is by compromise, or mutual concession,—that is to say, one party cedes half of its claims, and the other party half of its rights; he who grasps most gets most, and the whole is pronounced an equitable division, "perfectly honorable to both parties."

The latter mode was adopted in the present instance. The Yankees gave up claims to vast tracts of the Nieuw Nederlands which they had never seen, and all right to the land of Manna-hata and the city of New Amsterdam, to which they had no right at all; while the Dutch, in return, agreed that the Yankees should retain possession of the frontier places where they had squatted, and of both sides of the Connecticut river.

21. **tarpauling:** belonging to a sailor or mariner.

When the news of this treaty arrived at New Amsterdam, the whole city was in an uproar of exultation. The old women rejoiced that there was to be no war, the old men that their cabbage-gardens were safe from invasion; while the political sages pronounced the treaty a great triumph over the Yankees, considering how much they had claimed, and how little they had been "fobbed off with."

And now my worthy reader is, doubtless, like the great and good Peter, congratulating himself with the idea that his feelings will no longer be harassed by afflicting details of stolen horses, broken heads, impounded hogs, and all the other catalogue of heart-rending cruelties that disgraced these border wars. But if he should indulge in such expectations, it is a proof that he is but little versed in the paradoxical ways of cabinets; to convince him of which, I solicit his serious attention to my next chapter, wherein I will show that Peter Stuyvesant has already committed a great error in politics, and, by effecting a peace, has materially hazarded the tranquillity of the province.

CHAPTER 4

CONTAINING DIVERS SPECULATIONS ON WAR AND NEGOTIATIONS—SHOWING THAT A TREATY OF PEACE IS A GREAT NATIONAL EVIL

IT WAS the opinion of that poetical philosopher, Lucretius, that war was the original state of man, whom he described as being primitively a savage beast of prey, engaged in a constant state of hostility with his own species, and that this ferocious spirit was tamed and ameliorated by society. The same opinion has been advocated by Hobbes,[22] nor have there been wanting many other philosophers to admit and defend.

For my part, though prodigiously fond of these valuable speculations, so complimentary to human nature, yet, in this instance, I am inclined to take the proposition by halves, believing with Horace,[23] that, though war may have been originally the favorite amusement and industrious employ-

22. **advocated by Hobbes:** "Hobbes's Leviathan. Part i. ch. 13" [I].
23. **Horace:** "*Quum prorepserunt primis animalia terris,/Mutuum ac turpe pecus, glandem atque cubilia propter,/Unguibus et pugnis, dein fustibus, atque ita porro/Pugnabant armis, quae post fabricaverat usus.*/Hor. Sat. L. i. S. 3" [I]. The substance of this passage from the third satire in Horace's first book is given in the first three sentences of the ensuing paragraph.

ment of our progenitors, yet, like many other excellent habits, so far from being ameliorated, it has been cultivated and confirmed by refinement and civilization, and increases in exact proportion as we approach towards that state of perfection which is the *ne plus ultra* of modern philosophy.

The first conflict between man and man was the mere exertion of physical force, unaided by auxiliary weapons; his arm was his buckler, his fist was his mace, and a broken head the catastrophe of his encounters. The battle of unassisted strength was succeeded by the more rugged one of stones and clubs, and war assumed a sanguinary aspect. As man advanced in refinement, as his faculties expanded, and as his sensibilities became more exquisite, he grew rapidly more ingenious and experienced in the art of murdering his fellow-beings. He invented a thousand devices to defend and to assault: the helmet, the cuirass, and the buckler, the sword, the dart, and the javelin, prepared him to elude the wound as well as to launch the blow. Still urging on, in the career of philanthropic invention, he enlarges and heightens his powers of defence and injury:—The Aries,[24] the Scorpio,[25] the Balista, and the Catapulta, give a horror and sublimity to war, and magnify its glory, by increasing its desolation. Still insatiable, though armed with machinery that seemed to reach the limits of destructive invention, and to yield a power of injury commensurate even with the desires of revenge,—still deeper researches must be made in the diabolical arcana. With furious zeal he dives into the bowels of the earth; he toils midst poisonous minerals and deadly salts, —the sublime discovery of gunpowder blazes upon the world—and finally the dreadful art of fighting by proclamation [26] seems to endow the demon of war with ubiquity and omnipotence!

This, indeed, is grand!—this, indeed, marks the powers of mind, and bespeaks that divine endowment of reason, which distinguishes us from the animals, our inferiors. The unenlightened brutes content themselves with the native force which Providence has assigned them. The angry bull butts with his horns, as did his progenitors before him; the lion, the leopard, and the tiger seek only with their talons and their fangs to gratify their sanguinary fury; and even the subtle serpent darts the same venom, and uses the same wiles, as did his sire before the flood. Man alone, blessed with the inventive mind, goes on from discovery to discovery,—enlarges and multiplies his powers of destruction,—arrogates the tremendous weapons of Deity itself, and tasks creation to assist him in murdering his brother-worm!

In proportion as the art of war has increased in improvement has the art of preserving peace advanced in equal ratio; and as we have discovered, in this age of wonders and inventions, that proclamation is the most formidable engine in war, so have we discovered the no less ingenious mode of maintaining peace by perpetual negotiations.

A treaty, or, to speak more correctly, a negotiation, therefore, according to the acceptation of experienced statesmen, learned in these matters, is no longer an attempt to accommodate differences, to ascertain rights, and to establish an equitable exchange of kind offices, but a contest of skill between two powers, which shall over-reach and take in the other. It is a cunning endeavor to obtain by peaceful manœuvre, and the chicanery of cabinets, those advantages which a nation would otherwise have wrested by force of arms,—in the same manner as a conscientious highwayman reforms and becomes a quiet and praiseworthy citizen, contenting himself with cheating his neighbor out of that property he would formerly have seized with open violence.

In fact, the only time when two nations can be said to be in a state of perfect amity is, when a negotiation is open, and a treaty pending. Then, when there are no stipulations entered into, no bonds to restrain the will, no specific limits to awaken the captious jealousy of right implanted in our nature, when each party has some advantage to hope and expect from the other, then it is that the two nations are wonderfully gracious and friendly,—their ministers professing the highest mutual regard, exchanging billets-doux, making fine speeches, and indulging in all those little diplomatic flirtations, coquetries, and fondlings, that do so marvellously tickle the good-humor of the respective nations. Thus it may paradoxically be said, that there is never so good an understanding between two nations as when there is a little misunderstanding,—and that so long as they are on no terms at all, they are on the best terms in the world!

I do not by any means pretend to claim the merit of having made the above discovery. It has, in fact, long been secretly acted upon by certain enlightened cabinets, and is, together with divers other notable theories, privately copied out of the commonplace book of an illustrious gentleman, who has been member of congress, and enjoyed the unlimited confidence of heads of departments. To this principle may be ascribed the wonderful

24. **Aries:** battering-ram. 25. **Scorpio:** instrument for projecting stones. 26. **art . . . proclamation:** an art invented by Kieft. The allusion is part of the satire on Jefferson's foreign policy.

ingenuity shown of late years in protracting and interrupting negotiations. Hence the cunning measure of appointing as ambassador some political pettifogger skilled in delays, sophisms, and misapprehensions, and dexterous in the art of baffling argument,—or some blundering statesman, whose errors and misconstructions may be a plea for refusing to ratify his engagements. And hence, too, that most notable expedient, so popular with our government, of sending out a brace of ambassadors,—between whom, having each an individual will to consult, character to establish, and interest to promote, you may as well look for unanimity and concord as between two lovers with one mistress, two dogs with one bone, or two naked rogues with one pair of breeches. This disagreement, therefore, is continually breeding delays and impediments, in consequence of which the negotiation goes on swimmingly—inasmuch as there is no prospect of its ever coming to a close. Nothing is lost by these delays and obstacles but time; and in a negotiation, according to the theory I have exposed, all time lost is in reality so much time gained:—with what delightful paradoxes does modern political economy abound!

Now all that I have here advanced is so notoriously true, that I almost blush to take up the time of my readers with treating of matters which must many a time have stared them in the face. But the proposition to which I would most earnestly call their attention is this, that, though a negotiation be the most harmonizing of all national transactions, yet a treaty of peace is a great political evil, and one of the most fruitful sources of war.

I have rarely seen an instance of any special contract between individuals that did not produce jealousies, bickerings, and often downright ruptures between them; nor did I ever know of a treaty between two nations that did not occasion continual misunderstandings. How many worthy country neighbors have I known, who, after living in peace and good-fellowship for years, have been thrown into a state of distrust, cavilling, and animosity, by some ill-starred agreement about fences, runs of water, and stray cattle! And how many well-meaning nations, who would otherwise have remained in the most amicable disposition towards each other, have been brought to swords' points about the infringement or misconstruction of some treaty, which in an evil hour they had concluded, by way of making their amity more sure!

Treaties at best are but complied with so long as interest requires their fulfilment; consequently they are virtually binding on the weaker party only, or, in plain truth, they are not binding at all. No nation will wantonly go to war with another if it has nothing to gain thereby, and therefore needs no treaty to restrain it from violence; and if it have anything to gain, I much question, from what I have witnessed of the righteous conduct of nations, whether any treaty could be made so strong that it could not thrust the sword through,—nay, I would hold ten to one, the treaty itself would be the very source to which resort would be had to find a pretext for hostilities.

Thus, therefore, I conclude,—that, though it is the best of all policies for a nation to keep up a constant negotiation with its neighbors, yet it is the summit of folly for it ever to be beguiled into a treaty; for then comes on non-fulfilment and infraction, then remonstrance, then altercation, then retaliation, then recrimination, and finally open war. In a word, negotiation is like courtship, a time of sweet words, gallant speeches, soft looks, and endearing caresses,—but the marriage ceremony is the signal for hostilities.

If my painstaking reader be not somewhat perplexed by the ratiocination of the foregoing passage, he will perceive, at a glance, that the Great Peter, in concluding a treaty with his eastern neighbors, was guilty of lamentable error in policy. In fact, to this unlucky agreement may be traced a world of bickerings and heart-burnings, between the parties, about fancied or pretended infringements of treaty-stipulations; in all which the Yankees were prone to indemnify themselves by a "dig into the sides" of the New Netherlands. But, in sooth, these border feuds, albeit they gave great annoyance to the good burghers of Mannahata, were so pitiful in their nature, that a grave historian like myself, who grudges the time spent in anything less than the revolutions of states and fall of empires, would deem them unworthy of being inscribed on his page. The reader is, therefore, to take it for granted, though I scorn to waste, in the detail, that time which my furrowed brow and trembling hand inform me is invaluable, that all the while the Great Peter was occupied in those tremendous and bloody contests which I shall shortly rehearse; there was a continued series of little, dirty, snivelling scourings, broils, and maraudings, kept up on the eastern frontiers by the moss-troopers of Connecticut. But, like that mirror of chivalry, the sage and valorous Don Quixote, I leave these petty contests for some future Sancho Panza of an historian, while I reserve my prowess and my pen for achievements of higher dignity; for at this moment I hear a direful and portentous note issuing from the bosom of the great council of the league, and resounding throughout the regions of the east, menacing the fame and fortunes of Peter Stuyvesant. I call, therefore, upon the reader to leave behind him all the paltry brawls of the Connecticut borders, and to press forward with me to the relief of our favorite hero, who, I foresee, will be wofully beset by the implacable Yankees in the next chapter.

CHAPTER 5

HOW PETER STUYVESANT WAS GRIEVOUSLY BELIED BY THE GREAT COUNCIL OF THE LEAGUE; AND HOW HE SENT ANTONY THE TRUMPETER TO TAKE TO THE COUNCIL A PIECE OF HIS MIND

THAT THE reader may be aware of the peril at this moment menacing Peter Stuyvesant and his capital, I must remind him of the old charge advanced in the council of the league in the time of William the Testy, that the Nederlanders were carrying on a trade "damnable and injurious to the colonists," in furnishing the savages with "guns, powther and shott." This, as I then suggested, was a crafty device of the Yankee confederacy to have a snug cause of war *in petto,* in case any favorable opportunity should present of attempting the conquest of the New Nederlands: the great object of Yankee ambition.

Accordingly we now find, when every other ground of complaint had apparently been removed by treaty, this nefarious charge revived with tenfold virulence, and hurled like a thunderbolt at the very head of Peter Stuyvesant; happily his head, like that of the great bull of the Wabash, was proof against such missiles.

To be explicit, we are told that, in the year 1651, the great confederacy of the east accused the immaculate Peter, the soul of honor and heart of steel, of secretly endeavoring, by gifts and promises, to instigate the Narroheganset, Mohaque, and Pequot Indians, to surprise and massacre the Yankee settlements. "For," as the grand council observed, "the Indians round about for divers hundred miles cercute seeme to have drunk deepe of an intoxicating cupp, att or from the Manhattoes against the English, whoe have sought their good, both in bodily and spirituall respects."

This charge they pretended to support by the evidence of divers Indians, who were probably moved by that spirit of truth which is said to reside in the bottle, and who swore to the fact as sturdily as though they had been so many Christian troopers.[27]

Though descended from a family which suffered much injury from the losel Yankees of those times, my great-grandfather having had a yoke of oxen and his best pacer stolen, and having received a pair of black eyes and a bloody nose in one of these border wars, and my grandfather, when a very little boy tending pigs, having been kidnapped and severely flogged by a long-sided Connecticut schoolmaster,—yet I should have passed over all these wrongs with forgiveness and oblivion,—I could even have suffered them to have broken Everet Ducking's head,—to have kicked the doughty Jacobus Van Curlet and his ragged regiment out of doors,[28]—to have carried every hog into captivity, and depopulated every henroost on the face of the earth with perfect impunity,—but this wanton attack upon one of the most gallant and irreproachable heroes of modern times is too much even for me to digest, and has overset, with a single puff, the patience of the historian, and the forbearance of the Dutchman.

Oh, reader, it was false! I swear to thee, it was false!—if thou hast any respect to my word,—if the undeviating character for veracity, which I have endeavored to maintain throughout this work, has its due weight upon thee, thou wilt not give thy faith to this tale of slander; for I pledge my honor and my immortal fame to thee, that the gallant Peter Stuyvesant was not only innocent of this foul conspiracy, but would have suffered his right arm or even his wooden leg to consume with slow and everlasting flames, rather than attempt to destroy his enemies in any other way than open, generous warfare;—beshrew those caitiff scouts, that conspired to sully his honest name by such an imputation!

Peter Stuyvesant, though haply he may never have heard of a knight-errant, had as true a heart of chivalry as ever beat at the round table of King Arthur. In the honest bosom of this heroic Dutchman dwelt the seven noble virtues of knighthood, flourishing among his hardy qualities like wild flowers among rocks. He was, in truth, a hero of chivalry struck off by nature at a single heat, and though little care may have been taken to refine her workmanship, he stood forth a miracle of her skill. In all his dealings he was headstrong perhaps, but open and aboveboard; if there was anything in the whole world he most loathed and despised, it was cunning and secret wile; "straight forward" was his motto; and he would at any time

27. troopers: Irving, in revising, has omitted the following detail: "And to be more sure of their veracity, the knowing council previously made every mother's son of them devoutly drunk. . . ." **28. could . . . doors:** These are references to earlier conflicts between the Yankees and the Dutch. "Ducking" is a pun on the family name of Irving's friend E. A. Duyckinck, the New York editor.

rather run his hard head against a stone wall than attempt to get round it.

Such was Peter Stuyvesant; and if my admiration of him has on this occasion transported my style beyond the sober gravity which becomes the philosophic recorder of historic events, I must plead as an apology, that, though a little gray-headed Dutchman, arrived almost at the downhill of life, I still retain a lingering spark of that fire which kindles in the eye of youth when contemplating the virtues of ancient worthies. Blessed, thrice and nine times blessed be the good St. Nicholas, if I have indeed escaped that apathy which chills the sympathies of age and paralyzes every glow of enthusiasm.

The first measure of Peter Stuyvesant, on hearing of this slanderous charge, would have been worthy of a man who had studied for years in the chivalrous library of Don Quixote. Drawing his sword and laying it across the table, to put him in proper tune, he took pen in hand and indited a proud and lofty letter to the council of the league, reproaching them with giving ear to the slanders of heathen savages against a Christian, a soldier, and a cavalier; declaring, that, whoever charged him with the plot in question, lied in his throat; to prove which he offered to meet the president of the council or any of his compeers, or their champion, Captain Alicxsander Partridg, that mighty man of Rhodes, in single combat,—wherein he trusted to vindicate his honor by the prowess of his arm.

This missive was intrusted to his trumpeter and squire, Antony Van Corlear, that man of emergencies, with orders to travel night and day, sparing neither whip nor spur, seeing that he carried the vindication of his patron's fame in his saddle-bags.

The loyal Antony accomplished his mission with great speed and considerable loss of leather. He delivered his missive with becoming ceremony, accompanying it with a flourish of defiance on his trumpet to the whole council, ending with a significant and nasal twang full in the face of Captain Partridg, who nearly jumped out of his skin in an ecstasy of astonishment.

The grand council was composed of men too cool and practical to be put readily in a heat, or to indulge in knight-errantry; and above all to run a tilt with such a fiery hero as Peter the Headstrong. They knew the advantage, however, to have always a snug, justifiable cause of war in reserve with a neighbor, who had territories worth invading; so they devised a reply to Peter Stuyvesant, calculated to keep up the "raw" which they had established.

On receiving this answer, Antony Van Corlear remounted the Flanders mare which he always rode, and trotted merrily back to the Manhattoes, solacing himself by the way according to his wont; twanging his trumpet like a very devil, so that the sweet valleys and banks of the Connecticut resounded with the warlike melody; bringing all the folks to the windows as he passed through Hartford and Pyquag, and Middletown, and all the other border towns, ogling and winking at the women, and making aërial wind-mills from the end of his nose at their husbands, and stopping occasionally in the villages to eat pumpkin-pies, dance at country frolics, and bundle with the Yankee lasses—whom he rejoiced exceedingly with his soul-stirring instrument.

CHAPTER 6

HOW PETER STUYVESANT DEMANDED A COURT OF HONOR—AND WHAT THE COURT OF HONOR AWARDED TO HIM

THE REPLY of the grand council to Peter Stuyvesant was couched in the coolest and most diplomatic language. They assured him that "his confident denials of the barbarous plot alleged against him would weigh little against the testimony of divers sober and respectable Indians"; that "his guilt was proved to their perfect satisfaction," so that they must still require and seek due *satisfaction and security;* ending with—"so we rest, sir—Yours in ways of righteousness."

I forbear to say how the lion-hearted Peter roared and ramped at finding himself more and more entangled in the meshes thus artfully drawn round him by the knowing Yankees. Impatient, however, of suffering so gross an aspersion to rest upon his honest name, he sent a second messenger to the council, reiterating his denial of the treachery imputed to him, and offering to submit his conduct to the scrutiny of a court of honor. His offer was readily accepted; and now he looked forward with confidence to an august tribunal to be assembled at the Manhattoes, formed of high-minded cavaliers, peradventure governors and commanders of the confederate plantations, when the matter might be investigated by his peers, in a manner befitting his rank and dignity.

While he was awaiting the arrival of such high functionaries, behold, one sunshiny afternoon there rode into the great gate of the Manhattoes two lean, hungry-looking Yankees, mounted on Narragansett pacers, with saddle-bags under their bottoms, and green satchels under their arms, who looked marvellously like two pettifogging attorneys beating the hoof from one county court to another in quest of lawsuits; and, in sooth, though they may have passed under different names at the time, I have reason to suspect they were the identical varlets who had negotiated the worthy Dutch commissioners out of the Connecticut river.

It was a rule with these indefatigable missionaries never to let the grass grow under their feet. Scarce had they, therefore, alighted at the inn and deposited their saddle-bags, than they made their way to the residence of the governor. They found him, according to custom, smoking his afternoon pipe on the "stoop," or bench at the porch of his house, and announced themselves, at once, as commissioners sent by the grand council of the east to investigate the truth of certain charges advanced against him.

The good Peter took his pipe from his mouth, and gazed at them for a moment in mute astonishment. By way of expediting business, they were proceeding on the spot to put some preliminary questions,—asking him, peradventure, whether he pleaded guilty or not guilty, considering him something in the light of a culprit at the bar,—when they were brought to a pause by seeing him lay down his pipe and begin to fumble with his walking-staff. For a moment those present would not have given half a crown for both the crowns of the commissioners; but Peter Stuyvesant repressed his mighty wrath and stayed his hand; he scanned the varlets from head to foot, satchels and all, with a look of ineffable scorn; then strode into the house, slammed the door after him, and commanded that they should never again be admitted to his presence.

The knowing commissioners winked to each other, and made a certificate on the spot that the governor had refused to answer their interrogatories or to submit to their examination. They then proceeded to rummage about the city for two or three days, in quest of what they called evidence, perplexing Indians and old women with their cross-questioning until they had stuffed their satchels and saddle-bags with all kinds of apocryphal tales, rumors, and calumnies; with these they mounted their Narraganset pacers and travelled back to the grand council; neither did the proud-hearted Peter trouble himself to hinder their researches nor impede their departure; he was too mindful of their sacred character as envoys; but I warrant me, had they played the same tricks with William the Testy, he would have had them tucked up by the waistband and treated to an aërial gambol on his patent gallows.

CHAPTER 7

HOW "DRUM ECCLESIASTIC" WAS BEATEN THROUGHOUT CONNECTICUT FOR A CRUSADE AGAINST THE NEW NETHERLANDS, AND HOW PETER STUYVESANT TOOK MEASURES TO FORTIFY HIS CAPITAL

THE GRAND COUNCIL of the east held a solemn meeting on the return of their envoys. As no advocate appeared in behalf of Peter Stuyvesant, everything went against him. His haughty refusal to submit to the questioning of the commissioners was construed into a consciousness of guilt. The contents of the satchels and saddle-bags were poured forth before the council and appeared a mountain of evidence. A pale, bilious orator took the floor, and declaimed for hours and in belligerent terms. He was one of those furious zealots who blows the bellows of faction until the whole furnace of politics is red-hot with sparks and cinders. What was it to him if he should set the house on fire, so that he might boil his pot by the blaze. He was from the borders of Connecticut; his constituents lived by marauding their Dutch neighbors, and were the greatest poachers in Christendom, excepting the Scotch border nobles. His eloquence had its effect, and it was determined to set on foot an expedition against the Nieuw Nederlands.

It was necessary, however, to prepare the public mind for this measure. Accordingly the arguments of the orator were echoed from the pulpit for several succeeding Sundays, and a crusade was preached up against Peter Stuyvesant and his devoted city.

This is the first we hear of the "drum ecclesiastic" [29] beating up for recruits in worldly warfare in our country. It has since been called into frequent use. A cunning politician often lurks under the clerical robe; things spiritual and things temporal are strangely jumbled together, like drugs on an apothecary's shelf; and instead of a peaceful sermon, the simple seeker after righteousness has often a political pamphlet thrust down his throat, labelled with a pious text from Scripture.

And now nothing was talked of but an expedition against the Manhattoes. It pleased the populace, who had a vehement prejudice against the Dutch, considering them a vastly inferior race,

29. **"drum ecclesiastic"**: Cf. Samuel Butler, *Hudibras* (1662), Part I, Canto I, l. 11.

who had sought the new world for the lucre of gain, not the liberty of conscience; who were mere heretics and infidels, inasmuch as they refused to believe in witches and sea-serpents, and had faith in the virtues of horse-shoes nailed to the door; ate pork without molasses; held pumpkins in contempt, and were in perpetual breach of the eleventh commandment of all true Yankees, "Thou shalt have codfish dinners on Saturdays."

No sooner did Peter Stuyvesant get wind of the storm that was brewing in the east, than he set to work to prepare for it. He was not one of those economical rulers, who postpone the expense of fortifying until the enemy is at the door. There is nothing, he would say, that keeps off enemies and crows more than the smell of gunpowder. He proceeded, therefore, with all diligence, to put the province and its metropolis in a posture of defence.

Among the remnants which remained from the days of William the Testy were the militia laws,—by which the inhabitants were obliged to turn out twice a year, with such military equipments as it pleased God,—and were put under the command of tailors and man-milliners, who, though on ordinary occasions they might have been the meekest, most pippin-hearted little men in the world, were very devils at parade, when they had cocked hats on their heads and swords by their sides. Under the instructions of these periodical warriors, the peaceful burghers of the Manhattoes were schooled in iron war, and became so hardy in the process of time, that they could march through sun and rain, from one end of the town to the other, without flinching,—and so intrepid and adroit, that they could face to the right, wheel to the left, and fire without winking or blinking.

Peter Stuyvesant, like all old soldiers who have seen service and smelt gunpowder, had no great respect for militia troops; however, he determined to give them a trial, and accordingly called for a general muster, inspection, and review. But, oh Mars and Bellona! what a turning-out was here! Here came old Roelant Cuckaburt, with a short blunderbuss on his shoulder, and a long horseman's sword trailing by his side; and Barent Dirkson, with something that looked like a copper kettle turned upsidedown on his head, and a couple of old horse-pistols in his belt; and Dirk Volkertson, with a long duck fowling-piece without any ramrod; and a host more, armed higgledy-piggledy,—with swords, hatchets, snickersnees, crowbars, broomsticks, and what not; the officers distinguished from the rest by having their slouched hats cocked up with pins, and surmounted with cocktail feathers.

The sturdy Peter eyed this nondescript host with some such rueful aspect as a man would eye the devil, and determined to give his featherbed soldiers a seasoning. He accordingly put them through their manual exercise over and over again; trudged them backwards and forwards about the streets of New Amsterdam until their short legs ached and their fat sides sweated again; and finally encamped them in the evening on the summit of a hill without the city, to give them a taste of camp life, intending the next day to renew the toils and perils of the field. But so it came to pass that in the night there fell a great and heavy rain, and melted away the army, so that in the morning, when Gaffer Phœbus shed his first beams upon the camp, scarce a warrior remained except Peter Stuyvesant and his trumpeter Van Corlear.

This awful desolation of a whole army would have appalled a commander of less nerve; but it served to confirm Peter's want of confidence in the militia system, which he thenceforward used to call, in joke,—for he sometimes indulged in a joke,—William the Testy's broken reed. He now took into his service a goodly number of burly, broad-shouldered, broad-bottomed Dutchmen; whom he paid in good silver and gold, and of whom he boasted, that, whether they could stand fire or not, they were at least water-proof. He fortified the city, too, with pickets and palisadoes, extending across the island from river to river, and, above all, cast up mud batteries, or redoubts, on the point of the island where it divided the beautiful bosom of the bay.

These latter redoubts, in process of time, came to be pleasantly overrun by a carpet of grass and clover, and overshadowed by wide-spreading elms and sycamores, among the branches of which the birds would build their nests and rejoice the ear with their melodious notes. Under these trees, too, the old burghers would smoke their afternoon pipe, contemplating the golden sun as he sank in the west, an emblem of the tranquil end toward which they were declining. Here, too, would the young men and maidens of the town take their evening stroll, watching the silver moonbeams as they trembled along the calm bosom of the bay, or lit up the sail of some gliding bark, and peradventure interchanging the soft vows of honest affection,—for to evening strolls in this favored spot were traced most of the marriages in New Amsterdam.

Such was the origin of that renowned promenade, THE BATTERY, which, though ostensibly devoted to the stern purposes of war, has ever been consecrated to the sweet delights of peace. The scene of many a gambol in happy childhood, —of many a tender assignation in riper years,— of many a soothing walk in declining age,—the healthful resort of the feeble invalid,—the Sunday refreshment of the dusty tradesman,—in fine, the ornament and delight of New York, and the pride of the lovely island of Manna-hata.

CHAPTER 8

HOW THE YANKEE CRUSADE AGAINST THE NEW NETHERLANDS WAS BAFFLED BY THE SUDDEN OUTBREAK OF WITCH-CRAFT AMONG THE PEOPLE OF THE EAST

HAVING THUS provided for the temporary security of New Amsterdam, and guarded it against any sudden surprise, the gallant Peter took a hearty pinch of snuff, and snapping his fingers, set the great council of Amphictyons and their champion, the redoubtable Alicxsander Patridg, at defiance. In the mean time the moss-troopers of Connecticut, the warriors of New Haven and Hartford, and Pyquag, otherwise called Weathersfield, famous for its onions and its witches, and of all the other border-towns, were in a prodigious turmoil, furbishing up their rusty weapons, shouting aloud for war, and anticipating easy conquests, and glorious rummaging of the fat little Dutch villages.

In the midst of these warlike preparations, however, they received the chilling news that the colony of Massachusetts refused to back them in this righteous war. It seems that the gallant conduct of Peter Stuyvesant, the generous warmth of his vindication, and the chivalrous spirit of his defiance, though lost upon the grand council of the league, had carried conviction to the general court of Massachusetts, which nobly refused to believe him guilty of the villainous plot laid at his door.[30]

The defection of so important a colony paralyzed the councils of the leaguc, some such dissension arose among its members as prevailed of yore in the camp of the brawling warriors of Greece, and in the end the crusade against the Manhattoes was abandoned.

It is said that the moss-troopers of Connecticut were sorely disappointed; but well for them that their belligerent cravings were not gratified: for by my faith, whatever might have been the ultimate result of a conflict with all the powers of the east, in the interim the stomachful heroes of Pyquag would have been choked with their own onions, and all the border-towns of Connecticut would have had such a scouring from the lion-hearted Peter and his robustious myrmidons, that I warrant me they would not have had the stomach to squat on the land or invade the henroost of a Nederlander for a century to come.

But it was not merely the refusal of Massachusetts to join in their unholy crusade that confounded the councils of the league; for about this time broke out in the New-England provinces the awful plague of witchcraft, which spread like pestilence through the land. Such a howling abomination could not be suffered to remain long unnoticed; it soon excited the fiery indignation of those guardians of the commonwealth who whilom had evinced such active benevolence in the conversion of Quakers and Anabaptists.[31] The grand council of the league publicly set their faces against the crime, and bloody laws were enacted against all "Solem conversing or compacting with the divil by way of conjuracion or the like." [32] Strict search, too, was made after witches, who were easily detected by devil's pinches,— by being able to weep but three tears, and those out of the left eye,—and by having a most suspicious predilection for black cats and broomsticks! What is particularly worthy of admiration is, that this terrible art, which has baffled the studies and researches of philosophers, astrologers, theurgists, and other sages, was chiefly confined to the most ignorant, decrepit, and ugly old women in the community, with scarce more brains than the broomsticks they rode upon.

When once an alarm is sounded, the public, who dearly love to be in a panic, are always ready to keep it up. Raise but the cry of yellow fever, and immediately every headache, indigestion, and overflowing of the bile is pronounced the terrible epidemic; cry out mad dog, and every unlucky cur in the street is in jeopardy: so in the present instance, whoever was troubled with colic or lumbago was sure to be bewitched,—and woe to any unlucky old woman living in the neighborhood!

It is incredible the number of offences that were detected, "for every one of which," says the reverend Cotton Mather, in that excellent work the *History of New England,* "we have such a

30. **door:** "Hazard's State Papers" [I].

31. **Quakers and Anabaptists:** ironic reference to the persecution of these sects by the seventeenth-century New England Puritans.

32. "New Plymouth record" [I]: Irving was probably using Hazard, I, 415.

sufficient evidence, that no reasonable man in this whole country ever did question them; *and it will be unreasonable to do it in any other*." [33]

Indeed, that authentic and judicious historian John Josselyn, Gent., furnishes us with unquestionable facts on this subject. "There are none," observes he, "that beg in this country, but there be witches too many,—bottle-bellied witches, and others, that produce many strange apparitions, if you will believe report, of a shallop at sea manned with women,—and of a ship and great red horse standing by the main-mast; the ship being in a small cove to the eastward, vanished of a sudden," etc.

The number of delinquents, however, and their magical devices, were not more remarkable than their diabolical obstinacy. Though exhorted in the most solemn, persuasive, and affectionate manner to confess themselves guilty, and be burnt for the good of religion and the entertainment of the public, yet did they most pertinaciously persist in asserting their innocence. Such incredible obstinacy was in itself deserving of immediate punishment, and was sufficient proof, if proof were necessary, that they were in league with the devil, who is perverseness itself. But their judges were just and merciful, and were determined to punish none that were not convicted on the best of testimony; not that they needed any evidence to satisfy their own minds,—for, like true and experienced judges, their minds were perfectly made up, and they were thoroughly satisfied of the guilt of the prisoners before they proceeded to try them,—but still something was necessary to convince the community at large,—to quiet those prying quidnuncs who should come after them,—in short, the world must be satisfied. Oh, the world—the world!—all the world knows the world of trouble the world is eternally occasioning! The worthy judges, therefore, were driven to the necessity of sifting, detecting, and making evident as noonday, matters which were at the commencement all clearly understood and firmly decided upon in their own pericraniums,—so that it may truly be said, that the witches were burnt to gratify the populace of the day, but were tried for the satisfaction of the whole world that should come after them!

Finding, therefore, that neither exhortation, sound reason, nor friendly entreaty had any avail on these hardened offenders, they resorted to the more urgent arguments of torture; and having thus absolutely wrung the truth from their stubborn lips, they condemned them to undergo the roasting due unto the heinous crimes they had confessed. Some even carried their perverseness so far as to expire under the torture, protesting their innocence to the last; but these were looked upon as thoroughly and absolutely possessed by the devil: and the pious by-standers only lamented that they had not lived a little longer, to have perished in the flames.

In the city of Ephesus, we are told that the plague was expelled by stoning a ragged old beggar to death, whom Apollonius [34] pointed out as being the evil spirit that caused it, and who actually showed himself to be a demon, by changing into a shagged dog. In like manner, and by measures equally sagacious, a salutary check was given to this growing evil. The witches were all burnt, banished, or panic-struck, and in a little while there was not an ugly old woman to be found throughout New England,—which is doubtless one reason why all the young women there are so handsome. Those honest folk who had suffered from their incantations gradually recovered, excepting such as had been afflicted with twitches and aches, which, however, assumed the less alarming aspects of rheumatisms, sciatics and lumbagos; and the good people of New England, abandoning the study of the occult sciences, turned their attention to the more profitable hocus-pocus of trade, and soon became expert in the legerdemain art of turning a penny. Still, however, a tinge of the old leaven is discernible, even unto this day, in their characters: witches occasionally start up among them in different disguises, as physicians, civilians, and divines. The people at large show a keenness, a cleverness, and a profundity of wisdom, that savors strongly of witchcraft; and it has been remarked, that, whenever any stones fall from the moon,[35] the greater part of them is sure to tumble into New England!

1809, 1812, 1848

33. "Mather's Hist. New Eng. B.6, ch.7" [I], a reference to Mather's *Magnalia Christi Americana: or, The Ecclesiastical History of New England* (1702).

34. **Apollonius:** Apollonius of Tyăna, in Cappadocia, who figures prominently in the well-known story on which Keats's *Lamia* is based. 35. **stones . . . moon:** Several instances of stone showers were reported by early New England writers, including Cotton Mather, who looked on them as sure signs of the presence of demons or witches. This chapter shows Irving stretching history to fit fiction and intensify satire. No witches were burned in New England. The account here, though it ostensibly describes the minor disturbance in Connecticut in 1662, more closely parallels the Salem delusion of 1692, during which nineteen convicted witches were hanged, and one, who pleaded neither guilty nor not guilty, was pressed to death.

FROM BOOK VI [1809]

CHAPTER 7

CONTAINING THE MOST HORRIBLE BATTLE EVER RECORDED IN POETRY OR PROSE; WITH THE ADMIRABLE EXPLOITS OF PETER THE HEADSTRONG

"NOW HAD the Dutchmen snatch'd a huge repast," and finding themselves wonderfully encouraged and animated thereby, prepared to take the field. Expectation, says a faithful matter of fact dutch poet, whose works were unfortunately destroyed in the conflagration of the Alexandrian library [1]—Expectation now stood on stilts.[2] The world forgot to turn round, or rather stood still, that it might witness the affray; like a fat round bellied alderman, watching the combat of two chivalric flies upon his jerkin. The eyes of all mankind, as usual in such cases, were turned upon Fort Christina.[3] The sun, like a little man in a crowd, at a puppet shew, scampered about the heavens, popping his head here and there, and endeavouring to get a peep between the unmannerly clouds, that obtruded themselves in his way. The historians filled their ink-horns—the poets went without their dinners, either that they might buy paper and goose-quills, or because they could not get any thing to eat—antiquity scowled sulkily out of its grave, to see itself outdone—while even posterity stood mute, gazing in gaping extacy of retrospection, on the eventful field!

The immortal deities, who whilome had seen service at the "affair" of Troy——now mounted their feather-bed clouds, and sailed over the plain, or mingled among the combatants in different disguises, all itching to have a finger in the pie. Jupiter sent off his thunderbolt to a noted copper-smith, to have it furbished up for the direful occasion. Venus, swore by her chastity she'd patronize the Swedes, and in semblance of a blear eyed trull, paraded the battlements of Fort Christina, accompanied by Diana, as a serjeant's widow, of cracked reputation—The noted bully Mars, stuck two horse pistols into his belt, shouldered a rusty firelock, and gallantly swaggered at their elbow, as a drunken corporal—while Apollo trudged in their rear, as a bandy-legged fifer, playing most villainously out of tune.

On the other side, the ox-eyed Juno, who had won a pair of black eyes over night, in one of her curtain lectures with old Jupiter, displayed her haughty beauties on a baggage waggon——Minerva, as a brawny gin suttler, tucked up her skirts, brandished her fists, and swore most heroically, in exceeding bad dutch, (having but lately studied the language) by way of keeping up the spirits of the soldiers; while Vulcan halted as a club-footed blacksmith, lately promoted to be a captain of militia. All was silent horror, or bustling preparation; war reared his horrid front, gnashed loud his iron fangs, and shook his direful crest of bristling bayonets.

And now the mighty chieftans marshalled out their hosts. Here stood stout Risingh,[4] firm as a thousand rocks——encrusted with stockades, and entrenched to the chin in mud batteries—His artillery consisting of two swivels and a carronade, loaded to the muzzle, the touch holes primed, and a whiskered bombardier stationed at each, with lighted match in hand, waiting the word. His valiant infantry, that had never turned back upon an enemy (having never seen any before)——lined the breast work in grim array, each having his mustachios fiercely greased, and his hair pomatumed back, and queued so stiffly, that he grinned above the ramparts like a grizly death's head.

There came on the intrepid Hard-koppig Piet,—a second Bayard, without fear or reproach—his brows knit, his teeth clenched, his breath held hard, rushing on like ten thousand bellowing bulls of Bashan.[5] His faithful squire Van Corlear, trudging valiantly at his heels, with his trumpet gorgeously bedecked with red and yellow ribbands, the remembrances of his fair mistresses at the Manhattoes. Then came waddling on his sturdy comrades, swarming like the myrmidons of Achilles. There were the Van Wycks and the Van Dycks and the Ten Eycks—the Van Nesses, the Van Tassels, the Van Grolls; the Van Hœsens, the Van Giesons, and the Van Blarcoms—The Van Warts, the Van Winkles, the Van Dams; the Van Pelts, the Van Rippers, and the Van Brunts.—There were the Van Horns, the Van Borsums, the Van Bunschotens; the Van Gelders, the Van Arsdales, and the Van Bummels—The Vander Belts, the Vander Hoofs, the Vander Voorts, the Vander Lyns, the Vander Pools and the Vander Spiegels.—There came the Hoffmans, the Hooglands, the Hoppers, the Cloppers, the Oothouts, the Quackenbosses, the Roerbacks, the Garrebrantzes, the Onderdonks, the Varra Vangers, the Schermerhorns, the Brinkerhoffs, the Bontecous, the

Book VI. **1. conflagration . . . library:** The great library of ancient learning at Alexandria, Egypt, was largely destroyed by fire in 391 A. D. **2. Expectation . . . stilts:** Cf. *Henry V*, II, Prologue, l. 8. **3. Fort Christina:** chief fort of New Sweden, located between what are now Baltimore and Philadelphia.

4. Risingh: Johan Classon Rising, governor of New Sweden.
5. bulls of Bashan: Cf. Ps. 22:12.

Knickerbockers, the Hockstrassers, the Ten Breecheses and the Tough Breecheses, with a host more of valiant worthies, whose names are too crabbed to be written, or if they could be written, it would be impossible for man to utter—all fortified with a mighty dinner, and to use the words of a great Dutch poet

—"Brimful of wrath and cabbage!"

For an instant the mighty Peter paused in the midst of his career, and mounting on a rotten stump addressed his troops in eloquent low dutch, exhorting them to fight like *duyvels,* and assuring them that if they conquered, they should get plenty of booty—if they fell they should be allowed the unparalleled satisfaction, while dying, of reflecting that it was in the service of their country—and after they were dead, of seeing their names inscribed in the temple of renown and handed down, in company with all the other great men of the year, for the admiration of posterity. —Finally he swore to them, on the word of a governor (and they knew him too well to doubt it for a moment) that if he caught any mother's son of them looking pale, or playing craven, he'd curry his hide till he made him run out of it like a snake in spring time.—Then lugging out his direful snickersnee, he brandished it three times over his head, ordered Van Corlear to sound a tremendous charge, and shouting the words "St. Nicholas and the Manhattoes!" courageously dashed forwards. His warlike followers, who had employed the interval in lighting their pipes, instantly stuck them in their mouths, gave a furious puff, and charged gallantly, under cover of the smoke.

The Swedish garrison, ordered by the cunning Risingh not to fire until they could distinguish the whites of their assailants' eyes, stood in horrid silence on the covert-way; until the eager dutchmen had half ascended the glacis. Then did they pour into them such a tremendous volley, that the very hills quaked around, and were terrified even unto an incontinence of water, insomuch that certain springs burst forth from their sides, which continue to run unto the present day. Not a dutchman but would have bit the dust, beneath that dreadful fire, had not the protecting Minerva kindly taken care, that the Swedes should one and all, observe their usual custom of shutting their eyes and turning away their heads, at the moment of discharge.

But were not the muskets levelled in vain, for the balls, winged with unerring fate, went point blank into a flock of wild geese, which, like geese as they were, happened at that moment to be flying past——and brought down seventy dozen of them—which furnished a luxurious supper to the conquerors, being well seasoned and stuffed with onions.

Neither was the volley useless to the musqueteers, for the hostile wind, commissioned by the implacable Juno, carried the smoke and dust full in the faces of the dutchmen, and would inevitably have blinded them, had their eyes been open. The Swedes followed up their fire, by leaping the counterscarp, and falling tooth and nail upon the foe, with furious outcries. And now might be seen prodigies of valour, of which neither history nor song have ever recorded a parallel. Here was beheld the sturdy Stoffel Brinkerhoff brandishing his lusty quarter staff, like the terrible giant Blanderon his oak tree (for he scorned to carry any other weapon,) and drumming a horrific tune upon the heads of whole squadrons of Swedes. There were the crafty Van Courtlandts, posted at a distance, like the little Locrian archers [6] of yore, and plying it most potently with the long bow, for which they were so justly renowned. At another place were collected on a rising knoll the valiant men of Sing-Sing, who assisted marvellously in the fight, by chaunting forth the great song of St. Nicholas. In a different part of the field might be seen the Van Grolls of Anthony's Nose; but they were horribly perplexed in a defile between two little hills, by reason of the length of their noses. There were the Van Bunschotens of Nyack and Kakiat, so renowned for kicking with the left foot, but their skill availed them little at present, being short of wind in consequence of the hearty dinner they had eaten—and they would irretrievably have been put to rout, had they not been reinforced by a gallant corps of *Voltigeurs* [7] composed of the Hoppers, who advanced to their assistance nimbly on one foot. At another place might you see the Van Arsdales, and the Van Bummels, who ever went together, gallantly pressing forward to bombard the fortress—but as to the Gardeniers of Hudson, they were absent from the battle, having been sent out on a marauding party, to lay waste the neighbouring water-melon patches. Nor must I omit to mention the incomparable atchievement of Antony Van Corlear, who, for a good quarter of an hour waged horrid fight with a little pursy Swedish drummer, whose hide he drummed most magnificently; and had he not come into the battle with no other weapon but his trumpet, would infallibly have put him to an untimely end.

But now the combat thickened—on came the

6. Locrian archers: ancient Greeks renowned for their ferocity.
7. ***Voltigeurs:*** picked French riflemen.

mighty Jacobus Varra Vanger and the fighting men of the Wael Bogtig; after them thundered the Van Pelts of Esopus, together with the Van Rippers and the Van Brunts, bearing down all before them—then the Suy Dams and the Van Dams, pressing forward with many a blustering oath, at the head of the warriors of Hell-gate, clad in their thunder and lightning gaberdines; and lastly the standard bearers and body guards of Peter Stuyvesant, bearing the great beaver of the Manhattoes.

And now commenced the horrid din, the desperate struggle, the maddening ferocity, the frantic desperation, the confusion and self abandonment of war. Dutchman and Swede commingled, tugged, panted and blowed. The heavens were darkened with a tempest of missives.[8] Carcasses, fire balls, smoke balls, stink balls and hand grenades, jostling each other, in the air. Bang! went the guns—whack! struck the broad swords—thump! went the cudgels—crash! went the musket stocks—blows—kicks—cuffs——scratches——black eyes and bloody noses swelling the horrors of the scene! Thick-thwack, cut and hack, helter-skelter, higgledy-piggledy, hurley-burley, head over heels, klip-klap, slag op slag, hob over bol, rough and tumble!——Dunder and blixum! swore the dutchmen, splitter and splutter! cried the Swedes—Storm the works! shouted Hard-koppig Piet—fire the mine! roared stout Risingh—Tantara-ra-ra! twang'd the trumpet of Antony Van Corlear—until all voice and sound became unintelligible—grunts of pain, yells of fury, and shouts of triumph commingling in one hideous clamour. The earth shook as if struck with a paralytic stroke—the trees shrunk aghast, and wilted at the sight—the rocks burrowed in the ground like rabbits, and even Christina creek turned from its course, and ran up a mountain in breathless terror!

Nothing, save the dullness of their weapons, the damaged condition of their powder, and the singular accident of one and all striking with the flat instead of the edge of their swords, could have prevented a most horrible carnage—As it was, the sweat prodigiously streaming, ran in rivers on the field, fortunately without drowning a soul, the combatants being to a man, expert swimmers, and furnished with cork jackets for the occasion—but many a valiant head was broken, many a stubborn rib belaboured, and many a broken winded hero drew short breath that day!

Long hung the contest doubtful, for though a heavy shower of rain, sent by the "cloud compelling Jove," in some measure cooled their ardour, as doth a bucket of water thrown on a group of fighting mastiffs, yet did they but pause for a moment, to return with tenfold fury to the charge, belabouring each other with black and bloody bruises. Just at this juncture was seen a vast and dense column of smoke, slowly rolling towards the scene of battle, which for a while made even the furious combatants to stay their arms in mute astonishment—but the wind for a moment dispersing the murky cloud, from the midst thereof emerged the flaunting banner of the immortal Michael Paw. This noble chieftain came fearlessly on, leading a solid phalanx of oyster-fed Pavonians,[9] who had remained behind, partly as a *corps de reserve,* and partly to digest the enormous dinner they had eaten. These sturdy yeomen, nothing daunted, did trudge manfully forward, smoaking their pipes with outrageous vigour, so as to raise the awful cloud that has been mentioned; but marching exceedingly slow, being short of leg and of great rotundity in the belt.

And now the protecting deities of the army of New Amsterdam, having unthinkingly left the field and stept into a neighbouring tavern to refresh themselves with a pot of beer, a direful catastrophe had well nigh chanced to befall the Nederlanders. Scarcely had the myrmidons of the puissant Paw attained the front of battle, before the Swedes, instructed by the cunning Risingh, levelled a shower of blows, full at their tobacco pipes. Astounded at this unexpected assault, and totally discomfited at seeing their pipes broken by this "d——d nonsense," the valiant dutchmen fall in vast confusion——already they begin to fly——like a frightened drove of unwieldy Elephants they throw their own army in an uproar——bearing down a whole legion of little Hoppers——the sacred banner on which is blazoned the gigantic oyster of Communipaw is trampled in the dirt——The Swedes pluck up new spirits and pressing on their rear, apply their feet *a parte poste*[10] with a vigour that prodigiously accelerates their motions—nor doth the renowned Paw himself, fail to receive divers grievous and intolerable visitations of shoe leather!

But what, Oh muse! was the rage of the gallant Peter, when from afar he saw his army yield? With a voice of thunder did he roar after his recreant warriors, putting up such a war whoop, as did the stern Achilles, when the Trojan troops were on the point of burning all his gunboats. The dreadful

8. **missives:** missiles.

9. **Pavonians:** "Pavonia" was the early name for the coastal section of New Jersey below New York City. 10. ***a parte poste:*** *a parte post,* a Scholastic phrase meaning posteriorly or from behind.

shout rung in long echoes through the woods—trees toppled at the noise; bears, wolves and panthers jumped out of their skins, in pure affright; several wild looking hills bounced clear over the Delaware; and all the small beer in Fort Christina, turned sour at the sound! [11]

The men of the Manhattoes plucked up new courage when they heard their leader——or rather they dreaded his fierce displeasure, of which they stood in more awe than of all the Swedes in Christendom—but the daring Peter, not waiting for their aid, plunged sword in hand, into the thickest of the foe. Then did he display some such incredible atchievements, as have never been known since the miraculous days of the giants. Wherever he went the enemy shrunk before him—with fierce impetuosity he pushed forward, driving the Swedes, like dogs, into their own ditch—but as he fearlessly advanced, the foe, like rushing waves which close upon the scudding bark, thronged in his rear, and hung upon his flank with fearful peril. One desperate Swede, who had a mighty heart, almost as large as a pepper-corn, drove his dastard sword full at the hero's heart. But the protecting power that watches over the safety of all great and good men turned aside the hostile blade, and directed it to a large side pocket, where reposed an enormous Iron Tobacco Box, endowed like the shield of Achilles with supernatural powers——no doubt in consequence of its being piously decorated with a portrait of the blessed St. Nicholas. Thus was the dreadful blow repelled, but not without occasioning to the great Peter a fearful loss of wind.

Like as a furious bear, when gored by worrying curs, turns fiercely round, shews his dread teeth, and springs upon the foe, so did our hero turn upon the treacherous Swede.[12] The miserable varlet sought in flight, for safety——but the active Peter, seizing him by an immeasurable queue, that dangled from his head—"Ah Whoreson Caterpillar!" roared he, "here is what shall make dog's meat of thee!" [13] So saying he whirled his trusty sword, and made a blow, that would have decapitated him, had he, like Briareus, half a hundred heads, but that the pitying steel struck short and shaved the queue forever from his crown. At this very moment a cunning arquebusier, perched on the summit of a neighbouring mound, levelled his deadly instrument, and would have sent the gallant Stuyvesant, a wailing ghost to haunt the Stygian shore——had not the watchful Minerva, who had just stopped to tie up her garter, seen the great peril of her favourite chief, and dispatched old Boreas with his bellows; who in the very nick of time, just as the direful match descended to the pan, gave such a lucky blast, as blew all the priming from the touch hole!

Thus waged the horrid fight——when the stout Risingh, surveying the battle from the top of a little ravelin, perceived his faithful troops, banged, beaten and kicked by the invincible Peter. Language cannot describe the choler with which he was seized at the sight——he only stopped for a moment to disburthen himself of five thousand anathemas; and then drawing his immeasurable cheese toaster,[14] straddled down to the field of combat, with some such thundering strides, as Jupiter is said by old Hesiod to have taken, when he strode down the spheres, to play off his sky rockets at the Titans.

No sooner did these two rival heroes come face to face, than they each made a prodigious start of fifty feet, (flemish measure) such as is made by your most experienced stage champions. Then did they regard each other for a moment, with bitter aspect, like two furious ram cats, on the very point of a clapper clawing. Then did they throw themselves in one attitude, then in another, striking their swords on the ground, first on the right side, then on the left, at last at it they went, like five hundred houses on fire! Words cannot tell the prodigies of strength and valour, displayed in this direful encounter—an encounter, compared to which the far famed battles of Ajax with Hector, of Eneas with Turnus, Orlando with Rodomont,[15] Guy of Warwick with Colbrand the Dane, or of that renowned Welsh Knight Sir Owen [16] of the mountains with the giant Guylon, were all gentle sports and holliday recreations. At length the valiant Peter watching his opportunity, aimed a fearful blow with the full intention of cleaving his adversary to the very chine; but Risingh nimbly raising his sword, warded it off so narrowly, that glancing on one side, it shaved away a huge canteen full of fourth proof brandy, that he always carried swung on one side; thence pursuing its tranchant [17] course, it severed off a deep coat pocket, stored with bread and cheese—all which dainties rolling among the armies, occasioned a

11. **With . . . sound!:** This entire passage is omitted in the revision. 12. **Like . . . Swede:** The hyperbole of the epic simile is dropped in the revision. 13. **"Ah . . . thee!":** Cf. Falstaff in *I Henry IV*, II.ii.88, and Mercutio in *Romeo and Juliet*, III.i.112. Irving later changed "dog's" to Mercutio's "worms'."

14. **cheese toaster:** humorous designation for a sword. 15. **Ajax . . . Rodomont:** allusions to the *Iliad*, VII, and the *Aeneid*, XII, and an apparently confused reference to Ariosto's *Orlando Furioso* (1532). 16. **Guy . . . Owen:** Guy and Owen were heroes of medieval romances. 17. **tranchant:** cutting; an early form of "trenchant."

fearful scrambling between the Swedes and Dutchmen, and made the general battle to wax ten times more furious than ever.

Enraged to see his military stores thus wofully laid waste, the stout Risingh collecting all his forces, aimed a mighty blow, full at the hero's crest. In vain did his fierce little cocked hat oppose its course; the biting steel clove through the stubborn ram beaver, and would infallibly have cracked his gallant crown, but that the scull was of such adamantine hardness that the brittle weapon shivered into five and twenty pieces, shedding a thousand sparks, like beams of glory, round his grizly visage.

Stunned with the blow the valiant Peter reeled, turned up his eyes and beheld fifty thousand suns, besides moons and stars, dancing Scotch reels about the firmament [18]—at length, missing his footing, by reason of his wooden leg, down he came, on his seat of honour, with a crash that shook the surrounding hills, and would infallibly have wracked his anatomical system, had he not been received into a cushion softer than velvet, which providence, or Minerva, or St. Nicholas, or some kindly cow, had benevolently prepared for his reception.

The furious Risingh, in despight of that noble maxim, cherished by all true knights, that "fair play is a jewel," hastened to take advantage of the hero's fall; but just as he was stooping to give the fatal blow, the ever vigilant Peter bestowed him a sturdy thwack over the sconce, with his wooden leg, that set some dozen chimes of bells ringing triple bob-majors [19] in his cerebellum. The bewildered Swede staggered with the blow, and in the mean time the wary Peter, espying a pocket pistol lying hard by (which had dropped from the wallet of his faithful squire and trumpeter Van Corlear during his furious encounter with the drummer) discharged it full at the head of the reeling Risingh—Let not my reader mistake—it was not a murderous weapon loaded with powder and ball, but a little sturdy stone pottle, charged to the muzzle with a double dram of true dutch courage, which the knowing Van Corlear always carried about him by way of replenishing his valour. The hideous missive sung through the air, and true to its course, as was the mighty fragment of a rock, discharged at Hector by bully Ajax, encountered the huge head of the gigantic Swede with matchless violence.

18. **beheld . . . firmament:** In the revision this passage reads simply, "beheld a thousand suns, besides moons and stars, dancing about the firmament." 19. **set . . . bob-majors:** A bob-major is a change rung upon eight bells. In revising, Irving reduced the "dozen chimes" to one.

This heaven directed blow decided the eventful battle. The ponderous pericranium of general Jan Risingh sunk upon his breast; his knees tottered under him; a deathlike torpor seized upon his Titan frame, and he tumbled to the earth with such tremendous violence, that old Pluto started with affright, lest he should have broken through the roof of his infernal palace.

His fall, like that of Goliath, was the signal for defeat and victory——The Swedes gave way—the Dutch pressed forward; the former took to their heels, the latter hotly pursued—Some entered with them, pell mell, through the sally port—others stormed the bastion, and others scrambled over the curtain. Thus in a little while the impregnable fortress of Fort Christina, which like another Troy had stood a siege of full ten *hours,* was finally carried by assault, without the loss of a single man on either side. Victory in the likeness of a gigantic ox fly, sat perched upon the little cocked hat of the gallant Stuyvesant, and it was universally declared, by all the writers, whom he hired to write the history of his expedition, that on this memorable day he gained a sufficient quantity of glory to immortalize a dozen of the greatest heroes in Christendom!

CHAPTER 8

IN WHICH THE AUTHOR AND THE READER, WHILE REPOSING AFTER THE BATTLE, FALL INTO A VERY GRAVE AND INSTRUCTIVE DISCOURSE——AFTER WHICH IS RECORDED THE CONDUCT OF PETER STUYVESANT IN RESPECT TO HIS VICTORY.

THANKS to St. Nicholas! I have fairly got through this tremendous battle: let us sit down, my worthy reader, and cool ourselves, for truly I am in a prodigious sweat and agitation—Body o' me, but this fighting of battles is hot work! and if your great commanders, did but know what trouble they give their historians, they would not have the conscience to atchieve so many horrible victories. I already hear my reader complaining, that throughout all this boasted battle, there is not the least slaughter, nor a single individual maimed, if we except the unhappy Swede, who was shorn of his queue by the tranchant blade of Peter Stuyvesant——all which is a manifest outrage on probability, and highly injurious to the interest of the narrative.

For once I candidly confess my captious reader has some grounds for his murmuring—But though

I could give a variety of substantial reasons for not having deluged my whole page with blood, and swelled the cadence of every sentence with dying groans, yet I will content myself with barely mentioning one; which if it be not sufficient to satisfy every reasonable man on the face of the earth, I will consent that my book shall be cast into the flames—The simple truth then is this, that on consulting every history, manuscript and tradition, which relates to this memorable, though long forgotten battle, I cannot find that a single man was killed, or even wounded, throughout the whole affair!

My readers, if they have any bowels, must easily feel the distressing situation in which I was placed. I had already promised to furnish them with a hideous and unparalleled battle——I had made incredible preparations for the same——and had moreover worked myself up into a most warlike and blood-thirsty state of mind——my honour, as a historian, and my feelings, as a man of spirit, were both too deeply engaged in the business, to back out. Beside, I had transported a great and powerful force of warriors from the Nederlandts, at vast trouble and expense, and I could not reconcile it to my own conscience, or to that reverence which I entertain for them, and their illustrious descendants, to have suffered them to return home, like a renowned British expedition—with a flea in their ears.

How to extract myself from this dilemma was truly perplexing. Had the inexorable fates only allowed me half a dozen dead men, I should have been contented, for I would have made them such heroes as abounded in the olden time, but whose race is now unfortunately extinct. Men, who, if we may believe those authentic writers, the poets, could drive great armies like sheep before them, and conquer and desolate whole cities by their single arm. I'd have given every mother's son of them as many lives as a cat, and made them die hard, I warrant you.

But seeing that I had not a single carcass at my disposal, all that was left for me, was to make the most I could of my battle, by means of kicks and cuffs, and bruises—black eyes, and bloody noses, and such like ignoble wounds. My greatest difficulty however, was, when I had once put my warriors in a passion, and let them loose into the midst of the enemy; to keep them from doing mischief. Many a time had I to restrain the sturdy Peter, from cleaving a gigantic Swede, to the very waist-band, or spitting half a dozen little fellows on his sword, like so many sparrows—And when I had set some hundreds of missives flying in the air, I did not dare to suffer one of them to reach the ground, lest it should have put an end to some unlucky Dutchman.

The reader cannot conceive how much I suffered from thus in a manner having my hands tied, and how many tempting opportunities I had to wink at, where I might have made as fine a death blow, as any recorded in history or song.

From my own experience, I begin to doubt most potently of the authenticity of many of Dan Homer's stories. I verily believe, that when he had once launched one of his hearty blades among a crowd of the enemy, he cut down many an honest fellow, without any authority for so doing, excepting that he presented a fair mark—and that often a poor devil was sent to grim Pluto's domains, merely because he had a name that would give a sounding turn to a period. But I disclaim all such unprincipled liberties—let me but have truth and the law on my side, and no man would fight harder than myself—but since the various records I consulted did not warrant it, I had too much conscience to kill a single soldier.—By St. Nicholas, but it would have been a pretty piece of business! My enemies the critics, who I foresee will be ready enough to lay any crime they can discover, at my door, might have charged me with murder outright—and I should have esteemed myself lucky to escape, with no harsher verdict than manslaughter!

And now gentle reader that we are tranquilly sitting down here, smoking our pipes, permit me to indulge in a melancholy reflection which at this moment passes across my mind.—How vain, how fleeting, how uncertain are all those gaudy bubbles after which we are panting and toiling in this world of fair delusions. The wealthy store which the hoary miser has painfully amassed with so many weary days, so many sleepless nights, a spendthrift heir shall squander away in joyless prodigality—The noblest monuments which pride has ever reared to perpetuate a name, the hand of time shall shortly tumble into promiscuous ruins——and even the brightest laurels, gained by hardiest feats of arms, may wither and be forever blighted by the chilling neglect of mankind. —"How many illustrious heroes," says the good Boëtius, "who were once the pride and glory of the age, hath the silence of historians buried in eternal oblivion!" And this it was, that made the Spartans when they went to battle, solemnly to sacrifice to the muses, supplicating that their atchievements should be worthily recorded. Had not Homer tuned his lofty lyre, observes the elegant Cicero, the valour of Achilles had remained unsung.—And such too, after all the toils and perils he had braved, after all the gallant actions he had achieved, such too had nearly been the fate of the chivalric Peter Stuyvesant, but that I fortunately stepped in and engraved his name on the indelible tablet of history, just as the caitiff Time was silently brushing it away forever!

The more I reflect, the more am I astonished to think, what important beings are we historians! We are the sovereign censors who decide upon the renown or infamy of our fellow mortals—We are the public almoners of fame, dealing out her favours according to our judgment or caprice—we are the benefactors of kings——we are the guardians of truth—we are the scourgers of guilt—we are the instructors of the world—we are—in short, what are we not!—And yet how often does the lofty patrician or lordly Burgomaster stalk contemptuously by the little, plodding, dusty historian like myself, little thinking that this humble mortal is the arbiter of his fate, on whom it shall depend whether he shall live in future ages, or be forgotten in the dirt, as were his ancestors before him. "Insult not the dervise" [20] said a wise caliph to his son, "lest thou offend thine historian;" and many a mighty man of the olden time, had he observed so obvious a maxim, would have escaped divers cruel wipes of the pen, which have been drawn across his character.

But let not my readers think I am indulging in vain glorious boasting, from the consciousness of my own power and importance. On the contrary I shudder to think what direful commotions, what heart rending calamities we historians occasion in the world—I swear to thee, honest reader, as I am a man, I weep at the very idea!—Why, let me ask, are so many illustrious men daily tearing themselves away from the embraces of their distracted families——slighting the smiles of beauty—despising the allurements of fortune, and exposing themselves to all the miseries of war?——Why are renowned generals cutting the throats of thousands who never injured them in their lives?—Why are kings desolating empires and depopulating whole countries? in short, what induces all great men, of all ages and countries to commit so many horrible victories and misdeeds, and inflict so many miseries upon mankind and on themselves; but the mere hope that we historians will kindly take them into notice, and admit them into a corner of our volumes. So that the mighty object of all their toils, their hardships and privations is nothing but *immortal fame*——and what is immortal fame?—why, half a page of dirty paper!——alas! alas! how humiliating the idea—that the renown of so great a man as Peter Stuyvesant, should depend upon the pen of so little a man, as Diedrich Knickerbocker!

And now, having refreshed ourselves after the fatigues and perils of the field, it behoves us to return once more to the scene of conflict, and inquire what were the results of this renowned conquest. The Fortress of Christina being the fair metropolis and in a manner the Key to New Sweden, its capture was speedily followed by the entire subjugation of the province. This was not a little promoted by the gallant and courteous deportment of the chivalric Peter. Though a man terrible in battle, yet in the hour of victory was he endued with a spirit generous, merciful and humane—He vaunted not over his enemies, nor did he make defeat more galling by unmanly insults; for like that mirror of Knightly virtue, the renowned Paladin Orlando, he was more anxious to do great actions, than to talk of them after they were done. He put no man to death; ordered no houses to be burnt down; permitted no ravages to be perpetrated on the property of the vanquished, and even gave one of his bravest staff officers a severe rib-roasting, who was detected in the act of sacking a hen roost.

He moreover issued a proclamation inviting the inhabitants to submit to the authority of their high mightinesses; but declaring, with unexampled clemency, that whoever refused, should be lodged at the public expense, in a goodly castle provided for the purpose, and have an armed retinue to wait on them in the bargain. In consequence of these beneficent terms, about thirty Swedes stepped manfully forward and took the oath of allegiance; in reward for which they were graciously permitted to remain on the banks of the Delaware, where their descendants reside at this very day. But I am told by sundry observant travellers, that they have never been able to get over the chap-fallen looks of their ancestors, and do still unaccountably transmit from father to son, manifest marks of the sound drubbing given them by the sturdy Amsterdammers.

The whole country of New Sweden, having thus yielded to the arms of the triumphant Peter, was reduced to a colony called South River, and placed under the superintendance of a lieutenant governor; subject to the controul of the supreme government at New Amsterdam. This great dignitary, was called Mynheer William Beekman, or rather *Beck*man, who derived his surname, as did Ovidius Naso [21] of yore, from the lordly dimensions of his nose, which projected from the centre of his countenance, like the beak of a parrot. Indeed, it

20. **dervise**: dervish.

21. **Ovidius Naso**: the Latin poet Ovid (43 B.C.–17 A.D.).

is furthermore insinuated by various ancient records, that this was not only the origin of his name, but likewise the foundation of his fortune, for, as the city was as yet unprovided with a clock, the public made use of Mynheer Beckman's face, as a sundial. Thus did this romantic, and truly picturesque feature, first thrust itself into public notice, dragging its possessor along with it, who in his turn dragged after him the whole Beckman family—These, as the story further adds, were for a long time among the most ancient and honourable families of the province, and gratefully commemorated the origin of their dignity, not as your noble families in England would do, by having a glowing proboscis emblazoned in their escutcheon, but by one and all, wearing a right goodly nose, stuck in the very middle of their faces.

Thus was this perilous enterprise gloriously terminated, with the loss of only two men; Wolfert Van Horne, a tall spare man, who was knocked overboard by the boom of a sloop, in a flaw of wind, and fat Brom Van Bummel, who was suddenly carried off by a villainous indigestion; both, however, were immortalized, as having bravely fallen in the service of their country. True it is, Peter Stuyvesant had one of his limbs terribly fractured, being shattered to pieces in the act of storming the fortress; but as it was fortunately his wooden leg the wound was promptly and effectually healed.

And now nothing remains to this branch of my history, but to mention, that this immaculate hero, and his victorious army, returned joyously to the Manhattoes, marching under the shade of their laurels, as did the followers of young Malcolm, under the moving forest of Dunsinane.[22] Thus did they make a solemn and triumphant entry into New Amsterdam, bearing with them the conquered Risingh, and the remnant of his battered crew, who had refused allegiance. For it appears that the gigantic Swede, had only fallen into a swound, at the end of the battle, from whence he was speedily restored by a wholesome tweak of the nose.

These captive heroes were lodged, according to the promise of the governor, at the public expense, in a fair and spacious castle; being the prison of state, of which Stoffel Brinkerhoff, the immortal conqueror of Oyster Bay, was appointed Lord Lieutenant; and which has ever since remained in the possession of his descendants.[23]

It was a pleasant and goodly sight to witness the joy of the people of New Amsterdam, at beholding their warriors once more returned, from this war in the wilderness. The old women thronged round Antony Van Corlear, who gave the whole history of the campaign with matchless accuracy; saving that he took the credit of fighting the whole battle himself, and especially of vanquishing the stout Risingh, which he considered himself as clearly entitled to, seeing that it was effected by his own stone pottle. The schoolmasters throughout the town gave holliday to their little urchins, who followed in droves after the drums, with paper caps on their heads and sticks in their breeches, thus taking the first lesson in vagabondizing. As to the sturdy rabble they thronged at the heels of Peter Stuyvesant wherever he went, waving their greasy hats in the air, and shouting "Hard-koppig Piet forever!"

It was indeed a day of roaring rout and jubilee. A huge dinner was prepared at the Stadt-house in honour of the conquerors, where were assembled in one glorious constellation, the great and the little luminaries of New Amsterdam. There were the lordly Schout and his obsequious deputy—the Burgomasters with their officious Schepens at their elbows—the subaltern officers at the elbows of the Schepens, and so on to the lowest grade of illustrious hangers-on of police; every Tag having his Rag at his side, to finish his pipe, drink off his heeltaps, and laugh at his flights of immortal dulness. In short—for a city feast is a city feast all the world over, and has been a city feast ever since the creation—the dinner went off much the same as do our great corporation junkettings and fourth of July banquets. Loads of fish, flesh and fowl were devoured, oceans of liquor drank, thousands of pipes smoked, and many a dull joke honoured with much obstreperous fat sided laughter.

I must not omit to mention that to this far-famed victory Peter Stuyvesant was indebted for another of his many titles—for so hugely delighted were the honest burghers with his atchievements, that they unanimously honoured him with the name of *Pieter ede Groodt,* that is to say Peter the Great, or as it was translated by the people of New Amsterdam, *Piet de Pig*—an appellation which he maintained even unto the day of his death.

1809

22. followers . . . Dunsinane: See *Macbeth,* V.iv. **23. These . . . descendants:** "This castle though very much altered and modernized is still in being. And stands at the corner of Pearl Street, facing Coentie's slip" [I].

FROM

THE SKETCH BOOK
OF GEOFFREY CRAYON, GENT.

THE AUTHOR'S ACCOUNT OF HIMSELF

> "I am of this mind with Homer, that as the snaile that crept out of her shel was turned eftsoons into a toad, and thereby was forced to make a stoole to sit on; so the traveller that stragleth from his owne country is in a short time transformed into so monstrous a shape, that he is faine to alter his mansion with his manners, and to live where he can, not where he would."
>
> LYLY'S *Euphues*.[1]

I WAS always fond of visiting new scenes, and observing strange characters and manners. Even when a mere child I began my travels, and made many tours of discovery into foreign parts and unknown regions of my native city, to the frequent alarm of my parents, and the emolument of the town-crier. As I grew into boyhood, I extended the range of my observations. My holiday afternoons were spent in rambles about the surrounding country. I made myself familiar with all its places famous in history or fable. I knew every spot where a murder or robbery had been committed, or a ghost seen. I visited the neighboring villages, and added greatly to my stock of knowledge, by noting their habits and customs, and conversing with their sages and great men. I even journeyed one long summer's day to the summit of the most distant hill, whence I stretched my eye over many a mile of terra incognita, and was astonished to find how vast a globe I inhabited.

This rambling propensity strengthened with my years. Books of voyages and travels became my passion, and in devouring their contents, I neglected the regular exercises of the school. How wistfully would I wander about the pier-heads in fine weather, and watch the parting ships, bound to distant climes—with what longing eyes would I gaze after their lessening sails, and waft myself in imagination to the ends of the earth!

Further reading and thinking, though they brought this vague inclination into more reasonable bounds, only served to make it more decided. I visited various parts of my own country; and had I been merely a lover of fine scenery, I should have felt little desire to seek elsewhere its gratification, for on no country have the charms of nature been more prodigally lavished. Her mighty lakes, like oceans of liquid silver; her mountains, with their bright aerial tints; her valleys, teeming with wild fertility; her tremendous cataracts, thundering in their solitudes; her boundless plains, waving with spontaneous verdure; her broad deep rivers, rolling in solemn silence to the ocean; her trackless forests, where vegetation puts forth all its magnificence; her skies, kindling with the magic of summer clouds and glorious sunshine;—no, never need an American look beyond his own country for the sublime and beautiful of natural scenery.

But Europe held forth the charms of storied and poetical association. There were to be seen the masterpieces of art, the refinements of highly-cultivated society, the quaint peculiarities of ancient and local custom. My native country was full of youthful promise: Europe was rich in the accumulated treasures of age. Her very ruins told the history of times gone by, and every mouldering stone was a chronicle. I longed to wander over the scenes of renowned achievement—to tread, as it were, in the footsteps of antiquity—to loiter about the ruined castle—to meditate on the falling tower—to escape, in short, from the commonplace realities of the present, and lose myself among the shadowy grandeurs of the past.

I had, beside all this, an earnest desire to see the great men of the earth. We have, it is true, our great men in America: not a city but has an ample share of them. I have mingled among them in my time, and been almost withered by the shade into which they cast me; for there is nothing so baleful to a small man as the shade of a great one, particularly the great man of a city. But I was anxious to see the great men of Europe; for I had read in the works of various philosophers, that all animals degenerated in America, and man among the number.[2] A great man of Europe, thought I, must therefore be as superior to a great man of America, as a peak of the Alps to a highland of the Hudson; and in this idea I was confirmed, by observing the comparative importance and swelling magnitude of many English travellers among us, who, I was assured, were very little people in their own country. I will visit this land of wonders, thought I, and see the gigantic race from which I am degenerated.

THE SKETCH BOOK. **The Author's Account of Himself.** 1. John Lyly, *Euphues and His England* (1580).

2. for . . . number: Dr. Samuel Johnson, for instance, had spoken of Americans as "a race of convicts," destined for "ages of barbarism."

It has been either my good or evil lot to have my roving passion gratified. I have wandered through different countries, and witnessed many of the shifting scenes of life. I cannot say that I have studied them with the eye of a philosopher; but rather with the sauntering gaze with which humble lovers of the picturesque stroll from the window of one print-shop to another; caught sometimes by the delineations of beauty, sometimes by the distortions of caricature, and sometimes by the loveliness of landscape. As it is the fashion for modern tourists to travel pencil in hand, and bring home their portfolios filled with sketches, I am disposed to get up a few for the entertainment of my friends. When, however, I look over the hints and memorandums I have taken down for the purpose, my heart almost fails me at finding how my idle humor has led me aside from the great objects studied by every regular traveller who would make a book. I fear I shall give equal disappointment with an unlucky landscape painter, who had travelled on the continent, but, following the bent of his vagrant inclination, had sketched in nooks, and corners, and by-places. His sketch book was accordingly crowded with cottages, and landscapes, and obscure ruins; but he had neglected to paint St. Peter's, or the Coliseum; the cascade of Terni,[3] or the bay of Naples; and had not a single glacier or volcano in his whole collection.

1819, 1848

RIP VAN WINKLE

A Posthumous Writing of Diedrich Knickerbocker

◇

ALTHOUGH "Rip Van Winkle," like most of Irving's American stories, is attributed to Knickerbocker, its style is essentially Crayon's. Holding the "truthful" Knickerbocker responsible is a warning against a literal-minded reading.

By the time of *The Sketch Book* Irving had developed great admiration for writers, like Shakespeare, who utilize and imaginatively supplement local folk materials in such a way as to give expression to distinctive national or regional qualities. He tried himself to incorporate native folklore elements in his American stories, but, as his concluding note suggests, when they did not suffice he did not hesitate to use importations from abroad.

◇

By Woden,[1] God of Saxons,
From whence comes Wensday, that is Wodensday.
Truth is a thing that ever I will keep
Unto thylke day in which I creep into
My sepulchre—

CARTWRIGHT [2]

[The following Tale was found among the papers of the late Diedrich Knickerbocker, an old gentleman of New York, who was very curious in the Dutch history of the province, and the manners of the descendants from its primitive settlers. His historical researches, however, did not lie so much among books as among men; for the former are lamentably scanty on his favorite topics; whereas he found the old burghers, and still more their wives, rich in that legendary lore so invaluable to true history. Whenever, therefore, he happened upon a genuine Dutch family, snugly shut up in its low-roofed farmhouse, under a spreading sycamore, he looked upon it as a little clasped volume of black-letter, and studied it with the zeal of a bookworm.

The result of all these researches was a history of the province during the reign of the Dutch governors, which he published some years since. There have been various opinions as to the literary character of his work, and, to tell the truth, it is not a whit better than it should be. Its chief merit is its scrupulous accuracy, which indeed was a little questioned on its first appearance, but has since been completely established; and it is now admitted into all historical collections as a book of unquestionable authority.

The old gentleman died shortly after the publication of his work; and now that he is dead and gone, it cannot do much harm to his memory to say that his time might have been much better employed in weightier labors. He, however, was apt to ride his hobby his own way; and though it did now and then kick up the dust a little in the eyes of his neighbors, and grieve the spirit of some friends, for whom he felt the truest deference and affection, yet his errors and follies are remembered "more in sorrow than in anger," and it begins to be suspected that he never intended to injure or offend. But however his memory may be appreciated by critics, it is still held dear by many folk whose good opinion is well worth having; particularly by certain biscuit-bakers, who have gone so far as to imprint his likeness on their New-Year cakes; and have thus given him a chance for immortality, almost equal to the being stamped on a Waterloo Medal, or a Queen Anne's Farthing.]

3. **cascade of Terni:** artificial waterfalls in Perugia, Italy.

Rip Van Winkle. 1. **Woden:** Germanic god of war and storms. 2. **Cartwright:** The lines are spoken by Moth, the pedantic antiquarian in William Cartwright's *The Ordinary* (1651), III.i.1050–54.

WHOEVER has made a voyage up the Hudson must remember the Kaatskill mountains. They are a dismembered branch of the great Appalachian family, and are seen away to the west of the river, swelling up to a noble height, and lording it over the surrounding country. Every change of season, every change of weather, indeed, every hour of the day, produces some change in the magical hues and shapes of these mountains, and they are regarded by all the good wives, far and near, as perfect barometers. When the weather is fair and settled, they are clothed in blue and purple, and print their bold outlines on the clear evening sky; but sometimes, when the rest of the landscape is cloudless, they will gather a hood of gray vapors about their summits, which, in the last rays of the setting sun, will glow and light up like a crown of glory.

At the foot of these fairy mountains, the voyager may have descried the light smoke curling up from a village, whose shingle-roofs gleam among the trees, just where the blue tints of the upland melt away into the fresh green of the nearer landscape. It is a little village, of great antiquity, having been founded by some of the Dutch colonists in the early times of the province, just about the beginning of the government of the good Peter Stuyvesant (may he rest in peace!), and there were some of the houses of the original settlers standing within a few years, built of small yellow bricks brought from Holland, having latticed windows and gable fronts, surmounted with weathercocks.

In that same village, and in one of these very houses (which, to tell the precise truth, was sadly time-worn and weather-beaten), there lived, many years since, while the country was yet a province of Great Britain, a simple, good-natured fellow, of the name of Rip Van Winkle. He was a descendant of the Van Winkles who figured so gallantly in the chivalrous days of Peter Stuyvesant, and accompanied him to the siege of Fort Christina. He inherited, however, but little of the martial character of his ancestors. I have observed that he was a simple, good-natured man; he was, moreover, a kind neighbor, and an obedient, hen-pecked husband. Indeed, to the latter circumstance might be owing that meekness of spirit which gained him such universal popularity; for those men are most apt to be obsequious and conciliating abroad, who are under the discipline of shrews at home. Their tempers, doubtless, are rendered pliant and malleable in the fiery furnace of domestic tribulation; and a curtain-lecture is worth all the sermons in the world for teaching the virtues of patience and long-suffering. A termagant wife may, therefore, in some respects be considered a tolerable blessing; and if so, Rip Van Winkle was thrice blessed.

Certain it is, that he was a great favorite among all the good wives of the village, who, as usual with the amiable sex, took his part in all family squabbles; and never failed, whenever they talked those matters over in their evening gossipings, to lay all the blame on Dame Van Winkle. The children of the village, too, would shout with joy whenever he approached. He assisted at their sports, made their playthings, taught them to fly kites and shoot marbles, and told them long stories of ghosts, witches and Indians. Whenever he went dodging about the village, he was surrounded by a troop of them, hanging on his skirts, clambering on his back, and playing a thousand tricks on him with impunity; and not a dog would bark at him throughout the neighborhood.

The great error in Rip's composition was an insuperable aversion to all kinds of profitable labor. It could not be from the want of assiduity or perseverance; for he would sit on a wet rock, with a rod as long and heavy as a Tartar's lance, and fish all day without a murmur, even though he should not be encouraged by a single nibble. He would carry a fowling-piece on his shoulder for hours together, trudging through woods and swamps, and up hill and down dale, to shoot a few squirrels or wild pigeons. He would never refuse to assist a neighbor even in the roughest toil, and was a foremost man at all country frolics for husking Indian corn, or building stone fences; the women of the village, too, used to employ him to run their errands, and to do such little odd jobs as their less obliging husbands would not do for them. In a word, Rip was ready to attend to anybody's business but his own; but as to doing family duty, and keeping his farm in order, he found it impossible.

In fact, he declared it was of no use to work on his farm; it was the most pestilent little piece of ground in the whole country; everything about it went wrong, and would go wrong, in spite of him. His fences were continually falling to pieces; his cow would either go astray, or get among the cabbages; weeds were sure to grow quicker in his fields than anywhere else; the rain always made a point of setting in just as he had some out-door work to do; so that though his patrimonial estate had dwindled away under his management, acre by acre, until there was little more left than a mere patch of Indian corn and potatoes, yet it was the worst conditioned farm in the neighborhood.

His children, too, were as ragged and wild as if they belonged to nobody. His son Rip, an urchin begotten in his own likeness, promised to inherit the habits, with the old clothes, of his father. He was generally seen trooping like a colt at his mother's heels, equipped in a pair of his father's cast-off galligaskins, which he had much ado to hold up with one hand, as a fine lady does her train in bad weather.

Rip Van Winkle, however, was one of those happy mortals, of foolish, well-oiled dispositions, who take the world easy, eat white bread or brown, whichever can be got with least thought or trouble, and would rather starve on a penny than work for a pound. If left to himself, he would have whistled life away in perfect contentment; but his wife kept continually dinning in his ears about his idleness, his carelessness, and the ruin he was bringing on his family. Morning, noon, and night, her tongue was incessantly going, and everything he said or did was sure to produce a torrent of household eloquence. Rip had but one way of replying to all lectures of the kind, and that, by frequent use, had grown into a habit. He shrugged his shoulders, shook his head, cast up his eyes, but said nothing. This, however, always provoked a fresh volley from his wife; so that he was fain to draw off his forces, and take to the outside of the house—the only side which, in truth, belongs to a hen-pecked husband.

Rip's sole domestic adherent was his dog Wolf, who was as much hen-pecked as his master; for Dame Van Winkle regarded them as companions in idleness, and even looked upon Wolf with an evil eye, as the cause of his master's going so often astray. True it is, in all points of spirit befitting an honorable dog, he was as courageous an animal as ever scoured the woods; but what courage can withstand the ever-during and all-besetting terrors of a woman's tongue? The moment Wolf entered the house his crest fell, his tail drooped to the ground, or curled between his legs, he sneaked about with a gallows air, casting many a sidelong glance at Dame Van Winkle, and at the least flourish of a broomstick or ladle he would fly to the door with yelping precipitation.

Times grew worse and worse with Rip Van Winkle as years of matrimony rolled on; a tart temper never mellows with age, and a sharp tongue is the only edged tool that grows keener with constant use. For a long while he used to console himself, when driven from home, by frequenting a kind of perpetual club of the sages, philosophers, and other idle personages of the village, which held its sessions on a bench before a small inn, designated by a rubicund portrait of His Majesty George the Third. Here they used to sit in the shade through a long, lazy summer's day, talking listlessly over village gossip, or telling endless sleepy stories about nothing. But it would have been worth any statesman's money to have heard the profound discussions that sometimes took place, when by chance an old newspaper fell into their hands from some passing traveller. How solemnly they would listen to the contents, as drawled out by Derrick Van Bummel, the schoolmaster, a dapper learned little man, who was not to be daunted by the most gigantic word in the dictionary; and how sagely they would deliberate upon public events some months after they had taken place.

The opinions of this junto were completely controlled by Nicholas Vedder, a patriarch of the village, and landlord of the inn, at the door of which he took his seat from morning till night, just moving sufficiently to avoid the sun and keep in the shade of a large tree; so that the neighbors could tell the hour by his movements as accurately as by a sun-dial. It is true he was rarely heard to speak, but smoked his pipe incessantly. His adherents, however (for every great man has his adherents), perfectly understood him, and knew how to gather his opinions. When anything that was read or related displeased him, he was observed to smoke his pipe vehemently, and to send forth short, frequent, and angry puffs; but when pleased, he would inhale the smoke slowly and tranquilly, and emit it in light and placid clouds; and sometimes, taking the pipe from his mouth, and letting the fragrant vapor curl about his nose, would gravely nod his head in token of perfect approbation.

From even this stronghold the unlucky Rip was at length routed by his termagant wife, who would suddenly break in upon the tranquillity of the assemblage and call the members all to naught; nor was that august personage, Nicholas Vedder himself, sacred from the daring tongue of this terrible virago, who charged him outright with encouraging her husband in habits of idleness.

Poor Rip was at last reduced almost to despair; and his only alternative, to escape from the labor of the farm and clamor of his wife, was to take gun in hand and stroll away into the woods. Here he would sometimes seat himself at the foot of a tree, and share the contents of his wallet with Wolf, with whom he sympathized as a fellow-sufferer in persecution. "Poor Wolf," he would say, "thy mistress leads thee a dog's life of it; but never mind, my lad, whilst I live thou shalt never want a friend to stand by thee!" Wolf would wag his tail, look wistfully in his master's face; and if dogs can feel pity, I verily believe he reciprocated the sentiment with all his heart.

In a long ramble of the kind on a fine autumnal day, Rip had unconsciously scrambled to one of the highest parts of the Kaatskill mountains. He was after his favorite sport of squirrel-shooting, and the still solitudes had echoed and re-echoed with the reports of his gun. Panting and fatigued, he threw himself, late in the afternoon, on a green knoll, covered with mountain herbage, that crowned the brow of a precipice. From an opening between the trees he could overlook all the lower country for many a mile of rich woodland. He saw at a distance the lordly Hudson, far, far below him, moving on its silent but majestic course, with the reflection of a purple cloud, or the sail of a lagging bark, here and there sleeping on its glassy bosom, and at last losing itself in the blue highlands.

On the other side he looked down into a deep mountain glen, wild, lonely, and shagged, the bottom filled with fragments from the impending cliffs, and scarcely lighted by the reflected rays of the setting sun. For some time Rip lay musing on this scene; evening was gradually advancing; the mountains began to throw their long blue shadows over the valleys; he saw that it would be dark long before he could reach the village, and he heaved a heavy sigh when he thought of encountering the terrors of Dame Van Winkle.

As he was about to descend, he heard a voice from a distance, hallooing, "Rip Van Winkle, Rip Van Winkle!" He looked round, but could see nothing but a crow winging its solitary flight across the mountain. He thought his fancy must have deceived him, and turned again to descend, when he heard the same cry ring through the still evening air: "Rip Van Winkle! Rip Van Winkle!"—at the same time Wolf bristled up his back, and giving a low growl, skulked to his master's side, looking fearfully down into the glen. Rip now felt a vague apprehension stealing over him; he looked anxiously in the same direction, and perceived a strange figure slowly toiling up the rocks, and bending under the weight of something he carried on his back. He was suprised to see any human being in this lonely and unfrequented place; but supposing it to be some one of the neighborhood in need of his assistance, he hastened down to yield it.

On nearer approach he was still more surprised at the singularity of the stranger's appearance. He was a short, square-built old fellow, with thick bushy hair, and a grizzled beard. His dress was of the antique Dutch fashion,—a cloth jerkin strapped round the waist—several pair of breeches, the outer one of ample volume, decorated with rows of buttons down the sides, and bunches at the knees. He bore on his shoulder a stout keg, that seemed full of liquor, and made signs for Rip to approach and assist him with the load. Though rather shy and distrustful of this new acquaintance, Rip complied with his usual alacrity; and mutually relieving one another, they clambered up a narrow gully, apparently the dry bed of a mountain torrent. As they ascended, Rip every now and then heard long, rolling peals, like distant thunder, that seemed to issue out of a deep ravine, or rather cleft, between lofty rocks, toward which their rugged path conducted. He paused for an instant, but supposing it to be the muttering of one of those transient thunder-showers which often take place in mountain heights, he proceeded. Passing through the ravine, they came to a hollow, like a small amphitheatre, surrounded by perpendicular precipices, over the brinks of which impending trees shot their branches, so that you only caught glimpses of the azure sky and the bright evening cloud. During the whole time Rip and his companion had labored on in silence; for though the former marvelled greatly what could be the object of carrying a keg of liquor up this wild mountain, yet there was something strange and incomprehensible about the unknown, that inspired awe and checked familiarity.

On entering the amphitheatre, new objects of wonder presented themselves. On a level spot in the centre was a company of odd-looking personages playing at ninepins. They were dressed in a quaint, outlandish fashion; some wore short doublets, others jerkins, with long knives in their belts, and most of them had enormous breeches, of similar style with that of the guide's. Their visages, too, were peculiar: one had a large beard, broad face, and small piggish eyes; the face of another seemed to consist entirely of nose, and was surmounted by a white sugar-loaf hat, set off with a little red cock's tail. They all had beards, of various shapes and colors. There was one who seemed to be the commander. He was a stout old gentleman, with a weather-beaten countenance; he wore a laced doublet, broad belt and hanger, high crowned hat and feather, red stockings, and high-heeled shoes, with roses in them. The whole group reminded Rip of the figures in an old Flemish painting, in the parlor of Dominie Van Shaick, the village parson, and which had been brought over from Holland at the time of the settlement.

What seemed particularly odd to Rip was, that, though these folks were evidently amusing themselves, yet they maintained the gravest faces, the most mysterious silence, and were, withal, the most melancholy party of pleasure he had ever witnessed. Nothing interrupted the stillness of the scene but the noise of the balls, which, whenever they were rolled, echoed along the mountains like rumbling peals of thunder.

As Rip and his companion approached them, they suddenly desisted from their play, and stared at him with such fixed, statue-like gaze, and such strange, uncouth, lack-lustre countenances, that his heart turned within him, and his knees smote together. His companion now emptied the contents of the keg into large flagons, and made signs to him to wait upon the company. He obeyed with fear and trembling; they quaffed the liquor in profound silence, and then returned to their game.

By degrees Rip's awe and apprehension subsided. He even ventured, when no eye was fixed upon him, to taste the beverage, which he found had much of the flavor of excellent Hollands. He was naturally a thirsty soul, and was soon tempted to repeat the draught. One taste provoked another; and he reiterated his visits to the flagon so often that at length his senses were overpowered, his eyes swam in his head, his head gradually declined, and he fell into a deep sleep.

On waking, he found himself on the green knoll whence he had first seen the old man of the glen. He rubbed his eyes—it was a bright sunny morning. The birds were hopping and twittering among the bushes, and the eagle was wheeling aloft, and breasting the pure mountain breeze. "Surely," thought Rip, "I have not slept here all night." He recalled the occurrences before he fell asleep. The strange man with a keg of liquor—the mountain ravine—the wild retreat among the rocks—the woe-begone party at ninepins—the flagon—"Oh! that flagon! that wicked flagon!" thought Rip,—"what excuse shall I make to Dame Van Winkle?"

He looked round for his gun, but in place of the clean, well-oiled fowling-piece, he found an old firelock lying by him, the barrel incrusted with rust, the lock falling off, and the stock worm-eaten. He now suspected that the grave roisters of the mountain had put a trick upon him, and, having dosed him with liquor, had robbed him of his gun. Wolf, too, had disappeared, but he might have strayed away after a squirrel or partridge. He whistled after him, and shouted his name, but all in vain; the echoes repeated his whistle and shout, but no dog was to be seen.

He determined to revisit the scene of the last evening's gambol, and if he met with any of the party, to demand his dog and gun. As he rose to walk, he found himself stiff in the joints, and wanting in his usual activity. "These mountain beds do not agree with me," thought Rip, "and if this frolic should lay me up with a fit of the rheumatism, I shall have a blessed time with Dame Van Winkle." With some difficulty he got down into the glen: he found the gully up which he and his companion had ascended the preceding evening; but to his astonishment a mountain stream was now foaming down it, leaping from rock to rock, and filling the glen with babbling murmurs. He, however, made shift to scramble up its sides, working his toilsome way through thickets of birch, sassafras, and witch-hazel, and sometimes tripped up or entangled by the wild grape-vines that twisted their coils or tendrils from tree to tree, and spread a kind of network in his path.

At length he reached to where the ravine had opened through the cliffs to the amphitheatre; but no traces of such opening remained. The rocks presented a high, impenetrable wall, over which the torrent came tumbling in a sheet of feathery foam, and fell into a broad deep basin, black from the shadows of the surrounding forest. Here, then, poor Rip was brought to a stand. He again called and whistled after his dog; he was only answered by the cawing of a flock of idle crows, sporting high in air about a dry tree that overhung a sunny precipice; and who, secure in their elevation, seemed to look down and scoff at the poor man's perplexities. What was to be done? the morning was passing away, and Rip felt famished for want of his breakfast. He grieved to give up his dog and gun; he dreaded to meet his wife; but it would not do to starve among the mountains. He shook his head, shouldered the rusty firelock, and, with a heart full of trouble and anxiety, turned his steps homeward.

As he approached the village he met a number of people, but none whom he knew, which some what surprised him, for he had thought himself acquainted with every one in the country round. Their dress, too, was of a different fashion from that to which he was accustomed. They all stared at him with equal marks of surprise, and whenever they cast their eyes upon him, invariably stroked their chins. The constant recurrence of this gesture induced Rip, involuntarily, to do the same, when, to his astonishment, he found his beard had grown a foot long!

He had now entered the skirts of the village. A troop of strange children ran at his heels, hooting after him, and pointing at his gray beard. The dogs, too, not one of which he recognized for an old acquaintance, barked at him as he passed. The very village was altered; it was larger and more populous. There were rows of houses which he had never seen before, and those which had been his familiar haunts had disappeared. Strange names were over the doors—strange faces at the windows—everything was strange. His mind now misgave him; he began to doubt whether both he and the world around him were not bewitched. Surely this was his native village, which he had left but the day before. There stood the Kaatskill mountains—there ran the silver Hudson at a distance—there was every hill and dale precisely as it had always been. Rip was sorely perplexed. "That flagon last night," thought he, "has addled my poor head sadly!"

It was with some difficulty that he found the way to his own house, which he approached with silent awe, expecting every moment to hear the shrill voice of Dame Van Winkle. He found the house gone to decay—the roof fallen in, the windows shattered, and the doors off the hinges. A half-starved dog that looked like Wolf was skulking about it. Rip called him by name, but the cur snarled, showed his teeth, and passed on. This was an unkind cut indeed. "My very dog," sighed poor Rip, "has forgotten me!"

He entered the house, which, to tell the truth, Dame Van Winkle had always kept in neat order. It was empty, forlorn, and apparently abandoned. This desolateness overcame all his connubial fears—he called loudly for his wife and children—the lonely chambers rang for a moment with his voice, and then all again was silence.

He now hurried forth, and hastened to his old resort, the village inn—but it too was gone. A large rickety wooden building stood in its place, with great gaping windows, some of them broken and mended with old hats and petticoats, and over the door was painted, "The Union Hotel, by Jonathan Doolittle." Instead of the great tree that used to shelter the quiet little Dutch inn of yore, there now was reared a tall naked pole, with something on the top that looked like a red nightcap,[3] and from it was fluttering a flag, on which was a singular assemblage of stars and stripes;—all this was strange and incomprehensible. He recognized on the sign, however, the ruby face of King George, under which he had smoked so many a peaceful pipe; but even this was singularly metamorphosed. The red coat was changed for one of blue and buff, a sword was held in the hand instead of a sceptre, the head was decorated with a cocked hat, and underneath was painted in large characters, GENERAL WASHINGTON.

There was, as usual, a crowd of folk about the door, but none that Rip recollected. The very character of the people seemed changed. There was a busy, bustling, disputatious tone about it, instead of the accustomed phlegm and drowsy tranquillity. He looked in vain for the sage Nicholas Vedder, with his broad face, double chin, and fair long pipe, uttering clouds of tobacco-smoke instead of idle speeches; or Van Bummel, the schoolmaster, doling forth the contents of an ancient newspaper. In place of these, a lean, bilious-looking fellow, with his pockets full of hand-bills, was haranguing vehemently about rights of citizens—elections—members of congress—liberty—Bunker's Hill—heroes of seventy-six—and other words, which were a perfect Babylonish[4] jargon to the bewildered Van Winkle.

The appearance of Rip, with his long, grizzled beard, his rusty fowling-piece, his uncouth dress, and an army of women and children at his heels, soon attracted the attention of the tavern-politicians. They crowded round him, eying him from head to foot with great curiosity. The orator bustled up to him, and, drawing him partly aside, inquired "On which side he voted?" Rip stared in vacant stupidity. Another short but busy little fellow pulled him by the arm, and, rising on tiptoe, inquired in his ear, "Whether he was Federal or Democrat?" Rip was equally at a loss to comprehend the question; when a knowing, self-important old gentleman, in a sharp cocked hat, made his way through the crowd, putting them to the right and left with his elbows as he passed, and planting himself before Van Winkle, with one arm akimbo, the other resting on his cane, his keen eyes and sharp hat penetrating, as it were, into his very soul, demanded, in an austere tone, "What brought him to the election with a gun on his shoulder, and a mob at his heels; and whether he meant to breed a riot in the village?"—"Alas! gentlemen," cried Rip, somewhat dismayed, "I am a poor quiet man, a native of the place, and a loyal subject of the King, God bless him!"

Here a general shout burst from the by-standers—"A tory! a tory! a spy! a refugee! hustle him! away with him!" It was with great difficulty that the self-important man in the cocked hat restored order; and, having assumed a tenfold austerity of brow, demanded again of the unknown culprit, what he came there for, and whom he was seeking? The poor man humbly assured him that he meant no harm, but merely came there in search of some of his neighbors, who used to keep about the tavern.

"Well—who are they?—name them."

Rip bethought himself a moment, and inquired, "Where's Nicholas Vedder?"

There was a silence for a little while, when an old man replied, in a thin piping voice, "Nicholas Vedder! why, he is dead and gone these eighteen years! There was a wooden tombstone in the churchyard that used to tell all about him, but that's rotten and gone too."

3. **tall . . . nightcap:** liberty pole and liberty cap, symbols used in the American and French Revolutions.

4. **Babylonish:** Babel-like.

"Where's Brom Dutcher?"

"Oh, he went off to the army in the beginning of the war; some say he was killed at the storming of Stony Point—others say he was drowned in a squall at the foot of Antony's Nose. I don't know —he never came back again."

"Where's Van Bummel, the schoolmaster?"

"He went off to the wars too, was a great militia general, and is now in congress."

Rip's heart died away at hearing of these sad changes in his home and friends, and finding himself thus alone in the world. Every answer puzzled him too, by treating of such enormous lapses of time, and of matters which he could not understand: war—congress—Stony Point;—he had no courage to ask after any more friends, but cried out in despair, "Does nobody here know Rip Van Winkle?"

"Oh, Rip Van Winkle!" exclaimed two or three, "oh, to be sure! that's Rip Van Winkle yonder, leaning against the tree."

Rip looked, and beheld a precise counterpart of himself, as he went up the mountain; apparently as lazy, and certainly as ragged. The poor fellow was now completely confounded. He doubted his own identity, and whether he was himself or another man. In the midst of his bewilderment, the man in the cocked hat demanded who he was, and what was his name.

"God knows," exclaimed he, at his wit's end; "I'm not myself—I'm somebody else—that's me yonder—no—that's somebody else got into my shoes—I was myself last night, but I fell asleep on the mountain, and they've changed my gun, and everything's changed, and I'm changed, and I can't tell what's my name, or who I am!"

The by-standers began now to look at each other, nod, wink significantly, and tap their fingers against their foreheads. There was a whisper, also, about securing the gun, and keeping the old fellow from doing mischief, at the very suggestion of which the self-important man in the cocked hat retired with some precipitation. At this critical moment a fresh, comely woman pressed through the throng to get a peep at the gray-bearded man. She had a chubby child in her arms, which, frightened at his looks, began to cry. "Hush, Rip," cried she, "hush, you little fool; the old man won't hurt you." The name of the child, the air of the mother, the tone of her voice, all awakened a train of recollections in his mind. "What is your name, my good woman?" asked he.

"Judith Gardenier."

"And your father's name?"

"Ah, poor man, Rip Van Winkle was his name, but it's twenty years since he went away from home with his gun, and never has been heard of since,—his dog came home without him; but whether he shot himself, or was carried away by the Indians, nobody can tell. I was then but a little girl."

Rip had but one question more to ask; but he put it with a faltering voice:

"Where's your mother?"

"Oh, she too had died but a short time since; she broke a bloodvessel in a fit of passion at a New-England peddler."

There was a drop of comfort, at least, in this intelligence. The honest man could contain himself no longer. He caught his daughter and her child in his arms. "I am your father!" cried he—"Young Rip Van Winkle once—old Rip Van Winkle now! —Does nobody know poor Rip Van Winkle?"

All stood amazed, until an old woman, tottering out from among the crowd, put her hand to her brow, and peering under it in his face for a moment, exclaimed, "Sure enough! it is Rip Van Winkle—it is himself! Welcome home again, old neighbor. Why, where have you been these twenty long years?"

Rip's story was soon told, for the whole twenty years had been to him but as one night. The neighbors stared when they heard it; some were seen to wink at each other, and put their tongues in their cheeks: and the self-important man in the cocked hat, who, when the alarm was over, had returned to the field, screwed down the corners of his mouth, and shook his head—upon which there was a general shaking of the head throughout the assemblage.

It was determined, however, to take the opinion of old Peter Vanderdonk, who was seen slowly advancing up the road. He was a descendant of the historian of that name, who wrote one of the earliest accounts of the province. Peter was the most ancient inhabitant of the village, and well versed in all the wonderful events and traditions of the neighborhood. He recollected Rip at once, and corroborated his story in the most satisfactory manner. He assured the company that it was a fact, handed down from his ancestor the historian, that the Kaatskill mountains had always been haunted by strange beings. That it was affirmed that the great Hendrick Hudson, the first discoverer of the river and country, kept a kind of vigil there every twenty years, with his crew of the Half-moon; being permitted in this way to revisit the scenes of his enterprise, and keep a guardian eye upon the river and the great city called by his name. That his father had once seen them in their old Dutch dresses playing at ninepins in a hollow of the mountain; and that he himself had heard, one summer afternoon, the sound of their balls, like distant peals of thunder.

To make a long story short, the company broke up and returned to the more important concerns of the election. Rip's daughter took him home to live with her; she had a snug, well-furnished house, and a stout, cheery farmer for a husband, whom Rip recollected for one of the urchins that used to climb upon his back. As to Rip's son and heir, who was the ditto of himself, seen leaning against the tree, he was employed to work on the farm; but evinced an hereditary disposition to attend to anything else but his business.

Rip now resumed his old walks and habits; he soon found many of his former cronies, though all rather the worse for the wear and tear of time; and preferred making friends among the rising generation, with whom he soon grew into great favor.

Having nothing to do at home, and being arrived at that happy age when a man can be idle with impunity, he took his place once more on the bench at the inn-door, and was reverenced as one of the patriarchs of the village, and a chronicle of the old times "before the war." It was some time before he could get into the regular track of gossip, or could be made to comprehend the strange events that had taken place during his torpor. How that there had been a revolutionary war,—that the country had thrown off the yoke of old England,—and that, instead of being a subject of his Majesty George the Third, he was now a free citizen of the United States. Rip, in fact, was no politician; the changes of states and empires made but little impression on him; but there was one species of despotism under which he had long groaned, and that was—petticoat government. Happily that was at an end; he had got his neck out of the yoke of matrimony, and could go in and out whenever he pleased, without dreading the tyranny of Dame Van Winkle. Whenever her name was mentioned, however, he shook his head, shrugged his shoulders, and cast up his eyes; which might pass either for an expression of resignation to his fate, or joy at his deliverance.

He used to tell his story to every stranger that arrived at Mr. Doolittle's hotel. He was observed, at first, to vary on some points every time he told it, which was, doubtless, owing to his having so recently awaked. It at last settled down precisely to the tale I have related, and not a man, woman, or child in the neighborhood but knew it by heart. Some always pretended to doubt the reality of it, and insisted that Rip had been out of his head, and that this was one point on which he always remained flighty. The old Dutch inhabitants, however, almost universally gave it full credit. Even to this day they never hear a thunder-storm of a summer afternoon about the Kaatskill, but they say Hendrick Hudson and his crew are at their game of ninepins; and it is a common wish of all henpecked husbands in the neighborhood, when life hangs heavy on their hands, that they might have a quieting draught out of Rip Van Winkle's flagon.

NOTE

The foregoing Tale, one would suspect, had been suggested to Mr. Knickerbocker by a little German superstition about the Emperor Frederick *der Rothbart,* and the Kypphäuser mountain: [5] the subjoined note, however, which he had appended to the tale, shows that it is an absolute fact, narrated with his usual fidelity.

"The story of Rip Van Winkle may seem incredible to many, but nevertheless I give it my full belief, for I know the vicinity of our old Dutch settlements to have been very subject to marvellous events and appearances. Indeed, I have heard many stranger stories than this, in the villages along the Hudson; all of which were too well authenticated to admit of a doubt. I have even talked with Rip Van Winkle myself, who, when last I saw him, was a very venerable old man, and so perfectly rational and consistent on every other point, that I think no conscientious person could refuse to take this into the bargain; nay, I have seen a certificate on the subject taken before a country justice and signed with a cross, in the justice's own handwriting. The story, therefore, is beyond the possibility of doubt.

"D. K."

POSTSCRIPT

The following are travelling notes from a memorandum-book of Mr. Knickerbocker.

The Kaatsberg, or Catskill Mountains, have always been a region full of fable. The Indians considered them the abode of spirits, who influenced the weather, spreading sunshine or clouds over the landscape, and sending good or bad hunting-seasons. They were ruled by an old squaw spirit, said to be their mother. She dwelt on the highest peak of the Catskills, and had charge of the doors of day and night to open and shut them at the proper hour. She hung up the new moons in the skies, and cut up the old ones into stars. In times of drought, if properly propitiated, she would spin light summer clouds out of cobwebs and morning dew, and send them off from the crest of the mountain, flake after flake, like flakes of carded cotton, to float in the air; until, dissolved by the heat of the sun, they would fall in gentle showers, causing the grass to spring, the fruits to ripen, and the corn to grow an inch an hour. If displeased, however, she would brew up clouds black as ink, sitting in the midst of them like a bottle-

5. **The . . . mountain:** For a full account of Irving's indebtedness, see Pochmann's "Irving's German Sources in *The Sketch Book.*"

bellied spider in the midst of its web; and when these clouds broke, woe betide the valleys!

In old times, say the Indian traditions, there was a kind of Manitou or Spirit, who kept about the wildest recesses of the Catskill Mountains, and took a mischievous pleasure in wreaking all kinds of evils and vexations upon the red men. Sometimes he would assume the form of a bear, a panther, or a deer, lead the bewildered hunter a weary chase through tangled forests and among ragged rocks; and then spring off with a loud ho! ho! leaving him aghast on the brink of a beetling precipice or raging torrent.

The favorite abode of this Manitou is still shown. It is a great rock or cliff on the loneliest part of the mountains, and, from the flowering vines which clamber about it, and the wild flowers which abound in its neighborhood, is known by the name of the Garden Rock. Near the foot of it is a small lake, the haunt of the solitary bittern, with water-snakes basking in the sun on the leaves of the pond-lilies which lie on the surface. This place was held in great awe by the Indians, insomuch that the boldest hunter would not pursue his game within its precincts. Once upon a time, however, a hunter who had lost his way, penetrated to the Garden Rock, where he beheld a number of gourds placed in the crotches of trees. One of these he seized and made off with it, but in the hurry of his retreat he let it fall among the rocks, when a great stream gushed forth, which washed him away and swept him down precipices, where he was dashed to pieces, and the stream made its way to the Hudson, and continues to flow to the present day; being the identical stream known by the name of the Kaaters-kill.

1819, 1848

WESTMINSTER ABBEY

◇

IRVING did not himself discover Westminster Abbey as a literary subject. Goldsmith (*Citizen of the World*, Letter XII) and Addison (*Spectator*, No. 26) were his chief predecessors. His performance is worth comparing with theirs.

◇

When I behold, with deep astonishment,
To famous Westminster how there resorte
Living in brasse or stoney monument,
The princes and the worthies of all sorte:
Doe not I see reformde nobilitie,
Without contempt, or pride, or ostentation,
And looke upon offenselesse majesty,
Naked of pomp or earthly domination?
And how a play-game of a painted stone
Contents the quiet now and silent sprites,
Whome all the world which late they stood upon
Could not content or quench their appetites.
Life is a frost of cold felicitie,
And death the thaw of all our vanitie.

CHRISTOLERO'S *Epigrams*, by T. B.,[1] 1598

ON ONE of those sober and rather melancholy days, in the latter part of Autumn, when the shadows of morning and evening almost mingle together, and throw a gloom over the decline of the year, I passed several hours in rambling about Westminster Abbey. There was something congenial to the season in the mournful magnificence of the old pile; and, as I passed its threshold, seemed like stepping back into the regions of antiquity, and losing myself among the shades of former ages.

I entered from the inner court of Westminster School, through a long, low, vaulted passage, that had an almost subterranean look, being dimly lighted in one part by circular perforations in the massive walls. Through this dark avenue I had a distant view of the cloisters, with the figure of an old verger, in his black gown, moving along their shadowy vaults, and seeming like a spectre from one of the neighboring tombs. The approach to the abbey through these gloomy monastic remains prepares the mind for its solemn contemplation. The cloisters still retain something of the quiet and seclusion of former days. The gray walls are discolored by damps, and crumbling with age; a coat of hoary moss has gathered over the inscriptions of the mural monuments, and obscured the death's-heads, and other funereal emblems. The sharp touches of the chisel are gone from the rich tracery of the arches; the roses which adorned the key-stones have lost their leafy beauty; everything bears marks of the gradual dilapidations of time, which yet has something touching and pleasing in its very decay.

The sun was pouring down a yellow autumnal ray into the square of the cloisters; beaming upon a scanty plot of grass in the centre, and lighting up an angle of the vaulted passage with a kind of dusky splendor. From between the arcades, the eye glanced up to a bit of blue sky or a passing cloud, and beheld the sun-gilt pinnacles of the abbey towering into the azure heaven.

As I paced the cloisters, sometimes contemplating this mingled picture of glory and decay, and sometimes endeavoring to decipher the inscriptions on the tombstones, which formed the pavement

Westminster Abbey. 1. **Christolero's . . . T. B.:** *Chrestoleros: Seuen Bookes of Epigrames*, by Thomas Bastard. The stanza quoted is the thirty-second epigram.

beneath my feet, my eye was attracted to three figures, rudely carved in relief, but nearly worn away by the footsteps of many generations. They were the effigies of three of the early abbots; the epitaphs were entirely effaced; the names alone remained, having no doubt been renewed in later times. (Vitalis Abbas. 1082, and Gislebertus Crispinus. Abbas. 1114, and Laurentius. Abbas. 1176.) I remained some little while, musing over these casual relics of antiquity, thus left like wrecks upon this distant shore of time, telling no tale but that such beings had been, and had perished; teaching no moral but the futility of that pride which hopes still to exact homage in its ashes, and to live in an inscription. A little longer, and even these faint records will be obliterated, and the monument will cease to be a memorial. Whilst I was yet looking down upon these gravestones, I was roused by the sound of the abbey clock, reverberating from buttress to buttress, and echoing among the cloisters. It is almost startling to hear this warning of departed time sounding among the tombs, and telling the lapse of the hour, which, like a billow, has rolled us onward towards the grave. I pursued my walk to an arched door opening to the interior of the abbey. On entering here, the magnitude of the building breaks fully upon the mind, contrasted with the vaults of the cloisters. The eyes gaze with wonder at clustered columns of gigantic dimensions, with arches springing from them to such an amazing height; and man wandering about their bases, shrunk into insignificance in comparison with his own handiwork. The spaciousness and gloom of this vast edifice produce a profound and mysterious awe. We step cautiously and softly about, as if fearful of disturbing the hallowed silence of the tomb; while every footfall whispers along the walls, and chatters among the sepulchres, making us more sensible of the quiet we have interrupted.

It seems as if the awful nature of the place presses down upon the soul, and hushes the beholder into noiseless reverence. We feel that we are surrounded by the congregated bones of the great men of past times, who have filled history with their deeds, and the earth with their renown.

And yet it almost provokes a smile at the vanity of human ambition, to see how they are crowded together and jostled in the dust; what parsimony is observed in doling out a scanty nook, a gloomy corner, a little portion of earth, to those, whom, when alive, kingdoms could not satisfy; and how many shapes, and forms, and artifices are devised to catch the casual notice of the passenger, and save from forgetfulness, for a few short years, a name which once aspired to occupy ages of the world's thought and admiration.

I passed some time in Poet's Corner, which occupies an end of one of the transepts or cross aisles of the abbey. The monuments are generally simple; for the lives of literary men afford no striking themes for the sculptor. Shakespeare and Addison have statues erected to their memories; but the greater part have busts, medallions, and sometimes mere inscriptions. Notwithstanding the simplicity of these memorials, I have always observed that the visitors to the abbey remained longest about them. A kinder and fonder feeling takes place of that cold curiosity or vague admiration with which they gaze on the splendid monuments of the great and the heroic. They linger about these as about the tombs of friends and companions; for indeed there is something of companionship between the author and the reader. Other men are known to posterity only through the medium of history, which is continually growing faint and obscure; but the intercourse between the author and his fellowmen is ever new, active, and immediate. He has lived for them more than for himself; he has sacrificed surrounding enjoyments, and shut himself up from the delights of social life, that he might the more intimately commune with distant minds and distant ages. Well may the world cherish his renown; for it has been purchased, not by deeds of violence and blood, but by the diligent dispensation of pleasure. Well may posterity be grateful to his memory; for he has left it an inheritance, not of empty names and sounding actions, but whole treasures of wisdom, bright gems of thought, and golden veins of language.

From Poet's Corner I continued my stroll towards that part of the abbey which contains the sepulchres of the kings. I wandered among what once were chapels, but which are now occupied by the tombs and monuments of the great. At every turn I met with some illustrious name, or the cognizance of some powerful house renowned in history. As the eye darts into these dusky chambers of death, it catches glimpses of quaint effigies; some kneeling in niches, as if in devotion; others stretched upon the tombs, with hands piously pressed together; warriors in armor, as if reposing after battle; prelates with crosiers and mitres; and nobles in robes and coronets, lying as it were in state. In glancing over this scene, so strangely populous, yet where every form is so still and silent, it seems almost as if we were treading a mansion of that fabled city, where every being had been suddenly transmuted into stone.

I paused to contemplate a tomb on which lay the effigy of a knight in complete armor. A large buckler was on one arm; the hands were pressed together in supplication upon the breast; the face was almost covered by the morion; the legs were crossed in token of the warrior's having been engaged in the holy war. It was the tomb of a Crusader; of one of those military enthusiasts who so strangely mingled religion and romance, and whose exploits form the connecting link between fact and fiction; between the history and the fairy tale. There is something extremely picturesque in the tombs of these adventurers, decorated as they are with rude armorial bearings and Gothic sculpture. They comport with the antiquated chapels in which they are generally found; and in considering them, the imagination is apt to kindle with the legendary associations, the romantic fiction, the chivalrous pomp and pageantry, which poetry has spread over the wars for the sepulchre of Christ. They are the relics of times utterly gone by; of beings passed from recollection; of customs and manners with which ours have no affinity. They are like objects from some strange and distant land, of which we have no certain knowledge, and about which all our conceptions are vague and visionary. There is something extremely solemn and awful in those effigies on Gothic tombs, extended as if in the sleep of death, or in the supplication of the dying hour. They have an effect infinitely more impressive on my feelings than the fanciful attitudes, the over-wrought conceits, and allegorical groups, which abound on modern monuments. I have been struck, also, with the superiority of many of the old sepulchral inscriptions. There was a noble way, in former times, of saying things simply, and yet saying them proudly; and I do not know an epitaph that breathes a loftier consciousness of family worth and honorable lineage than one which affirms, of a noble house, that "all the brothers were brave, and all the sisters virtuous."

In the opposite transept to Poet's Corner stands a monument which is among the most renowned achievements of modern art; but which to me appears horrible rather than sublime. It is the tomb of Mrs. Nightingale, by Roubillac.[2] The bottom of the monument is represented as throwing open its marble doors, and a sheeted skeleton is starting forth. The shroud is falling from his fleshless frame as he launches his dart at his victim. She is sinking into her affrighted husband's arms, who strives, with vain and frantic effort, to avert the blow. The whole is executed with terrible truth and spirit; we almost fancy we hear the gibbering yell of triumph bursting from the distended jaws of the spectre.—But why should we thus seek to clothe death with unneccessary terrors, and to spread horrors round the tomb of those we love? The grave should be surrounded by everything that might inspire tenderness and veneration for the dead; or that might win the living to virtue. It is the place, not of disgust and dismay, but of sorrow and meditation.

While wandering about those gloomy vaults and silent aisles, studying the records of the dead, the sound of busy existence from without occasionally reaches the ear;—the rumbling of the passing equipage; the murmur of the multitude; or perhaps the light laugh of pleasure. The contrast is striking with the deathlike repose around: and it has a strange effect upon the feelings, thus to hear the surges of active life hurrying along, and beating against the very walls of the sepulchre.

I continued in this way to move from tomb to tomb, and from chapel to chapel. The day was gradually wearing away; the distant tread of loiterers about the abbey grew less and less frequent; the sweet-tongued bell was summoning to evening prayers; and I saw at a distance the choristers, in their white surplices, crossing the aisle and entering the choir. I stood before the entrance to Henry the Seventh's chapel. A flight of steps lead up to it, through a deep and gloomy, but magnificent arch. Great gates of brass, richly and delicately wrought, turn heavily upon their hinges, as if proudly reluctant to admit the feet of common mortals into this most gorgeous of sepulchres.

On entering, the eye is astonished by the pomp of architecture, and the elaborate beauty of sculptured detail. The very walls are wrought into universal ornament, incrusted with tracery, and scooped into niches, crowded with the statues of saints and martyrs. Stone seems, by the cunning labor of the chisel, to have been robbed of its weight and density, suspended aloft, as if by magic, and the fretted roof achieved with the wonderful minuteness and airy security of a cobweb.

Along the sides of the chapel are the lofty stalls of the Knights of the Bath, richly carved of oak, though with the grotesque decorations of Gothic architecture. On the pinnacles of the stalls are affixed the helmets and crests of the knights, with their scarfs and swords; and above them are suspended their banners, emblazoned with armorial bearings, and contrasting the splendor of gold and purple and crimson with the cold gray fretwork of the roof. In the midst of this grand mausoleum stands the sepulchre of its founder,—his effigy, with that of his queen, extended on a sumptuous tomb, and the whole surrounded by a superbly wrought brazen railing.

There is a sad dreariness in this magnificence,

2. Roubillac: Louis François Roubillas, or Roubiliac (1695–1762), sculptor of several other monuments in the Abbey; popular in his time for his flamboyant style.

this strange mixture of tombs and trophies; these emblems of living and aspiring ambition, close beside mementos which show the dust and oblivion in which all must sooner or later terminate. Nothing impresses the mind with a deeper feeling of loneliness than to tread the silent and deserted scene of former throng and pageant. On looking round on the vacant stalls of the knights and their esquires, and on the rows of dusty but gorgeous banners that were once borne before them, my imagination conjured up the scene when this hall was bright with the valor and beauty of the land; glittering with the splendor of jewelled rank and military array; alive with the tread of many feet and the hum of an admiring multitude. All had passed away; the silence of death had settled again upon the place, interrupted only by the casual chirping of birds, which had found their way into the chapel, and built there nests among its friezes and pendants—sure signs of solitariness and desertion.

When I read the names inscribed on the banners, they were those of men scattered far and wide about the world; some tossing upon distant seas; some under arms in distant lands; some mingling in the busy intrigues of courts and cabinets; all seeking to deserve one more distinction in this mansion of shadowy honors: the melancholy reward of a monument.

Two small aisles on each side of this chapel present a touching instance of the equality of the grave; which brings down the oppressor to a level with the oppressed, and mingles the dust of the bitterest enemies together. In one is the sepulchre of the haughty Elizabeth; in the other is that of her victim, the lovely and unfortunate Mary.[3] Not an hour in the day but some ejaculation of pity is uttered over the fate of the latter, mingled with indignation at her oppressor. The walls of Elizabeth's sepulchre continually echo with the sighs of sympathy heaved at the grave of her rival.

A peculiar melancholy reigns over the aisle where Mary lies buried. The light struggles dimly through windows darkened by dust. The greater part of the place is in deep shadow, and the walls are stained and tinted by time and weather. A marble figure of Mary is stretched upon the tomb, round which is an iron railing, much corroded, bearing her national emblem—the thistle. I was weary with wandering, and sat down to rest myself by the monument, revolving in my mind the checkered and disastrous story of poor Mary.

The sound of casual footsteps had ceased from the abbey. I could only hear, now and then, the distant voice of the priest repeating the evening service, and the faint responses of the choir; these paused for a time, and all was hushed. The stillness, the desertion and obscurity that were gradually prevailing around, gave a deeper and more solemn interest to the place.

> For in the silent grave no conversation,
> No joyful tread of friends, no voice of lovers.
> No careful father's counsel—nothing's heard,
> For nothing is, but all oblivion,
> Dust, and an endless darkness.[4]

Suddenly the notes of the deep-laboring organ burst upon the ear, falling with doubled and redoubled intensity, and rolling, as it were, huge billows of sound. How well do their volume and grandeur accord with this mighty building! With what pomp do they swell through its vast vaults, and breathe their awful harmony through these caves of death, and make the silent sepulchre vocal!—And now they rise in triumph and acclamation, heaving higher and higher their accordant notes, and piling sound on sound.—And now they pause, and the soft voices of the choir break out into sweet gushes of melody; they soar aloft, and warble along the roof, and seem to play about these lofty vaults like the pure airs of heaven. Again the pealing organ heaves its thrilling thunders, compressing air into music, and rolling it forth upon the soul. What long-drawn cadences! What solemn sweeping concords! It grows more and more dense and powerful—it fills the vast pile, and seems to jar the very walls—the ear is stunned—the senses are overwhelmed. And now it is winding up in full jubilee—it is rising from the earth to heaven—the very soul seems rapt away and floated upwards on this swelling tide of harmony!

I sat for some time lost in that kind of reverie which a strain of music is apt sometimes to inspire: the shadows of evening were gradually thickening round me; the monuments began to cast deeper and deeper gloom; and the distant clock again gave token of the slowly waning day.

I rose and prepared to leave the abbey. As I descended the flight of steps which lead into the body of the building, my eye was caught by the shrine of Edward the Confessor, and I ascended the small staircase that conducts to it, to take from thence a general survey of this wilderness of tombs. The shrine is elevated upon a kind of platform, and close around it are the sepulchres of various kings

3. **Mary:** Mary Stuart, Queen of Scotland, executed 1587, for allegedly plotting against Elizabeth.

4. **For . . . darkness:** Beaumont and Fletcher, *Thierry and Theodoret* (1621), IV.i.

and queens. From this eminence the eye looks down between pillars and funeral trophies to the chapels and chambers below, crowded with tombs, —where warriors, prelates, courtiers, and statesmen lie mouldering in their "beds of darkness." Close by me stood the great chair of coronation, rudely carved of oak, in the barbarous taste of a remote and Gothic age. The scene seemed almost as if contrived, with theatrical artifice, to produce an effect upon the beholder. Here was a type of the beginning and the end of human pomp and power; here it was literally but a step from the throne to the sepulchre. Would not one think that these incongruous mementos had been gathered together as a lesson to living greatness?—to show it, even in the moment of its proudest exaltation, the neglect and dishonor to which it must soon arrive; how soon that crown which encircles its brow must pass away, and it must lie down in the dust and disgraces of the tomb, and be trampled upon by the feet of the meanest of the multitude. For, strange to tell, even the grave is here no longer a sanctuary. There is a shocking levity in some natures, which leads them to sport with awful and hallowed things; and there are base minds, which delight to revenge on the illustrious dead the abject homage and grovelling servility which they pay to the living. The coffin of Edward the Confessor has been broken open, and his remains despoiled of their funereal ornaments; the sceptre has been stolen from the hand of the imperious Elizabeth, and the effigy of Henry the Fifth lies headless. Not a royal monument but bears some proof how false and fugitive is the homage of mankind. Some are plundered; some mutilated; some covered with ribaldry and insult,—all more or less outraged and dishonored!

The last beams of day were now faintly streaming through the painted windows in high vaults above me; the lower parts of the abbey were already wrapped in the obscurity of twilight. The chapels and aisles grew darker and darker. The effigies of the kings faded into shadows; the marble figures of the monuments assumed strange shapes in the uncertain light; the evening breeze crept through the aisles like the cold breath of the grave; and even the distant footfall of a verger, traversing the Poet's Corner, had something strange and dreary in its sound. I slowly retraced my morning's walk, and as I passed out at the portal of the cloisters, the door, closing with a jarring noise behind me, filled the whole building with echoes.

I endeavored to form some arrangement in my mind of the objects I had been contemplating, but found they were already fallen into indistinctness and confusion. Names, inscriptions, trophies, had all become confounded in my recollection, though I had scarcely taken my foot from off the threshold. What, thought I, is this vast assemblage of sepulchres but a treasury of humiliation; a huge pile of reiterated homilies on the emptiness of renown, and the certainty of oblivion! It is, indeed, the empire of death—his great shadowy palace, where he sits in state, mocking at the relics of human glory, and spreading dust and forgetfulness on the monuments of princes. How idle a boast, after all, is the immortality of a name. Time is ever silently turning over his pages; we are too much engrossed by the story of the present, to think of the characters and anecdotes that gave interest to the past; and each age is a volume thrown aside to be speedily forgotten. The idol of to-day pushes the hero of yesterday out of our recollection; and will, in turn, be supplanted by his successor of to-morrow. "Our fathers," says Sir Thomas Browne, "find their graves in our short memories, and sadly tell us how we may be buried in our survivors." History fades into fable; fact becomes clouded with doubt and controversy; the inscription moulders from the tablet; the statue falls from the pedestal. Columns, arches, pyramids, what are they but heaps of sand; and their epitaphs, but characters written in the dust? What is the security of a tomb, or the perpetuity of an embalmment? The remains of Alexander the Great have been scattered to the wind, and his empty sarcophagus is now the mere curiosity of a museum. "The Egyptian mummies, which Cambyses or time hath spared, avarice now consumeth; Mizraim cures wounds, and Pharaoh is sold for balsams." [5]

What then is to insure this pile which now towers above me from sharing the fate of mightier mausoleums? The time must come when its gilded vaults, which now spring so loftily, shall lie in rubbish beneath the feet; when, instead of the sound of melody and praise, the wind shall whistle through the broken arches, and the owl hoot from the shattered tower,—when the garish sunbeam shall break into these gloomy mansions of death, and the ivy twine round the fallen column; and the foxglove hang its blossoms about the nameless urn, as if in mockery of the dead. Thus man passes away; his name perishes from record and recollection; his history is as a tale that is told,[6] and his very monument becomes a ruin.

1820, 1848

5. **"The . . . balsams":** "Sir T. Browne" [I]. Both this and the preceding quotation are from Sir Thomas Browne's *Hydriotaphia, or Urn Burial* (1658), Chap. 5. **Mizraim:** Hebrew name for Egypt. In the Middle Ages mummies were thought to have medicinal properties. 6. **as . . . told:** Ps. 90:9.

JOHN BULL

◇

⁋ IN "John Bull," reverting to the tradition of periodical-essay personification and allegory, Irving tempers his admiration for English character with satire. The mixed attitude, as well as some of the imagery, anticipates *Bracebridge Hall.*

◇

An old song, made by an aged old pate,
Of an old worshipful gentleman who had a great estate,
That kept a brave old house at a bountiful rate,
And an old porter to relieve the poor at his gate.
With an old study fill'd full of learned old books,
With an old reverend chaplain, you might know him by his looks,
With an old buttery hatch worn quite off the hooks,
And an old kitchen that maintained half-a-dozen old cooks.
Like an old courtier, etc.
OLD SONG.[1]

THERE is no species of humor in which the English more excel, than that which consists in caricaturing and giving ludicrous appellations, or nicknames. In this way they have whimsically designated, not merely individuals, but nations; and, in their fondness for pushing a joke, they have not spared even themselves. One would think that, in personifying itself, a nation would be apt to picture something grand, heroic, and imposing; but it is characteristic of the peculiar humor of the English, and of their love for what is blunt, comic, and familiar, that they have embodied their national oddities in the figure of a sturdy, corpulent old fellow, with a three-cornered hat, red waistcoat, leather breeches, and stout oaken cudgel. Thus they have taken a singular delight in exhibiting their most private foibles in a laughable point of view; and have been so successful in their delineations, that there is scarcely a being in actual existence more absolutely present to the public mind than that eccentric personage, John Bull.

Perhaps the continual contemplation of the character thus drawn of them has contributed to fix it upon the nation; and thus to give reality to what at first may have been painted in a great measure from the imagination. Men are apt to acquire peculiarities that are continually ascribed to them. The common orders of English seem wonderfully captivated with the *beau ideal* which they have formed of John Bull, and endeavor to act up to the broad caricature that is perpetually before their eyes. Unluckily, they sometimes make their boasted Bull-ism an apology for their prejudice or grossness; and this I have especially noticed among those truly homebred and genuine sons of the soil who have never migrated beyond the sound of Bow-bells.[2] If one of these should be a little uncouth in speech, and apt to utter impertinent truths, he confesses that he is a real John Bull, and always speaks his mind. If he now and then flies into an unreasonable burst of passion about trifles, he observes, that John Bull is a choleric old blade, but then his passion is over in a moment, and he bears no malice. If he betrays a coarseness of taste, and an insensibility to foreign refinements, he thanks heaven for his ignorance—he is a plain John Bull, and has no relish for frippery and nicknacks. His very proneness to be gulled by strangers, and to pay extravagantly for absurdities, is excused under the plea of munificence—for John is always more generous than wise.

Thus, under the name of John Bull, he will contrive to argue every fault into a merit, and will frankly convict himself of being the honestest fellow in existence.

However little, therefore, the character may have suited in the first instance, it has gradually adapted itself to the nation, or rather they have adapted themselves to each other; and a stranger who wishes to study English peculiarities, may gather much valuable information from the innumerable portraits of John Bull, as exhibited in the windows of the caricature-shops. Still, however, he is one of those fertile humorists,[3] that are continually throwing out new portraits, and presenting different aspects from different points of view; and, often as he has been described, I cannot resist the temptation to give a slight sketch of him, such as he has met my eye.

John Bull, to all appearance, is a plain downright matter-of-fact fellow, with much less of poetry about him than rich prose. There is little of romance in his nature, but a vast deal of strong natural feeling. He excels in humor more than in wit; is jolly rather than gay; melancholy rather than morose; can easily be moved to a sudden tear, or surprised into a broad laugh; but he

John Bull. 1. **Old Song:** "The Old and Young Courtier," attributed to Thomas Dekker (1572?–1632?).

2. **those . . . Bow-bells:** cockneys, who allegedly live near enough to St. Mary-le-Bow to hear the bells. 3. **humorists:** persons subject to "humors," whims, or fancies.

loathes sentiment, and has no turn for light pleasantry. He is a boon companion, if you allow him to have his humor, and to talk about himself; and he will stand by a friend in a quarrel, with life and purse, however soundly he may be cudgelled.

In this last respect, to tell the truth, he has a propensity to be somewhat too ready. He is a busy-minded personage, who thinks not merely for himself and family, but for all the country round, and is most generously disposed to be everybody's champion. He is continually volunteering his services to settle his neighbors' affairs, and takes it in great dudgeon if they engage in any matter of consequence without asking his advice; though he seldom engages in any friendly office of the kind without finishing by getting into a squabble with all parties, and then railing bitterly at their ingratitude. He unluckily took lessons in his youth in the noble science of defence, and having accomplished himself in the use of his limbs and his weapons, and become a perfect master at boxing and cudgel-play, he has had a troublesome life of it ever since. He cannot hear of a quarrel between the most distant of his neighbors, but he begins incontinently to fumble with the head of his cudgel, and consider whether his interest or honor does not require that he should meddle in the broil. Indeed he has extended his relations of pride and policy so completely over the whole country, that no event can take place, without infringing some of his finely-spun rights and dignities. Couched in his little domain, with these filaments stretching forth in every direction, he is like some choleric, bottle-bellied old spider, who has woven his web over a whole chamber, so that a fly cannot buzz, nor a breeze blow, without startling his repose, and causing him to sally forth wrathfully from his den.

Though really a good-hearted, good-tempered old fellow at bottom, yet he is singularly fond of being in the midst of contention. It is one of his peculiarities, however, that he only relishes the beginning of an affray; he always goes into a fight with alacrity, but comes out of it grumbling even when victorious; and though no one fights with more obstinacy to carry a contested point, yet, when the battle is over, and he comes to the reconciliation, he is so much taken up with the mere shaking of hands, that he is apt to let his antagonist pocket all that they have been quarrelling about. It is not, therefore, fighting that he ought so much to be on his guard against, as making friends. It is difficult to cudgel him out of a farthing; but put him in a good humor, and you may bargain him out of all the money in his pocket. He is like a stout ship, which will weather the roughest storm uninjured, but roll its masts overboard in the succeeding calm.

He is a little fond of playing the magnifico abroad; of pulling out a long purse; flinging his money bravely about at boxing matches, horse races, cock fights, and carrying a high head among "gentlemen of the fancy":[4] but immediately after one of these fits of extravagance, he will be taken with violent qualms of economy; stop short at the most trivial expenditure; talk desperately of being ruined and brought upon the parish; and, in such moods, will not pay the smallest tradesman's bill, without violent altercation. He is in fact the most punctual and discontented paymaster in the world; drawing his coin out of his breeches pocket with infinite reluctance; paying to the uttermost farthing, but accompanying every guinea with a growl.

With all his talk of economy, however, he is a bountiful provider, and a hospitable housekeeper. His economy is of a whimsical kind, its chief object being to devise how he may afford to be extravagant; for he will begrudge himself a beefsteak and pint of port one day, that he may roast an ox whole, broach a hogshead of ale, and treat all his neighbors on the next.

His domestic establishment is enormously expensive: not so much from any great outward parade, as from the great consumption of solid beef and pudding; the vast number of followers he feeds and clothes; and his singular disposition to pay hugely for small services. He is a most kind and indulgent master, and, provided his servants humor his peculiarities, flatter his vanity a little now and then, and do not peculate grossly on him before his face, they may manage him to perfection. Every thing that lives on him seems to thrive and grow fat. His house-servants are well paid, and pampered, and have little to do. His horses are sleek and lazy, and prance slowly before his state carriage; and his house-dogs sleep quietly about the door, and will hardly bark at a housebreaker.

His family mansion is an old castellated manor-house, gray with age, and of a most venerable, though weather-beaten appearance. It has been built upon no regular plan, but is a vast accumulation of parts, erected in various tastes and ages. The centre bears evident traces of Saxon architecture, and is as solid as ponderous stone and old English oak can make it. Like all the relics of that style, it is full of obscure passages, intricate mazes, and dusky chambers; and though these have been partially lighted up in modern days, yet there are many places where you must still grope in the

4. **"gentlemen . . . fancy"**: sporting enthusiasts.

dark. Additions have been made to the original edifice from time to time, and great alterations have taken place; towers and battlements have been erected during wars and tumults: wings built in time of peace; and out-houses, lodges, and offices, run up according to the whim or convenience of different generations, until it has become one of the most spacious, rambling tenements imaginable. An entire wing is taken up with the family chapel, a reverend pile, that must have been exceedingly sumptuous, and, indeed, in spite of having been altered and simplified at various periods, has still a look of solemn religious pomp. Its walls within are storied with the monuments of John's ancestors; and it is snugly fitted up with soft cushions and well-lined chairs, where such of his family as are inclined to church services, may doze comfortably in the discharge of their duties.

To keep up this chapel has cost John much money; but he is stanch in his religion, and piqued in his zeal, from the circumstance that many dissenting chapels have been erected in his vicinity, and several of his neighbors, with whom he has had quarrels, are strong papists.

To do the duties of the chapel he maintains, at a large expense, a pious and portly family chaplain. He is a most learned and decorous personage, and a truly well-bred Christian, who always backs the old gentleman in his opinions, winks discreetly at his little peccadilloes, rebukes the children when refractory, and is of great use in exhorting the tenants to read their Bibles, say their prayers, and, above all, to pay their rents punctually, and without grumbling.

The family apartments are in a very antiquated taste, somewhat heavy, and often inconvenient, but full of the solemn magnificence of former times; fitted up with rich, though faded tapestry, unwieldy furniture, and loads of massy gorgeous old plate. The vast fireplaces, ample kitchens, extensive cellars, and sumptuous banqueting halls, all speak of the roaring hospitality of days of yore, of which the modern festivity at the manor-house is but a shadow. There are, however, complete suites of rooms apparently deserted and time-worn; and towers and turrets that are tottering to decay; so that in high winds there is danger of their tumbling about the ears of the household.

John has frequently been advised to have the old edifice thoroughly overhauled; and to have some of the useless parts pulled down, and the others strengthened with their materials; but the old gentleman always grows testy on this subject. He swears the house is an excellent house—that it is tight and weather proof, and not to be shaken by tempests—that it has stood for several hundred years, and, therefore, is not likely to tumble down now—that as to its being inconvenient, his family is accustomed to the inconveniences, and would not be comfortable without them—that as to its unwieldy size and irregular construction, these result from its being the growth of centuries, and being improved by the wisdom of every generation—that an old family, like his, requires a large house to dwell in; new, upstart families may live in modern cottages and snug boxes; but an old English family should inhabit an old English manor-house. If you point out any part of the building as superfluous, he insists that it is material to the strength or decoration of the rest, and the harmony of the whole; and swears that the parts are so built into each other, that if you pull down one, you run the risk of having the whole about your ears.

The secret of the matter is, that John has a great disposition to protect and patronize. He thinks it indispensable to the dignity of an ancient and honorable family, to be bounteous in its appointments, and to be eaten up by dependents; and so, partly from pride, and partly from kind-heartedness, he makes it a rule always to give shelter and maintenance to his superannuated servants.

The consequence is, that, like many other venerable family establishments, his manor is encumbered by old retainers whom he cannot turn off, and an old style which he cannot lay down. His mansion is like a great hospital of invalids, and, with all its magnitude, is not a whit too large for its inhabitants. Not a nook or corner but is of use in housing some useless personage. Groups of veteran beef-eaters, gouty pensioners, and retired heroes of the buttery and the larder, are seen lolling about its walls, crawling over its lawns, dozing under its trees, or sunning themselves upon the benches at its doors. Every office and out-house is garrisoned by these supernumeraries and their families; for they are amazingly prolific, and when they die off, are sure to leave John a legacy of hungry mouths to be provided for. A mattock cannot be struck against the most mouldering tumble-down tower, but out pops, from some cranny or loop-hole, the gray pate of some superannuated hanger-on, who has lived at John's expense all his life, and makes the most grievous outcry at their pulling down the roof from over the head of a worn-out servant of the family. This is an appeal that John's honest heart never can withstand; so that a man, who has faithfully eaten his beef and pudding all his life, is sure to be rewarded with a pipe and tankard in his old days.

A great part of his park, also, is turned into paddocks, where his broken-down chargers are turned loose to graze undisturbed for the remainder of their existence—a worthy example of grateful recollection, which if some of his neighbors were to imitate, would not be to their discredit. Indeed, it is one of his great pleasures to point out these old steeds to his visitors, to dwell on their good qualities, extol their past services, and boast, with some little vainglory, of the perilous adventures and hardy exploits through which they have carried him.

He is given, however, to indulge his veneration for family usages, and family incumbrances, to a whimsical extent. His manor is infested by gangs of gipsies; yet he will not suffer them to be driven off, because they have infested the place time out of mind, and been regular poachers upon every generation of the family. He will scarcely permit a dry branch to be lopped from the great trees that surround the house, lest it should molest the rooks, that have bred there for centuries. Owls have taken possession of the dovecote; but they are hereditary owls, and must not be disturbed. Swallows have nearly choked up every chimney with their nests; martins build in every frieze and cornice; crows flutter about the towers, and perch on every weather-cock; and old gray-headed rats may be seen in every quarter of the house, running in and out of their holes undauntedly in broad daylight. In short, John has such a reverence for every thing that has been long in the family, that he will not hear even of abuses being reformed, because they are good old family abuses.

All these whims and habits have concurred wofully to drain the old gentleman's purse; and as he prides himself on punctuality in money matters, and wishes to maintain his credit in the neighborhood, they have caused him great perplexity in meeting his engagements. This, too, has been increased by the altercations and heart-burnings which are continually taking place in his family. His children have been brought up to different callings, and are of different ways of thinking; and as they have always been allowed to speak their minds freely, they do not fail to exercise the privilege most clamorously in the present posture of his affairs. Some stand up for the honor of the race, and are clear that the old establishment should be kept up in all its state, whatever may be the cost; others, who are more prudent and considerate, entreat the old gentleman to retrench his expenses, and to put his whole system of housekeeping on a more moderate footing. He has, indeed, at times, seemed inclined to listen to their opinions, but their wholesome advice has been completely defeated by the obstreperous conduct of one of his sons. This is a noisy, rattle-pated fellow, of rather low habits, who neglects his business to frequent ale-houses—is the orator of village clubs, and a complete oracle among the poorest of his father's tenants. No sooner does he hear any of his brothers mention reform or retrenchment, than up he jumps, takes the words out of their mouths, and roars out for an overturn. When his tongue is once going nothing can stop it. He rants about the room; hectors the old man about his spendthrift practices; ridicules his tastes and pursuits; insists that he shall turn the old servants out of doors; give the broken-down horses to the hounds; send the fat chaplain packing, and take a field-preacher in his place—nay, that the whole family mansion shall be levelled with the ground, and a plain one of brick and mortar built in its place. He rails at every social entertainment and family festivity, and skulks away growling to the ale-house whenever an equipage drives up to the door. Though constantly complaining of the emptiness of his purse, yet he scruples not to spend all his pocket-money in these tavern convocations, and even runs up scores for the liquor over which he preaches about his father's extravagance.

It may readily be imagined how little such thwarting agrees with the old cavalier's fiery temperament. He has become so irritable, from repeated crossings, that the mere mention of retrenchment or reform is a signal for a brawl between him and the tavern oracle. As the latter is too sturdy and refractory for paternal discipline, having grown out of all fear of the cudgel, they have frequent scenes of wordy warfare, which at times run so high, that John is fain to call in the aid of his son Tom, an officer who has served abroad, but is at present living at home, on half-pay. This last is sure to stand by the old gentleman, right or wrong; likes nothing so much as a racketing, roistering life; and is ready at a wink or nod, to out sabre, and flourish it over the orator's head, if he dares to array himself against paternal authority.

These family dissensions, as usual, have got abroad, and are rare food for scandal in John's neighborhood. People begin to look wise, and shake their heads, whenever his affairs are mentioned. They all "hope that matters are not so bad with him as represented; but when a man's own children begin to rail at his extravagance, things must be badly managed. They understand he is mortgaged over head and ears, and is continually dabbling with money lenders. He is certainly an open-handed old gentleman, but they fear he has lived too fast; indeed, they never knew any good come of this fondness for hunting, racing, revelling and prize-fighting. In short, Mr. Bull's estate is a very fine one, and has been in the family a long time; but, for all that, they have known many finer estates come to the hammer."

What is worst of all, is the effect which these pecuniary embarrassments and domestic feuds have had on the poor man himself. Instead of that jolly round corporation, and smug rosy face, which he used to present, he has of late become as shrivelled and shrunk as a frost-bitten apple. His scarlet gold-laced waistcoat, which bellied out so bravely in those prosperous days when he sailed before the wind, now hangs loosely about him like a mainsail in a calm.[5] His leather breeches are all in folds and wrinkles, and apparently have much ado to hold up the boots that yawn on both sides of his once sturdy legs.

Instead of strutting about as formerly, with his three-cornered hat on one side; flourishing his cudgel, and bringing it down every moment with a hearty thump upon the ground; looking every one sturdily in the face, and trolling out a stave of a catch or a drinking song; he now goes about whistling thoughtfully to himself, with his head drooping down, his cudgel tucked under his arm, and his hands thrust to the bottom of his breeches pockets, which are evidently empty.

Such is the plight of honest John Bull at present; yet for all this the old fellow's spirit is as tall and as gallant as ever. If you drop the least expression of sympathy or concern, he takes fire in an instant; swears that he is the richest and stoutest fellow in the country; talks of laying out large sums to adorn his house or buy another estate; and with a valiant swagger and grasping of his cudgel, longs exceedingly to have another bout at quarter-staff.

Though there may be something rather whimsical in all this, yet I confess I cannot look upon John's situation without strong feelings of interest. With all his odd humors and obstinate prejudices, he is a sterling-hearted old blade. He may not be so wonderfully fine a fellow as he thinks himself, but he is at least twice as good as his neighbors represent him. His virtues are all his own; all plain, homebred, and unaffected. His very faults smack of the raciness of his good qualities. His extravagance savors of his generosity; his quarrelsomeness of his courage; his credulity of his open faith; his vanity of his pride; and his bluntness of his sincerity. They are all the redundancies of a rich and liberal character. He is like his own oak, rough without, but sound and solid within; whose bark abounds with excrescences in proportion to the growth and grandeur of the timber; and whose branches make a fearful groaning and murmuring in the least storm, from their very magnitude and luxuriance. There is something, too, in the appearance of his old family mansion that is extremely poetical and picturesque; and, as long as it can be rendered comfortably habitable, I should almost tremble to see it meddled with, during the present conflict of tastes and opinions. Some of his advisers are no doubt good architects, that might be of service; but many, I fear, are mere levellers, who, when they had once got to work with their mattocks on this venerable edifice, would never stop until they had brought it to the ground, and perhaps buried themselves among the ruins. All that I wish is, that John's present troubles may teach him more prudence in future. That he may cease to distress his mind about other people's affairs; that he may give up the fruitless attempt to promote the good of his neighbors, and the peace and happiness of the world, by dint of the cudgel; that he may remain quietly at home; gradually get his house into repair; cultivate his rich estate according to his fancy; husband his income—if he thinks proper; bring his unruly children into order—if he can; renew the jovial scenes of ancient prosperity; and long enjoy, on his paternal lands, a green, an honorable, and a merry old age.

1820, 1848

5. **Instead . . . calm:** Shakespearean echoes contribute to the raciness of Irving's style in parts of *The Sketch Book*. Cf. *I Henry IV*, III.iii.1–5.

THE LEGEND OF SLEEPY HOLLOW

Found Among the Papers of the Late Diedrich Knickerbocker

◇

ORIGINALLY Irving juxtaposed this story with an excessively sentimental piece, "The Pride of the Village," at the end of the sixth installment of *The Sketch Book*. Subsequently, however, he made "Sleepy Hollow" the final story in the entire book.

Irving's use of German sources here, though less significant than in "Rip Van Winkle," has been carefully documented by Henry A. Pochmann.

◇

A pleasing land of drowsy head it was,
  Of dreams that wave before the half-shut eye;
And of gay castles in the clouds that pass,
  For ever flushing round a summer sky.
Castle of Indolence[1]

In the bosom of one of those spacious coves which indent the eastern shore of the Hudson, at that broad expansion of the river denominated by the ancient Dutch navigators the Tappan Zee, and where they always prudently shortened sail, and implored the protection of St. Nicholas when they crossed, there lies a small market-town or rural port, which by some is called Greensburgh, but which is more generally and properly known by the name of Tarry Town. This name was given, we are told, in former days, by the good housewives of the adjacent country, from the inveterate propensity of their husbands to linger about the village tavern on market-days. Be that as it may, I do not vouch for the fact, but merely advert to it for the sake of being precise and authentic. Not far from this village, perhaps about two miles, there is a little valley, or rather lap of land, among high hills, which is one of the quietest places in the whole world. A small brook glides through it, with just murmur enough to lull one to repose; and the occasional whistle of a quail, or tapping of a woodpecker, is almost the only sound that ever breaks in upon the uniform tranquillity.

I recollect that, when a stripling, my first exploit in squirrel-shooting was in a grove of tall walnut-trees that shades one side of the valley. I had wandered into it at noon-time, when all nature is peculiarly quiet, and was startled by the roar of my own gun, as it broke the Sabbath stillness around, and was prolonged and reverberated by the angry echoes. If ever I should wish for a retreat, whither I might steal from the world and its distractions, and dream quietly away the remnant of a troubled life, I know of none more promising than this little valley.

From the listless repose of the place, and the peculiar character of its inhabitants, who are descendants from the original Dutch settlers, this sequestered glen has long been known by the name of Sleepy Hollow, and its rustic lads are called the Sleepy Hollow Boys throughout all the neighboring country. A drowsy, dreamy influence seems to hang over the land, and to pervade the very atmosphere. Some say that the place was bewitched by a high German doctor, during the early days of the settlement; others, that an old Indian chief, the prophet or wizard of his tribe, held his pow-wows there before the country was discovered by Master Hendrick Hudson. Certain it is, the place still continues under the sway of some witching power, that holds a spell over the minds of the good people, causing them to walk in a continual reverie. They are given to all kinds of marvellous beliefs; are subject to trances and visions; and frequently see strange sights, and hear music and voices in the air. The whole neighborhood abounds with local tales, haunted spots, and twilight superstitions; stars shoot and meteors glare oftener across the valley than in any other part of the country, and the nightmare, with her whole nine fold[2] seems to make it the favorite scene of her gambols.

The dominant spirit, however, that haunts this enchanted region, and seems to be commander-in-chief of all the powers of the air, is the apparition of a figure on horseback without a head. It is said by some to be the ghost of a Hessian trooper, whose head had been carried away by a cannon-ball, in some nameless battle during the Revolutionary War, and who is ever and anon seen by the country folk, hurrying along in the gloom of night, as if on the wings of the wind. His haunts are not confined to the valley, but extend at times to the adjacent roads, and especially to the vicinity of a church at no great distance. Indeed certain of the most authentic historians of those parts, who have been careful in collecting and collating the floating facts concerning this spectre, allege that the body of the trooper, having been buried in the church-yard, the ghost rides forth to the scene of battle in nightly quest of his head; and that the rushing speed with which he sometimes passes along the Hollow, like a midnight blast, is owing to his being belated, and in a hurry to get back to the church yard before daybreak.

Such is the general purport of this legendary superstition, which has furnished materials for many a wild story in that region of shadows; and the spectre is known, at all the country firesides, by the name of the Headless Horseman of Sleepy Hollow.

It is remarkable that the visionary propensity I have mentioned is not confined to the native inhabitants of the valley, but is unconsciously imbibed by every one who resides there for a time. However wide awake they may have been before they entered that sleepy region, they are sure, in a little time, to inhale the witching influence of the air, and begin to grow imaginative, to dream dreams, and see apparitions.

I mention this peaceful spot with all possible

The Legend of Sleepy Hollow. **1.** ***Castle of Indolence:*** poem by James Thomson (1748), I.vi.1–4.

2. nightmare . . . fold: Cf. *King Lear*, III.iv.126.

laud; for it is in such little retired Dutch valleys, found here and there embosomed in the great State of New York, that population, manners, and customs remain fixed; while the great torrent of migration and improvement, which is making such incessant changes in other parts of this restless country, sweeps by them unobserved. They are like those little nooks of still water which border a rapid stream; where we may see the straw and bubble riding quietly at anchor, or slowly revolving in their mimic harbor, undisturbed by the rush of the passing current. Though many years have elapsed since I trod the drowsy shades of Sleepy Hollow, yet I question whether I should not still find the same trees and the same families vegetating in its sheltered bosom.

In this by-place of nature, there abode, in a remote period of American history, that is to say, some thirty years since, a worthy wight of the name of Ichabod Crane; who sojourned, or, as he expressed it, "tarried," in Sleepy Hollow, for the purpose of instructing the children of the vicinity. He was a native of Connecticut, a State which supplies the Union with pioneers for the mind as well as for the forest, and sends forth yearly its legions of frontier woodsmen and country schoolmasters. The cognomen of Crane was not inapplicable to his person. He was tall, but exceedingly lank, with narrow shoulders, long arms and legs, hands that dangled a mile out of his sleeves, feet that might have served for shovels, and his whole frame most loosely hung together. His head was small, and flat at top, with huge ears, large green glassy eyes, and a long snipe nose, so that it looked like a weathercock perched upon his spindle neck, to tell which way the wind blew. To see him striding along the profile of a hill on a windy day, with his clothes bagging and fluttering about him, one might have mistaken him for the genius of famine descending upon the earth, or some scarecrow eloped from a cornfield.

His school-house was a low building of one large room, rudely constructed of logs; the windows partly glazed, and partly patched with leaves of old copy-books. It was most ingeniously secured at vacant hours by a withe twisted in the handle of the door, and stakes set against the window-shutters; so that, though a thief might get in with perfect ease, he would find some embarrassment in getting out: an idea most probably borrowed by the architect, Yost Van Houten, from the mystery of an eel-pot. The school-house stood in a rather lonely but pleasant situation, just at the foot of a woody hill, with a brook running close by, and a formidable birch-tree growing at one end of it. From hence the low murmur of his pupils' voices, conning over their lessons, might be heard in a drowsy summer's day, like the hum of a bee-hive; interrupted now and then by the authoritative voice of the master, in the tone of menace or command; or, peradventure, by the appalling sound of the birch, as he urged some tardy loiterer along the flowery path of knowledge. Truth to say, he was a conscientious man, and ever bore in mind the golden maxim, "Spare the rod and spoil the child."—Ichabod Crane's scholars certainly were not spoiled.

I would not have it imagined, however, that he was one of those cruel potentates of the school, who joy in the smart of their subjects; on the contrary, he administered justice with discrimination rather than severity, taking the burden off the backs of the weak, and laying it on those of the strong. Your mere puny stripling, that winced at the least flourish of the rod, was passed by with indulgence; but the claims of justice were satisfied by inflicting a double portion on some little, tough, wrong-headed, broad-skirted Dutch urchin, who sulked and swelled and grew dogged and sullen beneath the birch. All this he called "doing his duty" by their parents; and he never inflicted a chastisement without following it by the assurance, so consolatory to the smarting urchin, that "he would remember it, and thank him for it the longest day he had to live."

When school-hours were over, he was even the companion and playmate of the larger boys; and on holiday afternoons would convoy some of the smaller ones home, who happened to have pretty sisters, or good housewives for mothers, noted for the comforts of the cupboard. Indeed it behooved him to keep on good terms with his pupils. The revenue arising from his school was small, and would have been scarcely sufficient to furnish him with daily bread, for he was a huge feeder,[3] and, though lank, had the dilating powers of an anaconda; but to help out his maintenance, he was, according to country custom in those parts, boarded and lodged at the houses of the farmers, whose children he instructed. With these he lived successively a week at a time; thus going the rounds of the neighborhood, with all his worldly effects tied up in a cotton handkerchief.

That all this might not be too onerous on the purses of his rustic patrons, who are apt to consider the costs of schooling a grievous burden, and schoolmasters as mere drones, he had various ways of rendering himself both useful and agreeable. He assisted the farmers occasionally in the lighter labors of their farms; helped to make hay;

3. **huge feeder:** Cf. *Merchant of Venice,* II.v.46.

mended the fences; took the horses to water; drove the cows from pasture; and cut wood for the winter fire. He laid aside, too, all the dominant dignity and absolute sway with which he lorded it in his little empire, the school, and became wonderfully gentle and ingratiating. He found favor in the eyes of the mothers, by petting the children, particularly the youngest; and like the lion bold, which whilom so magnanimously the lamb did hold,[4] he would sit with a child on one knee, and rock a cradle with his foot for whole hours together.

In addition to his other vocations, he was the singing-master of the neighborhood, and picked up many bright shillings by instructing the young folks in psalmody. It was a matter of no little vanity to him, on Sundays, to take his station in front of the church-gallery, with a band of chosen singers; where, in his own mind, he completely carried away the palm from the parson. Certain it is, his voice resounded far above all the rest of the congregation; and there are peculiar quavers still to be heard in that church, and which may even be heard half a mile off, quite to the opposite side of the mill-pond, on a still Sunday morning, which are said to be legitimately descended from the nose of Ichabod Crane. Thus, by divers little makeshifts in that ingenious way which is commonly denominated "by hook and by crook," the worthy pedagogue got on tolerably enough, and was thought, by all who understood nothing of the labor of headwork, to have a wonderfully easy life of it.

The schoolmaster is generally a man of some importance in the female circle of a rural neighborhood; being considered a kind of idle, gentleman-like personage, of vastly superior taste and accomplishments to the rough country swains, and, indeed, inferior in learning only to the parson. His appearance, therefore, is apt to occasion some little stir at the tea-table of a farm-house, and the addition of a supernumerary dish of cakes or sweetmeats, or, peradventure, the parade of a silver teapot. Our man of letters, therefore, was peculiarly happy in the smiles of all the country damsels. How he would figure among them in the churchyard, between services on Sundays! gathering grapes for them from the wild vines that overrun the surrounding trees; reciting for their amusement all the epitaphs on the tombstones; or sauntering, with a whole bevy of them, along the banks of the adjacent mill-pond; while the more bashful country bumpkins hung sheepishly back, envying his superior elegance and address.

From his half-itinerant life, also, he was a kind of travelling gazette, carrying the whole budget of local gossip from house to house: so that his appearance was always greeted with satisfaction. He was, moreover, esteemed by the women as a man of great erudition, for he had read several books quite through, and was a perfect master of Cotton Mather's "History of New England Witchcraft," [5] in which, by the way, he most firmly and potently believed.

He was, in fact, an odd mixture of small shrewdness and simple credulity. His appetite for the marvellous, and his powers of digesting it, were equally extraordinary; and both had been increased by his residence in this spellbound region. No tale was too gross or monstrous for his capacious swallow. It was often his delight, after his school was dismissed in the afternoon, to stretch himself on the rich bed of clover bordering the little brook that whimpered by his school-house, and there con over old Mather's direful tales, until the gathering dusk of the evening made the printed page a mere mist before his eyes. Then, as he wended his way, by swamp and stream, and awful woodland, to the farm-house where he happened to be quartered, every sound of nature, at that witching hour, fluttered his excited imagination; the moan of the whippoorwill [6] from the hill-side; the boding cry of the tree-toad, that harbinger of storm; the dreary hooting of the screech-owl, or the sudden rustling in the thicket of birds frightened from their roost. The fire-flies, too, which sparkled most vividly in the darkest places, now and then startled him, as one of uncommon brightness would stream across his path; and if, by chance, a huge blockhead of a beetle came winging his blundering flight against him, the poor varlet was ready to give up the ghost, with the idea that he was struck with a witch's token. His only resource on such occasions, either to drown thought or drive away evil spirits, was to sing psalm-tunes; and the good people of Sleepy Hollow, as they sat by their doors of an evening, were often filled with awe, at hearing his nasal melody, "in linked sweetness long drawn out," [7] floating from the distant hill, or along the dusky road.

Another of his sources of fearful pleasure was, to pass long winter evenings with the old Dutch wives, as they sat spinning by the fire, with a row of apples roasting and spluttering along the hearth,

4. **lion . . . hold**: an allusion to the couplet under the letter *L* in the *New England Primer:* "The lion bold/The lamb doth hold."

5. **"History . . . Witchcraft"**: This is not an actual title. Mather wrote on the subject in *Wonders of the Invisible World* (1693), *Memorable Providences, Relating to Witchcraft* (1689), and in the *Magnalia*, Book VI, Chap. 7.

6. **Whippoorwill**: "The whippoorwill is a bird which is only heard at night. It receives its name from its note, which is thought to resemble these words" [I].

7. **"in . . . out"**: Milton, "L'Allegro," l. 140.

and listen to their marvellous tales of ghosts and goblins, and haunted fields, and haunted brooks, and haunted bridges, and haunted houses, and particularly of the headless horseman, or Galloping Hessian of the Hollow, as they sometimes called him. He would delight them equally by his anecdotes of witchcraft, and of the direful omens and portentous sights and sounds in the air, which prevailed in the earlier times of Connecticut; and would frighten them wofully with speculations upon comets and shooting stars, and with the alarming fact that the world did absolutely turn round, and that they were half the time topsy-turvy!

But if there was a pleasure in all this, while snugly cuddling in the chimney-corner of a chamber that was all of a ruddy glow from the crackling wood-fire, and where, of course, no spectre dared to show his face, it was dearly purchased by the terrors of his subsequent walk homewards. What fearful shapes and shadows beset his path amidst the dim and ghastly glare of a snowy night!—With what wistful look did he eye every trembling ray of light streaming across the waste fields from some distant window!—How often was he appalled by some shrub covered with snow, which, like a sheeted spectre, beset his very path!—How often did he shrink with curdling awe at the sound of his own steps on the frosty crust beneath his feet; and dread to look over his shoulder, lest he should behold some uncouth being tramping close behind him!—and how often was he thrown into complete dismay by some rushing blast, howling among the trees, in the idea that it was the Galloping Hessian on one of his nightly scourings!

All these, however, were mere terrors of the night, phantoms of the mind that walk in darkness; and though he had seen many spectres in his time, and been more than once beset by Satan in divers shapes, in his lonely perambulations, yet daylight put an end to all these evils; and he would have passed a pleasant life of it, in despite of the devil and all his works, if his path had not been crossed by a being that causes more perplexity to mortal man than ghosts, goblins, and the whole race of witches put together, and that was—a woman.

Among the musical disciples who assembled, one evening in each week, to receive his instructions in psalmody, was Katrina Van Tassel, the daughter and only child of a substantial Dutch farmer. She was a blooming lass of fresh eighteen; plump as a partridge; ripe and melting and rosy-cheeked as one of her father's peaches, and universally famed, not merely for her beauty, but her vast expectations. She was withal a little of a coquette, as might be perceived even in her dress, which was a mixture of ancient and modern fashions, as most suited to set off her charms. She wore the ornaments of pure yellow gold, which her great-great-grandmother had brought over from Saardam; the tempting stomacher of the olden time; and withal a provokingly short petticoat, to display the prettiest foot and ankle in the country round.

Ichabod Crane had a soft and foolish heart towards the sex; and it is not to be wondered at that so tempting a morsel soon found favor in his eyes; more especially after he had visited her in her paternal mansion. Old Baltus Van Tassel was a perfect picture of a thriving, contented, liberal-hearted farmer. He seldom, it is true, sent either his eyes or his thoughts beyond the boundaries of his own farm; but within those everything was snug, happy, and well-conditioned. He was satisfied with his wealth, but not proud of it; and piqued himself upon the hearty abundance rather than the style in which he lived. His stronghold was situated on the banks of the Hudson, in one of those green, sheltered, fertile nooks in which the Dutch farmers are so fond of nestling. A great elm-tree spread its broad branches over it; at the foot of which bubbled up a spring of the softest and sweetest water, in a little well, formed of a barrel; and then stole sparkling away through the grass, to a neighboring brook, that bubbled along among alders and dwarf willows. Hard by the farm-house was a vast barn, that might have served for a church; every window and crevice of which seemed bursting forth with the treasures of the farm; the flail was busily resounding within it from morning till night; swallows and martins skimmed twittering about the eaves; and rows of pigeons, some with one eye turned up, as if watching the weather, some with their heads under their wings, or buried in their bosoms, and others swelling, and cooing, and bowing about their dames, were enjoying the sunshine on the roof. Sleek unwieldly porkers were grunting in the repose and abundance of their pens; whence sallied forth, now and then, troops of sucking pigs, as if to snuff the air. A stately squadron of snowy geese were riding in an adjoining pond, convoying whole fleets of ducks; regiments of turkeys were gobbling through the farm-yard, and guinea fowls fretting about it, like ill-tempered housewives, with their peevish discontented cry. Before the barn-door strutted the gallant cock, that pattern of a husband, a warrior, and a fine gentleman, clapping his burnished wings, and crowing in the pride and gladness of his heart—sometimes tearing up the earth with his feet, and then generously calling his ever-hungry family of wives and children to enjoy the rich morsel which he had discovered.

The pedagogue's mouth watered, as he looked upon this sumptuous promise of luxurious winter fare. In his devouring mind's eye he pictured to himself every roasting-pig running about with a pudding in his belly,[8] and an apple in his mouth; the pigeons were snugly put to bed in a comfortable pie, and tucked in with a coverlet of crust; the geese were swimming in their own gravy; and the ducks pairing cosily in dishes, like snug married couples, with a decent competency of onion-sauce. In the porkers he saw carved out the future sleek side of bacon, and juicy relishing ham; not a turkey but he beheld daintily trussed up, with its gizzard under its wing, and, peradventure, a necklace of savory sausages; and even bright chanticleer himself lay sprawling on his back, in a side-dish, with uplifted claws, as if craving that quarter which his chivalrous spirit disdained to ask while living.

As the enraptured Ichabod fancied all this, and as he rolled his great green eyes over the fat meadow-lands, the rich fields of wheat, of rye, of buckwheat, and Indian corn, and the orchard burdened with ruddy fruit, which surrounded the warm tenement of Van Tassel, his heart yearned after the damsel who was to inherit these domains, and his imagination expanded with the idea how they might be readily turned into cash, and the money invested in immense tracts of wild land, and shingle palaces in the wilderness. Nay, his busy fancy already realized his hopes, and presented to him the blooming Katrina, with a whole family of children, mounted on the top of a wagon loaded with household trumpery, with pots and kettles dangling beneath; and he beheld himself bestriding a pacing mare, with a colt at her heels, setting out for Kentucky, Tennessee, or the Lord knows where.

When he entered the house, the conquest of his heart was complete. It was one of those spacious farm-houses, with high-ridged, but lowly-sloping roofs, built in the style handed down from the first Dutch settlers; the low projecting eaves forming a piazza along the front, capable of being closed up in bad weather. Under this were hung flails, harness, various utensils of husbandry, and nets for fishing in the neighboring river. Benches were built along the sides for summer use; and a great spinning-wheel at one end, and a churn at the other, showed the various uses to which this important porch might be devoted. From this piazza the wondering Ichabod entered the hall, which formed the centre of the mansion and the place of usual residence. Here, rows of resplendent pewter, ranged on a long dresser, dazzled his eyes. In one corner stood a huge bag of wool ready to be spun; in another a quantity of linsey-woolsey just from the loom; ears of Indian corn, and strings of dried apples and peaches, hung in gay festoons along the walls, mingled with the gaud of red peppers; and a door left ajar gave him a peep into the best parlor, where the claw-footed chairs and dark mahogany tables shone like mirrors; and irons, with their accompanying shovel and tongs, glistened from their covert of asparagus tops; mock-oranges and conch-shells decorated the mantel-piece; strings of various colored birds' eggs were suspended above it; a great ostrich egg was hung from the centre of the room, and a corner-cupboard, knowingly left open, displayed immense treasures of old silver and well-mended china.

From the moment Ichabod laid his eyes upon these regions of delight, the peace of his mind was at an end, and his only study was how to gain the affections of the peerless daughter of Van Tassel. In this enterprise, however, he had more real difficulties than generally fell to the lot of a knight-errant of yore, who seldom had anything but giants, enchanters, fiery dragons, and such like easily conquered adversaries, to contend with; and had to make his way merely through gates of iron and brass, and walls of adamant, to the castle-keep, where the lady of his heart was confined; all which he achieved as easily as a man would carve his way to the centre of a Christmas pie; and then the lady gave him her hand as a matter of course. Ichabod, on the contrary, had to win his way to the heart of a country coquette, beset with a labyrinth of whims and caprices, which were forever presenting new difficulties and impediments; and he had to encounter a host of fearful adversaries of real flesh and blood, the numerous rustic admirers, who beset every portal to her heart; keeping a watchful and angry eye upon each other, but ready to fly out in the common cause against any new competitor.

Among these the most formidable was a burly, roaring, roistering blade, of the name of Abraham, or, according to the Dutch abbreviation, Brom Van Brunt, the hero of the country round, which rang with his feats of strength and hardihood. He was broad-shouldered, and double-jointed, with short curly black hair, and a bluff but not unpleasant countenance, having a mingled air of fun and arrogance. From his Herculean frame and great powers of limb, he had received the nickname of BROM BONES, by which he was universally known. He was famed for great

8. **roasting-pig . . . belly:** Cf. *I Henry IV*, II.iv.498.

knowledge and skill in horsemanship, being as dexterous on horseback as a Tartar. He was foremost at all races and cockfights; and, with the ascendancy which bodily strength acquires in rustic life, was the umpire in all disputes, setting his hat on one side, and giving his decisions with an air and tone admitting of no gainsay or appeal. He was always ready for either a fight or a frolic; but had more mischief than ill-will in his composition; and, with all his overbearing roughness, there was a strong dash of waggish good-humor at bottom. He had three or four boon companions, who regarded him as their model, and at the head of whom he scoured the country, attending every scene of feud or merriment for miles round. In cold weather he was distinguished by a fur cap, surmounted with a flaunting fox's tail; and when the folks at a country gathering descried this well-known crest at a distance, whisking about among a squad of hard riders, they always stood by for a squall. Sometimes his crew would be heard dashing along past the farm-houses at midnight, with whoop and halloo, like a troop of Don Cossacks; and the old dames, startled out of their sleep, would listen for a moment till the hurry-scurry had clattered by, and then exclaim, "Ay, there goes Brom Bones and his gang!" The neighbors looked upon him with a mixture of awe, admiration, and good-will; and when any madcap prank, or rustic brawl, occurred in the vicinity, always shook their heads, and warranted Brom Bones was at the bottom of it.

This rantipole [9] hero had for some time singled out the blooming Katrina for the object of his uncouth gallantries; and though his amorous toyings were something like the gentle caresses and endearments of a bear, yet it was whispered that she did not altogether discourage his hopes. Certain it is, his advances were signals for rival candidates to retire, who felt no inclination to cross a lion in his amours; insomuch, that, when his horse was seen tied to Van Tassel's paling, on a Sunday night, a sure sign that his master was courting, or, as it is termed, "sparking," within, all other suitors passed by in despair, and carried the war into other quarters.

Such was the formidable rival with whom Ichabod Crane had to contend, and, considering all things, a stouter man than he would have shrunk from the competition, and a wiser man would have despaired. He had, however, a happy mixture of pliability and perseverance in his nature; he was in form and spirit like a supplejack—yielding, but tough; though he bent, he never broke; and though he bowed beneath the slightest pressure, yet, the moment it was away—jerk! he was as erect, and carried his head as high as ever.

To have taken the field openly against his rival would have been madness; for he was not a man to be thwarted in his amours, any more than that stormy lover, Achilles. Ichabod, therefore, made his advances in a quiet and gently insinuating manner. Under cover of his character of singing-master, he had made frequent visits at the farm-house; not that he had anything to apprehend from the meddlesome interference of parents, which is so often a stumbling-block in the path of lovers. Balt Van Tassel was an easy, indulgent soul; he loved his daughter better even than his pipe, and, like a reasonable man and an excellent father, let her have her way in everything. His notable little wife, too, had enough to do to attend to her housekeeping and manage her poultry; for, as she sagely observed, ducks and geese are foolish things, and must be looked after, but girls can take care of themselves. Thus while the busy dame bustled about the house, or plied her spinning-wheel at one end of the piazza, honest Balt would sit smoking his evening pipe at the other, watching the achievements of a little wooden warrior, who, armed with a sword in each hand, was most valiantly fighting the wind on the pinnacle of the barn. In the mean time, Ichabod would carry on his suit with the daughter by the side of the spring under the great elm, or sauntering along in the twilight,—that hour so favorable to the lover's eloquence.

I profess not to know how women's hearts are wooed and won. To me they have always been matters of riddle and admiration. Some seem to have but one vulnerable point, or door of access; while others have a thousand avenues, and may be captured in a thousand different ways. It is a great triumph of skill to gain the former, but a still greater proof of generalship to maintain possession of the latter, for the man must battle for his fortress at every door and window. He who wins a thousand common hearts is therefore entitled to some renown; but he who keeps undisputed sway over the heart of a coquette, is indeed a hero. Certain it is, this was not the case with the redoubtable Brom Bones; and from the moment Ichabod Crane made his advances, the interests of the former evidently declined; his horse was no longer seen tied at the palings on Sunday nights, and a deadly feud gradually arose between him and the preceptor of Sleepy Hollow.

Brom, who had a degree of rough chivalry in his nature, would fain have carried matters to open warfare, and have settled their pretensions to the

9. **rantipole:** wild, reckless.

lady according to the mode of those most concise and simple reasoners, the knights-errant of yore—by single combat; but Ichabod was too conscious of the superior might of his adversary to enter the lists against him: he had overheard a boast of Bones, that he would "double the schoolmaster up, and lay him on a shelf of his own schoolhouse;" and he was too wary to give him an opportunity. There was something extremely provoking in this obstinately pacific system; it left Brom no alternative but to draw upon the funds of rustic waggery in his disposition, and to play off boorish practical jokes upon his rival. Ichabod became the object of whimsical persecution to Bones and his gang of rough riders. They harried his hitherto peaceful domains; smoked out his singing-school, by stopping up the chimney; broke into the school-house at night, in spite of its formidable fastenings of withe and window-stakes, and turned everything topsy-turvy: so that the poor schoolmaster began to think all the witches in the country held their meetings there. But what was still more annoying, Brom took opportunities of turning him into ridicule in presence of his mistress, and had a scoundrel dog whom he taught to whine in the most ludicrous manner, and introduced as a rival of Ichabod's to instruct her in psalmody.

In this way matters went on for some time, without producing any material effect on the relative situation of the contending powers. On a fine autumnal afternoon, Ichabod, in pensive mood, sat enthroned on the lofty stool whence he usually watched all the concerns of his little literary realm. In his hand he swayed a ferule, that sceptre of despotic power; the birch of justice reposed on three nails, behind the throne, a constant terror to evil-doers; while on the desk before him might be seen sundry contraband articles and prohibited weapons, detected upon the persons of idle urchins; such as half-munched apples, popguns, whirligigs, fly-cages, and whole legions of rampant little paper game-cocks. Apparently there had been some appalling act of justice recently inflicted, for his scholars were all busily intent upon their books, or slyly whispering behind them with one eye kept upon the master; and a kind of buzzing stillness reigned throughout the school-room. It was suddenly interrupted by the appearance of a negro, in tow-cloth jacket and trousers, a round-crowned fragment of a hat, like the cap of Mercury, and mounted on the back of a ragged, wild, half-broken colt, which he managed with a rope by way of halter. He came clattering up to the school-door with an invitation to Ichabod to attend a merry-making or "quilting frolic," to be held that evening at Mynheer Van Tassel's; and having delivered his message with that air of importance, and effort at fine language, which a negro is apt to display on petty embassies of the kind, he dashed over the brook, and was seen scampering away up the Hollow, full of the importance and hurry of his mission.

All was now bustle and hubbub in the late quiet school-room. The scholars were hurried through their lessons, without stopping at trifles; those who were nimble skipped over half with impunity, and those who were tardy had a smart application now and then in the rear, to quicken their speed, or help them over a tall word. Books were flung aside without being put away on the shelves, inkstands were overturned, benches thrown down, and the whole school was turned loose an hour before the usual time, bursting forth like a legion of young imps, yelping and racketing about the green, in joy at their early emancipation.

The gallant Ichabod now spent at least an extra half-hour at his toilet, brushing and furbishing up his best and indeed only suit of rusty black, and arranging his looks by a bit of broken looking-glass, that hung up in the school-house. That he might make his appearance before his mistress in the true style of a cavalier, he borrowed a horse from the farmer with whom he was domiciliated, a choleric old Dutchman, of the name of Hans Van Ripper, and, thus gallantly mounted, issued forth, like a knight-errant in quest of adventures. But it is meet I should, in the true spirit of romantic story, give some account of the looks and equipments of my hero and his steed. The animal he bestrode was a broken-down plough-horse, that had outlived almost everything but his viciousness. He was gaunt and shagged, with a ewe neck and a head like a hammer; his rusty mane and tail were tangled and knotted with burrs; one eye had lost its pupil, and was glaring and spectral; but the other had the gleam of a genuine devil in it. Still he must have had fire and mettle in his day, if we may judge from the name he bore of Gunpowder. He had, in fact, been a favorite steed of his master's, the choleric Van Ripper, who was a furious rider, and had infused, very probably, some of his own spirit into the animal; for, old and broken-down as he looked, there was more of the lurking devil in him than in any young filly in the country.

Ichabod was a suitable figure for such a steed. He rode with short stirrups, which brought his knees nearly up to the pommel of the saddle; his sharp elbows stuck out like grasshoppers'; he carried his whip perpendicularly in his hand, like a sceptre, and, as his horse jogged on, the motion of his arms was not unlike the flapping of a pair of wings. A small wool hat rested on the top of his nose, for so his scanty strip of forehead might be called; and the skirts of his black coat fluttered out almost to the horse's tail. Such was the appearance of Ichabod and his steed, as they shambled out of the gate of Hans Van Ripper, and it was altogether such an apparition as is seldom to be met with in broad daylight.

It was, as I have said, a fine autumnal day, the sky was clear and serene, and nature wore that rich and golden livery which we always associate with the idea of abundance. The forests had put on their sober brown and yellow, while some trees of the tenderer kind had been nipped by the frosts into brilliant dyes of orange, purple, and scarlet. Streaming files of wild ducks began to make their appearance high in the air; the bark of the squirrel might be heard from the groves of beech and hickory nuts, and the pensive whistle of the quail at intervals from the neighboring stubble-field.

The small birds were taking their farewell banquets. In the fulness of their revelry, they fluttered, chirping and frolicking, from bush to bush, and tree to tree, capricious from the very profusion and variety around them. There was the honest cockrobin, the favorite game of stripling sportsmen, with its loud querulous notes; and the twittering blackbirds flying in sable clouds; and the golden-winged woodpecker, with his crimson crest, his broad black gorget, and splendid plumage; and the cedar-bird, with its red-tipt wings and yellow-tipt tail, and its little montero cap of feathers; and the blue jay, that noisy coxcomb, in his gay light-blue coat and white under-clothes, screaming and chattering, nodding and bobbing and bowing, and pretending to be on good terms with every songster of the grove.

As Ichabod jogged slowly on his way, his eye, ever open to every symptom of culinary abundance, ranged with delight over the treasures of jolly autumn. On all sides he beheld vast store of apples; some hanging in oppressive opulence on the trees; some gathered into baskets and barrels for the market; others heaped up in rich piles for the cider-press. Farther on he beheld great fields of Indian corn, with its golden ears peeping from their leafy coverts, and holding out the promise of cakes and hasty-pudding; and the yellow pumpkins lying beneath them, turning up their fair round bellies [10] to the sun, and giving ample prospects of the most luxurious of pies; and anon he passed the fragrant buckwheat fields, breathing the odor of the bee-hive, and as he beheld them, soft anticipations stole over his mind of dainty slapjacks, well buttered, and garnished with honey or treacle, by the delicate little dimpled hand of Katrina Van Tassel.

Thus feeding his mind with many sweet thoughts and "sugared suppositions," he journeyed along the sides of a range of hills which look out upon some of the goodliest scenes of the mighty Hudson. The sun gradually wheeled his broad disk down into the west. The wide bosom of the Tappan Zee lay motionless and glassy, excepting that here and there a gentle undulation waved and prolonged the blue shadow of the distant mountain. A few amber clouds floated in the sky, without a breath of air to move them. The horizon was of a fine golden tint, changing gradually into a pure apple-green, and from that into the deep blue of the mid-heaven. A slanting ray lingered on the woody crests of the precipices that overhung some parts of the river, giving greater depth to the dark-gray and purple of their rocky sides. A sloop was loitering in the distance, dropping slowly down with the tide, her sail hanging uselessly against the mast; and as the reflection of the sky gleamed along the still water, it seemed as if the vessel was suspended in the air.

It was toward evening that Ichabod arrived at the castle of the Heer Van Tassel, which he found thronged with the pride and flower of the adjacent country. Old farmers, a spare leathern-faced race, in homespun coats and breeches, blue stockings, huge shoes, and magnificent pewter buckles. Their brisk withered little dames, in close crimped caps, long-waisted shortgowns, homespun petticoats, with scissors and pincushions, and gay calico pockets hanging on the outside. Buxom lasses, almost as antiquated as their mothers, excepting where a straw hat, a fine ribbon, or perhaps a white frock, gave symptoms of city innovation. The sons, in short square-skirted coats with rows of stupendous brass buttons, and their hair generally queued in the fashion of the times, especially if they could procure an eel-skin for the purpose, it being esteemed, throughout the country, as a potent nourisher and strengthener of the hair.

Brom Bones, however, was the hero of the scene, having come to the gathering on his favorite steed, Daredevil, a creature, like himself, full of mettle and mischief, and which no one but himself could manage. He was, in fact, noted for preferring vicious animals, given to all kinds of tricks, which kept the rider in constant risk of his neck, for he held a tractable well-broken horse as unworthy of a lad of spirit.

Fain would I pause to dwell upon the world of charms that burst upon the enraptured gaze of my hero, as he entered the state parlor of Van Tas-

10. **fair round bellies:** Cf. *As You Like It*, II.vii.154.

sel's mansion. Not those of the bevy of buxom lasses, with their luxurious display of red and white; but the ample charms of a genuine Dutch country tea-table, in the sumptuous time of autumn. Such heaped-up platters of cakes of various and almost indescribable kinds, known only to experienced Dutch housewives! There was the doughty doughnut, the tenderer oly koek, and the crisp and crumbling cruller; sweet cakes and short cakes, ginger-cakes and honey-cakes, and the whole family of cakes. And then there were apple-pies and peach-pies and pumpkin-pies; besides slices of ham and smoked beef; and moreover delectable dishes of preserved plums, and peaches, and pears, and quinces; not to mention broiled shad and roasted chickens; together with bowls of milk and cream, all mingled higgledy-piggledy, pretty much as I have enumerated them, with the motherly tea-pot sending up its clouds of vapor from the midst—Heaven bless the mark! I want breath and time to discuss this banquet as it deserves, and am too eager to get on with my story. Happily, Ichabod Crane was not in so great a hurry as his historian, but did ample justice to every dainty.

He was a kind and thankful creature, whose heart dilated in proportion as his skin was filled with good cheer; and whose spirits rose with eating as some men's do with drink. He could not help, too, rolling his large eyes round him as he ate, and chuckling with the possibility that he might one day be lord of all this scene of almost unimaginable luxury and splendor. Then, he thought, how soon he'd turn his back upon the old school-house; snap his fingers in the face of Hans Van Ripper, and every other niggardly patron, and kick any itinerant pedagogue out-of-doors that should dare to call him comrade!

Old Baltus Van Tassel moved about among his guests with a face dilated with content and good-humor, round and jolly as the harvest-moon. His hospitable attentions were brief, but expressive, being confined to a shake of the hand, a slap on the shoulder, a loud laugh, and a pressing invitation to "fall to, and help themselves."

And now the sound of the music from the common room, or hall, summoned to the dance. The musician was an old gray-headed negro, who had been the itinerant orchestra of the neighborhood for more than half a century. His instrument was as old and battered as himself. The greater part of the time he scraped on two or three strings accompanying every movement of the bow with a motion of the head; bowing almost to the ground and stamping with his foot whenever a fresh couple were to start.

Ichabod prided himself upon his dancing as much as upon his vocal powers. Not a limb, not a fibre about him was idle; and to have seen his loosely hung frame in full motion, and clattering about the room, you would have thought Saint Vitus himself, that blessed patron of the dance, was figuring before you in person. He was the admiration of all the negroes; who, having gathered, of all ages and sizes, from the farm and the neighborhood, stood forming a pyramid of shining black faces at every door and window, gazing with delight at the scene, rolling their white eyeballs, and showing grinning rows of ivory from ear to ear. How could the flogger of urchins be otherwise than animated and joyous? the lady of his heart was his partner in the dance, and smiling graciously in reply to all his amorous oglings; while Brom Bones, sorely smitten with love and jealousy, sat brooding by himself in one corner.

When the dance was at an end, Ichabod was attracted to a knot of the sager folks, who, with old Van Tassel, sat smoking at one end of the piazza, gossiping over former times, and drawing out long stories about the war.

This neighborhood, at the time of which I am speaking, was one of those highly favored places which abound with chronicle and great men. The British and American line had run near it during the war; it had, therefore, been the scene of marauding, and infested with refugees, cow-boys,[11] and all kinds of border chivalry. Just sufficient time had elapsed to enable each story-teller to dress up his tale with a little becoming fiction, and, in the indistinctness of his recollection, to make himself the hero of every exploit.

There was the story of Doffue Martling, a large blue-bearded Dutchman, who had nearly taken a British frigate with an old iron nine-pounder from a mud breastwork, only that his gun burst at the sixth discharge. And there was an old gentleman who shall be nameless, being too rich a mynheer to be lightly mentioned, who, in the battle of Whiteplains, being an excellent master of defence, parried a musket-ball with a small sword, insomuch that he absolutely felt it whiz round the blade, and glance off at the hilt; in proof of which he was ready at any time to show the sword, with the hilt a little bent. There were several more that had been equally great in the field, not one of whom but was persuaded that he had a considerable hand in bringing the war to a happy termination.

But all these were nothing to the tales of ghosts and apparitions that succeeded. The neighborhood is rich in legendary treasures of the kind. Local

11. **cow-boys:** guerilla troops in the region during the American Revolution.

tales and superstitions thrive best in these sheltered long-settled retreats; but are trampled underfoot by the shifting throng that forms the population of most of our country places. Besides, there is no encouragement for ghosts in most of our villages, for they have scarcely had time to finish their first nap, and turn themselves in their graves, before their surviving friends have travelled away from the neighborhood; so that when they turn out at night to walk their rounds, they have no acquaintance left to call upon. This is perhaps the reason why we so seldom hear of ghosts, except in our long-established Dutch communities.

The immediate cause, however, of the prevalence of supernatural stories in these parts was doubtless owing to the vicinity of Sleepy Hollow. There was a contagion in the very air that blew from that haunted region; it breathed forth an atmosphere of dreams and fancies infecting all the land. Several of the Sleepy Hollow people were present at Van Tassel's, and, as usual, were doling out their wild and wonderful legends. Many dismal tales were told about funeral trains, and mourning cries and wailings heard and seen about the great tree where the unfortunate Major André [12] was taken, and which stood in the neighborhood. Some mention was made also of the woman in white, that haunted the dark glen at Raven Rock, and was often heard to shriek on winter nights before a storm, having perished there in the snow. The chief part of the stories, however, turned upon the favorite spectre of Sleepy Hollow, the headless horseman, who had been heard several times of late, patrolling the country; and, it was said, tethered his horse nightly among the graves in the churchyard.

The sequestered situation of this church seems always to have made it a favorite haunt of troubled spirits. It stands on a knoll, surrounded by locust-trees and lofty elms, from among which its decent whitewashed walls shine modestly forth, like Christian purity beaming through the shades of retirement. A gentle slope descends from it to a silver sheet of water, bordered by high trees, between which, peeps may be caught at the blue hills of the Hudson. To look upon its grass-grown yard, where the sunbeams seem to sleep so quietly, one would think that there at least the dead might rest in peace. On one side of the church extends a wide woody dell, along which raves a large brook among broken rocks and trunks of fallen trees. Over a deep black part of the stream, not far from the church, was formerly thrown a wooden bridge; the road that led to it, and the bridge itself, were thickly shaded by overhanging trees, which cast a gloom about it, even in the daytime, but occasioned a fearful darkness at night. This was one of the favorite haunts of the headless horseman; and the place where he was most frequently encountered. The tale was told of old Brouwer, a most heretical disbeliever in ghosts, how he met the horseman returning from his foray into Sleepy Hollow, and was obliged to get up behind him; how they galloped over bush and brake, over hill and swamp, until they reached the bridge; when the horseman suddenly turned into a skeleton, threw old Brouwer into the brook, and sprang away over the tree-tops with a clap of thunder.

This story was immediately matched by a thrice marvellous adventure of Brom Bones, who made light of the galloping Hessian as an arrant jockey. He affirmed that, on returning one night from the neighboring village of Sing Sing, he had been overtaken by this midnight trooper; that he had offered to race with him for a bowl of punch, and should have won it too, for Daredevil beat the goblin horse all hollow, but, just as they came to the church-bridge, the Hessian bolted, and vanished in a flash of fire.

All these tales, told in that drowsy undertone with which men talk in the dark, the countenances of the listeners only now and then receiving a casual gleam from the glare of a pipe, sank deep in the mind of Ichabod. He repaid them in kind with large extracts from his invaluable author, Cotton Mather, and added many marvellous events that had taken place in his native State of Connecticut, and fearful sights which he had seen in his nightly walks about the Sleepy Hollow.

The revel now gradually broke up. The old farmers gathered together their families in their wagons, and were heard for some time rattling along the hollow roads, and over the distant hills. Some of the damsels mounted on pillions behind their favorite swains, and their light-hearted laughter, mingling with the clatter of hoofs, echoed along the silent woodlands, sounding fainter and fainter until they gradually died away—and the late scene of noise and frolic was all silent and deserted. Ichabod only lingered behind, according to the custom of country lovers, to have a *tête-à-tête* with the heiress, fully convinced that he was now on the high road to success. What passed at this interview I will not pretend to say, for in fact I do not know. Something, however, I fear me, must have gone wrong, for he certainly sallied forth, after no very great interval, with an air quite desolate and chopfallen.—Oh, these women! these women! Could that girl have been play-

12. **André:** British officer executed as a spy in the Revolution.

ing off any of her coquettish tricks?—Was her encouragement of the poor pedagogue all a mere sham to secure her conquest of his rival?—Heaven only knows, not I!—Let it suffice to say, Ichabod stole forth with the air of one who had been sacking a henroost, rather than a fair lady's heart. Without looking to the right or left to notice the scene of rural wealth on which he had so often gloated, he went straight to the stable, and with several hearty cuffs and kicks, roused his steed most uncourteously from the comfortable quarters in which he was soundly sleeping, dreaming of mountains of corn and oats, and whole valleys of timothy and clover.

It was the very witching time of night [13] that Ichabod, heavy-hearted and crestfallen, pursued his travel homewards, along the sides of the lofty hills which rise above Tarry Town, and which he had traversed so cheerily in the afternoon. The hour was as dismal as himself. Far below him, the Tappan Zee spread its dusky and indistinct waste of waters, with here and there the tall mast of a sloop riding quietly at anchor under the land. In the dead hush of midnight he could even hear the barking of the watch-dog from the opposite shore of the Hudson; but it was so vague and faint as only to give an idea of his distance from this faithful companion of man. Now and then, too, the long-drawn crowing of a cock, accidentally awakened, would sound far, far off, from some farmhouse away among the hills—but it was like a dreaming sound in his ear. No signs of life occurred near him, but occasionally the melancholy chirp of a cricket, or perhaps the guttural twang of a bull-frog, from a neighboring marsh, as if sleeping uncomfortably, and turning suddenly in his bed.

All the stories of ghosts and goblins that he had heard in the afternoon, now came crowding upon his recollection. The night grew darker and darker; the stars seemed to sink deeper in the sky, and driving clouds occasionally hid them from his sight. He had never felt so lonely and dismal. He was, moreover, approaching the very place where many of the scenes of the ghost-stories had been laid. In the centre of the road stood an enormous tulip-tree, which towered like a giant above all the other trees of the neighborhood, and formed a kind of landmark. Its limbs were gnarled, and fantastic, large enough to form trunks for ordinary trees, twisting down almost to the earth, and rising again into the air. It was connected with the tragical story of the unfortunate André, who had been taken prisoner hard by; and was universally known by the name of Major André's tree. The common people regarded it with a mixture of respect and superstition, partly out of sympathy for the fate of its ill-starred namesake, and partly from the tales of strange sights and doleful lamentations told concerning it.

As Ichabod approached this fearful tree, he began to whistle: he thought his whistle was answered,—it was but a blast sweeping sharply through the dry branches. As he approached a little nearer, he thought he saw something white, hanging in the midst of the tree,—he paused and ceased whistling; but on looking more narrowly, perceived that it was a place where the tree had been scathed by lightning, and the white wood laid bare. Suddenly he heard a groan,—his teeth chattered and his knees smote against the saddle: it was but the rubbing of one huge bough upon another, as they were swayed about by the breeze. He passed the tree in safety; but new perils lay before him.

About two hundred yards from the tree a small brook crossed the road, and ran into a marshy and thickly wooded glen, known by the name of Wiley's swamp. A few rough logs, laid side by side, served for a bridge over this stream. On that side of the road where the brook entered the wood, a group of oaks and chestnuts, matted thick with wild grape-vines, threw a cavernous gloom over it. To pass this bridge was the severest trial. It was at this identical spot that the unfortunate André was captured, and under the covert of those chestnuts and vines were the sturdy yeomen concealed who surprised him. This has ever since been considered a haunted stream, and fearful are the feelings of the school boy who has to pass it alone after dark.

As he approached the stream, his heart began to thump; he summoned up, however, all his resolution, gave his horse half a score of kicks in the ribs, and attempted to dash briskly across the bridge; but instead of starting forward, the perverse old animal made a lateral movement, and ran broadside against the fence. Ichabod, whose fears increased with the delay, jerked the reins on the other side, and kicked lustily with the contrary foot: it was all in vain; his steed started, it is true, but it was only to plunge to the opposite side of the road into a thicket of brambles and alder bushes. The schoolmaster now bestowed both whip and heel upon the starveling ribs of old Gunpowder, who dashed forward, snuffling and snorting, but came to a stand just by the bridge, with a suddenness that had nearly sent his rider sprawling over his head. Just at this moment a plashy tramp by the side of the bridge caught the sensitive ear of Ichabod. In the dark shadow of the

13. **very . . . night:** from *Hamlet*, III.ii.406.

grove, on the margin of the brook, he beheld something huge, misshapen, black, and towering. It stirred not, but seemed gathered up in the gloom, like some gigantic monster ready to spring upon the traveller.

The hair of the affrighted pedagogue rose upon his head with terror. What was to be done? To turn and fly was now too late; and besides, what chance was there of escaping ghost or goblin, if such it was, which could ride upon the wings of the wind? Summoning up, therefore, a show of courage, he demanded in stammering accents—"Who are you?" He received no reply. He repeated his demand in a still more agitated voice. Still there was no answer. Once more he cudgelled the sides of the inflexible Gunpowder, and, shutting his eyes, broke forth with involuntary fervor into a psalm-tune. Just then the shadowy object of alarm put itself in motion, and, with a scramble and a bound, stood at once in the middle of the road. Though the night was dark and dismal, yet the form of the unknown might now in some degree be ascertained. He appeared to be a horseman of large dimensions, and mounted on a black horse of powerful frame. He made no offer of molestation or sociability, but kept aloof on one side of the road, jogging along on the blind side of old Gunpowder, who had now got over his fright and waywardness.

Ichabod, who had no relish for this strange midnight companion, and bethought himself of the adventure of Brom Bones with the Galloping Hessian, now quickened his steed, in hopes of leaving him behind. The stranger, however, quickened his horse to an equal pace. Ichabod pulled up, and fell into a walk, thinking to lag behind,—the other did the same. His heart began to sink within him; he endeavored to resume his psalm-tune, but his parched tongue clove to the roof of his mouth, and he could not utter a stave. There was something in the moody and dogged silence of this pertinacious companion, that was mysterious and appalling. It was soon fearfully accounted for. On mounting a rising ground, which brought the figure of his fellow-traveller in relief against the sky, gigantic in height, and muffled in a cloak, Ichabod was horror-struck, on perceiving that he was headless!—but his horror was still more increased, on observing that the head, which should have rested on his shoulders, was carried before him on the pommel of the saddle: his terror rose to desperation; he rained a shower of kicks and blows upon Gunpowder, hoping, by a sudden movement, to give his companion the slip,—but the spectre started full jump with him. Away then they dashed, through thick and thin; stones flying, and sparks flashing at every bound. Ichabod's flimsy garments fluttered in the air, as he stretched his long lank body away over his horse's head, in the eagerness of his flight.

They had now reached the road which turns off to Sleepy Hollow; but Gunpowder, who seemed possessed with a demon, instead of keeping up it, made an opposite turn, and plunged headlong downhill to the left. This road leads through a sandy hollow, shaded by trees for about a quarter of a mile, where it crosses the bridge famous in goblin story, and just beyond swells the green knoll on which stands the whitewashed church.

As yet the panic of the steed had given his unskilful rider an apparent advantage in the chase; but just as he had got half-way through the hollow, the girths of the saddle gave way, and he felt it slipping from under him. He seized it by the pommel, and endeavored to hold it firm, but in vain; and had just time to save himself by clasping old Gunpowder round the neck, when the saddle fell to the earth, and he heard it trampled underfoot by his pursuer. For a moment the terror of Hans Van Ripper's wrath passed across his mind—for it was his Sunday saddle; but this was no time for petty fears; the goblin was hard on his haunches; and (unskilful rider that he was!) he had much ado to maintain his seat; sometimes slipping on one side, sometimes on another, and sometimes jolted on the high ridge of his horse's backbone, with a violence that he verily feared would cleave him asunder.

An opening in the trees now cheered him with the hopes that the church-bridge was at hand. The wavering reflection of a silver star in the bosom of the brook told him that he was not mistaken. He saw the walls of the church dimly glaring under the trees beyond. He recollected the place where Brom Bones's ghostly competitor had disappeared. "If I can but reach that bridge," thought Ichabod, "I am safe." Just then he heard the black steed panting and blowing close behind him; he even fancied that he felt his hot breath. Another convulsive kick in the ribs, and old Gunpowder sprang upon the bridge; he thundered over the resounding planks; he gained the opposite side; and now Ichabod cast a look behind to see if his pursuer should vanish, according to rule, in a flash of fire and brimstone. Just then he saw the goblin rising in his stirrups, and in the very act of hurling his head at him. Ichabod endeavored to dodge the horrible missile, but too late. It encountered his cranium with a tremendous crash,—he was tumbled headlong into the dust, and Gunpowder, the black steed, and the goblin rider, passed by like a whirlwind.

The next morning the old horse was found without his saddle, and with the bridle under his feet, soberly cropping the grass at his master's gate. Ichabod did not make his appearance at breakfast;—dinner-hour came, but no Ichabod. The boys assembled at the school-house, and strolled idly about the banks of the brook; but no schoolmaster. Hans Van Ripper now began to feel some uneasiness about the fate of poor Ichabod, and his saddle. An inquiry was set on foot, and after diligent investigation they came upon his traces. In one part of the road leading to the church was found the saddle trampled in the dirt; the tracks of horses' hoofs deeply dented in the road, and evidently at furious speed, were traced to the bridge, beyond which, on the bank of a broad part of the brook, where the water ran deep and black, was found the hat of the unfortunate Ichabod, and close beside it a shattered pumpkin.

The brook was searched, but the body of the schoolmaster was not to be discovered. Hans Van Ripper, as executor of his estate, examined the bundle which contained all his worldly effects. They consisted of two shirts and a half; two stocks for the neck; a pair or two of worsted stockings; an old pair of corduroy small-clothes; a rusty razor; a book of psalm-tunes, full of dogs' ears, and a broken pitchpipe. As to the books and furniture of the school-house, they belonged to the community, excepting Cotton Mather's *History of Witchcraft,* a *New England Almanac,* and a book of dreams and fortune-telling; in which last was a sheet of foolscap much scribbled and blotted in several fruitless attempts to make a copy of verses in honor of the heiress of Van Tassel. These magic books and the poetic scrawl were forthwith consigned to the flames by Hans Van Ripper; who from that time forward determined to send his children no more to school; observing, that he never knew any good come of this same reading and writing. Whatever money the schoolmaster possessed, and he had received his quarter's pay but a day or two before, he must have had about his person at the time of his disappearance.

The mysterious event caused much speculation at the church on the following Sunday. Knots of gazers and gossips were collected in the churchyard, at the bridge, and at the spot where the hat and pumpkin had been found. The stories of Brouwer, of Bones, and a whole budget of others, were called to mind; and when they had diligently considered them all, and compared them with the symptoms of the present case, they shook their heads, and came to the conclusion that Ichabod had been carried off by the Galloping Hessian. As he was a bachelor, and in nobody's debt, nobody troubled his head any more about him. The school was removed to a different quarter of the Hollow, and another pedagogue reigned in his stead.

It is true, an old farmer, who had been down to New York on a visit several years after, and from whom this account of the ghostly adventure was received, brought home the intelligence that Ichabod Crane was still alive; that he had left the neighborhood, partly through fear of the goblin and Hans Van Ripper, and partly in mortification at having been suddenly dismissed by the heiress; that he had changed his quarters to a distant part of the country; had kept school and studied law at the same time, had been admitted to the bar, turned politician, electioneered, written for the newspapers, and finally had been made a justice of the Ten Pound Court. Brom Bones too, who shortly after his rival's disappearance conducted the blooming Katrina in triumph to the altar, was observed to look exceeding knowing whenever the story of Ichabod was related, and always burst into a hearty laugh at the mention of the pumpkin; which led some to suspect that he knew more about the matter than he chose to tell.

The old country wives, however, who are the best judges of these matters, maintain to this day that Ichabod was spirited away by supernatural means; and it is a favorite story often told about the neighborhood round the winter evening fire. The bridge became more than ever an object of superstitious awe, and that may be the reason why the road has been altered of late years, so as to approach the church by the border of the mill-pond. The school-house, being deserted, soon fell to decay, and was reported to be haunted by the ghost of the unfortunate pedagogue; and the ploughboy, loitering homeward of a still summer evening, has often fancied his voice at a distance, chanting a melancholy psalm-tune among the tranquil solitudes of Sleepy Hollow.

POSTSCRIPT,

Found in the Handwriting of Mr. Knickerbocker

The preceding Tale is given, almost in the precise words in which I heard it related at a Corporation meeting of the ancient city of Manhattoes, at which were present many of its sagest and most illustrious burghers. The narrator was a pleasant, shabby, gentlemanly old fellow, in pepper-and-salt clothes, with a sadly humorous face; and one whom I strongly suspected of being poor,—he made such efforts to be entertaining. When his story was concluded, there was much laughter and approbation, particularly from two or three deputy aldermen, who had been asleep the greater part of the time.

There was, however, one tall, dry-looking old gentleman, with beetling eyebrows, who maintained a grave and rather severe face throughout: now and then folding his arms, inclining his head, and looking down upon the floor, as if turning a doubt over in his mind. He was one of your wary men, who never laugh, but upon good grounds—when they have reason and the law on their side. When the mirth of the rest of the company had subsided and silence was restored, he leaned one arm on the elbow of his chair, and, sticking the other akimbo, demanded, with a slight but exceedingly sage motion of the head, and contraction of the brow, what was the moral of the story, and what it went to prove?

The story-teller, who was just putting a glass of wine to his lips, as a refreshment after his toils, paused for a moment, looked at his inquirer with an air of infinite deference, and, lowering the glass slowly to the table, observed, that the story was intended most logically to prove:—

"That there is no situation in life but has its advantages and pleasures—provided we will but take a joke as we find it:

"That, therefore, he that runs races with goblin troopers is likely to have rough riding of it.

"Ergo, for a country schoolmaster to be refused the hand of a Dutch heiress, is a certain step to high preferment in the state."

The cautious old gentleman knit his brows tenfold closer after this explanation, being sorely puzzled by the ratiocination of the syllogism; while, methought, the one in pepper-and-salt eyed him with something of a triumphant leer. At length he observed, that all this was very well, but still he thought the story a little on the extravagant—there were one or two points on which he had his doubts.

"Faith, sir," replied the story-teller, "as to that matter, I don't believe one half of it myself."

D. K.

1820, 1848

FROM

BRACEBRIDGE HALL

THE STOUT GENTLEMAN

A STAGE-COACH ROMANCE

¶ OF THE narrator of this story Crayon says, "He was a thin, pale, weazen-faced man, extremely nervous," who "offered to give some account of a mysterious personage . . . whom he thought fully entitled to being classed with the Man with the Iron Mask." This account, Crayon adds, "has in it all the elements of that mysterious and romantic narrative so greatly sought after at the present day."

I'll cross it, though it blast me!
Hamlet [1]

IT WAS a rainy Sunday in the gloomy month of November. I had been detained, in the course of a journey, by a slight indisposition, from which I was recovering; but was still feverish, and obliged to keep within doors all day, at an inn of the small town of Derby. A wet Sunday in a country inn!—whoever has had the luck to experience one can alone judge of my situation. The rain pattered against the casements; the bells tolled for church with a melancholy sound. I went to the windows in quest of something to amuse the eye; but it seemed as if I had been placed completely out of the reach of all amusement. The windows of my bedroom looked out among tiled roofs and stacks of chimneys, while those of my sitting-room commanded a full view of the stable-yard. I know of nothing more calculated to make a man sick of this world than a stable-yard on a rainy day. The place was littered with wet straw that had been kicked about by travellers and stable-boys. In one corner was a stagnant pool of water, surrounding an island of muck; there were several half-drowned fowls crowded together under a cart, among which was a miserable, crestfallen cock, drenched out of all life and spirit; his drooping tail matted, as it were, into a single feather, along which the water trickled from his back; near the cart was a half-dozing cow, chewing the cud, and standing patiently to be rained on, with wreaths of vapor rising from her reeking hide; a wall-eyed horse, tired of the loneliness of the stable, was poking his spectral head out of a window, with the rain dripping on it from the eaves; an unhappy cur, chained to a dog-house hard by, uttered something, every now and then, between a bark and a yelp; a drab of a kitchen-wench tramped backwards and forwards through the yard in pattens, looking as sulky as the weather itself; everything, in short, was comfortless and forlorn, excepting a crew of hardened ducks, assembled like boon companions round a puddle, and making a riotous noise over their liquor.

I was lonely and listless, and wanted amusement. My room soon became insupportable. I abandoned it, and sought what is technically called the travellers'-room. This is a public room set apart at most inns for the accommodation of a class of wayfarers called travellers, or riders; a kind of commercial knights-errant, who are in-

THE STOUT GENTLEMAN. 1. *Hamlet:* I.i.127.

cessantly scouring the kingdom in gigs, on horseback, or by coach. They are the only successors that I know of at the present day to the knights-errant of yore. They lead the same kind of roving, adventurous life, only changing the lance for a driving-whip, the buckler for a pattern-card, and the coat of mail for an upper Benjamin.[2] Instead of vindicating the charms of peerless beauty, they rove about, spreading the fame and standing of some substantial tradesman, or manufacturer, and are ready at any time to bargain in his name; it being the fashion nowadays to trade, instead of fight, with one another. As the room of the hostel, in the good old fighting-times, would be hung round at night with the armor of way-worn warriors, such as coats of mail, falchions, and yawning helmets, so the travellers'-room is garnished with the harnessing of their successors, with box-coats, whips of all kinds, spurs, gaiters, and oil-cloth covered hats.

I was in hopes of finding some of these worthies to talk with, but was disappointed. There were, indeed, two or three in the room; but I could make nothing of them. One was just finishing his breakfast, quarrelling with his bread and butter, and huffing the waiter; another buttoned on a pair of gaiters, with many execrations at Boots for not having cleaned his shoes well; a third sat drumming on the table with his fingers and looking at the rain as it streamed down the window-glass; they all appeared infected by the weather, and disappeared, one after the other, without exchanging a word.

I sauntered to the window, and stood gazing at the people, picking their way to church, with petticoats hoisted midleg high, and dripping umbrellas. The bell ceased to toll, and the streets became silent. I then amused myself with watching the daughters of a tradesman opposite; who, being confined to the house for fear of wetting their Sunday finery, played off their charms at the front windows, to fascinate the chance tenants of the inn. They at length were summoned away by a vigilant vinegar-faced mother, and I had nothing further from without to amuse me.

What was I to do to pass away the long-lived day? I was sadly nervous and lonely; and everything about an inn seems calculated to make a dull day ten times duller. Old newspapers, smelling of beer and tobacco-smoke, and which I had already read half a dozen times. Good-for-nothing books, that were worse than rainy weather. I bored myself to death with an old volume of the Lady's Magazine. I read all the commonplace names of ambitious travellers scrawled on the panes of glass; the eternal families of the Smiths, and the Browns, and the Jacksons, and the Johnsons, and all the other sons; and I deciphered several scraps of fatiguing inn-window poetry which I have met with in all parts of the world.

The day continued lowering and gloomy; the slovenly, ragged, spongy cloud drifted heavily along; there was no variety even in the rain: it was one dull, continued, monotonous patter—patter—patter, excepting that now and then I was enlivened by the idea of a brisk shower, from the rattling of the drops upon a passing umbrella.

It was quite *refreshing* (if I may be allowed a hackneyed phrase of the day) when, in the course of the morning, a horn blew, and a stage-coach whirled through the street, with outside passengers stuck all over it, cowering under cotton umbrellas, and seethed together, and reeking with the steams of wet box-coats and upper Benajmins.

The sound brought out from their lurking-places a crew of vagabond boys, and vagabond dogs, and the carroty-headed hostler, and that nondescript animal ycleped Boots, and all the other vagabond race that infest the purlieus of an inn; but the bustle was transient; the coach again whirled on its way; and boy and dog, and hostler and Boots, all slunk back again to their holes; the street again became silent, and the rain continued to rain on. In fact, there was no hope of its clearing up; the barometer pointed to rainy weather; mine hostess's tortoise-shell cat sat by the fire washing her face, and rubbing her paws over her ears; and, on referring to the Almanac, I found a direful prediction stretching from the top of the page to the bottom through the whole month, "expect—much—rain—about—this—time!"

I was dreadfully hipped. The hours seemed as if they would never creep by. The very ticking of the clock became irksome. At length the stillness of the house was interrupted by the ringing of a bell. Shortly after I heard the voice of a waiter at the bar: "The stout gentleman in No. 13 wants his breakfast. Tea and bread and butter, with ham and eggs; the eggs not to be too much done."

In such a situation as mine, every incident is of importance. Here was a subject of speculation presented to my mind, and ample exercise for my imagination. I am prone to paint pictures to myself, and on this occasion I had some materials to work upon. Had the guest up-stairs been mentioned as Mr. Smith, or Mr. Brown, or Mr. Jackson, or Mr. Johnson, or merely as "the gentleman in No. 13," it would have been a perfect blank to me. I should have thought nothing of it; but "The stout gentleman!"—the very name had something

2. **upper Benjamin:** an overcoat.

in it of the picturesque. It at once gave the size; it embodied the personage to my mind's eye, and my fancy did the rest.

He was stout, or, as some term it, lusty; in all probability, therefore, he was advanced in life, some people expanding as they grow old. By his breakfasting rather late, and in his own room, he must be a man accustomed to live at his ease, and above the necessity of early rising; no doubt a round, rosy, lusty old gentleman.

There was another violent ringing. The stout gentleman was impatient for his breakfast. He was evidently a man of importance; "well to do in the world;" accustomed to be promptly waited upon; of a keen appetite, and a little cross when hungry; "perhaps," thought I, "he may be some London Alderman; or who knows but he may be a Member of Parliament?"

The breakfast was sent up, and there was a short interval of silence; he was, doubtless, making the tea. Presently there was a violent ringing; and before it could be answered, another ringing still more violent. "Bless me! what a choleric old gentleman!" The waiter came down in a huff. The butter was rancid, the eggs were overdone, the ham was too salt;—the stout gentleman was evidently nice in his eating; one of those who eat and growl, and keep the waiter on the trot, and live in a state militant with the household.

The hostess got into a fume. I should observe that she was a brisk, coquettish woman; a little of a shrew, and something of a slammerkin,[3] but very pretty withal; with a nincompoop for a husband, as shrews are apt to have. She rated the servants roundly for their negligence in sending up so bad a breakfast, but said not a word against the stout gentleman; by which I clearly perceived that he must be a man of consequence, entitled to make a noise and to give trouble at a country inn. Other eggs, and ham, and bread and butter were sent up. They appeared to be more graciously received; at least there was no further complaint.

I had not made many turns about the travellers'-room, when there was another ringing. Shortly afterwards there was a stir and an inquest about the house. The stout gentleman wanted the Times or the Chronicle newspaper. I set him down, therefore, for a Whig; or rather, from his being so absolute and lordly where he had a chance, I suspected him of being a Radical. Hunt, I had heard, was a large man; "who knows," thought I, "but it is Hunt himself!" [4]

My curiosity began to be awakened. I inquired of the waiter who was this stout gentleman that was making all this stir; but I could get no information: nobody seemed to know his name. The landlords of bustling inns seldom trouble their heads about the names or occupations of their transient guests. The color of a coat, the shape or size of the person, is enough to suggest a travelling name. It is either the tall gentleman, or the short gentleman, or the gentleman in black, or the gentleman in snuff-color; or, as in the present instance, the stout gentleman. A designation of the kind once hit on, answers every purpose, and saves all further inquiry.

Rain—rain—rain! pitiless, ceaseless rain! No such thing as putting a foot out of doors, and no occupation nor amusement within. By and by I heard some one walking overhead. It was in the stout gentleman's room. He evidently was a large man by the heaviness of his tread; and an old man from his wearing such creaking soles. "He is doubtless," thought I, "some rich old square-toes of regular habits, and is now taking exercise after breakfast."

I now read all the advertisements of coaches and hotels that were stuck about the mantelpiece. The Lady's Magazine had become an abomination to me; it was as tedious as the day itself. I wandered out, not knowing what to do, and ascended again to my room. I had not been there long, when there was a squall from a neighboring bedroom. A door opened and slammed violently; a chamber-maid, that I had remarked for having a ruddy, good-humored face, went down stairs in a violent flurry. The stout gentleman had been rude to her!

This sent a whole host of my deductions to the deuce in a moment. This unknown personage could not be an old gentleman; for old gentlemen are not apt to be so obstreperous to chambermaids. He could not be a young gentleman; for young gentlemen are not apt to inspire such indignation. He must be a middle-aged man, and confounded ugly into the bargain, or the girl would not have taken the matter in such terrible dudgeon. I confess I was sorely puzzled.

In a few minutes I heard the voice of my landlady. I caught a glance of her as she came tramping up-stairs,—her face glowing, her cap flaring, her tongue wagging the whole way. "She'd have no such doings in her house, she'd warrant. If gentlemen did spend money freely, it was no rule. She'd have no servant-maids of hers treated in that way, when they were about their work, that's what she wouldn't."

As I hate squabbles, particularly with women, and above all with pretty women, I slunk back into

3. **slammerkin:** a slovenly female. 4. **Hunt himself:** Henry Hunt (1773–1835), a politician known in his day as "Radical Hunt."

my room, and partly closed the door; but my curiosity was too much excited not to listen. The landlady marched intrepidly to the enemy's citadel, and entered it with a storm: the door closed after her. I heard her voice in high windy clamor for a moment or two. Then it gradually subsided, like a gust of wind in a garret; then there was a laugh; then I heard nothing more.

After a little while my landlady came out with an odd smile on her face, adjusting her cap, which was a little on one side. As she went down stairs, I heard the landlord ask her what was the matter; she said, "Nothing at all, only the girl's a fool."—I was more than ever perplexed what to make of this unaccountable personage, who could put a good-natured chamber-maid in a passion, and send away a termagant landlady in smiles. He could not be so old, nor cross, nor ugly either.

I had to go to work at his picture again, and to paint him entirely different. I now set him down for one of those stout gentlemen that are frequently met with swaggering about the doors of country inns. Moist, merry fellows, in Belcher handkerchiefs,[5] whose bulk is a little assisted by malt-liquors. Men who have seen the world, and been sworn at Highgate; who are used to tavern-life; up to all the tricks of tapsters, and knowing in the ways of sinful publicans. Free-livers on a small scale; who are prodigal within the compass of a guinea; who call all the waiters by name, tousle the maids, gossip with the landlady at the bar, and prose over a pint of port, or a glass of negus, after dinner.

The morning wore away in forming these and similar surmises. As fast as I wove one system of belief, some movement of the unknown would completely overturn it, and throw all my thoughts again into confusion. Such are the solitary operations of a feverish mind. I was, as I have said, extremely nervous; and the continual meditation on the concerns of this invisible personage began to have its effect:—I was getting a fit of the fidgets.

Dinner-time came. I hoped the stout gentleman might dine in the travellers'-room, and that I might at length get a view of his person; but no—he had dinner served in his own room. What could be the meaning of this solitude and mystery? He could not be a radical; there was something too aristocratical in thus keeping himself apart from the rest of the world, and condemning himself to his own dull company throughout a rainy day. And then, too, he lived too well for a discontented politician. He seemed to expatiate on a variety of dishes, and to sit over his wine like a jolly friend of good living. Indeed, my doubts on this head were soon at an end; for he could not have finished his first bottle before I could faintly hear him humming a tune; and on listening I found it to be "God save the King." 'Twas plain, then, he was no radical, but a faithful subject; one who grew loyal over his bottle, and was ready to stand by king and constitution, when he could stand by nothing else. But who could he be? My conjectures began to run wild. Was he not some personage of distinction travelling incog.? "God knows!" said I, at my wit's end; "it may be one of the royal family for aught I know, for they are all stout gentlemen!"

The weather continued rainy. The mysterious unknown kept his room, and, as far as I could judge, his chair, for I did not hear him move. In the mean time, as the day advanced, the travellers' room began to be frequented. Some, who had just arrived, came in buttoned up in box-coats; others came home who had been dispersed about the town; some took their dinners, and some their tea. Had I been in a different mood, I should have found entertainment in studying this peculiar class of men. There were two especially, who were regular wags of the road, and up to all the standing jokes of travellers. They had a thousand sly things to say to the waiting-maid, whom they called Louisa, and Ethelinda, and a dozen other fine names, changing the name every time, and chuckling amazingly at their own waggery. My mind, however, had been completely engrossed by the stout gentleman. He had kept my fancy in chase during a long day, and it was not now to be diverted from the scent.

The evening gradually wore away. The travellers read the papers two or three times over. Some drew round the fire and told long stories about their horses, about their adventures, their overturns, and breakings-down. They discussed the credit of different merchants and different inns; and the two wags told several choice anecdotes of pretty chamber-maids and kind landladies. All this passed as they were quietly taking what they called their night-caps, that is to say, strong glasses of brandy and water and sugar, or some other mixture of the kind; after which they one after another rang for "Boots" and the chamber-maid, and walked off to bed in old shoes cut down into marvellously uncomfortable slippers.

There was now only one man left: a short-legged, long-bodied, plethoric fellow, with a very large, sandy head. He sat by himself, with a glass of port-wine negus, and a spoon; sipping and stirring, and meditating and sipping, until nothing was left but the spoon. He gradually fell asleep bolt up-

5. **Belcher handkerchiefs**: large particolored neckerchiefs.

right in his chair, with the empty glass standing before him; and the candle seemed to fall asleep too, for the wick grew long, and black, and cabbaged at the end, and dimmed the little light that remained in the chamber. The gloom that now prevailed was contagious. Around hung the shapeless, and almost spectral, box-coats of departed travellers, long since buried in deep sleep. I only heard the ticking of the clock, with the deep-drawn breathings of the sleeping topers, and the drippings of the rain, drop—drop—drop, from the eaves of the house. The church-bells chimed midnight. All at once the stout gentleman began to walk overhead, pacing slowly backwards and forwards. There was something extremely awful in all this, especially to one in my state of nerves. These ghastly great-coats, these guttural breathings, and the creaking footsteps of this mysterious being. His steps grew fainter and fainter, and at length died away. I could bear it no longer. I was wound up to the desperation of a hero of romance. "Be he who or what he may," said I to myself, "I'll have a sight of him!" I seized a chamber-candle, and hurried up to No. 13. The door stood ajar. I hesitated—I entered: the room was deserted. There stood a large, broad-bottomed elbow-chair at a table, on which was an empty tumbler, and a "Times," newspaper, and the room smelt powerfully of Stilton cheese.

The mysterious stranger had evidently but just retired. I turned off, sorely disappointed, to my room, which had been changed to the front of the house. As I went along the corridor, I saw a large pair of boots, with dirty, waxed tops, standing at the door of a bedchamber. They doubtless belonged to the unknown; but it would not do to disturb so redoubtable a personage in his den: he might discharge a pistol, or something worse, at my head. I went to bed, therefore, and lay awake half the night in a terribly nervous state; and even when I fell asleep, I was still haunted in my dreams by the idea of the stout gentleman and his wax-topped boots.

I slept rather late the next morning, and was awakened by some stir and bustle in the house, which I could not at first comprehend; until getting more awake, I found there was a mail-coach starting from the door. Suddenly there was a cry from below, "The gentleman has forgot his umbrella! Look for the gentleman's umbrella in No. 13!" I heard an immediate scampering of a chambermaid along the passage, and a shrill reply as she ran, "Here it is! here's the gentleman's umbrella!"

The mysterious stranger then was on the point of setting off. This was the only chance I should ever have of knowing him. I sprang out of bed, scrambled to the window, snatched aside the curtains, and just caught a glimpse of the rear of a person getting in at the coach-door. The skirts of a brown coat parted behind, and gave me a full view of the broad disk of a pair of drab breeches. The door closed—"all right!" was the word—the coach whirled off;—and that was all I ever saw of the stout gentleman!

1822, 1848

FROM

TALES OF A TRAVELLER

ADVENTURE OF THE GERMAN STUDENT

¶ EARLY in *Tales of a Traveller* the reader is introduced to "an old gentleman, one side of whose face was no match for the other. The eye-lid drooped and hung down like an unhinged window-shutter. Indeed the whole side of his head was dilapidated, and seemed like the wing of a house shut up and haunted." This decidedly odd personage is the appropriate narrator for "Adventure of the German Student." First observing that the previous tales in Part I of *Tales of a Traveller* have "had a rather burlesque tendency," he offers the "German Student" as a "very grave and singular," but truthful, story.

ON A STORMY night, in the tempestuous times of the French revolution, a young German was returning to his lodgings, at a late hour, across the old part of Paris. The lightning gleamed, and the loud claps of thunder rattled through the lofty narrow streets—but I should first tell you something about this young German.

Gottfried Wolfgang was a young man of good family. He had studied for some time at Göttingen, but being of a visionary and enthusiastic character, he had wandered into those wild and speculative doctrines which have so often bewildered German students. His secluded life, his intense application, and the singular nature of his studies, had an effect on both mind and body. His health was impaired; his imagination diseased. He had been indulging in fanciful speculations on spiritual essences, until, like Swedenborg, he had an ideal world of his own around him. He took up a notion, I do not know from what cause, that there was an evil influence hanging over him; an evil genius or spirit seeking to ensnare him and ensure his perdition. Such an idea working on his melancholy temperament, produced the most gloomy effects. He became haggard and desponding. His friends discovered the mental malady preying upon him, and determined that the best cure was a change of scene; he was sent, therefore, to finish his studies amidst the splendors and gayeties of Paris.

Wolfgang arrived at Paris at the breaking out of the revolution. The popular delirium at first caught his enthusiastic mind, and he was captivated by the political and philosophical theories of the day: but the scenes of blood which followed shocked his sensitive nature, disgusted him with society and the world, and made him more than ever a recluse. He shut himself up in a solitary apartment in the *Pays Latin,*[1] the quarter of students. There, in a gloomy street not far from the monastic walls of the Sorbonne, he pursued his favorite speculations. Sometimes he spent hours together in the great libraries of Paris, those catacombs of departed authors, rummaging among their hoards of dusty and obsolete works in quest of food for his unhealthy appetite. He was, in a manner, a literary ghoul, feeding in the charnel-house of decayed literature.

Wolfgang, though solitary and recluse, was of an ardent temperament, but for a time it operated merely upon his imagination. He was too shy and ignorant of the world to make any advances to the fair, but he was a passionate admirer of female beauty, and in his lonely chamber would often lose himself in reveries on forms and faces which he had seen, and his fancy would deck out images of loveliness far surpassing the reality.

While his mind was in this excited and sublimated state, a dream produced an extraordinary effect upon him. It was of a female face of transcendent beauty. So strong was the impression made, that he dreamt of it again and again. It haunted his thoughts by day, his slumbers by night; in fine, he became passionately enamoured of this shadow of a dream. This lasted so long that it became one of those fixed ideas which haunt the minds of melancholy men, and are at times mistaken for madness.

Such was Gottfried Wolfgang, and such his situation at the time I mentioned. He was returning home late one stormy night, through some of the old and gloomy streets of the *Marais,* the ancient part of Paris. The loud claps of thunder rattled among the high houses of the narrow streets. He came to the Place de Grève, the square where public executions are performed. The lightning quivered about the pinnacles of the ancient Hôtel de Ville, and shed flickering gleams over the open space in front. As Wolfgang was crossing the square, he shrank back with horror at finding himself close by the guillotine. It was the height of the reign of terror, when this dreadful instrument of death stood ever ready, and its scaffold was continually running with the blood of the virtuous and the brave. It had that very day been actively employed in the work of carnage, and there it stood in grim array, amidst a silent and sleeping city, waiting for fresh victims.

Wolfgang's heart sickened within him, and he was turning shuddering from the horrible engine, when he beheld a shadowy form, cowering as it were at the foot of the steps which led up to the scaffold. A succession of vivid flashes of lightning revealed it more distinctly. It was a female figure, dressed in black. She was seated on one of the lower steps of the scaffold, leaning forward, her face hid in her lap; and her long dishevelled tresses hanging to the ground, streaming with the rain which fell in torrents. Wolfgang paused. There was something awful in this solitary monument of woe. The female had the appearance of being above the common order. He knew the times to be full of vicissitude, and that many a fair head, which had once been pillowed on down, now wandered houseless. Perhaps this was some poor mourner whom the dreadful axe had rendered desolate, and who sat here heart-broken on the strand of existence, from which all that was dear to her had been launched into eternity.

He approached, and addressed her in the accents of sympathy. She raised her head and gazed wildly at him. What was his astonishment at beholding, by the bright glare of the lightning, the very face which had haunted him in his dreams. It was pale and disconsolate, but ravishingly beautiful.

Trembling with violent and conflicting emotions, Wolfgang again accosted her. He spoke something of her being exposed at such an hour of the night, and to the fury of such a storm, and offered to conduct her to her friends. She pointed to the guillotine with a gesture of dreadful signification.

"I have no friend on earth!" said she.

"But you have a home," said Wolfgang.

"Yes—in the grave!"

The heart of the student melted at the words.

"If a stranger dare make an offer," said he, "without danger of being misunderstood, I would offer my humble dwelling as a shelter; myself as a devoted friend. I am friendless myself in Paris, and a stranger in the land; but if my life could be of

TALES OF A TRAVELLER. **Adventure of the German Student.**

1. *Pays Latin:* the Latin Quarter.

service, it is at your disposal, and should be sacrificed before harm or indignity should come to you."

There was an honest earnestness in the young man's manner that had its effect. His foreign accent, too, was in his favor; it showed him not to be a hackneyed inhabitant of Paris. Indeed, there is an eloquence in true enthusiasm that is not to be doubted. The homeless stranger confided herself implicitly to the protection of the student.

He supported her faltering steps across the Pont Neuf,[2] and by the place where the statue of Henry the Fourth had been overthrown by the populace. The storm had abated, and the thunder rumbled at a distance. All Paris was quiet; that great volcano of human passion slumbered for a while, to gather fresh strength for the next day's eruption. The student conducted his charge through the ancient streets of the *Pays Latin,* and by the dusky walls of the Sorbonne, to the great dingy hotel which he inhabited. The old portress who admitted them stared with surprise at the unusual sight of the melancholy Wolfgang with a female companion.

On entering his apartment, the student, for the first time, blushed at the scantiness and indifference of his dwelling. He had but one chamber—an old-fashioned saloon—heavily carved, and fantastically furnished with the remains of former magnificence, for it was one of those hotels in the quarter of the Luxembourg palace, which had once belonged to nobility. It was lumbered with books and papers, and all the usual apparatus of a student, and his bed stood in a recess at one end.

When lights were brought, and Wolfgang had a better opportunity of contemplating the stranger, he was more than ever intoxicated by her beauty. Her face was pale, but of a dazzling fairness, set off by a profusion of raven hair that hung clustering about it. Her eyes were large and brilliant, with a singular expression approaching almost to wildness. As far as her black dress permitted her shape to be seen, it was of perfect symmetry. Her whole appearance was highly striking, though she was dressed in the simplest style. The only thing approaching to an ornament which she wore, was a broad black band round her neck, clasped by diamonds.

The perplexity now commenced with the student how to dispose of the helpless being thus thrown upon his protection. He thought of abandoning his chamber to her, and seeking shelter for himself elsewhere. Still he was so fascinated by her charms, there seemed to be such a spell upon his thoughts and senses, that he could not tear himself from her presence. Her manner, too, was singular and unaccountable. She spoke no more of the guillotine. Her grief had abated. The attentions of the student had first won her confidence, and then, apparently, her heart. She was evidently an enthusiast like himself, and enthusiasts soon understand each other.

In the infatuation of the moment, Wolfgang avowed his passion for her. He told her the story of his mysterious dream, and how she had possessed his heart before he had even seen her. She was strangely affected by his recital, and acknowledged to have felt an impulse towards him equally unaccountable. It was the time for wild theory and wild actions. Old prejudices and superstitions were done away; everything was under the sway of the "Goddess of Reason." Among other rubbish of the old times, the forms and ceremonies of marriage began to be considered superfluous bonds for honorable minds. Social compacts were the vogue. Wolfgang was too much of a theorist not to be tainted by the liberal doctrines of the day.

"Why should we separate?" said he: "our hearts are united; in the eye of reason and honor we are as one. What need is there of sordid forms to bind high souls together?"

The stranger listened with emotion: she had evidently received illumination at the same school.

"You have no home nor family," continued he; "let me be everything to you, or rather let us be everything to one another. If form is necessary, form shall be observed—there is my hand. I pledge myself to you forever."

"Forever?" said the stranger, solemnly.

"Forever!" repeated Wolfgang.

The stranger clasped the hand extended to her: "Then I am yours," murmured she, and sank upon his bosom.

The next morning the student left his bride sleeping, and sallied forth at an early hour to seek more spacious apartments suitable to the change in his situation. When he returned, he found the stranger lying with her head hanging over the bed, and one arm thrown over it. He spoke to her, but received no reply. He advanced to awaken her from her uneasy posture. On taking her hand, it was cold—there was no pulsation—her face was pallid and ghastly. In a word, she was a corpse.

Horrified and frantic, he alarmed the house. A scene of confusion ensued. The police was summoned. As the officer of police entered the room, he started back on beholding the corpse.

"Great heaven!" cried he, "how did this woman come here?"

"Do you know anything about her?" said Wolfgang eagerly.

2. **Pont Neuf**: bridge across the Seine River.

"Do I?" exclaimed the officer: "she was guillotined yesterday."

He stepped forward; undid the black collar round the neck of the corpse, and the head rolled on the floor!

The student burst into a frenzy. "The fiend! the fiend has gained possession of me!" shrieked he: "I am lost forever."

They tried to soothe him, but in vain. He was possessed with the frightful belief that an evil spirit had reanimated the dead body to ensnare him. He went distracted, and died in a mad-house.

Here the old gentleman with the haunted head finished his narrative.

"And is this really a fact?" said the inquisitive gentleman.

"A fact not to be doubted," replied the other. "I had it from the best authority. The student told it me himself. I saw him in a mad-house in Paris."

1825, 1849

THE DEVIL AND TOM WALKER

◊

"The Devil and Tom Walker" is one of "The Money-Diggers" series, Part IV, of *Tales of a Traveller*. All of Part IV is said by Crayon to "have been found among the papers of the late Diedrich Knickerbocker."

◊

A FEW miles from Boston in Massachusetts, there is a deep inlet, winding several miles into the interior of the country from Charles Bay, and terminating in a thickly-wooded swamp or morass. On one side of this inlet is a beautiful dark grove; on the opposite side the land rises abruptly from the water's edge into a high ridge, on which grow a few scattered oaks of great age and immense size. Under one of these gigantic trees, according to old stories, there was a great amount of treasure buried by Kidd the pirate. The inlet allowed a facility to bring the money in a boat secretly and at night to the very foot of the hill; the elevation of the place permitted a good look-out to be kept that no one was at hand; while the remarkable trees formed good landmarks by which the place might easily be found again. The old stories add, moreover, that the devil presided at the hiding of the money, and took it under his guardianship; but this, it is well known, he always does with buried treasure, particularly when it has been ill-gotten. Be that as it may, Kidd never returned to recover his wealth; being shortly after seized at Boston, sent out to England, and there hanged for a pirate.

About the year 1727, just at the time that earthquakes were prevalent in New England, and shook many tall sinners down upon their knees, there lived near this place a meagre, miserly fellow, of the name of Tom Walker. He had a wife as miserly as himself: they were so miserly that they even conspired to cheat each other. Whatever the woman could lay hands on, she hid away; a hen could not cackle but she was on the alert to secure the new-laid egg. Her husband was continually prying about to detect her secret hoards, and many and fierce were the conflicts that took place about what ought to have been common property. They lived in a forlorn-looking house that stood alone, and had an air of starvation. A few straggling savin-trees, emblems of sterility, grew near it; no smoke ever curled from its chimney; no traveller stopped at its door. A miserable horse, whose ribs were as articulate as the bars of a gridiron, stalked about a field, where a thin carpet of moss, scarcely covering the ragged beds of puddingstone, tantalized and balked his hunger; and sometimes he would lean his head over the fence, look piteously at the passer-by, and seem to petition deliverance from this land of famine.

The house and its inmates had altogether a bad name. Tom's wife was a tall termagant, fierce of temper, loud of tongue, and strong of arm. Her voice was often heard in wordy warfare with her husband; and his face sometimes showed signs that their conflicts were not confined to words. No one ventured, however, to interfere between them. The lonely wayfarer shrunk within himself at the horrid clamor and clapper-clawing; eyed the den of discord askance; and hurried on his way, rejoicing, if a bachelor, in his celibacy.

One day that Tom Walker had been to a distant part of the neighborhood, he took what he considered a short cut homeward, through the swamp. Like most short cuts, it was an ill-chosen route. The swamp was thickly grown with great gloomy pines and hemlocks, some of them ninety feet high, which made it dark at noonday, and a retreat for all the owls of the neighborhood. It was full of pits and quagmires, partly covered with weeds and mosses, where the green surface often betrayed the traveller into a gulf of black, smothering mud: there were also dark and stagnant pools, the abodes of the tadpole, the bull-frog, and the water-snake; where the trunks of pines and hemlocks lay half-drowned, half-rotting, looking like alligators sleeping in the mire.

Tom had long been picking his way cautiously through this treacherous forest; stepping from tuft to tuft of rushes and roots, which afforded precarious footholds among deep sloughs; or pacing carefully, like a cat, along the prostrate trunks of trees; startled now and then by the sudden screaming of the bittern, or the quacking of a wild duck rising on the wing from some solitary pool. At length he arrived at a firm piece of ground, which ran out like a peninsula into the deep bosom of the swamp. It had been one of the strongholds of the Indians during their wars with the first colonists. Here they had thrown up a kind of fort, which they had looked upon as almost impregnable, and had used as a place of refuge for their squaws and children. Nothing remained of the old Indian fort but a few embankments, gradually sinking to the level of the surrounding earth, and already overgrown in part by oaks and other forest trees, the foliage of which formed a contrast to the dark pines and hemlocks of the swamp.

It was late in the dusk of evening when Tom Walker reached the old fort, and he paused there awhile to rest himself. Any one but he would have felt unwilling to linger in this lonely, melancholy place, for the common people had a bad opinion of it, from the stories handed down from the time of the Indian wars; when it was asserted that the savages held incantations here, and made sacrifices to the evil spirit.

Tom Walker, however, was not a man to be troubled with any fears of the kind. He reposed himself for some time on the trunk of a fallen hemlock, listening to the boding cry of the treetoad, and delving with his walking-staff into a mound of black mould at his feet. As he turned up the soil unconsciously, his staff struck against something hard. He raked it out of the vegetable mould, and lo! a cloven skull, with an Indian tomahawk buried deep in it, lay before him. The rust on the weapon showed the time that had elapsed since this death-blow had been given. It was a dreary memento of the fierce struggle that had taken place in this last foothold of the Indian warriors.

"Humph!" said Tom Walker, as he gave it a kick to shake the dirt from it.

"Let that skull alone!" said a gruff voice. Tom lifted up his eyes, and beheld a great black man seated directly opposite him, on the stump of a tree. He was exceedingly surprised, having neither heard nor seen any one approach; and he was still more perplexed on observing, as well as the gathering gloom would permit, that the stranger was neither negro nor Indian. It is true he was dressed in a rude half Indian garb, and had a red belt or sash swathed round his body; but his face was neither black nor copper-color, but swarthy and dingy, and begrimed with soot, as if he had been accustomed to toil among fires and forges. He had a shock of coarse black hair, that stood out from his head in all directions, and bore an axe on his shoulder.

He scowled for a moment at Tom with a pair of great red eyes.

"What are you doing on my grounds?" said the black man, with a hoarse growling voice.

"Your grounds!" said Tom with a sneer, "no more your grounds than mine; they belong to Deacon Peabody."

"Deacon Peabody be d——d," said the stranger, "as I flatter myself he will be, if he does not look more to his own sins and less to those of his neighbors. Look yonder, and see how Deacon Peabody is faring."

Tom looked in the direction that the stranger pointed, and beheld one of the great trees, fair and flourishing without, but rotten at the core, and saw that it had been nearly hewn through, so that the first high wind was likely to blow it down. On the bark of the tree was scored the name of Deacon Peabody, an eminent man, who had waxed wealthy by driving shrewd bargains with the Indians. He now looked around, and found most of the tall trees marked with the name of some great man of the colony, and all more or less scored by the axe. The one on which he had been seated, and which had evidently just been hewn down, bore the name of Crowninshield; and he recollected a mighty rich man of that name, who made a vulgar display of wealth, which it was whispered he had acquired by buccaneering.

"He's just ready for burning!" said the black man, with a growl of triumph. "You see I am likely to have a good stock of firewood for winter."

"But what right have you," said Tom, "to cut down Deacon Peabody's timber?"

"The right of a prior claim," said the other. "This woodland belonged to me long before one of your white-faced race put foot upon the soil."

"And pray, who are you, if I may be so bold?" said Tom.

"Oh, I go by various names. I am the wild huntsman in some countries; the black miner in others. In this neighborhood I am known by the name of the black woodsman. I am he to whom the red men consecrated this spot, and in honor of whom they now and then roasted a white man, by way of sweet-smelling sacrifice. Since the red men have been exterminated by you white savages, I amuse myself by presiding at the persecutions of Quakers and Anabaptists; I am the great patron and prompter of slave-dealers, and the grand-master of the Salem witches."

"The upshot of all which is, that, if I mistake not," said Tom, sturdily, "you are he commonly called Old Scratch."

"The same, at your service!" replied the black man, with a half civil nod.

Such was the opening of this interview, according to the old story; though it has almost too familiar an air to be credited. One would think that to meet with such a singular personage, in this wild, lonely place, would have shaken any man's nerves; but Tom was a hard-minded fellow, not easily daunted, and he had lived so long with a termagant wife, that he did not even fear the devil.

It is said that after this commencement they had a long and earnest conversation together, as Tom returned homeward. The black man told him of great sums of money buried by Kidd the pirate, under the oak-trees on the high ridge, not far from the morass. All these were under his command, and protected by his power, so that none could find them but such as propitiated his favor. These he offered to place within Tom Walker's reach, having conceived an especial kindness for him; but they were to be had only on certain conditions. What these conditions were may be easily surmised, though Tom never disclosed them publicly. They must have been very hard, for he required time to think of them, and he was not a man to stick at trifles when money was in view. When they had reached the edge of the swamp, the stranger paused—"What proof have I that all you have been telling me is true?" said Tom. "There's my signature," said the black man, pressing his finger on Tom's forehead. So saying, he turned off among the thickets of the swamp, and seemed, as Tom said, to go down, down, down, into the earth, until nothing but his head and shoulders could be seen, and so on, until he totally disappeared.

When Tom reached home, he found the black print of a finger burnt, as it were, into his forehead, which nothing could obliterate.

The first news his wife had to tell him was the sudden death of Absalom Crowninshield, the rich buccaneer. It was announced in the papers with the usual flourish, that "A great man had fallen in Israel." [1]

Tom recollected the tree which his black friend had just hewn down, and which was ready for burning. "Let the freebooter roast," said Tom, "who cares!" He now felt convinced that all he had heard and seen was no illusion.

He was not prone to let his wife into his confidence; but as this was an uneasy secret, he willingly shared it with her. All her avarice was awakened at the mention of hidden gold, and she urged her husband to comply with the black man's terms, and secure what would make them wealthy for life. However Tom might have felt disposed to sell himself to the Devil, he was determined not to do so to oblige his wife; so he flatly refused, out of the mere spirit of contradiction. Many and bitter were the quarrels they had on the subject; but the more she talked, the more resolute was Tom not to be damned to please her.

At length she determined to drive the bargain on her own account, and if she succeeded, to keep all the gain to herself. Being of the same fearless temper as her husband, she set off for the old Indian fort towards the close of a summer's day. She was many hours absent. When she came back, she was reserved and sullen in her replies. She spoke something of a black man, whom she had met about twilight, hewing at the root of a tall tree. He was sulky, however, and would not come to terms: she was to go again with a propitiatory offering, but what it was she forbore to say.

The next evening she set off again for the swamp, with her apron heavily laden. Tom waited and waited for her, but in vain; midnight came, but she did not make her appearance: morning, noon, night returned, but still she did not come. Tom now grew uneasy for her safety, especially as he found she had carried off in her apron the silver teapot and spoons, and every portable article of value. Another night elapsed, another morning came; but no wife. In a word, she was never heard of more.

What was her real fate nobody knows, in consequence of so many pretending to know. It is one of those facts which have become confounded by a variety of historians. Some asserted that she lost her way among the tangled mazes of the swamp, and sank into some pit or slough; others, more uncharitable, hinted that she had eloped with the household booty, and made off to some other province; while others surmised that the tempter had decoyed her into a dismal quagmire, on the top of which her hat was found lying. In confirmation of this, it was said a great black man, with an axe on his shoulder, was seen late that very evening coming out of the swamp, carrying a bundle tied in a check apron, with an air of surly triumph.

The most current and probable story, however, observes, that Tom Walker grew so anxious about the fate of his wife and his property, that he set out

The Devil and Tom Walker. 1. "A . . . Israel": II Sam. 3:38.

at length to seek them both at the Indian fort. During a long summer's afternoon he searched about the gloomy place, but no wife was to be seen. He called her name repeatedly, but she was nowhere to be heard. The bittern alone responded to his voice, as he flew screaming by; or the bull-frog croaked dolefully from a neighboring pool. At length, it is said, just in the brown hour of twilight, when the owls began to hoot, and the bats to flit about, his attention was attracted by the clamor of carrion crows hovering about a cypress-tree. He looked up, and beheld a bundle tied in a check apron, and hanging in the branches of the tree, with a great vulture perched hard by, as if keeping watch upon it. He leaped with joy; for he recognized his wife's apron, and supposed it to contain the household valuables.

"Let us get hold of the property," said he, consolingly to himself, "and we will endeavor to do without the woman."

As he scrambled up the tree, the vulture spread its wide wings, and sailed off screaming into the deep shadows of the forest. Tom seized the checked apron, but woeful sight! found nothing but a heart and liver tied up in it!

Such, according to this most authentic old story, was all that was to be found of Tom's wife. She had probably attempted to deal with the black man as she had been accustomed to deal with her husband; but though a female scold is generally considered a match for the devil, yet in this instance she appears to have had the worst of it. She must have died game, however; for it is said Tom noticed many prints of cloven feet deeply stamped about the tree, and found handfuls of hair, that looked as if they had been plucked from the coarse black shock of the woodman. Tom knew his wife's prowess by experience. He shrugged his shoulders, as he looked at the signs of a fierce clapper-clawing. "Egad," said he to himself, "Old Scratch must have had a tough time of it!"

Tom consoled himself for the loss of his property, with the loss of his wife, for he was a man of fortitude. He even felt something like gratitude towards the black woodman, who, he considered, had done him a kindness. He sought, therefore, to cultivate a further acquaintance with him, but for some time without success; the old black-legs played shy, for whatever people may think, he is not always to be had for calling for: he knows how to play his cards when pretty sure of his game.

At length, it is said, when delay had whetted Tom's eagerness to the quick, and prepared him to agree to any thing rather than not gain the promised treasure, he met the black man one evening in his usual woodman's dress, with his axe on his shoulder, sauntering along the swamp, and humming a tune. He affected to receive Tom's advances with great indifference, made brief replies, and went on humming his tune.

By degrees, however, Tom brought him to business, and they began to haggle about the terms on which the former was to have the pirate's treasure. There was one condition which need not be mentioned, being generally understood in all cases where the devil grants favors; but there were others about which, though of less importance, he was inflexibly obstinate. He insisted that the money found through his means should be employed in his service. He proposed, therefore, that Tom should employ it in the black traffick; that is to say, that he should fit out a slave-ship. This, however, Tom resolutely refused: he was bad enough in all conscience; but the devil himself could not tempt him to turn slave-trader.

Finding Tom so squeamish on this point, he did not insist upon it, but proposed, instead, that he should turn usurer; the devil being extremely anxious for the increase of usurers, looking upon them as his peculiar people.

To this no objections were made, for it was just to Tom's taste.

"You shall open a broker's shop in Boston next month," said the black man.

"I'll do it to-morrow, if you wish," said Tom Walker.

"You shall lend money at two per cent. a month."

"Egad, I'll charge four!" replied Tom Walker.

"You shall extort bonds, foreclose mortgages, drive the merchants to bankruptcy——"

"I'll drive them to the d——l," cried Tom Walker.

"You are the usurer for my money!" said black-legs with delight. "When will you want the rhino?"

"This very night."

"Done!" said the devil.

"Done!" said Tom Walker.—So they shook hands and struck a bargain.

A few days' time saw Tom Walker seated behind his desk in a counting-house in Boston.

His reputation for a ready-moneyed man, who would lend money out for a good consideration, soon spread abroad. Everybody remembers the time of Governor Belcher,[2] when money was particularly scarce. It was a time of paper credit. The country had been deluged with government bills; the famous Land Bank [3] had been established;

2. Governor Belcher: Jonathan Belcher, governor of Massachusetts, 1730–41. **3. Land Bank:** a bank of credit issuing notes against land security.

there had been a rage for speculating; the people had run mad with schemes for new settlements; for building cities in the wilderness; land-jobbers went about with maps of grants, and townships, and Eldorados, lying nobody knew where, but which everybody was ready to purchase. In a word, the great speculating fever which breaks out every now and then in the country, had raged to an alarming degree, and everybody was dreaming of making sudden fortunes from nothing. As usual the fever had subsided; the dream had gone off, and the imaginary fortunes with it; the patients were left in doleful plight, and the whole country resounded with the consequent cry of "hard times."

At this propitious time of public distress did Tom Walker set up as usurer in Boston. His door was soon thronged by customers. The needy and adventurous; the gambling speculator; the dreaming land-jobber; the thriftless tradesman; the merchant with cracked credit; in short, every one driven to raise money by desperate means and desperate sacrifices, hurried to Tom Walker.

Thus Tom was the universal friend of the needy, and acted like a "friend in need;" that is to say, he always exacted good pay and good security. In proportion to the distress of the applicant was the hardness of his terms. He accumulated bonds and mortgages; gradually squeezed his customers closer and closer: and sent them at length, dry as a sponge, from his door.

In this way he made money hand over hand; became a rich and mighty man, and exalted his cocked hat upon 'Change. He built himself, as usual, a vast house, out of ostentation; but left the greater part of it unfinished and unfurnished, out of parsimony. He even set up a carriage in the fulness of his vainglory, though he nearly starved the horses which drew it; and as the ungreased wheels groaned and screeched on the axle-trees, you would have thought you heard the souls of the poor debtors he was squeezing.

As Tom waxed old, however, he grew thoughtful. Having secured the good things of this world, he began to feel anxious about those of the next. He thought with regret on the bargain he had made with his black friend, and set his wits to work to cheat him out of the conditions. He became, therefore, all of a sudden, a violent churchgoer. He prayed loudly and strenuously, as if heaven were to be taken by force of lungs. Indeed, one might always tell when he had sinned most during the week, by the clamor of his Sunday devotion. The quiet Christians who had been modestly and steadfastly travelling Zionward, were struck with self-reproach at seeing themselves so suddenly outstripped in their career by this new-made convert. Tom was as rigid in religious as in money matters; he was a stern supervisor and censurer of his neighbors, and seemed to think every sin entered up to their account became a credit on his own side of the page. He even talked of the expediency of reviving the persecution of Quakers and Anabaptists. In a word, Tom's zeal become as notorious as his riches.

Still, in spite of all this strenuous attention to forms, Tom had a lurking dread that the devil, after all, would have his due. That he might not be taken unawares, therefore, it is said he always carried a small Bible in his coat-pocket. He had also a great folio Bible on his counting-house desk, and would frequently be found reading it when people called on business; on such occasions he would lay his green spectacles in the book, to mark the place, while he turned round to drive some usurious bargain.

Some say that Tom grew a little crack-brained in his old days, and that fancying his end approaching, he had his horse new shod, saddled and bridled, and buried with his feet uppermost; because he supposed that at the last day the world would be turned upside down; in which case he should find his horse standing ready for mounting, and he was determined at the worst to give his old friend a run for it. This, however, is probably a mere old wives' fable. If he really did take such a precaution, it was totally superfluous; at least so says the authentic old legend; which closes his story in the following manner.

One hot summer afternoon in the dog-days, just as a terrible black thundergust was coming up, Tom sat in his counting house in his white linen cap and India silk morning-gown. He was on the point of foreclosing a mortgage, by which he would complete the ruin of an unlucky land speculator for whom he had professed the greatest friendship. The poor land-jobber begged him to grant a few months' indulgence. Tom had grown testy and irritated, and refused another day.

"My family will be ruined, and brought upon the parish," said the land-jobber. "Charity begins at home," replied Tom; "I must take care of myself in these hard times."

"You have made so much money out of me," said the speculator.

Tom lost his patience and his piety—"The devil take me," said he, "if I have made a farthing!"

Just then there were three loud knocks at the street door. He stepped out to see who was there. A black man was holding a black horse, which neighed and stamped with impatience.

"Tom, you're come for," said the black fellow,

gruffly. Tom shrank back, but too late. He had left his little Bible at the bottom of his coat-pocket, and his big Bible on the desk buried under the mortgage he was about to foreclose: never was sinner taken more unawares. The black man whisked him like a child into the saddle, gave the horse the lash, and away he galloped, with Tom on his back, in the midst of the thunderstorm. The clerks stuck their pens behind their ears, and stared after him from the windows. Away went Tom Walker, dashing down the streets; his white cap bobbing up and down; his morning-gown fluttering in the wind, and his steed striking fire out of the pavement at every bound. When the clerks turned to look for the black man he had disappeared.

Tom Walker never returned to foreclose the mortgage. A countryman who lived on the border of the swamp, reported that in the height of the thundergust he had heard a great clattering of hoofs and a howling along the road, and running to the window caught sight of a figure, such as I have described, on a horse that galloped like mad across the fields, over the hills, and down into the black hemlock swamp towards the old Indian fort; and that shortly after a thunder-bolt falling in that direction seemed to set the whole forest in a blaze.

The good people of Boston shook their heads and shrugged their shoulders, but had been so much accustomed to witches and goblins, and tricks of the devil, in all kinds of shapes, from the first settlement of the colony, that they were not so much horror-struck as might have been expected. Trustees were appointed to take charge of Tom's effects. There was nothing, however, to administer upon. On searching his coffers all his bonds and mortgages were found reduced to cinders. In place of gold and silver his iron chest was filled with chips and shavings; two skeletons lay in his stable instead of his half-starved horses, and the very next day his great house took fire and was burnt to the ground.

Such was the end of Tom Walker and his ill-gotten wealth. Let all griping money-brokers lay this story to heart. The truth of it is not to be doubted. The very hole under the oak-trees, whence he dug Kidd's money, is to be seen to this day; and the neighboring swamp and old Indian fort are often haunted in stormy nights by a figure on horseback, in morning-gown and white cap, which is doubtless the troubled spirit of the usurer. In fact, the story has resolved itself into a proverb, and is the origin of that popular saying, so prevalent throughout New England, of "The Devil and Tom Walker."

1825, 1849

FROM

THE ALHAMBRA

THE MYSTERIOUS CHAMBERS

ANOTHER example of the sketch as first-person narrative, "The Mysterious Chambers" shows Irving shrugging off his early fears and almost literally withdrawing into the past. The moonlight and nostalgia with which the sketch is saturated epitomize *The Alhambra.*

As I was rambling one day about the Moorish halls, my attention was, for the first time, attracted to a door in a remote gallery, communicating apparently with some part of the Alhambra which I had not yet explored. I attempted to open it, but it was locked. I knocked, but no one answered, and the sound seemed to reverberate through empty chambers. Here then was a mystery. Here was the haunted wing of the castle. How was I to get at the dark secrets here shut up from the public eye? Should I come privately at night with lamp and sword, according to the prying custom of heroes of romance; or should I endeavor to draw the secret from Pépe the stuttering gardener; or the ingenuous Dolores,[1] or the loquacious Mateo? [2] Or should I go frankly and openly to Dame Antonia the chatelaine, and ask her all about it? I chose the latter course, as being the simplest though the least romantic; and found, somewhat to my disappointment, that there was no mystery in the case. I was welcome to explore the apartment, and there was the key.

Thus provided, I returned forthwith to the door. It opened, as I had surmised, to a range of vacant chambers; but they were quite different from the rest of the palace. The architecture, though rich and antiquated, was European. There was nothing Moorish about it. The first two rooms were lofty; the ceilings, broken in many places, were of cedar, deeply panelled and skillfully carved with fruits and flowers, intermingled with grotesque masks or faces.

The walls had evidently in ancient times been hung with damask, but now were naked, and scrawled over by that class of aspiring travellers who defile noble monuments with their worthless names. The windows, dismantled and open to wind and weather, looked out into a charming little

THE MYSTERIOUS CHAMBERS. 1. **Dolores:** the niece of Tia, "Antonia, the chatelaine." 2. **Mateo:** Irving's guide, handy man, and "gossiping squire."

secluded garden, where an alabaster fountain sparkled among roses and myrtles, and was surrounded by orange and citron trees, some of which flung their branches into the chambers. Beyond these rooms were two saloons, longer but less lofty, looking also into the garden. In the compartments of the panelled ceilings were baskets of fruit and garlands of flowers, painted by no mean hand, and in tolerable preservation. The walls also had been painted in fresco in the Italian style, but the paintings were nearly obliterated; the windows were in the same shattered state with those of the other chambers. This fanciful suite of rooms terminated in an open gallery with balustrades, running at right angles along another side of the garden. The whole apartment, so delicate and elegant in its decorations, so choice and sequestered in its situation along this retired little garden, and so different in architecture from the neighboring halls, awakened an interest in its history. I found on inquiry that it was an apartment fitted up by Italian artists in the early part of the last century, at the time when Philip V.[3] and his second wife, the beautiful Elizabetta of Farnese, daughter of the duke of Parma, were expected at the Alhambra. It was destined for the queen and the ladies of her train. One of the loftiest chambers had been her sleeping-room. A narrow staircase, now walled up, led up to a delightful belvidere, originally a mirador[4] of the Moorish sultanas, communicating with the harem, but which was fitted up as a boudoir for the fair Elizabetta, and still retains the name of *el tocador de la Reyna,* or the queen's toilette.

One window of the royal sleeping-room commanded a prospect of the Generalife[5] and its embowered terraces, another looked out into the little secluded garden I have mentioned, which was decidedly Moorish in its character, and also had its history. It was in fact the garden of Lindaraxa, so often mentioned in descriptions of the Alhambra; but who this Lindaraxa was I had never heard explained. A little research gave me the few particulars known about her. She was a Moorish beauty who flourished in the court of Muhamed the Left-Handed,[6] and was the daughter of his loyal adherent, the alcayde of Malaga, who sheltered him in his city when driven from the throne. On regaining his crown, the alcayde was rewarded for his fidelity. His daughter had her apartment in the Alhambra, and was given by the king in marriage to Nasar, a young Cetimerien prince descended from Aben Hud[7] the Just. Their espousals were doubtless celebrated in the royal palace, and their honey-moon may have passed among these very bowers.[8]

Four centuries had elapsed since the fair Lindaraxa passed away, yet how much of the fragile beauty of the scenes she inhabited remained! The garden still bloomed in which she delighted; the fountain still presented the crystal mirror in which her charms may once have been reflected; the alabaster, it is true, had lost its whiteness; the basin beneath, overrun with weeds had become the lurking-place of the lizard, but there was something in the very decay that enhanced the interest of the scene, speaking as it did of that mutability, the irrevocable lot of man and all his works.

The desolation too of these chambers, once the abode of the proud and elegant Elizabetta, had a more touching charm for me than if I had beheld them in their pristine splendor, glittering with the pageantry of a court.

When I returned to my quarters in the governor's apartment, everything seemed tame and common place after the poetic region I had left. The thought suggested itself: Why could I not change my quarters to these vacant chambers? that would indeed be living in the Alhambra, surrounded by its gardens and fountains, as in the time of the Moorish sovereigns. I proposed the change to Dame Antonia and her family, and it occasioned vast surprise. They could not conceive any rational inducement for the choice of an apartment so forlorn, remote, and solitary. Dolores exclaimed at its frightful loneliness—nothing but bats and owls flitting about; and then a fox and wild-cat kept in the vaults of the neighboring baths and roamed about at night. The good Tia had more reasonable objections. The neighborhood was infested by vagrants; gipsies swarmed in the caverns of the adjacent hills; the palace was ruinous and easy to be entered in many places; the rumor of a stranger quartered alone in one of the remote and ruined apartments, out of the hearing of the rest of the inhabitants, might tempt unwelcome visitors in the night, especially as foreigners were always supposed to be well stocked with money. I was not to be diverted from my humor, however, and my will was law with these good people. So, calling in the assistance of a carpenter, and the ever-officious Mateo Ximenes, the doors and win-

3. **Philip V:** King of Spain (1700–46). 4. **mirador:** a gallery or balcony. 5. **Generalife:** the summer palace. 6. **Muhamed the Left-Handed:** Mohammed VII (1395–1450), King of Granada. 7. **Aben Hud:** King of Granada (d. 1238).

8. **Their . . . bowers:** "One of the things in which the Moorish kings interfered was in the marriage of their nobles: hence it came that all the señors attached to the royal person were married in the palace; and there was always a chamber destined for the ceremony.—Paseos por Granada, *Paseo* XXI" [I]. This is Irving's translation from the original Spanish, here omitted. The author of *Paseos* (Madrid, 1814) was Padre Juan de Echeverría.

dows were soon placed in a state of tolerable security, and the sleeping-room of the stately Elizabetta prepared for my reception. Mateo kindly volunteered as a body-guard to sleep in my antechamber; but I did not think it worth while to put his valor to the proof.

With all the hardihood I had assumed and all the precautions I had taken, I must confess the first night passed in these quarters was inexpressibly dreary. I do not think it was so much the apprehension of dangers from without that affected me, as the character of the place itself, with all its strange associations: the deeds of violence committed there; the tragical ends of many of those who had once reigned there in splendor. As I passed beneath the fated halls of the tower of Comares on the way to my chamber, I called to mind a quotation that used to thrill me in the days of boyhood:

> "Fate sits on these dark battlements and frowns;
> And, as the portal opens to receive me,
> A voice in sullen echoes through the courts
> Tells of a nameless deed!"

The whole family escorted me to my chamber, and took leave of me as of one engaged on a perilous enterprise; and when I heard their retreating steps die away along the waste antechambers and echoing galleries; and turned the key of my door, I was reminded of those hobgoblin stories, where the hero is left to accomplish the adventure of an enchanted house.

Even the thoughts of the fair Elizabetta and the beauties of her court, who had once graced these chambers, now, by a perversion of fancy, added to the gloom. Here was the scene of their transient gayety and loveliness; here were the very traces of their elegance and enjoyment; but what and where were they?—Dust and ashes! tenants of the tomb! phantoms of the memory!

A vague and indescribable awe was creeping over me. I would fain have ascribed it to the thoughts of robbers awakened by the evening's conversation, but I felt it was something more unreal and absurd. The long-buried superstitions of the nursery were reviving, and asserting their power over my imagination. Every thing began to be affected by the working of my mind. The whispering of the wind among the citron-trees beneath my window had something sinister. I cast my eyes into the garden of Lindaraxa; the groves presented a gulf of shadows; the thickets, indistinct and ghastly shapes. I was glad to close the window, but my chamber itself became infected. There was a slight rustling noise overhead; a bat suddenly emerged from a broken panel of the ceiling, flitting about the room and athwart my solitary lamp, and as the fateful bird almost flouted my face with his noiseless wing, the grotesque faces carved in high relief in the cedar ceiling, whence he had emerged, seemed to mope and mow at me.

Rousing myself and half smiling at this temporary weakness, I resolved to brave it out in the true spirit of the hero of the enchanted house; so, taking lamp in hand, I sallied forth to make a tour of the palace. Notwithstanding every mental exertion, the task was a severe one. I had to traverse waste halls and mysterious galleries, where the rays of the lamp extended but a short distance around me. I walked, as it were, in a mere halo of light, walled in by impenetrable darkness. The vaulted corridors were as caverns; the ceilings of the halls were lost in gloom. I recalled all that had been said of the danger from interlopers in these remote and ruined apartments. Might not some vagrant foe be lurking before or behind me, in the outer darkness? My own shadow, cast upon the wall, began to disturb me. The echoes of my own footsteps along the corridors made me pause and look round. I was traversing scenes fraught with dismal recollections. One dark passage led down to the mosque where Yusef,[9] the Moorish monarch, the finisher of the Alhambra, had been basely murdered. In another place, I trod the gallery where another monarch had been struck down by the poniard of a relative whom he had thwarted in his love.

A low murmuring sound, as of stifled voices and clanking chains, now reached me. It seemed to come from the Hall of the Abencerrages.[10] I knew it to be the rush of water through subterranean channels, but it sounded strangely in the night and reminded me of the dismal stories to which it had given rise.

Soon, however, my ear was assailed by sounds too fearfully real to be the work of fancy. As I was crossing the Hall of Ambassadors, low moans and broken ejaculations rose, as it were, from beneath my feet. I paused and listened. They then appeared to be outside of the tower—then again within. Then broke forth howlings as of an animal—then stifled shrieks and inarticulate ravings. Heard in that dead hour and singular place, the effect was thrilling. I had no desire for further perambulation; but returned to my chamber with infinitely more alacrity than I had sallied forth, and drew my breath more freely when once more within its walls and the door bolted behind me. When I awoke in the morning, with the sun shining in at

9. **Yusef:** Yusef Abul Hagig, King of Granada, 1333–54.
10. **Abencerrages:** family of the Beni Serraj, a group of whom were allegedly massacred in the Hall referred to, during civil wars in Granada in the fifteenth century.

my window and lighting up every part of the building with his cheerful and truth-telling beams, I could scarcely recall the shadows and fancies conjured up by the gloom of the preceding night; or believe that the scenes around me, so naked and apparent, could have been clothed with such imaginary horrors.

Still, the dismal howlings and ejaculations I had heard were not ideal; they were soon accounted for, however, by my handmaid Dolores: being the ravings of a poor maniac, a brother of her aunt, who was subject to violent paroxysms, during which he was confined in a vaulted room beneath the Hall of Ambassadors.

In the course of a few evenings a thorough change took place in the scene and its associations. The moon, which when I took possession of my new apartments was invisible, gradually gained each evening upon the darkness of the night, and at length rolled in full splendor above the towers, pouring a flood of tempered light into every court and hall. The garden beneath my window, before wrapped in gloom, was gently lighted up; the orange and citron trees were tipped with silver; the fountain sparkled in the moonbeams, and even the blush of the rose was faintly visible.

I now felt the poetic merit of the Arabic inscription on the walls,—"How beauteous is this garden; where the flowers of the earth vie with the stars of heaven. What can compare with the vase of yon alabaster fountain filled with crystal water? Nothing but the moon in her fulness shining in the midst of an unclouded sky!"

On such heavenly nights I would sit for hours at my window inhaling the sweetness of the garden, and musing on the checkered fortunes of those whose history was dimly shadowed out in the elegant memorials around. Sometimes, when all was quiet and the clock from the distant cathedral of Granada struck the midnight hour, I have sallied out on another tour and wandered over the whole building; but how different from my first tour! No longer dark and mysterious; no longer peopled with shadowy foes; no longer recalling scenes of violence and murder; all was open, spacious, beautiful; every thing calling up pleasing and romantic fancies. Lindaraxa once more walked in her garden; the gay chivalry of Moslem Granada once more glittered about the Court of Lions. Who can do justice to a moonlight night in such a climate and such a place? The temperature of a summer midnight in Andalusia is perfectly ethereal. We seem lifted up into a purer atmosphere; we feel a serenity of soul, a buoyancy of spirits, an elasticity of frame, which render mere existence happiness. But when moonlight is added to all this, the effect is like enchantment. Under its plastic sway the Alhambra seems to regain its pristine glories. Every rent and chasm of time; every mouldering tint and weather-stain is gone; the marble resumes its original whiteness; the long colonnades brighten in the moonbeams; the halls are illuminated with a softened radiance,—we tread the enchanted palace of an Arabian tale!

What a delight, at such a time, to ascend to the little airy pavilion of the queen's toilette (*el tocador de la Reyna*), which, like a bird-cage, overhangs the valley of the Darro,[11] and gaze from its light arcades upon the moonlight prospect! To the right, the swelling mountains of the Sierra Nevada, robbed of their ruggedness and softened into a fairy land, with their snowy summits gleaming like silver clouds against the deep blue sky. And then to lean over the parapet of the Tocador and gaze down upon Granada and the Albaycin [12] spread out like a map below; all buried in deep repose; the white palaces and convents sleeping in the moonshine, and beyond all these the vapory Vega [13] fading away like a dream-land in the distance.

Sometimes the faint click of castanets rises from the Alameda, where some gay Andalusians are dancing away the summer night. Sometimes the dubious tones of a guitar and the notes of an amorous voice, tell perchance the whereabout of some moonstruck lover serenading his lady's window.

Such is a faint picture of the moonlight nights I have passed loitering about the courts and halls and balconies of this most suggestive pile; "feeding my fancy with sugared suppositions," and enjoying that mixture of reverie and sensation which steal away existence in a southern climate; so that it has been almost morning before I have retired to bed, and been lulled to sleep by the falling waters of the fountain of Lindaraxa.

1832, 1850

FROM

A TOUR ON THE PRAIRIES

◊

¶ IRVING's one-month trip west of Fort Gibson, on the Neosho River in what is now Oklahoma, was made

11. **Darro:** the river at Granada. 12. **Albaycin:** a nearby height on which a fortress formerly stood. 13. **Vega:** an open plain.

possible by Henry L. Ellsworth, newly appointed Indian Commissioner in the region, who invited the author and his two traveling companions, Charles Joseph Latrobe and the Count de Pourtalès, to accompany him on an official tour of the Pawnee country in the fall of 1832. Ellsworth's party had as escort a contingent of United States Army Rangers.

The interval between Chapters 5 and 10 is two days.

◇

CHAPTER 5

FRONTIER SCENES—A LYCURGUS OF THE BORDER—LYNCH'S LAW—THE DANGER OF FINDING A HORSE—THE YOUNG OSAGE

ON THE following morning (Oct. 11), we were on the march by half-past seven o'clock, and rode through deep rich bottoms of alluvial soil, overgrown with redundant vegetation, and trees of an enormous size. Our route lay parallel to the west bank of the Arkansas, on the borders of which river, near the confluence of the Red Fork, we expected to overtake the main body of rangers. For some miles the country was sprinkled with Creek villages and farm-houses; the inhabitants of which appeared to have adopted, with considerable facility, the rudiments of civilization, and to have thriven in consequence. Their farms were well stocked, and their houses had a look of comfort and abundance.

We met with numbers of them returning from one of their grand games of ball, for which their nation is celebrated. Some were on foot, some on horseback; the latter, occasionally, with gaylydressed females behind them. They are a well-made race, muscular and closely knit, with well-turned thighs and legs. They have a Gipsy fondness for brilliant colors and gay decorations, and are bright and fanciful objects when seen at a distance on the prairies. One had a scarlet handkerchief bound round his head, surmounted with a tuft of black feathers like a cock's tail. Another had a white handkerchief, with red feathers; while a third, for want of a plume, had stuck in his turban a brilliant bunch of sumach.

On the verge of the wilderness we paused to inquire our way at a log house, owned by a white settler or squatter, a tall raw-boned old fellow, with red hair, a lank lantern visage, and an inveterate habit of winking with one eye, as if every thing he said was of knowing import. He was in a towering passion. One of his horses was missing; he was sure it had been stolen in the night by a straggling party of Osages encamped in a neighboring swamp; but he would have satisfaction! He would make an example of the villains. He had accordingly caught down his rifle from the wall, that invariable enforcer of right or wrong upon the frontiers, and, having saddled his steed, was about to sally forth on a foray into the swamp; while a brother squatter, with rifle in hand, stood ready to accompany him.

We endeavored to calm the old campaigner of the prairies, by suggesting that his horse might have strayed into the neighboring woods; but he had the frontier propensity to charge every thing to the Indians, and nothing could dissuade him from carrying fire and sword into the swamp.

After riding a few miles further we lost the trail of the main body of rangers, and became perplexed by a variety of tracks made by the Indians and settlers. At length coming to a log house, inhabited by a white man, the very last on the frontier, we found that we had wandered from our true course. Taking us back for some distance, he again brought us to the right trail; putting ourselves upon which, we took our final departure, and launched into the broad wilderness.

The trail kept on like a straggling footpath, over hill and dale, through brush and brake, and tangled thicket, and open prairie. In traversing the wilds it is customary for a party either of horse or foot to follow each other in single file like the Indians; so that the leaders break the way for those who follow, and lessen their labor and fatigue. In this way, also, the number of a party is concealed, the whole leaving but one narrow well trampled track to mark their course.

We had not long regained the trail, when, on emerging from a forest, we beheld our raw-boned, hard-winking, hard-riding knight-errant of the frontier, descending the slope of a hill, followed by his companion in arms. As he drew near to us, the gauntness of his figure and ruefulness of his aspect reminded me of the description of the hero of La Mancha,[1] and he was equally bent on affairs of doughty enterprise, being about to penetrate the thickets of the perilous swamp, within which the enemy lay ensconced.

While we were holding a parley with him on the slope of the hill, we descried an Osage on horseback issuing out of a skirt of wood about half a mile off, and leading a horse by a halter. The latter was immediately recognized by our hard-winking friend as the steed of which he was in quest. As the Osage drew near, I was struck with his ap-

A TOUR ON THE PRAIRIES. **Chapter 5.** **1. hero of La Mancha:** Don Quixote.

pearance. He was about nineteen or twenty years of age, but well grown, with the fine Roman countenance common to his tribe, and as he rode with his blanket wrapped round his loins, his naked bust would have furnished a model for a statuary. He was mounted on a beautiful piebald horse, a mottled white and brown, of the wild breed of the prairies, decorated with a broad collar, from which hung in front a tuft of horse-hair dyed of a bright scarlet.

The youth rode slowly up to us with a frank open air, and signified by means of our interpreter Beatte,[2] that the horse he was leading had wandered to their camp, and he was now on his way to conduct him back to his owner.

I had expected to witness an expression of gratitude on the part of our hard-favored cavalier, but to my surprise the old fellow broke out into a furious passion. He declared that the Indians had carried off his horse in the night, with the intention of bringing him home in the morning, and claiming a reward for finding him; a common practice, as he affirmed, among the Indians. He was, therefore, for tying the young Indian to a tree and giving him a sound lashing; and was quite surprised at the burst of indignation which this novel mode of requiting a service drew from us. Such, however, is too often the administration of law on the frontier, "Lynch's law," as it is technically termed, in which the plaintiff is apt to be witness, jury, judge, and executioner, and the defendant to be convicted and punished on mere presumption; and in this way, I am convinced, are occasioned many of those heart-burnings and resentments among the Indians, which lead to retaliation, and end in Indian wars. When I compared the open, noble countenance and frank demeanor of the young Osage, with the sinister visage and high-handed conduct of the frontiersman, I felt little doubt on whose back a lash would be most meritoriously bestowed.

Being thus obliged to content himself with the recovery of his horse, without the pleasure of flogging the finder into the bargain, the old Lycurgus, or rather Draco, of the frontier, set off growling on his return homeward, followed by his brother squatter.

As for the youthful Osage, we were all prepossessed in his favor; the young Count [3] especially, with the sympathies proper to his age and incident to his character, had taken quite a fancy to him. Nothing would suit but he must have the young Osage as a companion and squire in his expedition into the wilderness. The youth was easily tempted, and, with the prospect of a safe range over the buffalo prairies and the promise of a new blanket, he turned his bridle, left the swamp and the encampment of his friends behind him, and set off to follow the Count in his wanderings in quest of the Osage hunters.

Such is the glorious independence of man in a savage state. This youth, with his rifle, his blanket, and his horse, was ready at a moment's warning to rove the world; he carried all his worldly effects with him, and in the absence of artificial wants, possessed the great secret of personal freedom. We of society are slaves, not so much to others as to ourselves; our superfluities are the chains that bind us, impeding every movement of our bodies and thwarting every impulse of our souls. Such, at least, were my speculations at the time, though I am not sure but that they took their tone from the enthusiasm of the young Count, who seemed more enchanted than ever with the wild chivalry of the prairies, and talked of putting on the Indian dress and adopting the Indian habits during the time he hoped to pass with the Osages.

CHAPTER 10

AMUSEMENTS IN THE CAMP—CONSULTATIONS—HUNTERS' FARE AND FEASTING —EVENING SCENES—CAMP MELODY —THE FATE OF AN AMATEUR OWL

On returning to the camp, we found it a scene of the greatest hilarity. Some of the rangers were shooting at a mark, others were leaping, wrestling, and playing at prison-bars.[1] They were mostly young men, on their first expedition, in high health and vigor, and buoyant with anticipations; and I can conceive nothing more likely to set the youthful blood into a flow than a wild wood-life of the kind, and the range of a magnificent wilderness, abounding with game, and fruitful of adventure. We send our youth abroad to grow luxurious and effeminate in Europe; it appears to me that a previous tour on the prairies would be more likely to produce that manliness, simplicity, and self-dependence most in unison with our political institutions.[2]

While the young men were engaged in these boisterous amusements, a graver set, composed of

2. Beatte: Pierre Beatte, half-breed hunter and guide to the party. **3. Count:** Albert-Alexandre de Pourtales (1812–61), a Swiss, one of Irving's traveling companions. They had met on board ship on Irving's trip home in 1832.

Chapter 10. **1. prison-bars:** the game of prisoner's base. **2. We . . . institutions:** Irving's capacity for responding to the impressions of the moment makes him here begin to sound like Emerson in "The American Scholar" two years later.

the Captain,[3] the Doctor,[4] and other sages and leaders of the camp, were seated or stretched out on the grass, round a frontier map, holding a consultation about our position, and the course we were to pursue.

Our plan was to cross the Arkansas just above where the Red Fork falls into it, then to keep westerly, until we should pass through a grand belt of open forest, called the Cross Timber, which ranges nearly north and south from the Arkansas to Red River; after which we were to keep a southerly course towards the latter river.

Our half-breed, Beatte, being an experienced Osage hunter, was called into the consultation. "Have you ever hunted in this direction?" said the Captain. "Yes," was the laconic reply.

"Perhaps, then, you can tell us in which direction lies the Red Fork?"

"If you keep along yonder, by the edge of the prairie, you will come to a bald hill, with a pile of stones upon it."

"I have noticed that hill as I was hunting," said the Captain.

"Well! those stones were set up by the Osages as a landmark: from that spot you may have a sight of the Red Fork."

"In that case," cried the Captain, "we shall reach the Red Fork to-morrow; then cross the Arkansas above it, into the Pawnee country, and then in two days we shall crack buffalo bones!"

The idea of arriving at the adventurous hunting-grounds of the Pawnees, and of coming upon the traces of the buffaloes, made every eye sparkle with animation. Our further conversation was interrupted by the sharp report of a rifle at no great distance from the camp.

"That's old Ryan's rifle," exclaimed the Captain; "there's a buck down, I'll warrant!" nor was he mistaken; for, before long, the veteran made his appearance, calling upon one of the younger rangers to return with him, and aid in bringing home the carcass.

The surrounding country, in fact, abounded with game, so that the camp was overstocked with provisions, and, as no less than twenty bee-trees had been cut down in the vicinity, every one revelled in luxury. With the wasteful prodigality of hunters, there was a continual feasting, and scarce any one put by provision for the morrow. The cooking was conducted in hunters' style: the meat was stuck upon tapering spits of dogwood, which were thrust perpendicularly into the ground, so as to sustain the joint before the fire, where it was roasted or broiled with all its juices retained in it in a manner that would have tickled the palate of the most experienced gourmand. As much could not be said in favor of the bread. It was little more than a paste made of flour and water, and fried like fritters, in lard: though some adopted a ruder style, twisting it round the ends of sticks, and thus roasting it before the fire. In either way, I have found it extremely palatable on the prairies. No one knows the true relish of food until he has a hunter's appetite.

Before sunset, we were summoned by little Tonish [5] to a sumptuous repast. Blankets had been spread on the ground near to the fire, upon which we took our seats. A large dish, or bowl, made from the root of a maple-tree, and which we had purchased at the Indian village, was placed on the ground before us, and into it were emptied the contents of one of the camp-kettles, consisting of a wild turkey hashed, together with slices of bacon and lumps of dough. Beside it was placed another bowl of similar ware, containing an ample supply of fritters. After we had discussed [6] the hash, two wooden spits, on which the ribs of a fat buck were broiling before the fire, were removed and planted in the ground before us, with a triumphant air, by little Tonish. Having no dishes, we had to proceed in hunters' style, cutting off strips and slices with our hunting knives, and dipping them in salt and pepper. To do justice to Tonish's cookery, however, and to the keen sauce of the prairies, never have I tasted venison so delicious. With all this, our beverage was coffee, boiled in a camp-kettle, sweetened with brown sugar, and drunk out of tin cups: and such was the style of our banqueting throughout this expedition, whenever provisions were plenty, and as long as flour and coffee and sugar held out.

As the twilight thickened into night, the sentinels were marched forth to their stations around the camp: an indispensable precaution in a country infested by Indians. The encampment now presented a picturesque appearance. Camp-fires were blazing and smouldering here and there among the trees, with groups of rangers round them; some seated or lying on the ground, others standing in the ruddy glare of the flames, or in shadowy relief. At some of the fires there was much boisterous mirth, where peals of laughter were mingled with loud ribald jokes and uncouth exclamations; for the troop was evidently a raw, undisciplined band, levied among the wild youngsters of the frontier, who had enlisted, some for the sake of

3. **Captain:** Captain Jesse Bean, commander of the company of Rangers. 4. **Doctor:** Dr. David Holt, surgeon hired by the Army.

5. **Tonish:** Antoine Deshetres, Creole cook and general factotum, counterpart of Mateo in *The Alhambra*. 6. **discussed:** an ironic usage: investigated or tried the quality of; consumed.

roving adventure, and some for the purpose of getting a knowledge of the country. Many of them were the neighbors of their officers, and accustomed to regard them with the familiarity of equals and companions. None of them had any idea of the restraint and decorum of a camp, or ambition to acquire a name for exactness in a profession in which they had no intention of continuing.

While this boisterous merriment prevailed at some of the fires, there suddenly rose a strain of nasal melody from another, at which a choir of "vocalists" were uniting their voices in a most lugubrious psalm-tune. This was led by one of the lieutenants; a tall, spare man, who we were informed had officiated as school-master, singing-master, and occasionally as Methodist preacher, in one of the villages of the frontier. The chant rose solemnly and sadly in the night air, and reminded me of the description of similar canticles in the camps of the Covenanters; and, indeed, the strange medley of figures and faces and uncouth garbs congregated together in our troop would not have disgraced the banners of Praise-God Barebones.[7]

In one of the intervals of this nasal psalmody an amateur owl, as if in competition, began his dreary hooting. Immediately there was a cry throughout the camp of "Charley's owl! Charley's owl!" It seems this "obscure bird" had visited the camp every night, and had been fired at by one of the sentinels, a half-witted lad named Charley; who, on being called up for firing when on duty, excused himself by saying, that he understood that owls made uncommonly good soup.

One of the young rangers mimicked the cry of this bird of wisdom, who, with a simplicity little consonant with his character, came hovering within sight, and alighted on the naked branch of a tree lit up by the blaze of our fire. The young Count immediately seized his fowling-piece, took fatal aim, and in a twinkling the poor bird of ill omen came fluttering to the ground. Charley was now called upon to make and eat his dish of owl-soup, but declined, as he had not shot the bird.

In the course of the evening I paid a visit to the Captain's fire. It was composed of huge trunks of trees, and of sufficient magnitude to roast a buffalo whole. Here were a number of the prime hunters and leaders of the camp, some sitting, some standing, and others lying on skins or blankets before the fire, telling old frontier stories about hunting and Indian warfare.

As the night advanced, we perceived above the trees, to the west, a ruddy glow flushing up the sky.

"That must be a prairie set on fire by the Osage hunters," said the Captain.

"It is at the Red Fork," said Beatte, regarding the sky. "It seems but three miles distant, yet it perhaps is twenty."

About half-past eight o'clock, a beautiful pale light gradually sprang up in the east, a precursor of the rising moon. Drawing off from the Captain's lodge, I now prepared for the night's repose. I had determined to abandon the shelter of the tent, and henceforth to bivouac like the rangers. A bear-skin spread at the foot of a tree was my bed, with a pair of saddle-bags for a pillow. Wrapping myself in blankets, I stretched myself on this hunter's couch, and soon fell into a sound and sweet sleep, from which I did not awake until the bugle sounded at daybreak.

1835, 1849

7. **Praise-God Barebones:** Praisegod Barbon, or Barebone, a London leather-seller and Anabaptist preacher, noted for his long sermons. Cromwell's parliament of 1653, in which Barebone served, was named after him.

MARIUS BEWLEY
Editor

James Fenimore Cooper

1789–1851

William Cullen Bryant

1794–1878

It is a commonplace of literary history that the 1850's represent the most brilliant period of achievement in American literature. *The Scarlet Letter*, *Moby-Dick*, *Walden*, and *Leaves of Grass*, to mention only the most obvious books, were produced during the first five years of the decade. The nineteenth century had seen nothing like it before, nor would it again as the nation moved through the Civil War into the genteel vulgarity of the Gilded Age. As we look back on the 1850's from the present time, the very magnitude of those achievements, which have given a characteristic stamp to the American literary sensibility, acts as a kind of watershed—dividing us from a remoter American past which one may be more inclined to visit from motives of historical interest than from any compelling sense of kinship. But in the case of James Fenimore Cooper, a kinship does exist.

Cooper died at the beginning of the 1850's, but there are aspects of his mind and writings that place him in a more direct relationship with the great writers who came after him than with his strict contemporaries. Today he is commonly regarded as a writer of boys' books. As a recent American critic has pointed out, most of the great American classics may be regarded as boys' books. But this is only one way, and a very narrow way, of looking at them: and there is more than one way of looking at Cooper. Quantitatively, a good deal has been written about him in the past, but contemporary criticism, which has had so much to say about Melville and James, has tended to shy away from him. This is unfortunate, for there is a great deal in Cooper to repay scrutiny. With the exception of Hugh Henry Brackenridge, whose satirical novel on early American politics, *Modern Chivalry*, also goes unread, Cooper was the first American writer to use the novel form seriously as a vehicle of social and political criticism. He wished to argue and to communicate his ideas about society and American manners, politics, and economics. This new note of seriousness that he brought to his role as a novelist (even when he tried to disclaim it) was in itself a new recognition of the possibilities of fiction. His satiric examination of American life, and his exploration of the contrast between American and European attitudes, in novels like *Homeward Bound* (1838) and *Home as Found* (1838), look forward to Henry James, while such characters as Steadfast Dodge and Aristabulus Bragg (the names are descriptive) anticipate the Babbitts and Dodsworths of a later literary generation.

One of the functions and responsibilities of literature is to define nationality in the act of describing or dramatizing it. Without Shakespeare, Milton, Jane Austen, and Dickens, it is difficult to imagine that the English would know how to think and act like Englishmen. The novels of Cooper are an exercise in national definition. He sets out to tell his countrymen what it should be to think and act like an American, and if he is often too self-conscious in his mission, he nevertheless extends the range of our self-knowledge. In the great figure of Natty Bumppo he has given us a symbolic character who seems in ways almost mysterious to embody the very genius of America itself: at any rate, of that America stretching backward in time toward that early moment when, as Scott Fitzgerald said, "a fresh, green breast of the new world" presented man "for the last time in history with something commensurate to his capacity for wonder." It is essential that in an age of concrete and chrome the lines of imaginative communication with that earlier world should not be destroyed.

The American writer during the first half of the nineteenth century was in a vulnerable position. He was exposed to two dangers. He might be tempted to consider the whole idea of an American literature invalid and content himself with a servile imitation of English models. An anonymous author was not a solitary voice when he wrote, in 1807:

We know that in this land, where the spirit of democracy is everywhere diffused, we are exposed as it were to a poisonous atmosphere, which blasts everything beautiful in nature, and corrodes everything elegant in art; we know that with us "the rose leaves fall ungathered," and we believe that there is little to praise and nothing to admire in most of the objects which would first present themselves to the view of a stranger.

On the other hand, he might react in the opposite direction and think the United States culturally independent of the Old World, and so abandon himself to a suffocating literary provincialism. As the Connecticut poet, John Trumbull, put it much earlier in *An Essay on the Use and Advantages of the Fine Arts* (1770):

This land her Steele and Addison shall view,
The former glories equalled by the new;
Some future Shakespeare charm the rising age,
And hold in magic charm the listening page.

In either case there would have been little truth involved in the literature that resulted, and America would not have discovered her true image in such distorting mirrors.

It is a tribute to Cooper's intelligence that he successfully avoided these two pitfalls. His novels usually show a deep sympathy with his country, and a strong faith in its possibilities: but this is always accompanied by an insight into the limitations surrounding the conditions of life in America that prevents him from falling into the kind of inflationary writing that marred the work of many of his contemporaries. One of the characters in the late novel, *The Redskins*, makes a measured assessment of the American cultural scene that clarifies Cooper's lifelong attitude:

"Will New York ever be a capital? Yes—out of all question, yes. But the day will not come until after the sudden changes of condition which immediately and so naturally succeeded the revolution, have ceased to influence ordinary society, and those above again impart to those below more than they receive. This restoration to the natural state of things must take place as soon as society gets settled; and there will be nothing to prevent a town living under our own institutions—spirit, *tendencies*, and all—from obtaining the highest tone that ever yet prevailed in a capital. The folly is in anticipating the natural course of events. Nothing will more hasten these events, however, than a literature that is controlled, not by the lower, but by the higher opinion of the country; which literature is yet, in a great degree, to be created." [CHAP. 1]

This was written in 1846, shortly before the 1850's that were to go far toward creating such a literature as Cooper envisages here. The literature of that decade was no accident. More than a half-century of national history leads up to it, during which the foundations of a literary tradition were established. Without the substantial beginnings of such a tradition the later accomplishments would have been impossible, and it was Cooper who did more than any other writer to give it scope and dignity. He enlarged the function and range of the novel by making it an organ of serious intellectual criticism; he gave it a peculiarly national flavor by his celebration of American scenery and by his treatment of distinctively American problems. In some ways what Henry James was to say of Hawthorne might even more truthfully be said of Cooper: that he showed "to what a use American matter could be put by an American hand: a consummation involving, it appeared, the happiest moral. For the moral was that an American could be an artist, one of the finest, without going 'outside' about it. . . ." Above all, the international reputation Cooper achieved as an artist lent a sense of security to a new literature that was both brash and unsure of itself.

In our own time we have witnessed several notable literary revivals. When Melville died in 1891 he had already been long forgotten. "Probably, if the truth were known," said a newspaper obituary, "even his own generation has long thought him dead. . . ." But today no other American writer of the nineteenth century speaks as profoundly and intimately to us as Melville. Similarly, Henry James is no longer considered an esoteric craftsman, writing only for a small audience. It is not fashion that dictates these shifts in taste, but fundamental changes in our problems and needs. Shortly after Cooper died in 1851, Melville wrote that "a grateful posterity will take the best care of Fenimore Cooper." Cooper has never been forgotten to the extent that Melville was until the 1920's; nevertheless, Melville's words have not proved prophetic. If Cooper is conventionally honored, he is seldom read; and today very little of his enormous production is in print. What likelihood is there of a Cooper revival, even on a moderate scale? There is this to recommend it: under his old-fashioned prose, the questions that engage his attention are similar to many that trouble us. They are not the same torturing problems of metaphysical anxiety and doubt that we share with Melville. Rather, they are political in character.

The central preoccupation, seen under a variety of aspects, that troubles Cooper in his most representative novels is the threat to democracy in action as it exists in a country where traditional values are in the process of being supplanted by economic motives; where manners and cultural standards are in the process of being reduced to the lowest common denominator, and where the intolerant tyranny of the majority threatens the liberalism of the few. In an age vitiated by concepts of conformity, Cooper's better novels demonstrate the healthfulness of a patriotic subversiveness that does not regard flank-rubbing with the herd the most satisfactory form of social contact. Our age has been described as one of mass civilization and minority culture. In *The American Democrat* (1838) Cooper had explained why democracies are especially prone to this cultural affliction:

> The tendency of democracies is, in all things, to mediocrity, since the tastes, knowledge and principles of the majority form the tribunal of appeal. This circumstance, while it certainly serves to elevate the average qualities of a nation, renders the introduction of a high standard difficult. Thus do we find in literature, the arts, architecture and all acquired knowledge, a tendency in America to gravitate towards the common centre in this, as in other things; lending a value and estimation to mediocrity that are not elsewhere given. It is fair to expect, however, that a foundation so broad, may in time sustain a superstructure of commensurate proportions, and that the influence of masses will in this, as in other interests, have a generally beneficial effect. Still . . . the mass of no community is qualified to decide the most correctly on anything, which, in its nature, is above its reach.
>
> ["On the Disadvantages of Democracy"]

This recognition is pervasive throughout Cooper's books. It is an attitude that is easy to misinterpret unless it is focused in the full context of his political credo, and the Americans of his day did misinterpret it. "The most intense lover of his country," wrote Thomas R. Lounsbury, his first biographer, "he became the most unpopular man of letters to whom it has ever given birth." Cooper believed in the ascendency of the uncommon man, and today it would be unwise for us to forget our first major novelist who was centrally concerned in his work with a truth that has become even more urgent with the passage of time.

But it must be confessed that certain qualities in Cooper's prose militate against a widespread revival of interest in his work. At his best, Cooper is a great writer. When he describes the wilderness or the sea, few can surpass him. As Joseph Conrad said of him:

> His descriptions have the magistral ampleness of a gesture indicating the sweep of a vast horizon. They embrace the colours of sunset, the peace of starlight, the aspects of storm and calm, the great loneliness of the waters, the stillness of watchful coasts. . . .[1]

But in local passages the prose is sometimes archaic and stilted, the dialogue wooden, the humor debatable. In the beginning, the reader must have patience and generous sympathy if he is to realize that Mark Twain's insulting essay, "The Literary Offenses of Fenimore Cooper," tells more about Twain's critical incapacity than it does about Cooper's limitations. In the end, one can do nothing better than remember Conrad's words: "He wrote before the great American language was born, and he wrote as well as any novelist of his time."

II

A YEAR before he died, Cooper is reported to have said that "it takes a first class aristocrat to make a first class Democrat." This might be taken as the motto of his life. It not only affected his practical political thinking to the end, but it left its mark on most of his writing, which was always a reflection of his deepest political and social convictions. It was to argue and further the cause of these convictions that it seemed worthwhile to him to write at all. There has sometimes been confusion about Cooper's politics because it has appeared to many literary historians that a man of his aristocratic predilections had no business being a Jacksonian Democrat, especially when his father had been one of the New York state partisan leaders of the Federalists—that party out of which the Whig party grew. One Cooper scholar put it this way a number of years ago:

> Cooper was a country gentleman, a Whig squire. . . . He wanted to be and was loyal to the United States and its form of government, but his social ideals were in conflict with the "levelling" and "majority" tendencies present in Jacksonian America—a most uncomfortable time for a traditionalist!

But Cooper was never a Whig. He was, though perhaps with qualifications towards the end of his life, an ardent supporter of Jackson's policies, seeing in the Whig party a powerful oligarchy of vested interests based on business and financial speculation. In a political pamphlet attacking the Whigs, *A Letter to His Countrymen* (1834), Cooper described in general terms the political tendencies of his time, but he meant the application to be made to the Whigs in particular:

> I had had abundant occasion to observe that the great political contest of the age was not, as is usually pretended, between the antagonist principles of monarchy and democracy, but in reality between those who, under the shallow pretence of limiting power to the *elite* of society, were contending for exclusive advantage at the expense of their fellow creatures.

In other words, Cooper in 1834 was very much in the position of the liberal of today who may well believe that standards must be maintained by a minority of informed and disciplined leaders, but who refuses to accept as an adequate substitute an "aristocracy" of intrenched capitalists intent on augmenting their own power and resources. Cooper, like Hawthorne, William Cullen Bryant, Horatio Greenough, Hiram Powers, George Bancroft, James K. Paulding, and most of the other intellectuals and artists of the day, knew that one could be a Jacksonian Democrat without being a Vandal, but that it was very difficult to be a Whig without being a Philistine. The

[1] Joseph Conrad, "Tales of the Sea," *Notes on Life and Letters* (1921).

leveling tendencies and the emphasis on majority opinion were certainly present in Jacksonian America, and a reading of Cooper's political primer, *The American Democrat* (1838), will reveal how painful these were to Cooper; but they were imperfections of the political surface, not of the heart, and they might be corrected. Cooper believed that such a corrective mission could be accomplished only by men who were equally devoted to democratic principles and to standards of personal conduct and taste that were popularly described as "aristocratic" in the new equalitarian atmosphere of his America.

Perhaps it would really be more accurate to describe Cooper as a Jeffersonian Democrat, for his faith was in the land, and like Jefferson he envisaged America as a republic whose wealth consisted in farms and landed estates rather than in business and finance. It was natural that landed wealth should appear the best kind of wealth to him—in his boyhood he had lived with it under almost idyllic circumstances, or so it seemed when he looked back on those years from mature manhood. It seemed to him that the most precious human values attached themselves, in the course of time, to inherited property, and so were transmitted from one generation to the next. Land was the basis of social solidarity and the guarantee of social and cultural continuity. As opposed to wealth accumulated through business and financial speculation (the principal sources of Whig prosperity), landed property supported character, encouraged responsibility, and fostered tradition. Cooper knew this from the example of his father.

Judge William Cooper had been one of the most successful land agents of the Revolutionary years. By 1786 he had acquired 40,000 acres of land in western New York near Otsego Lake, and here, in 1790, he brought his family from New Jersey. The child James (Cooper took his mother's family name, Fenimore, only later in life) was then only thirteen months old. The mansion house which Judge Cooper soon built is described in a history of Cooperstown as "a great rectangular stone house with castellated roof and gothic windows, surrounded by box hedges and wide lawns trimmed precisely by black gardeners, far surpassing any other home in the far west." Growing up between the frontier freedom of the woods and the lake—the Glimmerglass of *The Deerslayer*—and the spacious ease of Otsego Hall with its retinue of slaves and servants, it is not remarkable that Cooper found his democratic and aristocratic propensities at mutual ease in later life.

Cooper's education was suitable for the son of a Congressman and the wealthiest man in his county. It culminated at Yale, from which he was expelled in his third year for an undistinguished undergraduate performance involving gunpowder in a keyhole and a donkey in the classroom. At home again, young Cooper had thoughts of the sea which his father, at this point, was willing to encourage. He sailed at first before the mast of a merchant vessel, and in 1808 entered the United States Navy as a midshipman. During these years he acquired that love of the sea and detailed knowledge of ships and sailing that enabled him to become the first great sea novelist before Conrad. By the time he resigned from the Navy in 1810 his father was dead, having been struck over the head by a political opponent, and Cooper himself was about to be married. He had chosen Miss Susan Augusta De Lancey, whose ancestors had distinguished themselves in the service of the king, and whose grandfather had been royal lieutenant governor of New York. The marriage was a happy one, and almost certainly his wife's upper-class Tory background confirmed those tendencies in Cooper's character that we have already noted.

At his father's death Cooper was very well off financially, but, for whatever reasons, within a few years his circumstances were considerably reduced. "Accident first made me a writer," Cooper once wrote, but the fact that it held out promise of financial reward undoubtedly encouraged him to continue on a course so casually begun. His first novel, *Precaution* (1820), was written as the result of a bet with his wife. Apparently he intended it to be an imitation of Jane Austen's *Persuasion*. It is not surprising that the future master of the American wilderness showed limited command of the English drawing room. His second novel, *The Spy* (1821), is one of the earliest of the American classics, and its success—eight thousand copies in four months—must have persuaded Cooper to continue in his new role. It is the story of a colonial family, the Whartons, living in Westchester during the Revolution, and the plot becomes a kind of debate in action between the American and the British points of view. Cooper returned to the Revolution in later novels, and, in his use of the theme of divided loyalties, one occasionally has anticipations of the later international novel with its dialectical pattern of American and European attitudes. The most famous character in the novel is Harvey Birch, the Yankee peddler, who is Washington's favorite spy. He accomplishes his missions for the Americans by posing as a spy for the British, and this device of the superimposed identity, the assumed role, becomes a favorite one with Cooper in later books. He utilizes it in a variety of ways, but usually for the purpose of maintaining an aloofness from his material and exercising superior control over it. Though he made little of it technically, Cooper, like Henry James, was attracted to the role of the detached observer, as all writers must be whose interest is intellectual and analytic.

Cooper's third novel, *The Pioneers* (1823), sold thirty-five hundred copies on the day of publication. Natty Bumppo, who has been called the most memorable character in American fiction, was first introduced in this novel. Cooper was to pursue Natty's career in the wilderness and on the prairies through four more books, but these must be discussed as a unit later. The same year saw *The Pilot*, the first of a series of sea stories in which Cooper drew on his naval experience. By this time he had become, with the possible exception of Irving, the best-known writer in America, both at home and abroad, and his income had been greatly augmented. He was now ready to fulfill an old ambition by taking his family to Europe. The extended visit lasted over seven years during which time Cooper, with characteristic but scarcely credible energy, published seven novels, a long book of American social criticism, *The Travelling Bachelor: or Notions of the Americans*, and collected the material for five travel books which he published shortly after his return in 1833. Cooper moved through Europe, not as an obscure American, but as a literary lion who was everywhere considered to be the peer of Sir Walter Scott. Lafayette was his friend, and through the American minister in Paris he secured entry into the most influential governing circles and fashionable coteries. He was an indefatigable observer of foreign manners and attitudes, and always a tireless champion of America. Yet it is probable that in subtle ways these splendid years in Europe disqualified him from ever happily settling down in the United States when he came home again.

Cooper returned to America with a more detached attitude than ever, determined to instruct his countrymen in the basic rudiments of what makes a *good* American. It is not altogether surprising that the Americans objected. The period of Cooper's popularity came to an end. After the publication of *Homeward Bound*, a review of it appeared in the *North American Review* which indicates the new response:

> Professing to be a sturdy republican, he has exhausted his powers of invective upon the manners and characters of his countrymen, who are, taking his own descriptions for truth, ignorant of the first principles of social refinement, and no better than a nation of brutes and savages. If such are the friends of Republicanism, she may well pray heaven to save her from them.

Cooper's admiration for aristocratic values came to a patriotic focus in his concept of the American gentleman. The American gentleman, so far as outward manners, spiritual refinement, and cultivated tastes went, was not to be distinguished from the finest flower of European nobility. Eve Effingham, the heroine of *Homeward Bound* and *Home as Found*—both published in 1838—reflected perfectly Cooper's faith in a natural aristocracy in the United States:

> Eve actually fancied that the position of an American gentleman might really become, nay, that it *ought* to be the highest of all human stations short of that of sovereigns. Such a man had no superior, with the exception of those who actually ruled, in her eyes, and this fact, she conceived rendered him more than noble, as nobility is usually graduated. She had been accustomed to

seeing her father and John Effingham moving in the best circles of Europe, respected for their information and independence, undistinguished by their manners, admired for their personal appearance, manly, courteous, and of noble bearing and principles, if not set apart from the rest of mankind by an arbitrary rule connected with rank. Rich, and possessing all the habits that properly mark refinement, of gentle extraction, of liberal attainments, walking abroad in the dignity of manhood, and with none between them and the Deity, Eve had learned to regard the gentlemen of her race as the equals in station of any of their European associates, and as the superiors of most, in everything that is necessary to true distinction. [*Home as Found*, CHAP. 13]

This was naturally not the breed of American Cooper found most in evidence when he returned home, and the two Effingham novels are filled with satiric portraits, often scathing and penetrating, of less admirable national types who still ring as painfully true as Sinclair Lewis's gallery. Cooper was always better when he attacked than when he praised. Here is a description of Mr. Steadfast Dodge:

Mr. Dodge came from that part of the country in which men were accustomed to think, act, almost to eat and drink and sleep, in common; or, in any other words, from one of those regions in America, in which there was so much community, that few had the moral courage, even when they possessed the knowledge, and all the other necessary means, to cause their individuality to be respected. When the usual process of conventions, sub-conventions, caucuses, and public meetings did not supply the means of a "concentrated action," he and his neighbors had long been in the habit of having recourse to societies, by way of obtaining "energetic means," as it was termed; and from his tenth year up to his twenty-fifth, this gentleman had been either a president, vice-president, manager, or committee-man, of some philosophical, political, or religious expedient to fortify human wisdom, make men better, and resist error and despotism. His experience had rendered him expert in what may well enough be termed the language of association. No man of his years, in the twenty-six States, could more readily apply the terms of "taking up"—"excitement"—"unqualified hostility"—"public opinion"—"spreading before the public"—or any other of those generic phrases that imply the privileges of all, and the rights of none.
[*Homeward Bound*, CHAP. 4]

But to appreciate Cooper's cruel mastery of the meannesses and hypocrisies of these Americans, it is necessary to see them in action. The social analysis in the Effingham novels, particularly of the New York scene in *Home as Found*, can occasionally be Jamesian in the quality of its comedy, and it is both accurate and ruthless with its barbs. Steadfast Dodge and Aristabulus Bragg are comic characters, but in Cooper's eyes they posed a real threat to America. Only a class of disinterested intellectuals and democrats like Edward Effingham, Eve's father, could counteract it, and today it is difficult to say that Cooper was wrong. The concentrated creative outburst of 1838 is clearly symptomatic of a crisis of mind and heart. After the long years abroad, Cooper was equipped to look at his countrymen with a sharper, more critical vision than he had possessed before. The tremendous energy that he brought to the task of revaluation is amply exhibited in *Homeward Bound*, *Home as Found*, and *The American Democrat*, which, with a fourth book, *Gleanings in Europe: Italy*, all belong to this one extraordinary year. Cooper summed the situation up admirably in this passage from *The American Democrat:*

The democrat, recognizing the right of all to participate in power, will be more liberal in his general sentiments, a quality of superiority in itself; but, in conceding this much to his fellow man, he will proudly maintain his own independence of vulgar domination, as indispensable to his personal habits. The same principle and manliness that would induce him to depose a royal despot would induce him to resist a vulgar tyrant.
["An Aristocrat and a Democrat"]

We have seen that for Cooper a great protection against such vulgar domination had been a landed gentry. From colonial days New York had been dotted with large manorial estates of which the largest, Rensselaerwyck on the Hudson, comprised a million acres. Vast numbers of farmers rented small holdings on long leases from these great landlords for which, in addition to their yearly rent, they often performed services that were feudal in character. During the 1840's agitation became widespread in the state to force the large landowners to sell the farms outright to their tenants, and Anti-Rent societies that were formed had recourse to violence to prevent foreclosures and the collection of rents that had fallen in arrears.

Cooper wrote the Littlepage trilogy in defense of the landed gentry among whom he had grown up. After the Leatherstocking Tales, it is one of Cooper's most interesting achievements. These three novels, *Satanstoe, The Chainbearer*, and *The Redskins*, were all published in 1845 and 1846. They carry the story of the Littlepage family from colonial times, through three generations living on their landed estates or sometimes in Europe, down to Cooper's own day when such holdings were threatened by mob violence and by state law. For once Cooper had misjudged the situation. Whatever abuses the Anti-Rent agitators may have been guilty of, the land laws against which they were rebelling established wealth and poverty on a permanent basis. If the old system guaranteed that the great estates and the incomes deriving from them should be handed on from father to son, they guaranteed no less the continuity of poverty on the small, often stony and infertile holdings. Tenants frequently were able to escape from the terms of their leases only into absolute and hopeless poverty. Nor were the great landowners whom Cooper supported so bravely any longer the chivalric natural aristocracy whom he seemed to remember from his youth. A fusion had already taken place between the great speculators and businessmen among the Whigs and the landed gentry of an earlier period. But Cooper was desperate in the middle forties to hold back that tidal wave of leveling influences which he saw sweeping everything before it. "The secret of this change among ourselves," he wrote in *The Redskins*, "is the innate dislike which is growing up in the country to see any man distinguished from the mass around him in anything, even though it should be in merit." Property appeared to be the last defense, and Cooper was ready to champion it, even on the most feudal of terms. "It is pretended the durable leases are feudal in their nature," he wrote. "We do not conceive this to be true; but, admitting it to be so, it would only prove that feudality, to this extent, is a part of the institutions of the state." It was an unfortunate position for a man of Cooper's liberal instincts and intelligence to find himself in, but in the total context of his thought it was understandable and forgivable. In any event, he was championing a lost cause. Nevertheless, the Littlepage trilogy remains a solid achievement. Only *The Redskins*, written when the Anti-Rent movement was reaching its peak, is violently propagandistic. *Satanstoe*, taking its title from the name of the Littlepage estate in Westchester, is an indispensable book for any student of Cooper. It is mainly concerned with giving us a pastoral picture of colonial New York when the great estates had only recently been acquired. The title of *The Chainbearer* has reference to the surveyor's chains with the aid of which land is surveyed, boundaries laid out, and property rights guaranteed. These chains are symbolic of order and inheritance; but despite excellent parts, the argument of *The Chainbearer* begans to grow heavy. Each successive generation of the Littlepages, even if they do not admit it, finds it more difficult to reconcile the claims of democracy and aristocracy.

Cooper died in 1851 on the eve of his sixty-second birthday. His life, so energetically lived, had been all of a piece, dedicated passionately to certain principles and ideals from which he never deviated for a moment in the face of that public opinion which he held in such contempt as the source of American weakness. It has been impossible to relate here the long history of Cooper's successful libel suits against the Whig newspaper editors of his day, who liked nothing more than to slander an important and articulate Jacksonian Democrat. He reduced them to glowering silence in the end, and made it clear to all that a man and a writer of integrity, at least if he were Cooper, had means of redress against the Steadfast Dodges of the time, even if they were newspaper editors. Cooper is a major artist in the American literary tradition, but not the least of his importance to us today is that he possessed, in a high degree, that beautiful attribute of being, in whatever he did, a seriously controversial figure.

III

THE Leatherstocking Tales were written over a period of eighteen years, from 1823 when *The*

Pioneers was published, to 1841 when *The Deerslayer* appeared. Nevertheless, an unusual consistency of tone and intention informs these five novels. This arises mainly from the character of Natty Bumppo, who also goes under the names of Deerslayer, Hawkeye, Pathfinder, and Leatherstocking. The creation of Leatherstocking is probably the most significant thing that happened in American literature during the first half-century of its national history. Leatherstocking belongs to that small group of fictional characters which includes Melville's Ishmael and Ahab, Huckleberry Finn, and perhaps Jay Gatsby, who seem to be related in some special way to the deepest meaning of the American experience itself. Critics have sometimes described these characters as "mythic," and for Leatherstocking they have often added the word "epic." D. H. Lawrence was among them when he said that the Leatherstocking books formed "a sort of American Odyssey, with Natty Bumppo for Odysseus." The "epic" quality of these novels is almost too obvious for comment. They create for us the primeval American wilderness as no art will ever be able to create it again. It is not, certainly, the wilderness as it ever existed, but a wilderness heroically imagined, belonging to a kind of American Golden Age. There is something undeniably Homeric about this faraway world of forest solitudes and more than life-size figures engaged in mortal combat: of Indians who have the bearing of ancient kings and can speak in poetry that would do no discredit to J. M. Synge's Irish peasants. It is a world of great but uncomplicated contrasts between cruelty and nobility, between the silence of endless woods and the sudden tumult of Indian ambuscade. All but one of the Leatherstocking Tales, *The Pioneers*, is concerned with bloody conflict, yet the fighting is always interpolated with passages of quiet beauty when that yet unspoiled American world glows on Cooper's pages like an earthly paradise.

By counterpointing his pattern of conflict and violence with scenes of forest loveliness, Cooper is not merely taking time out from action for descriptive detail. He is a master of pace and timing, and he disposes these blocks of prose in such way as to achieve the maximum of effect. The bloodcurdling cries of his savages are the more terrifying because he first creates with great artistry the awful stillness of the woods. Scenes of violence and bloodshed in Cooper are regularly followed by interludes in which the calmness of the natural world is reasserted, when the claims of battle and death give way for a time before the regenerative forces of life. It is Cooper's wonderful ability to handle these shifts of tone and viewpoint that is responsible for the sustained intensity of his actions through many chapters, and for the sense of universality he imparts so often to his incidents of forest warfare.

Cooper has a splendidly pictorial imagination that was fostered by his interest in painting. He has a habit of framing his scenes as if they were enclosed in a picture space, circumscribing the action on a visually composed stage with concentrated effect, and intensifying emotion by accents of color and skillfully deployed areas of light and shadow. Here is a night scene of an Indian encampment from *The Deerslayer* (1841) that Natty views from the safety of an offshore canoe which is concealed by darkness from the Indians themselves:

The canoe lay in front of a natural vista, not only through the bushes that lined the shore but of the trees also, that afforded a clear view of the camp. . . . In consequence of their recent change of ground, the Indians had not yet retired to their huts, but had been delayed by their preparations, which included lodging as well as food. A large fire had been made, as much to answer the purposes of torches, as for the use of their simple cookery, and at this precise moment it was blazing high and bright, having recently received a large supply of dried brush. The effect was to illuminate the arches of the forest, and to render the whole area occupied by the camp as light as if hundreds of tapers were burning. . . .

Deerslayer saw at a glance that many of the warriors were absent. His acquaintance, Rivenoak, however, was present, being seated in the foreground of a picture that Salvator Rosa would have delighted to draw, his swarthy features illuminated as much by pleasure as by the torch-like flame. . . . A boy was looking over his shoulder, in dull curiosity, completing the group. More in the background, eight or ten warriors lay half recumbent on the ground, or sat with their backs inclining against trees, so many types of indolent repose. Their arms were near them, sometimes leaning against the same tree as themselves, or were lying across their bodies, in indolent preparation. [CHAP. 16]

Cooper handles this kind of composition almost plastically, and the result is not static, as one might fear. It confers on the action that occurs in such carefully composed scenes both tightness of form and an unforgettable theatricality. These novels are not meant to be realistic. Consider Chapter 30 from *The Deerslayer* (see p. 328) in which the ex-pirate's beautiful daughter, Judith Hutter, attempts to rescue Deerslayer from the torture stake by emerging from the surrounding forests into the Indian encampment dressed in a magnificently regal brocade gown, which Cooper has gone to great pains in the plot to place at her disposal. The Indians are almost, but not quite, awed into submission by this glittering vision of majestic beauty. It makes no difference that the whole incident could scarcely have happened, at least in the way Cooper describes it. It has an imaginative quality that is like some ballet of the American wilderness. One thinks, perhaps, of Dryden's heroic tragedies, yet the high-colored extravagance matters even less with Cooper because the whole action of the episode is not only adequately imagined, the moral stature of the hero is exalted enough, and of a character proper to sustain this kind of baroque stylization in the plotting. The scene is composed in the grand manner, and the accents of color are exactly right:

Objects became visible among the trees of the background, and a body of troops was seen advancing with measured tread. They came upon the charge, the scarlet of the king's livery shining among the bright green foliage of the forest.

But the choreographic mastery with which Cooper controls the rapid action of the Leatherstocking Tales would not in itself be enough to insure their preeminent status in American literature before the 1850's. The real source of their appeal and power lies in Natty Bumppo's character. It is as uncomplicated as the solitudes in which he dwells, as heroic as the actions he performs. Yet there is nothing primitive in his nature. Natty cannot read, but in contrast with this philosopher of the woods, the Effinghams themselves appear a little unsophisticated. Natty is never at a loss, for his wisdom seems as old as the continent, as enduring as the hills. At twenty-three in *The Deerslayer* (1841) he is as wise as he is in *The Prairie* (1827) when he is in his eighties. In his extraordinary death scene from that novel we feel that we are in the presence of some hero of the ancient world about to be raised to the status of an immortal.

Deerslayer can catch a tomahawk in mid-air and return it to the sender, and his feats of marksmanship with Killdeer, his rifle, have never been equaled. But it is not on these feats that Cooper builds up Natty's stature. Natty is a living incarnation of the natural moral law. One of the characters in *The Prairie* describes him in these words:

"The man I speak of was of great simplicity of mind, but of sterling worth. Unlike most of those who live a border life, he united the better, instead of the worst, qualities of the two people. He was a man endowed with the choicest and perhaps rarest gift of nature; that of distinguishing good from evil." [CHAP. 10]

It is not the least remarkable thing about the Leatherstocking Tales that, in the end, the reader actively and warmly shares this opinion of Natty. In attempting to present such a man, Cooper might have given us a prig and a bore; but, as D. H. Lawrence has said, Natty is a saint with a gun. His moralizing, without which he would not be Natty, is never offensive, and rarely tedious. There is nothing righteous about Leatherstocking, but—and this is something quite different—an aura of goodness seems to invest this aloof but talkative celibate of the wilderness. It has seemed ironical to some that Natty, who shows more concern for the sanctity of life than any other great character in our literature, should be responsible, as hunter and fighter, for so many deaths. But the irony is in the facts of existence, not in Leatherstocking, and Chapter 7, in which Natty kills his first Indian (see p. 308), is an astonishing depiction of conscience struggling with brutal necessity. Natty's reverence for life is preserved through seas of blood, and the lifelong effort involved renders it for us in the concrete. We observe it as an integral part of Natty's character and behavior, even in the act of killing. The old hunter of *The Pioneers*, who is angered by the wanton slaughter of the pigeons (see p. 346), is in a direct line with the young Deerslayer of Chapter 7.

Related to this reverence for life is Leatherstocking's greatest gift, which is uniquely his among our fictional characters: a profound understanding, which goes deeper than generosity and tolerance, of the genius of race. Natty is always proud of his white "gifts," but by these he means nothings racist. He has an almost mystical insight into those universal laws which ordain that each species, each race, shall exist according to its own nature, or as he calls it, its own "gifts." In his intuitive understanding and loving acceptance of "differences" that are according to nature, Natty's attitude is basically religious, though in a sense that looks toward the natural law rather than toward any specific theology. The friendship between Natty and Chingachgook that runs through the five Leatherstocking Tales is symbolic of this deep understanding of "differences." Like Ishmael and Queequeg, like Huck and Jim, it is one of the great friendships of literature, and it exists because of, not in despite of, their contrasting "gifts."

Natty is a kind of tutelary spirit of the American land. It is essential to his conception that he should stand aloof and detached, with no closer, more enduring relation than his friendship for Chingachgook, who himself symbolizes the aboriginal life and culture of America. But if Cooper has created Natty in an almost mythic dimension, he has also succeeded in imparting great warmth to him, and a capacity for emotion without which his virtues might seem a little forbidding. It would have done violence to Cooper's conception of Leatherstocking to have given him a wife. There is something priestly about his role that domestic ties would have violated and rendered absurd. But in *The Pathfinder* (1840) Natty falls deeply and hopelessly in love. Cooper shows a sure control over his material here, for so far from appearing out of character, Natty's moral nature grows in stature. The final effect is to add still greater weight to the wisdom he embodies by showing as its human source a nature that is no less passionately than nobly alive. Critics often say that American literature, at least until recently, has not seriously attempted to treat of love and the relationship between the sexes, and the Leatherstocking Tales are sometimes mentioned as partial substantiation of the charge. The charge in general is probably true, but it should be said that Natty's interview with Mabel Dunham on the shores of Lake Ontario, in Chapter 18 of *The Pathfinder* (see p. 339), is the most impressive scene between a man and a woman in American literature until Hawthorne in *The Scarlet Letter* brings Hester Prynne and Dimmesdale together in the woods. Mabel Dunham is also a refutation, along with Judith Hutter, of the charge that Cooper is always hopeless in the creation of female character.

Poised between love of America and disillusionment with her course, Cooper was able to create in Leatherstocking a symbolic character who resolved artistically the tension he had come to feel in himself between patriotic devotion and disaffection. In his old age, Leatherstocking flees to the western prairies to escape the advance of a civilization he distrusts as much as Cooper. In words that sound like Cooper's own, the old man says:

> What the world of America is coming to, and where the machinations of its people are to end, the Lord, He only knows. . . . towns and villages, farms and highways, churches and schools, in short all the inventions and deviltries of man, are spread across the region.

Cooper had become deeply discouraged, but with the creation of Leatherstocking—particularly as presented in the last three novels—he expressed his ultimate, his only hope: that the wisdom of natural virtue, and a purifying love of the land and forests and water, might yet redeem the American from the selfishness of the settlements: by which he meant the greed for money and power that he felt was corrupting the Republic. Unlike the Effingham novels, the Leatherstocking Tales are not polemical. It is rather through poetry and discreetly symbolic action that they embody the complex tensions we have spoken of. And it is because they exist as art adequately realized that they remain, both below and above the levels of conscious argument, the best vindication we have in his work of Cooper's deepest convictions.

IV

LEATHERSTOCKING is a richly original creation, but the originality resides in the fact that Cooper was able to realize his conception with such mastery, creating him from the inside out. Leatherstocking is no lay figure dressed in a fringed green hunting shirt and a fur cap, but, as we have already said, he gives tangible form to Cooper's most searching quest for the meaning of American experience. He does not illustrate any set conclusions at which Cooper had already arrived when he began these novels. It would be more correct to say that Natty *is* Cooper's conclusion about the American world, its limitations and its possibilities, and that he arrived at it *in the process* of writing. All of Cooper's hopes and fears about America, his love and his disgust, are realized in this one symbolic character whose "great simplicity" is of that superlative kind that represents the resolution of opposed tensions in the transcendant unity of art. But it is essential to Leatherstocking's greatness that the final distillation of his wisdom be concerned with the lot of man in an inscrutable universe rather than with the lot of the American gentleman in the America of Cooper's time. In *The Prairie* Leatherstocking says:

"Here have I been a dweller on the earth for fourscore and six changes of the seasons, and all that time have I looked at the growing and the dying trees, and yet do I not know the reasons why the bud starts under the summer sun, or the leaf falls when it is pinched by the frosts. Your larning, though it is man's boast, is folly in the eyes of Him, who sits in the clouds, and looks down in sorrow at the pride and vanity of his creatures. Many is the hour that I've passed, lying in the shades of the woods, or stretched upon the hills of these open fields, looking up into the blue skies, where I could fancy the Great One had taken his stand, and was solemnizing on the waywardness of man and brute below, as I myself had often looked at the ants tumbling over each other in their eagerness, though in a way and a fashion more suited to His mightiness and power. Knowledge! It is a plaything. Say, you who think it is so easy to climb into the judgment-seat above, can you tell me anything of the beginning and the end? . . . What is life, and what is death? Why does the eagle live so long, and why is the time of the butterfly so short?"

[CHAP. 17]

Cooper's unhappiness with the American social and political patterns of his day is seen to be absorbed here into universal questions of the human situation itself. Leatherstocking thus becomes the means by which the problems of the narrowly national scene that agitated the Effinghams are refocused against the background of the eternal.

It has already been suggested that this universalizing process is achieved largely through Leatherstocking's intimate communication with nature. In *The Deerslayer*, Cooper says of Natty:

He loved the woods for their freshness, their sublime solitudes, their vastness, and the impress that they everywhere bore of the divine hand of their Creator. He rarely moved through them without pausing to dwell on some peculiar beauty that gave him pleasure, though seldom attempting to investigate the causes; and never did a day pass without his communing in spirit, and this, too, without the aid of forms or language, with the infinite Source of all he saw, felt, and beheld.

[CHAP. 16]

We have said that Leatherstocking is a richly original creation, but that the originality exists in the art with which Cooper gave him concrete embodiment, and not in any paraphrasable ideas that went into his making. The above passage is quoted to illustrate, not what is original in the conception of Leatherstocking, but what he shares in common with the ideology of much American writing and art in Cooper's day.

Compare this passage from *The Deerslayer* with the opening paragraph of William Cullen Bryant's "A Forest Hymn" (1825) (see p. 365). The attitudes toward nature in both appear nearly identical. Nature is the symbol of the Creator, the mighty Cause, the infinite Source. Nature, for Bryant, is a temple, and the metaphor is carried out in some detail: the forest trees are venerable columns, the forest paths are winding aisles, the overarching branches are dim vaults. In this solemn cathedral atmosphere the heart is filled with awe of the "Maker." Bryant uses the term advisedly, for nature is an artifact whose purpose is to keep man's mind directed to the Supreme Craftsman. Nature should impart moral instruction, and it should elevate; but it should also be able to keep man suitably depressed, on occasion, with its lessons of decay and death:

> Written on thy works I read
> The lesson of thy own eternity.
> Lo! all grow old and die. . . .

To communicate this moral lesson, which he never substantially enlarged in his poetry after composing the first version of "Thanatopsis" at the age of seventeen, Bryant developed a sonorous blank verse that, for short passages, can be remarkably effective. But its effect depends too much on sound alone, which cannot, in the end, compensate for the usual commonplaceness of its imagery. Bryant is orotund without magniloquence, and if we read "Thanatopsis" with a subdued and valid pleasure, to follow this by, say, "Hymn to Death," "The Antiquity of Freedom," "An Evening Revery," "A Forest Hymn," and "The Flood of Years," becomes a little like listening to a harmonium with the pedal stuck.

Natty also looks upon the woods as a temple which everywhere bears the impress "of the divine hand of their Creator." In a passage from *The Deerslayer* in which Natty is speaking to Judith Hutter, we find a concentration of themes which both Cooper and Bryant share with their time:

"As for farms, they have their uses, and there's them that like to pass their lives on 'em; but what comfort can a man look for in a clearin', that he can't find in double quantities in the forest? If air, and room, and light, are a little craved, the windrows and the streams will furnish 'em, or here are the lakes for such as have bigger longings in that way; but where are you to find your shades and laughing springs, and leaping brooks, and vinerable trees, a thousand years old, in a clearin'? You don't find *them*, but you find their disabled trunks, marking the 'arth like headstones in a graveyard. It seems to me that the people who live in such places must be always thinkin' of their own inds, and of universal decay that is brought about by time and natur', but the decay that follows waste and violence. They call 'em the temples of the Lord; but, Judith, the whole 'arth is a temple of the Lord to such as have the right mind." [CHAP. 15]

The decay of nature—the mutability theme —is a favorite one with Bryant. His sonnet, "Mutation," is inferior to Wordsworth's "Mutability" sonnet, but not greatly so:

They talk of short-lived pleasure—be it so—
  Pain dies as quickly: stern, hard-featured pain
Expires, and lets her weary prisoner go.
  The fiercest agonies have shortest reign;
  And after dreams of horror, comes again
The welcome morning with its rays of peace.
  Oblivion, softly wiping out the stain,
Makes the strong secret pangs of shame to cease.
Remorse is virtue's root; its fair increase
  Are fruits of innocence and blessedness:
Thus joy, o'erborne and bound, doth still release
  His young limbs from the chains that round him press.
Weep not that the world changes—did it keep
A stable, changeless state, 'twere cause indeed to weep.

Generations and civilizations are born, flourish, decay, and die. This endlessly repeated cycle should teach us to look behind the passing show for that which alone is immutable and eternal, and which reverberates through Bryant's poetry as a kind of Supreme Abstraction personified. Bryant repeatedly, like many other writers and painters of his generation, invoked the vanished Indian civilization as an example of the transitoriness of earthly things, and he liked nothing better than to point out, as in the concluding stanzas of "An Indian at the Burial-Place of His Fathers" (see p. 365), that as they are now, so we shall be. Mutability is a universal theme in literature, and to see what magnificent things American poets would do with it later, one should consider Whitman's "Song of Myself," or "When Lilacs Last in the Dooryard Bloom'd," or Wallace Stevens' "Sunday Morning," or even Emily Dickinson's "The Chariot." Why then does Bryant's treatment of the theme seem so thin to us? For one thing, he characteristically approaches it under the aspect of death, and Bryant's attitude to death was a little morbid, immature, and imaginatively delimiting. Frail health in his youth, combined with an enthusiasm for the graveyard school of poetry, did a good deal of damage. But more important is the fact that Bryant's poetry rarely seems to be in touch with his vital interest in life. Poetry often seems for Bryant something hallowed and set apart, like a best parlor filled with marmoreal statuary that is only opened up on Sundays. It is a little difficult to speak naturally or breathe very deeply in it.

This is sad because Bryant was one of the most worthwhile men of his generation, intelligent and beautifully generous, and courageous enough physically to thrash William Leete Stone, the editor of the New York *Commercial Advertiser*, with a cowhide whip on Broadway for some insulting anti-Jackson statements he had published. Bryant was the editor of the New York *Evening Post* for half a century, from 1829 until his death in 1878, and his editorial record is one of distinguished liberalism. He was an ardent Jacksonian Democrat until the slavery question drove him temporarily into the ranks of the Republicans, and in 1860 his editorials, by influencing New York opinion, greatly assisted the nomination of Lincoln. Parrington, in his excellent sketch of Bryant in *Main Currents in American Thought* (1927–30), says that a serious injustice has been done to him because critics have neglected the liberal journalist for "the youthful versifier who described American scenery." This may be true, but unfortunately we must contribute to that injustice here.

From several of our quotations it is clear that Bryant and Cooper shared certain central attitudes in common beyond the fact that they were both Democrats. Nevertheless, there were differences. Cooper, with no editorial outlet to express his political convictions or assuage the intensity of his feelings about America, poured them creatively into his novels. Even when Leatherstocking is expressing conventionally held views about nature and mutability and the infinite Source which are indistinguishable in substance from Bryant's, we never confuse them. If Natty as a symbolic character is partly forged from certain current attitudes, those attitudes are metamorphosed by Cooper, in the process of creatively imagining Natty, into something original and new, and closely related to life. The Leatherstocking Tales grow directly out of Cooper's passionate concern with life; and where could he express that concern, being neither an active politician nor a newspaper editor, except in his art? On the other hand, Bryant tends to withdraw in his poems from the real field of his later interest, which is politics and journalism, into a genteel heaven of moral sublimity that is as unrelated to life as Bryant's daily editorial tasks were intimately a part of it. The result is that Cooper gives us major art, at least in the Leatherstocking novels, and Bryant gives us conventional, rather bloodless verse.

Bryant's was a limited genius. "To a Waterfowl" is a superb poem, and there are others as well. But something went wrong somewhere. Many of his poems are combinations of highly successful passages with sandy tracts. Consider these three verses:

The path we planned beneath October's sky,
  Along the hillside, through the woodland shade,
Is finished; thanks to thee, whose kindly eye
  Has watched me, as I plied the busy spade;
Else had I wearied, ere this path of ours
Had pierced the woodland to its inner bowers.

Yet, 'twas a pleasant toil to trace and beat,
  Among the glowing trees, this winding way,
While the sweet autumn sunshine, doubly sweet,
  Flushed with the ruddy foliage, round us lay,
As if some gorgeous cloud of morning stood,
In glory, mid the arches of the wood.

A path! what beauty doth a path bestow
  Even on the dreariest wild! its savage nooks
Seem homelike where accustomed footsteps go,
  And the grim rock puts on familar looks.
The tangled swamp, through which a pathway strays,
Becomes a garden with strange flowers and sprays.

This is a completely successful poem. The tone is quietly personal, easily modulating to the natural speaking voice. There is no deliberate elevation or rhetorical gesturing about it. At the same time there is a great deal of genuine style and elegance, imparting color and character to the sensitively restrained mode of expression. The path itself becomes a subtly suggestive symbol of some hinted wisdom not explicitly defined but capable of wonderful extensions in the imagination. The poem reminds one of Robert Frost at his best, with echoes from the seventeenth century—Marvell perhaps. The poem is a perfect little whole. Unfortunately, there are nine more verses in "The Path." They are by no means bad, but they deteriorate rapidly from the level established here, and end in the higher moralizing. Even that fine little path becomes a highway overburdened with rather heavy allegorical freight.

It is more often like that than not with Bryant's poems. If the motive behind them is more sensitive and complex than the sustained organ note can cope with, if the rhetorical posture and the conventional sublime prove inadequate to express his meaning, he is inclined to look for an allegorical escape clause. But in doing so he manages to escape from what is finest in his own genius. And it would be difficult to quote three finer verses of poetry from the American nineteenth century before Whitman than these. Bryant's limitations are in great part the limitations of his time, but he was no more exposed to them than Cooper; and we have seen that, for various reasons, Cooper managed to surmount them.

It is easy to denigrate Bryant's poetry, as Poe confessed as long ago as 1846 in a criticism that is still pertinent:

> But although it may be said, in general, that Mr. Bryant's position is *comparatively* well settled, still for some time past there has been a growing tendency to underestimate him. . . .
>
> It will never do to claim for Bryant a genius of the loftiest order, but there has been latterly . . . a growing disposition to deny him genius in any respect. He is now commonly spoken of as "a man of high poetical *talent*, very '*correct*,' with a warm appreciation of the beauty of nature and great descriptive powers, but rather too much of the old-school manner of Cowper, Goldsmith, and Young." This is the truth, but not the whole truth. Mr. Bryant has genius, and that of a marked character, but it has been overlooked by modern schools, because deficient in those externals which have become in a measure symbolical of those schools.

Bryant has been called the father of American poetry, and he probably deserves the title as much as such preposterous labels can ever be deserved. In 1821, when Bryan was twenty-seven years old, a small volume of eight of his poems was published in Cambridge. It contains some of his best work: "To a Waterfowl," "Inscription for the Entrance to a Wood," "The Yellow Violet," "Green River," and "Thanatopsis." To appreciate Bryant's achievement one only has to consider American poetry up to that point. The early Puritans, when they wrote poetry at all, wrote in an older European tradition. If we make a large exception of Philip Freneau, the American neoclassic poets (by whom we mean chicfly the Connecticut Wits) wrote competent but uninspired imitations of Pope and the later English eighteenth-century poets. In such a tradition, Bryant's poetry represented the most solid and refreshing work that had so far been produced by an American poet. The reverberations of his more solemn music, in those interminable forest aisles of his, tend to drown out his better poems, but if we listen long and hard, some sweet, distinguished notes come through.

READING SUGGESTIONS

COOPER

The Works of James Fenimore Cooper, 33 vols. (1895–1900).

The Leatherstocking Saga, ed. by Allan Nevins (1954). This is an admirable presentation of the five Leatherstocking novels with those parts eliminated which do not specially pertain to Natty Bumppo. The Introduction is useful.

All of the Leatherstocking novels are available in popular reprints. *The American Democrat* is in a paperback edition.

James Fenimore Cooper: Representative Selections, ed. by Robert E. Spiller (1936). Presents Cooper's nonfiction prose.

Since Thomas R. Lounsbury published the first biography of Cooper in 1882, there have been many studies of his life and particular aspects of his thought and activity. The most useful general biography to begin with is James Grossman's *James Fenimore Cooper*, in the American Men of Letters series (1949). *The Letters and Journals of James Fenimore Cooper*, ed. by James Franklin Beard (1960), gives a vivid firsthand impression of Cooper's career until his return from Europe in 1833 with the aid of lucid editorial comment. Books dealing with special aspects of Cooper include *The Whig Myth of Feni-*

more Cooper by Dorothy Waples (1938). Cooper's political thought is briefly but admirably treated in *The Age of Jackson* by Arthur M. Schlesinger, Jr. (1945), chap. 29. Robert E. Spiller's *Fenimore Cooper: Critic of His Times* (1931) also treats Cooper's political and social thought. The Anti-Rent agitation in New York, which forms the background of the Littlepage trilogy, is the subject of Henry Christman's *Tin Horns and Calico* (1945). There has been a good deal of work done on Cooper and the Indian. See in particular *The Savages of America* by Roy Harvey Pearce (1953).

Critical comment on Cooper as an artist is invariably joined to comment on his political and social thought. However, the emphasis in the following books and articles tends to be literary:

MARIUS BEWLEY, *The Eccentric Design* (1959). Chaps. 3, 4, and 5 are devoted to Cooper and expand certain ideas in the present Introduction.

EDWIN H. CADY, *The Gentleman in America* (1949), chaps. 5, 6.

RICHARD CHASE, *The American Novel and Its Tradition* (1957), chap. 3.

HOWARD MUMFORD JONES, "James Fenimore Cooper: Prose and Picture," *Tulane Studies in English*, III (1952).

D. H. LAWRENCE, *Studies in Classic American Literature* (1924), chaps. 4, 5. This extraordinary book is both personal and extreme in its judgments, but the chapter on the Leatherstocking novels is one of the most valuable and illuminating series of insights into them that we have.

HENRY NASH SMITH, *Virgin Land* (1950), chap. 6.

YVOR WINTERS, "Fenimore Cooper, or the Ruins of Time," *Maule's Curse* (1938). Reprinted in *In Defense of Reason* (1947).

Among estimates of Cooper by other artists, that of D. H. Lawrence has already been cited. Conrad's short essay, "Tales of the Sea," reprinted in *Notes on Life and Letters* (1921), is well worth looking up. Balzac has an appraisal, translated in Katherine Prescott Wormeley's *Personal Opinions of Balzac* (1923). "Discourse on the Life and Genius of Cooper" was delivered as a commemorative address by Bryant in 1852. It is to be found in Bryant's *Orations and Addresses* (1872), and in Tremaine McDowell's *William Cullen Bryant: Representative Selections* (1935).

BRYANT

The standard text for Bryant's poems is *The Poetical Works of William Cullen Bryant*, ed. by Parke Godwin, 2 vols. (1883).

The most convenient text is Tremaine McDowell's *William Cullen Bryant: Representative Selections, with Introduction, Bibliography, and Notes* (1935).

Biographies include William A. Bradley, *William Cullen Bryant*, English Men of Letters Series (1905); and *Gotham Yankee*, by Harry Houston Peckham (1950). Allan Nevins, *The Evening Post: A Century of Journalism* (1920), gives the best account of Bryant's newspaper career. A good summary of Bryant's liberal attitudes is contained in Vernon Louis Parrington's *Main Currents in American Thought* (1927–30).

The absence of any really satisfactory contemporary criticism of Bryant's poetry is in itself suggestive. The best work on him is that which treats of his historical significance in the American literary tradition. From this point of view particular mention should be made of two comparatively recent articles: "Kindred Spirits: Bryant and Cole," by Donald A. Ringe, *American Quarterly*, VI (1954); and "The Concept of the Sublime in Bryant and Cole," by Charles Sanford, *American Literature*, XXVII (1957). Two useful studies of the literary taste of the period are "The Decline of Neoclassicism, 1801–1848," by M. F. Heiser, and "The Rise of Romanticism, 1805–1855," by G. Harrison Orians. Both are included in *Transitions in American Literary History*, ed. by Harry Hayden Clark (1953).

James Fenimore Cooper

FROM

THE LEATHERSTOCKING TALES

◇

¶ IT IS NOT commonly a satisfactory procedure to offer excerpts from novels in an anthology. But aside from the fact that Cooper leaves us no alternative if he is to be presented at all in the role of artist, the Leatherstocking Tales are primarily concerned with the presentation of a character, Natty Bumppo, whose essential meaning may be grasped by considering a number of episodes and scenes from his life detached from the specific plot or sequence of events in which they occur. In Section III of the Introduction we have tried to suggest what this meaning is. Perhaps we might go so far as to say that Cooper's conception of Leatherstocking anticipates in practice Matthew Arnold's description of poetry as a criticism of life, for that is really Leatherstocking's final effect on us. We have chosen most of the selections from *The Deerslayer,* and in this one instance some attempt has been made to convey an idea of the total action by means of interpolated synopses of omitted chapters.

The dates of the Leatherstocking Tales are: 1823, *The Pioneers;* 1826, *The Last of the Mohicans;* 1827, *The Prairie;* 1840, *The Pathfinder;* and 1841, *The Deerslayer.* Our excerpts are presented in the chronological order of Leatherstocking's life, not in the chronological order in which Cooper wrote them. It is the last of these novels that shows Natty to us for the first time as a young man. This is probably the best of the Leatherstocking Tales, and Cooper's conception of Natty is here brought to its most rounded statement. As James Grossman says in his life of Cooper: "Time has mercifully run backward for Natty Bumppo and Chingachgook, and they are half a century younger than when we met them on this very spot in *The Pioneers.*" Cooper's order of composition leaves us with a sense of Natty's immortal youth, and this is the way it ought to be.

◇

FROM

THE DEERSLAYER

CHAPTER 1

On the human imagination events produce the effects of time. Thus, he who has travelled far and seen much is apt to fancy that he has lived long and the history that most abounds in important incidents soonest assumes the aspect of antiquity. In no other way can we account for the venerable air that is already gathering around American annals. When the mind reverts to the earliest days of colonial history, the period seems remote and obscure, the thousand changes that thicken along the links of recollections, throwing back the origin of the nation to a day so distant as seemingly to reach the mists of time; and yet four lives of ordinary duration would suffice to transmit, from mouth to mouth, in the form of tradition, all that civilized man has achieved within the limits of the republic. Although New York alone possesses a population materially exceeding that of either of the four smallest kingdoms of Europe, or materially exceeding that of the entire Swiss Confederation, it is little more than two centuries since the Dutch commenced their settlement, rescuing the region from the savage state. Thus, what seems venerable by an accumulation of changes is reduced to familiarity when we come seriously to consider it solely in connection with time.

This glance into the perspective of the past will prepare the reader to look at the pictures we are about to sketch, with less surprise than he might otherwise feel; and a few additional explanations may carry him back in imagination to the precise condition of society that we desire to delineate. It is matter of history that the settlements on the eastern shores of the Hudson, such as Claverack, Kinderhook, and even Poughkeepsie, were not regarded as safe from Indian incursions a century since; and there is still standing on the banks of the same river, and within musket-shot of the wharves of Albany, a residence of a younger branch [1] of the Van Rensselaers, that has loopholes constructed for defence against the same crafty enemy, although it dates from a period scarcely so distant. Other similar memorials of the infancy of the country are to be found, scattered through what is now deemed the very centre of American civilization, affording the plainest proofs that all we possess of security from invasion and hostile violence is the growth of but little more than the time that is frequently filled by a single human life.

The incidents of this tale occurred between the years 1740 and 1745, when the settled portions of the colony of New York were confined to the four Atlantic counties, a narrow belt of country on each side of the Hudson, extending from its mouth to the falls near its head, and to a few advanced "neighborhoods" on the Mohawk and the Schoharie. Broad belts of the virgin wilderness not only reached the shores of the first river, but they even crossed it, stretching away into New England, and affording forest covers to the noiseless moccasin of the native warrior, as he trod the secret and bloody war-path. A bird's-eye view of the whole region east of the Mississippi must then have offered one vast expanse of woods, relieved by a comparatively narrow fringe of cultivation along the sea, dotted by the glittering surfaces of lakes, and intersected by the waving lines of river. In such a vast picture of solemn solitude, the district of country we design to paint sinks into insignificance, though we feel encouraged to proceed by the conviction that, with slight and immaterial distinctions, he who succeeds in giving an accurate idea of any portion of this wild region must necessarily convey a tolerably correct notion of the whole.

Whatever may be the changes produced by man, the eternal round of the seasons is unbroken.

THE DEERSLAYER. 1. "It is no more than justice to say that the Greenbush Van Rensselaers claim to be the oldest branch of that ancient and respectable family" [Cooper's note].

Summer and winter, seed-time and harvest, return in their stated order with a sublime precision, affording to man one of the noblest of all the occasions he enjoys of proving the high powers of his far-reaching mind, in compassing the laws that control their exact uniformity, and in calculating their never-ending revolutions. Centuries of summer suns had warmed the tops of the same noble oaks and pines, sending their heats even to the tenacious roots, when voices were heard calling to each other, in the depths of a forest, of which the leafy surface lay bathed in the brilliant light of a cloudless day in June, while the trunks of the trees rose in gloomy grandeur in the shades beneath. The calls were in different tones, evidently proceeding from two men who had lost their way, and were searching in different directions for their path. At length a shout proclaimed success, and presently a man of gigantic mould broke out of the tangled labyrinth of a small swamp, emerging into an opening that appeared to have been formed partly by the ravages of the wind, and partly by those of fire. This little area, which afforded a good view of the sky, although it was pretty well filled with dead trees, lay on the side of one of the high hills, or low mountains, into which nearly the whole surface of the adjacent country was broken.

"Here is room to breathe in!" exclaimed the liberated forester, as soon as he found himself under a clear sky, shaking his huge frame like a mastiff that has just escaped from a snowbank. "Hurrah! Deerslayer; here is daylight, at last, and yonder is the lake."

These words were scarcely uttered when the second forester dashed aside the bushes of the swamp, and appeared in the area. After making a hurried adjustment of his arms and disordered dress, he joined his companion, who had already begun his disposition for a halt.

"Do you know this spot?" demanded the one called Deerslayer, "or do you shout at the sight of the sun?"

"Both, lad, both; I know the spot, and am not sorry to see so useful a fri'nd as the sun. Now we have got the p'ints of the compass in our minds once more, and 't will be our own faults if we let anything turn them topsy-turvy ag'in, as has just happened. My name is not Hurry Harry, if this be not the very spot where the land-hunters 'camped the last summer, and passed a week. See! yonder are the dead bushes of their bower, and here is the spring. Much as I like the sun, boy, I've no occasion for it to tell me it is noon; this stomach of mine is as good a time-piece as is to be found in the colony, and it already p'ints to half-past twelve. So open the wallet, and let us wind up for another six hours' run."

At this suggestion, both set themselves about making the preparations necessary for their usual frugal but hearty meal. We will profit by this pause in the discourse to give the reader some idea of the appearance of the men, each of whom is destined to enact no insignificant part in our legend. It would not have been easy to find a more noble specimen of vigorous manhood than was offered in the person of him who called himself Hurry Harry. His real name was Henry March; but the frontiermen having caught the practice of giving *sobriquets* from the Indians, the appellation of Hurry was far oftener applied to him than his proper designation, and not unfrequently he was termed Hurry Skurry, a nickname he had obtained from a dashing, reckless, off-hand manner, and a physical restlessness that kept him so constantly on the move, as to cause him to be known along the whole line of scattered habitations that lay between the province and the Canadas. The stature of Hurry Harry exceeded six feet four, and being unusually well proportioned, his strength fully realized the idea created by his gigantic frame. The face did no discredit to the rest of the man, for it was both good-humored and handsome. His air was free, and though his manner necessarily partook of the rudeness of a border life, the grandeur that pervaded so noble a physique prevented it from becoming altogether vulgar.

Deerslayer, as Hurry called his companion, was a very different person in appearance, as well as in character. In stature he stood about six feet in his moccasins, but his frame was comparatively light and slender, showing muscles, however, that promised unusual agility, if not unusual strength. His face would have had little to recommend it except youth, were it not for an expression that seldom failed to win upon those who had leisure to examine it, and to yield to the feeling of confidence it created. This expression was simply that of guileless truth, sustained by an earnestness of purpose, and a sincerity of feeling, that rendered it remarkable. At times this air of integrity seemed to be so simple as to awaken the suspicion of a want of the usual means to discriminate between artifice and truth; but few came in serious contact with the man, without losing this distrust in respect for his opinions and motives.

Both these frontiermen were still young, Hurry having reached the age of six or eight and twenty, while Deerslayer was several years his junior. Their attire needs no particular description, though it may be well to add that it was composed in no small degree of dressed deer-skins, and had the usual signs of belonging to those who pass their time between the skirts of civilized society and the boundless forests. There was, notwithstanding, some attention to smartness and the picturesque in the arrangements of Deerslayer's dress, more particularly in the part connected with his arms and accoutrements. His rifle was in perfect condition, the handle of his hunting-knife was neatly carved, his powder-horn was ornamented with suitable devices lightly cut into the material, and his shot-pouch was decorated with wampum. On the other hand, Hurry Harry, either from constitutional recklessness, or from a secret consciousness how little his appearance required artificial aids, wore everything in a careless, slovenly manner, as if he felt a noble scorn for the trifling accessories of dress and ornaments. Perhaps the peculiar effect of his fine form and great stature was increased rather than lessened, by this unstudied and disdainful air of indifference.

"Come, Deerslayer, fall to, and prove that you have a Delaware stomach, as you say you have had a Delaware edication," cried Hurry, setting the example by opening his mouth to receive a slice of cold venison steak that would have made an entire meal for a European peasant; "fall to, lad, and prove your manhood on this poor devil of a doe with your teeth, as you've already done with your rifle."

"Nay, nay, Hurry, there's little manhood in killing a doe, and that too out of season; though there might be some in bringing down a painter or a catamount," returned the other, disposing himself to comply. "The Delawares have given me my name, not so much on account of a bold heart, as on account of a quick eye, and an actyve foot. There may not be any cowardyce in overcoming a deer, but sartain it is, there's no great valor."

"The Delawares themselves are no heroes," muttered Hurry through his teeth, the mouth being too full to permit it to be fairly opened, "or they would never have allowed them loping vagabonds, the Mingos, to make them women."

"That matter is not rightly understood—has never been rightly explained," said Deerslayer earnestly, for he was as zealous a friend as his companion was dangerous as an enemy; "the Mengwe fill the woods with their lies, and misconstruct words and treaties. I have now lived ten years with the Delawares, and know them to be as manful as any other nation, when the proper time to strike comes."

"Harkee, Master Deerslayer, since we are on the subject, we may as well open our minds to each other in a man-to-man way; answer me one question; you have had so much luck among the game as to have gotten a title, it would seem, but did you ever hit anything human or intelligible: did you ever pull trigger on an inimy that was capable of pulling one upon you?"

This question produced a singular collision between mortification and correct feeling, in the bosom of the youth, that was easily to be traced in the workings of his ingenuous countenance. The struggle was short, however; uprightness of heart soon getting the better of false pride and frontier boastfulness.

"To own the truth, I never did," answered Deerslayer; "seeing that a fitting occasion never offered. The Delawares have been peaceable since my sojourn with 'em, and I hold it to be onlawful to take the life of man, except in open and generous warfare."

"What! did you never find a fellow thieving among your traps and skins, and do the law on him with your own hands, by way of saving the magistrates trouble in the settlements, and the rogue himself the cost of the suit?"

"I am no trapper, Hurry," returned the young man proudly: "I live by the rifle, a we'pon at which I will not turn my back on any man of my years, atween the Hudson and the St. Lawrence. I never offer a skin that has not a hole in its head besides them which natur' made to see with or to breathe through."

"Ay, ay, this is all very well, in the animal way, though it makes but a poor figure alongside of scalps and ambushes. Shooting an Indian from an ambush is acting up to his own principles, and now we have what you call a lawful war on our hands, the sooner you wipe that disgrace off your character, the sounder will be your sleep; if it only come from knowing there is one inimy the less prowling in the woods. I shall not frequent your society long, friend Natty, unless you look higher than four-footed beasts to practyse your rifle on."

"Our journey is nearly ended, you say, Master March, and we can part to-night, if you see occasion. I have a fri'nd waiting for me, who will think it no disgrace to consort with a fellow-creatur' that has never yet slain his kind."

"I wish I knew what has brought that skulking Delaware into this part of the country so early in the season," muttered Hurry to himself, in a way to show equally distrust and a recklessness of its betrayal. "Where did you say the young chief was to give you the meeting?"

"At a small round rock, near the foot of the

lake, where, they tell me, the tribes are given to resorting to make their treaties, and to bury their hatchets. This rock have I often heard the Delawares mention, though lake and rock are equally strangers to me. The country is claimed by both Mingos and Mohicans, and is a sort of common territory to fish and hunt through, in time of peace, though what it may become in war-time, the Lord only knows!"

"Common territory!" exclaimed Hurry, laughing aloud. "I should like to know what Floating Tom Hutter would say to that? He claims the lake as his own property, in vartue of fifteen years' possession, and will not be likely to give it up to either Mingo or Delaware without a battle for it."

"And what will the colony say to such a quarrel? All this country must have some owner, the gentry pushing their cravings into the wilderness, even where they never dare to ventur', in their own persons, to look at the land they own."

"That may do in other quarters of the colony, Deerslayer, but it will not do here. Not a human being, the Lord excepted, owns a foot of sile in this part of the country. Pen was never put to paper consarning either hill or valley hereaway, as I've heard old Tom say time and ag'in, and so he claims the best right to it of any man breathing; and what Tom claims, he'll be very like to maintain."

"By what I've heard you say, Hurry, this Floating Tom must be an oncommon mortal; neither Mingo, Delaware, nor pale-face. His possession, too, has been long, by your tell, and altogether beyond frontier endurance. What's the man's history and natur'?"

"Why, as to old Tom's human natur', it is not much like other men's human natur', but more like a muskrat's human natur', seeing that he takes more to the ways of that animal than to the ways of any other fellow-creatur'. Some think he was a free liver on the salt water, in his youth, and a companion of a sartain Kidd, who was hanged for piracy, long afore you and I were born or acquainted, and that he came up into these regions, thinking that the king's cruisers could never cross the mountains, and that he might enjoy the plunder peaceably in the woods."

"Then he was wrong, Hurry; very wrong. A man can enjoy plunder *peaceably* nowhere."

"That's much as his turn of mind may happen to be. I've known them that never could enjoy it at all, unless it was in the midst of a jollification, and them ag'in that enjoyed it best in a corner. Some men have no peace if they don't find plunder, and some if they do. Human natur' is crooked in these matters. Old Tom seems to belong to neither set, as he enjoys his, if plunder he has really got, with his darters, in a very quiet and comfortably way, and wishes for no more."

"Ay, he has darters, too; I've heard the Delawares who've hunted this a way, tell their histories of these young women. Is there no mother, Hurry?"

"There was *once,* as in reason; but she has now been dead and sunk these two good years."

"Anan?" said Deerslayer, looking up at his companion in a little surprise.

"Dead and sunk, I say, and I hope that's good English. The old fellow lowered his wife into the lake, by way of seeing the last of her, as I can testify, being an eye-witness of the ceremony; but whether Tom did it to save digging, which is no easy job among roots, or out of a consait that water washes away sin sooner than 'arth, is more than I can say."

"Was the poor woman oncommon wicked, that her husband should take so much pains with her body?"

"Not onreasonable; though she had her faults. I consider Judith Hutter to have been as graceful, and about as likely to make a good ind as any woman who had lived so long beyond the sound of church bells; and I conclude old Tom sunk her as much by way of *saving* pains, as by way of *taking* it. There was a little steel in her temper, it's true, and, as old Hutter is pretty much flint, they struck out sparks once-and-a-while; but, on the whole, they might be said to live amicable like. When they did kindle, the listeners got some such insights into their past lives, as one gets into the darker parts of the woods, when a stray gleam of sunshine finds its way down to the roots of the trees. But Judith I shall always esteem, as it's recommend enough to one woman to be the mother of such a creatur' as her darter, Judith Hutter!"

"Ay, Judith was the name the Delawares mentioned, though it was pronounced after a fashion of their own. From their discourse, I do not think the girl would much please my fancy."

"Thy fancy!" exclaimed March, taking fire equally at the indifference and at the presumption of his companion, "what the devil have you to do with a fancy, and that, too, consarning one like Judith? You are but a boy—a sapling, that has scarce got root. Judith has had *men* among her suitors, ever since she was fifteen; which is now near five years; and will not be apt even to cast a look upon a half-grown creatur' like you!"

"It is June, and there is not a cloud atween us and the sun, Hurry, so all this heat is not wanted," answered the other, altogether undisturbed; "any one may have a fancy, and a squirrel has a right to make up his mind touching a catamount."

"Ay, but it might not be wise, always, to let the catamount know it," growled March. "But you're young and thoughtless, and I'll overlook your ignorance. Come, Deerslayer," he added, with a good-natured laugh, after pausing a moment to reflect, "come, Deerslayer, we are sworn fri'nds, and will not quarrel about a light-minded, jilting jade, just because she happens to be handsome; more especially as you have never seen her. Judith is only for a man whose teeth show the full marks, and it's foolish to be afeard of a boy. What *did* the Delawares say of the hussy? for an Indian, after all, has his notions of womankind, as well as a white man."

"They said she was fair to look on, and pleasant of speech; but over-given to admirers, and light-minded."

"They are devils incarnate! After all, what schoolmaster is a match for an Indian, in looking into natur'? Some people think they are only good on a trail or the war-path, but I say that they are philosophers, and understand a man as well as they understand a beaver, and a woman as well as they understand either. Now that's Judith's character to a ribbon! To own the truth to you, Deerslayer, I should have married the gal two years since, if it had not been for two particular things, one of which was this very light-mindedness."

"And what may have been the other?" demanded the hunter, who continued to eat like one that took very little interest in the subject.

"T'other was an insartainty about her having *me*. The hussy is handsome, and she knows it. Boy, not a tree that is growing in these hills is straighter, or waves in the wind with an easier bend, nor did you ever see the doe that bounded with a more nat'ral motion. If that was all, every tongue would sound her praises; but she has such failings that I find it hard to overlook them, and sometimes I swear I'll never visit the lake ag'in."

"Which is the reason that you always come back? Nothing is ever made more sure by swearing about it."

"Ah, Deerslayer, you are a novelty in these partic'lars; keeping as true to edication as if you had never left the settlements. With me the case is different, and I never want to clinch an idee, that I do not feel a wish to swear about it. If you know'd all that I know consarning Judith, you'd find a justification for a little cussing. Now, the officers sometimes stray over to the lake, from the forts on the Mohawk, to fish and hunt, and then the creatur' seems beside herself! You can see in the manner which she wears her finery, and the airs she gives herself with the gallants."

"That is unseemly in a poor man's darter," returned Deerslayer gravely, "the officers are all gentry, and can only look on such as Judith with evil intentions."

"There's the unsartainty, and the damper! I have my misgivings about a particular captain, and Jude has no one to blame but her own folly, if I'm right. On the whole, I wish to look upon her as modest and becoming, and yet the clouds that drive among these hills are not more unsartain. Not a dozen white men have ever laid eyes upon her since she was a child, and yet her airs, with two or three of these officers, are extinguishers!"

"I would think no more of such a woman, but turn my mind altogether to the forest; *that* will not deceive you, being ordered and ruled by a hand that never wavers."

"If you know'd Judith, you would see how much easier it is to say this than it would be to do it. Could I bring my mind to be easy about the officers, I would carry the gal off to the Mohawk by force, make her marry me in spite of her whiffling, and leave old Tom to the care of Hetty, his other child, who, if she be not as handsome or as quick-witted as her sister, is much the most dutiful."

"Is there another bird in the same nest?" asked Deerslayer, raising his eyes with a species of half-awakened curiosity—"the Delawares spoke to me only of one."

"That's nat'ral enough, when Judith Hutter and Hetty Hutter are in question. Hetty is only comely, while her sister, I tell thee, boy, is such another as is not to be found atween this and the sea: Judith is as full of wit, and talk, and cunning, as an old Indian orator, while poor Hetty is at the best but 'compass meant us.' "

"Anan?" inquired, again, the Deerslayer.

"Why, what the officers call 'compass meant us,' which I understand to signify that she means always to go in the right direction, but sometimes doesn't know how. 'Compass' for the p'int, and 'meant us' for the intention. No, poor Hetty is what I call on the varge of ignorance, and sometimes she stumbles on one side of the line, and sometimes on t'other."

"Them are beings that the Lord has in his 'special care," said Deerslayer, solemnly; "for he looks carefully to all who fall short of their proper share of reason. The redskins honor and respect them who are so gifted, knowing that the Evil Spirit delights more to dwell in an artful body, than in one that has no cunning to work upon."

"I'll answer for it, then, that he will not remain long with poor Hetty; for the child is just 'compass meant us,' as I have told you. Old Tom has a feeling for the gal, and so has Judith, quick-witted and glorious as she is herself; else would I not answer for her being altogether safe among the sort of men that sometimes meet on the lake shore."

"I thought this water an onknown and little-frequented sheet," observed the Deerslayer, evidently uneasy at the idea of being too near the world.

"It's all that, lad, the eyes of twenty white men never having been laid on it; still, twenty true-bred frontiermen—hunters and trappers, and scouts, and the like,—can do a deal of mischief if they try. 'Twould be an awful thing to me, Deerslayer, did I find Judith married, after an absence of six months!"

"Have you the gal's faith, to encourage you to hope otherwise?"

"Not at all. I know not how it is: I'm good-looking, boy,—that much I can see in any spring on which the sun shines,—and yet I could not get the hussy to a promise, or even a cordial willing smile, though she will laugh by the hour. If she *has* dared to marry in my absence, she'll be like to know the pleasures of widowhood afore she is twenty!"

"You would not harm the man she has chosen, Hurry, simply because she found him more to her liking than yourself?"

"Why not? If an inimy crosses my path, will I not beat him out of it! Look at me! am I a man like to let any sneaking, crawling, skin-trader get the better of me in a matter that touches me as near as the kindness of Judith Hutter? Besides, when we live beyond law, we must be our own judges and executioners. And if a man *should* be found dead in the woods, who is there to say who slew him, even admitting that the colony took the matter in hand and made a stir about it?"

"If that man should be Judith Hutter's husband, after what has passed, I might tell enough, at least, to put the colony on the trail."

"You!—half-grown, venison-hunting bantling! You dare to think of informing against Hurry Harry in so much as a matter touching a mink or a woodchuck!"

"I would dare to speak truth, Hurry, consarning you or any man that ever lived."

March looked at his companion, for a moment, in silent amazement; then seizing him by the throat with both hands, he shook his comparatively slight frame with a violence that menaced the dislocation of some of the bones. Nor was this done jocularly, for anger flashed from the giant's eyes, and there were certain signs that seemed to threaten much more earnestness than the occasion would appear to call for. Whatever might be the real intention of March, and it is probable there was none settled in his mind, it is certain that he was unusually aroused; and most men who found themselves throttled by one of a mould so gigantic, in such a mood, and in a solitude so deep and helpless, would have felt intimidated, and tempted to yield even the right. Not so, however, with Deerslayer. His countenance remained unmoved; his hand did not shake, and his answer was given in a voice that did not resort to the artifice of louder tones, even by way of proving its owner's resolution.

"You may shake, Hurry, until you bring down the mountain," he said quietly, "but nothing beside truth will you shake from me. It is probable that Judith Hutter has no husband to slay, and you may never have a chance to waylay one, else would I tell her of your threat, in the first conversation I held with the gal."

March released his gripe, and sat regarding the other in silent astonishment.

"I thought we had been friends," he at length added; "but you've got the last secret of mine that will ever enter your ears."

"I want none, if they are to be like this. I know we live in the woods, Hurry, and are thought to be beyond human laws,—and perhaps we are so, in fact, whatever it may be in right,—but there is a law and a law-maker, that rule across the whole continent. He that flies in the face of either need not call me a friend."

"Damme, Deerslayer, if I do not believe you are at heart a Moravian, and no fair-minded, plain-dealing hunter, as you've pretended to be!"

"Fair-minded or not, Hurry, you will find me as plain-dealing in deeds as I am in words. But this giving way to sudden anger is foolish, and proves how little you have sojourned with the redman. Judith Hutter no doubt is still single, and you spoke but as the tongue ran, and not as the heart felt. There's my hand, and we will say and think no more about it."

Hurry seemed more surprised than ever; then he burst forth in a loud, good-natured laugh, which brought tears to his eyes. After this he accepted the offered hand, and the parties became friends.

" 'Twould have been foolish to quarrel about an idee," March cried, as he resumed his meal, "and more like lawyers in the towns than like sensible men in the woods. They tell me, Deerslayer, much ill-blood grows out of idees among the people in the lower counties, and that they sometimes get to extremities upon them."

"That do they,—that do they; and about other matters that might better be left to take care of themselves. I have heard the Moravians say that there are lands in which men quarrel even consarning their religion; and if they can get their tempers up on such a subject, Hurry, the Lord have marcy on 'em. Howsever, there is no occasion for our following their example, and more especially about a husband that this Judith Hutter may never see, or never wish to see. For my part, I feel more cur'osity about the feeble-witted sister than about your beauty. There's something that comes close to a man's feelin's, when he meets with a fellow-creatur' that has all the outward show of an accountable mortal, and who fails of being what he seems, only through a lack of reason. This is bad enough in a man, but when it comes to a woman, and she a young, and maybe a winning creatur' it touches all the pitiful thoughts his natur' has. God knows, Hurry, that such poor things be defenceless enough with all their wits about 'em; but it's a cruel fortun' when that great protector and guide fails 'em."

"Harkee, Deerslayer,—you know what the hunters, and trappers, and peltry-men in general be; and their best friends will not deny that they are headstrong and given to having their own way, without much bethinking 'em of other people's rights or feelin's,—and yet I don't think the man is to be found, in all this region, who would harm Hetty Hutter, if he could; no, not even a redskin."

"Therein, fri'nd Hurry, you do the Delawares, at least, and all their allied tribes, only justice, for a redskin looks upon a being thus struck by God's power as especially under his care. I rejoice to hear what you say, however, I rejoice to hear it; but as the sun is beginning to turn towards the a'ternoon's sky, had we not better strike the trail ag'in, and make forward, that we may get an opportunity of seeing these wonderful sisters?"

Harry March giving a cheerful assent, the remnants of the meal were soon collected; then the travellers shouldered their packs, resumed their arms, and, quitting the little area of light, they again plunged into the deep shadows of the forest.

CHAPTER 2

OUR TWO adventurers had not far to go. Hurry knew the direction, as soon as he had found the open spot and the spring, and he now led on with the confident step of a man assured of his object. The forest was dark, as a matter of course, but it was no longer obstructed by underbrush, and the footing was firm and dry. After proceeding near a mile, March stopped, and began to cast about him with an inquiring look, examining the different objects with care, and occasionally turning his eyes on the trunks of the fallen trees, with which the ground was well sprinkled, as is usually the case in an American wood, especially in those parts of the country where timber has not yet become valuable.

"*This* must be the place, Deerslayer," March at length observed; "here is a beech by the side of a hemlock, with three pines at hand, and yonder is a white birch with a broken top; and yet I see no rock, nor any of the branches bent down, as I told you would be the case."

"Broken branches are onskilful landmarks, as the least exper'enced know that branches don't often break of themselves," returned the other; "and they also lead to suspicion and discoveries. The Delawares never trust to broken branches, unless it is in friendly times, and on an open trail. As for the beeches, and pines, and hemlocks, why, they are to be seen on all sides of us, not only by twos and threes, but by forties, and fifties, and hundreds."

"Very true, Deerslayer, but you never calculate on position. Here is a beech and a hemlock—"

"Yes, and there is another beech and a hemlock, as loving as two brothers, or, for that matter, more loving than some brothers; and yonder are others, for neither tree is a rarity in these woods. I fear me, Hurry, you are better at trapping beaver and shooting bears, than at leading on a blindish sort of a trail. Ha! there's what you wish to find, a'ter all!"

"Now, Deerslayer, this is one of your Delaware pretensions, for hang me if I see anything but these trees, which do seem to start up around us in a most onaccountable and perplexing manner."

"Look this a way, Hurry—here, in a line with the black oak—don't you see the crooked sapling that is hooked up in the branches of the bass-wood, near it? Now, that sapling was once snow-ridden, and got the bend by its weight; but it never straightened itself, and fastened itself in among the bass-wood branches in the way you see. The hand of man did that act of kindness for it."

"That hand was mine!" exclaimed Hurry; "I found the slender young thing bent to the airth, like an unfortunate creatur' borne down by misfortune, and stuck it up where you see it. After all, Deerslayer, I must allow, you're getting to have an oncommon good eye for the woods!"

"'Tis improving, Hurry—'tis improving, I will acknowledge; but 'tis only a child's eye, compared to some I know. There's Tamenund, now, though a man so old that few remember when he was in his prime, Tamenund lets nothing escape his look, which is more like the scent of a hound than the sight of an eye. Then Uncas,[2] the father of Chingachgook, and the lawful chief of the Mohicans, is another that it is almost hopeless to pass unseen. I'm improving, I will allow—I'm improving, but far from being perfect, as yet."

"And who is this Chingachgook, of whom you talk so much, Deerslayer?" asked Hurry, as he moved off in the direction of the righted sapling; "a loping redskin, at the best, I make no question."

"Not so, Hurry, but the best of loping redskins, as you call 'em. If he had his rights, he would be a great chief; but, as it is, he is only a brave and just-minded Delaware; respected, and even obeyed in some things, 'tis true, but of a fallen race, and belonging to a fallen people. Ah! Harry March, 'twould warm the heart within you to sit in their lodges of a winter's night, and listen to the traditions of the ancient greatness and power of the Mohicans!"

"Harkee, fri'nd Nathaniel," said Hurry, stopping short to face his companion, in order that his words might carry greater weight with them, "if a man believed all that other people choose to say in their own favor, he might get an oversized opinion of them, and an undersized opinion of himself. These redskins are notable boasters, and I set down more than half of their traditions as pure talk."

"There is truth in what you say, Hurry, I'll not deny it, for I've seen it, and believe it. They *do* boast, but then that is a gift from natur'; and it's sinful to withstand nat'ral gifts. See; this is the spot you come to find!"

This remark cut short the discourse, and both the men now gave all their attention to the object immediately before them. Deerslayer pointed out to his companion the trunk of a huge linden, or bass-wood, as it is termed in the language of the country, which had filled its time, and fallen by its own weight. This tree, like so many millions of its brethren, lay where it had fallen, and was mouldering under the slow but certain influence of the seasons. The decay, however, had attacked its centre, even while it stood erect in the pride of vegetation, hollowing out its heart, as disease sometimes destroys the vitals of animal life, even while a fair exterior is presented to the observer. As the trunk lay stretched for near a hundred feet along the earth, the quick eye of the hunter detected this peculiarity, and, from this and other circumstances, he knew it to be the tree of which March was in search.

"Ay, here we have what we want," cried Hurry, looking in at the larger end of the linden; "everything is as snug as if it had been left in an old woman's cupboard. Come, lend me a hand, Deerslayer, and we'll be afloat in half an hour."

At this call the hunter joined his companion, and the two went to work deliberately and regularly, like men accustomed to the sort of thing in which they were employed. In the first place, Hurry removed some pieces of bark that lay before the large opening in the tree, and which the other declared to be disposed in a way that would have been more likely to attract attention than to conceal the cover, had any straggler passed that way. The two then drew out a bark canoe, containing its seats, paddles, and other appliances, even to fishing-lines and rods. This vessel was by no means small; but such was its comparative lightness, and so gigantic was the strength of Hurry, that the latter shouldered it with seeming ease, declining all assistance, even in the act of raising it to the awkward position in which he was obliged to hold it.

"Lead ahead, Deerslayer," said March, "and open the bushes; the rest I can do for myself."

The other obeyed, and the men left the spot, Deerslayer clearing the way for his companion, and inclining to the right or to the left, as the latter directed. In about ten minutes they both broke suddenly into the brilliant light of the sun, on a low gravelly point, that was washed by water on quite half its outline.

An exclamation of surprise broke from the lips of Deerslayer, an exclamation that was low and guardedly made, however, for his habits were much more thoughtful and regulated than those of the reckless Hurry, when, on reaching the margin of the lake, he beheld the view that unexpectedly met his gaze. It was, in truth, sufficiently striking to merit a brief description. On a level with the point lay a broad sheet of water, so placid and limpid that it resembled a bed of the pure mountain atmosphere, compressed into a setting of hills and woods. Its length was about three leagues, while its breadth was irregular, expanding to half a league, or even more, opposite to the point, and contracting to less than half that distance, more to the southward. Of course, its margin was irregular, being indented

2. "Lest the similarity of the names should produce confusion, it may be well to say that the Uncas here mentioned is the grandfather of him who plays so conspicuous a part in *The Last of the Mohicans*" [C].

by bays, and broken by many projecting, low points. At its northern, or nearest end, it was bounded by an isolated mountain, lower land falling off east and west, gracefully relieving the sweep of the outline. Still the character of the country was mountainous; high hills, or low mountains, rising abruptly from the water, on quite nine tenths of its circuit. The exceptions, indeed, only served a little to vary the scene; and even beyond the parts of the shore that were comparatively low, the background was high, though more distant.

But the most striking peculiarities of this scene were its solemn solitude and sweet repose. On all sides, wherever the eye turned, nothing met it but the mirror-like surface of the lake, the placid view of heaven, and the dense setting of woods. So rich and fleecy were the outlines of the forest, that scarce an opening could be seen, the whole visible earth, from the rounded mountain-top to the water's edge, presenting one unvaried hue of unbroken verdure. As if vegetation were not satisfied with a triumph so complete, the trees overhung the lake itself, shooting out towards the light; and there were miles along its eastern shore, where a boat might have pulled beneath the branches of dark Rembrandt-looking hemlocks, "quivering aspens," and melancholy pines. In a word, the hand of man had never yet defaced or deformed any part of this native scene, which lay bathed in the sunlight, a glorious picture of affluent forest-grandeur, softened by the balminess of June, and relieved by the beautiful variety afforded by the presence of so broad an expanse of water.

"This is grand!—'tis solemn!—'tis an edication of itself, to look upon!" exclaimed Deerslayer, as he stood leaning on his rifle, and gazing to the right and left, north and south, above and beneath, in whichever direction his eye could wander; "not a tree disturbed even by redskin hand, as I can discover, but everything left in the ordering of the Lord, to live and die according to his own designs and laws! Hurry, your Judith ought to be a moral and well-disposed young woman, if she has passed half the time you mention in the centre of a spot so favored."

"That's naked truth; and yet the gal has the vagaries. *All* her time has not been passed here, howsever, old Tom having the custom, afore I know'd him, of going to spend the winters in the neighborhood of the settlers, or under the guns of the forts. No, no, Jude has caught more than is for her good from the settlers, and especially from the gallantifying officers."

"If she has—if she has, Hurry, this is a school to set her mind right ag'in. But what is this I see off here, abreast of us, that seems too small for an island, and too large for a boat, though it stands in the midst of the water?"

"Why, that is what these gallanting gentry from the forts call Muskrat Castle; and old Tom himself will grin at the name, though it bears so hard on his own natur' and character. 'Tis the stationary house, there being two; this, which never moves, and the other, that floats, being sometimes in one part of the lake and sometimes in another. The last goes by the name of the ark, though what may be the meaning of the word is more than I can tell you."

"It must come from the missionaries, Hurry, whom I have heard speak and read of such a thing. They say that the 'arth was once covered with water, and that Noah, with his children, was saved from drowning by building a vessel called an ark, in which he embarked in season. Some of the Delawares believe this tradition, and some deny it; but it behooves you and me, as white men born, to put our faith in its truth. Do you see anything of this ark?"

"'Tis down south, no doubt, or anchored in some of the bays. But the canoe is ready, and fifteen minutes will carry two such paddles as your'n and mine to the castle."

At this suggestion, Deerslayer helped his companion to place the different articles in the canoe, which was already afloat. This was no sooner done than the two frontiersmen embarked, and by a vigorous push sent the light bark some eight or ten rods from the shore. Hurry now took the seat in the stern, while Deerslayer placed himself forward, and by leisurely but steady strokes of the paddles, the canoe glided across the placid sheet, towards the extraordinary-looking structure that the former had styled Muskrat Castle. Several times the men ceased paddling, and looked about them at the scene, as new glimpses opened from behind points, enabling them to see farther down the lake, or to get broader views of the wooded mountains. The only changes, however, were in the new forms of the hills, the varying curvature of the bays, and the wider reaches of the valley south; the whole earth apparently being clothed in a gala-dress of leaves.

"This *is* a sight to warm the heart!" exclaimed Deerslayer, when they had thus stopped for the fourth or fifth time; "the lake seems made to let us get an insight into the noble forests; and land and water alike stand in the beauty of God's providence! Do you say, Hurry, that there is no man who calls himself lawful owner of all these glories?"

"None but the King, lad. He may pretend to some right of that natur', but he is so far away that his claim will never trouble old Tom Hutter, who has got possession, and is like to keep it as long as his life lasts. Tom is no squatter, not being on land; I call him a floater."

"I inv*y* that man! I know it's wrong, and I strive ag'in the feelin', but I inv*y* that man! Don't think, Hurry, that I'm consarting any plan to put myself in his moccasins, for such a thought doesn't harbor in my mind; but I can't help a little inv*y*? 'Tis a nat'ral feelin', and the best of us are but nat'ral a'ter all and give way to such feelin's at times."

"You've only to marry Hetty to inherit half the estate," cried Hurry, laughing; "the gal is comely; nay, if it wasn't for her sister's beauty she would be even handsome; and then her wits are so small that you may easily convart her into one of your own way of thinking, in all things. Do *you* take Hetty off the old fellow's hands, and *I*'ll engage he'll give you an interest in every deer you can knock over within five miles of his lake."

"Does game abound?" suddenly demanded the other, who paid but little attention to March's raillery.

"It has the country to itself. Scarce a trigger is pulled on it; and as for the trappers, this is not a region they greatly frequent. I ought not to be so much here myself, but Jude pulls one way, while the beaver pulls another. More than a hundred Spanish dollars has that creatur' cost me the last two seasons, and yet I could not forego the wish to look upon her face once more."

"Do the redmen often visit this lake, Hurry?" continued Deerslayer, pursuing his own train of thought.

"Why, they come and go; sometimes in parties, and sometimes singly. The country seems to belong to no native tribe in particular; and so it has fallen into the hands of the Hutter tribe. The old man tells me that some sharp ones have been wheedling the Mohawks for an Indian deed, in order to get a title out of the colony; but nothing has come of it, seeing that no one heavy enough for such a trade has yet meddled with the matter. The hunters have a good life-lease still of this wilderness."

"So much the better, so much the better, Hurry. If I was King of England, the man that felled one of these trees without good occasion for the timber, should be banished to a desarted and forlorn region, in which no four-footed animal ever trod. Right glad am I that Chingachgook ap-p'inted our meeting on this lake, for hitherto eye of mine never looked on such a glorious spectacle."

"That's because you've kept so much among the Delawares, in whose country there are no lakes. Now, farther north and farther west these bits of water abound; and you're young, and may yet live to see 'em. But though there be other lakes, Deerslayer, there's no other Judith Hutter!"

At this remark his companion smiled, and then he dropped his paddle into the water, as if in consideration of a lover's haste. Both now pulled vigorously until they got within a hundred yards of the "castle," as Hurry familiarly called the house of Hutter, when they again ceased paddling; the admirer of Judith restraining his impatience the more readily, as he perceived that the building was untenanted, at the moment. This new pause was to enable Deerslayer to survey the singular edifice, which was of a construction so novel as to merit a particular description.

Muskrat Castle, as the house had been facetiously named by some waggish officer, stood in the open lake, at a distance of fully a quarter of a mile from the nearest shore. On every other side the water extended much farther, the precise position being distant about two miles from the northern end of the sheet, and near, if not quite, a mile from its eastern shore. As there was not the smallest appearance of any island, but the house stood on piles, with the water flowing beneath it, and Deerslayer had already discovered that the lake was of a great depth, he was fain to ask an explanation of this singular circumstance. Hurry solved the difficulty by telling him that on this spot alone, a long, narrow shoal, which extended for a few hundred yards in a north and south direction, rose within six or eight feet of the surface of the lake, and that Hutter had driven piles into it, and placed his habitation on them, for the purpose of security.

"The old fellow was burnt out three times, atween the Indians and the hunters; and in one affray with the redskins he lost his only son, since which time he has taken to the water for safety. No one can attack him here, without coming in a boat, and the plunder and scalps would scarce be worth the trouble of digging out canoes. Then it's by no means sartain which would whip in such a scrimmage, for old Tom is well supplied with arms and ammunition, and the castle, as you may see, is a tight breastwork ag'in light shot."

Deerslayer had some theoretical knowledge of frontier warfare, though he had never yet been called on to raise his hand in anger against a fellow-creature. He saw that Hurry did not overrate the strength of this position in a military point of view, since it would not be easy to attack it without exposing the assailants to the fire of the besieged. A good deal of art had also been manifested in the disposition of the timber of which the building was constructed and which afforded a protection much greater than was usual to the ordinary log-cabins of the frontier. The sides and ends were composed of the trunks of large pines, cut about nine feet long, and placed upright, instead of being laid horizontally, as was the practice of the country. These logs were squared on three sides, and had large tenons on each end. Massive sills were secured on the heads of the piles, with suitable grooves dug out of their upper surfaces, which had been squared for the purpose, and the lower tenons of the upright pieces were placed in these grooves, giving them a secure fastening below. Plates had been laid on the upper ends of the upright logs, and were kept in their places by a similar contrivance; the several corners of the structure being well fastened by scarfing and pinning the sills and plates. The floors were made of smaller logs, similarly squared, and the roof was composed of light poles, firmly united, and well covered with bark. The effect of this ingenious arrangement was to give its owner a house that could be approached only by water, the sides of which were composed of logs closely wedged together, which were two feet thick in their thinnest parts, and which could be separated only by a deliberate and laborious use of human hands, or by the slow operation of time. The outer surface of the building was rude and uneven, the logs being of unequal sizes; but the squared surfaces within gave both the sides and floor as uniform an appearance as was desired, either for use or show. The chimney was not the least singular portion of the castle, as Hurry made his companion observe, while he explained the process by which it had been made. The material was a stiff clay, properly worked, which had been put together in a mould of sticks, and suffered to harden, a foot or two at a time, commencing at the bottom. When the entire chimney had thus been raised, and had been properly bound in with outward props, a brisk fire was kindled, and kept going until it was burned to something like a brick-red. This had not been an easy operation, nor had it succeeded entirely; but by dint of filling the cracks with fresh clay, a safe fireplace and chimney had been obtained in the end. This part of the work stood on the log-floor, secured beneath by an extra pile. There were a few other peculiarities about this dwelling, which will better appear in the course of the narrative.

"Old Tom is full of contrivances," added Hurry, "and he set his heart on the success of his chimney, which threatened more than once to give out altogether; but parseverance will even overcome smoke; and now he has a comfortable cabin of it, though it did promise, at one time, to be a chinky sort of a flue to carry flames and fire."

"You seem to know the whole history of the castle, Hurry, chimney and sides," said Deerslayer, smiling; "is love so overcoming that it causes a man to study the story of his sweetheart's habitation?"

"Partly that, lad, and partly eyesight," returned the good-natured giant, laughing; "there was a large gang of us in the lake, the summer the old fellow built, and we helped him along with the job. I raised no small part of the weight of them uprights with my own shoulders, and the axes flew, I can inform you, Master Natty, while we were bee-ing it among the trees ashore. The old devil is no way stingy about food, and as we had often eat at his hearth, we thought we would just house him comfortably, afore we went to Albany with our skins. Yes, many is the meal I've swallowed in Tom Hutter's cabins; and Hetty, though so weak in the way of wits, has a wonderful particular way about a frying-pan or a gridiron!"

While the parties were thus discoursing, the canoe had been gradually drawing nearer to the "castle," and was now so close as to require but a single stroke of a paddle to reach the landing. This was at a floored platform in front of the entrance, that might have been some twenty feet square.

"Old Tom calls this sort of a wharf his dooryard," observed Hurry, as he fastened the canoe, after he and his companion had left it; "and the gallants from the forts have named it the 'castle court,' though what a 'court' can have to do here is more than I can tell you, seeing that there is no law. 'Tis as I supposed; not a soul within, but the whole family is off on a v'y'age of discovery!"

While Hurry was bustling about the "dooryard," examining the fishing-spears, rods, nets, and other similar appliances of a frontier cabin, Deerslayer, whose manner was altogether more rebuked and quiet, entered the building with a curiosity that was not usually exhibited by one so long trained in Indian habits. The interior of the "castle" was as faultlessly neat as its exterior was novel. The entire space, some twenty feet by forty, was subdivided into several small sleeping-rooms; the apartment into which he first entered, serving equally for the ordinary uses of its inmates, and a kitchen. The furniture was of the strange mixture that it is not uncommon to find in the remotely situated log-tenements of the interior. Most of it was rude, and to the last degree rustic; but there was a clock, with a handsome case of dark wood, in a corner, and two or three chairs, with a table and bureau, that had evidently come from some dwelling of more than usual pretension. The clock was industriously ticking, but its leaden-looking hands did no discredit to their dull aspect, for they pointed to the hour of eleven, though the sun plainly showed it was some time past the turn of the day. There was also a dark, massive chest. The kitchen utensils were of the simplest kind, and far from numerous, but every article was in its place, and showed the nicest care in its condition.

After Deerslayer had cast a look about him in the outer room, he raised a wooden latch, and entered a narrow passage that divided the inner end of the house into two equal parts. Frontier usages being no way scrupulous, and his curiosity being strongly excited, the young man now opened a door, and found himself in a bedroom. A single glance sufficed to show that the apartment belonged to females. The bed was of the feathers of wild geese, and filled nearly to overflowing; but it lay in a rude bunk, raised only a foot from the floor. On one side of it were arranged, on pegs, various dresses, of a quality much superior to what one would expect to meet in such a place, with ribbons and other similar articles to correspond. Pretty shoes, with handsome silver buckles, such as were then worn by females in easy circumstances, were not wanting; and no less than six fans, of gay colors, were placed half open, in a way to catch the eye by their conceits and hues. Even the pillow, on this side of the bed, was covered with finer linen than its companion, and it was ornamented with a small ruffle. A cap, coquettishly decorated with ribbons, hung above it, and a pair of long gloves, such as were rarely used in those days by persons of the laboring classes, were pinned ostentatiously to it, as if with an intention to exhibit them there, if they could not be shown on the owner's arms.

All this Deerslayer saw, and noted with a degree of minuteness that would have done credit to the habitual observation of his friends, the Delawares. Nor did he fail to perceive the distinction that existed between the appearances on the different sides of the bed, the head of which stood against the wall. On that opposite to the one just described, everything was homely and uninviting, except through its perfect neatness. The few garments that were hanging from the pegs were of the coarsest materials and of the commonest forms, while nothing seemed made for show. Of ribbons there was not one; nor was there either cap or kerchief beyond those which Hutter's daughters might be fairly entitled to wear.

It was now several years since Deerslayer had been in a spot especially devoted to the uses of females of his own color and race. The sight brought back to his mind a rush of childish recollections; and he lingered in the room with a tenderness of feeling to which he had long been a stranger. He bethought him of his mother, whose homely vestments he remembered to have been hanging on pegs like those which he felt must belong to Hetty Hutter; and he bethought himself of a sister, whose incipient and native taste for finery had exhibited itself somewhat in the manner of that of Judith, though necessarily in a less degree. These little resemblances opened a long hidden vein of sensations; and as he quitted the room, it was with a saddened mien. He looked no further, but returned slowly and thoughtfully towards the "door-yard."

"Old Tom has taken to a new calling, and has been trying his hand at the traps," cried Hurry, who had been coolly examining the borderer's implements; "if that is his humor, and you're disposed to remain in these parts, we can make an oncommon comfortable season of it; for, while the old man and I out-knowledge the beaver, you can fish, and knock down the deer, to keep body and soul together. We always give the poorest hunters half a share, but one as actyve and sartain as yourself might expect a full one."

"Thank'ee, Hurry; thank'ee, with all my heart—but I do a little beavering for myself as occasions offer. 'Tis true, the Delawares call me Deerslayer, but it's not so much because I'm pretty fatal with the venison as because that while I kill so many bucks and does, I've never yet taken the life of a fellow-creatur'. They say their traditions do not tell of another who had shed so much blood of animals that had not shed the blood of man."

"I hope they don't account you chicken-hearted, lad? A faint-hearted man is like a no-tailed beaver."

"I don't believe, Hurry, that they account me as out-of-the-way timorsome, even though they may not account me as out-of-the-way brave. But I'm not quarrelsome; and that goes a great way towards keeping blood off the hands, among the hunters and redskins; and then, Harry March, it keeps blood off the conscience, too."

"Well, for my part I account game, a redskin, and a Frenchman as pretty much the same thing; though I'm as onquarrelsome a man, too, as there is in all the colonies. I despise a quarreller as I do a cur-dog; but one has no need to be overscrupulsome when it's the right time to show the flint."

"I look upon him as the most of a man who acts nearest the right, Hurry. But this is a glorious spot, and my eyes never a-weary looking at it!"

"'Tis your first acquaintance with a lake; and these idees come over us all at such times. Lakes have a general character, as I say, being pretty much water and land, and points and bays."

As this definition by no means met the feelings that were uppermost in the mind of the young hunter, he made no immediate answer, but stood gazing at the dark hills and the glassy water in silent enjoyment.

"Have the Governor's or the King's people given this lake a name?" he suddenly asked, as if struck with a new idea. "If they've not begun to blaze their trees, and set up their compasses, and line off their maps, it's likely they've not bethought them to disturb natur' with a name."

"They've not got to that, yet; and the last time I went in with skins, one of the King's surveyors was questioning me consarning all the region hereabouts. He had heard that there was a lake in this quarter, and had got some general notions about it, such as that there was water and hills; but how much of either, he know'd no more than you know of the Mohawk tongue. I didn't open the trap any wider than was necessary, giving him but poor encouragement in the way of farms and clearings. In short, I left on his mind some such opinion of this country as a man gets of a spring of dirty water, with a path to it that is so muddy that one mires afore he sets out. He told me they hadn't got the spot down yet, on their maps; though I conclude that is a mistake, for he showed me his parchment, and there is a lake down on it where there is no lake in fact, and which is about fifty miles from the place where it ought to be, if they meant it for this. I don't think my account will encourage him to mark down another, by way of improvement."

Here Hurry laughed heartily, such tricks being particularly grateful to a set of men who dreaded the approaches of civilization as a curtailment of their own lawless empire. The egregious errors that existed in the maps of the day, all of which were made in Europe, were, moreover, a standing topic of ridicule among them; for, if they had not science enough to make any better themselves, they had sufficient local information to detect the gross blunders contained in those that existed. Any one who will take the trouble to compare these unanswerable evidences of the topographical skill of our fathers a century since, with the more accurate sketches of our own time, will at once perceive that the men of the woods had a sufficient justification for all their criticism on this branch of the skill of the colonial governments, which did not at all hesitate to place a river or a lake a degree or two out of the way, even though they lay within a day's march of the inhabited parts of the country.

"I'm glad it has no name," resumed Deerslayer, "or, at least, no pale-face name; for their christenings always foretell waste and destruction. No doubt, howsever, the redskins have their modes of knowing it, and the hunters and trappers, too; they are likely to call the place by something reasonable and resembling."

"As for the tribes, each has its own tongue, and its own way of calling things; and they treat this part of the world just as they treat all others. Among ourselves, we've got to calling the place the 'Glimmerglass,' seeing that its whole basin is so often fringed with pines, cast upward from its face; as if it would throw back the hills that hang over it."

"There is an outlet, I know, for all lakes have outlets, and the rock at which I am to meet Chingachgook stands near an outlet. Has *that* no colony-name yet?"

"In that particular they've got the advantage of us, having one end, and that the biggest, in their own keeping: they've given it a name which has found its way up to its source; names nat'rally working up stream. No doubt, Deerslayer, you've seen the Susquehannah, down in the Delaware country?"

"That have I, and hunted along its banks a hundred times."

"That and this are the same in fact, and, I suppose, the same in sound. I am glad they've been compelled to keep the redmen's name, for it would be too hard to rob them of both land and name!"

Deerslayer made no answer; but he stood leaning on his rifle, gazing at the view which so much delighted him. The reader is not to suppose, however, that it was the picturesque alone which so strongly attracted his attention. The spot was very lovely, of a truth, and it was then seen in one of its most favorable moments, the surface of the lake being as smooth as glass and as limpid as pure air, throwing back the mountains, clothed in dark pines, along the whole of its eastern boundary, the points thrusting forward their trees even to nearly horizontal lines, while the bays were seen glittering through an occasional arch beneath, left by a vault fretted with branches and leaves. It was the air of deep repose—the solitudes, that spoke of scenes and forests untouched by the hands of man—the reign of nature, in a word, that gave so much pure delight to one of his habits and turn of mind. Still, he felt, though it was unconsciously, like a poet also. If he found a pleasure in studying this large, and to him unusual opening into the mysteries and forms of the woods, as one is gratified in getting broader views of any subject that has long occupied his thoughts, he was not insensible to the innate loveliness of such a landscape neither, but felt a portion of that soothing of the spirit which is a common attendant of a scene so thoroughly pervaded by the holy calm of nature.

[HURRY HARRY and Deerslayer find old Tom Hutter's ark concealed in a stream opening from the far end of the lake where he has gone trapping. Judith proves to be as beautiful and gracious as Hurry has described her, and she soon shows a strong preference for Deerslayer over his companion. It is the beginning of King George's War and a band of Hurons or Mingos, allies of the French, who have been hunting on the Glimmerglass, have already received word of the new hostilities between the French and the English. They determine not to leave the territory without some white enemy scalps for trophies, and they make an attack on the ark which is unsuccessful. In the face of the common danger, Deerslayer and Hurry join forces with Hutter. The colony offers a bounty for each Indian scalp, and as there is an encampment of Hurons on the lake, including many women and children, Hutter and Hurry decide to go on a scalping expedition, against which Deerslayer strongly protests:

> "My gifts are not scalpers' gifts, but such as belong to my religion and color. I'll stand by you, old man, in the ark or in the castle, but I'll not unhumanize my natur' by falling into ways that God intended for another race. If you and Hurry have got any thoughts that lean towards the colony's gold, go by yourselves in s'arch of it, and leave the females to my care."

But Deerslayer consents to help Hutter and Hurry recover two canoes that are concealed on the shores of the Glimmerglass. "The great object for people posted like ourselves," says Hutter, "is to command the water." Under cover of darkness, the three paddle to shore; but unknown to Deerslayer, the other two plan a side excursion into the Huron camp for scalps while he awaits their return in the canoe offshore. During their expedition, Hutter and Hurry are taken prisoners by the Huron warriors, and Deerslayer, unable to help them, sleeps that night on the lake in the bottom of the canoe.]

CHAPTER 7

DAY HAD fairly dawned before the young man . . . again opened his eyes. This was no sooner done, than he started up, and looked about him with the eagerness of one who suddenly felt the importance of accurately ascertaining his precise position. His rest had been deep and undisturbed; and when he awoke, it was with a clearness of intellect and a readiness of resources that were very much needed at that particular moment. The sun had not risen, it is true, but the vault of heaven was rich with the winning softness that "brings and shuts the day," while the whole air was filled with the carols of birds, the hymns of the feathered tribe. These sounds first told Deerslayer the risks he ran. The air, for wind it could scarce be called, was still light, it is true, but it had increased a little in the course of the night, and as the canoes were mere feathers on the water, they had drifted twice the expected distance; and, what was still more dangerous, had approached so near the base of the mountain that here rose precipitously from the eastern shore, as to render the carols of the birds plainly audible. This was not the worst. The third canoe had taken the same direction, and was slowly drifting towards a point where it must inevitably touch, unless turned aside by a shift of wind, or human hands. In other respects, nothing presented itself to attract attention, or to awaken alarm. The castle stood on its shoal, nearly abreast of the canoes, for the drift had amounted to miles in the course of the night, and the ark lay fastened to its piles, as both had been left so many hours before.

As a matter of course, Deerslayer's attention was first given to the canoe ahead. It was already quite near the point, and a very few strokes of the paddle sufficed to tell him that it must touch before he could possibly overtake it. Just at this moment, too, the wind inopportunely freshened, rendering the drift of the light craft much more rapid than certain. Feeling the impossibility of preventing a contact with the land, the young man wisely determined not to heat himself with unnecessary exertions; but first looking to the priming of his piece, he proceeded slowly and warily towards the point, taking care to make a little circuit, that he might be exposed on only one side, as he approached.

The canoe adrift being directed by no such intelligence, pursued its proper way, and grounded on a small sunken rock, at the distance of three or four yards from the shore. Just at that moment, Deerslayer had got abreast of the point, and turned the bows of his own boat to the land; first casting loose his tow, that his movements might be unencumbered. The canoe hung an instant on the rock; then it rose a hair's breadth on an almost imperceptible swell of the water, swung round, floated clear, and reached the strand. All this the young man noted, but it neither quickened his pulses, nor hastened his hand. If any one had been lying in wait for the arrival of the waif, he must be seen, and the utmost caution in approaching the shore became indispensable; if no one was in ambush, hurry was unnecessary. The point being nearly diagonally opposite to the Indian encampment, he hoped the last, though the former was not only possible, but probable; for the savages were prompt in adopting all the expedients of their particular modes of warfare, and quite likely had many scouts searching the shores for craft to carry them off to the castle. As a glance at the lake from any height or projection would expose the smallest object on its surface, there was little hope that either of the canoes would pass unseen; and Indian sagacity needed no instruction to tell which way a boat or a log would drift, when the direction of the wind was known. As Deerslayer drew nearer and nearer to the land, the stroke of his paddle grew slower, his eye became more watchful, and his ears and nostrils almost dilated with the effort to detect any lurking danger. 'Twas a trying moment for a novice, nor was there the encouragement which even the timid sometimes feel, when conscious of being observed and commended. He was entirely alone, thrown on his own resources, and was cheered by no friendly eye, emboldened by no encouraging voice. Notwithstanding all these circumstances, the most experienced veteran in forest warfare could not have behaved better. Equally free from recklessness and hesitation, his advance was marked by a sort of philosophical prudence, that appeared to render him superior to all motives but those which were best calculated to effect his purpose. Such was the commencement of a career in forest exploits, that afterwards rendered this man, in his way, and under the limits of his habits and opportunities, as renowned as many a hero whose name has adorned the pages of works more celebrated than legends simple as ours can ever become.

When about a hundred yards from the shore, Deerslayer rose in the canoe, gave three or four vigorous strokes with the paddle, sufficient of themselves to impel the bark to land, and then quickly laying aside the instrument of labor, he seized that of war. He was in the very act of raising the rifle, when a sharp report was followed by the buzz of a bullet that passed so near his body as to cause him involuntarily to start. The next instant Deerslayer staggered, and fell his whole length in the bottom of the canoe. A yell—it came from a single voice—followed, and an Indian leaped from the bushes upon the open area of the point, bounding towards the canoe. This was the moment the young man desired. He rose on the instant, and levelled his own rifle at his uncovered foe; but his finger hesitated about pulling the trigger on one whom he held at such a disadvantage. This little delay, probably, saved the life of the Indian, who bounded back into the cover as swiftly as he had broken out of it. In the meantime Deerslayer had been swiftly approaching the land, and his own canoe reached the point just as his enemy disappeared. As its movements had not been directed, it touched the shore a few yards from the other boat; and though the rifle of his foe had to be loaded, there was not time to secure his prize, and carry it beyond danger, before he would be exposed to another shot. Under the circumstances, therefore, he did not pause an instant, but dashed into the woods and sought a cover.

On the immediate point there was a small open area, partly in native grass, and partly beach, but a dense fringe of bushes lined its upper side. This narrow belt of dwarf vegetation passed, one issued immediately into the high and gloomy vaults of the forest. The land was tolerably level for a few hundred feet, and then it rose precipitously in a mountain-side. The trees were tall, large, and so free from underbrush, that they resembled vast columns, irregularly scattered, upholding a dome of leaves. Although they stood tolerably close together, for their ages and size, the eye could penetrate to considerable distances; and bodies of men, even, might have engaged beneath their cover, with concert and intelligence.

Deerslayer knew that his adversary must be employed in reloading, unless he had fled. The former proved to be the case, for the young man had no sooner placed himself behind a tree, than he caught a glimpse of the arm of the Indian, his body being concealed by an oak, in the very act of forcing the leathered bullet home. Nothing would have been easier than to spring forward, and decide the affair by a close assault on his unprepared foe; but every feeling of Deerslayer revolted at such a step, although his own life had just been attempted from a cover. He was yet unpractised in the ruthless expedients of savage warfare, of which he knew nothing except by tradition and theory, and it struck him as an unfair advantage to assail an unarmed foe. His color had heightened, his eye frowned, his lips were compressed, and all his energies were collected and ready; but, instead of advancing to fire, he dropped his rifle to the usual position of a sportsman in readiness to catch his aim, and muttered to himself, unconscious that he was speaking—

"No, no—that may be redskin warfare, but it's not a Christian's gifts. Let the miscreant charge, and then we'll take it out like men; for the canoe he *must* not, and *shall* not have. No, no; let him have time to load, and God will take care of the right!"

All this time the Indian had been so intent on his own movements, that he was even ignorant that his enemy was in the woods. His only apprehension was, that the canoe would be recovered and carried away before he might be in readiness to prevent it. He had sought the cover from habit, but was within a few feet of the fringe of bushes, and could be at the margin of the forest in readiness to fire in a moment. The distance between him and his enemy was about fifty yards, and the trees were so arranged by nature that the line of sight was not interrupted, except by the particular trees behind which each party stood.

His rifle was no sooner loaded, than the savage glanced around him, and advanced incautiously as regarded the real, but stealthily as respected the fancied position of his enemy, until he was fairly exposed. Then Deerslayer stepped from behind his own cover, and hailed him.

"This a way, redskin; this a way, if you're looking for me," he called out. "I'm young in war, but not so young as to stand on an open beach to be shot down like an owl, by daylight. It rests on yourself whether it's peace or war atween us; for my gifts are white gifts, and I'm not one of them that thinks it valiant to slay human mortals, singly, in the woods."

The savage was a good deal startled by this sudden discovery of the danger he ran. He had a little knowledge of English, however, and caught the drift of the other's meaning. He was also too well schooled to betray alarm, but, dropping the butt of his rifle to the earth, with an air of confidence, he made a gesture of lofty courtesy. All this was done with the ease and self-possession of one accustomed to consider no man his superior. In the midst of this consummate acting, however, the volcano that raged within caused his eyes to glare, and his nostrils to dilate, like those of some wild beast that is suddenly prevented from taking the fatal leap.

"Two canoes," he said, in the deep guttural tones of his race, holding up the number of fingers he mentioned, by way of preventing mistakes; "one for you—one for me."

"No, no, Mingo, that will never do. You own neither; and neither shall you have, as long as I can prevent it. I know it's war atween your people and mine, but that's no reason why human mortals should slay each other, like savage creatur's that meet in the woods; go your way, then, and leave me to go mine. The world is large enough for us both; and when we meet fairly in battle, why, the Lord will order the fate of each of us."

"Good!" exclaimed the Indian; "my brother missionary—great talk; all about Manitou."

"Not so—not so, warrior. I'm not good enough for the Moravians, and am too good for most of the other vagabonds that preach about in the woods. No, no; I'm only a hunter, as yet, though afore the peace is made, 'tis like enough there'll be occasion to strike a blow at some of your people. Still, I wish it to be done in fair fight, and not in a quarrel about the ownership of a miserable canoe."

"Good! My brother very young—but he is very wise. Little warrior—great talker. Chief, sometimes, in council."

"I don't know this, nor do I say it, Injin," returned Deerslayer, coloring a little at the ill-concealed sarcasm of the other's manner; "I look forward to a life in the woods, and I only hope it may be a peaceable one. All young men must go on the war-path, when there's occasion, but war isn't needfully massacre. I've seen enough of the last, this very night, to know that Providence frowns on it; and I now invite you to go your own way, while I go mine; and hope that we may part fri'nds."

"Good! My brother has two scalp—gray hair under t'other. Old wisdom—young tongue."

Here the savage advanced with confidence, his hand extended, his face smiling, and his whole bearing denoting amity and respect. Deerslayer met his offered friendship in a proper spirit, and they shook hands cordially, each endeavoring to assure the other of his sincerity and desire to be at peace.

"All have his own," said the Indian; "my canoe, mine; your canoe, your'n. Go look; if your'n, you keep; if mine, I keep."

"That's just, redskin; thought you must be wrong in thinking the canoe your property. Hows'ever, seein' is believin', and we'll go down to the shore, where you may look with your own eyes; for it's likely you'll object to trustin' altogether to mine."

The Indian uttered his favorite exclamation of "Good!" and then they walked side by side, towards the shore. There was no apparent distrust in the manner of either, the Indian moving in advance, as if he wished to show his companion that he did not fear turning his back to him. As they reached the open ground, the former pointed towards Deerslayer's boat, and said emphatically—

"No mine—pale-face canoe. *This* redman's. No want other man's canoe—want his own."

"You're wrong, redskin, you're altogether wrong. This canoe was left in old Hutter's keeping, and is his'n according to law, red or white, till its owner comes to claim it. Here's the seats and the stitching of the bark to speak for themselves. No man ever know'd an Injin to turn off such work."

"Good! My brother little old—big wisdom. Injin no make him. White man's work."

"I'm glad you think so, for holding out to the contrary might have made ill blood atween us, every one having a right to take possession of his own. I'll just shove the canoe out of reach of dispute at once, as the quickest way of settling difficulties."

While Deerslayer was speaking, he put a foot against the end of the light boat, and giving a vigorous shove, he sent it out into the lake a hundred feet or more, where, taking the true current, it would necessarily float past the point, and be in no further danger of coming ashore. The savage started at this ready and decided expedient, and his companion saw that he cast a hurried and fierce glance at his own canoe, or that which contained the paddles. The change of manner, however, was but momentary, and then the Iroquois resumed his air of friendliness, and a smile of satisfaction.

"Good!" he repeated, with stronger emphasis than ever. "Young head, old mind. Know how to settle quarrel. Farewell, brother. He go to house in water—muskrat house—Injin go to camp; tell chiefs no find canoe."

Deerslayer was not sorry to hear this proposal, for he felt anxious to join the females, and he took the offered hand of the Indian very willingly. The parting words were friendly, and while the red-man walked calmly towards the wood, with the rifle in the hollow of his arm, without once looking back in uneasiness or distrust, the white man moved towards the remaining canoe, carrying his piece in the same pacific manner, it is true, but keeping his eye fastened on the movements of the other. This distrust, however, seemed to be altogether uncalled for, and as if ashamed to have entertained it, the young man averted his look, and stepped carelessly up to his boat. Here he began to push the canoe from the shore, and to make his other preparations for departing. He might have been thus employed a minute, when, happening to turn his face towards the land, his quick and certain eye told him, at a glance, the imminent jeopardy in which his life was placed. The black, ferocious eyes of the savage were glancing on him, like those of the crouching tiger, through a small opening in the bushes, and the muzzle of his rifle seemed already to be opening in a line with his own body.

Then, indeed, the long practice of Deerslayer, as a hunter, did him good service. Accustomed to fire with the deer on the bound, and often when the precise position of the animal's body had in a manner to be guessed at, he used the same expedients here. To cock and poise his rifle were the acts of a single moment and at single motion; then aiming almost without sighting, he fired into the bushes where he knew a body ought to be, in order to sustain the appaling countenance which alone was visible. There was not time to raise the piece any higher, or to take a more deliberate aim. So rapid were his movements that both parties discharged their pieces at the same instant, the concussions mingling in one report. The mountains, indeed, gave back but a single echo. Deerslayer dropped his piece, and stood with head erect, steady as one of the pines in the calm of a June morning, watching the result; while the savage gave the yell that has become historical for its appalling influence, leaped through the bushes, and came bounding across the open ground, flourishing a tomahawk. Still Deerslayer moved not, but stood with his unloaded rifle fallen against his shoulders, while, with a hunter's habits, his hands were mechanically feeling for the powder-horn and charger. When about forty feet from his enemy, the savage hurled his keen weapon; but it was with an eye so vacant, and a hand so unsteady and feeble, that the young man caught it by the handle as it was flying past him. At that instant the Indian staggered and fell his whole length on the ground.

"I know'd it—I know'd it!" exclaimed Deerslayer, who was already preparing to force a fresh bullet into his rifle; "I know'd it must come to this, as soon as I had got the range from the creatur's eyes. A man sights suddenly, and fires quick when his own life's in danger; yes, I know'd it would come to this. I was about the hundredth part of a second too quick for him, or it might have been bad for me! The riptyle's bullet has just grazed my side—but say what you will for or ag'in 'em, a redskin is by no means as sartain with powder and ball as a white man. Their gifts don't seem to lie that a way. Even Chingachgook, great as he is in other matters, isn't downright deadly with the rifle."

By this time the piece was reloaded, and Deerslayer, after tossing the tomahawk into the canoe, advanced to his victim, and stood over him, leaning on his rifle, in melancholy attention. It was the first instance in which he had seen a man fall in battle—it was the first fellow-creature against whom he had ever seriously raised his own hand. The sensations were novel; and regret, with the freshness of our better feelings, mingled with his triumph. The Indian was not dead, though shot directly through the body. He lay on his back motionless, but his eyes, now full of consciousness, watched each action of his victor—as the fallen bird regards the fowler—jealous of every movement. The man probably expected the fatal blow which was to precede the loss of his scalp; or perhaps he anticipated that this latter act of cruelty would precede his death. Deerslayer read his thoughts; and he found a melancholy satisfaction in relieving the apprehensions of the helpless savage.

"No, no, redskin," he said; "you've nothing more to fear from me. I am of a Christian stock, and scalping is not of my gifts. I'll just make sartain of your rifle, and then come back and do you what sarvice I can. Though here I can't stay much longer, as the crack of three rifles will be apt to bring some of your devils down upon me."

The close of this was said in a sort of a soliloquy, as the young man went in quest of the fallen rifle. The piece was found where its owner had dropped it, and was immediately put into the canoe. Laying his own rifle at its side, Deerslayer then returned and stood over the Indian again.

"All inmity atween you and me's at an ind, redskin," he said; "and you may set your heart at rest on the score of the scalp, or any further injury. My gifts are white, as I've told you; and I hope my conduct will be white also!"

Could looks have conveyed all they meant, it is probable Deerslayer's innocent vanity on the subject of color would have been rebuked a little; but he comprehended the gratitude that was expressed in the eyes of the dying savage, without in the least detecting the bitter sarcasm that struggled with the better feeling.

"Water!" ejaculated the thirsty and unfortunate creature; "give poor Injin water."

"Ay, water you shall have, if you drink the lake dry. I'll just carry you down to it, that you may take your fill. This is the way, they tell me, with all wounded people—water is their greatest comfort and delight."

So saying, Deerslayer raised the Indian in his arms, and carried him to the lake. Here he first helped him to take an attitude in which he could appease his burning thirst; after which he seated himself on a stone, and took the head of his wounded adversary in his own lap, and endeavored to soothe his anguish in the best manner he could.

"It would be sinful in me to tell you your time hadn't come, warror," he commenced, "and therefore I'll not say it. You've passed the middle age already, and, considerin' the sort of lives ye lead, your days have been pretty well filled. The principal thing now, is to look forward to what comes next. Neither redskin nor paleface, on the whole, calculates much on sleepin' forever; but both expect to live in another world. Each has his gifts, and will be judged by 'em, and I suppose you've thought these matters over enough not to stand in need of sarmons when the trial comes. You'll find your happy hunting-grounds, if you've been a just Injin; if an onjust, you'll meet your desarts in another way. I've my own idees about these things; but you're too old and exper'enced to need any explanations from one as young as I."

"Good!" ejaculated the Indian, whose voice retained its depth even as life ebbed away; "young head—old wisdom!"

"It's sometimes a consolation, when the ind comes, to know that them we've harmed, or *tried* to harm, forgive us. I suppose natur' seeks this relief, by way of getting a pardon on 'arth; as we never can know whether He pardons, who is all in all, till judgment itself comes. It's soothing to know that *any* pardon at such times; and that, I conclude, is the secret. Now, as for myself, I overlook altogether your designs ag'in my life; first, because no harm came of 'em; next, because it's your gifts, and natur', and trainin', and I ought not to have trusted you at all; and, finally and chiefly, because I can bear no ill-will to a dying man, whether heathen or Christian. So put your heart at ease, so far as I'm consarned; you know best what other matters ought to trouble you, or what ought to give you satisfaction in so trying a moment."

It is probable that the Indian had some of the fearful glimpses of the unknown state of being which God, in mercy, seems at times to afford to all the human race; but they were necessarily in conformity with his habits and prejudices. Like most of his people, and like too many of our own, he thought more of dying in a way to gain applause among those he left than to secure a better state of existence hereafter. While Deerslayer was speaking, his mind was a little bewildered, though he felt that the intention was good; and when he had done, a regret passed over his spirit that none of his own tribe were present to witness his stoicism, under extreme bodily suffering, and the firmness with which he met his end. With the high innate courtesy that so often distinguishes the Indian warrior before he becomes corrupted by too much intercourse with the worst class of the white men, he endeavored to express his thankfulness for the other's good intentions, and to let him understand that they were appreciated.

"Good!" he repeated, for this was an English word much used by the savages, "good! young head; young *heart,* too. *Old* heart tough; no shed tear. Hear Indian when he die, and no want to lie—what he call him?"

"Deerslayer is the name I bear now, though the Delawares have said that when I get back from this war-path, I shall have a more manly title, provided I can 'arn one."

"That good name for boy—poor name for warrior. He get better quick. No fear *there,"*—the savage had strength sufficient, under the strong excitement he felt, to raise a hand and tap the young man on his breast,—"eye sartain—finger lightning—aim, death—great warrior soon. No Deerslayer—Hawkeye—Hawkeye—Hawkeye. Shake hand."

Deerslayer—or Hawkeye, as the youth was then first named, for in after years he bore the appellation throughout all that region—Deerslayer took the hand of the savage, whose last breath was drawn in that attitude, gazing in admiration at the countenance of a stranger, who had shown so much readiness, skill, and firmness, in a scene that was equally trying and novel. When the reader remembers it is the highest gratification an Indian can receive to see his enemy betray weakness, he will be better able to appreciate the conduct which had extorted so great a concession at such a moment.

"His spirit has fled!" said Deerslayer, in a suppressed, melancholy voice. "Ah's me! Well, to this we must all come, sooner or later; and he is happiest, let his skin be what color it may, who is best fitted to meet it. Here lies the body of no doubt a brave warrior, and the soul is already flying towards its heaven or hell, whether that be a happy hunting-ground, a place scant of game, regions of glory, according to Moravian doctrine, or flames of fire! So it happens, too, as regards other matters! Here have old Hutter and Hurry Harry got themselves into difficulty, if they haven't got themselves into torment and death, and all for a bounty that luck offers to me in what many would think a lawful and suitable manner. But not a farthing of such money shall cross my hand. White I was born, and white will I die; clinging to color to the last, even though the King's majesty, his governors, and all his councils, both at home and in the colonies, forget from what they come, and where they hope to go, and all for a little advantage in warfare. No, no, warrior, hand of mine shall never molest your scalp, and so your soul may rest in peace on the p'int of making a decent appearance when the body comes to join it, in your own land of spirits."

Deerslayer arose as soon as he had spoken. Then he placed the body of the dead man in a sitting posture, with its back against the little rock, taking the necessary care to prevent it from falling or in any way settling into an attitude that might be thought unseemly by the sensitive, though wild notions of a savage. When this duty was performed, the young man stood gazing at the grim countenance of his fallen foe, in a sort of melancholy abstraction. As was his practice, however, a habit gained by living so much alone in the forest, he then began again to give utterance to his thoughts and feelings aloud.

"I didn't wish your life, redskin," he said, "but you left me no choice atween killing or being killed. Each party acted according to his gifts, I suppose, and blame can light on neither. You were treacherous, according to your natur' in war, and I was a little oversightful, as I'm apt to be in trusting others. Well, this is my first battle with a human mortal, though it's not likely to be the last. I have fou't most of the creatur's of the forest, such as bears, wolves, painters, and catamounts, but this is the beginning with the redskins. If I was Injin born, now, I might tell of this, or carry in the scalp, and boast of the expl'ite afore the whole tribe; or, if my inimy had only been even a bear, 'twould have been nat'ral and proper to let everybody know what had happened; but I don't well see how I'm to let even Chingachgook into this secret, so long as it can be done only by boasting with a white tongue. And why should I wish to boast of it a'ter all? It's slaying a human, although he was a savage; and how do I know that he was a just Injin; and that he has not been taken away suddenly to anything but happy hunting-grounds. When it's onsartain whether good or evil has been done, the wisest way is not to be boastful—still, I *should* like Chingachgook to know that I haven't discredited the Delawares, or my training!"

Part of this was uttered aloud, while part was merely muttered between the speaker's teeth; his more confident opinions enjoying the first advantage, while his doubts were expressed in the latter mode. Soliloquy and reflection received a startling interruption, however, by the sudden appearance of a second Indian on the lake shore, a few hundred yards from the point. This man, evidently another scout, who had probably been drawn to the place by the reports of the rifles, broke out of the forest with so little caution that Deerslayer caught a view of his person before he was himself discovered. When the latter event did occur, as was the case a moment later, the savage gave a loud yell, which was answered by a dozen voices from different parts of the mountain-side. There was no longer any time for delay; in another minute the boat was quitting the shore under long and steady sweeps of the paddle.

As soon as Deerslayer believed himself to be at a safe distance, he ceased his efforts, permitting the little bark to drift, while he leisurely took a survey of the state of things. The canoe first sent adrift was floating before the air, quite a quarter of a mile above him, and a little nearer to the shore than he wished, now that he knew more of the savages were so near at hand. The canoe shoved from the point was within a few yards of him, he having directed his own course towards it on quitting the land. The dead Indian lay in grim quiet where he had left him, the warrior who had shown himself from the forest had already vanished, and the woods themselves were as silent and seemingly deserted as the day they came fresh from the hands of their great Creator. This profound stillness, however, lasted but a moment. When time had been given to the scouts of the enemy to reconnoitre, they burst out of the thicket upon the naked point, filling the air with yells of fury at discovering the death of their companion. These cries were immediately succeeded by shouts of delight when they reached the body and clustered eagerly around it. Deerslayer was a sufficient adept in the usages of the natives to understand the reason of the change. The yell was the customary lamentation at the loss of a warrior, the shout a sign of rejoicing that the conqueror had not been able to secure the scalp; the trophy, without which a victory is never considered complete. The distance at which the canoes lay probably prevented any attempts to injure the conqueror, the American Indian, like the panther of his own woods, seldom making any effort against his foe unless tolerably certain it is under circumstances that may be expected to prove effective.

As the young man had no longer any motive to remain near the point, he prepared to collect his canoes, in order to tow them off to the castle. That nearest was soon in tow, when he proceeded in quest of the other, which was all this time floating up the lake. The eye of Deerslayer was no sooner fastened on this last boat, than it struck him that it was nearer to the shore than it would have been had it merely followed the course of the gentle current of air. He began to suspect the influence of some unseen current in the water, and he quickened his exertions, in order to regain possession of it before it could drift into a dangerous proximity to the woods. On getting nearer, he thought that the canoe had a perceptible motion through the water, and, as it lay broadside to the air, that this motion was taking it towards the land. A few vigorous strokes of the paddle carried him still nearer, when the mystery was explained. Something was evidently in motion on the off-side of the canoe, or that which was farthest from himself, and closer scrutiny showed that it was a naked human arm. An Indian was lying in the bottom of the canoe, and was propelling it slowly but certainly to the shore, using his hand as a paddle. Deerslayer understood the whole artifice at a glance. A savage had swum off to the boat while he was occupied with his enemy on the point, got possession, and was using these means to urge it to the shore.

Satisfied that the man in the canoe could have no arms, Deerslayer did not hesitate to dash close alongside of the retiring boat, without deeming it necessary to raise his own rifle. As soon as the wash of the water, which he made in approaching, became audible to the prostrate savage, the latter sprang to his feet, and uttered an exclamation that proved how completely he was taken by surprise.

"If you've enj'yed yourself enough in that canoe, redskin," Deerslayer coolly observed, stopping his own career in sufficient time to prevent an absolute collision between the two boats,—"if you've enj'yed yourself enough in that canoe, you'll do a prudent act by taking to the lake ag'in. I'm reasonable in these matters, and don't crave your blood, though there's them about that would look upon you more as a due-bill for the bounty than a human mortal. Take to the lake this minute, afore we get to hot words."

The savage was one of those who did not understand a word of English, and he was indebted to the gestures of Deerslayer, and to the expression of an eye that did not often deceive, for an imperfect comprehension of his meaning. Perhaps, too, the sight of the rifle that lay so near the hand of the white man quickened his decision. At all events, he crouched like a tiger about to take his leap, uttered a yell, and the next instant his naked body disappeared in the water.

When he rose to take breath, it was at the distance of several yards from the canoe, and the hasty glance he threw behind him denoted how much he feared the arrival of a fatal messenger from the rifle of his foe. But the young man made no indication of any hostile intention. Deliberately securing the canoe to the others, he began to paddle from the shore; and by the time the Indian reached the land, and had shaken himself, like a spaniel, on quitting the water, his dreaded enemy was already beyond rifleshot on his way to the castle. As was so much his practice, Deerslayer did not fail to soliloquize on what had just occurred, while steadily pursuing his course towards the point of destination.

"Well, well,"—he commenced,—"'twould have been wrong to kill a human mortal without an object. Scalps are of no account with me, and life is sweet, and ought not to be taken marcilessly by them that have white gifts. The savage was a Mingo, it's true; and I make no doubt he is, and will be as long as he lives, a ra'al riptyle and vagabond; but that's no reason I should forget my gifts and color. No, no,—let him go; if ever we meet ag'in, rifle in hand, why then 'twill be seen which has the stoutest heart and the quickest eye. Hawkeye! That's not a bad name for a warrior, sounding much more manful and valiant than Deerslayer! 'Twouldn't be a bad title to begin with, and it has been fairly 'arned. If 'twas Chingachgook, now, he might go home and boast of his deeds, and the chiefs would name him Hawkeye in a minute; but it don't become white blood to brag, and 'tisn't easy to see how the matter can be known unless I do. Well, well—everything is in the hands of Providence; this affair as well as another; I'll trust to that for getting my desarts in all things."

Having thus betrayed what might be termed his weak spot, the young man continued to paddle in silence, making his way diligently, and as fast as his tows would allow him, towards the castle. By this time the sun had not only risen, but it had appeared over the eastern mountains, and was shedding a flood of glorious light on this as yet unchristened sheet of water. The whole scene was radiant with beauty; and no one unaccustomed to the ordinary history of the woods would fancy it had so lately witnessed incidents so ruthless and barbarous. As he approached the building of old Hutter, Deerslayer thought, or rather *felt,* that its appearance was in singular harmony with all the rest of the scene. Although nothing had been consulted but strength and security, the rude, massive logs, covered with their rough bark, the projecting roof, and the form, would contribute to render the building picturesque in almost any situation, while its actual position added novelty and piquancy to its other points of interest.

When Deerslayer drew nearer to the castle, however, objects of interest presented themselves that at once eclipsed any beauties that might have distinguished the scenery of the lake, and the site of the singular edifice. Judith and Hetty stood on the platform before the door, Hurry's door-yard, awaiting his approach with manifest anxiety; the former, from time to time, taking a survey of his person and of the canoes through the old ship's spy-glass that has been already mentioned. Never probably did this girl seem more brilliantly beautiful than at that moment; the flush of anxiety and alarm increasing her color to its richest tints, while the softness of her eyes, a charm that even poor Hetty shared with her, was deepened by intense concern. Such, at least, without pausing or pretending to analyze motives, or to draw any other very nice distinction between cause and effect, were the opinions of the young man, as his canoes reached the side of the ark, where he carefully fastened all three before he put his foot on the platform.

[Chingachgook, according to plan, now joins Deerslayer. We learn that his trip to the Glimmerglass is principally motivated by his desire to rescue the Indian maiden, Wah-ta-Wah, whom he loves. She has been abducted by Briarthorne, a renegade Delaware, and evidence suggests she has been brought among the Hurons on the lake shore. In the meantime plans are laid to gain the freedom of Hurry and Hutter. An old locked chest that had once belonged to Judith's mother is part of the furniture of Muskrat Castle. In the hope of finding suitable ransom, Judith and Deerslayer now open it. Among its contents are found letters which prove that the two girls are not the children of old Hutter; a rich brocade dress which will play a significant part in Chapter 30, and a handsome set of ivory chessmen. The castles stand on the backs of elephants, and these small carvings of an animal (which the Indians have never seen) prove the ideal ransom. After negotiations with the Indians, Hurry and Hutter are returned, but later the two men, through Mingo treachery, are ambushed in the castle. Hurry again escapes, but Hutter is scalped while still alive, and later dies.

It has been ascertained by this time that Wah-ta-Wah, or Hist, is indeed a prisoner in the Huron camp, and, during the night, Deerslayer accompanies Chingachgook to the shore to recover the girl. When Judith tries to dissuade him from so dangerous a mission, he pleads his deep friendship for Chingachgook, or the Great Serpent. In the episode that follows, Chingachgook with Natty's help brings Hist safely off, but Deerslayer himself is now captured. However, the Hurons wish desperately to secure the return of Hist, with whom one of their young braves has fallen in love, and they release Deerslayer on a furlough to carry certain peace terms to those gathered in the castle, with the understanding that he is to return to captivity voluntarily when he has accomplished the mission. In taking this risk, the Mingos have interpreted Deerslayer's character correctly, as the following exchange between Hurry and Deerslayer proves:

"What's an Injin, or a word passed, or a furlough taken from creatur's like them, that have neither souls nor names?"

"If they've got neither souls nor names, you and I have both, Harry March, and one is accountable for the other. This furlough is not, as you seem to think, a matter 'atween me and the Mingos, seeing it is a solemn bargain 'atween me and God. He who thinks he can say what he pleases, in his distress, and that 'twill all pass for nothing, because 'tis uttered in the forest, and into red men's ears, knows little of his situation, and hopes, and wants. The words are said to the ears of the Almighty. The air is his breath, and the light of the sun is little more than a glance of his eye."

Deerslayer returns to the Huron camp on the lake shore at the appointed hour. "The canoe now glided ahead, holding its way towards the point, where Deerslayer well knew that his enemies expected him, and where he now began to be afraid he might not arrive in season to redeem his plighted faith."]

CHAPTER 27

ONE EXPERIENCED in the signs of the heavens would have seen that the sun wanted but two or three minutes of the zenith, when Deerslayer landed on the point where the Hurons were now encamped, nearly abreast of the castle. This spot was similar to the one already described, with the exception that the surface of the land was less broken and less crowded with trees. Owing to these two circumstances, it was all the better suited to the purpose for which it had been selected, the space beneath the branches bearing some resemblance to a densely wooded lawn. Favored by its position and its spring, it had been much resorted to by savages and hunters, and the natural grasses had succeeded their fires, leaving an appearance of sward in places, a very unusual accompaniment of the virgin forest. Nor was the margin of water fringed with bushes as on so much of its shore, but the eye penetrated the woods immediately on reaching the strand, commanding nearly the whole area of the projection.

If it was a point of honor with the Indian warrior to redeem his word, when pledged to return and meet his death at a given hour, so was it a point of characteristic pride to show no womanish impatience, but to reappear as nearly as possible at the appointed moment. It was well not to exceed the grace accorded by the generosity of the enemy, but it was better to meet it to a minute. Something of this dramatic effect mingles with most of the graver usages of the American aborigines, and no doubt, like the prevalence of a similar feeling among people more sophisticated and refined, may be referred to a principle of nature. We all love the wonderful, and when it comes attended by chivalrous self-devotion and a rigid regard to honor, it presents itself to our admiration in a shape doubly attractive. As respects Deerslayer, though he took a pride in showing his white blood, by often deviating from the usages of the redmen, he frequently dropped into their customs, and oftener into their feelings, unconsciously to himself, in consequence of having no other arbiters to appeal to, than their judgments and tastes. On the present occasion, he would have abstained from betraying a feverish haste by a too speedy return, since it would have contained a tacit admission that the time asked for was more than had been wanted; but, on the other hand, had the idea occurred to him, he would have quickened his movements a little in order to avoid the dramatic appearance of returning at the precise instant set as the utmost limit of his absence. Still, accident had interfered to defeat the last intention, for when the young man put his foot on the point, and advanced with a steady tread towards the group of chiefs that was seated in grave array on a fallen tree, the oldest of their number cast his eye upward at an opening in the trees, and pointed out to his companions the startling fact that the sun was just entering a space that was known to mark the zenith. A common, but low exclamation of surprise and admiration escaped every mouth, and the grim warriors looked at each other; some with envy and disappointment, some with astonishment, at the precise accuracy of their victim, and others with a more generous and liberal feeling. The American Indian always deemed his moral victories the noblest, prizing the groans and yielding of his victim under torture more than the trophy of his scalp; and the trophy itself more than his life. To slay, and not to bring off the proof of victory, indeed, was scarcely deemed honorable; even these rude and fierce tenants of the forest, like their more nurtured brethren of the court and the camp, having set up for themselves imaginary and arbitrary points of honor, to supplant the conclusions of the right, and the decisions of reason.

The Hurons had been divided in their opinions concerning the probability of their captive's return. Most among them, indeed, had not expected it possible for a pale-face to come back voluntarily, and meet the known penalties of an Indian torture; but a few of the seniors expected better things from one who had already shown himself so singularly cool, brave, and upright. The party had come to its decision, however, less in the expectation of finding the pledge redeemed, than in the hope of disgracing the Delawares by casting into their teeth the delinquency of one bred in their villages. They would have greatly preferred that Chingachgook should be their prisoner, and prove the traitor; but the pale-face scion of the hated stock was no bad substitute for their purposes, failing in their designs against the ancient stem. With a view to render the triumph as signal as possible, in the event of the hour's passing without the reappearance of the hunter, all the warriors and scouts of the party had been called in; and the whole band, men, women, and children, was now assembled at this single point, to be a witness of the expected scene. As the castle was in plain view, and by no means distant, it was easily watched by daylight; and it being thought that its inmates were now limited to Hurry, the Delaware, and the two girls, no apprehensions were felt of their being able to escape unseen. A large raft, having a breast-work of logs, had been prepared, and was in actual readiness to be used against either ark or castle, as occasion might require, as soon as the fate of Deerslayer was determined; the seniors of the party having come to the opinion that it was getting to be hazardous to delay their departure for Canada beyond the coming night. In short, the band awaited merely to dispose of this single affair, ere it brought matters to a crisis, and prepared to commence its retreat towards the distant waters of Ontario.

It was an imposing scene, into which Deerslayer now found himself advancing. All the older warriors were seated on the trunk of the fallen tree, waiting his approach with grave decorum. On the right stood the young men, armed, while the left was occupied by the women and children. In the centre was an open space of considerable extent, always canopied by leaves, but from which the underbrush, dead wood, and other obstacles had been carefully removed. The more open area had probably been much used by former parties, for this was the place where the appearance of a sward was the most decided. The arches of the woods, even at high noon, cast their sombre shadows on the spot, which the brilliant rays of the sun that struggled through the leaves contributed to mellow, and, if such an expression can be used, to illuminate. It was probably from a similar scene that the mind of man first got its idea of the effects of Gothic tracery and churchly hues; this temple of nature producing some such effect, so far as light and shadows were concerned, as the well-known offspring of human invention.

As was not unusual among the tribes and wandering bands of the aborigines, two chiefs shared, in nearly equal degrees, the principal and primitive authority that was wielded over these children of the forest. There were several who might claim the distinction of being chief men, but the two in question were so much superior to all the rest in influence, that when they agreed, no one disputed their mandates; and when they were divided, the band hesitated, like men who had lost their governing principle of action. It was also in conformity with practice—perhaps we might add, in conformity with nature, that one of the chiefs was indebted to his mind for his influence, whereas the other owed his distinction altogether to qualities that were physical. One was a senior, well known for eloquence in debate, wisdom in council, and prudence in measures; while his competitor, if not his rival, was a brave, distinguished in war, notorious for ferocity, and remarkable, in the way of intellect, for nothing but the cunning and expedients of the war-path. The first was Rivenoak, who has already been introduced to the reader, while the last was called Le Panthère, in the language of the Canadas; or the Panther, to resort to the vernacular of the English colonies. The appellation of the fighting chief was supposed to indicate the qualities of the warrior, agreeably to a practice of the redman's nomenclature; ferocity, cunning, and treachery being, perhaps, the distinctive features of his character. The title had been received from the French, and was prized so much the more from that circumstance, the Indian submitting profoundly to the greater intelligence of his pale-face allies, in most things of this nature. How well the *sobriquet* was merited, will be seen in the sequel.

Rivenoak and the Panther sat side by side, awaiting the approach of their prisoner, as Deerslayer put his moccasined foot on the strand; nor did either move or utter a syllable until the young man had advanced into the centre of the area, and proclaimed his presence with his voice. This was done firmly, though in a simple manner that marked the character of the individual.

"Here I am, Mingos," he said, in the dialect of the Delawares, a language that most present understood; "here I am, and there is the sun. One is not more true to the laws of natur', than the other has proved true to his word. I am your prisoner; do with me what you please. My business with man and 'arth is settled; nothing remains now but to meet the white man's God, accordin' to a white man's duties and gifts."

A murmur of approbation escaped even the women at this address, and, for an instant, there was a strong and pretty general desire to adopt into the tribe one who owned so brave a spirit. Still there were dissenters from this wish, among the principal of whom might be classed the Panther, and his sister, Le Sumach, so called from the number of her children, who was the widow of Le Loup Cervier, now known to have fallen by the hand of the captive. Native ferocity held one in subjection, while the corroding passion of revenge prevented the other from admitting any gentler feeling at the moment. Not so with Rivenoak. This chief arose, stretched his arm before him, in a gesture of courtesy, and paid his compliments with an ease and dignity that a prince might have envied. As, in that band, his wisdom and eloquence were confessedly without rivals, he knew that on himself would properly fall the duty of first replying to the speech of the pale-face.

"Pale-face, you are honest," said the Huron orator. "My people are happy in having captured a man, and not a skulking fox. We now know you; we shall treat you like a brave. If you have slain one of our warriors, and helped to kill others, you have a life of your own ready to give away in return. Some of my young men thought that the blood of a pale-face was too thin; that it would refuse to run under the Huron knife. You will show them it is not so; your heart is stout as well as your body. It is a pleasure to make such a prisoner; should my warriors say that the death of Le Loup Cervier ought not to be forgotten, and that he cannot travel towards the land of spirits alone, that his enemy must be sent to overtake him, they will remember that he fell by the hand of a brave, and send you after him with such signs of our friendship as shall not make him ashamed to keep your company. I have spoken; you know what I have said."

"True enough, Mingo, all true as the Gospel," returned the simple-minded hunter; "you *have* spoken, and I *do* know not only what you have *said,* but, what is still more important, what you *mean.* I dare say your warrior, the Lynx, was a stout-hearted brave, and worthy of your fri'ndship and respect, but I do not feel unworthy to keep his company, without any passport from your hands. Nevertheless, I am ready to receive judgment from your council, if, indeed, the matter was not determined among you, afore I got back."

"My old men would not sit in council over a pale-face until they saw him among them," answered Rivenoak, looking around him a little ironically; "they said it would be like sitting in council over the winds; they go where they will, and come back as they see fit, and not otherwise. There was one voice that spoke in your favor, Deerslayer, but it was alone, like the wren whose mate has been struck by the hawk."

"I thank that voice, whosever it may have been, Mingo, and will say it was as true a voice, as the rest were lying voices. A furlough is as binding on a pale-face, if he be honest, as it is on a redskin; and was it not so, I would never bring disgrace on the Delawares, among whom I may be said to have received my edication. But words are useless, and lead to braggin' feelin's; here I am; act your will on me."

Rivenoak made a sign of acquiescence, and then a short conference was privately held among the chiefs. As soon as the latter ended, three or four young men fell back from among the armed group, and disappeared. Then it was signified to the prisoner that he was at liberty to go at large on the point, until a council was held concerning his fate. There was more of seeming, than of real confidence, however, in this apparent liberality, inasmuch as the young men mentioned already formed a line of sentinels across the breadth of the point, inland, and escape from any other part was out of the question. Even the canoe was removed beyond this line of sentinels, to a spot where it was considered safe from any sudden attempt. These precautions did not proceed from a failure of confidence, but from the circumstance that the prisoner had now complied with all the required conditions of his parole, and it would have been considered a commendable and honorable exploit to escape from his foes. So nice, indeed, were the distinctions drawn by the savages, in cases of this nature, that they often gave their victims a chance to evade the torture, deeming it as creditable to the captors to overtake, or to outwit a fugitive, when his exertions were supposed to be quickened by the extreme jeopardy of his situation, as it was for him to get clear from so much extraordinary vigilance.

Nor was Deerslayer unconscious of, or forgetful of, his rights, and of his opportunities. Could he now have seen any probable opening for an escape, the attempt would not have been delayed a minute. But the case seemed desperate. He was aware of the line of sentinels, and felt the difficulty of breaking through it, unharmed. The lake offered no advantages, as the canoe would have given his foes the greatest facilities for overtaking him; else would he have found it no difficult task to swim as far as the castle. As he walked about the point, he even examined the spot to ascertain if it offered no place of concealment; but its openness, its size, and the hundred watchful glances that were turned towards him, even while those who made them affected not to see him, prevented any such expedient from succeeding. The dread and disgrace of failure had no influence on Deerslayer, who deemed it ever a point of honor to reason and feel like white men, rather than as an Indian, and who felt it as a sort of duty to do all he could, that did not involve a dereliction from principle, in order to save his life. Still he hesitated about making the effort, for he also felt that he ought to see the chance of success before he committed himself.

In the meantime the business of the camp appeared to proceed in its regular train. The chiefs consulted apart, admitting no one but the Sumach to their councils; for she, the widow of the fallen warrior, had an exclusive right to be heard on such an occasion. The young men strolled about in indolent listlessness, awaiting the result with Indian impatience, while the females prepared the feast that was to celebrate the termination of the affair, whether it proved fortunate or otherwise for our hero. No one betrayed feeling; and an indifferent observer, beyond the extreme watchfulness of the sentinels, would have detected no extraordinary movement or sensation to denote the real state of things. Two or three old women put their heads together, and it appeared unfavorably to the prospect of Deerslayer, by their scowling looks and angry gestures; but a group of Indian girls were evidently animated by a different impulse, as was apparent by stolen glances that expressed pity and regret. In this condition of the camp, an hour soon glided away.

Suspense is, perhaps, the feeling of all others, that is most difficult to be supported. When Deerslayer landed, he fully expected in the course of a few minutes to undergo the tortures of an Indian revenge, and he was prepared to meet his fate manfully; but the delay proved far more trying than the nearer approach of suffering, and the intended victim began seriously to meditate some desperate effort at escape, as it might be from sheer anxiety to terminate the scene, when he was suddenly summoned to appear, once more, in front of his judges, who had already arranged the band in its former order, in readiness to receive him.

"Killer of the Deer," commenced Rivenoak, as soon as his captive stood before him, "my aged men have listened to wise words; they are ready to speak. You are a man whose fathers came from beyond the rising sun; we are children of the setting sun; we turn our faces towards the Great Sweet Lakes when we look towards our villages. It may be a wise country and full of riches towards the morning, but it is very pleasant towards the evening. We love most to look in that direction. When we gaze at the east we feel afraid, canoe after canoe bringing more and more of your people in the track of the sun, as if their land was so full as to run over. The redmen are few already; they have need of help. One of our best lodges has lately been emptied by the death of its master; it will be a long time before his son can grow big enough to sit in his place. There is his widow! she will want venison to feed her and her children, for her sons are yet like the young of the robin before they quit the nest. By your hand has this great calamity befallen her. She has two duties; one to Le Loup Cervier, and one to his children. Scalp for scalp, life for life, blood for blood, is one law; to feed her young another. We know you, Killer of the Deer. You are honest; when you say a thing it is so. You have but one tongue and that is not forked like a snake's. Your head is never hid in the grass; all can see it. What you say that will you do. You are just. When you have done wrong, it is your wish to do right again as soon as you can. Here is the Sumach; she is alone in her wigwam, with children crying around her for food; yonder is a rifle, it is loaded and ready to be fired. Take the gun; go forth and shoot a deer; bring the venison and lay it before the widow of Le Loup Cervier; feed her children; call yourself her husband. After which, your heart will no longer be Delaware but Huron; Le Sumach's ears will not hear the cries of her children; my people will count the proper number of warriors."

"I feared this, Rivenoak," answered Deerslayer, when the other had ceased speaking; "yes, I did dread that it would come to this. Howsever, the truth is soon told, and that will put an end to all expectations on this head. Mingo, I'm white, and Christian-born; 'twould ill become me to take a wife, under redskin forms, from among heathen. That which I wouldn't do in peaceable times, and under a bright sun, still less would I do behind clouds, in order to save my life. I may never marry; most likely Providence, in putting me up here in the woods, has intended I should live single, and without a lodge of my own; but should such a thing come to pass, none but a woman of my own color and gifts shall darken the door of my wigwam. As for feeding the young of your dead warrior, I would do that cheerfully, could it be done without discredit; but it cannot, seeing that I can never live in a Huron village. Your own young men must find the Sumach in venison, and the next time she marries, let her take a husband whose legs are not long enough to overrun territory that don't belong to him. We fou't a fair battle, and he fell; in this there is nothin' but what a brave expects, and should be ready to meet. As for getting a Mingo heart, as well might you expect to see gray hairs on a boy, or the blackberry growing on the pine. No, no, Huron; my gifts are white, so far as wives are consarned; it is Delaware in all things touchin' Injins."

These words were scarcely out of the mouth of Deerslayer, before a common murmur betrayed the dissatisfaction with which they had been heard. The aged women, in particular, were loud in their expressions of disgust; and the gentle Sumach herself, a woman quite old enough to be our hero's mother, was not the least pacific in her denunciations. But all the other manifestations of disappointment and discontent were thrown into the background, by the fierce resentment of the Panther. This grim chief had thought it a degradation to permit his sister to become the wife of a paleface of the Yengeese, at all, and had only given a reluctant consent to the arrangement—one by no means unusual among the Indians, however—at the earnest solicitations of the bereaved widow; and it goaded him to the quick to find his condescension slighted, the honor he had with so much regret been persuaded to accord, contemned. The animal from which he got his name does not glare on his intended prey with more frightful ferocity, than his eyes gleamed on the captive; nor was his arm backward in seconding the fierce resentment that almost consumed his breast.

"Dog of the pale-faces!" he exclaimed, in Iroquois, "go yell among the curs of your own evil hunting-grounds!"

The denunciation was accompanied by an appropriate action. Even while speaking his arm was lifted and the tomahawk hurled. Luckily the loud tones of the speaker had drawn the eye of Deerslayer towards him, else would that moment have probably closed his career. So great was the dexterity with which this dangerous weapon was thrown, and so deadly the intent, that it would have riven the skull of the prisoner, had he not stretched forth an arm, and caught the handle in one of its turns, with a readiness quite as remarkable as the skill with which the missile had been hurled. The projectile force was so great, notwithstanding, that when Deerslayer's arm was arrested, his hand was raised above and behind his own head, and in the very attitude necessary to return the attack. It is not certain whether the circumstance of finding himself unexpectedly in this menacing posture and armed, tempted the young man to retaliate, or whether sudden resentment overcame his forbearance and prudence. His eye kindled, however, and a small red spot appeared on each cheek, while he cast all his energy into the effort of his arm, and threw back the weapon at his assailant. The unexpectedness of this blow contributed to its success; the Panther neither raising an arm nor bending his head to avoid it. The keen little axe struck the victim in a perpendicular line with the nose, directly between the eyes, literally braining him on the spot. Sallying forward, as the serpent darts at its enemy even while receiving its own death-wound, this man of powerful frame fell his length into the open area formed by the circle, quivering in death. A common rush to his relief left the captive, for a single instant, quite without the crowd; and, willing to make one desperate effort for life, he bounded off with the activity of a deer. There was but a breathless instant, when the whole band, old and young, women and children, abandoning the lifeless body of the Panther where it lay, raised the yell of alarm, and followed in pursuit.

Sudden as had been the event which induced Deerslayer to make this desperate trial of speed, his mind was not wholly unprepared for the fearful emergency. In the course of the past hour, he had pondered well on the chances of such an experiment, and had shrewdly calculated all the details of success and failure. At the first leap, therefore, his body was completely under the direction of an intelligence that turned all its efforts to the best account, and prevented everything like hesitation or indecision, at the important instant of the start. To this alone was he indebted for the first great advantage, that of getting through the line of sentinels unharmed. The manner in which this was done, though sufficiently simple, merits a description.

Although the shores of the point were not fringed with bushes, as was the case with most of the others on the lake, it was owing altogether to the circumstance that the spot had been so much used by hunters and fishermen. This fringe commenced on what might be termed the mainland, and was dense as usual, extending in long lines both north and south. In the latter direction, then, Deerslayer held his way; and, as the sentinels were a little without the commencement of this thicket before the alarm was clearly communicated to them, the fugitive had gained its cover. To run among the bushes, however, was out of the question, and Deerslayer held his way for some forty or fifty yards in the water, which was barely knee deep, offering as great an obstacle to the speed of his pursuers as it did to his own. As soon as a favorable spot presented, he darted through the line of bushes, and issued into the open woods.

Several rifles were discharged at Deerslayer while in the water, and more followed as he came out into the comparative exposure of the clear forest. But the direction of his line of flight which partially crossed that of the fire, the haste with which the weapons had been aimed, and the general confusion that prevailed in the camp, prevented any harm from being done. Bullets whistled past him, and many cut twigs from the branches at his side, but not one touched even his dress. The delay caused by these fruitless attempts was of great service to the fugitive, who had gained more than a hundred yards on even the leading men of the Hurons, ere something like concert and order had entered into the chase. To think of following with rifle in hand was out of the question; and after emptying their pieces in vague hope of wounding their captive, the best runners of the Indians threw them aside, calling out to the women and boys to recover and load them again, as soon as possible.

Deerslayer knew too well the desperate nature of the struggle in which he was engaged, to lose one of the precious moments. He also knew that his only hope was to run in a straight line, for as soon as he began to turn, or double, the greater number of his pursuers would put escape out of the question. He held his way, therefore, in a diagonal direction up the acclivity, which was neither very high nor very steep, in this part of the mountain, but which was sufficiently toilsome for one contending for life, to render it painfully oppressive. There, however, he slackened his speed, to recover breath, proceeding even at a quick walk, or a slow trot, along the more difficult parts of the way. The Hurons were whooping and leaping behind him; but this he disregarded, well knowing they must overcome the difficulties he had surmounted, ere they could reach the elevation to which he had attained. The summit of the first hill was now quite near him, and he saw, by the formation of the land, that a deep glen intervened, before the base of a second hill could be reached. Walking deliberately to the summit, he glanced eagerly about him, in every direction, in quest of a cover. None offered in the ground; but a fallen tree lay near him, and desperate circumstances required desperate remedies. This tree lay in a line parallel to the glen, at the brow of the hill; to leap on it, and then to force his person as close as possible under its lower side, took but a moment. Previously to disappearing from his pursuers, however, Deerslayer stood on the height, and gave a cry of triumph, as if exulting at the sight of the descent that lay before him. In the next instant he was stretched beneath the tree.

No sooner was this expedient adopted, than the young man ascertained how desperate had been his own efforts, by the violence of the pulsation in his frame. He could hear his heart beat, and his breathing was like the action of a bellows in quick motion. Breath was gained, however, and the heart soon ceased to throb as if about to break through its confinement. The footsteps of those who toiled up the opposite side of the acclivity were now audible, and presently voices and treads announced the arrival of the pursuers. The foremost shouted as they reached the height; then, fearful that their enemy would escape under favor of the descent, each leaped upon the fallen tree, and plunged into the ravine, trusting to get a sight of the pursued, ere he reached the bottom. In this manner, Huron followed Huron, until Natty began to hope the whole had passed. Others succeeded, however, until quite forty had leaped over the tree; and then he counted them, as the surest mode of ascertaining how many could be behind. Presently all were in the bottom of the glen, quite a hundred feet below him, and some had even ascended part of the opposite hill, when it became evident an inquiry was making, as to the direction he had taken. This was the critical moment; and one of nerves less steady, or of a training that had been neglected, would have seized it to rise and fly. Not so with Deerslayer. He still lay quiet, watching with jealous vigilance every movement below, and fast regaining his breath.

The Hurons now resembled a pack of hounds at fault. Little was said, but each man ran about, examining the dead leaves, as the hound hunts for the lost scent. The great number of moccasins that had passed made the examination difficult, though the in-toe of an Indian was easily to be distinguished from the freer and wider step of a white man. Believing that no more pursuers remained behind, and hoping to steal away unseen, Deerslayer suddenly threw himself over the tree, and fell on the upper side. This achievement appeared to be effected successfully, and hope beat high in the bosom of the fugitive. Rising to his hands and feet, after a moment lost in listening to the sounds in the glen, in order to ascertain if he had been seen, the young man next scrambled to the top of the hill, a distance of only ten yards, in the expectation of getting its brow between him and his pursuers, and himself so far under cover. Even this was effected, and he rose to his feet, walking swiftly but steadily along the summit, in a direction opposite to that in which he had first fled. The nature of the calls in the glen, however, soon made him uneasy, and he sprang upon the summit, again, in order to reconnoitre. No sooner did he reach the height than he was seen, and the chase renewed. As it was better footing on the level ground, Deerslayer now avoided the side-hill, holding his flight along the ridge; while the Hurons, judging from the general formation of the land, saw that the ridge would soon melt into the hollow, and kept to the latter, as the easiest mode of heading the fugitive. A few, at the same time, turned south, with a view to prevent his escaping in that direction; while some crossed his trail towards the water, in order to prevent his retreat by the lake, running southerly.

The situation of Deerslayer was now more critical than it ever had been. He was virtually surrounded on three sides, having the lake on the fourth. But he had pondered well on all the chances, and took his measures with coolness, even while at the top of his speed. As is generally the case with the vigorous border-men, he could outrun any single Indian among his pursuers, who were principally formidable to him on account of their numbers, and the advantages they possessed in position; and he would not have hesitated to break off, in a straight line, at any spot, could he have got the whole band again fairly behind him. But no such chance did, or indeed could now offer; and when he found that he was descending towards the glen, by the melting away of the ridge, he turned short at right angles to his previous course, and went down the declivity with tremendous velocity, holding his way towards the shore. Some of his pursuers came panting up the hill, in direct chase, while most still kept on, in the ravine, intending to head him at its termination. Deerslayer had now a different, though a desperate project in view. Abandoning all thoughts of escape by the woods, he made the best of his way towards the canoe. He knew where it lay: could it be reached, he had only to run the gauntlet of a few rifles, and success would be certain. None of the warriors had kept their weapons, which would have retarded their speed, and the risk would come either from the uncertain hands of the women, or from those of some well-grown boy; though most of the latter were already out in hot pursuit. Everything seemed propitious to the execution of this plan, and the course being a continued descent, the young man went over the ground at a rate that promised a speedy termination to his toil.

As Deerslayer approached the point, several women and children were passed, but, though the former endeavored to cast dried branches between his legs, the terror inspired by his bold retaliation on the redoubted Panther was so great, that none dared come near enough seriously to molest him. He went by all triumphantly, and reached the fringe of bushes. Plunging through these, our hero found himself once more in the lake and within fifty feet of the canoe. Here he ceased to run, for he well understood that his breath was now all-important to him. He even stooped, as he advanced, and cooled his parched mouth, by scooping up water in his hand to drink. Still the moments pressed, and he soon stood at the side of the canoe. The first glance told him that the paddles had been removed! This was a sore disappointment after all his efforts, and, for a single moment, he thought of turning and of facing his foes by walking with dignity into the centre of the camp again. But an infernal yell, such as the American savage alone can raise, proclaimed the quick approach of the nearest of his pursuers, and the instinct of life triumphed. Preparing himself duly, and giving a right direction to its bows, he ran off into the water bearing the canoe before him, threw all his strength and skill into a last effort, and cast himself forward so as to fall into the bottom of the light craft, without materially impeding its way. Here he remained on his back, both to regain his breath and to cover his person from the deadly rifle. The lightness, which was such an advantage in paddling the canoe, now operated unfavorably. The material was so like a feather that the boat had no momentum; else would the impulse in that smooth and placid sheet have impelled it to a distance from the shore, that would have rendered paddling with the hands safe. Could such a point once be reached, Deerslayer thought he might get far enough out to attract the attention of Chingachgook and Judith, who would not fail to come to his relief with other canoes, a circumstance that promised everything. As the young man lay in the bottom of the canoe he watched its movements, by studying the tops of the trees on the mountain-side, and judged of his distance by the time and the motion. Voices on the shore were now numerous, and he heard something said about manning the raft, which fortunately for the fugitive lay at a considerable distance on the other side of the point.

Perhaps the situation of Deerslayer had not been more critical that day than it was at this moment. It certainly had not been one half as tantalizing. He lay perfectly quiet for two or three minutes, trusting to the single sense of hearing, confident that the noise on the lake would reach his ears, did any one approach by swimming. Once or twice he fancied that the element was stirred by the cautious movement of an arm, and then he perceived it was the wash of the water on the pebbles of the strand; for in mimicry of the ocean, it is seldom that those little lakes are so totally tranquil, as not to possess a slight heaving and setting on their shores. Suddenly all the voices ceased, and a death-like stillness pervaded the spot; a quietness as profound as if all lay in the repose of inanimate life. By this time the canoe had drifted so far as to render nothing visible to Deerslayer, as he lay on his back, except the blue void of space, and a few of those brighter rays that proceed from the effulgence of the sun, marking his proximity. It was not possible to endure this uncertainty long. The young man well knew that the profound stillness foreboded evil, the savages never being so silent as when about to strike a blow; resembling the stealthy foot of the panther ere he takes his leap. He took out a knife, and was about to cut a hole through the bark in order to get a view of the shore, when he paused from a dread of being seen in the operation, which would direct the enemy where to aim their bullets. At this instant a rifle *was* fired, and the ball pierced both sides of the canoe, within eighteen inches of the spot where his head lay. This was close work, but our hero had too lately gone through that which was closer, to be appalled. He lay still half a minute longer, and then he saw the summit of an oak coming slowly within his narrow horizon.

Unable to account for this change, Deerslayer could restrain his impatience no longer. Hitching his body along, with the utmost caution, he got his eye at the bullet-hole, and fortunately commanded a very tolerable view of the point. The canoe, by one of those imperceptible impulses that so often decide the fate of men, as well as the course of things, had inclined southerly, and was slowly drifting down the lake. It was lucky that Deerslayer had given it a shove sufficiently vigorous to send it past the end of the point ere it took this inclination, or it must have gone ashore again. As it was, it drifted so near it as to bring the tops of two or three of the trees within the range of the young man's view, as has been mentioned, and, indeed, to come in quite as close proximity with the extremity of the point as was at all safe. The distance could not much have exceeded a hundred feet, though fortunately a light current of air from the southwest began to set it slowly off shore.

Deerslayer now felt the urgent necessity of resorting to some expedient to get farther from his foes, and, if possible, to apprise his friends of his situation. The distance rendered the last difficult, while the proximity to the point rendered the first indispensable. As was usual in such a craft, a large, round, smooth stone was in each end of the canoe, for the double purpose of seats and ballast; one of these was within reach of his feet. The stone he contrived to get so far between his legs as to reach it with his hands, and then he managed to roll it to the side of its fellow in the bows, where the two served to keep the trim of the light boat, while he worked his own body as far aft as possible. Before quitting the shore, and as soon as he perceived that the paddles were gone, Deerslayer had thrown a bit of dead branch into the canoe, and this was within the reach of his arm. Removing the cap he wore, he put it on the end of this stick, and just let it appear over the edge of the canoe, as far as possible from his own person. This *ruse* was scarcely adopted, before the young man had proof how much he had underrated the intelligence of his enemies. In contempt of an artifice so shallow and commonplace, a bullet was fired directly through another part of the canoe, which actually razed his skin. He dropped the cap, and instantly raised it immediately over his head, as a safeguard. It would seem that this second artifice was unseen, or what was more probable, the Hurons, feeling certain of recovering their captive, wished to take him alive.

Deerslayer lay passive a few minutes longer, his eye at the bullet-hole, however, and much did he rejoice at seeing that he was drifting gradually farther and farther from the shore. When he looked upwards, the tree-tops had disappeared, but he soon found that the canoe was slowly turning, so as to prevent his getting a view of anything at his peep-hole, but of the two extremities of the lake. He now bethought him of the stick, which was crooked, and offered some facilities for rowing, without the necessity of rising. The experiment succeeded, on trial, better even than he had hoped, though his great embarrassment was to keep the canoe straight. That his present manœuvre was seen soon became apparent by the clamor on the shore, and a bullet entering the stern of the canoe, traversed its length, whistling between the arms of our hero, and passed out at the head. This satisfied the fugitive that he was getting away with tolerable speed, and induced him to increase his efforts. He was making a stronger push than common, when another messenger from the point broke the stick out-board, and at once deprived him of his oar. As the sound of voices seemed to grow more and more distant, however, Deerslayer determined to leave all to the drift, until he believed himself beyond the reach of bullets. This was nervous work, but it was the wisest of all the expedients that offered; and the young man was encouraged to persevere in it, by the circumstance that he felt his face fanned by the air, a proof that there was a little more wind.

from CHAPTER 28

BY THIS TIME, Deerslayer had been twenty minutes in the canoe, and he began to grow a little impatient for some signs of relief from his friends. The position of the boat still prevented his seeing in any direction, unless it were up or down the lake; and, though he knew that this line of sight must pass within a hundred yards of the castle, it, in fact, passed that distance to the westward of the buildings. The profound stillness troubled him also, for he knew not whether to ascribe it to the increasing space between him and the Indians, or to some new artifice. At length, wearied with fruitless watchfulness, the young man turned himself on his back, closed his eyes, and awaited the result in determined acquiescence. If the savages could so completely control their thirst for revenge, he was resolved to be as calm as themselves, and to trust his fate to the interposition of the currents and air.

Some additional ten minutes may have passed in this quiescent manner, on both sides, when Deerslayer thought he heard a slight noise, like a low rubbing against the bottom of his canoe. He opened his eyes of course, in expectation of seeing the face or arm of an Indian rising from the water, and found that a canopy of leaves was impending directly over his head. Starting to his feet, the first object that met his eyes was Rivenoak, who had so far aided the slow progress of the boat, as to draw it on the point, the grating on the strand being the sound that had first given our hero the alarm. The change in the drift of the canoe had been altogether owing to the baffling nature of the light currents of air, aided by some eddies in the water. . . .

"Come," said the Huron, with a quiet gesture of authority to order his prisoner to land; "my young friend has sailed about till he is tired; he will forget how to run again, unless he uses his legs.". . .

CHAPTER 29

IT WAS one of the common expedients of the savages, on such occasions, to put the nerves of their victims to the severest proofs. On the other hand, it was a matter of Indian pride to betray no yielding to terror or pain; but for the prisoner to provoke his enemies to such acts of violence as would soonest produce death. Many a warrior had been known to bring his own sufferings to a more speedy termination, by taunting reproaches and reviling language, when he found that his physical system was giving way under the agony of sufferings, produced by a hellish ingenuity, that might well eclipse all that has been said of the infernal devices of religious persecution. This happy expedient of taking refuge from the ferocity of his foes in their passions, was denied Deerslayer, however, by his peculiar notions of the duty of a white man; and he had stoutly made up his mind to endure everything, in preference to disgracing his color.

No sooner did the young men understand that they were at liberty to commence, than some of the boldest and most forward among them sprang into the arena, tomahawk in hand. Here they prepared to throw that dangerous weapon, the object being to strike the tree as near as possible to the victim's head, without absolutely hitting him. This was so hazardous an experiment, that none but those who were known to be exceedingly expert with the weapon were allowed to enter the lists at all, lest an early death might interfere with the expected entertainment. In the truest hands, it was seldom that the captive escaped injury in these trials; and it often happened that death followed even when the blow was not premeditated. In the particular case of our hero, Rivenoak and the older warriors were apprehensive that the example of the Panther's fate might prove a motive with some fiery spirit, suddenly to sacrifice his conqueror, when the temptation of effecting it in precisely the same manner, and possibly with the identical weapon with which the warrior had fallen, offered. This circumstance, of itself, rendered the ordeal of the tomahawk doubly critical for the Deerslayer.

It would seem, however, that all who now entered what we shall call the lists, were more disposed to exhibit their own dexterity than to resent the deaths of their comrades. Each prepared himself for the trial, with the feelings of rivalry, rather than with the desire for vengeance; and for the first few minutes, the prisoner had little more connection with the result, than grew out of the interest that necessarily attached itself to a living target. The young men were eager, instead of being fierce, and Rivenoak thought he still saw signs of being able to save the life of the captive, when the vanity of the young men had been gratified; always admitting, that it was not sacrificed to the delicate experiments that were about to be made.

The first youth who presented himself for the trial, was called the Raven, having as yet had no opportunity of obtaining a more warlike *sobriquet*. He was remarkable for high pretension rather than for skill or exploits; and those who knew his character, thought the captive in imminent danger, when he took his stand, and poised the tomahawk. Nevertheless, the young man was good-natured, and no thought was uppermost in his mind, other than the desire to make a better cast than any of his fellows. Deerslayer got an inkling of this warrior's want of reputation, by the injunctions that he had received from the seniors; who, indeed, would have objected to his appearing in the arena at all, but for an influence derived from his father, an aged warrior of great merit, who was then in the lodges of the tribe. Still, our hero maintained an appearance of self-possession. He had made up his mind that his hour was come, and it would have been a mercy, instead of a calamity, to fall by the unsteadiness of the first hand that was raised against him. After a suitable number of flourishes and gesticulations, that promised much more than he could perform, the Raven let the tomahawk quit his hand. The weapon whirled through the air, with the usual evolutions, cut a chip from the sapling to which the prisoner was bound, within a few inches of his cheek, and stuck in a large oak that grew several yards behind him. This was decidedly a bad effort, and a common sneer proclaimed as much, to the great mortification of the young man. On the other hand, there was a general, but suppressed murmur of admiration, at the steadiness with which the captive stood the trial. The head was the only part he could move, and this had been purposely left free, that the tormentors might have the amusement, and the tormented endure the shame, of dodging, and otherwise attempting to avoid the blows. Deerslayer disappointed these hopes, by a command of nerve that rendered his whole body as immovable as the tree to which he was bound. Nor did he even adopt the natural and usual expedient of shutting his eyes: the firmest and oldest warrior of the redmen never having more disdainfully denied himself this advantage, under similar circumstances.

The Raven had no sooner made his unsuccessful and puerile effort than he was succeeded by Le Daim-Mose, or the Moose; a middle-aged warrior, who was particularly skilful in the use of the tomahawk, and from whose attempt the spectators confidently looked for gratification. This man had none of the good-nature of the Raven, but he would gladly have sacrificed the captive to his hatred of the pale-faces generally, were it not for the greater interest he felt in his own success as one particularly skilful in the use of this weapon. He took his stand quietly, but with an air of confidence, poised his little axe but a single instant, advanced a foot with a quick motion, and threw. Deerslayer saw the keen instrument whirling towards him, and believed all was over; still he was not touched. The tomahawk had actually bound the head of the captive to the tree, by carrying before it some of his hair; having buried itself deep beneath the soft bark. A general yell expressed the delight of the spectators, and the Moose felt his heart soften a little towards the prisoner, whose steadiness of nerve alone enabled him to give this evidence of his consummate skill.

Le Daim-Mose was succeeded by the Bounding Boy, or Le Garçon qui Bondi, who came leaping into the circle, like a hound or a goat at play. This was one of those elastic youths, whose muscles seemed always in motion, and who either affected, or who from habit was actually unable to move in any other manner, than by showing the antics just mentioned. Nevertheless, he was both brave and skilful, and had gained the respect of his people by deeds in war as well as success in the hunts. A far nobler name would long since have fallen to his share, had not a Frenchman of rank inadvertently given him this *sobriquet,* which he religiously preserved as coming from his great father, who lived beyond the wide salt lake. The Bounding Boy skipped about in front of the captive, menacing him with his tomahawk, now on one side and now on another, and then again in front, in the vain hope of being able to extort some sign of fear, by this parade of danger. At length Deerslayer's patience became exhausted by all this mummery, and he spoke for the first time since the trial had actually commenced.

"Throw away, Huron!" he cried, "or your tomahawk will forget its arr'nd. Why do you keep loping about like a fa'an that's showing its dam how well it can skip, when you're a warrior grown, yourself, and a warrior grown defies you and all your silly antics? Throw, or the Huron gals will laugh in your face."

Although not intended to produce such an effect, the last words aroused the "Bounding" warrior to fury. The same nervous excitability which rendered him so active in his person, made it difficult to repress his feelings, and the words were scarcely past the lips of the speaker, than the tomahawk left the hand of the Indian. Nor was it cast without goodwill, and a fierce determination to slay. Had the intention been less deadly, the danger might have been greater. The aim was uncertain, and the weapon glanced near the cheek of the captive, slightly cutting the shoulder in its evolutions. This was the first instance in which any other object than that of terrifying the prisoner, and of displaying skill, had been manifested; and the Bounding Boy was immediately led from the arena, and was warmly rebuked for his intemperate haste, which had come so near defeating all the hopes of the band.

To this irritable person succeeded several other young warriors, who not only hurled the tomahawk but who cast the knife, a far more dangerous experiment, with reckless indifference; yet they always manifested a skill that prevented any injury to the captive. Several times Deerslayer was grazed, but in no instance did he receive what might be termed a wound. The unflinching firmness with which he faced his assailants, more especially in the sort of rally with which this trial terminated, excited a profound respect in the spectators; and when the chiefs announced that the prisoner had well withstood the trials of the knife and the tomahawk, there was not a single individual in the band who really felt any hostility towards him, with the exception of Sumach and the Bounding Boy. These two discontented spirits got together, it is true, feeding each other's ire; but, as yet, their malignant feelings were confined very much to themselves, though there existed the danger that the others, ere long, could not fail to be excited by their own efforts into that demoniacal state which usually accompanied all similar scenes among the redmen.

Rivenoak now told his people that the pale-face had proved himself to be a man. He might live with the Delawares, but he had not been made woman with that tribe. He wished to know whether it was the desire of the Hurons to proceed any further. Even the gentlest of the females, however, had received too much satisfaction in the late trials to forego their expectations of a gratifying exhibition; and there was but one voice in the request to proceed. The politic chief, who had some such desire to receive so celebrated a hunter into his tribe as a European minister has to devise a new and available means of taxation, sought every plausible means of arresting the trial in season; for he well knew, if permitted to go far enough to arouse the more ferocious passions of the tormentors, it would be as easy to dam the waters of the great lakes of his own region, as to attempt to arrest them in their bloody career. He therefore called four or five of the best marksmen to him, and bid them put the captive to the proof of the rifle, while, at the same time, he cautioned them touching the necessity of their maintaining their own credit, by the closest attention to the manner of exhibiting their skill.

When Deerslayer saw the chosen warriors step into the circle, with their arms prepared for service, he felt some such relief as the miserable sufferer, who had long endured the agonies of disease, feels at the certain approach of death. Any trifling variance in the aim of this formidable weapon would prove fatal; since, the head being the target, or rather the point it was desired to graze without injury, an inch or two of difference in the line of projection must at once determine the question of life or death.

In the torture by the rifle there was none of the latitude permitted that appeared in the case of even Gesler's apple, a hair'sbreadth being, in fact, the utmost limits that an expert marksman would allow himself on an occasion like this. Victims were frequently shot through the head by too eager or unskilful hands; and it often occurred that, exasperated by the fortitude and taunts of the prisoner, death was dealt intentionally in a moment of ungovernable irritation. All this Deerslayer well knew, for it was in relating the traditions of such scenes, as well as of the battles and victories of their people, that the old men beguiled the long winter evenings in their cabins. He now fully expected the end of his career, and experienced a sort of melancholy pleasure in the idea that he was to fall by a weapon as much beloved as the rifle. A slight interruption, however, took place before the business was allowed to proceed. . . .

The warriors, as soon as this interruption had ceased, resumed their places, and again prepared to exhibit their skill, as there was a double object in view, that of putting the constancy of the captive to the proof, and that of showing how steady were the hands of the marksmen under circumstances of excitement. The distance was small, and, in one sense, safe. But in diminishing the distance taken by the tormentors, the trial to the nerves of the captive was essentially increased. The face of Deerslayer, indeed, was just removed sufficiently from the ends of the guns to escape the effects of the flash, and his steady eye was enabled to look directly into their muzzles, as it might be, in anticipation of the fatal messenger that was to issue from each. The cunning Hurons well knew this fact; and scarce one levelled his piece without first causing it to point as near as possible at the forehead of the prisoner, in the hope that his fortitude would fail him, and that the band would enjoy the triumph of seeing a victim quail under their ingenious cruelty. Nevertheless, each of the competitors was still careful not to injure; the disgrace of striking prematurely being second only to that of failing altogether in attaining the object. Shot after shot was made; all the bullets coming in close proximity to the Deerslayer's head, without touching it. Still, no one could detect even the twitching of a muscle on the part of the captive, or the slightest winking of an eye. This indomitable resolution, which so much exceeded everything of its kind that any present had before witnessed, might be referred to three distinct causes. The first was resignation to his fate, blended with natural steadiness of deportment; for our hero had calmly made up his mind that he must die, and preferred this mode to any other; the second was his great familiarity with this particular weapon, which deprived it of all the terror that is usually connected with the mere form of the danger; and the third was this familiarity carried out in practice, to a degree so nice as to enable the intended victim to tell, within an inch, the precise spot where each bullet must strike, for he calculated its range by looking in at the bore of the piece. So exact was Deerslayer's estimation of the line of fire, that his pride of feeling finally got the better of his resignation, and, when five or six had discharged their bullets into the trees, he could not refrain from expressing his contempt at their want of hand and eye.

"You may call this shooting, Mingos," he exclaimed, "but we've squaws among the Delawares, and I have known Dutch gals on the Mohawk, that could outdo your greatest indivors. Ondo these arms of mine, put a rifle into my hands, and I'll pin the thinnest warlock in your party to any tree you can show me; and this at a hundred yards: ay, or at two hundred, if the object can be seen, nineteen shots in twenty: or, for that matter, twenty in twenty if the piece is creditable and trusty!"

A low, menacing murmur followed this cool taunt; the ire of the warriors kindled at listening to such a reproach from one who so far disdained their efforts as to refuse even to wink, when a rifle was discharged as near his face as could be done without burning it. Rivenoak perceived that the moment was critical, and, still retaining his hope of adopting so noted a hunter into his tribe, the politic old chief interposed in time, probably, to prevent an immediate resort to that portion of the torture which must necessarily have produced death, through extreme bodily suffering, if in no other manner. Moving into the centre of the irritated group, he addressed them with his usual wily logic and plausible manner, at once suppressing the fierce movement that had commenced.

"I see how it is," he said. "We have been like the pale-faces when they fasten their doors at night, out of fear of the redman. They use so many bars, that the fire comes and burns them before they can get out. We have bound the Deerslayer too tight; the thongs keep his limbs from shaking, and his eyes from shutting. Loosen him; let us see what his own body is really made of."

It is often the case when we are thwarted in a cherished scheme, that any expedient, however unlikely to succeed, is gladly resorted to, in preference to a total abandonment of the project. So it was with the Hurons. The proposal of the chief found instant favor; and several hands were immediately at work cutting and tearing the ropes of bark from the body of our hero. In half a minute, Deerslayer stood as free from bonds, as when, an hour before, he had commenced his flight on the side of the mountain. Some little time was necessary that he should recover the use of his limbs, the circulation of the blood having been checked by the tightness of the ligatures; and this was accorded to him by the politic Rivenoak, under the pretence that his body would be more likely to submit to apprehension, if his true tone were restored; though really with a view to give time to the fierce passions which had been awakened in the bosoms of his young men, to subside. This *ruse* succeeded; and Deerslayer, by rubbing his limbs, stamping his feet, and moving about, soon regained the circulation; recovering all his physical powers as effectually as if nothing had occurred to disturb them.

It is seldom men think of death in the pride of their health and strength. So it was with Deerslayer. Having been helplessly bound, and, as he had every reason to suppose, so lately on the very verge of the other world, to find himself so unexpectedly liberated, in possession of his strength, and with a full command of limb, acted on him like a sudden restoration to life, re-animating hopes that he had once absolutely abandoned. From that instant all his plans changed. In this he simply obeyed a law of nature; for while we have wished to represent our hero as being resigned to his fate, it has been far from our intention to represent him as anxious to die. From the instant that his buoyancy of feeling revived, his thoughts were keenly bent on the various projects that presented themselves as modes of evading the designs of his enemies; and he again became the quick-witted, ingenious, and determined woodsman, alive to all his own powers and resources. The change was so great, that his mind resumed its elasticity; and, no longer thinking of submission, it dwelt only on the devices of the sort of warfare in which he was engaged.

As soon as Deerslayer was released, the band divided itself in a circle around him, in order to hedge him in; and the desire to break down his spirit grew in them, precisely as they saw proofs of the difficulty there would be in subduing it. The honor of the band was now involved in the issue; and even the sex lost all its sympathy with suffering, in the desire to save the reputation of the tribe. The voices of the girls, soft and melodious as nature had made them, were heard mingling with the menaces of the men; and the wrongs of Sumach suddenly assumed the character of injuries inflicted on every Huron female. Yielding to this rising tumult, the men drew back a little, signifying to the females that they left the captive, for a time, in their hands; it being a common practice, on such occasions, for the women to endeavor to throw the victim into a rage, by their taunts and revilings, and then to turn him suddenly over to the men, in a state of mind that was little favorable to resisting the agony of bodily suffering. Nor was this party without the proper instruments for effecting such a purpose. Sumach had a notoriety as a scold; and one or two crones, like the Shebear, had come out with the party, most probably as the conservators of its decency and moral discipline; such things occurring in savage as well as civilized life. It is unnecessary to repeat all that ferocity and ignorance could invent for such a purpose; the only difference between this outbreaking of feminine anger, and a similar scene among ourselves, consisting in the figures of speech and the epithets; the Huron women calling their prisoner by the names of the lower and least respected animals that were known to themselves.

But Deerslayer's mind was too much occupied to permit him to be disturbed by the abuse of excited hags; and their rage necessarily increasing with his indifference, as his indifference increased with their rage, the furies soon rendered themselves impotent by their own excesses. Perceiving that the attempt was a complete failure, the warriors interfered to put a stop to this scene; and this so much the more, because preparations were now seriously making for the commencement of the real tortures, or that which would put the fortitude of the sufferer to the test of severe bodily pain. A sudden and unlooked-for announcement that proceeded from one of the look-outs, a boy ten or twelve years old, however, put a momentary check to the whole proceedings. As this interruption has a close connection with the *dénouement* of our story, it shall be given in a separate chapter.

CHAPTER 30

IT EXCEEDED Deerslayer's power to ascertain what had produced the sudden pause in the movements of his enemies, until the fact was revealed in the due course of events. He perceived that much agitation prevailed among the women in particular, while the warriors rested on their arms, in a sort of dignified expectation. It was plain no alarm was excited, though it was not equally apparent that a friendly occurrence produced the delay. Rivenoak was evidently apprised of all, and by a gesture of his arm he appeared to direct the circle to remain unbroken, and for each person to await the issue in the situation he or she then occupied. It required but a minute or two to bring an explanation of this singular and mysterious pause, which was soon terminated by the appearance of Judith, on the exterior of the line of bodies, and her ready admission within its circle.

If Deerslayer was startled by this unexpected arrival, well knowing that the quick-witted girl would claim none of that exemption from the penalties of captivity that was so cheerfully accorded to her feeble-minded sister, he was equally astonished at the guise in which she came. All her ordinary forest attire, neat and becoming as this usually was, had been laid aside for the brocade that has been already mentioned, and which had once before wrought so great and magical an effect in her appearance. Nor was this all. Accustomed to see the ladies of the garrison, in the formal gala attire of the day, and familiar with the more critical niceties of these matters, the girl had managed to complete her dress, in a way to leave nothing strikingly defective in its details, or even to betray an incongruity that would have been detected by one practised in the mysteries of the toilet. Head, feet, arms, hands, bust, and drapery, were all in harmony, as female attire was then deemed attractive and harmonious: and the end she aimed at, that of imposing on the uninstructed senses of the savages, by causing them to believe their guest was a woman of rank and importance, might well have succeeded with those whose habits had taught them to discriminate between persons. Judith, in addition to her rare native beauty, had a singular grace of person, and her mother had imparted enough of her own deportment to prevent any striking or offensive vulgarity of manner; so that, sooth to say, the gorgeous dress might have been worse bestowed in nearly every particular. Had it been displayed in a capital, a thousand might have worn it before one could have been found to do more credit to its gay colors, glossy satins, and rich laces, than the beautiful creature whose person it now aided to adorn.

The effect of such an apparition had not been miscalculated. The instant Judith found herself within the circle, she was, in a degree, compensated for the fearful personal risk she ran, by the unequivocal sensation of surprise and admiration produced by her appearance. The grim old warriors uttered their favorite exclamation, "Hugh!" The younger men were still more sensibly overcome, and even the women were not backward in letting open manifestations of pleasure escape them. It was seldom that these untutored children of the forest had ever seen any white female above the commonest sort, and as to dress, never before had so much splendor shone before their eyes. The gayest uniforms of both French and English seemed dull compared with the lustre of the brocade; and while the rare personal beauty of the wearer added to the effect produced by its hues, the attire did not fail to adorn that beauty in a way which surpassed even the hopes of its wearer. Deerslayer himself was astounded, and this quite as much by the brilliant picture the girl presented, as at the indifference to consequences with which she had braved the danger of the step she had taken. Under such circumstances, all waited for the visitor to explain her object, which to most of the spectators seemed as inexplicable as her appearance.

"Which of these warriors is the principal chief?" demanded Judith of Deerslayer, as soon as she found it was expected that she should open the communication; "my errand is too important to be delivered to any of inferior rank. First explain to the Hurons what I say; then give an answer to the question I have put."

Deerslayer quietly complied, his auditors greedily listening to the interpretation of the first words that fell from so extraordinary a vision. The demand seemed perfectly in character for one who had every appearance of an exalted rank herself. Rivenoak gave an appropriate reply, by presenting himself before his fair visitor in a way to leave no doubt that he was entitled to all the consideration he claimed.

"I can believe this, Huron," resumed Judith, enacting her assumed part with a steadiness and dignity that did credit to her powers of imitation, for she strove to impart to her manner the condescending courtesy she had once observed in the wife of a general officer, at a similar though a more amicable scene: "I can believe you to be the principal person of this party; I see in your countenance the marks of thought and reflection. To you, then, I must make my communication."

"Let the Flower of the Woods speak," returned the old chief, courteously, as soon as her address had been translated so that all might understand it. "If her words are as pleasant as her looks, they will never quit my ears; I shall hear them long after the winter in Canada has killed the flowers, and frozen all the speeches of summer."

This admiration was grateful to one constituted like Judith, and contributed to aid her self-possession, quite as much as it fed her vanity. Smiling involuntarily, or in spite of her wish to seem reserved, she proceeded in her plot.

"Now, Huron," she continued, "listen to my words. Your eyes tell you that I am no common woman. I will not say I am queen of this country; *she* is afar off, in a distant land; but under our gracious monarchs there are many degrees of rank; one of these I fill. What that rank is precisely it is unnecessary for me to say, since you would not understand it. For that information you must trust your eyes. You *see* what I am; you must *feel* that in listening to my words, you listen to one who can be your friend or your enemy, as you treat her."

This was well uttered, with a due attention to manner and a steadiness of tone that was really surprising, considering all the circumstances of the case. It was well, though simply rendered into the Indian dialect, too, and it was received with a respect and gravity that augured favorably for the girl's success. But Indian thought is not easily traced to its sources. Judith waited with anxiety to hear the answer, filled with hope even while she doubted. Rivenoak was a ready speaker, and he answered as promptly as comported with the notions of Indian decorum; that peculiar people seeming to think a short delay respectful, inasmuch as it manifests that the words already heard have been duly weighed.

"My daughter is handsomer than the wild roses of Ontario; her voice as pleasant to the ear as the song of the wren," answered the cautious and wily chief, who of all the band stood alone in not being being fully imposed on by the magnificent and unusual appearance of Judith, but who distrusted even while he wondered; "the humming-bird is not much larger than the bee; yet its feathers are as gay as the tail of the peacock. The Great Spirit sometimes puts very bright clothes on very little animals. Still, he covers the moose with coarse hair. These things are beyond the understanding of poor Indians, who can only comprehend what they see and hear. No doubt my daughter has a very large wigwam somewhere about the lake: the Hurons have not found it on account of their ignorance?"

"I have told you, chief, that it would be useless to state my rank and residence, inasmuch as you would not comprehend them. You must trust to your eyes for this knowledge; what redman is there that cannot see? This blanket that I wear is not the blanket of a common squaw; these ornaments are such as the wives and daughters of chiefs only appear in. Now listen and hear why I have come alone among your people, and hearken to the errand that has brought me here. The Yengeese have young men as well as the Hurons; and plenty of them, too; this you well know."

"The Yengeese are as plenty as the leaves on the trees! This every Huron knows and feels."

"I understand you, chief. Had I brought a party with me it might have caused trouble. My young men and your young men would have looked angrily at each other; especially had my young men seen that pale-face bound for the tortures. He is a great hunter, and is much loved by all the garrisons, far and near. There would have been blows about him, and the trail of the Iroquois back to the Canadas would have been marked with blood."

"There is so much blood on it now," returned the chief, gloomily, "that it blinds our eyes. My young men see that it is all Huron."

"No doubt; and more Huron blood would be spilt, had I come surrounded with pale-faces. I have heard of Rivenoak, and have thought it would be better to send him back in peace to his village, that he might leave his women and children behind him; if he then wished to come for our scalps, we would meet him. He loves animals made of ivory, and little rifles. See; I have brought some with me to show him. I am his friend. When he has packed up these things among his goods, he will start for his village, before any of my young men can overtake him; and then he will show his people in Canada what riches they can come to seek, now that our great fathers, across the salt lake, have sent each other the warhatchet. I will lead back with me, this great hunter, of whom I have need to keep my house in venison."

Judith, who was sufficiently familiar with Indian phraseology, endeavored to express her ideas in the sententious manner common to those people; and she succeeded even beyond her own expectations. Deerslayer did her full justice in the translation, and this so much the more readily, since the girl carefully abstained from uttering any direct untruth; a homage she paid to the young man's known aversion to falsehood, which he deemed a meanness altogether unworthy of a white man's gifts. The offering of the two remaining elephants, and of the pistols already mentioned, one of which was all the worse for the recent accident, produced a lively sensation among the Hurons generally, though Rivenoak received it coldly, notwithstanding the delight with which he had first discovered the probable existence of a creature with two tails. In a word, this cool and sagacious savage was not so easily imposed on as his followers; and with a sentiment of honor, that half the civilized world would have deemed supererogatory, he declined the acceptance of a bribe that he felt no disposition to earn by a compliance with the donor's wishes.

"Let my daughter keep her two-tailed hog, to eat when venison is scarce," he dryly answered; "and the little gun, which has two muzzles. The Hurons will kill deer when they are hungry; and they have long rifles to fight with. This hunter cannot quit my young men now; they wish to know if he is as stout-hearted as he boasts himself to be."

"That I deny, Huron," interrupted Deerslayer, with warmth; "yes, that I downright deny, as ag'in truth and reason. No man has heard me *boast,* and no man shall, though ye flay me alive, and then roast the quivering flesh, with your own infarnal devices and cruelties! I may be humble, and misfortunate, and your prisoner; but I'm no boaster, by my very gifts."

"My young pale-face *boasts* he is *no* boaster," returned the crafty chief; "he *must* be right. I hear a strange bird singing. It has very rich feathers. No Huron ever before saw such feathers. They will be ashamed to go back to their village and tell their people that they let their prisoner go on account of the song of this strange bird, and not be able to give the *name* of the bird. They do not know how to say whether it is a wren or a catbird. This would be a great disgrace; my young men would not be allowed to travel in the woods, without taking their mothers with them to tell them the names of the birds."

"You can ask my name of your prisoner," returned the girl. "It is Judith; and there is a great deal of the history of Judith in the pale-faces' best book, the Bible. If I am a bird of fine feathers, I have also my name."

"No," answered the wily Huron, betraying the artifice he had so long practised, by speaking in English, with tolerable accuracy; "I not ask prisoner. He tired; he want rest. I ask my daughter, with feeble-mind. She speak truth. Come here, daughter; you answer. *Your* name, Hetty?"

"Yes, that's what they call me," returned the girl, "though it's written Esther, in the Bible."

"He write *him* in Bible, too? All write in Bible. No matter—what *her* name?"

"That's Judith, and it's so written in the Bible, though father sometimes called her Jude. That's my sister Judith, Thomas Hutter's daughter—Thomas Hutter, whom you called the Muskrat; though he was *no* muskrat, but a man, like yourselves—he lived in a house on the water, and that was enough for *you.*"

A smile of triumph gleamed on the hard wrinkled countenance of the chief, when he found how completely his appeal to the truth-loving Hetty had succeeded. As for Judith herself, the moment her sister was questioned, she saw that all was lost; for no sign, or even treaty, could have induced the right-feeling girl to utter a falsehood. To attempt to impose a daughter of the Muskrat on the savages, as a princess or a great lady, she knew would be idle; and she saw her bold and ingenious expedient for liberating the captive fail, through one of the simplest and most natural causes that could be imagined. She turned her eye on Deerslayer, therefore, as if imploring him to interfere, to save them both.

"It will not do, Judith," said the young man, in answer to this appeal, which he understood, though he saw its uselessness; "it will not do. 'Twas a bold idee, and fit for a general's lady; but yonder Mingo"—Rivenoak had withdrawn to a little distance, and was out of ear-shot—"but yonder Mingo is an oncommon man, and not to be deceived by any unnat'ral sarcumventions. Things must come afore him in their right order to draw a cloud afore *his* eyes! 'Twas too much to attempt making him fancy that a queen or a great lady lived in these mountains, and no doubt he thinks the fine clothes you wear are some of the plunder of your own father—or, at least, of him who once passed for your father; as quite likely it was, if all they say is true."

"At all events, Deerslayer, my presence here will save you for a time. They will hardly attempt torturing you before my face!"

"Why not, Judith? Do you think they will treat a woman of the pale-faces more tenderly than they treat their own? It's true that your sex will most likely save you from the torments, but it will not save your liberty, and may not save your scalp. I wish you hadn't come, my good Judith; it can do no good to me, while it may do great harm to yourself."

"I can share your fate," the girl answered, with generous enthusiasm. "That shall not injure you while I stand by, if in my power to prevent it—besides—"

"Besides what, Judith? What means have you to stop Injin cruelties, or to avart Injin deviltries?"

"None, perhaps, Deerslayer," answered the girl, with firmness; "but I can suffer with my friends—die with them, if necessary."

"Ah! Judith—suffer you may; but die you will not until the Lord's time shall come. It's little likely that one of your sex and beauty will meet with a harder fate than to become the wife of a chief, if indeed your white inclinations can stoop to match with an Injin. 'Twould have been better had you stayed in the ark or the castle; but what has been done, is done. You was about to say something, when you stopped at 'besides?' "

"It might not be safe to mention it here, Deerslayer," the girl hurriedly answered, moving past him carelessly that she might speak in a low tone; "half an hour is all in all to us. None of your friends are idle."

The hunter replied merely by a grateful look. Then he turned towards his enemies, as if ready again to face the torments. A short consultation had passed among the elders of the band, and by this time they also were prepared with their decision. The merciful purpose of Rivenoak had been much weakened by the artifice of Judith, which, failing of its real object, was likely to produce results the very opposite of those she had anticipated. This was natural; the feeling being aided by the resentment of an Indian, who found how near he had been to becoming the dupe of an inexperienced girl. By this time Judith's real character was fully understood—the widespread reputation of her beauty contributed to the exposure. As for the unusual attire, it was confounded with the profound mystery of the animals with two tails, and, for the moment, lost its influence.

When Rivenoak, therefore, faced the captive again, it was with an altered countenance. He had abandoned the wish of saving him, and was no longer disposed to retard the more serious part of the torture. This change of sentiment was, in effect, communicated to the young men, who were already eagerly engaged in making their preparations for the contemplated scene. Fragments of dried wood were rapidly collected near the sapling, the splinters which it was intended to thrust into the flesh of the victim, previously to lighting, were all collected, and the thongs were already produced that were again to bind him to the tree. All this was done in profound silence, Judith watching every movement with breathless expectation, while Deerslayer himself stood seemingly as unmoved as one of the pines of the hills. When the warriors advanced to bind him, however, the young man glanced at Judith, as if to inquire whether resistance or submission were most advisable. By a significant gesture she counselled the last; and, in a minute he was once more fastened to the tree, a helpless object of any insult or wrong that might be offered. So eagerly did every one now act, that nothing was said. The fire was immediately lighted in the pile, and the end of all was anxiously expected.

It was not the intention of the Hurons absolutely to destroy the life of their victim by means of fire. They designed merely to put his physical fortitude to the severest proofs it could endure, short of that extremity. In the end, they fully intended to carry his scalp with them into their village, but it was their wish first to break down his resolution, and to reduce him to the level of a complaining sufferer. With this view, the pile of brush and branches had been placed at a proper distance, or one at which it was thought the heat would soon become intolerable, though it might not be immediately dangerous. As often happened, however, on these occasions, this distance had been miscalculated, and the flames began to wave their forked tongues in a proximity to the face of the victim that would have proved fatal in another instant, had not Hetty rushed through the crowd, armed with a stick, and scattered the blazing pile in a dozen directions. More than one hand was raised to strike the presumptuous intruder to the earth; but the chiefs prevented the blows, by reminding their irritated followers of the state of her mind. Hetty, herself, was insensible to the risk she ran; but, as soon as she had performed this bold act, she stood looking about her in frowning resentment, as if to rebuke the crowd of attentive savages for their cruelty.

"God bless you, dearest sister, for that brave and ready act," murmured Judith, herself unnerved so much as to be incapable of exertion;

"Heaven itself has sent you on its holy errand."

" 'Twas well meant, Judith," rejoined the victim; " 'twas excellently meant, and 'twas timely, though it may prove ontimely in the ind! What is to come to pass must come to pass soon, or 'twill quickly be too late. Had I drawn in one mouthful of that flame in breathing, the power of man couldn't save my life; and you see that this time they've so bound my forehead as not to leave my head the smallest chance. 'Twas well-meant; but it might have been more marciful to let the flames act their part."

"Cruel, heartless Hurons!" exclaimed the still indignant Hetty; "would you burn a man and a Christian as you would burn a log of wood! Do you never read your Bibles? or do you think God will forget such things?"

A gesture from Rivenoak caused the scattered brands to be collected; fresh wood was brought, even the women and children busying themselves eagerly in the gathering of dried sticks. The flame was just kindling a second time, when an *Indian* female pushed through the circle, advanced to the heap, and with her foot dashed aside the lighted twigs in time to prevent the conflagration. A yell followed this second disappointment; but when the offender turned towards the circle, and presented the countenance of Hist, it was succeeded by a common exclamation of pleasure and surprise. For a minute, all thought of pursuing the business in hand was forgotten, and young and old crowded around the girl, in haste to demand an explanation of her sudden and unlooked-for return. It was at this critical instant that Hist spoke to Judith in a low voice, placed some small object, unseen, in her hand, and then turned to meet the salutations of the Huron girls, with whom she was personally a great favorite. Judith recovered her self-possession and acted promptly. The small, keen-edged knife, that Hist had given to the other, was passed by the latter into the hands of Hetty, as the safest and least-suspected medium of transferring it to Deerslayer. But the feeble intellect of the last defeated the well-grounded hopes of all three. Instead of first cutting loose the hands of the victim, and then concealing the knife in his clothes, in readiness for action at the most available instant, she went to work herself, with earnestness and simplicity, to cut the thongs that bound his head, that he might not again be in danger of inhaling flames. Of course this deliberate procedure was seen, and the hands of Hetty were arrested ere she had more than liberated the upper portion of the captive's body, not including his arms, below the elbows. This discovery at once pointed distrust towards Hist; and, to Judith's surprise, when questioned on the subject, that spirited girl was not disposed to deny her agency in what had passed.

"Why should I not help the Deerslayer?" the girl demanded, in the tones of a firm-minded woman. "He is the brother of a Delaware chief; my heart is all Delaware. Come forth, miserable Briarthorn, and wash the Iroquois paint from your face; stand before the Hurons, the crow that you are; you would eat the carrion of your own dead rather than starve. Put him face to face with Deerslayer, chiefs and warriors; I will show you how great a knave you have been keeping in your tribe."

This bold language, uttered in their own dialect, and with a manner full of confidence, produced a deep sensation among the Hurons. Treachery is always liable to distrust; and though the recreant Briarthorn had endeavored to serve the enemy well, his exertions and assiduities had gained for him little more than toleration. His wish to obtain Hist for a wife had first induced him to betray her and his own people; but serious rivals to his first project had risen up among his new friends, weakening still more their sympathies with treason. In a word, Briarthorn had been barely permitted to remain in the Huron encampment, where he was as closely and as jealously watched as Hist herself; seldom appearing before the chiefs, and sedulously keeping out of view of Deerslayer, who, until this moment, was ignorant even of his presence. Thus summoned, however, it was impossible to remain in the background. "Wash the Iroquois paint from his face," he did not; for when he stood in the centre of the circle, he was so disguised in these new colors, that, at first, the hunter did not recognize him. He assumed an air of defiance, notwithstanding, and haughtily demanded what any could say against Briarthorn.

"Ask yourself that," continued Hist, with spirit, though her manner grew less concentrated; and there was a slight air of abstraction that became observable to Deerslayer and Judith, if to no others. "Ask that of your own heart, sneaking woodchuck of the Delawares; come not here with the face of an innocent man. Go look in the spring; see the colors of your enemies on your lying skin; and then come back and boast how you ran from your tribe, and took the blanket of the French for your covering. Paint yourself as bright as a humming-bird, you will still be black as the crow."

Hist had been so uniformly gentle while living with the Hurons, that they now listened to her language with surprise. As for the delinquent, his blood boiled in his veins; and it was well for the pretty speaker that it was not in his power to execute the revenge he burned to inflict on her, in spite of his pretended love.

"Who wishes Briarthorn?" he sternly asked. "If this pale-face is tired of life; if afraid of Indian torments, speak, Rivenoak; I will send him after the warriors we have lost."

"No, chief,—no, Rivenoak," eagerly interrupted Hist. "The Deerslayer fears nothing; least of all a crow! Unbind him—cut his withes—place him face to face with this cawing bird; then let us see which is tired of life."

Hist made a forward movement, as if to take a knife from a young man, and perform the office she had mentioned in person; but an aged warrior interposed, at a sign from Rivenoak. The chief watched all the girl did, with distrust; for, even while speaking in her most boastful language and in the steadiest manner, there was an air of uncertainty and expectation about her, that could not escape so close an observer. She acted well; but two or three of the old men were equally satisfied that it was merely acting. Her proposal to release Deerslayer, therefore, was rejected; and the disappointed Hist found herself driven back from the sapling at the very moment she fancied herself about to be successful. At the same time the circle, which had got to be crowded and confused, was enlarged, and brought once more into order. Rivenoak now announced the intention of the old men again to proceed; the delay having been continued long enough, and leading to no result.

"Stop, Huron; stay, chiefs!" exclaimed Judith, scarce knowing what she said, or why she interposed, unless to obtain time; "for God's sake, a single minute longer—"

The words were cut short by another and a still more extraordinary interruption. A young Indian came bounding through the Huron ranks, leaping into the very centre of the circle, in a way to denote the utmost confidence, or a temerity bordering on foolhardiness. Five or six sentinels were still watching the lake at different and distant points; and it was the first impression of Rivenoak that one of these had come in with tidings of import. Still, the movements of the stranger were so rapid, and his war-dress, which scarcely left him more drapery than an antique statue, had so little distinguishing about it, that, at the first moment, it was impossible to ascertain whether he were friend or foe. Three leaps carried this warrior to the side of Deerslayer, whose withes were cut in the twinkling of an eye, with a quickness and precision that left the prisoner perfect master of his limbs. Not till this was effected did the stranger bestow a glance on any other object; then he turned and showed the astonished Hurons the noble brow, fine person, and eagle eye of a young warrior, in the paint and panoply of a Delaware. He held a rifle in each hand, the butts of both resting on the earth, while from one dangled its proper pouch and horn. This was Killdeer, which even as he looked boldly and in defiance on the crowd around him, he suffered to fall back into the hands of the proper owner. The presence of two armed men, though it was in their midst, startled the Hurons. Their rifles were scattered about against the different trees, and their only weapons were their knives and tomahawks. Still, they had too much self-possession to betray fear. It was little likely that so small a force would assail so strong a band; and each man expected some extraordinary proposition to succeed so decisive a step. The stranger did not seem disposed to disappoint them; he prepared to speak.

"Hurons," he said, "this earth is very big. The great lakes are big, too; there is room beyond them for the Iroquois; there is room for the Delawares on this side. I am Chingachgook, the son of Uncas; the kinsman of Tamenund. This is my betrothed; that pale-face is my friend. My heart was heavy when I missed him. All the Delaware girls are waiting for Wah; they wonder that she stays away so long. Come, let us say farewell, and go on our path."

"Hurons, this is your mortal enemy, the Great Serpent of them you hate!" cried Briarthorn. "If he escape, blood will be in your moccasin prints from this spot to the Canadas. *I* am *all* Huron."

As the last words were uttered, the traitor cast his knife at the naked breast of the Delaware. A quick movement of the arm, on the part of Hist, who stood near, turned aside the blow, the dangerous weapon burying its point in a pine. At the next instant, a similar weapon glanced from the hand of the Serpent, and quivered in the recreant's heart. A minute had scarcely elapsed from the moment in which Chingachgook bounded into the circle, and that in which Briarthorn fell, like a dog, dead in his tracks. The rapidity of events prevented the Hurons from acting; but this catastrophe permitted no further delay. A common exclamation followed, and the whole party was in motion. At this instant, a sound unusual to the woods was heard, and every Huron, male and female, paused to listen, with ears erect and faces filled with expectation. The sound was regular and heavy, as if the earth were struck with beetles. Objects became visible among the trees of the background, and a body of troops was seen advancing with measured tread. They came upon the charge, the scarlet of the king's livery shining among the bright green foliage of the forest.

The scene that followed is not easily described. It was one in which wild confusion, despair, and frenzied efforts were so blended as to destroy the unity and distinctness of the action. A general yell burst from the inclosed Hurons; it was succeeded by the hearty cheers of England. Still, not a musket or rifle was fired, though that steady, measured tramp continued, and the bayonet was seen gleaming in advance of a line that counted nearly sixty men. The Hurons were taken at a fearful disadvantage. On three sides was the water, while their formidable and trained foes cut them off from flight on the fourth. Each warrior rushed for his arms, and then all on the point, man, woman, and child, eagerly sought the covers. In this scene of confusion and dismay, however, nothing could surpass the discretion and coolness of Deerslayer. His first care was to place Judith and Hist behind trees, and he looked for Hetty; but she had been hurried away in the crowd of Huron women. This effected, he threw himself on a flank of the retiring Hurons, who were inclining off towards the southern margin of the point, in the hope of escaping through the water. Deerslayer watched his opportunity, and finding two of his recent tormentors in a range, his rifle first broke the silence of the terrific scene. The bullet brought down both at one discharge. This drew a general fire from the Hurons, and the rifle and war-cry of the Serpent were heard in the clamor. Still, the trained men returned no answering volley, the whoop and piece of Hurry alone being heard on their side, if we except the short, prompt word of authority, and that heavy, measured, and menacing tread. Presently, however, the shrieks, groans, and denunciations that usually accompany the use of the bayonet, followed. That terrible and deadly weapon was glutted in vengeance. The scene that succeeded was one of those, of which so many have occurred in our own times, in which neither age nor sex forms an exemption to the lot of a savage warfare.

CHAPTER 32

THE DAY that followed proved to be melancholy, though one of much activity. The soldiers, who had so lately been employed in interring their victims, were now called on to bury their own dead. The scene of the morning had left a saddened feeling on all the gentlemen of the party, and the rest felt the influence of a similar sensation, in a variety of ways, and from many causes. Hour dragged on after hour until evening arrived, and then came the last melancholy offices, in honor of poor Hetty Hutter. Her body was laid in the lake by the side of that of the mother she had so loved and reverenced; the surgeon, though actually an unbeliever, so far complying with the received decencies of life, as to read the funeral service over her grave, as he had previously done over those of the other *Christian* slain. It mattered not; that all-seeing eye which reads the heart, could not fail to discriminate between the living and the dead, and the gentle soul of the unfortunate girl was already far removed beyond the errors or deceptions of any human ritual. These simple rites, however, were not wholly wanting in suitable accompaniments. The tears of Judith and Hist were shed freely, and Deerslayer gazed upon the limpid water that now flowed over one whose spirit was even purer than its own mountain springs, with glistening eyes. Even the Delaware turned aside to conceal his weakness, while the common men gazed on the ceremony with wondering eyes and chastened feelings.

The business of the day closed with this pious office. By order of the commanding officer all retired early to rest, for it was intended to begin the march homewards with the return of light. One party indeed, bearing the wounded, the prisoners, and the trophies, had left the castle in the middle of the day, under the guidance of Hurry, intending to reach the fort by shorter marches. It had been landed on the point so often mentioned, or that described in our opening pages; and when the sun set, was already encamped on the brow of the long, broken, and ridgy hills that fell away towards the valley of the Mohawk. The departure of this detachment had greatly simplified the duty of the succeeding day, disencumbering its march of its baggage and wounded, and otherwise leaving him who had issued the order greater liberty of action.

Judith held no communication with any but Hist, after the death of her sister, until she retired for the night. Her sorrow had been respected, and both the females had been left with the body, unintruded on to the last moment. The rattling of the drum broke the silence of that tranquil water, and the echoes of the tattoo were heard among the mountains so soon after the ceremony was over, as to preclude the danger of interruption. That star which had been the guide of Hist, rose on a scene as silent as if the quiet of nature had never yet been disturbed by the labors or passions of man. One solitary sentinel, with his relief, paced the platform throughout the night; and morning was ushered in, as usual, by the martial beat of the reveille.

Military precision succeeded to the desultory proceedings of border-men, and when a hasty and frugal breakfast was taken, the party began its movement towards the shore, with a regularity and order that prevented noise or confusion. Of all the officers, Warley alone remained. Craig headed the detachment in advance, Thornton was with the wounded, and Graham accompanied his patients, as a matter of course. Even the chest of Hutter, with all the more valuable of his effects, was borne away, leaving nothing behind that was worth the labor of a removal. Judith was not sorry to see that the captain respected her feelings, and that he occupied himself entirely with the duty of his command, leaving her to her own discretion and feelings. It was understood by all, that the place was to be totally abandoned; but beyond this no explanations were asked or given.

The soldiers embarked in the ark, with the captain at their head. He had inquired of Judith in what way she chose to proceed, and understanding her wish to remain with Hist to the last moment, he neither molested her with requests, or offended her with advice. There was but one safe and familiar trail to the Mohawk; and on that, at the proper hour, he doubted not that they should meet in amity, if not in renewed intercourse.

When all were on board, the sweeps were manned, and the ark moved in its sluggish manner towards the distant point. Deerslayer and Chingachgook now lifted two of the canoes from the water, and placed them in the castle. The windows and door were then barred, and the house was left, by means of the trap, in the manner already described. On quitting the palisades, Hist was seen in the remaining canoe, where the Delaware immediately joined her, and paddled away, leaving Judith standing alone on the platform. Owing to this prompt proceeding Deerslayer found himself alone with the beautiful, and still weeping mourner. Too simple to suspect anything, the young man swept the light boat round, and received its mistress in it, when he followed the course already taken by his friend.

The direction to the point led diagonally past, and at no great distance from, the graves of the dead. As the canoe glided by, Judith, for the first time that morning, spoke to her companion. She said but little, merely uttering a simple request to stop for a minute or two, ere she left the place.

"I may never see this spot again, Deerslayer," she said, "and it contains the bodies of my mother and sister! Is it not possible, think you, that the innocence of one of these beings may answer, in the eyes of God, for the salvation of both?"

"I don't understand it so, Judith; though I'm no missionary, and am but poorly taught. Each spirit answers for its own backslidings; though a hearty repentance will satisfy God's laws."

"Then *must* my poor, poor mother be in heaven! Bitterly—bitterly has she repented of her sins; and surely her sufferings in this life ought to count as something against her sufferings in the next!"

"All this goes beyond me, Judith. I strive to do right, here, as the surest means of keeping all right, hereafter. Hetty was oncommon, as all that know'd her must allow; and her soul was as fit to consort with angels, the hour it left its body, as that of any saint in the Bible!"

"I do believe you only do her justice! Alas! alas!—that there should be so great differences between those who were nursed at the same breast, slept in the same bed, and dwelt under the same roof! But, no matter,—move the canoe a little farther east, Deerslayer; the sun so dazzles my eyes that I cannot see the graves. This is Hetty's, on the right of mother's?"

"Sartain—you asked that of us; and all are glad to do as you wish, Judith, when you do that which is right."

The girl gazed at him near a minute, in silent attention; then she turned her eyes backward, at the castle.

"This lake will soon be entirely deserted," she said, "and this, too, at a moment when it will be a more secure dwelling-place than ever. What has so lately happened will prevent the Iroquois from venturing again to visit it, for a long time to come."

"That it will!—yes, that may be set down as settled. I do not mean to pass thisaway, ag'in, so long as the war lasts; for, to my mind, no Huron moccasin will leave its print on the leaves of this forest, until their traditions have forgotten to tell their young men of their disgrace and rout."

"And do you so delight in violence and bloodshed? I had thought better of *you*, Deerslayer—believed you one who could find his happiness in a quiet domestic home, with an attached and loving wife, ready to study your wishes, and healthy and dutiful children, anxious to follow in your footsteps, and to become as honest and just as yourself."

"Lord, Judith, what a tongue you're mistress of! Speech and looks go hand in hand, like; and what one can't do, the other is pretty sartain to perform! Such a gal, in a month, might spoil the stoutest warrior in the colony."

"And am I then so mistaken? Do you really love war, Deerslayer, better than the hearth and the affections?"

"I understand your meaning, gal; yes, I do understand what you mean, I believe, though I don't think you altogether understand *me*. Warrior I may now call myself, I suppose, for I've both fou't and conquered, which is sufficient for the name; neither will I deny that I've feelin's for the callin', which is both manful and honorable, when carried on accordin' to nat'ral gifts—but I've no relish for blood. Youth is youth, howsever, and a Mingo is a Mingo. If the young men of this region stood by, and suffered the vagabonds to overrun the land, why, we might as well all turn Frenchers at once, and give up country and kin. I'm no fire-eater, Judith, or one that likes fightin' for fightin's sake; but I can see no great difference atween *givin' up territory afore a war, out of a dread of war, and givin' it up a'ter a war, because we can't help it—onless it be that the last is the most manful and honorable.*"

"No woman would ever wish to see her husband or brother stand by, and submit to insult and wrong, Deerslayer, however she might mourn the necessity of his running into the dangers of battle. But you've done enough already, in clearing this region of the Hurons; since to you is principally owing the credit of our late victory. Now listen to me patiently, and answer me with that native honesty, which it is as pleasant to regard in one of your sex as it is unusual to meet with."

Judith paused; for now that she was on the very point of explaining herself, native modesty asserted its power, notwithstanding the encouragement and confidence she derived from the great simplicity of her companion's character. Her cheeks, which had so lately been pale, flushed, and her eyes lighted with some of their former brilliancy. Feeling gave expression to her countenance, and softness to her voice, rendering her who was always beautiful, trebly seductive and winning.

"Deerslayer," she said, after a considerable pause, "this is not a moment for affectation, deception, or a want of frankness of any sort. Here, over my mother's grave, and over the grave of truth-loving, truth-telling Hetty, everything like unfair dealing seems to be out of place. I will therefore speak to you without any reserve, and without any dread of being misunderstood. You are not an acquaintance of a week, but it appears to me as if I had known you for years. So much, and so much that is important, has taken place within that short time, that the sorrows, and dangers, and escapes of a whole life have been crowded into a few days; and they who have suffered and acted together in such scenes, ought not to feel like strangers. I know that what I am about to say might be misunderstood by most men, but I hope for a generous construction of my course from you. We are not here dwelling among the arts and deceptions of the settlements, but young people who have no occasion to deceive each other, in any manner or form. I hope I make myself understood?"

"Sartain, Judith; few convarse better than yourself, and none more agreeable, like. Your words are as pleasant as your looks."

"It is the manner in which you have so often praised those looks, that gives me courage to proceed. Still, Deerslayer, it is not easy for one of my sex and years to forget all her lessons of infancy, all her habits, and her natural diffidence, and say openly what her heart feels!"

"Why not, Judith? Why shouldn't women as well as men deal fairly and honestly by their fellow-creatur's? I see no reason why you should not speak as plainly as myself, when there is anything ra'ally important to be said."

This indomitable diffidence, which still prevented the young man from suspecting the truth, would have completely discouraged the girl, had not her whole soul, as well as her whole heart, been set upon making a desperate effort to rescue herself from a future that she dreaded with a horror as vivid as the distinctness with which she fancied she foresaw it. This motive, however, raised her above all common considerations, and she persevered even to her own surprise, if not to her great confusion.

"I will—I *must* deal as plainly with you, as I would with poor, dear Hetty, were that sweet child living!" she continued, turning pale, instead of blushing, the high resolution by which she was prompted reversing the effect that such a procedure would ordinarily produce on one of her sex; "yes, I will smother all other feelings, in the one that is now uppermost! You love the woods and the life that we pass, here, in the wilderness, away from the dwellings and towns of the whites."

"As I loved my parents, Judith, when they was living! This very spot would be all creation to me, could this war be fairly over, once; and the settlers kept at a distance."

"Why quit it, then? It has no owner—at least none who can claim a better right than mine, and *that* I freely give to you. Were it a kingdom, Deerslayer, I think I should delight to say the same. Let us then return to it, after we have seen the priest at the fort, and never quit it again, until God calls us away to that world where we shall find the spirits of my poor mother and sister."

A long, thoughtful pause succeeded; Judith having covered her face with both her hands, after forcing herself to utter so plain a proposal, and Deerslayer musing equally in sorrow and surprise, on the meaning of the language he had just heard. At length the hunter broke the silence, speaking in a tone that was softened to gentleness by his desire not to offend.

"You haven't thought well of this, Judith," he said; "no, your feelin's are awakened by all that has lately happened, and believin' yourself to be without kindred in the world, you are in too great a haste to find some to fill the places of them that's lost."

"Were I living in a crowd of friends, Deerslayer, I should still think as I now think,—say as I now say," returned Judith, speaking with her hands still shading her lovely face.

"Thank you, gal—thank you, from the bottom of my heart. Howsever, I am not one to take advantage of a weak moment, when you're forgetful of your own great advantages, and fancy 'arth and all it holds is in this little canoe. No—no—Judith, 'twould be ongin'rous in me; what you've offered can never come to pass!"

"It all may be, and that without leaving cause of repentance to any," answered Judith, with an impetuosity of feeling and manner, that at once unveiled her eyes. "We can cause the soldiers to leave our goods on the road, till we return, when they can easily be brought back to the house; the lake will be no more visited by the enemy, this war at least; all your skins may be readily sold at the garrison; there *you* can buy the few necessaries we shall want, for I wish never to see the spot again; and Deerslayer," added the girl, smiling with a sweetness and nature that the young man found it hard to resist, "as a proof how wholly I am and wish to be yours—how completely I desire to be nothing but your wife, the very first fire that we kindle, after our return, shall be lighted with the brocade dress, and fed by every article I have that you may think unfit for the woman you wish to live with!"

"Ah's me!—you're a winning and a lovely creatur', Judith; yes, you *are* all that, and no one can deny it, and speak truth. These pictur's are pleasant to the thoughts, but they mightn't prove so happy as you now think 'em. Forget it all, therefore, and let us paddle after the Sarpent and Hist, as if nothing had been said on the subject."

Judith was deeply mortified, and what is more, she was profoundly grieved. Still there was a steadiness and quiet in the manner of Deerslayer, that completely smothered her hopes, and told her that for once, her exceeding beauty had failed to excite the admiration and homage it was wont to receive. Women are said seldom to forgive those who slight their advances; but this high-spirited and impetuous girl entertained no shadow of resentment, then or ever, against the fair-dealing and ingenuous hunter. At the moment, the prevailing feeling was the wish to be certain that there was no misunderstanding. After another painful pause, therefore, she brought the matter to an issue, by a question too direct to admit of equivocation.

"God forbid that we lay up regrets in after life, through any want of sincerity now," she said. "I hope we understand each other at least. You will not accept me for a wife, Deerslayer?"

" 'Tis better for both that I shouldn't take advantage of your own forgetfulness, Judith. We can never marry."

"You do not love me,—cannot find it in your heart, perhaps, to esteem me, Deerslayer!"

"Everything in the way of fri'ndship, Judith—everything, even to sarvices and life itself. Yes, I'd risk as much for you, at this moment, as I would risk in behalf of Hist; and that is sayin' as much as I can say of any darter of woman. I do not think I feel towards either—mind I say *either,* Judith—as if I wished to quit father and mother—if father and mother was livin'; which, however, neither is—but if both was livin', I do not feel towards any woman as if I wish'd to quit 'em in order to cleave unto *her.*"

"This is enough!" answered Judith, in a rebuked and smothered voice; "I understand all that you mean. Marry you cannot, without loving; and that love you do not feel for me. Make no answer if I am right, for I shall understand your silence. *That* will be painful enough of itself."

Deerslayer obeyed her, and he made no reply. For more than a minute the girl riveted her bright eyes on him as if to read his soul; while he sat playing with the water, like a corrected schoolboy. Then Judith herself dropped the end of her paddle, and urged the canoe away from the spot, with a movement as reluctant as the feelings which controlled it. Deerslayer quietly aided the effort, however, and they were soon on the trackless line taken by the Delaware.

In their way to the point, not another syllable was exchanged between Deerslayer and his fair companion. As Judith sat in the bow of the canoe, her back was turned towards him, else it is probable the expression of her countenance might have induced him to venture some soothing terms of friendship and regard. Contrary to what would have been expected, resentment was still absent, though the color frequently changed from the deep flush of mortification to the paleness of disappointment. Sorrow, deep, heartfelt sorrow, however, was the predominant emotion, and this was betrayed in a manner not to be mistaken.

As neither labored hard at the paddle, the ark had already arrived, and the soldiers had disembarked before the canoe of the two loiterers reached the point. Chingachgook had preceded it, and was already some distance in the wood, at a spot where the two trails, that to the garrison, and that to the villages of the Delawares, separated. The soldiers, too, had taken up their line of march; first setting the ark adrift again, with a reckless disregard of its fate. All this Judith saw, but she heeded it not. The Glimmerglass had no longer any charms for her; and when she put her foot on the strand, she immediately proceeded on the trail of the soldiers, without casting a single glance behind her. Even Hist was passed unnoticed; that modest young creature shrinking from the averted face of Judith, as if guilty herself of some wrong-doing.

"Wait you here, Sarpent," said Deerslayer, as he followed in the footsteps of the dejected beauty, while passing his friend. "I will just see Judith among her party, and come and j'ine you."

A hundred yards had hid the couple from those in front, as well as those in the rear, when Judith turned and spoke.

"This will do, Deerslayer," she said, sadly. "I understand your kindness, but shall not need it. In a few minutes I shall reach the soldiers. As you cannot go with me on the journey of life, I do not wish you to go farther on this. But stop; before we part I would ask you a single question. And I require of you as you fear God, and reverence the truth, not to deceive me in your answer. I know you do not love another; and I can see but one reason why you cannot, *will* not love me. Tell me, then, Deerslayer—" The girl paused, the words she was about to utter, seeming to choke her. Then rallying all her resolution, with a face that flushed and paled at every breath she drew, she continued: "Tell me, then, Deerslayer, if anything light of me, that Henry March has said, may not have influenced your feelings?"

Truth was the Deerslayer's polar star. He ever kept it in view; and it was nearly impossible for him to avoid uttering it, even when prudence demanded silence. Judith read his answer in his countenance; and with a heart nearly broken by the consciousness of undeserving, she signed to him an adieu, and buried herself in the woods. For some time Deerslayer was irresolute as to his course; but in the end, he retraced his steps and joined the Delaware. That night, the three "camped" on the head-waters of their own river, and the succeeding evening they entered the village of the tribe; Chingachgook and his betrothed, in triumph; their companion honored and admired, but in a sorrow that it required months of activity to remove.

The war that then had its rise was stirring and bloody. The Delaware chief rose among his people, until his name was never mentioned without eulogiums; while another Uncas, the last of his race, was added to the long line of warriors who bore that distinguished appellation. As for the Deerslayer, under the *sobriquet* of Hawkeye, he made his fame spread far and near, until the crack of his rifle became as terrible to the ears of the Mingos, as the thunders of the Manitou. His services were soon required by the officers of the Crown, and he especially attached himself, in the field, to one in particular, with whose after-life he had a close and important connection.

Fifteen years had passed away, ere it was in the power of the Deerslayer to revisit the Glimmerglass. A peace had intervened, and it was on the eve of another, and still more important war, when he and his constant friend, Chingachgook, were hastening to the forts to join their allies. A stripling accompanied them, for Hist already slumbered beneath the pines of the Delawares, and the three survivors had now become inseparable. They reached the lake just as the sun was setting. Here all was unchanged; the river still rushed through its bower of trees; the little rock was wasting away by the slow action of the waves in the course of centuries; the mountains stood in their native dress, dark, rich, and mysterious; while the sheet glistened in its solitude, a beautiful gem of the forest.

The following morning the youth discovered one of the canoes drifted on the shore, in a state of decay. A little labor put it in a state for service, and they all embarked, with a desire to examine the place. All the points were passed, and Chingachgook pointed out to his son the spot where the Hurons had first encamped, and the point whence he had succeeded in stealing his bride. Here they even landed; but all trace of the former visit had disappeared. Next they proceeded to the scene of the battle, and there they found a few of the signs that linger around such localities. Wild beasts had disinterred many of the bodies, and human bones were bleaching in the rains of summer. Uncas regarded all with reverence and pity, though traditions were already rousing his young mind to the ambition and sternness of a warrior.

From the point, the canoe took its way towards the shoal, where the remains of the castle were still visible, a picturesque ruin. The storms of winter had long since unroofed the house, and decay had eaten into the logs. All the fastenings were untouched, but the seasons rioted in the place, as if in mockery at the attempt to exclude them. The palisades were rotting, as were the piles; and it was evident that a few more recurrences of winter, a few more gales and tempests, would sweep all into the lake, and blot the building from the face of that magnificent solitude. The graves could not be found. Either the elements had obliterated their traces, or time had caused those who looked for them to forget their position.

The ark was discovered stranded on the eastern shore, where it had long before been driven, with the prevalent northwest winds. It lay on the sandy extremity of a long, low point, that is situated about two miles from the outlet, and which is itself fast disappearing before the action of the elements. The scow was filled with water, the cabin unroofed, and the logs were decaying. Some of its coarser furniture still remained, and the heart of Deerslayer beat quick as he found a ribbon of Judith's fluttering from a log. It recalled all her beauty, and we may add, all her failings. Although the girl had never touched his heart, the Hawkeye, for so we ought now to call him, still retained a kind and sincere interest in her welfare. He tore away the ribbon and knotted it to the stock of Killdeer, which had been the gift of the girl herself.

A few miles farther up the lake another of the canoes was discovered; and on the point where the party finally landed, were found those which had been left there upon the shore. That in which the present navigation was made, and the one discovered on the eastern shore, had dropped through the decayed floor of the castle, drifted past the falling palisades, and had been thrown as waifs upon the beach.

From all these signs, it was probable the lake had not been visited since the occurrence of the final scene of our tale. Accident or tradition had rendered it again a spot sacred to nature; the frequent wars, and the feeble population of the colonies, still confining the settlements within narrow boundaries. Chingachgook and his friend left the spot with melancholy feelings. It had been the region of their First War-Path, and it carried back the minds of both to scenes of tenderness as well as to hours of triumph. They held their way towards the Mohawk in silence, however, to rush into new adventures, as stirring and as remarkable as those which had attended their opening career on this lovely lake. At a later day they returned to the place, where the Indian found a grave.

Time and circumstances have drawn an impenetrable mystery around all else connected with the Hutters. They lived, erred, died, and are forgotten. None connected have felt sufficient interest in the disgraced and disgracing, to withdraw the veil; and a century is about to erase even the recollection of their names. The history of crime is ever revolting, and it is fortunate that few love to dwell on its incidents. The sins of the family have long since been arraigned at the judgment-seat of God, or are registered for the terrible settlement of the last great day.

The same fate attended Judith. When Hawkeye reached the garrison on the Mohawk, he inquired anxiously after that lovely, but misguided creature. None knew her—even her person was no longer remembered. Other officers had again and again succeeded the Warleys and Craigs and Grahams; though an old sergeant of the garrison, who had lately come from England, was enabled to tell our hero that Sir Robert Warley lived on his paternal estates, and that there was a lady of rare beauty in the lodge, who had great influence over him, though she did not bear his name. Whether this was Judith, relapsed into her early failing, or some other victim of the soldier's, Hawkeye never knew, nor would it be pleasant or profitable to inquire. We live in a world of transgressions and selfishness, and no pictures that represent us otherwise can be true; though happily for human nature, gleamings of that pure spirit in whose likeness man has been fashioned, are to be seen, relieving its deformities, and mitigating, if not excusing its crimes.

FROM

THE PATHFINDER

[THE action of *The Pathfinder* occurs about fifteen years after *The Deerslayer,* when Leatherstocking is in his late thirties. The story is concerned with events centered around the British Fort Oswego on Lake Ontario, to which Leatherstocking has helped escort Mabel Dunham, the daughter of his old friend Sergeant Dunham. Encouraged by the sergeant, who wishes his daughter to marry the hunter, Leatherstocking falls in love with Mabel; but she is already in love with Jasper Western, a young fresh-water sailor.]

from CHAPTER 18

IT WAS near noon when the gale broke; and then its force abated as suddenly as its violence had arisen. In less than two hours after the wind fell, the surface of the lake, though still agitated, was no longer glittering with foam; and in double that time, the entire sheet presented the ordinary scene of disturbed water, that was unbroken by the violence of a tempest. Still the waves came rolling incessantly towards the shore, and the lines of breakers remained, though the spray had ceased to fly; the combing of the swells was more moderate, and all that there was of violence proceeded from the impulsion of wind which had abated.

As it was impossible to make head against the sea that was still up, with the light opposing air that blew from the eastward, all thoughts of getting under way that afternoon were abandoned. Jasper, who had now quietly resumed the command of the *Scud,* busied himself, however, in heaving-up the anchors, which were lifted in succession; the kedges that backed them were weighed, and everything was got in readiness for a prompt departure, as soon as the state of the weather would allow. In the meantime, they who had no concern with these duties sought such means of amusement as their peculiar circumstances allowed.

As is common with those who are unused to the confinement of a vessel, Mabel cast wistful eyes towards the shore; nor was it long before she expressed a wish that it were possible to land. The Pathfinder was near her at the time, and he assured her that nothing would be easier, as they had a bark canoe on deck, which was the best possible mode of conveyance to go through a surf. After the usual doubts and misgivings, the Sergeant was appealed to; his opinion proved to be favorable, and preparations to carry the whim into effect were immediately made.

The party which was to land consisted of Sergeant Dunham, his daughter, and the Pathfinder. Accustomed to the canoe, Mabel took her seat in the centre with great steadiness, her father was placed in the bows, while the guide assumed the office of conductor, by steering in the stern. There was little need of impelling the canoe by means of the paddle, for the rollers sent it forward at moments with a violence that set every effort to govern its movements at defiance. More than once, before the shore was reached, Mabel repented of her temerity, but Pathfinder encouraged her, and really manifested so much self-possession, coolness, and strength of arm himself, that even a female might have hesitated about owning all her apprehensions. Our heroine was no coward; and while she felt the novelty of her situation, in landing through a surf, she also experienced a fair proportion of its wild delight. At moments, indeed, her heart was in her mouth, as the bubble of a boat floated on the very crest of a foaming breaker, appearing to skim the water like a swallow, and then she flushed and laughed, as, left by the glancing element, they appeared to linger behind as if ashamed of having been outdone in the headlong race. A few minutes sufficed for this excitement; for though the distance between the cutter and the land considerably exceeded a quarter of a mile, the intermediate space was passed in a very few minutes.

On landing, the Sergeant kissed his daughter kindly, for he was so much of a soldier as always to feel more at home on *terra firma* than when afloat; and, taking his gun, he announced his intention to pass an hour in quest of game.

"Pathfinder will remain near you, girl, and no doubt he will tell you some of the traditions of this part of the world, or some of his own experiences with the Mingos."

The guide laughed, promised to have a care of Mabel, and in a few minutes the father had ascended a steep acclivity and disappeared in the forest. The others took another direction, which, after a few minutes of a sharp ascent also, brought them to a small naked point on the promontory, where the eye overlooked an extensive and very peculiar panorama. Here Mabel seated herself on a fragment of fallen rock to recover her breath and strength, while her companion, on whose sinews no personal exertion seemed to make any impression, stood at her side, leaning in his own and not ungraceful manner on his long rifle. Several minutes passed, and neither spoke; Mabel, in particular, being lost in admiration of the view.

The position the two had obtained was sufficiently elevated to command a wide reach of the lake, which stretched away towards the north-east in a boundless sheet, glittering beneath the rays of an afternoon's sun, and yet betraying the remains of that agitation which it had endured while tossed by the late tempest. The land set bounds to its limits in a huge crescent, disappearing in distance towards the south-east and the north. Far as the eye could reach, nothing but forest was visible, not even a solitary sign of civilization breaking in upon the uniform and grand magnificence of nature. The gale had driven the *Scud* beyond the line of those forts with which the French were then endeavoring to gird the English North American possessions; for, following the channels of communication between the great lakes, their posts were on the banks of the Niagara, while our adventurers had reached a point many leagues westward of that celebrated strait. The cutter rode at single anchor, without the breakers, resembling some well-imagined and accurately-executed toy, intended rather for a glass case than for struggles with the elements which she had so lately gone through, while the canoe lay on the narrow beach, just out of reach of the waves that came booming upon the land, a speck upon the shingles.

"We are very far here from human habitations!" exclaimed Mabel, when, after a long survey of the scene, its principal peculiarities forced themselves on her active and ever brilliant imagination; "this is indeed being on a frontier."

"Have they more sightly scenes than this nearer the sea and around their large towns?" demanded Pathfinder, with an interest he was apt to discover in such a subject.

"I will not say that: there is more to remind one of his fellow-beings there than here; less, perhaps, to remind one of God."

"Ay, Mabel, that is what my own feelings say. I am but a poor hunter, I know, untaught and unlarned; but God is as near me, in this my home, as he is near the king in his royal palace."

"Who can doubt it?" returned Mabel, looking from the view up into the hard-featured but honest face of her companion, though not without surprise at the energy of his manner. "One feels nearer to God in such a spot, I think, than when the mind is distracted by the objects of the towns."

"You say all I wish to say myself, Mabel, but in so much plainer speech, that you make me ashamed of wishing to let others know what I feel on such matters. I have coasted this lake in search of skins afore the war, and have been here already; not at this very spot, for we landed yonder, where you may see the blasted oak that stands above the cluster of hemlocks—"

"How, Pathfinder, can you remember all these trifles so accurately?"

"These are our streets and houses, our churches and palaces. Remember them, indeed! I once made an appointment with the Big Sarpent, to meet at twelve o'clock at noon, near the foot of a certain pine, at the end of six months, when neither of us was within three hundred miles of the spot. The tree stood, and stands still, unless the judgment of Providence has lighted on that too, in the midst of the forest, fifty miles from any settlement, but in a most extraordinary neighborhood for beaver."

"And did you meet at that very spot and hour?"

"Does the sun rise and set? When I reached the tree, I found the Sarpent leaning against its trunk with torn leggings and muddied moccasins. The Delaware had got into a swamp, and it worried him not a little to find his way out of it; but as the sun which comes over the eastern hills in the morning goes down behind the western at night, so was he true to time and place. No fear of Chingachgook when there is either a friend or an enemy in the case. He is equally sartain with each."

"And where is the Delaware now? why is he not with us to-day?"

"He is scouting on the Mingo trail, where I ought to have been too, but for a great human infirmity."

"You seem above, beyond, superior to all infirmity, Pathfinder; I never yet met with a man who appeared to be so little liable to the weaknesses of nature."

"If you mean in the way of health and strength, Mabel, Providence has been kind to me; though I fancy the open air, long hunts, active scoutings, forest fare, and the sleep of a good conscience, may always keep the doctors at a distance. But I am human after all; yes, I find I'm very human in some of my feelings."

Mabel looked surprised, and it would be no more than delineating the character of her sex, if we added that her sweet countenance expressed a good deal of curiosity, too, though her tongue was more discreet.

"There is something bewitching in this wild life of yours, Pathfinder," she exclaimed, a tinge of enthusiasm mantling her cheeks. "I find I'm fast getting to be a frontier girl, and am coming to love all this grand silence of the woods. The towns seem tame to me; and, as my father will probably pass the remainder of his days here, where he has already lived so long, I begin to feel that I should be happy to continue with him, and not to return to the sea-shore."

"The woods are never silent, Mabel, to such as understand their meaning. Days at a time have I travelled them alone, without feeling the want of company; and, as for conversation, for such as can comprehend their language, there is no want of rational and instructive discourse."

"I believe you are happier when alone, Pathfinder, than when mingling with your fellow-creatures."

"I will not say that, I will not say exactly that. I have seen the time when I have thought that God was sufficient for me in the forest, and that I have craved no more than His bounty and His care. But other feelings have got uppermost, and I suppose natur' will have its way. All other creaturs mate, Mabel, and it was intended man should do so too."

"And have you never bethought you of seeking a wife, Pathfinder, to share your fortunes?" inquired the girl, with the directness and simplicity that the pure of heart and the undesigning are the most apt to manifest, and with that feeling of affection which is inbred in her sex. "To me it seems you only want a home to return to from your wanderings to render your life completely happy. Were I a man, it would be my delight to roam through these forests at will, or to sail over this beautiful lake."

"I understand you, Mabel; and God bless you for thinking of the welfare of men as humble as we are. We have our pleasures, it is true, as well as our gifts, but we might be happier; yes, I do think we might be happier."

"Happier! in what way, Pathfinder? In this pure air, with these cool and shaded forests to wander through, this lovely lake to gaze at and sail upon, with clear consciences, and abundance for all their real wants, men ought to be nothing less than as perfectly happy as their infirmities will allow."

"Every creatur' has its gifts, Mabel, and men have theirs," answered the guide, looking stealthily at his beautiful companion, whose cheeks had flushed and eyes brightened under the ardor of feelings excited by the novelty of her striking situation; "and all must obey them. Do you see yonder pigeon that is just alightin' on the beach—here in a line with the fallen chestnut?"

"Certainly; it is the only thing stirring with life in it, besides ourselves, that is to be seen in this vast solitude."

"Not so, Mabel, not so; Providence makes nothing that lives to live quite alone. Here is its mate, just rising on the wing; it has been feeding near the other beach, but it will not long be separated from its companion."

"I understand you, Pathfinder," returned Mabel, smiling sweetly, though as calmly as if the discourse was with her father. "But a hunter may find a mate, even in this wild region. The Indian girls are affectionate and true, I know; for such was the wife of Arrowhead, to a husband who oftener frowned than smiled."

"That would never do, Mabel, and good would never come of it. Kind must cling to kind, and country to country, if one would find happiness. If, indeed, I could meet with one like you, who would consent to be a hunter's wife, and who would not scorn my ignorance and rudeness, then, indeed, would all the toil of the past appear like the sporting of the young deer, and all the future like sunshine."

"One like me! A girl of my years and indiscretion would hardly make a fit companion for the boldest scout and surest hunter on the lines."

"Ah, Mabel! I fear me that I have been improving a redskin's gifts with a pale-face's natur'? Such a character would insure a wife in an Indian village."

"Surely, surely, Pathfinder, you would not think of choosing one so ignorant, so frivolus, so vain, and so inexperienced as I for your wife?" Mabel would have added, "and as young"; but an instinctive feeling of delicacy repressed the words.

"Any why not, Mabel? If you are ignorant of frontier usages, you know more than all of us of pleasant anecdotes and town customs: as for frivolous, I know not what it means; but if it signifies beauty, ah's me! I fear it is no fault in my eyes. Vain you are not, as is seen by the kind manner in which you listen to all my idle tales about scoutings and trails; and as for experience, that will come with years. Besides, Mabel, I fear men think little of these matters when they are about to take wives: I do."

"Pathfinder, your words—your looks—surely, all this is meant in trifling; you speak in pleasantry?"

"To me it is always agreeable to be near you, Mabel; and I should sleep sounder this blessed night than I have done for a week past, could I think that you find such discourse as pleasant as I do."

We shall not say that Mabel Dunham had not believed herself a favorite with the guide. This her quick feminine sagacity had early discovered; and perhaps she had occasionally thought there had mingled with his regard and friendship some of that manly tenderness which the ruder sex must be coarse, indeed, not to show on occasions to the gentler; but the idea that he seriously sought her for his wife had never before crossed the mind of the spirited and ingenuous girl. Now, however, a gleam of something like the truth broke in upon her imagination, less induced by the words of her companion, perhaps, than by his manner. Looking earnestly into the rugged, honest countenance of the scout, Mabel's own features became concerned and grave; and when she spoke again, it was with a gentleness of manner that attracted him to her even more powerfully than the words themselves were calculated to repel.

"You and I should understand each other, Pathfinder," said she with an earnest sincerity; "nor should there be any cloud between us. You are too upright and frank to meet with anything but sincerity and frankness in return. Surely, surely, all this means nothing—has no other connection with your feelings than such a friendship as one of your wisdom and character would naturally feel for a girl like me?"

"I believe it's all nat'ral, Mabel; yes, I do: the Sergeant tells me he had such feelings towards your own mother, and I think I've seen something like it in the young people I have from time to time guided through the wilderness. Yes, yes, I daresay it's all nat'ral enough, and that makes it come so easy, and is a great comfort to me."

"Pathfinder, your words make me uneasy. Speak plainer, or change the subject for ever. You do not, cannot mean that—you cannot wish me to understand"—even the tongue of the spirited Mabel faltered, and she shrank, with maiden shame, from adding what she wished so earnestly to say. Rallying her courage, however, and determined to know all as soon and as plainly as possible, after a moment's hesitation, she continued—"I mean, Pathfinder, that you do not wish me to understand that you seriously think of me as a wife?"

"I do, Mabel; that's it, that's just it; and you have put the matter in a much better point of view than I with my forest gifts and frontier ways would ever be able to do. The Sergeant and I have concluded on the matter, if it is agreeable to you, as he thinks is likely to be the case; though I doubt my own power to please one who deserves the best husband America can produce."

Mabel's countenance changed from uneasiness to surprise; and then, by a transition still quicker, from surprise to pain.

"My father!" she exclaimed—"my dear father has thought of my becoming your wife, Pathfinder?"

"Yes, he has, Mabel, he has, indeed. He has even thought such a thing might be agreeable to you, and has almost encouraged me to fancy it might be true."

"But you yourself—you certainly can care nothing whether this singular expectation shall ever be realized or not?"

"Anan?"

"I mean, Pathfinder, that you have talked of this match more to oblige my father than anything else; that your feelings are no way concerned, let my answer be what it may?"

The scout looked earnestly into the beautiful face of Mabel, which had flushed with the ardor and novelty of her sensations, and it was not possible to mistake the intense admiration that betrayed itself in every lineament of his ingenuous countenance.

"I have often thought myself happy, Mabel, when ranging the woods on a successful hunt, breathing the pure air of the hills, and filled with vigor and health; but I now know that it has all been idleness and vanity compared with the delight it would give me to know that you thought better of me than you think of most others."

"Better of you!—I do, indeed, think better of you, Pathfinder, than of most others: I am not certain that I do not think better of you than of any other; for your truth, honesty, simplicity, justice, and courage are scarcely equalled by any of earth."

"Ah, Mabel, these are sweet and encouraging words from you! and the Sergeant, after all, was not so near wrong as I feared."

"Nay, Pathfinder, in the name of all that is sacred and just, do not let us misunderstand each other in a matter of so much importance. While I esteem, respect, nay, reverence you, almost as much as I reverence my own dear father, it is impossible that I should ever become your wife—that I—"

The change in her companion's countenance was so sudden and so great, that the moment the effect of what she had uttered became visible in the face of the Pathfinder, Mabel arrested her own words, notwithstanding her strong desire to be explicit, the reluctance with which she could at any time cause pain being sufficient of itself to induce the pause. Neither spoke for some time, the shade of disappointment that crossed the rugged lineaments of the hunter amounting so nearly to anguish as to frighten his companion, while the sensation of choking became so strong in the Pathfinder that he fairly griped his throat, like one who sought physical relief for physical suffering. The convulsive manner in which his fingers worked actually struck the alarmed girl with a feeling of awe.

"Nay, Pathfinder," Mabel eagerly added, the instant she could command her voice—"I may have said more than I mean; for all things of this nature are possible, and women, they say, are never sure of their own minds. What I wish you to understand is, that it is not likely that you and I should ever think of each other as man and wife ought to think of each other."

"I do not—I shall never think in that way again, Mabel," gasped forth the Pathfinder, who appeared to utter his words like one just raised above the pressure of some suffocating substance. "No, no, I shall never think of you, or any one else, again in that way."

"Pathfinder, dear Pathfinder, understand me; do not attach more meaning to my words than I do myself: a match like that would be unwise, unnatural, perhaps."

"Yes, unnat'ral—ag'in natur'; and so I told the Sergeant, but he *would* have it otherwise."

"Pathfinder! oh, this is worse than I could have imagined! Take my hand, excellent Pathfinder, and let me see that you do not hate me. For God's sake, smile upon me again."

"Hate you, Mabel! Smile upon you! Ah's me!"

"Nay, give me your hand; your hardy, true, and manly hand—both, both, Pathfinder! for I shall not be easy until I feel certain that we are friends again, and that all this has been a mistake."

"Mabel!" said the guide, looking wistfully into the face of the generous and impetuous girl, as she held his two hard and sunburnt hands in her own pretty and delicate fingers, and laughing in his own silent and peculiar manner, while anguish gleamed over lineaments which seemed incapable of deception, even while agitated with emotions so conflicting—"Mabel! the Sergeant was wrong."

The pent-up feelings could endure no more, and the tears rolled down the cheeks of the scout like rain. His fingers again worked convulsively at his throat; and his breast heaved, as if it possessed a tenant of which it would be rid, by any effort, however desperate.

"Pathfinder! Pathfinder!" Mabel almost shrieked; "anything but this, anything but this! Speak to me, Pathfinder! smile again, say one kind word, anything to prove you can forgive me."

"The Sergeant was wrong!" exclaimed the guide, laughing amid his agony, in a way to terrify his companion by the unnatural mixture of anguish and light-heartedness. "I knew it, I knew it, and said it; yes, the Sergeant was wrong after all."

"We can be friends, though we cannot be man and wife," continued Mabel, almost as much disturbed as her companion, scarcely knowing what she said; "we can always be friends, and always will."

"I thought the Sergeant was mistaken," resumed the Pathfinder, when a great effort had enabled him to command himself, "for I did not think my gifts were such as would please the fancy of a town-bred girl. It would have been better, Mabel, had he not over-persuaded me into a different notion; and it might have been better, too, had you not been so pleasant and confiding like; yes, it would."

"If I thought any error of mine had raised false expectations in you, Pathfinder, however unintentionally on my part, I should never forgive myself; for, believe me, I would rather endure pain in my own feelings than you should suffer."

"That's just it, Mabel, that's just it. These speeches and opinions, spoken in so soft a voice, and in a way I'm so unused to in the woods, have done the mischief. But I now see plainly, and begin to understand the difference between us better, and will strive to keep down thought, and to go abroad again as I used to do, looking for the game and the inimy. Ah's me, Mabel! I have indeed been on a false trail since we met."

"In a little while you will forget all this, and think of me as a friend, who owes you her life."

"This may be the way in the towns, but I doubt if it's nat'ral to the woods. With us, when the eye sees a lovely sight, it is apt to keep it long in view, or when the mind takes in an upright and proper feeling, it is loath to part with it."

"You will forget it all, when you come seriously to recollect that I am altogether unsuited to be your wife."

"So I told the Sergeant; but he would have it otherwise. I knew you was too young and beautiful for one of middle age, like myself, and who never was comely to look at even in youth; and then your ways have not been my ways; nor would a hunter's cabin be a fitting place for one who was edicated among chiefs, as it were. If I were younger and comelier, though, like Jasper Eau-douce—"

"Never mind Jasper Eau-douce," interrupted Mabel impatiently; "we can talk of something else."

"Jasper is a worthy lad, Mabel; ay, and a comely," returned the guileless guide, looking earnestly at the girl, as if he distrusted her judgment in speaking slightingly of his friend. "Were I only half as comely as Jasper Western, my misgivings in this affair would not have been so great, and they might not have been so true."

"We will not talk of Jasper Western," repeated Mabel, the color mounting to her temples; "he may be good enough in a gale, or on the lake, but he is not good enough to talk of here."

"I fear me, Mabel, he is better than the man who is likely to be your husband, though the Sergeant says that never can take place. But the Sergeant was wrong once, and he may be wrong twice."

"And who is likely to be my husband, Pathfinder! This is scarcely less strange than what has just passed between us."

"I know it is nat'ral for like to seek like, and for them that have consorted much with officers' ladies to wish to be officers' ladies themselves. But, Mabel, I may speak plainly to you, I know; and I hope my words will not give you pain; for, now I understand what it is to be disappointed in such feelings, I wouldn't wish to cause even a Mingo sorrow on this head. But happiness is not always to be found in a marquee, any more than in a tent; and though the officers' quarters may look more tempting than the rest of the barracks, there is often great misery between husband and wife inside of their doors."

"I do not doubt it in the least, Pathfinder; and, did it rest with me to decide, I would sooner follow you to some cabin in the woods, and share your fortune, whether it might be better or worse, than go inside the door of any officer I know, with an intention of remaining there as its master's wife."

"Mabel, this is not what Lundie hopes, or Lundie thinks."

"And what care I for Lundie? He is major of the 55th, and may command his men to wheel and march about as he pleases; but he cannot compel me to wed the greatest or the meanest of his mess. Besides, what can you know of Lundie's wishes on such a subject?"

"From Lundie's own mouth. The Sergeant had told him that he wished me for a son-in-law; and the Major, being an old and a true friend, conversed with me on the subject. He put it to me plainly, whether it would not be more ginerous in me to let an officer succeed, than to strive to make you share a hunter's fortune. I owned the truth, I did; and that was, that I thought it might; but when he told me that the Quartermaster would be his choice, I would not abide by the conditions. No, no Mabel; I know Davy Muir well, and though he may make you a lady, he can never make you a happy woman, or himself a gentleman."

"My father has been very wrong if he has said or done aught to cause you sorrow, Pathfinder; and so great is my respect for you, so sincere my friendship, that were it not for one—I mean that no person need fear Lieutenant Muir's influence with me—I would rather remain as I am to my dying day than become a lady at the cost of being his wife."

"I do not think you would say that which you do not feel, Mabel," returned Pathfinder earnestly.

"Not at such a moment, on such a subject, and least of all to you. No; Lieutenant Muir may find wives where he can—my name shall never be on his catalogue."

"Thank you, thank you for that, Mabel; for, though there is no longer any hope for me, I could never be happy were you to take to the Quartermaster. I feared the commission might count for something, I did; and I know the man. It is not jealousy that makes me speak in this manner, but truth, for I know the man. Now, were you to fancy a desarving youth, one like Jasper Western, for instance—"

"Why always mention Jasper Eau-douce, Pathfinder? he can have no concern with our friendship; let us talk of yourself, and of the manner in which you intend to pass the winter."

"Ah's me!—I'm little worth at the best, Mabel, unless it may be on a trail or with the rifle; and less worth now that I have discovered the Sergeant's mistake. There is no need, therefore, of talking of me. It has been very pleasant to me to be near you so long, and even to fancy that the Sergeant was right; but that is all over now. I shall go down the lake with Jasper, and then there will be business to occupy us, and that will keep useless thoughts out of the mind."

"And you will forget this—forget me—no, not forget me, either, Pathfinder; but you will resume your old pursuits, and cease to think a girl of sufficient importance to disturb your peace?"

"I never knowed it afore, Mabel; but girls are of more account in this life than I could have believed. Now, afore I knowed you, the new-born babe did not sleep more sweetly than I used; my head was no sooner on the root, or the stone, or mayhap on the skin, than all was lost to the senses, unless it might be to go over in the night the business of the day in a dream like; and there I lay till the moment came to be stirring, and the swallows were not more certain to be on the wing with the light, than I to be afoot at the moment I wished to be. All this seemed a gift, and might be calculated on even in the midst of a Mingo camp; for I've been outlying in my time, in the very villages of the vagabonds."

"And all this will return to you, Pathfinder, for one so upright and sincere will never waste his happiness on a mere fancy. You will dream again of your hunts, of the deer you have slain, and of the beaver you have taken."

"Ah's me, Mabel, I wish never to dream again! Before we met, I had a sort of pleasure in following up the hounds, in fancy, as it might be; and even in striking a trail of the Iroquois—nay, I've been in scrimmages and ambushments, in thought like, and found satisfaction in it, according to my gifts; but all those things have lost their charms since I've made acquaintance with you. Now, I think no longer of anything rude in my dreams; but the very last night we stayed in the garrison I imagined I had a cabin in a grove of sugar maples, and at the root of every tree was a Mabel Dunham, while the birds among the branches sang ballads instead of the notes that natur' gave, and even the deer stopped to listen. I tried to shoot a fa'n, but Killdeer missed fire, and the creatur' laughed in my face, as pleasantly as a young girl laughs in her merriment, and then it bounded away, looking back as if expecting me to follow."

"No more of this, Pathfinder; we'll talk no more of these things," said Mabel, dashing the tears from her eyes; for the simple, earnest manner in which this hardy woodsman betrayed the deep hold she had taken of his feelings nearly proved too much for her own generous heart. "Now, let us look for my father; he cannot be distant, as I heard his gun quite near.". . .

FROM

THE PIONEERS

[IN *The Pioneers* Natty is in his early seventies. Lake Otsego, the Glimmerglass of *The Deerslayer,* has now been settled, and in this first novel of the series Cooper gives us a picture of Cooperstown as he remembered it from childhood. In the novel the town is called Templeton. The pastoral pictures Cooper has given us of frontier life—a more civilized frontier, it should be said, than the western frontier of a later date—adjusting itself harmoniously to the rhythm of the seasons as the year runs its course, are vivid, and often of great beauty. The character of Leatherstocking is not yet fully developed, but the outline is already firmly sketched in, and Leatherstocking's hatred of the waste and brutality of the settlements is nowhere better pictured than in the following chapter.]

CHAPTER 22

FROM THIS time to the close of April, the weather continued to be a succession of great and rapid changes. One day, the soft airs of spring would seem to be stealing along the valley, and, in unison with an invigorating sun, attempting, covertly, to rouse the dormant powers of the vegetable world; while on the next, the surly blasts from the north would sweep across the lake, and erase every impression left by their gentle adversaries. The snow, however, finally disappeared, and the green wheat fields were seen in every direction, spotted with the dark and charred stumps that had, the preceding season, supported some of the proudest trees of the forest. Ploughs were in motion, wherever those useful implements could be used, and the smokes of the sugar-camps were no longer seen issuing from the summits of the woods of maple. The lake had lost all the characteristic beauty of a field of ice, but still a dark and gloomy covering concealed its waters, for the absence of currents left them yet hid under a porous crust, which, saturated with the fluid, barely retained enough of its strength to preserve the contiguity of its parts. Large flocks of wild geese were seen passing over the country, which hovered, for a time, around the hidden sheet of water, apparently searching for an opening, where they might find a resting-place; and then, on finding themselves excluded by the chill covering, would soar away to the north, filling the air with their discordant screams, as if venting their complaints at the tardy operations of nature.

For a week, the dark covering of the Otsego was left to the undisturbed possession of two eagles, who alighted on the centre of its field, and sat proudly eyeing the extent of their undisputed territory. During the presence of these monarchs of the air, the flocks of migrating birds avoided crossing the plain of ice, by turning into the hills, apparently seeking the protection of the forests, while the white and bald heads of the tenants of the lake were turned upward, with a look of majestic contempt, as if penetrating to the very heavens with the acuteness of their vision. But the time had come, when even these kings of birds were to be dispossessed. An opening had been gradually increasing, at the lower extremity of the lake, and around the dark spot where the current of the river had prevented the formation of ice, during even the coldest weather; and the fresh southerly winds, that now breathed freely up the valley, obtained an impression on the waters. Mimic waves began to curl over the margin of the frozen field, which exhibited an outline of crystallizations, that slowly receded towards the north. At each step the power of the winds and the waves increased, until, after a struggle of a few hours, the turbulent little billows succeeded in setting the whole field in an undulating motion, when it was driven beyond the reach of the eye, with a rapidity that was as magical as the change produced in the scene by this expulsion of the lingering remnant of winter. Just as the last sheet of agitated ice was disappearing in the distance, the eagles rose over the border of crystals, and soared with a wide sweep far above the clouds, while the waves tossed their little caps of snow into the air, as if rioting in their release from a thraldom of five months' duration.

The following morning Elizabeth was awakened by the exhilarating sounds of the martins, who were quarreling and chattering around the little boxes that were suspended above her windows, and the cries of Richard, who was calling, in tones as animating as the signs of the season itself—

"Awake! awake! my lady fair! the gulls are hovering over the lake already, and the heavens are alive with the pigeons. You may look an hour before you can find a hole, through which to get a peep at the sun. Awake! awake! lazy ones! Benjamin is overhauling the ammunition, and we only wait for our breakfasts, and away for the mountains and pigeon shooting."

There was no resisting this animated appeal, and in a few minutes Miss Temple and her friend descended to the parlor. The doors of the hall were thrown open, and the mild, balmy air of a clear spring morning was ventilating the apartment, where the vigilance of the ex-steward had been so long maintaining an artificial heat with such unremitted diligence. The gentlemen were impatiently waiting for their morning's repast, each being equipt in the garb of a sportsman. Mr. Jones made many visits to the southern door, and would cry—

"See, cousin Bess! see, 'duke, the pigeon-roosts of the south have broken up! They are growing more thick every instant. Here is a flock that the eye cannot see the end of. There is food enough in it to keep the army of Xerxes for a month, and feathers enough to make beds for the whole county. Xerxes, Mr. Edwards, was a Grecian king, who—no, he was a Turk, or a Persian, who wanted to conquer Greece, just the same as these rascals will overrun our wheat-fields, when they come back in the fall. Away! away! Bess, I long to pepper them from the mountain."

In this wish both Marmaduke and young Edwards seemed equally to participate, for the sight was most exhilarating to a sportsman; and the ladies soon dismissed the party, after a hasty breakfast.

If the heavens were alive with pigeons, the whole village seemed equally in motion, with men, women, and children. Every species of fire-arms, from the French ducking-gun, with its barrel of near six feet in length, to the common horseman's pistol, was to be seen in the hands of the men and boys; while bows and arrows, some made of the simple stick of a walnut sapling, and others in a rude imitation of the ancient crossbows, were carried by many of the latter.

The houses and the signs of life apparent in the village, drove the alarmed birds from the direct line of their flight, towards the mountains, along the sides and near the bases of which they were glancing in dense masses, that were equally wonderful by the rapidity of their motion, as by their incredible numbers.

We have already said, that across the inclined plane which fell from the steep ascent of the mountain to the banks of the Susquehanna, ran the highway, on either side of which a clearing of many acres had been made at a very early day. Over those clearings, and up the eastern mountain, and along the dangerous path that was cut into its side, the different individuals posted themselves, as suited their inclinations; and in a few moments the attack commenced.

Among the sportsmen was to be seen the tall, gaunt form of Leatherstocking, who was walking over the field, with his rifle hanging on his arm, his dogs following close at his heels, now scenting the dead or wounded birds, that were beginning to tumble from the flocks, and then crouching under the legs of their master, as if they participated in his feelings at this wasteful and unsportsmenlike execution.

The reports of the fire-arms became rapid, whole volleys rising from the plain, as flocks of more than ordinary numbers darted over the opening, covering the field with darkness, like an interposing cloud; and then the light smoke of a single piece would issue from among the leafless bushes on the mountain, as death was hurled on the retreat of the affrighted birds, who were rising from a volley, for many feet into the air, in a vain effort to escape the attacks of man. Arrows, and missiles of every kind, were seen in the midst of the flocks; and so numerous were the birds, and so low did they take their flight, that even long poles, in the hands of those on the sides of the mountain, were used to strike them to earth.

During all this time, Mr. Jones, who disdained the humble and ordinary means of destruction used by his companions, was busily occupied, aided by Benjamin, in making arrangements for an assault of a more than ordinarily fatal character. Among the relics of the old military excursions, that occasionally are discovered throughout the different districts of New York, there had been found in Templeton, at its settlement, a small swivel, which would carry a ball of a pound weight. It was thought to have been deserted by a war party of the whites, in one of their inroads into the Indian settlements, when, perhaps their convenience or the necessities induced them to leave such an encumbrance behind them in the woods. This miniature cannon had been released from the rust, and being mounted on little wheels, was now in a state for actual service. For several years, it was the sole organ for extraordinary rejoicings that was used in those mountains. On the mornings of the Fourths of July, it would be heard, with its echoes ringing among the hills, and telling forth its sounds, for thirteen times, with all the dignity of a two-and-thirty pounder; and even Captain Hollister, who was the highest authority in that part of the country on all such occasions, affirmed that considering its dimensions, it was no despicable gun for a salute. It was somewhat the worse for the service it had performed, it is true, there being but a trifling difference in size between the touch-hole and the muzzle. Still, the grand conceptions of Richard had suggested the importance of such an instrument, in hurling death at his nimble enemies. The swivel was dragged by a horse into a part of the open space, that the Sheriff thought most eligible for planting a battery of the kind, and Mr. Pump proceeded to load it. Several handfuls of duck-shot were placed on top of the powder, and the Major-domo soon announced that his piece was ready for service.

The sight of such an implement collected all the

idle spectators to the spot, who, being mostly boys, filled the air with their cries of exultation and delight. The gun was pointed on high and Richard, holding a coal of fire in a pair of tongs, patiently took his seat on a stump, awaiting the appearance of a flock that was worthy of his notice.

So prodigious was the number of the birds, that the scattering fire of the guns, with the hurling of missiles, and the cries of the boys, had no other effect than to break off small flocks from the immense masses that continued to dart along the valley, as if the whole creation of the feathered tribe were pouring through that one pass. None pretended to collect the game, which lay scattered over the fields in such profusion as to cover the very ground with the fluttering victims.

Leatherstocking was a silent, but uneasy spectator of all these proceedings, but was able to keep his sentiments to himself until he saw the introduction of the swivel into the sports.

"This comes of settling a country!" he said—"here have I known the pigeons to fly for forty long years, and, till you made your clearings, there was nobody to skear or to hurt them. I loved to see them come into the woods, for they were company to a body; hurting nothing; being, as it was, as harmless as a garter-snake. But now it gives me sore thoughts when I hear the frighty things whizzing through the air, for I know its only a motion to bring out all the brats in the village at them. Well! the Lord won't see the waste of his creaters for nothing, and right will be done to the pigeons, as well as others, by-and-by. There's Mr. Oliver, as bad as the rest of them, firing into the flocks as if he was shooting down nothing but the Mingo warriors."

Among the sportsmen was Billy Kirby, who, armed with an old musket, was leading, and without even looking into the air, was firing and shouting as his victims fell even on his own person. He heard the speech of Natty, and took upon himself to reply—

"What's that, old Leatherstocking!" he cried, "grumbling at the loss of a few pigeons! If you had to sow your wheat twice, and three times, as I have done, you wouldn't be so massyfully feeling'd to'ards the divils.—Hurrah, boys! scatter the feathers. This is better than shooting at a turkey's head and neck, old fellow."

"It's better for you, maybe, Billy Kirby," replied the indignant old hunter, "and all them as don't know how to put a ball down a rifle barrel, or how to bring it up ag'n with a true aim; but it's wicked to be shooting into flocks in this wasty manner; and none do it, who know how to knock over a single bird. If a body has a craving for pigeon's flesh, why! it's made the same as all other creater's, for man's eating, but not to kill twenty and eat one. When I want such a thing I go into the woods till I find one to my liking, and then I shoot him off the branches without touching a feather of another, though there might be a hundred on the same tree. But you couldn't do such a thing, Billy Kirby—you couldn't do it if you tried."

"What's that you say, you old dried cornstalk! you sapless stub!" cried the wood-chopper. "You've grown mighty boasting, sin' you killed the turkey; but if you're for a single shot, here goes at that bird which comes on by himself."

The fire from the distant part of the field had driven a single pigeon below the flock to which it had belonged, and frightened with the constant reports of the muskets, it was approaching the spot where the disputants stood, darting first from one side, and then to the other, cutting the air with the swiftness of lightning, and making a noise with its wings, not unlike the rushing of a bullet. Unfortunately for the wood-chopper, notwithstanding his vaunt, he did not see his bird until it was too late for him to fire as it approached, and he pulled his trigger at the unlucky moment when it was darting immediately over his head. The bird continued its course with incredible velocity.

Natty lowered the rifle from his arm, when the challenge was made, and, waiting a moment, until the terrified victim had got in a line with his eyes, and had dropped near the bank of the lake, he raised it again with uncommon rapidity, and fired. It might have been chance, or it might have been skill, that produced the result; it was probably a union of both; but the pigeon whirled over in the air, and fell into the lake with a broken wing. At the sound of his rifle, both his dogs started from his feet, and in a few minutes the "slut" brought out the bird, still alive.

The wonderful exploit of Leatherstocking was noised through the field with great rapidity, and the sportsmen gathered in to learn the truth of the report.

"What," said young Edwards, "have you really killed a pigeon on the wing, Natty, with a single ball?"

"Haven't I killed loons before now, lad, that dive at the flash?" returned the hunter. "It's much better to kill only such as you want, without wasting your powder and lead, than to be firing into God's creaters in such a wicked manner. But I come out for a bird, and you know the reason why I like small game, Mr. Oliver, and now I have got one I will go home, for I don't relish to see these wasty ways that you are all practysing, as if the least thing wasn't made for use, and not to destroy."

"Thou sayest well, Leatherstocking," cried Marmaduke, "and I begin to think it time to put an end to this work of destruction."

"Put an ind, Judge, to your clearings. An't the woods His work as well as the pigeons? Use, but don't waste. Wasn't the woods made for the beasts and birds to harbour in? and when man wanted their flesh, their skins, or their feathers, there's the place to seek them. But I'll go to the hut with my own game, for I wouldn't touch one of the harmless things that kiver the ground here, looking up with their eyes on me, as if they only wanted tongues to say their thoughts."

With this sentiment in his mouth, Leatherstocking threw his rifle over his arm, and followed by his dogs, stepping across the clearing with great caution, taking care not to tread on one of the wounded birds that lay in his path, he soon entered the bushes on the margin and was hid from view.

Whatever impression the morality of Natty made on the Judge, it was utterly lost on Richard. He availed himself of the gathering of the sportsmen, to lay a plan for one "fell swoop" of destruction. The musket-men were drawn up in battle array, in a line extending on each side of his artillery, with orders to await the signal of firing from himself.

"Stand by, my lads," said Benjamin, who acted as an aid-de-camp on this momentous occasion, "stand by, my hearties, and when Squire Dickens heaves out the signal for to begin firing, d'ye see, you may open upon them in a broadside. Take care and fire low, boys, and you'll be sure to hull the flock."

"Fire low!" shouted Kirby—"hear the old fool! If we fire low we may hit the stumps, but not ruffle a pigeon."

"How should you know, you lubber?" cried Benjamin, with a very unbecoming heat for an officer on the eve of battle—"how should you know, you grampus? Haven't I sailed aboard of the Boadishy for five years? and wasn't it a standing order to fire low, and to hull your enemy? Keep silence at your guns, boys, and mind the order that is passed."

The loud laughs of the musket-men were silenced by the authoritative voice of Richard, who called to them for attention and obedience to his signals.

Some millions of pigeons were supposed to have already passed, that morning over the valley of Templeton; but nothing like the flock that was now approaching had been seen before. It extended from mountain to mountain in one solid blue mass, and the eye looked in vain over the southern hills to find its termination. The front of this living column was distinctly marked by a line, but very slightly indented, so regular and even was the flight. Even Marmaduke forgot the morality of Leatherstocking as it approached, and, in common with the rest, brought his musket to his shoulder.

"Fire!" cried the Sheriff, clapping his coal to the priming of the cannon. As half of Benjamin's charge escaped through the touch-hole, the whole volley of the musketry preceded the report of the swivel. On receiving this united discharge of small arms, the front of the flock darted upward, while, at the same instant, myriads of those in their rear rushed with amazing rapidity into their places, so that when the column of white smoke gushed from the mouth of the little cannon, an accumulated mass of objects was gliding over its point of direction.—The roar of the gun echoed along the mountains, and died away to the north, like distant thunder, while the whole flock of alarmed birds seemed, for a moment, thrown into one disorderly and agitated mass. The air was filled with their irregular flights, layer rising over layer, far above the tops of the highest pines, none daring to advance beyond the dangerous pass; when, suddenly, some of the leaders of the feathered tribe shot across the valley, taking their flight directly over the village, and the hundreds of thousands in their rear followed their example, deserting the eastern side of the plain to their persecutors and their fallen.

"Victory!" shouted Richard, "victory! we have driven the enemy from the field."

"Not so, Dickon," said Marmaduke, "the field is covered with them; and like the Leatherstocking, I see nothing but eyes, in every direction, as the innocent sufferers turn their heads in terror to examine my movements. Full one half of those that have fallen are yet alive: and I think it is time to end the sport; if sport it be."

"Sport!" cried the Sheriff; "it is princely sport! There are some thousands of the blue-coated boys on the ground, so that every old woman in the village may have a pot-pie for the asking."

"Well, we happily frightened the birds from this side of the valley," said Marmaduke, "and our carnage must of necessity end, for the present. Boys, I will give you sixpence a hundred for the pigeons' heads only; so go to work, and bring them into the village, where I will pay you."

This expedient produced the desired effect, for every urchin on the ground went industriously to work to wring the necks of the wounded birds.

Judge Temple retired towards his dwelling with that kind of feeling, that many a man has experienced before him, who discovers, after the excitement of the moment has passed, that he has purchased pleasure at the price of misery to others. Horses were loaded with the dead; and, after the first burst of sporting, the shooting of pigeons became a business, for the remainder of the season, more in proportion to the people. Richard, however, boasted for many a year, of his shot with the "cricket;" and Benjamin gravely asserted, that he thought they killed nearly as many pigeons on that day, as there were Frenchmen destroyed on the memorable occasion of Rodney's victory.

FROM

THE AMERICAN DEMOCRAT

◇

THERE is a long line of distinguished books that have attempted to analyze and define the political and social genius of this country at various points in its history. The list includes the early *Letters from an American Farmer* (1782) by St. Jean de Crèvecoeur, Alexis de Tocqueville's *Democracy in America* (1835), and Henry James's *The American Scene* (1907). Among these *The American Democrat*, published in 1838, should hold an honored place. It is as relevant to contemporary America as to Cooper's own day. It is a short book of forty-six chapters (probably intended by Cooper originally as an elementary school text) in which he analyzes the form of the American government and points out political dangers and social illusions which attend it. Although a Jacksonian Democrat, Cooper often sounds here very much like the Federalist John Adams, a man whose political philosophy in the end resembled Jeffersonian agrarianism more closely than it did the brand of capitalism sponsored by his own party under Hamilton. Cooper's Introduction makes his intention clear:

> The writer believes himself to be as good a democrat as there is in America. But his democracy is not of the impracticable school. He prefers a democracy to any other system, on account of its comparative advantages, and not on account of its perfection. He knows it has evils; great and increasing evils, and evils peculiar to itself; but he believes that monarchy and aristocracy have more. It will be very apparent to all who read this book, that he is not a believer in the scheme of raising men very far above their natural propensities.

◇

ADVANTAGES OF A DEMOCRACY

THE PRINCIPAL advantage of a democracy, is a general elevation in the character of the people. If few are raised to a very great height, few are depressed very low. As a consequence, the average of society is much more respectable than under any other form of government. The vulgar charge that the tendency of democracies is to levelling, meaning to drag all down to the level of the lowest, is singularly untrue, its real tendency being to elevate the depressed to a condition not unworthy of their manhood. In the absence of privileged orders, entails and distinctions, devised permanently to separate men into social castes, it is true none are great but those who become so by their acts, but, confining the remark to the upper classes of society, it would be much more true to say that democracy refuses to lend itself to unnatural and arbitrary distinctions, than to accuse it of a tendency to level those who have a just claim to be elevated. A denial of a favor, is not an invasion of a right.

Democracies are exempt from the military charges, both pecuniary and personal, that become necessary in governments in which the majority are subjects, since no force is required to repress those who, under other systems, are dangerous to the state, by their greater physical power.

As the success of democracies is mainly dependant on the intelligence of the people, the means of preserving the government are precisely those which most conduce to the happiness and social progress of man. Hence we find the state endeavoring to raise its citizens in the scale of being, the certain means of laying the broadest foundation of national prosperity. If the arts are advanced in aristocracies, through the taste of patrons, in democracies, though of slower growth, they will prosper as a consequence of general information; or as a superstructure reared on a wider and more solid foundation.

Democracies being, as nearly as possible, founded in natural justice, little violence is done to the sense of right by the institutions, and men have less occasion than usual, to resort to fallacies and false principles in cultivating the faculties. As a consequence, common sense is more encouraged, and the community is apt to entertain juster notions of all moral truths, than under systems that are necessarily sophisticated. Society is thus a gainer in the greatest element of happiness, or in the right perception of the different relations between men and things.

Democracies being established for the common interests, and the publick agents being held in constant check by the people, their general tendency is to serve the whole community, and not small portions of it, as is the case in narrow governments. It is as rational to suppose that a hungry man will first help his neighbor to bread, when master of his own acts, as to suppose that any but those who feel themselves to be truly public servants, will first bethink themselves of the publick, when in situations of publick trust. In a government of one, that one and his parasites will be the first and best served; in a government of a few, the few; and in a government of many, the many. Thus the general tendency of democratical institutions is to equalize advantages, and to spread its blessings over the entire surface of society.

Democracies, other things being equal, are the cheapest form of government, since little money is lavished in representation, and they who have to pay the taxes, have also, directly or indirectly, a voice in imposing them.

Democracies are less liable to popular tumults than any other polities, because the people, having legal means in their power to redress wrongs, have little inducement to employ any other. The man who can right himself by a vote, will seldom resort to a musket. Grievances, moreover, are less frequent, the most corrupt representatives of a democratick constituency generally standing in awe of its censure.

As men in bodies usually defer to the right, unless acting under erroneous impressions, or excited by sudden resentments, democracies pay more respect to abstract justice, in the management of their foreign concerns, than either aristocracies or monarchies, an appeal always lying against abuses, or violations of principle, to a popular sentiment, that, in the end, seldom fails to decide in favor of truth.

In democracies, with a due allowance for the workings of personal selfishness, it is usually a motive with those in places of trust, to consult the interests of the mass, there being little doubt, that in this system, the entire community has more regard paid to its wants and wishes, than in either of the two others.

ON THE DISADVANTAGES OF DEMOCRACY

DEMOCRACIES are liable to popular impulses, which, necessarily arising from imperfect information, often work injustice from good motives. Tumults of the people are less apt to occur in democracies than under any other form of government, for, possessing the legal means of redressing themselves, there is less necessity to resort to force, but, public opinion constituting, virtually, the power of the state, measures are more apt to be influenced by sudden mutations of sentiment, than under systems where the rulers have better opportunities and more leisure for examination. There is more feeling and less design in the movements of masses than in those of small bodies, except as design emanates from demagogues and political managers.

The efforts of the masses that are struggling to obtain their rights, in monarchies and aristocracies, however, are not to be imputed to democracy; in such cases, the people use their natural weapon, force, merely because they are denied any participation in the legal authority.

When democracies are small, these impulses frequently do great injury to the public service, but in large states they are seldom of sufficient extent to produce results before there is time to feel the influence of reason. It is, therefore, one of the errors of politicians to imagine democracies more practicable in small than in large communities, an error that has probably arisen from the fact that, the ignorance of masses having hitherto put men at the mercy of the combinations of the affluent and intelligent, democracies have been permitted to exist only in countries insignificant by their wealth and numbers.

Large democracies, on the other hand, while less exposed to the principal evil of this form of government, than smaller, are unable to scrutinize and understand character with the severity and intelligence that are of so much importance in all representative governments, and consequently the people are peculiarly exposed to become the dupes of demagogues and political schemers, most of the crimes of democracies arising from the faults and designs of men of this character, rather than from the propensities of the people, who, having little temptation to do wrong, are seldom guilty of crimes except through ignorance.

Democracies are necessarily controlled by publick opinion, and failing of the means of obtaining power more honestly, the fraudulent and ambitious find a motive to mislead, and even to corrupt the common sentiment, to attain their ends. This is the greatest and most pervading danger of all large democracies, since it is sapping the foundations of society, by undermining its virtue. We see the effects of this baneful influence, in the openness and audacity with which men avow improper motives and improper acts, trusting to find support in a popular feeling, for while vicious influences are perhaps more admitted in other countries, than in America, in none are they so openly avowed.

It may also be urged against democracies, that,

nothing being more corrupting than the management of human affairs, which are constantly demanding sacrifices of permanent principles to interests that are as constantly fluctuating, their people are exposed to assaults on their morals from this quarter, that the masses of other nations escape. It is probable, however, that this evil, while it ought properly to be enumerated as one of the disadvantages of the system, is more than counterbalanced by the main results, even on the score of morals.

The constant appeals to public opinion in a democracy, though excellent as a corrective of public vices, induce private hypocrisy, causing men to conceal their own convictions when opposed to those of the mass, the latter being seldom wholly right, or wholly wrong. A want of national manliness is a vice to be guarded against, for the man who would dare to resist a monarch, shrinks from opposing an entire community. That the latter is quite often wrong, however, is abundantly proved by the fact, that its own judgments fluctuate, as it reasons and thinks differently this year, or this month even, from what it reasoned and thought the last.

The tendency of democracies is, in all things, to mediocrity, since the tastes, knowledge and principles of the majority form the tribunal of appeal. This circumstance, while it certainly serves to elevate the average qualities of a nation, renders the introduction of a high standard difficult. Thus do we find in literature, the arts, architecture and in all acquired knowledge, a tendency in America to gravitate towards the common center in this, as in other things; lending a value and estimation to mediocrity that are not elsewhere given. It is fair to expect, however, that a foundation so broad, may in time sustain a superstructure of commensurate proportions, and that the influence of masses will in this, as in the other interests, have a generally beneficial effect. Still it should not be forgotten that, with the exception of those works, of which, as they appeal to human sympathies or the practices of men, an intelligent public is the best judge, the mass of no community is qualified to decide the most correctly on any thing, which, in its nature, is above its reach.

It is a besetting vice of democracies to substitute publick opinion for law. This is the usual form in which masses of men exhibit their tyranny. When the majority of the entire community commits this fault it is a sore grievance, but when local bodies, influenced by local interests, pretend to style themselves the publick, they are assuming powers that properly belong to the whole body of the people, and to them only under constitutional limitations. No tyranny of one, nor any tyranny of the few, is worse than this. All attempts in the publick, therefore, to do that which the publick has no right to do, should be frowned upon as the precise form in which tyranny is the most apt to be displayed in a democracy.

Democracies, depending so much on popular opinion are more liable to be influenced to their injury, through the management of foreign and hostile nations, than other governments. It is generally known that, in Europe, secret means are resorted to, to influence sentiment in this way, and we have witnessed in this country open appeals to the people, against the acts of their servants, in matters of foreign relations, made by foreign, not to say, hostile agents. Perhaps no stronger case can be cited of this weakness on the part of democracies, than is shown in this fact, for here we find men sufficiently audacious to build the hope of so far abusing opinion, as to persuade a people to act directly against their own dignity and interests.

The misleading of publick opinion in one way or another, is the parent of the principal disadvantages of a democracy, for in most instances it is first corrupting a community in order that it may be otherwise injured. Were it not for the counteracting influence of reason, which, in the end, seldom, perhaps never fails to assert its power, this defect would of itself, be sufficient to induce all discreet men to decide against this form of government. The greater the danger, the greater the necessity that all well-intentioned and right-minded citizens should be on their guard against its influence.

It would be hazardous, however, to impute all the peculiar faults of American character, to the institutions, the country existing under so many unusual influences. If the latter were overlooked, one might be induced to think frankness and sincerity of character were less encouraged by popular institutions than was formerly supposed, close observers affirming that these qualities are less frequent here, than in most other countries. When the general ease of society is remembered, there is unquestionably more deception of opinion practised than one would naturally expect, but this failing is properly to be imputed to causes that have no necessary connection with democratical institutions, though men defer to publick opinion, right or wrong, quite as submissively as they defer to princes. Although truths are not smothered altogether in democracies, they are often temporarily abandoned under this malign influence, unless there is a powerful motive to sustain them at the moment. While we see in our own democracy this manifest disposition to defer to the wrong, in matters that are not properly subject to the common sentiment, in deference to the popular will of the hour, there is a singular boldness in the use of personalities, as if men avenged themselves for the restraints of the one case by a licentiousness that is without hazard.

The base feelings of detraction and envy have more room for exhibition, and perhaps a stronger incentive in a democracy, than in other forms of government, in which the people get accustomed to personal deference by the artificial distinctions of the institutions. This is the reason that men become impatient of all superiority in a democracy, and manifest a wish to prefer those who affect a deference to the publick, rather than those who are worthy.

ON STATION

STATION may be divided into that which is political, or publick, and that which is social, or private. In monarchies and aristocracies the two are found united, since the higher classes, as a matter of course, monopolize all the offices of consideration; but, in democracies, there is not, nor is it proper that there should be, any intimate connexion between them.

Political, or publick station, is that which is derived from office, and, in a democracy, must embrace men of very different degrees of leisure, refinement, habits and knowledge. This is characteristick of the institutions, which, under a popular government, confer on political station more power than rank, since the latter is expressly avoided in this system.

Social station is that which one possesses in the ordinary associations, and is dependent on birth, education, personal qualities, property, tastes, habits, and, in some instances, on caprice, or fashion. Although the latter undeniably is sometimes admitted to control social station, it generally depends, however, on the other considerations named.

Social station, in the main, is a consequence of property. So long as there is civilization there must be the rights of property, and so long as there are the rights of property, their obvious consequences must follow. All that democracies legitimately attempt is to prevent the advantages which accompany social station from accumulating rights that do not properly belong to the condition, which is effected by pronouncing that it shall have no factitious political aids.

They who have reasoned ignorantly, or who have aimed at effecting their personal ends by flattering the popular feeling, have boldly affirmed that "one man is as good as another;" a maxim that is true in neither nature, revealed morals, nor political theory.

That one man is not as good as another in natural qualities, is proved on the testimony of our senses. One man is stronger than another; he is handsomer, taller, swifter, wiser, or braver, than all his fellows. In short, the physical and moral qualities are unequally distributed, and, as a necessary consequence, in none of them, can one man be justly said to be as good as another. Perhaps no two human beings can be found so precisely equal in every thing, that one shall not be pronounced the superior of the other; which, of course, establishes the fact that there is no natural equality.

The advocates of exclusive political privileges reason on this circumstance by assuming, that as nature has made differences between men, those institutions which create political orders, are no more than carrying out the great designs of providence. The error of their argument is in supposing it a confirmation of the designs of nature to attempt to supplant her, for, while the latter has rendered men unequal, it is not from male to male, according to the order of primogeniture, as is usually established by human ordinances. In order not to interfere with the inequality of nature, her laws must be left to their own operations, which is just what is done in democracies, after a proper attention has been paid to the peace of society, by protecting the weak against the strong.

That one man is not deemed as good as another in the grand moral system of providence, is revealed to us in Holy Writ, by the scheme of future rewards and punishments, as well as by the whole history of those whom God has favored in this world, for their piety, or punished for their rebellion. As compared with perfect holiness, all men are frail; but, as compared with each other, we are throughout the whole of sacred history made to see, that, in a moral sense, one man is not as good as another. The evil doer is punished, while they who are distinguished for their qualities and acts, are intended to be preferred.

The absolute moral and physical equality that are inferred by the maxim, that "one man is as good as another," would at once do away with the elections, since a lottery would be both simpler, easier and cheaper than the present mode of selecting representatives. Men, in such a case, would draw lots for office, as they are now drawn for juries. Choice supposes a preference, and preference inequality of merit, or of fitness.

We are then to discard all visionary theories on this head, and look at things as they are. All that the most popular institutions attempt, is to prohibit that one *race* of men shall be made better than another by law, from father to son, which would be defeating the intentions of providence, creating a superiority that exists in neither physical nor moral nature, and substituting a political scheme for the will of God and the force of things.

As a principle, one man is as good as another in rights. Such is the extent of the most liberal institutions of this country, and this provision is not general. The slave is not as good as his owner, even in rights. But in those states where slavery does not exist, all men have essentially the same rights, an equality, which, so far from establishing that "one man is as good as another," in a social sense, is the very means of producing the inequality of condition that actually exists. By possessing the same rights to exercise their respective faculties, the active and frugal become more wealthy than the idle and dissolute; the wise and gifted more trusted than the silly and ignorant; the polished and refined more respected and sought, than the rude and vulgar.

In most countries, birth is a principal source of social distinction, society being divided into castes, the noble having an hereditary claim to be the superior of the plebeian. This is an unwise and an arbitrary distinction that has led to most of the social diseases of the old world, and from which America is happily exempt. But great care must be had in construing the principles which have led to this great change, for America is the first important country of modern times, in which such positive distinctions have been destroyed.

Still some legal differences, and more social advantages, are produced by birth, even in America. The child inherits the property, and a portion of the consideration of the parent. Without the first of these privileges, men would not exert themselves to acquire more property than would suffice for their own personal necessities, parental affection being one of the most powerful incentives to industry. Without such an inducement, then, it would follow that civilization would become stationary, or, it would recede; the incentives of individuality and of the affections, being absolutely necessary to impel men to endure the labor and privations that alone can advance it.

The hereditary consideration of the child, so long as it is kept within due bounds, by being confined to a natural sentiment, is also productive of good, since no more active inducement to great and glorious deeds can offer, than the deeply seated interest that man takes in his posterity. All that reason and justice require is effected, by setting bounds to such advantages, in denying hereditary claims to trusts and power; but evil would be the day, and ominous the symptom, when a people shall deny that any portion of the consideration of the ancestor is due to the descendant.

It is as vain to think of altogether setting aside sentiment and the affections, in regulating human affairs, as to imagine it possible to raise a nature, known to be erring and weak, to the level of perfection.

The Deity, in that terrible warning delivered from the mount, where he declares that he "will visit the sins of the fathers upon the children, unto the third and fourth generation," does no more than utter one of those sublime moral truths, which, in conformity with his divine providence, pervade nature. It is merely an announcement of a principle that cannot safely be separated from justice, and one that is closely connected with all the purest motives and highest aspirations of man.

There would be a manifest injustice in visiting the offence of the criminal on his nearest of kin, by making the innocent man participate in the disgrace of a guilty relative, as is notoriously done most, by those most disposed to rail at reflected renown, and not to allow of the same participation in the glory. Both depend upon a sentiment deeper than human laws, and have been established for purposes so evidently useful as to require no explanation. All that is demanded of us, is to have a care that this sentiment do not degenerate to a prejudice, and that, in the one case, we do not visit the innocent too severely, or, in the other, exalt the unworthy beyond the bounds of prudence.

It is a natural consequence of the rights of property and of the sentiment named, that birth should produce some advantages, in a social sense, even in the most democratical of the American communities. The son imbibes a portion of the intelligence, refinement and habits of the father, and he shares in his associations. These must be enumerated as the legitimate advantages of birth, and without invading the private arrangements of families and individuals, and establishing a perfect community of education, they are unavoidable. Men of the same habits, the same degree of cultivation and refinement, the same opinions, naturally associate together, in every class of life. The day laborer will not mingle with the slave; the skilful mechanic feels his superiority over the mere laborer, claims higher wages and has a pride in his craft; the man in trade justly fancies that his habits elevate him above the mechanic, so far as social position is concerned, and the man of refinement, with his education, tastes and sentiments, is superior to all. Idle declamation on these points, does not impair the force of things, and life is a series of facts. These inequalities of condition, of manners, of mental cultivation must exist, unless it be intended to reduce all to a common level of ignorance and vulgarity, which would be virtually to return to a condition of barbarism.

The result of these undeniable facts, is the inequalities of social station, in America, as elsewhere, though it is an inequality that exists without any more arbitrary distinctions than are indispensably connected with the maintenance of civilization. In a social sense, there are orders here, as in all other countries, but the classes run into each other more easily, the lines of separation are less strongly drawn, and their shadows are more intimately blended.

This social inequality of America is an unavoidable result of the institutions, though nowhere proclaimed in them, the different constitutions maintaining a profound silence on the subject, they who framed them probably knowing that it is as much a consequence of civilized society, as breathing is a vital function of animal life.

ON LANGUAGE

LANGUAGE being the medium of thought, its use enters into our most familiar practices. A just, clear and simple expression of our ideas is a necessary accomplishment for all who aspire to be classed with gentlemen and ladies. It renders all more respectable, besides making intercourse more intelligible, safer and more agreeable.

The common faults of American language are an ambition of effect, a want of simplicity, and a turgid abuse of terms. To these may be added ambiguity of expression. Many perversions of significations also exist, and a formality of speech, which, while it renders conversation ungraceful, and destroys its playfulness, seriously weakens the power of the language, by applying to ordinary ideas, words that are suited only to themes of gravity and dignity.

While it is true that the great body of the American people use their language more correctly than the mass of any other considerable nation, it is equally true that a smaller proportion than common attain to elegance in this accomplishment, especially in speech. Contrary to the general law in such matters, the women of the country have a less agreeable utterance than the men, a defect that great care should be taken to remedy, as the nursery is the birthplace of so many of our habits.

The limits of this work will not permit an enumeration of the popular abuses of significations, but a few shall be mentioned, in order that the student may possess a general clue to the faults. "Creek," a word that signifies an *inlet* of the sea, or of a lake, is misapplied to running streams, and frequently to the *outlets* of lakes. A "square," is called a "park;" "lakes," are often called "ponds;" and "arms of the sea," are sometimes termed "rivers."

In pronunciation, the faults are still more numerous, partaking decidedly of provincialisms. The letter *u,* sounded like double *o,* or *oo,* or like *i,* as in vir*too,* for*tin,* for*tinate;* and *ew,* pronounced also like *oo,* are common errors. This is an exceedingly vicious pronunciation, rendering the language mean and vulgar. "New," pronounced as *"noo,"* is an example, and "few," as *"foo;"* the true sounds are *"nu"* and *"fu,"* the *u* retaining its proper soft sound, and not that of *"oo."*

The attempt to reduce the pronunciation of the English language to a common rule, produces much confusion, and taking the usages of polite life as the standard, many uncouth innovations. All know the pronunciation of plough; but it will scarcely do to take this sound as the only power of the same combination of final letters, for we should be compelled to call though, thou; through, throu; and tough, tou.

False accentuation is a common American fault. Ensign (insin,) is called en*syne,* and engine (injin,) en*gyne.* Indeed, it is a common fault of narrow associations, to suppose that words are to be pronounced as they are spelled.

Many words are in a state of mutation, the pronunciation being unsettled even in the best society, a result that must often arise where language is as variable and undetermined as the English. To this class belong "clerk," "cucumber" and "gold," which are often pronounced as spelt, though it were better and more in conformity with polite usage to say "clark," *"cow*cumber," (not cow*cum*ber,) and "goold." For *looten*ant (lieutenant) there is not sufficient authority, the true pronunciation being *"levten*ant." By making a familiar compound of this word, we see the uselessness of attempting to reduce the language to any other laws than those of the usages of polite life, for they who affect to say *looten*ant, do not say *"looten*ant-co-lo-nel," but *"looten*ant-kurnel."

The polite pronunciation of "either" and "neither," is "i-ther" and "ni-ther," and not "eether" and "neether." This is a case in which the better usage of the language has respected derivations, for *"ei,"* in German are pronounced as in "height" and "sleight," *"ie"* making the sound of *"ee."* We see the arbitrary usages of the English, however, by comparing these legitimate sounds with those of the words "lieutenant colonel," which are derived from the French, in which language the latter word is called *"co-lo-nel."*

Some changes of the language are to be regretted, as they lead to false inferences, and society is always a loser by mistaking names for things. Life is a fact, and it is seldom any good arises from a misapprehension of the real circumstances under which we exist. The word "gentleman" has a positive and limited signification. It means one elevated above the mass of society by his birth, manners, attainments, character and social condition. As no civilized society can exist without these social differences, nothing is gained by denying the use of the term. If blackguards were to be *called* "gentlemen," and "gentlemen," "blackguards," the difference between them would be as obvious as it is today.

The word "gentleman," is derived from the French *gentilhomme,* which originally signified one of noble birth. This was at a time when the characteristics of the condition were never found beyond a caste. As society advanced, ordinary men attained the qualifications of nobility, without that of birth, and the meaning of the word was extended. It is now possible to be a gentleman without birth, though, even in America, where such distinctions are purely conditional, they who have birth, except in extraordinary instances, are classed with gentlemen. To call a laborer, one who has neither education, manners, accomplishments, tastes, associations, nor any one of the ordinary requisites, a gentleman, is just as absurd as to call one who is thus qualified, a fellow. The word must have some especial signification, or it would be synonymous with man. One may have gentleman-like feelings, principles and appearance, without possessing the liberal attainments that distinguish the gentleman. Least of all does money alone make a gentleman, though, as it becomes a means of obtaining the other requisites, it is usual to give it a place in the claims of the class. Men may be, and often are, very rich, without having the smallest title to be deemed gentlemen. A man may be a distinguished gentleman, and not possess as much money as his own footman.

This word, however, is sometimes used instead of the old terms, "sirs," "my masters," &c. &c., as in addressing bodies of men. Thus we say "gentlemen," in addressing a publick meeting, in complaisance, and as, by possibility, some gentlemen may be present. This is a license that may be tolerated, though he who should insist that all present were, as individuals, gentlemen, would hardly escape ridicule.

What has just been said of the word gentleman, is equally true with that of lady. The standard of these two classes, rises as society becomes more civilized and refined; the man who might pass for a gentleman in one nation, or community, not being able to maintain the same position in another.

The inefficiency of the effort to subvert things by names, is shown in the fact that, in all civilized communities, there is a class of men, who silently and quietly recognize each other, as gentlemen; who associate together freely and without reserve, and who admit each other's claims without scruple or distrust. This class may be limited by prejudice and arbitrary enactments, as in Europe, or it may have no other rules than those of taste, sentiment and the silent laws of usage, as in America.

The same observations may be made in relation to the words master and servant. He who employs laborers, with the right to command, is a master, and he who lets himself to work, with an obligation to obey, a servant. Thus there are house, or domestic servants, farm servants, shop servants, and various other servants; the term master being in all these cases the correlative.

In consequence of the domestic servants of America having once been Negro slaves, a prejudice has arisen among the laboring classes of the whites, who not only dislike the term servant, but have also reejcted that of master. So far has this prejudice gone, that in lieu of the latter, they have resorted to the use of the word *boss,* which has precisely the same meaning in Dutch! How far a subterfuge of this nature is worthy of a manly and common sense people, will admit of question.

A similar objection may be made to the use of the word "help," which is not only an innovation on a just and established term, but which does not properly convey the meaning intended. They who aid their masters in the toil may be deemed "helps," but they who perform all the labor do not assist, or help to do the thing, but they do it themselves. A man does not usually hire his cook to *help* him cook his dinner, but to cook it herself. Nothing is therefore gained, while something is lost in simplicity and clearness by the substitution of new and imperfect terms, for the long established words of the language. In all cases in which the people of America have retained the *things* of their ancestors, they should not be ashamed to keep the *names.*

The love of turgid expressions is gaining ground, and ought to be corrected. One of the most certain evidences of a man of high breeding, is his simplicity of speech; a simplicity that is equally removed from vulgarity and exaggeration. He calls a spade, a "spade." His enunciation, while clear, deliberate and dignified, is totally without strut, showing his familiarity with the world, and, in some degree, reflecting the qualities of his mind, which is polished without being addicted to sentimentalism, or any other bloated feeling. He never calls his wife, "his lady," but "his wife," and he is not afraid of lessening the dignity of the human race, by styling the most elevated and refined of his fellow creatures, "men and women." He does not say, in speaking of a dance, that "the attire of the ladies was exceedingly elegant and peculiarly becoming at the late assembly," but that "the women were well dressed at the last ball;" nor is he apt to remark, "that the Rev. Mr. G——gave us an elegant and searching discourse the past sabbath," but, that "the parson preached a good sermon last sunday."

The utterance of a gentleman ought to be deliberate and clear, without being measured. All idea of effort should be banished, though nothing lost for want of distinctness. His emphasis ought to be almost imperceptible; never halting, or abrupt; and least of all, so placed as to give an idea of his own sense of cleverness; but regulated by those slight intonations that give point to wit, and force to reason. His language should rise with the subject, and, as he must be an educated and accomplished man, he cannot but know that the highest quality of eloquence, and all sublimity, is in the thought, rather than in the words, though there must be an adaptation of the one to the other.

This is still more true of women than of men, since the former are the natural agents in maintaining the refinement of a people.

All cannot reach the highest standard in such matters, for it depends on early habit, and particularly on early associations. The children of gentlemen are as readily distinguished from other children by these peculiarities, as by the greater delicacy of their minds, and higher tact in breeding. But we are not to abandon all improvement, because perfection is reached but by few. Simplicity should be the first aim, after one is removed from vulgarity, and let the finer shades of accomplishment be acquired as they can be attained. In no case, however, can one who aims at turgid language, exaggerated sentiment, or pedantic utterance, lay claim to be either a man or a woman of the world.

ON THE AMERICAN PRESS

THE NEWSPAPER press of this country is distinguished from that of Europe in several essential particulars. While there are more prints, they are generally of a lower character. It follows that in all in which they are useful, their utility is more diffused through society, and in all in which they are hurtful, the injury they inflict is more widespread and corrupting.

The great number of newspapers in America, is a cause of there being so little capital, and consequently so little intelligence, employed in their management. It is also a reason of the inexactitude of much of the news they circulate. It requires a larger investment of capital than is usual in this country, to obtain correct information; while, on the other hand, the great competition renders editors reckless and impatient to fill their columns. To these circumstances may be added the greater influence of vague and unfounded rumours in a vast and thinly settled country, than on a compact population, covering a small surface.

Discreet and observing men have questioned, whether, after excluding the notices of deaths and marriages, one half of the circumstances that are related in the newspapers of America, as facts, are true in their essential features; and, in cases connected with party politics, it may be questioned if even so large a proportion can be set down as accurate.

This is a terrible picture to contemplate, for when the number of prints is remembered, and the avidity with which they are read is brought into the account, we are made to perceive that the entire nation, in a moral sense, breathes an atmosphere of falsehoods. There is little use, however, in concealing the truth; on the contrary, the dread in which publick men and writers commonly stand of the power of the press to injure them, has permitted the evil to extend so far, that it is scarcely exceeding the bounds of a just alarm, to say that the country cannot much longer exist in safety, under the malign influence that now overshadows it. Any one, who has lived long enough to note changes of the sort, must have perceived how fast men of probity and virtue are loosing their influence in the country, to be superseded by those who scarcely deem an affectation of the higher qualities necessary to their success. This fearful change must, in a great measure, be ascribed to the corruption of the publick press, which, as a whole, owes its existence to the schemes of interested political adventurers.

Those who are little acquainted with the world are apt to imagine that a fact, or an argument, that is stated publickly in print, is entitled to more credit and respect, than the same fact or argument presented orally, or in conversation. So far from this being true, however, in regard to the press of this country, it would be safer to infer the very reverse. Men who are accustomed daily to throw off their mistatements, become reckless of the consequences, and he who would hesitate about committing himself by an allegation made face to face, and as it were on his personal responsibility, would indite a paragraph, behind the impersonality of his editorial character, to be uttered to the world in the irresponsible columns of a journal. It is seldom, in cases which admit of doubt, that men are required to speak on the moment; but, with the compositor in waiting, the time pressing, and the moral certainty that a rival establishment will circulate the questionable statement if he decline, the editor too often throws himself into the breach. The contradiction of to-day, will make a paragraph, as well as the lie of yesterday, though he who sees the last and not the first, unless able to appreciate the character of his authority, carries away an untruth.

Instead of considering the editor of a newspaper, as an abstraction, with no motive in view but that of maintaining principles and disseminating facts, it is necessary to remember that he is a man, with all the interests and passions of one who has chosen this means to advance his fortunes, and of course, with all the accompanying temptations to abuse his opportunities, and this too, usually, with the additional drawback of being a partisan in politics, religion, or literature. If the possession of power, in ordinary cases, is a constant inducement to turn it to an unjust profit, it is peculiarly so in the extraordinary case of the control of a public press.

Editors praise their personal friends, and abuse their enemies in print, as private individuals praise their friends, and abuse their enemies with their tongues. Their position increases the number of each, and the consequence is, that the readers obtain inflated views of the first, and unjust notions of the last.

If newspapers are useful in overthrowing tyrants, it is only to establish a tyranny of their own. The press tyrannizes over publick men, letters, the arts, the stage, and even over private life. Under the pretence of protecting publick morals, it is corrupting them to the core, and under the semblance of maintaining liberty, it is gradually establishing a despotism as ruthless, as grasping, and one that is quite as vulgar as that of any christian state known. With loud professions of freedom of opinion, there is no tolerance; with a parade of patriotism, no sacrifice of interests; and with fulsome panegyrics on propriety, too frequently, no decency.

There is but one way of extricating the mind from the baneful influence of the press of this country, and that is by making a rigid analysis of its nature and motives. By remembering that all statements that involve disputed points are *ex parte;* that there is no impersonality, except in professions; that all the ordinary passions and interests act upon its statements with less than the ordinary responsibilities; and that there is the constant temptation to abuse, which ever accompanies power, one may come, at last, to a just appreciation of its merits, and in a degree, learn to neutralize its malignant influence. But this is a freedom of mind that few attain, for few have the means of arriving at these truths!

The admixture of truth and falsehood in the intelligence circulated by the press, is one of the chief causes of its evils. A journal that gave utterance to nothing but untruths, would loose its influence with its character, but there are none so ignorant as not to see the necessity of occasionally issuing truths. It is only in cases in which the editor has a direct interest to the contrary, in which he has not the leisure or the means of ascertaining facts, or in which he is himself misled by the passions, cupidity and interests of others, that untruths find a place in his columns. Still these instances may, perhaps, include a majority of the cases.

In a country like this, it is indispensable to mental independence, that every man should have a clear perception of the quality of the political news, and of the political opinions circulated by the press, for, he who confides implicitly to its statements is yielding himself blindly to either the designed and exaggerated praises of friends, or to the calculated abuse of opponents. As no man is either as good, or as bad, as vulgar report makes him, we can, at once, see the value that ought to be given to such statements.

All representations that dwell wholly on merits, or on faults, are to be distrusted, since none are perfect, and it may, perhaps, be added, none utterly without some redeeming qualities.

Whenever the papers unite to commend, without qualification, it is safe to believe in either venality, or a disposition to defer to a preconceived notion of excellence, most men choosing to float with the current, rather than to resist it, when no active motive urges a contrary course, feeding falsehood, because it flatters a predilection; and whenever censure is general and sweeping, one may be almost certain it is exaggerated and false.

Puffs, political, literary, personal and national, can commonly be detected by their *ex parte* statements, as may be their counterpart, detraction. Dishonesty of intention is easily discovered by the man of the world, in both, by the tone; and he who blindly receives either eulogium or censure, because they stand audaciously in print, demonstrates that his judgment is still in its infancy.

Authors review themselves, or friends are employed to do it for them; political adventurers have their dependants, who build their fortunes on those of their patrons; artists, players, and even religionists, are not above having recourse to such expedients to advance their interests and reputations. The world would be surprised to learn the tyranny that the press has exercised, in our own times, over some of the greatest of modern names, few men possessing the manliness and moral courage that are necessary to resist its oppression.

The people that has overturned the throne of a monarch, and set up a government of opinion in its stead, and which blindly yields its interests to the designs of those who would rule through the instrumentality of newspapers, has only exchanged one form of despotism for another.

It is often made a matter of boasting, that the United States contain so many publick journals. It were wiser to make it a cause of mourning, since the quality, in this instance, diminishes in an inverse ratio to the quantity.

Another reason may be found for the deleterious influence of the American press, in the peculiar physical condition of the country. In all communities, the better opinion, whether as relates to moral or scientific truths, tastes, manners and facts, is necessarily in the keeping of a few; the great majority of mankind being precluded by their opportunities from reaching so high in the mental scale. The proportion between the intelligent and whole numbers, after making a proper allowance on account of the differences in civilization, is probably as great in this country, as in any other; possibly it is greater among the males; but the great extent of the territory prevents its concentration, and consequently, weakens its influence. Under such circumstances, the press has less to contend with than in other countries, where designing and ignorant men would stand rebuked before the collected opinion of those who, by their characters and information, are usually too powerful to be misled by vulgarity, sophistry and falsehood. Another reason is to be found in the popular character of the government, bodies of men requiring to be addressed in modes suited to the average qualities of masses.

In America, while the contest was for great principles, the press aided in elevating the common character, in improving the common mind, and in maintaining the common interests; but, since the contest has ceased, and the struggle has become one purely of selfishness and personal interests, it is employed, as a whole, in fast undermining its own work, and in preparing the nation for some terrible reverses, if not in calling down upon it, a just judgment of God.

As the press of this country now exists, it would seem to be expressly devised by the great agent of mischief, to depress and destroy all that is good, and to elevate and advance all that is evil in the nation. The little truth that is urged, is usually urged coarsely, weakened and rendered vicious, by personalities; while those who live by falsehoods, fallacies, enmities, partialities and the schemes of the designing, find the press the very instrument that the devils would invent to effect their designs.

A witty, but unprincipled statesman of our own times, has said that "speech was bestowed on man to conceal his thoughts;" judging from its present condition, he might have added, "and the press to pervert truth."

ON PROPERTY

As PROPERTY is the base of all civilization, its existence and security are indispensable to social improvement. Were it possible to have a community of property, it would soon be found that no one would toil, but that men would be disposed to be satisfied with barely enough for the supply of their physical wants, since none would exert themselves to obtain advantages solely for the use of others. The failure of all attempts to form communities, even on a small scale, with a common interest, goes to prove this. Where there is a rigid equality of condition, as well as of rights, that condition must necessarily be one of a low scale of mediocrity, since it is impossible to elevate those who do not possess the requisite qualities any higher. Thus we see that the societies, or religious sects, in which a community of property prevails, are content with merely supplying the wants of life, knowing little or nothing of its elegancies, refinements, or mental pleasures. These communities, moreover, possess an outlet for their idle and dissolute, by resorting to expulsion, a remedy that society itself cannot apply.

The principle of individuality, or to use a less winning term, of selfishness, lies at the root of all voluntary human exertion. We toil for food, for clothes, for houses, lands, and for property, in general. This is done, because we know that the fruits of our labor will belong to ourselves, or to those who are most dear to us. It follows, that all which society enjoys beyond the mere supply of its first necessities, is dependant on their rights of property.

It is not known that man exists anywhere without establishing rules for the protection of property. Even insects, reptiles, beasts and birds, have their several possessions, in their nests, dens and supplies. So completely is animal exertion, in general, whether in man or beast, dependant on the enjoyment of this right, under limitations which mark their several conditions, that we may infer that the rights of property, to a certain extent, are founded in nature. The food obtained by his toil, cannot be taken from the mouth of man, or beast, without doing violence to one of the first of our natural rights. We apply the term of robber, or despoiler, to the reptile or bird, that preys on the aliment of another animal, as well as to the human thief. So long as natural justice is admitted to exist, the party assailed, in such cases, has a right to defend his own.

The rights of property become artificial and extended, as society becomes civilized. In the savage state the land is without owners, property consisting in the hut, the food, and the arms used in war and in the chase. In pastoral, or semi-barbarous states, use gives claims, not to individuals, but to tribes, and flocks are pastured on grounds that belong to one entire community, but to that one only. Private property is composed of cattle, sheep, tents, horses, camels, with the common claims to share in the common fields.

Civilization has established various, and in some cases, arbitrary and unjust distinctions, as pertaining to the rights of property. These are abuses, the tendency of man being to convert into curses things that Providence designed to prove benefits. Still, most of the ordinances of civilized society, that are connected with this interest, are founded in reason, and ought to be rigidly maintained.

The first great principle connected with the rights of property, is its inviolability in all cases in which the laws leave it in possession of the proprietor. Every child should be taught to respect the sanctity of his neighbour's house, garden, fields and all that is his. On those parts of another's possessions, where it is permitted to go, he should go with care not to abuse the privilege, and from those parts which he is forbidden to use, he should religiously abstain. The child that is properly impressed in infancy, with the rights of property, is in little danger of committing theft in after life, or, in any other manner of invading that which is the just possession of another.

The doctrine that any one "may do what he please with his own," however, is false. One may do with his own, whatever the laws and institutions of his country allow, and no more. One may even respect the letter, and yet violate the spirit of those laws and institutions, committing a moral, if not a legal offence, in so doing. Thus, he, who would bring his money to bear upon the elections of a country like this, abuses his situation, unless his efforts are confined to fair and manly discussions before the body of the people.

In nations where the mass have no political rights, means have been found to accumulate power by the aid of wealth. The pretence has been that none but the rich have a stake in society. Every man who has wants, feelings, affections and character, has a stake in society. Of the two, perhaps, the necessities of men are a greater corrective of political abuses, than their surplus means. Both may lead to evil, beyond a doubt, but, as laws which are framed by all, must be tolerably impartial and general in their operation, less danger arises from the rule of the former, than from the rule of the latter. When property rules, it rules alone; but when the poor are admitted to have a voice in government, the rich are never excluded. Such is the nature of man, that all exclusive power is uniformly directed to exclusive purposes. Property always carries with it a portion of indirect political influence, and it is unwise, and even dangerous, to strengthen this influence by adding to it constitutional privileges; the result always being to make the strong stronger, and the weak weaker.

On the other hand, all who love equal justice, and, indeed, the safety of free institutions, should understand that property has its rights, and the necessity of rigidly respecting them. It is the right of the posessor of property to be placed on an equal footing with all his fellow citizens, in every respect. If he is not to be exalted on account of his wealth, neither is he to be denounced. In this country, it is the intention of the institutions, that money should neither increase nor lessen political influence.

There are habits that belong to every condition of life. The man of hereditary wealth, is usually a man of leisure, and he little understands the true spirit of democracy, who supposes that such a man is not to enjoy the tastes and inclinations, which are the fruits of leisure and cultivation, without let or hindrance. Democracy leaves every man the master of his acts and time, his tastes and habits, so long as he discharges his duty to the publick, and respects the laws. He who declaims against another for holding himself aloof from general association, arrogates to himself a power of censure that he does not rightly possess, and betrays his own consciousness of inferiority. Men of really high social station never make this complaint, for they are above jealousy; and they who do, only discover a feeling that is every way removed from the manliness and spirit of true independence.

One may certainly be purse-proud, and of all the sources of human pride, mere wealth is the basest and most vulgar minded. Real gentlemen are almost invariably above this low feeling, and they who attribute habits, that have their rise in sentiment, tastes, knowledge and refinement, to such a cause, usually make the mistake of letting their own ignorance of the existence of motives so elevated, be known. In a word, if the man of property has no more personal legal immunities, than the man who has none, neither has he fewer. He is privileged to use his own means, under the general regulations of society, in the pursuit of his own happiness, and they who would interfere with him, so far from appreciating liberty, are ignorant of its vital principles.

If left to itself, unsupported by factitious political aid, but sufficiently protected against the designs and rapacity of the dishonest, property is an instrument of working most of the good that society enjoys. It elevates a national character, by affording the means of cultivating knowledge and the tastes; it introduces all above barbarism into society; and it encourages and sustains laudable and useful efforts in individuals. Like every other great good, its abuses are in proportion to its benefits.

The possessor of property is not, half the time, as much the object of envy as the needy imagine, for its corrupting influence endangers eternal peace. Great estates are generally of more benefit to the community than to their owners. They bring with them anxiety, cares, demands, and, usually, exaggerated notions, on the part of the publick, of the duties of the rich. So far from being objects of envy, their possessors are oftener the subjects of commiseration; he who has enough for his rational wants, agreeably to his habits and education, always proving the happier man.

The possessions of new families are commonly exaggerated in the publick mind, while those of long established families are as commonly diminished.

A people that deems the possession of riches its highest source of distinction, admits one of the most degrading of all influences to preside over its opinions. At no time, should money be ever ranked as more than a means, and he who lives as if the acquisition of property were the sole end of his existence, betrays the dominion of the most sordid, base, and grovelling motive, that life offers.

Property is desirable as the ground work of moral independence, as a means of improving the faculties, and of doing good to others, and as the agent in all that distinguishes the civilized man from the savage.

Property has been made the test of political rights, in two distinct forms. It has been *represented,* and it has been established as a *qualification.* The *representation* of property is effected in two modes; first, by giving the proprietor more votes than one, according to the number and situation of his freeholds; and, secondly, by raising the test of qualification so high, as to exclude all but the affluent from the franchise. The first was the English system, previously to the recent changes; the last, is the actual system of France.

A government founded on the representation of property, however direct or indirect, is radically vicious, since it is a union of two of the most corrupting influences to which man is subject. It is the proper business of government to resist the corruptions of money, and not to depend on them.

To a qualification of property, if placed so low as to embrace the great majority of the people, there is no very serious objection, though better tests might, perhaps, be devised. Residence, character, information, and fixed relations with society, ought to be added to this qualification; and it might be better, even, could they be made entirely to supersede it. In local governments, or those of towns and villages, which do little more than control property, a low property qualification is the true test of the franchise, though even in these cases, it might be well to add information and character.

William Cullen Bryant

THE YELLOW VIOLET

◇

THE CULTURAL time lag between America and England prevented any widespread enthusiasm for the English romantic poets, or, indeed, any considerable knowledge of them, during the first quarter of the century, and for some time later. Nevertheless, several of Bryant's poems are indebted to Wordsworth. Among these is "The Yellow Violet," written when Bryant was twenty years old. It is one of his best poems. R. H. Dana has written of Bryant's response to Wordsworth:

> I shall never forget with what feeling my friend Bryant some years ago described to me the effect produced upon him by his meeting for the first time with Wordsworth's *Ballads.* He lived, when quite young, where but few works of poetry were to be had: at a period, too, when Pope was still the great idol

in the Temple of Art. He said that upon opening Wordsworth a thousand springs seemed to gush up at once in his heart, and the face of nature of a sudden to change into a strange freshness and life.

◇

When beechen buds begin to swell,
    And woods the blue-bird's warble know,
The yellow violet's modest bell
    Peeps from the last year's leaves below.

Ere russet fields their green resume,
    Sweet flower, I love, in forest bare,
To meet thee, when thy faint perfume
    Alone is in the virgin air.

Of all her train, the hands of Spring
    First plant thee in the watery mould,
And I have seen thee blossoming
    Beside the snow-bank's edges cold.

Thy parent sun, who bade thee view
    Pale skies, and chilling moisture sip,
Has bathed thee in his own bright hue,
    And streaked with jet thy glowing lip.

Yet slight thy form, and low thy seat,
    And earthward bent thy gentle eye,
Unapt the passing view to meet
    When loftier flowers are flaunting nigh.

Oft, in the sunless April day,
    Thy early smile has stayed my walk;
But midst the gorgeous blooms of May,
    I passed thee on thy humble stalk.

So they, who climb to wealth, forget
    The friends in darker fortunes tried.
I copied them—but I regret
    That I should ape the ways of pride.

And when again the genial hour
    Awakes the painted tribes of light,
I'll not o'erlook the modest flower
    That made the woods of April bright.

1821 *1814*

TO A WATERFOWL

◇

IN DECEMBER, 1815, Bryant was walking toward the village of Plainfield, Massachusetts, where he intended to set up a law practice. Parke Godwin in his early life (1883) described what happened on that walk:

> As he walked up the hills, very forlorn and desolate indeed, not knowing what was to become of him in the big world which grew bigger as he ascended and yet darker with the coming on of night. The sun had already set, leaving behind it one of those brilliant seas of chrysolite and opal which often flood the New England skies. While he was looking on the rosy splendor with rapt admiration, a solitary bird made wing along the illuminated horizon. He watched the lone wanderer until it was lost in the distance, asking himself whither it had come and to what far home it was flying. When he went to the house where he was to stop for the night, his mind was still full of what he had seen and felt, and he wrote those lines . . . "To a Waterfowl."

◇

    Whither, midst falling dew,
While glow the heavens with the last steps of day,
Far, through their rosy depths, dost thou pursue
    Thy solitary way?

    Vainly the fowler's eye
Might mark thy distant flight to do thee wrong,
As, darkly seen against the crimson sky,
    Thy figure floats along.

    Seek'st thou the plashy brink
Of weedy lake, or marge of river wide,
Or where the rocking billows rise and sink
    On the chafed ocean-side?

    There is a Power whose care
Teaches thy way along that pathless coast—
The desert and illimitable air—
    Lone wandering, but not lost.

    All day thy wings have fanned,
At that far height, the cold, thin atmosphere,
Yet stoop not, weary, to the welcome land,
    Though the dark night is near.

    And soon that toil shall end;
Soon shalt thou find a summer home, and rest,
And scream among thy fellows; reeds shall bend,
    Soon, o'er thy sheltered nest.

    Thou'rt gone, the abyss of heaven
Hath swallowed up thy form; yet, on my heart
Deeply hath sunk the lesson thou hast given,
    And shall not soon depart.

    He who, from zone to zone,
Guides through the boundless sky thy certain flight,

In the long way that I must tread alone
    Will lead my steps aright.

1818 *1815*

THANATOPSIS

◇

THE FOLLOWING letter was written by Bryant in 1855 in reply to an enquiry concerning "Thanatopsis":

> I cannot give you any information of the occasion which suggested to my mind the idea of my poem Thanatopsis. It was written when I was seventeen or eighteen years old—I have not now at hand the memorandums which would enable me to be precise—and I believe it was composed in my solitary rambles in the woods. As it was first committed to paper, it began with the half-line—"Yet a few days, and thee"—and ended with the beginning of another line with the words—"And make their bed with thee." The rest of the poem—the introduction and the close—was added some years afterward, in 1821, when I published a little collection of my poems at Cambridge.

◇

To him who in the love of Nature holds
Communion with her visible forms, she speaks
A various language: for his gayer hours
She has a voice of gladness, and a smile
And eloquence of beauty; and she glides
Into his darker musings with a mild
And healing sympathy that steals away
Their sharpness ere he is aware. When thoughts
Of the last bitter hour come like a blight
Over thy spirit, and sad images
Of the stern agony and shroud and pall
And breathless darkness and the narrow house
Make thee to shudder and grow sick at heart,
Go forth under the open sky and list
To Nature's teachings, while from all around—
Earth and her waters and the depths of air—
Comes a still voice—Yet a few days, and thee
The all-beholding sun shall see no more
In all his course; nor yet in the cold ground,
Where thy pale form was laid with many tears,
Nor in the embrace of ocean, shall exist
Thy image. Earth, that nourished thee, shall claim
Thy growth, to be resolved to earth again,
And, lost each human trace, surrendering up
Thine individual being, shalt thou go
To mix for ever with the elements,
To be a brother to the insensible rock
And to the sluggish clod, which the rude swain
Turns with his share and treads upon; the oak
Shall send his roots abroad and pierce thy mould.

Yet not to thine eternal resting-place
Shalt thou retire alone, nor couldst thou wish
Couch more magnificent. Thou shalt lie down
With patriarchs of the infant world, with kings,
The powerful of the earth, the wise, the good,
Fair forms, and hoary seers of ages past,
All in one mighty sepulchre. The hills
Rock-ribbed and ancient as the sun; the vales
Stretching in pensive quietness between;
The venerable woods, rivers that move
In majesty, and the complaining brooks
That make the meadows green; and, poured round all,
Old Ocean's gray and melancholy waste,—
Are but the solemn decorations all
Of the great tomb of man. The golden sun,
The planets, all the infinite host of heaven,
Are shining on the sad abodes of death,
Through the still lapse of ages. All that tread
The globe are but a handful to the tribes
That slumber in its bosom. Take the wings
Of morning, pierce the Barcan wilderness,
Or lose thyself in the continuous woods
Where rolls the Oregon, and hears no sound
Save his own dashings; yet the dead are there,
And millions in those solitudes, since first
The flight of years began, have laid them down
In their last sleep: the dead reign there alone.
So shalt thou rest; and what if thou withdraw
In silence from the living, and no friend
Take note of thy departure? All that breathe
Will share thy destiny. The gay will laugh
When thou art gone, the solemn brood of care
Plod on, and each one as before will chase
His favorite phantom; yet all these shall leave
Their mirth and their employments, and shall come
And make their bed with thee. As the long train
Of ages glide away, the sons of men—
The youth in life's green spring, and he who goes
In the full strength of years, matron and maid,
The speechless babe, and the gray-headed man—
Shall one by one be gathered to thy side
By those who in their turn shall follow them.

So live that when thy summons comes to join
The innumerable caravan which moves
To that mysterious realm where each shall take
His chamber in the silent halls of death,
Thou go not, like the quarry-slave at night,
Scourged to his dungeon, but, sustained and soothed

By an unfaltering trust, approach thy grave
Like one who wraps the drapery of his couch
About him and lies down to pleasant dreams.

1817, 1821 *1811*

INSCRIPTION FOR THE ENTRANCE TO A WOOD

Stranger, if thou has learned a truth which needs
No school of long experience, that the world
Is full of guilt and misery, and hast seen
Enough of all its sorrows, crimes, and cares,
To tire thee of it, enter this wild wood
And view the haunts of Nature. The calm shade
Shall bring a kindred calm, and the sweet breeze
That makes the green leaves dance, shall waft a balm
To thy sick heart. Thou will find nothing here
Of all that pained thee in the haunts of men,
And made thee loathe thy life. The primal curse
Fell, it is true, upon the unsinning earth,
But not in vengeance. God hath yoked to guilt
Her pale tormentor, misery. Hence, these shades
Are still the abodes of gladness; the thick roof
Of green and stirring branches is alive
And musical with birds, that sing and sport
In wantonness of spirit; while below
The squirrel, with raised paws and form erect,
Chirps merrily. Throngs of insects in the shade
Try their thin wings and dance in the warm beam
That waked them into life. Even the green trees
Partake the deep contentment; as they bend
To the soft winds, the sun from the blue sky
Looks in and sheds a blessing on the scene.
Scarce less the cleft-born wild-flower seems to enjoy
Existence, than the wingèd plunderer
That sucks its sweets. The mossy rocks themselves
And the old and ponderous trunks of prostrate trees
That lead from knoll to knoll a causey rude
Or bridge the sunken brook, and their dark roots,
With all their earth upon them, twisting high,
Breathe fixed tranquillity. The rivulet
Sends forth glad sounds, and tripping o'er its bed
Of pebbly sands, or leaping down the rocks,
Seems, with continuous laughter, to rejoice
In its own being. Softly tread the marge,
Lest from her midway perch thou scare the wren
That dips her bill in water. The cool wind,
That stirs the stream in play, shall come to thee,
Like one that loves thee nor will let thee pass
Ungreeted, and shall give its light embrace.

1817 *1816*

OH FAIREST OF THE RURAL MAIDS

◇

¶ Poe said of these stanzas that they "will strike every poet as the truest *poem* ever written by Bryant." The "rural maid" of the poem is Frances Fairchild, whom Bryant met in the spring of 1820 while unhappily practising law at Great Barrington, Massachusetts. They were married the following year. The obvious literary influence is Wordsworth's "Lucy" poems.

◇

Oh fairest of the rural maids!
Thy birth was in the forest shades;
Green boughs, and glimpses of the sky,
Were all that met thine infant eye.

Thy sports, thy wanderings, when a child,
Were ever in the sylvan wild;
And all the beauty of the place
Is in thy heart and on thy face.

The twilight of the trees and rocks
Is in the light shade of thy locks;
Thy step is as the wind that weaves
Its playful way among the leaves.

Thine eyes are springs, in whose serene
And silent waters heaven is seen;
Their lashes are the herbs that look
On their young figures in the brook.

The forest depths, by foot unpressed,
Are not more sinless than thy breast;
The holy peace, that fills the air
Of those calm solitudes, is there.

1832 *1820*

AN INDIAN AT THE BURIAL-PLACE OF HIS FATHERS

It is the spot I came to seek—
My father's ancient burial-place,
Ere from these vales, ashamed and weak,
Withdrew our wasted race.
It is the spot—I know it well—
Of which our old traditions tell.

For here the upland bank sends out
A ridge toward the riverside;
I know the shaggy hills about,
The meadows smooth and wide,
The plains, that, toward the southern sky,
Fenced east and west by mountains lie.

A white man, gazing on the scene,
Would say a lovely spot was here,
And praise the lawns, so fresh and green,
Between the hills so sheer.
I like it not—I would the plain
Lay in its tall old groves again.

The sheep are on the slopes around,
The cattle in the meadows feed,
And laborers turn the crumbling ground,
Or drop the yellow seed,
And prancing steeds, in trappings gay,
Whirl the bright chariot o'er the way.

Methinks it were a nobler sight
To see these vales in woods arrayed,
Their summits in the golden light,
Their trunks in grateful shade,
And herds of deer that bounding go
O'er hills and prostrate trees below.

And then to mark the lord of all,
The forest hero, trained to wars,
Quivered and plumed, and lithe and tall,
And seamed with glorious scars,
Walk forth, amid his reign, to dare
The wolf, and grapple with the bear.

This bank, in which the dead were laid,
Was sacred when its soil was ours;
Hither the silent Indian maid
Brought wreaths of beads and flowers,
And the gray chief and gifted seer
Worshipped the god of thunders here.

But now the wheat is green and high
On clods that hid the warrior's breast,
And scattered in the furrows lie
The weapons of his rest;
And there, in the loose sand, is thrown
Of his large arm the mouldering bone.

Ah, little thought the strong and brave
Who bore their lifeless chieftain forth—
Or the young wife that weeping gave
Her first-born to the earth,
That the pale race who waste us now
Among their bones should guide the plough.

They waste us—ay—like April snow
In the warm noon, we shrink away;
And fast they follow, as we go
Toward the setting day—
Till they shall fill the land, and we
Are driven into the Western sea.

But I behold a fearful sign,
To which the white men's eyes are blind;
Their race may vanish hence, like mine,
And leave no trace behind,
Save ruins o'er the region spread,
And the white stones above the dead.

Before these fields were shorn and tilled,
Full to the brim our rivers flowed;
The melody of waters filled
The fresh and boundless wood;
And torrents dashed and rivulets played,
And fountains spouted in the shade.

Those grateful sounds are heard no more,
The springs are silent in the sun;
The rivers, by the blackened shore,
With lessening current run;
The realm our tribes are crushed to get
May be a barren desert yet.

1824

A FOREST HYMN

The groves were God's first temples. Ere man
learned

To hew the shaft, and lay the architrave,
And spread the roof above them—ere he framed
The lofty vault, to gather and roll back
The sound of anthems; in the darkling wood,
Amid the cool and silence, he knelt down,
And offered to the Mightiest solemn thanks
And supplication. For his simple heart
Might not resist the sacred influence
Which, from the stilly twilight of the place,
And from the gray old trunks that high in heaven
Mingled their mossy boughs, and from the sound
Of the invisible breath that swayed at once
All their green tops, stole over him, and bowed
His spirit with the thought of boundless power
And inaccessible majesty. Ah, why
Should we, in the world's riper years, neglect
God's ancient sanctuaries, and adore
Only among the crowd, and under roofs
That our frail hands have raised? Let me, at least,
Here, in the shadow of this aged wood,
Offer one hymn—thrice happy, if it find
Acceptance in His ear.

Father, thy hand
Hath reared these venerable columns, thou
Didst weave this verdant roof. Thou didst look down
Upon the naked earth, and, forthwith, rose
All these fair ranks of trees. They, in thy sun,
Budded, and shook their green leaves in thy breeze,
And shot toward heaven. The century-living crow
Whose birth was in their tops, grew old and died
Among their branches, till, at last, they stood,
As now they stand, massy, and tall, and dark,
Fit shrine for humble worshiper to hold
Communion with his Maker. These dim vaults,
These winding aisles, of human pomp or pride
Report not. No fantastic carvings show
The boast of our vain race to change the form
Of thy fair works. But thou art here—thou fill'st
The solitude. Thou art in the soft winds
That run along the summit of these trees
In music; thou art in the cooler breath
That from the inmost darkness of the place
Comes, scarcely felt; the barky trunks, the ground,
The fresh moist ground, are all instinct with thee.
Here is continual worship;—Nature, here,
In the tranquillity that thou dost love,
Enjoys thy presence. Noiselessly, around,
From perch to perch, the solitary bird
Passes; and yon clear spring, that, midst its herbs,
Wells softly forth and wandering steeps the roots
Of half the mighty forest, tells no tale
Of all the good it does. Thou hast not left
Thyself without a witness, in the shades,
Of thy perfections. Grandeur, strength, and grace
Are here to speak of thee. This mighty oak—
By whose immovable stem I stand and seem
Almost annihilated—not a prince,
In all that proud old world beyond the deep,
E'er wore his crown as loftily as he
Wears the green coronal of leaves with which
Thy hand has graced him. Nestled at his root
Is beauty, such as blooms not in the glare
Of the broad sun. That delicate forest flower,
With scented breath and look so like a smile,
Seems, as it issues from the shapeless mold,
An emanation of the indwelling Life,
A visible token of the upholding Love,
That are the soul of this great universe.

My heart is awed within me when I think
Of the great miracle that still goes on,
In silence, round me—the perpetual work
Of thy creation, finished, yet renewed
Forever. Written on thy works I read
The lesson of thy own eternity.
Lo! all grow old and die—but see again,
How on the faltering footsteps of decay
Youth presses—ever gay and beautiful youth
In all its beautiful forms. These lofty trees
Wave not less proudly that their ancestors
Molder beneath them. Oh, there is not lost
One of earth's charms: upon her bosom yet,
After the flight of untold centuries,
The freshness of her far beginning lies
And yet shall lie. Life mocks the idle hate
Of his arch-enemy Death—yea, seats himself
Upon the tyrant's throne—the sepulcher,
And of the triumphs of his ghastly foe
Makes his own nourishment. For he came forth
From thine own bosom, and shall have no end.

There have been holy men who hid themselves
Deep in the woody wilderness, and gave
Their lives to thought and prayer, till they outlived
The generation born with them, nor seemed
Less aged than the hoary trees and rocks
Around them;—and there have been holy men
Who deemed it were not well to pass life thus.
But let me often to these solitudes
Retire, and in thy presence reassure
My feeble virtue. Here its enemies,
The passions, at thy plainer footsteps shrink
And tremble and are still. O God! when thou
Dost scare the world with tempests, set on fire
The heavens with falling thunderbolts, or fill,
With all the waters of the firmament,
The swift dark whirlwind that uproots the woods
And drowns the villages; when, at thy call,
Uprises the great deep and throws himself

Upon the continent, and overwhelms
Its cities—who forgets not, at the sight
Of these tremendous tokens of thy power,
His pride, and lays his strifes and follies by?
Oh, from these sterner aspects of thy face
Spare me and mine, nor let us need the wrath
Of the mad unchained elements to teach
Who rules them. Be it ours to meditate,
In these calm shades, thy milder majesty,
And to the beautiful order of thy works
Learn to conform the order of our lives.

1825 *1825*

TO COLE, THE PAINTER DEPARTING FOR EUROPE

◊

¶ THOMAS COLE (1801–48) founded the Hudson River school of painting. He was a friend of Cooper and a close friend of Bryant, with whom he took walking tours in the Catskills, and whose attitude toward nature he shared. The Hudson River school, which included such painters as Thomas Doughty and Asher Brown Durand, developed a moral philosophy of landscape that corresponds closely to that expressed, for example, in "A Forest Hymn." These painters had a contemplative and religious vision of American scenery. Their fondness for dead, decaying trees was intended to proclaim the mutability of all things. They used sweeping effects of storm cloud and streaming light to suggest the brooding presence of the Eternal, and they liked introducing tiny human figures into panoramic vistas to suggest the smallness of man before his Creator. At the same time they endeavored to make their landscapes distinctively American, for the American earth was new, and uncontaminated by the guilty European past. It is easy to trace parallels between the landscape vision of these painters and American scenery as described by Bryant and Cooper. Cooper's ability to describe vast panoramic tracts of forest, prairie, or river valley, as seen from some lofty peak, is indebted to the paintings of this school. One of its best known pictures, "Kindred Spirits" by Durand, shows Bryant and Cole as two small frock-coated figures standing above a Catskill gorge, with mountains, forest trees, a waterfall and a turbulent stream, in the background. The two correct little figures, who are soberly enjoying these wild but solemn aspects of nature, provide a commentary on the whole school.

◊

Thine eyes shall see the light of distant skies;
  Yet, COLE! thy heart shall bear to Europe's strand
  A living image of our own bright land,
Such as upon thy glorious canvas lies;
Lone lakes—savannas where the bison roves—
  Rocks rich with summer garlands—solemn streams—
  Skies, where the desert eagle wheels and screams—
Spring bloom and autumn blaze of boundless groves.
Fair scenes shall greet thee where thou goest—fair,
  But different—everywhere the trace of men,
  Paths, homes, graves, ruins, from the lowest glen
To where life shrinks from the fierce Alpine air.
  Gaze on them, till the tears shall dim thy sight,
  But keep that earlier, wilder image bright.

1830 *1829*

RICHARD WILBUR
Editor

Edgar Allan Poe

1809–1849

EDGAR POE was born in Boston, Massachusetts on January 19, 1809. His mother, Elizabeth Arnold Poe, was an actress of some talent and much charm, who in the year of Edgar's birth was to reach the peak of her career, playing Ophelia to the Hamlet of John Howard Payne. Her husband David, an indifferent actor often humiliated by the critics, began in the same year to render himself unemployable through drink; at last, in July of 1810, he abandoned his family and vanished utterly from record. Soon after, Elizabeth Poe's fortunes and health declined, and in December of 1811, at the age of twenty-four, she died of consumption in a theatrical rooming house in Richmond, Virginia.

She left three children to the world. William Henry, the elder son, had long since been adopted by his grandfather, General David Poe of Baltimore: gifted and unbalanced, he was to become a sailor, a poet, and a drunkard, and then to die at twenty-four of the disease which had carried off his mother. Rosalie, the youngest child, about whom there were rumors of illegitimacy, was taken into the charitable Richmond household of William MacKenzie: she would live into her sixties as a markedly eccentric spinster. Three-year-old Edgar, whose life was to be both better and worse than these, was also taken from his mother's death chamber into a charitable Richmond family.

The charity seems to have been chiefly Frances Allan's; she was a soft-natured woman, and had no children of her own to love. John Allan, her husband, was a shrewd, handsome, ambitious merchant given to choler and self-righteousness, whose reception of Edgar must have been at best a matter of cold principle. But whatever the motives and intentions of his foster-parents, the orphan boy found himself living, as a son, in the fine house of a family fast rising in Virginia's commercial aristocracy. When John Allan's business took him to England in 1815, Edgar was placed in the Manor House School at Stoke Newington, near London, where, as "Master Allan," he studied until his eleventh year. On the family's return to Richmond, John Allan continued to provide his ward with the education of a young Virginia gentleman; moreover, the Allans gave polite parties for Edgar, to which the children of Richmond's best families were invited. The boy was also encouraged to learn the rudiments of the family business, so that, although his name had now reverted to "Master Poe," it became his and Richmond's presumption that he was, or would become, John Allan's adopted son and heir.

Nevertheless, there are indications that Richmond's acceptance of Edgar Poe was frankly provisional, and that the boy could never have felt a comfortable assurance as to his place in the world. In discussing Poe's school days, a Colonel Preston recalled that of Edgar Poe it was known that his parents had been players, and that he was dependent upon the bounty that is bestowed upon an adopted son. All this had the effect of making the boys decline his leadership; and on looking backward on it since, I fancy it gave him a fierceness he would otherwise not have had.

It doubtless moved him to such feats as his Byronic seven-mile swim in the James River; insecurity may also have prompted, in some measure, his intense attachment to Mrs. Jane Stith Stanard, the mother of a schoolmate; and perhaps it was one cause of that growing moodiness which John Allan noted and disapproved.

As Edgar entered young manhood, there was a progressive collapse of sympathy between him and his guardian, who often accused him of idleness and a surly ingratitude. Too little is known of the substance of their differences to permit of any present adjudication, but certain things seem clear: John Allan was contemptuous of Edgar's developing literary ambition; he was disappointed by Edgar's want of interest in a mercantile career; and he was, for these and other reasons, impatient of supporting a troublesome ward with whom he had no temperamental affinity. This impatience was soon translated into action. When the respectable Royster family, in 1826, put an end to Edgar's courtship of their daughter Sarah Elmira, it was undoubtedly done on the basis of authoritative information that Edgar Poe was not to be John Allan's heir. And when Edgar, in that same year, entered the newly opened University of Virginia, it was with an allowance inadequate to his minimum needs. In an effort to escape the embarrassments which such malevolent parsimony made inevitable, he took to gambling, and in eight months lost some two thousand dollars. Since Allan then refused to pay both his legitimate debts and his "debts of honor," Edgar could not return to the university. After a violent quarrel with Allan, he left home and Richmond in March, 1827, with the vague project of "finding some place in the wide world."

In later years, Poe sometimes improved upon his life between 1827 and 1830 by tall tales of fighting in Greece, writing in Paris, or dueling in Spain. The truth is that the eighteen-year-old adventurer worked his way to Boston on a coal barge, under the alias of Henri le Rennet, found no employment there, and so enlisted in the U.S. Army as Edgar A. Perry. During the early months of his enlistment, he published at Boston a small volume entitled *Tamerlane and Other Poems*. The poems were few, the edition extremely small, and the public impact negligible.

Poe had always done honorably as a scholar; he now did honorably as a soldier, and by January of 1829 reached the highest noncommissioned grade, that of sergeant major. However, the thought of completing a five-year hitch had already become intolerable to him ("the prime of my life would be wasted"), and he now sought to secure his discharge. This was finally effected, through the kind concern of his officers and the grudging consent of his guardian, on the understanding that Sergeant Major Perry would seek appointment to the U.S. Military Academy at West Point.

While waiting for his appointment to come through, Poe shared for a time the poverty of his Grandmother Poe's household in Baltimore. Under that roof were his tubercular and dissipated brother William Henry, his aunt Maria Clemm, and a seven-year-old cousin, Virginia, who six years thereafter was to become his "child-bride." In December Poe rejoiced in the publication of *Al Aaraaf, Tamerlane and Minor Poems* by the Baltimore house of Hatch and Dunning, and in its immediate favorable notice by the novelist and critic John Neal. This literary recognition, together with his ward's obedient intention of becoming a West Point officer, moved John Allan to permit him a visit to Richmond, and there Poe remained until yet another quarrel forced his return to Baltimore in May of 1830.

The appointment, however, had at last been wangled, and in June he went on to West Point. It is plain that Poe, who was overage for a cadet and had no relish for a military future, entered the academy in the desperate hope of recovering John Allan's favor and patronage. As always, he proceeded to distinguish himself in his studies; but Allan's refusal to write, or to send him any expense money, gave reason to doubt that diligence would be rewarded. Indeed, Poe was not even notified when his guardian—then nineteen months a widower—was married in October to a woman quite young enough to give him an heir. On learning of this fatal development, Poe relinquished his hopes of an inheritance and, lacking his guardian's permission to resign from the academy, sought and gained a prompt dismissal for "gross neglect of duty" and "disobedience of orders."

During his last days at West Point, Poe wrote Allan a letter which was full, as usual, of half-truth and self-pity, of alternate accusation and entreaty. "My future life," he said, "(Which thank God will not endure long) must be passed in indigence and sickness." The prophecy was correct, and the remaining eighteen years of his existence were—despite his more romantic biographers—a Sahara of dreariness, pain, and drudgery. To be sure, Poe's marriage, in 1836, to his girl-cousin Virginia secured him an oasis of affection and solicitude. If, as seems possible, Poe was sexually incapable, it was nevertheless a marriage; and Virginia's mother, Mrs. Clemm, who ran the always impoverished household until the end, was, as one lady visitor put it, "a sort of Universal Providence for her strange children." There was also the satisfaction of winning an occasional prize—fifty dollars for "Ms. Found in a Bottle," one hundred for "The Gold Bug,"—and of publishing an occasional collection of poems or tales.

But Poe was never able to support his small family by his poetry and fiction—"Ligeia" sold for ten dollars—and it was not until the celebrity of "The Raven," in 1845, that he enjoyed any real reputation as an artist. Prior to that time he was known for, and subsisted by means of, his editorial and critical labors for a series of periodicals in Richmond, Philadelphia, and New York. He was a good editor. Among other achievements, he quintupled the circulation of the *Southern Literary Messenger*, and in six months built up the subscription list of *Graham's Magazine* from five thousand to twenty thousand—thus enriching his employers, but never, unfortunately, quite freeing his family from the necessity for supplemental begging. As a critic, Poe produced a great quantity of conscientious work, and in a period of puffery, chauvinism, and literary gang-warfare, was outstanding for his insistence on definite, high, and specifically aesthetic criteria. Because, as an editor of periodicals, he was obliged to review the books which came to his desk, Poe inevitably wasted much thought on unworthy subjects; it is lamentable that so fine a critical intellect had to concern itself, not only with Hawthorne and Bryant, but also, and mostly, with such titles as *The Canons of Good Breeding*, and *Poetical Remains of the Late Lucretia Maria Davidson.*

The romantic legend of Poe minimizes the hard-plugging professional writer and editor in favor of the drunkard whose excesses cost him the editorship of the *Messenger*, and later, of *Burton's*. What should be compassionately remembered is that Poe was always unstable, and often underfed and exhausted; his usual frame of mind, as his depressing correspondence shows, was never very far from panic. Whenever his perilous balance was disturbed—as by the first signs of Virginia's fatal consumption, in 1842—he fell into a distraction of mind which, when it became insufferable, he blacked out by means of drink. It is doubtful that Poe consumed any great amount of alcohol in his lifetime, since his constitution would not tolerate it, even in modest quantities; and it seems best, as Poe himself advised, to refer the drink to the insanity, rather than the insanity to the drink.

Poe's last years were not without stable periods and literary achievements; out of them came "Ulalume," "The Domain of Arnheim," and the remarkable cosmological prose poem *Eureka*. But Virginia's decline and death robbed him of his one refuge from a world with which he could not steadily cope. It was not, as some have supposed, a burning-eyed libertine who conducted overlapping "affairs" with Mrs. Osgood, Mrs. Whitman, Mrs. Richmond, and his widowed childhood sweetheart, Elmira Royster Shelton. As W. H. Auden bluntly puts it, Poe was "an unmanly sort of man whose love-life seems to have been largely confined to crying in laps and playing house." What he sought from all these women, with the frantic anxiety of a lost child, was the equivalent of adoption.

A series of paranoid articles on Longfellow's "plagiarism," which Poe published in the *Broadway Journal* during 1845, would from a fully sane man have been dishonest, and Longfellow's decent and perceptive response was to say that the articles must have arisen from "the irritation of a sensitive nature, chafed by some indefinite sense of wrong." Thereafter the symptoms became clearer and more frequent: brain fever, fugue, persecutory hallucinations. . . . The circumstances which led to Poe's death are not fully known, and most scholars mistrust the story—eloquently evoked by Hart Crane in "The Bridge"—that Poe had been dragged, sick and drunk, from one polling place to another as a "repeater." But if his end, in October of 1849, was the result of foul play, those who left him dying in torn clothing, on a rainy Baltimore sidewalk, had only abetted an inevitable process of disintegration.

II

POE's fiction is full of allusions to his own history, some of them relatively open, as when he assigns his birthday to William Wilson, and some of them—as when he borrows the name of Usher from an early benefactor of his mother—obscure both in reference and in point. Such personal allusions cannot well be ignored, but the reader should be warned against concluding from their frequency that Poe's fiction is nothing but murky autobiography or psychodrama. To say that Virginia Poe equals Ligeia, or that Ligeia equals Virginia Poe, is to shed little light on either. We shall not go wrong, however, if we take Poe's autobiographical references as indicative of a taste for covert significance, and approach him with the hypothesis that his meaning lies, where he said it should, in an "under current." It would also be safe to suppose, on the basis of so many private allusions, that Poe's vision of the world was personally come by, and that he is not to be explained as an American imitator of, for example, E. T. A. Hoffmann. The often terrible substance of his tales, as Poe himself said, is "not of Germany, but of the soul."

While detailed analogies between Poe's life and work are not of much use, there were constants in his life which, together with the prevalent literary influences, may be thought to have determined his themes and attitudes. For one thing, Poe at no time enjoyed a definite social identity. In childhood and youth, he was an orphan of "low" parentage half-assimilated to the Virginia aristocracy. In manhood, despite his gentleman's training, he found himself doomed to a life of shabbiness, loan-begging, and hack work. One consequence was that he came to think of himself as a fallen aristocrat among "low ruffians and boobies, . . . men . . . without a shadow . . . of caste." In politics, he grew aristocratic *à outrance*, hating the tyrant "Mob" and laying it down that "democracy is a very admirable form of government—for dogs." To a sense of fallen greatness we may also ascribe his continual fabrications about his family origins and European travels, and his pretensions to more linguistic knowledge than he possessed. (The knowledge of languages was still, in Poe's day, one mark of a gentleman; the Prince Regent had once asked regarding a stranger, "Is he a gentleman? Has he any Greek?")

But Poe's radical solution to the problem of his place in the world was, quite simply, to secede from it. "The sole unquestionable aristocracy," he announced, was that of the intellect, and by this he intended the poetic intellect only. Scientists, in his view, were mere "diggers and pedlars of minute facts," who belonged in the "sculleries" rather than the "parlors" of Mind. And since Poe thought of poetry as concerned, not with earthly and human things, but with the pursuit of unearthly beauty, the superiority of the poet, like that of the mystic, consisted in a rapt disrelation to other men. He was monarch of the domain of his own visions, as Crusoe of his desert island; his aristocracy was not social and comparative, but spiritual and absolute.

It was this Poe who told James Russell Lowell, in answer to a request for biographical data,

> I live continually in a reverie of the future. . . . You speak of "an estimate of my life,"—and, from what I have already said, you will see that I have none to give. . . . My life has been *whim*—impulse—passion—a longing for solitude—a scorn of all things present, in an earnest longing for the future.

It was this Poe who wrote to a lady admirer, "My existence has been the merest Romance

—in the sense of the most utter unworldliness." And it was this Poe who embodied his isolate "real self," his poetic or visionary faculty, in such high-born, rich, solitary, and visionary figures as Egaeus and Roderick Usher.

If Poe's galling sense of social anomaly inclined him toward a species of *contemptus mundi,* so also did his outrageous hunger to be loved and cared for. "The want of parental affection," he wrote, "has been the heaviest of my trials," and his letters exhibit a lifelong effort to secure too late, and from almost any quarter, the various psychic benefits of a happy childhood. The world could not answer his exorbitant emotional demands, and he was therefore, one suspects, the more disposed to look for happiness beyond it—in the shadows of memory, in the valleys of dream, in glimpses of a past or future heavenly existence.

Another constant in Poe's life was extreme emotional conflict. This was manifested in the helpless ambivalence of his letters, and also, at times, of his criticism. Elizabeth Barrett noted how Poe, in a review of her poems, oscillated between "the two extremes of laudation and reprehension." "You would have thought," she told her husband-to-be, "that it had been written by a friend and foe, each stark mad with love and hate and writing the alternate paragraphs . . ." In his conduct, as every biographer has observed, Poe was at all times his own worst enemy; he had a genius for self-defeat, and the imminence of any success, whether professional or amatory, led him to frustrate his apparent desires by doing or saying the fatal thing. He might have cried out with St. Paul, "I do not understand my own actions. For I do not do what I want, but I do the very thing I hate." In his fiction, the theater of which was the individual soul, Poe sought to understand, and succeeded at least in portraying, that conflict and perversity from which all men have suffered, but few more fearfully than he.

That Poe was socially dislocated, emotionally starved, and torn in spirit, does not explain his art. Yet these facts may help us to understand why, as a continuator of English and European romanticism, he could carry some of its tendencies to unprecedented extremes, demanding of poetry that it totally repudiate this earthly life and making, in his psychological fiction, a vast and original contribution to that movement which Erich Heller has called "the discovery and colonisation of inwardness." [1]

III

FROM first to last, from "Al Aaraaf" to *Eureka,* Poe's vision of things was cosmic in extent, and any approach to his work must be prefaced by a brief synthetic account of that vision. The universe, as Poe conceived it, is a poetic or artistic creation, a "plot of God." It has come about through God's breaking-up of His original unity, and His self-radiation into space; it is presently at the point of maximum diffusion, and will soon begin to contract toward a final reassembly in—and as—God. Since God, in creating the universe, fragmented Himself into His creatures, and now exists only in those "infinite individualizations of Himself," it is they who must, by some counterimpulse, restore the original oneness of things.

What must this counterimpulse be? Since "the source of all motion is thought," it must be intellectual or spiritual in character. And since the creation is a work of art, the counterimpulse which can reunify it must be imaginative. In short, the duty of God's creatures is to think God together again by discovering, through the fusing power of poetic imagination, the primal unity in the present diversity.

The one true response to the creation, then, is to take an imaginative delight in its beauty and harmony, seen and unseen. To deny the validity and holiness of poetic intuition, to prefer some other mode of knowledge, would be to deny God and fall away from Him. Unfortunately, the planet Earth has done just that, by succumbing to the spirit of scientific rationalism, and by preferring material "fact" to visionary truth. As a result, the souls of men have grown dark, diseased, and insensitive, and even physical nature has by contagion "fallen" from its original divine beauty and order. Before the earth can rejoin the cosmic process, and assist the other stars in reconstituting God, it will have to be redeemed from rationalism and materialism by that purifying fire which the Bible foretells.

[1] Erich Heller, *The Hazard of Modern Poetry* (1953), p. 18.

Meanwhile, our fallen planet is not a happy environment for a poet. In him alone, of all the inhabitants of Earth, the divine spark of imagination still burns brightly; his soul alone vaguely remembers, from a previous existence, a divine harmony and beauty, and yearns to return thither. Yet everything around him conspires to reduce him to its own degraded level: the scientist and "utilitarian" discredit and abuse him, their corrupt and prosaic thought invades his consciousness, and nowhere in the human or natural environment can he find suitable objects for contemplation. His only means of escape is the suspension of outward consciousness, and a deliberate retreat from the temporal, rational, physical world into the visionary depths of his mind. There, in the immaterial regions of dream, he can purge himself of all earthly taint, and deliver himself to visions of that heavenly beauty which is the thought of God.

Poe's poet is thus at war with the external world. But he is also, unfortunately, at war within himself. As a pre-existent soul, or as a happy child, he once enjoyed a perfect psychic harmony; his consciousness was purely imaginative, and he knew the universe for the poem that it is. However, as he grew older on this corrupted Earth, and entered the society of men, it was unavoidable that his integrity of being should be compromised and destroyed. His intellect learned a respect for logic and prosaic fact; his awakening passions drew him toward the merely physical; conscience began its contests with desire; and there arose in him a mysterious spirit of perversity. Like Poe's universe, the poet's soul has lost its original unity; and like that universe, it will not regain that unity save in death. Till then, the poet's imagination must struggle not only against the mundane and physical world around him, but also against the mundane and physical aspects of his divided nature; he will not now find it easy to disengage his spirit from earthly things, and commune with that heavenly harmony which is symbolized, in Poe's fiction, by such figures as the Lady Ligeia.

IV

THE *Oxford Companion to American Literature* summarizes "Ligeia" as follows:

An aristocratic young man marries Ligeia, a woman of strange, dark beauty and great learning. They are deeply in love, and share an interest in the occult, until a wasting illness triumphs over Ligeia's passionate will to live, and she dies. In melancholy grief, her husband leaves his lonely home on the Rhine to purchase an English abbey, where he grows mentally deranged under the influence of opium. He marries fair-haired Lady Rowena Trevanion, although they are not in love, and Rowena soon dies in a strange manner. Her husband watches by the bier, and sees signs of returning life in the body, but considers these to be hallucinations. At last she rises to her feet and looses the cerements from her head, so that masses of long black hair stream forth. When she opens her eyes, he realizes that the lost Ligeia's will to live has triumphed, for she has assumed what was formerly the body of Rowena.

Considering its purpose and the difficulties involved, this summary is admirable, and yet it seems ludicrously unrelated to the actual experience of reading "Ligeia." It is as if some dark prophecy of Nostradamus had been translated into the straightforward language of Walter Lippmann. An examination of the disparities between summary and story may serve to set in relief some of Poe's characteristics as a writer of fiction.

In the first place, the summary necessarily exaggerates the prominence of plot in Poe's story, the first two-thirds of which consists mainly of rumination and brooding description. Only with the onset of Rowena's illness does narrative predominate, and the effect of the whole is not to leave us with any secure sense of fact or of causal sequence. Again, the summary confers on the persons of the story a credibility of character, motive, and feeling which they do not possess. We do not experience the narrator as "an aristocratic young man," but as a monstrous and unclassifiable sensibility. Ligeia does not strike us as a strangely beautiful and learned woman, but as an omniscient goddess. It does not seem adequate to say that the characters are "deeply in love" or "not in love," because their emotional frequencies are simply not ours: we cannot attune ourselves to a man who, looking into his beloved's eyes, is both "delighted and appalled," nor can we accept "mental alienation" as sufficient explanation of a perfectly motiveless remarriage. The fact is that Poe's characters escape our everyday understanding, and are meant to.

The main thing ignored in the summary is, of course, that "Ligeia" is not objectively told, but narrated—as so often in Poe—by a hero not quite in his ordinary mind. Such a narrative strategy has various effects, the chief one being this: that it encourages the reader to doubt that the ostensible story is the real or only one. Having come to doubt the ostensible story, the reader will perhaps decide to take it as a madman's misconstruction of doubtless prosaic events; but if he is familiar with Poe's criticism, he may more fruitfully decide to treat it as a cunning allegory, and look for some "mystic or secondary" meaning beneath it. Imaginative literature, Poe said, is "that class of composition in which there lies beneath the transparent upper current of meaning, an under or *suggestive* one." Since Poe thought "Ligeia" his best story, we may confidently sound it for an undercurrent.

The story begins with the narrator's confession that he "cannot remember how, when, or even precisely where" he first met Ligeia; moreover, he has never learned his beloved's surname, and cannot remember why not. Such a paroxysm of noninformativeness is potentially comic (and Poe later burlesqued the passage in "The Man Who Was Used Up"), but the intention here is serious. Vagueness and indefinitiveness were, in Poe's aesthetic theory, indispensable to the highest art, because they estrange the reader from mundane fact and meaning, and presumably set him adrift toward the spiritual and dim. This process of estrangement begins early and emphatically in "Ligeia," and is sustained throughout by the narrator's uncertainties, as well as by his repeated assertions that "words are impotent to convey" his subject matter.

But the more immediate effect of the opening paragraph is to detach Ligeia from the realm of actualities—from "when" and "where," from time and place—and thus, to suggest that she is really an idea. The hero speculates that he may have forgotten his first meeting with Ligeia "because, in truth, the character of my beloved, her rare learning, her singular yet placid cast of beauty, and the thrilling and enthralling eloquence of her low musical language, made their way into my heart by paces so steadily and stealthily progressive, that they have been unnoticed and unknown." It is true that people may "grow on us," but so sourceless and insensible a process as the hero describes would better characterize the development of some taste, or faculty, or idea within the soul. Let us see what idea is embodied in Ligeia.

Poe borrowed her name—as so much else—from Milton: in *Comus,* when the Attendant Spirit summons the nymph Sabrina to free the chaste Lady from Comus's spell, he adjures her in the name of the siren Ligea (l. 880 ff.) and other sea-immortals. Poe first used the borrowed name in his cosmic poem "Al Aaraaf," where Ligeia is one of the two presiding spirits of a wandering star, the function of which is to mediate between Heaven and the scattered worlds of the universe, conveying to the latter a redemptive awareness of divine beauty and harmony. Like Milton's siren, she is associated with song; she governs, in fact, "the music of things" (II.127), and has properly been described as "the personified harmony of nature."

If one tries the experiment of identifying the heroine of "Ligeia" with her namesake in "Al Aaraaf," one finds that the story begins at once to make sense, and that all its apparent hyperbole becomes sober statement. If Ligeia is not a woman, but a mediatory spirit embodying the Platonic idea of harmony, she quite naturally has "the beauty of beings either above or apart from the earth," and speaks with "a melody more than mortal." Being immaterial, she might be expected to come and go "as a shadow," with a step of "incomprehensible lightness." And since she is the principle of harmony which pervades all things, it is understandable that the hero should discover "in the commonest objects of the universe, a circle of analogies" to the expression of her eyes.

Ligeia's eyes are her major feature, and hidden within them, the hero says, is a "something more profound than the well of Democritus." The nature of this mystery is readily discovered, since Poe was here quoting a passage which he attributed to Joseph Glanvill, and later used as the epigraph of "A Descent into the Maelström":

The ways of God in Nature, as in Providence, are not as our ways; nor are the models that we frame in any way commensurate to the vastness, profundity, and unsearchableness of His works, which have a depth in them greater than the well of Democritus.

It is now understandable why the narrator, looking into Ligeia's eyes, should be "delighted and appalled"; what he dimly glimpses there is nothing less than "the ways of God."

In short, Ligeia is not distinguishable from what Poe called, in his review of R. H. Horne's *Orion*, "the sentiment of the beautiful—that divine sixth sense which is yet so faintly understood . . . that sense which speaks of GOD through his purest, if not his *sole* attribute—which proves, and which alone proves his existence." Because the principle of harmony belongs to all those arts through which the spirit intuits supernal beauty, Ligeia's attributes are not merely musical: her hand is marble; her skin is ivory; she resembles the Venus de' Medici; her hair interprets the Homeric epithet "hyacinthine," and she herself is a poet. She evokes Greek, Graeco-Roman, or Hebrew art —as do all her many counterparts, including Helen and the Marchesa Aphrodite—because such art was produced before the "fall" of Earth, in a golden time when man's soul was attuned to universal beauty.

The "gigantic" learning of Ligeia, which encompasses "*all* the wide areas of moral, physical, and mathematical science," must be understood in some mystic sense, because heavenly spirits cannot be supposed to study books. Here it is enlightening to recall a passage from "The Colloquy of Monos and Una," in which Monos is lamenting the corruption of Earth by the disease of rationalism. Alas, cries Monos, "alas for the pure contemplative spirit and majestic intuition of Plato! Alas for the Μουσικη [Music] which he justly regarded as an all sufficient education for the soul!"

In a footnote to this passage, Poe quotes the *Republic* twice, once to the effect that music is educationally all-sufficient, and again (from III.401) as follows:

For this reason is a musical education most essential; since it causes Rhythm and Harmony to penetrate most intimately into the soul, taking the strongest hold upon it, filling it with *beauty* and making the man *beautiful-minded* . . . He will praise and admire *the beautiful;* will receive it with joy into his soul, will feed upon it, and *assimilate his own condition with it.*

Poe then goes on to say:

Music Μουσικη had, among the Athenians, a far more comprehensive signification than with us. It included not only the harmonies of time and of tune, but the poetic diction, sentiment and creation, each in its widest sense. The study of *music* was with them, in fact, the general cultivation of the taste—of that which recognizes the beautiful —in contradistinction from reason, which deals only with the true.

We may now interpret Ligeia's universal "learning" in this way: she is the inspirer and heavenly goal of a kind of knowledge, purely aesthetic and superior to the rational, which soars intuitively toward the Forms of things, and assimilates the soul to transcendental Beauty. Such knowledge is "all sufficient" and all-inclusive, because it proceeds, by direct visionary means, toward those great answers which the trammeled reason will never reach. Such knowledge is also infallible because, the universe being an infinitely harmonious work of art, any perception of beauty or harmony must be true. The Keatsian idea that Beauty guarantees Truth was most boldly expressed by Poe in *Eureka*, where he argued that

symmetry and consistency are convertible terms: —thus Poetry and Truth are one. A thing is consistent in the ratio of its truth—true in the ratio of its consistency. *A perfect consistency, I repeat, can be nothing but an absolute truth.*

So long as Ligeia is with him as his "wife," the hero's harmonious soul is untouched by his diseased Earthly environment, and devotes itself to unbroken poetic visions of ultramundane harmony and beauty. In the superficial story, this happy period belongs to his adult life, but there are strong hints of another chronology: as Ligeia bends over the hero at his studies, he "resigns himself, with a childlike confidence, to her guidance"; when she falls ill, he is "but as a child groping benighted"; and her death leaves him with "feelings of utter abandonment." It is, in fact, as a child that the hero dwells with Ligeia and the heavenly harmony she confers; he is Wordsworth's "Mighty prophet! Seer blest!" and the passing of Ligeia is the passing of childhood and its "visionary gleam." As Poe put it in his juvenile poem "Tamerlane,"

> . . . boyhood is a summer sun
> Whose waning is the dreariest one.
> For all we live to know is known,
> And all we seek to keep hath flown.

The remainder of the story is an allegory of the efforts of the poetic soul, once compromised and disrupted by exposure to the world, to overcome the world and itself, and recover the imaginative absolutism of childhood. The poet-hero's retreat into a "remote and unsocial" English abbey, his addiction to opium, and his "incipient madness," symbolize the retreat from waking consciousness—from bodily, moral, and intellectual consciousness—into the imaginative freedom of reverie and dream. Like "The Haunted Palace," the House of Usher, and all such edifices in Poe, the abbey represents the hero's isolated and self-absorbed mind. Its decay, like that of the Usher mansion, signifies that the consciousness within is disengaging itself from the material world and the material self, and will soon (in a subjective sense) destroy them. As for the interior, which the hero has decorated in a spirit of "child-like perversity," it is, like the apartment of the hero of "The Assignation," quite literally "a bower of dreams."

The abbey's bridal chamber—the one room fully described—is pentagonal in shape, but the angles are hidden by sarcophagi, and the walls are hung with a figured material continually agitated by an artificial current of wind. The effect, therefore, is generally circular, but there is a perpetual ambiguity of form. The room thus avoids—as all Poe's dream-rooms do—that "rectangular obscenity" which Poe associated with the "harsh mathematical reason" now prevalent on Earth. The furnishings, like those of "The Assignation," reflect a scorn for "proprieties of place, and of time": the juxtaposition of Venetian, Saracenic, Druidical, and Egyptian objects exhibits the richness and daring of the hero's imagination, and very concretely expresses one idea of Poe's poem "Dream-Land," that in dreams we are "out of SPACE—out of TIME."

Entering dream, one escapes not only from local and temporal limitations, but also from external sensation. "It is as if," Poe says, "the five senses were supplanted by five others alien to mortality." Therefore Poe's dreamers lead a strictly indoor or sheltered existence, and their perceptions are wholly intramural. "Ligeia's" bridal chamber has a window of "leaden hue," which denatures the daylight to a "ghastly lustre"; the wind which rushes behind the draperies is "artificial"; and the changeable figures of the agitated draperies suggest those vivid and ever-shifting images of the hypnagogic state which Poe took to be "glimpses of the spirit's outer world."

The bridal chamber is not only a dreaming mind, but a mind obsessed with a mournful longing for Ligeia. A vine—first in the hero's catalogue of natural objects reminiscent of his beloved—shadows the gray window; the walls, like Ligeia's intellect, are "gigantic"; the fires of the pendant censer "writhe" like Ligeia's fierce spirit; and the gold-and-black décor recalls her radiant eyes and jet-black hair. Plainly, the chamber does not contain a consciousness hospitable to Rowena.

What, on the allegorical plane, does the fair-haired Rowena stand for? She is beautiful, but unlike Ligeia she is earthly, temporal, material. She is, in fact, what Poe elsewhere calls "the type of physical beauty," and she stands also for that part of the hero's compromised nature which adheres to such beauty. The progressive wasting-away of Rowena enacts, therefore, a Platonic version of the art process, in which beauty is imaginatively extricated from the temporal and physical, and may at last be glimpsed in its bodiless essence. Rowena's decomposition is a progress toward the immateriality of Ligeia; her *rigor mortis* is an approach to the timeless and ideal condition of statuary; and when Rowena becomes Ligeia, and the hero is "chilled into stone" by the transformation, we perceive that he has momentarily purified his consciousness of everything earthly, attained once more to the Beautiful, and "assimilated his own condition with it."

Ostensibly, the transformation is effected by the "gigantic volition" of Ligeia, but the narrator is, in truth, the sole agent in the tale; [1]

[1] See Roy P. Basler, *Sex, Symbolism, and Psychology in Literature* (1948).

the waning of Rowena and the waxing of Ligeia are governed by his mind's gradual movement from reverie to the visionary brink of sleep. "The night waned," he tells us, "and still, with a bosom full of bitter thoughts of the one only and supremely beloved, I remained gazing upon the body of Rowena." It is this remorseless and dematerializing gaze which alters Rowena—just as Berenice is withered by the gaze of Egaeus, or the bride of "The Oval Portrait" by that of her painter-husband.

Ligeia appears in proportion as Rowena fades, and we first see her as "a faint, indefinite shadow of angelic aspect" in the pool of light beneath the censer. Of this censer, which hangs on its golden chain in the center of the chamber, something must be said. It derives ultimately from the *Iliad* (VIII.18–26), but Poe plainly found it in *Paradise Lost* (II.1004 ff., 1051 ff.), where the created universe depends from Heaven by a golden chain which serves also as the pathway of angels. In Poe's "Al Aaraaf" (II.20 ff.), Milton's chain is incorporated into the description of the palace of Nesace, spirit of Beauty:

A dome, by linkèd light from Heaven let down,
Sat gently on these columns as a crown—
A window of one circular diamond, there,
Looked out above into the purple air,
And rays from God shot down that meteor chain
And hallowed all the beauty twice again,
Save when, between th' Empyrean and that ring,
Some eager spirit flapped his dusky wing.

The golden chain reappears, as a chandelier, in a number of Poe's interiors, signifying always the linkage between poetic imagination and the divine mind. The particolored flames of the censer in "Ligeia" are the purifying fire of imagination, and consist of diffracted "rays from God." Because the golden chain is the pathway of angels, it is beneath the censer that we first spy Ligeia's "dusky wing"; and it is there, again, "in the middle of the apartment," that she at last reopens her profound eyes.

The foregoing discussion of "Ligeia" would be disproportionate were the story not so central to Poe's thought, so characteristic of his method, and so much an index of his symbolism, that it opens up the fiction in general. The typical Poe story is, in its action, an allegory of dream-experience: it occurs within the mind of a poet; the characters are not distinct personalities, but principles or faculties of the poet's divided nature; the steps of the action correspond to the successive states of a mind moving into sleep; and the end of the action is the end of a dream. Sometimes, as in "William Wilson," the narrative will have a strong admixture of realism and of credible psychology; elsewhere, as in "The Fall of the House of Usher," there will be no such admixture, and the one available coherence will be allegorical.

Generally, Poe offers the reader some suggestion that his characters are but aspects of a single personality: they will be bound together by marriage, or kinship, or old and intimate acquaintance; or perhaps they will share a common height, eye color, or birthday; or perhaps their names will have some obvious or sly similarity. In "Usher," which is essentially a retelling of "Ligeia," the narrator has been a boyhood companion of Roderick Usher and is now "his only personal friend," while Lady Madeline, the third character of the story, is Usher's twin sister and "sole companion for long years." The narrator's journey to Usher's domain is a dream-journey into his own mind, in the depths of which, and on the brink of sleep, he encounters in Roderick Usher his visionary soul. Usher embodies, in his tremulousness and in his variations of voice and mood, the incertitude of the hypnagogic state, that borderline condition wherein "the confines of the waking world blend with those of the world of dreams." Like the hero of "Ligeia," Usher is struggling to purge himself of waking and worldly consciousness, and Lady Madeline's "wasting-away," like Rowena's, enacts this process of purgation. Once dead and encoffined —once "death-refined"—Lady Madeline can rise again as a Ligeia-figure, climb to the turret room where Roderick awaits her, and "in her violent and now final death-agonies, bear him to the floor a corpse." Grisly as their death-embrace may seen, it actually symbolizes the momentary reunion of a divided soul; and, since "by sleep and its world alone is *Death* imaged," it also symbolizes the final restoration and purification of that soul in the life to come.

The dematerialization of Usher's whirlwind-shaken house, and its collapse into its reflection in the tarn, express these same ideas; and they express as well the descent of the dreaming mind into unconscious sleep. "Ligeia" similarly ends, if not with a fall, at least with the vertigo which precedes and accompanies a fall. Its narrator's mind becomes "a helpless prey to a whirl of violent emotions," and the wind-current which circles the vast room, agitating the lofty draperies, intensifies at the close, so that Ligeia's unbound hair "streams forth into the rushing atmosphere of the chamber."

The violent whirlings which conclude both "Ligeia" and "Usher" put one in mind of the dizzy windings and final plunge of "The Domain of Arnheim," and of the whirlpools of "Ms. Found in a Bottle" and "A Descent into the Maelström." The comparison is fruitful, because such tales prove, upon examination, to tell in their own way the essential "Ligeia" story. In them, the dreaming mind's movement toward unearthly visions is geared, not to the stages of a woman's dissolution, but to the stages of a journey. The visitor to Arnheim moves, during his river-journey, into an ever-increasing solitude and strangeness, leaving behind him first the city, and then the river-boat with its passengers and crew; transferred to a "fairy" canoe, he floats for a time in a circular basin which, in its perfect mirroring of nature, symbolizes the double consciousness of the hypnagogic state; then, drawn by the current, he glides down a dizzily winding stream until—a golden door swinging wide to the accompaniment of mysterious music—he plunges into "the circumscribed Eden of his dreams." The aspect of nature, during the journey, has undergone a gradual change from commonplace rustic charm to paradisal beauty, and this change corresponds precisely to the gradual transformation of the earthly Rowena into the heavenly Ligeia. "Ms. Found in a Bottle" tells the same story in terms of an ocean voyage, and in the key of terror.

V

OF ALL Poe's stories, those of detection seem most complete in their "upper current," and least in need of allegorical interpretation. They have on the face of it a clear point: the superiority of intuition to reason. In *Eureka,* following a denunciation of Aristotelian and Baconian reasoning as "creeping and crawling," Poe asserts that Kepler's laws, from which Newton deduced the law of gravitation, were initially pure guesses, which Kepler then tailored into self-consistency and a consequent absolute truth.

> Yes!—these vital laws Kepler *guessed*—that is to say, he *imagined* them. Had he been asked to point out either the *de*ductive or *in*ductive route by which he attained them, his reply might have been—"I know nothing about *routes*—but I *do* know the machinery of the Universe. Here it is. I grasped it with *my soul*—I reached it through mere dint of *intuition*."

It is the Prefect of Police, in the three Dupin stories, who stands for that methodical reason which "creeps and crawls" and blinds itself with the "Scotch snuff of *detail*." Dupin, although Poe describes his mental operations as "analytic," and as based on a psychological calculus of probabilities, is actually representative of a pure poetic intuition bordering on omniscience. He *dreams* his solutions, and it sometimes appears that in solving a problem he can dispense, not only with reason, but with the problem itself. In "The Mystery of Marie Roget," Dupin sleeps in his armchair for seven or eight hours during the Prefect's recital of the evidence, his eyes hidden by green-glassed spectacles reminiscent of the tinted windows of Poe's dream-chambers. In "The Purloined Letter," Dupin invites the Prefect to give him the facts of the case—"or not"; just as he likes. The implication is that Dupin can somehow do without the mere facts; and indeed, within his first six speeches—well before the Prefect has told him anything—Dupin has intuitively solved the problem in all but its details. So confident is he of his principle of solution that he teases the Prefect by repeating it thrice.

It may be objected that Poe does also present Dupin as a reasoner, who offers his conclusions logically and at length. There are several answers to that objection, one being that a flat ascription of preterhuman powers, as in *Superman Comics,* makes for dull fiction. It is characteristic of Dupin that he first arrives at some conclusion, and then explains it logically to the narrator. In so doing, he is not reproducing his original mode of thought, any more than Poe, in his "Philosophy of Composition," gives a true account of the writing of "The

Raven." Rather, he is translating an ineffable process into lay terms; or demonstrating that intuition includes and obviates reason; or—like some Kepler—investigating the possibility that there was an implicit logic in his intuitive leap. This we know because, while Dupin's conclusions are always correct, the logic by which he claims to have reached them is generally faulty.[1] Readers would be more critical of Dupin's reasoning were they not disarmed by the correctness of his conclusions.

Insofar as Dupin has any method, it consists in identifying his intellect with that of another, and thereby divining what that person must think or do. Everyone has this power, in some degree, but with Dupin it is so strong that he can infallibly read the thoughts of a hypothetical Maltese sailor. In short, Dupin's power of divination is unlimited, and quite outflies the capabilities of his method; we are to see him not as a psychologist but as a seer. Poe said in his "Marginalia" that "poetic genius . . . in its supreme development, embodies all orders of intellectual capacity," and the statement applies to Dupin. He is a godlike genius who, possessing the highest and most comprehensive order of mind, includes in himself all possible lesser minds, and can therefore fathom any man—indeed, any primate—by mere introspection. How this omniscient solipsism is related to Poe's thought in general may be seen by a footnote to *Eureka,* in which Poe is remarking on his theory that the Universe, through its own imaginative efforts, is to be reabsorbed in God:

> The pain of the reflection that we shall lose our individual identity, ceases at once when we further reflect that the process, as above described, is neither more nor less than that of the absorption, by each individual intelligence, of all other intelligences (that is, of the Universe) into its own. That God may be all in all, each must become God.

The poet-detective Dupin is in the vanguard of that movement.

"The Purloined Letter," despite its adequacy as a detective tale, and as a vindication of pure intuition, is also an allegory of conflict within a single soul. As allegory, it belongs to a class of tales—"The Man of the Crowd," "Murders in the Rue Morgue"—in which the soul of a poet "detects" and confronts the evil or brutal principle in itself. By hint upon hint, Poe invites the reader to play detective himself, and to discover that the Minister D—— is the worldly, unprincipled "brother" or double of Auguste Dupin. And who is the queen, whom Dupin liberates from the Minister's power? Like the Lady Fortunato, like the Marchesa Aphrodite, like Di Broglio's wife, like Ligeia, she is that sense of beauty which must not be the captive of our lower natures.

VI

THE BODY of Poe's poetry is very small in proportion to his total work, partly because he had to neglect poetry in favor of better-paid literary labors, and partly because his conception of poetry, as it evolved, was so exclusive and extreme as to preclude any great productivity. Here are some random snippets from his criticism:

> The phrase, "A long poem," is simply a flat contradiction in terms . . . didactic subjects are utterly *beyond,* or rather beneath, the province of true poesy . . . A satire is, of course, *no* poem . . . we agree with Coleridge, that poetry and *passion* are discordant . . . Poetry, in elevating, tranquillizes the soul. With the *heart* it has nothing to do . . . With the Intellect or with the Conscience it has only collateral relations. Unless incidentally, it has no concern whatever with Duty or Truth . . . Give it any undue decision—imbue it with any very determinate tone—and you deprive it, at once, of its ethereal, its ideal, its intrinsic and essential character. You dispel its luxury of dream.

To the short story, which Poe regarded as a lower form than poetry, "and more appreciable by the mass of mankind," he permitted some measure of verisimilitude, and a logical clarity of plot and idea. But the function of poetry being not to organize and interpret earthly experience, but to induce a mood in which the soul soars toward supernal beauty, Poe excluded from poetry everything which might detain the soul on Earth. Thus, poetry must be disembarrassed of that moral sense which involves us with humanity; it must throw overboard that factuality, and that narrative or logical clarity,

[1] See Denis Marion, *La Méthode Intellectuelle d'Edgar Poe* (1952).

which would render it compassable by the mundane intellect; and it must eschew all human emotions, since, when compared to the sense of beauty, they are—as Poe said in reviewing Horne's *Orion*—"vapid and insignificant" and "trammel the soul in its flight to an ideal Helusion."

In practice, these principles resulted in a remorseless elaboration of those techniques of "estrangement" which we have already noted in "Ligeia." We must not, Poe warns us in a review of Macaulay, "confound obscurity of expression with the expression of obscurity," and surely the best of his tales may be defended as illuminations of a subject matter essentially obscure. But the poems, with few exceptions, do not truly illuminate, and what brilliance they have is like that of a Fourth-of-July rocket destroying itself in the void.

When one of Poe's poems has a narrative basis, as in "The Valley of Unrest," the reader will often struggle in vain to derive it from the poem proper, and will arrive at a plot, if at all, by interpolation from related prose works. "The Haunted Palace" and "The Raven" are, among Poe's verse-narratives, relatively clear, yet even they have a tantalizing incompleteness which one does not find in the better tales. Although the "plots" of Poe's poems always bear on his inveterate concerns, they mostly seem to be there not for plot's sake, or for meaning's sake, but to furnish a substance which the poem may "waste away" and etherealize.

The celebrated vagueness of Milton's *Paradise Lost*, whereby he conveys the impression of shadowing-forth things unknowable in themselves, was appropriated by Poe for purposes fundamentally opposed to Milton's. Poe was not interested in giving a qualified concreteness to divine things, but rather in verbally destroying the concreteness of earthly things. From Milton's description of Chaos as a "dark Illimitable ocean without bound," Poe learned how to write of "seas without a shore" and "boundless floods"; likewise, Milton's "dark unbottomed infinite Abyss" begot the "bottomless vales" of Poe's "Dream-Land." In Poe, the effect of such paradoxes is quite simply to annihilate the words "seas," "floods," and "vales," as we understand them, and so magically to deprive the reader of a part of the world he knows. In so doing, Poe's paradoxes support his continual explicit stress on disappearance, silence, oblivion, and all ideas which suggest nonbeing. It was the notion of approximating nothingness which most excited him in his own poetry, and in that of others. As a critic, he quoted approvingly almost any use of such words as "dim" and "unseen," and in reviewing Joseph Rodman Drake's *Culprit Fay* he characteristically observed that "in the expression 'glimmers and dies' . . . the imagination is exalted by the moral sentiment of beauty heightened in dissolution."

In an 1843 review of Rufus Griswold's *Poets and Poetry of America*, Poe scanned the first line of his "Haunted Palace" as follows:

In the/ greenest/ of our/ valleys

This supports a considerable body of contemporary testimony to the effect that Poe's reading of his poems was metronomic. There are several explanations for this feature of his poetry, aside from the relative indelicacy of Poe's ear. Expressive rhythm in poetry derives either from the things and movements described, or from the emotions embodied. The first source of rhythm was not altogether denied to Poe; we have, for instance, the line, "Down, down that town shall settle hence." But the second was precluded by Poe's having banished from his poetry all emotion save that "tremulous delight" which attends an imaginary destruction of the physical world. Poe's rhythmic regularity is not, however, wholly the result of such exclusion. He thought of the poem not as an object for contemplation but as a means of engendering "sensations which bewilder while they enthrall—and which would *not* so enthrall if they did not so bewilder." In short, he thought of the poem as casting a spell, and accordingly endowed it with the brevity, repetitiveness, sonority, and the impressive rhythmic monotony of a charm or incantation. In a charm we are far less concerned with the sense than with the effect—nonsense will do, if it only works—and therefore Poe's incantatory techniques further the general effort of his poetry to nullify—in a logical and denotative sense—the words with which it is made.

Poe's poetry is pure negation; it does not and

cannot acquaint us with supernal beauty, and the reader may well question whether there is anything very spiritual about a program of estranging us from the known by subverting the words through which we know it. A number of Poe's poems are enchanting in much the way they mean to be, but the present writer reserves his respect for the major tales, which, for all the secretiveness of their allegory, are great and trail-blazing realizations of inner experience.

NOTE

The editor wishes to thank Professor T. O. Mabbott for his great kindness in reading the Introduction and notes to this section, correcting several errors of fact, and supplying a number of data which the editor did not possess.

READING SUGGESTIONS

The best and most comprehensive edition of Poe's works is still the seventeen-volume *Complete Works*, ed. by James A. Harrison (1902). A new and complete edition, ed. by T. O. Mabbott, is underway at the Harvard University Press. Killis Campbell's *The Poems of Edgar Allan Poe* (1917) is the best edition of the poems, and the present editor is much indebted to Campbell's annotations. A two-volume *Letters of Edgar Allan Poe* has been edited by John Ward Ostrom (1948).

ARTHUR HOBSON QUINN's *Edgar Allan Poe: A Critical Biography* (1941) is an accurate and scholarly life which, however, does not wholly supersede G. E. Woodberry's *Life* (1885; revised, 2 vols., 1909). More popular biographies are Hervey Allen's semi-fictional *Israfel*, 2 vols. (1926; revised, 1 vol., 1934) and Frances Winwar's *The Haunted Palace* (1959).

There is so much criticism of Poe, and so little of it in the form of general book-length studies, that the student must be referred to such bibliographies as those in Spiller *et al.*, *Literary History of the United States* (1948), Vol. III, and in the *Bibliography Supplement* to that work (1959), ed. by Richard M. Ludwig. Four recent studies of some generality are N. B. Fagin's *The Histrionic Mr. Poe* (1949), Patrick F. Quinn's *The French Face of Edgar Poe* (1957), Edward H. Davidson's *Poe: A Critical Study* (1957), and Harry Levin's *The Power of Blackness* (1958).

POEMS

EVENING STAR

¶ IN "Evening Star" the poet rejects a "lowly" and relatively earthly Beauty (the moon) in favor of a "distant" and heavenly Beauty (Venus). Note that the enshrouding of the moon increases the visibility of Venus, as the death of Rowena makes possible a vision of Ligeia. This early poem embodies Poe's basic formula of destructive transcendence.

Critics have rightly pointed out Poe's debt to Thomas Moore's "While Gazing on the Moon's Light." However, Poe's poem is better than Moore's, and significantly reverses Moore's preference for the "smiling" moon over the "proud" and "distant" stars.

'T was noontide of summer,
  And mid-time of night;
And stars, in their orbits,
  Shone pale, thro' the light
Of the brighter, cold moon,
  'Mid planets her slaves,
Herself in the Heavens,
  Her beam on the waves.
  I gaz'd a while
  On her cold smile;
Too cold—too cold for me.
  There pass'd as a shroud,
  A fleecy cloud,
And I turn'd away to thee,
  Proud Evening Star,
  In thy glory afar,
And dearer thy beam shall be;
  For joy to my heart
  Is the proud part
Thou bearest in Heav'n at night,
  And more I admire
  Thy distant fire
Than that colder, lowly light.

1827

A DREAM

"A DREAM" expresses the poet's fidelity to aesthetic and visionary knowledge, despite the claims of what Poe calls in *Eureka* the "conventional World-Reason." The "lovely beam" of line 11 is opposed to "Truth's day-star" (the sun) as Venus to the moon in "Evening Star." The poem is indebted to Byron's "I Would I Were a Careless Child."

In visions of the dark night
I have dreamed of joy departed,
But a waking dream of life and light
Hath left me broken-hearted.

Ah! what is not a dream by day
To him whose eyes are cast
On things around him with a ray
Turned back upon the past?

That holy dream—that holy dream,
While all the world were chiding,
Hath cheered me as a lovely beam
A lonely spirit guiding.

What though that light, thro' storm and night,
So trembled from afar,
What could there be more purely bright
In Truth's day-star?

1827

THE LAKE: TO ——

THIS lake anticipates all the gulfs, tarns and whirlpools through which Poe's dreaming heroes plunge into eternity. The "tremulous delight" which attends the idea of annihilation is the primary feeling—or sensation—which Poe's poetry seeks to produce.

Some scholars think that the model for Poe's lake may have been the Lake of the Dismal Swamp, near Norfolk. Its waters are believed to be poisonous, and it is said to be haunted by the ghost of a lover who, maddened by the death of his sweetheart, ran into the swamp and was lost. Thomas Moore wrote a poem on the subject in 1803.

In spring of youth it was my lot
To haunt of the wide world a spot
The which I could not love the less—
So lovely was the loneliness
Of a wild lake, with black rock bound,
And the tall pines that towered around.

But when the Night had thrown her pall
Upon that spot, as upon all,
And the mystic wind went by
Murmuring in melody,
Then—ah, then—I would awake
To the terror of the lone lake.

Yet that terror was not fright,
But a tremulous delight—
A feeling not the jewelled mine
Could teach or bribe me to define—
Nor Love—although the Love were thine.

Death was in that poisonous wave,
And in its gulf a fitting grave
For him who thence could solace bring
To his lone imagining,
Whose solitary soul could make
An Eden of that dim lake.

1827

SONNET—TO SCIENCE

AN INDUBITABLE source for the sestet of this sonnet has lately been discovered. In the Hunter translation of Bernadin de St. Pierre's *Studies in Nature* (1808) the following sentence appears: "It is Science which has dragged down the chaste Diana from her nocturnal car; she has banished the Hamadryads from the antique forests, and the gentle Naiads from the fountains."

Whether Poe knew Keats's *Lamia* in 1829 is uncertain. In any case, the student will find interesting parallels to this sonnet in I.1–6 and II.229–38, as well as in the final alteration of Lamia by the "demon eyes" of the philosopher Apollonius. Whereas Keats's poem finds neither dream nor "cold philosophy" adequate to the truth of things, Poe's sonnet approves the first and denounces the second. Indeed, it sees the Earth as so corrupted by rationalism that the poet can discover beauty only in visions of "some happier star."

Science! true daughter of Old Time thou art!
Who alterest all things with thy peering eyes.
Why preyest thou thus upon the poet's heart,
Vulture, whose wings are dull realities?
How should he love thee? or how deem thee wise,
Who wouldst not leave him in his wandering
To seek for treasure in the jewelled skies,
Albeit he soared with an undaunted wing?
Hast thou not dragged Diana from her car?
And driven the Hamadryad from the wood
To seek a shelter in some happier star?
Hast thou not torn the Naiad from her flood,
The Elfin from the green grass, and from me
The summer dream beneath the tamarind tree?

1829

SONNET—TO SCIENCE. 3–4. Why . . . realities?: The poet is likened here to Prometheus and in the second quatrain to Icarus.

ROMANCE

THIS poem is about how time deprives the soul of its early visionary wholeness. Poe's dark-plumaged carrion birds (condor, vulture, raven) are symbols of devouring time.

Romance, who loves to nod and sing,
With drowsy head and folded wing,
Among the green leaves as they shake
Far down within some shadowy lake,
To me a painted paroquet
Hath been—a most familiar bird—
Taught me my alphabet to say,
To lisp my very earliest word,
While in the wild wood I did lie,
A child—with a most knowing eye.

Of late, eternal Condor years
So shake the very Heaven on high
With tumult as they thunder by,
I have no time for idle cares
Through gazing on the unquiet sky.
And when an hour with calmer wings
Its down upon my spirit flings—
That little time with lyre and rhyme
To while away—forbidden things!
My heart would feel to be a crime
Unless it trembled with the strings.

1829

ALONE

THOUGH never published by Poe, this poem has lately been proven authentic.

From childhood's hour I have not been
As others were—I have not seen
As others saw—I could not bring
My passions from a common spring—
From the same source I have not taken
My sorrow—I could not awaken
My heart to joy at the same tone—
And all I lov'd—*I* lov'd alone.
Then—in my childhood—in the dawn
Of a most stormy life—was drawn
From ev'ry depth of good and ill
The mystery which binds me still—
From the torrent, or the fountain—
From the red cliff of the mountain—
From the sun that round me roll'd
In its autumn tint of gold—
From the lightning in the sky
As it pass'd me flying by—
From the thunder, and the storm—
And the cloud that took the form
(When the rest of Heaven was blue)
Of a demon in my view.

FAIRY-LAND

A LIGHT treatment of Poe's customary material, in which there are deliberate and humorous collapses into the prosaic (ll. 13–14, 33–38).

Dim vales—and shadowy floods—
And cloudy-looking woods,
Whose forms we can't discover
For the tears that drip all over:
Huge moons there wax and wane—
Again—again—again—
Every moment of the night—
Forever changing places—
And they put out the star-light
With the breath from their pale faces.
About twelve by the moon-dial,
One more filmy than the rest
(A kind which, upon trial,
They have found to be the best)
Comes down—still down—and down
With its centre on the crown
Of a mountain's eminence,
While its wide circumference
In easy drapery falls
Over hamlets, over halls,
Wherever they may be—
O'er the strange woods—o'er the sea—
Over spirits on the wing—
Over every drowsy thing—
And buries them up quite
In a labyrinth of light—
And then, how deep!—O, deep,
Is the passion of their sleep!
In the morning they arise,
And their moony covering
Is soaring in the skies,
With the tempests as they toss,
Like—almost any thing—
Or a yellow Albatross.
They use that moon no more
For the same end as before,
Videlicet, a tent—
Which I think extragavant:
Its atomies, however,
Into a shower dissever,

FAIRY-LAND. 1–4. **Dim . . . over**: These lines reappear, with modifications, in "Dreamland," ll. 9–12. 11. **moon-dial**: "A dial for showing the hours of the night by the moon" (*OED*).

Of which those butterflies
Of Earth, who seek the skies,
And so come down again
(Never-contented things!)
Have brought a specimen
Upon their quivering wings.

1829

TO HELEN

❡ THE ADDRESSEE of this famous poem may or may not be a mortal woman; but she is, in any case, ideally perceived, and endowed with all the attributes of a Ligeia. As Psyche, the goddess of the soul, she carries the poet back to the visionary integrity which characterized his youth (l. 5) and that of the Earth (ll. 9–10).

Helen, thy beauty is to me
  Like those Nicéan barks of yore,
That gently, o'er a perfumed sea,
  The weary, way-worn wanderer bore
  To his own native shore.

On desperate seas long wont to roam,
  Thy hyacinth hair, thy classic face,
Thy Naiad airs have brought me home
  To the glory that was Greece,
And the grandeur that was Rome.

Lo! in yon brilliant window-niche
  How statue-like I see thee stand,
  The agate lamp within thy hand!
Ah, Psyche, from the regions which
  Are Holy-Land!

1831

ISRAFEL

❡ "ISRAFEL" expresses Poe's aspiration toward a supernal beauty which should mediate—like the gardens of Arnheim—between the earthly and the divine. The epigraph is taken, not from the Koran, but from George Sale's introduction to his translation of the Koran (1743). Poe modified Sale's language, and inserted the phrase "whose heart-strings are a lute," which seems to have been suggested, immediately, by Poe's own poem "Romance," ll. 20–21.

And the angel Israfel, whose
heart-strings are a lute, and
who has the sweetest voice
of all God's creatures.
KORAN

In Heaven a spirit doth dwell
  "Whose heart-strings are a lute;"
None sing so wildly well
As the angel Israfel,
And the giddy stars (so legends tell),
Ceasing their hymns, attend the spell
  Of his voice, all mute.

Tottering above
  In her highest noon,
  The enamoured moon
Blushes with love,
  While, to listen, the red levin
  (With the rapid Pleiads, even,
  Which were seven,)
  Pauses in Heaven.

And they say (the starry choir
  And the other listening things)
That Israfeli's fire
Is owing to that lyre
  By which he sits and sings—
The trembling living wire
  Of those unusual strings.

41–42. Of . . . skies: See "The Poetic Principle," 1 n. TO HELEN. **2. Nicéan:** What Poe intended by this word is not clear. An interesting recent discovery is the use of "Nicean"—signifying "victorious"—in the Langhorne translation of Plutarch (1770). The source of ll. 2–5 may be a vague recollection of Book XIII of the *Odyssey*, in which a Phaeacian bark carries the sleeping Odysseus to his native Ithaca. This supposition is supported by the fact that Homer (in VI.231 and elsewhere) likens Odysseus' hair to the hyacinth. However, the word "Nicéan" may well derive from the "Nyseian isle" mentioned by Milton in a catalogue of Edenic places (*Paradise Lost*, IV.275). This supposition is supported by the fact that, twenty-six lines thereafter, Milton is describing the "hyacinthine locks" of Adam. **7. Thy . . . face:** The hair of the Marchesa Aphrodite, in "The Assignation," clusters "round and round her classical head, in curls like those of the young hyacinth." And Ligeia has "raven-black . . . glossy . . . luxuriant, and naturally curling tresses, setting forth the full force of the Homeric epithet, 'hyacinthine!' " **9–10. To . . . Rome:** Poe often applies the terms "glory," "grandeur" and "gloom" to his Edens or havens of imaginative freedom. The valley of "Eleonora," which symbolizes the dreamy insulation of childhood, is "a magic prison-house of grandeur and of glory." The Coliseum, in the poem of that name, is described as having "grandeur, gloom, and glory." And the château of "The Oval Portrait" is a pile of "commingled gloom and grandeur." **12. How . . . stand:** Something is said, in Part IV of the Introduction, of "Ligeia's" symbolic use of sculpture; see also 7 n. and 12 n. to that story. Not only Helen and Ligeia, but many other Poe heroines, possess or acquire the ideal and timeless characteristics of sculpture. **14. Ah . . . which:** Poe's conception of Psyche, and of her relationship to visionary poetry, accords with that of Keats's "Ode to Psyche." ISRAFEL. **5–7. And . . . mute:** Keats's Lamia, who is likened in I.265 to a "descended Pleiad," sings "A song of love, too sweet for earthly lyres,/While, like held breath, the stars drew in their panting fires (I.299–300). **12. levin:** lightning. **13–14. With . . . seven:** Thomas Holley Chivers, and several other nineteenth-century poets, wrote poems based on a story of "the lost Pleiad."

But the skies that angel trod,
    Where deep thoughts are a duty—
Where Love's a grown-up God—
    Where the Houri glances are
Imbued with all the beauty
    Which we worship in a star.

Therefore, thou are not wrong,
    Israfeli, who despisest
An unimpassioned song;
To thee the laurels belong,
    Best bard, because the wisest!
Merrily live, and long!

The ecstasies above
    With thy burning measures suit—
Thy grief, thy joy, thy hate, thy love,
    With the fervour of thy lute—
    Well may the stars be mute!

Yes, Heaven is thine; but this
    Is a world of sweets and sours;
    Our flowers are merely—flowers,
And the shadow of thy perfect bliss
    Is the sunshine of ours.

If I could dwell
Where Israfel
    Hath dwelt, and he where I,
He might not sing so wildly well
    A mortal melody,
While a bolder note than this might swell
    From my lyre within the sky.

1831

THE CITY IN THE SEA

❡ WHATEVER this poem may owe to Byron's "Darkness," Shelley's "Lines Written Among the Euganean Hills," or Flavius Josephus' account of the engulfment of Gomorrah in the Dead Sea, it is very much Poe's own, and amounts to a vague and eccentric apocalyptic vision. The sleeping inhabitants of the city are not, as line 4 makes plain, the wicked dead alone. Perhaps they are the dead in general, awaiting Judgment and the destruction of the symbolic Babylon. More likely still, they may be that race of dreamers described in "Al Aaraaf," who in life and after-life prefer their dreams of beauty to any "truth," human or divine, and must therefore pay the price of final annihilation.

Lo! Death has reared himself a throne
In a strange city lying alone
Far down within the dim West,
Where the good and the bad and the worst and the
    best
Have gone to their eternal rest.
There shrines and palaces and towers
(Time-eaten towers that tremble not!)
Resemble nothing that is ours.
Around, by lifting winds forgot,
Resignedly beneath the sky
The melancholy waters lie.

No rays from the holy heaven come down
On the long night-time of that town;
But light from out the lurid sea
Streams up the turrets silently—
Gleams up the pinnacles far and free—
Up domes—up spires—up kingly halls—
Up fanes—up Babylon-like walls—
Up shadowy long-forgotten bowers
Of sculptured ivy and stone flowers—
Up many and many a marvellous shrine
Whose wreathèd friezes intertwine
The viol, the violet, and the vine.

Resignedly beneath the sky
The melancholy waters lie.
So blend the turrets and shadows there
That all seem pendulous in air,
While from a proud tower in the town
Death looks gigantically down.

There open fanes and gaping graves
Yawn level with the luminous waves;
But not the riches there that lie
In each idol's diamond eye—
Not the gaily-jewelled dead
Tempt the waters from their bed;
For no ripples curl, alas!
Along that wilderness of glass—
No swellings tell that winds may be
Upon some far-off happier sea—
No heavings hint that winds have been
On seas less hideously serene.

But lo, a stir is in the air!
The wave—there is a movement there!
As if the towers had thrust aside,
In slightly sinking, the dull tide—
As if their tops had feebly given
A void within the filmy Heaven.

23. **skies**: the object of "trod."

THE CITY IN THE SEA. 7. **Time-eaten . . . not!**: The city is a whole community of those ornate and decomposing structures in which the dreamer-heroes of Poe's fiction dwell. It especially resembles the Usher mansion, to which it corresponds in all details of atmosphere and lighting and in its final descent into the waters.

The waves have now a redder glow—
The hours are breathing faint and low—
And when, amid no earthly moans,
Down, down that town shall settle hence,
Hell, rising from a thousand thrones,
Shall do it reverence.

1831

THE SLEEPER

❡ IN HIS "Philosophy of Composition," Poe declared "the death of a beautiful woman" to be "the most poetical topic in the world." The dead and enshrouded lady of this poem is described as sleeping, because Poe imagined death as a "conscious slumber."

At midnight, in the month of June,
I stand beneath the mystic moon.
An opiate vapour, dewy, dim,
Exhales from out her golden rim,
And, softly dripping, drop by drop,
Upon the quiet mountain top,
Steals drowsily and musically
Into the universal valley.
The rosemary nods upon the grave;
The lily lolls upon the wave;
Wrapping the fog about its breast,
The ruin moulders into rest;
Looking like Lethe, see! the lake
A conscious slumber seems to take,
And would not, for the world, awake.
All Beauty sleeps!—and lo! where lies
Irene, with her Destinies!

Oh, lady bright! can it be right—
This window open to the night?
The wanton airs, from the tree-top,
Laughingly through the lattice drop—
The bodiless airs, a wizard rout,
Flit through thy chamber in and out,
And wave the curtain canopy
So fitfully—so fearfully—
Above the closed and fringèd lid
'Neath which thy slumb'ring soul lies hid,
That, o'er the floor and down the wall,
Like ghosts the shadows rise and fall!
Oh, lady dear, hast thou no fear?
Why and what art thou dreaming here?
Sure thou art come o'er far-off seas,
A wonder to these garden trees!
Strange is thy pallor! strange thy dress!
Strange, above all, thy length of tress,
And this all solemn silentness!

The lady sleeps! Oh, may her sleep,
Which is enduring, so be deep!
Heaven have her in its sacred keep!
This chamber changed for one more holy,
This bed for one more melancholy,
I pray to God that she may lie
Forever with unopened eye,
While the pale sheeted ghosts go by!

My love, she sleeps! Oh, may her sleep,
As it is lasting, so be deep!
Soft may the worms about her creep!
Far in the forest, dim and old,
For her may some tall vault unfold—
Some vault that oft hath flung its black
And wingèd panels fluttering back,
Triumphant, o'er the crested palls
Of her grand family funerals—

Some sepulchre, remote, alone,
Against whose portal she hath thrown,
In childhood, many an idle stone—
Some tomb from out whose sounding door
She ne'er shall force an echo more,
Thrilling to think, poor child of sin!
It was the dead who groaned within.

1831

LENORE

❡ THE FIRST and third stanzas are spoken by the family priest, or by some false friend of the dead Lenore; her lover, Guy de Vere, speaks the second and last stanzas.

Ah, broken is the golden bowl!—the spirit flown
  forever!
Let the bell toll!—a saintly soul floats on the
  Stygian river:—
And, Guy de Vere, hast *thou* no tear?—weep now
  or never more!
See! on yon drear and rigid bier low lies thy love,
  Lenore!

52–53. **Hell . . . reverence:** Isaiah says, in his prophecy of the fall of Babylon (14:9), "Hell from beneath is moved for thee to meet thee at thy coming: it stirreth up the dead for thee, even all the chief ones of the earth; it hath raised up from their thrones all the kings of the nations." See also Rev. 20:14–15. THE SLEEPER. 1–8. **At . . . valley:** Compare the lighter treatment of this idea in "Fairy-Land," l. 11 ff., and see "The Oval Portrait," 8 n. 9–10. **The . . . wave:** The rosemary and lily conventionally symbolize remembrance and purity. 18–36. **Oh . . . silentness!:** This verse-paragraph was, in an earlier version of the poem, hummed into the lady's ear by the moon. So assigned, the lines made better dramatic sense.

LENORE. 1. **Ah . . . forever!:** See Eccles. 12:6.

Come, let the burial rite be read—the funeral song be sung!—
An anthem for the queenliest dead that ever died so young—
A dirge for her the doubly dead in that she died so young.

"Wretches! ye loved her for her wealth, and ye hated her for her pride;
And, when she fell in feeble health, ye blessed her—that she died:—
How *shall* the ritual, then, be read—the requiem how be sung
By you—by yours, the evil eye,—by yours, the slanderous tongue
That did to death the innocence that died, and died so young?"

Peccavimus; yet rave not thus! but let a Sabbath song
Go up to God so solemnly the dead may feel no wrong!
The sweet Lenore hath gone before, with Hope that flew beside,
Leaving thee wild for the dear child that should have been thy bride—
For her, the fair and debonair, that now so lowly lies,
The life upon her yellow hair, but not within her eyes—
The life still there upon her hair, the death upon her eyes.

"Avaunt!—avaunt! to friends from fiends the indignant ghost is riven—
From Hell unto a high estate within the utmost Heaven—
From moan and groan to a golden throne beside the king of Heaven:—
Let *no* bell toll, then, lest her soul, amid its hallowed mirth,
Should catch the note as it doth float up from the damnèd Earth!
And I—tonight my heart is light:—no dirge will I upraise,
But waft the angel on her flight with a Paean of old days!"

1831

THE VALLEY OF UNREST

❡ "THE VALLEY OF UNREST" obscurely tells a part of Poe's fundamental tale: a soul loses its original harmony through exposure to the corrupt world of men. "Eleonora" and "Silence—A Fable" contain passages which illuminate this poem.

Once it smiled a silent dell
Where the people did not dwell;
They had gone unto the wars,
Trusting to the mild-eyed stars,
Nightly, from their azure towers,
To keep watch above the flowers,
In the midst of which all day
The red sun-light lazily lay.
Now each visitor shall confess
The sad valley's restlessness.
Nothing there is motionless—
Nothing save the airs that brood
Over the magic solitude.
Ah, by no wind are stirred those trees
That palpitate like the chill seas
Around the misty Hebrides!
Ah, by no wind those clouds are driven
That rustle through the unquiet Heaven
Uneasily, from morn till even,
Over the violets there that lie
In myriad types of the human eye—
Over the lilies there that wave
And weep above a nameless grave!
They wave:—from out their fragrant tops
Eternal dews come down in drops.
They weep:—from off their delicate stems
Perennial tears descend in gems.

1831

THE COLISEUM

❡ THIS, Poe's first effort at blank verse, leans here and there on Byron's *Childe Harold,* but is best clarified by comparison with "Ms. Found in a Bottle," also published in 1833. The thirst for Ruin, in both story and poem, is ultimately a thirst for what Shelley's *Alastor* called "the world's youth"—for the early and unfallen condition of Earth and of the soul.

Type of the antique Rome! Rich reliquary
Of lofty contemplation left to Time
By buried centuries of pomp and power!
At length—at length—after so many days
Of weary pilgrimage and burning thirst
(Thirst for the springs of lore that in thee lie),

13. *Peccavimus:* "we have sinned."

THE VALLEY OF UNREST. **20–23. Over . . . grave!:** Violets signify faithfulness, and are associated with early death. Laertes says of Ophelia (*Hamlet*, V.1), "Lay her i' the earth;/And from her fair and unpolluted flesh/May violets spring." Lilies signify purity. The grave contains a dead Ligeia or Eleonora; that is, the principle of harmony has departed.

I kneel, an altered and an humble man,
Amid thy shadows, and so drink within
My very soul thy grandeur, gloom, and glory!

Vastness! and Age! and Memories of Eld!
Silence! and Desolation! and dim Night!
I feel ye now—I feel ye in your strength—
O spells more sure than e'er Judaean king
Taught in the gardens of Gethsemane!
O charms more potent than the rapt Chaldee
Ever drew down from out the quiet stars!

Here, where a hero fell, a column falls!
Here, where the mimic eagle glared in gold,
A midnight vigil holds the swarthy bat!
Here, where the dames of Rome their gilded hair
Waved to the wind, now wave the reed and thistle!
Here, where on golden throne the monarch lolled,
Glides, spectre-like, unto his marble home,
Lit by the wan light of the hornèd moon,
The swift and silent lizard of the stones!

But stay! these walls—these ivy-clad arcades—
These mouldering plinths—these sad and blackened shafts—
These vague entablatures—this crumbling frieze—
These shattered cornices—this wreck—this ruin—
These stones—alas! these gray stones—are they all—
All of the famed and the colossal left
By the corrosive Hours to Fate and me?

"Not all"—the Echoes answer me—"not all!
Prophetic sounds and loud, arise forever
From us, and from all Ruin, unto the wise,
As melody from Memnon to the Sun.
We rule the hearts of mightiest men—we rule
With a despotic sway all giant minds.
We are not impotent—we pallid stones.
Not all our power is gone—not all our fame—
Not all the magic of our high renown—
Not all the wonder that encircles us—
Not all the mysteries that in us lie—
Not all the memories that hang upon
And cling around about us as a garment,
Clothing us in a robe of more than glory."

1833

THE COLISEUM. **9. My . . . glory!**: See "To Helen," 9–10 n. **13. O . . . king**: A reference to Christ. **36. As . . . Sun**: The Memnon statue near Thebes, in Egypt, was said to greet the dawn with music. **44–46. Not . . . glory**: Compare "The Sleeper," ll. 11–12.

TO ONE IN PARADISE

ORIGINALLY, and with some textual differences, this poem was a part of Poe's story "The Assignation." Two lines from Shelley's "Lines Written Among the Euganean Hills"—

Many a green isle needs must be
In the deep wide sea of Misery—

may have prompted Poe's third line.

Thou wast that all to me, love,
  For which my soul did pine—
A green isle in the sea, love,
  A fountain and a shrine,
All wreathed with fairy fruits and flowers,
  And all the flowers were mine.

Ah, dream too bright to last!
  Ah, starry Hope! that didst arise
But to be overcast!
  A voice from out the Future cries,
"On! on!"—but o'er the Past
  (Dim gulf!) my spirit hovering lies
Mute, motionless, aghast!

For, alas! alas! with me
  The light of Life is o'er!
No more—no more—no more—
  (Such language holds the solemn sea
To the sands upon the shore)
  Shall bloom the thunder-blasted tree,
 Or the stricken eagle soar!

And all my days are trances,
  And all my nightly dreams
 Are where thy grey eye glances,
  And where thy footstep gleams—
In what ethereal dances,
  By what eternal streams.

1834

THE HAUNTED PALACE

THIS poem, first published separately and later incorporated in "The Fall of the House of Usher," is a key to Poe's architectural symbolism. "By 'The Haunted Palace,' " Poe wrote Rufus Griswold in 1841, "I mean to imply a mind haunted by phantoms—a disordered brain." The reader will readily see that the palace is a head, that its windows are eyes, its banners golden hair, its pearl and ruby door teeth and lips. Within the palace-head is a harmonious and imaginative consciousness, which expresses itself in "wit and wisdom." The corruption of that consciousness, which blights the palace and its valley, is not explained in the poem, but

Poe is obviously retelling his basic story, as outlined in Part III of the Introduction.

In the greenest of our valleys,
By good angels tenanted,
Once a fair and stately palace—
Radiant palace—reared its head.
In the monarch Thought's dominion—
It stood there!
Never seraph spread a pinion
Over fabric half so fair!

Banners yellow, glorious, golden,
On its roof did float and flow,
(This—all this—was in the olden
Time long ago,)
And every gentle air that dallied,
In that sweet day,
Along the ramparts plumed and pallid,
A wingèd odor went away.

Wanderers in that happy valley,
Through two luminous windows, saw
Spirits moving musically
To a lute's well-tunèd law,
Round about a throne, where sitting,
Porphyrogene!
In state his glory well befitting,
The ruler of the realm was seen.

And all with pearl and ruby glowing
Was the fair palace door,
Through which came flowing, flowing, flowing,
And sparkliing evermore,
A troop of Echoes, whose sweet duty
Was but to sing,
In voices of surpassing beauty,
The wit and wisdom of their king.

But evil things, in robes of sorrow,
Assailed the monarch's high estate.
(Ah, let us mourn!—for never morrow
Shall dawn upon him, desolate!)
And round about his home the glory
That blushed and bloomed,
Is but a dim-remembered story
Of the old time entombed.

And travellers, now, within that valley,
Through the red-litten windows see
Vast forms that move fantastically
To a discordant melody,

THE HAUNTED PALACE. **8. fabric:** building. **15. pallid:** yellow (Latin *pallidus*). **22. Porphyrogene:** Poe's invented form of "porphyrogenite," meaning "born in the purple."

While, like a ghastly rapid river,
Through the pale door
A hideous throng rush out forever,
And laugh—but smile no more.

1839

SONNET—SILENCE

❡ THIS "sonnet"—which has a nine-line octave, irregularly rhymed—is unusual in Poe's poetry, since it logically develops an idea. By "corporate Silence" (l. 10) Poe means bodily death; its incorporate or immaterial "shadow" (l. 13) is the death of the soul.

There are some qualities—some incorporate things,
That have a double life, which thus is made
A type of that twin entity which springs
From matter and light, evinced in solid and shade.
There is a two-fold *Silence*—sea and shore—
Body and soul. One dwells in lonely places,
Newly with grass o'ergrown; some solemn graces,
Some human memories and tearful lore,
Render him terrorless: his name's "No More."
He is the corporate Silence: dread him not!
No power hath he of evil in himself;
But should some urgent fate (untimely lot!)
Bring thee to meet his shadow (nameless elf,
That haunteth the lone regions where hath trod
No foot of man,) commend thyself to God!

1840

THE CONQUEROR WORM

❡ THE COMPASSIONATE angel audience of this poem contemplates the madness and horror of human life, at that point in cosmic history where the Universe has reached maximum diffusion and the "lonesome" Earth is at its remotest from God's original harmony. Earthly life has become "formless," the music of the spheres is but "fitfully" heard, and mankind—though made "in the form of God on high"—must perish before the Universe can regather toward its primal unity. The conclusion of *Eureka* (see p. 474) takes an optimistic view of what is here considered tragic.

Lo! 't is a gala night
Within the lonesome latter years!

THE CONQUEROR WORM. **2. Within . . . years!:** An addendum to *Eureka* states that the reassembly and annihilation of the Universe "may take place not until the planets have become flaming suns—*from an accumulation of their own Sun's caloric,*

An angel throng, bewinged, bedight
In veils, and drowned in tears,
Sit in a theatre, to see
A play of hopes and fears,
While the orchestra breathes fitfully
The music of the spheres.

Mimes, in the form of God on high,
Mutter and mumble low,
And hither and thither fly—
Mere puppets they, who come and go
At bidding of vast formless things
That shift the scenery to and fro,
Flapping from out their Condor wings
Invisible Wo!

That motley drama—oh, be sure
It shall not be forgot!
With its Phantom chased for evermore
By a crowd that seize it not,
Through a circle that ever returneth in
To the self-same spot,
And much of Madness, and more of Sin,
And Horror the soul of the plot.

But see, amid the mimic rout,
A crawling shape intrude!
A blood-red thing that writhes from out
The scenic solitude!
It writhes!—it writhes!—with mortal pangs
The mimes become its food,
And seraphs sob at vermin fangs
In human gore imbued.

Out—out are the lights—out all!
And, over each quivering form,
The curtain, a funeral pall,
Comes down with the rush of a storm,
While the angels, all pallid and wan,
Uprising, unveiling, affirm
That the play is the tragedy, "Man,"
And its hero, the Conqueror Worm.

1843

DREAM-LAND

SINCE to dream is to escape the material world, Poe's fictional descriptions of the dream process are full of the breaking-down of matter and the dissolution of finite forms. It is understandable that a poem like "Dream-Land" should borrow so much from the prospect of Chaos in *Paradise Lost* (II.890 ff.):

Before their eyes in sudden view appear
The secrets of the hoary deep, a dark
Illimitable ocean without bound,
Without dimension, where length, breadth, and
highth,
And time and place are lost; where eldest Night
And Chaos, *Ancestors of Nature, hold*
Eternal Anarchy . . .

By a route obscure and lonely,
Haunted by ill angels only,
Where an Eidolon, named NIGHT,
On a black throne reigns upright,
I have reached these lands but newly
From an ultimate dim Thule—
From a wild weird clime that lieth, sublime,
Out of SPACE—out of TIME.

Bottomless vales and boundless floods,
And chasms, and caves, and Titan woods,
With forms that no man can discover
For the tears that drip all over;
Mountains toppling evermore
Into seas without a shore;
Seas that restlessly aspire,
Surging, unto skies of fire;
Lakes that endlessly outspread
Their lone waters—lone and dead,—
Their still waters—still and chilly
With the snows of the lolling lily.

By the lakes that thus outspread
Their lone waters, lone and dead,—
Their sad waters, sad and chilly
With the snows of the lolling lily—
By the mountains—near the river
Murmuring lowly, murmuring ever,—
By the grey woods,—by the swamp
Where the toad and the newt encamp,—
By the dismal tarns and pools
Where dwell the Ghouls,—
By each spot the most unholy—
In each nook most melancholy,—
There the traveller meets, aghast,
Sheeted Memories of the Past—
Shrouded forms that start and sigh
As they pass the wanderer by—
White-robed forms of friends long given,
In agony, to the Earth—and Heaven.

For the heart whose woes are legion
'T is a peaceful, soothing region—
For the spirit that walks in shadow
'T is—oh, 't is an Eldorado!

reaching from centre to surface, which shall in the lonesome latter days melt all the 'elements' and dissipate the solid foundations out as a scroll."

DREAM-LAND. **3. an Eidolon:** a phantom. **6. From . . . Thule:** See "The Pit and the Pendulum," 15 n.

But the traveller, travelling through it,
May not—dare not openly view it;
Never its mysteries are exposed
To the weak human eye unclosed;
So wills its King, who hath forbid
The uplifting of the fringèd lid;
And thus the sad Soul that here passes
Beholds it but through darkened glasses.

By a route obscure and lonely,
Haunted by ill angels only,
Where an Eidolon, named NIGHT,
On a black throne reigns upright,
I have wandered home but newly
From this ultimate dim Thule.

1844

THE RAVEN

¶ "THE RAVEN" is the clearest and most developed of Poe's verse-narratives, and one of a very few Poe poems which possess any dramatic variation of tone: it progresses from mournfulness to trepidation, thence to jocularity and finally, by way of hysterical self-torture, to despair. It has therefore been much declaimed in the schoolrooms of America. Despite the completeness of "The Raven" as narrative, the reader is left with a feeling that certain meanings—perhaps because of the difficulties of the chosen stanza form—have not been adequately suggested. Considering what symbolic force sculpture usually has for Poe, it is hard to believe that the bust of Pallas signifies merely the scholarship of the lover; yet no other supposition is encouraged. Similarly, one does not know how much, if anything, to make of the resemblance between the final tableaux of "The Raven" and "The Black Cat."

Once upon a midnight dreary, while I pondered, weak and weary,
Over many a quaint and curious volume of forgotten lore—
While I nodded, nearly napping, suddenly there came a tapping,
As of some one gently rapping, rapping at my chamber door.
" 'Tis some visitor," I muttered, "tapping at my chamber door—
Only this and nothing more."

Ah, distinctly I remember it was in the bleak December;
And each separate dying ember wrought its ghost upon the floor.
Eagerly I wished the morrow;—vainly I had sought to borrow
From my books surcease of sorrow—sorrow for the lost Lenore—
For the rare and radiant maiden whom the angels name Lenore—
Nameless *here* for evermore.

And the silken, sad, uncertain rustling of each purple curtain
Thrilled me—filled me with fantastic terrors never felt before;
So that now, to still the beating of my heart, I stood repeating,
" 'Tis some visitor entreating entrance at my chamber door—
Some late visitor entreating entrance at my chamber door;—
This it is and nothing more."

Presently my soul grew stronger; hesitating then no longer,
"Sir," said I, "or Madam, truly your forgiveness I implore;
But the fact is I was napping, and so gently you came rapping,
And so faintly you came tapping, tapping at my chamber door,
That I scarce was sure I heard you"—here I opened wide the door;—
Darkness there and nothing more.

Deep into that darkness peering, long I stood there wondering, fearing,
Doubting, dreaming dreams no mortal ever dared to dream before;
But the silence was unbroken, and the stillness gave no token,
And the only word there spoken was the whispered word, "Lenore?"
This I whispered, and an echo murmured back the word "Lenore!"
Merely this and nothing more.

Back into the chamber turning, all my soul within me burning,
Soon again I heard a tapping somewhat louder than before.
"Surely," said I, "surely that is something at my window lattice;
Let me see, then, what thereat is, and this mystery explore—
Let my heart be still a moment and this mystery explore;—
'Tis the wind and nothing more!"

THE RAVEN. **12. Nameless . . . evermore:** The beloved's earthly name no longer applies to her, since she has left the earth for Aidenn (heaven), and is there known by the angelic name of Lenore.

Open here I flung the shutter, when, with many a flirt and flutter,
In there stepped a stately Raven of the saintly days of yore;
Not the least obeisance made he; not a minute stopped or stayed he;
But, with mien of lord or lady, perched above my chamber door—
Perched upon a bust of Pallas just above my chamber door—
Perched, and sat, and nothing more.

Then this ebony bird beguiling my sad fancy into smiling,
By the grave and stern decorum of the countenance it wore,
"Though thy crest be shorn and shaven, thou," I said, "art sure no craven,
Ghastly grim and ancient Raven wandering from the Nightly shore—
Tell me what thy lordly name is on the Night's Plutonian shore!"
Quoth the Raven, "Nevermore."

Much I marvelled this ungainly fowl to hear discourse so plainly,
Though its answer little meaning—little relevancy bore;
For we cannot help agreeing that no living human being
Ever yet was blessed with seeing bird above his chamber door—
Bird or beast upon the sculptured bust above his chamber door,
With such name as "Nevermore."

But the Raven, sitting lonely on the placid bust, spoke only
That one word, as if his soul in that one word he did outpour.
Nothing farther then he uttered—not a feather then he fluttered—
Till I scarcely more than muttered, "Other friends have flown before—
On the morrow *he* will leave me, as my Hopes have flown before."
Then the bird said, "Nevermore."

Startled at the stillness broken by reply so aptly spoken,
"Doubtless," said I, "what it utters is its only stock and store
Caught from some unhappy master whom unmerciful Disaster
Followed fast and followed faster till his songs one burden bore—
Till the dirges of his Hope that melancholy burden bore
Of 'Never—nevermore.' "

But the Raven still beguiling all my fancy into smiling,
Straight I wheeled a cushioned seat in front of bird, and bust and door;
Then, upon the velvet sinking, I betook myself to linking
Fancy unto fancy, thinking what this ominous bird of yore—
What this grim, ungainly, ghastly, gaunt, and ominous bird of yore
Meant in croaking "Nevermore."

This I sat engaged in guessing, but no syllable expressing
To the fowl whose fiery eyes now burned into my bosom's core;
This and more I sat divining, with my head at ease reclining
On the cushion's velvet lining that the lamp-light gloated o'er,
But whose velvet-violet lining with the lamp-light gloating o'er,
She shall press, ah, nevermore!

Then, methought, the air grew denser, perfumed from an unseen censer
Swung by Seraphim whose foot-falls tinkled on The tufted floor.
"Wretch," I cried, "thy God hath lent thee—by these angels he hath sent thee
Respite—respite and nepenthe from thy memories of Lenore;
Quaff, oh, quaff this kind nepenthe and forget this lost Lenore!"
Quoth the Raven, "Nevermore."

"Prophet!" said I, "thing of evil!—prophet still, if bird or devil!—
Whether Tempter sent, or whether tempest tossed thee here ashore,
Desolate yet all undaunted, on this desert land enchanted—
On this home by Horror haunted—tell me truly, I implore—

74. To . . . core: See "Sonnet—to Science," ll. 2–4. "The Black Cat" also had an "eye of fire." **79–80. Then . . . floor:** Compare the censer and the "gentle foot-fall upon the carpet" in "Ligeia." **87–88. Desolate . . . haunted:** As in "The Haunted Palace" or "The Fall of the House of Usher," the environs of the lover's house have become wasteland.

Is there—*is* there balm in Gilead?—tell me—tell me, I implore!"
Quoth the Raven, "Nevermore."

"Prophet!" said I, "thing of evil!—prophet still, if bird or devil!
By that Heaven that bends above us—by that God we both adore—
Tell this soul with sorrow laden if, within the distant Aidenn,
It shall clasp a sainted maiden whom the angels name Lenore—
Clasp a rare and radiant maiden whom the angels name Lenore."
Quoth the Raven, "Nevermore."

"Be that word our sign of parting, bird or fiend!" I shrieked, upstarting—
"Get thee back into the tempest and the Night's Plutonian shore!
Leave no black plume as a token of that lie thy soul hath spoken!
Leave my loneliness unbroken!—quit the bust above my door!
Take thy beak from out my heart, and take thy form from off my door!"
Quoth the Raven, "Nevermore."

And the Raven, never flitting, still is sitting, *still* is sitting
On the pallid bust of Pallas just above my chamber door;
And his eyes have all the seeming of a demon's that is dreaming,
And the lamp-light o'er him streaming throws his shadow on the floor;
And my soul from out that shadow that lies floating on the floor
Shall be lifted—nevermore!

1845

ULALUME—A BALLAD

THIS poem represents a conflict and reconciliation between the poet's self and his "Psyche," or soul. The poet owes eternal fidelity to Ulalume, his dead beloved, but in stanzas 4–7 he is forgetfully attracted to a new love and seeks to persuade his soul that the new love is redemptive and ideal. The soul then forcibly reminds the poet of his Ulalume, and prevails. In the final stanza of the poem, which has taken the form of a dream-allegory, self and soul are united in rejecting the new love as "sinful," and in supposing that the powers of dream have deluded them with false hope out of pity for their sorrow.

The skies they were ashen and sober;
The leaves they were crispèd and sere—
The leaves they were withering and sere:
It was night, in the lonesome October
Of my most immemorial year:
It was hard by the dim lake of Auber,
In the misty mid region of Weir—
It was down by the dank tarn of Auber,
In the ghoul-haunted woodland of Weir.

Here once, through an alley Titanic,
Of cypress, I roamed with my Soul—
Of cypress, with Psyche, my Soul.
These were days when my heart was volcanic
As the scoriac rivers that roll—
As the lavas that restlessly roll
Their sulphurous currents down Yaanek
In the ultimate climes of the Pole—
That groan as they roll down Mount Yaanek
In the realms of the Boreal Pole.

Our talk had been serious and sober,
But our thoughts they were palsied and sere—
Our memories were treacherous and sere—
For we knew not the month was October,
And we marked not the night of the year
(Ah, night of all nights in the year!)—
We noted not the dim lake of Auber
(Though once we had journeyed down here)—
We remembered not the dank tarn of Auber,
Nor the ghoul-haunted woodland of Weir.

And now, as the night was senescent
And star-dials pointed to morn—
As the star-dials hinted of morn—
At the end of our path a liquescent
And nebulous lustre was born,
Out of which a miraculous crescent
Arose with a duplicate horn—
Astarte's bediamonded crescent
Distinct with its duplicate horn.

And I said: "She is warmer than Dian;
She rolls through an ether of sighs—

89. Is . . . implore: See Jer. 8:22. **101. Take . . . door!:** See "Sonnet—to Science," l. 3.

ULALUME. 6–7. It . . . Weir: Critics suggest that Poe may have borrowed "Auber" from Jean François Auber, composer of the "Lac des Fées," and "Weir" from Robert Walter Weir, a painter of the Hudson River school. **14. scoriac:** scoria are volcanic cinders. **39. Dian:** Diana, the moon. Compare Poe's contrast of moon and Venus in "Evening Star."

She revels in a region of sighs.
She has seen that the tears are not dry on
These cheeks, where the worm never dies,
And has come past the stars of the Lion,
To point us the path to the skies—
To the Lethean peace of the skies—
Come up, in despite of the Lion,
To shine on us with her bright eyes—
Come up through the lair of the Lion,
With love in her luminous eyes."

But Psyche, uplifting her finger,
Said: "Sadly this star I mistrust—
Her pallor I strangely mistrust:
Ah, hasten!—ah, let us not linger!
Ah, fly!—let us fly!—for we must."
In terror she spoke, letting sink her
Wings until they trailed in the dust—
In agony sobbed, letting sink her
Plumes till they trailed in the dust—
Till they sorrowfully trailed in the dust.

I replied: "This is nothing but dreaming:
Let us on by this tremulous light!
Let us bathe in this crystalline light!
Its Sibyllic splendor is beaming
With Hope and in Beauty to-night:—
See!—it flickers up the sky through the night!
Ah, we safely may trust to its gleaming,
And be sure it will lead us aright—
We surely may trust to a gleaming
That cannot but guide us aright,
Since it flickers up to Heaven through the night."

Thus I pacified Psyche and kissed her,
And tempted her out of her gloom—
And conquered her scruples and gloom;
And we passed to the end of the vista,
But were stopped by the door of a tomb—
By the door of a legended tomb;
And I said—"What is written, sweet sister,
On the door of this legended tomb?"
She replied: "Ulalume—Ulalume!—
'Tis the vault of thy lost Ulalume!"

Then my heart it grew ashen and sober
As the leaves that were crispèd and sere—
As the leaves that were withering and sere;
And I cried: "It was surely October
On *this* very night of last year
That I journeyed—I journeyed down here!—
That I brought a dread burden down here—
On this night of all nights in the year,
Ah, what demon has tempted me here?

43. **These . . . dies:** See Isa. 66:2–4.

Well I know, now, this dim lake of Auber—
This misty mid region of Weir—
Well I know, now, this dank tarn of Auber,
This ghoul-haunted woodland of Weir."

Said we, then,—the two, then: "Ah, can it
Have been that the woodlandish ghouls—
The pitiful, the merciful ghouls—
To bar up our way and to ban it
From the secret that lies in these wolds—
From the thing that lies hidden in these wolds—
Have drawn up the spectre of a planet
From the limbo of lunary souls—
This sinfully scintillant planet
From the Hell of the planetary souls?"

1847

TO —— —— ——

¶ A TRIBUTE to Mrs. Marie Louise Shew, who had come to the aid of the Poes in 1846–47, during Virginia's last illness and Poe's subsequent collapse.

Not long ago, the writer of these lines,
In the mad pride of intellectuality,
Maintained "the power of words"—denied that ever
A thought arose within the human brain
Beyond the utterance of the human tongue;
And now, as if in mockery of that boast,
Two words—two foreign soft dissyllables—
Italian tones made only to be murmured
By angels dreaming in the moonlit "dew
That hangs like chains of pearl on Hermon hill"—
Have stirred from out the abysses of his heart,
Unthought-like thoughts that are the souls of thought,
Richer, far wilder, far diviner visions
Than even the seraph harper, Israfel,
Who has "the sweetest voice of all God's creatures,"
Could hope to utter. And I! my spells are broken.
The pen falls powerless from my shivering hand.
With thy dear name as text, though bidden by thee,
I cannot write—I cannot speak or think,
Alas, I cannot feel; for 't is not feeling,

TO —— —— ——. 3. **Maintained . . . ever:** This refers to the first selection from "Marginalia" (see p. 471). 7. **Two . . . dissyllables:** Since Poe later says that Mrs. Shew's name is his text, the two words must be "Marie Louise." 9–10. **"dew . . . hill":** The quotation has been traced to a passage (based on Ps. 133:3) in Peele's *David and Bethsabe.* 12. **Unthought-like . . . thought:** hypnagogic images. 15. **Who . . . creatures:** See the epigraph to "Israfel."

This standing motionless upon the golden
Threshold of the wide-open gate of dreams,
Gazing, entranced, adown the gorgeous vista,
And thrilling as I see upon the right,
Upon the left, and all the way along
Amid empurpled vapors, far away
To where the prospect terminates—*thee only.*

1848

ELDORADO

THE WORD "Eldorado" had much appeal in 1849, the year of the California gold fever. Poe's poem mocks that fever, asserting that true riches are not to be found in this world.

Gaily bedight,
A gallant knight,
In sunshine and in shadow,
Had journeyed long,
Singing a song,
In search of Eldorado.

But he grew old—
This knight so bold—
And o'er his heart a shadow
Fell as he found
No spot of ground
That looked like Eldorado.

And, as his strength
Failed him at length,
He met a pilgrim shadow—
"Shadow," said he,
"Where can it be—
This land of Eldorado?"

"Over the Mountains
Of the Moon,
Down the Valley of the Shadow,
Ride, boldly ride,"
The shade replied,—
"If you seek for Eldorado!"

1849

21–27. This . . . *only*: It is said of Ellison's bride, in "The Domain of Arnheim," that her "loveliness and love enveloped his existence in the purple atmosphere of paradise." These lines also recall the prospect of Arnheim with which the story ends.
ELDORADO. **19–20. Over . . . Moon:** Claudius Ptolemy, the great geographer of the second century A.D., portrayed the Nile as rising from two lakes watered by a snowy range called "The Mountains of the Moon." In 1848–49, several missionaries returned from the unexplored East-African interior with reports of snow-capped mountains, thus stimulating a widespread interest in the mystery of the sources of the Nile. Poe's public therefore had a lively awareness of Ptolemy's "Mountains of the Moon" at the time of the publication of "Eldorado."

FOR ANNIE

THE ADDRESSEE of this poem was Mrs. Richmond of Lowell, Massachusetts, with whom Poe had a fervent Platonic relationship in 1848–49. In a letter of November 7, 1848, Poe reminded her of "that last holy promise . . . the promise that, under all circumstances, you would come to me on my bed of death . . ."

Thank Heaven! the crisis,
The danger, is past,
And the lingering illness
Is over at last—
And the fever called "Living"
Is conquered at last.

Sadly, I know
I am shorn of my strength,
And no muscle I move
As I lie at full length—
But no matter!—I feel
I am better at length.

And I rest so composedly,
Now, in my bed,
That any beholder
Might fancy me dead—
Might start at beholding me,
Thinking me dead.

The moaning and groaning,
The sighing and sobbing,
Are quieted now,
With that horrible throbbing
At heart:—ah, that horrible,
Horrible throbbing!

The sickness—the nausea—
The pitiless pain—
Have ceased, with the fever
That maddened my brain—
With the fever called "Living"
That burned in my brain.

And oh! of all tortures
That torture the worst
Has abated—the terrible
Torture of thirst
For the naphthaline river

FOR ANNIE. **22. With . . . throbbing:** This "horrible throbbing" is the normal heartbeat, just as the madness of l. 28 is normal consciousness. They are described here as aspects of illness, because in this poem life itself is a tormenting "fever."
35–36. For . . . accurst: Naphtha is an inflammable fluid, and Poe is thinking here of Phlegethon, a flaming river in Hades. In "The Poetic Principle" Poe wrote that "in regard to Passion, alas! its tendency is to degrade rather than to elevate the Soul."

Of Passion accurst:—
I have drank of a water
That quenches all thirst:—

Of a water that flows,
With a lullaby sound,
From a spring but a very few
Feet under ground—
From a cavern not very far
Down under ground.

And ah! let it never
Be foolishly said
That my room it is gloomy
And narrow my bed;
For man never slept
In a different bed—
And, to *sleep*, you must slumber
In just such a bed.

My tantalized spirit
Here blandly reposes,
Forgetting, or never
Regretting, its roses—
Its old agitations
Of myrtles and roses:

For now, while so quietly
Lying, it fancies
A holier odor
About it, of pansies—
A rosemary odor,
Commingled with pansies—
With rue and the beautiful
Puritan pansies.

And so it lies happily,
Bathing in many
A dream of the truth
And the beauty of Annie—
Drowned in a bath
Of the tresses of Annie.

She tenderly kissed me,
She fondly caressed,
And then I fell gently
To sleep on her breast—
Deeply to sleep
From the heaven of her breast.

When the light was extinguished,
She covered me warm,
And she prayed to the angels
To keep me from harm—
To the queen of the angels
To shield me from harm.

And I lie so composedly,
Now, in my bed,
(Knowing her love),
That you fancy me dead—
And I rest so contentedly,
Now, in my bed
(With her love at my breast),
That you fancy me dead—
That you shudder to look at me,
Thinking me dead:—

But my heart it is brighter
Than all of the many
Stars of the sky,
For it sparkles with Annie—
It glows with the light
Of the love of my Annie—
With the thought of the light
Of the eyes of my Annie.

1849

39–44. Of . . . ground: This suggests Lethe, the river of purification and forgetfulness in Hades. See "The Sleeper," ll. 13–15, and "Ulalume," l. 46. **53. My . . . spirit:** The word "tantalized" derives from Tantalus, who was punished in Hades by thirst, and by his hunger for the unreachable fruit. **55–58. Forgetting . . . roses:** In the "language of flowers" myrtle and rose symbolize love and beauty. **61–66. A . . . pansies:** Pansies mean "thoughts" or "think of me"; rosemary means "remembrance"; rue means "grace," or "purification."

ANNABEL LEE

THE ARTFUL and incantatory use of repetition, which steadily increased in Poe's later poetry—"Eldorado," "For Annie"—reached an extreme in "Annabel Lee." Here there is not only repetition of word and line, but sustained recapitulation, as in ll. 21–26.

It was many and many a year ago,
In a kingdom by the sea,
That a maiden there lived whom you may know
By the name of ANNABEL LEE;
And this maiden she lived with no other thought
Than to love and be loved by me.

I was a child and *she* was a child,
In this kingdom by the sea,
But we loved with a love that was more than love—
I and my ANNABEL LEE—
With a love that the wingèd seraphs of Heaven
Coveted her and me.

ANNABEL LEE. **3–4. That . . . Lee:** The poet is withholding her heavenly name, and perhaps her earthly name as well. See "The Raven," ll. 11–12.

And this was the reason that, long ago,
In this kingdom by the sea,
A wind blew out of a cloud, chilling
My beautiful ANNABEL LEE;
So that her highborn kinsmen came
And bore her away from me,
To shut her up in a sepulchre
In this kingdom by the sea.

The angels, not half so happy in Heaven,
Went envying her and me:—
Yes!—that was the reason (as all men know,
In this kingdom by the sea)
That the wind came out of the cloud by night,
Chilling and killing my ANNABEL LEE.

But our love it was stronger by far than the love
Of those who were older than we—
Of many far wiser than we—
And neither the angels in Heaven above,
Nor the demons down under the sea,
Can ever dissever my soul from the soul
Of the beautiful ANNABEL LEE:—

For the moon never beams, without bringing me dreams
Of the beautiful ANNABEL LEE;
And the stars never rise, but I feel the bright eyes
Of the beautiful ANNABEL LEE:
And so, all the night-tide, I lie down by the side
Of my darling—my darling—my life and my bride,
In the sepulchre there by the sea—
In her tomb by the sounding sea.

1849

17. So . . . came: Annabel Lee's "highborn kinsmen" are "the wingèd seraphs of Heaven," in line 11. For Poe's association of spirituality with aristocracy, see Part II of the Introduction.

MS. FOUND IN A BOTTLE

◇

❡ THIS story was awarded a fifty-dollar prize by the Baltimore *Saturday Visiter,* and published there in October, 1833. It reflects Poe's excitement, and that of his contemporaries, about polar exploration. In 1835, Poe's fictional hero Hans Pfaall observed a northern "polar gulf" from his balloon; in 1836, Poe supported J. N. Reynolds' long-standing campaign for an American expedition to the South Seas; in 1838, Poe's Arthur Gordon Pym plunged, like the narrator of "Ms.," into a watery abyss at the South Pole; and as Poe lay dying in a Baltimore hospital, he cried out again and again for "Reynolds!" While he shared and exploited the public interest in the actual exploration of the poles, Poe also assimilated the subject to his private vision; a sea voyage ending in a whirlpool became his great metaphor for the soul's conquest of the unknown.

◇

Qui n'a plus qu'un moment à vivre
N'a plus rien à dissimuler.
QUINAULT, *Atys*[1]

OF MY country and of my family I have little to say. Ill usage and length of years have driven me from the one, and estranged me from the other. Hereditary wealth afforded me an education of no common order, and a contemplative turn of mind enabled me to methodize the stores which early study very diligently garnered up. Beyond all things the works of the German moralists gave me great delight; not from any ill-advised admiration of their eloquent madness, but from the ease with which my habits of rigid thought enabled me to detect their falsities. I have often been reproached with the aridity of my genius—a deficiency of imagination has been imputed to me as a crime—and the Pyrrhonism[2] of my opinions has at all times rendered me notorious. Indeed a strong relish for physical philosophy has, I fear, tinctured my mind with a very common error of this age—I mean the habit of referring occurrences, even the least susceptible of such reference, to the principles of that science. Upon the whole, no person could be less liable than myself to be led away from the severe precincts of truth by the *ignes fatui*[3] of superstition. I have thought proper to premise thus much lest the incredible tale I have to tell should be considered rather the raving of a crude imagination, than the positive experience of a mind to which the reveries of fancy have been a dead letter and a nullity.

After many years spent in foreign travel, I sailed in the year 18—, from the port of Batavia,

MS. FOUND IN A BOTTLE. 1. **Quinault—*Atys:*** These lines from *Atys,* a tragedy by Philippe Quinault (1635–88), may be translated, "He who has no longer than a moment to live/Has no longer anything to hide." 2. **Pyrrhonism:** radical skepticism, as taught by the Greek philosopher Pyrrho (365–275 B.C.). By having a skeptical man tell his "incredible tale," Poe somewhat disarms the reader and achieves some interesting contrasts between prosaic style and marvelous matter. That the narrator is scientifically inclined helps to motivate his "report." 3. ***ignes fatui:*** will-o'-the-wisps; delusions.

in the rich and populous island of Java, on a voyage to the Archipelago of the Sunda islands. I went as passenger—having no other inducement than a kind of nervous restlessness which haunted me like a fiend.

Our vessel was a beautiful ship of about four hundred tons, copper-fastened, and built at Bombay of Malabar teak. She was freighted with cotton-wool and oil, from the Lachadive islands. We had also on board coir, jaggeree, ghee, cocoa-nuts, and a few cases of opium. The stowage was clumsily done, and the vessel consequently crank.[4]

We got under way with a mere breath of wind, and for many days stood along the eastern coast of Java, without any other incident to beguile the monotony of our course than the occasional meeting with some of the small grabs[5] of the Archipelago to which we were bound.

One evening, leaning over the taffrail, I observed a very singular, isolated cloud, to the N. W. It was remarkable, as well for its color, as from its being the first we had seen since our departure from Batavia. I watched it attentively until sunset, when it spread all at once to the eastward and westward, girting in the horizon with a narrow strip of vapor, and looking like a long line of low beach. My notice was soon afterwards attracted by the dusky-red appearance of the moon, and the peculiar character of the sea. The latter was undergoing a rapid change, and the water seemed more than usually transparent. Although I could distinctly see the bottom, yet, heaving the lead, I found the ship in fifteen fathoms. The air now became intolerably hot, and was loaded with spiral exhalations similar to those arising from heated iron. As night came on, every breath of wind died away, and a more entire calm it is impossible to conceive.[6] The flame of a candle burned upon the poop without the least perceptible motion, and a long hair, held between the finger and thumb, hung without the possibility of detecting a vibration. However, as the captain said he could perceive no indication of danger, and as we were drifting in bodily to shore, he ordered the sails to be furled, and the anchor let go. No watch was set, and the crew, consisting principally of Malays, stretched themselves deliberately upon deck. I went below—not without a full presentiment of evil. Indeed every appearance warranted me in apprehending a Simoom. I told the captain my fears—but he paid no attention to what I said, and left me without deigning to give a reply. My uneasiness, however, prevented me from sleeping, and about midnight I went upon deck. As I placed my foot upon the upper step of the companion-ladder, I was startled with a loud, humming noise, like that occasioned by the rapid revolution of a mill-wheel,[7] and before I could ascertain its meaning, I found the ship quivering to its centre. In the next instant, a wilderness of foam hurled us upon our beam-ends, and, rushing over us fore and aft, swept the entire decks from stem to stern.

The extreme fury of the blast proved in a great measure the salvation of the ship. Although completely water-logged, yet, as all her masts had gone by the board, she rose, after a minute, heavily from the sea, and, staggering awhile beneath the immense pressure of the tempest, finally righted.

By what miracle I escaped destruction, it is impossible to say. Stunned by the shock of the water, I found myself, upon recovery, jammed in between the stern-post and rudder. With great difficulty I gained my feet, and looking dizzily around, was, at first, struck with the idea of our being among breakers, so terrific beyond the wildest imagination was the whirlpool of mountainous and foaming ocean within which we were engulfed. After a while, I heard the voice of an old Swede, who had shipped with us at the moment of our leaving port. I hallooed to him with all my strength, and presently he came reeling aft. We soon discovered that we were the sole survivors of the accident. All on deck, with the exception of ourselves, had been swept overboard, and the captain and mates must have perished as they slept, for the cabins were deluged with water. Without assistance, we could expect to do little for the security of the ship, and our exertions were at first paralyzed by the momentary expectation of going down. Our cable had, of course, parted like pack-thread, at the first breath of the hurricane, or we should have been instantaneously overwhelmed. We scudded with frightful velocity before the sea, and the water made clear breaches over us. The frame-work of our stern was shattered excessively, and, in almost every respect, we had received considerable injury—but to our extreme joy we found the pumps unchoked, and that we had made no great shifting of our ballast. The main fury of the Simoom had already blown over,

4. **We . . . crank:** coir is cocoanut fiber, jaggeree is crude palm sugar, ghee is a liquid butter, and "crank" means "unsteady."
5. **grabs:** a grab is a two-masted coasting vessel of the Orient.
6. The foregoing description may be correct (Joseph Conrad praised the accuracy of Poe's nautical knowledge), but it also involves the roof of cloud, the dimmed light, the transparent water and the airlessness which Poe used throughout his work to give natural scenes the qualities of reverie or dream.

7. **loud . . . mill-wheel:** such hummings or buzzings are frequent in Poe, as auditory symbols of the transition to dream (see "The Pit and the Pendulum," 3 n.). The "mill-wheel," like the earlier "spiral exhalations," anticipates the tale's whirling and vertiginous close.

and we apprehended little danger from the violence of the wind—but we looked forward to its total cessation with dismay, well believing, that, in our shattered condition, we should inevitably perish in the tremendous swell which would ensue. But this very just apprehension seemed by no means likely to be soon verified. For five entire days and nights—during which our only subsistence was a small quantity of jaggeree, procured with great difficulty from the forecastle—the hulk flew at a rate defying computation, before rapidly succeeding flaws of wind, which, without equalling the first violence of the Simoom, were still more terrific than any tempest I had before encountered. Our course for the first four days was, with trifling variations, S. E. and by South; and we must have run down the coast of New Holland.[8] On the fifth day the cold became extreme, although the wind had hauled round a point more to the northward. The sun arose with a sickly yellow lustre, and clambered a very few degrees above the horizon—emitting no decisive light. There were no clouds whatever apparent, yet the wind was upon the increase, and blew with a fitful and unsteady fury. About noon, as nearly as we could guess, our attention was again arrested by the appearance of the sun. It gave out no light, properly so called, but a dull and sullen glow unaccompanied by any ray. Just before sinking within the turgid sea its central fires suddenly went out, as if hurriedly extinguished by some unaccountable power. It was a dim, silver-like rim, alone, as it rushed down the unfathomable ocean.

We waited in vain for the arrival of the sixth day—that day to me has not arrived—to the Swede, never did arrive. Thenceforward we were enshrouded in pitchy darkness, so that we could not have seen an object at twenty paces from the ship. Eternal night continued to envelop us, all unrelieved by the phosphoric sea-brilliancy to which we had been accustomed in the tropics. We observed too, that, although the tempest continued to rage with unabated violence, there was no longer to be discovered the usual appearance of surf, or foam, which had hitherto attended us. All around was horror, and thick gloom, and a black sweltering desert of ebony. Superstitious terror crept by degrees into the spirit of the old Swede, and my own soul was wrapped up in silent wonder. We neglected all care of the ship, as worse than useless, and securing ourselves as well as possible to the stump of the mizen-mast, looked out bitterly into the world of ocean. We had no means of calculating time, nor could we form any guess of our situation. We were, however, well aware of having made farther to the southward than any previous navigators, and felt extreme amazement at not meeting with the usual impediments of ice. In the meantime every moment threatened to be our last—every mountainous billow hurried to overwhelm us. The swell surpassed anything I had imagined possible, and that we were not instantly buried is a miracle. My companion spoke of the lightness of our cargo, and reminded me of the excellent qualities of our ship—but I could not help feeling the utter hopelessness of hope itself, and prepared myself gloomily for that death which I thought nothing could defer beyond an hour, as, with every knot of way the ship made, the swelling of the black stupendous seas became more dismally appalling. At times we gasped for breath at an elevation beyond the Albatross—at times became dizzy with the velocity of our descent into some watery hell, where the air grew stagnant, and no sound disturbed the slumbers of the Kraken.[9]

We were at the bottom of one of these abysses, when a quick scream from my companion broke fearfully upon the night. "See! see!"—cried he, shrieking in my ears,—"Almighty God! see! see!" As he spoke, I became aware of a dull, sullen glare of red light which streamed down the sides of the vast chasm where we lay, and threw a fitful brilliancy upon our deck. Casting my eyes upwards, I beheld a spectacle which froze the current of my blood. At a terrific height directly above us, and upon the very verge of the precipitous descent, hovered a gigantic ship of nearly four thousand tons. Although upreared upon the summit of a wave of more than a hundred times her own altitude, her apparent size still exceeded that of any ship of the line or East Indiaman in existence. Her huge hull was of a deep dingy black, unrelieved by any of the customary carvings of a ship. A single row of brass cannon protruded from her open ports, and dashed off from their polished surfaces the fires of innumerable battle-lanterns, which swung to and fro about her rigging. But what mainly inspired us with horror and astonishment, was that she bore up under a press of sail in the very teeth of that supernatural sea, and of that ungovernable hurricane. When we first discovered her, her stupendous bows were alone to be seen, as she rose up, like a demon of the deep, slowly from the dim and horrible gulf beyond her. For a moment of intense terror she paused upon the giddy pinnacle, as if in contemplation of her own sublimity, then trembled and tottered, and—came down.

8. **New Holland**: Australia.

9. **Kraken**: a fabulous sea monster.

At this instant, I know not what sudden self-possession came over my spirit. Staggering as far aft as I could, I awaited fearlessly the ruin that was to overwhelm. Our own vessel was at length ceasing from her struggles, and sinking with her head to the sea. The shock of the descending mass struck her, consequently, in that portion of her frame which was already under water, and the inevitable result was to hurl me with irresistible violence upon the rigging of the stranger.

As I fell, the ship hove in stays, and went about, and to the confusion ensuing I attributed my escape from the notice of the crew. With little difficulty I made my way unperceived to the main hatchway, which was partially open, and soon found an opportunity of secreting myself in the hold. Why I did so I can hardly tell. A nameless and indefinite sense of awe, which at first sight of the navigators of the ship had taken hold of my mind, was perhaps the principle of my concealment. I was unwilling to trust myself with a race of people who had offered, to the cursory glance I had taken, so many points of vague novelty, doubt, and apprehension. I therefore thought proper to contrive a hiding-place in the hold. This I did by removing a small portion of the shifting-boards in such a manner as to afford me a convenient retreat between the huge timbers of the ship.

I had scarcely completed my work, when a foot-step in the hold forced me to make use of it. A man passed by my place of concealment with a feeble and unsteady gait. I could not see his face, but had an opportunity of observing his general appearance. There was about it an evidence of great age and infirmity. His knees tottered beneath a load of years, and his entire frame quivered under the burthen.[10] He muttered to himself, in a low broken tone, some words of a language which I could not understand, and groped in a corner among a pile of singular-looking instruments, and decayed charts of navigation. His manner was a wild mixture of the peevishness of second childhood, and the solemn dignity of a god. He at length went on deck, and I saw him no more.

* * *

A feeling, for which I have no name, has taken possession of my soul—a sensation which will admit of no analysis, to which the lessons of by-gone time are inadequate, and for which I fear futurity itself will offer me no key. To a mind constituted like my own the latter consideration is an evil. I shall never,—I know that I shall never—be satisfied with regard to the nature of my conceptions. Yet it is not wonderful that these conceptions are indefinite, since they have their origin in sources so utterly novel. A new sense, a new entity is added to my soul.

* * *

It is long since I first trod the deck of this terrible ship, and the rays of my destiny are, I think, gathering to a focus. Incomprehensible men! Wrapped up in meditations of a kind which I cannot divine, they pass me by unnoticed. Concealment is utter folly on my part, for the people *will not* see. It was but just now that I passed directly before the eyes of the mate,—it was no long while ago that I ventured into the captain's own private cabin, and took thence the materials with which I write, and have written. I shall from time to time continue this journal. It is true that I may not find an opportunity of transmitting it to the world, but I will not fail to make the endeavor. At the last moment I will enclose the MS. in a bottle, and cast it within the sea.

* * *

An incident has occurred which has given me new room for meditation. Are such things the operations of ungoverned Chance? I had ventured upon deck and thrown myself down, without attracting any notice, among a pile of ratlin-stuff and old sails in the bottom of the yawl. While musing upon the singularity of my fate, I unwittingly daubed with a tar-brush the edges of a neatly-folded studding-sail which lay near me on a barrel. The studding-sail is now bent upon the ship, and the thoughtless touches of the brush are spread out into the word DISCOVERY.[11]

* * *

I have made many observations lately upon the structure of the vessel. Although well armed, she is not, I think, a ship of war. Her rigging, build, and general equipment, all negative a supposition of this kind. What she *is not* I can easily perceive, what she *is* I fear it is impossible to say. I know not how it is, but in scrutinizing her strange model and singular cast of spars, her huge size and overgrown suits of canvass, her severely simple bow and antiquated stern, there will occasionally flash

10. **His . . . burthen:** Tremulousness is variously explained in Poe. Here the assigned cause is age and infirmity; with Roderick Usher it is fear. Fundamentally, however, tremulousness means that the person perceived is an immaterial vision, and partakes of the instability of dream.

11. **I . . . DISCOVERY:** Such gradual acquisition of significance is found in "Silence—A Fable," where indecipherable characters reshape themselves into the words "DESOLATION" and "SILENCE"; also in "Ligeia," where arabesque tapestry figures take on pictorial meaning, and in "The Black Cat," where a cat's white marking becomes, "by degrees nearly imperceptible," an image of the gallows. In these and similar passages, Poe is imitating the fluid development of meaning and direction in dream.

across my mind a sensation of familiar things, and there is always mixed up with such indistinct shadows of recollection, an unaccountable memory of old foreign chronicles and ages long ago.[12]

* * *

I have been looking at the timbers of the ship. She is built of a material to which I am a stranger. There is a peculiar character about the wood which strikes me as rendering it unfit for the purpose to which it has been applied. I mean its extreme *porousness,* considered independently of the worm-eaten condition which is a consequence of navigation in these seas, and apart from the rottenness attendant upon age. It will appear perhaps an observation somewhat over-curious, but this wood has every characteristic of Spanish oak, *if Spanish oak were distended or swelled by any unnatural means.*

In reading the above sentence a curious apothegm of an old weather-beaten Dutch navigator comes full upon my recollection. "It is as sure," he was wont to say, when any doubt was entertained of his veracity, "as sure as there is a sea where the ship itself will grow in bulk like the living body of the seaman."

* * *

About an hour ago, I made bold to thrust myself among a group of the crew. They paid me no manner of attention, and, although I stood in the very midst of them all, seemed utterly unconscious of my presence. Like the one I had at first seen in the hold, they all bore about them the marks of a hoary old age. Their knees trembled with infirmity, their shoulders were bent double with decrepitude, their shrivelled skins rattled in the wind, their voices were low, tremulous, and broken, their eyes glistened with the rheum of years, and their gray hairs streamed terribly in the tempest. Around them on every part of the deck lay scattered mathematical instruments of the most quaint and obsolete construction.

* * *

I mentioned some time ago the bending of a studding-sail. From that period the ship, being thrown dead off the wind, has held her terrific course due south, with every rag of canvass packed upon her from her trucks to her lower-studding-sail booms, and rolling every moment her top-gallant yard-arms into the most appalling hell of water which it can enter into the mind of man to imagine. I have just left the deck, where I find it impossible to maintain a footing, although the crew seem to experience little inconvenience. It appears to me a miracle of miracles that our enormous bulk is not buried up at once and forever. We are surely doomed to hover continually upon the brink of Eternity, without taking a final plunge into the abyss. From billows a thousand times more stupendous than any I have ever seen, we glide away with the facility of the arrowy sea-gull; and the colossal waters rear their heads above us like demons of the deep, but like demons confined to simple threats and forbidden to destroy. I am led to attribute these frequent escapes to the only natural cause which can account for such effect. I must suppose the ship to be within the influence of some strong current, or impetuous under-tow.

* * *

I have seen the captain face to face, and in his own cabin—but, as I expected, he paid me no attention. Although in his appearance there is, to a casual observer, nothing which might bespeak him more or less than man—still a feeling of irrepressible reverence and awe mingled with the sensation of wonder with which I regarded him. In stature he is nearly my own height, that is, about five feet eight inches.[13] He is of a well-knit and compact frame of body, neither robust nor remarkably otherwise. But it is the singularity of the expression which reigns upon the face, it is the intense, the wonderful, the thrilling evidence of old age so utter, so extreme, which excites within my spirit a sense—a sentiment ineffable. His forehead, although little wrinkled, seems to bear upon it the stamp of a myriad of years. His gray hairs are records of the past, and his grayer eyes are sybils of the future.[14] The cabin floor was thickly strewn with strange, iron-clasped folios, and mouldering instruments of science, and obsolete long-forgotten charts. His head was bowed down upon his hands, and he pored with a fiery unquiet eye over a paper which I took to be a commission, and which, at all events, bore the signature of a monarch. He muttered to himself, as did the first seaman whom I saw in the hold, some low peevish syllables of a foreign tongue, and although the speaker was close at my elbow, yet his voice seemed to reach my ears from the distance of a mile.[15]

12. **sensation . . . ago:** The narrator of "The Fall of the House of Usher" finds the interior of the Usher mansion strangely "familiar," and William Wilson's double brings to Wilson's mind "wild, confused and thronging memories of a time when memory herself was yet unborn." The narrator's sense of old familiarity means that he has rejoined, by way of dream, that visionary faculty which presided over his soul during its earthly infancy and previous unearthly existence.

13. **five . . . inches:** This was Poe's own height, as recorded at the time of his enlistment in the Army. The narrator and the captain are "doubles." 14. **His . . . future:** Poe here echoes Byron's poem "The Dream" (ll. 12–13), in which dreams are thus described: "They pass like spirits of the past, they speak Like Sybils of the future . . ." Poe's own eyes were gray. 15. **his . . . mile:** Dupin, when at his most imaginative, ad-

* * *

The ship and all in it are imbued with the spirit of Eld. The crew glide to and fro like the ghosts of buried centuries, their eyes have an eager and uneasy meaning, and when their figures fall athwart my path in the wild glare of the battle-lanterns, I feel as I have never felt before, although I have been all my life a dealer in antiquities, and have imbibed the shadows of fallen columns at Balbec, and Tadmor, and Persepolis,[16] until my very soul has become a ruin.

* * *

When I look around me I feel ashamed of my former apprehensions. If I trembled at the blast which has hitherto attended us, shall I not stand aghast at a warring of wind and ocean, to convey any idea of which the words tornado and simoom are trivial and ineffective! All in the immediate vicinity of the ship is the blackness of eternal night, and a chaos of foamless water; but, about a league on either side of us, may be seen, indistinctly and at intervals, stupendous ramparts of ice, towering away into the desolate sky, and looking like the walls of the universe.

* * *

As I imagined, the ship proves to be in a current; if that appellation can properly be given to a tide which, howling and shrieking by the white ice, thunders on to the southward with a velocity like the headlong dashing of a cataract.

* * *

To conceive the horror of my sensations is, I presume, utterly impossible—yet a curiosity to penetrate the mysteries of these awful regions predominates even over my despair, and will reconcile me to the most hideous aspect of death.[17] It is evident that we are hurrying onwards to some exciting knowledge—some never-to-be-imparted secret, whose attainment is destruction.[18] Perhaps this current leads us to the southern pole itself—it must be confessed that a supposition apparently so wild has every probability in its favor.

* * *

The crew pace the deck with unquiet and tremulous step, but there is upon their countenances an expression more of the eagerness of hope than of the apathy of despair.

In the meantime the wind is still in our poop, and as we carry a crowd of canvass, the ship is at times lifted bodily from out the sea—Oh, horror upon horror! the ice opens suddenly to the right, and to the left, and we are whirling dizzily, in immense concentric circles, round and round the borders of a gigantic amphitheatre, the summit of whose walls is lost in the darkness and the distance. But little time will be left me to ponder upon my destiny—the circles rapidly grow small —we are plunging madly within the grasp of the whirlpool—and amid a roaring, and bellowing, and shrieking of ocean and of tempest, the ship is quivering, oh God! and—going down.[19]

LIGEIA

◇

¶ "LIGEIA" was first published in the Baltimore *American Museum* of September 18, 1838. For an interpretation of the story, see the Introduction, Part IV. The reader should notice how the story is knit together by the ideas of remembering and of transmutation; also how, during the description of Rowena's illness, the reappearance of Ligeia is suggestively anticipated by the recurrence of certain words—such as "shadow," "low," "gentle," "marble," and "utterly"—which have early been associated with her.

◇

> And the will therein lieth, which dieth not. Who knoweth the mysteries of the will, with its vigor? For God is but a great will pervading all things by nature of its intentness. Man doth not yield himself to the angels, nor unto death utterly, save only through the weakness of his feeble will.
>
> JOSEPH GLANVILL [1]

I CANNOT, for my soul, remember how, when, even precisely where, I first became acquainted

dresses the narrator of "Murders in the Rue Morgue" in a high abstracted voice which, "although by no means loud, has that intonation which is commonly employed in speaking to someone at a great distance." **16. Balbec . . . Persepolis:** Nesace's palace in "Al Aaraaf," which is an anthology of the architectural beauties of antiquity, has "Friezes from Tadmor and Persepolis —/From Balbec, and the stilly clear abyss/Of Beautiful Gomorrah! . . ." The narrator's thirst for the ruins of Earth's early and "unfallen" ages anticipates the "Amphitheatre" of ice at the close. **17. curiosity . . . death:** See "The Pit and the Pendulum," 12 n. **18. some . . . destruction:** The narrator of "Ligeia" seeks "a wisdom too divinely precious not to be forbidden."

19. "The 'Ms. Found in a Bottle' was originally published in 1831, and it was not until many years afterwards that I became acquainted with the maps of Mercator, in which the ocean is represented as rushing, by four months, into the (northern) Polar Gulf, to be absorbed into the bowels of the earth; the Pole itself being represented by a black rock, towering to a prodigious height" [Poe's note]. LIGEIA. **1. Glanvill:** English ecclesiastic (1636–80) believer in witchcraft and the pre-existence of souls, author of *The Vanity of Dogmatizing*. The epigraph has not yet been found in Glanvill's works.

with the lady Ligeia. Long years have since elapsed, and my memory is feeble through much suffering. Or, perhaps, I cannot *now* bring these points to mind, because, in truth, the character of my beloved, her rare learning, her singular yet placid cast of beauty, and the thrilling and enthralling eloquence of her low musical language, made their way into my heart by paces so steadily and stealthily progressive that they have been unnoticed and unknown. Yet I believe that I met her first and most frequently in some large, old, decaying city near the Rhine. Of her family—I have surely heard her speak. That it is of a remotely ancient date cannot be doubted. Ligeia! Ligeia! Buried in studies of a nature more than all else adapted to deaden impressions of the outward world, it is by that sweet word alone—by Ligeia—that I bring before mine eyes in fancy the image of her who is no more. And now, while I write, a recollection flashes upon me that I have *never known* the paternal name of her who was my friend and my betrothed, and who became the partner of my studies, and finally the wife of my bosom. Was it a playful charge on the part of my Ligeia? or was it a test of my strength of affection, that I should institute no inquiries upon this point? or was it rather a caprice of my own—a wildly romantic offering on the shrine of the most passionate devotion? I but indistinctly recall the fact itself—what wonder that I have utterly forgotten the circumstances which originated or attended it? And, indeed, if ever that spirit which is entitled *Romance*—if ever she, the wan and the misty-winged *Ashtophet* [2] of idolatrous Egypt, presided, as they tell, over marriages ill-omened, then most surely she presided over mine.

There is one dear topic, however, on which my memory fails me not. It is the *person* of Ligeia. In stature she was tall, somewhat slender, and, in her latter days, even emaciated. I would in vain attempt to portray the majesty, the quiet ease of her demeanor, or the incomprehensible lightness and elasticity of her footfall. She came and departed as a shadow. I was never made aware of her entrance into my closed study save by the dear music of her low sweet voice, as she placed her marble hand upon my shoulder. In beauty of face no maiden ever equalled her. It was the radiance of an opium-dream—an airy and spirit-lifting vision more wildly divine than the phantasies which hovered about the slumbering souls of the daughters of Delos.[3] Yet her features were not of that regular mould which we have been falsely taught to worship in the classical labors of the heathen. "There is no exquisite beauty," says Bacon, Lord Verulam, speaking truly of all the forms and *genera* of beauty, "without some *strangeness* in the proportion." [4] Yet, although I saw that the features of Ligeia were not of a classic regularity—although I perceived that her loveliness was indeed "exquisite," and felt that there was much of "strangeness" pervading it, yet I have tried in vain to detect the irregularity and to trace home my own perception of "the strange." I examined the contour of the lofty and pale forehead—it was faultless—how cold indeed that word when applied to a majesty so divine!—the skin rivalling the purest ivory, the commanding extent and repose, the gentle prominence of the regions above the temples; [5] and then the raven-black, the glossy, the luxuriant and naturally-curling tresses, setting forth the full force of the Homeric epithet, "hyacinthine!" [6] I looked at the delicate outlines of the nose—and nowhere but in the graceful medallions of the Hebrews had I beheld a similar perfection. There were the same luxurious smoothness of surface, the same scarcely perceptible tendency to the aquiline, the same harmoniously curved nostrils speaking the free spirit. I regarded the sweet mouth. Here was indeed the triumph of all things heavenly—the magnificent turn of the short upper lip—the soft, voluptuous slumber of the under—the dimples which sported, and the color which spoke—the teeth glancing back, with a brilliancy almost startling, every ray of the holy light which fell upon them in her serene and placid yet most exultingly radiant of all smiles. I scrutinized the formation of the chin—and, here too, I found the gentleness of breadth, the softness and the majesty, the fullness and the spirituality, of the Greek—the contour which the god Apollo revealed but in a dream, to Cleomenes,[7] the son of the Athenian. And then I peered into the large eyes of Ligeia.

For eyes we have no models in the remotely antique. It might have been, too, that in these eyes of my beloved lay the secret to which Lord Verulam alludes. They were, I must believe, far larger than the ordinary eyes of our own race. They were even fuller than the fullest of the gazelle eyes of the tribe of the valley of Nourjahad.[8] Yet it was

2. ***Ashtophet:*** doubtless refers to an Egyptian version of the Syrian love goddess Ashtoreth, identified with Astarte. Milton speaks of her in *Paradise Lost*, I.438 ff. 3. **Delos:** an Aegean island, birthplace and shrine of Apollo, god of music and poetry.

4. **"There . . . proportion":** slightly misquoted from Francis Bacon's essay "Of Beauty." Bacon wrote not "exquisite" but "excellent." 5. **the . . . temples:** In phrenology, a science which much interested Poe, such a protuberance would argue "ideality" or imagination. 6. **"hyacinthine!":** See "To Helen," 7 n. The *curliness* of the hyacinth is the basis of comparison. 7. **Cleomenes:** Athenian sculptor of the Venus de' Medici. 8. **Nourjahad:** The name is taken from Mrs. Frances

only at intervals—in moments of intense excitement—that this peculiarity became more than slightly noticeable in Ligeia. And at such moments was her beauty—in my heated fancy thus it appeared perhaps—the beauty of beings either above or apart from the earth—the beauty of the fabulous Houri of the Turk. The hue of the orbs was the most brilliant of black, and, far over them, hung jetty lashes of great length. The brows, slightly irregular in outline, had the same tint. The "strangeness," however, which I found in the eyes, was of a nature distinct from the formation, or the color, or the brilliancy of the features, and must, after all, be referred to the *expression*. Ah, word of no meaning! behind whose vast latitude of mere sound we intrench our ignorance of so much of the spiritual. The expression of the eyes of Ligeia! How for long hours have I pondered upon it! How have I, through the whole of a midsummer night, struggled to fathom it! What was it—that something more profound than the well of Democritus [9]—which lay far within the pupils of my beloved? What *was* it? I was possessed with a passion to discover. Those eyes! those large, those shining, those divine orbs! they became to me twin stars of Leda, and I to them devoutest of astrologers.

There is no point, among the many incomprehensible anomalies of the science of mind, more thrillingly exciting than the fact—never, I believe, noticed in the schools—that in our endeavors to recall to memory something long forgotten, we often find ourselves *upon the very verge* of remembrance, without being able, in the end, to remember. And thus how frequently, in my intense scrutiny of Ligeia's eyes, have I felt approaching the full knowledge of their expression—felt it approaching—yet not quite be mine—and so at length entirely depart! And (strange, oh strangest mystery of all!) I found, in the commonest objects of the universe, a circle of analogies to that expression. I mean to say that, subsequently to the period when Ligeia's beauty passed into my spirit, there dwelling as in a shrine, I derived, from many existences in the material world, a sentiment such as I felt always aroused, within me, by her large and luminous orbs. Yet not the more could I define that sentiment, or analyze, or even steadily view it. I recognized it, let me repeat, sometimes in the survey of a rapidly growing vine—in the contemplation of a moth, a butterfly, a chrysalis, a stream of running water. I have felt it in the ocean; in the falling of a meteor. I have felt it in the glances of unusually aged people. And there are one or two stars in heaven—(one especially, a star of the sixth magnitude, double and changeable, to be found near the large star in Lyra) in a telescopic scrutiny of which I have been made aware of the feeling. I have been filled with it by certain sounds from stringed instruments, and not unfrequently by passages from books. Among innumerable other instances, I well remember something in a volume of Joseph Glanvill, which (perhaps from its quaintness—who shall say?) never failed to inspire me with the sentiment;—"And the will therein lieth, which dieth not. Who knoweth the mysteries of the will, with its vigor? For God is but a great will pervading all things by nature of its intentness. Man doth not yield him to the angels, nor unto death utterly, save only through the weakness of his feeble will."

Length of years and subsequent reflection, have enabled me to trace, indeed, some remote connection between this passage in the English moralist and a portion of the character of Ligeia. An *intensity* in thought, action, or speech, was possibly, in her, a result, or at least an index, of that gigantic volition which, during our long intercourse, failed to give other and more immediate evidence of its existence. Of all the women whom I have even known, she, the outwardly calm, the ever-placid Ligeia, was the most violently a prey to the tumultuous vultures of stern passion. And of such passion I could form no estimate, save by the miraculous expansion of those eyes which at once so delighted and appalled me—by the almost magical melody, modulation, distinctness, and placidity of her very low voice—and by the fierce energy (rendered doubly effective by contrast with her manner of utterance) of the wild words which she habitually uttered.

I have spoken of the learning of Ligeia; it was immense—such as I have never known, in woman. In the classical tongues was she deeply proficient, and as far as my own acquaintance extended in regard to the modern dialects of Europe, I have never known her at fault. Indeed upon any theme of the most admired, because simply the most abstruse of the boasted erudition of the academy, have I *ever* found Ligeia at fault? How singularly—how thrillingly, this one point in the nature of my wife has forced itself, at this late period only, upon my attention! I said her knowledge was such as I have never known in woman—but where breathes the man who has traversed, and successfully, *all* the wide areas of moral, physical, and mathematical science? I saw not then what I now clearly perceive, that the acquisitions of Ligeia

Sheridan's oriental tale, *The History of Nourjahad* (1767).
9. In *The Advancement of Learning* (III.iii) Bacon writes, "It was well said by Democritus, 'that the truth of nature lies hid in certain deep mines and caves.' "

were gigantic, were astounding; yet I was sufficiently aware of her infinite supremacy to resign myself, with a child-like confidence, to her guidance through the chaotic world of metaphysical investigation at which I was most busily occupied during the earlier years of our marriage. With how vast a triumph—with how vivid a delight—with how much of all that is ethereal in hope—did I *feel,* as she bent over me in studies but little sought—but less known—that delicious vista by slow degrees expanding before me, down whose long, gorgeous, and all untrodden path, I might at length pass onward to the goal of a wisdom too divinely precious not to be forbidden!

How poignant, then, must have been the grief with which, after some years, I beheld my well-grounded expectations take wings to themselves and fly away! Without Ligeia I was but as a child groping benighted. Her presence, her readings alone, rendered vividly luminous the many mysteries of the transcendentalism in which we were immersed. Wanting the radiant lustre of her eyes, letters, lambent and golden, grew duller than Saturnian lead.[10] And now those eyes shone less and less frequently upon the pages over which I pored. Ligeia grew ill. The wild eyes blazed with a too—too glorious effulgence; the pale fingers became of the transparent waxen hue of the grave; and the blue veins upon the lofty forehead swelled and sank impetuously with the tides of the most gentle emotion. I saw that she must die—and I struggled desperately in spirit with the grim Azrael. And the struggles of the passionate wife were, to my astonishment, even more energetic than my own. There had been much in her stern nature to impress me with the belief that, to her, death would have come without its terrors; but not so. Words are impotent to convey any just idea of the fierceness of resistance with which she wrestled with the Shadow. I groaned in anguish at the pitiable spectacle. I would have soothed—I would have reasoned; but, in the intensity of her wild desire for life,—for life—*but* for life—solace and reason were alike the uttermost folly. Yet not until the last instance, amid the most convulsive writhings of her fierce spirit, was shaken the external placidity of her demeanor. Her voice grew more gentle—grew more low—yet I would not wish to dwell upon the wild meaning of the quietly uttered words. My brain reeled as I hearkened entranced, to a melody more than mortal—to assumptions and aspirations which mortality had never before known.

That she loved me I should not have doubted; and I might have been easily aware that, in a bosom such as hers, love would have reigned no ordinary passion. But in death only was I fully impressed with the strength of her affection. For long hours, detaining my hand, would she pour out before me the overflowing of a heart whose more than passionate devotion amounted to idolatry. How had I deserved to be so blessed by such confessions?—how had I deserved to be so cursed with the removal of my beloved in the hour of her making them? But upon this subject I cannot bear to dilate. Let me say only, that in Ligeia's more than womanly abandonment to a love, alas! all unmerited, all unworthily bestowed, I at length recognized the principle of her longing with so wildly earnest a desire for the life which was now fleeing so rapidly away. It is this wild longing—it is this eager vehemence of desire for life—*but* for life—that I have no power to portray—no utterance capable of expressing.

At high noon of the night in which she departed, beckoning me, peremptorily, to her side, she bade me repeat certain verses composed by herself not many days before. I obeyed her.—They were these:

Lo! 'tis a gala night
  Within the lonesome latter years!
An angel throng, bewinged, bedight
  In veils, and drowned in tears,
Sit in a theatre, to see
  A play of hopes and fears,
While the orchestra breathes fitfully
  The music of the spheres.

Mimes, in the form of God on high,
  Mutter and mumble low,
And hither and thither fly—
  Mere puppets they, who come and go
At bidding of vast formless things
  That shift the scenery to and fro,
Flapping from out their Condor wings
  Invisible Wo!

That motley drama!—oh, be sure
  It shall not be forgot!
With its Phantom chased forever more,
  By a crowd that seize it not,
Through a circle that ever returneth in
  To the self-same spot,
And much of Madness and more of Sin
  And Horror the soul of the plot.

10. **Wanting . . . lead:** In medieval alchemy, which sought to transmute the baser metals into gold, *Saturnus* or Saturn was the technical term for lead. Poe is comparing the hero's loss of Ligeia's enlightening presence to a reversal of the alchemical process. Lead and gold will reappear in the leaden-hued window and golden draperies of Rowena's bridal chamber.

But see, amid the mimic rout,
A crawling shape intrude!
A blood-red thing that writhes from out
The scenic solitude!
It writhes!—it writhes!—with mortal pangs
The mimes become its food,
And the seraphs sob at vermin fangs
In human gore imbued.

Out—out are the lights—out all!
And over each quivering form,
The curtain, a funeral pall,
Comes down with the rush of a storm,
And the angels, all pallid and wan,
Uprising, unveiling, affirm
That the play is the tragedy, "Man,"
And its hero the Conqueror Worm.

"O God!" half shrieked Ligeia, leaping to her feet and extending her arms aloft with a spasmodic movement, as I made an end of these lines —"O God! O Divine Father!—shall these things be undeviatingly so?—shall this Conqueror be not once conquered? Are we not part and parcel in Thee? Who—who knoweth the mysteries of the will with its vigor? Man doth not yield him to the angels, *nor unto death utterly,* save only through the weakness of his feeble will."

And now, as if exhausted with emotion, she suffered her white arms to fall, and returned solemnly to her bed of death. And as she breathed her last sighs, there came mingled with them a low murmur from her lips. I bent to them my ear, and distinguished, again, the concluding words of the passage in Glanvill—*"Man doth not yield him to the angels, nor unto death utterly, save only through the weakness of his feeble will."*

She died;—and I, crushed into the very dust with sorrow, could no longer endure the lonely desolation of my dwelling in the dim and decaying city by the Rhine. I had no lack of what the world calls wealth. Ligeia had brought me far more, very far more than ordinarily falls to the lot of mortals. After a few months, therefore, of weary and aimless wandering, I purchased, and put in some repair, an abbey, which I shall not name, in one of the wildest and least frequented portions of fair England. The gloomy and dreary grandeur of the building, the almost savage aspect of the domain, the many melancholy and time-honored memories connected with both, had much in unison with the feelings of utter abandonment which had driven me into that remote and unsocial region of the country. Yet although the external abbey, with its verdant decay hanging about it, suffered but little alteration, I gave way, with a child-like perversity, and perchance with a faint hope of alleviating my sorrows, to a display of more than regal magnificence within.—For such follies, even in childhood, I had imbibed a taste, and now they came back to me as if in the dotage of grief. Alas, I feel how much even of incipient madness might have been discovered in the gorgeous and fantastic draperies, in the solemn carvings of Egypt, in the wild cornices and furniture, in the Bedlam patterns of the carpets of tufted gold! I had become a bounden slave in the trammels of opium, and my labors and orders had taken a coloring from my dreams. But these absurdities I must not pause to dctail. Let me speak only of that one chamber, ever accursed, whither, in a moment of mental alienation, I led from the altar as my bride—as the successor of the unforgotten Ligeia—the fair-haired and blue-eyed Lady Rowena Trevanion, of Tremaine.

There is no individual portion of the architecture and decoration of that bridal chamber which is not now visibly before me. Where were the souls of the haughty family of the bride, when, through thirst of gold, they permitted to pass the threshold of an apartment *so* bedecked, a maiden and a daughter so beloved? I have said that I minutely remember the details of the chamber—yet I am sadly forgetful on topics of deep moment—and here there was no system, no keeping, in the fantastic display, to take hold upon the memory. The room lay in a high turret of the castellated abbey, was pentagonal in shape, and of capacious size. Occupying the whole southern face of the pentagon was the sole window—an immense sheet of unbroken glass from Venice—a single pane, and tinted of a leaden hue, so that the rays of either the sun or moon, passing through it, fell with a ghastly lustre on the objects within. Over the upper portion of this huge window, extended the trellis-work of an aged vine, which clambered up the massy walls of the turret. The ceiling, of gloomy-looking oak, was excessively lofty, vaulted, and elaborately fretted with the wildest and most grotesque specimens of a semi-Gothic, semi-Druidical device. From out the most central recess of this melancholy vaulting, depended, by a single chain of gold with long links, a huge censer of the same metal, Saracenic in pattern, and with many perforations so contrived that there writhed in and out of them, as if endued with a serpent vitality, a continual succession of parti-colored fires.

Some few ottomans and golden candelabra, of Eastern figure, were in various stations about—and there was the couch, too—the bridal couch—of an Indian model, and low, and sculptured of solid ebony, with a pall-like canopy above. In each of the angles of the chamber stood on end a gigantic sarcophagus of black granite, from the tombs of the kings over against Luxor, with their aged lids full of immemorial sculpture. But in the draping of the apartment lay, alas! the chief phantasy of all. The lofty walls, gigantic in height—even unproportionably so—were hung from summit to foot, in vast folds, with a heavy and massive-looking tapestry—tapestry of a material which was found alike as a carpet on the floor, as a covering for the ottomans and the ebony bed, as a canopy for the bed and as the gorgeous volutes of the curtains which partially shaded the window. The material was the richest cloth of gold. It was spotted all over, at irregular intervals, with arabesque figures, about a foot in diameter, and wrought upon the cloth in patterns of the most jetty black. But these figures partook of the true character of the arabesque only when regarded from a single point of view. By a contrivance now common, and indeed traceable to a very remote period of antiquity, they were made changeable in aspect. To one entering the room, they bore the appearance of simple monstrosities; but upon a farther advance, this appearance gradually departed; and step by step, as the visiter moved his station in the chamber, he saw himself surrounded by an endless succession of the ghastly forms which belong to the superstition of the Norman, or arise in the guilty slumbers of the monk.[11] The phantasmagoric effect was vastly heightened by the artificial introduction of a strong continual current of wind behind the draperies—giving a hideous and uneasy animation to the whole.

In halls such as these—in a bridal chamber such as this—I passed, with the Lady of Tremaine, the unhallowed hours of the first month of our marriage—passed them with but little disquietude. That my wife dreaded the fierce moodiness of my temper—that she shunned me and loved me but little—I could not help perceiving; but it gave me rather pleasure than otherwise. I loathed her with a hatred belonging more to demon than to man. My memory flew back, (oh, with what intensity of regret!) to Ligeia, the beloved, the august, the beautiful, the entombed. I revelled in recollections of her purity, of her widom, of her lofty, her ethereal nature, of her passionate, her idolatrous love. Now, then, did my spirit fully and freely burn with more than all the fires of her own. In the excitement of my opium dreams (for I was habitually fettered in the shackles of the drug) I would call aloud upon her name, during the silence of the night, or among the sheltered recesses of the glens by day, as if, through the wild eagerness, the solemn passion, the consuming ardor of my longing for the departed, I could restore her to the pathways she had abandoned—ah, *could* it be forever?—upon the earth.

About the commencement of the second month of the marriage, the Lady Rowena was attacked with sudden illness, from which her recovery was slow. The fever which consumed her rendered her nights uneasy; and in her perturbed state of half-slumber, she spoke of sounds, and of motions, in and above the chamber of the turret, which I concluded had no origin save in the distemper of her fancy, or perhaps in the phantasmagoric influences of the chamber itself. She became at length convalescent—finally well. Yet but a brief period elapsed, ere a second more violent disorder again threw her upon a bed of suffering; and from this attack her frame, at all times feeble, never altogether recovered. Her illnesses were, after this epoch, of alarming character, and of more alarming recurrence, defying alike the knowledge and the great exertions of her physicians. With the increase of the chronic disease which had thus, apparently, taken too sure hold upon her constitution to be eradicated by human means, I could not fail to observe a similar increase in the nervous irritation of her temperament, and in her excitability by trivial causes of fear. She spoke again, and now more frequently and pertinaciously, of the sounds—of the slight sounds—and of the unusual motions among the tapestries, to which she had formerly alluded.

One night, near the closing in of September, she pressed this distressing subject with more than usual emphasis upon my attention. She had just awakened from an unquiet slumber, and I had been watching, with feelings half of anxiety, half of vague terror, the workings of her emaciated countenance. I sat by the side of her ebony bed, upon one of the ottomans of India. She partly arose, and spoke, in an earnest low whisper, of sounds which she *then* heard, but which I could not hear—of motions which she *then* saw, but which I could not perceive. The wind was rushing hurriedly behind the tapestries, and I wished to show her (what, let me confess it, I could not *all* believe) that those almost inarticulate breathings, and those very gentle variations of the figures upon the wall, were but the natural effects of that customary rushing of the wind. But a deadly pallor, overspreading her face, had proved to me that my

11. The walls of the torture chamber in "The Pit and the Pendulum" are "daubed in all the hideous and repulsive devices to which the charnel superstition of the monks has given rise." The tapestry figures of "Ligeia," like the painted devices of "The Pit and the Pendulum," represent hypnagogic images. Their changeable character anticipates the transmutation of Rowena.

exertions to reassure her would be fruitless. She appeared to be fainting, and no attendants were within call. I remembered where was deposited a decanter of light wine which had been ordered by her physicians, and hastened across the chamber to procure it. But, as I stepped beneath the light of the censer, two circumstances of a startling nature attracted my attention. I had felt that some palpable although invisible object had passed lightly by my person; and I saw that there lay upon the golden carpet, in the very middle of the rich lustre thrown from the censer, a shadow—a faint, indefinite shadow of angelic aspect—such as might be fancied for the shadow of a shade. But I was wild with the excitement of an immoderate dose of opium, and heeded these things but little, nor spoke of them to Rowena. Having found the wine, I recrossed the chamber, and poured out a gobletful, which I held to the lips of the fainting lady. She had now partially recovered, however, and took the vessel herself, while I sank upon an ottoman near me, with my eyes fastened upon her person. It was then that I became distinctly aware of a gentle foot-fall upon the carpet, and near the couch; and in a second thereafter, as Rowena was in the act of raising the wine to her lips, I saw, or may have dreamed that I saw, fall within the goblet, as if from some invisible spring in the atmosphere of the room, three or four large drops of a brilliant and ruby colored fluid. If this I saw—not so Rowena. She swallowed the wine unhesitatingly, and I forbore to speak to her of a circumstance which must, after all, I considered, have been but the suggestion of a vivid imagination, rendered morbidly active by the terror of the lady, by the opium, and by the hour.

Yet I cannot conceal it from my own perception that, immediately subsequent to the fall of the ruby-drops, a rapid change for the worse took place in the disorder of my wife; so that, on the third subsequent night, the hands of her menials prepared her for the tomb, and on the fourth, I sat alone, with her shrouded body, in that fantastic chamber which had received her as my bride.—Wild visions, opium-engendered, flitted, shadow-like, before me. I gazed with unquiet eye upon the sarcophagi in the angles of the room, upon the varying figures of the drapery, and upon the writhing of the parti-colored fires in the censer overhead. My eyes then fell, as I called to mind the circumstances of a former night, to the spot beneath the glare of the censer where I had seen the faint traces of the shadow. It was there, however, no longer; and breathing with greater freedom, I turned my glances to the pallid and rigid figure upon the bed. Then rushed upon me a thousand memories of Ligeia—and then came back upon my heart, with the turbulent violence of a flood, the whole of that unutterable wo with which I had regarded *her* thus enshrouded. The night waned; and still, with a bosom full of bitter thoughts of the one only and supremely beloved, I remained gazing upon the body of Rowena.

It might have been midnight, or perhaps earlier, or later, for I had taken no note of time, when a sob, low, gentle, but very distinct, startled me from my revery.—I *felt* that it came from the bed of ebony—the bed of death. I listened in an agony of superstitious terror—but there was no repetition of the sound. I strained my vision to detect any motion in the corpse—but there was not the slightest perceptible. Yet I could not have been deceived. I *had* heard the noise, however faint, and my soul was awakened within me. I resolutely and perseveringly kept my attention riveted upon the body. Many minutes elapsed before any circumstance occurred tending to throw light upon the mystery. At length it became evident that a slight, a very feeble, and barely noticeable tinge of color had flushed up within the cheeks, and along the sunken small veins of the eyelids. Through a species of unutterable horror and awe, for which the language of mortality has no sufficiently energetic expression, I felt my heart cease to beat, my limbs grow rigid where I sat. Yet a sense of duty finally operated to restore my self-possession. I could no longer doubt that we had been precipitate in our preparations—that Rowena still lived. It was necessary that some immediate exertion be made; yet the turret was altogether apart from the portion of the abbey tenanted by the servants—there were none within call—I had no means of summoning them to my aid without leaving the room for many minutes—and this I could not venture to do. I therefore struggled alone in my endeavors to call back the spirit still hovering. In a short period it was certain, however, that a relapse had taken place; the color disappeared from both eyelid and cheek, leaving a wanness even more than that of marble; the lips became doubly shrivelled and pinched up in the ghastly expression of death; a repulsive clamminess and coldness overspread rapidly the surface of the body; and all the usual rigorous stiffness immediately supervened. I fell back with a shudder upon the couch from which I had been so startlingly aroused, and again gave myself up to passionate waking visions of Ligeia.

An hour thus elapsed when (could it be possible?) I was a second time aware of some vague sound issuing from the region of the bed. I listened—in extremity of horror. The sound came again—it was a sigh. Rushing to the corpse, I saw—distinctly saw—a tremor upon the lips. In a minute afterward they relaxed, disclosing a bright line of the pearly teeth. Amazement now struggled in my bosom with the profound awe which had hitherto reigned there alone. I felt that my vision grew dim, that my reason wandered; and it was only by a violent effort that I at length succeeded in nerving myself to the task which duty thus once more had pointed out. There was now a partial glow upon the forehead and upon the cheek and throat; a perceptible warmth pervaded the whole frame; there was even a slight pulsation at the heart. The lady *lived;* and with redoubled ardor I betook myself to the task of restoration. I chafed and bathed the temples and the hands, and used every exertion which experience, and no little medical reading, could suggest. But in vain. Suddenly, the color fled, the pulsation ceased, the lips resumed the expression of the dead, and, in an instant afterward, the whole body took upon itself the icy chilliness, the livid hue, the intense rigidity, the sunken outline, and all the loathsome peculiarities of that which has been, for many days, a tenant of the tomb.

And again I sunk into visions of Ligeia—and again, (what marvel that I shudder while I write?) *again* there reached my ears a low sob from the region of the ebony bed. But why shall I minutely detail the unspeakable horrors of that night? Why shall I pause to relate how, time after time, until near the period of the gray dawn, this hideous drama of revivification was repeated; how each terrific relapse was only into a sterner and apparently more irredeemable death; how each agony wore the aspect of a struggle with some invisible foe; and how each struggle was succeeded by I know not what of wild change in the personal appearance of the corpse? Let me hurry to a conclusion.

The greater part of the fearful night had worn away, and she who had been dead once again stirred—and now more vigorously than hitherto, although arousing from a dissolution more appalling in its utter hopelessness than any. I had long ceased to struggle or to move, and remained sitting rigidly upon the ottoman, a helpless prey to a whirl of violent emotions, of which extreme awe was perhaps the least terrible, the least consuming. The corpse, I repeat, stirred, and now more vigorously than before. The hues of life flushed up with unwonted energy into the countenance—the limbs relaxed—and, save that the eyelids were yet pressed heavily together, and that the bandages and draperies of the grave still imparted their charnel character to the figure, I might have dreamed that Rowena had indeed shaken off, utterly, the fetters of Death. But if this idea was not, even then, altogether adopted, I could at least doubt no longer, when, arising from the bed, tottering, with feeble steps, with closed eyes, and with the manner of one bewildered in a dream, the thing that was enshrouded advanced boldly and palpably into the middle of the apartment.

I trembled not—I stirred not—for a crowd of unutterable fancies connected with the air, the stature, the demeanor of the figure, rushing hurriedly through my brain, had paralyzed—had chilled me into stone.[12] I stirred not—but gazed upon the apparition. There was a mad disorder in my thoughts—a tumult unappeasable. Could it, indeed, be the *living* Rowena who confronted me? Could it, indeed, be Rowena *at all*—the fair-haired, the blue-eyed Lady Rowena Trevanion of Tremaine? Why, *why* should I doubt it? The bandage lay heavily about the mouth—but then might it not be the mouth of the breathing Lady of Tremaine? And the cheeks—there were the roses as in her noon of life—yes, these might indeed be the fair cheeks of the living Lady of Tremaine. And the chin, with its dimples, as in health, might it not be hers?—but *had she then grown taller since her malady?* What inexpressible madness seized me with that thought? One bound, and I had reached her feet! Shrinking from my touch, she let fall from her head, unloosened, the ghastly cerements which had confined it, and there streamed forth into the rushing atmosphere of the chamber huge masses of long and dishevelled hair; *it was blacker than the raven wings of midnight!* And now slowly opened *the eyes* of the figure which stood before me. "Here then, at least," I shrieked aloud, "can I never—can I never be mistaken—these are the full, and the black, and the wild eyes—of my lost love—of the Lady—of the LADY LIGEIA."

THE FALL OF THE HOUSE OF USHER

◇

¶ "THE FALL OF THE HOUSE OF USHER" was first published in *Burton's Gentleman's Magazine* (September

12. **chilled . . . stone:** Compare Poe's use of sculpture-symbolism to that of Keats in "The Eve of St. Agnes." Especially relevant are ll. 289–324, in which Porphyro becomes first like "sculptured stone" and then like a "throbbing star," thus passing into an ideal reality and assimilating himself to Madeline's dream.

18, 1839). For comment on this story, see the Introduction, Part IV.

◇

Son cœur est un luth suspendu;
Sitôt qu'on le touche il résonne.
DE BÉRANGER [1]

DURING the whole of a dull, dark, and soundless day in the autumn of the year, when the clouds hung oppressively low in the heavens, I had been passing alone, on horseback, through a singularly dreary tract of country, and at length found myself, as the shades of the evening drew on, within view of the melancholy House of Usher.[2] I know not how it was—but, with the first glimpse of the building, a sense of insufferable gloom pervaded my spirit. I say insufferable; for the feeling was unrelieved by any of that half-pleasurable, because poetic, sentiment with which the mind usually receives even the sternest natural images of the desolate or terrible. I looked upon the scene before me—upon the mere house, and the simple landscape features of the domain—upon the bleak walls—upon the vacant eye-like windows—upon a few rank sedges—and upon a few white trunks of decayed trees—with an utter depression of soul which I can compare to no earthly sensation more properly than to the after-dream of the reveller upon opium—the bitter lapse into every-day life—the hideous dropping off of the veil. There was an iciness, a sinking, a sickening of the heart—an unredeemed dreariness of thought which no goading of the imagination could torture into aught of the sublime. What was it—I paused to think—what was it that so unnerved me in the contemplation of the House of Usher? It was a mystery all insoluble; nor could I grapple with the shadowy fancies that crowded upon me as I pondered. I was forced to fall back upon the unsatisfactory conclusion, that while, beyond doubt, there *are* combinations of very simple natural objects which have the power of thus affecting us, still the analysis of this power lies among considerations beyond our depth. It was possible, I reflected, that a mere different arrangement of the particulars of the scene, of the details of the picture, would be sufficient to modify, or perhaps to annihilate its capacity for sorrowful impression; and, acting upon this idea, I reined my horse to the precipitous brink of a black and lurid tarn that lay in unruffled lustre by the dwelling, and gazed down—but with a shudder even more thrilling than before—upon the remodelled and inverted images of the gray sedge, and the ghastly tree-stems, and the vacant and eye-like windows.

Nevertheless, in this mansion of gloom I now proposed to myself a sojourn of some weeks. Its proprietor, Roderick Usher, had been one of my boon companions in boyhood; but many years had elapsed since our last meeting. A letter, however, had lately reached me in a distant part of the country—a letter from him—which, in its wildly importunate nature, had admitted of no other than a personal reply. The MS. gave evidence of nervous agitation. The writer spoke of acute bodily illness—of a mental disorder which oppressed him—and of an earnest desire to see me, as his best and indeed his only personal friend, with a view of attempting, by the cheerfulness of my society, some alleviation of his malady. It was the manner in which all this, and much more, was said—it was the apparent *heart* that went with his request—which allowed me no room for hesitation; and I accordingly obeyed forthwith what I still considered a very singular summons.

Although, as boys, we had been even intimate associates, yet I really knew little of my friend. His reserve had been always excessive and habitual. I was aware, however, that his very ancient family had been noted, time out of mind, for a peculiar sensibility of temperament, displaying itself, through long ages, in many works of exalted art, and manifested, of late, in repeated deeds of munificent yet unobtrusive charity, as well as in a passionate devotion to the intricacies, perhaps even more than to the orthodox and easily recognizable beauties, of musical science. I had learned, too, the very remarkable fact, that the stem of the Usher race, all time-honoured as it was, had put forth, at no period, any enduring branch; in other words, that the entire family lay in the direct line of descent, and had always, with very trifling and very temporary variation, so lain. It was this deficiency, I considered, while running over in thought the perfect keeping of the character of the premises with the accredited character of the people, and while speculating upon the possible influence which the one, in the long lapse of centuries, might have exercised upon the other—it was this deficiency, perhaps, of collateral issue, and the consequent undeviating transmission, from sire to son, of the patrimony with the name, which had, at length, so identified the two as to merge the original title of the estate in the quaint and equivocal appellation

THE FALL OF THE HOUSE OF USHER. 1. **De Béranger:** The verses are taken from "Le Refus," a poem by Pierre Jean de Béranger (1780–1857), and might be translated: "His heart is a hanging lute;/If it be but touched, it resounds." See "Israfel," l. 2. 2. **Usher:** Mr. and Mrs. Luke Usher, a theatrical couple, were unofficial guardians of Elizabeth Arnold, Poe's mother, when the latter was an orphaned child-actress.

of the "House of Usher"—an appellation which seemed to include, in the minds of the peasantry who used it, both the family and the family mansion.

I have said that the sole effect of my somewhat childish experiment—that of looking down within the tarn—had been to deepen the first singular impression. There can be no doubt that the consciousness of the rapid increase of my superstition—for why should I not so term it?—served mainly to accelerate the increase itself. Such, I have long known, is the paradoxical law of all sentiments having terror as a basis. And it might have been for this reason only, that, when I again uplifted my eyes to the house itself, from its image in the pool, there grew in my mind a strange fancy—a fancy so ridiculous, indeed, that I but mention it to show the vivid force of the sensations which oppressed me. I had so worked upon my imagination as really to believe that about the whole mansion and domain there hung an atmosphere peculiar to themselves and their immediate vicinity—an atmosphere which had no affinity with the air of heaven, but which had reeked up from the decayed trees, and the gray wall, and the silent tarn—a pestilent and mystic vapour, dull, sluggish, faintly discernible, and leaden-hued.

Shaking off from my spirit what *must* have been a dream, I scanned more narrowly the real aspect of the building. Its principal feature seemed to be that of an excessive antiquity. The discoloration of ages had been great. Minute fungi overspread the whole exterior, hanging in a fine tangled web-work from the eaves. Yet all this was apart from any extraordinary dilapidation. No portion of the masonry had fallen; and there appeared to be a wild inconsistency between its still perfect adaptation of parts, and the crumbling condition of the individual stones. In this there was much that reminded me of the specious totality of old wood-work which has rotted for long years in some neglected vault, with no disturbance from the breath of the external air.[3] Beyond this indication of extensive decay, however, the fabric gave little token of instability. Perhaps the eye of a scrutinizing observer might have discovered a barely perceptible fissure, which, extending from the roof of the building in front, made its way down the wall in a zigzag direction, until it became lost in the sullen waters of the tarn.

Noticing these things, I rode over a short causeway to the house. A servant in waiting took my horse, and I entered the Gothic archway of the hall. A valet, of stealthy step, thence conducted me, in silence, through many dark and intricate passages in my progress to the *studio* of his master. Much that I encountered on the way contributed, I know not how, to heighten the vague sentiments of which I have already spoken. While the objects around me—while the carvings of the ceilings, the sombre tapestries of the walls, the ebon blackness of the floors, and the phantasmagoric armorial trophies which rattled as I strode, were but matters to which, or to such as which, I had been accustomed from my infancy—while I hesitated not to acknowledge how familiar was all this—I still wondered to find how unfamiliar were the fancies which ordinary images were stirring up. On one of the staircases, I met the physician of the family. His countenance, I thought, wore a mingled expression of low cunning and perplexity. He accosted me with trepidation and passed on. The valet now threw open a door and ushered me into the presence of his master.

The room in which I found myself was very large and lofty. The windows were long, narrow, and pointed, and at so vast a distance from the black oaken floor as to be altogether inaccessible from within. Feeble gleams of encrimsoned light made their way through the trellised panes, and served to render sufficiently distinct the more prominent objects around; the eye, however, struggled in vain to reach the remoter angles of the chamber, or the recesses of the vaulted and fretted ceiling. Dark draperies hung upon the walls. The general furniture was profuse, comfortless, antique, and tattered. Many books and musical instruments lay scattered about, but failed to give any vitality to the scene. I felt that I breathed an atmosphere of sorrow. An air of stern, deep, and irredeemable gloom hung over and pervaded all.

Upon my entrance, Usher arose from a sofa on which he had been lying at full length, and greeted me with a vivacious warmth which had much in it, I at first thought, of an overdone cordiality—of the constrained effort of the *ennuyé* man of the world. A glance, however, at his countenance convinced me of his perfect sincerity. We sat down; and for some moments, while he spoke not, I gazed upon him with a feeling half of pity, half of awe. Surely, man had never before so terribly altered, in so brief a period, as had Roderick Usher! It was with difficulty that I could bring myself to admit the identity of the wan being before me with the companion of my early boyhood. Yet the character of his face had been at all times remarkable. A cadaverousness of complexion; an eye large, liquid, and luminous beyond comparison; lips somewhat thin and very pallid, but of a surpassingly beautiful curve; a nose of a delicate Hebrew model, but with a

3. **In . . . air:** Compare the "rottenness" and "worm-eaten condition" of the phantom ship in "Ms. Found in a Bottle."

breadth of nostril unusual in similar formations; a finely moulded chin, speaking, in its want of prominence, of a want of moral energy; hair of a more than web-like softness and tenuity; these features, with an inordinate expansion above the regions of the temple,[4] made up altogether a countenance not easily to be forgotten. And now in the mere exaggeration of the prevailing character of these features, and of the expression they were wont to convey, lay so much of change that I doubted to whom I spoke. The now ghastly pallor of the skin, and the now miraculous lustre of the eye, above all things startled and even awed me. The silken hair, too, had been suffered to grow all unheeded, and as, in its wild gossamer texture, it floated rather than fell about the face. I could not, even with effort, connect its Arabesque expression with any idea of simple humanity.

In the manner of my friend I was at once struck with an incoherence—an inconsistency; and I soon found this to arise from a series of feeble and futile struggles to overcome an habitual trepidancy—an excessive nervous agitation. For something of this nature I had indeed been prepared, no less by his letter, than by reminiscences of certain boyish traits, and by conclusions deduced from his peculiar physical conformation and temperament. His action was alternately vivacious and sullen. His voice varied rapidly from a tremulous indecision (when the animal spirits seemed utterly in abeyance) to that species of energetic concision—that abrupt, weighty, unhurried, and hollow-sounding enunciation—that leaden, self-balanced, and perfectly modulated guttural utterance, which may be observed in the lost drunkard, or the irreclaimable eater of opium, during the periods of his most intense excitement.

It was thus that he spoke of the object of my visit, of his earnest desire to see me, and of the solace he expected me to afford him. He entered, at some length, into what he conceived to be the nature of his malady. It was, he said, a constitutional and a family evil, and one for which he despaired to find a remedy—a mere nervous affection, he immediately added, which would undoubtedly soon pass off. It displayed itself in a host of unnatural sensations. Some of these, as he detailed them, interested and bewildered me; although, perhaps, the terms and the general manner of their narration had their weight. He suffered much from a morbid acuteness of the senses; the most insipid food was alone endurable; he could wear only garments of certain texture; the odours of all flowers were oppressive; his eyes were tortured by even a faint light; and there were but peculiar sounds, and these from stringed instruments, which did not inspire him with horror.[5]

To an anomalous species of terror I found him a bounden slave. "I shall perish," said he, "I *must* perish in this deplorable folly. Thus, thus, and not otherwise, shall I be lost. I dread the events of the future, not in themselves, but in their results. I shudder at the thought of any, even the most trivial, incident, which may operate upon this intolerable agitation of soul. I have, indeed, no abhorrence of danger, except in its absolute effect—in terror. In this unnerved—in this pitiable condition—I feel that the period will sooner or later arrive when I must abandon life and reason together, in some struggle with the grim phantasm, FEAR."

I learned, moreover, at intervals, and through broken and equivocal hints, another singular feature of his mental condition. He was enchained by certain superstitious impressions in regard to the dwelling which he tenanted, and whence, for many years, he had never ventured forth—in regard to an influence whose supposititious force was conveyed in terms too shadowy here to be re-stated—an influence which some peculiarities in the mere form and substance of his family mansion had, by dint of long sufferance, he said, obtained over his spirit—an effect which the *physique* of the gray walls and turrets, and of the dim tarn into which they all looked down, had, at length, brought about upon the *morale* of his existence.

He admitted, however, although with hesitation, that much of the peculiar gloom which thus afflicted him could be traced to a more natural and far more palpable origin—to the severe and long-continued illness—indeed to the evidently approaching dissolution—of a tenderly beloved sister, his sole companion for long years, his last and only relative on earth. "Her decease," he said, with a bitterness which I can never forget, "would leave him (him, the hopeless and the frail) the last of the ancient race of the Ushers." While he spoke, the lady Madeline (for so was she called) passed slowly through a remote portion of the apartment, and, without having noticed my presence, disappeared. I regarded her with an utter astonishment not unmingled with dread; and yet I found it impossible to account for such feelings. A sensation of stupor oppressed me, as my eyes followed her retreating steps. When a door, at length, closed upon her, my glance sought instinctively and eagerly the

4. **with . . . temple:** See "Ligeia," 5 n. Usher also resembles Ligeia in his large, luminous eyes and Hebrew nose.

5. **He . . . horror:** Usher has almost wholly dispensed with the bodily or "rudimentary" senses which perceive the external world.

countenance of the brother—but he had buried his face in his hands, and I could only perceive that a far more than ordinary wanness had overspread the emaciated fingers through which trickled many passionate tears.

The disease of the lady Madeline had long baffled the skill of her physicians. A settled apathy, a gradual wasting away of the person, and frequent although transient affections of a partially cataleptical character were the unusual diagnosis. Hitherto she had steadily borne up against the pressure of her malady, and had not betaken herself finally to bed; but on the closing in of the evening of my arrival at the house, she succumbed (as her brother told me at night with inexpressible agitation) to the prostrating power of the destroyer; and I learned that the glimpse I had obtained of her person would thus probably be the last I should obtain—that the lady, at least while living, would be seen by me no more.

For several days ensuing, her name was unmentioned by either Usher or myself: and during this period I was busied in earnest endeavours to alleviate the melancholy of my friend. We painted and read together, or I listened, as if in a dream, to the wild improvisations of his speaking guitar. And thus, as a closer and still closer intimacy admitted me more unreservedly into the recesses of his spirit, the more bitterly did I perceive the futility of all attempt at cheering a mind from which darkness, as if an inherent positive quality, poured forth upon all objects of the moral and physical universe in one unceasing radiation of gloom.

I shall ever bear about me a memory of the many solemn hours I thus spent alone with the master of the House of Usher. Yet I should fail in any attempt to convey an idea of the exact character of the studies, or of the occupations, in which he involved me, or led me the way. An excited and highly distempered ideality threw a sulphureous lustre over all. His long improvised dirges will ring forever in my ears. Among other things, I hold painfully in mind a certain singular perversion and amplification of the wild air of the last waltz of Von Weber.[6] From the paintings over which his elaborate fancy brooded, and which grew, touch by touch, into vaguenesses at which I shuddered the more thrillingly, because I shuddered knowing not why;—from these paintings (vivid as their images now are before me) I would in vain endeavour to educe more than a small portion which should lie within the compass of merely written words.[7] By the utter simplicity, by the nakedness of his designs, he arrested and overawed attention. If ever mortal painted an idea, that mortal was Roderick Usher. For me at least, in the circumstances then surrounding me, there arose out of the pure abstractions which the hypochondriac contrived to throw upon his canvas, an intensity of intolerable awe, no shadow of which felt I ever yet in the contemplation of the certainly glowing yet too concrete reveries of Fuseli.[8]

One of the phantasmagoric conceptions of my friend, partaking not so rigidly of the spirit of abstraction, may be shadowed forth, although feebly, in words. A small picture presented the interior of an immensely long and rectangular vault or tunnel, with low walls, smooth, white, and without interruption or device. Certain accessory points of the design served well to convey the idea that this excavation lay at an exceeding depth below the surface of the earth. No outlet was observed in any portion of its vast extent, and no torch or other artificial source of light was discernible; yet a flood of intense rays rolled throughout, and bathed the whole in a ghastly and inappropriate splendour.[9]

I have just spoken of that morbid condition of the auditory nerve which rendered all music intolerable to the sufferer, with the exception of certain effects of stringed instruments. It was, perhaps, the narrow limits to which he thus confined himself upon the guitar which gave birth, in great measure, to the fantastic character of his performances. But the fervid *facility* of his *impromptus* could not be so accounted for. They must have been, and were, in the notes, as well as in the words of his wild fantasias (for he not unfrequently accompanied himself with rhymed verbal improvisations), the result of that intense mental collectedness and concentration to which I have previously alluded as observable only in particular moments of the highest artificial excitement. The words of one of these rhapsodies I have easily remembered. I was, perhaps, the more forcibly impressed with it as he gave it, because, in the under or mystic current of its meaning, I fancied that I perceived, and for the first time, a full consciousness on the part of Usher of the tottering of his lofty reason upon her throne. The verses, which were entitled "The Haunted Palace," ran very nearly, if not accurately, thus:

6. Von Weber: German Romantic composer (1786–1826). **7. From . . . words:** In one of his "Marginalia" (see p. 471), Poe asserts that, whereas "no thought, properly so called" is "beyond the compass of words," he has found it "absolutely impossible to adapt language" to the description of hypnagogic images. **8. Fuseli:** Henry Fuseli (1741–1825), Swiss-born professor at the Royal Academy in London, was a great painter of the fantastic and terrible. **9. One . . . splendour:** "A grave? Oh, no, a lantern, slaughtered youth;/For here lies Juliet, and her beauty makes/This vault a feasting presence full of light" (*Romeo and Juliet,* V.iii.84–86).

I

In the greenest of our valleys,
By good angels tenanted,
Once a fair and stately palace—
Radiant palace—reared its head.
In the monarch Thought's dominion—
It stood there!
Never seraph spread a pinion
Over fabric half so fair.

II

Banners yellow, glorious, golden,
On its roof did float and flow
(This—all this—was in the olden
Time long ago)
And every gentle air that dallied,
In that sweet day,
Along the ramparts plumed and pallid,
A winged odour went away.

III

Wanderers in that happy valley
Through two luminous windows saw
Spirits moving musically
To a lute's well-tunèd law,
Round about a throne, where sitting
(Porphyrogene!)
In state his glory well befitting,
The ruler of the realm was seen.

IV

And all with pearl and ruby glowing
Was the fair palace door,
Through which came flowing, flowing, flowing
And sparkling evermore,
A troop of Echoes whose sweet duty
Was but to sing,
In voices of surpassing beauty,
The wit and wisdom of their king.

V

But evil things, in robes of sorrow,
Assailed the monarch's high estate;
(Ah, let us mourn, for never morrow
Shall dawn upon him, desolate!)
And, round about his home, the glory
That blushed and bloomed
Is but a dim-remembered story
Of the old time entombed.

VI

And travellers now within that valley,
Through the red-litten windows see
Vast forms that move fantastically
To a discordant melody;
While, like a rapid ghastly river,
Through the pale door,
A hideous throng rush out forever,
And laugh—but smile no more.

I well remember that suggestions arising from this ballad, led us into a train of thought, wherein there became manifest an opinion of Usher's which I mention not so much on account of its novelty, (for other men have thought thus,) as on account of the pertinacity with which he maintained it. This opinion, in its general form, was that of the sentience of all vegetable things. But, in his disordered fancy, the idea had assumed a more daring character, and trespassed, under certain conditions, upon the kingdom of inorganization.[10] I lack words to express the full extent, or the earnest *abandon* of his persuasion. The belief, however, was connected (as I have previously hinted) with the gray stones of the home of his forefathers. The conditions of the sentience had been here, he imagined, fulfilled in the method of collocation of these stones—in the order of their arrangement, as well as in that of the many *fungi* which overspread them, and of the decayed trees which stood around —above all, in the long undisturbed endurance of this arrangement, and in its reduplication in the still waters of the tarn. Its evidence—the evidence of the sentience—was to be seen, he said (and I here started as he spoke), in the gradual yet certain condensation of an atmosphere of their own about the waters and the walls. The result was discoverable, he added, in that silent yet importunate and terrible influence which for centuries had moulded the destinies of his family, and which made *him* what I now saw him—what he was. Such opinions need no comment, and I will make none.

Our books—the books which, for years, had formed no small portion of the mental existence of the invalid—were, as might be supposed, in strict keeping with this character of phantasm. We pored together over such works as the *Ververt et Chartreuse* of Gresset; the *Belphegor* of Machiavelli; the *Heaven and Hell* of Swedenborg; the *Subterranean Voyage of Nicholas Klimm* of Holberg; the *Chiromancy* of Robert Fludd, of Jean D'Indaginé, and of De la Chambre; the *Journey into the Blue Distance* of Tieck; and the *City of the Sun* of Campanella. One favourite volume was a small octavo edition of the *Directorium Inquisitorum,* by the Dominican Eymeric de Gironne; and there were passages in Pomponius Mela, about the old African Satyrs and Œgipans, over which Usher would sit dreaming for hours. His chief delight,

10. **kingdom of inorganization:** the realm of inorganic matter.

however, was found in the perusal of an exceedingly rare and curious book in quarto Gothic—the manual of a forgotten church—the *Vigiliæ Mortuorum secundum Chorum Ecclesiæ Maguntinæ*.[11]

I could not help thinking of the wild ritual of this work, and of its probable influence upon the hypochondriac, when, one evening, having informed me abruptly that the lady Madeline was no more, he stated his intention of preserving her corpse for a fortnight, (previously to its final interment,) in one of the numerous vaults within the main walls of the building. The worldly reason, however, assigned for this singular proceeding, was one which I did not feel at liberty to dispute. The brother had been led to his resolution (so he told me) by consideration of the unusual character of the malady of the deceased, of certain obtrusive and eager inquiries on the part of her medical men, and of the remote and exposed situation of the burial-ground of the family. I will not deny that when I called to mind the sinister countenance of the person whom I met upon the staircase, on the day of my arrival at the house, I had no desire to oppose what I regarded as at best but a harmless, and by no means an unnatural, precaution.

At the request of Usher, I personally aided him in the arrangements for the temporary entombment. The body having been encoffined, we two alone bore it to its rest. The vault in which we placed it (and which had been so long unopened that our torches, half smothered in its oppressive atmosphere, gave us little opportunity for investigation) was small, damp, and entirely without means of admission for light; lying, at great depth, immediately beneath that portion of the building in which was my own sleeping apartment. It had been used, apparently, in remote feudal times, for the worst purposes of a donjon-keep, and, in later days, as a place of deposit for powder, or some other highly combustible substance, as a portion of its floor, and the whole interior of a long archway through which we reached it, were carefully sheathed with copper. The door, of massive iron, had been, also, similarly protected. Its immense weight caused an unusually sharp grating sound, as it moved upon its hinges.

Having deposited our mournful burden upon tressels within this region of horror, we partially turned aside the yet unscrewed lid of the coffin, and looked upon the face of the tenant. A striking similitude between the brother and sister now first arrested my attention; and Usher, divining, perhaps, my thoughts, murmured out some few words from which I learned that the deceased and himself had been twins, and that sympathies of a scarcely intelligible nature had always existed between them. Our glances, however, rested not long upon the dead—for we could not regard her unawed. The disease which had thus entombed the lady in the maturity of youth, had left, as usual in all maladies of a strictly cataleptical character, the mockery of a faint blush upon the bosom and the face, and that suspiciously lingering smile upon the lip which is so terrible in death. We replaced and screwed down the lid, and, having secured the door of iron, made our way, with toil, into the scarcely less gloomy apartments of the upper portion of the house.

And now, some days of bitter grief having elapsed, an observable change came over the features of the mental disorder of my friend. His ordinary manner had vanished. His ordinary occupations were neglected or forgotten. He roamed from chamber to chamber with hurried, unequal, and objectless step. The pallor of his countenance had assumed, if possible, a more ghastly hue—but the luminousness of his eye had utterly gone out. The once occasional huskiness of his tone was heard no more; and a tremulous quaver, as if of extreme terror, habitually characterized his utterance. There were times, indeed, when I thought his unceasingly agitated mind was labouring with some oppressive secret, to divulge which he struggled for the necessary courage. At times, again, I was obliged to resolve all into the mere inexplicable vagaries of madness, for I beheld him gazing upon vacancy for long hours, in an attitude of the profoundest attention, as if listening to some imaginary sound. It was no wonder that his condition

11. **Our . . . *Maguntinæ:*** Jean Baptiste Louis Gresset wrote the two poems *Vert-Vert* (1734) and *La Chartreuse* (1735). Nicolló Machiavelli's novel *Belfagor* appeared in 1545. Emanuel Swedenborg, Swedish philosopher, scientist, and mystic, published *De Coelo . . . et de Inferno* in 1758. The Danish historian and dramatist Ludwig Holberg was the author of *Nicolai Klimii Iter Subterraneum* (1741), an imaginary-voyage tale. Robert Fludd (1574–1637) was an English physician and cabalist. D'Indaginé's *Chiromantia* (1522) and De la Chambre's *Discours sur les Principes de la Chiromancie* (1653) were studies of palmistry. Johann Ludwig Tieck (1773–1853) was a celebrated German novelist and critic: the book referred to is an English translation of Tieck's volume, *Das Alte Buch.* Tommaso Campanella, who shared Usher's belief in the sentience of all things, was the author of *Civitas Solis*, a Utopian work (1643). Eymeric, fourteenth-century Spanish Inquisitor-General, left a record of his Inquisitorial proceedings, which became the guide of Torquemada. Pomponius Mela was the author of *De Situ Orbis*, a geographical treatise of the first century A.D.: Poe pretends to quote from the work in his "Island of the Fay," but is actually quoting from Hugh Murray's *Encyclopaedia of Geography.* The manual of *Vigiliae Mortuorum*, or rites of the dead, was printed at Basel, *c.* 1500. The collective effect of this catalogue of Usher's books is to certify that their owner, like Ligeia, has "gigantic" learning, that his consciousness is not limited by place or time, and that his thoughts dwell upon imaginary worlds and the afterlife. Such thoughts are the direct cause of Lady Madeline's dissolution.

terrified—that it infected me. I felt creeping upon me, by slow yet certain degrees, the wild influences of his own fantastic yet impressive superstitions.

It was, especially, upon retiring to bed late in the night of the seventh or eighth day after the placing of the lady Madeline within the donjon, that I experienced the full power of such feelings. Sleep came not near my couch—while the hours waned and waned away. I struggled to reason off the nervousness which had dominion over me. I endeavoured to believe that much, if not all of what I felt, was due to the bewildering influence of the gloomy furniture of the room—of the dark and tattered draperies, which, tortured into motion by the breath of a rising tempest, swayed fitfully to and fro upon the walls, and rustled uneasily about the decorations of the bed. But my efforts were fruitless. An irrepressible tremour gradually pervaded my frame; and, at length, there sat upon my very heart an incubus of utterly causeless alarm. Shaking this off with a gasp and a struggle, I uplifted myself upon the pillows, and, peering earnestly within the intense darkness of the chamber, hearkened—I know not why, except that an instinctive spirit prompted me—to certain low and indefinite sounds [12] which came, through the pauses of the storm, at long intervals, I knew not whence. Overpowered by an intense sentiment of horror, unaccountable yet unendurable, I threw on my clothes with haste, (for I felt that I should sleep no more during the night,) and endeavoured to arouse myself from the pitiable condition into which I had fallen, by pacing rapidly to and fro through the apartment.

I had taken but few turns in this manner, when a light step on an adjoining staircase arrested my attention. I presently recognized it as that of Usher. In an instant afterward he rapped, with a gentle touch, at my door, and entered, bearing a lamp. His countenance was, as usual, cadaverously wan—but, moreover, there was a species of mad hilarity in his eyes—an evidently restrained *hysteria* in his whole demeanour. His air appalled me—but anything was preferable to the solitude which I had so long endured, and I even welcomed his presence as a relief.

"And you have not seen it?" he said abruptly, after having stared about him for some moments in silence—"you have not then seen it?—but, stay! you shall." Thus speaking, and having carefully shaded his lamp, he hurried to one of the casements, and threw it freely open to the storm.

The impetuous fury of the entering gust nearly lifted us from our feet. It was, indeed, a tempestuous yet sternly beautiful night, and one wildly singular in its terror and its beauty. A whirlwind had apparently collected its force in our vicinity; for there were frequent and violent alterations in the direction of the wind; and the exceeding density of the clouds (which hung so low as to press upon the turrets of the house) did not prevent our perceiving the life-like velocity with which they flew careering from all points against each other, without passing away into the distance. I say that even their exceeding density did not prevent our perceiving this—yet we had no glimpse of the moon or stars—nor was there any flashing forth of the lightning. But the under surfaces of the huge masses of agitated vapour, as well as all terrestrial objects immediately around us, were glowing in the unnatural light of a faintly luminous and distinctly visible gaseous exhalation which hung about and enshrouded the mansion.

"You must not—you shall not behold this!" said I, shuddering, to Usher, as I led him, with a gentle violence, from the window to a seat. "These appearances, which bewilder you, are merely electrical phenomena not uncommon—or it may be that they have their ghastly origin in the rank miasma of the tarn. Let us close this casement;—the air is chilling and dangerous to your frame. Here is one of your favourite romances. I will read, and you shall listen;—and so we will pass away this terrible night together."

The antique volume which I had taken up was the *Mad Trist* [13] of Sir Launcelot Canning; but I had called it a favourite of Usher's more in sad jest than in earnest; for, in truth, there is little in its uncouth and unimaginative prolixity which could have had interest for the lofty and spiritual ideality of my friend. It was, however, the only book immediately at hand; and I indulged a vague hope that the excitement which now agitated the hypochondriac, might find relief (for the history of mental disorder is full of similar anomalies) even in the extremeness of the folly which I should read. Could I have judged, indeed, by the wild overstrained air of vivacity with which he hearkened, or apparently hearkened, to the words of the tale, I might well have congratulated myself upon the success of my design.

I had arrived at that well-known portion of the story where Ethelred, the hero of the Trist, having sought in vain for peaceable admission into the dwelling of the hermit, proceeds to make good an entrance by force. Here, it will be remembered, the words of the narrative run thus:

12. **certain . . . sounds:** These sounds correspond to the "slight sounds" and "unusual motions" which trouble Rowena in the first stages of her illness.

13. ***Mad Trist:*** The book has not been found and is surely of Poe's invention.

"And Ethelred, who was by nature of a doughty heart, and who was now mighty withal, on account of the powerfulness of the wine which he had drunken, waited no longer to hold parley with the hermit, who, in sooth, was of an obstinate and maliceful turn, but, feeling the rain upon his shoulders, and fearing the rising of the tempest, uplifted his mace outright, and, with blows, made quickly room in the plankings of the door for his gauntleted hand; and now pulling therewith sturdily, he so cracked, and ripped, and tore all asunder, that the noise of the dry and hollow-sounding wood alarumed and reverberated throughout the forest."

At the termination of this sentence I started and; for a moment, paused; for it appeared to me (although I at once concluded that my excited fancy had deceived me)—it appeared to me that, from some very remote portion of the mansion, there came, indistinctly, to my ears, what might have been, in its exact similarity of character, the echo (but a stifled and dull one certainly) of the very cracking and ripping sound which Sir Launcelot had so particularly described. It was, beyond doubt, the coincidence alone which had arrested my attention; for, amid the rattling of the sashes of the casements, and the ordinary commingled noises of the still increasing storm, the sound, in itself, had nothing, surely, which should have interested or disturbed me. I continued the story:

"But the good champion Ethelred, now entering within the door, was sore enraged and amazed to perceive no signal of the maliceful hermit; but, in the stead thereof, a dragon of a scaly and prodigious demeanour, and of a fiery tongue, which sate in guard before a palace of gold, with a floor of silver; and upon the wall there hung a shield of shining brass with this legend enwritten—

> Who entereth herein, a conqueror hath bin;
> Who slayeth the dragon, the shield he shall win.

And Ethelred uplifted his mace, and struck upon the head of the dragon, which fell before him, and gave up his pesty breath, with a shriek so horrid and harsh, and withal so piercing, that Ethelred had fain to close his ears with his hands against the dreadful noise of it, the like whereof was never before heard."

Here again I paused abruptly, and now with a feeling of wild amazement—for there could be no doubt whatever that, in this instance, I did actually hear (although from what direction it proceeded I found it impossible to say) a low and apparently distant, but harsh, protracted, and most unusual screaming or grating sound—the exact counterpart of what my fancy had already conjured up for the dragon's unnatural shriek as described by the romancer.

Oppressed, as I certainly was, upon the occurrence of this second and most extraordinary coincidence, by a thousand conflicting sensations, in which wonder and extreme terror were predominant, I still retained sufficient presence of mind to avoid exciting, by any observation, the sensitive nervousness of my companion. I was by no means certain that he had noticed the sounds in question; although, assuredly, a strange alteration had, during the last few minutes, taken place in his demeanour. From a position fronting my own, he had gradually brought round his chair, so as to sit with his face to the door of the chamber; and thus I could but partially perceive his features, although I saw that his lips trembled as if he were murmuring inaudibly. His head had dropped upon his breast—yet I knew that he was not asleep, from the wide and rigid opening of the eye as I caught a glance of it in profile. The motion of his body, too, was at variance with this idea—for he rocked from side to side with a gentle yet constant and uniform sway. Having rapidly taken notice of all this, I resumed the narrative of Sir Launcelot, which thus proceeded:

"And now, the champion, having escaped from the terrible fury of the dragon, bethinking himself of the brazen shield, and of the breaking up of the enchantment which was upon it, removed the carcass from out of the way before him, and approached valorously over the silver pavement of the castle to where the shield was upon the wall; which in sooth tarried not for his full coming, but fell down at his feet upon the silver floor, with a mighty great and terrible ringing sound."

No sooner had these syllables passed my lips, than—as if a shield of brass had indeed, at the moment, fallen heavily upon a floor of silver—I became aware of a distinct, hollow, metallic, and clangorous, yet apparently muffled, reverberation. Completely unnerved, I leaped to my feet; but the measured rocking movement of Usher was undisturbed. I rushed to the chair in which he sat. His eyes were bent fixedly before him, and throughout his whole countenance there reigned a stony rigidity. But, as I placed my hand upon his shoulder, there came a strong shudder over his whole person; a sickly smile quivered about his lips; and I saw that he spoke in a low, hurried, and gibbering murmur, as if unconscious of my presence. Bending closely over him, I at length drank in the hideous import of his words.

"Not hear it?—yes, I hear it, and *have* heard it. Long—long—long—many minutes, many hours, many days, have I heard it—yet I dared not—oh, pity me, miserable wretch that I am!—I dared not —I *dared* not speak! *We have put her living in the tomb!* Said I not that my senses were acute? I *now* tell you that I heard her first feeble movements in the hollow coffiin. I heard them—many, many days ago—yet I dared not—I *dared not speak!* And now—to-night—Ethelred—ha! ha!—the breaking of the hermit's door, and the death-cry of the dragon, and the clangour of the shield!—say, rather, the rending of her coffin, and the grating of the iron hinges of her prison, and her struggles within the coppered archway of the vault! Oh whither shall I fly? [14] Will she not be here anon? Is she not hurrying to upbraid me for my haste? Have I not heard her footstep on the stair? Do I not distinguish that heavy and horrible beating of her heart? MADMAN!"—here he sprang furiously to his feet, and shrieked out his syllables, as if in the effort he were giving up his soul—"MADMAN! I TELL YOU THAT SHE NOW STANDS WITHOUT THE DOOR!"

As if in the superhuman energy of his utterance there had been found the potency of a spell, the huge antique panels to which the speaker pointed threw slowly back, upon the instant, their ponderous and ebony jaws.[15] It was the work of the rushing gust—but then without those doors there DID stand the lofty and enshrouded figure of the lady Madeline of Usher. There was blood upon her white robes, and the evidence of some bitter struggle upon every portion of her emaciated frame. For a moment she remained trembling and reeling to and fro upon the threshold, then, with a low moaning cry, fell heavily inward upon the person of her brother, and in her violent and now final death-agonies, bore him to the floor a corpse, and a victim to the terrors he had anticipated.

From that chamber, and from that mansion, I fled aghast. The storm was still abroad in all its wrath as I found myself crossing the old causeway. Suddenly there shot along the path a wild light, and I turned to see whence a gleam so unusual could have issued; for the vast house and its shadows were alone behind me. The radiance was that of the full, setting, and blood-red moon, which now shone vividly through that once barely discernible fissure, of which I have before spoken as extending from the roof of the building, in a zigzag direction, to the base. While I gazed, this fissure rapidly widened—there came a fierce breath of the whirlwind —the entire orb of the satellite burst at once upon my sight—my brain reeled as I saw the mighty walls rushing asunder—there was a long tumultuous shouting sound like the voice of a thousand waters [16]—and the deep and dank tarn at my feet closed sullenly and silently over the fragments of the "HOUSE OF USHER."

14. Oh . . . fly?: "Whither shall I go from thy spirit? Or whither shall I flee from thy presence?" (Ps. 139:7). **15. the huge . . . jaws:** This echoes "The Sleeper," ll. 50–51: "Some vault that oft hath flung its black/And wingèd panels fluttering back."

WILLIAM WILSON

◊

THIS story was first published in *Burton's Gentleman's Magazine* for October, 1839. It represents Poe's most open use of the theme of the "double," and describes the conflict, within a single personality, of soul, or conscience, and worldly passion. The name "William Wilson" suggests *will* and *wilfulness,* and the rival "wills" of Wilson and his double are frequently mentioned in the narrative.

◊

What say of it? what say [of] CONSCIENCE grim,
That spectre in my path?

CHAMBERLAYNE'S *"Pharronida"* [1]

LET ME call myself, for the present, William Wilson. The fair page now lying before me need not be sullied with my real appellation. This has been already too much an object for the scorn—for the horror—for the detestation of my race. To the uttermost regions of the globe have not the indignant winds bruited its unparalleled infamy? Oh, outcast of all outcasts most abandoned! —to the earth art thou not for ever dead? to its honors, to its flowers, to its golden aspirations?—and a cloud, dense, dismal, and limitless, does it not hang eternally between thy hopes and heaven?

I would not, if I could, here or to-day, embody a record of my later years of unspeakable misery, and unpardonable crime. This epoch—these later years—took unto themselves a sudden elevation in turpitude, whose origin alone it is my present pur-

16. the voice . . . waters: This alludes to the "voice from heaven, as the voice of many waters" (Rev. 14), which precedes the fall of Babylon. Poe's myths of the cosmos and of the human soul have the same pattern, the former being an analogical extension of the latter: both cosmos and soul proceed from unity to diversity and then, through purification, back to the original unity. By comparing the fall of the Usher mansion to the symbolic fall of Babylon, Poe is indicating the destined role of the poetic soul in the purification of Earth. WILLIAM WILSON. **1. *Pharronida:*** The epigraph, ascribed to William Chamberlayne's heroic poem of 1659, has not been found there.

pose to assign. Men usually grow base by degrees. From me, in an instant, all virtue dropped bodily as a mantle. From comparatively trivial wickedness I passed, with the stride of a giant, into more than the enormities of an Elah-Gabalus.[2] What chance—what one event brought this evil thing to pass, bear with me while I relate. Death approaches; and the shadow which foreruns him has thrown a softening influence over my spirit. I long, in passing through the dim valley, for the sympathy—I had nearly said for the pity—of my fellow men. I would fain have them believe that I have been, in some measure, the slave of circumstances beyond human control.[3] I would wish them to seek out for me, in the details I am about to give, some little oasis of *fatality* amid a wilderness of error. I would have them allow—what they cannot refrain from allowing—that, although temptation may have erewhile existed as great, man was never *thus*, at least, tempted before—certainly, never *thus* fell. And is it therefore that he has never thus suffered? Have I not indeed been living in a dream? And am I not now dying a victim to the horror and the mystery of the wildest of all sublunary visions?

I am the descendant of a race whose imaginative and easily excitable temperament has at all times rendered them remarkable; and, in my earliest infancy, I gave evidence of having fully inherited the family character. As I advanced in years it was more strongly developed; becoming, for many reasons, a cause of serious disquietude to my friends, and of positive injury to myself. I grew self-willed, addicted to the wildest caprices, and a prey to the most ungovernable passions. Weak-minded, and beset with constitutional infirmities akin to my own, my parents could do but little to check the evil propensities which distinguished me. Some feeble and ill-directed efforts resulted in complete failure on their part, and, of course, in total triumph on mine. Thenceforward my voice was a household law; and at an age when few children have abandoned their leading-strings, I was left to the guidance of my own will, and became, in all but name, the master of my own actions.

My earliest recollections of a school-life,[4] are connected with a large, rambling, Elizabethan house, in a misty-looking village of England, where were a vast number of gigantic and gnarled trees, and where all the houses were excessively ancient. In truth, it was a dream-like and spirit-soothing place, that venerable old town. At this moment, in fancy, I feel the refreshing chilliness of its deeply-shadowed avenues, inhale the fragrance of its thousand shrubberies, and thrill anew with undefinable delight, at the deep hollow note of the church-bell, breaking, each hour, with sullen and sudden roar, upon the stillness of the dusky atmosphere in which the fretted Gothic steeple lay imbedded and asleep.

It gives me, perhaps, as much of pleasure as I can now in any manner experience, to dwell upon minute recollections of the school and its concerns. Steeped in misery as I am—misery, alas! only too real—I shall be pardoned for seeking relief, however slight and temporary, in the weakness of a few rambling details. These, moreover, utterly trivial, and even ridiculous in themselves, assume, to my fancy, adventitious importance, as connected with a period and a locality when and where I recognize the first ambiguous monitions of the destiny which afterward so fully overshadowed me. Let me then remember.

The house, I have said, was old and irregular. The grounds were extensive, and a high and solid brick wall, topped with a bed of mortar and broken glass, encompassed the whole. This prison-like rampart formed the limit of our domain; beyond it we saw but thrice a week—once every Saturday afternoon, when, attended by two ushers, we were permitted to take brief walks in a body through some of the neighbouring fields—and twice during Sunday, when we were paraded in the same formal manner to the morning and evening service in the one church of the village. Of this church the principal of our school was pastor. With how deep a spirit of wonder and perplexity was I wont to regard him from our remote pew in the gallery, as, with step solemn and slow, he ascended the pulpit! This reverend man, with countenance so demurely benign, with robes so glossy and so clerically flowing, with wig so minutely powdered, so rigid and so vast,—could this be he who, of late, with sour visage, and in snuffy habiliments, administered, ferule in hand, the Draconian Laws of the academy? Oh, gigantic paradox, too utterly monstrous for solution!

At an angle of the ponderous wall frowned a more ponderous gate. It was riveted and studded with iron bolts, and surmounted with jagged iron spikes. What impressions of deep awe did it inspire! It was never opened save for the three peri-

2. **Elah-Gabalus:** Elagabalus, or Heliogabalus, was a profligate Roman emperor who reigned during 218–22 A.D. 3. **I . . . control:** Reviewing Mrs. L. Miles's *Phrenology* in 1836, Poe wrote: "We must not consider the possession of particular and instinctive propensities, as acquitting us of responsibility in the indulgence of culpable actions. On the contrary, it is the perversion of our faculties which causes the greatest misery we endure, and for which (having the free exercise of *reason*) we are accountable to God." 4. **school-life:** The following description is based upon Poe's recollections of the Manor House School in Stoke Newington, now a part of London.

odical egressions and ingressions already mentioned; then, in every creak of its mighty hinges, we found a plenitude of mystery—a world of matter for solemn remark, or for more solemn meditation.

The extensive enclosure was irregular in form, having many capacious recesses. Of these, three or four of the largest constituted the play-ground. It was level, and covered with fine hard gravel. I well remember it had no trees, nor benches, nor any thing similar within it. Of course it was in the rear of the house. In front lay a small parterre, planted with box and other shrubs, but through this sacred division we passed only upon rare occasions indeed—such as a first advent to school or final departure thence, or perhaps, when a parent or friend having called for us, we joyfully took our way home for the Christmas or Midsummer holidays.

But the house!—how quaint an old building was this!—to me how veritably a palace of enchantment! There was really no end to its windings—to its incomprehensible subdivisions. It was difficult, at any given time, to say with certainty upon which of its two stories one happened to be. From each room to every other there were sure to be found three or four steps either in ascent or descent. Then the lateral branches were innumerable—inconceivable—and so returning in upon themselves, that our most exact ideas in regard to the whole mansion were not very far different from those with which we pondered upon infinity. During the five years of my residence here, I was never able to ascertain with precision, in what remote locality lay the little sleeping apartment assigned to myself and some eighteen or twenty other scholars.

The school-room was the largest in the house—I could not help thinking, in the world. It was very long, narrow, and dismally low, with pointed Gothic windows and a ceiling of oak. In a remote and terror-inspiring angle was a square enclosure of eight or ten feet, comprising the *sanctum,* "during hours," of our principal, the Reverend Dr. Bransby.[5] It was a solid structure, with massy door, sooner than open which in the absence of the "Dominie," we would all have willingly perished by the *peine forte et dure.*[6] In other angles were two other similar boxes, far less reverenced, indeed, but still greatly matters of awe. One of these was the pulpit of the "classical" usher, one of the "English and mathematical." Interspersed about the room, crossing and recrossing in endless irregularity, were innumerable benches and desks, black, ancient, and time-worn, piled desperately with much-bethumbed books, and so beseamed with initial letters, names at full length, grotesque figures, and other multiplied efforts of the knife, as to have entirely lost what little of original form might have been their portion in days long departed. A huge bucket with water stood at one extremity of the room, and a clock of stupendous dimensions at the other.

Encompassed by the massy walls of this venerable academy, I passed, yet not in tedium or disgust, the years of the third lustrum of my life. The teeming brain of childhood requires no external world of incident to occupy or amuse it; and the apparently dismal monotony of a school was replete with more intense excitement than my riper youth has derived from luxury, or my full manhood from crime. Yet I must believe that my first mental development had in it much of the uncommon—even much of the *outré.* Upon mankind at large the events of very early existence rarely leave in mature age any definite impression. All is gray shadow—a weak and irregular remembrance—an indistinct regathering of feeble pleasures and phantasmagoric pains. With me this is not so. In childhood I must have felt with the energy of a man what I now find stamped upon memory in lines as vivid, as deep, and as durable as the *exergues* of the Carthaginian medals.

Yet in fact—in the fact of the world's view—how little was there to remember! The morning's awakening, the nightly summons to bed; the connings, the recitations; the periodical half-holidays, and perambulations; the play-ground, with its broils, its pastimes, its intrigues;—these, by a mental sorcery long forgotten, were made to involve a wilderness of sensation, a world of rich incident, an universe of varied emotion, of excitement the most passionate and spirit-stirring. *"Oh, le bon temps, que ce siècle de fer!"* [7]

In truth, the ardor, the enthusiasm, and the imperiousness of my disposition, soon rendered me a marked character among my schoolmates, and by slow, but natural gradations, gave me an ascendancy over all not greatly older than myself;—over all with a single exception. This exception was found in the person of a scholar, who, although no relation, bore the same Christian and surname as myself;—a circumstance, in fact, little remarkable; for, notwithstanding a noble descent, mine was one of those everyday appellations which seem, by prescriptive right, to have been, time out of mind, the

5. **Bransby:** the actual name of Poe's principal at the Manor House School. 6. ***peine . . . dure:*** a punishment in which the victim was pressed to death.

7. ***"Oh . . . fer!":*** The quotation, from Voltaire's "Le Mondain," might be rendered, "Oh, what a good time it is, this iron age!" The iron age, according to the Greek and Roman poets, succeeded those of gold, silver, and bronze, and brought in wickedness and war.

common property of the mob. In this narrative I have therefore designated myself as William Wilson,—a fictitious title not very dissimilar to the real. My namesake alone, of those who in school phraseology constituted "our set," presumed to compete with me in the studies of the class—in the sports and broils of the play-ground—to refuse implicit belief in my assertions, and submission to my will—indeed, to interfere with my arbitrary dictation in any respect whatsoever. If there is on earth a supreme and unqualified despotism, it is the despotism of a mastermind in boyhood over the less energetic spirits of its companions.

Wilson's rebellion was to me a source of the greatest embarrassment;—the more so as, in spite of the bravado with which in public I made a point of treating him and his pretensions, I secretly felt that I feared him, and could not help thinking the equality which he maintained so easily with myself, a proof of his true superiority; since not to be overcome, cost me a perpetual struggle. Yet this superiority—even this equality—was in truth acknowledged by no one but myself; our associates, by some unaccountable blindness, seemed not even to suspect it. Indeed, his competition, his resistance, and especially his impertinent and dogged interference with my purposes, were not more pointed than private. He appeared to be destitute alike of the ambition which urged, and of the passionate energy of the mind which enabled me to excel. In his rivalry he might have been supposed actuated solely by a whimsical desire to thwart, astonish, or mortify myself; although there were times when I could not help observing, with a feeling made up of wonder, abasement, and pique, that he mingled with his injuries, his insults, or his contradictions, a certain most inappropriate, and assuredly most unwelcome affectionateness of manner.[8] I could only conceive this singular behavior to arise from a consummate self-conceit assuming the vulgar airs of patronage and protection.

Perhaps it was this latter trait in Wilson's conduct, conjoined with our identity of name, and the mere accident of our having entered the school upon the same day, which set afloat the notion that we were brothers, among the senior classes in the academy.[9] These do not usually inquire with much strictness into the affairs of their juniors. I have before said, or should have said, that Wilson was not, in a most remote degree, connected with my family. But assuredly if we *had* been brothers we must have been twins; for, after leaving Dr. Bransby's, I casually learned that my namesake was born on the nineteenth of January, 1813[10]—and this is a somewhat remarkable coincidence; for the day is precisely that of my own nativity.

It may seem strange that in spite of the continual anxiety occasioned me by the rivalry of Wilson, and his intolerable spirit of contradiction, I could not bring myself to hate him altogether. We had, to be sure, nearly every day a quarrel in which, yielding me publicly the palm of victory, he, in some manner, contrived to make me feel that it was he who had deserved it; yet a sense of pride on my part, and a veritable dignity on his own, kept us always upon what are called "speaking terms," while there were many points of strong congeniality in our tempers, operating to awake in me a sentiment which our position alone, perhaps, prevented from ripening into friendship. It is difficult, indeed, to define, or even to describe, my real feelings toward him. They formed a motley and heterogeneous admixture;—some petulant animosity, which was not yet hatred, some esteem, more respect, much fear, with a world of uneasy curiosity. To the moralist it will be unnecessary to say, in addition, that Wilson and myself were the most inseparable of companions.

It was no doubt the anomalous state of affairs existing between us, which turned all my attacks upon him, (and there were many, either open or covert) into the channel of banter or practical joke (giving pain while assuming the aspect of mere fun) rather than into a more serious and determined hostility. But my endeavours on this head were by no means uniformly successful, even when my plans were the most wittily concocted; for my namesake had much about him, in character, of that unassuming and quiet austerity which, while enjoying the poignancy of its own jokes, has no heel of Achilles in itself, and absolutely refuses to be laughed at. I could find, indeed, but one vulnerable point, and that, lying in a personal peculiarity, arising, perhaps, from constitutional disease, would have been spared by any antagonist less at his wit's end than myself;—my rival had a weakness in the faucial or guttural organs, which precluded him from raising his voice at any time *above a very low whisper*.[11] Of this defect I did not fail to take what poor advantage lay in my power.

8. In . . . manner: Wilson's namesake has the same paradoxical mixture of benevolence and repressiveness which earlier characterized the principal. **9. Perhaps . . . academy:** Brothers have been known to bear identical names; however, as P. F. Quinn observes, "identity of name" would argue *against* the notion that the two Wilsons are brothers. This faulty logic casts doubt on the narrator's claim that his double was known to others.

10. Poe's birthday was January 19, 1809. In different printings of the story, the year appeared as 1809, 1811, and 1813. **11. I . . . *whisper*:** Poe is alluding to the "still small voice" of I Kings 19:12. The expression has come to be a synonym of "conscience."

Wilson's retaliations in kind were many; and there was one form of his practical wit that disturbed me beyond measure. How his sagacity first discovered at all that so petty a thing would vex me, is a question I never could solve; but having discovered, he habitually practised the annoyance. I had always felt aversion to my uncourtly patronymic, and its very common, if not plebeian prænomen. The words were venom in my ears; and when, upon the day of my arrival, a second William Wilson came also to the academy, I felt angry with him for bearing the name, and doubly disgusted with the name because a stranger bore it, who would be the cause of its twofold repetition, who would be constantly in my presence, and whose concerns, in the ordinary routine of the school business, must inevitably, on account of the detestable coincidence, be often confounded with my own.

The feeling of vexation thus engendered grew stronger with every circumstance tending to show resemblance, moral or physical, between my rival and myself. I had not then discovered the remarkable fact that we were of the same age; but I saw that we were of the same height, and I perceived that we were even singularly alike in general contour of person and outline of feature. I was galled, too, by the rumor touching a relationship, which had grown current in the upper forms. In a word, nothing could more seriously disturb me, (although I scrupulously concealed such disturbance,) than any allusions to a similarity of mind, person, or condition existing between us. But, in truth, I had no reason to believe that (with the exception of the matter of relationship, and in the case of Wilson himself) this similarity had ever been made a subject of comment, or even observed at all by our schoolfellows. That *he* observed it in all its bearings, and as fixedly as I, was apparent; but that he could discover in such circumstances so fruitful a field of annoyance, can only be attributed, as I said before, to his more than ordinary penetration.

His cue, which was to perfect an imitation of myself, lay both in words and in actions; and most admirably did he play his part. My dress it was an easy matter to copy; my gait and general manner were, without difficulty, appropriated; in spite of his constitutional defect, even my voice did not escape him. My louder tones were, of course, unattempted, but then the key, it was identical; *and his singular whisper, it grew the very echo of my own.*[12]

12. Both Roderick Usher and C. Auguste Dupin are double-voiced, the higher voice being spiritual and the lower, physical.

How greatly this most exquisite portraiture harassed me, (for it could not justly be termed a caricature,) I will not now venture to describe. I had but one consolation—in the fact that the imitation, apparently, was noticed by myself alone, and that I had to endure only the knowing and strangely sarcastic smiles of my namesake himself. Satisfied with having produced in my bosom the intended effect, he seemed to chuckle in secret over the sting he had inflicted, and was characteristically disregardful of the public applause which the success of his witty endeavours might have so easily elicited. That the school, indeed, did not feel his design, perceive its accomplishment, and participate in his sneer, was, for many anxious months, a riddle I could not resolve. Perhaps the *gradation* of his copy rendered it not so readily perceptible; or, more possibly, I owed my security to the masterly air of the copyist, who, disdaining the letter, (which in a painting is all the obtuse can see,) gave but the full spirit of his original for my individual contemplation and chagrin.

I have already more than once spoken of the disgusting air of patronage which he assumed toward me, and of his frequent officious interference with my will. This interference often took the ungracious character of advice; advice not openly given, but hinted or insinuated. I received it with a repugnance which gained strength as I grew in years. Yet, at this distant day, let me do him the simple justice to acknowledge that I can recall no occasion when the suggestions of my rival were on the side of those errors or follies so usual to his immature age and seeming inexperience; that his moral sense, at least, if not his general talents and worldly wisdom, was far keener than my own; and that I might, to-day, have been a better and thus a happier man, had I less frequently rejected the counsels embodied in those meaning whispers which I then but too cordially hated and too bitterly despised.

As it was, I at length grew restive in the extreme under his distasteful supervision, and daily resented more and more openly what I considered his intolerable arrogance. I have said that, in the first years of our connection as schoolmates, my feelings in regard to him might have been easily ripened into friendship: but, in the latter months of my residence at the academy, although the intrusion of his ordinary manner had, beyond doubt, in some measure, abated, my sentiments, in nearly similar proportion, partook very much of positive hatred. Upon one occasion he saw this, I think, and afterward avoided, or made a show of avoiding me.

It was about the same period, if I remember

aright, that, in an altercation of violence with him, in which he was more than usually thrown off his guard, and spoke and acted with an openness of demeanor rather foreign to his nature, I discovered, or fancied I discovered, in his accent, in his air, and general appearance, a something which first startled, and then deeply interested me, by bringing to mind dim visions of my earliest infancy—wild, confused and thronging memories of a time when memory herself was yet unborn. I cannot better describe the sensation which oppressed me than by saying that I could with difficulty shake off the belief of my having been acquainted with the being who stood before me, at some epoch very long ago—some point of the past even infinitely remote.[13] The delusion, however, faded rapidly as it came; and I mention it at all but to define the day of the last conversation I there held with my singular namesake.

The huge old house, with its countless subdivisions, had several large chambers communicating with each other, where slept the greater number of the students. There were, however, (as must necessarily happen in a building so awkwardly planned,) many little nooks or recesses, the odds and ends of the structure; and these the economic ingenuity of Dr. Bransby had also fitted up as dormitories; although, being the merest closets, they were capable of accommodating but a single individual. One of these small apartments was occupied by Wilson.

One night, about the close of my fifth year at the school, and immediately after the altercation just mentioned, finding every one wrapped in sleep, I arose from bed, and, lamp in hand, stole through a wilderness of narrow passages, from my own bedroom to that of my rival. I had long been plotting one of those ill-natured pieces of practical wit at his expense in which I had hitherto been so uniformly unsuccessful. It was my intention, now, to put my scheme in operation, and I resolved to make him feel the whole extent of the malice with which I was imbued. Having reached his closet, I noiselessly entered, leaving the lamp, with a shade over it, on the outside. I advanced a step and listened to the sound of his tranquil breathing. Assured of his being asleep, I returned, took the light, and with it again approached the bed. Close curtains were around it, which, in the prosecution of my plan, I slowly and quietly withdrew, when the bright rays fell vividly upon the sleeper, and my eyes, at the same moment, upon his countenance. I looked;—and a numbness, an iciness of feeling instantly pervaded my frame. My breast heaved, my knees tottered, my whole spirit became possessed with an objectless yet intolerable horror. Gasping for breath, I lowered the lamp in still nearer proximity to the face. Were these—*these* the lineaments of William Wilson? I saw, indeed, that they were his, but I shook as if with a fit of the ague in fancying they were not. What *was* there about them to confound me in this manner? I gazed;—while my brain reeled with a multitude of incoherent thoughts. Not thus he appeared—assuredly not *thus*—in the vivacity of his waking hours. The same name! the same contour of person! the same day of arrival at the academy! And then his dogged and meaningless imitation of my gait, my voice, my habits, and my manner! Was it, in truth, within the bounds of human possibility, that *what I now saw* was the result, merely, of the habitual practice of this sarcastic imitation? Awe-stricken, and with a creeping shudder, I extinguished the lamp, passed silently from the chamber, and left, at once, the halls of that old academy, never to enter them again.

After a lapse of some months, spent at home in mere idleness, I found myself a student at Eton. The brief interval had been sufficient to enfeeble my remembrance of the events at Dr. Bransby's, or at least to effect a material change in the nature of the feelings with which I remembered them. The truth—the tragedy—of the drama was no more. I could now find room to doubt the evidence of my senses; and seldom called up the subject at all but with wonder at the extent of human credulity, and a smile at the vivid force of the imagination which I hereditarily possessed. Neither was this species of skepticism likely to be diminished by the character of the life I led at Eton. The vortex of thoughtless folly into which I there so immediately and so recklessly plunged, washed away all but the froth of my past hours, engulfed at once every solid or serious impression, and left to memory only the veriest levities of a former existence.

I do not wish, however, to trace the course of my miserable profligacy here—a profligacy which set at defiance the laws, while it eluded the vigilance of the institution. Three years of folly, passed without profit, had but given me rooted habits of vice, and added, in a somewhat unusual degree, to my bodily stature, when, after a week of soulless dissipation, I invited a small party of the most dissolute students to a secret carousal in my chambers. We met at a late hour of the night; for our debaucheries were to be faithfully protracted until morning. The wine flowed freely, and there were not wanting other and perhaps more

13. **It . . . remote:** In infancy, and perhaps in a prior existence, Wilson's soul was undivided; the passions were either unawakened or under spiritual control, and conscience was not distinguishable from the aesthetic sense.

dangerous seductions; so that the grey dawn had already faintly appeared in the east while our delirious extravagance was at its height. Madly flushed with cards and intoxication, I was in the act of insisting upon a toast of more than wonted profanity, when my attention was suddenly diverted by the violent, although partial, unclosing of the door of the apartment, and by the eager voice of a servant from without. He said that some person, apparently in great haste, demanded to speak with me in the hall.

Wildly excited with wine, the unexpected interruption rather delighted than surprised me. I staggered forward at once, and a few steps brought me to the vestibule of the building. In this low and small room there hung no lamp; and now no light at all was admitted, save that of the exceedingly feeble dawn which made its way through the semi-circular window. As I put my foot over the threshold, I became aware of the figure of a youth about my own height, and habited in a white kerseymere morning frock, cut in the novel fashion of the one I myself wore at the moment. This the faint light enabled me to perceive; but the features of his face I could not distinguish. Upon my entering he strode hurriedly up to me, and, seizing me by the arm with a gesture of petulant impatience, whispered the words "William Wilson!" in my ear.

I grew perfectly sober in an instant.

There was that in the manner of the stranger, and in the tremulous shake of his uplifted finger,[14] as he held it between my eyes and the light, which filled me with unqualified amazement; but it was not this which had so violently moved me. It was the pregnancy of solemn admonition in the singular, low, hissing utterance; and, above all, it was the character, the tone, *the key,* of those few, simple, and familiar, yet *whispered* syllables, which came with a thousand thronging memories of bygone days, and struck upon my soul with the shock of a galvanic battery. Ere I could recover the use of my senses he was gone.

Although this event failed not of a vivid effect upon my disordered imagination, yet was it evanescent as vivid. For some weeks, indeed, I busied myself in earnest enquiry, or was wrapped in a cloud of morbid speculation. I did not pretend to disguise from my perception the identity of the singular individual who thus perseveringly interfered with my affairs, and harassed me with his insinuated counsel. But who and what was this Wilson?—and whence came he?—and what were his purposes? Upon neither of these points could I be satisfied; merely ascertaining, in regard to him, that a sudden accident in his family had caused his removal from Dr. Bransby's academy on the afternoon of the day in which I myself had eloped. But in a brief period I ceased to think upon the subject; my attention being all absorbed in a contemplated departure for Oxford. Thither I soon went, the uncalculating vanity of my parents furnishing me with an outfit and annual establishment, which would enable me to indulge at will in the luxury already so dear to my heart,—to vie in profuseness of expenditure with the haughtiest heirs of the wealthiest earldoms in Great Britain.

Excited by such appliances to vice, my constitutional temperament broke forth with redoubled ardor, and I spurned even the common restraints of decency in the mad infatuation of my revels. But it were absurd to pause in the detail of my extravagance. Let it suffice, that among spendthrifts I out-Heroded Herod, and that, giving name to a multitude of novel follies, I added no brief appendix to the long catalogue of vices then usual in the most dissolute university of Europe.

It could hardly be credited, however, that I had, even here, so utterly fallen from the gentlemanly estate, as to seek acquaintance with the vilest arts of the gambler by profession, and, having become an adept in his despicable science, to practice it habitually as a means of increasing my already enormous income at the expense of the weak-minded among my fellow-collegians. Such, nevertheless, was the fact. And the very enormity of this offence against all manly and honourable sentiment proved, beyond doubt, the main if not the sole reason of the impunity with which it was committed. Who, indeed, among my most abandoned associates, would not rather have disputed the clearest evidence of his senses, than have suspected of such courses, the gay, the frank, the generous William Wilson—the noblest and most liberal commoner at Oxford—him whose follies (said his parasites) were but the follies of youth and unbridled fancy—whose errors but inimitable whim—whose darkest vice but a careless and dashing extravagance?

I had been now two years successfully busied in this way, when there came to the university a young *parvenu* nobleman, Glendinning—rich, said report, as Herodes Atticus[15]—his riches, too, as easily acquired. I soon found him of weak intellect, and, of course, marked him as a fitting sub-

14. tremulous . . . finger: Compare the fingers of the spirit-crew of "Ms. Found in a Bottle," which the narrator perceives, against "the wild glare of the battle-lanterns." They are tremulous and translucent because spectral.

15. Herodes Atticus: Greek rhetorician of the second century A.D. A teacher of Marcus Aurelius, a consul, and a man of vast wealth.

ject for my skill. I frequently engaged him in play, and contrived, with the gambler's usual art, to let him win considerable sums, the more effectually to entangle him in my snares. At length, my schemes being ripe, I met him (with the full intention that this meeting should be final and decisive) at the chambers of a fellow-commoner, (Mr. Preston,) [16] equally intimate with both, but who, to do him justice, entertained not even a remote suspicion of my design. To give to this a better colouring, I had contrived to have assembled a party of some eight or ten, and was solicitously careful that the introduction of cards should appear accidental, and originate in the proposal of my contemplated dupe himself. To be brief upon a vile topic, none of the low finesse was omitted, so customary upon similar occasions, that it is a just matter for wonder how any are still found so besotted as to fall its victim.

We had protracted our sitting far into the night, and I had at length effected the manœuvre of getting Glendinning as my sole antagonist. The game, too, was my favourite *écarté*. The rest of the company, interested in the extent of our play, had abandoned their own cards, and were standing around us as spectators. The *parvenu,* who had been induced by my artifices in the early part of the evening, to drink deeply, now shuffled, dealt, or played, with a wild nervousness of manner for which his intoxication, I thought, might partially, but could not altogether account. In a very short period he had become my debtor to a large amount, when, having taken a long draught of port, he did precisely what I had been coolly anticipating—he proposed to double our already extravagant stakes. With a well-feigned show of reluctance, and not until after my repeated refusal had seduced him into some angry words which gave a color of *pique* to my compliance, did I finally comply. The result, of course, did but prove how entirely the prey was in my toils; in less than an hour he had quadrupled his debt. For some time his countenance had been losing the florid tinge lent it by the wine; but now, to my astonishment, I perceived that it had grown to a pallor truly fearful. I say, to my astonishment. Glendinning had been represented to my eager inquiries as immeasurably wealthy; and the sums which he had as yet lost, although in themselves vast, could not, I supposed, very seriously annoy, much less so violently affect him. That he was overcome by the wine just swallowed, was the idea which most readily presented itself; and, rather with a view to the preservation of my own character in the eyes of my associates, than from any less interested motive, I was about to insist, peremptorily, upon a discontinuance of the play, when some expressions at my elbow from among the company, and an ejaculation evincing utter despair on the part of Glendinning, gave me to understand that I had effected his total ruin under circumstances which, rendering him an object for the pity of all, should have protected him from the ill offices even of a fiend.

What now might have been my conduct it is difficult to say. The pitiable condition of my dupe had thrown an air of embarrassed gloom over all; and, for some moments, a profound silence was maintained, during which I could not help feeling my cheeks tingle with the many burning glances of scorn or reproach cast upon me by the less abandoned of the party. I will even own that an intolerable weight of anxiety was for a brief instant lifted from my bosom by the sudden and extraordinary interruption which ensued. The wide, heavy folding doors of the apartment were all at once thrown open, to their full extent, with a vigorous and rushing impetuosity that extinguished, as if by magic, every candle in the room. Their light, in dying, enabled us just to perceive that a stranger had entered, about my own height, and closely muffled in a cloak. The darkness, however, was not total; and we could only *feel* that he was standing in our midst. Before any one of us could recover from the extreme astonishment into which this rudeness had thrown all, we heard the voice of the intruder.

"Gentlemen," he said, in a low, distinct, and never-to-be-forgotten *whisper* which thrilled to the very marrow of my bones, "Gentlemen, I make no apology for this behaviour, because in thus behaving, I am fulfilling a duty. You are, beyond doubt, uninformed of the true character of the person who has to-night won at *écarté* a large sum of money from Lord Glendinning. I will therefore put you upon an expeditious and decisive plan of obtaining this very necessary information. Please to examine, at your leisure, the inner linings of the cuff of his left sleeve, and the several little packages which may be found in the somewhat capacious pockets of his embroidered morning wrapper."

While he spoke, so profound was the stillness that one might have heard a pin drop upon the floor. In ceasing, he departed at once, and as abruptly as he had entered. Can I—shall I describe my sensations?—must I say that I felt all the horrors of the damned? Most assuredly I had little time given for reflection. Many hands roughly seized me upon the spot, and lights were imme-

16. **Preston:** John Preston was a friend and fellow student of Poe's at the University of Virginia, where Poe lost large sums by gambling.

diately reprocured. A search ensued. In the lining of my sleeve were found all the court cards essential in *écarté,* and, in the pockets of my wrapper, a number of packs, fac-similes of those used at our sittings, with the single exception that mine were of the species called, technically, *arrondées;* the honors being slightly convex at the ends, the lower cards slightly convex at the sides. In this disposition, the dupe who cuts, as customary, at the length of the pack, will invariably find that he cuts his antagonist an honor; while the gambler, cutting at the breadth, will, as certainly, cut nothing for his victim which may count in the records of the game.

Any burst of indignation upon this discovery would have affected me less than the silent contempt, or the sarcastic composure, with which it was received.

"Mr. Wilson," said our host, stooping to remove from beneath his feet an exceedingly luxurious cloak of rare furs, "Mr. Wilson, this is your property." (The weather was cold; and, upon quitting my own room, I had thrown a cloak over my dressing wrapper, putting it off upon reaching the scene of play.) "I presume it is supererogatory to seek here (eyeing the folds of the garment with a bitter smile) for any farther evidence of your skill. Indeed, we have had enough. You will see the necessity, I hope, of quitting Oxford—at all events, of quitting instantly my chambers."

Abased, humbled to the dust as I then was, it is probable that I should have resented this galling language by immediate personal violence, had not my whole attention been at the moment arrested by a fact of the most startling character. The cloak which I had worn was of a rare description of fur; how rare, how extravagantly costly, I shall not venture to say. Its fashion, too, was of my own fantastic invention; for I was fastidious to an absurd degree of coxcombry, in matters of this frivolous nature. When, therefore, Mr. Preston reached me that which he had picked up upon the floor, and near the folding doors of the apartment, it was with an astonishment nearly bordering upon terror, that I perceived my own already hanging on my arm, (where I had no doubt unwittingly placed it,) and that the one presented me was but its exact counterpart in every, in even the minutest possible particular. The singular being who had so disastrously exposed me, had been muffled, I remembered, in a cloak; and none had been worn at all by any of the members of our party with the exception of myself. Retaining some presence of mind, I took the one offered me by Preston; placed it, unnoticed, over my own; left the apartment with a resolute scowl of defiance; and, next morning ere dawn of day, commenced a hurried journey from Oxford to the continent, in a perfect agony of horror and of shame.

I fled in vain. My evil destiny pursued me as if in exultation, and proved, indeed, that the exercise of its mysterious dominion had as yet only begun. Scarcely had I set foot in Paris, ere I had fresh evidence of the detestable interest taken by this Wilson in my concerns. Years flew, while I experienced no relief. Villain!—at Rome, with how untimely, yet with how spectral an officiousness, stepped he in between me and my ambition! at Vienna, too—at Berlin—and at Moscow! Where, in truth, had I *not* bitter cause to curse him within my heart? From his inscrutable tyranny did I at length flee, panic-stricken, as from a pestilence; and to the very ends of the earth [17] *I fled in vain.*

And again, and again, in secret communion with my own spirit, would I demand the questions "Who is he?—whence came he?—and what are his objects?" But no answer was there found. And then I scrutinized, with a minute scrutiny, the forms, and the methods, and the leading traits of his impertinent supervision. But even here there was very little upon which to base a conjecture. It was noticeable, indeed, that, in no one of the multiplied instances in which he had of late crossed my path, had he so crossed it except to frustrate those schemes, or to disturb those actions, which, if fully carried out, might have resulted in bitter mischief. Poor justification this, in truth, for an authority so imperiously assumed! Poor indemnity for natural rights of self-agency so pertinaciously, so insultingly denied!

I had also been forced to notice that my tormentor, for a very long period of time, (while scrupulously and with miraculous dexterity maintaining his whim of an identity of apparel with myself,) had so contrived it, in the execution of his varied interference with my will, that I saw not, at any moment, the features of his face. Be Wilson what he might, *this,* at least, was but the veriest of affectation, or of folly. Could he, for an instant, have supposed that, in my admonisher at Eton—in the destroyer of my honor at Oxford,—in him who thwarted my ambition at Rome, my revenge at Paris, my passionate love at Naples, or what he falsely termed my avarice in Egypt,—that in this, my arch-enemy and evil genius, I could fail to recognize the William Wilson of my schoolboy days,—the namesake, the companion, the rival,—the

17. **ends of the earth:** echoes many Biblical passages concerning the omnipotence and omnipresence of God. These qualities are later attributed to Wilson's double, who as "conscience" is God's agent.

hated and dreaded rival at Dr. Bransby's? Impossible!—But let me hasten to the last eventful scene of the drama.

Thus far I had succumbed supinely to this imperious domination. The sentiment of deep awe with which I habitually regarded the elevated character, the majestic wisdom, the apparent omnipresence and omnipotence of Wilson, added to a feeling of even terror, with which certain other traits in his nature and assumptions inspired me, had operated, hitherto, to impress me with an idea of my own utter weakness and helplessness, and to suggest an implicit, although bitterly reluctant submission to his arbitrary will. But, of late days, I had given myself up entirely to wine; and its maddening influence upon my hereditary temper rendered me more and more impatient of control. I began to murmur,—to hesitate,—to resist. And was it only fancy which induced me to believe that, with the increase of my own firmness, that of my tormentor underwent a proportional diminution? Be this as it may, I now began to feel the inspiration of a burning hope, and at length nurtured in my secret thoughts a stern and desperate resolution that I would submit no longer to be enslaved.

It was at Rome, during the Carnival of 18—, that I attended a masquerade in the palazzo of the Neapolitan Duke Di Broglio. I had indulged more freely than usual in the excesses of the wine-table; and now the suffocating atmosphere of the crowded rooms irritated me beyond endurance. The difficulty, too, of forcing my way through the mazes of the company contributed not a little to the ruffling of my temper; for I was anxiously seeking (let me not say with what unworthy motive) the young, the gay, the beautiful wife of the aged and doting Di Broglio.[18] With a too unscrupulous confidence she had previously communicated to me the secret of the costume in which she would be habited and now, having caught a glimpse of her person, I was hurrying to make my way into her presence.—At this moment I felt a light hand placed upon my shoulder, and that ever-remembered, low, damnable *whisper* within my ear.

In an absolute frenzy of wrath, I turned at once upon him who had thus interrupted me, and seized him violently by the collar. He was attired, as I had expected, in a costume altogether similar to my own; wearing a Spanish cloak of blue velvet, begirt about the waist with a crimson belt sustaining a rapier. A mask of black silk entirely covered his face.

"Scoundrel!" I said, in a voice husky with rage, while every syllable I uttered seemed as new fuel to my fury, "scoundrel! impostor! accursed villain! you shall not—you *shall not* dog me unto death! Follow me, or I stab you where you stand!" —and I broke my way from the ballroom into a small antechamber adjoining, dragging him unresistingly with me as I went.

Upon entering, I thrust him furiously from me. He staggered against the wall, while I closed the door with an oath, and commanded him to draw. He hesitated but for an instant; then, with a slight sigh, drew in silence, and put himself upon his defence.

The contest was brief indeed. I was frantic with every species of wild excitement, and felt within my single arm the energy and power of a multitude. In a few seconds I forced him by sheer strength against the wainscotting, and thus, getting him at mercy, plunged my sword, with brute ferocity, repeatedly through and through his bosom.

At that instant some person tried the latch of the door. I hastened to prevent an intrusion, and then immediately returned to my dying antagonist. But what human language can adequately portray *that* astonishment, *that* horror which possessed me at the spectacle then presented to view? The brief moment in which I averted my eyes had been sufficient to produce, apparently, a material change in the arrangements at the upper or farther end of the room. A large mirror,—so at first it seemed to me in my confusion—now stood where none had been perceptible before; and as I stepped up to it in extremity of terror, mine own image, but with features all pale and dabbled in blood, advanced to meet me with a feeble and tottering gait.

Thus it appeared, I say, but was not. It was my antagonist—it was Wilson, who then stood before me in the agonies of his dissolution. His mask and cloak lay, where he had thrown them, upon the floor. Not a thread in all his raiment—not a line in all the marked and singular lineaments of his face which was not, even in the most absolute identity, *mine own!*

It was Wilson; but he spoke no longer in a whisper,[19] and I could have fancied that I myself was speaking while he said:

18. **the . . . Di Broglio:** The Marchesa Aphrodite, in "The Assignation," is described as "the gayest of the gay—the most lovely where all were beautiful—but still the young wife of the old and intriguing Mentoni." Similarity of language, in Poe, generally indicates similarity of substance, and Di Broglio's wife is doubtless, like the Marchesa, "the type of spiritual beauty." Wilson's passionate designs upon her therefore create a crescendo of conflict between him and his conscience.

19. **no . . . whisper:** Wilson's voice earlier grew "husky with rage" (thus approximating the double's "whisper") in anticipation of the latter's adoption, here, of Wilson's stronger voice. The effect is to demonstrate their identity and common fate.

"You have conquered, and I yield. Yet, henceforward art thou also dead—dead to the World, to Heaven, and to Hope! In me didst thou exist [20]*—and, in my death, see by this image, which is thine own, how utterly thou hast murdered thyself."*

THE MAN OF THE CROWD

◊

"THE MAN OF THE CROWD" was published in *Burton's Gentleman's Magazine* for December, 1840, and its narrator possesses those extraordinary observant and intuitive faculties with which, in the following year, Poe was to endow his detective-hero Dupin. Superficially, the story is a kind of detective-tale, in which the narrator "shadows" for twenty-four hours the one Londoner whose social and moral identity he cannot fathom at a glance. Actually, as the tale's progressive improbability invites the reader to divine, the narrator (like Dupin) is engaged in a wholly inward adventure—the "detection" and confrontation of the principle of evil in himself. In general, the narrative moves from the possible to the incredible, from the morally and socially respectable to the utterly degraded, and from twilight into an ever-deeper darkness. It is a black and wandering mental journey, lit by bright clearings of dream; in it, the narrator learns what he can of that part of his fallen nature which is, like William Wilson, "dead to the World, to Heaven, and to Hope," and which seeks by frantic imposture to escape the sense of its own nonentity.

◊

Ce grand malheur, de ne pouvoir être seul.
LA BRUYÈRE [1]

IT WAS well said of a certain German book that *"es lässt sich nicht lesen"*—it does not permit itself to be read. There are some secrets which do not permit themselves to be told. Men die nightly in their beds, wringing the hands of ghostly confessors, and looking them piteously in the eyes—die with despair of heart and convulsion of throat, on account of the hideousness of mysteries which will not *suffer themselves* to be revealed. Now and then, alas, the conscience of man takes up a burden so heavy in horror that it can be thrown down only into the grave. And thus the essence of all crime is undivulged.[2]

Not long ago, about the closing in of an evening in autumn, I sat at the large bow window of the D—— Coffee-House in London. For some months I had been ill in health, but was now convalescent, and, with returning strength, found myself in one of those happy moods which are so precisely the converse of *ennui*—moods of the keenest appetency, when the film from the mental vision departs—the ἀχλὺς ἥ πρὶν ἐπῆεν [3]—and the intellect, electrified, surpasses as greatly its every-day condition, as does the vivid yet candid reason of Leibnitz, the mad and flimsy rhetoric of Gorgias.[4] Merely to breathe was enjoyment; and I derived positive pleasure even from many of the legitimate sources of pain. I felt a calm but inquisitive interest in every thing. With a cigar in my mouth and a newspaper in my lap, I had been amusing myself for the greater part of the afternoon, now in poring over advertisements, now in observing the promiscuous company in the room, and now in peering through the smoky panes into the street.

This latter is one of the principal thoroughfares of the city, and had been very much crowded during the whole day. But, as the darkness came on, the throng momently increased; and, by the time the lamps were well lighted, two dense and continuous tides of population were rushing past the door. At this particular period of the evening I had never before been in a similar situation, and the tumultuous sea of human heads filled me, therefore, with a delicious novelty of emotion. I gave up, at length, all care of things within the hotel, and became absorbed in contemplation of the scene without.

At first my observations took an abstract and generalizing turn. I looked at the passengers in masses, and thought of them in their aggregate relations. Soon, however, I descended to details, and regarded with minute interest the innumerable varieties of figure, dress, air, gait, visage, and expression of countenance.

20. *In . . . exist:* The words recall St. Paul's words to the Athenians: "For in him we live, and move, and have our being" (Acts 18:28). The irrevocable deadness of Wilson is perhaps explained by Matt. 12:32. **THE MAN OF THE CROWD. 1. La Bruyère:** The epigraph is slightly misquoted from Jean de la Bruyère (1645–96), who actually wrote: *"Tout nôtre mal vient de ne pouvoir être seuls."* This might be translated, "All our ills come from our inability to be alone."

2. And . . . undivulged: In "The Imp of the Perverse," Poe says that man's inclination to evil, the "unfathomable longing of the soul to *vex* itself," is a "radical, primitive impulse" and an utter mystery. "Nor will this overwhelming tendency to do wrong for the wrong's sake, admit of analysis . . ." **3. the . . . ἐπῆεν:** "the mist that before was upon it . . ." (*Iliad*, V.127). **4. Leibnitz . . . Gorgias:** Gottfried Wilhelm von Leibnitz, German philosopher (1646–1716). Gorgias, Sicilian rhetorician of the fifth century B.C.

By far the greater number of those who went by had a satisfied business-like demeanor, and seemed to be thinking only of making their way through the press. Their brows were knit, and their eyes rolled quickly; when pushed against by fellow-wayfarers they evinced no symptom of impatience, but adjusted their clothes and hurried on. Others, still a numerous class, were restless in their movements, had flushed faces, and talked and gesticulated to themselves, as if feeling in solitude on account of the very denseness of the company around. When impeded in their progress, these people suddenly ceased muttering, but redoubled their gesticulations, and awaited, with an absent and overdone smile upon the lips, the course of the persons impeding them. If jostled, they bowed profusely to the jostlers, and appeared overwhelmed with confusion.—There was nothing very distinctive about these two large classes beyond what I have noted. Their habiliments belonged to that order which is pointedly termed decent. They were undoubtedly noblemen, merchants, attorneys, tradesmen, stock-jobbers—the Eupatrids and the common-places of society—men of leisure and men actively engaged in affairs of their own—conducting business upon their own responsibility. They did not greatly excite my attention.

The tribe of clerks was an obvious one; and here I discerned two remarkable divisions. There were the junior clerks of flash houses—young gentlemen with tight coats, bright boots, well-oiled hair, and supercilious lips. Setting aside a certain dapperness of carriage, which may be termed *deskism* for want of a better word, the manner of these persons seemed to me an exact facsimile of what had been the perfection of *bon ton* about twelve or eighteen months before. They wore the cast-off graces of the gentry;—and this, I believe, involves the best definition of the class.

The division of the upper clerks of staunch firms, or of the "steady old fellows," it was not possible to mistake. These were known by their coats and pantaloons of black or brown, made to sit comfortably, with white cravats and waistcoats, broad solid-looking shoes, and thick hose or gaiters.—They had all slightly bald heads, from which the right ears, long used to pen-holding, had an odd habit of standing off on end.[5] I observed that they always removed or settled their hats with both hands, and wore watches, with short gold chains of a substantial and ancient pattern. Theirs was the affectation of respectability;—if indeed there be an affectation so honorable.

There were many individuals of dashing appearance, whom I easily understood as belonging to the race of swell pick-pockets, with which all great cities are infested. I watched these gentry with much inquisitiveness, and found it difficult to imagine how they should ever be mistaken for gentlemen by gentlemen themselves. Their voluminousness of wristband, with an air of excessive frankness, should betray them at once.

The gamblers, of whom I descried not a few, were still more easily recognisable. They wore every variety of dress, from that of the desperate thimble-rig[6] bully, with velvet waistcoat, fancy neckerchief, gilt chains, and filigreed buttons, to that of the scrupulously inornate clergyman than which nothing could be less liable to suspicion. Still all were distinguished by a certain sodden swarthiness of complexion, a filmy dimness of eye, and pallor and compression of lip. There were two other traits, moreover, by which I could always detect them;—a guarded lowness of tone in conversation, and a more than ordinary extension of the thumb in a direction at right angles with the fingers.—Very often, in company with these sharpers, I observed an order of men somewhat different in habits, but still birds of a kindred feather. They may be defined as the gentlemen who live by their wits. They seem to prey upon the public in two battalions—that of the dandies and that of the military men. Of the first grade the leading features are long locks and smiles; of the second, frogged coats and frowns.

Descending in the scale of what is termed gentility, I found darker and deeper themes for speculation. I saw Jew peddlers, with hawk eyes flashing from countenances whose every other feature wore only an expression of abject humility; sturdy professional street beggars scowling upon mendicants of a better stamp, whom despair alone had driven forth into the night for charity; feeble and ghastly invalids, upon whom death had placed a sure hand, and who sidled and tottered through the mob, looking every one beseechingly in the face, as if in search of some chance consolation, some lost hope; modest young girls returning from long and late labor to a cheerless home, and shrinking more tearfully than indignantly from the glances of ruffians, whose direct contact, even, could not be avoided; women of the town of all kinds and of all ages—the unequivocal beauty in the prime of her womanhood, putting one in mind of the statue in Lucian,[7] with the surface of Parian marble, and the interior filled with filth—the loath-

5. **the . . . end:** first of a number of improbable perceptions, the effect of which is to suggest that the narrator is not observing but envisioning.

6. **thimble-rig:** swindling. 7. **Lucian:** Greek writer of the second century A.D., author of the *Dialogues.*

some and utterly lost leper in rags—the wrinkled, bejewelled and paint-begrimed beldame, making a last effort at youth—the mere child of immature form, yet, from long association, an adept in the dreadful coquetries of her trade, and burning with a rabid ambition to be ranked the equal of her elders in vice; drunkards innumerable and indescribable—some in shreds and patches, reeling, inarticulate, with bruised visage and lack-lustre eyes—some in whole although filthy garments, with a slightly unsteady swagger, thick sensual lips, and hearty-looking rubicund faces—others clothed in materials which had once been good, and which even now were scrupulously well brushed—men who walked with a more than naturally firm and springy step, but whose countenances were fearfully pale, whose eyes were hideously wild and red, and who clutched with quivering fingers, as they strode through the crowd, at every object which came within their reach; beside these, pie-men, porters, coal-heavers, sweeps; organ-grinders, monkey-exhibitors and ballad-mongers, those who vended with those who sang; ragged artizans and exhausted laborers of every description, and all full of a noisy and inordinate vivacity which jarred discordantly upon the ear, and gave an aching sensation to the eye.

As the night deepened, so deepened to me the interest of the scene; for not only did the general character of the crowd materially alter (its gentler features retiring in the gradual withdrawal of the more orderly portion of the people, and its harsher ones coming out into bolder relief, as the late hour brought forth every species of infamy from its den,) but the rays of the gas-lamps, feeble at first in their struggle with the dying day, had now at length gained ascendancy, and threw over every thing a fitful and garish lustre. All was dark yet splendid—as that ebony to which has been likened the style of Tertullian.[8]

The wild effects of the light enchained me to an examination of individual faces; and although the rapidity with which the world of light flitted before the window, prevented me from casting more than a glance upon each visage, still it seemed that, in my then peculiar mental state, I could frequently read, even in that brief interval of a glance, the history of long years.

With my brow to the glass, I was thus occupied in scrutinizing the mob, when suddenly there came into view a countenance (that of a decrepid old man, some sixty-five or seventy years of age,)—a countenance which at once arrested and absorbed my whole attention, on account of the absolute idiosyncrasy of its expression. Any thing even remotely resembling that expression I had never seen before. I well remember that my first thought, upon beholding it, was that Retzsch,[9] had he viewed it, would have greatly preferred it to his own pictural incarnations of the fiend. As I endeavored, during the brief minute of my original survey, to form some analysis of the meaning conveyed, there arose confusedly and paradoxically within my mind, the ideas of vast mental power, of caution, of penuriousness, of avarice, of coolness, of malice, of blood-thirstiness, of triumph, of merriment, of excessive terror, of intense—of supreme despair. I felt singularly aroused, startled, fascinated. "How wild a history," I said to myself, "is written within that bosom!" Then came a craving desire to keep the man in view—to know more of him. Hurriedly putting on an overcoat, and seizing my hat and cane, I made my way into the street, and pushed through the crowd in the direction which I had seen him take; for he had already disappeared. With some little difficulty I at length came within sight of him, approached, and followed him closely, yet cautiously, so as not to attract his attention.

I had now a good opportunity of examining his person. He was short in stature, very thin, and apparently very feeble. His clothes, generally, were filthy and ragged; but as he came, now and then, within the strong glare of a lamp, I perceived that his linen, although dirty, was of beautiful texture; and my vision deceived me, or, through a rent in a closely-buttoned and evidently second-handed *roquelaire*[10] which enveloped him, I caught a glimpse both of a diamond and of a dagger. These observations heightened my curiosity, and I resolved to follow the stranger whithersoever he should go.

It was now fully night-fall, and a thick humid fog hung over the city, soon ending in a settled and heavy rain. This change of weather had an odd effect upon the crowd, the whole of which was at once put into new commotion, and overshadowed by a world of umbrellas. The waver, the jostle, and the hum increased in a tenfold degree. For my own part I did not much regard the rain—the lurking of an old fever in my system rendering the moisture somewhat too dangerously pleasant. Tying a handkerchief about my mouth, I kept on.[11]

8. **Tertullian:** one of the Latin church fathers (160?–230?), author of the *Apology*.

9. **Retzsch:** Moritz Retzsch (1779–1857), German artist who illustrated Goethe's *Faust*. 10. *roquelaire:* rare spelling of French *roquelaure* (cloak). 11. **Tying . . . on:** In "King Pest," "Loss of Breath," and "The Premature Burial," Poe refers to the practice of binding up the jaws of the dead. When the narrator of "The Man of the Crowd" binds up his jaws, and so

For half an hour the old man held his way with difficulty along the great thoroughfare; and I here walked close at his elbow through fear of losing sight of him. Never once turning his head to look back, he did not observe me. By and by he passed into a cross street, which, although densely filled with people, was not quite so much thronged as the main one he had quitted. Here a change in his demeanor became evident. He walked more slowly and with less object than before—more hesitatingly. He crossed and re-crossed the way repeatedly, without apparent aim; and the press was still so thick, that, at every such movement, I was obliged to follow him closely. The street was a narrow and long one, and his course lay within it for nearly an hour, during which the passengers had gradually diminished to about that number which is ordinarily seen at noon on Broadway near the park—so vast a difference is there between a London populace and that of the most frequented American city. A second turn brought us into a square, brilliantly lighted, and overflowing with life. The old manner of the stranger re-appeared. His chin fell upon his breast, while his eyes rolled wildly from under his knit brows, in every direction, upon those who hemmed him in.[12] He urged his way steadily and perseveringly. I was surprised, however, to find, upon his having made the circuit of the square, that he turned and retraced his steps. Still more was I astonished to see him repeat the same walk several times—once nearly detecting me as he came round with a sudden movement.

In this exercise he spent another hour, at the end of which we met with far less interruption from passengers than at first. The rain fell fast; the air grew cool; and the people were retiring to their homes. With a gesture of impatience, the wanderer passed into a by-street comparatively deserted. Down this, some quarter of a mile long, he rushed with an activity I could not have dreamed of seeing in one so aged, and which put me to much trouble in pursuit. A few minutes brought us to a large and busy bazaar, with the localities of which the stranger appeared well acquainted, and where his original demeanor again became apparent, as he forced his way to and fro, without aim, among the host of buyers and sellers.

During the hour and a half, or thereabouts, which we passed in this place, it required much caution on my part to keep him within reach without attracting his observation. Luckily I wore a pair of caoutchouc over-shoes, and could move about in perfect silence. At no moment did he see that I watched him. He entered shop after shop, priced nothing, spoke no word, and looked at all objects with a wild and vacant stare. I was now utterly amazed at his behaviour, and firmly resolved that we should not part until I had satisfied myself in some measure respecting him.

A loud-toned clock struck eleven, and the company were fast deserting the bazaar. A shopkeeper, in putting up a shutter, jostled the old man, and at the instant I saw a strong shudder come over his frame. He hurried into the street, looked anxiously around him for an instant, and then ran with incredible swiftness through many crooked and people-less lanes, until we emerged once more upon the great thoroughfare whence we had started—the street of the D—— Hotel. It no longer wore, however, the same aspect. It was still brilliant with gas; but the rain fell fiercely, and there were few persons to be seen. The stranger grew pale. He walked moodily some paces up the once populous avenue, then, with a heavy sigh, turned in the direction of the river, and, plunging through a great variety of devious ways, came out, at length, in view of one of the principal theatres. It was about being closed, and the audience were thronging from the doors. I saw the old man gasp as if for breath while he threw himself amid the crowd; but I thought that the intense agony of his countenance had, in some measure, abated. His head again fell upon his breast; he appeared as I had seen him at first. I observed that he now took the course in which had gone the greater number of the audience—but, upon the whole, I was at a loss to comprehend the waywardness of his actions.

As he proceeded, the company grew more scattered, and his old uneasiness and vacillation were resumed. For some time he followed closely a party of some ten or twelve roisterers; but from this number one by one dropped off, until three only remained together, in a narrow and gloomy lane little frequented. The stranger paused, and, for a moment, seemed lost in thought; then, with every mark of agitation, pursued rapidly a route which brought us to the verge of the city, amid regions very different from those we had hitherto traversed. It was the most noisome quarter of London, where every thing wore the worst impress of the most deplorable poverty, and of the most desperate crime. By the dim light of an accidental lamp, tall, antique, worm-eaten, wooden tenements were seen tottering to their fall, in directions

comes to resemble a corpse, it is as when the hero of "Ligeia" finds himself "chilled into stone." The point is that the narrator is now "dead to the world," having entered fully into dream, and moves—like the traveler of "Dream-Land"—among phantoms.

12. His . . . in: Here the stranger is impersonating the "businesslike" persons described in the fifth paragraph.

so many and capricious that scarce the semblance of a passage was discernible between them. The paving-stones lay at random, displaced from their beds by the rankly growing grass. Horrible filth festered in the dammed-up gutters. The whole atmosphere teemed with desolation. Yet, as we proceeded, the sounds of human life revived by sure degrees, and at length large bands of the most abandoned of a London populace were seen reeling to and fro. The spirits of the old man again flickered up, as a lamp which is near its death-hour. Once more he strode onward with elastic tread. Suddenly a corner was turned, a blaze of light burst upon our sight, and we stood before one of the huge suburban temples of Intemperance —one of the palaces of the fiend, Gin.

It was now nearly day-break; but a number of wretched inebriates still pressed in and out of the flaunting entrance. With a half shriek of joy the old man forced a passage within, resumed at once his original bearing, and stalked backward and forward, without apparent object, among the throng. He had not been thus long occupied, however, before a rush to the doors gave token that the host was closing them for the night. It was something even more intense than despair that I then observed upon the countenance of the singular being whom I had watched so pertinaciously. Yet he did not hesitate in his career, but, with a mad energy, retraced his steps at once, to the heart of the mighty London. Long and swiftly he fled, while I followed him in the wildest amazement, resolute not to abandon a scrutiny in which I now felt an interest all-absorbing. The sun arose while we proceeded, and, when we had once again reached that most thronged mart of the populous town, the street of the D—— Hotel, it presented an appearance of human bustle and activity scarcely inferior to what I had seen on the evening before. And here, long, amid the momently increasing confusion, did I persist in my pursuit of the stranger. But, as usual, he walked to and fro, and during the day did not pass from out the turmoil of that street. And, as the shades of the second evening came on, I grew wearied unto death, and, stopping fully in front of the wanderer, gazed at him steadfastly in the face. He noticed me not,[13] but resumed his solemn walk, while I, ceasing to follow, remained absorbed in contemplation. "This old man," I said at length, "is the type and the genius of deep crime. He refuses to be alone. *He is the man of the crowd.* It will be in vain to follow; for I shall learn no more of him, nor of his deeds. The worst heart of the world is a grosser book than the *Hortulus Animæ,* and perhaps it is but one of the great mercies of God that *'es lässt sich nicht lesen.'* "[14]

THE OVAL PORTRAIT

◇

Graham's Magazine first published this brief story, under the title of "Life in Death," in April, 1842. The relationships of narrator, painter, and bride correspond to those of the principals in "The Fall of the House of Usher," while the concluding history of the portrait, in which the bride is transmuted into Art, is a simpler version of "Ligeia." As in several of his shorter prose works, and certain of his poems, Poe here permits his style to become highly rhetorical and repetitive.

◇

THE CHÂTEAU in which my valet had ventured to make forcible entrance, rather than permit me, in my desperately wounded condition, to pass a night in the open air, was one of those piles of commingled gloom and grandeur which have so long frowned among the Apennines, not less in fact than in the fancy of Mrs. Radcliffe.[1] To all appearance it had been temporarily and very lately abandoned. We established ourselves in one of the smallest and least sumptuously furnished apartments. It lay in a remote turret of the building. Its decorations were rich, yet tattered and antique. Its walls were hung with tapestry and bedecked with manifold and multiform armorial trophies, together with an unusually great number of very spirited modern paintings in frames of rich golden arabesque. In these paintings, which depended from the walls not only in their main surfaces, but in very many nooks which the bizarre architecture of the château rendered

13. **He . . . not:** The stranger is "a decrepid old man," like the captain of "Ms. Found in a Bottle," because he derives from that remote and forgotten period at which the narrator's harmony of soul was first disrupted by the principle of evil. He is also like the absorbed captain of "Ms." in not perceiving the narrator—perhaps, in his case, because the essence of evil is an incorrigible solitude.

14. **The . . . *lesen:*** This closing sentiment is elaborated in the third and fourth selections from "Marginalia" (see pp. 472–73). Poe identifies the book mentioned as "The *Hortulus Animae cum Oratiunculos Aliquibus Superadditis* of Grünninger." The Strasbourg printer Johannes Grüninger printed the *Hortulus Animae* ("Little Garden of the Soul") in 1500. THE OVAL PORTRAIT. 1. **Mrs. Radcliffe:** Ann Radcliffe, author of *The Mysteries of Udolpho* (1794) and other Gothic fiction.

necessary—in these paintings my incipient delirium,[2] perhaps, had caused me to take deep interest; so that I bade Pedro to close the heavy shutters of the room—since it was already night—to light the tongues of a tall candelabrum which stood by the head of my bed—and to throw open far and wide the fringed curtains of black velvet which enveloped the bed itself. I wished all this done that I might resign myself, if not to sleep, at least alternately to the contemplation of these pictures, and the perusal of a small volume which had been found upon the pillow, and which purported to criticise and describe them.

Long—long I read—and devoutly, devotedly I gazed. Rapidly and gloriously the hours flew by, and the deep midnight came. The position of the candelabrum displeased me, and outstretching my hand with difficulty, rather than disturb my slumbering valet, I placed it so as to throw its rays more fully upon the book.

But the action produced an effect altogether unanticipated. The rays of the numerous candles (for there were many) now fell within a niche of the room which had hitherto been thrown into deep shade by one of the bed-posts. I thus saw in vivid light a picture all unnoticed before.[3] It was the portrait of a young girl just ripening into womanhood. I glanced at the painting hurriedly, and then closed my eyes. Why I did this was not at first apparent even to my own perception. But while my lids remained thus shut, I ran over in mind my reason for so shutting them. It was an impulsive movement to gain time for thought—to make sure that my vision had not deceived me—to calm and subdue my fancy for a more sober and more certain gaze. In a very few moments I again looked fixedly at the painting.

That I now saw aright I could not and would not doubt; for the first flashing of the candles upon that canvas had seemed to dissipate the dreamy stupor which was stealing over my senses, and to startle me at once into waking life.

The portrait, I have already said, was that of a young girl. It was a mere head and shoulders, done in what is technically termed a *vignette* manner; much in the style of the favorite heads of Sully.[4] The arms, the bosom and even the ends of the radiant hair, melted imperceptibly into the vague yet deep shadow which formed the background of the whole. The frame was oval, richly gilded and filagreed in *Moresque*.[5] As a thing of art nothing could be more admirable than the painting itself. But it could have been neither the execution of the work, nor the immortal beauty[6] of the countenance, which had so suddenly and so vehemently moved me. Least of all, could it have been that my fancy, shaken from its half slumber, had mistaken the head for that of a living person. I saw at once that the peculiarities of the design, of the *vignetting*, and of the frame, must have instantly dispelled such idea—must have prevented even its momentary entertainment. Thinking earnestly upon these points, I remained, for an hour perhaps, half sitting, half reclining, with my vision riveted upon the portrait. At length, satisfied with the true secret of its effect, I fell back within the bed. I had found the spell of the picture in an absolute *life-likeliness* of expression, which at first startling, finally confounded, subdued and appalled me. With deep and reverent awe I replaced the candelabrum in its former position. The cause of my deep agitation being thus shut from view, I sought eagerly the volume which discussed the paintings and their histories. Turning to the number which designated the oval portrait, I there read the vague and quaint words which follow:

"She was a maiden of rarest beauty, and not more lovely than full of glee. And evil was the hour when she saw, and loved, and wedded the painter. He, passionate, studious, austere, and having already a bride in his Art; she a maiden of rarest beauty, and not more lovely than full of glee; all light and smiles, and frolicksome as the young fawn: loving and cherishing all things: hating only the Art which was her rival: dreading only the palette and brushes and other untoward instruments which deprived her of the countenance of her lover. It was thus a terrible thing for this lady to hear the painter speak of his desire to portray even his young bride. But she was humble and obedient, and sat meekly for many weeks in the dark high turret-chamber where the light dripped upon the pale canvas only from overhead.[7] But he, the painter, took glory in his work, which went on from hour to hour and from day to day. And he was a passionate, and wild and moody man, who became lost in reveries; so that he *would* not see that the light which fell so ghastlily in that lone turret withered the health and the spirits of his bride, who pined visibly to all but him. Yet she smiled on and still on, uncomplain-

2. **incipient delirium:** Compare the "incipient madness" which motivates the bizarre decoration of the abbey in "Ligeia."
3. **The . . . before:** See "Ms. Found in a Bottle," 11 n.
4. ***vignette* . . . Sully:** A vignette is a head-and-shoulders portrait with an indefinite or shadowy border. Thomas Sully (1783–1872) was a celebrated American portrait painter.

5. **in *Moresque:*** in the intricate Moorish decorative style.
6. **immortal beauty:** See the remarks, in Part IV of the Introduction, on apparent hyperbole in "Ligeia."
7. **light . . . overhead:** This dripping light combines the meanings and functions of the censer and the "ruby drops" in "Ligeia."

ingly, because she saw that the painter, (who had high renown,) took a fervid and burning pleasure in his task, and wrought day and night to depict her who so loved him, yet who grew daily more dispirited and weak. And in sooth some who beheld the portrait spoke of its resemblance in low words, as of a mighty marvel, and a proof not less of the power of the painter than of his deep love for her whom he depicted so surpassingly well. But at length, as the labor drew nearer to its conclusion, there were admitted none into the turret; for the painter had grown wild with the ardor of his work, and turned his eyes from the canvas rarely, even to regard the countenance of his wife. And he *would* not see that the tints which he spread upon the canvas were drawn from the cheeks of her who sate beside him. And when many weeks had passed, and but little remained to do, save one brush upon the mouth and one tint upon the eye, the spirit of the lady again flickered up as the flame within the socket of the lamp. And then the brush was given, and then the tint was placed; and, for one moment, the painter stood entranced before the work which he had wrought; but in the next, while he yet gazed, he grew tremulous and very pallid, and aghast, and crying with a loud voice, 'This is indeed *Life* itself!' turned suddenly to regard his beloved:—*She was dead!*"

THE MASQUE OF THE RED DEATH

◊

FIRST published in *Graham's Magazine* for May, 1842, this is one of Poe's best-made tales and one of his more explicit allegories. A man escapes from "diseased" temporal reality into dream, yet his clock-like heart beats on, binding him to time and to the world. The final confrontation, like that of "William Wilson," is a meeting of doubles: the dreamer resists his temporal self, and the latter's summons to awaken. The story also resembles "William Wilson" in rhythm: in each case the dream is episodic, its license being interrupted as if by the Freudian "censor." Comparison with Keats's *Lamia*, Part II, is illuminating.

◊

THE "Red Death" had long devastated the country. No pestilence had ever been so fatal, or so hideous. Blood was its Avatar and its seal—the redness and the horror of blood. There were sharp pains, and sudden dizziness, and then profuse bleeding at the pores, with dissolution. The scarlet stains upon the body and especially upon the face of the victim, were the pest ban which shut him out from the aid and from the sympathy of his fellow-men. And the whole seizure, progress and termination of the disease, were the incidents of half an hour.

But the Prince Prospero [1] was happy and dauntless and sagacious. When his dominions were half depopulated, he summoned to his presence a thousand hale and light-hearted friends from among the knights and dames of his court, and with these retired to the deep seclusion of one of his castellated abbeys. This was an extensive and magnificent structure, the creation of the prince's own eccentric yet august taste. A strong and lofty wall girdled it in. This wall had gates of iron. The courtiers, having entered, brought furnaces and massy hammers and welded the bolts. They resolved to leave means neither of ingress or egress to the sudden impulses of despair or frenzy from within. The abbey was amply provisioned. With such precautions the courtiers might bid defiance to contagion. The external world could take care of itself.[2] In the meantime it was folly to grieve, or to think. The prince had provided all the appliances of pleasure. There were buffoons, there were improvisatori, there were ballet-dancers, there were musicians, there was Beauty, there was wine. All these and security were within. Without was the "Red Death."

It was toward the close of the fifth or sixth month of his seclusion, and while the pestilence raged most furiously abroad, that the Prince Prospero entertained his thousand friends at a masked ball of the most unusual magnificence.

It was a voluptuous scene, that masquerade. But first let me tell of the rooms in which it was held. There were seven—an imperial suite. In many palaces, however, such suites form a long and straight vista, while the folding doors slide back nearly to the walls on either hand, so that the view of the whole extent is scarcely impeded. Here the case was very different; as might have been expected from the duke's love of the *bizarre*. The apartments were so irregularly disposed that the vi-

THE MASQUE OF THE RED DEATH. 1. **Prospero:** The name recalls the duke-magician of Shakespeare's *Tempest* and in its implication of wealth resembles "Fortunato" and "Montresor" in "The Cask of Amontillado." The significance of wealth in Poe's fiction is crystallized in his phrase, "luxury of dream." 2. **The . . . itself:** Compare the narrator in "Ligeia," who is "buried in studies of a nature more than all else adapted to deaden impressions of the outward world."

sion embraced but little more than one at a time. There was a sharp turn at every twenty or thirty yards, and at each turn a novel effect. To the right and left, in the middle of each wall, a tall and narrow Gothic window looked out upon a closed corridor which pursued the windings of the suite. These windows were of stained glass whose color varied in accordance with the prevailing hue of the decorations of the chamber into which it opened. That at the eastern extremity was hung, for example, in blue—and vividly blue were its windows. The second chamber was purple in its ornaments and tapestries, and here the panes were purple. The third was green throughout, and so were the casements. The fourth was furnished and lighted with orange—the fifth with white—the sixth with violet. The seventh apartment was closely shrouded in black velvet tapestries that hung all over the ceiling and down the walls, falling in heavy folds upon a carpet of the same material and hue. But in this chamber only, the color of the windows failed to correspond with the decorations. The panes here were scarlet—a deep blood color. Now in no one of the seven apartments was there any lamp or candelabrum, amid the profusion of golden ornaments that lay scattered to and fro or depended from the roof. There was no light of any kind emanating from lamp or candle within the suite of chambers. But in the corridors that followed the suite, there stood, opposite to each window a heavy tripod, bearing a brazier of fire, that projected its rays through the tinted glass and so glaringly illumined the room. And thus were produced a multitude of gaudy and fantastic appearances. But in the western or black chamber the effect of the fire-light that streamed upon the dark hangings through the blood-tinted panes, was ghastly in the extreme, and produced so wild a look upon the countenances of those who entered, that there were few of the company bold enough to set foot within its precincts at all.

It was in this apartment, also, that there stood against the western wall, a gigantic clock of ebony. Its pendulum swung to and fro with a dull, heavy, monotonous clang; and when the minute-hand made the circuit of the face, and the hour was to be stricken, there came from the brazen lungs of the clock a sound which was clear and loud and deep and exceedingly musical, but of so peculiar a note and emphasis that, at each lapse of an hour, the musicians of the orchestra were constrained to pause, momentarily, in their performance, to hearken to the sound; and thus the waltzers perforce ceased their evolutions; and there was a brief disconcert of the whole gay company; and, while the chimes of the clock yet rang, it was observed that the giddiest grew pale, and the more aged and sedate passed their hands over their brows as if in confused revery or meditation. But when the echoes had fully ceased, a light laughter at once pervaded the assembly; the musicians looked at each other and smiled as if at their own nervousness and folly, and made whispering vows, each to the other, that the next chiming of the clock should produce in them no similar emotion; and then, after the lapse of sixty minutes, (which embrace three thousand and six hundred seconds of the Time that flies,) there came yet another chiming of the clock, and then were the same disconcert and tremulousness and meditation as before.

But, in spite of these things, it was a gay and magnificent revel. The tastes of the duke were peculiar. He had a fine eye for colors and effects. He disregarded the *decora* of mere fashion. His plans were bold and fiery, and his conceptions glowed with barbaric lustre. There are some who would have thought him mad. His followers felt that he was not. It was necessary to hear and see and touch him to be *sure* that he was not.

He had directed, in great part, the moveable embellishments of the seven chambers, upon occasion of this great *fête;* and it was his own guiding taste which had given character to the masqueraders. Be sure they were grotesque. There were much glare and glitter and piquancy and phantasm —much of what has been since seen in *Hernani.*[3] There were arabesque figures with unsuited limbs and appointments. There were delirious fancies such as the madman fashions. There were much of the beautiful, much of the wanton, much of the *bizarre,* something of the terrible, and not a little of that which might have excited disgust. To and fro in the seven chambers there stalked, in fact, a multitude of dreams. And these—the dreams—writhed in and about, taking hue from the rooms, and causing the wild music of the orchestra to seem as the echo of their steps. And, anon, there strikes the ebony clock which stands in the hall of the velvet. And then, for a moment, all is still, and all is silent save the voice of the clock. The dreams are stiff-frozen as they stand. But the echoes of the chime die away—they have endured but an instant—and a light, half-subdued laughter floats after them as they depart. And now again the music swells, and the dreams live, and writhe to and fro more merrily than ever, taking hue from the many-tinted windows through which stream the rays from the tripods. But to the chamber which lies most westwardly of the seven, there are

3. *Hernani:* controversial tragedy by Victor Hugo (1830).

now none of the maskers who venture; for the night is waning away; and there flows a ruddier light through the blood-colored panes; and the blackness of the sable drapery appals; and to him whose foot falls upon the sable carpet, there comes from the near clock of ebony a muffled peal more solemnly emphatic than any which reaches *their* ears who indulge in the more remote gaieties of the other apartments.

But these other apartments were densely crowded, and in them beat feverishly the heart of life. And the revel went whirlingly on, until at length there commenced the sounding of midnight upon the clock. And then the music ceased, as I have told; and the evolutions of the waltzers were quieted; and there was an uneasy cessation of all things as before. But now there were twelve strokes to be sounded by the bell of the clock; and thus it happened, perhaps, that more of thought crept, with more of time, into the meditations of the thoughtful among those who revelled. And thus, too, it happened, perhaps, that before the last echoes of the last chime had utterly sunk into silence, there were many individuals in the crowd who had found leisure to become aware of the presence of a masked figure which had arrested the attention of no single individual before. And the rumor of this new presence having spread itself whisperingly around, there arose at length from the whole company a buzz, or murmur, expressive of disapprobation and surprise—then, finally, of terror, of horror, and of disgust.

In an assembly of phantasms such as I have painted, it may well be supposed that no ordinary appearance could have excited such sensation. In truth the masquerade license of the night was nearly unlimited; but the figure in question had out-Heroded Herod, and gone beyond the bounds of even the prince's indefinite decorum. There are chords in the hearts of the most reckless which cannot be touched without emotion. Even with the utterly lost, to whom life and death are equally jests, there are matters of which no jest can be made. The whole company, indeed, seemed now deeply to feel that in the costume and bearing of the stranger neither wit nor propriety existed. The figure was tall and gaunt, and shrouded from head to foot in the habiliments of the grave. The mask which concealed the visage was made so nearly to resemble the countenance of a stiffened corpse that the closest scrutiny must have had difficulty in detecting the cheat. And yet all this might have been endured, if not approved, by the mad revellers around. But the mummer had gone so far as to assume the type of the Red Death. His vesture was dabbled in *blood*—and his broad brow, with all the features of the face, was besprinkled with the scarlet horror.

When the eyes of Prince Prospero fell upon this spectral image (which with a slow and solemn movement, as if more fully to sustain its *rôle,* stalked to and fro among the waltzers) he was seen to be convulsed, in the first moment with a strong shudder either of terror or distaste; but, in the next, his brow reddened with rage.

"Who dares?" he demanded hoarsely of the courtiers who stood near him—"who dares insult us with this blasphemous mockery? Seize him and unmask him—that we may know whom we have to hang at sunrise, from the battlements!"

It was in the eastern or blue chamber in which stood the Prince Prospero as he uttered these words. They rang throughout the seven rooms loudly and clearly—for the prince was a bold and robust man, and the music had become hushed at the waving of his hand.

It was in the blue room where stood the prince, with a group of pale courtiers by his side. At first, as he spoke, there was a slight rushing movement of this group in the direction of the intruder, who at the moment was also near at hand, and now, with deliberate and stately step, made closer approach to the speaker. But from a certain nameless awe with which the mad assumptions of the mummer had inspired the whole party, there were found none who put forth hand to seize him; so that, unimpeded, he passed within a yard of the prince's person; and, while the vast assembly, as if with one impulse, shrank from the centres of the rooms to the walls, he made his way uninterruptedly, but with the same solemn and measured step which had distinguished him from the first, through the blue chamber to the purple—through the purple to the green—through the green to the orange—through this again to the white—and even thence to the violet, ere a decided movement had been made to arrest him. It was then, however, that the Prince Prospero, maddening with rage and the shame of his own momentary cowardice, rushed hurriedly through the six chambers, while none followed him on account of a deadly terror that had seized upon all. He bore aloft a drawn dagger, and had approached, in rapid impetuosity, to within three or four feet of the retreating figure, when the latter, having attained the extremity of the velvet apartment, turned suddenly and confronted his pursuer. There was a sharp cry—and the dagger dropped gleaming upon the sable carpet, upon which, instantly afterwards, fell prostrate in death the Prince Prospero. Then, summoning the wild courage of despair, a throng of the revellers at once threw themselves into the black apartment, and, seizing the mummer, whose tall figure stood erect and motionless within the shadow of the ebony clock, gasped in unutterable horror at finding the grave-cerements and corpse-like mask which they handled with so violent a rudeness, untenanted by any tangible form.

And now was acknowledged the presence of the Red Death. He had come like a thief in the night. And one by one dropped the revellers in the blood-bedewed halls of their revel, and died each in the despairing posture of his fall. And the life of the ebony clock went out with that of the last of the gay. And the flames of the tripods expired. And Darkness and Decay and the Red Death held illimitable dominion over all.

THE PIT AND THE PENDULUM

◇

THIS WAS first published in *The Gift* (1843). Poe thought of dream-experience as unlocking the secrets of death and afterlife, and the story is therefore a triple narrative. First, it is a story of torture at the hands of the Inquisition. Second, it is an account of a nightmare in which the dreamer is spiritually impotent, and cannot free his soul of the temporal—the pendulum—and the physical—the "charnal" paintings of the chamber wall. Finally, it is a horrible vision of Judgment Day, in which a fallen soul is all but sent to damnation or annihilation.

◇

Impia tortorum longos hic turba furores
Sanguinis innocui, non satiata, aluit.
Sospite nunc patriâ, fracto nunc funeris antro,
Mors ubi dira fuit vita salusque patent.[1]

QUATRAIN COMPOSED FOR THE GATES OF A MARKET TO BE ERECTED UPON THE SITE OF THE JACOBIN CLUB HOUSE AT PARIS.

I WAS sick—sick unto death [2] with that long agony; and when they at length unbound me, and I was permitted to sit, I felt that my senses were leaving me. The sentence—the dread sentence of death—was the last of distinct accentuation which reached my ears. After that, the sound of the inquisitorial voices seemed merged in one dreamy indeterminate hum. It conveyed to my soul the idea of *revolution*—perhaps from its association in fancy with the burr of a mill-wheel.[3] This only for a brief period; for presently I heard no more. Yet, for a while, I saw; but with how terrible an exaggeration! I saw the lips of the black-robed judges. They appeared to me white—whiter than the sheet upon which I trace these words—and thin even to grotesqueness; thin with the intensity of their expression of firmness—of immovable resolution—of stern contempt of human torture. I saw that the decrees of what to me was Fate were still issuing from those lips. I saw them writhe with a deadly locution. I saw them fashion the syllables of my name; and I shuddered because no sound succeeded. I saw, too, for a few moments of delirious horror, the soft and nearly imperceptible waving of the sable draperies which enwrapped the walls of the apartment. And then my vision fell upon the seven tall candles [4] upon the table. At first they wore the aspect of charity, and seemed white slender angels who would save me; but then, all at once, there came a most deadly nausea over my spirit, and I felt every fibre in my frame thrill as if I had touched the wire of a galvanic battery, while the angel forms became meaningless spectres, with heads of flame, and I saw that from them there would be no help. And then there stole into my fancy, like a rich musical note, the thought of what sweet rest there must be in the grave. The thought came gently and stealthily, and it seemed long before it attained full appreciation; but just as my spirit came at length properly to feel and entertain it, the figures of the judges vanished, as if magically, from before me; the tall candles sank into nothingness; their flames went out utterly; the blackness of darkness [5] supervened; all sensations appeared swallowed up in a mad rushing descent as of the soul into Hades.[6] Then silence, and stillness, and night were the universe.

THE PIT AND THE PENDULUM. 1. *Impia . . . patent:* "Here an ungodly pack of executioners long nourished their insatiable appetite for innocent blood. The fatherland is free of them now, their bloody dungeons are destroyed, and life and happiness possess the ground where fearful death once reigned." **2. sick unto death:** In Isa. 38, Hezekiah is "sick unto death," but the Lord relents and restores him. Hezekiah then says to the Lord, "thou hast in love to my soul delivered it from the pit of corruption . . . they that go down into the pit cannot hope for thy truth."

3. After . . . mill-wheel: Poe is describing the same auditory phenomenon as Emily Dickinson treats in her poem, "I heard a fly buzz–when I died." See the Dickinson poem, Vol. II, p. 24, and see also "Ms. Found in a Bottle," 7 n. **4. seven . . . candles:** These are the "seven golden candlesticks" of Rev. 1:12. See also the "seven lamps of fire" (4:5) and the "seven angels" (15:1). **5. the blackness of darkness:** In Jude, Christians are warned against "ungodly men" and "filthy dreamers" who are "sensual, having not the Spirit." Such are described as "wandering stars, to whom is reserved the blackness of darkness forever." **6. mad . . . Hades:** In

I had swooned; but still will not say that all of consciousness was lost. What of it there remained I will not attempt to define, or even to describe; yet all was not lost. In the deepest slumber—no! In delirium—no! In a swoon—no! In death—no! even in the grave all *is not* lost. Else there is no immortality for man. Arousing from the most profound of slumbers, we break the gossamer web of *some* dream.[7] Yet in a second afterward, (so frail may that web have been) we remember not that we have dreamed. In the return to life from the swoon there are two stages; first, that of the sense of mental or spiritual; secondly, that of the sense of physical, existence. It seems probable that if, upon reaching the second stage, we could recall the impressions of the first, we should find these impressions eloquent in memories of the gulf beyond. And that gulf is—what? How at least shall we distinguish its shadows from those of the tomb? But if the impressions of what I have termed the first stage, are not, at will, recalled, yet, after long interval, do they not come unbidden, while we marvel whence they come? He who has never swooned, is not he who finds strange palaces and wildly familiar faces in coals that glow; is not he who beholds floating in mid-air the sad visions that the many may not view; is not he who ponders over the perfume of some novel flower; is not he whose brain grows bewildered with the meaning of some musical cadence which has never before arrested his attention.[8]

Amid frequent and thoughtful endeavors to remember, amid earnest struggles to regather some token of the state of seeming nothingness into which my soul had lapsed, there have been moments when I have dreamed of success; there have been brief, very brief periods when I have conjured up remembrances which the lucid reason of a later epoch assures me could have had reference only to that condition of seeming unconsciousness. These shadows of memory tell, indistinctly, of tall figures that lifted and bore me in silence down —down—still down—till a hideous dizziness oppressed me at the mere idea of the interminableness of the descent. They tell also of a vague horror at my heart, on account of that heart's unnatural stillness. Then comes a sense of sudden motionlessness throughout all things; as if those who bore me (a ghastly train!) had outrun, in their descent, the limits of the limitless, and paused from the wearisomeness of their toil. After this I call to mind flatness and dampness; and then all is *madness*—the madness of a memory which busies itself among forbidden things.

Very suddenly there came back to my soul motion and sound—the tumultuous motion of the heart, and, in my ears, the sound of its beating. Then a pause in which all is blank. Then again sound, and motion, and touch—a tingling sensation pervading my frame. Then the mere consciousness of existence, without thought—a condition which lasted long. Then, very suddenly, *thought,* and shuddering terror, and earnest endeavor to comprehend my true state. Then a strong desire to lapse into insensibility. Then a rushing revival of soul and a successful effort to move. And now a full memory of the trial, of the judges, of the sable draperies, of the sentence, of the sickness, of the swoon. Then entire forgetfulness of all that followed; of all that a later day and much earnestness of endeavor have enabled me vaguely to recall.

So far, I had not opened my eyes. I felt that I lay upon my back, unbound. I reached out my hand, and it fell heavily upon something damp and hard. There I suffered it to remain for many minutes, while I strove to imagine where and *what* I could be. I longed, yet dared not, to employ my vision. I dreaded the first glance at objects around me. It was not that I feared to look upon things horrible, but that I grew aghast lest there should be *nothing* to see. At length, with a wild desperation at heart, I quickly unclosed my eyes. My worst thoughts, then, were confirmed. The blackness of eternal night encompassed me. I struggled for breath. The intensity of the darkness seemed to oppress and stifle me. The atmosphere was intolerably close. I still lay quietly, and made effort to exercise my reason. I brought to mind the inquisitorial proceedings, and attempted from that point to deduce my real condition. The sentence had passed; and it appeared to me that a very long interval of time had since elapsed. Yet not for a moment did I suppose myself actually dead. Such a supposition, notwithstanding what we read in fiction, is altogether inconsistent with real existence; —but where and in what state was I? The condemned to death, I knew, perished usually at the *autos-da-fé,* and one of these had been held on the very night of the day of my trial. Had I been remanded to my dungeon, to await the next sacrifice, which would not take place for many months? This I at once saw could not be. Victims had been in immediate demand. Moreover, my dungeon, as well as all the condemned cells at Toledo, had

"The Conversation of Eiros and Charmion," Eiros describes his death (which coincided with the purification of Earth by fire) as having been accompanied by "a mad, rushing, horrible sound, like the 'voice of many waters.' " See "The Fall of the House of Usher," 16 n. **7. Arousing . . . dream:** See the second selection from "Marginalia," p. 472. **8. perfume . . . attention:** Poe refers here to the unearthly flowers and music of "Al Aaraaf" and "Israfel."

stone floors, and light was not altogether excluded.

A fearful idea now suddenly drove the blood in torrents upon my heart, and for a brief period I once more relapsed into insensibility. Upon recovering, I at once started to my feet, trembling convulsively in every fibre. I thrust my arms wildly above and around me in all directions. I felt nothing; yet dreaded to move a step, lest I should be impeded by the walls of a *tomb*. Perspiration burst from every pore, and stood in cold big beads upon my forehead. The agony of suspense grew at length intolerable, and I cautiously moved forward, with my arms extended, and my eyes straining from their sockets in the hope of catching some faint ray of light. I proceeded for many paces; but still all was blackness and vacancy. I breathed more freely. It seemed evident that mine was not, at least, the most hideous of fates.[9]

And now, as I still continued to step cautiously onward, there came thronging upon my recollection a thousand vague rumors of the horrors of Toledo. Of the dungeons there had been strange things narrated—fables I had always deemed them,—but yet strange, and too ghastly to repeat, save in a whisper. Was I left to perish of starvation in this subterranean world of darkness; or what fate, perhaps even more fearful, awaited me? That the result would be death, and a death of more than customary bitterness, I knew too well the character of my judges to doubt. The mode and the hour were all that occupied or distracted me.

My outstretched hands at length encountered some solid obstruction. It was a wall, seemingly of stone masonry—very smooth, slimy, and cold. I followed it up; stepping with all the careful distrust with which certain antique narratives had inspired me. This process, however, afforded me no means of ascertaining the dimensions of my dungeon, as I might make its circuit and return to the point whence I set out without being aware of the fact, so perfectly uniform seemed the wall. I therefore sought the knife which had been in my pocket, when led into the inquisitorial chamber; but it was gone; my clothes had been exchanged for a wrapper of coarse serge. I had thought of forcing the blade in some minute crevice of the masonry, so as to identify my point of departure. The difficulty, nevertheless, was but trivial; although, in the disorder of my fancy, it seemed at first insuperable. I tore a part of the hem from the robe and placed the fragment at full length, and at right angles to the wall. In groping my way around the prison, I could not fail to encounter this rag upon completing the circuit. So, at least, I thought; but I had not counted upon the extent of the dungeon, or upon my own weakness. The ground was moist and slippery. I staggered onward for some time, when I stumbled and fell. My excessive fatigue induced me to remain prostrate; and sleep soon overtook me as I lay.

Upon awaking, and stretching forth an arm, I found beside me a loaf and a pitcher with water. I was too much exhausted to reflect upon this circumstance, but ate and drank with avidity. Shortly afterward, I resumed my tour around the prison, and with much toil, came at last upon the fragment of the serge. Up to the period when I fell, I had counted fifty-two paces, and, upon resuming my walk, I had counted forty-eight more—when I arrived at the rag. There were in all, then, a hundred paces; and, admitting two paces to the yard, I presumed the dungeon to be fifty yards in circuit. I had met, however, with many angles in the wall, and thus I could form no guess at the shape of the vault, for vault I could not help supposing it to be.

I had little object—certainly no hope—in these researches; but a vague curiosity prompted me to continue them. Quitting the wall, I resolved to cross the area of the enclosure. At first, I proceeded with extreme caution, for the floor, although seemingly of solid material, was treacherous with slime. At length, however, I took courage, and did not hesitate to step firmly; endeavoring to cross in as direct a line as possible. I had advanced some ten or twelve paces in this manner, when the remnant of the torn hem of my robe became entangled between my legs. I stepped on it, and fell violently on my face.

In the confusion attending my fall, I did not immediately apprehend a somewhat startling circumstance, which yet, in a few seconds afterward, and while I still lay prostrate, arrested my attention. It was this—my chin rested upon the floor of the prison, but my lips, and the upper portion of my head, although seemingly at a less elevation than the chin, touched nothing. At the same time, my forehead seemed bathed in a clammy vapor, and the peculiar smell of decayed fungus arose to my nostrils.[10] I put forward my arm, and shuddered to find that I had fallen at the very brink of a circular pit, whose extent, of course, I had no means of ascertaining at the moment. Groping about the masonry just below the margin, I succeeded in dislodging a small fragment, and let it fall into the abyss. For many seconds I hearkened to its reverberations as it dashed against the sides of the

9. **most . . . fates:** Poe touches often on this theme, in "The Premature Burial" and elsewhere.

10. **my . . . nostrils:** "A pestilent and mystic vapor" surrounds the House of Usher, and "minute fungi overspread the whole exterior."

chasm in its descent; at length there was a sullen plunge into water, succeeded by loud echoes. At the same moment, there came a sound resembling the quick opening and as rapid closing of a door overhead, while a faint gleam of light [11] flashed suddenly through the gloom, and as suddenly faded away.

I saw clearly the doom which had been prepared for me, and congratulated myself upon the timely accident by which I had escaped. Another step before my fall, and the world had seen me no more. And the death just avoided was of that very character which I had regarded as fabulous and frivolous in the tales respecting the Inquisition. To the victims of its tyranny, there was the choice of death with its direst physical agonies, or death with its most hideous moral horrors. I had been reserved for the latter. By long suffering my nerves had been unstrung, until I trembled at the sound of my own voice, and had become in every respect a fitting subject for the species of torture which awaited me.

Shaking in every limb, I groped my way back to the wall—resolving there to perish rather than risk the terrors of the wells, of which my imagination now pictured many in various positions about the dungeon. In other conditions of mind, I might have had courage to end my misery at once, by a plunge into one of these abysses; but now I was the veriest of cowards. Neither could I forget what I had read of these pits—that the *sudden* extinction of life formed no part of their most horrible plan.

Agitation of spirit kept me awake for many long hours, but at length I again slumbered. Upon arousing, I found by my side, as before, a loaf and a pitcher of water. A burning thirst consumed me, and I emptied the vessel at a draught. It must have been drugged—for scarcely had I drunk, before I became irresistibly drowsy. A deep sleep fell upon me—a sleep like that of death. How long it lasted of course, I know not; but when, once again, I unclosed my eyes, the objects around me were visible. By a wild, sulphurous lustre, the origin of which I could not at first determine, I was enabled to see the extent and aspect of the prison.

In its size I had been greatly mistaken. The whole circuit of its walls did not exceed twenty-five yards. For some minutes this fact occasioned me a world of vain trouble; vain indeed—for what could be of less importance, under the terrible circumstances which environed me, than the mere dimensions of my dungeon? But my soul took a wild interest in trifles, and I busied myself in endeavors to account for the error I had committed in my measurement.[12] The truth at length flashed upon me. In my first attempt at exploration I had counted fifty-two paces, up to the period when I fell: I must then have been within a pace or two of the fragment of serge; in fact, I had nearly performed the circuit of the vault. I then slept—and, upon awaking, I must have returned upon my steps—thus supposing the circuit nearly double what it actually was. My confusion of mind prevented me from observing that I began my tour with the wall to the left, and ended it with the wall to the right.

I had been deceived, too, in respect to the shape of the enclosure. In feeling my way I had found many angles, and thus deduced an idea of great irregularity; so potent is the effect of total darkness upon one arousing from lethargy or sleep! The angles were simply those of a few slight depressions, or niches, at odd intervals. The general shape of the prison was square.[13] What I had taken for masonry seemed now to be iron, or some other metal, in huge plates, whose sutures or joints occasioned the depression. The entire surface of this metallic enclosure was rudely daubed in all the hideous and repulsive devices to which the charnel superstition of the monks has given rise.[14] The figures of fiends in aspects of menace, with skeleton forms, and other more really fearful images, overspread and disfigured the walls. I observed that the outlines of these monstrosities were sufficiently distinct, but that the colors seemed faded and blurred, as if from the effects of a damp atmosphere. I now noticed the floor, too, which was of stone. In the centre yawned the circular pit from whose jaws I had escaped; but it was the only one in the dungeon.

All this I saw indistinctly and by much effort: for my personal condition had been greatly changed during slumber. I now lay upon my back, and at full length, on a species of low framework of wood. To this I was securely bound by a long strap resembling a surcingle. It passed in many convolutions about my limbs and body, leaving at

11. **faint . . . light:** This light and the pendulum that later descends correspond to the censer and chain of "Ligeia."

12. **But . . . measurement:** In "Ms. Found in a Bottle" and "A Descent into the Maelström," Poe depicts the same emotional paradox of curiosity in the midst of terror. This paradox expresses the doubleness of hypnagogic experience, in which we can at once dream and watch ourselves dream. Wherever Poe's narrator is not the hero, as in "Usher," he embodies the mind's power to witness the dream, as well as suffer it. 13. **The . . . square:** Since this story records a dream which is not redemptive but the very reverse, its "dream-room" has what Poe called, in "The Colloquy of Monos and Una," a "rectangular obscenity." See Introduction, Part IV. 14. **The . . . rise:** See "Ligeia," 11 n.

liberty only my head, and my left arm to such extent that I could, by dint of much exertion, supply myself with food from an earthen dish which lay by my side on the floor. I saw, to my horror, that the pitcher had been removed. I say to my horror —for I was consumed with intolerable thirst. This thirst it appeared to be the design of my persecutors to stimulate: for the food in the dish was meat pungently seasoned.

Looking upward, I surveyed the ceiling of my prison. It was some thirty or forty feet overhead, and constructed much as the side walls. In one of its panels a very singular figure riveted my whole attention. It was the painted figure of Time as he is commonly represented, save that, in lieu of a scythe, he held what, at a casual glance, I supposed to be the pictured image of a huge pendulum, such as we see on antique clocks. There was something, however, in the appearance of this machine which caused me to regard it more attentively. While I gazed directly upward at it (for its position was immediately over my own) I fancied that I saw it in motion. In an instant afterward the fancy was confirmed. Its sweep was brief, and of course slow. I watched it for some minutes, somewhat in fear, but more in wonder. Wearied at length with observing its dull movement, I turned my eyes upon the other objects in the cell.

A slight noise attracted my notice, and, looking to the floor, I saw several enormous rats traversing it. They had issued from the well which lay just within view to my right. Even then, while I gazed, they came up in troops, hurriedly, with ravenous eyes, allured by the scent of the meat. From this it required much effort and attention to scare them away.

It might have been half an hour, perhaps even an hour, (for I could take but imperfect note of time) before I again cast my eyes upward. What I then saw confounded and amazed me. The sweep of the pendulum had increased in extent by nearly a yard. As a natural consequence its velocity was also much greater. But what mainly disturbed me was the idea that it had perceptibly *descended.* I now observed—with what horror it is needless to say—that its nether extremity was formed of a crescent of glittering steel, about a foot in length from horn to horn; the horns upward, and the under edge evidently as keen as that of a razor. Like a razor also, it seemed massy and heavy, tapering from the edge into a solid and broad structure above. It was appended to a weighty rod of brass, and the whole *hissed* as it swung through the air.

I could no longer doubt the doom prepared for me by monkish ingenuity in torture. My cognizance of the pit had become known to the inquisitorial agents—*the pit,* whose horrors had been destined for so bold a recusant as myself—*the pit,* typical of hell, and regarded by rumor as the Ultima Thule [15] of all their punishments. The plunge into this pit I had avoided by the merest of accidents, and I knew that surprise, or entrapment into torment, formed an important portion of all the grotesquerie of these dungeon deaths. Having failed to fall, it was no part of the demon plan to hurl me into the abyss; and thus (there being no alternative) a different and a milder destruction awaited me. Milder! I half smiled in my agony as I thought of such application of such a term.

What boots it to tell of the long, long hours of horror more than mortal, during which I counted the rushing oscillations of the steel! Inch by inch—line by line—with a descent only appreciable at intervals that seemed ages—down and still down it came! Days passed—it might have been that many days passed—ere it swept so closely over me as to fan me with its acrid breath. The odor of the sharp steel forced itself into my nostrils. I prayed —I wearied heaven with my prayer for its more speedy descent. I grew frantically mad, and struggled to force myself upward against the sweep of the fearful scimitar. And then I fell suddenly calm, and lay smiling at the glittering death, as a child at some rare bauble.[16]

There was another interval of utter insensibility; it was brief; for, upon again lapsing into life, there had been no perceptible descent in the pendulum. But it might have been long—for I knew there were demons who took note of my swoon, and who could have arrested the vibration at pleasure. Upon my recovery, too, I felt very—oh, inexpressibly sick and weak, as if through long inanition. Even amid the agonies of that period, the human nature craved food. With painful effort I outstretched my left arm as far as my bonds permitted, and took possession of the small remnant which had been spared me by the rats. As I put a portion of it within my lips, there rushed to my mind a half formed thought of joy—of hope. Yet what business had *I* with hope? It was, as I say, a half formed thought—man has many such which are never completed. I felt that it was of joy—of hope; but I felt also that it had perished in its formation. In vain I struggled to perfect—to regain it. Long suffering had nearly annihilated all my or-

15. **Ultima Thule:** in ancient geography, the extreme limit of travel and discovery; figuratively, the ultimate in anything.
16. **bauble:** The chandelier chain of the Devil's apartment in "The Duc de l'Omelette" concludes in a blazing ruby; compare also the "window of one circular diamond" in "Al Aaraaf" (quoted in Introduction, Part IV).

dinary powers of mind. I was an imbecile—an idiot.

The vibration of the pendulum was at right angles to my length. I saw that the crescent was designed to cross the region of the heart.[17] It would fray the serge of my robe—it would return and repeat its operations—again—and again. Notwithstanding its terrifically wide sweep (some thirty feet or more) and the hissing vigor of its descent, sufficient to sunder these very walls of iron, still the fraying of my robe would be all that, for several minutes, it would accomplish. And at this thought I paused. I dared not go further than this reflection. I dwelt upon it with a pertinacity of attention—as if, in so dwelling, I could arrest *here* the descent of the steel. I forced myself to ponder upon the sound of the crescent as it should pass across the garment—upon the peculiar thrilling sensation which the friction of cloth produces on the nerves. I pondered upon all this frivolity until my teeth were on edge.

Down—steadily down it crept. I took a frenzied pleasure in contrasting its downward with its lateral velocity. To the right—to the left—far and wide—with the shriek of a damned spirit; to my heart with the stealthy pace of a tiger! I alternately laughed and howled, as the one or the other idea grew predominant.[18]

Down—certainly, relentlessly down! It vibrated within three inches of my bosom! I struggled violently—furiously—to free my left arm. This was free only from the elbow to the hand. I could reach the latter, from the platter beside me, to my mouth, with great effort, but no farther. Could I have broken the fastenings above the elbow, I would have seized and attempted to arrest the pendulum. I might as well have attempted to arrest an avalanche!

Down—still unceasingly—still inevitably down! I gasped and struggled at each vibration. I shrunk convulsively at its every sweep. My eyes followed its outward or upward whirls with the eagerness of the most unmeaning despair; they closed themselves spasmodically at the descent, although death would have been a relief, oh! how unspeakable! Still I quivered in every nerve to think how slight a sinking of the machinery would precipitate that keen, glistening axe upon my bosom. It was *hope* that prompted the nerve to quiver—the frame to shrink. It was *hope*—the hope that triumphs on the rack—that whispers to the death-condemned even in the dungeons of the Inquisition.

I saw that some ten or twelve vibrations would bring the steel in actual contact with my robe—and with this observation there suddenly came over my spirit all the keen, collected calmness of despair. For the first time during many hours—or perhaps days—I *thought*. It now occurred to me, that the bandage, or surcingle, which enveloped me, was *unique*.[19] I was tied by no separate cord. The first stroke of the razor-like crescent athwart any portion of the band would so detach it that it might be unwound from my person by means of my left hand. But how fearful, in that case, the proximity of the steel! The result of the slightest struggle, how deadly! Was it likely, moreover, that the minions of the torturer had not foreseen and provided for this possibility! Was it probable that the bandage crossed my bosom in the track of the pendulum? Dreading to find my faint, and, as it seemed, my last hope frustrated, I so far elevated my head as to obtain a distinct view of my breast. The surcingle enveloped my limbs and body close in all directions—*save in the path of the destroying crescent.*

Scarcely had I dropped my head back into its original position, when there flashed upon my mind what I cannot better describe than as the unformed half of that idea of deliverance to which I have previously alluded, and of which a moiety only floated inderminately through my brain when I raised food to my burning lips. The whole thought was now present—feeble, scarcely sane, scarcely definite—but still entire. I proceeded at once, with the nervous energy of despair, to attempt its execution.

For many hours the immediate vicinity of the low framework upon which I lay had been literally swarming with rats. They were wild, bold, ravenous; their red eyes glaring upon me as if they waited but for motionlessness on my part to make me their prey. "To what food," I thought, "have they been accustomed in the well?"

They had devoured, in spite of all my efforts to prevent them, all but a small remnant of the contents of the dish. I had fallen into an habitual seesaw or wave of the hand about the platter. and, at length, the unconscious uniformity of the movement deprived it of effect. In their voracity, the

17. **crescent . . . heart:** See "Sonnet—to Science," ll. 1–3.
18. **Down . . . predominant:** Poe's piece "A Predicament" (1838), ostensibly a take-off on *Blackwood's* stories but in great part self-mockery, burlesqued this passage before it was ever written. The narrator of "A Predicament" is being decapitated by "the huge, glittering, scimitar-like minute-hand" of a clock. "Meantime the ponderous and terrific *Scythe of Time* (for I now discovered the literal import of that classical phrase) had not stopped, nor was it likely to stop, in its career. Down and still down, it came. It had already buried its sharp edge a full inch in my flesh, and my sensations grew indistinct and confused . . . The ticking of the machinery amused me. *Amused me*, I say, for my sensations now bordered upon perfect happiness . . ."

19. ***unique:*** all of one piece.

vermin frequently fastened their sharp fangs in my fingers. With the particles of the oily and spicy viand which now remained, I thoroughly rubbed the bandage wherever I could reach it; then, raising my hand from the floor, I lay breathlessly still.

At first, the ravenous animals were startled and terrified at the change—at the cessation of movement. They shrank alarmedly back; many sought the well. But this was only for a moment. I had not counted in vain upon their voracity. Observing that I remained without motion, one or two of the boldest leaped upon the framework, and smelt at the surcingle. This seemed the signal for a general rush. Forth from the well they hurried in fresh troops. They clung to the wood—they overran it, and leaped in hundreds upon my person. The measured movement of the pendulum disturbed them not at all. Avoiding its strokes, they busied themselves with the anointed bandage. They pressed—they swarmed upon me in ever accumulating heaps. They writhed upon my throat; their cold lips sought my own; I was half stifled by their thronging pressure; disgust, for which the world has no name, swelled my bosom, and chilled, with a heavy clamminess, my heart. Yet one minute, and I felt that the struggle would be over. Plainly I perceived the loosening of the bandage. I knew that in more than one place it must be already severed. With a more than human resolution I lay *still.*

Nor had I erred in my calculations—nor had I endured in vain. I at length felt that I was *free.* The surcingle hung in ribands from my body. But the stroke of the pendulum already pressed upon my bosom. It had divided the serge of the robe. It had cut through the linen beneath. Twice again it swung, and a sharp sense of pain shot through every nerve. But the moment of escape had arrived. At a wave of my hand my deliverers hurried tumultuously away. With a steady movement—cautious, sidelong, shrinking, and slow—I slid from the embrace of the bandage and beyond the reach of the scimitar. For the moment, at least, *I was free.*

Free!—and in the grasp of the Inquisition! I had scarcely stepped from my wooden bed of horror upon the stone floor of the prison, when the motion of the hellish machine ceased, and I beheld it drawn up, by some invisible force, through the ceiling. This was a lesson which I took desperately to heart. My every motion was undoubtedly watched. Free!—I had but escaped death in one form of agony, to be delivered unto worse than death in some other. With that thought I rolled my eyes nervously around on the barriers of iron that hemmed me in. Something unusual—some change which, at first, I could not appreciate distinctly—it was obvious, had taken place in the apartment. For many minutes of a dreamy and trembling abstraction, I busied myself in vain, unconnected conjecture. During this period, I became aware, for the first time, of the origin of the sulphurous light which illumined the cell. It proceeded from a fissure, about half an inch in width, extending entirely around the prison at the base of the walls, which thus appeared, and were, completely separated from the floor. I endeavored, but of course in vain, to look through the aperture.

As I arose from the attempt, the mystery of the alteration in the chamber broke at once upon my understanding. I have observed that, although the outlines of the figures upon the walls were sufficiently distinct, yet the colors seemed blurred and indefinite. These colors had now assumed, and were momentarily assuming, a startling and most intense brilliancy, that gave to the spectral and fiendish portraitures an aspect that might have thrilled even firmer nerves than my own. Demon eyes, of a wild and ghastly vivacity, glared upon me in a thousand directions, where none had been visible before, and gleamed with the lurid lustre of a fire that I could not force my imagination to regard as unreal.

Unreal!—Even while I breathed there came to my nostrils the breath of the vapor of heated iron! A suffocating odour pervaded the prison! A deeper glow settled each moment in the eyes that glared at my agonies! A richer tint of crimson diffused itself over the pictured horrors of blood. I panted! I gasped for breath! There could be no doubt of the design of my tormentors—oh! most unrelenting! oh! most demoniac of men! I shrank from the glowing metal to the centre of the cell. Amid the thought of the fiery destruction that impended, the idea of the coolness of the well came over my soul like balm. I rushed to its deadly brink. I threw my straining vision below. The glare from the enkindled roof illumined its inmost recesses. Yet, for a wild moment, did my spirit refuse to comprehend the meaning of what I saw. At length it forced—it wrestled its way into my soul—it burned itself in upon my shuddering reason. Oh! for a voice to speak!—oh! horror!—oh! any horror but this! With a shriek, I rushed from the margin, and buried my face in my hands—weeping bitterly.

The heat rapidly increased, and once again I looked up, shuddering as with a fit of the ague. There had been a second change in the cell—and now the change was obviously in the *form.* As before, it was in vain that I at first endeavoured to appreciate or understand what was taking place.

But not long was I left in doubt. The Inquisitorial vengeance had been hurried by my two-fold escape, and there was to be no more dallying with the King of Terrors. The room had been square. I saw that two of its iron angles were now acute—two, consequently, obtuse. The fearful difference quickly increased with a low rumbling or moaning sound. In an instant the apartment had shifted its form into that of a lozenge. But the alteration stopped not here—I neither hoped nor desired it to stop. I could have clasped the red walls to my bosom as a garment of eternal peace. "Death," I said, "any death but that of the pit!" Fool! might I not have known that *into the pit* it was the object of the burning iron to urge me? Could I resist its glow? or, if even that, could I withstand its pressure? And now, flatter and flatter grew the lozenge, with a rapidity that left me no time for contemplation. Its centre, and of course, its greatest width, came just over the yawning gulf. I shrank back—but the closing walls pressed me resistlessly onward. At length for my seared and writhing body there was no longer an inch of foothold on the firm floor of the prison. I struggled no more, but the agony of my soul found vent in one loud, long, and final scream of despair. I felt that I tottered upon the brink—I averted my eyes—

There was a discordant hum of human voices! There was a loud blast as of many trumpets! There was a harsh grating as of a thousand thunders! The fiery walls rushed back! An outstretched-arm caught my own as I fell, fainting, into the abyss. It was that of General Lasalle.[20] The French army had entered Toledo. The Inquisition was in the hands of its enemies.

THE PURLOINED LETTER

◇

FIRST published in *The Gift* (January, 1845), "The Purloined Letter" was Poe's third story about his detective-hero Dupin. For comment, see the Introduction, Part V.

◇

Nil sapientiæ odiosius acumine nimio.
SENECA [1]

AT PARIS, just after dark one gusty evening in the autumn of 18—, I was enjoying the twofold luxury of meditation and a meerschaum, in company with my friend C. Auguste Dupin, in his little back library, or book-closet, *au troisième, No. 33 Rue Dunôt, Faubourg St. Germain.*[2] For one hour at least we had maintained a profound silence; while each, to any casual observer, might have seemed intently and exclusively occupied with the curling eddies of smoke that oppressed the atmosphere of the chamber. For myself, however, I was mentally discussing certain topics which had formed matter for conversation between us at an earlier period of the evening; I mean the affair of the Rue Morgue, and the mystery attending the murder of Marie Rogêt. I looked upon it, therefore, as something of a coincidence, when the door of our apartment was thrown open and admitted our old acquaintance, Monsieur G——, the Prefect of the Parisian police.

We gave him a hearty welcome; for there was nearly half as much of the entertaining as of the contemptible about the man, and we had not seen him for several years. We had been sitting in the dark, and Dupin now arose for the purpose of lighting a lamp, but sat down again, without doing so, upon G.'s saying that he had called to consult us, or rather to ask the opinion of my friend, about some official business which had occasioned a great deal of trouble.

"If it is any point requiring reflection," observed Dupin, as he forbore to enkindle the wick, "we shall examine it to better purpose in the dark."

"That is another of your odd notions," said the Prefect, who had a fashion of calling every thing "odd" that was beyond his comprehension, and thus lived amid an absolute legion of "oddities."

"Very true," said Dupin, as he supplied his visiter with a pipe, and rolled towards him a comfortable chair.

"And what is the difficulty now?" I asked. "Nothing more in the assassination way, I hope?"

"Oh no; nothing of that nature. The fact is, the business is *very* simple indeed, and I make no

20. General Lasalle: the Comte de Lasalle (1775–1809), a divisional general in the Peninsular War. Only on the literal level does the General's rescue of the hero constitute a "U.S. Cavalry" ending. As a record of nightmare, the story has reached that point where the dreamer must "escape" by awakening.

THE PURLOINED LETTER. **1. Seneca**: The epigraph, not located in Seneca, means, "Nothing is more repugnant to learning than too much insight." **2. At . . . *St. Germain:*** As established in "The Murders in the Rue Morgue" (1841), Dupin and the narrator live in a "time-eaten and grotesque mansion . . . tottering to its fall in a retired and desolate portion of the Faubourg St. Germain." They occupy the fourth floor only and go out only at night; during the day, they shutter the windows and in feeble candlelight, "busy their souls in dreams." Dupin is, in short, a Roderick Usher.

doubt that we can manage it sufficiently well ourselves; but then I thought Dupin would like to hear the details of it, because it is so excessively *odd.*"

"Simple and odd," said Dupin.

"Why, yes; and not exactly that either. The fact is, we have all been a good deal puzzled because the affair *is* so simple, and yet baffles us altogether."

"Perhaps it is the very simplicity of the thing which puts you at fault," said my friend.

"What nonsense you *do* talk!" replied the Prefect, laughing heartily.

"Perhaps the mystery is a little *too* plain," said Dupin.

"Oh, good heavens! who ever heard of such an idea?"

"A little *too* self-evident."

"Ha! ha! ha!—ha! ha! ha!—ho! ho! ho!"—roared our visiter, profoundly amused, "oh, Dupin, you will be the death of me yet!"

"And what, after all, *is* the matter on hand?" I asked.

"Why, I will tell you," replied the Prefect, as he gave a long, steady, and contemplative puff, and settled himself in his chair. "I will tell you in a few words; but, before I begin, let me caution you that this is an affair demanding the greatest secrecy, and that I should most probably lose the position I now hold, were it known that I confided it to any one."

"Proceed," said I.

"Or not," said Dupin.

"Well, then; I have received personal information, from a very high quarter, that a certain document of the last importance, has been purloined from the royal apartments. The individual who purloined it is known; this beyond a doubt; he was seen to take it. It is known, also, that it still remains in his possession."

"How is this known?" asked Dupin.

"It is clearly inferred," replied the Prefect, "from the nature of the document, and from the non-appearance of certain results which would at once arise from its passing *out* of the robber's possession;—that is to say, from his employing it as he must design in the end to employ it."

"Be a little more explicit," I said.

"Well, I may venture so far as to say that the paper gives its holder a certain power in a certain quarter where such power is immensely valuable." The Prefect was fond of the cant of diplomacy.

"Still I do not quite understand," said Dupin.

"No? Well; the disclosure of the document to a third person, who shall be nameless, would bring in question the honor of a personage of most exalted station; and this fact gives the holder of the document an ascendancy over the illustrious personage whose honor and peace are so jeopardized."

"But this ascendancy," I interposed, "would depend upon the robber's knowledge of the loser's knowledge of the robber. Who would dare—"

"The thief," said G., "is the Minister D——, who dares all things, those unbecoming as well as those becoming a man. The method of the theft was not less ingenious than bold. The document in question—a letter, to be frank—had been received by the personage robbed while alone in the royal *boudoir*. During its perusal she was suddenly interrupted by the entrance of the other exalted personage from whom especially it was her wish to conceal it. After a hurried and vain endeavor to thrust it in a drawer, she was forced to place it, open it was, upon a table. The address, however was uppermost, and, the contents thus unexposed, the letter escaped notice. At this juncture enters the Minister D——. His lynx eye immediately perceives the paper, recognizes the handwriting of the address, observes the confusion of the personage addressed, and fathoms her secret.[3] After some business transactions, hurried through in his ordinary manner, he produces a letter somewhat similar to the one in question, opens it, pretends to read it, and then places it in close juxtaposition to the other. Again he converses, for some fifteen minutes, upon the public affairs. At length, in taking leave, he takes also from the table the letter to which he had no claim. Its rightful owner saw, but, of course, dared not call attention to the act, in the presence of the third personage who stood at her elbow. The minister decamped; leaving his own letter—one of no importance—upon the table."

"Here, then," said Dupin to me, "you have precisely what you demand to make the ascendancy complete—the robber's knowledge of the loser's knowledge of the robber."

"Yes," replied the Prefect; "and the power thus attained has, for some months past, been wielded, for political purposes, to a very dangerous extent. The personage robbed is more thoroughly convinced, every day, of the necessity of reclaiming her letter. But this, of course, cannot be done openly. In fine, driven to despair, she has committed the matter to me."

"Than whom," said Dupin, amid a perfect whirlwind of smoke, "no more sagacious agent could, I suppose, be desired, or even imagined."

"You flatter me," replied the Prefect; "but it

3. **At . . . secret:** The Minister D—— here gives a demonstration of the instant and intuitive penetration which characterizes Dupin.

is possible that some such opinion may have been entertained."

"It is clear," said I, "as you observe, that the letter is still in the possession of the Minister; since it is this possession, and not any employment of the letter, which bestows the power. With the employment the power departs."

"True," said G.; "and upon this conviction I proceeded. My first care was to make thorough search of the Minister's hotel; and here my chief embarrassment lay in the necessity of searching without his knowledge. Beyond all things, I have been warned of the danger which would result from giving him reason to suspect our design."

"But," said I, "you are quite *au fait* in these investigations. The Parisian police have done this thing often before."

"O yes; and for this reason I did not despair. The habits of the Minister gave me, too, a great advantage. He is frequently absent from home all night. His servants are by no means numerous. They sleep at a distance from their master's apartment, and, being chiefly Neapolitans, are readily made drunk. I have keys, as you know, with which I can open any chamber or cabinet in Paris. For three months a night has not passed, during the greater part of which I have not been engaged, personally, in ransacking the D—— Hôtel. My honor is interested, and, to mention a great secret, the reward is enormous. So I did not abandon the search until I had become fully satisfied that the thief is a more astute man than myself. I fancy that I have investigated every nook and corner of the premises in which it is possible that the paper can be concealed."

"But is it not possible," I suggested, "that although the letter may be in possession of the Minister, as it unquestionably is, he may have concealed it elsewhere than upon his own premises?"

"This is barely possible," said Dupin. "The present peculiar condition of affairs at court, and especially of those intrigues in which D—— is known to be involved, would render the instant availability of the document—its susceptibility of being produced at a moment's notice—a point of nearly equal importance with its possession."

"Its susceptibility of being produced?" said I.

"That is to say, of being *destroyed,*" said Dupin.

"True," I observed; "the paper is clearly then upon the premises. As for its being upon the person of the Minister, we may consider that as out of the question."

"Entirely," said the Prefect. "He has been twice waylaid, as if by foot-pads, and his person rigorously searched under my own inspection."

"You might have spared yourself this trouble," said Dupin. "D——, I presume, is not altogether a fool, and, if not, must have anticipated these waylayings, as a matter of course."

"Not *altogethe*r a fool," said G., "but then he is a poet, which I take to be only one remove from a fool."

"True," said Dupin, after a long and thoughtful whiff from his meerschaum, "although I have been guilty of certain doggerel myself."

"Suppose you detail," said I, "the particulars of your search."

"Why the fact is, we took our time, and we searched *everywhere.* I have had long experience in these affairs. I took the entire building, room by room; devoting the nights of a whole week to each. We examined, first, the furniture of each apartment. We opened every possible drawer; and I presume you know that, to a properly trained police agent, such a thing as a *secret* drawer is impossible. Any man is a dolt who permits a 'secret' drawer to escape him in a search of this kind. The thing is *so* plain. There is a certain amount of bulk —of space—to be accounted for in every cabinet. Then we have accurate rules. The fiftieth part of a line could not escape us. After the cabinets we took the chairs. The cushions we probed with the fine long needles you have seen me employ. From the tables we removed the tops."

"Why so?"

"Sometimes the top of a table, or other similarly arranged piece of furniture, is removed by the person wishing to conceal an article; then the leg is excavated, the article deposited within the cavity, and the top replaced. The bottoms and tops of bed-posts are employed in the same way."

"But could not the cavity be detected by sounding?" I asked.

"By no means, if, when the article is deposited, a sufficient wadding of cotton be placed around it. Besides, in our case, we were obliged to proceed without noise."

"But you could not have removed—you could not have taken to pieces *all* articles of furniture in which it would have been possible to make a deposit in the manner you mention. A letter may be compressed into a thin spiral roll, not differing much in shape or bulk from a large knitting-needle, and in this form it might be inserted into the rung of a chair, for example. You did not take to pieces all the chairs?"

"Certainly not; but we did better—we examined the rungs of every chair in the hotel, and, indeed the jointings of every description of furniture, by the aid of a most powerful microscope. Had there been any traces of recent disturbance we should not have failed to detect it instantly. A single grain of gimlet-dust, for example, would have been as obvious as an apple. Any disorder in the glueing—any unusual gaping in the joints—would have sufficed to insure detection."

"I presume you looked to the mirrors, between the boards and the plates, and you probed the beds and the bed-clothes, as well as the curtains and carpets."

"That of course; and when we had absolutely completed every particle of the furniture in this way, then we examined the house itself. We divided its entire surface into compartments, which we numbered, so that none might be missed; then we scrutinized each individual square inch throughout the premises, including the two houses immediately adjoining, with the microscope as before."

"The two houses adjoining!" I exclaimed; "you must have had a great deal of trouble."

"We had; but the reward offered is prodigious."

"You include the *grounds* about the houses?"

"All the grounds are paved with brick. They gave us comparatively little trouble. We examined the moss between the bricks, and found it undisturbed."

"You looked among D——'s papers, of course, and into the books of the library?"

"Certainly; we opened every package and parcel; we not only opened every book, but we turned over every leaf in each volume, not contenting ourselves with a mere shake, according to the fashion of some of our police officers. We also measured the thickness of every book-*cover,* with the most accurate admeasurement, and applied to each the most jealous scrutiny of the microscope. Had any of the bindings been recently meddled with, it would have been utterly impossible that the fact should have escaped observation. Some five or six volumes, just from the hands of the binder, we carefully probed, longitudinally, with the needles."

"You explored the floors beneath the carpets?"

"Beyond doubt. We removed every carpet, and examined the boards with the microscope."

"And the paper on the walls?"

"Yes."

"You looked into the cellars?"

"We did."

"Then," I said; "you have been making a miscalculation, and the letter is *not* upon the premises, as you suppose."

"I fear you are right there," said the Prefect. "And now, Dupin, what would you advise me to do?"

"To make a thorough re-search of the premises."

"That is absolutely needless," replied G——. "I am not more sure that I breathe than I am that the letter is not at the hotel."

"I have no better advice to give you," said Dupin. "You have, of course, an accurate description of the letter?"

"Oh, yes!"—And here the Prefect, producing a memorandum-book, proceeded to read aloud a minute account of the internal, and especially of the external, appearance of the missing document. Soon after finishing the perusal of this description, he took his departure, more entirely depressed in spirits than I had ever known the good gentleman before.

In about a month afterward he paid us another visit, and found us occupied very nearly as before. He took a pipe and a chair and entered into some ordinary conversation. At length I said;—

"Well, but G——, what of the purloined letter? I presume you have at last made up your mind that there is no such thing as overreaching the Minister?"

"Confound him, say I—yes; I made the re-examination, however, as Dupin suggested—but it was all labor lost, as I knew it would be."

"How much was the reward offered, did you say?" asked Dupin.

"Why, a very great deal—a *very* liberal reward—I don't like to say how much, precisely; but one thing I *will* say, that I wouldn't mind giving my individual check for fifty-thousand francs to any one who could obtain me that letter. The fact is, it is becoming of more and more importance every day; and the reward has been lately doubled. If it were trebled, however, I could do no more than I have done."

"Why, yes," said Dupin, drawlingly, between the whiffs of his meerschaum, "I really—think, G——, you have not exerted yourself—to the utmost in this matter. You might—do a little more, I think, eh?"

"How?—in what way?"

"Why—puff, puff—you might—puff, puff—employ counsel in the matter, eh?—puff, puff, puff. Do you remember the story they tell of Abernethy?" [4]

"No; hang Abernethy!"

"To be sure! hang him and welcome. But, once upon a time, a certain rich miser conceived the design of spunging upon this Abernethy for a medical opinion. Getting up, for this purpose, an ordinary conversation in a private company, he insinuated his case to the physician, as that of an imaginary individual.

4. **Abernethy:** John Abernethy, celebrated English surgeon (1764–1831).

" 'We will suppose,' said the miser, 'that his symptoms are such and such; now, doctor, what would *you* have directed him to take?'

" 'Take!' said Abernethy, 'why, take *advice,* to be sure.' "

"But," said the Prefect, a little discomposed, "*I* am *perfectly* willing to take advice, and to pay for it. I would *really* give fifty-thousand francs to any one who would aid me in the matter."

"In that case," replied Dupin, opening a drawer, and producing a check-book, "you may as well fill me up a check for the amount mentioned. When you have signed it, I will hand you the letter."

I was astounded. The Prefect appeared absolutely thunder-stricken. For some minutes he remained speechless and motionless, looking incredulously at my friend with open mouth, and eyes that seemed starting from their sockets; then, apparently recovering himself in some measure, he seized a pen, and after several pauses and vacant stares, finally filled up and signed a check for fifty-thousand francs, and handed it across the table to Dupin. The latter examined it carefully and deposited it in his pocket-book; then, unlocking an *escritoire,* took thence a letter and gave it to the Prefect. This functionary grasped it in a perfect agony of joy, opened it with a trembling hand, cast a rapid glance at its contents, and then, scrambling and struggling to the door, rushed at length unceremoniously from the room and from the house, without having uttered a syllable since Dupin had requested him to fill up the check.

When he had gone, my friend entered into some explanations.

"The Parisian police," he said, "are exceedingly able in their way. They are persevering, ingenious, cunning, and thoroughly versed in the knowledge which their duties seem chiefly to demand. Thus, when G—— detailed to us his mode of searching the premises at the Hôtel D——, I felt entire confidence in his having made a satisfactory investigation—so far as his labors extended."

"So far as his labors extended?" said I.

"Yes," said Dupin. "The measures adopted were not only the best of their kind, but carried out to absolute perfection. Had the letter been deposited within the range of their search, these fellows would, beyond a question, have found it."

I merely laughed—but he seemed quite serious in all that he said.

"The measures, then," he continued, "were good in their kind, and well executed; their defect lay in their being inapplicable to the case, and to the man. A certain set of highly ingenious resources are, with the Prefect, a sort of Proscrustean bed, to which he forcibly adapts his designs. But he perpetually errs by being too deep or too shallow, for the matter in hand; and many a schoolboy is a better reasoner than he. I knew one about eight years of age, whose success at guessing in the game of 'even and odd' attracted universal admiration. This game is simple, and is played with marbles. One player holds in his hand a number of these toys, and demands of another whether that number is even or odd. If the guess is right, the guesser wins one; if wrong, he loses one. The boy to whom I allude won all the marbles of the school. Of course he had some principle of guessing; and this lay in mere observation and admeasurement of the astuteness of his opponents. For example, an arrant simpleton is his opponent, and, holding up his closed hand, asks, 'Are they even or odd?' Our schoolboy replies, 'Odd,' and loses; but upon the second trial he wins, for he then says to himself, 'The simpleton had them even upon the first trial, and his amount of cunning is just sufficient to make him have them odd upon the second; I will therefore guess odd;'—he guesses odd, and wins. Now, with a simpleton a degree above the first, he would have reasoned thus: 'This fellow finds that in the first instance I guessed odd, and, in the second, he will propose to himself upon the first impulse, a simple variation from even to odd, as did the first simpleton; but then a second thought will suggest that this is too simple a variation, and finally he will decide upon putting it even as before. I will therefore guess even;'—he guesses even, and wins. Now this mode of reasoning in the schoolboy, whom his fellows termed 'lucky,'—what, in its last analysis, is it?"

"It is merely," I said, "an identification of the reasoner's intellect with that of his opponent."

"It is," said Dupin; "and, upon inquiring of the boy by what means he effected the *thorough* identification in which his success consisted, I received answer as follows: 'When I wish to find out how wise, or how stupid, or how good, or how wicked is any one, or what are his thoughts at the moment, I fashion the expression of my face, as accurately as possible, in accordance with the expression of his, and then wait to see what thoughts or sentiments arise in my mind or heart, as if to match or correspond with the expression.' This response of the schoolboy lies at the bottom of all the spurious profundity which has been attributed to Rochefoucault, to La Bougive, to Machiavelli, and to Campanella." [5]

5. **spurious . . . Campanella:** The Duc de La Rochefoucauld (1613–80) was the author of *Moral Maxims and Reflections.* The name "La Bougive" is probably an error of transcription for "La Bruyère." Jean de la Bruyère (1645–96) was a brilliant

"And the identification," I said, "of the reasoner's intellect with that of his opponent, depends, if I understand you aright, upon the accuracy with which the opponent's intellect is admeasured."

"For its practical value it depends upon this," replied Dupin; "and the Prefect and his cohort fail so frequently, first, by default of this identification, and, secondly, by ill-admeasurement, or rather through non-admeasurement, of the intellect with which they are engaged. They consider only their *own* ideas of ingenuity; and, in searching for anything hidden, advert only to the modes in which *they* would have hidden it. They are right in this much—that their own ingenuity is a faithful representative of that of *the mass;* but when the cunning of the individual felon is diverse in character from their own, the felon foils them, of course. This always happens when it is above their own, and very usually when it is below. They have no variation of principle in their investigations; at best, when urged by some unusual emergency—by some extraordinary reward—they extend or exaggerate their old modes of *practice,* without touching their principles. What, for example, in this case of D——, has been done to vary the principle of action? What is all this boring, and probing, and sounding, and scrutinizing with the microscope, and dividing the surface of the building into registered square inches—what is it all but an exaggeration *of the application* of the one principle or set of principles of search, which are based upon the one set of notions regarding human ingenuity, to which the Prefect, in the long routine of his duty, has been accustomed? Do you not see he has taken it for granted that *all* men proceed to conceal a letter,—not exactly in a gimlet-hole bored in a chair-leg—but, at least, in *some* out-of-the-way hole or corner suggested by the same tenor of thought which would urge a man to secrete a letter in a gimlet-hole bored in a chair-leg? And do you not see also, that such *recherchés* nooks for concealment are adapted only for ordinary occasions, and would be adopted only by ordinary intellects; for, in all cases of concealment, a disposal of the article concealed—a disposal of it in this *recherché* manner,—is, in the very first instance, presumable and presumed; and thus its discovery depends, not at all upon the acumen, but altogether upon the mere care, patience, and determination of the seekers; and where the case is of importance—or, what amounts to the same thing in the policial eyes, when the reward is of magnitude,—the qualities in question have *never* been known to fail. You will now understand what I meant in suggesting that, had the purloined letter been hidden anywhere within the limits of the Prefect's examination—in other words, had the principle of its concealment been comprehended within the principles of the Prefect—its discovery would have been a matter altogether beyond question. This functionary, however, has been thoroughly mystified; and the remote source of his defeat lies in the supposition that the Minister is a fool, because he has acquired renown as a poet. All fools are poets; this the Prefect *feels;* and he is merely guilty of a *non distributio medii* [6] in thence inferring that all poets are fools."

"But is this really the poet?" I asked. "There are two brothers, I know; and both have attained reputation in letters. The Minister I believe has written learnedly on the Differential Calculus. He is a mathematician, and no poet."

"You are mistaken; I know him well; he is both. As poet *and* mathematician, he would reason well; as mere mathematician, he could not have reasoned at all, and thus would have been at the mercy of the Prefect."

"You surprise me," I said, "by these opinions, which have been contradicted by the voice of the world. You do not mean to set at naught the well-digested idea of centuries. The mathematical reason has long been regarded as *the* reason *par excellence.*"

" '*Il y a à parier,*' " replied Dupin, quoting from Chamfort,[7] " '*que toute idée publique, toute convention reçue, est une sottise, car elle a convenue au plus grand nombre.*' The mathematicians, I grant you, have done their best to promulgate the popular error to which you allude, and which is none the less an error for its promulgation as truth. With an art worthy a better cause, for example, they have insinuated the term 'analysis' into application to algebra. The French are the originators of this particular deception; but if a term is of any importance—if words derive any value from applicability—then 'analysis' conveys 'algebra' about as much as, in Latin, '*ambitus*' implies 'ambition,' '*religio*' 'religion,' or '*homines honesti,*' a set of *honorable* men."

"You have a quarrel on hand, I see," said I, "with some of the algebraists of Paris; but proceed."

depicter of manners and character. Niccolò Machiavelli wrote his study of statecraft, *The Prince,* in 1513. Tommaso Campanella wrote *The City of the Sun* (1643). What these authors represent to Poe is "psychological insight."

6. *non . . . medii:* an undistributed middle; a failure of logic.

7. **Chamfort:** Nicolas Chamfort (1741–94). The quotation means, "The chances are that any popular idea, any accepted notion, is foolishness, since it has proved agreeable to the mass of mankind."

"I dispute the availability, and thus the value, of that reason which is cultivated in any especial form other than the abstractly logical. I dispute, in particular, the reason educed by mathematical study. The mathematics are the science of form and quantity; mathematical reasoning is merely logic applied to observation upon form and quantity. The great error lies in supposing that even the truths of what is called *pure* algebra, are abstract or general truths. And this error is so egregious that I am confounded at the universality with which it has been received. Mathematical axioms are *not* axioms of general truth. What is true of *relation*— of form and quantity—is often grossly false in regard to morals, for example. In this latter science it is very usually *un*true that the aggregated parts are equal to the whole. In chemistry also the axiom fails. In the consideration of motive it fails; for two motives, each of a given value, have not, necessarily, a value when united, equal to the sum of their values apart. There are numerous other mathematical truths which are only truths within the limits of *relation*. But the mathematician argues from his *finite truths,* through habit, as if they were of an absolutely general applicability—as the world indeed imagines them to be. Bryant, in his very learned 'Mythology,' mentions an analogous source of error, when he says that 'although the Pagan fables are not believed, yet we forget ourselves continually, and make inferences from them as existing realities.' With the algebraists, however, who are Pagans themselves, the 'Pagan fables' *are* believed, and the inferences are made, not so much through lapse of memory as through an unaccountable addling of the brains. In short, I never yet encountered the mere mathematician who would be trusted out of equal roots, or one who did not clandestinely hold it as a point of his faith that $x^2 + px$ was absolutely and unconditionally equal to q. Say to one of these gentlemen, by way of experiment, if you please, that you believe occasions may occur where $x^2 + px$ is *not* altogether equal to q, and, having made him understand what you mean, get out of his reach as speedily as convenient, for, beyond doubt, he will endeavor to knock you down.

"I mean to say," continued Dupin, while I merely laughed at his last observations, "that if the Minister had been no more than a mathematician, the Prefect would have been under no necessity of giving me this check. I knew him, however, as both mathematician and poet, and my measures were adapted to his capacity, with reference to the circumstances by which he was surrounded. I knew him as a courtier, too, and as a bold *intriguant.* Such a man, I considered, could not fail to be aware of the ordinary policial modes of action. He could not have failed to anticipate—and events have proved that he did not fail to anticipate—the waylayings to which he was subjected. He must have foreseen, I reflected, the secret investigations of his premises. His frequent absences from home at night, which were hailed by the Prefect as certain aids to his success, I regarded only as *ruses,* to afford opportunity for thorough search to the police, and thus the sooner to impress them with the conviction to which G——, in fact, did finally arrive—the conviction that the letter was not upon the premises. I felt, also, that the whole train of thought, which I was at some pains in detailing to you just now, concerning the invariable principle of policial action in searches for articles concealed—I felt that this whole train of thought would necessarily pass through the mind of the Minister. It would imperatively lead him to despise all the ordinary *nooks* of concealment. *He* could not, I reflected, be so weak as not to see that the most intricate and remote recess of his hotel would be as open as his commonest closets to the eyes, to the probes, to the gimlets, and to the microscopes of the Prefect. I saw, in fine, that he would be driven, as a matter of course, to *simplicity,* if not deliberately induced to it as a matter of choice. You will remember, perhaps, how desperately the Prefect laughed when I suggested, upon our first interview, that it was just possible this mystery troubled him so much on account of its being so *very* self-evident."

"Yes," said I, "I remember his merriment well. I really thought he would have fallen into convulsions."

"The material world," continued Dupin, "abounds with very strict analogies to the immaterial; and thus some color of truth has been given to the rhetorical dogma, that metaphor, or simile, may be made to strengthen an argument as well as to embellish a description. The principle of the *vis inertiæ,* for example, seems to be identical in physics and metaphysics. It is not more true in the former, that a large body is with more difficulty set in motion than a smaller one, and that its subsequent *momentum* is commensurate with this difficulty, than it is, in the latter, that intellects of the vaster capacity, while more forcible, more constant, and more eventful in their movements than those of inferior grade, are yet the less readily moved, and more embarrassed and full of hesitation in the first few steps of their progress. Again: have you ever noticed which of the street signs, over the shop doors, are the most attractive of attention?"

"I have never given the matter a thought," I said.

"There is a game of puzzles," he resumed, "which is played upon a map. One party playing requires another to find a given word—the name of town, river, state or empire—any word, in short, upon the motley and perplexed surface of the chart. A novice in the game generally seeks to embarrass his opponents by giving them the most minutely lettered names; but the adept selects such words as stretch, in large characters, from one end of the chart to the other. These, like the over-largely lettered signs and placards of the street, escape observation by dint of being excessively obvious; and here the physical oversight is precisely analogous with the moral inapprehension by which the intellect suffers to pass unnoticed those considerations which are too obtrusively and too palpably self-evident. But this is a point, it appears, somewhat above or beneath the understanding of the Prefect. He never once thought it probable, or possible, that the Minister had deposited the letter immediately beneath the nose of the whole world, by way of best preventing any portion of that world from perceiving it.

"But the more I reflected upon the daring, dashing, and discriminating ingenuity of D——; upon the fact that the document must always have been *at hand,* if he intended to use it to good purpose; and upon the decisive evidence, obtained by the Prefect, that it was not hidden within the limits of that dignitary's ordinary search—the more satisfied I became that, to conceal this letter, the Minister had resorted to the comprehensive and sagacious expedient of not attempting to conceal it at all.

"Full of these ideas, I prepared myself with a pair of green spectacles,[8] and called one fine morning, quite by accident, at the Ministerial hotel. I found D—— at home, yawning, lounging, and dawdling, as usual, and pretending to be in the last extremity of *ennui*. He is, perhaps, the most really energetic human being now alive—but that is only when nobody sees him.

"To be even with him, I complained of my weak eyes, and lamented the necessity of the spectacles, under cover of which I cautiously and thoroughly surveyed the whole apartment, while seemingly intent only upon the conversation of my host.

"I paid especial attention to a large writing-table near which he sat, and upon which lay confusedly, some miscellaneous letters and other papers, with one or two musical instruments and a few books. Here, however, after a long and a very deliberate scrutiny, I saw nothing to excite particular suspicion.

"At length my eyes, in going the circuit of the room, fell upon a trumpery filigree card-rack of pasteboard, that hung dangling by a dirty blue ribbon, from a little brass knob just beneath the middle of the mantel-piece. In this rack, which had three or four compartments, were five or six visiting cards and a solitary letter. This last was much soiled and crumpled. It was torn nearly in two, across the middle—as if a design, in the first instance, to tear it entirely up as worthless, had been altered, or stayed, in the second. It had a large black seal, bearing the D—— cipher *very* conspicuously, and was addressed, in a diminutive female hand, to D——, the Minister, himself. It was thrust carelessly, and even, as it seemed, contemptuously, into one of the upper divisions of the rack.

"No sooner had I glanced at this letter than I concluded it to be that of which I was in search. To be sure, it was, to all appearance, radically different from the one of which the Prefect had read us so minute a description. Here the seal was large and black, with the D—— cipher; there it was small and red, with the ducal arms of the S—— family. Here, the address, to the Minister, was diminutive and feminine; there the superscription, to a certain royal personage, was markedly bold and decided; the size alone formed a point of correspondence. But, then, the *radicalness* of these differences, which was excessive; the dirt; the soiled and torn condition of the paper, so inconsistent with the *true* methodical habits of D——, and so suggestive of a design to delude the beholder into an idea of the worthlessness of the document;—these things, together with the hyper-obtrusive situation of this document, full in the view of every visiter, and thus exactly in accordance with the conclusions to which I had previously arrived; these things, I say, were strongly corroborative of suspicion, in one who came with the intention to suspect.

"I protracted my visit as long as possible, and, while I maintained a most animated discussion with the Minister, upon a topic which I knew well had never failed to interest and excite him, I kept my attention really riveted upon the letter. In this examination, I committed to memory its external appearance and arrangement in the rack; and also fell, at length, upon a discovery which set at rest whatever trivial doubt I might have entertained. In scrutinizing the edges of the paper, I observed them to be more *chafed* than seemed

8. **green spectacles:** Such spectacles are also worn by Dupin in "The Mystery of Marie Roget," and by the Devil in "Bon-Bon." The implication is that Dupin's visit to the Minister is an act of introspection.

necessary. They presented the *broken* appearance which is manifested when a stiff paper, having been once folded and pressed with a folder, is refolded in a reversed direction, in the same creases or edges which had formed the original fold. This discovery was sufficient. It was clear to me that the letter had been turned, as a glove, inside out, re-directed, and re-sealed. I bade the Minister good morning, and took my departure at once, leaving a gold snuff-box upon the table.

"The next morning I called for the snuff-box, when we resumed, quite eagerly, the conversation of the preceding day. While thus engaged, however, a loud report, as if of a pistol, was heard immediately beneath the windows of the hotel, and was succeeded by a series of fearful screams, and the shoutings of a mob. D—— rushed to a casement, threw it open, and looked out. In the meantime I stepped to the card-rack, took the letter, put it in my pocket, and replaced it by a *fac-simile,* (so far as regards externals) which I had carefully prepared at my lodgings; imitating the D— cipher, very readily, by means of a seal formed of bread.

"The disturbance in the street had been occasioned by the frantic behavior of a man with a musket. He had fired it among a crowd of women and children. It proved, however, to have been without ball, and the fellow was suffered to go his way as a lunatic or a drunkard. When he had gone, D—— came from the window, whither I had followed him immediately upon securing the object in view. Soon afterward I bade him farewell. The pretended lunatic was a man in my own pay."

"But what purpose had you," I asked, "in replacing the letter by a *fac-simile?* Would it not have been better, at the first visit, to have seized it openly, and departed?"

"D——," replied Dupin, "is a desperate man, and a man of nerve. His hotel, too, is not without attendants devoted to his interests. Had I made the wild attempt you suggest, I might never have left the Ministerial presence alive. The good people of Paris might have heard of me no more. But I had an object apart from these considerations. You know my political prepossessions. In this matter, I act as a partisan of the lady concerned. For eighteen months the Minister has had her in his power. She has now him in hers; since, being unaware that the letter is not in his possession, he will proceed with his exactions as if it was. Thus will he inevitably commit himself, at once, to his political destruction. His downfall, too, will not be more precipitate than awkward. It is all very well to talk about the *facilis descensus Averni;* [9] but in all kinds of climbing, as Catalani [10] said of singing, it is far more easy to get up than to come down. In the present instance I have no sympathy—at least no pity—for him who descends. He is that *monstrum horrendum,*[11] an unprincipled man of genius. I confess, however, that I should like very well to know the precise character of his thoughts, when, being defied by her whom the Prefect terms 'a certain personage,' he is reduced to opening the letter which I left for him in the card-rack."

"How? did you put any thing particular in it?"

"Why—it did not seem altogether right to leave the interior blank—that would have been insulting. D——, at Vienna once, did me an evil turn, which I told him, quite good-humoredly, that I should remember. So, as I knew he would feel some curiosity in regard to the identity of the person who had outwitted him, I thought it a pity not to give him a clew. He is well acquainted with my MS., and I just copied into the middle of the blank sheet the words—

——Un dessein si funeste,
S'il n'est digne d'Atrée, est digne de Thyeste.[12]

They are to be found in Crébillon's *Atrée.*"

THE DOMAIN OF ARNHEIM

◇

THE FIRST part of "The Domain of Arnheim" appeared in 1842, under the title "The Landscape Garden"; Andrew Jackson Downing had just published his *Treatise on the Theory and Practice of Landscape-Gardening,* and there was widespread interest in the subject. With a few revisions, and with the addition of the river journey to Arnheim, the piece reappeared as now titled in the *Columbian Lady's and Gentleman's Magazine* for March, 1847. For comment, see the Introduction, Part IV.

◇

9. ***facilis . . . Averni:*** a quotation from Vergil, meaning "the descent to the infernal regions is easy" (*Aeneid,* VI.126)
10. **Catalani:** Angelica Catalani, Italian singer (1780–1849).
11. ***monstrum horrendum:*** "fearful monster." Also Vergilian.
12. **Un . . . Thyeste:** The quotation is taken from Prosper Jolyot de Crébillon's tragedy of 1707, *Atrée et Thyeste,* V.iv. It may be translated, "So dreadful a plot, / If unworthy of Atreus, is quite worthy of Thyestes." Crébillon's play is based upon the bloody rivalry of King Atreus of Mycenae and his brother Thyestes, and Poe's citation of it is a final hint that Dupin and the Minister are "brothers" or doubles.

The garden like a lady fair was cut,
  That lay as if she slumbered in delight,
And to the open skies her eyes did shut.
  The azure fields of Heaven were 'sembled right
  In a large round set with the flowers of light.
The flowers de luce and the round sparks of dew
That hung upon their azure leaves did shew
Like twinkling stars that sparkle in the evening blue.

GILES FLETCHER [1]

FROM his cradle to his grave a gale of prosperity bore my friend Ellison along. Nor do I use the word prosperity in its mere worldly sense. I mean it as synonymous with happiness. The person of whom I speak seemed born for the purpose of foreshadowing the doctrines of Turgot, Price, Priestley and Condorcet [2]—of exemplifying by individual instance what has been deemed the chimera of the perfectionists. In the brief existence of Ellison I fancy that I have seen refuted the dogma, that in man's very nature lies some hidden principle, the antagonist of bliss. An anxious examination of his career has given me to understand that, in general, from the violation of a few simple laws of humanity arises the wretchedness of mankind—that as a species we have in our possession the as yet unwrought elements of content—and that, even now, in the present darkness and madness of all thought on the great question of the social condition, it is not impossible that man, the individual, under certain unusual and highly fortuitous conditions, may be happy.

With opinions such as these my young friend, too, was fully imbued; and thus it is worthy of observation that the uninterrupted enjoyment which distinguished his life was, in great measure, the result of preconcert. It is, indeed, evident that with less of the instinctive philosophy which, now and then, stands so well in the stead of experience, Mr. Ellison would have found himself precipitated, by the very extraordinary success of his life, into the common vortex of unhappiness which yawns for those of pre-eminent endowments. But it is by no means my object to pen an essay on happiness. The ideas of my friend may be summed up in a few words. He admitted but four elementary principles, or, more strictly, conditions, of bliss. That which he considered chief was (strange to say!) the simple and purely physical one of free exercise in the open air. "The health," he said, "attainable by other means is scarcely worth the name." He instanced the ecstasies of the fox-hunter, and pointed to the tillers of the earth, the only people who, as a class, can be fairly considered happier than others. His second condition was the love of woman. His third, and most difficult of realization, was the contempt of ambition. His fourth was an object of unceasing pursuit; and he held that, other things being equal, the extent of attainable happiness was in proportion to the spirituality of this object.

Ellison was remarkable in the continuous profusion of good gifts lavished upon him by fortune. In personal grace and beauty he exceeded all men. His intellect was of that order to which the acquisition of knowledge is less a labor than an intuition and a necessity. His family was one of the most illustrious of the empire. His bride was the loveliest and most devoted of women. His possessions had been always ample; but, on the attainment of his majority, it was discovered that one of those extraordinary freaks of fate had been played in his behalf which startle the whole social world amid which they occur, and seldom fail radically to alter the moral constitution of those who are their objects.

It appears that, about a hundred years before Mr. Ellison's coming of age, there had died, in a remote province, one Mr. Seabright Ellison. This gentleman had amassed a princely fortune, and, having no immediate connections, conceived the whim of suffering his wealth to accumulate for a century after his decease. Minutely and sagaciously directing the various modes of investment, he bequeathed the aggregate amount to the nearest of blood, bearing the name Ellison, who should be alive at the end of the hundred years. Many attempts had been made to set aside this singular bequest; their *ex post facto* character rendered them abortive; but the attention of a jealous government was aroused, and a legislative act finally obtained, forbidding all similar accumulations. This act, however, did not prevent young Ellison from entering into possession, on his twenty-first birth-day, as the heir of his ancestor Seabright, of a fortune of *four hundred and fifty millions of dollars.*[3]

THE DOMAIN OF ARNHEIM. 1. **The . . . Fletcher:** The epigraph is Stanza 42 of Fletcher's allegorical poem, "Christ's Victorie on Earth" (1610). 2. **doctrines . . . Condorcet:** Anne Robert Jacques Turgot, Richard Price, Joseph Priestley, and the Marquis de Condorcet were eighteenth-century political economists. Poe reeled off the same names, in the same order, in his early burlesque, "Lionizing." Collectively, they stood in Poe's mind for the idea—antipathetic to him—of human perfectibility.

3. **It . . . *dollars:*** "An incident, similar in outline to the one here imagined, occurred, not very long ago, in England. The name of the fortunate heir was Thelluson. I first saw an account of this matter in the 'Tour' of Prince Pückler-Muskau, who makes the sum inherited *ninety millions of pounds*, and justly observes that 'in the contemplation of so vast a sum, and of the services to which it might be applied, there is something even of the sublime.' To suit the views of this article I have followed the Prince's statement, although a grossly exaggerated one. The germ, and, in fact, the commencement of the present paper was published many years ago—previous to the issue of the first number of Sue's admirable '*Juif Errant*,' which may possibly have been suggested to him by Muskau's account" [P]. The name Ellison may have derived from a coalescence, in Poe's mind, of

When it had become known that such was the enormous wealth inherited, there were, of course, many speculations as to the mode of its disposal. The magnitude and the immediate availability of the sum bewildered all who thought on the topic. The possessor of any *appreciable* amount of money might have been imagined to perform any one of a thousand things. With riches merely surpassing those of any citizen, it would have been easy to suppose him engaging to supreme excess in the fashionable extravagances of his time—or busying himself with political intrigue—or aiming at ministerial power—or purchasing increase of nobility—or collecting large museums of *virtù*—or playing the munificent patron of letters, of science, of art—or endowing, and bestowing his name upon, extensive institutions of charity. But for the inconceivable wealth in the actual possession of the heir, these objects and all ordinary objects were felt to afford too limited a field. Recourse was had to figures, and these but sufficed to confound. It was seen that, even at three per cent, the annual income of the inheritance amounted to no less than thirteen millions and five hundred thousand dollars; which was one million and one hundred and twenty-five thousand per month; or thirty-six thousand nine hundred and eighty-six per day; or one thousand five hundred and forty-one per hour; or six and twenty dollars for every minute that flew. Thus the usual track of supposition was thoroughly broken up. Men knew not what to imagine. There were some who even conceived that Mr. Ellison would divest himself of at least one half of his fortune, as of utterly superfluous opulence—enriching whole troops of his relatives by division of his superabundance. To the nearest of these he did, in fact, abandon the very unusual wealth which was his own before the inheritance.

I was not surprised, however, to perceive that he had long made up his mind on a point which had occasioned so much discussion to his friends. Nor was I greatly astonished at the nature of his decision. In regard to individual charities he had satisfied his conscience. In the possibility of any improvement, properly so called, being effected by man himself in the general condition of man, he had (I am sorry to confess it) little faith. Upon the whole, whether happily or unhappily, he was thrown back, in very great measure, upon self.

In the widest and noblest sense he was a poet. He comprehended, moreover, the true character, the august aims, the supreme majesty and dignity of the poetic sentiment. The fullest, if not the sole proper satisfaction of this sentiment he instinctively felt to lie in the creation of novel forms of beauty. Some peculiarities, either in his early education, or in the nature of his intellect, had tinged with what is termed materialism all his ethical speculations; and it was this bias, perhaps, which led him to believe that the most advantageous at least, if not the sole legitimate field for the poetic exercise, lies in the creation of novel moods of purely *physical* loveliness. Thus it happened he became neither musician nor poet—if we use this latter term in its every-day acceptation. Or it might have been that he neglected to become either, merely in pursuance of his idea that in contempt of ambition is to be found one of the essential principles of happiness on earth. Is it not, indeed, possible that, while a high order of genius is necessarily ambitious, the highest is above that which is termed ambition? And may it not thus happen that many far greater than Milton have contentedly remained "mute and inglorious?" I believe that the world has never seen—and that, unless through some series of accidents goading the noblest order of mind into distasteful exertion, the world will never see—that full extent of triumphant execution, in the richer domains of art, of which the human nature is absolutely capable.

Ellison became neither musician nor poet; although no man lived more profoundly enamored of music and poetry. Under other circumstances than those which invested him, it is not impossible that he would have become a painter. Sculpture, although in its nature rigorously poetical, was too limited in its extent and consequences, to have occupied, at any time, much of his attention. And I have now mentioned all the provinces in which the common understanding of the poetic sentiment has declared it capable of expatiating. But Ellison maintained that the richest, the truest, and most natural, if not altogether the most extensive province, had been unaccountably neglected. No definition had spoken of the landscape-gardener as of the poet; yet it seemed to my friend that the creation of the landscape-garden offered to the proper Muse the most magnificent of opportunities. Here, indeed, was the fairest field for the display of imagination in the endless combining of forms of novel beauty; the elements to enter into combination being, by a vast superiority, the most glorious which the earth could afford. In the multiform and multicolor of the flower and the trees, he recognized the most direct and energetic efforts of Nature at physi-

"Thellusson" and "T. H. Ellis." The latter name belonged to the son of John Allan's business partner. Unlike Poe, T. H. Ellis derived an inheritance from the profits of the firm of Ellis & Allan. Across from the Ellis's Richmond dwelling was a large and beautiful garden, owned by John Allan but tended by the Ellis gardener. The young Poe, and his young friend Ellis, frequently played there.

cal loveliness. And in the direction or concentration of this effort—or, more properly, in its adaptation to the eyes which were to behold it on earth—he perceived that he should be employing the best means—laboring to the greatest advantage—in the fulfilment, not only of his own destiny as poet, but of the august purposes for which the Deity had implanted the poetic sentiment in man.

"Its adaptation to the eyes which were to behold it on earth." In his explanation of this phraseology, Mr. Ellison did much toward solving what has always seemed to me an enigma:—I mean the fact (which none but the ignorant dispute) that no such combination of scenery exists in nature as the painter of genius may produce. No such paradises are to be found in reality as have glowed on the canvas of Claude. In the most enchanting of natural landscapes, there will always be found a defect or an excess—many excesses and defects. While the component parts may defy, individually, the highest skill of the artist, the arrangement of these parts will always be susceptible of improvement. In short, no position can be attained on the wide surface of the *natural* earth, from which an artistical eye, looking steadily, will not find matter of offence in what is termed the "composition" of the landscape. And yet how unintelligible is this! In all other matters we are justly instructed to regard nature as supreme. With her details we shrink from competition. Who shall presume to imitate the colors of the tulip, or to improve the proportions of the lily of the valley? The criticism which says, of sculpture or portraiture, that here nature is to be exalted or idealized rather than imitated, is in error. No pictorial or sculptural combinations of points of human loveliness do more than approach the living and breathing beauty. In landscape alone is the principle of the critic true, and, having felt its truth here, it is but the headlong spirit of generalization which has led him to pronounce it true throughout all the domains of art. Having, I say, *felt* its truth here; for the feeling is no affectation or chimera. The mathematics afford no more absolute demonstrations than the sentiment of his art yields the artist. He not only believes, but positively knows, that such and such apparently arbitrary arrangements of matter constitute and alone constitute the true beauty. His reasons, however, have not yet been matured into expression. It remains for a more profound analysis than the world has yet seen, fully to investigate and express them. Nevertheless he is confirmed in his instinctive opinions by the voice of all his brethren. Let a "composition" be defective; let an emendation be wrought in its mere arrangement of form; let this emendation be submitted to every artist in the world; by each will its necessity be admitted. And even far more than this:—in remedy of the defective composition, each insulated member of the fraternity would have suggested the identical emendation.

I repeat that in landscape arrangements alone is the physical nature susceptible of exaltation, and that, therefore, her susceptibility of improvement at this one point, was a mystery I had been unable to solve. My own thoughts on the subject had rested in the idea that the primitive intention of nature would have so arranged the earth's surface as to have fulfilled at all points man's sense of perfection in the beautiful, the sublime, or the picturesque; but that this primitive intention had been frustrated by the known geological disturbances—disturbances of form and color-grouping, in the correction or allaying of which lies the soul of art. The force of this idea was much weakened, however, by the necessity which it involved of considering the disturbances abnormal and unadapted to any purpose. It was Ellison who suggested that they were prognostic of *death*. He thus explained:—Admit the earthly immortality of man to have been the first intention. We have then the primitive arrangement of the earth's surface adapted to his blissful estate, as not existent but designed. The disturbances were the preparations for his subsequently conceived deathful condition.

"Now," said my friend, "what we regard as exaltation of the landscape may be really such, as respects only the moral or human *point of view*. Each alteration of the natural scenery may possibly effect a blemish in the picture, if we can suppose this picture viewed at large—in mass—from some point distant from the earth's surface, although not beyond the limits of its atmosphere. It is easily understood that what might improve a closely scrutinized detail, may at the same time injure a general or more distinctly observed effect. There *may* be a class of beings, human once, but now invisible to humanity, to whom, from afar, our disorder may seem order—our unpicturesqueness picturesque; in a word, the earth-angels, for whose scrutiny more especially than our own, and for whose death-refined appreciation of the beautiful, may have been set in array by God the wide landscape-gardens of the hemispheres."

In the course of discussion, my friend quoted some passages from a writer on landscape-gardening, who has been supposed to have well treated his theme:

" 'There are properly but two styles of landscape-gardening, the natural and the artificial. One seeks to recall the original beauty of the country, by adapting its means to the surrounding scenery; cultivating trees in harmony with the hills or plains of the neighboring land; detecting and bringing into practice those nice relations of size, proportion and color which, hid from the common observer, are revealed everywhere to the experienced student of nature. The result of the natural style of gardening, is seen rather in the absence of all defects and incongruities—in the prevalence of a healthy harmony and order—than in the creation of any special wonders or miracles. The artificial style has as many varieties as there are different tastes to gratify. It has a certain general relation to the various styles of building. There are the stately avenues and retirements of Versailles; Italian terraces; and a various mixed old English style, which bears some relation to the domestic Gothic or English Elizabethan architecture. Whatever may be said against the abuses of the artificial landscape-gardening, a mixture of pure art in the garden scene adds to it a great beauty. This is partly pleasing to the eye, by the show of order and design, and partly moral. A terrace, with an old moss-covered balustrade, calls up at once to the eye the fair forms that have passed there in other days. The slightest exhibition of art is an evidence of care and human interest.'

"From what I have already observed," said Ellison, "you will understand that I reject the idea, here expressed, of recalling the original beauty of the country. The original beauty is never so great as that which may be introduced. Of course, everything depends on the selection of a spot with capabilities. What is said about detecting and bringing into practice nice relations of size, proportion, and color, is one of those mere vaguenesses of speech which serve to veil inaccuracy of thought. The phrase quoted may mean anything, or nothing, and guides in no degree. That the true result of the natural style of gardening is seen rather in the absence of all defects and incongruities than in the creation of any special wonders or miracles, is a proposition better suited to the grovelling apprehension of the herd than to the fervid dreams of the man of genius. The negative merit suggested appertains to that hobbling criticism which, in letters, would elevate Addison into apotheosis. In truth, while that virtue which consists in the mere avoidance of vice appeals directly to the understanding, and can thus be circumscribed in *rule,* the loftier virtue, which flames in creation, can be apprehended in its results alone. Rule applies but to the merits of denial—to the excellencies which refrain. Beyond these the critical art can but suggest. We may be instructed to build a "Cato," but we are in vain told *how* to conceive a Parthenon or an *Inferno.* The thing done, however; the wonder accomplished; and the capacity for apprehension becomes universal. The sophists of the negative school who, through inability to create, have scoffed at creation, are now found the loudest in applause. What, in its chrysalis condition of principle, affronted their demure reason, never fails, in its maturity of accomplishment, to extort admiration from their instinct of beauty.

"The author's observations on the artificial style," continued Ellison, "are less objectionable. A mixture of pure art in a garden scene adds to it a great beauty. This is just; as also is the reference to the sense of human interest. The principle expressed is incontrovertible—but there *may* be something beyond it. There may be an object in keeping with the principle—an object unattainable by the means ordinarily possessed by individuals, yet which, if attained, would lend a charm to the landscape-garden far surpassing that which a sense of merely human interest could bestow. A poet, having very unusual pecuniary resources, might, while retaining the necessary idea of art, or culture, or, as our author expresses it, of interest, so imbue his designs at once with extent and novelty of beauty, as to convey the sentiment of spiritual interference. It will be seen that, in bringing about such result, he secures all the advantages of interest or *design*, while relieving his work of the harshness or technicality of the worldly *art*. In the most rugged of wildernesses—in the most savage of the scenes of pure nature—there is apparent the *art* of a creator; yet this art is apparent to reflection only; in no respect has it the obvious force of a feeling. Now let us suppose this sense of the Almighty design to be *one step depressed*—to be brought into something like harmony or consistency with the sense of human art—to form an intermedium between the two:—let us imagine, for example, a landscape whose combined vastness and definitiveness—whose united beauty, magnificence, and *strangeness,* shall convey the idea of care, or culture, or superintendence, on the part of beings superior, yet akin to humanity—then the sentiment of *interest* is preserved, while the art intervolved is made to assume the air of an intermediate or secondary nature—a nature which is not God, nor an emanation from God, but which still is nature in the sense of the handiwork of the angels that hover between man and God." [4]

It was in devoting his enormous wealth to the embodiment of a vision such as this—in the free exercise in the open air ensured by the personal superintendence of his plans—in the unceasing object which these plans afforded—in the high spiritu-

4. **"Now . . . God":** Ellison's choice of an art which mediates between the human and the divine accords with the implicit ideas of "Ligeia" and "Israfel," and the explicit thought of "Al Aaraaf."

ality of the object—in the contempt of ambition which it enabled him truly to feel—in the perennial springs with which it gratified, without possibility of satiating, that one master passion of his soul, the thirst for beauty; above all, it was in the sympathy of a woman, not unwomanly, whose loveliness and love enveloped his existence in the purple atmosphere of Paradise, that Ellison thought to find, *and found*, exemption from the ordinary cases of humanity, with a far greater amount of positive happiness than ever glowed in the rapt day-dreams of De Staël.

I despair of conveying to the reader any distinct conception of the marvels which my friend did actually accomplish. I wish to describe, but am disheartened by the difficulty of description, and hesitate between detail and generality. Perhaps the better course will be to unite the two in their extremes.

Mr. Ellison's first step regarded, of course, the choice of a locality; and scarcely had he commenced thinking on this point, when the luxuriant nature of the Pacific Islands arrested his attention. In fact, he had made up his mind for a voyage to the South Seas, when a night's reflection induced him to abandon the idea. "Were I misanthropic," he said, "such a *locale* would suit me. The thoroughness of its insulation and seclusion, and the difficulty of ingress and egress, would in such case be the charm of charms; but as yet I am not Timon.[5] I wish the composure but not the depression of solitude. There must remain with me a certain control over the extent and duration of my repose. There will be frequent hours in which I shall need, too, the sympathy of the poetic in what I have done. Let me seek, then, a spot not far from a populous city—whose vicinity, also, will best enable me to execute my plans."

In search of a suitable place so situated, Ellison travelled for several years, and I was permitted to accompany him. A thousand spots with which I was enraptured he rejected without hesitation, for reasons which satisfied me, in the end, that he was right. We came at length to an elevated table-land of wonderful fertility and beauty, affording a panoramic prospect very little less in extent than that of Ætna, and, in Ellison's opinion as well as my own, surpassing the far-famed view from that mountain in all the true elements of the picturesque.

"I am aware," said the traveller, as he drew a sigh of deep delight after gazing on this scene, entranced, for nearly an hour, "I know that here, in my circumstances, nine-tenths of the most fastidious of men would rest content. This panorama is indeed glorious, and I should rejoice in it but for the excess of its glory. The taste of all the architects I have ever known leads them, for the sake of 'prospect,' to put up buildings on hill-tops. The error is obvious. Grandeur in any of its moods, but especially in that of extent, startles, excites—and then fatigues, depresses. For the occasional scene nothing can be better—for the constant view nothing worse. And, in the constant view, the most objectionable phase of grandeur is that of extent; the worst phase of extent, that of distance. It is at war with the sentiment and with the sense of *seclusion*—the sentiment and sense which we seek to humor in 'retiring to the country.' In looking from the summit of a mountain we cannot help feeling *abroad* in the world. The heart-sick avoid distant prospects as a pestilence."

It was not until toward the close of the fourth year of our search that we found a locality with which Ellison professed himself satisfied. It is, of course, needless to say *where* was the locality. The late death of my friend, in causing his domain to be thrown open to certain classes of visitors, has given to *Arnheim* a species of secret and subdued if not solemn celebrity, similar in kind, although infinitely superior in degree, to that which so long distinguished Fonthill.[6]

The usual approach to Arnheim was by the river. The visitor left the city in the early morning. During the forenoon he passed between shores of a tranquil and domestic beauty, on which grazed innumerable sheep, their white fleeces spotting the vivid green of rolling meadows. By degrees the idea of cultivation subsided into that of merely pastoral care. This slowly became merged in a sense of retirement—this again in a consciousness of solitude. As the evening approached the channel grew more narrow; the banks more and more precipitous; and these latter were clothed in richer, more profuse, and more sombre foliage. The water increased in transparency. The stream took a thousand turns, so that at no moment could its gleaming surface be seen for a greater distance than a furlong. At every instant the vessel seemed imprisoned within an enchanted circle, having insuperable and impenetrable walls of foliage, a roof of ultra-marine satin, and *no* floor—the keel balancing itself with admirable nicety on that of a phantom bark which, by some accident having been turned upside down, floated in constant company with the substantial one, for the purpose of sustaining it. The channel now became a *gorge*—although the term is somewhat inapplicable, and I employ it merely because

5. **Timon:** misanthropic hero of Shakespeare's play, *Timon of Athens.*

6. **Fonthill:** a secluded and fantastic mansion built by the wealthy and eccentric Englishman William Beckford (1759–1844), author of *Vathek.*

the language has no word which better represents the most striking—not the most distinctive—feature of the scene. The character of gorge was maintained only in the height and parallelism of the shores; it was lost altogether in their other traits. The walls of the ravine (through which the clear water still tranquilly flowed) arose to an elevation of a hundred and occasionally of a hundred and fifty feet, and inclined so much toward each other as, in a great measure, to shut out the light of day; while the long plume-like moss which depended densely from the intertwining shrubberies overhead, gave the whole chasm an air of funereal gloom. The windings became more frequent and intricate, and seemed often as if returning in upon themselves, so that the voyager had long lost all idea of direction. He was, moreover, enwrapt in an exquisite sense of the strange. The thought of nature still remained, but her character seemed to have undergone modification: there was a weird symmetry, a thrilling uniformity, a wizard propriety in these her works. Not a dead branch—not a withered leaf—not a stray pebble—not a patch of the brown earth was anywhere visible. The crystal water welled up against the clean granite, or the unblemished moss, with a sharpness of outline that delighted while it bewildered the eye.

Having threaded the mazes of this channel for some hours, the gloom deepening every moment, a sharp and unexpected turn of the vessel brought it suddenly, as if dropped from heaven, into a circular basin of very considerable extent when compared with the width of the gorge. It was about two hundred yards in diameter, and girt in at all points but one—that immediately fronting the vessel as it entered—by hills equal in general height to the walls of the chasm, although of a thoroughly different character. Their sides sloped from the water's edge at an angle of some forty-five degrees, and they were clothed from base to summit—not a perceptible point escaping—in a drapery of the most gorgeous flower-blossoms; scarcely a green leaf being visible among the sea of odorous and fluctuating color. This basin was of great depth, but so transparent was the water that the bottom, which seemed to consist of a thick mass of small round alabaster pebbles, was distinctly visible by glimpses—that is to say, whenever the eye could permit itself *not* to see, far down in the inverted Heaven, the duplicate blooming of the hills. On these latter there were no trees, nor even shrubs of any size. The impressions wrought on the observer were those of richness, warmth, color, quietude, uniformity, softness, delicacy, daintiness, voluptuousness, and a miraculous extremeness of culture that suggested dreams of a new race of fairies, laborious, tasteful, magnificent and fastidious; but as the eye traced upward the myriad-tinted slope, from its sharp junction with the water to its vague termination amid the folds of overhanging cloud, it became, indeed, difficult not to fancy a panoramic cataract of rubies, sapphires, opals and golden onyxes, rolling silently out of the sky.

The visiter, shooting suddenly into this bay from out the gloom of the ravine, is delighted but astounded by the full orb of the declining sun, which he had supposed to be already far below the horizon, but which now confronts him, and forms the sole termination of an otherwise limitless vista seen through another chasm-like rift in the hills.

But here the voyager quits the vessel which has borne him so far, and descends into a light canoe of ivory, stained with arabesque devices in vivid scarlet, both within and without. The poop and beak of this boat arise high above the water, with sharp points, so that the general form is that of an irregular crescent. It lies on the surface of the bay with the proud grace of a swan. On its ermined floor reposes a single feathery paddle of satin-wood; but no oarsman or attendant is to be seen. The guest is bidden to be of good cheer—that the fates will take care of him. The larger vessel disappears, and he is left along in the canoe, which lies apparently motionless in the middle of the lake. While he considers what course to pursue, however, he becomes aware of a gentle movement in the fairy bark. It slowly swings itself around until its prow points toward the sun. It advances with a gentle but gradually accelerated velocity, while the slight ripples it creates seem to break about the ivory side in divinest melody—seem to offer the only possible explanation of the soothing yet melancholy music for whose unseen origin the bewildered voyager looks around him in vain.

The canoe steadily proceeds, and the rocky gate of the vista is approached, so that its depths can be more distinctly seen. To the right arise a chain of lofty hills rudely and luxuriantly wooded. It is observed, however, that the trait of exquisite *cleanness* where the bank dips into the water, still prevails. There is not one token of the usual river *débris*. To the left the character of the scene is softer and more obviously artificial. Here the bank slopes upward from the stream in a very gentle ascent, forming a broad sward of grass of a texture resembling nothing so much as velvet, and of a brilliancy of green which would bear comparison with the tint of the purest emerald. This *plateau* varies in width from ten to three hundred yards; reaching from the river-bank to a wall, fifty feet high, which extends, in an infinity of curves, but following the general direction of the river, until lost in the distance to the westward. This wall is of one continuous rock, and has been formed by cutting perpendicularly the once rugged precipice of the stream's southern bank; but no trace of the labor has been suffered to remain. The chiselled stone has the hue of ages and is profusely overhung and overspread with the ivy, the coral honeysuckle, the eglantine, and the clematis. The uniformity of the top and bottom lines of the wall is fully relieved by occasional trees of gigantic height, growing singly or in small groups, both along the *plateau* and in the domain behind the wall, but in close proximity to it; so that frequent limbs (of the black walnut especially) reach over and dip their pendent extremities into the water. Farther back within the domain, the vision is impeded by an impenetrable screen of foliage.

These things are observed during the canoe's gradual approach to what I have called the gate of the vista. On drawing nearer to this, however, its chasm-like appearance vanishes; a new outlet from the bay is discovered to the left—in which direction the wall is also seen to sweep, still following the general course of the stream. Down this new opening the eye cannot penetrate very far; for the stream, accompanied by the wall, still bends to the left, until both are swallowed up by the leaves.

The boat, nevertheless, glides magically into the winding channel; and here the shore opposite the wall is found to resemble that opposite the wall in the straight vista. Lofty hills, rising occasionally into mountains, and covered with vegetation in wild luxuriance, still shut in the scene.

Floating gently onward, but with a velocity slightly augmented, the voyager, after many short turns, finds his progress apparently barred by a gigantic gate or rather door of burnished gold, elaborately carved and fretted, and reflecting the direct rays of the now fast-sinking sun with an effulgence that seems to wreathe the whole surrounding forest in flames. This gate is inserted in the lofty wall; which here appears to cross the river at right angles. In a few moments, however, it is seen that the main body of the water still sweeps in a gentle and extensive curve to the left, the wall following it as before, while a stream of considerable volume, diverging from the principal one, makes its way, with a slight ripple, under the door, and is thus hidden from sight. The canoe falls into the lesser channel and approaches the gate. Its ponderous wings are slowly and musically expanded. The boat glides between them, and commences a rapid descent into a vast amphitheatre entirely begirt with purple mountains, whose bases are laved by a gleaming river throughout the full extent of their circuit. Meantime the whole Paradise of Arnheim bursts upon the view. There is a gush of entrancing melody; there is an oppressive sense of strange sweet odor; —there is a dream-like intermingling to the eye of tall slender Eastern trees—bosky shrubberies—flocks of golden and crimson birds—lily-fringed lakes—meadows of violets, tulips, poppies, hyacinths, and tuberoses—long intertangled lines of silver streamlets—and, upspringing confusedly from amid all, a mass of semi-Gothic, semi-Saracenic architecture, sustaining itself by miracle in mid-air, glittering in the red sunlight with a hundred oriels, minarets, and pinnacles; and seeming the phantom handiwork, conjointly, of the Sylphs, of the Fairies, of the Genii, and of the Gnomes.

FROM

REVIEW OF THOMAS MOORE'S ALCIPHRON

◇

¶ POE's review of Moore's poem appeared in *Burton's Gentleman's Magazine* for January, 1840. The following effort to distinguish the fanciful from the imaginative prepared for the conclusion that in some respects —in his frequent use of the simile, for example—Moore was merely fanciful, but that he was nevertheless "suggestive" or imaginative "in no little degree."

◇

A NEW poem from Moore calls to mind that critical opinion respecting him which had its origin, we believe, in the dogmatism of Coleridge—we mean the opinion that he is essentially the poet of *fancy*—the term being employed in contradistinction to *imagination*. "The fancy," says the author of the "Ancient Mariner," in his *Biographia Literaria*, "the fancy combines, the imagination creates." And this was intended, and has been received, as a distinction. If so at all, it is one without a difference; without even a difference of *degree*. The fancy as nearly creates as the imagination; and neither creates in any respect.[1] All novel

REVIEW OF MOORE. **1. The . . . respect:** In "The Poetic Principle" (1850), Poe describes poetry as striving toward, and sometimes achieving, "the creation of supernal Beauty." But Poe's later criticism does not truly contradict the review of *Alciphron* in regard to the imagination's power to create. When, as described in the fifth selection from "Marginalia," a novel combination of earthly ideas results in a glimpse conceptions are merely unusual combinations. The mind of man can *imagine* nothing which has not really existed; and this point is susceptible of the most positive demonstration—see the Baron de Bielfeld, in his *Premiers Traits de L'Erudition Universelle,* 1767. It will be said, perhaps, that we can imagine a *griffin,* and that a griffin does not exist. Not the griffin certainly, but its component parts. It is a mere compendium of known limbs and features—of known qualities. Thus with all which seems to be *new*—which appears to be a *creation* of intellect. It is resoluble into the old. The wildest and most vigorous effort of mind cannot stand the test of this analysis.

We might make a distinction, *of degree,* between the fancy and the imagination, in saying that the latter is the former *loftily employed.* But experience proves this distinction to be unsatisfactory. What we *feel* and *know* to be fancy, will be found still only *fanciful,* whatever be the theme which engages it. It retains its idiosyncrasy under all circumstances. No *subject* exalts it into the ideal. We might exemplify this by reference to the writings of one whom our patriotism, rather than our judgment, has elevated to a niche in the Poetic Temple which he does not becomingly fill, and which he cannot long uninterruptedly hold. We allude to the late Dr. Rodman Drake, whose puerile abortion, *The Culprit Fay,* we examined, at some length, in a *critique* elsewhere,[2] proving it, we think, beyond all question, to belong to that class of the pseudo-ideal, in dealing with which we find ourselves embarrassed between a kind of half-consciousness that we ought to admire, and the certainty that we do not. Dr. Drake was employed upon a good subject—at least it is a subject precisely identical with those which Shakespeare was wont so happily to treat, and in which, especially, the author of *Lilian* [3] has so wonderfully succeeded. But the American has brought to his task a mere *fancy,* and has grossly failed in doing what many suppose him to have done—in writing an ideal or imaginative poem. There is not one particle of the true ποίησις[4] about *The Culprit Fay.* We say that the subject, even at its best points, did not aid Dr. Drake in the slightest degree. He was never more than *fanciful.* The passage, for example, chiefly cited by his admirers, is the account of the "Sylphid Queen"; and to show the difference between the false and true ideal, we collated, in the review just alluded to, this, the most admired passage, with one upon a similar topic by Shelley. We shall be pardoned for repeating here, as nearly as we remember them, some words of what we then said.

The description of the Sylphid Queen runs thus:—

But oh, how fair the shape that lay
  Beneath a rainbow bending bright;
She seemed to the entranced Fay
  The loveliest of the forms of light;
Her mantle was the purple rolled
  At twilight in the west afar;
'Twas tied with threads of dawning gold,
  And buttoned with a sparkling star.
Her face was like the lily roon
  That veils the vestal planet's hue;
Her eyes two beamlets from the moon
  Set floating in the welkin blue.
Her hair is like the sunny beam,
And the diamond gems which round it gleam
Are the pure drops of dewy even
That ne'er have left their native heaven.

In the "Queen Mab" of Shelley, a Fairy is thus introduced:—

Those who had looked upon the sight,
  Passing all human glory,
Saw not the yellow moon,
Saw not the mortal scene,
Heard not the night-wind's rush,
Heard not an earthly sound,
Saw but the fairy pageant,
Heard but the heavenly strains
That filled the lonely dwelling—

And thus described—

The Fairy's frame was slight; yon fibrous cloud
That catches but the palest tinge of even,
And which the straining eye can hardly seize,
When melting into eastern twilight's shadow,
Were scarce so thin, so slight; but the fair star
That gems the glittering coronet of morn,
Sheds not a light so mild, so powerful,
As that which, bursting from the Fairy's form
Spread a purpureal halo round the scene,
  Yet with an undulating motion,
  Swayed to her outline gracefully.

In these exquisite lines the faculty of mere comparison is but little exercised—that of ideality in a wonderful degree. It is probable that in a similar case Dr. Drake would have formed the face of the fairy of the "fibrous cloud," her arms of the "pale tinge of even," her eyes of the "fair stars," and her body of the "twilight shadow." Having so done, his admirers would have congratulated him upon his *imagination,* not taking the trouble to think that

of unearthly beauty, such beauty has not been created from nothing but rather remembered, or rediscovered. The function of the poet is, in fact, to *uncreate* the diffused Universe by intuiting its original oneness. **2. a *critique* elsewhere:** For the *Southern Literary Messenger* of April, 1836, Poe wrote a double review of Joseph Rodman Drake's *The Culprit Fay* and Fitz-Greene Halleck's *Alnwick Castle.* **3. *Lilian:*** refers not to Tennyson's lyric (1830) but to W. M. Praed's verse fairy tale (1823). **4. ποίησις:** here best translated "poetic spirit."

they themselves could at any moment *imagine* a fairy of materials equally as good, and conveying an equally distinct idea. Their mistake would be precisely analogous to that of many a schoolboy who admires the imagination displayed in Jack the Giant-Killer, and is finally rejoiced at discovering his own imagination to surpass that of the author, since the monsters destroyed by Jack are only about forty feet in height, and he himself has no trouble in imagining some of one hundred and forty. It will be seen that the fairy of Shelley is not a mere compound of incongruous natural objects, inartificially put together, and unaccompanied by any *moral* [5] sentiment; but a being, in the illustration of whose nature some physical elements are used collaterally as adjuncts, while the main conception springs immediately, *or thus apparently springs,* from the brain of the poet, enveloped in the moral sentiments of grace, of colour, of motion—of the beautiful, of the *mystical,* of the august—in short, of the ideal.

The truth is that the just distinction between the fancy and the imagination (and which is still but a distinction of *degree*) is involved in the consideration of the *mystic*. We give this as an idea of our own, altogether. We have no authority for our opinion—but do not the less firmly hold it. The term *mystic* is here employed in the sense of Augustus William Schlegel, and of most other German critics. It is applied by them to that class of composition in which there lies beneath the transparent upper current of meaning an under or *suggestive* one. What we vaguely term the *moral* of any sentiment is its mystic or secondary expression. It has the vast force of an accompaniment in music. This vivifies the air; that spiritualizes the *fanciful* conception, and lifts it into the *ideal.*

This theory will bear, we think, the most rigorous tests which can be made applicable to it, and will be acknowledged as tenable by all who are themselves imaginative. If we carefully examine those poems, or portions of poems, or those prose romances, which mankind have been accustomed to designate as *imaginative* (for an instinctive feeling leads us to employ properly the term whose full import we have still never been able to define), it will be seen that all so designated are remarkable for the *suggestive* character which we have discussed. They are strongly *mystic,* in the proper sense of the word. We will here only call to the reader's mind, the *Prometheus Vinctus* of Aeschylus; the *Inferno* of Dante; the *Destruction of Numantia* by Cervantes; the *Comus* of Milton; the "Ancient Mariner," the "Christabel," and the "Kubla Khan" of Coleridge; the "Nightingale" of Keats; and, most especially, the "Sensitive Plant" of Shelley, and the *Undine* of De la Motte Fouqué.[6] These two latter poems (for we call them both such) are the finest possible examples of the purely *ideal.* There is little of fancy here, and everything of imagination. With each note of the lyre is heard a ghostly, and not always a distinct, but an august and soul-exalting *echo.* In every glimpse of beauty presented, we catch, through long and wild vistas, dim bewildering visions of a far more ethereal beauty *beyond.* But not so in poems which the world has always persisted in terming *fanciful.* Here the upper current is often exceedingly brilliant and beautiful; but then men feel that this upper current *is all.* No Naiad voice addresses them from *below*. The notes of the air of the song do not tremble with the according tones of the accompaniment.

5. *moral:* Here, as often in Poe, the word means "spiritual."

EXORDIUM

◇

THIS statement on the function of criticism preceded the critical notices in *Graham's Magazine* for January, 1842.

◇

IN COMMENCING, with the New Year, a New Volume, we shall be permitted to say a very few words by way of *exordium* to our usual chapter of Reviews, or, as we should prefer calling them, of Critical Notices. Yet we speak *not* for the sake of *exordium,* but because we have really something to say, and know not when or where better to say it.

That the public attention, in America, has, of late days, been more than usually directed to the matter of literary criticism, is plainly apparent. Our periodicals are beginning to acknowledge the importance of the science (shall we so term it?), and to disdain the flippant *opinion* which so long has been made its substitute.

Time was when we imported our critical decisions from the mother country. For many years we

6. **We . . . Fouqué:** The works mentioned are familiar, save perhaps for *La Numancia*, a tragedy by Miguel de Cervantes (1547–1616), and *Undine*, a prose romance by Friedrich de La Motte-Fouqué (1777–1843). Poe reviewed a translation of the latter in *Burton's* (September, 1839).

enacted a perfect farce of subserviency to the *dicta* of Great Britain. At last a revulsion of feeling, with self-disgust, necessarily ensued. Urged by these, we plunged into the opposite extreme. In throwing *totally* off that "authority," whose voice had so long been so sacred, we even surpassed, and by much, our original folly. But the watchword now was, "A national literature!"—as if any true literature *could be* "national"—as if the world at large were not the only proper stage for the literary *histrio*.[1] We became, suddenly, the merest and maddest *partizans* in letters. Our papers spoke of "tariffs" and "protection." Our Magazines had habitual passages about that "truly native novelist, Mr. Cooper," or that "staunch American genius, Mr. Paulding." Unmindful of the spirit of the axioms that "a prophet has no honor in his own land" and that "a hero is never a hero to his *valet-de-chambre*"—axioms founded in reason and in truth—our reviews urged the propriety—our booksellers the necessity, of strictly "American" themes. A foreign subject, at this epoch, was a weight more than enough to drag down into the very depths of critical damnation the finest writer owning nativity in the States; while, on the reverse, we found ourselves daily in the paradoxical dilemma of liking, or pretending to like, a stupid book the better because (sure enough) its stupidity was of our own growth, and discussed our own affairs.

It is, in fact, but very lately that this anomalous state of feeling has shown any signs of subsidence. Still it *is* subsiding. Our views of literature in general having expanded, we begin to demand the use —to inquire into the offices and provinces of criticism—to regard it more as an art based immoveably in nature, less as a mere system of fluctuating and conventional dogmas. And, with the prevalence of these ideas, has arrived a distaste even to the home-dictation of the bookseller-*coteries*. If our editors are not as yet *all* independent of the will of a publisher, a majority of them scruple, at least, *to confess* a subservience, and enter into no positive combinations against the minority who despise and discard it. And this is a *very* great improvement of exceedingly late date.

Escaping these quicksands, our criticism is nevertheless in some danger—some very little danger —of falling into the pit of a most detestable species of cant—the cant of *generality*. This tendency has been given it, in the first instance, by the onward and tumultuous spirit of the age. With the increase of the thinking-material comes the desire, if not the necessity, of abandoning particulars for masses. Yet in our individual case, as a nation, we seem merely to have adopted this bias from the British Quarterly Reviews, upon which our own Quarterlies have been slavishly and pertinaciously modelled. In the foreign journal, the review or criticism properly so termed has gradually yet steadily degenerated into what we see it at present—that is to say, into anything but criticism. Originally a "review" was not so called as *lucus a non lucendo*.[2] Its name conveyed a just idea of its design. It reviewed, or surveyed the book whose title formed its text, and, giving an analysis of its contents, passed judgment upon its merits or defects. But, through the system of anonymous contribution, this natural process lost ground from day to day. The name of a writer being known only to a few, it became to him an object not so much to write well, as to write fluently, at so many guineas per sheet. The analysis of a book is a matter of time and of mental exertion. For many classes of composition there is required a deliberate perusal, with notes, and subsequent generalization. An easy substitute for this labor was found in a digest or compendium of the work noticed, with copious extracts—or a still easier, in random comments upon such passages as accidentally met the eye of the critic, with the passages themselves copied at full length. The mode of reviewing most in favor, however, because carrying with it the greatest *semblance* of care, was that of diffuse essay upon the subject matter of the publication, the reviewer (?) using the facts alone which the publication supplied, and using them as material for some theory, the sole concern, bearing, and intention of which, was mere difference of opinion with the author. These came at length to be understood and habitually practised as the customary or conventional *fashions* of review; and although the nobler order of intellects did not fall into the full heresy of these fashions—we may still assert that even Macaulay's nearest approach to criticism in its legitimate sense, is to be found in his article upon Ranke's *History of the Popes*—an article in which the whole strength of the reviewer is put forth *to account* for a single fact—the progress of Romanism—which the book under discussion has established.

Now, while we do not mean to deny that a good essay is a good thing, we yet assert that these papers on general topics have nothing whatever to do with that *criticism* which their evil example has nevertheless infected *in se*. Because these dogmatising pamphlets, which *were once* "Reviews," have lapsed from their original faith, it does not follow that the faith itself is extinct—that "there shall be

EXORDIUM. 1. *histrio:* performer.

2. *lucus a non lucendo:* literally, "a grove is so called because it is not lighted"; any absurd derivation or misnomer.

no more cakes and ale"—that criticism, in its old acceptation, does not exist. But we complain of a growing inclination on the part of our lighter journals to believe, on such grounds, that such is the fact—that because the British Quarterlies, through supineness, and our own, through a degrading imitation, have come to merge all varieties of vague generalization in the one title of "Review," it therefore results that criticism, being everything in the universe, is, consequently, nothing whatever in fact. For to this end, and to none other conceivable, is the tendency of such propositions, for example, as we find in a late number of that very clever monthly magazine, *Arcturus.*

"But *now*" (the emphasis on the *now* is our own)—"But *now,*" says Mr. Mathews,[3] in the preface to the first volume of his journal, "criticism has a wider scope and a universal interest. It dismisses errors of grammar, and hands over an imperfect rhyme or a false quantity to the proof-reader; it looks *now* to the heart of the subject and the author's design. It is a test of opinion. Its acuteness is not pedantic, but philosophical; it unravels the web of the author's mystery to interpret his meaning to others; it detects his sophistry, because sophistry is injurious to the heart and life; it promulgates his beauties with liberal, generous praise, because this is its true duty as the servant of truth. Good criticism may be well asked for, since it is the type of literature of the day. It gives method to the universal inquisitiveness on every topic relating to life or action. A criticism, *now,* includes every form of literature except perhaps the imaginative and the strictly dramatic. It is an essay, a sermon, an oration, a chapter in history, a philosophical speculation, a prose-poem, an art-novel, a dialogue; it admits of humor, pathos, the personal feelings of autobiography, the broadest views of statesmanship. As the ballad and the epic were the productions of the days of Homer, the review is the native characteristic growth of the nineteenth century."

We respect the talent of Mr. Mathews, but must dissent from nearly all that he here says. The species of "review" which he designates as the "characteristic growth of the nineteenth century" is only the growth of the last twenty or thirty years *in Great Britain.* The French Reviews, for example, which are *not* anonymous, are very different things, and preserve the *unique* spirit of true criticism. And what need we say of the Germans?—what of Winckelmann, of Novalis, of Schelling, of Goethe, of Augustus William, and of Frederick Schlegel?—that their magnificent *critiques raisonnées* differ from those of Kames, of Johnson, and of Blair,[4] in principle not at all, (for the principles of these artists will not fail until Nature herself expires,) but solely in their more careful elaboration, their greater thoroughness, their more profound analysis and application of the principles themselves. That a criticism *"now"* should be different in spirit, as Mr. Mathews supposes, from a criticism at any previous period, is to insinuate a charge of variability in laws that cannot vary—the laws of man's heart and intellect—for these are the sole basis upon which the true critical art is established. And this art *"now"* no more than in the days of the "Dunciad," can, without neglect of its duty, "dismiss errors of grammar," or "hand over an imperfect rhyme or a false quantity to the proof-reader." What is meant by a "test of opinion" in the connexion here given the words by Mr. M., we do not comprehend as clearly as we could desire. By this phrase we are as completely enveloped in doubt as was Mirabeau in the castle of *If.*[5] To our imperfect appreciation it seems to form a portion of that general vagueness which is the *tone* of the whole philosophy at this point:—but all that which our journalist describes a criticism to be, is all that which we sturdily maintain it *is not.* Criticism is *not,* we think, an essay, nor a sermon, nor an oration, nor a chapter in history, nor a philosophical speculation, nor a prose-poem, nor an art-novel, nor a dialogue. In fact, it *can be* nothing in the world but —a criticism. But if it were all that *Arcturus* imagines, it is not very clear why it might not be equally "imaginative" or "dramatic"—a romance or a melodrama, or both. That it would be a farce cannot be doubted.

It is against this frantic spirit of *generalization* that we protest. We have a word, "criticism," whose import is sufficiently distinct, through long usage, at least; and we have an art of high importance and clearly-ascertained limit, which this word is quite well enough understood to represent. Of that conglomerate science to which Mr. Mathews so eloquently alludes, and of which we are instructed that it is anything and everything at once—of this science we know nothing, and really wish to know less; but we object to our contemporary's appropriation in its behalf, of a term to which we, in common with a large majority of mankind, have been accustomed to attach a cer-

3. **Mr. Mathews:** Cornelius Mathews (1817–89), poet, playwright, and founder, in 1840, with Evert A. Duyckinck, of *Arcturus: A Journal of Books and Opinion.*

4. **And . . . Blair:** The less familiar names are those of Friedrich von Hardenberg (1772–1801), whose pen-name was "Novalis"; Henry Home, Lord Kames (1696–1782), author of *Elements of Criticism*; and Hugh Blair (1718–1800), author of *Lectures on Rhetoric.*

5. **Mirabeau . . . If:** The Comte de Mirabeau (1749–91), French orator and statesman, was confined, in 1774, in the Chateau d'If. Poe is playing on the English sense of *if.*

tain and very definite idea. Is there no word but "criticism" which may be made to serve the purposes of *Arcturus?* Has it any objection to Orphicism,[6] or Dialism, or Emersonism, or any other pregnant compound indicative of confusion worse confounded?

Still, we must not pretend a total misapprehension of the idea of Mr. Mathews, and we should be sorry that he misunderstood *us.* It may be granted that we differ only in terms—although the difference will yet be found not unimportant in effect. Following the highest authority, we would wish, in a word, to limit literary criticism to comment upon *Art.* A book is written—and it is only *as the book* that we subject it to review. With the opinions of the work, considered otherwise than in their relation to the work itself, the critic has really nothing to do. It is his part simply to decide upon *the mode* in which these opinions are brought to bear. Criticism is thus no "test of opinion." For this test, the work, divested of its pretensions as an *art-product,* is turned over for discussion to the world at large—and first, to that class which it especially addresses—if a history, to the historian—if a metaphysical treatise, to the moralist. In this, the only true and intelligible sense, it will be seen that criticism, the test or analysis of *Art,* (*not* of opinion,) is only properly employed upon productions which have their basis in art itself, and although the journalist (whose duties and objects are multiform) may turn aside, at pleasure, from the *mode* or vehicle of opinion to discussion of the opinion conveyed—it is still clear that he is *"critical"* only in so much as he deviates from his true province not at all.

And of the critic himself what shall we say?—for as yet we have spoken only the *proem* to the true *epopea.* What *can* we better say of him than, with Bulwer, that "he must have courage to blame boldly, magnanimity to eschew envy, genius to appreciate, learning to compare, an eye for beauty, an ear for music, and a heart for feeling." [7] Let us add, a talent for analysis and a solemn indifference to abuse.

6. **Orphicism:** refers to Bronson Alcott's "Orphic Sayings," published 1840–44 in the Transcendentalist periodical the *Dial.*
7. **"he . . . feeling":** quoted from *Critical and Miscellaneous Writings of Sir Edward Lytton Bulwer,* which Poe had reviewed for *Graham's* in November, 1841.

REVIEW OF NATHANIEL HAWTHORNE'S TWICE-TOLD TALES

◇

¶ IN THIS review (*Graham's Magazine,* May, 1842), Poe proves his discernment by recognizing the merits of his contemporary. The review also offers a theory of the short story, a distinction between the provinces of poem and tale, and some observations on Hawthorne's use of "suggestion" which throw light on Poe's own intentions as a writer of fiction.

◇

THE PIECES in the volumes entitled *Twice-Told Tales,* are now in their third republication, and, of course, are thrice-told. Moreover, they are by no means *all* tales, either in the ordinary or in the legitimate understanding of the term. Many of them are pure essays; for example, "Sights from a Steeple," "Sunday at Home," "Little Annie's Ramble," "A Rill from the Town Pump," "The Toll-Gatherer's Day," "The Haunted Mind," "The Sister Years," "Snow-Flakes," "Night Sketches," and "Foot-Prints on the Sea-Shore." I mention these matters chiefly on account of their discrepancy with that marked precision and finish by which the body of the work is distinguished.

Of the Essays just named, I must be content to speak in brief. They are each and all beautiful, without being characterized by the polish and adaptation so visible in the tales proper. A painter would at once note their leading or predominant feature, and style it *repose.* There is no attempt at effect. All is quiet, thoughtful, subdued. Yet this repose may exist simultaneously with high originality of thought; and Mr. Hawthorne has demonstrated the fact. At every turn we meet with novel combination; yet these combinations never surpass the limits of the quiet. We are soothed as we read; and with all is a calm astonishment that ideas so apparently obvious have never occurred or been presented to us before. Herein our author differs materially from Lamb or Hunt or Hazlitt—who, with vivid originality of manner and expression, have less of the true novelty of thought than is generally supposed, and whose originality, at best, has an uneasy and meretricious quaintness, replete with startling effects unfounded in nature, and inducing trains of reflection which lead to no satisfactory result. The Essays of Hawthorne have much of the character of Irving, with more of originality, and less of finish; while, compared with the *Spectator,*[1] they have a vast superiority at all points. The *Spectator,* Mr. Irving, and Hawthorne have in common that tranquil and subdued manner which I have chosen to denominate *repose;* but, in the case of the two former, this repose is attained rather by the absence of novel combination, or of originality, than otherwise, and consists chiefly in the calm, quiet, unostentatious expression of commonplace thoughts, in an unambitious, unadulterated Saxon. In them, by strong effort, we are made to conceive the absence of all. In the essays before me the absence of effort is too obvious to be mistaken, and a strong undercurrent of *suggestion* runs continuously beneath the upper stream of the tranquil thesis.[2] In short, these effusions of Mr. Hawthorne are the product of a truly imaginative intellect, restrained, and in some measure repressed, by fastidiousness of taste, by constitutional melancholy, and by indolence.

But it is of his tales that I desire principally to speak. The tale proper, in my opinion, affords unquestionably the fairest field for the exercise of the loftiest talent, which can be afforded by the wide domains of mere prose. Were I bidden to say how the highest genius could be most advantageously employed for the best display of its own powers, I should answer, without hesitation—in the composition of a rhymed poem, not to exceed in length what might be perused in an hour. Within this limit alone can the highest order of true poetry exist. I need only here say, upon this topic, that, in almost all classes of composition, the unity of effect or impression is a point of the greatest importance. It is clear, moreover, that this unity cannot be thoroughly preserved in productions whose perusal cannot be completed at one sitting. We may continue the reading of a prose composition, from the very nature of prose itself, much longer than we can persevere, to any good purpose, in the perusal of a poem. This latter, if truly fulfilling the demands of the poetic sentiment, induces an exaltation of the soul which cannot be long sustained. All high excitements are necessarily transient. Thus a long poem is a paradox. And, without unity of impression, the deepest effects cannot be brought about. Epics were the offspring of an imperfect sense of Art, and their reign is no more. A poem *too* brief may produce a vivid, but never an intense or enduring impression. Without a certain continuity of effort—without a certain duration of repetition or purpose—the soul is never deeply moved. There must be the dropping of the water upon the rock. De Béranger has wrought brilliant things—pungent and spirit-stirring—but, like all immassive bodies, they lack *momentum,* and thus fail to satisfy the poetic Sentiment. They sparkle and excite, but, from want of continuity, fail deeply to impress. Extreme brevity will degenerate into epigrammatism; but the sin of extreme length is more unpardonable. *In medio tutissimus ibis.*[3]

Were I called upon, however, to designate that class of composition which, next to such a poem as I have suggested, should best fulfil the demands of high genius—should offer it the most advantageous field of exertion—I should unhesitatingly speak of the prose tale as Mr. Hawthorne has here exemplified it. I allude to the short prose narrative, requiring from a half-hour to one or two hours in its perusal. The ordinary novel is objectionable, from its length, for reasons already stated in substance. As it cannot be read at one sitting, it deprives itself, of course, of the immense force derivable from *totality*. Worldly interests intervening during the pauses of perusal, modify, annul, or counteract, in a greater or less degree, the impressions of the book. But simple cessation in reading would, of itself, be sufficient to destroy the true unity. In the brief tale, however, the author is enabled to carry out the fulness of his intention, be it what it may. During the hour of perusal the soul of the reader is at the writer's control. There are no external or extrinsic influences—resulting from weariness or interruption.

A skilful literary artist has constructed a tale. If wise, he has not fashioned his thoughts to accommodate his incidents; but having conceived, with deliberate care, a certain unique or single *effect* to be wrought out, he then invents such incidents—he then combines such events as may best aid him in establishing this preconceived effect. If his very initial sentence tend not to the outbringing of this effect, then he has failed in his first step. In the whole composition there should be no word written, of which the tendency, direct or indirect, is not to the one pre-established design. And by such means, with such care and skill, a picture is at length painted which leaves in the mind of him who contemplates it with a kindred art, a sense of the fullest satisfaction. The idea of the tale has been presented unblemished, because undisturbed; and this is an end unattainable by the novel. Undue brevity is just as exceptionable here as in the poem; but undue length is yet more to be avoided.

We have said that the tale has a point of superi-

REVIEW OF HAWTHORNE. **1. the** ***Spectator:*** The *Spectator* was written and published, during 1711–14, by Joseph Addison and Richard Steele. **2. strong . . . thesis:** See the latter paragraphs of Poe's review of Moore's *Alciphron,* p. 462.

3. ***In medio . . . ibis:*** "It is safest to keep to the middle way."

ority even over the poem. In fact, while the *rhythm* of this latter is an essential aid in the development of the poem's highest idea—the idea of the Beautiful—the artificialities of this rhythm are an inseparable bar to the development of all points of thought or expression which have their basis in *Truth*. But Truth is often, and in very great degree, the aim of the tale. Some of the finest tales are tales of ratiocination. Thus the field of this species of composition, if not in so elevated a region on the mountain of Mind, is a table-land of far vaster extent than the domain of the mere poem. Its products are never so rich, but infinitely more numerous, and more appreciable by the mass of mankind. The writer of the prose tale, in short, may bring to his theme a vast variety of modes or inflections of thought and expression—(the ratiocinative, for example, the sarcastic or the humorous) which are not only antagonistical to the nature of the poem, but absolutely forbidden by one of its most peculiar and indispensable adjuncts; we allude, of course, to rhythm. It may be added, here, *par parenthèse,* that the author who aims at the purely beautiful in a prose tale is laboring at a great disadvantage. For Beauty can be better treated in the poem. Not so with terror, or passion, or horror, or a multitude of such other points. And here it will be seen how full of prejudice are the usual animadversions against those *tales of effect,* many fine examples of which were found in the earlier numbers of Blackwood. The impressions produced were wrought in a legitimate sphere of action, and constituted a legitimate although sometimes an exaggerated interest. They were relished by every man of genius: although there were found many men of genius who condemned them without just ground. The true critic will but demand that the design intended be accomplished, to the fullest extent, by means most advantageously applicable.

We have very few American tales of real merit —we may say, indeed, none, with the exception of *The Tales of a Traveller* of Washington Irving, and these *Twice-Told Tales* of Mr. Hawthorne. Some of the pieces of Mr. John Neal [4] abound in vigor and originality; but in general, his compositions of this class are excessively diffuse, extravagant, and indicative of an imperfect sentiment of Art. Articles at random are, now and then, met with in our periodicals which might be advantageously compared with the best effusions of the British Magazines; but, upon the whole, we are far behind our progenitors in this department of literature.

4. **John Neal:** novelist, poet and critic (1793–1876), who in December, 1829, wrote an appreciative notice of Poe's "Al Aaraaf" in his literary periodical the *Yankee.*

Of Mr. Hawthorne's Tales we would say, emphatically, that they belong to the highest region of Art—an Art subservient to genius of a very lofty order. We had supposed, with good reason for so supposing, that he had been thrust into his present position by one of the impudent *cliques* which beset our literature, and whose pretensions it is our full purpose to expose at the earliest opportunity; but we have been most agreeably mistaken. We know of few compositions which the critic can more honestly commend than these *Twice-Told Tales.* As Americans, we feel proud of the book.

Mr. Hawthorne's distinctive trait is invention, creation, imagination, originality—a trait which, in the literature of fiction, is positively worth all the rest. But the nature of the originality, so far as regards its manifestation in letters, is but imperfectly understood. The inventive or original mind as frequently displays itself in novelty of *tone* as in novelty of matter. Mr. Hawthorne is original in *all* points.

It would be a matter of some difficulty to designate the best of these tales; we repeat that, without exception, they are beautiful. "Wakefield" is remarkable for the skill with which an old idea—a well-known incident—is worked up or discussed. A man of whims conceives the purpose of quitting his wife and residing *incognito,* for twenty years in her immediate neighborhood. Something of this kind actually happened in London. The force of Mr. Hawthorne's tale lies in the analysis of the motives which must or might have impelled the husband to such folly, in the first instance, with the possible causes of his perseverance. Upon this thesis a sketch of singular power has been constructed. "The Wedding Knell" is full of the boldest imagination—an imagination fully controlled by taste. The most captious critic could find no flaw in this production. "The Minister's Black Veil" is a masterly composition of which the sole defect is that to the rabble its exquisite skill will be *caviare.* The *obvious* meaning of this article will be found to smother its insinuated one.[5] The *moral* put into the mouth of the dying minister will be supposed to convey the *true* import of the narrative; and that a crime of dark dye, (having reference to the "young lady") has been committed, is a point which only minds congenial with that of the author will perceive. "Mr. Higginbotham's Catastrophe" is vividly original and managed most dexterously.

5. **The . . . one:** On the other hand, the insinuated meaning must not be too clear: in "The Philosophy of Composition," Poe wrote, "It is the *excess* of the suggested meaning—it is the rendering this the upper instead of the under current of the theme—which turns into prose (and that of the very flattest kind) the so-called poetry of the so-called transcendentalists."

"Dr. Heidegger's Experiment" is exceedingly well imagined, and executed with surpassing ability. The artist breathes in every line of it. "The White Old Maid" is objectionable, even more than the "Minister's Black Veil," on the score of its mysticism. Even with the thoughtful and analytic, there will be much trouble in penetrating its entire import.

"The Hollow of the Three Hills" we would quote in full, had we space;—not as evincing higher talent than any of the other pieces, but as affording an excellent example of the author's peculiar ability. The subject is commonplace. A witch subjects the Distant and the Past to the view of a mourner. It has been the fashion to describe, in such cases, a mirror in which the images of the absent appear; or a cloud of smoke is made to arise, and thence the figures are gradually unfolded. Mr. Hawthorne has wonderfully heightened his effect by making the ear, in place of the eye, the medium by which the fantasy is conveyed. The head of the mourner is enveloped in the cloak of the witch, and within its magic folds there arise sounds which have an all-sufficient intelligence. Throughout this article also, the artist is conspicuous—not more in positive than in negative merits. Not only is all done that should be done, but (what perhaps is an end with more difficulty attained) there is nothing done which should not be. Every word *tells,* and there is not a word which does *not* tell.

In "Howe's Masquerade" we observe something which resembles a plagiarism—but which *may* be a very flattering coincidence of thought. We quote the passage in question.

> *With a dark flush of wrath* upon his brow they saw the general *draw his sword* and *advance to meet* the figure *in the cloak* before the latter had stepped one pace upon the floor. *"Villian, unmuffle yourself,"* cried he, "you pass no farther!" The figure, without blenching a hair's breadth from the sword which was pointed at his breast, made a solemn pause, and *lowered the cape of the cloak* from his face, yet not sufficiently for the spectators to catch a glimpse of it. But Sir William Howe had evidently seen enough. The sternness of his countenance gave place to a look of wild amazement, if not horror, while he recoiled several steps from the figure, *and let fall his sword upon the floor.*—See vol. 2, p. 20.

The idea here is, that the figure in the cloak is the phantom or reduplication of Sir William Howe; but in an article called "William Wilson," one of the "Tales of the Grotesque and Arabesque," we have not only the same idea, but the same idea similarly presented in several respects. We quote two paragraphs, which our readers may compare with what has been already given. We have italicized, above, the immediate particulars of resemblance.

> The brief moment in which I averted my eyes had been sufficient to produce, apparently, a material change in the arrangement at the upper or farther end of the room. A large mirror, it appeared to me, now stood where none had been perceptible before; and as I stepped up to it in extremity of terror, mine own image, but with features all pale and dabbled in blood, *advanced* with a feeble and tottering gait to meet me. Thus it appeared I say, but was not. It was Wilson, who then stood before me in the agonies of dissolution. Not a line in all the marked and singular lineaments of that face which was not even identically mine own. *His mask and cloak lay where he had thrown them, upon the floor.* Vol. 2, p. 336.

Here, it will be observed that, not only are the two general conceptions identical, but there are various *points* of similarity. In each case the figure seen is the wraith or duplication of the beholder. In each case the scene is a masquerade. In each case the figure is cloaked. In each, there is a quarrel—that is to say, angry words pass between the parties. In each the beholder is enraged. In each the cloak and sword fall upon the floor. The "villain, unmuffle yourself," of Mr. H. is precisely paralleled [6] by a passage at page 56, of "William Wilson."

I must hasten to conclude this paper with a summary of Mr. Hawthorne's merits and demerits.

He is peculiar and *not* original—unless in those detailed fancies and detached thoughts which his want of general originality will deprive of the appreciation due to them, in preventing them from ever reaching the *public* eye. He is infinitely too fond of allegory, and can never hope for popularity so long as he persists in it. This he will not do, for allegory is at war with the whole tone of his nature, which disports itself never so well as when escaping from the mysticism of his Goodman Browns and White Old Maids into the hearty, genial, but still Indian-summer sunshine of his Wakefields and Little Annie's Rambles. Indeed, *his* spirit of "metaphor run-mad" is clearly imbibed from the phalanx and phalanstery [7] atmosphere in which he has been so long struggling for breath. He has not half the material for the exclusiveness of authorship that he possesses for its universality. He has the purest style, the finest taste, the most

6. **precisely paralleled:** Hawthorne could not have plagiarized, since his story appeared in the *Democratic Review* of May, 1838, and "William Wilson" in *Burton's* for October, 1839. 7. **phalanx and phalanstery:** The communal experiment at Brook Farm had begun in 1841.

available scholarship, the most delicate humor, the most touching pathos, the most radiant imagination, the most consummate ingenuity; and with these varied good qualities he has done *well* as a mystic. But is there any one of these qualities which should prevent his doing doubly as well in a career of honest, upright, sensible, prehensible and comprehensible things? Let him mend his pen, get a bottle of visible ink, come out from the Old Manse, cut Mr. Alcott, hang (if possible) the editor of the *Dial*, and throw out of the window to the pigs all his odd numbers of the *North American Review*.[8]

PREFACE TO THE RAVEN AND OTHER POEMS

◊

THE FOLLOWING is a prefatory note to Poe's last volume of poems, published in 1845.

◊

THESE trifles are collected and republished chiefly with a view to their redemption from the many improvements to which they have been subjected while going "the rounds of the press." I am naturally anxious that if what I have written is to circulate at all, it should circulate as I wrote it. In defence of my own taste, nevertheless, it is incumbent on me to say that I think nothing in this volume of much value to the public, or very creditable to myself. Events not to be controlled have prevented me from making, at any time, any serious effort in what, under happier circumstances, would have been the field of my choice. With me poetry has not been a purpose, but a passion; and the passions should be held in reverence; they must not—they cannot at will be excited, with an eye to the paltry compensations, or the more paltry commendations, of mankind.

E. A. P.

8. **Let . . . *Review*:** Poe refers to Bronson Alcott (1799–1888), Transcendentalist philosopher, and to Margaret Fuller (1810–50), editor of the *Dial*. The *North American Review*, while not a Transcendentalist organ, did publish some members of the group.

FROM

THE POETIC PRINCIPLE

◊

POE gave this lecture a number of times toward the end of his life, in Providence, Richmond, and elsewhere. It was published after his death in the New York *Home Journal* for August 31, 1850. The text derives, in great part, from Poe's review of Longfellow's *Ballads* in *Graham's Magazine* for April, 1842.

◊

WHILE the epic mania—while the idea that, to merit in poetry, prolixity is indispensable—has, for some years past, been gradually dying out of the public mind, by mere dint of its own absurdity, we find it succeeded by a heresy too palpably false to be long tolerated, but one which, in the brief period it has already endured, may be said to have accomplished more in the corruption of our Poetical Literature than all its other enemies combined. I allude to the heresy of *The Didactic*. It has been assumed, tacitly and avowedly, directly and indirectly, that the ultimate object of all Poetry is Truth. Every poem, it is said, should inculcate a moral; and by this moral is the poetical merit of the work to be adjudged. We Americans especially have patronised this happy idea; and we Bostonians, very especially, have developed it in full. We have taken it into our heads that to write a poem simply for the poem's sake, and to acknowledge such to have been our design, would be to confess ourselves radically wanting in the true Poetic dignity and force:—but the simple fact is, that, would we but permit ourselves to look into our own souls, we should immediately there discover that under the sun there neither exists nor *can* exist any work more thoroughly dignified—more supremely noble—than this very poem—this poem *per se*—this poem which is a poem and nothing more—this poem written solely for the poem's sake.

With as deep a reverence for the True as ever inspired the bosom of man, I would, nevertheless, limit, in some measure, its modes of inculcation. I would limit to enforce them. I would not enfeeble them by dissipation. The demands of Truth are severe. She has no sympathy with the myrtles. All *that* which is so indispensable in Song, is precisely all *that* with which *she* has nothing whatever to do. It is but making her a flaunting paradox, to wreathe her in gems and flowers. In enforcing a truth, we need severity rather than efflorescence of language. We must be simple, precise, terse. We must be cool, calm, unimpassioned. In a word, we must be in that mood which, as nearly as possible, is the exact converse of the poetical. *He* must be blind indeed who does not perceive the radical and chasmal differences between the truthful and the poetical modes of inculcation. He must be theory-mad beyond redemption who, in spite of these differences, shall still persist in attempting to reconcile the obstinate oils and waters of Poetry and Truth.

Dividing the world of mind into its three most immediately obvious distinctions, we have the Pure Intellect, Taste, and the Moral Sense. I place Taste in the middle, because it is just this position which, in the mind, it occupies. It holds intimate relations with either extreme; but from the Moral Sense is separated by so faint a difference that Aristotle has not hesitated to place some of its operations among the virtues themselves. Nevertheless, we find the offices of the trio marked with a sufficient distinction. Just as the Intellect concerns itself with Truth, so Taste informs us of the Beautiful while the Moral Sense is regardful of Duty. Of this latter, while Conscience teaches the obligation, and Reason the expediency, Taste contents herself with displaying the charms:—waging war upon Vice solely on the ground of her deformity—her disproportion—her animosity to the fitting, to the appropriate, to the harmonious—in a word, to Beauty.

An immortal instinct, deep within the spirit of man, is thus, plainly, a sense of the Beautiful. This it is which administers to his delight in the manifold forms, and sounds, and odours, and sentiments amid which he exists. And just as the lily is repeated in the lake, or the eyes of Amaryllis in the mirror, so is the mere oral or written repetition of these forms, and sounds, and colours, and odours, and sentiments, a duplicate source of delight. But this mere repetition is not poetry. He who shall simply sing, with however glowing enthusiasm, or with however vivid a truth of description, of the sights, and sounds, and odours, and colours, and sentiments, which greet *him* in common with all mankind—he, I say, has yet failed to prove his divine title. There is still a something in the distance which he has been unable to attain. We have still a thirst unquenchable, to allay which he has not shown us the crystal springs. This thirst belongs to the immortality of Man. It is at once a consequence and an indication of his perennial existence. It is the desire of the moth for the star.[1] It is no mere appreciation of the Beauty before us—but a wild effort to reach the Beauty above. Inspired by an ecstatic prescience of the glories beyond the grave, we struggle, by multiform combinations among the things and thoughts of Time, to attain a portion of that Loveliness whose very elements, perhaps, appertain to eternity alone.[2] And thus when by Poetry—or when by Music, the most entrancing of the Poetic moods—we find ourselves melted into tears—we weep then—not as the Abbate Gravina [3] supposes—through excess of pleasure, but through a certain petulant, impatient sorrow at our inability to grasp *now* wholly, here on earth, at once and for ever, those divine and rapturous joys, of which *through* the poem, or *through* the music, we attain to but brief and indeterminate glimpses.

The struggle to apprehend the supernal Loveliness—this struggle, on the part of souls fittingly constituted—has given to the world all *that* which it (the world) has ever been enabled at once to understand and to *feel* as poetic.

The Poetic Sentiment, of course, may develope itself in various modes—in Painting, in Sculpture, in Architecture, in the Dance—very especially in Music,—and very peculiarly, and with a wide field, in the composition of the Landscape Garden. Our present theme, however, has regard only to its manifestation in words. And here let me speak briefly on the topic of rhythm. Contenting myself with the certainty that Music, in its various modes of metre, rhythm, and rhyme, is of so vast a moment in Poetry as never to be wisely rejected—is so vitally important an adjunct, that he is simply silly who declines its assistance, I will not now pause to maintain its absolute essentiality. It is in Music, perhaps, that the soul most nearly attains the great end for which, when inspired by the Poetic Sentiment, it struggles—the creation of supernal Beauty. It *may* be, indeed, that here this sublime end is, now and then, attained *in fact*. We are often made to feel, with a shivering delight, that from an earthly harp are stricken notes which *cannot* have been unfamiliar to the angels.[4] And thus there can be little doubt that in the union of Poetry with Music in its popular sense, we shall find the widest field for the Poetic development. The old Bards and Minnesingers had advantages which we do not possess—and Thomas Moore, singing his own songs, was, in the most legitimate manner, perfecting them as poems.

THE POETIC PRINCIPLE. **1. desire . . . star:** echoes Shelley's poem, "One word is too often profaned."

2. Inspired . . . alone: See the analogy between chemistry and poetry in the fifth selection from "Marginalia," p. 473. **3. Gravina:** Gian Vincenzo Gravina, author of *Della Ragion Poetica* (1708). **4. We . . . angels:** recalls Poe's poem "Israfel," p. 385.

To recapitulate, then:—I would define, in brief, the Poetry of words as *The Rhythmical Creation of Beauty*. Its sole arbiter is Taste. With the Intellect or with the Conscience, it has only collateral relations. Unless incidentally, it has no concern whatever either with Duty or with Truth.

A few words, however, in explanation. *That* pleasure which is at once the most pure, the most elevating, and the most intense, is derived, I maintain, from the contemplation of the Beautiful. In the contemplation of Beauty we alone find it possible to attain that pleasurable elevation, or excitement, *of the soul,* which we recognize as the Poetic Sentiment, and which is so easily distinguished from Truth, which is the satisfaction of the Reason, or from Passion, which is the excitement of the heart. I make Beauty, therefore—using the word as inclusive of the sublime—I make Beauty the province of the poem, simply because it is an obvious rule of Art that effects should be made to spring as directly as possible from their causes—no one as yet having been weak enough to deny that the peculiar elevation in question is at least *most readily* attainable in the poem. It by no means follows, however, that the incitements of Passion, or the precepts of Duty, or even the lessons of Truth, may not be introduced into a poem, and with advantage; for they may subserve, incidentally, in various ways, the general purposes of the work:—but the true artist will always contrive to tone them down in proper subjection to that *Beauty* which is the atmosphere and the real essence of the poem. . . .

. . . While this [the poetic] Principle itself is, strictly and simply, the Human Aspiration for Supernal Beauty, the manifestation of the Principle is always found in *an elevating excitement of the Soul*—quite independent of that passion which is the intoxication of the Heart—or of that Truth which is the satisfaction of the Reason. For, in regard to Passion, alas! its tendency is to degrade rather than elevate the Soul. Love, on the contrary—Love—the true, the divine Eros—the Uranian, as distinguished from the Dionaean Venus [5]—is unquestionably the purest and truest of all poetical themes. And in regard to Truth—if, to be sure, through the attainment of a truth, we are led to perceive a harmony where none was apparent before, we experience, at once, the true poetical effect—but this effect is referable to the harmony alone, and not in the least degree to the truth which merely served to render the harmony manifest.

5. **Uranian . . . Venus:** The Uranian Aphrodite represents heavenly or spiritual love and beauty; Aphrodite regarded as the offspring of Zeus and the Titaness Dione is a lower or earthly principle. Milton invokes Urania, in preference to the Muses of Helicon, in his *Paradise Lost,* I and VII. Compare the opposition of moon and Venus in Poe's poem "Evening Star," p. 382.

FROM

MARGINALIA

◊

THE "Marginalia" were published in various magazines during the period 1844–49. Often they were culled from Poe's earlier reviews, but more often they were fresh observations. The first selection below is most important to an understanding of Poe, dealing as it does with what W. B. Yeats called "that marchland between waking and dreaming where our thoughts begin to have a life of their own—the region where art is nurtured and inspiration born." The fifth selection is also of peculiar importance, as an explicit statement of Poe's destructive and negative aesthetic: the highest imagination, he felt, achieves the ideal not *through* the real, but by the annihilation of the real.

◊

HOW very commonly we hear it remarked, that such and such thoughts are beyond the compass of words! I do not believe that any thought, properly so called, is out of the reach of language. I fancy, rather, that where difficulty in expression is experienced, there is, in the intellect which experiences it, a want either of deliberateness or of method. For my own part, I have never had a thought which I could not set down in words, with even more distinctness than that with which I conceived it:—as I have before observed, the thought is logicalized by the effort at (written) expression.

There is, however, a class of fancies, of exquisite delicacy, which are *not* thoughts, and to which, *as yet,* I have found it absolutely impossible to adapt language. I use the word *fancies* at random, and merely because I must use *some* word; but the idea commonly attached to the term is not even remotely applicable to the shadows of shadows in question. They seem to me rather psychal than intellectual. They arise in the soul (alas, how rarely!) only at its epochs of most intense tranquillity—when the bodily and mental health are in perfection—and at those mere points of time where the confines of the waking world blend with those of the world of dreams. I am aware of these "fancies" only when I am upon the very brink of sleep, with the consciousness that I am so. I have satisfied myself that this condition exists but for an inappreciable *point* of time—yet it is crowded with these "shadows of shadows"; and for absolute *thought* there is demanded time's *endurance*. These "fancies" have in them a pleasurable ecstasy, as far beyond the most pleasurable of the world of wakefulness, or of dreams, as the Heaven of the Northman theology is beyond its Hell. I regard the visions, even as they arise, with an awe which, in some measure, moderates or tranquillizes the ecstasy—I so regard them, through a conviction (which seems a portion of the ecstasy itself) that this ecstasy, in itself, is of a character supernal to the Human Nature—is a glimpse of the spirit's outer world; and I arrive at this conclusion—if this term is at all applicable to instantaneous intuition—by a perception that the delight experienced has, as its element, but *the absoluteness of novelty*. I say the absoluteness—for in these fancies—let me now term them psychal impressions—there is really nothing even approximate in character to impressions ordinarily received. It is as if the five senses were supplanted by five myriad others alien to mortality.

Now, so entire is my faith in the *power of words*, that, at times, I have believed it possible to embody even the evanescence of fancies such as I have attempted to describe. In experiments with this end in view, I have proceeded so far as, first, to control (when the bodily and mental health are good) the existence of the condition:—that is to say, I can now (unless when ill) be sure that the condition will supervene, if I so wish it, at the point of time already described: of its supervention, until lately, I could never be certain, even under the most favorable circumstances. I mean to say, merely, that now I can be sure, when all circumstances are favorable, of the supervention of the condition, and feel even the capacity of inducing or compelling it:—the favorable circumstances, however, are not the less rare—else had I compelled, already, the Heaven into the earth.

I have proceeded so far, secondly, as to prevent the lapse from *the point* of which I speak—the point of blending between wakefulness and sleep—as to prevent at will, I say, the lapse from this border-ground into the dominion of sleep. Not that I can *continue* the condition—not that I can render the point more than a point—but that I can startle myself from the point into wakefulness—and *thus transfer the point itself into the realm of Memory*—convey its impressions, or more properly their recollections, to a situation where (although still for a brief period) I can survey them with the eye of analysis.

For these reasons—that is to say, because I have been enabled to accomplish thus much—I do not altogether despair of embodying in words at least enough of the fancies in question to convey, to certain classes of intellect, a shadowy conception of their character.

In saying this I am not to be understood as supposing that the fancies, or psychal impressions, to which I allude, are confined to my individual self—are not, in a word, common to all mankind—for on this point it is quite impossible that I should form an opinion—but nothing can be more certain than that even a partial record of the impressions would startle the universal intellect of mankind, by the *supremeness of the novelty* of the material employed, and of its consequent suggestions. In a word—should I ever write a paper on this topic, the world will be compelled to acknowledge that, at last, I have done an original thing.

WE might contrive a very poetical and very suggestive, although, perhaps, no very tenable philosophy, by supposing that the virtuous live while the wicked suffer annihilation, hereafter; and that the danger of the annihilation (which would be in the ratio of the sin) might be indicated nightly by slumber, and occasionally, with more distinctness, by a swoon. In proportion to the dreamlessness of the sleep, for example, would be the degree of the soul's liability to annihilation. In the same way, to swoon and awake in utter unconsciousness of any lapse of time during the syncope, would demonstrate the soul to be then in such condition that, had death occurred, annihilation would have followed. On the other hand, when the revival is attended with the remembrance of visions, (as is now and then the case, in fact,) then the soul is to be considered in such condition as would insure its existence after the bodily death—the bliss or wretchedness of the existence to be indicated by the character of the visions.

THERE are moments when, even to the sober eye of Reason, the world of our sad humanity must assume the aspect of Hell; but the Imagination of Man is no Carathis,[1] to explore with impunity its every cavern. Alas! the grim legion of sepulchral terrors can*not* be regarded as altogether fanciful; but like the Demons in whose company Afrasiab [2] made his voyage down the

MARGINALIA. 1. **Carathis:** mother of the Caliph Vathek, in William Beckford's oriental tale, *Vathek* (1786). 2. **Afrasiab:** the King of Turan, defeated by Rustum in the *Shahnameh*, an epic composed by the Persian poet Firdusi (950–1020).

Oxus, they must sleep, or they will devour us—they must be suffered to slumber, or we perish.

IF any ambitious man have a fancy to revolutionize, at one effort, the universal world of human thought, human opinion, and human sentiment, the opportunity is his own—the road to immortal renown lies straight, open, and unencumbered before him. All that he has to do is write and publish a very little book. Its title should be simple—a few plain words—*My Heart Laid Bare*. But—this little book must be *true to its title*.

Now, is it not very singular that, with the rabid thirst for notoriety which distinguishes so many of mankind—so many, too, who care not a fig what is thought of them after death, there should not be found one man having sufficient hardihood to write this little book? To *write,* I say. There are ten thousand men who, if the book were once written, would laugh at the notion of being disturbed by its publication during their life, and who could not even conceive *why* they should object to its being published after their death. But to write it—*there* is the rub. No man dare write it. No man ever will dare write it. No man *could* write it, even if he dared. The paper would shrivel and blaze at every touch of the fiery pen.

THE *pure Imagination* chooses, from *either Beauty or Deformity,* only the most combinable things hitherto uncombined; the compound, as a general rule, partaking, in character, of beauty, or sublimity, in the ratio of the respective beauty or sublimity of the things combined—which are themselves still to be considered as atomic—that is to say, as previous combinations. But, as often analogously happens in physical chemistry, so not unfrequently does it occur in this chemistry of the intellect, that the admixture of two elements results in a something that has nothing of the qualities of one of them, or even nothing of the qualities of either. . . . Thus, the range of Imagination is unlimited. Its materials extend throughout the universe. Even out of deformities it fabricates that *Beauty* which is at once its sole object and its inevitable test. But, in general, the richness or force of the matters combined; the facility of discovering combinable novelties worth combining; and, especially, the absolute "chemical combination" of the completed mass—are the particulars to be regarded in our estimate of Imagination. It is this thorough harmony of an imaginative work which so often causes it to be undervalued by the thoughtless, through the character of *obviousness* which is superinduced. We are apt to find ourselves asking *why* it is that these combinations have never been imagined before.

THE theorizers on Government, who pretend always to "begin with the beginning," commence with Man in what they call his *natural* state—the savage. What right have they to suppose this his natural state? Man's chief idiosyncrasy being reason, it follows that his savage condition—his condition of action *without* reason—is his *unnatural* state. The more he reasons, the nearer he approaches the position to which this chief idiosyncrasy impels him; and not until he attains this position with exactitude—not until his reason has exhausted itself for his improvement—not until he has stepped upon the highest pinnacle of civilization—will his *natural* state be ultimately reached, or thoroughly determined.

THE sense of high birth is a moral force whose value the democrats, albeit compact of mathematics, are never in condition to calculate. *"Pour savoir ce qu'est Dieu,"* says the Baron de Bielfeld,[3] *"il faut etre Dieu même."*

THAT man is not truly brave who is afraid either to seem or to be, when it suits him, a coward.

NOT only do I think it paradoxical to speak of a man of *genius* as personally ignoble, but I confidently maintain that the *highest* genius is but the loftiest moral nobility.

I HAVE sometimes amused myself by endeavoring to fancy what would be the fate of any individual gifted, or rather accursed, with an intellect *very* far superior to that of his race. Of course, he would be conscious of his superiority; nor could he (if otherwise constituted as man is) help manifesting his consciousness. Thus he would make himself enemies at all points. And since his opinions and speculations would widely differ from those of *all* mankind—that he would be considered a madman, is evident. How horribly painful such a condition! Hell could invent no greater torture than that of being charged with abnormal weakness on account of being abnormally strong.

In like manner, nothing can be clearer than that a *very* generous spirit—*truly* feeling what all merely profess—must inevitably find itself misconceived in every direction—its motives misinterpreted. Just as extremeness of intelligence would be thought fatuity, so excess of chivalry could not fail of being

3. **Bielfeld:** the Baron von Bielefeld (1712–70), author of *The Elements of Universal Erudition.* The quotation means "To understand God one must be God himself."

looked upon as meanness in its last degree:—and so on with other virtues. This subject is a painful one indeed. That individuals *have* so soared above the plane of their race, is scarcely to be questioned; but, in looking back through history for traces of their existence, we should pass over all biographies of "the good and the great," while we search carefully the slight records of wretches who died in prison, in Bedlam, or upon the gallows.

FROM

EUREKA

◇

THE FOLLOWING are the concluding paragraphs of Poe's cosmological prose poem of 1848, the general outlines of which are sketched in Part III of the Introduction. This closing passage is particularly valuable for its account of the soul's history: its previous existence, during which it was cognizant of divine harmony; its dreamy youth on Earth; its corruption by the "conventional World-Reason"; its occasional glimpses or memories, during manhood, of its cosmic destiny; its preordained escape from material diversity into the spiritual oneness of God. All of Poe's fiction is in some measure based on this myth of the soul.

◇

I REPEAT then—Let us endeavor to comprehend that the final globe of globes will instantaneously disappear, and that God will remain all in all.

But are we here to pause? Not so. On the Universal agglomeration and dissolution, we can readily conceive that a new and perhaps totally different series of conditions may ensue—another creation and irradiation, returning into itself—another action and reaction of the Divine Will. Guiding our imaginations by that omniprevalent law of laws, the law of periodicity, are we not, indeed, more than justified in entertaining a belief—let us say, rather, in indulging a hope—that the processes we have here ventured to contemplate will be renewed forever, and forever, and forever; a novel Universe swelling into existence, and then subsiding into nothingness, at every throb of the Heart Divine?

And now—this Heart Divine—what is it? *It is our own.*

Let not the merely seeming irreverence of this idea frighten our souls from that cool exercise of consciousness—from that deep tranquillity of self-inspection—through which alone we can hope to attain the presence of this, the most sublime of truths, and look it leisurely in the face.

The *phaenomena* on which our conclusions must at this point depend, are merely spiritual shadows, but not the less thoroughly substantial.

We walk about, amid the destinies of our world-existence, encompassed by dim but ever present *Memories* of a Destiny more vast—very distant in the bygone time, and infinitely awful.

We live out a Youth peculiarly haunted by such dreams; yet never mistaking them for dreams. As Memories we *know* them. *During our Youth* the distinction is too clear to deceive us even for a moment.

So long as this Youth endures, the feeling *that we exist,* is the most natural of all feelings. We understand it *thoroughly*. That there was a period at which we did *not* exist—or, that it might so have happened that we never had existed at all—are the considerations, indeed, which *during this youth,* we find difficulty in understanding. Why we should *not* exist, is, *up to the epoch of our Manhood,* of all queries the most unanswerable. Existence—self-existence—existence from all Time and to all Eternity—seems, up to the epoch of Manhood, a normal and unquestionable condition:—*seems, because it is.*

But now comes the period at which a conventional World-Reason awakens us from the truth of our dream. Doubt, Surprise and Incomprehensibility arrive at the same moment. They say:—"You live and the time was when you lived not. You have been created. An Intelligence exists greater than your own; and it is only through this Intelligence you live at all." These things we struggle to comprehend and cannot:—*cannot,* because these things, being untrue, are thus, of necessity, incomprehensible.

No thinking being lives who, at some luminous point of his life of thought, has not felt himself lost amid the surges of futile efforts at understanding, or believing, that anything exists *greater than his own soul.* The utter impossibility of any one's soul feeling itself inferior to another; the intense, overwhelming dissatisfaction and rebellion at the thought;—these, with the omniprevalent aspirations at perfection, are but the spiritual, coincident with the material, struggles towards the original Unity—are, to my mind at least, a species of proof far surpassing what Man terms demonstration, that no one soul *is* inferior to another—that nothing is, or can be, superior to any one soul—that each soul is, in part, its own God—its own Creator:—in a word, that God—the material *and* spiritual God—*now* exists solely in the diffused Matter and Spirit of the Universe; and that the regathering of this diffused Matter and Spirit will be but the reconstitution of the *purely* Spiritual and Individual God.

In this view, and in this view alone, we comprehend the riddles of Divine Injustice—of Inexorable Fate. In this view alone the existence of Evil becomes intelligible; but in this view it becomes more—it becomes endurable. Our souls no longer rebel at a *Sorrow* which we ourselves have imposed upon ourselves, in furtherance of our own purposes—with a view—if even with a futile view —to the extension of our own *Joy*.

I have spoken of *Memories* that haunt us during our youth. They sometimes pursuc us even in our Manhood:—assume gradually less and less indefinite shapes:—now and then speak to us with low voices, saying:

"There was an epoch in the Night of Time, when a still-existent Being existed—one of an absolutely infinite number of similar Beings that people the absolutely infinite domains of the absolutely infinite space. It was not and is not in the power of this Being—any more than it is in your own—to extend, by actual increase, the joy of his Existence; but just as it *is* in your power to expand or to concentrate your pleasures (the absolute amount of happiness remaining always the same) so did and does a similar capability appertain to this Divine Being, who thus passes his Eternity in perpetual variation of Concentrated Self and almost Infinite Self-Diffusion. What you call The Universe is but his present expansive existence. He now feels his life through an infinity of imperfect pleasures—the partial and pain-entangled pleasures of those inconceivably numerous things which you designate as his creatures, but which are really but infinite individualizations of Himself. All these creatures—*all*—those which you term animate, as well as those to whom you deny life for no better reason than that you do not behold it in operation—*all* these creatures have, in a greater or less degree, a capacity for pleasure and for pain:—*but the general sum of their sensations is precisely that amount of Happiness which appertains by right to the Divine Being when concentrated within Himself.* These creatures are all too, more or less conscious Intelligences; conscious, first, of a proper identity; conscious, secondly and by faint indeterminate glimpses, of an identity with the Divine Being of whom we speak—of an identity with God. Of the two classes of consciousness, fancy that the former will grow weaker, the latter stronger, during the long succession of ages which must elapse before these myriads of individual Intelligences become blended—when the bright stars become blended—into One. Think that the sense of individual identity will be gradually merged in the general consciousness—that Man, for example, ceasing imperceptibly to feel himself Man, will at length attain that awfully triumphant epoch when he shall recognize his existence as that of Jehovah. In the meantime bear in mind that all is Life—Life—Life within Life—the less within the greater, and all within the *Spirit Divine*.

NEWTON ARVIN
Editor

Ralph Waldo Emerson

1803–1882

EMERSON has had a curious fate, though by no means a unique one. To the older generation, at the beginning of his career, he seemed a propagator of dangerous and probably subversive ideas—"the latest form of infidelity," as a famous attack had it. The old ex-President, John Quincy Adams, wagging his head sadly over the heresies preached by this son of an old friend, could only describe them as "wild and visionary phantasies," clearly destructive of "the most important and solemn duties of the Christian faith." To the younger generation, on the contrary, he spoke as a liberator and a spurrer-on—a liberator from the handcuffs of convention and timidity, a spurrer-on to a life of rebellion, experiment, discovery, and heroic action. For younger men and women—and this over a period of decades—he played the roles both of a Socrates and of a Taillefer; of an emancipator and a warrior-bard, a questioner and an instigator to valor. He did more than any other man, said John Jay Chapman, "to rescue the youth of the next generation and fit them for the fierce times to follow. It will not be denied that he sent ten thousand sons to the war."

Time passed, however, and though this tonicity of Emerson's has probably never ceased to exercise, behind the scenes, its invigorating effect on responsive minds, a public process of dilution and vulgarization got under way: the inflammatory strains in his thought were conveniently banked over and damped down; his affirmations were translated into complacencies, his ardor into "strenuousness," and his philosophical optimism into Positive Thinking. The vulgarizers, to tell the truth, could always cite chapter and verse for their deformations of Emerson's teaching: their version is a caricature, but it is a caricature of something that is really there. In any case, his name gradually became synonymous with a shallow cheerfulness or a kind of Boy Scout gospel of essentially adolescent virility. The best minds of a later generation found less and less to make use of in Emerson, more and more to reject; and Yvor Winters was only, in his turn, caricaturing a serious and widespread view when he called Emerson "a fraud and a sentimentalist." It was quite as wrongheaded a judgment as John Quincy Adams's had been, and it will not stand up under questioning. But it can be seen through and set aside only if we return to what Emerson actually thought and wrote.

II

UNLIKE the lives of some other American writers—Melville, for example, or Mark Twain or Hemingway—Emerson's life was externally wanting in the stuff of vivid narrative: outwardly it was not very eventful or dramatic or *mouvementé*. His real life was, for the most part, an inward one, and in that sense his biography can be quickly summarized. "Great geniuses," he once said, "have the shortest biographies. Their cousins can tell you nothing about them." There may be some striking exceptions to this rule, but Emerson himself is not one of them. He was born in Boston in 1803, during Jefferson's first administration, to a highly respectable family of strongly anti-Jeffersonian and conservatively Federalist opinions. His father was a Unitarian minister, and indeed Emerson was the scion of an ancient ministerial stock: he was to be the eighth consecutive clergyman in a line reaching back to the seventeenth century—a line, to put it otherwise, stretching down from the pristine Calvinism of the first emigrants through the evangelical fervors of Edwards' generation to what Emerson called "the pale negations of Boston Unitarianism" as they were expounded by his father from the pulpit of the First Church. Emerson came by his priestly office as naturally as any young Levite or Brahmin, and, given his genius, it was equally natural that, when the time came, he should recoil upon this paternal heritage and cast it from him.

"My recollections of early life," he once wrote, "are not very pleasant." What he had in mind in saying this was at least partly the fact that his father, the Reverend William Emerson, died when he himself was only eight, and that the family life from then on was bound in by what he calls "the iron band of poverty, of necessity, of austerity." Emerson and his brothers were early inured to the rigors of something very like penury. But this did not mean that their education was neglected. Pinched as the family life was materially, Emerson was sent to the Boston Latin School and then, at the age of fourteen, to Harvard, where he graduated in the class of 1821. A few years of rather disconsolate schoolteaching followed, and in 1825, after a good deal of troubled uncertainty over the choice of a vocation, Emerson entered the Harvard Divinity School. The years that followed were made difficult not only by uncertain health but by much painful self-distrust and recurrent moods of dejection. In 1826, however, he obtained his "approbation" to preach in Unitarian churches, and three years later he became the pastor of the Second Church in Boston.

His career as a minister was to be a short one. The young Emerson was far too sensitive to the intellectual and literary changes that were taking place in Europe and, less conspicuously, in this country, to be long contented with the essentially eighteenth-century outlook of even the "liberal Christians." "From their orthodox kind of dissent he dissented," as Lowell said of another preacher, and in 1832, despite the protests of his affectionate congregation, he resigned his pastorate. The immediate occasion for Emerson's withdrawal from the ministry was his inability to continue conscientiously to administer the Lord's Supper, but his difficulties covered more ground than that. Both his reading and his independent thinking had driven Emerson farther and farther from *any* version of institutional religion, and though he continued for a few years to preach occasionally as a substitute for other ministers, it was with less and less conviction or satisfaction, and in 1839 he gave up the pulpit once and for all.

His resignation had confronted him again with the question of a vocation, both in the sternly practical and in the ideal sense. The answer had presented itself almost providentially: the age of the lecture platform—the lyceum system—had been ushered in only a few years earlier; and in 1833, after traveling for some months in Europe, Emerson gave his first lecture from a public platform to the Natural History Society in Boston. It was only the first of scores of lectures that were to follow, over a period of nearly forty years. Oratory, public speech, had from an early age been one of Emerson's abiding preoccupations (in college he is said to have been "especially happy . . . in declamation"). Despite his need of solitude and solitary meditation, he felt also the need of direct communication with a living audience, and in the long run he was to prove a deeply impressive and widely influential lecturer. Most of his essays were originally presented, though usually not in their final form, as lectures, and for many years he was a familiar figure to audiences not only in New England but in the Middle States and later in "the West"—in Cleveland and Cincinnati, in Chicago and St. Louis, in Madison and Milwaukee.

Meanwhile, to return to the thirties, Emerson's life, after the discontents, the indecisions, and the false starts of his youth, had gradually taken on an outward form that, in spite of practical anxieties and a series of personal bereavements, was to harmonize more and more with the inward serenity he had somehow attained, however precariously. In 1834 he had settled for good in Concord, the village that had been the home of his ancestors; in the following year he made a second marriage—his young and lovely first wife had died before his resignation—and bought the spacious house that was to be his permanent home; and in 1836, with the publication of his first book, *Nature,* he began to gather about him those like-minded contemporaries and then, as time went on, those younger admirers and even disciples who were to demonstrate to him that, in "thinking alone" and in "speaking his own mind," he was thinking and speaking for a whole age.

Despite the physical and material strenuousness of American society at the time, or because of it, a canopy of conventionality, of oppressive stuffiness, hung over its intellectual and spiritual life; and all the dissatisfied minds that were longing to see the canopy lifted were on the alert to recognize any voice that would speak out against the prevailing grayness. *Nature* did this; and the result was that Emerson was invited, almost at once, to deliver the annual Phi Beta Kappa oration at Harvard the following summer. "The American Scholar," as he called this oration, exhilarated his hearers, especially the younger men, with the eager sense that they were listening to a manifesto of intellectual independence; and when, a year later, in 1838, he was invited by the graduating class at the Harvard Divinity School to deliver an address to *them,* he responded with a discourse that identified him permanently with the forces that were making for moral and spiritual renovation.

Utterances such as these, and the orations at Dartmouth and Waterville that soon followed, made Emerson for a time a kind of storm center of the "Newness," as the movement of revolt came to be called. Controversy for its own sake, however, had no charms for Emerson; he was prepared to bear witness to the truths he saw, but he had no love of dispute, of hot-tempered argument, of the jangle of debate; and though he never merely retreated to the rear of the battle, he insisted quietly on his right to withdraw, for repose and restoration, to what his "admirable gossip," Montaigne, had called the back shop of his mind. His life in Concord, as time went on, came to resemble that of a forest philosopher or a Stoic sage or even a very unorthodox anchorite. No substance so magnetic as that of Emerson's mind, however, could fail to pull other minds toward itself, and he had perhaps more than his quota of visitors and votaries—some of them bores, some of them gentle lunatics, some of them (like Thoreau and Whitman) men of independent genius.

Much of his time was spent sauntering in the woods and fields, along the riverside or pond-sides of Concord, the low-pitched beauty of which he loved, and which he found an inexhaustible restorer. Much of his time, too, was spent writing in the journal that he had begun at the age of sixteen, while he was a Junior in college, and that he kept steadily, year after year, until his old age. One of the purposes of this journal was to serve as a kind of literary bank from the deposits in which he drew much of the material for his lectures and, later, his essays. But it had an independent value of its own for him. The private notebook or journal was a peculiarly natural form of literary expression for a writer who was both so sharply observant and so delicately introspective as Emerson was, and the ten volumes of his published *Journals* are an organic and indispensable part of his total literary achievement. It is impossible to know Emerson intimately without reading them, but it is impossible also to represent them adequately in a few pages of selections, and they are very regrettably not represented at all in this book.

Morally speaking, he never retreated an inch from the advanced positions he had taken in the thirties, though he enriched and deepened and tempered them intellectually. But the rest of the country, or much of it, caught up with him as time went on; his great distinction as a speaker and writer was not to be denied, nor the force and wisdom of his exhortations; and Emerson came to be recognized, in middle and later life, as one of the two or three most eminent men of letters in America. Predictable and proper honors, even of an official sort, came to him: though he was not invited back to Harvard for almost thirty years after the talk at the Divinity School, he was at last, in 1866, given an honorary degree by the college, and in 1867 the alumni elected him an "overseer." In the same year, with a pleasant symbolic fitness, he was invited once again to deliver an address ("Progress of Culture") to the Phi Beta Kappa society. He lived for another decade and a half, trimming himself, as he said, "to the storm of time," but determined to "obey the voice at eve obeyed at prime," and died peacefully in 1882.

III

THE immense value Emerson's teaching had for his own generation was due, on the level of ideas, partly to what he rejected and partly to what he affirmed. Earlier writers—Irving, Bryant, Cooper—had given expression in their work to one impulse or another of the romantic *sensibility;* Emerson, for the first time in this country, gave full and eloquent expression to the *philosophy* of romantic idealism—of what was soon known, though Emerson came to dislike the word, as "Transcendentalism." Fortunately he was never described as "the American Coleridge" or "the American Carlyle," though the service he performed for the American mind was not dissimilar to that which Coleridge and Carlyle had performed for the English. Like them, and partly under their spell, he had come to detest the whole system of ideas that had held sway over men's minds in Europe—and, somewhat less tyrannically, in America—for almost two centuries before his time, and to resolve that he would think and act in the light of truer insights and a profounder knowledge. One way to put this, though not a wholly just one, is to say that Emerson felt the world had had enough of Benjamin Franklin.

At any rate, he felt that the spiritual and intellectual biases of the seventeenth and eighteenth centuries, of the Age of Reason, however creative they might have been in their prime, had ended in sterility and denudation, and that the time had come for the reassertion of older wisdoms; still more, for the utterance of fresher ones. On the deepest level he was persuaded that the religious life had been impoverished and all but destroyed, partly by the empty traditionalism of the churches, partly by the dehydrated rationality of the Deists. He had ceased to believe, moreover, in that conception of knowledge and role of the mind formulated by Lockean empiricism, which was still the basis of philosophical teaching when he was an undergraduate and the underpinning of Unitarian doctrine when he studied at the Divinity School. The image of the world, of nature, that had been so dear to the imagination of the older materialists and mechanists—the image of a World Machine as beautifully, as delicately, constructed as a watch or an orrery, but quite as mechanical—had come to seem to Emerson, as to Goethe and Wordsworth, intolerable. In the sphere of morals, too, he was in full rebellion against the eighteenth century—against that calculus of pleasures and pains which it had made the test of right and wrong—against the tenet of what Carlyle called "the monster UTILITARIA" according to which the only criterion of good and evil in human life is the criterion of Utility. And finally, like the great European romantics, Emerson was ready to throw into the discard all those older views of beauty, of the arts, of poetry, of the role of the poet, that had been so congenial to the rationalistic mind and that have come to be known in literary history as the principles of neoclassicism.

The rationalistic mind seemed to him to have chilled and rigidified the whole of human existence, beginning with the life of the spirit on its profoundest levels. His own religious experience, like that of his grandfather in the days of Edwards and Whitefield, had taught him that religion has far less to do with the "understanding" than with what Edwards called "an affected fervent heart," and that without "a certain enthusiasm," as Emerson himself said, it is nothing. The cool, reasonable, philosophical beliefs of the Deists and of many Unitarians seemed to him a spiritless substitute for religion, not religion itself; this, for him, was "an influx of the Divine mind into our mind"—

an ecstasy, not an induction. With institutions, with churches, with creeds and liturgies, it has, at best, only secondary relations. Essentially it is a superrational communication between the individual soul and what Emerson came to call the Over-Soul; its truth, as he said to the young men at the Divinity School, "is guarded by one stern condition; this, namely; it is an intuition. It cannot be received at second hand." The religion of the sects, like the religion of the Deists, had ceased, for Emerson, to be a vehicle of spiritual experience.

His *own* experience, again—his meditations, his moments of vision, his immersion in the writings of Plato and the Neoplatonists, of Swedenborg, of the Hindu teachers—had carried him well beyond the frontiers of even a liberalized Christianity: in that sense John Quincy Adams was right enough. The Emersonian faith is a faith that, without indeed repudiating the whole Judaeo-Christian tradition, is no longer specifically either Judaic or Christian. It is a purely idealistic belief in an ultimate spiritual reality, an impersonal and timeless Absolute, a transcendent ONE. In its true nature this One is not to be described or defined; it eludes all attempts to confine it in a net of language or system; it is simply essential Being—"that Unity, that Over-Soul, within which every man's particular being is contained and made one with all other"—and in its presence all else is only relatively real, is transitional and somehow illusory. Yet this central Unity is not, as in some absolutist systems, destructive of all diversity or individuality: the reality of these may be only relative and in some ultimate sense illusory, but it is not a mere empty delusion. A mysterious contradiction is involved, but Emerson "knows" that the individual soul exists and that, without its ceasing to exist, it and the divine Soul are one. Divinity, as he says, is within as well as above: "God in us worships God." It is this divine principle that is the true self, not "the biographical Ego."

What follows from such convictions is that the physical world, real as it is empirically, is dependent for its reality on Spirit, and that the ultimate nature of things is not to be found, as materialists have always held, in matter, but in mind. In the strictest metaphysical sense, Emerson's thought probably does not hold together with perfect coherence on these levels, but he made no claim to being a system-builder, and the spirit of his teaching, its intrinsic direction, is plain enough. The philosophy that had given to the mind a dependent and secondary status in its relation to the external world, that had seen it as essentially passive in the process of knowing, that had denied to it an active, a creative role—this philosophy Emerson, like his European precursors, repudiated. What took its place for him was the conviction that the physical world is the *creation* of mind, not its formative context, and that, since mind has somehow brought that world into existence, our knowledge of it is the knowledge the artist has of his own handiwork: "the Intellect builds the universe and is the key to all it contains." As time went on, Emerson was to grow more and more doubtful about the certainty of our knowledge of particulars, of details, of "accidents"; but of the trustworthiness of the mind as the key to the Whole he felt no final skepticism.

Nor did he doubt for a moment that the whole mechanistic conception of Nature was a fallacious one. The World Machine had simply broken down, like so many machines, and what had taken its place, for the imagination, was the World Tree—or at any rate some metaphor of growth, of organic productivity, of creative burgeoning and fertility. Nature was no longer an ingenious and essentially lifeless contrivance: it was an animated and dynamic Life. "We can point nowhere," says Emerson, "to anything final; but tendency appears on all hands: planet, system, constellation, total nature is growing like a field of maize in July; is becoming somewhat else; is in rapid metamorphosis." So swift, indeed, so incessant is its movement that in order to express it in language we must avail ourselves of such metaphors not only as that of a tree but as that of a rushing stream or a series of circles rapidly expanding outward from an unchanging center.

Not only so: there is another aspect in which nature must be viewed—an aspect that follows from its dependence on mind. If, as Emerson says, "intellect is primary; nature, secondary; it is the memory of the mind," then it must follow that what are called the laws of nature are not merely objective and independent uniformities; properly conceived, they are laws of the intellect itself; they are, so to say, intellectual, not material laws, and a perfect correspondence will be discoverable between them and the laws of the human mind. What are called scientific facts will turn out to "correspond," as Swedenborg held, to spiritual facts, and indeed to be symbolic of them. "Everything transitory," said Goethe, "is only a symbol"; and for Emerson, too, the whole of physical nature, the cosmos itself, is one vast symbol of Spirit. Mere literalness, prosaic factuality, disappears from the cosmic scene; all things are metaphors, and symbolism, far from being a mere device of the poets or the theologians, is the clue to all immaterial reality. "We are symbols and inhabit symbols," says Emerson; "workman, work, and tools, words and things, birth and death, all are emblems": our knowledge of the world is inherently a symbolic knowledge, and language itself is essentially and necessarily a system of metaphors.

In all this Emerson was not only drawing upon his predecessors—Swedenborg and Goethe, Coleridge and Carlyle—but giving a turn to the doctrine of symbols that entitles him to be seen as himself a predecessor of more recent thinkers; of Ernst Cassirer, for one, with his view that "the special symbolic forms are not imitations, but *organs* of reality." In any case, by teaching that objects in nature are not merely measurable, weighable, mathematically describable facts, but emblems of the intangible, Emerson was making a complete break with the metaphysics of materialism. He made an equally complete break with its ethics. The older school of moralists—the hedonists and utilitarians—had sought to find a sanction for ethical distinctions in the experiences of pleasure and pain, and for ethical behavior in the criterion of utility. The result was of course, not only a materialistic but a relativistic theory of good and evil. To Emerson this theory was anathema; he described it once as "the stinking philosophy of the utilitarian." For him the distinction between virtue and vice is *relative* to nothing: it is an absolute distinction. Goodness is by no means merely that which conduces to the multiplication of pleasures or satisfactions: it is "the adherence in action to the nature of things." It is, in short, a purely ideal or transcendental conception, and what Emerson repeatedly calls the Moral Law is for him the eternal law of Being itself. As such, it is not simply a guide to conduct but an object of adoration; Emerson conceives of the Good indeed as identical with the One, and of religion as essentially its worship. "The progress of religion," he says, "is steadily to its identity with morals."

It might be supposed that, entertaining as he did so austerely ideal a conception of the good, Emerson's practical morality would be not *only* a very austere but a very safe and law-abiding one. And in fact it does make stern demands on the conscience and on personal conduct at every turn. Yet it is very far, in spirit and intention, from being an inculcation of cautious and conventional virtues; it is an inculcation, rather, of risky, unconventional, and heroic virtues—the virtues of the man who acts not in the light of received codes but in the light of the Moral Law itself. From the point of view of ordinary morality such a man is by no means sure to be "good." "I hate goodies," Emerson indeed wrote in his journal. "I hate goodness that preaches . . . Goodies make us very bad . . . We will almost sin to spite them." To the conformists who toe the harmless line of inherited morals, the Hero, the Great Man, is not always distinguishable from the law-breaker, and in practice he does often, in the merely legal sense, break the law. "The men who evince the force of the moral sentiment and of genius," says Emerson, "are not normal, canonical people, but wild and Ishmaelitish"; and his admiration went, again and again, though often with essential reservations, to men like Caesar and Cromwell and Napoleon rather than to more manageable characters. If we were to say, with a French philosophical writer,[1] that Emerson's doctrine is "an immoralism," we should be misrepresenting him to readers for whom that word has the familiar connotations. But as it is used in its special context it is not inapplicable.

Traditional systems of ethics have ordinarily found the sanctions of right and wrong in some appeal to the needs or demands of a group—

[1] Charles Andler, *Les Précurseurs de Nietzsche* (1920).

of a race, a class, a state, a people—in short, of society. Emerson is an "immoralist" chiefly because he finds those sanctions, or seems to find them, solely in the moral sense of the individual. Here, as elsewhere in Emerson, a contradiction is involved that could lead, and has led, to much misunderstanding. But there can be no doubt that, at one pole of his teaching, Emerson intended to disseminate a new and quite radical respect for the sacredness of individuality, for the incommensurable uniqueness of the "single man," and for the virtues of moral and intellectual independence. "Nature," he says, "never rhymes her children, nor makes two men alike"; and what follows from this, in his belief, is that a man's duty consists, first of all, in resisting all pressures from without, in refusing to measure his conduct by the accepted values of society, and in thinking and acting in the light of self-derived and self-warranted standards. Through all Emerson's early addresses and essays runs like a burden this "lesson of self-help": it was the principal secret of his immense effect as an ethical teacher, and it is quite true that the lesson could be interpreted not only as a call to heroic action but also as a kind of august authorization for various forms of "immoralism."

It could do so for the very good reason that one strain in Emerson's thought is in fact a love of the spectacle not only of Heroism but of Power. The fact of personal force, of superior vitality, of great individual energy, aroused such enthusiasm in him that he was willing to make many allowances for the irregularities to which these qualities might conduce. "Power first," he says, "or no leading class. In politics and in trade, bruisers and pirates are of better promise than talkers and clerks"; and elsewhere he lays it down that "We must fetch the pump with dirty water, if clean cannot be had." Pronouncements such as this might well be expected to give aid and comfort to forms of immoralism that even the unconventional and nonconforming will dread. And indeed the step from Emerson's cult of the strong man to Nietzsche's "Will to Power" would not seem to be a very great one: Nietzsche himself, on whom Emerson had a profound effect, did not find it so.

There is a genuinely hazardous quality in all this that cannot be cheerfully whistled away, just as there is in Whitman's comparable cult of strength—of what he calls "the power of personality just or unjust." Yet we turn from these passages in Emerson in which a doubtfully scrupulous individualism is celebrated, to other passages, apparently in baffling contradiction to them, in which the very reality of individuals, in any ultimate sense, is denied. "The study of many individuals," says one of these, "leads us to an elemental region wherein the individual is lost, or wherein all touch by their summits . . . All that respects the individual is temporary and prospective, like the individual himself, who is ascending out of his limits into a catholic existence." In short, and though real contradictions in Emerson's teaching remain, he himself was able to preach his gospel of self-trust so urgently, and sometimes so carelessly, only because his profoundest faith was not, after all, in "selfism," as he calls it scornfully, but in "the ever-blessed ONE." Whether the individual soul is really "lost" in the ONE or retains a mysterious independence is not wholly clear, but whatever its reality it is one that yields to the supreme reality of the Over-Soul, and, rightly understood, the man who relies on himself is not relying merely on his empirical self but on "the aboriginal Self, on which a universal reliance may be grounded." [1] From Emerson's point of view, this neither negates his defiant individualism nor furnishes any real ethical sanction for immoral conduct.

On the highest level the contradiction here is not at all a willful inconsistency but a special case of what holds for Emerson's thinking generally. He will never be understood by readers who fail to take it in that he is a consciously "dialectical" thinker—one, that is, who holds that contradiction is inherent in experience itself, that the natural order is through and through paradoxical, and that we shall never comprehend it truly until we have learned to "keep the diagonal line." This truth is what he calls, following other writers, Polarity: "The fact of two poles," he says, "of two forces, centripetal and centrifugal, is universal, and each force by its own activity develops the other." It was the great lesson he felt that he had

[1] See "Self-Reliance," p. 514.

learned from Plato, of whom he says, with humorous reverence, "a man who could see two sides of a thing was born"; though if Plato had in a sense taught him this, it was because the lesson was already lurking in the grain of his own mind. In any case, the most comprehensive and abstract manifestation of the principle of Polarity was for Emerson, as for Plato, the antithesis of Unity and Variety, the One and the Many, Oneness and Otherness. It is in the light of this true paradox that the reality and the rights of the individual can be asserted without our forgetting that the One also exists, and indeed, unlike the individual, has an absolute existence. For the principle of Polarity is not itself an ultimate truth; it is only an empirical one. A metaphysical choice is forced upon us, and in the end we see that Unity is a deeper fact than Variety. "We unite all things," says Emerson, "by perceiving the law which pervades them; by perceiving the superficial differences and the profound resemblances." It is his capacity for perceiving both the differences and the resemblances that, as much as anything, makes Emerson a permanently impressive as well as a bracing writer.

IV

TOO MUCH can hardly be made of Emerson's role as an awakener, an agitating and fermentative force, in his own time and potentially still; but it must not be forgotten that he was also a great writer, a great artist. As an artist in prose he did not quite invent a new form or mode, but he possessed himself of an inherited form, and shaped it so boldly and freely as an expressive medium for his own needs that the product has all the freshness of originality in the true sense. As a matter of fact, the derivation of Emerson's form is not perfectly simple. It was not until the appearance of his second published *volume, Essays: First Series*, in 1841, that Emerson had placed himself before his readers explicitly in the role of essayist. His earliest compositions had been sermons; he had turned from the sermon to the lecture, but in the order of *publication*, to ignore *Nature* for the moment, what he had begun with had been "discourses" (an "Historical Discourse at Concord" in 1835), or "orations" ("The American Scholar: An Oration . . ."), or "addresses" ("An Address Delivered Before the Senior Class in Divinity College"). In short, what he called the essay was the offspring, on one side, of some form or other of public speech—in the pulpit, on the lecture-platform, on the special occasion—and rather few of his "essays" fail to betray that their ancestry was partly in the spoken word. It was partly, too, in the written word, and his models here were such favorite authors of his, from early youth, as the Plutarch not only of the *Lives* but of the *Moralia* (or *Essays and Miscellanies*, as they were known in one translation), the beloved Montaigne of the *Essais*, and the Bacon of the English *Essays* (of which he said in an early lecture that "Few books ever written contain so much wisdom and will bear to be read so many times"). To the later Addisonian tradition, that of the "periodical" essay, in which Franklin had worked, Emerson owed little or nothing.

It has often been made a reproach to him that, brilliant as his sentences may be, Emerson had little feeling for the larger units of structure, and that his essays are perhaps glittering heaps of *sententiae* but not artistically ordered wholes. This criticism has been reinforced by the knowledge that both the lectures and the essays were "pieced together," like quilt-covers of variegated prose, from the journals—as though the sense of composition, if strong enough, could not produce an effect of beautiful coherence even by this process. Emerson himself, at any rate, certainly intended that his essays should have a structural firmness of their own, though not perhaps an easily obvious or rigidly logical one. Rhetoric for him, indeed, was a "species of architecture": he called it "the Building of Discourse," and was convinced that "Profoundest thoughts, sublime images, dazzling figures are squandered and lost in an immethodical harangue." Of the dangers of the "aphoristic style" he was fully conscious: he did not wish to frustrate his readers, as he felt that his friend Alcott sometimes did, with "a cord of chips for a cord of wood." Nor does he—with some exceptions—do this.

His feeling for compositional wholeness was in fact much stronger than it has usually been said to be, but if the impression remains, even in the minds of some intelligent readers, that he is a writer of aphorisms rather than of sustained discourses, the reasons are understandable. It is true that he is one of the most *quotable* of modern writers: again and again his sentences, and even his phrases, can be detached from their context, like jewels from a disregarded setting, and quoted with a delight that seems to set at naught their relation to other sentences. It is true, too, that the transition from one sentence, or even one paragraph, to another is not always explicitly made, and this produces an effect of apparent discontinuity. "It is not the masters," he said, however, "who spin the ostentatious continuity"—and if he habitually omitted the familiar connectives of logical discourse it was partly because he wished to leave some of the work of thinking to his readers, and partly because what he meant by continuity was not a logical but a superlogical principle.

It remains true that Emerson was a skilled and studious rhetorician, and that his sense of the architecture of an essay normally, and beautifully, triumphed over the tendency to dispersion or looseness. He had begun, after all, as a preacher in the tradition, however relaxed, of the Puritan homily, and his own early sermons are sometimes models of orderly discourse. The habit survived at least in his earliest publications: in *Nature*, in "The American Scholar," in "Self-Reliance," he is still, in certain sections, numbering his topics, and though he later abandoned this formality, he rarely abandoned the "building" principle it was based on. A careful scrutiny of almost any one of his characteristic essays will reveal, beneath the undulating surface, the actual firmness of the design.

The essay on "The Poet" is a fair example. Like so many of the essays it begins with an eloquent exordium (paragraph 1)—a kind of prelude in which Emerson, reiterating one of the themes of *Nature*, enounces the Transcendental doctrine of Beauty as essentially an ideal or spiritual, not a physical, reality. What follows is a passage (pars. 2–8) that characterizes the Poet as "the man of Beauty"—not a mere verse-maker or man of letters but a Seer and Sayer. The full development of this subject leads to another restatement of a theme in *Nature* (pars. 9–17)—the essentially symbolic character of all objects, and the necessary dependence of the Poet, therefore, on symbols. After a kind of digression (par. 18) on the inexhaustible fertility both of Nature and of poetic inspiration, Emerson moves on (pars. 19–27) to a treatment of the Imagination as the power that is at work in all true poetry; an account of the Imagination that makes much of its necessarily *organic* expression, its largely unconscious operations, its intoxicating powers, its liberating role, and its characteristic expression in the flowing rather than the fixed.

The remarks on Swedenborg (pars. 28 and 29) are simply illustrative of these generalizations; they are followed by the great passage (par. 30) in which Emerson laments the failure of America to produce the kind of bard he has been describing and voices his confidence that, nevertheless, the country "will not wait long for metres." One sentence (par. 31) serves as a bridge-passage from this inspiriting outburst to the long and characteristically eloquent peroration (pars. 32–34) in which Emerson, after affirming the dependence of the Poet on higher powers than his own, addresses him directly with earnest admonitions to the service of the ideal.

Such is the careful articulation of a not untypical essay: if it is compared with the really baroque "disordered order" of one of Montaigne's characteristic pieces, it will seem almost pedantically coherent. The abrupt beginnings, the repeated and unapologetic digressions, the unexplained transitions, the sudden anticlimactic terminations of the typical Montaignesque essay are far to seek in Emerson. A certain freedom from prim orderliness he had undoubtedly learned, along with other lessons, from the French writer, but it is only in occasional and mostly late essays that he even approaches Montaigne in discontinuity. Meanwhile, the excitation his prose begets depends not only on his mastery of design but on the wonderful resourcefulness of his rhetoric in the narrower sense, on his practised command over the whole range of expressive and captivating devices of style. It is true that he is a master of the aphorism—of the terse single sentence that seems to be saying, in the briefest and wittiest way, a particular thing so that it need never be said again. But to suppose that Emerson's powers are limited to the aphorism would be to ignore a dozen other aspects of his art—his mastery of the cumulative and ascending paragraph, his powerful uses of parallelism, reiteration, and antithesis, his love of even such "artificial" devices as anaphora and the tricolon, his frank resort to apostrophe and interrogation, and, what deserves much fuller treatment than is possible here, his feeling, both strong and delicate, for the rhythms of English prose.

A careful look at such a passage as the peroration of "The American Scholar" will reveal how much of its enkindling power, to speak only stylistically and not morally, depends on the brilliance with which a whole series of such "figures" are pressed into the service of Emerson's meaning. It will also reveal—but so indeed will a look at almost any page of Emerson—how much of his power and charm as a prose writer depends on the all but Shakesperean exhaustlessness of his metaphors. This is of course because he thought in metaphors, when he thought at all intensely, as he himself recognized: "All thinking," he said, "is analogizing," and certainly this holds for the kind of thinking that lies at the base of most of his writing. Abstraction was, for him, too likely to be falsification: only the living image, the seeable and touchable metaphor, could, in the usual course, do justice to the vigor and the suppleness of his thought.

What strikes one about Emerson's metaphors is not only their freshness, for the most part, their lesser dependence on literature than on experience, but their imaginative range—the fact that they stretch out over the whole space from the celestial to the common, from the lofty to the low, from "the thrones of angels" and "the whole garden of God" to "a wood-pile in the yard" or "the rats in the wall." But indeed it is not easy, beyond a certain point, to distinguish between Emerson's metaphorical language and his language generally; of *that* the catholicity, the all-inclusive hospitality, the elasticity in moving from the elevated or the learned to the colloquial and even the "vulgar" have long been recognized. It is what Lowell had in mind when he said that Emerson's diction is like "homespun cloth-of-gold." Only Melville and Whitman, among his contemporaries, have a comparable linguistic scope, and perhaps neither of them bestrews his pages with quite so generous or so various a shower of locutions as Emerson—locutions which can be erudite and even pedantic ("hodiernal," "pudency," "pleniloquence"), or familiar ("all stir and no go," "deny it up and down," "a drop too much"), or sometimes brutally plain ("this filthy enactment," "cathartic virtue," "snores and gastric noises," "all blab").

"Speak with the vulgar," he says, "think with the wise." It is a vivid way of expressing his love for actual speech, with its energy and its picturesqueness, but the witty form of the sentence is only half faithful to the truth of his practice. For him "the wise," it is true, were often the simple and unlettered, and that is why he speaks with them at times. But his diction, his imagery, and indeed his prose style generally have a versatility, a richness, and sometimes a grandeur that might equally well be described as "speaking with the noble." His writing, just as such, has polarities that "correspond" to the deep polarities of his thought.

V

WHAT has been said about the essay "The Poet" is enough to suggest that, in his aesthetics as well as in his metaphysics and his ethics, Emerson was a part of that powerful swing away from the older attitudes, the older materialisms, that occurred in Europe and then in this country in the generation before him, and in his own. The most characteristic conception of Beauty in the earlier time was a thoroughly hedonistic and, as Emerson would say, "sensual" one; a conception that associated it inextricably with pleasure. "Pleasure and pain," Hume had said, ". . . are not only necessary attendants of beauty and deformity, but constitute their very essence." In his rejection of this certainly rather simplistic hedonism, Emerson turned back to an older set of insights—those of Plato and the Neoplationists—and reaffirmed the transcendental conception of Beauty as pure Idea, as one of the eternal Forms on which all temporal things depend for what reality they have, or as one of the aspects, along with the True and the Good, of the Absolute itself. The Artist, in this view, is no mere craftsman but a servant, religious in his dedication, of the Idea; and the arts exist, not essentially to give pleasure ("As soon as beauty is sought, not from religion and love but for pleasure, it degrades the seeker"), but "to educate the perception of beauty" in this Platonic sense.

Poetry, like the other arts, according to this conception, quite loses its neoclassical character as Imitation of Nature, and becomes "creation"—the giving of form and verbal expression to intuitions into the reality that lies behind Nature and of which Nature is itself only an ephemeral vestment. A consequence of this is that one can no longer speak, as the neoclassical critics had done, in the light of imitational criteria—criteria of mere "verisimilitude," of propriety, of correctness, of "the rules," and the like. There are no "rules," and the test of genuinely poetic language and form is not its conformity to inherited standards of correctness, but its expressive truth to the ever-fresh and ever-unique themes with which the poet deals. No established forms or styles can possibly be prescribed to the poet; his subject itself must dictate the pattern. "Ask the fact for the form," says Emerson; and as for language, "Any word, every word in language, every circumstance, becomes poetic in the hands of a higher thought."

Such, very sketchily hinted at, was Emerson's poetics, and such were the criteria in the light of which his own poems were written. "I wish," he said, "to write such rhymes as shall not suggest a restraint, but contrariwise the wildest freedom." To readers now, Emerson's verse is probably less likely to suggest ideas of wildness or extravagance than of, if not "restraint," at least lowness of pitch, sobriety, and even sedateness. Yet there is more of the untamed in Emerson than meets the careless eye, and from the older point of view the truth is that he had thrown off many of the inhibitions that had been supposed to be essential to poetic form.

He had thrown them off quite consciously. As a youth he had written a fair amount of verse, but always in the conventional modes—an undergraduate poem on Hindu superstition was composed in the starchiest of pentameter couplets—but he had found these modes less and less bearable with the passage of time, and just as his prose began to shed its conventional qualities and to take on its recognizably "Emersonian" character in the year or two that followed his resignation from the ministry, so in the same years, with "Each and All" and "The Snow-Storm," he began to find his own voice, his own individual accent, as a poet. During the period of the celebrated early addresses he was also writing "The Humble-Bee," "The Problem," and "Uriel," and demonstrating that, in the one medium as in the other, he had achieved both a wonderful freshness and a wonderful ripeness of utterance.

If, in the formal and linguistic sense, Emerson's verse is typically untraditional and unprecedented, it is because he had new and unhackneyed things to say. No doubt in a sense they were also very old things, but if so, they were old things that had the novelty which always characterizes restatement in a new hour. The themes of eighteenth-century poetry had been suggested by the life of society, or by a very rational kind of reflection, or by nature and the seasons contemplated in a highly reasonable and Newtonian spirit. Most of Emerson's themes came to him, not from society, but from solitude; as the fruits, not of rational reflection, but of rapt meditation; or from nature and the seasons contemplated, not so much in a reasonable, as in an enthusiastic spirit. The mystery of the One and the Many, the falsity of "linear" thinking, the identity of the soul of nature and the individual soul, the vatic or prophetic character of poetry itself—such were a few of the subjects that Emerson typically treated in his verse; they need only to be "stated" in this prosaic manner to make it clear that they could not, without loss, have been treated in the older styles.

To be sure, it would be misleading to overstate the unconventionality of *all* Emerson's verse. Some of his most successful poems, both early and late, are composed in well-tried metrical and stanzaic forms, and their verbal texture by no means always represents an abrupt departure from tradition. The blank verse of "The Snow-Storm" or "Xenophanes," the quatrains of the "Boston Hymn" or "Brahma" or "Waldeinsamkeit," the octaves of "The World-Soul" or "The Sphinx"—these, in themselves, were familiar enough; and neither the language nor the imagery always suggests "the wildest freedom" from the practice of English poets in the late eighteenth century. The personal qualities here are subtler and more elusive than sweeping innovation would be likely to produce; but they are there, and it says much for Emerson's versatility as a poet that he could infuse with so much fresh life the blank verse he had inherited from Landor or Wordsworth, or the quatrains he had lifted out of the hymnals.

Meanwhile, it was on another track that he was moving toward a still more personal and idiosyncratic mode of expression in poetry. There had been a peculiar felicity for him, in so early a poem as "Each and All," in a pattern of freely-syllabled four-stress lines, where the rhymes might, but need not, fall in couplets; and during the next few years he revealed how congenial this pattern was to him in such poems as "The Problem," "Uriel," and parts of "Monadnoc," with their increasingly free gait and increasingly "anti-poetic" diction. The next step was to abandon any sort of syllable-counting or consistency of rhyming, and he took that step (perhaps with a recollection of the "Pindarics" of Cowley and Dryden, perhaps in emulation of Goethe's practice in *Faust*) in other parts of "Monadnoc," in the "Ode Inscribed to W. H. Channing," in "Give All to Love." If it were not for the rhymes—and they are not only irregular but sometimes missing—this verse might well be described simply as free verse; at all events, the peculiarly Emersonian note can be heard nowhere so unmistakably as in the poems composed in these "logaoedic," anti-lyrical, uneuphonious lines, intermediate as they are between verse and prose, with their suggestion of half-conversational improvisation, rising at times to a spirited recitatif and even, as in parts of "Threnody," to something like a solemn chant, but avoiding both lyricism and the familiar eloquence of traditional blank verse. The transition from this to the free verse of Pound and Eliot would not be a difficult one.

The real originality of these poems is enhanced, too, by what might be called the quiet boldness of Emerson's language and imagery. "Some of my first thinking about my own language," Robert Frost has said, "was certainly Emersonian"; and one can easily see how this might have been. The filiation between the two poets is evident enough when one does no more than glance at the opening lines of Emerson's "journal" poem, "The Adirondacs":

We crossed Champlain to Keeseville with our
  friends,
Thence, in strong country carts, rode up the forks
Of the Ausable stream, intent to reach
The Adirondac lakes. At Martin's Beach
We chose our boats; each man a boat and guide,—
Ten men, ten guides, our company all told.

The speaking tones here, to be sure, the Yankee cadences, are exceptional in Emerson, though they are to be found elsewhere too, as in the opening lines of "Hamatreya," but it is not hard to see how they might have served as a model to the young Frost in his search for a verse-rhythm and a diction that should be true to the natural speech of his own people. Emerson knew that speech well: he had listened to it in the post office at Concord, in the intervales of New Hampshire, in the village taverns at the base of Monadnock; and he had felt that he could spare "the learned lecture," "institutes and dictionaries," and the like, for "that hardy English root" which throve "unvalued, underfoot" among the unlettered country people of New England.

He never attempted, in any literal way, to reproduce that speech in his verse—any more, indeed, than Frost did—but he delighted in trying to catch some of its tart savor. He delighted in enriching the strong local quality of some poems with the imagery of the New England farm or field or wood—with "every windward stake," "coop or kennel," "hay, corn, roots, hemp, flax, apples, wool and wood," "clay, lime, gravel, granite-ledge," "the black ducks mounting from the lake," or "blue-vetch and trillium, hawkweed, sassafras." Nor did he hesitate, well before *Leaves of Grass,* to introduce into verse the unromantic imagery of nineteenth-century city or industrial or civic life—the imagery of "hotels," "railways," "a factory," "time-and-space conquering steam," "the light-outspeeding telegraph," "the mountain tunnelled," "the steamer built," "politics," "votes," and "polls."

He pointed the way here for Whitman, for

Emily Dickinson, and possibly for Melville. But, striking as Emerson's localism and modernism are, and useful as his example proved to later poets, these are not, in the end, the most important things to say about him as a poet. His own claims to the status of poet were over-modest, and all but two or three of his poems were little esteemed in his own time. Yet the truth is that Emerson left behind him a small but impressive body of verse that entitles him to be ranked, for freshness, intensity, and prophetic power, with the poets just alluded to and with few others in this country in his age. Small as the number of his successful poems is, his range within them is greater than any brief treatment can suggest: if the gnomic and unlyrical manner of certain poems seems to be his most idiosyncratic one, it should not be forgotten that he was also capable of the more excited strain of "The World-Soul," the "Ode to Beauty," and "Bacchus," the wail of "Threnody," the effortless lyricism of "Waldeinsamkeit," or the hymnic and public elevation of the "Concord Hymn," the "Boston Hymn," and the "Ode" sung in the town hall at Concord in 1857 ("O tenderly the haughty day/Fills his blue urn with fire"). His great authority as a writer generally derives, ultimately, from the wonderful reach of his polarity, from the length of the leap he could take in spirit from the atom to the All, from details to Unity, from the minute and even mean to the sublime. This holds for his verse as well as for his prose; the author of his best poems can justly be said to have done what he tells us his archetypal bard, Merlin, did; can be said to have reconciled "extremes of nature"; to have comprehended, and expressed, the most polar opposities. Only two or three of our other writers approach him in this achievement.

READING SUGGESTIONS

EDITIONS

The standard edition is the Centenary Edition, *Complete Works of Ralph Waldo Emerson*, ed. by Edward Waldo Emerson, 12 vols. (1903–04)—cited here as *Works*. It includes very full and useful notes in the appendices to the several volumes. This should be supplemented by the *Journals of Ralph Waldo Emerson*, ed. by Edward Waldo Emerson and Waldo Emerson Forbes, 10 vols. (1909–14)—cited here as *Journals*. A new and more reliable text of the journals is in process of publication under the title, *The Journals and Miscellaneous Notebooks of Ralph Waldo Emerson*, ed. by William H. Gilman, Alfred R. Ferguson, George P. Clark, and Merrill R. Davis (Vol. I, 1960). There are two volumes of selections from the journals, each of which has an emphasis and a value of its own: *The Heart of Emerson's Journals*, ed. by Bliss Perry (1926), and *The Journals of Ralph Waldo Emerson*, ed. by Robert N. Linscott (1960).

LETTERS

The great bulk of Emerson's letters are available in the *Letters of Ralph Waldo Emerson*, ed. by Ralph L. Rusk, 6 vols. (1939)—cited here as *Letters*. Not included, however, are the letters to be found in the *Correspondence of Thomas Carlyle and Ralph Waldo Emerson*, ed. by Charles Eliot Norton, 2 vols. (1883).

BIOGRAPHY

Ralph L. Rusk, *The Life of Ralph Waldo Emerson* (1949). The standard biography; thorough and informative.

James E. Cabot, *A Memoir of Ralph Waldo Emerson* (1887). Though superseded by Rusk, this memoir is still of great value as the work of a younger contemporary who was Emerson's literary executor.

Charles J. Woodbury, *Talks with Emerson* (1890). A vivid small book by a much younger contemporary.

CRITICISM

Frederic I. Carpenter, *Emerson Handbook* (1953). A useful reference work.

Critical books devoted either to Emerson's work as a whole or to special aspects are:

O. W. Firkins, *Ralph Waldo Emerson* (1915).
Vivian C. Hopkins, *Spires of Form* (1951).
Sherman Paul, *Emerson's Angle of Vision* (1952).
Stephen E. Whicher, *Freedom and Fate: An Inner Life of Ralph Waldo Emerson* (1953).

Various, and variously interesting, critical treatments of Emerson, over a period of two or three generations, may be found in essays in the following volumes:

Matthew Arnold, *Discourses in America* (1885).
Henry James, *Partial Portraits* (1888).
John Jay Chapman, *Emerson and Other Essays* (1898).
George Santayana, *Interpretations of Poetry and Religion* (1900).
William James, *Memories and Studies* (1911).
John Dewey, *Character and Events* (1929).
Yvor Winters, *Maule's Curse* (1938).
F. O. Matthiessen, *American Renaissance* (1941).
Charles Feidelson, Jr., *Symbolism and American Literature* (1953).
D. H. Lawrence, *Selected Literary Criticism*, ed. by Anthony Beal (1956).
Georges Poulet, *Studies in Human Time* (1956).
Perry Miller, *Errand into the Wilderness* (1956).
Harold C. Gardiner, s.j., editor, *American Classics Reconsidered* (1958).

NATURE

◇

THE idea of a book on the grand subject of Nature seems to have been in Emerson's mind for some time before he got round to writing it; in the journal he kept on shipboard when returning from England in 1833 he wrote: "I like my book about Nature, and wish I knew where and how I ought to live" (*Journals*, III, 196). He seems not to have been able to begin the book, however, until after he had gone to live as a boarder with his step-grandfather, Dr. Ripley, at the Manse in Concord, in 1834. It was not finished, short as it was, until late in the summer of 1836, and was published, anonymously, in Boston that September. The edition was a very small one—five hundred copies—but even so, a second edition was not needed for thirteen years: in 1849 the little book reappeared as the first piece in a volume entitled *Nature, Addresses, and Lectures* (*Works*, I). *Nature* may have had, during those years, very *few* readers, but they were important readers, the right readers; and the influence of the work was, as so often happens, quite out of proportion to its success in the bookshops. This was not because the insights expressed in it were all, in the literal sense, "original" with Emerson: they were the results primarily, it is true, of his own musings, but they had been strongly affected by the reading he had done during the preceding years, in Plato and the Neoplatonists, in such English Platonists as Ralph Cudworth (1617–88), in Swedenborg (1688–1772) and such American disciples of his as Sampson Reed (*Observations on the Growth of the Mind*, 1826), in Wordsworth and Coleridge, in Goethe and, mostly at second hand, in the German idealist philosophers. In that sense the book represented a kind of shimmering synthesis of ideas that had been floating about in the European and American mind for a generation or two, and indeed, in one sense, for many centuries; but the synthesis had, nevertheless, a powerful effect of freshness and novelty. It expressed a view of nature and the relations of the human spirit to it that seemed incomparably truer, to some men, than the views that had been dominant for a hundred years and more; and it became, for such men, a Prophetic Book. It is easy, even now, to see why this was true.

◇

A subtle chain of countless rings
The next unto the farthest brings;
The eye reads omens where it goes,
And speaks all languages the rose;
And, striving to be man, the worm
Mounts through all the spires of form.[1]

INTRODUCTION

OUR AGE is retrospective. It builds the sepulchres of the fathers. It writes biographies, histories, and criticism. The foregoing generations beheld God and nature face to face; we, through their eyes. Why should not we also enjoy an original relation to the universe? Why should not we have a poetry and philosophy of insight and not of tradition, and a religion by revelation to us, and not the history of theirs? Embosomed for a season in nature, whose floods of life stream around and through us, and invite us, by the powers they supply, to action proportioned to nature, why should we grope among the dry bones of the past, or put the living generation into masquerade out of its faded wardrobe? The sun shines to-day also. There is more wool and flax in the fields. There are new lands, new men, new thoughts. Let us demand our own works and laws and worship.

Undoubtedly we have no questions to ask which are unanswerable. We must trust the perfection of the creation so far as to believe that whatever curiosity the order of things has awakened in our minds, the order of things can satisfy. Every man's condition is a solution in hieroglyphic to those inquiries he would put. He acts it as life, before he apprehends it as truth. In like manner, nature is already, in its forms and tendencies, describing its own design. Let us interrogate the great apparition that shines so peacefully around us. Let us inquire, to what end is nature?

All science has one aim, namely, to find a theory of nature. We have theories of races and of functions, but scarcely yet a remote approach to an idea of creation. We are now so far from the road to truth, that religious teachers dispute and hate each other, and speculative men are esteemed unsound and frivolous. But to a sound judgment, the most abstract truth is the most practical. Whenever a true theory appears, it will be its own evidence. Its test is, that it will explain all phenomena. Now many are thought not only unexplained but inexplicable; as language, sleep, madness, dreams, beasts, sex.

Philosophically considered, the universe is composed of Nature and the Soul. Strictly speaking, therefore, all that is separate from us, all which Philosophy distinguishes as the NOT ME,[2] that

NATURE. 1. **A . . . form:** This "motto," which was the epigraph of *Nature* when it was republished in 1849 in the volume *Nature, Addresses, and Lectures*, was later incorporated in the poem "May-Day," in the 1867 volume entitled *May-Day and Other Pieces* (*Works*, IX, 165–66). 2. **The Not Me:** a distinction, derived from the German philosopher Fichte, which Emerson might have come upon in Carlyle's essay on Novalis (1829): "what Fichte means by his far-famed *Ich* and *Nicht-Ich* [I and Not-I]." Carlyle later used the expression, "the NOT ME," in *Sartor Resartus* (1833–34), Book II, Chap. 8

is, both nature and art, all other men and my own body, must be ranked under this name, NATURE. In enumerating the values of nature and casting up their sum, I shall use the word in both senses;—in its common and in its philosophical import. In inquiries so general as our present one, the inaccuracy is not material; no confusion of thought will occur. *Nature,* in the common sense, refers to essences unchanged by man; space, the air, the river, the leaf. *Art* is applied to the mixture of his will with the same things, as in a house, a canal, a statue, a picture. But his operations taken together are so insignificant, a little chipping, baking, patching, and washing, that in an impression so grand as that of the world on the human mind, they do not vary the result.

I. NATURE

TO GO into solitude, a man needs to retire as much from his chamber as from society. I am not solitary whilst I read and write, though nobody is with me. But if a man would be alone, let him look at the stars. The rays that come from those heavenly worlds will separate between him and what he touches. One might think the atmosphere was made transparent with this design, to give man, in the heavenly bodies, the perpetual presence of the sublime. Seen in the streets of cities, how great they are! If the stars should appear one night in a thousand years, how would men believe and adore; and preserve for many generations the remembrance of the city of God which had been shown! But every night come out these envoys of beauty, and light the universe with their admonishing smile.

The stars awaken a certain reverence, because though always present, they are inaccessible; but all natural objects make a kindred impression, when the mind is open to their influence. Nature never wears a mean appearance. Neither does the wisest man extort her secret, and lose his curiosity by finding out all her perfection. Nature never became a toy to a wise spirit. The flowers, the animals, the mountains, reflected the wisdom of his best hour, as much as they had delighted the simplicity of his childhood.

When we speak of nature in this manner, we have a distinct but most poetical sense in the mind. We mean the integrity of impression made by manifold natural objects. It is this which distinguishes the stick of timber of the wood-cutter from the tree of the poet. The charming landscape which I saw this morning is indubitably made up of some twenty or thirty farms. Miller owns this field, Locke that, and Manning the woodland beyond. But none of them owns the landscape. There is a property in the horizon which no man has but he whose eye can integrate all the parts, that is, the poet. This is the best part of these men's farms, yet to this their warranty-deeds give no title.

To speak truly, few adult persons can see nature. Most persons do not see the sun. At least they have a very superficial seeing. The sun illuminates only the eye of the man, but shines into the eye and the heart of the child. The lover of nature is he whose inward and outward senses are still truly adjusted to each other; who has retained the spirit of infancy even into the era of manhood. His intercourse with heaven and earth becomes part of his daily food. In the presence of nature a wild delight runs through the man, in spite of real sorrows. Nature says;—he is my creature, and maugre all his impertinent griefs, he shall be glad with me. Not the sun or the summer alone, but every hour and season yields its tribute of delight; for every hour and change corresponds to and authorizes a different state of the mind, from breathless noon to grimmest midnight. Nature is a setting that fits equally well a comic or a mourning piece. In good health, the air is a cordial of incredible virtue. Crossing a bare common, in snow puddles, at twilight, under a clouded sky, without having in my thoughts any occurrence of special good fortune, I have enjoyed a perfect exhilaration. I am glad to the brink of fear. In the woods, too, a man casts off his years, as the snake his slough, and at what period soever of life, is always a child. In the woods is perpetual youth. Within these plantations of God, a decorum and sanctity reign, a perennial festival is dressed, and the guest sees not how he should tire of them in a thousand years. In the woods, we return to reason and faith. There I feel that nothing can befall me in life,—no disgrace, no calamity (leaving me my eyes), which nature cannot repair. Standing on the bare ground,—my head bathed by the blithe air, and uplifted into infinite space,—all mean egotism vanishes. I become a transparent eyeball; I am nothing; I see all; the currents of the Universal Being circulate through me; I am part or parcel of God. The name of the nearest friend sounds then foreign and accidental: to be brothers, to be acquaintances,—master or servant, is then a trifle and a disturbance. I am the lover of uncontained and immortal beauty. In the wilderness, I find something more dear and connate than in streets or villages. In the tranquil landscape, and especially in the distant line of the horizon, man beholds somewhat as beautiful as his own nature.[3]

3. **In the woods . . . nature:** This passage is a revision and

The greatest delight which the fields and woods minister is the suggestion of an occult relation between man and the vegetable. I am not alone and unacknowledged. They nod to me, and I to them. The waving of the boughs in the storm is new to me and old. It takes me by surprise, and yet is not unknown. Its effect is like that of a higher thought or a better emotion coming over me, when I deemed I was thinking justly or doing right.

Yet it is certain that the power to produce this delight does not reside in nature, but in man, or in a harmony of both. It is necessary to use these pleasures with great temperance. For nature is not always tricked in holiday attire, but the same scene which yesterday breathed perfume and glittered as for the frolic of the nymphs, is overspread with melancholy to-day. Nature always wears the colors of the spirit. To a man laboring under calamity, the heat of his own fire hath sadness in it. Then there is a kind of contempt of the landscape felt by him who has just lost by death a dear friend. The sky is less grand as it shuts down over less worth in the population.

II. COMMODITY

[IN THE very short second chapter of *Nature* Emerson lays it down that the natural world has many "uses" for man, and that these may all be reduced to four general categories which he calls Commodity, Beauty, Language, and Discipline. In this chapter he treats the first of these, Commodity, a term by which he means to signify the merely physical or material, the practical, uses to which Nature may be put—"all those advantages," as he says, "which our senses owe to nature." He describes these with a glow of perhaps unexpected praise, but ends by remarking that of course "this mercenary benefit is one which has respect to a farther good"—the good he deals with in the ensuing chapters.]

III. BEAUTY

A NOBLER want of man is served by nature, namely, the love of Beauty.

The ancient Greeks called the world κόσμος,[4] beauty. Such is the constitution of all things, or such the plastic power of the human eye, that the primary forms, as the sky, the mountain, the tree, the animal, give us a delight *in and for themselves;* a pleasure arising from outline, color, motion, and grouping. This seems partly owing to the eye itself. The eye is the best of artists. By the mutual action of its structure and of the laws of light, perspective is produced, which integrates every mass of objects, of what character soever, into a well colored and shaded globe, so that where the particular objects are mean and unaffecting, the landscape which they compose is round and symmetrical. And as the eye is the best composer, so light is the first of painters. There is no object so foul that intense light will not make beautiful. And the stimulus it affords to the sense, and a sort of infinitude which it hath, like space and time, make all matter gay. Even the corpse has its own beauty. But besides this general grace diffused over nature, almost all the individual forms are agreeable to the eye, as is proved by our endless imitations of some of them, as the acorn, the grape, the pine-cone, the wheat-ear, the egg, the wings and forms of most birds, the lion's claw, the serpent, the butterfly, sea-shells, flames, clouds, buds, leaves, and the forms of many trees, as the palm.

For better consideration, we may distribute the aspects of Beauty in a threefold manner.

1. First, the simple perception of natural forms is a delight. The influence of the forms and actions in nature is so needful to man, that, in its lowest functions, it seems to lie on the confines of commodity and beauty. To the body and mind which have been cramped by noxious work or company, nature is medicinal and restores their tone. The tradesman, the attorney comes out of the din and craft of the street and sees the sky and the woods, and is a man again. In their eternal calm, he finds himself. The health of the eye seems to demand a horizon. We are never tired, so long as we can see far enough.

But in other hours, Nature satisfies by its loveliness, and without any mixture of corporeal benefit. I see the spectacle of morning from the hilltop over against my house, from daybreak to sunrise, with emotions which an angel might share. The long slender bars of cloud float like fishes in the sea of crimson light. From the earth, as a shore, I look out into that silent sea. I seem to partake its rapid transformations; the active enchantment reaches my dust, and I dilate and conspire[5] with the morning wind. How does Nature deify us with a few and cheap elements! Give me health and a day, and I will make the pomp of emperors ridiculous. The dawn is my Assyria; the sunset and moonrise my Paphos,[6] and unimaginable realms of faerie; broad noon shall be my England of the senses and the understanding; the night shall be my Germany of mystic philosophy and dreams.

Not less excellent, except for our less susceptibility in the afternoon, was the charm, last eve-

amplification of a passage in Emerson's journal for March 19, 1835 (*Journals*, III, 451–52). 4. κόσμος: *kosmos*, the Greek word signifying primarily "order."

5. **conspire**: breathe in unison. 6. **Paphos**: ancient city on the island of Cyprus, seat of a cult of Aphrodite.

ning, of a January sunset. The western clouds divided and subdivided themselves into pink flakes modulated with tints of unspeakable softness, and the air had so much life and sweetness that it was a pain to come within doors. What was it that nature would say? Was there no meaning in the live repose of the valley behind the mill, and which Homer or Shakespeare could not re-form for me in words? The leafless trees become spires of flame in the sunset, with the blue east for their background, and the stars of the dead calices of flowers, and every withered stem and stubble rimed with frost, contribute something to the mute music.

The inhabitants of cities suppose that the country landscape is pleasant only half the year. I please myself with the graces of the winter scenery, and believe that we are as much touched by it as by the genial influences of summer. To the attentive eye, each moment of the year has its own beauty, and in the same field, it beholds, every hour, a picture which was never seen before, and which shall never be seen again. The heavens change every moment, and reflect their glory or gloom on the plains beneath. The state of the crop in the surrounding farms alters the expression of the earth from week to week. The succession of native plants in the pastures and roadsides, which makes the silent clock by which time tells the summer hours, will make even the divisions of the day sensible to a keen observer. The tribes of birds and insects, like the plants punctual to their time, follow each other, and the year has room for all. By water-courses, the variety is greater. In July, the blue pontederia or pickerel-weed blooms in large beds in the shallow parts of our pleasant river, and swarms with yellow butterflies in continual motion. Art cannot rival this pomp of purple and gold. Indeed the river is a perpetual gala, and boasts each month a new ornament.

But this beauty of Nature which is seen and felt as beauty, is the least part. The shows of day, the dewy morning, the rainbow, mountains, orchards in blossom, stars, moonlight, shadows in still water, and the like, if too eagerly hunted, become shows merely, and mock us with their unreality. Go out of the house to see the moon, and 'tis mere tinsel; it will not please as when its light shines upon your necessary journey. The beauty that shimmers in the yellow afternoons of October, who ever could clutch it? Go forth to find it, and it is gone; 'tis only a mirage as you look from the windows of diligence.

2. The presence of a higher, namely, of the spiritual element is essential to its perfection. The high and divine beauty which can be loved without effeminacy, is that which is found in combination with the human will. Beauty is the mark God sets upon virtue. Every natural action is graceful. Every heroic act is also decent,[7] and causes the place and the bystanders to shine. We are taught by great actions that the universe is the property of every individual in it. Every rational creature has all nature for his dowry and estate. It is his, if he will. He may divest himself of it; he may creep into a corner, and abdicate his kingdom, as most men do, but he is entitled to the world by his constitution. In proportion to the energy of his thought and will, he takes up the world into himself. "All those things for which men plough, build, or sail, obey virtue;" said Sallust.[8] "The winds and waves," said Gibbon, "are always on the side of the ablest navigators." [9] So are the sun and moon and all the stars of heaven. When a noble act is done,—perchance in a scene of great natural beauty; when Leonidas [10] and his three hundred martyrs consume one day in dying, and the sun and moon come each and look at them once in the steep defile of Thermopylæ; when Arnold Winkelried,[11] in the high Alps, under the shadow of the avalanche, gathers in his side a sheaf of Austrian spears to break the line for his comrades; are not these heroes entitled to add the beauty of the scene to the beauty of the deed? When the bark of Columbus nears the shore of America;—before it, the beach lined with savages, fleeing out of all their huts of cane; the sea behind; and the purple mountains of the Indian Archipelago around, can we separate the man from the living picture? Does not the New World clothe his form with her palm-groves and savannahs as fit drapery? Ever does natural beauty steal in like air, and envelope great actions. When Sir Harry Vane [12] was dragged up the Tower-hill, sitting on a sled, to suffer death as the champion of the English laws, one of the multitude cried out to him, "You never sate on so glorious a seat!" Charles II, to intimidate the citizens of London, caused the patriot Lord Russell [13]

7. **decent:** becoming. 8. **"All . . . virtue":** See *The War with Catiline,* I.7. **Sallust:** C. Sallustius Crispus (86–34 B.C.), Roman historian, author of a history of Catiline's conspiracy and a history of the war between the Romans and Jugurtha, king of Numidia. 9. **"The . . . navigators":** See *History of the Decline and Fall of the Roman Empire,* Chap. 68. 10. **Leonidas:** King of Sparta and leader of the Spartan army at Thermopylae (see Herodotus, *History,* Book VII). 11. **Arnold Winkelried:** Swiss patriot who was traditionally said to have died heroically at the Battle of Sempach (1386), in which Austrian troops were routed. 12. **Sir Harry Vane:** Sir Henry Vane, the Younger (1613–62), fourth governor of the Massachusetts Bay Colony (1636–37); later a leader of the Parliamentary party in England; executed for high treason after the restoration of the Stuarts. 13. **Lord Russell:** William Russell, Lord Russell (1639–83), English statesman, executed for high treason under Charles II for his involvement in the so-called Rye House Plot.

to be drawn in an open coach through the principal streets of the city on his way to the scaffold. "But," his biographer says, "the multitude imagined they saw liberty and virtue sitting by his side." In private places, among sordid objects, an act of truth or heroism seems at once to draw to itself the sky as its temple, the sun as its candle. Nature stretches out her arms to embrace man, only let his thoughts be of equal greatness. Willingly does she follow his steps with the rose and the violet, and bend her lines of grandeur and grace to the decoration of her darling child. Only let his thoughts be of equal scope, and the frame will suit the picture. A virtuous man is in unison with her works, and makes the central figure of the visible sphere. Homer, Pindar, Socrates, Phocion,[14] associate themselves fitly in our memory with the geography and climate of Greece. The visible heavens and earth sympathize with Jesus. And in common life whosoever has seen a person of powerful character and happy genius, will have remarked how easily he took all things along with him,—the persons, the opinions, and the day, and nature became ancillary to a man.

3. There is still another aspect under which the beauty of the world may be viewed, namely, as it becomes an object of the intellect. Beside the relation of things to virtue, they have a relation to thought. The intellect searches out the absolute order of things as they stand in the mind of God, and without the colors of affection. The intellectual and the active powers seem to succeed each other, and the exclusive activity of the one generates the exclusive activity of the other. There is something unfriendly in each to the other, but they are like the alternate periods of feeding and working in animals; each prepares and will be followed by the other. Therefore does beauty, which, in relation to actions, as we have seen, comes unsought, and comes because it is unsought, remain for the apprehension and pursuit of the intellect; and then again, in its turn, of the active power. Nothing divine dies. All good is eternally reproductive. The beauty of nature re-forms itself in the mind, and not for barren contemplation, but for new creation.

All men are in some degree impressed by the face of the world; some men even to delight. This love of beauty is Taste. Others have the same love in such excess, that, not content with admiring, they seek to embody it in new forms. The creation of beauty is Art.

The production of a work of art throws a light upon the mystery of humanity. A work of art is an abstract or epitome of the world. It is the result or expression of nature, in miniature. For although the works of nature are innumerable and all different, the result or the expression of them all is similar and single. Nature is a sea of forms radically alike and even unique. A leaf, a sunbeam, a landscape, the ocean, make an analogous impression on the mind. What is common to them all,—that perfectness and harmony, is beauty. The standard of beauty is the entire circuit of natural forms,—the totality of nature; which the Italians expressed by defining beauty *il più nell' uno*.[15] Nothing is quite beautiful alone; nothing but is beautiful in the whole. A single object is only so far beautiful as it suggests this universal grace. The poet, the painter, the sculptor, the musician, the architect, seek each to concentrate this radiance of the world on one point, and each in his several work to satisfy the love of beauty which stimulates him to produce. Thus is Art a nature passed through the alembic of man. Thus in art does Nature work through the will of a man filled with the beauty of her first works.

The world thus exists to the soul to satisfy the desire of beauty. This element I call an ultimate end. No reason can be asked or given why the soul seeks beauty. Beauty, in its largest and profoundest sense, is one expression for the universe. God is the all-fair. Truth, and goodness, and beauty, are but different faces of the same All. But beauty in nature is not ultimate. It is the herald of inward and eternal beauty, and is not alone a solid and satisfactory good. It must stand as a part, and not as yet the last or highest expression of the final cause of Nature.

IV. LANGUAGE

LANGUAGE is a third use which Nature subserves to man. Nature is the vehicle of thought, and in a simple, double, and threefold degree.

1. Words are signs of natural facts.

2. Particular natural facts are symbols of particular spiritual facts.

3. Nature is the symbol of spirit.[16]

14. **Phocion:** Athenian general and statesman of the fourth century B.C., subject of one of Plutarch's *Lives*.

15. ***il più nell' uno:*** "the many in one." 16. **Words . . . spirit:** These ideas, as developed in this chapter, Emerson had made his own, but they have precedents in the work of earlier writers. One of Emerson's sources was the Swedish mystic and theologian, Emanuel Swedenborg (1688–1772), in whose thought he had been deeply interested for some years before and while writing *Nature.* In Swedenborg's great treatise, *Heaven and Its Wonders, the World of Spirit, and Hell,* for example, he would have come upon such passages as this: "The whole natural world corresponds to the spiritual world; and not only the natural world collectively, but also its individual parts. . . ."

1. Words are signs of natural facts. The use of natural history is to give us aid in supernatural history; the use of the outer creation, to give us language for the beings and changes of the inward creation. Every word which is used to express a moral or intellectual fact, if traced to its root, is found to be borrowed from some material appearance. *Right* means *straight; wrong* means *twisted. Spirit* primarily means *wind; transgression,* the crossing of a *line; supercilious,* the *raising of the eyebrow*. We say the *heart* to express emotion, the *head* to denote thought; and *thought* and *emotion* are words borrowed from sensible things, and now appropriated to spiritual nature. Most of the process by which this transformation is made, is hidden from us in the remote time when language was framed; but the same tendency may be daily observed in children. Children and savages use only nouns or names of things, which they convert into verbs, and apply to analogous mental acts.

2. But this origin of all words that convey a spiritual import,—so conspicuous a fact in the history of language,—is our least debt to nature. It is not words only that are emblematic; it is things which are emblematic. Every natural fact is a symbol of some spiritual fact. Every appearance in nature corresponds to some state of the mind, and that state of the mind can only be described by presenting that natural appearance as its picture. An enraged man is a lion, a cunning man is a fox, a firm man is a rock, a learned man is a torch. A lamb is innocence; a snake is subtle spite; flowers express to us the delicate affections. Light and darkness are our familiar expression for knowledge and ignorance; and heat for love. Visible distance behind and before us, is respectively our image of memory and hope.

Who looks upon a river in a meditative hour and is not reminded of the flux of all things? Throw a stone into the stream, and the circles that propagate themselves are the beautiful type of all influence. Man is conscious of a universal soul within or behind his individual life, wherein, as in a firmament, the natures of Justice, Truth, Love, Freedom, arise and shine. This universal soul he calls Reason: it is not mine, or thine, or his, but we are its; we are its property and men. And the blue sky in which the private earth is buried, the sky with its eternal calm, and full of everlasting orbs, is the type of Reason. That which intellectually considered we call Reason, considered in relation to nature, we call Spirit. Spirit is the Creator. Spirit hath life in itself. And man in all ages and countries embodies it in his language as the FATHER.

It is easily seen that there is nothing lucky or capricious in these analogies, but that they are constant, and pervade nature. These are not the dreams of a few poets, here and there, but man is an analogist, and studies relations in all objects. He is placed in the centre of beings, and a ray of relation passes from every other being to him. And neither can man be understood without these objects, nor these objects without man. All the facts in natural history taken by themselves, have no value, but are barren, like a single sex. But marry it to human history, and it is full of life. Whole floras, all Linnaeus' and Buffon's volumes,[17] are dry catalogues of facts; but the most trivial of these facts, the habit of a plant, the organs, or work, or noise of an insect, applied to the illustration of a fact in intellectual philosophy, or in any way associated to human nature, affects us in the most lively and agreeable manner. The seed of a plant,—to what affecting analogies in the nature of man is that little fruit made use of, in all discourse, up to the voice of Paul, who calls the human corpse a seed,—"It is sown a natural body; it is raised a spiritual body." [18] The motion of the earth round its axis and round the sun, makes the day and the year. These are certain amounts of brute light and heat. But is there no intent of an analogy between man's life and the seasons? And do the seasons gain no grandeur or pathos from that analogy? The instincts of the ant are very unimportant considered as the ant's; but the moment a ray of relation is seen to extend from it to man, and the little drudge is seen to be a monitor, a little body with a mighty heart, then all its habits, even that said to be recently observed, that it never sleeps, become sublime.

Because of this radical correspondence between visible things and human thoughts, savages, who have only what is necessary, converse in figures. As we go back in history, language becomes more picturesque, until its infancy, when it is all poetry; or all spiritual facts are represented by natural symbols. The same symbols are found to make the original elements of all languages. It has moreover been observed, that the idioms of all languages approach each other in passages of the greatest eloquence and power. And as this is the first language, so is it the last. This immediate dependence of language upon nature, this conversion of an outward phenomenon into a type of somewhat in human life, never loses its power to affect us. It is this which gives that piquancy to the con-

17. **all Linnaeus' and Buffon's volumes:** Carl von Linné, or Linnaeus (1707–78), author of the *Systema Naturae* and originator of the system of binomial nomenclature for plant and animal species. Comte de Buffon (1707–88), author of the immensely influential *Histoire Naturelle.* 18. **"It . . . body":** See I Cor. 15:44.

versation of a strong-natured farmer or backwoodsman, which all men relish.

A man's power to connect his thought with its proper symbol, and so to utter it, depends on the simplicity of his character, that is, upon his love of truth and his desire to communicate it without loss. The corruption of man is followed by the corruption of language. When simplicity of character and the sovereignty of ideas is broken up by the prevalence of secondary desires,—the desire of riches, of pleasure, of power, and of praise,—and duplicity and falsehood take place of simplicity and truth, the power over nature as an interpreter of the will is in a degree lost; new imagery ceases to be created, and old words are perverted to stand for things which are not; a paper currency is employed, when there is no bullion in the vaults. In due time the fraud is manifest, and words lose all power to stimulate the understanding or the affections. Hundreds of writers may be found in every long-civilized nation who for a short time believe and make others believe that they see and utter truths, who do not of themselves clothe one thought in its natural garment, but who feed unconsciously on the language created by the primary writers of the country, those, namely, who hold primarily on nature.

But wise men pierce this rotten diction and fasten words again to visible things; so that picturesque language is at once a commanding certificate that he who employs it is a man in alliance with truth and God. The moment our discourse rises above the ground line of familiar facts and is inflamed with passion or exalted by thought, it clothes itself in images. A man conversing in earnest, if he watch his intellectual processes, will find that a material image more or less luminous arises in his mind, contemporaneous with every thought, which furnishes the vestment of the thought. Hence, good writing and brilliant discourse are perpetual allegories. This imagery is spontaneous. It is the blending of experience with the present action of the mind. It is proper creation. It is the working of the Original Cause through the instruments he has already made.

These facts may suggest the advantage which the country-life possesses, for a powerful mind, over the artificial and curtailed life of cities. We know more from nature than we can at will communicate. Its light flows into the mind evermore, and we forget its presence. The poet, the orator, bred in the woods, whose senses have been nourished by their fair and appeasing changes, year after year, without design and without heed,—shall not lose their lesson altogether, in the roar of cities or the broil of politics. Long hereafter, amidst agitation and terror in national councils, —in the hour of revolution,—these solemn images shall reappear in their morning lustre, as fit symbols and words of the thoughts which the passing events shall awaken. At the call of a noble sentiment, again the woods wave, the pines murmur, the river rolls and shines, and the cattle low upon the mountains, as he saw and heard them in his infancy. And with these forms, the spells of persuasion, the keys of power are put into his hands.

3. We are thus assisted by natural objects in the expression of particular meanings. But how great a language to convey such pepper-corn informations! Did it need such noble races of creatures, this profusion of forms, this host of orbs in heaven, to furnish man with the dictionary and grammar of his municipal speech? Whilst we use this grand cipher to expedite the affairs of our pot and kettle, we feel that we have not yet put it to its use, neither are able. We are like travellers using the cinders of a volcano to roast their eggs. Whilst we see that it always stands ready to clothe what we would say, we cannot avoid the question whether the characters are not significant of themselves. Have mountains, and waves, and skies, no significance but what we consciously give them when we employ them as emblems of our thoughts? The world is emblematic. Parts of speech are metaphors, because the whole of nature is a metaphor of the human mind. The laws of moral nature answer to those of matter as face to face in a glass. "The visible world and the relation of its parts, is the dial plate of the invisible." The axioms of physics translate the laws of ethics. Thus, "the whole is greater than its part;" "reaction is equal to action;" "the smallest weight may be made to lift the greatest, the difference of weight being compensated by time;" and many the like propositions, which have an ethical as well as physical sense. These propositions have a much more extensive and universal sense when applied to human life, than when confined to technical use.

In like manner, the memorable words of history and the proverbs of nations consist usually of a natural fact, selected as a picture or parable of a moral truth. Thus; A rolling stone gathers no moss; A bird in the hand is worth two in the bush; A cripple in the right way will beat a racer in the wrong; Make hay while the sun shines; 'Tis hard to carry a full cup even; Vinegar is the son of wine; The last ounce broke the camel's back; Long-lived trees make roots first;—and the like. In their primary sense these are trivial facts, but we repeat them for the value of their analogical import. What is true of proverbs, is true of all fables, parables, and allegories.

This relation between the mind and matter is not fancied by some poet, but stands in the will of God, and so is free to be known by all men. It appears to men, or it does not appear. When in fortunate hours we ponder this miracle, the wise man doubts if at all other times he is not blind and deaf;

"Can such things be,
And overcome us like a summer's cloud,
Without our special wonder?" [19]

for the universe becomes transparent, and the light of higher laws than its own shines through it. It is the standing problem which has exercised the wonder and the study of every fine genius since the world began; from the era of the Egyptians and the Brahmins to that of Pythagoras, of Plato, of Bacon, of Leibnitz, of Swedenborg. There sits the Sphinx at the roadside, and from age to age, as each prophet comes by, he tries his fortune at reading her riddle. There seems to be a necessity in spirit to manifest itself in material forms; and day and night, river and storm, beast and bird, acid and alkali, preëxist in necessary Ideas in the mind of God, and are what they are by virtue of preceding affections in the world of spirit. A Fact is the end or last issue of spirit. The visible creation is the terminus or the circumference of the invisible world. "Material objects," said a French philosopher,[20] "are necessarily kinds of *scoriæ* [21] of the substantial thoughts of the Creator, which must always preserve an exact relation to their first origin; in other words, visible nature must have a spiritual and moral side."

This doctrine is abstruse, and though the images of "garment," "*scoriæ*," "mirror," etc., may stimulate the fancy, we must summon the aid of subtler and more vital expositors to make it plain. "Every scripture is to be interpreted by the same spirit which gave it forth,"—is the fundamental law of criticism. A life in harmony with Nature, the love of truth and of virtue, will purge the eyes to understand her text. By degrees we may come to know the primitive sense of the permanent objects of nature, so that the world shall be to us an open book, and every form significant of its hidden life and final cause.

A new interest surprises us, whilst, under the view now suggested, we contemplate the fearful extent and multitude of objects; since "every object rightly seen, unlocks a new faculty of the soul." That which was unconscious truth, becomes, when interpreted and defined in an object, a part of the domain of knowledge,—a new weapon in the magazine of power.

V. DISCIPLINE

[IN SPEAKING of the fourth "use" of nature, Discipline, Emerson has two things in mind: the training of the "understanding" (by which, following Coleridge's usage, he means the practical intelligence) in "intellectual truths," and the training of the "reason" (by which he means here principally the moral sense) in the workings of the moral law, that law which "lies at the center of nature and radiates to the circumference." Men achieve a material command over nature through the knowledge, and only through the knowledge, of her rigorous but beneficent regularities; and, on a higher level, they discover through this knowledge a sanction for the virtuous life in the fact that "sensible objects . . . reflect the conscience"; that is, that even the physical world is, in an emblematic way, pervaded through and through by morality.]

VI. IDEALISM

THUS is the unspeakable but intelligible and practicable meaning of the world conveyed to man, the immortal pupil, in every object of sense. To this one end of Discipline, all parts of nature conspire.

A noble doubt perpetually suggests itself,—whether this end be not the Final Cause of the Universe; and whether nature outwardly exists. It is a sufficient account of that Appearance we call the World, that God will teach a human mind, and so makes it the receiver of a certain number of congruent sensations, which we call sun and moon, man and woman, house and trade. In my utter impotence to test the authenticity of the report of my senses, to know whether the impressions they make on me correspond with outlying objects, what difference does it make, whether Orion is up there in heaven, or some god paints the image in the firmament of the soul? The relations of parts and the end of the whole remaining the same, what is the difference, whether land and sea interact, and worlds revolve and intermingle without number or end,—deep yawning under deep, and galaxy balancing galaxy, throughout absolute space,—or whether, without relations of time and space, the same appearances are inscribed in the constant faith of man? Whether nature enjoy a substantial existence without, or is only in the apocalypse of the mind, it is alike useful and alike venerable to me. Be it what it may, it is ideal to me so long as I cannot try the accuracy of my senses.

19. "Can . . . wonder?": Somewhat inaccurately quoted from *Macbeth*, III.iv.109–11. **20. a French philosopher:** J. G. E. Oegger (whose name appears in other forms and whose exact dates are uncertain), a French Swedenborgian writer, one of whose books, *Le Vrai Messie* (1829), was translated in part as *The True Messiah* by Elizabeth Peabody, a friend of Emerson's. Though her translation was not published until 1842, Emerson had read it in manuscript before he wrote *Nature*. **21. *scoriæ*:** dross, slag.

The frivolous make themselves merry with the Ideal theory, as if its consequences were burlesque; as if it affected the stability of nature. It surely does not. God never jests with us, and will not compromise the end of nature by permitting any inconsequence in its procession. Any distrust of the permanence of laws would paralyze the faculties of man. Their permanence is sacredly respected, and his faith therein is perfect. The wheels and springs of man are all set to the hypothesis of the permanence of nature. We are not built like a ship to be tossed, but like a house to stand. It is a natural consequence of this structure, that so long as the active powers predominate over the reflective, we resist with indignation any hint that nature is more short-lived or mutable than spirit. The broker, the wheelwright, the carpenter, the tollman, are much displeased at the intimation.

But whilst we acquiesce entirely in the permanence of natural laws, the question of the absolute existence of nature still remains open. It is the uniform effect of culture on the human mind, not to shake our faith in the stability of particular phenomena, as of heat, water, azote; [22] but to lead us to regard nature as phenomenon, not a substance; to attribute necessary existence to spirit; to esteem nature as an accident and an effect.

To the senses and the unrenewed understanding, belongs a sort of instinctive belief in the absolute existence of nature. In their view man and nature are indissolubly joined. Things are ultimates, and they never look beyond their sphere. The presence of Reason mars this faith. The first effort of thought tends to relax this despotism of the senses which binds us to nature as if we were a part of it, and shows us nature aloof, and, as it were, afloat. Until this higher agency intervened, the animal eye sees, with wonderful accuracy, sharp outlines and colored surfaces. When the eye of Reason opens, to outline and surface are at once added grace and expression. These proceed from imagination and affection, and abate somewhat of the angular distinctness of objects. If the Reason be stimulated to more earnest vision, outlines and surfaces become transparent, and are no longer seen; causes and spirits are seen through them. The best moments of life are these delicious awakenings of the higher powers, and the reverential withdrawing of nature before its God.

Let us proceed to indicate the effects of culture.

1. Our first institution [23] in the Ideal philosophy is a hint from Nature herself.

Nature is made to conspire with spirit to emancipate us. Certain mechanical changes, a small alteration in our local position, apprises us of a dualism. We are strangely affected by seeing the shore from a moving ship, from a balloon, or through the tints of an unusual sky. The least change in our point of view gives the whole world a pictorial air. A man who seldom rides, needs only to get into a coach and traverse his own town, to turn the street into a puppet-show. The men, the women,—talking, running, bartering, fighting,—the earnest mechanic, the lounger, the beggar, the boys, the dogs, are unrealized [24] at once, or, at least, wholly detached from all relation to the observer, and seen as apparent, not substantial beings. What new thoughts are suggested by seeing a face of country quite familiar, in the rapid movement of the railroad car! Nay, the most wonted objects, (make a very slight change in the point of vision,) please us most. In a camera obscura, the butcher's cart, and the figure of one of our own family amuse us. So a portrait of a well-known face gratifies us. Turn the eyes upside down, by looking at the landscape through your legs, and how agreeable is the picture, though you have seen it any time these twenty years!

In these cases, by mechanical means, is suggested the difference between the observer and the spectacle—between man and nature. Hence arises a pleasure mixed with awe; I may say, a low degree of the sublime is felt, from the fact, probably, that man is hereby apprised that whilst the world is a spectacle, something in himself is stable.

2. In a higher manner the poet communicates the same pleasure. By a few strokes he delineates, as on air, the sun, the mountain, the camp, the city, the hero, the maiden, not different from what we know them, but only lifted from the ground and afloat before the eye. He unfixes the land and the sea, makes them revolve around the axis of his primary thought, and disposes them anew. Possessed himself by a heroic passion, he uses matter as symbols of it. The sensual man conforms thoughts to things; the poet conforms things to his thoughts. The one esteems nature as rooted and fast; the other, as fluid, and impresses his being thereon. To him, the refractory world is ductile and flexible; he invests dust and stones with humanity, and makes them the words of the Reason. The Imagination may be defined to be the use which the Reason makes of the material world. Shakspeare possesses the power of subordinating nature for the purposes of expression, beyond all poets. His imperial muse tosses the creation like a bauble from hand to hand, and uses it to embody any caprice of thought that is uppermost in his

22. **azote:** nitrogen.

23. **institution:** instruction.

24. **unrealized:** rendered unreal.

mind. The remotest spaces of nature are visited, and the farthest sundered things are brought together, by a subtile spiritual connection. We are made aware that magnitude of material things is relative, and all objects shrink and expand to serve the passion of the poet. Thus in his sonnets, the lays of birds, the scents and dyes of flowers he finds to be the *shadow* of his beloved; time, which keeps her from him, is his *chest;* the suspicion she has awakened, is her *ornament;*

> The ornament of beauty is Suspect,
> A crow which flies in heaven's sweetest air.[25]

His passion is not the fruit of chance; it swells, as he speaks, to a city, or a state.

> No, it was builded far from accident;
> It suffers not in smiling pomp, nor falls
> Under the brow of thralling discontent;
> It fears not policy, that heretic,
> That works on leases of short numbered hours,
> But all alone stands hugely politic.[26]

In the strength of his constancy, the Pyramids seem to him recent and transitory. The freshness of youth and love dazzles him with its resemblance to morning;

> Take those lips away
> Which so sweetly were forsworn;
> And those eyes,—the break of day,
> Lights that do mislead the morn.[27]

The wild beauty of this hyperbole, I may say in passing, it would not be easy to match in literature.

This transfiguration which all material objects undergo through the passion of the poet,—this power which he exerts to dwarf the great, to magnify the small,—might be illustrated by a thousand examples from his Plays. I have before me the Tempest, and will cite only these few lines.

> ARIEL. The strong based promontory
> Have I made shake, and by the spurs plucked up
> The pine and cedar.

Prospero calls for music to soothe the frantic Alonzo, and his companions;

> A solemn air, and the best comforter
> To an unsettled fancy, cure my brains
> Now useless, boiled within thy skull.

Again;

> The charm dissolves apace,
> And, as the morning steals upon the night,
> Melting the darkness, so their rising senses
> Begin to chase the ignorant fumes that mantle
> Their clearer reason.
> Their understanding
> Begins to swell: and the approaching tide
> Will shortly fill the reasonable shores
> That now lie foul and muddy.[28]

The perception of real affinities between events (that is to say, of *ideal* affinities, for those only are real), enables the poet thus to make free with the most imposing forms and phenomena of the world, and to assert the predominance of the soul.

3. Whilst thus the poet animates nature with his own thoughts, he differs from the philosopher only herein, that the one proposes Beauty as his main end; the other Truth. But the philosopher, not less than the poet, postpones the apparent order and relations of things to the empire of thought. "The problem of philosophy," according to Plato, "is, for all that exists conditionally, to find a ground unconditioned and absolute." It proceeds on the faith that a law determines all phenomena, which being known, the phenomena can be predicted. That law, when in the mind, is an idea. Its beauty is infinite. The true philosopher and the true poet are one, and a beauty, which is truth, and a truth, which is beauty, is the aim of both. Is not the charm of one of Plato's or Aristotle's definitions strictly like that of the Antigone of Sophocles? It is, in both cases, that a spiritual life has been imparted to nature; that the solid seeming block of matter has been pervaded and dissolved by a thought; that this feeble human being has penetrated the vast masses of nature with an informing soul, and recognized itself in their harmony, that is, seized their law. In physics, when this is attained, the memory disburthens itself of its cumbrous catalogues of particulars, and carries centuries of observation in a single formula.

Thus even in physics, the material is degraded before the spiritual. The astronomer, the geometer, rely on their irrefragable analysis, and disdain the results of observation. The sublime remark of Euler on his law of arches, "This will be found contrary to all experience, yet is true;" [29] had already transferred nature into the mind, and left matter like an outcast corpse.

4. Intellectual science has been observed to beget invariably a doubt of the existence of matter. Turgot [30] said, "He that has never doubted the

25. The . . . air: See Shakespeare, Sonnet LXX, ll. 3–4. **26. No . . . politic:** *Idem,* Sonnet CXXIV, ll. 5–11: inaccurately quoted. **27. Take . . . morn:** freely quoted from the boy's song in *Measure for Measure,* IV.i.1–4.

28. Ariel . . . muddy: These quotations, with some inaccuracies, are all from *The Tempest,* V.i. The lines beginning, "The strong based promontory," however, are not Ariel's but Prospero's. **29. The . . . true:** Leonhard Euler (1707–83), Swiss mathematician. "The celebrated Euler," says Coleridge, "treating on some point respecting arches, makes this curious remark:—'All experience is in contradiction of this; *sed potius fidendum est analysi,* but this is no reason for doubting the analysis' " (*The Friend,* Section the Second, Essay VII). **30. Turgot:** A.R.J. Turgot, Baron de Laune (1727–81), French economist and statesman, comptroller-general of France under Louis XVI.

existence of matter, may be assured he has no aptitude for metaphysical inquiries." It fastens the attention upon immortal necessary uncreated natures, that is, upon Ideas; and in their presence we feel that the outward circumstance is a dream and a shade. Whilst we wait in this Olympus of gods, we think of nature as an appendix to the soul. We ascend into their region, and know that these are the thoughts of the Supreme Being. "These are they who were set up from everlasting, from the beginning, or ever the earth was. When he prepared the heavens, they were there; when he established the clouds above, when he strengthened the fountains of the deep. Then they were by him, as one brought up with him. Of them took he counsel." [31]

Their influence is proportionate. As objects of science they are accessible to few men. Yet all men are capable of being raised by piety or by passion, into their region. And no man touches these divine natures, without becoming, in some degree, himself divine. Like a new soul, they renew the body. We become physically nimble and lightsome; we tread on air; life is no longer irksome, and we think it will never be so. No man fears age or misfortune or death in their serene company, for he is transported out of the district of change. Whilst we behold unveiled the nature of Justice and Truth, we learn the difference between the absolute and the conditional or relative. We apprehend the absolute. As it were, for the first time, *we exist*. We become immortal, for we learn that time and space are relations of matter; that with a perception of truth or a virtuous will they have no affinity.

5. Finally, religion and ethics, which may be fitly called the practice of ideas, or the introduction of ideas into life, have an analogous effect with all lower culture, in degrading nature and suggesting its dependence on spirit. Ethics and religion differ herein; that the one is the system of human duties commencing from man; the other, from God. Religion includes the personality of God; Ethics does not. They are one to our present design. They both put nature under foot. The first and last lesson of religion is, "The things that are seen, are temporal; the things that are unseen, are eternal." [32] It puts an affront upon nature. It does that for the unschooled, which philosophy does for Berkeley and Viasa.[33] The uniform language that may be heard in the churches of the most ignorant sects is,—"Contemn the unsubstantial shows of the world; they are vanities, dreams, shadows, unrealities; seek the realities of religion." The devotee flouts nature. Some theosophists have arrived at a certain hostility and indignation towards matter, as the Manichean [34] and Plotinus.[35] They distrusted in themselves any looking back to these flesh-pots of Egypt. Plotinus was ashamed of his body.[36] In short, they might all say of matter, what Michael Angelo said of external beauty, "It is the frail and weary weed, in which God dresses the soul which he has called into time." [37]

It appears that motion, poetry, physical and intellectual science, and religion, all tend to affect our convictions of the reality of the external world. But I own there is something ungrateful in expanding too curiously the particulars of the general proposition, that all culture tends to imbue us with idealism. I have no hostility to nature, but a child's love to it. I expand and live in the warm day like corn and melons. Let us speak her fair. I do not wish to fling stones at my beautiful mother, nor soil my gentle nest. I only wish to indicate the true position of nature in regard to man, wherein to establish man all right education tends; as the ground which to attain is the object of human life, that is, of man's connection with nature. Culture inverts the vulgar views of nature, and brings the mind to call that apparent which it uses to call real, and that real which it uses to call visionary. Children, it is true, believe in the external world. The belief that it appears only, is an afterthought, but with culture this faith will as surely arise on the mind as did the first.

The advantage of the ideal theory over the popular faith is this, that it presents the world in precisely that view which is most desirable to the mind. It is, in fact, the view which Reason, both speculative and practical, that is, philosophy and virtue, take. For seen in the light of thought, the world always is phenomenal; and virtue subordinates it to the mind. Idealism sees the world in God. It beholds the whole circle of persons and things, of actions and events, of country and religion, not as painfully accumulated, atom after atom, act after act, in an aged creeping Past, but as one vast picture which God paints on the in-

31. **"These . . . counsel"**: paraphrased from Prov. 8:23, 27, 28, 30. 32. **"The . . . eternal"**: See II Cor. 4:18. 33. **Viasa**: legendary compiler of the Hindu Vedas.

34. **the Manichean**: Manichaeism, a widespread semi-Christian religion of the fourth century, mistakenly supposed to have taught that matter is essentially evil. 35. **Plotinus**: Neoplatonist philosopher of the third century A.D., one of Emerson's favorite philosophical writers, whose *Enneads* he had read in Thomas Taylor's translation. 36. **ashamed of his body**: Porphyry, a disciple of Plotinus, says in his life of that philosopher that he "seemed ashamed of being in the body" ("On the Life of Plotinus," 1). 37. **"It . . . time"**: a free translation of Michelangelo's Sonnet CXXIII, ll.9–11. A more literal translation of these lines would be: "You gave to time this divine soul, and in this fleshly garment, so frail and weary, did imprison it, and in a grim fate."

stant eternity for the contemplation of the soul. Therefore the soul holds itself off from a too trivial and microscopic study of the universal tablet. It respects the end too much to immerse itself in the means. It sees something more important in Christianity than the scandals of ecclesiastical history or the niceties of criticism; and, very incurious concerning persons or miracles, and not at all disturbed by chasms of historical evidence, it accepts from God the phenomenon, as it finds it, as the pure and awful form of religion in the world. It is not hot and passionate at the appearance of what it calls its own good or bad fortune, at the union or opposition of other persons. No man is its enemy. It accepts whatsoever befalls, as part of its lesson. It is a watcher more than a doer, and it is a doer, only that it may the better watch.

VII. SPIRIT

[THIS short chapter restates, in somewhat different terms, the themes of "Language" and "Idealism." It is doubtless true, says Emerson, that matter is only "a phenomenon [that is, an appearance], not a substance [that is, a self-existent reality]"; but the mere denial of the existence of matter, he goes on to say, is frustrating to the needs of the spirit; it seems to erect a desolating dualism between me and nature; but this dualism can be transcended by the reflection that not only in the soul of man but "behind nature, throughout nature, spirit is present"; and that therefore there is a profound harmony between the physical world and the human soul. "The world," he says, "proceeds from the same spirit as the body of man."

Emerson seems originally to have intended this chapter as a separate essay, to be published in the same volume with *Nature;* but in the end he decided to make a seventh chapter of it (*Letters,* II, 26).]

VIII. PROSPECTS

[THE last chapter of *Nature* is a kind of rhapsody or descant on the illimitable horizons that will open up before man when he learns to apply, not just half, but the whole of his force to nature; that is, when he reaches beyond the merely empirical knowledge accessible to the Understanding, and arrives at the higher knowledge accessible only to the Reason (see headnote to V, "Discipline," above). The chapter is diversified by two longish passages that, though they are in prose, purport to be quotations from "a certain poet," who is later described as "my Orphic poet." Partly because of the latter phrase, these paragraphs have sometimes been supposed to summarize the monologues of Emerson's friend, Bronson Alcott, who later published a series of "Orphic Sayings" in the *Dial* (1840); but it seems more probable that, though they are not unlike Alcott in drift and manner, they are Emerson's own work, and were intended by him simply to lend dramatic variety and a kind of detached character to his disquisition.]

THE AMERICAN SCHOLAR

AN ORATION DELIVERED BEFORE THE PHI BETA KAPPA SOCIETY, AT CAMBRIDGE, AUGUST 31, 1837

◇

¶ "THIS grand oration," said Oliver Wendell Holmes, "was our intellectual Declaration of Independence . . . the young men went out from it as if a prophet had been proclaiming to them 'Thus saith the Lord.'" Emerson had been invited, in 1834, to read a poem at the annual Phi Beta Kappa exercises at Harvard; he had done so, and now again, in 1837, he was asked, on short notice, when another person declined, to deliver the annual oration before the Society. He agreed, and "the most famous of all Phi Beta Kappa orations" was delivered to a large and expectant audience in the meetinghouse across from the Harvard Yard on August 31, shortly after noon. The impression it created was immense. Bronson Alcott remembered "the mixed confusion, consternation, surprise, and wonder" of some members of the audience, but Holmes was right at least about the young men, and Lowell describes the occasion as

> an event without any former parallel in our literary annals, a scene to be always treasured in the memory for its picturesqueness and its inspiration. What crowded and breathless aisles, what windows clustering with eager heads, what enthusiasm of approval, what grim silence of foregone dissent! It was our Yankee version of a lecture by Abelard, our Harvard parallel to the last public appearance of Schelling.

◇

MR. PRESIDENT AND GENTLEMEN:

I greet you on the recommencement of our literary year. Our anniversary is one of hope, and, perhaps, not enough of labor. We do not meet for games of strength or skill, for the recitation of histories, tragedies, and odes, like the ancient Greeks; for parliaments of love and poesy, like the Troubadours; nor for the advancement of science, like our contemporaries in the British and European capitals. Thus far, our holiday has been simply a friendly sign of the survival of the love of letters amongst a people too busy to give to letters any more. As such it is precious as the sign of an indestructible instinct. Perhaps the time is already come when it ought to be, and will be, something else; when the sluggard intellect of this continent will look from under its iron lids and fill the postponed expectation of the world with something better than the exertions of mechanical skill. Our day of dependence, our long apprenticeship to the learning of other lands, draws to a close. The millions that around us are rushing into life, cannot always be fed on the sere remains of foreign harvests. Events, actions arise, that must be sung, that will sing themselves. Who can doubt that poetry will revive and lead in a new age, as the star in the constellation Harp, which now flames in our zenith, astronomers announce, shall one day be the pole-star for a thousand years?

In this hope I accept the topic which not only usage but the nature of our association seem to prescribe to this day,—the AMERICAN SCHOLAR. Year by year we come up hither to read one more chapter of his biography. Let us inquire what light new days and events have thrown on his character and his hopes.

It is one of those fables which out of an unknown antiquity convey an unlooked-for wisdom, that the gods, in the beginning, divided Man into men,[1] that he might be more helpful to himself; just as the hand was divided into fingers, the better to answer its end.

The old fable covers a doctrine ever new and sublime; that there is One Man,—present to all particular men only partially, or through one faculty; and that you must take the whole society to find the whole man. Man is not a farmer, or a professor, or an engineer, but he is all. Man is priest, and scholar, and statesman, and producer, and soldier. In the *divided* or social state these functions are parcelled out to individuals, each of whom aims to do his stint of the joint work, whilst each other performs his. The fable implies that the individual, to possess himself, must sometimes return from his own labor to embrace all the other laborers. But, unfortunately, this original unit, this fountain of power, has been so distributed to multitudes, has been so minutely subdivided and peddled out, that it is spilled into drops, and cannot be gathered. The state of society is one in which the members have suffered amputation from the trunk, and strut about so many walking monsters, —a good finger, a neck, a stomach, an elbow, but never a man.

Man is thus metamorphosed into a thing, into many things. The planter, who is Man sent out into the field to gather food, is seldom cheered by any idea of the true dignity of his ministry. He sees his bushel and his cart, and nothing beyond, and sinks into the farmer, instead of Man on the farm. The tradesman scarcely ever gives an ideal worth to his work, but is ridden by the routine of his craft, and the soul is subject to dollars. The priest becomes a form; the attorney a statute-book; the mechanic a machine; the sailor a rope of the ship.

In this distribution of functions the scholar is the delegated intellect. In the right state he is *Man Thinking*. In the degenerate state, when the victim of society, he tends to become a mere thinker, or still worse, the parrot of other men's thinking.

In this view of him, as Man Thinking, the theory of his office is contained. Him Nature solicits with all her placid, all her monitory pictures; him the past instructs; him the future invites. Is not indeed every man a student, and do not all things exist for the student's behoof? And, finally, is not the true scholar the only true master? But the old oracle said, "All things have two handles: beware of the wrong one." In life, too often, the scholar errs with mankind and forfeits his privilege. Let us see him in his school, and consider him in reference to the main influences he receives.

I. The first in time and the first in importance of the influences upon the mind is that of nature. Every day, the sun; and, after sunset, Night and her stars. Ever the winds blow; ever the grass grows. Every day, men and women, conversing—beholding and beholden. The scholar is he of all men whom this spectacle most engages. He must settle its value in his mind. What is nature to him? There is never a beginning, there is never an end, to the inexplicable continuity of this web of God, but always circular power returning into itself. Therein it resembles his own spirit, whose beginning, whose ending, he never can find,—so entire, so boundless. Far too as her splendors shine, system on system shooting like rays, upward, downward, without centre, without circumference,—in the mass and in the particle, Nature hastens to render account of herself to the mind. Classification begins. To the young mind every thing is individual, stands by itself. By and by, it finds how to join two things and see in them one nature; then three, then three thousand; and so, tyrannized over by its own unifying instinct, it goes on tying things together, diminishing anomalies, discovering roots running under ground whereby contrary and remote things cohere and flower out from one stem. It presently learns that since the dawn of history there has been a constant accumulation and classifying of facts. But what is classi-

THE AMERICAN SCHOLAR. 1. **divided Man into men:** Emerson may be alluding here to the speech of Aristophanes in Plato's *Symposium* or perhaps to a passage in Plutarch's essay, "Of Brotherly Love": but in either case, his allusion is not pedantically precise.

fication but the perceiving that these objects are not chaotic, and are not foreign, but have a law which is also a law of the human mind? The astronomer discovers that geometry, a pure abstraction of the human mind, is the measure of planetary motion. The chemist finds proportions and intelligible method throughout matter; and science is nothing but the finding of analogy, identity, in the most remote parts. The ambitious soul sits down before each refractory fact; one after another reduces all strange constitutions, all new powers, to their class and their law, and goes on forever to animate the last fibre of organization, the outskirts of nature, by insight.

Thus to him, to this schoolboy under the bending dome of day, is suggested that he and it proceed from one root; one is leaf and one is flower; relation, sympathy, stirring in every vein. And what is that root? Is not that the soul of his soul? A thought too bold; a dream too wild. Yet when this spiritual light shall have revealed the law of more earthly natures,—when he has learned to worship the soul, and to see that the natural philosophy that now is, is only the first gropings of its gigantic hand, he shall look forward to an ever expanding knowledge as to a becoming creator. He shall see that nature is the opposite of the soul, answering to it part for part. One is seal and one is print. Its beauty is the beauty of his own mind. Its laws are the laws of his own mind. Nature then becomes to him the measure of his attainments. So much of nature as he is ignorant of, so much of his own mind does he not yet possess. And, in fine, the ancient precept, "Know thyself," and the modern precept, "Study nature," become at last one maxim.

II. The next great influence into the spirit of the scholar is the mind of the Past,—in whatever form, whether of literature, of art, of institutions, that mind is inscribed. Books are the best type of the influence of the past, and perhaps we shall get at the truth,—learn the amount of this influence more conveniently,—by considering their value alone.

The theory of books is noble. The scholar of the first age received into him the world around; brooded thereon; gave it the new arrangement of his own mind, and uttered it again. It came into him life; it went out from him truth. It came to him short-lived actions; it went out from him immortal thoughts. It came to him business; it went from him poetry. It was dead fact; now, it is quick thought. It can stand, and it can go. It now endures, it now flies, it now inspires. Precisely in proportion to the depth of mind from which it issued, so high does it soar, so long does it sing.

Or, I might say, it depends on how far the process had gone, of transmuting life into truth. In proportion to the completeness of the distillation, so will the purity and imperishableness of the product be. But none is quite perfect. As no air-pump can by any means make a perfect vacuum, so neither can any artist entirely exclude the conventional, the local, the perishable from his book, or write a book of pure thought, that shall be as efficient, in all respects, to a remote posterity, as to contemporaries, or rather to the second age. Each age, it is found, must write its own books; or rather, each generation for the next succeeding. The books of an older period will not fit this.

Yet hence arises a grave mischief. The sacredness which attaches to the act of creation, the act of thought, is transferred to the record. The poet chanting was felt to be a divine man: henceforth the chant is divine also. The writer was a just and wise spirit: henceforward it is settled the book is perfect; as love of the hero corrupts into worship of his statue. Instantly the book becomes noxious: the guide is a tyrant. The sluggish and perverted mind of the multitude, slow to open to the incursions of Reason, having once so opened, having once received this book, stands upon it, and makes an outcry if it is disparaged. Colleges are built on it. Books are written on it by thinkers, not by Man Thinking; by men of talent, that is, who start wrong, who set out from accepted dogmas, not from their own sight of principles. Meek young men grow up in libraries, believing it their duty to accept the views which Cicero, which Locke, which Bacon, have given; forgetful that Cicero, Locke, and Bacon were only young men in libraries when they wrote these books.

Hence, instead of Man Thinking, we have the bookworm. Hence the book-learned class, who value books, as such; not as related to nature and the human constitution, but as making a sort of Third Estate with the world and the soul. Hence the restorers of readings, the emendators, the bibliomaniacs of all degrees.

Books are the best of things, well used; abused, among the worst. What is the right use? What is the one end which all means go to effect? They are for nothing but to inspire. I had better never see a book than to be warped by its attraction clean out of my own orbit, and made a satellite instead of a system. The one thing in the world, of value, is the active soul. This every man is entitled to; this every man contains within him, although in almost all men obstructed and as yet unborn. The soul active sees absolute truth and utters truth, or creates. In this action it is genius; not the privilege of here and there a favorite, but the sound estate of every man. In its essence it is progressive. The book, the college, the school of art, the institution of any kind, stop with some past utterance of genius. This is good, say they,—let us hold by this. They pin me down. They look backward and not forward. But genius looks forward: the eyes of man are set in his forehead, not in his hind-head: man hopes: genius creates. Whatever talents may be, if the man create not, the pure efflux of the Deity is not his;—cinders and smoke there may be, but not yet flame. There are creative manners, there are creative actions, and creative words; manners, actions, words, that is, indicative of no custom or authority, but springing spontaneous from the mind's own sense of good and fair.

On the other part, instead of being its own seer, let it receive from another mind its truth, though it were in torrents of light, without periods of solitude, inquest, and self-recovery, and a fatal disservice is done. Genius is always sufficiently the enemy of genius by over-influence. The literature of every nation bears me witness. The English dramatic poets have Shakspearized now for two hundred years.

Undoubtedly there is a right way of reading, so it be sternly subordinated. Man Thinking must not be subdued by his instruments. Books are for the scholar's idle times. When he can read God directly, the hour is too precious to be wasted in other men's transcripts of their readings. But when the intervals of darkness come, as come they must,—when the sun is hid and the stars withdraw their shining,—we repair to the lamps which were kindled by their ray, to guide our steps to the East again, where the dawn is. We hear, that we may speak. The Arabian proverb says, "A fig tree, looking on a fig tree, becometh fruitful."

It is remarkable, the character of the pleasure we derive from the best books. They impress us with the conviction that one nature wrote and the same reads. We read the verses of one of the great English poets, of Chaucer, of Marvell, of Dryden, with the most modern joy,—with a pleasure, I mean, which is in great part caused by the abstraction of all *time* from their verses. There is some awe mixed with the joy of our surprise, when this poet, who lived in some past world, two or three hundred years ago, says that which lies close to my own soul, that which I also had well-nigh thought and said. But for the evidence thence afforded to the philosophical doctrine of the identity of all minds, we should suppose some preëstablished harmony, some foresight of souls that were to be, and some preparation of stores for their future wants, like the fact observed in insects, who lay up food before death for the young grub they shall never see.

I would not be hurried by any love of system, by any exaggeration of instincts, to underrate the Book. We all know, that as the human body can be nourished on any food, though it were boiled grass and the broth of shoes, so the human mind can be fed by any knowledge. And great and heroic men have existed who had almost no other information than by the printed page. I only would say that it needs a strong head to bear that diet. One must be an inventor to read well. As the proverb says, "He that would bring home the wealth of the Indies, must carry out the wealth of the Indies." There is then creative reading as well as creative writing. When the mind is braced by labor and invention, the page of whatever book we read becomes luminous with manifold allusion. Every sentence is doubly significant, and the sense of our author is as broad as the world. We then see, what is always true, that as the seer's hour of vision is short and rare among heavy days and months, so is its record, perchance, the least part of his volume. The discerning will read, in his Plato or Shakspeare, only that least part,—only the authentic utterances of the oracle;—all the rest he rejects, were it never so many times Plato's and Shakspeare's.

Of course there is a portion of reading quite indispensable to a wise man. History and exact science he must learn by laborious reading. Colleges, in like manner, have their indispensable office,—to teach elements. But they can only highly serve us when they aim not to drill, but to create; when they gather from far every ray of various genius to their hospitable halls, and by the concentrated fires, set the hearts of their youth on flame. Thought and knowledge are natures in which apparatus and pretension avail nothing. Gowns and pecuniary foundations, though of towns of gold, can never countervail the least sentence or syllable of wit. Forget this, and our American colleges will recede in their public importance, whilst they grow richer every year.

III. There goes in the world a notion that the scholar should be a recluse, a valetudinarian,—as unfit for any handiwork or public labor as a penknife for an axe. The so-called "practical men" sneer at speculative men, as if, because they speculate or *see,* they could do nothing. I have heard it said that the clergy,—who are always, more universally than any other class, the scholars of their day,—are addressed as women; that the rough, spontaneous conversation of men they do not hear, but only a mincing and diluted speech. They are often virtually disfranchised; and indeed there are advocates for their celibacy. As far as this is true of the studious classes, it is not just and wise. Action is with the scholar subordinate, but it is essential. Without it he is not yet man. Without it thought can never ripen into truth. Whilst the world hangs before the eye as a cloud of beauty, we cannot even see its beauty. Inaction is cowardice, but there can be no scholar without the heroic mind. The preamble of thought, the transition through which it passes from the unconscious to the conscious, is action. Only so much do I know, as I have lived. Instantly we know whose words are loaded with life, and whose not.

The world,—this shadow of the soul, or *other me,*—lies wide around. Its attractions are the keys which unlock my thoughts and make me acquainted with myself. I run eagerly into this resounding tumult. I grasp the hands of those next me, and take my place in the ring to suffer and to work, taught by an instinct that so shall the dumb abyss be vocal with speech. I pierce its order; I dissipate its fear; I dispose of it within the circuit of my expanding life. So much only of life as I know by experience, so much of the wilderness have I vanquished and planted, or so far have I extended my being, my dominion. I do not see how any man can afford, for the sake of his nerves and his nap, to spare any action in which he can partake. It is pearls and rubies to his discourse. Drudgery, calamity, exasperation, want, are instructors in eloquence and wisdom. The true scholar grudges every opportunity of action past by, as a loss of power. It is the raw material out of which the intellect moulds her splendid products. A strange process too, this by which experience is converted into thought, as a mulberry leaf is converted into satin. The manufacture goes forward at all hours.

The actions and events of our childhood and youth are now matters of calmest observation. They lie like fair pictures in the air. Not so with our recent actions,—with the business which we now have in hand. On this we are quite unable to speculate. Our affections as yet circulate through it. We no more feel or know it than we feel the feet, or the hand, or the brain of our body. The new deed is yet a part of life,—remains for a time immersed in our unconscious life. In some contemplative hour it detaches itself from the life like a ripe fruit, to become a thought of the mind. Instantly it is raised, transfigured; the corruptible has put on incorruption. Henceforth it is an object of beauty, however base its origin and neighborhood. Observe too the impossibility of antedating this act. In its grub state, it cannot fly, it cannot shine, it is a dull grub. But suddenly, without observation, the selfsame thing unfurls beautiful wings, and is an angel of wisdom. So is there no fact, no event, in our private history, which shall not, sooner or later, lose its adhesive, inert form, and astonish us by soaring from our body into the empyrean. Cradle and infancy, school and playground, the fear of boys, and dogs, and ferules, the love of little maids and berries, and many another fact that once filled the whole sky, are gone already; friend and relative, profession and party, town and country, nation and world, must also soar and sing.

Of course, he who has put forth his total strength in fit actions has the richest return of wisdom. I will not shut myself out of this globe of action, and transplant an oak into a flowerpot, there to hunger and pine; nor trust the revenue of some single faculty, and exhaust one vein of thought, much like those Savoyards, who, getting their livelihood by carving shepherds, shepherdesses, and smoking Dutchmen, for all Europe, went out one day to the mountain to find stock, and discovered that they had whittled up the last of their pine trees. Authors we have, in numbers, who have written out their vein, and who, moved by a commendable prudence, sail for Greece or Palestine, follow the trapper into the prairie, or ramble round Algiers, to replenish their merchantable stock.

If it were only for a vocabulary, the scholar would be covetous of action. Life is our dictionary. Years are well spent in country labors; in town; in the insight into trades and manufactures; in frank intercourse with many men and women; in science; in art; to the one end of mastering in all their facts a language by which to illustrate and embody our perceptions. I learn immediately from any speaker how much he has already lived, through the poverty or the splendor of his speech. Life lies behind us as the quarry from whence we get tiles and copestones for the masonry of to-day. This is the way to learn grammar. Colleges and books only copy the language which the field and the work-yard made.

But the final value of action, like that of books, and better than books, is that it is a resource. That great principle of Undulation in nature, that shows itself in the inspiring and expiring of the breath; in desire and satiety; in the ebb and flow of the sea; in day and night; in heat and cold; and, as yet more deeply ingrained in every atom and every fluid, is known to us under the name of Polarity,—these "fits of easy transmission and reflection," as Newton called them, are the law of nature because they are the law of spirit.

The mind now thinks, now acts, and each fit reproduces the other. When the artist has exhausted his materials, when the fancy no longer paints, when thoughts are no longer apprehended and books are a weariness,—he has always the resource *to live*. Character is higher than intellect. Thinking is the function. Living is the functionary. The stream retreats to its source. A great soul will be strong to live, as well as strong to think. Does he lack organ or medium to impart his truths? He can still fall back on this elemental force of living them. This is a total act. Thinking is a partial act. Let the grandeur of justice shine in his affairs. Let the beauty of affection cheer his lowly roof. Those "far from fame," who dwell and act with him, will feel the force of his constitution in the doings and passages of the day better than it can be measured by any public and designed display. Time shall teach him that the scholar loses no hour which the man lives. Herein he unfolds the sacred germ of his instinct, screened from influence. What is lost in seemliness is gained in strength. Not out of those on whom systems of education have exhausted their culture, comes the helpful giant to destroy the old or to build the new, but out of unhandselled [2] savage nature; out of terrible Druids and Berserkers come at last Alfred and Shakspeare.

I hear therefore with joy whatever is beginning to be said of the dignity and necessity of labor to every citizen. There is virtue yet in the hoe and the spade, for learned as well as for unlearned hands. And labor is everywhere welcome; always we are invited to work; only be this limitation observed, that a man shall not for the sake of wider activity sacrifice any opinion to the popular judgments and modes of action.

I have now spoken of the education of the scholar by nature, by books, and by action. It remains to say somewhat of his duties.

They are such as become Man Thinking. They may all be comprised in self-trust. The office of the scholar is to cheer, to raise, and to guide men by showing them facts amidst appearances. He plies the slow, unhonored, and unpaid task of observation. Flamsteed [3] and Herschel,[4] in their glazed observatories, may catalogue the stars with the praise of all men, and the results being splendid and useful, honor is sure. But he, in his private observatory, cataloguing obscure and nebulous stars of the human mind, which as yet no man has thought of as such,—watching days and months sometimes for a few facts; correcting still his old records;—must relinquish display and immediate fame. In the long period of his preparation he must betray often an ignorance and shiftlessness in popular arts, incurring the disdain of the able who shoulder him aside. Long he must stammer in his speech; often forego the living for the dead. Worse yet, he must accept—how often!—poverty and solitude. For the ease and pleasure of treading the old road, accepting the fashions, the education, the religion of society, he takes the cross of making his own, and, of course, the self-accusation, the faint heart, the frequent uncertainty and loss of time, which are the nettles and tangling vines in the way of the self-relying and self-directed; and the state of virtual hostility in which he seems to stand to society, and especially to educated society. For all this loss and scorn, what offset? He is to find consolation in exercising the highest functions of human nature. He is one who raises himself from private considerations and breathes and lives on public and illustrious thoughts. He is the world's eye. He is the world's heart. He is to resist the vulgar prosperity that retrogrades ever to barbarism, by preserving and communicating heroic sentiments, noble biographies, melodious verse, and the conclusions of history. Whatsoever oracles the human heart, in all emergencies, in all solemn hours, has uttered as its commentary on the world of actions,—these he shall receive and impart. And whatsoever new verdict Reason from her inviolable seat pronounces on the passing men and events of today,—this he shall hear and promulgate.

These being his functions, it becomes him to feel all confidence in himself, and to defer never to the popular cry. He and he only knows the world. The world of any moment is the merest appearance. Some great decorum, some fetish of a government, some ephemeral trade, or war, or man, is cried up by half mankind and cried down by the other half, as if all depended on this particular up or down. The odds are that the whole question is not worth the poorest thought which the scholar has lost in listening to the controversy. Let him not quit his belief that a popgun is a popgun, though the ancient and honorable of the earth affirm it to be the crack of doom. In silence, in steadiness, in severe abstraction, let him hold by himself; add observation to observation, patient of neglect, patient of reproach, and bide his own time,—happy enough if he can satisfy himself alone that this day he has seen something truly. Success treads on every right step. For the instinct is sure, that prompts him to tell his brother what he thinks. He then learns that in going down into the secrets of his own mind he has descended into the secrets of all minds. He learns that he who has mastered any law in his private thoughts, is master to that extent of all men whose language he speaks, and of all into whose language his own can be translated. The poet, in utter solitude remembering his spon-

2. **unhandselled**: a rare word (see *OED*), used by Emerson here, in a very unliteral sense, to mean something like "unequipped," "unfurnished," "unprovided for," with overtones of rawness, crudity, and primitiveness. 3. **Flamsteed**: John Flamsteed (1646–1719), English astronomer, author of *Historia Coelestis Britannica*. 4. **Herschel**: Emerson may be referring to either Sir Frederick William Herschel (1738–1822), German-born but English-adopted astronomer, discoverer of the planet Uranus, or to his son, Sir John Frederick William Herschel (1792–1871), English astronomer and chemist.

taneous thoughts and recording them, is found to have recorded that which men in crowded cities find true for them also. The orator distrusts at first the fitness of his frank confessions, his want of knowledge of the persons he addresses, until he finds that he is the complement of his hearers;—that they drink his words because he fulfils for them their own nature; the deeper he dives into his privatest, secretest presentiment, to his wonder he finds this is the most acceptable, most public, and universally true. The people delight in it; the better part of every man feels, This is my music; this is myself.

In self-trust all the virtues are comprehended. Free should the scholar be,—free and brave. Free even to the definition of freedom, "without any hindrance that does not arise out of his own constitution." [5] Brave; for fear is a thing which a scholar by his very function puts behind him. Fear always springs from ignorance. It is a shame to him if his tranquillity, amid dangerous times, arise from the presumption that like children and women his is a protected class; or if he seek a temporary peace by the diversion of his thoughts from politics or vexed questions, hiding his head like an ostrich in the flowering bushes, peeping into microscopes, and turning rhymes, as a boy whistles to keep his courage up. So is the danger a danger still; so is the fear worse. Manlike let him turn and face it. Let him look into its eye and search its nature, inspect its origin,—see the whelping of this lion,—which lies no great way back; he will then find in himself a perfect comprehension of its nature and extent; he will have made his hands meet on the other side, and can henceforth defy it and pass on superior. The world is his who can see through its pretension. What deafness, what stone-blind custom, what overgrown error you behold is there only by sufferance,—by your sufferance. See it to be a lie, and you have already dealt it its mortal blow.

Yes, we are the cowed,—we the trustless. It is a mischievous notion that we are come late into nature; that the world was finished a long time ago. As the world was plastic and fluid in the hands of God, so it is ever to so much of his attributes as we bring to it. To ignorance and sin, it is flint. They adapt themselves to it as they may; but in proportion as a man has any thing in him divine, the firmament flows before him and takes his signet and form. Not he is great who can alter matter, but he who can alter my state of mind. They are the kings of the world who give the color of their present thought to all nature and all art, and persuade men by the cheerful serenity of their carrying the matter, that this thing which they do is the apple which the ages have desired to pluck, now at last ripe, and inviting nations to the harvest. The great man makes the great thing. Wherever Macdonald sits, there is the head of the table. Linnaeus [6] makes botany the most alluring of studies, and wins it from the farmer and the herb-woman; Davy,[7] chemistry; and Cuvier,[8] fossils. The day is always his who works in it with serenity and great aims. The unstable estimates of men crowd to him whose mind is filled with a truth, as the heaped waves of the Atlantic follow the moon.

For this self-trust, the reason is deeper than can be fathomed,—darker than can be enlightened. I might not carry with me the feeling of my audience in stating my own belief. But I have already shown the ground of my hope, in adverting to the doctrine that man is one. I believe man has been wronged; he has wronged himself. He has almost lost the light that can lead him back to his prerogatives. Men are become of no account. Men in history, men in the world of to-day, are bugs, are spawn, and are called "the mass" and "the herd." In a century, in a millennium, one or two men; that is to say, one or two approximations to the right state of every man. All the rest behold in the hero or the poet their own green and crude being,—ripened; yes, and are content to be less, so *that* may attain to its full stature. What a testimony, full of grandeur, full of pity, is borne to the demands of his own nature, by the poor clansman, the poor partisan, who rejoices in the glory of his chief. The poor and the low find some amends to their immense moral capacity, for their acquiescence in a political and social inferiority. They are content to be brushed like flies from the path of a great person, so that justice shall be done by him to that common nature which it is the dearest desire of all to see enlarged and glorified. They sun themselves in the great man's light, and feel it to be their own element. They cast the dignity of man from their downtrod selves upon the shoulders of a hero, and will perish to add one drop of blood to make that great heart beat, those giant sinews combat and conquer. He lives for us, and we live in him.

Men, such as they are, very naturally seek money or power; and power because it is as good as money,—the "spoils," so called, "of office."

5. **"without . . . constitution":** freedom as defined by Immanuel Kant.

6. **Linnaeus:** See *Nature*, 17 n. 7. **Davy:** Sir Humphry Davy (1778–1829), English chemist, discoverer of potassium and sodium, professor of chemistry at the Royal Institution. 8. **Cuvier:** Baron Cuvier (1769–1832), French naturalist, palaeontologist, comparative anatomist, author of the *Règne Animal.*

And why not? for they aspire to the highest, and this, in their sleep-walking, they dream is highest. Wake them and they shall quit the false good and leap to the true, and leave governments to clerks and desks. This revolution is to be wrought by the gradual domestication of the idea of Culture. The main enterprise of the world for splendor, for extent, is the upbuilding of a man. Here are the materials strewn along the ground. The private life of one man shall be a more illustrious monarchy, more formidable to its enemy, more sweet and serene in its influence to its friend, than any kingdom in history. For a man, rightly viewed, comprehendeth the particular natures of all men. Each philosopher, each bard, each actor has only done for me, as by a delegate, what one day I can do for myself. The books which once we valued more than the apple of the eye, we have quite exhausted. What is that but saying that we have come up with the point of view which the universal mind took through the eyes of one scribe; we have been that man, and have passed on. First, one, then another, we drain all cisterns, and waxing greater by all these supplies, we crave a better and more abundant food. The man has never lived that can feed us ever. The human mind cannot be enshrined in a person who shall set a barrier on any one side to this unbounded, unboundable empire. It is one central fire, which, flaming now out of the lips of Etna, lightens the capes of Sicily, and now out of the throat of Vesuvius, illuminates the towers and vineyards of Naples. It is one light which beams out of a thousand stars. It is one soul which animates all men.

But I have dwelt perhaps tediously upon this abstraction of the Scholar. I ought not to delay longer to add what I have to say of nearer reference to the time and to this country.

Historically, there is thought to be a difference in the ideas which predominate over successive epochs, and there are data for marking the genius of the Classic, of the Romantic, and now of the Reflective or Philosophical age. With the views I have intimated of the oneness or the identity of the mind through all individuals, I do not much dwell on these differences. In fact, I believe each individual passes through all three. The boy is a Greek; the youth, romantic; the adult, reflective. I deny not, however, that a revolution in the leading idea may be distinctly enough traced.

Our age is bewailed as the age of Introversion. Must that needs be evil? We, it seems, are critical; we are embarrassed with second thoughts; we cannot enjoy any thing for hankering to know whereof the pleasures consists; we are lined with eyes; we see with our feet; the time is infected with Hamlet's unhappiness,—

> "Sicklied o'er with the pale cast of thought." [9]

It is so bad then? Sight is the last thing to be pitied. Would we be blind? Do we fear lest we should outsee nature and God, and drink truth dry? I look upon the discontent of the literary class as a mere announcement of the fact that they find themselves not in the state of mind of their fathers, and regret the coming state as untried; as a boy dreads the water before he has learned that he can swim. If there is any period one would desire to be born in, is it not the age of Revolution; when the old and the new stand side by side and admit of being compared; when the energies of all men are searched by fear and by hope; when the historic glories of the old can be compensated by the rich possibilities of the new era? This time, like all times, is a very good one, if we but know what to do with it.

I read with some joy of the auspicious signs of the coming days, as they glimmer already through poetry and art, through philosophy and science, through church and state.

One of these signs is the fact that the same movement which effected the elevation of what was called the lowest class in the state, assumed in literature a very marked and as benign an aspect. Instead of the sublime and beautiful, the near, the low, the common, was explored and poetized. That which had been negligently trodden under foot by those who were harnessing and provisioning themselves for long journeys into far countries, is suddenly found to be richer than all foreign parts. The literature of the poor, the feelings of the child, the philosophy of the street, the meaning of the household life, are the topics of the time. It is a great stride. It is a sign—is it not?—of new vigor when the extremities are made active, when currents of warm life run into the hands and the feet. I ask not for the great, the remote, the romantic; what is doing in Italy or Arabia; what is Greek art, or Provençal minstrelsy; I embrace the common, I explore and sit at the feet of the familiar, the low. Give me insight into to-day, and you may have the antique and future worlds. What would we really know the meaning of? The meal in the firkin; the milk in the pan; the ballad in the street; the news of the boat; the glance of the eye; the form and the gait of the body;—show me the ultimate reason of these matters; show me the sublime presence of the highest spiritual cause lurking, as always it does lurk, in these suburbs and extremities of nature; let me see every trifle bristling with the polarity that ranges it

9. **"Sicklied . . . thought":** *Hamlet*, III.i.85.

instantly on an eternal law; and the shop, the plough, and the ledger referred to the like cause by which light undulates and poets sing;—and the world lies no longer a dull miscellany and lumber-room, but has form and order; there is no trifle, there is no puzzle, but one design unites and animates the farthest pinnacle and the lowest trench.

This idea has inspired the genius of Goldsmith, Burns, Cowper, and, in a newer time, of Goethe, Wordsworth, and Carlyle. This idea they have differently followed and with various success. In contrast with their writing, the style of Pope, of Johnson, of Gibbon, looks cold and pedantic. This writing is blood-warm. Man is surprised to find that things near are not less beautiful and wondrous than things remote. The near explains the far. The drop is a small ocean. A man is related to all nature. This perception of the worth of the vulgar is fruitful in discoveries. Goethe, in this very thing the most modern of the moderns, has shown us, as none ever did, the genius of the ancients.

There is one man of genius who has done much for this philosophy of life, whose literary value has never yet been rightly estimated;—I mean Emanuel Swedenborg.[10] The most imaginative of men, yet writing with the precision of a mathematician, he endeavored to engraft a purely philosophical Ethics on the popular Christianity of his time. Such an attempt of course must have difficulty which no genius could surmount. But he saw and showed the connection between nature and the affections of the soul. He pierced the emblematic or spiritual character of the visible, audible, tangible world. Especially did his shade-loving muse hover over and interpret the lower parts of nature; he showed the mysterious bond that allies moral evil to the foul material forms, and has given in epical parables a theory of insanity, of beasts, of unclean and fearful things.

Another sign of our times, also marked by an analogous political movement, is the new importance given to the single person. Every thing that tends to insulate the individual,—to surround him with barriers of natural respect, so that each man shall feel the world is his, and man shall treat with man as a sovereign state with a sovereign state,—tends to true union as well as greatness. "I learned," said the melancholy Pestalozzi,[11] "that no man in God's wide earth is either willing or able to help any other man." Help must come from the bosom alone. The scholar is that man who must take up into himself all the ability of the time, all the contributions of the past, all the hopes of the future. He must be an university of knowledges. If there be one lesson more than another which should pierce his ear, it is, The world is nothing, the man is all; in yourself is the law of all nature, and you know not yet how a globule of sap ascends; in yourself slumbers the whole of Reason; it is for you to know all; it is for you to dare all. Mr. President and Gentlemen, this confidence in the unsearched might of man belongs, by all motives, by all prophecy, by all preparation, to the American Scholar. We have listened too long to the courtly muses of Europe. The spirit of the American freeman is already suspected to be timid, imitative, tame. Public and private avarice make the air we breathe thick and fat. The scholar is decent, indolent, complaisant. See already the tragic consequence. The mind of this country, taught to aim at low objects, eats upon itself. There is no work for any but the decorous and the complaisant. Young men of the fairest promise, who begin life upon our shores, inflated by the mountain winds, shined upon by all the stars of God, find the earth below not in unison with these, but are hindered from action by the disgust which the principles on which business is managed inspire, and turn drudges, or die of disgust, some of them suicides. What is the remedy? They did not yet see, and thousands of young men as hopeful now crowding to the barriers for the career do not yet see, that if the single man plant himself indomitably on his instincts, and there abide, the huge world will come round to him. Patience,—patience; with the shades of all the good and great for company; and for solace the perspective of your own infinite life; and for work the study and the communication of principles, the making those instincts prevalent, the conversion of the world. Is it not the chief disgrace in the world, not to be an unit;—not to be reckoned one character;—not to yield that peculiar fruit which each man was created to bear, but to be reckoned in the gross, in the hundred, or the thousand, of the party, the section, to which we belong; and our opinion predicted geographically, as the north, or the south? Not so, brothers and friends—please God, ours shall not be so. We will walk on our own feet; we will work with our own hands; we will speak our own minds. The study of letters shall be no longer a name for pity, for doubt, and for sensual indulgence. The dread of man and the love of man shall be a wall of defence and a wreath of joy around all. A nation of men will for the first time exist, because each believes himself inspired by the Divine Soul which also inspires all men.

10. **Emanuel Swedenborg:** See *Nature*, 17 n. 11. **the melancholy Pestalozzi:** Johann Heinrich Pestalozzi (1746–1827), Swiss educational reformer, much admired by the Transcendentalists. Pestalozzi's influence is discernible in Emerson's own essay "Education," in *Lectures and Biographical Sketches* (*Works*, X).

SELF-RELIANCE

◇

THIS famous discourse was first published in *Essays: First Series* (1841) (*Works*, II). The theme of moral independence, of resistance to external pressures, of non-conformity had been a favorite one with Emerson for many years before this essay was written: it was the subject, for example, of one of his best sermons, "Trust Yourself," which he had preached as early as 1830, and it is of course one of the major strains in "The American Scholar." Emerson's journals for the thirties abound in admonitions to himself to preserve his status as a free individual at all costs, and in the lectures he delivered in Boston and elsewhere he returned to the subject again and again. An interesting summary of the sources of "Self-Reliance" in Emerson's own journals and lectures may be found in Stephen E. Whicher, *Selections from Ralph Waldo Emerson* (1957), pp. 481–82.

◇

"Ne te quæsiveris extra." [1]

"Man is his own star; and the soul that can
Render an honest and a perfect man
Commands all light, all influence, all fate;
Nothing to him falls early or too late.
Our acts our angels are, or good or ill,
Our fatal shadows that walk by us still."

EPILOGUE TO BEAUMONT AND FLETCHER'S *Honest Man's Fortune* [2]

Cast the bantling on the rocks,
Suckle him with the she-wolf's teat,
Wintered with the hawk and fox,
Power and speed be hands and feet.

I READ the other day some verses written by an eminent painter which were original and not conventional.[3] The soul always hears an admonition in such lines, let the subject be what it may. The sentiment they instil is of more value than any thought they may contain. To believe your own thought, to believe that what is true for you in your private heart is true for all men,—that is genius. Speak your latent conviction, and it shall be the universal sense; for the inmost in due time becomes the outmost, and our first thought is rendered back to us by the trumpets of the Last Judgment. Familiar as the voice of the mind is to each, the highest merit we ascribe to Moses, Plato and Milton is that they set at naught books and traditions, and spoke not what men, but what *they* thought. A man should learn to detect and watch that gleam of light which flashes across his mind from within, more than the lustre of the firmament of bards and sages. Yet he dismisses without notice his thought, because it is his. In every work of genius we recognize our own rejected thoughts; they come back to us with a certain alienated majesty. Great works of art have no more affecting lesson for us than this. They teach us to abide by our spontaneous impression with good-humored inflexibility then most when the whole cry of voices is on the other side. Else to-morrow a stranger will say with masterly good sense precisely what we have thought and felt all the time, and we shall be forced to take with shame our own opinion from another.

There is a time in every man's education when he arrives at the conviction that envy is ignorance; that imitation is suicide; that he must take himself for better or worse as his portion; that though the wide universe is full of good, no kernel of nourishing corn can come to him but through his toil bestowed on that plot of ground which is given to him to till. The power which resides in him is new in nature, and none but he knows what that is which he can do, nor does he know until he has tried. Not for nothing one face, one character, one fact, makes much impression on him, and another none. This sculpture in the memory is not without preëstablished harmony. The eye was placed where one ray should fall, that it might testify of that particular ray. We but half express ourselves, and are ashamed of that divine idea which each of us represents. It may be safely trusted as proportionate and of good issues, so it be faithfully imparted, but God will not have his work made manifest by cowards. A man is relieved and gay when he has put his heart into his work and done his best; but what he has said or done otherwise shall give him no peace. It is a deliverance which does not deliver. In the attempt his genius deserts him; no muse befriends; no invention, no hope.

Trust thyself: every heart vibrates to that iron

SELF-RELIANCE. 1. ***"Ne . . . extra":*** "Do not seek yourself outside of yourself"; or perhaps, "ask for no man's opinion but your own" (Persius, *Satires*, I.7), a favorite quotation of Emerson. In a journal passage Emerson himself paraphrased the line thus: "Thou art sufficient unto thyself" (*Journals*, III, 337). (A more correct reading: "Nec te quaesiveris extra.") 2. **"Man . . . still":** See Beaumont and Fletcher, *The Honest Man's Fortune*, Epilogue, ll. 33–38. 3. **some . . . conventional:** These verses seem to have been some lines in a poem by Washington Allston (1779–1843), American painter and man of letters, with whom Emerson was acquainted. To judge from a journal entry of 1837 (*Journals*, IV, 295), he is referring here to a poem of Allston's entitled "To the Author of 'The Diary of an Ennuyée' [Mrs. Jameson], One of the Truest and Most Beautiful Books Ever Written on Italy" (Washington Allston, *Lectures on Art, and Poems*, 1850). The seventh and eighth stanzas of this poem, with their characterization of Nature as a loving ministrant to man, may have been particularly appealing to Emerson.

string. Accept the place the divine providence has found for you, the society of your contemporaries, the connection of events. Great men have always done so, and confided themselves childlike to the genius of their age, betraying their perception that the absolutely trustworthy was seated at their heart, working through their hands, predominating in all their being. And we are now men, and must accept in the highest mind the same transcendent destiny; and not minors and invalids in a protected corner, not cowards fleeing before a revolution, but guides, redeemers and benefactors, obeying the Almighty effort and advancing on Chaos and the Dark.

What pretty oracles nature yields us on this text in the face and behavior of children, babes, and even brutes! That divided and rebel mind, that distrust of a sentiment because our arithmetic has computed the strength and means opposed to our purpose, these have not. Their mind being whole, their eye is as yet unconquered, and when we look in their faces we are disconcerted. Infancy conforms to nobody; all conform to it; so that one babe commonly makes four or five out of the adults who prattle and play to it. So God has armed youth and puberty and manhood no less with its own piquancy and charm, and made it enviable and gracious and its claims not to be put by, if it will stand by itself. Do not think the youth has no force, because he cannot speak to you and me. Hark! in the next room his voice is sufficiently clear and emphatic. It seems he knows how to speak to his contemporaries. Bashful or bold then, he will know how to make us seniors very unnecessary.

The nonchalance of boys who are sure of a dinner, and would disdain as much as a lord or do or say aught to conciliate one, is the healthy attitude for human nature. A boy is in the parlor what the pit is in the playhouse; independent, irresponsible, looking out from his corner on such people and facts as pass by, he tries and sentences them on their merits, in the swift, summary way of boys, as good, bad, interesting, silly, eloquent, troublesome. He cumbers himself never about consequences, about interests; he gives an independent, genuine verdict. You must court him; he does not court you. But the man is as it were clapped into jail by his consciousness. As soon as he has once acted or spoken with *éclat* he is a committed person, watched by the sympathy or the hatred of hundreds, whose affections must now enter into his account. There is no Lethe [4] for this. Ah, that he could pass again into his neutrality! Who can thus avoid all pledges and, having observed, observe again from the same unaffected, unbiased, unbribable, unaffrighted innocence,—must always be formidable. He would utter opinions on all passing affairs, which being seen to be not private but necessary, would sink like darts into the ear of men and put them in fear.

These are the voices which we hear in solitude, but they grow faint and inaudible as we enter into the world. Society everywhere is in conspiracy against the manhood of every one of its members. Society is a joint-stock company, in which the members agree, for the better securing of his bread to each shareholder, to surrender the liberty and culture of the eater. The virtue in most request is conformity. Self-reliance is its aversion. It loves not realities and creators, but names and customs.

Whoso would be a man, must be a nonconformist. He who would gather immortal palms must not be hindered by the name of goodness, but must explore if it be goodness. Nothing is at last sacred but the integrity of your own mind. Absolve you to yourself, and you shall have the suffrage of the world. I remember an answer which when quite young I was prompted to make to a valued adviser who was wont to importune me with the dear old doctrines of the church. On my saying, "What have I to do with the sacredness of traditions, if I live wholly from within?" my friend suggested,—"But these impulses may be from below, not from above." I replied, "They do not seem to me to be such; but if I am the Devil's child, I will live then from the Devil." No law can be sacred to me but that of my nature. Good and bad are but names very readily transferable to that or this; the only right is what is after my constitution; the only wrong what is against it. A man is to carry himself in the presence of all opposition as if every thing were titular and ephemeral but he. I am ashamed to think how easily we capitulate to badges and names, to large societies and dead institutions. Every decent and well-spoken individual affects and sways me more than is right. I ought to go upright and vital, and speak the rude truth in all ways. If malice and vanity were the coat of philanthropy, shall that pass? If an angry bigot assumes this bountiful cause of Abolition, and comes to me with his last news from Barbadoes, why should I not say to him, "Go love thy infant; love thy wood-chopper; be good-natured and modest; have that grace; and never varnish your hard, uncharitable ambition with this incredible tenderness for black folk a thousand miles off. Thy love afar is spite at home." Rough and graceless would be such greeting, but truth is handsomer than the affectation of love. Your goodness must have some

4. **Lethe:** in classical mythology, the river of forgetfulness.

edge to it,—else it is none. The doctrine of hatred must be preached, as the counteraction of the doctrine of love, when that pules and whines. I shun father and mother and wife and brother when my genius calls me. I would write on the lintels of the door-post, *Whim*. I hope it is somewhat better than whim at last, but we cannot spend the day in explanation. Expect me not to show cause why I seek or why I exclude company. Then again, do not tell me, as a good man did to-day, of my obligation to put all poor men in good situations. Are they *my* poor? I tell thee, thou foolish philanthropist, that I grudge the dollar, the dime, the cent I give to such men as do not belong to me and to whom I do not belong. There is a class of persons to whom by all spiritual affinity I am bought and sold; for them I will go to prison if need be; but your miscellaneous popular charities; the education at college of fools; the building of meetinghouses to the vain end to which many now stand; alms to sots, and the thousand-fold Relief Societies;—though I confess with shame I sometimes succumb and give the dollar, it is a wicked dollar, which by and by I shall have the manhood to withhold.

Virtues are, in the popular estimate, rather the exception than the rule. There is the man *and* his virtues. Men do what is called a good action, as some piece of courage or charity, much as they would pay a fine in expiation of daily non-appearance on parade. Their works are done as an apology or extenuation of their living in the world,—as invalids and the insane pay a high board. Their virtues are penances. I do not wish to expiate, but to live. My life is for itself and not for a spectacle. I much prefer that it should be of a lower strain, so it be genuine and equal, than that it should be glittering and unsteady. I wish it to be sound and sweet, and not to need diet and bleeding. I ask primary evidence that you are a man, and refuse this appeal from the man to his actions. I know that for myself it makes no difference whether I do or forbear those actions which are reckoned excellent. I cannot consent to pay for a privilege where I have intrinsic right. Few and mean as my gifts may be, I actually am, and do not need for my own assurance or the assurance of my fellows any secondary testimony.

What I must do is all that concerns me, not what the people think. This rule, equally arduous in actual and in intellectual life, may serve for the whole distinction between greatness and meanness. It is the harder because you will always find those who think they know what is your duty better than you know it. It is easy in the world to live after the world's opinion; it is easy in solitude to live after our own; but the great man is he who in the midst of the crowd keeps with perfect sweetness the independence of solitude.

The objection to conforming to usages that have become dead to you is that it scatters your force. It loses your time and blurs the impression of your character. If you maintain a dead church, contribute to a dead Bible-society, vote with a great party either for the government or against it, spread your table like base housekeepers,—under all these screens I have difficulty to detect the precise man you are: and of course so much force is withdrawn from your proper life. But do your work, and I shall know you. Do your work, and you shall reinforce yourself. A man must consider what a blind-man's-buff is this game of conformity. If I know your sect I anticipate your argument. I hear a preacher announce for his text and topic the expediency of one of the institutions of his church. Do I not know beforehand that not possibly can he say a new and spontaneous word? Do I not know that with all this ostentation of examining the grounds of the institution he will do no such thing? Do I not know that he is pledged to himself not to look but at one side, the permitted side, not as a man, but as a parish minister? He is a retained attorney, and these airs of the bench are the emptiest affectation. Well, most men have bound their eyes with one or another handkerchief, and attached themselves to some one of these communities of opinion. This conformity makes them not false in a few particulars, authors of a few lies, but false in all particulars. Their every truth is not quite true. Their two is not the real two, their four not the real four; so that every word they say chagrins us and we know not where to begin to set them right. Meantime nature is not slow to equip us in the prison-uniform of the party to which we adhere. We come to wear one cut of face and figure, and acquire by degrees the gentlest asinine expression. There is a mortifying experience in particular, which does not fail to wreak itself also in the general history; I mean "the foolish face of praise,"[5] the forced smile which we put on in company where we do not feel at ease, in answer to conversation which does not interest us. The muscles, not spontaneously moved but moved by a low usurping wilfulness, grow tight about the outline of the face, with the most disagreeable sensation.

For nonconformity the world whips you with its displeasure. And therefore a man must know how to estimate a sour face. The by-standers look askance on him in the public street or in the

5. **"the foolish face of praise"**: "And wonder with a foolish face of praise" (Pope, "Epistle to Dr. Arbuthnot," l. 212).

friend's parlor. If this aversion had its origin in contempt and resistance like his own he might well go home with a sad countenance; but the sour faces of the multitude, like their sweet faces, have no deep cause, but are put on and off as the wind blows and a newspaper directs. Yet is the discontent of the multitude more formidable than that of the senate and the college. It is easy enough for a firm man who knows the world to brook the rage of the cultivated classes. Their rage is decorous and prudent, for they are timid, as being very vulnerable themselves. But when to their feminine rage the indignation of the people is added, when the ignorant and the poor are aroused, when the unintelligent brute force that lies at the bottom of society is made to growl and mow, it needs the habit of magnanimity and religion to treat it godlike as a trifle of no concernment.

The other terror that scares us from self-trust is our consistency; a reverence for our past act or word because the eyes of others have no other data for computing our orbit than our past acts, and we are loth to disappoint them.

But why should you keep your head over your shoulder? Why drag about this corpse of your memory, lest you contradict somewhat you have stated in this or that public place? Suppose you should contradict yourself; what then? It seems to be a rule of wisdom never to rely on your memory alone, scarcely even in acts of pure memory, but to bring the past for judgment into the thousand-eyed present, and live ever in a new day. In your metaphysics you have denied personality to the Deity, yet when the devout motions of the soul come, yield to them heart and life, though they should clothe God with shape and color. Leave your theory, as Joseph his coat in the hand of the harlot, and flee.[6]

A foolish consistency is the hobgoblin of little minds, adored by little statesmen and philosophers and divines. With consistency a great soul has simply nothing to do. He may as well concern himself with his shadow on the wall. Speak what you think now in hard words and to-morrow speak what to-morrow thinks in hard words again, though it contradict every thing you said to-day.—"Ah, so you shall be sure to be misunderstood."—Is it so bad then to be misunderstood? Pythagoras was misunderstood, and Socrates, and Jesus, and Luther, and Copernicus, and Galileo, and Newton, and every pure and wise spirit that ever took flesh. To be great is to be misunderstood.

I suppose no man can violate his nature. All the sallies of his will are rounded in by the law of his being, as the inequalities of Andes and Himmaleh are insignificant in the curve of the sphere. Nor does it matter how you gauge and try him. A character is like an acrostic or Alexandrian stanza;—read it forward, backward, or across, it still spells the same thing. In this pleasing contrite wood-life which God allows me, let me record day by day my honest thought without prospect or retrospect, and, I cannot doubt, it will be found symmetrical, though I mean it not and see it not. My book should smell of pines and resound with the hum of insects. The swallow over my window should interweave that thread or straw he carries in his bill into my web also. We pass for what we are. Character teaches above our wills. Men imagine that they communicate their virtue or vice only by overt actions, and do not see that virtue or vice emit a breath every moment.

There will be an agreement in whatever variety of actions, so they be each honest and natural in their hour. For of one will, the actions will be harmonious, however unlike they seem. These varieties are lost sight of at a little distance, at a little height of thought. One tendency unites them all. The voyage of the best ship is a zigzag line of a hundred tacks. See the line from a sufficient distance, and it strengthens itself to the average tendency. Your genuine action will explain itself and will explain your other genuine actions. Your conformity explains nothing. Act singly, and what you have already done singly will justify you now. Greatness appeals to the future. If I can be firm enough to-day to do right and scorn eyes, I must have done so much right before as to defend me now. Be it how it will, do right now. Always scorn appearances and you always may. The force of character is cumulative. All the foregone days of virtue work their health into this. What makes the majesty of the heroes of the senate and the field, which so fills the imagination? The consciousness of a train of great days and victories behind. They shed a united light on the advancing actor. He is attended as by a visible escort of angels. That is it which throws thunder into Chatham's[7] voice, and dignity into Washington's port, and America into Adams's eye. Honor is venerable to us because it is no ephemera. It is always ancient virtue. We worship it to-day because it is not of to-day. We love it and pay it homage because it is not a trap for our love and homage, but is self-dependent, self-derived, and therefore of an old immaculate pedigree, even if shown in a young person.

I hope in these days we have heard the last of

6. **Joseph . . . flee:** See Gen. 39:12.

7. **Chatham's voice:** William Pitt, Earl of Chatham (1708–78), English statesman and orator.

conformity and consistency. Let the words be gazetted [8] and ridiculous henceforward. Instead of the gong for dinner, let us hear a whistle from the Spartan fife. Let us never bow and apologize more. A great man is coming to eat at my house. I do not wish to please him; I wish that he should wish to please me. I will stand here for humanity, and though I would make it kind, I would make it true. Let us affront and reprimand the smooth mediocrity and squalid contentment of the times, and hurl in the face of custom and trade and office, the fact which is the upshot of all history, that there is a great responsible Thinker and Actor working wherever a man works; that a true man belongs to no other time or place, but is the centre of things. Where he is, there is nature. He measures you and all men and all events. Ordinarily, every body in society reminds us of somewhat else, or of some other person. Character, reality, reminds you of nothing else; it takes place of the whole creation. The man must be so much that he must make all circumstances indifferent. Every true man is a cause, a country, and an age; requires infinite spaces and numbers and time fully to accomplish his design;—and posterity seem to follow his steps as a train of clients. A man Cæsar is born, and for ages after we have a Roman Empire. Christ is born, and millions of minds so grow and cleave to his genius that he is confounded with virtue and the possible of man. An institution is the lengthened shadow of one man; as, Monachism,[9] of the Hermit Antony; the Reformation, of Luther; Quakerism, of Fox; Methodism, of Wesley; Abolition, of Clarkson.[10] Scipio, Milton called "the height of Rome;" and all history resolves itself very easily into the biography of a few stout and earnest persons.

Let a man then know his worth, and keep things under his feet. Let him not peep or steal, or skulk up and down with the air of a charity-boy, a bastard, or an interloper in the world which exists for him. But the man in the street, finding no worth in himself which corresponds to the force which built a tower or sculptured a marble god, feels poor when he looks on these. To him a palace, a statue, or a costly book have an alien and forbidding air, much like a gay equipage, and seem to say like that, "Who are you, Sir?" Yet they all are his, suitors for his notice, petitioners to his faculties that they will come out and take possession. The picture waits for my verdict; it is not to command me, but I am to settle its claims to praise. That popular fable of the sot who was picked up dead-drunk in the street, carried to the duke's house, washed and dressed and laid in the duke's bed, and, on his waking, treated with all obsequious ceremony like the duke, and assured that he had been insane,[11] owes its popularity to the fact that it symbolizes so well the state of man, who is in the world a sort of sot, but now and then wakes up, exercises his reason and finds himself a true prince.

Our reading is mendicant and sycophantic. In history our imagination plays us false. Kingdom and lordship, power and estate, are a gaudier vocabulary than private John and Edward in a small house and common day's work; but the things of life are the same to both; the sum total of both is the same. Why all this deference to Alfred and Scanderbeg [12] and Gustavus? [13] Suppose they were virtuous; did they wear out virtue? As great a stake depends on your private act to-day as followed their public and renowned steps. When private men shall act with original views, the lustre will be transferred from the actions of kings to those of gentlemen.

The world has been instructed by its kings, who have so magnetized the eyes of nations. It has been taught by this colossal symbol the mutual reverence that is due from man to man. The joyful loyalty with which men have everywhere suffered the king, the noble, or the great proprietor to walk among them by a law of his own, make his own scale of men and things and reverse theirs, pay for benefits not with money but with honor, and represent the law in his person, was the hieroglyphic by which they obscurely signified their consciousness of their own right and comeliness, the right of every man.

The magnetism which all original action exerts is explained when we inquire the reason of self-trust. Who is the Trustee? [14] What is the aboriginal Self, on which a universal reliance may be grounded? What is the nature and power of that science-baffling star, without parallax, without calculable elements, which shoots a ray of beauty even into trivial and impure actions, if the least

8. gazetted: retired from active service; tabooed; prohibited. Emerson's special use of the word is his own. **9. Monachism:** monasticism, of which St. Anthony (*c.* 250–350 A.D.) was the founder. **10. Clarkson:** Thomas Clarkson (1760–1846), English antislavery agitator.

11. That . . . insane: This is a very widespread folk tale, one version of which is Shakespeare's in the Induction to *The Taming of the Shrew*, sc. ii, in which Christopher Sly, a tinker, wakes up in a bedchamber in a Lord's house and is treated with great deference by the servants standing about. **12. Scanderbeg:** alternative spelling of Skanderbeg, otherwise known as George Castriota (1403–68), the national hero of the Albanians, who fought for the independence of Albania from the Turks; the subject of the Spanish Jew's Second Tale in Part Third of Longfellow's *Tales of a Wayside Inn.* **13. Gustavus:** Gustavus II, Adolphus (1594–1632), king of Sweden, one of the leaders of the Protestant cause in the Thirty Years' War. **14. Trustee:** he who is to be trusted or relied upon.

mark of independence appear? The inquiry leads us to that source, at once the essence of genius, of virtue, and of life, which we call Spontaneity or Instinct.[15] We denote this primary wisdom as Intuition, whilst all later teachings are tuitions.[16] In that deep force, the last fact behind which analysis cannot go, all things find their common origin. For the sense of being which in calm hours arises, we know not how, in the soul, is not diverse from things, from space, from light, from time, from man, but one with them and proceeds obviously from the same source whence their life and being also proceed. We first share the life by which things exist and afterwards see them as appearances in nature and forget that we have shared their cause. Here is the fountain of action and of thought. Here are the lungs of that inspiration which giveth man wisdom and which cannot be denied without impiety and atheism. We lie in the lap of immense intelligence, which makes us receivers of its truth and organs of its activity. When we discern justice, when we discern truth, we do nothing of ourselves, but allow a passage to its beams. If we ask whence this comes, if we seek to pry into the soul that causes, all philosophy is at fault. Its presence or its absence is all we can affirm. Every man discriminates between the voluntary acts of his mind and his involuntary perceptions, and knows that to his involuntary perceptions a perfect faith is due. He may err in the expression of them, but he knows that these things are so, like day and night, not to be disputed. My wilful actions and acquisitions are but roving;—the idlest reverie, the faintest native emotion, command my curiosity and respect. Thoughtless people contradict as readily the statement of perception as of opinions, or rather much more readily; for they do not distinguish between perception and notion. They fancy that I choose to see this or that thing. But perception is not whimsical, but fatal. If I see a trait, my children will see it after me, and in course of time all mankind,—although it may chance that no one has seen it before me. For my perception of it is as much a fact as the sun.

The relations of the soul to the divine spirit are so pure that it is profane to seek to interpose helps. It must be that when God speaketh he should communicate, not one thing, but all things; should fill the world with his voice; should scatter forth light, nature, time, souls, from the centre of the present thought; and new date and new create the whole. Whenever a mind is simple and receives a divine wisdom, old things pass away,—means, teachers, texts, temples fall; it lives now, and absorbs past and future into the present hour. All things are made sacred by relation to it,—one as much as another. All things are dissolved to their centre by their cause, and in the universal miracle petty and particular miracles disappear. If therefore a man claims to know and speak of God and carries you backward to the phraseology of some old mouldered nation in another country, in another world, believe him not. Is the acorn better than the oak which is its fulness and completion? Is the parent better than the child into whom he has cast his ripened being? Whence then this worship of the past? The centuries are conspirators against the sanity and authority of the soul. Time and space are but physiological colors which the eye makes, but the soul is light: where it is, is day; where it was, is night; and history is an impertinence and an injury if it be any thing more than a cheerful apologue or parable of my being and becoming.

Man is timid and apologetic; he is no longer upright; he dares not say "I think," "I am," but quotes some saint or sage. He is ashamed before the blade of grass or the blowing rose. These roses under my window make no reference to former roses or to better ones; they are for what they are; they exist with God to-day. There is no time to them. There is simply the rose; it is perfect in every moment of its existence. Before a leaf-bud has burst, its whole life acts; in the full-blown flower there is no more; in the leafless root there is no less. Its nature is satisfied and it satisfies nature in all moments alike. But man postpones or remembers; he does not live in the present, but with reverted eye laments the past, or, heedless of the riches that surround him, stands on tiptoe to foresee the future. He cannot be happy and strong until he too lives with nature in the present, above time.

This should be plain enough. Yet see what strong intellects dare not yet hear God himself unless he speak the phraseology of I know not what David, or Jeremiah, or Paul. We shall not always set so great a price on a few texts, on a few lives. We are like children who repeat by rote the sentences of grandames and tutors, and, as they grow older, of the men of talents and character they chance to see,—painfully recollecting the exact words they spoke; afterwards, when they come into the point of view which those had who uttered these sayings, they understand them and are will-

15. **Instinct:** a misunderstood and perhaps infelicitous word here. Emerson means by it, however, not, as has been unintelligently maintained, mere biological or animal drive, but an innate power of spiritual insight which is not and cannot be the product of any teaching or tuition. 16. **Intuition . . . tuitions:** a distinction (verbally striking, though without any literal etymological basis) between innate wisdom and the kinds of wisdom or knowledge that can be instilled or communicated from without.

ing to let the words go; for at any time they can use words as good when occasion comes. If we live truly, we shall see truly. It is as easy for the strong man to be strong, as it is for the weak to be weak. When we have new perception, we shall gladly disburden the memory of its hoarded treasures as old rubbish. When a man lives with God, his voice shall be as sweet as the murmur of the brook and the rustle of the corn.

And now at last the highest truth on this subject remains unsaid; probably cannot be said; for all that we say is the far-off remembering of the intuition. That thought by what I can now nearest approach to say it, is this. When good is near you, when you have life in yourself, it is not by any known or accustomed way; you shall not discern the footprints of any other; you shall not see the face of man; you shall not hear any name;—the way, the thought, the good, shall be wholly strange and new. It shall exclude example and experience. You take the way from man, not to man. All persons that ever existed are its forgotten ministers. Fear and hope are alike beneath it. There is somewhat low even in hope. In the hour of vision there is nothing that can be called gratitude, nor properly joy. The soul raised over passion beholds identity and eternal causation, perceives the self-existence of Truth and Right, and calms itself with knowing that all things go well. Vast spaces of nature, the Atlantic Ocean, the South Sea; long intervals of time, years, centuries, are of no account. This which I think and feel underlay every former state of life and circumstances, as it does underlie my present, and what is called life and what is called death.

Life only avails, not the having lived. Power ceases in the instant of repose; it resides in the moment of transition from a past to a new state, in the shooting of the gulf, in the darting to an aim. This one fact the world hates; that the soul *becomes;* for that forever degrades the past, turns all riches to poverty, all reputation to a shame, confounds the saint with the rogue, shoves Jesus and Judas equally aside. Why then do we prate of self-reliance? Inasmuch as the soul is present there will be power not confident but agent.[17] To talk of reliance is a poor external way of speaking. Speak rather of that which relies because it works and is. Who has more obedience than I masters me, though he should not raise his finger. Round him I must revolve by the gravitation of spirits. We fancy it rhetoric when we speak of eminent virtue. We do not yet see that virtue is Height, and that a man or a company of men, plastic and permeable to principles, by the law of nature must overpower and ride all cities, nations, kings, rich men, poets, who are not.

This is the ultimate fact which we so quickly reach on this, as on every topic, the resolution of all into the ever-blessed ONE.[18] Self-existence is the attribute of the Supreme Cause, and it constitutes the measure of good by the degree in which it enters into all lower forms. All things real are so by so much virtue as they contain. Commerce, husbandry, hunting, whaling, war, eloquence, personal weight, are somewhat,[19] and engage my respect as examples of its presence and impure action. I see the same law working in nature for conservation and growth. Power is, in nature, the essential measure of right. Nature suffers nothing to remain in her kingdoms which cannot help itself. The genesis and maturation of a planet, its poise and orbit, the bended tree recovering itself from the strong wind, the vital resources of every animal and vegetable, are demonstrations of the self-sufficing and therefore self-relying soul.

Thus all concentrates: let us not rove; let us sit at home with the cause. Let us stun and astonish the intruding rabble of men and books and institutions by a simple declaration of the divine fact. Bid the invaders take the shoes from off their feet, for God is here within. Let our simplicity judge them, and our docility to our own law demonstrate the poverty of nature and fortune beside our native riches.

But now we are a mob. Man does not stand in awe of man, nor is his genius admonished to stay at home, to put itself in communication with the internal ocean, but it goes abroad to beg a cup of water of the urns of other men. We must go alone. I like the silent church before the service begins, better than any preaching. How far off, how cool, how chaste the persons look, begirt each one with a precinct or sanctuary! So let us always sit. Why should we assume the faults of our friend, or wife, or father, or child, because they sit around our hearth, or are said to have the same blood? All men have my blood and I all men's. Not for that will I adopt their petulance or folly, even to the extent of being ashamed of it. But your isolation must not be mechanical, but spiritual, that is, must be elevation. At times the whole world seems to be in conspiracy to importune you with emphatic trifles. Friend, client, child, sickness, fear, want, charity, all knock at once at thy closet door and

17. **not confident but agent:** the two adjectives here have the force of participles (not *confiding* but *acting*), a touch of Emerson's verbal Latinism.

18. **the ever-blessed One:** the Over-Soul or spiritual Unity which lies at the center of all existence. 19. **somewhat:** an older substantive use of the word, signifying "something," "not a negligible quantity."

say,—"Come out unto us." But keep thy state; come not into their confusion. The power men possess to annoy me I give them by a weak curiosity. No man can come near me but through my act. "What we love that we have, but by desire we bereave ourselves of the love."

If we cannot at once rise to the sanctities of obedience and faith, let us at least resist our temptations; let us enter into the state of war and wake Thor and Woden, courage and constancy, in our Saxon breasts. This is to be done in our smooth times by speaking the truth. Check this lying hospitality and lying affection. Live no longer to the expectation of these deceived and deceiving people with whom we converse. Say to them, "O father, O mother, O wife, O brother, O friend, I have lived with you after appearances hitherto. Henceforward I am the truth's. Be it known unto you that henceforward I obey no law less than the eternal law. I will have no covenants but proximities. I shall endeavor to nourish my parents, to support my family, to be the chaste husband of one wife,—but these relations I must fill after a new and unprecedented way. I appeal from your customs. I must be myself. I cannot break myself any longer for you, or you. If you can love me for what I am, we shall be the happier. If you cannot, I will still seek to deserve that you should. I will not hide my tastes or aversions. I will so trust that what is deep is holy, that I will do strongly before the sun and moon whatever inly rejoices me and the heart appoints. If you are noble, I will love you; if you are not, I will not hurt you and myself by hypocritical attentions. If you are true, but not in the same truth with me, cleave to your companions; I will seek my own. I do this not selfishly but humbly and truly. It is alike your interest, and mine, and all men's, however long we have dwelt in lies, to live in truth. Does this sound harsh to-day? You will soon love what is dictated by your nature as well as mine, and if we follow the truth it will bring us out safe at last."—But so may you give these friends pain. Yes, but I cannot sell my liberty and my power, to save their sensibility. Besides, all persons have their moments of reason, when they look out into the region of absolute truth; then will they justify me and do the same thing.

The populace think that your rejection of popular standards is a rejection of all standard, and mere antinomianism; [20] and the bold sensualist will use the name of philosophy to gild his crimes. But the law of consciousness abides. There are two confessionals, in one or the other of which we must be shriven. You may fulfil your round of duties by clearing yourself in the *direct,* or in the *reflex* way. Consider whether you have satisfied your relations to father, mother, cousin, neighbor, town, cat and dog—whether any of these can upbraid you. But I may also neglect this reflex standard and absolve me to myself. I have my own stern claims and perfect circle. It denies the name of duty to many offices that are called duties. But if I can discharge its debts it enables me to dispense with the popular code. If any one imagines that this law is lax, let him keep its commandment one day.

And truly it demands something godlike in him who has cast off the common motives of humanity and has ventured to trust himself for a taskmaster. High be his heart, faithful his will, clear his sight, that he may in good earnest be doctrine, society, law, to himself, that a simple purpose may be to him as strong as iron necessity is to others!

If any man consider the present aspects of what is called by distinction *society,* he will see the need of these ethics. The sinew and heart of man seem to be drawn out, and we are become timorous, desponding whimperers. We are afraid of truth, afraid of fortune, afraid of death, and afraid of each other. Our age yields no great and perfect persons. We want men and women who shall renovate life and our social state, but we see that most natures are insolvent, cannot satisfy their own wants, have an ambition out of all proportion to their practical force and do lean and beg day and night continually. Our housekeeping is mendicant, our arts, our occupations, our marriages, our religion we have not chosen, but society has chosen for us. We are parlor soldiers. We shun the rugged battle of fate, where strength is born.

If our young men miscarry in their first enterprises they lose all heart. If the young merchant fails, men say he is *ruined.* If the finest genius studies at one of our colleges and is not installed in an office within one year afterwards in the cities or suburbs of Boston or New York, it seems to his friends and to himself that he is right in being disheartened and in complaining the rest of his life. A sturdy lad from New Hampshire or Vermont, who in turn tries all the professions, who *teams it, farms it, peddles,* keeps a school, preaches, edits a newspaper, goes to Congress, buys a township, and so forth, in successive years, and always like a cat falls on his feet, is worth a hundred of these city dolls. He walks abreast with his days and feels no shame in not "studying a profession," for he does not postpone his life, but lives already. He has not one chance, but a hundred chances. Let a Stoic

20. **antinomianism:** the doctrine of those who hold that the regenerate Christian, by the influx of divine grace, is set free from the moral law. See "New England Reformers," 3 n.

open the resources of man and tell men they are not leaning willows, but can and must detach themselves; that with the exercise of self-trust, new powers shall appear; that a man is the word made flesh, born to shed healing to the nations; that he should be ashamed of our compassion, and that the moment he acts for himself, tossing the laws, the books, idolatries and customs out of the window, we pity him no more but thank and revere him;—and that teacher shall restore the life of man to splendor and make his name dear to all history.

It is easy to see that a greater self-reliance must work a revolution in all the offices and relations of men; in their religion; in their education; in their pursuits; their modes of living; their association; in their property; in their speculative views.

1. In what prayers do men allow themselves! That which they call a holy office is not so much as brave and manly. Prayer looks abroad and asks for some foreign addition to come through some foreign virtue, and loses itself in endless mazes of natural and supernatural, and mediatorial and miraculous. Prayer that craves a particular commodity, anything less than all good, is vicious. Prayer is the contemplation of the facts of life from the highest point of view. It is the soliloquy of a beholding and jubilant soul. It is the spirit of God pronouncing his works good. But prayer as a means to effect a private end is meanness and theft. It supposes dualism and not a unity in nature and consciousness. As soon as the man is at one with God, he will not beg. He will then see prayer in all action. The prayer of the farmer kneeling in his field to weed it, the prayer of the rower kneeling with the stroke of his oar, are true prayers heard throughout nature, though for cheap ends. Cartach, in Fletcher's *Bonduca,* when admonished to inquire the mind of the god Audate, replies,—

> "His hidden meaning lies in our endeavors;
> Our valors are our best gods." [21]

Another sort of false prayers are our regrets. Discontent is the want of self-reliance: it is infirmity of will. Regret calamities if you can thereby help the sufferer; if not, attend your own work and already the evil begins to be repaired Our sympathy is just as base. We come to them who weep foolishly and sit down and cry for company, instead of imparting to them truth and health in rough electric shocks, putting them once more in communication with their own reason. The secret of fortune is joy in our hands. Welcome evermore to gods and men is the self-helping man. For him all doors are flung wide; him all tongues greet, all honors crown, all eyes follow with desire. Our love goes out to him and embraces him because he did not need it. We solicitously and apologetically caress and celebrate him because he held on his way and scorned our disapprobation. The gods love him because men hated him. "To the persevering mortal," said Zoroaster, "the blessed Immortals are swift."

As men's prayers are a disease of the will, so are their creeds a disease of the intellect. They say with those foolish Israelites, "Let not God speak to us, lest we die. Speak thou, speak any man with us, and we will obey." [22] Everywhere I am hindered of meeting God in my brother, because he has shut his own temple doors and recites fables merely of his brother's, or his brother's brother's God. Every new mind is a new classification. If it prove a mind of uncommon activity and power, a Locke, a Lavoisier,[23] a Hutton,[24] a Bentham, a Fourier,[25] it imposes its classification on other men, and lo! a new system. In proportion to the depth of the thought, and so to the number of the objects it touches and brings within reach of the pupil, is his complacency. But chiefly is this apparent in creeds and churches, which are also classifications of some powerful mind acting on the elemental thought of duty and man's relation to the Highest. Such is Calvanism, Quakerism, Swedenborgism. The pupil takes the same delight in subordinating everything to the new terminology as a girl who has just learned botany in seeing a new earth and new seasons thereby. It will happen for a time that the pupil will find his intellectual power has grown by the study of his master's mind. But in all unbalanced minds the classification is idolized, passes for the end and not for a speedily exhaustible means, so that the walls of the system blend to their eye in the remote horizon with the walls of the universe; the luminaries of heaven seem to them hung on the arch their master built. They cannot imagine how you aliens have any right to see,—how you can see; "It must be somehow that you stole the light from us." They do not yet perceive that light, unsystematic, indomitable, will break into any cabin, even into theirs. Let them chirp awhile and call it their own. If they are honest and do well, presently their neat new pin-

21. **When . . . gods:** See Beaumont and Fletcher, *Bonduca,* III.1. Emerson misquotes oddly here, perhaps from a bad text of the play. "The god Audate" should read "the goddess Andate," and the first line of the quotation should read, "Her hidden meaning dwels in our endeavors."

22. **"Let . . . obey":** freely quoted from Exod. 20:19. 23. **Lavoisier:** Antoine Laurent Lavoisier (1743–94), French chemist, discoverer of oxygen. 24. **Hutton:** James Hutton (1726–97), Scottish geologist, one of the founders of modern scientific geology. 25. **Fourier:** See "New England Reformers," 9 n.

fold will be too strait and low, will crack, will lean, will rot and vanish, and the immortal light, all young and joyful, million-orbed, million-colored, will beam over the universe as on the first morning.

2. It is for want of self-culture that the superstition of Travelling, whose idols are Italy, England, Egypt, retains its fascination for all educated Americans. They who made England, Italy, or Greece venerable in the imagination, did so by sticking fast where they were, like an axis of the earth. In manly hours we feel that duty is our place. The soul is no traveller; the wise man stays at home, and when his necessities, his duties, on any occasion call him from his house, or into foreign lands, he is at home still and shall make men sensible by the expression of his countenance that he goes, the missionary of wisdom and virtue, and visits cities and men like a sovereign and not like an interloper or a valet.

I have no churlish objection to the circumnavigation of the globe for the purposes of art, of study, and benevolence, so that the man is first domesticated, or does not go abroad with the hope of finding somewhat greater than he knows. He who travels to be amused, or get somewhat which he does not carry, travels away from himself, and grows old even in youth among old things. In Thebes, in Palmyra, his will and mind have become old and dilapidated as they. He carries ruins to ruins.

Travelling is a fool's paradise. Our first journeys discover to us the indifference of places. At home I dream that at Naples, at Rome, I can be intoxicated with beauty and lose my sadness. I pack my trunk, embrace my friends, embark on the sea and at last wake up in Naples, and there beside me is the stern fact, the sad self, unrelenting, identical, that I fled from. I seek the Vatican and the palaces. I affect to be intoxicated with sights and suggestions, but I am not intoxicated. My giant goes with me wherever I go.

3. But the rage of travelling is a symptom of a deeper unsoundness affecting the whole intellectual action. The intellect is vagabond, and our system of education fosters restlessness. Our minds travel when our bodies are forced to stay at home. We imitate; and what is imitation but the travelling of the mind? Our houses are built with foreign taste; our shelves are garnished with foreign ornaments; our opinions, our tastes, our faculties lean, and follow the Past and the Distant. The soul created the arts wherever they have flourished. It was in his own mind that the artist sought his model. It was an application of his own thought to the thing to be done and the conditions to be observed. And why need we copy the Doric or the Gothic model? Beauty, convenience, grandeur of thought and quaint expression are as near to us as to any, and if the American artist will study with hope and love the precise thing to be done by him, considering the climate, the soil, the length of the day, the wants of the people, the habit and form of the government, he will create a house in which all these will find themselves fitted, and taste and sentiment will be satisfied also.

Insist on yourself; never imitate. Your own gift you can present every moment with the cumulative force of a whole life's cultivation; but of the adopted talent of another you have only an extemporaneous half possession. That which each can do best, none but his Maker can teach him. No man yet knows what it is, nor can, till that person has exhibited it. Where is the master who could have taught Shakspeare? Where is the master who could have instructed Franklin, or Washington, or Bacon, or Newton? Every great man is a unique. The Scipionism of Scipio is precisely that part he could not borrow. Shakspeare will never be made by the study of Shakspeare. Do that which is assigned to you, and you cannot hope too much or dare too much. There is at this moment for you an utterance brave and grand as that of the colossal chisel of Phidias, or trowel of the Egyptians, or the pen of Moses or Dante, but different from all these. Not possibly will the soul, all rich, all eloquent, with thousand-cloven tongue, deign to repeat itself; but if you can hear what these patriarchs say, surely you can reply to them in the same pitch of voice; for the ear and the tongue are two organs of one nature. Abide in the simple and noble regions of thy life, obey thy heart, and thou shalt reproduce the Foreworld again.

4. As our Religion, our Education, our Art look abroad, so does our spirit of society. All men plume themselves on the improvement of society, and no man improves.

Society never advances. It recedes as fast on one side as it gains on the other. It undergoes continual changes; it is barbarous, it is civilized, it is christianized, it is rich, it is scientific; but this change is not amelioration. For every thing that is given something is taken. Society acquires new arts and loses old instincts. What a contrast between the well-clad, reading, writing, thinking American, with a watch, a pencil and a bill of exchange in his pocket, and the naked New Zealander, whose property is a club, a spear, a mat and an undivided twentieth of a shed to sleep under! But compare the health of the two men and you shall see that the white man has lost his aboriginal strength. If the traveller tell us truly, strike the savage with a broad-axe and in a day or two the flesh will unite and heal as if you struck the blow into soft pitch, and the same blow shall send the white to his grave.

The civilized man has built a coach, but has lost the use of his feet. He is supported on crutches, but lacks so much support of muscle. He has a fine Geneva watch, but he fails of the skill to tell the hour by the sun. A Greenwich nautical almanac he has, and so being sure of the information when he wants it, the man in the street does not know a star in the sky. The solstice he does not observe; the equinox he knows as little; and the whole bright calendar of the year is without a dial in his mind. His note-books impair his memory; his libraries overload his wit; the insurance-office increases the number of accidents; and it may be a question whether machinery does not encumber; whether we have not lost by refinement some energy, by a Christianity, entrenched in establishments and forms, some vigor of wild virtue. For every Stoic was a Stoic; but in Christendom where is the Christian?

There is no more deviation in the moral standard than in the standard of height or bulk. No greater men are now than ever were. A singular equality may be observed between the great men of the first and of the last ages; nor can all the science, art, religion, and philosophy of the nineteenth century avail to educate greater men than Plutarch's heroes, three or four and twenty centuries ago. Not in time is the race progressive. Phocion,[26] Socrates, Anaxagoras, Diogenes, are great men, but they leave no class. He who is really of their class will not be called by their name, but will be his own man, and in his turn the founder of a sect. The arts and inventions of each period are only its costume and do not invigorate men. The harm of the improved machinery may compensate its good. Hudson and Behring[27] accomplished so much in their fishing-boats as to astonish Parry[28] and Franklin, whose equipment exhausted the resources of science and art. Galileo, with an opera-glass, discovered a more splendid series of celestial phenomena than any one since. Columbus found the New World in an undecked boat. It is curious to see the periodical disuse and perishing of means and machinery which were introduced with loud laudation a few years or centuries before. The great genius returns to essential man. We reckoned the improvements of the art of war among the triumphs of science, and yet Napoleon conquered Europe by the bivouac, which consisted of falling back on naked valor and disencumbering it of all aids. The Emperor held it impossible to make a perfect army, says Las Cases,[29] "without abolishing our arms, magazines, commissaries and carriages, until, in imitation of the Roman custom, the soldier should receive his supply of corn, grind it in his hand-mill and bake his bread himself."

Society is a wave. The wave moves onward, but the water of which it is composed does not. The same particle does not rise from the valley to the ridge. Its unity is only phenomenal. The persons who make up a nation to-day, next year die, and their experience dies with them.

And so the reliance on Property, including the reliance on governments which protect it, is the want of self-reliance. Men have looked away from themselves and at things so long that they have come to esteem the religious, learned and civil institutions as guards of property, and they deprecate assaults on these, because they feel them to be assaults on property. They measure their esteem of each other by what each has, and not by what each is. But a cultivated man becomes ashamed of his property, out of new respect for his nature. Especially he hates what he has if he see that it is accidental,—came to him by inheritance, or gift, or crime; then he feels that it is not having; it does not belong to him, has no root in him and merely lies there because no revolution or no robber takes it away. But that which a man is, does always by necessity acquire; and what the man acquires, is living property, which does not wait the beck of rulers, or mobs, or revolutions, or fire, or storm, or bankruptcies, but perpetually renews itself wherever the man breathes. "Thy lot or portion of life," said the Caliph Ali, "is seeking after thee; therefore be at rest from seeking after it." Our dependence on these foreign goods leads us to our lavish respect for numbers. The political parties meet in numerous conventions; the greater the concourse and with each new uproar of announcement, The delegation from Essex![30] The Democrats from New Hampshire![31] The Whigs of Maine! the young patriot feels himself stronger than before by a new thousand of eyes and arms.

26. Phocion: See *Nature,* 14 n. **27. Behring:** alternative spelling of the surname of Vitus Jonassen Bering (1681–1741), Danish navigator and explorer, after whom Bering Strait was named. **28. Parry:** Sir William Edward Parry (1790–1855), English explorer, leader of a series of important voyages in the Arctic.

29. Las Cases: the Comte de Las Cases (1766–1842), a French official who became Napoleon's companion on St. Helena and wrote a famous book on Napoleon's last days, the *Mémorial de Ste-Hélène* (1822–23). **30. The delegation from Essex!:** that is, from Essex County, Mass. **31. The Democrats from New Hampshire!:** Emerson took a very dim view of the politicians of New Hampshire, perhaps particularly of the Democrats. See "Speech on Affairs in Kansas," 4 n., and "Ode Inscribed to W. H. Channing," 24–26 n.

In like manner the reformers summon conventions and vote and resolve in multitude. Not so, O friends! will the God deign to enter and inhabit you, but by a method precisely the reverse. It is only as a man puts off all foreign support and stands alone that I see him to be strong and to prevail. He is weaker by every recruit to his banner. Is not a man better than a town? Ask nothing of men, and, in the endless mutation, thou only firm column must presently appear the upholder of all that surrounds thee. He who knows what power is inborn, that he is weak because he has looked for good out of him and elsewhere, and, so perceiving, throws himself unhesitatingly on his thought, instantly rights himself, stands in the erect position, commands his limbs, works miracles; just as a man who stands on his feet is stronger than a man who stands on his head.

So use all that is called Fortune. Most men gamble with her, and gain all, and lose all, as her wheel rolls.[32] But do thou leave as unlawful these winnings, and deal with Cause and Effect, the chancellors of God. In the Will work and acquire, and thou hast chained the wheel of Chance, and shall sit hereafter out of fear from her rotations. A political victory, a rise of rents, the recovery of our sick or the return of your absent friend, or some other favorable event raises your spirits, and you think good days are preparing for you. Do not believe it. Nothing can bring you peace but yourself. Nothing can bring you peace but the triumph of principles.

NEW ENGLAND REFORMERS

A Lecture Read Before the Society in Amory Hall,[1] on Sunday, March 3, 1844

◇

THE inarticulate dissatisfaction which many persons felt with the conventionalities, the inequities, and the vices of American life had already, in the thirties, begun to find articulate expression in such reformist movements as temperance agitation and abolitionism. By the early forties the zeal for reform had gathered such head as to resemble a gale at sea or a prairie fire, and there was scarcely an aspect of nineteenth-century society—from the wage system to the shaving of men's beards, from factory production to the wearing of skirts by women—that did not come in for the most vigorous criticism, some of it intelligent and high-minded, some of it hardly short of insanity. Emerson's relation to this many-sided and passionate movement was necessarily an ambiguous one: he was torn between a natural sympathy with the spirit of innovation and amelioration and a distrust of the violent one-sidedness, the intellectual narrowness, and the pervasive humorlessness of many, perhaps most, of the actual reformers. In 1841, in a lecture on "Man the Reformer," he had already given expression to this characteristically contradictory and thoughtful attitude as probably no other man in the country could have done; in the present lecture, of 1844, while the movement was at its hottest, he came back to the subject and treated it with a still more rippling humor, on the one hand, and, on the other, with an even greater seriousness of sympathy.

◇

In the suburb, in the town,
On the railway, in the square,
Came a beam of goodness down
Doubling daylight everywhere:
Peace now each for malice takes,
Beauty for his sinful weeds,
For the angel Hope aye makes
Him an angel whom she leads.

WHOEVER has had opportunity of acquaintance with society in New England during the last twenty-five years, with those middle and with those leading sections that may constitute any just representation of the character and aim of the community, will have been struck with the great activity of thought and experimenting. His attention must be commanded by the signs that the Church, or religious party, is falling from the Church nominal, and is appearing in temperance and non-resistance societies; in movements of abolitionists and of socialists; and in very significant assemblies called Sabbath and Bible Conventions;[2] composed of ultraists, of seekers, of all the soul of the soldiery of dissent, and meeting to call in question the authority of the Sabbath, of the priesthood, and of the Church. In these movements nothing was more remarkable than the discontent they begot in the movers. The spirit of protest and of detachment

32. **as her wheel rolls:** Fortuna, the goddess of fortune, is usually represented in art as standing on a wheel, or resting her hand on one, to symbolize her fickleness.

NEW ENGLAND REFORMERS. 1. **the Society in Amory Hall:** the liberal Church of the Disciples in Boston, of which Emerson's friend, James Freeman Clarke, was minister.

2. **very . . . Conventions:** Emerson has in mind such gatherings of radicals and "come-outers" as the famous, or notorious, Chardon Street Convention, called by the Friends of Universal Reform in Boston in 1840, and the later Bible Convention of 1842. For an amusing account of the former, see his essay "Chardon Street Convention," in *Lectures and Biographical Sketches* (*Works*, X, 371–77).

drove the members of these Conventions to bear testimony against the Church, and immediately afterwards to declare their discontent with these Conventions, their independence of their colleagues, and their impatience of the methods whereby they were working. They defied each other, like a congress of kings, each of whom had a realm to rule, and a way of his own that made concert unprofitable. What a fertility of projects for the salvation of the world! One apostle thought all men should go to farming, and another that no man should buy or sell, that the use of money was the cardinal evil; another that the mischief was in our diet, that we eat and drink damnation. These made unleavened bread, and were foes to the death to fermentation. It was in vain urged by the housewife that God made yeast, as well as dough, and loves fermentation just as dearly as he loves vegetation; that fermentation develops the saccharine element in the grain, and makes it more palatable and more digestible. No; they wish the pure wheat, and will die but it shall not ferment. Stop, dear nature, these incessant advances of thine; let us scotch these ever-rolling wheels! Others attacked the system of agriculture, the use of animal manures in farming, and the tyranny of man over brute nature; these abuses polluted his food. The ox must be taken from the plough and the horse from the cart, the hundred acres of the farm must be spaded, and the man must walk, wherever boats and locomotives will not carry him. Even the insect world was to be defended—that had been too long neglected, and a society for the protection of ground-worms, slugs, and mosquitos was to be incorporated without delay. With these appeared the adepts of homœopathy, of hydropathy, of mesmerism, of phrenology, and their wonderful theories of the Christian miracles! Others assailed particular vocations, as that of the lawyer, that of the merchant, of the manufacturer, of the clergyman, of the scholar. Others attacked the institution of marriage as the fountain of social evils. Others devoted themselves to the worrying of churches and meetings for public worship; and the fertile forms of antinomianism [3] among the elder Puritans seemed to have their match in the plenty of the new harvest of reform.

With this din of opinion and debate there was a keener scrutiny of institutions and domestic life than any we had known; there was sincere protesting against existing evils, and there were changes of employment dictated by conscience. No doubt there was plentiful vaporing, and cases of backsliding might occur. But in each of these movements emerged a good result, a tendency to the adoption of simpler methods, and an assertion of the sufficiency of the private man. Thus it was directly in the spirit and genius of the age, what happened in one instance when a church censured and threatened to excommunicate one of its members on account of the somewhat hostile part to the church which his conscience led him to take in the anti-slavery business; the threatened individual immediately excommunicated the church, in a public and formal process. This has been several times repeated: it was excellent when it was done the first time, but of course loses all value when it is copied. Every project in the history of reform, no matter how violent and surprising, is good when it is the dictate of a man's genius and constitution, but very dull and suspicious when adopted from another. It is right and beautiful in any man to say, "I will take this coat, or this book, or this measure of corn of yours"—in whom we see the act to be original, and to flow from the whole spirit and faith of him; for then that taking will have a giving as free and divine; but we are very easily disposed to resist the same generosity of speech when we miss originality and truth to character in it.

There was in all the practical activities of New England for the last quarter of a century, a gradual withdrawal of tender consciences from the social organizations. There is observable throughout, the contest between mechanical and spiritual methods, but with a steady tendency of the thoughtful and virtuous to a deeper belief and reliance on spiritual facts.

In politics for example it is easy to see the progress of dissent. The country is full of rebellion; the country is full of kings. Hands off! let there be no control and no interference in the administration of the affairs of this kingdom of me. Hence the growth of the doctrine and of the party of Free Trade, and the willingness to try that experiment, in the face of what appear incontestable facts. I confess, the motto of the Globe newspaper [4] is so attractive to me that I can seldom find much appetite to read what is below it in its columns: "The world is governed too much." So the country is frequently affording solitary examples of resistance to the government, solitary nullifiers,[5] who throw themselves on their reserved rights; nay, who have

3. antinomianism: See "Self-Reliance," 20 n. Emerson is here alluding to Ann Hutchinson and other antinomian heretics in seventeenth-century Massachusetts Bay whose teachings proved a source of embarrassment and anxiety to the magistrates of the colony.

4. the Globe newspaper: the Washington *Daily Globe*.

5. solitary nullifiers: In 1843 Emerson's friend and neighbor, Bronson Alcott, had refused to pay his poll tax in Concord as a protest against government; he was arrested but not, to his chagrin, incarcerated. Thoreau's similar protest was made three years later, in 1846.

reserved all their rights; who reply to the assessor and to the clerk of court that they do not know the State, and embarrass the courts of law by non-juring and the commander-in-chief of the militia by non-resistance.[6]

The same disposition to scrutiny and dissent appeared in civil, festive, neighborly, and domestic society. A restless, prying, conscientious criticism broke out in unexpected quarters. Who gave me the money with which I bought my coat? Why should professional labor and that of the counting-house be paid so disproportionately to the labor of the porter and woodsawyer? This whole business of Trade gives me to pause and think, as it constitutes false relations between men; inasmuch as I am prone to count myself relieved of any responsibility to behave well and nobly to that person whom I pay with money; whereas if I had not that commodity, I should be put on my good behavior in all companies, and man would be a benefactor to man, as being himself his only certificate that he had a right to those aids and services which each asked of the other. Am I not too protected a person? is there not a wide disparity between the lot of me and the lot of thee, my poor brother, my poor sister? Am I not defrauded of my best culture in the loss of those gymnastics which manual labor and the emergencies of poverty constitute? I find nothing healthful or exalting in the smooth conventions of society; I do not like the close air of saloons.[7] I begin to suspect myself to be a prisoner, though treated with all this courtesy and luxury. I pay a destructive tax in my conformity.

The same insatiable criticism may be traced in the efforts for the reform of Education. The popular education has been taxed with a want of truth and nature. It was complained that an education to things was not given. We are students of words: we are shut up in schools, and colleges, and recitation-rooms, for ten or fifteen years, and come out at last with a bag of wind, a memory of words, and do not know a thing. We cannot use our hands, or our legs, or our eyes, or our arms. We do not know an edible root in the woods, we cannot tell our course by the stars, nor the hour of the day by the sun. It is well if we can swim and skate. We are afraid of a horse, of a cow, of a dog, of a snake, of a spider. The Roman rule was to teach a boy nothing that he could not learn standing. The old English rule was, "All summer in the field, and all winter in the study." And it seems as if a man should learn to plant, or to fish, or to hunt, that he might secure his subsistence at all events, and not be painful to his friends and fellow men. The lessons of science should be experimental also. The sight of a planet through a telescope is worth all the course on astronomy; the shock of the electric spark in the elbow outvalues all the theories; the taste of the nitrous oxide, the firing of an artificial volcano, are better than volumes of chemistry.

One of the traits of the new spirit is the inquisition it fixed on our scholastic devotion to the dead languages. The ancient languages, with great beauty of structure, contain wonderful remains of genius, which draw, and always will draw, certain like-minded men—Greek men, and Roman men—in all countries, to their study; but by a wonderful drowsiness of usage they had exacted the study of *all* men. Once (say two centuries ago), Latin and Greek had a strict relation to all the science and culture there was in Europe, and the Mathematics had a momentary importance at some era of activity in physical science. These things became stereotyped as *education,* as the manner of men is. But the Good Spirit never cared for the colleges, and though all men and boys were now drilled in Latin, Greek, and Mathematics, it had quite left these shells high and dry on the beach, and was now creating and feeding other matters at other ends of the world. But in a hundred high schools and colleges this warfare against common sense still goes on. Four, or six, or ten years, the pupil is parsing Greek and Latin, and as soon as he leaves the University, as it is ludicrously styled, he shuts those books for the last time. Some thousands of young men are graduated at our colleges in this country every year, and the persons who, at forty years, still read Greek, can all be counted on your hand. I never met with ten. Four or five persons I have seen who read Plato.

But is not this absurd, that the whole liberal talent of this country should be directed in its best years on studies which lead to nothing? What was the consequence? Some intelligent persons said or thought, "Is that Greek and Latin some spell to conjure with, and not words of reason? If the physician, the lawyer, the divine, never use it to come at their ends, I need never learn it to come at mine. Conjuring is gone out of fashion, and I will omit this conjugating, and go straight to affairs." So they jumped the Greek and Latin, and read law, medicine, or sermons, without it. To the astonishment of all, the self-made men took even ground at once with the oldest of the regular graduates, and in a few months the most conservative circles of Boston and New York had quite forgotten who of their gownsmen was college-bred, and who was not.

6. **non-resistance:** In 1839 a New England Non-Resistance Society was founded in Boston by William Lloyd Garrison, Edmund Quincy, and others, to advocate the principles of pacifism.
7. **saloons:** salons, drawing rooms.

One tendency appears alike in the philosophical speculation and in the rudest democratical movements, through all the petulance and all the puerility, the wish, namely, to cast aside the superfluous and arrive at short methods; urged, as I suppose, by an intuition that the human spirit is equal to all emergencies, alone, and that man is more often injured than helped by the means he uses.

I conceive this gradual casting off of material aids, and the indication of growing trust in the private self-supplied powers of the individual, to be the affirmative principle of the recent philosophy, and that it is feeling its own profound truth and is reaching forward at this very hour to the happiest conclusions. I readily concede that in this, as in every period of intellectual activity, there has been a noise of denial and protest; much was to be resisted, much was to be got rid of by those who were reared in the old, before they could begin to affirm and to construct. Many a reformer perishes in his removal of rubbish; and that makes the offensiveness of the class. They are partial; they are not equal to the work they pretend. They lose their way; in the assault on the kingdom of darkness they expend all their energy on some accidental evil, and lose their sanity and power of benefit. It is of little moment that one or two or twenty errors of our social system be corrected, but of much that the man be in his senses.

The criticism and attack on institutions, which we have witnessed, has made one thing plain, that society gains nothing whilst a man, not himself renovated, attempts to renovate things around him: he has become tediously good in some particular but negligent or narrow in the rest; and hypocrisy and vanity are often the disgusting result.

It is handsomer to remain in the establishment better than the establishment, and conduct that in the best manner, than to make a sally against evil by some single improvement, without supporting it by a total regeneration. Do not be so vain of your one objection. Do you think there is only one? Alas! my good friend, there is no part of society or of life better than any other part. All our things are right and wrong together. The wave of evil washes all our institutions alike. Do you complain of our Marriage? Our marriage is no worse than our education, our diet, our trade, our social customs. Do you complain of the laws of Property? It is a pedantry to give such importance to them. Can we not play the game of life with these counters, as well as with those? in the institution of property, as well as out of it? Let into it the new and renewing principle of love, and property will be universality. No one gives the impression of superiority to the institution, which he must give who will reform it. It makes no difference what you say, you must make me feel that you are aloof from it; by your natural and supernatural advantages do easily see to the end of it—do see how man can do without it. Now all men are on one side. No man deserves to be heard against property. Only Love, only an Idea, is against property as we hold it.

I cannot afford to be irritable and captious, nor to waste all my time in attacks. If I should go out of church whenever I hear a false sentiment I could never stay there five minutes. But why come out? the street is as false as the church, and when I get to my house, or to my manners, or to my speech, I have not got away from the lie. When we see an eager assailant of one of these wrongs, a special reformer, we feel like asking him, What right have you, sir, to your one virtue? Is virtue piecemeal? This is a jewel amidst the rags of a beggar.

In another way the right will be vindicated. In the midst of abuses, in the heart of cities, in the aisles of false churches, alike in one place and in another—wherever, namely, a just and heroic soul finds itself, there it will do what is next at hand, and by the new quality of character it shall put forth it shall abrogate that old condition, law or school in which it stands, before the law of its own mind.

If partiality was one fault of the movement party, the other defect was their reliance on Association.[8] Doubts such as those I have intimated drove many good persons to agitate the questions of social reform. But the revolt against the spirit of commerce, the spirit of aristocracy, and the inveterate abuses of cities, did not appear possible to individuals; and to do battle against numbers they armed themselves with numbers, and against concert they relied on new concert.

Following or advancing beyond the ideas of St. Simon, of Fourier, and of Owen,[9] three communities [10] have already been formed in Massachusetts on kindred plans, and many more in the country at large. They aim to give every member a share in the manual labor, to give an equal reward to labor and to talent, and to unite a liberal culture

8. **Association:** the name used by the Fourierist Socialists of the period to describe the form of cooperative or communitarian industry they advocated. 9. **St. Simon . . . Owen:** Comte de Saint-Simon (1760–1825), F. C. M. Fourier (1772–1837), and Robert Owen (1771–1858) were all pre-Marxist or "Utopian" Socialists who had a considerable influence on American radicals in the forties. 10. **three communities:** no doubt the communities at West Roxbury (Brook Farm, founded in 1841), at Milford (Hopedale, founded in 1842), and at Harvard (Fruitlands, founded also in 1842). When this lecture was written the two former were still in operation, but the community of Fruitlands, of which Bronson Alcott was one of the leaders, had come to grief, after a few months of very unstable existence, early in 1843.

with an education to labor. The scheme offers, by the economies of associated labor and expense, to make every member rich, on the same amount of property that, in separate families, would leave every member poor. These new associations are composed of men and women of superior talents and sentiments; yet it may easily be questioned whether such a community will draw, except in its beginnings, the able and the good; whether those who have energy will not prefer their chance of superiority and power in the world, to the humble certainties of the association; whether such a retreat does not promise to become an asylum to those who have tried and failed, rather than a field to the strong; and whether the members will not necessarily be fractions of men, because each finds that he cannot enter it without some compromise. Friendship and association are very fine things, and a grand phalanx [11] of the best of the human race, banded for some catholic object; yes, excellent; but remember that no society can ever be so large as one man. He, in his friendship, in his natural and momentary associations, doubles or multiplies himself; but in the hour in which he mortgages himself to two or ten or twenty, he dwarfs himself below the stature of one.

But the men of less faith could not thus believe, and to such, concert appears the sole specific of strength. I have failed, and you have failed, but perhaps together we shall not fail. Our housekeeping is not satisfactory to us, but perhaps a phalanx, a community, might be. Many of us have differed in opinion, and we could find no man who could make the truth plain, but possibly a college, or an ecclesiastical council, might. I have not been able either to persuade my brother or to prevail on myself to disuse the traffic or the potation of brandy, but perhaps a pledge of total abstinence might effectually restrain us. The candidate my party votes for is not to be trusted with a dollar, but he will be honest in the Senate, for we can bring public opinion to bear on him. Thus concert was the specific in all cases. But concert is neither better nor worse, neither more nor less potent, than individual force. All the men in the world cannot make a statue walk and speak, cannot make a drop of blood, or a blade of grass, any more than one man can. But let there be one man, let there be truth in two men, in ten men, then is concert for the first time possible; because the force which moves the world is a new quality, and can never be furnished by adding whatever quantities of a different kind. What is the use of the concert of the false and the disunited? There can be no concert in two, where there is no concert in one. When the individual is not *individual,*[12] but is dual; when his thoughts look one way and his actions another; when his faith is traversed by his habits; when his will, enlightened by reason, is warped by his sense; when with one hand he rows and with the other backs water, what concert can be?

I do not wonder at the interest these projects inspire. The world is awaking to the idea of union, and these experiments show what it is thinking of. It is and will be magic. Men will live and communicate, and plough, and reap, and govern, as by added ethereal power, when once they are united; as in a celebrated experiment, by expiration and respiration exactly together, four persons lift a heavy man from the ground by the little finger only, and without sense of weight. But this union must be inward, and not one of covenants, and is to be reached by a reverse of the methods they use. The union is only perfect when all the uniters are isolated. It is the union of friends who live in different streets or towns. Each man, if he attempts to join himself to others, is on all sides cramped and diminished of his proportion; and the stricter the union the smaller and the more pitiful he is. But leave him alone, to recognize in every hour and place the secret soul; he will go up and down doing the works of a true member, and, to the astonishment of all, the work will be done with concert, though no man spoke. Government will be adamantine without any governor. The union must be ideal in actual individualism.

I pass to the indication in some particulars of that faith in man, which the heart is preaching to us in these days, and which engages the more regard, from the consideration that the speculations of one generation are the history of the next following.

In alluding just now to our system of education, I spoke of the deadness of its details. But it is open to graver criticism than the palsy of its members: it is a system of despair. The disease with which the human mind now labors is want of faith. Men do not believe in a power of education. We do not think we can speak to divine sentiments in man, and we do not try. We renounce all high aims. We believe that the defects of so many perverse and so many frivolous people who make up society, are organic, and society is a hospital of incurables. A

11. **a grand phalanx:** Fourier had used the word "phalanx" for the smallest unit, sixteen hundred persons, into which his ideal society was to be organizationally divided. After the Brook Farm community turned Fourierist under the influence of Albert Brisbane, it was known as the "Phalanx," and the members published a periodical under that name.

12. ***individual:*** The etymological meaning of the word is "indivisible," "undivided."

man of good sense but of little faith, whose compassion seemed to lead him to church as often as he went there, said to me that "he liked to have concerts, and fairs, and churches, and other public amusements go on." I am afraid the remark is too honest, and comes from the same origin as the maxim of the tyrant, "If you would rule the world quietly, you must keep it amused." I notice too that the ground on which eminent public servants urge the claims of popular education is fear; "This country is filling up with thousands and millions of voters, and you must educate them to keep them from our throats." We do not believe that any education, any system of philosophy, any influence of genius, will ever give depth of insight to a superficial mind. Having settled ourselves into this infidelity, our skill is expended to procure alleviations, diversion, opiates. We adorn the victim with manual skill, his tongue with languages, his body with inoffensive and comely manners. So have we cunningly hid the tragedy of limitation and inner death we cannot avert. Is it strange that society should be devoured by a secret melancholy which breaks through all its smiles and all its gayety and games?

But even one step farther our infidelity has gone. It appears that some doubt is felt by good and wise men whether really the happiness and probity of men is increased by the culture of the mind in those disciplines to which we give the name of education. Unhappily too the doubt comes from scholars, from persons who have tried these methods. In their experience the scholar was not raised by the sacred thoughts amongst which he dwelt, but used them to selfish ends. He was a profane person, and became a showman, turning his gifts to a marketable use, and not to his own sustenance and growth. It was found that the intellect could be independently developed, that is, in separation from the man, as any single organ can be invigorated, and the result was monstrous. A canine appetite for knowledge was generated, which must still be fed but was never satisfied, and this knowledge, not being directed on action, never took the character of substantial, humane truth, blessing those whom it entered. It gave the scholar certain powers of expression, the power of speech, the power of poetry, of literary art, but it did not bring him to peace or to beneficence.

When the literary class betray a destitution of faith, it is not strange that society should be disheartened and sensualized by unbelief. What remedy? Life must be lifed on a higher plane. We must go up to a higher platform, to which we are always invited to ascend; there, the whole aspect of things changes. I resist the skepticism of our education and of our educated men. I do not believe that the differences of opinion and character in men are organic. I do not recognize, beside the class of the good and the wise, a permanent class of skeptics, or a class of conservatives, or of malignants, or of materialists. I do not believe in two classes. You remember the story of the poor woman who importuned King Philip of Macedon to grant her justice, which Philip refused: the woman exclaimed, "I appeal": the king, astonished, asked to whom she appealed: the woman replied, "From Philip drunk to Philip sober." [13] The text will suit me very well. I believe not in two classes of men, but in man in two moods, in Philip drunk and Philip sober. I think, according to the good-hearted word of Plato, "Unwillingly the soul is deprived of truth." Iron conservative, miser, or thief, no man is but by a supposed necessity which he tolerates by shortness or torpidity of sight. The soul lets no man go without some visitations and holy days of a diviner presence. It would be easy to show, by a narrow scanning of any man's biography, that we are not so wedded to our paltry performances of every kind but that every man has at intervals the grace to scorn his performances, in comparing them with his belief of what he should do—that he puts himself on the side of his enemies, listening gladly to what they say of him, and accusing himself of the same things.

What is it men love in Genius, but its infinite hope, which degrades all it has done? Genius counts all its miracles poor and short. Its own idea it never executed. The *Iliad,* the *Hamlet,* the Doric column, the Roman arch, the Gothic minster, the German anthem, when they are ended, the master casts behind him. How sinks the song in the waves of melody which the universe pours over his soul! Before that gracious Infinite out of which he drew these few strokes, how mean they look, though the praises of the world attend them. From the triumphs of his art he turns with desire to this greater defeat. Let those admire who will. With silent joy he sees himself to be capable of a beauty that eclipses all which his hands have done; all which human hands have ever done.

Well, we are all the children of genius, the children of virtue—and feel their inspirations in our happier hours. Is not every man sometimes a radical in politics? Men are conservatives when they are least vigorous, or when they are most luxurious. They are conservatives after dinner, or before taking their rest; when they are sick, or aged: in the morning, or when their intellect or their conscience has been aroused; when they hear music,

13. **You . . . sober:** This famous anecdote is told by Valerius Maximus in his *De Factis Dictisque Memorabilibus*, but it has long been familiar in English literary allusion.

or when they read poetry, they are radicals. In the circle of the rankest Tories that could be collected in England, Old or New, let a powerful and stimulating intellect, a man of great heart and mind act on them, and very quickly these frozen conservators will yield to the friendly influence, these hopeless will begin to hope, these haters will begin to love, these immovable statues will begin to spin and revolve. I cannot help recalling the fine anecdote which Warton relates of Bishop Berkeley,[14] when he was preparing to leave England with his plan of planting the gospel among the American savages. "Lord Bathurst told me that the members of the Scriblerus club being met at his house at dinner, they agreed to rally Berkeley, who was also his guest, on his scheme at Bermudas. Berkeley, having listened to the many lively things they had to say, begged to be heard in his turn, and displayed his plan with such an astonishing and animating force of eloquence and enthusiasm that they were struck dumb, and, after some pause, rose up all together with earnestness, exclaiming, 'Let us set out with him immediately.' " Men in all ways are better than they seem. They like flattery for the moment, but they know the truth for their own. It is a foolish cowardice which keeps us from trusting them and speaking to them rude truth. They resent your honesty for an instant, they will thank you for it always. What is it we heartily wish of each other? Is it to be pleased and flattered? No, but to be convicted and exposed, to be shamed out of our nonsense of all kinds, and made men of, instead of ghosts and phantoms. We are weary of gliding ghostlike through the world, which is itself so slight and unreal. We crave a sense of reality, though it come in strokes of pain. I explain so—by this manlike love of truth—those excesses and errors into which souls of great vigor, but not equal insight, often fall. They feel the poverty at the bottom of all the seeming affluence of the world. They know the speed with which they come straight through the thin masquerade, and conceive a disgust at the indigence of nature: Rousseau, Mirabeau, Charles Fox, Napoleon, Byron—and I could easily add names nearer home, of raging riders, who drive their steeds so hard, in the violence of living to forget its illusion: they would know the worst, and tread the floors of hell.[15] The heroes of ancient and modern fame, Cimon, Themistocles, Alcibiades, Alexander, Cæsar, have treated life and fortune as a game to be well and skilfully played, but the stake not to be so valued but that any time it could be held as a trifle light as air, and thrown up. Cæsar, just before the battle of Pharsalia, discourses with the Egyptian priest concerning the fountains of the Nile, and offers to quit the army, the empire, and Cleopatra, if he will show him those mysterious sources.[16]

The same magnanimity shows itself in our social relations, in the preference, namely, which each man gives to the society of superiors over that of his equals. All that a man has will he give for right relations with his mates. All that he has will he give for an erect demeanor in every company and on each occasion. He aims at such things as his neighbors prize, and gives his days and nights, his talents and his heart, to strike a good stroke, to acquit himself in all men's sight as a man. The consideration of an eminent citizen, of a noted merchant, of a man of mark in his profession; a naval and military honor, a general's commission, a marshal's baton, a ducal coronet, the laurel of poets, and, anyhow procured, the acknowledgment of eminent merit—have this lustre for each candidate that they enable him to walk erect and unashamed in the presence of some persons before whom he felt himself inferior. Having raised himself to this rank, having established his equality with class after class of those with whom he would live well, he still finds certain others before whom he cannot possess himself, because they have somewhat fairer, somewhat grander, somewhat purer, which extorts homage of him. Is his ambition pure? then will his laurels and his possessions seem worthless: instead of avoiding these men who make his fine gold dim, he will cast all behind him and seek their society only, woo and embrace this his humiliation and mortification, until he shall know why his eye sinks, his voice is husky, and his brilliant talents are paralyzed in this presence. He is sure that the soul which gives the lie to all things will tell none. His constitution will not mislead him. If it cannot carry itself as it ought, high and unmatchable in the presence of any man; if the secret oracles whose whisper makes the sweetness and dignity of his life do here withdraw and accompany him no longer—it is time to undervalue what he has valued, to dispossess himself of what he has acquired, and with Cæsar to take in his hand the army, the empire, and Cleopatra, and say, "All these will I relinquish, if you will show me the fountains of the Nile." [17] Dear to us are those who

14. **the . . . Berkeley:** Joseph Warton tells this story about Berkeley in his *Essay on the Genius and Writings of Pope*, II, 198 n. 15. **they . . . hell:** a fragment of Pindar preserved by Plutarch in his "Consolation to Apollonius." The sentence in Plutarch reads in English translation: "It is an expression of Pindar, that we are held to the dark bottom of hell by necessities as hard as iron" (*Essays and Miscellanies*, ed. by A. H. Clough and William W. Goodwin, I, 303).

16. **Cæsar . . . sources:** See Lucan, *De Bello Civili*, X.172–92. Emerson may have been familiar with Nicholas Rowe's translation of Lucan's poem as the *Pharsalia*. 17. **"All . . . Nile":**

love us; the swift moments we spend with them are a compensation for a great deal of misery; they enlarge our life—but dearer are those who reject us as unworthy, for they add another life: they build a heaven before us whereof we had not dreamed, and thereby supply to us new powers out of the recesses of the spirit, and urge us to new and unattempted performances.

As every man at heart wishes the best and not inferior society, wishes to be convicted of his error and to come to himself—so he wishes that the same healing should not stop in his thought, but should penetrate his will or active power. The selfish man suffers more from his selfishness than he from whom that selfishness withholds some important benefit. What he most wishes is to be lifted to some higher platform, that he may see beyond his present fear the trans-Alpine good, so that his fear, his coldness, his custom may be broken up like fragments of ice, melted and carried away in the great stream of good will. Do you ask my aid? I also wish to be a benefactor. I wish more to be a benefactor and servant than you wish to be served by me; and surely the greatest good fortune that could befall me is precisely to be so moved by you that I should say, "Take me and all mine, and use me and mine freely to your ends!" for I could not say it otherwise than because a great enlargement had come to my heart and mind, which made me superior to my fortunes. Here we are paralyzed with fear; we hold on to our little properties, house and land, office and money, for the bread which they have in our experience yielded us, although we confess that our being does not flow through them. We desire to be made great; we desire to be touched with that fire which shall command this ice to stream, and make our existence a benefit. If therefore we start objections to your project, O friend of the slave, or friend of the poor or of the race, understand well that it is because we wish to drive you to drive us into your measures. We wish to hear ourselves confuted. We are haunted with a belief that you have a secret which it would highliest advantage us to learn, and we would force you to impart it to us, though it should bring us to prison or to worse extremity.

Nothing shall warp me from the belief that every man is a lover of truth. There is no pure lie, no pure malignity in nature. The entertainment of the proposition of depravity [18] is the last profligacy and profanation. There is no skepticism, no atheism but that. Could it be received into common belief, suicide would unpeople the planet. It has had a name to live in some dogmatic theology, but each man's innocence and his real liking of his neighbor have kept it a dead letter. I remember standing at the polls one day when the anger of the political contest gave a certain grimness to the faces of the independent electors, and a good man at my side,[19] looking on the people, remarked, "I am satisfied that the largest part of these men, on either side, mean to vote right." I suppose considerate observers, looking at the masses of men in their blameless and in their equivocal actions, will assent, that in spite of selfishness and frivolity, the general purpose in the great number of persons is fidelity. The reason why anyone refuses his assent to your opinion, or his aid to your benevolent design, is in you: he refuses to accept you as a bringer of truth, because though you think you have it, he feels that you have it not. You have not given him the authentic sign.

If it were worth while to run into details this general doctrine of the latent but ever soliciting Spirit, it would be easy to adduce illustration in particulars of a man's equality to the Church, of his equality to the State, and of his equality to every other man. It is yet in all men's memory that, a few years ago, the liberal churches [20] complained that the Calvinistic Church denied to them the name of Christian. I think the complaint was confession: a religious church would not complain. A religious man, like Behmen,[21] Fox,[22] or Swedenborg is not irritated by wanting the sanction of the Church, but the Church feels the accusation of his presence and belief.

It only needs that a just man should walk in our streets to make it appear how pitiful and inartificial a contrivance is our legislation. The man whose part is taken and who does not wait for society in anything, has a power which society cannot choose but feel. The familiar experiment called the hydrostatic paradox, in which a capillary column of water balances the ocean, is a symbol of the relation of one man to the whole family of men. The wise Dandamis, on hearing the lives of Socrates, Pythagoras and Diogenes read, "judged them to be great men every way, excepting that they were too much subjected to the reverence of the laws, which to second and authorize, true virtue must abate very much of its original vigor."

And as a man is equal to the Church and equal

an allusion to the passage in Lucan drawn on above. **18. the proposition of depravity:** the Calvinist dogma of Total Depravity.

19. a good man at my side: Edmund Hosmer, a sagacious Concord farmer and great friend of Emerson's. **20. the liberal churches:** the Unitarian churches. **21. Behmen:** alternative spelling of the surname of Jakob Boehme, a German mystical writer of the late sixteenth and early seventeenth centuries, whose *Aurora* Emerson had read with enthusiasm in 1835. **22. Fox:** George Fox (1624–91), English religious leader, founder of the Society of Friends, the members of which very early came to be known as Quakers.

to the State, so he is equal to every other man. The disparities of power in men are superficial; and all frank and searching conversation, in which a man lays himself open to his brother, apprises each of their radical unity. When two persons sit and converse in a thoroughly good understanding, the remark is sure to be made, See how we have disputed about words! Let a clear, apprehensive mind, such as every man knows among his friends, converse with the most commanding poetic genius, I think it would appear that there was no inequality such as men fancy, between them; that a perfect understanding, a like receiving, a like perceiving, abolished differences; and the poet would confess that his creative imagination gave him no deep advantage, but only the superficial one that he could express himself and the other could not; that his advantage was a knack, which might impose on indolent men but could not impose on lovers of truth; for they know the tax of talent, or what a price of greatness the power of expression too often pays. I believe it is the conviction of the purest men that the net amount of man and man does not much vary. Each is incomparably superior to his companion in some faculty. His want of skill in other directions has added to his fitness for his own work. Each seems to have some compensation yielded to him by his infirmity, and every hindrance operates as a concentration of his force.

These and the like experiences intimate that man stands in strict connection with a higher fact never yet manifested. There is power over and behind us, and we are the channels of its communications. We seek to say thus and so, and over our head some spirit sits which contradicts what we say. We would persuade our fellow to this or that; another self within our eyes dissuades him. That which we keep back, this reveals. In vain we compose our faces and our words; it holds uncontrollable communication with the enemy, and he answers civilly to us, but believes the spirit. We exclaim, "There's a traitor in the house!" but at last it appears that he is the true man, and I am the traitor. This open channel to the highest life is the first and last reality, so subtle, so quiet, yet so tenacious, that although I have never expressed the truth, and although I have never heard the expression of it from any other, I know that the whole truth is here for me. What if I cannot answer your questions? I am not pained that I cannot frame a reply to the question. What is the operation we call Providence? There lies the unspoken thing, present, omnipresent. Every time we converse we seek to translate it into speech, but whether we hit or whether we miss, we have the fact. Every discourse is an approximate answer: but it is of small consequence that we do not get it into verbs and nouns, whilst it abides for contemplation forever.

If the auguries of the prophesying heart shall make themselves good in time, the man who shall be born, whose advent men and events prepare and foreshow, is one who shall enjoy his connection with a higher life, with the man within man; shall destroy distrust by his trust, shall use his native but forgotten methods, shall not take counsel of flesh and blood, but shall rely on the Law alive and beautiful which works over our heads and under our feet. Pitiless, it avails itself of our success when we obey it, and of our ruin when we contravene it. Men are all secret believers in it, else the word justice would have no meaning: they believe that the best is the true; that right is done at last; or chaos would come. It rewards actions after their nature, and not after the design of the agent. "Work," it saith to man, "in every hour, paid or unpaid, see only that thou work, and thou canst not escape the reward: whether thy work be fine or coarse, planting corn or writing epics, so only it be honest work, done to thine own approbation, it shall earn a reward to the senses as well as to the thought: no matter how often defeated, you are born to victory. The reward of a thing well done, is to have done it."

As soon as a man is wonted to look beyond surfaces, and to see how this high will prevails without an exception or an interval, he settles himself into serenity. He can already rely on the laws of gravity, that every stone will fall where it is due; the good globe is faithful, and carries us securely through the celestial spaces, anxious or resigned, we need not interfere to help it on: and he will learn one day the mild lesson they teach, that our own orbit is all our task, and we need not assist the administration of the universe. Do not be so impatient to set the town right concerning the unfounded pretensions and the false reputation of certain men of standing. They are laboring harder to set the town right concerning themselves, and will certainly succeed. Suppress for a few days your criticism on the insufficiency of this or that teacher or experimenter, and he will have demonstrated his insufficiency to all men's eyes. In like manner, let a man fall into the divine circuits, and he is enlarged. Obedience to his genius is the only liberating influence. We wish to escape from subjection and a sense of inferiority, and we make self-denying ordinances, we drink water, we eat grass, we refuse the laws, we go to jail: it is all in vain; only by obedience to his genius, only by the freest activity in the way constitutional to him, does an angel seem to arise before a man and lead him by the hand out of all the wards of the prison.

That which befits us, embosomed in beauty and wonder as we are, is cheerfulness and courage, and the endeavor to realize our aspirations. The life of man is the true romance, which when it is valiantly conducted will yield the imagination a higher joy than any fiction. All around us what powers are wrapped up under the coarse mattings of custom, and all wonder prevented. It is so wonderful to our neurologists that a man can see without his eyes, that it does not occur to them that it is just as wonderful that he should see with them; and that is ever the difference between the wise and the unwise: the latter wonders at what is unusual, the wise man wonders at the usual. Shall not the heart which has received so much, trust the Power by which it lives? May it not quit other leadings, and listen to the Soul that has guided it so gently and taught it so much, secure that the future will be worthy of the past?

THE POET

◇

ONE of the course of lectures Emerson delivered in Boston in the winter of 1841–42 was a lecture on the Poet. He seems to have composed the present essay in the latter year, making use of a few paragraphs from the lecture and drawing also, as usual with him, on his journals for the previous few years. The essay was published in *Essays: Second Series* (1844). Along with Poe's lecture "The Poetic Principle" (1848) and Whitman's preface to the first edition of *Leaves of Grass* (1855), it is one of the *loci classici* of romantic literary theory in American letters—the American counterpart of Schiller's "Naive and Sentimental Poetry" or Chapter 14 of Coleridge's *Biographia Literaria.*

◇

A moody child and wildly wise
Pursued the game with joyful eyes,
Which chose, like meteors, their way,
And rived the dark with private ray:
They overleapt the horizon's edge,
Searched with Apollo's privilege;
Through man, and woman, and sea, and star
Saw the dance of nature forward far;
Through worlds, and races, and terms, and times
Saw musical order, and pairing rhymes.[1]

Olympian bards who sung
  Divine ideas below,
Which always find us young,
  And always keep us so.[2]

THOSE who are esteemed umpires of taste are often persons who have acquired some knowledge of admired pictures or sculptures, and have an inclination for whatever is elegant; but if you inquire whether they are beautiful souls, and whether their own acts are like fair pictures, you learn that they are selfish and sensual. Their cultivation is local, as if you should rub a log of dry wood in one spot to produce fire, all the rest remaining cold. Their knowledge of the fine arts is some study of rules and particulars, or some limited judgment of color or form, which is exercised for amusement or for show. It is a proof of the shallowness of the doctrine of beauty as it lies in the minds of our amateurs, that men seem to have lost the perception of the instant dependence of form upon soul. There is no doctrine of forms in our philosophy. We were put into our bodies, as fire is put into a pan to be carried about; but there is no accurate adjustment between the spirit and the organ, much less is the latter the germination of the former. So in regard to other forms, the intellectual men do not believe in any essential dependence of the material world on thought and volition. Theologians think it a pretty air-castle to talk of the spiritual meaning of a ship or a cloud, of a city or a contract, but they prefer to come again to the solid ground of historical evidence; and even the poets are contented with a civil and conformed manner of living, and to write poems from the fancy, at a safe distance from their own experience. But the highest minds of the world have never ceased to explore the double meaning, or shall I say the quadruple or the centuple or much more manifold meaning, of every sensuous fact; Orpheus, Empedocles, Heraclitus, Plato, Plutarch, Dante, Swedenborg, and the masters of sculpture, picture and poetry. For we are not pans and barrows, nor even porters of the fire and torch-bearers, but children of the fire, made of it, and only the same divinity transmuted and at two or three removes, when we know least about it. And this hidden truth, that the fountains whence all this river of Time and its creatures floweth are intrinsically ideal and beautiful, draws us to the consideration of the nature and functions of the Poet, or the man of Beauty; to the means and materials he uses, and to the general aspect of the art in the present time.

The breadth of the problem is great, for the poet

THE POET. 1. **A . . . rhymes:** Another version of these lines appears in a posthumous poem, "The Poet" (*Works,* IX, 311).

2. **Olympian . . . so:** These lines occur also in "Ode to Beauty." See p. 579.

is representative. He stands among partial men for the complete man, and apprises us not of his wealth, but of the common wealth. The young man reveres men of genius, because, to speak truly, they are more himself than he is. They receive of the soul as he also receives, but they more. Nature enhances her beauty, to the eye of loving men, from their belief that the poet is beholding her shows at the same time. He is isolated among his contemporaries by truth and by his art, but with this consolation in his pursuits, that they will draw all men sooner or later. For all men live by truth and stand in need of expression. In love, in art, in avarice, in politics, in labor, in games, we study to utter our painful secret. The man is only half himself, the other half is his expression.

Notwithstanding this necessity to be published, adequate expression is rare. I know not how it is that we need an interpreter, but the great majority of men seem to be minors, who have not yet come into possession of their own, or mutes, who cannot report the conversation they have had with nature. There is no man who does not anticipate a supersensual utility in the sun and stars, earth and water. These stand and wait to render him a peculiar service. But there is some obstruction or some excess of phlegm in our constitution, which does not suffer them to yield the due effect. Too feeble fall the impressions of nature on us to make us artists. Every touch should thrill. Every man should be so much an artist that he could report in conversation what had befallen him. Yet, in our experience, the rays or appulses [3] have sufficient force to arrive at the senses, but not enough to reach the quick and compel the reproduction of themselves in speech. The poet is the person in whom these powers are in balance, the man without impediment, who sees and handles that which others dream of, traverses the whole scale of experience, and is representative of man, in virtue of being the largest power to receive and to impart.

For the Universe has three children, born at one time, which reappear under different names in every system of thought, whether they be called cause, operation and effect; or, more poetically, Jove, Pluto, Neptune; or, theologically, the Father, the Spirit and the Son; but which we will call here the Knower, the Doer and the Sayer. These stand respectively for the love of truth, for the love of good, and for the love of beauty. These three are equal. Each is that which he is, essentially, so that he cannot be surmounted or analyzed, and each of these three has the power of the others latent in him and his own, patent.

3. **appulses:** powerful driving motions toward something.

The poet is the sayer, the namer, and represents beauty. He is a sovereign, and stands on the center. For the world is not painted or adorned, but is from the beginning beautiful; and God has not made some beautiful things, but Beauty is the creator of the universe. Therefore the poet is not any permissive potentate, but is emperor in his own right. Criticism is infested with a cant of materialism, which assumes that manual skill and activity is the first merit of all men, and disparages such as say and do not, overlooking the fact that some men, namely poets, are natural sayers, sent into the world to the end of expression, and confounds them with those whose province is action but who quit it to imitate the sayers. But Homer's words are as costly and admirable to Homer as Agamemnon's victories are to Agamemnon. The poet does not wait for the hero or the sage, but, as they act and think primarily, so he writes primarily what will and must be spoken, reckoning the others, though primaries also, yet, in respect to him, secondaries and servants; as sitters or models in the studio of a painter, or as assistants who bring building-materials to an architect.

For poetry was all written before time was, and whenever we are so finely organized that we can penetrate into that region where the air is music, we hear those primal warblings and attempt to write them down, but we lose ever and anon a word or a verse and substitute something of our own, and thus miswrite the poem. The men of more delicate ear write down these cadences more faithfully, and these transcripts, though imperfect, become the songs of the nations. For nature is as truly beautiful as it is good, or as it is reasonable, and must as much appear as it must be done, or be known. Words and deeds are quite indifferent modes of the divine energy. Words are also actions, and actions are a kind of words.

The sign and credentials of the poet are that he announces that which no man foretold. He is the true and only doctor; [4] he knows and tells; he is the only teller of news, for he was present and privy to the appearance which he describes. He is a beholder of ideas and an utterer of the necessary and causal. For we do not speak now of men of poetical talents, or of industry and skill in meter, but of the true poet. I took part in a conversation the other day concerning a recent writer of lyrics,[5] a man of subtle mind, whose head appeared to be a music-box of delicate tunes and rhythms, and whose skill and command of language we could not sufficiently praise. But when the question arose

4. **doctor:** teacher. 5. **a recent writer of lyrics:** probably Tennyson, of whom Emerson later came to have a somewhat higher opinion.

whether he was not only a lyrist but a poet, we were obliged to confess that he is plainly a contemporary, not an eternal man. He does not stand out of our low limitations, like a Chimborazo under the line, running up from a torrid base through all the climates of the globe, with belts of the herbage of every latitude on its high and mottled sides; but this genius is the landscape-garden of a modern house, adorned with fountains and statues, with well-bred men and women standing and sitting in the walks and terraces. We hear, through all the varied music, the ground-tone of conventional life. Our poets are men of talents who sing, and not the children of music. The argument is secondary, the finish of the verses is primary.

For it is not meters, but a meter-making argument that makes a poem,—a thought so passionate and alive that like the spirit of a plant or an animal it has an architecture of its own, and adorns nature with a new thing. The thought and the form are equal in the order of time, but in the order of genesis the thought is prior to the form. The poet has a new thought; he has a whole new experience to unfold; he will tell us how it was with him, and all men will be the richer in his fortune. For the experience of each new age requires a new confession, and the world seems always waiting for its poet. I remember when I was young how much I was moved one morning by tidings that genius had appeared in a youth who sat near me at table. He had left his work and gone rambling none knew whither, and had written hundreds of lines, but could not tell whether that which was in him was therein told; he could tell nothing but that all was changed,—man, beast, heaven, earth and sea. How gladly we listened! how credulous! Society seemed to be compromised. We sat in the aurora of a sunrise which was to put out all the stars. Boston seemed to be at twice the distance it had the night before, or was much farther than that. Rome,—what was Rome? Plutarch and Shakspeare were in the yellow leaf,[6] and Homer no more should be heard of. It is much to know that poetry has been written this very day, under this very roof, by your side. What! that wonderful spirit has not expired! These stony moments are still sparkling and animated! I had fancied that the oracles were all silent, and nature had spent her fires; and behold! all night, from every pore, these fine auroras have been streaming. Every one has some interest in the advent of the poet, and no one knows how much it may concern him. We know that the secret of the world is profound, but who or what shall be our interpreter, we know not. A mountain ramble, a new style of face, a new person, may put the key into our hands. Of course the value of genius to us is in the veracity of its report. Talent may frolic and juggle; genius realizes and adds. Mankind in good earnest have availed so far in understanding themselves and their work, that the foremost watchman on the peak announces his news. It is the truest word ever spoken, and the phrase will be the fittest, most musical, and the unerring voice of the world for that time.

All that we call sacred history attests that the birth of a poet is the principal event in chronology. Man, never so often deceived, still watches for the arrival of a brother who can hold him steady to a truth until he has made it his own. With what joy I begin to read a poem which I confide in as an inspiration! And now my chains are to be broken; I shall mount above these clouds and opaque airs in which I live,—opaque, though they seem transparent,—and from the heaven of truth I shall see and comprehend my relations. That will reconcile me to life and renovate nature, to see trifles animated by a tendency, and to know what I am doing. Life will no more be a noise; now I shall see men and women, and know the signs by which they may be discerned from fools and satans. This day shall be better than my birthday: then I became an animal; now I am invited into the science of the real. Such is the hope, but the fruition is postponed. Oftener it falls that this winged man, who will carry me into the heaven, whirls me into mists, then leaps and frisks about with me as it were from cloud to cloud, still affirming that he is bound heavenward; and I, being myself a novice, am slow in perceiving that he does not know the way into the heavens, and is merely bent that I should admire his skill to rise like a fowl or a flying fish, a little way from the ground or the water; but the all-piercing, all-feeding and ocular air of heaven that man shall never inhabit. I tumble down again soon into my old nooks, and lead the life of exaggerations as before, and have lost my faith in the possibility of any guide who can lead me thither where I would be.

But, leaving these victims of vanity, let us, with new hope, observe how nature, by worthier impulses, has insured the poet's fidelity to his office of announcement and affirming, namely by the beauty of things, which becomes a new and higher beauty when expressed. Nature offers all her creatures to him as a picture-language. Being used as a type, a second wonderful value appears in the object, far better than its old value; as the carpenter's stretched cord, if you hold your ear close enough, is musical in the breeze. "Things more excellent than every image," says Jamblichus,[7] "are ex-

6. **the yellow leaf:** an echo of *Macbeth,* V.iii.23.

7. **Jamblichus:** or Iamblichus, a Neoplatonic philosopher of Syria

pressed through images." Things admit of being used as symbols because nature is a symbol, in the whole, and in every part. Every line we can draw in the sand has expression; and there is no body without its spirit or genius. All form is an effect of character; all condition, of the quality of the life; all harmony, of health; and for this reason a perception of beauty should be sympathetic, or proper only to the good. The beautiful rests on the foundations of the necessary. The soul makes the body, as the wise Spenser teaches:—

"So every spirit, as it is more pure,
And hath in it the more of heavenly light,
So it the fairer body doth procure
To habit in, and it more fairly dight,
With cheerful grace and amiable sight.
For, of the soul, the body form doth take,
For soul is form, and doth the body make." [8]

Here we find ourselves suddenly not in a critical speculation but in a holy place, and should go very warily and reverently. We stand before the secret of the world, there where Being passes into Appearance and Unity into Variety.

The Universe is the externization of the soul. Wherever the life is, that bursts into appearance around it. Our science is sensual, and therefore superficial. The earth and the heavenly bodies, physics and chemistry, we sensually treat, as if they were self-existent; but these are the retinue of that Being we have. "The mighty heaven," said Proclus,[9] "exhibits, in its transfigurations, clear images of the splendor of intellectual perceptions; being moved in conjunction with the unapparent periods of intellectual natures." Therefore science always goes abreast with the just elevation of the man, keeping step with religion and metaphysics; or the state of science is an index of our self-knowledge. Since every thing in nature answers to a moral power, if any phenomenon remains brute and dark it is because the corresponding faculty in the observer is not yet active.

No wonder then, if these waters be so deep, that we hover over them with a religious regard. The beauty of the fable proves the importance of the sense; to the poet, and to all others; or, if you please, every man is so far a poet as to be susceptible of these enchantments of nature; for all men have the thoughts whereof the universe is the celebration. I find that the fascination resides in the symbol. Who loves nature? Who does not? Is it only poets, and men of leisure and cultivation, who live with her? No; but also hunters, farmers, grooms and butchers, though they express their affection in their choice of life and not in their choice of words. The writer wonders what the coachman or the hunter values in riding, in horses and dogs. It is not superficial qualities. When you talk with him he holds these at as slight a rate as you. His worship is sympathetic; he has no definitions, but he is commanded in nature by the living power which he feels to be there present. No imitation or playing of these things would content him; he loves the earnest of the north wind, of rain, of stone and wood and iron. A beauty not explicable is dearer than a beauty which we can see to the end of. It is nature the symbol, nature certifying the supernatural, body overflowed by life which he worships with coarse but sincere rites.

The inwardness and mystery of this attachment drive men of every class to the use of emblems. The schools of poets and philosophers are not more intoxicated with their symbols than the populace with theirs. In our political parties, compute the power of badges and emblems. See the great ball which they roll from Baltimore to Bunker Hill! [10] In the political processions, Lowell goes in a loom, and Lynn in a shoe, and Salem in a ship.[11] Witness the cider-barrel, the log-cabin, the hickory-stick, the palmetto, and all the cognizances of party. See the power of national emblems. Some stars, lilies, leopards, a crescent, a lion, an eagle, or other figure which came into credit God knows how, on an old rag of bunting, blowing in the wind on a fort at the ends of the earth, shall make the blood tingle under the rudest or the most conventional exterior. The people fancy they hate poetry, and they are all poets and mystics!

Beyond this universality of the symbolic language, we are apprised of the divineness of this superior use of things, whereby the world is a temple whose walls are covered with emblems, pictures and commandments of the Deity,—in this, that there is no fact in nature which does not carry the whole sense of nature; and the distinctions which we make in events and in affairs, of low and high, honest and base, disappear when nature is used as a symbol. Thought makes everything fit for use. The vocabulary of an omniscient man would embrace words and images excluded from polite conversation. What would be base, or even obscene, to the obscene, becomes illustrious, spoken in a new connection of thought. The piety of the He-

in the fourth century A.D. **8. "So . . . make":** See Spenser's "Hymn in Honour of Beauty," ll. 127–33. The first line should read: "So every spirit, as it is most pure." **9. Proclus:** a Neoplatonic philosopher of the fifth century A.D.

10. See . . . Bunker Hill!: These rolling balls were a conspicuous feature of the Whig campaign for Harrison in 1840. **11. Lowell . . . Lynn . . . Salem:** three Massachusetts towns. Lowell was known for its textile mills, Lynn for its shoe factories, and Salem for its shipping and commerce.

brew prophets purges their grossness. The circumcision is an example of the power of poetry to raise the low and offensive. Small and mean things serve as well as great symbols. The meaner the type by which a law is expressed, the more pungent it is, and the more lasting in the memories of men; just as we choose the smallest box or case in which any needful utensil can be carried. Bare lists of words are found suggestive to an imaginative and excited mind, as it is related of Lord Chatham [12] that he was accustomed to read in Bailey's Dictionary when he was preparing to speak in Parliament. The poorest experience is rich enough for all the purposes of expressing thought. Why covet a knowledge of new facts? Day and night, house and garden, a few books, a few actions, serve us as well as would all trades and all spectacles. We are far from having exhausted the significance of the few symbols we use. We can come to use them yet with a terrible simplicity. It does not need that a poem should be long. Every word was once a poem. Every new relation is a new word. Also we use defects and deformities to a sacred purpose, so expressing our sense that the evils of the world are such only to the evil eye. In the old mythology, mythologists observe, defects are ascribed to divine natures, as lameness to Vulcan, blindness to Cupid, and the like,—to signify exuberances.

For as it is dislocation and detachment from the life of God that makes things ugly, the poet, who re-attaches things to nature and the Whole,—re-attaching even artificial things and violation of nature, to nature, by a deeper insight,—disposes very easily of the most disagreeable facts. Readers of poetry see the factory-village and the railway, and fancy that the poetry of the landscape is broken up by these; for these works of art are not yet consecrated in their reading; but the poet sees them fall within the great Order not less than the beehive or the spider's geometrical web. Nature adopts them very fast into her vital circles, and the gliding train of cars she loves like her own. Besides, in a centered mind, it signifies nothing how many mechanical inventions you exhibit. Though you add millions, and never so surprising, the fact of mechanics has not gained a grain's weight. The spiritual fact remains unalterable, by many or by few particulars; as no mountain is of any appreciable height to break the curve of the sphere. A shrewd country-boy goes to the city for the first time, and the complacent citizen is not satisfied with his little wonder. It is not that he does not see all the fine houses and know that he never saw such before, but he disposes of them as easily as the poet finds place for the railway. The chief value of the new fact is to enhance the great and constant fact of Life, which can dwarf any and every circumstance, and to which the belt of wampum and the commerce of America are alike.

The world being thus put under the mind for verb and noun, the poet is he who can articulate it. For though life is great, and fascinates and absorbs; and though all men are intelligent of the symbols through which it is named; yet they cannot originally use them. We are symbols and inhabit symbols; workmen, work, and tools, words and things, birth and death, all are emblems; but we sympathize with the symbols, and being infatuated with the economical uses of things, we do not know that they are thoughts. The poet, by an ulterior intellectual perception, gives them a power which makes their old use forgotten, and puts eyes and a tongue into every dumb and inanimate object. He perceives the independence of the thought on the symbol, the stability of the thought, the accidency [13] and fugacity [14] of the symbol. As the eyes of Lyncaeus [15] were said to see through the earth, so the poet turns the world to glass, and shows us all things in their right series and procession. For through that better perception he stands one step nearer to things, and sees the flowing or metamorphosis; perceives that thought is multiform; that within the form of every creature is a force impelling it to ascend into a higher form; and following with his eyes the life, uses the forms which express that life, and so his speech flows with the flowing of nature. All the facts of the animal economy, sex, nutriment, gestation, birth, growth, are symbols of the passage of the world into the soul of man, to suffer there a change and reappear a new and higher fact. He uses forms according to the life, and not according to the form. This is true science. The poet alone knows astronomy, chemistry, vegetation and animation, for he does not stop at these facts, but employs them as signs. He knows why the plain or meadow of space was strown with these flowers we call suns and moons and stars; why the great deep is adorned with animals, with men, and gods; for in every word he speaks he rides on them as the horses of thought.

By virtue of this science the poet is the Namer or Language-maker, naming things sometimes after their appearance, sometimes after their essence, and giving to every one its own name and not another's, thereby rejoicing the intellect, which de-

12. **Lord Chatham:** See "Self-Reliance," 7 n.

13. **accidency:** accidental or chance character. 14. **fugacity:** fleetingness, instability. 15. **Lyncaeus:** in Greek mythology, the lookout on the ship *Argo*.

lights in detachment or boundary. The poets made all the words, and therefore language is the archives of history, and, if we must say it, a sort of tomb of the muses. For though the origin of most of our words is forgotten, each word was at first a stroke of genius, and obtained currency because for the moment it symbolized the world to the first speaker and to the hearer. The etymologist finds the deadest word to have been once a brilliant picture. Language is fossil poetry. As the limestone of the continent consists of infinite masses of the shells of animalcules, so language is made up of images or tropes, which now, in their secondary use, have long ceased to remind us of their poetic origin. But the poet names the thing because he sees it, or comes one step nearer to it than any other. This expression or naming is not art, but a second nature, grown out of the first, as a leaf out of a tree. What we call nature is a certain self-regulated motion or change; and nature does all things by her own hands, and does not leave another to baptize her but baptizes herself; and this through the metamorphosis again. I remember that a certain poet [16] described it to me thus:—

Genius is the activity which repairs the decays of things, whether wholly or partly of a material and finite kind. Nature, through all her kingdoms, insures herself. Nobody cares for planting the poor fungus; so she shakes down from the gills of one agaric countless spores, any one of which, being preserved, transmits new billions of spores tomorrow or next day. The new agaric of this hour has a chance which the old one had not. This atom of seed is thrown into a new place, not subject to the accidents which destroyed its parent two rods off. She makes a man; and having brought him to ripe age, she will no longer run the risk of losing this wonder at a blow, but she detaches from him a new self, that the kind may be safe from accidents to which the individual is exposed. So when the soul of the poet has come to ripeness of thought, she detaches and sends away from it its poems or songs,—a fearless, sleepless, deathless progeny, which is not exposed to the accidents of the weary kingdom of time; a fearless, vivacious offspring, clad with wings (such was the virtue of the soul out of which they came) which carry them fast and far, and infix them irrecoverably into the hearts of men. These wings are the beauty of the poet's soul. The songs, thus flying immortal from their mortal parent, are pursued by clamorous flights of censures, which swarm in far greater numbers and threaten to devour them; but these last are not winged. At the end of a very short leap they fall plump down and rot, having received from the souls out of which they came no beautiful wings. But the melodies of the poet ascend and leap and pierce into the deeps of infinite time.

So far the bard taught me, using his freer speech. But nature has a higher end, in the production of new individuals, than security, namely *ascension,* or the passage of the soul into higher forms. I knew in my younger days the sculptor who made the statue of the youth which stands in the public garden. He was, as I remember, unable to tell directly what made him happy or unhappy, but by wonderful indirections he could tell. He rose one day, according to his habit, before the dawn, and saw the morning break, grand as the eternity out of which it came, and for many days after, he strove to express this tranquillity, and lo! his chisel had fashioned out of marble the form of a beautiful youth, Phosphorus, whose aspect is such that it is said all persons who look on it become silent. The poet also resigns himself to his mood, and that thought which agitated him is expressed, but *alter idem,*[17] in a manner totally new. The expression is organic, or the new type which things themselves take when liberated. As, in the sun, objects paint their images on the retina of the eye, so they, sharing the aspiration of the whole universe, tend to paint a far more delicate copy of their essence in his mind. Like the metamorphosis of things into higher organic forms is their change into melodies. Over everything stands its daemon or soul, and, as the form of the thing is reflected by the eye, so the soul of the thing is reflected by a melody. The sea, the mountain-ridge, Niagara, and every flower-bed, pre-exist, or superexist, in pre-cantations,[18] which sail like odors in the air, and when any man goes by with an ear sufficiently fine, he overhears them and endeavors to write down the notes without diluting or depraving them. And herein is the legitimation of criticism, in the mind's faith that the poems are a corrupt version of some text in nature with which they ought to be made to tally. A rhyme in one of our sonnets should not be less pleasing than the iterated nodes of a seashell, or the resembling difference of a group of flowers. The pairing of the birds is an idyl, not tedious as our idyls are; a tempest is a rough ode, without falsehood or rant; a summer, with its harvest sown, reaped and stored,

16. **a certain poet:** probably Emerson himself speaking in a slightly different tone.

17. ***alter idem:*** "another yet the same." 18. **pre-cantations:** prophetic incantations.

is an epic song, subordinating how many admirably executed parts. Why should not the symmetry and truth that modulate these, glide into our spirits, and we participate the invention of nature?

This insight, which expresses itself by what is called Imagination, is a very high sort of seeing, which does not come by study, but by the intellect being where and what it sees; by sharing the path or circuit of things through forms, and so making them translucid to others. The path of things is silent. Will they suffer a speaker to go with them? A spy they will not suffer; a lover, a poet, is the transcendency of their own nature,—him they will suffer. The condition of true naming, on the poet's part, is his resigning himself to the divine *aura* which breathes through forms, and accompanying that.

It is a secret which every intellectual man quickly learns, that beyond the energy of his possessed and conscious intellect he is capable of a new energy (as of an intellect doubled on itself), by abandonment to the nature of things; that beside his privacy of power as an individual man, there is a great public power on which he can draw, by unlocking, at all risks, his human doors, and suffering the ethereal tides to roll and circulate through him; then he is caught up into the life of the Universe, his speech is thunder, his thought is law, and his words are universally intelligible as the plants and animals. The poet knows that he speaks adequately then only when he speaks somewhat wildly, or "with the flower of the mind"; not with the intellect used as an organ, but with the intellect released from all service and suffered to take its direction from its celestial life; or as the ancients were wont to express themselves, not with intellect alone but with the intellect inebriated by nectar. As the traveler who has lost his way throws his reins on his horse's neck and trusts to the instinct of the animal to find his road, so must we do with the divine animal who carries us through this world. For if in any manner we can stimulate this instinct, new passages are opened for us into nature; the mind flows into and through things hardest and highest, and the metamorphosis is possible.

This is the reason why bards love wine, mead, narcotics, coffee, tea, opium, the fumes of sandalwood and tobacco, or whatever other procurers of animal exhilaration. All men avail themselves of such means as they can, to add this extraordinary power to their normal powers; and to this end they prize conversation, music, pictures, sculpture, dancing, theaters, traveling, war, mobs, fires, gaming, politics, or love, or science, or animal intoxication,—which are several coarser or finer *quasi*-mechanical substitutes for the true nectar, which is the ravishment of the intellect by coming nearer to the fact. These are auxiliaries to the centrifugal tendency of a man, to his passage out into free space, and they help him to escape the custody of that body in which he is pent up, and of that jail-yard of individual relations in which he is enclosed. Hence a great number of such as were professionally expressers of Beauty, as painters, poets, musicians and actors, have been more than others wont to lead a life of pleasure and indulgence; all but the few who received the true nectar; and, as it was a spurious mode of attaining freedom, as it was an emancipation not into the heavens but into the freedom of baser places, they were punished for that advantage they won, by a dissipation and deterioration. But never can any advantage be taken of nature by a trick. The spirit of the world, the great calm presence of the Creator, comes not forth to the sorceries of opium or of wine. The sublime vision comes to the pure and simple soul in a clean and chaste body. That is not an inspiration, which we owe to narcotics, but some counterfeit excitement and fury. Milton says that the lyric poet may drink wine and live generously, but the epic poet, he who shall sing of the gods and their descent unto men, must drink water out of a wooden bowl.[19] For poetry is not "Devil's wine," but God's wine. It is with this as it is with toys. We fill the hands and nurseries of our children with all manner of dolls, drums and horses; withdrawing their eyes from the plain face and sufficing objects of nature, the sun and moon, the animals, the water and stones, which should be their toys. So the poet's habit of living should be set on a key so low that the common influences should delight him. His cheerfulness should be the gift of the sunlight; the air should suffice for his inspiration, and he should be tipsy with water. That spirit which suffices quiet hearts, which seems to come forth to such from every dry knoll of sere grass, from every pine stump and half-imbedded stone on which the dull March sun shines, comes forth to the poor and hungry, and such as are of simple taste. If thou fill thy brain with Boston and New York, with fashion and covetousness, and wilt stimulate thy jaded senses with wine and French coffee, thou shalt find no radiance of wisdom in the lonely waste of the pine woods.

19. **Milton . . . bowl:** See *Elegia Sexta* (Elegy VI), one of Milton's Latin poems. Milton is, in fact, speaking here not of the lyric poet in the usual sense but of the writer of elegies. The phrase, "their descent unto men," or its Latin equivalent, is not to be found in Milton's verses.

If the imagination intoxicates the poet, it is not inactive in other men. The metamorphosis excites in the beholder an emotion of joy. The use of symbols has a certain power of emancipation and exhilaration for all men. We seem to be touched by a wand which makes us dance and run about happily, like children. We are like persons who come out of a cave or cellar into the open air. This is the effect on us of tropes, fables, oracles and all poetic forms. Poets are thus liberating gods. Men have really got a new sense, and found within their world another world, or nest of worlds; for, the metamorphosis once seen, we divine that it does not stop. I will not now consider how much this makes the charm of algebra and the mathematics, which also have their tropes, but it is felt in every definition; as when Aristotle defines *space* to be an immovable vessel in which things are contained; [20]—or when Plato defines a *line* to be a flowing point; or *figure* to be a bound of solid; and many the like. What a joyful sense of freedom we have when Vitruvius [21] announces the old opinion of artists that no architect can build any house well who does not know something of anatomy. When Socrates, in *Charmides,* tells us that the soul is cured of its maladies by certain incantations, and that these incantations are beautiful reasons, from which temperance is generated in souls; [22] when Plato calls the world an animal,[23] and Timaeus affirms that the plants also are animals; [24] or affirms a man to be a heavenly tree, growing with his root, which is his head, upward; and, as George Chapman, following him, writes,

> "So in our tree of man, whose nervie root
> Springs in his top;"— [25]

when Orpheus speaks of hoariness as "that white flower which marks extreme old age"; when Proclus [26] calls the universe the statue of the intellect; when Chaucer, in his praise of "Gentilesse," compares good blood in mean condition to fire, which, though carried to the darkest house betwixt this and the mount of Caucasus, will yet hold its natural office and burn as bright as if twenty thousand men did it behold; [27] when John saw, in the Apocalypse, the ruin of the world through evil, and the stars fall from heaven as the fig tree casteth her untimely fruit; [28] when Aesop reports the whole catalogue of common daily relations through the masquerade of birds and beasts; —we take the cheerful hint of the immortality of our essence and its versatile habit and escapes, as when the gypsies say of themselves "it is in vain to hang them, they cannot die."

The poets are thus liberating gods. The ancient British bards had for the title of their order, "Those who are free throughout the world." [29] They are free, and they make free. An imaginative book renders us much more service at first, by stimulating us through its tropes, than afterward when we arrive at the precise sense of the author. I think nothing is of any value in books excepting the transcendental and extraordinary. If a man is inflamed and carried away by his thought, to that degree that he forgets the authors and the public and heeds only this one dream which holds him like an insanity, let me read his paper, and you may have all the arguments and histories and criticism. All the value which attaches to Pythagoras, Paracelsus,[30] Cornelius Agrippa,[31] Cardan,[32] Kepler, Swedenborg, Schelling, Oken,[33] or any other who introduces questionable facts into his cosmogony, as angels, devils, magic, astrology, palmistry, mesmerism, and so on, is the certificate we have of departure from routine, and that here is a new witness. That also is the best success in conversation, the magic of liberty, which puts the world like a ball in our hands. How cheap even the liberty then seems; how mean to study, when an emotion communicates to the intellect the power to sap and upheave nature; how great the perspective! nations, times, systems, enter and disappear like threads in tapestry of large figure and many colors; dream delivers us to dream, and

20. as . . . contained: See Aristotle, *Physics*, Book IV.212a, 14. **21. Vitruvius:** Vitruvius Pollio, Roman engineer and architect of the Augustan period, author of a famous work, *On Architecture.* **22. When . . . souls:** See Plato, *Charmides*, 157. **23. when . . . animal:** See Plato, *Timaeus*, 30. **24. Timaeus . . . animals:** *Ibid.*, 77. **25. "So . . . top":** from the Dedication of Chapman's translation of the *Iliad* to Prince Henry, ll. 132–33. **26. Proclus:** See 9 n. **27. when . . . behold:** See "The Wife of Bath's Tale," ll. 1139–45. This, says his editor, was a favorite passage with Emerson (*Works*, III, 300).

28. when . . . fruit: See Rev. 6:13. **29. The . . . world:** According to William Owen (*The Heroic Elegies and Other Pieces of Llywarc Hen*, 1792), the British bards, when attending a bardic assembly outside of their own province or even outside of Britain, retained their appropriate titles, "The Bards of the Isle of Britain through the world," and "Those who are at liberty through the world." **30. Paracelsus:** Theophrastus Bombastus von Hohenheim (1493–1541), who took the surname of Paracelsus (that is, "superior to Celsus," a Platonic writer of the second century A.D.), German physician and writer on occult subjects, whose writings appear to be a mixture of sterile mystagogy and inspired insight into nature and man. **31. Cornelius Agrippa:** Henry Cornelius Agrippa von Nettesheim (1486–1535), German physician and writer on occult subjects, reputed in his time to be a magician. **32. Cardan:** Girolamo Cardano (1501–76), Italian physician and astrologer, author of a work, *De Subtilitate Rerum*, in which he expounded certain speculative views that anticipated modern scientific principles. **33. Oken:** Lorenz Oken (1779–1851), German naturalist, who, in a work entitled *Die Zeugung* ("Procreation"), set forth the theory that all organisms, both vegetable and animal, are derived from cells or vesicles.

while the drunkenness lasts we will sell our bed, our philosophy, our religion, in our opulence.

There is good reason why we should prize this liberation. The fate of the poor shepherd, who, blinded and lost in the snowstorm, perishes in a drift within a few feet of his cottage door, is an emblem of the state of man. On the brink of the waters of life and truth, we are miserably dying. The inaccessibleness of every thought but that we are in, is wonderful. What if you come near to it, you are as remote when you are nearest as when you are farthest. Every thought is also a prison; every heaven is also a prison. Therefore we love the poet, the inventor, who in any form, whether in an ode or in an action or in looks and behavior, has yielded us a new thought. He unlocks our chains and admits us to a new scene.

This emancipation is dear to all men, and the power to impart it, as it must come from greater depth and scope of thought, is a measure of intellect. Therefore all books of the imagination endure, all which ascend to that truth that the writer sees nature beneath him, and uses it as his exponent. Every verse or sentence possessing this virtue will take care of its own immortality. The religions of the world are the ejaculations of a few imaginative men.

But the quality of the imagination is to flow, and not to freeze. The poet did not stop at the color or the form, but read their meaning; neither may he rest in this meaning, but he makes the same objects exponents of his new thought. Here is the difference betwixt the poet and the mystic, that the last nails a symbol to one sense, which was a true sense for a moment, but soon becomes old and false. For all symbols are fluxional; [34] all language is vehicular [35] and transitive,[36] and is good, as ferries and horses are, for conveyance, not as farms and houses are, for homestead. Mysticism consists in the mistake of an accidental and individual symbol for an universal one. The morning-redness happens to be the favorite meteor to the eyes of Jacob Behmen,[37] and comes to stand to him for truth and faith; and, he believes, should stand for the same realities to every reader. But the first reader prefers as naturally the symbol of a mother and child, or a gardener and his bulb, or a jeweler polishing a gem. Either of these, or of a myriad more, are equally good to the person to whom they are significant. Only they must be held lightly, and be very willingly translated into the equivalent terms which others use. And the mystic must be steadily told,—All that you say is just as true without the tedious use of that symbol as with it. Let us have a little algebra, instead of this trite rhetoric,—universal signs, instead of these village symbols,—and we shall both be gainers. The history of hierarchies seems to show that all religious error consisted in making the symbol too stark and solid, and was at last nothing but an excess of the organ of language.

Swedenborg,[38] of all men in the recent ages, stands eminently for the translator of nature into thought. I do not know the man in history to whom things stood so uniformly for words. Before him the metamorphosis continually plays. Everything on which his eye rests, obeys the impulses of moral nature. The figs become grapes whilst he eats them. When some of his angels affirmed a truth, the laurel twig which they held blossomed in their hands. The noise which at a distance appeared like gnashing and thumping, on coming nearer was found to be the voice of disputants. The men in one of his visions, seen in heavenly light, appeared like dragons, and seemed in darkness; but to each other they appeared as men, and when the light from heaven shone into their cabin, they complained of the darkness, and were compelled to shut the window that they might see.

There was this perception in him which makes the poet or seer an object of awe and terror, namely that the same man or society of men may wear one aspect to themselves and their companions, and a different aspect to higher intelligences. Certain priests, whom he describes as conversing very learnedly together, appeared to the children who were at some distance, like dead horses; and many the like misappearances. And instantly the mind inquires whether these fishes under the bridge, yonder oxen in the pasture, those dogs in the yard, are immutably fishes, oxen and dogs, or only so appear to me, and perchance to themselves appear upright men; and whether I appear as a man to all eyes. The Brahmins and Pythagoras propounded the same question, and if any poet has witnessed the transformation he doubtless found it in harmony with various experiences. We have all seen changes as considerable in wheat and caterpillars. He is the poet and shall draw us with love and terror, who sees through the flowing vest the firm nature, and can declare it.

I look in vain for the poet whom I describe. We

34. **fluxional:** characterized by flux or flowing; not static, fixed, or rigid in their significance. 35. **vehicular:** capable of serving as a vehicle or mode of conveyance from one thing to another; here, from the literal to the intangible. 36. **transitive:** of the nature of what is transitional or intermediate between one thing and another. See preceding note. 37. **Behmen:** See "New England Reformers," 21 n.

38. **Swedenborg:** See *Nature*, 16 n.

do not with sufficient plainness or sufficient profoundness address ourselves to life, nor dare we chaunt our own times and social circumstance. If we filled the day with bravery, we should not shrink from celebrating it. Time and nature yield us many gifts, but not yet the timely man, the new religion, the reconciler, whom all things await. Dante's praise is that he dared to write his autobiography in colossal cipher, or into universality.[39] We have yet had no genius in America, with tyrannous eye, which knew the value of our incomparable materials, and saw, in the barbarism and materialism of the times, another carnival of the same gods whose picture he so much admires in Homer; then in the Middle Age; then in Calvanism. Banks and tariffs, the newspaper and caucus, Methodism and Unitarianism, are flat and dull to dull people, but rest on the same foundations of wonder as the town of Troy and the temple of Delphi, and are as swiftly passing away. Our log-rolling, our stumps and their politics, our fisheries, our Negroes and Indians, our boats and our repudiations,[40] the wrath of rogues and the pusillanimity of honest men, the northern trade, the southern planting, the western clearing, Oregon and Texas, are yet unsung. Yet America is a poem in our eyes; its ample geography dazzles the imagination, and it will not wait long for meters. If I have not found that excellent combination of gifts in my countrymen which I seek, neither could I aid myself to fix the idea of the poet by reading now and then in Chalmers's collection[41] of five centuries of English poets. These are wits more than poets, though there have been poets among them. But when we adhere to the ideal of the poet, we have our difficulties even with Milton and Homer. Milton is too literary, and Homer too literal and historical.

But I am not wise enough for a national criticism, and must use the old largeness a little longer, to discharge my errand from the muse to the poet concerning his art.

Art is the path of the creator to his work. The paths or methods are ideal and eternal, though few men ever see them; not the artist himself for years, or for a lifetime, unless he come into the conditions. The painter, the sculptor, the composer, the epic rhapsodist, the orator, all partake one desire, namely to express themselves symmetrically and abundantly, not dwarfishly and fragmentarily. They found or put themselves in certain conditions, as, the painter and sculptor before some impressive human figures; the orator into the assembly of the people; and the others in such scenes as each has found exciting to his intellect; and each presently feels the new desire. He hears a voice, he sees a beckoning. Then he is apprised, with wonder, what herds of daemons hem him in. He can no more rest; he says, with the old painter, "By God it is in me and must go forth of me." He pursues a beauty, half seen, which flies before him. The poet pours out verses in every solitude. Most of the things he says are conventional, no doubt; but by and by he says something which is original and beautiful. That charms him. He would say nothing else but such things. In our way of talking we say "That is yours, this is mine"; but the poet knows well that it is not his; that it is as strange and beautiful to him as to you; he would fain hear the like eloquence at length. Once having tasted this immortal ichor,[42] he cannot have enough of it, and as an admirable creative power exists in these intellections, it is of the last importance that these things get spoken. What a little of all we know is said! What drops of all the sea of our science are baled up! and by what accident it is that these are exposed, when so many secrets sleep in nature! Hence the necessity of speech and song; hence these throbs and heart-beatings in the orator, at the door of the assembly, to the end namely that thought may be ejaculated as Logos, or Word.

Doubt not, O poet, but persist. Say "It is in me, and shall out." Stand there, balked and dumb, stuttering and stammering, hissed and hooted, stand and strive, until at last rage draw out of thee that *dream*-power which every night shows thee is thine own; a power transcending all limit and privacy, and by virtue of which a man is the conductor of the whole river of electricity. Nothing walks, or creeps, or grows, or exists, which must not in turn arise and walk before him as exponent of his meaning. Comes he to that power, his genius is no longer exhaustible. All the creatures by pairs and by tribes pour into his mind as into a Noah's ark, to come forth again to people a new world. This is like the stock of air for our respiration or for the combustion of our fireplace; not a measure of gallons, but the entire atmosphere if wanted. And therefore the rich poets, as

39. **Dante's . . . universality:** Emerson is dwelling here on the personal or confessional aspect of the *Divine Comedy*. 40. **repudiations:** In the thirties and forties some of the states in the Union repudiated—that is to say, refused to pay—the debts they had contracted in the form of state bonds and the like. 41. **Chalmers's collection:** Alexander Chalmers (1759–1834), British editor and biographer, compiler of a once very familiar anthology, *The Works of the English Poets from Chaucer to Cowper,* in twenty-one volumes.

42. **ichor:** strictly, a mythological fluid that was supposed to flow in the blood of the Greek gods. Emerson seems here to be using the word as a synonym for "nectar," the drink of the gods, or for "ambrosia," their food.

Homer, Chaucer, Shakespeare, and Raphael, have obviously no limits to their works except the limits of their lifetime, and resemble a mirror carried through the street, ready to render an image of every created thing.

O poet! a new nobility is conferred in groves and pastures, and not in castles or by the sword-blade any longer. The conditions are hard, but equal. Thou shalt leave the world, and know the muse only. Thou shalt not know any longer the times, customs, graces, politics, or opinions of men, but shalt take all from the muse. For the time of towns is tolled from the world by funereal chimes, but in nature the universal hours are counted by succeeding tribes of animals and plants, and by growth of joy on joy. God wills also that thou abdicate a manifold and duplex life, and that thou be content that others speak for thee. Others shall be thy gentlemen and shall represent all courtesy and worldly life for thee; others shall do the great and resounding actions also. Thou shalt lie close hid with nature, and canst not be afforded to the Capitol or the Exchange. The world is full of renunciations and apprenticeships, and this is thine; thou must pass for a fool and a churl for a long season. This is the screen and sheath in which Pan has protected his well-beloved flower, and thou shalt be known only to thine own, and they shall console thee with tenderest love. And thou shalt not be able to rehearse the names of thy friends in thy verse, for an old shame before the holy ideal. And this is the reward; that the ideal shall be real to thee, and the impressions of the actual world shall fall like summer rain, copious, but not troublesome to thy invulnerable essence. Thou shalt have the whole land for thy park and manor, the sea for thy bath and navigation, without tax and without envy; the woods and the rivers thou shalt own, and thou shalt possess that wherein others are only tenants and boarders. Thou true landlord! sea-lord! air-lord! Wherever snow falls or water flows or birds fly, wherever day and night meet in twilight, wherever the blue heaven is hung by clouds or sown with stars, wherever are forms with transparent boundaries, wherever are outlets into celestial space, wherever is danger, and awe, and love,—there is Beauty, plenteous as rain, shed for thee, and though thou shouldst walk the world over, thou shalt not be able to find a condition inopportune or ignoble.

MONTAIGNE: OR, THE SKEPTIC

◇

¶ IN THE winter of 1845–46, before the Boston Lyceum, Emerson gave a course of seven lectures, the first of which was called "The Uses of Great Men"; this was followed by six lectures on as many representatives of greatness in its various manifestations—in philosophy, for example (Plato), in poetry (Shakespeare), in action (Napoleon). This series of lectures was repeated, under the general title "Representative Men," in England in the fall of 1847. The lecture on Montaigne as the embodiment of skepticism in its truest sense was one of these, and it appeared, along with the others (no doubt much revised), in 1850, in the volume similarly entitled *Representative Men* (*Works,* IV). Like the earlier essay "Experience" in the *Essays: Second Series* of 1844, the essay on Montaigne is interesting and important as a profoundly honest expression of that pole of Emerson's thought which stood at a diametrical remove from the apparently unqualified belief and hope expressed in *Nature* and in such discourses as the Divinity School "Address" and "The Over-Soul." Skepticism in the usual and merely negative sense was impossible for Emerson, but, as time went on, his thinking took more and more the form of what might be called faith-within-doubt—doubt of what man can know with any certainty in "experience," faith in what is revealed to him in moments of insight beyond experience. There is an excellent discussion of this essay in Stephen E. Whicher, *Freedom and Fate,* Chap. 6.

◇

EVERY fact is related on one side to sensation, and on the other to morals. The game of thought is, on the appearance of one of these two sides, to find the other: given the upper, to find the under side. Nothing so thin but has these two faces, and when the observer has seen the obverse, he turns it over to see the reverse. Life is a pitching of this penny,—heads or tails. We never tire of this game, because there is still a slight shudder of astonishment at the exhibition of the other face, at the contrast of the two faces. A man is flushed with success, and bethinks himself what this good luck signifies. He drives his bargain in the street; but it occurs that he also is bought and sold. He sees the beauty of a human face, and searches the cause of that beauty, which must be more beautiful. He builds his fortunes, maintains the laws, cherishes his children; but he asks himself, Why? and whereto? This head and this tail are called, in the language of philosophy, Infinite and Finite; Relative and Absolute; Apparent and Real; and many fine names beside.

Each man is born with a predisposition to one or the other of these sides of nature; and it will easily happen that men will be found devoted to one or the other. One class has the perception of difference, and is conversant with facts and surfaces, cities and persons, and the bringing certain things to pass;—the men of talent and action. Another class have the perception of identity, and are men of faith and philosophy, men of genius.

Each of these riders drives too fast. Plotinus [1] believes only in philosophers; Fenelon,[2] in saints; Pindar and Byron, in poets. Read the haughty language in which Plato and the Platonists speak of all men who are not devoted to their own shining abstractions: other men are rats and mice. The literary class is usually proud and exclusive. The correspondence of Pope and Swift describes mankind around them as monsters; and that of Goethe and Schiller, in our own time, is scarcely more kind.

It is easy to see how this arrogance comes. The genius is a genius by the first look he casts on any object. Is his eye creative? Does he not rest in angles and colors, but beholds the design?—he will presently undervalue the actual object. In powerful moments, his thought has dissolved the works of art and nature into their causes, so that the works appear heavy and faulty. He has a conception of beauty which the sculptor cannot embody.[3] Picture, statue, temple, railroad, steam-engine, existed first in an artist's mind, without flaw, mistake, or friction, which impair the executed models. So did the Church, the State, college, court, social circle, and all the institutions. It is not strange that these men, remembering what they have seen and hoped of ideas, should affirm disdainfully the superiority of ideas. Having at some time seen that the happy soul will carry all the arts in power, they say, Why cumber ourselves with superfluous realizations? and like dreaming beggars they assume to speak and act as if these values were already substantiated.

On the other part, the men of toil and trade and luxury,—the animal world, including the animal in the philosopher and poet also, and the practical world, including the painful drudgeries which are never excused to philosopher or poet any more than to the rest,—weigh heavily on the other side. The trade in our streets believes in no metaphysical causes, thinks nothing of the force which necessitated traders and a trading planet to exist: no, but sticks to cotton, sugar, wool and salt. The ward meetings, on election days, are not softened by any misgiving of the value of these ballotings. Hot life is streaming in a single direction. To the men of this world, to the animal strength and spirits, to the men of practical power, whilst immersed in it, the man of ideas appears out of his reason. They alone have reason.

Things always bring their own philosophy with them, that is, prudence. No man acquires property without acquiring with it a little arithmetic also. In England, the richest country that ever existed, property stands for more, compared with personal ability, than in any other. After dinner, a man believes less, denies more: verities have lost some charm. After dinner, arithmetic is the only science: ideas are disturbing, incendiary, follies of young men, repudiated by the solid portion of society: and a man comes to be valued by his athletic and animal qualities. Spence relates that Mr. Pope was with Sir Godfrey Kneller one day, when his nephew, a Guinea trader, came in. "Nephew," said Sir Godfrey, "you have the honor of seeing the two greatest men in the world." "I don't know how great men you may be," said the Guinea man, "but I don't like your looks. I have often bought a man much better than both of you, all muscles and bones, for ten guineas." [4] Thus the men of the senses revenge themselves on the professors and repay scorn for scorn. The first had leaped to conclusions not yet ripe, and say more than is true; the others make themselves merry with the philosopher, and weigh man by the pound. They believe that mustard bites the tongue, that pepper is hot, friction-matches incendiary, revolvers are to be avoided, and suspenders hold up pantaloons; that there is much sentiment in a chest of tea; and a man will be eloquent, if you give him good wine. Are you tender and scrupulous,—you must eat more mince-pie. They hold that Luther had milk in him when he said,—

> *"Wer nicht liebt Wein, Weiber, Gesang,*
> *Der bleibt ein Narr sein Leben lang;"*— [5]

and when he advised a young scholar, perplexed with fore-ordination and free-will, to get well

MONTAIGNE. **1. Plotinus:** See *Nature*, 36 n. **2. Fenelon:** François de La Mothe-Fénelon (1651–1715), Archbishop of Cambrai, French writer on theological and educational subjects; author of *Télémaque*, a didactic romance familiar to Emerson. **3. He . . . embody:** an echo of Michelangelo's Sonnet LXXXIII ("*Non ha l'ottimo artista alcun concetto*").

4. Spence . . . guineas: one of the "Supplemental Anecdotes" in Joseph Spence's *Anecdotes, Observations, and Characters, of Books and Men.* **5. "Wer . . . lang":** "Who loves not women, wine, and song, / Remains a fool his whole life long." These lines were fancifully attributed to Luther by an anonymous eighteenth-century German poet, and since then have often been supposed to be his.

drunk. "The nerves," says Cabanis,[6] "they are the man." My neighbor, a jolly farmer, in the tavern bar-room, thinks that the use of money is sure and speedy spending. For his part, he says, he puts his down his neck and gets the good of it.

The inconvenience of this way of thinking is that it runs into indifferentism and then into disgust. Life is eating us up. We shall be fables presently. Keep cool: it will be all one a hundred years hence. Life's well enough, but we shall be glad to get out of it, and they will all be glad to have us. Why should we fret and drudge? Our meat will taste tomorrow as it did yesterday, and we may at last have had enough of it. "Ah," said my languid gentleman at Oxford,[7] "there's nothing new or true,—and no matter."

With a little more bitterness, the cynic moans; our life is like an ass led to market by a bundle of hay being carried before him; he sees nothing but the bundle of hay. "There is so much trouble in coming into the world," said Lord Bolingbroke,[8] "and so much more, as well as meanness, in going out of it, that 'tis hardly worth while to be here at all." I knew a philosopher of this kidney who was accustomed briefly to sum up his experience of human nature in saying, "Mankind is a damned rascal": and the natural corollary is pretty sure to follow,—"The world lives by humbug, and so will I."

The abstractionist and the materialist thus mutually exasperating each other, and the scoffer expressing the worst of materialism, there arises a third party to occupy the middle ground between these two, the skeptic, namely. He finds both wrong by being in extremes. He labors to plant his feet, to be the beam of the balance. He will not go beyond his card. He sees the onesidedness of these men of the street; he will not be a Gibeonite;[9] he stands for the intellectual faculties, a cool head and whatever serves to keep it cool; no unadvised industry, no unrewarded self-devotion, no loss of the brains in toil. Am I an ox, or a dray?—You are both in extremes, he says. You that will have all solid, and a world of pig-lead, deceive yourselves grossly. You believe yourselves rooted and grounded on adamant; and yet, if we uncover the last facts of our knowledge, you are spinning like bubbles in a river, you know not whither or whence, and you are bottomed and capped and wrapped in delusions. Neither will he be betrayed to a book and wrapped in a gown.[10] The studious class are their own victims; they are thin and pale, their feet are cold, their heads are hot, the night is without sleep, the day a fear of interruption,—pallor, squalor, hunger and egotism. If you come near them and see what conceits they entertain,—they are abstractionists, and spend their days and nights in dreaming some dream; in expecting the homage of society to some precious scheme, built on a truth, but destitute of proportion in its presentment, of justness in its application, and of all energy of will in the schemer to embody and vitalize it.

But I see plainly, he says, that I cannot see. I know that human strength is not in extremes, but in avoiding extremes. I, at least, will shun the weakness of philosophizing beyond my depth. What is the use of pretending to powers we have not? What is the use of pretending to assurances we have not, respecting the other life? Why exaggerate the power of virtue? Why be an angel before your time? These strings, wound up too high, will snap. If there is a wish for immortality, and no evidence, why not say just that? If there are conflicting evidences, why not state them? If there is not ground for a candid thinker to make up his mind, yea or nay,—why not suspend the judgment? I weary of these dogmatizers. I tire of these hacks of routine, who deny the dogmas. I neither affirm nor deny. I stand here to try the case. I am here to consider, σκοπεῖν,[11] to consider how it is. I will try to keep the balance true. Of what use to take the chair and glibly rattle off theories of society, religion and nature, when I know that practical objections lie in the way, insurmountable by me and by my mates? Why so talkative in public, when each of my neighbors can pin me to my seat by arguments I cannot refute? Why pretend that life is so simple a game, when we know how subtle and elusive the Proteus[12] is? Why think to shut up all things in your narrow coop, when we know there are not one or two only, but ten, twenty, a thousand things, and unlike? Why fancy that you have all the truth in your keeping? There is much to say on all sides.

Who shall forbid a wise skepticism, seeing that

6. **Cabanis:** Pierre Jean Georges Cabanis (1757–1808), French physician and physiologist, author of a strongly materialistic work, *Relations between the Physical and the Moral Nature of Man* (*Rapports du physique et du moral de l'homme*, 1802). 7. **my languid gentleman at Oxford:** In April, 1848, Emerson visited friends at Oriel College, Oxford. His "languid gentleman" may have been Arthur Hugh Clough. 8. **Lord Bolingbroke:** Henry St. John, Viscount Bolingbroke (1678–1751), English statesman and writer on philosophical subjects. 9. **Gibeonite:** See Josh. 9:3–27.

10. **betrayed . . . gown:** an echo of George Herbert's poem, "Affliction (I)," ll. 39–40 ("Thou didst betray me to a lingring book / And wrap me in a gown"). 11. **σκοπεῖν:** *skopein*, to look at, contemplate, pay regard to. 12. **Proteus:** in Greek mythology, the old man of the sea, who had the power of assuming one shape after another in order to avoid the answering of questions put to him.

there is no practical question on which any thing more than an approximate solution can be had? Is not marriage an open question, when it is alleged, from the beginning of the world, that such as are in the institution wish to get out, and such as are out wish to get in? And the reply of Socrates, to him who asked whether he should choose a wife, still remains reasonable, that "whether he should choose one or not, he would repent it." [13] Is not the State a question? All society is divided in opinion on the subject of the State. Nobody loves it; great numbers dislike it and suffer conscientious scruples to allegiance; and the only defense set up, is the fear of doing worse in disorganizing. Is it otherwise with the Church? Or, to put any of the questions which touch mankind nearest,—shall the young man aim at a leading part in law, in politics, in trade? It will not be pretended that a success in either of these kinds is quite coincident with what is best and inmost in his mind. Shall he then, cutting the stays that hold him fast to the social state, put out to sea with no guidance but his genius? There is much to say on both sides. Remember the open question between the present order of "competition" and the friends of "attractive and associated labor." [14] The generous minds embrace the proposition of labor shared by all; it is the only honesty; nothing else is safe. It is from the poor man's hut alone that strength and virtue come: and yet, on the other side, it is alleged that labor impairs the form and breaks the spirit of man, and the laborers cry unanimously, "We have no thoughts." Culture, how indispensable! I cannot forgive you the want of accomplishments; and yet culture will instantly impair that chiefest beauty of spontaneousness. Excellent is culture for a savage; but once let him read in the book, and he is no longer able not to think of Plutarch's heroes. In short, since true fortitude of understanding consists "in not letting what we know be embarrassed by what we do not know," we ought to secure those advantages which we can command, and not risk them by clutching after the airy and unattainable. Come, no chimeras! Let us go abroad; let us mix in affairs; let us learn and get and have and climb. "Men are a sort of moving plants, and, like trees, receive a great part of their nourishment from the air. If they keep too much at home, they pine." Let us have a robust, manly life; let us know what we know, for certain; what we have, let it be solid and seasonable and our own. A world in the hand is worth two in the bush. Let us have to do with real men and women, and not with skipping ghosts.

This then is the right ground of the skeptic,—this of consideration, of self-containing; not at all of unbelief; not at all of universal denying, nor of universal doubting,—doubting even that he doubts; least of all of scoffing and profligate jeering at all that is stable and good. These are no more his moods than are those of religion and philosophy. He is the considerer, the prudent, taking in sail, counting stock, husbanding his means, believing that a man has too many enemies than that he can afford to be his own foe; that we cannot give ourselves too many advantages in this unequal conflict, with powers so vast and unweariable ranged on one side, and this little conceited vulnerable popinjay that a man is, bobbing up and down into every danger, on the other. It is a position taken up for better defense, as of more safety, and one that can be maintained; and it is one of more opportunity and range: as, when we build a house, the rule is to set it not too high nor too low, under the wind, but out of the dirt.

The philosophy we want is one of fluxions and mobility. The Spartan and Stoic schemes are too stark and stiff for our occasion. A theory of Saint John,[15] and of non-resistance, seems, on the other hand, too thin and aerial. We want some coat woven of elastic steel, stout as the first and limber as the second. We want a ship in these billows we inhabit. An angular, dogmatic house would be rent to chips and splinters in this storm of many elements. No, it must be tight, and fit to the form of man, to live at all; as a shell must dictate the architecture of a house founded on the sea. The soul of man must be the type of our scheme, just as the body of man is the type after which a dwelling-house is built. Adaptiveness is the peculiarity of human nature. We are golden averages, volitant stabilities, compensated or periodic errors, houses founded on the sea. The wise skeptic wishes to have a near view of the best game and the chief players; what is best in the planet; art and nature, places and events; but mainly men. Every thing that is excellent in mankind,—a form of grace, an arm of iron, lips of persuasion, a brain of resources, every one skilful to play and win,—he will see and judge.

The terms of admission to this spectacle are, that he have a certain solid and intelligible way of living of his own; some method of answering the

13. **"whether . . . it"**: This anecdote is told by Diogenes Laertius in his *Lives of the Philosophers*, II.xxxiii. 14. **"attractive and associated labor"**: terms used by the Fourieristic Socialists of the forties; see "New England Reformers," 8 n.

15. **a theory of Saint John**: probably a reference to the First Epistle of John, with its emphasis on the doctrine of love ("Beloved, if God so loved us, we ought also to love one another" [I John 4:11]).

inevitable needs of human life; proof that he has played with skill and success; that he has evinced the temper, stoutness and the range of qualities which, among his contemporaries and countrymen, entitle him to fellowship and trust. For the secrets of life are not shown except to sympathy and likeness. Men do not confide themselves to boys, or coxcombs, or pedants, but to their peers. Some wise limitation, as the modern phrase is; some condition between the extremes, and having, itself, a positive quality; some stark and sufficient man, who is not salt or sugar, but sufficiently related to the world to do justice to Paris or London, and, at the same time, a vigorous and original thinker, whom cities can not overawe, but who uses them,—is the fit person to occupy this ground of speculation.

These qualities meet in the character of Montaigne. And yet, since the personal regard which I entertain for Montaigne may be unduly great, I will, under the shield of this prince of egotists, offer, as an apology for electing him as the representative of skepticism, a word or two to explain how my love began and grew for this admirable gossip.[16]

A single odd volume of Cotton's translation [17] of the *Essays* remained to me from my father's library, when a boy. It lay long neglected, until, after many years, when I was newly escaped from college, I read the book, and procured the remaining volumes. I remember the delight and wonder in which I lived with it. It seemed to me as if I had myself written the book, in some former life, so sincerely it spoke to my thought and experience. It happened, when in Paris, in 1833, that, in the cemetery of Père Lachaise, I came to a tomb of Auguste Collignon, who died in 1830, aged sixty-eight years, and who, said the monument, "lived to do right, and had formed himself to virtue on the Essays of Montaigne." Some years later, I became acquainted with an accomplished English poet, John Sterling; [18] and, in prosecuting my correspondence, I found that, from a love of Montaigne, he had made a pilgrimage to his chateau, still standing near Castellan, in Périgord, and, after two hundred and fifty years, had copied from the walls of his library the inscriptions which Montaigne had written there. That Journal of Mr. Sterling's, published in the Westminster Review, Mr. Hazlitt has reprinted in the *Prolegomena* to his edition of the Essays.[19] I heard with pleasure that one of the newly-discovered autographs of William Shakespeare was in a copy of Florio's translation of Montaigne.[20] It is the only book which we certainly know to have been in the poet's library. And, oddly enough, the duplicate copy of Florio, which the British Museum purchased with a view of protecting the Shakespeare autograph (as I was informed in the Museum), turned out to have the autograph of Ben Jonson in the fly-leaf. Leigh Hunt relates of Lord Byron, that Montaigne was the only great writer of past times whom he read with avowed satisfaction.[21] Other coincidences, not needful to be mentioned here, concurred to make this old Gascon still new and immortal for me.

In 1571, on the death of his father,[22] Montaigne, then thirty-eight years old, retired from the practice of law at Bordeaux, and settled himself on his estate. Though he had been a man of pleasure and sometimes a courtier, his studious habits now grew on him, and he loved the compass, staidness and independence of the country gentleman's life. He took up his economy in good earnest, and made his farms yield the most. Downright and plain-dealing, and abhorring to be deceived or to deceive, he was esteemed in the country for his sense and probity. In the civil wars of the League,[23] which converted every house into a fort, Montaigne kept his gates open and his house without defense. All parties freely came and went, his courage and honor being universally esteemed. The neighboring lords and gentry brought jewels and papers to him for safe-keeping. Gibbon reckons, in these bigoted times, but two men of liberality in France,—Henry IV and Montaigne.

Montaigne is the frankest and honestest of all writers. His French freedom runs into grossness; but he has anticipated all censure by the bounty of his own confessions. In his times, books were written to one sex only, and almost all were written in Latin; so that in a humorist a certain nakedness of statement was permitted, which our manners, of a literature addressed equally to both sexes, do

16. **gossip**: a person given to easy and unrestrained conversation. 17. **Cotton's translation**: Charles Cotton (1630–87), English poet, was also one of the early translators of Montaigne. 18. **John Sterling**: English clergyman and poet (1806–44), friend of Carlyle and a great admirer of Emerson, with whom he carried on a correspondence for several years, though the two men never met (*A Correspondence between John Sterling and Ralph Waldo Emerson*, 1897).

19. **That . . . Essays**: William Hazlitt, the Younger, quotes from this Journal in the Preface to his edition of Montaigne's *Essays* (1842). 20. **I . . . Montaigne**: Giovanni (or John) Florio (1553?–1625) was the first translator of Montaigne into English (*Essays*, 1603). The Shakespeare autograph to which Emerson here refers is now regarded as a forgery. 21. **Leigh Hunt . . . satisfaction**: Hunt records this fact in *Lord Byron and Some of His Contemporaries* (I, 178). 22. **In . . . father**: In fact, Montaigne's father died in 1568, and it was in July, 1570, that Montaigne resigned his office as counsellor in the Parlement of Bordeaux. 23. **the League**: the Holy League, an alliance of Catholic leaders in France, active in the religious wars of the late sixteenth century.

not allow. But though a biblical plainness coupled with a most uncanonical levity may shut his pages to many sensitive readers, yet the offense is superficial. He parades it: he makes the most of it: nobody can think or say worse of him than he does. He pretends to most of the vices; and, if there be any virtue in him, he says, it got in by stealth. There is no man, in his opinion, who has not deserved hanging five or six times; and he pretends no exception in his own behalf. "Five or six as ridiculous stories," too, he says, "can be told of me, as of any man living." [24] But, with all this really superfluous frankness, the opinion of an invincible probity grows into every reader's mind. "When I the most strictly and religiously confess myself, I find that the best virtue I have has in it some tincture of vice; and I, who am as sincere and perfect a lover of virtue of that stamp as any other whatever, am afraid that Plato, in his purest virtue, if he had listened and laid his ear close to himself, would have heard some jarring sound of human mixture; but faint and remote and only to be perceived by himself." [25]

Here is an impatience and fastidiousness at color or pretence of any kind. He has been in courts so long as to have conceived a furious disgust at appearances; he will indulge himself with a little cursing and swearing; he will talk with sailors and gipsies, use flash and street ballads; he has stayed in-doors till he is deadly sick; he will to the open air, though it rain bullets. He has seen too much of gentlemen of the long robe, until he wishes for cannibals; and is so nervous, by factitious life, that he thinks the more barbarous man is, the better he is. He likes his saddle. You may read theology, and grammar, and metaphysics elsewhere. Whatever you get here shall smack of the earth and of real life, sweet, or smart, or stinging. He makes no hesitation to entertain you with the records of his disease, and his journey to Italy is quite full of that matter.[26] He took and kept this position of equilibrium. Over his name he drew an emblematic pair of scales, and wrote *Que sçais-je?* [27] under it. As I look at his effigy opposite the title-page, I seem to hear him say, "You may play old Poz,[28] if you will; you may rail and exaggerate,—I stand here for truth, and will not, for all the states and churches and revenues and personal reputations of Europe, overstate the dry fact, as I see it; I will rather mumble and prose about what I certainly know,—my house and barns; my father, my wife and my tenants; my old lean bald pate; my knives and forks; what meats I eat and what drinks I prefer, and a hundred straws just as ridiculous,—than I will write, with a fine crowquill, a fine romance. I like gray days, and autumn and winter weather. I am gray and autumnal myself, and think an undress and old shoes that do not pinch my feet, and old friends who do not constrain me, and plain topics where I do not need to strain myself and pump my brains, the most suitable. Our condition as men is risky and ticklish enough. One cannot be sure of himself and his fortune an hour, but he may be whisked off into some pitiable or ridiculous plight. Why should I vapor and play the philosopher, instead of ballasting, the best I can, this dancing balloon? So, at least, I live within compass, keep myself ready for action, and can shoot the gulf at last with decency. If there be anything farcical in such a life, the blame is not mine: let it lie at fate's and nature's door."

The Essays, therefore, are an entertaining soliloquy on every random topic that comes into his head; treating every thing without ceremony, yet with masculine sense. There have been men with deeper insight; but, one would say, never a man with such abundance of thoughts: he is never dull, never insincere, and has the genius to make the reader care for all that he cares for.

The sincerity and marrow of the man reaches to his sentences. I know not anywhere the book that seems less written. It is the language of conversation transferred to a book. Cut these words, and they would bleed; they are vascular and alive. One has the same pleasure in it that he feels in listening to the necessary speech of men about their work, when any unusual circumstance gives momentary importance to the dialogue. For blacksmiths and teamsters do not trip in their speech; it is a shower of bullets. It is Cambridge men who correct themselves and begin again at every half sentence, and, moreover, will pun, and refine too much, and swerve from the matter to the expression. Montaigne talks with shrewdness, knows the world and books and himself, and uses the positive degree; never shrieks, or protests, or prays: no weakness, no convulsion, no superlative: does not wish to jump out of his skin, or play any antics, or annihilate space or time, but is stout and solid; tastes every moment of the day; likes pain because it makes him feel himself and realize

24. **"Five . . . living"**: See Montaigne's essay, "Of Three Kinds of Society," *Essays*, Book III, Chap. 3. 25. **"When . . . himself"**: See Montaigne's essay, "We Taste Nothing in Its Pure State," *Essays*, Book II, Chap. 20. 26. **his . . . matter**: Montaigne made a long journey through Germany, Switzerland, and Italy in 1580–81; his journal account of these travels was published in 1774. 27. ***Que sçais-je:*** "What do I know?" 28. **old Poz**: anyone perfectly confident of the soundness of his own opinions. (In Maria Edgeworth's dramatic sketch, "Old Poz," in *The Parent's Assistant; or, Stories for Children*, one character, Justice Headstrong, who is constantly using the expression, "That's poz!" is given this nickname by one of the others.)

things; as we pinch ourselves to know that we are awake. He keeps the plain; he rarely mounts or sinks; likes to feel solid ground and the stones underneath. His writing has no enthusiasms,[29] no aspiration; contented, self-respecting and keeping the middle of the road. There is but one exception,—in his love for Socrates. In speaking of him, for once his cheek flushes and his style rises to passion.

Montaigne died of a quinsy, at the age of sixty, in 1592. When he came to die he caused the mass to be celebrated in his chamber. At the age of thirty-three, he had been married. "But," he says, "might I have had my own will, I would not have married Wisdom herself, if she would have had me: but 'tis to much purpose to evade it, the common custom and use of life will have it so. Most of my actions are guided by example, not choice." [30] In the hour of death, he gave the same weight to custom. *Que sçais-je?* What do I know?

This book of Montaigne the world has endorsed by translating it into all tongues and printing seventy-five editions of it in Europe; and that, too, a circulation somewhat chosen, namely among courtiers, soldiers, princes, men of the world and men of wit and generosity.

Shall we say that Montaigne has spoken wisely, and given the right and permanent expression of the human mind, on the conduct of life?

We are natural believers. Truth, or the connection between cause and effect, alone interests us. We are persuaded that a thread runs through all things: all worlds are strung on it, as beads; and men, and events, and life, come to us only because of that thread: they pass and repass only that we may know the direction and continuity of that line. A book or statement which goes to show that there is no line, but random and chaos, a calamity out of nothing, a prosperity and no account of it, a hero born from a fool, a fool from a hero,—dispirits us. Seen or unseen, we believe the tie exists. Talent makes counterfeit ties; genius finds the real ones. We hearken to the man of science, because we anticipate the sequence in natural phenomena which he uncovers. We love whatever affirms, connects, preserves; and dislike what scatters or pulls down. One man appears whose nature is to all men's eyes conserving and constructive; his presence supposes a well-ordered society, agriculture, trade, large institutions and empire. If these did not exist, they would begin to exist through his endeavors. Therefore he cheers and comforts men, who feel all this in him very readily. The nonconformist and the rebel say all manner of unanswerable things against the existing republic, but discover to our sense no plan of house or state of their own. Therefore, though the town and state and way of living, which our counsellor contemplated, might be a very modest or musty prosperity, yet men rightly go for him, and reject the reformer so long as he comes only with axe and crowbar.

But though we are natural conservers and causationists, and reject a sour, dumpish unbelief, the skeptical class, which Montaigne represents, have reason, and every man, at some time, belongs to it. Every superior mind will pass through this domain of equilibration,—I should rather say, will know how to avail himself of the checks and balances in nature, as a natural weapon against the exaggeration and formalism of bigots and blockheads.

Skepticism is the attitude assumed by the student in relation to the particulars which society adores, but which he sees to be reverend only in their tendency and spirit. The ground occupied by the skeptic is the vestibule of the temple. Society does not like to have any breath of question blown on the existing order. But the interrogation of custom at all points is an inevitable stage in the growth of every superior mind, and is the evidence of its perception of the flowing power which remains itself in all changes.

The superior mind will find itself equally at odds with the evils of society and with the projects that are offered to relieve them. The wise skeptic is a bad citizen; no conservative, he sees the selfishness of property and the drowsiness of institutions. But neither is he fit to work with any democratic party that ever was constituted; for parties wish every one committed, and he penetrates the popular patriotism. His politics are those of the "Soul's Errand" of Sir Walter Raleigh; [31] or of Krishna, in the Bhagavat, "There is none who is worthy of my love or hatred"; [32] whilst he sentences law, physic, divinity, commerce and custom. He is a reformer; yet he is no better member of the philanthropic association. It turns out that he is not the champion of the operative, the pauper, the prisoner, the slave. It stands in his

29. **no enthusiasms:** The essay "Of Friendship" (Book I, Chap. 28) would seem to suggest another exception. Montaigne's love for his friend Étienne de la Boétie. 30. **"But . . . choice":** See Montaigne's essay, "Of Some Verses of Virgil," *Essays*, Book III, Chap. 5.

31. **the "Soul's Errand" of Sir Walter Raleigh:** This poem is also entitled "The Lie" ("Go, soul, the body's guest, / Upon a thankless errand"). 32. **"There . . . hatred":** See Lecture IX of Sir Charles Wilkins's translation of the Bhagavad-Gita or Chap. 9 of the translation by Swami Prabhavanada and Christopher Isherwood (see "Brahma," 1–4 n.).

mind that our life in this world is not of quite so easy interpretation as churches and schoolbooks say. He does not wish to take ground against these benevolences, to play the part of devil's attorney, and blazon every doubt and sneer that darkens the sun for him. But he says, There are doubts.

I mean to use the occasion, and celebrate the calendar-day of our Saint Michel de Montaigne, by counting and describing these doubts or negations. I wish to ferret them out of their holes and sun them a little. We must do with them as the police do with old rogues, who are shown up to the public at the marshal's office. They will never be so formidable when once they have been identified and registered. But I mean honestly by them,—that justice shall be done to their terrors. I shall not take Sunday objections, made up on purpose to be put down. I shall take the worst I can find, whether I can dispose of them or they of me.

I do not press the skepticism of the materialist. I know the quadruped opinion will not prevail. 'Tis of no importance what bats and oxen think. The first dangerous symptom I report is, the levity of intellect; as if it were fatal to earnestness to know much. Knowledge is the knowing that we can not know. The dull pray; the geniuses are light mockers. How respectable is earnestness on every platform! but intellect kills it. Nay, San Carlo,[33] my subtle and admirable friend, one of the most penetrating of men, finds that all direct ascension, even of lofty piety, leads to this ghastly insight and sends back the votary orphaned. My astonishing San Carlo thought the lawgivers and saints infected. They found the ark empty; saw, and would not tell; and tried to choke off their approaching followers, by saying, "Action, action, my dear fellows, is for you!" Bad as was to me this detection by San Carlo, this frost in July, this blow from a bride, there was still a worse, namely the cloy or satiety of the saints. In the mount of vision, ere they have yet risen from their knees, they say, "We discover that this our homage and beatitude is partial and deformed: we must fly for relief to be suspected and reviled Intellect, to the Understanding, the Mephistopheles, to the gymnastics of talent."

This is hobgoblin the first; and though it has been the subject of much elegy in our nineteenth century, from Byron, Goethe and other poets of less fame, not to mention many distinguished private observers,—I confess it is not very affecting to my imagination; for it seems to concern the shattering of baby-houses and crockery-shops. What flutters the Church of Rome, or of England, or of Geneva, or of Boston, may yet be very far from touching any principle of faith. I think that the intellect and moral sentiment are unanimous; and that though philosophy extirpates bugbears, yet it supplies the natural checks of vice, and polarity to the soul. I think that the wiser a man is, the more stupendous he finds the natural and moral economy, and lifts himself to a more absolute reliance.

There is the power of moods, each setting at nought all but its own tissue of facts and beliefs. There is the power of complexions, obviously modifying the dispositions and sentiments. The beliefs and unbeliefs appear to be structural; and as soon as each man attains the poise and vivacity which allow the whole machinery to play, he will not need extreme examples, but will rapidly alternate all opinions in his own life. Our life is March weather, savage and serene in one hour. We go forth austere, dedicated, believing in the iron links of Destiny, and will not turn on our heel to save our life: but a book, or a bust, or only the sound of a name, shoots a spark through the nerves, and we suddenly believe in will: my finger-ring shall be the seal of Solomon;[34] fate is for imbeciles; all is possible to the resolved mind. Presently a new experience gives a new turn to our thoughts: common sense resumes its tyranny; we say, "Well, the army, after all, is the gate to fame, manners and poetry: and, look you,—on the whole, selfishness plants best, prunes best, makes the best commerce and the best citizen." Are the opinions of a man on right and wrong, on fate and causation, at the mercy of a broken sleep or an indigestion? Is his belief in God and Duty no deeper than a stomach evidence? And what guaranty for the permanence of his opinions? I like not the French celerity,—a new Church and State once a week. This is the second negation; and I shall let it pass for what it will. As far as it asserts rotation of states of mind, I suppose it suggests its own remedy, namely in the record of larger periods. What is the mean of many states; of all the states? Does the general voice of ages affirm any principle, or is no community of sentiment discoverable in distant times and places? And when it shows the power of self-interest, I accept that as part of the divine law and must reconcile it with aspiration the best I can.

33. **San Carlo:** Saint Charles, Emerson's affectionate nickname for Charles King Newcomb (1820–94), a young friend of his from Providence, R.I., much admired by him and the other Transcendentalists for his intellectual promise—a promise which was not fulfilled by Newcomb's later life.

34. **the seal of Solomon:** According to a Jewish legend, the Archangel Michael gave Solomon, during the building of the Temple in Jerusalem, a magic ring with a seal by means of which he could command all the demons of the earth and press them into his service.

The word Fate, or Destiny, expresses the sense of mankind, in all ages, that the laws of the world do not always befriend, but often hurt and crush us. Fate, in the shape of *Kinde* or nature,[35] grows over us like grass. We paint Time with a scythe; Love and Fortune, blind; and Destiny, deaf. We have too little power of resistance against this ferocity which champs us up. What front can we make against these unavoidable, victorious, maleficent forces? What can I do against the influence of Race, in my history? What can I do against hereditary and constitutional habits; against scrofula, lymph, impotence? against climate, against barbarism, in my country? I can reason down or deny every thing, except this perpetual Belly: feed he must and will, and I cannot make him respectable.

But the main resistance which the affirmative impulse finds, and one including all others, is in the doctrine of the Illusionists. There is a painful rumor in circulation that we have been practiced upon in all the principal performances of life, and free agency is the emptiest name. We have been sopped and drugged with the air, with food, with woman, with children, with sciences, with events, which leave us exactly where they found us. The mathematics, 'tis complained, leave the mind where they find it: so do all sciences; and so do all events and actions. I find a man who has passed through all the sciences, the churl he was; and, through all the offices, learned, civil and social, can detect the child. We are not the less necessitated to dedicate life to them. In fact we may come to accept it as the fixed rule and theory of our state of education, that God is a substance, and his method is illusion. The Eastern sages owned the goddess Yoganidra, the great illusory energy of Vishnu, by whom, as utter ignorance, the whole world is beguiled.[36]

Or shall I state it thus?—The astonishment of life is the absence of any appearance of reconciliation between the theory and practice of life. Reason, the prized reality, the Law, is apprehended, now and then, for a serene and profound moment amidst the hubbub of cares and works which have no direct bearing on it;—is then lost for months or years, and again found for an interval, to be lost again. If we compute it in time, we may, in fifty years, have half a dozen reasonable hours. But what are these cares and works the better? A method in the world we do not see, but this parallelism of great and little, which never react on each other, nor discover the smallest tendency to converge. Experiences, fortunes, governings, readings, writings, are nothing to the purpose; as when a man comes into the room it does not appear whether he has been fed on yams or buffalo,—he has contrived to get so much bone and fiber as he wants, out of rice or out of snow. So vast is the disproportion between the sky of law and the pismire of performance under it, that whether he is a man of worth or a sot is not so great a matter as we say. Shall I add, as one juggle of this enchantment, the stunning non-intercourse law which makes cooperation impossible? The young spirit pants to enter society. But all the ways of culture and greatness lead to solitary imprisonment. He has been often balked. He did not expect a sympathy with his thought from the village, but he went with it to the chosen and intelligent, and found no entertainment for it, but mere misapprehension, distaste and scoffing. Men are strangely mistimed and misapplied; and the excellence of each is an inflamed individualism which separates him more.

There are these, and more than these diseases of thought, which our ordinary teachers do not attempt to remove. Now shall we, because a good nature inclines us to virtue's side, say, There are no doubts,—and lie for the right? Is life to be led in a brave or in a cowardly manner? and is not the satisfaction of the doubts essential to all manliness? Is the name of virtue to be a barrier to that which is virtue? Can you not believe that a man of earnest and burly habit may find small good in tea, essays and catechism, and want a rougher instruction, want men, labor, trade, farming, war, hunger, plenty, love, hatred, doubt and terror to make things plain to him; and has he not a right to insist on being convinced in his own way? When he is convinced, he will be worth the pains.

Belief consists in accepting the affirmations of the soul; unbelief, in denying them. Some minds are incapable of skepticism. The doubts they profess to entertain are rather a civility or accommodation to the common discourse of their company. They may well give themselves leave to speculate, for they are secure of a return. Once admitted to the heaven of thought, they see no relapse into night, but infinite invitation on the other side. Heaven is within heaven, and sky over sky, and they are encompassed with divinities. Others there are to whom the heaven is brass, and it shuts down to the surface of the earth. It is a question of temperament, or of more or less immersion in nature. The last class must needs have a reflex or parasite faith; not a sight of realities, but an instinctive reliance on the seers and believers of realities. The manners and thoughts of believers astonish them and convince them that these have seen something

35. ***Kinde* or nature:** the archaic meaning of "kind." See *Hamlet*, I.ii.65. 36. **goddess . . . beguiled:** See the Vishnú Puráńa, Book V, Chap. 1. Yoganidra is also known as Máyá.

which is hid from themselves. But their sensual habit would fix the believer to his last position, whilst he as inevitably advances; and presently the unbeliever, for love of belief, burns the believer.

Great believers are always reckoned infidels, impracticable, fantastic, atheistic, and really men of no account. The spiritualist finds himself driven to express his faith by a series of skepticisms. Charitable souls come with their projects and ask his cooperation. How can he hesitate? It is the rule of mere comity and courtesy to agree where you can, and to turn your sentence with something auspicious, and not freezing and sinister. But he is forced to say, "O, these things will be as they must be: what can you do? These particular griefs and crimes are the foliage and fruit of such trees as we see growing. It is vain to complain of the leaf or the berry; cut it off, it will bear another just as bad. You must begin your cure lower down." The generosities of the day prove an intractable element for him. The people's questions are not his; their methods are not his; and against all the dictates of good nature he is driven to say he has no pleasure in them.

Even the doctrines dear to the hope of man, of the divine Providence and of the immortality of the soul, his neighbors can not put the statement so that he shall affirm it. But he denies out of more faith, and not less. He denies out of honesty. He had rather stand charged with the imbecility of skepticism, than with untruth. I believe, he says, in the moral design of the universe; it exists hospitably for the weal of souls; but your dogmas seem to me caricatures: why should I make believe them? Will any say, This is cold and infidel? The wise and magnanimous will not say so. They will exult in his far-sighted good-will that can abandon to the adversary all the ground of tradition and common belief, without losing a jot of strength. It sees to the end of all transgression. George Fox saw that there was "an ocean of darkness and death; but withal an infinite ocean of light and love which flowed over that of darkness." [37]

The final solution in which skepticism is lost, is in the moral sentiment, which never forfeits its supremacy. All moods may be safely tried, and their weight allowed to all objections: the moral sentiment as easily outweighs them all, as any one. This is the drop which balances the sea. I play with the miscellany of facts, and take those superficial views which we call skepticism; but I know that they will presently appear to me in that order which makes skepticism impossible. A man of thought must feel the thought that is parent of the universe; that the masses of nature do undulate and flow.

This faith avails to the whole emergency of life and objects. The world is saturated with deity and with law. He is content with just and unjust, with sots and fools, with the triumph of folly and fraud. He can behold with serenity the yawning gulf between the ambition of man and his power of performance, between the demand and supply of power, which makes the tragedy of all souls.

Charles Fourier [38] announced that "the attractions of man are proportioned to his destinies"; in other words, that every desire predicts its own satisfaction. Yet all experience exhibits the reverse of this; the incompetency of power is the universal grief of young and ardent minds. They accuse the divine Providence of a certain parsimony. It has shown the heaven and earth to every child and filled him with a desire for the whole; a desire raging, infinite; a hunger, as of space to be filled with planets; a cry of famine, as of devils for souls. Then for the satisfaction,—to each man is administered a single drop, a bead of dew of vital power, *per day*,—a cup as large as space, and one drop of the water of life in it. Each man woke in the morning with an appetite that could eat the solar system like a cake; a spirit for action and passion without bounds; he could lay his hand on the morning star; he could try conclusions with gravitation or chemistry; but, on the first motion to prove his strength,—hands, feet, senses, gave way and would not serve him. He was an emperor deserted by his states, and left to whistle by himself, or thrust into a mob of emperors, all whistling: and still the sirens sang, "The attractions are proportioned to the destinies." In every house, in the heart of each maiden and of each boy, in the soul of the soaring saint, this chasm is found,—between the largest promise of ideal power, and the shabby experience.

The expansive nature of truth comes to our succor, elastic, not to be surrounded. Man helps himself by larger generalizations. The lesson of life is practically to generalize; to believe what the years and the centuries say, against the hours; to resist the usurpation of particulars; to penetrate to their catholic sense. Things seem to say one thing, and say the reverse. The appearance is immoral; the result is moral. Things seem to tend downward, to justify despondency, to promote rogues, to defeat the just; and by knaves as by martyrs the just cause is carried forward. Although knaves win in every political struggle, although society seems to be delivered over from the hands of one set of

37. "an . . . darkness": See *The Journal of George Fox*, Chap. 1. Emerson adds the word "withal."

38. Charles Fourier: See "New England Reformers," 9 n.

criminals into the hands of another set of criminals, as fast as the government is changed, and the march of civilization is a train of felonies,—yet, general ends are somehow answered. We see, now, events forced on which seem to retard or retrograde the civility of ages. But the world-spirit is a good swimmer, and storms and waves cannot drown him. He snaps his finger at laws: and so, throughout history, heaven seems to affect low and poor means. Through the years and the centuries, through evil agents, through toys and atoms, a great and beneficent tendency irresistibly streams.

Let a man learn to look for the permanent in the mutable and fleeting; let him learn to bear the disappearance of things he was wont to reverence without losing his reverence; let him learn that he is here, not to work but to be worked upon; and that, though abyss open under abyss, and opinion displace opinion, all are at last contained in the Eternal Cause:—

> "If my bark sink, 'tis to another sea." [39]

39. **"If . . . sea"**: from "A Poet's Hope," a poem by Emerson's young friend, Ellery Channing, a poet whom Emerson admired with qualification.

SPEECH ON AFFAIRS IN KANSAS

◇

TEMPERAMENTALLY Emerson was deeply disinclined to engage in controversy and still more averse to taking an active and public part in any sort of reformist agitation, as he confessed in the "Ode Inscribed to W. H. Channing" in 1846 (see p. 577). Despite this intense reluctance on his part, however, to step up into the ring, the adoption in 1850 of the famous Compromise of that year, including as it did a brutally proslavery Fugitive Slave Law, roused such anger in him that he began to find it more and more difficult to hold himself aloof. "This filthy enactment," he wrote in his journal, "was made in the nineteenth century, by people who could read and write. I will not obey it, by God" (*Journals*, VIII, 236). In 1851 he spoke against the law at a public meeting in Concord, and, three years later, he made an even more eloquent address on the subject at a meeting in New York, in which his genius for invective manifested itself in a passionate diatribe against his former idol, Daniel Webster (*Works*, XI, 215–44). The passage in the same year, 1854, of the Kansas-Nebraska Act, repealing the Missouri Compromise and opening up the new territories to the possibility of slavery, aroused him still further, and he followed with alarm and indignation the events that ensued in the territory of Kansas, the virtual civil war between proslavery and free-soil partisans. The violence and bloodshed had not come to an end in the fall of 1856 when Emerson made the following speech at a meeting in Cambridge to raise money for the free state settlers in Kansas.

◇

SPEECH AT THE KANSAS RELIEF MEETING IN CAMBRIDGE WEDNESDAY EVENING, SEPTEMBER 10, 1856

> And ye shall succor men;
> 'T is nobleness to serve;
> Help them who cannot help again:
> Beware from right to swerve.[1]

I REGRET, with all this company, the absence of Mr. Whitman of Kansas, whose narrative was to constitute the interest of this meeting. Mr. Whitman is not here; but knowing, as we all do, why he is not, what duties kept him at home, he is more than present. His vacant chair speaks for him. For quite other reasons, I had been wiser to have stayed at home, unskilled as I am to address a political meeting, but it is impossible for the most recluse to extricate himself from the questions of the times.

There is this peculiarity about the case of Kansas, that all the right is on one side. We hear the screams of hunted wives and children answered by the howl of the butchers. The testimony of the telegraphs from St. Louis and the border confirm the worst details. The printed letters of border ruffians [2] avow the facts. When pressed to look at the cause of the mischief in the Kansas laws, the President [3] falters and declines the discussion; but his supporters in the Senate, Mr. Cass,[4] Mr. Geyer,[5]

AFFAIRS IN KANSAS. 1. **And . . . swerve**: This stanza from the "Boston Hymn" (1863) (see p. 586) was inserted by Emerson's editors as a motto to this speech when it was included, after his death, in the volume entitled *Miscellanies* (1884) (*Works*, XI, 254). 2. **border ruffians**: the free soilers' epithet for the proslavery guerilla bands, mostly from the slave state of Missouri, who poured into Kansas after the passage of the Kansas-Nebraska Act. 3. **the President**: Franklin Pierce (1804–69), a New Hampshire Democrat who had been elected to the presidency in 1852 with strong proslavery support, and who had acted, throughout the Kansas troubles, in undisguised sympathy with that side. Emerson had a very low opinion of Pierce: he described him later in his journal as "that paltry Franklin Pierce" (*Journals*, X, 41) and regarded him as either the worst or the weakest of all the presidents down to that period (*Ibid.*, IX, 528). 4. **Mr. Cass**: Lewis Cass (1782–1866), leading Democratic politician, Senator from Michigan at this time. 5. **Mr. Geyer**: Henry S. Geyer (1790–1859), Senator from Missouri; defended the "border ruffians" and was later the leading attorney for the slave-owner in the Dred Scott case.

Mr. Hunter,[6] speak out, and declare the intolerable atrocity of the code. It is a maxim that all party spirit produces the incapacity to receive natural impressions from facts; and our recent political history has abundantly borne out the maxim. But these details that have come from Kansas are so horrible, that the hostile press have but one word in reply, namely, that it is all exaggeration, 't is an Abolition lie. Do the Committee of Investigation say that the outrages have been overstated? Does their dismal catalogue of private tragedies show it? Do the private letters? Is it an exaggeration, that Mr. Hopps of Somerville, Mr. Hoyt of Deerfield, Mr. Jennison of Groton, Mr. Phillips of Berkshire, have been murdered? That Mr. Robinson of Fitchburg[7] has been imprisoned? Rev. Mr. Nute of Springfield seized, and up to this time we have no tidings of his fate?

In these calamities under which they suffer, and the worst which threaten them, the people of Kansas ask for bread, clothes, arms and men, to save them alive, and enable them to stand against these enemies of the human race. They have a right to be helped, for they have helped themselves.

This aid must be sent, and this is not to be doled out as an ordinary charity; but bestowed up to the magnitude of the want, and, as has been elsewhere said, "on the scale of a national action." I think we are to give largely, lavishly, to these men. And we must prepare to do it. We must learn to do with less, live in a smaller tenement, sell our apple-trees, our acres, our pleasant houses. I know people who are making haste to reduce their expenses and pay their debts, not with a view to new accumulations, but in preparation to save and earn for the benefit of the Kansas emigrants.

We must have aid from individuals,—we must also have aid from the state. I know that the last legislature refused that aid. I know that lawyers hesitate on technical grounds, and wonder what method of relief the legislature will apply. But I submit that, in a case like this, where citizens of Massachusetts, legal voters here, have emigrated to national territory under the sanction of every law, and are then set on by highwaymen, driven from their new homes, pillaged, and numbers of them killed and scalped, and the whole world knows that this is no accidental brawl, but a systematic war to the knife, and in defiance of all laws and liberties,—I submit that the governor and legislature should neither slumber nor sleep till they have found out how to send effectual aid and comfort to these poor farmers, or else should resign their seats to those who can. But first let them hang the halls of the state-house with black crape, and order funeral service to be said for the citizens whom they were unable to defend.

We stick at the technical difficulties. I think there never was a people so choked and stultified by forms. We adore the forms of law, instead of making them vehicles of wisdom and justice. I like the primary assembly. I own I have little esteem for governments. I esteem them only good in the moment when they are established. I set the private man first. He only who is able to stand alone is qualified to be a citizen. Next to the private man, I value the primary assembly, met to watch the government and to correct it. That is the theory of the American State, that it exists to execute the will of the citizens, is always responsible to them, and is always to be changed when it does not. First, the private citizen, then the primary assembly, and the government last.

In this country for the last few years the government has been the chief obstruction to the common weal. Who doubts that Kansas would have been very well settled, if the United States had let it alone? The government armed and led the ruffians against the poor farmers. I do not know any story so gloomy as the politics of this country for the last twenty years, centralizing ever more manifestly round one spring, and that a vast crime, and ever more plainly, until it is notorious that all promotion, power and policy are dictated from one source,—illustrating the fatal effects of a false position to demoralize legislation and put the best people always at an disadvantage;—one crime always present, always to be varnished over, to find fine names for; and we free statesmen,[8] as accomplices to the guilt, ever in the power of the grand offender.

Language has lost its meaning in the universal cant. *Representative Government* is really misrepresentative; *Union* is a conspiracy against the Northern States which the Northern States are to have the privilege of paying for; the *adding of Cuba and Central America* to the slave marts is *enlarging the area of Freedom. Manifest Destiny, Democracy, Freedom,* fine names for an ugly thing. They call it otto of rose[9] and lavender,—I

6. Mr. Hunter: Robert M. T. Hunter (1809–87), Senator from Virginia; along with Jefferson Davis and Robert Toombs a member of the so-called "Southern Triumvirate" in the Senate; later, during the Civil War, Secretary of State of the Confederacy. **7. Mr. Robinson of Fitchburg:** Charles Robinson (1818–94), formerly a physician in Fitchburg, Mass.; in 1854 a resident agent of the New England Emigrant Aid Company (a free-soil organization) in Kansas; commander-in-chief of the free state troops in 1855; free state governor for a few months in 1856; arrested and imprisoned at Lecompton by the proslavery state government. **8. we free statesmen:** we citizens of the free states. **9. otto of rose:** attar of rose, a perfume.

call it bilge-water. They call it Chivalry and Freedom; I call it the stealing all the earnings of a poor man and the earnings of his little girl and boy, and the earnings of all that shall come from him, his children's children forever.

But this is Union, and this is Democracy; and our poor people, led by the nose by these fine words, dance and sing, ring bells and fire cannon, with every new link of the chain which is forged for their limbs by the plotters in the Capitol.

What are the results of law and union? There is no Union. Can any citizen of Massachusetts travel in honor through Kentucky and Alabama and speak his mind? Or can any citizen of the Southern country who happens to think kidnapping a bad thing, say so? Let Mr. Underwood of Virginia [10] answer. Is it to be supposed that there are no men in Carolina who dissent from the popular sentiment now reigning there? It must happen, in the variety of human opinions, that there are dissenters. They are silent as the grave. Are there no women in that country,—women, who always carry the conscience of a people? Yet we have not heard one discordant whisper.

In the free states, we give a snivelling support to slavery. The judges give cowardly interpretations to the law, in direct opposition to the known foundations of all law, that *every immoral statute is void.* And here of Kansas, the President says: "Let the complainants go to the courts;" though he knows that when the poor plundered farmer comes to the court, he finds the ringleader who has robbed him dismounting from his own horse, and unbuckling his knife to sit as his judge.

The President told the Kansas Committee that the whole difficulty grew from "the factious spirit of the Kansas people respecting institutions which they need not have concerned themselves about." A very remarkable speech from a Democratic President to his fellow citizens, that they are not to concern themselves with institutions which they alone are to create and determine. The President is a lawyer, and should know the statutes of the land. But I borrow the language of an eminent man, used long since, with far less occasion: "If that be law, let the ploughshare be run under the foundations of the Capitol;"—and if that be Government, extirpation is the only cure.

I am glad to see that the terror at disunion and anarchy is disappearing. Massachusetts, in its heroic day, had no government—was an anarchy. Every man stood on his own feet, was his own governor; and there was no breach of peace from Cape Cod to Mount Hoosac. California, a few years ago, by the testimony of all people at that time in the country, had the best government that ever existed. Pans of gold lay drying outside of every man's tent, in perfect security. The land was measured into little strips of a few feet wide, all side by side. A bit of ground that your hand could cover was worth one or two hundred dollars, on the edge of your strip; and there was no dispute. Every man throughout the country was armed with knife and revolver, and it was known that instant justice would be administered to each offence, and perfect peace reigned. For the Saxon man, when he is well awake, is not a pirate but a citizen, all made of hooks and eyes, and links himself naturally to his brothers, as bees hook themselves to one another and to their queen in a loyal swarm.

But the hour is coming when the strongest will not be strong enough. A harder task will the new revolution of the nineteenth century be than was the revolution of the eighteenth century. I think the American Revolution bought its glory cheap. If the problem was new, it was simple. If there were few people, they were united, and the enemy three thousand miles off. But now, vast property, gigantic interests, family connections, webs of party, cover the land with a network that immensely multiplies the dangers of war.

Fellow citizens, in these times full of the fate of the Republic, I think the towns should hold town meetings, and resolve themselves into Committees of Safety, go into permanent sessions, adjourning from week to week, from month to month. I wish we could send the sergeant-at-arms to stop every American who is about to leave the country. Send home every one who is abroad, lest they should find no country to return to. Come home and stay at home, while there is a country to save. When it is lost it will be time enough for any who are luckless enough to remain alive to gather up their clothes and depart to some land where freedom exists.

10. **Mr. Underwood of Virginia:** John Curtiss Underwood (1809–73), though a Northerner by birth, was a resident and property owner in Virginia, but as a very outspoken Free-soiler, he found life in that state so uncomfortable for a man of his views that he was forced to give up his residence there.

FATE

◆

¶ IN December, 1851, Emerson gave a lecture on Fate at the Masonic Temple in Boston; it was the first lecture in a course he called "The Conduct of Life," but he seems not to have been satisfied with its original form, for he spoke in a letter to his wife from Cincinnati, a year later, of the "chapter" on Fate as not yet written; presumably, that is, not written in such a form as to satisfy him. In the spring of 1853 he spoke of the essay in a letter to Carlyle as if it were at last satisfactorily composed, but, although he seems to have delivered it as a lecture several times during the following years, Emerson did not publish it until 1860, when it appeared as the first essay in a volume called by the old title, *The Conduct of Life* (*Works*, VI). It is his most sustained treatment of the age-old problem of destiny —or "determinism"—and the freedom of the will, and one of the best illustrations, among his essays, of his dialectical method of dealing with such problems: indeed, he makes that method more explicit in the third paragraph than anywhere else in his published work. Nowhere else, moreover, does he put so emphatically—almost so insistently—the case for a determinist interpretation of experience, as well as for a rather grimly realistic one. But he does so only to move, after many pages, to the antithetical pole, and put the case, however "illogically," for freedom. The distinction he makes is that between physical nature, including human life on one level, as the realm of determinism, and the intellectual and moral world as the realm of free volition. His last word—"Let us build altars to the Beautiful Necessity" (see p. 565)—is one of characteristically chastened hopefulness; of what Stephen E. Whicher has well called Emerson's "agnostic optimism."

◇

Delicate omens traced in air,
To the lone bard true witness bare;
Birds with auguries on their wings
Chanted undeceiving things,
Him to beckon, him to warn;
Well might then the poet scorn
To learn of scribe or courier
Hints writ in vaster character;
And on his mind, at dawn of day,
Soft shadows of the evening lay.
For the prevision is allied
Unto the thing so signified;
Or say, the foresight that awaits
Is the same Genius that creates.

IT CHANCED during one winter a few years ago, that our cities were bent on discussing the theory of the Age. By an odd coincidence, four or five noted men were each reading a discourse to the citizens of Boston or New York, on the Spirit of the Times.[1] It so happened that the subject had the same prominence in some remarkable pamphlets and journals issued in London in the same season.[2] To me, however, the question of the times resolved itself into a practical question of the conduct of life. How shall I live? We are incompetent to solve the times. Our geometry cannot span the huge orbits of the prevailing ideas, behold their return and reconcile their opposition. We can only obey our own polarity. 'Tis fine for us to speculate and elect our course, if we must accept an irresistible dictation.

In our first steps to gain our wishes we come upon immovable limitations. We are fired with the hope to reform men. After many experiments we find that we must begin earlier,—at school. But the boys and girls are not docile; we can make nothing of them. We decide that they are not of good stock. We must begin our reform earlier still,—at generation: that is to say, there is Fate, or laws of the world.

But if there be irresistible dictation, this dictation understands itself. If we must accept Fate, we are not less compelled to affirm liberty, the significance of the individual, the grandeur of duty, the power of character. This is true, and that other is true. But our geometry cannot span these extreme points and reconcile them. What to do? By obeying each thought frankly, by harping, or, if you will, pounding on each string, we learn at last its power. By the same obedience to other thoughts we learn theirs, and then comes some reasonable hope of harmonizing them. We are sure that, though we know not how, necessity does comport with liberty, the individual with the world, my polarity with the spirit of the times. The riddle of the age has for each a private solution. If one would study his own time, it must be by this method of taking up in turn each of the leading topics which belong to our scheme of human life, and by firmly stating all that is agreeable to experience on one, and doing the same justice to the opposing facts in the others, the true limitations will appear. Any excess of emphasis on one part would be corrected, and a just balance would be made.

But let us honestly state the facts. Our America has a bad name for superficialness. Great men, great nations, have not been boasters and buffoons, but perceivers of the terror of life, and have manned themselves to face it. The Spartan, embodying his religion in his country, dies before its majesty without a question. The Turk, who believes his doom is written on the iron leaf in the moment when he entered the world, rushes on the enemy's saber with undivided will. The Turk, the Arab, the Persian, accepts the foreordained fate:—

FATE. 1. **By . . . Times:** On January 29, 1850, Emerson himself had lectured on "The Spirit of the Times" to a large audience in New York (see Jeanne Kronman, "Three Unpublished Lectures of Ralph Waldo Emerson," *New England Quarterly*, XIX [1946], 98 ff.). 2. **in the same season:** This phrase is very approximate if Emerson has in mind *The Spirit of the Age*, by William Hazlitt (1825), and R. H. Horne's *A New Spirit of the Age* (1844).

"On two days, it steads not to run from thy grave,
The appointed, and the unappointed day;
On the first, neither balm nor physician can save,
Nor thee, on the second, the Universe slay." [3]

The Hindu under the wheel is as firm. Our Calvinists in the last generation had something of the same dignity. They felt that the weight of the Universe held them down to their place. What could *they* do? Wise men feel that there is something which cannot be talked or voted away,—a strap or belt which girds the world:—

"The Destinee, ministre general,
That executeth in the world over al,
The purveiance that God hath seen beforne,
So strong it is, that though the world had sworne
The contrary of a thing by yea or nay,
Yet sometime it shall fallen on a day
That falleth not oft in a thousand yeer;
For certainly, our appetités here,
Be it of warre, or pees, or hate, or love,
All this is ruled by the sight above." [4]

CHAUCER: *The Knighte's Tale.*

The Greek Tragedy expressed the same sense. "Whatever is fated that will take place. The great immense mind of Jove is not to be transgressed." [5]

Savages cling to a local god of one tribe or town. The broad ethics of Jesus were quickly narrowed to village theologies, which preach an election or favoritism. And now and then an amiable parson, like Jung Stilling [6] or Robert Huntington,[7] believes in a pistareen-Providence,[8] which, whenever the good man wants a dinner, makes that somebody shall knock at his door and leave a half-dollar. But Nature is no sentimentalist,—does not cosset or pamper us. We must see that the world is rough and surly, and will not mind drowning a man or a woman, but swallows your ship like a grain of dust. The cold, inconsiderate of persons, tingles your blood, benumbs your feet, freezes a man like an apple. The diseases, the elements, fortune, gravity, lightning, respect no persons. The way of Providence is a little rude. The habit of snake and spider, the snap of the tiger and other leapers and bloody jumpers, the crackle of the bones of his prey in the coil of the anaconda,—these are in the system, and our habits are like theirs. You have just dined, and however scrupulously the slaughterhouse is concealed in the graceful distance of miles, there is complicity, expensive races,—race living at the expense of race. The planet is liable to shocks from comets, perturbations from planets, rendings from earthquake and volcano, alterations of climate, precessions of equinoxes. Rivers dry up by opening of the forest. The sea changes its bed. Towns and counties fall into it. At Lisbon an earthquake killed men like flies.[9] At Naples three years ago ten thousand persons were crushed in a few minutes.[10] The scurvy at sea, the sword of the climate in the west of Africa, at Cayenne, at Panama, at New Orleans, cut off men like a massacre. Our western prairie shakes with fever and ague. The cholera, the small-pox, have proved as mortal to some tribes as a frost to the crickets, which, having filled the summer with noise, are silenced by a fall of the temperature of one night. Without uncovering what does not concern us, or counting how many species of parasites hang on a bombyx,[11] or groping after intestinal parasites or infusory [12] biters, or the obscurities of alternate generation,—the forms of the shark, the *labrus,*[13] the jaw of the sea-wolf paved with crushing teeth, the weapons of the grampus, and other warriors hidden in the sea, are hints of ferocity in the interiors of nature. Let us not deny it up and down. Providence has a wild, rough, incalculable road to its end, and it is of no use to try to whitewash its huge, mixed instrumentalities, or to dress up that terrific benefactor in a clean shirt and white neckcloth of a student in divinity.

Will you say, the disasters which threaten mankind are exceptional, and one need not lay his account for cataclysms every day? Aye, but what happens once may happen again, and so long as these strokes are not to be parried by us they must be feared.

But these shocks and ruins are less destructive to us than the stealthy power of other laws which act on us daily. An expense of ends to means is fate;

3. **"On . . . slay"**: From the Persian poet Ali ben Abu as translated by Emerson from the German translation by von Hammer-Purgstall. 4. **"The . . . above"**: See "The Knight's Tale," ll. 805–14. Emerson quotes the passage with several changes in the spelling—deliberately, says his editor (*Works*, VI, 338). 5. **"Whatever . . . transgressed"**: See Aeschylus, *The Suppliants*, ll. 1047–49. 6. **Jung Stilling:** Johann Heinrich Jung (1740–1817), better-known by his assumed name, Heinrich Stilling; German physician and mystical writer, a friend of Goethe, who gives a kindly account of him in his autobiography, *Poetry and Truth.* 7. **Robert Huntington:** probably a slip of memory for William Huntington (1745–1813), an eccentric but popular English preacher, who appended to his name the initials S. S.—Sinner Saved—and, among other prophecies, predicted the downfall of the papacy in about the year 1870. 8. **pistareen-Providence:** A pistareen is a Spanish coin of trifling value.

9. **At . . . flies:** the earthquake of 1755 which destroyed virtually the whole city and was one of the events that impelled Voltaire to write *Candide.* 10. **At . . . minutes:** On December 17, 1857, the whole Kingdom of Naples was shaken by a severe earthquake which partly destroyed several villages, caused widespread ruin in the city of Naples, and killed some thousands of people. 11. **bombyx:** the moth of the silkworm. 12. **infusory:** pertaining to the Infusoria, microscopic marine animals. 13. ***labrus:*** a kind of predatory fish, thick-lipped (whence the name), belonging to the rockfish family, of which Emerson might have read in Cuvier's *Règne Animal.*

—organization tyrannizing over character. The menagerie, or forms and powers of the spine, is a book of fate; the bill of the bird, the skull of the snake, determines tyrannically its limits. So is the scale of races, of temperaments; so is sex; so is climate; so is the reaction of talents imprisoning the vital power in certain directions. Every spirit makes its house; but afterwards the house confines the spirit.

The gross lines are legible to the dull; the cabman is phrenologist so far, he looks in your face to see if his shilling is sure. A dome of brow denotes one thing, a pot-belly another; a squint, a pug-nose, mats of hair, the pigment of the epidermis, betray character. People seem sheathed in their tough organization. Ask Spurzheim,[14] ask the doctors, ask Quételet [15] if temperaments decide nothing?—or if there be anything they do not decide? Read the description in medical books of the four temperaments [16] and you will think you are reading your own thoughts which you had not yet told. Find the part which black eyes and which blue eyes play severally in the company. How shall a man escape from his ancestors, or draw off from his veins the black drop which he drew from his father's or his mother's life? It often appears in a family as if all the qualities of the progenitors were potted in several jars,—some ruling quality in each son or daughter of the house; and sometimes the unmixed temperament, the rank unmitigated elixir, the family vice is drawn off in a separate individual and the others are proportionally relieved. We sometimes see a change of expression in our companion and say his father or his mother comes to the windows of his eyes, and sometimes a remote relative. In different hours a man represents each of several of his ancestors, as if there were seven or eight of us rolled up in each man's skin,—seven or eight ancestors at least; and they constitute the variety of notes for that new piece of music which his life is. At the corner of the street you read the possibility of each passenger in the facial angle, in the complexion, in the depth of his eye. His parentage determines it. Men are what their mothers made them. You may as well ask a loom which weaves huckabuck [17] why it does not make cashmere, as expect poetry from this engineer, or a chemical discovery from that jobber. Ask the digger in the ditch to explain Newton's laws; the fine organs of his brain have been pinched by overwork and squalid poverty from father to son for a hundred years. When each comes forth from his mother's womb, the gate of gifts closes behind him. Let him value his hands and feet, he has but one pair. So he has but one future, and that is already predetermined in his lobes and described in that little fatty face, pig-eye, and squat form. All the privilege and all the legislation of the world cannot meddle or help to make a poet or a prince of him.

Jesus said, "When he looketh on her, he hath committed adultery." [18] But he is an adulterer before he has yet looked on the woman, by the superfluity of animal and the defect of thought in his constitution. Who meets him, or who meets her, in the street, sees that they are ripe to be each other's victim.

In certain men digestion and sex absorb the vital force, and the stronger these are, the individual is so much weaker. The more of these drones perish, the better for the hive. If, later, they give birth to some superior individual, with force enough to add to this animal a new aim and a complete apparatus to work it out, all the ancestors are gladly forgotten. Most men and most women are merely one couple more. Now and then one has a new cell or camarilla [19] opened in his brain,—an architectural, a musical, or a philological knack; some stray taste or talent for flowers, or chemistry, or pigments, or story-telling; a good hand for drawing, a good foot for dancing, an athletic frame for wide journeying, etc.—which skill nowise alters rank in the scale of nature, but serves to pass the time; the life of sensation going on as before. At last these hints and tendencies are fixed in one or in a succession. Each absorbs so much food and force as to become itself a new center. The new talent draws off so rapidly the vital force that not enough remains for the animal functions, hardly enough for health; so that in the second generation, if the like genius appear, the health is visibly deteriorated and the generative force impaired.

People are born with the moral or with the material bias;—uterine brothers with this diverging destination; and I suppose, with high magnifiers, Mr. Frauenhofer [20] or Dr. Carpenter [21] might come to distinguish in the embryo, at the fourth day,—this is a Whig, and that a Free-soiler.

14. **Spurzheim:** Johann Kaspar Spurzheim (1776–1832), one of the principal disciples of F. J. Gall, founder of the pseudo-science of phrenology. 15. **Quételet:** Lambert-Adolphe-Jacques Quételet (1796–1874), Belgian mathematician, virtual founder of the science of statistics. 16. **the four temperaments:** the four psychological types into which classical medical theory divided human beings according to their constitutional make-up; an essentially deterministic doctrine. 17. **huckabuck:** also huckaback; a kind of linen fabric used for toweling.

18. **"When . . . adultery":** a paraphrase of Matt. 5:28. 19. **camarilla:** a small chamber. 20. **Mr. Frauenhofer:** Joseph Frauenhofer (1787–1826), German optician, inventor of improvements in the telescope. 21. **Dr. Carpenter:** William B. Carpenter (1813–85), English biologist, author of *The Microscope and Its Revelations* (1856).

It was a poetic attempt to lift this mountain of Fate, to reconcile this despotism of race with liberty, which led the Hindus to say, "Fate is nothing but the deeds committed in a prior state of existence." [22] I find the coincidence of the extremes of Eastern and Western speculation in the daring statement of Schelling,[23] "There is in every man a certain feeling that he has been what he is from all eternity, and by no means became such in time." To say it less sublimely,—in the history of the individual is always an account of his condition, and he knows himself to be a party to his present estate.

A good deal of our politics is physiological. Now and then a man of wealth in the heyday of youth adopts the tenet of broadest freedom. In England there is always some man of wealth and large connection, planting himself, during all his years of health, on the side of progress, who, as soon as he begins to die, checks his forward play, calls in his troops and becomes conservative. All conservatives are such from personal defects. They have been effeminated by position or nature, born halt and blind, through luxury of their parents, and can only, like invalids, act on the defensive. But strong natures, backwoodsmen, New Hampshire giants, Napoleons, Burkes, Broughams,[24] Websters, Kossuths,[25] are inevitable patriots, until their life ebbs and their defects and gout, palsy and money, warp them.

The strongest idea incarnates itself in majorities and nations, in the healthiest and strongest. Probably the election goes by avoirdupois weight, and if you could weigh bodily the tonnage of any hundred of the Whig and the Democratic party in a town on the Dearborn balance,[26] as they passed the hay-scales, you could predict with certainty which party would carry it. On the whole it would be rather the speediest way of deciding the vote, to put the selectmen or the mayor and aldermen at the hay-scales.

In science we have to consider two things: power and circumstance. All we know of the egg, from each successive discovery, is, *another vesicle;* and if, after five hundred years you get a better observer or a better glass, he finds, within the last observed, another. In vegetable and animal tissue it is just alike, and all that the primary power or spasm operates is still vesicles, vesicles. Yes,—but the tyrannical Circumstance! A vesicle in new circumstances, a vesicle lodged in darkness, Oken [27] thought, became animal; in light, a plant. Lodged in the parent animal, it suffers changes which end in unsheathing miraculous capability in the unaltered vesicle, and it unlocks itself to fish, bird, or quadruped, head and foot, eye and claw. The Circumstance is Nature. Nature is what you may do. There is much you may not. We have two things, —the circumstance, and the life. Once we thought positive power was all. Now we learn that negative power, or circumstance, is half. Nature is the tyrannous circumstance, the thick skull, the sheathed snake, the ponderous, rock-like jaw; necessitated activity; violent direction; the conditions of a tool, like the locomotive, strong enough on its track, but which can do nothing but mischief off of it; or skates, which are wings on the ice but fetters on the ground.

The book of Nature is the book of Fate. She turns the gigantic pages,—leaf after leaf,—never re-turning one. One leaf she lays down, a floor of granite; then a thousand ages, and a bed of slate; a thousand ages, and a measure of coal; a thousand ages, and a layer of marl and mud: vegetable forms appear; her first misshapen animals, zoöphyte, trilobium, fish; then, saurians,—rude forms, in which she has only blocked her future statue, concealing under these unwieldy monsters the fine type of her coming king. The face of the planet cools and dries, the races meliorate, and man is born. But when a race has lived its term, it comes no more again.

The population of the world is a conditional population; not the best, but the best that could live now; and the scale of tribes, and the steadiness with which victory adheres to one tribe and defeat to another, is as uniform as the superposition of strata. We know in history what weight belongs to race. We see the English, French, and Germans planting themselves on every shore and market of America and Australia, and monopolizing the commerce of these countries. We like the nervous and victorious habit of our own branch of the family. We follow the step of the Jew, of the Indian, of the Negro. We see how much will has been expended to extinguish the Jew, in vain. Look at the

22. **"Fate . . . existence"**: probably not a direct quotation from any particular Hindu source, but Emerson's terse summary of the cardinal doctrine of Karma. 23. **Schelling**: Friedrich Wilhelm Joseph von Schelling (1775–1854), German philosopher, author of *A System of Transcendental Idealism* (1800), who had an important influence on Coleridge and, largely through him, on Emerson. 24. **Broughams**: Henry Peter Brougham, Baron Brougham and Vaux (1778–1868), English Whig statesman, proponent of the Reform Bill of 1832, and Lord Chancellor. 25. **Kossuths**: Louis Kossuth (1802–94), Hungarian patriot and statesman, who was the principal leader of the Hungarian revolution in 1848, and who, after the suppression of that revolution, made a visit to the United States. During this trip Kossuth visited Concord, where he met with a cordial reception (May, 1852); Emerson made the address of welcome to him in the Town Hall (see *Miscellanies; Works*, XI). 26. **the Dearborn balance**: the spring balance invented by Henry Dearborn.

27. **Oken**: See "The Poet," 33 n.

unpalatable conclusions of Knox,[28] in his *Fragment of Races;*—a rash and unsatisfactory writer, but charged with pungent and unforgetable truths. "Nature respects race, and not hybrids." "Every race has its own *habitat.*" "Detach a colony from the race, and it deteriorates to the crab." [29] See the shades of the picture. The German and Irish millions, like the Negro, have a great deal of guano in their destiny. They are ferried over the Atlantic and carted over America, to ditch and to drudge, to make corn cheap and then to lie down prematurely to make a spot of green grass on the prairie.

One more fagot of these adamantine bandages is the new science of Statistics.[30] It is a rule that the most casual and extraordinary events, if the basis of population is broad enough, become matter of fixed calculation. It would not be safe to say when a captain like Bonaparte, a singer like Jenny Lind, or a navigator like Bowditch [31] would be born in Boston; but, on a population of twenty or two hundred millions, something like accuracy may be had.

'Tis frivolous to fix pedantically the date of particular inventions. They have all been invented over and over fifty times. Man is the arch machine of which all these shifts drawn from himself are toy models. He helps himself on each emergency by copying or duplicating his own structure, just so far as the need is. 'Tis hard to find the right Homer, Zoroaster, or Menu; [32] harder still to find the Tubal Cain,[33] or Vulcan, or Cadmus, or Copernicus, or Fust,[34] or Fulton; the indisputable inventor. There are scores and centuries of them. "The air is full of men." This kind of talent so abounds, this constructive tool-making efficiency, as if it adhered to the chemic atoms; as if the air he breathes were made of Vaucansons,[35] Franklins, and Watts.

Doubtless in every million there will be an astronomer, a mathematician, a comic poet, a mystic. No one can read the history of astronomy without perceiving that Copernicus, Newton, Laplace,[36] are not new men, or a new kind of men, but that Thales, Anaximenes, Hipparchus, Empedocles, Aristarchus, Pythagoras, Oenipodes,[37] had anticipated them; each had the same tense geometrical brain, apt for the same vigorous computation and logic; a mind parallel to the movement of the world. The Roman mile probably rested on a measure of a degree of the meridian. Mahometan and Chinese know what we know of leap-year, of the Gregorian calendar, and of the precession of the equinoxes. As in every barrel of cowries brought to New Bedford there shall be one *orangia,*[38] so there will, in a dozen millions of Malays and Mahometans, be one or two astronomical skulls. In a large city, the most casual things, and things whose beauty lies in their casualty, are produced as punctually and to order as the baker's muffin for breakfast. *Punch* makes exactly one capital joke a week; and the journals contrive to furnish one good piece of news every day.

And not less work the laws of repression, the penalties of violated functions. Famine, typhus, frost, war, suicide and effete races must be reckoned calculable parts of the system of the world.

These are pebbles from the mountains, hints of the terms by which our life is walled up, and which show a kind of mechanical exactness, as of a loom or mill in what we call casual or fortuitous events.

The force with which we resist these torrents of tendency looks so ridiculously inadequate that it amounts to little more than a criticism or protest made by a minority of one, under compulsion of millions. I seemed in the height of a tempest to see men overboard struggling in the waves, and driven about here and there. They glanced intelligently at each other, but 'twas little they could do for one another; 'twas much if each could keep afloat alone. Well, they had a right to their eye-beams, and all the rest was Fate.

28. Knox: Robert Knox (1791–1862), Scottish anatomist and ethnologist, who, in *The Races of Men, A Fragment* (1850), set forth the view that the various human races are as sharply distinct from one another as animal species. **29. the crab:** the crab apple. **30. the new science of Statistics:** Emerson's son, his editor, quotes from Quételet (see 15 n.): "Everything which pertains to the human species, considered as a whole, belongs to the order of physical facts. The greater the number of individuals, the more does the influence of the individual will disappear, leaving predominance to a series of general facts dependent on causes by which society exists and is preserved" (*Works,* VI, 341–42). Emerson had written in his journal for 1854: "I accept the Quételet statistics. In a million men, one Homer, and in every million [one], and Homer requires Homer to read him" (*Journals,* VIII, 478). **31. Bowditch:** Nathaniel Bowditch (1773–1838), American mathematician, author of the widely used *New American Practical Navigator* (1802). **32. Menu:** more correctly, Manu, legendary author of the Hindu code, *The Laws of Manu,* which in translation proved intensely interesting to both Emerson and Thoreau. **33. Tubal Cain:** See Gen. 4:22. **34. Fust:** Johann Fust (*c.* 1400–66), an early German printer, associated with Gutenberg. **35. Vaucansons:** Jacques de Vaucanson (1709–82), French mathematician and inventor, who made important improvements in the hand-loom, but was perhaps better known in his own time for the ingenious automata he invented, including a mechanical duck that could pick up grains, swallow them, and even digest them. Voltaire called him "the rival of Prometheus." **36. Laplace:** Marquis de Laplace (1749–1827), French mathematician and astronomer, author of the great systematic work, *Mécanique Céleste,* and first propounder of the nebular hypothesis for the origin of the solar system. **37. Thales . . . Oenipodes:** Thales, Anaximenes, Empedocles, and Pythagoras were pre-Socratic Greek philosophers of the fifth and sixth centuries B.C.; Hipparchus was an astronomer of the second century B.C.; Aristarchus, a grammarian of the same period; Oenopides (incorrectly spelled here), a Greek astronomer and mathematician of the fifth century B.C. **38. cowries . . . *orangia*:** kinds of seashell.

•

We cannot trifle with this reality, this cropping-out in our planted gardens of the core of the world. No picture of life can have any veracity that does not admit the odious facts. A man's power is hooped in by a necessity which, by many experiments, he touches on every side until he learns its arc.

The element running through entire nature, which we popularly call Fate, is known to us as limitation. Whatever limits us we call Fate. If we are brute and barbarous, the fate takes a brute and dreadful shape. As we refine, our checks become finer. If we rise to spiritual culture, the antagonism takes a spiritual form. In the Hindu fables, Vishnu follows Maya through all her ascending changes, from insect and crawfish up to elephant; whatever form she took, he took the male form of that kind, until she became at last woman and goddess, and he a man and a god.[39] The limitations refine as the soul purifies, but the ring of necessity is always perched at the top.

When the gods in the Norse heaven were unable to bind the Fenris Wolf with steel or with weight of mountains,—the one he snapped and the other he spurned with his heel,—they put round his foot a limp band softer than silk or cobweb, and this held him; the more he spurned it the stiffer it drew.[40] So soft and so stanch is the ring of Fate. Neither brandy, nor nectar, nor sulphuric ether, nor hell-fire, nor ichor, nor poetry, nor genius, can get rid of this limp band. For if we give it the high sense in which the poets use it, even thought itself is not above Fate; that too must act according to eternal laws, and all that is wilful and fantastic in it is in opposition to its fundamental essence.

And last of all, high over thought, in the world of morals, Fate appears as vindicator, leveling the high, lifting the low, requiring justice in man, and always striking soon or late when justice is not done. What is useful will last, what is hurtful will sink. "The doer must suffer," said the Greeks; "you would soothe a Deity not to be soothed." "God himself cannot procure good for the wicked," said the Welsh triad.[41] "God may consent, but only for a time," said the bard of Spain. The limitation is impassable by any insight of man. In its last and loftiest ascensions, insight itself and the freedom of the will is one of its obedient members. But we must not run into generalizations too large, but show the natural bounds on essential distinctions, and seek to do justice to the other elements as well.

Thus we trace Fate in matter, mind, and morals; in race, in retardations of strata, and in thought and character as well. It is everywhere bound or limitation. But Fate has its lord; limitation its limits,—is different seen from above and from below, from within and from without. For though Fate is immense, so is Power, which is the other fact in the dual world, immense. If Fate follows and limits Power, Power attends and antagonizes Fate. We must respect Fate as natural history, but there is more than natural history. For who and what is this criticism that pries into the matter? Man is not order of nature, sack and sack, belly and members, link in a chain, nor any ignominious baggage; but a stupendous antagonism, a dragging together of the poles of the Universe. He betrays his relation to what is below him,—thick-skulled, small-brained, fishy, quadrumanous, quadruped ill-disguised, hardly escaped into biped,—and has paid for the new powers by loss of some of the old ones. But the lightning which explodes and fashions planets, maker of planets and suns, is in him. On one side elemental order, sandstone and granite, rock-ledges, peat-bog, forest, sea and shore; and on the other part thought, the spirit which composes and decomposes nature,—here they are, side by side, god and devil, mind and matter, king and conspirator, belt and spasm, riding peacefully together in the eye and brain of every man.

Nor can he blink the freewill. To hazard the contradiction,—freedom is necessary. If you please to plant yourself on the side of Fate, and say, Fate is all; then we say, a part of Fate is the freedom of man. Forever wells up the impulse of choosing and acting in the soul. Intellect annuls Fate. So far as a man thinks, he is free. And though nothing is more disgusting than the crowing about liberty by slaves, as most men are, and the flippant mistaking for freedom of some paper preamble like a Declaration of Independence or the statute right to vote, by those who have never dared to think or to act, —yet it is wholesome to man to look not at Fate, but the other way: the practical view is the other.

39. **In . . . god:** Vishnu was one of the three gods of the Hindu Trinity (along with Brahma and Siva) who saved mankind in a series of ten avatars or incarnations. Máyá (otherwise known as Yoganidra) was the goddess of illusion (see "Montaigne," 36 n.).

40. **When . . . drew:** This story of the Fenriswolf or Fenrir is told in the *Younger Edda* ("Gylfi's Mocking," 34). The "limp band" with which the monster was bound was made, we are told, of six things, including the beard of a woman, the breath of a fish, and the spittle of a bird.

41. **God . . . triad:** See Edward Davies, *The Mythology and Rites of the British Druids* (1809), p. 79. A triad, in Welsh poetics, is "a form of composition characterized by an arrangement of subjects or statements in groups of three" (*OED*). William Owen (see "The Poet," 29 n.), in a work which Emerson knew, quotes a typical triad that might well have struck him: "the three primary requisites of Genius: an eye that can see nature, a heart that can feel nature, and boldness that dares follow nature."

His sound relation to these facts is to use and command, not to cringe to them. "Look not on Nature, for her name is fatal," said the oracle. The too much contemplation of these limits induces meanness. They who talk much of destiny, their birth-star, etc., are in a lower dangerous plane, and invite the evils they fear.

I cited the instinctive and heroic races as proud believers in Destiny. They conspire with it; a loving resignation is with the event. But the dogma makes a different impression when it is held by the weak and lazy. 'Tis weak and vicious people who cast the blame on Fate. The right use of Fate is to bring up our conduct to the loftiness of nature. Rude and invincible except by themselves are the elements. So let man be. Let him empty his breast of his windy conceits, and show his lordship by manners and deeds on the scale of nature. Let him hold his purpose as with the tug of gravitation. No power, no persuasion, no bribe shall make him give up his point. A man ought to compare advantageously with a river, an oak, or a mountain. He shall have not less the flow, the expansion, and the resistance of these.

'Tis the best use of Fate to teach a fatal courage. Go face the fire at sea, or the cholera in your friend's house, or the burglar in your own, or what danger lies in the way of duty,—knowing you are guarded by the cherubim of Destiny. If you believe in Fate to your harm, believe it at least for your good.

For if Fate is so prevailing, man also is part of it, and can confront fate with fate. If the Universe have these savage accidents, our atoms are as savage in resistance. We should be crushed by the atmosphere, but for the reaction of the air within the body. A tube made of a film of glass can resist the shock of the ocean if filled with the same water. If there be omnipotence in the stroke, there is omnipotence of recoil.

1. But Fate against Fate is only parrying and defence: there are also the noble creative forces. The revelation of Thought takes man out of servitude into freedom. We rightly say of ourselves, we were born and afterward we were born again, and many times. We have successive experiences so important that the new forgets the old, and hence the mythology of the seven or the nine heavens. The day of days, the great day of the feast of life, is that in which the inward eye opens to the Unity in things, to the omnipresence of law:—sees that what is must be and ought to be, or is the best. This beatitude dips from on high down on us and we see. It is not in us so much as we are in it. If the air come to our lungs, we breathe and live; if not, we die. If the light come to our eyes, we see; else not. And if truth come to our mind we suddenly expand to its dimensions, as if we grew to worlds. We are as lawgivers; we speak for Nature; we prophesy and divine.

This insight throws us on the party and interest of the Universe, against all and sundry; against ourselves as much as others. A man speaking from insight affirms of himself what is true of the mind: seeing its immortality, he says, I am immortal; seeing its invincibility, he says, I am strong. It is not in us, but we are in it. It is of the maker, not of what is made. All things are touched and changed by it. This uses and is not used. It distances those who share it from those who share it not. Those who share it not are flocks and herds. It dates from itself; not from former men or better men, gospel, or constitution, or college, or custom. Where it shines, Nature is no longer intrusive, but all things make a musical or pictorial impression. The world of men show like a comedy without laughter: populations, interests, government, history; 'tis all toy figures in a toy house. It does not overvalue particular truths. We hear eagerly every thought and word quoted from an intellectual man. But in his presence our own mind is roused to activity, and we forget very fast what he says, much more interested in the new play of our own thought than in any thought of his. 'Tis the majesty into which we have suddenly mounted, the impersonality, the scorn of egotisms, the sphere of laws, that engage us. Once we were stepping a little this way and a little that way; now we are as men in a balloon, and do not think so much of the point we have left, or the point we would make, as of the liberty and glory of the way.

Just as much intellect as you add, so much organic power. He who sees through the design, presides over it, and must will that which must be. We sit and rule, and, though we sleep, our dream will come to pass. Our thought, though it were only an hour old, affirms an oldest necessity, not to be separated from thought, and not to be separated from will. They must always have coexisted. It apprises us of its sovereignty and godhead, which refuse to be severed from it. It is not mine or thine, but the will of all mind. It is poured into the souls of all men, as the soul itself which constitutes them men. I know not whether there be, as is alleged, in the upper region of our atmosphere, a permanent westerly current which carries with it all atoms which rise to that height, but I see that when souls reach a certain clearness of perception they accept a knowledge and motive above selfishness. A breath of will blows eternally through the universe of souls in the direction of the Right and Necessary. It is the air which all intellects inhale and exhale, and it is the wind which blows the worlds into order and orbit.

Thought dissolves the material universe by carrying the mind up into a sphere where all is plastic. Of two men, each obeying his own thought, he whose thought is deepest will be the strongest character. Always one man more than another represents the will of Divine Providence to the period.

2. If thought makes free, so does the moral sentiment. The mixtures of spiritual chemistry refuse to be analyzed. Yet we can see that with the perception of truth is joined the desire that it shall prevail; that affection is essential to will. Moreover, when a strong will appears, it usually results from a certain unity of organization, as if the whole energy of body and mind flowed in one direction. All great force is real and elemental. There is no manufacturing a strong will. There must be a pound to balance a pound. Where power is shown in will, it must rest on the universal force. Alaric [42] and Bonaparte must believe they rest on a truth, or their will can be bought or bent. There is a bribe possible for any finite will. But the pure sympathy with universal ends is an infinite force, and cannot be bribed or bent. Whoever has had experience of the moral sentiment cannot choose but believe in unlimited power. Each pulse from that heart is an oath from the Most High. I know not what the word *sublime* means, if it be not the intimations, in this infant, of a terrific force. A text of heroism, a name and anecdote of courage, are not arguments but sallies of freedom. One of these is the verse of the Persian Hafiz, " 'Tis written on the gate of Heaven, 'Woe unto him who suffers himself to be betrayed by Fate!' " [43] Does the reading of history make us fatalists? What courage does not the opposite opinion show! A little whim of will to be free gallantly contending against the universe of chemistry.

But insight is not will, nor is affection will. Perception is cold, and goodness dies in wishes. As Voltaire said, 'tis the misfortune of worthy people that they are cowards; *"un des plus grands malheurs des honnêtes gens c'est qu'ils sont des lâches."* [44] There must be a fusion of these two to generate the energy of will. There can be no driving force except through the conversion of the man into his will, making him the will, and the will him. And one may say boldly that no man has a right perception of any truth who has not been reacted on by it so as to be ready to be its martyr.

The one serious and formidable thing in nature is a will. Society is servile from want of will, and therefore the world wants saviours and religions. One way is right to go; the hero sees it, and moves on that aim, and has the world under him for root and support. He is to others as the world. His approbation is honor; his dissent, infamy. The glance of his eye has the force of sunbeams. A personal influence towers up in memory only worthy, and we gladly forget numbers, money, climate, gravitation, and the rest of Fate.

We can afford to allow the limitation, if we know it is the meter of the growing man. We stand against Fate, as children stand up against the wall in their father's house and notch their height from year to year. But when the boy grows to man, and is master of the house, he pulls down that wall and builds a new and bigger. 'Tis only a question of time. Every brave youth is in training to ride and rule this dragon. His science is to make weapons and wings of these passions and retarding forces. Now whether, seeing these two things, fate and power, we are permitted to believe in unity? The bulk of mankind believe in two gods. They are under one dominion here in the house, as friend and parent, in social circles, in letters, in art, in love, in religion; but in mechanics, in dealing with steam and climate, in trade, in politics, they think they come under another; and that it would be a practical blunder to transfer the method and way of working of one sphere into the other. What good, honest, generous men at home, will be wolves and foxes on 'Change! What pious men in the parlor will vote for what reprobates at the polls! To a certain point, they believe themselves the care of a Providence. But in a steamboat, in an epidemic, in war, they believe a malignant energy rules.

But relation and connection are not somewhere and sometimes, but everywhere and always. The divine order does not stop where their sight stops. The friendly power works on the same rules in the next farm and the next planet. But where they have not experience they run against it and hurt themselves. Fate then is a name for facts not yet passed under the fire of thought; for causes which are unpenetrated.

But every jet of chaos which threatens to exterminate us is convertible by intellect into wholesome force. Fate is unpenetrated causes. The water drowns ship and sailor like a grain of dust. But learn to swim, trim your bark, and the wave which drowned it will be cloven by it and carry it like its own foam, a plume and a power. The cold is in-

42. **Alaric**: King of the Visigoths (*c.* 370–410), conqueror of Rome in 410 A.D. 43. **One . . . Fate!**: Hafiz, the fourteenth-century Persian poet, whom Emerson read in German translation, was one of his favorite poets. For a slightly different version of these lines see Emerson's essay "Persian Poetry" in *Letters and Social Aims* (*Works*, VIII, 245). 44. ***"un . . . lâches"***: "one of the greatest misfortunes of worthy people is that they are cowards."

considerate of persons, tingles your blood, freezes a man like a dewdrop. But learn to skate, and the ice will give you a graceful, sweet, and poetic motion. The cold will brace your limbs and brain to genius, and make you foremost men of time. Cold and sea will train an imperial Saxon race, which nature cannot bear to lose, and after cooping it up for a thousand years in yonder England, gives a hundred Englands, a hundred Mexicos. All the bloods it shall absorb and domineer: and more than Mexicos, the secrets of water and steam, the spasms of electricity, the ductility of metals, the chariot of the air, the ruddered balloon are awaiting you.

The annual slaughter from typhus far exceeds that of war; but right drainage destroys typhus. The plague in the sea-service from scurvy is healed by lemon juice and other diets portable or procurable; the depopulation by cholera and small-pox is ended by drainage and vaccination; and every other pest is not less in the chain of cause and effect, and may be fought off. And whilst art draws out the venom, it commonly extorts some benefit from the vanquished enemy. The mischievous torrent is taught to drudge for man; the wild beasts he makes useful for food, or dress, or labor; the chemic explosions are controlled like his watch. These are now the steeds on which he rides. Man moves in all modes, by legs of horses, by wings of wind, by steam, by gas of balloon, by electricity, and stands on tiptoe threatening to hunt the eagle in his own element. There's nothing he will not make his carrier.

Steam was till the other day the devil which we dreaded. Every pot made by any human potter or brazier had a hole in its cover, to let off the enemy, lest he should lift pot and roof and carry the house away. But the Marquis of Worcester,[45] Watt, and Fulton bethought themselves that where was power was not devil, but was God; that it must be availed of, and not by any means let off and wasted. Could he lift pots and roofs and houses so handily? He was the workman they were in search of. He could be used to lift away, chain and compel other devils far more reluctant and dangerous, namely, cubic miles of earth, mountains, weight or resistance of water, machinery, and the labors of all men in the world; and time he shall lengthen, and shorten space.

It has not fared much otherwise with higher kinds of steam. The opinion of the million was the terror of the world, and it was attempted either to dissipate it, by amusing nations, or to pile it over with strata of society,—a layer of soldiers, over that a layer of lords, and a king on the top; with clamps and hoops of castles, garrisons, and police. But sometimes the religious principle would get in and burst the hoops and rive every mountain laid on top of it. The Fultons and Watts of politics, believing in unity, saw that it was a power, and by satisfying it (as justice satisfies everybody), through a different disposition of society,—grouping it on a level instead of piling it into a mountain,—they have contrived to make of this terror the most harmless and energetic form of a State.

Very odious, I confess, are the lessons of Fate. Who likes to have a dapper phrenologist pronouncing on his fortunes? Who likes to believe that he has, hidden in his skull, spine, and pelvis, all the vices of a Saxon or Celtic race, which will be sure to pull him down,—with what grandeur of hope and resolve he is fired,—into a selfish, huckstering, servile, dodging animal? A learned physician tells us the fact is invariable with the Neapolitan, that when mature he assumes the forms of the unmistakable scoundrel. That is a little overstated,—but may pass.

But these are magazines and arsenals. A man must thank his defects, and stand in some terror of his talents. A transcendent talent draws so largely on his forces as to lame him; a defect pays him revenues on the other side. The sufferance which is the badge of the Jew, has made him, in these days, the ruler of the rulers of the earth. If Fate is ore and quarry, if evil is good in the making, if limitation is power that shall be, if calamities, oppositions, and weights are wings and means,—we are reconciled.

Fate involves the melioration. No statement of the Universe can have any soundness which does not admit its ascending effort. The direction of the whole and of the parts is toward benefit, and in proportion to the health. Behind every individual closes organization; before him opens liberty,—the Better, the Best. The first and worse races are dead. The second and imperfect races are dying out, or remain for the maturing of higher. In the latest race, in man, every generosity, every new perception, the love and praise he extorts from his fellows, are certificates of advance out of fate into freedom. Liberation of the will from the sheaths and clogs of organization which he has outgrown, is the end and aim of this world. Every calamity is a spur and valuable hint; and where his endeavors do not yet fully avail, they tell as tendency. The whole circle of animal life—tooth against tooth, devouring war, war for food, a yelp of pain and a grunt of triumph, until at last the whole menagerie,

45. the Marquis of Worcester: Edward Somerset, Marquis of Worcester (1601–67), author of *Century of . . . Inventions* (1663); described, among other possible inventions, a kind of primitive steam engine.

the whole chemical mass is mellowed and refined for higher use—pleases at a sufficient perspective.

But to see how fate slides into freedom and freedom into fate, observe how far the roots of every creature run, or find if you can a point where there is no thread of connection. Our life is consentaneous and far-related. This knot of nature is so well tied that nobody was ever cunning enough to find the two ends. Nature is intricate, overlapped, interweaved and endless. Christopher Wren [46] said of the beautiful King's College chapel, that "if anybody would tell him where to lay the first stone, he would build such another." But where shall we find the first atom in this house of man, which is all consent, inosculation and balance of parts?

The web of relation is shown in *habitat,* shown in hibernation. When hibernation was observed, it was found that whilst some animals became torpid in winter, others were torpid in summer: hibernation then was a false name. The *long sleep* is not an effect of cold, but is regulated by the supply of food proper to the animal. It becomes torpid when the fruit or prey it lives on is not in season, and regains its activity when its food is ready.

Eyes are found in light; ears in auricular air; feet on land; fins in water; wings in air; and each creature where it was meant to be, with a mutual fitness. Every zone has its own *Fauna.* There is adjustment between the animal and its food, its parasite, its enemy. Balances are kept. It is not allowed to diminish in numbers, nor to exceed. The like adjustments exist for man. His food is cooked when he arrives; his coal in the pit; the house ventilated; the mud of the deluge dried; his companions arrived at the same hour, and awaiting him with love, concert, laughter and tears. These are coarse adjustments, but the invisible are not less. There are more belongings to every creature than his air and his food. His instincts must be met, and he has predisposing power that bends and fits what is near him to his use. He is not possible until the invisible things are right for him, as well as the visible. Of what changes then in sky and earth, and in finer skies and earths, does the appearance of some Dante or Columbus apprise us!

How is this effected? Nature is no spendthrift, but takes the shortest way to her ends. As the general says to his soldiers, "If you want a fort, build a fort," so nature makes every creature do its own work and get its living,—is it planet, animal or tree. The planet makes itself. The animal cell makes itself;—then, what it wants. Every creature, wren or dragon, shall make its own lair. As soon as there is life, there is self-direction and absorbing and using of material. Life is freedom, —life in the direct ratio of its amount. You may be sure the new-born man is not inert. Life works both voluntarily and supernaturally in its neighborhood. Do you suppose he can be estimated by his weight in pounds, or that he is contained in his skin,—this reaching, radiating, jaculating [47] fellow? The smallest candle fills a mile with its rays, and the papillae of a man run out to every star.

When there is something to be done, the world knows how to get it done. The vegetable eye makes leaf, pericarp, root, bark, or thorn, as the need is; the first cell converts itself into stomach, mouth, nose, or nail, according to the want; the world throws its life into a hero or a shepherd, and puts him where he is wanted. Dante and Columbus were Italians, in their time; they would be Russians or Americans today. Things ripen, new men come. The adaptation is not capricious. The ulterior aim, the purpose beyond itself, the correlation by which planets subside and crystallize, then animate beasts and men,—will not stop but will work into finer particulars, and from finer to finest.

The secret of the world is the tie between person and event. Person makes event, and event person. The "times," "the age," what is that but a few profound persons and a few active persons who epitomize the times?—Goethe, Hegel, Metternich, Adams, Calhoun, Guizot, Peel, Cobden, Kossuth, Rothschild, Astor, Brunel,[48] and the rest. The same fitness must be presumed between a man and the time and event, as between the sexes, or between a race of animals and the food it eats, or the inferior races it uses. He thinks his fate alien, because the copula is hidden. But the soul contains the event that shall befall it; for the event is only the actualization of its thoughts, and what we pray to ourselves for is always granted.[49] The event is the print of your form. It fits you like your skin. What each does is proper to him. Events are the children of his body and mind. We learn that the soul of Fate is the soul of us, as Hafiz sings,—

> "Alas! till now I had not known,
> My guide and fortune's guide are one." [50]

46. **Christopher Wren:** English architect (1632–1723), designer of the restored St. Paul's Cathedral in London.

47. **jaculating:** hurling or darting. 48. **Brunel:** Isambard Kingdom Brunel (1806–59), engineer and inventor who designed the first Atlantic steamer, the *Great Western.* 49. **what . . . granted:** The first sermon Emerson preached, in 1826, was inspired by a remark he had heard, while working in the hayfields, made by a Methodist farm laborer, who said that "*men were always praying*, and that *their prayers were answered*" (*Journals*, II, 98 n.). This first sermon, "Pray Without Ceasing," may be found in *Young Emerson Speaks*, ed. by Arthur C. McGiffert (1938). 50. **"Alas! . . . one":** quoted also in "Persian

All the toys that infatuate men and which they play for,—houses, land, money, luxury, power, fame, are the selfsame things, with a new gauze or two of illusion overlaid. And of all the drums and rattles by which men are made willing to have their heads broke, and are led out solemnly every morning to parade,—the most admirable is this by which we are brought to believe that events are arbitrary and independent of actions. At the conjuror's, we detect the hair by which he moves his puppet, but we have not eyes sharp enough to descry the thread that ties cause and effect.

Nature magically suits the man to his fortunes, by making these the fruit of his character. Ducks take to the water, eagles to the sky, waders to the sea margin, hunters to the forest, clerks to counting-rooms, soldiers to the frontier. Thus events grow on the same stem with persons; are subpersons. The pleasure of life is according to the man that lives it, and not according to the work or the place. Life is an ecstasy. We know what madness belongs to love,—what power to paint a vile object in hues of heaven. As insane persons are indifferent to their dress, diet, and other accommodations, and as we do in dreams, with equanimity, the most absurd acts, so a drop more of wine in our cup of life will reconcile us to strange company and work. Each creature puts forth from itself its own condition and sphere, as the slug sweats out its slimy house on the pear-leaf, and the woolly aphides on the apple perspire their own bed, and the fish its shell. In youth we clothe ourselves with rainbows and go as brave as the zodiac. In age we put out another sort of perspiration,—gout, fever, rheumatism, caprice, doubt, fretting and avarice.

A man's fortunes are the fruit of his character. A man's friends are his magnetisms. We go to Herodotus and Plutarch for examples of Fate; but we are examples. "*Quisque suos patimur manes.*" [51] The tendency of every man to enact all that is in his constitution is expressed in the old belief that the efforts which we make to escape from our destiny only serve to lead us into it: and I have noticed a man likes better to be complimented on his position, as the proof of the last or total excellence, than on his merits.

A man will see his character emitted in the events that seem to meet, but which exude from and accompany him. Events expand with the character. As once he found himself among toys, so now he plays a part in colossal systems, and his growth is declared in his ambition, his companions and his performance. He looks like a piece of luck, but is a piece of causation; the mosaic, angulated [52] and ground to fit into the gap he fills. Hence in each town there is some man who is, in his brain and performance, an explanation of the tillage, production, factories, banks, churches, ways of living and society of that town. If you do not chance to meet him, all that you see will leave you a little puzzled; if you see him it will become plain. We know in Massachusetts who built New Bedford, who built Lynn, Lowell, Lawrence, Clinton, Fitchburg, Holyoke, Portland, and many another noisy mart. Each of these men, if they were transparent, would seem to you not so much men as walking cities, and wherever you put them they would build one.

History is the action and reaction of these two, —Nature and Thought; two boys pushing each other on the curbstone of the pavement. Everything is pusher or pushed; and matter and mind are in perpetual tilt and balance, so. Whilst the man is weak, the earth takes up him. He plants his brain and affections. By and by he will take up the earth, and have his gardens and vineyards in the beautiful order and productiveness of his thought. Every solid in the universe is ready to become fluid on the approach of the mind, and the power to flux [53] it is the measure of the mind. If the wall remain adamant, it accuses the want of thought. To a subtle force it will stream into new forms, expressive of the character of the mind. What is the city in which we sit here, but an aggregate of incongruous materials which have obeyed the will of some man? The granite was reluctant, but his hands were stronger, and it came. Iron was deep in the ground and well combined with stone, but could not hide from his fires. Wood, lime, stuffs, fruits, gums, were dispersed over the earth and sea, in vain. Here they are, within reach of every man's day-labor,—what he wants of them. The whole world is the flux of matter over the wires of thought to the poles or points where it would build. The races of men rise out of the ground preoccupied with a thought which rules them, and divided into parties ready armed and angry to fight for this metaphysical abstraction. The quality of the thought differences the Egyptian and the Roman, the Austrian and the American. The men who come on the stage at one period are all found to be related to each other. Certain ideas are in the

Poetry" (*Works*, VIII, 245). **51. "*Quisque suos patimur manes*":** See *Aeneid*, VI.743. The line occurs in the speech of Anchises to Aeneas in the Underworld on the life history of the soul. It may be translated: "Each of us undergoes his own particular penalty." For Emerson here the line clearly signifies the fatality of every man's individual constitution and innate character.

52. angulated: constructed with corners. **53. flux:** used here as a verb; to make fluid.

air. We are all impressionable, for we are made of them; all impressionable, but some more than others, and these first express them. This explains the curious contemporaneousness of inventions and discoveries. The truth is in the air, and the most impressionable brain will announce it first, but all will announce it a few minutes later. So women, as most susceptible, are the best index of the coming hour. So the great man, that is, the man most imbued with the spirt of the time, is the impressionable man;—of a fiber irritable and delicate, like iodine to light. He feels the infinitesimal attractions. His mind is righter than others because he yields to a current so feeble as can be felt only by a needle delicately poised.

The correlation is shown in defects. Möller, in his *Essay on Architecture*,[54] taught that the building which was fitted accurately to answer its end would turn out to be beautiful though beauty had not been intended. I find the like unity in human structures rather virulent and pervasive; that a crudity in the blood will appear in the argument; a hump in the shoulder will appear in the speech and handiwork. If his mind could be seen, the hump would be seen. If a man has a see-saw in his voice, it will run into his sentences, into his poem, into the structure of his fable, into his speculation, into his charity. And as every man is hunted by his own daemon, vexed by his own disease, this checks all his activity.

So each man, like each plant, has his parasites. A strong, astringent, bilious nature has more truculent enemies than the slugs and moths that fret my leaves. Such an one has curculios, borers, knife-worms; a swindler ate him first, then a client, then a quack, then smooth, plausible gentlemen, bitter and selfish as Moloch.

This correlation really existing can be divined. If the threads are there, thought can follow and show them. Especially when a soul is quick and docile, as Chaucer sings:—

> "Or if the soule of proper kind
> Be so parfite as men find,
> That it wot what is to come,
> And that he warneth all and some
> Of everiche of hir aventures,
> By avisions or figures;
> But that our flesh hath no might
> To understand it aright
> For it is warned too derkely." [55]

Some people are made up of rhyme, coincidence, omen, periodicity, and presage: they meet the person they seek; what their companion prepares to say to them, they first say to him; and a hundred signs apprise them of what is about to befall.

Wonderful intricacy in the web, wonderful constancy in the design this vagabond life admits. We wonder how the fly finds its mate, and yet year after year, we find two men, two women, without legal or carnal tie, spend a great part of their best time within a few feet of each other. And the moral is that what we seek we shall find;[56] what we flee from flees from us; as Goethe said, "what we wish for in youth, comes in heaps on us in old age,"[57] too often cursed with the granting of our prayer: and hence the high caution, that since we are sure of having what we wish, we beware to ask only for high things.

One key, one solution to the mysteries of human condition, one solution to the old knots of fate, freedom, and foreknowledge, exists; the propounding, namely, of the double consciousness. A man must ride alternately on the horses of his private and his public nature, as the equestrians in the circus throw themselves nimbly from horse to horse, or plant one foot on the back of one and the other foot on the back of the other. So when a man is the victim of his fate, has sciatica in his loins and cramp in his mind; a club-foot and a club in his wit; a sour face and a selfish temper; a strut in his gait and a conceit in his affection; or is ground to powder by the vice of his race;—he is to rally on his relation to the Universe, which his ruin benefits. Leaving the daemon who suffers, he is to take sides with the Deity who secures universal benefit by his pain.

To offset the drag of temperament and race, which pulls down, learn this lesson, namely, that by the cunning co-presence of two elements, which is throughout nature, whatever lames or paralyzes you draws in with it the divinity, in some form, to repay. A good intention clothes itself with sudden power. When a god wishes to ride, any chip or pebble will bud and shoot out winged feet and serve him for a horse.

Let us build altars to the Blessed Unity which holds nature and souls in perfect solution, and compels every atom to serve an universal end. I do not wonder at a snow-flake, a shell, a summer landscape, or the glory of the stars; but at the necessity of beauty under which the universe lies; that all is and must be pictorial; that the rainbow

54. Möller, in his *Essay on Architecture*: probably Georg Moller (not Möller) (1784–1852), German architect, author of *Denkmäler der deutschen Baukunst*, translated into English as *Essay on the Origin and Progress of Gothic Architecture* (1825).

55. "Or . . . derkely": See Chaucer, *The House of Fame*, Proem, ll. 43–51. The lines are quoted by Emerson with some inaccuracy.

56. what . . . find: See Matt. 7:7.

57. as . . . age: the motto to the Second Part of Goethe's autobiography, *Poetry and Truth*. "In heaps" is a rather colloquial translation of Goethe's more restrained expression, "*die Fülle*" (abundance).

and the curve of the horizon and the arch of the blue vault are only results from the organism of the eye. There is no need for foolish amateurs to fetch me to admire a garden of flowers, or a sun-gilt cloud, or a waterfall, when I cannot look without seeing splendor and grace. How idle to choose a random sparkle here or there, when the indwelling necessity plants the rose of beauty on the brow of chaos, and discloses the central intention of Nature to be harmony and joy.

Let us build altars to the Beautiful Necessity. If we thought men were free in the sense that in a single exception one fantastical will could prevail over the law of things, it were all one as if a child's hand could pull down the sun. If in the least particular one could derange the order of nature, —who would accept the gift of life?

Let us build altars to the Beautiful Necessity, which secures that all is made of one piece; that plaintiff and defendant, friend and enemy, animal and planet, food and eater are of one kind. In astronomy is vast space but no foreign system; in geology, vast time but the same laws as today. Why should we be afraid of Nature, which is no other than "philosophy and theology embodied"? Why should we fear to be crushed by savage elements, we who are made up of the same elements? Let us build to the Beautiful Necessity, which makes man brave in believing that he cannot shun a danger that is appointed, nor incur one that is not; to the Necessity which rudely or softly educates him to the perception that there are no contingencies; that Law rules throughout existence; a Law which is not intelligent but intelligence;— not personal nor impersonal—it disdains words and passes understanding; it dissolves persons; it vivifies nature; yet solicits the pure in heart to draw on all its omnipotence.

ILLUSIONS

◇

❡ LIKE the essay "Fate," this essay appeared first in *The Conduct of Life* in 1860. It is too short to have been, as it stands, a lecture in "The Conduct of Life" series which Emerson had been delivering off and on during the fifties, and its unity of form seems too complete to justify the assumption that it is a mere fragmentary version of one of them. In any case, it is the most poetic expression in his works of Emerson's quasi-Oriental doctrine of Máyá—the illusoriness, the merely phenomenal character, of the world of "experience," and the "central reality" of the Unity that lies behind it. Carlyle was much moved by the beauty of the essay. "The finale of all," he said in a letter to Emerson, "that of 'Illusions' falling on us like snow-showers, but again of 'the gods sitting steadfast on their thrones' all the while,—what a *Fiat Lux* is there, into the deeps of philosophy, which the vulgar has not, which hardly three men living *have*, yet dreamt of!" (*Carlyle-Emerson Correspondence*, II, 276.)

◇

Flow, flow the waves hated,
Accursed, adored,
The waves of mutation:
No anchorage is.
Sleep is not, death is not;
Who seem to die live.
House you were born in,
Friends of your spring-time,
Old man and young maid,
Day's toil and its guerdon,
They are all vanishing,
Fleeing to fables,
Cannot be moored.
See the stars through them,
Through treacherous marbles.
Know, the stars yonder,
The stars everlasting,
Are fugitive also,
And emulate, vaulted,
The lambent heat-lightning,
And fire-fly's flight.

When thou dost return
On the wave's circulation,
Beholding the shimmer,
The wild dissipation,
And, out of endeavor
To change and to flow,
The gas become solid,
And phantoms and nothings
Return to be things,
And endless imbroglio
Is law and the world,—
Then first shalt thou know,
That in the wild turmoil,
Horsed on the Proteus,[1]
Thou ridest to power,
And to endurance.

SOME YEARS ago, in company with an agreeable party, I spent a long summer day in exploring the

ILLUSIONS. 1. **Proteus:** See "Montaigne," 12 n.

Mammoth Cave in Kentucky.[2] We traversed, through spacious galleries affording a solid masonry foundation for the town and country overhead, the six or eight black miles from the mouth of the cavern to the innermost recess which tourists visit,—a niche or grotto made of one seamless stalactite, and called, I believe, Serena's Bower. I lost the light of one day. I saw high domes and bottomless pits; heard the voice of unseen waterfalls; paddled three quarters of a mile in the deep Echo River, whose waters are peopled with the blind fish; crossed the streams "Lethe" and "Styx;" plied with music and guns the echoes in these alarming galleries; saw every form of stalagmite and stalactite in the sculptured and fretted chambers;—icicle, orange-flower, acanthus, grapes and snowball. We shot Bengal lights into the vaults and groins of the sparry cathedrals and examined all the masterpieces which the four combined engineers, water, limestone, gravitation and time, could make in the dark.

The mysteries and scenery of the cave had the same dignity that belongs to all natural objects, and which shames the fine things to which we foppishly compare them. I remarked especially the mimetic habit with which nature, on new instruments, hums her old tunes, making night to mimic day, and chemistry to ape vegetation. But I then took notice and still chiefly remember that the best thing which the cave had to offer was an illusion. On arriving at what is called the "Star-Chamber," our lamps were taken from us by the guide and extinguished or put aside, and, on looking upwards, I saw or seemed to see the night heaven thick with stars glimmering more or less brightly over our heads, and even what seemed a comet flaming among them. All the party were touched with astonishment and pleasure. Our musical friends sung with much feeling a pretty song, "The stars are in the quiet sky," [3] etc., and I sat down on the rocky floor to enjoy the serene picture. Some crystal specks in the black ceiling high overhead, reflecting the light of a half-hid lamp, yielded this magnificent effect.

I own I did not like the cave so well for eking out its sublimities with this theatrical trick. But I have had many experiences like it, before and since; and we must be content to be pleased without too curiously analyzing the occasions. Our conversation with nature is not just what it seems. The cloudrack, the sunrise and sunset glories, rainbows and Northern Lights are not quite so spheral as our childhood thought them, and the part our organization plays in them is too large. The senses interfere everywhere and mix their own structure with all they report of. Once we fancied the earth a plane, and stationary. In admiring the sunset we do not yet deduct the rounding, coördinating, pictorial powers of the eye.

The same interference from our organization creates the most of our pleasure and pain. Our first mistake is the belief that the circumstance gives the joy which we give to the circumstance. Life is an ecstasy. Life is sweet as nitrous oxide; and the fisherman dripping all day over a cold pond, the switchman at the railway intersection, the farmer in the field, the negro in the rice-swamp, the fop in the street, the hunter in the woods, the barrister with the jury, the belle at the ball, all ascribe a certain pleasure to their employment, which they themselves give it. Health and appetite impart the sweetness to sugar, bread, and meat. We fancy that our civilization has got on far, but we still come back to our primers.

We live by our imaginations, by our admirations, by our sentiments. The child walks amid heaps of illusions, which he does not like to have disturbed. The boy, how sweet to him in his fancy! how dear the story of barons and battles! What a hero he is, whilst he feeds on his heroes! What a debt is his to imaginative books! He has no better friend or influence than Scott, Shakespeare, Plutarch and Homer. The man lives to other objects, but who dare affirm that they are more real? Even the prose of the streets is full of refractions. In the life of the dreariest alderman, fancy enters into all details and colors them with rosy hue. He imitates the air and actions of people whom he admires, and is raised in his own eyes. He pays a debt quicker to a rich man than to a poor man. He wishes the bow and compliment of some leader in the state or in society; weighs what he says; perhaps he never comes nearer to him for that, but dies at last better contented for this amusement of his eyes and his fancy.

The world rolls, the din of life is never hushed. In London, in Paris, in Boston, in San Francisco, the carnival, the masquerade is at its height. Nobody drops his domino. The unities, the fictions of the piece it would be an impertinence to break. The chapter of fascinations is very long. Great is paint; nay, God is the painter; and we rightly accuse the critic who destroys too many illusions.

2. **the Mammoth Cave in Kentucky:** In June, 1850, Emerson, on a lecture tour in the West, visited the Mammoth Cave, near Brownsville, Kentucky. His impressions at the time were recorded in a letter to his wife of June 16 (*Letters*, IV, 209–14). In September, 1857, he observed in his journal: "Curious that the best thing I saw in Mammoth Cave was an illusion. But I have had many experiences like that and many men have" (*Journals*, IX, 113). 3. **"The . . . sky":** the song, "Night and Love," beginning "When stars are in the quiet skies," from Bulwer-Lytton's *Ernest Maltravers*, Book III, Chap. 1.

Society does not love its unmaskers. It was wittily if somewhat bitterly said by D'Alembert,[4] *"qu'un état de vapeur était un état très fâcheux, parcequ'il nous faisait voir les choses comme elles sont."* [5] I find men victims of illusion in all parts of life. Children, youths, adults and old men, all are led by one bawble or another. Yoganidra, the goddess of illusion,[6] Proteus, or Momus,[7] or Gylfi's Mocking,[8]—for the Power has many names,—is stronger than the Titans, stronger than Apollo. Few have overheard the gods or surprised their secret. Life is a succession of lessons which must be lived to be understood. All is riddle, and the key to a riddle is another riddle. There are as many pillows of illusion as flakes in a snow-storm. We wake from one dream into another dream. The toys to be sure are various, and are graduated in refinement to the quality of the dupe. The intellectual man requires a fine bait; the sots are easily amused. But everybody is drugged with his own frenzy, and the pageant marches at all hours, with music and banner and badge.

Amid the joyous troop who give in to the charivari, comes now and then a sad-eyed boy whose eyes lack the requisite refractions to clothe the show in due glory, and who is afflicted with a tendency to trace home the glittering miscellany of fruits and flowers to one root. Science is a search after identity, and the scientific whim is lurking in all corners. At the State Fair a friend of mine complained that all the varieties of fancy pears in our orchards seem to have been selected by somebody who had a whim for a particular kind of pear, and only cultivated such as had that perfume; they were all alike. And I remember the quarrel of another youth [9] with the confectioners, that when he racked his wit to choose the best comfits in the shops, in all the endless varieties of sweetmeat he could find only three flavors, or two. What then? Pears and cakes are good for something; and because you unluckily have an eye or nose too keen, why need you spoil the comfort which the rest of us find in them? I knew a humorist who in a good deal of rattle had a grain or two of sense. He shocked the company by maintaining that the attributes of God were two,—power and risibility, and that it was the duty of every pious man to keep up the comedy. And I have known gentlemen of great stake in the community, but whose sympathies were cold,—presidents of colleges and governors and senators,—who held themselves bound to sign every temperance pledge, and act with Bible societies and missions and peace-makers, and cry *Hist-a-boy!* to every good dog. We must not carry comity too far, but we all have kind impulses in this direction. When the boys come into my yard for leave to gather horse-chestnuts, I own I enter into nature's game, and affect to grant the permission reluctantly, fearing that any moment they will find out the imposture of that showy chaff. But this tenderness is quite unnecessary; the enchantments are laid on very thick. Their young life is thatched with them. Bare and grim to tears is the lot of the children in the hovel I saw yesterday; yet not the less they hung it round with frippery romance, like the children of the happiest fortune, and talked of "the dear cottage where so many joyful hours had flown." Well, this thatching of hovels is the custom of the country. Women, more than all, are the element and kingdom of illusion. Being fascinated, they fascinate. They see through Claude-Lorraines.[10] And how dare any one, if he could, pluck away the *coulisses*,[11] stage effects and ceremonies, by which they live? Too pathetic, too pitiable, is the region of affection, and its atmosphere always liable to *mirage*.

We are not very much to blame for our bad marriages. We live amid hallucinations; and this especial trap is laid to trip up our feet with, and all are tripped up first or last. But the mighty Mother who had been so sly with us, as if she felt that she owed us some indemnity, insinuates into the Pandora-box of marriage some deep and serious benefits and some great joys. We find a delight in the beauty and happiness of children that makes the heart too big for the body. In the worst-assorted connections there is ever some mixture of true marriage. Teague [12] and his jade get some just relations of mutual respect, kindly observation, and fostering of each other; learn something, and would carry themselves wiselier if they were now to begin.

4. **D'Alembert:** Jean le Rond d'Alembert (1717–83), French mathematician and philosopher, collaborator with Diderot on the *Encyclopaedia*. 5. ***"qu'un . . . sont":*** that a vaporous state is a very annoying one because it makes us see things as they are. 6. **Yoganidra, the goddess of illusion:** See "Montaigne," 36 n. 7. **Momus:** in Greek mythology, the god of mockery or fault-finding. 8. **Gylfi's Mocking:** The word "mocking" here might also be translated "delusion." Emerson is referring to the first part of the *Prose Edda*. Gylfi is a wise king of Sweden who journeys to Asgard, the abode of the gods, to learn the secret of their knowledge and power. But the gods conjure up a series of "false shows" to beguile him, and in the end, when these have all vanished, Gylfi is presumably unsure of the reality of what he has heard and seen. 9. **the quarrel of another youth:** This youth seems to have been Emerson's younger friend, Ellery Channing (see "Montaigne," 39 n.), who is said to have remarked that "whatever you asked for at a confectioner's, they brought you only one thing, *but there were two kinds of it*" (*Works*, VI, 429). 10. **Claude-Lorraines:** more properly, Claude Lorrain (1600–82), French landscape painter. 11. ***coulisses:*** spaces behind the scenes in a theater. 12. **Teague:** generic name for an immigrant Irish laborer.

'T is fine for us to point at one or another fine madman, as if there were any exempts. The scholar in his library is none. I, who have all my life heard any number of orations and debates, read poems and miscellaneous books, conversed with many geniuses, am still the victim of any new page; and if Marmaduke, or Hugh, or Moosehead, or any other, invent a new style or mythology, I fancy that the world will be all brave and right if dressed in these colors, which I had not thought of. Then at once I will daub with this new paint; but it will not stick. 'T is like the cement which the peddler sells at the door; he makes broken crockery hold with it, but you can never buy of him a bit of cement which will make it hold when he is gone.

Men who make themselves felt in the world avail themselves of a certain fate in their constitution which they know how to use. But they never deeply interest us unless they lift a corner of the curtain, or betray, never so slightly, their penetration of what is behind it. 'T is the charm of practical men that outside of their practicality are a certain poetry and play, as if they led the good horse Power by the bridle, and preferred to walk, though they can ride so fiercely. Bonaparte is intellectual, as well as Cæsar; and the best soldiers, sea-captains and railway men have a gentleness when off duty, a good-natured admission that there are illusions, and who shall say that he is not their sport? We stigmatize the cast-iron fellows who cannot so detach themselves, as "dragon-ridden," "thunder-stricken," and fools of fate, with whatever powers endowed.

Since our tuition is through emblems and indirections, it is well to know that there is method in it, a fixed scale and rank above rank in the phantasms. We begin low with coarse masks and rise to the most subtle and beautiful. The red men told Columbus "they had an herb which took away fatigue;" but he found the illusion of "arriving from the east at the Indies" more composing to his lofty spirit than any tobacco. Is not our faith in the impenetrability of matter more sedative than narcotics? You play with jackstraws, balls, bowls, horse and gun, estates and politics; but there are finer games before you. Is not time a pretty toy? Life will show you masks that are worth all your carnivals. Yonder mountain must migrate into your mind. The fine star-dust and nebulous blur in Orion, "the portentous year of Mizar and Alcor," [13] must come down and be dealt with in your household thought. What if you shall come to discern that the play and playground of all this pompous history are radiations from yourself, and that the sun borrows his beams? What terrible questions we are learning to ask! The former men believed in magic, by which temples, cities, and men were swallowed up, and all trace of them gone. We are coming on the secret of a magic which sweeps out of men's minds all vestige of theism and beliefs which they and their fathers held and were framed upon.

There are deceptions of the senses, deceptions of the passions, and the structural, beneficent illusions of sentiment and of the intellect. There is the illusion of love, which attributes to the beloved person all which that person shares with his or her family, sex, age or condition, nay, with the human mind itself. 'T is these which the lover loves, and Anna Matilda gets the credit of them. As if one shut up always in a tower, with one window through which the face of heaven and earth could be seen, should fancy that all the marvels he beheld belonged to that window. There is the illusion of time, which is very deep; who has disposed of it?—or come to the conviction that what seems the *succession* of thought is only the distribution of wholes into causal series? The intellect sees that every atom carries the whole of nature; that the mind opens to omnipotence; that, in the endless striving and ascents, the metamorphosis is entire, so that the soul doth not know itself in its own act when that act is perfected. There is illusion that shall deceive even the elect. There is illusion that shall deceive even the performer of the miracle. Though he makes his body, he denies that he makes it. Though the world exist from thought, thought is daunted in presence of the world. One after the other we accept the mental laws, still resisting those which follow, which however must be accepted. But all our concessions only compel us to new profusion. And what avails it that science has come to treat space and time as simply forms of thought, and the material world as hypothetical, and withal our pretension of *property* and even of self-hood are fading with the rest, if, at last, even our thoughts are not finalities, but the incessant flowing and ascension reach these also, and each thought which yesterday was a finality, to-day is yielding to a larger generalization?

With such volatile elements to work in, 't is no wonder if our estimates are loose and floating. We must work and affirm, but we have no guess of the value of what we say or do. The cloud is now as big as your hand, and now it covers a county. That story of Thor, who was set to drain the drinking-horn in Asgard and to wrestle with the old woman and to run with the runner Lok, and presently

13. **"the . . . Alcor"**: Mizar and Alcor, two stars in the "handle" of the Great Dipper, known together to the Arabs as "The Horse and Rider." Mizar is said to revolve around Alcor once every 190,000 years.

found that he had been drinking up the sea, and wrestling with Time, and racing with Thought,[14]—describes us, who are contending, amid these seeming trifles, with the supreme energies of nature. We fancy we have fallen into bad company and squalid condition, low debts, shoe-bills, broken glass to pay for, pots to buy, butcher's meat, sugar, milk and coal. "Set me some great task, ye gods! and I will show my spirit." "Not so," says the good Heaven; "plod and plough, vamp your old coats and hats, weave a shoestring; great affairs and the best wine by and by." Well, 't is all phantasm; and if we weave a yard of tape in all humility and as well as we can, long hereafter we shall see it was no cotton tape at all but some galaxy which we braided, and that the threads were Time and Nature.

We cannot write the order of the variable winds. How can we penetrate the law of our shifting moods and susceptibility? Yet they differ as all and nothing. Instead of the firmament of yesterday, which our eyes require, it is to-day an egg-shell which coops us in; we cannot even see what or where our stars of destiny are. From day to day the capital facts of human life are hidden from our eyes. Suddenly the mist rolls up and reveals them, and we think how much good time is gone that might have been saved had any hint of these things been shown. A sudden rise in the road shows us the system of mountains, and all the summits, which have been just as near us all the year, but quite out of mind. But these alternations are not without their order, and we are parties to our various fortune. If life seem a succession of dreams, yet poetic justice is done in dreams also. The visions of good men are good; it is the undisciplined will that is whipped with bad thoughts and bad fortunes. When we break the laws, we lose our hold on the central reality. Like sick men in hospitals, we change only from bed to bed, from one folly to another; and it cannot signify much what becomes of such castaways, wailing, stupid, comatose creatures, lifted from bed to bed, from the nothing of life to the nothing of death.

In this kingdom of illusions we grope eagerly for stays and foundations. There is none but a strict and faithful dealing at home and a severe barring out of all duplicity or illusion there. Whatever games are played with us, we must play no games with ourselves, but deal in our privacy with the last honesty and truth. I look upon the simple and childish virtues of veracity and honesty as the root of all that is sublime in character. Speak as you think, be what you are, pay your debts of all kinds. I prefer to be owned as sound and solvent, and my word as good as my bond, and to be what cannot be skipped, or dissipated, or undermined, to all the *éclat* in the universe. This reality is the foundation of friendship, religion, poetry, and art. At the top or at the bottom of all illusions, I set the cheat which still leads us to work and live for appearances; in spite of our conviction, in all sane hours, that it is what we really are that avails with friends, with strangers, and with fate or fortune.

One would think from the talk of men that riches and poverty were a great matter; and our civilization mainly respects it. But the Indians say that they do not think the white man, with his brow of care, always toiling, afraid of heat and cold, and keeping within doors, has any advantage of them. The permanent interest of every man is never to be in a false position, but to have the weight of nature to back him in all that he does. Riches and poverty are a thick or thin costume; and our life—the life of all of us—identical. For we transcend the circumstance continually and taste the real quality of existence; as in our employments, which only differ in the manifestations but express the same laws; or in our thoughts, which wear no silks and taste no ice-creams. We see God face to face every hour, and know the savor of nature.

The early Greek philosophers Heraclitus and Xenophanes [15] measured their force on this problem of identity. Diogenes of Apollonia [16] said that unless the atoms were made of one stuff, they could never blend and act with one another. But the Hindoos, in their sacred writings, express the liveliest feeling, both of the essential identity and of that illusion which they conceive variety to be. "The notions, *'I am,'* and *'This is mine,'* which influence mankind, are but delusions of the mother of the world. Dispel, O Lord of all creatures! the conceit of knowledge which proceeds from ignorance." [17] And the beatitude of man they hold to lie in being freed from fascination.

The intellect is stimulated by the statement of truth in a trope, and the will by clothing the laws of life in illusions. But the unities of Truth and of Right are not broken by the disguise. There need never be any confusion in these. In a crowded life of many parts and performers, on a stage of nations, or in the obscurest hamlet in Maine or Cali-

14. **That . . . Thought:** This tale is told in the *Prose Edda* (see 8 n.) ("Gylfi's Mocking," 46–47), but it is not in Asgard that Thor is subjected to these tests, but in the "burg" of the giant, Utgard-Loke.

15. **Xenophanes:** See the poem, "Xenophanes," p. 581.
16. **Diogenes of Apollonia:** Greek philosopher of the fifth century B.C. Emerson seems here to be summarizing Fragment 2 of Diogenes. 17. **"The . . . ignorance":** from Aditi's praise of Krishna in the Vishnú Puráña, Book V, Chap. 30. See note on "Brahma," p. 585.

fornia, the same elements offer the same choices to each new comer, and, according to his election, he fixes his fortune in absolute Nature. It would be hard to put more mental and moral philosophy than the Persians have thrown into a sentence,—

"Fooled thou must be, though wisest of the wise:
Then be the fool of virtue, not of vice."

There is no chance and no anarchy in the universe. All is system and gradation. Every god is there sitting in his sphere. The young mortal enters the hall of the firmament; there is he alone with them alone, they pouring on him benedictions and gifts, and beckoning him up to their thrones. On the instant, and incessantly, fall snow-storms of illusions. He fancies himself in a vast crowd which sways this way and that and whose movement and doings he must obey: he fancies himself poor, orphaned, insignificant. The mad crowd drives hither and thither, now furiously commanding this thing to be done, now that. What is he that he should resist their will, and think or act for himself? Every moment new changes and new showers of deceptions to baffle and distract him. And when, by and by, for an instant, the air clears and the cloud lifts a little, there are the gods still sitting around him on their thrones,—they alone with him alone.[18]

FROM

POEMS [1847]

◊

THOUGH he had written verse from a very early age, Emerson was singularly diffident about appearing publicly in the role of a poet; and with one or two exceptions, he published no poems until late in the thirties, when James Freeman Clarke, who had gone to Louisville as minister of the Unitarian Church there, persuaded him in 1839 to contribute "Each and All," "The Rhodora," and one or two other poems to the *Western Literary Messenger*, which Clarke was then editing in Kentucky. After the *Dial* was founded in 1840, with Emerson's blessing and cooperation, he naturally allowed still further poems ("The Problem," "Woodnotes," "The Snow-Storm," and others) to be published in its pages; and at last, in 1847, he made a collection of the verse he had written up to that point, and with considerable hesitation brought out his first volume of *Poems*. Not for twenty years did he publish another book of verse, but in 1867 appeared *May-Day and Other Pieces*, which contained most of the poems he had written in the interval (the title poem, "Brahma," "Boston Hymn," "Waldeinsamkeit," and others). In 1876 he published a third and final volume, *Selected Poems*, mostly made up of poems that had come out in the earlier volumes with the addition of five or six new but unimportant pieces. A scattering of other poems, unfinished or in Emerson's own view not worth publishing, were included posthumously by his editors in an Appendix.

◊

EACH AND ALL

THE theme of this poem—that composition is "more important than the beauty of individual forms to effect"—had been expressed by Emerson in his journal some months before it was written (*Journals*, III, 298); and he came back to the thought later that year (1834) in an entry which reads in part:

> Everything, to be appreciated, must be seen from the point where its rays converge to a focus . . . The shepherd or the beggar in his red cloak little knows what a charm he gives to the wide landscape that charms you on the mountain-top and whereof he makes the most agreeable feature, and I no more [than he know] that part my individuality plays in the All. [*Ibid.*, p. 373]

The reminiscence of the seashells was set down in the former of these entries, and the shepherd or the beggar in his red cloak seems to have lingered in Emerson's memory from his Italian travels in 1833:

> Italy is the country of beauty, but I think specially in the northern part. Everything is ornamented. A peasant wears a scarlet cloak. If he has no other ornament, he ties on a red garter or knee-band. [*Ibid.*, p. 140]

Little thinks, in the field, yon red-cloaked clown
Of thee from the hill-top looking down;
The heifer that lows in the upland farm,
Far-heard, lows not thine ear to charm;
The sexton, tolling his bell at noon,
Deems not that great Napoleon
Stops his horse, and lists with delight,
Whilst his files sweep round yon Alpine height;
Nor knowest thou what argument
Thy life to thy neighbor's creed has lent.
All are needed by each one;
Nothing is fair or good alone.
I thought the sparrow's note from heaven,

18. **they alone with him alone:** an echo of the famous and sublime passage in the *Enneads* of Plotinus (VI.ix), as translated by Thomas Taylor: "This, therefore, is the life of the Gods, and of divine and happy men, a liberation from all terrene concerns, a life unaccompanied with human pleasures, and a flight of the alone to the alone." The whole paragraph is reminiscent also of a passage in the *Phaedo* of Plato (79).

Singing at dawn on the alder bough;
I brought him home, in his nest, at even;
He sings the song, but it cheers not now,
For I did not bring home the river and sky;
He sang to my ear—they sang to my eye.
The delicate shells lay on the shore;
The bubbles of the latest wave
Fresh pearls to their enamel gave,
And the bellowing of the savage sea
Greeted their safe escape to me.
I wiped away the weeds and foam,
I fetched my sea-born treasures home;
But the poor, unsightly, noisome things
Had left their beauty on the shore
With the sun and the sand and the wild uproar.
The lover watched his graceful maid,
As 'mid the virgin train she strayed,
Nor knew her beauty's best attire
Was woven still by the snow-white choir.
At last she came to his hermitage,
Like the bird from the woodlands to the cage;
The gay enchantment was undone,
A gentle wife, but fairy none.
Then I said, "I covet truth;
Beauty is unripe childhood's cheat;
I leave it behind with the games of youth":
As I spoke, beneath my feet
The ground-pine curled its pretty wreath,
Running over the club-moss burrs;
I inhaled the violet's breath;
Around me stood the oaks and firs;
Pine-cones and acorns lay on the ground;
Over me soared the eternal sky,
Full of light and of deity;
Again I saw, again I heard,
The rolling river, the morning bird;
Beauty through my senses stole;
I yielded myself to the perfect whole.

THE PROBLEM

¶ ORIGINALLY entitled "The Priest," this poem expresses Emerson's preoccupation, during the late thirties, with the problem of vocation. He had resigned from the ministry seven years before the poem was written, and by this time he had ceased to preach even occasionally as a substitute for other clergymen, but the beauty and grandeur of the priestly vocation at its highest never ceased to exercise their claim upon his veneration. He came to believe, however, that the role of the priest could be played by other men than the ordained cleric, even by the lyceum lecturer, but especially by the artist. He also came to believe that the artist receives his deepest suggestion from nature herself; the structural forms the architect "creates," for example, owe their beauty and authority to their derivation from the organic forms in nature.

I like a church; I like a cowl;
I love a prophet of the soul;
And on my heart monastic aisles
Fall like sweet strains, or pensive smiles;
Yet not for all his faith can see
Would I that cowlèd churchman be.

Why should the vest on him allure,
Which I could not on me endure?
Not from a vain or shallow thought
His awful Jove young Phidias brought;
Never from lips of cunning fell
The thrilling Delphic oracle;
Out from the heart of nature rolled
The burdens of the Bible old;
The litanies of nations came,
Like the volcano's tongue of flame,
Up from the burning core below,—
The canticles of love and woe:
The hand that rounded Peter's dome
And groined the aisles of Christian Rome
Wrought in a sad sincerity;
Himself from God he could not free;
He builded better than he knew;—
The conscious stone to beauty grew.

Know'st thou what wove yon woodbird's nest
Of leaves, and feathers from her breast?
Or how the fish outbuilt her shell,
Painting with morn each annual cell?
Or how the sacred pine-tree adds
To her old leaves new myriads?
Such and so grew these holy piles,
Whilst love and terror laid the tiles.
Earth proudly wears the Parthenon,
As the best gem upon her zone,
And Morning opes with haste her lids
To gaze upon the Pyramids;
O'er England's abbeys bends the sky,
As on its friends, with kindred eye;
For out of Thought's interior sphere
These wonders rose to upper air;
And Nature gladly gave them place,
Adopted them into her race,
And granted them an equal date
With Andes and with Ararat.

These temples grew as grows the grass;
Art might obey, but not surpass.

THE PROBLEM. **10. His awful Jove:** the gold and ivory statue of Zeus at Olympia, the work of one of the greatest of Greek sculptors, the fifth-century artist Phidias. **19. The . . . dome:** The hand was Michelangelo's, the architect of St. Peter's at Rome.

The passive Master lent his hand
To the vast soul that o'er him planned;
And the same power that reared the shrine
Bestrode the tribes that knelt within.
Ever the fiery Pentecost
Girds with one flame the countless host,
Trances the heart through chanting choirs,
And through the priest the mind inspires.
The word unto the prophet spoken
Was writ on tables yet unbroken;
The word by seers or sibyls told,
In groves of oak, or fanes of gold,
Still floats upon the morning wind,
Still whispers to the willing mind.
One accent of the Holy Ghost
The heedless world hath never lost.
I know what say the fathers wise,—
The Book itself before me lies,
Old *Chrysostom*, best Augustine,
And he who blent both in his line,
The younger *Golden Lips* or mines,
Taylor, the Shakespeare of divines.
His words are music in my ear,
I see his cowlèd portrait dear;
And yet, for all his faith could see,
I would not the good bishop be.

URIEL

¶ THIS "greatest Western poem yet," as Robert Frost has called it with a certain humorous exaggeration in *A Masque of Reason* (1945), is a kind of mythologizing treatment, not without its own humor, of Emerson's challenge to theological orthodoxy in the Address of 1838 at the Divinity School and the alarm this caused in orthodox circles. Like Emerson, Uriel—who, in *Paradise Lost*, is the Archangel of the Sun, and is thus identified with the idea of illumination—startles both "the young deities" (the students at the Divinity School) and "the stern old war-gods" (Andrews Norton and other eminent clergymen) by pronouncing his "sentiment divine"—namely, that there are no straight lines in nature (the rationalism of the Unitarians, inherited from Locke and the eighteenth century, is false to reality); that all things—the universe itself—are round (reality is illogical or paradoxical in a manner of which only the circle or the sphere can be taken as emblematic). Uriel, like Emerson, withdraws temporarily from the tumult of controversy, but "now and then" his voice of "cherub scorn" is heard, like Emerson's voice on the lecture platform, uttering "truth-speaking things," and causing the gods to shake without quite knowing why. For an interesting commentary on "Uriel" see Stephen Whicher, *Freedom and Fate*, pp. 74–76.

It fell in the ancient periods
  Which the brooding soul surveys,
Or ever the wild Time coined itself
  Into calendar months and days.

This was the lapse of Uriel,
Which in Paradise befell.
Once, among the Pleiads walking,
Seyd overheard the young gods talking;
And the treason, too long pent,
To his ears was evident.
The young deities discussed
Laws of form, and metre just,
Orb, quintessence, and sunbeams,
What subsisteth, and what seems.
One, with low tones that decide,
And doubt and reverend use defied,
With a look that solved the sphere,
And stirred the devils everywhere,
Gave his sentiment divine
Against the being of a line.
"Line in nature is not found;
Unit and universe are round;
In vain produced, all rays return;
Evil will bless, and ice will burn."
As Uriel spoke with piercing eye,
A shudder ran around the sky;
The stern old war-gods shook their heads,
The seraphs frowned from myrtle-beds;
Seemed to the holy festival
The rash word boded ill to all;
The balance-beam of Fate was bent;
The bounds of good and ill were rent;
Strong Hades could not keep his own,
But all slid to confusion.

A sad self-knowledge, withering, fell
On the beauty of Uriel;
In heaven once eminent, the god
Withdrew, that hour, into his cloud;
Whether doomed to long gyration
In the sea of generation,
Or by knowledge grown too bright

55. the prophet: Moses; see Exod. 31:18. **65. Old *Chrysostom:*** St. John Chrysostom, bishop of Antioch in the fourth century. The sobriquet "Chrysostom," meaning "golden lips," was applied to him because of his eloquence as a preacher. **67–68. The . . . divines:** Jeremy Taylor (1613–67), bishop of Dromore, one of the greatest of Anglican pulpit orators. **mines:** that is, of golden eloquence.

URIEL. **7. the Pleiads:** perhaps a reminiscence of the Voice out of the Whirlwind in Job (38:31): "Canst thou bind the sweet influences of the Pleiades, or loose the bands of Orion?" **8. Seyd:** alternative spelling of the name of the Persian poet Saadi, used here and elsewhere by Emerson to signify the archetypal Poet. **23. In . . . return:** Frost paraphrases this line in *A Masque of Reason.*

To hit the nerve of feebler sight.
Straightway, a forgetting wind
Stole over the celestial kind,
And their lips the secret kept,
If in ashes the fire-seed slept.
But now and then, truth-speaking things
Shamed the angels' veiling wings;
And, shrilling from the solar course,
Or from fruit of chemic force,
Procession of a soul in matter,
Or the speeding change of water,
Or out of the good of evil born,
Came Uriel's voice of cherub scorn,
And a blush tinged the upper sky,
And the gods shook, they knew not why.

THE WORLD-SOUL

❡ THE conception of a Soul of the World—an *Anima Mundi* or living spirit pervading the whole cosmos and holding it together in unity—is one that Emerson inherited partly from Stoicism, partly from the Neoplatonists; he did not adhere to it literally but found it, as here, a usable symbol of the transcendent Unity he genuinely believed in. This poem gives expression to his sense of the contrast between the ignoble facts on the surface of reality, the meanness of so much of human life superficially contemplated, and the grandeur of the ideal as it shines through these facts in the form of heroic conduct or the beauty of the arts. It gives expression also to his philosophically optimistic conviction that evil is only "good in the making" (see "Fate," p. 561), and that the World-Soul or "patient Daemon" (l. 77) knows how to elicit goodness from everything, however disheartening it may seem to be just in itself.

Thanks to the morning light,
  Thanks to the foaming sea,
To the uplands of New Hampshire,
  To the green-haired forest free;
Thanks to each man of courage,
  To the maids of holy mind,
To the boy with his games undaunted
  Who never looks behind.

Cities of proud hotels,
  Houses of rich and great,
Vice nestles in your chambers,
  Beneath your roofs of slate.
It cannot conquer folly,—
  Time-and-space-conquering steam,—
And the light-outspeeding telegraph
  Bears nothing on its beam.

The politics are base;
  The letters do not cheer;
And 'tis far in the deeps of history,
  The voice that speaketh clear.
Trade and the streets ensnare us,
  Our bodies are weak and worn;
We plot and corrupt each other,
  And we despoil the unborn.

Yet there in the parlor sits
  Some figure of noble guise,—
Our angel, in a stranger's form,
  Or woman's pleading eyes;
Or only a flashing sunbeam
  In at the window-pane;
Or Music pours on mortals
  Its beautiful disdain.

The inevitable morning
  Finds them who in cellars be;
And be sure the all-loving Nature
  Will smile in a factory.
Yon ridge of purple landscape,
  Yon sky between the walls,
Hold all the hidden wonders
  In scanty intervals.

Alas! the Sprite that haunts us
  Deceives our rash desire;
It whispers of the glorious gods,
  And leaves us in the mire.
We cannot learn the cipher
  That's writ upon our cell;
Stars taunt us by a mystery
  Which we could never spell.

If but one hero knew it,
  The world would blush in flame;
The sage, till he hit the secret,
  Would hang his head for shame.
Our brothers have not read it,
  Not one has found the key;
And henceforth we are comforted,—
  We are but such as they.

Still, still the secret presses;
  The nearing clouds draw down;
The crimson morning flames into
  The fopperies of the town.
Within, without the idle earth,
  Stars weave eternal rings;
The sun himself shines heartily,
  And shares the joy he brings.

And what if Trade sow cities
  Like shells along the shore,
And thatch with towns the prairie broad
  With railways ironed o'er?—

They are but sailing foam-bells
Along Thought's causing stream,
And take their shape and sun-color
From him that sends the dream.

For Destiny never swerves
Nor yields to men the helm;
He shoots his thought, by hidden nerves,
Throughout the solid realm.
The patient Daemon sits,
With roses and a shroud;
He has his way, and deals his gifts,—
But ours is not allowed.

He is no churl nor trifler,
And his viceroy is none,—
Love-without-weakness,—
Of Genius sire and son.
And his will is not thwarted;
The seeds of land and sea
Are the atoms of his body bright,
And his behest obey.

He serveth the servant,
The brave he loves amain;
He kills the cripple and the sick,
And straight begins again;
For gods delight in gods,
And thrust the weak aside;
To him who scorns their charities
Their arms fly open wide.

When the old world is sterile
And the ages are effete,
He will from wrecks and sediment
The fairer world complete.
He forbids to despair;
His cheeks mantle with mirth;
And the unimagined good of men
Is yeaning at the birth.

Spring still makes spring in the mind
When sixty years are told;
Love wakes anew this throbbing heart,
And we are never old;
Over the winter glaciers
I see the summer glow,
And through the wild-piled snow-drift
The warm rosebuds below.

THE WORLD-SOUL. **104. yeaning:** bringing forth young.

THE SPHINX

❡ NOTORIOUSLY one of Emerson's more complex and difficult poems, "The Sphinx" has been variously interpreted. Thoreau wrote a long analysis of it in his journal for March, 1841 (*Writings,* VII, 229–37), and Emerson himself furnished a kind of clue in a journal passage quoted by his editor:

> I have often been asked the meaning of the 'Sphinx.' It is this,—The perception of identity unites all things and explains one by another, and the most rare and strange is equally facile as the most common. But if the mind live only in particulars, and see only differences (wanting the power to see the whole—all in each), then the world addresses to this mind a question it cannot answer, and each new fact tears it in pieces, and it is vanquished by the distracting variety. [*Works,* IX, 412]

If it is remembered that the Sphinx is to be thought of *both* as "the world," or the Spirit of Nature, and as, in Thoreau's phrase, "man's insatiable and questioning spirit" (ll. 111–12), and that the Poet has clearly perceived that all things, including the Sphinx and himself, are united in an ultimate identity (ll. 97–104), some of the difficulty of the poem will disappear. Thomas R. Whitaker has discussed it interestingly in "The Riddle of Emerson's 'Sphinx'" (*American Literature,* XXVII, 179 ff.).

The Sphinx is drowsy,
Her wings are furled:
Her ear is heavy,
She broods on the world.
"Who'll tell me my secret,
The ages have kept?—
I awaited the seer
While they slumbered and slept:—

"The fate of the man-child,
The meaning of man;
Known fruit of the unknown;
Dædalian plan;
Out of sleeping a waking,
Out of waking a sleep;
Life death overtaking;
Deep underneath deep?

"Erect as a sunbeam,
Upspringeth the palm;
The elephant browses,
Undaunted and calm;
In beautiful motion
The thrush plies his wings;

THE SPHINX. **12. Dædalian:** cunningly wrought; from the name of Daedalus, mythical builder of the labyrinth of Minos in Crete. "Daedalian," said Thoreau, "expresses both the skill and the inscrutable design of the builder."

Kind leaves of his covert,
    Your silence he sings.

"The waves, unashamèd,
    In difference sweet,
Play glad with the breezes,
    Old playfellows meet;
The journeying atoms,
    Primordial wholes,
Firmly draw, firmly drive,
    By their animate poles.

"Sea, earth, air, sound, silence,
    Plant, quadruped, bird,
By one music enchanted,
    One deity stirred,—
Each the other adorning,
    Accompany still;
Night veileth and morning,
    The vapor the hill.

"The babe by its mother
    Lies bathèd in joy;
Glide its hours uncounted,—
    The sun is its toy;
Shines the peace of all being,
    Without cloud, in its eyes;
And the sum of the world
    In soft miniature lies.

"But man crouches and blushes,
    Absconds and conceals;
He creepeth and peepeth,
    He palters and steals;
Infirm, melancholy,
    Jealous glancing around,
An oaf, an accomplice,
    He poisons the ground.

"Out spoke the great mother,
    Beholding his fear;—
At the sound of her accents
    Cold shuddered the sphere:—
'Who has drugged my boy's cup?
    Who has mixed my boy's bread?
Who, with sadness and madness,
    Has turned my child's head?' "

I heard a poet answer
    Aloud and cheerfully,
"Say on, sweet Sphinx! thy dirges
    Are pleasant songs to me.
Deep love lieth under
    These pictures of time;
They fade in the light of
    Their meaning sublime.

"The fiend that man harries
    Is love of the Best;
Yawns the pit of the Dragon,
    Lit by rays from the Blest.
The Lethe of Nature
    Can't trance him again,
Whose soul sees the perfect,
    Which his eyes seek in vain.

"To vision profounder,
    Man's spirit must dive;
His aye-rolling orb
    At no goal will arrive;
The heavens that now draw him
    With sweetness untold,
Once found,—for new heavens
    He spurneth the old.

"Pride ruined the angels,
    Their shame them restores;
Lurks the joy that is sweetest
    In stings of remorse.
Have I a lover
    Who is noble and free?—
I would he were nobler
    Than to love me.

"Eterne alternation
    Now follows, now flies;
And under pain, pleasure,—
    Under pleasure, pain lies.
Love works at the centre,
    Heart-heaving alway;
Forth speed the strong pulses
    To the borders of day.

"Dull Sphinx, Jove keep thy five wits;
    Thy sight is growing blear;
Rue, myrrh and cummin for the Sphinx,
    Her muddy eyes to clear!"
The old Sphinx bit her thick lip,—
    Said, "Who taught thee me to name?
I am thy spirit, yoke-fellow;
    Of thine eye I am eyebeam.

"Thou art the unanswered question;
    Couldst see thy proper eye,
Always it asketh, asketh;
    And each answer is a lie.
So take thy quest through nature,
    It through thousand natures ply;
Ask on, thou clothed eternity;
    Time is the false reply."

Uprose the merry Sphinx,
    And crouched no more in stone;

She melted into purple cloud,
  She silvered in the moon;
She spired into a yellow flame;
  She flowered in blossoms red;
She flowed into a foaming wave:
  She stood Monadnoc's head.

Through a thousand voices
  Spoke the universal dame;
"Who telleth one of my meanings,
  Is master of all I am."

HAMATREYA

¶ IN THE autumn of 1845 Emerson copied into his journal certain passages from the Vishńu Puráńa, one of the Hindu scriptures he had been reading in translation (*Works,* IX, 416–17). "Hamatreya" is a quietly humorous Yankee version of one of these—a passage from Book IV, Chap. 24, of the Puráńa which had evidently caught Emerson's fancy. The revered sage, Paráśara, is there represented as giving his disciple, Maitreya, a summary account—a kind of Book of the Kings—of the sovereigns who have held sway in the world; at the end of all this he remarks that these great monarchs, with their delusory belief that the earth itself was a possession of theirs and their dynasties' forever, have now all passed away. "Earth laughs," continues Paráśara, "as if smiling with autumnal flowers, to behold her kings unable to effect the subjugation of themselves." He then goes on to repeat to Maitreya the stanzas chanted, as he says, by Earth on the folly of princes, deluded as they are by the conviction of their absolute ownership. See *The Vishńu Puráńa,* translated by H. H. Wilson (1840), pp. 487–89.

Bulkeley, Hunt, Willard, Hosmer, Meriam, Flint,
Possessed the land which rendered to their toil
Hay, corn, roots, hemp, flax, apples, wool and
  wood.
Each of these landlords walked amidst his farm,
Saying, " 'Tis mine, my children's and my
  name's.
How sweet the west wind sounds in my own trees!
How graceful climb those shadows on my hill!
I fancy these pure waters and the flags
Know me, as does my dog: we sympathize;
And, I affirm, my actions smack of the soil."

Where are these men? Asleep beneath their
  grounds:
And strangers, fond as they, their furrows plough.
Earth laughs in flowers, to see her boastful boys
Earth-proud, proud of the earth which is not
  theirs;
Who steer the plough, but cannot steer their
  feet
Clear of the grave.
They added ridge to valley, brook to pond,
And sighed for all that bounded their domain;
"This suits me for a pasture; that's my park;
We must have clay, lime, gravel, granite-ledge,
And misty lowland, where to go for peat.
The land is well—lies fairly to the south.
'Tis good, when you have crossed the sea and back,
To find the sitfast acres where you left them."
Ah! the hot owner sees not Death, who adds
Him to his land, a lump of mold the more.
Hear what the Earth says:

EARTH-SONG

"Mine and yours;
Mine, not yours.
Earth endures;
Stars abide—
Shine down in the old sea;
Old are the shores;
But where are old men?
I who have seen much,
Such have I never seen.

"The lawyer's deed
Ran sure,
In tail,
To them, and to their heirs
Who shall succeed,
Without fail,
Forevermore.

"Here is the land,
Shaggy with wood,
With its old valley,
Mound and flood.
But the heritors?
Fled like the flood's foam.
The lawyer, and the laws,
And the kingdom,
Clean swept herefrom.

128. Monadnoc's head: Monadnock (the usual spelling) is a mountain in southern New Hampshire. "Monadnoc here," says Whitaker, "as in Emerson's poem about it, is the 'grand affirmer of the present tense.' " HAMATREYA. Why Emerson changed the name Maitreya to the form he uses here is not clear: perhaps he simply felt that this latter name was more euphonious; perhaps there is some echo in it of the word "hamadryad," though this would have no literal appropriateness. **1. Bulkeley . . . Flint:** names of some of the early settlers of Concord. One of them, Peter Bulkeley, was an ancestor of Emerson, and in his own time one of the people he most respected in Concord; Edmund Hosmer, a simple and sagacious farmer, was descended from another. (See "New England Reformers," 19 n.)

24. sitfast: sitting firmly, well-established, fixed; cf. steadfast. **39. In tail:** intail, entail; legal term for perpetual ownership of an estate by a succession of heirs.

"They called me theirs,
Who so controlled me;
Yet every one
Wished to stay, and is gone,
How am I theirs,
If they cannot hold me,
But I hold them?"

When I heard the Earth-song,
I was no longer brave;
My avarice cooled
Like lust in the chill of the grave.

THE RHODORA

ON BEING ASKED, WHENCE IS THE FLOWER?

In May, when sea-winds pierced our solitudes,
I found the fresh Rhodora in the woods,
Spreading its leafless blooms in a damp nook,
To please the desert and the sluggish brook.
The purple petals, fallen in the pool,
Made the black water with their beauty gay;
Here might the red-bird come his plumes to cool,
And court the flower that cheapens his array.
Rhodora! if the sages ask thee why
This charm is wasted on the earth and sky,
Tell them, dear, that if eyes were made for seeing,
Then Beauty is its own excuse for being:
Why thou wert there, O rival of the rose!
I never thought to ask, I never knew:
But, in my simple ignorance, suppose
The self-same Power that brought me there brought you.

1839

THE SNOW-STORM

ONE of Emerson's earliest successful poems, "The Snow-Storm" was probably written in 1835, commemorative of a great snowfall in Concord the preceding winter. The thought of the second part of the poem—the suggestiveness of natural forms to the artist, particularly (here) to the architect—is the thought that he also expressed in "The Problem," and it has an echo in his essay "History" in *Essays: First Series:* "I have seen a snow-drift along the sides of the stone wall which obviously gave the idea of the common architectural scroll to abut a tower" (*Works*, II, 19).

Announced by all the trumpets of the sky,
Arrives the snow, and, driving o'er the fields,
Seems nowhere to alight: the whited air
Hides hills and woods, the river, and the heaven,
And veils the farm-house at the garden's end.
The sled and traveler stopped, the courier's feet
Delayed, all friends shut out, the housemates sit
Around the radiant fireplace, enclosed
In a tumultuous privacy of storm.

Come see the north wind's masonry.
Out of an unseen quarry evermore
Furnished with tile, the fierce artificer
Curves his white bastions with projected roof
Round every windward stake, or tree, or door.
Speeding, the myriad-handed, his wild work
So fanciful, so savage, nought cares he
For number or proportion. Mockingly,
On coop or kennel he hangs Parian wreaths;
A swan-like form invests the hidden thorn;
Fills up the farmer's lane from wall to wall,
Maugre the farmer's sighs; and at the gate
A tapering turret overtops the work.
And when his hours are numbered, and the world
Is all his own, retiring, as he were not,
Leaves, when the sun appears, astonished Art
To mimic in slow structures, stone by stone,
Built in an age, the mad wind's night-work,
The frolic architecture of the snow.

ODE INSCRIBED TO W. H. CHANNING

THIS poem seems to have been written, some time after the declaration of war on Mexico, in the spring of 1846, as a result of some conversation or correspondence with Emerson's younger friend, W. H. Channing, a Unitarian minister and ardent abolitionist, who had spoken in Concord in the summer of 1845. Channing must have attempted to persuade Emerson to take a more vigorous and more public stand against the aggressions of the proslavery forces both in the South and in the North. At this period, though certainly not later, Emerson felt that active and absorbing participation in the public agitation of such questions was not his true role: "I have," he wrote, "quite other slaves to free than those negroes, to wit, imprisoned spirits, imprisoned thoughts" (*Works*, IX, 428).

Though loath to grieve
The evil time's sole patriot,
I cannot leave

THE SNOW-STORM. **9. In . . . storm:** Emily Dickinson was so much pleased by this line that she copied it on a sheet of stationery and enclosed it in a letter of her sister's to a friend (*Letters*, Johnson, III, 928). **18. Parian:** The finest marble used by Greek sculptors in antiquity was quarried on the Aegean island of Paros. ODE INSCRIBED TO W. H. CHANNING. **2. sole patriot:** Channing; a consciously hyperbolic description of a man for whom, however, Emerson did in fact have great respect.

My honied thought
For the priest's cant,
Or statesman's rant.

If I refuse
My study for their politique,
Which at the best is trick,
The angry Muse
Puts confusion in my brain.

But who is he that prates
Of the culture of mankind,
Of better arts and life?
Go, blindworm, go,
Behold the famous States
Harrying Mexico
With rifle and with knife!

Or who, with accent bolder,
Dare praise the freedom-loving mountaineer?
I found by thee, O rushing Contoocook!
And in thy valleys, Agiochook!
The jackals of the negro-holder.

The God who made New Hampshire
Taunted the lofty land
With little men;—
Small bat and wren
House in the oak:—
If earth-fire cleave
The upheaved land, and bury the folk,
The southern crocodile would grieve.
Virtue palters; Right is hence;
Freedom praised, but hid;
Funeral eloquence
Rattles the coffin-lid.

What boots thy zeal,
O glowing friend,
That would indignant rend
The northland from the south?
Wherefore? to what good end?
Boston Bay and Bunker Hill
Would serve things still;
Things are of the snake.

The horseman serves the horse,
The neatherd serves the neat,
The merchant serves the purse,
The eater serves his meat;
'Tis the day of the chattel,
Web to weave, and corn to grind;
Things are in the saddle,
And ride mankind.

There are two laws discrete,
Not reconciled,—
Law for man, and law for thing;
The last builds town and fleet,
But it runs wild,
And doth the man unking.

'Tis fit the forest fall,
The steep be graded,
The mountain tunneled,
The sand shaded,
The orchard planted,
The glebe tilled,
The prairie granted,
The steamer built.

Let man serve law for man;
Live for friendship, live for love,
For truth's and harmony's behoof;
The state may follow how it can,
As Olympus follows Jove.

Yet do not I implore
The wrinkled shopman to my sounding woods,
Nor bid the unwilling senator
Ask votes of thrushes in the solitudes.
Every one to his chosen work;—
Foolish hands may mix and mar;
Wise and sure the issues are.
Round they roll till dark is light,
Sex to sex, and even to odd;—
The over-god
Who marries Right to Might,
Who peoples, unpeoples,—
He who exterminates
Races by stronger races,
Black by white faces,—
Knows to bring honey
Out of the lion;
Grafts gentlest scion
On pirate and Turk.

The Cossack eats Poland,

21. Contoocook: a river in New Hampshire. **22. Agiochook:** the Indian name for the White Mountains. **23. The . . . negro-holder:** overseers, deputies, and the like sent in pursuit of fugitive slaves. **24–26. The . . . men:** This half-humorously low estimate of the men of New Hampshire is an echo of passages in Emerson's journal written during a vacation trip into that state in the summer of 1839 (*Journals*, V, 245–47). **41–42. Boston Bay . . . still:** that is, despite their associations with the heroic memories of the Revolution. **45. neat:** cattle.

52. discrete: distinct; not to be confused with one another. **64. granted:** disposed of by land grants. **86–87. honey . . . lion:** See Judg. 14:5–9. **90–93. The . . . mute:** an allusion to the "partitions" of Poland in the late eighteenth century, of which the lion's share went to Russia; and to the suppression of political and intellectual liberties there by the Russians.

Like stolen fruit;
Her last noble is ruined,
Her last poet mute:
Straight, into double band
The victors divide;
Half for freedom strike and stand;—
The astonished Muse finds thousands at her side.

ODE TO BEAUTY

¶ WHEN this poem appeared in the *Dial* for October, 1843, Thoreau, who was at the time living in the family of Emerson's brother William on Staten Island, wrote to Emerson: "I have a good deal of fault to find with your ode to Beauty"; and went on to specify some of his objections. "Yet I love your poetry," he added, "as I do little else that is near and recent" (Walter Harding and Carl Bode, editors, *Correspondence of Henry David Thoreau*, pp. 145–46). Together with the essay "Art" in *Essays: First Series* and the later essay "Beauty" in *The Conduct of Life*, this poem furnishes a key to Emerson's idealistic aesthetics.

Who gave thee, O Beauty,
The keys of this breast,—
Too credulous lover
Of blest and unblest?
Say, when in lapsed ages
Thee knew I of old?
Or what was the service
For which I was sold?
When first my eyes saw thee,
I found me thy thrall,
By magical drawings,
Sweet tyrant of all!
I drank at thy fountain
False waters of thirst;
Thou intimate stranger,
Thou latest and first!
Thy dangerous glances
Make women of men;
New-born, we are melting
Into nature again.

Lavish, lavish promiser,
Nigh persuading gods to err!
Guest of million painted forms,
Which in turn thy glory warms!
The frailest leaf, the mossy bark,
The acorn's cup, the raindrop's arc,
The swinging spider's silver line,
The ruby of the drop of wine,
The shining pebble of the pond,
Thou inscribest with a bond,
In thy momentary play,
Would bankrupt nature to repay.
Ah, what avails it
To hide or to shun
Whom the Infinite One
Hath granted his throne?
The heaven high over
Is the deep's lover;
The sun and sea,
Informed by thee,
Before me run
And draw me on,
Yet fly me still,
As Fate refuses
To me the heart Fate for me chooses.
Is it that my opulent soul
Was mingled from the generous whole;
Sea-valleys and the deep of skies
Furnished several supplies;
And the sands whereof I'm made
Draw me to them, self-betrayed?
I turn the proud portfolio
Which holds the grand designs
Of Salvator, of Guercino,
And Piranesi's lines.
I hear the lofty pæans
Of the masters of the shell,
Who heard the starry music
And recount the numbers well;
Olympian bards who sung
Divine Ideas below,
Which always find us young
And always keep us so.
Oft, in streets or humblest places,
I detect far-wandering graces,
Which, from Eden wide astray,
In lowly homes have lost their way.

Thee gliding through the sea of form,
Like the lightning through the storm,
Somewhat not to be possessed,
Somewhat not to be caressed,
No feet so fleet could ever find,
No perfect form could ever bind.

94–97. **Straight . . . side:** There was a nationalist insurrection in Poland in 1830–31 which had been plotted for some years by men who had been in touch with the "Decembrist" revolutionaries in Russia. "The astonished Muse" may refer to the role played in the struggle for Polish freedom by the patriot-poet, Adam Mickiewicz. ODE TO BEAUTY. 6. **Thee . . . old?:** one of the "stereotyped lines" Thoreau disliked.

54. **Of . . . Guercino:** Salvator Rosa (1615–73), Italian Baroque painter, much admired by the Romantics of the nineteenth century. **Guercino:** sobriquet of Giovanni Francesco Barbieri (1591–1666), Italian historical painter. 55. **Piranesi:** Giovanni Battista Piranesi (1720–78), Italian engraver of pictures of Roman antiquities and of fanciful architectural compositions of great power and strangeness. 57. **the shell:** musical instruments.

Thou eternal fugitive,
Hovering over all that live,
Quick and skilful to inspire
Sweet, extravagant desire,
Starry space and lily-bell
Filling with thy roseate smell,
Wilt not give the lips to taste
Of the nectar which thou hast.

All that's good and great with thee
Works in close conspiracy;
Thou hast bribed the dark and lonely
To report thy features only,
And the cold and purple morning
Itself with thoughts of thee adorning;
The leafy dell, the city mart,
Equal trophies of thine art;
E'en the flowing azure air
Thou hast touched for my despair;
And, if I languish into dreams,
Again I meet the ardent beams.
Queen of things! I dare not die
In Being's deeps past ear and eye;
Lest there I find the same deceiver
And be the sport of Fate forever.
Dread Power, but dear! if God thou be,
Unmake me quite, or give thyself to me!

GIVE ALL TO LOVE

¶ IN THIS poem, Robert Frost has said, "Emerson supplies the emancipating formula for giving an attachment up for an attraction, one nationality for another nationality, one love for another love . . . Left to myself I have gradually come to see what Emerson was meaning in 'Give All to Love' was, Give all to Meaning. The freedom is ours to insist on meaning" (see *Daedalus*, LXXXVIII [Fall, 1959], 715–16). The same apparently irresponsible but essentially Platonic doctrine is expressed in the essay "Love" (*Essays: First Series*) and at the end of the essay "Compensation" (*Ibid.*).

Give all to love;
Obey thy heart;
Friends, kindred, days,
Estate, good-fame,
Plans, credit and the Muse,—
Nothing refuse.

'Tis a brave master;
Let it have scope:
Follow it utterly,
Hope beyond hope:
High and more high
It dives into noon,
With wing unspent,
Untold intent;
But it is a god,
Knows its own path
And the outlets of the sky.

It was never for the mean;
It requireth courage stout.
Souls above doubt,
Valor unbending,
It will reward,—
They shall return
More than they were,
And every ascending.

Leave all for love;
Yet, hear me, yet,
One word more thy heart behoved,
One pulse more of firm endeavor,
Keep thee today,
Tomorrow, forever,
Free as an Arab
Of thy beloved.

Cling with life to the maid;
But when the surprise,
First vague shadow of surmise
Flits across her bosom young,
Of a joy apart from thee,
Free be she, fancy-free;
Nor thou detain her vesture's hem,
Nor the palest rose she flung
From her summer diadem.

Though thou loved her as thyself,
As a self of purer clay,
Though her parting dims the day,
Stealing grace from all alive;
Heartily know,
When half-gods go,
The gods arrive.

MEROPS

What care I, so they stand the same,—
Things of the heavenly mind,—
How long the power to give them name
Tarries yet behind?

GIVE ALL TO LOVE. 39. **fancy-free**: an echo of Shakespeare's line, "In maiden meditation, fancy-free" (*A Midsummer Night's Dream*, II.i.164). MEROPS. The Greek word means "endowed with speech, articulate-speaking." See also *Works*, IX, 445–46.

Thus far today your favors reach,
O fair, appeasing presences!
Ye taught my lips a single speech,
And a thousand silences.

Space grants beyond his fated road
No inch to the god of day;
And copious language still bestowed
One word, no more, to say.

XENOPHANES

❡ XENOPHANES was a pre-Socratic philosopher and poet who asserted that "There is one God, greatest among gods and men, neither in shape nor in thought like unto mortals." He is said also to have held that "The All is One and the One is God." Somewhat unhistorically, in all probability, Emerson is using Xenophanes here as the type of the philosopher whose insight into Unity is so powerful that it blinds him to the antithetical fact of Plurality—a state of mind which the poet represents himself for the moment as sharing. In *Nature*, V, Emerson remarks that "Xenophanes complained in his old age, that, look where he would, all things hastened back to Unity" (*Works*, I, 43).

By fate, not option, frugal Nature gave
One scent to hyson and to wall-flower,
One sound to pine-groves and to waterfalls,
One aspect to the desert and the lake.
It was her stern necessity: all things
Are of one pattern made; bird, beast and flower,
Song, picture, form, space, thought and character
Deceive us, seeming to be many things,
And are but one. Beheld far off, they part
As God and devil; bring them to the mind,
They dull its edge with their monotony.
To know one element, explore another,
And in the second reappears the first.
The specious panorama of a year
But multiplies the image of a day,—
A belt of mirrors round a taper's flame;
And universal Nature, through her vast
And crowded whole, an infinite paroquet,
Repeats one note.

THRENODY

❡ IN January, 1842, Emerson's five-year-old son Waldo, a beautiful and gifted child, died after a few days' illness. The bereavement was a terrible one, and in the first part of "Threnody" (ll. 1–175), which Emerson seems to have written during the early spring, shortly after the boy's death, he gives vent to a bitterness of grief such as one finds nowhere else in his verse or indeed, outside of his journal and his private letters, in his prose. The second part of the poem (ll. 176–289), which was written some months later, in 1843, expresses Emerson's recovery from the first anguish of loss and his acceptance of a calmer view of death and bereavement. The language and imagery throughout owe nothing to the tradition of the classical pastoral elegy, as most of the great elegiac poems in English have done; the poem is wholly native and unconventional.

The South-wind brings
Life, sunshine and desire,
And on every mount and meadow
Breathes aromatic fire;
But over the dead he has no power,
The lost, the lost, he cannot restore;
And, looking over the hills, I mourn
The darling who shall not return.

I see my empty house,
I see my trees repair their boughs;
And he, the wondrous child,
Whose silver warble wild
Outvalued every pulsing sound
Within the air's cerulean round,—
The hyacinthine boy, for whom
Morn well might break and April bloom,
The gracious boy, who did adorn
The world whereinto he was born,
And by his countenance repay
The favor of the loving Day,—
Has disappeared from the Day's eye;
Far and wide she cannot find him;
My hopes pursue, they cannot bind him.
Returned this day, the South-wind searches,
And finds young pines and budding birches;
But finds not the budding man;
Nature, who lost, cannot remake him;
Fate let him fall, Fate can't retake him;
Nature, Fate, men, him seek in vain.

And whither now, my truant wise and sweet,
O, whither tend thy feet?
I had the right, few days ago,
Thy steps to watch, thy place to know:
How have I forfeited the right?
Hast thou forgot me in a new delight?
I hearken for thy household cheer,
O eloquent child!
Whose voice, an equal messenger,
Conveyed thy meaning mild.

XENOPHANES. **2. hyson:** a kind of China tea.

THRENODY. **15. hyacinthine:** classically beautiful, like the Greek youth, Hyacinth, beloved by Apollo.

What though the pains and joys
Whereof it spoke were toys
Fitting his age and ken,
Yet fairest dames and bearded men,
Who heard the sweet request,
So gentle, wise and grave,
Bended with joy to his behest
And let the world's affairs go by,
A while to share his cordial game,
Or mend his wicker wagon-frame,
Still plotting how their hungry ear
That winsome voice again might hear;
For his lips could well pronounce
Words that were persuasions.

Gentlest guardians marked serene
His early hope, his liberal mien;
Took counsel from his guiding eyes
To make this wisdom earthly wise.
Ah, vainly do these eyes recall
The school-march, each day's festival,
When every morn my bosom glowed
To watch the convoy on the road;
The babe in willow wagon closed,
With rolling eyes and face composed;
With children forward and behind,
Like Cupids studiously inclined;
And he the chieftain paced beside,
The center of the troop allied,
With sunny face of sweet repose,
To guard the babe from fancied foes.
The little captain innocent
Took the eye with him as he went;
Each village senior paused to scan
And speak the lovely caravan.
From the window I look out
To mark thy beautiful parade,
Stately marching in cap and coat
To some tune by fairies played;—
A music heard by thee alone
To works as noble led thee on.

Now Love and Pride, alas! in vain,
Up and down their glances strain.
The painted sled stands where it stood;
The kennel by the corded wood;
His gathered sticks to stanch the wall
Of the snow-tower, when snow should fall;
The ominous hole he dug in the sand,
And childhood's castles built or planned;
His daily haunts I well discern,—
The poultry-yard, the shed, the barn,—
And every inch of garden ground
Paced by the blessed feet around,
From the roadside to the brook
Whereinto he loved to look.
Step the meek fowls where erst they ranged;
The wintry garden lies unchanged;
The brook into the stream runs on;
But the deep-eyed boy is gone.

On that shaded day,
Dark with more clouds than tempests are,
When thou didst yield thy innocent breath
In birdlike heavings unto death,
Night came, and Nature had not thee;
I said, "We are mates in misery."
The morrow dawned with needless glow;
Each snowbird chirped, each fowl must crow;
Each tramper started; but the feet
Of the most beautiful and sweet
Of human youth had left the hill
And garden,—they were bound and still.
There's not a sparrow or a wren,
There's not a blade of autumn grain,
Which the four seasons do not tend
And tides of life and increase lend;
And every chick of every bird,
And weed and rock-moss is preferred.
O ostrich-like forgetfulness!
O loss of larger in the less!
Was there no star that could be sent,
No watcher in the firmament,
No angel from the countless host
That loiters round the crystal coast,
Could stoop to heal that only child,
Nature's sweet marvel undefiled,
And keep the blossom of the earth,
Which all her harvests were not worth?
Not mine,—I never called thee mine,
But Nature's heir,—if I repine,
And seeing rashly torn and moved
Not what I made, but what I loved,
Grow early old with grief that thou
Must to the wastes of Nature go,—
'Tis because a general hope
Was quenched, and all must doubt and grope.
For flattering planets seemed to say
This child should ills of ages stay,
By wondrous tongue, and guided pen,
Bring the flown Muses back to men.
Perchance not he but Nature ailed,
The world and not the infant failed.
It was not ripe yet to sustain
A genius of so fine a strain,

48. **cordial:** in the sense of hearty, cheerful, or gay. 84. **stanch:** to make stanch; to support; not, of course, to stop the flow of.

96–97. **The . . . gone:** "If," wrote Emerson in his journal, "I go down to the bottom of the garden it seems as if some one had fallen into the brook. Every place is handsome or tolerable where he has been" (*Journals*, VI, 154).

Who gazed upon the sun and moon
As if he came unto his own,
And, pregnant with his grander thought,
Brought the old order into doubt.
His beauty once their beauty tried;
They could not feed him, and he died,
And wandered backward as in scorn,
To wait an aeon to be born.

Ill day which made this beauty waste,
Plight broken, this high face defaced!
Some went and came about the dead;
And some in books of solace read;
Some to their friends the tidings say;
Some went to write, some went to pray;
One tarried here, there hurried one;
But their heart abode with none.
Covetous death bereaved us all,
To aggrandize one funeral.
The eager fate which carried thee
Took the largest part of me:
For this losing is true dying;
This is lordly man's down-lying,
This his slow but sure reclining,
Star by star his world resigning.

O child of paradise,
Boy who made dear his father's home,
In whose deep eyes
Men read the welfare of the times to come,
I am too much bereft.
The world dishonored thou hast left.
O truth's and nature's costly lie!
O trusted broken prophecy!
O richest fortune sourly crossed!
Born for the future, to the future lost!

The deep Heart answered, "Weepest thou?
Worthier cause for passion wild
If I had not taken the child.
And deemest thou as those who pore,
With aged eyes, short way before,—
Think'st Beauty vanished from the coast
Of matter, and thy darling lost?
Taught he not thee—the man of eld,
Whose eyes within his eyes beheld
Heaven's numerous hierarchy span
The mystic gulf from God to man?
To be alone wilt thou begin
When worlds of lovers hem thee in?
Tomorrow, when the masks shall fall
That dizen Nature's carnival,
The pure shall see by their own will,
Which overflowing Love shall fill,
'Tis not within the force of fate
The fate-conjoined to separate.
But thou, my votary, weepest thou?
I gave thee sight—where is it now?
I taught thy heart beyond the reach
Of ritual, bible, or of speech;
Wrote in thy mind's transparent table,
As far as the incommunicable;
Taught thee each private sign to raise
Lit by the supersolar blaze.
Past utterance, and past belief,
And past the blasphemy of grief,
The mysteries of Nature's heart;
And though no Muse can these impart,
Throb thine with Nature's throbbing breast,
And all is clear from east to west.

"I came to thee as to a friend;
Dearest, to thee I did not send
Tutors, but a joyful eye,
Innocence that matched the sky,
Lovely locks, a form of wonder,
Laughter rich as woodland thunder,
That thou might'st entertain apart
The richest flowering of all art:
And, as the great all-loving Day
Through smallest chambers takes its way,
That thou might'st break thy daily bread
With prophet, savior and head;
That thou might'st cherish for thine own
The riches of sweet Mary's Son,
Boy-Rabbi, Israel's paragon.
And thoughtest thou such guest
Would in thy hall take up his rest?
Would rushing life forget her laws,
Fate's glowing revolution pause?
High omens ask diviner guess;
Not to be conned to tediousness
And know my higher gifts unbind
The zone that girds the incarnate mind.
When the scanty shores are full
With Thought's perilous, whirling pool;
When frail Nature can no more,
Then the Spirit strikes the hour:
My servant Death, with solving rite,
Pours finite into infinite.
Wilt thou freeze love's tidal flow,
Whose streams through Nature circling go?
Nail the wild star to its track
On the half-climbed zodiac?
Light is light which radiates,
Blood is blood which circulates,
Life is life which generates,

176. **The deep Heart:** the heart of Nature. 183. **the man of eld:** Emerson may have in mind the Plato of *Phaedo* (79–80).

236. **solving:** perhaps in the sense of "dissolving."

And many-seeming life is one,—
Wilt thou transfix and make it none?
Its onward force too starkly pent
In figure, bone and lineament?
Wilt thou, uncalled, interrogate,
Talker! the unreplying Fate?
Nor see the genius of the whole
Ascendant in the private soul,
Beckon it when to go and come,
Self-announced its hour of doom?
Fair the soul's recess and shrine,
Magic-built to last a season;
Masterpiece of love benign;
Fairer that expansive reason
Whose omen 'tis, and sign.
Wilt thou not ope thy heart to know
What rainbows teach, and sunsets show?
Verdict which accumulates
From lengthening scroll of human fates,
Voice of earth to earth returned,
Prayers of saints that inly burned,—
Saying, *What is excellent,*
As God lives, is permanent;
Hearts are dust, hearts' loves remain;
Heart's love will meet thee again.
Revere the Maker; fetch thine eye
Up to his style, and manners of the sky.
Not of adamant and gold
Built he heaven stark and cold;
No, but a nest of bending reeds,
Flowering grass and scented weeds;
Or like a traveler's fleeing tent,
Or bow above the tempest bent;
Built of tears and sacred flames,
And virtue reaching to its aims;
Built of furtherance and pursuing,
Not of spent deeds, but of doing.
Silent rushes the swift Lord
Through ruined systems still restored,
Broadsowing, bleak and void to bless,
Plants with worlds the wilderness;
Waters with tears of ancient sorrow
Apples of Eden ripe tomorrow.
House and tenant go to ground,
Lost in God, in Godhead found."

CONCORD HYMN

Sung at the Completion of the Battle Monument, July 4, 1837

❡ A MONUMENT to the Minute Men who had fought the British troops at Concord in 1775 was set up, in the middle thirties, on a piece of land which had been presented to the town by Emerson's step-grandfather, the Rev. Ezra Ripley, on whose property the skirmish had been fought—in a meadow just across the Concord River from his parsonage, the Manse. Although Emerson himself could not be present on the occasion of the dedication of the monument, the Fourth of July, 1837, the hymn he had composed for the event was sung by a choir to the tune of "Old Hundred." Holmes described the poem as "compact, expressive, serene, solemn, musical"; and Robert Frost has spoken of the first four lines as "surpassing anv other ever written about soldiers" (*Daedalus*, LXXXVIII [Fall, 1959], 718).

By the rude bridge that arched the flood,
  Their flag to April's breeze unfurled,
Here once the embattled farmers stood
  And fired the shot heard round the world.

The foe long since in silence slept;
  Alike the conqueror silent sleeps;
And Time the ruined bridge has swept
  Down the dark stream which seaward creeps.

On this green bank, by this soft stream,
  We set today a votive stone;
That memory may their deed redeem,
  When, like our sires, our sons are gone.

Spirit, that made those heroes dare
  To die, and leave their children free,
Bid Time and Nature gently spare
  The shaft we raise to them and thee.

FROM

MAY-DAY AND OTHER PIECES

BRAHMA

❡ THESE stanzas, which were published in the first issue of the *Atlantic Monthly* (November, 1857), and were supposed by many of their readers to be hopelessly opaque, present, in fact, few serious difficulties to the reader who has even a modest familiarity with the Hindu sacred books—books which Emerson had been poring over for years. He must have had particularly in mind, in writing "Brahma," two works, the Bhagavad-

247. too starkly pent: too rigidly confined. **284. bleak . . . bless:** to bless that which is bleak and empty; the two adjectives seem to be used as nouns.

Gita and the Katha Upanishad. In both there are passages which set forth the doctrine of the illusoriness of death, the deathlessness of the real Self. According to these passages, the Self cannot kill or be killed, as the body can, for it is not born nor does it die, but is indestructible and imperishable; it is indeed only a phase of the absolute and eternal Self, which is Brahma, the transcendent and undying One, in whom all contradictions are reconciled and all distinctions lost. These passages may be found, though not in the translations known to Emerson (see footnotes), in *Bhagavad-Gita: The Song of God*, translated by Swami Prabhavanandra and Christopher Isherwood (1944), Chap. 2; and in *The Ten Principal Upanishads*, put into English by Shree Purohit Swāmi and W. B. Yeats (1937), Katha Upanishad: Book I, 2. Emerson's late essay on "Immortality" (*Letters and Social Aims*) concludes with a paraphrase of the first and second sections of Book I of the Katha Upanishad, omitting some of the verses he had already echoed very closely in "Brahma."

If the red slayer think he slays,
    Or if the slain think he is slain,
They know not well the subtle ways
    I keep, and pass, and turn again.

Far or forgot to me is near;
    Shadow and sunlight are the same;
The vanished gods to me appear;
    And one to me are shame and fame.

They reckon ill who leave me out;
    When me they fly, I am the wings;
I am the doubter and the doubt,
    And I the hymn the Brahmin sings.

The strong gods pine for my abode,
    And pine in vain the sacred Seven;
But thou, meek lover of the good!
    Find me, and turn thy back on heaven.

BRAHMA. **1–4. If . . . again:** "The man who believeth that it is the soul which killeth, and he who thinketh that the soul may be destroyed, are both alike deceived; for it neither killeth, nor is killed" (Charles Wilkins, trans., *The Bhagavat-Geeta*, 1785). "If the slayer thinks I slay, if the slain thinks I am slain, then both of them do not know well. It (the soul) does not slay, nor is it slain" (E. Röer, trans., *Katha Upanishad*, 1853). These were the translations Emerson knew. **9. They . . . out:** When he wrote this line Emerson may have been remembering a Spanish proverb he had copied many years before (1832) in his journal: "He counts very unskilfully who leaves God out of his reckoning" (*Journals*, II, 480). **13. The strong gods:** Indra, the sky-god; Agni, the god of fire; and Yama, the god of death and immortality. All three are ultimately to be absorbed in Brahma. **14. the sacred Seven:** the seven highest saints. **15–16. But . . . heaven:** "Surrendering all the laws, come for refuge to me alone. I will deliver thee from all sins; grieve not" (Krishna to Arjuna, Bhagavad Gita, Lesson the Eighteenth, *Hindu Scriptures* [Everyman], p. 286).

BOSTON HYMN

Read in Music Hall, January 1, 1863

¶ AS THE subtitle indicates, Emerson read this poem at a great meeting in Boston to celebrate Lincoln's signing of the Emancipation Proclamation. Henry James, who as a young man was present at the meeting, describes Emerson's reading of the "Boston Hymn" in his fine essay on Emerson (*Partial Portraits*, pp. 27–28).

The word of the Lord by night
To the watching Pilgrims came,
As they sat by the seaside,
And filled their hearts with flame.

God said, I am tired of kings,
I suffer them no more;
Up to my ear the morning brings
The outrage of the poor.

Think ye I made this ball
A field of havoc and war,
Where tyrants great and tyrants small
Might harry the weak and poor?

My angel,—his name is Freedom,—
Choose him to be your king;
He shall cut pathways east and west
And fend you with his wing.

Lo! I uncover the land
Which I hid of old time in the West,
As the sculptor uncovers the statue
When he has wrought his best;

I show Columbia, of the rocks
Which dip their foot in the seas
And soar to the air-borne flocks
Of clouds and the boreal fleece.

I will divide my goods;
Call in the wretch and slave:
None shall rule but the humble,
And none but Toil shall have.

I will have never a noble,
No lineage counted great;
Fishers and choppers and ploughmen
Shall constitute a state.

Go, cut down trees in the forest
And trim the straightest boughs;

BOSTON HYMN. **1–4. The . . . flame:** "That night [at Delftshaven] was spent with little sleep by the most, but with friendly entertainment and Christian discourse and other real expressions of true Christian love" (William Bradford, *Of Plymouth Plantation*, Chap. 7). See p. 15 of this volume. **16. fend:** defend.

Cut down trees in the forest
And build me a wooden house.

Call the people together,
The young men and the sires,
The digger in the harvest field,
Hireling and him that hires;

And here in a pine state-house
They shall choose men to rule
In every needful faculty,
In church and state and school.

Lo, now! if these poor men
Can govern the land and sea
And make just laws below the sun,
As planets faithful be.

And ye shall succor men;
'T is nobleness to serve;
Help them who cannot help again:
Beware from right to swerve.

I break your bonds and masterships,
And I unchain the slave:
Free be his heart and hand henceforth
As wind and wandering wave.

I cause from every creature
His proper good to flow:
As much as he is and doeth,
So much he shall bestow.

But, laying hands on another
To coin his labor and sweat,
He goes in pawn to his victim
For eternal years in debt.

To-day unbind the captive,
So only are ye unbound;
Lift up a people from the dust,
Trump of their rescue, sound!

Pay ransom to the owner
And fill the bag to the brim.
Who is the owner? The slave is owner,
And ever was. Pay him.

O North! give him beauty for rags,
And honor, O South! for his shame;
Nevada! coin thy golden crags
With Freedom's image and name.

Up! and the dusky race
That sat in darkness long,—
Be swift their feet as antelopes,
And as behemoth strong.

Come, East and West and North,
By races, as snow-flakes,
And carry my purpose forth,
Which neither halts nor shakes.

My will fulfilled shall be,
For, in daylight or in dark,
My thunderbolt has eyes to see
His way home to the mark.

49–52. **And . . . swerve:** See motto of "Speech on Affairs in Kansas," p. 550. 69–70. **Pay . . . brim:** See passage from an address by Emerson before the Anti-Slavery Society in New York in 1855 (*Works*, IX, 469).

80. **behemoth:** a huge and powerful beast; see Job 40:15.

VOLUNTARIES

THE poem of which this is the third section was written as a eulogy of Colonel Robert Gould Shaw, a young Harvard man who had taken command of the first regiment of Negro soldiers in the Union Army, and had been killed in action at Fort Wagner, South Carolina, in June, 1863. "Voluntaries" appeared in the *Atlantic Monthly* in October.

III

In an age of fops and toys,
Wanting wisdom, void of right,
Who shall nerve heroic boys
To hazard all in Freedom's fight,—
Break sharply off their jolly games,
Forsake their comrades gay
And quit proud homes and youthful dames
For famine, toil and fray?
Yet on the nimble air benign
Speed nimbler messages,
That waft the breath of grace divine
To hearts in sloth and ease.
So nigh is grandeur to our dust,
So near is God to man,
When Duty whispers low, *Thou must,*
The youth replies, *I can.*

DAYS

Daughters of Time, the hypocritic Days,
Muffled and dumb like barefoot dervishes,
And marching single in an endless file,
Bring diadems and fagots in their hands.
To each they offer gifts after his will,
Bread, kingdoms, stars, and sky that holds them all.

I, in my pleachèd garden, watched the pomp,
Forgot my morning wishes, hastily
Took a few herbs and apples, and the Day
Turned and departed silent. I, too late,
Under her solemn fillet saw the scorn.

TWO RIVERS

THE thought of this poem—that the actual river is a symbol of the ideal river or the stream of Being itself—was first expressed, in this special form, in an entry in Emerson's journal for the early summer of 1856. The closeness of the poetic version to the prose original may be illustrated by the first sentence of the latter: "Thy voice is sweet, Musketaquid, and repeats the music of the rain, but sweeter is the silent stream which flows even through thee, as thou through the land" (*Works*, IX, 487). Long before this, however, the symbol of the river had been a characteristic one for Emerson: see, for example, the chapter "Language" in *Nature* (pp. 494–97), the essay "The Over-Soul" in *Essays: First Series* (*Works*, II, 268), or the essay "Nature" in *Essays: Second Series* (*Ibid.*, III, 178–79).

Thy summer voice, Musketaquit,
Repeats the music of the rain;
But sweeter rivers pulsing flit
Through thee, as thou through Concord Plain.

Thou in thy narrow banks art pent:
The stream I love unbounded goes
Through flood and sea and firmament;
Through light, through life, it forward flows.

I see the inundation sweet,
I hear the spending of the stream
Through years, through men, through Nature fleet,
Through love and thought, through power and dream.

Musketaquit, a goblin strong,
Of shard and flint makes jewels gay;
They lose their grief who hear his song,
And where he winds is the day of day.

So forth and brighter fares my stream,—
Who drink it shall not thirst again;
No darkness stains its equal gleam,
And ages drop in it like rain.

TWO RIVERS. **1. Musketaquit:** Indian name for the Concord River. **18. Who . . . again:** See John 4:14 ("But whosoever drinketh of the water that I shall give him shall never thirst; but the water that I shall give him shall be in him a well of water springing up into everlasting life").

WALDEINSAMKEIT

I do not count the hours I spend
In wandering by the sea;
The forest is my loyal friend,
Like God it useth me.

In plains that room for shadows make
Of skirting hills to lie,
Bound in by streams which give and take
Their colors from the sky;

Or on the mountain-crest sublime,
Or down the oaken glade,
O what have I to do with time?
For this the day was made.

Cities of mortals woe-begone
Fantastic care derides,
But in the serious landscape lone
Stern benefit abides.

Sheen will tarnish, honey cloy,
And merry is only a mask of sad,
But, sober on a fund of joy,
The woods at heart are glad.

There the great Planter plants
Of fruitful worlds the grain,
And with a million spells enchants
The souls that walk in pain.

Still on the seeds of all he made
The rose of beauty burns;
Through times that wear and forms that fade,
Immortal youth returns.

The black ducks mounting from the lake,
The pigeon in the pines,
The bittern's boom, a desert make
Which no false art refines.

Down in yon watery nook,
Where bearded mists divide,
The gray old gods whom Chaos knew,
The sires of Nature, hide.

Aloft, in secret veins of air,
Blows the sweet breath of song,
O, few to scale those uplands dare,
Though they to all belong!

WALDEINSAMKEIT. "solitude of the forest." **1–2. I . . . sea:** "They [the English] think . . . with the Arabs, that the days spent in the chase are not counted in the length of life" (*English Traits*, Chap. 4 [*Works*, V, 70]).

See thou bring not to field or stone
The fancies found in books;
Leave authors' eyes, and fetch your own,
To brave the landscape's looks.

Oblivion here thy wisdom is,
Thy thrift, the sleep of cares;
For a proud idleness like this
Crowns all thy mean affairs.

TERMINUS

It is time to be old,
To take in sail:
The god of bounds,
Who sets to seas a shore,
Came to me in his fatal rounds,
And said: "No more!
No farther shoot
Thy broad ambitious branches, and thy root.
Fancy departs: no more invent;
Contract thy firmament
To compass of a tent.
There's not enough for this and that,
Make thy option which of two;
Economize the failing river,
Not the less revere the Giver,
Leave the many and hold the few.
Timely wise accept the terms,
Soften the fall with wary foot;
A little while
Still plan and smile,
And—fault of novel germs—
Mature the unfallen fruit.
Curse, if thou wilt, thy sires,
Bad husbands of their fires,
Who, when they gave thee breath,
Failed to bequeath
The needful sinew stark as once,
The Baresark marrow to thy bones,
But left a legacy of ebbing veins,
Inconstant heat and nerveless reins,
Amid the Muses, left thee deaf and dumb,
Amid the gladiators, halt and numb."

As the bird trims her to the gale,
I trim myself to the storm of time,
I man the rudder, reef the sail,
Obey the voice at eve obeyed at prime:
"Lowly faithful, banish fear,
Right onward drive unharmed;
The port, well worth the cruise, is near,
And every wave is charmed."

FROM

ELEMENTS AND MOTTOES

[IN *May-Day and Other Pieces* Emerson included, under the title "Elements," a group of short gnomic poems which had already appeared as epigraphs to the prose essays. This group was later expanded by his editors and entitled "Elements and Mottoes." Of the poems that follow here, one ("Compensation") is taken from *Essays: First Series,* two ("Politics" and "Nature") from *Essays: Second Series,* and three ("Beauty," "Worship," and "Wealth") from *The Conduct of Life.*

COMPENSATION

The wings of Time are black and white,
Pied with morning and with night.
Mountain tall and ocean deep
Trembling balance duly keep.
In changing moon and tidal wave,
Glows the feud of Want and Have.
Gauge of more and less through space,
Electric star or pencil plays.
The lonely Earth amid the balls
That hurry through the eternal halls,
A makeweight flying to the void,
Supplemental asteroid,
Or compensatory spark,
Shoots across the neutral Dark.

POLITICS

Gold and iron are good
To buy iron and gold;
All earth's fleece and food
For their like are sold.
Boded Merlin wise,
Proved Napoleon great,—
Nor kind nor coinage buys
Aught above its rate.
Fear, Craft and Avarice
Cannot rear a State.
Out of dust to build
What is more than dust,—
Walls Amphion piled
Phœbus stablish must.

TERMINUS. In Roman mythology Terminus is the god of boundaries and frontiers. The name here, however, has also the strong connotation of the English word, "termination," and an association with old age or the end of life. **21. fault:** in default. **24. husbands:** economizers. **28. Baresark:** berserker; in Norse mythology, a superhumanly powerful and energetic warrior.

36. prime: the first hour of the day. POLITICS. **5–6. Boded . . . great:** If Merlin prophesied wisely, if Napoleon proved to be great, it was because . . . **13. Amphion:** in Greek mythology, one of the rulers of Thebes, who had received a lyre from Hermes; he played on this with such magical power that he charmed the very stones into moving and forming the wall of the city.

When the Muses nine
With the Virtues meet,
Find to their design
An Atlantic seat,
By green orchard boughs
Fended from the heat,
Where the statesman ploughs
Furrow for the wheat;
When the Church is social worth,
When the state-house is the hearth,
Then the perfect State is come,
The republican at home.

NATURE

The rounded world is fair to see,
Nine times folded in mystery:
Though baffled seers cannot impart
The secret of its laboring heart,
Throb thine with Nature's throbbing breast,
And all is clear from east to west.
Spirit that lurks each form within
Beckons to spirit of its kin;
Self-kindled every atom glows
And hints the future which it owes.

BEAUTY

Was never form and never face
So sweet to SEYD as only grace
Which did not slumber like a stone
But hovered gleaming and was gone.
Beauty chased he everywhere,
In flame, in storm, in clouds of air.
He smote the lake to feed his eye
With the beryl beam of the broken wave.
He flung in pebbles well to hear
The moment's music which they gave.
Oft pealed for him a lofty tone
From nodding pole and belting zone.
He heard a voice none else could hear
From centred and from errant sphere.
The quaking earth did quake in rhyme,
Seas ebbed and flowed in epic chime.
In dens of passion, and pits of woe,
He saw strong Eros struggling through,
To sun the dark and solve the curse,
And beam to the bounds of the universe.
While thus to love he gave his days
In loyal worship, scorning praise,
How spread their lures for him, in vain,
Thieving Ambition and paltering Gain!
He thought it happier to be dead,
To die for Beauty, than live for bread.

NATURE. **2. Nine times folded:** perhaps an allusion to the nine concentric spheres or heavens of Ptolemaic astronomy.
BEAUTY. **2. Seyd:** See "Uriel," l. 8. **19. solve:** See "Threnody," l. 236.

WORSHIP

This is he, who, felled by foes,
Sprung harmless up, refreshed by blows:
He to captivity was sold,
But him no prison-bars would hold:
Though they sealed him in a rock,
Mountain chains he can unlock:
Thrown to lions for their meat,
The crouching lion kissed his feet:
Bound to the stake, no flames appalled,
But arched o'er him an honoring vault.
This is he men miscall Fate,
Threading dark ways, arriving late,
But ever coming in time to crown
The truth, and hurl wrongdoers down.
He is the oldest, and best known,
More near than aught thou call'st thy own,
Yet, greeted in another's eyes,
Disconcerts with glad surprise.
This is Jove, who, deaf to prayers,
Floods with blessings unawares.
Draw, if thou canst, the mystic line
Severing rightly his from thine,
Which is human, which divine.

WEALTH

Who shall tell what did befall,
Far away in time, when once,
Over the lifeless ball,
Hung idle stars and suns?
What god the element obeyed?
Wings of what wind the lichen bore,
Wafting the puny seeds of power,
Which, lodged in rock, the rock abrade?
And well the primal pioneer
Knew the strong task to it assigned,
Patient through Heaven's enormous year
To build in matter home for mind.
From air the creeping centuries drew
The matted thicket low and wide,
This must the leaves of ages strew
The granite slab to clothe and hide,
Ere wheat can wave its golden pride.
What smiths, and in what furnace, rolled
(In dizzy aeons dim and mute
The reeling brain can ill compute)
Copper and iron, lead and gold?
What oldest star the fame can save
Of races perishing to pave
The planet with a floor of lime?
Dust is their pyramid and mole:
Who saw what ferns and palms were pressed

WORSHIP. **7–8. Thrown . . . feet:** An allusion to the familiar story of Androcles and the lion, told by Aulus Gellius in his *Noctes Atticae*.

Under the tumbling mountain's breast,
In the safe herbal of the coal?
But when the quarried means were piled,
All is waste and worthless, till
Arrives the wise selecting will,
And, out of slime and chaos, Wit
Draws the threads of fair and fit.
Then temples rose, and towns, and marts,
The shop of toil, the hall of arts;
Then flew the sail across the seas
To feed the North from tropic trees;
The storm-wind wove, the torrent span,
Where they were bid, the rivers ran;
New slaves fulfilled the poet's dream,
Galvanic wire, strong-shouldered steam.
Then docks were built, and crops were stored,
And ingots added to the hoard.
But though light-headed man forget,
Remembering Matter pays her debt:
Still, through her motes and masses, draw
Electric thrills and ties of law,
Which bind the strengths of Nature wild
To the conscience of a child.

FROM

QUATRAINS

THIS was the title of a group of four-line (and in one case five-line) poems in *May-Day and Other Pieces.* Landor, one of his favorite English poets, may have suggested this terse and gnomic form to Emerson, who had also been much interested in the use of a similar form by the Persian poets whom he read in German translation.

GARDENER

True Brahmin, in the morning meadows wet,
Expound the Vedas of the violet,
Or, hid in vines, peeping through many a loop,
See the plum redden, and the beurré stoop.

CLIMACTERIC

I am not wiser for my age,
Nor skilful by my grief;
Life loiters at the book's first page,—
Ah! could we turn the leaf.

ΑΔΑΚΡΥΝ ΝΕΜΟΝΤΑΙ ΑΙΩΝΑ

'A new commandment,' said the smiling Muse,
'I give my darling son, Thou shalt not preach';—
Luther, Fox, Behmen, Swedenborg, grew pale,
And, on the instant, rosier clouds upbore
Hafiz and Shakespeare with their shining choirs.

GARDENER. **2. Vedas:** the earliest of the Hindu sacred books; collections of hymns and prayers. **4. beurré:** a kind of pear. ΑΔΑΚΡΥΝ ΝΕΜΟΝΤΑΙ ΑΙΩΝΑ. The Greek phrase, which means "they lead a tearless life," is taken from a passage in Pindar's Second Olympian Ode describing the future life of good men.

FROM

APPENDIX

THE four following poems were never published by Emerson but were included by his editors in posthumous editions of his works.

TRANSITION

See yonder leafless trees against the sky,
How they diffuse themselves into the air,
And, ever subdividing, separate
Limbs into branches, branches into twigs,
As if they loved the element, and hasted
To dissipate their being into it.

NAHANT

All day the waves assailed the rock,
I heard no church-bell chime,
The sea-beat scorns the minster clock
And breaks the glass of Time.

GRACE

"GRACE" was published anonymously in the *Dial* for January, 1842. Ten years after this Emerson collaborated on a volume of *Memoirs of Margaret Fuller Ossoli* with W. H. Channing and James Freeman Clarke. Channing, in the manuscript of his contribution, used the poem as a motto to one of his chapters and apparently attributed it to the seventeenth-century poet,

3. Behmen: See "New England Reformers," 21 n. **5. Hafiz:** See "Fate," 43 n. GRACE. **1. preventing:** anticipating. Emerson has in mind here the theological phrase, "prevenient grace"; that is, God's grace when it anticipates the repentance of the sinner and predisposes his heart to turn to God. In the context of this poem, however, the word also has much of its normal modern connotation of "hindering" or "inhibiting."

George Herbert (*Works,* IX, 510). Herbert was indeed one of Emerson's favorite poets, and Emerson was amused by Channing's error—amused and pleased by what he called, in a letter to Channing, an "infinite honor." The style of "Grace" does in fact somewhat recall that of Herbert.

How much, preventing God, how much I owe
To the defenses thou hast round me set;
Example, custom, fear, occasion slow,—
These scornèd bondmen were my parapet.
I dare not peep over this parapet
To gauge with glance the roaring gulf below,
The depths of sin to which I had descended,
Had not these me against myself defended.

LIMITS

Who knows this or that?
Hark in the wall to the rat:
Since the world was, he has gnawed;
Of his wisdom, of his fraud
What dost thou know?
In the wretched little beast
Is life and heart,
Child and parent,
Not without relation
To fruitful field and sun and moon.
What art thou? His wicked eye
Is cruel to thy cruelty.

KENNETH S. LYNN
Editor

Henry David Thoreau

1817–1862

LIKE John Brown, whom he deeply admired, and whose raid on Harper's Ferry he defended with unforgettable eloquence, Thoreau was possessed by a vision of perfect freedom to which he gave his life. In everything he did and said, he tested what it was like to be one's own master; his writings both record his experiments and call on us to be experimental, too.

In the fall of 1837, shortly after his graduation from Harvard College, when he was living once more with his family in Concord, Thoreau wrote in the journal he had just begun to keep regularly, "The world is a fit theatre today in which any part may be acted. There is this moment proposed to me every kind of life that men lead anywhere, or that imagination can paint." South African planter, Greenland whaler, soldier in Florida, navigator of any sea, were among the occupations he conjectured for himself. Yet when a friend proposed to him that they work their passage across the Atlantic and travel through Europe, the celebrator of perfect freedom turned him down. The decision was characteristic. For if all the world was a theater to Thoreau, it is important to note that he seldom went on the road. The only other book besides *Walden* which he published in his lifetime was a travel book, to be sure, but it only recorded *A Week on the Concord and Merrimack Rivers*. That many of his posthumous publications bear place names as titles—*The Maine Woods, Cape Cod, A Yankee in Canada*—is indicative of the fact that occasionally he *did* leave Concord, but his absences were not for long and did not take him far. Even when he was living at Walden Pond he often returned home for week ends.

Part of the explanation for his home-bodiness is that Thoreau was very dependent, emotionally speaking, on his family. He lived a great part of his life under his parents' roof and he died in his mother's house. He never married. When he was twenty-six he wrote a letter to his mother in which he confessed, "Methinks I should be content to sit at the back-door in Concord, under the poplar-tree, henceforth forever." But perhaps the most poignant instance of his attachment occurred when he was a Senior at Harvard. He asked his mother what occupation he should choose, and when she replied, "You can buckle on your knapsack, and roam abroad to seek your fortune," he wept until his sister Helen embraced him and said, comfortingly, "No, Henry, you shall not go; you shall stay at home and live with us."

The main reason, however, that he never went anywhere is that Thoreau deliberately lived a life of paradox. He insisted that there was society in solitude, that silence was a mode of communication, that idleness was productive, that one could go far by staying put.

Freedom, he said repeatedly, was not what his neighbors construed it to be; he found it difficult, he confessed, to exaggerate their error. To force them to redefine their terms by making them acknowledge the truth of his outrageous paradoxes was his consistent strategy. Like the cow he spoke of in *Walden*, "which kicks over the pail, leaps the cowyard fence, and runs after her calf in milking time," he lived a life of adventure in native pastures.

Thoreau, then, never went in search of his fortune, and never, in a certain sense, amounted to anything. For a time he taught school; he worked for the Emersons as a gardener and general handyman, and helped to edit the *Dial*; off and on, he was a surveyor; and he made pencils in his father's pencil factory. For a Harvard graduate it was an extravagant performance, and some of those who were witness to his behavior were disgusted by it. James Russell Lowell, who lived for a year in Concord, found Thoreau difficult and unpleasant, thought there was no excuse for his unbounded egotism, and contemptuously dismissed him as a failure who was spending his life picking up the windfalls in Emerson's orchard.

The wisecrack was not only directed against the scandalous means of livelihood Thoreau had chosen, but against the independence of his mind as well; in Lowell's view, Thoreau lived off Emerson's intellect as well as his charity. There is no doubt, of course, that Emerson's essays, especially *Nature* (1836)—which was published in the fall of Thoreau's senior year at Harvard—had an enormous impact on the younger man, stirring him to the depths of his being. He imbibed so many of Emerson's ideas that Emerson himself believed that his mind was mirrored in Thoreau's, the one significant difference being that his own was more metaphysical and Thoreau's more concrete; it was right that Thoreau, not Emerson, should write the "Natural History of Massachusetts" (1842), because Thoreau knew the facts of the subject as well as its truth. Yet this difference hardly exhausted the contrast between the two men. Emerson proclaimed that "whoso would be a man, must be a nonconformist," but Emerson's nonconformity had its distinct limits. If the authorities of the Harvard Divinity School turned their backs on him for the heresy of his 1838 address, Emerson was still invited to Boston for meetings of the Saturday Club, an organization which was as proper as it was literary, and he was both a respectable and respected citizen of the Concord community. Although he was prepared to acknowledge that "for nonconformity the world whips you with its displeasure," he was nevertheless distressed at the news that Thoreau had carried his disapproval of America's war with Mexico to the point where he had been put in jail for refusing to pay a tax. Emerson was generous to Thoreau in a hundred ways—he encouraged him in his writing by persuading the editors of the *Dial* to print one of his poems; he gave him permission to live on some property he owned at Walden Pond; and he habitually referred to his lesser-known friend as "*the* man of Concord." But Emerson also patronized Thoreau, and nowhere more so than in his fond assumption that Thoreau's intransigent radicalism and intensity of spirit were merely personal idiosyncrasies and that when all was said and done their ideas of life were the same. As the years passed, the relationship with Emerson became increasingly unbearable for Thoreau. The latter years of his journal do not present a flattering portrait of the man who first proposed that he keep it. "I doubt," runs a scornful entry of 1852, "if Emerson could trundle a wheelbarrow through the streets." In 1856 Thoreau wrote of their friendship that it had been "one long tragedy."

For his part, Emerson was finally somewhat disappointed in his protégé. He had taken up Thoreau when the younger man was unknown because he had recognized his rare combination of qualities. Thoreau, Emerson perceived, was steeped in English poetry, especially in the works of the seventeenth-century metaphysicals in whom Emerson was also interested; he possessed a knowledge of languages, of Greek, Latin, French, Italian, Spanish, German, and Anglo-Saxon, that was astonishing; his acquaintance with the writings of the Hindu mystics eventually rivaled Emerson's. In the woods, Thoreau was unsurpassed. He saw everything; he knew everything; he could ice-skate thirty miles a day over the frozen rivers; he could sniff the smoke of a man's pipe a third of a mile away. In the oration which Emerson gave at Thoreau's funeral (subsequently enlarged for publication in the *Atlantic Monthly*), the list of his physical achievements makes him seem almost legendary, like a figure out of a *Davy Crockett Almanack.*

> His senses were acute, his frame well-knit and hardy . . . and there was a wonderful fitness of body and mind. He could pace sixteen rods more accurately than another man could measure them with rod and chain. He could find his path in the woods at night . . . better by his feet than his eyes. He could estimate the measure of a tree very well by his eye; he could estimate the weight of a calf or a pig, like a dealer . . . He was a good swimmer, runner, skater, boatman, and would probably outwalk most countrymen in a day's journey.

Thoreau also was accomplished in a variety of mechanical skills and could do any kind of handyman's job. He was, in Emerson's eyes, the potentially perfect example of the American scholar whom he had envisaged in his 1837 address, the man of books who was also the man of action, the "helpful giant" who would build a new American culture. But Thoreau never turned his talents to great enterprise and command. "I so much regret the loss," wrote Emerson, "that I cannot help counting it a fault in him that he had no ambition. Wanting this, instead of engineering for all America, he was the captain of a huckleberry-party. Pounding beans is good to the end of pounding empires one of these days; but if, at the end of years, it is still only beans!"

II

FOR YOUNG college graduates who would engineer for all America, the nation of the 1830's offered two great opportunities: Religion and Business. The trouble was, as Thoreau said, that "neither the New Testament nor Poor Richard speaks to our condition." The job problem as he saw it was "how to make the getting our living poetic! for if it is not poetic it is not life but death that we get." Christianity, he conceded, conceived of life poetically. "Seek first the kingdom of heaven." "Lay not up for yourselves treasures on earth." "For what is a man profited, if he shall gain the whole world and lose his own soul?" Such statements were so challenging that Thoreau could not believe any Yankee had ever read them. But the hypocrisy of New England churchgoers aside, Thoreau felt that the New Testament did not speak to his generation because it was too exclusively concerned with man's spiritual affairs. Tough-minded and practical, a shrewd Yankee for all his hatred of the type, Thoreau was convinced that Christ had imperfectly taught mankind how to live. Christ's thoughts were all directed toward another world, and for Thoreau this was unsatisfactory. "There is another kind of success than his," he said. "Even here we have a sort of living to get, and must buffet it somewhat longer. There are various tough problems to solve, and we must make shift to live, betwixt spirit and matter, such a human life as we can."

As for Business, Thoreau was graduated from college in the midst of the financial panic of 1837, a time hardly calculated to make Poor Richard's philosophy of life seem attractive. In a commencement debate on the virtues of the Commercial Spirit, Thoreau chose to speak on the negative side, and he continued to do so all his adult life, most notably in his journals and in *Walden.* Even as a small boy he had known how he felt about the American dream of success. For Thoreau's father, once a prosperous storekeeper, had gone bankrupt and been forced into the business of manufacturing pencils. Thereafter the family took in boarders in order to make ends meet. The son they sent to Harvard was always neatly dressed, but his classmates noted that his clothes were unfashionable and occasionally patched. The Thoreaus, in sum, were shabby genteel. Now, life in America has a way of driving such people into a corner, of draining them emotionally, of sniffing out their pathetic pretenses with cruel skill; their tragedy has been one of the major concerns of the American novel from Howells on, and it has furnished the theme of the two most important American plays of our time, *Death of a Salesman* and *The Glass Menagerie.* Yet the experience of failing in a success-mad society has sometimes proved to be a liberation. For one of the striking facts about American literature is the number of our writers who have emerged from shabby-genteel backgrounds. Irving, Poe, Hawthorne, Melville, Emerson—to take only writers of Thoreau's time—all came from families of declining status, and the triumph of their art is in a variety of ways related to this circumstance. In Thoreau's case, the experience of wearing patches helped him to understand that "wealth and the approbation of man" constituted a hollow definition of success. "The *terra firma* of my existence," he affirmed, "lies far beyond."

III

IN ORDER to reach the firm ground that lay beyond, Thoreau struck upon the idea—the year was 1840—of going to live at Walden Pond. Not until 1845, however, was he sufficiently clear of debts to carry out his plan. By doing a little farming on some acres that Emerson owned near the Pond, and by cutting his personal needs to the bone, he was able—as he told Horace Greeley—to get a year's living for six weeks of work. There he remained for two and a half years. His move to Walden was for a brief season the scandal of Concord, but the real drama of his sojourn by the Pond consisted of an action the town gossips never saw: the play of his mind and imagination. What he proposed to do was to explore the "Farthest Indies," not by actually going there, but by "other routes and other methods of travel."

Thoreau's passage to India began with his intense awareness of himself, with his terrific concentration on the resources of his own personality. So self-conscious was Thoreau that all his life he was aware of a certain doubleness in himself. He could all but literally stand aside and watch himself in action and in thought. "However intense my experience," he said, "I am conscious of the presence and criticism of a part of me which, as it were, is not a part of me, but spectator, sharing no experience, but taking note of it, and that is no more I than you." Along with his self-centeredness went a faith that everything he thought and did was important. As a Transcendentalist, he believed that every fact could flower into truth; therefore, each experience of Henry Thoreau could be made to yield up a more heroic significance. It is scarcely accidental that the lines from the Elizabethan poet Samuel Daniel that are quoted both in the *Week on the Concord and Merrimack* and in "A Plea for Captain John Brown" were on Thoreau's lips, according to some of his friends, more often than any other poem—

Unless above himself he can
Erect himself, how poor a thing is man.

To Nature he paid as unremitting attention as he did to Self. The naturalist John Burroughs, among others, has not been impressed by Thoreau as an observer of plants and animals, and has berated him for his sloppy classifications; such criticisms, however, are almost totally irrelevant because they fail to take into account Thoreau's real aim in studying the natural world. If there was anyone whom Thoreau hated it was the scientific observer who carefully recorded and classified biological phenomena and did nothing more. He specifically attacked Humboldt and Darwin for their automatic habit of minutely careful observation, followed by notebook citation, followed by nothing. He urged those who loved Nature to avoid their example. "Do not tread upon the heels of your experience," he said. "Be impressed without making a minute of it. Poetry puts an interval between the impression and the expression,—waits till the seed germinates naturally." The germination of the seed was an event the naturalists failed to wait for. They had no sense of awe or delight in the out-of-doors, and Thoreau dismissed them with sweeping contempt: "Most of our modern authors have not imagined the actual beasts which they presume to describe."

Underlying the bitterness of Thoreau's attack on the naturalists was the fear that in his own investigations of Nature his imagination would someday fail him—that he, too, would be caught in a morass of facts which would refuse to surrender their ultimate meaning to him. As the later volumes of his journals reveal, this was in fact the tragedy that lay in wait for him. But in the years of full intellectual power, and especially in the Walden period, every walk in the woods became "a sort of crusade . . . to go forth and reconquer this Holy Land from the hands of the Infidels." His favorite direction for walking was west, because the West meant Wildness, and Wildness was "the preservation of the world . . . From the forest and wilderness come the tonics and barks which brace mankind." Yet if he literally walked westward, he reached the Wild only by an act of imagination. Once, in the primeval Maine woods, Thoreau declared that "we have not seen pure Nature, unless we have seen her thus vast and drear and inhuman, though in the midst of cities. Nature was here something savage and awful, though beautiful." Concord woods, however, were not the forests of Maine, and Thoreau knew it. He was fully aware that there were no cougars or panthers or lynxes or wolverines in eastern Massachusetts in the 1840's. As he once admitted,

> I cannot but feel as if I lived in a tamed, and, as it were, emasculated country . . . Is it not a maimed and imperfect nature that I am conversant with? . . . I take infinite pains to know all the phenomena of spring, for instance, thinking that I have here the entire poem, and then, to my chagrin, I hear that it is but an imperfect copy that I possess, and have read, that my ancestors have torn out many of the first leaves and grandest passages and mutilated it in many places.

But the tameness of Concord woods did not put bracing tonics and barks beyond mankind's reach. "I shall never find in the wilds of Labrador," Thoreau triumphantly proclaimed, "any greater wildness than in some recess in Concord, i.e., than I import into it." Even in a woods where the wolf and the lynx no longer roamed, a walker could penetrate to the anarchic, wild freedom that lay at the heart of Nature if only his imagination were sufficiently extravagant; one could apprehend it, for example, simply by listening, with all one's faculties intensely concentrated, to a blue jay:

> The unrelenting steel cold scream of a jay, unmelted, that never flows into a song, a sort of wintry trumpet, screaming cold; hard, tense, frozen music, like the winter sky itself; in the blue livery of winter's bands.

Another route to the farthest Indies lay in reading. Like every other activity, reading for Thoreau involved an absolute self-consciousness. "Books," he said, "must be read as deliberately and reservedly as they were written." He disliked novels and was acquainted with few of them; he preferred travel books (Josselyn's *New England Rarities Discovered* was one of his favorites) and philosophy. If walking took him Westward, his reading often took him East, toward Greece, India, and China. Indeed, the classics of Hindu and Buddhist thought absorbed him so completely that they made him feel as if he were living in another world. Thus in May of 1841, after reading the book of the Hindu god Menu, Thoreau observed in his journal:

> That title, "The Laws of Menu with the Gloss of Culluca," comes to me with such a volume of sound as if it had swept unobstructed over the plains of Hindostan; and when my eye rests on yonder birches, or the sun in the water, or the shadows of the trees, it seems to signify the laws of them all. They are the laws of you and me, a fragrance wafted down from those old times, and no more to be refuted than the wind. When my imagination travels eastward and backward to those remote years of the gods, I seem to draw near to the habitation of the morning, and the dawn at length has a place. I remember the book as an hour before sunrise.

Thoreau's study of a book was an action that involved his whole being.

IV

VIVIDLY aware in the face of every experience, Thoreau was more self-conscious, which in his terms is to say more alive, when he was writing than at any other time. His poetry and his prose both reflect a careful, deliberate craftsman whose remarkable ability to detach himself from his work and judge its quality with dispassionate objectivity is best summarized in his remark that an artist's work primarily consists of performing "post-mortem examinations of himself before he is dead." Thoreau's writing can seem spontaneous, but it is not; it is highly wrought, cunningly contrived; it is the supreme expression of his doubleness. His journals, in which he recorded his daily crusades, are more artful than Emerson's, and like the latter's journals they served a larger artfulness. For Thoreau's private works were a great sourcebook, a mine, out of which he extracted ideas and expressions which were then carefully reset, often after an immense amount of lapidary effort, in the mosaic of the more ambitious and more intricate designs of his public essays.

The two full-length books that Thoreau published in his lifetime are the products of the most beautifully disciplined writing talent of the age in America. *A Week on the Concord and Merrimack* is, however, a more experimental, less finished design, inasmuch as it represents the trying-out of the method of presentation that Thoreau would follow in *Walden*. As his masterpiece would, the *Week* recalls an experience of the author's past. In the summer of 1839, Thoreau, in company with his brother John, had taken a canoe trip on the Concord and Merrimack. Two years later, his brother died horribly of lockjaw. Thereafter, Thoreau's recollections of their idyllic river journey had a special poignance. Four years after John's death, Thoreau went to live by Walden Pond and wrote the *Week*. He continued to work on the manuscript, revising and adding to it, after he left the Pond. When the book was finally published—at Thoreau's personal expense—in 1849, the *Week* represented ten years of meditation and work.

Purporting to be a simple record of the 1839 trip, the *Week* in fact contains poems which Thoreau had printed in the *Dial*, journal entries, fragments of essays, and whole lectures written in periods both before and long after the journey. Though the actual trip took a good deal longer, the artful trip lasts seven days, with one chapter for each day. The book seems casually organized, and to a certain extent this is true. But if the thought wanders, there is a transcendental, an organic, rationale for digression in the meandering flow of the rivers. The use of a drifting rhythm as the matrix for the thought and action of a book would not be exploited as successfully again by an American author until *Huckleberry Finn* (1885). Besides its stream-like movement, the book is held together by a rising and falling movement, the cycle of sunrise and sunset, which is repeated each day. The subjects which Thoreau discusses en route are not fortuitous, but are organically related to the unfolding panorama of the journey and to the particular day of the week. (World mythologies, for example, are discussed on Sunday.) Beneath its seeming looseness, the *Week* has the tightness and the economy for which Thoreau always strove.

V

Walden (1854) is even more artful, and more deceptive; the supreme creation of Thoreau's self-consciousness, it lauds simplicity by means of complexity. In substance as well as in mode of expression, the "humor" of the book is paradoxical.

Thus the author asserts that neither the New Testament nor Poor Richard speaks to our condition, but the opening of *Walden* sounds remarkably like Benjamin Franklin's *Autobiography*. There is, first of all, the same disarmingly candid explanation as to why the author happened to write this book; in Thoreau's case, he insists that he has been prompted to authorship partly because so many of his townsmen have asked him questions about his sojourn at the Pond, just as Franklin claims that one of the reasons he became an author was that he felt his son might be interested in learning something about his ancestors. And just as Franklin is charmingly frank about his egotistic desire to talk about himself, so Thoreau admits in a delightful phrase, "I should not talk so much about myself if there were anybody else whom I knew as well." The title of the first chapter would surely have been approved of by Poor Richard: "Economy."

What Thoreau is doing, however, is to destroy the enemy with the enemy's own weapons. He deliberately appropriates the language of the success ethic in order to expose it. In the immemorial manner of the businessman, he talks about "conditions," except that he does not judge them by the standard of economic prosperity. Prosperity, indeed, is ruining the country. The mass of men lead lives of quiet desperation. Their fingers tremble from the hard work they do. They are nothing but machines. They are gasping for breath; they must lie and flatter to get ahead. Published two years after Harriet Beecher Stowe had made Simon Legree a national byword, *Walden* asserts that "it is hard to have a Southern overseer; it is worse to have a Northern one, but worst of all when you are the slave-driver of yourself." The unluckiest of all are those who succeed, for farms, houses, barns, and cattle—in sum, possessions—make horrible demands upon their owners, and are more easily acquired than got rid of. As for luxuries and the so-called comforts of life, they have been throughout history positive hindrances to the elevation of mankind.

Against this appalling picture of the economy of his neighbors, Thoreau sets forth his own economy, his personal plan of living, in a series of elaborate financial metaphors which appear at first glance to be an attempt to justify his plan in terms of the Poor Richard civilization he has just been scorning. The decision to go to the woods is spoken of as the determination "to go into business at oncc." Over the years, he has "well-nigh sunk all his capital" into listening to the wind, therefore why should he not turn to this new "enterprise"? For a long time he had felt that Walden Pond "would be a good place for business, not solely on account of the railroad and the ice trade; it offers advantages which it may not be good policy to divulge; it is a good port and a good foundation." Having always endeavored "to acquire strict business habits," he of course keeps ledgers and accounts during his sojourn. *Walden* contains itemized lists which outdo anything in the collected works of Franklin. The cost of the things Thoreau buys is given in meticulous detail, down to the half penny—even the quarter penny. And if Franklin's economies, his ability to cut his meals down to a glass of water and a handful of raisins, seem awesome, Thoreau's tall tale of economy reduces Ben Franklin to a spendthrift. On food for the first eight months of his stay Thoreau spent $8.74; on clothing, $8.40¾; on housing, $28.12½. Once again, however, this ruthless application of the principles of Poor Richard to the practical problems of daily living is made with an anti-Poor Richard purpose.

Poor Richard believed that early to bed and early to rise makes a man healthy, wealthy, and wise. Poor Richard was ascetic in the present, kept his shop now, so that in the future his shop would keep him. But the "Yankee shrewdness" of which Thoreau speaks is directed toward avoiding, not attaining, "the splendid mausoleum" where Poor Richard dreamed of living. The asceticism of Thoreau is directed toward the goal of a greater awareness, a superior intensity, a more and more absolute self-consciousness.

> It occurred to me when I awoke this morning, feeling regret of the day before in eating fruit, which had dulled my sensibilities, that man was to be treated as a musical instrument, and if any viol was to be made of sound timber and kept well-tuned always, it was he, so that when the bow of events is drawn across him he may vibrate and resound in perfect harmony. A sensitive soul will be continually trying its strings to see if they are in tune. A man's body must be rasped down exactly to a shaving. It is of far more importance than the wood of a Cremona violin.

Thoreau accepts the frugality of Poor Richard, but to the end that he will achieve the sensitivity of a Cremona violin, not that he will make a fortune. Thoreau cuts down on costs because "the cost of a thing is the amount of what I will call life which is required to be exchanged for it, immediately or in the long run," and, therefore, a cost reduction is not money saved but a life saved. He gets up at sunrise not for the purpose of getting ahead, but because "poetry and art date from such an hour." In perhaps the clearest indication that Thoreau had Franklin in mind when he wrote *Walden*, he says that one of his prime motives for early rising was so that he could hear the crowing of the wild cocks in the woods—for to hear those birds "who would not be early to rise, and rise earlier and earlier every successive day of his life, till he became unspeakably healthy, wealthy, and wise?" In this juxtaposition of the wild chanticleer of the woods with the most famous of Poor Richard's aphorisms is contained the essence of Thoreau's defiance of Franklin's America.

The bulk of the chapter "Economy" is taken up with an elaboration of his objections to the way in which his neighbors feed, clothe, and house themselves, and of his alternative ideas. His critique is largely centered on the habits of the group which Thorstein Veblen would forty-five years later call the leisure class. The Poor Richard who has made his pile can think of nothing to do except eat more and richer food, build larger and more splendid houses, and wear more abundant clothing. The result is that the rich are not simply comfortably warm, but unnaturally hot; they are in fact cooked—"of course *à la mode*." Thoreau's concern is to strip away all these superfluities. "Fanciful clothes are our epidermis, or false skin, which partakes not of our life, and may be stripped off here and there without fatal injury." As for housing, Thoreau maintained that "before we can adorn our houses with beautiful objects the walls must be stripped, and beautiful housekeeping and beautiful living laid for a foundation." He wants to get rid of all pretense and display, he wants to get to the heart of things and start growing outward from there. He comes to the Pond to confront experience directly, to make a fresh start, to shuck off the dead skin of a materialistic civilization. This is the "private business" he wishes to transact, and *Walden* is the story of his metamorphosis.

In this light, the practical details of economy can be seen to have a transcendental significance. The stripping away of the layers of clothing and housing in which modern man is cooking to death is the symbolic first step in the act of metamorphosis—as Nature herself witnesses.

> Our moulting season, like that of the fowls, must be a crisis in our lives. The loon retires to solitary ponds to spend it. Thus also the snake casts its slough, and the caterpillar its wormy coat, by an internal industry and expansion; for clothes are but our outmost cuticle and coil.

Yet if the casting of the old coat and the creation of a new one are accomplished in solitude, this does not mean that the new coat has no significance for society. In one of the first paragraphs of the book, Thoreau remarks that he hopes his readers will accept such portions of his narrative as apply to them, and that he trusts "none will stretch the seams in putting on the coat, for it may do good service to him whom it fits." *Walden* itself is a new "garment" for mankind as well as for the man who made it, and by donning it mankind can accomplish collective rebirth and renewal. For "if there is not a new man, how can the new clothes be made to fit?"

With that question we reach the heart of the chapter on economy, the building of Thoreau's house. The conception of Thoreau's dream house is at the other end of the scale from Poe's fantastic "Domain of Arnheim" (see pp. 453–60), but both are equally removed from middle-class, mid-nineteenth-century America. Poe had built luxuriously in the name of Art and Beauty and Taste; Thoreau defines true luxury as the employment of Nature as the "raw material of tropes and symbols" in the creation of an object. In the spring of 1845, Thoreau tells us, he had gone out to Walden and cut down some "tall, arrowy white pines, still in their youth, for timber." He bleached and purified the boards in the sun. He dug his cellar where a woodchuck had a hole. Thus his house had grown from the inside out, like an organism. If all men built their own houses, says Thoreau, they would perhaps be poets. But his self-conscious purification of the boards in the sun is not merely poetic, it is religious. While Poor Richard did not speak to Thoreau's condition, *Walden* nonetheless has a Yankee economy to it; the New Testament did not speak to his condition either, and yet *Walden* has a Christian economy too. Christ's forty days in the wilderness were a process of purification, and to Thoreau, who regarded Christ as "a sublime actor on the stage of the world," such a retreat from the world was an act of supreme self-consciousness which he self-consciously wished to repeat. The Christian parallel by no means exhausted Thoreau's awareness of the religious nature of his sojourn at the Pond. The fable of withdrawal and renewal was one which was common to all the great religions of the world. ("It is interesting to observe," he wrote in the *Week*, "with what singular unanimity the farthest sundered nations and generations consent to give completeness and roundness to an ancient fable.") Thus his retreat to the Pond had Hindu as well as Christian overtones. The doctrine of Yoga, to which Emerson had introduced Thoreau, urged a complete abstraction from all worldly objects. Work must be done without the hope of material reward; sacrifice, mortification of the flesh, and controlling the breath were the indispensable preliminaries to a higher state of being. "Depend upon it that, rude and careless as I am," Thoreau wrote, "I would fain practice the yoga faithfully . . . To some extent, and at rare intervals, even I am a yogi." On another occasion he said, "One may discover the root of a Hindoo religion in his own private history, when, in the silent intervals of the day or the night, he does sometimes inflict on himself like austerities with a stern satisfaction."

It would be a mistake to think that Thoreau carried these Christian and Hindu analogies beyond the point of general resemblance. Thoreau was not a Yogi, of course, if for no other reason than that the Hindu mystic wishes release from the unending cycle of rebirth, whereas *Walden* glorifies it. But he did act in conscious knowledge of the general similarity between Eastern religion and his own reenactment of a universal fable; his invocations of Christ and the gods of Greece had the same general analogical purpose. While many of the fabulous parallels are drawn in a spirit of self-deflationary humor which rescues the book from the dangers of both egotism and blasphemy, in a very real sense the author of *Walden* is always serious. The prosaic details of cutting down trees and hewing timbers and digging a cellar, of paying an Irishman named Collins $4.25 for the lumber in a shanty that Collins had occupied, are quite deliberately arranged in such a way as to reveal their religious meaning. Thoreau's ideal was—

> Facts should only be as the frame to my pictures; they should be material to the mythology which I am writing; not facts to assist men to make money, farmers to farm profitably, in any common sense; facts to tell who I am and where I have been or what I have thought . . . My facts shall be falsehoods to the common sense. I would so state facts that they shall be significant, shall be mythic or mythologic.

He cuts down young trees in the spring and he bleaches boards in the sun: these are preliminary steps in building a house. They are also a part of the religious ceremony of purification and renewal.

The fourth chapter of *Walden*, "Sounds," introduces another major aspect of the renewal theme: the seeding, planting, fertilizing, flowering, and harvesting of crops. The progress of his bean field is a conversational topic of which Thoreau never grows tired; it also furnishes him with a rhythm that finally imposes an order on the entire book. The structure of the *Week* is a sequence of seven days; in *Walden*, the action begins in early summer and ends the following spring; the twenty-six months which Thoreau actually spent at the Pond are compressed into the cycle of a year; his account of his life in the woods follows the elemental pattern of the flowering, death, and replanting of a bean crop. Throughout the book one is constantly being reminded of the continuing drama of vegetation. In the chapter "Visitors," for example, after he has talked at some length about the people who have come to see him—the most memorable visitor being the French woodchopper, and the most fascinating being the runaway slave, whom "I helped to forward toward the north star"—Thoreau suddenly breaks off the description, and the next chapter begins: "Meanwhile my beans . . . were impatient to be hoed." And in the second half of the book, in the chapters which follows the crucial chapter "The Ponds," the seasonal cycle comes more and more to dominate the action.

Yet, far down inside Thoreau's submission of his life to Nature, there is an ambiguity. The chapter "Higher Laws" begins with the famous sentence,

> As I came home through the woods with my string of fish, trailing my pole, it being now quite dark, I caught a glimpse of a woodchuck, stealing across my path, and felt a strange thrill of savage delight, and was strongly tempted to seize and devour him raw; not that I was hungry then, except for that wildness which he represented.

Here, seemingly, is the statement of the natural man who likes to spend his days up to his chin in a swamp, of the primitivist who wants to tear apart a woodchuck as if he were an animal himself. But there was an invincible fastidiousness about Thoreau, an abhorrence of dirt and filth that was very deep in him. As the chapter "Higher Laws" makes clear, his adherence to a simple diet sprang as much from his loathing of the unclean as it did from any positive belief in the spiritual efficacy of moderation. Despite the fantasy about the woodchuck, Thoreau was a vegetarian; as he says in "Higher Laws," "the practical objection to animal food in my case was its uncleanness." Such food had no ill effect on his body, but it disagreed, as he says, with his imagination. In revulsion, Thoreau compared meat-eaters to the gluttonous maggot and the gross larva of the caterpillar. The same thing was true of his drinking habits. Thoreau found that water was the only drink worth stomaching, again because his imagination revolted at anything stronger.

Thoreau could be self-consciously earthy and announce that "the poet writes the history of his own body," but no description could be more inapplicable to the poet that Thoreau in fact was. As reported in Emerson's biography of Thoreau, one of Thoreau's friends once said, "I love Henry, but . . . as for taking his arm, I should as soon think of taking the arm of an elm tree." Thoreau wrote that "there is no remedy for love but to love more," but he never married. While he carried Whitman's *Leaves of Grass* around Concord "like a red flag," his response to Whitman's sexuality was decidedly squeamish:

> There are two or three pieces in the book which are disagreeable to say the least; simply sensual. He does not celebrate love at all. It is as if the beasts spoke. I think that men have not been ashamed of themselves without reason.

Thoreau worshiped the sun, its life-giving powers; over and over again in *Walden* he contrasts the clear sunlight with the "smoke of opinion" of misguided men which obscures it from sight, or with the "smoke and steam and hissing" of the railroad train which threatens man's whole relation to the sun. He talks of pouring water on the floor of his unfinished house and letting the sun dry it. The sun in all these connections is a symbol of purification and light. But the sun is also a corrupter, the agent of overripeness, taint, putrefaction. Therefore, the sun, the fundamental source of all transcendental correspondences between man and Nature, was for Thoreau an uneasy subject. Constantly in *Walden*, when Thoreau is talking about the sun, one has the feeling that he is about to break through Emerson's formulation that Nature is the present expositor of the divine mind and confront the fact that Nature is not always so reassuringly disposed. But in the end he does not. He is merely squeamish, and averts his eyes from the full import of the solar correspondence. Thoreau could triumphantly proclaim that he "dreamed of purity last night," but he said very little about his nightmares. Only a more audacious voyager like Melville would be willing to stare into the sun and then tell all that he saw there.

The closest Thoreau came to facing up to the possible existence of ambiguity within the virtues he celebrated was in his discussion of poverty. Throughout *Walden* he glorifies poverty. "By poverty, i.e., simplicity of life and fewness of incidents, I am solidified and crystallized, as a vapor or liquid by cold. It is a singular concentration of strength and energy and flavor." But on the Baker Farm near Walden he discovers John Field, an Irishman, and his family living in a miserable rented hut. Poverty has not crystallized the Fields, it has degraded them. The roof of the hut leaks, they are all cold and miserable. Field works hard and so does his wife, but to no avail; the family is starving and filthy. Yet for all his recognition of what poverty has done to them, Thoreau clings to the belief that defiance is the solution. He tells them they must build a simple house of their own, cut out tea, coffee, butter, and meat, and then they will all be as healthy, wealthy, and wise as he is. Melville's story, "Cock-a-Doodle-Doo!", published the year before *Walden*, both prophesies and parodies the naïve belief that Self-Reliance is a solution to the problem of human want.

In the dramatic structure of *Walden*, "The Ponds" is the central chapter. Coming in the exact center of the book, it looks back on the more worldly first half and looks forward to the more seasonal, more mythological second half. In rejecting both the New Testament and Poor Richard, Thoreau had said, "We must make shift to live, betwixt spirit and matter, such a human life as we can," and "The Ponds" maintains an exquisite balance between these two realms of existence. Walden Pond, Thoreau tells us here, has two colors. Viewed at a certain distance on a certain day, the Pond is "a clear and deep green well." At other times it is a "matchless and indescribable blue, such as watered or changeable silks and sword blades suggest." Blue and green, the color of the sky and the color of the earth, of this world and the next, Walden Pond brings together the rejected values of the New Testament and Poor Richard in a new synthesis which transforms both.

Both the "earth's eye" and "sky water," the Pond is also the supreme object of correspondence between the mind and Nature, between the soul and God. So profound is the correspondence that, fishing in the Pond one dark night, Thoreau feels that he might almost cast his line upward into the air as downward into the Pond. Sounding the bottom of the Pond corresponds to sounding the soul, for the Pond is "God's Drop." "Heaven," says Thoreau, speaking of Walden, "is under our feet as well as over our heads." For a man to whom Self-Reliance was a Bible, there was profound meaning in the fact that the Pond has no visible inlet or outlet; it maintains itself by an inner energy, its own fresh springs. Unlike the ambiguous sun, the Pond is an unmitigated "vision of serenity and purity." It is a great crystal on the surface of the earth, a lake of light. It is very old, older than America; Thoreau remembers having heard that a potter lived on its banks before the Revolution; indeed, it is older than mankind:

> Perhaps on that spring morning when Adam and Eve were driven out of Eden, Walden Pond was already in existence, and even then breaking up in a gentle spring rain accompanied by mist and a southerly wind, and covered with myriads of ducks and geese, which had not heard of the fall, when still such pure lakes sufficed them.

The clean, wild ducks still come to the Pond in the course of their migrations, and in the fall the loon comes as always to Walden "to moult and bathe in the pond, making the woods ring with his wild laughter." The loon, with whose moulting Thoreau had already identified himself, is the great embodiment of the spirit of the Pond. The loon can soar and swoop in the sky; it can also dive under water all the way to the bottom and swim under water for great distances. Quite the most extraordinary event in *Walden* is the game which Thoreau plays with the loon, watching to see where it will dive and then rowing madly to the place where he anticipates the bird will come up, a magnificent game of tag played through the elements of air and water, lasting for an hour or more, while the bird makes the woods ring with its demoniac laughter. As Thoreau once wrote in his journals, "Not by constraint or severity shall you have access to true wisdom, but by abandonment, and childlike mirthfulness. If you would know aught, be gay before it."

If the Pond is old, it is also "perennially young." "It has not acquired one permanent wrinkle after all its ripples." The villagers think of piping its waters into Concord, but Walden's inexhaustibility is proof against such desecration. Although the Fitchburg Railway, that "devilish Iron Horse," muddies the waters with its foot, Walden can absorb the engine's soot, wash out State Street in the bargain, and still retain its purity. The woods around the lake may be cut down, but after a season another forest "is springing up by its shore as lustily as ever." Surely such a Pond could never die.

But the great drama of the book is that it does. On the night of December 22, 1845, Walden freezes over. To be sure, the ice looks alternately blue and green, just as the water had; and even in the depths of winter a fisherman can bring up on an anchor from the bottom of the pond a bright green weed, a symbol of life and an object of correspondence: "Methinks my own soul must be a bright invisible green." But the ice-locked Pond is dying, nonetheless, and the sequence of four chapters beginning with "House-Warming" records its progressive strangulation. As for Thoreau, he slowly retreats into himself as winter sets in. In "House-Warming" he builds a chimney and plasters his house. When the snow covers the ground, "I withdrew yet farther into my shell and endeavored to keep a bright fire within my house and within my breast." The book becomes more and more elemental. Thoreau's movements outdoors are constricted; fewer animals and birds are seen. The book has been full of sounds, but suddenly a silence falls over everything. "Even the hooting of the owl was hushed." There are fewer visitors than before.

But in his shut-in solitude, Thoreau has at last reached the vital center from which true outward growth can begin. He has cast off his wormy coat and woven for himself "a silken web or chrysalis, and nymph-like shall ere long burst forth a more perfect creature, fitted for a higher society." In the chapter called "Spring" the ritual of renewal reaches its climactic stage, and Thoreau's transmutation, his recovery of life, is completed. In the warm sun, the ice on the Pond rots; here, for once, rottenness does not run counter to the over-all symbolism of the book; rottenness here means not decay but fertility, a fertility out of which death flows back into life; soon the air is filled with the cheerful music of "a thousand tinkling rills and rivulets whose veins are filled with the blood of winter they are bearing off." "The symbol of perpetual youth, the grassblade," is seen again, the sun shines bright and warm, "recreating the world." In May, the loon returns to the Pond. "Walden," says Thoreau, "was dead and is alive again." With its rebirth, Thoreau changes "from the lumpish grub in the earth to the airy and fluttering butterfly." Gathering together all the metamorphic symbolism of the book, Thoreau concludes *Walden* with the triumphant fable of the bug:

> Every one has heard the story which has gone the rounds of New England, of a strong and beautiful bug which came out of the dry leaf of an old table of apple-tree wood, which had stood in a farmer's kitchen for sixty years, first in Connecticut, and afterward in Massachusetts,—from an egg deposited in the living tree many years earlier still . . . Who does not feel his faith in a resurrection and an immortality strengthened by hearing of this?

By his refusal to hurry, by the heroism of his patience and his singleness of purpose and his resolution, Thoreau in *Walden* triumphs over the tyranny of time. A gasping, clock-watching, hurrying America is enslaved by time, but Thoreau, like the Hindu artist Kouroo to whom he compares himself, has made no compromise with time, and therefore time has kept out of his way. Kouroo's resolve had been to create one perfect work of art—a beautiful staff—though it take his entire lifetime, and that had been Thoreau's resolve too. By the time that Kouroo had selected the stick on which to begin his carving, all his friends had grown old and died. Before he had given it proper shape, the dynasty of the Candahars was at an end; by the time he had smoothed and polished the staff, Kalpa was no longer the polestar; ere he had adorned the head with precious stones, Brahma had awoke and slumbered many times. But when the finishing stroke was put to his work, it suddenly expanded before the eyes of the astonished artist into the fairest of all the creations of Brahma. He had made a new system in making a staff, a world with full and fair proportions; in which, though the old cities and dynasties had passed away, fairer and more glorious ones had taken their places. And now he saw by the heap of shavings still fresh at his feet, that, for him and his work, the former lapse of time had been an illusion, and that no more time had elapsed than is required for a single scintillation from the brain of Brahma to fall on and inflame the tinder of a mortal brain.

The revisions, the years of meditation and devotion which Thoreau had poured into his great book, made it a veritable staff of Kouroo. Of all the gods with whom Thoreau compared himself, he seems perhaps most like Narcissus. At Walden Pond, he gazed down into the deep green well of the water and stared at his own reflection. He stared long and hard; he looked at no one else. But by that intense concentration on himself, his refusal to write about anyone else but himself, Thoreau transcended himself and wrote about humanity and for other people. Unlike Narcissus, he did not die as a result of gazing overly long into the water of Walden. Instead, he created a book about the Pond which cheated time and death and became as immortal as Brahma.

READING SUGGESTIONS

EDITIONS

The Writings of Henry David Thoreau, 20 vols. (1906). The standard edition.

CARL BODE, editor, *Collected Poems of Henry Thoreau* (1943). Definitive.

CARL BODE AND WALTER HARDING, editors, *The Correspondence of Henry David Thoreau* (1958). The most complete collection of letters to and from Thoreau.

Journals, ed. by Bradford Torrey and Francis H. Allen, with a foreword by Henry Seidel Canby, 14 vols. (1949).

The Heart of Thoreau's Journals, ed. by Odell Shepard (1927).

PERRY MILLER, *Consciousness in Concord* (1958). Includes the text of the "Lost Journal" (1840–41).

J. LYNDON SHANLEY, *The Making of Walden* (1957). Includes the first version of Thoreau's masterpiece and an analysis of his revisions.

BIOGRAPHY AND CRITICISM

HENRY SEIDEL CANBY, *Thoreau* (1939). The best biography.

WILLIAM ELLERY CHANNING, *Thoreau: The Poet-Naturalist* (1873, revised and enlarged by Frank Sanborn, 1902). Thoreau as seen by a friend and fellow excursionist.

WALTER HARDING, editor, *Thoreau: A Century of Criticism* (1954). A collection of critical essays on Thoreau from his own time to ours. Includes pieces by James Russell Lowell, Havelock Ellis, Paul Elmer More, Sinclair Lewis, and Henry Miller.

WALTER HARDING, *A Thoreau Handbook* (1959). A comprehensive bibliographical guide.

F. O. MATTHIESSEN, *American Renaissance* (1941). The most sensitive study of Thoreau's expression.

SHERMAN PAUL, *The Shores of America: Thoreau's Inward Exploration* (1958). An exhaustive discussion of Thoreau's mind and art.

LEO STOLLER, *After Walden* (1957). Analyzes Thoreau's changing views of "economic man."

MARK VAN DOREN, *Henry David Thoreau* (1916). A hostile report.

A WINTER WALK

◇

IN THE spring of 1843, Thoreau left Concord for Staten Island, New York, to become the tutor of the family of William Emerson. Ralph Waldo Emerson encouraged him to make the move, on the theory that it would bring the aspiring author in contact with the literary world of New York City. But Thoreau's attempts to sell his work in New York were unsuccessful, and he found tutoring rather a bore. Not surprisingly, he became very homesick. Out of his yearning for Concord came "A Winter Walk." Emerson accepted it for publication in the *Dial* (it appeared in the October, 1843 issue), but with something less than complete approval. "I had some hesitation about it," he wrote to Thoreau,

> notwithstanding its faithful observation and its fine sketches of the pickerelfisher and of the woodchopper, on account of *mannerism*, an old charge of mine,—as if, by attention, one could get the trick of the rhetoric; for example, to call a cold place sultry, a solitude public, a wilderness *domestic* (a favorite word), and in the woods to insult over cities, armies, etc.

To many modern readers, however, the essay is one of Thoreau's finest early efforts. That he chose to organize his observations into what he termed an "excursion" foreshadows the characteristic structure of his later and more famous work.

◇

THE WIND has gently murmured through the blinds, or puffed with feathery softness against the windows, and occasionally sighed like a summer zephyr lifting the leaves along, the livelong night. The meadow mouse has slept in his snug gallery in the sod, the owl has sat in a hollow tree in the depth of the swamp, the rabbit, the squirrel, and the fox have all been housed. The watch-dog has lain quiet on the hearth, and the cattle have stood silent in their stalls. The earth itself has slept, as it were its first, not its last sleep, save when some street sign or woodhouse door has faintly creaked upon its hinge, cheering forlorn nature at her midnight work—the only sound awake 'twixt Venus and Mars—advertising us of a remote inward warmth, a divine cheer and fellowship, where gods are met together, but where it is very bleak for men to stand. But while the earth has slumbered, all the air has been alive with feathery flakes descending, as if some northern Ceres reigned, showering her silvery grain over all the fields.

We sleep, and at length awake to the still reality of a winter morning. The snow lies warm as cotton or down upon the window sill; the broadened sash and frosted panes admit a dim and private light, which enhances the snug cheer within. The stillness of the morning is impressive. The floor creaks under our feet as we move toward the window to look abroad through some clear space over the fields. We see the roofs stand under their snow burden. From the eaves and fences hang stalactites of snow, and in the yard stand stalagmites covering some concealed core. The trees and shrubs rear white arms to the sky on every side; and where were walls and fences, we see fantastic forms stretching in frolic gambols across the dusky landscape, as if Nature had strewn her fresh designs over the fields by night as models for man's art.

Silently we unlatch the door, letting the drift fall in, and step abroad to face the cutting air. Already the stars have lost some of their sparkle, and a dull, leaden mist skirts the horizon. A lurid brazen light in the east proclaims the approach of day, while the western landscape is dim and spectral still, and clothed in a somber Tartarean light,[1] like the shadowy realms. They are Infernal sounds only that you hear—the crowing of cocks, the barking of dogs, the chopping of wood, the lowing of kine, all seem to come from Pluto's barnyard and beyond the Styx—not for any melancholy they suggest, but their twilight bustle is too solemn and mysterious for earth. The recent tracks of the fox or otter, in the yard, remind us that each hour of the night is crowded with events, and the primeval nature is still working and making tracks in the snow. Opening the gate, we tread briskly along the lone country road, crunching the dry and crisped snow under our feet, or aroused by the sharp, clear creak of the wood sled, just starting for the distant market, from the early farmer's door, where it has lain the summer long, dreaming amid the chips and stubble; while far through the drifts and powdered windows we see the farmer's early candle, like a paled star, emitting a lonely beam, as if some severe virtue were at its matins there. And one by one the smokes begin to ascend from the chimneys amid the trees and snows.

The sluggish smoke curls up from some deep dell,
The stiffened air exploring in the dawn,
And making slow acquaintance with the day
Delaying now upon its heavenward course,
In wreathèd loiterings dallying with itself,
With as uncertain purpose and slow deed
As its half-awakened master by the hearth,
Whose mind still slumbering and sluggish thoughts
Have not yet swept into the onward current
Of the new day—and now it streams afar,
The while the chopper goes with step direct,
And mind intent to swing the early axe.
First in the dusky dawn he sends abroad
His early scout, his emissary, smoke,
The earliest, latest pilgrim from the roof,
To feel the frosty air, inform the day;
And while he crouches still beside the hearth,
Nor musters courage to unbar the door,
It has gone down the glen with the light wind,
And o'er the plain unfurled its venturous wreath,
Draped the treetops, loitered upon the hill,
And warmed the pinions of the early bird;
And now, perchance, high in the crispy air,
Has caught sight of the day o'er the earth's edge,
And greets its master's eye at his low door,
As some refulgent cloud in the upper sky.

We hear the sound of woodchopping at the farmers' doors, far over the frozen earth, the baying of the house-dog, and the distant clarion of the cock—though the thin and frosty air conveys only the finer particles of sound to our ears, with short and sweet vibrations, as the waves subside soonest on the purest and lightest liquids, in which gross substances sink to the bottom. They come clear and bell-like, and from a greater distance in the horizon, as if there were fewer impediments than in summer to make them faint and ragged. The ground is sonorous, like seasoned wood, and even the ordinary rural sounds are melodious, and the jingling of the ice on the trees is sweet and liquid. There is the least possible moisture in the atmosphere, all being dried up or congealed, and it is of such extreme tenuity and elasticity that it becomes a source of delight. The withdrawn and tense sky seems groined like the aisles of a cathedral, and the polished air sparkles as if there were crystals of ice floating in it. As they who have resided in Greenland tell us that when it freezes "the sea smokes like burning turf-land, and a fog or mist arises, called frost-smoke," which "cutting smoke frequently raises blisters on the face and hands, and is very pernicious to the health." But this pure, stinging cold is an elixir to the lungs, and not so much a frozen mist as a crystallized midsummer haze, refined and purified by cold.

The sun at length rises through the distant woods, as if with the faint clashing, swinging sound of cymbals, melting the air with his beams, and with such rapid steps the morning travels, that already his rays are gilding the distant western mountains. Meanwhile we step hastily along through the powdery snow, warmed by an inward heat, enjoying an Indian summer still, in the increased glow of thought and feeling. Probably if our lives were more conformed to nature, we should not need to defend ourselves against her heats and colds, but find her our constant nurse and friend, as do plants and quadrupeds. If our bodies were fed with pure and simple elements, and not with a stimulating and heating diet, they would afford no more pasture for cold than a leafless twig, but thrive like the trees, which find even winter genial to their expansion.

The wonderful purity of nature at this season is a most pleasing fact. Every decayed stump and moss-grown stone and rail, and the dead leaves of autumn, are concealed by a clean napkin of snow. In the bare fields and tinkling woods, see what virtue survives. In the coldest and bleakest places, the warmest charities still maintain a foothold. A cold and searching wind drives away all contagion, and nothing can withstand it but what has a virtue in it, and accordingly, whatever we meet with in cold and bleak places, as the tops of mountains, we respect for a sort of sturdy innocence, a Puritan

A WINTER WALK. **1. Tartarean light:** In the *Iliad*, Tartarus is the infernal region below Hades.

toughness. All things beside seem to be called in for shelter, and what stays out must be part of the original frame of the universe, and of such valor as God himself. It is invigorating to breathe the cleansed air. Its greater fineness and purity are visible to the eye, and we would fain stay out long and late, that the gales may sigh through us, too, as through the leafless trees, and fit us for the winter—as if we hoped so to borrow some pure and steadfast virtue, which will stead us in all seasons.

There is a slumbering subterranean fire in nature which never goes out, and which no cold can chill. It finally melts the great snow, and in January or July is only buried under a thicker or thinner covering. In the coldest day it flows somewhere, and the snow melts around every tree. This field of winter rye, which sprouted late in the fall, and now speedily dissolves the snow, is where the fire is very thinly covered. We feel warmed by it. In the winter, warmth stands for all virtue, and we resort in thought to a trickling rill, with its bare stones shining in the sun, and to warm springs in the woods, with as much eagerness as rabbits and robins. The steam which rises from swamps and pools is as dear and domestic as that of our own kettle. What fire could ever equal the sunshine of a winter's day, when the meadow mice come out by the wall-sides, and the chickadee lisps in the defiles of the wood? The warmth comes directly from the sun, and is not radiated from the earth, as in summer; and when we feel his beams on our backs as we are treading some snowy dell, we are grateful as for a special kindness, and bless the sun which has followed us into that by-place.

This subterranan fire has its altar in each man's breast; for in the coldest day, and on the bleakest hill, the traveler cherishes a warmer fire within the folds of his cloak than is kindled on any hearth. A healthy man, indeed, is the complement of the seasons, and in winter, summer is in his heart. There is the south. Thither have all birds and insects migrated, and around the warm springs in his breast are gathered the robin and the lark.

At length, having reached the edge of the woods, and shut out the gadding town, we enter within their covert as we go under the roof of a cottage, and cross its threshold, all ceiled and banked up with snow. They are glad and warm still, and as genial and cheery in winter as in summer. As we stand in the midst of the pines in the flickering and checkered light which straggles but little way into their maze, we wonder if the towns have ever heard their simple story. It seems to us that no traveler has ever explored them, and notwithstanding the wonders which science is elsewhere revealing every day, who would not like to hear their annals? Our humble villages in the plain are their contribution. We borrow from the forest the boards which shelter and the sticks which warm us. How important is their evergreen to the winter, that portion of the summer which does not fade, the permanent year, the unwithered grass! Thus simply, and with little expense of altitude, is the surface of the earth diversified. What would human life be without forests, those natural cities? From the tops of mountains they appear like smooth-shaven lawns, yet whither shall we walk but in this taller grass?

In this glade covered with bushes of a year's growth, see how the silvery dust lies on every seared leaf and twig, deposited in such infinite and luxurious forms as by their very variety atone for the absence of color. Observe the tiny tracks of mice around every stem, and the triangular tracks of the rabbit. A pure elastic heaven hangs over all, as if the impurities of the summer sky, refined and shrunk by the chaste winter's cold, had been winnowed from the heavens upon the earth.

Nature confounds her summer distinctions at this season. The heavens seem to be nearer the earth. The elements are less reserved and distinct. Water turns to ice, rain to snow. The day is but a Scandinavian night. The winter is an arctic summer.

How much more living is the life that is in nature, the furred life which still survives the stinging nights, and, from amidst fields and woods covered with frost and snow, sees the sun rise!

"The foodless wilds
Pour forth their brown inhabitants."

The gray squirrel and rabbit are brisk and playful in the remote glens, even on the morning of the cold Friday. Here is our Lapland and Labrador, and for our Esquimaux and Knistenaux, Dog-ribbed Indians, Novazemblaites, and Spitzbergeners, are there not the ice-cutter and woodchopper, the fox, muskrat, and mink?

Still, in the midst of the arctic day, we may trace the summer to its retreats, and sympathize with some contemporary life. Stretched over the brooks, in the midst of the frost-bound meadows, we may observe the submarine cottages of the caddis-worms, the larvae of the Plicipennes; their small cylindrical cases built around themselves, composed of flags, sticks, grass, and withered leaves, shells, and pebble, in form and color like the wrecks which strew the bottom,—now drifting along over the pebbly bottom, now whirling in tiny eddies and dashing down steep falls, or sweeping rapidly along with the current, or else swaying to and fro at the end of some grass-blade or root.

Anon they will leave their sunken habitations, and, crawling up the stems of plants, or to the surface, like gnats, as perfect insects henceforth, flutter over the surface of the water, or sacrifice their short lives in the flame of our candles at evening. Down yonder little glen the shrubs are drooping under their burden, and the red alderberries contrast with the white ground. Here are the marks of a myriad feet which have already been abroad. The sun rises as proudly over such a glen as over the valley of the Seine or the Tiber, and it seems the residence of a pure and self-subsistent valor, such as they never witnessed—which never knew defeat nor fear. Here reign the simplicity and purity of a primitive age, and a health and hope far remote from towns and cities. Standing quite alone, far in the forest, while the wind is shaking down snow from the trees, and leaving the only human tracks behind us, we find our reflections of a richer variety than the life of cities. The chickadee and nuthatch are more inspiring society than statesmen and philosophers, and we shall return to these last as to more vulgar companions. In this lonely glen, with its brook draining the slopes, its creased ice and crystals of all hues, where the spruces and hemlocks stand up on either side, and the rush and sere wild oats in the rivulet itself, our lives are more serene and worthy to contemplate.

As the day advances, the heat of the sun is reflected by the hillsides, and we hear a faint but sweet music, where flows the rill released from its fetters, and the icicles are melting on the trees; and the nuthatch and partridge are heard and seen. The south wind melts the snow at noon, and the bare ground appears with its withered grass and leaves, and we are invigorated by the perfume which exhales from it, as by the scent of strong meats.

Let us go into this deserted woodman's hut, and see how he has passed the long winter nights and the short and stormy days. For here man has lived under this south hillside, and it seems a civilized and public spot. We have such associations as when the traveler stands by the ruins of Palmyra or Hecatompolis. Singing birds and flowers perchance have begun to appear here, for flowers as well as weeds follow in the footsteps of man. These hemlocks whispered over his head, these hickory logs were his fuel, and these pitch pine roots kindled his fire; yonder fuming rill in the hollow, whose thin and airy vapor still ascends as busily as ever, though he is far off now, was his well. These hemlock boughs, and the straw upon this raised platform, were his bed, and this broken dish held his drink. But he has not been here this season, for the phoebes built their nest upon this shelf last summer. I find some embers left as if he had but just gone out, where he baked his pot of beans; and while at evening he smoked his pipe, whose stemless bowl lies in the ashes, chatted with his only companion, if perchance he had any, about the depth of the snow on the morrow, already falling fast and thick without, or disputed whether the last sound was the screech of an owl, or the creak of a bough, or imagination only; and through his broad chimney-throat, in the late winter evening, ere he stretched himself upon the straw, he looked up to learn the progress of the storm, and, seeing the bright stars of Cassiopeia's Chair shining brightly down upon him, fell contentedly asleep.

See how many traces from which we may learn the chopper's history! From this stump we may guess the sharpness of his axe, and from the slope of the stroke, on which side he stood, and whether he cut down the tree without going round it or changing hands; and, from the flexure of the splinters, we may know which way it fell. This one chip contains inscribed on it the whole history of the woodchopper and of the world. On this scrap of paper, which held his sugar or salt, perchance, or was the wadding of his gun, sitting on a log in the forest, with what interest we read the tattle of cities, of those larger huts, empty and to let, like this, in High Streets and Broadways. The eaves are dripping on the south side of this simple roof, while the titmouse lisps in the pine and the genial warmth of the sun around the door is somewhat kind and human.

After two seasons, this rude dwelling does not deform the scene. Already the birds resort to it, to build their nests, and you may track to its door the feet of many quadrupeds. Thus, for a long time, nature overlooks the encroachment and profanity of man. The wood still cheerfully and unsuspiciously echoes the strokes of the axe that fells it, and while they are few and seldom, they enhance its wildness, and all the elements strive to naturalize the sound.

Now our path begins to ascend gradually to the top of this high hill, from whose precipitous south side we can look over the broad country of forest and field and river, to the distant snowy mountains. See yonder thin column of smoke curling up through the woods from some invisible farmhouse, the standard raised over some rural homestead. There must be a warmer and more genial spot there below, as where we detect the vapor from a spring forming a cloud above the trees. What fine relations are established between the traveler who discovers this airy column from some eminence in the forest and him who sits below! Up goes the smoke as silently and naturally as the vapor exhales from the leaves, and as busy disposing itself in wreaths as the housewife on the hearth below. It is a hieroglyphic of man's life, and suggests more intimate and important things than the boiling of a pot. Where its fine column rises above the forest, like an ensign, some human life has planted itself—and such is the beginning of Rome, the establishment of the arts, and the foundation of empires, whether on the prairies of America or the steppes of Asia.

And now we descend again, to the brink of this woodland lake,[2] which lies in a hollow of the hills, as if it were their expressed juice, and that of the leaves which are annually steeped in it. Without outlet or inlet to the eye, it has still its history, in the lapse of its waves, in the rounded pebbles on its shore, and in the pines which grow down to its brink. It has not been idle, though sedentary, but, like Abu Musa, teaches that "sitting still at home is the heavenly way; the going out is the way of the world." Yet in its evaporation it travels as far as any. In summer it is the earth's liquid eye, a mirror in the breast of nature. The sins of the wood are washed out in it. See how the woods form an amphitheater about it, and it is an arena for all the genialness of nature. All trees direct the traveler to its brink, all paths seek it out, birds fly to it, quadrupeds flee to it, and the very ground inclines toward it. It is nature's saloon, where she has sat down to her toilet. Consider her silent economy and tidiness; how the sun comes with his evaporation to sweep the dust from its surface each morning, and a fresh surface is constantly welling up; and annually, after whatever impurities have accumulated herein, its liquid transparency appears again in the spring. In summer a hushed music seems to sweep across its surface. But now a plain sheet of snow conceals it from our eyes, except where the wind has swept the ice bare, and the sere leaves are gliding from side to side, tacking and veering on their tiny voyages. Here is one just keeled up against a pebble on shore, a dry beech leaf, rocking still, as if it would start again. A skillful engineer, methinks, might project its course since it fell from the parent stem. Here are all the elements for such a calculation. Its present position, the direction of the wind, the level of the pond, and how much more is given. In its scarred edges and veins is its log rolled up.

We fancy ourselves in the interior of a larger house. The surface of the pond is our deal table or sanded floor, and the woods rise abruptly from its edge, like the walls of a cottage. The lines set to catch pickerel through the ice look like a larger culinary preparation, and the men stand about on the white ground like pieces of forest furniture. The actions of these men, at the distance of half a mile over the ice and snow, impress us as when we read the exploits of Alexander in history. They seem not unworthy of the scenery, and as momentous as the conquest of kingdoms.

Again we have wandered through the arches of the wood, until from its skirts we hear the distant booming of ice from yonder bay [3] of the river, as if it were moved by some other and subtler tide than oceans know. To me it has a strange sound of home, thrilling as the voice of one's distant and noble kindred. A mild summer sun shines over forest and lake, and though there is but one green leaf for many rods, yet nature enjoys a serene health. Every sound is fraught with the same mysterious assurance of health, as well now the creaking of the boughs in January, as the soft sough of the wind in July.

When Winter fringes every bough
  With his fantastic wreath,
And puts the seal of silence now
  Upon the leaves beneath;

When every stream in its penthouse
  Goes gurgling on its way,
And in his gallery the mouse
  Nibbleth the meadow hay;

Methinks the summer still is nigh,
  And lurketh underneath,
At that same meadow mouse doth lie
  Snug in that last year's heath.

And if perchance the chickadee
  Lisp a faint note anon,
The snow is summer's canopy,
  Which she herself put on.

Fair blossoms deck the cheerful trees,
  And dazzling fruits depend;
The north wind sighs a summer breeze,
  The nipping frosts to fend,

Bringing glad tidings unto me,
  The while I stand all ear,
Of a serene eternity,
  Which need not winter fear.

Out on the silent pond straightway
  The restless ice doth crack,

2. **woodland lake:** Walden Pond.

3. **yonder bay:** Fair Haven Bay.

And pond sprites merry gambols play
  Amid the deafening rack.

Eager I hasten to the vale,
  As if I heard brave news,
How nature held high festival,
  Which it were hard to lose.

I gambol with my neighbor ice,
  And sympathizing quake,
As each new crack darts in a trice
  Across the gladsome lake.

One with the cricket in the ground,
  And fagot on the hearth,
Resounds the rare domestic sound
  Along the forest path.

Before night we will take a journey on skates along the course of this meandering river,[4] as full of novelty to one who sits by the cottage fire all the winter's day, as if it were over the polar ice, with Captain Parry [5] or Franklin; [6] following the winding of the stream, now flowing amid hills, now spreading out into fair meadows, and forming a myriad coves and bays where the pine and hemlock overarch. The river flows in the rear of the towns, and we see all things from a new and wilder side. The fields and gardens come down to it with a frankness, and freedom from pretension, which they do not wear on the highway. It is the outside and edge of the earth. Our eyes are not offended by violent contrasts. The last rail of the farmer's fence is some swaying willow bough, which still preserves its freshness, and here at length all fences stop, and we no longer cross any road. We may go far up within the country now by the most retired and level road, never climbing a hill, but by broad levels ascending to the upland meadows. It is a beautiful illustration of the law of obedience, the flow of a river; the path for a sick man, a highway down which an acorn cup may float secure with its freight. Its slight occasional falls, whose precipices would not diversify the landscape, are celebrated by mist and spray, and attract the traveler from far and near. From the remote interior, its current conducts him by broad and easy steps, or by one gentler inclined plane, to the sea. Thus by an early and constant yielding to the inequalities of the ground it secures itself the easiest passage.

4. **meandering river:** Concord River. 5. **Captain Parry:** William Parry (*fl.* 1601), a traveler and author of a famous account of a trip to Turkey, Persia, and Russia. 6. **Franklin:** Sir John Franklin (1786–1847), Arctic explorer.

No domain of nature is quite closed to man at all times, and now we draw near to the empire of the fishes. Our feet glide swiftly over unfathomed depths, where in summer our line tempted the pout and perch, and where the stately pickerel lurked in the long corridors formed by the bulrushes. The deep, impenetrable marsh, where the heron waded and bittern squatted, is made pervious to our swift shoes, as if a thousand railroads had been made into it. With one impulse we are carried to the cabin of the muskrat, that earliest settler, and see him dart away under the transparent ice, like a furred fish, to his hole in the bank; and we glide rapidly over meadows where lately "the mower whet his scythe," through beds of frozen cranberries mixed with meadow-grass. We skate near to where the blackbird, the pewee, and the kingbird hung their nests over the water, and the hornets builded from the maple in the swamp. How many gay warblers, following the sun, have radiated from this nest of silver birch and thistledown! On the swamp's outer edge was hung the supermarine village, where no foot penetrated. In this hollow tree the wood duck reared her brood, and slid away each day to forage in yonder fen.

In winter, nature is a cabinet of curiosities, full of dried specimens, in their natural order and position. The meadows and forests are a *hortus siccus*. The leaves and grasses stand perfectly pressed by the air without screw or gum, and the birds' nests are not hung on an artificial twig, but where they builded them. We go about dry-shod to inspect the summer's work in the rank swamp, and see what a growth have got the alders, the willows, and the maples; testifying to how many warm suns, and fertilizing dews and showers. See what strides their boughs took in the luxuriant summer —and anon these dormant buds will carry them onward and upward another span into the heavens.

Occasionally we wade through fields of snow, under whose depths the river is lost for many rods, to appear again to the right or left, where we least expected; still holding on its way underneath, with a faint, stertorous, rumbling sound, as if, like the bear and marmot, it too had hibernated, and we had followed its faint summer trail to where it earthed itself in snow and ice. At first we should have thought that rivers would be empty and dry in midwinter, or else frozen solid till the spring thawed them; but their volume is not diminished even, for only a superficial cold bridges their surfaces. The thousand springs which feed the lakes and streams are flowing still. The issues of a few surface springs only are closed, and they go to swell the deep reservoirs. Nature's wells are below the frost. The summer brooks are not filled with snow-water, nor does the mower quench his thirst with that alone. The streams are swollen when the snow melts in the spring, because nature's work has been delayed, the water being turned into ice and snow, whose particles are less smooth and round, and do not find their level so soon.

Far over the ice, between the hemlock woods and snow-clad hills, stands the pickerel-fisher, his lines set in some retired cove, like a Finlander, with his arms thrust into the pouches of his dreadnaught; with dull, snowy, fishy thoughts, himself a finless fish, separated a few inches from his race; dumb, erect, and made to be enveloped in clouds and snows, like the pines on shore. In these wild scenes, men stand about in the scenery, or move deliberately and heavily, having sacrificed the sprightliness and vivacity of towns to the dumb sobriety of nature. He does not make the scenery less wild, more than the jays and muskrats, but stands there as a part of it, as the natives are represented in the voyages of early navigators, at Nootka Sound, and on the Northwest coast, with their furs about them, before they were tempted to loquacity by a scrap of iron. He belongs to the natural family of man, and is planted deeper in nature and has more root than the inhabitants of towns. Go to him, ask what luck, and you will learn that he too is a worshiper of the unseen. Hear with what sincere deference and waving gesture in his tone he speaks of the lake pickerel, which he has never seen, his primitive and ideal race of pickerel. He is connected with the shore still, as by a fishline, and yet remembers the season when he took fish through the ice on the pond, while the peas were up in his garden at home.

But now, while we have loitered, the clouds have gathered again, and a few straggling snowflakes are beginning to descend. Faster and faster they fall, shutting out the distant objects from sight. The snow falls on every wood and field, and no crevice is forgotten; by the river and the pond, on the hill and in the valley. Quadrupeds are confined to their coverts and the birds sit upon their perches this peaceful hour. There is not so much sound as in fair weather, but silently and gradually every slope, and the gray walls and fences, and the polished ice, and the sere leaves, which were not buried before, are concealed, and the tracks of men and beasts are lost. With so little effort does nature reassert her rule and blot out the traces of men. Hear how Homer has described the same: "The snowflakes fall thick and fast on a winter's day. The winds are lulled, and the snow falls incessant, covering the tops of the mountains, and the hills, and the plains where the lotus tree grows, and the cultivated fields, and they are falling by the inlets and shores of the foaming sea, but are silently dissolved by the waves." The snow levels all things, and infolds them deeper in the bosom of nature, as, in the slow summer, vegetation creeps up to to the entablature of the temple, and the turrets of the castle, and helps her to prevail over art.

The surly night wind rustles through the wood, and warns us to retrace our steps, while the sun goes down behind the thickening storm, and birds seek their roosts, and cattle their stalls.

> "Drooping the lab'rer ox
> Stands covered o'er with snow, and *now* demands
> The fruit of all his toil."

Though winter is represented in the almanac as an old man, facing the wind and sleet, and drawing his cloak about him, we rather think of him as a merry woodchopper, and warm-blooded youth, as blithe as summer. The unexplored grandeur of the storm keeps up the spirits of the traveler. It does not trifle with us, but has a sweet earnestness. In winter we lead a more inward life. Our hearts are warm and cheery, like cottages under drifts, whose windows and doors are half concealed, but from whose chimneys the smoke cheerfully ascends. The imprisoning drifts increase the sense of comfort which the house affords, and in the coldest days we are content to sit over the hearth and see the sky through the chimney-top, enjoying the quiet and serene life that may be had in a warm corner by the chimney-side, or feeling our pulse by listening to the low of cattle in the street, or the sound of the flail in distant barns all the long afternoon. No doubt a skillful physician could determine our health by observing how these simple and natural sounds affected us. We enjoy now, not an Oriental, but a Boreal leisure, around warm stoves and fireplaces, and watch the shadow of motes in the sunbeams.

Sometimes our fate grows too homely and familiarly serious ever to be cruel. Consider how for three months the human destiny is wrapped in furs. The good Hebrew Revelation takes no cognizance of all this cheerful snow. Is there no religion for the temperate and frigid zones? We know of no scripture which records the pure benignity of the gods on a New England winter night. Their praises have never been sung, only their wrath deprecated. The best scripture, after all, records but a meager faith. Its saints live reserved and austere. Let a brave, devout man spend the year in the woods of Maine or Labrador, and see if the Hebrew Scriptures speak adequately to his condition and experience, from the setting in of winter to the breaking up of the ice.

Now commences the long winter evening around the farmer's hearth, when the thoughts of the indwellers travel far abroad, and men are by nature and necessity charitable and liberal to all creatures. Now is the happy resistance to cold, when the farmer reaps his reward, and thinks of his preparedness for winter, and, through the glittering panes, sees with equanimity "the mansion of the northern bear," for now the storm is over,

> "The full ethereal round,
> Infinite worlds disclosing to the view,
> Shines out intensely keen; and all one cope
> Of starry glitter glows from pole to pole."

CIVIL DISOBEDIENCE

◇

¶ IN THE course of his odd-job career, Thoreau sometimes gave lectures. Although he was not an effective speaker, some of his most powerful pieces were first enunciated in the Concord Lyceum, including "Civil Disobedience," which he delivered in February, 1848. The following year it was published in Elizabeth Peabody's *Aesthetic Papers*, a volume which also included Emerson's essay "War" and Hawthorne's "Main Street." Well-known throughout the nineteenth century, "Civil Disobedience" became world-famous in the twentieth century when Mahatma Gandhi acknowledged it as the chief inspiration of his doctrine of passive resistance. Liberal critics who view big government as the chief agent of social justice have been embarrassed by the essay's notoriety and have attempted to play down its importance in the Thoreau canon, just as they have tried to de-emphasize Thoreau's dramatic refusal to pay his tax by pointing out that Bronson Alcott had done the same thing four years previously. But in the era of Martin Luther King and the "sit-ins," the dynamic, revolutionary power of individual protest cannot be denied. "Civil Disobedience" is surely an essay for our times.

◇

I HEARTILY accept the motto, "That government is best which governs least"; and I should like to see it acted up to more rapidly and systematically. Carried out, it finally amounts to this, which also I believe—"That government is best which governs not at all"; and when men are prepared for it, that will be the kind of government which they will have. Government is at best but an expedient; but most governments are usually, and all governments are sometimes, inexpedient. The objections which have been brought against a standing army, and they are many and weighty, and deserve to prevail, may also at last be brought against a standing government. The standing army is only an arm of the standing government. The government itself, which is only the mode which the people have chosen to execute their will, is equally liable to be abused and perverted before the people can act through it. Witness the present Mexican war, the work of comparatively a few individuals using the standing government as their tool; for, in the outset, the people would not have consented to this measure.

This American government—what is it but a tradition, though a recent one, endeavoring to transmit itself unimpaired to posterity, but each instant losing some of its integrity? It has not the vitality and force of a single living man; for a single man can bend it to his will. It is a sort of wooden gun to the people themselves. But it is not the less necessary for this; for the people must have some complicated machinery or other, and hear its din, to satisfy that idea of government which they have. Governments show thus how successfully men can be imposed on, even impose on themselves, for their own advantage. It is excellent, we must all allow. Yet this government never of itself furthered any enterprise, but by the alacrity with which it got out of its way. *It* does not keep the country free. *It* does not settle the West. *It* does not educate. The character inherent in the American people has done all that has been accomplished; and it would have done somewhat more, if the government had not sometimes got in its way. For government is an expedient by which men would fain succeed in letting one another alone; and, as has been said, when it is most expedient, the governed are most let alone by it. Trade and commerce, if they were not made of india-rubber, would never manage to bounce over the obstacles which legislators are continually putting in their way; and, if one were to judge these men wholly by the effects of their actions and not partly by their intentions, they would deserve to be classed and punished with those mischievous persons who put obstructions on the railroads.

But, to speak practically and as a citizen, unlike those who call themselves no-government men, I ask for, not at once no government, but *at once* a better government. Let every man make known what kind of government would command his respect, and that will be one step toward obtaining it.

After all, the practical reason why, when the power is once in the hands of the people, a majority are permitted, and for a long period continue, to rule is not because they are most likely to be in the right, nor because this seems fairest to the minority, but because they are physically the strongest. But a government in which the majority rule in all cases cannot be based on justice, even as far as men understand it. Can there not be a government in which majorities do not virtually decide right and wrong, but conscience?—in which majorities decide only those questions to which the rule of expediency is applicable? Must the citizen ever for a moment, or in the least degree, resign his conscience to the legislator? Why has every man a conscience, then? I think that we should be men first, and subjects afterward. It is not desirable to cultivate a respect for the law, so much as for the right. The only obligation which I have a right to assume is to do at any time what I think right. It is truly enough said that a corporation has no conscience; but a corporation of conscientious men is a corporation *with* a conscience. Law never made men a whit more just; and, by means of their respect for it, even the well-disposed are daily made the agents of injustice. A common and natural result of an undue respect for law is, that you may see a file of soldiers, colonel, captain, corporal, privates, powder-monkeys, and all, marching in admirable order over hill and dale to the wars, against their wills, ay, against their common sense and consciences, which makes it very steep marching indeed, and produces a palpitation of the heart. They have no doubt that it is a damnable business in which they are concerned; they are all peaceably inclined. Now, what are they? Men at all? or small movable forts and magazines, at the service of some unscrupulous man in power? Visit the Navy Yard, and behold a marine, such a man as an American government can make, or such as it can make a man with its black arts—a mere shadow and reminiscence of humanity, a man laid out alive and standing, and already, as one may say, buried under arms with funeral accompaniments, though it may be,

"Not a drum was heard, not a funeral note,
  As his corse to the rampart we hurried;
Not a soldier discharged his farewell shot
  O'er the grave where our hero we buried." [1]

The mass of men serve the state thus, not as men mainly, but as machines, with their bodies. They are the standing army, and the militia, jailers, constables, *posse comitatus,* etc. In most cases there is no free exercise whatever of the judgment or of the moral sense; but they put themselves on a level with wood and earth and stones; and wooden men can perhaps be manufactured that will serve the purpose as well. Such command no more respect than men of straw or a lump of dirt. They have the same sort of worth only as horses and dogs. Yet such as these even are commonly esteemed good citizens. Others—as most legislators, politicians, lawyers, ministers, and office-holders—serve the state chiefly with their heads; and, as they rarely make any moral distinctions, they are as likely to serve the devil, without *intending* it, as God. A very few—as heroes, patriots, martyrs, reformers in the great sense, and *men*—serve the state with their consciences also, and so necessarily resist it for the most part; and they are commonly treated as enemies by it. A wise man will only be useful as a man, and will not submit to be "clay," and "stop a hole to keep the wind away," [2] but leave that office to his dust at least:

"I am too high-born to be propertied,
To be a secondary at control,
Or useful serving-man and instrument
To any sovereign state throughout the world." [3]

He who gives himself entirely to his fellow men appears to them useless and selfish; but he who gives himself partially to them is pronounced a benefactor and philanthropist.

How does it become a man to behave toward this American government today? I answer, that he cannot without disgrace be associated with it. I cannot for an instant recognize that political organization as *my* government which is the *slave's* government also.

All men recognize the right of revolution; that is, the right to refuse allegiance to, and to resist, the government, when its tyranny or its inefficiency are great and unendurable. But almost all say that such is not the case now. But such was the case, they think, in the Revolution of '75. If one were to tell me that this was a bad government because it taxed certain foreign commodities brought to its ports, it is most probable that I should not make an ado about it, for I can do without them. All machines have their friction; and possibly this does enough good to counterbalance the evil. At any rate, it is a great evil to make a stir about it. But when the friction comes to have its machine, and oppression and robbery are organized, I say, let us not have such a machine any longer. In other words, when a sixth of the population of a nation which has undertaken to be the refuge of liberty are slaves, and a whole country is unjustly overrun and conquered by a foreign army, and

CIVIL DISOBEDIENCE. **1. "Not . . . buried"**: The opening lines of "Burial of Sir John Moore at Corunna," by the Irish clergyman-poet Charles Wolfe (1791–1823).

2. A . . . away: Cf. Shakespeare, *Hamlet*, V.i.236–37. **3. "I . . . world"**: Cf. Shakespeare, *King John*, V.ii.79–82.

subjected to military law, I think that it is not too soon for honest men to rebel and revolutionize. What makes this duty the more urgent is the fact that the country so overrun is not our own, but ours is the invading army.

Paley,[4] a common authority with many on moral questions, in his chapter on the "Duty of Submission to Civil Government," resolves all civil obligation into expediency; and he proceeds to say that "so long as the interest of the whole society requires it, that is, so long as the established government cannot be resisted or changed without public inconveniency, it is the will of God . . . that the established government be obeyed—and no longer. This principle being admitted, the justice of every particular case of resistance is reduced to a computation of the quantity of the danger and grievance on the one side, and of the probability and expense of redressing it on the other." Of this, he says, every man shall judge for himself. But Paley appears never to have contemplated those cases to which the rule of expediency does not apply, in which a people, as well as an individual, must do justice, cost what it may. If I have unjustly wrested a plank from a drowning man, I must restore it to him though I drown myself. This, according to Paley, would be inconvenient. But he that would save his life, in such a case, shall lose it. This people must cease to hold slaves, and to make war on Mexico, though it cost them their existence as a people.

In their practice, nations agree with Paley; but does anyone think that Massachusetts does exactly what is right at the present crisis?

"A drab of state, a cloth-o'-silver slut,
To have her train borne up, and her soul trail in the dirt."

Practically speaking, the opponents to a reform in Massachusetts are not a hundred thousand politicians at the South, but a hundred thousand merchants and farmers here, who are more interested in commerce and agriculture than they are in humanity, and are not prepared to do justice to the slave and to Mexico, *cost what it may*. I quarrel not with far-off foes, but with those who, near at home, co-operate with, and do the bidding of, those far away, and without whom the latter would be harmless. We are accustomed to say, that the mass of men are unprepared; but improvement is slow, because the few are not materially wiser or better than the many. It is not so important that many should be as good as you, as that there be some absolute goodness somewhere; for that will leaven the whole lump. There are thousands who are *in opinion* opposed to slavery and to the war, who yet in effect do nothing to put an end to them; who, esteeming themselves children of Washington and Franklin, sit down with their hands in their pockets, and say that they know not what to do, and do nothing; who even postpone the question of freedom to the question of free trade, and quietly read the prices-current along with the latest advices from Mexico, after dinner, and, it may be, fall asleep over them both. What is the price-current of an honest man and patriot today? They hesitate, and they regret, and sometimes they petition; but they do nothing in earnest and with effect. They will wait, well disposed, for others to remedy the evil, that they may no longer have it to regret. At most, they give only a cheap vote, and a feeble countenance and Godspeed, to the right, as it goes by them. There are nine hundred and ninety-nine patrons of virtue to one virtuous man. But it is easier to deal with the real possessor of a thing than with the temporary guardian of it.

All voting is a sort of gaming, like checkers or backgammon, with a slight moral tinge to it, a playing with right and wrong, with moral questions; and betting naturally accompanies it. The character of the voters is not staked. I cast my vote, perchance, as I think right; but I am not vitally concerned that that right should prevail. I am willing to leave it to the majority. Its obligation, therefore, never exceeds that of expediency. Even voting *for the right* is *doing* nothing for it. It is only expressing to men feebly your desire that it should prevail. A wise man will not leave the right to the mercy of chance, nor wish it to prevail through the power of the majority. There is but little virtue in the action of masses of men. When the majority shall at length vote for the abolition of slavery, it will be because they are indifferent to slavery, or because there is but little slavery left to be abolished by their vote. *They* will then be the only slaves. Only *his* vote can hasten the abolition of slavery who asserts his own freedom by his vote.

I hear of a convention to be held at Baltimore, or elsewhere, for the selection of a candidate for the Presidency, made up chiefly of editors, and men who are politicians by profession; but I think, what is it to any independent, intelligent, and respectable man what decision they may come to? Shall we not have the advantage of his wisdom and honesty, nevertheless? Can we not count upon some independent votes? Are there not many individuals in the country who do not attend conventions? But no: I find that the respectable man,

4. **Paley:** William Paley (1743–1805), British philosopher, whose moral utilitarianism is exemplified by this quotation from his *Principles of Moral and Political Philosophy* (1785).

so called, has immediately drifted from his position, and despairs of his country, when his country has more reason to despair of him. He forthwith adopts one of the candidates thus selected as the only *available* one, thus proving that he is himself *available* for any purposes of the demagogue. His vote is of no more worth than that of any unprincipled foreigner or hireling native, who may have been bought. O for a man who is a *man*, and, as my neighbor says, has a bone in his back which you cannot pass your hand through! Our statistics are at fault: the population has been returned too large. How many *men* are there to a square thousand miles in this country? Hardly one. Does not America offer any inducement for men to settle here? The American has dwindled into an Odd Fellow—one who may be known by the development of his organ of gregariousness, and a manifest lack of intellect and cheerful self-reliance; whose first and chief concern, on coming into the world, is to see that the almshouses are in good repair; and, before yet he has lawfully donned the virile garb, to collect a fund for the support of the widows and orphans that may be; who, in short, ventures to live only by the aid of the Mutual Insurance company, which has promised to bury him decently.

It is not a man's duty, as a matter of course, to devote himself to the eradication of any, even the most enormous, wrong; he may still properly have other concerns to engage him; but it is his duty, at least, to wash his hands of it, and, if he gives it no thought longer, not to give it practically his support. If I devote myself to other pursuits and contemplations, I must first see, at least, that I do not pursue them sitting upon another man's shoulders. I must get off him first, that he may pursue his contemplations too. See what gross inconsistency is tolerated. I have heard some of my townsmen say, "I should like to have them order me out to help put down an insurrection of the slaves, or to march to Mexico—see if I would go"; and yet these very men have each, directly by their allegiance, and so indirectly, at least, by their money, furnished a substitute. The soldier is applauded who refuses to serve in an unjust war by those who do not refuse to sustain the unjust government which makes the war; is applauded by those whose own act and authority he disregards and sets at naught; as if the state were penitent to that degree that it hired one to scourge it while it sinned, but not to that degree that it left off sinning for a moment. Thus, under the name of Order and Civil Government, we are all made at last to pay homage to and support our own meanness. After the first blush of sin comes its indifference; and from immoral it becomes, as it were, *unmoral*, and not quite unnecessary to that life which we have made.

The broadest and most prevalent error requires the most disinterested virtue to sustain it. The slight reproach to which the virtue of patriotism is commonly liable, the noble are most likely to incur. Those who, while they disapprove of the character and measures of a government, yield to it their allegiance and support are undoubtedly its most conscientious supporters, and so frequently the most serious obstacles to reform. Some are petitioning the State to dissolve the Union, to disregard the requisitions of the President. Why do they not dissolve it themselves—the union between themselves and the State—and refuse to pay their quota into its treasury? Do not they stand in the same relation to the State that the State does to the Union? And have not the same reasons prevented the State from resisting the Union which have prevented them from resisting the State?

How can a man be satisfied to entertain an opinion merely, and enjoy *it?* Is there any enjoyment in it, if his opinion is that he is aggrieved? If you are cheated out of a single dollar by your neighbor, you do not rest satisfied with knowing that you are cheated, or with saying that you are cheated, or even with petitioning him to pay you your due; but you take effectual steps at once to obtain the full amount, and see that you are never cheated again. Action from principle, the perception and the performance of right, changes things and relations; it is essentially revolutionary, and does not consist wholly with anything which was. It not only divides States and churches, it divides families; ay, it divides the *individual,* separating the diabolical in him from the divine.

Unjust laws exist: shall we be content to obey them, or shall we endeavor to amend them, and obey them until we have succeeded, or shall we transgress them at once? Men generally, under such a government as this, think that they ought to wait until they have persuaded the majority to alter them. They think that, if they should resist, the remedy would be worse than the evil. But it is the fault of the government itself that the remedy *is* worse than the evil. *It* makes it worse. Why is it not more apt to anticipate and provide for reform? Why does it not cherish its wise minority? Why does it cry and resist before it is hurt? Why does it not encourage its citizens to be on the alert to point out its faults, and *do* better than it would have them? Why does it always crucify Christ, and excommunicate Copernicus and Luther, and pronounce Washington and Franklin rebels?

One would think, that a deliberate and practical

denial of its authority was the only offence never contemplated by government; else, why has it not assigned its definite, its suitable and proportionate, penalty? If a man who has no property refuses but once to earn nine shillings for the State, he is put in prison for a period unlimited by any law that I know, and determined only by the discretion of those who placed him there; but if he should steal ninety times nine shillings from the State, he is soon permitted to go at large again.

If the injustice is part of the necessary friction of the machine of government, let it go, let it go: perchance it will wear smooth—certainly the machine will wear out. If the injustice has a spring, or a pulley, or a rope, or a crank, exclusively for itself, then perhaps you may consider whether the remedy will not be worse than the evil; but if it is of such a nature that it requires you to be the agent of injustice to another, then, I say, break the law. Let your life be a counter-friction to stop the machine. What I have to do is to see, at any rate, that I do not lend myself to the wrong which I condemn.

As for adopting the ways which the State has provided for remedying the evil, I know not of such ways. They take too much time, and a man's life will be gone. I have other affairs to attend to. I came into this world, not chiefly to make this a good place to live in, but to live in it, be it good or bad. A man has not everything to do, but something; and because he cannot do *everything,* it is not necessary that he should do *something* wrong. It is not my business to be petitioning the Governor or the Legislature any more than it is theirs to petition me; and if they should not hear my petition, what should I do then? But in this case the State has provided no way: its very Constitution is the evil. This may seem to be harsh and stubborn and unconciliatory; but it is to treat with the utmost kindness and consideration the only spirit that can appreciate or deserves it. So is all change for the better, like birth and death, which convulse the body.

I do not hesitate to say, that those who call themselves Abolitionists should at once effectually withdraw their support, both in person and property, from the government of Massachusetts, and not wait till they constitute a majority of one, before they suffer the right to prevail through them. I think that it is enough if they have God on their side, without waiting for that other one. Moreover, any man more right than his neighbors constitutes a majority of one already.

I meet this American government, or its representative, the State government, directly, and face to face, once a year—no more—in the person of its tax-gatherer; this is the only mode in which a man situated as I am necessarily meets it; and it then says distinctly, Recognize me; and the simplest, the most effectual, and, in the present posture of affairs, the indispensablest mode of treating with it on this head, of expressing your little satisfaction with and love for it, is to deny it then. My civil neighbor, the tax-gatherer, is the very man I have to deal with—for it is, after all, with men and not with parchment that I quarrel—and he has voluntarily chosen to be an agent of the government. How shall he ever know well what he is and does as an officer of the government, or as a man, until he is obliged to consider whether he shall treat me, his neighbor, for whom he has respect, as a neighbor and well-disposed man, or as a maniac and disturber of the peace, and see if he can get over this obstruction to his neighborliness without a ruder and more impetuous thought or speech corresponding with his action. I know this well, that if one thousand, if one hundred, if ten men whom I could name—if ten *honest* men only—ay, if *one* HONEST man, in this State of Massachusetts, *ceasing to hold slaves,* were actually to withdraw from this copartnership, and be locked up in the county jail therefor, it would be the abolition of slavery in America. For it matters not how small the beginning may seem to be: what is once well done is done forever. But we love better to talk about it: that we say is our mission. Reform keeps many scores of newspapers in its service, but not one man. If my esteemed neighbor, the State's ambassador,[5] who will devote his days to the settlement of the question of human rights in the Council Chamber, instead of being threatened with the prisons of Carolina, were to sit down the prisoner of Massachusetts, that State which is so anxious to foist the sin of slavery upon her sister—though at present she can discover only an act of inhospitality to be the ground of a quarrel with her—the Legislature would not wholly waive the subject the following winter.

Under a government which imprisons any unjustly, the true place for a just man is also a prison. The proper place today, the only place which Massachusetts has provided for her freer and less desponding spirits, is in her prisons, to be put out and locked out of the State by her own act, as they have already put themselves out by their principles. It is there that the fugitive slave, and the Mexican prisoner on parole, and the Indian come to plead

5. **the State's ambassador:** Samuel Hoar (1778–1856), Concord lawyer and Congressman, was sent to Charleston, S.C., to represent Negro seamen from Massachusetts threatened with arrest and enslavement. Hoar was forcibly expelled from the port.

the wrongs of his race should find them; on that separate, but more free and honorable, ground, where the State places those who are not *with* her, but *against* her—the only house in a slave State in which a free man can abide with honor. If any think that their influence would be lost there, and their voices no longer afflict the ear of the State, that they would not be as an enemy within its walls, they do not know by how much truth is stronger than error, nor how much more eloquently and effectively he can combat injustice who has experienced a little in his own person. Cast your whole vote, not a strip of paper merely, but your whole influence. A minority is powerless while it conforms to the majority; it is not even a minority then; but it is irresistible when it clogs by its whole weight. If the alternative is to keep all just men in prison, or give up war and slavery, the State will not hesitate which to choose. If a thousand men were not to pay their tax-bills this year, that would not be a violent and bloody measure, as it would be to pay them, and enable the State to commit violence and shed innocent blood. This is, in fact, the definition of a peaceable revolution, if any such is possible. If the tax-gatherer, or any other public officer, asks me, as one has done, "But what shall I do?" my answer is, "If you really wish to do anything, resign your office." When the subject has refused allegiance, and the officer has resigned his office, then the revolution is accomplished. But even suppose blood should flow. Is there not a sort of blood shed when the conscience is wounded? Through this wound a man's real manhood and immortality flow out, and he bleeds to an everlasting death. I see this blood flowing now.

I have contemplated the imprisonment of the offender, rather than the seizure of his goods—though both will serve the same purpose—because they who assert the purest right, and consequently are most dangerous to a corrupt State, commonly have not spent much time in accumulating property. To such the State renders comparatively small service, and a slight tax is wont to appear exorbitant, particularly if they are obliged to earn it by special labor with their hands. If there were one who lived wholly without the use of money, the State itself would hesitate to demand it of him. But the rich man—not to make any invidious comparison—is always sold to the institution which makes him rich. Absolutely speaking, the more money, the less virtue; for money comes between a man and his objects, and obtains them for him; and it was certainly no great virtue to obtain it. It puts to rest many questions which he would otherwise be taxed to answer; while the only new question which it puts is the hard but superfluous one, how to spend it. Thus his moral ground is taken from under his feet. The opportunities of living are diminished in proportion as what are called the "means" are increased. The best thing a man can do for his culture when he is rich is to endeavor to carry out those schemes which he entertained when he was poor. Christ answered the Herodians according to their condition. "Show me the tribute-money," said he—and one took a penny out of his pocket—if you use money which has the image of Caesar on it, and which he has made current and valuable, that is, *if you are men of the State,* and gladly enjoy the advantages of Caesar's government, then pay him back some of his own when he demands it. "Render therefore to Caesar that which is Caesar's, and to God those things which are God's"—leaving them no wiser than before as to which was which; for they did not wish to know.

When I converse with the freest of my neighbors, I perceive that, whatever they may say about the magnitude and seriousness of the question, and their regard for the public tranquillity, the long and the short of the matter is, that they cannot spare the protection of the existing government, and they dread the consequences to their property and families of disobedience to it. For my own part, I should not like to think that I ever rely on the protection of the State. But, if I deny the authority of the State when it presents its tax bill, it will soon take and waste all my property, and so harass me and my children without end. This is hard. This makes it impossible for a man to live honestly, and at the same time comfortably, in outward respects. It will not be worth the while to accumulate property; that would be sure to go again. You must hire or squat somewhere, and raise but a small crop, and eat that soon. You must live within yourself, and depend upon yourself always tucked up and ready for a start, and not have many affairs. A man may grow rich in Turkey even, if he will be in all respects a good subject of the Turkish government. Confucius said: "If a state is governed by the principles of reason, poverty and misery are subjects of shame; if a state is not governed by the principles of reason, riches and honors are the subjects of shame." No: until I want the protection of Massachusetts to be extended to me in some distant Southern port, where my liberty is endangered, or until I am bent solely on building up an estate at home by peaceful enterprise, I can afford to refuse allegiance to Massachusetts, and her right to my property and life. It costs me less in every sense to incur the penalty of disobedience to the State than it would to obey. I should feel as if I were worth less in that case.

Some years ago, the State met me in behalf of the Church, and commanded me to pay a certain sum toward the support of a clergyman whose preaching my father attended, but never I myself. "Pay," it said, "or be locked up in the jail." I declined to pay.[6] But, unfortunately, another man saw fit to pay it. I did not see why the schoolmaster should be taxed to support the priest, and not the priest the schoolmaster; for I was not the State's schoolmaster, but I supported myself by voluntary subscription. I did not see why the lyceum should not present its tax bill, and have the State to back its demand, as well as the Church. However, at the request of the selectmen, I condescended to make some such statement as this in writing: "Know all men by these presents, that I, Henry Thoreau, do not wish to be regarded as a member of any incorporated society which I have not joined." This I gave to the town clerk; and he has it. The State, having thus learned that I did not wish to be regarded as a member of that church, has never made a like demand on me since; though it said that it must adhere to its original presumption that time. If I had known how to name them, I should then have signed off in detail from all the societies which I never signed on to; but I did not know where to find a complete list.

I have paid no poll-tax for six years. I was put into a jail once on this account, for one night; and, as I stood considering the walls of solid stone, two or three feet thick, the door of wood and iron, a foot thick, and the iron grating which strained the light, I could not help being struck with the foolishness of that institution which treated me as if I were mere flesh and blood and bones, to be locked up. I wondered that it should have concluded at length that this was the best use it could put me to, and had never thought to avail itself of my services in some way. I saw that, if there was a wall of stone between me and my townsmen, there was a still more difficult one to climb or break through before they could get to be as free as I was. I did not for a moment feel confined, and the walls seemed a great waste of stone and mortar. I felt as if I alone of all my townsmen had paid my tax. They plainly did not know how to treat me, but behaved like persons who are underbred. In every threat and in every compliment there was a blunder; for they thought that my chief desire was to stand the other side of that stone wall. I could not but smile to see how industriously they locked the door on my meditations, which followed them out again without let or hindrance, and *they* were really all that was dangerous. As they could not reach me, they had resolved to punish my body; just as boys, if they cannot come at some person against whom they have a spite, will abuse his dog. I saw that the State was half-witted, that it was timid as a lone woman with her silver spoons, and that it did not know its friends from its foes, and I lost all my remaining respect for it, and pitied it.

Thus the State never intentionally confronts a man's sense, intellectual or moral, but only his body, his senses. It is not armed with superior wit or honesty, but with superior physical strength. I was not born to be forced. I will breathe after my own fashion. Let us see who is the strongest. What force has a multitude? They only can force me who obey a higher law than I. They force me to become like themselves. I do not hear of *men* being *forced* to live this way or that by masses of men. What sort of life were that to live? When I meet a government which says to me, "Your money or your life," why should I be in haste to give it my money? It may be in a great strait, and not know what to do: I cannot help that. It must help itself; do as I do. It is not worth the while to snivel about it. I am not responsible for the successful working of the machinery of society. I am not the son of the engineer. I perceive that, when an acorn and a chestnut fall side by side, the one does not remain inert to make way for the other, but both obey their own laws, and spring and grow and flourish as best they can, till one, perchance, overshadows and destroys the other. If a plant cannot live according to its nature, it dies; and so a man.

The night in prison was novel and interesting enough. The prisoners in their shirtsleeves were enjoying a chat and the evening air in the doorway, when I entered. But the jailer said, "Come, boys, it is time to lock up"; and so they dispersed, and I heard the sound of their steps returning into the hollow apartments. My room-mate was introduced to me by the jailer as "a first-rate fellow and a clever man." When the door was locked, he showed me where to hang my hat, and how he managed matters there. The rooms were whitewashed once a month; and this one, at least, was the whitest, most simply furnished, and probably the neatest apartment in the town. He naturally wanted to know where I came from, and what brought me there; and, when I had told him, I asked him in my turn how he came there, presuming him to be an honest man, of course; and, as the world goes, I believe he was. "Why," said he, "they accuse me of burning a barn; but I never did it." As near as I could discover, he had prob-

6. **I . . . pay:** Thoreau signed off from church taxes in 1838 and went to jail in July, 1846, for refusing to pay his poll tax.

ably gone to bed in a barn when drunk, and smoked his pipe there; and so a barn was burnt. He had the reputation of being a clever man, had been there some three months waiting for his trial to come on, and would have to wait as much longer; but he was quite domesticated and contented, since he got his board for nothing, and thought that he was well treated.

He occupied one window, and I the other; and I saw that if one stayed there long, his principal business would be to look out the window. I had soon read all the tracts that were left there, and examined where former prisoners had broken out, and where a grate had been sawed off, and heard the history of the various occupants of that room; for I found that even here there was a history and a gossip which never circulated beyond the walls of the jail. Probably this is the only house in the town where verses are composed, which are afterward printed in a circular form, but not published. I was shown quite a long list of verses which were composed by some young men who had been detected in an attempt to escape, who avenged themselves by singing them.

I pumped my fellow-prisoner as dry as I could, for fear I should never see him again; but at length he showed me which was my bed, and left me to blow out the lamp.

It was like traveling into a far country, such as I had never expected to behold, to lie there for one night. It seemed to me that I never had heard the town clock strike before, nor the evening sounds of the village; for we slept with the windows open, which were inside the grating. It was to see my native village in the light of the Middle Ages, and our Concord was turned into a Rhine stream, and visions of knights and castles passed before me. They were the voices of old burghers that I heard in the streets. I was an involuntary spectator and auditor of whatever was done and said in the kitchen of the adjacent village inn—a wholly new and rare experience to me. It was a closer view of my native town. I was fairly inside of it. I never had seen its institutions before. This is one of its peculiar institutions; for it is a shire town. I began to comprehend what its inhabitants were about.

In the morning, our breakfasts were put through the hole in the door, in small oblong-square tin pans, made to fit, and holding a pint of chocolate, with brown bread, and an iron spoon. When they called for the vessels again, I was green enough to return what bread I had left; but my comrade seized it, and said that I should lay that up for lunch or dinner. Soon after he was let out to work at haying in a neighboring field, whither he went every day, and would not be back till noon; so he bade me good-day, saying that he doubted if he should see me again.

When I came out of prison—for some one interfered, and paid that tax—I did not perceive that great changes had taken place on the common, such as he observed who went in a youth and emerged a tottering and gray-headed man; and yet a change had to my eyes come over the scene—the town, and State, and country—greater than any that mere time could effect. I saw yet more distinctly the State in which I lived. I saw to what extent the people among whom I lived could be trusted as good neighbors and friends; that their friendship was for summer weather only; that they did not greatly propose to do right; that they were a distinct race from me by their prejudices and superstitions, as the Chinamen and Malays are; that in their sacrifices to humanity they ran no risks, not even to their property; that after all they were not so noble but they treated the thief as he had treated them, and hoped, by a certain outward observance and a few prayers, and by walking in a particular straight though useless path from time to time, to save their souls. This may be to judge my neighbors harshly; for I believe that many of them are not aware that they have such an institution as the jail in their village.

It was formerly the custom in our village, when a poor debtor came out of jail, for his acquaintances to salute him, looking through their fingers, which were crossed to represent the grating of a jail window, "How do ye do?" My neighbors did not thus salute me, but first looked at me, and then at one another, as if I had returned from a long journey. I was put into jail as I was going to the shoemaker's to get a shoe which was mended. When I was let out the next morning, I proceeded to finish my errand, and, having put on my mended shoe, joined a huckleberry party, who were impatient to put themselves under my conduct; and in half an hour—for the horse was soon tackled—was in the midst of a huckleberry field, on one of our highest hills, two miles off, and then the State was nowhere to be seen.

This is the whole history of "My Prisons." [7]

I have never declined paying the highway tax, because I am as desirous of being a good neighbor as I am of being a bad subject; and as for supporting schools, I am doing my part to educate my fellow-countrymen now. It is for no particular item in the tax bill that I refuse to pay it. I simply

7. **"My Prisons"**: English translation of the title *Le Mie Prigioni*, a record of his Austrian incarceration by the Italian patriot and poet Silvio Pellico (1789–1854).

wish to refuse allegiance to the State, to withdraw and stand aloof from it effectually. I do not care to trace the course of my dollar, if I could, till it buys a man or a musket to shoot one with—the dollar is innocent—but I am concerned to trace the effects of my allegiance. In fact, I quietly declare war with the State, after my fashion, though I will still make what use and get what advantage of her I can, as is usual in such cases.

If others pay the tax which is demanded of me, from a sympathy with the State, they do but what they have already done in their own case, or rather they abet injustice to a greater extent than the State requires. If they pay the tax from a mistaken interest in the individual taxed, to save his property, or prevent his going to jail, it is because they have not considered wisely how far they let their private feelings interfere with the public good.

This, then, is my position at present. But one cannot be too much on his guard in such a case, lest his action be biased by obstinacy or an undue regard for the opinions of men. Let him see that he does only what belongs to himself and to the hour.

I think sometimes, Why, this people mean well, they are only ignorant; they would do better if they knew how: why give your neighbors this pain to treat you as they are not inclined to? But I think again, This is no reason why I should do as they do, or permit others to suffer much greater pain of a different kind. Again, I sometimes say to myself, When many millions of men, without heat, without ill will, without personal feeling of any kind, demand of you a few shillings only, without the possibility, such is their constitution, of retracting or altering their present demand, and without the possibility, on your side, of appeal to any other millions, why expose yourself to this overwhelming brute force? You do not resist cold and hunger, the winds and the waves, thus obstinately; you quietly submit to a thousand similar necessities. You do not put your head into the fire. But just in proportion as I regard this as not wholly a brute force, but partly a human force, and consider that I have relations to those millions as to so many millions of men, and not of mere brute or inanimate things, I see that appeal is possible, first and instantaneously, from them to the Maker of them, and, secondly, from them to themselves. But if I put my head deliberately into the fire, there is no appeal to fire or to the Maker of fire, and I have only myself to blame. If I could convince myself that I have any right to be satisfied with men as they are, and to treat them accordingly, and not according, in some respects, to my requisitions and expectations of what they and I ought to be, then, like a good Mussulman and fatalist, I should endeavor to be satisfied with things as they are, and say it is the will of God. And, above all, there is this difference between resisting this and a purely brute or natural force, that I can resist this with some effect; but I cannot expect, like Orpheus, to change the nature of the rocks and trees and beasts.

I do not wish to quarrel with any man or nation. I do not wish to split hairs, to make fine distinctions, or set myself up as better than my neighbors. I seek rather, I may say, even an excuse for conforming to the laws of the land. I am but too ready to conform to them. Indeed, I have reason to suspect myself on this head; and each year, as the tax-gatherer comes round, I find myself disposed to review the acts and position of the general and State governments, and the spirit of the people, to discover a pretext for conformity.

> "We must affect our country as our parents,
> And if at any time we alienate
> Our love or industry from doing it honor,
> We must respect effects and teach the soul
> Matter of conscience and religion,
> And not desire of rule or benefit."

I believe that the State will soon be able to take all my work of this sort out of my hands, and then I shall be no better a patriot than my fellow-countrymen. Seen from a lower point of view, the Constitution, with all its faults, is very good; the law and the courts are very respectable; even this State and this American government are, in many respects, very admirable, and rare things, to be thankful for, such as a great many have described them; but seen from a point of view a little higher, they are what I have described them; seen from a higher still, and the highest, who shall say what they are, or that they are worth looking at or thinking of at all?

However, the government does not concern me much, and I shall bestow the fewest possible thoughts on it. It is not many moments that I live under a government, even in this world. If a man is thought-free, fancy-free, imagination-free, that which *is not* never for a long time appearing *to be* to him, unwise rulers or reformers cannot fatally interrupt him.

I know that most men think differently from myself; but those whose lives are by profession devoted to the study of these or kindred subjects content me as little as any. Statesmen and legislators, standing so completely within the institution, never distinctly and nakedly behold it. They speak of moving society, but have no resting-place without it. They may be men of a certain experience and discrimination, and have no doubt invented ingenious and even useful systems, for which we sincerely thank them; but all their wit and usefulness lie within certain not very wide limits. They are wont to forget that the world is not governed by policy and expediency. Webster never goes behind government, and so cannot speak with authority about it. His words are wisdom to those legislators who contemplate no essential reform in the existing government; but for thinkers, and those who legislate for all time, he never once glances at the subject. I know of those whose serene and wise speculations on this theme would soon reveal the limits of his mind's range and hospitality. Yet, compared with the cheap professions of most reformers, and the still cheaper wisdom and eloquence of politicians in general, his are almost the only sensible and valuable words, and we thank Heaven for him. Comparatively, he is always strong, original, and, above all, practical. Still, his quality is not wisdom, but prudence. The lawyer's truth is not Truth, but consistency or a consistent expediency. Truth is always in harmony with herself, and is not concerned chiefly to reveal the justice that may consist with wrong-doing. He well deserves to be called, as he has been called, the Defender of the Constitution. There are really no blows to be given by him but defensive ones. He is not a leader, but a follower. His leaders are the men of '87. "I have never made an effort," he says, "and never propose to make an effort; I have never countenanced an effort, and never mean to countenance an effort, to disturb the arrangement as originally made, by which the various States came into the Union." Still thinking of the sanction which the Constitution gives to slavery, he says, "Because it was a part of the original compact—let it stand." Notwithstanding his special acuteness and ability, he is unable to take a fact out of its merely political relations, and behold it as it lies absolutely to be disposed of by the intellect—what, for instance, it behooves a man to do here in America today with regard to slavery—but ventures, or is driven, to make some such desperate answer as the following, while professing to speak absolutely, and as a private man—from which what new and singular code of social duties might be inferred? "The manner," says he, "in which the governments of those States where slavery exists are to regulate it is for their own consideration, under their responsibility to their constituents, to the general laws of propriety, humanity, and justice, and to God. Associations formed elsewhere, springing from a feeling of humanity, or any other cause, have nothing whatever to do with it. They have never received any encouragement from me, and they never will." [8]

They who know of no purer sources of truth, who have traced up its stream no higher, stand, and wisely stand, by the Bible and the Constitution, and drink at it there with reverence and humility; but they who behold where it comes trickling into this lake or that pool, gird up their loins once more, and continue their pilgrimage toward its fountainhead.

No man with a genius for legislation has appeared in America. They are rare in the history of the world. There are orators, politicians, and eloquent men, by the thousand; but the speaker has not yet opened his mouth to speak who is capable of settling the much-vexed questions of the day. We love eloquence for its own sake, and not for any truth which it may utter, or any heroism it may inspire. Our legislators have not yet learned the comparative value of free trade and of freedom, of union, and of rectitude, to a nation. They have no genius or talent for comparatively humble questions of taxation and finance, commerce and manufactures and agriculture. If we were left solely to the wordy wit of legislators in Congress for our guidance, uncorrected by the seasonable experience and the effectual complaints of the people, America would not long retain her rank among the nations. For eighteen hundred years, though perchance I have no right to say it, the New Testament has been written; yet where is the legislator who has wisdom and practical talent enough to avail himself of the light which it sheds on the science of legislation?

The authority of government, even such as I am willing to submit to—for I will cheerfully obey those who know and can do better than I, and in many things even those who neither know nor can do so well—is still an impure one: to be strictly just, it must have the sanction and consent of the governed. It can have no pure right over my person and property but what I concede to it. The progress from an absolute to a limited monarchy, from a limited monarchy to a democracy, is a progress toward a true respect for the individual. Even the Chinese philosopher was wise enough to regard the individual as the basis of the empire. Is a democracy, such as we know it, the last improvement possible in government? Is it not possible to take a step further towards recognizing and organizing the rights of man? There will never be a really free and enlightened State until the State comes to recognize the individual as a higher and independent power, from which all its own power

8. "These extracts have been inserted since the lecture was read" [Thoreau's note].

and authority are derived, and treats him accordingly. I please myself with imagining a State at last which can afford to be just to all men, and to treat the individual with respect as a neighbor; which even would not think it inconsistent with its own repose if a few were to live aloof from it, not meddling with it, nor embraced by it, who fulfilled all the duties of neighbors and fellow men. A State which bore this kind of fruit, and suffered it to drop off as fast as it ripened, would prepare the way for a still more perfect and glorious State, which also I have imagined, but not yet anywhere seen.

WALKING

◇

¶ ORIGINALLY entitled "The Wild," and first delivered before the Concord Lyceum in 1851, "Walking" was somewhat revised during Thoreau's final illness. It was published posthumously in the *Atlantic Monthly* in 1862. To a nation that was completing a transcontinental expansion, Thoreau set forth in this essay a vision of another West which could forever replenish and rejuvenate American culture with its "absolute freedom and wildness." This mythological West could not be located geographically; it did not lie beyond the Alleghenies or across the wide Missouri; a state of mind, not a place, it was present wherever man was willing to trust the untrammeled responses of his own genius.

◇

I WISH to speak a word for Nature, for absolute freedom and wildness, as contrasted with a freedom and culture merely civil—to regard man as an inhabitant, or a part and parcel of Nature, rather than a member of society. I wish to make an extreme statement, if so I may make an emphatic one, for there are enough champions of civilization: the minister and the school committee and every one of you will take care of that.

I have met with but one or two persons in the course of my life who understood the art of Walking, that is, of taking walks—who had a genius, so to speak, for *sauntering,* which word is beautifully derived "from idle people who roved about the country, in the Middle Ages, and asked charity, under pretense of going *à la Sainte Terre,*" to the Holy Land, till the children exclaimed, "There goes a *Sainte-Terrer,*" a Saunterer, a Holy-Lander. They who never go to the Holy Land in their walks, as they pretend, are indeed mere idlers and vagabonds; but they who do go there are saunterers in the good sense, such as I mean. Some, however, would derive the word from *sans terre,* without land or a home, which, therefore, in the good sense, will mean, having no particular home, but equally at home everywhere. For this is the secret of successful sauntering. He who sits still in a house all the time may be the greatest vagrant of all; but the saunterer, in the good sense, is no more vagrant than the meandering river, which is all the while sedulously seeking the shortest course to the sea. But I prefer the first, which, indeed, is the most probable derivation. For every walk is a sort of crusade, preached by some Peter the Hermit in us, to go forth and reconquer this Holy Land from the hands of the Infidels.

It is true, we are but faint-hearted crusaders, even the walkers, nowadays, who undertake no persevering, never-ending enterprises. Our expeditions are but tours, and come round again at evening to the old hearthside from which we set out. Half the walk is but retracing our steps. We should go forth on the shortest walk, perchance, in the spirit of undying adventure, never to return, prepared to send back our embalmed hearts only as relics to our desolate kingdoms. If you are ready to leave father and mother, and brother and sister, and wife and child and friends, and never see them again—if you have paid your debts, and made your will, and settled all your affairs, and are a free man—then you are ready for a walk.

To come down to my own experience, my companion and I, for I sometimes have a companion, take pleasure in fancying ourselves knights of a new, or rather an old, order—not Equestrians or Chevaliers, not Ritters or Riders, but Walkers, a still more ancient and honorable class, I trust. The chivalric and heroic spirit which once belonged to the Rider seems now to reside in, or perchance to have subsided into, the Walker—not the Knight, but Walker, Errant. He is a sort of fourth estate, outside of Church and State and People.

We have felt that we almost alone hereabouts practiced this noble art; though, to tell the truth, at least if their own assertions are to be received, most of my townsmen would fain walk sometimes, as I do, but they cannot. No wealth can buy the requisite leisure, freedom, and independence which are the capital in this profession. It comes only by the grace of God. It requires a direct dispensation from Heaven to become a walker. You must be born into the family of the Walkers. *Ambulator nascitur, non fit.* Some of my townsmen, it is true, can remember and have described to me some walks which they took ten years ago, in which they were so blessed as to lose themselves for half an hour in the woods; but I know very well that they have confined themselves to the highway ever since, whatever pretensions they may make to belong to this select class. No doubt they were elevated for a moment as by the reminiscence of a previous state of existence, when even they were foresters and outlaws.

"When he came to grene wode,
 In a mery mornynge,
There he herde the notes small
 Of byrdes mery syngynge.

"It is ferre gone, sayd Robyn,
 That I was last here;
Me lyste a lytell for to shote
 At the donne dere." [1]

I think that I cannot preserve my health and spirits, unless I spend four hours a day at least—and it is commonly more than that—sauntering through the woods and over the hills and fields, absolutely free from all worldly engagements. You may safely say, A penny for your thoughts, or a thousand pounds. When sometimes I am reminded that the mechanics and shopkeepers stay in their shops not only all the forenoon, but all the afternoon too, sitting with crossed legs, so many of them—as if the legs were made to sit upon, and not to stand or walk upon—I think that they deserve some credit for not having all committed suicide long ago.

I, who cannot stay in my chamber for a single day without acquiring some rust, and when sometimes I have stolen forth for a walk at the eleventh hour, or four o'clock in the afternoon, too late to redeem the day, when the shades of night were already beginning to be mingled with the daylight, have felt as if I had committed some sin to be atoned for—I confess that I am astonished at the power of endurance, to say nothing of the moral insensibility, of my neighbors who confine themselves to shops and offices the whole day for weeks and months, aye, and years almost together. I know not what manner of stuff they are of, sitting there now at three o'clock in the afternoon, as if it were three o'clock in the morning. Bonaparte may talk of the three-o'clock-in-the-morning courage, but it is nothing to the courage which can sit down cheerfully at this hour in the afternoon over against one's self whom you have known all the morning, to starve out a garrison to whom you are bound by such strong ties of sympathy. I wonder that about this time, or say between four and five o'clock in the afternoon, too late for the morning papers and too early for the evening ones, there is not a general explosion heard up and down the street, scattering a legion of antiquated and house-bred notions and whims to the four winds for an airing—and so the evil cure itself.

How womankind, who are confined to the house still more than men, stand it I do not know; but I have ground to suspect that most of them do not *stand* it at all. When, early in a summer afternoon, we have been shaking the dust of the village from the skirts of our garments, making haste past those houses with purely Doric or Gothic fronts, which have such an air of repose about them, my companion whispers that probably about these times their occupants are all gone to bed. Then it is that I appreciate the beauty and the glory of architecture, which itself never turns in, but forever stands out and erect, keeping watch over the slumberers.

No doubt temperament, and, above all, age, have a good deal to do with it. As a man grows older, his ability to sit still and follow indoor occupations increases. He grows vespertinal in his habits as the evening of life approaches, till at last he comes forth only just before sundown, and gets all the walk that he requires in half an hour.

But the walking of which I speak has nothing in it akin to taking exercise, as it is called, as the sick take medicine at stated hours—as the swinging of dumbbells or chairs; but is itself the enterprise and adventure of the day. If you would get exercise, go in search of the springs of life. Think of a man's swinging dumbbells for his health, when those springs are bubbling up in far-off pastures unsought by him!

Moreover, you must walk like a camel, which is said to be the only beast which ruminates when walking. When a traveler asked Wordsworth's servant to show him her master's study, she answered, "Here is his library, but his study is out of doors."

Living much out of doors, in the sun and wind, will no doubt produce a certain roughness of character—will cause a thicker cuticle to grow over some of the finer qualities of our nature, as on the face and hands, or as severe manual labor robs the hands of some of their delicacy of touch. So staying in the house, on the other hand, may produce a softness and smoothness, not to say thinness of skin, accompanied by an increased sensibility to certain impressions. Perhaps we should be more susceptible to some influences important to our intellectual and moral growth, if the sun had shone and the wind blown on us a little less; and no doubt it is a nice matter to proportion

WALKING. 1. "When . . . dere": the Robin Hood Ballads.

rightly the thick and thin skin. But methinks that is a scurf that will fall off fast enough—that the natural remedy is to be found in the proportion which the night bears to the day, the winter to the summer, thought to experience. There will be so much the more air and sunshine in our thoughts. The callous palms of the laborer are conversant with finer tissues of self-respect and heroism, whose touch thrills the heart, than the languid fingers of idleness. That is mere sentimentality that lies abed by day and thinks itself white, far from the tan and callus of experience.

When we walk, we naturally go to the fields and woods: what would become of us, if we walked only in a garden or a mall? Even some sects of philosophers have felt the necessity of importing the woods to themselves, since they did not go to the woods. "They planted groves and walks of Platanes," where they took *subdiales ambulationes* in porticos open to the air. Of course it is of no use to direct our steps to the woods, if they do not carry us thither. I am alarmed when it happens that I have walked a mile into the woods bodily, without getting there in spirit. In my afternoon walk I would fain forget all my morning occupations and my obligations to society. But it sometimes happens that I cannot easily shake off the village. The thought of some work will run in my head and I am not where my body is—I am out of my senses. In my walks I would fain return to my senses. What business have I in the woods, if I am thinking of something out of the woods? I suspect myself, and cannot help a shudder, when I find myself so implicated even in what are called good works—for this may sometimes happen.

My vicinity affords many good walks; and though for so many years I have walked almost every day, and sometimes for several days together, I have not yet exhausted them. An absolutely new prospect is a great happiness, and I can still get this any afternoon. Two or three hours' walking will carry me to as strange a country as I expect ever to see. A single farmhouse which I had not seen before is sometimes as good as the dominions of the King of Dahomey. There is in fact a sort of harmony discoverable between the capabilities of the landscape within a circle of ten miles' radius, or the limits of an afternoon walk, and the threescore years and ten of human life. It will never become quite familiar to you.

Nowadays almost all man's improvements, so called, as the building of houses and the cutting down of the forest and of all large trees, simply deform the landscape, and make it more and more tame and cheap. A people who would begin by burning the fences and let the forest stand! I saw the fences half consumed, their ends lost in the middle of the prairie, and some worldly miser with a surveyor looking after his bounds, while heaven had taken place around him, and he did not see the angels going to and fro, but was looking for an old post-hole in the midst of paradise. I looked again, and saw him standing in the middle of a boggy Stygian fen, surrounded by devils, and he had found his bounds without a doubt, three little stones, where a stake had been driven, and looking nearer, I saw that the Prince of Darkness was his surveyor.

I can easily walk ten, fifteen, twenty, any number of miles, commencing at my own door, without going by any house, without crossing a road except where the fox and the mink do: first along by the river, and then the brook, and then the meadow and the woodside. There are square miles in my vicinity which have no inhabitant. From many a hill I can see civilization and the abodes of man afar. The farmers and their works are scarcely more obvious than woodchucks and their burrows. Man and his affairs, church and state and school, trade and commerce, and manufactures and agriculture, even politics, the most alarming of them all—I am pleased to see how little space they occupy in the landscape. Politics is but a narrow field, and that still narrower highway yonder leads to it. I sometimes direct the traveler thither. If you would go to the political world, follow the great road, follow that market-man, keep his dust in your eyes, and it will lead you straight to it; for it, too, has its place merely, and does not occupy all space. I pass from it as from a bean field into the forest, and it is forgotten. In one half-hour I can walk off to some portion of the earth's surface where a man does not stand from one year's end to another, and there, consequently, politics are not, for they are but as the cigar-smoke of a man.

The village is the place to which the roads tend, a sort of expansion of the highway, as a lake of a river. It is the body of which roads are the arms and legs—a trivial or quadrivial place, the thoroughfare and ordinary of travelers. The word is from the Latin *villa,* which together with *via,* a way, or more anciently *ved* and *vella,* Varro derives from veho, to carry, because the villa is the place to and from which things are carried. They who got their living by teaming were said *vellaturam facere*. Hence, too, the Latin word *vilis* and our vile, also *villain*. This suggests what kind of degeneracy villagers are liable to. They are wayworn by the travel that goes by and over them, without traveling themselves.

Some do not walk at all; others walk in the highways; a few walk across lots. Roads are made for horses and men of business. I do not travel in them much, comparatively, because I am not in a hurry to get to any tavern or grocery or livery-stable or depot to which they lead. I am a good horse to travel, but not from choice a roadster. The landscape-painter uses the figures of men to mark a road. He would not make that use of my figure. I walk out into a nature such as the old prophets and poets, Menu, Moses, Homer, Chaucer, walked in. You may name it America, but it is not America; neither Americus Vespucius, nor Columbus, nor the rest were the discoverers of it. There is a truer account of it in mythology than in any history of America, so called, that I have seen.

However, there are a few old roads that may be trodden with profit, as if they led somewhere now that they are nearly discontinued. There is the Old Marlborough Road, which does not go to Marlborough now, methinks, unless that is Marlborough where it carries me. I am the bolder to speak of it here, because I presume that there are one or two such roads in every town.

THE OLD MARLBOROUGH ROAD

Where they once dug for money,
But never found any;
Where sometimes Martial Miles
Singly files,
And Elijah Wood,
I fear for no good:
No other man,
Save Elisha Dugan—
O man of wild habits,
Partridges and rabbits,
Who hast no cares
Only to set snares,
Who liv'st all alone,
Close to the bone,
And where life is sweetest
Constantly eatest.
When the spring stirs my blood
With the instinct to travel,
I can get enough gravel
On the Old Marlborough Road.
Nobody repairs it,
For nobody wears it;
It is a living way,
As the Christians say.
Not many there be
Who enter therein,
Only the guests of the
Irishman Quin.
What is it, what is it,
But a direction out there,
And the bare possibility
Of going somewhere?
Great guide-boards of stone,
But travelers none;
Cenotaphs of the towns
Named on their crowns.
It is worth going to see
Where you *might* be.
What king
Did the thing,
I am still wondering;
Set up how or when,
By what selectmen,
Gourgas or Lee,
Clark or Darby?
They're a great endeavor
To be something forever;
Blank tablets of stone,
Where a traveler might groan,
And in one sentence
Grave all that is known;
Which another might read,
In his extreme need.
I know one or two
Lines that would do,
Literature that might stand
All over the land,
Which a man could remember
Till next December,
And read again in the spring,
After the thawing.
If with fancy unfurled
You leave your abode,
You may go round the world
By the Old Marlborough Road.

At present, in this vicinity, the best part of the land is not private property; the landscape is not owned, and the walker enjoys comparative freedom. But possibly the day will come when it will be partitioned off into so-called pleasure-grounds, in which a few will take a narrow and exclusive pleasure only—when fences shall be multiplied, and man-traps and other engines invented to confine men to the *public* road, and walking over the surface of God's earth shall be construed to mean trespassing on some gentleman's grounds. To enjoy a thing exclusively is commonly to exclude yourself from the true enjoyment of it. Let us improve our opportunities, then, before the evil days come.

What is it that makes it so hard sometimes to determine whither we will walk? I believe that there is a subtle magnetism in Nature, which, if we unconsciously yield to it, will direct us aright. It is not indifferent to us which way we walk. There is a right way; but we are very liable from heedlessness and stupidity to take the wrong one. We would fain take that walk, never yet taken by us through this actual world, which is perfectly symbolical of the path which we love to travel in the interior and ideal world; and sometimes, no doubt, we find it difficult to choose our direction, because it does not yet exist distinctly in our idea.

When I go out of the house for a walk, uncertain as yet whither I will bend my steps, and submit myself to my instinct to decide for me, I find, strange and whimsical as it may seem, that I finally and inevitably settle southwest, toward some particular wood or meadow or deserted pasture or hill in that direction. My needle is slow to settle, varies a few degrees, and does not always point due southwest, it is true, and it has good authority for this variation, but it always settles between west and south-southwest. The future lies that way to me, and the earth seems more unexhausted and richer on that side. The outline which would bound my walks would be, not a circle, but a parabola, or rather like one of those cometary orbits which have been thought to be non-returning curves, in this case opening westward, in which my house occupies the place of the sun. I turn round and round irresolute sometimes for a quarter of an hour, until I decide, for a thousandth time, that I will walk into the southwest or west. Eastward I go only by force; but westward I go free. Thither no business leads me. It is hard for me to believe that I shall find fair landscapes or sufficient wildness and freedom behind the eastern horizon. I am not excited by the prospect of a walk thither; but I believe that the forest which I see in the western horizon stretches uninterruptedly toward the setting sun, and there are no towns nor cities in it of enough consequence to disturb me. Let me live where I will, on this side is the city, on that the wilderness, and ever I am leaving the city more and more, and withdrawing into the wilderness. I should not lay so much stress on this fact, if I did not believe that something like this is the prevailing tendency of my countrymen. I must walk toward Oregon, and not toward Europe. And that way the nation is moving, and I may say that mankind progress from east to west. Within a few years we have witnessed the phenomenon of a southeastward migration, in the settlement of Australia; but this affects us as a retrograde movement, and, judging from the moral and physical character of the first generation of Australians, has not yet proved a successful experiment. The eastern Tartars think that there is nothing west beyond Thibet. "The world ends there," say they; "beyond there is nothing but a shoreless sea." It is unmitigated East where they live.

We go eastward to realize history and study the works of art and literature, retracing the steps of the race; we go westward as into the future, with a spirit of enterprise and adventure. The Atlantic is a Lethean stream, in our passage over which we have had an opportunity to forget the Old World and its institutions. If we do not succeed this time, there is perhaps one more chance for the race left before it arrives on the banks of the Styx; and that is in the Lethe of the Pacific, which is three times as wide.

I know not how significant it is, or how far it is an evidence of singularity, that an individual should thus consent in his pettiest walk with the general movement of the race; but I know that something akin to the migratory instinct in birds and quadrupeds—which, in some instances, is known to have affected the squirrel tribe, impelling them to a general and mysterious movement, in which they were seen, say some, crossing the broadest rivers, each on its particular chip, with its tail raised for a sail, and bridging narrower streams with their dead—that something like the *furor* which affects the domestic cattle in the spring, and which is referred to a worm in their tails, affects both nations and individuals, either perennially or from time to time. Not a flock of wild geese cackles over our town, but it to some extent unsettles the value of real estate here, and, if I were a broker, I should probably take that disturbance into account.

"Than longen folk to gon on pilgrimages,
And palmeres for to seken strange strondes." [2]

Every sunset which I witness inspires me with the desire to go to a West as distant and as fair as that into which the sun goes down. He appears to migrate westward daily, and tempt us to follow him. He is the Great Western Pioneer whom the nations follow. We dream all night of those mountain-ridges in the horizon, though they may be of vapor only, which were last gilded by his rays. The island of Atlantis, and the islands and gardens of the Hesperides, a sort of terrestrial paradise, appear to have been the Great West of the ancients, enveloped in mystery and poetry. Who has not seen in imagination, when looking into the sunset sky, the gardens of the Hesperides, and the foundation of all those fables?

Columbus felt the westward tendency more strongly than any before. He obeyed it, and found a New World for Castile and León. The herd of men in those days scented fresh pastures from afar.

"And now the sun had stretched out all the hills,
And now was dropped into the western bay;
At last *he* rose, and twitched his mantle blue;
Tomorrow to fresh woods and pastures new." [3]

2. **"Than . . . strondes"**: Chaucer, Prologue to *The Canterbury Tales*, ll. 12–13.
3. **"And . . . new"**: John Milton, *Lycidas*, ll. 190–93.

Where on the globe can there be found an area of equal extent with that occupied by the bulk of our States, so fertile and so rich and varied in its productions, and at the same time so habitable by the European, as this is? Michaux, who knew but part of them, says that "the species of large trees are much more numerous in North America than in Europe; in the United States there are more than one hundred and forty species that exceed thirty feet in height; in France there are but thirty that attain this size." Later botanists more than confirm his observations. Humboldt came to America to realize his youthful dreams of a tropical vegetation, and he beheld it in its greatest perfection in the primitive forests of the Amazon, the most gigantic wilderness on the earth, which he has so eloquently described. The geographer Guyot, himself a European, goes farther—farther than I am ready to follow him; yet not when he says: "As the plant is made for the animal, as the vegetable world is made for the animal world, America is made for the man of the Old World. . . . The man of the Old World sets out upon his way. Leaving the highlands of Asia, he descends from station to station towards Europe. Each of his steps is marked by a new civilization superior to the preceding, by a greater power of development. Arrived at the Atlantic, he pauses on the shore of this unknown ocean, the bounds of which he knows not, and turns upon his footprints for an instant." When he has exhausted the rich soil of Europe, and reinvigorated himself, "then recommences his adventurous career westward as in the earliest ages." So far Guyot.

From this western impulse coming in contact with the barrier of the Atlantic sprang the commerce and enterprise of modern times. The younger Michaux, in his *Travels West of the Alleghanies in 1802,* says that the common inquiry in the newly settled West was, " 'From what part of the world have you come?' As if these vast and fertile regions would naturally be the place of meeting and common country of all the inhabitants of the globe."

To use an obsolete Latin word, I might say, *Ex Oriente lux; ex Occidente* FRUX. From the East light; from the West fruit.

Sir Francis Head, an English traveler and a Governor-General of Canada, tells us that "in both the northern and southern hemispheres of the New World, Nature has not only outlined her works on a larger scale, but has painted the whole picture with brighter and more costly colors than she used in delineating and in beautifying the Old World. . . . The heavens of America appear infinitely higher, the sky is bluer, the air is fresher, the cold is intenser, the moon looks larger, the stars are brighter, the thunder is louder, the lightning is vivider, the wind is stronger, the rain is heavier, the mountains are higher, the rivers longer, the forests bigger, the plains broader." This statement will do at least to set against Buffon's account of this part of the world and its productions.

Linnaeus said long ago, "*Nescio quae facies* laeta, glabra *plantis Americanis*" (I know not what there is of joyous and smooth in the aspect of American plants); and I think that in this country there are no, or at most very few, *Africanae bestiae,* African beasts, as the Romans called them, and that in this respect also it is peculiarly fitted for the habitation of man. We are told that within three miles of the center of the East-Indian city of Singapore, some of the inhabitants are annually carried off by tigers; but the traveler can lie down in the woods at night almost anywhere in North America without fear of wild beasts.

These are encouraging testimonies. If the moon looks larger here than in Europe, probably the sun looks larger also. If the heavens of America appear infinitely higher, and the stars brighter, I trust that these facts are symbolical of the height to which the philosophy and poetry and religion of her inhabitants may one day soar. At length, perchance, the immaterial heaven will appear as much higher to the American mind, and the intimations that star it as much brighter. For I believe that climate does thus react on man—as there is something in the mountain air that feeds the spirit and inspires. Will not man grow to greater perfection intellectually as well as physically under these influences? Or is it unimportant how many foggy days there are in his life? I trust that we shall be more imaginative, that our thoughts will be clearer, fresher, and more ethereal, as our sky—our understanding more comprehensive and broader, like our plains—our intellect generally on a grander scale, like our thunder and lightning, our rivers and mountains and forests—and our hearts shall even correspond in breadth and depth and grandeur to our inland seas. Perchance there will appear to the traveler something, he knows not what, of *laeta* and *glabra,* of joyous and serene, in our very faces. Else to what end does the world go on, and why was America discovered?

To Americans I hardly need to say,

> "Westward the star of empire takes its way." [4]

As a true patriot, I should be ashamed to think

4. **"Westward . . . way"**: From the sixth stanza of *Verses on the Prospect of Planting Arts and Learning in America,* by Bishop George Berkeley (1685–1753). Thoreau replaced Berkeley's "course" with "star."

that Adam in paradise was more favorably situated on the whole than the backwoodsman in this country.

Our sympathies in Massachusetts are not confined to New England; though we may be estranged from the South, we sympathize with the West. There is the home of the younger sons, as among the Scandinavians they took to the sea for their inheritance. It is too late to be studying Hebrew; it is more important to understand even the slang of today.

Some months ago I went to see a panorama of the Rhine. It was like a dream of the Middle Ages. I floated down its historic stream in something more than imagination, under bridges built by the Romans, and repaired by later heroes, past cities and castles whose very names were music to my ears, and each of which was the subject of a legend. There were Ehrenbreitstein and Rolandseck and Coblentz, which I knew only in history. They were ruins that interested me chiefly. There seemed to come up from its waters and its vine-clad hills and valleys a hushed music as of Crusaders departing for the Holy Land. I floated along under the spell of enchantment, as if I had been transported to an heroic age, and breathed an atmosphere of chivalry.

Soon after, I went to see a panorama of the Mississippi, and as I worked my way up the river in the light of today, and saw the steamboats wooding up, counted the rising cities, gazed on the fresh ruins of Nauvoo, beheld the Indians moving west across the stream, and, as before I had looked up the Moselle, now looked up the Ohio and the Missouri and heard the legends of Dubuque and of Wenona's Cliff—still thinking more of the future than of the past or present—I saw that this was a Rhine stream of a different kind; that the foundations of castles were yet to be laid, and the famous bridges were yet to be thrown over the river; and I felt that *this was the heroic age itself,* though we know it not, for the hero is commonly the simplest and obscurest of men.

The West of which I speak is but another name for the Wild; and what I have been preparing to say is, that in Wildness is the preservation of the World. Every tree sends its fibers forth in search of the Wild. The cities import it at any price. Men plow and sail for it. From the forest and wilderness come the tonics and barks which brace mankind. Our ancestors were savages. The story of Romulus and Remus being suckled by a wolf is not a meaningless fable. The founders of every state which has risen to eminence have drawn their nourishment and vigor from a similar wild source. It was because the children of the Empire were not suckled by the wolf that they were conquered and displaced by the children of the northern forests who were.

I believe in the forest, and in the meadow, and in the night in which the corn grows. We require an infusion of hemlock, spruce or arbor vitae in our tea. There is a difference between eating and drinking for strength and from mere gluttony. The Hottentots eagerly devour the marrow of the koodoo and other antelopes raw, as a matter of course. Some of our northern Indians eat raw the marrow of the Arctic reindeer, as well as various other parts, including the summits of the antlers, as long as they are soft. And herein, perchance, they have stolen a march on the cooks of Paris. They get what usually goes to feed the fire. This is probably better than stall-fed beef and slaughterhouse pork to make a man of. Give me a wildness whose glance no civilization can endure—as if we lived on the marrow of koodoos devoured raw.

There are some intervals which border the strain of the wood thrush, to which I would migrate—wild lands where no settler has squatted; to which, methinks, I am already acclimated.

The African hunter Cumming tells us that the skin of the eland, as well as that of most other antelopes just killed, emits the most delicious perfume of trees and grass. I would have every man so much like a wild antelope, so much a part and parcel of nature, that his very person should thus sweetly advertise our senses of his presence, and remind us of those parts of nature which he most haunts. I feel no disposition to be satirical, when the trapper's coat emits the odor of musquash even; it is a sweeter scent to me than that which commonly exhales from the merchant's or the scholar's garments. When I go into their wardrobes and handle their vestments, I am reminded of no grassy plains and flowery meads which they have frequented, but of dusty merchants' exchanges and libraries rather.

A tanned skin is something more than respectable, and perhaps olive is a fitter color than white for a man—a denizen of the woods. "The pale white man!" I do not wonder that the African pitied him. Darwin the naturalist says, "A white man bathing by the side of a Tahitian was like a plant bleached by the gardener's art, compared with a fine, dark green one, growing vigorously in the open fields."

Ben Jonson exclaims,

> "How near to the good is what is fair!"

So I would say,

> How near to good is what is *wild!*

Life consists with wildness. The most alive is the wildest. Not yet subdued to man, its presence refreshes him. One who pressed forward incessantly and never rested from his labors, who grew fast and made infinite demands on life, would always find himself in a new country or wilderness, and surrounded by the raw material of life. He would be climbing over the prostrate stems of primitive forest-trees.

Hope and the future for me are not in lawns and cultivated fields, not in towns and cities, but in the impervious and quaking swamps. When, formerly, I have analyzed my partiality for some farm which I had contemplated purchasing, I have frequently found that I was attracted solely by a few square rods of impermeable and unfathomable bog—a natural sink in one corner of it. That was the jewel which dazzled me. I derive more of my subsistence from the swamps which surround my native town than from the cultivated gardens in the village. There are no richer parterres to my eyes than the dense beds of dwarf andromeda (*Cassandra calyculata*) which cover these tender places on the earth's surface. Botany cannot go farther than tell me the names of the shrubs which grow there—the high blueberry, panicled andromeda, lambkill, azalea, and rhodora—all standing in the quaking sphagnum. I often think that I should like to have my house front on this mass of dull red bushes, omitting other flower plots and borders, transplanted spruce and trim box, even graveled walks—to have this fertile spot under my windows, not a few imported barrowfuls of soil only to cover the sand which was thrown out in digging the cellar. Why not put my house, my parlor, behind this plot, instead of behind that meager assemblage of curiosities, that poor apology for a Nature and Art, which I call my front yard? It is an effort to clear up and make a decent appearance when the carpenter and mason have departed, though done as much for the passer-by as the dweller within. The most tasteful front-yard fence was never an agreeable object of study to me; the most elaborate ornaments, acorn tops, or what not, soon wearied and disgusted me. Bring your sills up to the very edge of the swamp, then (though it may not be the best place for a dry cellar), so that there be no access on that side to citizens. Front yards are not made to walk in, but, at most, through, and you could go in the back way.

Yes, though you may think me perverse, if it were proposed to me to dwell in the neighborhood of the most beautiful garden that ever human art contrived, or else of a Dismal Swamp, I should certainly decide for the swamp. How vain, then, have been all your labors, citizens, for me!

My spirits infallibly rise in proportion to the outward dreariness. Give me the ocean, the desert, or the wilderness! In the desert, pure air and solitude compensate for want of moisture and fertility. The traveler Burton says of it: "Your *morale* improves; you become frank and cordial, hospitable and single-minded. . . . In the desert, spirituous liquors excite only disgust. There is a keen enjoyment in a mere animal existence." They who have been traveling long on the steppes of Tartary say, "On re-entering cultivated lands, the agitation, perplexity, and turmoil of civilization oppressed and suffocated us; the air seemed to fail us, and we felt every moment as if about to die of asphyxia." When I would recreate myself, I seek the darkest wood, the thickest and most interminable and, to the citizen, most dismal, swamp. I enter a swamp as a sacred place, a *sanctum sanctorum*. There is the strength, the marrow, of Nature. The wild-wood covers the virgin mould, and the same soil is good for men and for trees. A man's health requires as many acres of meadow to his prospect as his farm does loads of muck. There are the strong meats on which he feeds. A town is saved, not more by the righteous men in it than by the woods and swamps that surround it. A township where one primitive forest waves above while another primitive forest rots below—such a town is fitted to raise not only corn and potatoes, but poets and philosophers for the coming ages. In such a soil grew Homer and Confucius and the rest, and out of such a wilderness comes the Reformer eating locusts and wild honey.

To preserve wild animals implies generally the creation of a forest for them to dwell in or resort to. So it is with man. A hundred years ago they sold bark in our streets peeled from our own woods. In the very aspect of those primitive and rugged trees there was, methinks, a tanning principle which hardened and consolidated the fibers of men's thoughts. Ah! already I shudder for these comparatively degenerate days of my native village, when you cannot collect a load of bark of good thickness, and we no longer produce tar and turpentine.

The civilized nations—Greece, Rome, England—have been sustained by the primitive forests which anciently rotted where they stand. They survive as long as the soil is not exhausted. Alas for human culture! little is to be expected of a nation, when the vegetable mould is exhausted, and it is compelled to make manure of the bones of its fathers. There the poet sustains himself merely by his own superfluous fat, and the philosopher comes down on his marrow-bones.

It is said to be the task of the American "to

work the virgin soil," and that "agriculture here already assumes proportions unknown everywhere else." I think that the farmer displaces the Indian even because he redeems the meadow, and so makes himself stronger and in some respects more natural. I was surveying for a man the other day a single straight line one hundred and thirty-two rods long, through a swamp at whose entrance might have been written the words which Dante read over the entrance to the infernal regions, "Leave all hope, ye that enter"—that is, of ever getting out again; where at one time I saw my employer actually up to his neck and swimming for his life in his property, though it was still winter. He had another similar swamp which I could not survey at all, because it was completely under water, and nevertheless, with regard to a third swamp, which I did *survey* from a distance, he remarked to me, true to his instincts, that he would not part with it for any consideration, on account of the mud which it contained. And that man intends to put a girdling ditch round the whole in the course of forty months, and so redeem it by the magic of his spade. I refer to him only as the type of a class.

The weapons with which we have gained our most important victories, which should be handed down as heirlooms from father to son, are not the sword and the lance, but the bushwhack, the turf-cutter, the spade, and the bog hoe, rusted with the blood of many a meadow, and begrimed with the dust of many a hard-fought field. The very winds blew the Indian's cornfield into the meadow, and pointed out the way which he had not the skill to follow. He had no better implement with which to intrench himself in the land than a clam-shell. But the farmer is armed with plow and spade.

In literature it is only the wild that attracts us. Dullness is but another name for tameness. It is the uncivilized free and wild thinking in Hamlet and the Iliad, in all the scriptures and mythologies, not learned in the schools, that delights us. As the wild duck is more swift and beautiful than the tame, so is the wild—the mallard—thought, which 'mid falling dews wings its way above the fens. A truly good book is something as natural, and as unexpectedly and unaccountably fair and perfect, as a wild-flower discovered on the prairies of the West or in the jungles of the East. Genius is a light which makes the darkness visible, like the lightning's flash, which perchance shatters the temple of knowledge itself—and not a taper lighted at the hearthstone of the race, which pales before the light of common day.

English literature, from the days of the minstrels to the Lake Poets—Chaucer and Spenser and Milton, and even Shakespeare, included—breathes no quite fresh and, in this sense, wild strain. It is an essentially tame and civilized literature, reflecting Greece and Rome. Her wilderness is a greenwood, her wild man a Robin Hood. There is plenty of genial love of Nature, but not so much of Nature herself. Her chronicles inform us when her wild animals, but not when the wild man in her, became extinct.

The science of Humboldt is one thing, poetry is another thing. The poet today, notwithstanding all the discoveries of science, and the accumulated learning of mankind, enjoys no advantage over Homer.

Where is the literature which gives expression to Nature? He would be a poet who could impress the winds and streams into his service, to speak for him; who nailed words to their primitive senses, as farmers drive down stakes in the spring, which the frost has heaved; who derived his words as often as he used them—transplanted them to his page with earth adhering to their roots; whose words were so true and fresh and natural that they would appear to expand like the buds at the approach of spring, though they lay half smothered between two musty leaves in a library—aye, to bloom and bear fruit there, after their kind, annually, for the faithful reader, in sympathy with surrounding Nature.

I do not know of any poetry to quote which adequately expresses this yearning for the Wild. Approached from this side, the best poetry is tame. I do not know where to find in any literature, ancient or modern, any account which contents me of that Nature with which even I am acquainted. You will perceive that I demand something which no Augustan nor Elizabethan age, which no *culture,* in short, can give. Mythology comes nearer to it than anything. How much more fertile a Nature, at least, has Grecian mythology its root in than English literature! Mythology is the crop which the Old World bore before its soil was exhausted, before the fancy and imagination were affected with blight; and which it still bears, wherever its pristine vigor is unabated. All other literatures endure only as the elms which overshadow our houses; but this is like the great dragon-tree of the Western Isles, as old as mankind, and, whether that does or not, will endure as long; for the decay of other literatures makes the soil in which it thrives.

The West is preparing to add its fables to those of the East. The valleys of the Ganges, the Nile, and the Rhine having yielded their crop, it remains to be seen what the valleys of the Amazon, the

Plate, the Orinoco, the St. Lawrence, and the Mississippi will produce. Perchance, when, in the course of ages, American liberty has become a fiction of the past—as it is to some extent a fiction of the present—the poets of the world will be inspired by American mythology.

The wildest dreams of wild men, even, are not the less true, though they may not recommend themselves to the sense which is most common among Englishmen and Americans today. It is not every truth that recommends itself to the common sense. Nature has a place for the wild clematis as well as for the cabbage. Some expressions of truth are reminiscent, others merely *sensible,* as the phrase is, others prophetic. Some forms of disease, even, may prophesy forms of health. The geologist has discovered that the figures of serpents, griffins, flying dragons, and other fanciful embellishments of heraldry, have their prototypes in the forms of fossil species which were extinct before man was created, and hence "indicate a faint and shadowy knowledge of a previous state of organic existence." The Hindus dreamed that the earth rested on an elephant, and the elephant on a tortoise, and the tortoise on a serpent; and though it may be an unimportant coincidence, it will not be out of place here to state, that a fossil tortoise has lately been discovered in Asia large enough to support an elephant. I confess that I am partial to these wild fancies, which transcend the order of time and development. They are the sublimest recreation of the intellect. The partridge loves peas, but not those that go with her into the pot.

In short, all good things are wild and free. There is something in a strain of music, whether produced by an instrument or by the human voice—take the sound of a bugle in a summer night, for instance—which by its wildness, to speak without satire, reminds me of the cries emitted by wild beasts in their native forests. It is so much of their wildness as I can understand. Give me for my friends and neighbors wild men, not tame ones. The wildness of the savage is but a faint symbol of the awful ferity with which good men and lovers meet.

I love even to see the domestic animals reassert their native rights—any evidence that they have not wholly lost their original wild habits and vigor; as when my neighbor's cow breaks out of her pasture early in the spring and boldly swims the river, a cold, gray tide, twenty-five or thirty rods wide, swollen by the melted snow. It is the buffalo crossing the Mississippi. This exploit confers some dignity on the herd in my eyes—already dignified. The seeds of instinct are preserved under the thick hides of cattle and horses, like seeds in the bowels of the earth, an indefinite period.

Any sportiveness in cattle is unexpected. I saw one day a herd of a dozen bullocks and cows running about and frisking in unwieldy sport, like huge rats, even like kittens. They shook their heads, raised their tails, and rushed up and down a hill, and I perceived by their horns, as well as by their activity, their relation to the deer tribe. But, alas! a sudden loud *Whoa!* would have damped their ardor at once, reduced them from venison to beef, and stiffened their sides and sinews like the locomotive. Who but the Evil One has cried "Whoa!" to mankind? Indeed, the life of cattle, like that of many men, is but a sort of locomotiveness; they move a side at a time, and man, by his machinery, is meeting the horse and the ox halfway. Whatever part the whip has touched is thenceforth palsied. Who would ever think of a *side* of any of the supple cat tribe, as we speak of a *side* of beef?

I rejoice that horses and steers have to be broken before they can be made the slaves of men, and that men themselves have some wild oats still left to sow before they become submissive members of society. Undoubtedly, all men are not equally fit subjects for civilization; and because the majority, like dogs and sheep, are tame by inherited disposition, this is no reason why the others should have their natures broken that they may be reduced to the same level. Men are in the main alike, but they were made several in order that they might be various. If a low use is to be served, one man will do nearly or quite as well as another; if a high one, individual excellence is to be regarded. Any man can stop a hole to keep the wind away, but no other man could serve so rare a use as the author of this illustration did. Confucius says, "The skins of the tiger and the leopard, when they are tanned, are as the skins of the dog and the sheep tanned." But it is not the part of a true culture to tame tigers, any more than it is to make sheep ferocious; and tanning their skins for shoes is not the best use to which they can be put.

When looking over a list of men's names in a foreign language, as of military officers, or of authors who have written on a particular subject, I am reminded once more that there is nothing in a name. The name Menschikoff, for instance, has nothing in it to my ears more human than a whisker, and it may belong to a rat. As the names of the Poles and Russians are to us, so are ours to them. It is as if they had been named by the child's rigmarole, *Iery wiery ichery van, tittle-tol-tan.* I see in my mind a herd of wild creatures swarming over the earth, and to each the herdsman has affixed some barbarous sound in his own dialect. The names of men are, of course, as cheap and meaningless as *Bose* and *Tray,* the names of dogs.

Methinks it would be some advantage to philosophy if men were named merely in the gross, as they are known. It would be necessary only to know the genus and perhaps the race or variety, to know the individual. We are not prepared to believe that every private soldier in a Roman army had a name of his own—because we have not supposed that he had a character of his own.

At present our only true names are nicknames. I knew a boy who, from his peculiar energy, was called "Buster" by his playmates, and this rightly supplanted his Christian name. Some travelers tell us that an Indian had no name given him at first, but earned it, and his name was his fame; and among some tribes he acquired a new name with every new exploit. It is pitiful when a man bears a name for convenience merely, who has earned neither name nor fame.

I will not allow mere names to make distinctions for me, but still see men in herds for all them. A familiar name cannot make a man less strange to me. It may be given to a savage who retains in secret his own wild title earned in the woods. We have a wild savage in us, and a savage name is perchance somewhere recorded as ours. I see that my neighbor, who bears the familiar epithet William or Edwin, takes it off with his jacket. It does not adhere to him when asleep or in anger, or aroused by any passion or inspiration. I seem to hear pronounced by some of his kin at such a time his original wild name in some jaw-breaking or else melodious tongue.

Here is this vast, savage, howling mother of ours, Nature, lying all around, with such beauty, and such affection for her children, as the leopard; and yet we are so early weaned from her breast to society, to that culture which is exclusively an interaction of man on man—a sort of breeding in and in, which produces at most a merely English nobility, a civilization destined to have a speedy limit.

In society, in the best institutions of men, it is easy to detect a certain precocity. When we should still be growing children, we are already little men. Give me a culture which imports much muck from the meadows, and deepens the soil—not that which trusts to heating manures, and improved implements and modes of culture only!

Many a poor sore-eyed student that I have heard of would grow faster, both intellectually and physically, if, instead of sitting up so very late, he honestly slumbered a fool's allowance.

There may be an excess even of informing light. Niepce, a Frenchman, discovered "actinism," that power in the sun's rays which produces a chemical effect; that granite rocks, and stone structures, and statues of metal "are all alike destructively acted upon during the hours of sunshine, and, but for provisions of Nature no less wonderful, would soon perish under the delicate touch of the most subtile of the agencies of the universe." But he observed that "those bodies which underwent this change during the daylight possessed the power of restoring themselves to their original conditions during the hours of night, when this excitement was no longer influencing them." Hence it has been inferred that "the hours of darkness are as necessary to the inorganic creation as we know night and sleep are to the organic kingdom." Not even does the moon shine every night, but gives place to darkness.

I would not have every man nor every part of a man cultivated, any more than I would have every acre of earth cultivated: part will be tillage, but the greater part will be meadow and forest, not only serving an immediate use, but preparing a mould against a distant future, by the annual decay of the vegetation which it supports.

There are other letters for the child to learn than those which Cadmus invented. The Spaniards have a good term to express this wild and dusky knowledge, *Gramática parda,* tawny grammar, a kind of mother-wit derived from that same leopard to which I have referred.

We have heard of a Society for the Diffusion of Useful Knowledge. It is said that knowledge is power, and the like. Methinks there is equal need of a Society for the Diffusion of Useful Ignorance, what we will call Beautiful Knowledge, a knowledge useful in a higher sense: for what is most of our boasted so-called knowledge but a conceit that we know something, which robs us of the advantage of our actual ignorance? What we call knowledge is often our positive ignorance; ignorance our negative knowledge. By long years of patient industry and reading of the newspapers—for what are the libraries of science but files of newspapers?—a man accumulates a myriad facts, lays them up in his memory, and then when in some spring of his life he saunters abroad into the Great Fields of thought, he, as it were, goes to grass like a horse and leaves all his harness behind in the stable. I would say to the Society for the Diffusion of Useful Knowledge, sometimes, Go to grass. You have eaten hay long enough. The spring has come with its green crop. The very cows are driven to their country pastures before the end of May; though I have heard of one unnatural farmer who kept his cow in the barn and fed her on hay all the year round. So, frequently, the Society for the Diffusion of Useful Knowledge treats its cattle.

A man's ignorance sometimes is not only useful, but beautiful—while his knowledge, so called, is oftentimes worse than useless, besides being ugly. Which is the best man to deal with—he who knows nothing about a subject, and, what is extremely rare, knows that he knows nothing, or he who really knows something about it, but thinks that he knows all?

My desire for knowledge is intermittent, but my desire to bathe my head in atmospheres unknown to my feet is perennial and constant. The highest that we can attain to is not Knowledge, but Sympathy with Intelligence. I do not know that this higher knowledge amounts to anything more definite than a novel and grand surprise on a sudden revelation of the insufficiency of all that we called Knowledge before—a discovery that there are more things in heaven and earth than are dreamed of in our philosophy. It is the lighting up of the mist by the sun. Man cannot *know* in any higher sense than this, any more than he can look serenely and with impunity in the face of the sun: Ὡς τὶ νοῶν, οὐ χεῖνον νοήσεις, "You will not perceive that, as perceiving a particular thing," say the Chaldean Oracles.

There is something servile in the habit of seeking after a law which we may obey. We may study the laws of matter at and for our convenience, but a successful life knows no law. It is an unfortunate discovery certainly, that of a law which binds us where we did not know before that we were bound. Live free, child of the mist—and with respect to knowledge we are all children of the mist. The man who takes the liberty to live is superior to all the laws, by virtue of his relation to the lawmaker. "That is active duty," says the Vishnu Purana, "which is not for our bondage; that is knowledge which is for our liberation: all other duty is good only unto weariness; all other knowledge is only the cleverness of an artist."

It is remarkable how few events or crises there are in our histories, how little exercised we have been in our minds, how few experiences we have had. I would fain be assured that I am growing apace and rankly, though my very growth disturb this dull equanimity—though it be with struggle through long, dark, muggy nights or seasons of gloom. It would be well if all our lives were a divine tragedy even, instead of this trivial comedy or farce. Dante, Bunyan, and others appear to have been exercised in their minds more than we: they were subjected to a kind of culture such as our district schools and colleges do not contemplate. Even Mahomet, though many may scream at his name, had a good deal more to live for, aye, and to die for, than they have commonly.

When, at rare intervals, some thought visits one, as perchance he is walking on a railroad, then, indeed, the cars go by without his hearing them. But soon, by some inexorable law, our life goes by and the cars return.

"Gentle breeze, that wanderest unseen,
And bendest the thistles round Loira of storms,
Traveler of the windy glens,
Why hast thou left my ear so soon?"

While almost all men feel an attraction drawing them to society, few are attracted strongly to Nature. In their reaction to Nature men appear to me for the most part, notwithstanding their arts, lower than the animals. It is not often a beautiful relation, as in the case of the animals. How little appreciation of the beauty of the landscape there is among us! We have to be told that the Greeks called the world Κόσμος, Beauty, or Order, but we do not see clearly why they did so, and we esteem it at best only a curious philological fact.

For my part, I feel that with regard to Nature I live a sort of border life, on the confines of a world into which I make occasional and transient forays only, and my patriotism and allegiance to the state into whose territories I seem to retreat are those of a moss-trooper. Unto a life which I call natural I would gladly follow even a will-o'-the-wisp through bogs and sloughs unimaginable, but no moon nor firefly has shown me the causeway to it. Nature is a personality so vast and universal that we have never seen one of her features. The walker in the familiar fields which stretch around my native town sometimes finds himself in another land than is described in their owners' deeds, as it were in some faraway field on the confines of the actual Concord, where her jurisdiction ceases, and the idea which the word Concord suggests ceases to be suggested. These farms which I have myself surveyed, these bounds which I have set up, appear dimly still as through a mist; but they have no chemistry to fix them; they fade from the surface of the glass, and the picture which the painter painted stands out dimly from beneath. The world with which we are commonly acquainted leaves no trace, and it will have no anniversary.

I took a walk on Spaulding's Farm the other afternoon. I saw the setting sun lighting up the opposite side of a stately pine wood. Its golden rays straggled into the aisles of the wood as into some noble hall. I was impressed as if some ancient and altogether admirable and shining family had settled there in that part of the land called Concord, unknown to me—to whom the sun was servant—who had not gone into society in the village—who had not been called on. I saw their park, their pleasure-ground, beyond through the wood, in Spaulding's cranberry-meadow. The pines furnished them with gables as they grew. Their house was not obvious to vision; the trees grew through it. I do not know whether I heard the sounds of a suppressed hilarity or not. They seemed to recline on the sunbeams. They have sons and daughters. They are quite well. The farmer's cart-path, which leads directly through their hall, does not in the least put them out, as the muddy bottom of a pool is sometimes seen through the reflected skies. They never heard of Spaulding, and do not know that he is their neighbor—notwithstanding I heard him whistle as he drove his team through the house. Nothing can equal the serenity of their lives. Their coat-of-arms is simply a lichen. I saw it painted on the pines and oaks. Their attics were in the tops of the trees. They are of no politics. There was no noise of labor. I did not perceive that they were weaving or spinning. Yet I did detect, when the wind lulled and hearing was done away, the finest imaginable sweet musical hum—as of a distant hive in May—which perchance was the sound of their thinking. They had no idle thoughts, and no one without could see their work, for their industry was not as in knots and excrescences embayed.

But I find it difficult to remember them. They fade irrevocably out of my mind even now while I speak, and endeavor to recall them and recollect myself. It is only after a long and serious effort to recollect my best thoughts that I become again aware of their cohabitancy. If it were not for such families as this, I think I should move out of Concord.

We are accustomed to say in New England that few and fewer pigeons visit us every year. Our forests furnish no mast for them. So, it would seem, few and fewer thoughts visit each growing man from year to year, for the grove in our minds is laid waste—sold to feed unnecessary fires of ambition, or sent to mill—and there is scarcely a twig left for them to perch on. They no longer build nor breed with us. In some more genial season, perchance, a faint shadow flits across the landscape of the mind, cast by the *wings* of some thought in its vernal or autumnal migration, but, looking up, we are unable to detect the substance of the thought itself. Our winged thoughts are turned to poultry. They no longer soar, and they attain only to a Shanghai and Cochin-China grandeur. Those *gra-a-ate thoughts,* those *gra-a-ate men* you hear of!

We hug the earth—how rarely we mount! Methinks we might elevate ourselves a little more. We might climb a tree, at least. I found my account in climbing a tree once. It was a tall white pine, on the top of a hill; and though I got well pitched, I was well paid for it, for I discovered new mountains in the horizon which I had never seen before—so much more of the earth and the heavens. I might have walked about the foot of the tree for three-score years and ten, and yet I certainly should never have seen them. But, above all, I discovered around me—it was near the end of June—on the ends of the topmost branches only, a few minute and delicate red conelike blossoms, the fertile flower of the white pine looking heavenward. I carried straightway to the village the topmost spire, and showed it to stranger jurymen who walked the streets—for it was court week—and to farmers and lumber-dealers and woodchoppers and hunters, and not one had ever seen the like before, but they wondered as at a star dropped down. Tell of ancient architects finishing their works on the tops of columns as perfectly as on the lower and more visible parts! Nature has from the first expanded the minute blossoms of the forest only toward the heavens, above men's heads and unobserved by them. We see only the flowers that are under our feet in the meadows. The pines have developed their delicate blossoms on the highest twigs of the wood every summer for ages, as well over the heads of Nature's red children as of her white ones; yet scarcely a farmer or hunter in the land has ever seen them.

Above all, we cannot afford not to live in the present. He is blessed over all mortals who loses no moment of the passing life in remembering the past. Unless our philosophy hears the cock crow in every barnyard within our horizon, it is belated. That sound commonly reminds us that we are growing rusty and antique in our employments and habits of thought. His philosophy comes down to a more recent time than ours. There is something suggested by it that is a newer testament—the gospel according to this moment. He has not fallen astern; he has got up early and kept up early, and to be where he is is to be in season, in the foremost rank of time. It is an expression of the health and soundness of Nature, a brag for all the world—healthiness as of a spring burst forth, a new fountain of the Muses, to celebrate this last instant of time. Where he lives no fugitive slave laws are passed. Who has not betrayed his master many times since last he heard that note?

The merit of this bird's strain is in its freedom

from all plaintiveness. The singer can easily move us to tears or to laughter, but where is he who can excite in us a pure morning joy? When, in doleful dumps, breaking the awful stillness of our wooden sidewalk on a Sunday, or, perchance, a watcher in the house of mourning, I hear a cockerel crow far or near, I think to myself, "There is one of us well, at any rate," and with a sudden gush return to my senses.

We had a remarkable sunset one day last November. I was walking in a meadow, the source of a small brook, when the sun at last, just before setting, after a cold, gray day, reached a clear stratum in the horizon, and the softest, brightest morning sunlight fell on the dry grass and on the stems of the trees in the opposite horizon and on the leaves of the shrub oaks on the hillside, while our shadows stretched long over the meadow eastward, as if we were the only motes in its beams. It was such a light as we could not have imagined a moment before, and the air also was so warm and serene that nothing was wanting to make a paradise of that meadow. When we reflected that this was not a solitary phenomenon, never to happen again, but that it would happen forever and ever, an infinite number of evenings, and cheer and reassure the latest child that walked there, it was more glorious still.

The sun sets on some retired meadow, where no house is visible, with all the glory and splendor that it lavishes on cities, and perchance as it has never set before—where there is but a solitary marsh hawk to have his wings gilded by it, or only a musquash looks out from his cabin, and there is some little black-veined brook in the midst of the marsh, just beginning to meander, winding slowly round a decaying stump. We walked in so pure and bright a light, gilding the withered grass and leaves, so softly and serenely bright, I thought I had never bathed in such a golden flood, without a ripple or a murmur to it. The west side of every wood and rising ground gleamed like the boundary of Elysium, and the sun on our backs seemed like a gentle herdsman driving us home at evening.

So we saunter toward the Holy Land, till one day the sun shall shine more brightly than ever he has done, shall perchance shine into our minds and hearts, and light up our whole lives with a great awakening light, as warm and serene and golden as on a bankside in autumn.

FROM

WALDEN

◊

THE SECOND chapter of Thoreau's masterpiece—which was published in 1854—contrasts the serene fullness of life at the Pond with the frenetic dissatisfactions of town life he had described in the first chapter. "Where I Lived" also includes one of Thoreau's most eloquent assertions of the importance of leading a Transcendental life: "We are able to apprehend at all what is sublime and noble only by the perpetual instilling and drenching of the reality that surrounds us."

◊

WHERE I LIVED AND WHAT I LIVED FOR

AT A CERTAIN season of our life we are accustomed to consider every spot as the possible site of a house. I have thus surveyed the country on every side within a dozen miles of where I live. In imagination I have bought all the farms in succession, for all were to be bought, and I knew their price. I walked over each farmer's premises, tasted his wild apples, discoursed on husbandry with him, took his farm at his price, at any price, mortgaging it to him in my mind; even put a higher price on it—took everything but a deed of it—took his word for his deed, for I dearly loved to talk—cultivated it, and him too to some extent, I trust, and withdrew when I had enjoyed it long enough, leaving him to carry it on. This experience entitled me to be regarded as a sort of real-estate broker by my friends. Wherever I sat, there I might live, and the landscape radiated from me accordingly. What is a house but a *sedes,* a seat?—better if a country seat. I discovered many a site for a house not likely to be soon improved, which some might have thought too far from the village, but to my eyes the village was too far from it. Well, there I might live, I said; and there I did live, for an hour, a summer and a winter life; saw how I could let the years run off, buffet the winter through, and see the spring come in. The future inhabitants of this region, wherever they may place their houses, may be sure that they have been anticipated. An afternoon sufficed to lay out the land into orchard, woodlot, and pasture, and to decide what fine oaks or pines should be left to stand before the door, and whence each blasted tree could be seen to the best advantage; and then I let it lie, fallow perchance, for a man is rich in proportion to the number of things which he can afford to let alone.

My imagination carried me so far that I even had the refusal of several farms—the refusal was all I wanted—but I never got my fingers burned by actual possession. The nearest that I came to actual possession was when I bought the Hollowell place, and had begun to sort my seeds, and collected materials with which to make a wheelbarrow to carry it on or off with; but before the owner gave me a deed of it, his wife—every man has such a wife—changed her mind and wished to keep it, and he offered me ten dollars to release him. Now, to speak the truth, I had but ten cents in the world, and it surpassed my arithmetic to tell, if I was that man who had ten cents, or who had a farm, or ten dollars, or all together. However, I let him keep the ten dollars and the farm too, for I had carried it far enough; or rather, to be generous, I sold him the farm for just what I gave for it, and, as he was not a rich man, made him a present of ten dollars, and still had my ten cents, and seeds, and materials for a wheelbarrow left. I found thus that I had been a rich man without any damage to my poverty. But I retained the landscape, and I have since annually carried off what it yielded without a wheelbarrow. With respect to landscapes,

"I am monarch of all I *survey*,
My right there is none to dispute."[1]

I have frequently seen a poet withdraw, having enjoyed the most valuable part of a farm, while the crusty farmer supposed that he had got a few wild apples only. Why, the owner does not know it for many years when a poet has put his farm in rhyme, the most admirable kind of invisible fence, has fairly impounded it, milked it, skimmed it, and got all the cream, and left the farmer only the skimmed milk.

The real attractions of the Hollowell farm, to me, were: its complete retirement, being about two miles from the village, half a mile from the nearest neighbor, and separated from the highway by a broad field; its bounding on the river, which the owner said protected it by its fogs from frosts in the spring, though that was nothing to me; the gray color and ruinous state of the house and barn, and the dilapidated fences, which put such an interval between me and the last occupant; the hollow and lichen-covered apple trees, gnawed by rabbits, showing what kind of neighbors I should have; but above all, the recollection I had of it from my earliest voyages up the river, when the house was concealed behind a dense grove of red maples, through which I heard the house-dog bark. I was in haste to buy it, before the proprietor finished getting out some rocks, cutting down the hollow apple trees, and grubbing up some young birches which had sprung up in the pasture, or, in short, had made any more of his improvements. To enjoy these advantages I was ready to carry it on; like Atlas, to take the world on my shoulders—I never heard what compensation he received for that—and do all those things which had no other motive or excuse but that I might pay for it and be unmolested in my possession of it; for I knew all the while that it would yield the most abundant crop of the kind I wanted if I could only afford to let it alone. But it turned out as I have said.

All that I could say, then, with respect to farming on a large scale (I have always cultivated a garden), was, that I had had my seeds ready. Many think that seeds improve with age. I have no doubt that time discriminates between the good and the bad; and when at last I shall plant, I shall be less likely to be disappointed. But I would say to my fellows, once for all, As long as possible live free and uncommitted. It makes but little difference whether you are committed to a farm or the county jail.

Old Cato, whose *De Re Rusticâ* is my "Cultivator," says, and the only translation I have seen makes sheer nonsense of the passage, "When you think of getting a farm turn it thus in your mind, not to buy greedily; nor spare your pains to look at it, and do not think it enough to go round it once. The oftener you go there the more it will please you, if it is good." I think I shall not buy greedily, but go round and round it as long as I live, and be buried in it first, that it may please me the more at last.

The present was my next experiment of this kind, which I purpose to describe more at length, for convenience, putting the experience of two years into one. As I have said, I do not propose to write an ode to dejection, but to brag as lustily as chanticleer in the morning, standing on his roost, if only to wake my neighbors up.

When first I took up my abode in the woods, that is, began to spend my nights as well as days there, which, by accident, was on Independence Day, or the Fourth of July, 1845, my house was not finished for winter, but was merely a defense against the rain, without plastering or chimney, the walls being of rough weather-stained boards, with wide chinks, which made it cool at night. The upright white hewn studs and freshly planed door and win-

WALDEN. 1. **"I . . . dispute"**: From the first stanza of "Verses Supposed to be Written by Alexander Selkirk," by William Cowper (1731–1800). Selkirk was the prototype Defoe had in mind when he wrote *Robinson Crusoe.*

dow casings gave it a clean and airy look, especially in the morning, when its timbers were saturated with dew, so that I fancied that by noon some sweet gum would exude from them. To my imagination it retained throughout the day more or less of this auroral character, reminding me of a certain house on a mountain which I had visited a year before. This was an airy and unplastered cabin, fit to entertain a traveling god, and where a goddess might trail her garments. The winds which passed over my dwelling were such as sweep over the ridges of mountains, bearing the broken strains, or celestial parts only, of terrestrial music. The morning wind forever blows, the poem of creation is uninterrupted; but few are the ears that hear it. Olympus is but the outside of the earth everywhere.

The only house I had been the owner of before, if I except a boat, was a tent, which I used occasionally when making excursions in the summer, and this is still rolled up in my garret; but the boat, after passing from hand to hand, has gone down the stream of time. With this more substantial shelter about me, I had made some progress toward settling in the world. This frame, so slightly clad, was a sort of crystallization around me, and reacted on the builder. It was suggestive somewhat as a picture in outlines. I did not need to go outdoors to take the air, for the atmosphere within had lost none of its freshness. It was not so much within doors as behind a door where I sat, even in the rainiest weather. The Harivansa says, "An abode without birds is like a meat without seasoning." Such was not my abode, for I found myself suddenly neighbor to the birds; not by having imprisoned one, but having caged myself near them. I was not only nearer to some of those which commonly frequent the garden and the orchard, but to those wilder and more thrilling songsters of the forest which never, or rarely, serenade a villager—the wood-thrush, the veery, the scarlet tanager, the field-sparrow, the whippoorwill, and many others.

I was seated by the shore of a small pond, about a mile and a half south of the village of Concord and somewhat higher than it, in the midst of an extensive wood between that town and Lincoln, and about two miles south of that our only field known to fame, Concord Battle Ground; but I was so low in the woods that the opposite shore, half a mile off, like the rest, covered with wood, was my most distant horizon. For the first week, whenever I looked out on the pond it impressed me like a tarn high up on the side of a mountain, its bottom far above the surface of other lakes, and, as the sun arose, I saw it throwing off its nightly clothing of mist, and here and there, by degrees, its soft ripples or its smooth reflecting surface was revealed, while the mists, like ghosts, were stealthily withdrawing in every direction into the woods, as at the breaking up of some nocturnal conventicle. The very dew seemed to hang upon the trees later into the day than usual, as on the sides of mountains.

This small lake was of most value as a neighbor in the intervals of a gentle rainstorm in August, when, both air and water being perfectly still, but the sky overcast, mid-afternoon had all the serenity of evening, and the wood-thrush sang around, and was heard from shore to shore. A lake like this is never smoother than at such a time; and the clear portion of the air above it being shallow and darkened by clouds, the water, full of light and reflections, becomes a lower heaven itself so much the more important. From a hilltop near by, where the wood had been recently cut off, there was a pleasing vista southward across the pond, through a wide indentation in the hills which form the shore there, where their opposite sides sloping toward each other suggested a stream flowing out in that direction through a wooded valley, but stream there was none. That way I looked between and over the near green hills to some distant and higher ones in the horizon, tinged with blue. Indeed, by standing on tiptoe I could catch a glimpse of some of the peaks of the still bluer and more distant mountain ranges in the northwest, those true-blue coins from heaven's own mint, and also of some portion of the village. But in other directions, even from this point, I could not see over or beyond the woods which surrounded me. It is well to have some water in your neighborhood, to give buoyancy to and float the earth. One value even of the smallest well is, that when you look into it you see that earth is not continent but insular. This is as important as that it keeps butter cool. When I looked across the pond from this peak toward the Sudbury meadows, which in time of flood I distinguished elevated perhaps by a mirage in their seething valley, like a coin in a basin, all the earth beyond the pond appeared like a thin crust insulated and floated even by this small sheet of intervening water, and I was reminded that this on which I dwelt was but *dry land*.

Though the view from my door was still more contracted, I did not feel crowded or confined in the least. There was pasture enough for my imagination. The low shrub-oak plateau to which the opposite shore arose, stretched away toward the prairies of the West and the steppes of Tartary, affording ample room for all the roving families of men. "There are none happy in the world but beings who enjoy freely a vast horizon," said Damodara, when his herds required new and larger pastures.

Both place and time were changed, and I dwelt nearer to those parts of the universe and to those eras in history which had most attracted me. Where I lived was as far off as many a region viewed nightly by astronomers. We are wont to imagine rare and delectable places in some remote and more celestial corner of the system, behind the constellation of Cassiopeia's Chair, far from noise and disturbance. I discovered that my house actually had its site in such a withdrawn, but forever new and unprofaned, part of the universe. If it were worth the while to settle in those parts near to the Pleiades or the Hyades, to Aldebaran or Altair, then I was really there, or at an equal remoteness from the life which I had left behind, dwindled and twinkling with as fine a ray to my nearest neighbor, and to be seen only in moonless nights by him. Such was that part of creation where I had squatted;

> "There was a shepherd that did live,
> And held his thoughts as high
> As were the mounts whereon his flocks
> Did hourly feed him by."

What should we think of the shepherd's life if his flocks always wandered to higher pastures than his thoughts?

Every morning was a cheerful invitation to make my life of equal simplicity, and I may say innocence, with Nature herself. I have been as sincere a worshiper of Aurora as the Greeks. I got up early and bathed in the pond; that was a religious exercise, and one of the best things which I did. They say that characters were engraven on the bathing tub of King Tching-thang to this effect: "Renew thyself completely each day; do it again, and again, and forever again." I can understand that. Morning brings back the heroic ages. I was as much affected by the faint hum of a mosquito making its invisible and unimaginable tour through my apartment at earliest dawn, when I was sitting with door and windows open, as I could be by any trumpet that ever sang of fame. It was Homer's requiem; itself an Iliad and Odyssey in the air, singing its own wrath and wanderings. There was something cosmical about it; a standing advertisement, till forbidden, of the everlasting vigor and fertility of the world. The morning, which is the most memorable season of the day, is the awakening hour. Then there is least somnolence in us; and for an hour, at least, some part of us awakes which slumbers all the rest of the day and night. Little is to be expected of that day, if it can be called a day, to which we are not awakened by our Genius, but by the mechanical nudgings of some servitor, are not awakened by our own newly acquired force and aspirations from within, accompanied by the undulations of celestial music, instead of factory bells, and a fragrance filling the air—to a higher life than we fell asleep from; and thus the darkness bear its fruit, and prove itself to be good, no less than the light. That man who does not believe that each day contains an earlier, more sacred and auroral hour than he has yet profaned, has despaired of life, and is pursuing a descending and darkening way. After a partial cessation of his sensuous life, the soul of man, or its organs rather, are reinvigorated each day, and his Genius tries again what noble life it can make. All memorable events, I should say, transpire in morning time and in a morning atmosphere. The Vedas say, "All intelligences awake with the morning." Poetry and art, and the fairest and most memorable of the actions of men, date from such an hour. All poets and heroes, like Memnon, are the children of Aurora, and emit their music at sunrise. To him whose elastic and vigorous thought keeps pace with the sun, the day is a perpetual morning. It matters not what the clocks say or the attitudes and labors of men. Morning is when I am awake and there is a dawn in me. Moral reform is the effort to throw off sleep. Why is it that men give so poor an account of their day if they have not been slumbering? They are not such poor calculators. If they had not been overcome with drowsiness they would have performed something. The millions are awake enough for physical labor; but only one in a million is awake enough for effective intellectual exertion, only one in a hundred millions to a poetic or divine life. To be awake is to be alive. I have never yet met a man who was quite awake. How could I have looked him in the face?

We must learn to reawaken and keep ourselves awake, not by mechanical aids, but by an infinite expectation of the dawn, which does not forsake us in our soundest sleep. I know of no more encouraging fact than the unquestionable ability of man to elevate his life by a conscious endeavor. It is something to be able to paint a particular picture, or to carve a statue, and so to make a few objects beautiful; but it is far more glorious to carve and paint the very atmosphere and medium through which we look, which morally we can do. To affect the quality of the day, that is the highest of arts. Every man is tasked to make his life, even in its details, worthy of the contemplation of his most elevated and critical hour. If we refused, or rather used up, such paltry information as we get, the oracles would distinctly inform us how this might be done.

I went to the woods because I wished to live deliberately, to front only the essential facts of life, and see if I could not learn what it had to teach, and not, when I came to die, discover that I had not lived. I did not wish to live what was not life, living is so dear; nor did I wish to practice resignation, unless it was quite necessary. I wanted to live deep and suck out all the marrow of life, to live so sturdily and Spartan-like as to put to rout all that was not life, to cut a broad swath and shave close, to drive life into a corner, and reduce it to its lowest terms, and, if it proved to be mean, why then to get the whole and genuine meanness of it, and publish its meanness to the world; or if it were sublime, to know it by experience, and be able to give a true account of it in my next excursion. For most men, it appears to me, are in a strange uncertainty about it, whether it is of the devil or of God, and have *somewhat hastily* concluded that it is the chief end of man here to "glorify God and enjoy him forever."

Still we live meanly, like ants; though the fable tells us that we were long ago changed into men; like pygmies we fight with cranes; it is error upon error, and clout upon clout, and our best virtue has for its occasion a superfluous and evitable wretchedness. Our life is frittered away by detail. An honest man has hardly need to count more than his ten fingers, or in extreme cases he may add his ten toes, and lump the rest. Simplicity, simplicity, simplicity! I say, let your affairs be as two or three, and not a hundred or a thousand; instead of a million count half a dozen, and keep your accounts on your thumb nail. In the midst of this chopping sea of civilized life, such are the clouds and storms and quicksands and thousand-and-one items to be allowed for, that a man has to live, if he would not founder and go to the bottom and not make his port at all, by dead reckoning, and he must be a great calculator indeed who succeeds. Simplify, simplify. Instead of three meals a day, if it be necessary eat but one; instead of a hundred dishes, five; and reduce other things in proportion. Our life is like a German Confederacy, made up of petty states, with its boundary forever fluctuating, so that even a German cannot tell you how it is bounded at any moment. The nation itself, with all its so-called internal improvements, which, by the way are all external and superficial, is just such an unwieldy and overgrown establishment, cluttered with furniture and tripped up by its own traps, ruined by luxury and heedless expense, by want of calculation and a worthy aim, as the million households in the land; and the only cure for it as for them is in a rigid economy, a stern and more than Spartan simplicity of life and elevation of purpose. It lives too fast. Men think that it is essential that the *Nation* have commerce, and export ice, and talk through a telegraph, and ride thirty miles an hour, without a doubt, whether *they* do or not; but whether we should live like baboons or like men, is a little uncertain. If we do not get out sleepers, and forge rails, and devote days and nights to the work, but go to tinkering upon our *lives* to improve *them,* who will build railroads? And if railroads are not built, how shall we get to heaven in season? But if we stay at home and mind our business, who will want railroads? We do not ride on the railroad; it rides upon us. Did you ever think what those sleepers [2] are that underlie the railroad? Each one is a man, an Irishman, or a Yankee man. The rails are laid on them, and they are covered with sand, and the cars run smoothly over them. They are sound sleepers, I assure you. And every few years a new lot is laid down and run over; so that, if some have the pleasure of riding on a rail, others have the misfortune to be ridden upon. And when they run over a man that is walking in his sleep, a supernumerary sleeper in the wrong position, and wake him up, they suddenly stop the cars, and make a hue and cry about it, as if this were an exception. I am glad to know that it takes a gang of men for every five miles to keep the sleepers down and level in their beds as it is, for this is a sign that they may sometime get up again.

Why should we live with such hurry and waste of life? We are determined to be starved before we are hungry. Men say that a stitch in time saves nine, and so they take a thousand stitches today to save nine tomorrow. As for *work,* we haven't any of any consequence. We have the Saint Vitus' dance, and cannot possibly keep our heads still. If I should only give a few pulls at the parish bell-rope, as for a fire, that is, without setting the bell, there is hardly a man on his farm in the outskirts of Concord, notwithstanding that press of engagements which was his excuse so many times this morning, nor a boy, nor a woman, I might almost say, but would forsake all and follow that sound, not mainly to save property from the flames, but, if we will confess the truth, much more to see it burn, since burn it must, and we, be it known, did not set it on fire—or to see it put out, and have a hand in it, if that is done as handsomely; yes, even if it were the parish church itself. Hardly a man takes a half hour's nap after dinner, but when he wakes he holds up his head and asks, "What's the news?" as if the rest of mankind had stood his sentinels. Some give directions to be waked every half hour, doubtless for no other purpose; and then, to pay for it, they tell what they have dreamed. After a

2. **sleepers:** railroad ties.

night's sleep the news is as indispensable as the breakfast. "Pray tell me anything new that has happened to a man anywhere on this globe"—and he reads it over his coffee and rolls, that a man has had his eyes gouged out this morning on the Wachito River; never dreaming the while that he lives in the dark unfathomed mammoth cave of this world, and has but the rudiment of an eye himself.

For my part, I could easily do without the post-office. I think that there are very few important communications made through it. To speak critically, I never received more than one or two letters in my life—I wrote this some years ago—that were worth the postage. The penny-post is, commonly, an institution through which you seriously offer a man that penny for his thoughts which is so often safely offered in jest. And I am sure that I never read any memorable news in a newspaper. If we read of one man robbed, or murdered, or killed by accident, or one house burned, or one vessel wrecked, or one steamboat blown up, or one cow run over on the Western Railroad, or one mad dog killed, or one lot of grasshoppers in the winter—we never need read of another. One is enough. If you are acquainted with the principle, what do you care for a myriad instances and applications? To a philosopher all *news,* as it is called, is gossip, and they who edit and read it are old women over their tea. Yet not a few are greedy after this gossip. There was such a rush, as I hear, the other day at one of the offices to learn the foreign news by the last arrival, that several large squares of plate glass belonging to the establishment were broken by the pressure—news which I seriously think a ready wit might write a twelvemonth or twelve years beforehand with sufficient accuracy. As for Spain, for instance, if you know how to throw in Don Carlos and the Infanta, and Don Pedro and Seville and Granada, from time to time in the right proportions—they may have changed the names a little since I saw the papers—and serve up a bull-fight when other entertainments fail, it will be true to the letter, and give us as good an idea of the exact state or ruin of things in Spain as the most succinct and lucid reports under this head in the newspapers: and as for England, almost the last significant scrap of news from that quarter was the revolution of 1649; and if you have learned the history of her crops for an average year, you never need attend to that thing again, unless your speculations are of a merely pecuniary character. If one may judge who rarely looks into the newspapers, nothing new does ever happen in foreign parts, a French revolution not excepted.

What news! how much more important to know what that is which was never old! "Kieou-he-yu (great dignitary of the state of Wei) sent a man to Khoung-tseu to know his news. Khoung-tseu caused the messenger to be seated near him, and questioned him in these terms: What is your master doing? The messenger answered with respect: My master desires to diminish the number of his faults, but he cannot come to the end of them. The messenger being gone, the philosopher remarked: What a worthy messenger! What a worthy messenger!" The preacher, instead of vexing the ears of drowsy farmers on their day of rest at the end of the week—for Sunday is the fit conclusion of an ill-spent week, and not the fresh and brave beginning of a new one—with this one other draggle-tail of a sermon, should shout with thundering voice—"Pause! Avast! Why so seeming fast, but deadly slow?"

Shams and delusions are esteemed for soundest truths, while reality is fabulous. If men would steadily observe realities only, and not allow themselves to be deluded, life, to compare it with such things as we know, would be like a fairy tale and the Arabian Nights' Entertainments. If we respected only what is inevitable and has a right to be, music and poetry would resound along the streets. When we are unhurried and wise, we perceive that only great and worthy things have any permanent and absolute existence—that petty fears and petty pleasures are but the shadow of the reality. This is always exhilarating and sublime. By closing the eyes and slumbering, and consenting to be deceived by shows, men establish and confirm their daily life of routine and habit everywhere, which still is built on purely illusory foundations. Children, who play life, discern its true law and relations more clearly than men, who fail to live it worthily, but who think that they are wiser by experience, that is, by failure. I have read in a Hindu book that "there was a king's son, who, being expelled in infancy from his native city, was brought up by a forester, and, growing up to maturity in that state, imagined himself to belong to the barbarous race with which he lived. One of his father's ministers, having discovered him, revealed to him what he was, and the misconception of his character was removed, and he knew himself to be a prince. So soul," continues the Hindu philosopher, "from the circumstances in which it is placed, mistakes its own character, until the truth is revealed to it by some holy teacher, and then it knows itself to be *Brahme.*" I perceive that we inhabitants of New England live this mean life that we do because our vision does not penetrate the surface of things. We think that that *is* which *appears* to be. If a man should walk through this town and see only the reality, where, think you, would the "Mill-dam" go to? If he should give us an account of the realities he beheld there, we should not recognize the place in his description. Look at a meeting-house, or a courthouse, or a jail, or a shop, or a dwelling-house, and say what that thing really is before a true gaze, and they would all go to pieces in your account of them. Men esteem truth remote, in the outskirts of the system, behind the farthest star, before Adam and after the last man. In eternity there is indeed something true and sublime. But all these times and places and occasions are now and here. God himself culminates in the present moment, and will never be more divine in the lapse of all the ages. And we are enabled to apprehend at all what is sublime and noble only by the perpetual instilling and drenching of the reality that surrounds us. The universe constantly and obediently answers to our conceptions; whether we travel fast or slow, the track is laid for us. Let us spend our lives in conceiving then. The poet or the artist never yet had so fair and noble a design but some of his posterity at least could accomplish it.

Let us spend one day as deliberately as Nature, and not be thrown off the track by every nutshell and mosquito's wing that falls on the rails. Let us rise early and fast, or break fast, gently and without perturbation; let company come and let company go, let the bells ring and the children cry—determined to make a day of it. Why should we knock under and go with the stream? Let us not be upset and overwhelmed in that terrible rapid and whirlpool called a dinner, situated in the meridian shallows. Weather this danger and you are safe, for the rest of the way is down hill. With unrelaxed nerves, with morning vigor, sail by it, looking another way, tied to the mast like Ulysses. If the engine whistles, let it whistle till it is hoarse for its pains. If the bell rings, why should we run? We will consider what kind of music they are like. Let us settle ourselves, and work and wedge our feet downward through the mud and slush of opinion, and prejudice, and tradition, and delusion, and appearance, that alluvion which covers the globe, through Paris and London, through New York and Boston and Concord, through church and state, through poetry and philosophy and religion, till we come to a hard bottom and rocks in place, which we can call *reality,* and say, This is, and no mistake; and then begin, having a *point d'appui,*[3] below freshet and frost and fire, a place where you might found a wall or a state, or set a lamppost safely, or perhaps a gauge, not a Nilometer,[4] but a Realometer, that future ages might know how deep a freshet of shams and appearances had gathered from time to time. If you stand right fronting and face to face to a fact, you will see the sun glimmer on both its surfaces, as if it were a cimeter, and feel its sweet edge dividing you through the heart and marrow, and so you will happily conclude your mortal career. Be it life or death, we crave only reality. If we are really dying, let us hear the rattle in our throats and feel cold in the extremities; if we are alive, let us go about our business.

Time is but the stream I go a-fishing in. I drink at it; but while I drink I see the sandy bottom and detect how shallow it is. Its thin current slides away, but eternity remains. I would drink deeper; fish in the sky, whose bottom is pebbly with stars. I cannot count one. I know not the first letter of the alphabet. I have always been regretting that I was not as wise as the day I was born. The intellect is a cleaver; it discerns and rifts its way into the secret of things. I do not wish to be any more busy with my hands than is necessary. My head is hands and feet. I feel all my best faculties concentrated in it. My instinct tells me that my head is an organ for burrowing, as some creatures use their snout and forepaws, and with it I would mine and burrow my way through these hills. I think that the richest vein is somewhere hereabouts; so by the divining rod and thin rising vapors I judge; and here I will begin to mine.

3. *point d'appui:* foundation. 4. **Nilometer:** an ancient device used to record the rise and fall of the Nile.

FROM

CAPE COD

◊

Cape Cod was published posthumously in 1865. The first four chapters had already been printed by Thoreau in *Putnam's Magazine* in 1855; two other chapters, including this one, were printed during the autumn preceding publication of the book in the *Atlantic Monthly.* The book takes its outline from the first trip Thoreau made to Cape Cod, in 1849, accompanied by his friend William Ellery Channing; but it also includes elements from two later trips, one alone and one again with Channing.

Thoreau had a fondness for queer, quirky, eccentric New England characters; he enjoyed their vivid independence and spectacular self-reliance. "The Wellfleet Oysterman" sketches an old man whom he obviously relished.

◊

THE WELLFLEET OYSTERMAN

HAVING walked about eight miles since we struck the beach, and passed the boundary between Wellfleet and Truro, a stone post in the sand—for even this sand comes under the jurisdiction of one town or another—we turned inland over barren hills and valleys, whither the sea, for some reason, did not follow us, and, tracing up a Hollow, discovered two or three sober-looking houses within half a mile, uncommonly near the eastern coast. Their garrets were apparently so full of chambers, that their roofs could hardly lie down straight, and we did not doubt that there was room for us there. Houses near the sea are generally low and broad. These were a story and a half high; but if you merely counted the windows in their gable ends, you would think that there were many stories more, or, at any rate, that the half-story was the only one thought worthy of being illustrated. The great number of windows in the ends of the houses, and their irregularity in size and position, here and elsewhere on the Cape, struck us agreeably—as if each of the various occupants who had their *cunabula* behind had punched a hole where his necessities required it, and according to his size and stature, without regard to outside effect. There were windows for the grown folks, and windows for the children—three or four apiece; as a certain man had a large hole cut in his barn door for the cat, and another smaller one for the kitten. Sometimes they were so low under the eaves that I thought they must have perforated the plate beam for another apartment, and I noticed some which were triangular, to fit that part more exactly. The ends of the houses had thus as many muzzles as a revolver, and, if the inhabitants have the same habit of staring out the windows that some of our neighbors have, a traveler must stand a small chance with them.

Generally, the old-fashioned and unpainted houses on the Cape looked more comfortable, as well as picturesque, than the modern and more pretending ones, which were less in harmony with the scenery, and less firmly planted.

These houses were on the shores of a chain of ponds, seven in number, the source of a small stream called Herring River, which empties into the Bay. There are many Herring Rivers on the Cape; they will, perhaps, be more numerous than herrings soon. We knocked at the door of the first house, but its inhabitants were all gone away. In the meanwhile, we saw the occupants of the next one looking out the window at us, and before we reached it an old woman came out and fastened the door of her bulkhead, and went in again. Nevertheless, we did not hesitate to knock at her door, when a grizzly-looking man appeared, whom we took to be sixty or seventy years old. He asked us, at first, suspiciously, where we were from, and what our business was; to which we returned plain answers.

"How far is Concord from Boston?" he inquired.

"Twenty miles by railroad."

"Twenty miles by railroad," he repeated.

"Didn't you ever hear of Concord of Revolutionary fame?"

"Didn't I ever hear of Concord? Why, I heard guns fire at the battle of Bunker Hill. [They hear the sound of heavy cannon across the Bay.] I am almost ninety; I am eighty-eight year old. I was fourteen year old at the time of Concord Fight—and where were you then?"

We were obliged to confess that we were not in the fight.

"Well, walk in, we'll leave it to the women," said he.

So we walked in, surprised, and sat down, an old woman taking our hats and bundles, and the old man continued, drawing up to the large, old-fashioned fireplace:

"I am a poor, good-for-nothing crittur, as Isaiah says; I am all broken down this year. I am under petticoat government here."

The family consisted of the old man, his wife, and his daughter, who appeared nearly as old as her mother, a fool, her son (a brutish-looking, middle-aged man, with a prominent lower face, who was standing by the hearth when we entered, but immediately went out), and a little boy of ten.

While my companion talked with the women, I talked with the old man. They said that he was old and foolish, but he was evidently too knowing for them.

"These women," said he to me, "are both of them poor good-for-nothing critturs. This one is my wife. I married her sixty-four years ago. She is eighty-four years old, and as deaf as an adder, and the other is not much better."

He thought well of the Bible, or at least he *spoke* well, and did not *think* ill, of it, for that would not have been prudent for a man of his age. He said that he had read it attentively for many years, and he had much of it at his tongue's end. He seemed deeply impressed with a sense of his own nothingness, and would repeatedly exclaim:

"I am a nothing. What I gather from my Bible is just this; that man is a poor good-for-nothing crittur, and everything is just as God sees fit and disposes."

"May I ask your name?" I said.

"Yes," he answered, "I am not ashamed to tell my name. My name is ——. My great-grandfather came over from England and settled here."

He was an old Wellfleet oysterman, who had acquired a competency in that business, and had sons still engaged in it.

Nearly all the oyster shops and stands in Massachusetts, I am told, are supplied and kept by natives of Wellfleet, and a part of this town is still called Billingsgate from the oysters having been formerly planted there; but the native oysters are said to have died in 1770. Various causes are assigned for this, such as a ground frost, the carcasses of blackfish, kept to rot in the harbor, and the like, but the most common account of the matter is—and I find that a similar superstition with regard to the disappearance of fishes exists almost everywhere—that when Wellfleet began to quarrel with the neighboring towns about the right to gather them, yellow specks appeared in them, and Providence caused them to disappear. A few years ago sixty thousand bushels were annually brought from the South and planted in the harbor of Wellfleet till they attained "the proper relish of Billingsgate"; but now they are imported commonly full-grown, and laid down near their markets, at Boston and elsewhere, where the water, being a mixture of salt and fresh, suits them better. The business was said to be still good and improving.

The old man said that the oysters were liable to freeze in the winter, if planted too high; but if it were not "so cold as to strain their eyes" they were not injured. The inhabitants of New Brunswick have noticed that "ice will not form over an oyster-bed, unless the cold is very intense indeed, and when the bays are frozen over the oyster-beds are easily discovered by the water above them remaining unfrozen, or as the French residents say, *dégelée*." Our host said that they kept them in cellars all winter.

"Without anything to eat or drink?" I asked.

"Without anything to eat or drink," he answered.

"Can the oysters move?"

"Just as much as my shoe."

But when I caught him saying that they "bedded themselves down in the sand, flat side up, round side down," I told him that my shoe could not do that, without the aid of my foot in it; at which he said that they merely settled down as they grew; if put down in a square they would be found so; but the clam could move quite fast. I have since been told by oystermen of Long Island, where the oyster is still indigenous and abundant, that they are found in large masses attached to the parent in their midst, and are so taken up with their tongs; in which case, they say, the age of the young proves that there could have been no motion for five or six years at least. And Buckland in his *Curiosities of Natural History* (page 50) says: "An oyster, who has once taken up his position and fixed himself when quite young, can never make a change. Oysters, nevertheless, that have not fixed themselves, but remain loose at the bottom of the sea, have the power of locomotion; they open their shells to their fullest extent, and then suddenly contracting them, the expulsion of the water forwards gives a motion backwards. A fisherman at Guernsey told me that he had frequently seen oysters moving in this way."

Some still entertain the question "whether the oyster was indigenous in Massachusetts Bay," and whether Wellfleet Harbor was a "natural habitat" of this fish; but, to say nothing of the testimony of old oystermen, which, I think, is quite conclusive, though the native oyster may now be extinct there, I saw that their shells, opened by the Indians, were strewn all over the Cape. Indeed, the Cape was at first thickly settled by Indians on account of the abundance of these and other fish. We saw many traces of their occupancy after this, in Truro, near Great Hollow, and at High Head, near East Harbor River—oysters, clams, cockles, and other shells, mingled with ashes and the bones of deer and other quadrupeds. I picked up half a dozen arrow-heads, and in an hour or two could have filled my pockets with them. The Indians lived about the edges of the swamps, then probably in some instances ponds, for shelter and water. Moreover, Champlain, in the edition of his "Voyages" printed in 1613, says that in the year 1606 he and Poitrincourt explored a harbor (Barnstable Harbor?) in the southerly part of what is now called Massachusetts Bay, in latitude 42°, about five leagues south, one point west of *Cap Blanc* (Cape Cod), and there they found many good oysters, and they named it *"le Port aux Huistres"* [sic] (Oyster Harbor). In one edition of his map (1632), the *"R. aux Escailles"* is drawn emptying into the same part of the bay, and on the map *"Novi Belgii,"* in Ogilby's America (1670), the words *"Port aux Huistres"* are placed against the same place. Also William Wood, who left New England in 1633, speaks, in his *New England's Prospect,* published in 1634, of "a great oyster-bank" in Charles River, and of another in the Mistick, each of which obstructed the navigation of its river. "The oysters," says he, "be great ones in form of a shoe-horn; some be a foot long; these breed on certain banks that are bare every spring tide. This fish without the shell is so big, that it must admit of a division before you can well get it into your mouth." Oysters are still found there.

Our host told us that the sea-clam, or hen, was not easily obtained; it was raked up, but never on the Atlantic side, only cast ashore there in small quantities in storms. The fisherman sometimes wades in water several feet deep, and thrusts a pointed stick into the sand before him. When this enters between the valves of a clam, he closes them on it, and is drawn out. It has been known to catch and hold coot and teal which were preying on it. I chanced to be on the bank of the Acushnet at New Bedford one day since this, watching some ducks, when a man informed me that, having let out his young ducks to seek their food amid the samphire (*Salicornia*) and other weeds along the riverside at low tide that morning, at length he noticed that one remained stationary, amid the weeds, something preventing it from following the others, and going to it he found its foot tightly shut in a quahog's shell. He took up both together, carried them to his home, and his wife opening the shell with a knife released the duck and cooked the quahog. The old man said that the great clams were good to eat, but that they always took out a certain part which was poisonous, before they cooked them. "People said it would kill a cat." I did not tell him that I had eaten a large one entire that afternoon, but began to think that I was tougher than a cat. He stated that peddlers came round there, and sometimes tried to sell the women folks a skimmer, but he told them that their women had got a better skimmer than *they* could make, in the shell of their clams; it was shaped just right for this purpose. They call them "skim-alls" in some places. He also said that the sun-squall was poisonous to handle, and when the sailors came across it, they did not meddle with it, but heaved it out of their way. I told him that I had handled it that afternoon, and had felt no ill effects as yet. But he said it made the hands itch, especially if they had previously been scratched, or if I put it into my bosom, I should find out what it was.

He informed us that no ice ever formed on the back side of the Cape, or not more than once in a century, and but little snow lay there, it being either absorbed or blown or washed away. Sometimes in winter, when the tide was down, the beach was frozen, and afforded a hard road up the back side for some thirty miles, as smooth as a floor. One winter when he was a boy, he and his father "took right out into the Back Side before daylight, and walked to Provincetown and back to dinner."

When I asked what they did with all that barren-looking land, where I saw so few cultivated fields—"Nothing," he said.

"Then why fence your fields?"

"To keep the sand from blowing and covering up the whole."

"The yellow sand," said he, "has some life in it, but the white little or none."

When, in answer to his questions, I told him that I was a surveyor, he said that they who surveyed his farm were accustomed, where the ground was uneven, to loop up each chain as high as their elbows; that was the allowance they made, and he wished to know if I could tell him why they did not come out according to his deed, or twice alike. He seemed to have more respect for surveyors of the old school, which I did not wonder at. "King George the Third," said he, "laid out a road four rods wide and straight, the whole length of the Cape," but where it was now he could not tell.

This story of the surveyors reminded me of a Long Islander, who once, when I had made ready to jump from the bow of his boat to the shore, and he thought that I underrated the distance and would fall short—though I found afterward that he judged of the elasticity of my joints by his own—told me that when he came to a brook which he wanted to get over, he held up one leg, and then, if his foot appeared to cover any part of the opposite bank, he knew that he could jump it. "Why," I told him, "to say nothing of the Mississippi, and other small watery streams, I could blot out a star with my foot, but I would not engage to jump that distance," and asked how he knew when he had got his leg at the right elevation. But he regarded his legs as no less accurate than a pair of screw dividers or an ordinary quadrant, and appeared to have a painful recollection of every degree and minute in the arc which they described; and he would have had me believe that there was a kind of hitch in his hip-joint which answered the purpose. I suggested that he should connect his two ankles by a string of the proper length, which should be the chord of an arc, measuring his jumping ability on horizontal surfaces—assuming one leg to be a perpendicular to the plane of the horizon, which, however, may have been too bold an assumption in this case. Nevertheless, this was a kind of geometry in the legs which it interested me to hear of.

Our host took pleasure in telling us the names of the ponds, most of which we could see from his windows, and making us repeat them after him, to see if we had got them right. They were Gull Pond, the largest and a very handsome one, clear and deep, and more than a mile in circumference, Newcomb's, Swett's, Slough, Horse-Leech, Round, and Herring Ponds, all connected at high water, if I do not mistake. The coast-surveyors had come to him for their names, and he told them of one which they had not detected. He said that they were not so high as formerly. There was an earthquake about four years before he was born, which cracked the pans of the ponds, which were of iron, and caused them to settle. I did not remember to have read of this. Innumerable gulls used to resort to them; but the large gulls were now very scarce, for, as he said, the English robbed their nests far in the north, where they breed. He remembered well when gulls were taken in the gull-house, and when small birds were killed by means of a frying-pan and fire at night. His father once lost a valuable horse from this cause. A party from Wellfleet having lighted their fire for this purpose, one dark night, on Billingsgate Island, twenty horses which were pastured there, and this colt among them, being frightened by it, and endeavoring in the dark to cross the passage which separated them from the neighboring beach, and which was then fordable at low tide, were all swept out to sea and drowned. I observed that many horses were still turned out to pasture all summer on the islands and beaches in Wellfleet, Eastham, and Orleans, as a kind of common. He also described the killing of what he called "wild hens," here, after they had gone to roost in the woods, when he was a boy. Perhaps they were "prairie hens" (pinnated grouse).

He liked the beach pea (*Lathyrus maritimus*), cooked green, as well as the cultivated. He had seen it growing very abundantly in Newfoundland, where also the inhabitants ate them, but he had never been able to obtain any ripe for seed. We read, under the head of Chatham, that "in 1555, during a time of great scarcity, the people about Orford, in Sussex [England] were preserved from perishing by eating the seeds of this plant, which grew there in great abundance upon the sea coast. Cows, horses, sheep, and goats eat it." But the writer who quoted this could not learn that they had been used in Barnstable County.

He had been a voyager, then? Oh, he had been about the world in his day. He once considered himself a pilot for all our coast; but now they had changed the names so he might be bothered.

He gave us to taste what he called the Summer Sweeting, a pleasant apple which he raised, and frequently grafted from, but had never seen growing elsewhere, except once—three trees on Newfoundland, or at the bay of Chaleur, I forget which, as he was sailing by. He was sure that he could tell the tree at a distance.

At length the fool, whom my companion called the wizard, came in, muttering between his teeth, "Damn book-peddlers—all the time talking about books. Better do something. Damn 'em. I'll shoot 'em. Got a doctor down here. Damn him, I'll get a gun and shoot him"; never once holding up his head. Whereat the old man stood up and said in a loud voice, as if he was accustomed to command, and this was not the first time he had been obliged to exert his authority there: "John, go sit down, mind your business—we've heard you talk before—precious little you'll do—your bark is worse than your bite." But, without minding, John muttered the same gibberish over again, and then sat down at the table which the old folks had left. He ate all there was on it, and then turned to the apples, which his aged mother was paring, that she might give her guests some applesauce for breakfast, but she drew them away and sent him off.

When I approached this house the next summer, over the desolate hills between it and the shore, which are worthy to have been the birthplace of Ossian, I saw the wizard in the midst of a corn field on the hillside, but, as usual, he loomed so strangely, that I mistook him for a scarecrow.

This was the merriest old man that we had ever seen, and one of the best preserved. His style of conversation was coarse and plain enough to have suited Rabelais. He would have made a good Panurge. Or rather he was a sober Silenus, and we were the boys Chromis and Mnasilus, who listened to his story.

> "Not by Haemonian hills the Thracian bard,
> Nor awful Phoebus was on Pindus heard
> With deeper silence or with more regard."

There was a strange mingling of past and present in his conversation, for he had lived under King George, and might have remembered when Napoleon and the moderns generally were born. He said that one day, when the troubles between the Colonies and the mother country first broke out, as he, a boy of fifteen, was pitching hay out of a cart, one Donne, an old Tory, who was talking with his father, a good Whig, said to him, "Why, Uncle Bill, you might as well undertake to pitch that pond into the ocean with a pitchfork, as for the Colonies to undertake to gain their independence." He remembered well General Washington, and how he rode his horse along the streets of Boston, and he stood up to show us how he looked.

"He was a r—a—ther large and portly-looking man, a manly and resolute-looking officer, with a pretty good leg as he sat on his horse."—"There, I'll tell you, this was the way with Washington." Then he jumped up again, and bowed gracefully to right and left, making show as if he were waving his hat. Said he, "*That* was Washington."

He told us many anecdotes of the Revolution, and was much pleased when we told him that we had read the same in history, and that his account agreed with the written.

"Oh," he said, "I know, I know! I was a young fellow of sixteen, with my ears wide open; and a fellow of that age, you know, is pretty wide awake, and likes to know everything that's going on. Oh, I know!"

He told us the story of the wreck of the Franklin, which took place there the previous spring; how a boy came to his house early in the morning to know whose boat that was by the shore, for there was a vessel in distress, and he, being an old man, first ate his breakfast, and then walked over to the top of the hill by the shore, and sat down there, having found a comfortable seat, to see the ship wrecked. She was on the bar, only a quarter of a mile from him, and still nearer to the men on the beach, who had got a boat ready, but could render no assistance on account of the breakers, for there was a pretty high sea running. There were the passengers all crowded together in the forward part of the ship, and some were getting out of the cabin windows and were drawn on deck by the others.

"I saw the captain get out his boat," said he; "he had one little one; and then they jumped into it one after another, down as straight as an arrow. I counted them. There were nine. One was a woman, and she jumped as straight as any of them. Then they shoved off. The sea took them back, one wave went over them, and when they came up there were six still clinging to the boat; I counted them. The next wave turned the boat bottom upward, and emptied them all out. None of them ever came ashore alive. There were the rest of them all crowded together on the forecastle, the other parts of the ship being under water. They had seen all that happened to the boat. At length a heavy sea separated the forecastle from the rest of the wreck, and set it inside of the worst breaker, and the boat was able to reach them, and it saved all that were left, but one woman."

He also told us of the steamer Cambria's getting aground on this shore a few months before we were there, and of her English passengers who roamed over his grounds, and who, he said, thought the prospect from the high hill by the shore, "the most delightsome they had ever seen," and also of the pranks which the ladies played with his scoop-net in the ponds. He spoke of these travelers with their purses full of guineas, just as our provincial fathers used to speak of British bloods in the time of King George the Third.

Quid loquar? Why repeat what he told us?

> *"Aut Scyllam Nisi, quam fama secuta est,*
> *Candida succinctam latrantibus inguina monstris,*
> *Dulichias vexâsse rates, et gurgite in alto*
> *Ah! timidos nautas canibus lacerâsse marinis?"* [1]

In the course of the evening I began to feel the potency of the clam which I had eaten, and I was obliged to confess to our host that I was no tougher than the cat he told of; but he answered, that he was a plain-spoken man, and he could tell me that it was all imagination. At any rate, it proved an emetic in my case, and I was made quite sick by it for a short time, while he laughed at my expense. I was pleased to read afterward, in Mourt's Relation of the landing of the Pilgrims in Provincetown Harbor, these words: "We found great muscles [the old editor says that they were undoubtedly sea-clams] and very fat and full of sea-pearl; but we could not eat them, for they made us all sick that did eat, as well sailors as passengers, . . . but they were soon well again." It brought me nearer to the Pilgrims to be thus reminded by a similar experience that I was so like them. Moreover, it was a valuable confirmation of their story, and I am prepared now to believe every word of Mourt's Relation. I was also pleased to find that man and the clam lay still at the same angle to one another. But I did not notice sea-pearl. Like Cleopatra, I must have swallowed it. I have since dug these clams on a flat in the Bay and observed them. They could squirt full ten feet before the wind, as appeared by the marks of the drops on the sand.

"Now I am going to ask you a question," said the old man, "and I don't know as you can tell me; but you are a learned man, and I never had any learning, only what I got by natur."—It was in vain that we reminded him that he could quote Josephus to our confusion.—"I've thought, if I ever met a learned man I should like to ask him this question. Can you tell me how *Axy* is spelt, and what it means? *Axy,"* says he; "there's a girl over here is named *Axy*. Now what is it? What does it mean? Is it Scripture? I've read my Bible twenty-five years over and over, and I never came across it."

"Did you read it twenty-five years for this object?" I asked.

"Well, *how* is it spelt? Wife, how is it spelt?"

She said, "It is in the Bible; I've seen it."

"Well, how do you spell it?"

"I don't know. A c h, ach, s e h, seh,—Achseh."

"Does that spell Axy? Well, do *you* know what it means?" asked he, turning to me.

CAPE COD. 1. **"Aut . . . marinis?"**: Virgil, *Ecologues*, VI.74–77:

> "Or the tale of Scylla, daughter of Nisus, whom report has followed to the effect that
> She girt as to her white loins with barking dogs
> Did afflict the Dulichian ships and in the deep surge
> Ah! did she mangle the fearful sailors with marine dogs."

"No," I replied, "I never heard the sound before."

"There was a schoolmaster down here once, and they asked him what it meant, and he said it had no more meaning than a bean-pole."

I told him that I held the same opinion with the schoolmaster. I had been a schoolmaster myself, and had had strange names to deal with. I also heard of such names as Zoheth, Beriah, Amaziah, Bethuel, and Shearjashub, hereabouts.

At length the little boy, who had a seat quite in the chimney-corner, took off his stockings and shoes, warmed his feet, and having had his sore leg freshly salved, went off to bed; then the fool made bare his knotty-looking feet and legs, and followed him; and finally the old man exposed his calves also to our gaze. We had never had the good fortune to see an old man's legs before, and were surprised to find them fair and plump as an infant's, and we thought that he took a pride in exhibiting them. He then proceeded to make preparations for retiring, discoursing meanwhile with Panurgic plainness of speech on the ills to which old humanity is subject. We were a rare haul for him. He could commonly get none but ministers to talk to, though sometimes ten of them at once, and he was glad to meet some of the laity at leisure. The evening was not long enough for him. As I had been sick, the old lady asked if I would not go to bed—it was getting late for old people; but the old man, who had not yet done his stories, said, "You ain't particular, are you?"

"Oh, no," said I, "I am in no hurry. I believe I have weathered the Clam cape."

"They are good," said he; "I wish I had some of them now."

"They never hurt me," said the old lady.

"But then you took out the part that killed a cat," said I.

At last we cut him short in the midst of his stories, which he promised to resume in the morning. Yet, after all, one of the old ladies who came into our room in the night to fasten the fire-board, which rattled, as she went out took the precaution to fasten us in. Old women are by nature more suspicious than old men. However, the winds howled around the house, and made the fire-boards as well as the casements rattle well that night. It was probably a windy night for any locality, but we could not distinguish the roar which was proper to the ocean from that which was due to the wind alone.

The sounds which the ocean makes must be very significant and interesting to those who live near it. When I was leaving the shore at this place the next summer, and had got a quarter of a mile distant, ascending a hill, I was startled by a sudden, loud sound from the sea, as if a large steamer were letting off steam by the shore, so that I caught my breath and felt my blood run cold for an instant, and I turned about, expecting to see one of the Atlantic steamers thus far out of her course, but there was nothing unusual to be seen. There was a low bank at the entrance of the Hollow, between me and the ocean, and suspecting that I might have risen into another stratum of air in ascending the hill—which had wafted to me only the ordinary roar of the sea—I immediately descended again, to see if I lost hearing of it; but, without regard to my ascending or descending, it died away in a minute or two, and yet there was scarcely any wind all the while. The old man said that this was what they called the "rut," a peculiar roar of the sea before the wind changes, which, however, he could not account for. He thought that he could tell all about the weather from the sounds which the sea made.

Old Josselyn, who came to New England in 1638, has it among his weather-signs, that "the resounding of the sea from the shore, and murmuring of the winds in the woods, without apparent wind, sheweth wind to follow."

Being on another part of the coast one night since this, I heard the roar of the surf a mile distant, and the inhabitants said it was a sign that the wind would work round east, and we should have rainy weather. The ocean was heaped up somewhere at the eastward, and this roar was occasioned by its effort to preserve its equilibrium, the wave reaching the shore before the wind. Also the captain of a packet between this country and England told me that he sometimes met with a wave on the Atlantic coming against the wind, perhaps in a calm sea, which indicated that at a distance the wind was blowing from an opposite quarter, but the undulation had traveled faster than it. Sailors tell of "tide-rips" and "ground-swells," which they suppose to have been occasioned by hurricanes and earthquakes, and to have traveled many hundred, and sometimes even two or three thousand miles.

Before sunrise the next morning they let us out again, and I ran over to the beach to see the sun come out of the ocean. The old woman of eighty-four winters was already out in the cold morning wind, bareheaded, tripping about like a young girl, and driving up the cow to milk. She got the breakfast with dispatch, and without noise or bustle; and meanwhile the old man resumed his stories, standing before us, who were sitting, with his back to the chimney, and ejecting his tobacco-juice right and left into the fire behind him, without regard to the various dishes which were there preparing. At breakfast we had eels, buttermilk cake, cold bread, green beans, doughnuts, and tea. The old man talked a steady stream; and when his wife told him he had better eat his breakfast, he said, "Don't hurry me; I have lived too long to be hurried." I ate of the applesauce and the doughnuts, which I thought had sustained the least detriment from the old man's shots, but my companion refused the applesauce, and ate of the hot cake and green beans, which had appeared to him to occupy the safest part of the hearth. But on comparing notes afterward, I told him that the buttermilk cake was particularly exposed, and I saw how it suffered repeatedly, and therefore I avoided it; but he declared that, however that might be, he witnessed that the applesauce was seriously injured, and had therefore declined that. After breakfast we looked at his clock, which was out of order, and oiled it with some "hen's grease," for want of sweet oil, for he scarcely could believe that we were not tinkers or peddlers; meanwhile, he told a story about visions, which had reference to a crack in the clock-case made by frost one night. He was curious to know to what religious sect we belonged. He said that he had been to hear thirteen kinds of preaching in one month, when he was young, but he did not join any of them—he stuck to his Bible. There was nothing like any of them in his Bible. While I was shaving in the next room, I heard him ask my companion to what sect he belonged, to which he answered,—

"Oh, I belong to the Universal Brotherhood."

"What's that?" he asked, "Sons o' Temperance?"

Finally, filling our pockets with doughnuts, which he was pleased to find that we called by the same name that he did, and paying for our entertainment, we took our departure; but he followed us out of doors, and made us tell him the names of the vegetables which he had raised from seeds that came out of the Franklin. They were cabbage, broccoli, and parsley. As I had asked him the names of so many things, he tried me in turn with all the plants which grew in his garden, both wild and cultivated. It was about half an acre, which he cultivated wholly himself. Besides the common garden vegetables, there were yellow dock, lemon balm, hyssop, gill-go-over-the-ground, mouse-ear, chick-weed, Roman wormwood, elecampane, and other plants. As we stood there, I saw a fish hawk stoop to pick a fish out of his pond.

"There," said I, "he has got a fish."

"Well," said the old man, who was looking all the while, but could see nothing, "he didn't dive, he just wet his claws."

And, sure enough, he did not this time, though it is said that they often do, but he merely stooped low enough to pick him out with his talons; but as he bore his shining prey over the bushes, it fell to the ground, and we did not see that he recovered it. That is not their practice.

Thus, having had another crack with the old man, he standing bareheaded under the eaves, he directed us "athwart the fields," and we took to the beach again for another day, it being now late in the morning.

It was but a day or two after this that the safe of the Provincetown Bank was broken open and robbed by two men from the interior, and we learned that our hospitable entertainers did at least transiently harbor the suspicion that we were the men.

A PLEA FOR CAPTAIN JOHN BROWN

◇

THOREAU met John Brown twice. Their meetings were brief, but Thoreau recognized what kind of a man he was. Later, the bravery of the raid on Harper's Ferry and the moral courage Brown showed before his captors moved Thoreau profoundly. As he said,

> If any one who has seen Brown in Concord can now pursue any other train of thought, I do not know what he is made of. If he gets his usual allowance of sleep, I will warrant him to fatten easily, under any circumstances which do not touch his body or purse. I put a piece of paper and a pencil under my pillow, and when I could not sleep, I wrote in the dark.

From these notes Thoreau wrote his "Plea for Captain John Brown," which he then delivered in Concord, Worcester, and finally in Boston before Theodore Parker's great audience at the Fraternity Lectures. Toward the end of the same year, 1859, Thoreau set down in his journal some further thoughts about Brown which were read aloud at Brown's grave in the Adirondacks the following Fourth of July:

> What avail all your scholarly accomplishments and learning, compared with wisdom and manhood? To omit his other behavior, see what a work this comparatively unread and unlettered man wrote within six weeks. He wrote in prison, not a History of the World, like Raleigh, but an American book which I think will live longer than that. I do not know of such words, uttered under such circumstances, and so copiously withal, in Roman or English or any his-

tory. The *art* of composition is as simple as the discharge of a bullet from a rifle, and its masterpieces imply an infinitely greater force behind them. This unlettered man's speaking and writing are standard English. Some words and phrases deemed vulgarisms and Americanisms before, he has made standard American.

Of all the men who were said to be my contemporaries, it seemed to me that John Brown was the only one who *had not died*. I meet him at every turn. He is more alive than ever he was. He has earned immortality. He is not confined to North Elba [1] nor to Kansas. He is no longer working in secret. He works in public, and in the clearest light that shines on this land.

◇

I TRUST that you will pardon me for being here. I do not wish to force my thoughts upon you, but I feel forced myself. Little as I know of Captain Brown, I would fain do my part to correct the tone and the statements of the newspapers, and of my countrymen generally, respecting his character and actions. It costs us nothing to be just. We can at least express our sympathy with, and admiration of, him and his companions, and that is what I now propose to do.

First, as to his history. I will endeavor to omit, as much as possible, what you have already read. I need not describe his person to you, for probably most of you have seen and will not soon forget him. I am told that his grandfather, John Brown, was an officer in the Revolution; that he himself was born in Connecticut about the beginning of this century, but early went with his father to Ohio. I heard him say that his father was a contractor who furnished beef to the army there, in the War of 1812; that he accompanied him to the camp, and assisted him in that employment, seeing a good deal of military life,—more, perhaps, than if he had been a soldier; for he was often present at the councils of the officers. Especially, he learned by experience how armies are supplied and maintained in the field,—a work which, he observed, requires at least as much experience and skill as to lead them in battle. He said that few persons had any conception of the cost, even the pecuniary cost, of firing a single bullet in war. He saw enough, at any rate, to disgust him with a military life; indeed, to excite in him a great abhorrence of it; so much so, that though he was tempted by the offer of some petty office in the army, when he was about eighteen, he not only declined that, but he also refused to train when warned, and was fined for it. He then resolved that he would never have anything to do with any war, unless it were a war for liberty.

When the troubles in Kansas began, he sent several of his sons thither to strengthen the party of the Free State men, fitting them out with such weapons as he had, telling them that if the troubles should increase, and there should be need of him, he would follow, to assist them with his hand and counsel. This, as you all know, he soon after did; and it was through his agency, far more than any other's, that Kansas was made free.

For a part of his life he was a surveyor, and at one time he was engaged in wool-growing, and he went to Europe as an agent about that business. There, as everywhere, he had his eyes about him, and made many original observations. He said, for instance, that he saw why the soil of England was so rich, and that of Germany (I think it was) so poor, and he thought of writing to some of the crowned heads about it. It was because in England the peasantry live on the soil which they cultivate, but in Germany they are gathered into villages at night. It is a pity that he did not make a book of his observations.

I should say that he was an old-fashioned man in his respect for the Constitution, and his faith in the permanence of this Union. Slavery he deemed to be wholly opposed to these, and he was its determined foe.

He was by descent and birth a New England farmer, a man of great common sense, deliberate and practical as that class is, and tenfold more so. He was like the best of those who stood at Concord Bridge once, on Lexington Common, and on Bunker Hill, only he was firmer and higher principled than any that I have chanced to hear of as there. It was no abolition lecturer that converted him. Ethan Allen and Stark, with whom he may in some respects be compared, were rangers in a lower and less important field. They could bravely face their country's foes, but he had the courage to face his country herself when she was in the wrong. A Western writer says, to account for his escape from so many perils, that he was concealed under a "rural exterior"; as if, in that prairie land, a hero should, by good rights, wear a citizen's dress only.

He did not go to the college called Harvard, good old Alma Mater as she is. He was not fed on the pap that is there furnished. As he phrased it, "I know no more of grammar than one of your calves." But he went to the great university of the West, where he sedulously pursued the study of Liberty, for which he had early betrayed a fondness, and having taken many degrees, he finally commenced the public practice of Humanity in

A PLEA FOR CAPTAIN JOHN BROWN. 1. **North Elba**: where Brown was buried.

Kansas, as you all know. Such were *his humanities,* and not any study of grammar. He would have left a Greek accent slanting the wrong way, and righted up a falling man.

He was one of that class of whom we hear a great deal, but, for the most part, see nothing at all,—the Puritans. It would be in vain to kill him. He died lately in the time of Cromwell, but he reappeared here. Why should he not? Some of the Puritan stock are said to have come over and settled in New England. They were a class that did something else than celebrate their forefathers' day, and eat parched corn in remembrance of that time. They were neither Democrats nor Republicans, but men of simple habits, straightforward, prayerful; not thinking much of rulers who did not fear God, not making many compromises, nor seeking after available candidates.

"In his camp," as one has recently written, and as I have myself heard him state, "he permitted no profanity; no man of loose morals was suffered to remain there, unless, indeed, as a prisoner of war. 'I would rather,' said he, 'have the small-pox, yellow fever, and cholera, all together in my camp, than a man without principle . . . It is a mistake, sir, that our people make, when they think that bullies are the best fighters, or that they are the fit men to oppose these Southerners. Give me men of good principles,—God-fearing men,—men who respect themselves, and with a dozen of them I will oppose any hundred such men as these Buford ruffians.' " He said that if one offered himself to be a soldier under him, who was forward to tell what he could or would do if he could only get sight of the enemy, he had but little confidence in him.

He was never able to find more than a score or so of recruits whom he would accept, and only about a dozen, among them his sons, in whom he had perfect faith. When he was here, some years ago, he showed to a few a little manuscript book, —his "orderly book" I think he called it,—containing the names of his company in Kansas, and the rules by which they bound themselves; and he stated that several of them had already sealed the contract with their blood. When some one remarked that, with the addition of a chaplain, it would have been a perfect Cromwellian troop, he observed that he would have been glad to add a chaplain to the list, if he could have found one who could fill that office worthily. It is easy enough to find one for the United States Army. I believe that he had prayers in his camp morning and evening, nevertheless.

He was a man of Spartan habits, and at sixty was scrupulous about his diet at your table, excusing himself by saying that he must eat sparingly and fare hard, as became a soldier, or one who was fitting himself for difficult enterprises, a life of exposure.

A man of rare common sense and directness of speech, as of action; a transcendentalist above all, a man of ideas and principles,—that was what distinguished him. Not yielding to a whim or transient impulse, but carrying out the purpose of a life. I noticed that he did not overstate anything, but spoke within bounds. I remember, particularly, how, in his speech here, he referred to what his family had suffered in Kansas, without ever giving the least vent to his pent-up fire. It was a volcano with an ordinary chimney-flue. Also referring to the deeds of certain Border Ruffians, he said, rapidly paring away his speech, like an experienced soldier, keeping a reserve of force and meaning, "They had a perfect right to be hung." He was not in the least a rhetorician, was not talking to Buncombe or his constituents anywhere, had no need to invent anything but to tell the simple truth, and communicate his own resolution; therefore he appeared incomparably strong, and eloquence in Congress and elsewhere seemed to me at a discount. It was like the speeches of Cromwell compared with those of an ordinary king.

As for his tact and prudence, I will merely say, that at a time when scarcely a man from the Free States was able to reach Kansas by any direct route, at least without having his arms taken from him, he, carrying what imperfect guns and other weapons he could collect, openly and slowly drove an ox-cart through Missouri, apparently in the capacity of a surveyor, with his surveying compass exposed in it, and so passed unsuspected, and had ample opportunity to learn the designs of the enemy. For some time after his arrival he still followed the same profession. When, for instance, he saw a knot of ruffians on the prairie, discussing, of course, the single topic which then occupied their minds, he would, perhaps, take his compass and one of his sons, and proceed to run an imaginary line right through the very spot on which that conclave had assembled, and when he came up to them, he would naturally pause and have some talk with them, learning their news, and, at last, all their plans perfectly; and having thus completed his real survey he would resume his imaginary one, and run on his line till he was out of sight.

When I expressed surprise that he could live in Kansas at all, with a price set upon his head, and so large a number, including the authorities, exasperated against him, he accounted for it by saying, "It is perfectly well understood that I will not be taken." Much of the time for some years he has had to skulk in swamps, suffering from poverty, and from sickness which was the consequence of exposure, befriended only by Indians and a few whites. But though it might be known that he was lurking in a particular swamp, his foes commonly did not care to go in after him. He could even come out into a town where there were more Border Ruffians than Free State men, and transact some business, without delaying long, and yet not be molested; for, said he, "no little handful of men were willing to undertake it, and a large body could not be got together in season."

As for his recent failure, we do not know the facts about it. It was evidently far from being a wild and desperate attempt. His enemy, Mr. Vallandigham,[2] is compelled to say that "it was among the best planned and executed conspiracies that ever failed."

Not to mention his other successes, was it a failure, or did it show a want of good management, to deliver from bondage a dozen human beings, and walk off with them by broad daylight, for weeks if not months, at a leisurely pace, through one state after another, for half the length of the North, conspicuous to all parties, with a price set upon his head, going into a court-room on his way and telling what he had done, thus convincing Missouri that it was not profitable to try to hold slaves in his neighborhood?—and this, not because the government menials were lenient, but because they were afraid of him.

Yet he did not attribute his success, foolishly, to "his star," or to any magic. He said, truly, that the reason why such greatly superior numbers quailed before him was, as one of his prisoners confessed, because they *lacked a cause,*—a kind of armor which he and his party never lacked. When the time came, few men were found willing to lay down their lives in defense of what they knew to be wrong; they did not like that this should be their last act in this world.

But to make haste to *his* last act, and its effects.

The newspapers seem to ignore, or perhaps are really ignorant of the fact that there are at least as many as two or three individuals to a town throughout the North who think much as the present speaker does about him and his enterprise. I do not hesitate to say that they are an important and growing party. We aspire to be something more than stupid and timid chattels, pretending to read history and our Bibles, but desecrating every house and every day we breathe in. Perhaps anxious politicians may prove that only seventeen white men and five negroes were concerned in the late enterprise; but their very anxiety to prove this might suggest to themselves that all is not told. Why do they still dodge the truth? They are so anxious because of a dim consciousness of the fact, which they do not distinctly face, that at least a million of the free inhabitants of the United States would have rejoiced if it had succeeded. They at most only criticize the tactics. Though we wear no crape, the thought of that man's position and probable fate is spoiling many a man's day here at the North for other thinking. If any one who has seen him here can pursue successfully any other train of thought, I do not know what he is made of. If there is any such who gets his usual allowance of sleep, I will warrant him to fatten easily under any circumstances which do not touch his body or purse. I put a piece of paper and pencil under my pillow, and when I could not sleep I wrote in the dark.

On the whole, my respect for my fellow-men, except as one may outweigh a million, is not being increased these days. I have noticed the cold-blooded way in which newspaper writers and men generally speak of this event, as if an ordinary malefactor, though one of unusual "pluck,"—as the Governor of Virginia is reported to have said, using the language of the cock-pit, "the gamest man he ever saw,"—had been caught, and were about to be hung. He was not dreaming of his foes when the governor thought he looked so brave. It turns what sweetness I have to gall, to hear, or hear of, the remarks of some of my neighbors. When we heard at first that he was dead, one of my townsmen observed that "he died as the fool dieth"; which, pardon me, for an instant suggested a likeness in him dying to my neighbor living. Others, craven-hearted, said disparagingly, that "he threw his life away," because he resisted the government. Which way have they thrown *their* lives, pray?—such as would praise a man for attacking singly an ordinary band of thieves or murderers. I hear another ask, Yankee-like, "What will he gain by it?" as if he expected to fill his pockets by this enterprise. Such a one has no idea of gain but in this worldly sense. If it does not lead to a "surprise" party, if he does not get a new pair of boots, or a vote of thanks, it must be a failure. "But he won't gain anything by it." Well, no, I don't suppose he could get four-and-six pence a day for being hung, take the year around; but then he stands a chance to save a considerable part of his soul,—and *such* a soul!—when *you* do not. No doubt you can get more in your market for a quart of milk than for a quart of blood, but that is not the market that heroes carry their blood to.

2. **Mr. Vallandigham:** Clement L. Vallandigham (1820–71), an Ohio Democrat but pro-Southern in his sympathies.

Such do not know that like the seed is the fruit, and that, in the moral world, when good seed is planted, good fruit is inevitable, and does not depend on our watering and cultivating; that when you plant, or bury, a hero in his field, a crop of heroes is sure to spring up. This is a seed of such force and vitality, that it does not ask our leave to germinate.

The momentary charge at Balaklava, in obedience to a blundering command, proving what a perfect machine the soldier is, has, properly enough, been celebrated by a poet laureate; but the steady, and for the most part successful, charge of this man, for some years, against the legions of Slavery, in obedience to an infinitely higher command, is as much more memorable than that as an intelligent and conscientious man is superior to a machine. Do you think that that will go unsung?

"Served him right,"—"A dangerous man,"—"He is undoubtedly insane." So they proceed to live their sane, and wise, and altogether admirable lives, reading their Plutarch a little, but chiefly pausing at that feat of Putnam,[3] who was let down into a wolf's den; and in this wise they nourish themselves for brave and patriotic deeds some time or other. The Tract Society could afford to print that story of Putnam. You might open the district schools with the reading of it, for there is nothing about Slavery of the Church in it; unless it occurs to the reader that some pastors are *wolves* in sheep's clothing. "The American Board of Commissioners for Foreign Missions," even, might dare to protest against *that* wolf. I have heard of boards, and of American boards, but it chances that I never heard of this particular lumber till lately. And yet I hear of Northern men, and women, and children, by families, buying a "life-membership" in such societies as these. A life-membership in the grave! You can get buried cheaper than that.

Our foes are in our midst and all about us. There is hardly a house but is divided against itself, for our foe is the all but universal woodenness of both head and heart, the want of vitality in man, which is the effect of our vice; and hence are begotten fear, superstition, bigotry, persecution, and slavery of all kinds. We are mere figure-heads upon a hulk, with livers in the place of hearts. The curse is the worship of idols, which at length changes the worshipper into a stone image himself; and the New Englander is just as much an idolater as the Hindoo. This man was an exception, for he did not set up even a political graven image between him and his God.

3. **Putnam:** Israel Putnam (1718–90), a famous soldier in the American Revolution.

A church that can never have done with excommunicating Christ while it exists! Away with your broad and flat churches, and your narrow and tall churches! Take a step forward, and invent a new style of out-houses. Invent a salt that will save you, and defend our nostrils.

The modern Christian is a man who has consented to say all the prayers in the liturgy, provided you will let him go straight to bed and sleep quietly afterward. All his prayers begin with "Now I lay me down to sleep," and he is forever looking forward to the time when he shall go to his *"long* rest." He has consented to perform certain old-established charities, too, after a fashion, but he does not wish to hear of any new-fangled ones; he doesn't wish to have any supplementary articles added to the contract, to fit it to the present time. He shows the whites of his eyes on the Sabbath, and the blacks all the rest of the week. The evil is not merely a stagnation of blood, but a stagnation of spirit. Many, no doubt, are well disposed, but sluggish by constitution and by habit, and they cannot conceive of a man who is actuated by higher motives than they are. Accordingly they pronounce this man insane, for they know that *they* could never act as he does, as long as they are themselves.

We dream of foreign countries, of other times and races of men, placing them at a distance in history or space; but let some significant event like the present occur in our midst, and we discover, often, this distance and this strangeness between us and our nearest neighbors. *They* are our Austrias, and Chinas, and South Sea Islands. Our crowded society becomes well spaced all at once, clean and handsome to the eye,—a city of magnificent distances. We discover why it was that we never got beyond compliments and surfaces with them before; we become aware of as many versts between us and them as there are between a wandering Tartar and a Chinese town. The thoughtful man becomes a hermit in the thoroughfares of the market-place. Impassable seas suddenly find their level between us, or dumb steppes stretch themselves out there. It is the difference of constitution, of intelligence, and faith, and not streams and mountains, that makes the true and impassable boundaries between individuals and between states. None but the like-minded can come plenipotentiary to our court.

I read all the newspapers I could get within a

week after this event and I do not remember in them a single expression of sympathy for these men. I have since seen one noble statement, in a Boston paper, not editorial. Some voluminous sheets decided not to print the full report of Brown's words to the exclusion of other matter. It was as if a publisher should reject the manuscript of the New Testament, and print Wilson's last speech. The same journal which contained this pregnant news was chiefly filled, in parallel columns, with the reports of the political conventions that were being held. But the descent to them was too steep. They should have been spared this contrast,—being printed in an extra, at least. To turn from the voices and deeds of earnest men to the *cackling* of political conventions! Office-seekers and speech-makers, who do not so much as lay an honest egg, but wear their breasts bare upon an egg of chalk. Their great game is the game of straws, or rather that universal aboriginal game of the platter, at which the Indians cried *hub, bub!* Exclude the reports of religious and political conventions, and publish the words of a living man.

But I object not so much to what they have omitted as to what they have inserted. Even the *Liberator* [4] called it "a misguided, wild, and apparently insane—effort." As for the herd of newspapers and magazines, I do not chance to know an editor in the country who will deliberately print anything which he knows will ultimately and permanently reduce the number of his subscribers. They do not believe that it would be expedient. How then can they print truth? If we do not say pleasant things, they argue, nobody will attend to us. And so they do like some traveling auctioneers who sing an obscene song, in order to draw a crowd around them. Republican editors, obliged to get their sentences ready for the morning edition, and accustomed to look at everything by the twilight of politics, express no admiration, nor true sorrow even, but call these men "deluded fanatics," —"mistaken men,"—"insane," or "crazed." It suggests what a *sane* set of editors we are blessed with, *not* "mistaken men;" who know very well on which side their bread is buttered, at least.

A man does a brave and humane deed, and at once, on all sides, we hear people and parties declaring, "I didn't do it, nor countenance *him* to do it, in any conceivable way. It can't be fairly inferred from my past career." I, for one, am not interested to hear you define your position. I don't know that I ever was or ever shall be. I think it is mere egotism, or impertinence at this time. Ye needn't take so much pains to wash your skirts of him. No intelligent man will ever be convinced that he was any creature of yours. He went and came, as he himself informs us, "under the auspices of John Brown and nobody else." The Republican Party does not perceive how many his *failure* will make to vote more correctly than they would have them. They have counted the votes of Pennsylvania & Co., but they have not correctly counted Captain Brown's vote. He has taken the wind out of their sails,—the little wind they had,— and they may as well lie to and repair.

What though he did not belong to your clique! Though you may not approve of his method or his principles, recognize his magnanimity. Would you not like to claim kindredship with him in that, though in no other thing he is like, or likely, to you? Do you think that you would lose your reputation so? What you lost at the spile, you would gain at the bung.

If they do not mean all this, then they do not speak the truth, and say what they mean. They are simply at their old tricks still.

"It was always conceded to him," *says one who calls him crazy,* "that he was a conscientious man, very modest in his demeanor, apparently inoffensive, until the subject of Slavery was introduced, when he would exhibit a feeling of indignation unparalleled."

The slave-ship is on her way, crowded with its dying victims; new cargoes are being added in mid-ocean; a small crew of slaveholders, countenanced by a large body of passengers, is smothering four million under the hatches, and yet the politician asserts that the only proper way by which deliverance is to be obtained is by "the quiet diffusion of the sentiments of humanity," without any "outbreak." As if the sentiments of humanity were ever found unaccompanied by its deeds, and you could disperse them, all finished to order, the pure article, as easily as water with a watering-pot, and so lay the dust. What is that that I hear cast overboard? The bodies of the dead that have found deliverance. That is the way we are "diffusing" humanity, and its sentiments with it.

Prominent and influential editors, accustomed to deal with politicians, men of an infinitely lower grade, say, in their ignorance, that he acted "on the principle of revenge." They do not know the man. They must enlarge themselves to conceive of him. I have no doubt that the time will come when they will begin to see him as he was. They have got to conceive of a man of faith and of religious principle, and not a politician or an Indian; of a man who did not wait till he was personally interfered with or thwarted in some harmless business

4. **the *Liberator*:** The newspaper of the famous abolitionist agitator William Lloyd Garrison (1805–79).

before he gave his life to the cause of the oppressed.

If Walker may be considered the representative of the South, I wish I could say that Brown was the representative of the North. He was a superior man. He did not value his bodily life in comparison with ideal things. He did not recognize unjust human laws, but resisted them as he was bid. For once we are lifted out of the trivialness and dust of politics into the region of truth and manhood. No man in America has ever stood up so persistently and effectively for the dignity of human nature, knowing himself for a man, and the equal of any and all governments. In that sense he was the most American of us all. He needed no babbling lawyer, making false issues, to defend him. He was more than a match for all the judges that American voters, or office-holders of whatever grade, can create. He could not have been tried by a jury of his peers, because his peers did not exist. When a man stands up serenely against the condemnation and vengeance of mankind, rising above them literally *by a whole body,*—even though he were of late the vilest murderer, who has settled that matter with himself,—the spectacle is a sublime one,—didn't ye know it, *ye Liberators, ye Tribunes, ye Republicans?*—and we become criminal in comparison. Do yourselves the honor to recognize him. He needs none of your respect.

As for the Democratic journals, they are not human enough to affect me at all. I do not feel indignation at anything they may say.

I am aware that I anticipate a little,—that he was still, at the last accounts, alive in the hands of his foes; but that being the case, I have all along found myself thinking and speaking of him as physically dead.

I do not believe in erecting statues to those who still live in our hearts, whose bones have not yet crumbled in the earth around us, but I would rather see the statue of Captain Brown in the Massachusetts State-House yard than that of any other man whom I know. I rejoice that I live in this age, that I am his contemporary.

What a contrast, when we turn to that political party which is so anxiously shuffling him and his plot out of its way, and looking around for some available slaveholder, perhaps, to be its candidate, at least for one who will execute the Fugitive Slave Law, and all those other unjust laws which he took up arms to annul!

Insane! A father and six sons, and one son-in-law, and several more men besides,—as many at least as twelve disciples,—all struck with insanity at once; while the sane tyrant holds with a firmer gripe than ever his four millions of slaves, and a thousand sane editors, his abettors, are saving their country and their bacon! Just as insane were his efforts in Kansas. Ask the tyrant who is his most dangerous foe, the sane man or the insane? Do the thousands who know him best, who have rejoiced at his deeds in Kansas, and have afforded him material aid there, think him insane? Such a use of this word is a mere trope with most who persist in using it, and I have no doubt that many of the rest have already in silence retracted their words.

Read his admirable answers to Mason and others. How they are dwarfed and defeated by the contrast! On the one side, half-brutish, half-timid questioning; on the other, truth, clear as lightning, crashing into their obscene temples. They are made to stand with Pilate, and Gessler, and the Inquisition. How ineffectual their speech and action! and what a void their silence! They are but helpless tools in this great work. It was no human power that gathered them about this preacher.

What have Massachusetts and the North sent a few *sane* representatives to Congress for, of late years?—to declare with effect what kind of sentiments? All their speeches put together and boiled down—and probably they themselves will confess it—do not match for manly directness and force, and for simple truth, the few casual remarks of crazy John Brown on the floor of the Harper's Ferry engine-house,—that man whom you are about to hang, to send to the other world, though not to represent *you* there. No, he was not our representative in any sense. He was too fair a specimen of a man to represent the like of us. Who, then, *were* his constituents? If you read his words understandingly you will find out. In his case there is no idle eloquence, no made, nor maiden speech, no compliments to the oppressor. Truth is his inspirer, and earnestness the polisher of his sentences. He could afford to lose his Sharp's rifles, while he retained his faculty of speech,—a Sharp's rifle of infinitely surer and longer range.

And the New York *Herald* reports the conversation *verbatim!* It does not know of what undying words it is made the vehicle.

I have no respect for the penetration of any man who can read the report of that conversation and still call the principal in it insane. It has the ring of a saner sanity than an ordinary discipline and habits of life, than an ordinary organization, secure. Take any sentence of it,—"Any questions that I can honorably answer, I will; not otherwise. So far as I am myself concerned, I have told everything truthfully. I value my word, sir." The few who talk about his vindictive spirit, while they really admire his heroism, have no test by which to detect a noble man, no amalgam to combine with his pure gold. They mix their own dross with it.

It is a relief to turn from these slanders to the testimony of his more truthful, but frightened jailers and hangmen. Governor Wise [5] speaks far more justly and appreciatingly of him than any Northern editor, or politician, or public personage, that I chance to have heard from. I know that you can afford to hear him again on this subject. He says: "They are themselves mistaken who take him to be a madman. . . . He is cool, collected, and indomitable, and it is but just to him to say that he was humane to his prisoners. . . . And he inspired me with great trust in his integrity as a man of truth. He is a fanatic, vain and garrulous" (I leave that part to Mr. Wise), "but firm, truthful, and intelligent. His men, too, who survive, are like him. . . . Colonel Washington says that he was the coolest and firmest man he ever saw in defying danger and death. With one son dead by his side, and another shot through, he felt the pulse of his dying son with one hand, and held his rifle with the other, and commanded his men with the utmost composure, encouraging them to be firm, and to sell their lives as dear as they could. Of the three white prisoners, Brown, Stevens, and Coppoc, it was hard to say which was most firm."

Almost the first Northern men whom the slaveholder has learned to respect!

The testimony of Mr. Vallandigham, though less valuable, is of the same purport, that "it is vain to underrate either the man or his conspiracy. . . . He is the farthest possible removed from the ordinary ruffian, fanatic, or madman."

"All is quiet at Harper's Ferry," say the journals. What is the character of that calm which follows when the law and the slaveholder prevail? I regard this event as a touchstone designed to bring out, with glaring distinctness, the character of this government. We needed to be thus assisted to see it by the light of history. It needed to see itself. When a government puts forth its strength on the side of injustice, as ours to maintain slavery and kill the liberators of the slave, it reveals itself a merely brute force, or worse, a demoniacal force. It is the head of the Plug-Uglies. It is more manifest than ever that tyranny rules. I see this government to be effectually allied with France and Austria in oppressing mankind. There sits a tyrant holding fettered four millions of slaves; here comes their heroic liberator. This most hypocritical and diabolical government looks up from its seat on the gasping four millions, and inquires with an assumption of innocence: "What do you assault me for? Am I not an honest man? Cease agitation on this subject, or I will make a slave of you, too, or else hang you."

We talk about a *representative* government; but what a monster of a government is that where the noblest faculties of the mind, and the *whole heart,* are not *represented!* A semi-human tiger or ox, stalking over the earth, with its heart taken out and the top of its brain shot away. Heroes have fought well on their stumps when their legs were shot off, but I never heard of any good done by such a government as that.

The only government that I recognize—and it matters not how few are at the head of it, or how small its army—is that power that establishes justice in the land, never that which establishes injustice. What shall we think of a government to which all the truly brave and just men in the land are enemies, standing between it and those whom it oppresses? A government that pretends to be Christian and crucifies a million Christs every day!

Treason! Where does such treason take its rise? I cannot help thinking of you as you deserve, ye governments. Can you dry up the fountains of thought? High treason, when it is resistance to tyranny here below, has its origin in, and is first committed by, the power that makes and forever recreates man. When you have caught and hung all these human rebels, you have accomplished nothing but your own guilt, for you have not struck at the fountain-head. You presume to contend with a foe against whom West Point cadets and rifled cannon *point not.* Can all the art of the cannon founder tempt matter to turn against its makers? Is the form in which the founder thinks he casts it more essential than the constitution of it and of himself?

The United States have a coffle of four millions of slaves. They are determined to keep them in this condition; and Massachusetts is one of the confederated overseers to prevent their escape. Such are not all the inhabitants of Massachusetts, but such are they who rule and are obeyed here. It was Massachusetts, as well as Virginia, that put down this insurrection at Harper's Ferry. She sent the marines there, and she will have *to pay the penalty of her sin.*

Suppose that there is a society in this State that out of its own purse and magnanimity saves all the fugitive slaves that run to us, and protects our colored fellow-citizens, and leaves the other work to

5. **Governor Wise:** Governor Henry Alexander Wise (1806–76) of Virginia, an outspoken defender of slavery.

the government, so called. Is not that government fast losing its occupation, and becoming contemptible to mankind? If private men are obliged to perform the offices of government, to protect the weak and dispense justice, then the government becomes only a hired man, or clerk, to perform menial or indifferent services. Of course, that is but the shadow of a government whose existence necessitates a Vigilant Committee. What should we think of the Oriental Cadi even, behind whom worked in secret a Vigilant Committee? But such is the character of our Northern States generally; each has its Vigilant Committee. And, to a certain extent, these crazy governments recognize and accept this relation. They say, virtually, "We'll be glad to work for you on these terms, only don't make a noise about it." And thus the government, its salary being insured, withdraws into the back shop, taking the Constitution with it, and bestows most of its labor on repairing that. When I hear it at work sometimes, as I go by, it reminds me, at its best, of those farmers who in winter contrive to turn a penny by following the coopering business. And what kind of spirit is their barrel made to hold? They speculate in stocks, and bore holes in mountains, but they are not competent to lay out even a decent highway. The only *free* road, the Underground Railroad, is owned and managed by the Vigilant Committee. *They* have tunneled under the whole breadth of the land. Such a government is losing its power and respectability as surely as water runs out of a leaky vessel, and is held by one that can contain it.

I hear many condemn these men because they were so few. When were the good and the brave ever in a majority? Would you have had him wait till that time came?—till you and I came over to him? The very fact that he had no rabble or troop of hirelings about him would alone distinguish him from ordinary heroes. His company was small indeed, because few could be found worthy to pass muster. Each one who there laid down his life for the poor and oppressed was a picked man, culled out of many thousands, if not millions; apparently a man of principle, of rare courage, and devoted humanity; ready to sacrifice his life at any moment for the benefit of his fellow-man. It may be doubted if there were as many more their equals in these respects in all the country,—I speak of his followers only,—for their leader, no doubt, scoured the land far and wide, seeking to swell his troop. These alone were ready to step between the oppressor and the oppressed. Surely they were the very best men you could select to be hung. That was the greatest compliment which this country could pay them. They were ripe for her gallows. She has tried a long time, she has hung a good many, but never found the right one before.

When I think of him, and his six sons, and his son-in-law, not to enumerate the others, enlisted for this fight, proceeding coolly, reverently, humanely to work, for months if not years, sleeping, and waking upon it, summering and wintering the thought, without expecting any reward but a good conscience, while almost all America stood ranked on the other side,—I say again that it affects me as a sublime spectacle. If he had had any journal advocating *"his cause,"* any organ, as the phrase is, monotonously and wearisomely playing the same old tune, and then passing round the hat, it would have been fatal to his efficiency. If he had acted in any way so as to be let alone by the government, he might have been suspected. It was the fact that the tyrant must give place to him, or he to the tyrant, that distinguished him from all the reformers of the day that I know.

It was his peculiar doctrine that a man has a perfect right to interfere by force with the slaveholder, in order to rescue the slave. I agree with him. They who are continually shocked by slavery have some right to be shocked by the violent death of the slaveholder, but no others. Such will be more shocked by his life than by his death. I shall not be forward to think him mistaken in his method who quickest succeeds to liberate the slave. I speak for the slave when I say that I prefer the philanthropy of Captain Brown to that philanthropy which neither shoots me nor liberates me. At any rate, I do not think it is quite sane for one to spend his whole life in talking or writing about this matter, unless he is continuously inspired, and I have not done so. A man may have other affairs to attend to. I do not wish to kill nor to be killed, but I can foresee circumstances in which both these things would be by me unavoidable. We preserve the so-called peace of our community by deeds of petty violence every day. Look at the policeman's billy and handcuffs! Look at the jail! Look at the gallows! Look at the chaplain of the regiment! We are hoping only to live safely on the outskirts of *this* provisional army. So we defend ourselves and our hen-roosts, and maintain slavery. I know that the mass of my countrymen think that the only righteous use that can be made of Sharp's rifles and revolvers is to fight duels with them, when we are insulted by other nations, or to hunt Indians, or shoot fugitive slaves with them, or the like. I think that for once the Sharp's rifles and the revolvers were employed in a righteous cause. The tools were in the hands of one who could use them.

The same indignation that is said to have cleared

the temple once will clear it again. The question is not about the weapon, but the spirit in which you use it. No man has appeared in America, as yet, who loved his fellow-man so well, and treated him so tenderly. He lived for him. He took up his life and he laid it down for him. What sort of violence is that which is encouraged, not by soldiers, but by peaceable citizens, not so much by laymen as by ministers of the Gospel, not so much by the fighting sects as by the Quakers, and not so much by Quaker men as by Quaker women?

This event advertises me that there is such a fact as death,—the possibility of a man's dying. It seems as if no man had ever died in America before; for in order to die you must first have lived. I don't believe in the hearses, and palls, and funerals that they have had. There was no death in the case, because there had been no life; they merely rotted or sloughed off, pretty much as they had rotted or sloughed along. No temple's veil was rent, only a hole dug somewhere. Let the dead bury their dead. The best of them fairly ran down like a clock. Franklin,—Washington,—they were left off without dying; they were merely missing one day. I hear a good many pretend that they are going to die; or that they have died, for aught that I know. Nonsense! I'll defy them to do it. They haven't got life enough in them. They'll deliquesce like fungi, and keep a hundred eulogists mopping the spot where they left off. Only half a dozen or so have died since the world began. Do you think that you are going to die, sir? No! there's no hope of you. You haven't got your lesson yet. You've got to stay after school. We make a needless ado about capital punishment,—taking lives, when there is no life to take. *Memento mori.* We don't understand that sublime sentence which some worthy got sculptured on his gravestone once. We've interpreted it in a groveling and sniveling sense; we've wholly forgotten how to die.

But be sure you do die nevertheless. Do your work, and finish it. If you know how to begin, you will know when to end.

These men, in teaching us how to die, have at the same time taught us how to live. If this man's acts and words do not create a revival, it will be the severest possible satire on the acts and words that do. It is the best news that America has ever heard. It has already quickened the feeble pulse of the North, and infused more and more generous blood into her veins and heart than any number of years of what is called commercial and political prosperity could. How many a man who was lately contemplating suicide has now something to live for!

One writer says that Brown's peculiar monomania made him to be "dreaded by the Missourians as a supernatural being." Sure enough, a hero in the midst of us cowards is always so dreaded. He is just that thing. He shows himself superior to nature. He has a spark of divinity in him.

"Unless above himself he can
Erect himself, how poor a thing is man!"

Newspaper editors argue also that it is a proof of his *insanity* that he thought he was appointed to do this work which he did,—that he did not suspect himself for a moment! They talk as if it were impossible that a man could be "divinely appointed" in these days to do any work whatever; as if vows and religion were out of date as connected with any man's daily work; as if the agent to abolish slavery could only be somebody appointed by the President, or by some political party. They talk as if a man's death were a failure, and his continued life, be it of whatever character, were a success.

When I reflect to what a cause this man devoted himself, and how religiously, and then reflect to what cause his judges and all who condemn him so angrily and fluently devote themselves, I see that they are as far apart as the heavens and earth are asunder.

The amount of it is, our *"leading men"* are a harmless kind of folk, and they know *well enough* that they were not divinely appointed, but elected by the votes of their party.

Who is it whose safety requires that Captain Brown be hung? Is it indispensable to any Northern man? Is there no resource but to cast this man also to the Minotaur? If you do not wish it, say so distinctly. While these things are being done, beauty stands veiled and music is a screeching lie. Think of him,—of his rare qualities!—such a man as it takes ages to make, and ages to understand; no mock hero, nor the representative of any party. A man such as the sun may not rise upon again in this benighted land. To whose making went the costliest material, the finest adamant; sent to be the redeemer of those in captivity; and the only use to which you can put him is to hang him at the end of a rope! You who pretend to care for Christ Crucified, consider what you are about to do to him who offered himself to be the saviour of four millions of men.

Any man knows when he is justified, and all the wits in the world cannot enlighten him on that point. The murderer always knows that he is justly punished; but when a government takes the life of a man without the consent of his conscience, it is an audacious government, and is taking a step towards its own dissolution. It is not possible that an individual may be right and a government wrong? Are laws to be enforced simply because they were made? or declared by any number of men to be good, if they are *not* good? Is there any necessity for a man's being a tool to perform a deed of which his better nature disapproves? Is it the intention of lawmakers that *good* men shall be hung ever? Are judges to interpret the law according to the letter, and not the spirit? What right have *you* to enter into a compact with yourself that you *will* do thus or so, against the light within you? Is it for *you* to *make up* your mind,—to form any resolution whatever,—and not accept the convictions that are forced upon you, and which ever pass your understanding? I do not believe in lawyers, in that mode of attacking or defending a man, because you descend to meet the judge on his own ground, and, in cases of the highest importance, it is of no consequence whether a man breaks a human law or not. Let lawyers decide trivial cases. Business men may arrange that among themselves. If they were the interpreters of the everlasting laws which rightfully bind a man, that would be another thing. A counterfeiting law-factory, standing half in a slave land and half in a free! What kind of laws for free men can you expect from that?

I am here to plead his cause with you. I plead not for his life, but for his character,—his immortal life; and so it becomes your cause wholly, and is not his in the least. Some eighteen hundred years ago Christ was crucified; this morning, perchance, Captain Brown was hung. These are the two ends of a chain which is not without its links. He is not Old Brown any longer; he is an angel of light.

I see now that it was necessary that the bravest and humanest man in all the country should be hung. Perhaps he saw it himself. I *almost fear* that I may yet hear of his deliverance, doubting if a prolonged life, if *any* life, can do as much good as his death.

"Misguided!" "Garrulous!" "Insane!" "Vindictive!" So ye write in your easy-chairs, and thus he wounded responds from the floor of the armory, clear as a cloudless sky, true as the voice of nature is: "No man sent me here; it was my own prompting and that of my Maker. I acknowledge no master in human form."

And in what a sweet and noble strain he proceeds, addressing his captors, who stand over him: "I think, my friends, you are guilty of a great wrong against God and humanity, and it would be perfectly right for any one to interfere with you so far as to free those you willfully and wickedly hold in bondage."

And, referring to his movement: "It is, in my opinion, the greatest service a man can render to God."

"I pity the poor in bondage that have none to help them; that is why I am here; not to gratify any personal animosity, revenge, or vindictive spirit. It is my sympathy with the oppressed and the wronged, that are as good as you, and as precious in the sight of God."

You don't know your testament when you see it.

"I want you to understand that I respect the rights of the poorest and weakest of colored people, oppressed by the slave power, just as much as I do those of the most wealthy and powerful."

"I wish to say, furthermore, that you had better, all you people at the South, prepare yourself for a settlement of that question, that must come up for settlement sooner than you are prepared for it. The sooner you are prepared the better. You may dispose of me very easily. I am nearly disposed of now; but this question is still to be settled,—this Negro question, I mean; the end of that is not yet."

I foresee the time when the painter will paint that scene, no longer going to Rome for a subject; the poet will sing it; the historian record it; and, with the Landing of the Pilgrims and the Declaration of Independence, it will be the ornament of some future national gallery, when at least the present form of slavery shall be no more here. We shall then be at liberty to weep for Captain Brown. Then, and not till then, we will take our revenge.

WILD APPLES

◊

THIS essay was first delivered as a lecture before the Concord Lyceum in February, 1860, and was published posthumously in the *Atlantic Monthly* in 1862. It represents a fragment of a "Kalendar" that Thoreau had planned to write, in which he proposed to study all the natural phenomena that occurred in a year's time. Of all the correspondences that Thoreau discovered between Nature and himself, the wild apple tree was a singularly apt one—for what was Thoreau if not a scrubby growth which yet bore his "own peculiar fruit in triumph"?

◊

THE HISTORY OF THE APPLE TREE

IT IS remarkable how closely the history of the apple tree is connected with that of man. The geologist tells us that the order of the *Rosaceae,* which includes the apple, also the true grasses, and the *Labiatae,* or mints, were introduced only a short time previous to the appearance of man on the globe.

It appears that apples made a part of the food of that unknown primitive people whose traces have lately been found at the bottom of the Swiss lakes, supposed to be older than the foundation of Rome, so old that they had no metallic implements. An entire black and shrivelled crab-apple has been recovered from their stores.

Tacitus says of the ancient Germans that they satisfied their hunger with wild apples (*agrestia poma*), among other things.

Niebuhr observes that 'the words for a house, a field, a plow, plowing, wine, oil, milk, sheep, apples, and others relating to agriculture and the gentler way of life, agree in Latin and Greek, while the Latin words for all objects pertaining to war or the chase are utterly alien from the Greek.' Thus the apple tree may be considered a symbol of peace no less than the olive.

The apple was early so important, and generally distributed, that its name traced to its root in many languages signifies fruit in general. Μῆλον, in Greek, means an apple, also the fruit of other trees, also a sheep and any cattle, and finally riches in general.

The apple tree has been celebrated by the Hebrews, Greeks, Romans, and Scandinavians. Some have thought that the first human pair was tempted by its fruit. Goddesses are fabled to have contended for it, dragons were set to watch it, and heroes were employed to pluck it.

The tree is mentioned in at least three places in the Old Testament, and its fruit in two or three more. Solomon sings, 'As the apple-tree among the trees of the wood, so is my beloved among the sons.' And again, 'Stay me with flagons, comfort me with apples.' The noblest part of man's noblest feature is named from this fruit, 'the apple of the eye.'

The apple tree is also mentioned by Homer and Herodotus. Ulysses saw in the glorious garden of Alcinoüs 'pears and pomegranates, and apple trees bearing beautiful fruit' (Καὶ μηλέαι ἀγλαόκαρποι). And according to Homer, apples were among the fruits which Tantalus could not pluck, the wind ever blowing their boughs away from him. Theophrastus knew and described the apple tree as a botanist.

According to the Prose Edda, 'Iduna keeps in a box the apples which the gods, when they feel old age approaching, have only to taste of to become young again. It is in this manner that they will be kept in renovated youth until Ragnarok' (or the destruction of the gods).

I learn from Loudon that 'the ancient Welsh bards were rewarded for excelling in song by the token of the apple-spray;' and 'in the Highlands of Scotland the apple-tree is the badge of the clan Lamont.'

The apple tree (*Pyrus malus*) belongs chiefly to the northern temperate zone. Loudon says that 'it grows spontaneously in every part of Europe except the frigid zones, and throughout Western Asia, China, and Japan.' We have also two or three varieties of the apple indigenous in North America. The cultivated apple tree was first introduced into this country by the earliest settlers, and is thought to do as well or better here than anywhere else. Probably some of the varieties which are now cultivated were first introduced into Britain by the Romans.

Pliny, adopting the distinction of Theophrastus, says, 'Of trees there are some which are altogether wild (*sylvestres*), some more civilized (*urbaniores*).' Theophrastus includes the apple among the last; and, indeed, it is in this sense the most civilized of all trees. It is as harmless as a dove, as beautiful as a rose, and as valuable as flocks and herbs. It has been longer cultivated than any other, and so is more humanized; and who knows but, like the dog, it will at length be no longer traceable to its wild original? It migrates with man, like the dog and horse and cow: first, perchance, from Greece to Italy, thence to England, thence to America; and our Western emigrant is still marching steadily toward the setting sun with the seeds of the apple in his pocket, or perhaps a few young trees strapped to his load. At least a million apple trees are thus set farther westward this year than any cultivated ones grew last year. Consider how the Blossom Week, like the Sabbath, is thus annually spreading over the prairies; for when man migrates, he carries with him not only his birds, quadrupeds, insects, vegetables, and his very sward, but his orchard also.

The leaves and tender twigs are an agreeable food to many domestic animals, as the cow, horse, sheep, and goat; and the fruit is sought after by the first, as well as by the hog. Thus there appears to have existed a natural alliance between these animals and this tree from the first. 'The fruit of the crab in the forests of France' is said to be 'a great resource for the wild boar.'

Not only the Indian, but many indigenous insects, birds, and quadrupeds, welcome the apple tree to these shores. The tent caterpillar saddled her eggs on the very first twig that was formed, and it has since shared her affections with the wild cherry; and the canker-worm also in a measure abandoned the elm to feed on it. As it grew apace, the bluebird, robin, cherrybird, kingbird, and many more came with haste and built their nests and warbled in its boughs, and so became orchard-birds, and multiplied more than ever. It was an era in the history of their race. The downy woodpecker found such a savory morsel under its bark that he perforated it in a ring quite round the tree, before he left it—a thing which he had never done before, to my knowledge. It did not take the partridge long to find out how sweet its buds were, and every winter eve she flew, and still flies, from the wood, to pluck them, much to the farmer's sorrow. The rabbit, too, was not slow to learn the taste of its twigs and bark; and when the fruit was ripe, the squirrel half rolled, half carried it to his hole; and even the musquash crept up the bank from the brook at evening, and greedily devoured it, until he had worn a path in the grass there; and when it was frozen and thawed, the crow and the jay were glad to taste it occasionally. The owl crept into the first apple tree that became hollow, and fairly hooted with delight, finding it just the place for him; so, settling down into it, he has remained there ever since.

My theme being the Wild Apple, I will merely glance at some of the seasons in the annual growth of the cultivated apple, and pass on to my special province.

The flowers of the apple are perhaps the most beautiful of any tree's, so copious and so delicious to both sight and scent. The walker is frequently tempted to turn and linger near some more than usually handsome one, whose blossoms are two-thirds expanded. How superior it is in these respects to the pear, whose blossoms are neither colored nor fragrant!

By the middle of July, green apples are so large as to remind us of coddling, and of the autumn. The sward is commonly strewed with little ones which fall still-born, as it were—Nature thus thinning them for us. The Roman writer Palladius said, 'If apples are inclined to fall before their time, a stone placed in a split root will retain them.' Some such notion, still surviving, may account for some of the stones which we see placed, to be overgrown, in the forks of trees. They have a saying, in Suffolk, England,—

> 'At Michaelmas time, or a little before,
> Half an apple goes to the core.'

Early apples begin to be ripe about the first of August; but I think that none of them are so good to eat as some to smell. One is worth more to scent your handkerchief with than any perfume which they sell in the shops. The fragrance of some fruits is not to be forgotten, along with that of flowers. Some gnarly apple which I pick up in the road reminds me by its fragrance of all the wealth of Pomona—carrying me forward to those days when they will be collected in golden and ruddy heaps in the orchards and about the cider-mills.

A week or two later, as you are going by orchards or gardens, especially in the evenings, you pass through a little region possessed by the fragrance of ripe apples and thus enjoy them without price, and without robbing anybody.

There is thus about all natural products a certain volatile and ethereal quality which represents their highest value, and which cannot be vulgarized, or bought and sold. No mortal has ever enjoyed the perfect flavor of any fruit, and only the godlike among men begin to taste its ambrosial qualities. For nectar and ambrosia are only those fine flavors of every earthly fruit which our coarse palates fail to perceive—just as we occupy the heaven of the gods without knowing it. When I see a particularly mean man carrying a load of fair and fragrant early apples to market, I seem to see a contest going on between him and his horse, on the one side, and the apples on the other, and, to my mind, the apples always gain it. Pliny says that apples are the heaviest of all things, and that the oxen begin to sweat at the mere sight of a load of them. Our driver begins to lose his load the moment he tries to transport them to where they do not belong, that is, to any but the most beautiful. Though he gets out from time to time, and feels of them, and thinks they are all there, I see the stream of their evanescent and celestial qualities going to heaven from his cart, while the pulp and skin and core only are going to market. They are not apples, but pomace. Are not these still Iduna's apples, the taste of which keeps the gods forever young? and think you that they will let Loki or Thjassi carry them off to Jotunheim, while they grow wrinkled and gray? No, for Ragnarok, or the destruction of the gods, is not yet.

There is another thinning of the fruit, commonly near the end of August or in September, when the ground is strewn with windfalls; and this happens especially when high winds occur after rain. In some orchards you may see fully three quarters of the whole crop on the ground, lying in a circular form beneath the trees, yet hard and green, or if it is a hillside, rolled far down the hill. However, it is an ill wind that blows nobody any good. All the country over, people are busy picking up the windfalls, and this will make them cheap for early apple pies.

In October, the leaves falling, the apples are more distinct on the trees. I saw one year in a neighboring town some trees fuller of fruit than I remember to have ever seen before, small yellow apples hanging over the road. The branches were gracefully drooping with their weight, like a barberry bush, so that the whole tree acquired a new character. Even the topmost branches, instead of standing erect, spread and drooped in all directions; and there were so many poles supporting the lower ones that they looked like pictures of banyan trees. As an old English manuscript says, 'The mo appelen the tree bereth the more sche boweth to the folk.'

Surely the apple is the noblest of fruits. Let the most beautiful or the swiftest have it. That should be the 'going' price of apples.

Between the 5th and 20th of October I see the barrels lie under the trees. And perhaps I talk with one who is selecting some choice barrels to fulfill an order. He turns a specked one over many times before he leaves it out. If I were to tell what is passing in my mind, I should say that every one was specked which he had handled; for he rubs off all the bloom and those fugacious ethereal qualities leave it. Cool evenings prompt the farmers to make haste, and at length I see only the ladders here and there left leaning against the trees.

It would be well, if we accepted these gifts with more joy and gratitude, and did not think it enough simply to put a fresh load of compost about the tree. Some old English customs are suggestive at least. I find them described chiefly in Brand's *Popular Antiquities*. It appears that 'on Christmas Eve the farmers and their men in Devonshire take a large bowl of cider, with a toast in it, and carrying it in state to the orchard, they salute the apple-trees with much ceremony, in order to make them bear well the next season.' This salutation consists in 'throwing some of the cider about the roots of the tree, placing bits of the toast on the branches,' and then, 'encircling one of the best bearing trees in the orchard, they drink the following toast three several times:

> 'Here's to thee, old apple tree,
> Whence thou mayst bud, and whence thou mayst blow,
> And whence thou mayst bear apples enow!
> Hat-full! caps-full!
> Bushel, bushel, sacks-full!
> And my pockets full, too! Hurra!'

Also what was called 'apple-howling' used to be practiced in various counties of England on New Year's Eve. A troop of boys visited the different orchards, and, encircling the apple trees, repeated the following words:

> 'Stand fast, root! Bear well, top!
> Pray God send us a good howling crop!
> Every twig, apples big!
> Every bough, apples enow!'

'They then shout in chorus, one of the boys accompanying them on a cow's horn. During this ceremony they rap the trees with their sticks.' This is called 'wassailing' the trees, and is thought by some to be 'a relic of the heathen sacrifice to Pomona.'

Herrick sings—

> 'Wassaile the trees that they may beare
> You many a plum and many a peare;
> For more or less fruits they will bring
> As you so give them wassailing.'

Our poets have as yet a better right to sing of cider than of wine; but it behooves them to sing better than English Phillips did, else they will do no credit to their Muse.

THE WILD APPLE

SO MUCH for the more civilized apple trees (*urbaniores*, as Pliny calls them). I love better to go through the old orchards of ungrafted apple trees, at what ever season of the year—so irregularly planted: sometimes two trees standing close together; and the rows so devious that you would think that they not only had grown while the owner was sleeping, but had been set out by him in a somnambulic state. The rows of grafted fruit will never tempt me to wander amid them like these. But I now, alas, speak rather from memory than from any recent experience, such ravages have been made!

Some soils, like a rocky tract called the Easterbrooks Country in my neighborhood, are so suited to the apple, that it will grow faster in them without any care, or if only the ground is broken up once a year, than it will in many places with any amount of care. The owners of this tract allow that the soil is excellent for fruit, but they say that it is so rocky that they have not patience to plough it, and that, together with the distance, is the reason why it is not cultivated. There are, or were recently, extensive orchards there standing without order. Nay, they spring up wild and bear well there in the midst of pines, birches, maples, and oaks. I am often surprised to see rising amid these trees the rounded tops of apple trees glowing with red or yellow fruit, in harmony with the autumnal tints of the forest.

Going up the side of a cliff about the first of November, I saw a vigorous young apple tree, which, planted by birds or cows, had shot up amid the rocks and open woods there, and had now much fruit on it, uninjured by the frosts, when all cultivated apples were gathered. It was a rank, wild growth, with many green leaves on it still, and made an impression of thorniness. The fruit was hard and green, but looked as if it would be palatable in the winter. Some was dangling on the twigs, but more half buried in the wet leaves under the tree, or rolled far down the hill amid the rocks. The owner knows nothing of it. The day was not observed when it first blossomed, nor when it first bore fruit, unless by the chickadee. There was no dancing on the green beneath it in its honor, and now there is no hand to pluck its fruit—which is only gnawed by squirrels, as I perceive. It has done double duty—not only borne this crop, but each twig has grown a foot into the air. And this is *such* fruit! bigger than many berries, we must admit, and carried home will be sound and palatable next spring. What care I for Iduna's apples so long as I can get these?

When I go by this shrub thus late and hardy, and see its dangling fruit, I respect the tree and I am grateful for Nature's bounty, even though I cannot eat it. Here on this rugged and woody hillside has grown an apple tree, not planted by man, no relic of a former orchard, but a natural growth, like the pines and oaks. Most fruits which we prize and use depend entirely on our care. Corn and grain, potatoes, peaches, melons, etc., depend altogether on our planting; but the apple emulates man's independence and enterprise. It is not simply carried, as I have said, but, like him, to some extent, it has migrated to this New World, and is even, here and there, making its way amid the aboriginal trees; just as the ox and dog and horse sometimes run wild and maintain themselves.

Even the sourest and crabbedest apple, growing in the most unfavorable position, suggests such thoughts as these, it is so noble a fruit.

THE CRAB

NEVERTHELESS, *our* wild apple is wild only like myself, perchance, who belong not to the aboriginal race here, but have strayed into the woods from the cultivated stock. Wilder still, as I have said, there grows elsewhere in this country a native and aboriginal crab-apple, *Malus coronaria,* 'whose nature has not yet been modified by cultivation.' It is found from western New York to Minnesota, and southward. Michaux says that its ordinary height "is fifteen or eighteen feet, but it is sometimes found twenty-five or thirty feet high,' and that the large ones, 'exactly resemble the common apple tree.' 'The flowers are white mingled with rose color, and are collected in corymbs.' They are remarkable for their delicious odor. The fruit, according to him, is about an inch and a half in diameter, and is intensely acid. Yet they make fine sweetmeats and also cider of them. He concludes that 'if, on being cultivated, it does not yield new and palatable varieties, it will at least be celebrated for the beauty of its flowers, and for the sweetness of its perfume.'

I never saw the crab-apple till May, 1861. I had heard of it through Michaux, but more modern botanists, so far as I know, have not treated it as of peculiar importance. Thus it was a half-fabulous tree to me. I contemplated a pilgrimage to the 'Glades,' a portion of Pennsylvania where it was said to grow to perfection. I thought of sending to a nursery for it, but doubted if they had it, or would distinguish it from European varieties. At last I had occasion to go to Minnesota, and on entering Michigan I began to notice from the cars a tree with handsome rose-colored flowers. At first I thought it some variety of thorn; but it was not long before the truth flashed on me, that this was my long-sought crab-apple. It was the prevailing flowering shrub or tree to be seen from the cars at that season of the year—about the middle of May. But the cars never stopped before one, and so I was launched on the bosom of the Mississippi without having touched one, experiencing the fate of Tantalus. On arriving at St. Anthony's Falls, I was sorry to be told that I was too far north for the crab-apple. Nevertheless I succeeded in finding it about eight miles west of the Falls; touched it and smelled it, and secured a lingering corymb of flowers for my herbarium. This must have been near its northern limit.

HOW THE WILD APPLE GROWS

BUT THOUGH these are indigenous, like the Indians, I doubt whether they are any hardier than those backwoodsmen among the apple trees, which, though descended from cultivated stocks, plant themselves in distant fields and forests, where the soil is favorable to them. I know of no trees which have more difficulties to contend with, and which more sturdily resist their foes. These are the ones whose story we have to tell. It oftentimes reads thus:

Near the beginning of May, we notice little thickets of apple trees just springing up in the pastures where cattle have been—as the rocky ones of our Easterbrooks Country, or the top of Nobscot Hill, in Sudbury. One or two of these, perhaps, survive the drought and other accidents—

their very birthplace defending them against the encroaching grass and some other dangers, at first.

In two years' time 't had thus
  Reached the level of the rocks,
Admired the stretching world,
  Nor feared the wandering flocks.

But at this tender age
  Its sufferings began:
There came a browsing ox
  And cut it down a span.

This time, perhaps, the ox does not notice it amid the grass; but the next year, when it has grown more stout, he recognizes it for a fellow-emigrant from the old country, the flavor of whose leaves and twigs he well knows; and though at first he pauses to welcome it, and express his surprise, and gets for answer, 'The same cause that brought you here brought me,' he nevertheless browses it again, reflecting, it may be, that he has some title to it.

Thus cut down annually, it does not despair; but, putting forth two short twigs for every one cut off, it spreads out low along the ground in the hollows or between the rocks, growing more stout and scrubby, until it forms, not a tree as yet, but a little pyramidal, stiff, twiggy mass, almost as solid and impenetrable as a rock. Some of the densest and most impenetrable clumps of bushes that I have ever seen, as well on account of the closeness and stubbornness of their branches as of their thorns, have been these wild apple scrubs. They are more like the scrubby fir and black spruce on which you stand, and sometimes walk, on the tops of mountains, where cold is the demon they contend with, than anything else. No wonder they are prompted to grow thorns at last, to defend themselves against such foes. In their thorniness, however, there is no malice, only some malic acid.

The rocky pastures of the tract I have referred to—for they maintain their ground best in a rocky field—are thickly sprinkled with these little tufts, reminding you often of some rigid gray mosses or lichens, and you see thousands of little trees just springing up between them, with the seed still attached to them.

Being regularly clipped all around each year by the cows, as a hedge with shears, they are often of a perfect conical or pyramidal form, from one to four feet high, and more or less sharp, as if trimmed by the gardener's art. In the pastures on Nobscot Hill and its spurs, they make fine dark shadows when the sun is low. They are also an excellent covert from hawks for many small birds that roost and build in them. Whole flocks perch in them at night, and I have seen three robins' nests in one which was six feet in diameter.

No doubt many of these are already old trees, if you reckon from the day they were planted, but infants still when you consider their development and the long life before them. I counted the annual rings of some which were just one foot high, and as wide as high, and found that they were about twelve years old, but quite sound and thrifty! They were so low that they were unnoticed by the walker, while many of their contemporaries from the nurseries were already bearing considerable crops. But what you gain in time is perhaps in this case, too, lost in power—that is, in the vigor of the tree. This is their pyramidal state.

The cows continue to browse them thus for twenty years or more, keeping them down and compelling them to spread, until at last they are so broad that they become their own fence, when some interior shoot, which their foes cannot reach, darts upward with joy: for it has not forgotten its high calling, and bears its own peculiar fruit in triumph.

Such are the tactics by which it finally defeats its bovine foes. Now, if you have watched the progress of a particular shrub, you will see that it is no longer a simple pyramid or cone, but that out of its apex there rises a sprig or two, growing more lustily perchance than an orchard-tree, since the plant now devotes the whole of its repressed energy to these upright parts. In a short time these become a small tree, an inverted pyramid resting on the apex of the other, so that the whole has now the form of a vast hour-glass. The spreading bottom, having served its purpose, finally disappears, and the generous tree permits the now harmless cows to come in and stand in its shade, and rub against and redden its trunk, which has grown in spite of them, and even to taste a part of its fruit, and so disperse the seed.

Thus the cows create their own shade and food; and the tree, its hour-glass being inverted, lives a second life, as it were.

It is an important question with some nowadays, whether you should trim young apple trees as high as your nose or as high as your eyes. The ox trims them up as high as he can reach, and that is about the right height, I think.

In spite of wandering kine, and other adverse circumstances, that despised shrub, valued only by small birds as a covert and shelter from hawks, has its blossom week at last, and in course of time its harvest, sincere, though small.

By the end of some October, when its leaves have fallen, I frequently see such a central sprig, whose progress I have watched, when I thought it had forgotten its destiny, as I had, bearing its first crop of small green or yellow or rosy fruit, which the cows cannot get at over the bushy and thorny hedge which surrounds it, and I make haste to taste the new and undescribed variety. We have all heard of the numerous varieties of fruit invented by Van Mons and Knight. This is the system of Van Cow, and she has invented far more and more memorable varieties than both of them.

Through what hardships it may attain to bear a sweet fruit! Though somewhat small, it may prove equal, if not superior, in flavor to that which has grown in a garden—will perchance be all the sweeter and more palatable for the very difficulties it has had to contend with. Who knows but this chance wild fruit, planted by a cow or a bird on some remote and rocky hillside, where it is as yet unobserved by man, may be the choicest of all its kind, and foreign potentates shall hear of it, and royal societies seek to propagate it, though the virtues of the perhaps truly crabbed owner of the soil may never be heard of—at least, beyond the limits of his village? It was thus the Porter and the Baldwin grew.

Every wild apple shrub excites our expectation thus, somewhat as every wild child. It is, perhaps, a prince in disguise. What a lesson to man! So are human beings, referred to the highest standard, the celestial fruit which they suggest and aspire to bear, browsed on by fate; and only the most persistent and strongest genius defends itself and prevails, sends a tender scion upward at last, and drops its perfect fruit on the ungrateful earth. Poets and philosophers and statesmen thus spring up in the country pastures, and outlast the hosts of unoriginal men.

Such is always the pursuit of knowledge. The celestial fruits, the golden apples of the Hesperides, are ever guarded by a hundred-headed dragon which never sleeps, so that it is an Herculean labor to pluck them.

This is one, and the most remarkable way in which the wild apple is propagated; but commonly it springs up at wide intervals in woods and swamp, and by the sides of roads, as the soil may suit it, and grows with comparative rapidity. Those which grow in dense woods are very tall and slender. I frequently pluck from these trees a perfectly mild and tamed fruit. As Palladius says, '*Et injussu consternitur ubere mali.* And the ground is strewn with the fruit of an unbidden apple tree.

It is an old notion that, if these wild trees do not bear a valuable fruit of their own, they are the best stocks by which to transmit to posterity the most highly prized qualities of others. However, I am not in search of stocks, but the wild fruit itself, whose fierce gust has suffered no 'inteneration.' It is not my

> 'highest plot
> To plant the Bergamot.'

THE FRUIT, AND ITS FLAVOR

THE TIME for wild apples is the last of October and the first of November. They then get to be palatable, for they ripen late, and they are still perhaps as beautiful as ever. I make a great account of these fruits, which the farmers do not think it worth the while to gather—wild flavors of the Muse, vivacious and inspiriting. The farmer thinks that he has better in his barrels, but he is mistaken, unless he has a walker's appetite and imagination, neither of which can he have.

Such as grow quite wild, and are left out till the first of November, I presume that the owner does not mean to gather. They belong to children as wild as themselves—to certain active boys that I know—to the wild-eyed woman of the fields, to whom nothing comes amiss, who gleans after all the world, and, moreover, to us walkers. We have met with them, and they are ours. These rights, long enough insisted upon, have come to be an institution in some old countries, where they have learned how to live. I hear that 'the custom of grippling, which may be called apple-gleaning, is, or was formerly, practised in Herefordshire. It consists in leaving a few apples, which are called the gripples, on every tree, after the general gathering, for the boys, who go with climbing-poles and bags to collect them.'

As for those I speak of, I pluck them as a wild fruit, native to this quarter of the earth—fruit of old trees that have been dying ever since I was a boy and are not yet dead, frequented only by the woodpecker and the squirrel, deserted now by the owner, who has not faith enough to look under their boughs. From the appearance of the tree-top, at a little distance, you would expect nothing but lichens to drop from it, but your faith is rewarded by finding the grown strewn with spirited fruit—some of it, perhaps, collected at squirrel-holes, with the marks of their teeth by which they carried them—some containing a cricket or two silently feeding within, and some, especially in damp days, a shell-less snail. The very sticks and stones lodged in the tree-top might have convinced you of the savoriness of the fruit which has been so eagerly sought after in past years.

I have seen no account of these among the 'Fruits and Fruit-Trees of America,' though they are more memorable to my taste than the grafted kinds; more racy and wild American flavors do they possess when October and November, when December and January, and perhaps February and March even, have assuaged them somewhat. An old farmer in my neighborhood, who always selects the right word, says that 'they have a kind of bow-arrow tang.'

Apples for grafting appear to have been selected commonly, not so much for their spirited flavor, as for their mildness, their size, and bearing qualities—not so much for their beauty, as for their fairness and soundness. Indeed, I have no faith in the selected lists of pomological gentlemen. Their 'Favorites' and 'Nonesuches' and 'Seek-no-farthers,' when I have fruited them, commonly turn out very tame and forgettable. They are eaten with comparatively little zest, and have no real *tang* nor *smack* to them.

What if some of these wildings are acrid and puckery, genuine *verjuice,* do they not still belong to the *Pomaceae,* which are uniformly innocent and kind to our race? I still begrudge them to the cider-mill. Perhaps they are not fairly ripe yet.

No wonder that these small and high-colored apples are thought to make the best cider. Loudon quotes from the *Herefordshire Report,* that 'apples of a small size are always, if equal in quality, to be preferred to those of a larger size, in order that the rind and kernel may bear the greatest porportion to the pulp, which affords the weakest and most watery juice.' And he says that, 'to prove this, Dr. Symonds, of Hereford, about the year 1800, made one hogshead of cider entirely from the rinds and cores of apples, and another from the pulp only, when the first was found of extraordinary strength and flavor, while the latter was sweet and insipid.'

Evelyn says that the 'Red-strake' was the favorite cider-apple in his day; and he quotes one Dr. Newburg as saying, 'In Jersey 'tis a general observation, as I hear, that the more of red any apple has in its rind, the more proper it is for this use. Pale-faced apples they exclude as much as may be from their cider-vat.' This opinion still prevails.

All apples are good in November. Those which the farmer leaves out as unsalable and unpalatable to those who frequent the markets are choicest fruit to the walker. But it is remarkable that the wild apple, which I praise as so spirited and racy when eaten in the fields or woods, being brought into the house has frequently a harsh and crabbed taste. The Saunterer's Apple not even the saunterer can eat in the house. The palate rejects it there, as it does haws and acorns, and demands a tamed one; for there you miss the November air, which is the sauce it is to be eaten with. Accordingly, when Tityrus, seeing the lengthening shadows, invites Meliboeus to go home and pass the night with him, he promises him *mild* apples and soft chestnuts—*Mitia poma, castaneae molles.* I frequently pluck wild apples of so rich and spicy a flavor that I wonder all orchardists do not get a scion from that tree, and I fail not to bring home my pockets full. But perchance, when I take one out of my desk and taste it in my chamber, I find it unexpectedly crude—sour enough to set a squirrel's teeth on edge and make a jay scream.

These apples have hung in the wind and frost and rain till they have absorbed the qualities of the weather or season, and thus are highly *seasoned,* and they *pierce* and *sting* and *permeate* us with their spirit. They must be eaten in *season,* accordingly—that is, out-of-doors.

To appreciate the wild and sharp flavors of these October fruits, it is necessary that you be breathing the sharp October or November air. The outdoor air and exercise which the walker gets give a different tone to his palate, and he craves a fruit which the sedentary would call harsh and crabbed. They must be eaten in the fields, when your system is all aglow with exercise, when the frosty weather nips your fingers, the wind rattles the bare boughs or rustles the few remaining leaves, and the jay is heard screaming around. What is sour in the house a bracing walk makes sweet. Some of these apples might be labelled, 'To be eaten in the wind.'

Of course no flavors are thrown away; they are intended for the taste that is up to them. Some apples have two distinct flavors, and perhaps one half of them must be eaten in the house, the other outdoors. One Peter Whitney wrote from Northborough in 1782, for the Proceedings of the Boston Academy, describing an apple tree in that town 'producing fruit of opposite qualities, part of the same apple being frequently sour and the other sweet;' also, some all sour, and others all sweet, and this diversity on all parts of the tree.

There is a wild apple on Nawshawtuct Hill in my town which has to me a peculiarly pleasant bitter tang, not perceived till it is three-quarters tasted. It remains on the tongue. As you eat it, it smells exactly like a squash-bug. It is a sort of triumph to eat and relish it.

I hear that the fruit of a kind of plum tree in Provence is 'called *Prunes sibarelles,* because it is impossible to whistle after having eaten them, from their sourness.' But perhaps they were only eaten in the house and in summer, and if tried out-of-doors in a stinging atmosphere, who knows but you could whistle an octave higher and clearer?

In the fields only are the sours and bitters of

Nature appreciated; just as the woodchopper eats his meal in a sunny glade, in the middle of a winter day, with content, basks in a sunny ray there, and dreams of summer in a degree of cold which, experienced in a chamber, would make a student miserable. They who are at work abroad are not cold, but rather it is they who sit shivering in houses. As with temperatures, so with flavors; as with cold and heat, so with sour and sweet. This natural raciness, the sours and bitters which the diseased palate refuses, are the true condiments.

Let your condiments be in the condition of your senses. To appreciate the flavor of these wild apples requires vigorous and healthy senses, *papillae* firm and erect on the tongue and palate, not easily flattened and tamed.

From my experience with wild apples, I can understand that there may be reasons for a savage's preferring many kinds of food which the civilized man rejects. The former has the palate of an outdoor man. It takes a savage or wild taste to appreciate a wild fruit.

What a healthy out-of-door appetite it takes to relish the apple of life, the apple of the world, then!

> 'Nor is it every apple I desire,
> Nor that which pleases every palate best;
> 'Tis not the lasting Deuxan I require,
> Nor yet the red-cheeked Greening I request,
> Nor that which first beshrewed the name of wife,
> Nor that whose beauty caused the golden strife:
> No, no! bring me an apple from the tree of life.'

So there is one *thought* for the field, another for the house. I would have my thoughts, like wild apples, to be food for walkers, and will not warrant them to be palatable if tasted in the house.

THEIR BEAUTY

ALMOST all wild apples are handsome. They cannot be too gnarly and crabbed and rusty to look at. The gnarliest will have some redeeming traits even to the eye. You will discover some evening redness dashed or sprinkled on some protuberance or in some cavity. It is rare that the summer lets an apple go without streaking or spotting it on some part of its sphere. It will have some red stains, commemorating the mornings and evenings it has witnessed; some dark and rusty blotches, in memory of the clouds and foggy, mildewy days that have passed over it; and a spacious field of green reflecting the general face of nature—green even as the fields; or a yellow ground, which implies a milder flavor—yellow as the harvest, or russet as the hills.

Apples, these I mean, unspeakably fair—apples not of Discord, but of Concord! Yet not so rare but that the homeliest may have a share. Painted by the frosts, some a uniform clear bright yellow, or red, or crimson, as if their spheres had regularly revolved, and enjoyed the influence of the sun on all sides alike—some with the faintest pink blush imaginable—some brindled with deep red streaks like a cow, or with hundreds of fine blood-red rays running regularly from the stem-dimple to the blossom end, like meridional lines, on a straw-colored ground—some touched with a greenish rust, like a fine lichen, here and there, with crimson blotches or eyes more or less confluent and fiery when wet—and others gnarly, and freckled or peppered all over on the stem side with fine crimson spots on a white ground, as if accidentally sprinkled from the brush of Him who paints the autumn leaves. Others, again, are sometimes red inside, perfused with a beautiful blush, fairy food, too beautiful to eat—apple of the Hesperides, apple of the evening sky! But like shells and pebbles on the seashore, they must be seen as they sparkle amid the withering leaves in some dell in the woods, in the autumnal air, or as they lie in the wet grass, and not when they have wilted and faded in the house.

THE NAMING OF THEM

IT WOULD be a pleasant pastime to find suitable names for the hundred varieties which go to a single heap at the cider-mill. Would it not tax a man's invention—no one to be named after a man, and all in the *lingua vernacula?* Who shall stand godfather at the christening of the wild apples? It would exhaust the Latin and Greek languages, if they were used, and make the *lingua vernacula* flag. We should have to call in the sunrise and the sunset, the rainbow and the autumn woods and the wild-flowers, and the woodpecker and the purple finch and the squirrel and the jay and the butterfly, the November traveller and the truant boy, to our aid.

In 1836 there were in the garden of the London Horticultural Society more than fourteen hundred distinct sorts. But here are species which they have not in their catalogue, not to mention the varieties which our crab might yield to cultivation.

Let us enumerate a few of these. I find myself compelled, after all, to give the Latin names of some for the benefit of those who live where English is not spoken—for they are likely to have a world-wide reputation.

There is, first of all, the Wood Apple (*Malus sylvatica*); the Blue-Jay Apple; the Apple which grows in Dells in the Woods (*sylvestrivallis*), also in Hollows in Pastures (*campestrivallis*); the Apple that grows in an old Cellar-Hole (*Malus cellaris*); the Meadow Apple; the Partridge Apple;

the Truant's Apple (*cessatoris*), which no boy will ever go by without knocking off some, however *late* it may be; the Saunterer's Apple—you must lose yourself before you can find the way to that; the Beauty of the Air; (*decus aeris*); December-Eating; the Frozen-Thawed (*gelato-soluta*), good only in that state; the Concord Apple, possibly the same with the *Musketaquidensis;* the Assabet Apple; the Brindled Apple; Wine of New England; the Chickaree Apple; the Green Apple (*Malus viridis*)—this has many synonyms: in an imperfect state, it is the *choleramorbifera aut dysenterifera, puerulis dilectissima;* the Apple which Atalanta stopped to pick up; the Hedge Apple (*Malus sepium*); the Slug Apple (*limacea*); the Railroad Apple, which perhaps came from a core thrown out of the cars; the Apple whose Fruit we tasted in our Youth; our Particular Apple not to be found in any catalogue; *pedestrium solatium;* also the Apple where hangs the forgotten Scythe; Iduna's Apples, and the Apples which Loki found in the Wood; and a great many more I have on my list, too numerous to mention—all of them good. As Bodaeus exclaims, referring to the cultivated kinds, and adapting Virgil to his case, so I, adapting Bodaeus,

'Not if I had a hundred tongues, a hundred mouths,
An iron voice, could I describe all the forms
And reckon up all the names of these *wild apples.*'

THE LAST GLEANING

BY THE middle of November the wild apples have lost some of their brilliancy, and have chiefly fallen. A great part are decayed on the ground, and the sound ones are more palatable than before. The note of the chickadee sounds now more distinct, as you wander amid the old trees, and the autumnal dandelion is half closed and tearful. But still, if you are a skillful gleaner, you may get many a pocketful even of grafted fruit, long after apples are supposed to be gone out-of-doors. I know a Blue Pearmain tree, growing within the edge of a swamp, almost as good as wild. You would not suppose that there was any fruit left there, on the first survey, but you must look according to system. Those which lie exposed are quite brown and rotten now, or perchance a few still show one blooming cheek here and there amid the wet leaves. Nevertheless, with experienced eyes, I explore amid the bare alders and the huckleberry bushes and the withered sedge, and in the crevices of the rocks, which are full of leaves, and pry under the fallen and decaying ferns, which, with apple and alder leaves, thickly strew the ground. For I know that they lie concealed, fallen into hollows long since and covered up by the leaves of the tree itself—a proper kind of packing. From these lurking-places, anywhere within the circumference of the tree, I draw forth the fruit, all wet and glossy, maybe nibbled by rabbits and hollowed out by crickets, and perhaps with a leaf or two cemented to it (as Curzon an old manuscript from a monastery's mouldy cellar), but still with a rich bloom on it, and at least as ripe and well-kept, if not better than those in barrels, more crisp and lively than they. If these resources fail to yield anything, I have learned to look between the bases of the suckers which spring thickly from some horizontal limb, for now and then one lodges there, or in the very midst of an alder-clump, where they are covered by leaves, safe from cows which may have smelled them out. If I am sharp-set, for I do not refuse the Blue Pearmain, I fill my pockets on each side; and as I retrace my steps in the frosty eve, being perhaps four or five miles from home, I eat one first from this side, and then from that, to keep my balance.

I learn from Topsell's Gesner, whose authority appears to be Albertus, that the following is the way in which the hedgehog collects and carries home his apples. He says—'His meat is apples, worms, or grapes: when he findeth apples or grapes on the earth, he rolleth himself upon them, until he have filled all his prickles, and then he carrieth them home to his den, never bearing above one in his mouth; and if it fortune that one of them fall off by the way, he likewise shaketh off all the residue, and wallowth upon them afresh, until they be all settled upon his back again. So, forth he goeth, making a noise like a cart-wheel; and if he have any young ones in his nest, they pull off his load wherewithal he is loaded, eating thereof what they please, and laying up the residue for the time to come.'

THE 'FROZEN-THAWED APPLE'

TOWARD the end of November, though some of the sound ones are yet more mellow and perhaps more edible, they have generally, like the leaves, lost their beauty, and are beginning to freeze. It is finger-cold, and prudent farmers get in their barrelled apples, and bring you the apples and cider which they have engaged; for it is time to put them into the cellar. Perhaps a few on the ground show their red cheeks above the early snow, and occasionally some even preserve their color and soundness under the snow throughout the winter. But generally at the beginning of the winter they freeze hard, and soon, though undecayed, acquire the color of a baked apple.

Before the end of December, generally, they

experience their first thawing. Those which a month ago were sour, crabbed, and quite unpalatable to the civilized taste, such at least as were frozen while sound, let a warmer sun come to thaw them—for they are extremely sensitive to its rays —are found to be filled with a rich, sweet cider, better than any bottled cider that I know of, and with which I am better acquainted than with wine. All apples are good in this state, and your jaws are the cider-press. Others, which have more substance, are a sweet and luscious food—in my opinion of more worth than the pineapples which are imported from the West Indies. Those which lately even I tasted only to repent of it—for I am semicivilized—which the farmer willingly left on the tree, I am now glad to find have the property of hanging on like the leaves of the young oaks. It is a way to keep cider sweet without boiling. Let the frost come to freeze them first, solid as stones, and then the rain or a warm winter day to thaw them, and they will seem to have borrowed a flavor from heaven through the medium of the air in which they hang. Or perchance you find, when you get home, that those which rattled in your pocket have thawed, and the ice is turned to cider. But after the third or fourth freezing and thawing they will not be found so good.

What are the imported half-ripe fruits of the torrid south, to this fruit matured by the cold of the frigid north? There are those crabbed apples with which I cheated my companion, and kept a smooth face that I might tempt him to eat. Now we both greedily fill our pockets with them—bending to drink the cup and save our lappets from the overflowing juice—and grow more social with their wine. Was there one that hung so high and sheltered by the tangled branches that our sticks could not dislodge it?

It is a fruit never carried to market, that I am aware of—quite distinct from the apple of the markets, as from dried apple and cider—and it is not every winter that produces it in perfection.

The era of the Wild Apple will soon be past. It is a fruit which will probably become extinct in New England. You may still wander through old orchards of native fruit of great extent, which for the most part went to the cider-mill, now all gone to decay. I have heard of an orchard in a distant town, on the side of a hill, where the apples rolled down and lay four feet deep against a wall on the lower side, and this the owner cut down for fear they should be made into cider. Since the temperance reform and the general introduction of grafted fruit, no native apple trees, such as I see everywhere on deserted pastures, and where the woods have grown up around them, are set out. I fear that he who walks over these fields a century hence will not know the pleasure of knocking off wild apples. Ah, poor man, there are many pleasures which he will not know! Notwithstanding the prevalence of the Baldwin and the Porter, I doubt if so extensive orchards are set out today in my town as there were a century ago, when those vast straggling cider-orchards were planted, when men both ate and drank apples, when the pomace-heap was the only nursery, and trees cost nothing but the trouble of setting them out. Men could afford then to stick a tree by every wall-side and let it take its chance. I see nobody planting trees today in such out of the way places, along the lonely roads and lanes, and at the bottom of dells in the wood. Now that they have grafted trees, and pay a price for them, they collect them into a plat by their houses, and fence them in—and the end of it all will be that we shall be compelled to look for our apples in a barrel.

THIS is 'The word of the Lord that came to Joel the son of Pethuel.

'Hear this, ye old men, and give ear, all ye inhabitants of the land! Hath this been in your days, or even in the days of your fathers? . . .

'That which the palmerworm hath left hath the locust eaten; and that which the locust hath left hath the cankerworm eaten; and that which the cankerworm hath left hath the caterpillar eaten.

'Awake, ye drunkards, and weep; and howl, all ye drinkers of wine, because of the new wine; for it is cut off from your mouth.

'For a nation is come upon my land, strong, and without number, whose teeth are the teeth of a lion, and he hath the cheek teeth of a great lion.

'He hath laid my vine waste, and barked my fig tree: he hath made it clean bare, and cast it away; the branches thereof are made white . . .

'Be ye ashamed, O ye husbandmen; howl, O ye vinedressers . . .

'The vine is dried up, and the fig tree languisheth; the pomegranate tree, the palm tree also, and the apple tree, even all the trees of the field, are withered: because joy is withered away from the sons of men.'

LIFE WITHOUT PRINCIPLE

◇

⁋ THIS was published posthumously in the *Atlantic Monthly* in 1863.

◇

AT A LYCEUM, not long since, I felt that the lecturer had chosen a theme too foreign to himself, and so failed to interest me as much as he might have done. He described things not in or near to his heart, but toward his extremities and superficies. There was, in this sense, no truly central or centralizing thought in the lecture. I would have had him deal with privatest experience, as the poet does. The greatest compliment that was ever paid me was when one asked me what *I thought,* and attended to my answer. I am surprised, as well as delighted, when this happens, it is such a rare use he would make of me, as if he were acquainted with the tool. Commonly, if men want anything of me, it is only to know how many acres I make of their land—since I am a surveyor—or, at most, what trivial news I have burdened myself with. They never will go to law for my meat; they prefer the shell. A man once came a considerable distance to ask me to lecture on Slavery; but on conversing with him, I found that he and his clique expected seven eighths of the lecture to be theirs, and only one eighth mine; so I declined. I take it for granted, when I am invited to lecture anywhere—for I have had a little experience in that business—that there is a desire to hear what *I think* on some subject, though I may be the greatest fool in the country, and not that I should say pleasant things merely, or such as the audience will assent to; and I resolve, accordingly, that I will give them a strong dose of myself. They have sent for me, and engaged to pay for me, and I am determined that they shall have me, though I bore them beyond all precedent.

So now I would say something similar to you, my readers. Since *you* are my readers, and I have not been much of a traveler, I will not talk about people a thousand miles off, but come as near home as I can. As the time is short, I will leave out all the flattery, and retain all the criticism.

Let us consider the way in which we spend our lives.

This world is a place of business. What an infinite bustle! I am awaked almost every night by the panting of the locomotive. It interrupts my dreams. There is no sabbath. It would be glorious to see mankind at leisure for once. It is nothing but work, work, work. I cannot easily buy a blank-book to write thoughts in; they are commonly ruled for dollars and cents. An Irishman, seeing me making a minute in the fields, took it for granted that I was calculating my wages. If a man was tossed out of a window when an infant, and so made a cripple for life, or scared out of his wits by the Indians, it is regretted chiefly because he was thus incapacitated for—business! I think that there is nothing, not even crime, more opposed to poetry, to philosophy, ay, to life itself, than this incessant business.

There is a coarse and boisterous money-making fellow in the outskirts of our town, who is going to build a bank-wall under the hill along the edge of his meadow. The powers have put this into his head to keep him out of mischief, and he wishes me to spend three weeks digging there with him. The result will be that he will perhaps get some more money to hoard, and leave for his heirs to spend foolishly. If I do this, most will commend me as an industrious and hard-working man; but if I choose to devote myself to certain labors which yield more real profit, though but little money, they may be inclined to look on me as an idler. Nevertheless, as I do not need the police of meaningless labor to regulate me, and do not see anything absolutely praiseworthy in this fellow's undertaking any more than in many an enterprise of our own or foreign governments, however amusing it may be to him or them, I prefer to finish my education at a different school.

If a man walk in the woods for love of them half of each day, he is in danger of being regarded as a loafer; but if he spends his whole day as a speculator, shearing off those woods and making earth bald before her time, he is esteemed an industrious and enterprising citizen. As if a town had no interest in its forests but to cut them down!

Most men would feel insulted if it were proposed to employ them in throwing stones over a wall, and then in throwing them back, merely that they might earn their wages. But many are no more worthily employed now. For instance: just after sunrise, one summer morning, I noticed one of my neighbors walking beside his team, which was slowly drawing a heavy hewn stone swung under the axle, surrounded by an atmosphere of industry—his day's work begun, his brow commenced to sweat—a reproach to all sluggards and idlers—pausing abreast the shoulders of his oxen, and half turning round with a flourish of his merciful whip, while they gained their length on him. And I thought, Such is the labor which the American Congress exists to protect—honest, manly toil—honest as the day is long—that makes his bread taste sweet, and keeps society sweet—which all men respect and have consecrated; one of the sacred band, doing the needful but irksome drudgery. Indeed, I felt a slight reproach, because I observed this from a window, and was not abroad and stirring about a similar business. The day went by, and at evening I passed the yard of another neighbor, who keeps many servants, and spends much money foolishly, while he adds nothing to the common stock, and there I saw the stone of the morning lying beside a whimsical structure intended to adorn this Lord Timothy Dexter's [1] premises, and the dignity forthwith departed from the teamster's labor, in my eyes. In my opinion, the sun was made to light worthier toil than this. I may add that his employer has since run off, in debt to a good part of the town, and, after passing through Chancery, has settled somewhere else, there to become once more a patron of the arts.

The ways by which you may get money almost without exception lead downward. To have done anything by which you earned money *merely* is to have been truly idle or worse. If the laborer gets no more than the wages which his employer pays him, he is cheated, he cheats himself. If you would get money as a writer or lecturer, you must be popular, which is to go down perpendicularly. Those services which the community will most readily pay for, it is most disagreeable to render. You are paid for being something less than a man. The state does not commonly reward a genius any more wisely. Even the poet laureate would rather not have to celebrate the accidents of royalty. He must be bribed with a pipe of wine; and perhaps another poet is called away from his muse to gauge that very pipe. As for my own business, even that kind of surveying which I could do with most satisfaction my employers do not want. They would prefer that I should do my work coarsely and not too well, ay, not well enough. When I observe that there are different ways of surveying, my employer commonly asks which will give him the most land, not which is most correct. I once invented a rule for measuring cordwood, and tried to introduce it in Boston; but the measurer there told me that the sellers did not wish to have their wood measured correctly—that he was already too accurate for them, and therefore they commonly got their wood measured in Charlestown before crossing the bridge.

The aim of the laborer should be, not to get his living, to get "a good job," but to perform well a certain work; and, even in a pecuniary sense, it would be economy for a town to pay its laborers so well that they would not feel that they were working for low ends, as for a livelihood merely, but for scientific, or even moral ends. Do not hire a man who does your work for money, but him who does it for love of it.

It is remarkable that there are few men so well employed, so much to their minds, but that a little money or fame would commonly buy them off from their present pursuit. I see advertisements for *active* young men, as if activity were the whole of a young man's capital. Yet I have been surprised when one has with confidence proposed to me, a grown man, to embark in some enterprise of his, as if I had absolutely nothing to do, my life having been a complete failure hitherto. What a doubtful compliment this to pay me! As if he had met me halfway across the ocean beating up against the wind, but bound nowhere, and proposed to me to go along with him! If I did, what do you think the underwriters would say? No, no! I am not without employment at this stage of the voyage. To tell the truth, I saw an advertisement for able-bodied seamen, when I was a boy, sauntering in my native port, and as soon as I came of age I embarked.

The community has no bribe that will tempt a wise man. You may raise money enough to tunnel a mountain, but you cannot raise money enough to hire a man who is minding *his own* business. An efficient and valuable man does what he can, whether the community pay him for it or not. The inefficient offer their inefficiency to the highest bidder, and are forever expecting to be put into office. One would suppose that they were rarely disappointed.

Perhaps I am more than usually jealous with respect to my freedom. I feel that my connection with and obligation to society are still very slight and transient. Those slight labors which afford me a livelihood, and by which it is allowed that I am to some extent serviceable to my contemporaries, are as yet commonly a pleasure to me, and I am not often reminded that they are a necessity. So far I am successful. But I foresee that if my wants should be much increased, the labor required to supply them would become a drudgery. If I should sell both my forenoons and afternoons to society, as most appear to do, I am sure that for me there

LIFE WITHOUT PRINCIPLE. 1. **Lord Timothy Dexter's:** "Lord" Timothy Dexter (1747–1806) was an eccentric merchant of Newburyport, Mass., who established himself in a splendid mansion, the front yard of which was decorated by more than forty life-sized statues of famous men.

would be nothing left worth living for. I trust that I shall never thus sell my birthright for a mess of pottage. I wish to suggest that a man may be very industrious, and yet not spend his time well. There is no more fatal blunderer than he who consumes the greater part of his life getting his living. All great enterprises are self-supporting. The poet, for instance, must sustain his body by his poetry, as a steam planing-mill feeds its boilers with the shavings it makes. You must get your living by loving. But as it is said of the merchants that ninety-seven in a hundred fail, so the life of men generally, tried by this standard, is a failure, and bankruptcy may be surely prophesied.

Merely to come into the world the heir of a fortune is not to be born, but to be stillborn, rather. To be supported by the charity of friends, or a government pension—provided you continue to breathe—by whatever fine synonyms you describe these relations, is to go into the almshouse. On Sundays the poor debtor goes to church to take an account of stock, and finds, of course, that his outgoes have been greater than his income. In the Catholic Church, especially, they go into chancery, make a clean confession, give up all, and think to start again. Thus men will lie on their backs, talking about the fall of man, and never make an effort to get up.

As for the comparative demand which men make on life, it is an important difference between two, that the one is satisfied with a level success, that his marks can all be hit by point-blank shots, but the other, however low and unsuccessful his life may be, constantly elevates his aim, though at a very slight angle to the horizon. I should much rather be the last man, though, as the Orientals say, "Greatness doth not approach him who is forever looking down; and all those who are looking high are growing poor."

It is remarkable that there is little or nothing to be remembered written on the subject of getting a living; how to make getting a living not merely honest and honorable, but altogether inviting and glorious; for if *getting* a living is not so, then living is not. One would think, from looking at literature, that this question had never disturbed a solitary individual's musings. Is it that men are too much disgusted with their experience to speak of it? The lesson of value which money teaches, which the Author of the Universe has taken so much pains to teach us, we are inclined to skip altogether. As for the means of living, it is wonderful how indifferent men of all classes are about it, even reformers, so called—whether they inherit, or earn, or steal it. I think that Society has done nothing for us in this respect, or at least has undone what she has done. Cold and hunger seem more friendly to my nature than those methods which men have adopted and advise to ward them off.

The title *wise* is, for the most part, falsely applied. How can one be a wise man, if he does not know any better how to live than other men?—if he is only more cunning and intellectually subtle? Does Wisdom work in a treadmill? or does she teach how to succeed *by her example?* Is there any such thing as wisdom not applied to life? Is she merely the miller who grinds the finest logic? It is pertinent to ask if Plato got his *living* in a better way or more successfully than his contemporaries —or did he succumb to the difficulties of life like other men? Did he seem to prevail over some of them merely by indifference, or by assuming grand airs? or find it easier to live, because his aunt remembered him in her will? The ways in which most men get their living, that is, live, are mere makeshifts, and a shirking of the real business of life—chiefly because they do not know, but partly because they do not mean, any better.

The rush to California, for instance, and the attitude, not merely of merchants, but of philosophers and prophets, so called, in relation to it, reflect the greatest disgrace on mankind. That so many are ready to live by luck, and so get the means of commanding the labor of others less lucky, without contributing any value to society! And that is called enterprise! I know of no more startling development of the immorality of trade, and all the common modes of getting a living. The philosophy and poetry and religion of such a mankind are not worth the dust of a puffball. The hog that gets his living by rooting, stirring up the soil so, would be ashamed of such company. If I could command the wealth of all the worlds by lifting my finger, I would not pay *such* a price for it. Even Mahomet knew that God did not make this world in jest. It makes God to be a moneyed gentleman who scatters a handful of pennies in order to see mankind scramble for them. The world's raffle! A subsistence in the domains of Nature a thing to be raffled for! What a comment, what a satire, on our institutions! The conclusion will be, that mankind will hang itself upon a tree. And have all the precepts in all the Bibles taught men only this? and is the last and most admirable invention of the human race only an improved muck-rate? Is this the ground on which Orientals and Occidentals meet? Did God direct us so to get our living, digging where we never planted—and He would, perchance, reward us with lumps of gold?

God gave the righteous man a certificate entitling him to food and raiment, but the unrighteous man found a facsimile of the same in God's coffers, and appropriated it, and obtained food and raiment like the former. It is one of the most extensive systems of counterfeiting that the world has seen. I did not know that mankind was suffering for want of gold. I have seen a little of it. I know that it is very malleable, but not so malleable as wit. A grain of gold will gild a great surface, but not so much as a grain of wisdom.

The gold digger in the ravines of the mountains is as much a gambler as his fellow in the saloons of San Francisco. What difference does it make whether you shake dirt or shake dice? If you win, society is the loser. The gold digger is the enemy of the honest laborer, whatever checks and compensations there may be. It is not enough to tell me that you worked hard to get your gold. So does the Devil work hard. The way of transgressors may be hard in many respects. The humblest observer who goes to the mines sees and says that gold digging is of the character of a lottery; the gold thus obtained is not the same thing with the wages of honest toil. But, practically, he forgets what he has seen, for he has seen only the fact, not the principle, and goes into trade there, that is, buys a ticket in what commonly proves another lottery, where the fact is not so obvious.

After reading Howitt's account [2] of the Australian gold diggings one evening, I had in my mind's eye, all night, the numerous valleys, with their streams, all cut up with foul pits, from ten to one hundred feet deep, and half a dozen feet across, as close as they can be dug, and partly filled with water—the locality to which men furiously rush to probe for their fortunes—uncertain where they shall break ground—not knowing but the gold is under their camp itself—sometimes digging one hundred and sixty feet before they strike the vein, or then missing it by a foot—turned into demons, and regardless of each others' rights, in their thirst for riches—whole valleys, for thirty miles, suddenly honeycombed by the pits of the miners, so that even hundreds are drowned in them—standing in water, and covered with mud and clay, they work night and day, dying of exposure and disease. Having read this, and partly forgotten it, I was thinking, accidentally, of my own unsatisfactory life, doing as others do; and with that vision of the diggings still before me, I asked myself why *I* might not be washing some gold daily, though it were only the finest particles—why *I* might not sink a shaft down to the gold within me, and work that mine. *There* is a Ballarat, a Bendigo for you—what though it were a sulky-gully? At any rate, I might pursue some path, however solitary and narrow and crooked, in which I could walk with love and reverence. Wherever a man separates from the multitude, and goes his own way in this mood, there indeed is a fork in the road, though ordinary travelers may see only a gap in the paling. His solitary path across lots will turn out the *higher way* of the two.

Men rush to California and Australia as if the true gold were to be found in that direction; but that is to go to the very opposite extreme to where it lies. They go prospecting farther and farther away from the true lead, and are most unfortunate when they think themselves most successful. Is not our *native* soil auriferous? Does not a stream from the golden mountains flow through our native valley? and has not this for more than geologic ages been bringing down the shining particles and forming the nuggets for us? Yet, strange to tell, if a digger steal away, prospecting for this true gold, into the unexplored solitudes around us, there is no danger that any will dog his steps, and endeavor to supplant him. He may claim and undermine the whole valley even, both the cultivated and the uncultivated portions, his whole life long in peace, for no one will ever dispute his claim. They will not mind his cradles or his toms. He is not confined to a claim twelve feet square, as at Ballarat, but may mine anywhere, and wash the whole wide world in his tom.

Howitt says of the man who found the great nugget which weighed twenty-eight pounds, at the Bendigo diggings in Australia: "He soon began to drink; got a horse, and rode all about, generally at full gallop, and, when he met people, called out to inquire if they knew who he was, and then kindly informed them that he was 'the bloody wretch that had found the nugget.' At last he rode full speed against a tree, and nearly knocked his brains out." I think, however, there was no danger of that, for he had already knocked his brains out against the nugget. Howitt adds, "He is a hopelessly ruined man." But he is a type of the class. They are all fast men. Hear some of the names of the places where they dig: "Jackass Flat"—"Sheep's-Head Gully"—"Murderer's Bar," etc. Is there no satire in these names? Let them carry their ill-gotten wealth where they will, I am thinking it will still be "Jackass Flat," if not "Murderer's Bar," where they live.

The last resource of our energy has been the robbing of graveyards on the Isthmus of Darien, an enterprise which appears to be but in its infancy; for, according to late accounts, an act has passed its second reading in the legislature of New Granada, regulating this kind of mining; and a cor-

2. **Howitt's account:** Richard Howitt (1799–1869), an English poet and author of *Impressions of Australia* (1845).

respondent of the *Tribune* writes: "In the dry season, when the weather will permit of the country being properly prospected, no doubt other rich *guacas* [that is, graveyards] will be found." To emigrants he says: "Do not come before December; take the Isthmus route in preference to the Boca del Toro one; bring no useless baggage, and do not cumber yourself with a tent; but a good pair of blankets will be necessary; a pick, shovel, and axe of good material will be almost all that is required": advice which might have been taken from the "Burker's Guide." And he concludes with this line in italics and small capitals: *"If you are doing well at home,* STAY THERE," which may fairly be interpreted to mean, "If you are getting a good living by robbing graveyards at home, stay there."

But why go to California for a text? She is the child of New England, bred at her own school and church.

It is remarkable that among all the preachers there are so few moral teachers. The prophets are employed in excusing the ways of men. Most reverend seniors, the *illuminati* of the age, tell me, with a gracious, reminiscent smile, betwixt an aspiration and a shudder, not to be too tender about these things—to lump all that, that is, make a lump of gold of it. The highest advice I have heard on these subjects was groveling. The burden of it was—It is not worth your while to undertake to reform the world in this particular. Do not ask how your bread is buttered; it will make you sick, if you do—and the like. A man had better starve at once than lose his innocence in the process of getting his bread. If within the sophisticated man there is not an unsophisticated one, then he is but one of the devil's angels. As we grow old, we live more coarsely, we relax a little in our disciplines, and, to some extent, cease to obey our finest instincts. But we should be fastidious to the extreme of sanity, disregarding the gibes of those who are more unfortunate than ourselves.

In our science and philosophy, even, there is commonly no true and absolute account of things. The spirit of sect and bigotry has planted its hoof amid the stars. You have only to discuss the problem, whether the stars are inhabited or not, in order to discover it. Why must we daub the heavens as well as the earth? It was an unfortunate discovery that Dr. Kane [3] was a Mason, and that Sir John Franklin [4] was another. But it was a more cruel suggestion that possibly that was the reason why the former went in search of the latter. There is not a popular magazine in this country that would dare to print a child's thought on important subjects without comment. It must be submitted to the D.D.'s. I would it were the chickadee-dees.

You come from attending the funeral of mankind to attend to a natural phenomenon. A little thought is sexton to all the world.

I hardly know an *intellectual* man, even, who is so broad and truly liberal that you can think aloud in his society. Most with whom you endeavor to talk soon come to a stand against some institution in which they appear to hold stock, that is, some particular, not universal, way of viewing things. They will continually thrust their own low roof, with its narrow skylight, between you and the sky, when it is the unobstructed heavens you would view. Get out of the way with your cobwebs; wash your windows, I say! In some lyceums they tell me that they have voted to exclude the subject of religion. But how do I know what their religion is, and when I am near to or far from it? I have walked into such an arena and done my best to make a clean breast of what religion I have experienced, and the audience never suspected what I was about. The lecture was as harmless as moonshine to them. Whereas, if I had read to them the biography of the greatest scamps in history, they might have thought that I had written the lives of the deacons of their church. Ordinarily, the inquiry is, Where did you come from? or, Where are you going? That was a more pertinent question which I overheard one of my auditors put to another once—"What does he lecture for?" It made me quake in my shoes.

To speak impartially, the best men that I know are not serene, a world in themselves. For the most part, they dwell in forms, and flatter and study effect only more finely than the rest. We select granite for the underpinning of our houses and barns; we build fences of stone; but we do not ourselves rest on an underpinning of granitic truth, the lowest primitive rock. Our sills are rotten. What stuff is the man made of who is not co-existent in our thought with the purest and subtilest truth? I often accuse my finest acquaintances of an immense frivolity; for, while there are manners and compliments we do not meet, we do not teach one another the lessons of honesty and sincerity that the brutes do, or of steadiness and solidity that the rocks do. The fault is commonly mutual, however; for we do not habitually demand any more of each other.

That excitement about Kossuth, consider how characteristic, but superficial, it was!—only another kind of politics or dancing. Men were making speeches to him all over the country, but each expressed only the thought, or the want of thought, of the multitude. No man stood on truth. They

3. Dr. Kane: Sir Robert Kane (1809–90), an eminent Irish chemist and author of *Elements of Chemistry* (1841). **4. Sir John Franklin:** See "A Winter Walk," 6 n.

were merely banded together, as usual one leaning on another, and all together on nothing; as the Hindus made the world rest on an elephant, the elephant on a tortoise, and the tortoise on a serpent, and had nothing to put under the serpent. For all fruit of that stir we have the Kossuth hat.

Just so hollow and ineffectual, for the most part, is our ordinary conversation. Surface meets surface. When our life ceases to be inward and private, conversation degenerates into mere gossip. We rarely meet a man who can tell us any news which he has not read in a newspaper, or been told by his neighbor; and, for the most part, the only difference between us and our fellow is that he has seen the newspaper, or been out to tea, and we have not. In proportion as our inward life fails, we go more constantly and desperately to the post office. You may depend on it, that the poor fellow who walks away with the greatest number of letters, proud of his extensive correspondence, has not heard from himself this long while.

I do not know but it is too much to read one newspaper a week. I have tried it recently, and for so long it seems to me that I have not dwelt in my native region. The sun, the clouds, the snow, the trees say not so much to me. You cannot serve two masters. It requires more than a day's devotion to know and to possess the wealth of a day.

We may well be ashamed to tell what things we have read or heard in our day. I do not know why my news should be so trivial—considering what one's dreams and expectations are, why the developments should be so paltry. The news we hear, for the most part, is not news to our genius. It is the stalest repetition. You are often tempted to ask why such stress is laid on a particular experience which you have had—that, after twenty-five years, you should meet Hobbins, Registrar of Deeds, again on the sidewalk. Have you not budged an inch, then? Such is the daily news. Its facts appear to float in the atmosphere, insignificant as the sporules of fungi, and impinge on some neglected *thallus,* or surface of our minds, which affords a basis for them, and hence a parasitic growth. We should wash ourselves clean of such news. Of what consequence, though our planet explode, if there is no character involved in the explosion? In health we have not the least curiosity about such events. We do not live for idle amusement. I would not run round a corner to see the world blow up.

All summer, and far into the autumn, perchance, you unconsciously went by the newspapers and the news, and now you find it was because the morning and the evening were full of news to you. Your walks were full of incidents. You attended, not to the affairs of Europe, but to your own affairs in Massachusetts fields. If you chance to live and move and have your being in that thin stratum in which the events that make the news transpire—thinner than the paper on which it is printed—then these things will fill the world for you; but if you soar above or dive below that plane, you cannot remember nor be reminded of them. Really to see the sun rise or go down every day, so to relate ourselves to a universal fact, would preserve us sane forever. Nations! What are nations? Tartars, and Huns, and Chinamen! Like insects, they swarm. The historian strives in vain to make them memorable. It is for want of a man that there are so many men. It is individuals that populate the world. Any man thinking may say with the Spirit of Lodin,

> "I look down from my height on nations,
> And they become ashes before me;—
> Calm is my dwelling in the clouds;
> Pleasant are the great fields of my rest."

Pray, let us live without being drawn by dogs, Esquimaux-fashion, tearing over hill and dale, and biting each other's ears.

Not without a slight shudder at the danger, I often perceive how near I had come to admitting into my mind the details of some trivial affair—the news of the street; and I am astonished to observe how willing men are to lumber their minds with such rubbish—to permit idle rumors and incidents of the most insignificant kind to intrude on ground which should be sacred to thought. Shall the mind be a public arena, where the affairs of the street and the gossip of the tea-table chiefly are discussed? Or shall it be a quarter of heaven itself—an hypethral temple, consecrated to the service of the gods? I find it so difficult to dispose of the few facts which to me are significant, that I hesitate to burden my attention with those which are insignificant, which only a divine mind could illustrate. Such is, for the most part, the news in newspapers and conversation. It is important to preserve the mind's chastity in this respect. Think of admitting the details of a single case of the criminal court into our thoughts, to stalk profanely through their very *sanctum sanctorum* for an hour, ay, for many hours! to make a very barroom of the mind's inmost apartment, as if for so long the dust of the street had occupied us—the very street itself, with all its travel, its bustle, and filth, had passed through our thoughts' shrine! Would it not be an intellectual and moral suicide? When I have been compelled to sit spectator and auditor in a courtroom for some hours, and have seen my neighbors, who were not compelled, stealing in from time to time, and tiptoeing about with washed hands and faces, it has appeared to my mind's eye, that, when they took off their hats, their ears suddenly expanded into vast hoppers for sound, between which even their narrow heads were crowded. Like the vanes of windmills, they caught the broad but shallow stream of sound, which, after a few titillating gyrations in their coggy brains, passed out the other side. I wondered if, when they got home, they were as careful to wash their ears as before their hands and faces. It has seemed to me, at such a time, that the auditors and the witnesses, the jury and the counsel, the judge and the criminal at the bar—if I may presume him guilty before he is convicted—were all equally criminal, and a thunderbolt might be expected to descend and consume them all together.

By all kinds of traps and signboards, threatening the extreme penalty of the divine law, exclude such trespassers from the only ground which can be sacred to you. It is so hard to forget what it is worse than useless to remember! If I am to be a thoroughfare, I prefer that it be of the mountain brooks, the Parnassian streams, and not the town sewers. There is inspiration, that gossip which comes to the ear of the attentive mind from the courts of heaven. There is the profane and stale revelation of the barroom and the police court. The same ear is fitted to receive both communications. Only the character of the hearer determines to which it shall be open, and to which closed. I believe that the mind can be permanently profaned by the habit of attending to trivial things, so that all our thoughts shall be tinged with triviality. Our very intellect shall be macadamized, as it were, its foundation broken into fragments for the wheels of travel to roll over; and if you would know what will make the most durable pavement, surpassing rolled stones, spruce blocks; and asphaltum, you have only to look into some of our minds which have been subjected to this treatment so long.

If we have thus desecrated ourselves—as who has not?—the remedy will be by wariness and devotion to reconsecrate ourselves, and make once more a fane of the mind. We should treat our minds, that is, ourselves, as innocent and ingenuous children, whose guardians we are, and be careful what objects and what subjects we thrust on their attention. Read not the Times. Read the Eternities. Conventionalities are at length as bad as impurities. Even the facts of science may dust the mind by their dryness, unless they are in a sense effaced each morning, or rather rendered fertile by the dews of fresh and living truth. Knowledge does not come to us by details, but in flashes of light from heaven. Yes, every thought that passes through the mind helps to wear and tear it, and to deepen the ruts, which, as in the streets of Pompeii, evince how much it has been used. How many things there are concerning which we might well deliberate whether we had better know them—had better let their peddling-carts be driven, even at the slowest trot or walk, over that bridge of glorious span by which we trust to pass at last from the farthest brink of time to the nearest shore of eternity! Have we no culture, no refinement—but skill only to live coarsely and serve the Devil?—to acquire a little worldly wealth, or fame, or liberty, and make a false show with it, as if we were all husk and shell, with no tender and living kernel to us? Shall our institutions be like those chestnut burs which contain abortive nuts, perfect only to prick the fingers?

America is said to be the arena on which the battle of freedom is to be fought; but surely it cannot be freedom in a merely political sense that is meant. Even if we grant that the American has freed himself from a political tyrant, he is still the slave of an economical and moral tyrant. Now that the republic—the *res-publica*—has been settled, it is time to look after the *res-privata*—the private state—to see, as the Roman senate charged its consuls, *"ne quid res*-PRIVATA *detrimenti caperet,"* that the *private* state receive no detriment.

Do we call this the land of the free? What is it to be free from King George and continue the slaves of King Prejudice? What is it to be born free and not to live free? What is the value of any political freedom, but as a means to moral freedom? Is it a freedom to be slaves, or a freedom to be free, of which we boast? We are a nation of politicians, concerned about the outmost defenses only of freedom. It is our children's children who may perchance be really free. We tax ourselves unjustly. There is a part of us which is not represented. It is taxation without representation. We quarter troops, we quarter fools and cattle of all sorts upon ourselves. We quarter our gross bodies on our poor souls, till the former eat up all the latter's substance.

With respect to a true culture and manhood, we are essentially provincial still, not metropolitan—mere Jonathans. We are provincial, because we do not find at home our standards; because we do not worship truth, but the reflection of truth; because we are warped and narrowed by an exclusive devotion to trade and commerce and manufactures and agriculture and the like, which are but means, and not the end.

So is the English Parliament provincial. Mere country bumpkins, they betray themselves, when any more important question arises for them to settle, the Irish question, for instance—the English question why did I not say? Their natures are subdued to what they work in. Their "good breeding" respects only secondary objects. The finest manners in the world are awkwardness and fatuity when contrasted with a finer intelligence. They appear but as the fashions of past days—mere courtliness, knee-buckles and smallclothes, out of date. It is the vice, but not the excellence of manners, that they are continually being deserted by the character; they are cast-off clothes or shells, claiming the respect which belonged to the living creature. You are presented with the shells instead of the meat, and it is no excuse generally, that, in the case of some fishes, the shells are of more worth than the meat. The man who thrusts his manners upon me does as if he were to insist on introducing me to his cabinet of curiosities, when I wished to see himself. It was not in this sense that the poet Decker called Christ "the first true gentleman that ever breathed." I repeat that in this sense the most splendid court in Christendom is provincial, having authority to consult about Transalpine interests only, and not the affairs of Rome. A praetor or proconsul would suffice to settle the questions which absorb the attention of the English Parliament and the American Congress.

Government and legislation! these I thought were respectable professions. We have heard of heaven-born Numas, Lycurguses, and Solons, in the history of the world, whose *names* at least may stand for ideal legislators; but think of legislating to *regulate* the breeding of slaves, or the exportation of tobacco! What have divine legislators to do with the exportation or the importation of tobacco? what humane ones with the breeding of slaves? Suppose you were to submit the question to any son of God—and has He no children in the Nineteenth Century? is it a family which is extinct?—in what condition would you get it again? What shall a State like Virginia say for itself at the last day, in which these have been the principal, the staple productions? What ground is there for patriotism in such a State? I derive my facts from statistical tables which the States themselves have published.

A commerce that whitens every sea in quest of nuts and raisins, and makes slaves of its sailors for this purpose! I saw, the other day, a vessel which had been wrecked, and many lives lost, and her cargo of rags, juniper berries, and bitter almonds were strewn along the shore. It seemed hardly worth the while to tempt the dangers of the sea between Leghorn and New York for the sake of a cargo of juniper berries and bitter almonds. America sending to the Old World for her bitters! Is not the sea-brine, is not shipwreck, bitter enough to make the cup of life go down here? Yet such, to a great extent, is our boasted commerce; and there are those who style themselves statesmen and philosophers who are so blind as to think that progress and civilization depend on precisely this kind of interchange and activity—the activity of flies about a molasses-hogshead. Very well, observes one, if men were oysters. And very well, answer I, if men were mosquitoes.

Lieutenant Herndon,[5] whom our government sent to explore the Amazon, and, it is said, to extend the area of slavery, observed that there was wanting there "an industrious and active population, who know what the comforts of life are, and who have artificial wants to draw out the great resources of the country." But what are the "artificial wants" to be encouraged? Not the love of luxuries, like the tobacco and slaves of, I believe, his native Virginia, nor the ice and granite and other material wealth of our native New England; nor are "the great resources of a country" that fertility or barrenness of soil which produces these. The chief want, in every State that I have been into, was a high and earnest purpose in its inhabitants. This alone draws out "the great resources" of Nature, and at last taxes her beyond her resources; for man naturally dies out of her. When we want culture more than potatoes, and illumination more than sugar-plums, then the great resources of a world are taxed and drawn out, and the result, or staple production, is, not slaves, nor operatives, but men—those rare fruits called heroes, saints, poets, philosophers, and redeemers.

In short, as a snowdrift is formed where there is a lull in the wind, so, one would say, where there is a lull of truth, an institution springs up. But the truth blows right on over it, nevertheless, and at length blows it down.

What is called politics is comparatively something so superficial and inhuman, that practically I have never fairly recognized that it concerns me at all. The newspapers, I perceive, devote some of their columns specially to politics or government without charge; and this, one would say, is all that saves it; but as I love literature and to some extent the truth also, I never read those columns at any rate. I do not wish to blunt my sense of right so much. I have not got to answer for having read a single President's Message. A strange age of the world this, when empires, kingdoms, and republics come a-begging to a private man's door, and utter their complaints at his elbow! I cannot take up a newspaper but I find that some wretched gov-

5. **Lieutenant Herndon:** William Lewis Herndon (1813–57), a naval officer who made a complete survey of the Amazon river system.

ernment or other, hard pushed and on its last legs, is interceding with me, the reader, to vote for it—more importunate than an Italian beggar; and if I have a mind to look at its certificate, made, perchance, by some benevolent merchant's clerk, or the skipper that brought it over, for it cannot speak a word of English itself, I shall probably read of the eruption of some Vesuvius, or the overflowing of some Po, true or forged, which brought it into this condition. I do not hesitate, in such a case, to suggest work, or the almshouse; or why not keep its castle in silence, as I do commonly? The poor President, what with preserving his popularity and doing his duty, is completely bewildered. The newspapers are the ruling power. Any other government is reduced to a few marines at Fort Independence. If a man neglects to read the Daily Times, government will go down on its knees to him, for this is the only treason in these days.

Those things which now most engage the attention of men, as politics and the daily routine, are, it is true, vital functions of human society, but should be unconsciously performed, like the corresponding functions of the physical body. They are *infra*-human, a kind of vegetation. I sometimes awake to a half-consciousness of them going on about me, as a man may become conscious of some of the processes of digestion in a morbid state, and so have the dyspepsia, as it is called. It is as if a thinker submitted himself to be rasped by the great gizzard of creation. Politics is, as it were, the gizzard of society, full of grit and gravel, and the two political parties are its two opposite halves—sometimes split into quarters, it may be, which grind on each other. Not only individuals, but states, have thus a confirmed dyspepsia, which expresses itself, you can imagine by what sort of eloquence. Thus our life is not altogether a forgetting, but also, alas! to a great extent, a remembering, of that which we should never have been conscious of, certainly not in our waking hours. Why should we not meet, not always as dyspeptics, to tell our bad dreams, but sometimes as *eu*peptics, to congratulate each other on the ever-glorious morning? I do not make an exorbitant demand, surely.

POEMS

◊

¶ SOME of Thoreau's poems were published in H. S. Salt's and F. B. Sanborn's *Poems of Nature* in 1895, and in 1943 Carl Bode brought out *Collected Poems of Henry Thoreau.* During Thoreau's lifetime, however, the only poems he managed to publish in book form were those which he included in the *Week* and *Walden.* While an undergraduate at Harvard, Thoreau had observed that the Greek poets had an "appetite for visible images," whereas the poetry of northern Europe tended toward the "dark and mysterious." In his poetic practice, he usually attempted to follow the Greek ideal, and his best poems are distinguished by the firm grounding of their thought in a Nature that one can see.

◊

SYMPATHY

¶ "SYMPATHY" was written in June, 1839, and published in the *Dial,* I (July, 1840), 71. Emerson said of this poem that it "reveals the tenderness under that triple steel of stoicism, and the intellectual subtility it could animate."

Lately, alas, I knew a gentle boy,
  Whose features all were cast in Virtue's mould,
As one she had designed for Beauty's toy,
  But after manned him for her own stronghold.

On every side he open was as day,
  That you might see no lack of strength within,
For walls and ports do only serve alway
  For a pretense to feebleness and sin.

Say not that Caesar was victorious,
  With toil and strike who stormed the House of
    Fame,
In other sense this youth was glorious,
  Himself a kingdom wheresoe'er he came.

No strength went out to get him victory,
  When all was income of its own accord;
For where he went none other was to see,
  But all were parcel of their noble lord.

He forayed like the subtile haze of summer,
  That stilly shows fresh landscapes to our eyes,
And revolutions work without a murmur,
  Or rustling of a leaf beneath the skies.

So was I taken unawares by this,
I quite forgot my homage to confess;
Yet now am forced to know, though hard it is,
I might have loved him had I loved him less.

Each moment as we nearer drew to each,
A stern respect withheld us farther yet,
So that we seemed beyond each other's reach,
And less acquainted than when first we met.

We two were one while we did sympathize,
So could we not the simplest bargain drive;
And what avails it now that we are wise,
If absence doth this doubleness contrive?

Eternity may not the chance repeat,
But I must tread my single way alone,
In sad remembrance that we once did meet,
And know that bliss irrevocably gone.

The spheres henceforth my elegy shall sing,
For elegy has other subject none;
Each strain of music in my ears shall ring
Knell of departure from that other one.

Make haste and celebrate my tragedy;
With fitting strain resound ye woods and fields;
Sorrow is dearer in such case to me
Than all the joys other occasion yields.

Is 't then too late the damage to repair?
Distance, forsooth, from my weak grasp hath reft
The empty husk, and clutched the useless tare,
But in my hands the wheat and kernel left.

If I but love that virtue which he is,
Though it be scented in the morning air,
Still shall we be truest acquaintances,
Nor mortals know a sympathy more rare.

SIC VITA

["SIC VITA" was published in the *Dial*, II (July, 1841), 81–82 and reprinted in the *Week* (1849). Written while Thoreau was still a Harvard undergraduate, this poem was then thrown into the window of a friend wrapped round a bunch of violets and tied loosely with straw. The friend was Mrs. Lucy Jackson Brown, a sister of Emerson's second wife, Lidian. Compare the sentence in the *Week* which immediately precedes "Sic Vita": "I have seen a bunch of violets in a glass vase, tied loosely with a straw, which reminded me of myself."

I am a parcel of vain strivings tied
By a chance bond together,
Dangling this way and that, their links
Were made so loose and wide,
Methinks,
For milder weather.

A bunch of violets without their roots,
And sorrel intermixed,
Encircled by a wisp of straw
Once coiled about their shoots,
The law
By which I'm fixed.

A nosegay which Time clutched from out
Those fair Elysian fields,
With weeds and broken stems, in haste,
Doth make the rabble rout
That waste
The day he yields.

And here I bloom for a short hour unseen,
Drinking my juices up,
With no root in the land
To keep my branches green,
But stand
In a bare cup.

Some tender buds were left upon my stem
In mimicry of life,
But ah! the children will not know,
Till time has withered them,
The woe
With which they're rife.

But now I see I was not plucked for naught,
And after in life's vase
Of glass set while I might survive,
But by a kind hand brought
Alive
To a strange place.

That stock thus thinned will soon redeem its hours,
And by another year,
Such as God knows, with freer air,
More fruits and fairer flowers
Will bear,
While I droop here.

THE INWARD MORNING

["THE INWARD MORNING" was written as two separate lyrics in 1841, but published as one poem in the *Dial*, III (October, 1842), 198–99. Compare this poem to the section "Idealism" in Emerson's 1836 *Nature* (see pp. 497–501).

Packed in my mind lie all the clothes
  Which outward nature wears,
And in its fashion's hourly change
  It all things else repairs.

In vain I look for change abroad,
  And can no difference find,
Till some new ray of peace uncalled
  Illumes my inmost mind.

What is it gilds the trees and clouds,
  And paints the heavens so gay,
But yonder fast-abiding light
  With its unchanging ray?

Lo, when the sun streams through the wood,
  Upon a winter's morn,
Where'er his silent beams intrude
  The murky night is gone.

How could the patient pine have known
  The morning breeze would come,
Or humble flowers anticipate
  The insect's noonday hum,—

Till the new light with morning cheer
  From far streamed through the aisles,
And nimbly told the forest trees
  For many stretching miles?

I've heard within my inmost soul
  Such cheerful morning news,
In the horizon of my mind
  Have seen such orient hues,

As in the twilight of the dawn,
  When the first birds awake,
Are heard within some silent wood,
  Where they the small twigs break,

Or in the eastern skies are seen,
  Before the sun appears,
The harbingers of summer heats
  Which from afar he bears.

WINTER MEMORIES

❡ "WINTER MEMORIES" was published in "Natural History of Massachusetts," the *Dial*, III (July, 1842), 19. The first version of this poem appears as an entry in Thoreau's journal, for December 30, 1841.

Within the circuit of this plodding life
There enter moments of an azure hue,
Untarnished fair as is the violet
Or anemone, when the spring strews them
By some meandering rivulet, which make
The best philosophy untrue that aims
But to console man for his grievances.
I have remembered when the winter came,
High in my chamber in the frosty nights,
When in the still light of the cheerful moon,
On every twig and rail and jutting spout,
The icy spears were adding to their length
Against the arrows of the coming sun,
How in the shimmering noon of summer past
Some unrecorded beam slanted across
The upland pastures where the Johnswort grew;
Or heard, amid the verdure of my mind,
The bee's long smothered hum, on the blue flag
Loitering amidst the mead; or busy rill,
Which now through all its course stands still and dumb
Its own memorial,—purling at its play
Along the slopes, and through the meadows next,
Until its youthful sound was hushed at last
In the staid current of the lowland stream;
Or seen the furrows shine but late upturned,
And where the fieldfare followed in the rear,
When all the fields around lay bound and hoar
Beneath a thick integument of snow.
So by God's cheap economy made rich
To go upon my winter's task again.

TO THE MAIDEN IN THE EAST

❡ "TO THE MAIDEN IN THE EAST" was published in the *Dial*, III (October, 1842), 222, and reprinted in the *Week* (1849).

  Low in the eastern sky
Is set thy glancing eye;
And though its gracious light
Ne'er riseth to my sight,
Yet every star that climbs
Above the gnarled limbs
    Of yonder hill,
Conveys thy gentle will.

Believe I knew thy thought,
And that the zephyrs brought
Thy kindest wishes through,
As mine they bear to you,
That some attentive cloud
Did pause amid the crowd
    Over my head,
While gentle things were said.

Believe the thrushes sung,
And that the flower-bells rung,

That herbs exhaled their scent,
And beasts knew what was meant,
The trees a welcome waved,
And lakes their margins laved,
        When thy free mind
To my retreat did wind.

It was a summer eve,
The air did gently heave
While yet a low-hung cloud
Thy eastern skies did shroud;
The lightning's silent gleam,
Startling my drowsy dream,
        Seemed like the flash
Under thy dark eyelash.

Still will I strive to be
As if thou wert with me;
Whatever path I take,
It shall be for thy sake,
Of gentle slope and wide,
As thou wert by my side,
        Without a root
To trip thy gentle foot.

I'll walk with gentle pace,
And choose the smoothest place,
And careful dip the oar,
And shun the winding shore,
And gently steer my boat
Where water-lilies float,
        And cardinal flowers
Stand in their sylvan bowers.

MIST

❨["MIST" was probably written in 1842 and was first published in the *Week* (1849).

   Low-anchored cloud,
Newfoundland air,
Fountain-head and source of rivers,
Dew-cloth, dream drapery,
And napkin spread by fays;
Drifting meadow of the air,
Where bloom the daisied banks and violets,
And in whose fenny labyrinth
The bittern booms and heron wades;
Spirit of lakes and seas and rivers,
Bear only perfumes and the scent
Of healing herbs to just men's fields!

SMOKE

❨["SMOKE" was published in the *Dial*, III (April, 1843), 505–06, and reprinted in *Walden* (1854). This was one of the poems which Thoreau called "Orphics," a name which calls attention to its Grecian form and content.

   Light-winged Smoke, Icarian bird,
Melting thy pinions in thy upward flight,
Lark without song, and messenger of dawn,
Circling above the hamlets at thy nest;
Or else, departing dream, and shadowy form
Of midnight vision, gathering up thy skirts;
By night star-veiling, and by day
Darkening the light and blotting out the sun;
Go thou my incense upward from this hearth,
And ask the gods to pardon this clear flame

INSPIRATION

❨["INSPIRATION" was posthumously published in *Commonwealth* (June 19, 1863), a Boston weekly newspaper, edited by F. B. Sanborn.

Whate'er we leave to God, God does,
   And blesses us;
The work we choose should be our own,
   God lets alone.

If with light head erect I sing,
   Though all the muses lend their force,
From my poor love of anything,
   The verse is weak and shallow as its source.

But if with bended neck I grope,
   Listening behind me for my wit,
With faith superior to hope,
   More anxious to keep back than forward it,

Making my soul accomplice there
   Unto the flame my heart hath lit,
Then will the verse forever wear,—
   Time cannot bend the line which God hath writ.

Always the general show of things
   Floats in review before my mind,
And such true love and reverence brings,
   That sometimes I forget that I am blind.

But now there comes unsought, unseen,
   Some clear, divine electuary,
And I who had but sensual been,
   Grow sensible, and as God is, am wary.

I hearing get who had but ears,
  And sight, who had but eyes before,
I moments live who lived but years,
  And truth discern who knew but learning's lore.

I hear beyond the range of sound,
  I see beyond the range of sight,
New earths and skies and seas around,
  And in my day the sun doth pale his light.

A clear and ancient harmony
  Pierces my soul through all its din,
As through its utmost melody,—
  Farther behind than they—farther within.

More swift its bolt than lightning is,
  Its voice than thunder is more loud,
It doth expand my privacies
  To all, and leave me single in the crowd.

It speaks with such authority,
  With so serene and lofty tone,
That idle Time runs gadding by,
  And leaves me with Eternity alone.

Then chiefly is my natal hour,
  And only then my prime of life,
Of manhood's strength it is the flower,
  'Tis peace's end and war's beginning strife.

'T hath come in summer's broadest noon,
  By a grey wall or some chance place,
Unseasoned time, insulted June,
  And vexed the day with its presuming face.

Such fragrance round my couch it makes,
  More rich than are Arabian drugs,
That my soul scents its life and wakes
  The body up beneath its perfumed rugs.

Such is the Muse—the heavenly maid,
  The star that guides our mortal course,
Which shows where life's true kernel's laid,
  Its wheat's fine flower, and its undying force.

She with one breath attunes the spheres,
  And also my poor human heart,
With one impulse propels the years
  Around, and gives my throbbing pulse its start.

I will not doubt forever more,
  Nor falter from a steadfast faith,
For though the system be turned o'er,
  God takes not back the word which once he saith.

I will then trust the love untold
  Which not my worth nor want has bought,
Which wooed me young and woos me old,
  And to this evening hath me brought.

My memory I'll educate
  To know the one historic truth,
Remembering to the latest date
  The only true and sole immortal youth.

Be but thy inspiration given,
  No matter through what danger sought,
I'll fathom hell or climb to heaven,
  And yet esteem that cheap which love has bought.

Fame cannot tempt the bard
  Who's famous with his God,
Nor laurel him reward
  Who hath his Maker's nod.

MANHOOD

"MANHOOD" was first published in Carl Bode, *Collected Poems of Henry Thoreau* (1943), p. 225.

I love to see the man, a long-lived child,
As yet uninjured by all worldly taint
As the fresh infant whose whole life is play.
'Tis a serene spectacle for a serene day;
But better still I love to contemplate
The mature soul of lesser innocence,
Who hath traveled far on life's dusty road
Far from the starting point of infancy
And proudly bears his small degen'racy
Blazon'd on his memorial standard high
Who from the sad experience of his fate
Since his bark struck on that unlucky rock
Has proudly steered his life with his own hands.
Though his face harbors less of innocence
Yet there do chiefly lurk within its depths
Furrowed by care, but yet all over spread
With the ripe bloom of a self-wrought content
Noble resolves which do reprove the gods
And it doth more assert man's eminence
Above the happy level of the brute
And more doth advertise me of the heights
To which no natural path doth ever lead
No natural light can ever light our steps,
—But the far-piercing ray that shines
From the recesses of a brave man's eye.

EDWARD H. DAVIDSON
Editor

Nathaniel Hawthorne

1804–1864

THAT a century after he lived he should be included in a collection of major writers of America would have baffled and amused Hawthorne. During his lifetime the profession of letters was so poorly rewarded, and Hawthorne himself had been so consistently ignored, that to be a subject for literary study and analysis, to be termed a "classic" among American writers, would have seemed nothing short of grotesque. Yet, aside from the poor pay and the lack of recognition—certainly he had far less to complain of than did Poe—Hawthorne has not suffered the slow or sudden loss of popularity which befell many of his contemporaries, nor has he been made into a fashionable mode, a literary cliché in our own time. Indeed, his literary reputation has maintained its high place more steadily than has that of any other major American writer: Poe has never earned from critics the plaudits he has received from the general reading public, and Whitman could not win the place he wanted in the minds and hearts of his countrymen. If Hawthorne never found the quick surge of acceptance, the extraordinarily favorable critical reception which Melville has gained during the past forty years, he has sustained his reputation as a classic American writer virtually unchanged since his *Scarlet Letter* was published in 1850.

It is difficult to account for a reputation which has remained so well established amid the fluctuating moods of history and the quixotic shifts in literary taste. Some critics have charged that Hawthorne's genius was thin and narrow: one can count the distinguished novels on the fingers of one hand—and the memorable short stories on the fingers of two. Others have supposed that Hawthorne's art was deep, not broad, as no doubt it was; and in our day, when depth and ambiguity are much admired in writing, Hawthorne has continued to offer enough complexity and mystery to hold a wide variety of readers. His writings seem to be very simple: schoolchildren read them with profit and, perhaps, some pleasure. Yet the tales are most skillfully contrived: they offer problems and require intense critical analysis which, once it is performed, suggests that Hawthorne is not a mere tale-teller but a skilled artist who can take his place with the leading writers of the world. There is something deceptive about the writings and the man who produced them; they appear to be both simple and meaningful, cautious and yet intense, remote and still formidable, as indeed they are.

In the life history of Nathaniel Hawthorne are no high surges of drama and excitement, no flaming and sulfurous sins over which biographers can exercise their rhetoric and pseudo-psychologists ponder the inhibition, the trauma, the concealed loathing which might, if one looks far enough, color the writings. The story is quite otherwise: Hawthorne's life was commonplace, even dull. He had the distinction of being born on Independence Day in 1804 of a family which could boast colorful ancestors. William Hathorne—the *w* was added by Hawthorne himself, apparently to make the spelling conform to the pronunciation of the name—was that "steeple-crowned progenitor" who had come to Massachusetts with Governor Winthrop in 1630 and had played a prominent role in the early colony. His son, John Hathorne, became a lawyer and a judge of the special court which heard the evidence and passed sentences of death on nineteen witches in the famous trials held in Salem in 1692. Thereafter, the family had declined from positions of importance; Hawthorne's father lingered in the boy's memory as the sea captain who had been lost off Surinam, leaving a widow with three children to rear and educate. Years afterward Hawthorne admitted that little remained of a once-proud family except a mere scribbler of tales who might be making better and more lucrative use of his time than sitting at a writing desk.

Young Hawthorne attended the Salem schools and then, from 1821 to 1825, Bowdoin College in the far-off woods of Brunswick, Maine. The college was new; it looked as if its several buildings had been placed intact in the endless wilderness where a river flowed nearby. Yet Bowdoin would never again have students who would become quite so famous: Longfellow was to be the distinguished professor of modern languages and the equally distinguished poet; Franklin Pierce rose to be President of the United States. And, of course, there was Hawthorne, who, when he graduated, was in the middle of his class; his only high marks were in the courses which, more often than not, are the bane of the undergraduate—rhetoric and composition. In every other respect he showed little promise: he had not prepared to study law; he seemed in no way destined for the ministry—the law and the ministry were then the two main paths of adventure for ambitious college graduates—and he had even less interest in teaching school than would, a few years later, his friend Henry Thoreau. He had only one thing he really wanted to do, and he did it: he returned to his mother's home on Charter Street, Salem, and became a writer.

To become a writer was no easier in 1825 than it is in a later time. Then as now the young writer would need more patience and endurance than most people have, and sacrifice months and years to producing what the outside world seldom reads or even hears of; the rewards may come, but they usually come late, as they did for Hawthorne. In the meantime, the youthful writer must do the best he can, constantly practice to perfect his craft and style, and gain a maturity of mind which may someday reveal to him his true self and his true subject. Hawthorne's years of practice and experimentation were spent on a novel, *Fanshawe* (1828), which presented some of his undergraduate life behind a rather opaque disguise, and on a great number of short stories, some of which were printed and many of which were undoubtedly destroyed.

If a writer ever becomes a craftsman of distinction, he must find his true, his special genius. If he never finds his way during his impressionable years, he had better abandon writing altogether. The period in Hawthorne's life between twenty-one and thirty-three was the crucial time: Hawthorne found his special voice and style and fashioned the particular lines and colors of his art.

These "twelve dark years," as he afterward called them, have attracted a great deal of critical attention—those years from his graduation in 1825 until his "emergence" in 1837. Hawthorne himself helped to create the legend of his solitary existence, his withdrawal from the world, his lonely night walks along the deserted streets of Salem or down to the dark shoreline. In some of his notebook entries and in the letters he wrote to his fiancée, Sophia Peabody, he called up those months of self-denial and dedication to a useless literary indulgence for which the outside world had scant use or reward. One should always be wary of the confessions a young man puts in a letter to the woman he loves, especially if he is a literary young man. A young man in love is not necessarily a liar, but, like Huck Finn, he "stretches the truth" a little. Actually, throughout those twelve years Hawthorne lived a quite active life; he visited his friends; he took extensive summer tours to the New England mountains and as far west as Niagara Falls; he watched with fascination long and sensational murder trials; he attended the local taverns, and, in general, he behaved much as a young man between the ages of twenty-one and thirty-three is likely to behave.

Yet there is enough truth in the legend of the "twelve dark years" to give it literary significance. That a young man is taking trips or visiting taverns and murder trials does not obviate the possibility that he is thinking and living quite differently within himself. It is not important that a writer sit in an upstairs room and practice his craft for twelve years: what is important is that he open a negotiation with a world—not the world of actuality in which he lives and moves, but that other world of his imagination, of his deepest sensibility, of what Hawthorne called "the interior of the heart." Hawthorne early discovered what was his world of the imagination, and he was wise to remain in it for the rest of his life. It was not within the boundaries of Salem, or of Massachusetts, or even anywhere in the western hemisphere, though it had recognizable place names. It was that region within the human heart and consciousness where sin and guilt reside, where dark secrets are hidden from the peering eyes of men, where the deep festerings of remorse and conscience work to destroy, and where the eternal questions of men never quite find the answers which comfort and satisfy. Whether or not "twelve dark years" were needed to form this world, Hawthorne had lived, and was thereafter to live, with a dimension of blackness lodged in his work, for he was especially gifted with the insight to perceive, and the craft to disclose, the drama of human suffering which forever exists as a rule of existence.

The year 1837 was important in Hawthorne's life. He collected a number of short stories he had published in magazines and issued them in a volume entitled *Twice-Told Tales*. The book had little sale and attracted only modest critical attention; its odd title suggested that the author was doing nothing more than retell the same weary narratives which men had long known. In that same year Hawthorne met and became engaged to Sophia Peabody of Salem and Boston. In days when young lovers did not think that they had to be married at once, Hawthorne and Sophia waited —waited from 1839 to 1841 while Hawthorne had a dull job in the Boston customhouse. They continued to wait through the seven months from April to November, 1841, when Hawthorne was a member of the famous Brook Farm community: there a group of people with high literary and grandly reformist social aspirations—many of them Transcendentalists, but not Emerson or Thoreau—tried to prove that men need not grind their lives away at monotonous, senseless work. Unfortunately for Hawthorne, the work on the farm was monotonous and unrewarding, and he found little interest in turning a wicked world to rights. He left the farm wiser than he had been in the ways of men and women; later he would recast the adventure in his novel *The Blithedale Romance* (1852).

In the summer of 1842 Hawthorne and Sophia Peabody were married and moved into the Old Manse in Concord, already made famous by Emerson's residence and the writing of *Nature* (1836). For a time the sales of stories supported the husband and wife and the children as they arrived. Yet, quite evidently, a life devoted to literature became ever more precarious: Hawthorne could not earn a living from his writing. Accordingly, out of need rather than desire, he accepted a political appointment from the Massachusetts Democrats who had been victorious in the election of 1844 and became surveyor in the Salem customhouse. For three years he drew his salary and had very little to do: Salem was in a commercial decline; it was not even in competition with the whaling ports New Bedford and Nantucket which Melville would celebrate a few years later. Then, in one of those political upheavals which regularly marked the early Republic, the Whigs triumphed; the Democrats must go, and in June, 1849, Hawthorne lost his place as surveyor.

Although Hawthorne tried to get back his job, he knew that his only hope was his writing. Between that summer of 1849 and the opening of 1850 he produced his masterwork, *The Scar-*

let Letter. The Preface, which he entitled "The Custom House," was a wry, backhanded attempt to get even with the political enemies who had made him lose his place; it also tells us something of what was going on in that other self, the imagination, during the dull hours and years in the customhouse. The book was at once a striking success and made Hawthorne's name known in literary circles. Six months later, in the summer of 1850, he first met Melville, who found in Hawthorne a writer who dared to investigate the dark underside of human sin and suffering. Perhaps the meeting and subsequent friendship encouraged Melville to go his own extraordinary way in *Moby-Dick*.

Even though Hawthorne published *The House of the Seven Gables* (1851), compiled another collection of short stories, *The Snow-Image and Other Twice-Told Tales* (1851), and issued *The Blithedale Romance* (1852), he was still driven to earn more money. After his friend, Franklin Pierce, was elected President, Hawthorne in 1853 accepted an appointment as consul at Liverpool, one of the most lucrative positions in the State Department. Throughout four years he worked diligently in the grimy consulate by the waterfront; he also found time to travel up and down the English countryside, to gaze at quaint English villages and churches, to explore the byways of London, and to receive the honors due a visiting literary man. In 1858, again with the change of a political administration, Hawthorne resigned from the consulate and for a year resided in Italy before returning to England. The results of these travels were the notebooks he kept and *The Marble Faun* (1860), which he published shortly before he returned to the United States.

Hawthorne's last years were clouded by a nagging worry over money: his savings from the consulate did not last as long as he had hoped. The Civil War threatened and then began; Hawthorne could only sit and watch the collapse of a world, both real and imaginary, that he had once known. As he worked desperately to complete one last novel, he seemed visibly to weaken and to waste away. His friends and family were deeply concerned. A short journey to Washington and even to the scene of the war in 1862 was to no avail. In May, 1864, Hawthorne died in his sleep while staying in Plymouth, New Hampshire. Of his generation of distinguished literary men, only Thoreau had gone before him; those who survived were at the funeral in Concord to pay him tribute.

II

HAWTHORNE's lifelong dedication to his art puts him in the company of other American writers who were similarly dedicated and who were deeply concerned with the question of the artist in America. One of the curiosities of any reading of Hawthorne is that he tended to raise this question as if it were a joke. His wry and mordant comments on the folly of dreaming dreams and writing stories only to fascinate children are among the most devastating in our literary history: they reveal the misplacement of a writer in a society which has scant use for him. Henry James cogently remarked on the thinness of American life in the time Hawthorne lived; the suggestion is true if we suppose that Hawthorne was less an artist than he might otherwise have been had he had a deep past and lived in a land with the storied enchantment of history as his daily imaginative fare.

If a writer does feel misplaced in his native land, then perforce, he must solve his private dilemma as best he can or renounce his vocation. One of Hawthorne's ways was to project an alter ego, as though he lived with "another Hawthorne." One side of Hawthorne lived comfortably and unspectacularly in the world; it wisely abandoned the daily submission to the paper on the writing desk and went to work at desks in the Boston and Salem customhouses; it bought property, paid taxes, and lived a decorous and dignified life. This side showed to the world a bland, retiring, even shy gentleman. Holmes once remarked that Hawthorne was like a candle burning on a mantelpiece; it did not give off much heat, but its light was clear. This Hawthorne baffles any reader, as it baffled Henry James, who took too literally the jocularity, the transparent and not very funny jokes, the rather trite commonplaces on man's folly, and the nearly total absence of any interest in the burning issues of Hawthorne's own day. The mood of jest, of bantering indifference, even colors Hawthorne's remarks on what was most important to him—his writings. The Prefaces to *The Scarlet Letter* and to *The House of the Seven Gables* are expressions of that side of a man who presumes to think that the profession of letters in America is a ludicrous joke.

Then there was the "other Hawthorne" which the tales and novels portray—the intensely brooding mind, the inquiring imagination, the speculator on the dark ambiguity of man's being. None of Hawthorne's friends and associates could quite reconcile these two differing aspects of the same man; Emerson professed to be delighted with the raffish satire of "The Celestial Railroad" and preferred to let the darker nature of his friend remain unpenetrated. Melville saw more clearly than anyone else that Hawthorne was not simply a shy artist whose delicate tales masked a profound moral understanding; for Melville, Hawthorne was a grand "No-sayer" who undercut the deceptive illusions by which men live comfortably and dully.

Any answer to the question of a dual Hawthorne might solve one aspect and ignore the other. The man and the artist were two quite separate beings. To attempt to find Hawthorne, the man, in his writings is to misjudge Hawthorne, the writer; and to read the writings as a mirror of the man is to falsify both the man and the writer. The man and the artist lived and worked together, but they were two quite differing expressions not only of the man but of the literary situation in America.

The question of a writer's displacement, whether real or imagined, is different every time a writer lives. The America in which Hawthorne lived lacked a tragic heritage and a tragic vision. Even though there had been powerful and profound inquiries into man's suffering and tragic situation, the adventure into the depths of man's moral nature had been customarily undertaken by clergymen, who, if they were marvelously skilled in revealing the terror of existence, were not competent to deal with the single human life as itself tragic. For the Puritan, man was tragic because God had so willed the human destiny; for a Deist of the eighteenth century the question of tragedy was academic and even slightly absurd: man's reason could overcome the "tragic" circumstance. For the Unitarian and the religious idealist of the nineteenth century, tragedy had long ceased to have any meaning. The later Emerson faced the dark implications of human disenfranchisement from a universe which was not all good, but that teaching was concealed by that other, the smiling-faced Emerson whom everyone already knew.

Yet, however Hawthorne lacked an imaginative and intellectual heritage of literary tragedy, he was aware of the extent of the world's moral tragedy. He early discovered, almost as if it were his unique domain, a world inhabited by the sin-sick and guilty who may find peace, not in illumination or redemption, but in the awareness of their suffering. The very lack of a literary and an artistic heritage, and his admission that as a writer he lived ill at ease in his own homeland, turned Hawthorne into an anatomist of "the interior of the heart." His consciousness of the isolation of man in the universe, of the ring of darkness which encircles all joy, and the need of men, at least a few men, to see into their own souls was for Hawthorne, as it was for Melville and Mark Twain, the ethical substitution for the tragic vision which the English literary tradition had possessed since the time of Shakespeare.

If America has seldom had a tradition of literary tragedy, it can boast of a heritage of moral inquiry in its literature which is still one of the surprises of the world of letters. Europeans are always entranced by the startling discrepancy between a country which appears to bend its energies wholly on practical, technical accomplishments and yet, by contrast, whose writers seek out and uncover the dark abysm of human evil and suffering. Hawthorne is representative of one half of our tradition of moral inquiry; Emerson and Thoreau may well represent another. *Nature* and *Walden* are masterworks of inquiry in the quest of human thought for self-understanding. Yet, at the same time that they present a profound moral search, they are effectively disclosing the autobiography of moral understanding; they skillfully unfold the vagaries of a single self and at every moment chart for us the "psychology" of individual moral existence. To read *Nature* and *Walden* we must come to terms with and intimately know the brooding introspection and the moral ideas of Emerson and Thoreau.

When we read Hawthorne, we are not dealing with the "autobiography" of Hawthorne; his tales and novels are not about the man Hawthorne slowly approaching an understanding of human experience. Like their creator, the writings present an elaborate masquerade; they have a double life. The protagonists of the tales —Robin Molineux, Goodman Brown, Parson Hooper, to name a few—are forced to live by introspection, by the most private self-consciousness, and by some vision of a moral destiny of the universe. Yet they are never allowed to know what is happening in their minds at the moments of crucial thought and action. They are driven, even destroyed—yet they are forbidden to know their own ideas. This masquerade of consciousness is one of the most haunting aspects of Hawthorne's art.

Not only are Hawthorne's protagonists denied the power of introspection, but the movement of the story is away from the man or the woman under investigation and toward what Hawthorne himself called the "moral universe." Robin, Brown, and Hooper are placed in some nebulous, even timeless moral comprehension or blindness and then go the way they must go, not because their minds will that direction, but because every thought they have is but part of an infinitely larger "thought," the timeless, moral understanding of the universe. The knowledge of sin becomes a vantage point from which to establish a most intimate relation with the world and to find the truest knowledge of this world, for the universe has been sinful and guilt-ridden long before man came to exist.

"The Maypole of Merry Mount" introduces us not merely to a strangely misplaced scene of jollity and dancing but rather to a comprehension that merrymaking is some vestige of ancient harmony which man lost in the long ages since he has had the power of thought. Man may once have been joyful, in ages past, but darkness and gloom have by now become the measures of historical time. Only by understanding how temporary and fleeting are the joys of this world can men come to know that sin and evil are not acts of mind or motions of the body or even the breaking of a Puritan law. Sin and evil are the moral constants which link all men in the continuity of time past, present, and future. The "strange feeling" which Edith feels in her heart the moment she asks a question is the bond she establishes with the suffering and evil of the ages. Similarly, in the tales on art and artists Hawthorne considers this this theme: in "The Prophetic Pictures" and in "The Artist of the Beautiful" the moral element of art is not its relation to contemporary society. Art does not reflect the present and the actual; indeed, for Hawthorne, the artist is like every other morally comprehending man: he is continually engaged, in ways far beyond his knowing, in uncovering the "pastness" of any act in the present. A picture presents a question in human consciousness and is a revelation of the inscrutable ways by which any action, no matter how trivial, is related to all other actions in the past. The portraits of the husband and wife were "prophetic" because they unmasked the long-concealed evil which all men carry with them behind their comfortable masquerade of success.

In nearly all Hawthorne's stories something keeps us at a distance, prevents us from discovering at once what the stories are about, and teases us into reading them more deeply than we might otherwise do. The tales are ambiguous because they present a very considerable gap between what the characters in the stories know about themselves and, by contrast, what is required of us as readers to know. We must exercise the privilege of penetrating the mystery and unravelling the secret. Hawthorne's artistic excellence is nowhere better demonstrated than in his power of deepening the commonplace, simple truths of human life. Mystery is a part of understanding, for knowledge of his moral truths never comes easily and no matter how far it goes, knowledge is always incomplete.

III

SOME have said that Hawthorne was not really interested in living human beings but in men and women only as types or moral objects. The charge is true if we recognize that the characters in the tales and novels are always in intimate association with the scene in which they live and move: the village, the church, the study, the forest, the hill—these are outward projections of inward states of being and perhaps are themselves, as objects in the world, not very "real" either. "My Kinsman, Major Molineux," a quite early story, shows clearly how intimately the scene acts in concert with the unfolding plot. As we follow Robin's night walk, we move through scenic disclosures which tell us as much as Robin himself ever can about what is really happening. The noisy confusion in the tavern, the leering enticement of the young girl, the deepening terror of the streets, and the quiet enclosure Robin finds in the portico of the church take us deeper and deeper into a mood of foreboding and terror and into the darkening of Robin's own mind as he slowly understands the evil of an evil world. With "Young Goodman Brown" Hawthorne's method of bringing the "moral universe" into association with human figures has been deepened and refined. The farther Brown journeys into the forest, the more suggestive and even prophetic the scene becomes. The dusky forest, the withered branch on the tree, the gnarled figures, and the red-lit fire all suggest the guilty heart of Brown himself. At the climax of the story Brown screams, the scene instantly dissolves, and Brown is back in Salem once more. What Brown eventually realized was that he had undertaken a journey which was not real: everything he experienced and everything he saw was but an outward manifestation of his own inner state of mind.

When Hawthorne wrote "The Maypole of Merry Mount," this method of objectifying inner states of being had become a key to his craft. The forest, the shower of withering rose petals, and the groan of the falling tree are not so much actions in nature as they are signs of what is occurring in the minds and hearts of Edith and Edgar. Indeed, the world "becomes psychology" for the characters. They are incapable of expressing their own inner states and so must have much of their private thought expressed by means other than the direct dialogue and straightforward expository devices common to the novel when Hawthorne began to write fiction. Hawthorne's craft so deepened that by the time he wrote "Ethan Brand" and *The Scarlet Letter*, both published in 1850, this gauzy, suggestive, "moral universe" would be one of our best ways of knowing what was truly happening to his men and women in their innermost hearts.

Hawthorne's men and women live in a strange, dark world; they are burdened with sin and guilt which they are incapable of expressing on their own. Yet Hawthorne did not reduce his characters to puppets in a highly colored scene. He was not trying, as was Poe, to bring human life and the natural world into some unified, or convulsive, relationship. Nor was he trying to illustrate profound moral truths by moving human beings through a carefully contrived moral allegory to reach a fitting moral conclusion. Otherwise, he would have been a sermonizer or, like Franklin, a propounder of moral axioms as in "The Way to Wealth." Rather, he was a symbolist and, if the definition can be made more precisely, a "Puritan symbolist."

A symbolist is different every time he occurs or every time he has a thought. Hawthorne was symbolist different from Melville, Whitman, or Emily Dickinson. No one can say what makes a symbolist writer or what forms the special symbolic imagination a writer may have. Certain times are favorable to the appearance of symbolist thought: the Middle Ages, the early seventeenth century, the period of the Puritan migration to Massachusetts, and the first half of the nineteenth century in America were propitious to a symbolist method of feeling, thinking, and making meaning known. Hawthorne came, therefore, at a time in the artistic and imaginative life of America which encouraged a form of thinking which is symbolist. However much Hawthorne differed from Emerson, he nonetheless was not too far from the questions which Emerson asked and even some of the answers which Emerson—or Thoreau, Whitman, and Melville too—obtained.

Symbols are ways of making meaning known. A falling leaf, a ray of sunshine, a smile, a mark on a young woman's cheek, a fire, a veil over a face—these and the infinite variety of objects and motions in nature are what become symbols when men see in them meanings beyond their mere experience as objects or events. Artists and writers are symbolists when they seek to interpret the world of fact according to ideas and premises which are not implicit in those objects. A burning bush is ostensibly a bush on fire, but it "becomes meaning" when it is interpreted and is known to offer a sign to men.

We should also understand that symbols are not invented; writers do not make up objects and then conveniently assign meanings to them. If a writer does so, he is a faker and soon detected. Furthermore, a symbol does not exist alone or as a single object of meaning; rather, symbols are always in relationship, context, association; they organize a wide variety of ideas into single, and sometimes simple, acts of understanding. A country's flag is a host of memories, historical events, emotional complexities which a rectangular cloth in varying colors and designs may embody. Again: symbols are part of a culture; certain symbols are very meaningful to Frenchmen, Germans, and Americans; objects may assume symbolic importance in differing times and places. Indeed, every writer lives in a unique historical situation which has its own complex of symbols, and he may express himself in ways, and according to designs of meaning, of which he is himself unknowing. A writer is virtually in the grip of his time and the symbolic situation which he inherits: what he writes is an unconscious reflection of the moral tone, the principal desires, the underlying directions which his age gives him, and, quite unaware of what he is doing, he may be mirroring some of the most tenuous and some of the most profound ideas of his age. Chiefly because he reflected a long-ago Puritan way of thinking about and looking at the world; because, in a real sense, he made his fiction out of "cases of conscience"; and, because he reflected certain moral ideas of his own time, Hawthorne can rightly be regarded as a latter-day Puritan, a moral symbolist.

Hawthorne's best subjects and his clearest vision were derived from the New England Puritan past—that long and memorable roll-call of themes, historical events, and significant men who had played their roles in the early colony and commonwealth. What that past gave Hawthorne was what his own times could not, namely, a valid artistic subject matter and a range of imaginative speculation. If the contemporary soil of nineteenth-century America was thin, as Henry James believed, the older Puritan earth was deep and rich enough for a thousand tales. In this special imaginative, symbolic spectrum Hawthorne found his best work, "The Minister's Black Veil," "Young Goodman Brown," "Ethan Brand," and *The Scarlet Letter*.

Hawthorne rediscovered what another Puritan, Jonathan Edwards, had long ago known: the world contains meaning. Men may know or be ignorant—in theological Puritaism the terms were "saved" or "condemned"—insofar as they are provided with the perception to read and understand that world of sign, symbol, and meaning all around them. Edwards, as he informs us in his "Personal Narrative," rode into the woods and saw Christ in a vision; Goodman Brown took his night journey into the woods and returned forever a changed man. The understanding of what took place in both events could be presented only as an imaginative speculation, with all its tenuous hints and its partial answers. The problem both for Edwards and for Goodman Brown is essentially the same: How does a man come to know what he truly is, and what is his place in the world? Edwards had asked this question as a theologian; another Puritan, the poet Edward Taylor, had found his answers in the objects of everyday life wherein God reveals His ways to men: "Huswifery" is a model of immediately known images as signs of God's presence.

Hawthorne was neither a theologian nor a poet; his symbolism is, however, rightly called "Puritan," for the objects of this our world must necessarily be read aright. One obvious difference between Hawthorne and his Puritan antecedents is that, for a seventeenth- or eighteenth-century mind, a symbol is an invitation, even a demand, to further deeper meaning and understanding. For Hawthorne a symbol is not so much an idea or a meaning which the human mind slowly comes to know; rather, a symbol is a dimension of nature. The symbol fulfills itself; it contains all that is to be known; it does not promise that farther vision in Edwards' search for understanding in this world or Taylor's reverent privilege to glorify a spinning wheel. When we have completed one of Hawthorne's tales or novels, we know all that we shall ever know about the falling leaf, the hand over the heart, the veil over the face; these symbols have been our only way to understand the people who have sinned and who suffer and our only way whereby we have known the world in which they live.

Hawthorne's symbolism so encloses the action and so fully determines what the characters shall be that a symbol becomes "psychology"; it is our way of learning the motives and purposes of men and women who are denied the right to know themselves. In "The Maypole of Merry Mount" what the people feel and think is almost nothing; yet the physical objects—the gaudily decorated tree, the masks, the dark lowering forest all around—"think" for them: every mood and whim is contained in and mirrored by that scene. Edith does not really think when she wonders about the mystery of sadness in her heart; by contrast, the shower of withering rose petals thinks for her; it shows that, however sad she may be, the world itself exists on the principle of universal suffering. Parson Hooper does not come to a knowledge of secret sin until he sees that all other faces and even the earth have their black veils. And when Goodman Brown has left his youthful innocence and truly matured, he knows that the most pious people and the most serene earth are cankered by what he has discovered in himself.

Hawthorne's symbolism, even his ideas which are behind those symbols, creates a closed world. Men and women are not capable of thinking about or shaping their destiny; the world and its symbols do that shaping for them. They are in the control of a mysterious, active force which has existed long before they lived and will continue to be exerted long after they are gone. If Hawthorne accepted most of Puritan thought and its symbolism, he did not show life as moving toward a Puritan self-enlightenment and peace. The characters suffer from a Puritan's troubled conscience, the need for self-scrutiny and self-understanding, and from the loneliness which is all men's history; yet they are without any sense that the divine hand is at work for ill or good in their lives. They exist as if every law in the universe were as rigid and exacting as for a seventeenth-century Puritan; yet God long ago removed Himself from His world. Here, in brief, is the paradox of Hawthorne's writings: the perdurable laws and the timeless symbols still remain as remorselessly in force as in a time long past; but man, alone, has somehow lost all sense of a God of law or a God of understanding.

IV

HAWTHORNE was a latter-day Puritan. He was also a citizen of the literary world of his own time. If his symbolism was framed in the thinking of Puritanism, it was also investigating the most cogent thought of his own day. "Young Goodman Brown" appeared in 1835, the year before the publication of Emerson's *Nature*. Hawthorne's short story might be read as a mildly prefiguring dramatization of Emerson's thesis. Brown walks from the ostensibly real world of Salem and into the test or "discipline" of the night meeting; once there, he is in a shimmering world of fact fused with dream, of wisdom compounded of insanity, of certainty mingled with fear, until he finally emerges with a cry—not into the enlightenment of Emersonian "prospects" but into that dark "ambiguity of sin or sorrow," the unresolved doubt which never answers the question which Emerson answered so affirmatively. "Know then," Emerson said triumphantly, "that the world exists for you. For you is the phenomenon perfect. . . . Build therefore your own world." For Brown, not the world, but man's own knowledge of his deceptions and self-delusions is all that exists. To be sure, one builds his own world, but it is one fashioned only in the awareness that nothing, not even one's self, is certain. In such a story as "The Celestial Railroad" and in his novels, Hawthorne raised the Emersonian, the major nineteenth-century questions: Is the world real, or is it merely what we want it to be? Is human life formed in accordance with a divine destiny which man may come to know if he seeks hard and far enough? Does man ever gain self-knowledge, or is he thrust ever deeper into the loneliness of his private speculation?

These and similar issues are the bases for the tales from the earliest, in the eighteen-thirties, to the last, in 1850. Like his friend Melville, Hawthorne wrote a testament of rejection. For both writers the world is an unquiet place, and most men live in it their lives of wonder, searching, and piecemeal despair. Yet, if the two men are alike in their themes, they were quite unlike in other ways. Hawthorne's "double mind" spared him: he lived somehow free, as a man, of the perils which a vision of darkness might bring; his imagination seldom seems to have impinged on his everyday, practical life. By contrast, Melville lived as a private man precisely what he thought and presented as a writer; his was the truer vocation of the man to his art, for what he saw in his imagination he believed in his daily life. When the two friends met in 1856, after a separation of several years, Hawthorne's journal entry (see p. 769) vividly shows the ravages which the imagination of Melville had produced in the author of *Moby-Dick* and *Pierre,* a man whose thinking and imagination were one. Hawthorne was, by contrast, forever distanced from his art; his double mind was his insurance against the crippling effects of hypersensitivity and morbidity of conscience.

Yet, for all that one may admire in Hawthorne's thought, it is his art which has survived and gained the greatest favor in our own time. Hawthorne as a man is, accordingly, less interesting than Hawthorne as a craftsman and symbolist who, almost in spite of himself, became a major writer. One says "in spite of himself" because Hawthorne was, as a person, curiously unwilling to talk about his art or about the problems of writing. The long hours he spent with Melville were filled with Hawthorne's monosyllables and Melville's tireless sentences which wove around and through the questions of man as a writer, as a thinker, as a citizen of the domain of art. Hawthorne's notebooks have been much admired for presenting the inner life of Hawthorne the man. They do so only on those rare and unexpected occasions when Hawthorne is at ease or when he does not have any other writing to do. The jottings of ideas for tales—a representative group is presented in these selections—are so hesitatingly and even waggishly noted that one can only be puzzled. Hawthorne was not an interesting keeper of a notebook because he kept his notebook as if he did not take it very seriously. He seems to have understood that he had only a scant amount of imaginative energy; he husbanded it with care and discretion. Even his Prefaces to the collections of short stories and to the novels were written in a mood of apology, as if the writer had his nerve intruding upon the privacy of the reader.

Hawthorne was a major writer not because of what he was as a man, a social thinker, or as a judge of his own writings, but because, from first to last, he saw each human life as a single unit, a separate, isolated case of conscience which—just as for a Puritan of the seventeenth century or for Jonathan Edwards—was faced with its own unique destiny and had to find its own unique way. Hawthorne's men and women are always undertaking a journey of consciousness—the walk of Goodman Brown through the darkening forest; the heedless strolling of Robin Molineux through a balefully lit town; the haunted steps of Parson Hooper to his death; the endless wandering of Ethan Brand until he came home; the pilgrimage of Hester Prynne from the scaffold and back to it again. Along the route of these journeys there are no guides such as directed Bunyan's Christian to the Celestial City, and there are not even the inner promptings of conscience to distinguish between a safe and a dangerous step.

The route of these journeys was, as we have seen, not shaped by or known to the persons undertaking them; rather, the journeys were prescribed and determined by the iron ring which Fate sets against each human Will. Emerson's "Fate" and "Illusions" are a commentary on Hawthorne's vision of human life: to think is to press against the enclosing ring of destiny, for not an atom moves or a shadow flickers but in accordance with the unyielding fate of everything to do what it must. Human thinking can go only so far as it is privileged to thrust itself and then breaks against the overmastering Necessity which binds it. To think is to be free only at that instant of thinking: Parson Hooper was free on the moment of his assuming the black veil; the artist Aylmer was free when he decided that he would paint a perfect picture. But the free act of thought was itself the end of freedom, for that thought thereafter necessitated the inevitable destiny which came to Hooper, Aylmer, Hester Prynne, and the others. Man lives, therefore, in his freedom, but his freedom is, as Emerson showed, his fate: every act of willing is a narrowing of the ring of one's life until, as Goodman Brown discovered, one lives in silence.

Such a view of life puts Hawthorne near Emerson—the Emerson, not of *Nature* or "The American Scholar," but of the later writings and of the poems like "Uriel" (see p. 572) and "Fate" (see p. 552). It links him even more closely than friendship could to Melville, who subtitled one of his novels "or, The Ambiguities," and whose wanderings within his own dark mind brought Ahab to the tightened circle of the whale rope and Billy Budd to the noose at the end of the yardarm. It places Hawthorne within the tradition of American writing from Edwards to Emily Dickinson and to Faulkner and beyond. He was one among many who were gifted with "the power of blackness"—the search into and beyond the mysterious underside of human thought, into that interior heart of man where secrets remain forever hidden and into the narrowing distance between what men hope they can do and what little they eventually accomplish. Hawthorne's world was, to be sure, not a "real" world: it was fashioned of the ephemeral dreams, the chiaroscuros of human thinking set against the rigidity of time and chance. Hawthorne's was a profoundly moral vision which, if it were denied the grandeur of tragedy, was nonetheless sensitive to those shapes of emotion and thought which his symbolism displayed and made memorable.

Thus the key to Hawthorne is his symbolic imagination and his moral insight. His writings have remained alive and his artistic reputation continues unassailed through more than a century of changing literary taste. He has been able to outshine names of apparently greater brilliance because his writings, however simple they may appear and however limited their themes may be, have continually demanded that they be read anew with a quickening response to discover what must be known if one is to understand them fully. Our journey of understanding is like that of a Puritan of another age, or like that of one of Hawthorne's own men and women: we are given the signs, the symbols of human thought, and we are privileged to know them as best we can. Yet their final revelation will forever escape us, because men's deepest beliefs are themselves symbolic and, being so, are wrapped in mysteries.

READING SUGGESTIONS

EDITIONS

The Complete Works of Nathaniel Hawthorne, ed. by George P. Lathrop, 12 vols. (1883). Still the standard edition. An enlarged "Autograph Edition," 22 vols., was published in 1900.

A complete, authoritative edition of Hawthorne's writings, ed. by William Charvat, Roy Harvey Pearce, and Fredson Bowers, is under way and will be published by the Ohio State University Press.

BIOGRAPHY

RANDALL STEWART, *Nathaniel Hawthorne* (1948). A compact and virtually definitive account of the novelist's life.

NOTEBOOKS AND LETTERS

The American Notebooks by Nathaniel Hawthorne, ed. by Randall Stewart (1932); *The English Notebooks by Nathaniel Hawthorne*, ed. by Randall Stewart (1941). Both establish the definitive texts.

The French and Italian Notebooks are being re-edited, and a complete edition of Hawthorne's letters is forthcoming.

CRITICISM

HENRY JAMES, *Hawthorne* (1879). Remains one of the most illuminating critical discussions of one novelist by another.

D. H. LAWRENCE, *Studies in Classic American Literature* (1923). Provided one of the most stimulating and argumentative theories of Hawthorne's Puritanism.

NEWTON ARVIN, *Hawthorne* (1929). A very perceptive biographical and critical study.

AUSTIN WARREN, *Nathaniel Hawthorne: Representative Selections* (1934). Contains an early and significant critical analysis which helped to establish the more recent approach to Hawthorne's writings.

F. O. MATTHIESSEN, *American Renaissance: Art and Expression in the Age of Emerson and Whitman* (1941). Includes a brilliant analysis of Hawthorne in terms of his symbolic imagination.

In recent years Hawthorne has received critical attention from many points of view; among the most illuminating studies are the following:

AUSTIN WARREN, *Rage for Order* (1948).

MARK VAN DOREN, *Nathaniel Hawthorne* (1949). A graceful survey of the writings.

MARIUS BEWLEY, *The Complex Fate* (1952).

RICHARD HARTER FOGLE, *Hawthorne's Fiction: The Light and the Dark* (1952).

CHARLES FEIDELSON, JR., *Symbolism and American Literature* (1953).

R. W. B. Lewis, *The American Adam* (1955).
Hyatt H. Waggoner, *Hawthorne: A Critical Study* (1955).
Richard Chase, *The American Novel and Its Tradition* (1957).
Roy R. Male, *Hawthorne's Tragic Vision* (1957).
Harry Levin, *The Power of Blackness* (1958).

MY KINSMAN, MAJOR MOLINEUX

THE STORY may treat a number of ideas: the silencing of Major Molineux as a spokesman for New England's rights under the oppressive Crown governor; the disillusionment of a young colonial democrat who valued titles or inherited rank; the journey of an innocent country youth through an education into the world's evil. For all its apparent allegory of Good and Evil, of man and Satan, of light and darkness, the story is one of the most ambiguous and interesting Hawthorne wrote. It first appeared in *The Token* for 1832 and was not included in Hawthorne's collections of tales until *The Snow-Image* volume of 1852.

AFTER the kings of Great Britain had assumed the right of appointing the colonial governors, the measures of the latter seldom met with the ready and generous approbation which had been paid to those of their predecessors, under the original charters. The people looked with most jealous scrutiny to the exercise of power which did not emanate from themselves, and they usually rewarded their rulers with slender gratitude for the compliances by which, in softening their instructions from beyond the sea, they had incurred the reprehension of those who gave them. The annals of Massachusetts Bay will inform us, that of six governors in the space of about forty years from the surrender of the old charter, under James II., two were imprisoned by a popular insurrection; a third, as Hutchinson inclines to believe, was driven from the province by the whizzing of a musket-ball; a fourth, in the opinion of the same historian, was hastened to his grave by continual bickerings with the House of Representatives; and the remaining two, as well as their successors, till the Revolution, were favored with few and brief intervals of peaceful sway.[1] The inferior members of the court party, in times of high political excitement, led scarcely a more desirable life. These remarks may serve as a preface to the following adventures, which chanced upon a summer night, not far from a hundred years ago. The reader, in order to avoid a long and dry detail of colonial affairs, is requested to dispense with an account of the train of circumstances that had caused much temporary inflammation of the popular mind.

It was near nine o'clock of a moonlight evening, when a boat crossed the ferry with a single passenger, who had obtained his conveyance at that unusual hour by the promise of an extra fare. While he stood on the landing place, searching in either pocket for the means of fulfilling his agreement, the ferryman lifted a lantern, by the aid of which, and the newly-risen moon, he took a very accurate survey of the stranger's figure. He was a youth of barely eighteen years, evidently country-bred, and now, as it should seem, upon his first visit to town. He was clad in a coarse gray coat, well worn, but in excellent repair; his under garments were durably constructed of leather, and fitted tight to a pair of serviceable and well-shaped limbs; his stockings of blue yarn were the incontrovertible work of a mother or a sister; and on his head was a three-cornered hat, which in its better days had perhaps sheltered the graver brow of the lad's father. Under his left arm was a heavy cudgel, formed of an oak sapling, and retaining a part of the hardened root; and his equipment was completed by a wallet, not so abundantly stocked as to incommode the vigorous shoulders on which it hung. Brown, curly hair, well-shaped features, and bright, cheerful eyes, were nature's gifts, and worth all that art could have done for his adornment.

The youth, one of whose names was Robin, finally drew from his pocket the half of a little

MY KINSMAN, MAJOR MOLINEUX. 1. **The . . . sway:** The historical summary concerns the people of Massachusetts who, by appeal to the charter, sought to control the colonial governors appointed by the Crown. After more than half a century, the Crown finally annulled the Massachusetts charter in 1684. The "six governors" who followed each other "in the space of about forty years" were Simon Bradstreet (1679–86, 1689–92), Sir Edmund Andros (1686–89), Sir William Phips (1692–94), Richard Coote, Earl of Bellomont (1697–1700), Joseph Dudley (1702–15), and Samuel Shute (1716–22). Hawthorne's authority for these matters is Thomas Hutchinson, *The History of the Colony of Massachusetts Bay* (1764–1828).

province bill of five shillings, which, in the depreciation of that sort of currency, did but satisfy the ferryman's demand, with the surplus of a sexangular piece of parchment, valued at three pence. He then walked forward into the town, with as light a step as if his day's journey had not already exceeded thirty miles, and with as eager an eye as if he were entering London city, instead of the little metropolis of a New England colony. Before Robin had proceeded far, however, it occurred to him that he knew not whither to direct his steps; so he paused, and looked up and down the narrow street, scrutinizing the small and mean wooden buildings that were scattered on either side.

"This low hovel cannot be my kinsman's dwelling," thought he, "nor yonder old house, where the moonlight enters at the broken casement; and truly I see none hereabouts that might be worthy of him. It would have been wise to inquire my way of the ferryman, and doubtless he would have gone with me, and earned a shilling from the Major for his pains. But the next man I meet will do as well."

He resumed his walk, and was glad to perceive that the street now became wider, and the houses more respectable in their appearance. He soon discerned a figure moving on moderately in advance, and hastened his steps to overtake it. As Robin drew nigh, he saw that the passenger was a man in years, with a full periwig of gray hair, a wide-skirted coat of dark cloth, and silk stockings rolled above his knees. He carried a long and polished cane, which he struck down perpendicularly before him at every step; and at regular intervals he uttered two successive hems, of a peculiarly solemn and sepulchral intonation. Having made these observations, Robin laid hold of the skirt of the old man's coat, just when the light from the open door and windows of a barber's shop fell upon both their figures.

"Good evening to you, honored sir," said he, making a low bow, and still retaining his hold of the skirt. "I pray you tell me whereabouts is the dwelling of my kinsman, Major Molineux."

The youth's question was uttered very loudly; and one of the barbers, whose razor was descending on a well-soaped chin, and another who was dressing a Ramillies wig,[2] left their occupations, and came to the door. The citizen, in the mean time, turned a long-favored countenance upon Robin, and answered him in a tone of excessive anger and annoyance. His two sepulchral hems, however, broke into the very centre of his rebuke, with most singular effect, like a thought of the cold grave obtruding among wrathful passions.

"Let go my garment, fellow! I tell you, I know not the man you speak of. What! I have authority, I have—hem, hem—authority; and if this be the respect you show for your betters, your feet shall be brought acquainted with the stocks by daylight, tomorrow morning!"

Robin released the old man's skirt, and hastened away, pursued by an ill-mannered roar of laughter from the barber's shop. He was at first considerably surprised by the result of his question, but, being a shrewd youth, soon thought himself able to account for the mystery.

"This is some country representative," was his conclusion, "who has never seen the inside of my kinsman's door, and lacks the breeding to answer a stranger civilly. The man is old, or verily—I might be tempted to turn back and smite him on the nose. Ah, Robin, Robin! even the barber's boys laugh at you for choosing such a guide! You will be wiser in time, friend Robin."

He now became entangled in a succession of crooked and narrow streets, which crossed each other, and meandered at no great distance from the water-side. The smell of tar was obvious to his nostrils, the masts of vessels pierced the moonlight above the tops of the buildings, and the numerous signs, which Robin paused to read, informed him that he was near the centre of business. But the streets were empty, the shops were closed, and lights were visible only in the second stories of a few dwelling-houses. At length, on the corner of a narrow lane, through which he was passing, he beheld the broad countenance of a British hero swinging before the door of an inn, whence proceeded the voices of many guests. The casement of one of the lower windows was thrown back, and a very thin curtain permitted Robin to distinguish a party at supper, round a well-furnished table. The fragrance of the good cheer steamed forth into the outer air, and the youth could not fail to recollect that the last remnant of his travelling stock of provision had yielded to his morning appetite, and that noon had found, and left him, dinnerless.

"Oh, that a parchment three-penny might give me a right to sit down at yonder table!" said Robin, with a sigh. "But the Major will make me welcome to the best of his victuals; so I will even step boldly in, and inquire my way to his dwelling."

He entered the tavern, and was guided by the murmur of voices, and the fumes of tobacco, to the public room. It was a long and low apartment, with oaken walls, grown dark in the continual smoke, and a floor, which was thickly sanded, but

2. **Ramillies wig:** from Ramillies, Belgium, famous for its cloth-making; the allusion is to a plaited wig with a bow of ribbon tied at top and bottom.

of no immaculate purity. A number of persons—the larger part of whom appeared to be mariners, or in some way connected with the sea—occupied the wooden benches, or leather-bottomed chairs, conversing on various matters, and occasionally lending their attention to some topic of general interest. Three or four little groups were draining as many bowls of punch, which the West India trade had long since made a familiar drink in the colony. Others, who had the appearance of men who lived by regular and laborious handicraft, preferred the insulated bliss of an unshared potation, and became more taciturn under its influence. Nearly all, in short, evinced a predilection for the Good Creature in some of its various shapes, for this is a vice to which, as Fast Day sermons [3] of a hundred years ago will testify, we have a long hereditary claim. The only guests to whom Robin's sympathies inclined him were two or three sheepish countrymen, who were using the inn somewhat after the fashion of a Turkish caravansary; they had gotten themselves into the darkest corner of the room, and heedless of the Nicotian atmosphere,[4] were supping on the bread of their own ovens, and the bacon cured in their own chimney-smoke. But though Robin felt a sort of brotherhood with these strangers, his eyes were attracted from them to a person who stood near the door, holding whispered conversation with a group of ill-dressed associates. His features were separately striking almost to grotesqueness, and the whole face left a deep impression on the memory. The forehead bulged out into a double prominence, with a vale between; the nose came boldly forth in an irregular curve, and its bridge was of more than a finger's breadth; the eyebrows were deep and shaggy, and the eyes glowed beneath them like fire in a cave.

While Robin deliberated of whom to inquire respecting his kinsman's dwelling, he was accosted by the innkeeper, a little man in a stained white apron, who had come to pay his professional welcome to the stranger. Being in the second generation from a French Protestant,[5] he seemed to have inherited the courtesy of his parent nation; but no variety of circumstances was ever known to change his voice from the one shrill note in which he now addressed Robin.

"From the country, I presume, sir?" said he, with a profound bow. "Beg leave to congratulate you on your arrival, and trust you intend a long stay with us. Fine town here, sir, beautiful buildings, and much that may interest a stranger. May I hope for the honor of your commands in respect to supper?"

"The man sees a family likeness! the rogue has guessed that I am related to the Major!" thought Robin, who had hitherto experienced little superfluous civility.

All eyes were now turned on the country lad, standing at the door, in his worn three-cornered hat, gray coat, leather breeches, and blue yarn stockings, leaning on an oaken cudgel, and bearing a wallet on his back.

Robin replied to the courteous innkeeper, with such an assumption of confidence as befitted the Major's relative. "My honest friend," he said, "I shall make it a point to patronize your house on some occasion, when"—here he could not help lowering his voice—"when I may have more than a parchment three-pence in my pocket. My present business," continued he, speaking with lofty confidence, "is merely to inquire my way to the dwelling of my kinsman, Major Molineux."

There was a sudden and general movement in the room, which Robin interpreted as expressing the eagerness of each individual to become his guide. But the innkeeper turned his eyes to a written paper on the wall, which he read, or seemed to read, with occasional recurrences to the young man's figure.

"What have we here?" said he, breaking his speech into little dry fragments. "Left the house of the subscriber, bounden servant,[6] Hezekiah Mudge,—had on, when he went away, gray coat, leather breeches, master's third-best hat. One pound currency reward to whosoever shall lodge him in any jail of the province. Better trudge, boy; better trudge!"

Robin had begun to draw his hand towards the lighter end of the oak cudgel, but a strange hostility in every countenance induced him to relinquish his purpose of breaking the courteous innkeeper's head. As he turned to leave the room, he encountered a sneering glance from the bold-featured personage whom he had before noticed; and no sooner was he beyond the door, than he heard a general laugh, in which the innkeeper's voice might be distinguished, like the dropping of small stones into a kettle.

"Now, is it not strange," thought Robin, with his usual shrewdness,—"is it not strange that the confession of an empty pocket should outweigh the name of my kinsman, Major Molineux? Oh, if I

3. **Fast Day sermons:** the addresses delivered by the New England clergy on special days of public penance. 4. **Nicotian atmosphere:** the air of "nicotiana," i.e., nicotine or tobacco. 5. **second . . . Protestant:** the child of a Huguenot refugee from France, a few of whom made their way to New England.

6. **bounden servant:** an indentured servant who served his master for a period of seven years and then gained his freedom. To break an indenture was a serious crime.

had one of those grinning rascals in the woods, where I and my oak sapling grew up together, I would teach him that my arm is heavy though my purse be light!"

On turning the corner of the narrow lane, Robin found himself in a spacious street, with an unbroken line of lofty houses on each side, and a steepled building at the upper end, whence the ringing of a bell announced the hour of nine. The light of the moon, and the lamps from the numerous shop-windows, discovered people promenading on the pavement, and amongst them Robin had hoped to recognize his hitherto inscrutable relative. The result of his former inquiries made him unwilling to hazard another, in a scene of such publicity, and he determined to walk slowly and silently up the street, thrusting his face close to that of every elderly gentleman, in search of the Major's lineaments. In his progress, Robin encountered many gay and gallant figures. Embroidered garments of showy colors, enormous periwigs, gold-laced hats, and silver-hilted swords glided past him and dazzled his optics. Travelled youths, imitators of the European fine gentlemen of the period, trod jauntily along, half dancing to the fashionable tunes which they hummed, and making poor Robin ashamed of his quiet and natural gait. At length, after many pauses to examine the gorgeous display of goods in the shop-windows, and after suffering some rebukes for the impertinence of his scrutiny into people's faces, the Major's kinsman found himself near the steepled building, still unsuccessful in his search. As yet, however, he had seen only one side of the thronged street; so Robin crossed, and continued the same sort of inquisition down the opposite pavement, with stronger hopes than the philosopher seeking an honest man, but with no better fortune. He had arrived about midway towards the lower end, from which his course began, when he overheard the approach of some one, who struck down a cane on the flagstones at every step, uttering, at regular intervals, two sepulchral hems.

"Mercy on us!" quoth Robin, recognizing the sound.

Turning a corner, which chanced to be close at his right hand, he hastened to pursue his researches in some other part of the town. His patience now was wearing low, and he seemed to feel more fatigue from his rambles since he crossed the ferry, than from his journey of several days on the other side. Hunger also pleaded loudly within him, and Robin began to balance the propriety of demanding, violently, and with lifted cudgel, the necessary guidance from the first solitary passenger whom he should meet. While a resolution to this effect was gaining strength, he entered a street of mean appearance, on either side of which a row of ill-built houses was straggling towards the harbor. The moonlight fell upon no passenger along the whole extent, but in the third domicile which Robin passed there was a half-opened door, and his keen glance detected a woman's garment within.

"My luck may be better here," said he to himself.

Accordingly, he approached the door, and beheld it shut closer as he did so; yet an open space remained, sufficing for the fair occupant to observe the stranger, without a corresponding display on her part. All that Robin could discern was a strip of scarlet petticoat, and the occasional sparkle of an eye, as if the moonbeams were trembling on some bright thing.

"Pretty mistress," for I may call her so with a good conscience, thought the shrewd youth, since I know nothing to the contrary,—"my sweet pretty mistress, will you be kind enough to tell me whereabouts I must seek the dwelling of my kinsman, Major Molineux?"

Robin's face was plaintive and winning, and the female, seeing nothing to be shunned in the handsome country youth, thrust open the door, and came forth into the moonlight. She was a dainty little figure, with a white neck, round arms, and a slender waist, at the extremity of which her scarlet petticoat jutted out over a hoop, as if she were standing in a balloon. Moreover, her face was oval and pretty, her hair dark beneath the little cap, and her bright eyes possessed a sly freedom, which triumphed over those of Robin.

"Major Molineux dwells here," said this fair woman.

Now, her voice was the sweetest Robin had heard that night, yet he could not help doubting whether that sweet voice spoke Gospel truth. He looked up and down the mean street, and then surveyed the house before which they stood. It was a small, dark edifice of two stories, the second of which projected over the lower floor, and the front apartment had the aspect of a shop for petty commodities.

"Now, truly, I am in luck," replied Robin, cunningly, "and so indeed is my kinsman, the Major, in having so pretty a housekeeper. But I prithee trouble him to step to the door; I will deliver him a message from his friends in the country, and then go back to my lodgings at the inn."

"Nay, the Major has been abed this hour or more," said the lady of the scarlet petticoat; "and it would be to little purpose to disturb him tonight, seeing his evening drought was of the strongest. But he is a kind-hearted man, and it would be as much as my life's worth to let a kinsman of his turn away from the door. You are the good old gentleman's very picture, and I could swear that was his rainy-weather hat. Also he has garments very much resembling those leather small-clothes. But come in, I pray, for I bid you hearty welcome in his name."

So saying, the fair and hospitable dame took our hero by the hand; and the touch was light, and the force was gentleness, and though Robin read in her eyes what he did not hear in her words, yet the slender-waisted woman in the scarlet petticoat proved stronger than the athletic country youth. She had drawn his half-willing footsteps nearly to the threshold, when the opening of a door in the neighborhood startled the Major's housekeeper, and, leaving the Major's kinsman, she vanished speedily into her own domicile. A heavy yawn preceded the appearance of a man, who, like the Moonshine of Pyramus and Thisbe,[7] carried a lantern, needlessly aiding his sister luminary in the heavens. As he walked sleepily up the street, he turned his broad, dull face on Robin, and displayed a long staff, spiked at the end.

"Home, vagabond, home!" said the watchman, in accents that seemed to fall asleep as soon as they were uttered. "Home, or we'll set you in the stocks, by peep of day!"

"This is the second hint of the kind," thought Robin. "I wish they would end my difficulties, by setting me there to-night."

Nevertheless, the youth felt an instinctive antipathy towards the guardian of midnight order, which at first prevented him from asking his usual question. But just when the man was about to vanish behind the corner, Robin resolved not to lose the opportunity, and shouted lustily after him,—

"I say, friend! will you guide me to the house of my kinsman, Major Molineux?"

The watchman made no reply, but turned the corner and was gone; yet Robin seemed to hear the sound of drowsy laughter stealing along the solitary street. At that moment, also, a pleasant titter saluted him from the open window above his head; he looked up, and caught the sparkle of a saucy eye; a round arm beckoned to him, and next he heard light footsteps descending the staircase within. But Robin, being of the household of a New England clergyman, was a good youth, as well as a shrewd one; so he resisted temptation, and fled away.

He now roamed desperately, and at random, through the town, almost ready to believe that a spell was on him, like that by which a wizard of his country had once kept three pursuers wandering, a whole winter night, within twenty paces of the cottage which they sought. The streets lay before him, strange and desolate, and the lights were extinguished in almost every house. Twice, however, little parties of men, among whom Robin distinguished individuals in outlandish attire, came hurrying along; but, though on both occasions, they paused to address him, such intercourse did not at all enlighten his perplexity. They did but utter a few words in some language of which Robin knew nothing, and perceiving his inability to answer, bestowed a curse upon him in plain English and hastened away. Finally, the lad determined to knock at the door of every mansion that might appear worthy to be occupied by his kinsman, trusting that perseverance would overcome the fatality that had hitherto thwarted him. Firm in this resolve, he was passing beneath the walls of a church, which formed the corner of two streets, when, as he turned into the shade of its steeple, he encountered a bulky stranger, muffled in a cloak. The man was proceeding with the speed of earnest business, but Robin planted himself full before him, holding the oak cudgel with both hands across his body as a bar to further passage.

"Halt, honest man, and answer me a question," said he, very resolutely. "Tell me, this instant, whereabouts is the dwelling of my kinsman, Major Molineux!"

"Keep your tongue between your teeth, fool, and let me pass!" said a deep, gruff voice, which Robin partly remembered. "Let me pass, or I'll strike you to the earth!"

"No, no, neighbor!" cried Robin, flourishing his cudgel, and then thrusting its larger end close to the man's muffled face. "No, no, I'm not the fool you take me for, nor do you pass till I have an answer to my question. Whereabouts is the dwelling of my kinsman, Major Molineux?"

The stranger, instead of attempting to force his passage, stepped back into the moonlight, unmuffled his face, and stared full into that of Robin.

"Watch here an hour, and Major Molineux will pass by," said he.

Robin gazed with dismay and astonishment on the unprecedented physiognomy of the speaker. The forehead with its double prominence, the broad hooked nose, the shaggy eyebrows, and fiery eyes, were those which he had noticed at the inn, but the man's complexion had undergone a singular, or, more properly, a two-fold change. One side of the face blazed an intense red, while the other was black as midnight, the division line

7. **Moonshine . . . Thisbe:** See Shakespeare, *Midsummer Night's Dream,* V.i.130 ff.

being in the broad bridge of the nose; and a mouth which seemed to extend from ear to ear was black or red, in contrast to the color of the cheek. The effect was as if two individual devils, a fiend of fire and a fiend of darkness, had united themselves to form this infernal visage. The stranger grinned in Robin's face, muffled his particolored features, and was out of sight in a moment.

"Strange things we travellers see!" ejaculated Robin.

He seated himself, however, upon the steps of the church-door, resolving to wait the appointed time for his kinsman. A few moments were consumed in philosophical speculations upon the species of man who had just left him; but having settled this point shrewdly, rationally, and satisfactorily, he was compelled to look elsewhere for his amusement. And first he threw his eyes along the street. It was of more respectable appearance than most of those into which he had wandered, and the moon, creating, like the imaginative power, a beautiful strangeness in familiar objects, gave something of romance to a scene that might not have possessed it in the light of day. The irregular and often quaint architecture of the houses, some of whose roofs were broken into numerous little peaks, while others ascended, steep and narrow, into a single point, and others again were square; the pure snow-white of some of their complexions, the aged darkness of others, and the thousand sparklings, reflected from bright substances in the walls of many; these matters engaged Robin's attention for a while, and then began to grow wearisome. Next he endeavored to define the forms of distant objects, starting away, with almost ghostly indistinctness, just as his eye appeared to grasp them; and finally he took a minute survey of an edifice which stood on the opposite side of the street, directly in front of the church-door, where he was stationed. It was a large, square mansion, distinguished from its neighbors by a balcony, which rested on tall pillars, and by an elaborate Gothic window, communicating therewith.

"Perhaps this is the very house I have been seeking," thought Robin.

Then he strove to speed away the time, by listening to a murmur which swept continually along the street, yet was scarcely audible, except to an unaccustomed ear like his; it was a low, dull, dreamy sound, compounded of many noises, each of which was at too a great a distance to be separately heard. Robin marvelled at this snore of a sleeping town, and marvelled more whenever its continuity was broken by now and then a distant shout, apparently loud where it originated. But altogether it was a sleep-inspiring sound, and, to shake off its drowsy influence, Robin arose, and climbed a window-frame, that he might view the interior of the church. There the moonbeams came trembling in, and fell down upon the deserted pews, and extended along the quiet aisles. A fainter yet more awful radiance was hovering around the pulpit, and one solitary ray had dared to rest upon the open page of the great Bible. Had nature, in that deep hour, become a worshipper in the house which man had builded? Or was that heavenly light the visible sanctity of the place,—visible because no earthly and impure feet were within the walls? The scene made Robin's heart shiver with a sensation of loneliness stronger than he had ever felt in the remotest depths of his native woods; so he turned away and sat down again before the door. There were graves around the church, and now an uneasy thought obtruded into Robin's breast. What if the object of his search, which had been so often and so strangely thwarted, were all the time mouldering in his shroud? What if his kinsman should glide through yonder gate, and nod and smile to him in dimly passing by?

"Oh that any breathing thing were here with me!" said Robin.

Recalling his thoughts from this uncomfortable track, he sent them over forest, hill, and stream, and attempted to imagine how that evening of ambiguity and weariness had been spent by his father's household. He pictured them assembled at the door, beneath the tree, the great old tree, which had been spared for its huge twisted trunk, and venerable shade, when a thousand leafy brethren fell. There, at the going down of the summer sun, it was his father's custom to perform domestic worship, that the neighbors might come and join with him like brothers of the family, and that the wayfaring man might pause to drink at that fountain, and keep his heart pure by freshening the memory of home. Robin distinguished the seat of every individual of the little audience; he saw the good man in the midst, holding the Scriptures in the golden light that fell from the western clouds; he beheld him close the book and all rise up to pray. He heard the old thanksgivings for daily mercies, the old supplications for their continuance, to which he had so often listened in weariness, but which were now among his dear remembrances. He perceived the slight inequality of his father's voice when he came to speak of the absent one; he noted how his mother turned her face to the broad and knotted trunk; how his elder brother scorned, because the beard was rough upon his upper lip, to permit his features to be moved; how the younger sister drew down a low hanging branch before her eyes; and how the little one of all, whose sports had hitherto broken the decorum of the scene, understood the prayer for her playmate, and burst into clamorous grief. Then he saw them go in at the door; and when Robin would have entered also, the latch tinkled into its place, and he was excluded from his home.

"Am I here, or there?" cried Robin, starting; for all at once, when his thoughts had become visible and audible in a dream, the long, wide, solitary street shone out before him.

He aroused himself, and endeavored to fix his attention steadily upon the large edifice which he had surveyed before. But still his mind kept vibrating between fancy and reality; by turns, the pillars of the balcony lengthened into the tall, bare stems of pines, dwindled down to human figures, and settled again into their true shape and size, and then commenced a new succession of changes. For a single moment, when he deemed himself awake, he could have sworn that a visage—one which he seemed to remember, yet could not absolutely name as his kinsman's—was looking towards him from the Gothic window. A deeper sleep wrestled with and nearly overcame him, but fled at the sound of footsteps along the opposite pavement. Robin rubbed his eyes, discerned a man passing at the foot of the balcony, and addressed him in a loud, peevish, and lamentable cry.

"Hallo, friend! must I wait here all night for my kinsman, Major Molineux?"

The sleeping echoes awoke, and answered the voice; and the passenger, barely able to discern a figure sitting in the oblique shade of the steeple, traversed the street to obtain a nearer view. He was himself a gentleman in his prime, of open, intelligent, cheerful, and altogether prepossessing countenance. Perceiving a country youth, apparently homeless and without friends, he accosted him in a tone of real kindness, which had become strange to Robin's ears.

"Well, my good lad, why are you sitting here?" inquired he. "Can I be of service to you in any way?"

"I am afraid not, sir," replied Robin, despondingly; "yet I shall take it kindly, if you'll answer me a single question. I've been searching, half the night, for one Major Molineux; now, sir, is there really such a person in these parts, or am I dreaming?"

"Major Molineux! The name is not altogether strange to me," said the gentleman, smiling. "Have you any objection to telling me the nature of your business with him?"

Then Robin briefly related that his father was a clergyman, settled on a small salary, at a long distance back in the country, and that he and Major Molineux were brothers' children. The Major, having inherited riches, and acquired civil and military rank, had visited his cousin, in great pomp, a year or two before; had manifested much interest in Robin and an elder brother, and, being childless himself, had thrown out hints respecting the future establishment of one of them in life. The elder brother was destined to succeed to the farm which his father cultivated in the interval of sacred duties; it was therefore determined that Robin should profit by his kinsman's generous intentions, especially as he seemed to be rather the favorite, and was thought to possess other necessary endowments.

"For I have the name of being a shrewd youth," observed Robin, in this part of his story.

"I doubt not you deserve it," replied his new friend, good-naturedly; "but pray proceed."

"Well, sir, being nearly eighteen years old, and well-grown, as you see," continued Robin, drawing himself up to his full height, "I thought it high time to begin the world. So my mother and sister put me in handsome trim, and my father gave me half the remnant of his last year's salary, and five days ago I started for this place, to pay the Major a visit. But, would you believe it, sir! I crossed the ferry a little after dark, and have yet found nobody that would show me the way to his dwelling; —only, an hour or two since, I was told to wait here, and Major Molineux would pass by."

"Can you describe the man who told you this?" inquired the gentleman.

"Oh, he was a very ill-favored fellow, sir," replied Robin, "with two great bumps on his forehead, a hook nose, fiery eyes,—and, what struck me as the strangest, his face was of two different colors. Do you happen to know such a man, sir?"

"Not intimately," answered the stranger, "but I chanced to meet him a little time previous to your stopping me. I believe you may trust his word, and that the Major will very shortly pass through this street. In the mean time, as I have a singular curiosity to witness your meeting, I will sit down here upon the steps, and bear you company."

He seated himself accordingly, and soon engaged his companion in animated discourse. It was but of brief continuance, however, for a noise of shouting, which had long been remotely audible, drew so much nearer that Robin inquired its cause.

"What may be the meaning of this uproar?" asked he. "Truly, if your town be always as noisy, I shall find little sleep, while I am an inhabitant."

"Why, indeed, friend Robin, there do appear to

be three or four riotous fellows abroad to-night," replied the gentleman. "You must not expect all the stillness of your native woods, here in our streets. But the watch will shortly be at the heels of these lads, and—"

"Ay, and set them in the stocks by peep of day," interrupted Robin, recollecting his own encounter with the drowsy lantern-bearer. "But, dear sir, if I may trust my ears, an army of watchmen would never make head against such a multitude of rioters. There were at least a thousand voices went up to make that one shout."

"May not a man have several voices, Robin, as well as two complexions?" said his friend.

"Perhaps a man may; but Heaven forbid that a woman should!" responded the shrewd youth, thinking of the seductive tones of the Major's housekeeper.

The sounds of a trumpet in some neighboring street now became so evident and continual, that Robin's curiosity was strongly excited. In addition to the shouts, he heard frequent bursts from many instruments of discord, and a wild and confused laughter filled up the intervals. Robin rose from the steps, and looked wistfully towards a point whither people seemed to be hastening.

"Surely some prodigious merry-making is going on," exclaimed he. "I have laughed very little since I left home, sir, and should be sorry to lose an opportunity. Shall we step round the corner by the darkish house, and take our share of the fun?"

"Sit down again, sit down, good Robin," replied the gentleman, laying his hand on the skirt of the gray coat. "You forget that we must wait here for your kinsman; and there is reason to believe that he will pass by, in the course of a very few moments."

The near approach of the uproar had now disturbed the neighborhood; windows flew open on all sides; and many heads, in the attire of the pillow, and confused by sleep suddenly broken, were protruded to the gaze of whoever had leisure to observe them. Eager voices hailed each other from house to house, all demanding the explanation, which not a soul could give. Half-dressed men hurried towards the unknown commotion, stumbling as they went over the stone steps that thrust themselves into the narrow foot-walk. The shouts, the laughter, and the tuneless bray, the antipodes of music, came onwards with increasing din, till scattered individuals, and then denser bodies, began to appear round a corner at the distance of a hundred yards.

"Will you recognize your kinsman, if he passes in this crowd?" inquired the gentleman.

"Indeed, I can't warrant it, sir; but I'll take my stand here, and keep a bright look-out," answered Robin, descending to the outer edge of the pavement.

A mighty stream of people now emptied into the street, and came rolling slowly towards the church. A single horseman wheeled the corner in the midst of them, and close behind him came a band of fearful wind-instruments, sending forth a fresher discord, now that no interveing buildings kept it from the ear. Then a redder light disturbed the moonbeams, and a dense multitude of torches shone along the street, concealing, by their glare, whatever object they illuminated. The single horseman, clad in a military dress, and bearing a drawn sword, rode onward as the leader, and, by his fierce and variegated countenance, appeared like war personified: the red of one cheek was an emblem of fire and sword; the blackness of the other betokened the mourning that attends them. In his train were wild figures in the Indian dress, and many fantastic shapes without a model, giving the whole march a visionary air, as if a dream had broken forth from some feverish brain, and were sweeping visibly through the midnight streets. A mass of people, inactive, except as applauding spectators, hemmed the procession in; and several women ran along the side-walk, piercing the confusion of heavier sounds with their shrill voices of mirth or terror.

"The double-faced fellow has his eye upon me," muttered Robin, with an indefinite but an uncomfortable idea that he was himself to bear a part in the pageantry.

The leader turned himself in the saddle, and fixed his glance full upon the country youth, as the steed went slowly by. When Robin had freed his eyes from those fiery ones, the musicians were passing before him, and the torches were close at hand; but the unsteady brightness of the latter formed a veil which he could not penetrate. The rattling of wheels over the stones sometimes found its way to his ear, and confused traces of a human form appeared at intervals, and then melted into the vivid light. A moment more, and the leader thundered a command to halt: the trumpets vomited a horrid breath, and then held their peace; the shouts and laughter of the people died away, and there remained only a universal hum, allied to silence. Right before Robin's eyes was an uncovered cart. There the torches blazed the brightest, there the moon shone out like day, and there, in tar-and-feathery dignity, sat his kinsman, Major Molineux!

He was an elderly man, of large and majestic person, and strong, square features, betokening a steady soul; but steady as it was, his enemies had found means to shake it. His face was pale as death, and far more ghastly; the broad forehead was contracted in his agony, so that his eyebrows formed one grizzled line; his eyes were red and wild, and the foam hung white upon his quivering lip. His whole frame was agitated by a quick and continual tremor, which his pride strove to quell, even in those circumstances of overwhelming humiliation. But perhaps the bitterest pang of all was when his eyes met those of Robin; for he evidently knew him on the instant, as the youth stood witnessing the foul disgrace of a head grown gray in honor. They stared at each other in silence, and Robin's knees shook, and his hair bristled, with a mixture of pity and terror. Soon, however, a bewildering excitement began to seize upon his mind; the preceding adventures of the night, the unexpected appearance of the crowd, the torches, the confused din and the hush that followed, the spectre of his kinsman reviled by that great multitude,—all this, and, more than all, a perception of tremendous ridicule in the whole scene, affected him with a sort of mental inebriety. At that moment a voice of sluggish merriment saluted Robin's ears; he turned instinctively, and just behind the corner of the church stood the lantern-bearer, rubbing his eyes, and drowsily enjoying the lad's amazement. Then he heard a peal of laughter like the ringing of silvery bells; a woman twitched his arm, a saucy eye met his, and he saw the lady of the scarlet petticoat. A sharp, dry cachinnation appealed to his memory, and, standing on tiptoe in the crowd, with his white apron over his head, he beheld the courteous little innkeeper. And lastly, there sailed over the heads of the multitude a great, broad laugh, broken in the midst by two sepulchral hems; thus, "Haw, haw, haw,—hem, hem,—haw, haw, haw, haw!"

The sound proceeded from the balcony of the opposite edifice, and thither Robin turned his eyes. In front of the Gothic window stood the old citizen, wrapped in a wide gown, his gray periwig exchanged for a night-cap, which was thrust back from his forehead, and his silk stockings hanging about his legs. He supported himself on his polished cane in a fit of convulsive merriment, which manifested itself on his solemn old features like a funny inscription on a tomb-stone. Then Robin seemed to hear the voices of the barbers, of the guests of the inn, and of all who had made sport of him that night. The contagion was spreading among the multitude, when, all at once, it seized upon Robin, and he sent forth a shout of laughter that echoed through the street;—every man shook his sides, every man emptied his lungs, but Robin's shout was the loudest there. The cloud-spirits peeped from their silvery islands, as the congregated mirth went roaring up the sky! The Man in the Moon heard the far bellow. "Oho," quoth he, "the old earth is frolicsome tonight!"

When there was a momentary calm in that tempestuous sea of sound, the leader gave the sign, the procession resumed its march. On they went, like fiends that throng in mockery around some dead potentate, mighty no more, but majestic still in his agony. On they went, in counterfeited pomp, in senseless uproar, in frenzied merriment, trampling all on an old man's heart. On swept the tumult, and left a silent street behind.

* * *

"Well, Robin, are you dreaming?" inquired the gentleman, laying his hand on the youth's shoulder.

Robin started, and withdrew his arm from the stone post to which he had instinctively clung, as the living stream rolled by him. His cheek was somewhat pale, and his eye not quite as lively as in the earlier part of the evening.

"Will you be kind enough to show me the way to the ferry?" said he, after a moment's pause.

"You have, then, adopted a new subject of inquiry?" observed his companion, with a smile.

"Why, yes, sir," replied Robin, rather dryly. "Thanks to you, and to my other friends, I have at last met my kinsman, and he will scarce desire to see my face again. I begin to grow weary of a town life, sir. Will you show me the way to the ferry?"

"No, my good friend Robin,—not to-night, at least," said the gentleman. "Some few days hence, if you wish it, I will speed you on your journey. Or, if you prefer to remain with us, perhaps, as you are a shrewd youth, you may rise in the world without the help of your kinsman, Major Molineux."

YOUNG GOODMAN BROWN

◊

¶ THIS tale first appeared in the *New England Magazine* (April, 1835), and was reprinted in *Mosses from an Old Manse* (1846). The locale of Salem and the use of well-known persons who suffered in the witchcraft delusion of 1692 would seem to give the narrative a solid historical basis. Actually, however, the persons who appear from history are of less consequence than the ambiguous study of an inquiring Puritan who discovers the extent and depth of evil both in society and in himself.

◇

YOUNG Goodman [1] Brown came forth at sunset into the street at Salem village; but put his head back, after crossing the threshold, to exchange a parting kiss with his young wife. And Faith, as the wife was aptly named, thrust her own pretty head into the street, letting the wind play with the pink ribbons of her cap while she called to Goodman Brown.

"Dearest heart," whispered she, softly and rather sadly, when her lips were close to his ear, "prithee put off your journey until sunrise and sleep in your own bed to-night. A lone woman is troubled with such dreams and such thoughts that she's afeared of herself sometimes. Pray tarry with me this night, dear husband, of all nights in the year."

"My love and my Faith," replied young Goodman Brown, "of all nights in the year, this one night must I tarry away from thee. My journey, as thou callest it, forth and back again, must needs be done 'twixt now and sunrise. What, my sweet, pretty wife, dost thou doubt me already, and we but three months married?"

"Then God bless you!" said Faith, with the pink ribbons; "and may you find all well when you come back."

"Amen!" cried Goodman Brown. "Say thy prayers, dear Faith, and go to bed at dusk, and no harm will come to thee."

So they parted; and the young man pursued his way until, being about to turn the corner by the meeting-house, he looked back and saw the head of Faith still peeping after him with a melancholy air, in spite of her pink ribbons.

"Poor little Faith!" thought he, for his heart smote him. "What a wretch am I to leave her on such an errand! She talks of dreams, too. Methought as she spoke there was trouble in her face, as if a dream had warned her what work is to be done to-night. But no, no; 't would kill her to think it. Well, she's a blessed angel on earth; and after this one night I'll cling to her skirts and follow her to heaven."

With this excellent resolve for the future, Goodman Brown felt himself justified in making more haste on his present evil purpose. He had taken a dreary road, darkened by all the gloomiest trees of the forest, which barely stood aside to let the narrow path creep through, and closed immediately behind. It was all as lonely as could be; and there is this peculiarity in such a solitude, that the traveller knows not who may be concealed by the innumerable trunks and the thick boughs overhead; so that with lonely footsteps he may yet be passing through an unseen multitude.

"There may be a devilish Indian behind every tree," said Goodman Brown to himself; and he glanced fearfully behind him as he added, "What if the devil himself should be at my very elbow!"

His head being turned back, he passed a crook of the road, and, looking forward again, beheld the figure of a man, in grave and decent attire, seated at the foot of an old tree. He arose at Goodman Brown's approach and walked onward side by side with him.

"You are late, Goodman Brown," said he. "The clock of the Old South [2] was striking as I came through Boston, and that is full fifteen minutes agone."

"Faith kept me back a while," replied the young man, with a tremor in his voice, caused by the sudden appearance of his companion, though not wholly unexpected.

It was now deep dusk in the forest, and deepest in that part of it where these two were journeying. As nearly as could be discerned, the second traveller was about fifty years old, apparently in the same rank of life as Goodman Brown, and bearing a considerable resemblance to him, though perhaps more in expression than features. Still they might have been taken for father and son. And yet, though the elder person was as simply clad as the younger, and as simple in manner too, he had an indescribable air of one who knew the world, and who would not have felt abashed at the governor's dinner table or in King William's [3] court, were it possible that his affairs should call him thither. But the only thing about him that could be fixed upon as remarkable was his staff, which bore the likeness of a great black snake, so curiously wrought that it might almost be seen to twist and wriggle itself like a living serpent. This, of course, must have been an ocular deception, assisted by the uncertain light.

"Come, Goodman Brown," cried his fellow-traveller, "this is a dull pace for the beginning of a journey. Take my staff, if you are so soon weary."

"Friend," said the other, exchanging his slow pace for a full stop, "having kept covenant by meeting thee here, it is my purpose now to return

YOUNG GOODMAN BROWN. 1. **Goodman:** The term referred to a man of middle estate; "Mr." referred to a man of position.

2. **Old South:** the Boston church organized in 1669. The "clock" is an anachronism: the bell tower and clock were not erected until the new church structure was built in 1730—some time after the events in the story take place. 3. **King William's:** William III, King of England, 1689–1702.

whence I came. I have scruples touching the matter thou wot'st of."

"Sayest thou so?" replied he of the serpent, smiling apart. "Let us walk on, nevertheless, reasoning as we go; and if I convince thee not thou shalt turn back. We are but a little way in the forest yet."

"Too far! too far!" exclaimed the goodman, unconsciously resuming his walk. "My father never went into the woods on such an errand, nor his father before him. We have been a race of honest men and good Christians since the days of the martyrs; and shall I be the first of the name of Brown that ever took this path and kept"—

"Such company, thou wouldst say," observed the elder person, interpreting his pause. "Well said, Goodman Brown! I have been as well acquainted with your family as with ever a one among the Puritans; and that's no trifle to say. I helped your grandfather, the constable, when he lashed the Quaker woman [4] so smartly through the streets of Salem; and it was I that brought your father a pitch-pine knot, kindled at my own hearth, to set fire to an Indian village, in King Philip's war.[5] They were my good friends, both; and many a pleasant walk have we had along this path, and returned merrily after midnight. I would fain be friends with you for their sake."

"If it be as thou sayest," replied Goodman Brown, "I marvel they never spoke of these matters; or, verily, I marvel not, seeing that the least rumor of the sort would have driven them from New England. We are a people of prayer, and good works to boot, and abide no such wickedness."

"Wickedness or not," said the traveller with the twisted staff, "I have a very general acquaintance here in New England. The deacons of many a church have drunk the communion wine with me; the selectmen of divers towns make me their chairman; and a majority of the Great and General Court [6] are firm supporters of my interest. The governor and I, too—But these are state secrets."

"Can this be so?" cried Goodman Brown, with a stare of amazement at his undisturbed companion. "Howbeit, I have nothing to do with the governor and council; they have their own ways, and are no rule for a simple husbandman like me. But, were I to go on with thee, how should I meet the eye of that good old man, our minister, at Salem village? Oh, his voice would make me tremble both Sabbath day and lecture day."

Thus far the elder traveller had listened with due gravity; but now burst into a fit of irrepressible mirth, shaking himself so violently that his snake-like staff actually seemed to wriggle in sympathy.

"Ha! ha! ha!" shouted he again and again; then composing himself, "Well, go on, Goodman Brown, go on; but, prithee, don't kill me with laughing."

"Well, then, to end the matter at once," said Goodman Brown, considerably nettled, "there is my wife, Faith. It would break her dear little heart; and I'd rather break my own."

"Nay, if that be the case," answered the other, "e'en go thy ways, Goodman Brown. I would not for twenty old women like the one hobbling before us that Faith should come to any harm."

As he spoke he pointed his staff at a female figure on the path, in whom Goodman Brown recognized a very pious and exemplary dame, who had taught him his catechism in youth, and was still his moral and spiritual adviser, jointly with the minister and Deacon Gookin.[7]

"A marvel, truly, that Goody Cloyse [8] should be so far in the wilderness at nightfall," said he. "But with your leave, friend, I shall take a cut through the woods until we have left this Christian woman behind. Being a stranger to you, she might ask whom I was consorting with and whither I was going."

"Be it so," said his fellow-traveller. "Betake you to the woods, and let me keep the path."

Accordingly the young man turned aside, but took care to watch his companion, who advanced softly along the road until he had come within a staff's length of the old dame. She, meanwhile, was making the best of her way, with singular speed for so aged a woman, and mumbling some indistinct words—a prayer, doubtless—as she went. The traveller put forth his staff and touched her withered neck with what seemed the serpent's tail.

"The devil!" screamed the pious old lady.

"Then Goody Cloyse knows her old friend?" observed the traveller, confronting her and leaning on his writhing stick.

"Ah, forsooth, and is it your worship indeed?" cried the good dame. "Yea, truly is it, and in the very image of my old gossip, Goodman Brown, the grandfather of the silly fellow that now is. But

4. **lashed . . . woman:** William Hathorne (1607?–81) was reputed to have driven Quaker women out of Salem. 5. **King Philip's war:** a desperate and futile stand by the Indians in 1676. 6. **Great and General Court:** the legislative body of colonial Massachusetts.

7. **Deacon Gookin:** Daniel Gookin (1612–87), who was superintendent of the Indians and author of the *Historical Collections of the Indians of Massachusetts* (1674). 8. **Goody Cloyse:** She was sentenced to death for witchcraft in 1692, as were Goody Cory and Martha Carrier.

—would your worship believe it?—my broomstick hath strangely disappeared, stolen, as I suspect, by that unhanged witch, Goody Cory, and that, too, when I was all anointed with the juice of smallage, and cinquefoil, and wolf's bane"—[9]

"Mingled with fine wheat and the fat of a new-born babe," said the shape of old Goodman Brown.

"Ah, your worship knows the recipe," cried the old lady, cackling aloud. "So, as I was saying, being all ready for the meeting, and no horse to ride on, I made up my mind to foot it; for they tell me there is a nice young man to be taken into communion to-night. But now your good worship will lend me your arm, and we shall be there in a twinkling."

"That can hardly be," answered her friend. "I may not spare you my arm, Goody Cloyse; but here is my staff, if you will."

So saying, he threw it down at her feet, where, perhaps, it assumed life, being one of the rods which its owner had formerly lent to the Egyptian magi.[10] Of this fact, however, Goodman Brown could not take cognizance. He had cast up his eyes in astonishment, and, looking down again, beheld neither Goody Cloyse nor the serpentine staff, but this fellow-traveller alone, who waited for him as calmly as if nothing had happened.

"That old woman taught me my catechism," said the young man; and there was a world of meaning in this simple comment.

They continued to walk onward, while the elder traveller exhorted his companion to make good speed and persevere in the path, discoursing so aptly that his arguments seemed rather to spring up in the bosom of his auditor than to be suggested by himself. As they went, he plucked a branch of maple to serve for a walking stick, and began to strip it of the twigs and little boughs, which were wet with evening dew. The moment his fingers touched them they became strangely withered and dried up as with a week's sunshine. Thus the pair proceeded, at a good free pace, until suddenly, in a gloomy hollow of the road, Goodman Brown sat himself down on the stump of a tree and refused to go any farther.

"Friend," said he, stubbornly, "my mind is made up. Not another step will I budge on this errand. What if a wretched old woman do choose to go to the devil when I thought she was going to heaven: is that any reason why I should quit my dear Faith and go after her?"

"You will think better of this by and by," said his acquaintance, composedly. "Sit here and rest yourself a while; and when you feel like moving again, there is my staff to help you along."

Without more words, he threw his companion the maple stick, and was as speedily out of sight as if he had vanished into the deepening gloom. The young man sat a few moments by the roadside, applauding himself greatly, and thinking with how clear a conscience he should meet the minister in his morning walk, nor shrink from the eye of good old Deacon Gookin. And what calm sleep would be his that very night, which was to have been spent so wickedly, but so purely and sweetly now, in the arms of Faith! Amidst these pleasant and praiseworthy meditations, Goodman Brown heard the tramp of horses along the road, and deemed it advisable to conceal himself within the verge of the forest, conscious of the guilty purpose that had brought him thither, though now so happily turned from it.

On came the hoof tramps and the voices of the riders, two grave old voices, conversing soberly as they drew near. These mingled sounds appeared to pass along the road, within a few yards of the young man's hiding-place; but, owing doubtless to the depth of the gloom at that particular spot, neither the travellers nor their steeds were visible. Though their figures brushed the small boughs by the wayside, it could not be seen that they intercepted, even for a moment, the faint gleam from the strip of bright sky athwart which they must have passed. Goodman Brown alternately crouched and stood on tiptoe, pulling aside the branches and thrusting forth his head as far as he durst without discerning so much as a shadow. It vexed him the more, because he could have sworn, were such a thing possible, that he recognized the voices of the minister and Deacon Gookin, jogging along quietly, as they were wont to do, when bound to some ordination or ecclesiastical council. While yet within hearing, one of the riders stopped to pluck a switch.

"Of the two, reverend sir," said the voice like the deacon's, "I had rather miss an ordination dinner than to-night's meeting. They tell me that some of our community are to be here from Falmouth and beyond, and others from Connecticut and Rhode Island, besides several of the Indian powwows, who, after their fashion, know almost as much deviltry as the best of us. Moreover, there is a goodly young woman to be taken into communion."

"Mighty well, Deacon Gookin!" replied the solemn old tones of the minister. "Spur up, or we shall be late. Nothing can be done, you know, until I get on the ground."

9. **smallage . . . bane:** "smallage" is parsley; "cinquefoil" is a plant of the rose family; "wolf's bane" is aconite or monkshood.
10. **Egyptian magi:** See Exod. 7:8–12.

The hoofs clattered again; and the voices, talking so strangely in the empty air, passed on through the forest, where no church had ever been gathered or solitary Christian prayed. Whither, then, could these holy men be journeying so deep into the heathen wilderness? Young Goodman Brown caught hold of a tree for support, being ready to sink down on the ground, faint and overburdened with the heavy sickness of his heart. He looked up to the sky, doubting whether there really was a heaven above him. Yet there was the blue arch, and the stars brightening in it.

"With heaven above and Faith below, I will yet stand firm against the devil!" cried Goodman Brown.

While he still gazed upward into the deep arch of the firmament and had lifted his hands to pray, a cloud, though no wind was stirring, hurried across the zenith and hid the brightening stars. The blue sky was still visible, except directly overhead, where this black mass of cloud was sweeping swiftly northward. Aloft in the air, as if from the depths of the cloud, came a confused and doubtful sound of voices. Once the listener fancied that he could distinguish the accents of towns-people of his own, men and women, both pious and ungodly, many of whom he had met at the communion table, and had seen others rioting at the tavern. The next moment, so indistinct were the sounds, he doubted whether he had heard aught but the murmur of the old forest, whispering without a wind. Then came a stronger swell of those familiar tones, heard daily in the sunshine at Salem village, but never until now from a cloud of night. There was one voice, of a young woman, uttering lamentations, yet with an uncertain sorrow, and entreating for some favor, which, perhaps, it would grieve her to obtain; and all the unseen multitude, both saints and sinners, seemed to encourage her onward.

"Faith!" shouted Goodman Brown, in a voice of agony and desperation; and the echoes of the forest mocked him, crying, "Faith! Faith!" as if bewildered wretches were seeking her all through the wilderness.

The cry of grief, rage, and terror was yet piercing the night, when the unhappy husband held his breath for a response. There was a scream, drowned immediately in a louder murmur of voices, fading into far-off laughter, as the dark cloud swept away, leaving the clear and silent sky above Goodman Brown. But something fluttered lightly down through the air and caught on the branch of a tree. The young man seized it, and beheld a pink ribbon.

"My Faith is gone!" cried he, after one stupefied moment. "There is no good on earth; and sin is but a name. Come, devil; for to thee is this world given."

And, maddened with despair, so that he laughed loud and long, did Goodman Brown grasp his staff and set forth again, at such a rate that he seemed to fly along the forest path rather than to walk or run. The road grew wilder and drearier and more faintly traced, and vanished at length, leaving him in the heart of the dark wilderness, still rushing onward with the instinct that guides mortal man to evil. The whole forest was peopled with frightful sounds—the creaking of the trees, the howling of wild beasts, and the yell of Indians; while sometimes the wind tolled like a distant church bell, and sometimes gave a broad roar around the traveller, as if all Nature were laughing him to scorn. But he was himself the chief horror of the scene, and shrank not from its other horrors.

"Ha! ha! ha!" roared Goodman Brown when the wind laughed at him. "Let us hear which will laugh loudest. Think not to frighten me with your deviltry. Come witch, come wizard, come Indian powwow, come devil himself, and here comes Goodman Brown. You may as well fear him as he fear you."

In truth, all through the haunted forest there could be nothing more frightful than the figure of Goodman Brown. On he flew among the black pines, brandishing his staff with frenzied gestures, now giving vent to an inspiration of horrid blasphemy, and now shouting forth such laughter as set all the echoes of the forest laughing like demons around him. The fiend in his own shape is less hideous than when he rages in the breast of man. Thus sped the demoniac on his course, until, quivering among the trees, he saw a red light before him, as when the felled trunks and branches of a clearing have been set on fire, and throw up their lurid blaze against the sky, at the hour of midnight. He paused, in a lull of the tempest that had driven him onward, and heard the swell of what seemed a hymn, rolling solemnly from a distance with the weight of many voices. He knew the tune; it was a familiar one in the choir of the village meeting-house. The verse died heavily away, and was lengthened by a chorus, not of human voices, but of all the sounds of the benighted wilderness pealing in awful harmony together. Goodman Brown cried out, and his cry was lost to his own ear by its unison with the cry of the desert.

In the interval of silence he stole forward until the light glared full upon his eyes. At one extremity of an open space, hemmed in by the dark wall of the forest, arose a rock, bearing some rude, natural resemblance either to an altar or a pulpit, and surrounded by four blazing pines, their tops aflame, their stems untouched, like candles at an evening meeting. The mass of foliage that had overgrown the summit of the rock was all on fire, blazing high into the night and fitfully illuminating the whole field. Each pendent twig and leafy festoon was in a blaze. As the red light arose and fell, a numerous congregation alternately shone forth, then disappeared in shadow, and again grew, as it were, out of the darkness, peopling the heart of the solitary woods at once.

"A grave and dark-clad company," quoth Goodman Brown.

In truth they were such. Among them, quivering to and fro between gloom and splendor, appeared faces that would be seen next day at the council board of the province, and others which, Sabbath after Sabbath, looked devoutly heavenward, and benignantly over the crowded pews, from the holiest pulpits in the land. Some affirm that the lady of the governor was there. At least there were high dames well known to her, and wives of honored husbands, and widows, a great multitude, and ancient maidens, all of excellent repute, and fair young girls, who trembled lest their mothers should espy them. Either the sudden gleams of light flashing over the obscure field bedazzled Goodman Brown, or he recognized a score of the church members of Salem village famous for their especial sanctity. Good old Deacon Gookin had arrived, and waited at the skirts of that venerable saint, his revered pastor. But, irreverently consorting with these grave, reputable, and pious people, these elders of the church, these chaste dames and dewy virgins, there were men of dissolute lives and women of spotted fame, wretches given over to all mean and filthy vice, and suspected even of horrid crimes. It was strange to see that the good shrank not from the wicked, nor were the sinners abashed by the saints. Scattered also among their pale-faced enemies were the Indian priests, or powwows, who had often scared their native forest with more hideous incantations than any known to English witchcraft.

"But where is Faith?" thought Goodman Brown; and, as hope came into his heart, he trembled.

Another verse of the hymn arose, a slow and mournful strain, such as the pious love, but joined to words which expressed all that our nature can conceive of sin, and darkly hinted at far more. Unfathomable to mere mortals is the lore of fiends. Verse after verse was sung; and still the chorus of the desert swelled between like the deepest tone of a mighty organ; and with the final peal of that dreadful anthem there came a sound, as if the roaring wind, the rushing streams, the howling beasts, and every other voice of the unconcerted wilderness were mingling and according with the voice of guilty man in homage to the prince of all. The four blazing pines threw up a loftier flame, and obscurely discovered shapes and visages of horror on the smoke wreaths above the impious assembly. At the same moment the fire on the rock shot redly forth and formed a glowing arch above its base, where now appeared a figure. With reverence be it spoken, the figure bore no slight similitude, both in garb and manner, to some grave divine of the New England churches.

"Bring forth the converts!" cried a voice that echoed through the field and rolled into the forest.

At the word, Goodman Brown stepped forth from the shadow of the trees and approached the congregation, with whom he felt a loathful brotherhood by the sympathy of all that was wicked in his heart. He could have well-nigh sworn that the shape of his own dead father beckoned him to advance, looking downward from a smoke wreath, while a woman, with dim features of despair, threw out her hand to warn him back. Was it his mother? But he had no power to retreat one step, nor to resist, even in thought, when the minister and good old Deacon Gookin seized his arms and led him to the blazing rock. Thither came also the slender form of a veiled female, led between Goody Cloyse, that pious teacher of the catechism, and Martha Carrier, who had received the devil's promise to be queen of hell. A rampant hag was she. And there stood the proselytes beneath the canopy of fire.

"Welcome, my children," said the dark figure, "to the communion of your race. Ye have found thus young your nature and your destiny. My children, look behind you!"

They turned; and flashing forth, as it were, in a sheet of flame, the fiend worshippers were seen; the smile of welcome gleamed darkly on every visage.

"There," resumed the sable form, "are all whom ye have reverenced from youth. Ye deemed them holier than yourselves, and shrank from your own sin, contrasting it with their lives of righteousness and prayerful aspirations heavenward. Yet here are they all in my worshipping assembly. This night it shall be granted you to know their secret deeds: how hoary-bearded elders of the church have whispered wanton words to the young maids of their households; how many a woman, eager for widows' weeds, has given her husband a drink at bedtime and let him sleep his last sleep in her bosom; how beardless youths have made haste to inherit their fathers' wealth; and how fair damsels—blush not, sweet ones—have dug little graves in the garden, and bidden me, the sole guest, to an infant's funeral. By the sympathy of your human hearts for sin ye shall scent out all the places—whether in church, bed-chamber, street, field, or forest—where crime has been committed, and shall exult to behold the whole earth one stain of guilt, one mighty blood spot. Far more than this. It shall be yours to penetrate, in every bosom, the deep mystery of sin, the fountain of all wicked arts, and which inexhaustibly supplies more evil impulses than human power—than my power at its utmost—can make manifest in deeds. And now, my children, look upon each other."

They did so; and, by the blaze of the hell-kindled torches, the wretched man beheld his Faith, and the wife her husband, trembling before that unhallowed altar.

"Lo, there ye stand, my children," said the figure, in a deep and solemn tone, almost sad with its despairing awfulness, as if his once angelic nature could yet mourn for our miserable race. "Depending upon one another's hearts, ye had still hoped that virtue were not all a dream. Now are ye undeceived. Evil is the nature of mankind. Evil must be your only happiness. Welcome again, my children, to the communion of your race."

"Welcome," repeated the fiend worshippers, in one cry of despair and triumph.

And there they stood, the only pair, as it seemed, who were yet hesitating on the verge of wickedness in this dark world. A basin was hollowed, naturally, in the rock. Did it contain water, reddened by the lurid light? or was it blood? or, perchance, a liquid flame? Herein did the shape of evil dip his hand and prepare to lay the mark of baptism upon their foreheads, that they might be partakers of the mystery of sin, more conscious of the secret guilt of others, both in deed and thought, than they could now be of their own. The husband cast one look at his pale wife, and Faith at him. What polluted wretches would the next glance show them to each other, shuddering alike at what they disclosed and what they saw!

"Faith! Faith!" cried the husband, "look up to heaven, and resist the wicked one."

Whether Faith obeyed he knew not. Hardly had he spoken when he found himself amid calm night and solitude, listening to a roar of the wind which died heavily away through the forest. He staggered against the rock, and felt it chill and damp; while a hanging twig, that had been all on fire, besprinkled his cheek with the coldest dew.

The next morning young Goodman Brown came slowly into the street of Salem village, staring around him like a bewildered man. The good old minister was taking a walk along the graveyard to get an appetite for breakfast and meditate his sermon, and bestowed a blessing, as he passed, on Goodman Brown. He shrank from the venerable saint as if to avoid an anathema. Old Deacon Gookin was at domestic worship, and the holy words of his prayer were heard through the open window. "What God doth the wizard pray to?" quoth Goodman Brown. Goody Cloyse, that excellent old Christian, stood in the early sunshine at her own lattice, catechizing a little girl who had brought her a pint of morning's milk. Goodman Brown snatched away the child as from the grasp of the fiend himself. Turning the corner by the meeting-house, he spied the head of Faith, with the pink ribbons, gazing anxiously forth, and bursting into such joy at sight of him that she skipped along the street and almost kissed her husband before the whole village. But Goodman Brown looked sternly and sadly into her face, and passed on without a greeting.

Had Goodman Brown fallen asleep in the forest and only dreamed a wild dream of a witch-meeting?

Be it so if you will; but, alas! it was a dream of evil omen for young Goodman Brown. A stern, a sad, a darkly meditative, a distrustful, if not a desperate man did he become from the night of that fearful dream. On the Sabbath day, when the congregation were singing a holy psalm, he could not listen because an anthem of sin rushed loudly upon his ear and drowned all the blessed strain. When the minister spoke from the pulpit with power and fervid eloquence, and, with his hand on the open Bible, of the sacred truths of our religion, and of saint-like lives and triumphant deaths, and of future bliss or misery unutterable, then did Goodman Brown turn pale, dreading lest the roof should thunder down upon the gray blasphemer and his hearers. Often, awaking suddenly at midnight, he shrank from the bosom of Faith; and at morning or eventide, when the family knelt down at prayer, he scowled and muttered to himself, and gazed sternly at his wife, and turned away. And when he had lived long, and was borne to his grave a hoary corpse, followed by Faith, an aged woman, and children and grandchildren, a goodly procession, besides neighbors not a few, they carved no hopeful verse upon his tombstone, for his dying hour was gloom.

WAKEFIELD

◇

HAWTHORNE tells us that he found the anecdote which suggested "Wakefield" in "some old magazine or newspaper." He may have read it in Dr. William King's *Anecdotes of His Own Times* (1818): a man named Howe arose early one morning, bid his wife goodbye, and disappeared for seventeen years. By changing his name and disguising his appearance, he frequented the section of London where his wife lived; he even attended church where he could observe her. At the end of his absence he returned home but never confessed "what was the real cause of such a singular conduct." Hawthorne's story is even more ambiguous: no reason is given for Wakefield's departure; the exile may be self-imposed, but its true secret lies beyond Wakefield's knowing. His place in society is so precarious, as is perhaps any man's, that one step astray may make him an "Outcast of the Universe." The story appeared first in the *New England Magazine* for May, 1835, and was afterward included in the *Twice-Told Tales* (1837).

◇

IN SOME old magazine or newspaper I recollect a story, told as truth, of a man—let us call him Wakefield—who absented himself for a long time from his wife. The fact, thus abstractedly stated, is not very uncommon, nor—without a proper distinction of circumstances—to be condemned either as naughty or nonsensical. Howbeit, this, though far from the most aggravated, is perhaps the strangest, instance on record, of marital delinquency; and, moreover, as remarkable a freak as may be found in the whole list of human oddities. The wedded couple lived in London. The man, under pretence of going a journey, took lodgings in the next street to his own house, and there, unheard of by his wife or friends, and without the shadow of a reason for such self-banishment, dwelt upwards of twenty years. During that period, he beheld his home every day, and frequently the forlorn Mrs. Wakefield. And after so great a gap in his matrimonial felicity—when his death was reckoned certain, his estate settled, his name dismissed from memory, and his wife, long, long ago, resigned to her autumnal widowhood—he entered the door one evening, quietly, as from a day's absence, and became a loving spouse till death.

This outline is all that I remember. But the incident, though of the purest originality, unexampled, and probably never to be repeated, is one, I think, which appeals to the generous sympathies of mankind. We know, each for himself, that none of us would perpetrate such a folly, yet feel as if some other might. To my own contemplations, at least, it has often recurred, always exciting wonder, but with a sense that the story must be true, and a conception of its hero's character. Whenever any subject so forcibly affects the mind, time is well spent in thinking of it. If the reader choose, let him do his own meditation; or if he prefer to ramble with me through the twenty years of Wakefield's vagary, I bid him welcome; trusting that there will be a pervading spirit and a moral, even should we fail to find them, done up neatly, and condensed into the final sentence. Thought has always its efficacy, and every striking incident its moral.

What sort of a man was Wakefield? We are free to shape out our own idea, and call it by his name. He was now in the meridian of life; his matrimonial affections, never violent, were sobered into a calm, habitual sentiment; of all husbands, he was likely to be the most constant, because a certain sluggishness would keep his heart at rest, wherever it might be placed. He was intellectual, but not actively so; his mind occupied itself in long and lazy musings, that ended to no purpose, or had not vigor to attain it; his thoughts were seldom so energetic as to seize hold of words. Imagination, in the proper meaning of the term, made no part of Wakefield's gifts. With a cold but not depraved nor wandering heart, and a mind never feverish with riotous thoughts, nor perplexed with originality, who could have anticipated that our friend would entitle himself to a foremost place among the doers of eccentric deeds? Had his acquaintances been asked, who was the man in London the surest to perform nothing to-day which should be remembered on the morrow, they would have thought of Wakefield. Only the wife of his bosom might have hesitated. She, without having analyzed his character, was partly aware of a quiet selfishness, that had rusted into his inactive mind; of a peculiar sort of vanity, the most uneasy attribute about him; of a disposition to craft, which had seldom produced more positive effects than the keeping of petty secrets, hardly worth revealing; and, lastly, of what she called a little strangeness, sometimes, in the good man. This latter quality is indefinable, and perhaps non-existent.

Let us now imagine Wakefield bidding adieu to his wife. It is the dusk of an October evening. His equipment is a drab greatcoat, a hat covered with an oilcloth, top-boots, an umbrella in one hand and a small portmanteau in the other. He has informed Mrs. Wakefield that he is to take the night coach into the country. She would fain inquire the length of his journey, its object, and the probable time of his return; but, indulgent to his harmless love of mystery, interrogates him only by a look. He tells her not to expect him positively by the return coach, nor to be alarmed should he tarry three or four days; but, at all events, to look for him at supper on Friday evening. Wakefield himself, be it considered, has no suspicion of what is before him. He holds out his hand, she gives her own, and meets his parting kiss in the matter-of-course way of a ten years' matrimony; and forth goes the middle-aged Mr. Wakefield, almost resolved to perplex his good lady by a whole week's absence. After the door has closed behind him, she perceives it thrust partly open, and a vision of her husband's face, through the aperture, smiling on her, and gone in a moment. For the time, this little incident is dismissed without a thought. But, long afterwards, when she has been more years a widow than a wife, that smile recurs, and flickers across all her reminiscences of Wakefield's visage. In her many musings, she surrounds the original smile with a multitude of fantasies, which make it strange and awful: as, for instance, if she imagines him in a coffin, that parting look is frozen on his pale features; or, if she dreams of him in heaven, still his blessed spirit wears a quiet and crafty smile. Yet, for its sake, when all others have given him up for dead, she sometimes doubts whether she is a widow.

But our business is with the husband. We must hurry after him along the street, ere he lose his individuality, and melt into the great mass of London life. It would be vain searching for him there. Let us follow close at his heels, therefore, until, after several superfluous turns and doublings, we find him comfortably established by the fireside of a small apartment, previously bespoken. He is in the next street to his own, and at his journey's end. He can scarcely trust his good fortune, in having got thither unperceived—recollecting that, at one time, he was delayed by the throng, in the very focus of a lighted lantern; and, again, there were footsteps that seemed to tread behind his own, distinct from the multitudinous tramp around him; and, anon, he heard a voice shouting afar, and fancied that it called his name. Doubtless, a dozen busybodies had been watching him, and told his wife the whole affair. Poor Wakefield! Little knowest thou thine own insignificance in this great world! No mortal eye but mine has traced thee. Go quietly to thy bed, foolish man; and, on the morrow, if thou wilt be wise, get thee home to good Mrs. Wakefield, and tell her the truth. Remove not thyself, even for a little week, from thy place in her chaste bosom. Were she, for a single moment, to deem thee dead, or lost, or lastingly divided from her, thou wouldst be wofully conscious of a change in thy true wife forever after. It is perilous to make a chasm in human affections; not that they gape so long and wide—but so quickly close again!

Almost repenting of his frolic, or whatever it may be termed, Wakefield lies down betimes, and starting from his first nap, spreads forth his arms into the wide and solitary waste of the unaccustomed bed. "No,"—thinks he, gathering the bedclothes about him,—"I will not sleep alone another night."

In the morning he rises earlier than usual, and sets himself to consider what he really means to do. Such are his loose and rambling modes of thought that he has taken this very singular step with the consciousness of a purpose, indeed, but without being able to define it sufficiently for his own contemplation. The vagueness of the project, and the convulsive effort with which he plunges into the execution of it, are equally characteristic of a feeble-minded man. Wakefield sifts his ideas, however, as minutely as he may, and finds himself curious to know the progress of matters at home —how his exemplary wife will endure her widowhood of a week; and, briefly, how the little sphere of creatures and circumstances, in which he was a central object, will be affected by his removal. A morbid vanity, therefore, lies nearest the bottom of the affair. But, how is he to attain his ends? Not, certainly, by keeping close in this comfortable lodging, where, though he slept and awoke in the next street to his home, he is as effectually abroad as if the stage-coach had been whirling him away all night. Yet, should he reappear, the whole project is knocked in the head. His poor brains being hopelessly puzzled with this dilemma, he at length ventures out, partly resolving to cross the head of the street, and send one hasty glance towards his forsaken domicile. Habit—for he is a man of habits—takes him by the hand, and guides him, wholly unaware, to his own door, where, just at the critical moment, he is aroused by the scraping of his foot upon the step. Wakefield! whither are you going?

At that instant his fate was turning on the pivot. Little dreaming of the doom to which his first backward step devotes him, he hurries away, breathless with agitation hitherto unfelt, and hardly dares turn his head at the distant corner. Can it be that nobody caught sight of him? Will not the whole household—the decent Mrs. Wakefield, the smart maid-servant, and the dirty little footboy—raise a hue and cry, through London streets, in pursuit of their fugitive lord and master?

Wonderful escape! He gathers courage to pause and look homeward, but is perplexed with a sense of change about the familiar edifice, such as affects us all, when, after a separation of months or years, we again see some hill or lake, or work of art, with which we were friends of old. In ordinary cases, this indescribable impression is caused by the comparison and contrast between our imperfect reminiscences and the reality. In Wakefield, the magic of a single night has wrought a similar transformation, because, in that brief period, a great moral change has been effected. But this is a secret from himself. Before leaving the spot, he catches a far and momentary glimpse of his wife, passing athwart the front window, with her face turned towards the head of the street. The crafty nincompoop takes to his heels, scared with the idea that, among a thousand such atoms of mortality, her eye must have detected him. Right glad is his heart, though his brain be somewhat dizzy, when he finds himself by the coal fire of his lodgings.

So much for the commencement of this long whim-wham. After the initial conception, and the stirring up of the man's sluggish temperament to put it in practice, the whole matter evolves itself in a natural train. We may suppose him, as the result of deep deliberation, buying a new wig, of reddish hair, and selecting sundry garments, in a fashion unlike his customary suit of brown, from a Jew's old-clothes bag. It is accomplished. Wakefield is another man. The new system being now established, a retrograde movement to the old would be almost as difficult as the step that placed him in his unparalleled position. Furthermore, he is rendered obstinate by a sulkiness occasionally incident to his temper, and brought on at present by the inadequate sensation which he conceives to have been produced in the bosom of Mrs. Wakefield. He will not go back until she be frightened half to death. Well; twice or thrice has she passed before his sight, each time with a heavier step, a paler cheek, and more anxious brow; and in the third week of his non-appearance he detects a portent of evil entering the house, in the guise of an apothecary. Next day the knocker is muffled. Towards nightfall comes the chariot of a physician, and deposits its big-wigged and solemn burden at Wakefield's door, whence, after a quarter of an hour's visit, he emerges, perchance the herald of a funeral. Dear woman! Will she die? By this time, Wakefield is excited to something like energy of feeling, but still lingers away from his wife's bedside, pleading with his conscience that she must not be disturbed at such a juncture. If aught else restrains him, he does not know it. In the course of a few weeks she gradually recovers; the crisis is over; her heart is sad, perhaps, but quiet; and, let him return soon or late, it will never be feverish for him again. Such ideas glimmer through the mist of Wakefield's mind, and render him indistinctly conscious that an almost impassable gulf divides his hired apartment from his former home. "It is but in the next street!" he sometimes says. Fool! it is in another world. Hitherto, he has put off his return from one particular day to another; henceforward, he leaves the precise time undetermined. Not to-morrow—probably next week—pretty soon. Poor man! The dead have nearly as much chance of revisiting their earthly homes as the self-banished Wakefield.

Would that I had a folio to write, instead of an article of a dozen pages! Then might I exemplify how an influence beyond our control lays its strong hand on every deed which we do, and weaves its consequences into an iron tissue of necessity. Wakefield is spell-bound. We must leave him, for ten years or so, to haunt around his house, without once crossing the threshold, and to be faithful to his wife, with all the affection of which his heart is capable, while he is slowly fading out of hers. Long since, it must be remarked, he had lost the perception of singularity in his conduct.

Now for a scene! Amid the throng of a London street we distinguish a man, now waxing elderly, with few characteristics to attract careless observers, yet bearing, in his whole aspect, the handwriting of no common fate, for such as have the skill to read it. He is meagre; his low and narrow forehead is deeply wrinkled; his eyes, small and lustreless, sometimes wander apprehensively about him, but oftener seem to look inward. He bends his head, and moves with an indescribable obliquity of gait, as if unwilling to display his full front to the world. Watch him long enough to see what we have described, and you will allow that circumstances—which often produce remarkable men from nature's ordinary handiwork—have produced one such here. Next, leaving him to sidle along the footwalk, cast your eyes in the opposite direction, where a portly female, considerably in the wane of life, with a prayer-book in her hand, is proceeding to yonder church. She has the placid mien of settled widowhood. Her regrets have either died away, or have become so essential to her heart, that they would be poorly exchanged for joy. Just as the lean man and well-conditioned woman are passing, a slight obstruction occurs, and brings these two figures directly in contact. Their hands touch; the pressure of the crowd forces her bosom against his shoulder; they stand, face to face, staring into each other's eyes. After a ten years' separation, thus Wakefield meets his wife!

The throng eddies away, and carries them asunder. The sober widow, resuming her former pace, proceeds to church, but pauses in the portal, and throws a perplexed glance along the street. She passes in, however, opening her prayer-book as she goes. And the man! with so wild a face that busy and selfish London stands to gaze after him, he hurries to his lodgings, bolts the door, and throws himself upon the bed. The latent feelings of years break out; his feeble mind acquires a brief energy from their strength; all the miserable strangeness of his life is revealed to him at a glance: and he cries out, passionately, "Wakefield! Wakefield! You are mad!"

Perhaps he was so. The singularity of his situation must have so moulded him to himself, that, considered in regard to his fellow-creatures and the business of life, he could not be said to possess his right mind. He had contrived, or rather he had happened, to dissever himself from the world—to vanish—to give up his place and privileges with living men, without being admitted among the dead. The life of a hermit is nowise parallel to his. He was in the bustle of the city, as of old, but the crowd swept by and saw him not; he was, we may figuratively say, always beside his wife and at his hearth, yet must never feel the warmth of the one nor the affection of the other. It was Wakefield's unprecedented fate to retain his original share of human sympathies, and to be still involved in human interests, while he had lost his reciprocal influence on them. It would be a most curious speculation to trace out the effect of such circumstances on his heart and intellect, separately, and in unison. Yet, changed as he was, he would seldom be conscious of it, but deem himself the same man as ever; glimpses of the truth, indeed, would come, but only for the moment; and still he would keep saying, "I shall soon go back!"—nor reflect that he had been saying so for twenty years.

I conceive, also, that these twenty years would appear, in the retrospect, scarcely longer than the week to which Wakefield had at first limited his absence. He would look on the affair as no more than an interlude in the main business of his life. When, after a little while more, he should deem it time to reënter his parlor, his wife would clap her hands for joy, on beholding the middle-aged Mr. Wakefield. Alas, what a mistake! Would Time but await the close of our favorite follies, we should be young men, all of us, and till Doomsday.

One evening, in the twentieth year since he vanished, Wakefield is taking his customary walk towards the dwelling which he still calls his own. It is a gusty night of autumn, with frequent showers that patter down upon the pavement, and are gone before a man can put up his umbrella. Pausing near the house, Wakefield discerns, through the parlor windows of the second floor, the red glow and the glimmer and fitful flash of a comfortable fire. On the ceiling appears a grotesque shadow of good Mrs. Wakefield. The cap, the nose and chin, and the broad waist, form an admirable caricature, which dances, moreover, with the up-flickering and down-sinking blaze, almost too merrily for the shade of an elderly widow. At this instant a shower chances to fall, and is driven, by the unmannerly gust, full into Wakefield's face and bosom. He is quite penetrated with its autumnal chill. Shall he stand, wet and shivering here, when his own hearth has a good fire to warm him, and his own wife will run to fetch the gray coat and small-clothes, which, doubtless, she has kept carefully in the closet of their bed chamber? No! Wakefield is no such fool. He ascends the steps—heavily!—for twenty years have stiffened his legs since he came down—but he knows it not. Stay, Wakefield! Would you go to the sole home that is left you? Then step into your grave! The door opens. As he passes in, we have a parting glimpse of his visage, and recognize the crafty smile, which was the precursor of the little joke that he has ever since been playing off at his wife's expense. How unmercifully has he quizzed the poor woman! Well, a good night's rest to Wakefield!

This happy event—supposing it to be such—could only have occurred at an unpremeditated moment. We will not follow our friend across the threshold. He has left us much food for thought, a portion of which shall lend its wisdom to a moral, and be shaped into a figure. Amid the seeming confusion of our mysterious world, individuals are so nicely adjusted to a system, and systems to one another and to a whole, that, by stepping aside for a moment, a man exposes himself to a fearful risk of losing his place forever. Like Wakefield, he may become, as it were, the Outcast of the Universe.

THE MAYPOLE OF MERRY MOUNT

◇

❡ SUBTITLED "A Parable" and first published in *The Token* for 1836, this story was included in the *Twice-Told Tales* (1837). Thomas Morton, the presumed villain of the story, was a London lawyer who was charged with selling rum and firearms to the Indians. In 1628 Captain Miles Standish arrested Morton, jailed him for a time, and caused him to be deported. John Endicott and a party of Pilgrims cut down the maypole and, according to Governor Bradford, rebuked the merrymakers "for their profaneness and admonished them to look there should be better walking." The name of the place was changed to Mount Dagon. The best account is that of Bradford in *Of Plymouth Plantation* (see pp. 44–47 of this volume). Morton's narrative and defense appeared in his *New English Canaan* (1637), Book III, Chap. 14.

◇

There is an admirable foundation for a philosophic romance in the curious history of the early settlement of Mount Wollaston, or Merry Mount. In the slight sketch here attempted, the facts, recorded on the grave pages of our New England annalists, have wrought themselves, almost spontaneously, into a sort of allegory. The masques, mummeries, and festive customs, described in the text, are in accordance with the manners of the age. Authority on these points may be found in Strutt's Book [1] *of English Sports and Pastimes.*

BRIGHT were the days at Merry Mount, when the Maypole was the banner staff of that gay colony! They who reared it, should their banner be triumphant, were to pour sunshine over New England's rugged hills, and scatter flower seeds throughout the soil. Jollity and gloom were contending for an empire. Midsummer eve had come, bringing deep verdure to the forest, and roses in her lap, of a more vivid hue than the tender buds of Spring. But May, or her mirthful spirit, dwelt all the year round at Merry Mount, sporting with the Summer months, and revelling with Autumn, and basking in the glow of Winter's fireside. Through a world of toil and care she flitted with a dreamlike smile, and came hither to find a home among the lightsome hearts of Merry Mount.

Never had the Maypole been so gayly decked as at sunset on midsummer eve. This venerated emblem was a pine-tree, which had preserved the slender grace of youth, while it equalled the loftiest height of the old wood monarchs. From its top streamed a silken banner, colored like the rainbow. Down nearly to the ground the pole was dressed with birchen boughs, and others of the liveliest green, and some with silvery leaves, fastened by ribbons that fluttered in fantastic knots of twenty different colors, but no sad ones. Garden flowers, and blossoms of the wilderness, laughed gladly forth amid the verdure, so fresh and dewy that they must have grown by magic on that happy pine-tree. Where this green and flowery splendor terminated, the shaft of the Maypole was stained with the seven brilliant hues of the banner at its top. On the lowest green bough hung an abundant wreath of roses, some that had been gathered in the sunniest spots of the forest, and others, of still richer blush, which the colonists had reared from English seed. O, people of the Golden Age,[2] the chief of your husbandry was to raise flowers!

But what was the wild throng that stood hand in hand about the Maypole? It could not be that the fauns and nymphs, when driven from their classic groves and homes of ancient fable, had sought refuge, as all the persecuted did, in the fresh woods of the West. These were Gothic monsters, though perhaps of Grecian ancestry. On the shoulders of a comely youth uprose the head and branching antlers of a stag; a second, human in all other points, had the grim visage of a wolf; a third, still with the trunk and limbs of a mortal man, showed the beard and horns of a venerable he-goat. There was the likeness of a bear erect, brute in all but his hind legs, which were adorned with pink silk stockings. And here again, almost as wondrous, stood a real bear of the dark forest, lending each of his fore paws to the grasp of a human hand, and as ready for the dance as any in that circle. His inferior nature rose half way, to meet his companions as they stooped. Other faces wore the similitude of man or woman, but distorted or extravagant, with red noses pendulous before their mouths, which seemed of awful depth, and stretched from ear to ear in an eternal fit of laughter. Here might be seen the Salvage Man, well known in heraldry, hairy as a baboon, and girdled with green leaves. By his side, a noble figure, but still a counterfeit, appeared an Indian hunter, with feathery crest and wampum belt. Many of this strange company wore foolscaps, and had little bells appended to their garments, tinkling with a silvery sound, responsive to the inaudible music of their gleesome spirits. Some youths and maidens were of soberer garb, yet well maintained their places in the irregular throng by the expression of wild revelry upon their features. Such were the colonists of Merry Mount, as they stood in the broad smile of sunset round their venerated Maypole.

Had a wanderer, bewildered in the melancholy

THE MAYPOLE OF MERRY MOUNT. 1. **Strutt's Book:** Joseph Strutt (1749–1802), author of *The Sports and Pastimes of the People of England* (1801).

2. **Golden Age:** in the mythical history of the world, that time of pure happiness, joy, and love which was, in the inevitable decay, followed by the silver, the brass, and finally the iron age.

forest, heard their mirth, and stolen a half-affrighted glance, he might have fancied them the crew of Comus,[3] some already transformed to brutes, some midway between man and beast, and the others rioting in the flow of tipsy jollity that foreran the change. But a band of Puritans, who watched the scene, invisible themselves, compared the masques to those devils and ruined souls with whom their superstition peopled the black wilderness.

Within the ring of monsters appeared the two airiest forms that had ever trodden on any more solid footing than a purple and golden cloud. One was a youth in glistening apparel, with a scarf of the rainbow pattern crosswise on his breast. His right hand held a gilded staff, the ensign of high dignity among the revellers, and his left grasped the slender fingers of a fair maiden, not less gayly decorated than himself. Bright roses glowed in contrast with the dark and glossy curls of each, and were scattered round their feet, or had sprung up spontaneously there. Behind this lightsome couple, so close to the Maypole that its boughs shaded his jovial face, stood the figure of an English priest, canonically dressed, yet decked with flowers, in heathen fashion, and wearing a chaplet of the native vine leaves. By the riot of his rolling eye, and the pagan decorations of his holy garb, he seemed the wildest monster here, and the very Comus of the crew.

"Votaries of the Maypole," cried the flower-decked priest, "merrily, all day long, have the woods echoed to your mirth. But be this your merriest hour, my hearts! Lo, here stand the Lord and Lady of the May, whom I, a clerk of Oxford, and high priest of Merry Mount, am presently to join in holy matrimony. Up with your nimble spirits, ye morris-dancers, green men, and glee maidens, bears and wolves, and horned gentlemen! Come; a chorus now, rich with the old mirth of Merry England, and the wilder glee of this fresh forest; and then a dance, to show the youthful pair what life is made of, and how airily they should go through it! All ye that love the Maypole, lend your voices to the nuptial song of the Lord and Lady of the May!"

This wedlock was more serious than most affairs of Merry Mount, where jest and delusion, trick and fantasy, kept up a continual carnival. The Lord and Lady of the May, though their titles must be laid down at sunset, were really and truly to be partners for the dance of life, beginning the measure that same bright eve. The wreath of roses, that hung from the lowest green bough of the Maypole, had been twined for them, and would be thrown over both their heads, in symbol of their flowery union. When the priest had spoken, therefore, a riotous uproar burst from the rout of monstrous figures.

"Begin you the stave, reverend Sir," cried they all; "and never did the woods ring to such a merry peal as we of the Maypole shall send up!"

Immediately a prelude of pipe, cithern, and viol, touched with practised minstrelsy, began to play from a neighboring thicket, in such a mirthful cadence that the boughs of the Maypole quivered to the sound. But the May Lord, he of the gilded staff, chancing to look into his Lady's eyes, was wonder struck at the almost pensive glance that met his own.

"Edith, sweet Lady of the May," whispered he reproachfully, "is yon wreath of roses a garland to hang above our graves, that you look so sad? O, Edith, this is our golden time! Tarnish it not by any pensive shadow of the mind; for it may be that nothing of futurity will be brighter than the mere remembrance of what is now passing."

"That was the very thought that saddened me! How came it in your mind too?" said Edith, in a still lower tone than he, for it was high treason to be sad at Merry Mount. "Therefore do I sigh amid this festive music. And besides, dear Edgar, I struggle as with a dream, and fancy that these shapes of our jovial friends are visionary, and their mirth unreal, and that we are no true Lord and Lady of the May. What is the mystery in my heart?"

Just then, as if a spell had loosened them, down came a little shower of withering rose leaves from the Maypole. Alas, for the young lovers! No sooner had their hearts glowed with real passion than they were sensible of something vague and unsubstantial in their former pleasures, and felt a dreary presentiment of inevitable change. From the moment that they truly loved, they had subjected themselves to earth's doom of care and sorrow, and troubled joy, and had no more a home at Merry Mount. That was Edith's mystery. Now leave we the priest to marry them, and the masquers to sport round the Maypole, till the last sunbeam be withdrawn from its summit, and the shadows of the forest mingle gloomily in the dance. Meanwhile, we may discover who these gay people were.

Two hundred years ago, and more, the old world and its inhabitants became mutually weary of each other. Men voyaged by thousands to the West: some to barter glass beads, and such like jewels, for the furs of the Indian hunter; some to conquer virgin empires; and one stern band to

3. **crew of Comus:** See Milton, *Comus*, l. 92 ff.

pray. But none of these motives had much weight with the colonists of Merry Mount. Their leaders were men who had sported so long with life, that when Thought and Wisdom came, even these unwelcome guests were led astray by the crowd of vanities which they should have put to flight. Erring Thought and perverted Wisdom were made to put on masques, and play the fool. The men of whom we speak, after losing the heart's fresh gayety, imagined a wild philosophy of pleasure, and came hither to act out their latest daydream. They gathered followers from all that giddy tribe whose whole life is like the festal days of soberer men. In their train were minstrels, not unknown in London streets: wandering players, whose theatres had been the halls of noblemen; mummers, rope-dancers, and mountebanks, who would long be missed at wakes, church-ales, and fairs; in a word, mirth makers of every sort, such as abounded in that age, but now began to be discountenanced by the rapid growth of Puritanism. Light had their footsteps been on land, and as lightly they came across the sea. Many had been maddened by their previous troubles into a gay despair; others were as madly gay in the flush of youth, like the May Lord and his Lady; but whatever might be the quality of their mirth, old and young were gay at Merry Mount. The young deemed themselves happy. The elder spirits, if they knew that mirth was but the counterfeit of happiness, yet followed the false shadow wilfully, because at least her garments glittered brightest. Sworn triflers of a lifetime, they would not venture among the sober truths of life not even to be truly blest.

All the hereditary pastimes of Old England were transplanted hither. The King of Christmas was duly crowned, and the Lord of Misrule bore potent sway. On the eve of St. John,[4] they felled whole acres of the forest to make bonfires, and danced by the blaze all night, crowned with garlands, and throwing flowers into the flame. At harvest time, though their crop was of the smallest, they made an image with the sheaves of Indian corn, and wreathed it with autumnal garlands, and bore it home triumphantly. But what chiefly characterized the colonists of Merry Mount was their veneration for the Maypole. It has made their true history a poet's tale. Spring decked the hallowed emblem with young blossoms and fresh green boughs; Summer brought roses of the deepest blush, and the perfected foliage of the forest; Autumn enriched it with that red and yellow gorgeousness which converts each wildwood leaf into a painted flower; and Winter silvered it with sleet, and hung it round with icicles, till it flashed in the cold sunshine, itself a frozen sunbeam. Thus each alternate season did homage to the Maypole, and paid it a tribute of its own richest splendor. Its votaries danced round it, once, at least, in every month; sometimes they called it their religion, or their altar; but always, it was the banner staff of Merry Mount.

Unfortunately, there were men in the new world of a sterner faith than these Maypole worshippers. Not far from Merry Mount was a settlement of Puritans, most dismal wretches, who said their prayers before daylight, and then wrought in the forest or the cornfield till evening made it prayer time again. Their weapons were always at hand to shoot down the straggling savage. When they met in conclave, it was never to keep up the old English mirth, but to hear sermons three hours long, or to proclaim bounties on the heads of wolves and the scalps of Indians. Their festivals were fast days, and their chief pastime the singing of psalms. Woe to the youth or maiden who did but dream of a dance! The selectman nodded to the constable; and there sat the light-heeled reprobate in the stocks; or if he danced, it was round the whipping-post, which might be termed the Puritan Maypole.

A party of these grim Puritans, toiling through the difficult woods, each with a horseload of iron armor to burden his footsteps, would sometimes draw near the sunny precincts of Merry Mount. There were the silken colonists, sporting round their Maypole; perhaps teaching a bear to dance, or striving to communicate their mirth to the grave Indian; or masquerading in the skins of deer and wolves, which they had hunted for that especial purpose. Often, the whole colony were playing at blindman's buff, magistrates and all, with their eyes bandaged, except a single scapegoat, whom the blinded sinners pursued by the tinkling of the bells at his garments. Once, it is said, they were seen following a flower-decked corpse, with merriment and festive music, to his grave. But did the dead man laugh? In their quietest times, they sang ballads and told tales, for the edification of their pious visitors; or perplexed them with juggling tricks; or grinned at them through horse collars; and when sport itself grew wearisome, they made game of their own stupidity, and began a yawning match. At the very least of these enormities, the men of iron shook their heads and frowned so darkly that the revellers looked up, imagining that a momentary cloud had overcast the sunshine, which was to be perpetual there. On the other hand, the Puritans affirmed that, when a

4. **eve of St. John:** Midsummer's Eve, June 23, an occasion for celebration throughout centuries in Old England.

psalm was pealing from their place of worship, the echo which the forest sent them back seemed often like the chorus of a jolly catch, closing with a roar of laughter. Who but the fiend, and his bond slaves, the crew of Merry Mount, had thus disturbed them? In due time, a feud arose, stern and bitter on one side, and as serious on the other as anything could be among such light spirits as had sworn allegiance to the Maypole. The future complexion of New England was involved in this important quarrel. Should the grizzly saints establish their jurisdiction over the gay sinners, then would their spirits darken all the clime, and make it a land of clouded visages, of hard toil, of sermon and psalm forever. But should the banner staff of Merry Mount be fortunate, sunshine would break upon the hills, and flowers would beautify the forest, and late posterity do homage to the Maypole.

After these authentic passages from history, we return to the nuptials of the Lord and Lady of the May. Alas! we have delayed too long, and must darken our tale too suddenly. As we glance again at the Maypole, a solitary sunbeam is fading from the summit, and leaves only a faint, golden tinge blended with the hues of the rainbow banner. Even that dim light is now withdrawn, relinquishing the whole domain of Merry Mount to the evening gloom, which has rushed so instantaneously from the black surrounding woods. But some of these black shadows have rushed forth in human shape.

Yes, with the setting sun, the last day of mirth had passed from Merry Mount. The ring of gay masquers was disordered and broken; the stag lowered his antlers in dismay; the wolf grew weaker than a lamb; the bells of the morris-dancers tinkled with tremulous affright. The Puritans had played a characteristic part in the Maypole mummeries. Their darksome figures were intermixed with the wild shapes of their foes, and made the scene a picture of the moment, when waking thoughts start up amid the scattered fantasies of a dream. The leader of the hostile party stood in the centre of the circle, while the rout of monsters cowered around him, like evil spirits in the presence of a dread magician. No fantastic foolery could look him in the face. So stern was the energy of his aspect, that the whole man, visage, frame, and soul, seemed wrought of iron, gifted with life and thought, yet all of one substance with his headpiece and breastplate. It was the Puritan of Puritans: it was Endicott [5] himself!

"Stand off, priest of Baal!" said he, with a grim frown, and laying no reverent hand upon the surplice. "I know thee, Blackstone! [6] Thou art the man who couldst not abide the rule even of thine own corrupted church, and hast come hither to preach iniquity, and to give example of it in thy life. But now shall it be seen that the Lord hath sanctified this wilderness for his peculiar people. Woe unto them that would defile it! And first, for this flower-decked abomination, the altar of thy worship!"

And with his keen sword Endicott assaulted the hallowed Maypole. Nor long did it resist his arm. It groaned with a dismal sound; it showered leaves and rosebuds upon the remorseless enthusiast; and finally, with all its green boughs and ribbons and flowers, symbolic of departed pleasures, down fell the banner staff of Merry Mount. As it sank, tradition says, the evening sky grew darker, and the woods threw forth a more sombre shadow.

"There," cried Endicott, looking triumphantly on his work, "there lies the only Maypole in New England! The thought is strong within me that, by its fall, is shadowed forth the fate of light and idle mirth makers, amongst us and our posterity. Amen, saith John Endicott."

"Amen!" echoed his followers.

But the votaries of the Maypole gave one groan for their idol. At the sound, the Puritan leader glanced at the crew of Comus, each a figure of broad mirth, yet, at this moment, strangely expressive of sorrow and dismay.

"Valiant captain," quoth Peter Palfrey,[7] the Ancient [8] of the band, "what order shall be taken with the prisoners?"

"I thought not to repent me of cutting down a Maypole," replied Endicott, "yet now I could find in my heart to plant it again, and give each of these bestial pagans one other dance round their idol. It would have served rarely for a whipping-post!"

"But there are pine-trees enow," suggested the lieutenant.

"True, good Ancient," said the leader. "Wherefore, bind the heathen crew, and bestow on them a small matter of stripes apiece, as earnest of our future justice. Set some of the rogues in the stocks

5. **Endicott:** John Endicott (1589?–1665), governor of the Massachusetts Bay Colony.

6. **Blackstone:** "Did Governor Endicott speak less positively, we should suspect a mistake here. The Rev. Mr. Blackstone, though an eccentric, is not known to have been an immoral man. We rather doubt his identity with the priest of Merry Mount" [Hawthorne's note]. Blackstone was an Anglican priest who remained on good terms with the Pilgrims. 7. **Peter Palfrey:** identified by Hawthorne in "Main Street" as one of the first settlers in Salem. 8. **Ancient:** the standard-bearer or ensign of the troop.

to rest themselves, so soon as Providence shall bring us to one of our own well-ordered settlements, where such accommodations may be found. Further penalties, such as branding and cropping of ears, shall be thought of hereafter."

"How many stripes for the priest?" inquired Ancient Palfrey.

"None as yet," answered Endicott, bending his iron frown upon the culprit. "It must be for the Great and General Court to determine, whether stripes and long imprisonment, and other grievous penalty, may atone for his transgressions. Let him look to himself! For such as violate our civil order, it may be permitted us to show mercy. But woe to the wretch that troubleth our religion!"

"And this dancing bear," resumed the officer. "Must he share the stripes of his fellows?"

"Shoot him through the head!" said the energetic Puritan. "I suspect witchcraft in the beast."

"Here be a couple of shining ones," continued Peter Palfrey, pointing his weapon at the Lord and Lady of the May. "They seem to be of high station among these misdoers. Methinks their dignity will not be fitted with less than a double share of stripes."

Endicott rested on his sword, and closely surveyed the dress and aspect of the hapless pair. There they stood, pale, downcast, and apprehensive. Yet there was an air of mutual support, and of pure affection, seeking aid and giving it, that showed them to be man and wife, with the sanction of a priest upon their love. The youth, in the peril of the moment, had dropped his gilded staff, and thrown his arm about the Lady of the May, who leaned against his breast, too lightly to burden him, but with weight enough to express that their destinies were linked together, for good or evil. They looked first at each other, and then into the grim captain's face. There they stood, in the first hour of wedlock, while the idle pleasures, of which their companions were the emblems, had given place to the sternest cares of life, personified by the dark Puritans. But never had their youthful beauty seemed so pure and high as when its glow was chastened by adversity.

"Youth," said Endicott, "ye stand in an evil case, thou and thy maiden wife. Make ready presently, for I am minded that ye shall both have a token to remember your wedding day!"

"Stern man," cried the May Lord, "how can I move thee? Were the means at hand, I would resist to the death. Being powerless, I entreat! Do with me as thou wilt, but let Edith go untouched!"

"Not so," replied the immitigable zealot. "We are not wont to show an idle courtesy to that sex, which requireth the stricter discipline. What sayest thou, maid? Shall thy silken bridegroom suffer thy share of the penalty, besides his own?"

"Be it death," said Edith, "and lay it all on me!"

Truly, as Endicott had said, the poor lovers stood in a woful case. Their foes were triumphant, their friends captive and abased, their home desolate, the benighted wilderness around them, and a rigorous destiny, in the shape of the Puritan leader, their only guide. Yet the deepening twilight could not altogether conceal that the iron man was softened; he smiled at the fair spectacle of early love; he almost sighed for the inevitable blight of early hopes.

"The troubles of life have come hastily on this young couple," observed Endicott. "We will see how they comport themselves under their present trials ere we burden them with greater. If, among the spoil, there be any garments of a more decent fashion, let them be put upon this May Lord and his Lady, instead of their glistening vanities. Look to it, some of you."

"And shall not the youth's hair be cut?" asked Peter Palfrey, looking with abhorrence at the lovelock and long glossy curls of the young man.

"Crop it forthwith, and that in the true pumpkin-shell fashion," answered the captain. "Then bring them along with us, but more gently than their fellows. There be qualities in the youth, which may make him valiant to fight, and sober to toil, and pious to pray; and in the maiden, that may fit her to become a mother in our Israel, bringing up babes in better nurture than her own hath been. Nor think ye, young ones, that they are the happiest, even in our lifetime of a moment, who misspend it in dancing round a Maypole!"

And Endicott, the severest Puritan of all who laid the rock foundation of New England, lifted the wreath of roses from the ruin of the Maypole, and threw it, with his own gauntleted hand, over the heads of the Lord and Lady of the May. It was a deed of prophecy. As the moral gloom of the world overpowers all systematic gayety, even so was their home of wild mirth made desolate amid the sad forest. They returned to it no more. But as their flowery garland was wreathed of the brightest roses that had grown there, so, in the tie that united them, were intertwined all the purest and best of their early joys. They went heavenward, supporting each other along the difficult path which it was their lot to tread, and never wasted one regretful thought on the vanities of Merry Mount.

THE MINISTER'S BLACK VEIL

A Parable [1]

◇

THE STORY appeared first in *The Token* (1836) and was included in the *Twice-Told Tales* (1837). The interest and literary value of the tale may not be so much its inquiry into the depths of human conscience—we may well take for granted that Parson Hooper is guiltless of any real sin—but rather the continual unfolding of the narrative. Men sin, not according to law, but "within." The Rev. Mr. Dimmesdale would learn in *The Scarlet Letter*—for Parson Hooper is Dimmesdale in an earlier guise—that each man is all his life "loathsomely treasuring up the secret of his [own] sin."

◇

THE SEXTON stood in the porch of Milford meeting-house, pulling busily at the bell-rope. The old people of the village came stooping along the street. Children, with bright faces, tripped merrily beside their parents, or mimicked a graver gait, in the conscious dignity of their Sunday clothes. Spruce bachelors looked sidelong at the pretty maidens, and fancied that the Sabbath sunshine made them prettier than on week days. When the throng had mostly streamed into the porch, the sexton began to toll the bell, keeping his eye on the Reverend Mr. Hooper's door. The first glimpse of the clergyman's figure was the signal for the bell to cease its summons.

"But what has good Parson Hooper got upon his face?" cried the sexton in astonishment.

All within hearing immediately turned about, and beheld the semblance of Mr. Hooper, pacing slowly his meditative way towards the meeting-house. With one accord they started, expressing more wonder than if some strange minister were coming to dust the cushions of Mr. Hooper's pulpit.

"Are you sure it is our parson?" inquired Goodman Gray of the sexton.

"Of a certainty it is good Mr. Hooper," replied the sexton. "He was to have exchanged pulpits with Parson Shute, of Westbury; but Parson Shute sent to excuse himself yesterday, being to preach a funeral sermon."

The cause of so much amazement may appear sufficiently slight. Mr. Hooper, a gentlemanly person, of about thirty, though still a bachelor, was dressed with due clerical neatness, as if a careful wife had starched his band, and brushed the weekly dust from his Sunday's garb. There was but one thing remarkable in his appearance. Swathed about his forehead, and hanging down over his face, so low as to be shaken by his breath, Mr. Hooper had on a black veil. On a nearer view it seemed to consist of two folds of crape, which entirely concealed his features, except the mouth and chin, but probably did not intercept his sight, further than to give a darkened aspect to all living and inanimate things. With this gloomy shade before him, good Mr. Hooper walked onward, at a slow and quiet pace, stooping somewhat, and looking on the ground, as is customary with abstracted men, yet nodding kindly to those of his parishioners who still waited on the meeting-house steps. But so wonder-struck were they that his greeting hardly met with a return.

"I can't really feel as if good Mr. Hooper's face was behind that piece of crape," said the sexton.

"I don't like it," muttered an old woman, as she hobbled into the meeting-house. "He has changed himself into something awful, only by hiding his face."

"Our parson has gone mad!" cried Goodman Gray, following him across the threshold.

A rumor of some unaccountable phenomenon had preceded Mr. Hooper into the meeting-house, and set all the congregation astir. Few could refrain from twisting their heads towards the door; many stood upright, and turned directly about; while several little boys clambered upon the seats, and came down again with a terrible racket. There was a general bustle, a rustling of the women's gowns and shuffling of the men's feet, greatly at variance with that hushed repose which should attend the entrance of the minister. But Mr. Hooper appeared not to notice the perturbation of his people. He entered with an almost noiseless step, bent his head mildly to the pews on each side, and bowed as he passed his oldest parishioner, a white-haired great-grandsire, who occupied an arm-chair in the centre of the aisle. It was strange to observe how slowly this venerable man became conscious of something singular in the appearance of his pastor. He seemed not fully to partake of

THE MINISTER'S BLACK VEIL. 1. **A Parable:** "Another clergyman in New England, Mr. Joseph Moody, of York, Maine, who died about eighty years since, made himself remarkable by the same eccentricity that is here related of the Reverend Mr. Hooper. In his case, however, the symbol had a different import. In early life he had accidentally killed a beloved friend; and from that day till the hour of his death, he hid his face from men" [H]. The story of the Rev. Joseph Moody (1700–53) is told in William Sprague's *Annals of the American Pulpit* (1804).

the prevailing wonder, till Mr. Hooper had ascended the stairs, and showed himself in the pulpit, face to face with his congregation, except for the black veil. That mysterious emblem was never once withdrawn. It shook with his measured breath, as he gave out the psalm; it threw its obscurity between him and the holy page, as he read the Scriptures; and while he prayed, the veil lay heavily on his uplifted countenance. Did he seek to hide it from the dread Being whom he was addressing?

Such was the effect of this simple piece of crape, that more than one woman of delicate nerves was forced to leave the meeting-house. Yet perhaps the pale-faced congregation was almost as fearful a sight to the minister, as his black veil to them.

Mr. Hooper had the reputation of a good preacher, but not an energetic one: he strove to win his people heavenward by mild, persuasive influences, rather than to drive them thither by the thunders of the Word. The sermon which he now delivered was marked by the same characteristics of style and manner as the general series of his pulpit oratory. But there was something, either in the sentiment of the discourse itself, or in the imagination of the auditors, which made it greatly the most powerful effort that they had ever heard from their pastor's lips. It was tinged, rather more darkly than usual, with the gentle gloom of Mr. Hooper's temperament. The subject had reference to secret sin, and those sad mysteries which we hide from our nearest and dearest, and would fain conceal from our own consciousness, even forgetting that the Omniscient can detect them. A subtle power was breathed into his words. Each member of the congregation, the most innocent girl, and the man of hardened breast, felt as if the preacher had crept upon them, behind his awful veil, and discovered their hoarded iniquity of deed or thought. Many spread their clasped hands on their bosoms. There was nothing terrible in what Mr. Hooper said, at least, no violence; and yet, with every tremor of his melancholy voice, the hearers quaked. An unsought pathos came hand in hand with awe. So sensible were the audience of some unwonted attribute in their minister, that they longed for a breath of wind to blow aside the veil, almost believing that a stranger's visage would be discovered, though the form, gesture, and voice were those of Mr. Hooper.

At the close of the services, the people hurried out with indecorous confusion, eager to communicate their pent-up amazement, and conscious of lighter spirits the moment they lost sight of the black veil. Some gathered in little circles, huddled closely together, with their mouths all whispering in the centre; some went homeward alone, wrapt in silent meditation; some talked loudly, and profaned the Sabbath day with ostentatious laughter. A few shook their sagacious heads, intimating that they could penetrate the mystery; while one or two affirmed that there was no mystery at all, but only that Mr. Hooper's eyes were so weakened by the midnight lamp, as to require a shade. After a brief interval, forth came good Mr. Hooper also, in the rear of his flock. Turning his veiled face from one group to another, he paid due reverence to the hoary heads, saluted the middle aged with kind dignity as their friend and spiritual guide, greeted the young with mingled authority and love, and laid his hands on the little children's heads to bless them. Such was always his custom on the Sabbath day. Strange and bewildered looks repaid him for his courtesy. None, as on former occasions, aspired to the honor of walking by their pastor's side. Old Squire Saunders, doubtless by an accidental lapse of memory, neglected to invite Mr. Hooper to his table, where the good clergyman had been wont to bless the food, almost every Sunday since his settlement. He returned, therefore, to the parsonage, and, at the moment of closing the door, was observed to look back upon the people, all of whom had their eyes fixed upon the minister. A sad smile gleamed faintly from beneath the black veil, and flickered about his mouth, glimmering as he disappeared.

"How strange," said a lady, "that a simple black veil, such as any woman might wear on her bonnet should become such a terrible thing on Mr. Hooper's face!"

"Something must surely be amiss with Mr. Hooper's intellects," observed her husband, the physician of the village. "But the strangest part of the affair is the effect of this vagary, even on a sober-minded man like myself. The black veil, though it covers only our pastor's face, throws its influence over his whole person, and makes him ghostlike from head to foot. Do you not feel it so?"

"Truly do I," replied the lady; "and I would not be alone with him for the world. I wonder he is not afraid to be alone with himself!"

"Men sometimes are so," said her husband.

The afternoon service was attended with similar circumstances. At its conclusion, the bell tolled for the funeral of a young lady. The relatives and friends were assembled in the house, and the more distant acquaintances stood about the door, speaking of the good qualities of the deceased, when their talk was interrupted by the appearance of Mr. Hooper, still covered with his black veil. It was now an appropriate emblem. The clergyman stepped into the room where the corpse was laid, and bent over the coffin, to take a last farewell of his deceased parishioner. As he stooped, the veil hung straight down from his forehead, so that, if her eyelids had not been closed forever, the dead maiden might have seen his face. Could Mr. Hooper be fearful of her glance, that he so hastily caught back the black veil? A person who watched the interview between the dead and living, scrupled not to affirm, that, at the instant when the clergyman's features were disclosed, the corpse had slightly shuddered, rustling the shroud and muslin cap, though the countenance retained the composure of death.[2] A superstitious old woman was the only witness of this prodigy. From the coffin Mr. Hooper passed into the chamber of the mourners, and thence to the head of the staircase, to make the funeral prayer. It was a tender and heart-dissolving prayer, full of sorrow, yet so imbued with celestial hopes, that the music of a heavenly harp, swept by the fingers of the dead, seemed faintly to be heard among the saddest accents of the minister. The people trembled, though they but darkly understood him when he prayed that they, and himself, and all of mortal race, might be ready, as he trusted this young maiden had been, for the dreadful hour that should snatch the veil from their faces. The bearers went heavily forth, and the mourners followed, saddening all the street, with the dead before them, and Mr. Hooper in his black veil behind.

"Why do you look back?" said one in the procession to his partner.

"I had a fancy," replied she, "that the minister and the maiden's spirit were walking hand in hand."

"And so had I, at the same moment," said the other.

That night, the handsomest couple in Milford village were to be joined in wedlock. Though reckoned a melancholy man, Mr. Hooper had a placid cheerfulness for such occasions, which often excited a sympathetic smile where livelier merriment would have been thrown away. There was no quality of his disposition which made him more beloved than this. The company at the wedding awaited his arrival with impatience, trusting that the strange awe, which had gathered over him throughout the day, would now be dispelled. But such was not the result. When Mr. Hooper came, the first thing that their eyes rested on was the same horrible black veil, which had added deeper gloom to the funeral, and could portend nothing but evil to the wedding. Such was its immediate effect on the guests that a cloud seemed to have rolled duskily from beneath the black crape, and dimmed the light of the candles. The bridal pair stood up before the minister. But the bride's cold fingers quivered in the tremulous hand of the bridegroom, and her deathlike paleness caused a whisper that the maiden who had been buried a few hours before was come from her grave to be married. If ever another wedding were so dismal, it was that famous one where they tolled the wedding knell. After performing the ceremony, Mr. Hooper raised a glass of wine to his lips, wishing happiness to the new-married couple in a strain of mild pleasantry that ought to have brightened the features of the guests, like a cheerful gleam from the hearth. At that instant, catching a glimpse of his figure in the looking-glass, the black veil involved his own spirit in the horror with which it overwhelmed all others. His frame shuddered, his lips grew white, he spilt the untasted wine upon the carpet, and rushed forth into the darkness. For the Earth, too, had on her Black Veil.

The next day, the whole village of Milford talked of little else than Parson Hooper's black veil. That, and the mystery concealed behind it, supplied a topic for discussion between acquaintances meeting in the street, and good women gossiping at their open windows. It was the first item of news that the tavern-keeper told to his guests. The children babbled of it on their way to school. One imitative little imp covered his face with an old black handkerchief, thereby so affrighting his playmates that the panic seized himself, and he well-nigh lost his wits by his own waggery.

It was remarkable that of all the busybodies and impertinent people in the parish, not one ventured to put the plain question to Mr. Hooper, wherefore he did this thing. Hitherto, whenever there appeared the slightest call for such interference, he had never lacked advisers, nor shown himself averse to be guided by their judgment. If he erred at all, it was by so painful a degree of self-distrust, that even the mildest censure would lead him to consider an indifferent action as a crime. Yet, though so well acquainted with this amiable weakness, no individual among his parishioners chose to make the black veil a subject of friendly remonstrance. There was a feeling of dread, nei-

2. **composure of death:** In his review of the *Twice-Told Tales* Poe suggested that Parson Hooper had assumed the black veil because of the wrong he had done this young woman: "The moral put into the mouth of the dying minister will be supposed to convey the true import of the narrative; and that a crime of dark dye (having reference to the 'young lady') has been committed, is a point which only minds congenial with that of the author will perceive." Poe's explanation may be plausible, but it does not solve the moral problem which the story raises.

ther plainly confessed nor carefully concealed, which caused each to shift the responsibility upon another, till at length it was found expedient to send a deputation of the church, in order to deal with Mr. Hooper about the mystery, before it should grow into a scandal. Never did an embassy so ill discharge its duties. The minister received them with friendly courtesy, but became silent, after they were seated, leaving to his visitors the whole burden of introducing their important business. The topic, it might be supposed, was obvious enough. There was the black veil swathed round Mr. Hooper's forehead, and concealing every feature above his placid mouth, on which, at times, they could perceive the glimmering of a melancholy smile. But that piece of crape, to their imagination, seemed to hang down before his heart, the symbol of a fearful secret between him and them. Were the veil but cast aside, they might speak freely of it, but not till then. Thus they sat a considerable time, speechless, confused, and shrinking uneasily from Mr. Hooper's eye, which they felt to be fixed upon them with an invisible glance. Finally, the deputies returned abashed to their constituents, pronouncing the matter too weighty to be handled, except by a council of the churches, if, indeed, it might not require a general synod.

But there was one person in the village unappalled by the awe with which the black veil had impressed all beside herself. When the deputies returned without an explanation, or even venturing to demand one, she, with the calm energy of her character, determined to chase away the strange cloud that appeared to be settling round Mr. Hooper, every moment more darkly than before. As his plighted wife, it should be her privilege to know what the black veil concealed. At the minister's first visit, therefore, she entered upon the subject with a direct simplicity, which made the task easier both for him and her. After he had seated himself, she fixed her eyes steadfastly upon the veil, but could discern nothing of the dreadful gloom that had so overawed the multitude: it was but a double fold of crape, hanging down from his forehead to his mouth, and slightly stirring with his breath.

"No," said she aloud, and smiling, "there is nothing terrible in this piece of crape, except that it hides a face which I am always glad to look upon. Come, good sir, let the sun shine from behind the cloud. First lay aside your black veil: then tell me why you put it on."

Mr. Hooper's smile glimmered faintly.

"There is an hour to come," said he, "when all of us shall cast aside our veils. Take it not amiss, beloved friend, if I wear this piece of crape till then."

"Your words are a mystery, too," returned the young lady. "Take away the veil from them, at least."

"Elizabeth, I will," said he, "so far as my vow may suffer me. Know, then, this veil is a type and a symbol, and I am bound to wear it ever, both in light and darkness, in solitude and before the gaze of multitudes, and as with strangers, so with my familiar friends. No mortal eye will see it withdrawn. This dismal shade must separate me from the world: even you, Elizabeth, can never come behind it!"

"What grievous affliction hath befallen you," she earnestly inquired, "that you should thus darken your eyes forever?"

"If it be a sign of mourning," replied Mr. Hooper, "I, perhaps, like most other mortals, have sorrows dark enough to be typified by a black veil."

"But what if the world will not believe that it is the type of an innocent sorrow?" urged Elizabeth. "Beloved and respected as you are, there may be whispers that you hide your face under the consciousness of secret sin. For the sake of your holy office, do away this scandal!"

The color rose into her cheeks as she intimated the nature of the rumors that were already abroad in the village. But Mr. Hooper's mildness did not forsake him. He even smiled again—that same sad smile, which always appeared like a faint glimmering of light, proceeding from the obscurity beneath the veil.

"If I hide my face for sorrow, there is cause enough," he merely replied; "and if I cover it for secret sin, what mortal might not do the same?"

And with this gentle, but unconquerable obstinacy did he resist all her entreaties. At length Elizabeth sat silent. For a few moments she appeared lost in thought, considering, probably, what new methods might be tried to withdraw her lover from so dark a fantasy, which, if it had no other meaning, was perhaps a symptom of mental disease. Though of a firmer character than his own, the tears rolled down her cheeks. But, in an instant, as it were, a new feeling took the place of sorrow: her eyes were fixed insensibly on the black veil, when, like a sudden twilight in the air, its terrors fell around her. She arose, and stood trembling before him.

"And do you feel it then, at last?" said he mournfully.

She made no reply, but covered her eyes with her hand, and turned to leave the room. He rushed forward and caught her arm.

"Have patience with me, Elizabeth!" cried he, passionately. "Do not desert me, though this veil must be between us here on earth. Be mine, and hereafter there shall be no veil over my face, no darkness between our souls! It is but a mortal veil —it is not for eternity! O! you know not how lonely I am, and how frightened, to be alone behind my black veil. Do not leave me in this miserable obscurity forever!"

"Lift the veil but once, and look me in the face," said she.

"Never! It cannot be!" replied Mr. Hooper.

"Then farewell!" said Elizabeth.

She withdrew her arm from his grasp, and slowly departed, pausing at the door, to give one long shuddering gaze, that seemed almost to penetrate the mystery of the black veil. But, even amid his grief, Mr. Hooper smiled to think that only a material emblem had separated him from happiness, though the horrors, which it shadowed forth, must be drawn darkly between the fondest of lovers.

From that time no attempts were made to remove Mr. Hooper's black veil, or, by a direct appeal, to discover the secret which it was supposed to hide. By persons who claimed a superiority to popular prejudice, it was reckoned merely an eccentric whim, such as often mingles with the sober actions of men otherwise rational, and tinges them all with its own semblance of insanity. But with the multitude, good Mr. Hooper was irreparably a bugbear. He could not walk the street with any peace of mind, so conscious was he that the gentle and timid would turn aside to avoid him, and that others would make it a point of hardihood to throw themselves in his way. The impertinence of the latter class compelled him to give up his customary walk at sunset to the burial ground; for when he leaned pensively over the gate, there would always be faces behind the gravestones, peeping at his black veil. A fable went the rounds that the stare of the dead people drove him thence. It grieved him, to the very depth of his kind heart, to observe how the children fled from his approach, breaking up their merriest sports, while his melancholy figure was yet afar off. Their instinctive dread caused him to feel more strongly than aught else, that a preternatural horror was interwoven with the threads of the black crape. In truth, his own antipathy to the veil was known to be so great, that he never willingly passed before a mirror, nor stooped to drink at a still fountain, lest, in its peaceful bosom, he should be affrighted by himself. This was what gave plausibility to the whispers, that Mr. Hooper's conscience tortured him for some great crime too horrible to be entirely concealed, or otherwise than so obscurely intimated. Thus, from beneath the black veil, there rolled a cloud into the sunshine, and ambiguity of sin or sorrow, which enveloped the poor minister, so that love or sympathy could never reach him. It was said that ghost and fiend consorted with him there. With self-shudderings and outward terrors, he walked continually in its shadow, groping darkly within his own soul, or gazing through a medium that saddened the whole world. Even the lawless wind, it was believed, respected his dreadful secret, and never blew aside the veil. But still good Mr. Hooper sadly smiled at the pale visages of the worldly throng as he passed by.

Among all its bad influences, the black veil had the one desirable effect, of making its wearer a very efficient clergyman. By the aid of his mysterious emblem—for there was no other apparent cause—he became a man of awful power over souls that were in agony for sin. His converts always regarded him with a dread peculiar to themselves, affirming, though but figuratively, that, before he brought them to celestial light, they had been with him behind the black veil. Its gloom, indeed, enabled him to sympathize with all dark affections. Dying sinners cried aloud for Mr. Hooper, and would not yield their breath till he appeared; though ever, as he stooped to whisper consolation, they shuddered at the veiled face so near their own. Such were the terrors of the black veil, even when Death had bared his visage! Strangers came long distances to attend service at his church, with the mere idle purpose of gazing at his figure, because it was forbidden them to behold his face. But many were made to quake ere they departed! Once, during Governor Belcher's [3] administration, Mr. Hooper was appointed to preach the election sermon.[4] Covered with his black veil, he stood before the chief magistrate, the council, and the representatives, and wrought so deep an impression, that the legislative measures of that year were characterized by all the gloom and piety of our earliest ancestral sway.

In this manner Mr. Hooper spent a long life, irreproachable in outward act, yet shrouded in dismal suspicions; kind and loving, though unloved, and dimly feared; a man apart from men, shunned in their health and joy, but ever sum-

3. **Governor Belcher's:** Jonathan Belcher (1682–1757), royal governor of the Massachusetts Bay Colony, 1730–41. 4. **election sermon:** a formal address by a clergyman who thereby earned one of the highest rewards the colony could bestow upon him. The climax of *The Scarlet Letter* is on the occasion of the Rev. Mr. Dimmesdale's preaching the election sermon before the officers and the assembled citizens of the colony.

moned to their aid in mortal anguish. As years wore on, shedding their snows above his sable veil, he acquired a name throughout the New England churches, and they called him Father Hooper. Nearly all his parishioners, who were of mature age when he was settled, had been borne away by many a funeral: he had one congregation in the church, and a more crowded one in the church-yard; and having wrought so late into the evening, and done his work so well, it was now good Father Hooper's turn to rest.

Several persons were visible by the shaded candlelight, in the death chamber of the old clergyman. Natural connections he had none. But there was the decorously grave, though unmoved physician, seeking only to mitigate the last pangs of the patient whom he could not save. There were the deacons, and other eminently pious members of his church. There, also, was the Reverend Mr. Clark, of Westbury, a young and zealous divine, who had ridden in haste to pray by the bedside of the expiring minister. There was the nurse, no hired handmaiden of death, but one whose calm affection had endured thus long in secrecy, in solitude, amid the chill of age, and would not perish, even at the dying hour. Who, but Elizabeth! And there lay the hoary head of good Father Hooper upon the death pillow, with the black veil still swathed about his brow, and reaching down over his face, so that each more difficult gasp of his faint breath caused it to stir. All through life that piece of crape had hung between him and the world: it had separated him from cheerful brotherhood and woman's love, and kept him in that saddest of all prisons, his own heart; and still it lay upon his face, as if to deepen the gloom of his darksome chamber, and shade him from the sunshine of eternity.

For some time previous, his mind had been confused, wavering doubtfully between the past and the present, and hovering forward, as it were, at intervals, into the indistinctness of the world to come. There had been feverish turns, which tossed him from side to side, and wore away what little strength he had. But in his most convulsive struggles, and in the wildest vagaries of his intellect, when no other thought retained its sober influence, he still showed an awful solicitude lest the black veil should slip aside. Even if his bewildered soul could have forgotten, there was a faithful woman at his pillow, who, with averted eyes, would have covered that aged face, which she had last beheld in the comeliness of manhood. At length the death-stricken old man lay quietly in the torpor of mental and bodily exhaustion, with an imperceptible pulse, and breath that grew fainter and fainter, except when a long, deep, and irregular inspiration seemed to prelude the flight of his spirit.

The minister of Westbury approached the bedside.

"Venerable Father Hooper," said he, "the moment of your release is at hand. Are you ready for the lifting of the veil that shuts in time from eternity?"

Father Hooper at first replied merely by a feeble motion of his head; then, apprehensive, perhaps, that his meaning might be doubtful, he exerted himself to speak.

"Yea," said he, in faint accents, "my soul hath a patient weariness until that veil be lifted."

"And is it fitting," resumed the Reverend Mr. Clark, "that a man so given to prayer, of such a blameless example, holy in deed and thought, so far as mortal judgment may pronounce; is it fitting that a father in the church should leave a shadow on his memory, that may seem to blacken a life so pure? I pray you, my venerable brother, let not this thing be! Suffer us to be gladdened by your triumphant aspect as you go to your reward. Before the veil of eternity be lifted, let me cast aside this black veil from your face!"

And thus speaking, the Reverend Mr. Clark bent forward to reveal the mystery of so many years. But, exerting a sudden energy, that made all the beholders stand aghast, Father Hooper snatched both his hands from beneath the bedclothes, and pressed them strongly on the black veil, resolute to struggle, if the minister of Westbury would contend with a dying man.

"Never!" cried the veiled clergyman. "On earth, never!"

"Dark old man!" exclaimed the affrighted minister, "with what horrible crime upon your soul are you now passing to the judgment?"

Father Hooper's breath heaved; it rattled in his throat; but, with a mighty effort, grasping forward with his hands, he caught hold of life, and held it back till he should speak. He even raised himself in bed; and there he sat, shivering with the arms of death around him, while the black veil hung down, awful, at that last moment, in the gathered terrors of a lifetime. And yet the faint, sad smile, so often there, now seemed to glimmer from its obscurity, and linger on Father Hooper's lips.

"Why do you tremble at me alone?" cried he, turning his veiled face round the circle of pale spectators. "Tremble also at each other! Have men avoided me, and women shown no pity, and children screamed and fled, only for my black veil? What, but the mystery which it obscurely typifies, has made this piece of crape so awful? When the friend shows his inmost heart to his friend; the lover to his best beloved; when man does not vainly shrink from the eye of his Creator, loathsomely treasuring up the secret of his sin; then deem me a monster, for the symbol beneath which I have lived, and die! I look around me, and, lo! on every visage a Black Veil!"

While his auditors shrank from one another, in mutual affright, Father Hooper fell back upon his pillow, a veiled corpse, with a faint smile lingering on the lips. Still veiled, they laid him in his coffin, and a veiled corpse they bore him to the grave. The grass of many years has sprung up and withered on that grave, the burial stone is moss-grown, and good Mr. Hooper's face is dust; but awful is still the thought that it mouldered beneath the Black Veil!

THE PROPHETIC PICTURES [1]

◊

THIS story, first published in *The Token* for 1837 and afterward included in the *Twice-Told Tales* (1837), may have been based on the age-old idea of the painter who explores his sitters' minds and discovers what they seek most earnestly to hide from the world, and also on a partial portrait of Hawthorne himself: "Like all other men around whom an engrossing purpose wreathes itself, he was insulated from the mass of mankind. . . . It is not good for a man to cherish a solitary ambition." Occasionally the hidden side of Hawthorne—that portion which belonged exclusively to the writer—broke through the mask which Hawthorne presented to the world. But, as in the last paragraph of the tale, the question of identity is raised and then passed by: "some would call it Fate, and hurry onward." Hawthorne's allegorizing genius seldom served him better than in this unfolding of the dark recesses of human consciousness, all the while that the people so revealed are quite unaware of what is being done to them. Hawthorne himself may have been sometimes capable of such self-analysis.

◊

"BUT this painter!" cried Walter Ludlow, with animation. "He not only excels in his peculiar art, but possesses vast acquirements in all other learning and science. He talks Hebrew with Dr. Mather,[2] and gives lectures in anatomy to Dr. Boylston.[3] In a word, he will meet the best instructed man among us on his own ground. Moreover, he is a polished gentleman—a citizen of the world—yes, a true cosmopolite; for he will speak like a native of each clime and country of the globe, except our own forests, whither he is now going. Nor is all this what I most admire in him."

"Indeed!" said Elinor, who had listened with a woman's interest to the description of such a man. "Yet this is admirable enough."

"Surely it is," replied her lover, "but far less so than his natural gift of adapting himself to every variety of character, insomuch that all men—and all women too, Elinor—shall find a mirror of themselves in this wonderful painter. But the greatest wonder is yet to be told."

"Nay, if he have more wonderful attributes than these," said Elinor, laughing, "Boston is a perilous abode for the poor gentleman. Are you telling me of a painter, or a wizard?"

"In truth," answered he, "that question might be asked much more seriously than you suppose. They say that he paints not merely a man's features, but his mind and heart. He catches the secret sentiments and passions, and throws them upon the canvas, like sunshine—or perhaps, in the portraits of dark-souled men, like a gleam of infernal fire. It is an awful gift," added Walter, lowering his voice from its tone of enthusiasm. "I shall be almost afraid to sit to him."

"Walter, are you in earnest?" exclaimed Elinor.

"For Heaven's sake, dearest Elinor, do not let him paint the look which you now wear," said her lover, smiling, though rather perplexed. "There:

THE PROPHETIC PICTURES. 1. **Prophetic Pictures:** "This story was suggested by an anecdote of Stuart, related in Dunlap's *History of the Arts of Design*—a most entertaining book to the general reader, and a most deeply interesting one, we should think, to the artist" [H]. The reference is to the work by William Dunlap, published in 1834, concerning an incident in the life of Gilbert Stuart, the portraitist: "Lord Mulgrave employed Stuart to paint the portrait of his brother, General Phipps, previous to his going abroad. On seeing the picture, . . . Mulgrave exclaimed, 'What is this?—this is very strange!' and stood gazing at the portrait. 'I have painted your brother as I saw him,' said the artist. 'I see insanity in that face,' was the brother's reply. The General went to India, and the first account his brother had of him was that of suicide from insanity. He went mad and cut his throat. It is that that the real portrait-painter dives into the recesses of his sitters' minds" (I, 187).

2. **Dr. Mather:** Cotton Mather (1663–1728), the learned divine of Boston who, though he may be charged with having incited some of the witchcraft delusion of 1692, was a learned scholar, the author of the *Magnalia Christi Americana* (1702), and an enlightened scientific investigator of the phenomena of this world. In 1712 he was elected an honorary fellow of the Royal Society.

3. **Dr. Boylston:** Zabdiel Boylston (1679–1766), the famed physician who in 1721 first introduced the practice of inoculation for smallpox into the colonies. When he met with abuse and the opposition of the citizens of Massachusetts, he was ably supported by Cotton Mather.

it is passing away now, but when you spoke you seemed frightened to death, and very sad besides. What were you thinking of?"

"Nothing, nothing," answered Elinor hastily. "You paint my face with your own fantasies. Well, come for me to-morrow, and we will visit this wonderful artist."

But when the young man had departed, it cannot be denied that a remarkable expression was again visible on the fair and youthful face of his mistress. It was a sad and anxious look, little in accordance with what should have been the feelings of a maiden on the eve of wedlock. Yet Walter Ludlow was the chosen of her heart.

"A look!" said Elinor to herself. "No wonder that it startled him, if it expressed what I sometimes feel. I know, by my own experience, how frightful a look may be. But it was all fancy. I thought nothing of it at the time—I have seen nothing of it since—I did but dream it."

And she busied herself about the embroidery of a ruff, in which she meant that her portrait should be taken.

The painter, of whom they had been speaking, was not one of those native artists who, at a later period than this, borrowed their colors from the Indians, and manufactured their pencils of the furs of wild beasts. Perhaps, if he could have revoked his life and prearranged his destiny, he might have chosen to belong to that school without a master, in the hope of being at least original, since there were no works of art to imitate nor rules to follow. But he had been born and educated in Europe. People said that he had studied the grandeur or beauty of conception, and every touch of the master hand, in all the most famous pictures, in cabinets and galleries, and on the walls of churches, till there was nothing more for his powerful mind to learn. Art could add nothing to its lessons, but Nature might. He had therefore visited a world whither none of his professional brethren had preceded him, to feast his eyes on visible images that were noble and picturesque, yet had never been transferred to canvas. America was too poor to afford other temptations to an artist of eminence, though many of the colonial gentry, on the painter's arrival, had expressed a wish to transmit their lineaments to posterity by means of his skill. Whenever such proposals were made, he fixed his piercing eyes on the applicant, and seemed to look him through and through. If he beheld only a sleek and comfortable visage, though there were a gold-laced coat to adorn the picture and golden guineas to pay for it, he civilly rejected the task and the reward. But if the face were the index of any thing uncommon, in thought, sentiment, or experience, or if he met a beggar in the street, with a white beard and a furrowed brow; or if sometimes a child happened to look up and smile, he would exhaust all the art on them that he denied to wealth.

Pictorial skill being so rare in the colonies, the painter became an object of general curiosity. If few or none could appreciate the technical merit of his productions, yet there were points, in regard to which the opinion of the crowd was as valuable as the refined judgment of the amateur. He watched the effect that each picture produced on such untutored beholders, and derived profit from their remarks, while they would as soon have thought of instructing Nature herself as him who seemed to rival her. Their admiration, it must be owned, was tinctured with the prejudices of the age and country. Some deemed it an offence against the Mosaic law, and even a presumptuous mockery of the Creator, to bring into existence such lively images of his creatures. Others, frightened at the art which could raise phantoms at will, and keep the form of the dead among the living, were inclined to consider the painter as a magician, or perhaps the famous Black Man,[4] of old witch times, plotting mischief in a new guise. These foolish fancies were more than half believed among the mob. Even in superior circles his character was invested with a vague awe, partly rising like smoke wreaths from the popular superstitions, but chiefly caused by the varied knowledge and talents which he made subservient to his profession.

Being on the eve of marriage, Walter Ludlow and Elinor were eager to obtain their portraits, as the first of what, they doubtless hoped, would be a long series of family pictures. The day after the conversation above recorded they visited the painter's rooms. A servant ushered them into an apartment, where, though the artist himself was not visible, there were personages whom they could hardly forbear greeting with reverence. They knew, indeed, that the whole assembly were but pictures, yet felt it impossible to separate the idea of life and intellect from such striking counterfeits. Several of the portraits were known to them, either as distinguished characters of the day or their private acquaintances. There was Governor Burnet,[5] looking as if he had just received an undutiful communication from the House of Representatives, and were inditing a most sharp response. Mr. Cooke [6] hung beside the ruler whom he opposed,

4. **Black Man:** Satan, who roamed the world in order to tempt men to their doom. 5. **Governor Burnet:** William Burnet (1688–1729), colonial governor, first of New York and New Jersey (1720–28), and later of Massachusetts (1728–29). 6. **Mr. Cook:** Elisha Cooke (1678–1737), physician and colonial statesman who opposed such royal governors as Shute and Burnet and their power of the veto over colonial legislation.

sturdy, and somewhat puritanical, as befitted a popular leader. The ancient lady of Sir William Phipps [7] eyed them from the wall, in ruff and farthingale,—an imperious old dame, not unsuspected of witchcraft. John Winslow,[8] then a very young man, wore the expression of warlike enterprise, which long afterwards made him a distinguished general. Their personal friends were recognized at a glance. In most of the pictures, the whole mind and character were brought out on the countenance, and concentrated into a single look, so that, to speak paradoxically, the originals hardly resembled themselves so strikingly as the portraits did.

Among these modern worthies there were two old bearded Saints, who had almost vanished into the darkening canvas. There was also a pale, but unfaded Madonna, who had perhaps been worshipped in Rome, and now regarded the lovers with such a mild and holy look that they longed to worship too.

"How singular a thought," observed Walter Ludlow, "that this beautiful face has been beautiful for above two hundred years! Oh, if all beauty would endure so well! Do you not envy her, Elinor?"

"If earth were heaven, I might," she replied. "But where all things fade, how miserable to be the one that could not fade!"

"This dark old St. Peter has a fierce and ugly scowl, saint though he be," continued Walter. "He troubles me. But the Virgin looks kindly at us."

"Yes; but very sorrowfully, methinks," said Elinor.

The easel stood beneath these three old pictures, sustaining one that had been recently commenced. After a little inspection, they began to recognize the features of their own minister, the Rev. Dr. Colman,[9] growing into shape and life, as it were, out of a cloud.

"Kind old man!" exclaimed Elinor. "He gazes at me as if he were about to utter a word of paternal advice."

"And at me," said Walter, "as if he were about to shake his head and rebuke me for some suspected iniquity. But so does the original. I shall never feel quite comfortable under his eye till we stand before him to be married."

They now heard a footstep on the floor, and turning, beheld the painter, who had been some moments in the room, and had listened to a few of their remarks. He was a middle-aged man, with a countenance well worthy of his own pencil. Indeed, by the picturesque, though careless arrangement of his rich dress, and, perhaps, because his soul dwelt always among painted shapes, he looked somewhat like a portrait himself. His visitors were sensible of a kindred between the artist and his works, and felt as if one of the pictures had stepped from the canvas to salute them.

Walter Ludlow, who was slightly known to the painter, explained the object of their visit. While he spoke, a sunbeam was falling athwart his figure and Elinor's, with so happy an effect that they also seemed living pictures of youth and beauty, gladdened by bright fortune. The artist was evidently struck.

"My easel is occupied for several ensuing days, and my stay in Boston must be brief," said he, thoughtfully; then, after an observant glance, he added: "but your wishes shall be gratified, though I disappoint the Chief Justice and Madam Oliver.[10] I must not lose this opportunity, for the sake of painting a few ells of broadcloth and brocade."

The painter expressed a desire to introduce both their portraits into one picture, and represent them engaged in some appropriate action. This plan would have delighted the lovers, but was necessarily rejected, because so large a space of canvas would have been unfit for the room which it was intended to decorate. Two half-length portraits were therefore fixed upon. After they had taken leave, Walter Ludlow asked Elinor, with a smile, whether she knew what an influence over their fates the painter was about to acquire.

"The old women of Boston affirm," continued he, "that after he has once got possession of a person's face and figure, he may paint him in any act or situation whatever—and the picture will be prophetic. Do you believe it?"

"Not quite," said Elinor, smiling. "Yet if he has such magic, there is something so gentle in his manner that I am sure he will use it well."

It was the painter's choice to proceed with both the portraits at the same time, assigning as a reason, in the mystical language which he sometimes used, that the faces threw light upon each other.

7. **lady . . . Phipps:** Mary Spencer Hull Phips, a wealthy lady and wife of Sir William Phips (1651–95). See "My Kinsman, Major Molineux," 1 n. Phips was the first royal governor of Massachusetts under the charter of 1691, which was procured following the overthrow of the Stuart dynasty. 8. **John Winslow:** the distinguished colonial soldier (1703–74) who, under Governor Shirley, built forts in defense against the Indians and who fought in Canada and Nova Scotia in the French and Indian War. 9. **the Rev. Dr. Colman:** Benjamin Colman (1673–1747), the distinguished pastor of the Brattle Street Church in Boston.

10. **Chief . . . Oliver:** Peter Oliver (1713–91), a judge in the Massachusetts lower courts who became chief justice in 1771. His wife was Mary Clarke Oliver of a distinguished New England family.

Accordingly he gave now a touch to Walter, and now to Elinor, and the features of one and the other began to start forth so vividly that it appeared as if his triumphant art would actually disengage them from the canvas. Amid the rich light and deep shade, they beheld their phantom selves. But, though the likeness promised to be perfect, they were not quite satisfied with the expression; it seemed more vague than in most of the painter's works. He, however, was satisfied with the prospect of success, and being much interested in the lovers, employed his leisure moments, unknown to them, in making a crayon sketch of their two figures. During their sittings, he engaged them in conversation, and kindled up their faces with characteristic traits, which, though continually varying, it was his purpose to combine and fix. At length he announced that at their next visit both the portraits would be ready for delivery.

"If my pencil will but be true to my conception, in the few last touches which I meditate," observed he, "these two pictures will be my very best performances. Seldom, indeed, has an artist such subjects."

While speaking, he still bent his penetrative eye upon them, nor withdrew it till they had reached the bottom of the stairs.

Nothing, in the whole circle of human vanities, takes stronger hold of the imagination than this affair of having a portrait painted. Yet why should it be so? The looking-glass, the polished globes of the andirons, the mirror-like water, and all other reflecting surfaces, continually present us with portraits, or rather ghosts of ourselves, which we glance at, and straightway forget them. But we forget them only because they vanish. It is the idea of duration—of earthy immortality—that gives such a mysterious interest to our own portraits. Walter and Elinor were not insensible to this feeling, and hastened to the painter's room, punctually at the appointed hour, to meet those pictured shapes which were to be their representatives with posterity. The sunshine flashed after them into the apartment, but left it somewhat gloomy as they closed the door.

Their eyes were immediately attracted to their portraits, which rested against the farthest wall of the room. At the first glance, through the dim light and the distance, seeing themselves in precisely their natural attitudes, and with all the air that they recognized so well, they uttered a simultaneous exclamation of delight.

"There we stand," cried Walter, enthusiastically, "fixed in sunshine forever! No dark passions can gather on our faces!"

"No," said Elinor, more calmly; "no dreary change can sadden us."

This was said while they were approaching, and had yet gained only an imperfect view of the pictures. The painter, after saluting them, busied himself at a table in completing a crayon sketch, leaving his visitors to form their own judgment as to his perfected labors. At intervals, he sent a glance from beneath his deep eyebrows, watching their countenances in profile, with his pencil suspended over the sketch. They had now stood some moments, each in front of the other's picture, contemplating it with entranced attention, but without uttering a word. At length, Walter stepped forward—then back—viewing Elinor's portrait in various lights, and finally spoke.

"Is there not a change?" said he, in a doubtful and meditative tone. "Yes; the perception of it grows more vivid the longer I look. It is certainly the same picture that I saw yesterday; the dress—the features—all are the same; and yet something is altered."

"Is then the picture less like than it was yesterday?" inquired the painter, now drawing near, with irrepressible interest.

"The features are perfect, Elinor," answered Walter, "and, at the first glance, the expression seemed also hers. But, I could fancy that the portrait has changed countenance, while I have been looking at it. The eyes are fixed on mine with a strangely sad and anxious expression. Nay, it is grief and terror! Is this like Elinor?"

"Compare the living face with the pictured one," said the painter.

Walter glanced sidelong at his mistress, and started. Motionless and absorbed—fascinated, as it were—in contemplation of Walter's portrait, Elinor's face had assumed precisely the expression of which he had just been complaining. Had she practised for whole hours before a mirror, she could not have caught the look so successfully. Had the picture itself been a mirror, it could not have thrown back her present aspect with stronger and more melancholy truth. She appeared quite unconscious of the dialogue between the artist and her lover.

"Elinor," exclaimed Walter, in amazement, "what change has come over you?"

She did not hear him, nor desist from her fixed gaze, till he seized her hand, and thus attracted her notice; then, with a sudden tremor, she looked from the picture to the face of the original.

"Do you see no change in your portrait?" asked she.

"In mine?—None!" replied Walter, examining it. "But let me see! Yes; there is a slight change—

an improvement, I think, in the picture, though none in the likeness. It has a livelier expression than yesterday, as if some bright thought were flashing from the eyes, and about to be uttered from the lips. Now that I have caught the look, it becomes very decided."

While he was intent on these observations, Elinor turned to the painter. She regarded him with grief and awe, and felt that he repaid her with sympathy and commiseration, though wherefore, she could but vaguely guess.

"That look!" whispered she, and shuddered. "How came it there?"

"Madam," said the painter, sadly, taking her hand, and leading her apart, "in both these pictures, I have painted what I saw. The artist—the true artist—must look beneath the exterior. It is his gift—his proudest, but often a melancholy one—to see the inmost soul, and, by a power indefinable even to himself, to make it glow or darken upon the canvas, in glances that express the thought and sentiment of years. Would that I might convince myself of error in the present instance!"

They had now approached the table, on which were heads in chalk, hands almost as expressive as ordinary faces, ivied church towers, thatched cottages, old thunder-stricken trees, Oriental and antique costume, and all such picturesque vagaries of an artist's idle moments. Turning them over, with seeming carelessness, a crayon sketch of two figures was disclosed.

"If I have failed," continued he—"if your heart does not see itself reflected in your own portrait—if you have no secret cause to trust my delineation of the other—it is not yet too late to alter them. I might change the action of these figures too. But would it influence the event?"

He directed her notice to the sketch. A thrill ran through Elinor's frame; a shriek was upon her lips; but she stifled it, with the self-command that becomes habitual to all who hide thoughts of fear and anguish within their bosoms. Turning from the table, she perceived that Walter had advanced near enough to have seen the sketch, though she could not determine whether it had caught his eye.

"We will not have the pictures altered," said she, hastily. "If mine is sad, I shall but look the gayer for the contrast."

"Be it so," answered the painter, bowing. "May your griefs be such fanciful ones that only your picture may mourn for them! For your joys—may they be true and deep, and paint themselves upon this lovely face till it quite belie my art!"

After the marriage of Walter and Elinor, the pictures formed the two most splendid ornaments of their abode. They hung side by side, separated by a narrow panel, appearing to eye each other constantly, yet always returning the gaze of the spectator. Travelled gentlemen, who professed a knowledge of such subjects, reckoned these among the most admirable specimens of modern portraiture; while common observers compared them with the originals, feature by feature, and were rapturous in praise of the likeness. But it was on a third class—neither travelled connoisseurs nor common observers, but people of natural sensibility—that the pictures wrought their strongest effect. Such persons might gaze carelessly at first, but, becoming interested, would return day after day, and study these painted faces like the pages of a mystic volume. Walter Ludlow's portrait attracted their earliest notice. In the absence of himself and his bride, they sometimes disputed as to the expression which the painter had intended to throw upon the features; all agreeing that there was a look of earnest import, though no two explained it alike. There was less diversity of opinion in regard to Elinor's picture. They differed, indeed, in their attempts to estimate the nature and depth of the gloom that dwelt upon her face, but agreed that it was gloom, and alien from the natural temperament of their youthful friend. A certain fanciful person announced, as the result of much scrutiny, that both these pictures were parts of one design, and that the melancholy strength of feeling, in Elinor's countenance, bore reference to the more vivid emotion, or, as he termed it, the wild passion, in that of Walter. Though unskilled in the art, he even began a sketch, in which the action of the two figures was to correspond with their mutual expression.

It was whispered among friends that, day by day, Elinor's face was assuming a deeper shade of pensiveness, which threatened soon to render her too true a counterpart of her melancholy picture. Walter, on the other hand, instead of acquiring the vivid look which the painter had given him on the canvas, became reserved and downcast, with no outward flashes of emotion, however it might be smouldering within. In course of time, Elinor hung a gorgeous curtain of purple silk, wrought with flowers and fringed with heavy golden tassels, before the pictures, under pretence that the dust would tarnish their hues, or the light dim them. It was enough. Her visitors felt, that the massive folds of the silk must never be withdrawn, nor the portraits mentioned in her presence.

Time wore on; and the painter came again. He had been far enough to the north to see the silver cascade of the Crystal Hills, and to look over the vast round of cloud and forest from the summit of New England's loftiest mountain. But he did not profane that scene by the mockery of his art. He had also lain in a canoe on the bosom of Lake George, making his soul the mirror of its loveliness and grandeur, till not a picture in the Vatican was more vivid than his recollection. He had gone with the Indian hunters to Niagara, and there, again, had flung his hopeless pencil down the precipice, feeling that he could as soon paint the roar, as aught else that goes to make up the wondrous cataract. In truth, it was seldom his impulse to copy natural scenery, except as a framework for the delineations of the human form and face, instinct with thought, passion, or suffering. With store of such his adventurous ramble had enriched him: the stern dignity of Indian chiefs; the dusky loveliness of Indian girls; the domestic life of wigwams; the stealthy march; the battle beneath gloomy pine-trees; the frontier fortress with its garrison; the anomaly of the old French partisan, bred in courts, but grown gray in shaggy deserts; such were the scenes and portraits that he had sketched. The glow of perilous moments; flashes of wild feeling; struggles of fierce power,—love, hate, grief, frenzy; in a word, all the worn-out heart of the old earth had been revealed to him under a new form. His portfolio was filled with graphic illustrations of the volume of his memory, which genius would transmute into its own substance, and imbue with immortality. He felt that the deep wisdom in his art, which he had sought so far, was found.

But amid stern or lovely nature, in the perils of the forest or its overwhelming peacefulness, still there had been two phantoms, the companions of his way. Like all other men around whom an engrossing purpose wreathes itself, he was insulated from the mass of human kind. He had no aim—no pleasure—no sympathies—but what were ultimately connected with his art. Though gentle in manner and upright in intent and action, he did not possess kindly feelings; his heart was cold; no living creature could be brought near enough to keep him warm. For these two beings, however, he had felt, in its greatest intensity, the sort of interest which always allied him to the subjects of his pencil. He had pried into their souls with his keenest insight, and pictured the result upon their features with his utmost skill, so as barely to fall short of that standard which no genius ever reached, his own severe conception. He had caught from the duskiness of the future—at least, so he fancied—a fearful secret, and had obscurely revealed it on the portraits. So much of himself—of his imagination and all other powers—had been lavished on the study of Walter and Elinor, that he almost regarded them as creations of his own, like the thousands with which he had peopled the realms of Picture. Therefore did they flit through the twilight of the woods, hover on the mist of waterfalls, look forth from the mirror of the lake, nor melt away in the noontide sun. They haunted his pictorial fancy, not as mockeries of life, nor pale goblins of the dead, but in the guise of portraits, each with the unalterable expression which his magic had evoked from the caverns of the soul. He could not recross the Atlantic till he had again beheld the originals of those airy pictures.

"O glorious Art!" thus mused the enthusiastic painter as he trod the street, "thou art the image of the Creator's own. The innumerable forms, that wander in nothingness, start into being at thy beck. The dead live again. Thou recallest them to their old scenes, and givest their gray shadows the lustre of a better life, at once earthly and immortal. Thou snatchest back the fleeting moments of History. With thee there is no Past, for, at thy touch, all that is great becomes forever present; and illustrious men live through long ages, in the visible performance of the very deeds which made them what they are. O potent Art! as thou bringest the faintly revealed Past to stand in that narrow strip of sunlight, which we call Now, canst thou summon the shrouded Future to meet her there? Have I not achieved it? Am I not thy Prophet?"

Thus, with a proud, yet melancholy fervor, did he almost cry aloud, as he passed through the toilsome street, among people that knew not of his reveries, nor could understand nor care for them. It is not good for man to cherish a solitary ambition. Unless there be those around him by whose example he may regulate himself, his thoughts, desires, and hopes will become extravagant, and he the semblance, perhaps the reality, of a madman. Reading other bosoms with an acuteness almost preternatural, the painter failed to see the disorder of his own.

"And this should be the house," said he, looking up and down the front, before he knocked. "Heaven help my brains! That picture! Methinks it will never vanish. Whether I look at the windows or the door, there it is framed within them, painted strongly, and glowing in the richest tints—the faces of the portraits—the figures and action of the sketch!"

He knocked.

"The Portraits! Are they within?" inquired he of the domestic; then recollecting himself—"your master and mistress! Are they at home?"

"They are, sir," said the servant, adding, as he noticed that picturesque aspect of which the painter could never divest himself, "and the Portraits too!"

The guest was admitted into a parlor, communicating by a central door with an interior room of the same size. As the first apartment was empty, he passed to the entrance of the second, within which his eyes were greeted by those living personages, as well as their pictured representatives, who had long been the objects of so singular an interest. He involuntarily paused on the threshold.

They had not perceived his approach. Walter and Elinor were standing before the portraits, whence the former had just flung back the rich and voluminous folds of the silken curtain, holding its golden tassel with one hand, while the other grasped that of his bride. The pictures, concealed for months, gleamed forth again in undiminished splendor, appearing to throw a sombre light across the room, rather than to be disclosed by a borrowed radiance. That of Elinor had been almost prophetic. A pensiveness, and next a gentle sorrow, had successively dwelt upon her countenance, deepening, with the lapse of time, into a quiet anguish. A mixture of affright would now have made it the very expression of the portrait. Walter's face was moody and dull, or animated only by fitful flashes, which left a heavier darkness for their momentary illumination. He looked from Elinor to her portrait, and thence to his own, in the contemplation of which he finally stood absorbed.

The painter seemed to hear the step of Destiny approaching behind him, on its progress towards its victims. A strange thought darted into his mind. Was not his own the form in which that destiny had embodied itself, and he a chief agent of the coming evil which he had foreshadowed?

Still, Walter remained silent before the picture, communing with it as with his own heart, and abandoning himself to the spell of evil influence that the painter had cast upon the features. Gradually his eyes kindled; while as Elinor watched the increasing wildness of his face, her own assumed a look of terror; and when at last he turned upon her, the resemblance of both to their portraits was complete.

"Our fate is upon us!" howled Walter. "Die!"

Drawing a knife, he sustained her, as she was sinking to the ground, and aimed it at her bosom. In the action, and in the look and attitude of each, the painter beheld the figures of his sketch. The picture, with all its tremendous coloring, was finished.

"Hold, madman!" cried he, sternly.

He had advanced from the door, and interposed himself between the wretched beings, with the same sense of power to regulate their destiny as to alter a scene upon the canvas. He stood like a magician, controlling the phantoms which he had evoked.

"What!" muttered Walter Ludlow, as he relapsed from fierce excitement into silent gloom. "Does Fate impede its own decree?"

"Wretched lady!" said the painter, "did I not warn you?"

"You did," replied Elinor, calmly, as her terror gave place to the quiet grief which it had disturbed. "But—I love him!"

Is there not a deep moral in the tale? Could the result of one, or all our deeds, be shadowed forth and set before us, some would call it Fate, and hurry onward, others be swept along by their passionate desires, and none be turned aside by the PROPHETIC PICTURES.

THE BIRTHMARK

◇

¶ THE TWO notebook entries for 1837 (see p. 767) were probably the beginnings for this story which was first published in the *Pioneer* (March, 1843) and included in the *Mosses from an Old Manse* (1846). The theme of the tale is suggested in the notebook entries: although man directs his energy toward the most lovely and perfect thing he can create, the very nature of beauty is its being flawed, and that which, in this life, is most pure and ethereal is so only in its imperfection. If our humanity loses its imperfection, it may cease to be human and become even subhuman. Man's dreams and the Ideal are the measure of a perfection which can never be attained.

◇

IN THE latter part of the last century there lived a man of science, an eminent proficient in every branch of natural philosophy, who not long before our story opens had made experience of a spiritual affinity more attractive than any chemical one. He had left his laboratory to the care of an assistant, cleared his fine countenance from the furnace smoke, washed the stain of acids from his fingers, and persuaded a beautiful woman to become his wife. In those days when the comparatively recent discovery of electricity and other kindred mysteries of Nature seemed to open paths into the region of miracle, it was not unusual for the love of science to rival the love of woman in its depth and absorbing energy. The higher intellect, the imagination, the spirit, and even the heart might all find their congenial aliment in pursuits which, as some of their ardent votaries believed, would ascend from one step of powerful intelligence to another, until the philosopher should lay his hand on the secret of creative force and perhaps make new worlds for himself. We know not whether Aylmer possessed this degree of faith in man's ultimate control over Nature. He had devoted himself, however, too unreservedly to scientific studies ever to be weaned from them by any second passion. His love for his young wife might prove the stronger of the two; but it could only be by intertwining itself with his love of science, and uniting the strength of the latter to his own.

Such a union accordingly took place, and was attended with truly remarkable consequences and a deeply impressive moral. One day, very soon after their marriage, Aylmer sat gazing at his wife with a trouble in his countenance that grew stronger until he spoke.

"Georgiana," said he, "has it never occurred to you that the mark upon your cheek might be removed?"

"No, indeed," said she, smiling; but perceiving the seriousness of his manner, she blushed deeply. "To tell the truth it has been so often called a charm that I was simple enough to imagine it might be so."

"Ah, upon another face perhaps it might," replied her husband; "but never on yours. No, dearest Georgiana, you came so nearly perfect from the hand of Nature that this slightest possible defect, which we hesitate whether to term a defect or a beauty, shocks me, as being the visible mark of earthly imperfection."

"Shocks you, my husband!" cried Georgiana, deeply hurt; at first reddening with momentary anger, but then bursting into tears. "Then why did you take me from my mother's side? You cannot love what shocks you!"

To explain this conversation it must be mentioned that in the centre of Georgiana's left cheek there was a singular mark, deeply interwoven, as it were, with the texture and substance of her face. In the usual state of her complexion—a healthy though delicate bloom—the mark wore a tint of deeper crimson, which imperfectly defined its shape amid the surrounding rosiness. When she blushed it gradually became more indistinct, and finally vanished amid the triumphant rush of blood that bathed the whole cheek with its brilliant glow. But if any shifting motion caused her to turn pale there was the mark again, a crimson stain upon the snow, in what Aylmer sometimes deemed an almost fearful distinctness. Its shape bore not a little similarity to the human hand, though of the smallest pygmy size. Georgiana's lovers were wont to say that some fairy at her birth hour had laid her tiny hand upon the infant's cheek, and left this impress there in token of the magic endowments that were to give her such sway over all hearts. Many a desperate swain would have risked life for the privilege of pressing his lips to the mysterious hand. It must not be concealed, however, that the impression wrought by this fairy sign manual varied exceedingly, according to the difference of temperament in the beholders. Some fastidious persons—but they were exclusively of her own sex—affirmed that the bloody hand, as they chose to call it, quite destroyed the effect of Georgiana's beauty, and rendered her countenance even hideous. But it would be as reasonable to say that one of those small blue stains which sometimes occur in the purest statuary marble would convert the Eve of Powers [1] to a monster. Masculine observers, if the birthmark did not heighten their admiration, contented themselves with wishing it away, that the world might possess one living specimen of ideal loveliness without the semblance of a flaw. After his marriage,—for he thought little or nothing of the matter before,—Aylmer discovered that this was the case with himself.

Had she been less beautiful,—if Envy's self could have found aught else to sneer at,—he might have felt his affection heightened by the prettiness of this mimic hand, now vaguely portrayed, now lost, now stealing forth again and glimmering to and fro with every pulse of emotion that throbbed within her heart; but seeing her otherwise so perfect, he found this one defect grow more and more intolerable with every moment of their united lives. It was the fatal flaw of humanity which Nature, in one shape or another, stamps ineffaceably on all her productions, either to imply that they are temporary and finite, or that their perfection must be wrought by toil and pain. The crimson hand expressed the ineludible gripe in which mortality clutches the highest and purest of earthly mould, degrading them into kindred with the lowest, and even with the very brutes, like whom their visible frames return to dust. In this manner, selecting it as the symbol of his wife's liability to sin, sorrow, decay, and death, Aylmer's sombre imagination was not long in rendering the birthmark a frightful object, causing him more trouble and horror than ever

THE BIRTHMARK. 1. **Eve of Powers:** Hiram Powers (1805–73), the American sculptor, created a life-size figure, "Eve Before the Fall."

Georgiana's beauty, whether of soul or sense, had given him delight.

At all the seasons which should have been their happiest, he invariably and without intending it, nay, in spite of a purpose to the contrary, reverted to this one disastrous topic. Trifling as it at first appeared, it so connected itself with innumerable trains of thought and modes of feeling that it became the central point of all. With the morning twilight Aylmer opened his eyes upon his wife's face and recognized the symbol of imperfection; and when they sat together at the evening hearth his eyes wandered stealthily to her cheek, and beheld, flickering with the blaze of the wood fire, the spectral hand that wrote mortality where he would fain have worshipped. Georgiana soon learned to shudder at his gaze. It needed but a glance with the peculiar expression that his face often wore to change the roses of her cheek into a deathlike paleness, amid which the crimson hand was brought strongly out, like a bass-relief of ruby on the whitest marble.

Late one night when the lights were growing dim, so as hardly to betray the stain on the poor wife's cheek, she herself, for the first time, voluntarily took up the subject.

"Do you remember, my dear Aylmer," said she, with a feeble attempt at a smile, "have you any recollection of a dream last night about this odious hand?"

"None! none whatever!" replied Aylmer, starting; but then he added, in a dry, cold tone, affected for the sake of concealing the real depth of his emotion, "I might well dream of it; for before I fell asleep it had taken a pretty firm hold of my fancy."

"And you did dream of it?" continued Georgiana, hastily; for she dreaded lest a gush of tears should interrupt what she had to say. "A terrible dream! I wonder that you can forget it. Is it possible to forget this one expression?—'It is in her heart now; we must have it out!' Reflect, my husband; for by all means I would have you recall that dream."

The mind is in a sad state when Sleep, the all-involving, cannot confine her spectres within the dim region of her sway, but suffers them to break forth, affrighting this actual life with secrets that perchance belong to a deeper one. Aylmer now remembered his dream. He had fancied himself with his servant Aminadab, attempting an operation for the removal of the birthmark; but the deeper went the knife, the deeper sank the hand, until at length its tiny grasp appeared to have caught hold of Georgiana's heart; whence, however, her husband was inexorably resolved to cut or wrench it away.

When the dream had shaped itself perfectly in his memory, Aylmer sat in his wife's presence with a guilty feeling. Truth often finds its way to the mind close muffled in robes of sleep, and then speaks with uncompromising directness of matters in regard to which we practise an unconscious self-deception during our waking moments. Until now he had not been aware of the tyrannizing influence acquired by one idea over his mind, and of the lengths which he might find in his heart to go for the sake of giving himself peace.

"Aylmer," resumed Georgiana, solemnly, "I know not what may be the cost to both of us to rid me of this fatal birthmark. Perhaps its removal may cause cureless deformity; or it may be the stain goes as deep as life itself. Again: do we know that there is a possibility, on any terms, of unclasping the firm gripe of this little hand which was laid upon me before I came into the world?"

"Dearest Georgiana, I have spent much thought upon the subject," hastily interrupted Aylmer. "I am convinced of the perfect practicability of its removal."

"If there be the remotest possibility of it," continued Georgiana, "let the attempt be made at whatever risk. Danger is nothing to me; for life, while this hateful mark makes me the object of your horror and disgust,—life is a burden which I would fling down with joy. Either remove this dreadful hand, or take my wretched life! You have deep science. All the world bears witness of it. You have achieved great wonders. Cannot you remove this little, little mark, which I cover with the tips of two small fingers? Is this beyond your power, for the sake of your own peace, and to save your poor wife from madness?"

"Noblest, dearest, tenderest wife," cried Aylmer, rapturously, "doubt not my power. I have already given this matter the deepest thought—thought which might almost have enlightened me to create a being less perfect than yourself. Georgiana, you have led me deeper than ever into the heart of science. I feel myself fully competent to render this dear cheek as faultless as its fellow; and then, most beloved, what will be my triumph when I shall have corrected what Nature left imperfect in her fairest work! Even Pygmalion,[2] when his sculptured woman assumed life, felt not greater ecstasy than mine will be."

"It is resolved, then," said Georgiana, faintly smiling. "And, Aylmer, spare me not, though you should find the birthmark take refuge in my heart at last."

2. **Pygmalion:** a mythical king of Cyprus who fell in love with the ivory statue of Galatea; his prayers to Aphrodite brought the statue to life.

Her husband tenderly kissed her cheek—her right cheek—not that which bore the impress of the crimson hand.

The next day Aylmer apprised his wife of a plan that he had formed whereby he might have opportunity for the intense thought and constant watchfulness which the proposed operation would require; while Georgiana, likewise, would enjoy the perfect repose essential to its success. They were to seclude themselves in the extensive apartments occupied by Aylmer as a laboratory, and where, during his toilsome youth, he had made discoveries in the elemental powers of Nature that had roused the admiration of all the learned societies in Europe. Seated calmly in this laboratory, the pale philosopher had investigated the secrets of the highest cloud region and of the profoundest mines; he had satisfied himself of the causes that kindled and kept alive the fires of the volcano; and had explained the mystery of fountains, and how it is that they gush forth, some so bright and pure, and others with such rich medicinal virtues, from the dark bosom of the earth. Here, too, at an earlier period, he had studied the wonders of the human frame, and attempted to fathom the very process by which Nature assimilates all her precious influences from earth and air, and from the spiritual world, to create and foster man, her masterpiece. The latter pursuit, however, Aylmer had long laid aside in unwilling recognition of the truth—against which all seekers sooner or later stumble—that our great creative Mother, while she amuses us with apparently working in the broadest sunshine, is yet severely careful to keep her own secrets, and, in spite of her pretended openness, shows us nothing but results. She permits us, indeed, to mar, but seldom to mend, and, like a jealous patentee, on no account to make. Now, however, Aylmer resumed these half-forgotten investigations; not, of course, with such hopes or wishes as first suggested them; but because they involved much physiological truth and lay in the path of his proposed scheme for the treatment of Georgiana.

As he led her over the threshold of the laboratory, Georgiana was cold and tremulous. Aylmer looked cheerfully into her face, with intent to reassure her, but was so startled with the intense glow of the birthmark upon the whiteness of her cheek that he could not restrain a strong convulsive shudder. His wife fainted.

"Aminadab! Aminadab!" shouted Aylmer, stamping violently on the floor.

Forthwith there issued from an inner apartment a man of low stature, but bulky frame, with shaggy hair hanging about his visage, which was grimed with the vapors of the furnace. This personage had been Aylmer's underworker during his whole scientific career, and was admirably fitted for that office by his great mechanical readiness, and the skill with which, while incapable of comprehending a single principle, he executed all the details of his master's experiments. With his vast strength, his shaggy hair, his smoky aspect, and the indescribable earthiness that incrusted him, he seemed to represent man's physical nature; while Aylmer's slender figure, and pale, intellectual face, were no less apt a type of the spiritual element.

"Throw open the door of the boudoir, Aminadab," said Aylmer, "and burn a pastil."

"Yes, master," answered Aminadab, looking intently at the lifeless form of Georgiana; and then he muttered to himself, "If she were my wife, I'd never part with that birthmark."

When Georgiana recovered consciousness she found herself breathing an atmosphere of penetrating fragrance, the gentle potency of which had recalled her from her deathlike faintness. The scene around her looked like enchantment. Aylmer had converted those smoky, dingy, sombre rooms, where he had spent his brightest years in recondite pursuits, into a series of beautiful apartments not unfit to be the secluded abode of a lovely woman. The walls were hung with gorgeous curtains, which imparted the combination of grandeur and grace that no other species of adornment can achieve; and as they fell from the ceiling to the floor, their rich and ponderous folds, concealing all angles and straight lines, appeared to shut in the scene from infinite space. For aught Georgiana knew, it might be a pavilion among the clouds. And Aylmer, excluding the sunshine, which would have interfered with his chemical processes, had supplied its place with perfumed lamps, emitting flames of various hue, but all uniting in a soft, impurpled radiance. He now knelt by his wife's side, watching her earnestly, but without alarm; for he was confident in his science, and felt that he could draw a magic circle round her within which no evil might intrude.

"Where am I? Ah, I remember," said Georgiana, faintly; and she placed her hand over her cheek to hide the terrible mark from her husband's eyes.

"Fear not, dearest!" exclaimed he. "Do not shrink from me! Believe me, Georgiana, I even rejoice in this single imperfection, since it will be such a rapture to remove it."

"Oh, spare me!" sadly replied his wife. "Pray do not look at it again. I never can forget that convulsive shudder."

In order to soothe Georgiana, and, as it were,

to release her mind from the burden of actual things, Aylmer now put in practice some of the light and playful secrets which science had taught him among its profounder lore. Airy figures, absolutely bodiless ideas, and forms of unsubstantial beauty came and danced before her, imprinting their momentary footsteps on beams of light. Though she had some indistinct idea of the method of these optical phenomena, still the illusion was almost perfect enough to warrant the belief that her husband possessed sway over the spiritual world. Then again, when she felt a wish to look forth from her seclusion, immediately, as if her thoughts were answered, the procession of external existence flitted across a screen. The scenery and the figures of actual life were perfectly represented, but with that bewitching, yet indescribable difference which always makes a picture, an image, or a shadow so much more attractive than the original. When wearied of this, Aylmer bade her cast her eyes upon a vessel containing a quantity of earth. She did so, with little interest at first; but was soon startled to perceive the germ of a plant shooting upward from the soil. Then came the slender stalk; the leaves gradually unfolded themselves; and amid them was a perfect and lovely flower.

"It is magical!" cried Georgiana. "I dare not touch it."

"Nay, pluck it," answered Aylmer,—"pluck it, and inhale its brief perfume while you may. The flower will wither in a few moments and leave nothing save its brown seed vessels; but thence may be perpetuated a race as ephemeral as itself."

But Georgiana had no sooner touched the flower than the whole plant suffered a blight, its leaves turning coal-black as if by the agency of fire.

"There was too powerful a stimulus," said Aylmer, thoughtfully.

To make up for this abortive experiment, he proposed to take her portrait by a scientific process of his own invention. It was to be effected by rays of light striking upon a polished plate of metal. Georgiana assented; but, on looking at the result, was affrighted to find the features of the portrait blurred and indefinable; while the minute figure of a hand appeared where the cheek should have been. Aylmer snatched the metallic plate and threw it into a jar of corrosive acid.

Soon, however, he forgot these mortifying failures. In the intervals of study and chemical experiment he came to her flushed and exhausted, but seemed invigorated by her presence, and spoke in glowing language of the resources of his art. He gave a history of the long dynasty of the alchemists,[3] who spent so many ages in quest of the universal solvent by which the golden principle might be elicited from all things vile and base. Aylmer appeared to believe that, by the plainest scientific logic, it was altogether within the limits of possibility to discover this long-sought medium; "but," he added, "a philosopher who should go deep enough to acquire the power would attain too lofty a wisdom to stoop to the exercise of it." Not less singular were his opinions in regard to the elixir vitæ. He more than intimated that it was at his option to concoct a liquid that should prolong life for years, perhaps interminably; but that it would produce a discord in Nature which all the world, and chiefly the quaffer of the immortal nostrum, would find cause to curse.

"Aylmer, are you in earnest?" asked Georgiana, looking at him with amazement and fear. "It is terrible to possess such power, or even to dream of possessing it."

"Oh, do not tremble, my love," said her husband. "I would not wrong either you or myself by working such inharmonious effects upon our lives; but I would have you consider how trifling, in comparison, is the skill requisite to remove this little hand."

At the mention of the birthmark, Georgiana, as usual, shrank as if a redhot iron had touched her cheek.

Again Aylmer applied himself to his labors. She could hear his voice in the distant furnace room giving directions to Aminadab, whose harsh, uncouth, misshapen tones were audible in response, more like the grunt or growl of a brute than human speech. After hours of absence, Aylmer reappeared and proposed that she should now examine his cabinet of chemical products and natural treasures of the earth. Among the former he showed her a small vial, in which, he remarked, was contained a gentle yet most powerful fragrance, capable of impregnating all the breezes that blow across a kingdom. They were of inestimable value, the contents of that little vial; and, as he said so, he threw some of the perfume into the air and filled the room with piercing and invigorating delight.

"And what is this?" asked Georgiana, pointing to a small crystal globe containing a gold-colored liquid. "It is so beautiful to the eye that I could imagine it the elixir of life."

3. **He . . . alchemists:** Alchemy, the predecessor of modern medical science, was the medieval chemistry which sought to transmute base metals into gold and to discover the universal cure for diseases. The search for the "elixir Vitae" was to discover the magical nostrum which would indefinitely prolong life. Aylmer's experiments, however modern they may be, are mostly of the "black arts" associated with alchemy.

"In one sense it is," replied Aylmer; "or, rather, the elixir of immortality. It is the most precious poison that ever was concocted in this world. By its aid I could apportion the lifetime of any mortal at whom you might point your finger. The strength of the dose would determine whether he were to linger out years, or drop dead in the midst of a breath. No king on his guarded throne could keep his life if I, in my private station, should deem that the welfare of millions justified me in depriving him of it."

"Why do you keep such a terrific drug?" inquired Georgiana in horror.

"Do not mistrust me, dearest," said her husband, smiling; "its virtuous potency is yet greater than its harmful one. But see! here is a powerful cosmetic. With a few drops of this in a vase of water, freckles may be washed away as easily as the hands are cleansed. A stronger infusion would take the blood out of the cheek, and leave the rosiest beauty a pale ghost."

"Is it with this lotion that you intend to bathe my cheek?" asked Georgiana, anxiously.

"Oh, no," hastily replied her husband; "this is merely superficial. Your case demands a remedy that shall go deeper."

In his interviews with Georgiana, Aylmer generally made minute inquiries as to her sensations and whether the confinement of the rooms and the temperature of the atmosphere agreed with her. These questions had such a particular drift that Georgiana began to conjecture that she was already subjected to certain physical influences, either breathed in with the fragrant air or taken with her food. She fancied likewise, but it might be altogether fancy, that there was a stirring up of her system—a strange, indefinite sensation creeping through her veins, and tingling, half painfully, half pleasurably, at her heart. Still, whenever she dared to look into the mirror, there she beheld herself pale as a white rose and with the crimson birthmark stamped upon her cheek. Not even Aylmer now hated it so much as she.

To dispel the tedium of the hours which her husband found it necessary to devote to the processes of combination and analysis, Georgiana turned over the volumes of his scientific library. In many dark old tomes she met with chapters full of romance and poetry. They were the works of the philosophers of the middle ages, such as Albertus Magnus, Cornelius Agrippa, Paracelsus, and the famous friar who created the prophetic Brazen Head.[4] All these antique naturalists stood in advance of their centuries, yet were imbued with some of their credulity, and therefore were believed, and perhaps imagined themselves to have acquired from the investigation of Nature a power above Nature, and from physics a sway over the spiritual world. Hardly less curious and imaginative were the early volumes of the Transactions of the Royal Society,[5] in which the members, knowing little of the limits of natural possibility, were continually recording wonders or proposing methods whereby wonders might be wrought.

But to Georgiana the most engrossing volume was a large folio from her husband's own hand, in which he had recorded every experiment of his scientific career, its original aim, the methods adopted for its development, and its final success or failure, with the circumstances to which either event was attributable. The book, in truth, was both the history and emblem of his ardent, ambitious, imaginative, yet practical and laborious life. He handled physical details as if there were nothing beyond them; yet spiritualized them all, and redeemed himself from materialism by his strong and eager aspiration towards the infinite. In his grasp the veriest clod of earth assumed a soul. Georgiana, as she read, reverenced Aylmer and loved him more profoundly than ever, but with a less entire dependence on his judgment than heretofore. Much as he had accomplished, she could not but observe that his most splendid successes were almost invariably failures, if compared with the ideal at which he aimed. His brightest diamonds were the merest pebbles, and felt to be so by himself, in comparison with the inestimable gems which lay hidden beyond his reach. The volume, rich with achievements that had won renown for its author, was yet as melancholy a record as ever mortal hand had penned. It was the sad confession and continual exemplification of the shortcomings of the composite man, the spirit burdened with clay and working in matter, and of the despair that assails the higher nature at finding itself so miserably thwarted by the earthly part. Perhaps every man of genius in whatever sphere might recognize the image of his own experience in Aylmer's journal.

So deeply did these reflections affect Georgiana that she laid her face upon the open volume and burst into tears. In this situation she was found by her husband.

4. **Albertus . . . Head:** Albertus Magnus (1193?–1280), German saint, philosopher, and alchemist. Cornelius Agrippa (1486?–1535), German physician, theologian, and writer. Paracelsus (1493–1541), Swiss-born alchemist and physician. **Brazen Head:** the English philosopher and man of science, Roger Bacon (1214–94), was reputed to have made a head of brass.

5. **Transactions . . . Society:** the *Philosophical Transactions* of The Royal Society for Improving Natural Knowledge, the famous scientific body founded in 1660.

"It is dangerous to read in a sorcerer's books," said he, with a smile, though his countenance was uneasy and displeased. "Georgiana, there are pages in that volume which I can scarcely glance over and keep my senses. Take heed lest it prove as detrimental to you."

"It has made me worship you more than ever," said she.

"Ah, wait for this one success," rejoined he, "then worship me if you will. I shall deem myself hardly unworthy of it. But come, I have sought you for the luxury of your voice. Sing to me, dearest."

So she poured out the liquid music of her voice to quench the thirst of his spirit. He then took his leave with a boyish exuberance of gayety, assuring her that her seclusion would endure but a little longer, and that the result was already certain. Scarcely had he departed when Georgiana felt irresistibly impelled to follow him. She had forgotten to inform Aylmer of a symptom which for two or three hours past had begun to excite her attention. It was a sensation in the fatal birthmark, not painful, but which induced a restlessness throughout her system. Hastening after her husband, she intruded for the first time into the laboratory.

The first thing that struck her eye was the furnace, that hot and feverish worker, with the intense glow of its fire, which by the quantities of soot clustered above it seemed to have been burning for ages. There was a distilling apparatus in full operation. Around the room were retorts, tubes, cylinders, crucibles, and other apparatus of chemical research. An electrical machine stood ready for immediate use. The atmosphere felt oppressively close, and was tainted with gaseous odors which had been tormented forth by the processes of science. The severe and homely simplicity of the apartment, with its naked walls and brick pavement, looked strange, accustomed as Georgiana had become to the fantastic elegance of her boudoir. But what chiefly, indeed almost solely, drew her attention, was the aspect of Aylmer himself.

He was pale as death, anxious and absorbed, and hung over the furnace as if it depended upon his utmost watchfulness whether the liquid which it was distilling should be the draught of immortal happiness or misery. How different from the sanguine and joyous mien that he had assumed for Georgiana's encouragement!

"Carefully now, Aminadab; carefully, thou human machine; carefully, thou man of clay!" muttered Aylmer, more to himself than his assistant. "Now, if there be a thought too much or too little, it is all over."

"Ho! ho!" mumbled Aminadab. "Look, master! look!"

Aylmer raised his eyes hastily, and at first reddened, then grew paler than ever, on beholding Georgiana. He rushed towards her and seized her arm with a gripe that left the print of his fingers upon it.

"Why do you come hither? Have you no trust in your husband?" cried he, impetuously. "Would you throw the blight of that fatal birthmark over my labors? It is not well done. Go, prying woman, go!"

"Nay, Aylmer," said Georgiana with the firmness of which she possessed no stinted endowment, "it is not you that have a right to complain. You mistrust your wife; you have concealed the anxiety with which you watch the development of this experiment. Think not so unworthily of me, my husband. Tell me all the risk we run, and fear not that I shall shrink; for my share in it is far less than your own."

"No, no, Georgiana!" said Aylmer, impatiently; "it must not be."

"I submit," replied she calmly. "And, Aylmer, I shall quaff whatever draught you bring me; but it will be on the same principle that would induce me to take a dose of poison if offered by your hand."

"My noble wife," said Aylmer, deeply moved, "I knew not the height and depth of your nature until now. Nothing shall be concealed. Know, then, that this crimson hand, superficial as it seems, has clutched its grasp into your being with a strength of which I had no previous conception. I have already administered agents powerful enough to do aught except to change your entire physical system. Only one thing remains to be tried. If that fail us we are ruined."

"Why did you hesitate to tell me this?" asked she.

"Because, Georgiana," said Aylmer, in a low voice, "there is danger."

"Danger? There is but one danger—that this horrible stigma shall be left upon my cheek!" cried Georgiana. "Remove it, remove it, whatever be the cost, or we shall both go mad!"

"Heaven knows your words are too true," said Aylmer, sadly. "And now, dearest, return to your boudoir. In a little while all will be tested."

He conducted her back and took leave of her with a solemn tenderness which spoke far more than his words how much was now at stake. After his departure Georgiana became rapt in musings. She considered the character of Aylmer, and did it completer justice than at any previous moment. Her heart exulted, while it trembled, at his honorable love—so pure and lofty that it would accept nothing less than perfection nor miserably make itself contented with an earthlier nature than he had dreamed of. She felt how much more precious was such a sentiment than that meaner kind which would have borne with the imperfection for her sake, and have been guilty of treason to holy love by degrading its perfect idea to the level of the actual; and with her whole spirit she prayed that, for a single moment, she might satisfy his highest and deepest conception. Longer than one moment she well knew it could not be; for his spirit was ever on the march, ever ascending, and each instant required something that was beyond the scope of the instant before.

The sound of her husband's footsteps aroused her. He bore a crystal goblet containing a liquor colorless as water, but bright enough to be the draught of immortality. Aylmer was pale; but it seemed rather the consequence of a highly-wrought state of mind and tension of spirit than of fear or doubt.

"The concoction of the draught has been perfect," said he, in answer to Georgiana's look. "Unless all my science have deceived me, it cannot fail."

"Save on your account, my dearest Aylmer," observed his wife, "I might wish to put off this birthmark of mortality by relinquishing mortality itself in preference to any other mode. Life is but a sad possession to those who have attained precisely the degree of moral advancement at which I stand. Were I weaker and blinder it might be happiness. Were I stronger, it might be endured hopefully. But, being what I find myself, methinks I am of all mortals the most fit to die."

"You are fit for heaven without tasting death!" replied her husband. "But why do we speak of dying? The draught cannot fail. Behold its effect upon this plant."

On the window seat there stood a geranium diseased with yellow blotches, which had overspread all its leaves. Aylmer poured a small quantity of the liquid upon the soil in which it grew. In a little time, when the roots of the plant had taken up the moisture, the unsightly blotches began to be extinguished in a living verdure.

"There needed no proof," said Georgiana, quietly. "Give me the goblet. I joyfully stake all upon your word."

"Drink, then, thou lofty creature!" exclaimed Aylmer, with fervid admiration. "There is no taint of imperfection on thy spirit. Thy sensible frame, too, shall soon be all perfect."

She quaffed the liquid and returned the goblet to his hand.

"It is grateful," said she with a placid smile. "Methinks it is like water from a heavenly fountain; for it contains I know not what of unobtrusive fragrance and deliciousness. It allays a feverish thirst that had parched me for many days. Now, dearest, let me sleep. My earthly senses are closing over my spirit like the leaves around the heart of a rose at sunset."

She spoke the last words with a gentle reluctance, as if it required almost more energy than she could command to pronounce the faint and lingering syllables. Scarcely had they loitered through her lips ere she was lost in slumber. Aylmer sat by her side, watching her aspect with the emotions proper to a man the whole value of whose existence was involved in the process now to be tested. Mingled with this mood, however, was the philosophic investigation characteristic of the man of science. Not the minutest symptom escaped him. A heightened flush of the cheek, a slight irregularity of breath, a quiver of the eyelid, a hardly perceptible tremor through the frame,—such were the details which, as the moments passed, he wrote down in his folio volume. Intense thought had set its stamp upon every previous page of that volume, but the thoughts of years were all concentrated upon the last.

While thus employed, he failed not to gaze often at the fatal hand, and not without a shudder. Yet once, by a strange and unaccountable impulse, he pressed it with his lips. His spirit recoiled, however, in the very act; and Georgiana, out of the midst of her deep sleep, moved uneasily and murmured as if in remonstrance. Again Aylmer resumed his watch. Nor was it without avail. The crimson hand, which at first had been strongly visible upon the marble paleness of Georgiana's cheek, now grew more faintly outlined. She remained not less pale than ever; but the birthmark, with every breath that came and went, lost somewhat of its former distinctness. Its presence had been awful; its departure was more awful still. Watch the stain of the rainbow fading out of the sky, and you will know how that mysterious symbol passed away.

"By Heaven! it is well-nigh gone!" said Aylmer to himself, in almost irrepressible ecstasy. "I can scarcely trace it now. Success! success! And now it is like the faintest rose color. The lightest flush of blood across her cheek would overcome it. But she is so pale!"

He drew aside the window curtain and suffered the light of natural day to fall into the room and rest upon her cheek. At the same time he heard a gross, hoarse chuckle, which he had long known as his servant Aminadab's expression of delight.

"Ah, clod! ah, earthly mass!" cried Aylmer, laughing in a sort of frenzy, "you have served me well! Matter and spirit—earth and heaven—have both done their part in this! Laugh, thing of the senses! You have earned the right to laugh."

These exclamations broke Georgiana's sleep. She slowly unclosed her eyes and gazed into the mirror which her husband had arranged for that purpose. A faint smile flitted over her lips when she recognized how barely perceptible was now that crimson hand which had once blazed forth with such disastrous brilliancy as to scare away all their happiness. But then her eyes sought Aylmer's face with a trouble and anxiety that he could by no means account for.

"My poor Aylmer!" murmured she.

"Poor? Nay, richest, happiest, most favored!" exclaimed he. "My peerless bride, it is successful! You are perfect!"

"My poor Aylmer," she repeated, with a more than human tenderness, "you have aimed loftily; you have done nobly. Do not repent that with so high and pure a feeling, you have rejected the best the earth could offer. Aylmer, dearest Aylmer, I am dying!"

Alas! it was too true! The fatal hand had grappled with the mystery of life, and was the bond by which an angelic spirit kept itself in union with a mortal frame. As the last crimson tint of the birthmark—that sole token of human imperfection—faded from her cheek, the parting breath of the now perfect woman passed into the atmosphere, and her soul, lingering a moment near her husband, took its heavenward flight. Then a hoarse, chuckling laugh was heard again! Thus ever does the gross fatality of earth exult in its invariable triumph over the immortal essence which, in this dim sphere of half development, demands the completeness of a higher state. Yet, had Aylmer reached a profounder wisdom, he need not thus have flung away the happiness which would have woven his mortal life of the selfsame texture with the celestial. The momentary circumstance was too strong for him; he failed to look beyond the shadowy scope of time, and, living once for all in eternity, to find the perfect future in the present.

THE CELESTIAL RAILROAD

◇

¶ THIS humorous, satiric story—published in the *Democratic Review* (May, 1843) and afterward in the *Mosses from an Old Manse* (1846)—is quite obviously based on John Bunyan's *Pilgrim's Progress* (1678). In its time the story attracted much attention among those who objected to Modernism in religion and relished Hawthorne's sly hits at New Thought. It was widely reprinted and circulated as a pamphlet issued by an evangelical tract society. While Hawthorne's purpose was to satirize Emersonian idealism, Transcendentalism, German philosophy, and liberal Protestantism, one cannot be entirely certain that the old-fashioned and sturdy faith of New England Puritanism is meant to be the last bulwark of truth. The bridge over the Slough of Despond, the burden of sin which is deposited in the baggage car, the tunnel through the Hill Difficulty, and the gas lamps which illumine the Valley of the Shadow may demonstrate that modern "improvements" do not make the journey from sin to redemption an easy and sure one.

◇

NOT a great while ago, passing through the gate of dreams, I visited that region of the earth in which lies the famous City of Destruction. It interested me much to learn that by the public spirit of some of the inhabitants a railroad has recently been established between this populous and flourishing town and the Celestial City. Having a little time upon my hands, I resolved to gratify a liberal curiosity by making a trip thither. Accordingly, one fine morning after paying my bill at the hotel, and directing the porter to stow my luggage behind a coach, I took my seat in the vehicle and set out for the station-house. It was my good fortune to enjoy the company of a gentleman—one Mr. Smooth-it-away—who, though he had never actually visited the Celestial City, yet seemed as well acquainted with its laws, customs, policy, and statistics, as with those of the City of Destruction, of which he was a native townsman. Being, moreover, a director of the railroad corporation and one of its largest stockholders, he had it in his power to give me all desirable information respecting that praiseworthy enterprise.

Our coach rattled out of the city, and at a short distance from its outskirts passed over a bridge of elegant construction, but somewhat too slight, as I imagined, to sustain any considerable weight. On both sides lay an extensive quagmire, which could not have been more disagreeable, either to sight or smell, had all the kennels of the earth emptied their pollution there.

"This," remarked Mr. Smooth-it-away, "is the famous Slough of Despond—a disgrace to all the neighborhood; and the greater that it might so easily be converted into firm ground."

"I have understood," said I, "that efforts have been made for that purpose from time immemorial. Bunyan mentions that above twenty thousand cartloads of wholesome instructions had been thrown in here without effect."

"Very probably! And what effect could be anticipated from such unsubstantial stuff?" cried Mr. Smooth-it-away. "You observe this convenient bridge. We obtained a sufficient foundation for it by throwing into the slough some editions of books of morality; volumes of French philosophy and German rationalism; tracts, sermons, and essays of modern clergymen; extracts from Plato, Confucius, and various Hindoo sages, together with a few ingenious commentaries upon texts of Scripture,—all of which by some scientific process, have been converted into a mass like granite. The whole bog might be filled up with similar matter."

It really seemed to me, however, that the bridge vibrated and heaved up and down in a very formidable manner; and, spite of Mr. Smooth-it-away's testimony to the solidity of its foundation, I should be loath to cross it in a crowded omnibus, especially if each passenger were encumbered with as heavy luggage as that gentleman and myself. Nevertheless we got over without accident, and soon found ourselves at the station-house. This very neat and spacious edifice is erected on the site of the little wicket gate, which formerly, as all old pilgrims will recollect, stood directly across the highway, and, by its inconvenient narrowness, was a great obstruction to the traveller of liberal mind and expansive stomach. The reader of John Bunyan will be glad to know that Christian's old friend Evangelist, who was accustomed to supply each pilgrim with a mystic roll,[1] now presides at the ticket office. Some malicious persons it is true deny the identity of this reputable character with the Evangelist of old times, and even pretend to bring competent evidence of an imposture. Without involving myself in a dispute I shall merely observe that, so far as my experience goes, the square pieces of pasteboard now delivered to passengers are much more convenient and useful along the road than the antique roll of parchment. Whether they will be as readily received at the gate of the Celestial City I decline giving an opinion.

A large number of passengers were already at the station-house awaiting the departure of the cars. By the aspect and demeanor of these persons it was easy to judge that the feelings of the community had undergone a very favorable change in reference to the celestial pilgrimage. It would have done Bunyan's heart good to see it. Instead of a lonely and ragged man with a huge burden on his back, plodding along sorrowfully on foot while the whole city hooted after him, here were parties of the first gentry and most respectable people in the neighborhood setting forth towards the Celestial City as cheerfully as if the pilgrimage were merely a summer tour. Among the gentlemen were characters of deserved eminence—magistrates, politicians, and men of wealth, by whose example religion could not but be greatly recommended to their meaner brethren. In the ladies' apartment, too, I rejoiced to distinguish some of those flowers of fashionable society who are so well fitted to adorn the most elevated circles of the Celestial City. There was much pleasant conversation about the news of the day, topics of business and politics, or the lighter matters of amusement; while religion, though indubitably the main thing at heart, was thrown tastefully into the background. Even an infidel would have heard little or nothing to shock his sensibility.

One great convenience of the new method of going on pilgrimage I must not forget to mention. Our enormous burdens, instead of being carried on our shoulders as had been the custom of old,[2] were all snugly deposited in the baggage car, and, as I was assured, would be delivered to their respective owners at the journey's end. Another thing, likewise, the benevolent reader will be delighted to understand. It may be remembered that there was an ancient feud between Prince Beelzebub [3] and the keeper of the wicket gate, and that the adherents of the former distinguished personage were accustomed to shoot deadly arrows at honest pilgrims while knocking at the door. This dispute, much to the credit as well of the illustrious potentate above mentioned as of the worthy and enlightened directors of the railroad, has been pacifically arranged on the principle of mutual compromise. The

THE CELESTIAL RAILROAD. 1. **Evangelist . . . roll:** "Then he [Evangelist] gave him a parchment roll, and there was written within, 'Flee from the wrath to come.' " (*Pilgrim's Progress*).

2. **burdens . . . old:** "I dreamed, and behold I saw a man clothed with rags, standing in a certain place, . . . and a great burden upon his back" (*Pilgrim's Progress*). 3. **Beelzebub:** "the prince of devils," Matt. 12:24; in Milton's *Paradise Lost*, he is second only to Satan; in *Pilgrim's Progress* he is captain of the castle near the Wicket-Gate.

prince's subjects are now pretty numerously employed about the station-house, some in taking care of the baggage, others in collecting fuel, feeding the engines, and such congenial occupations; and I can conscientiously affirm that persons more attentive to their business, more willing to accommodate, or more generally agreeable to the passengers, are not to be found on any railroad. Every good heart must surely exult at so satisfactory an arrangement of an immemorial difficulty.

"Where is Mr. Greatheart?" [4] inquired I. "Beyond a doubt the directors have engaged that famous old champion to be chief conductor on the railroad?"

"Why, no," said Mr. Smooth-it-away, with a dry cough. "He was offered the situation of brakeman; but, to tell you the truth, our friend Greatheart has grown preposterously stiff and narrow in his old age. He has so often guided pilgrims over the road on foot that he considers it a sin to travel in any other fashion. Besides, the old fellow had entered so heartily into the ancient feud with Prince Beelzebub that he would have been perpetually at blows or ill language with some of the prince's subjects, and thus have embroiled us anew. So, on the whole, we were not sorry when honest Greatheart went off to the Celestial City in a huff and left us at liberty to choose a more suitable and accommodating man. Yonder comes the engineer of the train. You will probably recognize him at once."

The engine at this moment took its station in advance of the cars, looking, I must confess, much more like a sort of mechanical demon that would hurry us to the infernal regions than a laudable contrivance for smoothing our way to the Celestial City. On its top sat a personage almost enveloped in smoke and flame, which, not to startle the reader, appeared to gush from his own mouth and stomach as well as from the engine's brazen abdomen.

"Do my eyes deceive me?" cried I. "What on earth is this! A living creature? If so, he is own brother to the engine he rides upon!"

"Poh, poh, you are obtuse!" said Mr. Smooth-it-away, with a hearty laugh. "Don't you know Apollyon,[5] Christian's old enemy, with whom he fought so fierce a battle in the Valley of Humiliation? He was the very fellow to manage the engine; and so we have reconciled him to the custom of going on pilgrimage, and engaged him as chief engineer."

"Bravo, bravo!" exclaimed I, with irrepressible enthusiasm; "this shows the liberality of the age; this proves, if anything can, that all musty prejudices are in a fair way to be obliterated. And how will Christian rejoice to hear of this happy transformation of his old antagonist! I promise myself great pleasure in informing him of it when we reach the Celestial City."

The passengers being all comfortably seated, we now rattled away merrily, accomplishing a greater distance in ten minutes than Christian probably trudged over in a day. It was laughable, while we glanced along, as it were, at the tail of a thunderbolt, to observe two dusty foot travellers in the old pilgrim guise, with cockle shell and staff, their mystic rolls of parchment in their hands and their intolerable burdens on their backs. The preposterous obstinacy of these honest people in persisting to groan and stumble along the difficult pathway rather than take advantage of modern improvements, excited great mirth among our wiser brotherhood. We greeted the two pilgrims with many pleasant gibes and a roar of laughter; whereupon they gazed at us with such woful and absurdly compassionate visages that our merriment grew tenfold more obstreperous. Apollyon also entered heartily into the fun, and contrived to flirt the smoke and flame of the engine, or of his own breath, into their faces, and envelop them in an atmosphere of scalding steam. These little practical jokes amused us mightily, and doubtless afforded the pilgrims the gratification of considering themselves martyrs.

At some distance from the railroad Mr. Smooth-it-away pointed to a large, antique edifice, which, he observed, was a tavern of long standing, and had formerly been a noted stopping-place for pilgrims. In Bunyan's road-book it is mentioned as the Interpreter's House.

"I have long had a curiosity to visit that old mansion," remarked I.

"It is not one of our stations, as you perceive," said my companion. "The keeper was violently opposed to the railroad; and well he might be, as the track left his house of entertainment on one side, and thus was pretty certain to deprive him of all his reputable customers. But the footpath still passes his door, and the old gentleman now and then receives a call from some simple traveller, and entertains him with fare as old-fashioned as himself."

Before our talk on this subject came to a conclusion we were rushing by the place where Christian's burden fell from his shoulders at the sight of

4. **Mr. Greatheart:** the guide of Christiana in the second part of *Pilgrim's Progress.* 5. **Apollyon:** Apollyon is described in *Pilgrim's Progress:* "Now the monster was hideous to behold; he was clothed with scales, like a fish . . . , he had wings like a dragon, feet like a bear, and out of his belly came fire and smoke, and his mouth was as the mouth of a lion."

the Cross. This served as a theme for Mr. Smooth-it-away, Mr. Live-for-the-world, Mr. Hide-sin-in-the-heart, Mr. Scaly-conscience, and a knot of gentlemen from the town of Shun-repentance, to descant upon the inestimable advantages resulting from the safety of our baggage. Myself, and all the passengers indeed, joined with great unanimity in this view of the matter; for our burdens were rich in many things esteemed precious throughout the world; and, especially, we each of us possessed a great variety of favorite Habits, which we trusted would not be out of fashion even in the polite circles of the Celestial City. It would have been a sad spectacle to see such an assortment of valuable articles tumbling into the sepulchre. Thus pleasantly conversing on the favorable circumstances of our position as compared with those of past pilgrims and of narrow-minded ones at the present day, we soon found ourselves at the foot of the Hill Difficulty.[6] Through the very heart of this rocky mountain a tunnel has been constructed of most admirable architecture, with a lofty arch and a spacious double track; so that, unless the earth and rocks should chance to crumble down, it will remain an eternal monument of the builder's skill and enterprise. It is a great though incidental advantage that the materials from the heart of the Hill Difficulty have been employed in filling up the Valley of Humiliation, thus obviating the necessity of descending into that disagreeable and unwholesome hollow.

"This is a wonderful improvement, indeed," said I. "Yet I should have been glad of an opportunity to visit the Palace Beautiful and be introduced to the charming young ladies—Miss Prudence, Miss Piety, Miss Charity, and the rest—who have the kindness to entertain pilgrims there."

"Young ladies!" cried Mr. Smooth-it-away, as soon as he could speak for laughing. "And charming young ladies! Why, my dear fellow, they are old maids, every soul of them—prim, starched, dry, and angular; and not one of them, I will venture to say, has altered so much as the fashion of her gown since the days of Christian's pilgrimage."

"Ah, well," said I, much comforted, "then I can very readily dispense with their acquaintance."

The respectable Apollyon was now putting on the steam at a prodigious rate, anxious, perhaps, to get rid of the unpleasant reminiscences connected with the spot where he had so disastrously encountered Christian. Consulting Mr. Bunyan's road-book, I perceived that we must now be within a few miles of the Valley of the Shadow of Death,[7] into which doleful region, at our present speed, we should plunge much sooner than seemed at all desirable. In truth, I expected nothing better than to find myself in the ditch on one side or the quag on the other; but on communicating my apprehensions to Mr. Smooth-it-away, he assured me that the difficulties of this passage, even in its worst condition, had been vastly exaggerated, and that, in its present state of improvement, I might consider myself as safe as on any railroad in Christendom.

Even while we were speaking the train shot into the entrance of this dreaded Valley. Though I plead guilty to some foolish palpitations of the heart during our headlong rush over the causeway here constructed, yet it were unjust to withhold the highest encomiums on the boldness of its original conception and the ingenuity of those who executed it. It was gratifying, likewise, to observe how much care had been taken to dispel the everlasting gloom and supply the defect of cheerful sunshine, not a ray of which has ever penetrated among these awful shadows. For this purpose, the inflammable gas which exudes plentifully from the soil is collected by means of pipes, and thence communicated to a quadruple row of lamps along the whole extent of the passage. Thus a radiance has been created even out of the fiery and sulphurous curse that rests forever upon the Valley—a radiance hurtful, however, to the eyes, and somewhat bewildering, as I discovered by the changes which it wrought in the visages of my companions. In this respect, as compared with natural daylight, there is the same difference as between truth and falsehood; but if the reader have ever travelled through the Dark Valley, he will have learned to be thankful for any light that he could get—if not from the sky above, then from the blasted soil beneath. Such was the red brilliancy of these lamps that they appeared to build walls of fire on both sides of the track, between which we held our course at lightning speed, while a reverberating thunder filled the Valley with its echoes. Had the engine run off the track,—a catastrophe, it is whispered, by no means unprecedented,—the bottomless pit, if there be any such place, would undoubtedly have received us. Just as some dismal fooleries of this nature had made my heart quake there came a tre-

6. High Difficulty: In *Pilgrim's Progress* there are "two other ways" than the proper one: "one turned to the left hand, and the other to the right, at the bottom of the hill; but the narrow way led right up the side of the hill."

7. Valley . . . Death: "Now . . . was . . . called the Valley of the Shadow of Death. . . . Now this Valley is a very solitary place. . . . About the midst of this Valley, I perceived the mouth of hell to be. . . . And ever and anon the flame and smoke would come out in such abundance, with sparks and hideous noises. . . . Also he heard doleful voices, and rushings to and fro, so that sometimes he thought he should be torn to pieces, or trodden down like mire in the streets" (*Pilgrim's Progress*).

mendous shriek, careering along the Valley as if a thousand devils had burst their lungs to utter it, but which proved to be merely the whistle of the engine on arriving at a stopping-place.

The spot where we had now paused is the same that our friend Bunyan—a truthful man, but infected with many fantastic notions—has designated, in terms plainer than I like to repeat, as the mouth of the infernal region. This, however, must be a mistake, inasmuch as Mr. Smooth-it-away, while we remained in the smoky and lurid cavern, took occasion to prove that Tophet [8] has not even a metaphorical existence. The place, he assured us, is no other than the crater of a half-extinct volcano, in which the directors had caused forges to be set up for the manufacture of railroad iron. Hence, also, is obtained a plentiful supply of fuel for the use of the engines. Whoever had gazed into the dismal obscurity of the broad cavern mouth, whence ever and anon darted huge tongues of dusky flame, and had seen the strange, half-shaped monsters, and visions of faces horribly grotesque, into which the smoke seemed to wreathe itself, and had heard the awful murmurs, and shrieks, and deep, shuddering whispers of the blast, sometimes forming themselves into words almost articulate, would have seized upon Mr. Smooth-it-away's comfortable explanation as greedily as we did. The inhabitants of the cavern, moreover, were unlovely personages, dark, smoke-begrimed, generally deformed, with misshapen feet, and a glow of dusky redness in their eyes as if their hearts had caught fire and were blazing out of the upper windows. It struck me as a peculiarity that the laborers at the forge and those who brought fuel to the engine, when they began to draw short breath, positively emitted smoke from their mouth and nostrils.

Among the idlers about the train, most of whom were puffing cigars which they had lighted at the flame of the crater, I was perplexed to notice several who, to my certain knowledge, had heretofore set forth by railroad for the Celestial City. They looked dark, wild, and smoky, with a singular resemblance, indeed, to the native inhabitants, like whom, also, they had a disagreeable propensity to ill-natured gibes and sneers, the habit of which had wrought a settled contortion of their visages. Having been on speaking terms with one of these persons,—an indolent, good-for-nothing fellow, who went by the name of Take-it-easy,—I called him, and inquired what was his business there.

"Did you not start," said I, "for the Celestial City?"

"That's a fact," said Mr. Take-it-easy, carelessly puffing some smoke into my eyes. "But I heard such bad accounts that I never took pains to climb the hill on which the city stands. No business doing, no fun going on, nothing to drink, and no smoking allowed, and a thrumming of church music from morning till night. I would not stay in such a place if they offered me house room and living free."

"But, my good Mr. Take-it-easy," cried I, "why take up your residence here, of all places in the world?"

"Oh," said the loafer, with a grin, "it is very warm hereabouts, and I meet with plenty of old acquaintances, and altogether the place suits me. I hope to see you back again some day soon. A pleasant journey to you."

While he was speaking the bell of the engine rang, and we dashed away after dropping a few passengers, but receiving no new ones. Rattling onward through the Valley, we were dazzled with the fiercely gleaming gas lamps, as before. But sometimes, in the dark of intense brightness, grim faces, that bore the aspect and expression of individual sins, or evil passions, seemed to thrust themselves through the veil of light, glaring upon us, and stretching forth a great, dusky hand, as if to impede our progress. I almost thought that they were my own sins that appalled me there. These were freaks of imagination—nothing more, certainly—mere delusions, which I ought to be heartily ashamed of; but all through the Dark Valley I was tormented, and pestered, and dolefully bewildered with the same kind of waking dreams. The mephitic gases of that region intoxicate the brain. As the light of natural day, however, began to struggle with the glow of the lanterns, these vain imaginations lost their vividness, and finally vanished with the first ray of sunshine that greeted our escape from the Valley of the Shadow of Death. Ere we had gone a mile beyond it I could wellnigh have taken my oath that this whole gloomy passage was a dream.

At the end of the Valley, as John Bunyan mentions, is a cavern, where, in his days, dwelt two cruel giants, Pope and Pagan, who had strown the ground about their residence with the bones of slaughtered pilgrims. These vile old troglodytes are no longer there; but into their deserted cave another terrible giant has thrust himself, and makes it his business to seize upon honest travellers and fatten them for his table with plentiful meals of smoke, mist, moonshine, raw potatoes, and sawdust. He is a German by birth, and is called Giant Transcendentalist; but as to his form, his features, his substance, and his nature generally, it is the chief peculiarity of this huge miscreant that nei-

8. **Tophet:** in the Old Testament a valley where human sacrifices of children to Moloch were performed. Here it refers to hell.

ther he for himself, nor anybody for him, has ever been able to describe them. As we rushed by the cavern's mouth we caught a hasty glimpse of him, looking somewhat like an ill-proportioned figure, but considerably more like a heap of fog and duskiness. He shouted [9] after us, but in so strange a phraseology that we knew not what he meant, nor whether to be encouraged or affrighted.

It was late in the day when the train thundered into the ancient city of Vanity, where Vanity Fair is still at the height of prosperity, and exhibits an epitome of whatever is brilliant, gay, and fascinating beneath the sun. As I purposed to make a considerable stay here, it gratified me to learn that there is no longer the want of harmony between the town's-people and pilgrims, which impelled the former to such lamentably mistaken measures as the persecution of Christian and the fiery martyrdom of Faithful. On the contrary, as the new railroad brings with it great trade and a constant influx of strangers, the lord of Vanity Fair is its chief patron, and the capitalists of the city are among the largest stockholders. Many passengers stop to take their pleasure or make their profit in the Fair, instead of going onward to the Celestial City. Indeed, such are the charms of the place that people often affirm it to be the true and only heaven; stoutly contending that there is no other, that those who seek further are mere dreamers, and that, if the fabled brightness of the Celestial City lay but a bare mile beyond the gates of Vanity, they would not be fools enough to go thither. Without subscribing to these perhaps exaggerated encomiums, I can truly say that my abode in the city was mainly agreeable, and my intercourse with the inhabitants productive of much amusement and instruction.

Being naturally of a serious turn, my attention was directed to the solid advantages derivable from a residence here, rather than to the effervescent pleasures which are the grand object with too many visitants. The Christian reader, if he have had no accounts of the city later than Bunyan's time, will be surprised to hear that almost every street has its church, and that the reverend clergy are nowhere held in higher respect than at Vanity Fair. And well do they deserve such honorable estimation; for the maxims of wisdom and virtue which fall from their lips come from as deep a spiritual source, and tend to as lofty a religious aim, as those of the sagest philosophers of old. In justification of this high praise I need only mention the names of the Rev. Mr. Shallow-deep, the Rev. Mr. Stumble-at-truth, that fine old clerical character the Rev. Mr. This-to-day, who expects shortly to resign his pulpit to the Rev. Mr. That-to-morrow; together with the Rev. Mr. Bewilderment, the Rev. Mr. Clog-the-spirit, and, last and greatest, the Rev. Dr. Wind-of-doctrine. The labors of these eminent divines are aided by those of innumerable lecturers, who diffuse such a various profundity, in all subjects of human or celestial science, that any man may acquire an omnigenous erudition without the trouble of even learning to read. Thus literature is etherealized by assuming for its medium the human voice; and knowledge, depositing all its heavier particles, except, doubtless, its gold, becomes exhaled into a sound, which forthwith steals into the ever-open ear of the community. These ingenious methods constitute a sort of machinery, by which thought and study are done to every person's hand without his putting himself to the slightest inconvenience in the matter. There is another species of machine for the wholesale manufacture of individual morality. This excellent result is effected by societies for all manner of virtuous purposes, with which a man has merely to connect himself, throwing, as it were, his quota of virtue into the common stock, and the president and directors will take care that the aggregate amount be well applied. All these, and other wonderful improvements in ethics, religion, and literature, being made plain to my comprehension by the ingenious Mr. Smooth-it-away, inspired me with a vast admiration of Vanity Fair.

It would fill a volume, in an age of pamphlets, were I to record all my observations in this great capital of human business and pleasure. There was an unlimited range of society—the powerful, the wise, the witty, and the famous in every walk of life; princes, presidents, poets, generals, artists, actors, and philanthropists,—all making their own market at the Fair, and deeming no price too exorbitant for such commodities as hit their fancy. It was well worth one's while, even if he had no idea of buying or selling, to loiter through the bazaars and observe the various sorts of traffic that were going forward.

Some of the purchasers, I thought, made very foolish bargains. For instance, a young man having inherited a splendid fortune, laid out a considerable portion of it in the purchase of diseases, and finally spent all the rest for a heavy lot of repentance and a suit of rags. A very pretty girl bartered a heart as clear as crystal, and which seemed her most valuable possession, for another

9. **He shouted:** ". . . at the sight of the Old Man that sat in the mouth of the cave, he [Christian] could not tell what to think, especially because he spake to him . . . saying, 'You will never mend till more of you be burned.' But Christian held his peace, and set a good face on it, and so went by and catched no hurt" *Pilgrim's Progress*).

jewel of the same kind, but so worn and defaced as to be utterly worthless. In one shop there were a great many crowns of laurel and myrtle, which soldiers, authors, statesmen, and various other people pressed eagerly to buy; some purchased these paltry wreaths with their lives, others by a toilsome servitude of years, and many sacrificed whatever was most valuable, yet finally slunk away without the crown. There was a sort of stock or scrip, called Conscience, which seemed to be in great demand, and would purchase almost anything. Indeed, few rich commodities were to be obtained without paying a heavy sum in this particular stock, and a man's business was seldom very lucrative unless he knew precisely when and how to throw his hoard of conscience into the market. Yet as this stock was the only thing of permanent value, whoever parted with it was sure to find himself a loser in the long run. Several of the speculations were of a questionable character. Occasionally a member of Congress recruited his pocket by the sale of his constituents; and I was assured that public officers have often sold their country at very moderate prices. Thousands sold their happiness for a whim. Gilded chains were in great demand, and purchased with almost any sacrifice. In truth, those who desired, according to the old adage, to sell anything valuable for a song, might find customers all over the Fair; and there were innumerable messes of pottage, piping hot, for such as chose to buy them with their birthrights.[10] A few articles, however, could not be found genuine at Vanity Fair. If a customer wished to renew his stock of youth the dealers offered him a set of false teeth and an auburn wig; if he demanded peace of mind, they recommended opium or a brandy bottle.

Tracts of land and golden mansions, situate in the Celestial City, were often exchanged, at very disadvantageous rates, for a few years' lease of small, dismal, inconvenient tenements in Vanity Fair. Prince Beelzebub himself took great interest in this sort of traffic, and sometimes condescended to meddle with smaller matters. I once had the pleasure to see him bargaining with a miser for his soul, which, after much ingenious skirmishing on both sides, his highness succeeded in obtaining at about the value of sixpence. The prince remarked with a smile, that he was a loser by the transaction.

Day after day, as I walked the streets of Vanity, my manners and deportment became more and more like those of the inhabitants. The place began to seem like home; the idea of pursuing my travels to the Celestial City was almost obliterated from my mind. I was reminded of it, however, by the sight of the same pair of simple pilgrims at whom we had laughed so heartily when Apollyon puffed smoke and steam into their faces at the commencement of our journey. There they stood amidst the densest bustle of Vanity; the dealers offering them their purple and fine linen and jewels, the men of wit and humor gibing at them, a pair of buxom ladies ogling them askance, while the benevolent Mr. Smooth-it-away whispered some of his wisdom at their elbows, and pointed to a newly-erected temple; but there were these worthy simpletons, making the scene look wild and monstrous, merely by their sturdy repudiation of all part in its business or pleasures.

One of them—his name was Stick-to-the-right—perceived in my face, I suppose, a species of sympathy and almost admiration, which, to my own great surprise, I could not help feeling for this pragmatic couple. It prompted him to address me.

"Sir," inquired he, with a sad, yet mild and kindly voice, "do you call yourself a pilgrim?"

"Yes," I replied, "my right to that appellation is indubitable. I am merely a sojourner here in Vanity Fair, being bound to the Celestial City by the new railroad."

"Alas, friend," rejoined Mr. Stick-to-the-right, "I do assure you, and beseech you to receive the truth of my words, that that whole concern is a bubble. You may travel on it all your lifetime, were you to live thousands of years, and yet never get beyond the limits of Vanity Fair. Yea, though you should deem yourself entering the gates of the blessed city, it will be nothing but a miserable delusion."

"The Lord of the Celestial City," began the other pilgrim, whose name was Mr. Foot-it-to-heaven, "has refused, and will ever refuse, to grant an act of incorporation for this railroad; and unless that be obtained, no passenger can ever hope to enter his dominions. Wherefore every man who buys a ticket must lay his account with losing the purchase money, which is the value of his own soul."

"Poh, nonsense!" said Mr. Smooth-it-away, taking my arm and leading me off, "these fellows ought to be indicted for a libel. If the law stood as it once did in Vanity Fair we should see them grinning through the iron bars of the prison window."

This incident made a considerable impression on my mind, and contributed with other circumstances to indispose me to a permanent residence in the city of Vanity; although, of course, I was

10. **messes . . . birthrights:** Esau sold his birthright to Jacob for a mess of pottage; see Gen. 25:29–34.

not simple enough to give up my original plan of gliding along easily and commodiously by railroad. Still, I grew anxious to be gone. There was one strange thing that troubled me. Amid the occupations or amusements of the Fair, nothing was more common than for a person—whether at feast, theatre, or church, or trafficking for wealth and honors, or whatever he might be doing, and however unseasonable the interruption—suddenly to vanish like a soap bubble, and be never more seen of his fellows; and so accustomed were the latter to such little accidents that they went on with their business as quietly as if nothing had happened. But it was otherwise with me.

Finally, after a pretty long residence at the Fair, I resumed my journey towards the Celestial City, still with Mr. Smooth-it-away at my side. At a short distance beyond the suburbs of Vanity we passed the ancient silver mine, of which Demas was the first discoverer, and which is now wrought to great advantage, supplying nearly all the coined currency of the world. A little further onward was the spot where Lot's wife [11] had stood forever under the semblance of a pillar of salt. Curious travellers have long since carried it away piecemeal. Had all regrets been punished as rigorously as this poor dame's were, my yearning for the relinquished delights of Vanity Fair might have produced a similar change in my own corporeal substance, and left me a warning to future pilgrims.

The next remarkable object was a large edifice, constructed of mossgrown stone, but in a modern and airy style of architecture. The engine came to a pause in its vicinity, with the usual tremendous shriek.

"This was formerly the castle of the redoubted giant Despair," observed Mr. Smooth-it-away; "but since his death Mr. Flimsy-faith has repaired it, and keeps an excellent house of entertainment here. It is one of our stopping-places."

"It seems but slightly put together," remarked I, looking at the frail yet ponderous walls. "I do not envy Mr. Flimsy-faith his habitation. Some day it will thunder down upon the heads of the occupants."

"We shall escape at all events," said Mr. Smooth-it-away, "for Apollyon is putting on the steam again."

The road now plunged into a gorge of the Delectable Mountains, and traversed the field where in former ages the blind men wandered and stumbled among the tombs. One of these ancient tombstones had been thrust across the track by some malicious person, and gave the train of cars a terrible jolt. Far up the rugged side of a mountain I perceived a rusty iron door, half overgrown with bushes and creeping plants, but with smoke issuing from its crevices.

"Is that," inquired I, "the very door in the hillside which the shepherds assured Christian was a by-way to hell?"

"That was a joke on the part of the shepherds," said Mr. Smooth-it-away, with a smile. "It is neither more nor less than the door of a cavern which they use as a smoke-house for the preparation of mutton hams."

My recollections of the journey are now, for a little space, dim and confused, inasmuch as a singular drowsiness here overcame me, owing to the fact that we were passing over the enchanted ground, the air of which encourages a disposition to sleep. I awoke, however, as soon as we crossed the borders of the pleasant land of Beulah. All the passengers were rubbing their eyes, comparing watches, and congratulating one another on the prospect of arriving so seasonably at the journey's end. The sweet breezes of this happy clime came refreshingly to our nostrils; we beheld the glimmering gush of silver fountains, overhung by trees of beautiful foliage and delicious fruit, which were propagated by grafts from the celestial gardens. Once, as we dashed onward like a hurricane, there was a flutter of wings and the bright appearance of an angel in the air, speeding forth on some heavenly mission. The engine now announced the close vicinity of the final station-house by one last and horrible scream, in which there seemed to be distinguishable every kind of wailing and woe, and bitter fierceness of wrath, all mixed up with the wild laughter of a devil or a madman. Throughout our journey, at every stopping-place, Apollyon had exercised his ingenuity in screwing the most abominable sounds out of the whistle of the steam-engine; but in this closing effort he outdid himself and created an infernal uproar, which, besides disturbing the peaceful inhabitants of Beulah, must have sent its discord even through the celestial gates.

While the horrid clamor was still ringing in our ears we heard an exulting strain, as if a thousand instruments of music, with height and depth and sweetness in their tones, at once tender and triumphant, were struck in unison, to greet the approach of some illustrious hero, who had fought the good fight [12] and won a glorious victory, and was come to lay aside his battered arms forever. Looking to ascertain what might be the occasion

11. **Lot's wife:** in fleeing from Sodom, the wicked city, she looked back and was turned into a pillar of salt; see Gen. 19:26.

12. **fought . . . fight:** the Christian ideal of self-denying service; see Tim. 4:7.

of this glad harmony, I perceived, on alighting from the cars, that a multitude of shining ones had assembled on the other side of the river, to welcome two poor pilgrims, who were just emerging from its depths. They were the same whom Apollyon and ourselves had persecuted with taunts, and gibes, and scalding steam, at the commencement of our journey—the same whose unworldly aspect and impressive words had stirred my conscience amid the wild revellers of Vanity Fair.

"How amazingly well those men have got on," cried I to Mr. Smooth-it-away. "I wish we were secure of as good a reception."

"Never fear, never fear!" answered my friend. "Come, make haste; the ferry boat will be off directly, and in three minutes you will be on the other side of the river. No doubt you will find coaches to carry you up to the city gates."

A steam ferry boat, the last improvement on this important route, lay at the river side, puffing, snorting, and emitting all those other disagreeable utterances which betoken the departure to be immediate. I hurried on board with the rest of the passengers, most of whom were in great perturbation: some bawling out for their baggage; some tearing their hair and exclaiming that the boat would explode or sink; some already pale with the heaving of the stream; some gazing affrighted at the ugly aspect of the steersman; and some still dizzy with the slumberous influences of the Enchanted Ground. Looking back to the shore, I was amazed to discern Mr. Smooth-it-away waving his hand in token of farewell.

"Don't you go over to the Celestial City?" exclaimed I.

"Oh, no!" answered he with a queer smile, and that same disagreeable contortion of visage which I had remarked in the inhabitants of the Dark Valley. "Oh, no! I have come thus far only for the sake of your pleasant company. Good-by! We shall meet again."

And then did my excellent friend Mr. Smooth-it-away laugh outright, in the midst of which cachinnation a smoke-wreath issued from his mouth and nostrils, while a twinkle of lurid flame darted out of either eye, proving indubitably that his heart was all of a red blaze. The impudent fiend! To deny the existence of Tophet, when he felt its fiery tortures raging within his breast. I rushed to the side of the boat, intending to fling myself on shore; but the wheels, as they began their revolutions, threw a dash of spray over me so cold—so deadly cold, with the chill that will never leave those waters until Death be drowned in his own river—that with a shiver and a heartquake I awoke. Thank Heaven it was a Dream!

THE ARTIST OF THE BEAUTIFUL

◊

¶ THIS story first appeared in the *Democratic Review* (June, 1844) and was gathered in *Mosses from an Old Manse* (1846). The narrative may be taken as a commentary on the nature of the artist, who, by his devotion to the artistic ideal, isolates himself from the community of men. His creation of art, however ephemeral and even useless, is its own reward. Some have thought that the story is an allegory of Hawthorne's idea of his own art. Whatever the interpretation, the action of the narrative goes counter to generally accepted ideas of art: art is here not a representation of nature nor is it a Platonic transcending of the physical world wherein, as Emerson proposed, the realm of "essence" is apprehended or reached. Indeed, the story is of interest for its opposition to principles of art in Hawthorne's day and for its linkages with some of Melville's ideas.

◊

AN ELDERLY man, with his pretty daughter on his arm, was passing along the street, and emerged from the gloom of the cloudy evening into the light that fell across the pavement from the window of a small shop. It was a projecting window; and on the inside were suspended a variety of watches, pinchbeck,[1] silver, and one or two of gold, all with their faces turned from the streets, as if churlishly disinclined to inform the wayfarers what o'clock it was. Seated within the shop, sidelong to the window, with his pale face bent earnestly over some delicate piece of mechanism on which was thrown the concentrated lustre of a shade lamp, appeared a young man.

"What can Owen Warland be about?" muttered old Peter Hovenden, himself a retired watchmaker, and the former master of this same young man whose occupation he was now wondering at. "What can the fellow be about? These six months past I have never come by his shop without seeing him just as steadily at work as now. It would be a flight beyond his usual foolery to seek for the perpetual motion; and yet I know enough of my old business to be certain that what he is now so busy with is no part of the machinery of a watch."

"Perhaps, father," said Annie, without showing

THE ARTIST OF THE BEAUTIFUL. 1. **pinchbeck:** an alloy of copper and zinc, used to imitate gold in cheap jewelry; hence, anything counterfeit or spurious.

much interest in the question, "Owen is inventing a new kind of timekeeper. I am sure he has ingenuity enough."

"Poh, child! He has not the sort of ingenuity to invent anything better than a Dutch toy," answered her father, who had formerly been put to much vexation by Owen Warland's irregular genius. "A plague on such ingenuity! All the effect that ever I knew of it was to spoil the accuracy of some of the best watches in my shop. He would turn the sun out of its orbit and derange the whole course of time, if, as I said before, his ingenuity could grasp anything bigger than a child's toy!"

"Hush, father! He hears you!" whispered Annie, pressing the old man's arm. "His ears are as delicate as his feelings; and you know how easily disturbed they are. Do let us move on."

So Peter Hovenden and his daughter Annie plodded on without further conversation, until in a by-street of the town they found themselves passing the open door of a blacksmith's shop. Within was seen the forge, now blazing up and illuminating the high and dusky roof, and now confining its lustre to a narrow precinct of the coal-strewn floor, according as the breath of the bellows was puffed forth or again inhaled into its vast leathern lungs. In the intervals of brightness it was easy to distinguish objects in remote corners of the shop and the horseshoes that hung upon the wall; in the momentary gloom the fire seemed to be glimmering amidst the vagueness of unenclosed space. Moving about in this red glare and alternate dusk was the figure of the blacksmith, well worthy to be viewed in so picturesque an aspect of light and shade, where the bright blaze struggled with the black night, as if each would have snatched his comely strength from the other. Anon he drew a white-hot bar of iron from the coals, laid it on the anvil, uplifted his arm of might, and was soon enveloped in the myriads of sparks which the strokes of his hammer scattered into the surrounding gloom.

"Now, that is a pleasant sight," said the old watchmaker. "I know what it is to work in gold; but give me the worker in iron after all is said and done. He spends his labor upon a reality. What say you, daughter Annie?"

"Pray don't speak so loud, father," whispered Annie, "Robert Danforth will hear you."

"And what if he should hear me?" said Peter Hovenden. "I say again, it is a good and a wholesome thing to depend upon main strength and reality, and to earn one's bread with the bare and brawny arm of a blacksmith. A watchmaker gets his brain puzzled by his wheels within a wheel, or loses his health or the nicety of his eyesight, as was my case, and finds himself at middle age, or a little after, past labor at his own trade and fit for nothing else, yet too poor to live at his ease. So I say once again, give me main strength for my money. And then, how it takes the nonsense out of a man! Did you ever hear of a blacksmith being such a fool as Owen Warland yonder?"

"Well said, uncle Hovenden!" shouted Robert Danforth from the forge, in a full, deep, merry voice, that made the roof reëcho. "And what says Miss Annie to that doctrine? She, I suppose, will think it a genteeler business to tinker up a lady's watch than to forge a horseshoe or make a gridiron."

Annie drew her father onward without giving him time for reply.

But we must return to Owen Warland's shop, and spend more meditation upon his history and character than either Peter Hovenden, or probably his daughter Annie, or Owen's old schoolfellow, Robert Danforth, would have thought due to so slight a subject. From the time that his little fingers could grasp a penknife, Owen had been remarkable for a delicate ingenuity, which sometimes produced pretty shapes in wood, principally figures of flowers and birds, and sometimes seemed to aim at the hidden mysteries of mechanism. But it was always for purposes of grace, and never with any mockery of the useful. He did not, like the crowd of school-boy artisans, construct little windmills on the angle of a barn or watermills across the neighboring brook. Those who discovered such peculiarity in the boy as to think it worth their while to observe him closely, sometimes saw reason to suppose that he was attempting to imitate the beautiful movements of Nature as exemplified in the flight of birds or the activity of little animals. It seemed, in fact, a new development of the love of the beautiful, such as might have made him a poet, a painter, or a sculptor, and which was as completely refined from all utilitarian coarseness as it could have been in either of the fine arts. He looked with singular distaste at the stiff and regular processes of ordinary machinery. Being once carried to see a steam-engine, in the expectation that his intuitive comprehension of mechanical principles would be gratified, he turned pale and grew sick, as if something monstrous and unnatural had been presented to him. This horror was partly owing to the size and terrible energy of the iron laborer; for the character of Owen's mind was microscopic, and tended naturally to the minute, in accordance with his diminutive frame and the marvellous smallness and delicate power of his fingers. Not that his sense of beauty was thereby diminished into a sense of prettiness. The beautiful idea has no relation to size, and may be as perfectly developed in a space too minute for any but microscopic investigation as within the ample verge that is measured by the arc of the rainbow. But, at all events, this characteristic minuteness in his objects and accomplishments made the world even more incapable than it might otherwise have been of appreciating Owen Warland's genius. The boy's relatives saw nothing better to be done—as perhaps there was not—than to bind him apprentice to a watchmaker, hoping that his strange ingenuity might thus be regulated and put to utilitarian purposes.

Peter Hovenden's opinion of his apprentice has already been expressed. He could make nothing of the lad. Owen's apprehension of the professional mysteries, it is true, was inconceivably quick; but he altogether forgot or despised the grand object of a watchmaker's business, and cared no more for the measurement of time than if it had been merged into eternity. So long, however, as he remained under his old master's care, Owen's lack of sturdiness made it possible, by strict injunctions and sharp oversight, to restrain his creative eccentricity within bounds; but when his apprenticeship was served out, and he had taken the little shop which Peter Hovenden's failing eyesight compelled him to relinquish, then did people recognize how unfit a person was Owen Warland to lead old blind Father Time along his daily course. One of his most rational projects was to connect a musical operation with the machinery of his watches, so that all the harsh dissonances of life might be rendered tuneful, and each flitting moment fall into the abyss of the past in golden drops of harmony. If a family clock was intrusted to him for repair,—one of those tall, ancient clocks that have grown nearly allied to human nature by measuring out the lifetime of many generations,—he would take upon himself to arrange a dance or funeral procession of figures across its venerable face, representing twelve mirthful or melancholy hours. Several freaks of this kind quite destroyed the young watchmaker's credit with that steady and matter-of-fact class of people who hold the opinion that time is not to be trifled with, whether considered as the medium of advancement and prosperity in this world or preparation for the next. His custom rapidly diminished—a misfortune, however, that was probably reckoned among his better accidents by Owen Warland, who was becoming more and more absorbed in a secret occupation which drew all his science and manual dexterity into itself, and likewise gave full employment to the characteristic tendencies of his genius. This pursuit had already consumed many months.

After the old watchmaker and his pretty daughter had gazed at him out of the obscurity of the street, Owen Warland was seized with a fluttering of the nerves, which made his hand tremble too violently to proceed with such delicate labor as he was now engaged upon.

"It was Annie herself!" murmured he. "I should have known it, by this throbbing of my heart, before I heard her father's voice. Ah, how it throbs! I shall scarcely be able to work again on this exquisite mechanism to-night. Annie! dearest Annie! thou shouldst give firmness to my heart and hand, and not shake them thus; for if I strive to put the very spirit of beauty into form and give it motion, it is for thy sake alone. O throbbing heart, be quiet! If my labor be thus thwarted, there will come vague and unsatisfied dreams which will leave me spiritless to-morrow."

As he was endeavoring to settle himself again to his task, the shop door opened and gave admittance to no other than the stalwart figure which Peter Hovenden had paused to admire, as seen amid the light and shadow of the blacksmith's shop. Robert Danforth had brought a little anvil of his own manufacture, and peculiarly constructed, which the young artist had recently bespoken. Owen examined the article and pronounced it fashioned according to his wish.

"Why, yes," said Robert Danforth, his strong voice filling the shop as with the sound of a bass viol, "I consider myself equal to anything in the way of my own trade; though I should have made but a poor figure at yours with such a fist as this," added he, laughing, as he laid his vast hand beside the delicate one of Owen. "But what then? I put more main strength into one blow of my sledge hammer than all that you have expended since you were a 'prentice. Is not that the truth?"

"Very probably," answered the low and slender voice of Owen. "Strength is an earthly monster. I make no pretensions to it. My force, whatever there may be of it, is altogether spiritual."

"Well, but, Owen, what are you about?" asked his old schoolfellow, still in such a hearty volume of tone that it made the artist shrink, especially as the question related to a subject so sacred as the absorbing dream of his imagination. "Folks do say that you are trying to discover the perpetual motion."

"The perpetual motion? Nonsense!" replied Owen Warland, with a movement of disgust; for he was full of little petulances. "It can never be discovered. It is a dream that may delude men whose brains are mystified with matter, but not me. Besides, if such a discovery were possible, it would not be worth my while to make it only to have the secret turned to such purposes as are now effected by steam and water power. I am not ambitious to be honored with the paternity of a new kind of cotton machine."

"That would be droll enough!" cried the blacksmith, breaking out into such an uproar of laughter that Owen himself and the bell glasses on his workboard quivered in unison. "No, no, Owen! No child of yours will have iron joints and sinews. Well, I won't hinder you any more. Good night, Owen, and success, and if you need any assistance, so far as a downright blow of hammer upon anvil will answer the purpose, I'm your man."

And with another laugh the man of main strength left the shop.

"How strange it is," whispered Owen Warland to himself, leaning his head upon his hand, "that all my musings, my purposes, my passion for the beautiful, my consciousness of power to create it, —a finer, more ethereal power, of which this earthly giant can have no conception,—all, all, look so vain and idle whenever my path is crossed by Robert Danforth! He would drive me mad were I to meet him often. His hard, brute force darkens and confuses the spiritual element within me; but I, too, will be strong in my own way. I will not yield to him."

He took from beneath a glass a piece of minute machinery, which he set in the condensed light of his lamp, and, looking intently at it through a magnifying glass, proceeded to operate with a delicate instrument of steel. In an instant, however, he fell back in his chair and clasped his hands, with a look of horror on his face that made its small features as impressive as those of a giant would have been.

"Heaven! What have I done?" exclaimed he. "The vapor, the influence of that brute force,—it has bewildered me and obscured my perception. I have made the very stroke—the fatal stroke—that I have dreaded from the first. It is all over—the toil of months, the object of my life. I am ruined!"

And there he sat, in strange despair, until his lamp flickered in the socket and left the Artist of the Beautiful in darkness.

Thus it is that ideas, which grow up within the imagination and appear so lovely to it and of a value beyond whatever men call valuable, are exposed to be shattered and annihilated by contact with the practical. It is requisite for the ideal artist to possess a force of character that seems hardly compatible with its delicacy; he must keep his faith in himself while the incredulous world assails him with its utter disbelief; he must stand up against mankind and be his own sole disciple, both as respects his genius and the objects to which it is directed.

For a time Owen Warland succumbed to this severe but inevitable test. He spent a few sluggish weeks with his head so continually resting in his hands that the towns-people had scarcely an opportunity to see his countenance. When at last it was again uplifted to the light of day, a cold, dull, nameless change was perceptible upon it. In the opinion of Peter Hovenden, however, and that order of sagacious understandings who think that life should be regulated, like clockwork, with leaden weights, the alteration was entirely for the better. Owen now, indeed, applied himself to business with dogged industry. It was marvellous to witness the obtuse gravity with which he would inspect the wheels of a great old silver watch; thereby delighting the owner, in whose fob it had been worn till he deemed it a portion of his own life, and was accordingly jealous of its treatment. In consequence of the good report thus acquired, Owen Warland was invited by the proper authorities to regulate the clock in the church steeple. He succeeded so admirably in this matter of public interest that the merchants gruffly acknowledged his merits on 'Change;[2] the nurse whispered his praises as she gave the potion in the sick-chamber; the lover blessed him at the hour of appointed interview; and the town in general thanked Owen for the punctuality of dinner time. In a word, the heavy weight upon his spirits kept everything in order, not merely within his own system, but wheresoever the iron accents of the church clock were audible. It was a circumstance, though minute, yet characteristic of his present state, that, when employed to engrave names or initials on silver spoons, he now wrote the requisite letters in the plainest possible style, omitting a variety of fanciful flourishes that had heretofore distinguished his work in this kind.

One day, during the era of this happy transformation, old Peter Hovenden came to visit his former apprentice.

"Well, Owen," said he, "I am glad to hear such good accounts of you from all quarters, and especially from the town clock yonder, which speaks in your commendation every hour of the twenty-four. Only get rid altogether of your nonsensical trash about the beautiful, which I nor nobody else, nor yourself to boot, could ever under-

2. **'Change:** a shortened form of "Exchange"; in England the place in a town or city where merchants, bankers, brokers, and citizens met to do business.

stand,—only free yourself of that, and your success in life is as sure as daylight. Why, if you go on in this way, I should even venture to let you doctor this precious old watch of mine; though, except my daughter Annie, I have nothing else so valuable in the world."

"I should hardly dare touch it, sir," replied Owen, in a depressed tone; for he was weighed down by his old master's presence.

"In time," said the latter,—"in time, you will be capable of it."

The old watchmaker, with the freedom naturally consequent on his former authority, went on inspecting the work which Owen had in hand at the moment, together with other matters that were in progress. The artist, meanwhile, could scarcely lift his head. There was nothing so antipodal to his nature as this man's cold, unimaginative sagacity, by contact with which everything was converted into a dream except the densest matter of the physical world. Owen groaned in spirit and prayed fervently to be delivered from him.

"But what is this?" cried Peter Hovenden abruptly, taking up a dusty bell glass, beneath which appeared a mechanical something, as delicate and minute as the system of a butterfly's anatomy. "What have we here? Owen! Owen! there is witchcraft in these little chains, and wheels, and paddles. See! with one pinch of my finger and thumb I am going to deliver you from all future peril."

"For Heaven's sake," screamed Owen Warland, springing up with wonderful energy, "as you would not drive me mad, do not touch it! The slightest pressure of your finger would ruin me forever."

"Aha, young man! And is it so?" said the old watchmaker, looking at him with just enough of penetration to torture Owen's soul with the bitterness of worldly criticism. "Well, take your own course; but I warn you again that in this small piece of mechanism lives your evil spirit. Shall I exorcise him?"

"You are my evil spirit," answered Owen, much excited,—"you and the hard, coarse world! The leaden thoughts and the despondency that you fling upon me are my clogs, else I should long ago have achieved the task that I was created for."

Peter Hovenden shook his head, with the mixture of contempt and indignation which mankind, of whom he was partly a representative, deem themselves entitled to feel towards all simpletons who seek other prizes than the dusty one along the highway. He then took his leave, with an uplifted finger and a sneer upon his face that haunted the artist's dreams for many a night afterwards. At the time of his old master's visit, Owen was probably on the point of taking up the relinquished task; but, by this sinister event, he was thrown back into the state whence he had been slowly emerging.

But the innate tendency of his soul had only been accumulating fresh vigor during its apparent sluggishness. As the summer advanced he almost totally relinquished his business, and permitted Father Time, so far as the old gentleman was represented by the clocks and watches under his control, to stray at random through human life, making infinite confusion among the train of bewildered hours. He wasted the sunshine, as people said, in wandering through the woods and fields and along the banks of streams. There, like a child, he found amusement in chasing butterflies or watching the motions of water insects. There was something truly mysterious in the intentness with which he contemplated these living playthings as they sported on the breeze or examined the structure of an imperial insect whom he had imprisoned. The chase of butterflies was an apt emblem of the ideal pursuit in which he had spent so many golden hours; but would the beautiful idea ever be yielded to his hand like the butterfly that symbolized it? Sweet, doubtless, were these days, and congenial to the artist's soul. They were full of bright conceptions, which gleamed through his intellectual world as the butterflies gleamed through the outward atmosphere, and were real to him, for the instant, without the toil, and perplexity, and many disappointments of attempting to make them visible to the sensual eye. Alas that the artist, whether in poetry, or whatever other material, may not content himself with the inward enjoyment of the beautiful, but must chase the flitting mystery beyond the verge of his ethereal domain, and crush its frail being in seizing it with a material grasp. Owen Warland felt the impulse to give external reality to his ideas as irresistibly as any of the poets or painters who have arrayed the world in a dimmer and fainter beauty, imperfectly copied from the richness of their visions.

The night was now his time for the slow progress of re-creating the one idea to which all his intellectual activity referred itself. Always at the approach of dusk he stole into the town, locked himself within his shop, and wrought with patient delicacy of touch for many hours. Sometimes he was startled by the rap of the watchman, who, when all the world should be asleep, had caught the gleam of lamplight through the crevices of Owen Warland's shutters. Daylight, to the morbid sensibility of his mind, seemed to have an intrusiveness that interfered with his pursuits. On cloudy and inclement days, therefore, he sat with his head upon his hands, muffling, as it were, his sensitive brain in a mist of indefinite musings; for it was a relief to escape from the sharp distinctness with which he was compelled to shape out his thoughts during his nightly toil.

From one of these fits of torpor he was aroused by the entrance of Annie Hovenden, who came into the shop with the freedom of a customer, and also with something of the familiarity of a childish friend. She had worn a hole through her silver thimble, and wanted Owen to repair it.

"But I don't know whether you will condescend to such a task," said she, laughing, "now that you are so taken up with the notion of putting spirit into machinery."

"Where did you get that idea, Annie?" said Owen, starting in surprise.

"Oh, out of my own head," answered she, "and from something that I heard you say, long ago, when you were but a boy and I a little child. But come; will you mend this poor thimble of mine?"

"Anything for your sake, Annie," said Owen Warland,—"anything, even were it to work at Robert Danforth's forge."

"And that would be a pretty sight!" retorted Annie, glancing with imperceptible slightness at the artist's small and slender frame. "Well; here is the thimble."

"But that is a strange idea of yours," said Owen, "about the spiritualization of matter."

And then the thought stole into his mind that this young girl possessed the gift to comprehend him better than all the world besides. And what a help and strength would it be to him in his lonely toil if he could gain the sympathy of the only being whom he loved! To persons whose pursuits are insulated from the common business of life—who are either in advance of mankind or apart from it—there often comes a sensation of moral cold that makes the spirit shiver as if it had reached the frozen solitudes around the pole. What the prophet, the poet, the reformer, the criminal, or any other man with human yearnings, but separated from the multitude by a peculiar lot, might feel, poor Owen felt.

"Annie," cried he, growing pale as death at the thought, "how gladly would I tell you the secret of my pursuit! You, methinks, would estimate it rightly. You, I know, would hear it with a reverence that I must not expect from the harsh, material world."

"Would I not? to be sure I would!" replied Annie Hovenden, lightly laughing. "Come; explain to me quickly what is the meaning of this little whirligig, so delicately wrought, that it might be a plaything for Queen Mab.[3] See! I will put it in motion."

"Hold!" exclaimed Owen, "hold!"

Annie had but given the slightest possible touch, with the point of a needle, to the same minute portion of complicated machinery which has been more than once mentioned, when the artist seized her by the wrist with a force that made her scream aloud. She was affrighted at the convulsion of intense rage and anguish that writhed across his features. The next instant he let his head sink upon his hands.

"Go, Annie," murmured he; "I have deceived myself, and must suffer for it. I yearned for sympathy and thought, and fancied, and dreamed that you might give it me; but you lack the talisman, Annie, that should admit you into my secrets. That touch has undone the toil of months and the thought of a lifetime! It was not your fault, Annie; but you have ruined me!"

Poor Owen Warland! He had indeed erred, yet pardonably; for if any human spirit could have sufficiently reverenced the processes so sacred in his eyes, it must have been a woman's. Even Annie Hovenden, possibly, might not have disappointed him had she been enlightened by the deep intelligence of love.

The artist spent the ensuing winter in a way that satisfied any persons who had hitherto retained a hopeful opinion of him that he was, in truth, irrevocably doomed to inutility as regarded the world, and to an evil destiny on his own part. The decease of a relative had put him in possession of a small inheritance. Thus freed from the necessity of toil, and having lost the steadfast influence of a great purpose,—great, at least, to him,—he abandoned himself to habits from which it might have been supposed the mere delicacy of his organization would have availed to secure him. But when the ethereal portion of a man of genius is obscured, the earthly part assumes an influence the more uncontrollable, because the character is now thrown off the balance to which Providence had so nicely adjusted it, and which, in coarser natures, is adjusted by some other method. Owen Warland made proof of whatever show of bliss may be found in riot. He looked at the world through the golden medium of wine, and contemplated the visions that bubble up so gayly around the brim of the glass, and that people the air with shapes of pleasant madness, which so soon grow ghostly and forlorn. Even when this dismal and inevitable change had taken place, the young man might still have continued to quaff

3. **Queen Mab**: "the fairies' midwife" who delivers men of their dreams; see *Romeo and Juliet*, I.iv.53–94.

the cup of enchantments, though its vapor did but shroud life in gloom and fill the gloom with spectres that mocked at him. There was a certain irksomeness of spirit, which, being real, and the deepest sensation of which the artist was now conscious, was more intolerable than any fantastic miseries and horrors that the abuse of wine could summon up. In the latter case he could remember, even out of the midst of his trouble, that all was but a delusion; in the former, the heavy anguish was his actual life.

From this perilous state he was redeemed by an incident which more than one person witnessed, but of which the shrewdest could not explain or conjecture the operation on Owen Warland's mind. It was very simple. On a warm afternoon of spring, as the artist sat among his riotous companions with a glass of wine before him, a splendid butterfly flew in at the open window and fluttered about his head.

"Ah," exclaimed Owen, who had drank freely, "are you alive again, child of the sun and playmate of the summer breeze, after your dismal winter's nap? Then it is time for me to be at work!"

And, leaving his unemptied glass upon the table, he departed and was never known to sip another drop of wine.

And now, again, he resumed his wanderings in the woods and fields. It might be fancied that the bright butterfly, which had come so spirit-like into the window as Owen sat with the rude revellers, was indeed a spirit commissioned to recall him to the pure, ideal life that had so etherealized him among men. It might be fancied that he went forth to seek this spirit in its sunny haunts; for still, as in the summer time gone by, he was seen to steal gently up wherever a butterfly had alighted, and lose himself in contemplation of it. When it took flight his eyes followed the winged vision, as if its airy track would show the path to heaven. But what could be the purpose of the unseasonable toil, which was again resumed, as the watchman knew by the lines of lamplight through the crevices of Owen Warland's shutters? The towns-people had one comprehensive explanation of all these singularities. Owen Warland had gone mad! How universally efficacious—how satisfactory, too, and soothing to the injured sensibility of narrowness and dulness—is this easy method of accounting for whatever lies beyond the world's most ordinary scope! From St. Paul's [4] days down to our poor little Artist of the Beautiful, the same talisman had been applied to the elucidation of all mysteries in the words or deeds of men who spoke or acted too wisely or too well. In Owen Warland's case the judgment of his towns-people may have been correct. Perhaps he was mad. The lack of sympathy—that contrast between himself and his neighbors which took away the restraint of example—was enough to make him so. Or possibly he had caught just so much of ethereal radiance as served to bewilder him, in an earthly sense, by its intermixture with the common daylight.

One evening, when the artist had returned from a customary ramble and had just thrown the lustre of his lamp on the delicate piece of work so often interrupted, but still taken up again, as if his fate were embodied in its mechanism, he was surprised by the entrance of old Peter Hovenden. Owen never met this man without a shrinking of the heart. Of all the world he was most terrible, by reason of a keen understanding which saw so distinctly what it did see, and disbelieved so uncompromisingly in what it could not see. On this occasion the old watchmaker had merely a gracious word or two to say.

"Owen, my lad," said he, "we must see you at my house to-morrow night."

The artist began to mutter some excuse.

"Oh, but it must be so," quoth Peter Hovenden, "for the sake of the days when you were one of the household. What, my boy! don't you know that my daughter Annie is engaged to Robert Danforth? We are making an entertainment, in our humble way, to celebrate the event."

"Ah!" said Owen.

That little monosyllable was all he uttered; its tone seemed cold and unconcerned to an ear like Peter Hovenden's; and yet there was in it the stifled outcry of the poor artist's heart, which he compressed within him like a man holding down an evil spirit. One slight outbreak, however, imperceptible to the old watchmaker, he allowed himself. Raising the instrument with which he was about to begin his work, he let it fall upon the little system of machinery that had, anew, cost him months of thought and toil. It was shattered by the stroke!

Owen Warland's story would have been no tolerable representation of the troubled life of those who strive to create the beautiful, if, amid all other thwarting influences, love had not interposed to steal the cunning from his hand. Outwardly he had been no ardent or enterprising lover; the career of his passion had confined its tumults and vicissitudes so entirely within the artist's imagination that Annie herself had scarcely more than a woman's intuitive perception of it; but, in Owen's view, it covered the whole field

4. **St. Paul's:** See Acts 26:24: "Festus said with a loud voice, Paul, thou art beside thyself; much learning doth make thee mad."

of his life. Forgetful of the time when she had shown herself incapable of any deep response, he had persisted in connecting all his dreams of artistical success with Annie's image; she was the visible shape in which the spiritual power that he worshipped, and on whose altar he hoped to lay a not unworthy offering, was made manifest to him. Of course he had deceived himself; there were no such attributes in Annie Hovenden as his imagination had endowed her with. She, in the aspect which she wore to his inward vision, was as much a creature of his own as the mysterious piece of mechanism would be were it ever realized. Had he become convinced of his mistake through the medium of successful love,—had he won Annie to his bosom, and there beheld her fade from angel into ordinary woman,—the disappointment might have driven him back, with concentrated energy, upon his sole remaining object. On the other hand, had he found Annie what he fancied, his lot would have been so rich in beauty that out of its mere redundancy he might have wrought the beautiful into many a worthier type than he had toiled for; but the guise in which his sorrow came to him, the sense that the angel of his life had been snatched away and given to a rude man of earth and iron, who could neither need nor appreciate her ministrations,—this was the very perversity of fate that makes human existence appear too absurd and contradictory to be the scene of one other hope or one other fear. There was nothing left for Owen Warland but to sit down like a man that had been stunned.

He went through a fit of illness. After his recovery his small and slender frame assumed an obtuser garniture of flesh than it had ever before worn. His thin cheeks became round; his delicate little hand, so spiritually fashioned to achieve fairy task-work, grew plumper than the hand of a thriving infant. His aspect had a childishness such as might have induced a stranger to pat him on the head—pausing, however, in the act, to wonder what manner of child was here. It was as if the spirit had gone out of him, leaving the body to flourish in a sort of vegetable existence. Not that Owen Warland was idiotic. He could talk, and not irrationally. Somewhat of a babbler, indeed, did people begin to think him; for he was apt to discourse at wearisome length of marvels of mechanism that he had read about in books, but which he had learned to consider as absolutely fabulous. Among them he enumerated the Man of Brass, constructed by Albertus Magnus, and the Brazen Head of Friar Bacon; [5] and, coming down to later times, the automata of a little coach and horses, which it was pretended had been manufactured for the Dauphin of France; [6] together with an insect that buzzed about the ear like a living fly, and yet was but a contrivance of minute steel springs. There was a story, too, of a duck that waddled, and quacked, and ate; though, had any honest citizen purchased it for dinner, he would have found himself cheated with the mere mechanical apparition of a duck.

"But all these accounts," said Owen Warland, "I am now satisfied are mere impositions."

Then, in a mysterious way, he would confess that he once thought differently. In his idle and dreamy days he had considered it possible, in a certain sense, to spiritualize machinery, and to combine with the new species of life and motion thus produced a beauty that should attain to the ideal which Nature has proposed to herself in all her creatures, but has never taken pains to realize. He seemed, however, to retain no very distinct perception either of the process of achieving this object or of the design itself.

"I have thrown it all aside now," he would say. "It was a dream such as young men are always mystifying themselves with. Now that I have acquired a little common sense, it makes me laugh to think of it."

Poor, poor and fallen Owen Warland! These were the symptoms that he had ceased to be an inhabitant of the better sphere that lies unseen around us. He had lost his faith in the invisible, and now prided himself, as such unfortunates invariably do, in the wisdom which rejected much that even his eye could see, and trusted confidently in nothing but what his hand could touch. This is the calamity of men whose spiritual part dies out of them and leaves the grosser understanding to assimilate them more and more to the things of which alone it can take cognizance; but in Owen Warland the spirit was not dead nor passed away; it only slept.

How it awoke again is not recorded. Perhaps the torpid slumber was broken by a convulsive pain. Perhaps, as in a former instance, the butterfly came and hovered about his head and reinspired him,—as indeed this creature of the sunshine had always a mysterious mission for the artist,—reinspired him with the former purpose of his life. Whether it were pain or happiness that thrilled through his veins, his first impulse was to thank Heaven for rendering him again the being of thought, imagination, and keenest sensibility that he had long ceased to be.

5. **Man . . . Bacon:** See "The Birthmark," 4 n.

6. **Dauphin of France:** the son of Louis XVI, known as Louis XVII (1785–95).

"Now for my task," said he. "Never did I feel such strength for it as now."

Yet, strong as he felt himself, he was incited to toil the more diligently by an anxiety lest death should surprise him in the midst of his labors. This anxiety, perhaps, is common to all men who set their hearts upon anything so high, in their own view of it, that life becomes of importance only as conditional to its accomplishment. So long as we love life for itself, we seldom dread the losing it. When we desire life for the attainment of an object, we recognize the frailty of its texture. But, side by side with this sense of insecurity, there is a vital faith in our invulnerability to the shaft of death while engaged in any task that seems assigned by Providence as our proper thing to do, and which the world would have cause to mourn for should we leave it unaccomplished. Can the philosopher, big with the inspiration of an idea that is to reform mankind, believe that he is to be beckoned from this sensible existence at the very instant when he is mustering his breath to speak the word of light? Should he perish so, the weary ages may pass away—the world's, whose life sand may fall, drop by drop—before another intellect is prepared to develop the truth that might have been uttered then. But history affords many an example where the most precious spirit, at any particular epoch manifested in human shape, has gone hence untimely, without space allowed him, so far as mortal judgment could discern, to perform his mission on the earth. The prophet dies, and the man of torpid heart and sluggish brain lives on. The poet leaves his song half sung, or finishes it, beyond the scope of mortal ears, in a celestial choir. The painter—as Allston [7] did—leaves half his conception on the canvas to sadden us with its imperfect beauty, and goes to picture forth the whole, if it be no irreverence to say so, in the hues of heaven. But rather such incomplete designs of this life will be perfected nowhere. This so frequent abortion of man's dearest projects must be taken as a proof that the deeds of earth, however etherealized by piety or genius, are without value, except as exercises and manifestations of the spirit. In heaven, all ordinary thought is higher and more melodious than Milton's song. Then, would he add another verse to any strain that he had left unfinished here?

But to return to Owen Warland. It was his fortune, good or ill, to achieve the purpose of his life. Pass we over a long space of intense thought, yearning effort, minute toil, and wasting anxiety, succeeded by an instant of solitary triumph: let all this be imagined; and then behold the artist, on a winter evening, seeking admittance to Robert Danforth's fireside circle. There he found the man of iron, with his massive substance thoroughly warmed and attempered by domestic influences. And there was Annie, too, now transformed into a matron, with much of her husband's plain and sturdy nature, but imbued, as Owen Warland still believed, with a finer grace, that might enable her to be the interpreter between strength and beauty. It happened, likewise, that old Peter Hovenden was a guest this evening at his daughter's fireside, and it was his well-remembered expression of keen, cold criticism that first encountered the artist's glance.

"My old friend Owen!" cried Robert Danforth, starting up, and compressing the artist's delicate fingers within a hand that was accustomed to gripe bars of iron. "This is kind and neighborly to come to us at last. I was afraid your perpetual motion had bewitched you out of the remembrance of old times."

"We are glad to see you," said Annie, while a blush reddened her matronly cheek. "It was not like a friend to stay from us so long."

"Well, Owen," inquired the old watchmaker, as his first greeting, "how comes on the beautiful? Have you created it at last?"

The artist did not immediately reply, being startled by the apparition of a young child of strength that was tumbling about on the carpet,—a little personage who had come mysteriously out of the infinite but with something so sturdy and real in his composition that he seemed moulded out of the densest substance which earth could supply. This hopeful infant crawled towards the newcomer, and setting himself on end, as Robert Danforth expressed the posture, stared at Owen with a look of such sagacious observation that the mother could not help exchanging a proud glance with her husband. But the artist was disturbed by the child's look, as imagining a resemblance between it and Peter Hovenden's habitual expression. He could have fancied that the old watchmaker was compressed into this baby shape, and looking out of those baby eyes, and repeating, as he now did, the malicious question:—

"The beautiful, Owen! How comes on the beautiful? Have you succeeded in creating the beautiful?"

"I have succeeded," replied the artist, with a momentary light of triumph in his eyes and a smile of sunshine, yet steeped in such depth of thought that it was almost sadness. "Yes, my friends, it is the truth. I have succeeded."

7. **Allston:** Washington Allston (1779–1843), the American painter who left his picture "Belshazzar's Feast" unfinished at his death.

"Indeed!" cried Annie, a look of maiden mirthfulness peeping out of her face again. "And is it lawful, now, to inquire what the secret is?"

"Surely; it is to disclose it that I have come," answered Owen Warland. "You shall know, and see, and touch, and possess the secret! For, Annie, —if by that name I may still address the friend of my boyish years,—Annie, it is for your bridal gift that I have wrought this spiritualized mechanism, this harmony of motion, this mystery of beauty. It comes late, indeed; but it is as we go onward in life, when objects begin to lose their freshness of hue and our souls their delicacy of perception, that the spirit of beauty is most needed. If,—forgive me, Annie,—if you know how to value this gift, it can never come too late."

He produced, as he spoke, what seemed a jewel box. It was carved richly out of ebony by his own hand, and inlaid with a fanciful tracery of pearl, representing a boy in pursuit of a butterfly, which, elsewhere, had become a winged spirit, and was flying heavenward; while the boy, or youth, had found such efficacy in his strong desire that he ascended from earth to cloud, and from cloud to celestial atmosphere, to win the beautiful. This case of ebony the artist opened, and bade Annie place her finger on its edge. She did so, but almost screamed as a butterfly fluttered forth, and, alighting on her finger's tip, sat waving the ample magnificence of its purple and gold-speckled wings, as if in prelude to a flight. It is impossible to express by words the glory, the splendor, the delicate gorgeousness which were softened into the beauty of this object. Nature's ideal butterfly was here realized in all its perfection; not in the pattern of such faded insects as flit among earthly flowers, but of those which hover across the meads of paradise for child-angels and the spirits of departed infants to disport themselves with. The rich down was visible upon its wings; the lustre of its eyes seemed instinct with spirit. The firelight glimmered around this wonder—the candles gleamed upon it; but it glistened apparently by its own radiance, and illuminated the finger and outstretched hand on which it rested with a white gleam like that of precious stones. In its perfect beauty, the consideration of size was entirely lost. Had its wings overreached the firmament, the mind could not have been more filled or satisfied.

"Beautiful! beautiful!" exclaimed Annie. "Is it alive? Is it alive?"

"Alive? To be sure it is," answered her husband. "Do you suppose any mortal has skill enough to make a butterfly, or would put himself to the trouble of making one, when any child may catch a score of them in a summer's afternoon? Alive? Certainly! But this pretty box is undoubtedly of our friend Owen's manufacture; and really it does him credit."

At this moment the butterfly waved its wings anew, with a motion so absolutely lifelike that Annie was startled, and even awe-stricken; for, in spite of her husband's opinion, she could not satisfy herself whether it was indeed a living creature or a piece of wondrous mechanism.

"Is it alive?" she repeated, more earnestly than before.

"Judge for yourself," said Owen Warland, who stood gazing in her face with fixed attention.

The butterfly now flung itself upon the air, fluttered round Annie's head, and soared into a distant region of the parlor, still making itself perceptible to sight by the starry gleam in which the motion of its wings enveloped it. The infant on the floor followed its course with his sagacious little eyes. After flying about the room, it returned in a spiral curve and settled again on Annie's finger.

"But is it alive?" exclaimed she again; and the finger on which the gorgeous mystery had alighted was so tremulous that the butterfly was forced to balance himself with his wings. "Tell me if it be alive, or whether you created it."

"Wherefore ask who created it, so it be beautiful?" replied Owen Warland. "Alive? Yes, Annie; it may well be said to possess life, for it has absorbed my own being into itself; and in the secret of that butterfly, and in its beauty,—which is not merely outward, but deep as its whole system,—is represented the intellect, the imagination, the sensibility, the soul of an Artist of the Beautiful! Yes; I created it. But"—and here his countenance somewhat changed—"this butterfly is not now to me what it was when I beheld it afar off in the daydreams of my youth."

"Be it what it may, it is a pretty plaything," said the blacksmith, grinning with childlike delight. "I wonder whether it would condescend to alight on such a great clumsy finger as mine? Hold it hither, Annie."

By the artist's direction, Annie touched her finger's tip to that of her husband; and, after a momentary delay, the butterfly fluttered from one to the other. It preluded a second flight by a similar, yet not precisely the same, waving of wings as in the first experiment; then, ascending from the blacksmith's stalwart finger, it rose in a gradually enlarging curve to the ceiling, made one wide sweep around the room, and returned with an undulating movement to the point whence it had started.

"Well, that does beat all nature!" cried Robert Danforth, bestowing the heartiest praise that he could find expression for; and, indeed, had he paused there, a man of finer words and nicer perception could not easily have said more. "That goes beyond me, I confess. But what then? There is more real use in one downright blow of my sledge hammer than in the whole five years' labor that our friend Owen has wasted on this butterfly."

Here the child clapped his hands and made a great babble of indistinct utterance, apparently demanding that the butterfly should be given him for a plaything.

Owen Warland, meanwhile, glanced sidelong at Annie, to discover whether she sympathized in her husband's estimate of the comparative value of the beautiful and the practical. There was, amid all her kindness towards himself, amid all the wonder and admiration with which she contemplated the marvellous work of his hands and incarnation of his idea, a secret scorn—too secret, perhaps, for her own consciousness, and perceptible only to such intuitive discernment as that of the artist. But Owen, in the latter stages of his pursuit, had risen out of the region in which such a discovery might have been torture. He knew that the world, and Annie as the representative of the world, whatever praise might be bestowed, could never say the fitting word nor feel the fitting sentiment which should be the perfect recompense of an artist who, symbolizing a lofty moral by a material trifle,—converting what was earthly to spiritual gold,—had won the beautiful into his handiwork. Not at this latest moment was he to learn that the reward of all high performance must be sought within itself, or sought in vain. There was, however, a view of the matter which Annie and her husband, and even Peter Hovenden, might fully have understood, and which would have satisfied them that the toil of years had here been worthily bestowed. Owen Warland might have told them that this butterfly, this plaything, this bridal gift of a poor watchmaker to a blacksmith's wife, was, in truth, a gem of art that a monarch would have purchased with honors and abundant wealth, and have treasured it among the jewels of his kingdom as the most unique and wondrous of them all. But the artist smiled and kept the secret to himself.

"Father," said Annie, thinking that a word of praise from the old watchmaker might gratify his former apprentice, "do come and admire this pretty butterfly."

"Let us see," said Peter Hovenden, rising from his chair, with a sneer upon his face that always made people doubt, as he himself did, in everything but a material existence. "Here is my finger for it to alight upon. I shall understand it better when once I have touched it."

But, to the increased astonishment of Annie, when the tip of her father's finger was pressed against that of her husband, on which the butterfly still rested, the insect drooped its wings and seemed on the point of falling to the floor. Even the bright spots of gold upon its wings and body, unless her eyes deceived her, grew dim, and the glowing purple took a dusky hue, and the starry lustre that gleamed around the blacksmith's hand became faint and vanished.

"It is dying! it is dying!" cried Annie, in alarm.

"It has been delicately wrought," said the artist, calmly. "As I told you, it has imbibed a spiritual essence—call it magnetism, or what you will. In an atmosphere of doubt and mockery its exquisite susceptibility suffers torture, as does the soul of him who instilled his own life into it. It has already lost its beauty; in a few moments more its mechanism would be irreparably injured."

"Take away your hand, father!" entreated Annie, turning pale. "Here is my child; let it rest on his innocent hand. There, perhaps, its life will revive and its colors grow brighter than ever."

Her father, with an acrid smile, withdrew his finger. The butterfly then appeared to recover the power of voluntary motion, while its hues assumed much of their original lustre, and the gleam of starlight, which was its most ethereal attribute, again formed a halo round about it. At first, when transferred from Robert Danforth's hand to the small finger of the child, this radiance grew so powerful that it positively threw the little fellow's shadow back against the wall. He, meanwhile, extended his plump hand as he had seen his father and mother do, and watched the waving of the insect's wings with infantine delight. Nevertheless, there was a certain odd expression of sagacity that made Owen Warland feel as if here were old Peter Hovenden, partially, and but partially, redeemed from his hard scepticism into childish faith.

"How wise the little monkey looks!" whispered Robert Danforth to his wife.

"I never saw such a look on a child's face," answered Annie, admiring her own infant, and with good reason, far more than the artistic butterfly. "The darling knows more of the mystery than we do."

As if the butterfly, like the artist, were conscious of something not entirely congenial in the child's nature, it alternately sparkled and grew dim. At length it arose from the small hand of the infant with an airy motion that seemed to bear it upward without an effort, as if the ethereal instincts with which its master's spirit had endowed it impelled this fair vision involuntarily to a higher sphere. Had there been no obstruction, it might have soared into the sky and grown immortal. But its lustre gleamed upon the ceiling; the exquisite texture of its wings brushed against that earthly medium; and a sparkle or two, as of stardust, floated downward and lay glimmering on the carpet. Then the butterfly came fluttering down, and, instead of returning to the infant, was apparently attracted towards the artist's hand.

"Not so! not so!" murmured Owen Warland, as if his handiwork could have understood him. "Thou has gone forth out of thy master's heart. There is no return for thee."

With a wavering movement, and emitting a tremulous radiance, the butterfly struggled, as it were, towards the infant, and was about to alight upon his finger; but while it still hovered in the air, the little child of strength, with his grandsire's sharp and shrewd expression in his face, made a snatch at the marvellous insect and compressed it in his hand. Annie screamed. Old Peter Hovenden burst into a cold and scornful laugh. The blacksmith, by main force, unclosed the infant's hand, and found within the palm a small heap of glittering fragments, whence the mystery of beauty had fled forever. And as for Owen Warland, he looked placidly at what seemed the ruin of his life's labor, and which was yet no ruin. He had caught a far other butterfly than this. When the artist rose high enough to achieve the beautiful, the symbol by which he made it perceptible to mortal senses became of little value in his eyes while his spirit possessed itself in the enjoyment of the reality.

ETHAN BRAND

A Chapter from an Abortive Romance

◊

PUBLISHED in the *Boston Museum* (January, 1850) and in *Holden's Dollar Magazine* (May, 1851), and reprinted in the *Snow-Image and Other Twice-Told Tales* (1852), this story is anticipated in a notebook entry for 1844: "The search of an investigator for the Unpardonable Sin;—he at last finds it in his own heart and practice." The background of the story derives from Hawthorne's description of a trip to North Adams, Massachusetts, from July to September, 1836, especially the details for the lime-kiln, Lawyer Giles, the one-armed soap maker, the boy Joe, and the German and his diorama. The narrative quite evidently treats the theme of the hardness of heart which isolates and destroys a man's whole being. It may also concern that danger of the intellect which separates the Head from the Heart and inevitably brings about the annihilation of an otherwise sentient being.

◊

BARTRAM the lime-burner, a rough, heavy-looking man, begrimed with charcoal, sat watching his kiln at nightfall, while his little son played at building houses with the scattered fragments of marble, when, on the hill-side below them, they heard a roar of laughter, not mirthful, but slow, and even solemn, like a wind shaking the boughs of the forest.

"Father, what is that?" asked the little boy, leaving his play, and pressing betwixt his father's knees.

"Oh, some drunken man, I suppose," answered the lime-burner; "some merry fellow from the bar-room in the village, who dared not laugh loud enough within doors lest he should blow the roof of the house off. So here he is, shaking his jolly sides at the foot of Graylock." [1]

"But, father," said the child, more sensitive than the obtuse, middle-aged clown, "he does not laugh like a man that is glad. So the noise frightens me!"

"Don't be a fool, child!" cried his father, gruffly. "You will never make a man, I do believe; there is too much of your mother in you. I have known the rustling of a leaf startle you. Hark! Here comes the merry fellow now. You shall see that there is no harm in him."

Bartram and his little son, while they were talking thus, sat watching the same lime-kiln that had been the scene of Ethan Brand's solitary and meditative life, before he began his search for the Unpardonable Sin. Many years, as we have seen, had now elapsed, since that portentous night when the IDEA was first developed. The kiln, however, on the mountain-side, stood unimpaired, and was in nothing changed since he had thrown his dark thoughts into the intense glow of its furnace, and melted them, as it were, into the one thought that took possession of his life. It was a rude, round, tower-like structure about twenty feet high, heavily built of rough stones, and with a hillock of earth heaped about the larger part of its circumference;

ETHAN BRAND. 1. **Graylock:** Mt. Graylock, or Saddle Mountain, the highest peak in the Berkshires.

so that the blocks and fragments of marble might be drawn by cart-loads, and thrown in at the top. There was an opening at the bottom of the tower, like an oven-mouth, but large enough to admit a man in a stooping posture, and provided with a massive iron door. With the smoke and jets of flame issuing from the chinks and crevices of this door, which seemed to give admittance into the hill-side, it resembled nothing so much as the private entrance to the infernal regions, which the shepherds of the Delectable Mountains [2] were accustomed to show to pilgrims.

There are many such lime-kilns in that tract of country, for the purpose of burning the white marble which composes a large part of the substance of the hills. Some of them, built years ago, and long deserted, with weeds growing in the vacant round of the interior, which is open to the sky, and grass and wildflowers rooting themselves into the chinks of the stones, look already like relics of antiquity, and may yet be overspread with the lichens of centuries to come. Others, where the lime-burner still feeds his daily and night-long fire, afford points of interest to the wanderer among the hills, who seats himself on a log of wood or a fragment of marble, to hold a chat with the solitary man. It is a lonesome, and, when the character is inclined to thought, may be an intensely thoughtful occupation; as it proved in the case of Ethan Brand, who had mused to such strange purpose, in days gone by, while the fire in this very kiln was burning.

The man who now watched the fire was of a different order, and troubled himself with no thoughts save the very few that were requisite to his business. At frequent intervals, he flung back the clashing weight of the iron door, and, turning his face from the insufferable glare, thrust in huge logs of oak, or stirred the immense brands with a long pole. Within the furnace were seen the curling and riotous flames, and the burning marble, almost molten with the intensity of heat; while without, the reflection of the fire quivered on the dark intricacy of the surrounding forest, and showed in the foreground a bright and ruddy little picture of the hut, the spring beside its door, the athletic and coal-begrimed figure of the lime-burner, and the half-frightened child, shrinking into the protection of his father's shadow. And when, again, the iron door was closed, then reappeared the tender light of the half-full moon, which vainly strove to trace out the indistinct shapes of the neighboring mountains; and, in the upper sky, there was a flitting congregation of clouds, still faintly tinged with the rosy sunset, though thus far down into the valley the sunshine had vanished long and long ago.

The little boy now crept still closer to his father, as footsteps were heard ascending the hill-side, and a human form thrust aside the bushes that clustered beneath the trees.

"Halloo! who is it?" cried the lime-burner, vexed at his son's timidity, yet half infected by it. "Come forward, and show yourself, like a man, or I'll fling this chunk of marble at your head!"

"You offer me a rough welcome," said a gloomy voice, as the unknown man drew nigh. "Yet I neither claim nor desire a kinder one, even at my own fireside."

To obtain a distincter view, Bartram threw open the iron door of the kiln, whence immediately issued a gush of fierce light, that smote full upon the stranger's face and figure. To a careless eye there appeared nothing very remarkable in his aspect, which was that of a man in a coarse, brown, country-made suit of clothes, tall and thin, with the staff and heavy shoes of a wayfarer. As he advanced, he fixed his eyes—which were very bright —intently upon the brightness of the furnace, as if he beheld, or expected to behold, some object worthy of note within it.

"Good evening, stranger," said the lime-burner; "whence come you, so late in the day?"

"I come from my search," answered the wayfarer; "for, at last, it is finished."

"Drunk!—or crazy!" muttered Bartram to himself. "I shall have trouble with the fellow. The sooner I drive him away, the better."

The little boy, all in a tremble, whispered to his father, and begged him to shut the door of the kiln, so that there might not be so much light; for that there was something in the man's face which he was afraid to look at, yet could not look away from. And, indeed, even the lime-burner's dull and torpid sense began to be impressed by an indescribable something in that thin, rugged, thoughtful visage, with the grizzled hair hanging wildly about it, and those deeply sunken eyes, which gleamed like fires within the entrance of a mysterious cavern. But, as he closed the door, the stranger turned towards him, and spoke in a quiet, familiar way, that made Bartram feel as if he were a sane and sensible man, after all.

"Your task draws to an end, I see," said he. "This marble has already been burning three days. A few hours more will convert the stone to lime."

"Why, who are you?" exclaimed the lime-burner. "You seem as well acquainted with my business as I am myself."

2. **Delectable Mountains:** in Bunyan's *Pilgrim's Progress* the mountains from which Christian first sees the Celestial City.

"And well I may be," said the stranger; "for I followed the same craft many a long year, and here, too, on this very spot. But you are a newcomer in these parts. Did you never hear of Ethan Brand?"

"The man that went in search of the Unpardonable Sin?" asked Bartram, with a laugh.

"The same," answered the stranger. "He has found what he sought, and therefore he comes back again."

"What! then you are Ethan Brand himself?" cried the lime-burner, in amazement. "I am a newcomer here, as you say, and they call it eighteen years since you left the foot of Graylock. But, I can tell you, the good folks still talk about Ethan Brand, in the village yonder, and what a strange errand took him away from his lime-kiln. Well, and so you have found the Unpardonable Sin?"

"Even so!" said the stranger, calmly.

"If the question is a fair one," proceeded Bartram, "where might it be?"

Ethan Brand laid his finger on his own heart.

"Here!" replied he.

And then, without mirth in his countenance, but as if moved by an involuntary recognition of the infinite absurdity of seeking throughout the world for what was the closest of all things to himself, and looking into every heart, save his own, for what was hidden in no other breast, he broke into a laugh of scorn. It was the same slow, heavy laugh, that had almost appalled the lime-burner when it heralded the wayfarer's approach.

The solitary mountain-side was made dismal by it. Laughter, when out of place, mistimed, or bursting forth from a disordered state of feeling, may be the most terrible modulation of the human voice. The laughter of one asleep, even if it be a little child,—the madman's laugh,—the wild, screaming laugh of a born idiot,—are sounds that we sometimes tremble to hear, and would always willingly forget. Poets have imagined no utterance of fiends or hobgoblins so fearfully appropriate as a laugh. And even the obtuse lime-burner felt his nerves shaken, as this strange man looked inward at his own heart, and burst into laughter that rolled away into the night, and was indistinctly reverberated among the hills.

"Joe," said he to his little son, "scamper down to the tavern in the village, and tell the jolly fellows there that Ethan Brand has come back, and that he has found the Unpardonable Sin!"

The boy darted away on his errand, to which Ethan Brand made no objection, nor seemed hardly to notice it. He sat on a log of wood, looking steadfastly at the iron door of the kiln. When the child was out of sight, and his swift and light footsteps ceased to be heard treading first on the fallen leaves and then on the rocky mountain-path, the lime-burner began to regret his departure. He felt that the little fellow's presence had been a barrier between his guest and himself, and that he must now deal, heart to heart, with a man who, on his own confession, had committed the one only crime for which Heaven could afford no mercy. That crime, in its indistinct blackness, seemed to overshadow him. The lime-burner's own sins rose up within him, and made his memory riotous with a throng of evil shapes that asserted their kindred with the Master Sin, whatever it might be, which it was within the scope of man's corrupted nature to conceive and cherish. They were all of one family; they went to and fro between his breast and Ethan Brand's, and carried dark greetings from one to the other.

Then Bartram remembered the stories which had grown traditionally in reference to this strange man, who had come upon him like a shadow of the night, and was making himself at home in his old place, after so long absence, that the dead people, dead and buried for years, would have had more right to be at home, in any familiar spot, than he. Ethan Brand, it was said, had conversed with Satan himself in the lurid blaze of this very kiln. The legend had been matter of mirth heretofore, but looked grisly now. According to this tale, before Ethan Brand departed on his search, he had been accustomed to evoke a fiend from the hot furnace of the lime-kiln, night after night, in order to confer with him about the Unpardonable Sin; the man and the fiend each laboring to frame the image of some mode of guilt which could neither be atoned for nor forgiven. And, with the first gleam of light upon the mountain-top, the fiend crept in at the iron door, there to abide the intensest element of fire until again summoned forth to share in the dreadful task of extending man's possible guilt beyond the scope of Heaven's else infinite mercy.

While the lime-burner was struggling with the horror of these thoughts, Ethan Brand rose from the log, and flung open the door of the kiln. The action was in such accordance with the idea in Bartram's mind, that he almost expected to see the Evil One issue forth, red-hot, from the raging furnace.

"Hold! hold!" cried he, with a tremulous attempt to laugh; for he was ashamed of his fears, although they overmastered him. "Don't, for mercy's sake, bring out your Devil now!"

"Man!" sternly replied Ethan Brand, "what need have I of the Devil? I have left him behind me, on my track. It is with such half-way sinners as you that he busies himself. Fear not, because I open the door, I do but act by old custom, and am going to trim your fire, like a lime-burner, as I was once."

He stirred the vast coals, thrust in more wood, and bent forward to gaze into the hollow prison-house of the fire, regardless of the fierce glow that reddened upon his face. The lime-burner sat watching him, and half suspected this strange guest of a purpose, if not to evoke a fiend, at least to plunge bodily into the flames, and thus vanish from the sight of man. Ethan Brand, however, drew quietly back, and closed the door of the kiln.

"I have looked," said he, "into many a human heart that was seven times hotter with sinful passions than yonder furnace is with fire. But I found not there what I sought. No, not the Unpardonable Sin!"

"What is the Unpardonable Sin?" asked the lime-burner; and then he shrank farther from his companion, trembling lest his question should be answered.

"It is a sin that grew within my own breast," replied Ethan Brand, standing erect, with a pride that distinguishes all enthusiasts of his stamp. "A sin that grew nowhere else! The sin of an intellect that triumphed over the sense of brotherhood with man and reverence for God, and sacrificed everything to its own mighty claims! The only sin that deserves a recompense of immortal agony! Freely, were it to do again, would I incur the guilt. Unshrinkingly I accept the retribution!"

"The man's head is turned," muttered the lime-burner to himself. "He may be a sinner like the rest of us,—nothing more likely,—but, I'll be sworn, he is a madman too."

Nevertheless, he felt uncomfortable at his situation, alone with Ethan Brand on the wild mountain-side, and was right glad to hear the rough murmur of tongues, and the footsteps of what seemed a pretty numerous party, stumbling over the stones and rustling through the underbrush. Soon appeared the whole lazy regiment that was wont to infest the village tavern, comprehending three or four individuals who had drunk flip beside the bar-room fire through all the winters, and smoked their pipes beneath the stoop through all the summers, since Ethan Brand's departure. Laughing boisterously, and mingling all their voices together in unceremonious talk, they now burst into the moonshine and narrow streaks of firelight that illuminated the open space before the lime-kiln. Bartram set the door ajar again, flooding the spot with light, that the whole company might get a fair view of Ethan Brand, and he of them.

There, among other old acquaintances, was a once ubiquitous man, now almost extinct, but whom we were formerly sure to encounter at the hotel of every thriving village throughout the country. It was the stage-agent. The present specimen of the genus was a wilted and smoke-dried man, wrinkled and red-nosed, in a smartly cut, brown, bobtailed coat, with brass buttons, who, for a length of time unknown, had kept his desk and corner in the bar-room, and was still puffing what seemed to be the same cigar that he had lighted twenty years before. He had great fame as a dry joker, though, perhaps, less on account of any intrinsic humor than from a certain flavor of brandy-toddy and tobacco-smoke, which impregnated all his ideas and expressions, as well as his person. Another well-remembered, though strangely altered, face was that of Lawyer Giles, as people still called him in courtesy; an elderly ragamuffin, in his soiled shirt-sleeves and tow-cloth trousers. This poor fellow had been an attorney, in what he called his better days, a sharp practitioner, and in great vogue among the village litigants; but flip, and sling, and toddy, and cocktails, imbibed at all hours, morning, noon, and night, had caused him to slide from intellectual to various kinds and degrees of bodily labor, till at last, to adopt his own phrase, he slid into a soap-vat. In other words, Giles was now a soap-boiler, in a small way. He had come to be but the fragment of a human being, a part of one foot having been chopped off by an axe, and an entire hand torn away by the devilish grip of a steam-engine. Yet, though the corporeal hand was gone, a spiritual member remained; for, stretching forth the stump, Giles steadfastly averred that he felt an invisible thumb and fingers with as vivid a sensation as before the real ones were amputated. A maimed and miserable wretch he was; but one, nevertheless, whom the world could not trample on, and had no right to scorn, either in this or any previous stage of his misfortunes, since he had still kept up the courage and spirit of a man, asked nothing in charity, and with his one hand—and that the left one—fought a stern battle against want and hostile circumstances.

Among the throng, too, came another personage, who, with certain points of similarity to Lawyer Giles, had many more of difference. It was the village doctor; a man of some fifty years, whom, at an earlier period of his life, we introduced as paying a professional visit to Ethan Brand during the latter's supposed insanity. He was now a purple-visaged, rude, and brutal, yet half-gentlemanly figure, with something wild, ruined, and desperate in his talk, and in all the details of his gesture and manners. Brandy possessed this man like an evil spirit, and made him as surly and savage as a wild beast, and as miserable as a lost soul; but there was supposed to be in him such wonderful skill, such native gifts of healing, beyond any which medical science could impart, that society caught hold of him, and would not let him sink out of its reach. So, swaying to and fro upon his horse, and grumbling thick accents at the bedside, he visited all the sick-chambers for miles about among the mountain towns, and sometimes raised a dying man, as it were, by miracle, or quite as often, no doubt, sent his patient to a grave that was dug many a year too soon. The doctor had an everlasting pipe in his mouth, and, as somebody said, in allusion to his habit of swearing, it was always alight with hell-fire.

These three worthies pressed forward, and greeted Ethan Brand each after his own fashion, earnestly inviting him to partake of the contents of a certain black bottle, in which, as they averred, he would find something far better worth seeking for than the Unpardonable Sin. No mind, which has wrought itself by intense and solitary meditation into a high state of enthusiasm, can endure the kind of contact with low and vulgar modes of thought and feeling to which Ethan Brand was now subjected. It made him doubt—and, strange to say, it was a painful doubt—whether he had indeed found the Unpardonable Sin, and found it within himself. The whole question on which he had exhausted life, and more than life, looked like a delusion.

"Leave me," he said bitterly, "ye brute beasts, that have made yourselves so, shrivelling up your souls with fiery liquors! I have done with you. Years and years ago, I groped into your hearts and found nothing there for my purpose. Get ye gone!"

"Why, you uncivil scoundrel," cried the fierce doctor, "is that the way you respond to the kindness of your best friends? Then let me tell you the truth. You have no more found the Unpardonable Sin than yonder boy Joe has. You are but a crazy fellow,—I told you so twenty years ago,—neither better nor worse than a crazy fellow, and the fit companion of old Humphrey, here!"

He pointed to an old man, shabbily dressed, with long white hair, thin visage, and unsteady eyes. For some years past this aged person had been wandering about among the hills, inquiring of all travellers whom he met for his daughter. The girl, it seemed, had gone off with a company of circus-performers, and occasionally tidings of her came to the village, and fine stories were told of her glittering appearance as she rode on horseback in the ring, or performed marvellous feats on the tight-rope.

The white-haired father now approached Ethan Brand, and gazed unsteadily into his face.

"They tell me you have been all over the earth," said he, wringing his hands with earnestness. "You must have seen my daughter, for she makes a grand figure in the world, and everybody goes to see her. Did she send any word to her old father, or say when she was coming back?"

Ethan Brand's eye quailed beneath the old man's. That daughter, from whom he so earnestly desired a word of greeting, was the Esther of our tale, the very girl whom, with such cold and remorseless purpose, Ethan Brand had made the subject of a psychological experiment, and wasted, absorbed, and perhaps annihilated her soul, in the process.

"Yes," murmured he, turning away from the hoary wanderer, "it is no delusion. There is an Unpardonable Sin!"

While these things were passing, a merry scene was going forward in the area of cheerful light, beside the spring and before the door of the hut. A number of the youth of the village, yound men and girls, had hurried up the hill-side, impelled by curiosity to see Ethan Brand, the hero of so many a legend familiar to their childhood. Finding nothing, however, very remarkable in his aspect, —nothing but a sunburnt wayfarer, in plain garb and dusty shoes, who sat looking into the fire as if he fancied pictures among the coals,—these young people speedily grew tired of observing him. As it happened, there was other amusement at hand. An old German Jew travelling with a diorama on his back, was passing down the mountain-road towards the village just as the party turned aside from it, and, in hopes of eking out the profits of the day, the showman had kept them company to the lime-kiln.

"Come, old Dutchman," cried one of the young men, "let us see your pictures, if you can swear they are worth looking at!"

"Oh yes, Captain," answered the Jew,—whether as a matter of courtesy or craft, he styled everybody Captain,—"I shall show you, indeed, some very superb pictures!"

So, placing his box in a proper position, he invited the young men and girls to look through the glass orifices of the machine, and proceeded to exhibit a series of the most outrageous scratchings and daubings, as specimens of the fine arts, that ever an itinerant showman had the face to impose upon his circle of spectators. The pictures were worn out, moreover, tattered, full of cracks and wrinkles, dingy with tobacco-smoke, and otherwise in a most pitiable condition. Some purported to be cities, public edifices, and ruined castles in Europe; others represented Napoleon's battles and Nelson's sea-fights; and in the midst of these would be seen a gigantic, brown, hairy hand,—which might have been mistaken for the Hand of Destiny, though, in truth, it was only the showman's,—pointing its forefinger to various scenes of the conflict, while its owner gave historical illustrations. When, with much merriment at its abominable deficiency of merit, the exhibition was concluded, the German bade little Joe put his head into the box. Viewed through the magnifying-glasses, the boy's round, rosy visage assumed the strangest imaginable aspect of an immense Titanic child, the mouth grinning broadly, and the eyes and every other feature overflowing with fun at the joke. Suddenly, however, that merry face turned pale, and its expression changed to horror, for this easily impressed and excitable child had become sensible that the eye of Ethan Brand was fixed upon him through the glass.

"You make the little man to be afraid, Captain," said the German Jew, turning up the dark and strong outline of his visage from his stooping posture. "But look again, and, by chance, I shall cause you to see somewhat that is very fine, upon my word!"

Ethan Brand gazed into the box for an instant, and then starting back, looked fixedly at the German. What had he seen? Nothing, apparently; for a curious youth, who had peeped in almost at the same moment, beheld only a vacant space of canvas.

"I remember you now," muttered Ethan Brand to the showman.

"Ah, Captain," whispered the Jew of Nuremburg, with a dark smile, "I find it to be a heavy matter in my show-box,—this Unpardonable Sin! By my faith, Captain, it has wearied my shoulders, this long day, to carry it over the mountain."

"Peace," answered Ethan Brand, sternly, "or get thee into the furnace yonder!"

The Jew's exhibition had scarcely concluded, when a great, elderly dog—who seemed to be his own master, as no person in the company laid claim to him—saw fit to render himself the object of public notice. Hitherto, he had shown himself a very quiet, well-disposed old dog, going round from one to another, and, by way of being sociable, offering his rough head to be patted by any kindly hand that would take so much trouble. But now, all of a sudden, this grave and venerable quadruped, of his own mere motion, and without the slightest suggestion from anybody else, began to run round after his tail, which, to heighten the absurdity of the proceeding, was a great deal shorter than it should have been. Never was seen such headlong eagerness in pursuit of an object that could not possibly be attained; never was heard such a tremendous outbreak of growling, snarling, barking, and snapping,—as if one end of the ridiculous brute's body were at deadly and most unforgivable enmity with the other. Faster and faster, round about went the cur; and faster and still faster fled the unapproachable brevity of his tail; and louder and fiercer grew his yells of rage and animosity; until, utterly exhausted, and as far from the goal as ever, the foolish old dog ceased his performance as suddenly as he had begun it. The next moment he was as mild, quiet, sensible, and respectable in his deportment, as when he first scraped acquaintance with the company.

As may be supposed, the exhibition was greeted with universal laughter, clapping of hands, and shouts of encore, to which the canine performer responded by wagging all that there was to wag of his tail, but appeared totally unable to repeat his very successful effort to amuse the spectators.

Meanwhile, Ethan Brand had resumed his seat upon the log, and moved, it might be, by a perception of some remote analogy between his own case and that of this self-pursuing cur, he broke into the awful laugh, which, more than any other token, expressed the condition of his inward being. From that moment, the merriment of the party was at an end; they stood aghast, dreading lest the inauspicious sound should be reverberated around the horizon, and that mountain would thunder it to mountain, and so the horror be prolonged upon their ears. Then, whispering one to another that it was late,—that the moon was almost down,—that the August night was growing chill,—they hurried homewards, leaving the lime-burner and little Joe to deal as they might with their unwelcome guest. Save for these three human beings, the open space on the hill-side was a solitude, set in a vast gloom of forest. Beyond that darksome verge, the firelight glimmered on the stately trunks and almost black foliage of pines, intermixed with the lighter verdure of sapling oaks, maples, and poplars, while here and there lay the gigantic corpses of dead trees, decaying on the leaf-strewn soil. And it seemed to little Joe—a timorous and imaginative child—that the silent forest was holding its breath until some fearful thing should happen.

Ethan Brand thrust more wood into the fire, and closed the door of the kiln, then looking over his shoulder at the lime-burner and his son, he bade, rather than advised, them to retire to rest.

"For myself, I cannot sleep," said he. "I have matters that it concerns me to meditate upon. I will watch the fire, as I used to do in the old time."

"And call the Devil out of the furnace to keep you company, I suppose," muttered Bartram, who had been making intimate acquaintance with the black bottle above mentioned. "But watch, if you like, and call as many devils as you like! For my part, I shall be all the better for a snooze. Come, Joe!"

As the boy followed his father into the hut, he looked back at the wayfarer, and the tears came into his eyes, for his tender spirit had an intuition of the bleak and terrible loneliness in which this man had enveloped himself.

When they had gone, Ethan Brand sat listening to the crackling of the kindled wood, and looking at the little spirits of fire that issued through the chinks of the door. These trifles, however, once so familiar, had but the slightest hold of his attention, while deep within his mind he was reviewing the gradual but marvellous change that had been wrought upon him by the search to which he had devoted himself. He remembered how the night dew had fallen upon him,—how the dark forest had whispered to him,—how the stars had gleamed upon him,—a simple and loving man, watching his fire in the years gone by, and ever musing as it burned. He remembered with what tenderness, with what love and sympathy for mankind, and what pity for human guilt and woe, he had first begun to contemplate those ideas which afterwards became the inspiration of his life; with what reverence he had then looked into the heart of man, viewing it as a temple originally divine, and, however desecrated, still to be held sacred by a brother; with what awful fear he had deprecated the success of his pursuit, and prayed that the Unpardonable Sin might never be revealed to him. Then ensued that vast intellectual development, which, in its progress, disturbed the counterpoise between his mind and heart. The Idea that possessed his life had operated as a means of education; it had gone on cultivating his powers to the highest point of which they were susceptible; it had raised him from the level of an unlettered laborer to stand on a star-lit eminence, whither the philosophers of the earth, laden with the lore of universities, might vainly strive to clamber after him. So much for the intellect! But where was the heart? That, indeed, had withered,—had contracted,—had hardened,—had perished! It had ceased to partake of the universal throb. He had lost his hold of the magnetic chain of humanity. He was no longer a brother-man, opening the chambers or the dungeons of our common nature by the key of holy sympathy, which gave him a right to share in all its secrets; he was now a cold observer, looking on mankind as the subject of his experiment, and, at length, converting man and woman to be his puppets, and pulling the wires that moved them to such degrees of crime as were demanded for his study.

Thus Ethan Brand became a fiend. He began to be so from the moment that his moral nature had ceased to keep the pace of improvement with his intellect. And now, as his highest effort and inevitable development,—as the bright and gorgeous flower, and rich, delicious fruit of his life's labor,—he had produced the Unpardonable Sin!

"What more have I to seek? what more to achieve?" said Ethan Brand to himself. "My task is done, and well done!"

Starting from the log with a certain alacrity in his gait and ascending the hillock of earth that was raised against the stone circumference of the lime-kiln, he thus reached the top of the structure. It was a space of perhaps ten feet across, from edge to edge, presenting a view of the upper surface of the immense mass of broken marble with which the kiln was heaped. All these innumerable blocks and fragments of marble were red-hot and vividly on fire, sending up great spouts of blue flame, which quivered aloft and danced madly, as within a magic circle, and sank and rose again, with continual and multitudinous activity. As the lonely man bent forward over this terrible body of fire, the blasting heat smote up against his person with a breath that, it might be supposed, would have scorched and shrivelled him up in a moment.

Ethan Brand stood erect, and raised his arms on high. The blue flames played upon his face, and imparted the wild and ghastly light which alone could have suited its expression; it was that of a fiend on the verge of plunging into his gulf of intensest torment.

"O Mother Earth," cried he, "who art no more my Mother, and into whose bosom this frame shall never be resolved! O mankind, whose brotherhood I have cast off, and trampled thy great heart beneath my feet! O stars of heaven, that shone on me of old, as if to light me onward and upward!—farewell all, and forever. Come, deadly element of Fire,—henceforth my familiar friend! Embrace me, as I do thee!"

That night the sound of a fearful peal of laughter rolled heavily through the sleep of the lime-burner and his little son; dim shapes of horror and anguish haunted their dreams, and seemed still present in the rude hovel, when they opened their eyes to the daylight.

"Up, boy, up!" cried the lime-burner, staring about him. "Thank Heaven, the night is gone, at last; and rather than pass such another, I would watch my lime-kiln, wide awake, for a twelvemonth. This Ethan Brand, with his humbug of an Unpardonable Sin, has done me no such mighty favor, in taking my place!"

He issued from the hut, followed by little Joe, who kept fast hold of his father's hand. The early sunshine was already pouring its gold upon the mountaintops, and though the valleys were still in shadow, they smiled cheerfully in the promise of the bright day that was hastening onward. The village, completely shut in by hills, which swelled away gently about it, looked as if it had rested peacefully in the hollow of the great hand of providence. Every dwelling was distinctly visible; the little spires of the two churches pointed upwards, and caught a fore-glimmering of brightness from the sun-gilt skies upon their gilded weathercocks. The tavern was astir, and the figure of the old, smoke-dried stage-agent, cigar in mouth, was seen beneath the stoop. Old Graylock was glorified with a golden cloud upon his head. Scattered likewise over the breasts of the surrounding mountains, there were heaps of hoary mist, in fantastic shapes, some of them far down into the valley, others high up towards the summits, and still others, of the same family of mist or cloud, hovering in the gold radiance of the upper atmosphere. Stepping from one to another of the clouds that rested on the hills, and thence to the loftier brotherhood that sailed in air, it seemed almost as if a mortal man might thus ascend into the heavenly regions. Earth was so mingled with sky that it was a day-dream to look at it.

To supply that charm of the familiar and homely, which Nature so readily adopts into a scene like this, the stage-coach was rattling down the mountain-road, and the driver sounded his horn, while Echo caught up the notes, and intertwined them into a rich and varied and elaborate harmony, of which the original performer could lay claim to little share. The great hills played a concert among themselves, each contributing a strain of airy sweetness.

Little Joe's face brightened at once.

"Dear father," cried he, skipping cheerily to and fro, "that strange man is gone, and the sky and the mountains all seem glad of it!"

"Yes," growled the lime-burner, with an oath, "but he had let the fire go down, and no thanks to him if five hundred bushels of lime are not spoiled. If I catch the fellow hereabouts again, I shall feel like tossing him into the furnace!"

With his long pole in his hand, he ascended to the top of the kiln. After a moment's pause, he called to his son.

"Come up here, Joe!" said he.

So little Joe ran up the hillock, and stood by his father's side. The marble was all burnt into perfect, snow-white lime. But on its surface, in the midst of the circle,—snow-white too, and thoroughly converted into lime,—lay a human skeleton, in the attitude of a person who, after long toil, lies down to long repose. Within the ribs—strange to say—was the shape of a human heart.

"Was the fellow's heart made of marble?" cried Bartram, in some perplexity at this phenomenon. "At any rate, it is burnt into what looks like special good lime, and, taking all the bones together, my kiln is half a bushel the richer for him."

So saying, the rude lime-burner lifted his pole, and, letting it fall upon the skeleton, the relics of Ethan Brand were crumbled into fragments.

FROM

THE AMERICAN AND ENGLISH NOTEBOOKS

◇

HAWTHORNE'S notebooks were a narrative of his life, a record of his friendships and his travels, and a collection of ideas for tales. A representative selection of entries offers many glimpses into a writer's workshop: we can see that Hawthorne's mind was continually playing with moral hypotheses—those nebulous themes of good and evil which, once they could be dramatized in the lives of men and women, would offer insights into man's place in the total moral universe. Hawthorne's portraits of his friends, Thoreau and Melville, are the most vivid that we have.

◇

[1835]

A SKETCH to be given of a modern reformer,—a type of the extreme doctrines on the subject of slaves, cold water, and other such topics. He goes about the streets haranguing most eloquently, and is on the point of making many converts, when his labors are suddenly interrupted by the appearance of the keeper of a madhouse, whence he has escaped. Much may be made of this idea.

A CHANGE from a gay young girl to an old

woman; the melancholy events, the effects of which have clustered around her character, and gradually imbued it with their influence, till she becomes a lover of sick-chambers, taking pleasure in receiving dying breaths and in laying out the dead; also having her mind full of funeral reminiscences, and possessing more acquaintances beneath the burial turf than above it.

A WELL-CONCERTED train of events to be thrown into confusion by some misplaced circumstance, unsuspected till the catastrophe, yet exerting its influence from beginning to end.

ON THE common, at dusk, after a salute from two field-pieces, the smoke lay long and heavily on the ground, without much spreading beyond the original space over which it had gushed from the guns. It was about the height of a man. The evening clear, but with an autumnal chill.

THE WORLD is so sad and solemn, that things meant in jest are liable, by an overpowering influence, to become dreadful earnest,—gayly dressed fantasies turning to ghostly and black-clad images of themselves.

A STORY, the hero of which is to be represented as naturally capable of deep and strong passion, and looking forward to the time when he shall feel passionate love, which is to be the great event of his existence. But it so chances that he never falls in love, and although he gives up the expectation of so doing, and marries calmly, yet it is somewhat sadly, with sentiments merely of esteem for his bride. The lady might be one who had loved him early in life, but whom then, in his expectation of passionate love, he had scorned.

THE SCENE of a story or sketch to be laid within the light of a street-lantern; the time, when the lamp is near going out; and the catastrophe to be simultaneous with the last flickering gleam.

THE PECULIAR weariness and depression of spirits which is felt after a day wasted in turning over a magazine or other light miscellany, different from the state of the mind after severe study; because there has been no excitement, no difficulties to be overcome, but the spirits have evaporated insensibly.

TO REPRESENT the process by which sober truth gradually strips off all the beautiful draperies with which imagination has enveloped a beloved object, till from an angel she turns out to be a merely ordinary woman. This to be done without caricature, perhaps with a quiet humor interfused, but the prevailing impression to be a sad one. The story might consist of the various alterations in the feelings of the absent lover, caused by successive events that display the true character of his mistress; and the catastrophe should take place at their meeting, when he finds himself equally disappointed in her person; or the whole spirit of the thing may here be reproduced.

TWO PERSONS might be bitter enemies through life, and mutually cause the ruin of one another, and of all that were dear to them. Finally, meeting at the funeral of a grandchild, the offspring of a son and daughter married without their consent,—and who, as well as the child, had been the victims of their hatred,—they might discover that the supposed ground of the quarrel was altogether a mistake, and then be wofully reconciled.

TWO PERSONS, by mutual agreement, to make their wills in each other's favor, then to wait impatiently for one another's death, and both to be informed of the desired event at the same time. Both, in most joyous sorrow, hasten to be present at the funeral, meet, and find themselves both hoaxed.

THE STORY of a man, cool and hard-hearted, and acknowledging no brotherhood with mankind. At his death they might try to dig him a grave, but, at a little space beneath the ground, strike upon a rock, as if the earth refused to receive the unnatural son into her bosom. Then they would put him into an old sepulchre, where the coffins and corpses were all turned to dust, and so he would be alone. Then the body would petrify; and he having died in some characteristic act and expression, he would seem, through endless ages of death, to repel society as in life, and no one would be buried in that tomb forever.

IN AN old house, a mysterious knocking might be heard on the wall, where had formerly been a doorway, now bricked up.

IT MIGHT be stated, as the closing circumstance of a tale, that the body of one of the characters had been petrified, and still existed in that state.

A YOUNG man to win the love of a girl, without any serious intentions, and to find that in that love, which might have been the greatest blessing of his life, he had conjured up a spirit of mischief which pursued him throughout his whole career,—and this without any revengeful purposes on the part of the deserted girl.

TWO LOVERS, or other persons, on the most private business, to appoint a meeting in what they supposed to be a place of the utmost solitude, and to find it thronged with people.

SOME treasure or other thing to be buried, and a tree planted directly over the spot, so as to embrace it with its roots.

A TREE, tall and venerable, to be said by tradition to have been the staff of some famous man, who happened to thrust it into the ground, where it took root.

A FELLOW without money, having a hundred and seventy miles to go, fastened a chain and padlock to his legs, and lay down to sleep in a field. He was apprehended, and carried gratis to a jail in the town whither he desired to go.

AN OLD volume in a large library,—every one to be afraid to unclasp and open it, because it was said to be a book of magic.

A GHOST seen by moonlight; when the moon was out, it would shine and melt through the airy substance of the ghost, as through a cloud.

TO MAKE one's own reflection in a mirror the subject of a story.

IN A DREAM to wander to some place where may be heard the complaints of all the miserable on earth.

SOME common quality or circumstance that should bring together people the most unlike in all other respects, and make a brotherhood and sisterhood of them,—the rich and the proud finding themselves in the same category with the mean and the despised.

A PERSON to consider himself as the prime mover of certain remarkable events, but to discover that his actions have not contributed in the least thereto. Another person to be the cause, without suspecting it.

A PERSON or family long desires some particular good. At last it comes in such profusion as to be the great pest of their lives.

A MAN, perhaps with a persuasion that he shall make his fortune by some singular means, and with an eager longing so to do, while digging or boring for water, to strike upon a salt-spring.

TO HAVE one event operate in several places,—as, for example, if a man's head were to be cut off in one town, men's heads to drop off in several towns.

FOLLOW out the fantasy of a man taking his life by instalments, instead of at one payment,—say ten years of life alternately with ten years of suspended animation.

SENTIMENTS in a foreign language, which merely convey the sentiment without retaining to the reader any graces of style or harmony of sound, have somewhat of the charm of thoughts in one's own mind that have not yet been put into words. No possible words that we might adapt to them could realize the unshaped beauty that they appear to possess. This is the reason that translations are never satisfactory,—and less so, I should think, to one who cannot than to one who can pronounce the language.

A PERSON to be writing a tale, and to find that it shapes itself against his intentions; that the characters act otherwise than he thought; that unforeseen events occur; and a catastrophe comes which he strives in vain to avert. It might shadow forth his own fate,—he having made himself one of the personages.

[*1836*]

IN THIS dismal chamber FAME was won. (Salem, Union Street.)

THE RACE of mankind to be swept away, leaving all their cities and works. Then another human pair to be placed in the world, with native intelligence like Adam and Eve, but knowing nothing of their predecessors or of their own nature and destiny. They, perhaps, to be described as working out this knowledge by their sympathy with what they saw, and by their own feelings.

CURIOUS to imagine what murmurings and discontent would be excited, if any of the great so-called calamities of human beings were to be abolished,—as, for instance, death.

TRIFLES to one are matters of life and death to another. As, for instance, a farmer desires a brisk breeze to winnow his grain; and mariners, to blow them out of the reach of pirates.

A RECLUSE, like myself, or a prisoner, to measure time by the progress of sunshine through his chamber.

WOULD it not be wiser for people to rejoice at all that they now sorrow for, and *vice versa?* To put on bridal garments at funerals, and mourning at weddings? For their friends to condole with them when they attained riches and honor, as only so much care added?

FAME! Some very humble persons in a town may be said to possess it,—as, the penny-post, the town-crier, the constable,—and they are known to everybody; while many richer, more intellectual, worthier persons are unknown by the majority of their fellow-citizens. Something analogous in the world at large.

NOBODY will use other people's experience, nor have any of his own till it is too late to use it.

A GIRL'S lover to be slain and buried in her flower-garden, and the earth levelled over him. That particular spot, which she happens to plant with some peculiar variety of flowers, produces them of admirable splendor, beauty, and perfume; and she delights, with an indescribable impulse, to wear them in her bosom, and scent her chamber with them. Thus the classic fantasy would be realized, of dead people transformed to flowers.

OUR BODY to be possessed by two different spirits; so that half of the visage shall express one mood, and the other half another.

[*1837*]

A PERSON to be in the possession of something as perfect as mortal man has a right to demand; he tries to make it better, and ruins it entirely.

A PERSON to spend all his life and splendid talents in trying to achieve something naturally impossible,—as to make a conquest over Nature.

[*1842*]

SOME MAN of powerful character to command a person, morally subjected to him, to perform some act. The commanding person to suddenly die; and, for all the rest of his life, the subjected one continues to perform that act.

TO TRACE out the influence of a frightful and disgraceful crime, in debasing and destroying a character naturally high and noble—the guilty person being alone conscious of the crime.

A MAN to swallow a small snake—and it to be a symbol of a cherished sin.

A PERSON with an ice-cold hand—his right hand; which people ever afterwards remember, when once they have grasped it.

A PHYSICIAN for the cure of moral diseases.

A MORAL philosopher to buy a slave, or otherwise get possession of a human being, and to use him for the sake of experiment, by trying the operation of a certain vice on him.

THE HUMAN Heart to be allegorized as a cavern; at the entrance there is sunshine, and flowers growing about it. You step within, but a short distance, and begin to find yourself surrounded with a terrible gloom, and monsters of divers kinds; it seems like Hell itself. You are bewildered, and wander long without hope. At last a light strikes upon you. You peep towards it, and find yourself in a region that seems, in some sort, to reproduce the flowers and sunny beauty of the entrance, but all perfect. These are the depths of the heart, or of a human nature, bright and peaceful; the gloom and terror may lie deep; but deeper still is the eternal beauty.

TO ALLEGORIZE life with a masquerade, and represent mankind generally as masquers. Here and there, a natural face may appear.

THE ADVANTAGES of a longer life than is allotted to mortals—the many things that might then be accomplished;—to which one life-time is inadequate, and for which the time spent is therefore lost; a successor being unable to take up the task when we drop it.

PEARL—the English of Margaret—a pretty name for a girl in a story.

A MAN seeks for something excellent, and seeks it in the wrong way, and in a wrong spirit, and finds something horrible—as for instance, he seeks for treasure, and finds a dead body—for the gold that somebody has hidden, and brings to light his accumulated sins.

THE SEARCH of an investigator for the Unpardonable Sin;—he at last finds it in his own heart and practice.

The Unpardonable Sin might consist in a want of love and reverence for the Human Soul; in consequence of which, the investigator pried into its dark depths, not with a hope or purpose of making it better, but from a cold philosophical curiosity. . . . Would not this, in other words, be the separation of the intellect from the heart?

The life of a woman, who, by the old colony law, was condemned always to wear the letter A, sewed on her garment, in token of her having committed adultery.

Mr. Thorow dined with us yesterday.[1] He is a singular character—a young man with much of wild original stuff still remaining in him; and so far as he is sophisticated, it is in a way and method of his own. He is as ugly as sin, long-nosed, queer-mouthed, and with uncouth and somewhat rustic, although courteous manners, corresponding very well with such an exterior. But his ugliness is of an honest and agreeable fashion, and becomes him much better than beauty. He was educated, I believe at Cambridge, and formerly kept school in this town; but for two or three years back, he has repudiated all regular modes of getting a living, and seems inclined to lead a sort of Indian life among civilized men—an Indian life, I mean, as respects the absence of any systematic effort for a livelihood. He has been for sometime an inmate of Mr. Emerson's family; and, in requital, he labors in the garden, and performs such other offices as may suit him—being entertained by Mr. Emerson for the sake of what true manhood there is in him. Mr. Thorow is a keen and delicate observer of nature—a genuine observer, which, I suspect, is almost as rare a character as even an original poet; and Nature, in return for his love, seems to adopt him as her special child, and shows him secrets which few others are allowed to witness. He is familiar with beast, fish, fowl, and reptile, and has strange stories to tell of his adventures, and friendly passages with these lower brethren of mortality. . . . With all this he has more than a tincture of literature—a deep and true taste for poetry, especially the elder poets. . . . On the whole I find him a healthy and wholesome man to know.

October 9th [1854]

My ancestor left England in 1635. I return in 1853. I sometimes feel as if I myself had been absent these two hundred and eighteen years—leaving England just emerging from the feudal system, and finding it on the verge of Republicanism. It brings the two far separated points of time very closely together, to view the matter thus.

December 28th [1854]

I think I have been happier, this Christmas, than ever before,—by our own fireside, and with my wife and children about me. More content to enjoy what I had; less anxious for anything beyond it, in this life. My early life was perhaps a good preparation for the declining half of life, it having been such a blank that any possible thereafter would compare favorably with it. For a long, long while, I have occasionally been visited with a singular dream; and I have an impression that I have dreamed it, even since I have been in England. It is, that I am still at college—or, sometimes, even at school—and there is a sense that I have been there unconscionably long, and have quite failed to make such progress in life as my contemporaries have; and I seem to meet some of them with a feeling of shame and depression that broods over me, when I think of it, even at this moment. This dream, recurring all through these twenty or thirty years, must be one of the effects of that heavy seclusion in which I shut myself up, for twelve years, after leaving college, when everybody moved onward and left me behind. How strange that it should come now, when I may call myself famous, and prosperous!—when I am happy, too!—still that same dream of life hopelessly a failure!

September 14th [1855]

Speaking of Thackeray, I cannot but wonder at his coolness in respect to his own pathos, and compare it with my emotions when I read the last scene of the Scarlet Letter to my wife, just after writing it—tried to read it, rather, for my voice swelled and heaved, as if I were tossed up and down on an ocean, as it subsided after a storm. But I was in a very nervous state, then, having gone through a great diversity and severity of emotion, for many months past. I think I have never overcome my own adamant in any other instance.

November 20th [1856]

A week ago last Monday, Herman Melville came to see me at the Consulate, looking much as he used to do (a little paler, and perhaps a little

NOTEBOOKS. 1. **Mr. Thorow . . . yesterday:** Hawthorne's phonetic spelling of Thoreau suggests that the name was pronounced with the accent on the first syllable. The occasion was August 30, 1842.

sadder), in a rough outside coat, and with his characteristic gravity and reserve of manner. He had crossed from New York to Glasgow in a screw steamer, about a fortnight before, and had since been seeing Edinburgh and other interesting places. I felt rather awkward at first; because this is the first time I have met him since my ineffectual attempt to get him a consular appointment from General Pierce. However, I failed only from real lack of power to serve him; so there was no reason to be ashamed, and we soon found ourselves on pretty much our former terms of sociability and confidence. Melville has not been well, of late; he has been affected with neuralgic complaints in his head and limbs, and no doubt has suffered from too constant literary occupation, pursued without much success, latterly; and his writings, for a long while past, have indicated a morbid state of mind. So he left his place at Pittsfield, and has established his wife and family, I believe, with his father-in-law in Boston, and is thus far on his way to Constantinople. I do not wonder that he found it necessary to take an airing through the world, after so many years of toilsome pen-labor and domestic life, following upon so wild and adventurous a youth as his was. I invited him to come and stay with us at Southport, as long as he might remain in this vicinity; and accordingly, he did come, the next day, taking with him, by way of baggage, the least little bit of a bundle, which, he told me, contained a night-shirt and a tooth-brush. He is a person of very gentlemanly instincts in every respect, save that he is a little heterodox in the matter of clean linen.

He stayed with us from Tuesday till Thursday; and, on the intervening day, we took a pretty long walk together, and sat down in a hollow among the sand hills (sheltering ourselves from the high, cool wind) and smoked a cigar. Melville, as he always does, began to reason of Providence and futurity, and of everything that lies beyond human ken, and informed me that he had "pretty much made up his mind to be annihilated"; but still he does not seem to rest in that anticipation; and, I think, will never rest until he gets hold of a definite belief. It is strange how he persists—and has persisted ever since I knew him, and probably long before—in wandering to-and-fro over these deserts, as dismal and monotonous as the sand hills amid which we were sitting. He can neither believe, nor be comfortable in his unbelief; and he is too honest and courageous not to try to do one or the other. If he were a religious man, he would be one of the most truly religious and reverential; he has a very high and noble nature, and better worth immortality than most of us.

THE OLD MANSE

The Author Makes the Reader Acquainted with His Abode

◇

THIS introductory essay to *Mosses from an Old Manse* (1846) may have been written as a record of Hawthorne's first years of marriage to Sophia Peabody, from 1842 to 1846. It was also a series of comments on Hawthorne's contemporaries who formed the Concord group and who, particularly under the guidance of Emerson, were churning with the ideas which Hawthorne found either amusing or slightly absurd. The essay presents the problem of a writer in a situation which was inimical, if not dangerous: the very charm of the Manse, the slow-moving river nearby, the inducements to absent one's self from work and linger among the piles of musty books in the attic or with the squashes in the garden—these were, as they so often became for Hawthorne, the obstacles which seemed to block one's vision but which, in the end, were the means whereby the daily routine was made into the stuff of Romance. If Hawthorne was an indifferent keeper of a daily journal, he was a splendid memorialist of his own private life and of that other life which belongs to the writer alone.

◇

BETWEEN two tall gate-posts of rough-hewn stone (the gate itself having fallen from its hinges at some unknown epoch) we beheld the gray front of the old parsonage terminating the vista of an avenue of black ash-trees. It was now a twelvemonth since the funeral procession of the venerable clergyman,[1] its last inhabitant, had turned from that gateway towards the village burying-ground. The wheel-track leading to the door, as well as the whole breadth of the avenue, was almost overgrown with grass, affording dainty mouthfuls to two or three vagrant cows and an old white horse who had his own living to pick up along the roadside. The glimmering shadows that lay half asleep between the door of the house and the public highway were a kind of spiritual medium, seen through which the edifice had not quite the aspect of belonging to the material world. Certainly it had little in common with those ordinary abodes which stand so imminent upon the road that every passer-by can thrust his head, as it were,

THE OLD MANSE. 1. **venerable clergyman:** the Rev. Ezra Ripley, who planted the apple trees and who died in 1841.

into the domestic circle. From these quiet windows the figures of passing travelers looked too remote and dim to disturb the sense of privacy. In its near retirement and accessible seclusion it was the very spot for the residence of a clergyman, —a man not estranged from human life, yet enveloped in the midst of it with a veil woven of intermingled gloom and brightness. It was worthy to have been one of the time-honored parsonages of England in which, through many generations, a succession of holy occupants pass from youth to age, and bequeath each an inheritance of sanctity to pervade the house and hover over it as with an atmosphere.

Nor, in truth, had the Old Manse ever been profaned by a lay occupant until that memorable summer afternoon when I entered it as my home. A priest [2] had built it; a priest had succeeded to it; other priestly men from time to time had dwelt in it; and children born in its chambers had grown up to assume the priestly character. It was awful to reflect how many sermons must have been written there. The latest inhabitant alone—he by whose translation to paradise the dwelling was left vacant—had penned nearly three thousand discourses, besides the better, if not the greater, number that gushed living from his lips. How often, no doubt, had he paced to and fro along the avenue, attuning his meditations to the sighs and gentle murmurs and deep and solemn peals of the wind among the lofty tops of the trees! In that variety of natural utterances he could find something accordant with every passage of his sermon, were it of tenderness or reverential fear. The boughs over my head seemed shadowy with solemn thoughts as well as with rustling leaves. I took shame to myself for having been so long a writer of idle stories, and ventured to hope that wisdom would descend upon me with the falling leaves of the avenue, and that I should light upon an intellectual treasure in the Old Manse well worth those hoards of long-hidden gold which people seek for in moss-grown houses. Profound treatises of morality; a layman's unprofessional, and therefore unprejudiced, views of religion; histories (such as Bancroft [3] might have written had he taken up his abode here as he once proposed) bright with picture, gleaming over a depth of philosophic thought, —these were the works that might fitly have flowed from such a retirement. In the humblest event, I resolved at least to achieve a novel that should evolve some deep lesson, and should possess physical substance enough to stand alone.

In furtherance of my design, and as if to leave me no pretext for not fulfilling it, there was in the rear of the house the most delightful little nook of a study that ever afforded its snug seclusion to a scholar. It was here that Emerson wrote *Nature;* for he was then an inhabitant of the Manse, and used to watch the Assyrian dawn and Paphian sunset [4] and moonrise from the summit of our eastern hill. When I first saw the room its walls were blackened with the smoke of unnumbered years, and made still blacker by the grim prints of Puritan ministers that hung around. These worthies looked strangely like bad angels, or at least like men who had wrestled so continually and so sternly with the devil that somewhat of his sooty fierceness had been imparted to their own visages. They had all vanished now; a cheerful coat of paint and golden-tinted paper-hangings lighted up the small apartment; while the shadow of a willow-tree that swept against the overhanging eaves attempered the cheery western sunshine. In place of the grim prints there was the sweet and lovely head of one of Raphael's Madonnas and two pleasant little pictures of the Lake of Como. The only other decorations were a purple vase of flowers, always fresh, and a bronze one containing graceful ferns. My books (few, and by no means choice; for they were chiefly such waifs as chance had thrown in my way) stood in order about the room, seldom to be disturbed.

The study had three windows, set with little, old-fashioned panes of glass, each with a crack across it. The two on the western side looked, or rather peeped, between the willow branches down into the orchard, with glimpses of the river through the trees. The third, facing northward, commanded a broader view of the river at a spot where its hitherto obscure waters gleam forth into the light of history. It was at this window that the clergyman who then dwelt in the Manse stood watching the outbreak of a long and deadly struggle between two nations; he saw the irregular array of his parishioners on the farther side of the river and the glittering line of the British on the hither bank. He awaited in an agony of suspense the rattle of the musketry. It came, and there needed but a gentle wind to sweep the battle smoke around this quiet house.

Perhaps the reader, whom I cannot help considering as my guest in the Old Manse and en-

2. **A priest:** Emerson's grandfather, the Rev. William Emerson, who witnessed the battle of Concord Bridge and who had built the house in 1765. 3. **Bancroft:** George Bancroft (1800–91), author of the *History of the United States* (1834–75). He secured for Hawthorne the appointment, in 1839, to the position in the Boston customhouse.

4. **Assyrian . . . sunset:** an allusion to the passage in Emerson's *Nature* (see p. 492).

titled to all courtesy in the way of sight-showing, —perhaps he will choose to take a nearer view of the memorable spot. We stand now on the river's brink. It may well be called the Concord, the river of peace and quietness; for it is certainly the most unexcitable and sluggish stream that ever loitered imperceptibly towards its eternity—the sea. Positively I had lived three weeks beside it before it grew quite clear to my perception which way the current flowed. It never has a vivacious aspect except when a northwestern breeze is vexing its surface on a sunshiny day. From the incurable indolence of its nature, the stream is happily incapable of becoming the slave of human ingenuity, as is the fate of so many a wild, free mountain torrent. While all things else are compelled to subserve some useful purpose, it idles its sluggish life away in lazy liberty, without turning a solitary spindle or affording even water power enough to grind the corn that grows upon its banks. The torpor of its movement allows it nowhere a bright, pebbly shore, nor so much as a narrow strip of glistening sand, in any part of its course. It slumbers between broad prairies, kissing the long meadow grass, and bathes the overhanging boughs of elder bushes and willows, or the roots of elms and ash trees and clumps of maples. Flags and rushes grow along its plashy shore; the yellow water-lily spreads its broad, flat leaves on the margin; and the fragrant white pond-lily abounds, generally selecting a position just so far from the river's brink that it cannot be grasped save at the hazard of plunging in.

It is a marvel whence this perfect flower derives its loveliness and perfume, springing as it does from the black mud over which the river sleeps, and where lurk the slimy eel, and speckled frog, and the mud turtle, whom continual washing cannot cleanse. It is the very same black mud out of which the yellow lily sucks its obscene life and noisome odor. Thus we see too in the world, that some persons assimilate only what is ugly and evil from the same moral circumstances which supply good and beautiful results—the fragrance of celestial flowers—to the daily life of others.

The reader must not, from any testimony of mine, contract a dislike towards our slumberous stream. In the light of a calm and golden sunset it becomes lovely beyond expression; the more lovely for the quietude that so well accords with the hour, when even the wind, after blustering all day long, usually hushes itself to rest. Each tree and rock, and every blade of grass, is distinctly imaged, and, however unsightly in reality, assumes ideal beauty in the reflection. The minutest things of earth and the broad aspect of the firmament are pictured equally without effort and with the same felicity of success. All the sky glows downward at our feet; the rich clouds float through the unruffled bosom of the stream like heavenly thoughts through a peaceful heart. We will not, then, malign our river as gross and impure while it can glorify itself with so adequate a picture of the heaven that broods above it; or, if we remember its tawny hue and the muddiness of its bed, let it be a symbol that the earthliest human soul has an infinite spiritual capacity and may contain the better world within its depths. But, indeed, the same lesson might be drawn out of any mud puddle in the streets of a city; and, being taught us everywhere, it must be true.

Come, we have pursued a somewhat devious track in our walk to the battle-ground. Here we are, at the point where the river was crossed by the old bridge, the possession of which was the immediate object of the contest. On the hither side grow two or three elms, throwing a wide circumference of shade, but which must have been planted at some period within the three-score years and ten that have passed since the battle day. On the farther shore, overhung by a clump of elder bushes, we discern the stone abutment of the bridge. Looking down into the river, I once discovered some heavy fragments of the timbers, all green with half a century's growth of water-moss; for during that length of time the tramp of horses and human footsteps have ceased along this ancient highway. The stream has here about the breadth of twenty strokes of a swimmer's arm,—a space not too wide when the bullets were whistling across. Old people who dwell hereabouts will point out the very spots on the western bank where our countrymen fell down and died; and on this side of the river an obelisk of granite has grown up from the soil that was fertilized with British blood. The monument, not more than twenty feet in height, is such as it befitted the inhabitants of a village to erect in illustration of a matter of local interest rather than what was suitable to commemorate an epoch of national history. Still, by the fathers of the village this famous deed was done; and their descendants might rightfully claim the privilege of building a memorial.

A humbler token of the fight, yet a more interesting one than the granite obelisk, may be seen close under the stone-wall which separates the battle-ground from the precincts of the parsonage. It is the grave—marked by a small, moss-grown fragment of stone at the head and another at the foot—the grave of two British soldiers who were slain in the skirmish, and have ever since slept peacefully where Zechariah Brown and Thomas

Davis buried them. Soon was their warfare ended; a weary night march from Boston, a rattling volley of musketry across the river, and then these many years of rest. In the long procession of slain invaders who passed into eternity from the battle-fields of the revolution, these two nameless soldiers led the way.

Lowell, the poet, as we were once standing over this grave, told me a tradition in reference to one of the inhabitants below. The story has something deeply impressive, though its circumstances cannot altogether be reconciled with probability. A youth in the service of the clergymen happened to be chopping wood, that April morning, at the back door of the Manse, and when the noise of battle rang from side to side of the bridge he hastened across the intervening field to see what might be going forward. It is rather strange, by the way, that this lad should have been so diligently at work when the whole population of town and country were startled out of their customary business by the advance of the British troops. Be that as it might, the tradition says that the lad now left his task and hurried to the battle-field with the axe still in his hand. The British had by this time retreated, the Americans were in pursuit; and the late scene of strife was thus deserted by both parties. Two soldiers lay on the ground—one was a corpse; but, as the young New Englander drew nigh, the other Briton raised himself painfully upon his hands and knees and gave a ghastly stare into his face. The boy,—it must have been a nervous impulse, without purpose, without thought, and betokening a sensitive and impressible nature rather than a hardened one,—the boy uplifted his axe and dealt the wounded soldier a fierce and fatal blow upon the head.

I could wish that the grave might be opened; for I would fain know whether either of the skeleton soldiers has the mark of an axe in his skull. The story comes home to me like truth. Oftentimes, as an intellectual and moral exercise, I have sought to follow that poor youth through his subsequent career, and observe how his soul was tortured by the blood stain, contracted as it had been before the long custom of war had robbed human life of its sanctity, and while it still seemed murderous to slay a brother man. This one circumstance has borne more fruit for me than all that history tells us of the fight. . . .

. . . The Old Manse! We had almost forgotten it, but will return thither through the orchard. This was set out by the last clergyman, in the decline of his life, when the neighbors laughed at the hoary-headed man for planting trees from which he could have no prospect of gathering fruit. Even had that been the case, there was only so much the better motive for planting them, in the pure and unselfish hope of benefiting his successors,—an end so seldom achieved by more ambitious efforts. But the old minister, before reaching his patriarchal age of ninety, ate the apples from this orchard during many years, and added silver and gold to his annual stipend by disposing of the superfluity. It is pleasant to think of him walking among the trees in the quiet afternoons of early autumn and picking up here and there a windfall, while he observes how heavily the branches are weighed down, and computes the number of empty flour barrels that will be filled by their burden. He loved each tree, doubtless, as if it had been his own child. An orchard has a relation to mankind, and readily connects itself with matters of the heart. The trees possess a domestic character; they have lost the wild nature of their forest kindred, and have grown humanized by receiving the care of man as well as by contributing to his wants. There is so much individuality of character, too, among apple trees that it gives them an additional claim to be the objects of human interest. One is harsh and crabbed in its manifestations; another gives us fruit as mild as charity. One is churlish and illiberal, evidently grudging the few apples that it bears; another exhausts itself in free-hearted benevolence. The variety of grotesque shapes into which apple trees contort themselves has its effect on those who get acquainted with them: they stretch out their crooked branches, and take such hold of the imagination that we remember them as humorists and odd-fellows. And what is more melancholy than the old apple trees that linger about the spot where once stood a homestead, but where there is now only a ruined chimney rising out of a grassy and weed-grown cellar? They offer their fruit to every wayfarer,—apples that are bitter sweet with the moral of Time's vicissitude.

I have met with no other such pleasant trouble in the world as that of finding myself, with only the two or three mouths which it was my privilege to feed, the sole inheritor of the old clergyman's wealth of fruits. Throughout the summer there were cherries and currants; and then came autumn, with his immense burden of apples, dropping them continually from his overladen shoulders as he trudged along. In the stillest afternoon, if I listened, the thump of a great apple was audible, falling without a breath of wind, from the mere necessity of perfect ripeness. And, besides, there were pear trees, that flung down bushels upon bushels of heavy pears; and peach trees, which, in a good year, tormented me with peaches, neither to be eaten nor kept, nor, without labor and perplexity, to be given away. The idea of an infinite generosity and exhaustless bounty on the part of our Mother Nature was well worth obtaining through such cares as these. That feeling can be enjoyed in perfection only by the natives of summer islands, where the bread-fruit, the cocoa, the palm, and the orange grow spontaneously and hold forth the ever-ready meal; but likewise almost as well by a man long habituated to city life, who plunges into such a solitude as that of the Old Manse, where he plucks the fruit of trees that he did not plant, and which therefore, to my heterodox taste, bear the closest resemblance to those that grew in Eden. It has been an apothegm these five thousand years, that toil sweetens the bread it earns. For my part, (speaking from hard experience, acquired while belaboring the rugged furrows of Brook Farm), I relish best the free gifts of Providence.

Not that it can be disputed that the light toil requisite to cultivate a moderately-sized garden imparts such zest to kitchen vegetables as is never found in those of the market gardener. Childless men, if they would know something of the bliss of paternity, should plant a seed,—be it squash, bean, Indian corn, or perhaps a mere flower or worthless weed,—should plant it with their own hands, and nurse it from infancy to maturity altogether by their own care. If there be not too many of them, each individual plant becomes an object of separate interest. My garden, that skirted the avenue of the Manse, was of precisely the right extent. An hour or two of morning labor was all that it required. But I used to visit and revisit it a dozen times a day, and stand in deep contemplation over my vegetable progeny with a love that nobody could share or conceive of, who had never taken part in the process of creation. It was one of the most bewitching sights in the world to observe a hill of beans thrusting aside the soil, or a row of early peas just peeping forth sufficiently to trace a line of delicate green. Later in the season the humming-birds were attracted by the blossoms of a peculiar variety of bean; and they were a joy to me, those little spiritual visitants, for deigning to sip airy food out of my nectar cups. Multitudes of bees used to bury themselves in the yellow blossoms of the summer squashes. This, too, was a deep satisfaction; although, when they had laden themselves with sweets, they flew away to some unknown hive, which would give back nothing in requital of what my garden had contributed. But I was glad thus to fling a benefaction upon the passing breeze with the certainty that somebody must profit by it, and that there would be a little more honey in the world to allay the sourness and bitterness which mankind is always complaining of. Yes, indeed; my life was the sweeter for that honey.

Speaking of summer squashes, I must say a word of their beautiful and varied forms. They presented an endless diversity of urns and vases, shallow or deep, scalloped or plain, moulded in patterns which a sculptor would do well to copy, since Art has never invented anything more graceful. A hundred squashes in the garden were worthy, in my eyes at least, of being rendered indestructible in marble. If ever Providence (but I know it never will) should assign me a superfluity of gold, part of it shall be expended for a service of plate, or most delicate porcelain, to be wrought into the shapes of summer squashes gathered from vines which I will plant with my own hands. As dishes for containing vegetables they would be peculiarly appropriate.

But not merely the squeamish love of the beautiful was gratified by my toil in the kitchen garden. There was a hearty enjoyment, likewise, in observing the growth of the crook-necked winter squashes, from the first little bulb, with the withered blossom adhering to it, until they lay strewn upon the soil, big, round fellows, hiding their heads beneath the leaves, but turning up their great yellow rotundities to the noontide sun. Gazing at them, I felt that by my agency something worth living for had been done. A new substance was born into the world. They were real and tangible existences, which the mind could seize hold of and rejoice in. A cabbage, too,—especially the early Dutch cabbage, which swells to a monstrous circumference, until its ambitious heart often bursts asunder,—is a matter to be proud of when we can claim a share with the earth and sky in producing it. But, after all, the hugest pleasure is reserved until these vegetable children of ours are smoking on the table, and we, like Saturn, make a meal of them.

What with the river, the battle-field, the orchard and the garden, the reader begins to despair of finding his way back into the Old Manse. But in agreeable weather it is the truest hospitality to keep him out-of-doors. I never grew quite acquainted with my habitation till a long spell of sulky rain had confined me beneath its roof. There could not be a more sombre aspect of external Nature than as then seen from the windows of my study. The great willow tree had caught and retained among its leaves a whole cataract of water, to be shaken down at intervals by the frequent gusts of wind. All day long, and for a week together, the rain was drip-drip-dripping and splash-splash-

splashing from the eaves, and bubbling and foaming into the tubs beneath the spouts. The old, unpainted shingles of the house and out-buildings were black with moisture; and the mosses of ancient growth upon the walls looked green and fresh, as if they were the newest things and afterthought of Time. The usually mirrored surface of the river was blurred by an infinity of raindrops; the whole landscape had a completely water-soaked appearance, conveying the impression that the earth was wet through like a sponge; while the summit of a wooded hill, about a mile distant, was enveloped in a dense mist, where the demon of the tempest seemed to have his abiding-place and to be plotting still direr inclemencies.

Nature has no kindness, no hospitality, during a rain. In the fiercest heat of sunny days she retains a secret mercy, and welcomes the wayfarer to shady nooks of the woods whither the sun cannot penetrate; but she provides no shelter against her storms. It makes us shiver to think of those deep, umbrageous recesses, those overshadowing banks, where we found such enjoyment during the sultry afternoons. Not a twig of foliage there but would dash a little shower into our faces. Looking reproachfully towards the impenetrable sky,—if sky there be above that dismal uniformity of cloud,—we are apt to murmur against the whole system of the universe, since it involves the extinction of so many summer days in so short a life by the hissing and spluttering rain. In such spells of weather—and it is to be supposed such weather came—Eve's bower in paradise must have been but a cheerless and aguish kind of shelter, nowise comparable to the old parsonage, which had resources of its own to beguile the week's imprisonment. The idea of sleeping on a couch of wet roses!

Happy the man who in a rainy day can betake himself to a huge garret, stored, like that of the Manse, with lumber that each generation has left behind it from a period before the revolution. Our garret was an arched hall, dimly illuminated through small and dusty windows; it was but a twilight at the best; and there were nooks, or rather caverns, of deep obscurity, the secrets of which I never learned, being too reverent of their dust and cobwebs. The beams and rafters, roughly hewn and with strips of bark still on them, and the rude masonry of the chimneys, made the garret look wild and uncivilized,—an aspect unlike what was seen elsewhere in the quiet and decorous old house. But on one side there was a little white-washed apartment which bore the traditionary title of the Saint's Chamber, because holy men in their youth had slept and studied and prayed there. With its elevated retirement, its one window, its small fireplace, and its closet, convenient for an oratory, it was the very spot where a young man might inspire himself with solemn enthusiasm and cherish saintly dreams. The occupants, at various epochs, had left brief records and ejaculations inscribed upon the walls. There, too, hung a tattered and shrivelled roll of canvas, which on inspection proved to be the forcibly wrought picture of a clergyman, in wig, band, and gown, holding a Bible in his hand. As I turned his face towards the light he eyed me with an air of authority such as men of his profession seldom assume in our days. The original had been pastor of the parish more than a century ago, a friend of Whitefield,[5] and almost his equal in fervid eloquence. I bowed before the effigy of the dignified divine, and felt as if I had now met face to face with the ghost by whom, as there was reason to apprehend, the Manse was haunted.

Houses of any antiquity in New England are so invariably possessed with spirits that the matter seems hardly worth alluding to. Our ghost used to heave deep sighs in a particular corner of the parlor, and sometimes rustled paper, as if he were turning over a sermon in the long upper entry,—where nevertheless he was invisible in spite of the bright moonshine that fell through the eastern window. Not improbably he wished me to edit and publish a selection from a chest full of manuscript discourses that stood in the garret. Once, while Hilliard [6] and other friends sat talking with us in the twilight, there came a rustling noise as of a minister's silk gown, sweeping through the very midst of the company, so closely as almost to brush against the chairs. Still there was nothing visible. A yet stranger business was that of a ghostly servant maid, who used to be heard in the kitchen at deepest midnight, grinding coffee, cooking, ironing,—performing, in short, all kinds of domestic labor,—although no traces of anything accomplished could be detected the next morning. Some neglected duty of her servitude—some ill-starched ministerial band—disturbed the poor damsel in her grave and kept her at work without any wages.

But to return from this digression. A part of my predecessor's library was stored in the garret,—no unfit receptacle indeed for such dreary trash as comprised the greater number of volumes. The

5. original . . . Whitefield: George Whitefield (1714–70), the English evangelist and associate of John Wesley, twice preached at Concord at the invitation of the Rev. Daniel Bliss, an ancestor of Emerson and the "original" referred to. **6. Hilliard:** George Hilliard (1808–79), a Boston lawyer, minor author, and friend of Hawthorne.

old books would have been worth nothing at an auction. In this venerable garret, however, they possessed an interest, quite apart from their literary value, as heirlooms, many of which had been transmitted down through a series of consecrated hands from the days of the mighty Puritan divines. Autographs of famous names were to be seen in faded ink on some of their flyleaves; and there were marginal observations or interpolated pages closely covered with manuscript in illegible shorthand, perhaps concealing matter of profound truth and wisdom. The world will never be the better for it. A few of the books were Latin folios, written by Catholic authors; others demolished Papistry, as with a sledge-hammer, in plain English. A dissertation on the book of Job—which only Job himself could have had patience to read—filled at least a score of small, thickset quartos, at the rate of two or three volumes to a chapter. Then there was a vast folio body of divinity—too corpulent a body, it might be feared, to comprehend the spiritual element of religion. Volumes of this form dated back two-hundred years or more, and were generally bound in black leather, exhibiting precisely such an appearance as we should attribute to books of enchantment. Others equally antique were of a size proper to be carried in the large waistcoat pockets of old times,—diminutive, but as black as their bulkier brethren, and abundantly interfused with Greek and Latin quotations. These little old volumes impressed me as if they had been intended for very large ones, but had been unfortunately blighted at an early stage of their growth.

The rain pattered upon the roof and the sky gloomed through the dusty garret windows, while I burrowed among these venerable books in search of any living thought which should burn like a coal of fire, or glow like an inextinguishable gem, beneath the dead trumpery that had long hidden it. But I found no such treasure; all was dead alike; and I could not but muse deeply and wonderingly upon the humiliating fact that the works of man's intellect decay like those of his hands. Thought grows mouldy. What was good and nourishing food for the spirits of one generation affords no sustenance for the next. Books of religion, however, cannot be considered a fair test of the enduring and vivacious properties of human thought, because such books so seldom really touch upon their ostensible subject, and have, therefore, so little business to be written at all. So long as an unlettered soul can attain to saving grace, there would seem to be no deadly error in holding theological libraries to be accumulations of, for the most part, stupendous impertinence.

Many of the books had accrued in the latter years of the last clergyman's lifetime. These threatened to be of even less interest than the elder works, a century hence, to any curious inquirer who should then rummage them as I was doing now. Volumes of the *Liberal Preacher* and *Christian Examiner,*[7] occasional sermons, controversial pamphlets, tracts, and other productions of a like fugitive nature took the place of the thick and heavy volumes of past time. In a physical point of view there was much the same difference as between a feather and a lump of lead; but, intellectually regarded, the specific gravity of old and new was about upon a par. Both also were alike frigid. The elder books, nevertheless, seemed to have been earnestly written, and might be conceived to have possessed warmth at some former period; although, with the lapse of time, the heated masses had cooled down even to the freezing point. The frigidity of the modern productions, on the other hand, was characteristic and inherent, and evidently had little to do with the writer's qualities of mind and heart. In fine, of this whole dusty heap of literature I tossed aside all the sacred part, and felt myself none the less a Christian for eschewing it. There appeared no hope of either mounting to the better world on a Gothic staircase of ancient folios or of flying thither on the wings of a modern tract.

Nothing, strange to say, retained any sap except what had been written for the passing day and year without the remotest pretension or idea of permanence. There were a few old newspapers, and still older almanacs, which reproduced to my mental eye the epochs when they had issued from the press with a distinctness that was altogether unaccountable. It was as if I had found bits of magic looking-glass among the books, with the images of a vanished century in them. I turned my eyes towards the tattered picture above mentioned, and asked of the austere divine wherefore it was that he and his brethren, after the most painful rummaging and groping into their minds, had been able to produce nothing half so real as these newspaper scribblers and almanac makers had thrown off in the effervescence of a moment. The portrait responded not; so I sought an answer for myself. It is the age itself that writes newspapers and almanacs, which, therefore, have a distinct purpose and meaning at the time, and a kind of intelligible truth for all times; whereas most other works—being written by men who, in the very act,

7. *Liberal Preacher . . . Examiner:* the *Liberal Preacher*, a monthly magazine of sermons, published 1827–30 and 1831–36; the *Christian Examiner*, a theological review designed for clergymen, published 1824–69.

set themselves apart from their age—are likely to possess little significance when new, and none at all when old. Genius, indeed, melts many ages into one, and thus effects something permanent, yet still with a similarity of office to that of the more ephemeral writer. A work of genius is but the newspaper of a century, or perchance of a hundred centuries.

Lightly as I have spoken of these old books, there yet lingers with me a superstitious reverence for literature of all kinds. A bound volume has a charm in my eyes similar to what scraps of manuscript possess for the good Mussulman. He imagines that those wind-wafted records are perhaps hallowed by some sacred verse; and I, that every new book or antique one may contain the 'open sesame,'—the spell to disclose treasures hidden in some unsuspected cave of Truth. Thus it was not without sadness that I turned away from the library of the Old Manse.

Blessed was the sunshine when it came again at the close of another stormy day, beaming from the edge of the western horizon; while the massive firmament of clouds threw down all the gloom it could, but served only to kindle the golden light into a more brilliant glow by the strongly contrasted shadows. Heaven smiled at the earth, so long unseen, from beneath its heavy eyelid. Tomorrow for the hill-tops and the wood-paths.

Or it might be that Ellery Channing [8] came up the avenue to join me in a fishing excursion on the river. Strange and happy times were those when we cast aside all irksome forms and strait-laced habitudes, and delivered ourselves up to the free air, to live like the Indians or any less conventional race during one bright semicircle of the sun. Rowing our boat against the current, between wide meadows, we turned aside into the Assabeth.[9] A more lovely stream than this, for a mile above its junction with the Concord, has never flowed on earth,—nowhere, indeed, except to lave the interior regions of a poet's imagination. It is sheltered from the breeze by woods and a hillside; so that elsewhere there might be a hurricane, and here scarcely a ripple across the shaded water. The current lingers along so gently that the mere force of the boatman's will seems sufficient to propel his craft against it. It comes flowing softly through the midmost privacy and deepest heart of a wood which whispers it to be quiet; while the stream whispers back again from its sedgy borders, as if river and wood were hushing one another to sleep. Yes; the river sleeps along its course and dreams of the sky and of the clustering foliage, amid which fall showers of broken sunlight, imparting specks of vivid cheerfulness, in contrast with the quiet depth of the prevailing tint. Of all this scene, the slumbering river has a dream picture in its bosom. Which, after all, was the most real—the picture, or the original?—the objects palpable to our grosser senses, or their apotheosis in the stream beneath? Surely the disembodied images stand in closer relation to the soul. But both the original and the reflection had here an ideal charm; and, had it been a thought more wild, I could have fancied that this river had strayed forth out of the rich scenery of my companion's inner world; only the vegetation along its banks should then have had an Oriental character.[10]

Gentle and unobtrusive as the river is, yet the tranquil woods seem hardly satisfied to allow it passage. The trees are rooted on the very verge of the water, and dip their pendent branches into it. At one spot there is a lofty bank, on the slope of which grow some hemlocks, declining across the stream with outstretched arms, as if resolute to take the plunge. In other places the banks are almost on a level with the water; so that the quiet congregation of trees set their feet in the flood, and are fringed with foliage down to the surface. Cardinal flowers kindle their spiral flames and illuminate the dark nooks among the shrubbery. The pond-lily grows abundantly along the margin—that delicious flower, which, as Thoreau tells me, opens its virgin bosom to the first sunlight and perfects its being through the magic of that genial kiss. He has beheld beds of them unfolding in due succession as the sunrise stole gradually from flower to flower—a sight not to be hoped for unless when a poet adjusts his inward eye to a proper focus with the outward organ. Grape-vines here and there twine themselves around shrub and tree and hang their clusters over the water within reach of the boatman's hand. Oftentimes they unite two trees of alien race in an inextricable twine, marrying the hemlock and the maple against their will, and enriching them with a purple offspring of which neither is the parent. One of these ambitious parasites has climbed into the upper branches of a tall, white pine, and is still ascending from bough to bough, unsatisfied till it shall crown the tree's airy summit with a wreath of its broad foliage and a cluster of its grapes.

The winding course of the stream continually shut out the scene behind us, and revealed as calm

8. **Ellery Channing:** William Ellery Channing, nephew of the distinguished Unitarian clergyman, friend of Thoreau, and one of the Transcendentalist poets of Concord. 9. **Assabeth:** the Assabeth River joins the Concord River at Concord.

10. **Oriental character:** the Concord Transcendentalists were reading the recently translated books of Oriental philosophy.

and lovely a one before. We glided from depth to depth, and breathed new seclusion at every turn. The shy kingfisher flew from the withered branch close at hand to another at a distance, uttering a shrill cry of anger or alarm. Ducks that had been floating there since the preceding eve were startled at our approach, and skimmed along the glassy river, breaking its dark surface with a bright streak. The pickerel leaped from among the lily-pads. The turtle, sunning itself upon a rock or at the root of a tree, slid suddenly into the water with a plunge. The painted Indian who paddled his canoe along the Assabeth three hundred years ago could hardly have seen a wilder gentleness displayed upon its banks and reflected in its bosom than we did. Nor could the same Indian have prepared his noontide meal with more simplicity. We drew up our skiff at some point where the overarching shade formed a natural bower, and there kindled a fire with the pine cones and decayed branches that lay strewn plentifully around. Soon the smoke ascended among the trees, impregnated with a savory incense, not heavy, dull, and surfeiting, like the steam of cookery within doors, but sprightly and piquant. The smell of our feast was akin to the woodland odors with which it mingled: there was no sacrilege committed by our intrusion there: the sacred solitude was hospitable, and granted us free leave to cook and eat in the recess that was at once our kitchen and banqueting hall. It is strange what humble offices may be performed in a beautiful scene without destroying its poetry. Our fire, red gleaming among the trees, and we beside it, busied with culinary rites and spreading out our meal on a moss-grown log, all seemed in unison with the river gliding by and the foliage rustling over us. And, what was strangest, neither did our mirth seem to disturb the propriety of the solemn woods; although the hobgoblins of the old wilderness and the will-of-the-wisps that glimmered in the marshy places might have come trooping to share our table-talk, and have added their shrill laughter to our merriment. It was the very spot in which to utter the extremest nonsense or the profoundest wisdom, or that ethereal product of the mind which partakes of both, and may become one or the other, in correspondence with the faith and insight of the auditor.

So amid sunshine and shadow, rustling leaves and sighing waters, up gushed our talk like the babble of a fountain. The evanescent spray was Ellery's; and his, too, the lumps of golden thought that lay glimmering in the fountain's bed and brightened both our faces by the reflection. Could he have drawn out that virgin gold and stamped it with the mint mark that alone gives currency, the world might have had the profit, and he the fame. My mind was the richer merely by the knowledge that it was there. But the chief profit of those wild days to him and me lay, not in any definite idea, not in any angular or rounded truth, which we dug out of the shapeless mass of problematical stuff, but in the freedom which we thereby won from all custom and conventionalism and fettering influences of man on man. We were so free to-day that it was impossible to be slaves again to-morrow. When we crossed the threshold of the house or trod the thronged pavements of a city, still the leaves of the trees that overhang the Assabeth were whispering to us, "Be free! be free!" Therefore along that shady river-bank there are spots, marked with a heap of ashes and half-consumed brands, only less sacred in my remembrance than the hearth of a household fire.

And yet how sweet, as we floated homeward adown the golden river at sunset,—how sweet was it to return within the system of human society, not as to a dungeon and a chain, but as to a stately edifice, whence we could go forth at will into statelier simplicity! How gently, too, did the sight of the Old Manse, best seen from the river, overshadowed with its willow and all environed about with the foliage of its orchard and avenue,—how gently did its gray, homely aspect rebuke the speculative extravagances of the day! It had grown sacred in connection with the artificial life against which we inveighed; it had been a home for many years in spite of all; it was my home too; and, with these thoughts, it seemed to me that all the artifice and conventionalism of life was but an impalpable thinness upon its surface, and that the depth below was none the worse for it. Once, as we turned our boat to the bank, there was a cloud, in the shape of an immensely gigantic figure of a hound, couched above the house, as if keeping guard over it. Gazing at this symbol, I prayed that the upper influences might long protect the institutions that had grown out of the heart of mankind.

If ever my readers should decide to give up civilized life, cities, houses, and whatever moral or material enormities in addition to these the perverted ingenuity of our race has contrived, let it be in the early autumn. Then Nature will love him better than at any other season, and will take him to her bosom with a more motherly tenderness. I could scarcely endure the roof of the old house above me in those first autumnal days. How early in the summer, too, the prophecy of autumn comes! Earlier in some years than in others; sometimes even in the first weeks of July. There is no other feeling like what is caused by this faint, doubtful, yet real perception—if it be not rather a foreboding—of the year's decay, so blessedly sweet and sad in the same breath.

Did I say that there was no feeling like it? Ah, but there is a half-acknowledged melancholy like to this when we stand in the perfected vigor of our life and feel that Time has now given us all his flowers, and that the next work of his never idle fingers must be to steal them one by one away.

I have forgotten whether the song of the cricket be not as early a token of autumn's approach as any other,—that song which may be called an audible stillness; for though very loud and heard afar, yet the mind does not take note of it as a sound, so completely is its individual existence merged among the accompanying characteristics of the season. Alas for the pleasant summer time! In August the grass is still verdant on the hills and in the valleys; the foliage of the trees is as dense as ever, and as green; the flowers gleam forth in richer abundance along the margin of the river, and by the stone walls, and deep among the woods; the days, too, are as fervid now as they were a month ago; and yet in every breath of wind and in every beam of sunshine we hear the whispered farewell and behold the parting smile of a dear friend. There is a coolness amid all the heat, a mildness in the blazing noon. Not a breeze can stir but it thrills us with the breath of autumn. A pensive glory is seen in the far golden gleams; among the shadows of the trees. The flowers—even the brightest of them, and they are the most gorgeous of the year—have this gentle sadness wedded to their pomp, and typify the character of the delicious time each within itself. The brilliant cardinal flower has never seemed gay to me.

Still later in the season Nature's tenderness waxes stronger. It is impossible not to be fond of our mother now; for she is so fond of us! At other periods she does not make this impression on me, or only at rare intervals; but in those genial days of autumn, when she has perfected her harvests and accomplished every needful thing that was given her to do, then she overflows with a blessed superfluity of love. She has leisure to caress her children now. It is good to be alive at such times. Thank Heaven for breath—yes, for mere breath—when it is made up of a heavenly breeze like this! It comes with a real kiss upon our cheeks; it would linger fondly around us if it might; but, since it must be gone, it embraces us with its whole kindly heart and passes onward to embrace likewise the next thing that it meets. A blessing is flung abroad and scattered far and wide over the earth, to be gathered up by all who choose. I recline upon the still unwithered grass and whisper to myself, "O perfect day! O beautiful world! O beneficent God!" And it is the promise of a blessed eternity; for our Creator would never have made such lovely days and have given us the deep hearts to enjoy them, above and beyond all thought, unless we were meant to be immortal. This sunshine is the golden pledge thereof. It beams through the gates of paradise and shows us glimpses far inward.

By and by, in a little time, the outward world puts on a drear austerity. On some October morning there is a heavy hoar-frost on the grass and along the tops of the fences; and at sunrise the leaves fall from the trees of our avenue without a breath of wind, quietly descending by their own weight. All summer long they have murmured like the noise of waters; they have roared loudly while the branches were wrestling with the thunder gust; they have made music both glad and solemn; they have attuned my thoughts by their quiet sound as I paced to and fro beneath the arch of intermingling boughs. Now they can only rustle under my feet. Henceforth the gray parsonage begins to assume a larger importance, and draws to its fireside,—for the abomination of the air-tight stove is reserved till wintry weather,—draws closer and closer to its fireside the vagrant impulses that had gone wandering about through the summer.

When summer was dead and buried the Old Manse became as lonely as a hermitage. Not that ever—in my time at least—it had been thronged with company; but, at no rare intervals, we welcomed some friend out of the dusty glare and tumult of the world, and rejoiced to share with him the transparent obscurity that was floating over us. In one respect our precincts were like the Enchanted Ground through which the pilgrim travelled on his way to the Celestial City! [11] The guests, each and all, felt a slumberous influence upon them; they fell asleep in chairs, or took a more deliberate siesta on the sofa, or were seen stretched among the shadows of the orchard, looking up dreamily through the boughs. They could not have paid a more acceptable compliment to my abode, nor to my own qualities as a host. I held it as a proof that they left their cares behind them as they passed between the stone gateposts at the entrance of our avenue, and that the so powerful opiate was the abundance of peace and quiet within and all around us. Others could give them pleasure and amusement or instruction—these could be picked up anywhere; but it was for me to give them rest—rest in a life of trouble. What better could be done for those weary and world-worn spirits?—for him [12] whose career of perpetual action was imped-

11. **Enchanted . . . City:** an allusion to the Delectable Mountains in John Bunyan's *Pilgrim's Progress* (1678). 12. **him:** Horatio Bridge (1806–93), a classmate of Hawthorne at Bowdoin

ed and harassed by the rarest of his powers and the richest of his acquirements?—for another [13] who had thrown his ardent heart from earliest youth into the strife of politics, and now, perchance, began to suspect that one lifetime is too brief for the accomplishment of any lofty aim?—for her [14] on whose feminine nature had been imposed the heavy gift of intellectual power, such as a strong man might have staggered under, and with it the necessity to act upon the world?—in a word, not to multiply instances, what better could be done for anybody who came within our magic circle than to throw the spell of a tranquil spirit over him? And when it had wrought its full effect, then we dismissed him, with but misty reminiscences, as if he had been dreaming of us.

Were I to adopt a pet idea, as so many people do, and fondle it in my embraces to the exclusion of all others, it would be, that the great want which mankind labors under at this present period is sleep. The world should recline its vast head on the first convenient pillow and take an age-long nap. It has gone distracted through a morbid activity, and, while preternaturally wide awake, is nevertheless tormented by visions that seem real to it now, but would assume their true aspect and character were all things once set right by an interval of sound repose. This is the only method of getting rid of old delusions and avoiding new ones; of regenerating our race, so that it might in due time awake as an infant out of dewy slumber; of restoring to us the simple perception of what is right, and the single-hearted desire to achieve it, both of which have long been lost in consequence of this weary activity of brain and torpor or passion of the heart that now afflict the universe. Stimulants, the only mode of treatment hitherto attempted, cannot quell the disease; they do but heighten the delirium.

Let not the above paragraph ever be quoted against the author; for, though tinctured with its modicum of truth, it is the result and expression of what he knew, while he was writing, to be but a distorted survey of the state and prospects of mankind. There were circumstances around me which made it difficult to view the world precisely as it exists; for, severe and sober as was the Old Manse, it was necessary to go but a little way beyond its threshold before meeting with stranger moral shapes of men than might have been encountered elsewhere in a circuit of a thousand miles.

These hobgoblins of flesh and blood were attracted thither by the widespreading influence of a great original thinker, who had his earthly abode at the opposite extremity of our village. His mind acted upon other minds of a certain constitution with wonderful magnetism, and drew many men upon long pilgrimages to speak with him face to face. Young visionaries—to whom just so much of insight had been imparted as to make life all a labyrinth around them—came to seek the clew that should guide them out of their self-involved bewilderment. Gray-headed theorists—whose systems, at first air, had finally imprisoned them in an iron frame-work—travelled painfully to his door, not to ask deliverance, but to invite the free spirit into their own thraldom. People that had lighted on a new thought, or a thought that they fancied new, came to Emerson, as the finder of a glittering gem hastens to a lapidary, to ascertain its quality and value. Uncertain, troubled, earnest wanderers through the midnight of the moral world beheld his intellectual fire as a beacon burning on a hill-top, and, climbing the difficult ascent, looked forth into the surrounding obscurity more hopefully than hitherto. The light revealed objects unseen before,—mountains, gleaming lakes, glimpses of a creation among the chaos; but also, as was unavoidable, it attracted bats and owls and the whole host of night birds, which flapped their dusky wings against the gazer's eyes, and sometimes were mistaken for fowls of angelic feather. Such delusions always hover nigh whenever a beacon fire of truth is kindled.

For myself, there had been epochs of my life when I, too, might have asked of this prophet the master word that should solve me the riddle of the universe; but now, being happy, I felt as if there were no question to be put, and therefore admired Emerson as a poet of deep beauty and austere tenderness, but sought nothing from him as a philosopher. It was good, nevertheless, to meet him in the wood-paths, or sometimes in our avenue, with that pure intellectual gleam diffused about his presence like the garment of a shining one; and he so quiet, so simple, so without pretension, encountering each man alive as if expecting to receive more than he could impart. And, in truth, the heart of many an ordinary man had, perchance, inscriptions which he could not read. But it was impossible to dwell in his vicinity without inhaling more or less the mountain atmosphere of his lofty thought, which, in the brains of some people, wrought a singular giddiness,—new truth being as heady as

and a lifelong friend. Just before moving into the Old Manse, Hawthorne had helped Bridge edit the *Journal of an African Cruiser* (1845), a narrative of a voyage. Bridge, it would appear, suffered the privations and difficulties of authorship, as did Hawthorne himself. **13. another:** Franklin Pierce (1804–69), another collegemate of Hawthorne and a lifelong friend who became President of the United States (1853–57) and appointed Hawthorne consul at Liverpool. **14. her:** Margaret Fuller (1810–50), a friend of Emerson, an important member of the Concord group, and, occasionally, a visitor in the Old Manse.

new wine. Never was a poor little country village infested with such a variety of queer, strangely-dressed, oddly-behaved mortals, most of whom took upon themselves to be important agents of the world's destiny, yet were simply bores of a very intense water. Such, I imagine, is the invariable character of persons who crowd so closely about an original thinker as to draw in his unuttered breath and thus become imbued with a false originality. This triteness of novelty is enough to make any man of common sense blaspheme at all ideas of less than a century's standing, and pray that the world may be petrified and rendered immovable in precisely the worst moral and physical state that it ever yet arrived at, rather than be benefited by such schemes of such philosophers.

And now I begin to feel—and perhaps should have sooner felt—that we have talked enough of the Old Manse. Mine honored reader, it may be, will vilify the poor author as an egotist for babbling through so many pages about a moss-grown country parsonage, and his life within its walls and on the river and in the woods, and the influences that wrought upon him from all these sources. My conscience, however, does not reproach me with betraying anything too sacredly individual to be revealed by a human spirit to its brother or sister spirit. How narrow—how shallow and scanty too—is the stream of thought that has been flowing from my pen, compared with the broad tide of dim emotions, ideas, and associations which swell around me from that portion of my existence! How little have I told! and of that little, how almost nothing is even tinctured with any quality that makes it exclusively my own! Has the reader gone wandering, hand in hand with me, through the inner passages of my being? and have we groped together into all its chambers and examined their treasures or their rubbish? Not so. We have been standing on the greensward, but just within the cavern's mouth, where the common sunshine is free to penetrate, and where every footstep is therefore free to come. I have appealed to no sentiment or sensibilities save such as are diffused among us all. So far as I am a man of really individual attributes I veil my face; nor am I, nor have I ever been, one of those supremely hospitable people who serve up their own hearts, delicately fried, with brain sauce, as a tidbit for their beloved public.

Glancing back over what I have written, it seems but the scattered reminiscences of a single summer. In fairyland there is no measurement of time; and, in a spot so sheltered from the turmoil of life's ocean, three years hastened away with a noiseless flight, as the breezy sunshine chases the cloud shadows across the depths of a still valley. Now came hints, growing more and more distinct, that the owner of the old house was pining for his native air. Carpenters next appeared, making a tremendous racket among the out-buildings, strewing the green grass with pine shavings and chips of chestnut joists, and vexing the whole antiquity of the place with their discordant renovations. Soon, moreover, they divested our abode of the veil of woodbine which had crept over a large portion of its southern face. All the aged mosses were cleared unsparingly away; and there were horrible whispers about brushing up the external walls with a coat of paint—a purpose as little to my taste as might be that of rouging the venerable cheeks of one's grandmother. But the hand that renovates is always more sacrilegious than that which destroys. In fine, we gathered up our household goods, drank a farewell cup of tea in our pleasant little breakfast-room,—delicately fragrant tea, an unpurchasable luxury, one of the many angel gifts that had fallen like dew upon us,—and passed forth between the tall stone gateposts as uncertain as the wandering Arabs where our tent might next be pitched. Providence took me by the hand, and —an oddity of dispensation which, I trust, there is no irreverence in smiling at—has led me, as the newspapers announce while I am writing, from the Old Manse into a custom house. As a story teller, I have often contrived strange vicissitudes for my imaginary personages, but none like this.

The treasure of intellectual good which I hoped to find in our secluded dwelling had never come to light. No profound treatise of ethics, no philosophic history, no novel even, that could stand unsupported on its edges. All that I had to show, as a man of letters, were these few tales and essays, which had blossomed out like flowers in the calm summer of my heart and mind. Save editing (an easy task) the journal of my friend of many years, the *African Cruiser,* I had done nothing else. With these idle weeds and withering blossoms I have intermixed some that were produced long ago,—old, faded things, reminding me of flowers pressed between the leaves of a book,—and now offer the bouquet, such as it is, to any whom it may please. These fitful sketches, with so little of external life about them, yet claiming no profundity of purpose,—so reserved, even while they sometimes seem so frank,—often but half in earnest, and never, even when most so, expressing satisfactorily the thoughts which they profess to image,—such trifles, I truly feel, afford no solid basis for a literary reputation. Nevertheless, the public—if my limited number of readers, whom I venture to regard rather as a circle of friends, may be termed a public—will receive them the more kindly, as the last offering, the last collection, of this nature which it is my purpose ever to put forth. Unless I could do better, I have done enough in this kind. For myself the book will always retain one charm—as reminding me of the river, with its delightful solitudes, and of the avenue, the garden, and the orchard, and especially the dear old Manse, with the little study on its western side, and the sunshine glimmering through the willow branches while I wrote.

Let the reader, if he will do me so much honor, imagine himself my guest, and that, having seen whatever may be worthy of notice within and about the Old Manse, he has finally been ushered into my study. There, after seating him in an antique elbow chair, an heirloom of the house, I take forth a roll of manuscript and entreat his attention to the following tales—an act of personal inhospitality, however, which I never was guilty of, nor ever will be, even to my worst enemy.

THE CUSTOM HOUSE

Introductory to *The Scarlet Letter*

◇

HAWTHORNE's Prefaces continue the theme of personal reminiscence which colors "The Old Manse." But the mood of recollection was deepened by Hawthorne's commitment to the life of art. In the Custom House Introduction to *The Scarlet Letter* Hawthorne was getting even with his political enemies who made him lose his position and, at the same time, offering an "apology" for writing a novel. In the legend of Surveyor Pue and of the red letter A, he may have been trying to fabricate history as a means of strengthening the historical structure of his moral tale; he may also have been proposing that a writer must find that strange and special place where the "Actual" and the "Imaginary" meet. If the real is too obtrusive, then the artistic expression is stifled; if the imaginary can slowly emerge and the theme of the novel become apparent, then the novel can virtually write itself.

◇

. . . IN MY native town of Salem, at the head of what, half a century ago, in the days of old King Derby,[1] was a bustling wharf,—but which is now burdened with decayed wooden warehouses, and exhibits few or no symptoms of commercial life; except, perhaps, a bark or brig, half-way down its melancholy length, discharging hides; or, nearer at hand, a Nova Scotia schooner, pitching out her cargo of fire-wood,—at the head, I say, of this dilapidated wharf, which the tide often overflows, and along which, at the base and in the rear of the row of buildings, the track of many languid years is seen in a border of unthrifty grass,—here, with a view from its front windows adown this not very enlivening prospect, and thence across the harbor, stands a spacious edifice of brick. From the loftiest point of its roof, during precisely three and a half hours of each forenoon, floats or droops, in breeze or calm, the banner of the republic; but with the thirteen stripes turned vertically, instead of horizontally, and thus indicating that a civil, and not a military post of Uncle Sam's government, is here established. Its front is ornamented with a portico of half a dozen wooden pillars, supporting a balcony, beneath which a flight of wide granite steps descends towards the street. Over the entrance hovers an enormous specimen of the American eagle, with outspread wings, a shield before her breast, and, if I recollect aright, a bunch of intermingled thunderbolts and barbed arrows in each claw. With the customary infirmity of temper that characterizes this unhappy fowl, she appears, by the fierceness of her beak and eye, and the general truculency of her attitude, to threaten mischief to the inoffensive community; and especially to warn all citizens, careful of their safety, against intruding on the premises which she overshadows with her wings. Nevertheless, vixenly as she looks, many people are seeking, at this very moment, to shelter themselves under the wing of the federal eagle; imagining, I presume, that her bosom has all the softness and snugness of an eider-down pillow. But she has no great tenderness, even in her best of moods, and, sooner or later,—oftener soon than late,—is apt to fling off her nestlings, with a scratch of her claw, a dab of her beak, or a rankling wound from her barbed arrows.

The pavement round about the above-described edifice—which we may as well name at once as the Custom House of the port—has grass enough growing in its chinks to show that it has not, of late days, been worn by any multitudinous resort of business. In some months of the year, however, there often chances a forenoon when affairs move onward with a livelier tread. Such occasions might

THE CUSTOM HOUSE. 1. **old King Derby:** Elias Hasket Derby (1739–99), a merchant and shipowner of Salem who helped raise arms for the Revolution and dispatched the first ships which opened trade with the Orient.

remind the elderly citizen of that period before the last war with England,[2] when Salem was a port by itself; not scorned, as she is now, by her own merchants and ship-owners, who permit her wharves to crumble to ruin, while their ventures go to swell, needlessly and imperceptibly, the mighty flood of commerce at New York or Boston. On some such morning, when three of four vessels happen to have arrived at once,—usually from Africa or South America,—or to be on the verge of their departure thitherward, there is a sound of frequent feet, passing briskly up and down the granite steps. Here, before his own wife has greeted him, you may greet the sea-flushed shipmaster, just in port, with his vessel's papers under his arm, in a tarnished tin box. Here, too, comes his owner, cheerful or sombre, gracious or in the sulks, accordingly as his scheme of the now accomplished voyage has been realized in merchandise that will readily be turned to gold, or has buried him under a bulk of incommodities, such as nobody will care to rid him of. Here, likewise,—the germ of the wrinkle-browed, grizzly-bearded, care-worn merchant,—we have the smart young clerk, who gets the taste of traffic as a wolf-cub does of blood, and already sends adventures in his master's ships, when he had better be sailing mimic-boats upon a mill-pond. Another figure in the scene is the outward-bound sailor, in quest of a protection; or the recently arrived one, pale and feeble, seeking a passport to the hospital. Nor must we forget the captains of the rusty little schooners that bring firewood from the British provinces; a rough-looking set of tarpaulins, without the alertness of the Yankee aspect, but contributing an item of no slight importance to our decaying trade. . . .

. . . This old town of Salem—my native place, though I have dwelt much away from it, both in boyhood and maturer years—possesses, or did possess, a hold on my affections, the force of which I have never realized during my seasons of actual residence here. Indeed, so far as its physical aspect is concerned, with its flat, unvaried surface, covered chiefly with wooden houses, few or none of which pretend to architectural beauty,—its irregularity, which is neither picturesque nor quaint, but only tame,—its long and lazy street lounging wearisomely through the whole extent of the peninsula, with Gallows Hill and New Guinea at one end, and a view of the almshouse at the other,—such being the features of my native town, it would be quite as reasonable to form a sentimental attachment to a disarranged checkerboard. And yet, though invariably happiest elsewhere, there is within me a feeling for old Salem, which, in lack of a better phrase, I must be content to call affection. The sentiment is probably assignable to the deep and aged roots which my family has struck into the soil. It is now nearly two centuries and a quarter since the original Briton, the earliest emigrant of my name,[3] made his appearance in the wild and forest-bordered settlement, which has since become a city. And here his descendants have been born and died, and have mingled their earthly substance with the soil, until no small portion of it must necessarily be akin to the mortal frame wherewith, for a little while, I walk the streets. In part, therefore, the attachment which I speak of is the mere sensuous sympathy of dust for dust. Few of my countrymen can know what it is; nor, as frequent transplantation is perhaps better for the stock, need they consider it desirable to know.

But the sentiment has likewise its moral quality. The figure of that first ancestor, invested by family tradition with a dim and dusky grandeur, was present to my boyish imagination, as far back as I can remember. It still haunts me, and induces a sort of home-feeling with the past, which I scarcely claim in reference to the present phase of the town. I seem to have a stronger claim to a residence here on account of this grave, bearded, sable-cloaked and steeple-crowned progenitor,—who came so early, with his Bible and his sword, and trode the unworn street with such a stately port, and made so large a figure, as a man of war and peace,—a stronger claim than for myself, whose name is seldom heard and my face hardly known. He was a soldier, legislator, judge; he was a ruler in the Church; he had all the Puritanic traits, both good and evil. He was likewise a better persecutor, as witness the Quakers, who have remembered him in their histories, and relate an incident of his hard severity towards a woman of their sect, which will last longer, it is to be feared, than any record of his better deeds, although these were many. His son,[4] too, inherited the persecuting spirit, and made himself so conspicuous in the martyrdom of the witches, that their blood may fairly be said to have left a stain upon him. So deep a stain, indeed, that his old dry bones, in the Charter-street burial-ground, must still retain it, if they have not crumbled utterly to dust! I know not whether these ancestors of mine bethought themselves to repent, and ask pardon of heaven for their cruelties; or whether they are now groaning under the heavy

2. **war with England:** the War of 1812 (to 1815).

3. **earliest . . . my name:** William Hathorne (1607?–81), who emigrated to New England in 1630 and afterward took a prominent part in Massachusetts politics. 4. **His son:** John Hathorne (1641–1717), the great-great-grandfather of Nathaniel, was one of the judges in the Salem witchcraft trials of 1692.

consequences of them, in another state of being. At all events, I, the present writer, as their representative, hereby take shame upon myself for their sakes, and pray that any curse incurred by them—as I have heard, and as the dreary and unprosperous condition of the race, for many a long year back, would argue to exist—may be now and henceforth removed.

Doubtless, however, either of these stern and black-browed Puritans would have thought it quite a sufficient retribution for his sins, that, after so long a lapse of years, the old trunk of the family tree, with so much venerable moss upon it, should have borne, as its topmost bough, an idler like myself. No aim, that I have ever cherished, would they recognize as laudable; no success of mine—if my life, beyond its domestic scope, had ever been brightened by success—would they deem otherwise than worthless, if not positively disgraceful. "What is he?" murmurs one gray shadow of my forefathers to the other. "A writer of story-books! What kind of a business in life,—what mode of glorifying God, or being serviceable to mankind in his day and generation,—may that be? Why, the degenerate fellow might as well have been a fiddler!" Such are the compliments bandied between my great-grandsires and myself, across the gulf of time! And yet, let them scorn me as they will, strong traits of their nature have intertwined themselves with mine.

Planted deep, in the town's earliest infancy and childhood, by these two earnest and energetic men, the race has ever since subsisted here; always, too, in respectability; never, so far as I have known, disgraced by a single unworthy member; but seldom or never, on the other hand, after the first two generations, performing any memorable deed, or so much as putting forward a claim to public notice. Gradually, they have sunk almost out of sight; as old houses, here and there about the streets, get covered half-way to the eaves by the accumulation of new soil. From father to son, for above a hundred years, they followed the sea; a gray-headed shipmaster, in each generation, retiring from the quarter-deck to the homestead, while a boy of fourteen took the hereditary place before the mast, confronting the salt spray and the gale, which had blustered against his sire and grandsire. The boy, also, in due time, passed from the forecastle to the cabin, spent a tempestuous manhood, and returned from his world-wanderings, to grow old, and die, and mingle his dust with the natal earth. This long connection of a family with one spot, as its place of birth and burial, creates a kindred between the human being and the locality, quite independent of any charm in the scenery or moral circumstances that surround him. It is not love, but instinct. The new inhabitant—who came himself from a foreign land, or whose father or grandfather came—has little claim to be called a Salemite; he has no conception of the oyster-like tenacity with which an old settler, over whom his third century is creeping, clings to the spot where his successive generations have been imbedded. It is no matter that the place is joyless for him; that he is weary of the old wooden houses, the mud and dust, the dead level of site and sentiment, the chill east wind, and the chillest of social atmospheres; —all these, and whatever faults besides he may see or imagine, are nothing to the purpose. The spell survives, and just as powerfully as if the natal spot were an earthly paradise. So has it been in my case. I felt it almost as a destiny to make Salem my home; so that the mould of features and cast of character which had all along been familiar here —ever, as one representative of the race lay down in his grave, another assuming, as it were, his sentry-march along the main street—might still in my little day be seen and recognized in the old town. Nevertheless, this very sentiment is an evidence that the connection, which has become an unhealthy one, should at least be severed. Human nature will not flourish, any more than a potato, if it be planted and replanted, for too long a series of generations, in the same worn-out soil. My children have had other birthplaces, and, so far as their fortunes may be within my control, shall strike their roots into unaccustomed earth. . . .

. . . Literature, its exertions and objects, were now of little moment in my regard. I cared not, at this period, for books; they were apart from me. Nature,—except it were human nature,—the nature that is developed in earth and sky, was, in one sense, hidden from me; and all the imaginative delight, wherewith it had been spiritualized, passed away out of my mind. A gift, a faculty, if it had not departed, was suspended and inanimate within me. There would have been something sad, unutterably dreary, in all this, had I not been conscious that it lay at my own option to recall whatever was valuable in the past. It might be true, indeed, that this was a life which could not with impunity be lived too long; else, it might have made me permanently other than I had been without transforming me into any shape which it would be worth my while to take. But I never considered it as other than a transitory life. There was always a prophetic instinct, a low whisper in my ear, that, within no long period, and whenever a new change of custom should be essential to my good, a change would come.

Meanwhile, there I was, a Surveyor of the Revenue,[5] and, so far as I have been able to understand, as good a Surveyor as need be. A man of thought, fancy, and sensibility (had he ten times the Surveyor's proportion of those qualities) may, at any time, be a man of affairs, if he will only choose to give himself the trouble. My fellow-officers, and the merchants and sea-captains, with whom my official duties brought me into any manner of connection, viewed me in no other light, and probably knew me in no other character. None of them, I presume, had ever read a page of my inditing, or would have cared a fig the more for me if they had read them all; nor would it have mended the matter, in the least, had those same unprofitable pages been written with a pen like that of Burns or of Chaucer, each of whom was a Custom Officer in his day, as well as I. It is a good lesson—though it may often be a hard one—for a man who has dreamed of literary fame, and of making for himself a rank among the world's dignitaries by such means, to step aside out of the narrow circle in which his claims are recognized, and to find how utterly devoid of significance, beyond that circle, is all that he achieves, and all he aims at. I know not that I especially needed the lesson, either in the way of warning or rebuke; but, at any rate, I learned it thoroughly: nor, it gives me pleasure to reflect, did the truth, as it came home to my perception, ever cost me a pang, or require to be thrown off in a sigh. In the way of literary talk, it is true, the Naval Officer—an excellent fellow, who came into office with me and went out only a little later—would often engage me in a discussion about one or the other of his favorite topics, Napoleon or Shakespeare. The Collector's junior clerk, too,—a young gentleman who, it was whispered, occasionally covered a sheet of Uncle Sam's letter-paper with what (at the distance of a few yards) looked very much like poetry,—used now and then to speak to me of books, as matters with which I might possibly be conversant. This was my all of lettered intercourse; and it was quite sufficient for my necessities.

No longer seeking or caring that my name should be blazoned abroad on title-pages, I smiled to think that it had now another kind of vogue. The Custom House marker imprinted it, with a stencil and black paint, on pepper-bags, and baskets of anatto, and cigar-boxes, and bales of all kinds of dutiable merchandise, in testimony that these commodities had paid the impost, and gone regularly through the office. Borne on such queer vehicle of fame, a knowledge of my existence, so far as a name conveys it, was carried where it had never been before, and, I hope, will never go again.

But the past was not dead. Once in a great while, the thoughts, that had seemed so vital and so active, yet had been put to rest so quietly, revived again. One of the most remarkable occasions, when the habit of bygone days awoke in me, was that which brings it within the law of literary propriety to offer the public the sketch which I am now writing.

In the second story of the Custom House, there is a large room, in which the brick-work and naked rafters have never been covered with panelling and plaster. The edifice—originally projected on a scale adapted to the old commercial enterprise of the port, and with an idea of subsequent prosperity destined never to be realized—contains far more space than its occupants know what to do with. This airy hall, therefore, over the Collector's apartments, remains unfinished to this day, and, in spite of the aged cobwebs that festoon its dusky beams, appears still to await the labor of the carpenter and mason. At one end of the room, in a recess, were a number of barrels, piled one upon another, containing bundles of official documents. Large quantities of similar rubbish lay lumbering the floor. It was sorrowful to think how many days, and weeks, and months, and years of toil, had been wasted on these musty papers, which were now only an encumbrance on earth, and were hidden away in this forgotten corner, never more to be glanced at by human eyes. But, then, what reams of other manuscripts—filled not with the dulness of official formalities, but with the thought of inventive brains and the rich effusion of deep hearts—had gone equally to oblivion; and that, moreover, without serving a purpose in their day, as these heaped-up papers had, and—saddest of all—without purchasing for their writers the comfortable livelihood which the clerks of the Custom House had gained by these worthless scratchings of the pen! Yet not altogether worthless, perhaps, as materials of local history. Here, no doubt, statistics of the former commerce of Salem might be discovered, and memorials of her princely merchants,—old King Derby,—old Billy Gray,[6]—old Simon Forrester,[7]—and many another magnate in his day; whose powdered head, however, was scarcely in the tomb, before his mountain pile of wealth began to dwindle. The founders of the greater part of the families which now compose the aristocracy of Salem might here be traced, from the petty and obscure beginnings of their traffic, at periods gener-

5. **Surveyor . . . Revenue:** Hawthorne's position in the custom-house, 1846–49.

6. **Billy Gray:** William Gray (1750–1825), a wealthy shipowner of Salem and lieutenant governor of Massachusetts. 7. **Simon Forrester:** another well-to-do shipowner (1776–1851) in Salem.

ally much posterior to the Revolution, upward to what their children look upon as long-established rank.

Prior to the Revolution, there is a dearth of records; the earlier documents and archives of the Custom House having, probably, been carried off to Halifax, when all the King's officials accompanied the British army in its flight from Boston. It has often been a matter of regret with me; for, going back, perhaps, to the days of the Protectorate, those papers must have contained many references to forgotten or remembered men, and to antique customs, which would have affected me with the same pleasure as when I used to pick up Indian arrow-heads in the field near the Old Manse.

But one idle and rainy day, it was my fortune to make a discovery of some little interest. Poking and burrowing into the heaped-up rubbish in the corner; unfolding one and another document, and reading the names of vessels that had long ago foundered at sea or rotted at the wharves, and those of merchants never heard of now on 'Change, nor very readily decipherable on their mossy tombstones; glancing at such matters with the saddened, weary, half-reluctant interest which we bestow on the corpse of dead activity,—and exerting my fancy, sluggish with little use, to raise up from dry bones an image of the old town's brighter aspect, when India was a new region, and only Salem knew the way thither,—I chanced to lay my hand on a small package, carefully done up in a piece of ancient yellow parchment. This envelope had the air of an official record of some period long past, when clerks engrossed their stiff and formal chirography on more substantial materials than at present. There was something about it that quickened an instinctive curiosity, and made me undo the faded red tape, that tied up the package, with the sense that a treasure would here be brought to light. Unbending the rigid folds of the parchment cover, I found it to be a commission, under the hand and seal of Governor Shirley,[8] in favor of one Jonathan Pue, as Surveyor of his Majesty's Customs for the port of Salem, in the Province of Massachusetts Bay. I remembered to have read (probably in Felt's *Annals* [9]) a notice of the decease of Mr. Surveyor Pue, about fourscore years ago; and likewise, in a newspaper of recent times, an account of the digging up of his remains in the little grave-yard of St. Peter's Church, during the renewal of that edifice. Nothing, if I rightly call to mind, was left of my respected predecessor, save an imperfect skeleton, and some fragments of apparel, and a wig of majestic frizzle; which, unlike the head that it once adorned, was in very satisfactory preservation. But, on examining the papers which the parchment commission served to envelop, I found more traces of Mr. Pue's mental part, and the internal operations of his head, than the frizzled wig had contained of the venerable skull itself.

They were documents, in short, not official, but of a private nature, or, at least, written in his private capacity, and apparently with his own hand. I could account for their being included in the heap of Custom House lumber only by the fact that Mr. Pue's death had happened suddenly; and that these papers, which he probably kept in his official desk, had never come to the knowledge of his heirs, or were supposed to relate to the business of the revenue. On the transfer of the archives to Halifax, this package proving to be of no public concern, was left behind and had remained ever since unopened.

The ancient Surveyor—being little molested, I suppose, at that early day, with business pertaining to his office—seems to have devoted some of his many leisure hours to researches as a local antiquarian, and other inquisitions of a similar nature. These supplied material for petty activity to a mind that would otherwise have been eaten up with rust. A portion of his facts, by the by, did me good service in the preparation of the article entitled "MAIN STREET," [10] included in the third volume of this edition. The remainder may perhaps be applied to purposes equally valuable hereafter; or not impossibly may be worked up, so far as they go, into a regular history of Salem, should my veneration for the natal soil ever impel me to so pious a task. Meanwhile, they shall be at the command of any gentleman, inclined, and competent, to take the unprofitable labor off my hands. As a final disposition, I contemplate depositing them with the Essex Historical Society.

But the object that most drew my attention, in the mysterious package, was a certain affair of fine red cloth, much worn and faded. There were traces about it of gold embroidery, which, however, was greatly frayed and defaced; so that none, or very little, of the glitter was left. It had been wrought, as was easy to perceive, with wonderful skill of needlework; and the stitch (as I am assured by ladies conversant with such mysteries) gives evidence of a now forgotten art, not to be recovered even by the process of picking out the threads. This

8. Governor Shirley: William Shirley (1694–1771), colonial governor of Massachusetts, 1741–57. **9. Felt's *Annals*:** Joseph Felt, *Annals of Salem from Its First Settlement* (1827). The death of Jonathan Pue is mentioned as occurring March 24, 1760.

10. "Main Street": a description of Old Salem published in 1849 and later included in *The Snow-Image and Other Twice-Told Tales* (1852).

rag of scarlet cloth,—for time and wear and a sacrilegious moth had reduced it to little other than a rag,—on careful examination, assumed the shape of a letter. It was the capital letter A. By an accurate measurement, each limb proved to be precisely three inches and a quarter in length. It had been intended, there could be no doubt, as an ornamental article of dress; but how it was to be worn, or what rank, honor, and dignity, in by-past times, were signified by it, was a riddle which (so evanescent are the fashions of the world in these particulars) I saw little hope of solving. And yet it strangely interested me. My eyes fastened themselves upon the old scarlet letter, and would not be turned aside. Certainly, there was some deep meaning in it, most worthy of interpretation, and which, as it were, streamed forth from the mystic symbol, subtly communicating itself to my sensibilities, but evading the analysis of my mind.

While thus perplexed,—and cogitating, among other hypotheses, whether the letter might not have been one of those decorations which the white men used to contrive, in order to take the eyes of Indians,—I happened to place it on my breast. It seemed to me,—the reader may smile, but must not doubt my word,—it seemed to me, then, that I experienced a sensation not altogether physical, yet almost so, as of burning heat; and as if the letter were not of red cloth, but red-hot iron. I shuddered, and involuntarily let it fall upon the floor.

In the absorbing contemplation of the scarlet letter, I had hitherto neglected to examine a small roll of dingy paper, around which it had been twisted. This I now opened, and had the satisfaction to find, recorded by the old Surveyor's pen, a reasonably complete explanation of the whole affair. There were several foolscap sheets, containing many particulars respecting the life and conversation of one Hester Prynne, who appeared to have been rather a noteworthy personage in the view of our ancestors. She had flourished during the period between the early days of Massachusetts and the close of the seventeenth century. Aged persons, alive in the time of Mr. Surveyor Pue, and from whose oral testimony he had made up his narrative, remembered her, in their youth, as a very old, but not decrepit woman, of a stately and solemn aspect. It had been her habit, from an almost immemorial date, to go about the country as a kind of voluntary nurse, and doing whatever miscellaneous good she might; taking upon herself, likewise, to give advice in all matters, especially those of the heart; by which means, as a person of such propensities inevitably must, she gained from many people the reverence due to an angel, but I should imagine, was looked upon by others as an intruder and a nuisance. Prying further into the manuscript, I found the record of other doings and sufferings of this singular woman, for most of which the reader is referred to the story entitled, "THE SCARLET LETTER"; and it should be borne carefully in mind, that the main facts of that story are authorized and authenticated by the document of Mr. Surveyor Pue. The original papers, together with the scarlet letter itself,—a most curious relic,—are still in my possession, and shall be freely exhibited to whomsoever, induced by the great interest of the narrative, may desire a sight of them. I must not be understood as affirming, that, in the dressing up of the tale, and imagining the motives and modes of passion that influenced the characters who figure in it, I have invariably confined myself within the limits of the old Surveyor's half a dozen sheets of foolscap. On the contrary, I have allowed myself, as to such points, nearly or altogether as much license as if the facts had been entirely of my own invention. What I contend for is the authenticity of the outline.

This incident recalled my mind, in some degree, to its old track. There seemed to be here the ground-work of a tale. It impressed me as if the ancient Surveyor, in his garb of a hundred years gone by, and wearing his immortal wig,—which was buried with him, but did not perish in the grave,—had met me in the deserted chamber of the Custom House. In his port was the dignity of one who had borne his Majesty's commission, and who was therefore illuminated by a ray of the splendor that shone so dazzlingly about the throne. How unlike, alas! the hang-dog look of a republican official, who, as the servant of the people, feels himself less than the least, and below the lowest, of his masters. With his own ghostly hand, the obscurely seen but majestic figure had imparted to me the scarlet symbol, and the little roll of explanatory manuscript. With his own ghostly voice, he had exhorted me, on the sacred consideration of my filial duty and reverence towards him,—who might reasonably regard himself as my official ancestor,—to bring his mouldy and moth-eaten lucubrations before the public. "Do this," said the ghost of Mr. Surveyor Pue, emphatically nodding the head that looked so imposing within its memorable wig, "do this, and the profit shall be all your own! You will shortly need it; for it is not in your days as it was in mine, when a man's office was a life-lease, and oftentimes an heirloom. But, I charge you, in this matter of old Mistress Prynne, give to your predecessor's memory the credit which will be rightfully due!" And I said to the ghost of Mr. Surveyor Pue, "I will!"

On Hester Prynne's story, therefore, I bestowed much thought. It was the subject of my meditations for many an hour, while pacing to and fro cross my room, or traversing with a hundred-fold repetition, the long extent from the front-door of the Custom House to the side-entrance, and back again. Great were the weariness and annoyance of the old Inspector and the Weighers and Gaugers, whose slumbers were disturbed by the unmercifully lengthened tramp of my passing and returning footsteps. Remembering their own former habits, they used to say that the Surveyor was walking the quarter-deck. They probably fancied that my sole object—and, indeed, the sole object for which a sane man could ever put himself into voluntary motion—was, to get an appetite for dinner. And to say the truth, an appetite, sharpened by the east wind that generally blew along the passage, was the only valuable result of so much indefatigable exercise. So little adapted is the atmosphere of a Custom House to the delicate harvest of fancy and sensibility, that, had I remained there through ten Presidencies yet to come, I doubt whether the tale of "The Scarlet Letter" would ever have been brought before the public eye. My imagination was a tarnished mirror. It would not reflect, or only with miserable dimness, the figures with which I did my best to people it. The characters of the narrative would not be warmed and rendered malleable by any heat that I could kindle at my intellectual forge. They would take neither the glow of passion nor the tenderness of sentiment, but retained all the rigidity of dead corpses, and stared me in the face with a fixed and ghastly grin of contemptuous defiance. "What have you to do with us?" that expression seemed to say. "The little power you might once have possessed over the tribe of unrealities is gone! You have bartered it for a pittance of the public gold. Go, then, and earn your wages!" In short, the almost torpid creatures of my own fancy twitted me with imbecility, and not without fair occasion.

It was not merely during the three hours and a half which Uncle Sam claimed as his share of my daily life, that this wretched numbness held possession of me. It went with me on my sea-shore walks, and rambles into the country, whenever—which was seldom and reluctantly—I bestirred myself to seek that invigorating charm of Nature, which used to give me such freshness and activity of thought, the moment that I stepped across the threshold of the Old Manse. The same torpor, as regarded the capacity for intellectual effort, accompanied me home, and weighed upon me in the chamber which I most absurdly termed my study. Nor did it quit me, when, late at night, I sat in the deserted parlor, lighted only by the glimmering coal-fire and the moon, striving to picture forth imaginary scenes, which, the next day, might flow out on the brightening page in many-hued description.

If the imaginative faculty refused to act at such an hour, it might well be deemed a hopeless case. Moonlight, in a familiar room, falling so white upon the carpet, and showing all its figures so distinctly,—making every object so minutely visible, yet so unlike a morning or noontide visibility,—is a medium the most suitable for a romance-writer to get acquainted with his illusive guests. There is the little domestic scenery of the well-known apartment; the chairs, with each its separate individuality; the centre-table, sustaining a work-basket, a volume or two, and an extinguished lamp; the sofa; the book-case; the picture on the wall;—all these details, so completely seen, are so spiritualized by the unusual light, that they seem to lose their actual substance, and become things of intellect. Nothing is too small or too trifling to undergo this change, and acquire dignity thereby. A child's shoe; the doll, seated in her little wicker carriage; the hobby-horse;—whatever, in a word, has been used or played with, during the day, is now invested with a quality of strangeness and remoteness, though still almost as vividly present as by daylight. Thus, therefore, the floor of our familiar room has become a neutral territory, somewhere between the real world and fairy-land, where the Actual and the Imaginary may meet, and each imbue itself with the nature of the other. Ghosts might enter here, without affrighting us. It would be too much in keeping with the scene to excite surprise, were we to look about us and discover a form beloved, but gone hence, now sitting quietly in a streak of this magic moonshine, with an aspect that would make us doubt whether it had returned from afar, or had never once stirred from our fireside.

The somewhat dim coal-fire has an essential influence in producing the effect which I would describe. It throws its unobtrusive tinge throughout the room, with a faint ruddiness upon the walls and ceiling, and a reflected gleam from the polish of the furniture. This warmer light mingles itself with the cold spirituality of the moonbeams, and communicates, as it were, a heart and sensibilities of human tenderness to the forms which fancy summons up. It converts them from snow-images into men and women. Glancing at the looking-glass, we behold—deep within its haunted verge—the smouldering glow of the half-extinguished anthracite, the white moonbeams on the floor, and a repetition of all the gleam and shadow of the picture, with one remove further from the actual, and nearer to the imaginative. Then, at such an hour, and with this scene before him, if a man, sitting all alone, cannot dream strange things, and make them look like truth, he need never try to write romances.

But, for myself, during the whole of my Custom House experience, moonlight and sunshine, and the glow of fire-light, were just alike in my regard; and neither of them was of one whit more avail than the twinkle of a tallow-candle. An entire class of susceptibilities, and a gift connected with them, —of no great richness or value, but the best I had, —was gone from me.

It is my belief, however, that, had I attempted a different order of composition, my faculties would not have been found so pointless and inefficacious. I might, for instance, have contented myself with writing out the narratives of a veteran shipmaster, one of the Inspectors, whom I should be most ungrateful not to mention, since scarcely a day passed that he did not stir me to laughter and admiration by his marvellous gifts as a story-teller. Could I have preserved the picturesque force of his style, and the humorous coloring which nature taught him how to throw over his descriptions, the result, I honestly believe, would have been something new in literature. Or I might readily have found a more serious task. It was a folly, with the materiality of this daily life pressing so intrusively upon me, to attempt to fling myself back into another age; or to insist on creating the semblance of a world out of airy matter, when, at every moment, the impalpable beauty of my soap-bubble was broken by the rude contact of some actual circumstance. The wiser effort would have been to diffuse thought and imagination through the opaque substance of today, and thus to make it a bright transparency; to spiritualize the burden that began to weigh so heavily; to seek, resolutely, the true and indestructible value that lay hidden in the petty and wearisome incidents, and ordinary characters, with which I was now conversant. The fault was mine. The page of life that was spread out before me seemed dull and commonplace, only because I had not fathomed its deeper import. A better book than I shall ever write was there; leaf after leaf presenting itself to me, just as it was written out by the reality of the flitting hour, and vanishing as fast as written, only because my brain wanted the insight and my hand the cunning to transcribe it. At some future day, it may be, I shall remember a few scattered fragments and broken paragraphs, and write them down, and find the letters turn to gold upon the page. . . .

. . . The life of the Custom House lies like a dream behind me. The old Inspector,—who, by the by, I regret to say, was overthrown and killed by a horse, some time ago; else he would certainly have lived forever,—he, and all those other venerable personages who sat with him at the receipt of custom, are but shadows in my view; white-headed and wrinkled images, which my fancy used to sport with, and has now flung aside forever. The merchants,—Pingree, Phillips, Shepard, Upton, Kimball, Bertram, Hunt,—these, and many other names, which had such a classic familiarity for my ear six months ago,—these men of traffic, who seemed to occupy so important a position in the world,—how little time has it required to disconnect me from them all, not merely in act, but recollection! It is with an effort that I recall the figures and appellations of these few. Soon, likewise, my old native town will loom upon me through the haze of memory, a mist brooding over and around it; as if it were no portion of the real earth, but an overgrown village in cloud-land, with only imaginary inhabitants to people its wooden houses, and walk its homely lanes, and the unpicturesque prolixity of its main street. Henceforth, it ceases to be a reality of my life. I am a citizen of somewhere else. My good townspeople will not much regret me; for—though it has been as dear an object as any, in my literary efforts, to be of some importance in their eyes, and to win myself a pleasant memory in this abode and burial-place of so many of my forefathers—there has never been, for me, the genial atmosphere which a literary man requires, in order to ripen the best harvest of his mind. I shall do better amongst other faces; and these familiar ones, it need hardly be said, will do just as well without me. . . .

1850

PREFACE TO TWICE-TOLD TALES, 1851 EDITION

THE AUTHOR of "TWICE-TOLD TALES" has a claim to one distinction, which, as none of his literary brethren will care about disputing it with him, he need not be afraid to mention. He was, for a good many years, the obscurest man of letters in America.

These stories were published in magazines and

annuals, extending over a period of ten or twelve years, and comprising the whole of the writer's young manhood, without making (so far as he has ever been aware) the slightest impression on the public. One or two among them, the "Rill from the Town Pump," in perhaps a greater degree than any other, had a pretty wide newspaper circulation; as for the rest, he had no grounds for supposing that, on their first appearance, they met with the good or evil fortune to be read by anybody. Throughout the time above specified, he had no incitement to literary effort in a reasonable prospect of reputation or profit, nothing but the pleasure itself of composition—an enjoyment not at all amiss in its way, and perhaps essential to the merit of the work in hand, but which, in the long run, will hardly keep the chill out of a writer's heart, or the numbness out of his fingers. To this total lack of sympathy, at the age when his mind would naturally have been most effervescent, the public owe it (and it is certainly an effect not to be regretted on either part) that the Author can show nothing for the thought and industry of that portion of his life, save the forty sketches, or thereabouts, included in these volumes.

Much more, indeed, he wrote; and some very small part of it might yet be rummaged out (but it would not be worth the trouble) among the dingy pages of fifteen-or-twenty-year-old periodicals, or within the shabby morocco covers of faded souvenirs. The remainder of the works alluded to had a very brief existence, but, on the score of brilliancy, enjoyed a fate vastly superior to that of their brotherhood, which succeeded in getting through the press. In a word, the Author burned them without mercy or remorse, and, moreover, without any subsequent regret, and had more than one occasion to marvel that such very dull stuff, as he knew his condemned manuscripts to be, should yet have possessed inflammability enough to set the chimney on fire!

After a long while the first collected volume of the "Tales" was published. By this time, if the Author had ever been greatly tormented by literary ambition (which he does not remember or believe to have been the case), it must have perished, beyond resuscitation, in the dearth of nutriment. This was fortunate; for the success of the volume was not such as would have gratified a craving desire for notoriety. A moderate edition was "got rid of" (to use the publisher's very significant phrase) within a reasonable time, but apparently without rendering the writer or his productions much more generally known than before. The great bulk of the reading public probably ignored the book altogether. A few persons read it, and liked it better than it deserved. At an interval of three or four years, the second volume was published, and encountered much the same sort of kindly, but calm, and very limited reception. The circulation of the two volumes was chiefly confined to New England; nor was it until long after this period, if it even yet be the case, that the Author could regard himself as addressing the American public, or, indeed, any public at all. He was merely writing to his known or unknown friends.

As he glances over these long-forgotten pages, and considers his way of life while composing them, the Author can very clearly discern why all this was so. After so many sober years, he would have reason to be ashamed if he could not criticise his own work as fairly as another man's; and, though it is little his business, and perhaps still less his interest, he can hardly resist a temptation to achieve something of the sort. If writers were allowed to do so, and would perform the task with perfect sincerity and unreserve, their opinions of their own productions would often be more valuable and instructive than the works themselves.

At all events, there can be no harm in the Author's remarking, that he rather wonders how the "TWICE-TOLD TALES" should have gained what vogue they did, than that it was so little and so gradual. They have the pale tint of flowers that blossomed in too retired a shade—the coolness of a meditative habit, which diffuses itself through the feeling and observation of every sketch. Instead of passion, there is sentiment; and, even in what purport to be pictures of actual life, we have allegory, not always so warmly dressed in its habiliments of flesh and blood, as to be taken into the reader's mind without a shiver. Whether from lack of power, or an unconquerable reserve, the Author's touches have often an effect of tameness; the merriest man can hardly contrive to laugh at his broadest humor; the tenderest woman, one would suppose, will hardly shed warm tears at his deepest pathos. The book, if you would see any thing in it, requires to be read in the clear, brown, twilight atmosphere in which it was written; if opened in the sunshine, it is apt to look exceedingly like a volume of blank pages.

With the foregoing characteristics, proper to the productions of a person in retirement, (which happened to be the Author's category at the time,) the book is devoid of others that we should quite as naturally look for. The sketches are not, it is hardly necessary to say, profound; but it is rather more remarkable that they so seldom, if ever, show any design on the writer's part to make them so. They have none of the abstruseness of idea, or obscurity of expression, which mark the written communications of a solitary mind with itself. They never need translation. It is, in fact, the style of a man of society. Every sentence, so far as it embodies thought or sensibility, may be understood and felt by anybody, who will give himself the trouble to read it, and will take up the book in a proper mood.

This statement of apparently opposite peculiarities leads us to a perception of what the sketches truly are. They are not the talk of a secluded man with his own mind and heart (had it been so, they could hardly have failed to be more deeply and permanently valuable), but his attempts, and very imperfectly successful ones, to open an intercourse with the world.

The Author would regret to be understood as speaking sourly or querulously of the slight mark made by his earlier literary efforts on the Public at large. It is so far the contrary, that he has been moved to write this Preface chiefly as affording him an opportunity to express how much enjoyment he has owed to these volumes, both before and since their publication. They are the memorials of very tranquil and not unhappy years. They failed, it is true,—nor could it have been otherwise,—in winning an extensive popularity. Occasionally, however, when he deemed them entirely forgotten, a paragraph or an article, from a native or foreign critic, would gratify his instincts of authorship with unexpected praise,—too generous praise, indeed, and too little alloyed with censure, which, therefore, he learned the better to inflict upon himself. And, by the by, it is a very suspicious symptom of a deficiency of the popular element in a book when it calls forth no harsh criticism. This has been particularly the fortune of the "TWICE-TOLD TALES." They made no enemies, and were so little known and talked about that those who read, and chanced to like them, were apt to conceive the sort of kindness for the book which a person naturally feels for a discovery of his own.

This kindly feeling (in some cases, at least) extended to the Author, who, on the internal evidence of his sketches, came to be regarded as a mild, shy, gentle, melancholic, exceedingly sensitive, and not very forcible man, hiding his blushes under an assumed name, the quaintness of which was supposed, somehow or other, to symbolize his personal and literary traits. He is by no means certain that some of his subsequent productions have not been influenced and modified by a natural desire to fill up so amiable an outline, and to act in consonance with the character assigned to him; nor, even now, could he forfeit it without a few tears of tender sensibility. To conclude, however: these volumes have opened the way to most agreeable associations, and to the formation of imperishable friendships; and there are many golden threads interwoven with his present happiness, which he can follow up more or less directly, until he finds their commencement here; so that his pleasant pathway among realities seems to proceed out of the Dreamland of his youth, and to be bordered with just enough of its shadowy foliage to shelter him from the heat of the day. He is therefore satisfied with what the "TWICE-TOLD TALES" have done for him, and feels it to be far better than fame.

PREFACE TO THE HOUSE OF THE SEVEN GABLES

WHEN a writer calls his work a Romance, it need hardly be observed that he wishes to claim a certain latitude, both as to its fashion and material, which he would not have felt himself entitled to assume, had he professed to be writing a Novel. The latter form of composition is presumed to aim at a very minute fidelity, not merely to the possible, but to the probable and ordinary course of man's experience. The former—while, as a work of art, it must rigidly subject itself to laws, and while it sins unpardonably so far as it may swerve aside from the truth of the human heart—has fairly a right to present that truth under circumstances, to a great extent, of the writer's own choosing or creation. If he thinks fit, also, he may so manage his atmospherical medium as to bring out or mellow the lights, and deepen and enrich the shadows, of the picture. He will be wise, no doubt, to make a very moderate use of the privileges here stated, and, especially, to mingle the Marvelous rather as a slight, delicate, and evanescent flavor, than as any portion of the actual substance of the dish offered to the public. He can hardly be said, however, to commit a literary crime, even if he disregard this caution.

In the present work the author has proposed to himself—but with what success, fortunately, it is not for him to judge—to keep undeviatingly within his immunities. The point of view in which this tale comes under the Romantic definition lies in the attempt to connect a bygone time with the very present that is flitting away from us. It is a legend, prolonging itself, from an epoch now gray in the distance down into our own broad daylight, and bringing along with it some of its legendary mist, which the reader, according to his pleasure, may either disregard or allow it to float almost imperceptibly about the characters and events for the sake of a picturesque effect. The narrative, it may be, is woven of so humble a texture as to require this advantage, and, at the same time, to render it the more difficult of attainment.

Many writers lay very great stress upon some definite moral purpose, at which they profess to aim their works. Not to be deficient in this particular, the author has provided himself with a moral;—the truth, namely, that the wrongdoing of one generation lives into the successive ones, and, divesting itself of every temporary advantage, becomes a pure and uncontrollable mischief,—and he would feel it a singular gratification, if this romance might effectually convince mankind—or, indeed, any one man—of the folly of tumbling down an avalanche of ill-gotten gold, or real estate, on the heads of an unfortunate posterity, thereby to maim and crush them, until the accumulated mass shall be scattered abroad in its original atoms. In good faith, however, he is not sufficiently imaginative to flatter himself with the slightest hope of this kind. When romances do really teach anything, or produce any effective operation, it is usually through a far more subtile process than the ostensible one. The author has considered it hardly worth his while, therefore, relentlessly to impale the story with its moral, as with an iron rod,—or, rather, as by sticking a pin through a butterfly,—thus at once depriving it of life, and causing it to stiffen in an ungainly and unnatural attitude. A high truth, indeed, fairly, finely, and skilfully wrought out, brightening at every step, and crowning the final development of a work of fiction, may add an artistic glory, but is never any truer, and seldom any more evident, at the last page than at the first.

The reader may perhaps choose to assign an actual locality to the imaginary events of this narrative. If permitted by the historical connection,—which, though slight, was essential to his plan,—the author would very willingly have avoided anything of this nature. Not to speak of other objections, it exposes the romance to an inflexible and exceedingly dangerous species of criticism, by bringing his fancy-pictures almost into positive contact with the realities of the moment. It has been no part of his object, however, to describe local manners, nor in any way to meddle with the characteristics of a community for whom he cherishes a proper respect and a natural regard. He trusts not to be considered as unpardonably offending, by laying out a street that infringes upon nobody's private rights, and appropriating a lot of land which had no visible owner, and building a house, of materials long in use for constructing castles in the air. The personages of the tale—though they give themselves out to be of ancient stability and considerable prominence—are really of the author's own making, or, at all events, of his own mixing; their virtues can shed no luster, nor their defects redound, in the remotest degree, to the discredit of the venerable town of which they profess to be inhabitants. He would be glad, therefore, if—especially in the quarter to which he alludes—the book may be read strictly as a romance, having a great deal more to do with the clouds overhead than with any portion of the actual soil of the County of Essex.

1851

PREFACE TO THE MARBLE FAUN

IT IS NOW seven or eight years (so many, at all events, that I cannot precisely remember the epoch) since the author of this Romance last appeared before the Public. It had grown to be a custom with him to introduce each of his humble publications with a familiar kind of Preface, addressed nominally to the Public at large, but really to a character with whom he felt entitled to use far greater freedom. He meant it for that one congenial friend,—more comprehensive of his purposes, more appreciative of his success, more indulgent of his shortcomings, and, in all respects, closer and kinder than a brother,—that all-sympathizing critic, in short, whom an author never actually meets, but to whom he implicitly makes his appeal whenever he is conscious of having done his best.

The antique fashion of Prefaces recognized this genial personage as the "Kind Reader," the "Gentle Reader," the "Beloved," the "Indulgent," or, at coldest, the "Honored Reader," to whom the prim old author was wont to make his preliminary explanations and apologies, with the certainty that they would be favorably received. I never personally encountered, nor corresponded through the post with this representative essence of all delightful and desirable qualities which a reader can possess. But, fortunately for myself, I never therefore concluded him to be merely a mythic character. I had always a sturdy faith in his actual existence, and wrote for him year after year, during which the great eye of the Public (as well it might) almost utterly overlooked my small productions.

Unquestionably, this gentle, kind, benevolent, indulgent, and most beloved and honored Reader did once exist for me, and (in spite of the infinite chances against a letter's reaching its destination without a definite address) duly received the scrolls which I flung upon whatever wind was blowing, in the faith that they would find him out. But, is he extant now? In these many years, since he last heard from me, may he not have deemed his earthly task accomplished, and have withdrawn to the paradise of gentle readers, wherever it may be, to the enjoyments of which his kindly charity on my behalf must surely have entitled him? I have a sad foreboding that this may be the truth. The "Gentle Reader," in the case of any individual author, is apt to be extremely short-lived; he seldom outlasts a literary fashion, and, except in very rare instances, closes his weary eyes before the writer was half done with him. If I find him at all, it will probably be under some mossy-gravestone, inscribed with a half-obliterated name which I shall never recognize.

Therefore, I have little heart or confidence (especially, writing as I do, in a foreign land, and after a long, long absence from my own) to presume upon the existence of that friend of friends, that unseen brother of the soul, whose apprehensive sympathy has so often encouraged me to be egotistical in my prefaces, careless though unkindly eyes should skim over what was never meant for them. I stand upon ceremony now; and, after stating a few particulars about the work which is here offered to the Public, must make my most reverential bow, and retire behind the curtain.

This Romance was sketched out during a residence of considerable length in Italy,[1] and has been re-written and prepared for the press in England. The author proposed to himself merely to write a fanciful story, evolving a thoughtful moral, and did not purpose attempting a portraiture of Italian manners and character. He has lived too long abroad not to be aware that a foreigner seldom acquires that knowledge of a country at once flexible and profound, which may justify him in endeavoring to idealize its traits.

Italy, as the site of his Romance, was chiefly valuable to him as affording a sort of poetic or fairy precinct, where actualities would not be so terribly insisted upon as they are, and must needs be, in America. No author, without a trial, can conceive of the difficulty of writing a romance about a country where there is no shadow, no antiquity, no mystery, no picturesque and gloomy wrong, nor anything but a commonplace prosperity, in broad and simple daylight, as is happily the case with my dear native land. It will be very long, I trust, before romance-writers may find congenial and easily handled themes, either in the annals of our stalwart republic, or in any characteristic and probable events of our individual lives. Romance and poetry, ivy, lichens, and wall-flowers need ruin to make them grow.

In re-writing these volumes, the author was somewhat surprised to see the extent to which he had introduced descriptions of various Italian objects, antique, pictorial, and statuesque. Yet these things fill the mind everywhere in Italy, and especially in Rome, and cannot easily be kept from flowing out upon the page when one writes freely, and with self-enjoyment. And, again, while reproducing the book, on the broad and dreary sands of Redcar,[2] with the gray German Ocean tumbling in upon me, and the northern blast always howling in my ears, the complete change of scene made these Italian reminiscences shine out so vividly that I could not find it in my heart to cancel them.

1860

THE MARBLE FAUN. 1. **residence . . . Italy**: the Hawthornes resided in Italy, 1858–59.

2. **Redcar**: a town in Yorkshire, England, on the North Sea.

WILLIAM CHARVAT
Editor

Henry Wadsworth Longfellow

1807–1882

James Russell Lowell

1819–1891

THE TERM "Fireside Poets" accurately describes a group of writers who were well known in New England in the 1840's, acquired a national audience after 1850, and were of unrivalled popularity in the quarter-century before World War I. The best-known members of the group were Henry Wadsworth Longfellow, James Russell Lowell, Oliver Wendell Holmes, John Greenleaf Whittier, and William Cullen Bryant. All were native New Englanders; indeed, all except Bryant lived in eastern Massachusetts, and the first three lived in the adjacent communities of Cambridge and Boston.

The word "fireside" indicates that they had a family audience—men, women, and children. It also implies that their verse was read aloud in the family circle . Their books were published in a variety of formats—from paperback to expensive, illustrated editions—at prices to suit every pocketbook. One or another of these editions was owned by most northern, western, and some southern, Americans who bought and read books.

In our time, there is no equivalent to this group of poets. The verse reading audience is now so stratified that there is no common bond between those who buy Eliot, Pound, and Stevens, and those who prefer Edgar Guest, James Whitcomb Riley, or the amateur verse which appears in thc Sunday edition of the local newspaper. The Fireside Poets, by contrast, were read alike by the highly educated and by some of the merely literate, though much of their work was beyond the comprehension of the latter.

It is to be expected that, writing for an audience both culturally mixed and family-centered, these poets emphasized certain subjects and avoided others. Their favorite themes were home, family, and children; nature; idealized love; religion—Protestant, but usually nondenominational; love of country, but rarely partisan politics; and they versified much story from history, legend, and anecdote, both native and foreign.

Their view of life can be described superficially by the soft term—common in nineteenth-century popular literature—"sunshine and shadow," which implies a balance of good and bad in human experience. The emphasis, one way or the other, varies somewhat from poet to poet. All had been taught to believe, through their heritage of eighteenth-century rationalism, that in the divine plan apparent evil was part of a total good. But Longfellow and Bryant, influenced by Puritanism or current Romantic attitudes, tended to put their fingers on the somber side of the scales. Balance is suggested in Longfellow's work by the recurrence of pairs of verbal opposites—sorrow-delight, toil-rest, soothe-affright.

> Our little lives are kept in equipoise
> By opposite attractions and desires

he wrote in "Haunted Houses." Yet a careful reading of even his supposedly optimistic—and worst—poems shows that though he believed in balance, he did not feel it. The village blacksmith at work looks picturesque to the children, and he begins and finishes something each day, but we get the impression that he toils and sorrows more than he rejoices. In "The Wreck of the Hesperus," the captain's will to act is favorably presented, but it leads to nothing but pointless sacrifice of life. "A Psalm of Life," in which we are told to "Trust no Future" and to "Learn to labor and to wait," is anything but a cheerful poem.

Longfellow's basic lessons, then, are austere ones. We are to work for work's own sake. We are to *accept* life's labors, deprivals, and sorrows. The reward is rest, and rest ultimately means death. The terror of death is mitigated by a serene but not very insistent assumption of immortality.

It is to be expected that, their audience being what it was, these poets should have certain forms and techniques in common. Their rhythms, though often skillfully varied, derive from traditional meters; their stanzas follow formal patterns; they favor either blank verse or conventional end-rhymes (rather than, for example, the elusive internal recurrences of sound one finds in Emily Dickinson and Walt Whitman); their language is traditional—their English usually British. They use inversions, and archaisms like "Thou see'st." Their images and metaphors are simple and familiar. Their symbolism is explicit, and their meanings and "lessons" are on the surface. The experienced reader of verse rarely has to read one of their poems twice to comprehend all that is in it.

All these writers used poetry as a vehicle for teaching. Most good poetry teaches in one way or another; the way the Fireside Poets had in common was that of explicit analogy. Some object or phenomenon in nature or some action is presented; an analogy with the human condition is then drawn; and usually—but not always—the meaning or moral of the analogy is explicitly stated.

This is not to say that all their verse is easy for the common reader of our own time. They were not "mass" poets in any sense of the word: the Edgar Guest fan would be puzzled by much of what they wrote, for they made demands on their audience as mass literature today does not. Their many allusions show that they expected readers to have some knowledge of classical myth, of European and American history and legend, of the story of Christianity and other religions, and of the Bible. They assumed, also, that readers had enough knowledge of formal grammar to be able to follow an extended syntactical structure, and to locate the remote antecedent of a pronoun. Some of them used foreign words and phrases without building in translations. And they were not afraid of what are now considered "big words." In short, the merely literate reader of today must use dictionaries, guides to mythology, gazetteers, and other tools in order to understand fully what the Fireside Poets are saying.

As "public" poets they had, of course, an advantage that has since diminished. Education in their time was relatively fixed and formalized. The very considerable number of readers who attended the academies, the denominational colleges, and even the better common schools, were likely to get some training in rhetoric, in Latin or French, and in moral philosophy, and to read some of the famous British classics—the work of Shakespeare, Milton, Pope, and *Pilgrim's Progress.* In other words, the poets could assume a far more homogeneous experience in literature and language in their readers than can be expected now.

Finally, they shared a belief or hope, held

by most serious American writers of the century, that it was possible, in Poe's phrase, "to suit at once the popular and the critical taste." From Poe and Emerson to Howells and the early Henry James, there was a general faith, often shaken but rarely wholly abandoned, that in a democracy writers could offer their best with some hope that even the culturally unsophisticated would accept them and support them sufficiently to make the literary life possible in America. Believing that the common reader was willing to exert himself, they did not resign themselves completely to his limitations. Moreover, all serious writers were conscious of belonging to the tradition—to the institution—of great Western literature, and made their readers aware that that tradition was being continued in America. In this respect, the Fireside Poets made a significant contribution. Much of their verse and prose is *about* the great writers of the past, and reading the work of the Poets was for their readers a kind of instruction in the history of literature.

II

ONE of the remarkable facts about this group is that though they appealed to literate people of every social class, they themselves—with one exception, Whittier—were members of the social elite—of what might be called the patrician level in the American social scale. None of them was independently wealthy, but they came from families whose names carried prestige; for whom a college education and membership in a respected profession were matters of course; and to whom public service of some sort—in the courts, churches, legislatures, and in the military during the Revolutionary War—was a source of pride. In a word, they "belonged"—had a sense of place in the social structure and in the American past. Perhaps partly for that reason they could attempt the risky profession of literature with a confidence that was denied to, say, an Edgar Allan Poe. In this democracy there was still a good deal of respect for the "high-born"—especially if the high-born earned their keep by achieving some sort of professional or public distinction. Everyone knew that Longfellow was a professor and a learned man, that he lived in a mansion, and that after his marriage to the daughter of Nathan Appleton he was increasingly well-to-do, but few readers resented his status. Though Holmes said that some people thought his verse writing impugned his ability as a physician, most of his readers were happy to think of him as Doctor Holmes of Boston. And Bryant lost no prestige as poet by being editor of a great New York newspaper and a translator of Greek classics.

Although Longfellow's immediate family was anything but rich, he was from the beginning exempt from the poverty and the galling sense of social inferiority which, long before Shakespeare's time, had exacerbated writers of humble origin who lived in cultures dominated by a hereditary or landed aristocracy. Longfellow's paternal grandfather was a state senator; his maternal grandfather was a Revolutionary general, a representative to Congress from Maine, and had a ten-thousand-acre estate which the boy often visited. His father was a Harvard graduate and a lawmaker for both his state and the nation. A boy from such a background knew that some sort of public service and leadership was expected of him, and although he had had literary ambitions even as a schoolchild, he dutifully considered entering the law or the ministry, the professions with which a literary career was usually combined. When he was seventeen (1824) his father wisely warned him that "there is not wealth enough in this country to afford encouragement to merely literary men. And as you have not had the fortune (I will not say whether good or ill) to be born rich, you must adopt a profession which will afford you subsistence as well as reputation. . . ." Here was the tough New England attitude which required that the ambition to *be* somebody in terms not primarily materialistic be based solidly on the ability to make one's own living by work. When Longfellow's alma mater, Bowdoin College, offered him its first professorship in modern languages, he found his solution: at the age of twenty-two he became the first American poet who supported his craft for any considerable length of time by being a teacher and scholar. Since about 1945 this arrangement has been common: most of our poets get employment in the universities.

Longfellow took his teaching seriously and for many years he put his major energies into academic chores. Essential to the spirit of his writings is the fact that, with no expectation of eventually inheriting wealth, he early assumed that his place was with the vast majority of the human race who must work for a living. As a teacher of foreign languages at Bowdoin (1829–34) and Harvard (1836–54), where much of his time was devoted to irksome elementary drilling, he knew the salaried worker's frustrations and dissatisfactions. Yet after his marriage into the affluent Appleton family, he continued to teach for eleven years. He left Harvard only when his reputation as a poet had become so firmly established that he knew he could earn at least a subsistence for himself through the hard work of writing poetry. Financially, what his marriage meant to him chiefly was that he need not give in to the pressures—which intensified as the century advanced—of publishers and of popular taste.

Essential also to the impact of his verse in his time was his passion for European culture. Even as his father was penning the letter of 1824, several students were establishing the American tradition of scholarship as a branch of the humane tradition of Europe. George Ticknor, already a teacher of modern languages at Harvard; George Bancroft, the future historian of America; Joseph Cogswell, our first scholarly librarian—all had studied or were studying in Germany, and were importing European scholarly techniques. From these men, Longfellow got letters of introduction to foreign writers and to Washington Irving in Spain.

Irving had already embodied much of his European experience in essays and tales. Longfellow combined Irving's belletristic interests with Ticknor's emphasis on scholarship. After his first sojourn abroad (1826–29) he was competent to write the foreign language textbooks he needed at Bowdoin, but he also prepared materials for an imitation of Irving's *Sketch Book*. *Outre-Mer* (1833–35) was the first of three semifictional, essay-structured prose works, all set in Europe, which in their time were as popular as his verse. *Hyperion* (1839) was the disguised autobiographical statement of an American teacher traveling in Europe who was making up his mind to be a professional poet in a culture which had hitherto not supported its poets. Glowing accounts of Europe's historic shrines, and long dialogues about European literature and art, suggest that, consciously or not, Longfellow was planning to make his literary life an extension of a long tradition.

For the rest of his career he was to find much of his poetic subject matter in European history, legend, art, and scenery. In the twentieth century he has been much criticized for not being more native, more contemporary in his interests. But there has been increasing recognition that in bringing to Americans the culture of Europe, in the form of translations and adaptations of its poetry, and in celebrating Old World history and story, he did much to mitigate the provincialism which, from the beginning to our own times, has narrowed and shallowed the American character. He softened much that he imported, but he made his readers aware not only of the grandeur and beauty but of some of the terror in their European heritage. If he sentimentalized Europe, as some critics have said, there are fewer quaint villages and carillons in his foreign settings than there are bloody battles, bigotry, wretched serfs, murders, and hovering menaces to life and liberty.

Longfellow has also been accused of being incapable of sympathy for the common man, yet he was deeply involved in a movement in the 1840's toward a literature about and for the common people. Orestes Brownson, a representative spokesman of the time, wrote that American "scholars"—there was a general assumption then that men of letters were also men of learning—must abandon their "lone reveries" and their "scholastic asceticism," and seek their inspiration in the "really living, moving, toiling and sweating, joying and sorrowing people around them." Longfellow had had his years of lonely reveries and scholastic asceticism, but from 1839 on his writings were informed by an awareness of the people, and he wished to reach the people as well as the cultured classes. In 1840 this scholarly gentleman of Cambridge wrote that he wanted to "work upon people's feelings," and that he contemplated printing "The Wreck of the Hesperus" on a broadside sheet, "with a coarse picture on it." He did not do so, but for years thereafter some of his work was published in our earliest mass magazines, and his verse was available in paperback editions selling for twelve and a half and fifty cents. The poet who could write about the

> weight of care,
> That crushes into dumb despair,
> One half the human race . . .
> Steeped to the lips in misery,
> Longing, and yet afraid to die

knew quite as well as Thoreau that the "mass of men lead lives of quiet desperation." The emotional weights in his vocabulary become obvious to one who reads enough of him. The endlessly reiterated words are "care," "weariness," "sorrow," "burden," "fear," "toil," and "defeat"—often in description of a man's work and a man's family. If, along with such words, we find a recurrence of others like "comfort," "balm," "cheer," and "soothe," it is because he felt that the need for comfort was great. But the comfort he offered was not delusive.

In 1839 he had said that the American artist "must wait." By 1850, in the "Dedication" to *The Seaside and the Fireside,* he could with confidence address his audience as "friends" and hope

> as no unwelcome guest,
> At your warm fireside, when the lamps are lighted,
> To have my place reserved among the rest,
> Nor stand as one unsought and uninvited!

This confidence was, in part, a result of the enthusiastic reception given to his first long poem, *Evangeline* (1847). Thereafter, long narratives in verse or dramatic form constituted the bulk of his writings. This fact brings up the problem of the long poem in modern literature. The epic had once been the poetic form in which the life of a whole nation or culture could be subsumed, but, after Milton, secular and religious cultures lost the homogeneity which made a *Paradise Lost* possible. Yet many nineteenth-century poets were not content to write lyrics only, and sought to create forms capable of carrying the weight of subjects of some magnitude. Increasingly, poets from Byron to Ezra Pound radically changed the tradition of the long poem by making it an exploration of the poet's self, Whitman's final version of *Leaves of Grass* being America's finest example. Longfellow and his imitators, however, attempted to continue the older tradition in poems about the lives of ethnic or religious or regional groups. *Evangeline* is the story of exiled Canadian villagers, *Hiawatha* (1855) of the myths of a group of Indian tribes, *The Courtship of Miles Standish* (1858) of a New England community. In *Tales of a Wayside Inn* (1863) he used Chaucerian devices to put twenty-two shorter tales, mostly about ancient Europe, into a framework resembling that of the *Canterbury Tales.*

Most of these pieces, however short or long, are in the anecdotal rather than in the epic strain. When, in his magnum opus—the three part verse drama, *Christus: A Mystery* (1872) —he attempted epic magnitude and unity, he failed. As early as 1842, in "Mezzo Cammin," he had lamented,

> Half of my life is gone, and I have not fulfilled
> The aspiration of my youth, to build
> Some tower of song with lofty parapet.

In the same year he planned the three parts of the *Christus*—I, "The Time of Christ (Hope)," II, "The Middle Ages (Faith)," III, "The Present (Charity)." Part II was published first as *The Golden Legend.* Part III, instead of dealing with "The Present" was limited to colonial New England under the title *The New England Tragedies* (1868). When the *Christus* was published as a whole it was a flat failure. Though it appeared in six different formats, variously priced, less than six thousand copies were printed. For the moment, Longfellow's public had deserted him.

The failure was intrinsic as well as commercial. To find the reason we must look into his whole philosophy of the history of religion in its relation to his belief in the idea of moral progress. Longfellow's historical assumptions were common in his generation: paganism, no matter what its virtues, was inferior to Catholicism; Catholicism, no matter what its strengths, was inferior to Protestantism; and a "religion of humanity" must eventually displace doctrinaire Protestantism. He had little trouble with the first part of the formula. The Jew, though better than the pagan, is excluded from the march of progress because, unlike the Christian, he looks backward in time even as he reads backwards in his books. (See "The Jewish Cemetery at Newport," p. 814.) The pagan American Indian can hardly be allowed to waste the soil of his hunting grounds while "downtrodden millions [of Christians] starve in the garrets of Europe." The old Norse gods failed because their "law of force" was challenged by the meek Christ's "law of love."

At this point the formula failed him. For his tales of Christianity imply not a meek Christ triumphant, but a suffering Christ who is worshiped by greedy and venal monks, vicious Torquemadas, and witch-hunting Puritans. The measure of his inability to reconcile his knowledge of history with his inherited convictions about progress was his intention to add a third drama to his two New England tragedies—the scene to be set among the Moravians of Bethlehem—in order to "harmonize the discord of the New England tragedies, and thus give a not unfitting close to the work." He intended, apparently, to attach a happy ending to what was obviously a tragic history, and "balance" the blight of Protestant fanaticism with the piety of a forgotten religious community. This is as far as he could let himself think toward the triumphant "Charity" of "The Present."

The *Christus* was a failure not only as a work of the intellect but as a work of art; yet its very weakness as art reveals the source of Longfellow's over-all success as a popular poet. Longfellow thought and felt in terms of parts rather than organically unified wholes. In 1849 he recorded in his journal his hope that his "broken melodies" would "unite themselves into a symphony not all unworthy [of] the sublime theme" of the *Christus*. Equally suggestive is his often repeated image of the poet as a builder, surrounded by blocks and yearning to build a tower with them. In *Michael Angelo*, his last long dramatic narrative—and one with moments of greatness in it—he described what he had been doing all his life:

Men build their houses from the masonry
  Of ruined tombs;
So from old chronicles, where sleep in dust
  Names that once filled the world with trumpet tones,
I build this verse; and flowers of song have thrust
Their roots among the loose disjointed stones,
  Which to this end I fashion as I must.
Quickened are those who touch the Prophet's bones.

Of course, "loose disjointed stones" no more unite themselves into a house or tower than melodies unite themselves into a symphony. We need not accept too literally Longfellow's modest implication that all he had to offer, in spite of his aspirations, was stones and flowers and melodies, but it is likely that his world-wide audience admired these rather than his attempts at symphonies and towers.

The quoted passage bears an interesting resemblance to Eliot's line near the end of *The Waste Land*, "These fragments I have shored against my ruins." Longfellow sensed what subsequent history made much clearer for Eliot forty years later: that modern man must search among the ruins of the past for the order and meaning that were going out of life even before the older poet died. Rome, says his Michael Angelo, is a

  malaria of the mind,
Out of this tomb of the majestic Past;
The fever to accomplish some great work
That will not let us sleep.

He repaid his debt to Europe by writing verse that was as eagerly read abroad as in America: there were at least seven hundred translations of his work into twenty-four languages. In England, where his poetry was as popular as Tennyson's, he was given honorary degrees by Oxford and Cambridge, and he was the first American whose bust was placed in the Poet's Corner of Westminster Abbey.

Among the Fireside Poets, Lowell was the most versatile, the most erudite, the least popular, and, in the broad terms of literary statesmanship, the most influential. His claim to membership in the group was based on a very few well-known poems, and on the fact that the publishers of the group, Ticknor & Fields, bracketed him with the others and printed his work in editions uniform with theirs. This is not to say that he was not widely known and respected by people who never read him, or that he did not earn such reputation as he achieved; rather, that there was much in his work that could not attract a popular audience. His learning was too conspicuous, his approach to life was too bookish, and he spread his many talents so thin that he never became really famous for any of them, except for his mastery of Yankee dialect in *The Biglow Papers* and for the charm, wit, and journalistic intimacy of his portraits of contemporaries in *A Fable for Critics*.

His background, and in some respects his career, were much like Longfellow's. His name was ancient and respected. His forebears went to Harvard, entered the law or ministry, and rendered public service. One branch of the family became rich in industry and commerce, but not the poet's. His father was a Harvard-educated Boston minister who bought a historic house, later called Elmwood; in this house Lowell was born and died. After Harvard ('38) from which he was once suspended for cutting classes, he studied law—because that was what was expected of him—but never practiced it. Instead he combined the literary life with humanitarian activities, mostly in the cause of abolition. But although he contributed much to antislavery periodicals in the 1840's, it is generally agreed that his interest in reform was inspired not by any deep-rooted radicalism of his own, but by the enthusiasms of the gentle bluestocking, Maria White, whom he met in 1839 and married in 1843. Even before she died in 1853, he had lost interest in radical politics, though not in liberal principles.

Yet it was during his years with her that he wrote his most popular and enduring works. In an extraordinary burst of creative energy, he published in a single year, 1848, *A Fable for Critics*, the First Series of *The Biglow Papers*, and *The Vision of Sir Launfal*, as well as the first large collection of his lyrics. Exhilarated by critical recognition of his ability and versatility, he began planning a series of linked verse tales ("The Nooning") in the tradition of the *Canterbury Tales* and similar to Longfellow's later and successful *Tales of a Wayside Inn*. A few parts of it, including "Fitz Adam's Story," were printed, but he never got very far with the project, perhaps fortunately, for he had little talent for sustained narrative.

Once he had passed through his radical period, his intellectual kinship with Longfellow became evident. Geographically, their horizons were the same—at once narrow and broad. Both were villagers deeply attached to the small town of Cambridge and to their historic homes, Elmwood and Craigie House. Neither had any interest in or liking for the West or the great and growing cities of the coast and of the Mississippi River basin. Like most of the American people in mid-century they were psychologically and intellectually agrarian—which is one reason why they became Household Poets.

On the other hand, both were dedicated to Harvard, the institution which was our greatest center for European studies. Both were enthusiastic European travelers: in 1851 Lowell made the first of his eight sojourns abroad, some of them prolonged. In his mind there was a vital similarity between the Cambridge of his boyhood and what survived of Old Europe. Cambridge had been "essentially an English village, quiet, unspeculative, without enterprise, sufficing to itself." Harvard had "in its intellectual atmosphere a repose which recalls that of grand old Oxford." Continuing, in his nostalgic "Cambridge Thirty Years Ago"—written in 1854 and addressed to a friend in Italy—he sees his boyhood community almost as an English hamlet:

> Thirty years ago, the town had indeed a character. Railways and omnibuses had not rolled flat all little social prominences and peculiarities, making every man as much a citizen everywhere as at home. . . . The penny newspaper had not yet silenced the tripod of the barber, oracle of news. Everybody knew everybody, and all about everybody, and village wit, whose high 'change was around the little market-house in the town square, had labelled every more marked individuality with nicknames that clung like burs. Things were established then, and men did not run through all the figures on the dial of society so swiftly as now, when hurry and competition seem to have quite unhung the modulating pendulum of steady thrift and competent training. Some slow-minded persons even followed their father's trade,—a humiliating spectacle, rarer every day.

We had our established loafers, topers, proverb-mongers, barber, parson, nay, postmaster, whose tenure was for life. The great political machine did not then come down at regular quadrennial intervals, like a nail-cutting machine, to make all official lives of a standard length, and to generate lazy and intriguing expectancy. Life flowed in recognized channels,—narrower, perhaps, but with all the more individuality and force.

No reader need be taken in by the obvious ironies in this passage. It celebrates the individual, but only as part of a community; it celebrates "the established," the "recognized channel"; and it deplores Jacksonian democracy, which was destroying the old order.

The death of his first wife in 1853, long and grievously anticipated, brought a hitherto lacking focus into his intellectual and professional life. He had had from college days a deep and personal interest in the history of English literature (in 1844 he had published a work entitled, *Conversations on Some of the Old Poets*), and he now returned with relief to his earlier studies. His new career began when a cousin, who was a trustee of the Lowell Institute, asked him to make use of his knowledge in a series of twelve lectures, given in 1854–55. These, ranging from the Old English ballads to Wordsworth, so impressed his Boston audience that he was appointed Longfellow's successor as Smith Professor of French and Spanish Languages and Literatures and Professor of Belles Lettres at Harvard University. The contrast of the two careers from this point on is remarkable. Longfellow, having established himself as a popular poet, resigned from Harvard in 1854, and the next year published one of the most popular of all nineteenth-century poems, *Hiawatha*. Lowell, having enjoyed much critical acclaim, if not popular success, for his works of 1848, took Longfellow's job and never again wrote a poem that had wide appeal.

Lowell had an important part in consolidating the literary prestige of New England, Massachusetts, Boston, Cambridge, and Harvard (the order is reversible). Before 1850 New England's provincial literary culture had little influence on the rest of the country. The region had a high literacy rate, and published more books and magazines in ratio to its population than any other section. But it published its writers' works for itself rather than for the country at large. Its readers accepted and respected cultural achievement and leadership; and just as today it tolerates more eccentricity of character in the private citizen than is permitted elsewhere, so in that day it gave its writers more latitude and freedom than was allowed in other regions. Emerson is a classic case in point. The least comprehensible of all lyceum speakers, he gave two and one-half times as many lectures inside New England as outside, and large local audiences patronized his most difficult lectures even while admitting they did not understand him. In other words, New England early accepted literature as an institution.

By 1850 New England had developed the greatest group of writers in the country, and had a publishing house which was eager to put its imprint on all their works, whether popular or not. When, about the same time, railroads made the West accessible, Ticknor & Fields gave its writers national circulation and publicity. Two years after the *Atlantic Monthly* was established (1857), the firm bought it. Lowell was its first editor and started it on its career as the greatest of all American literary magazines. The firm also bought the *North American Review* (1815–1940), our oldest magisterial review, which, when Lowell became its editor in 1864, had an authority out of all proportion to its tiny circulation.

Lowell was a professor at Harvard while he edited these magazines, and naturally looked to New England in general and Harvard in particular for his contributors. This fact opened the *Atlantic* to charges of provincialism, but these are hardly convincing, considering the fact that the New England writers had already been accepted by the country at large. Boston, Cambridge, and Concord had become the true literary if not the publishing center of the United States.

After his appointment at Harvard, Lowell put most of his writing energy into literary and political essays. The political pieces, which were of Republican persuasion and which called for educated, upper-class leadership to stay the downward leveling tendency in our democracy, led to his appointment as minister to Spain (1877–80) by Hayes, and minister to England (1880–85) by Garfield. Far from being mere rewards for services to a political party, these appointments were in harmony with an American tradition—the support of distinguished literary men in the form of federal jobs at home or abroad. And we must not forget those writings of Lowell in the 1850's and 1860's which made the *Atlantic Monthly* a force in the abolition of slavery, or the fact that in his "Ode Recited at the Harvard Commemoration" (1865) Lowell was one of the first of our writers to discern the true greatness of Abraham Lincoln.

The critical essays and addresses, which were often by-products of his Harvard lectures, fill five volumes and parts of two others in the collected editions. Ranging from Dante and Chaucer to Wordsworth and Keats, they made him the most influential academic critic in the later nineteenth century. One indication of his influence is that his hostile review of Thoreau's *Letters* in 1865 helped to delay the general acceptance of Thoreau for a generation or more.

His critical work has been the subject of endless controversy, partly because of his innumerable and unresolved internal conflicts between the claims of head and heart, reason and imagination, aristocracy and democracy, classicism and romanticism, humanism and humanitarianism, religion and science. All agree that much of his work is brilliant, scintillating, often generously and persuasively appreciative. It is also evident that he tended to reject the literature of his own century and to seek his values and principles in Dante, Chaucer, and Shakespeare—in other words, that he was uneasy among the multiplying confusions of the nineteenth century, and that he found peace and delight in the literatures of those older European societies whose cultures reflected stable and slowly changing orders in which each individual had his accepted place. Certainly, one of his central convictions was that literature which celebrates the ego of the individual, at the expense of the social values which civilize him, is unhealthy. This belief is at the center of two essays which are, historically, among the most important he wrote—"Rousseau and the Sentimentalists" (1867) and "Thoreau's Letters" (1865).

Much of Lowell's thinking about literature was perpetuated from the 1870's and 1880's to the 1920's by other critics, first by E. C. Stedman, George Edward Woodberry, and W. C. Brownell, and later by the New Humanists, Irving Babbitt, Paul Elmore More, and Paul Shorey, who were resisting the newer tendencies of twentieth-century literature.

Any modern reader who has a taste for good prose can get pleasure and profit from browsing through collections of Lowell's essays, both the critical—those on Dante, Chaucer, Shakespeare, Milton, and Wordsworth are among the best—and the familiar—"Cambridge Thirty Years Ago" and "On a Certain Condescension in Foreigners" are still enjoyable. He need not read the whole of an essay to get the good of it, for Lowell, brilliant, witty, and engagingly erudite as he was at his best, lacked the self-discipline to write a condensed, tightly constructed essay every part of which is essential to the whole. He was incurably digressive and discursive, and had no gift for unity. The Introduction to *The Biglow Papers* is an exception, perhaps because its subject is self-controlled.

In part, his diffuseness was the result of his extraordinary facility and versatility. Like Holmes, he could rhyme a lecture or a letter almost as easily as he could prose it; he was a brilliant and spontaneous punster; he found it hard to control the fireworks of his wit; and he had his foreign languages at his finger tips. At the same time, he could rarely achieve the density and intensity which characterize great poetry. There are fine lyrical passages in his verse, but many of his best and most characteristic pieces are long, rambling, rhymed personal essays rather than poems. "The Cathedral," for example, is studded with brilliant lines, but structurally it is a meandering, meditative essay on religion, science, and democracy. Lowell could achieve something like organization only when he donned the strait jacket of a rigid, established form like the ode.

He knew his faults—most of them. Scattered among his letters, which are among the most readable in American literature, are candid and perceptive statements about his own limitations. As of 1848, he was capable of saying of himself in *A Fable for Critics*,

There is Lowell, who's striving Parnassus to climb
With a whole bale of *isms* tied together with rhyme,
He might get on alone, spite of brambles and boulders,
But he can't with that bundle he has on his shoulders,
The top of the hill he will ne'er come nigh reaching
Till he learns the distinction 'twixt singing and preaching;
His lyre has some chords that would ring pretty well,
But he'd rather by half make a drum of the shell,
And rattle away till he's old as Methusalem,
At the head of a march to the last new Jerusalem.

Naturally, he did not advertise his strengths, but in spite of his dislike for much of the literature of his time, he contributed to the changes that were taking place. He took an important part in the shift from sentimentalism to realism in the American short story through his editorship of the *Atlantic*. His *A Fable for Critics* helped to establish a sense that America had, at last, a community of writers, and that these writers were strong enough to be evaluated on their own merits rather than on nationalistic or chauvinistic grounds. Moreover, the *Fable* helped to reduce the critical cliquishness, the regional bickering, and the political partisanship which were so harmful to American literature in the 1840's. This book by a New Englander, issued by an influential New York publisher, offered witty, kindly, balanced commentary on our writers without regard for the factions to which they had been assigned in the squalid quarrels of New York's Grub Street.

Finally, Lowell lent strong support to a movement which has profoundly affected the tone of modern literature. Before American writers could free themselves from the wrong kind of English influence, they needed assurance that native vernaculars and native speech rhythms were respectable substitutes for British language and rhetoric. It had always been granted that common speech was acceptable for the purpose of low comedy, but it was assumed that serious discourse needed the prop of traditional literary English. Lowell proved in *The Biglow Papers* that Yankee dialect was an effective instrument for impassioned political satire; and his Introduction to the Second Series is the most important document in the whole movement. In providing sound scholarly evidence that many Americanisms were of ancient European origin, and in demonstrating that the common speech is full of wit and colorful imagery, Lowell gave American vernaculars the academic support that they needed. In the crucial shift from the language of James Fenimore Cooper to that of Mark Twain, we find abundant evidence of the influence of James Russell Lowell.

READING SUGGESTIONS

THE FIRESIDE POETS

George Arms, *The Fields Were Green* (1953). Fresh critical studies of Bryant, Whittier, Holmes, Lowell, and Longfellow, with a selection of their poems.

Van Wyck Brooks, *The Flowering of New England* (1936). Much about the interrelations of this group and about the cultural atmosphere of Boston, Cambridge, and Concord.

Odell Shepard, "The New England Triumvirate: Longfellow, Holmes, Lowell," *Literary History of the United States* (1948), I, 587–606.

LONGFELLOW

Horace E. Scudder, editor, *The Complete Poetical Works of Henry Wadsworth Longfellow*, 1 vol. (1893). This is the Cambridge edition, still in print. It contains many of Longfellow's notes on the poems, and other useful apparatus.

Samuel Longfellow, editor, *The Works of Henry Wadsworth Longfellow*, 14 vols. (1886–91). This edition includes Longfellow's prose works.

Samuel Longfellow, *The Life of Henry W. Longfellow*, 2 vols. (1886). A third volume, Final Memorials, was added in 1887. This work is old-fashioned but still valuable for its use of letters and journals.

Lawrance Thompson, *Young Longfellow, 1807–1843* (1938). A lively departure from traditional estimates of Longfellow's youth; makes use of much new material.

Norman Holmes Pearson, "Both Longfellows," *University of Kansas City Review*, XVI (Summer, 1950), 245–53. Argues that Longfellow had two audiences—the "court" and the people.

LOWELL

Horace E. Scudder, editor, *The Complete Poetical Works of James Russell Lowell*, 1 vol. (1897). This is the Cambridge edition, still in print. Valuable for headnotes and chronology.

Charles E. Norton, editor, *The Complete Writings*

of James Russell Lowell, 16 vols. (1904). This edition includes Lowell's prose and three volumes of letters.

HORACE E. SCUDDER, *James Russell Lowell: A Biography*, 2 vols. (1901). Still the most complete and reliable biography.

NORMAN FOERSTER, *American Criticism* (1928), pp. 111–56. Still the best general estimate of Lowell as critic.

WALTER BLAIR, "A Brahmin Dons Homespun," *Horse Sense in American Humor* (1942). Deals with the relation of Lowell to American traditions of humor.

Henry Wadsworth Longfellow

THE BELEAGUERED CITY

◊

(SAMUEL LONGFELLOW, the poet's brother, explains that the suggestion for the poem came from a note in one of the volumes of Scott's *Border Minstrelsy*: "Similar to this was the *Nacht Lager*, or midnight camp, which seemed nightly to beleaguer the walls of Prague, but which disappeared upon the recitation of [certain] magical words."

◊

I have read, in some old, marvellous tale,
Some legend strange and vague,
That a midnight host of spectres pale
Beleaguered the walls of Prague.

Beside the Moldau's rushing stream,
With the wan moon overhead,
There stood, as in an awful dream,
The army of the dead.

White as a sea-fog, landward bound,
The spectral camp was seen,
And, with a sorrowful, deep sound,
The river flowed between.

No other voice nor sound was there,
No drum, nor sentry's pace;
The mist-like banners clasped the air
As clouds with clouds embrace.

But when the old cathedral bell
Proclaimed the morning prayer,
The white pavilions rose and fell
On the alarmèd air.

Down the broad valley fast and far
The troubled army fled;
Up rose the glorious morning star,
The ghastly host was dead.

I have read, in the marvellous heart of man,
That strange and mystic scroll,
That an army of phantoms vast and wan
Beleaguer the human soul.

Encamped beside Life's rushing stream,
In Fancy's misty light,
Gigantic shapes and shadows gleam
Portentous through the night.

Upon its midnight battle-ground
The spectral camp is seen,
And, with a sorrowful, deep sound,
Flows the River of Life between.

No other voice nor sound is there,
In the army of the grave;
No other challenge breaks the air,
But the rushing of Life's wave.

And when the solemn and deep church-bell
Entreats the soul to pray,
The midnight phantoms feel the spell,
The shadows sweep away.

Down the broad Vale of Tears afar
The spectral camp is fled;
Faith shineth as a morning star,
Our ghastly fears are dead.

1839 *1839*

THE SKELETON IN ARMOR

◊

(LONGFELLOW supposed a skeleton in armor, uncovered near Fall River, to be the remains of one of the old Northern sea rovers, who came to the northern coast of the Western Hemisphere in the tenth century. "Of course I make the tradition myself," he wrote. The date and origin of the Newport tower (l. 134) are controversial. As originally published in the *Knickerbocker* for January, 1841, the poem had marginal notes like those in Coleridge's "The Ancient Mariner."

◇

"Speak! speak! thou fearful guest!
Who, with thy hollow breast
Still in rude armor drest,
Comest to daunt me!
Wrapt not in Eastern balms,
But with thy fleshless palms
Stretched, as if asking alms,
Why dost thou haunt me?"

Then, from those cavernous eyes
Pale flashes seemed to rise,
As when the Northern skies
Gleam in December;
And, like the water's flow
Under December's snow,
Came a dull voice of woe
From the heart's chamber.

"I was a Viking old!
My deeds, though manifold,
No Skald in song has told,
No Saga taught thee!
Take heed, that in thy verse
Thou dost the tale rehearse,
Else dread a dead man's curse;
For this I sought thee.

"Far in the Northern Land,
By the wild Baltic's strand,
I, with my childish hand,
Tamed the gerfalcon;
And, with my skates fast-bound,
Skimmed the half-frozen Sound,
That the poor whimpering hound
Trembled to walk on.

"Oft to his frozen lair
Tracked I the grisly bear,
While from my path the hare
Fled like a shadow;
Oft through the forest dark
Followed the were-wolf's bark,
Until the soaring lark
Sang from the meadow.

"But when I older grew,
Joining a corsair's crew,
O'er the dark sea I flew
With the marauders.
Wild was the life we led;
Many the souls that sped,
Many the hearts that bled,
By our stern orders.

"Many a wassail-bout
Wore the long Winter out;
Often our midnight shout
Set the cocks crowing,
As we the Berserk's tale
Measured in cups of ale,
Draining the oaken pail,
Filled to o'erflowing.

"Once as I told in glee
Tales of the stormy sea,
Soft eyes did gaze on me,
Burning yet tender;
And as the white stars shine
On the dark Norway pine,
On that dark heart of mine
Fell their soft splendor.

"I wooed the blue-eyed maid,
Yielding, yet half afraid,
And in the forest's shade
Our vows were plighted.
Under its loosened vest
Fluttered her little breast,
Like birds within their nest
By the hawk frighted.

"Bright in her father's hall
Shields gleamed upon the wall,
Loud sang the minstrels all,
Chanting his glory;
When of old Hildebrand
I asked his daughter's hand,
Mute did the minstrels stand
To hear my story.

"While the brown ale he quaffed,
Loud then the champion laughed,
And as the wind-gusts waft
The sea-foam brightly,
So the loud laugh of scorn,
Out of those lips unshorn,
From the deep drinking-horn
Blew the foam lightly.

"She was a Prince's child,
I but a Viking wild,
And though she blushed and smiled
I was discarded!
Should not the dove so white
Follow the sea-mew's flight,

Why did they leave that night
  Her nest unguarded?

"Scarce had I put to sea,
Bearing the maid with me,
Fairest of all was she
  Among the Norsemen!
When on the white sea-strand,
Waving his armèd hand,
Saw we old Hildebrand,
  With twenty horsemen.

"Then launched they to the blast,
Bent like a reed each mast,
Yet we were gaining fast,
  When the wind failed us;
And with a sudden flaw
Came round the gusty Skaw,
So that our foe we saw
  Laugh as he hailed us.

"And as to catch the gale
Round veered the flapping sail,
'Death!' was the helmsman's hail,
  'Death without quarter!'
Mid-ships with iron keel
Struck we her ribs of steel;
Down her black hulk did reel
  Through the black water!

"As with his wings aslant,
Sails the fierce cormorant,
Seeking some rocky haunt,
  With his prey laden,—
So toward the open main,
Beating to sea again,
Through the wild hurricane,
  Bore I the maiden.

"Three weeks we westward bore,
And when the storm was o'er,
Cloud-like we saw the shore
  Stretching to leeward;
There for my lady's bower
Built I the lofty tower,
Which, to this very hour,
  Stands looking seaward.

"There lived we many years;
Time dried the maiden's tears;
She had forgot her fears,
  She was a mother;
Death closed her mild blue eyes,
Under that tower she lies;
Ne'er shall the sun arise
  On such another!

"Still grew my bosom then,
Still as a stagnant fen!
Hateful to me were men,
  The sunlight hateful!
In the vast forest here,
Clad in my warlike gear,
Fell I upon my spear,
  Oh, death was grateful!

"Thus, seamed with many scars,
Bursting these prison bars,
Up to its native stars
  My soul ascended!
There from the flowing bowl
Deep drinks the warrior's soul,
Skoal! to the Northland! *skoal!*"
  Thus the tale ended.

1841 *1840*

THE SKELETON IN ARMOR. 110. Skaw: Cape Skagen, northern point of Jutland in Denmark.

GOD'S-ACRE

I like that ancient Saxon phrase, which calls
  The burial-ground God's-Acre! It is just;
It consecrates each grave within its walls,
  And breathes a benison o'er the sleeping dust.

God's-Acre! Yes, that blessed name imparts
  Comfort to those who in the grave have sown
The seed that they had garnered in their hearts,
  Their bread of life, alas! no more their own.

Into its furrows shall we all be cast,
  In the sure faith, that we shall rise again
At the great harvest, when the archangel's blast
  Shall winnow like a fan, the chaff and grain.

Then shall the good stand in immortal bloom,
  In the fair gardens of that second birth;
And each bright blossom mingle its perfume
  With that of flowers, which never bloomed on earth.

With thy rude ploughshare, Death, turn up the sod,
  And spread the furrow for the seed we sow;
This is the field and Acre of our God,
  This is the place where human harvests grow.

1841 *1841*

THE GOBLET OF LIFE

Filled is Life's goblet to the brim;
And though my eyes with tears are dim,
I see its sparkling bubbles swim,
And chant a melancholy hymn
With solemn voice and slow.

No purple flowers,—no garlands green,
Conceal the goblet's shade or sheen,
Nor maddening draughts of Hippocrene,
Like gleams of sunshine, flash between
Thick leaves of mistletoe.

This goblet, wrought with curious art,
Is filled with waters, that upstart,
When the deep fountains of the heart,
By strong convulsions rent apart,
Are running all to waste.

And as it mantling passes round,
With fennel is it wreathed and crowned,
Whose seed and foliage sun-imbrowned
Are in its waters steeped and drowned,
And give a bitter taste.

Above the lowly plants it towers,
The fennel, with its yellow flowers,
And in an earlier age than ours
Was gifted with the wondrous powers,
Lost vision to restore.

It gave new strength, and fearless mood;
And gladiators, fierce and rude,
Mingled it in their daily food;
And he who battled and subdued,
A wreath of fennel wore.

Then in Life's goblet freely press
The leaves that give it bitterness,
Nor prize the colored waters less,
For in thy darkness and distress
New light and strength they give!

And he who has not learned to know
How false its sparkling bubbles show,
How bitter are the drops of woe,
With which its brim may overflow,
He has not learned to live.

The prayer of Ajax was for light;
Through all that dark and desperate fight,
The blackness of that noonday night,
He asked but the return of sight,
To see his foeman's face.

Let our unceasing, earnest prayer
Be, too, for light,—for strength to bear
Our portion of the weight of care,
That crushes into dumb despair
One half the human race.

O suffering, sad humanity!
O ye afflicted ones, who lie
Steeped to the lips in misery,
Longing, and yet afraid to die,
Patient, though sorely tried!

I pledge you in this cup of grief,
Where floats the fennel's bitter leaf!
The Battle of our Life is brief,
The alarm,—the struggle,—the relief,
Then sleep we side by side.

1842 *1841*

THE SLAVE IN THE DISMAL SWAMP

◊

[LONGFELLOW took little part in the reform programs of his time, but he contributed to the antislavery movement a little volume of eight poems, *Poems on Slavery* (1842). It made an impact—particularly on conservative friends, who disapproved of it.

◊

In dark fens of the Dismal Swamp
The hunted Negro lay;
He saw the fire of the midnight camp,
And heard at times a horse's tramp
And a bloodhound's distant bay.

Where will-o'-the-wisps and glow-worms shine,
In bulrush and in brake;
Where waving mosses shroud the pine,
And the cedar grows, and the poisonous vine
Is spotted like the snake;

Where hardly a human foot could pass,
Or a human heart would dare,
On the quaking turf of the green morass
He crouched in the rank and tangled grass,
Like a wild beast in his lair.

A poor old slave, infirm and lame;
Great scars deformed his face;
On his forehead he bore the brand of shame,
And the rags, that hid his mangled frame,
Were the livery of disgrace.

All things above were bright and fair,
All things were glad and free;
Lithe squirrels darted here and there,
And wild birds filled the echoing air
With songs of Liberty!

On him alone was the doom of pain,
From the morning of his birth;
On him alone the curse of Cain
Fell, like a flail on the garnered grain,
And struck him to the earth!

1842 *1842*

NUREMBERG

◇

THIS is a typical Longfellow travelogue. Many of the allusions are self-explanatory, but the curious student can find abundant further detail in Longfellow's notes printed in the *Complete Poetical Works* (Cambridge edition).

◇

In the valley of the Pegnitz, where across broad meadow-lands
Rise the blue Franconian mountains, Nuremberg, the ancient, stands.

Quaint old town of toil and traffic, quaint old town of art and song,
Memories haunt thy pointed gables, like the rooks that round them throng:

Memories of the Middle Ages, when the emperors, rough and bold,
Had their dwelling in thy castle, time-defying, centuries old;

And thy brave and thrifty burghers boasted, in their uncouth rhyme,
That their great imperial city stretched its hand through every clime.

In the court-yard of the castle, bound with many an iron band,
Stands the mighty linden planted by Queen Cunigunde's hand;

On the square the oriel window, where in old heroic days
Sat the poet Melchior singing Kaiser Maximilian's praise.

Everywhere I see around me rise the wondrous world of Art:
Fountains wrought with richest sculpture standing in the common mart;

And above cathedral doorways saints and bishops carved in stone,
By a former age commissioned as apostles to our own.

In the church of sainted Sebald sleeps enshrined his holy dust,
And in bronze the Twelve Apostles guard from age to age their trust;

In the church of sainted Lawrence stands a pix of sculpture rare,
Like the foamy sheaf of fountains, rising through the painted air.

Here, when Art was still religion, with a simple, reverent heart,
Lived and labored Albrecht Dürer, the Evangelist of Art;

Hence in silence and in sorrow, toiling still with busy hand,
Like an emigrant he wandered, seeking for the Better Land.

Emigravit is the inscription on the tombstone where he lies;
Dead he is not, but departed,—for the artist never dies.

Fairer seems the ancient city, and the sunshine seems more fair,
That he once has trod its pavement, that he once has breathed its air!

Through these streets so broad and stately, these obscure and dismal lanes,
Walked of yore the Mastersingers, chanting rude poetic strains.

From remote and sunless suburbs came they to the friendly guild,
Building nests in Fame's great temple, as in spouts the swallows build.

As the weaver plied the shuttle, wove he too the mystic rhyme,
And the smith his iron measures hammered to the anvil's chime;

Thanking God, whose boundless wisdom makes the flowers of poesy bloom
In the forge's dust and cinders, in the tissues of the loom.

Here Hans Sachs, the cobbler-poet, laureate of the gentle craft,
Wisest of the Twelve Wise Masters, in huge folios sang and laughed.

But his house is now an ale-house, with a nicely sanded floor,
And a garland in the window, and his face above the door;

Painted by some humble artist, as in Adam Puschman's song,
As the old man gray and dove-like, with his great beard white and long.

And at night the swart mechanic comes to drown his cark and care,
Quaffing ale from pewter tankards, in the master's antique chair.

Vanished is the ancient splendor, and before my dreamy eye
Wave these mingled shapes and figures, like a faded tapestry.

Not thy Councils, not thy Kaisers, win for thee the world's regard;
But thy painter, Albrecht Dürer, and Hans Sachs thy cobbler-bard.

Thus, O Nuremberg, a wanderer from a region far away,
As he paced thy streets and court-yards, sang in thought his careless lay:

Gathering from the pavement's crevice, as a floweret of the soil,
The nobility of labor,—the long pedigree of toil.

1844

THE ARSENAL AT SPRINGFIELD

◊

❡ THIS poem is related to the antiwar movement of the 1840's. One of the leaders, Charles Sumner, accompanied Longfellow on a visit to the arsenal.

◊

This is the Arsenal. From floor to ceiling,
Like a huge organ, rise the burnished arms;
But from their silent pipes no anthem pealing
Startles the villages with strange alarms.

Ah! what a sound will rise, how wild and dreary,
When the death-angel touches those swift keys!
What loud lament and dismal Miserere
Will mingle with their awful symphonies!

I hear even now the infinite fierce chorus,
The cries of agony, the endless groan,
Which, through the ages that have gone before us,
In long reverberations reach our own.

On helm and harness rings the Saxon hammer,
Through Cimbric forest roars the Norseman's song,
And loud, amid the universal clamor,
O'er distant deserts sounds the Tartar gong.

I hear the Florentine, who from his palace
Wheels out his battle-bell with dreadful din,
And Aztec priests upon their teocallis
Beat the wild war-drums made of serpent's skin;

The tumult of each sacked and burning village;
The shout that every prayer for mercy drowns;
The soldiers' revels in the midst of pillage;
The wail of famine in beleaguered towns;

The bursting shell, the gateway wrenched asunder,
The rattling musketry, the clashing blade;
And ever and anon, in tones of thunder
The diapason of the cannonade.

Is it, O man, with such discordant noises,
With such accursed instruments as these,
Thou drownest Nature's sweet and kindly voices,
And jarrest the celestial harmonies?

Were half the power that fills the world with terror,
Were half the wealth bestowed on camps and courts,
Given to redeem the human mind from error,
There were no need of arsenals or forts:

The warrior's name would be a name abhorrèd!
And every nation, that should lift again
Its hand against a brother, on its forehead
Would wear forevermore the curse of Cain!

Down the dark future, through long generations,
The echoing sounds grow fainter and then cease;
And like a bell, with solemn, sweet vibrations,
I hear once more the voice of Christ say, "Peace!"

Peace! and no longer from its brazen portals
The blast of War's great organ shakes the skies!
But beautiful as songs of the immortals,
The holy melodies of love arise.

1844 *1844*

SEAWEED

◊

LONGFELLOW here uses his method of teaching by analogy with mechanical precision. If one puts the eight stanzas into two parallel columns of four stanzas each, the analogies between the ocean and poetry become conspicuous.

◊

When descends on the Atlantic
The gigantic
Storm-wind of the equinox,
Landward in his wrath he scourges
The toiling surges,
Laden with seaweed from the rocks:

From Bermuda's reefs; from edges
Of sunken ledges,
In some far-off, bright Azore;
From Bahama, and the dashing,
Silver-flashing
Surges of San Salvador;

From the tumbling surf, that buries
The Orkneyan skerries,
Answering the hoarse Hebrides;
And from wrecks of ships, and drifting
Spars, uplifting
On the desolate, rainy seas;—

Ever drifting, drifting, drifting
On the shifting
Currents of the restless main;
Till in sheltered coves, and reaches
Of sandy beaches,
All have found repose again.

So when storms of wild emotion
Strike the ocean
Of the poet's soul, erelong
From each cave and rocky fastness,
In its vastness,
Floats some fragment of a song:

From the far-off isles enchanted,
Heaven has planted
With the golden fruit of Truth;
From the flashing surf, whose vision
Gleams Elysian
In the tropic clime of Youth;

From the strong Will, and the Endeavor
That forever
Wrestle with the tides of Fate;
From the wreck of Hopes far-scattered,
Tempest-shattered,
Floating waste and desolate;—

Ever drifting, drifting, drifting
On the shifting
Currents of the restless heart;
Till at length in books recorded,
They, like hoarded
Household words, no more depart.

1845 *1845*

TO THE DRIVING CLOUD

Gloomy and dark art thou, O chief of the mighty Omahas;
Gloomy and dark as the driving cloud, whose name thou hast taken!

Wrapped in thy scarlet blanket, I see thee stalk through the city's
Narrow and populous streets, as once by the margin of rivers
Stalked those birds unknown, that have left us only their footprints.
What, in a few short years, will remain of thy race but the footprints?

How canst thou walk these streets, who hast trod the green turf of the prairies?
How canst thou breathe this air, who hast breathed the sweet air of the mountains?
Ah! 't is in vain that with lordly looks of disdain thou dost challenge
Looks of disdain in return, and question these walls and these pavements,
Claiming the soil for thy hunting-grounds, while down-trodden millions
Starve in the garrets of Europe, and cry from its caverns that they, too,
Have been created heirs of the earth, and claim its division!

Back, then, back to thy woods in the regions west of the Wabash!
There as a monarch thou reignest. In autumn the leaves of the maple
Pave the floors of thy palace-halls with gold, and in summer
Pine-trees waft through its chambers the odorous breath of their branches.
There thou art strong and great, a hero, a tamer of horses!
There thou chasest the stately stag on the banks of the Elkhorn,
Or by the roar of the Running-Water, or where the Omaha
Calls thee, and leaps through the wild ravine like a brave of the Blackfeet!

Hark! what murmurs arise from the heart of those mountainous deserts?
Is it the cry of the Foxes and Crows, or the mighty Behemoth,
Who, unharmed, on his tusks once caught the bolts of the thunder,
And now lurks in his lair to destroy the race of the red man?
Far more fatal to thee and thy race than the Crows and the Foxes,
Far more fatal to thee and thy race than the tread of Behemoth,
Lo! the big thunder-canoe, that steadily breasts the Missouri's
Merciless current! and yonder, afar on the prairies, the camp-fires
Gleam through the night; and the cloud of dust in the gray of the daybreak
Marks not the buffalo's track, nor the Mandan's dexterous horse-race;
It is a caravan, whitening the desert where dwell the Camanches!
Ha! how the breath of these Saxons and Celts, like the blast of the east-wind,
Drifts evermore to the west the scanty smokes of thy wigwams!

1845 *1845*

WALTER VON DER VOGELWEID

◇

HORACE E. SCUDDER (Cambridge edition) says, "Walter von der Vogelweid, or Bird-Meadow, was one of the principal Minnesingers of the thirteenth century. He triumphed over Heinrich von Ofterdingen in that poetic contest at Wartburg Castle, known in literary history as the War of Wartburg."

◇

Vogelweid the Minnesinger,
When he left this world of ours,
Laid his body in the cloister,
Under Würtzburg's minster towers.

And he gave the monks his treasures,
Gave them all with this behest:
They should feed the birds at noontide
Daily on his place of rest;

Saying, "From these wandering minstrels
I have learned the art of song;
Let me now repay the lessons
They have taught so well and long."

Thus the bard of love departed;
And, fulfilling his desire,
On his tomb the birds were feasted
By the children of the choir.

Day by day, o'er tower and turret,
In foul weather and in fair,
Day by day, in vaster numbers,
Flocked the poets of the air.

On the tree whose heavy branches
  Overshadowed all the place,
On the pavement, on the tombstone,
  On the poet's sculptured face,

On the cross-bars of each window,
  On the lintel of each door,
They renewed the War of Wartburg,
  Which the bard had fought before.

There they sang their merry carols,
  Sang their lauds on every side;
And the name their voices uttered
  Was the name of Vogelweid.

Till at length the portly abbot
  Murmured, "Why this waste of food?
Be it changed to loaves henceforward
  For our fasting brotherhood."

Then in vain o'er tower and turret,
  From the walls and woodland nests,
When the minster bells rang noontide,
  Gathered the unwelcome guests.

Then in vain, with cries discordant,
  Clamorous round the Gothic spire,
Screamed the feathered Minnesingers
  For the children of the choir.

Time has long effaced the inscriptions
  On the cloister's funeral stones,
And tradition only tells us
  Where repose the poet's bones.

But around the vast cathedral,
  By sweet echoes multiplied,
Still the birds repeat the legend,
  And the name of Vogelweid.

1845 *1845*

THE FIRE OF DRIFT-WOOD

Devereux Farm, near Marblehead

We sat within the farm-house old,
  Whose windows, looking o'er the bay,
Gave to the sea-breeze damp and cold
  An easy entrance, night and day.

Not far away we saw the port,
  The strange, old-fashioned, silent town,
The lighthouse, the dismantled fort,
  The wooden houses, quaint and brown.

We sat and talked until the night,
  Descending, filled the little room;
Our faces faded from the sight,
  Our voices only broke the gloom.

We spake of many a vanished scene,
  Of what we once had thought and said,
Of what had been, and might have been,
  And who was changed, and who was dead;

And all that fills the hearts of friends,
  When first they feel, with secret pain,
Their lives thenceforth have separate ends,
  And never can be one again;

The first slight swerving of the heart,
  That words are powerless to express,
And leave it still unsaid in part,
  Or say it in too great excess.

The very tones in which we spake
  Had something strange, I could but mark;
The leaves of memory seemed to make
  A mournful rustling in the dark.

Oft died the words upon our lips,
  As suddenly, from out the fire
Built of the wreck of stranded ships,
  The flames would leap and then expire.

And, as their splendor flashed and failed,
  We thought of wrecks upon the main,
Of ships dismasted, that were hailed
  And sent no answer back again.

The windows, rattling in their frames,
  The ocean, roaring up the beach,
The gusty blast, the bickering flames,
  All mingled vaguely in our speech;

Until they made themselves a part
  Of fancies floating through the brain,
The long-lost ventures of the heart,
  That send no answers back again.

O flames that glowed! O hearts that yearned!
  They were indeed too much akin,
The drift-wood fire without that burned,
  The thoughts that burned and glowed within.

1849 *1848*

PRELUDE TO EVANGELINE

◊

[LONGFELLOW undertook this subject after his friend Hawthorne refused it. In history, the French colony known as Acadia, in Nova Scotia, was distrusted by the dominant British because of its neutrality and its friendliness with the Indians. In 1755 the British seized and deported most of the inhabitants. Longfellow built his tale on the resulting separation of a young husband and wife. The Prelude is presented here as a sample of Longfellow's tone in his handling of the story.

◊

This is the forest primeval. The murmuring pines and the hemlocks,
Bearded with moss, and in garments green, indistinct in the twilight,
Stand like Druids of eld, with voices sad and prophetic,
Stand like harpers hoar, with beards that rest on their bosoms.

Loud from its rocky caverns, the deep-voiced neighboring ocean
Speaks, and in accents disconsolate answers the wail of the forest.

This is the forest primeval; but where are the hearts that beneath it
Leaped like the roe, when he hears in the woodland the voice of the huntsman?

Where is the thatch-roofed village, the home of Acadian farmers,—
Men whose lives glided on like rivers that water the woodlands,
Darkened by shadows of earth, but reflecting an image of heaven?
Waste are those pleasant farms, and the farmers forever departed!
Scattered like dust and leaves, when the mighty blasts of October
Seize them, and whirl them aloft, and sprinkle them far o'er the ocean.
Naught but tradition remains of the beautiful village of Grand-Pré.

Ye who believe in affection that hopes, and endures, and is patient,
Ye who believe in the beauty and strength of woman's devotion,
List to the mournful tradition, still sung by the pines of the forest;
List to a Tale of Love in Acadie, home of the happy.

1847

KING WITLAF'S DRINKING-HORN

Witlaf, a king of the Saxons,
Ere yet his last he breathed,
To the merry monks of Croyland
His drinking-horn bequeathed,—

That, whenever they sat at their revels,
And drank from the golden bowl,
They might remember the donor,
And breathe a prayer for his soul.

So sat they once at Christmas,
And bade the goblet pass;
In their beards the red wine glistened
Like dew-drops in the grass.

They drank to the soul of Witlaf,
They drank to Christ the Lord,
And to each of the Twelve Apostles,
Who had preached his holy word.

They drank to the Saints and Martyrs
Of the dismal days of yore,
And as soon as the horn was empty
They remembered one Saint more.

And the reader droned from the pulpit,
Like the murmur of many bees,
The legend of good Saint Guthlac,
And Saint Basil's homilies;

Till the great bells of the convent,
From their prison in the tower,
Guthlac and Bartholomæus,
Proclaimed the midnight hour.

And the Yule-log cracked in the chimney,
And the Abbot bowed his head,
And the flamelets flapped and flickered,
But the Abbot was stark and dead.

Yet still in his pallid fingers
He clutched the golden bowl,
In which, like a pearl dissolving,
Had sunk and dissolved his soul.

But not for this their revels
The jovial monks forbore,
For they cried, "Fill high the goblet!
We must drink to one Saint more!"

1849 *1848*

DEDICATION

FROM *The Seaside and the Fireside*

As one who, walking in the twilight gloom,
Hears round about him voices as it darkens,
And seeing not the forms from which they come,
Pauses from time to time, and turns and hearkens;

So walking here in twilight, O my friends!
I hear your voices, softened by the distance,
And pause, and turn to listen, as each sends
His words of friendship, comfort, and assistance.

If any thought of mine, or sung or told,
Has ever given delight or consolation,
Ye have repaid me back a thousand-fold,
By every friendly sign and salutation.

Thanks for the sympathies that ye have shown!
Thanks for each kindly word, each silent token,
That teaches me, when seeming most alone,
Friends are around us, though no word be spoken.

Kind messages, that pass from land to land;
Kind letters, that betray the heart's deep history,
In which we feel the pressure of a hand,—
One touch of fire,—and all the rest is mystery!

The pleasant books, that silently among
Our household treasures take familiar places,
And are to us as if a living tongue
Spake from the printed leaves or pictured faces!

Perhaps on earth I shall never behold,
With eye of sense, your outward form and semblance;
Therefore to me ye never will grow old,
But live forever young in my remembrance!

Never grow old, nor change, nor pass away!
Your gentle voices will flow on forever,
When life grows bare and tarnished with decay,
As through a leafless landscape flows a river.

Not chance of birth or place has made us friends,
Being oftentimes of different tongues and nations,
But the endeavor for the selfsame ends,
With the same hopes, and fears, and aspirations.

Therefore I hope to join your seaside walk,
Saddened, and mostly silent, with emotion;
Not interrupting with intrusive talk
The grand, majestic symphonies of ocean.

Therefore I hope, as no unwelcome guest,
At your warm fireside, when the lamps are lighted,
To have my place reserved among the rest,
Nor stand as one unsought and uninvited!

1849

IN THE CHURCHYARD AT CAMBRIDGE

In the village churchyard she lies,
Dust is in her beautiful eyes,
No more she breathes, nor feels, nor stirs;
At her feet and at her head
Lies a slave to attend the dead,
But their dust is white as hers.

Was she, a lady of high degree,
So much in love with the vanity
And foolish pomp of this world of ours?
Or was it Christian charity,
And lowliness and humility,
The richest and rarest of all dowers?

Who shall tell us? No one speaks;
No color shoots into those cheeks,
Either of anger or of pride,

At the rude question we have asked;
Nor will the mystery be unmasked
By those who are sleeping at her side.

Hereafter?—And do you think to look
On the terrible pages of that Book
To find her failings, faults, and errors?
Ah, you will then have other cares,
In your own shortcomings and despairs,
In your own secret sins and terrors!

1853 *1851*

THE JEWISH CEMETERY AT NEWPORT

How strange it seems! These Hebrews in their graves,
Close by the street of this fair seaport town,
Silent beside the never-silent waves,
At rest in all this moving up and down!

The trees are white with dust, that o'er their sleep
Wave their broad curtains in the south-wind's breath,
While underneath these leafy tents they keep
The long, mysterious Exodus of Death.

And these sepulchral stones, so old and brown,
That pave with level flags their burial-place,
Seem like the tablets of the Law, thrown down
And broken by Moses at the mountain's base.

The very names recorded here are strange,
Of foreign accent, and of different climes;
Alvares and Rivera interchange
With Abraham and Jacob of old times.

"Blessed be God, for he created Death!"
The mourners said, "and Death is rest and peace;"
Then added, in the certainty of faith,
"And giveth Life that nevermore shall cease."

Closed are the portals of their Synagogue,
No Psalms of David now the silence break,
No Rabbi reads the ancient Decalogue
In the grand dialect the Prophets spake.

Gone are the living, but the dead remain,
And not neglected; for a hand unseen,
Scattering its bounty, like a summer rain,
Still keeps their graves and their remembrance green.

How came they here? What burst of Christian hate,
What persecution, merciless and blind,
Drove o'er the sea—that desert desolate—
These Ishmaels and Hagars of mankind?

They lived in narrow streets and lanes obscure,
Ghetto and Judenstrass, in mirk and mire;
Taught in the school of patience to endure
The life of anguish and the death of fire.

All their lives long, with the unleavened bread
And bitter herbs of exile and its fears,
The wasting famine of the heart they fed,
And slaked its thirst with marah of their tears.

Anathema maranatha! was the cry
That rang from town to town, from street to street:
At every gate the accursed Mordecai
Was mocked and jeered, and spurned by Christian feet.

Pride and humiliation hand in hand
Walked with them through the world where'er they went;
Trampled and beaten were they as the sand,
And yet unshaken as the continent.

For in the background figures vague and vast
Of patriarchs and of prophets rose sublime,
And all the great traditions of the Past
They saw reflected in the coming time.

And thus forever with reverted look
The mystic volume of the world they read,
Spelling it backward, like a Hebrew book,
Till life became a Legend of the Dead.

But ah! what once has been shall be no more!
The groaning earth in travail and in pain
Brings forth its races, but does not restore,
And the dead nations never rise again.

1852 *1852*

THE JEWISH CEMETERY AT NEWPORT. **32. Ishmaels and Hagars:** See Gen. 16:21. **34. Ghetto and Judenstrasse:** sections in which the Jews were segregated in European cities. **41. Anathema maranatha!:** a curse. See I Cor. 16:22. **43. Mordecai:** See the Book of Esther.

PROMETHEUS

Of Prometheus, how undaunted
On Olympus' shining bastions
His audacious foot he planted,
Myths are told and songs are chanted,
Full of promptings and suggestions.

Beautiful is the tradition
Of that flight through heavenly portals,
The old classic superstition
Of the theft and the transmission
Of the fire of the Immortals!

First the deed of noble daring,
Born of heavenward aspiration,
Then the fire with mortals sharing,
Then the vulture,—the despairing
Cry of pain on crags Caucasian.

All is but a symbol painted
Of the Poet, Prophet, Seer;
Only those are crowned and sainted
Who with grief have been acquainted,
Making nations nobler, freer.

In their feverish exultations,
In their triumph and their yearning,
In their passionate pulsations,
In their words among the nations,
The Promethean fire is burning.

Shall it, then, be unavailing,
All this toil for human culture?
Through the cloud-rack, dark and trailing
Must they see above them sailing
O'er life's barren crags the vulture?

Such a fate as this was Dante's,
By defeat and exile maddened;
Thus were Milton and Cervantes,
Nature's priests and Corybantes,
By affliction touched and saddened.

But the glories so transcendent
That around their memories cluster,
And, on all their steps attendant,
Make their darkened lives resplendent
With such gleams of inward lustre!

All the melodies mysterious,
Through the dreary darkness chanted;
Thoughts in attitudes imperious,
Voices soft, and deep, and serious,
Words that whispered, songs that haunted!

All the soul in rapt suspension,
All the quivering, palpitating
Chords of life in utmost tension,
With the fervor of invention,
With the rapture of creating!

Ah, Prometheus! heaven-scaling!
In such hours of exultation
Even the faintest heart, unquailing,
Might behold the vulture sailing
Round the cloudy crags Caucasian!

Though to all there be not given
Strength for such sublime endeavor,
Thus to scale the walls of heaven,
And to leaven with fiery leaven,
All the hearts of men forever;

Yet all bards, whose hearts unblighted
Honor and believe the presage,
Hold aloft their torches lighted,
Gleaming through the realms benighted,
As they onward bear the message!

1854

MY LOST YOUTH

Often I think of the beautiful town
That is seated by the sea;
Often in thought go up and down
The pleasant streets of that dear old town,
And my youth comes back to me.
And a verse of a Lapland song
Is haunting my memory still:
"A boy's will is the wind's will,
And the thoughts of youth are long, long thoughts."

I can see the shadowy lines of its trees,
And catch, in sudden gleams,
The sheen of the far-surrounding seas,
And islands that were the Hesperides
Of all my boyish dreams.
And the burden of that old song,
It murmurs and whispers still:
"A boy's will is the wind's will,

And the thoughts of youth are long, long thoughts."

I remember the black wharves and the slips,
And the sea-tides tossing free;
And Spanish sailors with bearded lips,
And the beauty and mystery of the ships,
And the magic of the sea.
And the voice of that wayward song
Is singing and saying still:
"A boy's will is the wind's will,
And the thoughts of youth are long, long thoughts."

I remember the bulwarks by the shore,
And the fort upon the hill;
The sunrise gun, with its hollow roar,
The drum-beat repeated o'er and o'er,
And the bugle wild and shrill.
And the music of that old song
Throbs in my memory still:
"A boy's will is the wind's will,
And the thoughts of youth are long, long thoughts."

I remember the sea-fight far away,
How it thundered o'er the tide!
And the dead captains, as they lay
In their graves, o'erlooking the tranquil bay
Where they in battle died.
And the sound of that mournful song
Goes through me with a thrill:
"A boy's will is the wind's will,
And the thoughts of youth are long, long thoughts."

I can see the breezy dome of groves,
The shadows of Deering's Woods;
And the friendships old and the early loves
Come back with a Sabbath sound, as of doves
In quiet neighborhoods.
And the verse of that sweet old song,
It flutters and murmurs still:
"A boy's will is the wind's will,
And the thoughts of youth are long, long thoughts."

I remember the gleams and glooms that dart
Across the school-boy's brain;
The song and the silence in the heart,
That in part are prophecies, and in part
Are longings wild and vain.
And the voice of that fitful song
Sings on, and is never still:
"A boy's will is the wind's will,
And the thoughts of youth are long, long thoughts."

There are things of which I may not speak;
There are dreams that cannot die;
There are thoughts that make the strong heart weak,
And bring a pallor into the cheek,
And a mist before the eye.
And the words of that fatal song
Come over me like a chill:
"A boy's will is the wind's will,
And the thoughts of youth are long, long thoughts."

Strange to me now are the forms I meet
When I visit the dear old town;
But the native air is pure and sweet,
And the trees that o'ershadow each well-known street,
As they balance up and down,
Are singing the beautiful song,
Are sighing and whispering still:
"A boy's will is the wind's will,
And the thoughts of youth are long, long thoughts."

And Deering's Woods are fresh and fair,
And with joy that is almost pain
My heart goes back to wander there,
And among the dreams of the days that were,
I find my lost youth again.
And the strange and beautiful song,
The groves are repeating it still:
"A boy's will is the wind's will,
And the thoughts of youth are long, long thoughts."

1855

THE SICILIAN'S TALE

King Robert of Sicily

◇

❡ "THE SICILIAN'S TALE" is from Part I of *Tales of a Wayside Inn* of 1863. In 1872 and 1873 Parts II and III were published, and it is from Part III that the three selections that follow "King Robert" have been taken. The pattern of the work as a whole—the relating of a succession of stories by a group of congenial acquaintances—follows that of Chaucer's *Canterbury Tales*. That "King Robert of Sicily," a story of a proud then penitent king, finds its plot in the *Gesta Romanorum* has been noted by Scudder, who further states: "Leigh Hunt, among moderns, has told the story in

A Jar of Honey from Mt. Hybla, from which source Mr. Longfellow seems to have drawn. Dante refers to the King in *Paradiso,* Canto VIII."

◇

Robert of Sicily, brother of Pope Urbane
And Valmond, Emperor of Allemaine,
Apparelled in magnificent attire,
With retinue of many a knight and squire,
On St. John's eve, at vespers, proudly sat
And heard the priests chant the Magnificat.
And as he listened, o'er and o'er again
Repeated, like a burden or refrain,
He caught the words, *"Deposuit potentes*
De sede, et exaltavit humiles;"
And slowly lifting up his kingly head
He to a learned clerk beside him said,
"What mean these words?" The clerk made answer meet,
"He has put down the mighty from their seat,
And has exalted them of low degree."
Thereat King Robert muttered scornfully,
" 'T is well that such seditious words are sung
Only by priests and in the Latin tongue;
For unto priests and people be it known,
There is no power can push me from my throne!"
And leaning back, he yawned and fell asleep, 21
Lulled by the chant monotonous and deep.

When he awoke, it was already night;
The church was empty, and there was no light,
Save where the lamps, that glimmered few and faint,
Lighted a little space before some saint.
He started from his seat and gazed around,
But saw no living thing and heard no sound.
He groped towards the door, but it was locked;
He cried aloud, and listened, and then knocked,
And uttered awful threatenings and complaints,
And imprecations upon men and saints. 32
The sounds reëchoed from the roof and walls
As if dead priests were laughing in their stalls.

At length the sexton, hearing from without
The tumult of the knocking and the shout,
And thinking thieves were in the house of prayer,
Came with his lantern, asking, "Who is there?"
Half choked with rage, King Robert fiercely said,
"Open: 't is I, the King! Art thou afraid?"
The frightened sexton, muttering, with a curse,
"This is some drunken vagabond, or worse!"
Turned the great key and flung the portal wide;
A man rushed by him at a single stride,
Haggard, half naked, without hat or cloak,
Who neither turned, nor looked at him, nor spoke,
But leaped into the blackness of the night,
And vanished like a spectre from his sight.

Robert of Sicily, brother of Pope Urbane
And Valmond, Emperor of Allemaine,
Despoiled of his magnificent attire,
Bareheaded, breathless, and besprent with mire,
With sense of wrong and outrage desperate,
Strode on and thundered at the palace gate;
Rushed through the courtyard, thrusting in his rage
To right and left each seneschal and page,
And hurried up the broad and sounding stair,
His white face ghastly in the torches' glare.
From hall to hall he passed with breathless speed;
Voices and cries he heard, but did not heed,
Until at last he reached the banquet-room,
Blazing with light, and breathing with perfume.

There on the dais sat another king,
Wearing his robes, his crown, his signet-ring,
King Robert's self in features, form, and height,
But all transfigured with angelic light!
It was an Angel; and his presence there
With a divine effulgence filled the air,
An exaltation, piercing the disguise,
Though none the hidden Angel recognize.

A moment speechless, motionless, amazed,
The throneless monarch on the Angel gazed,
Who met his look of anger and surprise
With the divine compassion of his eyes;
Then said, "Who art thou? and why com'st thou here?"
To which King Robert answered with a sneer,
"I am the King, and come to claim my own
From an impostor, who usurps my throne!"
And suddenly, at these audacious words,
Up sprang the angry guests, and drew their swords;
The Angel answered, with unruffled brow,
"Nay, not the King, but the King's Jester, thou
Henceforth shalt wear the bells and scalloped cape,
And for thy counsellor shalt lead an ape;
Thou shalt obey my servants when they call,
And wait upon my henchmen in the hall!"

Deaf to King Robert's threats and cries and prayers,
They thrust him from the hall and down the stairs;
A group of tittering pages ran before,
And as they opened wide the folding-door,
His heart failed, for he heard, with strange alarms,
The boisterous laughter of the men-at-arms,
And all the vaulted chamber roar and ring
With the mock plaudits of "Long live the King!"

Next morning, waking with the day's first beam,
He said within himself, "It was a dream!"
But the straw rustled as he turned his head,
There were the cap and bells beside his bed,
Around him rose the bare, discolored walls,
Close by, the steeds were champing in their stalls,
And in the corner, a revolting shape,
Shivering and chattering sat the wretched ape.
It was no dream; the world he loved so much
Had turned to dust and ashes at his touch!

Days came and went; and now returned again
To Sicily the old Saturnian reign;
Under the Angel's governance benign
The happy island danced with corn and wine,
And deep within the mountain's burning breast
Enceladus, the giant, was at rest.

Meanwhile King Robert yielded to his fate,
Sullen and silent and disconsolate.
Dressed in the motley garb that Jesters wear,
With look bewildered and a vacant stare,
Close shaven above the ears, as monks are shorn,
By courtiers mocked, by pages laughed to scorn,
His only friend the ape, his only food
What others left,—he still was unsubdued.
And when the Angel met him on his way,
And half in earnest, half in jest, would say,
Sternly, though tenderly, that he might feel
The velvet scabbard held a sword of steel,
"Art thou the King?" the passion of his woe
Burst from him in resistless overflow,
And, lifting high his forehead, he would fling
The haughty answer back, "I am, I am the King!"

Almost three years were ended; when there came
Ambassadors of great repute and name
From Valmond, Emperor of Allemaine,
Unto King Robert, saying that Pope Urbane
By letter summoned them forthwith to come
On Holy Thursday to his city of Rome.
The Angel with great joy received his guests,
And gave them presents of embroidered vests,
And velvet mantles with rich ermine lined,
And rings and jewels of the rarest kind.
Then he departed with them o'er the sea
Into the lovely land of Italy,
Whose loveliness was more resplendent made
By the mere passing of that cavalcade,
With plumes, and cloaks, and housings, and the stir
Of jewelled bridle and of golden spur.
And lo! among the menials, in mock state,
Upon a piebald steed, with shambling gait,
His cloak of fox-tails flapping in the wind,
The solemn ape demurely perched behind,
King Robert rode, making huge merriment
In all the country towns through which they went.

The Pope received them with great pomp and blare
Of bannered trumpets, on Saint Peter's square,
Giving his benediction and embrace,
Fervent, and full of apostolic grace.
While with congratulations and with prayers
He entertained the Angel unawares,
Robert, the Jester, bursting through the crowd,
Into their presence rushed, and cried aloud,
"I am the King! Look, and behold in me
Robert, your brother, King of Sicily!
This man, who wears my semblance to your eyes,
Is an impostor in a king's disguise.
Do you not know me? does no voice within
Answer my cry, and say we are akin?"

The Pope in silence, but with troubled mien,
Gazed at the Angel's countenance serene;
The Emperor, laughing, said, "It is strange sport
To keep a madman for thy Fool at court!"
And the poor, baffled Jester in disgrace
Was hustled back among the populace.

In solemn state the Holy Week went by,
And Easter Sunday gleamed upon the sky;
The presence of the Angel, with its light,
Before the sun rose, made the city bright,
And with new fervor filled the hearts of men,
Who felt that Christ indeed had risen again.
Even the Jester, on his bed of straw,
With haggard eyes the unwonted splendor saw,
He felt within a power unfelt before,
And, kneeling humbly on his chamber floor,
He heard the rushing garments of the Lord
Sweep through the silent air, ascending heavenward.

And now the visit ending, and once more
Valmond returning to the Danube's shore,
Homeward the Angel journeyed, and again
The land was made resplendent with his train,
Flashing along the towns of Italy
Unto Salerno, and from thence by sea.
And when once more within Palermo's wall,
And, seated on the throne in his great hall,
He heard the Angelus from convent towers,
As if the better world conversed with ours,
He beckoned to King Robert to draw nigher,
And with a gesture bade the rest retire;
And when they were alone, the Angel said,
"Art thou the King?" Then, bowing down his head,
King Robert crossed both hands upon his breast,
And meekly answered him: "Thou knowest best!

My sins as scarlet are; let me go hence,
And in some cloister's school of penitence,
Across those stones, that pave the way to heaven,
Walk barefoot, till my guilty soul be shriven!"

The Angel smiled, and from his radiant face
A holy light illumined all the place,
And through the open window, loud and clear,
They heard the monks chant in the chapel near,
Above the stir and tumult of the street:
"He has put down the mighty from their seat,
And has exalted them of low degree!"
And through the chant a second melody
Rose like the throbbing of a single string:
"I am an Angel, and thou art the King!"

King Robert, who was standing near the throne,
Lifted his eyes, and lo! he was alone!
But all apparelled as in days of old,
With ermined mantle and with cloth of gold;
And when his courtiers came, they found him there
Kneeling upon the floor, absorbed in silent prayer.

1863 *1862*

THE SPANISH JEW'S TALE

Azrael

King Solomon, before his palace gate
At evening, on the pavement tessellate
Was walking with a stranger from the East,
Arrayed in rich attire as for a feast,
The mighty Runjeet-Sing, a learned man,
And Rajah of the realms of Hindostan.
And as they walked the guest became aware
Of a white figure in the twilight air,
Gazing intent, as one who with surprise
His form and features seemed to recognize;
And in a whisper to the king he said:
"What is yon shape, that, pallid as the dead,
Is watching me, as if he sought to trace
In the dim light the features of my face?"

The king looked, and replied: "I know him well;
It is the Angel men call Azrael,
'T is the Death Angel; what hast thou to fear?"
And the guest answered: "Lest he should come near,
And speak to me, and take away my breath!
Save me from Azrael, save me from death!
O king, that hast dominion o'er the wind,
Bid it arise and bear me hence to Ind."

The king gazed upward at the cloudless sky,
Whispered a word, and raised his hand on high,
And lo! the signet-ring of chrysoprase
On his uplifted finger seemed to blaze
With hidden fire, and rushing from the west
There came a mighty wind, and seized the guest
And lifted him from earth, and on they passed,
His shining garments streaming in the blast,
A silken banner o'er the walls upreared,
A purple cloud, that gleamed and disappeared.
Then said the Angel, smiling: "If this man
Be Rajah Runjeet-Sing of Hindostan,
Thou hast done well in listening to his prayer;
I was upon my way to seek him there."

1873 *1872*

THE SPANISH JEW'S TALE. **Azrael.** Azrael is the Angel of Death in the Koran.

THE POET'S TALE

Charlemagne

Olger the Dane and Desiderio,
King of the Lombards, on a lofty tower
Stood gazing northward o'er the rolling plains,
League after league of harvests, to the foot
Of the snow-crested Alps, and saw approach
A mighty army, thronging all the roads
That led into the city. And the King
Said unto Olger, who had passed his youth
As hostage at the court of France, and knew
The Emperor's form and face: "Is Charlemagne
Among that host?" And Olger answered: "No."

And still the innumerable multitude
Flowed onward and increased, until the King
Cried in amazement: "Surely Charlemagne
Is coming in the midst of all these knights!"
And Olger answered slowly: "No; not yet;
He will not come so soon." Then much disturbed
King Desiderio asked: "What shall we do,
If he approach with a still greater army?"
And Olger answered: "When he shall appear,

You will behold what manner of man he is;
But what will then befall us I know not."

Then came the guard that never knew repose,
The Paladins of France; and at the sight
The Lombard King o'ercome with terror cried:
"This must be Charlemagne!" and as before
Did Olger answer: "No; not yet, not yet."

And then appeared in panoply complete
The Bishops and the Abbots and the Priests
Of the imperial chapel, and the Counts;
And Desiderio could no more endure
The light of day, nor yet encounter death,
But sobbed aloud and said: "Let us go down
And hide us in the bosom of the earth,
Far from the sight and anger of a foe
So terrible as this!" And Olger said:
"When you behold the harvests in the fields
Shaking with fear, the Po and the Ticino
Lashing the city walls with iron waves,
Then may you know that Charlemagne is come."
And even as he spake, in the northwest,
Lo! there uprose a black and threatening cloud,
Out of whose bosom flashed the light of arms
Upon the people pent up in the city;
A light more terrible than any darkness,
And Charlemagne appeared;—a Man of Iron!

His helmet was of iron, and his gloves
Of iron, and his breastplate and his greaves
And tassets were of iron, and his shield.
In his left hand he held an iron spear,
In his right hand his sword invincible.
The horse he rode on had the strength of iron,
And color of iron. All who went before him,
Beside him and behind him, his whole host,
Were armed with iron, and their hearts within them
Were stronger than the armor that they wore.
The fields and all the roads were filled with iron,
And points of iron glistened in the sun
And shed a terror through the city streets.

This at a single glance Olger the Dane
Saw from the tower, and turning to the King
Exclaimed in haste: "Behold! this is the man
You looked for with such eagerness!" and then
Fell as one dead at Desiderio's feet.

1873 *1872*

THE STUDENT'S TALE

Emma and Eginhard

◇

¶ THIS story is legendary. Eginhard (Einhard) (*c.* 770–840) studied in the school founded by Alcuin in Charlemagne's palace at Aachen. Eginhard, however, did marry a lady named Emma (although she was not a daughter of Charlemagne). He rose to high favor with the emperor, of whom he wrote a famous biography.

◇

When Alcuin taught the sons of Charlemagne,
In the free schools of Aix, how kings should reign,
And with them taught the children of the poor
How subjects should be patient and endure,
He touched the lips of some, as best befit,
With honey from the hives of Holy Writ;
Others intoxicated with the wine
Of ancient history, sweet but less divine;
Some with the wholesome fruits of grammar fed;
Others with mysteries of the stars o'erhead,
That hang suspended in the vaulted sky
Like lamps in some fair palace vast and high.

In sooth, it was a pleasant sight to see
That Saxon monk, with hood and rosary,
With inkhorn at his belt, and pen and book,
And mingled love and reverence in his look,
Or hear the cloister and the court repeat
The measured footfalls of his sandaled feet,
Or watch him with the pupils of his school,
Gentle of speech, but absolute of rule.

Among them, always earliest in his place,
Was Eginhard, a youth of Frankish race,
Whose face was bright with flashes that forerun
The splendors of a yet unrisen sun.
To him all things were possible, and seemed
Not what he had accomplished, but had dreamed,
And what were tasks to others were his play,
The pastime of an idle holiday.

Smaragdo, Abbot of St. Michael's, said,
With many a shrug and shaking of the head,
Surely some demon must possess the lad,
Who showed more wit than ever school-boy had,
And learned his Trivium thus without the rod;
But Alcuin said it was the grace of God.

THE STUDENT'S TALE. **Emma and Eginhard.** **2. Aix:** Aix-la Chapelle, the French name for Aachen.

Thus he grew up, in Logic point-device,
Perfect in Grammar, and in Rhetoric nice;
Science of Numbers, Geometric art,
And lore of Stars, and Music knew by heart;
A Minnesinger, long before the times
Of those who sang their love in Suabian rhymes.

The Emperor, when he heard this good report
Of Eginhard much buzzed about the court,
Said to himself, "This stripling seems to be
Purposely sent into the world for me;
He shall become my scribe, and shall be schooled
In all the arts whereby the world is ruled."
Thus did the gentle Eginhard attain
To honor in the court of Charlemagne;
Became the sovereign's favorite, his right hand,
So that his fame was great in all the land,
And all men loved him for his modest grace
And comeliness of figure and of face.
An inmate of the palace, yet recluse,
A man of books, yet sacred from abuse
Among the armèd knights with spur on heel
The tramp of horses and the clang of steel;
And as the Emperor promised he was schooled
In all the arts by which the world is ruled.
But the one art supreme, whose law is fate,
The Emperor never dreamed of till too late.

Home from her convent to the palace came
The lovely Princess Emma, whose sweet name,
Whispered by seneschal or sung by bard,
Had often touched the soul of Eginhard.
He saw her from his window, as in state
She came, by knights attended through the gate;
He saw her at the banquet of that day,
Fresh as the morn, and beautiful as May;
He saw her in the garden, as she strayed
Among the flowers of summer with her maid,
And said to him, "O Eginhard, disclose
The meaning and the mystery of the rose;"
And trembling he made answer: "In good sooth,
Its mystery is love, its meaning youth!"

How can I tell the signals and the signs
By which one heart another heart divines?
How can I tell the many thousand ways
By which it keeps the secret it betrays?

O mystery of love! O strange romance!
Among the Peers and Paladins of France,
Shining in steel, and prancing on gay steeds,
Noble by birth, yet nobler by great deeds,
The Princess Emma had no words nor looks
But for this clerk, this man of thought and books.

The summer passed, the autumn came; the stalks
Of lilies blackened in the garden walks;
The leaves fell, russet-golden and blood-red,
Love-letters, thought the poet, fancy-led,
Or Jove descending in a shower of gold
Into the lap of Danaë of old;
For poets cherish many a strange conceit,
And love transmutes all nature by its heat.
No more the garden lessons, nor the dark
And hurried meetings in the twilight park;
But now the studious lamp, and the delights
Of firesides in the silent winter nights,
And watching from his window hour by hour
The light that burned in Princess Emma's tower.

At length one night, while musing by the fire,
O'ercome at last by his insane desire,—
For what will reckless love not do and dare?
He crossed the court, and climbed the winding stair,
With some feigned message in the emperor's name;
But when he to the lady's presence came
He knelt down at her feet, until she laid
Her hand upon him, like a naked blade,
And whispered in his ear: "Arise, Sir Knight,
To my heart's level, O my heart's delight."

And there he lingered till the crowing cock,
The Alectryon of the farmyard and the flock,
Sang his aubade with lusty voice and clear,
To tell the sleeping world that dawn was near.
And then they parted; but at parting, lo!
They saw the palace courtyard white with snow,
And, placid as a nun, the moon on high
Gazing from cloudy cloisters of the sky.
"Alas!" he said, "how hide the fatal line
Of footprints leading from thy door to mine,
And none returning!" Ah, he little knew
What woman's wit, when put to proof, can do!

That night the Emperor, sleepless with the cares
And troubles that attend on state affairs,
Had risen before the dawn, and musing gazed
Into the silent night, as one amazed
To see the calm that reigned o'er all supreme,
When his own reign was but a troubled dream.
The moon lit up the gables capped with snow,
And the white roofs, and half the court below,
And he beheld a form, that seemed to cower
Beneath a burden, come from Emma's tower,—
A woman, who upon her shoulders bore
Clerk Eginhard to his own private door,
And then returned in haste, but still essayed
To tread the footprints she herself had made;
And as she passed across the lighted space,
The Emperor saw his daughter Emma's face!

He started not; he did not speak or moan,
But seemed as one who hath been turned to stone;
And stood there like a statue, nor awoke
Out of his trance of pain, till morning broke,
Till the stars faded, and the moon went down,
And o'er the towers and steeples of the town
Came the gray daylight; then the sun, who took
The empire of the world with sovereign look,
Suffusing with a soft and golden glow
All the dead landscape in its shroud of snow,
Touching with flame the tapering chapel spires,
Windows and roofs, and smoke of household fires,
And kindling park and palace as he came;
The stork's nest on the chimney seemed in flame.
And thus he stood till Eginhard appeared,
Demure and modest with his comely beard
And flowing flaxen tresses, come to ask,
As was his wont, the day's appointed task.
The Emperor looked upon him with a smile,
And gently said: "My son, wait yet awhile;
This hour my council meets upon some great
And very urgent business of the state.
Come back within the hour. On thy return
The work appointed for thee shalt thou learn."

Having dismissed this gallant Troubadour,
He summoned straight his council, and secure
And steadfast in his purpose, from the throne
All the adventure of the night made known;
Then asked for sentence; and with eager breath
Some answered banishment, and others death.

Then spake the king: "Your sentence is not mine;
Life is the gift of God, and is divine;
Nor from these palace walls shall one depart
Who carries such a secret in his heart;
My better judgment points another way.
Good Alcuin, I remember how one day
When my Pepino asked you, 'What are men?'
You wrote upon his tablets with your pen,
'Guests of the grave and travellers that pass!'
This being true of all men, we, alas!
Being all fashioned of the selfsame dust,
Let us be merciful as well as just;
This passing traveller who hath stolen away
The brightest jewel of my crown to-day,
Shall of himself the precious gem restore;
By giving it, I make it mine once more.
Over those fatal footprints I will throw
My ermine mantle like another snow."

Then Eginhard was summoned to the hall,
And entered, and in presence of them all,
The Emperor said: "My son, for thou to me
Hast been a son, and evermore shalt be,
Long hast thou served thy sovereign, and thy zeal
Pleads to me with importunate appeal,
While I have been forgetful to requite
Thy service and affection as was right.
But now the hour is come, when I, thy Lord,
Will crown thy love with such supreme reward,
A gift so precious kings have striven in vain
To win it from the hands of Charlemagne."

Then sprang the portals of the chamber wide,
And Princess Emma entered, in the pride
Of birth and beauty, that in part o'ercame
The conscious terror and the blush of shame.
And the good Emperor rose up from his throne,
And taking her white hand within his own
Placed it in Eginhard's, and said: "My son,
This is the gift thy constant zeal hath won;
Thus I repay the royal debt I owe,
And cover up the footprints in the snow."

1873 *1872*

DIVINA COMMEDIA

◇

[SIX sonnets, first published in the *Atlantic Monthly* (1864–66), served as prefaces to the three parts of Longfellow's translation of Dante's work. The poems reflect something of Longfellow's state of mind in the years following the tragic death of his second wife in 1861, and during the Civil War.

◇

I

Oft have I seen at some cathedral door
  A laborer, pausing in the dust and heat,
  Lay down his burden, and with reverent feet
  Enter, and cross himself, and on the floor
Kneel to repeat his paternoster o'er;
  Far off the noises of the world retreat;
  The loud vociferations of the street
  Become an undistinguishable roar.
So, as I enter here from day to day,
  And leave my burden at this minster gate,
  Kneeling in prayer, and not ashamed to pray,
The tumult of the time disconsolate
  To inarticulate murmurs dies away,
  While the eternal ages watch and wait.

1864

II

How strange the sculptures that adorn these towers!
This crowd of statues, in whose folded sleeves
Birds build their nests; while canopied with leaves
Parvis and portal bloom like trellised bowers,
And the vast minster seems a cross of flowers!
But fiends and dragons on the gargoyled eaves
Watch the dead Christ between the living thieves,
And, underneath, the traitor Judas lowers!
Ah! from what agonies of heart and brain,
What exultations trampling on despair,
What tenderness, what tears, what hate of wrong,
What passionate outcry of a soul in pain,
Uprose this poem of the earth and air,
This mediæval miracle of song!

1866

III

I enter, and I see thee in the gloom
Of the long aisles, O poet saturnine!
And strive to make my steps keep pace with thine.
The air is filled with some unknown perfume;
The congregation of the dead make room
For thee to pass; the votive tapers shine;
Like rooks that haunt Ravenna's groves of pine
The hovering echoes fly from tomb to tomb.
From the confessionals I hear arise
Rehearsals of forgotten tragedies,
And lamentations from the crypts below;
And then a voice celestial that begins
With the pathetic words, "Although your sins
As scarlet be," and ends with "as the snow."

1866

IV

With snow-white veil and garments as of flame,
She stands before thee, who so long ago
Filled thy young heart with passion and the woe
From which thy song and all its splendors came;
And while with stern rebuke she speaks thy name,
The ice about thy heart melts as the snow
On mountain heights, and in swift overflow
Comes gushing from thy lips in sobs of shame.
Thou makest full confession; and a gleam,
As of the dawn on some dark forest cast,
Seems on thy lifted forehead to increase;
Lethe and Eunoë—the remembered dream
And the forgotten sorrow—bring at last
That perfect pardon which is perfect peace.

1865

DIVINA COMMEDIA. **IV. 2. She:** Beatrice. **5. And . . . rebuke:** Beatrice's rebuke to Dante appears in Cantos XXX and XXXI of the *Purgatorio.*

12. Lethe and Eunoë: In the *Purgatorio* Dante drinks of Lethe, the river of forgetfulness, and of Eunoë, the river of memory of the good.

CHAUCER

An old man in a lodge within a park;
The chamber walls depicted all around
With portraitures of huntsman, hawk, and hound,
And the hurt deer. He listeneth to the lark,
Whose song comes with the sunshine through the dark
Of painted glass in leaden lattice bound;
He listeneth and he laugheth at the sound,
Then writeth in a book like any clerk.
He is the poet of the dawn, who wrote
The Canterbury Tales, and his old age
Made beautiful with song; and as I read
I hear the crowing cock, I hear the note
Of lark and linnet, and from every page
Rise odors of ploughed field or flowery mead.

1875 *1873*

SHAKESPEARE

A vision as of crowded city streets,
With human life in endless overflow;
Thunder of thoroughfares; trumpets that blow
To battle; clamor, in obscure retreats,
Of sailors landed from their anchored fleets;
Tolling of bells in turrets, and below
Voices of children, and bright flowers that throw
O'er garden-walls their intermingled sweets!
This vision comes to me when I unfold
The volume of the Poet paramount,
Whom all the Muses loved, not one alone;—

Into his hands they put the lyre of gold,
And, crowned with sacred laurel at their fount,
Placed him as Musagetes on their throne.

1875 *1873*

MILTON

I pace the sounding sea-beach and behold
How the voluminous billows roll and run,
Upheaving and subsiding, while the sun
Shines through their sheeted emerald far unrolled,
And the ninth wave, slow gathering fold by fold
All its loose-flowing garments into one,
Plunges upon the shore, and floods the dun
Pale reach of sands, and changes them to gold.
So in majestic cadence rise and fall
The mighty undulations of thy song,
O sightless bard, England's Mæonides!
And ever and anon, high over all
Uplifted, a ninth wave superb and strong,
Floods all the soul with its melodious seas.

1875 *1873*

THE TIDE RISES, THE TIDE FALLS

The tide rises, the tide falls,
The twilight darkens, the curlew calls;
Along the sea-sands damp and brown
The traveller hastens toward the town,
And the tide rises, the tide falls.

Darkness settles on roofs and walls,
But the sea, the sea in the darkness calls;
The little waves, with their soft, white hands,
Efface the footprints in the sand,
And the tide rises, the tide falls.

The morning breaks; the steeds in their stalls
Stamp and neigh, as the hostler calls;
The day returns, but nevermore
Returns the traveller to the shore,
And the tide rises, the tide falls.

1880 *1879*

SHAKESPEARE. 14. **Musagetes:** the leader of the Muses, i.e., Apollo. MILTON. 11. **Mæonides:** Homer. Like Homer, Milton was blind.

MORITURI SALUTAMUS

Poem for the Fiftieth Anniversary of the Class of 1825 in Bowdoin College

◇

THE TITLE is translated in the first two lines of the poem. Longfellow is said to have found his subject when he saw Gérome's famous painting of the gladiators saluting Caesar. The epigraph from Ovid may be translated: "Time passes away, we grow old with the silent years, and the days flee past with no delaying check."

◇

Tempora labuntur, tacitisque senescimus annis,
Et fugiunt freno non remorante dies.
OVID, *Fastorum,* Lib. vi.

"O Cæsar, we who are about to die
Salute you!" was the gladiators' cry
In the arena, standing face to face
With death and with the Roman populace.

O ye familiar scenes,—ye groves of pine,
That once were mine and are no longer mine,—
Thou river, widening through the meadows green
To the vast sea, so near and yet unseen,—
Ye halls, in whose seclusion and repose
Phantons of fame, like exhalations, rose
And vanished,—we who are about to die,
Salute you; earth and air and sea and sky,
And the Imperial Sun that scatters down
His sovereign splendors upon grove and town.

Ye do not answer us! ye do not hear!
We are forgotten; and in your austere
And calm indifference, ye little care
Whether we come or go, or whence or where.
What passing generations fill these halls,
What passing voices echo from these walls,
Ye heed not; we are only as the blast,
A moment heard, and then forever past.

Not so the teachers who in earlier days
Led our bewildered feet through learning's maze;
They answer us—alas! what have I said?
What greetings come there from the voiceless dead?
What salutation, welcome, or reply?
What pressure from the hands that lifeless lie?
They are no longer here; they all are gone
Into the land of shadows,—all save one.
Honor and reverence, and the good repute
That follows faithful service as its fruit,
Be unto him, whom living we salute.

The great Italian poet, when he made
His dreadful journey to the realms of shade,
Met there the old instructor of his youth,
And cried in tones of pity and of ruth:
"Oh, never from the memory of my heart
Your dear, paternal image shall depart,
Who while on earth, ere yet by death surprised,
Taught me how mortals are immortalized;
How grateful am I for that patient care
All my life long my language shall declare."

To-day we make the poet's words our own,
And utter them in plaintive undertone;
Nor to the living only be they said,
But to the other living called the dead,
Whose dear, paternal images appear
Not wrapped in gloom, but robed in sunshine here;
Whose simple lives, complete and without flaw,
Were in part and parcel of great Nature's law;
Who said not to their Lord, as if afraid,
"Here is thy talent in a napkin laid,"
But labored in their sphere, as men who live
In the delight that work alone can give.
Peace be to them; eternal peace and rest,
And the fulfilment of the great behest:
"Ye have been faithful over a few things,
Over ten cities shall ye reign as kings."
And ye who fill the places we once filled,
And follow in the furrows that we tilled,
Young men, whose generous hearts are beating high,
We who are old, and are about to die,
Salute you; hail you; take your hands in ours,
And crown you with our welcome as with flowers!

How beautiful is youth! how bright it gleams
With its illusions, aspirations, dreams!
Book of Beginnings, Story without End,
Each maid a heroine, and each man a friend!
Aladdin's Lamp, and Fortunatus' Purse,
That holds the treasures of the universe!
All possibilities are in its hands,
No danger daunts it, and no foe withstands;
In its sublime audacity of faith,
"Be thou removed!" it to the mountain saith,
And with ambitious feet, secure and proud,
Ascends the ladder leaning on the cloud!

As ancient Priam at the Scæan gate
Sat on the walls of Troy in regal state
With the old men, too old and weak to fight,
Chirping like grasshoppers in their delight
To see the embattled hosts, with spear and shield,
Of Trojans and Achaians in the field;
So from the snowy summits of our years
We see you in the plain, as each appears,
And question of you; asking, "Who is he
That towers above the others? Which may be
Atreides, Menelaus, Odysseus,
Ajax the great, or bold Idomeneus?"

Let him not boast who puts his armor on
As he who puts it off, the battle done.
Study yourselves; and most of all note well
Wherein kind Nature meant you to excel.
Not every blossom ripens into fruit;
Minerva, the inventress of the flute,
Flung it aside, when she her face surveyed
Distorted in a fountain as she played;
The unlucky Marsyas found it, and his fate
Was one to make the bravest hesitate.
Write on your doors the saying wise and old,
"Be bold! be bold!" and everywhere, "Be bold;
Be not too bold!" Yet better the excess
Than the defect; better the more than less;
Better like Hector in the field to die,
Than like a perfumed Paris turn and fly.

And now, my classmates; ye remaining few
That number not the half of those we knew,
Ye, against whose familiar names not yet
The fatal asterisk of death is set,
Ye I salute! The horologe of Time
Strikes the half-century with a solemn chime,
And summons us together once again,
The joy of meeting not unmixed with pain.

Where are the others? Voices from the deep
Caverns of darkness answer me: "They sleep!"
I name no names; instinctively I feel
Each at some well-remembered grave will kneel,

MORITURI SALUTAMUS. **30. all save one:** Professor A. S. Packard. **34–36. The . . . youth:** In the *Inferno*, XV.82–87, Dante addresses Bruno Latini. His words are translated in lines 38–43. **53. Here . . . talent:** See Matt. 25:14–30. **58–59. "Ye . . . kings":** See Luke 19:17.

98–99. The . . . hesitate: Marsyas, having found the flute, challenged Apollo to a contest. Marsyas lost, and was flayed alive. **101–102. "Be . . . bold!":** See Spencer's *Faerie Queene*, III.xi.54. **109. The . . . set:** The names of deceased members of a college class were marked with an asterisk.

And from the inscription wipe the weeds and moss,
For every heart best knoweth its own loss.
I see their scattered gravestones gleaming white
Through the pale dusk of the impending night;
O'er all alike the impartial sunset throws
Its golden liiies mingled with the rose;
We give to each a tender thought, and pass
Out of the graveyards with their tangled grass,
Unto these scenes frequented by our feet
When we were young, and life was fresh and sweet.

What shall I say to you? What can I say
Better than silence is? When I survey
This throng of faces turned to meet my own,
Friendly and fair, and yet to me unknown,
Transformed the very landscape seems to be;
It is the same, yet not the same to me.
So many memories crowd upon my brain,
So many ghosts are in the wooded plain,
I fain would steal away, with noiseless tread,
As from a house where some one lieth dead.
I cannot go;—I pause;—I hesitate;
My feet reluctant linger at the gate;
As one who struggles in a troubled dream
To speak and cannot, to myself I seem.

Vanish the dream! Vanish the idle fears!
Vanish the rolling mists of fifty years!
Whatever time or space may intervene,
I will not be a stranger in this scene.
Here every doubt, all indecision, ends;
Hail, my companions, comrades, classmates, friends!

Ah me! the fifty years since last we met
Seem to me fifty folios bound and set
By Time, the great transcriber, on his shelves,
Wherein are written the histories of ourselves.
What tragedies, what comedies, are there;
What joy and grief, what rapture and despair!
What chronicles of triumph and defeat,
Of struggle, and temptation, and retreat!
What records of regrets, and doubts, and fears!
What pages blotted, blistered by our tears!
What lovely landscapes on the margin shine,
What sweet, angelic faces, what divine
And holy images of love and trust,
Undimmed by age, unsoiled by damp or dust!

Whose hand shall dare to open and explore
These volumes, closed and clasped forevermore?
Not mine. With reverential feet I pass;
I hear a voice that cries, "Alas! alas!
Whatever hath been written shall remain,
Nor be erased nor written o'er again;
The unwritten only still belongs to thee:
Take heed, and ponder well what that shall be."

As children frightened by a thunder-cloud
Are reassured if some one reads aloud
A tale of wonder, with enchantment fraught,
Or wild adventure, that diverts their thought,
Let me endeavor with a tale to chase
The gathering shadows of the time and place,
And banish what we all too deeply feel
Wholly to say, or wholly to conceal.

In mediæval Rome, I know not where,
There stood an image with its arm in air,
And on its lifted finger, shining clear,
A golden ring with the device, "Strike here!"
Greatly the people wondered, though none guessed
The meaning that these words but half expressed,
Until a learned clerk, who at noonday
With downcast eyes was passing on his way,
Paused, and observed the spot, and marked it well,
Whereon the shadow of the finger fell;
And, coming back at midnight, delved, and found
A secret stairway leading underground.
Down this he passed into a spacious hall,
Lit by a flaming jewel on the wall;
And opposite, in threatening attitude,
With bow and shaft a brazen statue stood.
Upon its forehead, like a coronet,
Were these mysterious words of menace set:
"That which I am, I am; my fatal aim
None can escape, not even yon luminous flame!"

Midway the hall was a fair table placed,
With cloth of gold, and golden cups enchased
With rubies, and the plates and knives were gold,
And gold the bread and viands manifold.
Around it, silent, motionless, and sad,
Were seated gallant knights in armor clad,
And ladies beautiful with plume and zone,
But they were stone, their hearts within were stone;
And the vast hall was filled in every part
With silent crowds, stony in face and heart.

Long at the scene, bewildered and amazed,
The trembling clerk in speechless wonder gazed;
Then from the table, by his greed made bold,
He seized a goblet and a knife of gold,

174. Let . . . chase: The tale is from the medieval *Gesta Romanorum*, CVII.

And suddenly from their seats the guests upsprang,
The vaulted ceiling with loud clamors rang,
The archer sped his arrow, at their call,
Shattering the lambent jewel on the wall,
And all was dark around and overhead;—
Stark on the floor the luckless clerk lay dead!

The writer of this legend then records
Its ghostly application in these words:
The image is the Adversary old,
Whose beckoning finger points to realms of gold;
Our lusts and passions are the downward stair
That leads the soul from a diviner air;
The archer, Death; the flaming jewel, Life;
Terrestrial goods, the goblet and the knife;
The knights and ladies, all whose flesh and bone
By avarice have been hardened into stone;
The clerk, the scholar whom the love of pelf
Tempts from his books and from his nobler self.

The scholar and the world! The endless strife,
The discord in the harmonies of life!
The love of learning, the sequestered nooks,
And all the sweet serenity of books;
The market-place, the eager love of gain,
Whose aim is vanity, and whose end is pain!

But why, you ask me, should this tale be told
To men grown old, or who are growing old?
It is too late! Ah, nothing is too late
Till the tired heart shall cease to palpitate.
Cato learned Greek at eighty; Sophocles
Wrote his grand Œdipus, and Simonides
Bore off the prize of verse from his compeers,
When each had numbered more than fourscore years,
And Theophrastus, at fourscore and ten,
Had but begun his "Characters of Men."
Chaucer, at Woodstock with the nightingales,
At sixty wrote the Canterbury Tales;
Goethe at Weimar, toiling to the last,
Completed Faust when eighty years were past.
These are indeed exceptions; but they show
How far the gulf-stream of our youth may flow
Into the arctic regions of our lives,
Where little else than life itself survives.

As the barometer foretells the storm
While still the skies are clear, the weather warm,
So something in us, as old age draws near,
Betrays the pressure of the atmosphere.
The nimble mercury, ere we are aware,
Descends the elastic ladder of the air;
The telltale blood in artery and vein
Sinks from its higher levels in the brain;
Whatever poet, orator, or sage
May say of it, old age is still old age.
It is the waning, not the crescent moon;
The dusk of evening, not the blaze of noon;
It is not strength, but weakness; not desire,
But its surcease; not the fierce heat of fire,
The burning and consuming element,
But that of ashes and of embers spent,
In which some living sparks we still discern,
Enough to warm, but not enough to burn.

What then? Shall we sit idly down and say
The night hath come; it is no longer day?
The night hath not yet come; we are not quite
Cut off from labor by the failing light;
Something remains for us to do or dare;
Even the oldest tree some fruit may bear;
Not Œdipus Coloneus, or Greek Ode,
Or tales of pilgrims that one morning rode
Out of the gateway of the Tabard Inn,
But other something, would we but begin;
For age is opportunity no less
Than youth itself, though in another dress,
And as the evening twilight fades away
The sky is filled with stars, invisible by day.

1875 *1874*

THE CROSS OF SNOW

In the long, sleepless watches of the night,
  A gentle face—the face of one long dead—
  Looks at me from the wall, where round its head
  The night-lamp casts a halo of pale light.
Here in this room she died; and soul more white
  Never through martyrdom of fire was led
  To its repose; nor can in books be read
  The legend of a life more benedight.
There is a mountain in the distant West
  That, sun-defying, in its deep ravines
  Displays a cross of snow upon its side.
Such is the cross I wear upon my breast
  These eighteen years, through all the changing scenes
  And seasons, changeless since the day she died.

1885–86 *1879*

280. Tabard Inn: This inn, in Southwark, was the scene of the assembling of the pilgrims in Chaucer's *Canterbury Tales.* THE CROSS OF SNOW. **6. martyrdom of fire:** Longfellow's second wife died of burns suffered (before his eyes) in her home in 1861.

JUGURTHA

◊

❡ JUGURTHA (d. 104 B.C.) was a king of Numidia, defeated by the Romans. In Longfellow's source, Plutarch's life of Marius, Jugurtha addresses Hercules, not Apollo.

◊

How cold are thy baths, Apollo!
  Cried the African monarch, the splendid,
As down to his death in the hollow
  Dark dungeons of Rome he descended,
  Uncrowned, unthroned, unattended;
How cold are thy baths, Apollo!

How cold are thy baths, Apollo!
  Cried the Poet, unknown, unbefriended,
As the vision, that lured him to follow,
  With the mist and the darkness blended,
  And the dream of his life was ended;
How cold are thy baths, Apollo!

1880 *1879*

DEDICATION

FROM *Michael Angelo: A Fragment*

◊

❡ SOME of Longfellow's finest poetry is in his unfinished verse drama, *Michael Angelo,* which was posthumously published in 1883. For further information, see Horace E. Scudder's Cambridge edition of the poems.

◊

Nothing that is shall perish utterly,
  But perish only to revive again
  In other forms, as clouds restore in rain
  The exhalations of the land and sea.
Men build their houses from the masonry
  Of ruined tombs; the passion and the pain
  Of hearts, that long have ceased to beat, remain
  To throb in hearts that are, or are to be.
So from old chronicles, where sleep in dust
  Names that once filled the world with trumpet tones,
  I build this verse; and flowers of song have thrust
Their roots among the loose disjointed stones,
  Which to this end I fashion as I must.
  Quickened are they that touch the Prophet's bones.

1883

James Russell Lowell

FROM

A FABLE FOR CRITICS

◊

❡ DURING the 1840's Lowell knew many writers in New York and Philadelphia, and deplored the critical squabbles which stemmed from regional hostilities and political factionalism. Illuminating accounts of these frictions are to be found in Perry Miller's *The Raven and the Whale* (1956), and John Stafford's *The Literary Criticism of "Young America"* (1952). In *A Fable*— which owes something to Byron's *English Bards and Scotch Reviewers* and Leigh Hunt's *The Feast of the Poets*—Lowell surveyed the contemporary literary scene more effectively and sympathetically than Poe had done in his "Literati" papers several years earlier. The speaker in the poem is a critic who is giving an account of American writers to Apollo. In a Preface, Lowell wrote:

> This *jeu d'esprit* was extemporized, I may say, so rapidly was it written, purely for my own amusement and with no thought of publication. I sent daily instalments of it to a friend in New York, the late Charles F. Briggs. He urged me to let it be printed, and I at last consented to its anonymous publication. The secret was kept till after several persons laid claim to its authorship.

◊

. . . .
"There comes Emerson first, whose rich words, every one,
Are like gold nails in temples to hang trophies on,
Whose prose is grand verse, while his verse, the Lord knows,
Is some of it pr— No, 't is not even prose;
I 'm speaking of metres; some poems have welled
From those rare depths of soul that have ne'er been excelled;
They 're not epics, but that does n't matter a pin,
In creating, the only hard thing 's to begin;
A grass-blade 's no easier to make than an oak;
If you 've once found the way, you 've achieved the grand stroke;
In the worst of his poems are mines of rich matter,
But thrown in a heap with a crash and a clatter;
Now it is not one thing nor another alone
Makes a poem, but rather the general tone,
The something pervading, uniting the whole,
The before unconceived, unconceivable soul,
So that just in removing this trifle or that, you
Take away, as it were, a chief limb of the statue;
Roots, wood, bark, and leaves singly perfect may be,
But, clapt hodge-podge together, they don't make a tree.

"But, to come back to Emerson (whom, by the way,
I believe we left waiting),—his is, we may say,
A Greek head on right Yankee shoulders, whose range
Has Olympus for one pole, for t' other the Exchange;
He seems, to my thinking (although I 'm afraid
The comparison must, long ere this, have been made),
A Plotinus-Montaigne, where the Egyptian's gold mist
And the Gascon's shrewd wit cheek-by-jowl coexist;
All admire, and yet scarcely six converts he 's got
To I don't (nor they either) exactly know what;
For though he builds glorious temples, 't is odd
He leaves never a doorway to get in a god.
'T is refreshing to old-fashioned people like me
To meet such a primitive Pagan as he,
In whose mind all creation is duly respected
As parts of himself—just a little projected;
And who 's willing to worship the stars and the sun,
A convert to—nothing but Emerson.
So perfect a balance there is in his head,
That he talks of things sometimes as if they were dead;
Life, nature, love, God, and affairs of that sort,
He looks at as merely ideas; in short,
As if they were fossils stuck round in a cabinet,
Of such vast extent that our earth 's a mere dab in it;
Composed just as he is inclined to conjecture her,
Namely, one part pure earth, ninety-nine parts pure lecturer;
You are filled with delight at his clear demonstration,
Each figure, word, gesture, just fits the occasion,
With the quiet precision of science he 'll sort 'em,
But you can't help suspecting the whole a *post mortem.*

"There is Bryant, as quiet, as cool, and as dignified,
As a smooth, silent iceberg, that never is ignified,
Save when by reflection 't is kindled o' nights
With a semblance of flame by the chill Northern Lights.
He may rank (Griswold says so) first bard of your nation
(There 's no doubt that he stands in supreme iceolation),
Your topmost Parnassus he may set his heel on,
But no warm applauses come, peal following peal on,—
He 's too smooth and too polished to hang any zeal on:
Unqualified merits, I 'll grant, if you choose, he has 'em,
But he lacks the one merit of kindling enthusiasm;
If he stir you at all, it is just, on my soul,
Like being stirred up with the very North Pole.

"He is very nice reading in summer, but *inter Nos,* we don't want *extra* freezing in winter;
Take him up in the depth of July, my advice is,
When you feel an Egyptian devotion to ices.
But, deduct all you can, there 's enough that 's right good in him,
He has a true soul for field, river, and wood in him;
And his heart, in the midst of brick walls, or where'er it is,
Glows, softens, and thrills with the tenderest charities—

A FABLE FOR CRITICS. **2. gold nails:** See Eccles. 12:11. **27. Plotinus-Montaigne:** referring to the mixture of idealism and skepticism in Emerson.

55. Griswold: Rufus W. Griswold was the foremost anthologist, literary middleman, and critical logroller of the 1840's. **64–65.** ***inter Nos . . .*** : literally, "among ourselves"; however, with Lowell's addition of "*extra*" a mischief is begun which is compounded by punning.

To you mortals that delve in this trade-ridden planet?
No, to old Berkshire's hills, with their limestone and granite.
If you 're one who *in loco* (add *foco* here) *desipis,*
You will get of his outermost heart (as I guess) a piece;
But you 'd get deeper down if you came as a precipice,
And would break the last seal of its inwardest fountain,
If you only could palm yourself off for a mountain.
Mr. Quivis, or somebody quite as discerning,
Some scholar who 's hourly expecting his learning,
Calls B. the American Wordsworth; but Wordsworth
May be rated at more than your whole tuneful herd 's worth.
No, don't be absurd, he 's an excellent Bryant;
But, my friends, you 'll endanger the life of your client,
By attempting to stretch him up into a giant:
If you choose to compare him, I think there are two per-
-sons fit for a parallel—Thomson and Cowper;
I don't mean exactly,—there 's something of each,
There 's T.'s love of nature, C.'s penchant to preach;
Just mix up their minds so that C.'s spice of craziness
Shall balance and neutralize T.'s turn for laziness,
And it gives you a brain cool, quite frictionless, quiet,
Whose internal police nips the buds of all riot,—
A brain like a permanent strait-jacket put on
The heart that strives vainly to burst off a button,—
A brain which, without being slow or mechanic,
Does more than a larger less drilled, more volcanic;
He 's a Cowper condensed, with no craziness bitten,
And the advantage that Wordsworth before him had written.

"But, my dear little bardlings, don't prick up your ears
Nor suppose I would rank you and Bryant as peers;
If I call him an iceberg, I don't mean to say
There is nothing in that which is grand in its way;
He is almost the one of your poets that knows
How much grace, strength, and dignity lie in Repose;
If he sometimes fall short, he is too wise to mar
His thought's modest fulness by going too far;
'T would be well if your authors should all make a trial
Of what virtue there is in severe self-denial,
And measure their writings by Hesiod's staff,
Which teaches that all has less value than half.

. . . .

"There is Hawthorne, with genius so shrinking and rare
That you hardly at first see the strength that is there;
A frame so robust, with a nature so sweet,
So earnest, so graceful, so lithe and so fleet,
Is worth a descent from Olympus to meet;
'T is as if a rough oak that for ages had stood,
With his gnarled bony branches like ribs of the wood,
Should bloom, after cycles of struggle and scathe,
With a single anemone trembly and rathe;
His strength is so tender, his wildness so meek,
That a suitable parallel sets one to seek,—
He 's a John Bunyan Fouqué, a Puritan Tieck;
When Nature was shaping him, clay was not granted
For making so full-sized a man as she wanted,
So, to fill out her model, a little she spared
From some finer-grained stuff for a woman prepared,
And she could not have hit a more excellent plan
For making him fully and perfectly man.
The success of her scheme gave her so much delight,
That she tried it again, shortly after, in Dwight;
Only, while she was kneading and shaping the clay,
She sang to her work in her sweet childish way,

74. *in loco . . . desipis:* A complicated pun. *Loco desipis* refers to the saying, "You can be foolish in a particular place." "Locofoco" was the name applied to "liberal" political thinkers of the time. **86–87. If . . . Cowper:** "To demonstrate quickly and easily how per-/ -versely absurd 't is to sound this name *Cowper,*/ As people in general call him named *super,*/ I remark that he rhymes it himself with horse trooper" [Lowell's note]. **Cowper:** William Cowper (1731–1800), English poet. **Thomson:** James Thomson (1700–48), Scottish poet.

110–11. And . . . half: Hesiod, a Greek poet of the eighth century B.C., wrote in his *Works and Days:* "Fools! they know not how much half exceeds the whole." **123. John Bunyan . . . Tieck:** Lowell is here pairing opposites to suggest the contradictions in Hawthorne's temperament. The moral austerity of Bunyan and the Puritans is linked with the lush romanticism of the Germans, Baron de La Motte-Fouqué (1777–1843) and Ludwig Tieck (1773–1853). **131. Dwight:** J. S. Dwight (1813–93), Boston music critic, was, like Hawthorne, a member of the "transcendental" community, Brook Farm.

And found, when she 'd put the last touch to his soul,
That the music had somehow got mixed with the whole.

"Here 's Cooper, who 's written six volumes to show
He 's as good as a lord: well, let 's grant that he 's so;
If a person prefer that description of praise,
Why, a coronet 's certainly cheaper than bays;
But he need take no pains to convince us he 's not
(As his enemies say) the American Scott.
Choose any twelve men, and let C. read aloud
That one of his novels of which he 's most proud,
And I 'd lay any bet that, without ever quitting
Their box, they 'd be all, to a man, for acquitting.
He has drawn you one character, though, that is new,
One wildflower he 's plucked that is wet with the dew
Of this fresh Western world, and, the thing not to mince,
He has done naught but copy it ill ever since;
His Indians, with proper respect be it said,
Are just Natty Bumppo, daubed over with red,
And his very Long Toms are the same useful Nat,
Rigged up in duck pants and a sou'wester hat
(Though once in a Coffin, a good chance was found
To have slipped the old fellow away underground).
All his other men-figures are clothes upon sticks,
The *dernière chemise* of a man in a fix
(As a captain besieged, when his garrison 's small,
Sets up caps upon poles to be seen o'er the wall);
And the women he draws from one model don't vary,
All sappy as maples and flat as a prairie.
When a character 's wanted, he goes to the task
As a cooper would do in composing a cask;
He picks out the staves, of their qualities heedful,
Just hoops them together as tight as is needful,
And, if the best fortune should crown the attempt, he
Has made at the most something wooden and empty.

"Don't suppose I would underrate Cooper's abilities;
If I thought you 'd do that, I should feel very ill at ease;
The men who have given to *one* character life
And objective existence are not very rife;
You may number them all, both prose-writers and singers,
Without overrunning the bounds of your fingers,
And Natty won't go to oblivion quicker
Than Adams the parson or Primrose the vicar.

"There is one thing in Cooper I like, too, and that is
That on manners he lectures his countrymen gratis;
Not precisely so either, because, for a rarity,
He is paid for his tickets in unpopularity.
Now he may overcharge his American pictures.
But you 'll grant there 's a good deal of truth in his strictures;
And I honor the man who is willing to sink
Half his present repute for the freedom to think,
And, when he has thought, be his cause strong or weak,
Will risk t' other half for the freedom to speak,
Caring naught for what vengeance the mob has in store,
Let that mob be the upper ten thousand or lower.

"There are truths you Americans need to be told,
And it never 'll refute them to swagger and scold;
John Bull, looking o'er the Atlantic, in choler
At your aptness for trade, says you worship the dollar;
But to scorn such eye-dollar-try 's what very few do,
And John goes to that church as often as you do.
No matter what John says, don't try to outcrow him,
'T is enough to go quietly on and outgrow him;
Like most fathers, Bull hates to see Number One
Displacing himself in the mind of his son,
And detests the same faults in himself he 'd neglected
When he sees them again in his child's glass reflected;
To love one another you 're too like by half;
If he is a bull, you 're a pretty stout calf,
And tear your own pasture for naught but to show
What a nice pair of horns you 're beginning to grow.

"There are one or two things I should just like to hint,

152. Long Toms: Long Tom Coffin, the American sailor in Cooper's *The Pilot* (1823). **157.** ***dernière chemise:*** last shirt. **175. Than . . . vicar: Adams:** Parson Adams in Henry Fielding's *Joseph Andrews* (1742). **Primrose:** Dr. Primrose in Oliver Goldsmith's *The Vicar of Wakefield* (1766).

For you don't often get the truth told you in print;
The most of you (this is what strikes all beholders)
Have a mental and physical stoop in the shoulders;
Though you ought to be free as the winds and the waves,
You 've the gait and the manners of run-away slaves;
Though you brag of your New World, you don't half believe in it;
And as much of the Old as is possible weave in it;
Your goddess of freedom, a tight, buxom girl,
With lips like a cherry and teeth like a pearl,
With eyes bold as Herë's, and hair floating free,
And full of the sun as the spray of the sea,
Who can sing at a husking or romp at a shearing,
Who can trip through the forests alone without fearing,
Who can drive home the cows with a song through the grass,
Keeps glancing aside into Europe's cracked glass,
Hides her red hands in gloves, pinches up her lithe waist,
And makes herself wretched with transmarine taste;
She loses her fresh country charm when she takes
Any mirror except her own rivers and lakes.

"You steal Englishmen's books and think Englishmen's thought,
With their salt on her tail your wild eagle is caught;
Your literature suits its each whisper and motion
To what will be thought of it over the ocean;
The cast clothes of Europe your statesmanship tries
And mumbles again the old blarneys and lies;—
Forget Europe wholly, your veins throb with blood,
To which the dull current in hers is but mud:
Let her sneer, let her say your experiment fails,
In her voice there 's a tremble e'en now while she rails,
And your shore will soon be in the nature of things
Covered thick with gilt drift-wood of castaway kings,
Where alone, as it were in a Longfellow's Waif
Her fugitive pieces will find themselves safe.
O my friends, thank your god, if you have one, that he
'Twixt the Old World and you set the gulf of a sea;
Be strong-backed, brown-handed, upright as your pines,
By the scale of a hemisphere shape your designs,
Be true to yourselves and this new nineteenth age,
As a statue by Powers, or a picture by Page,
Plough, sail, forge, build, carve, paint, make all over new,
To your own New-World instincts contrive to be true,
Keep your ears open wide to the Future's first call,
Be whatever you will, but yourselves first of all,
Stand fronting the dawn on Toil's heaven-scaling peaks,
And become my new race of more practical Greeks.—
Hem! your likeness at present, I shudder to tell o't,
Is that you have your slaves, and the Greek had his helot."

"There comes Poe, with his raven, like Barnaby Rudge,
Three fifths of him genius and two fifths sheer fudge,
Who talks like a book of iambs and pentameters,
In a way to make people of common sense damn metres,
Who has written some things quite the best of their kind,
But the heart somehow seems all squeezed out by the mind,
Who— But hey-day! What 's this? Messieurs Mathews and Poe,
You must n't fling mud-balls at Longfellow so,
Does it make a man worse that his character's such
As to make his friends love him (as you think) too much?
Why, there is not a bard at this moment alive
More willing than he that his fellows should thrive;
While you are abusing him thus, even now
He would help either one of you out of a slough;
You may say that he 's smooth and all that till you 're hoarse,
But remember that elegance also is force;
After polishing granite as much as you will,
The heart keeps its tough old persistency still;
Deduct all you can, *that* still keeps you at bay;
Why, he 'll live till men weary of Collins and Gray.

214. Herë's: Herë, or Hera, the goddess of women, the sister and wife of Zeus.

243. Powers: Hiram Powers (1805–73), American sculptor. **Page:** William Page (1811–85), American historical and portrait painter. **252. Barnaby Rudge:** In Dickens' novel *Barnaby Rudge* (1841), as in Poe's poem, a raven is central to the action. **258. Mathews:** Cornelius Mathews (1817–89), a New Yorker who, like Poe, attacked Longfellow. **271. Why . . . Gray:** William Collins (1721–59) and Thomas Gray (1716–71) were representative pre-Romantic English poets.

I'm not over-fond of Greek metres in English,
To me rhyme 's a gain, so it be not too jinglish,
And your modern hexameter verses are no more
Like Greek ones than sleek Mr. Pope is like Homer;
As the roar of the sea to the coo of a pigeon is,
So, compared to your moderns, sounds old Melesigenes;
I may be too partial, the reason, perhaps, o't is
That I 've heard the old blind man recite his own rhapsodies,
And my ear with that music impregnate may be,
Like the poor exiled shell with the soul of the sea,
Or as one can't bear Strauss when his nature is cloven
To its deeps within deeps by the stroke of Beethoven;
But, set that aside, and 't is truth that I speak,
Had Theocritus written in English, not Greek,
I believe that his exquisite sense would scarce change a line
In that rare, tender, virgin-like pastoral Evangeline.
That 's not ancient nor modern, its place is apart
Where time has no sway, in the realm of pure Art,
'T is a shrine of retreat from Earth's hubbub and strife
As quiet and chaste as the author's own life.

"What! Irving? thrice welcome, warm heart and fine brain,
You bring back the happiest spirit from Spain,
And the gravest sweet humor, that ever were there
Since Cervantes met death in his gentle despair;
Nay, don't be embarrassed, nor look so beseeching,
I sha'n't run directly against my own preaching,
And, having just laughed at their Raphaels and Dantes,
Go to setting you up beside matchless Cervantes;
But allow me to speak what I honestly feel,—
To a true poet-heart add the fun of Dick Steele,
Throw in all of Addison, *minus* the chill,
With the whole of that partnership's stock and good-will,
Mix well, and while stirring, hum o'er, as a spell,
The fine *old* English Gentleman, simmer it well,
Sweeten just to your own private liking, then strain,
That only the finest and clearest remain,
Let it stand out of doors till a soul it receives
From the warm lazy sun loitering down through green leaves,
And you'll find a choice nature, not wholly deserving
A name either English or Yankee,—just Irving.

1848

275. Like . . . Homer: Alexander Pope (1688–1744) published translations of the *Iliad* and *Odyssey*, 1715–26. **277. Melesigenes:** Homer. **293. You . . . Spain:** Washington Irving returned from his ambassadorship to Spain in 1845.

AFTER THE BURIAL

◇

THIS poem and "The Darkened Mind" are examples of Lowell's more popular efforts. They also represent a staple theme of Fireside verse—domestic grief. Both poems are sentimental to the extent that the poet, as father and as son, expresses his emotions about pathetic situations in which there is loss but not demonstrated tragedy, but he does not soften either experience by seeking spurious comfort.

Lowell's second child, Rose, died after a week's illness in the spring of 1850. The implied speaker with whom the poet argues was his friend, Sydney Gay. The poem "has aroused," Lowell wrote in 1875, "strange echoes in men who assured me they were generally insensible to poetry."

◇

Yes, faith is a goodly anchor;
When skies are sweet as a psalm,
At the bows it lolls so stalwart,
In its bluff, broad-shouldered calm.

And when over breakers to leeward
The tattered surges are hurled,
It may keep our head to the tempest,
With its grip on the base of the world.

But, after the shipwreck, tell me
What help in its iron thews,
Still true to the broken hawser,
Deep down among sea-weed and ooze?

In the breaking gulfs of sorrow,
When the helpless feet stretch out
And find in the deeps of darkness
No footing so solid as doubt,

Then better one spar of Memory,
One broken plank of the Past,
That our human heart may cling to,
Though hopeless of shore at last!

To the spirit its splendid conjectures,
To the flesh its sweet despair,
Its tears o'er the thin-worn locket
With its anguish of deathless hair!

Immortal? I feel it and know it,
Who doubts it of such as she?
But that is the pang's very secret,—
Immortal away from me.

There 's a narrow ridge in the graveyard
Would scarce stay a child in his race,
But to me and my thought it is wider
Than the star-sown vague of Space.

Your logic, my friend, is perfect,
Your moral most drearily true;
But, since the earth clashed on *her* coffin,
I keep hearing that, and not you.

Console if you will, I can bear it;
'T is a well-meant alms of breath;
But not all the preaching since Adam
Has made Death other than Death.

It is pagan; but wait till you feel it,—
That jar of our earth, that dull shock
When the ploughshare of deeper passion
Tears down to our primitive rock.

Communion in spirit! Forgive me,
But I, who am earthly and weak,
Would give all my incomes from dream-
land
For a touch of her hand on my cheek.

That little shoe in the corner,
So worn and wrinkled and brown,
With its emptiness confutes you,
And argues your wisdom down.

1868 *1850*

EMERSON THE LECTURER

◊

¶ THIS was first published in the *Atlantic Monthly* (February, 1861) and revised for the *Nation* (November 12, 1868).

◊

IT IS a singular fact that Mr. Emerson is the most steadily attractive lecturer in America. Into that somewhat cold-waterish region adventurers of the sensational kind come down now and then with a splash, to become disregarded King Logs [1] before the next season. But Mr. Emerson always draws. A lecturer now for something like a third of a century, one of the pioneers of the lecturing system, the charm of his voice, his manner, and his matter has never lost its power over his earlier hearers, and continually winds new ones in its enchanting meshes. What they do not fully understand they take on trust, and listen, saying to themselves, as the old poet of Sir Philip Sidney,—

"A sweet, attractive, kind of grace,
A full assurance given by looks,
Continual comfort in a face,
The lineaments of gospel books." [2]

We call it a singular fact, because we Yankees are thought to be fond of the spread-eagle style, and nothing can be more remote from that than his. We are reckoned a practical folk, who would rather hear about a new air-tight stove than about Plato; yet our favorite teacher's practicality is not in the least of the Poor Richard variety. If he have any Buncombe constituency, it is that unrealized commonwealth of philosophers which Plotinus proposed to establish; and if he were to make an almanac, his directions to farmers would be something like this: "OCTOBER: *Indian Summer;* now is the time to get in your early Vedas." What, then, is his secret? Is it not that he out-Yankees us all? that his range includes us all? that he is equally at home with the potato-disease and original sin, with pegging shoes and the Over-Soul? that, as we try all trades, so has he tried all cultures? and above all, that his mysticism gives us a counterpoise to our super-practicality?

There is no man living to whom, as a writer, so many of us feel and thankfully acknowledge so great an indebtedness for ennobling impulses,—none whom so many cannot abide. What does he mean? ask these last. Where is his system? What is the use of it all? What the deuce have we to do with Brahma? I do not propose to write an essay on Emerson at this time. I will only say that one may find grandeur and consolation in a starlit night without caring to ask what it means, save grandeur and consolation; one may like Mon-

EMERSON THE LECTURER. 1. **King Logs**: In the Aesop fable, the frogs ask Jupiter for a king. He sends them a log, which they accept as a ruler until they realize what it is. 2. **"A . . . books"**: The verse is from Matthew Roydon's elegy to Sidney, published in *The Phoenix Nest* (1593).

taigne, as some ten generations before us have done, without thinking him so systematic as some more eminently tedious (or shall we say tediously eminent?) authors; one may think roses as good in their way as cabbages, though the latter would make a better show in the witness-box, if cross-examined as to their usefulness; and as for Brahma, why, he can take care of himself, and won't bite us at any rate.

The bother with Mr. Emerson is, that, though he writes in prose, he is essentially a poet. If you undertake to paraphrase what he says, and to reduce it to words of one syllable for infant minds, you will make as sad work of it as the good monk with his analysis of Homer in the *Epistolæ Obscurorum Virorum*.[3] We look upon him as one of the few men of genius whom our age has produced, and there needs no better proof of it than his masculine faculty of fecundating other minds. Search for his eloquence in his books and you will perchance miss it, but meanwhile you will find that it has kindled all your thoughts. For choice and pith of language he belongs to a better age than ours, and might rub shoulders with Fuller and Browne,—though he does use that abominable word *reliable*. His eye for a fine, telling phrase that will carry true is like that of a backwoodsman for a rifle; and he will dredge you up a choice word from the mud of Cotton Mather himself. A diction at once so rich and so homely as his I know not where to match in these days of writing by the page; it is like homespun cloth-of-gold. The many cannot miss his meaning, and only the few can find it. It is the open secret of all true genius. It is wholesome to angle in those profound pools, though one be rewarded with nothing more than the leap of a fish that flashes his freckled side in the sun and as suddenly absconds in the dark and dreamy waters again. There is keen excitement, though there be no ponderable acquisition. If we carry nothing home in our baskets, there is ample gain in dilated lungs and stimulated blood. What does he mean, quotha? He means inspiring hints, a divining-rod to your deeper nature. No doubt, Emerson, like all original men, has his peculiar audience, and yet I know none that can hold a promiscuous crowd in pleased attention so long as he. As in all original men, there is something for every palate. "Would you know," says Goethe, "the ripest cherries? Ask the boys and the blackbirds."

The announcement that such a pleasure as a new course of lectures by him is coming, to people as old as I am, is something like those forebodings of spring that prepare us every year for a familiar novelty, none the less novel, when it arrives, because it is familiar. We know perfectly well what we are to expect from Mr. Emerson, and yet what he says always penetrates and stirs us, as is apt to be the case with genius, in a very unlooked-for fashion. Perhaps genius is one of the few things which we gladly allow to repeat itself, —one of the few that multiply rather than weaken the force of their impression by iteration? Perhaps some of us hear more than the mere words, are moved by something deeper than the thoughts? If it be so, we are quite right, for it is thirty years and more of "plain living and high thinking" that speak to us in this altogether unique lay-preacher. We have shared in the beneficence of this varied culture, this fearless impartiality in criticism and speculation, this masculine sincerity, this sweetness of nature which rather stimulates than cloys, for a generation long. If ever there was a standing testimonial to the cumulative power and value of Character (and we need it sadly in these days), we have it in this gracious and dignified presence. What an antiseptic is a pure life! At sixty-five (or two years beyond his grand climacteric, as he would prefer to call it) he has that privilege of soul which abolishes the calendar, and presents him to us always the unwasted contemporary of his own prime. I do not know if he seem old to his younger hearers, but we who have known him so long wonder at the tenacity with which he maintains himself even in the outposts of youth. I suppose it is not the Emerson of 1868 to whom we listen. For us the whole life of the man is distilled in the clear drop of every sentence, and behind each word we divine the force of a noble character, the weight of a large capital of thinking and being. We do not go to hear what Emerson says so much as to hear Emerson. Not that we perceive any falling-off in anything that ever was essential to the charm of Mr. Emerson's peculiar style of thought or phrase. The first lecture,[4] to be sure, was more disjointed even than common. It was as if, after vainly trying to get his paragraphs into sequence and order, he had at last tried the desperate expedient of *shuffling* them. It was chaos come again, but it was a chaos full of shooting-stars, a jumble of creative forces. The second lecture, on "Criticism and Poetry," was quite up to the level of old times, full of that power of strangely subtle association whose indirect approaches startle the mind into almost painful attention, of those flashes of

3. ***Epistolæ Obscurorum Virorum:*** "*Letters of Obscure Men*," a sixteenth-century work.

4. **The first lecture:** Lowell refers here to Emerson's series of six Boston lectures beginning October 12, 1868. He revised and reprinted this essay before the series was completed.

mutual understanding between speaker and hearer that are gone ere one can say it lightens. The vice of Emerson's criticism seems to be, that while no man is so sensitive to what is poetical, few men are less sensible than he of what makes a poem. He values the solid meaning of thought above the subtler meaning of style. He would prefer Donne, I suspect, to Spenser, and sometimes mistakes the queer for the original.

To be young is surely the best, if the most precarious, gift of life; yet there are some of us who would hardly consent to be young again, if it were at the cost of our recollection of Mr. Emerson's first lectures during the consulate [5] of Van Buren. We used to walk in from the country to the Masonic Temple (I think it was), through the crisp winter night, and listen to that thrilling voice of his, so charged with subtle meaning and subtle music, as shipwrecked men on a raft to the hail of a ship that came with unhoped-for food and rescue. Cynics might say what they liked. Did our own imaginations transfigure dry remainder-biscuit [6] into ambrosia? At any rate, he brought us *life,* which, on the whole, is no bad thing. Was it all transcendentalism? magic-lantern pictures on mist? As you will. Those, then, were just what we wanted. But it was not so. The delight and the benefit were that he put us in communication with a larger style of thought, sharpened our wits with a more pungent phrase, gave us ravishing glimpses of an ideal under the dry husk of our New England; made us conscious of the supreme and everlasting originality of whatever bit of soul might be in any of us; freed us, in short, from the stocks of prose in which we had sat so long that we had grown well-nigh contented in our cramps. And who that saw the audience will ever forget it, where every one still capable of fire, or longing to renew in himself the half-forgotten sense of it, was gathered? Those faces, young and old, agleam with pale intellectual light, eager with pleased attention, flash upon me once more from the deep recesses of the years with an exquisite pathos. Ah, beautiful young eyes, brimming with love and hope, wholly vanished now in that other world we call the Past, or peering doubtfully through the pensive gloaming of memory, your light impoverishes these cheaper days! I hear again that rustle of sensation, as they turned to exchange glances over some pithier thought, some keener flash of that humor which always played about the horizon of his mind like heat-lightning, and it seems now like the sad whisper of the autumn leaves that are whirling around me. But would my picture be complete if I forgot that ample and vegete [7] countenance of Mr. R—— of W——,—how, from its regular post at the corner of the front bench, it turned in ruddy triumph to the profaner audience as if he were the inexplicably appointed fugleman of appreciation? I was reminded of him by those hearty cherubs in Titian's Assumption [8] that look at you as who should say, "Did you ever see a Madonna like *that?* Did you ever behold one hundred and fifty pounds of womanhood mount heavenward before like a rocket?"

To some of us that long-past experience remains as the most marvellous and fruitful we have ever had. Emerson awakened us, saved us from the body of this death. It is the sound of the trumpet that the young soul longs for, careless what breath may fill it. Sidney heard it in the ballad of "Chevy Chase," [9] and we in Emerson. Nor did it blow retreat, but called to us with assurance of victory. Did they say he was disconnected? So were the stars, that seemed larger to our eyes, still keen with that excitement, as we walked homeward with prouder stride over the creaking snow. And were *they* not knit together by a higher logic than our mere sense could master? Were we enthusiasts? I hope and believe we were, and am thankful to the man who made us worth something for once in our lives. If asked what was left? what we carried home? we should not have been careful for an answer. It would have been enough if we had said that something beautiful had passed that way. Or we might have asked in return what one brought away from a symphony of Beethoven? Enough that he had set that ferment of wholesome discontent at work in us. There is one, at least, of those old hearers, so many of whom are now in the fruition of that intellectual beauty of which Emerson gave them both the desire and the foretaste, who will always love to repeat:—

> *"Che in la mente m' è fitta, ed or m' accuora*
> *La cara e buona immagine paterna*
> *Di voi, quando nel mondo ad ora ad ora*
> *M' insegnavaste come l' uom s' eterna."* [10]

5. **consulate:** i.e., presidency. 6. **Did . . . remainder-biscuit:** See Shakespeare's *As You Like It*, II.vii.39.

7. **vegete:** ruddy, healthy. 8. **Titian's Assumption:** In this painting the amazed apostles gaze upward at the ascending Virgin. 9. **Sidney . . . Chase:** Sidney wrote in his *Defence of Poesie* (1595): "Certainly I must confess mine own barbarousness; I never heard the old song of Percy and Douglas that I found not my heart moved more than by a trumpet." 10. ***"Che . . . eterna":*** Dante's *Inferno*, XV.82–85. Longfellow's translation reads:

> "For in my mind is fixed, and touches now
> My heart, the dear and good paternal image
> Of you, when in the world from hour to hour
> You taught me how a man becomes eternal."

I am unconsciously thinking, as I write, of the third lecture of the present course, in which Mr. Emerson gave some delightful reminiscences of the intellectual influences in whose movement he had shared. It was like hearing Goethe read some passages of the *Wahrheit aus seinem Leben.*[11] Not that there was not a little *Dichtung,*[12] too, here and there, as the lecturer built up so lofty a pedestal under certain figures as to lift them into a prominence of obscurity, and seem to masthead them there. Everybody was asking his neighbor who this or that recondite great man was, in the faint hope that somebody might once have heard of him. There are those who call Mr. Emerson cold. Let them revise their judgment in presence of this loyalty of his that can keep warm for half a century, that never forgets a friendship, or fails to pay even a fancied obligation to the uttermost farthing. This substantiation of shadows was but incidental, and pleasantly characteristic of the man to those who know and love him. The greater part of the lecture was devoted to reminiscences of things substantial in themselves. He spoke of Everett, fresh from Greece and Germany; of Channing; of the translations of Margaret Fuller, Ripley, and Dwight; of the *Dial* and Brook Farm. To what he said of the latter an undertone of good-humored irony gave special zest. But what every one of his hearers felt was that the protagonist in the drama was left out. The lecturer was no Æneas to babble the *quorum magna pars fui,*[13] and, as one of his listeners, I cannot help wishing to say how each of them was commenting the story as it went along, and filling up the necessary gaps in it from his own private store of memories. His younger hearers could not know how much they owed to the benign impersonality, the quiet scorn of everything ignoble, the never-sated hunger of self-culture, that were personified in the man before them. But the older knew how much the country's intellectual emancipation was due to the stimulus of his teaching and example, how constantly he had kept burning the beacon of an ideal life above our lower region of turmoil. To him more than to all other causes together did the young martyrs of our civil war owe the sustaining strength of thoughtful heroism that is so touching in every record of their lives. Those who are grateful to Mr. Emerson, as many of us are, for what they feel to be most valuable in their culture, or perhaps I should say their impulse, are grateful not so much for any direct teachings of his as for that inspiring lift which only genius can give, and without which all doctrine is chaff.

This was something like the *caret* which some of us older boys wished to fill up on the margin of the master's lecture. Few men have been so much to so many, and through so large a range of aptitudes and temperaments and this simply because all of us value manhood beyond any or all other qualities of character. We may suspect in him, here and there, a certain thinness and vagueness of quality, but let the waters go over him as they list, this masculine fibre of his will keep its lively color and its toughness of texture. I have heard some great speakers and some accomplished orators, but never any that so moved and persuaded men as he. There is a kind of undertow in that rich baritone of his that sweeps our minds from their foothold into deeper waters with a drift we cannot and would not resist. And how artfully (for Emerson is a long-studied artist in these things) does the deliberate utterance, that seems waiting for the fit word, appear to admit us partners in the labor of thought and make us feel as if the glance of humor were a sudden suggestion, as if the perfect phrase lying written there on the desk were as unexpected to him as to us! In that closely filed speech of his at the Burns centenary dinner,[14] every word seemed to have just dropped down to him from the clouds. He looked far away over the heads of his hearers, with a vague kind of expectation, as into some private heaven of invention, and the winged period came at last obedient to his spell. "My dainty Ariel!"[15] he seemed murmuring to himself as he cast down his eyes as if in deprecation of the frenzy of approval and caught another sentence from the Sibylline leaves that lay before him, ambushed behind a dish of fruit and seen only by nearest neighbors. Every sentence brought down the house, as I never saw one brought down before,—and it is not so easy to hit Scotsmen with a sentiment that has no hint of native brogue in it. I watched, for it was an interesting study, how the quick sympathy ran flashing from face to face down the long tables, like an electric spark thrilling as it went, and then exploded in a thunder of plaudits. I watched till tables and faces vanished, for I, too, found myself caught up in the common enthusiasm, and my excited fancy set me under the *bema*[16] listening to him who fulmined over Greece. I can never help applying to him what Ben Jonson said of Bacon: "There happened in my time one noble speaker, who was full of gravity in his speaking. His lan-

11. ***Wahrheit aus seinem Leben:*** "Truth Out of His Life." The full title of Goethe's autobiography is *Dichtung und Wahrheit aus meinem Leben.* 12. ***Dichtung:*** Poetry. 13. ***quorum magna pars fui:*** "Of which things I was a great part" (*Aeneid,* II.6).

14. **In . . . dinner:** Emerson spoke at the Burns Festival, Boston, January 25, 1859. 15. **"My . . . Ariel!":** Shakespeare's *Tempest,* V.i.95. 16. ***bema:*** rostrum.

guage was nobly censorious. No man ever spake more neatly, more pressly, more weightily, or suffered less emptiness, less idleness, in what he uttered. No member of his speech but consisted of his own graces. His hearers could not cough, or look aside from him, without loss. He commanded where he spoke." Those who heard him while their natures were yet plastic, and their mental nerves trembled under the slightest breath of divine air, will never cease to feel and say:—

"Was never eye did see that face,
  Was never ear did hear that tongue,
Was never mind did mind his grace,
  That ever thought the travail long;
But eyes, and ears, and every thought,
Were with his sweet perfections caught."[17]

1861

SUNTHIN' IN THE PASTORAL LINE

FROM *The Biglow Papers,* SECOND SERIES

◇

¶ LOWELL began serializing the First Series of *The Biglow Papers* in a Boston newspaper in 1846. These dialect poems were a protest against the Mexican War, concerning which he wrote ten years later, it was "essentially a war of false pretences [which] would result in widening the boundaries and so prolonging the life of slavery." In the *Papers,* his "voice"—not to be completely identified with that of Lowell himself—was Hosea Biglow, a country Yankee whose common sense is "heated by conscience." Hosea's poems are "edited" by his pastor, Parson Wilbur, who sometimes serves as another "voice" for Lowell.

A Second Series, most of which appeared in the *Atlantic Monthly* between January, 1862, and May, 1866, offered commentary on issues connected with the Civil War. The sixth number, here printed, is an exception. Its descriptions of the New England scene are less dated than some of Lowell's political opinions.

◇

TO THE EDITORS OF THE *Atlantic Monthly*

Jaalam, 17th May, 1862.

GENTLEMEN,—

At the special request of Mr. Biglow, I intended to inclose, together with his own contribution, (into which, at my suggestion, he has thrown a little more of pastoral sentiment than usual,) some passages from my sermon on the day of the National Fast, from the text, "Remember them that are in bonds, as bound with them," Heb. xiii. 3. But I have not leisure sufficient at present for the copying of them, even were I altogether satisfied with the production as it stands. I should prefer, I confess, to contribute the entire discourse to the pages of your respectable miscellany, if it should be found acceptable upon perusal, especially as I find the difficulty in selection of greater magnitude than I had anticipated. What passes without challenge in the fervour of oral delivery, cannot always stand the colder criticism of the closet. I am not so great an enemy of Eloquence as my friend Mr. Biglow would appear to be from some passages in his contribution for the current month. I would not, indeed, hastily suspect him of covertly glancing at myself in his somewhat caustick animadversions, albeit some of the phrases he girds at are not entire strangers to my lips. I am a more hearty admirer of the Puritans than seems now to be the fashion, and believe, that, if they Hebraized a little too much in their speech, they showed remarkable practical sagacity as statesmen and founders. But such phenomena as Puritanism are the results rather of great religious than of merely social convulsions, and do not long survive them. So soon as an earnest conviction has cooled into a phrase, its work is over, and the best that can be done with it is to bury it. *Ite, missa est.*[1] I am inclined to agree with Mr. Biglow that we cannot settle the great political questions which are now presenting themselves to the nation by the opinions of Jeremiah or Ezekiel as to the wants and duties of the Jews in their time, nor do I believe that an entire community with their feelings and views would be practicable or even agreeable at the present day. At the same time I could wish that their habit of subordinating the actual to the moral, the flesh to the spirit, and this world to the other, were more common. They had found out, at least, the great military secret that soul weighs more than body.—But I am suddenly called to a sick-bed in the household of a valued parishioner.

With esteem and respect,
Your obedient servant,
HOMER WILBUR.

Once git a smell o' musk into a draw,
An' it clings hold like precerdents in law:

17. **"Was . . . caught":** Lowell quotes a second time from Roydon's "Elegie."

SUNTHIN' IN THE PASTORAL LINE. 1. ***Ite, missa est:*** "Go, the mass is finished." These words come just before the final blessing in the mass.

Your gra'ma'am put it there,—when, goodness knows,—
To jes' this-worldify her Sunday-clo'es;
But the old chist wun't sarve her gran'son's wife,
(For, 'thout new funnitoor, wut good in life?)
An' so ole clawfoot, from the precinks dread
O' the spare chamber, slinks into the shed
Where, dim with dust, it fust or last subsides
To holdin' seeds an' fifty things besides;
But better days stick fast in heart an' husk,
An' all you keep in 't gits a scent o' musk.

Jes' so with poets: wut they've airly read
Gits kind o' worked into their heart an' head,
So 's 't they can't seem to write but jest on sheers
With furrin countries or played-out ideers,
Nor hev a feelin', ef it doos n't smack
O' wut some critter chose to feel 'way back:
This makes 'em talk o' daisies, larks, an' things,
Ez though we 'd nothin' here that blows an' sings,—
(Why, I 'd give more for one live bobolink
Than a square mile o' larks in printer's ink,)—
This makes 'em think our fust o' May is May,
Which 't ain't, for all the almanicks can say.

O little city-gals, don't never go it
Blind on the word o' noospaper or poet!
They 're apt to puff, an' May-day seldom looks
Up in the country ez it doos in books;
They 're no more like than hornets'-nests an' hives,
Or printed sarmons be to holy lives.
I, with my trouses perched on cowhide boots,
Tuggin' my foundered feet out by the roots,
Hev seen ye come to fling on April's hearse
Your muslin nosegays from the milliner's,
Puzzlin' to find dry ground your queen to choose,
An' dance your throats sore in morocker shoes:
I 've seen ye an' felt proud, thet, come wut would,
Our Pilgrim stock wuz pethed with hardihood.
Pleasure doos make us Yankees kind o' winch,
Ez though 't wuz sunthin' paid for by the inch;
But yit we du contrive to worry thru,
Ef Dooty tells us thet the thing 's to du,
An' kerry a hollerday, ef we set out,
Ez stiddily ez though 't wuz a redoubt.

I, country-born an' bred, know where to find
Some blooms thet make the season suit the mind,
An' seem to metch the doubtin' bluebird's notes,—
Half-vent'rin' liverworts in furry coats,
Bloodroots, whose rolled-up leaves ef you oncurl,
Each on 'em 's cradle to a baby-pearl,—
But these are jes' Spring's pickets; sure ez sin,
The rebble frosts 'll try to drive 'em in;
For half our May 's so awfully like May n't,
't would rile a Shaker or an evrige saint;
Though I own up I like our back'ard springs
Thet kind o' haggle with their greens an' things,
An' when you 'most give up, 'uthout more words
Toss the fields full o' blossoms, leaves, an' birds;
Thet's Northun natur', slow an' apt to doubt,
But when it *doos* git stirred, ther' 's no ginout!

Fust come the blackbirds clatt'rin' in tall trees,
An' settlin' things in windy Congresses,—
Queer politicians, though, for I 'll be skinned
Ef all on 'em don't head aginst the wind.
'fore long the trees begin to show belief,—
The maple crimsons to a coral-reef,
Then saffern swarms swing off from all the willers
So plump they look like yaller caterpillars,
Then gray hossches'nuts leetle hands unfold
Softer 'n a baby's be at three days old:
Thet 's robin-redbreast's almanick; he knows
Thet arter this ther' 's only blossom-snows;
So, choosin' out a handy crotch an' spouse,
He goes to plast'rin' his adobe house.

Then seems to come a hitch,—things lag behind,
Till some fine mornin' Spring makes up her mind,
An' ez, when snow-swelled rivers cresh their dams
Heaped-up with ice thet dovetails in an' jams,
A leak comes spirtin' thru some pin-hole cleft,
Grows stronger, fercer, tears out right an' left,
Then all the waters bow themselves an' come,
Suddin, in one gret slope o' shedderin' foam,
Jes' so our Spring gits everythin' in tune
An' gives one leap from Aperl into June:
Then all comes crowdin' in; afore you think,
Young oak-leaves mist the side-hill woods with pink;
The catbird in the laylock-bush is loud:
The orchards turn to heaps o' rosy cloud;
Red-cedars blossom tu, though few folks know it,
An' look all dipt in sunshine like a poet;
The lime-trees pile their solid stacks o' shade
An' drows'ly simmer with the bees' sweet trade;
In ellum-shrouds the flashin' hangbird clings
An' for the summer vy'ge his hammock slings;
All down the loose-walled lanes in archin' bowers
The barb'ry droops its strings o' golden flowers,
Whose shrinkin' hearts the school-gals love to try
With pins,—they'll worry yourn so, boys, bimeby!
But I don't love your cat'logue style,—do you?—
Ez ef to sell off Natur' by vendoo;
One word with blood in 't 's twice ez good ez two:
'nuff sed, June's bridesman, poet o' the year,
Gladness on wings, the bobolink, is here;
Half-hid in tip-top apple-blooms he swings,

Or climbs aginst the breeze with quiverin' wings,
Or, givin' way to 't in a mock despair,
Runs down, a brook o' laughter, thru the air.

I ollus feel the sap start in my veins
In Spring, with curus heats an' prickly pains,
Thet drive me, when I git a chance, to walk
Off by myself to hev a privit talk
With a queer critter thet can't seem to 'gree
Along o' me like most folks,—Mister Me.
Ther' 's times when I'm unsoshle ez a stone,
An' sort o' suffercate to be alone,—
I 'm crowded jes' to think thet folks are nigh,
An' can't bear nothin' closer than the sky;
Now the wind 's full ez shifty in the mind
Ez wut it is ou'-doors, ef I ain't blind,
An' sometimes, in the fairest sou'west weather
My innard vane pints east for weeks together,
My natur' gits all goose-flesh, an' my sins
Come drizzlin' on my conscience sharp ez pins:
Wal, et sech times I jes' slip out o' sight
An' take it out in a fair stan'-up fight
With the one cuss I can't lay on the shelf,
The crook'dest stick in all the heap,—Myself.

'T wuz so las' Sabbath arter meetin'-time:
Findin' my feelin's would n't noways rhyme
With nobody's, but off the hendle flew
An' took things from an east-wind pint o' view,
I started off to lose me in the hills
Where the pines be, up back o' 'Siah's Mills:
Pines, ef you 're blue, are the best friends I know,
They mope an' sigh an' sheer your feelin's so,—
They hesh the ground beneath so, tu, I swan,
You half-forgit you 've gut a body on.
Ther' 's a small school'us' there where four roads meet,
The door-steps hollered out by little feet,
An' side-posts carved with names whose owners grew
To gret men, some on 'em, an' deacons, tu;
't ain't used no longer, coz the town hez gut
A high-school, where they teach the Lord knows wut:
Three-story larnin' 's pop'lar now; I guess
We thriv' ez wal on jes' two stories less,
For it strikes me ther' 's sech a thing ez sinnin'
By overloadin' children's underpinnin':
Wal, here it wuz I larned my A B C,
An' it's a kind o' favorite spot with me.

We 're curus critters: Now ain't jes' the minute
Thet ever fits us easy while we're in it;
Long ez 't wuz futur', 't would be perfect bliss,—
Soon ez it's past, *thet* time's wuth ten o' this;
An' yit there ain't a man thet need be told
Thet Now's the only bird lays eggs o' gold.
A knee-high lad, I used to plot an' plan
An' think 't wuz life's cap-sheaf to be a man;
Now, gittin' gray, there's nothin' I enjoy
Like dreamin' back along into a boy:
So the ole school'us' is a place I choose
Afore all others, ef I want to muse;
I set down where I used to set, an' git
My boyhood back, an' better things with it,—
Faith, Hope, an' sunthin', ef it is n't Cherrity,
It's want o' guile, an' thet 's ez gret a rerrity,—
While Fancy's cushin', free to Prince and Clown,
Makes the hard bench ez soft ez milkweed-down.

Now, 'fore I knowed, thet Sabbath arternoon
When I sot out to tramp myself in tune,
I found me in the school'us' on my seat,
Drummin' the march to No-wheres with my feet.
Thinkin' o' nothin', I've heerd ole folks say
Is a hard kind o' dooty in its way:
It's thinkin' everythin' you ever knew,
Or ever hearn, to make your feelin's blue.
I sot there tryin' thet on for a spell:
I thought o' the Rebellion, then o' Hell,
Which some folks tell ye now is jest a metterfor
(A the'ry, p'raps, it wun't *feel* none the better for);
I thought o' Reconstruction, wut we'd win
Patchin' our patent self-blow-up agin:
I thought ef this 'ere milkin' o' the wits,
So much a month, warn't givin' Natur' fits,—
Ef folks warn't druv, findin' their own milk fail,
To work the cow thet hez an iron tail,
An' ef idees 'thout ripenin' in the pan
Would send up cream to humor ary man:
From this to thet I let my worryin' creep,
Till finally I must ha' fell asleep.

Our lives in sleep are some like streams thet glide
'twixt flesh an' sperrit boundin' on each side,
Where both shores' shadders kind o' mix an' mingle
In sunthin' thet ain't jes' like either single;
An' when you cast off moorin's from To-day,
An' down towards To-morrer drift away,
The imiges thet tengle on the stream
Make a new upside-down'ard world o' dream:
Sometimes they seem like sunrise-streaks an' warnin's
O' wut 'll be in Heaven on Sabbath-mornin's,
An', mixed right in ez ef jest out o' spite,
Sunthin' thet says your supper ain't gone right.
I 'm gret on dreams, an' often when I wake,
I've lived so much it makes my mem'ry ache,
An' can't skurce take a cat-nap in my cheer
'thout hevin' 'em, some good, some bad, all queer.

Now I wuz settin' where I 'd ben, it seemed,
An' ain't sure yit whether I r'ally dreamed,
Nor, ef I did, how long I might ha' slep',
When I hearn some un stompin' up the step,
An' lookin' round, ef two an' two make four,
I see a Pilgrim Father in the door.
He wore a steeple-hat, tall boots, an' spurs
With rowels to 'em big ez ches'nut-burrs,
An' his gret sword behind him sloped away
Long 'z a man's speech thet dunno wut to say.—
"Ef your name 's Biglow, an' your given-name
Hosee," sez he, "it 's arter you I came;
I'm your gret-gran'ther multiplied by three."—
"My *wut?*" sez I.—"Your gret-gret-gret," sez he:
"You would n't ha' never ben here but for me.
Two hundred an' three year ago this May
The ship I come in sailed up Boston Bay;
I'd been a cunnle in our Civil War,—
But wut on airth hev *you* gut up one for?
Coz we du things in England, 't ain't for you
To git a notion you can du 'em tu:
I 'm told you write in public prints: ef true,
It's nateral you should know a thing or two."—
"Thet air 's an argymunt I can't endorse,—
't would prove, coz you wear spurs, you kep' a horse:
For brains," sez I, "wutever you may think,
Ain't boun' to cash the drafs o' pen-an'-ink,—
Though mos' folks write ez ef they hoped jes' quickenin'
The churn would argoo skim-milk into thickenin';
But skim-milk ain't a thing to change its view
O' wut it 's meant for more 'n a smoky flue.
But du pray tell me, 'fore we furder go,
How in all Natur' did you come to know
'bout our affairs," sez I, "in Kingdom-Come?"—
"Wal, I worked round at sperrit-rappin' some,
An' danced the tables till their legs wuz gone,
In hopes o' larnin' wut wuz goin' on,"
Sez he, "but mejums lie so like all-split
Thet I concluded it wuz best to quit.
But, come now, ef you wun't confess to knowin',
You've some conjectures how the thing's a-goin'."—
"Gran'ther," sez I, "a vane warn't never known
Nor asked to hev a jedgment of its own;
An' yit, ef 't ain't gut rusty in the jints,
It's safe to trust its say on certin pints:
It knows the wind's opinions to a T,
An' the wind settles wut the weather'll be."
"I never thought a scion of our stock
Could grow the wood to make a weathercock;
When I wuz younger 'n you, skurce more 'n a shaver,
No airthly wind," sez he, "could make me waver!"
(Ez he said this, he clinched his jaw an' forehead,
Hitchin' his belt to bring his sword-hilt forrard.)—
"Jes so it wuz with me," sez I, "I swow,
When *I* wuz younger 'n wut you see me now,—
Nothin' from Adam's fall to Huldy's bonnet,
Thet I warn't full-cocked with my jedgment on it;
But now I'm gittin' on in life, I find
It 's a sight harder to make up my mind,—
Nor I don't often try tu, when events
Will du it for me free of all expense.
The moral question 's ollus plain enough,—
It 's jes' the human-natur' side thet's tough;
Wut 's best to think may n't puzzle me nor you,—
The pinch comes in decidin' wut to *du;*
Ef you *read* History, all runs smooth ez grease,
Coz there the men ain't nothin' more 'n idees,—
But come to *make* it, ez we must to-day,
Th' idees hev arms an' legs an' stop the way:
It's easy fixin' things in facts an' figgers,—
They can't resist, nor warn't brought up with niggers;
But come to try your the'ry on,—why then
Your facts an' figgers change to ign'ant men
Actin' ez ugly—" —"Smite 'em hip an' thigh!"
Sez gran'ther, "and let every man-child die!
Oh for three weeks o' Crommle an' the Lord!
Up, Isr'el, to your tents an' grind the sword!"—
"Thet kind o' thing worked wal in ole Judee,
But you forgit how long it's ben A.D.;
You think thet 's ellerkence,—I call it shoddy,
A thing," sez I, "wun't cover soul nor body;
I like the plain all-wool o' common-sense,
Thet warms ye now, an' will a twelve-month hence.
You took to follerin' where the Prophets beckoned,
An', fust you knowed on, back come Charles the Second;
Now wut I want 's to hev all *we* gain stick,
An' not to start Millennium too quick;
We hain't to punish only, but to keep,
An' the cure 's gut to go a cent'ry deep."
"Wall, milk-an'-water ain't the best o' glue,"
Sez he, "an' so you'll find afore you're thru;
Ef reshness venters sunthin', shilly-shally
Loses ez often wut 's ten times the vally.
Thet exe of ourn, when Charles's neck gut split,
Opened a gap thet ain't bridged over yit:
Slav'ry 's your Charles, the Lord hez gin the exe"—
"Our Charles," sez I, "hez gut eight million necks.
The hardest question ain't the black man's right,
The trouble is to 'mancipate the white;
One 's chained in body an' can be sot free,
But t' other 's chained in soul to an idee:

It 's a long job, but we shall worry thru it;
Ef bagnets fail, the spellin'-book must du it."
"Hosee," sez he, "I think you 're goin' to fail:
The rettlesnake ain't dangerous in the tail;
This 'ere rebellion 's nothing but the rettle,—
You 'll stomp on thet an' think you've won the bettle;
It's Slavery thet 's the fangs an' thinkin' head,
An' ef you want selvation, cresh it dead,—
An' cresh it suddin, or you 'll larn by waitin'
Thet Chance wun't stop to listen to debatin'!"—
"God's truth!" sez I,—"an' ef *I* held the club,
An' knowed jes' where to strike,—but there 's the rub!"—
"Strike soon," sez he, "or you 'll be deadly ailin',—
Folks thet 's afeared to fail are sure o' failin';
God hates your sneakin' creturs thet believe
He'll settle things they run away an' leave!"
He brought his foot down fercely, ez he spoke,
An' give me sech a startle thet I woke.

1862

INTRODUCTION TO THE BIGLOW PAPERS, SECOND SERIES

◊

WHEN Lowell collected the several *Atlantic Monthly* installments of the Second Series of *The Biglow Papers* for publication as a separate book (1866), he prefixed this essay. It gives an account of the origin of the whole scheme, and a scholarly discussion of the historical backgrounds of American words.

◊

THOUGH prefaces seem of late to have fallen under some reproach, they have at least this advantage, that they set us again on the feet of our personal consciousness and rescue us from the gregarious mock-modesty or cowardice of that *we* which shrills feebly throughout modern literature like the shrieking of mice in the walls of a house that has passed its prime. Having a few words to say to the many friends whom the "Biglow Papers" have won me, I shall accordingly take the freedom of the first person singular of the personal pronoun. Let each of the good-natured unknown who have cheered me by the written communication of their sympathy look upon this Introduction as a private letter to himself.

When, more than twenty years ago, I wrote the first of the series, I had no definite plan and no intention of ever writing another. Thinking the Mexican war, as I think it still, a national crime committed in behoof of Slavery, our common sin, and wishing to put the feeling of those who thought as I did in a way that would tell, I imagined to myself such an upcountry man as I had often seen at antislavery gatherings, capable of district-school English, but always instinctively falling back into the natural stronghold of his homely dialect when heated to the point of self-forgetfulness. When I began to carry out my conception and to write in my assumed character, I found myself in a strait between two perils. On the one hand, I was in danger of being carried beyond the limit of my own opinions, or at least of that temper with which every man should speak his mind in print, and on the other I feared the risk of seeming to vulgarize a deep and sacred conviction. I needed on occasion to rise above the level of mere *patois,* and for this purpose conceived the Rev. Mr. Wilbur, who should express the more cautious element of the New England character and its pedantry, as Mr. Biglow should serve for its homely common-sense vivified and heated by conscience. The parson was to be the complement rather than the antithesis of his parishioner, and I felt or fancied a certain humorous element in the real identity of the two under a seeming incongruity. Mr. Wilbur's fondness for scraps of Latin, though drawn from the life, I adopted deliberately to heighten the contrast. Finding soon after that I needed some one as a mouthpiece of the mere drollery, for I conceive that true humor is never divorced from moral conviction, I invented Mr. Sawin for the clown of my little puppet-show. I meant to embody in him that half-conscious *un*morality which I had noticed as the recoil in gross natures from a puritanism that still strove to keep in its creed the intense savor which had long gone out of its faith and life. In the three I thought I should find room enough to express, as it was my plan to do, the popular feeling and opinion of the time. For the names of two of my characters, since I have received some remonstrances from very worthy persons who happen to bear them, I would say that they were purely fortuitous, probably mere unconscious memories of signboards or directories. Mr. Sawin's sprang from the accident of a rhyme at the end of his first epistle, and I purposely christened him by the impossible surname of Birdofredum not more to stigmatize him as the incarnation of "Manifest Destiny," in other words, of national recklessness as to right and wrong, than to avoid the chance of wounding any private sensitiveness.

The success of my experiment soon began not only to astonish me, but to make me feel the responsibility of knowing that I held in my hand a weapon instead of the mere fencing-stick I had supposed. Very far from being a popular author under my own name, so far, indeed, as to be almost unread, I found the verses of my pseudonym copied everywhere; I saw them pinned up in workshops; I heard them quoted and their authorship debated; I once even, when rumor had at length caught up my name in one of its eddies, had the satisfaction of overhearing it demonstrated, in the pauses of a concert, that *I* was utterly incompetent to have written anything of the kind. I had read too much not to know the utter worthlessness of contemporary reputation, especially as regards satire, but I knew also that by giving a certain amount of influence it also had its worth, if that influence were used on the right side. I had learned, too, that the first requisite of good writing is to have an earnest and definite purpose, whether aesthetic or moral, and that even good writing, to please long, must have more than an average amount either of imagination or common-sense. The first of these falls to the lot of scarcely one in several generations; the last is within the reach of many in every one that passes; and of this an author may fairly hope to become in part the mouthpiece. If I put on the cap and bells and made myself one of the court-fools of King Demos, it was less to make his majesty laugh than to win a passage to his royal ears for certain serious things which I had deeply at heart. I say this because there is no imputation that could be more galling to any man's self-respect than that of being a mere jester. I endeavored, by generalizing my satire, to give it what value I could beyond the passing moment and the immediate application. How far I have succeeded I cannot tell, but I have had better luck than I ever looked for in seeing my verses survive to pass beyond their nonage.

In choosing the Yankee dialect, I did not act without forethought. It had long seemed to me that the great vice of American writing and speaking was a studied want of simplicity, that we were in danger of coming to look on our mother-tongue as a dead language, to be sought in the grammar and dictionary rather than in the heart, and that our only chance of escape was by seeking it at its living sources among those who were, as Scottowe says of Major-General Gibbons, "divinely illiterate." President Lincoln, the only really great public man whom these latter days have seen, was great also in this, that he was master—witness his speech at Gettysburg—of a truly masculine English, classic because it was of no special period, and level at once to the highest and lowest of his countrymen. I learn from the highest authority that his favorite reading was in Shakespeare and Milton, to which, of course, the Bible should be added. But whoever should read the debates in Congress might fancy himself present at a meeting of the city council of some city of Southern Gaul in the decline of the Empire, where barbarians with a Latin varnish emulated each other in being more than Ciceronian. Whether it be want of culture, for the highest outcome of that is simplicity, or for whatever reason, it is certain that very few American writers or speakers wield their native language with the directness, precision, and force that are common as the day in the mother country. We use it like Scotsmen, not as if it belonged to us, but as if we wished to prove that we belonged to it, by showing our intimacy with its written rather than with its spoken dialect. And yet all the while our popular idiom is racy with life and vigor and originality, bucksome (as Milton used the word) to our new occasions, and proves itself no mere graft by sending up new suckers from the old root in spite of us. It is only from its roots in the living generations of men that a language can be reinforced with fresh vigor for its needs; what may be called a literate dialect grows ever more and more pedantic and foreign, till it becomes at last as unfitting a vehicle for living thought as monkish Latin. That we should all be made to talk like books is the danger with which we are threatened by the Universal Schoolmaster, who does his best to enslave the minds and memories of his victims to what he esteems the best models of English composition, that is to say, to the writers whose style is faultily correct and has no blood-warmth in it. No language after it has faded into *diction,* none that cannot suck up the feeding juices secreted for it in the rich mother-earth of common folk, can bring forth a sound and lusty book. True vigor and heartiness of phrase do not pass from page to page, but from man to man, where the brain is kindled and the lips suppled by downright living interests and by passion in its very throe. Language is the soil of thought, and our own especially is a rich leaf-mould, the slow deposit of ages, the shed foliage of feeling, fancy, and imagination, which has suffered an earth-change, that the vocal forest, as Howell called it, may clothe itself anew with living green. There is death in the dictionary; and, where language is too strictly limited by convention, the ground for expression to grow in is limited also; and we get a *potted* literature, Chinese dwarfs instead of healthy trees.

But while the schoolmaster has been busy starching our language and smoothing it flat with the mangle of a supposed classical authority, the newspaper reporter has been doing even more harm by stretching and swelling it to suit his occasions. A dozen years ago I began a list, which I have added to from time to time, of some of the changes which may be fairly laid at his door. I give a few of them as showing their tendency, all the more dangerous that their effect, like that of some poisons, is insensibly cumulative, and that they are sure at last of effect among a people whose chief reading is the daily paper. I give in two columns the old style and its modern equivalent.

OLD STYLE.	NEW STYLE.
Was hanged.	Was launched into eternity.
When the halter was put around his neck.	When the fatal noose was adjusted about the neck of the unfortunate victim of his own unbridled passions.
A great crowd came to see.	A vast concourse was assembled to witness.
Great fire.	Disastrous conflagration.
The fire spread.	The conflagration extended its devastating career.
House burned.	Edifice consumed.
The fire was got under.	The progress of the devouring element was arrested.
Man fell.	Individual was precipitated.
A horse and wagon ran against.	A valuable horse attached to a vehicle driven by J. S., in the employment of J. B., collided with.
The frightened horse.	The infuriated animal.
Sent for the doctor.	Called into requisition the services of the family physician.
The mayor of the city in a short speech welcomed.	The chief magistrate of the metropolis, in well-chosen and eloquent language, frequently interrupted by the plaudits of the surging multitude, officially tendered the hospitalities.
I shall say a few words.	I shall, with your permission, beg leave to offer some brief observations.
Began his answer.	Commenced his rejoinder.
Asked him to dine.	Tendered him a banquet.
A bystander advised.	One of those omnipresent characters who, as if in pursuance of some previous arrangement, are certain to be encountered in the vicinity when an accident occurs, ventured the suggestion.
He died.	He deceased, he passed out of existence, his spirit quitted its earthly habitation, winged its way to eternity, shook off its burden, etc.

In one sense this is nothing new. The school of Pope in verse ended by wire-drawing its phrase to such thinness that it could bear no weight of meaning whatever. Nor is fine writing by any means confined to America. All writers without imagination fall into it of necessity whenever they attempt the figurative. I take two examples from Mr. Merivale's "History of the Romans under the Empire," which, indeed, is full of such. "The last years of the age familiarly styled the Augustan were singularly barren of the literary glories from which its celebrity was chiefly derived. One by one the stars in its firmament had been lost to the world; Virgil and Horace, etc., had long since died; the charm which the imagination of Livy had thrown over the earlier annals of Rome had ceased to shine on the details of almost contemporary history; and if the flood of his eloquence still continued flowing, we can hardly suppose that the stream was as rapid, as fresh, and as clear as ever." I will not waste time in criticising the bad English or the mixture of metaphor in these sentences, but will simply cite another from the same author which is even worse. "The shadowy phantom of the Republic continued to flit before the eyes of the Cæsar. There was still, he apprehended, a germ of sentiment existing, on which a scion of his own house, or even a stranger, might boldly throw himself and raise the standard of patrician independence." Now a ghost may haunt a murderer, but hardly, I should think, to scare him with the threat of taking a new lease of its old tenement. And fancy the *scion* of a *house* in the act of *throwing itself* upon a *germ of sentiment* to *raise a standard!* I am glad, since we have so much in the same kind to answer for, that this bit of horticultural rhetoric is from beyond sea. I would not be supposed to condemn truly imaginative prose. There is a simplicity of splendor, no less than of plainness, and prose would be poor indeed if it could not find a tongue for that meaning of the mind which is behind the meaning of the words. It has sometimes seemed to me that in England there was a growing tendency to curtail language into a mere convenience, and to defecate it of all emotion as thoroughly as algebraic signs. This has arisen, no doubt, in part from that healthy national contempt of humbug which is characteristic of Englishmen, in part from that sensitiveness to the ludicrous which makes them so shy of expressing feeling, but in part also, it is to be feared, from a growing distrust, one might almost say hatred, of whatever is super-material. There is something sad in the scorn with which their journalists treat the notion of there being such a thing as a national ideal, seeming utterly to have forgotten that even in the affairs of this world the imagination is as much matter-of-fact as the understanding. If we were to trust the impression made on us by some of the cleverest and most characteristic of their periodical literature, we should think England hopelessly stranded on the good-humored cynicism of well-to-do middle-age, and should fancy it an enchanted nation, doomed to sit forever with its feet under the mahogany in that after-dinner mood which follows conscientious repletion, and which it is ill-manners to disturb with any topics more exciting than the quality of the wines. But there are already symptoms that a large class of Englishmen are getting weary of the dominion of consols and divine common-sense, and to believe that eternal three *per cent* is not the chief end of man, nor the highest and only kind of interest to which the powers and opportunities of England are entitled.

The quality of exaggeration has often been remarked on as typical of American character, and especially of American humor. In Dr. Petri's *Gedrängtes Handbuch der Fremdwörter,* we are told that the word *humbug* is commonly used for the exaggerations of the North-Americans. To be sure, one would be tempted to think the dream of Columbus half fulfilled, and that Europe had found in the West a nearer way to Orientalism, at least in diction. But it seems to me that a great deal of what is set down as mere extravagance is more fitly to be called intensity and picturesqueness, symptoms of the imaginative faculty in full health and strength, though producing, as yet, only the raw and formless material in which poetry is to work. By and by, perhaps, the world will see it fashioned into poem and picture, and Europe, which will be hard pushed for originality erelong, may have to thank us for a new sensation. The French continue to find Shakespeare exaggerated because he treated English just as our country-folk do when they speak of a "steep price," or say that they "freeze to" a thing. The first postulate of an original literature is that a people should use their language instinctively and unconsciously, as if it were a lively part of their growth and personality, not as the mere torpid boon of education or inheritance. Even Burns contrived to write very poor verse and prose in English. Vulgarisms are often only poetry in the egg. The late Mr. Horace Mann, in one of his public addresses, commented at some length on the beauty and moral significance of the French phrase *s'orienter,* and called on his young friends to practise upon it in life. There was not a Yankee in his audience whose problem had not always been to find out what was *about east,* and to shape his course accordingly. This charm which a familiar expression gains by being commented, as it were, and set in a new light by a foreign language, is curious and instructive. I cannot help thinking that Mr. Matthew Arnold forgets this a little too much sometimes when he writes of the beauties of French style. It would not be hard to find in the works of French Academicians phrases as coarse as those he cites from Burke, only they are veiled by the unfamiliarity of the language. But, however this may be, it is certain that poets and peasants please us in the same way by translating works back again to their primal freshness, and infusing them with a delightful strangeness which is anything but alienation. What, for example, is Milton's "*edge* of battle" but a doing into English of the Latin *acies? Was die Gans gedacht das der Schwan vollbracht,* what the goose but thought, that the swan full brought (or, to de-Saxonize it a little, what the goose conceived, that the swan achieved), and it may well be that the life, invention, and vigor shown by our popular speech, and the freedom with which it is shaped to the instant want of those who use it, are of the best omen for our having a swan at last. The part I have taken on myself is that of the humbler bird.

But it is affirmed that there is something innately vulgar in the Yankee dialect. M. Sainte-Beuve says, with his usual neatness: "*Je définis un patois une ancienne langue qui a eu des malheurs, ou encore une langue toute jeune et qui n'a pas fait fortune.*" [1] The first part of his definition applies to a dialect like the Provençal, the last to the Tuscan before Dante had lifted it into a classic, and neither, it seems to me, will quite fit a *patois,* which is not properly a dialect, but rather certain archaisms, proverbial phrases, and modes of pronunciation, which maintain themselves among the uneducated side by side with the finished and universally accepted language. Norman French, for example, or Scotch down to the time of James VI., could hardly be called *patois,* while I should be half inclined to name the Yankee a *lingo* rather than a dialect. It has retained a few words now fallen into disuse in the mother country, like *to tarry, to progress, fleshy, fall,* and some others; it has changed the meaning of some, as in *freshet;* and it has clung to what I suspect to have been the broad Norman pronunciation of *e* (which Molière puts into the mouth of his rustics) in such words as *sarvant, parfect, vartoo,* and the like. It maintains something of the French sound of *a* also in words like *chămber, dănger* (though the latter had certainly begun to take its present sound so early as 1636, when I find it sometimes spelt *dainger*). But in general it may be said that nothing can be found in it which does not still survive in some one or other of the English provincial dialects. There is, perhaps, a single exception in the verb to *sleeve.* To *sleeve* silk means to divide or ravel out a thread of silk with the point of a needle till it becomes *floss.* (A.-S. *sléfan,* to *cleave* = divide.) This, I think, explains the "*sleeveless* errand" in "Troilus and Cressida" so inadequately, sometimes so ludicrously darkened by the commentators. Is not a "sleeveless errand" one that cannot be unravelled, incomprehensible, and therefore bootless?

I am not speaking now of Americanisms properly so called, that is, of words or phrases which have grown into use here either through necessity, invention, or accident, such as a *carry,* a *one-horse affair,* a *prairie,* to *vamose.* Even these are fewer than is sometimes taken for granted. But I think some fair defence may be made against the charge of vulgarity. Properly speaking, vulgarity is in the thought, and not in the word or the way of pronouncing it. Modern French, the most polite of languages, is barbarously vulgar if compared with the Latin out of which it has been corrupted, or even with Italian. There is a wider gap, and one implying greater boorishness, between *ministerium* and *métier,* or *sapiens* and *sachant,* than between *druv* and *drove* or *agin* and *against,* which last is plainly an arrant superlative. Our rustic *coverlid* is nearer its French original than the diminutive cover*let,* into whith it has been ignorantly corrupted in politer speech. I obtained from three cultivated Englishmen at different times three diverse pronunciations of a single word,—*cowcumber, coocumber,* and *cucŭmber.* Of these the first, which is Yankee also, comes nearest to the nasality of *concombre.* Lord Ossory assures us that Voltaire saw the best society in England, and Voltaire tells his countrymen that *handkerchief* was pronounced *hankercher.* I find it so spelt in Hakluyt and elsewhere. This enormity the Yankee still persists in, and as there is always a reason for such deviations from the sound as represented by the spelling, may we not suspect two sources of derivation, and find an ancestor for *kercher* in *couverture* rather than in *couvrechef?* And what greater phonetic vagary (which Dryden, by the way, called *fegary*) in our *lingua rustica* than this *ker* for *couvre?* I copy from the fly-leaves of my books, where I have noted them from time to time, a few examples of pronunciation and phrase which will show that the Yankee often has antiquity and very respectable literary authority on his side. My list might be largely increased by referring to glossaries, but to them every one can go for himself, and I have gathered enough for my purpose.

I will take first those cases in which something like the French sound has been preserved in certain single letters and diphthongs. And this opens a curious question as to how long this Gallicism maintained itself in England. Sometimes a divergence in pronunciation has given us two words with different meanings, as in *genteel* and *jaunty,* which I find coming in toward the close of the seventeenth century, and wavering between *genteel* and *jantee.* It is usual in America to drop the *u* in words ending in *our,*—a very proper change recommended by Howell two centuries ago, and carried out by him so far as his printers would allow. This and the corresponding changes in *musique, musick,* and the like, which he also advocated, show that in his time the French accent indicated by the superfluous letters (for French had once nearly as strong an accent as Italian) had gone out of use. There is plenty of French accent down to the end of Elizabeth's reign. In Daniel we have *riches′* and *counsel′,* in Bishop Hall *comet′, chapëlain,* in Donne *pictures′, virtue′, presence′, mortal′, merit′, hainous′, giant′,* with many more, and Marston's satires are full of them. The two latter, however, are not to be relied on, as they may be suspected of Chaucerizing. Herrick writes *baptime.* The tendency to throw the accent back-

INTRODUCTION TO THE BIGLOW PAPERS. 1. *"Je . . . fortune":* "I define a *patois* as an old language that has had bad luck, or as a young language that has not made its fortune" [L].

ward began early. But the incongruities are perplexing, and perhaps mark the period of transition. In Warner's "Albion's England" we have *creator′* and *crëature′* side by side with the modern *creator* and *creature. E′nvy* and *e′nvying* occur in Campion (1602), and yet *envy′* survived Milton. In some cases we have gone back again nearer to the French, as in *rev′enue* for *reven′ue*. I had been so used to hearing *imbecile* pronounced with the accent on the first syllable, which is in accordance with the general tendency in such matters, that I was surprised to find *imbec′ile* in a verse of Wordsworth. The dictionaries all give it so. I asked a highly cultivated Englishman, and he declared for *imbeceel′*. In general it may be assumed that accent will finally settle on the syllable dictated by greater ease and therefore quickness of utterance. *Blas′phemous*, for example, is more rapidly pronounced than *blasphem′ous*, to which our Yankee clings, following in this the usage of many of the older poets. *Amer′ican* is easier than *Ameri′can*, and therefore the false quantity has carried the day, though the true one may be found in George Herbert, and even so late as Cowley.

To come back to the matter in hand. Our "uplandish man" retains the soft or thin sound of the *u* in some words, such as *rule, truth* (sometimes also pronounced *trŭth,* not *trooth*), while he says *noo* for *new,* and gives to *view* and *few* so indescribable a mixture of the two sounds with a slight nasal tincture that it may be called the Yankee shibboleth. Voltaire says that the English pronounce *true* as if it rhymed with *view,* and this is the sound our rustics give to it. Spenser writes *deow* (*dew*) which can only be pronounced with the Yankee nasality. In *rule* the least sound of *a* precedes the *u*. I find *reule* in Pecock's "Repressor." He probably pronounced it *rayoolë,* as the old French word from which it is derived was very likely to be sounded at first, with a reminiscence of its original *regula*. Tindal has *rueler,* and the Coventry Plays have *preudent*. In the "Parlyament of Byrdes" I find *reule*. As for *noo,* may it not claim some sanction in its derivation, whether from *nouveau* or *neuf,* the ancient sound of which may very well have been *noof,* as nearer *novus? Beef* would seem more like to have come from *buffe* than from *bœuf,* unless the two were mere varieties of spelling. The Saxon *few* may have caught enough from its French cousin *peu* to claim the benefit of the same doubt as to sound; and our slang phrase *a few* (as "I licked him a few") may well appeal to *un peu* for sense and authority. Nay, might not *lick* itself turn out to be the good old word *lam* in an English disguise, if the latter should claim descent as, perhaps, he fairly might, from the Latin *lambere?* The New England *ferce* for *fierce,* and *perce* for *pierce* (sometimes heard as *fairce* and *pairce*), are also Norman. For its antiquity I cite the rhyme of *verse* and *pierce* in Chapman and Donne, and in some commendatory verses by a Mr. Berkenhead before the poems of Francis Beaumont. Our *pairlous* for *perilous* is of the same kind, and is nearer Shakespeare's *parlous* than the modern pronunciation. One other Gallicism survives in our pronunciation. Perhaps I should rather call it a semi-Gallicism, for it is the result of a futile effort to reproduce a French sound with English lips. Thus for *joint, employ, royal,* we have *jynt, emply, rȳle,* the last differing only from *rile* (*roil*) in a prolongation of the *y* sound. I find *royal* so pronounced in the "Mirror for Magistrates." In Walter de Biblesworth I find *solives* Englished by *gistes*. This, it is true, may have been pronounced *jeests,* but the pronunciation *jystes* must have preceded the present spelling, which was no doubt adopted after the radical meaning was forgotten, as analogical with other words in *oi*. In the same way after Norman-French influence had softened the *l* out of *would* (we already find *woud* for *veut* in N. F. poems), *should* followed the example, and then an *l* was foisted into *could,* where it does not belong, to satisfy the logic of the eye, which has affected the pronunciation and even the spelling of English more than is commonly supposed. I meet with *eyster* for *oyster* as early as the fourteenth century. I find *viage* in Bishop Hall and Middleton the dramatist, *bile* for *boil* in Donne and Chrononhotonthologos, *line* for *loin* in Hall, *ryall* and *chyse* (for *choice*), *dystrye* for *destroy,* in the Coventry Plays. In Chapman's "All Fools" is the misprint of *employ* for *imply,* fairly inferring an identity of sound in the last syllable. Indeed, this pronunciation was habitual till after Pope, and Rogers tells us that the elegant Gray said *naise* for *noise* just as our rustics still do. Our *cornish* (which I find also in Herrick) remembers the French better than *cornice* does. While, clinging more closely to the Anglo-Saxon in dropping the *g* from the end of the present participle, the Yankee now and then pleases himself with an experiment in French nasality in words ending in *n*. It is not, so far as my experience goes, very common, though it may formerly have been more so. *Capting,* for instance, I never heard save in jest, the habitual form being *kepp'n*. But at any rate it is no invention of ours. In that delightful old volume, "Ane Compendious Buke of Godly and Spirituall Songs," in which I know not whether the piety itself or the simplicity of its expression be more charming, I find *burding, garding,* and *cousing,* and in the State Trials *un-*

certing used by a gentleman. I confess that I like the *n* better than the *ng*.

Of Yankee preterites I find *risse* and *rize* for *rose* in Beaumont and Fletcher, Middleton and Dryden, *clim* in Spenser, *chees* (*chose*) in Sir John Mandevil, *give* (*gave*) in the Coventry Plays, *shet* (*shut*) in Golding's Ovid, *het* in Chapman and in Weever's Epitaphs, *thriv* and *smit* in Drayton, *quit* in Ben Jonson and Henry More, and *pled* in the Paston Letters, nay, even in the fastidious Landor. *Rid* for *rode* was anciently common. So likewise was *see* for *saw,* but I find it in no writer of authority (except Golding), unless Chaucer's *seie* and Gower's *sigh* were, as I am inclined to think, so sounded. *Shew* is used by Hector Boece, Giles Fletcher, Drummond of Hawthornden, and in the Paston Letters. Similar strong preterites, like *snew, thew,* and even *mew,* are not without example. I find *sew* for *sewed* in "Piers Ploughman." Indeed, the anomalies in English preterites are perplexing. We have probably transferred *flew* from *flow* (as the preterite of which I have heard it) to *fly,* because we had another preterite in *fled.* Of weak preterites the Yankee retains *growed, blowed,* for which he has good authority, and less often *knowed.* His *sot* is merely a broad sounding of *sat,* no more inelegant than the common *got* for *gat,* which he further degrades into *gut.* When he says *darst,* he uses a form as old as Chaucer.

The Yankee has retained something of the long sound of the *a* in such words as *axe, wax,* pronouncing them *exe, wex* (shortened from *aix, waix*). He also says *hev* and *hed* (*hāve, hād*) for *have* and *had.* In most cases he follows an Anglo-Saxon usage. In *aix* for *axle* he certainly does. I find *wex* and *aisches* (*ashes*) in Pecock, and *exe* in the Paston Letters. Golding rhymes *wax* with *wexe* and spells *challenge chelenge.* Chaucer wrote *hendy.* Dryden rhymes *can* with *men,* as Mr. Biglow would. Alexander Gill, Milton's teacher, in his "Logonomia" cites *hez* for *hath* as peculiar to Lincolnshire. I find *hayth* in Collier's "Bibliographical Account of Early English Literature" under the date 1584, and Lord Cromwell so wrote it. Sir Christopher Wren wrote *belcony.* Our *fect* is only the O. F. *faict. Thaim* for *them* was common in the sixteenth century. We have an example of the same thing in the double form of the verb *thrash, thresh.* While the New-Englander cannot be brought to say *instead* for *instid* (commonly *'stid* where not the last word in a sentence), he changes the *i* into *e* in *red* for *rid, tell* for *till, hender* for *hinder, rense* for *rinse.* I find *red* in the old interlude of "Thersytes," *tell* in a letter of Daborne to Henslowe, and also, I shudder to mention it, in a letter of the great Duchess of Marlborough, Atossa herself! It occurs twice in a single verse of the Chester Plays,

> "*Tell* the day of dome, *tell* the beames blow."

From the word *blow* (in another sense) is formed *blowth,* which I heard again this summer after a long interval. Mr. Wright [2] explains it as meaning "a blossom." With us a single blossom is a *blow,* while *blowth* means the blossoming in general. A farmer would say that there was a good blowth on his fruit-trees. The word retreats farther inland and away from the railways, year by year. Wither rhymes *hinder* with *slender,* and Shakespeare and Lovelace have *renched* for *rinsed.* In "Gammer Gurton" and "Mirror for Magistrates" is *sence* for *since;* Marlborough's Duchess so writes it, and Donne rhymes *since* with *Amiens* and *patïence,* Bishop Hall and Otway with *pretence,* Chapman with *citizens,* Dryden with *providence.* Indeed, why should not *sithence* take that form? Dryden's wife (an earl's daughter) has *tell* for *till,* Margaret, mother of Henry VII., writes *seche* for *such,* and our *ef* finds authority in the old form *yeffe.*

E sometimes takes the place of *u,* as *jedge, tredge, bresh.* I find *tredge* in the interlude of "Jack Jugler," *bresh* in a citation by Collier from "London Cries" of the middle of the seventeenth century, and *resche* for *rush* (fifteenth century) in the very valuable "Volume of Vocabularies" edited by Mr. Wright. *Resce* is one of the Anglo-Saxon forms of the word in Bosworth's A.-S. Dictionary. Golding has *shet.* The Yankee always shortens the *u* in the ending *ture,* making *ventur, natur, pictur,* and so on. This was common, also, among the educated of the last generation. I am inclined to think it may have been once universal, and I certainly think it more elegant than the vile *vencher, naycher, pickcher,* that have taken its place, sounding like the invention of a lexicographer to mitigate a sneeze. Nash in his "Pierce Penniless" has *ventur,* and so spells it, and I meet it also in Spenser, Drayton, Ben Jonson, Herrick, and Prior. Spenser has *tort'rest,* which can be contracted only from *tortur* and not from *torcher.* Quarles rhymes *nature* with *creator,* and Dryden with *satire,* which he doubtless pronounced according to its older form of *satyr.* Quarles has also *torture* and *mortar.* Mary Boleyn writes *kreatur.* I find *pikter* in Izaak Walton's autograph will.

I shall now give some examples which cannot so easily be ranked under any special head. Gill charges the Eastern counties with *kiver* for *cover,* and *ta* for *to.* The Yankee pronounces both *too*

2. Mr. Wright: *Dictionary of Obsolete and Provincial English* [L].

and *to* like *ta* (like the *tou* in *touch*) where they are not emphatic. When they are, both become *tu.* In old spelling, *to* is the common (and indeed correct) form of *too,* which is only *to* with the sense of *in addition.* I suspect that the sound of our *too* has caught something from the French *tout,* and it is possible that the old *too too* is not a reduplication, but a reminiscence of the feminine form of the same word (*toute*) as anciently pronounced, with the *e* not yet silenced. Gill gives a Northern origin to *geaun* for *gown* and *waund* for *wound* (*vulnus*). Lovelace has *waund,* but there is something too dreadful in suspecting Spenser (who *borealized* in his pastorals) of having ever been guilty of *geaun!* And yet some delicate mouths even now are careful to observe the Hibernicism of *ge-ard* for *guard,* and *ge-url* for *girl.* Sir Philip Sidney (*credite posteri!*) wrote *furr* for *far.* I would hardly have believed it had I not seen it in *fac-simile.* As some consolation, I find *furder* in Lord Bacon and Donne, and Wither rhymes *far* with *cur.* The Yankee, who omits the final *d* in many words, as do the Scotch, makes up for it by adding one in *geound.* The purist does not feel the loss of the *d* sensibly in *lawn* and *yon,* from the former of which it has dropped again after a wrongful adoption (retained in *laundry*), while it properly belongs to the latter. But what shall we make of *git, yit,* and *yis?* I find *yis* and *git* in Warner's "Albion's England," *yet* rhyming with *wit, admit,* and *fit* in Donne, with *wit* in the "Revenger's Tragedy," Beaumont, and Suckling, with *writ* in Dryden, and latest of all with *wit* in Sir Hanbury Williams. Prior rhymes *fitting* and *begetting.* Worse is to come. Among others, Donne rhymes *again* with *sin,* and Quarles repeatedly with *in. Ben* for *been,* of which our dear Whittier is so fond, has the authority of Sackville, "Gammer Gurton" (the work of a bishop), Chapman, Dryden, and many more, though *bin* seems to have been the common form. Whittier's accenting the first syllable of *rom'ance* finds an accomplice in Drayton among others, and though manifestly wrong, is analogous with *Rom'ans.* Of other Yankeeisms, whether of form or pronunciation, which I have met with I add a few at random. Pecock writes *sowdiers* (*sogers, soudoyers*), and Chapman and Gill *sodder.* This absorption of the *l* is common in various dialects, especially in the Scottish. Pecock writes also *biyende,* and the authors of "Jack Jugler" and "Gammer Gurton" *yender.* The Yankee includes *"yon"* in the same category, and says "hither an' yen," for "to and fro." (Cf. German *jenseits.*) Pecock and plenty more have *wrastle.* Tindal has *agynste, gretter, shett, ondone, debytë* and *scace.* "Jack Jugler" has *scacely* (which I have often heard, though *skurce* is the common form), and Donne and Dryden make *great* rhyme with *set.* In the inscription on Caxton's tomb I find *ynd* for *end,* which the Yankee more often makes *eend,* still using familiarly the old phrase "right anend" for "continuously." His "stret (straight) along" in the same sense, which I thought peculiar to him, I find in Pecock. Tindal's *debytë* for *deputy* is so perfectly Yankee that I could almost fancy the brave martyr to have been deacon of the First Parish at Jaalam Centre. "Jack Jugler" further gives us *playsent* and *sartayne.* Dryden rhymes *certain* with *parting,* and Chapman and Ben Jonson use *certain,* as the Yankee always does, for *certainly.* The "Coventry Mysteries" have *occapied, massage, nateralle, materal* (*material*), and *meracles,*—all excellent Yankeeisms. In the "Quatre fils, Aymon" (1504),[3] is *vertus* for *virtuous.* Thomas Fuller called *volume vollum,* I suspect, for he spells it *volumne.* However, *per contra,* Yankees habitually say *colume* for *column.* Indeed, to prove that our ancestors brought their pronunciation with them from the Old Country, and have not wantonly debased their mother tongue, I need only to cite the words *scriptur, Israll, athists,* and *cherfulness* from Governor Bradford's "History." So the good man wrote them, and so the good descendants of his fellow-exiles still pronounce them. Brampton Gurdon writes *shet* in a letter to Winthrop. *Purtend* (*pretend*) has crept like a serpent into the "Paradise of Dainty Devices"; *purvide,* which is not so bad, is in Chaucer. These, of course, are universal vulgarisms, and not peculiar to the Yankee. Butler has a Yankee phrase, and pronunciation too, in "To which these *carr'ings-on* did tend." Langham or Laneham, who wrote an account of the festivities at Kenilworth in honor of Queen Bess, and who evidently tried to spell phonetically, makes *sorrows* into *sororz.* Herrick writes *hollow* for *halloo,* and perhaps pronounced it (*horresco suggerens!*) *holló,* as Yankees do. Why not, when it comes from *holà?* I find *ffelaschyppe* (*fellowship*) in the Coventry Plays. Spenser and his queen neither of them scrupled to write *afore,* and the former feels no inelegance even in *chaw* and *idee. 'Fore* was common till after Herrick. Dryden has *do's* for *does,* and his wife spells *worse wosce. Afeared* was once universal. Warner has *ery* for *ever a;* nay, he also has *illy,* with which we were once ignorantly reproached by persons more familiar with Murray's Grammar than with English

3. **"Quatre fils, Aymon" (1504):** "Cited in Collier. (I give my authority where I do not quote from the original book)" [L].

literature. And why not *illy?* Mr. Bartlett says it is "a word used by writers of an inferior class, who do not seem to perceive that *ill* is itself an adverb, without the termination *ly,*" and quotes Dr. Messer, President of Brown University, as asking triumphantly, "Why don't you say *welly?*" I should like to have had Dr. Messer answer his own question. It would be truer to say that it was used by people who still remembered that *ill* was an adjective, the shortened form of *evil,* out of which Shakespeare and the translators of the Bible ventured to make *evilly.* This slurred *evil* is "the dram of *eale*" in "Hamlet." I find *illy* in Warner. The objection to *illy* is not an etymological one, but simply that it is contrary to good usage,—a very sufficient reason. *Ill* as an adverb was at first a vulgarism, precisely like the rustic's when he says, "I was treated *bad.*" May not the reason of this exceptional form be looked for in that tendency to dodge what is hard to pronounce, to which I have already alluded? If the letters were distinctly uttered, as they should be, it would take too much time to say *ill-ly, well-ly,* and it is to be observed that we have avoided *smally* [4] and *tally* in the same way, though we add *ish* to them without hesitation in *smallish* and *tallish.* We have, to be sure, *dully* and *fully,* but for the one we prefer *stupidly,* and the other (though this may have come from eliding the *y* before *as*) is giving way to *full.* The uneducated, whose utterance is slower, still make adverbs when they will by adding *like* to all manner of adjectives. We have had *big* charged upon us, because we use it where an Englishman would now use *great.* I fully admit that it were better to distinguish between them, allowing to *big* a certain contemptuous quality; but as for authority, I want none better than that of Jeremy Taylor, who, in his noble sermon "On the Return of Prayer," speaks of "Jesus, whose spirit was meek and gentle up to the greatness of the *biggest* example." As for our double negative, I shall waste no time in quoting instances of it, because it was once as universal in English as it still is in the neo-Latin languages, where it does not strike us as vulgar. I am not sure that the loss of it is not to be regretted. But surely I shall admit the vulgarity of slurring or altogether eliding certain terminal consonants? I admit that a clear and sharp-cut enunciation is one of the crowning charms and elegancies of speech. Words so uttered are like coins fresh from the mint, compared with the worn and dingy drudges of long service,—I do not mean American coins, for those look less badly the more they lose of their original ugliness. No one is more painfully conscious than I of the contrast between the rifle-crack of an Englishman's *yes* and *no,* and the wet-fuse drawl of the same monosyllables in the mouths of my countrymen. But I do not find the dropping of final consonants disagreeable in Allan Ramsay or Burns, nor do I believe that our literary ancestors were sensible of that inelegance in the fusing them together of which we are conscious. How many educated men pronounce the *t* in *chestnut?* how many say *pentise* for *penthouse,* as they should. When a Yankee skipper says that he is "boun' for Gloster" (not Gloucëster, with the leave of the Universal Schoolmaster),[5] he but speaks like Chaucer or an old ballad-singer, though they would have pronounced it *boon.* This is one of the cases where the *d* is surreptitious, and has been added in compliment to the verb *bind,* with which it has nothing to do. If we consider the root of the word (though of course I grant that every race has a right to do what it will with what is so peculiarly its own as its speech), the *d* has no more right there than at the end of *gone,* where it is often put by children, who are our best guides to the sources of linguistic corruption, and the best teachers of its processes. Cromwell, minister of Henry VIII., writes *worle* for *world.* Chapman has *wan* for *wand,* and *lawn* has rightfully displaced *laund,* though with no thought, I suspect, of etymology. Rogers tells us that Lady Bathurst sent him some letters written to William III. by Queen Mary, in which she addresses him as "*Dear Husban.*" The old form *expoun',* which our farmers use, is more correct than the form with a barbarous *d* tacked on which has taken its place. Of the kind opposite to this, like our *gownd* for *gown,* and the London cockney's *wind* for *wine,* I find *drownd* for *drown* in the "Misfortunes of Arthur" (1584), and in Swift. And, by the way, whence came the long sound of *wind* which our poets still retain, and which survives in "winding" a horn, a totally different word from "winding" a kite-string? We say *behīnd* and *hīnder* (comparative) and yet *to hĭnder.* Shakespeare pronounced *kind kĭnd,* or what becomes of his play on that word and *kin* in "Hamlet"? Nay, did he not even (shall I dare to hint it?) drop the final *d* as the Yankee still does? John Lilly plays in the same way on *kindred* and *kindness.*

But to come to some other ancient instances. Warner rhymes *bounds* with *crowns, grounds* with *towns, text* with *sex, worst* with *crust, interrupts* with *cups;* Drayton, *defects* with *sex;* Chapman,

4. ***smally:*** "The word occurs in a letter of Mary Boleyn, in Golding, and Warner. Milton also was fond of the word" [L].

5. **When . . . Schoolmaster:** "Though I find Worcester in the *Mirror for Magistrates*" [L].

amends with *cleanse;* Webster, *defects* with *checks;* Ben Jonson, *minds* with *combines;* Marston, *trust* and *obsequious, clothes* and *shows;* Dryden gives the same sound to *clothes,* and has also *minds* with *designs.* Of course, I do not affirm that their ears may not have told them that these were imperfect rhymes (though I am by no means sure even of that), but they surely would never have tolerated any such had they suspected the least vulgarity in them. Prior has the rhyme *first* and *trust,* but puts it into the mouth of a landlady. Swift has *stunted* and *burnt it,* an intentionally imperfect rhyme, no doubt, but which I cite as giving precisely the Yankee pronunciation of *burned.* Donne couples in unhallowed wedlock *after* and *matter,* thus seeming to give to both the true Yankee sound; and it is not uncommon to find *after* and *daughter.* Worse than all, in one of Dodsley's Old Plays we have *onions* rhyming with *minions,*—I have tears in my eyes while I record it. And yet what is viler than the universal *Misses* (*Mrs.*) for *Mistress?* This was once a vulgarism, and in "The Miserics of Inforced Marriage" the rhyme (printed as prose in Dodsley's Old Plays by Collier),

"To make my young *mistress,*
Delighting in *kisses,*"

is put into the mouth of the clown. Our people say *Injun* for *Indian.* The tendency to make this change where *i* follows *d* is common. The Italian *giorno* and French *jour* from *diurnus* are familiar examples. And yet *Injun* is one of those depravations which the taste challenges peremptorily, though it have the authority of Charles Cotton—who rhymes *"Indies"* with *"cringes"*—and four English lexicographers, beginning with Dr. Sheridan, bid us say *invidgeous.* Yet after all it is no worse than the debasement which all our terminations in *tion* and *tience* have undergone, which yet we hear with *resignashun* and *payshunce,* though it might have aroused both *impat-i-ence* and *indigna-ti-on* in Shakespeare's time. When George Herbert tells us that if the sermon be dull,

"God takes a text and preacheth pati-ence,"

the prolongation of the word seems to convey some hint at the longanimity of the virtue. Consider what a poor curtal we have made of Ocean. There was something of his heave and expanse in *o-ce-an,* and Fletcher knew how to use it when he wrote so fine a verse as the second of these, the best deep-sea verse I know,—

"In desperate storms stem with a little rudder
The tumbling ruins of the oceän."

Oceanus was not then wholly shorn of his divine proportions, and our modern *oshun* sounds like the gush of small-beer in comparison. Some other contractions of ours have a vulgar air about them. *More 'n* for *more than,* as one of the worst, may stand for a type of such. Yet our old dramatists are full of such obscurations (elisions they can hardly be called) of the *th,* making *whe'r* of *whether, where* of *whither, here* of *hither, bro'r* of *brother, smo'r* of *smother, mo'r* of *mother,* and so on. And dear Brer Rabbit, can I forget him? Indeed, it is this that explains the word *rare* (which has Dryden's support), and which we say of meat where an Englishman would use *underdone.* I do not believe, with the dictionaries, that it had ever anything to do with the Icelandic *hrar* (*raw*), as it plainly has not in *rareripe,* which means earlier ripe. President Lincoln said of a precocious boy that "he was a *rareripe.*" And I do not believe it, for this reason, that the earliest form of the word with us was, and the commoner now in the inland parts still is, so far as I can discover, *rare-done.* Golding has "egs reere-rosted" which, whatever else it mean, cannot mean *raw*-roasted. I find *rather* as a monosyllable in Donne, and still better, as giving the sound, rhyming with *fair* in Warner. There is an epigram of Sir Thomas Browne in which the words *rather than* make a monosyllable:

"What furie is 't to take Death's part
And rather than by Nature, die by Art!"

The contraction *more 'n* I find in the old play "Fuimus Troes," in a verse where the measure is so strongly accented as to leave it beyond doubt,—

"A golden crown whose heirs
More than half the world subdue."

It may be, however, that the contraction is in "th' orld." It is unmistakable in the "Second Maiden's Tragedy":—

"It were but folly,
Dear soul, to boast of *more than* I can perform."

Is our *gin* for *given* more violent than *mar'l* for *marvel,* which was once common, and which I find as late as Herrick? Nay, Herrick has *gin* (spelling it *g'en*), too, as do the Scotch, who agree with us likewise in preferring *chimly* to *chimney.*

I will now leave pronunciation and turn to words or phrases which have been supposed peculiar to us, only pausing to pick up a single dropped stitch, in the pronunciation of the word *su'preme,* which I had thought native till I found it in the well-languaged Daniel. I will begin with a word of which I have never met with any example in any English writer of authority. We express the first stage of withering in a green plant suddenly cut down by the verb *to wilt*. It is, of course, own cousin of the German *welken,* but I have never come upon it in literary use, and my own books of reference give me faint help. Graff gives *welhèn, marcescere,* and refers to *weih* (*weak*), and conjecturally to A.-S. *hvelan*. The A.-S. *wealwian* (*to wither*) is nearer, but not so near as two words in the Icelandic, which perhaps put us on the track of its ancestry,—*velgi, tepefacere* (and *velki,* with the derivative) meaning *contaminare. Wilt,* at any rate, is a good word, filling, as it does, a sensible gap between drooping and withering, and the imaginative phrase "he wilted right down," like "he caved right in," is a true Americanism. *Wilt* occurs in English provincial glossaries, but is explained by *wither,* which with us it does not mean. We have a few words such as *cache, cohog, carry* (*portage*), *shoot* (*chute*), *timber* (*forest*), *bushwhack* (to pull a boat along by the bushes on the edge of a stream), *buckeye* (a picturesque word for the horse-chestnut); but how many can we be said to have fairly brought into the language, as Alexander Gill, who first mentions Americanisms, meant it when he said, *"Sed et ab Americanis nonnulla mutuamur ut* MAIZ *et* CANOA"? Very few, I suspect, and those mostly by borrowing from the French, German, Spanish, or Indian.[6] "The Dipper" for the "Great Bear" strikes me as having a native air. *Bogus,* in the sense of *worthless,* is undoubtedly ours, but is, I more than suspect, a corruption of the French *bagasse* (from low Latin *bagasea*), which travelled up the Mississippi from New Orleans, where it was used for the refuse of the sugar-cane. It is true, we have modified the meaning of some words. We use *freshet* in the sense of *flood,* for which I have not chanced upon any authority. Our New England cross between Ancient Pistol and Dugald Dalgetty, Captain Underhill, uses the word (1638) to mean a *current,* and I do not recollect it elsewhere in that sense. I therefore leave it with a ? for future explorers. *Crick* for *creek* I find in Captain John Smith and in the dedication of Fuller's "Holy Warre," and *run,* meaning a *small stream,* in Waymouth's "Voyage" (1605). *Humans* for *men,* which Mr. Bartlett includes in his "Dictionary of Americanisms," is Chapman's habitual phrase in his translation of Homer. I find it also in the old play of "The Hog hath lost his Pearl." *Dogs* for *andirons* is still current in New England, and in Walter de Biblesworth I find *chiens* glossed in the margin by *andirons. Gunning* for *shooting* is in Drayton. We once got credit for the poetical word *fall* for *autumn,* but Mr. Bartlett and the last edition of Webster's Dictionary refer us to Dryden. It is even older, for I find it in Drayton, and Bishop Hall has *autumn fall.* Middleton plays upon the word: "May'st thou have a reasonable good *spring,* for thou art like to have many dangerous foul *falls.*" Daniel does the same, and Coleridge uses it as we do. Gray uses the archaism *picked* for *peaked,* and the word *smudge* (as our backwoodsmen do) for a smothered fire. Lord Herbert of Cherbury (more properly perhaps than even Sidney, the last *preux chevalier*) has "the Emperor's folks" just as a Yankee would say it. *Loan* for *lend,* with which we have hitherto been blackened, I must retort upon the mother island, for it appears so long ago as in "Albion's England." *Fleshy,* in the sense of *stout,* may claim Ben Jonson's warrant, and I find it also so lately as in Francklin's "Lucian." *Chore* is also Jonson's word, and I am inclined to prefer it to *chare* and *char,* because I think that I see a more natural origin for it in the French *jour*—whence it might come to mean a day's work, and thence a job—than anywhere else.[7] *At onst* for *at once* I thought a corruption of our own, till I found it in the Chester Plays. I am now inclined to suspect it no corruption at all, but only an erratic and obsolete superlative *at onest. To progress′* was flung in our teeth till Mr. Pickering retorted with Shakespeare's "doth pro′gress down thy cheeks." I confess that I was never satisfied with this answer, because the accent was different, and because the word might here be reckoned a substantive quite as well as a verb. Mr. Bartlett (in his dictionary above cited) adds a surrebutter in a verse from Ford's "Broken Heart." Here the word is clearly a verb, but with the accent unhappily still on the first syllable. Mr. Bartlett says that he "cannot say whether the word was used in Bacon's time or not." It certainly was, and with the accent we give to it. Ben Jonson, in the "Alchemist," has this verse,

> "Progress′ so from extreme unto extreme,"

and Sir Philip Sidney,

> "Progressing then from fair Turias' golden place."

Surely we may now sleep in peace, and our English cousins will forgive us, since we have cleared ourselves from any suspicion of originality in the matter! Even after I had convinced myself that

6. **Very . . . Indian:** "This was written twenty years ago, and now (1890) I cannot open an English journal without coming upon an Americanism" [L].

7. ***Chore* . . . else:** "The Rev. A. L. Mayhew of Wadham College, Oxford has convinced me that I was astray in this" [L].

the chances were desperately against our having invented any of the *Americanisms* with which we are *faulted* and which we are in the habit of *voicing,* there were one or two which had so prevailingly indigenous an accent as to stagger me a little. One of these was "the biggest *thing out.*" Alas, even this slender comfort is denied me. Old Gower has

> "So harde an herte was none *oute,*"

and

> "That such merveile was none *oute.*"

He also, by the way, says "a *sighte* of flowres" as naturally as our up-country folk would say it. *Poor* for *lean, thirds* for *dower,* and *dry* for *thirsty* I find in Middleton's plays. *Dry* is also in Skelton and in the "World" (1754). In a note on Middleton, Mr. Dyce thinks it needful to explain the phrase *I can't tell* (universal in America) by the gloss *I could not say.* Middleton also uses *snecked,* which I had believed an Americanism till I saw it there. It is, of course, only another form of *snatch,* analogous to *theek* and *thatch* (cf. the proper names Dekker and Thacher), *break* (*brack*) and *breach, make* (still common with us) and *match. 'Long on* for *occasioned by* ("who is this 'long on?") occurs constantly in Gower and likewise in Middleton. *'Cause why* is in Chaucer. *Raising* (an English version of the French *leaven*) for *yeast* is employed by Gayton in his "Festivous Notes on Don Quixote." I have never seen an instance of our New England word *emptins* in the same sense, nor can I divine its original. Gayton has *limekill;* also *shuts* for *shutters,* and the latter is used by Mrs. Hutchinson in her "Life of Colonel Hutchinson." Bishop Hall, and Purchas in his "Pilgrims," have *chist* for *chest,* and it is certainly nearer *cista,* as well as to its form in the Teutonic languages, whence probably we got it. We retain the old sound from *cist,* but *chest* is as old as Chaucer. Lovelace says *wropt* for *wrapt.* "Musicianer" I had always associated with the militia-musters of my boyhood, and too hastily concluded it an abomination of our own, but Mr. Wright calls it a Norfolk word, and I find it to be as old as 1642 by an extract in Collier. "Not worth the time of day" had passed with me for native till I saw it in Shakespeare's "Pericles." For *slick* (which is only a shorter sound of *sleek,* like *crick* and the now universal *britches* for *breeches*) I will only call Chapman and Jonson. "That's a sure card!" and "That's a stinger!" both sound like modern slang, but you will find the one in the old interlude of "Thersytes" (1537), and the other in Middleton. "Right here," a favorite phrase with our orators and with a certain class of our editors, turns up *passim* in the Chester and Coventry plays. Mr. Dickens found something very ludicrous in what he considered our neologism *right away.* But I find a phrase very like it, and which I would gladly suspect to be a misprint for it, in "Gammer Gurton":—

> "Lyght it and bring it *tite away.*"

But *tite* is the true word in this case. After all, what is it but another form of *straightway? Cussedness,* meaning *wickedness, malignity,* and *cuss,* a sneaking, ill-natured fellow, in such phrases as "He donc it out o' pure cussedness," and "He is a nateral cuss," have been commonly thought Yankeeisms. To vent certain contemptuously indignant moods they are admirable in their rough-and-ready way. But neither is our own. *Cursydnesse,* in the same sense of malignant wickedness, occurs in the Coventry Plays, and *cuss* may perhaps claim to have come in with the Conqueror. At least the term is also French. Saint Simon uses it and confesses its usefulness. Speaking of the Abbé Dubois, he says, "Qui étoit en plein ce qu'un mauvais françois appelle un *sacre,* mais qui ne se peut guère exprimer autrement." "Not worth a cuss," though supported by "not worth a damn," may be a mere corruption, since "not worth a *cress*" is in "Piers Ploughman." "I don't see it" was the popular slang a year or two ago, and seemed to spring from the soil; but no, it is in Cibber's "Careless Husband." *Green sauce* for *vegetables* I meet in Beaumont and Fletcher, Gayton, and elsewhere. Our rustic pronunciation *sahce* (for either the dipthong *au* was anciently pronounced *ah,* or else we have followed abundant analogy in changing it to the latter sound, as we have in *chance, dance,* and so many more) may be the older one, and at least gives some hint at its ancestor *salsa. Warn,* in the sense of *notify,* is, I believe, now peculiar to us, but Pecock so employs it. I find *primmer* (*primer,* as we pronounce it) in Beaumont and Fletcher, and a "square eater" too (compare our *square* meal"), *heft* for *weight,* and "muchness" in the "Mirror for Magistrates," *bankbill* in Swift and Fielding, and *as* for *that* I might say *passim. To cotton to* is, I rather think, an Americanism. The nearest approach to it I have found is *cotton together,* in Congreve's "Love for Love." To *cotton* or *cotten,* in another sense, is old and common. Our word means to *cling,* and its origin, possibly, is to be sought in another direction, perhaps in A.-S. *cvead,* which means *mud, clay* (both proverbially clinging), or better yet, in the Icelandic *qvoda* (otherwise *kód*), meaning *resin* and *glue,* which are *κατ' ἐξοχήν,* sticky substances.

To *spit cotton* is, I think, American, and also, perhaps, *to flax* for *to beat*. *To the halves* still survives among us, though apparently obsolete in England. It means either to let or to hire a piece of land, receiving half the profit in money or in kind (*partibus locare*). I mention it because in a note by some English editor, to which I have lost my reference, I have seen it wrongly explained. The editors of Nares cite Burton. *To put,* in the sense of *to go,* as *Put!* for *Begone!* would seem our own, and yet it is strictly analogous to the French *se mettre à la voie,* and the Italian *mettersi in via.* Indeed, Dante has a verse,

> *"Io sarei* [for *mi sarei*] *già messo per lo sentiero,"*

which, but for the indignity, might be translated,

> "I should, ere this, have *put* along the way."

I deprecate in advance any share in General Banks's notions of international law, but we may all take a just pride in his exuberant eloquence as something distinctively American. When he spoke a few years ago of "letting the Union slide," even those who, for political purposes, reproached him with the sentiment, admired the indigenous virtue of his phrase. Yet I find "let the world slide" in Heywood's "Edward IV."; and in Beaumont and Fletcher's "Wit without Money," Valentine says,

> "Will you go drink,
> And let the world slide?"

So also in Sidney's "Arcadia,"

> "Let his dominion slide."

In the one case it is put into the mouth of a clown, in the other, of a gentleman, and was evidently proverbial. It has even higher sanction, for Chaucer writes,

> "Well nigh all other curës *let he slide.*"

Mr. Bartlett gives "above one's bend" as an Americanism; but compare Hamlet's "to the top of my bent." *In his tracks* for *immediately* has acquired an American accent, and passes where he can for a native, but is an importation nevertheless; for what is he but the Latin *e vestigio,* or at best the Norman French *eneslespas,* both which have the same meaning? *Hotfoot* (provincial also in England), I find in the old romance of "Tristan,"

> *"Si s'en parti* CHAUT PAS."

Like for *as* is never used in New England, but is universal in the South and West. It has on its side the authority of two kings (*ego sum rex Romanorum et supra grammaticam* [8]), Henry VIII. and Charles I. This were ample, without throwing into the scale the scholar and poet Daniel. *Them* was used as a nominative by the majesty of Edward VI., by Sir P. Hoby, and by Lord Paget (in Froude's "History"). I have never seen any passage adduced where *guess* was used as the Yankee uses it. The word was familiar in the mouths of our ancestors, but with a different shade of meaning from that we have given it, which is something like *rather think,* though the Yankee implies a confident certainty by it when he says, "I guess I *du!*" There are two examples in Otway, one of which ("So in the struggle, I guess the note was lost") perhaps might serve our purpose, and Coleridge's

> "I guess 't was fearful there to see"

certainly comes very near. But I have a higher authority than either in Selden, who, in one of his notes to the "Polyolbion," writes, "The first inventor of them (I *guess* you dislike not the addition) was one Berthold Swartz." Here he must mean by it, "I take it for granted." Robert Greene, in his "Quip for an Upstart Courtier," makes Cloth-breeches say, "but I *gesse* your maistership never tried what true honor meant." In this case the word seems to be used with a meaning precisely like that which we give it. Another peculiarity almost as prominent is the beginning sentences, especially in answer to questions, with "well." Put before such a phrase as "How d'e do?" it is commonly short, and has the sound of *wul,* but in reply it is deliberative, and the various shades of meaning which can be conveyed by difference of intonation, and by prolonging or abbreviating, I should vainly attempt to describe. I have heard *ooa-ahl, wahl, ahl, wăl,* and something nearly approaching the sound of the *le* in *able*. Sometimes before "I" it dwindles to a mere *l,* as " 'l *I* dunno." A friend of mine (why should I not please myself, though I displease him, by brightening my page with the initials of the most exquisite of humorists, J. H.? [9]) told me that he once heard five "wells," like pioneers, precede the answer to an inquiry about the price of land. The first was the ordinary *wul,* in deference to custom; the second, the long, perpending *ooahl,* with a falling inflection of the voice; the third, the same, but with the voice rising, as if in despair of a conclusion, into a plaintively nasal whine; the fourth, *wulh,* ending in the aspirate of a sigh; and then, fifth, came a short, sharp *wal,* showing that a conclusion had been reached. I have used this lat-

8. *ego . . . grammaticam:* "I am king of the Romans and above grammar." 9. J. H.: Probably John Holmes, brother of Oliver Wendell Holmes.

ter form in the "Biglow Papers," because, if enough nasality be added, it represents most nearly the average sound of what I may call the interjection.

A locution prevails in the Southern and Middle States which is so curious that, though never heard in New England, I will give a few lines to its discussion, the more readily because it is extinct elsewhere. I mean the use of *allow* in the sense of *affirm,* as "I allow that's a good horse." I find the word so used in 1558 by Anthony Jenkinson in Hakluyt: "Corne they sowe not, neither doe eate any bread, mocking the Christians for the same, and disabling our strengthe, saying we live by eating the toppe of a weede, and drinke a drinke made of the same, *allowing* theyr great devouring of flesh and drinking of milke to be the increase of theyr strength." That is, they undervalued our strength, and affirmed their own to be the result of a certain diet. In another passage of the same narrative the word has its more common meaning of approving or praising: "The said king, much *allowing* this declaration, said." Ducange quotes Bracton *sub voce* ADLOCARE for the meaning "to admit as proved," and the transition from this to "affirm" is by no means violent. Izaak Walton has "Lebault *allows* waterfrogs to be good meat," and here the word is equivalent to *affirms.* At the same time, when we consider some of the meanings of *allow* in old English, and of *allouer* in old French, and also remember that the verbs *prize* and *praise* are from one root, I think we must admit *allaudare* to a share in the paternity of *allow.* The sentence from Hakluyt would read equally well, "contemning our strengthe, . . . and praising (or valuing) their great eating of flesh as the cause of their increase in strength." After all, if we confine ourselves to *allocare,* it may turn out that the word was somewhere and somewhen used for *to bet,* analogously to *put up, put down, post* (cf. Spanish *apostar*), and the like. I hear boys in the street continually saying, "I bet that 's a good horse," or what not, meaning by no means to risk anything beyond their opinion in the matter.

The word *improve,* in the sense of "to occupy, make use of, employ," as Dr. Pickering defines it, he long ago proved to be no neologism. He would have done better, I think, had he substituted *profit by* for *employ.* He cites Dr. Franklin as saying that the word had never, so far as he knew, been used in New England before he left it in 1723, except in Dr. Mather's "Remarkable Providences," which he oddly calls a "very old book." Franklin, as Dr. Pickering goes on to show, was mistaken. Mr. Bartlett in his "Dictionary" merely abridges Pickering. Both of them should have confined the application of the word to material things, its extension to which is all that is peculiar in the supposed American use of it. For surely "Complete Letter-Writers" have been *"improving* this opportunity" time out of mind. I will illustrate the word a little further, because Pickering cites no English authorities. Skelton has a passage in his "Phyllyp Sparowe," which I quote the rather as it contains also the word *allowed,* and as it distinguishes *improve* from *employ:*—

> "His [Chaucer's] Englysh well alowed,
> So as it is *enprowed,*
> For as it is enployd,
> There is no English voyd."

Here the meaning is *to profit by.* In Fuller's "Holy Warre" (1647), we have "The Egyptians standing on the firm ground, were thereby enabled to *improve* and enforce their darts to the utmost." Here the word might certainly mean *to make use of.* Mrs. Hutchinson ("Life of Colonel H.") uses the word in the same way: "And therefore did not *emproove* his interest to engage the country in the quarrell." Swift in one of his letters says: "There is not an acre of land in Ireland turned to half its advantage; yet it is better *improved* than the people." I find it also in "Strength out of Weakness" (1652), and Plutarch's "Morals" (1714), but I know of only one example of its use in the purely American sense, and that is "a very good *improvement* for a mill" in the "State Trials" (Speech of the Attorney-General in the Lady Ivy's case, 1684). In the sense of *employ,* I could cite a dozen old English authorities.

In running over the fly-leaves of those delightful folios for this reference, I find a note which reminds me of another word, for our abuse of which we have been deservedly ridiculed. I mean *lady.* It is true I might cite the example of the Italian *donna* [10] (*domina*), which has been treated in the same way by a whole nation, and not, as *lady* among us, by the uncultivated only. It perhaps grew into use in the half-democratic republics of Italy in the same way and for the same reasons as with us. But I admit that our abuse of the word is villanous. I know of an orator who once said in a public meeting where bonnets preponderated, that "the ladies were last at the cross and first at the tomb"! But similar sins were committed before our day and in the mother country. In the "Harleian Miscellany" (vol. v. p. 455) I find "this *lady* is my servant; the hedger's daughter Ioan." In the "State Trials" I learn of "a *gentlewoman* that

10. *donna:* "*Dame,* in English as a decayed gentlewoman of the same family" [L].

lives cook with" such a one, and I hear the Lord High Steward speaking of the wife of a waiter at a bagnio as a *gentlewoman!* From the same authority, by the way, I can state that our vile habit of chewing tobacco had the somewhat unsavory example of Titus Oates, and I know by tradition from an eye-witness that the elegant General Burgoyne partook of the same vice. Howell, in one of his letters (dated 26 August, 1623), speaks thus of another "institution" which many have thought American: "They speak much of that boisterous Bishop of Halverstadt (for so they term him here), that, having taken a place wher ther were two Monasteries of Nuns and Friers, he caus'd divers feather-beds to be rip'd, and all the feathers to be thrown in a great Hall, whither the Nuns and Friers were thrust naked with their bodies oil'd and pitch'd, and to tumble among the feathers." Howell speaks as if the thing were new to him, and I know not if the "boisterous" Bishop was the inventor of it, but I find it practised in England before our Revolution.

Before leaving the subject, I will add a few comments made from time to time on the margin of Mr. Bartlett's excellent "Dictionary," to which I am glad thus publicly to acknowledge my many obligations. "Avails" is good old English, and the *vails* of Sir Joshua Reynolds's porter are famous. Averse *from,* averse *to,* and in connection with them the English vulgarism "different *to.*" The corrupt use of *to* in these cases, as well as in the Yankee "he lives to Salem," "to home," and others, must be a very old one, for in the one case it plainly arose from confounding the two French prepositions *à* (from Latin *ad* and *ab*), and in the other from translating the first of them. I once thought "different to" a modern vulgarism, and Mr. Thackeray, on my pointing it out to him in "Henry Esmond," confessed it to be an anachronism. Mr. Bartlett refers to "the old writers quoted in Richardson's Dictionary" for "different to," though in my edition of that work all the examples are with *from.* But I find *to* used invariably by Sir R. Hawkins in Hakluyt. *Banjo* is a negro corruption of O. E. *bandore. Bind-weed* can hardly be modern, for *wood-bind* is old and radically right, intertwining itself through *bindan* and *windan* with classic stems. *Bobolink:* is this a contraction for Bob o' Lincoln? I find *bobolynes,* in one of the poems attributed to Skelton, where it may be rendered *giddy-pate,* a term very fit for the bird in his ecstasies. *Cruel* for *great* is in Hakluyt. *Bowling-alley* is in Nash's "Pierce Pennilesse." *Curious,* meaning *nice,* occurs continually in old writers, and is as old as Pecock's "Repressor." *Droger* is O. E. *drugger. Educational* is in Burke. *Feeze* is only a form of *fizz. To fix,* in the American sense, I find used by the Commissioners of the United Colonies so early as 1675, "their arms well *fixed* and fit for service." *To take the foot in the hand* is German; so is *to go under. Gundalow* is old: I find *gundelo* in Hakluyt, and *gundello* in Booth's reprint of the folio Shakespeare of 1623. *Gonoff* is O. E. *gnoffe. Heap* is in "Piers Ploughman" ("and other names *an heep*"), and in Hakluyt ("seeing such a *heap* of their enemies ready to devour them"). *To liquor* is in the "Puritan" ("call 'em in, and liquor 'em a little"). *To loaf:* this, I think, is unquestionably German. *Laufen* is pronounced *lofen* in some parts of Germany, and I once heard one German student say to another, *Ich lauf' (lofe) hier bis du wiederkehrest,* and he began accordingly to saunter up and down, in short, to *loaf. To mull,* Mr. Bartlett says, means "to soften, to dispirit," and quotes from "Margaret,"—"There has been a pretty considerable *mullin* going on among the doctors,"—where it surely cannot mean what he says it does. We have always heard *mulling* used for *stirring, bustling,* sometimes in an underhand way. It is a metaphor derived probably from *mulling* wine, and the word itself must be a corruption of *mell,* from O. F. *mesler. Pair* of stairs is in Hakluyt. *To pull up stakes* is in Curwen's Journal, and therefore pre-Revolutionary. I think I have met with it earlier. *Raise:* under this word Mr. Bartlett omits "to raise a house," that is, the frame of a wooden one, and also the substantive formed from it, a *raisin'. Retire* for *go to bed* is in Fielding's "Amelia." *Setting-poles* cannot be new, for I find "some *set* [the boats] with long *poles*" in Hakluyt. *Shoulder-hitters:* I find that *shoulder-striker* is old. though I have lost the reference to my authority. *Snag* is no new word, though perhaps the Western application of it is so; but I find in Gill the proverb, "A bird in the bag is worth two on the snag." Dryden has *swop* and *to rights. Trail:* Hakluyt has "many wayes *traled* by the wilde beastes."

I subjoin a few phrases not in Mr. Bartlett's book which I have heard. *Bald-headed:* "to go it bald-headed"; in great haste, as where one rushes out without his hat. *Bogue:* "I don't git much done 'thout I *bogue* right in along 'th my men." *Carry:* a *portage. Cat-nap:* a short doze. *Cat-stick:* a small stick. *Chowder-head:* a muddle-brain. *Cling-john:* a soft cake of rye. *Cocoa-nut:* the head. *Cohees':* applied to the people of certain settlements in Western Pennsylvania, from their use of the archaic form *Quo' he. Dunnow'z I know:* the nearest your true Yankee ever comes *to* acknowledging ignorance. *Essence-pedler:* a skunk. *First-rate and a half. Fish-flakes,* for drying fish: O. E. *fleck* (*cratis*). *Gander-party:* a social gathering of men only. *Gawnicus:* a dolt. *Hawkins's whetstone:* rum; in derision of one Hawkins, a well-known temperance-lecturer. *Hyper:* to bustle: "I mus' *hyper* about an' git tea." *Keeler-tub:* one in which dishes are washed. ("And Greasy Joan doth *keel* the pot.") *Lap-tea:* where the guests are too many to sit at table. *Last of pea-time:* to be hard-up. *Lōse-laid* (loose-laid): a weaver's term, and probably English; weak-willed. *Malahack:* to cut up hastily or awkwardly. *Moonglade:* a beautiful word: for the track of moonlight on the water. *Off-ox:* an unmanageable, cross-grained fellow. *Old Driver, Old Splitfoot:* the Devil. *Onhitch:* to pull trigger (cf. Spanish *disparar*). *Popular:* conceited. *Rote:* sound of surf before a storm. *Rot-gut:* cheap whiskey; the word occurs in Heywood's "English Traveller" and Addison's "Drummer," for a poor kind of drink. *Seem:* it is habitual with the New-Englander to put this verb to strange uses, as, "I can't *seem* to be suited," "I could n't *seem* to know him." *Side-hill,* for *hillside*. *State-house:* this seems an Americanism, whether invented or derived from the Dutch *Stadhuys,* I know not. *Strike* and *string:* from the game of ninepins; to make a *strike* is to knock down all the pins with one ball, hence it has come to mean fortunate, successful. *Swampers:* men who break out roads for lumberers. *Tormented:* euphemism for damned, as, "not a tormented cent." *Virginia fence, to make a:* to walk like a drunken man.

It is always worth while to note down the erratic words or phrases which one meets with in any dialect. They may throw light on the meaning of other words, on the relationship of languages, or even on history itself. In so composite a language as ours they often supply a different form to express a different shade of meaning, as in *viol* and *fiddle, thrid* and *thread, smother* and *smoulder,* where the *l* has crept in by a false analogy with *would.* We have given back to England the excellent adjective *lengthy,* formed honestly like *earthy, drouthy,* and others, thus enabling their journalists to characterize our President's messages by a word civilly compromising between *long* and *tedious,* so as not to endanger the peace of the two countries by wounding our national sensitiveness to British criticism. Let me give two curious examples of the antiseptic property of dialects at which I have already glanced. Dante has *dindi* as a childish or low word for *danari* (money), and in Shropshire small Roman coins are still dug up which the peasants call *dinders.* This can hardly be a chance coincidence, but seems rather to carry the word back to the Roman soldiery. So our farmers say *chuk, chuk,* to their pigs, and *ciacco* is one of the Italian words for *hog.* When a countryman tells us that he "fell *all of a heap,*" I cannot help thinking that he unconsciously points to an affinity between our word *tumble,* and the Latin *tumulus,* that is older than most others. I believe that words, or even the mere intonation of them, have an astonishing vitality and power of propagation by the root, like the gardener's pest, quitch-grass,[11] while the application or combination of them may be new. It is in these last that my countrymen seem to me full of humor, invention, quickness of wit, and that sense of subtle analogy which needs only refining to become fancy and imagination. Prosaic as American life seems in many of its aspects to a European, bleak and bare as it is on the side of tradition, and utterly orphaned of the solemn inspiration of antiquity, I cannot help thinking that the ordinary talk of unlettered men among us is fuller of metaphor and of phrases that suggest lively images than that of any other people I have seen. Very many such will be found in Mr. Bartlett's book, though his short list of proverbs at the end seem to me, with one or two exceptions, as un-American as possible. Most of them have no character at all but coarseness, and are quite too long-skirted for working proverbs, in which language always "takes off its coat to it," as a Yankee would say. There are plenty that have a more native and puckery flavor, seedlings from the old stock often, and yet new varieties. One hears such not seldom among us Easterners, and the West would yield many more. "Mean enough to steal acorns from a blind hog"; "Cold as the north side of a Jenooary gravestone by starlight"; "Hungry as a graven image"; "Pop'lar as a hen with one chicken"; "A hen's time ain't much"; "Quicker 'n greased lightnin' "; "Ther's sech a thing ez bein' *tu*" (our Yankee paraphrase of μηδὲν ἄγαν); hence the phrase *tooin' round,* meaning a supererogatory activity like that of flies; "Stingy enough to skim his milk at both eends"; "Hot as the Devil's kitchen"; "Handy as a pocket in a shirt"; "He's a whole team and the dog under the wagon"; "All deacons are good, but there's odds in deacons" (to *deacon* berries is to put the largest atop); "So thievish they hev to take in their stone walls nights";[12] may serve as specimens. "I take my tea *barfoot,*" said a backwoodsman when asked if he would have cream and sugar. (I find *barfoot,* by the way, in the Coventry Plays.) A man speaking

11. **quitch-grass:** "Which whether in that form, or under its aliases *witch*-grass and *cooch*-grass, points us back to its original Saxon *quick*" [L]. 12. **"So . . . nights":** "And, by the way, the Yankee never says 'o' nights,' but uses the older adverbial form, analogous to the German *nachts*" [L].

to me once of a very rocky clearing said, "Stone's got a pretty heavy mortgage on that land," and I overheard a guide in the woods say to his companions who were urging him to sing, "Wal, I *did* sing once, but toons gut invented, an' thet spilt my trade." Whoever has driven over a stream by a bridge made of *slabs* will feel the picturesque force of the epithet *slab-bridged* applied to a fellow of shaky character. Almost every county has some good die-sinker in phrase, whose mintage passes into the currency of the whole neighborhood. Such a one described the county jail (the one stone building where all the dwellings are of wood) as "the house whose underpinnin' come up to the eaves," and called hell "the place where they did n't rake up their fires nights." I once asked a stage-driver if the other side of a hill were as steep as the one we were climbing: "Steep? chain lightnin' could n' go down it 'thout puttin' the shoe on!" And this brings me back to the exaggeration of which I spoke before. To me there is something very taking in the negro "so black that charcoal made a chalk-mark on him," and the wooden shingle "painted so like marble that it sank in water," as if its very consciousness or its vanity had been overpersuaded by the cunning of the painter. I heard a man, in order to give a notion of some very cold weather, say to another that a certain Joe, who had been taking mercury, found a lump of quicksilver in each boot, when he went home to dinner. This power of rapidly dramatizing a dry fact into flesh and blood and the vivid conception of Joe as a human thermometer strike me as showing a poetic sense that may be refined into faculty. At any rate there is humor here, and not mere quickness of wit,—the deeper and not the shallower quality. The *tendency* of humor is always towards overplus of expression, while the very essence of wit is its logical precision. Captain Basil Hall denied that our people had any humor, deceived, perhaps, by their gravity of manner. But this very seriousness is often the outward sign of that humorous quality of the mind which delights in finding an element of identity in things seemingly the most incongruous, and then again in forcing an incongruity upon things identical. Perhaps Captain Hall had no humor himself, and if so he would never find it. Did he always feel the point of what was said to himself? I doubt it, because I happen to know a chance he once had given him in vain. The Captain was walking up and down the veranda of a country tavern in Massachusetts while the coach changed horses. A thunder-storm was going on, and, with that pleasant European air of indirect self-compliment in condescending to be surprised by American merit, which we find so conciliating, he said to a countryman lounging against the door, "Pretty heavy thunder you have here." The other, who had divined at a glance his feeling of generous concession to a new country, drawled gravely, "Waal, we *du,* considerin' the number of inhabitants." This, the more I analyze it, the more humorous does it seem. The same man was capable of wit also, when he would. He was a cabinet-maker, and was once employed to make some commandment-tables for the parish meeting-house. The parson, a very old man, annoyed him by looking into his workshop every morning, and cautioning him to be very sure to pick out "clear mahogany without any *knots* in it." At last, wearied out, he retorted one day: "Wal, Dr. B., I guess ef I was to leave the *nots* out o' some o' the c'man'ments, 't 'ould soot you full ez wal!"

If I had taken the pains to write down the proverbial or pithy phrases I have heard, or if I had sooner thought of noting the Yankeeisms I met with in my reading, I might have been able to do more justice to my theme. But I have done all I wished in respect to pronunciation, if I have proved that where we are vulgar, we have the countenance of very good company. For, as to the *jus et norma loquendi,* I agree with Horace and those who have paraphrased or commented him, from Boileau to Gray. I think that a good rule for style is Galiani's definition of sublime oratory,—"l'art de tout dire sans être mis à la Bastille dans un pays où il est défendu de rien dire." [13] I profess myself a fanatical purist, but with a hearty contempt for the speech-gilders who affect purism without any thorough, or even pedagogic, knowledge of the engendure, growth, and affinities of the noble language about whose *mésalliances* they profess (like Dean Alford) to be so solicitous. If *they* had their way—! "Doch es sey," says Lessing, "dass jene gothische Höflichkeit eine unentbehrliche Tugend des heutigen Umganges ist. Soll sie darum unsere Schriften eben so schaal und falsch machen als unsern Umgang?" [14] And Drayton was not far wrong in affirming that

" 'T is possible to climb,
To kindle, or to slake,
Although in Skelton's rhyme."

Cumberland in his Memoirs tells us that when, in the midst of Admiral Rodney's great sea-fight,

13. **"l'art . . . dire"**: "The art of saying all without being put in jail in a country where it is forbidden to say anything."
14. **"Doch . . . Umgang?"**: "Even if it were true that this Gothic politeness is an indispensable virtue of our present-day social intercourse, should it therefore make our writings just as shallow and insincere as our social manners?"

Sir Charles Douglas said to him, "Behold, Sir George, the Greeks and Trojans contending for the body of Patroclus!" the Admiral answered, peevishly, "Damn the Greeks and damn the Trojans! I have other things to think of." After the battle was won, Rodney thus to Sir Charles, "Now, my dear friend, I am at the service of your Greeks and Trojans, and the whole of Homer's Iliad, or as much of it as you please!" I had some such feeling of the impertinence of our pseudo-classicality when I chose our homely dialect to work in. Should we be nothing, because somebody had contrived to be something (and that perhaps in a provincial dialect) ages ago? and to be nothing by our very attempt to be that something, which they had already been, and which therefore nobody could be again without being a bore? Is there no way left, then, I thought, of being natural, of being *naïf,* which means nothing more than native, of belonging to the age and country in which you are born? The Yankee, at least, is a new phenomenon; let us try to be *that.* It is perhaps a *pis aller,* but is not *No Thoroughfare* written up everywhere else? In the literary world, things seemed to me very much as they were in the latter half of the last century. Pope, skimming the cream of good sense and expression wherever he could find it, had made, not exactly poetry, but an honest, salable butter of worldly wisdom which pleasantly lubricated some of the drier morsels of life's daily bread, and, seeing this, scores of harmlessly insane people went on for the next fifty years coaxing his buttermilk with the regular up and down of the pentameter churn. And in our day do we not scent everywhere, and even carry away in our clothes against our will, that faint perfume of musk which Mr. Tennyson has left behind him, or worse, of Heine's *patchouli?* And might it not be possible to escape them by turning into one of our narrow New England lanes, shut in though it were by bleak stone walls on either hand, and where no better flowers were to be gathered than goldenrod and hardhack?

Beside the advantage of getting out of the beaten track, our dialect offered others hardly inferior. As I was about to make an endeavor to state them, I remembered something that the clear-sighted Goethe had said about Hebel's "Alemannische Gedichte," which, making proper deduction for special reference to the book under review, expresses what I would have said far better than I could hope to do: "Allen diesen innern guten Eigenschaften kommt die behagliche naive Sprache sehr zu statten. Man findet mehrere sinnlich bedeutende und wohlklingende Worte . . . von einem, zwei Buchstaben, Abbreviationen, Contractionen, viele kurze, leichte Sylben, neue Reime, welches, mehr als man glaubt, ein Vortheil für den Dichter ist. Diese Elemente werden durch glückliche Constructionen und lebhafte Formen zu einem Styl zusammengedrängt der zu diesem Zwecke vor unserer Büchersprache grosse Vorzüge hat." [15] Of course I do not mean to imply that *I* have come near achieving any such success as the great critic here indicates, but I think the success is *there,* and to be plucked by some more fortunate hand.

Nevertheless, I was encouraged by the approval of many whose opinions I valued. With a feeling too tender and grateful to be mixed with any vanity, I mention as one of these the late A. H. Clough, who more than any one of those I have known (no longer living), except Hawthorne, impressed me with the constant presence of that indefinable thing we call genius. He often suggested that I should try my hand at some Yankee Pastorals, which would admit of more sentiment and a higher tone without foregoing the advantage offered by the dialect. I have never completed anything of the kind, but, in this Second Series, both my remembrance of his counsel and the deeper feeling called up by the great interests at stake, led me to venture some passages nearer to what is called poetical than could have been admitted without incongruity into the former series. The time seemed calling to me, with the old poet,—

> "Leave, then, your wonted prattle
>   The oaten reed forbear;
> For I hear a sound of battle,
>   And trumpets rend the air!"

The only attempt I had ever made at anything like a pastoral (if that may be called an attempt which was the result almost of pure accident) was in "The Courtin'." While the introduction to the First Series was going through the press, I received word from the printer that there was a blank page left which must be filled. I sat down at once and improvised another fictitious "notice of the press," in which, because verse would fill up space more cheaply than prose, I inserted an extract from a supposed ballad of Mr. Biglow. I kept no copy of it, and the printer, as directed, cut it off when the gap was filled. Presently I began to re-

15. **"Allen . . . hat"**: "The homely, unsophisticated language brings out these inner merits to best advantage. One finds a number of sensuously meaningful and well-sounding words . . . of one or two letters, abbreviations, contractions, many short and light syllables, new rhymes, all of which is more advantageous to the poet than one might think. These elements are being condensed by felicitous constructions and vivid forms to create a style which for this purpose is far superior to our bookish language."

ceive letters asking for the rest of it, sometimes for the *balance* of it. I had none, but to answer such demands, I patched a conclusion upon it in a later edition. Those who had only the first continued to importune me. Afterward, being asked to write it out as an autograph for the Baltimore Sanitary Commission Fair, I added other verses, into some of which I infused a little more sentiment in a homely way, and after a fashion completed it by sketching in the characters and making a connected story. Most likely I have spoiled it, but I shall put it at the end of this Introduction, to answer once for all those kindly importunings.

As I have seen extracts from what purported to be writings of Mr. Biglow, which were not genuine, I may properly take this opportunity to say, that the two volumes now published contain every line I ever printed under that pseudonyme, and that I have never, so far as I can remember, written an anonymous article (elsewhere than in the "North American Review" and the "Atlantic Monthly," during my editorship of it) except a review of Mrs. Stowe's "Minister's Wooing," and, some twenty years ago, a sketch of the antislavery movement in America for an English journal.

A word more on pronunciation. I have endeavored to express this so far as I could by the types, taking such pains as, I fear, may sometimes make the reading harder than need be. At the same time, by studying uniformity I have sometimes been obliged to sacrifice minute exactness. The emphasis often modifies the habitual sound. For example, *for* is commonly *fer* (a shorter sound than *fur* for *far*), but when emphatic it always becomes *for,* as "wut *for!*" So *too* is pronounced like *to* (as it was anciently spelt), and *to* like *ta* (the sound as in the *tou* of *touch*), but *too,* when emphatic, changes into *tue,* and *to,* sometimes, in similar cases, into *toe,* as, "I did n' hardly know wut *toe* du!" Where vowels come together, or one precedes another following an aspirate, the two melt together, as was common with the older poets who formed their versification on French or Italian models. Drayton is thoroughly Yankee when he says "I 'xpect," and Pope when he says, "t' inspire." *With* becomes sometimes *'ith, 'ŭth,* or *'th,* or even disappears wholly where it comes before *the,* as, "I went along th' Square" (along with the Squire), the *are* sound being an archaism which I have noticed also in *choir,* like the old Scottish *quhair.*[16] (Herrick has, "Of flowers ne'er sucked by th' theeving bee.") *Without* becomes *athout* and *'thout. Afterwards* always retains its locative *s,* and is pronounced always *ahterwurds',* with a strong accent on the last syllable. This oddity has some support in the erratic *towards'* instead of *to'wards,* which we find in the poets and sometimes hear. The sound given to the first syllable of *to'wards,* I may remark, sustains the Yankee lengthening of the *o* in *to.* At the beginning of a sentence, *ahterwurds* has the accent on the first syllable; at the end of one, on the last; as, "*ah'terwurds'* he tol' me," "he tol' me *ahterwurds'.*" The Yankee never makes a mistake in his aspirates. *U* changes in many words to *e,* always in *such, brush, tush, hush, rush, blush,* seldom in *much,* oftener in *trust* and *crust,* never in *mush, gust, bust, tumble,* or (?) *flush,* in the latter case probably to avoid confusion with *flesh.* I have heard *flush* with the *ĕ* sound, however. For the same reason, I suspect, never in *gush* (at least, I never heard it), because we have already one *gesh* for *gash. A* and *i* short frequently become *e* short. *U* always becomes *o* in the prefix *un* (except *unto*), and *o* in return changes to *u* short in *uv* for *of,* and in some words beginning with *om. T* and *d, b* and *p, v* and *w,* remain intact. So much occurs to me in addition to what I said on this head in the preface to the former volume.

Of course in what I have said I wish to be understood as keeping in mind the difference between provincialisms properly so called and *slang. Slang* is always vulgar, because it is not a natural but an affected way of talking, and all mere tricks of speech or writing are offensive. I do not think that Mr. Biglow can be fairly charged with vulgarity, and I should have entirely failed in my design, if I had not made it appear that high and even refined sentiment may coexist with the shrewder and more comic elements of the Yankee character. I believe that what is essentially vulgar and mean-spirited in politics seldom has its source in the body of the people, but much rather among those who are made timid by their wealth or selfish by their love of power. A democracy can *afford* much better than an aristocracy to follow out its convictions, and is perhaps better qualified to build those convictions on plain principles of right and wrong, rather than on the shifting sands of expediency. I had always thought "Sam Slick" a libel on the Yankee character, and a complete falsification of Yankee modes of speech, though, for aught I know, it may be true in both respects so far as the British provinces are concerned. To me the dialect was native, was spoken all about me when a boy, at a time when an Irish day-laborer was as rare as an American one now. Since then I have made a study of it so far as opportunity allowed. But when I write in it, it is as in a mother tongue, and I am carried back far beyond any studies of it

16. *quhair:* "Greene in his *Quip for an Upstart Courtier* says, 'to *square* it up and downe the streetes before his mistresse' " [L].

to long-ago noonings in my father's hay-fields, and to the talk of Sam and Job over their jug of *black-strap* under the shadow of the ash-tree which still dapples the grass whence they have been gone so long.

But life is short, and prefaces should be. And so, my good friends, to whom this introductory epistle is addressed, farewell. Though some of you have remonstrated with me, I shall never write any more "Biglow Papers," however great the temptation,—great especially at the present time,—unless it be to complete the original plan of this Series by bringing out Mr. Sawin as an "original Union man." The very favor with which they have been received is a hindrance to me, by forcing on me a self-consciousness from which I was entirely free when I wrote the First Series. Moreover, I am no longer the same careless youth, with nothing to do but live to myself, my books, and my friends, that I was then. I always hated politics, in the ordinary sense of the word, and I am not likely to grow fonder of them, now that I have learned how rare it is to find a man who can keep principle clear from party and personal prejudice, or can conceive the possibility of another's doing so. I feel as if I could in some sort claim to be an *emeritus,* and I am sure that political satire will have full justice done it by that genuine and delightful humorist, the Rev. Petroleum V. Nasby. I regret that I killed off Mr. Wilbur so soon, for he would have enabled me to bring into this preface a number of learned quotations, which must now go a-begging, and also enabled me to dispersonalize myself into a vicarious egotism. He would have helped me likewise in clearing myself from a charge which I shall briefly touch on, because my friend Mr. Hughes has found it needful to defend me in his preface to one of the English editions of "The Biglow Papers." I thank Mr. Hughes heartily for his friendly care of my good name, and were his Preface accessible to my readers here (as I am glad it is not, for its partiality makes me blush), I should leave the matter where he left it. The charge is of profanity, brought in by persons who proclaimed African slavery of Divine institution, and is based (so far as I have heard) on two passages in the First Series—

"An' you 've gut to git up airly,
Ef you want to take in God,"

and,

"God 'll send the bill to you,"

and on some Scriptural illustrations by Mr. Sawin.

Now, in the first place, I was writing under an assumed character, and must talk as the person would whose mouthpiece I made myself. Will any one familiar with the New England countryman venture to tell me that he does *not* speak of sacred things familiarly? that Biblical allusions (allusions, that is, to the single book with whose language, from his church-going habits, he is intimate) are *not* frequent on his lips? If so, he cannot have pursued his studies of the character on so many long-ago muster-fields and at so many cattle-shows as I. But I scorn any such line of defence, and will confess at once that one of the things I am proud of in my countrymen is (I am not speaking now of such persons as I have assumed Mr. Sawin to be) that they do not put their Maker away far from them, or interpret the fear of God into being afraid of Him. The Talmudists had conceived a deep truth when they said, that "all things were in the power of God, save the fear of God"; and when people stand in great dread of an invisible power, I suspect they mistake quite another personage for the Deity. I might justify myself for the passages criticised by many parallel ones from Scripture, but I need not. The Reverend Homer Wilbur's note-books supply me with three apposite quotations. The first is from a Father of the Roman Church, the second from a Father of the Anglican, and the third from a Father of Modern English poetry. The Puritan divines would furnish me with many more such. St. Bernard says, *Sapiens nummularius est Deus: nummum fictum non recipiet;* "A cunning money-changer is God: he will take in no base coin." Latimer says, "You shall perceive that God, by this example, shaketh us by the noses and taketh us by the ears." Familiar enough, both of them, one would say! But I should think Mr. Biglow had verily stolen the last of the two maligned passages from Dryden's "Don Sebastian," where I find

"And beg of Heaven to charge the bill on me!"

And there I leave the matter, being willing to believe that the Saint, the Martyr, and even the Poet, were as careful of God's honor as my critics are ever likely to be.

FITZ ADAM'S STORY

◇

❡ AS EARLY as 1849 Lowell projected a long verse narrative, to be called "The Nooning," made up of stories told ostensibly by a group of his friends and himself, the framework and design of the whole resembling that of the *Canterbury Tales*. Only fragments of the work survive (see Scudder's note in the Cambridge edition, pp. 411–12), and of these "Fitz Adam's Story" is the only complete tale. It belongs not only to the American local color movement, but to the tradition, best exemplified in frontier humor, of the vernacular tale recorded by a cultivated observer.

◇

The next whose fortune 't was a tale to tell
Was one whom men, before they thought, loved well,
And after thinking wondered why they did,
For half he seemed to let them, half forbid,
And wrapped him so in humors, sheath on sheath,
'T was hard to guess the mellow soul beneath;
But, once divined, you took him to your heart,
While he appeared to bear with you as part
Of life's impertinence, and once a year
Betrayed his true self by a smile or tear,
Or rather something sweetly-shy and loath,
Withdrawn ere fully shown, and mixed of both.
A cynic? Not precisely: one who thrust
Against a heart too prone to love and trust,
Who so despised false sentiment he knew
Scarce in himself to part the false and true,
And strove to hide, by roughening-o'er the skin,
Those cobweb nerves he could not dull within.
Gentle by birth, but of a stem decayed,
He shunned life's rivalries and hated trade;
On a small patrimony and larger pride,
He lived uneaseful on the Other Side
(So he called Europe), only coming West
To give his Old-World appetite new zest;
Yet still the New World spooked it in his veins,
A ghost he could not lay with all his pains;
For never Pilgrims' offshoot scapes control
Of those old instincts that have shaped his soul.
A radical in thought, he puffed away
With shrewd contempt the dust of usage gray,
Yet loathed democracy as one who saw,
In what he longed to love, some vulgar flaw,
And, shocked through all his delicate reserves,
Remained a Tory by his taste and nerves.
His fancy's thrall, he drew all ergoes thence,
And thought himself the type of common sense;
Misliking women, not from cross or whim,
But that his mother shared too much in him,
And he half felt that what in them was grace
Made the unlucky weakness of his race.
What powers he had he hardly cared to know,
But sauntered through the world as through a show;
A critic fine in his haphazard way,
A sort of mild La Bruyère on half-pay.
For comic weaknesses he had an eye
Keen as an acid for an alkali,
Yet you could feel, through his sardonic tone,
He loved them all, unless they were his own.
You might have called him, with his humorous twist,
A kind of human entomologist:
As these bring home, from every walk they take,
Their hat-crowns stuck with bugs of curious make,
So he filled all the lining of his head
With characters impaled and ticketed,
And had a cabinet behind his eyes
For all they caught of mortal oddities.
He might have been a poet—many worse—
But that he had, or feigned, contempt of verse;
Called it tattooing language, and held rhymes
The young world's lullaby of ruder times.
Bitter in words, too indolent for gall,
He satirized himself the first of all,
In men and their affairs could find no law,
And was the ill logic that he thought he saw.

Scratching a match to light his pipe anew,
With eyes half shut some musing whiffs he drew
And thus began: "I give you all my word,
I think this mock-Decameron absurd;
Boccaccio's garden! how bring that to pass
In our bleak clime save under double glass?
The moral east-wind of New England life
Would snip its gay luxuriance like a knife;
Mile-deep the glaciers brooded here, they say,
Through æons numb; we feel their chill to-day.
These foreign plants are but half-hardy still,
Die on a south, and on a north wall chill.
Had we stayed Puritans! *They* had some heat,
(Though whence derived I have my own conceit,)
But you have long ago raked up their fires;
Where they had faith, you 've ten sham-Gothic spires.
Why more exotics? Try your native vines,
And in some thousand years you *may* have wines;
Your present grapes are harsh, all pulps and skins,
And want traditions of ancestral bins
That saved for evenings round the polished board
Old lava-fires, the sun-steeped hillside's hoard.
Without a Past, you lack that southern wall
O'er which the vines of Poesy should crawl;
Still they 're your only hope; no midnight oil
Makes up for virtue wanting in the soil;
Manure them well and prune them; 't won't be France,
Nor Spain, nor Italy, but there 's your chance.
You have one story-teller worth a score

FITZ ADAM'S STORY. 93–95. **story-teller . . . hawthorn:** The reference is to Nathaniel Hawthorne.

Of dead Boccaccios,—nay, add twenty more,—
A hawthorn asking spring's most dainty breath,
And him you 're freezing pretty well to death.
However, since you say so, I will tease
My memory to a story by degrees,
Though you will cry, 'Enough!' I'm well-nigh sure,
Ere I have dreamed through half my overture.
Stories were good for men who had no books,
(Fortunate race!) and built their nests like rooks
In lonely towers, to which the Jongleur brought
His pedler's-box of cheap and tawdry thought,
With here and there a fancy fit to see
Wrought in quaint grace in golden filigree,—
Some ring that with the Muse's finger yet
Is warm, like Aucassin and Nicolete;
The morning newspaper has spoilt his trade,
(For better or for worse, I leave unsaid,)
And stories now, to suit a public nice,
Must be half epigram, half pleasant vice.

"All tourists know Shebagog County: there
The summer idlers take their yearly stare,
Dress to see Nature in a well-bred way,
As 't were Italian opera, or play,
Encore the sunrise (if they 're out of bed),
And pat the Mighty Mother on the head:
These have I seen,—all things are good to see,—
And wondered much at their complacency.
This world's great show, that took in getting-up
Millions of years, they finish ere they sup;
Sights that God gleams through with soul-tingling force
They glance approvingly as things of course,
Say, 'That 's a grand rock,' 'This a pretty fall,'
Not thinking, 'Are we worthy?' What if all
The scornful landscape should turn round and say,
'This is a fool, and that a popinjay'?
I often wonder what the Mountain thinks
Of French boots creaking o'er his breathless brinks,
Or how the Sun would scare the chattering crowd,
If some fine day he chanced to think aloud.
I, who love Nature much as sinners can,
Love her where she most grandeur shows,—in man:
Here find I mountain, forest, cloud, and sun,
River and sea, and glows when day is done;
Nay, where she makes grotesques, and moulds in jest
The clown's cheap clay, I find unfading zest.
The natural instincts year by year retire,
As deer shrink northward from the settler's fire,
And he who loves the wild game-flavor more
Than city-feasts, where every man's a bore
To every other man, must seek it where
The steamer's throb and railway's iron blare
Have not yet startled with their punctual stir
The shy, wood-wandering brood of Character.

"There is a village, once the county town,
Through which the weekly mail rolled dustily down,
Where the courts sat, it may be, twice a year,
And the one tavern reeked with rustic cheer;
Cheeshogquesumscot erst, now Jethro hight,
Red-man and pale-face bore it equal spite.
The railway ruined it, the natives say,
That passed unwisely fifteen miles away,
And made a drain to which, with steady ooze,
Filtered away law, stage-coach, trade, and news.
The railway saved it; so at least think those
Who love old ways, old houses, old repose.
Of course the Tavern stayed: its genial host
Thought not of flitting more than did the post
On which high-hung the fading signboard creaks,
Inscribed, 'The Eagle Inn, by Ezra Weeks.'

"If in life's journey you should ever find
An inn medicinal for body and mind,
'T is sure to be some drowsy-looking house
Whose easy landlord has a bustling spouse:
He, if he like you, will not long forego
Some bottle deep in cobwebbed dust laid low,
That, since the War we used to call the 'Last,'
Has dozed and held its lang-syne memories fast:
From him exhales that Indian-summer air
Of hazy, lazy welcome everywhere,
While with her toil the napery is white,
The china dustless, the keen knife-blades bright,
Salt dry as sand, and bread that seems as though
'T were rather sea-foam baked than vulgar dough.

"In our swift country, houses trim and white
Are pitched like tents, the lodging of a night;
Each on its bank of baked turf mounted high
Perches impatient o'er the roadside dry,
While the wronged landscape coldly stands aloof,
Refusing friendship with the upstart roof.
Not so the Eagle; on a grass-green swell
That toward the south with sweet concessions fell
It dwelt retired, and half had grown to be
As aboriginal as rock or tree.
It nestled close to earth, and seemed to brood
O'er homely thoughts in a half-conscious mood,
As by the peat that rather fades than burns
The smouldering grandam nods and knits by turns,
Happy, although her newest news were old
Ere the first hostile drum at Concord rolled.
If paint it e'er had known, it knew no more

Than yellow lichens spattered thickly o'er
That soft lead-gray, less dark beneath the eaves
Which the slow brush of wind and weather leaves.
The ample roof sloped backward to the ground,
And vassal lean-tos gathered thickly round,
Patched on, as sire or son had felt the need,
Like chance growths sprouting from the old roof's seed,
Just as about a yellow-pine-tree spring
Its rough-barked darlings in a filial ring.
But the great chimney was the central thought
Whose gravitation through the cluster wrought;
For 't is not styles far-fetched from Greece or Rome,
But just the Fireside, that can make a home;
None of your spindling things of modern style,
Like pins stuck through to stay the card-built pile,
It rose broad shouldered, kindly, debonair,
Its warm breath whitening in the October air,
While on its front a heart in outline showed
The place it filled in that serene abode.

"When first I chanced the Eagle to explore,
Ezra sat listless by the open door;
One chair careened him at an angle meet,
Another nursed his hugely-slippered feet;
Upon a third reposed a shirt-sleeved arm,
And the whole man diffused tobacco's charm.
'Are you the landlord?' 'Wahl, I guess I be,'
Watching the smoke, he answered leisurely.
He was a stoutish man, and through the breast
Of his loose shirt there showed a brambly chest;
Streaked redly as a wind-foreboding morn,
His tanned cheeks curved to temples closely shorn;
Clean-shaved he was, save where a hedge of gray
Upon his brawny throat leaned every way
About an Adam's-apple, that beneath
Bulged like a boulder from a brambly heath.
The Western World's true child and nursling he,
Equipt with aptitudes enough for three:
No eye like his to value horse or cow,
Or gauge the contents of a stack or mow;
He could foretell the weather at a word,
He knew the haunt of every beast and bird,
Or where a two-pound trout was sure to lie,
Waiting the flutter of his home-made fly;
Nay, once in autumns five, he had the luck
To drop at fair-play range a ten-tined buck;
Of sportsmen true he favored every whim,
But never cockney found a guide in him;
A natural man, with all his instincts fresh,
Not buzzing helpless in Reflection's mesh,
Firm on its feet stood his broad-shouldered mind,
As bluffly honest as a northwest wind;
Hard-headed and soft-hearted, you 'd scarce meet
A kindlier mixture of the shrewd and sweet;
Generous by birth, and ill at saying 'No,'
Yet in a bargain he was all men's foe,
Would yield no inch of vantage in a trade,
And give away ere nightfall all he made.

" 'Can I have lodging here?' once more I said.
He blew a whiff, and, leaning back his head,
'You come a piece through Bailey's woods, I s'pose,
Acrost a bridge where a big swamp-oak grows?
It don't grow, neither; it 's ben dead ten year,
Nor th' ain't a livin' creetur, fur nor near,
Can tell wut killed it; but I some misdoubt
'T was borers, there 's sech heaps on 'em about.
You did n' chance to run ag'inst my son,
A long, slab-sided youngster with a gun?
He 'd oughto ben back more 'n an hour ago,
An' brought some birds to dress for supper—sho!
There he comes now. 'Say, Obed, wut ye got?
(He 'll hev some upland plover like as not.)
Wal, them 's real nice uns, an 'll eat A 1,
Ef I can stop their bein' over-done;
Nothin' riles *me* (I pledge my fastin' word)
Like cookin' out the natur' of a bird;
(Obed, you pick 'em out o' sight an' sound,
Your ma'am don't love no feathers cluttrin' round;)
Jes' scare 'em with the coals,—thet 's *my* idee.'
Then, turning suddenly about on me,
'Wal, Square, I guess so. Callilate to stay?
I'll ask Mis' Weeks; 'bout *thet* it's hern to say.'

"Well, there I lingered all October through,
In that sweet atmosphere of hazy blue,
So leisurely, so soothing, so forgiving,
That sometimes makes New England fit for living.
I watched the landscape, erst so granite glum,
Bloom like the south side of a ripening plum,
And each rock-maple on the hillside make
His ten days' sunset doubled in the lake;
The very stone walls draggling up the hills
Seemed touched, and wavered in their roundhead wills.
Ah! there 's a deal of sugar in the sun!
Tap me in Indian summer, I should run
A juice to make rock-candy of,—but then
We get such weather scarce one year in ten.

"There was a parlor in the house, a room
To make you shudder with its prudish gloom.
The furniture stood round with such an air,
There seemed an old maid's ghost in every chair,
Which looked as it had scuttled to its place
And pulled extempore a Sunday face,

Too smugly proper for a world of sin,
Like boys on whom the minister comes in.
The table, fronting you with icy stare,
Strove to look witless that its legs were bare,
While the black sofa with its horse-hair pall
Gloomed like a bier for Comfort's funeral.
Each piece appeared to do its chilly best
To seem an utter stranger to the rest,
As if acquaintanceship were deadly sin,
Like Britons meeting in a foreign inn.
Two portraits graced the wall in grimmest truth,
Mister and Mistress W. in their youth,—
New England youth, that seems a sort of pill,
Half wish-I-dared, half Edwards on the Will,
Bitter to swallow, and which leaves a trace
Of Calvinistic colic on the face.
Between them, o'er the mantel, hung in state
Solomon's temple, done in copperplate;
Invention pure, but meant, we may presume,
To give some Scripture sanction to the room.
Facing this last, two samplers you might see,
Each, with its urn and stiffly-weeping tree,
Devoted to some memory long ago
More faded than their lines of worsted woe;
Cut paper decked their frames against the flies,
Though none e'er dared an entrance who were wise,
And bushed asparagus in fading green
Added its shiver to the franklin clean.

"When first arrived, I chilled a half-hour there,
Nor dared deflower with use a single chair;
I caught no cold, yet flying pains could find
For weeks in me,—a rheumatism of mind.
One thing alone imprisoned there had power
To hold me in the place that long half-hour:
A scutcheon this, a helm-surmounted shield,
Three griffins argent on a sable field;
A relic of the shipwrecked past was here,
And Ezra held some Old-World lumber dear.
Nay, do not smile; I love this kind of thing,
These cooped traditions with a broken wing,
This freehold nook in Fancy's pipe-blown ball,
This less than nothing that is more than all!
Have I not seen sweet natures kept alive
Amid the humdrum of your business hive,
Undowered spinsters shielded from all harms,
By airy incomes from a coat of arms?"

He paused a moment, and his features took
The flitting sweetness of that inward look
I hinted at before; but, scarcely seen,
It shrank for shelter 'neath his harder mien,
And, rapping his black pipe of ashes clear,
He went on with a self-derisive sneer:
"No doubt we make a part of God's design,
And break the forest-path for feet divine;
To furnish foothold for this grand prevision
Is good, and yet—to be the mere transition,
That, you will say, is also good, though I
Scarce like to feed the ogre By-and-by.
Raw edges rasp my nerves; my taste is wooed
By things that are, not going to be, good,
Though were I what I dreamed two lustres gone,
I 'd stay to help the Consummation on,
Whether a new Rome than the old more fair,
Or a deadflat of rascal-ruled despair;
But *my* skull somehow never closed the suture
That seems to knit yours firmly with the future,
So you 'll excuse me if I 'm sometimes fain
To tie the Past's warm nightcap o'er my brain;
I 'm quite aware 't is not in fashion here,
But then your northeast winds are *so* severe!

"But to my story: though 't is truly naught
But a few hints in Memory's sketchbook caught,
And which may claim a value on the score
Of calling back some scenery now no more.
Shall I confess? The tavern's only Lar
Seemed (be not shocked!) its homely-featured bar
Here dozed a fire of beechen logs, that bred
Strange fancies in its embers golden-red,
And nursed the loggerhead whose hissing dip,
Timed by nice instinct, creamed the mug of flip
That made from mouth to mouth its genial round,
Nor left one nature wholly winter-bound;
Hence dropt the tinkling coal all mellow-ripe
For Uncle Reuben's talk-extinguished pipe;
Hence rayed the heat, as from an indoor sun,
That wooed forth many a shoot of rustic fun.
Here Ezra ruled as king by right divine;
No other face had such a wholesome shine,
No laugh like his so full of honest cheer;
Above the rest it crowed like Chanticleer.

"In this one room his dame you never saw,
Where reigned by custom old a Salic law;
Here coatless lolled he on his throne of oak,
And every tongue paused midway if he spoke.
Due mirth he loved, yet was his sway severe;
No blear-eyed driveller got his stagger here;
'Measure was happiness; who wanted more,
Must buy his ruin at the Deacon's store;'

308. the Will: the theologian Jonathan Edwards' famous treatise, *Freedom of the Will* (1754). **322. franklin:** an open iron stove invented by Benjamin Franklin.

369. Lar: singular of *lares* in Roman religion, images of household gods. Originally, the *lar* was a youth carrying a cup and a drinking horn. **385–86. In . . . law:** The code of laws of the Salian Franks excluded women from inheriting land.

None but his lodgers after ten could stay,
Nor after nine on eves of Sabbath-day.
He had his favorites and his pensioners,
The same that gypsy Nature owns for hers:
Loose-ended souls, whose skills bring scanty gold,
And whom the poor-house catches when they 're old;
Rude country-minstrels, men who doctor kine,
Or graft, and, out of scions ten, save nine;
Creatures of genius they, but never meant
To keep step with the civic regiment.
These Ezra welcomed, feeling in his mind
Perhaps some motions of the vagrant kind;
These paid no money, yet for them he drew
Special Jamaica from a tap they knew,
And, for their feelings, chalked behind the door
With solemn face a visionary score.
This thawed to life in Uncle Reuben's throat
A torpid shoal of jest and anecdote,
Like those queer fish that doze the droughts away,
And wait for moisture, wrapped in sun-baked clay;
This warmed the one-eyed fiddler to his task,
Perched in the corner on an empty cask,
By whose shrill art rapt suddenly, some boor
Rattled a double-shuffle on the floor;
'Hull's Victory' was, indeed, the favorite air,
Though 'Yankee Doodle' claimed its proper share.

"'T was there I caught from Uncle Reuben's lips,
In dribbling monologue 'twixt whiffs and sips,
The story I so long have tried to tell;
The humor coarse, the persons common,—well,
From Nature only do I love to paint,
Whether she send a satyr or a saint;
To me Sincerity 's the one thing good,
Soiled though she be and lost to maidenhood.
Quompegan is a town some ten miles south
From Jethro, at Nagumscot river-mouth,
A seaport town, and makes its title good
With lumber and dried fish and eastern wood.
Here Deacon Bitters dwelt and kept the Store,
The richest man for many a mile of shore;
In little less than everything dealt he,
From meeting-houses to a chest of tea;
So dextrous therewithal a flint to skin,
He could make profit on a single pin;
In business strict, to bring the balance true
He had been known to bite a fig in two,
And change a board-nail for a shingle-nail.
All that he had he ready held for sale,
His house, his tomb, whate'er the law allows,
And he had gladly parted with his spouse.
His one ambition still to get and get,
He would arrest your very ghost for debt.
His store looked righteous, should the Parson come,
But in a dark back-room he peddled rum,
And eased Ma'am Conscience, if she e'er would scold,
By christening it with water ere he sold.
A small, dry man he was, who wore a queue,
And one white neckcloth all the week-days through,—
On Monday white, by Saturday as dun
As that worn homeward by the prodigal son.
His frosted earlocks, striped with foxy brown,
Were braided up to hide a desert crown;
His coat was brownish, black perhaps of yore;
In summer-time a banyan loose he wore;
His trousers short, through many a season true,
Made no pretence to hide his stockings blue;
A waistcoat buff his chief adornment was,
Its porcelain buttons rimmed with dusky brass.
A deacon he, you saw it in each limb,
And well he knew to deacon-off a hymn,
Or lead the choir through all its wandering woes
With voice that gathered unction in his nose,
Wherein a constant snuffle you might hear,
As if with him 't were winter all the year.
At pew-head sat he with decorous pains,
In sermon-time could foot his weekly gains,
Or, with closed eyes and heaven-abstracted air,
Could plan a new investment in long-prayer.
A pious man, and thrifty too, he made
The psalms and prophets partners in his trade,
And in his orthodoxy straitened more
As it enlarged the business at his store;
He honored Moses, but, when gain he planned,
Had his own notion of the Promised Land.

"Soon as the winter made the sledding good,
From far around the farmers hauled him wood,
For all the trade had gathered 'neath his thumb.
He paid in groceries and New England rum,
Making two profits with a conscience clear,—
Cheap all he bought, and all he paid with dear.
With his own mete-wand measuring every load,
Each somehow had diminished on the road;
An honest cord in Jethro still would fail
By a good foot upon the Deacon's scale,
And, more to abate the price, his gimlet eye
Would pierce to cat-sticks that none else could spy;
Yet none dared grumble, for no farmer yet
But New Year found him in the Deacon's debt.

462. **deacon-off:** Part of "the office of deacon was to read aloud the hymns *given out* by the minister, one line at a time, the congregation singing each line as soon as read" [L]. 488. **cat-sticks:** Crooked logs concealed in a load of wood took up extra space and therefore prevented honest measure.

"While the first snow was mealy under feet,
A team drawled creaking down Quompegan street.
Two cords of oak weighed down the grinding sled,
And cornstalk fodder rustled overhead;
The oxen's muzzles, as they shouldered through,
Were silver-fringed; the driver's own was blue
As the coarse frock that swung below his knee.
Behind his load for shelter waded he;
His mittened hands now on his chest he beat,
Now stamped the stiffened cowhides of his feet,
Hushed as a ghost's; his armpit scarce could hold
The walnut whipstock slippery-bright with cold.
What wonder if, the tavern as he past,
He looked and longed, and stayed his beasts at last,
Who patient stood and veiled themselves in steam
While he explored the bar-room's ruddy gleam?

"Before the fire, in want of thought profound,
There sat a brother-townsman weather-bound:
A sturdy churl, crisp-headed, bristly-eared,
Red as a pepper; 'twixt coarse brows and beard
His eyes lay ambushed, on the watch for fools,
Clear, gray, and glittering like two bay-edged pools;
A shifty creature, with a turn for fun,
Could swap a poor horse for a better one,—
He 'd a high-stepper always in his stall;
Liked far and near, and dreaded therewithal.
To him the in-comer, 'Perez, how d' ye do?'
'Jest as I 'm mind to, Obed; how do you?'
Then, his eyes twinkling such swift gleams as run
Along the levelled barrel of a gun
Brought to his shoulder by a man you know
Will bring his game down, he continued, 'So,
I s'pose you're haulin' wood? But you 're too late;
The Deacon 's off; Old Splitfoot could n't wait;
He made a bee-line las' night in the storm
To where he won't need wood to keep him warm.
'Fore this he 's treasurer of a fund to train
Young imps as missionaries; hopes to gain
That way a contract that he has in view
For fireproof pitchforks of a pattern new.
It must have tickled him, all drawbacks weighed,
To think he stuck the Old One in a trade;
His soul, to start with, was n't worth a carrot,
And all he 'd left 'ould hardly serve to swear at.'

"By this time Obed had his wits thawed out,
And, looking at the other half in doubt,
Took off his fox-skin cap to scratch his head,
Donned it again, and drawled forth, 'Mean he 's dead?'
'Jesso; he 's dead and t' other *d* that follers
With folks that never love a thing but dollars.
He pulled up stakes last evening, fair and square,
And ever since there 's been a row Down There.
The minute the old chap arrived, you see,
Comes the Boss-devil to him, and says he,
"What are you good at? Little enough, I fear;
We callilate to make folks useful here."
"Well," says old Bitters, "I expect I can
Scale a fair load of wood with e'er a man."
"Wood we don't deal in; but perhaps you 'll suit,
Because we buy our brimstone by the foot:
Here, take this measurin'-rod, as smooth as sin,
And keep a reckonin' of what loads comes in.
You 'll not want business, for we need a lot
To keep the Yankees that you send us hot;
At firin' up they 're barely half as spry
As Spaniards or Italians, though they 're dry;
At first we have to let the draught on stronger,
But, heat 'em through, they seem to hold it longer."

" 'Bitters he took the rod, and pretty soon
A teamster comes, whistling an ex-psalm tune.
A likelier chap you would n't ask to see,
No different, but his limp, from you or me'—
'No different, Perez! Don't your memory fail?
Why, where in thunder was his horns and tail?'
'They 're only worn by some old-fashioned pokes;
They mostly aim at looking just like folks.
Sech things are scarce as queues and top-boots here;
'T would spoil their usefulness to look too queer.
Ef you could always know 'em when they come,
They 'd get no purchase on you: now be mum.
On come the teamster, smart as Davy Crockett,
Jinglin' the red-hot coppers in his pocket,
And clost behind, ('t was gold-dust, you 'd ha' sworn,)
A load of sulphur yallower 'n seed-corn;
To see it wasted as it is Down There
Would make a Friction-Match Co. tear its hair!
"Hold on!" says Bitters, "stop right where you be;
You can't go in athout a pass from me."
"All right," says t' other, "only step round smart;
I must be home by noon-time with the cart."
Bitters goes round it sharp-eyed as a rat,
Then with a scrap of paper on his hat
Pretends to cipher. "By the public staff,
That load scarce rises twelve foot and a half."
"There 's fourteen foot and over," says the driver,
"Worth twenty dollars, ef it 's worth a stiver;

Good fourth-proof brimstone, that 'll make 'em squirm,—
I leave it to the Headman of the Firm;
After we masure it, we always lay
Some on to allow for settlin' by the way.
Imp and full-grown, I 've carted sulphur here,
And gi'n fair satisfaction, thirty year."
With that they fell to quarrellin' so loud
That in five minutes they had drawed a crowd,
And afore long the Boss, who heard the row,
Comes elbowin' in with "What 's to pay here now?"
Both parties heard, the measurin'-rod he takes,
And of the load a careful survey makes.
"Sence I have bossed the business here," says he,
"No fairer load was ever seen by me."
Then, turnin' to the Deacon, "You mean cus,
None of your old Quompegan tricks with us!
They won't do here: we 're plain old-fashioned folks,
And don't quite understand that kind o' jokes.
I know this teamster, and his pa afore him,
And the hard-working Mrs. D. that bore him;
He would n't soil his conscience with a lie,
Though he might get the custom-house thereby.
Here, constable, take Bitters by the queue,
And clap him into furnace ninety-two,
And try this brimstone on him; if he 's bright,
He 'll find the masure honest afore night.
He is n't worth his fuel, and I 'll bet
The parish oven has to take him yet!" '

"This is my tale, heard twenty years ago
From Uncle Reuben, as the logs burned low,
Touching the walls and ceiling with that bloom
That makes a rose's calyx of a room.
I could not give his language, wherethrough ran
The gamy flavor of the bookless man
Who shapes a word before the fancy cools,
As lonely Crusoe improvised his tools.
I liked the tale,—'t was like so many told
By Rutebeuf and his brother Trouvères bold;
Nor were the hearers much unlike to theirs,
Men unsophisticate, rude-nerved as bears.
Ezra is gone and his large-hearted kind,
The landlords of the hospitable mind;
Good Warriner of Springfield was the last;
An inn is now a vision of the past;
One yet-surviving host my mind recalls,—
You 'll find him if you go to Trenton Falls."

1867

THE DARKENED MIND

◊

❡ Lowell's mother suffered from mental illness.

◊

The fire is burning clear and blithely,
Pleasantly whistles the winter wind;
We are about thee, thy friends and kindred,
On us all flickers the firelight kind;
There thou sittest in thy wonted corner
Lone and awful in thy darkened mind.

There thou sittest; now and then thou moanest;
Thou dost talk with what we cannot see,
Lookest at us with an eye so doubtful,
It doth put us very far from thee;
There thou sittest; we would fain be nigh thee,
But we know that it can never be.

We can touch thee, still we are no nearer;
Gather round thee, still thou art alone;
The wide chasm of reason is between us;
Thou confutest kindness with a moan;
We can speak to thee, and thou canst answer,
Like two prisoners through a wall of stone.

Hardest heart would call it very awful
When thou look'st at us and seest—oh, what?
If we move away, thou sittest gazing
With those vague eyes at the selfsame spot,
And thou mutterest, thy hands thou wringest,
Seeing something,—us thou seest not.

Strange it is that, in this open brightness,
Thou shouldst sit in such a narrow cell;
Strange it is that thou shouldst be so lonesome
Where those are who love thee all so well;
Not so much of thee is left among us
As the hum outliving the hushed bell.

1868

THE CATHEDRAL

◊

❡ This poem—which Lowell orginally intended to entitle "A Day at Chartres"—was inspired by a visit to the cathedral in 1855, but it was not written until 1869. After publishing it in the *Atlantic Monthly* (January, 1870), Lowell revised it for separate printing in the same year. The main theme of the poem begins at line 176.

◆

Far through the memory shines a happy day,
Cloudless of care, down-shod to every sense,
And simply perfect from its own resource,
As to a bee the new campanula's
Illuminate seclusion swung in air.
Such days are not the prey of setting suns,
Nor ever blurred with mist of afterthought;
Like words made magical by poets dead,
Wherein the music of all meaning is
The sense hath garnered or the soul divined,
They mingle with our life's ethereal part,
Sweetening and gathering sweetness evermore,
By beauty's franchise disenthralled of time.

I can recall, nay, they are present still,
Parts of myself, the perfume of my mind,
Days that seem farther off than Homer's now
Ere yet the child had loudened to the boy,
And I, recluse from playmates, found perforce
Companionship in things that not denied
Nor granted wholly; as is Nature's wont,
Who, safe in uncontaminate reserve,
Lets us mistake our longing for her love,
And mocks with various echo of ourselves.

These first sweet frauds upon our consciousness,
That blend the sensual with its imaged world,
These virginal cognitions, gifts of morn,
Ere life grow noisy, and slower-footed thought
Can overtake the rapture of the sense,
To thrust between ourselves and what we feel,
Have something in them secretly divine.
Vainly the eye, once schooled to serve the brain,
With pains deliberate studies to renew
The ideal vision: second-thoughts are prose;
For beauty's acme hath a term as brief
As the wave's poise before it break in pearl.
Our own breath dims the mirror of the sense,
Looking too long and closely: at a flash
We snatch the essential grace of meaning out,
And that first passion beggars all behind,
Heirs of a tamer transport prepossessed.
Who, seeing once, has truly seen again
The gray vague of unsympathizing sea
That dragged his Fancy from her moorings back
To shores inhospitable of eldest time,
Till blank foreboding of earth-gendered powers,
Pitiless seignories in the elements,
Omnipotences blind that darkling smite,
Misgave him, and repaganized the world?
Yet, by some subtler touch of sympathy,
These primal apprehensions, dimly stirred,
Perplex the eye with pictures from within.
This hath made poets dream of lives foregone
In worlds fantastical, more fair than ours;
So Memory cheats us, glimpsing half-revealed.
Even as I write she tries her wonted spell
In that continuous redbreast boding rain:
The bird I hear sings not from yonder elm;
But the flown ecstasy my childhood heard
Is vocal in my mind, renewed by him,
Haply made sweeter by the accumulate thrill
That threads my undivided life and steals
A pathos from the years and graves between.

I know not how it is with other men,
Whom I but guess, deciphering myself;
For me, once felt is so felt nevermore.
The fleeting relish at sensation's brim
Had in it the best ferment of the wine.
One spring I knew as never any since:
All night the surges of the warm southwest
Boomed intermittent through the wallowing elms,
And brought a morning from the Gulf adrift,
Omnipotent with sunshine, whose quick charm
Startled with crocuses the sullen turf
And wiled the bluebird to his whiff of song:
One summer hour abides, what time I perched,
Dappled with noonday, under simmering leaves,
And pulled the pulpy oxhearts, while aloof
An oriole clattered and the robins shrilled,
Denouncing me an alien and a thief:
One morn of autumn lords it o'er the rest,
When in the lane I watched the ash-leaves fall,
Balancing softly earthward without wind,
Or twirling with directer impulse down
On those fallen yesterday, now barbed with frost,
While I grew pensive with the pensive year:
And once I learned how marvellous winter was,
When past the fence-rails, downy-gray with rime,
I creaked adventurous o'er the spangled crust
That made familiar fields seem far and strange
As those stark wastes that whiten endlessly
In ghastly solitude about the pole,
And gleam relentless to the unsetting sun:
Instant the candid chambers of my brain
Were painted with these sovran images;
And later visions seem but copies pale
From those unfading frescos of the past,
Which I, young savage, in my age of flint,
Gazed at, and dimly felt a power in me
Parted from Nature by the joy in her
That doubtfully revealed me to myself.
Thenceforward I must stand outside the gate;

And paradise was paradise the more,
Known once and barred against satiety.

What we call Nature, all outside ourselves,
Is but our own conceit of what we see,
Our own reaction upon what we feel;
The world's a woman to our shifting mood,
Feeling with us, or making due pretence;
And therefore we the more persuade ourselves
To make all things our thought's confederates,
Conniving with us in whate'er we dream.
So when our Fancy seeks analogies,
Though she have hidden what she after finds,
She loves to cheat herself with feigned surprise.
I find my own complexion everywhere:
No rose, I doubt, was ever, like the first,
A marvel to the bush it dawned upon,
The rapture of its life made visible,
The mystery of its yearning realized,
As the first babe to the first woman born;
No falcon ever felt delight of wings
As when, an eyas, from the stolid cliff
Loosing himself, he followed his high heart
To swim on sunshine, masterless as wind;
And I believe the brown earth takes delight
In the new snowdrop looking back at her,
To think that by some vernal alchemy
It could transmute her darkness into pearl;
What is the buxom peony after that,
With its coarse constancy of hoyden blush?
What the full summer to that wonder new?

But, if in nothing else, in us there is
A sense fastidious hardly reconciled
To the poor makeshifts of life's scenery,
Where the same slide must double all its parts,
Shoved in for Tarsus and hitched back for Tyre.
I blame not in the soul this daintiness,
Rasher of surfeit than a humming-bird,
In things indifferent by sense purveyed;
It argues her an immortality
And dateless incomes of experience,
This unthrift housekeeping that will not brook
A dish warmed-over at the feast of life,
And finds Twice stale, served with whatever sauce.
Nor matters much how it may go with me
Who dwell in Grub Street and am proud to drudge
Where men, my betters, wet their crust with tears:
Use can make sweet the peach's shady side,
That only by reflection tastes of sun.

But she, my Princess, who will sometimes deign
My garret to illumine till the walls,
Narrow and dingy, scrawled with hackneyed thought
(Poor Richard slowly elbowing Plato out),
Dilate and drape themselves with tapestries
Nausikaa might have stooped o'er, while, between,
Mirrors, effaced in their own clearness, send
Her only image on through deepening deeps
With endless repercussion of delight,—
Bringer of life, witching each sense to soul,
That sometimes almost gives me to believe
I might have been a poet, gives at least
A brain desaxonized, an ear that makes
Music where none is, and a keener pang
Of exquisite surmise outleaping thought,—
Her will I pamper in her luxury:
No crumpled rose-leaf of too careless choice
Shall bring a northern nightmare to her dreams,
Vexing with sense of exile; hers shall be
The invitiate firstlings of experience,
Vibrations felt but once and felt life long:
Oh, more than half-way turn that Grecian front
Upon me, while with self-rebuke I spell,
On the plain fillet that confines thy hair
In conscious bounds of seeming unconstraint,
The *Naught in overplus,* thy race's badge!

One feast for her I secretly designed
In that Old World so strangely beautiful
To us the disinherited of eld,—
A day at Chartres, with no soul beside
To roil with pedant prate my joy serene
And make the minster shy of confidence.
I went, and, with the Saxon's pious care,
First ordered dinner at the pea-green inn,
The flies and I its only customers.
Eluding these, I loitered through the town,
With hope to take my minster unawares
In its grave solitude of memory.
A pretty burgh, and such as Fancy loves
For bygone grandeurs, faintly rumorous now

THE CATHEDRAL. **184. customers:** The following lines were omitted from every edition after the first because they offended Sir Leslie Stephen, an English friend of Lowell:

> Till by and by there came two Englishmen,
> Who made me feel, in their engaging way,
> I was a poacher on their self-preserve,
> Intent constructively on lese-anglicism.
> To them (in those old razor-ridden days)
> My beard translated me to hostile French;
> So they, desiring guidance in the town,
> Half condescended to my baser sphere,
> And clubbing in one mess their lack of phrase,
> Set their best man to grapple with the Gaul.
> '*Esker vous ate a nabitang?*' he asked;
> 'I never ate one; are they good?' asked I;
> Whereat they stared, then laughed, and we were friends,
> The seas, the wars, the centuries interposed,
> Abolished in the truce of common speech
> And mutual comfort of the mother-tongue.
> Like escaped convicts of Propriety,
> They furtively partook the joys of men,
> Glancing behind when buzzed some louder fly.

Upon the mind's horizon, as of storm
Brooding its dreamy thunders far aloof,
That mingle with our mood, but not disturb.
Its once grim bulwarks, tamed to lovers' walks,
Look down unwatchful on the sliding Eure,
Whose listless leisure suits the quiet place,
Lisping among his shallows homelike sounds
At Concord and by Bankside heard before.
Chance led me to a public pleasure-ground,
Where I grew kindly with the merry groups,
And blessed the Frenchman for his simple art
Of being domestic in the light of day.
His language has no word, we growl, for Home;
But he can find a fireside in the sun,
Play with his child, make love, and shriek his mind,
By throngs of strangers undisprivacied.
He makes his life a public gallery,
Nor feels himself till what he feels comes back
In manifold reflection from without;
While we, each pore alert with consciousness,
Hide our best selves as we had stolen them,
And each bystander a detective were,
Keen-eyed for every chink of undisguise.

So, musing o'er the problem which was best,—
A life wide-windowed, shining all abroad,
Or curtains drawn to shield from sight profane
The rites we pay to the mysterious I,—
With outward senses furloughed and head bowed
I followed some fine instinct in my feet,
Till, to unbend me from the loom of thought,
Looking up suddenly, I found mine eyes
Confronted with the minster's vast repose.
Silent and gray as forest-leaguered cliff
Left inland by the ocean's slow retreat,
That hears afar the breeze-borne rote and longs,
Remembering shocks of surf that clomb and fell,
Spume-sliding down the baffled decuman,
It rose before me, patiently remote
From the great tides of life it breasted once,
Hearing the noise of men as in a dream.
I stood before the triple northern port,
Where dedicated shapes of saints and kings,
Stern faces bleared with immemorial watch,
Looked down benignly grave and seemed to say,
Ye come and go incessant; we remain
Safe in the hallowed quiets of the past;
Be reverent, ye who flit and are forgot,
Of faith so nobly realized as this.
I seem to have heard it said by learnèd folk
Who drench you with æsthetics till you feel
As if all beauty were a ghastly bore,
The faucet to let loose a wash of words,
That Gothic is not Grecian, therefore worse;
But, being convinced by much experiment
How little inventiveness there is in man,
Grave copier of copies, I give thanks
For a new relish, careless to inquire
My pleasure's pedigree, if so it please,
Nobly, I mean, nor renegade to art.
The Grecian gluts me with its perfectness,
Unanswerable as Euclid, self-contained,
The one thing finished in this hasty world,
Forever finished, though the barbarous pit,
Fanatical on hearsay, stamp and shout
As if a miracle could be encored.
But ah! this other, this that never ends,
Still climbing, luring fancy still to climb,
As full of morals half-divined as life,
Graceful, grotesque, with ever new surprise
Of hazardous caprices sure to please,
Heavy as nightmare, airy-light as fern,
Imagination's very self in stone!
With one long sigh of infinite release
From pedantries past, present, or to come,
I looked, and owned myself a happy Goth.
Your blood is mine, ye architects of dream,
Builders of aspiration incomplete,
So more consummate, souls self-confident,
Who felt your own thought worthy of record
In monumental pomp! No Grecian drop
Rebukes these veins that leap with kindred thrill,
After long exile, to the mother-tongue.
Ovid in Pontus, puling for his Rome
Of men invirile and disnatured dames
That poison sucked from the Attic bloom decayed,
Shrank with a shudder from the blue-eyed race
Whose force rough-handed should renew the world,
And from the dregs of Romulus express
Such wine as Dante poured, or he who blew
Roland's vain blast, or sang the Campeador
In verse that clanks like armor in the charge,
Homeric juice, though brimmed in Odin's horn.
And they could build, if not the columned fane
That from the height gleamed seaward many-hued,
Something more friendly with their ruder skies:
The gray spire, molten now in driving mist,
Now lulled with the incommunicable blue;
The carvings touched to meaning new with snow,

224. rote: Scudder (Cambridge edition of the poems) quotes Lowell as follows: " '*Rote* is a familiar word all along our seaboard to express that dull and continuous burden of the sea heard inland before or after a great storm. The root of the word may be in *rumpere*, but it is more likely in *rotare*, from the identity of this sea-music with that of the rote—a kind of hurdy-gurdy with which the jongleurs accompanied their song. It is one of those Elizabethan words which we New-Englanders have preserved along with so many others. It occurs in the "Mirror for Magistrates," "the sea's rote," which Nares, not understanding, would change to rore! It is not to be found in any provincial glossary, but I caught it alive at Beverly and the Isles of Shoals.' "

Or commented with fleeting grace of shade;
The statues, motley as man's memory,
Partial as that, so mixed of true and false,
History and legend meeting with a kiss
Across this bound-mark where their realms confine;
The painted windows, freaking gloom with glow,
Dusking the sunshine which they seem to cheer,
Meet symbol of the senses and the soul,
And the whole pile, grim with the Northman's thought
Of life and death, and doom, life's equal fee,—
These were before me: and I gazed abashed,
Child of an age that lectures, not creates,
Plastering our swallow-nests on the awful Past,
And twittering round the work of larger men,
As we had builded what we but deface.
Far up the great bells wallowed in delight,
Tossing their clangors o'er the heedless town,
To call the worshippers who never came,
Or women mostly, in loath twos and threes.
I entered, reverent of whatever shrine
Guards piety and solace for my kind
Or gives the soul a moment's truce of God,
And shared decorous in the ancient rite
My sterner fathers held idolatrous.
The service over, I was tranced in thought:
Solemn the deepening vaults, and most to me,
Fresh from the fragile realm of deal and paint,
Or brick mock-pious with a marble front;
Solemn the lift of high-embowered roof,
The clustered stems that spread in boughs disleaved,
Through which the organ blew a dream of storm,
Though not more potent to sublime with awe
And shut the heart up in tranquillity,
Than aisles to me familiar that o'erarch
The conscious silences of brooding woods,
Centurial shadows, cloisters of the elk:
Yet here was sense of undefined regret,
Irreparable loss, uncertain what:
Was all this grandeur but anachronism,
A shell divorced of its informing life,
Where the priest housed him like a hermit-crab,
An alien to that faith of elder days
That gathered round it this fair shape of stone?
Is old Religion but a spectre now,
Haunting the solitude of darkened minds,
Mocked out of memory by the sceptic day?
Is there no corner safe from peeping Doubt,
Since Gutenberg made thought cosmopolite
And stretched electric threads from mind to mind?
Nay, did Faith build this wonder? or did Fear,
That makes a fetish and misnames it God
(Blockish or metaphysic, matters not),
Contrive this coop to shut its tyrant in,
Appeased with playthings, that he might not harm?

I turned and saw a beldame on her knees;
With eyes astray, she told mechanic beads
Before some shrine of saintly womanhood,
Bribed intercessor with the far-off Judge:
Such my first thought, by kindlier soon rebuked,
Pleading for whatsoever touches life
With upward impulse: be He nowhere else,
God is in all that liberates and lifts,
In all that humbles, sweetens, and consoles:
Blessèd the natures shored on every side
With landmarks of hereditary thought!
Thrice happy they that wander not life long
Beyond near succor of the household faith,
The guarded fold that shelters, not confines!
Their steps find patience in familiar paths,
Printed with hope by loved feet gone before
Of parent, child, or lover, glorified
By simple magic of dividing Time.
My lids were moistened as the woman knelt,
And—was it will, or some vibration faint
Of sacred Nature, deeper than the will?—
My heart occultly felt itself in hers,
Through mutual intercession gently leagued.

Or was it not mere sympathy of brain?
A sweetness intellectually conceived
In simpler creeds to me impossible?
A juggle of that pity for ourselves
In others, which puts on such pretty masks
And snares self-love with bait of charity?
Something of all it might be, or of none:
Yet for a moment I was snatched away
And had the evidence of things not seen;
For one rapt moment; then it all came back,
This age that blots out life with question-marks,
This nineteenth century with its knife and glass
That make thought physical, and thrust far off
The Heaven, so neighborly with man of old,
To voids sparse-sown with alienated stars.

'T is irrecoverable, that ancient faith,
Homely and wholesome, suited to the time,
With rod or candy for child-minded men:
No theologic tube, with lens on lens
Of syllogism transparent, brings it near,—
At best resolving some new nebula,
Or blurring some fixed-star of hope to mist.
Science was Faith once; Faith were Science now,
Would she but lay her bow and arrows by
And arm her with the weapons of the time.
Nothing that keeps thought out is safe from thought.
For there 's no virgin-fort but self-respect,

And Truth defensive hath lost hold on God.
Shall we treat Him as if He were a child
That knew not His own purpose? nor dare trust
The Rock of Ages to their chemic tests,
Lest some day the all-sustaining base divine
Should fail from under us, dissolved in gas?
The armèd eye that with a glance discerns
In a dry blood-speck between ox and man
Stares helpless at this miracle called life,
This shaping potency behind the egg,
This circulation swift of deity,
Where suns and systems inconspicuous float
As the poor blood-disks in our mortal veins.
Each age must worship its own thought of God,
More or less earthy, clarifying still
With subsidence continuous of the dregs;
Nor saint nor sage could fix immutably
The fluent image of the unstable Best,
Still changing in their very hands that wrought:
To-day's eternal truth To-morrow proved
Frail as frost-landscapes on a window-pane.
Meanwhile Thou smiledst, inaccessible,
At Thought's own substance made a cage for Thought,
And Truth locked fast with her own master-key;
Nor didst Thou reck what image man might make
Of his own shadow on the flowing world;
The climbing instinct was enough for Thee.
Or wast Thou, then, an ebbing tide that left
Strewn with dead miracle those eldest shores,
For men to dry, and dryly lecture on,
Thyself thenceforth incapable of flood?
Idle who hopes with prophets to be snatched
By virtue in their mantles left below;
Shall the soul live on other men's report,
Herself a pleasing fable of herself?
Man cannot be God's outlaw if he would,
Nor so abscond him in the caves of sense
But Nature still shall search some crevice out
With messages of splendor from that Source
Which, dive he, soar he, baffles still and lures.
This life were brutish did we not sometimes
Have intimation clear of wider scope,
Hints of occasion infinite, to keep
The soul alert with noble discontent
And onward yearnings of unstilled desire;
Fruitless, except we now and then divined
A mystery of Purpose, gleaming through
The secular confusions of the world,
Whose will we darkly accomplish, doing ours.
No man can think nor in himself perceive,
Sometimes at waking, in the street sometimes,
Or on the hillside, always unforewarned,
A grace of being, finer than himself,
That beckons and is gone,—a larger life
Upon his own impinging, with swift glimpse
Of spacious circles luminous with mind,
To which the ethereal substance of his own
Seems but gross cloud to make that visible,
Touched to a sudden glory round the edge.
Who that hath known these visitations fleet
Would strive to make them trite and ritual?
I, that still pray at morning and at eve,
Loving those roots that feed us from the past,
And prizing more than Plato things I learned
At that best academe, a mother's knee,
Thrice in my life perhaps have truly prayed,
Thrice, stirred below my conscious self, have felt
That perfect disenthralment which is God;
Nor know I which to hold worst enemy,
Him who on speculation's windy waste
Would turn me loose, stript of the raiment warm
By Faith contrived against our nakedness,
Or him who, cruel-kind, would fain obscure,
With painted saints and paraphrase of God,
The soul's east-window of divine surprise.
Where others worship I but look and long;
For, though not recreant to my fathers' faith,
Its forms to me are weariness, and most
That drony vacuum of compulsory prayer,
Still pumping phrases for the Ineffable,
Though all the valves of memory gasp and wheeze.
Words that have drawn transcendent meanings up
From the best passion of all bygone time,
Steeped through with tears of triumph and remorse,
Sweet with all sainthood, cleansed in martyr-fires,
Can they, so consecrate and so inspired,
By repetition wane to vexing wind?
Alas! we cannot draw habitual breath
In the thin air of life's supremer heights,
We cannot make each meal a sacrament,
Nor with our tailors be disbodied souls,—
We men, too conscious of earth's comedy,
Who see two sides, with our posed selves debate,
And only for great stakes can be sublime!
Let us be thankful when, as I do here,
We can read Bethel on a pile of stones,
And, seeing where God *has* been, trust in Him.

Brave Peter Fischer there in Nuremberg,
Moulding Saint Sebald's miracles in bronze,
Put saint and stander-by in that quaint garb
Familiar to him in his daily walk,
Not doubting God could grant a miracle
Then and in Nuremberg, if so He would;
But never artist for three hundred years
Hath dared the contradiction ludicrous
Of supernatural in modern clothes.
Perhaps the deeper faith that is to come
Will see God rather in the strenuous doubt,

Than in the creed held as an infant's hand
Holds purposeless whatso is placed therein.

Say it is drift, not progress, none the less,
With the old sextant of the fathers' creed,
We shape our courses by new-risen stars,
And, still lip-loyal to what once was truth,
Smuggle new meanings under ancient names,
Unconscious perverts of the Jesuit, Time.
Change is the mask that all Continuance wears
To keep us youngsters harmlessly amused;
Meanwhile some ailing or more watchful child,
Sitting apart, sees the old eyes gleam out,
Stern, and yet soft with humorous pity too.
Whilere, men burnt men for a doubtful point,
As if the mind were quenchable with fire,
And Faith danced round them with her war-paint on,
Devoutly savage as an Iroquois;
Now Calvin and Servetus at one board
Snuff in grave sympathy a milder roast,
And o'er their claret settle Comte unread.
Fagot and stake were desperately sincere:
Our cooler martyrdoms are done in types;
And flames that shine in controversial eyes
Burn out no brains but his who kindles them.
This is no age to get cathedrals built:
Did God, then, wait for one in Bethlehem?
Worst is not yet: lo, where his coming looms,
Of earth's anarchic children latest born,
Democracy, a Titan who hath learned
To laugh at Jove's old-fashioned thunderbolts,—
Could he not also forge them, if he would?
He, better skilled, with solvents merciless,
Loosened in air and borne on every wind,
Saps unperceived: the calm Olympian height
Of ancient order feels its bases yield,
And pale gods glance for help to gods as pale.
What will be left of good or worshipful,
Of spiritual secrets, mysteries,
Of fair religion's guarded heritage,
Heirlooms of soul, passed downward unprofaned
From eldest Ind? This Western giant coarse,
Scorning refinements which he lacks himself,
Loves not nor heeds the ancestral hierarchies,
Each rank dependent on the next above
In orderly gradation fixed as fate.
King by mere manhood, nor allowing aught
Of holier unction than the sweat of toil;
In his own strength sufficient; called to solve,
On the rough edges of society,
Problems long sacred to the choicer few,
And improvise what elsewhere men receive
As gifts of deity; tough foundling reared
Where every man 's his own Melchisedek,
How make him reverent of a King of kings?
Or Judge self-made, executor of laws
By him not first discussed and voted on?
For him no tree of knowledge is forbid,
Or sweeter if forbid. How save the ark,
Or holy of holies, unprofaned a day
From his unscrupulous curiosity
That handles everything as if to buy,
Tossing aside what fabrics delicate
Suit not the rough-and-tumble of his ways?
What hope for those fine-nerved humanities
That made earth gracious once with gentler arts,
Now the rude hands have caught the trick of thought
And claim an equal suffrage with the brain?

The born disciple of an elder time,
(To me sufficient, friendlier than the new,)
Who in my blood feel motions of the Past,
I thank benignant nature most for this,—
A force of sympathy, or call it lack
Of character firm-planted, loosing me
From the pent chamber of habitual self
To dwell enlarged in alien modes of thought,
Haply distasteful, wholesomer for that,
And through imagination to possess,
As they were mine, the lives of other men.
This growth original of virgin soil,
By fascination felt in opposites,
Pleases and shocks, entices and perturbs.
In this brown-fisted rough, this shirt-sleeved Cid,
This backwoods Charlemagne of empires new,
Whose blundering heel instinctively finds out
The goutier foot of speechless dignities,
Who, meeting Cæsar's self, would slap his back,
Call him "Old Horse," and challenge to a drink,
My lungs draw braver air, my breast dilates
With ampler manhood, and I front both worlds,
Of sense and spirit, as my natural fiefs,
To shape and then reshape them as I will.
It was the first man's charter; why not mine?
How forfeit? when deposed in other hands?

Thou shudder'st, Ovid? Dost in him forebode
A new avatar of the large-limbed Goth,
To break, or seem to break, tradition's clue,
And chase to dreamland back thy gods dethroned?
I think man's soul dwells nearer to the east,
Nearer to morning's fountains than the sun;
Herself the source whence all tradition sprang,
Herself at once both labyrinth and clue.
The miracle fades out of history,
But faith and wonder and the primal earth
Are born into the world with every child.
Shall this self-maker with the prying eyes,
This creature disenchanted of respect
By the New World's new fiend, Publicity,

Whose testing thumb leaves everywhere its smutch,
Not one day feel within himself the need
Of loyalty to better than himself,
That shall ennoble him with the upward look?
Shall he not catch the Voice that wanders earth,
With spiritual summons, dreamed or heard,
As sometimes, just ere sleep seals up the sense,
We hear our mother call from deeps of Time,
And, waking, find it vision,—none the less
The benediction bides, old skies return,
And that unreal thing, preëminent,
Makes air and dream of all we see and feel?
Shall he divine no strength unmade of votes,
Inward, impregnable, found soon as sought,
Not cognizable of sense, o'er sense supreme?
Else were he desolate as none before.
His holy places may not be of stone,
Nor made with hands, yet fairer far than aught
By artist feigned or pious ardor reared,
Fit altars for who guards inviolate
Gods chosen seat, the sacred form of man.
Doubtless his church will be no hospital
For superannuate forms and mumping shams,
No parlor where men issue policies
Of life-assurance on the Eternal Mind,
Nor his religion but an ambulance
To fetch life's wounded and malingerers in,
Scorned by the strong; yet he, unconscious heir
To the influence sweet of Athens and of Rome,
And old Judæa's gift of secret fire,
Spite of himself shall surely learn to know
And worship some ideal of himself,
Some divine thing, large-hearted, brotherly,
Not nice in trifles, a soft creditor,
Pleased with his world, and hating only cant.
And, if his Church be doubtful, it is sure
That, in a world, made for whatever else,
Not made for mere enjoyment, in a world
Of toil but half-requited, or, at best,
Paid in some futile currency of breath,
A world of incompleteness, sorrow swift
And consolation laggard, whatsoe'er
The form of building or the creed professed,
The Cross, bold type of shame to homage turned,
Of an unfinished life that sways the world,
Shall tower as sovereign emblem over all.

The kobold Thought moves with us when we shift
Our dwelling to escape him; perched aloft
On the first load of household-stuff he went;
For, where the mind goes, goes old furniture.
I, who to Chartres came to feed my eye
And give to Fancy one clear holiday,
Scarce saw the minster for the thoughts it stirred
Buzzing o'er past and future with vain quest.
Here once there stood a homely wooden church,
Which slow devotion nobly changed for this
That echoes vaguely to my modern steps.
By suffrage universal it was built,
As practised then, for all the country came
From far as Rouen, to give votes for God,
Each vote a block of stone securely laid
Obedient to the master's deep-mused plan.
Will what our ballots rear, responsible
To no grave forethought, stand so long as this?
Delight like this the eye of after days
Brightening with pride that here, at least, were men
Who meant and did the noblest thing they knew?
Can our religion cope with deeds like this?
We, too, build Gothic contract-shams, because
Our deacons have discovered that it pays,
And pews sell better under vaulted roofs
Of plaster painted like an Indian squaw.
Shall not that Western Goth, of whom we spoke,
So fiercely practical, so keen of eye,
Find out, some day, that nothing pays but God,
Served whether on the smoke-shut battlefield,
In work obscure done honestly, or vote
For truth unpopular, or faith maintained
To ruinous convictions, or good deeds
Wrought for good's sake, mindless of heaven or hell?
Shall he not learn that all prosperity,
Whose bases stretch not deeper than the sense,
Is but a trick of this world's atmosphere,
A desert-born mirage of spire and dome,
Or find too late, the Past's long lesson missed,
That dust the prophets shake from off their feet
Grows heavy to drag down both tower and wall?
I know not; but, sustained by sure belief
That man still rises level with the height
Of noblest opportunities, or makes
Such, if the time supply not, I can wait.
I gaze round on the windows, pride of France,
Each the bright gift of some mechanic guild
Who loved their city and thought gold well spent
To make her beautiful with piety;
I pause, transfigured by some stripe of bloom,
And my mind throngs with shining auguries,
Circle on circle, bright as seraphim,
With golden trumpets, silent, that await
The signal to blow news of good to men.

Then the revulsion came that always comes
After these dizzy elations of the mind:
And with a passionate pang of doubt I cried,
"O mountain-born, sweet with snow-filtered air
From uncontaminate wells of ether drawn
And never-broken secrecies of sky,
Freedom, with anguish won, misprized till lost,
They keep thee not who from thy sacred eyes

Catch the consuming lust of sensual good
And the brute's license of unfettered will.
Far from the popular shout and venal breath
Of Cleon blowing the mob's baser mind
To bubbles of wind-piloted conceit,
Thou shrinkest, gathering up thy skirts, to hide
In fortresses of solitary thought
And private virtue strong in self-restraint.
Must we too forfeit thee misunderstood,
Content with names, nor inly wise to know
That best things perish of their own excess,
And quality o'er-driven becomes defect?
Nay, is it thou indeed that we have glimpsed,
Or rather such illusion as of old
Through Athens glided menadlike and Rome,
A shape of vapor, mother of vain dreams
And mutinous traditions, specious plea
Of the glaived tyrant and long-memoried priest?"

I walked forth saddened; for all thought is sad,
And leaves a bitterish savor in the brain,
Tonic, it may be, not delectable,
And turned, reluctant, for a parting look
At those old weather-pitted images
Of bygone struggle, now so sternly calm.
About their shoulders sparrows had built nests,
And fluttered, chirping, from gray perch to perch,
Now on a mitre poising, now a crown,
Irreverently happy. While I thought
How confident they were, what careless hearts
Flew on those lightsome wings and shared the sun,
A larger shadow crossed; and looking up,
I saw where, nesting in the hoary towers,
The sparrow-hawk slid forth on noiseless air,
With sidelong head that watched the joy below,
Grim Norman baron o'er this clan of Kelts.
Enduring Nature, force conservative,
Indifferent to our noisy whims! Men prate
Of all heads to an equal grade cashiered
On level with the dullest, and expect
(Sick of no worse distemper than themselves)
A wondrous cure-all in equality;
They reason that To-morrow must be wise
Because To-day was not, nor Yesterday,
As if good days were shapen of themselves,
Not of the very lifeblood of men's souls;
Meanwhile, long-suffering, imperturbable,
Thou quietly complet'st thy syllogism,
And from the premise sparrow here below
Draw'st sure conclusion of the hawk above,
Pleased with the soft-billed songster, pleased no less
With the fierce beak of natures aquiline.

Thou beautiful Old Time, now hid away
In the Past's valley of Avilion,
Haply, like Arthur, till thy wound be healed,
Then to reclaim the sword and crown again!
Thrice beautiful to us; perchance less fair
To who possessed thee, as a mountain seems
To dwellers round its bases but a heap
Of barren obstacle that lairs the storm
And the avalanche's silent bolt holds back
Leashed with a hair,—meanwhile some far-off clown,
Hereditary delver of the plain,
Sees it an unmoved vision of repose,
Nest of the morning, and conjectures there
The dance of streams to idle shepherds' pipes,
And fairer habitations softly hung
On breezy slopes, or hid in valleys cool,
For happier men. No mortal ever dreams
That the scant isthmus he encamps upon
Between two oceans, one, the Stormy, passed,
And one, the Peaceful, yet to venture on,
Has been that future whereto prophets yearned
For the fulfilment of Earth's cheated hope,
Shall be that past which nerveless poets moan
As the lost opportunity of song.

O Power, more near my life than life itself
(Or what seems life to us in sense immured),
Even as the roots, shut in the darksome earth,
Share in the tree-top's joyance, and conceive
Of sunshine and wide air and wingèd things
By sympathy of nature, so do I
Have evidence of Thee so far above,
Yet in and of me! Rather Thou the root
Invisibly sustaining, hid in light,
Not darkness, or in darkness made by us.
If sometimes I must hear good men debate
Of other witness of Thyself than Thou,
As if there needed any help of ours
To nurse Thy flickering life, that else must cease,
Blown out, as 't were a candle, by men's breath,
My soul shall not be taken in their snare,
To change her inward surety for their doubt
Muffled from sight in formal robes of proof:
While she can only feel herself through Thee,
I fear not Thy withdrawal; more I fear,
Seeing, to know Thee not, hoodwinked with dreams
Of signs and wonders, while, unnoticed, Thou,
Walking Thy garden still commun'st with men,
Missed in the commonplace of miracle.

1870 *1869*

RICHARD CHASE
Editor

Herman Melville

1819–1891

NOWADAYS Melville is generally regarded as one of the greatest of American writers. We have no hesitation in placing him among, perhaps indeed at the head of, the "classic" American authors, as D. H. Lawrence called James Fenimore Cooper, Edgar Allan Poe, Nathaniel Hawthorne, and other tale-tellers, novelists, and poets who achieved their best work before the Civil War. Melville has found in recent decades a large number of American readers. He has exercised a strong influence on the minds of contemporary writers, as we see from such poems as Hart Crane's elegy "At Melville's Tomb" (1920); W. H. Auden's "Herman Melville" (1945); and Robert Lowell's "The Quaker Graveyard in Nantucket" (1946), in itself a great poem but deriving some of its most effective imagery from Melville's masterpiece, *Moby-Dick*. Many contemporary writers of fiction, looking for resources of the symbolic imagination, have turned to Melville, and many of them have found in his works the "allegories of moral consciousness" which William Faulkner tells us he has found there.

Melville's reputation is not only great; it seems also secure, for it is impossible to imagine an America of the future which will not honor and read this author. There is therefore much irony in the fact that when Melville died in 1891, he had long outlived the popularity and fame that he briefly enjoyed during the 1840's, when his South-Seas adventure tales—notably *Typee* (1846)—were in vogue. Although his later tales, novels, and poems had had a scattering of readers, perhaps more consistently in England than in his own country, he was virtually unknown at the time of his death, either to his fellow writers or to the world at large. Melville, one might think, should have occupied an important place in such an ambitious and influential survey of the American literary past as Van Wyck Brooks's *America's Coming of Age*, published in 1915. Yet he is not mentioned at all, so far had he sunk into obscurity. Nor, with the exception of Hawthorne, did the writers of his own century know him much better. Henry James, well versed in Whitman, Hawthorne and Emerson, seems to have known next to nothing about Melville, except that he retained in late years, as his essay of 1898 on American magazines shows, a dim memory of the author of *Typee*. James speaks in a rather uncomplimentary way of "the prose, as mild and easy as an Indian summer in the woods, of Herman Melville, of George William Curtis, and 'Ik Marvel.' " No one nowadays, surely, would put these three writers on a plane of equality or describe Melville's prose, even in *Typee*—let alone *Red-*

burn (1849), *Moby-Dick* (1851), "Bartleby the Scrivener" (1853), "Benito Cereno" (1855), *The Confidence Man* (1857), or *Billy Budd* (1924)—as James describes it. For this is a prose that knows more seasons than Indian summer and penetrates woods more deep, mysterious, and dangerous than those James had in mind.

It was not until the 1920's that Melville began to be salvaged from oblivion, as a part of the general historical and critical effort that Brooks had called for in order to "rediscover America" and to seek out our "usable past." Raymond Weaver, who gained access to many of Melville's papers, including the manuscript of the unpublished *Billy Budd*, published in 1921 the first full-scale biography. From this work the modern Melville scholarship flows, just as the criticism that sees Melville as a significant and representative figure in American culture flows from D. H. Lawrence's two chapters in his *Studies in Classic American Literature*, which appeared in 1923.

In his own lifetime Melville suffered much from a lack of recognition and doubtless also from the lack of a community of the literary life, a community, that is, of his peers, who might have given him encouragement and useful criticism. This kind of community he was to know only briefly in the 1840's. But he seems always to have felt the need of it and to have understood how it might foster the creative spirit. See, for example, his strong expostulation in "Hawthorne and His Mosses" (1850), urging Americans to acknowledge immediately Hawthorne's greatness:

> Give not over to future generations the glad duty of acknowledging him for what he is. Take that joy to yourself, in your own generation; and so shall he feel those grateful impulses on him, that may possibly prompt him to the full flower of some still greater achievement in your eyes. And by confessing him you thereby confess others; you brace the whole brotherhood. For genius, all over the world, stands hand in hand, and one shock of recognition runs the whole circle round.

Few enough people were to acknowledge Melville in his own time. Yet now, whether we are geniuses or not, we experience the shock of recognition of which he spoke whenever we look into his works.

II

WHEN Herman Melville was born in New York on August 1, 1819, one would not have suspected that his youth would be characterized by trouble, heartache, hard work, and restless voyagings to Europe and the South Seas as a common sailor. For both his father, Allan Melvill (as the name was then spelled), and his mother, Maria Gansevoort, came from well-to-do families that had some claim to aristocratic status. Allan Melvill's father and grandfather had been successful merchants and importers, and Maria Gansevoort's background was the Dutch landholding patriciate of the Hudson Valley. But the unsuspected destiny of Herman Melville began to unfold in 1830, when his father's business suffered severe financial reverses, and in 1832, when his father died. There is no doubt that the early death of Melville's father had a lifelong effect on his son's psychic constitution. There are good personal reasons why Melville calls himself Ishmael in *Moby-Dick*, for, like Abraham's son by Hagar (Gen. 16), Melville early learned to feel bereft both of patrimony and paternity; like the Biblical Ishmael, he could easily think of himself as a wanderer whose hand was turned against every man. And when we hear the Ishmael of *Moby-Dick* exclaim out of his loneliness: "Where is the foundling's father hidden?" we reflect that a part of the search for truth and certitude that makes the theme of many of Melville's books was a search for a father, or for those emotions of security and power associated with a boy's feelings for his father. Nor can there be any doubt that, democrat though he was, the loss of patrician status was not easy for Melville to take. The humiliations and sufferings of a youth brought up in genteel surroundings who suddenly finds himself among the callous and brutal sailors on a merchant ship are memorably described in *Redburn*, and in *Pierre* (1852) we observe the nostalgia and reverence with which the ill-fated hero regards his eminent ancestors.

In a sense it can be said that on the verge of his teens Melville lost not only a father but a mother, or at least the bonds of love and respect which he would have continued to form with his mother had the family destiny been a happier one. For Maria Melville seems, under the pressure of adversity, to have grown ever more harsh and morally overbearing. The imperious and frigid mother portrayed in *Pierre* is surely in some measure a portrait of Melville's own mother, and one suspects that the imperiousness and frigidity are more real than the fantasied idyl of affection between mother and son Melville describes in the opening chapters of this revealing novel. There are doubtless cultural as well as personal reasons why there are so few, indeed almost no, sympathetic or convincingly real women in Melville's books, but one may conjecture that an early failure of love between mother and son had something to do with it.

With Melville's mother must also be associated the influence of the Dutch Reformed Church, to which she belonged, on the youthful imagination of her son. Melville was early introduced, imaginatively and emotionally if not intellectually, to the strict Calvinism of this church, with its dark view of the human lot and its creed of predestination. As we shall see, Melville came later in life to believe that no deeply thinking mind, no matter what its specific doctrinal commitments, could ever be free of the profound sense of imperfection and fate which the Calvinist idea of original sin requires. This influence on Melville's imagination was certainly no less strong for the fact that he remained throughout his life an agnostic, though an unhappy one.

Melville's education was spotty; as he says in *Moby-Dick*, a whaling ship was his Yale and Harvard. He did, however, attend the Albany Academy for a time. Soon it was necessary for him to help the impoverished family by clerking in his elder brother's store, by working on his uncle's farm, and later by schoolteaching, which he did in Pittsfield, Massachusetts, and later in Greenbush, New York. But in the spring of 1839 he made a move that was to be decisive in the development of his character and genius: he embarked on the merchant ship *St. Lawrence*, bound for Liverpool. The literary result of this journey was *Redburn*, Melville's fourth book, published in 1849. There is undoubtedly much genuine autobiography in this book, although the hero is represented as being somewhat younger and more callow than Melville actually was at the time, and although the hard-bitten realism of the book is obviously mixed with elements of romance and fancy. But more important than the fact that the Liverpool trip later found literary representation is the fact that it inaugurated for Melville a period of nearly five years of restless wandering about the world that provided him with the material for his first six books, including *Moby-Dick*, and did much to give a definitive shape to his mind in all of its characteristic strength and weakness.

In January of 1841 Melville sailed out of Fairhaven, Massachusetts, on the whaler *Acushnet*, bound for the South Seas. We must suppose that the whaling ship, the South Seas, and the Marquesas Islands, where Melville underwent the experiences more or less accurately chronicled in *Typee*, roused his passions to their mature development and stirred, even in a sense created, his imagination. The whaling ship and the South Seas had a decisive effect on Melville's mind and his art, just as Europe stirred the mind of the young Henry James, Hannibal, Missouri, the mind of the young Mark Twain, Salem the mind of the young Hawthorne, or frontier New York State the mind of the young Fenimore Cooper. Melville had an affinity not shared in equal degree by these other writers for the exotic and the bizarre, for tumultuous passions, on the one hand, and erotic indolence on the other, for wild adventures, and for nature seen in its most spacious, magnificent, and mysterious aspects. Nowhere better than in the South Seas could these proclivities have been nurtured. There is no doubt, however, that Melville's experiences as a sailor, despite such idyllic friendships as may be mirrored in the stories of Ishmael and Queequeg in *Moby-Dick* or Tommo and Toby in *Typee*, confirmed in him, as a kind of fate, the loneliness he had learned to feel as a child. Despite his capacity for conviviality, despite his marriage and family, he was always to be what he calls in *Moby-Dick* an "isolato."

Melville was to make other journeys later in life, but none of course had the effect upon him of his years on whaling ships, although the trip of 1856–57 to England and the Near

East furnished him with fresh material and inspiration for the poetry he was to write during the 1860's and seventies. He returned in 1844 from the South Seas as a sailor in an American warship—as described in *White-Jacket* (1850)—and settled down to arduous years of writing. As I have said, Melville achieved considerable success and not a little notoriety with the publication of *Typee* in 1846. Yet only five years later, by which time he had written four other books and was in the midst of writing *Moby-Dick*, we find him ruefully conjecturing in a letter to Hawthorne that he was destined to be known only as "a man who had lived among the cannibals." "Dollars damn me," he says in another letter, "and the malicious Devil is forever grinning in upon me, holding the door ajar. . . . What I feel most moved to write, that is banned—it will not pay. Yet, altogether, write the *other* way I cannot." And again he says, "Try to get a living by the Truth—and go to the Soup Societies."

Elsewhere Melville exclaims: "There is the grand truth about Nathaniel Hawthorne. He says No! in thunder; but the Devil himself cannot make him say *yes*. For all men who say *yes*, lie." Although Melville was not exclusively a nay-sayer, his experiences and his reflections upon the quality of American civilization had taught him to utter the powerful "no" he attributes to Hawthorne. He had learned to say "no" to the boundlessly optimistic commercialized creed of most Americans, with its superficial and mean conception of the possibilities of human life, its denial of all the genuinely creative or heroic capacities of man, and its fear and dislike of any but the mildest truths. Melville's "no" finds expression in the tragic-comic tale "Bartleby the Scrivener." This story is too richly imaginative to be read simply as autobiography, at however great a remove. Yet in Bartleby's stubbornly repeated phrase, "I would prefer not to," we hear a version of Melville's "no." The story is a subtle study of the mystery, perhaps the pathology, of the fate of the dissenter or nay-sayer in a yea-saying culture.

By 1851, when he was only thirty-two, Melville had already largely lost the audience he had won with *Typee*. This was an audience which, as his letter to Hawthorne implies, wanted not truth but superficial and pleasant romance of the sort they took *Typee* to be. This audience, well enough pleased with *Omoo* (1847), the sequel to *Typee*, was disconcerted by *Mardi* (1849), with its allegories, its intellectuality, and ruminativeness. *Moby-Dick* was not to fare well either; too many readers regarded it as a potentially interesting adventure story spoiled by murky metaphysical speculations. And Melville's fate as an unappreciated and misunderstood writer was sealed with the publication in 1852 of *Pierre*, a novel about incest and suicide which was damned as not only obscure but morally reprehensible.

By this time Melville had become, as we look back upon him, the very archetype of the neglected and isolated writer in nineteenth-century America. Whitman and Henry James too suffered neglect and isolation, but never so drastically as did Melville. If any great American writer suffered an "ordeal," to borrow a word from Van Wyck Brooks's celebrated biography, *The Ordeal of Mark Twain* (1920), it was Melville. It is probable that his disappointment and feeling of isolation were deepened in 1851 by his failure to establish a close and lasting friendship with Hawthorne.

In 1847 Melville had married Elizabeth Shaw, the daughter of the chief justice of Massachusetts, and had settled in New York City. But for whatever reasons, personal or financial, the family—there were finally four children—moved in 1850 to a farm near Pittsfield, Massachusetts. At this time Hawthorne was living in nearby Lenox, and Melville felt an immediate affinity with him not only as a writer—as we see in "Hawthorne and His Mosses"—but, once he had met him, with Hawthorne himself. Melville's letters to Hawthorne are notable from an intellectual and literary point of view and tell us much about what was going on in the mind of the man who was engaged in writing *Moby-Dick*. But they are notable too for the community of feeling and mind which they invite, at times almost demand. Hawthorne's letters to Melville have not survived, but it is easy to conjecture that Melville's impulsiveness seemed excessive and was probably embarrassing to the reticent and retiring author of *The Scarlet Letter* (1850); he was not the man to match the ebullience of

Melville. And although the friendship ostensibly lasted for some time, it must soon have seemed abortive to Melville.

But it was not only public neglect and loneliness that Melville had to contend with in 1851. There was also his own premonition that even as he was completing *Moby-Dick* he had already exhausted his special material and, even worse, his genius. So we sense from this passage in a letter to Hawthorne:

> Until I was twenty-five I had no development at all. From my twenty-fifth year I date my life. Three weeks have scarcely passed, at any time between then and now, that I have not unfolded within myself. But I feel that I am now come to the inmost leaf of the bulb, and that shortly the flower will fall to the mould.

A sad premonition, especially when we reflect that under happier circumstances Melville might well have been looking forward to decades of further development, to the unfolding of ever more inward leaves. In a general way Melville's career seems to bear out F. Scott Fitzgerald's famous dictum that there are "no second acts" in American lives.

Fortunately, however, Melville's premonition was rather too pessimistic, for although he was never again to write a work that approaches the greatness of *Moby-Dick*, he did continue to write and even to find genuinely new and valuable subject matters and styles. But except for the magazine publication of stories like "Bartleby" and "Benito Cereno" and the meager body of readers who appreciated volumes like *The Confidence Man* (1857) and *Battle-Pieces* (1866), Melville was destined to write almost, one might say, in private. Certainly there was little money in it, and the image of Melville that haunts us from out of the past—the unsung author of *Moby-Dick* moving his family back to New York and working obscurely for almost twenty years as a customs inspector—has become legendary in the annals of our culture. That the customs inspector should have resolutely turned to the writing of poetry and, after his retirement in 1885, to the writing of *Billy Budd*, was surely an act of quiet heroism. Much of the poetry was privately printed and found virtually no readers. *Billy Budd*, completed in the year of the author's death, was not published until 1924. Yet Melville's posterity has learned to think highly of his poetry and to rank *Billy Budd*—as I am sure most readers would agree—second to *Moby-Dick* among his works. No doubt it is useless to speculate as to what Melville's development would have been had he met with a more fortunate reception and lived in a literary culture more immediately aware of true genius. We must content ourselves with what he left us, and that is a very great deal.

III

A PART of Melville's strength is the inclusiveness of his imagination. His work, especially *Moby-Dick*, constitutes a kind of culmination and synthesis of the various aspects of the American imagination as it developed before the Civil War. In some of the more melodramatic passages of *Pierre*, for example, we find the strain of Gothic romance that Charles Brockden Brown had brought into the American novel at the end of the eighteenth century. In sea stories like *Redburn* and *White-Jacket*, not to mention *Moby-Dick*, the influence not only of R. H. Dana's *Two Years Before the Mast* (1840) but also of the sea stories of Cooper has been absorbed. Indeed in a letter occasioned by a commemorative celebration in honor of Cooper, Melville wrote that "his works are among the earliest I remember, as in my boyhood producing a vivid, and awakening power upon my mind." Melville shares with Hawthorne an interest in the darker side of human nature and destiny, and like Hawthorne he is fascinated by the involutions of human psychology, by the ultimate alienation that may be the human lot—as in "Bartleby the Scrivener"—and by the distortions of the ego—as in the portrait of Captain Ahab in *Moby-Dick*. Hawthorne traced his own interest in the darker side of human nature to the background of New England Puritanism from which his family stemmed. Melville makes a similar association in "Hawthorne and His Mosses." Here he speaks of "the great power of blackness" in Hawthorne's imagination and speculates that it

> derives its force from its appeals to that Calvinistic sense of Innate Depravity and Original Sin, from whose visitations, in some shape or other, no deeply thinking mind is always and wholly

free. For, in certain moods, no man can weigh this world without throwing in something, somehow like Original Sin, to strike the uneven balance.

Clearly, the fertile resources of the Puritan imagination entered into the works of Melville as deeply as they did into Hawthorne's writings.

But of course there is much in Melville that is quite beyond the interest or capacity of Hawthorne. Especially there is the idyllic pastoral mood that permeates *Typee* and is invoked in many of the later tales and poems. Like Cooper's Leatherstocking tales—for example, *Deerslayer* (1841) and *The Last of the Mohicans* (1826)—*Typee* relies for its appeal, though in a very different setting, on the perennial romantic desire of modern man to escape from civilization with all of its complexities, injustices, and tensions and to recapture a lost state of innocence in a pastoral environment. It is a commonplace of criticism that this perennial impulse has had in America a special poignance, and found expression in a special form, because of the phenomenon of a rampant civilization driving west and a frontier forever retreating before it. The frontier has been written about in many different ways in American literature, and, as a symbol of human happiness and freedom, has been discovered in many different places. But the archetypal form of the story about the flight to the frontier is doubtless the one we see in the opening chapters of *Moby-Dick*, where Ishmael and his friend Queequeg are leaving civilization and setting sail, in a mood of perfect friendship and emotional release, for the far Pacific. The archetype, in other words, is of a white man or boy escaping to freedom with an Indian, or Negro, or Polynesian companion. This story has proven to be a rich resource of the American imagination, as we see if we recall, for example, Cooper's Natty Bumppo and Chingachgook, Mark Twain's Huckleberry Finn and Jim, and Faulkner's Ike McCaslin and Sam Fathers in "The Bear."

If, as there seems good reason for saying, the two forces that did most to shape the imagination of the classic writers were, first, the Calvinist sense of "blackness" and of moral and psychological complexity and, second, the pastoral idyl of the frontier, we see a major reason for Melville's greatness as a writer. Among the best writers older than himself, Cooper and Hawthorne were able to draw on only one of these forces, for there is no more Calvinism in Cooper than there is pastoral romance in Hawthorne. Melville was the first great writer who was able to draw on both these forces and in a measure to synthesize them.

But there is more to be said about the inclusiveness of Melville's mind. For one thing he was the first writer to make full use of the traditions of American folklore and "American humor," in Constance Rourke's phrase, forecasting in this way such writers as Mark Twain and William Faulkner, who were also to draw upon the accumulating fund of tall tales, legend and folk humor that had appeared in this country after the Revolution, mostly on the ever receding frontier, although Hawthorne had of course already found a source of materials in the more specialized and confined folklore of Puritan New England, just as Washington Irving had in the folklore of New York. One finds evidences of this influence throughout Melville, especially in *Moby-Dick* and the much neglected tale called *Israel Potter* (1855), with its semilegendary portraits of the hero himself and of Benjamin Franklin, Ethan Allen, and John Paul Jones. And *Moby-Dick* does what every epic does: it absorbs the native materials of the popular imagination—such as the tall tales about the white whale—into a work of art, conceived on a grand scale.

Finally, in considering the inclusiveness of Melville's mind, one should observe that both his tendency to draw on native materials and his view of art relate him to Whitman. Many critics, including D. H. Lawrence and Van Wyck Brooks, have said that Whitman's poetry is the first culmination of the American imagination because in this poetry the real and the ideal, or as Brooks put it, the lowbrow and the highbrow, were first brought into relationship and fused. Whitman, in other words, was able to endow the spiritual heritage of Puritanism and Transcendentalism with the body, as it were, of actual American life. He was able to bring into his poems not only spiritual aspiration and refinement but also the thriving realities of a vastly growing nation along with the American gusto for experience, experience of all facets of life without aristocratic scruple or moral inhibition. No doubt this is a true account of Whitman's poems. But it also applies to a certain extent to Melville. The passages in *Redburn* describing Liverpool certainly leave nothing to be desired on the score of realism. *White-Jacket* is full of realistic detail in its account of life aboard an American warship. And despite its metaphysical subtleties, transcendental flights, and symbolic poetry, *Moby-Dick* presents us with a panorama of richly thriving life, as well as meticulously detailed descriptions of the apparatus and techniques of the whaling industry. Without this panorama of real life, *Moby-Dick* would be a far different, and a far paler, book than it is. Melville sometimes compiles "epic" catalogues such as occur so often in Whitman's poems. The following passage from Chapter 54 of *Moby-Dick* resembles Whitman's catalogues in combining realistic details with an epic magnification and a vaunting Americanism:

> This Lakeman, in the land-locked heart of our America, had yet been nurtured by all those agrarian free-booting impressions popularly connected with the open ocean. For in their interflowing aggregate, those grand fresh-water seas of ours,—Erie, and Ontario, and Huron, and Superior, and Michigan,—possess an ocean-like expansiveness, with many of the ocean's noblest traits; with many of its rimmed varieties of races and of climes. They contain round archipelagoes of romantic isles, even as the Polynesian waters do; in large part, are shored by two great contrasting nations, as the Atlantic is; they furnish long maritime approaches to our numerous territorial colonies from the East, dotted all round their banks; here and there are frowned upon by batteries, and by the goat-like craggy guns of lofty Mackinaw; they have heard the fleet thunderings of naval victories; at intervals, they yield their beaches to wild barbarians, whose red painted faces flash from out their peltry wigwams; for leagues and leagues are flanked by ancient and unentered forests, where the gaunt pines stand like serried lines of kings in Gothic genealogies; those same woods harboring wild Afric beasts of prey, and silken creatures whose exported furs give robes to Tartar Emperors; they mirror the paved capitals of Buffalo and Cleveland, as well as Winnebago villages; they float alike the full-rigged merchant ship, the armed cruiser of the State, the steamer, and the beech canoe; they are swept by Borean and dismasting blasts as direful as any that lash the salted wave; they know what shipwrecks are, for out of sight of land, however inland, they have drowned full many a midnight ship with all its shrieking crew.

Despite his admiration for Hawthorne's nicely limned tales, Melville's own idea of art resembles that of Whitman. Hawthorne, judging from his works themselves, thought of the well-wrought tale as having a strict inner economy and as aiming to create a rather static, pictorial effect that would be complete in itself. Melville's idea of art is much more Promethean; he thought of a work of art as something never finished, something that remained living, organic, and emergent. "I have created the creative!" is the triumphant cry of the fanciful poet in *Mardi*. And at one point in *Moby-Dick* Melville bursts out with: "God keep me from ever completing anything. This whole book is but a draught—nay, but the draught of a draught." An exaggeration, of course, but reminding us of Whitman's account in his 1855 Preface to *Leaves of Grass* of the "organic" nature of poetry, and of his idea that "a great poem is no finish to a man or woman but rather a beginning."

Melville's mind, then, was capable of accommodating widely divergent ranges of experience and of projecting divergent images in the form of art. But if this power of inclusiveness contributed to the richness of his imagination, it did not give him inner serenity. Melville was in fact throughout his mature life a deeply divided, doubting, and troubled man. So Hawthorne noticed when Melville visited him in Liverpool in 1856. Melville, Hawthorne reports, discoursed ardently and eloquently about ultimate problems of truth and belief but despaired of finding any solution that would satisfy him. He could neither believe, Hawthorne writes, "nor be comfortable in his unbelief." Contradiction and alienation are of the essence in Melville's view of life and in his art. He saw human experience and the moral world man constructs for himself, indeed he saw nature itself, as riven by contradictions that could never be satisfactorily reconciled. Although his pessimism was modified in later years, he characteristically saw life as the quest of the individual for the truth and moral harmony that would always elude him, and he saw this quest as alienating the individual from the world, society, and himself.

The beginnings of this theme are to be seen in Melville's first book, *Typee. Typee* is not a great book, but in writing it Melville was performing a significant moral and psychological act which gives the story—on the surface so gay, romantic and jocose—a deep undercurrent of meaning. It is characteristic of Melville's art that *Typee* should have a pronounced rhythm or inner dramatic action. The events do not occur in a succession of static scenes, as usually happens in a story by Hawthorne or Poe. The rhythm of *Typee* consists of a series of imprisonments and liberations, of withdrawals from reality and of returns. The hero and his friend Toby escape from the ship. They are imprisoned among the thickly growing reeds as they flee inland. They escape from these to the mountains. Repeatedly they gain the top of a ridge and then plunge into a valley or dark defile. Then there is the long enforced stay among the seemingly benevolent Typees, with what might be called subrhythms of incipient escape. Finally there is the escape from the island at the end of the book. Despite the light tone of *Typee*, the action gives the effect of being cumulative, organic, morally and psychologically significant. In this respect it is different, say, from Poe's "Narrative of A. Gordon Pym" (1838), where the series of imprisonments and escapes does not culminate in anything but itself, and similar to *Huckleberry Finn* (1885), where the imprisonments and escapes do culminate in a significant meaning beyond the mere excitement of the various adventures described.

From the moral point of view the valley of Typee and its apparently idyllic life represent a kind of Eden, a state of innocence and happiness, and Melville's romanticized version of his stay among the cannibals is certainly one of the notable Eden fantasies of literature. But notwithstanding its pleasures, this Eden is seen to be illusory, not only because Eden is by nature illusory but because this is a partly fallen Eden, in which the effects of crime and violence, not to mention cannibalism, are real and present although held by the Typees furtively in the background. Hence, it is a fraudulent Eden and must be escaped. From the psychological point of view the valley of Typee represents the regressive impulses of escape, of prenatal comfort and safety, of a full indulgence of what Freud calls the pleasure principle. But in an adult—even so gay a youth as the author portrays himself as being—who belongs to the nervous, competitive, complicated Western world this indulgence produces anxiety and guilt and the fear of being unmanned—hence the symbolic leg injury of the hero. In a modern adult man the personality, in other words, must be integrated at a higher level than is afforded by Typee. The pleasure principle must be in part foresworn in favor of the reality principle.

The same parable is told in a different way by Hawthorne in such stories as "The Maypole of Merrymount" (1837) and *The Blithedale Romance* (1852). Hawthorne, however, was content, when he had rejected the Edenic ideal, to accept society pretty much as he found it, and he was content with such truths and solutions of man's dilemmas as did not too heavily tax his relatively serene skepticism. Not so Melville. Having rejected Typee as false, though not without retaining considerable nostalgia for it, he was determined to discover those truths—moral, philosophic, religious, political, aesthetic—which would make sense of the civilized world and provide a means of feeling in harmony with it. This quest, sometimes inspiring, sometimes agonized and despairing, is a central theme, though not necessarily the only theme, of Melville's writings at least through the late poem *Clarel* (1876).

Melville's third novel, *Mardi*, is a curious book which begins as a conventional adventure tale and then abruptly shifts into the realm of fantasy and allegory and depicts the imaginary voyage of a company of boon companions in search of truth, happiness, and experience in the fantasy world of Mardi. The story is an odd and not entirely successful amalgam of Rabelesian extravanganza, mildly Swiftian satire, and Melvillian jocosity. All the high spirits notwithstanding, there is no doubt that the book has a serious intent. This we see in the character of Taji, a distant prefiguration of the Ishmael of *Moby-Dick*, and his perplexed pursuit of certainty. At the end the world of Mardi seems to the hero to be characterized by unreason and ambiguity, and he sails off alone in an open boat over dangerous seas in search of other worlds.

It is not surprising, given his sense of the contradictoriness of things, that Melville should often employ symbolic oppositions as a part of his artistic technique. He noted interestedly that Hawthorne did the same—at least that seems to be what he is saying in "Hawthorne and His Mosses" when he writes: "For spite of all the Indian-summer sunlight on the hither side of Hawthorne's soul, the other side —like the dark half of the physical sphere—is shrouded in a blackness ten times black." Like the other classic writers Melville often uses symbolic lights and darks, a striking example of this being the great story "Benito Cereno." In *Mardi* the light and the dark are symbolized by two women: the angelic wraith Yillah, who seems to stand for innocence and reason, and the sinister, engrossing Hautia, the dark woman who suggests the destructive and irrational human impulses. In *Billy Budd*, the blond Billy and the dark villain Claggart are distant analogues to the symbolic women of *Mardi*, although the two girls in *Pierre*, Lucy and Isabel, are closer descendants of Yillah and Hautia.

We should not expect Yillah and Hautia to be "real," since they are frankly presented as figures in an allegory. But it may not be amiss to observe at this point that Melville was like a good many other of the most characteristic American writers from Cooper to Faulkner in being unable to present, even when he tried, a fully portrayed woman in whose reality we can quite believe—with the possible exception of Fayaway in *Typee*. *Pierre* is, at least by intention, the most "novelistic" of Melville's works, for in this book Melville was attempting to draw real characters in real situations without the element of romance, myth, or epic which we find in most of his writings. Yet Pierre's mother is never made believably real or female; she remains a kind of presiding magisterial presence, rather than a character. Lucy, though appealing, is impossibly pure and angelic. And Isabel, whom Melville tries to endow with sex and illicit intentions, is only a dim—sometimes, alas, almost a ludicrous—replica of a real *femme fatale*. The probability is that she was not intended to be a *femme fatale* at all but only an unfortunate and unhappy girl. Yet into Melville's portrait of her the element of melodrama and myth inevitably crept.

It was not in Melville's power to write the "novel of society" or the "novel of manners." In such novels the class to which the characters belong, and the actual day-to-day moral dilemmas and personal involvements in which they find themselves, are always at the center of the writer's attention. Melville does not write this kind of novel—nor do any of the other great American writers, with the exception of Henry James. Melville's finest achievement, *Moby-Dick*, is not really a novel, in the sense in which we are at present using the term; it is a kind of epic romance. It does not matter on board the *Pequod* that Ahab is a middle-class entrepreneur, that Starbuck is of the lower middle class, or that Ishmael has an aristocratic background. In his survey of human nature Melville practices what he calls in one of the letters to Hawthorne a "ruthless democracy." People are what they are because of some inner personal quality or fate. Writing to Hawthorne while he was still composing *Moby-Dick*, he speaks of "the tragedies of human thought in its own unbiased, native, and profounder workings." The embodiment of these inner tragedies of thought he purports to find in Hawthorne's *The House of the Seven Gables*, but it is obvious that the inner tragedies of his own characters—of Ahab and Ishmael—must also have been in his mind. Melville goes on to speak of the "visible truth" into which Hawthorne has entered so deeply, and then explains that "by visible truth, we mean the apprehension of the absolute condition of present things as they strike the eye of the man who fears them not." Melville's concern, be it noted, is not with the *circumstantial* condition of present things; that is the concern of the novelist, properly so called. Melville wants to plunge as directly as may be possible to the absolute. This, he suggests to us in

"Hawthorne and His Mosses," he has come to do not only by temperament but by emulating Hawthorne and Shakespeare. As Melville sees him, Shakespeare is primarily a truth-seeker: "It is those deep far-away things in him; those occasional flashings-forth of the intuitive truth in him; those short, quick probings at the very axis of reality;—these are the things that make Shakespeare, Shakespeare." Thus it is that Melville has given Captain Ahab a "Shakespearean" mind, as well as a good many Shakespearean words, particularly from *Macbeth* and *King Lear*. At the same time it is easy to see that Melville has endowed Ahab with some of the dire characteristics of vengefulness, thirst for the truth, and ultimate alienation which we find in Hawthorne's Chillingworth of *The Scarlet Letter* or in his Ethan Brand.

A part of the power of *Moby-Dick* is to be attributed to the whaling story which makes the narrative line. The whaling ships, the whalemen, and the hunt are fascinating phenomena in themselves, and despite his concern with the inner life of the mind and with the absolute, Melville does not, as I have noted before, stint himself in giving us the full cetological details. Perhaps more important is that in the unusual, indeed uncanny, phenomenon of the white whale Melville found a perfect unifying symbol for his various strands of meaning. The whale, with all of its ambiguity, its enormous power and its mildness, its horrendous violence and its beauty, is the perfect foil both for Ahab's tortured search for vengeance and truth and for Ishmael's reveries and speculations. Critics have argued at length about what the whale symbolizes. Obviously he is in one of his aspects a symbol, but it cannot be said with finality, though many people do, that Moby-Dick symbolizes Evil. Only Ahab in his growing madness sees him this way. To Starbuck the whale is only a "dumb brute." To Ishmael he is something very like nature itself: a thing of infinite inner contradiction, complexity, and paradox—the rich, endlessly protean but finally inscrutable object of human dream and thought. As the spectacle of the white whale and Ahab, Melville's most compelling portrait of the isolated man, is sifted through the musing mind of Ishmael, there unfolds before us a work of grandeur and beauty such as Melville was never to achieve again.

Despite the looseness, even the waywardness, of its composition, *Moby-Dick* brings the various strands of Melville's mind into an imaginative unity. The unity, however, is in the metaphors, the language, the symbols, the dramatic action, in other words, in the imaginative and aesthetic qualities of the book. It is not in its ideas. The conflicts between self and society, identity and nothingness, faith and doubt, free will and necessity are never resolved into a harmony or a solution. Thus R. W. B. Lewis is right in describing *Moby-Dick* as "an elaborate pattern of countercommentaries, the supreme instance of the dialectical novel—a novel of tensions without resolution." The Epilogue, in which Ishmael is saved from drowning by the coffin-lifebuoy, seems symbolically to affirm that a rebirth and a new life have been achieved. But the tone belies this, and at the very end, with its picture of the infinite mystery of the sea and the aloneness and helplessness of the hero, we cannot help seeing that Melville, in whom there is something both of Ahab and Ishmael, has not arrived at the certitude he sought.

There is no doubt that Melville, as the mildly skeptical Hawthorne seems to have thought, was *too* anxious to get at "the truth." He laid siege to the truth, one might say, and tried to take it by storm. Ideally what Melville wanted was that at some point in the dialectic of his mind a synthesis should occur between the truths of the imagination, or the aesthetic sense, and the truths of reason. But this did not happen, even in *Moby-Dick*. He felt, perhaps, the same dilemma that Ahab felt, who realized that in himself the "high perception," or rational faculty, was divorced from and at odds with "the low, enjoying power," or the aesthetic sense. Indeed the story of Ahab is basically the gradual alienation of the high perception from the low enjoying power and the mad, solipsistic view of the world that is the result of this alienation. Why aesthetic truth and rational truth *should* be expected to coincide perhaps does not strike us as a question that has to be immediately or even finally answered. Surely, it did not so strike other American writers less given to speculative thought than Melville—like Hawthorne and Henry

James. But for Melville the dilemma, in addition no doubt to the sheer fatigue he felt after his labors on *Moby-Dick*—he had after all published five books in five years—was nearly disastrous. For he had been led to the pessimistic conclusion that the aesthetic sense is mere illusion and that human reason is an alienating activity, leading to monomania and nihilism.

This state of mind is reflected in Melville's two most ambitious prose works of the 1850's after *Moby-Dick*—*Pierre: or, The Ambiguities* (1852) and *The Confidence Man* (1857). The hero of *Pierre*, an aspiring author with the highest of possible literary goals and a young man desperately given to the pursuit of truth, is finally defeated by the unbridgeable gap between his sense of what life ought to be and what it inexorably is. He is driven mad and dies a suicide, the victim, we are led to gather, of all those "ambiguities" of which the book's subtitle speaks. As in *Mardi*, the ambiguities are symbolized by two women—Lucy, the ever-faithful vessel of light, innocence, and truth, whom Pierre abandons, and Isabel, Pierre's half-sister and the dark woman of the novel, with whom Pierre enters into an incestuous relationship. *Pierre* is a painfully botched book which unsuccessfully tries to amalgamate literary conventions, such as those of the sentimental novel of seduction, the polite social novel, and the popular "uplifting" novel of vice and virtue, for which Melville had little aptitude. The book is all the more painful to read because of its ambitiousness. One suspects that only a Dostoevski could have done what Melville attempted—certainly no writer in mid-century America could have made a successful novel of the materials of *Pierre*.

Another side of Melville's pessimism is to be seen in *The Confidence Man*. Like *Pierre* it is a portrait of man imprisoned by the ambiguities of human nature and of the civilization man has made. But here the tone is of comedy and satire. Around the shifting, elusive quick-change artist and charlatan who is the book's main figure a rather bewildering succession of scenes occur, all designed to show in one way or another the contradiction, in the moral relationships of man, between appearance and reality. It is a "dark comedy" indeed, for Melville is not content merely to point out that men are often fakers and liars; he calls into question the very possibility of the human attempt to establish a reliable sense of meaning and value in a world where meaning and value can have no ultimate stability, or even a provisionally pragmatic stability. The central conception of the confidence man, who assumes so many guises with such deft agility, is a promising one, and in scattered passages of the book Melville has certainly created an impressive farcical comedy or masque of unreason. But he was unable to organize the book properly or to lay down his pen before he had made too much of a good thing. Still, the confidence man will always be associated in the minds of students of American literature with other portraits of master charlatans—possibly the Duke and the Dauphin in *Huckleberry Finn*, certainly with the Colonel Sellers of Mark Twain's *The Gilded Age*. What is missing in Melville's book is the geniality Mark Twain cannot help feeling for his charlatans. *The Confidence Man* is a deeply embittered book.

IV

WITH the exception of the months during which he was writing *Moby-Dick*, the decade of the 1850's, as we have noticed, was a dark and unhappy period for Melville. But *The Confidence Man* was to be the last of his overly ambitious attempts to confront his unhappiness. His writing in succeeding years was to be mostly verse—until he came in his last years to *Billy Budd*—and in his poetry we find, not serenity to be sure, but a new calmness and contemplativeness. Melville had scaled down his drastic Promethean efforts to storm the citadels of truth, and although he never learned to live at ease with his incurable skepticism about human affairs, neither did he react to them in later life with the fury displayed in *Pierre* and *The Confidence Man*—note, for example, the moderate, reflective tone of the long poem *Clarel* (1876).

The general modern opinion is that Melville, as an American poet, is second only to Whitman and Emily Dickinson in their century. It is true that apart from some isolated passages, and apart from a few short lyrics like "The Portent," "The Maldive Shark," and "Shiloh," he is not a highly accomplished artificer or master of poetic techniques. His poems are often rather awkward in their phrasing, and his determination to use only traditional stanzaic forms sometimes leads him into writing an infelicitous phrase in order to get the right rhyme. In all the superficial techniques of versification he is inferior to Longfellow or James Russell Lowell. But the fact remains that his mistakes are usually verbal and metrical; they are seldom mistakes or faults of the intelligence or of the imagination. This is why critics have often found similarities between Melville's poetry and that of Matthew Arnold and Thomas Hardy. At its characteristic best, Melville's verse is a body of serious poetry, deeply felt and courageously thought through by a mind that, if not entirely free of poetic cliché, turns naturally to the great problems of the time: the Civil War, the future of democracy, religion, history, politics, myth, nature, art, literature.

The Civil War elicited from Melville his first volume of poetry, *Battle-Pieces and Aspects of the War*, the only volume of verse in the meager body of distinguished writing about the war that may be favorably compared with Whitman's *Drum-Taps*. It is quite possible to say that the Civil War was a godsend to Melville, as it was to Whitman. Both poets had passed through a dark period of low spirits and self-doubt in the later 1850's, and the coming of the tragic national conflict gave both writers a new sense of purpose and dedication. Although he doubtless rightly suspected that *Battle-Pieces* would not be widely read, Melville nevertheless adopts a kind of public role as a poet of the war. "I muse upon my country's ills," he says in "Misgivings," and he thought it incumbent upon him to speak such words of compassion, admonition, and counsel as he could. Although against slavery and believing the South is in the wrong, Melville does not write as a partisan. The war as he sees it is a catastrophe that has happened, not so much because of a Southern insurrection, but because of innate imperfections in man's very nature, because of historical forces no man or group could fully control, and because of certain weaknesses in American democracy that the war itself has made ominously apparent. The general tendency of the war poems, as of all of Melville's poetry, is a somewhat skeptical yet gravely reassuring attitude toward the future of America and of mankind. "Let us pray," he writes in a prose Supplement to *Battle-Pieces*, "that the great historic tragedy of our time may not have been enacted without instructing our whole beloved country through terror and pity; and may fulfilment verify in the end those expectations which kindle the bards of Progress and Humanity."

The poem called "The Conflict of Conviction" contains in essence much of Melville's reaction to the war. It is a dialogue between an optimist and a pessimist—the "Yea" and "Nay" referred to at the end. On the optimistic side there is the enduring power of faith, the hope that the young—"The light is on the youthful brow"—will have more wisdom than their forebears, the assertion that God still exists, that nature is not governed by mere Necessity but that there is a "purpose strong" that "spins against" nature's destructive forces, that even though ugliness and evil have been loosed in the world—laying bare the gulfs with their "slimed foundations"—this fact in itself should allow man to build a better world on a deeper foundation. In rebuttal the pessimist, who in this poem at least seems to win the argument, says that the war is "man's latter fall," that Christianity is of no avail, that God has abdicated from human ken, leaving only "strong Necessity," and that the new iron dome of the Capitol building in Washington may symbolize not the realization of the aims of the founders of the country but the advent of a new iron age of injustice and oppression, that, in other words, the war may force an irreparable breach between America and all that it once stood for in its noble and youthful time.

Similar doubts are expressed as Melville ponders, in "The House-Top," the draft riots that occurred in New York. Here he fears that in breaking the relatively mild laws of a democratic nation the rioters are inviting a Draconian repression. In other poems, like "Dupont's Round Fight," the need for stable laws, not only in civil matters but in art and all of man's activities, is asserted. In "A Utilitarian View of the Monitor's Fight" Melville returns to the idea of the new iron age, this time dwelling on the fact that the Civil War is the first really modern war, in the sense that it has called into being mechanized weapons and that "warriors / Are now but operatives."

Yet even while lamenting the damage the war may have done to the continuity of civilization and of democratic institutions, Melville expresses a residual faith, in such poems as "Shiloh" and "Malvern Hill," that nature and time, with their restorative processes, will heal the breaches that have been made and reconcile man with man and the future with the past. In such later poems as "In a Bye-Canal" and "The Maldive Shark" Melville was to reflect upon nature much as he had in *Moby-Dick* and other prose works, stressing the precariousness of life and the presence in nature of sinister mysteries unknown to shallow philosophies. Yet he was to celebrate, in a poem like "The Bluebird," the transfiguring power of nature and its cycles of death and rebirth. He was also to turn to a topic unusual for him, as for most writers of his time—the relation of sex to human well-being and creative genius. This is the subject of the interesting if somewhat perplexing poem called "After the Pleasure Party." Except where the poet speaks directly, this poem is a dramatic monologue spoken, we gather, by a woman of intellectual attainments but frigid emotions—she is called Urania, the muse of astronomy. Her virginal life and the illusion of being "self-reliant, strong and free" she has built upon it are called into question in her own mind when she experiences a moment of passion at a pleasure party. Denying and repressing this upsurge of sexual emotion, she draws from the poet the warning that "Amor incensed" is a vindictive and destructive god. It is too bad that the conventions of the time did not allow Melville to speak more freely on a matter that obviously interested him all his life. He usually writes of sex very guardedly, although in some passages of *Typee* he allowed himself a sportive amorousness and in some chapters of *Moby-Dick* there is a strong erotic component—see also Melville's curious allegorical tale "The Paradise of Bachelors and the Tartarus of Maids" (1855).

V

Billy Budd, Melville's last work, carries on some of the themes of his poetry: the destruction of blameless youth; the necessity for law; the superiority from a human point of view of the heroic mode of warfare, typified by Lord Nelson, as opposed to grimly mechanized modern wars; the power of time and legend to bring about a perpetual rebirth of what is humanly valuable. Written between 1888 and 1891, when Melville was in his seventies, *Billy Budd* is understandably reminiscent and nostalgic. It might be said to be a Conradian tale. Captain Vere might imaginably appear in one of Conrad's books, for Conrad too liked to write about the dilemmas of a man in a position of responsibility whose duty conflicts with his humane impulses.

In reading *Billy Budd* one should keep in mind its *political* content, along with its broader moral and mythic themes. The French Revolution is the background of the tale, as Melville states in his Preface. He is writing of a time when the politics of insurgent democracy are very much in the air—when a hardheaded Dundee shipowner names his vessel the *Rights-of-Man*, because he is a "staunch admirer of Thomas Paine whose book in rejoinder to Burke's arraignment of the French Revolution had then been published for some time and had gone everywhere." The reference to Edmund Burke's *Reflections on the Revolution in France* (1790) is significant, for despite his undoubted sympathies with democratic libertarianism Melville is concerned, like Burke, with showing the necessity of law, the value of continuity in civilization, and the need for compromising extremes, such as are represented by the innocence of Billy and the evil of Claggart. For the political structure of a humane society is such that it can neither be perfectly good nor perfectly bad.

Claggart is the "given" quantity, in the sense that he is an example of "Natural Depravity: a depravity according to nature." True, Billy Budd is at first a kind of Adam in his innocence and then a kind of Christ in his sacrificial death, but we do not have the feeling that he is good by nature, or if he is, this is not where the emphasis falls. We would be surprised, in the light of Melville's general view of things, if it did. Given Claggart, Melville seems to have reflected, we must, if we are to preserve society, have Billy Budd with his goodness, his boyish hope and strength, and we must have Captain Vere, the stern father and magistrate whose duty it is to preserve order and rationality.

The political theme is enriched by the mythic and religious overtones of the story. For not only is Billy a kind of Adam and a kind of Christ; we are also reminded of the story of Abraham and Isaac, of the father who must be prepared to sacrifice the son and of the atonement between father and son. And the pathos of the story is enhanced by Melville's hint that the orphan Billy may actually be the son—"a presumable bye-blow"—of Captain Vere. The satanic or demonic quality of Claggart—here Melville is obviously influenced by Milton's portrait of Satan in *Paradise Lost*—does much to lend him the necessary mythic dimension which is given to the other characters. Moreover, the emotional implications of Claggart's acts are given a psychological eomplexity because of the perverse attraction he obviously feels for Billy.

The view of nature in *Billy Budd,* as we see from the many metaphors of devouring and eating ("The fleece of low-hanging vapor had vanished, licked up by the sun that late had so glorified it"), is the dark and dubious one we are accustomed to in Melville. What he had called in *Moby-Dick* "the horrible vulturism" of the world still obtains in *Billy Budd*. The metaphor becomes applicable to society in the suggestion of Melville's parable that civilization sustains itself only by feeding on youthful innocence and goodness, by the ritualistic sacrifice of the Christlike man. In this dark view of nature, as in his sense of the pain and evil in the world, Melville carried over into his last work what had been lifelong preoccupations. He also impresses us again with his powerful sense of the irreconcilable contradictions involved in life, and perhaps nowhere in his work did he find better or more vivid symbols for this sense of things than Billy and Claggart. In Melville's last work the light and the dark, good and evil, are still in dramatic and mortal conflict. But what we encounter in *Billy Budd* that we do not encounter in the other prose writings is the feeling of elegy and resignation, tinged with at least a minimal faith in the power of time and legend to right wrongs. For as we are told at the end, "the fresh young image of the Handsome Sailor" lives on in the minds and hearts of men.

Melville's story leaves us, as do such late Shakespearean plays as *The Winter's Tale,* with the faith that there is in the world a minimal principle of grace, redemption, and spiritual rebirth. It is possible, after all, that the terrible contradictions with which our experience confronts us may be absorbed in history, or assuaged by the beneficence and spiritual health of which human nature is capable. The tortured author of *Pierre* and *The Confidence Man* had found, late in life, at least some small measure of consolation.

READING SUGGESTIONS

EDITIONS

The Works of Herman Melville, 16 vols. (1922–24). It is a singular fact that this imperfect edition, published in London, is still the only full collection of Melville's writings. A projected complete works, under the imprint of Hendricks House, is in process of publication. Of the few volumes which have so far appeared, H. A. Murray's edition of *Pierre* is outstanding. But Melville's best-known books are readily available in reprints, paperback and hard cover.

BIOGRAPHY

Leon Howard, *Herman Melville* (1951). The best factual biography.

Jay Leyda, *The Melville Log: A Documentary Life of Herman Melville,* 2 vols. (1951). An enormous sourcebook of undigested materials and data bearing upon Melville's day-to-day life, so far as this can be known.

LETTERS

Merrill R. Davis and William H. Gilman, editors, *The Letters of Herman Melville* (1960). An excellent collection, which serves, however, to confirm one's impression of the striking superiority of Melville's letters to Hawthorne, as compared with those to other friends, to members of his family, and to publishers.

CRITICISM

D. H. Lawrence, *Studies in Classic American Literature* (1923). Contains a somewhat oracular but highly suggestive and influential analysis of Melville, particularly *Typee* and *Moby-Dick*.

Lewis Mumford, *Herman Melville* (1929).

F. O. MATTHIESSEN, *American Renaissance* (1941). The chapters on Melville are valuable, especially in relating him to the other classic American writers.

WILLIAM ELLERY SEDGWICK, *Herman Melville: the Tragedy of Mind* (1945). Stresses the philosophical and religious aspects of Melville's thought.

ROBERT PENN WARREN, "Melville the Poet," *Selected Essays* (1958). This essay did much to gain readers for Melville's poetry when it first appeared in 1946 and is still the best commentary.

CHARLES OLSON, *Call Me Ishmael* (1947). This is somewhat apocalyptic, in the Lawrence manner, but contains many interesting suggestions, especially those that relate Melville and Shakespeare.

RICHARD CHASE, *Herman Melville* (1949). An example of "myth criticism," usually described as "controversial."

HOWARD VINCENT, *The Trying-Out of Moby-Dick* (1949). *Moby-Dick* as seen against the background of the myths and facts of the whaling industry.

NEWTON ARVIN, *Herman Melville* (1950). This critical biography is the best and most balanced that has appeared. The first two-thirds of the book, taking Melville through the *Moby-Dick* period, are unsurpassed, although the concluding chapters somewhat slight Melville's later works.

LAWRANCE THOMPSON, *Melville's Quarrel with God* (1952). This perverse but interesting book asserts that Melville's ironies and symbolisms conceal an attack on God and religion.

CHARLES FEIDELSON, *Symbolism and American Literature* (1953). Part of this suggestive book is devoted to Melville, in the manner the title implies.

R. W. B. LEWIS, *The American Adam* (1955). Includes an excellent account of Melville in relation to the American myth of innocence.

EDWARD H. ROSENBERRY, *Melville and the Comic Spirit* (1955).

PERRY MILLER, *The Raven and the Whale* (1956). A vivid account of the younger Melville in relation to the literary life and the world of ideas and journalism in New York.

HAWTHORNE AND HIS MOSSES

THE FOLLOWING essay was published in two installments in August of 1850 in the *Literary World*, a magazine edited by Melville's friend Evert A. Duyckinck. Melville, acquainted with Hawthorne at the time but not yet a close friend, chose to sign the article "By a Virginian Spending July in Vermont" rather than by his own name. Both Hawthorne and his wife were much struck by the article and were anxious to know the identity of the author. "Hawthorne and His Mosses" is a review of Hawthorne's *Mosses from an Old Manse*. But it is interesting to us not only because of what Melville has to say about the book he is reviewing but because it reveals so much about the mind and imagination of the reviewer, who in the summer of 1850 was engaged in writing and rewriting *Moby-Dick*. One feels in Melville's review—in his comments on Hawthorne's tales, his remarks about the qualities of a great imagination, his hopes for a pre-eminent national literature and a fellowship of writers—some of the inner turmoil, ambition, and burgeoning creativity of the author at the time when his genius was flourishing most powerfully.

A PAPERED chamber in a fine old farm-house—a mile from any other dwelling, and dipped to the eaves in foliage—surrounded by mountains, old woods, and Indian ponds—this, surely, is the place to write of Hawthorne. Some charm is in this northern air, for love and duty seem both impelling to the task. A man of a deep and noble nature has seized me in this seclusion. His wild, witch voice rings through me; or, in softer cadences, I seem to hear it in the songs of the hill-side birds that sing in the larch trees at my window.

Would that all excellent books were foundlings, without father or mother, that so it might be, we could glorify them, without including their ostensible authors! Nor would any true man take exception to this—least of all, he who writes: "When the Artist rises high enough to achieve the Beautiful, the symbol by which he makes it perceptible to mortal senses becomes of little value in his eyes, while his spirit possesses itself in the enjoyment of the reality."

But more than this. I know not what would be the right name to put on the title page of an excelent book; but this I feel, that the names of all fine authors are fictitious ones, far more so than that of Junius [1]—simply standing, as they do, for the mystical, ever-eluding Spirit of all Beauty, which ubiquitously possesses men of genius. Purely imaginative as this fancy may appear, it nevertheless seems to receive some warranty from the fact that on a personal interview no great author has ever come

HAWTHORNE AND HIS MOSSES. 1. **Junius:** the pseudonym used by the author of a famous series of political "Letters" that appeared in England between 1769 and 1771.

up to the idea of his reader. But that dust of which our bodies are composed, how can it fitly express the nobler intelligence among us? With reverence be it spoken, that not even in the case of one deemed more than man, not even in our Savior, did his visible frame betoken anything of the augustness of the nature within. Else, how could those Jewish eye-witnesses fail to see heaven in his glance?

It is curious, how a man may travel along a country road, and yet miss the grandest or sweetest of prospects, by reason of an intervening hedge so like all other hedges as in no way to hint of the wide landscape beyond. So has it been with me concerning the enchanting landscape in the soul of this Hawthorne, this most excellent Man of Mosses. His *Old Manse* has been written now four years, but I never read it till a day or two since. I had seen it in the bookstores—heard of it often—even had it recommended to me by a tasteful friend, as a rare, quiet book, perhaps too deserving of popularity to be popular. But there are so many books called "excellent," and so much unpopular merit, that amid the thick stir of other things, the hint of my tasteful friend was disregarded; and for four years the Mosses on the Old Manse never refreshed me with their perennial green. It may be, however, that all this while, the book, like wine, was only improving in flavor and body. At any rate, it so chanced that this long procrastination eventuated in a happy result. At breakfast the other day, a mountain girl, a cousin of mine, who for the last two weeks has every morning helped me to strawberries and raspberries—which, like the roses and pearls in the fairy-tale, seemed to fall into the saucer from those strawberry-beds, her cheeks—this delightful creature, this charming Cherry, says to me—"I see you spend your mornings in the haymow; and yesterday I found there Dwight's *Travels in New England*. Now I have something far better than that—something more congenial to our summer on these hills. Take these raspberries, and then I will give you some moss."—"Moss!" said I.—"Yes, and you must take it to the barn with you, and good-by to 'Dwight.' "

With that she left me, and soon returned with a volume, verdantly bound, and garnished with a curious frontispiece in green—nothing less than a fragment of real moss cunningly pressed to a fly-leaf.—"Why this," said I, spilling my raspberries, "this is the *Mosses from an Old Manse*." "Yes," said cousin Cherry, "yes, it is that flowering Hawthorne."—"Hawthorne and Mosses," said I, "no more: it is morning: it is July in the country: and I am off for the barn."

Stretched on that new-mown clover, the hillside breeze blowing over me through the wide barn door, and soothed by the hum of the bees in the meadows around, how magically stole over me this Mossy Man! And how amply, how bountifully, did he redeem that delicious promise to his guests in the Old Manse, of whom it is written: "Others could give them pleasure and amusement, or instruction—these could be picked up anywhere—but it was for me to give them rest. Rest, in a life of trouble! What better could be done for those weary and world-worn spirits? . . . what better could be done for anybody, who came within our magic circle, than to throw the spell of a magic spirit over him?"—So all that day, half-buried in the new clover, I watched this Hawthorne's "Assyrian dawn and Paphian sunset and moonrise, from the summit of our eastern hill."

The soft ravishments of the man spun me round about in a web of dreams, and when the book was closed, when the spell was over, this wizard "dismissed me, with but misty reminiscences, as if I had been dreaming of him."

What a wild moonlight of contemplative humor bathes that Old Manse!—the rich and rare distillment of a spicy and slowly oozing heart. No rollicking rudeness, no gross fun fed on fat dinners, and bred in the lees of wine—but a humor so spiritually gentle, so high, so deep, and yet so richly relishable, that it were hardly inappropriate in an angel. It is the very religion of mirth; for nothing so human but it may be advanced to that. The orchard of the Old Manse seems the visible type of the fine mind that has described it. Those twisted and contorted old trees that "stretch out their crooked branches, and take such hold of the imagination, that we remember them as humorists and odd fellows." And then, as surrounded by these grotesque forms, and hushed in the noonday repose of this Hawthorne's spell, how aptly might the still fall of his ruddy thoughts into your soul be symbolized by "the thump of a great apple, in the stillest afternoon, falling without a breath of wind, from the mere necessity of perfect ripeness!" For no less ripe than ruddy are the apples of the thoughts and fancies in this sweet Man of Mosses.

"Buds and Bird-Voices"—What a delicious thing is that!—"Will the world ever be so decayed, that spring may not renew its greenness?"—And the "Fire-Worship." Was ever the hearth so glorified into an altar before? The mere title of that piece is better than any common work in fifty folio volumes. How exquisite is this:

> Nor did it lessen the charm of his soft, familiar courtesy and helpfulness, that the mighty spirit, were

opportunity offered him, would run riot through the peaceful house, wrap its inmates in his terrible embrace, and leave nothing of them save their whitened bones. This possibility of mad destruction only made his domestic kindness the more beautiful and touching. It was so sweet of him, being endowed with such power, to dwell, day after day, and one long, lonesome night after another, on the dusky hearth, only now and then betraying his wild nature, by thrusting his red tongue out of the chimney-top! True, he had done much mischief in the world, and was pretty certain to do more; but his warm heart atoned for all. He was kindly to the race of man. . . .

But he has still other apples, not quite so ruddy, though full as ripe—apples that have been left to wither on the tree, after the pleasant autumn gathering is past. The sketch of "The Old Apple-Dealer" is conceived in the subtlest spirit of sadness; he whose "subdued and nerveless boyhood prefigured his abortive prime, which, likewise, contained within itself the prophecy and image of his lean and torpid age." Such touches as are in this piece cannot proceed from any common heart. They argue such a depth of tenderness, such a boundless sympathy with all forms of being, such an omnipresent love, that we must needs say that this Hawthorne is here almost alone—in his generation at least—in the artistic manifestation of these things. Still more. Such touches as these—and many, very many similar ones, all through his chapters—furnish clues, whereby we enter a little way into the intricate, profound heart where they originated. And we see that suffering, some time or other and in some shape or other—this only can enable any man to depict it in others. All over him, Hawthorne's melancholy rests like an Indian summer, which, though bathing a whole country in one softness, still reveals the distinctive hue of every towering hill, and each far-winding vale.

But it is the least part of genius that attracts admiration. Where Hawthorne is known, he seems to be deemed a pleasant writer, with a pleasant style—a sequestered, harmless man, from whom any deep and weighty thing would hardly be anticipated: a man who means no meanings. But there is no man, in whom humor and love, like mountain peaks, soar to such a rapt height, as to receive the irradiations of the upper skies; there is no man in whom humor and love are developed in that high form called genius—no such man can exist without also possessing, as the indispensable complement of these, a great, deep intellect, which drops down into the universe like a plummet. Or, love and humor are only the eyes, through which such an intellect views this world. The great beauty in such a mind is but the product of its strength. What, to all readers, can be more charming than the piece entitled "Monsieur du Miroir"; and to a reader at all capable of fully fathoming it, what, at the same time, can possess more mystical depth of meaning?—Yes, there he sits, and looks at me—this "shape of mystery," this "identical Monsieur du Miroir."—"Methinks I should tremble now, were his wizard power, of gliding through all impediments in search of me, to place him suddenly before my eyes."

How profound, nay, appalling, is the moral evolved by the "Earth's Holocaust," where—beginning with the hollow follies and affectations of the world—all vanities and empty theories and forms are, one after another, and by an admirably graduated, growing comprehensiveness, thrown into the allegorical fire, till, at length, nothing is left but the all-engendering heart of man; which remaining still unconsumed, the great conflagration is naught.

Of a piece with this is "The Intelligence Office," a wondrous symbolizing of the secret workings in men's souls. There are other sketches, still more charged with ponderous import.

"The Christmas Banquet" and "The Bosom Serpent" would be fine subjects for a curious and elaborate analysis, touching the conjectural parts of the mind that produced them. For spite of all the Indian-summer sunlight on the hither side of Hawthorne's soul, the other side—like the dark half of the physical sphere—is shrouded in a blackness, ten times black. But this darkness but gives more effect to the ever-moving dawn, that forever advances through it, and circumnavigates his world. Whether Hawthorne has simply availed himself of this mystical blackness as a means to the wondrous effects he makes it to produce in his lights and shades; or whether there really lurks in him, perhaps unknown to himself, a touch of Puritanic gloom—this, I cannot altogether tell. Certain it is, however, that this great power of blackness in him derives its force from its appeals to that Calvinistic sense of Innate Depravity and Original Sin, from whose visitations, in some shape or other, no deeply thinking mind is always and wholly free. For, in certain moods, no man can weigh this world, without throwing in something, somehow like Original Sin, to strike the uneven balance. At all events, perhaps no writer has ever wielded this terrific thought with greater terror than this same harmless Hawthorne. Still more: this black conceit pervades him, through and through. You may be witched by his sunlight, transported by the bright gildings in the skies he builds over you, but there is the blackness of darkness beyond; and even his bright gildings but fringe and play upon the edges of thunder-clouds. —In one word, the world is mistaken in this Nathaniel Hawthorne. He himself must often have smiled at its absurd misconception of him. He is immeasurably deeper than the plummet of the mere critic. For it is not the brain that can test such a man; it is only the heart. You cannot come to know greatness by inspecting it; there is no glimpse to be caught of it, except by intuition; you need not ring it, you but touch it, and you find it is gold.

Now it is that blackness in Hawthorne, of which I have spoken, that so fixes and fascinates me. It may be, nevertheless, that it is too largely developed in him. Perhaps he does not give us a ray of his light for every shade of his dark. But however this may be, this blackness it is that furnishes the infinite obscure of his background—that background, against which Shakespeare plays his grandest conceits, the things that have made for Shakespeare his loftiest but most circumscribed renown, as the profoundest of thinkers. For by philosophers Shakespeare is not adored as the great man of tragedy and comedy.—"Off with his head! so much for Buckingham!" This sort of rant, interlined by another hand, brings down the house—those mistaken souls, who dream of Shakespeare as a mere man of Richard-the-Third humps, and Macbeth daggers. But it is those deep far-away things in him; those occasional flashings-forth of the intuitive Truth in him; those short, quick probings at the very axis of reality;—these are the things that make Shakespeare Shakespeare. Through the mouths of the dark characters of Hamlet, Timon, Lear, and Iago, he craftily says, or sometimes insinuates, the things which we feel to be so terrifically true that it were all but madness for any good man, in his own proper character, to utter, or even hint of them. Tormented into desperation, Lear the frantic king tears off the mask, and speaks the sane madness of vital truth. But, as I before said, it is the least part of genius that attracts admiration. And so, much of the blind, unbridled admiration that has been heaped upon Shakespeare has been lavished upon the least part of him. And few of his endless commentators and critics seem to have remembered, or even perceived, that the immediate products of a great mind are not so great as that undeveloped, and sometimes undevelopable yet dimly discernible greatness, to which these immediate products are but the infallible indices. In Shakespeare's tomb lies infinitely more than Shakespeare ever wrote. And if I magnify Shakespeare, it is not so much for what he did do, as for what he did not do, or refrained from doing. For in this world of lies, Truth is forced to fly like a scared white doe in the woodlands; and only by cunning glimpses will she reveal herself, as in Shakespeare and other masters of the great Art of Telling the Truth—even though it be covertly, and by snatches.

But if this view of the all-popular Shakespeare be seldom taken by his readers, and if very few who extol him have ever read him deeply, or, perhaps, only have seen him on the tricky stage (which alone made, and is still making, him his mere mob renown)—if few men have time, or patience, or palate, for the spiritual truth as it is in that great genius—it is, then, no matter of surprise that in a contemporaneous age, Nathaniel Hawthorne is a man as yet almost utterly mistaken among men. Here and there, in some quiet armchair in the noisy town, or some deep nook among the noiseless mountains, he may be appreciated for something of what he is. But unlike Shakespeare, who was forced to the contrary course by circumstances, Hawthorne (either from simple disinclination, or else from inaptitude) refrains from all the popularizing noise and show of broad farce, and blood-besmeared tragedy; content with the still, rich utterances of a great intellect in repose, and which sends few thoughts into circulation, except they be arterialized at his large warm lungs, and expanded in his honest heart.

Nor need you fix upon that blackness in him, if it suit you not. Nor, indeed, will all readers discern it, for it is, mostly, insinuated to those who may best understand it, and account for it; it is not obtruded upon every one alike.

Some may start to read of Shakespeare and Hawthorne on the same page. They may say, that if an illustration were needed, a lesser light might have sufficed to elucidate this Hawthorne, this small man of yesterday. But I am not, willingly, one of those who, as touching Shakespeare at least, exemplify the maxim of Rochefoucauld,[2] that "we exalt the reputation of some, in order to depress that of others"; who, to teach all noble-souled aspirants that there is no hope for them, pronounce Shakespeare absolutely unapproachable. But Shakespeare has been approached. There are minds that have gone as far as Shakespeare into the universe. And hardly a mortal man, who, at some time or other, has not felt as great thoughts in him as any you will find in *Hamlet*. We must not inferentially malign mankind for the sake of any one man, whoever he may be. This is too cheap a purchase of contentment for conscious mediocrity to make. Besides, this absolute and unconditional

2. **Rochefoucauld:** the Duc de La Rochefoucauld, who in the seventeenth century wrote his worldly and witty *Maximes*.

adoration of Shakespeare has grown to be a part of our Anglo-Saxon superstitions. The Thirty-Nine Articles [3] are now Forty. Intolerance has come to exist in this matter. You must believe in Shakespeare's unapproachability, or quit the country. But what sort of a belief is this for an American, a man who is bound to carry republican progressiveness into Literature, as well as into Life? Believe me, my friends, that men not very much inferior to Shakespeare are this day being born on the banks of the Ohio. And the day will come when you shall say; who reads a book by an Englishman that is a modern? The great mistake seems to be that even with those Americans who look forward to the coming of a great literary genius among us, they somehow fancy he will come in the costume of Queen Elizabeth's day, be a writer of dramas founded upon old English history, or the tales of Boccaccio.[4] Whereas great geniuses are parts of the times; they themselves are the times, and possess a correspondent coloring. It is of a piece with the Jews, who, while their Shiloh [5] was meekly walking in their streets, were still praying for his magnificent coming; looking for him in a chariot, who was already among them on an ass. Nor must we forget that, in his own lifetime, Shakespeare was not Shakespeare, but only Master William Shakespeare of the shrewd, thriving business firm of Condell, Shakespeare & Co., proprietors of the Globe Theatre in London, and by a courtly author, of the name of Chettle,[6] was looked at as an "upstart crow" beautified "with other birds' feathers." For, mark it well, imitation is often the first charge brought against real originality. Why this is so, there is not space to set forth here. You must have plenty of sea-room to tell the Truth in; especially when it seems to have an aspect of newness, as America did in 1492, though it was then just as old, and perhaps older than Asia, only those sagacious philosophers, the common sailors, had never seen it before, swearing it was all water and moonshine there.

Now, I do not say that Nathaniel of Salem is a greater than William of Avon, or as great. But the difference between the two men is by no means immeasurable. Not a very great deal more, and Nathaniel were verily William.

This, too, I mean—that if Shakespeare has not been equaled, give the world time, and he is sure to be surpassed, in one hemisphere or the other. Nor will it at all do to say that the world is getting gray and grizzled now, and has lost that fresh charm which she wore of old, and by virtue of which the great poets of past times made themselves what we esteem them to be. Not so. The world is as young today as when it was created and this Vermont morning dew is as wet to my feet as Eden's dew to Adam's. Nor has Nature been all over ransacked by our progenitors, so that no new charms and mysteries remain for this latter generation to find. Far from it. The trillionth part has not yet been said, and all that has been said but multiplies the avenues to what remains to be said. It is not so much paucity as superabundance of material that seems to incapacitate modern authors.

Let America then prize and cherish her writers; yea, let her glorify them. They are not so many in number as to exhaust her good will. And while she has good kith and kin of her own, to take to her bosom, let her not lavish her embraces upon the household of an alien. For believe it or not, England, after all, is, in many things, an alien to us. China has more bowels of real love for us than she. But even were there no strong literary individualities among us, as there are some dozen at least, nevertheless, let America first praise mediocrity even, in her own children, before she praises (for everywhere, merit demands acknowledgment from every one) the best excellence in the children of any other land. Let her own authors, I say, have the priority of appreciation. I was much pleased with a hot-headed Carolina cousin of mine, who once said, "If there were no other American to stand by, in Literature—why, then, I would stand by Pop Emmons and his *Fredoniad*,[7] and till a better epic came along, swear it was not very far behind the *Iliad*." Take away the words, and in spirit he was sound.

Not that American genius needs patronage in order to expand. For that explosive sort of stuff will expand though screwed up in a vise, and burst it, though it were triple steel. It is for the nation's sake, and not for her authors' sake, that I would have America be heedful of the increasing greatness among her writers. For how great the shame, if other nations should be before her, in crowning her heroes of the pen! But this is almost the case now. American authors have received more just and discriminating praise (however loftily and ridiculously given, in certain cases) even from some Englishmen, than from their own country-

3. **Thirty-Nine Articles:** These state the creed of the Anglican Church. 4. **Boccaccio:** Giovanni Boccaccio, the fourteenth-century Italian author of the *Decameron*. 5. **Shiloh:** a site of Jewish ritual and faith in Old Testament times. Melville uses the word in the sense of "Messiah." 6. **Chettle:** Henry Chettle, a minor playwright of Shakespeare's time. The words Melville attributes to Chettle, however, were actually those of Robert Greene, another writer of the time.

7. ***Fredoniad:*** Richard Emmons' poem was an abortive epic about the War of 1812.

men. There are hardly five critics in America; and several of them are asleep. As for patronage, it is the American author who now patronizes his country, and not his country him. And if at times some among them appeal to the people for more recognition, it is not always with selfish motives, but patriotic ones.

It is true that but few of them as yet have evinced that decided originality which merits great praise. But that graceful writer,[8] who perhaps of all Americans has received the most plaudits from his own country for his productions—that very popular and amiable writer, however good, and self-reliant in many things, perhaps owes his chief reputation to the self-acknowledged imitation of a foreign model, and to the studied avoidance of all topics but smooth ones. But it is better to fail in originality than to succeed in imitation. He who has never failed somewhere, that man can not be great. Failure is the true test of greatness. And if it be said that continual success is a proof that a man wisely knows his powers, it is only to be added that, in that case, he knows them to be small. Let us believe it, then, once for all, that there is no hope for us in these smooth, pleasing writers that know their powers. Without malice, but to speak the plain fact, they but furnish an appendix to Goldsmith, and other English authors. And we want no American Goldsmiths; nay, we want no American Miltons. It were the vilest thing you could say of a true American author, that he were an American Tompkins. Call him an American, and have done; for you cannot say a nobler thing of him.—But it is not meant that all American writers should studiously cleave to nationality in their writings; only this, no American writer should write like an Englishman, or a Frenchman; let him write like a man, for then he will be sure to write like an American. Let us away with this leaven of literary flunkyism towards England. If either must play the flunky in this thing, let England do it, not us. While we are rapidly preparing for that political supremacy among the nations, which prophetically awaits us at the close of the present century, in a literary point of view we are deplorably unprepared for it, and we seem studious to remain so. Hitherto, reasons might have existed why this should be; but no good reason exists now. And all that is requisite to amendment in this matter is simply this: that, while freely acknowledging all excellence, everywhere, we should refrain from unduly lauding foreign writers and, at the same time, duly recognize the meritorious writers that are our own; those writers who breathe that unshackled, democratic spirit of Christianity in all things, which now takes the practical lead in this world, though at the same time led by ourselves—us Americans. Let us boldly contemn all imitation, though it comes to us graceful and fragrant as the morning, and foster all originality, though, at first, it be crabbed and ugly as our own pine knots. And if any of our authors fail, or seem to fail, then, in the words of my enthusiastic Carolina cousin, let us clap him on the shoulder, and back him against all Europe for his second round. The truth is that, in our point of view, this matter of a national literature has come to such a pass with us that in some sense we must turn bullies, else the day is lost, or superiority so far beyond us, that we can hardly say it will ever be ours.

And now, my countrymen, as an excellent author, of your own flesh and blood—an unimitating, and, perhaps, in his way, an inimitable man—whom better can I commend to you, in the first place, than Nathaniel Hawthorne. He is one of the new and far better generation of your writers. The smell of your beeches and hemlocks is upon him; your own broad prairies are in his soul; and if you travel away inland into his deep and noble nature, you will hear the far roar of his Niagara. Give not over to future generations the glad duty of acknowledging him for what he is. Take that joy to yourself, in your own generation; and so shall he feel those grateful impulses in him that may possibly prompt him to the full flower of some still greater achievement in your eyes. And by confessing him, you thereby confess others; you brace the whole brotherhood. For genius, all over the world, stands hand in hand, and one shock of recognition runs the whole circle round.

In treating of Hawthorne, or rather of Hawthorne in his writings (for I never saw the man,[9] and in the chances of a quiet plantation life, remote from his haunts, perhaps never shall); in treating of his works, I say, I have thus far omitted all mention of his *Twice-Told Tales,* and *The Scarlet Letter*. Both are excellent, but full of such manifold, strange, and diffusive beauties, that time would all but fail me to point the half of them out. But there are things in those two books which, had they been written in England a century ago, Nathaniel Hawthorne had utterly displaced many of the bright names we now revere on authority. But I am content to leave Hawthorne to himself, and to the infallible finding of posterity; and however great may be the praise I have

8. **graceful writer:** undoubtedly an allusion to Washington Irving.

9. **for . . . man:** not strictly true, since Melville had been on a mountain hike and picnic with Hawthorne and other literary people shortly before he began the composition of "Hawthorne and His Mosses."

bestowed upon him, I feel, that in so doing, I have more served and honored myself than him. For, at bottom, great excellence is praise enough to itself; but the feeling of a sincere and appreciative love and admiration towards it—this is relieved by utterance; and warm, honest praise ever leaves a pleasant flavor in the mouth; and it is an honorable thing to confess to what is honorable in others.

But I cannot leave my subject yet. No man can read a fine author, and relish him to his very bones, while he reads, without subsequently fancying to himself some ideal image of the man and his mind. And if you rightly look for it, you will almost always find that the author himself has somewhere furnished you with his own picture. For poets (whether in prose or verse), being painters of Nature, are like their brethren of the pencil, the true portrait painters, who, in the multitude of likenesses to be sketched, do not invariably omit their own; and in all high instances, they paint them without any vanity, though, at times, with a lurking something, that would take several pages to properly define.

I submit it, then, to those best acquainted with the man personally, whether the following is not Nathaniel Hawthorne; and to himself, whether something involved in it does not express the temper of his mind—that lasting temper of all true, candid men—a seeker, not a finder yet:

> A man now entered, in neglected attire, with the aspect of a thinker, but somewhat too rough-hewn and brawny for a scholar. His face was full of sturdy vigor, with some finer and keener attribute beneath; though harsh at first, it was tempered with the glow of a large, warm heart, which had force enough to heat his powerful intellect through and through. He advanced to the Intelligencer, and looked at him with a glance of such stern sincerity, that perhaps few secrets were beyond its scope.
>
> "I seek for Truth," said he.

Twenty-four hours have elapsed since writing the foregoing. I have just returned from the haymow, charged more and more with love and admiration of Hawthorne. For I have just been gleaning through the *Mosses,* picking up many things here and there that had previously escaped me. And I found that but to glean after this man is better than to be in at the harvest of others. To be frank (though, perhaps, rather foolish), notwithstanding what I wrote yesterday of these Mosses, I had not then culled them all; but had, nevertheless, been sufficiently sensible of the subtle essences in them as to write as I did. To what infinite height of loving wonder and admiration I may yet be borne, when by repeatedly banqueting on these Mosses, I shall have thoroughly incorporated their whole stuff into my being—that, I can not tell. But already I feel that this Hawthorne has dropped germinous seeds into my soul. He expands and deepens down, the more I contemplate him; and further, and further, shoots his strong New England roots into the hot soil of my Southern soul.

By careful reference to the "Table of Contents," I now find that I have gone through all the sketches, but that when I yesterday wrote I had not at all read two particular pieces to which I now desire to call special attention—"A Select Party," and "Young Goodman Brown." Here be it said to all those whom this poor fugitive scrawl of mine may tempt to the perusal of the *Mosses* that they must on no account suffer themselves to be trifled with, disappointed, or deceived by the triviality of many of the titles to these Sketches. For in more than one instance the title utterly belies the piece. It is as if rustic demijohns containing the very best and costliest of Falernian and Tokay were labeled "Cider," "Perry," and "Elderberry Wine." The truth seems to be that, like many other geniuses, this Man of Mosses takes great delight in hoodwinking the world—at least with respect to himself. Personally, I doubt not that he rather prefers to be generally esteemed but a so-so sort of author; being willing to reserve the thorough and acute appreciation of what he is to that party most qualified to judge—that is, to himself. Besides, at the bottom of their natures, men like Hawthorne, in many things, deem the plaudits of the public such strong presumptive evidence of mediocrity in the object of them, that it would in some degree render them doubtful of their own powers, did they hear much and vociferous braying concerning them in the public pastures. True, I have been braying myself (if you please to be witty enough to have it so), but then I claim to be the first that has so brayed in this particular matter; and therefore, while pleading guilty to the charge, still claim all the merit due to originality.

But with whatever motive, playful or profound, Nathaniel Hawthorne has chosen to entitle his pieces in the manner he has, it is certain that some of them are directly calculated to deceive—egregiously deceive—the superficial skimmer of pages. To be downright and candid once more, let me cheerfully say that two of these titles did dolefully dupe no less an eagle-eyed reader than myself; and that, too, after I had been impressed with a sense of the great depth and breadth of this American man. "Who in the name of thunder" (as the country people say in this neighborhood), "who in the name of thunder," would anticipate any marvel in a piece entitled "Young Goodman Brown"? You would of course suppose that it was a simple little tale, intended as a supplement to "Goody Two-Shoes." Whereas it is deep as Dante; nor can you finish it, without addressing the author in his own words: "It is yours to penetrate, in every bosom, the deep mystery of sin." And with Young Goodman, too, in allegorical pursuit of his Puritan wife, you cry out in your anguish:

> "Faith!" shouted Goodman Brown, in a voice of agony and desperation; and the echoes of the forest mocked him, crying—"Faith! Faith!" as if bewildered wretches were seeking her, all through the wilderness.

Now this same piece, entitled "Young Goodman Brown," is one of the two that I had not at all read yesterday; and I allude to it now, because it is, in itself, such a strong positive illustration of of that blackness in Hawthorne which I had assumed from the mere occasional shadows of it, as revealed in several of the other sketches. But had I previously perused "Young Goodman Brown," I should have been at no pains to draw the conclusion which I came to at a time when I was ignorant that the book contained one such direct and unqualified manifestation of it.

The other piece of the two referred to is entitled "A Select Party," which, in my first simplicity upon originally taking hold of the book, I fancied must treat of some pumpkin-pie party in Old Salem, or some chowder party on Cape Cod. Whereas, by all the gods of Peedee! it is the sweetest and sublimest thing that has been written since Spenser wrote. Nay, there is nothing in Spenser that surpasses it, perhaps, nothing that equals it. And the test is this: read any canto in *The Faery Queen,* and then read "A Select Party," and decide which pleases you the most—that is, if you are qualified to judge. Do not be frightened at this; for when Spenser was alive, he was thought of very much as Hawthorne is now, was generally accounted just such a "gentle" harmless man. It may be that, to common eyes, the sublimity of Hawthorne seems lost in his sweetness—as perhaps in this same "Select Party" of his, for whom he has builded so august a dome of sunset clouds, and served them on richer plate than Belshazzar's when he banqueted his lords in Babylon.[10]

But my chief business now is to point out a particular page in this piece, having reference to an honored guest, who, under the name of "The Master Genius" but in the guise "of a young man of poor attire, with no insignia of rank or acknowledged eminence," is introduced to the Man of Fancy, who is the giver of the feast. Now the page having reference to this "Master Genius" so happily expresses much of what I yesterday wrote, touching the coming of the literary Shiloh of America, that I cannot but be charmed by the coincidence; especially, when it shows such a parity of ideas, at least in this one point, between a man like Hawthorne and a man like me.

And here, let me throw out another conceit of mine touching this American Shiloh, or "Master Genius," as Hawthorne calls him. May it not be, that this commanding mind has not been, is not, and never will be, individually developed in any one man? And would it, indeed, appear so unreasonable to suppose that this great fullness and overflowing may be, or may be destined to be, shared by a plurality of men of genius? Surely, to take the very greatest example on record, Shakespeare cannot be regarded as in himself the concretion of all the genius of his time, nor as so immeasurably beyond Marlowe, Webster, Ford, Beaumont, Jonson, that those great men can be said to share none of his power? For one, I conceive that there were dramatists in Elizabeth's day, between whom and Shakespeare the distance was by no means great. Let anyone, hitherto little acquainted with those neglected old authors, for the first time read them thoroughly, or even read Charles Lamb's *Specimens* of them, and he will be amazed at the wondrous ability of those Anaks [11] of men, and shocked at this renewed example of the fact that Fortune has more to do with fame than merit—though, without merit, lasting fame there can be none.

Nevertheless, it would argue too illy of my country were this maxim to hold good concerning Nathaniel Hawthorne, a man, who already, in some few minds, has shed "such a light as never illuminates the earth, save when a great heart burns as the household fire of a grand intellect."

The words are his—in "A Select Party"; and they are a magnificent setting to a coincident sentiment of my own, but ramblingly expressed yesterday, in reference to himself. Gainsay it who will, as I now write, I am Posterity speaking by proxy—and after times will make it more than good, when I declare that the American, who up to the present day, has evinced, in Literature, the largest brain with the largest heart—that man is Nathaniel Hawthorne. Moreover, that whatever Nathaniel Hawthorne may hereafter write, the *Mosses from an Old Manse* will be ultimately accounted his masterpiece. For there is a sure though a secret

10. **Belshazzar's . . . Babylon:** Dan. 5:1–4.

11. **Anaks:** a legendary race of giants; see Num. 13:33.

sign in some works which proves the culmination of the powers (only the developable ones, however) that produced them. But I am by no means desirous of the glory of a prophet. I pray Heaven that Hawthorne may *yet* prove me an impostor in this prediction. Especially, as I somehow cling to the strange fancy that, in all men, hiddenly reside certain wondrous, occult properties—as in some plants and minerals—which by some happy but very rare accident (as bronze was discovered by the melting of the iron and brass in the burning of Corinth) may chance to be called forth here on earth, not entirely waiting for their better discovery in the more congenial, blessed atmosphere of heaven.

Once more—for it is hard to be finite upon an infinite subject, and all subjects are infinite. By some people, this entire scrawl of mine may be esteemed altogether unnecessary, inasmuch, "as years ago" (they may say) "we found out the rich and rare stuff in this Hawthorne, whom you now parade forth as if only *yourself* were the discoverer of this Portuguese diamond in our Literature."—But even granting all this—and adding to it, the assumption that the books of Hawthorne have sold by the five thousand—what does that signify? They should be sold by the hundred thousand, and read by the million, and admired by every one who is capable of admiration.

LETTERS TO HAWTHORNE

◊

AS THEIR dates indicate, the first three of the following letters were written to Hawthorne before *Moby-Dick* was finished. The fourth is Melville's eloquent and grateful response to the letter (unfortunately not preserved) Hawthorne wrote to him after reading *Moby-Dick*. Like "Hawthorne and His Mosses," these impulsive and spontaneous letters are of inestimable value in understanding Melville's thoughts and feelings at this crucial point in his life.

◊

I

Pittsfield, Wednesday morning [April, 1851]

MY DEAR HAWTHORNE,

Concerning the young gentleman's shoes, I desire to say that a pair to fit him, of the desired pattern cannot be had in all Pittsfield,—a fact which sadly impairs that metropolitan pride I formerly took in the capital of Berkshire. Henceforth Pittsfield must hide its head. However, if a pair of *bootees* will at all answer, Pittsfield will be very happy to provide them. Pray mention all this to Mrs. Hawthorne, and command me.

"The House of the Seven Gables: A Romance. By Nathaniel Hawthorne. One vol. 16mo, pp. 344." The contents of this book do not belie its rich, clustering, romantic title. With great enjoyment we spent almost an hour in each separate gable. This book is like a fine old chamber, abundantly, but still judiciously, furnished with precisely that sort of furniture best fitted to furnish it. There are rich hangings, whereon are broidered scenes from tragedies. There is old china with rare devices, set about on the carved buffet; there are long and indolent lounges to throw yourself upon; there is an admirable sideboard, plentifully stored with good viands; there is a smell as of old wine in the pantry; and finally, in one corner, there is a dark little black-letter volume in golden clasps, entitled "Hawthorne: A Problem." It has delighted us; it has piqued a reperusal; it has robbed us of a day, and made us a present of a whole year of thoughtfulness; it has bred great exhilaration and exultation with the remembrance that the architect of the Gables resides only six miles off, and not three thousand miles away in England, say. We think the book, for pleasantness of running interest, surpasses the other works of the author. The curtains are now drawn; the sun comes in more; genialities peep out more. Were we to particularize what most struck us in the deeper passages, we would point out the scene where Clifford, for a moment, would fain throw himself forth from the window to join the procession; or the scene where the judge is left seated in his ancestral chair. Clifford is full of an awful truth throughout. He is conceived in the finest, truest spirit. He is no caricature. He is Clifford. And here we would say that, did circumstances permit, we should like nothing better than to devote an elaborate and careful paper to the full consideration and analysis of the purport and significance of what so strongly characterizes all of this author's writings. There is a certain tragic phase of humanity which, in our opinion, was never more powerfully embodied than by Hawthorne: we mean the tragicalness of human thought in its own unbiassed, native, and profounder workings. We think that into no recorded mind has the intense feeling of the visible truth ever entered more deeply than into this man's. By visible truth, we mean the apprehension of the absolute condition of present things as they strike the eye of the man who fears them not, though they do their worst to him,—the man who, like Russia or the British Empire, declares himself a sovereign nature (in himself) amid the powers of heaven, hell, and earth. He may perish; but so long as he exists he insists upon treating with all Powers upon an equal basis. If any of those other Powers choose to withhold certain secrets, let them; that does not impair my sovereignty in myself; that does not make me tributary. And perhaps, after all, there is *no* secret. We incline to think that the Problem of the Universe is like the Freemason's [1] mighty secret, so terrible to all children. It turns out, at last, to consist in a triangle, a mallet, and an apron,—nothing more! We incline to think that God cannot explain His own secrets, and that He would like a little information upon certain points Himself. We mortals astonish Him as much as He us. But it is this *Being* of the matter; there lies the knot with which we choke ourselves. As soon as you say *Me,* a *God,* a *Nature,* so soon you jump off from your stool and hang from the beam. Yes, that word is the hangman. Take God out of the dictionary, and you would have Him in the street.

There is the grand truth about Nathaniel Hawthorne. He says NO! in thunder; but the Devil himself cannot make him say *yes*. For all men who say *yes,* lie; and all men who say *no,* —why, they are in the happy condition of judicious, unincumbered travellers in Europe; they cross the frontiers into Eternity with nothing but a carpet-bag,—that is to say, the Ego. Whereas those *yes*-gentry, they travel with heaps of baggage, and, damn them! they will never get through the Custom House. What's the reason, Mr Hawthorne, that in the last stages of metaphysics a fellow always falls to *swearing* so? I could rip an hour. You see, I began with a little criticism extracted for your benefit from the "Pittsfield Secret Review," and here I have landed in Africa.

Walk down one of these mornings and see me. No nonsense; come. Remember me to Mrs. Hawthorne and the children.

H. MELVILLE

P.S. The marriage of Phoebe with the daguerreotypist is a fine stroke, because of his turning out to be a *Maule*. If you pass Hepzibah's cent-shop, buy me a Jim Crow (fresh) and send it to me by Ned Higgins.[2]

2

[June, 1851]

MY DEAR HAWTHORNE—

I should have been rumbling down to you in my pine-board chariot a long time ago, were it not that for some weeks past I have been more busy than you can well imagine,—out of doors,—building and patching and tinkering away in all directions. Besides, I had my crops to get in,—corn and potatoes (I hope to show you some famous ones by and by),—and many other things to attend to, all accumulating upon this one particular season. I work myself; and at night my bodily sensations are akin to those I have so often felt before, when a hired man, doing my day's work from sun to sun. But I mean to continue visiting you until you tell me that my visits are both supererogatory and superfluous. With no son of man do I stand upon any etiquette or ceremony, except the Christian ones of charity and honesty. I am told, my fellow-man, that there is an aristocracy of the brain. Some men have boldly advocated and asserted it. Schiller [3] seems to have done so, though I don't know much about him. At any rate, it is true that there have been those who, while earnest in behalf of political equality, still accept the intellectual estates. And I can well perceive, I think, how a man of superior mind can, by its intense cultivation, bring himself, as it were, into a certain spontaneous aristocracy of feeling,—exceedingly nice and fastidious,—similar to that which, in an English Howard,[4] conveys a torpedo-fish thrill at the slightest contact with a social plebian. So, when you see or hear of my ruthless democracy on all sides, you may possibly feel a touch of a shrink, or something of that sort. It is but nature to be shy of a mortal who boldly declares that a thief in jail is as honorable a personage as Gen. George Washington. This is ludicrous. But Truth is the silliest thing under the sun. Try to get a living by the Truth—and go to the Soup Societies. Heavens! Let any clergyman try to preach the Truth from its very stronghold, the pulpit, and they would ride him out of his church on his own pulpit bannister. It can hardly be doubted that all Reformers are bottomed upon the truth, more or less; and to the world at large are not reformers almost universally laughing-stocks? Why so? Truth is ridiculous to men. Thus easily in my room here do I, conceited and garrulous, reverse the test of my Lord Shaftesbury.[5]

LETTERS TO HAWTHORNE. 1. **Freemason:** a member of the fraternity of Freemasonry, a secret organization founded in the eighteenth century; it was devoted to the ideals of the brotherhood of man and agnosticism in religion and practiced the kind of fraternity ritual to which Melville refers. 2. **The . . . Higgins:** further allusions to characters in *The House of the Seven Gables.*

3. **Schiller:** J. C. F. von Schiller (1759–1805), the German poet and critic. 4. **Howard:** Melville uses the illustrious Howard family as a general symbol of aristocracy. 5. **Lord Shaftesbury:** In his *Characteristics* (1711) Shaftesbury proposes to test

It seems an inconsistency to assert unconditional democracy in all things, and yet confess a dislike to all mankind—in the mass. But not so.—But it's an endless sermon,—no more of it. I began by saying that the reason I have not been to Lenox is this,—in the evening I feel completely done up, as the phrase is, and incapable of the long jolting to get to your house and back. In a week or so, I go to New York, to bury myself in a third-story room, and work and slave on my "Whale"[6] while it is driving through the press. *That* is the only way I can finish it now,—I am so pulled hither and thither by circumstances. The calm, the coolness, the silent grass-growing mood in which a man *ought* always to compose,—that, I fear, can seldom be mine. Dollars damn me; and the malicious Devil is forever grinning in upon me, holding the door ajar. My dear Sir, a presentiment is on me,—I shall at last be worn out and perish, like an old nutmeg-grater, grated to pieces by the constant attrition of the wood, that is, the nutmeg. What I feel most moved to write, that is banned,—it will not pay. Yet, altogether, write the *other* way I cannot. So the product is a final hash, and all my books are botches. I'm rather sore, perhaps, in this letter; but see my hand! four blisters on this palm, made by hoes and hammers within the last few days. It is a rainy morning; so I am indoors, and all work suspended. I feel cheerfully disposed, and therefore I write a little bluely. Would the Gin[7] were here! If ever, my dear Hawthorne, in the eternal times that are to come, you and I shall sit down in Paradise, in some little shady corner by ourselves; and if we shall by any means be able to smuggle a basket of champagne there (I won't believe in a Temperance Heaven), and if we shall then cross our celestial legs in the celestial grass that is forever tropical, and strike our glasses and our heads together, till both musically ring in concert,—then, O my dear fellow-mortal, how shall we pleasantly discourse of all the things manifold which now so distress us,—when all the earth shall be but a reminiscence, yea, its final dissolution an antiquity. Then shall songs be composed as when wars are over: humorous, comic songs,—"Oh, when I lived in that queer little hole called the world," or, "Oh, when I toiled and sweated below," or, "Oh, when I knocked and was knocked in the fight"—yes, let us look forward to such things. Let us swear that, though now we sweat, yet it is because of the dry heat which is indispensable to the nourishment of the vine which is to bear the grapes that are to give us the champagne hereafter.

But I was talking about the "Whale." As the fishermen say, "he's in his flurry" when I left him some three weeks ago. I'm going to take him by his jaw, however, before long, and finish him up in some fashion or other. What's the use of elaborating what, in its very essence, is so short-lived as a modern book? Though I wrote the Gospels in this century, I should die in the gutter.—I talk all about myself, and this is selfishness and egotism. Granted. But how help it? I am writing to you; I know little about you, but something about myself. So I write about myself,—at least to you. Don't trouble yourself, though, about writing; and don't trouble yourself about visiting; and when you *do* visit, don't trouble yourself about talking. I will do all the writing and visiting and talking myself.—By the way, in the last "Dollar Magazine" I read "The Unpardonable Sin." He was a sad fellow, that Ethan Brand.[8] I have no doubt you are by this time responsible for many a shake and tremor of the tribe of "general readers." It is a frightful poetical creed that the cultivation of the brain eats out the heart. But it's my *prose* opinion that in most cases, in those men who have fine brains and work them well, the heart extends down to hams. And though you smoke them with the fire of tribulation, yet, like veritable hams, the head only gives the richer and the better flavor. I stand for the heart. To the dogs with the head! I had rather be a fool with a heart, than Jupiter Olympus with his head. The reason the mass of men fear God, and *at bottom dislike* Him, is because they rather distrust His Heart, and fancy Him all brain like a watch. (You perceive I employ a capital initial in the pronoun referring to the Deity; don't you think there is a slight dash of flunkeyism in that usage?) Another thing. I was in New York for four-and-twenty hours the other day, and saw a portrait of N.H. And I have seen and heard many flattering (in a publisher's point of view) allusions to the "Seven Gables." And I have seen "Tales" and "A New Volume" announced, by N.H. So upon the whole, I say to myself, this N.H. is in the

the truth by subjecting it to ridicule, rather than, as Melville somewhat perversely does, declaring it to *be* ridiculous. Melville, however, does not mean that truth is in itself ridiculous; he means that as compared with the conventional half-truths by which men live it must always seem so. **6. "Whale"**: While he was writing his book, Melville evidently thought of calling it *The Whale*, and it was in fact published in England under that title. The American edition, which soon followed, was called *Moby-Dick: or, The Whale*. **7. Gin**: A jinni is a spirit in Mohammedan mythology capable of performing services for (or doing evil to) human beings.

8. Ethan Brand: It is of interest that Melville was struck by Hawthorne's "Ethan Brand," for this is a tale of a restless truth-seeker somewhat resembling Melville himself. It cannot be a portrait of Melville, however, for it was written before Hawthorne had met him.

ascendant. My dear Sir, they begin to patronize. All Fame is patronage. Let me be infamous; there is no patronage in *that*. What "reputation" H.M. has is horrible. Think of it! To go down to posterity is bad enough, any way; but to go down as a "man who lived among the cannibals"! When I speak of posterity, in reference to myself, I only mean the babies who will probably be born in the moment immediately ensuing upon my giving up the ghost. I shall go down to some of them, in all likelihood. "Typee" will be given to them, perhaps, with their gingerbread. I have come to regard this matter of Fame as the most transparent of all vanities. I read Solomon [9] more and more, and every time see deeper and deeper and unspeakable meanings in him. I did not think of Fame, a year ago, as I do now. My development has been all within a few years past. I am like one of those seeds taken out of the Egyptian Pyramids, which, after being three thousand years a seed and nothing but a seed, being planted in English soil, it developed itself, grew to greenness, and then fell to mould. So I. Until I was twenty-five, I had no development at all. From my twenty-fifth year I date my life. Three weeks have scarcely passed, at any time between then and now, that I have not unfolded within myself. But I feel that I am now come to the inmost leaf of the bulb, and that shortly the flower must fall to the mould. It seems to me now that Solomon was the truest man who ever spoke, and yet that he a little *managed* the truth with a view to popular conservatism; or else there have been many corruptions and interpolations of the text.—In reading some of Goethe's sayings, so worshipped by his votaries, I came across this, *"Live in the all."* That is to say, your separate identity is but a wretched one,—good; but get out of yourself, spread and expand yourself, and bring to yourself the tinglings of life that are felt in the flowers and the woods, that are felt in the planets Saturn and Venus, and the Fixed Stars. What nonsense! Here is a fellow with a raging toothache. "My dear boy," Goethe says to him, "you are sorely afflicted with that tooth; but you must *live in the all,* and then you will be happy!" As with all great genius, there is an immense deal of flummery in Goethe, and in proportion to my own contact with him, a monstrous deal of it in me.

H. MELVILLE

P.S. "Amen!" saith Hawthorne.

N.B. This "all" feeling, though, there is some truth in. You must often have felt it, lying on the grass on a warm summer's day. Your legs seem to send out shoots into the earth. Your hair feels like leaves upon your head. This is the *all* feeling. But what plays the mischief with the truth is that men will insist upon the universal application of a temporary feeling or opinion.

P.S. You must not fail to admire my discretion in paying the postage on this letter.

9. **Solomon:** Ecclesiastes.

3

Pittsfield, June 29, 1851.

MY DEAR HAWTHORNE—

The clear air and open window invite me to write to you. For some time past I have been so busy with a thousand things that I have almost forgotten when I wrote you last, and whether I received an answer. This most persuasive season has now for weeks recalled me from certain crotchety and over-doleful chimeras, the like of which men like you and me, and some others, forming a chain of God's posts round the world, must be content to encounter now and then, and fight them the best way we can. But come they will,—for, in the boundless, trackless, but still glorious wild wilderness through which these outposts run, the Indians do sorely abound, as well as the insignificant but still stinging mosquitoes. Since you have been here, I have been building some shanties of houses (connected with the old one) and likewise some shanties of chapters and essays. I have been ploughing and sowing and raising and painting and printing and praying,—and now begin to come out upon a less bristling time, and to enjoy the calm prospect of things from a fair piazza at the north of the old farmhouse here.

Not entirely yet, tho', am I without something to be urgent with. The "Whale" is only half thro' the press; for, wearied with the long delays of the printers, and disgusted with the heat and dust of the Babylonish brick-kiln of New York, I came back to the country to feel the grass—and end the book reclining on it, if I may.—I am sure you will pardon this speaking all about myself; for if I *say* so much on that head, be sure all the rest of the world are thinking about themselves ten times as much. Let us speak, tho' we show all our faults and weaknesses,—for it is a sign of strength to be weak, to know it, and out with it,—not in set way and ostentatiously, tho', but incidentally and without premeditation.——But I am falling into my old foible,—preaching. I am busy, but shall not be very long. Come and spend a day here, if you can and want to; if not, stay in Lenox, and God give you long life. When I am quite free of my present engagements, I am going to treat myself to a ride and a visit to you. Have ready a bottle of brandy, because I always feel like drinking that heroic drink when we talk ontological heroics together. This is rather a crazy letter in some respects, I apprehend. If so, ascribe it to the intoxicating effects of the latter end of June operating upon a very susceptible and peradventure feeble temperament.

Shall I send you a fin of the "Whale" by way of a specimen mouthful? The tail is not yet cooked—tho' the hell-fire in which the whole book is broiled might not unreasonably have cooked it all ere this. This is the book's motto (the secret one), Ego non baptiso te in nomine—but make out the rest yourself.[10]

H.M.

4

Pittsfield, Monday afternoon [November, 1851]

MY DEAR HAWTHORNE—

People think that if a man has undergone any hardship, he should have a reward; but for my part, if I have done the hardest possible day's work, and then come to sit down in a corner and eat my supper comfortably—why, then I don't think I deserve any reward for my hard day's work—for am I not now at peace? Is not my supper good? My peace and my supper are my reward, my dear Hawthorne. So your joy-giving and exultation-breeding letter is not my reward for my ditcher's work with that book, but is the good goddess's bonus over and above what was stipulated for—for not one man in five cycles, who is wise, will expect appreciative recognition from his fellows, or any one of them. Appreciation! Recognition! Is love appreciated? Why, ever since Adam, who has got to the meaning of his great allegory—the world? Then we pygmies must be content to have our paper allegories but ill comprehended. I say your appreciation is my glorious gratuity. In my proud, humble way,—a shepherd-king,—I was lord of a little vale in the solitary Crimea; but you have now given me the crown of India. But on trying it on my head, I found it fell down on my ears, notwithstanding their asinine length—for it's only such ears that sustain such crowns.

Your letter was handed me last night on the road going to Mr Morewood's, and I read it there. Had I been at home, I would have sat down at once and answered it. In me divine magnanimities are spontaneous and instantaneous—catch them while you can. The world goes round, and the other side comes up. So now I can't write what I felt. But I felt pantheistic then—your heart beat in my ribs and mine in yours, and both in God's. A sense of unspeakable security is in me this moment, on account of your having understood the book. I have written a wicked book,[11] and feel spotless as the lamb. Ineffable socialities are in me. I would sit down and dine with you and all the gods in old Rome's Pantheon. It is a strange feeling—no hopefulness is in it, no despair. Content—that is it; and irresponsibility; but without licentious inclination. I speak now of my profoundest sense of being, not of an incidental feeling.

Whence come you, Hawthorne? By what right do you drink from my flagon of life? And when I put it to my lips—lo, they are yours and not mine. I feel that the Godhead is broken up like the bread at the Supper, and that we are the pieces. Hence this infinite fraternity of feeling. Now, sympathizing with the paper, my angel turns over another page. You did not care a penny for the book. But, now and then as you read, you understood the pervading thought that impelled the book—and that you praised. Was it not so? You were archangel enough to despise the imperfect body, and embrace the soul. Once you hugged the ugly Socrates because you saw the flame in the mouth, and heard the rushing of the demon,—the familiar,—and recognized the sound; for you have heard it in your own solitudes.

My dear Hawthorne, the atmospheric skepticisms steal into me now, and make me doubtful of my sanity in writing you thus. But, believe me, I am not mad, most noble Festus! [12] But truth is ever incoherent, and when the big hearts strike together, the concussion is a little stunning. Farewell. Don't write a word about the book. That would be robbing me of my miserly delight. I am heartily sorry I ever wrote anything about you—it was paltry. Lord, when shall we be done growing? As long as we have anything more to do, we have done nothing. So, now, let us add Moby Dick to our blessing, and step from that. Leviathan is not the biggest fish;—I have heard of Krakens.[13]

This is a long letter, but you are not at all bound

10. **Ego . . . yourself:** The sense of Melville's words is made clear by Chapter 113 of *Moby-Dick*, where Ahab declares: "*Ego non baptizo te in nomine patris, sed in nomine diaboli*" ("I do not baptize you in the name of the Father, but in the name of the Devil").

11. **wicked book:** This pronouncement has occasioned much argument among critics of Melville, some holding that in *Moby-Dick* he surrendered to a kind of Black Magic (as 10 n. on baptism might also suggest) and that covertly he was out to annihilate God and all moral values from a purely atheistic point of view. Perhaps he had that impulse, but the passage about having written a wicked book may simply mean that *Moby-Dick* releases passions and deals with subject matters certain to prove shocking to the conventional readers of Melville's time.

12. **I . . . Festus!:** the words of the prisoner, St. Paul, before the magistrate. See Acts 26:25. 13. **Krakens:** sea monsters in Norwegian mythology.

to answer it. Possibly, if you do answer it, and direct it to Herman Melville, you will missend it—for the very fingers that now guide this pen are not precisely the same that just took it up and put it on this paper. Lord, when shall we be done changing? Ah! it's a long stage, and no inn in sight, and night coming, and the body cold. But with you for a passenger, I am content and can be happy. I shall leave the world, I feel, with more satisfaction for having come to know you. Knowing you persuades me more than the Bible of our immortality.

What a pity, that, for your plain, bluff letter, you should get such gibberish! Mention me to Mrs. Hawthorne and to the children, and so, good-by to you, with my blessing.

HERMAN

P.S. I can't stop yet. If the world was entirely made up of Magians,[14] I'll tell you what I should do. I should have a paper-mill established at one end of the house, and so have an endless riband of foolscap rolling in upon my desk; and upon that endless riband I should write a thousand—a million—billion thoughts, all under the form of a letter to you. The divine magnet is on you, and my magnet responds. Which is the biggest? A foolish question—they are *One*.

P.P.S. Don't think that by writing me a letter, you shall always be bored with an immediate reply to it—and so keep both of us delving over a writing-desk eternally. No such thing! I sha'n't always answer your letters, and you may do just as you please.

14. **Magians:** Persian priests, but Melville uses the word to mean magicians or conjurors.

BARTLEBY THE SCRIVENER

A STORY OF WALL STREET

◊

¶ THIS short story was first published in two installments in November and December of 1853 in *Putnam's Monthly Magazine*. When it was republished in Melville's *Piazza Tales* (1856), it was called by one reviewer "the most original story in the volume" and another pronounced it a "portrait from life" and "one of the best bits of writing which ever came from the author's pen." Time has amply confirmed these high estimates of Melville's haunting tale. The extent to which "Bartleby" is a "portrait from life" is a matter of conjecture. But if, as I suggested in the Introduction above, Melville is projecting some of his own impulses and attitudes in the figure of Bartleby, it is of further interest that both Melville's brother Allan and his father-in-law Judge Shaw were lawyers, and that both had, at various times and in various ways, come to the aid of Herman Melville and his shakily financed family.

◊

I AM a rather elderly man. The nature of my avocations, for the last thirty years, has brought me into more than ordinary contact with what would seem an interesting and somewhat singular set of men, of whom, as yet, nothing, that I know of, has ever been written—I mean, the law-copyists, or scriveners. I have known very many of them, professionally and privately, and, if I pleased, could relate divers histories, at which good-natured gentlemen might smile, and sentimental souls might weep. But I waive the biographies of all other scriveners, for a few passages in the life of Bartleby, who was a scrivener, the strangest I ever saw, or heard of. While, of other law-copyists, I might write the complete life, of Bartleby nothing of that sort can be done. I believe that no materials exist for a full and satisfactory biography of this man. It is an irreparable loss to literature. Bartleby was one of those beings of whom nothing is ascertainable, except from the original sources, and, in his case, those are very small. What my own astonished eyes saw of Bartleby, *that* is all I know of him, except, indeed, one vague report, which will appear in the sequel.

Ere introducing the scrivener, as he first appeared to me, it is fit I make some mention of myself, my *employés,* my business, my chambers, and general surroundings; because some such description is indispensable to an adequate understanding of the chief character about to be presented. Imprimis: I am a man who, from his youth upwards, has been filled with a profound conviction that the easiest way of life is the best. Hence, though I belong to a profession proverbially energetic and nervous, even to turbulence, at times, yet nothing of that sort have I ever suffered to invade my peace. I am one of those unambitious lawyers who never addresses a jury, or in any way draws down public applause; but, in the cool tranquillity of a snug retreat, do a snug business among rich men's bonds, and mortgages, and title-deeds. All who know me, consider me an eminently *safe* man. The late John Jacob Astor, a personage little given to poetic enthusiasm, had no hesitation in pronouncing my first grand point to be prudence; my next, method. I do not speak it in vanity, but simply record the fact, that I was not unemployed in my profession by the late John Jacob Astor; a name which, I admit, I love to repeat; for it hath a rounded and orbicular sound to it, and rings like unto bullion. I will freely add, that I was not insensible to the late John Jacob Astor's good opinion.

Some time prior to the period at which this little history begins, my avocations had been largely increased. The good old office, now extinct in the State of New York, of a Master in Chancery, had been conferred upon me. It was not a very arduous office, but very pleasantly remunerative. I seldom lose my temper; much more seldom indulge in dangerous indignation at wrongs and outrages; but, I must be permitted to be rash here, and declare, that I consider the sudden and violent abrogation of the office of Master in Chancery, by the new Constitution, as a —— premature act; inasmuch as I had counted upon a life-lease of the profits, whereas I only received those of a few short years. But this is by the way.

My chambers were up stairs, at No. — Wall Street. At one end, they looked upon the white wall of the interior of a spacious sky-light shaft, penetrating the building from top to bottom.

This view might have been considered rather tame than otherwise, deficient in what landscape painters call "life." But, if so, the view from the other end of my chambers offered, at least, a contrast, if nothing more. In that direction, my windows commanded an unobstructed view of a lofty brick wall, black by age and everlasting shade; which wall required no spy-glass to bring out its lurking beauties, but, for the benefit of all near-sighted spectators, was pushed up to within ten feet of my window panes. Owing to the great height of the surrounding buildings, and my chambers being on the second floor, the interval between this wall and mine not a little resembled a huge square cistern.

At the period just preceding the advent of Bartleby, I had two persons as copyists in my employment, and a promising lad as an office-boy. First, Turkey; second, Nippers; third, Ginger Nut. These may seem names, the like of which are not usually found in the Directory. In truth, they were nicknames, mutually conferred upon each other by my three clerks, and were deemed expressive of their respective persons or characters. Turkey was a short, pursy Englishman, of about my own age —that is, somewhere not far from sixty. In the morning, one might say, his face was of a fine florid hue, but after twelve o'clock, meridian—his dinner hour—it blazed like a grate full of Christmas coals; and continued blazing—but, as it were, with a gradual wane—till six o'clock P.M., or thereabouts; after which, I saw no more of the proprietor of the face, which, gaining its meridian with the sun, seemed to set with it, to rise, culminate, and decline the following day, with the like regularity and undiminished glory. There are many singular coincidences I have known in the course of my life, not the least among which was the fact, that, exactly when Turkey displayed his fullest beams from his red and radiant countenance, just then, too, at that critical moment, began the daily period when I considered his business capacities as seriously disturbed for the remainder of the twenty-four hours. Not that he was absolutely idle, or averse to business, then; far from it. The difficulty was, he was apt to be altogether too energetic. There was a strange, inflamed, flurried, flighty recklessness of activity about him. He would be incautious in dipping his pen into his inkstand. All his blots upon my documents were dropped there after twelve o'clock meridian. Indeed, not only would he be reckless, and sadly given to making blots in the afternoon, but, some days, he went further, and was rather noisy. At such times, too, his face flamed with augmented blazonry, as if cannel coal had been heaped on anthracite. He made an unpleasant racket with his chair; spilled his sand-box; in mending his pens, impatiently split them all to pieces, and threw them on the floor in a sudden passion; stood up, and leaned over his table, boxing his papers about in a most indecorous manner, very sad to behold in an elderly man like him. Nevertheless, as he was in many ways a most valuable person to me, and all the time before twelve o'clock meridian, was the quickest, steadiest creature, too, accomplishing a great deal of work in a style not easily to be matched—for these reasons, I was willing to overlook his eccentricities, though, indeed, occasionally, I remonstrated with him. I did this very gently, however, because, though the civilest, nay, the blandest and most reverential of men in the morning, yet, in the afternoon, he was disposed, upon provocation, to be slightly rash with his tongue—in fact, insolent. Now, valuing his morning services as I did, and resolved not to lose them —yet, at the same time, made uncomfortable by his inflamed ways after twelve o'clock—and being a man of peace, unwilling by my admonitions to call forth unseemly retorts from him, I took upon me, one Saturday noon (he was always worse on Saturdays) to hint to him, very kindly, that, perhaps, now that he was growing old, it might be well to abridge his labors; in short, he need not come to my chambers after twelve o'clock, but, dinner over, had best go home to his lodgings, and rest himself till tea-time. But no; he insisted upon his afternoon devotions. His countenance became intolerably fervid, as he oratorically assured me—gesticulating with a long ruler at the other end of the room—that if his services in the morning were useful, how indispensable, then, in the afternoon?

"With submission, sir," said Turkey, on this occasion, "I consider myself your right-hand man. In the morning I but marshal and deploy my columns; but in the afternoon I put myself at their head and gallantly charge the foe, thus"—and he made a violent thrust with the ruler.

"But the blots, Turkey," intimated I.

"True; but, with submission, sir, behold these hairs! I am getting old. Surely, sir, a blot or two of a warm afternoon is not to be severely urged against gray hairs. Old age—even if it blot the page—is honorable. With submission, sir, we *both* are getting old."

This appeal to my fellow-feeling was hardly to be resisted. At all events, I saw that go he would not. So, I made up my mind to let him stay, resolving, nevertheless, to see to it that, during the afternoon, he had to do with my less important papers.

Nippers, the second on my list, was a whiskered, sallow, and, upon the whole, rather piratical-looking young man, of about five and twenty. I always deemed him the victim of two evil powers—ambition and indigestion. The ambition was evinced by a certain impatience of the duties of a mere copyist, an unwarrantable usurpation of strictly professional affairs, such as the original drawing up of legal documents. The indigestion seemed betokened in an occasional nervous testiness and grinning irritability, causing the teeth to audibly grind together over mistakes committed in copying; unnecessary maledictions, hissed, rather than spoken, in the heat of business; and especially by a continual discontent with the height of the table where he worked. Though of a very ingenious, mechanical turn, Nippers could never get this table to suit him. He put chips under it, blocks of various sorts, bits of pasteboard, and at last went so far as to attempt an exquisite adjustment, by final pieces of folded blotting-paper. But no invention would answer. If, for the sake of easing his back, he brought the table lid at a sharp angle well up towards his chin, and wrote there like a man using the steep roof of a Dutch house for his desk, then he declared that it stopped the circulation in his arms. If now he lowered the table to his waistbands, and stooped over it in writing, then there was a sore aching in his back. In short, the truth of the matter was, Nippers knew not what he wanted. Or, if he wanted anything, it was to be rid of a scrivener's table altogether. Among the manifestations of his diseased ambition was a fondness he had for receiving visits from certain ambiguous-looking fellows in seedy coats, whom he called his clients. Indeed, I was aware that not only was he, at times, considerable of a ward-politician, but he occasionally did a little business at the Justices' courts, and was not unknown on the steps of the Tombs. I have good reason to believe, however, that one individual who called upon him at my chambers, and who, with a grand air, he insisted was his client, was no other than a dun, and the alleged title-deed, a bill. But, with all his failings, and the annoyances he caused me, Nippers, like his compatriot Turkey, was a very useful man to me; wrote a neat, swift hand; and, when he chose, was not deficient in a gentlemanly sort of deportment. Added to this, he always dressed in a gentlemanly sort of way; and so, incidentally, reflected credit upon my chambers. Whereas, with respect to Turkey, I had much ado to keep him from being a reproach to me. His clothes were apt to look oily, and smell of eating-houses. He wore his pantaloons very loose and baggy in summer. His coats were execrable; his hat not to be handled. But while the hat was a thing of indifference to me, inasmuch as his natural civility and deference, as a dependent Englishman, always led him to doff it the moment he entered the room, yet his coat was another matter. Concerning his coats, I reasoned with him; but with no effect. The truth was, I suppose, that a man with so small an income could not afford to sport such a lustrous face and a lustrous coat at one and the same time. As Nippers once observed, Turkey's money went chiefly for red ink. One winter day, I presented Turkey with a highly respectable-looking coat of my own—a padded gray coat, of a most comfortable warmth, and which buttoned straight up from the knee to the neck. I thought Turkey would appreciate the favor, and abate his rashness and obstreperousness of afternoons. But no; I verily believe that buttoning himself up in so downy and blanket-like a coat had a pernicious effect upon him—upon the same principle that too much oats are bad for horses. In fact, precisely as a rash, restive horse is said to feel his oats, so Turkey felt his coat. It made him insolent. He was a man whom prosperity harmed.

Though, concerning the self-indulgent habits of Turkey, I had my own private surmises, yet, touching Nippers, I was well persuaded that, whatever might be his faults in other respects, he was, at least, a temperate young man. But, indeed, nature herself seemed to have been his vintner, and, at his birth, charged him so thoroughly with an irritable, brandy-like disposition, that all subsequent potations were needless. When I consider how, amid the stillness of my chambers, Nippers would sometimes impatiently rise from his seat, and stooping over his table, spread his arms wide apart, seize the whole desk, and move it, and jerk it, with a grim, grinding motion on the floor, as if the table were a perverse voluntary agent and vexing him, I plainly perceive that, for Nippers, brandy-and-water were altogether superfluous.

It was fortunate for me that, owing to its peculiar cause—indigestion—the irritability and consequent nervousness of Nippers were mainly observable in the morning, while in the afternoon he was comparatively mild. So that, Turkey's paroxysms only coming on about twelve o'clock, I never had to do with their eccentricities at one time. Their fits relieved each other, like guards. When Nippers's was on, Turkey's was off; and *vice versa.* This was a good natural arrangement, under the circumstances.

Ginger Nut, the third on my list, was a lad, some twelve years old. His father was a car-man, ambitious of seeing his son on the bench instead of a cart, before he died. So he sent him to my office, as student at law, errand-boy, cleaner and sweeper, at the rate of one dollar a week. He had a little desk to himself; but he did not use it much. Upon inspection, the drawer exhibited a great array of the shells of various sorts of nuts. Indeed, to this quick-witted youth, the whole noble science of the law was contained in a nutshell. Not the least among the employments of Ginger Nut, as well as one which he discharged with the most alacrity, was his duty as cake and apple purveyor for Turkey and Nippers. Copying law-papers being proverbially a dry, husky sort of business, my two scriveners were fain to moisten their mouths very often with Spitzenbergs,[1] to be had at the numerous stalls nigh the Custom House and Post Office. Also, they sent Ginger Nut very frequently for that peculiar cake—small, flat, round, and very spicy—after which he had been named by them. Of a cold morning, when business was but dull, Turkey would gobble up scores of these cakes, as if they were mere wafers—indeed, they sell them at the rate of six or eight for a penny—the scrape of his pen blending with the crunching of the crisp particles in his mouth. Rashest of all the fiery afternoon blunders and flurried rashnesses of Turkey, was his once moistening a ginger-cake between his lips, and clapping it on to a mortgage, for a seal. I came within an ace of dismissing him then. But he mollified me by making an oriental bow, and saying—

"With submission, sir, it was generous of me to find you in stationery on my own account."

Now my original business—that of a conveyancer and title hunter, and drawer-up of recondite documents of all sorts—was considerably increased by receiving the master's office. There was now great work for scriveners. Not only must I push the clerks already with me, but I must have additional help.

In answer to my advertisement, a motionless young man one morning stood upon my office threshold, the door being open, for it was summer. I can see that figure now—pallidly neat, pitiably respectable, incurably forlorn! It was Bartleby.

After a few words touching his qualifications, I engaged him, glad to have among my corps of copyists a man of so singularly sedate an aspect, which I thought might operate beneficially upon the flighty temper of Turkey, and the fiery one of Nippers.

I should have stated before that ground glass folding-doors divided my premises into two parts, one of which was occupied by my scriveners, the other by myself. According to my humor, I threw open these doors, or closed them. I resolved to assign Bartleby a corner by the folding-doors, but on my side of them, so as to have this quiet man within easy call, in case any trifling thing was to be done. I placed his desk close up to a small side-window in that part of the room, a window which originally had afforded a lateral view of certain grimy backyards and bricks, but which, owing to subsequent erections, commanded at present no view at all, though it gave some light. Within three feet of the panes was a wall, and the light came down from far above, between two lofty buildings, as from a very small opening in a dome. Still further to a satisfactory arrangement, I procured a high green folding screen, which might entirely isolate Bartleby from my sight, though not remove him from my voice. And thus, in a manner, privacy and society were conjoined.

At first, Bartleby did an extraordinary quantity of writing. As if long famishing for something to copy, he seemed to gorge himself on my documents. There was no pause for digestion. He ran a day and night line, copying by sun-light and by candle-light. I should have been quite delighted with his application, had he been cheerfully industrious. But he wrote on silently, palely, mechanically.

It is, of course, an indispensable part of a scrive-

BARTLEBY THE SCRIVENER. 1. **Spitzenbergs:** spitzenburgs; a variety of apple.

ner's business to verify the accuracy of his copy, word by word. Where there are two or more scriveners in an office, they assist each other in this examination, one reading from the copy, the other holding the original. It is a very dull, wearisome, and lethargic affair. I can readily imagine that, to some sanguine temperaments, it would be altogether intolerable. For example, I cannot credit that the mettlesome poet, Byron, would have contentedly sat down with Bartleby to examine a law document of, say five hundred pages, closely written in a crimpy hand.

Now and then, in the haste of business, it had been my habit to assist in comparing some brief document myself, calling Turkey or Nippers for this purpose. One object I had, in placing Bartleby so handy to me behind the screen, was to avail myself of his services on such trivial occasions. It was on the third day, I think, of his being with me, and before any necessity had arisen for having his own writing examined, that, being much hurried to complete a small affair I had in hand, I abruptly called to Bartleby. In my haste and natural expectancy of instant compliance, I sat with my head bent over the original on my desk, and my right hand sideways, and somewhat nervously extended with the copy, so that, immediately upon emerging from his retreat, Bartleby might snatch it and proceed to business without the least delay.

In this very attitude did I sit when I called to him, rapidly stating what it was I wanted him to do —namely, to examine a small paper with me. Imagine my surprise, nay, my consternation, when, without moving from his privacy, Bartleby, in a singularly mild, firm voice, replied, "I would prefer not to."

I sat awhile in perfect silence, rallying my stunned faculties. Immediately it occurred to me that my ears had deceived me, or Bartleby had entirely misunderstood my meaning. I repeated my request in the clearest tone I could assume; but in quite as clear a one came the previous reply, "I would prefer not to."

"Prefer not to," echoed I, rising in high excitement, and crossing the room with a stride. "What do you mean? Are you moon-struck? I want you to help me compare this sheet here—take it," and I thrust it towards him.

"I would prefer not to," said he.

I looked at him steadfastly. His face was leanly composed; his gray eye dimly calm. Not a wrinkle of agitation rippled him. Had there been the least uneasiness, anger, impatience, or impertinence in his manner; in other words, had there been any thing ordinarily human about him, doubtless I should have violently dismissed him from the premises. But as it was, I should have as soon thought of turning my pale plaster-of-paris bust of Cicero out of doors. I stood gazing at him awhile, as he went on with his own writing, and then reseated myself at my desk. This is very strange, thought I. What had one best do? But my business hurried me. I concluded to forget the matter for the present, reserving it for my future leisure. So calling Nippers from the other room, the paper was speedily examined.

A few days after this, Bartleby concluded four lengthy documents, being quadruplicates of a week's testimony taken before me in my High Court of Chancery. It became necessary to examine them. It was an important suit, and great accuracy was imperative. Having all things arranged, I called Turkey, Nippers, and Ginger Nut from the next room, meaning to place the four copies in the hands of my four clerks, while I should read from the original. Accordingly, Turkey, Nippers, and Ginger Nut had taken their seats in a row, each with his document in his hand, when I called to Bartleby to join this interesting group.

"Bartleby! quick, I am waiting."

I heard a slow scrape of his chair legs on the uncarpeted floor, and soon he appeared standing at the entrance of his hermitage.

"What is wanted?" said he, mildly.

"The copies, the copies," said I, hurriedly. "We are going to examine them. There—" and I held towards him the fourth quadruplicate.

"I would prefer not to," he said, and gently disappeared behind the screen.

For a few moments I was turned into a pillar of salt, standing at the head of my seated column of clerks. Recovering myself, I advanced towards the screen, and demanded the reason for such extraordinary conduct.

"*Why* do you refuse?"

"I would prefer not to."

With any other man I should have flown outright into a dreadful passion, scorned all further words, and thrust him ignominiously from my presence. But there was something about Bartleby that not only strangely disarmed me, but in a wonderful manner, touched and disconcerted me. I began to reason with him.

"These are your own copies we are about to examine. It is labor saving to you, because one examination will answer for your four papers. It is common usage. Every copyist is bound to help examine his copy. Is it not so? Will you not speak? Answer!"

"I prefer not to," he replied in a flutelike tone. It seemed to me that, while I had been addressing him, he carefully revolved every statement that I made; fully comprehended the meaning; could not gainsay the irresistible conclusion; but, at the same time, some paramount consideration prevailed with him to reply as he did.

"You are decided, then, not to comply with my request—a request made according to common usage and common sense?"

He briefly gave me to understand, that on that point my judgment was sound. Yes: his decision was irreversible.

It is not seldom the case that, when a man is browbeaten in some unprecedented and violently unreasonable way, he begins to stagger in his own plainest faith. He begins, as it were, vaguely to surmise that, wonderful as it may be, all the justice and all the reason is on the other side. Accordingly, if any disinterested persons are present, he turns to them for some reinforcement of his own faltering mind.

"Turkey," said I, "what do you think of this? Am I not right?"

"With submission, sir," said Turkey, in his blandest tone, "I think that you are."

"Nippers," said I, "what do *you* think of it?"

"I think I should kick him out of the office."

(The reader, of nice [2] perceptions, will here perceive that, it being morning, Turkey's answer is couched in polite and tranquil terms, but Nippers replies in ill-tempered ones. Or, to repeat a previous sentence, Nippers's ugly mood was on duty, and Turkey's off.)

"Ginger Nut," said I, willing to enlist the smallest suffrage in my behalf, "what do *you* think of it?"

"I think, sir, he's a little *luny,*" replied Ginger Nut, with a grin.

"You hear what they say," said I, turning towards the screen, "come forth and do your duty."

But he vouchsafed no reply. I pondered a moment in sore perplexity. But once more business hurried me. I determined again to postpone the consideration of this dilemma to my future leisure. With a little trouble we made out to examine the papers without Bartleby, though at every page or two Turkey deferentially dropped his opinion, that this proceeding was quite out of the common; while Nippers, twitching in his chair with a dyspeptic nervousness, ground out, between his set teeth, occasional hissing maledictions against the stubborn oaf behind the screen. And for his (Nippers's) part, this was the first and the last time he would do another man's business without pay.

Meanwhile Bartleby sat in his hermitage, oblivious to everything but his own peculiar business there.

Some days passed, the scrivener being employed upon another lengthy work. His late remarkable conduct led me to regard his ways narrowly. I observed that he never went to dinner; indeed, that he never went anywhere. As yet I had never, of my personal knowledge, known him to be outside of my office. He was a perpetual sentry in the corner. At about eleven o'clock though, in the morning, I noticed that Ginger Nut would advance toward the opening in Bartleby's screen, as if silently beckoned thither by a gesture invisible to me where I sat. The boy would then leave the office, jingling a few pence, and reappear with a handful of ginger-nuts, which he delivered in the hermitage, receiving two of the cakes for his trouble.

He lives, then, on ginger-nuts, thought I; never eats a dinner, properly speaking; he must be a vegetarian, then; but no; he never eats even vegetables; he eats nothing but ginger-nuts. My mind then ran on in reveries concerning the probable effects upon the human constitution of living entirely on ginger-nuts. Ginger-nuts are so called, because they contain ginger as one of their peculiar constituents, and the final flavoring one. Now, what was ginger? A hot, spicy thing. Was Bartleby hot and spicy? Not at all. Ginger, then, had no effect upon Bartleby. Probably he preferred it should have none.

Nothing so aggravates an earnest person as a passive resistance. If the individual so resisted be of a not inhumane temper, and the resisting one perfectly harmless in his passivity, then, in the better moods of the former, he will endeavor charitably to construe to his imagination what proves impossible to be solved by his judgment. Even so, for the most part, I regarded Bartleby and his ways. Poor fellow! thought I, he means no mischief; it is plain he intends no insolence; his aspect sufficiently evinces that his eccentricities are involuntary. He is useful to me. I can get along with him. If I turn him away, the chances are he will fall in with some less-indulgent employer, and then he will be rudely treated, and perhaps driven forth miserably to starve. Yes. Here I can cheaply purchase a delicious self-approval. To befriend Bartleby; to humor him in his strange willfulness, will cost me little or nothing, while I lay up in my soul what will eventually prove a sweet morsel for my conscience. But this mood was not invariable with me. The passiveness of Bartleby sometimes irritated me. I felt strangely goaded on to encounter him in new opposition—to elicit some angry spark from him answerable to my own. But,

2. **nice**: precise.

indeed, I might as well have essayed to strike fire with my knuckles against a bit of Windsor soap. But one afternoon the evil impulse in me mastered me, and the following little scene ensued:

"Bartleby," said I, "when those papers are all copied, I will compare them with you."

"I would prefer not to."

"How? Surely you do not mean to persist in that mulish vagary?"

No answer.

I threw open the folding-doors near by, and, turning upon Turkey and Nippers, exclaimed:

"Bartleby a second time says, he won't examine his papers. What do you think of it, Turkey?"

It was afternoon, be it remembered. Turkey sat glowing like a brass boiler; his bald head steaming; his hands reeling among his blotted papers.

"Think of it?" roared Turkey; "I think I'll just step behind his screen, and black his eyes for him!"

So saying, Turkey rose to his feet and threw his arms into a pugilistic position. He was hurrying away to make good his promise, when I detained him, alarmed at the effect of incautiously rousing Turkey's combativeness after dinner.

"Sit down, Turkey," said I, "and hear what Nippers has to say. What do you think of it, Nippers? Would I not be justified in immediately dismissing Bartleby?"

"Excuse me, that is for you to decide, sir. I think his conduct quite unusual, and, indeed, unjust, as regards Turkey and myself. But it may only be a passing whim."

"Ah," exclaimed I, "you have strangely changed your mind, then—you speak very gently of him now."

"All beer," cried Turkey; "gentleness is effects of beer—Nippers and I dined together to-day. You see how gentle *I* am, sir. Shall I go and black his eyes?"

"You refer to Bartleby, I suppose. No, not to-day, Turkey," I replied; "pray, put up your fists."

I closed the doors, and again advanced towards Bartleby. I felt additional incentives tempting me to my fate. I burned to be rebelled against again. I remembered that Bartleby never left the office.

"Bartleby," said I, "Ginger Nut is away; just step around to the Post Office, won't you? (it was but a three minutes' walk), and see if there is anything for me."

"I would prefer not to."

"You *will* not?"

"I *prefer* not."

I staggered to my desk, and sat there in a deep study. My blind inveteracy returned. Was there any other thing in which I could procure myself to be ignominiously repulsed by this lean, penniless wight?—my hired clerk? What added thing is there, perfectly reasonable, that he will be sure to refuse to do?

"Bartleby!"

No answer.

"Bartleby," in a louder tone.

No answer.

"Bartleby," I roared.

Like a very ghost, agreeably to the laws of magical invocation, at the third summons, he appeared at the entrance of his hermitage.

"Go to the next room, and tell Nippers to come to me."

"I prefer not to," he respectfully and slowly said, and mildly disappeared.

"Very good, Bartleby," said I, in a quiet sort of serenely-severe, self-possessed tone, intimating the unalterable purpose of some terrible retribution very close at hand. At the moment I half intended something of the kind. But upon the whole, as it was drawing towards my dinner-hour, I thought it best to put on my hat and walk home for the day, suffering much from perplexity and distress of mind.

Shall I acknowledge it? The conclusion of this whole business was, that it soon became a fixed fact of my chambers, that a pale young scrivener, by the name of Bartleby, had a desk there; that he copied for me at the usual rate of four cents a folio (one hundred words); but he was permanently exempt from examining the work done by him, that duty being transferred to Turkey and Nippers, out of compliment, doubtless, to their superior acuteness; moreover, said Bartleby was never, on any account, to be dispatched on the most trivial errand of any sort; and that even if entreated to take upon him such a matter, it was generally understood that he would "prefer not to"—in other words, that he would refuse point-blank.

As days passed on, I became considerably reconciled to Bartleby. His steadiness, his freedom from all dissipation, his incessant industry (except when he chose to throw himself into a standing revery behind his screen), his great stillness, his unalterableness of demeanor under all circumstances, made him a valuable acquisition. One prime thing was this—*he was always there*—first in the morning, continually through the day, and the last at night. I had a singular confidence in his honesty. I felt my most precious papers perfectly safe in his hands. Sometimes, to be sure, I could not, for the very soul of me, avoid falling into sudden spasmodic passions with him. For it was exceeding difficult to bear in mind all the time those strange peculiarities, privileges, and unheard of exemptions, forming the tacit stipulations on Bartleby's part under which he remained in my office. Now and then, in the eagerness of dispatching pressing business, I would inadvertently summon Bartleby, in a short, rapid tone, to put his finger, say, on the incipient tie of a bit of red tape with which I was about compressing some papers. Of course, from behind the screen the usual answer, "I prefer not to," was sure to come; and then, how could a human creature, with the common infirmities of our nature, refrain from bitterly exclaiming upon such perverseness—such unreasonableness. However, every added repulse of this sort which I received only tended to lessen the probability of my repeating the inadvertence.

Here it must be said, that according to the custom of most legal gentlemen occupying chambers in densely-populated law buildings, there were several keys to my door. One was kept by a woman residing in the attic, which person weekly scrubbed and daily swept and dusted my apartments. Another was kept by Turkey for convenience sake. The third I sometimes carried in my own pocket. The fourth I knew not who had.

Now, one Sunday morning I happened to go to Trinity Church, to hear a celebrated preacher, and finding myself rather early on the ground I thought I would walk around to my chambers for a while. Luckily I had my key with me; but upon applying it to the lock, I found it resisted by something inserted from the inside. Quite surprised, I called out; when to my consternation a key was turned from within; and thrusting his lean visage at me, and holding the door ajar, the apparition of Bartleby appeared, in his shirt sleeves, and otherwise in a strangely tattered *déshabille,* saying quietly that he was sorry, but he was deeply engaged just then, and—preferred not admitting me at present. In a brief word or two, he moreover added, that perhaps I had better walk around the block two or three times, and by that time he would probably have concluded his affairs.

Now, the utterly unsurmised appearance of Bartleby, tenanting my law-chambers of a Sunday morning, with his cadaverously gentlemanly *nonchalance,* yet withal firm and self-possessed, had such a strange effect upon me, that incontinently I slunk away from my own door, and did as desired. But not without sundry twinges of impotent rebellion against the mild effrontery of this unaccountable scrivener. Indeed, it was his wonderful mildness chiefly, which not only disarmed me, but unmanned me as it were. For I consider that one, for the time, is somehow unmanned when he tranquilly permits his hired clerk to dictate to him, and order him away from his own premises. Furthermore, I was full of uneasiness as to what Bartleby could possibly be doing in my office in his shirt sleeves, and in an otherwise dismantled condition of a Sunday morning. Was anything amiss going on? Nay, that was out of the question. It was not to be thought of for a moment that Bartleby was an immoral person. But what could he be doing there?—copying? Nay again, whatever might be his eccentricities, Bartleby was an eminently decorous person. He would be the last man to sit down to his desk in any state approaching to nudity. Besides, it was Sunday; and there was something about Bartleby that forbade the supposition that he would by any secular occupation violate the proprieties of the day.

Nevertheless, my mind was not pacified; and full of a restless curiosity, at last I returned to the door. Without hindrance I inserted my key, opened it, and entered. Bartleby was not to be seen. I looked round anxiously, peeped behind his screen; but it was very plain that he was gone. Upon more closely examining the place, I surmised that for an indefinite period Bartleby must have eaten, dressed, and slept in my office, and that, too, without plate, mirror, or bed. The cushioned seat of a ricketty old sofa in one corner bore the faint impress of a lean, reclining form. Rolled away under his desk, I found a blanket; under the empty grate, a blacking box and brush; on a chair, a tin basin, with soap and a ragged towel; in a newspaper a few crumbs of ginger-nuts and a morsel of cheese. Yes, thought I, it is evident enough that Bartleby has been making his home here, keeping bachelor's hall all by himself. Immediately then the thought came sweeping across me, what miserable friendlessness and loneliness are here revealed! His poverty is great; but his solitude, how horrible! Think of it. Of a Sunday, Wall Street is deserted as Petra;[3] and every night of every day it is an emptiness. This building, too, which of weekdays hums with industry and life, at nightfall echoes with sheer vacancy, and all through Sunday is forlorn. And here Bartleby makes his home; sole spectator of a solitude which he has seen all populous—a sort of innocent and transformed Marius[4] brooding among the ruins of Carthage!

For the first time in my life a feeling of overpowering stinging melancholy seized me. Before, I had never experienced aught but a not unpleasing sadness. The bond of a common humanity now drew me irresistibly to gloom. A fraternal melan-

3. **Petra:** the ruins of an ancient city in Palestine.

4. **Marius:** Gaius Marius (155?–186 B.C.), a Roman general. He is brooding because although he had won great victories in Africa, he had been banished from Rome as a result of political maneuvers.

choly! For both I and Bartleby were sons of Adam. I remembered the bright silks and sparkling faces I had seen that day, in gala trim, swan-like sailing down the Mississippi of Broadway; and I contrasted them with the pallid copyist, and thought to myself, Ah, happiness courts the light, so we deem the world is gay; but misery hides aloof, so we deem that misery there is none. These sad fancyings—chimeras, doubtless, of a sick and silly brain—led on to other and more special thoughts, concerning the eccentricities of Bartleby. Presentiments of strange discoveries hovered round me. The scrivener's pale form appeared to me laid out, among uncaring strangers, in its shivering winding sheet.

Suddenly I was attracted by Bartleby's closed desk, the key in open sight left in the lock.

I mean no mischief, seek the gratification of no heartless curiosity, thought I; besides, the desk is mine, and its contents, too, so I will make bold to look within. Everything was methodically arranged, the papers smoothly placed. The pigeon holes were deep, and removing the files of documents, I groped into their recesses. Presently I felt something there, and dragged it out. It was an old bandanna handkerchief, heavy and knotted. I opened it, and saw it was a savings's bank.

I now recalled all the quiet mysteries which I had noted in the man. I remembered that he never spoke but to answer; that, though at intervals he had considerable time to himself, yet I had never seen him reading—no, not even a newspaper; that for long periods he would stand looking out, at his pale window behind the screen, upon the dead brick wall; I was quite sure he never visited any refectory or eating house; while his pale face clearly indicated that he never drank beer like Turkey, or tea and coffee even, like other men; that he never went anywhere in particular that I could learn; never went out for a walk, unless, indeed, that was the case at present; that he had declined telling who he was, or whence he came, or whether he had any relatives in the world; that though so thin and pale, he never complained of ill health. And more than all, I remembered a certain unconscious air of pallid—how shall I call it?—of pallid haughtiness, say, or rather an austere reserve about him, which had positively awed me into my tame compliance with his eccentricities, when I had feared to ask him to do the slightest incidental thing for me, even though I might know, from his long-continued motionlessness, that behind his screen he must be standing in one of those dead-wall reveries of his.

Revolving all these things, and coupling them with the recently discovered fact, that he made my office his constant abiding place and home, and not forgetful of his morbid moodiness; revolving all these things, a prudential feeling began to steal over me. My first emotions had been those of pure melancholy and sincerest pity; but just in proportion as the forlornness of Bartleby grew and grew to my imagination, did that same melancholy merge into fear, that pity into repulsion. So true it is, and so terrible, too, that up to a certain point the thought or sight of misery enlists our best affections; but, in certain special cases, beyond that point it does not. They err who would assert that invariably this is owing to the inherent selfishness of the human heart. It rather proceeds from a certain hopelessness of remedying excessive and organic ill. To a sensitive being, pity is not seldom pain. And when at last it is perceived that such pity cannot lead to effectual succor, common sense bids the soul be rid of it. What I saw that morning persuaded me that the scrivener was the victim of innate and incurable disorder. I might give alms to his body; but his body did not pain him; it was his soul that suffered, and his soul I could not reach.

I did not accomplish the purpose of going to Trinity Church that morning. Somehow, the things I had seen disqualified me for the time from church-going. I walked homeward, thinking what I would do with Bartleby. Finally, I resolved upon this—I would put certain calm questions to him the next morning, touching his history, etc., and if he declined to answer them openly and unreservedly (and I supposed he would prefer not), then to give him a twenty dollar bill over and above whatever I might owe him, and tell him his services were no longer required; but that if in any other way I could assist him, I would be happy to do so, especially if he desired to return to his native place, wherever that might be, I would willingly help to defray the expenses. Moreover, if, after reaching home, he found himself at any time in want of aid, a letter from him would be sure of a reply.

The next morning came.

"Bartleby," said I, gently calling to him behind his screen.

No reply.

"Bartleby," said I, in a still gentler tone, "come here; I am not going to ask you to do anything you would prefer not to do—I simply wish to speak to you."

Upon this he noiselessly slid into view.

"Will you tell me, Bartleby, where you were born?"

"I would prefer not to."

"Will you tell me *anything* about yourself?"

"I would prefer not to."

"But what reasonable objection can you have to speak to me? I feel friendly towards you."

He did not look at me while I spoke, but kept his glance fixed upon my bust of Cicero, which, as I then sat, was directly behind me, some six inches above my head.

"What is your answer, Bartleby," said I, after waiting a considerable time for a reply, during which his countenance remained immovable, only there was the faintest conceivable tremor of the white attenuated mouth.

"At present I prefer to give no answer," he said, and retired into his hermitage.

It was rather weak in me I confess, but his manner, on this occasion, nettled me. Not only did there seem to lurk in it a certain calm disdain, but his perverseness seemed ungrateful, considering the undeniable good usage and indulgence he had received from me.

Again I sat ruminating what I should do. Mortified as I was at his behavior, and resolved as I had been to dismiss him when I entered my office, nevertheless I strangely felt something superstitious knocking at my heart, and forbidding me to carry out my purpose, and denouncing me for a villain if I dared to breathe one bitter word against this forlornest of mankind. At last, familiarly drawing my chair behind his screen, I sat down and said: "Bartleby, never mind, then, about revealing your history; but let me entreat you, as a friend, to comply as far as may be with the usages of this office. Say now, you will help to examine papers to-morrow or next day: in short, say now, that in a day or two you will begin to be a little reasonable: —say so, Bartleby."

"At present I would prefer not to be a little reasonable," was his mildly cadaverous reply.

Just then the folding-doors opened, and Nippers approached. He seemed suffering from an unusually bad night's rest, induced by severer indigestion than common. He overheard those final words of Bartleby.

"*Prefer not,* eh?" gritted Nippers—"I'd *prefer* him, if I were you, sir," addressing me—"I'd *prefer* him; I'd give him preferences, the stubborn mule! What is it, sir, pray, that he *prefers* not to do now?"

Bartleby moved not a limb.

"Mr. Nippers," said I, "I'd prefer that you would withdraw for the present."

Somehow, of late, I had got into the way of involuntarily using this word "prefer" upon all sorts of not exactly suitable occasions. And I trembled to think that my contact with the scrivener had already and seriously affected me in a mental way. And what further and deeper aberration might it not yet produce? This apprehension had not been without efficacy in determining me to summary measures.

As Nippers, looking very sour and sulky, was departing, Turkey blandly and deferentially approached.

"With submission, sir," said he, "yesterday I was thinking about Bartleby here, and I think that if he would but prefer to take a quart of good ale every day, it would do much towards mending him, and enabling him to assist in examining his papers."

"So you have got the word, too," said I, slightly excited.

"With submission, what word, sir," asked Turkey, respectfully crowding himself into the contracted space behind the screen, and by so doing, making me jostle the scrivener. "What word, sir?"

"I would prefer to be left alone here," said Bartleby, as if offended at being mobbed in his privacy.

"*That's* the word, Turkey," said I—"*that's* it."

"Oh, *prefer?* oh yes—queer word. I never use it myself. But, sir, as I was saying, if he would but prefer—"

"Turkey," interrupted I, "you will please withdraw."

"Oh certainly, sir, if you prefer that I should."

As he opened the folding-door to retire, Nippers at his desk caught a glimpse of me, and asked whether I would prefer to have a certain paper copied on blue paper or white. He did not in the least roguishly accent the word prefer. It was plain that it involuntarily rolled from his tongue. I thought to myself, surely I must get rid of a demented man, who already has in some degree turned the tongues, if not the heads of myself and clerks. But I thought it prudent not to break the dismission at once.

The next day I noticed that Bartleby did nothing but stand at his window in his dead-wall revery. Upon asking him why he did not write, he said that he had decided upon doing no more writing.

"Why, how now? what next?" exclaimed I, "do no more writing?"

"No more."

"And what is the reason?"

"Do you not see the reason for yourself," he indifferently replied.

I looked steadfastly at him, and perceived that his eyes looked dull and glazed. Instantly it occurred to me, that his unexampled diligence in copying by his dim window for the first few weeks of his stay with me might have temporarily impaired his vision.

I was touched. I said something in condolence

with him. I hinted that of course he did wisely in abstaining from writing for a while; and urged him to embrace that opportunity of taking wholesome exercise in the open air. This, however, he did not do. A few days after this, my other clerks being absent, and being in a great hurry to dispatch certain letters by the mail, I thought that, having nothing else earthly to do, Bartleby would surely be less inflexible than usual, and carry these letters to the post-office. But he blankly declined. So, much to my inconvenience, I went myself.

Still added days went by. Whether Bartleby's eyes improved or not, I could not say. To all appearance I thought they did. But when I asked him if they did, he vouchsafed no answer. At all events, he would do no copying. At last, in reply to my urgings, he informed me that he had permanently given up copying.

"What!" exclaimed I; "suppose your eyes should get entirely well—better than ever before—would you not copy then?"

"I have given up copying," he answered, and slid aside.

He remained as ever, a fixture in my chamber. Nay—if that were possible—he became still more of a fixture than before. What was to be done? He would do nothing in the office; why should he stay there? In plain fact, he had now become a millstone to me, not only useless as a necklace, but afflictive to bear. Yet I was sorry for him. I speak less than truth when I say that, on his own account, he occasioned me uneasiness. If he would but have named a single relative or friend, I would instantly have written, and urged their taking the poor fellow away to some convenient retreat. But he seemed alone, absolutely alone in the universe. A bit of wreck in the mid Atlantic. At length, necessities connected with my business tyrannized over all other considerations. Decently as I could, I told Bartleby that in six days time he must unconditionally leave the office. I warned him to take measures, in the interval, for procuring some other abode. I offered to assist him in his endeavor, if he himself would but take the first step towards a removal. "And when you finally quit me, Bartleby," added I, "I shall see that you go not away entirely unprovided. Six days from this hour, remember."

At the expiration of that period, I peeped behind the screen, and lo! Bartleby was there.

I buttoned up my coat, balanced myself; advanced slowly towards him, touched his shoulder, and said, "The time has come; you must quit this place; I am sorry for you; here is money; but you must go."

"I would prefer not," he replied, with his back still towards me.

"You *must*."

He remained silent.

Now I had an unbounded confidence in this man's common honesty. He had frequently restored to me sixpences and shillings carelessly dropped upon the floor, for I am apt to be very reckless in such shirt-button affairs. The proceeding, then, which followed will not be deemed extraordinary.

"Bartleby," said I, "I owe you twelve dollars on account; here are thirty-two; the odd twenty are yours—Will you take it?" and I handed the bills towards him.

But he made no motion.

"I will leave them here, then," putting them under a weight on the table. Then taking my hat and cane and going to the door, I tranquilly turned and added—"After you have removed your things from these offices, Bartleby, you will of course lock the door—since every one is now gone for the day but you—and if you please, slip your key underneath the mat, so that I may have it in the morning. I shall not see you again; so good-by to you. If, hereafter, in your new place of abode, I can be of any service to you, do not fail to advise me by letter. Good-by, Bartleby, and fare you well.

But he answered not a word; like the last column of some ruined temple, he remained standing mute and solitary in the middle of the otherwise deserted room.

As I walked home in a pensive mood, my vanity got the better of my pity. I could not but highly plume myself on my masterly management in getting rid of Bartleby. Masterly I call it, and such it must appear to any dispassionate thinker. The beauty of my procedure seemed to consist in its perfect quietness. There was no vulgar bullying, no bravado of any sort, no choleric hectoring, and striding to and fro across the apartment, jerking out vehement commands for Bartleby to bundle himself off with his beggarly traps. Nothing of the kind. Without loudly bidding Bartleby depart—as an inferior genius might have done—I *assumed* the ground that depart he must; and upon that assumption built all I had to say. The more I thought over my procedure, the more I was charmed with it. Nevertheless, next morning, upon awakening, I had my doubts—I had somehow slept off the fumes of vanity. One of the coolest and wisest hours a man has, is just after he awakes in the morning. My procedure seemed as sagacious as ever—but only in theory. How it would prove in practice—there was the rub. It was truly a beautiful thought to have assumed Bartleby's departure; but, after all, that assumption was simply my own, and none of Bartleby's. The great point was, not whether I had assumed that he would quit me, but whether he would prefer so to do. He was more a man of preferences than assumptions.

After breakfast, I walked down town, arguing the probabilities *pro* and *con*. One moment I thought it would prove a miserable failure, and Bartleby would be found all alive at my office as usual; the next moment it seemed certain that I should find his chair empty. And so I kept veering about. At the corner of Broadway and Canal Street, I saw quite an excited group of people standing in earnest conversation.

"I'll take odds he doesn't," said a voice as I passed.

"Doesn't go?—done!" said I; "put up your money."

I was instinctively putting my hand in my pocket to produce my own, when I remembered that this was an election day. The words I had overheard bore no reference to Bartleby, but to the success or non-success of some candidate for the mayoralty. In my intent frame of mind, I had, as it were, imagined that all Broadway shared in my excitement, and were debating the same question with me. I passed on, very thankful that the uproar of the street screened my momentary absent-mindedness.

As I had intended, I was earlier than usual at my office door. I stood listening for a moment. All was still. He must be gone. I tried the knob. The door was locked. Yes, my procedure had worked to a charm; he indeed must be vanished. Yet a certain melancholy mixed with this: I was almost sorry for my brilliant success. I was fumbling under the door mat for the key, which Bartleby was to have left there for me, when accidentally my knee knocked against a panel, producing a summoning sound, and in response a voice came to me from within—"Not yet; I am occupied."

It was Bartleby.

I was thunderstruck. For an instant I stood like the man who, pipe in mouth, was killed one cloudless afternoon long ago in Virginia, by summer lightning; at his own warm open window he was killed, and remained leaning out there upon the dreamy afternoon, till some one touched him, when he fell.

"Not gone!" I murmured at last. But again obeying that wondrous ascendancy which the inscrutable scrivener had over me, and from which ascendancy, for all my chafing, I could not completely escape, I slowly went down stairs and out into the street, and while walking round the block, considered what I should next do in this unheard-of perplexity. Turn the man out by an actual thrusting I could not; to drive him away by calling him hard names would not do; calling in the police was an unpleasant idea; and yet, permit him to enjoy his cadaverous triumph over me—this, too, I could not think of. What was to be done? or, if nothing could be done, was there anything further that I could *assume* in the matter? Yes, as before I had prospectively assumed that Bartleby would depart, so now I might retrospectively assume that departed he was. In the legitimate carrying out of this assumption, I might enter my office in a great hurry, and pretending not to see Bartleby at all, walk straight against him as if he were air. Such a proceeding would in a singular degree have the appearance of a home-thrust. It was hardly possible that Bartleby could withstand such an application of the doctrine of assumptions. But upon second thoughts the success of the plan seemed rather dubious. I resolved to argue the matter over with him again.

"Bartleby," said I, entering the office, with a quietly severe expression, "I am seriously displeased. I am pained, Bartleby. I had thought better of you. I had imagined you of such a gentlemanly organization, that in any delicate dilemma a slight hint would suffice—in short, an assumption. But it appears I am deceived. Why," I added, unaffectedly starting, "you have not even touched that money yet," pointing to it, just where I had left it the evening previous.

He answered nothing.

"Will you, or will you not, quit me?" I now demanded in a sudden passion, advancing close to him.

"I would prefer *not* to quit you," he replied, gently emphasizing the *not*.

"What earthly right have you to stay here? Do you pay any rent? Do you pay my taxes? Or is this property yours?"

He answered nothing.

"Are you ready to go on and write now? Are your eyes recovered? Could you copy a small paper for me this morning? or help examine a few lines? or step round to the post-office? In a word, will you do anything at all, to give a coloring to your refusal to depart the premises?"

He silently retired into his hermitage.

I was now in such a state of nervous resentment that I thought it but prudent to check myself at present from further demonstrations. Bartleby and I were alone. I remembered the tragedy of the unfortunate Adams and the still more unfortunate Colt in the solitary office of the latter; and how poor Colt, being dreadfully incensed by

Adams, and imprudently permitted himself to get wildy excited, was at unawares hurried into his fatal act—an act which certainly no man could possibly deplore more than the actor himself. Often it had occurred to me in my ponderings upon the subject, that had that altercation taken place in the public street, or at a private residence, it would not have terminated as it did. It was the circumstance of being alone in a solitary office, up stairs, of a building entirely unhallowed by humanizing domestic associations—an uncarpeted office, doubtless, of a dusty, haggard sort of appearance—this it must have been, which greatly helped to enhance the irritable desperation of the hapless Colt.

But when this old Adam of resentment rose in me and tempted me concerning Bartleby, I grappled him and threw him. How? Why, simply by recalling the divine injunction: "A new commandment give I unto you, that ye love one another." [5] Yes, this it was that saved me. Aside from higher considerations, charity often operates as a vastly wise and prudent principle—a great safeguard to its possessor. Men have committed murder for jealousy's sake, and anger's sake, and hatred's sake, and selfishness' sake, and spiritual pride's sake; but no man, that ever I heard of, ever committed a diabolical murder for sweet charity's sake. Mere self-interest, then, if no better motive can be enlisted, should, especially with high-tempered men, prompt all beings to charity and philanthropy. At any rate, upon the occasion in question, I strove to drown my exasperated feelings towards the scrivener by benevolently construing his conduct. Poor fellow, poor fellow! thought I, he don't mean anything; and besides, he has seen hard times, and ought to be indulged.

I endeavored, also, immediately to occupy myself, and at the same time to comfort my despondency. I tried to fancy, that in the course of the morning, at such time as might prove agreeable to him, Bartleby, of his own free accord, would emerge from his hermitage and take up some decided line of march in the direction of the door. But no. Half-past twelve o'clock came; Turkey began to glow in the face, overturn his inkstand, and become generally obstreperous; Nippers abated down into quietude and courtesy; Ginger Nut munched his noon apple; and Bartleby remained standing at his window in one of his profoundest dead-wall reveries. Will it be credited? Ought I to acknowledge it? That afternoon I left the office without saying one further word to him.

Some days now passed, during which, at leisure intervals I looked a little into "Edwards [6] on the Will," and "Priestley [7] on Necessity." Under the circumstances, those books induced a salutary feeling. Gradually I slid into the persuasion that these troubles of mine, touching the scrivener, had been all predestinated from eternity, and Bartleby was billeted upon me for some mysterious purpose of an allwise Providence, which it was not for a mere mortal like me to fathom. Yes, Bartleby, stay there behind your screen, thought I; I shall persecute you no more; you are harmless and noiseless as any of these old chairs; in short, I never feel so private as when I know you are here. At last I see it, I feel it; I penetrate to the predestinated purpose of my life. I am content. Others may have loftier parts to enact; but my mission in this world, Bartleby, is to furnish you with office-room for such period as you may see fit to remain.

I believe that this wise and blessed frame of mind would have continued with me, had it not been for the unsolicited and uncharitable remarks obtruded upon me by my professional friends who visited the rooms. But thus it often is, that the constant friction of illiberal minds wears out at last the best resolves of the more generous. Though to be sure, when I reflected upon it, it was not strange that people entering my office should be struck by the peculiar aspect of the unaccountable Bartleby, and so be tempted to throw out some sinister observations concerning him. Sometimes an attorney, having business with me, and calling at my office, and finding no one but the scrivener there, would undertake to obtain some sort of precise information from him touching my whereabouts; but without heeding his idle talk, Bartleby would remain standing immovable in the middle of the room. So after contemplating him in that position for a time, the attorney would depart, no wiser than he came.

Also, when a reference was going on, and the room full of lawyers and witnesses, and business driving fast, some deeply-occupied legal gentleman present, seeing Bartleby wholly unemployed, would request him to run round to his (the legal gentleman's) office and fetch some papers for him. Thereupon, Bartleby would tranquilly decline, and yet remain idle as before. Then the lawyer would give a great stare, and turn to me. And what could I say? At last I was made aware that all through the circle of my professional acquaintance, a whisper of wonder was running round, having reference to the strange creature I kept at my office. This worried me very much. And as the idea came upon me of his possibly turning out a long-lived man, and keep occupying my cham-

5. **love one another:** John 13:24.

6. **Edwards:** Jonathan Edwards, *The Freedom of the Will* (1754).

7. **Priestley:** Joseph Priestley (1733–1804). It is not clear to which of this author's voluminous writings Melville refers.

bers, and denying my authority; and perplexing my visitors; and scandalizing my professional reputation; and casting a general gloom over the premises; keeping soul and body together to the last upon his savings (for doubtless he spent but half a dime a day), and in the end perhaps outlive me, and claim possession of my office by right of his perpetual occupancy: as all these dark anticipations crowded upon me more and more, and my friends continually intruded their relentless remarks upon the apparition in my room; a great change was wrought in me. I resolved to gather all my faculties together, and forever rid me of this intolerable incubus.

Ere revolving any complicated project, however, adapted to this end, I first simply suggested to Bartleby the propriety of his permanent departure. In a calm and serious tone, I commended the idea to his careful and mature consideration. But, having taken three days to meditate upon it, he apprised me, that his original determination remained the same; in short, that he still preferred to abide with me.

What shall I do? I now said to myself, buttoning up my coat to the last button. What shall I do? what ought I to do? what does conscience say I *should* do with this man, or, rather, ghost. Rid myself of him, I must; go, he shall. But how? You will not thrust him, the poor, pale, passive mortal —you will not thrust such a helpless creature out of your door? you will not dishonor yourself by such cruelty? No, I will not, I cannot do that. Rather would I let him live and die here, and then mason up his remains in the wall. What, then, will you do? For all your coaxing, he will not budge. Bribes he leaves under your own paper-weight on your table; in short, it is quite plain that he prefers to cling to you.

Then something severe, something unusual must be done. What! surely you will not have him collared by a constable, and commit his innocent pallor to the common jail? And upon what ground could you procure such a thing to be done?—a vagrant, is he? What! he a vagrant, a wanderer, who refuses to budge? It is because he will *not* be a vagrant, then, that you seek to count him *as* a vagrant. That is too absurd. No visible means of support: there I have him. Wrong again: for indubitably he *does* support himself, and that is the only unanswerable proof that any man can show of his possessing the means so to do. No more, then. Since he will not quit me, I must quit him. I will change my offices; I will move elsewhere, and give him fair notice, that if I find him on my new premises I will then proceed against him as a common trespasser.

Acting accordingly, next day I thus addressed him: "I find these chambers too far from the City Hall; the air is unwholesome. In a word, I propose to remove my offices next week, and shall no longer require your services. I tell you this now, in order that you may seek another place."

He made no reply; and nothing more was said.

On the appointed day I engaged carts and men, proceeded to my chambers, and, having but little furniture, everything was removed in a few hours. Throughout, the scrivener remained standing behind the screen, which I directed to be removed the last thing. It was withdrawn; and, being folded up like a huge folio, left him the motionless occupant of a naked room. I stood in the entry watching him a moment, while something from within me upbraided me.

I re-entered, with my hand in my pocket—and —and my heart in my mouth.

"Good-by, Bartleby; I am going—good-by, and God some way bless you; and take that," slipping something in his hand. But it dropped upon the floor, and then—strange to say—I tore myself from him whom I had so longed to be rid of.

Established in my new quarters, for a day or two I kept the door locked, and started at every footfall in the passages. When I returned to my rooms, after any little absence, I would pause at the threshold for an instant, and attentively listen, ere applying my key. But these fears were needless. Bartleby never came nigh me.

I thought all was going well, when a perturbed-looking stranger visited me, inquiring whether I was the person who had recently occupied rooms at No. — Wall Street.

Full of forebodings, I replied that I was.

"Then, sir," said the stranger, who proved a lawyer, "you are responsible for the man you left there. He refuses to do any copying; he refuses to do anything; he says he prefers not to; and he refuses to quit the premises."

"I am very sorry, sir," said I, with assumed tranquillity, but an inward tremor, "but, really, the man you allude to is nothing to me—he is no relation or apprentice of mine, that you should hold me responsible for him."

"In mercy's name, who is he?"

"I certainly cannot inform you. I know nothing about him. Formerly I employed him as a copyist; but he has done nothing for me now for some time past."

"I shall settle him, then—good morning, sir."

Several days passed, and I heard nothing more; and, though I often felt a charitable prompting to call at the place and see poor Bartleby, yet a certain squeamishness, of I know not what, withheld me.

All is over with him, by this time, thought I, at last, when, through another week, no further intelligence reached me. But, coming to my room the day after, I found several persons waiting at my door in a high state of nervous excitement.

"That's the man—here he comes," cried the foremost one, whom I recognized as the lawyer who had previously called upon me alone.

"You must take him away, sir, at once," cried a portly person among them, advancing upon me, and whom I knew to be the landlord of No. — Wall Street. "These gentlemen, my tenants, cannot stand it any longer; Mr. B——," pointing to the lawyer, "has turned him out of his room, and he now persists in haunting the building generally, sitting upon the banisters of the stairs by day, and sleeping in the entry by night. Everybody is concerned; clients are leaving the offices; some fears are entertained of a mob; something you must do, and that without delay."

Aghast at this torrent, I fell back before it, and would fain have locked myself in my new quarters. In vain I persisted that Bartleby was nothing to me—no more than to any one else. In vain—I was the last person known to have anything to do with him, and they held me to the terrible account. Fearful, then, of being exposed in the papers (as one person present obscurely threatened), I considered the matter, and, at length, said, that if the lawyer would give me a confidential interview with the scrivener, in his (the lawyer's) own room, I would, that afternoon, strive my best to rid them of the nuisance they complained of.

Going up stairs to my old haunt, there was Bartleby silently sitting upon the banister at the landing.

"What are you doing here, Bartleby?" said I.

"Sitting upon the banister," he mildly replied.

I motioned him into the lawyer's room, who then left us.

"Bartleby," said I, "are you aware that you are the cause of great tribulation to me, by persisting in occupying the entry after being dismissed from the office?"

No answer.

"Now one of two things must take place. Either you must do something, or something must be done to you. Now what sort of business would you like to engage in? Would you like to re-engage in copying for some one?"

"No; I would prefer not to make any change."

"Would you like a clerkship in a dry-goods store?"

"There is too much confinement about that. No, I would not like a clerkship; but I am not particular."

"Too much confinement," I cried, "why you keep yourself confined all the time!"

"I would prefer not to take a clerkship," he rejoined, as if to settle that little item at once.

"How would a bar-tender's business suit you? There is no trying of the eye-sight in that."

"I would not like it at all; though, as I said before, I am not particular."

His unwonted wordiness inspirited me. I returned to the charge.

"Well, then, would you like to travel through the country collecting bills for the merchants? That would improve your health."

"No, I would prefer to be doing something else."

"How, then, would going as a companion to Europe, to entertain some young gentleman with your conversation—how would that suit you?"

"Not at all. It does not strike me that there is anything definite about that. I like to be stationary. But I am not particular."

"Stationary you shall be, then," I cried, now losing all patience, and, for the first time in all my exasperating connection with him, fairly flying into a passion. "If you do not go away from these premises before night, I shall feel bound—indeed, I *am* bound—to—to—to quit the premises myself!" I rather absurdly concluded, knowing not with what possible threat to try to frighten his immobility into compliance. Despairing of all further efforts, I was precipitately leaving him, when a final thought occurred to me—one which had not been wholly unindulged before.

"Bartleby," said I, in the kindest tone I could assume under such exciting circumstances, "will you go home with me now—not to my office, but my dwelling—and remain there till we can conclude upon some convenient arrangement for you at our leisure? Come, let us start now, right away."

"No: at present I would prefer not to make any change at all."

I answered nothing; but, effectually dodging every one by the suddenness and rapidity of my flight, rushed from the building, ran up Wall Street towards Broadway, and, jumping into the first omnibus, was soon removed from pursuit. As soon as tranquillity returned, I distinctly perceived that I had now done all that I possibly could, both in respect to the demands of the landlord and his tenants, and with regard to my own desire and sense of duty, to benefit Bartleby, and shield him from rude persecution. I now strove to be entirely care-free and quiescent; and my conscience justified me in the attempt; though, indeed, it was not so successful as I could have wished. So fearful was I of being again hunted out by the incensed landlord and his exasperated tenants, that, surrendering my business to Nippers, for a few days, I drove about the upper part of the town and through the suburbs, in my rockaway; crossed over to Jersey City and Hoboken, and paid fugitive visits to Manhattanville and Astoria. In fact, I almost lived in my rockaway for the time.

When again I entered my office, lo, a note from the landlord lay upon the desk. I opened it with trembling hands. It informed me that the writer had sent to the police, and had Bartleby removed to the Tombs as a vagrant. Moreover, since I knew more about him than any one else, he wished me to appear at that place, and make a suitable statement of the facts. These tidings had a conflicting effect upon me. At first I was indignant; but, at last, almost approved. The landlord's energetic, summary disposition, had led him to adopt a procedure which I do not think I would have decided upon myself; and yet, as a last resort, under such peculiar circumstances, it seemed the only plan.

As I afterwards learned, the poor scrivener, when told that he must be conducted to the Tombs, offered not the slightest obstacle, but, in his pale, unmoving way, silently acquiesced.

Some of the compassionate and curious bystanders joined the party; and headed by one of the constables arm in arm with Bartleby, the silent procession filed its way through all the noise, and heat, and joy of the roaring thoroughfares at noon.

The same day I received the note, I went to the Tombs, or, to speak more properly, the Halls of Justice. Seeking the right officer, I stated the purpose of my call, and was informed that the individual I described was, indeed, within. I then assured the functionary that Bartleby was a perfectly honest man, and greatly to be compassionated, however unaccountably eccentric. I narrated all I knew, and closed by suggesting the idea of letting him remain in as indulgent confinement as possible, till something less harsh might be done—though, indeed, I hardly knew what. At all events, if nothing else could be decided upon, the almshouse must receive him. I then begged to have an interview.

Being under no disgraceful charge, and quite serene and harmless in all his ways, they had permitted him freely to wander about the prison, and, especially, in the inclosed grass-platted yards thereof. And so I found him there, standing all alone in the quietest of the yards, his face towards a high wall, while all around, from the narrow slits of the jail windows, I thought I saw peering out upon him the eyes of murderers and thieves.

"Bartleby!"

"I know you," he said, without looking round—"and I want nothing to say to you."

"It was not I that brought you here, Bartleby," said I, keenly pained at his implied suspicion. "And to you, this should not be so vile a place. Nothing reproachful attaches to you by being here. And see, it is not so sad a place as one might think. Look, there is the sky, and here is the grass."

"I know where I am," he replied, but would say nothing more, and so I left him.

As I entered the corridor again, a broad meatlike man, in an apron, accosted me, and jerking his thumb over his shoulder, said—"Is that your friend?"

"Yes."

"Does he want to starve? If he does, let him live on the prison fare, that's all."

"Who are you?" asked I, not knowing what to make of such an unofficially speaking person in such a place.

"I am the grub-man. Such gentlemen as have friends here, hire me to provide them with something good to eat."

"Is this so?" said I, turning to the turnkey.

He said it was.

"Well, then," said I, slipping some silver into the grub-man's hands (for so they called him), "I want you to give particular attention to my friend there; let him have the best dinner you can get. And you must be as polite to him as possible."

"Introduce me, will you?" said the grub-man, looking at me with an expression which seemed to say he was all impatience for an opportunity to give a specimen of his breeding.

Thinking it would prove of benefit to the scrivener, I acquiesced; and, asking the grub-man his name, went up with him to Bartleby.

"Bartleby, this is a friend; you will find him very useful to you."

"Your sarvant, sir, your sarvant," said the grubman, making a low salutation behind his apron. "Hope you find it pleasant here, sir; nice grounds—cool apartments—hope you'll stay with us sometime—try to make it agreeable. What will you have for dinner to-day?"

"I prefer not to dine to-day," said Bartleby, turning away. "It would disagree with me; I am unused to dinners." So saying, he slowly moved to the other side of the inclosure, and took up a position fronting the dead-wall.

"How's this?" said the grub-man, addressing me with a stare of astonishment. "He's odd, ain't he?"

"I think he is a little deranged," said I, sadly.

"Deranged? deranged is it? Well, now, upon my word, I thought that friend of yourn was a gentleman forger; they are always pale and genteel-like, them forgers. I can't help pity 'em—can't help it, sir. Did you know Monroe Edwards?" he added, touchingly, and paused. Then, laying his hand piteously on my shoulder, sighed, "he died of consumption at Sing-Sing. So you weren't acquainted with Monroe?"

"No, I was never socially acquainted with any forgers. But I cannot stop longer. Look to my friend yonder. You will not lose by it. I will see you again."

Some few days after this, I again obtained admission to the Tombs, and went through the corridors in quest of Bartleby; but without finding him.

"I saw him coming from his cell not long ago," said a turnkey, "may be he's gone to loiter in the yards."

So I went in that direction.

"Are you looking for the silent man?" said another turnkey, passing me. "Yonder he lies—sleeping in the yard there. 'Tis not twenty minutes since I saw him lie down."

The yard was entirely quiet. It was not accessible to the common prisoners. The surrounding walls, of amazing thickness, kept off all sounds behind them. The Egyptian character of the masonry weighed upon me with its gloom. But a soft imprisoned turf grew under foot. The heart of the eternal pyramids, it seemed, wherein, by some strange magic, through the clefts, grass-seed, dropped by birds, had sprung.

Strangely huddled at the base of the wall, his knees drawn up, and lying on his side, his head touching the cold stones, I saw the wasted Bartleby. But nothing stirred. I paused; then went close up to him; stooped over, and saw that his dim eyes were open; otherwise he seemed profoundly sleeping. Something prompted me to touch him. I felt his hand, when a tingling shiver ran up my arm and down my spine to my feet.

The round face of the grub-man peered upon me now. "His dinner is ready. Won't he dine to-day, either? Or does he live without dining?"

"Lives without dining," said I, and closed the eyes.

"Eh!—He's asleep, ain't he?"

"With kings and counselors," [8] murmured I.

* * *

8. kings . . . counselors: See Job 3:13–14.

There would seem little need for proceeding further in this history. Imagination will readily supply the meagre recital of poor Bartleby's interment. But, ere parting with the reader, let me say, that if this little narrative has sufficiently interested him, to awaken curiosity as to who Bartleby was, and what manner of life he led prior to the present narrator's making his acquaintance, I can only reply, that in such curiosity I fully share, but am wholly unable to gratify it. Yet here I hardly know whether I should divulge one little item of rumor, which came to my ear a few months after the scrivener's decease. Upon what basis it rested, I could never ascertain; and hence, how true it is I cannot now tell. But, inasmuch as this vague report has not been without a certain suggestive interest to me, however said, it may prove the same with some others; and so I will briefly mention it. The report was this: that Bartleby had been a subordinate clerk in the Dead Letter Office at Washington, from which he had been suddenly removed by a change in the administration. When I think over this rumor, hardly can I express the emotions which seize me. Dead letters! does it not sound like dead men? Conceive a man by nature and misfortune prone to a pallid hopelessness, can any business seem more fitted to heighten it than that of continually handling these dead letters, and assorting them for the flames? For by the cart-load they are annually burned. Sometimes from out the folded paper the pale clerk takes a ring—the finger it was meant for, perhaps, moulders in the grave; a bank-note sent in swiftest charity—he whom it would relieve, nor eats nor hungers any more; pardon for those who died despairing; hope for those who died unhoping; good tidings for those who died stifled by unrelieved calamities. On errands of life, these letters speed to death.

Ah, Bartleby! Ah, humanity!

FROM

BATTLE-PIECES AND ASPECTS OF THE WAR

THE FOLLOWING group of poems, up to and including "Shiloh," are from *Battle-Pieces*, published in 1866. There is little evidence bearing upon the precise date of composition of most of Melville's later poetry, but concerning the Civil War poems we are on firmer ground. In his prefatory note to *Battle-Pieces* Melville wrote that "with few exceptions, the Pieces in this volume originated in an impulse imparted by the fall of Richmond." The "few exceptions" are presumably those which Melville himself dated in parentheses placed under the titles. As the present representative selection suggests, many of the best poems are among the relative few he wrote before the fall of Richmond, which took place on April 3, 1865.

◇

THE PORTENT
(1859)

Hanging from the beam,
Slowly swaying (such the law),
Gaunt the shadow on your green,
Shenandoah!
The cut is on the crown
(Lo, John Brown),
And the stabs shall heal no more.

Hidden in the cap
Is the anguish none can draw;
So your future veils its face,
Shenandoah!
But the streaming beard is shown
(Weird John Brown),
The meteor of the war.

MISGIVINGS
(1860)

When ocean-clouds over inland hills
Sweep storming in late autumn brown,
And horror the sodden valley fills,
And the spire falls crashing in the town,
I muse upon my country's ills—
The tempest bursting from the waste of Time
On the world's fairest hope linked with man's foulest crime.
Nature's dark side is heeded now—
(Ah! optimist-cheer disheartened flown)—
A child may read the moody brow
Of yon black mountain lone.
With shouts the torrents down the gorges go,
And storms are formed behind the storm we feel:
The hemlock shakes in the rafter, the oak in the driving keel.

THE PORTENT. 6. **John Brown:** John Brown (1800–59) was the leader of an abortive attempt to liberate the Southern Negroes. He briefly captured the Federal Arsenal at Harper's Ferry on the Shenandoah River, but was soon made prisoner and hanged.

THE CONFLICT OF CONVICTIONS
(1860–1861)

On starry heights
A bugle wails the long recall;
Derision stirs the deep abyss,
Heaven's ominous silence over all.
Return, return, O eager Hope,
And face man's latter fall.
Events, they make the dreamers quail;
Satan's old age is strong and hale,
A disciplined captain, gray in skill,
And Raphael a white enthusiast still;
Dashed aims, at which Christ's martyrs pale,
Shall Mammon's slaves fulfill?

(Dismantle the fort,
Cut down the fleet—
Battle no more shall be!
While the fields for fight in aeons to come
Congeal beneath the sea.)

The terrors of truth and dart of death
To faith alike are vain;
Though comets, gone a thousand years,
Return again,
Patient she stands—she can no more—
And waits, nor heeds she waxes hoar.

(At a stony gate,
A statue of stone,
Weed overgrown—
Long 'twill wait!)

But God his former mind retains,
Confirms his old decree;
The generations are inured to pains,
And strong Necessity
Surges, and heaps Time's strand with wrecks.
The People spread like a weedy grass,
The thing they will they bring to pass,
And prosper to the apoplex.
The rout it herds around the heart,
The ghost is yielded in the gloom;
Kings wag their heads—Now save thyself
Who wouldst rebuild the world in bloom.

(Tide-mark
And top of the ages' strife,

THE CONFLICT OF CONVICTIONS. 10. **Raphael:** in Hebrew religion, the archangel of healing. There is little doubt, however, that Melville is thinking of the Raphael of Milton's *Paradise Lost*, where he is the angel sent by God to Adam and Eve to admonish and counsel them and to explain to them His divine purpose. By calling him a "white enthusiast," Melville means that Raphael is now powerless to act. 12. **Mammon:** a personified Aramaic word, meaning inordinate wealth and greed; see Luke 6:24.

Verge where they called the world to come,
The last advance of life—
Ha ha, the rust on the Iron Dome!)

Nay, but revere the hid event;
In the cloud a sword is girded on,
I mark a twinkling in the tent
Of Michael the warrior one.
Senior wisdom suits not now,
The light is on the youthful brow.

(*Ay, in caves the miner see:*
His forehead bears, a blinking light;
Darkness so he feebly braves,
A meagre wight!)

But He who rules is old—is old;
Ah! faith is warm, but heaven with age is cold.

(*Ho ho, ho ho,*
The cloistered doubt
Of olden times
Is blurted out!)

The Ancient of Days forever is young,
Forever the scheme of Nature thrives;
I know a wind in purpose strong—
It spins *against* the way it drives
What if the gulfs their slimed foundations bare?
So deep must the stones be hurled
Whereon the throes of ages rear
The final empire and the happier world.

(*The poor old Past,*
The Future's slave,
She drudged through pain and crime
To bring about the blissful Prime,
Then—perished. There's *a grave!*)

Power unanointed may come—
Dominion (unsought by the free)
And the Iron Dome,
Stronger for stress and strain,
Fling her huge shadow athwart the main;
But the Founders' dream shall flee.
Age after age shall be
As age after age has been,
(From man's changeless heart their way they win);
And death be busy with all who strive—
Death, with silent negative.

48. Michael: in Jewish religion the most powerful of the archangels, but here again Melville is taking his characterization of angels from *Paradise Lost.* **61. The Ancient of Days:** Melville takes this apocalyptic name for God from Dan. 7:9.

YEA AND NAY—
EACH HATH HIS SAY;
BUT GOD HE KEEPS THE MIDDLE WAY.
NONE WAS BY
WHEN HE SPREAD THE SKY;
WISDOM IS VAIN, AND PROPHESY.

NOTE: "The gloomy lull of the early part of the winter of 1860–1861, seeming big with final disaster to our institutions, affected some minds that believed them to constitute one of the great hopes of mankind, much as the eclipse which came over the promise of the first French Revolution affected kindred natures, throwing them for the time into doubts and misgivings universal" [Melville's note].

THE MARCH INTO VIRGINIA

Ending in the First Manassas

(July, 1861)

Did all the lets and bars appear
To every just or larger end,
Whence should come the trust and cheer?
Youth must its ignorant impulse lend—
Age finds place in the rear.
All wars are boyish, and are fought by boys,
The champions and enthusiasts of the state:
Turbid ardors and vain joys
Not barrenly abate—
Stimulants to the power mature,
Preparatives of fate.

Who here forecasteth the event?
What heart but spurns at precedent
And warnings of the wise,
Contemned foreclosures of surprise?
The banners play, the bugles call,
The air is blue and prodigal.
No berrying party, pleasure-wooed,
No picnic party in the May,
Ever went less loth than they
Into that leafy neighborhood.
In Bacchic glee they file toward Fate,
Moloch's uninitiate;
Expectancy, and glad surmise
Of battle's unknown mysteries.
All they feel is this: 'tis glory,
A rapture sharp, though transitory,

THE MARCH INTO VIRGINIA. Melville refers to the Battle of Bull Run—a Federal disaster—which occurred in and around Manassas Junction, Va. **22. Bacchic:** adjective form of one of the names of Dionysus, the Greek god of wine. Melville uses the word to suggest a festive or holiday spirit. **23. Moloch:** a Semitic deity (mentioned in Lev. 18:21 and Amos 5:26) to whom parents sacrificed their children by burning.

Yet lasting in belaureled story.
So they gayly go to fight,
Chatting left and laughing right.

But some who this blithe mood present,
As on in lightsome files they fare,
Shall die experienced ere three days be spent—
Perish, enlightened by the vollied glare;
Or shame survive, and like to adamant,
The throe of Second Manassas share.

DUPONT'S ROUND FIGHT
(November, 1861)

In time and measure perfect moves
All Art whose aim is sure;
Evolving rhyme and stars divine
Have rules, and they endure.

Nor less the Fleet that warred for Right,
And, warring so, prevailed,
In geometric beauty curved,
And in an orbit sailed.

The rebel at Port Royal felt
The Unity overawe,
And rued the spell. A type was here,
And victory of LAW.

A UTILITARIAN VIEW OF THE MONITOR'S FIGHT

Plain be the phrase, yet apt the verse,
More ponderous than nimble;
For since grimed War here laid aside
His Orient pomp, 'twould ill befit
Overmuch to ply
The rhyme's barbaric cymbal.

Hail to victory without the gaud
Of glory; zeal that needs no fans
Of banners; plain mechanic power
Plied cogently in War now placed—
Where War belongs—
Among the trades and artisans.

Yet this was battle, and intense—
Beyond the strife of fleets heroic;
Deadlier, closer, calm 'mid storm;
No passion; all went on by crank,
Pivot, and screw,
And calculations of caloric.

Needless to dwell; the story's known.
The ringing of those plates on plates
Still ringeth round the world—
The clangor of that blacksmiths' fray.
The anvil-din
Resounds this message from the Fates:

War shall yet be, and to the end;
But war-paint shows the streaks of weather;
War yet shall be, but warriors
Are now but operatives; War's made
Less grand than Peace,
And a singe runs through lace and feather.

MALVERN HILL
(July, 1862)

Ye elms that wave on Malvern Hill
In prime of morn and May,
Recall ye how McClellan's men
Here stood at bay?
While deep within yon forest dim
Our rigid comrades lay—
Some with the cartridge in their mouth,
Others with fixed arms lifted South—
Invoking so
The cypress glades? Ah wilds of woe!

The spires of Richmond, late beheld
Through rifts in musket-haze,
Were closed from view in clouds of dust
On leaf-walled ways,
Where streamed our wagons in caravan;
And the Seven Nights and Days
Of march and fast, retreat and fight,
Pinched our grimed faces to ghastly plight—
Does the elm wood
Recall the haggard beards of blood?

The battle-smoked flag, with stars eclipsed,
We followed (it never fell!)—

DUPONT'S ROUND FIGHT. On November 7, 1861, Commodore S. F. Dupont succeeded in reducing the Confederate forts of Port Royal, S.C., and establishing a blockade. In the skillful naval maneuver or "round fight" of Dupont's ships Melville perceives an archetype of all form and law. A UTILITARIAN VIEW OF THE MONITOR'S FIGHT. On March 8–9, 1862, the Federal ship *Monitor* defeated the Confederate *Merrimack* off Hampton Roads, Va. Melville sees in this first battle of ironclad vessels the advent of new conceptions of both the tactics and the moral meaning of war. **4. Orient:** colorful.

18. caloric: what would now be called thermodynamics, or the calculation of the relation of heat to energy. MALVERN HILL. **1. Malvern Hill:** site of a battle on July 1, 1862, in which General G. B. McClellan won a victory over Lee's forces. **16. Seven Nights and Days:** refers to the battle preceding that of Malvern Hill, where, in his effort to defend Richmond, Lee won temporarily over McClellan.

In silence husbanded our strength—
  Received their yell;
Till on this slope we patient turned
  With cannon ordered well;
Reverse we proved was not defeat;
But ah, the sod what thousands meet!—
      Does Malvern Wood
Bethink itself, and muse and brood?

We elms of Malvern Hill
  Remembered every thing;
But sap the twig will fill:
Wag the world how it will,
  Leaves must be green in Spring.

IN THE PRISON PEN
(1864)

Listless he eyes the palisades
  And sentries in the glare;
'Tis barren as a pelican-beach—
  But his world is ended there.

Nothing to do; and vacant hands
  Bring on the idiot-pain;
He tries to think—to recollect,
  But the blur is on his brain.

Around him swarm the plaining ghosts
  Like those on Virgil's shore—
A wilderness of faces dim,
  And pale ones gashed and hoar.

A smiting sun. No shed, no tree;
  He totters to his lair—
A den that sick hands dug in earth
  Ere famine wasted there,

Or, dropping in his place, he swoons,
  Walled in by throngs that press,
Till forth from the throngs they bear him dead—
  Dead in his meagreness.

THE COLLEGE COLONEL

He rides at their head;
  A crutch by his saddle just slants in view,
One slung arm is in splints, you see,
  Yet he guides his strong steed—how coldly too.

He brings his regiment home—
  Not as they filed two years before,
But a remnant half-tattered, and battered, and worn,
Like castaway sailors, who—stunned
  By the surf's loud roar,
  Their mates dragged back and seen no more—
Again and again breast the surge,
  And at last crawl, spent, to shore.

A still rigidity and pale—
  An Indian aloofness lones his brow;
He has lived a thousand years
Compressed in battle's pains and prayers,
  Marches and watches slow.
There are welcoming shouts, and flags;
  Old men off hat to the Boy,
Wreaths from gay balconies fall at his feet,
  But to *him*—there comes alloy.

It is not that a leg is lost,
  It is not that an arm is maimed,
It is not that the fever has racked—
  Self he has long disclaimed.

But all through the Seven Days' Fight,
  And deep in the Wilderness grim,
And in the field-hospital tent,
  And Petersburg crater, and dim
Lean brooding in Libby, there came—
  Ah heaven!—what *truth* to him.

"THE COMING STORM"

A Picture by S. R. Gifford, and Owned by E. B. Included in the N. A. Exhibition, April, 1865

All feeling hearts must feel for him
  Who felt this picture. Presage dim—
Dim inklings from the shadowy sphere
  Fixed him and fascinated here.

A demon-cloud like the mountain one
  Burst on a spirit as mild
As this urned lake, the home of shades,
  But Shakespeare's pensive child.

IN THE PRISON PEN. **9. plaining:** mourning or lamenting. **10. Virgil's shore:** a reference to the *Aeneid*, VI.320 ff., where Aeneas, descending into Hades, encounters a multitude of restless and tormented ghosts of those who were not buried with proper rites.

THE COLLEGE COLONEL. **26. Seven Days' Fight:** "Malvern Hill," 16 n. above. **27. Wilderness:** The Battle of the Wilderness took place between the forces of Generals Grant and Lee in May, 1864, in an area north of Richmond between the Shenandoah and Rappahannock Rivers. **29. Petersburg crater:** a crater formed by a Federal mine that blew up the Confederate fortifications at Petersburg, Va., in July of 1864. **30. Libby:** a prison in Richmond, a converted warehouse where Federal officers were incarcerated, often under conditions of great hardship.

Never the lines had lightly scanned,
  Steeped in fable, steeped in fate;
The Hamlet in his heart was 'ware,
  Such hearts can antedate.

No utter surprise can come to him
  Who reaches Shakespeare's core;
That which we seek and shun is there—
    Man's final lore.

ON THE SLAIN COLLEGIANS

Youth is the time when hearts are large,
  And stirring wars
Appeal to the spirit which appeals in turn
  To the blade it draws.
If woman incite, and duty show
  (Though made the mask of Cain),
Or whether it be Truth's sacred cause,
  Who can aloof remain
That shares youth's ardor, uncooled by the snow
  Of wisdom or sordid gain?

The liberal arts and nurture sweet
Which give his gentleness to man—
  Train him to honor, lend him grace
Through bright examples meet—
That culture which makes never wan
With underminings deep, but holds
  The surface still, its fitting place,
  And so gives sunniness to the face
And bravery to the heart; what troops
  Of generous boys in happiness thus bred—
  Saturnians through life's Tempe led,
Went from the North and came from the South,
With golden mottoes in the mouth,
  To lie down midway on a bloody bed.

Woe for the homes of the North,
And woe for the seats of the South:
All who felt life's spring in prime,
And were swept by the wind of their place and time—
  All lavish hearts, on whichever side,
Of birth urbane or courage high,
Armed them for the stirring wars—
  Armed them—some to die.
    Apollo-like in pride,
Each would slay his Python—caught
The maxims in his temple taught—
  Aflame with sympathies whose blaze
Perforce enwrapped him—social laws,
  Friendship and kin, and by-gone days—
Vows, kisses—every heart unmoors,
And launches into the seas of wars.
What could they else—North or South?
Each went forth with blessings given
By priests and mothers in the name of Heaven;
  And honor in all was chief.
Warred one for Right, and one for Wrong?
So be it; but they both were young—
Each grape to his cluster clung,
All their elegies are sung.

The anguish of maternal hearts
  Must search for balm divine;
But well the striplings bore their fated parts
  (The heavens all parts assign)—
Never felt life's care or cloy.
Each bloomed and died an unabated Boy;
Nor dreamed what death was—thought it mere
Sliding into some vernal sphere.
They knew the joy, but leaped the grief,
Like plants that flower ere comes the leaf—
Which storms lay low in kindly doom,
And kill them in their flush of bloom.

NOTE: "The records of Northern colleges attest what numbers of our noblest youth went from them to the battle-field. Southern members of the same classes arrayed themselves on the side of Secession; while Southern seminaries contributed large quotas. Of all these, what numbers marched who never returned except on the shield" [M].

ON THE SLAIN COLLEGIANS. **5–6. duty . . . Cain:** suggesting that in the Civil War what appeared to be the call of duty was actually an incitement to fratricide. **21. Saturnians:** those who are supposed to have lived in the age of the Roman god Saturn, a "golden age" of happiness and prosperity. **21. Tempe:** a vale in Thessaly at the foot of Mt. Olympus, home of the gods, much celebrated for its beauty. **33–34. Apollo-like . . . Python:** In Greek myth Apollo proved his divine powers by slaying the dragon Python. In the great festival held every eight years at Delphi, the seat of Apollo, a young man impersonated the god and re-enacted the slaying of the dragon; he then journeyed to the Vale of Tempe, where he was purified and crowned with laurel.

THE HOUSE-TOP

A Night Piece

(July, 1863)

No sleep. The sultriness pervades the air
And binds the brain—a dense oppression, such
As tawny tigers feel in matted shades,
Vexing their blood and making apt for ravage.
Beneath the stars the roofy desert spreads
Vacant as Libya. All is hushed near by.
Yet fitfully from far breaks a mixed surf

Of muffled sound, the Atheist roar of riot.
Yonder, where parching Sirius set in drought,
Balefully glares red Arson—there—and there.
The Town is taken by its rats—ship-rats
And rats of the wharves. All civil charms
And priestly spells which late held hearts in awe—
Fear-bound, subjected to a better sway
Than sway of self; these like a dream dissolve,
And man rebounds whole aeons back in nature.
Hail to the low dull rumble, dull and dead,
And ponderous drag that shakes the wall.
Wise Draco comes, deep in the midnight roll
Of black artillery; he comes, though late;
In code corroborating Calvin's creed
And cynic tyrannies of honest kings;
He comes, nor parlies; and the Town, redeemed,
Give thanks devout; nor, being thankful, heeds
The grimy slur on the Republic's faith implied,
Which holds that Man is naturally good,
And—more—is Nature's Roman, never to be
  scourged.

NOTE: "'I dare not write the horrible and inconceivable atrocities committed,' says Froissart, in alluding to the remarkable sedition in France during his time. The like may be hinted of some proceedings of the draft-rioters" [M].

THE APPARITION

(*A Retrospect*)

Convulsions came; and, where the field
  Long slept in pastoral green,
A goblin-mountain was upheaved
(Sure the scared sense was all deceived),
  Marl-glen and slag-ravine.

The unreserve of Ill was there,
  The clinkers in her last retreat;
But, ere the eye could take it in,
Or mind could comprehension win,
  It sunk!—and at our feet.

So, then, Solidity's a crust—
  The core of fire below;
All may go well for many a year,
But who can think without a fear
  Of horrors that happen so?

ON THE PHOTOGRAPH OF A CORPS COMMANDER

Ay, man is manly. Here you see
  The warrior-carriage of the head,
And brave dilation of the frame;
  And lighting all, the soul that led
In Spottsylvania's charge to victory,
  Which justifies his fame.

A cheering picture. It is good
  To look upon a Chief like this,
In whom the spirit moulds the form.
  Here favoring Nature, oft remiss,
With eagle mien expressive has endued
  A man to kindle strains that warm.

Trace back his lineage, and his sires,
  Yeoman or noble, you shall find
Enrolled with men of Agincourt,
  Heroes who shared great Harry's mind.
Down to us come the knightly Norman fires,
  And front the Templars bore.

Nothing can lift the heart of man
  Like manhood in a fellow-man.
The thought of heaven's great King afar
But humbles us—too weak to scan;
But manly greatness men can span,
  And feel the bonds that draw.

THE HOUSE-TOP. **9. Sirius:** the dog-star in the constellation Canis Major. **11–12. The Town . . . wharves:** Mobs of rioters, largely Irish born, terrorized the city. **13. priestly spells:** The reference is to John Hughes, Roman Catholic bishop of New York, whose authority and blunt speech were unable to prevent the outbreak of rioting, but whose advice and courage later did much to end the four days of fire, looting, and the lynching of Negroes. **19. Draco:** an Athenian legislator of the seventh century B.C., whose codification of the laws of his time gave him the reputation of a harsh and relentless oppressor. **21. Calvin's creed:** Melville refers to the inexorable Calvinist idea of the predestination of the elect and the damned. **27. Nature's . . . scourged:** Roman citizens by law could not be whipped. THE APPARITION. **5. marl-glen:** a pit in which is found marl, a kind of earthy deposit useful as fertilizer.

ON THE PHOTOGRAPH OF A CORPS COMMANDER. **5. Spottsylvania's:** Many famous battles were fought in Spotsylvania County, Va. Presumably the reference here is to the Battle of Spotsylvania Court House in May, 1864. **16–17. Heroes . . . fires:** Henry V won a momentous victory over the French at Agincourt in 1415. **18. Templars:** The Knights Templars was a religious and military order formed in the twelfth century to guard the Holy Sepulchre at Jerusalem and protect pilgrims to the Holy Land.

SHILOH

A Requiem

(April, 1862)

Skimming lightly, wheeling still,
  The swallows fly low
Over the field in clouded days,
  The forest-field of Shiloh—
Over the field where April rain
Solaced the parched ones stretched in pain
Through the pause of night
That followed the Sunday fight
  Around the church of Shiloh—
The church so lone, the log-built one,
That echoed to many a parting groan
    And natural prayer
  Of dying foemen mingled there—
Foemen at morn, but friends at eve—
  Fame or country least their care:
(What like a bullet can undeceive!)
  But now they lie low,
While over them the swallows skim,
  And all is hushed at Shiloh.

FROM

JOHN MARR AND OTHER SAILORS [1888]

THE AEOLIAN HARP

At the Surf Inn

List the harp in window wailing
  Stirred by fitful gales from sea:
Shrieking up in mad crescendo—
  Dying down in plaintive key!

Listen: less a strain ideal
  Than Ariel's rendering of the Real.
What that Real is, let hint
  A picture stamped in memory's mint.

Braced well up, with beams aslant,
Betwixt the continents sails the *Phocion,*
To Baltimore bound from Alicant.
Blue breezy skies white fleeces fleck
Over the chill blue white-capped ocean:
From yard-arm comes—"Wreck ho, a wreck!"
Dismasted and adrift,
Long time a thing forsaken:
Overwashed by every wave
Like the slumbering kraken;
Heedless if the billow roar,
Oblivious of the lull,
Leagues and leagues from shoal or shore,
It swims—a levelled hull:
Bulwarks gone—a shaven wreck,
Nameless, and a grass-green deck.
A lumberman: perchance, in hold
Prostrate pines with hemlocks rolled.

It has drifted, waterlogged,
Till by trailing weeds beclogged:
  Drifted, drifted, day by day,
  Pilotless on pathless way.
It has drifted till each plank
Is oozy as the oyster-bank:
  Drifted, drifted, night by night,
  Craft that never shows a light;
Nor ever, to prevent worse knell,
Tolls in fog the warning bell.

From collision never shrinking,
Drive what may through darksome smother;
Saturate, but never sinking,
Fatal only to the *other!*
  Deadlier than the sunken reef
Since still the snare it shifteth,
  Torpid in dumb ambuscade
Waylayingly it drifteth.

  O, the sailors—O, the sails!
  O, the lost crews never heard of!
  Well the harp of Ariel wails
  Thoughts that tongue can tell no word of!

THE BERG

A Dream

I saw a ship of martial build
(Her standards set, her brave apparel on)

SHILOH. Shiloh, Tenn., was the site of a costly but indecisive battle between the Federal armies under Grant and Buell and the Confederates under Johnston and Beauregard. THE AEOLIAN HARP. The harp gets its name from Aeolus, the Greek god of the winds, and makes musical sounds when air currents play upon the strings. **6. Ariel's . . . Real:** Melville associates the airy spirit of magic and music, Ariel, in Shakespeare's *The Tempest,* with the Aeolian harp. In Act I of *The Tempest* Ariel causes a shipwreck at the bidding of his master Prospero. Melville suggests that in human experience the Real is often more dangerous and deadly than the Appearance men take to be reality. One of the main themes of *The Tempest* is the difference between the Real and the Apparent. **11. Alicant:** Alicante is a port in Spain. **18. kraken:** See 13 n. above, on Melville's letters to Hawthorne.

Directed as by madness mere
Against a stolid iceberg steer,
Nor budge it, though the infatuate ship went down.
The impact made huge ice-cubes fall
Sullen, in tons that crashed the deck;
But that one avalanche was all—
No other movement save the foundering wreck.

Along the spurs of ridges pale,
Not any slenderest shaft and frail,
A prism over glass-green gorges lone,
Toppled; or lace of traceries fine,
Nor pendant drops in grot or mine
Were jarred, when the stunned ship went down.
Nor sole the gulls in cloud that wheeled
Circling one snow-flanked peak afar,
But nearer fowl the floes that skimmed
And crystal beaches, felt no jar.
No thrill transmitted stirred the lock
Of jack-straw needle-ice at base;
Towers undermined by waves—the block
Atilt impending—kept their place.
Seals, dozing sleek on sliddery ledges
Slipt never, when by loftier edges
Through very inertia overthrown,
The impetuous ship in bafflement went down.

Hard Berg (methought), so cold, so vast,
With mortal damps self-overcast;
Exhaling still thy dankish breath—
Adrift dissolving, bound for death;
Though lumpish thou, a lumbering one—
A lumbering lubbard loitering slow,
Impingers rue thee and go down,
Sounding thy precipice below,
Nor stir the slimy slug that sprawls
Along thy dead indifference of walls.

THE TUFT OF KELP

All dripping in tangles green,
Cast up by a lonely sea
If purer for that, O Weed,
Bitterer, too, are ye?

THE MALDIVE SHARK

About the Shark, phlegmatical one,
Pale sot of the Maldive sea,
The sleek little pilot-fish, azure and slim,
How alert in attendance be.
From his saw-pit of mouth, from his charnel of maw
They have nothing of harm to dread,
But liquidly glide on his ghastly flank
Or before his Gorgonian head;
Or lurk in the port of serrated teeth
In white triple tiers of glittering gates,
And there find a haven when peril's abroad,
An asylum in jaws of the Fates!
They are friends; and friendly they guide him to prey,
Yet never partake of the treat—
Eyes and brains to the dotard lethargic and dull,
Pale ravener of horrible meat.

TO NED

Where is the world we roved, Ned Bunn?
Hollows thereof lay rich in shade
By voyagers old inviolate thrown
Ere Paul Pry cruised with Pelf and Trade.
To us old lads some thoughts come home
Who roamed a world young lads no more shall roam.

Nor less the satiate year impends
When, wearying of routine-resorts,
The pleasure-hunter shall break loose,
Ned, for our Pantheistic ports:—
Marquesas and glenned isles that be
Authentic Edens in a Pagan sea.

The charm of scenes untried shall lure,
And, Ned, a legend urge the flight—
The Typee-truants under stars
Unknown to Shakespeare's *Midsummer-Night;*
And man, if lost to Saturn's Age,
Yet feeling life no Syrian pilgrimage.

But, tell, shall he, the tourist, find
Our isles the same in violet-glow

THE BERG. **21. jack-straw:** refers to the game in which straws or strips of wire are put in a jumbled pile, the object being to remove each one singly without disturbing the others. **33. lubbard:** a lubber or lazy lout. THE MALDIVE SHARK. **2. Maldive sea:** a part of the Indian Ocean southwest of India. **3. pilot-fish:** a small, bluish fish often found accompanying, if not "piloting," sharks. **8. Gorgonian head:** The name Gorgon was given to three sisters in Greek myth whose heads were covered with snakes instead of hair and the mere sight of whom turned the beholder to stone. TO NED. **1. Ned Bunn:** Melville's fictitious name for Richard Tobias Greene, who had been his companion in the adventures related in *Typee*; he is called Toby in that book. **4. Paul Pry:** a proverbial name for any meddlesome, petty-minded, inquisitive person. The name comes from the farce *Paul Pry* by John Poole, produced in 1825. **10. Pantheistic:** Melville is not using this word in an exact theological sense; he is saying that the ports are suffused with a spirit of felicity, harmony, and pleasure. **17. Saturn's Age:** See "On the Slain Collegians," 21 n.

Enamoring us what years and years—
  Ah, Ned, what years and years ago!
Well, Adam advances, smart in pace,
But scarce by violets that advance you trace.

But we, in anchor-watches calm,
  The Indian Psyche's languor won,
And, musing, breathed primeval balm
  From Edens ere yet overrun;
Marvelling mild if mortal twice,
Here and hereafter, touch a Paradise.

FROM

TIMOLEON [1891]

IN A BYE-CANAL

A swoon of noon, a trance of tide,
The hushed siesta brooding wide
  Like calms far off Peru;
No floating wayfarer in sight,
Dumb noon, and haunted like the night
  When Jael the wiled one slew.
A languid impulse from the oar
Plied by my indolent gondolier
Tinkles against a palace hoar,
  And, hark, response I hear!
A lattice clicks; and lo, I see
Between the slats, mute summoning me,
What loveliest eyes of scintillation,
What basilisk glance of conjuration!
  Fronted I have, part taken the span
Of portents in nature and peril in man.
I have swum—I have been
'Twixt the whale's black flukes
        and the white shark's fin;
The enemy's desert have wandered in,
And there have turned, have turned and scanned,
Following me how noiselessly,
Envy and Slander, lepers hand in hand.
All this. But at the latticed eye—
"Hey! Gondolier, you sleep, my man;
Wake up!" And, shooting by, we ran;
The while I mused, This, surely now,
Confutes the Naturalists, allow!
Sirens, true sirens verily be,
Sirens, waylayers in the sea.
Well, wooed by these same deadly misses,
Is it shame to run?
No! flee them did divine Ulysses,
  Brave, wise, and Venus' son.

FRAGMENTS OF A LOST GNOSTIC POEM OF THE 12TH CENTURY

* * *

Found a family, build a state,
The pledged event is still the same:
Matter in end will never abate
His ancient brutal claim.

* * *

Indolence is heaven's ally here,
And energy the child of hell:
The Good Man pouring from his pitcher clear,
But brims the poisoned well.

MONODY

To have known him, to have loved him
  After loneness long;
And then to be estranged in life,
  And neither in the wrong;
And now for death to set his seal—
  Ease me, a little ease, my song!

By wintry hills his hermit-mound
  The sheeted snow-drifts drape,
And houseless there the snow-bird flits
  Beneath the fir-trees' crape:
Glazed now with ice the cloistral vine
  That hid the shyest grape.

26. **Indian Psyche's languor:** In Greek "psyche" means breath, soul, or mind. In Greek myth Psyche is a beautiful princess beloved by Eros (Cupid). Perhaps Melville's curious phrase is meant to suggest a languorous pleasure of the spirit, tinged with erotic feeling, which he associates with the East or Indies. IN A BYE-CANAL. 6. **Jael:** the wife of Heber the Kenite, who slew Sisera by driving a tent nail through his head after she had fed him and lulled him to sleep. See Judg. 2:17–22. 14. **basilisk:** a mythological serpent or dragon said to be able to kill by looking at its victim.

30–34. **wooed . . . son:** See *Odyssey*, XII, where Odysseus (Ulysses) is tempted by the Sirens. FRAGMENTS OF A LOST GNOSTIC POEM OF THE 12TH CENTURY. Melville's title is rather fanciful, but the brief poems under it do state the Gnostic belief in the ineradicable evil of the material world. MONODY. An elegy on Hawthorne, who died May 19, 1864.

AFTER THE PLEASURE PARTY

Lines Traced Under an Image of
Amor Threatening

Fear me, virgin whosoever
Taking pride from love exempt,
Fear me, slighted. Never, never
Brave me, nor my fury tempt:
Downy wings, but wroth they beat
Tempest even in reason's seat.

Behind the house the upland falls
With many an odorous tree—
White marbles gleaming through green halls,
Terrace by terrace, down and down,
And meets the starlit Mediterranean Sea.

'Tis Paradise. In such an hour
Some pangs that rend might take release.
Nor less perturbed who keeps this bower
Of balm, nor finds balsamic peace?
From whom the passionate words in vent
After long revery's discontent?

Tired of the homeless deep,
Look how their flight yon hurrying billows urge,
Hitherward but to reap
Passive repulse from the iron-bound verge!
Insensate, can they never know
'Tis mad to wreck the impulsion so?

An art of memory is, they tell:
But to forget! forget the glade
Wherein Fate sprung Love's ambuscade,
To flout pale years of cloistral life
And flush me in this sensuous strife.
'Tis Vesta struck with Sappho's smart.
No fable her delirious leap:
With more of cause in desperate heart,
Myself could take it—but to sleep!

Now first I feel, what all may ween,
That soon or late, if faded e'en,
One's sex asserts itself. Desire,
The dear desire through love to sway,
Is like the Geysers that aspire—
Through cold obstruction win their fervid way.
But baffled here—to take disdain,
To feel rule's instinct, yet not reign;
To dote, to come to this drear shame—
Hence the winged blaze that sweeps my soul
Like prairie fires that spurn control,
Where withering weeds incense the flame.

And kept I long heaven's watch for this,
Contemning love, for this, even this?
O terrace chill in Northern air,
O reaching ranging tube I placed
Against yon skies, and fable chased
Till, fool, I hailed for sister there
Starred Cassiopeia in Golden Chair.
In dream I throned me, nor I saw
In cell the idiot crowned with straw.

And yet, ah yet scarce ill I reigned,
Through self-illusion self-sustained,
When now—enlightened, undeceived—
What gain I barrenly bereaved!
Than this can be yet lower decline—
Envy and spleen, can these be mine?

The peasant girl demure that trod
Beside our wheels that climbed the way,
And bore along a blossoming rod
That looked the sceptre of May-day—
On her—to fire this petty hell,
His softened glance how moistly fell!
The cheat! on briars her buds were strung;
And wiles peeped forth from mien how meek.
The innocent bare-foot! young, so young!
To girls, strong man's a novice weak.
To tell such beads! And more remain,
Sad rosary of belittling pain.

When after lunch and sallies gay,
Like the Decameron folk we lay
In sylvan groups; and I—let be!
O, dreams he, can he dream that one
Because not roseate feels no sun?
The plain lone bramble thrills with Spring
As much as vines that grapes shall bring.

Me now fair studies charm no more.
Shall great thoughts writ, or high themes sung
Damask wan cheeks—unlock his arm

AFTER THE PLEASURE PARTY. *Amor:* Melville's personification of the Latin word for sexual love. A Renaissance poet would doubtless have used the word Cupid; a modern poet would be likely to use the Greek "Eros." **29. Vesta:** among the ancient Romans the goddess of the hearth-fire. A fire in her temple was kept alive by the vestal virgins: hence, as in Melville's usage, the word Vesta came to signify virginity. **Sappho:** a poet who flourished in Lesbos about 610 B.C. A legend says that she flung herself into the sea in despair because of an unrequited love.

51. Cassiopeia: in classical mythology the wife of an Ethiopian king and mother of Andromeda. After her death she was placed among the stars in the constellation bearing her name; the constellation is supposed to resemble a chair. The speaker in the poem is given the name Urania (see l. 111), the muse of astronomy. In calling herself Cassiopeia's sister the speaker means that she has tried to live a life free of the emotional entanglements of the world. **73. Decameron folk:** the characters in Boccaccio's *Decameron* (cf. 4 n. above under "Hawthorne and His Mosses").

About some radiant ninny flung?
How glad with all my starry lore,
I'd buy the veriest wanton's rose
Would but my bee therein repose.

Could I remake me! or set free
This sexless bound in sex, then plunge
Deeper than Sappho, in a lunge
Piercing Pan's paramount mystery!
For, Nature, in no shallow surge
Against thee either sex may urge,
Why hast thou made us but in halves—
Co-relatives? This makes us slaves.
If these co-relatives never meet
Self-hood itself seems incomplete.
And such the dicing of blind fate
Few matching halves here meet and mate.
What Cosmic jest or Anarch blunder
The human integral clove asunder
And shied the fractions through life's gate?

Ye stars that long your votary knew
Rapt in her vigil, see me here!
Whither is gone the spell ye threw
When rose before me Cassiopeia?
Usurped on by love's stronger rein—
But lo, your very selves do wane:
Light breaks—truth breaks! Silvered no more,
But chilled by dawn that brings the gale
Shivers yon bramble above the vale,
And disillusion opens all the shore.

One knows not if Urania yet
The pleasure-party may forget;
Or whether she lived down the strain
Of turbulent heart and revel brain;
For Amor so resents a slight,
And hers had been such haught disdain,
He long may wreak his boyish spite,
And boy-like, little reck the pain.

One knows not, no. But late in Rome
(For queens discrowned a congruous home)
Entering Albani's porch she stood
Fixed by an antique pagan stone
Colossal carved. No anchorite seer,
Not Thomas à Kempis, monk austere,
Religious more are in their tone;
Yet far, how far from Christian heart
That form august of heathen Art.
Swayed by its influence, long she stood,
Till surged emotion seething down,
She rallied and this mood she won:

Languid in frame for me,
To-day by Mary's convent shrine,
Touched by her picture's moving plea
In that poor nerveless hour of mine,
I mused—A Wanderer still must grieve.
Half I resolved to kneel and believe,
Believe and submit, the veil take on.
But thee, armed Virgin! less benign,
Thee now I invoke, thou mightier one.
Helmeted woman—if such term
Befit thee, far from strife
Of that which makes the sexual feud
And clogs the aspirant life—
O self-reliant, strong and free,
Thou in whom power and peace unite,
Transcender! raise me up to thee,
Raise me and arm me!

Fond appeal.
For never passion peace shall bring,
Nor Art inanimate for long
Inspire. Nothing my help or heal
While Amor incensed remembers wrong.
Vindictive, not himself he'll spare;
For scope to give his vengeance play
Himself he'll blaspheme and betray.

Then for Urania, virgins everywhere,
O pray! Example take too, and have care.

89. **Pan:** in Greek mythology the god of pastures and flocks; Melville makes him stand more generally for the mystery of nature and of the powerful unconscious instincts. 92–100. **Why . . . gate:** These lines refer to the ancient myth, found in Plato's *Symposium*, that in primeval times human beings individually were of both sexes and that this happy state of things was lost when they were divided into male and female. 121. **Albani's porch:** the porch of a villa in Rome. It is not clear what "antique pagan stone" so aroused Urania's passions. But Melville himself visited the Villa Albani in 1857 and recorded in his *Journal Up the Straits* his interest in statues he had seen there, among them one of the beautiful youth Antinoüs and another a caryatid, or supporting pillar, carved in the shape of a bacchante (that is, a female devotee of Bacchus).

IN A GARRET

Gems and jewels let them heap—
Wax sumptuous as the Sophi:
For me, to grapple from Art's deep
One dripping trophy!

ART

In placid hours well pleased we dream
Of many a brave unbodied scheme.

124. **Thomas à Kempis:** a monk who lived from 1380 to 1471 and wrote *The Imitation of Christ.* 138. **armed Virgin:** Athena, the austere goddess of wisdom, whose statue is also to be seen at the Villa Albani. IN A GARRET. 2. **Sophi:** a title once given to the shahs of Persia.

But form to lend, pulsed life create,
What unlike things must meet and mate:
A flame to melt—a wind to freeze;
Sad patience—joyous energies;
Humility—yet pride and scorn;
Instinct and study; love and hate;
Audacity—reverence. These must mate,
And fuse with Jacob's mystic heart,
To wrestle with the angel—Art.

THE ATTIC LANDSCAPE

Tourist, spare the avid glance
  That greedy roves the sight to see:
Little here of "Old Romance,"
  Or Picturesque of Tivoli.

No flushful tint the sense to warm—
Pure outline pale, a linear charm.
The clear-cut hills carved temples face,
Respond, and share their sculptural grace.

'Tis Art and Nature lodged together,
  Sister by sister, cheek to cheek;
Such Art, such Nature, and such weather
  The All-in-All seems here a Greek.

GREEK ARCHITECTURE

Not magnitude, not lavishness,
But Form—the Site;
Not innovating wilfulness,
But reverence for the Archetype.

THE RAVAGED VILLA

In shards the sylvan vases lie,
  Their links of dance undone,
And brambles wither by thy brim,
  Choked fountain of the sun!
The spider in the laurel spins,
  The weed exiles the flower:
And, flung to kiln, Apollo's bust
  Makes lime for Mammon's tower.

ART. **10. Jacob's mystic heart:** Jacob wrestles all night with an angel until convinced that it is the Lord (Gen. 32:24–30). THE ATTIC LANDSCAPE. **4. Tivoli:** a town outside of Rome about which Melville jotted down some notes in his *Journal Up the Straits*. THE RAVAGED VILLA. **7–8. Apollo's . . . tower:** The meaning is that beauty and tradition have been sacrificed to the rapacious purposes of man (see 33–34 n. above under "On the Slain Collegians" and 12 n. under "The Conflict of Convictions").

FROM

WEEDS AND WILDINGS

◇

THIS poem was included in a projected volume of poems on which Melville was working at the time of his death and so never published. It first appeared in 1922.

◇

THE BLUE-BIRD

Beneath yon Larkspur's azure bells
That sun their bees in balmy air
In mould no more the Blue-Bird dwells
Tho' late he found interment there.

All stiff he lay beneath the Fir
When shrill the March piped overhead,
And Pity gave him sepulchre
Within the Garden's sheltered bed.

And soft she sighed—Too soon he came;
On wings of hope he met the knell;
His heavenly tint the dust shall tame;
Ah, some misgiving had been well!

But, look, the clear etherial hue
In June it makes the Larkspur's dower;
It is the self-same welkin-blue—
The Bird's transfigured in the Flower.

BILLY BUDD, FORETOPMAN

◇

Billy Budd, found among Melville's effects in manuscript and not published until 1924, is in part inspired by the case of the American naval brig *Somers*, which in 1842 became for many interested persons a *cause célèbre*. A young midshipman, named Philip Spencer, was convicted of mutiny and hanged on board, along with a boatswain's mate and a common seaman. The executive officer who presided over the drumhead court which meted out the punishment was Guert Gansevoort, a cousin of Melville. There was much controversy at the time over the justice or injustice of the harsh sentence, and the case seems to have thrown a cloud over Gansevoort for the rest of his life. As we see from Melville's treatment of a similar case in *Billy Budd,* he had pondered long and deeply over its moral implications. The general subject of the story also stirred up in the aging Melville many memories and thoughts about his own days at sea, when, as he felt, sailing was still in its golden age. He had found a rich source of materials, and as he wrote and rewrote *Billy Budd* it grew from short story to novel, as we have it. F. Barron Freeman, in his *Melville's Billy Budd* (1948), has described the difficulty of establishing an accurate text, because of the chaotic condition of the manuscript and the frequent illegibility of Melville's handwriting. It is Mr. Freeman's version of the text, as amended by subsequent corrigenda, that is followed below. (Copyright by the President and Fellows of Harvard College.)

◇

DEDICATED
TO
JACK CHACE [1]
Englishman

Wherever that great heart may now be Here on earth or harbored in Paradise Captain of the main-top in the year 1843 in the U.S. Frigate "United States"

PREFACE

THE YEAR 1797, the year of this narrative, belongs to a period which as every thinker now feels, involved a crisis for Christendom not exceeded in its undetermined momentousness at the time by any other era whereof there is record. The opening proposition made by the Spirit of that Age, involved the rectification of the Old World's hereditary wrongs. In France to some extent this was bloodily effected. But what then? Straightway the Revolution itself became a wrongdoer, one more oppressive than the kings. Under Napoleon it enthroned upstart Kings, and initiated that prolonged agony of continual war whose final throe was Waterloo. During those years not the wisest could have foreseen that the outcome of all would be what to some thinkers apparently it has since turned out to be, a political advance along nearly the whole line for Europeans.

Now, as elsewhere hinted, it was something caught from the Revolutionary Spirit that at Spithead emboldened the man-of-war's men to rise against real abuses, long-standing ones, and afterwards at the Nore [2] to make inordinate and aggressive demands, successful resistance to which was confirmed only when the ringleaders were hung for an admonitory spectacle to the anchored fleet. Yet in a way analogous to the operation of the Revolution at large the Great Mutiny, though by Englishmen naturally deemed monstrous at the time, doubtless gave the first latent prompting to most important reforms in the British Navy.

BILLY BUDD
SAILOR

(*An inside narrative.*)

I

IN THE time before steamships, or then more frequently than now, a stroller along the docks of any considerable sea-port would occasionally have his attention arrested by a group of bronzed mariners, man-of-war's men or merchant-sailors in holiday attire ashore on liberty. In certain instances they would flank, or, like a body-guard quite surround some superior figure of their own class, moving along with them like Aldebaran among the lesser lights of his constellation. That signal object was the "Handsome Sailor" of the less prosaic time alike of the military and merchant navies. With no perceptible trace of the vainglorious about him, rather with the off-hand unaffectedness of natural regality, he seemed to accept the spontaneous homage of his shipmates. A somewhat remarkable instance recurs to me. In Liverpool, now half a century ago I saw under the shadow of the great dingy street-wall of Prince's Dock (an obstruction long since removed) a common sailor, so intensely black that he must needs have been a native African of the unadulterate blood of Ham. A symmetric figure much above the average height. The two ends of a gay silk handkerchief thrown loose about the neck danced upon the displayed ebony of his chest; in his ears were big hoops of gold, and a Scotch Highland bonnet with a tartan band set off his shapely head.

It was a hot noon in July; and his face, lustrous with perspiration, beamed with barbaric good humor. In jovial sallies right and left his white teeth flashing into view, he rollicked along, the centre of a company of his shipmates. These were made up of such an assortment of tribes and complexions as would have well fitted them to be marched up by Anacharsis Cloots [3] before the bar of the first

BILLY BUDD. 1. **Jack Chace:** Chace, to whom Melville dedicates his book, is described at length in *White-Jacket.* 2. **the Nore:** anchorage at the mouth of the Thames where the mutiny of 1797 in the British Navy took place.

3. **Cloots:** the Baron de Cloots (1755–94), who made a declaration of the rights of man before the French Assembly.

French Assembly as Representatives of the Human Race. At each spontaneous tribute rendered by the wayfarers to this black pagod of a fellow—the tribute of a pause and stare, and less frequent an exclamation,—the motley retinue showed that they took that sort of pride in the evoker of it which the Assyrian priests doubtless showed for their grand sculptured Bull when the faithful prostrated themselves.

To return.

If in some cases a bit of a nautical Murat[4] in setting forth his person ashore, the handsome sailor of the period in question evinced nothing of the dandified Billy-be-Dam, an amusing character all but extinct now, but occasionally to be encountered, and in a form yet more amusing than the original, at the tiller of the boats on the tempestuous Erie Canal or, more likely, vaporing in the groggeries along the tow-path. Invariably a proficient in his perilous calling, he was also more or less of a mighty boxer or wrestler. It was strength and beauty. Tales of his prowess were recited. Ashore he was the champion; afloat the spokesman; on every suitable occasion always foremost. Close-reefing topsails in a gale, there he was, astride the weather yard-arm-end, foot in the Flemish horse as "stirrup," both hands tugging at the "earring" as at a bridle, in very much the attitude of young Alexander curbing the fiery Bucephalus.[5] A superb figure, tossed up as by the horns of Taurus against the thunderous sky, cheerily hallooing to the strenuous file along the spar.

The moral nature was seldom out of keeping with the physical make. Indeed, except as toned by the former, the comeliness and power, always attractive in masculine conjunction, hardly could have drawn the sort of honest homage the Handsome Sailor in some examples received from his less gifted associates.

Such a cynosure, at least in aspect, and something such too in nature, though with important variations made apparent as the story proceeds, was welkin-eyed Billy Budd, or Baby Budd as more familiarly under circumstances hereafter to be given he at last came to be called, aged twenty-one, a foretopman of the British fleet toward the close of the last decade of the eighteenth century. It was not very long prior to the time of the narration that follows that he had entered the King's Service, having been impressed on the Narrow Seas from a homeward-bound English merchantman into a seventy-four outward-bound, H.M.S. *Indomitable;* which ship, as was not unusual in those hurried days having been obliged to put to sea short of her proper complement of men. Plump upon Billy at first sight in the gangway the boarding officer Lieutenant Ratcliffe pounced, even before the merchantman's crew was formally mustered on the quarter-deck for his deliberate inspection. And him only he elected. For whether it was because the other men who ranged before him showed to ill advantage after Billy, or whether he had some scruples in view of the merchantman being rather short-handed, however it might be, the officer contented himself with his first spontaneous choice. To the surprise of the ship's company, though much to the Lieutenant's satisfaction Billy made no demur. But, indeed, any demur would have been as idle as the protest of a goldfinch popped into a cage.

Noting his uncomplaining acquiescence, all but cheerful one might say, the shipmates turned a surprised glance of silent reproach at the sailor. The shipmaster was one of those worthy mortals found in every vocation even the humbler ones—the sort of person whom everybody agrees in calling "a respectable man." And—nor so strange to report as it may appear to be—though a ploughman of the troubled waters, life-long contending with the intractable elements, there was nothing this honest soul at heart loved better than simple peace and quiet. For the rest, he was fifty or thereabouts, a little inclined to corpulence, a prepossessing face, unwhiskered, and of an agreeable color—a rather full face, humanely intelligent in expression. On a fair day with a fair wind and all going well, a certain musical chime in his voice seemed to be the veritable unobstructed outcome of the innermost man. He had much prudence, much conscientiousness, and there were occasions when these virtues were the cause of overmuch disquietude in him. On a passage, so long as his craft was in any proximity to land, no sleep for Captain Graveling. He took to heart those serious responsibilities not so heavily borne by some shipmasters.

Now while Billy Budd was down in the forecastle getting his kit together, the *Indomitable's* lieutenant, burly and bluff, nowise disconcerted by Captain Graveling's omitting to proffer the customary hospitalities on an occasion so unwelcome to him, an omission simply caused by preoccupation of thought, unceremoniously invited himself into the cabin, and also to a flask from the spirit-locker, a receptacle which his experienced eye instantly discovered. In fact he was one of those sea-dogs in whom all the hardship and peril of naval life in the great prolonged wars of his time never impaired the natural instinct for sensuous enjoyment. His duty he always faithfully did; but duty

4. **Murat:** Joachim Murat (1767–1815) was one of Napoleon's generals. 5. **Bucephalus:** the horse of Alexander the Great.

is sometimes a dry obligation, and he was for irrigating its aridity, whensoever possible with a fertilizing decoction of strong waters. For the cabin's proprietor there was nothing left but to play the part of the enforced host with whatever grace and alacrity were practicable. As necessary adjuncts to the flask, he silently placed tumbler and water-jug before the irrepressible guest. But excusing himself from partaking just then, he dismally watched the unembarrassed officer deliberately diluting his grog a little, then tossing it off in three swallows, pushing the empty tumbler away, yet not so far as to be beyond easy reach, at the same time settling himself in his seat and smacking his lips with high satisfaction, looking straight at the host.

These proceedings over, the Master broke the silence; and there lurked a rueful reproach in the tone of his voice: "Lieutenant, you are going to take my best man from me, the jewel of 'em."

"Yes, I know" rejoined the other, immediately drawing back the tumbler preliminary to a replenishing; "Yes, I know. Sorry."

"Beg pardon, but you don't understand, Lieutenant. See here now. Before I shipped that young fellow, my forecastle was a rat-pit of quarrels. It was black times, I tell you, aboard the '*Rights*' here. I was worried to that degree my pipe had no comfort for me. But Billy came; and it was like a Catholic priest striking peace in an Irish shindy. Not that he preached to them or said or did anything in particular; but a virtue went out of him, sugaring the sour ones. They took to him like hornets to treacle; all but the buffer of the gang, the big shaggy chap with the fire-red whiskers. He indeed out of envy, perhaps, of the newcomer, and thinking such a 'sweet and pleasant fellow,' as he mockingly designated him to the others, could hardly have the spirit of a game-cock, must needs bestir himself in trying to get up an ugly row with him. Billy forebore with him and reasoned with him in a pleasant way—he is something like myself, Lieutenant, to whom aught like a quarrel is hateful—but nothing served. So, in the second dog-watch one day the Red Whiskers in presence of the others, under pretence of showing Billy just whence a sirloin steak was cut—for the fellow had once been a butcher—insultingly gave him a dig under the ribs. Quick as lightning Billy let fly his arm. I dare say he never meant to do quite as much as he did, but anyhow he gave the burly fool a terrible drubbing. It took about half a minute, I should think. And, lord bless you, the lubber was astonished at the celerity. And will you believe it, Lieutenant, the Red Whiskers now really loves Billy—loves him, or is the biggest hypocrite that ever I heard of. But they all love him. Some of 'em do his washing, darn his old trousers for him; the carpenter is at odd times making a pretty little chest of drawers for him. Anybody will do anything for Billy Budd; and it's the happy family here. But now Lieutenant, if that young fellow goes—I know how it will be aboard the '*Rights*.' Not again very soon shall I, coming up from dinner, lean over the capstan smoking a quiet pipe—no, not very soon again, I think. Ay, Lieutenant, you are going to take away the jewel of 'em; you are going to take away my peacemaker!" And with that the good soul had really some ado in checking a rising sob.

"Well," said the officer who had listened with amused interest to all this, and now waxing merry with his tipple; "Well, blessed are the peacemakers especially the fighting peacemakers! And such are the seventy-four beauties some of which you see poking their noses out at the port-holes of yonder war-ship lying-to for me" pointing through the cabin window of the *Indomitable*. "But courage! don't look so downhearted, man. Why, I pledge you in advance the royal approbation. Rest assured that His Majesty will be delighted to know that in a time when his hard tack is not sought for by sailors with such avidity as should be; a time also when some shipmasters privily resent the borrowing from them a tar or two for the service; His Majesty, I say, will be delighted to learn that *one* shipmaster at least cheerfully surrenders to the King, the flower of his flock, a sailor who with equal loyalty makes no dissent.—But where's my beauty? Ah," looking through the cabin's open door "Here he comes; and, by Jove—lugging along his chest—Apollo with his portmanteau!—My man," stepping out to him, "you can't take that big box aboard a war-ship. The boxes there are mostly shot-boxes. Put your duds in a bag, lad. Boot and saddle for the cavalryman, bag and hammock for the man-of-war's man."

The transfer from chest to bag was made. And, after seeing his man into the cutter and then following him down, the lieutenant pushed off from the *Rights-of-Man*. That was the merchant-ship's name; though by her master and crew abbreviated in sailor fashion into *The Rights*. The hard-headed Dundee owner was a staunch admirer of Thomas Paine whose book in rejoinder to Burke's arraignment of the French Revolution [6] had then been published for some time and had gone everywhere. In christening his vessel after the title of Paine's volume the man of Dundee was something like his contemporary shipowner, Stephen Girard of Philadelphia, whose sympathies, alike with his

6. **Burke's . . . Revolution:** See Introduction.

native land and its liberal philosophers, he evinced by naming his ships after Voltaire, Diderot, and so forth.

But now, when the boat swept under the merchant-man's stern, and officer and oarsmen were noting—some bitterly and others with a grin,—the name emblazoned there; just then it was that the new recruit jumped up from the bow where the coxswain had directed him to sit, and waving his hat to his silent shipmates sorrowfully looking over at him from the taffrail, bade the lads a genial good-bye. Then, making a salutation as to the ship herself, "And good bye to you too, old *Rights of Man.*"

"Down, Sir!" roared the lieutenant, instantly assuming all the rigor of his rank, though with difficulty repressing a smile.

To be sure Billy's action was a terrible breach of naval decorum. But in that decorum he had never been instructed; in consideration of which the lieutenant would hardly have been so energetic in reproof but for the concluding farewell to the ship. This he rather took as meant to convey a covert sally on the new recruit's part, a sly slur at impressment in general, and that of himself in especial. And yet, more likely, if satire it was in effect, it was hardly so by intention, for Billy though happily endowed with the gayety of high health, youth, and a free heart, was yet by no means of a satirical turn. The will to it and the sinister dexterity were alike wanting. To deal in double meanings and insinuations of any sort was quite foreign to his nature.

As to his enforced enlistment, that he seemed to take pretty much as he was wont to take any vicissitude of weather. Like the animals, though no philosopher, he was, without knowing it, practically a fatalist. And, it may be, that he rather liked this adventurous turn in his affairs, which promised an opening into novel scenes and martial excitements.

Aboard the *Indomitable* our merchant-sailor was forthwith rated as an able-seaman and assigned to the starboard watch of the fore-top. He was soon at home in the service, not at all disliked for his unpretentious good looks and a sort of genial happy-go-lucky air. No merrier man in his mess: in marked contrast to certain other individuals included like himself among the impressed portion of the ship's company; for these when not actively employed were sometimes, and more particularly in the last dog-watch when the drawing near of twilight induced revery, apt to fall into a saddish mood which in some partook of sullenness. But they were not so young as our foretopman, and no few of them must have known a hearth of some sort, others may have had wives and children left, too probably, in uncertain circumstances, and hardly any but must have had acknowledged kith and kin, while for Billy, as will shortly be seen, his entire family was practically invested in himself.

2

THOUGH our new-made foretopman was well received in the top and on the gun-decks, hardly here was he that cynosure he had previously been among those minor ship's companies of the merchant marine, with which companies only had he hitherto consorted.

He was young; and despite his all but fully developed frame in aspect looked even younger than he really was, owing to a lingering adolescent expression in the as yet smooth face all but feminine in purity of natural complexion but where, thanks to his seagoing, the lily was quite suppressed and the rose had some ado visibly to flush through the tan.

To one essentially such a novice in the complexities of factitious life, the abrupt transition from his former and simpler sphere to the ampler and more knowing world of a great war-ship; this might well have abashed him had there been any conceit or vanity in his composition. Among her miscellaneous multitude, the *Indomitable* mustered several individuals who however inferior in grade were of no common natural stamp, sailors more signally susceptive of that air which continuous martial discipline and repeated presence in battle can in some degree impart even to the average man. As the *handsome sailor* Billy Budd's position aboard the seventy-four was something analogous to that of a rustic beauty transplanted from the provinces and brought into competition with the high-born dames of the court. But this change of circumstances he scarce noted. As little did he observe that something about him provoked an ambiguous smile in one or two harder faces among the blue-jackets. Nor less unaware was he of the peculiar favorable effect of his person and demeanor had upon the more intelligent gentlemen of the quarter-deck. Nor could this well have been otherwise. Cast in a mould peculiar to the finest physical examples of those Englishmen in whom the Saxon strain would seem not at all to partake of any Norman or other admixture, he showed in face that humane look of reposeful good nature which the Greek sculptor in some instances gave to his heroic strong man, Hercules. But this again was subtly modified by another and pervasive quality. The ear, small and shapely, the arch of the foot, the curve in mouth and nostril, even the indurated hand dyed to the orange-tawny of the toucan's bill, a hand telling alike of the halyards and tar-bucket; but, above all, something in the mobile expression, and every chance attitude and movement, something suggestive of a mother eminently favored by Love and the Graces; all this strangely indicated a lineage in direct contradiction to his lot. The mysteriousness here, became less mysterious through a matter-of-fact elicited when Billy at the capstan was being formally mustered into the service. Asked by the officer, a small brisk little gentleman as it chanced among other questions, his place of birth, he replied, "Please, Sir, I don't know."

"Don't know where you were born?—Who was your father?"

"God knows, Sir."

Struck by the straightforward simplicity of these replies, the officer next asked "Do you know anything about your beginning?"

"No, Sir. But I have heard that I was found in a pretty silk-lined basket hanging one morning from the knocker of a good man's door in Bristol."

"Found say you? Well," throwing back his head and looking up and down the new recruit; "Well it turns out to have been a pretty good find. Hope they'll find some more like you, my man; the fleet sadly needs them."

Yes, Billy Budd was a foundling, a presumable bye-blow, and, evidently, no ignoble one. Noble descent was as evident in him as in a blood horse.

For the rest, with little or no sharpness of faculty or any trace of the wisdom of the serpent, nor yet quite a dove, he possessed that kind and degree of intelligence going along with the unconventional rectitude of a sound human creature, one to whom not yet has been proffered the questionable apple of knowledge. He was illiterate; he could not read, but he could sing, and like the illiterate nightingale was sometimes the composer of his own song.

Of self-consciousness he seemed to have little or none, or about as much as we may reasonably impute to a dog of Saint Bernard's breed.

Habitually living with the elements and knowing little more of the land than as a beach, or, rather, that portion of the terraqueous globe providentially set apart for dance-houses doxies and tapsters, in short what sailors call a "fiddlers' green," his simple nature remained unsophisticated by those moral obliquities which are not in every case incompatible with that manufacturable thing known as respectability. But are sailors, frequenters of "fiddlers'-greens," without vices? No; but less often than with landsmen do their vices, so called, partake of crookedness of heart, seeming less to proceed from viciousness than exuberance of vitality after long constraint; frank manifestations in accordance with natural law. By his original constitution aided by the cooperating influences of his lot, Billy in many respects was little more than a sort of upright barbarian, much such perhaps as Adam presumably might have been ere the urbane Serpent wriggled himself into his company.

And here be it submitted that apparently going to corroborate the doctrine of man's fall, a doctrine now popularly ignored, it is observable that where certain virtues pristine and unadulterate peculiarly characterize anybody in the external uniform of civilization, they will upon scrutiny seem not to be derived from custom or convention, but rather to be out of keeping with these, as if indeed exceptionally transmitted from a period prior to Cain's city and citified man. The character marked by such qualities has to an unvitiated taste an untampered-with flavor like that of berries, while the man thoroughly civilized even in a fair specimen of the breed has to the same moral palate a questionable smack as of a compounded wine. To any stray inheritor of these primitive qualities found, like Caspar Hauser,[7] wandering dazed in any Christian capital of our time the good-natured poet's famous invocation, near two thousand years ago, of the good rustic out of his latitude in the Rome of the Cesars, still appropriately holds:—

> "Honest and poor, Faithful in word and thought
> What has thee, Fabian, to the city brought." [8]

Though our Handsome Sailor had as much of masculine beauty as one can expect anywhere to see; nevertheless, like the beautiful woman in one of Hawthorne's minor tales,[9] there was just one thing amiss in him. No visible blemish indeed, as with the lady; no, but an occasional liability to a vocal defect. Though in the hour of elemental uproar or peril, he was everything that a sailor should be, yet under sudden provocation of strong heart-feeling his voice otherwise singularly musical, as if expressive of the harmony within, was apt to develop an organic hesitancy, in fact more or less of a stutter or even worse. In this particular Billy was a striking instance that the arch interferer, the envious marplot of Eden still has more or less to do

7. **Caspar Hauser:** a youth discovered in Germany in 1828 who seemingly had been brought up without any exposure to society. His case caused much interest, raising the question: What is human nature like without any (as we would now say) acculturation? 8. **"Honest . . . brought":** Martial, *Epigrams*, IV.5. 9. **tales:** Melville is thinking of "The Birthmark."

with every human consignment to this planet of earth. In every case, one way or another he is sure to slip in his little card as much as to remind us—I too have a hand here.

The avowal of such an imperfection in the Handsome Sailor should be evidence not alone that he is not presented as a conventional hero, but also that the story in which he is the main figure is no romance.

3

AT THE TIME of Billy Budd's arbitrary enlistment into the *Indomitable* that ship was on her way to join the Mediterranean fleet. No long time elapsed before the junction was effected. As one of that fleet the seventy-four participated in its movements, though at times on account of her superior sailing qualities, in the absence of frigates, despatched on separate duty as a scout and at times on less temporary service. But with all this the story has little concernment, restricted as it is to the inner life of one particular ship and the career of an individual sailor.

It was the summer of 1797. In the April of that year had occurred the commotion at Spithead followed in May by a second and yet more serious outbreak in the fleet at the Nore. The latter is known, and without exaggeration in the epithet, as the Great Mutiny. It was indeed a demonstration more menacing to England than the contemporary manifestoes and conquering and proselyting armies of the French Directory.

To the British Empire the Nore Mutiny was what a strike in the fire-brigade would be to London threatened by general arson. In a crisis when the kingdom might well have anticipated the famous signal that some years later published along the navál line of battle what it was that upon occasion England expected of Englishmen; *that* was the time when at the mast-heads of the three-deckers and seventy-fours moored in her own roadstead—a fleet, the right arm of a Power then all but the sole free conservative one of the Old World, the blue-jackets, to be numbered by thousands ran up with huzzas the British colors with the union and cross wiped out; by that cancellation transmuting the flag of founded law and freedom defined, into the enemy's red meteor of unbridled and unbounded revolt. Reasonable discontent growing out of practical grievances in the fleet had been ignited into irrational combustion as by live cinders blown across the Channel from France in flames.

The event converted into irony for a time those spirited strains of Dibdin—as a song-writer no mean auxiliary to the English Government at the European conjuncture—strains celebrating, among other things, the patriotic devotion of the British tar:

"And as for my life, 'tis the King's!"

Such an episode in the Island's grand naval story her naval historians naturally abridge; one of them (G. P. R. James [10]) candidly acknowledging that fain would he pass it over did not "impartiality forbid fastidiousness." And yet his mention is less a narration than a reference, having to do hardly at all with details. Nor are these readily to be found in the libraries. Like some other events in every age befalling states everywhere including America the Great Mutiny was of such character that national pride along with views of policy would fain shade it off into the historical background. Such events can not be ignored, but there is a considerate way of historically treating them. If a well-constituted individual refrains from blazoning aught amiss or calamitous in his family; a nation in the like circumstance may without reproach be equally discreet.

Though after parleyings between Government and the ringleaders, and concessions by the former as to some glaring abuses, the first uprising—that at Spithead—with difficulty was put down, or matters for the time pacified; yet at the Nore the unforeseen renewal of insurrection on a yet larger scale, and emphasized in the conferences that ensued by demands deemed by the authorities not only inadmissible but aggressively insolent, indicated—if the Red Flag did not sufficiently do so, what was the spirit animating the men. Final suppression, however, there was; but only made possible perhaps by the unswerving loyalty of the marine corps and a voluntary resumption of loyalty among influential sections of the crews.

To some extent the Nore Mutiny may be regarded as analogous to the distempering irruption of contagious fever in a frame constitutionally sound, and which anon throws it off.

At all events, of these thousands of mutineers were some of the tars who not so very long afterwards—whether wholly prompted thereto by patriotism, or pugnacious instinct, or by both,—helped to win a coronet for Nelson at the Nile, and the naval crown of crowns for him at Trafalgar. To the mutineers those battles and especially Trafalgar were a plenary absolution and a grand one: For all that goes to make up scenic naval display, heroic magnificence in arms, those battles especially Trafalgar stand unmatched in human annals.

10. **G. P. R. James:** apparently a mistake for William James, author of *The Naval History of Great Britain* (1860).

4

Concerning "The greatest sailor since the world began." TENNYSON?

IN THIS MATTER of writing, resolve as one may to keep to the main road, some by-paths have an enticement not readily to be withstood. I am going to err into such a by-path. If the reader will keep me company I shall be glad. At the least we can promise ourselves that pleasure which is wickedly said to be in sinning, for a literary sin the divergence will be.

Very likely it is no new remark that the inventions of our time have at last brought about a change in sea-warfare in degree corresponding to the revolution in all warfare effected by the original introduction from China into Europe of gunpowder. The first European fire-arm, a clumsy contrivance, was, as is well known, scouted by no few of the knights as a base implement, good enough peradventure for weavers too craven to stand up crossing steel with steel in frank fight. But as ashore knightly valor though shorn of its blazonry did not cease with the knights, neither on the seas though nowadays in encounters there a certain kind of displayed gallantry be fallen out of date as hardly applicable under changed circumstances, did the nobler qualities of such naval magnates as Don John of Austria, Doria, Van Tromp, Jean Bart, the long line of British Admirals and the American Decaturs of 1812 become obsolete with their wooden walls.

Nevertheless, to anybody who can hold the Present at its worth without being inappreciative of the Past, it may be forgiven, if to such an one the solitary old hulk at Portsmouth, Nelson's *Victory*, seems to float there, not alone as the decaying monument of a fame incorruptible, but also as a poetic reproach, softened by its picturesqueness, to the *Monitors* and yet mightier hulls of the European iron-clads. And this not altogether because such craft are unsightly, unavoidably lacking the symmetry and grand lines of the old battle-ships, but equally for other reasons.

There are some, perhaps, who while not altogether inaccessible to that poetic reproach just alluded to, may yet on behalf of the new order, be disposed to parry it; and this to the extent of iconoclasm, if need be. For example, prompted by the sight of the star inserted in the *Victory's* quarter-deck designating the spot where the Great Sailor fell, these martial utilitarians may suggest considerations implying that Nelson's ornate publication of his person in battle was not only unnecessary, but not military, nay savored of foolhardiness and vanity. They may add, too, that at Trafalgar it was in effect nothing less than a challenge to death; and death came; and that but for his bravado the victorious Admiral might possibly have survived the battle, and so, instead of having his sagacious dying injunctions overruled by his immediate successor in command he himself when the contest was decided might have brought his shattered fleet to anchor, a proceeding which might have averted the deplorable loss of life by shipwreck in the elemental tempest that followed the martial one.

Well, should we set aside the more disputable point whether for various reasons it was possible to anchor the fleet, then plausibly enough the Benthamites [11] of war may urge the above.

But the *might-have-been* is but boggy ground to build on. And, certainly, in foresight as to the larger issue of an encounter, and anxious preparations for it—buoying the deadly way and mapping it out, as at Copenhagen—few commanders have been so painstakingly circumspect as this same reckless declarer of his person in fight.

Personal prudence even when dictated by quite other than selfish considerations surely is no special virtue in a military man; while an excessive love of glory, impassioning a less burning impulse the honest sense of duty, is the first. If the name *Wellington* is not so much of a trumpet to the blood as the simpler name *Nelson,* the reason for this may perhaps be inferred from the above. Alfred in his funeral ode [12] on the victor of Waterloo ventures not to call him the greatest soldier of all time, though in the same ode he invokes Nelson as "the greatest sailor since the world began."

At Trafalgar Nelson on the brink of opening the fight sat down and wrote his last brief will and testament. If under the presentiment of the most magnificent of all victories to be crowned by his own glorious death, a sort of priestly motive led him to dress his person in the jewelled vouchers of his own shining deeds; if thus to have adorned himself for the altar and the sacrifice were indeed vain-glory, then affectation and fustian is each more heroic line in the great epics and dramas, since in such lines the poet but embodies in verse those exaltations of sentiment that a nature like Nelson, the opportunity being given, vitalizes into acts.

11. **Benthamites:** Jeremy Bentham (1748–1832), the philosopher of utilitarianism. 12. **ode:** Tennyson's "Ode on the Death of the Duke of Wellington." Tennyson's line reads, "The greatest sailor since our world began."

5

YES, THE OUTBREAK at the Nore was put down. But not every grievance was redressed. If the contractors, for example, were no longer permitted to ply some practices peculiar to their tribe everywhere, such as providing shoddy cloth, rations not sound, or false in the measure; not the less impressment, for one thing, went on. By custom sanctioned for centuries, and judicially maintained by a Lord Chancellor as late as Mansfield, that mode of manning the fleet, a mode now fallen into a sort of abeyance but never formally renounced, it was not practicable to give up in those years. Its abrogation would have crippled the indispensable fleet, one wholly under canvas, no steam-power, its innumerable sails and thousands of cannon, everything in short, worked by muscle alone; a fleet the more insatiate in demand for men, because then multiplying its ships of all grades against contingencies present and to come of the convulsed Continent.

Discontent foreran the Two Mutinies, and more or less it lurkingly survived them. Hence it was not unreasonable to apprehend some return of trouble sporadic or general. One instance of such apprehensions: In the same year with this story, Nelson, then Vice Admiral Sir Horatio, being with the fleet off the Spanish coast, was directed by the Admiral in command to shift his pennant from the *Captain* to the *Theseus;* and for this reason: that the latter ship having newly arrived on the station from home where it had taken part in the Great Mutiny, danger was apprehended from the temper of the men; and it was thought that an officer like Nelson was the one, not indeed to terrorize the crew into base subjection, but to win them, by force of his mere presence back to an allegiance if not as enthusiastic as his own, yet as true. So it was that for a time on more than one quarter-deck anxiety did exist. At sea precautionary vigilance was strained against relapse. At short notice an engagement might come on. When it did, the lieutenants assigned to batteries felt it uncumbent on them, in some instances to stand with drawn swords behind the men working the guns.

6

BUT ON BOARD the seventy-four in which Billy now swung his hammock, very little in the manner of the men and nothing obvious in the demeanor of the officers would have suggested to an ordinary observer that the Great Mutiny was a recent event. In their general bearing and conduct the commissioned officers of a war-ship naturally take their tone from the commander, that is if he have that ascendancy of character that ought to be his.

Captain the Honorable Edward Fairfax Vere, to give his full title, was a bachelor of forty or thereabouts, a sailor of distinction even in a time prolfic of renowned seamen. Though allied to the higher nobility his advancement had not been altogether owing to influences connected with that circumstance. He had seen much service, been in various engagements, always acquitting himself as an officer mindful of the welfare of his men, but never tolerating an infraction of discipline; thoroughly versed in the science of his profession, and intrepid to the verge of temerity, though never injudiciously so. For his gallantry in the West Indian waters as flag-lieutenant under Rodney [13] in that Admiral's crowning victory over De Grasse, he was made a post-captain.

Ashore in the garb of a civilian scarce anyone would have taken him for a sailor, more especially that he never garnished unprofessional talk with nautical terms, and grave in his bearing, evinced little appreciation of mere humor. It was not out of keeping with these traits that on a passage when nothing demanded his paramount action, he was the most undemonstrative of men. Any landsman observing this gentleman not conspicuous by his stature and wearing no pronounced insignia, emerging from his cabin retreat to the open deck, and noting the silent deference of the officers retiring to leeward, might have taken him for the King's guest, a civilian aboard the King's-ship, some highly honorable discreet envoy on his way to an important post. But in fact this unobtrusiveness of demeanor may have proceeded from a certain unaffected modesty of manhood sometimes accompanying a resolute nature, a modesty evinced at all times not calling for pronounced action, and which shown in any rank of life suggests a virtue aristocratic in kind.

As with some others engaged in various departments of the world's more heroic activities, Captain Vere though practical enough upon occasion would at times betray a certain dreaminess of mood. Standing alone on the weather-side of the quarter deck, one hand holding by the rigging he would absently gaze off at the blank sea. At the presentation to him then of some minor matter interrupting the current of his thoughts he would show more or less irascibility; but instantly he would control it.

In the navy he was popularly known by the appellation—Starry Vere. How such a designation happened to fall upon one who whatever his ster-

13. **Rodney:** Admiral George Brydges Rodney (1719–92) defeated the French Admiral de Grasse off Martinique in 1782.

ling qualities was without any brilliant ones was in this wise: A favorite kinsman, Lord Denton, a free-hearted fellow, had been the first to meet and congratulate him upon his return to England from his West Indian cruise; and but the day previous turning over a copy of Andrew Marvell's poems had lighted, not for the first time however, upon the lines entitled *Appleton House,* the name of one of the seats of their common ancestor, a hero in the German wars of the seventeenth century, in which poem occur the lines,

> "This 'tis to have been from the first
> In a domestic heaven nursed,
> Under the discipline severe
> Of Fairfax and the starry Vere."

And so, upon embracing his cousin fresh from Rodney's great victory wherein he had played so gallant a part, brimming over with just family pride in the sailor of their house, he exuberantly exclaimed, "Give ye joy, Ed; give ye joy, my starray Vere!" This got currency, and the novel prefix serving in familiar parlance readily to distinguish the *Indomitable's* Captain from another Vere his senior, a distant relative an officer of like rank in the navy, it remained permanently attached to the surname.

7

IN VIEW of the part that the commander of the *Indomitable* plays in scenes shortly to follow, it may be well to fill out that sketch of him outlined in the previous chapter.

Aside from his qualities as a sea-officer Captain Vere was an exceptional character. Unlike no few of England's renowned sailors, long and arduous service with signal devotion to it, had not resulted in absorbing and *salting* the entire man. He had a marked leaning toward everything intellectual. He loved books, never going to sea without a newly replenished library, compact but of the best. The isolated leisure, in some cases so wearisome, falling at intervals to commanders even during a war-cruise, never was tedious to Captain Vere. With nothing of that literary taste which less heeds the thing conveyed than the vehicle, his bias was toward those books to which every serious mind of superior order occupying any active post of authority in the world, naturally inclines: books treating of actual men and events no matter of what era—history, biography and unconventional writers, who, free from cant and convention, like Montaigne, honestly and in the spirit of common sense philosophize upon realities.

In this love of reading he found confirmation of his own more reserved thoughts—confirmation which he had vainly sought in social converse, so that as touching most fundamental topics, there had got to be established in him some positive convictions, which he forefelt would abide in him essentially unmodified so long as his intelligent part remained unimpaired. In view of the troubled period in which his lot was cast this was well for him. His settled convictions were as a dyke against those invading waters of novel opinion social political and otherwise, which carried away as in a torrent no few minds in those days, minds by nature not inferior to his own. While other members of that aristocracy to which by birth he belonged were incensed at the innovators mainly because their theories were inimical to the privileged classes, not alone Captain Vere disinterestedly opposed them because they seemed to him incapable of embodiment in lasting institutions, but at war with the peace of the world and the true welfare of mankind.

With minds less stored than his and less earnest, some officers of his rank, with whom at times he would necessarily consort, found him lacking in the companionable quality, a dry and bookish gentleman, as they deemed. Upon any chance withdrawal from their company one would be apt to say to another, something like this: "Vere is a noble fellow, Starry Vere. Spite the gazettes, Sir Horatio" meaning him with the Lord title "is at bottom scarce a better seaman or fighter. But between you and me now don't you think there is a queer streak of the pedantic running through him? Yes, like the King's yarn in a coil of navy-rope?"

Some apparent ground there was for this sort of confidential criticism; since not only did the Captain's discourse never fall into the jocosely familiar, but in illustrating of any point touching the stirring personages and events of the time as that he would be as apt to cite some historic character or incident of antiquity as he would to cite from the moderns. He seemed unmindful of the circumstance that to his bluff company such remote allusions however pertinent they might really be were altogether alien to men whose reading was mainly confined to the journals. But considerateness in such matters is not easy to natures constituted like Captain Vere's. Their honesty prescribes to them directness, sometimes far-reaching like that of a migratory fowl that in its flight never heeds when it crosses a frontier.

8

THE LIEUTENANTS and other commissioned gentlemen forming Captain Vere's staff it is not necessary here to particularize, nor needs it to make any mention of any of the warrant-officers. But among the petty-officers was one who having much to do with the story, may as well be forthwith introduced. His portrait I essay, but shall never hit it. This was John Claggart, the Master-at-arms. But that sea-title may to landsmen seem somewhat equivocal. Originally doubtless that petty-officer's function was the instruction of the men in the use of arms, sword or cutlas. But very long ago, owing to the advance in gunnery making hand-to-hand encounters less frequent and giving to nitre and sulphur the preeminence over steel, that function ceased; the Master-at-arms of a great war-ship becoming a sort of Chief of Police charged among other matters with the duty of preserving order on the populous lower gun-decks.

Claggart was a man about five and thirty, somewhat spare and tall, yet of no ill figure upon the whole. His hand was too small and shapely to have been accustomed to hard toil. The face was a notable one; the features all except the chin cleanly cut as those on a Greek medallion; yet the chin, beardless as Tecumseh's,[14] had something of strange protuberant heaviness in its make that recalled the prints of the Rev. Dr. Titus Oates, the historic deponent with the clerical drawl in the time of Charles II and the fraud of the alleged Popish Plot.[15] It served Claggart in his office that his eye could cast a tutoring glance. His brow was of the sort phrenologically associated with more than average intellect; silken jet curls partly clustering over it, making a foil to the pallor below, a pallor tinged with a faint shade of amber akin to the hue of time-tinted marbles of old. This complexion, singularly contrasting with the red or deeply bronzed visages of the sailors, and in part the result of his official seclusion from the sunlight, though it was not exactly displeasing, nevertheless seemed to hint of something defective or abnormal in the constitution and blood. But his general aspect and manner were so suggestive of an education and career incongruous with his naval function that when not actively engaged in it he looked like a man of high quality, social and moral, who for reasons of his own was keeping incog. Nothing was known of his former life. It might be that he was an Englishman; and yet there lurked a bit of accent in his speech suggesting that possibly he was not such by birth, but through naturalization in early childhood. Among certain grizzled sea-gossips of the gun-decks and forecastle went a rumor perdue that the master-at-arms was a *chevalier* who had volunteered into the King's navy by way of compounding for some mysterious swindle whereof he had been arraigned at the King's Bench. The fact that nobody could substantiate this report was, of course, nothing against its secret currency. Such a rumor once started on the gun-decks in reference to almost anyone below the rank of a commissioned officer would, during the period assigned to this narrative, have seemed not altogether wanting in credibility to the tarry old wiseacres of a man-of-war crew. And indeed a man of Claggart's accomplishments, without prior nautical experience entering the navy at mature life, as he did, and necessarily allotted at the start to the lowest grade in it; a man too who never made allusion to his previous life ashore; these were circumstances which in the dearth of exact knowledge as to his true antecedents opened to the invidious a vague field for unfavorable surmise.

But the sailors' dog-watch gossip concerning him derived a vague plausibility from the fact that now for some period the British Navy could so little afford to be squeamish in the matter of keeping up the muster-rolls, that not only were press-gangs notoriously abroad both afloat and ashore, but there was little or no secret about another matter, namely that the London police were at liberty to capture any able-bodied suspect, any questionable fellow at large and summarily ship him to the dock-yard or fleet. Furthermore, even among voluntary enlistments there were instances where the motive thereto partook neither of patriotic impulse nor yet of a random desire to experience a bit of sea-life and martial adventure. Insolvent debtors of minor grade, together with the promiscuous lame ducks of morality found in the Navy a convenient and secure refuge. Secure, because once enlisted aboard a King's-Ship, they were as much in sanctuary, as the transgressor of the Middle Ages harboring himself under the shadow of the altar. Such sanctioned irregularities which for obvious reasons the Government would hardly think to parade at the time and which consequently, and as affecting the least influential class of mankind, have all but dropped into oblivion, lend color to something for the truth whereof I do not vouch, and hence have some scruple in stating; something I remember having seen in print though the book I can not recall; but the same thing was personally communicated to me now more than forty years ago by an old pensioner in a cocked hat with whom I had a most interesting talk on the terrace at Greenwich, a Baltimore Negro, a Trafalgar man. It was to this effect: In the case of a warship short of hands

14. **Tecumseh:** American Indian chief (1768?–1813).

15. **Popish Plot:** In 1687 the Reverend Titus Oates caused a great stir in London by alleging that the Catholics were about to subvert England.

whose speedy sailing was imperative, the deficient quota in lack of any other way of making it good, would be eked out by draughts culled direct from the jails. For reasons previously suggested it would not perhaps be easy at the present day directly to prove or disprove the allegation. But allowed as a verity, how significant would it be of England's straits at the time confronted by those wars which like a flight of harpies rose shrieking from the din and dust of the fallen bastille. That era appears measurably clear to us who look back at it, and but read of it. But to the grandfathers of us graybeards, the more thoughtful of them, the genius of it presented an aspect like that of Camoen's[16] Spirit of the Cape, an eclipsing menace mysterious and prodigious. Not America was exempt from apprehension. At the height of Napoleon's unexampled conquests, there were Americans who had fought at Bunker Hill who looked forward to the possibility that the Atlantic might prove no barrier against the ultimate schemes of this French portentous upstart from the revolutionary chaos who seemed in act of fulfilling judgment prefigured in the Apocalypse.[17]

But the less credence was to be given to the gun-deck talk touching Claggart, seeing that no man holding his office in a man-of-war can ever hope to be popular with the crew. Besides, in derogatory comments upon anyone against whom they have a grudge, or for any reason or no reason mislike, sailors are much like landsmen, they are apt to exaggerate or romance it.

About as much was really known to the *Indomitable's* tars of the master-at-arms' career before entering the service as an astronomer knows about a comet's travels prior to its first observable appearance in the sky. The verdict of the sea quidnuncs has been cited only by way of showing what sort of moral impression the man made upon rude uncultivated natures whose conceptions of human wickedness were necessarily of the narrowest, limited to ideas of vulgar rascality,—a thief among the swinging hammocks during a night-watch, or the man-brokers and land-sharks of the sea-ports.

It was no gossip, however, but fact, that though, as before hinted, Claggart upon his entrance into the navy was, as a novice, assigned to the least honorable section of a man-of-war's crew, embracing the drudgery, he did not long remain there.

The superior capacity he immediately evinced, his constitutional sobriety, ingratiating deference to superiors, together with a peculiar ferreting genius manifested on a singular occasion, all this capped by a certain austere patriotism abruptly advanced him to the position of master-at-arms.

Of this maritime Chief of Police the ship's-corporals, so called, were the immediate subordinates, and compliant ones; and this, as is to be noted in some business departments ashore, almost to a degree inconsistent with entire moral volition. His place put various converging wires of underground influence under the Chief's control, capable when astutely worked through his understrappers of operating to the mysterious discomfort if nothing worse, of any of the sea-commonalty.

16. **Camoen's:** Melville was fond of the epic poem the *Lusiads* by Luis de Camoëns (1524–80). 17. **Apocalypse:** Revelation, the last book of the Bible.

9

LIFE in the fore-top well agreed with Billy Budd. There, when not actually engaged on the yards yet higher aloft, the topmen, who as such had been picked out for youth and activity, constituted an aerial club lounging at ease against the smaller stun'sails rolled up into cushions, spinning yarns like the lazy gods, and frequently amused with what was going on in the busy world of the decks below. No wonder then that a young fellow of Billy's disposition was well content in such society. Giving no cause of offence to anybody, he was always alert at a call. So in the merchant service it had been with him. But now such a punctiliousness in duty was shown that his topmates would sometimes good-naturedly laugh at him for it. This heightened alacrity had its cause, namely, the impression made upon him by the first formal gangway-punishment he had ever witnessed, which befell the day following his impressment. It had been incurred by a little fellow, young, a novice, an after-guardsman absent from his assigned post when the ship was being put about; a dereliction resulting in a rather serious hitch to that manœuvre, one demanding instantaneous promptitude in letting go and making fast. When Billy saw the culprit's naked back under the scourge gridironed with red welts, and worse; when he marked the dire expression on the liberated man's face as with his woolen shirt flung over him by the executioner he rushed forward from the spot to bury himself in the crowd, Billy was horrified. He resolved that never through remissness would he make himself liable to such a visitation or do or omit aught that might merit even verbal reproof. What then was his surprise and concern when ultimately he found himself getting into petty trouble occasionally about such matters as the stowage of his bag or something amiss in his hammock, matters under the police oversight of the ship's-corporals of the lower decks, and which brought down on him a vague threat from one of them.

So heedful in all things as he was, how could this be? He could not understand it, and it more than vexed him. When he spoke to his young topmates about it they were either lightly incredulous or found something comical in his unconcealed anxiety. "Is it your bag, Billy?" said one "well, sew yourself up in it, bully boy, and then you'll be sure to know if anybody meddles with it."

Now there was a veteran aboard who because his years began to disqualify him for more active work had been recently assigned duty as mainmast-man in his watch, looking to the gear belayed at the rail roundabout that great spar near the deck. At off-times the foretopman had picked up some acquaintance with him, and now in his trouble it occurred to him that he might be the sort of person to go to for wise counsel. He was an old Dansker [18] long anglicized in the service, of few words, many wrinkles and some honorable scars. His wizened face, time-tinted and weather-stained to the complexion of an antique parchment, was here and there peppered blue by the chance explosion of a gun-cartridge in action. He was an *Agamemnon*-man; some two years prior to the time of this story having served under Nelson when but Sir Horatio in that ship immortal in naval memory, and which dismantled and in part broken up to her bare ribs is seen a grand skeleton in Haydon's etching. As one of a boarding-party from the *Agamemnon* he had received a cut slantwise along one temple and cheek leaving a long pale scar like a streak of dawn's light falling athwart the dark visage. It was on account of that scar and the affair in which it was known that he had received it, as well as from his blue-peppered complexion that the Dansker went among the *Indomitable's* crew by the name of "Board-her-in-the-smoke."

Now the first time that his small weazel-eyes happened to light on Billy Budd, a certain grim internal merriment set all his ancient wrinkles into antic play. Was it that his eccentric unsentimental old sapience primitive in its kind saw or thought it saw something which in contrast with the warship's environment looked oddly incongruous in the handsome sailor? But after slyly studying him at intervals, the old Merlin's [19] equivocal merriment was modified; for now when the twain would meet, it would start in his face a quizzing sort of look, but it would be but momentary and sometimes replaced by an expression of speculative query as to what might eventually befall a nature like that, dropped into a world not without some man-traps and against whose subtleties simple courage lacking experience and address and without any touch of defensive ugliness, is of little avail; and where such innocence as man is capable of does yet in a moral emergency not always sharpen the faculties or enlighten the will.

However it was the Dansker in his ascetic way rather took to Billy. Nor was this only because of a certain philosophic interest in such a character. There was another cause. While the old man's eccentricities, sometimes bordering on the ursine, repelled the juniors, Billy, undeterred thereby, revering him as a salt hero would make advances, never passing the old Agamemnon-man without a salutation marked by that respect which is seldom lost on the aged however crabbed at times or whatever their station in life.

There was a vein of dry humor, or what not, in the mastman; and, whether in freak of patriarchal irony touching Billy's youth and athletic frame, or for some other and more recondite reason, from the first in addressing him he always substituted Baby for Billy. The Dansker in fact being the originator of the name by which the foretopman eventually became known aboard ship.

Well then, in his mysterious little difficulty going in quest of the wrinkled one, Billy found him off duty in a dog-watch ruminating by himself seated on a shot-box of the upper gun-deck now and then surveying with a somewhat cynical regard certain of the more swaggering promenaders there. Billy recounted his trouble, again wondering how it all happened. The salt seer attentively listened, accompanying the foretopman's recital with queer twitchings of his wrinkles and problematical little sparkles of his small ferret eyes. Making an end of his story, the foretopman asked, "And now, Dansker, do tell me what you think of it."

The old man, shoving up the front of his tarpaulin and deliberately rubbing the long slant scar at the point where it entered the thin hair, laconically said, "Baby Budd, *Jimmy Legs*" (meaning the master-at-arms) "is down on you."

"Jimmy Legs!" ejaculated Billy, his welkin eyes expanding; "what for? Why he calls me *the sweet and pleasant young fellow,* they tell me."

"Does he so?" grinned the grizzled one; then said "Ay Baby Lad a sweet voice has *Jimmy Legs."*

"No, not always. But to me he has. I seldom pass him but there comes a pleasant word."

"And that's because he's down upon you, Baby Budd."

Such reiteration along with the manner of it, incomprehensible to a novice, disturbed Billy almost as much as the mystery for which he had

18. **Dansker:** Dane. 19. **Merlin:** the magician who figures in the legends of King Arthur.

sought explanation. Something less unpleasingly oracular he tried to extract; but the old sea-Chiron thinking perhaps that for the nonce he had sufficiently instructed his young Achilles, pursed his lips, gathered all his wrinkles together and would commit himself to nothing further.

Years, and those experiences which befall certain shrewder men subordinated life-long to the will of superiors, all this had developed in the Dansker the pithy guarded cynicism that was his leading characteristic.

10

THE NEXT DAY an incident served to confirm Billy Budd in his incredulity as to the Dansker's strange summing up of the case submitted. The ship at noon going large before the wind was rolling on her course, and he below at dinner and engaged in some sportful talk with the members of his mess, chanced in a sudden lurch to spill the entire contents of his soup-pan upon the new scrubbed deck. Claggart, the Master-at-arms, offical rattan in hand, happened to be passing along the battery in a bay of which the mess was lodged, and the greasy liquid streamed just across his path. Stepping over it, he was proceeding on his way without comment, since the matter was nothing to take notice of under the circumstances, when he happened to observe who it was that had done the spilling. His countenance changed. Pausing, he was about to ejaculate something hasty at the sailor, but checked himself, and pointing down to the streaming soup, playfully tapped him from behind with his rattan, saying in a low musical voice peculiar to him at times "Handsomely done, my lad! And handsome is as handsome did it too!" And with that passed on. Not noted by Billy as not coming within his view was the involuntary smile, or rather grimace, that accompanied Claggart's equivocal words. Aridly it drew down the thin corners of his shapely mouth. But everybody taking his remark as meant for humorous, and at which therefore as coming from a superior they were bound to laugh, "with counterfeited glee" acted accordingly; and Billy tickled, it may be, by the allusion to his being the handsome sailor, merrily joined in; then addressing his messmates exclaimed "There now, who says that Jimmy Legs is down on me!" "And who said he was, Beauty?" demanded one Donald with some surprise. Whereat the foretopman looked a little foolish recalling that it was only one person, Board-her-in-the-smoke, who had suggested what to him was the smoky idea that this master-at-arms was in any peculiar way hostile to him. Meantime that functionary resuming his path must have momentarily worn some expression less guarded than that of the bitter smile, and usurping the face from the heart, some distorting expression perhaps, for a drummer-boy heedlessly frolicking along from the opposite direction and chancing to come into light collision with his person was strangely disconcerted by his aspect. Nor was the impression lessened when the official impulsively giving him a sharp cut with the rattan, vehemently exclaimed "Look where you go!"

11

WHAT was the matter with the master-at-arms? And, be the matter what it might, how could it have direct relation to Billy Budd with whom prior to the affair of the spilled soup he had never come into any special contact official or otherwise? What indeed could the trouble have to do with one so little inclined to give offence as the merchant-ship's *peacemaker,* even him who in Claggart's own phrase was "the sweet and pleasant young fellow"? Yes, why should *Jimmy Legs,* to borrow the Dansker's expression, be *down* on the Handsome Sailor? But, at heart and not for nothing, as the later chance encounter may indicate to the discerning, down on him, secretly down on him, he assuredly was.

Now to invent something touching the more private career of Claggart, something involving Billy Budd, of which something the latter should be wholly ignorant, some romantic incident implying that Claggart's knowledge of the young blue-jacket began at some period anterior to catching sight of him on board the seventy-four—all this, not so difficult to do, might avail in a way more or less interesting to account for whatever of enigma may appear to lurk in the case. But in fact there was nothing of the sort. And yet the cause, necessarily to be assumed as the sole one assignable, is in its very realism as much charged with that prime element of Radcliffian [20] romance, *the mysterious,* as any that the ingenuity of the author of the *Mysteries of Udolpho* could devise. For what can more partake of the mysterious than an antipathy spontaneous and profound such as is evoked in certain exceptional mortals by the mere aspect of some other mortal, however harmless he may be? if not called forth by this very harmlessness itself.

Now there can exist no irritating juxtaposition of dissimilar personalities comparable to that

20. **Radcliffian:** Ann Radcliffe (1764–1823), author of *The Mysteries of Udolpho* and other Gothic romances.

which is possible aboard a great war-ship fully manned and at sea. There, every day among all ranks almost every man comes into more or less of contact with almost every other man. Wholly there to avoid even the sight of an aggravating object one must needs give it Jonah's toss or jump overboard himself. Imagine how all this might eventually operate on some peculiar human creature the direct reverse of a saint?

But for the adequate comprehending of Claggart by a normal nature these hints are insufficient. To pass from a normal nature to him one must cross "the deadly space between." And this is best done by indirection.

Long ago an honest scholar my senior, said to me in reference to one who like himself is now no more, a man so unimpeachably respectable that against him nothing was ever openly said though among the few something was whispered, "Yes, X—— is a nut not to be cracked by the tap of a lady's fan. You are aware that I am the adherent of no organized religion much less of any philosophy built into a system. Well, for all that, I think that to try and get into X——, enter his labyrinth and get out again, without a clue derived from some source other than what is known as *knowledge of the world*—that were hardly possible, at least for me."

"Why," said I, "X—— however singular a study to some, is yet human, and knowledge of the world assuredly implies the knowledge of human nature, and in most of its varieties."

"Yes, but a superficial knowledge of it, serving ordinary purposes. But for anything deeper, I am not certain whether to know the world and to know human nature be not two distinct branches of knowledge, which while they may coexist in the same heart, yet either may exist with little or nothing of the other. Nay, in an average man of the world, his constant rubbing with it blunts that fine spiritual insight indispensable to the understanding of the essential in certain exceptional characters, whether evil ones or good. In a matter of some importance I have seen a girl wind an old lawyer about her little finger. Nor was it the dotage of senile love. Nothing of the sort. But he knew law better than he knew the girl's heart. Coke and Blackstone hardly shed so much light into obscure spiritual places as the Hebrew prophets. And who were they? Mostly recluses."

At the time my inexperience was such that I did not quite see the drift of all this. It may be that I see it now. And, indeed, if that lexicon which is based on Holy Writ were any longer popular, one might with less difficulty define and denominate certain phenomenal men. As it is, one must turn to some authority not liable to the charge of being tinctured with the Biblical element.

In a list of definitions included in the authentic translation of Plato, a list attributed to him, occurs this: "Natural Depravity: a depravity according to nature." A definition which though savoring of Calvinism, by no means involves Calvin's dogma as to total mankind. Evidently its intent makes it applicable but to individuals. Not many are the examples of this depravity which the gallows and jail supply. At any rate for notable instances, since these have no vulgar alloy of the brute in them, but invariably are dominated by intellectuality, one must go elsewhere. Civilization, especially if of the austerer sort, is auspicious to it. It folds itself in the mantle of respectability. It has its certain negative virtues serving as silent auxiliaries. It never allows wine to get within in its guard. It is not going too far to say that it is without vices or small sins. There is a phenomenal pride in it that excludes them from anything mercenary or avaricious. In short the depravity here meant partakes nothing of the sordid or sensual. It is serious, but free from acerbity. Though no flatterer of mankind it never speaks ill of it.

But the thing which in eminent instances signalizes so exceptional a nature is this: though the man's even temper and discreet bearing would seem to intimate a mind peculiarly subject to the law of reason, not the less in his heart he would seem to riot in complete exemption from that law having apparently little to do with reason further than to employ it as an ambidexter implement for effecting the irrational. That is to say: Toward the accomplishment of an aim which in wantonness of malignity would seem to partake of the insane, he will direct a cool judgement sagacious and sound.

These men are true madmen, and of the most dangerous sort, for their lunacy is not continuous but occasional evoked by some special object; it is probably secretive, which is as much to say it is self-contained, so that when moreover, most active it is to the average mind not distinguishable from sanity, and for the reason above suggested that whatever its aims may be, and the aim is never declared—the method and the outward proceeding are always perfectly rational.

Now something such an one was Claggart, in whom was the mania of an evil nature, not engendered by vicious training or corrupting books or licentious living, but born with him and innate, in short "a depravity according to nature."

12

Lawyers, Experts, Clergy

AN EPISODE

BY THE WAY, can it be the phenomenon, disowned or at least concealed, that in some criminal cases puzzles the courts? For this cause have our juries at times not only to endure the prolonged contentions of lawyers with their fees, but also the yet more perplexing strife of the medical experts with theirs?—But why leave it to them? why not subpoena(?) as well the clerical proficients? Their vocation bringing them into peculiar contact with so many human beings, and sometimes in their least guarded hour, in interviews very much more confidential than those of physician and patient; this would seem to qualify them to know something about those intricacies involved in the question of moral responsibility; whether in a given case, say, the crime proceeded from mania in the brain or rabies of the heart. As to any differences among themselves these clerical proficients might develop on the stand, these could hardly be greater than the direct contradictions exchanged between the remunerated medical experts.

Dark sayings are these, some will say. But why? Is it because they somewhat savor of Holy Writ in its phrase "mysteries of iniquity"? If they do, such savor was far enough from being intended for little will it commend these pages to many a reader of to-day.

The point of the present story turning on the hidden nature of the master-at-arms has necessitated this chapter. With an added hint or two in connection with the incident at the mess, the resumed narrative must be left to vindicate, as it may, its own credibility.

13

Pale ire, envy and despair [21]

THAT Claggart's figure was not amiss, and his face, save the chin, well moulded, has already been said. Of these favorable points he seemed not insensible, for he was not only neat but careful in his dress. But the form of Billy Budd was heroic; and if his face was without the intellectual look of the pallid Claggart's, not the less was it lit, like his, from within, though from a different source. The bonfire in his heart made luminous the rose-tan in his cheek.

In view of the marked contrast between the persons of the twain, it is more than probable that when the master-at-arms in the scene last given applied to the sailor the proverb *Handsome is as handsome does;* he there let escape an ironic inkling, not caught by the young sailors who heard it, as to what it was that had first moved him against Billy, namely, his significant personal beauty.

Now envy and antipathy passions irreconcilable in reason, nevertheless in fact may spring conjoined like Chang and Eng [22] in one birth. Is Envy then such a monster? Well, though many an arraigned mortal has in hopes of mitigated penalty pleaded guilty to horrible actions, did ever anybody seriously confess to envy? Something there is in it universally felt to be more shameful than even felonious crime. And not only does everbody disown it but the better sort are inclined to incredulity when it is in earnest imputed to an intelligent man. But since its lodgement is in the heart not the brain, no degree of intellect supplies a guarantee against it. But Claggart's was no vulgar form of the passion. Nor, as directed toward Billy Budd did it partake of that streak of apprehensive jealousy that marred Saul's visage perturbedly brooding on the comely young David.[23] Claggart's envy struck deeper. If askance he eyed the good looks, cheery health and frank enjoyment of young life in Billy Budd, it was because these went along with a nature that as Claggart magnetically felt, had in its simplicity never willed malice or experienced the reactionary bite of that serpent. To him, the spirit lodged within Billy, and looking out from his welkin eyes as from windows, that ineffability it was which made the dimple in his dyed cheek, suppled his joints, and dancing in his yellow curls made him preeminently the Handsome Sailor. One person excepted the master-at-arms was perhaps the only man in the ship intellectually capable of adequately appreciating the moral phenomenon presented in Billy Budd. And the insight but intensified his passion, which assuming various secret forms within him, at times assumed that of cynic disdain—disdain of innocence—To be nothing more than innocent! Yet in an aesthetic way he saw the charm of it, the courageous free-and-easy temper of it, and fain would have shared it, but he despaired of it.

With no power to annul the elemental evil in him, though readily enough he could hide it; apprehending the good, but powerless to be it; a nature like Claggart's surcharged with energy as such natures almost invariably are, what recourse

21. ***Pale . . . despair:*** description of Satan in Milton's *Paradise Lost,* IV.115.

22. **Chang and Eng:** Siamese twins famous in Melville's time.

23. **Saul's . . . David:** I Sam. 18:9 ff.

is left to it but to recoil upon itself and like the scorpion for which the Creator alone is responsible, act out to the end the part allotted it.

14

PASSION, and passion in its profoundest, is not a thing demanding a palatial stage whereon to play its part. Down among the groundlings, among the beggars and rakers of the garbage, profound passion is enacted. And the circumstances that provoke it, however trivial or mean, are no measure of its power. In the present instance the stage is a scrubbed gun-deck, and one of the external provocations a man-of-war's-man's spilled soup.

Now when the Master-at-arms noticed whence came that greasy fluid streaming before his feet, he must have taken it—to some extent wilfully, perhaps—not for the mere accident it assuredly was, but for the sly escape of a spontaneous feeling on Billy's part more or less answering to the antipathy on his own. In effect a foolish demonstration he must have thought, and very harmless, like the futile kick of a heifer, which yet were the heifer a shod stallion, would not be so harmless. Even so was it that into the gall of Claggart's envy he infused the vitriol of his contempt. But the incident confirmed to him certain tell-tale reports purveyed to his ear by *Squeak,* one of his more cunning Corporals, a grizzled little man, so nicknamed by the sailors on account of his squeaky voice, and sharp visage ferreting about the dark corners of the lower decks after interlopers, satirically suggesting to them the idea of a rat in a cellar.

From his Chief's employing him as an implicit tool in laying little traps for the worriment of the Foretopman—for it was from the Master-at-arms that the petty persecutions heretofore adverted to had proceeded—the corporal having naturally enough concluded that his master could have no love for the sailor, made it his business, faithful understrapper that he was, to foment the ill blood by perverting to his Chief certain innocent frolics of the good natured Foretopman, besides inventing for his mouth sundry contumelious epithets he claimed to have overheard him let fall. The Master-at-arms never suspected the veracity of these reports, more especially as to the epithets, for he well knew how secretly unpopular may become a master-at-arms at least a master-at-arms of those days zealous in his function, and how the bluejackets shoot at him in private their raillery and wit; the nickname by which he goes among them (*Jimmy Legs*) implying under the form of merriment their cherished disrespect and dislike.

But in view of the greediness of hate for patrolmen it hardly needed a purveyor to feed Claggart's passion. An uncommon prudence is habitual with the subtler depravity, for it has everything to hide. And in case of an injury but suspected, its secretiveness voluntarily cuts it off from enlightenment or disillusion; and, not unreluctantly, action is taken upon surmise as upon certainty. And the retaliation is apt to be in monstrous disproportion to the supposed offence; for when in anybody was revenge in its exactions aught else but an inordinate usurer. But how with Claggart's conscience? for though consciences are unlike as foreheads, every intelligence, not excluding the Scriptural devils who "believe and tremble," has one. But Claggart's conscience being but the lawyer to his will, made ogres of trifles, probably arguing that the motive imputed to Billy in spilling the soup just when he did, together with the epithets alleged, these, if nothing more, made a strong case against him; nay, justified animosity into a sort of retributive righteousness. The Pharisee is the Guy Fawkes [24] prowling in the hid chambers underlying the Claggarts. And they can really form no conception of an unreciprocated malice. Probably, the master-at-arms' clandestine persecution of Billy was started to try the temper of the man; but it had not developed any quality in him that enmity could make official use of or even pervert into even plausible self-justification; so that the occurrence at the mess, petty if it were, was a welcome one to that peculiar conscience assigned to be the private mentor of Claggart; and, for the rest, not improbably it put him upon new experiments.

15

NOT MANY DAYS after the last incident narrated something befell Billy Budd that more gravelled him than aught that had previously occurred.

It was a warm night for the latitude; and the Foretopman, whose watch at the time was properly below, was dozing on the uppermost deck whither he had ascended from his hot hammock one of hundreds suspended so closely wedged together over a lower gun-deck that there was little or no swing to them. He lay as in the shadow of a hill-side, stretched under the lee of the *booms,* a piled ridge of spare spars amidships between foremast and mainmast and among which the ship's largest boat, the launch, was stowed. Alongside of three other slumberers from below, he lay near

24. **Guy Fawkes:** Fawkes plotted to blow up the Houses of Parliament in 1605.

that end of the booms which approaches the foremast; his station aloft on duty as a foretopman being just over the deck-station of the forecastlemen, entitling him according to usage to make himself more or less at home in that neighborhood.

Presently he was stirred into semi-consciousness by somebody, who must have previously sounded the sleep of the others, touching his shoulder, and then as the Foretopman raised his head, breathing into his ear in a quick whisper, "Slip into the lee forechains, Billy; there is something in the wind. Don't speak. Quick, I will meet you there;" and disappeared.

Now Billy like sundry other essentially good natured ones had some of the weaknesses inseparable from essential good nature; and among these was a reluctance, almost an incapacity of plumply saying *no* to an abrupt proposition not obviously absurd, on the face of it, nor obviously unfriendly, nor iniquitous. And being of warm blood he had not the phlegm tacitly to negative any proposition by unresponsive inaction. Like his sense of fear, his apprehension as to aught outside of the honest and natural was seldom very quick. Besides, upon the present occasion, the drowse from his sleep still hung upon him.

However it was, he mechanically rose, and sleepily wondering what could be in the wind, betook himself to the designated place, a narrow platform, one of six, outside of the high bulwarks and screened by the great dead-eyes and multiple columned lanyards of the shrouds and backstays; and, in a great war-ship of that time, of dimensions commensurate to the hull's magnitude; a tarry balcony in short overhanging the sea, and so secluded that one mariner of the *Indomitable,* a non-conformist old tar of a serious turn, made it even in daytime his private oratory.

In this retired nook the stranger soon joined Billy Budd. There was no moon as yet; a haze obscured the star-light. He could not distinctly see the stranger's face. Yet from something in the outline and carriage, Billy took him to be, and correctly, for one of the afterguard.

"Hist! Billy," said the man in the same quick cautionary whisper as before; "You were impressed, weren't you? Well, so was I;" and he paused, as to mark the effect. But Billy not knowing exactly what to make of this said nothing. Then the other: "We are not the only impressed ones, Billy. There's a gang of us.—Couldn't you—help—at a pinch?"

"What do you mean?" demanded Billy here shaking off his drowse.

"Hist, hist!" the hurried whisper now growing husky, "see here;" and the man held up two small objects faintly twinkling in the nightlight; "see, they are yours, Billy, if you'll only—"

But Billy broke in, and in his resentful eagerness to deliver himself his vocal infirmity somewhat intruded: "D-D-Damme, I don't know what you are d-d-driving at, or what you mean, but you had better g-g-go where you belong!" For the moment the fellow, as confounded, did not stir; and Billy springing to his feet, said "If you d-don't start I'll t-t-toss you back over the r-rail!" There was no mistaking this and the mysterious emissary decamped disappearing in the direction of the mainmast in the shadow of the booms.

"Hallo, what's the matter?" here came growling from a forecastleman awakened from his deck-doze by Billy's raised voice. And as the foretopman reappeared and was recognized by him; "Ah, *Beauty,* is it you? Well, something must have been the matter for you st-st-stuttered."

"O," rejoined Billy, now mastering the impediment; "I found an afterguardsman in our part of the ship here and I bid him be off where he belongs."

"And is that all you did about it, foretopman?" gruffly demanded another, an irascible old fellow of brick-colored visage and hair, and who was known to his associate forecastlemen as *Red Pepper;* "such sneaks I should like to marry to the gunner's daughter!" by that expression meaning that he would like to subject them to disciplinary castigation over a gun.

However, Billy's rendering of the matter satisfactorily accounted to these inquirers for the brief commotion, since of all the sections of a ship's company the forecastlemen, veterans for the most part and bigoted in their sea-prejudices, are the most jealous in resenting territorial encroachments, especially on the part of any of the afterguard, of whom they have but a sorry opinion, chiefly landsmen, never going aloft except to reef or furl the mainsail, and in no wise competent to handle a marline spike or turn in a *dead-eye,* say.

16

THIS INCIDENT sorely puzzled Billy Budd. It was an entirely new experience; the first time in his life that he had ever been personally approached in underhand intriguing fashion. Prior to this encounter he had known nothing of the afterguardsman, the two men being stationed wide apart, one forward and aloft during his watch, the other on deck and aft.

What could it mean? And could they really be guineas, those two glittering objects the interloper had held up to his (Billy's) eyes? Where could the fellow get guineas? Why even buttons spare buttons are not so plentiful at sea. The more he turned the matter over, the more he was non-plussed, and made uneasy and discomforted. In his disgustful recoil from an overture which though he but ill comprehended he instinctively knew must involve evil of some sort, Billy Budd was like a young horse fresh from the pasture suddenly inhaling a vile whiff from some chemical factory and by repeated snortings tries to get it out of his nostrils and lungs. This frame of mind barred all desire of holding further parley with the fellow, even were it but for the purpose of gaining some enlightenment as to his design in approaching him. And yet he was not without natural curiosity to see how such a visitor in the dark would look in broad day.

He espied him the following afternoon in his first dog-watch below one of the smokers on that forward part of the upper gun deck allotted to the pipe. He recognized him by his general cut and build, more than by his round freckled face and glassy eyes of pale blue, veiled with lashes all but white. And yet Billy was a bit uncertain whether indeed it were he—yonder chap about his own age chatting and laughing in free-hearted way, leaning against a gun; a genial young fellow enough to look at, and something of a rattle-brain, to all appearance. Rather chubby too for a sailor even an afterguardsman. In short the last man in the world, one would think, to be overburthened with thoughts, especially those perilous thoughts that must needs belong to a conspirator in any serious project, or even to the underling of such a conspirator.

Although Billy was not aware of it, the fellow, with a sidelong watchful glance had perceived Billy first, and then noting that Billy was looking at him, thereupon nodded a familiar sort of friendly recognition as to an old acquaintance, without interrupting the talk he was engaged in with the group of smokers. A day or two afterwards chancing in the evening promenade on a gun deck, to pass Billy, he offered a flying word of good-fellowship as it were, which by its unexpectedness, and equivocalness under the circumstances so embarrassed Billy that he knew not how to respond to it, and let it go unnoticed.

Billy was now left more at a loss than before. The ineffectual speculations into which he was led were so disturbingly alien to him that he did his best to smother them. It never entered his mind that here was a matter which from its extreme questionableness, it was his duty as a loyal bluejacket to report in the proper quarter. And, probably, had such a step been suggested to him, he would have been deterred from taking it by the thought, one of novice-magnanimity, that it would savor overmuch of the dirty work of a tell-tale. He kept the thing to himself. Yet upon one occasion, he could not forbear a little disburthening himself to the old Dansker, tempted thereto perhaps by the influence of a balmy night when the ship lay becalmed; the twain, silent for the most part, sitting together on deck, their heads propped against the bulwarks. But it was only a partial and anonymous account that Billy gave, the unfounded scruples above referred to preventing full disclosure to anybody. Upon hearing Billy's version, the sage Dansker seemed to divine more than he was told; and after a little meditation during which his wrinkles were pursed as into a point, quite effacing for the time that quizzing expression his face sometimes wore,—"Didn't I say so, Baby Budd?"

"Say what?" demanded Billy.

"Why, *Jimmy Legs* is *down* on you."

"And what" rejoined Billy in amazement, "has *Jimmy Legs* to do with that cracked afterguardsman?"

"Ho, it was an afterguardsman then. A cat's-paw, a cat's-paw!" And with that exclamation, which, whether it had reference to a light puff of air just then coming over the calm sea, or subtler relation to the afterguardsman, there is no telling, the old Merlin gave a twisting wrench with his black teeth at his plug of tobacco, vouchsafing no reply to Billy's impetuous question, though now repeated, for it was his wont to relapse into grim silence when interrogated in skeptical sort as to any of his sententious oracles, not always very clear ones, rather partaking of that obscurity which invests most Delphic deliverances from any quarter.

Long experience had very likely brought this old man to that bitter prudence which never interferes in aught and never gives advice.

17

YES, DESPITE the Dansker's pithy insistence as to the Master-at-arms being at the bottom of these strange experiences of Billy on board the *Indomitable,* the young sailor was ready to ascribe them to almost anybody but the man who, to use Billy's own expression, "always had a pleasant word for him." This is to be wondered at. Yet not so much to be wondered at. In certain matters, some sailors even in mature life remain unsophisticated enough. But a young seafarer of the disposition of our athletic Foretopman, is much of a child-man. And yet a child's utter innocence is but its blank ignorance, and the innocence more or less wanes as intelligence waxes. But in Billy Budd intelligence, such as it was, had advanced, while yet his simplemindedness remained for the most part unaffected. Experience is a teacher indeed; yet did Billy's years make his experience small. Besides, he had none of that intuitive knowledge of the bad which in natures not good or incompletely so foreruns experience, and therefore may pertain, as in some instances it too clearly does pertain, even to youth.

And what could Billy know of man except of man as a mere sailor? And the old-fashioned sailor, the veritable man-before-the-mast, the sailor from from boyhood up, he, though indeed of the same species as a landsman is in some respects singularly distinct from him. The sailor is frankness, the landsman is finesse. Life is not a game with the sailor, demanding the long head; no intricate game of chess where few moves are made in straightforwardness, and ends are attained by indirection; an oblique, tedious, barren game hardly worth that poor candle burnt out in playing it.

Yes, as a class, sailors are in character a juvenile race. Even their deviations are marked by juvenility. And this more especially holding true with the sailors of Billy's time. Then, too, certain things which apply to all sailors, do more pointedly operate here and there, upon the junior one. Every sailor, too is accustomed to obey orders without debating them; his life afloat is externally ruled for him; he is not brought into that promiscuous commerce with mankind where unobstructed free agency on equal terms—equal superficially, at least—soon teaches one that unless upon occasion he exercise a distrust keen in proportion to the fairness of the appearance, some foul turn may be served him. A ruled undemonstrative distrustfulness is so habitual, not with business-men so much, as with men who know their kind in less shallow relations than business, namely, certain men-of-the-world, that they come at last to employ it all but unconsciously; and some of them would very likely feel real surprise at being charged with it as one of their general characteristics.

18

BUT AFTER the little matter at the mess Billy Budd no more found himself in strange trouble at times about his hammock or his clothes-bag or what not. While, as to that smile that occasionally sunned him, and the pleasant passing word, these were if not more frequent, yet if anything more pronounced than before.

But for all that, there were certain other demonstrations now. When Claggart's unobserved glance happened to light on belted Billy rolling along the upper gun-deck in the leisure of the second dog-watch exchanging passing broadsides of fun with other young promenaders in the crowd; that glance would follow the cheerful sea-Hyperion[25] with a settled meditative and melancholy expression, his eyes strangely suffused with incipient feverish tears. Then would Claggart look like the man of sorrows. Yes, and sometimes the melancholy expression would have in it a touch of soft yearning, as if Claggart could even have loved Billy but for fate and ban. But this was an evanescence, and quickly repented of, as it were, by an immitigable look, pinching and shrivelling the visage into the momentary semblance of a wrinkled walnut. But sometimes catching sight in advance of the foretopman coming in his direction, he would, upon their nearing, step aside a little to let him pass, dwelling upon Billy for the moment with the glittering dental satire of a Guise.[26] But upon any abrupt unforeseen encounter a red light would flash forth from his eye like a spark from an anvil in a dusk smithy. That quick fierce light was a strange one, darted from orbs which in repose were of a color nearest approaching a deeper violet, the softest of shades.

Though some of these caprices of the pit could not but be observed by their object, yet were they beyond the construing of such a nature. And the *thews* of Billy were hardly compatible with that sort of sensitive spiritual organisation which in some cases instinctively conveys to ignorant innocence an admonition of the proximity of the malign. He thought the master-at-arms acted in a manner rather queer at times. That was all. But the occasional frank air and pleasant word went for what they purported to be, the young sailor never having heard as yet of the "too fair-spoken man."

Had the foretopman been conscious of having done or said anything to provoke the ill will of the official, it would have been different with him, and his sight might have been purged if not sharpened. As it was innocence was his blinder.

So was it with him in yet another matter. Two minor officers—the Armorer and Captain of the Hold, with whom he had never exchanged a word, his position in the ship not bringing him into contact with them; these men now for the first began to cast upon Billy when they chanced to encounter him, that peculiar glance which evidences that the man from whom it comes has been some way tampered with and to the prejudice of him upon

25. **sea-Hyperion:** Melville may have in mind the hero of Keats's unfinished poem *Hyperion*, rather than the dim figure of Greek myth. 26. **Guise:** a French family of the sixteenth century, often embroiled in plots.

whom the glance lights. Never did it occur to Billy as a thing to be noted or a thing suspicious, though he well knew the fact, that the Armorer and Captain of the Hold, with the ship's-yeoman, apothecary, and others of that grade, were by naval usage, mess-mates of the master-at-arms, men with ears convenient to his confidential tongue.

But the general popularity that our *Handsome Sailor's* manly forwardness upon occasion, and irresistible good nature indicating no mental superiority tending to excite an invidious feeling; this good will on the part of most of his shipmates made him the less to concern himself about such mute aspects toward him as those whereto allusion has just been made.

As to the afterguardsman, though Billy for reasons already given necessarily saw little of him, yet when the two did happen to meet, invariably came the fellow's off-hand cheerful recognition, sometimes accompanied by a passing pleasant word or two. Whatever that equivocal young person's original design may really have been, or the design of which he might have been the deputy, certain it was from his manner upon these occasions, that he had wholly dropped it.

It was as if his precocity of crookedness (and every vulgar villain is precocious) had for once deceived him, and the man he had sought to entrap as a simpleton had, through his very simplicity ignominiously baffled him.

But shrewd ones may opine that it was hardly possible for Billy to refrain from going up to the afterguardsman and bluntly demanding to know his purpose in the initial interview, so abruptly closed in the fore-chains. Shrewd ones may also think it but natural in Billy to set about sounding some of the other impressed men of the ship in order to discover what basis, if any, there was for the emissary's obscure suggestions as to plotting disaffection aboard. Yes, the shrewd may so think. But something more, or rather, something else than mere shrewdness is perhaps needful for the due understanding of such a character as Billy Budd's.

As to Claggart, the monomania in the man—if that indeed it were—as involuntarily disclosed by starts in the manifestations detailed, yet in general covered over by his self-contained and rational demeanor; this, like a subterranean fire was eating its way deeper and deeper in him. Something decisive must come of it.

19

AFTER the mysterious interview in the fore-chains, the one so abruptly ended there by Billy, nothing especially German to the story occurred until the events now about to be narrated.

Elsewhere it has been said that in the lack of frigates (of course better sailers than line-of-battle ships) in the English squadron up the Straits at that period, the *Indomitable* was occasionally employed not only as an available substitute for a scout, but at times on detached service of more important kind. This was not alone because of her sailing qualities, not common in a ship of her rate, but quite as much, probably, that the character of her commander, it was thought, specially adapted him for any duty where under unforeseen difficulties a prompt initiative might have to be taken in some matter demanding knowledge and ability in addition to those qualities implied in good seamanship. It was on an expedition of the latter sort, a somewhat distant one, and when the *Indomitable* was almost at her furthest remove from the fleet that in the latter part of an afternoon-watch she unexpectedly came in sight of a ship of the enemy. It proved to be a frigate. The latter perceiving through the glass that the weight of men and metal would be heavily against her, invoking her light heels crowded sail to get away. After a chace urged almost against hope and lasting until about the middle of the first dog-watch, she signally succeeded in effecting her escape.

Not long after the pursuit had been given up, and ere the excitement incident thereto had altogether waned away, the master-at-arms ascending from his cavernous sphere made his appearance cap in hand by the mainmast respectfully waiting the notice of Captain Vere then solitary walking the weatherside of the quarter-deck, doubtless somewhat chafed at the failure of the pursuit. The spot where Claggart stood was the place allotted to men of lesser grades seeking some more particular interview either with the officer-of-the-deck or the Captain himself. But from the latter it was not often that a sailor or petty-officer of those days would seek a hearing; only some exceptional cause, would, according to established custom, have warranted that.

Presently, just as the Commander absorbed in his reflections was on the point of turning aft in his promenade, he became sensible of Claggart's presence, and saw the doffed cap held in deferential expectancy. Here be it said that Captain Vere's personal knowledge of this petty-officer had only begun at the time of the ship's last sailing from home, Claggart then for the first, in transfer from a ship detained for repairs, supplying on board the *Indomitable* the place of a previous master-at-arms disabled and ashore.

No sooner did the Commander observe who it

was that now deferentially stood awaiting his notice, than a peculiar expression came over him. It was not unlike that which uncontrollably will flit across the countenance of one at unawares encountering a person who though known to him indeed has hardly been long enough known for thorough knowledge, but something in whose aspect nevertheless now for the first provokes a vaguely repellent distaste. But coming to a stand, and resuming much of his wonted official manner, save that a sort of impatience lurked in the intonation of the opening word, he said, "Well? what is it, Master-at-Arms?"

With the air of a subordinate grieved at the necessity of being a messenger of ill tidings, and while conscientiously determined to be frank, yet equally resolved upon shunning overstatement, Claggart at this invitation or rather summons to disburthen, spoke up. What he said, conveyed in the language of no uneducated man, was to the effect following if not altogether in these words, namely, that during the chace and preparations for the possible encounter he had seen enough to convince him that at least one sailor aboard was a dangerous character in a ship mustering some who not only had taken a guilty part in the late serious troubles, but others also who, like the man in question, had entered His Majesty's service under another form than enlistment.

At this point Captain Vere with some impatience interrupted him: "Be direct, man; say impressed men."

Claggart made a gesture of subservience, and proceeded.

Quite lately, he (Claggart) had begun to suspect that on the gun-decks some sort of movement prompted by the sailor in question was covertly going on, but he had not thought himself warranted in reporting the suspicion so long as it remained indistinct. But from what he had that afternoon observed in the man referred to the suspicion of something clandestine going on had advanced to a point less removed from certainty. He deeply felt, he added, the serious responsibility assumed in making a report involving such possible consequences to the individual mainly concerned, besides tending to augment those natural anxieties which every naval commander must feel in view of extraordinary outbreaks so recent as those which, he sorrowfully said it, it needed not to name.

Now at the first broaching of the matter Captain Vere taken by surprise could not wholly dissemble his disquietude. But as Claggart went on, the former's aspect changed into restiveness under something in the witness' manner in giving his testimony. However, he refrained from interrupting him. And Claggart, continuing, concluded with this:

"God forbid, your honor, that the *Indomitable's* should be the experience of the——"

"Never mind that!" here preemptorily broke in the superior, his face altering with anger, instinctively divining the ship that the other was about to name, one in which the Nore Mutiny had assumed a singularly tragical character that for a time jeopardized the life of its commander. Under the circumstances he was indignant at the purposed allusion. When the commissioned officers themselves were on all occasions very heedful how they referred to the recent events, for a petty-officer unnecessarily to allude to them in the presence of his Captain, this struck him as a most immodest presumption. Besides, to his quick sense of self-respect, it even looked under the circumstances something like an attempt to alarm him. Nor at first was he without some surprise that one who so far as he had hitherto come under his notice had shown considerable tact in his function should in this particular evince such lack of it.

But these thoughts and kindred dubious ones flitting across his mind were suddenly replaced by an intuitional surmise which though as yet obscure in form served practically to affect his reception of the ill tidings. Certain it is, that long versed in everything pertaining to the complicated gun-deck life, which like every other form of life, has its secret mines and dubious side, the side popularly disclaimed, Captain Vere did not permit himself to be unduly disturbed by the general tenor of his subordinate's report. Furthermore, if in view of recent events prompt action should be taken at the first palpable sign of recurring insubordination, for all that, not judicious would it be, he thought, to keep the idea of lingering disaffection alive by undue forwardness in crediting an informer even if his own subordinate and charged among other things with police surveillance of the crew. This feeling would not perhaps have so prevailed with him were it not that upon a prior occasion the patriotic zeal officially evinced by Claggart had somewhat irritated him as appearing rather supersensible and strained. Furthermore something even in the official's self-possessed and somewhat ostentatious manner in making his specifications strangely reminded him of a bandsman, a perjurous witness in a capital case before a court-martial ashore of which when a lieutenant he Captain Vere had been a member.

Now the peremptory check given to Claggart in the matter of the arrested allusion was quickly followed up by this: "You say that there is at least one dangerous man aboard. Name him."

"William Budd. A foretopman, your honor—"

"William Budd" repeated Captain Vere with unfeigned astonishment; "and mean you the man that Lieutenant Ratcliffe took from the merchantman not very long ago—the young fellow who seems to be so popular with the men—Billy, the Handsome Sailor, as they call him?"

"The same, your honor; but for all his youth and good looks, a deep one. Not for nothing does he insinuate himself into the good will of his shipmates, since at the least all hands will at a pinch say a good word for him at all hazards. Did Lieutenant Ratcliffe happen to tell your honor of that adroit fling of Budd's, jumping up in the cutter's bow under the merchantman's stern when he was being taken off? It is even masqued by that sort of good humored air that at heart he resents his impressment. You have but noted his fair cheek. A man-trap may be under his ruddy-tipped daisies."

Now the *Handsome Sailor* as a signal figure among the crew had naturally enough attracted the Captain's attention from the first. Though in general not very demonstrative to his officers, he had congratulated Lieutenant Ratcliffe upon his good fortune in lighting on such a fine specimen of the genus homo, who in the nude might have posed for a statue of young Adam before the Fall. As to Billy's adieu to the ship *Rights-of-Man,* which the boarding lieutenant had indeed reported to him, but in a deferential way more as a good story than aught else, Captain Vere, though mistakenly understanding it as a satiric sally, had but thought so much the better of the impressed man for it; as a military sailor, admiring the spirit that could take an arbitrary enlistment so merrily and sensibly. The foretopman's conduct, too, so far as it had fallen under the Captain's notice had confirmed the first happy augury, while the new recruit's qualities as a *sailor-man* seemed to be such that he had thought of recommending him to the executive officer for promotion to a place that would more frequently bring him under his own observation, namely, the captaincy of the mizzen-top, replacing there in the starboard watch a man not so young whom partly for that reason he deemed less fitted for the post. Be it parenthesized here that since the mizzen-topmen having not to handle such breadths of heavy canvas as the lower sails on the main-mast and fore-mast, a young man if of the right stuff not only seems best adapted to duty there, but in fact is generally selected for the captaincy of that top, and the company under him are light hands and often but striplings. In sum, Captain Vere had from the beginning deemed Billy Budd to be what in the naval parlance of the time was called a *"King's bargain"* that is to say, for His Britannic Majesty's navy a capital investment at small outlay or none at all.

After a brief pause during which the reminiscences above mentioned passed vividly through his mind and he weighed the import of Claggart's last suggestion conveyed in the phrase "pitfall under the clover," and the more he weighed it the less reliance he felt in the informer's good faith. Suddenly he turned upon him and in a low voice: "Do you come to me, master-at-arms, with so foggy a tale? As to Budd, cite me an act or spoken word of his confirmatory of what you in general charge against him. Stay," drawing nearer to him "heed what you speak. Just now, and in a case like this, there is a yard-arm-end for the false-witness."

"Ah, your honor!" sighed Claggart mildly shaking his shapely head as in sad deprecation of such unmerited severity of tone. Then, bridling—erecting himself as in virtuous self-assertion, he circumstantially alleged certain words and acts, which collectively, if credited, led to presumptions mortally inculpating Budd. And for some of these averments, he added, substantiating proof was not far.

With gray eyes impatient and distrustful essaying to fathom to the bottom Claggart's calm violet ones, Captain Vere again heard him out; then for the moment stood ruminating. The mood he evinced, Claggart—himself for the time liberated from the other's scrutiny—steadily regarded with a look difficult to render,—a look curious of the operation of his tactics, a look such as might have been that of the spokesman of the envious children of Jacob deceptively imposing upon the troubled patriarch the blood-dyed coat of young Joseph.[27]

Though something exceptional in the moral quality of Captain Vere made him, in earnest encounter with a fellow-man, a veritable touch-stone of that man's essential nature, yet now as to Claggart and what was really going on in him his feeling partook less of intuitional conviction than of strong suspicion clogged by strange dubieties. The perplexity he evinced proceeded less from aught touching the man informed against—as Claggart doubtless opined—than from considerations how best to act in regard to the informer. At first indeed he was naturally for summoning that substantiation of his allegations which Claggart said was at hand. But such a proceeding would result in the matter at once getting abroad, which in the present stage of it, he thought, might undesirably affect the ship's company. If Claggart was a

27. **Joseph:** Gen. 37:31–34.

false witness,—that closed the affair. And therefore before trying the accusation, he would first practically test the accuser; and he thought this could be done in a quiet undemonstrative way.

The measure he determined upon involved a shifting of the scene, a transfer to a place less exposed to observation than the broad quarter-deck. For although the few gun-room officers there at the time had, in due observance of naval etiquette, withdrawn to leeward the moment Captain Vere had begun his promenade on the deck's weather-side; and though during the colloquy with Claggart they of course ventured not to diminish the distance; and though throughout the interview Captain Vere's voice was far from high, and Claggart's silvery and low; and the wind in the cordage and the wash of the sea helped the more to put them beyond ear-shot; nevertheless, the interview's continuance already had attracted observation from some topmen aloft and other sailors in the waist or further forward.

Having determined upon his measures, Captain Vere forthwith took action. Abruptly turning to Claggart he asked "Master-at-arms, is it now Budd's watch aloft?"

"No, your honor." Whereupon, "Mr. Wilkes!" summoning the nearest midshipman, "tell Albert to come to me." Albert was the Captain's hammockboy, a sort of sea-valet in whose discretion and fidelity his master had much confidence. The lad appeared. "You know Budd the foretopman?"

"I do, Sir."

"Go find him. It is his watch off. Manage to tell him out of ear-shot that he is wanted aft. Contrive it that he speaks to nobody. Keep him in talk yourself. And not till you get well aft here, not till then let him know that the place where he is wanted is my cabin. You understand. Go.—master-at-arms, show yourself on the decks below, and when you think it time for Albert to be coming with his man, stand by quietly to follow the sailor in."

20

NOW WHEN the foretopman found himself closeted there, as it were, in the cabin with the Captain and Claggart, he was surprised enough. But it was a surprise unaccompanied by apprehension or distrust. To an immature nature essentially honest and humane, forewarning intimations of subtler danger from one's kind come tardily if at all. The only thing that took shape in the young sailor's mind was this: Yes, the Captain, I have always thought, looks kindly upon me. Wonder if he's going to make me his coxswain. I should like that. And maybe now he is going to ask the master-at-arms about me.

"Shut the door there, sentry," said the commander; "stand without, and let nobody come in. —Now, master-at-arms, tell this man to his face what you told of him to me;" and stood prepared to scrutinize the mutually confronting visages.

With the measured step and calm collected air of an asylum-physician approaching in the public hall some patient beginning to show indications of a coming paradoxysm, Claggart deliberately advanced within short range of Billy, and mesmerically looking him in the eye, briefly recapitulated the accusation.

Not at first did Billy take it in. When he did, the rose-tan of his cheek looked struck as by white leprosy. He stood like one impaled and gagged. Meanwhile the accuser's eyes removing not as yet from the blue dilated ones, underwent a phenomenal change, their wonted rich violet color blurring into a muddy purple. Those lights of human intelligence losing human expression, gelidly protruding like the alien eyes of certain uncatalogued creatures of the deep. The first mesmeric glance was one of serpent fascination; the last was as the hungry lurch of the torpedo-fish.

"Speak, man!" said Captain Vere to the transfixed one struck by his aspect even more than by Claggart's, "Speak! defend yourself." Which appeal caused but a strange dumb gesturing and gurgling in Billy; amazement at such an accusation so suddenly sprung on inexperienced nonage; this, and, it may be, horror of the accuser, serving to bring out his lurking defect and in this instance for the time intensifying it into a convulsed tongue-tie; while the intent head and entire form straining forward in an agony of ineffectual eagerness to obey the injunction to speak and defend himself, gave an expression to the face like that of a condemned Vestal priestess in the moment of being buried alive, and in the first struggle against suffocation.

Though at the time Captain Vere was quite ignorant of Billy's liability to vocal impediment, he now immediately divined it, since vividly Billy's aspect recalled to him that of a bright young schoolmate of his whom he had once seen struck by much the same startling impotence in the act of eagerly rising in the class to be foremost in response to a testing question put to it by the master. Going close up to the young sailor, and laying a soothing hand on his shoulder, he said: "There is no hurry, my boy. Take your time, take your time." Contrary to the effect intended, these words so fatherly in tone, doubtless touching Billy's heart to the quick, prompted yet more violent efforts at utterance—efforts soon ending for the time in confirming the paralysis, and bringing to his face an expression which was as a crucifixion to behold. The next instant, quick as the flame from a discharged cannon at night, his right arm shot out, and Claggart dropped to the deck. Whether intentionally or but owing to the young athlete's superior height, the blow had taken effect full upon the forehead, so shapely and intellectual-looking a feature in the master-at-arms; so that the body fell over lengthwise, like a heavy plank tilted from erectness. A gasp or two, and he lay motionless.

"Fated boy," breathed Captain Vere in tone so low as to be almost a whisper, "what have you done! But here, help me."

The twain raised the felled one from the loins up into a sitting position. The spare form flexibly acquiesced, but inertly. It was like handling a dead snake. They lowered it back. Regaining erectness Captain Vere with one hand covering his face stood to all appearance as impassive as the object at his feet. Was he absorbed in taking in all the bearings of the event and what was best not only now at once to be done, but also in the sequel? Slowly he uncovered his face; and the effect was as if the moon emerging from eclipse should reappear with quite another aspect than that which had gone into hiding. The father in him, manifested towards Billy thus far in the scene, was replaced by the military disciplinarian. In his official tone he bade the foretopman retire to a state-room aft (pointing it out) and there remain till thence summoned. This order Billy in silence mechanically obeyed. Then going to the cabin-door where it opened on the quarter-deck, Captain Vere said to the sentry without, "Tell somebody to send Albert here." When the lad appeared his master so contrived it that he should not catch sight of the prone one. "Albert," he said to him, "tell the Surgeon I wish to see him. You need not come back till called." When the Surgeon entered—a self-poised character of that grave sense and experience that hardly anything could take him aback, —Captain Vere advanced to meet him, thus unconsciously intercepting his view of Claggart and interrupting the other's wonted ceremonious salutation, said, "Nay, tell me how it is with yonder man," directing his attention to the prostrate one.

The Surgeon looked, and for all his self-command, somewhat started at the abrupt revelation. On Claggart's always pallid complexion, thick black blood was now oozing from nostril and ear. To the gazer's professional eye it was unmistakably no living man that he saw.

"Is it so then?" said Captain Vere intently watching him. "I thought it. But verify it." Whereupon the customary tests confirmed the Surgeon's first glance, who now looking up in unfeigned concern, cast a look of intense inquisitiveness upon his superior. But Captain Vere, with one hand to his brow, was standing motionless. Suddenly, catching the Surgeon's arm convulsively, he exclaimed, pointing down to the body—"It is the divine judgement on Ananias! [28] Look!"

Disturbed by the excited manner he had never before observed in the *Indomitable's* Captain, and as yet wholly ignorant of the affair, the prudent Surgeon nevertheless held his peace, only again looking an earnest interrogation as to what it was that had resulted in such a tragedy.

But Captain Vere was now again motionless standing absorbed in thought. But again starting, he vehemently exclaimed—"Struck dead by an angel of God! Yet the angel must hang!"

At these passionate interjections, mere incoherences to the listener as yet unapprised of the antecedents, the Surgeon was profoundly discomposed. But now as recollecting himself, Captain Vere in less passionate tone briefly related the circumstances leading up to the event.

"But come; we must despatch" he added. "Help me to remove him (meaning the body) to yonder compartment," designating one opposite that where the foretopman remained immured. Anew disturbed by a request that as implying a desire for secrecy, seemed unaccountably strange to him, there was nothing for the subordinate to do but comply.

"Go now" said Captain Vere with something of his wonted manner—"Go now. I shall presently call a drum-head court. Tell the lieutenants what has happened, and tell Mr. Mordant," meaning the captain of marines, "and charge them to keep the matter to themselves."

21

FULL OF disquietude and misgiving the Surgeon left the cabin. Was Captain Vere suddenly affected in his mind, or was it but a transient excitement, brought about by so strange and extraordinary a happening? As to the drum-head court, it struck the Surgeon as impolitic, if nothing more. The thing to do, he thought, was to place Billy Budd in confinement and in a way dictated by usage, and postpone further action in so extraordinary a case, to such time as they should rejoin the squadron, and then refer it to the Admiral. He recalled the unwonted agitation of Captain Vere and his excited exclamations so at variance with his normal manner. Was he unhinged? But

28. **Ananias:** Acts 5:5.

assuming that he is, it is not so susceptible of proof. What then can he do? No more trying situation is conceivable than that of an officer subordinate under a Captain whom he suspects to be, not mad indeed, but yet not quite unaffected in his intellect. To argue his order to him would be insolence. To resist him would be mutiny.

In obedience to Captain Vere he communicated what had happened to the lieutenants and captain of marines; saying nothing as to the Captain's state. They fully shared his own surprise and concern. Like him too they seemed to think that such a matter should be referred to the Admiral.

22

WHO IN the rainbow can show the line where the violet tint ends and the orange tint begins? Distinctly we see the difference of the colors, but when exactly does the one first blendingly enter into the other? So with sanity and insanity. In pronounced cases there is no question about them. But in some supposed cases, in various degrees supposedly less pronounced, to draw the exact line of demarkation few will undertake though for a fee some professional experts will. There is nothing namable but that some men will undertake to do it for pay.

Whether Captain Vere, as the Surgeon professionally and privately surmised, was really the sudden victim of any degree of aberration, one must determine for himself by such light as this narrative may afford.

That the unhappy event which has been narrated could not have happened at a worse juncture was but too true. For it was close on the heel of the suppressed insurrections, an after-time very critical to naval authority, demanding from every English sea-commander two qualities not readily interfusable—prudence and rigor. Moreover there was something crucial in the case.

In the jugglery of circumstances preceding and attending the event on board the *Indomitable* and in the light of that martial code whereby it was formally to be judged, innocence and guilt personified in Claggart and Budd in effect changed places. In a legal view the apparent victim of the tragedy was he who had sought to victimize a man blameless; and the indisputable deed of the latter, navally regarded, constituted the most heinous of military crimes. Yet more. The essential right and wrong involved in the matter, the clearer that might be, so much the worse for the responsibility of a loyal sea-commander inasmuch as he was not authorized to determine the matter on that primitive basis.

Small wonder then that the *Indomitable's* Captain though in general a man of rapid decision, felt that circumspectness not less than promptitude was necessary. Until he could decide upon his course, and in each detail; and not only so, but until the concluding measure was upon the point of being enacted, he deemed it advisable, in view of all the circumstances to guard as much as possible against publicity. Here he may or may not have erred. Certain it is however that subsequently in the confidential talk of more than one or two gun-rooms and cabins he was not a little criticized by some officers, a fact imputed by his friends and vehemently by his cousin Jack Denton to professional jealousy of Starry Vere. Some *imaginative* ground for invidious comment there was. The maintenance of secrecy in the matter, the confining all knowledge of it for a time to the place where the homicide occurred, the quarter-deck cabin; in these particulars lurked some resemblance to the policy adopted in those tragedies of the palace which have occurred more than once in the capital founded by Peter the Barbarian.[29]

The case indeed was such that fain would the *Indomitable's* Captain have deferred taking any action whatever respecting it further than to keep the foretopman a close prisoner till the ship rejoined the squadron and then submitting the matter to the judgement of his Admiral.

But a true military officer is in one particular like a true monk. Not with more of self-abnegation will the latter keep his vows of monastic obedience than the former his vows of allegiance to martial duty.

Feeling that unless quick action was taken on it, the deed of the foretopman, so soon as it should be known on the gun-decks would tend to awaken any slumbering embers of the Nore among the crew, a sense of the urgency of the case overruled in Captain Vere every other consideration. But though a conscientious disciplinarian he was no lover of authority for mere authority's sake. Very far was he from embracing opportunities for monopolizing to himself the perils of moral responsibility none at least that could properly be referred to an official superior or shared with him by his official equals or even subordinates. So thinking he was glad it would not be at variance with usage to turn the matter over to a summary court of his own officers, reserving to himself as the one on whom the ultimate accountability would rest, the right of maintaining a supervision of it, or formally or informally interposing at need. Accordingly a drum-head court was summarily convened,

29. **Peter the Barbarian:** Peter the Great of Russia (1672–1725).

he electing the individuals composing it, the First Lieutenant, the Captain of marines, and the Sailing Master.

In associating an officer of marines with the sea-lieutenants in a case having to do with a sailor the Commander perhaps deviated from general custom. He was prompted thereto by the circumstance that he took that soldier to be a judicious person, thoughtful, and not altogether incapable of grappling with a difficult case unprecedented in his prior experience. Yet even as to him he was not without some latent misgiving, for withal he was an extremely good-natured man, an enjoyer of his dinner, a sound sleeper, and inclined to obesity. A man who though he would always maintain his manhood in battle might not prove altogether reliable in a moral dilemma involving aught of the tragic. As to the First Lieutenant and the Sailing Master Captain Vere could not but be aware that though honest natures, of approved gallantry upon occasion their intelligence was mostly confined to the matter of active seamanship and the fighting demands of their profession. The court was held in the same cabin where the unfortunate affair had taken place. This cabin, the Commander's, embraced the entire area under the poop-deck. Aft, and on either side was a small state-room the one room temporarily a jail and the other a dead-house and a yet smaller compartment leaving a space between, expanding forward into a goodly oblong of length coinciding with the ship's beam. A skylight of moderate dimension was overhead and at each end of the oblong space were two sashed port-hole windows easily convertible back into embrasures for short carronades.

All being quickly in readiness, Billy Budd was arraigned, Captain Vere necessarily appearing as the sole witness in the case, and as such temporarily sinking his rank, though singularly maintaining it in a matter apparently trivial, namely, that he testified from the ship's weather-side with that object having caused the court to sit on the leeside. Concisely he narrated all that had led up to the catastrophe, omitting nothing in Claggart's accusation and deposing as to the manner in which the prisoner had received it. At this testimony the three officers glanced with no little surprise at Billy Budd, the last man they would have suspected either of the mutinous design alleged by Claggart or the undeniable deed he himself had done.

The First Lieutenant taking judicial primacy and turning toward the prisoner, said, "Captain Vere has spoken. Is it or is it not as Captain Vere says?" In response came syllables not so much impeded in the utterance as might have been anticipated. They were these: "Captain Vere tells the truth. It is just as Captain Vere says, but it is not as the Master-at-Arms said. I have eaten the King's bread and I am true to the King."

"I believe you, my man," said the witness, his voice indicating a suppressed emotion not otherwise betrayed.

"God will bless you for that, Your Honor!" not without stammering said Billy, and all but broke down. But immediately was recalled to self-control by another question, to which with the same emotional difficulty of utterance he said "No, there was no malice between us. I never bore malice against the Master-at-arms. I am sorry that he is dead. I did not mean to kill him. Could I have used my tongue I would not have struck him. But he foully lied to my face and in presence of my Captain, and I had to say something, and I could only say it with a blow, God help me!"

In the impulsive above-board manner of the frank one the court saw confirmed all that was implied in words that just previously had perplexed them coming as they did from the testifier to the tragedy and promptly following Billy's impassioned disclaimer of mutinous intent—Captain Vere's words, "I believe you, my man."

Next it was asked of him whether he knew of or suspected aught savoring of incipient trouble (meaning mutiny, though the explicit term was avoided) going on in any section of the ship's company.

The reply lingered. This was naturally imputed by the court to the same vocal embarrassment which had retarded or obstructed previous answers. But in main it was otherwise here; the question immediately recalling to Billy's mind the interview with the afterguardsman in the fore-chains. But an innate repugnance to playing a part at all approaching that of an informer against one's own shipmates—the same erring sense of uninstructed honor which had stood in the way of his reporting the matter at the time though as a loyal man-of-war-man it was incumbent on him and failure so to do if charged against him and proven, would have subjected him to the heaviest of penalties; this, with the blind feeling now his, that nothing really was being hatched, prevailed with him. When the answer came it was a negative.

"One question more," said the officer of marines now first speaking and with a troubled earnestness. "You tell us that what the master-at-arms said against you was a lie. Now why should he have so lied, so maliciously lied, since you declare there was no malice between you?"

At that question unintentionally touching on a spiritual sphere wholly obscure to Billy's thoughts, he was nonplussed, evincing a confusion indeed that some observers, such as can readily be imagined, would have construed into involuntary evidence of hidden guilt. Nevertheless he strove some way to answer, but all at once relinquished the vain endeavor, at the same time turning an appealing glance towards Captain Vere as deeming him his best helper and friend. Captain Vere who had been seated for a time rose to his feet, addressing the interrogator. "The question you put to him comes naturally enough. But how can he rightly answer it? or anybody else? unless indeed it be he who lies within there" designating the compartment where lay the corpse. "But the prone one there will not rise to our summons. In effect, though, as it seems to me, the point you make is hardly material. Quite aside from any conceivable motive actuating the master-at-arms, and irrespective of the provocation to the blow, a martial court must needs in the present case confine its attention to the blow's consequence, which consequence justly is to be deemed not otherwise than as the striker's deed."

This utterance the full significance of which it was not at all likely that Billy took in, nevertheless caused him to turn a wistful interrogative look toward the speaker, a look in its dumb expressiveness not unlike that which a dog of generous breed might turn upon his master seeking in his face some elucidation of a previous gesture ambiguous to the canine intelligence. Nor was the same utterance without marked effect upon the three officers, more especially the soldier. Couched in it seemed to them a meaning unanticipated, involving a prejudgement on the speaker's part. It served to augment a mental disturbance previously evident enough.

The soldier once more spoke; in a tone of suggestive dubiety addressing at once his associates and Captain Vere: "Nobody is present—none of the ship's company, I mean, who might shed lateral light, if any is to be had, upon what remains mysterious in this matter."

"That is thoughtfully put" said Captain Vere; "I see your drift. Ay, there is a mystery; but, to use a Scriptural phrase, it is 'a mystery of iniquity,' [30] a matter for psychologic theologians to discuss. But what has a military court to do with it? Not to add that for us any possible investigation of it is cut off by the lasting tongue-tie of—him—in yonder," again designating the mortuary state-room. "The prisoner's deed,—with that alone we have to do."

To this, and particularly the closing reiteration, the marine soldier knowing not how aptly to reply, sadly abstained from saying aught. The First Lieutenant who at the outset had not unnaturally assumed primacy in the court, now overrulingly instructed by a glance from Captain Vere, a glance more effective than words, resumed that primacy. Turning to the prisoner, "Budd," he said, and scarce in equable tones, "Budd, if you have aught further to say for yourself, say it now."

Upon this the young sailor turned another quick glance toward Captain Vere; then, as taking a hint from that aspect, a hint confirming his own instinct that silence was now best, replied to the Lieutenant, "I have said all, Sir."

The marine—the same who had been the sentinel without the cabin-door at the time that the foretopman followed by the master-at-arms, entered it—he, standing by the sailor throughout these judicial proceedings, was now directed to take him back to the after compartment originally assigned to the prisoner and his custodian. As the twain disappeared from view, the three officers as partially liberated from some inward constraint associated with Billy's mere presence, simultaneously stirred in their seats. They exchanged looks of troubled indecision, yet feeling that decide they must and without long delay. For Captain Vere, he for the time stood unconsciously with his back toward them, apparently in one of his absent fits, gazing out from a sashed port-hole to windward upon the monotonous blank of the twilight sea. But the court's silence continuing, broken only at moments by brief consultations in low earnest tones, this seemed to assure him and encourage him. Turning, he to-and-fro paced the cabin athwart; in the returning ascent to windward, climbing the slant deck in the ship's lee roll; without knowing it symbolizing thus in his action a mind resolute to surmount difficulties even if against primitive instincts strong as the wind and the sea. Presently he came to a stand before the three. After scanning their faces he stood less as mustering his thoughts for expression, than as one inly deliberating how best to put them to well-meaning men not intellectually mature, men with whom it was necessary to demonstrate certain principles that were axioms to himself. Similar impatience as to talking is perhaps one reason that deters some minds from addressing any popular assemblies.

When speak he did, something both in the substance of what he said and his manner of saying it, showed the influence of unshared studies modifying and tempering the practical training of an active career. This, along with his phraseology now and then was suggestive of the grounds whereon rested that imputation of a certain pedantry so-

30. **'a . . . iniquity'**: II Thess. 2:7.

cially alleged against him by certain naval men of wholly practical cast, captains who nevertheless would frankly concede that His Majesty's navy mustered no more efficient officer of their grade than *Starry Vere.*

What he said was to this effect: "Hitherto I have been but the witness, little more; and I should hardly think now to take another tone, that of your coadjutor, for the time, did I not perceive in you,—at the crisis too—a troubled hesitancy, proceeding, I doubt not from the clash of military duty with moral scruple—scruple vitalized by compassion. For the compassion how can I otherwise than share it. But, mindful of paramount obligations I strive against scruples that may tend to enervate decision. Not, gentlemen, that I hide from myself that the case is an exceptional one. Speculatively regarded, it well might be referred to a jury of casuists. But for us here acting not as casuists or moralists, it is a case practical, and under martial law practically to be dealt with.

"But your scruples: do they move as in a dusk? Challenge them. Make them advance and declare themselves. Come now: do they import something like this: If, mindless of palliating circumstances, we are bound to regard the death of the Master-at-arms as the prisoner's deed, then does that deed constitute a capital crime whereof the penalty is a mortal one. But in natural justice is nothing but the prisoner's overt act to be considered? How can we adjudge to summary and shameful death a fellow-creature innocent before God, and whom we feel to be so?—Does that state it aright? You sign sad assent. Well, I too feel that, the full force of that. It is Nature. But do these buttons that we wear attest that our allegiance is to Nature? No, to the King. Though the ocean, which is inviolate Nature primeval, though this be the element where we move and have our being as sailors, yet as the King's officers lies our duty in a sphere correspondingly natural? So little is that true, that in receiving our commissions we in the most important regards ceased to be natural free-agents. When war is declared are we the commissioned fighters previously consulted? We fight at command. If our judgements approve the war, that is but coincidence. So in other particulars. So now. For suppose condemnation to follow these present proceedings. Would it be so much we ourselves that would condemn as it would be martial law operating through us? For that law and the rigor of it, we are not responsible. Our avowed responsibility is in this: That however pitilessly that law may operate, we nevertheless adhere to it and administer it.

"But the exceptional in the matter moves the hearts within you. Even so too is mine moved. But let not warm hearts betray heads that should be cool. Ashore in a criminal case will an upright judge allow himself off the bench to be waylaid by some tender kinswoman of the accused seeking to touch him with her tearful plea? Well the heart here denotes the feminine in man, is as that piteous woman, and hard though it be, she must here be ruled out."

He paused, earnestly studying them for a moment; then resumed.

"But something in your aspect seems to urge that it is not solely the heart that moves in you, but also the conscience, the private conscience. But tell me whether or not, occupying the position we do, private conscience should not yield to that imperial one formulated in the code under which alone we officially proceed?"

Here the three men moved in their seats, less convinced than agitated by the course of an argument troubling but the more the spontaneous conflict within.

Perceiving which, the speaker paused for a moment; then abruptly changing his tone, went on.

"To steady us a bit, let us recur to the facts.—In wartime at sea a man-of-war's-man strikes his superior in grade, and the blow kills. Apart from its effect the blow itself is, according to the Articles of War, a capital crime. Furthermore—"

"Ay, Sir," emotionally broke in the officer of marines, "in one sense it was. But surely Budd proposed neither mutiny nor homicide."

"Surely not, my good man. And before a court less arbitrary and more merciful than a martial one, that plea would largely extenuate. At the Last Assizes it shall acquit. But how here? We proceed under the law of the Mutiny Act. In feature no child can resemble his father more than that Act resembles in spirit the the thing from which it derives—War. In His Majesty's service—in this ship indeed—there are Englishmen forced to fight for the King against their will. Against their conscience, for aught we know. Though as their fellow-creatures some of us may appreciate their position, yet as navy officers, what reck we of it? Still less recks the enemy. Our impressed men he would fain cut down in the same swath with our volunteers. As regards the enemy's naval conscripts, some of whom may even share our own abhorrence of the regicidal French Directory, it is the same on our side. War looks but to the frontage, the appearance. And the Mutiny Act, War's child, takes after the father. Budd's intent or non-intent is nothing to the purpose.

"But while, put to it by those anxieties in you which I can not but respect, I only repeat myself—

while thus strangely we prolong proceedings that should be summary—the enemy may be sighted and an engagement result. We must do; and one of two things must we do—condemn or let go."

"Can we not convict and yet mitigate the penalty?" asked the junior Lieutenant here speaking, and falteringly, for the first.

"Lieutenant, were that clearly lawful for us under the circumstances consider the consequences of such clemency. The people" (meaning the ship's company) "have native-sense; most of them are familiar with our naval usage and tradition; and how would they take it? Even could you explain to them—which our official position forbids—they, long moulded by arbitrary discipline have not that kind of intelligent responsiveness that might qualify them to comprehend and discriminate. No, to the people the foretopman's deed however it be worded in the announcement will be plain homicide committed in a flagrant act of mutiny. What penalty for that should follow, they know. But it does not follow. *Why?* they will ruminate. You know what sailors are. Will they not revert to the recent outbreak at the Nore? Ay. They know the well-founded alarm—the panic it struck throughout England. Your clement sentence they would account pusillanimous. They would think that we flinch, that we are afraid of them—afraid of practising a lawful rigor singularly demanded at this juncture lest it should provoke new troubles. What shame to us such a conjecture on their part, and how deadly to discipline. You see then, whither prompted by duty and the law I steadfastly drive. But I beseech you, my friends, do not take me amiss. I feel as you do for this unfortunate boy. But did he know our hearts, I take him to be of that generous nature that he would feel even for us on whom in this military necessity so heavy a compulsion is laid."

With that, crossing the deck he resumed his place by the sashed port-hole, tacitly leaving the three to come to a decision. On the cabin's opposite side the troubled court sat silent. Loyal lieges, plain and practical, though at bottom they dissented from some points Captain Vere had put to them, they were without the faculty, hardly had the inclination to gainsay one whom they felt to be an earnest man, one too not less their superior in mind than in naval rank. But it is not improbable that even such of his words as were not without influence over them, less came home to them than his closing appeal to their instinct as sea-officers in the forethought he threw out as to the practical consequences to discipline, considering the unconfirmed tone of the fleet at the time, should a man-of-war's-man's violent killing at sea of a superior in grade be allowed to pass for aught else than a capital crime demanding prompt infliction of the penalty.

Not unlikely they were brought to something more or less akin to that harrassed frame of mind which in the year 1842 actuated the commander of the U.S. brig-of-war *Somers* [31] to resolve, under the so-called Articles of War, Articles modelled upon the English Mutiny Act, to resolve upon the execution at sea of a midshipman and two petty-officers as mutineers designing the seizure of the brig. Which resolution was carried out though in a time of peace and within not many days sail of home. An act vindicated by a naval court of inquiry subsequently convened ashore. History, and here cited without comment. True, the circumstances on board the *Somers* were different from those on board the *Indomitable*. But the urgency felt, well-warranted or otherwise, was much the same.

Says a writer whom few know, "Forty years after a battle it is easy for a non-combatant to reason about how it ought to have been fought. It is another thing personally and under fire to direct the fighting while involved in the obscuring smoke of it. Much so with respect to other emergencies involving considerations both practical and moral, and when it is imperative promptly to act. The greater the fog the more it imperils the steamer, and speed is put on though at the hazard of running somebody down. Little ween the snug card-players in the cabin of the responsibilities of the sleepless man on the bridge."

In brief, Billy Budd was formally convicted and sentenced to be hung at the yard-arm in the early morning-watch, it being now night. Otherwise, as is customary in such cases, the sentence would forthwith have been carried out. In war-time on the field or in the fleet, a mortal punishment decreed by a drum-head court—on the field sometimes decreed by but a nod from the General—follows without delay on the heel of conviction without appeal.

23

IT WAS Captain Vere himself who of his own motion communicated the finding of the court to the prisoner; for that purpose going to the compartment where he was in custody and bidding the marine there to withdraw for the time.

Beyond the communication of the sentence what took place at this interview was never

31. *Somers:* See headnote.

known. But in view of the character of the twain briefly closeted in that state-room, each radically sharing in the rarer qualities of our nature—so rare indeed as to be all but incredible to average minds however much cultivated—some conjectures may be ventured.

It would have been in consonance with the spirit of Captain Vere should he on this occasion have concealed nothing from the condemned one —should he indeed have frankly disclosed to him the part he himself had played in bringing about the decision, at the same time revealing his actuating motives. On Billy's side it is not improbable that such a confession would have been received in much the same spirit that prompted it. Not without a sort of joy indeed he might have appreciated the brave opinion of him implied in his Captain making such a confidant of him. Nor, as to the sentence itself could he have been insensible that it was imparted to him as to one not afraid to die. Even more may have been. Captain Vere in the end may have developed the passion sometimes latent under an exterior stoical or indifferent. He was old enough to have been Billy's father. The austere devotee of military duty letting himself melt back into what remains primeval in our formalized humanity may in the end have caught Billy to his heart even as Abraham may have caught young Isaac on the brink of resolutely offering him up in obedience to the exacting behest. But there is no telling the sacrament, seldom if in any case revealed to the gadding world wherever under circumstances at all akin to those here attempted to be set forth two of great Nature's nobler order embrace. There is privacy at the time, inviolable to the survivor, and holy oblivion the sequel to each diviner magnanimity, providentially covers all at last.

The first to encounter Captain Vere in act of leaving the compartment was the senior Lieutenant. The fact he beheld, for the moment one expressive of the agony of the strong, was to that officer, though a man of fifty, a startling revelation. That the condemned one suffered less than he who mainly had effected the condemnation was apparently indicated by the former's exclamation in the scene soon perforce to be touched upon.

24

OF A SERIES of incidents within a brief term rapidly following each other, the adequate narration may take up a term less brief, especially if explanation or comment here and there seem requisite to the better understanding of such incidents. Between the entrance into the cabin of him who never left it alive, and him who when he did leave it left it as one condemned to die; between this and the closeted interview just given less than an hour and a half had elapsed. It was an interval long enough however to awaken speculations among no few of the ship's company as to what it was that could be detaining in the cabin the master-at-arms and the sailor; for a rumor that both of them had been seen to enter it and neither of them had been seen to emerge, this rumor had got abroad upon the gun-decks and in the tops; the people of a great war-ship being in one respect like villagers taking microscopic note of every outward movement or non-movement going on. When therefore in weather not at all tempestuous all hands were called in the second dog-watch, a summons under such circumstances not usual in those hours, the crew were not wholly unprepared for some announcement extraordinary, one having connection too with the continued absence of the two men from their wonted haunts.

There was a moderate sea at the time; and the moon, newly risen and near to being at its full, silvered the white spar-deck wherever not blotted by the clear-cut shadows horizontally thrown of fixtures and moving men. On either side the quarter-deck the marine guard under arms was drawn up; and Captain Vere standing in his place surrounded by all the ward-room officers, addressed his men. In so doing his manner showed neither more nor less than that properly pertaining to his supreme position aboard his own ship. In clear terms and concise he told them what had taken place in the cabin; that the master-at-arms was dead; that he who had killed him had been already tried by a summary court and condemned to death; and that the execution would take place in the early morning watch. The word *mutiny* was not named in what he said. He refrained too from making the occasion an opportunity for any preachment as to the maintenance of discipline, thinking perhaps that under existing circumstances in the navy the consequence of violating discipline should be made to speak for itself.

Their captain's announcement was listened to by the throng of standing sailors in a dumbness like that of a seated congregation of believers in hell listening to the clergyman's announcement of his Calvinistic text.

At the close, however, a confused murmur went up. It began to wax. All but instantly, then, at a sign, it was pierced and suppressed by shrill whistles of the Boatswain and his Mates piping down one watch.

To be prepared for burial Claggart's body was delivered to certain petty-officers of his mess. And here, not to clog the sequel with lateral matters, it may be added that at a suitable hour, the master-at-arms was committed to the sea with every funeral honor properly belonging to his naval grade.

In this proceeding as in every public one growing out of the tragedy strict adherence to usage was observed. Nor in any point could it have been at all deviated from, either with respect to Claggart or Billy Budd without begetting undesirable speculations in the ship's company, sailors, and more particularly men-of-war's men, being of all men the greatest sticklers for usage.

For similar cause, all communication between Captain Vere and the condemned one ended with the closeted interview already given, the latter being now surrendered to the ordinary routine preliminary to the end. This transfer under guard from the Captain's quarters was effected without unusual precautions—at least no visible ones.

If possible not to let the men so much as surmise that their officers anticipate aught amiss from them is the tacit rule in a military ship. And the more that some sort of trouble should really be apprehended the more do the officers keep that apprehension to themselves; though not the less unostentatious vigilance may be augmented.

In the present instance the sentry placed over the prisoner had strict orders to let no one have communication with him but the Chaplain. And certain unobtrusive measures were taken absolutely to insure this point.

25

IN A seventy-four of the old order the deck known as the upper gun-deck was the one covered over by the spar-deck which last though not without its armament was for the most part exposed to the weather. In general it was at all hours free from hammocks; those of the crew swinging on the lower gun-deck, and berth-deck, the latter being not only a dormitory but also the place for the stowing of the sailors' bags, and on both sides lined with the large chests or movable pantries of the many messes of the men.

On the starboard side of the *Indomitable's* upper gun-deck, behold Billy Budd under sentry lying prone in irons in one of the bays formed by the regular spacing of the guns comprising the batteries on either side. All these pieces were of the heavier calibre of that period. Mounted on lumbering wooden carriages they were hampered with cumbersome harness of breechen and strong side-tackles for running them out. Guns and carriages, together with the long rammers and shorter lintstocks lodged in loops overhead—all these, as customary, were painted black; and the heavy hempen breechens tarred to the same tint, wore the like livery of the undertakers. In contrast with the funeral hue of these surroundings the prone sailor's exterior apparel, white *jumper* and white duck trousers, each more or less soiled, dimly glimmered in the obscure light of the bay like a patch of discolored snow in early April lingering at some upland cave's black mouth. In effect he is already in his shroud or the garments that shall serve him in lieu of one. Over him but scarce illuminating him, two battle-lanterns swing from two massive beams of the deck above. Fed with the oil supplied by the war-contractors (whose gains, honest or otherwise, are in every land an anticipated portion of the harvest of death) with flickering splashes of dirty yellow light they pollute the pale moonshine all but ineffectually struggling in obstructed flecks through the open ports from which the tompioned cannon protrude. Other lanterns at intervals serve but to bring out somewhat the obscurer bays which like small confessionals or side-chapels in a cathedral branch from the long dim-vistaed broad aisle between the two batteries of that covered tier.

Such was the deck where now lay the Handsome Sailor. Through the rose-tan of his complexion, no pallor could have shown. It would have taken days of sequestration from the winds and the sun to have brought about the effacement of that. But the skeleton in the cheek-bone at the point of its angle was just beginning delicately to be defined under the warm-tinted skin. In fervid hearts self-contained some brief experiences devour our human tissue as secret fire in a ship's hold consumes cotton in the bale.

But now lying between the two guns, as nipped in the vice of fate, Billy's agony, mainly proceeding from a generous young heart's virgin experience of the diabolical incarnate and effective in some men—the tension of that agony was over now. It survived not the something healing in the closeted interview with Captain Vere. Without movement, he lay as in a trance. That adolescent expression previously noted as his, taking on something akin to the look of a slumbering child in the cradle when the warm hearth-glow of the still chamber at night plays on the dimples that at whiles mysteriously form in the cheek, silently coming and going there. For now and then in the gyved one's trance a serene happy light born of some wandering reminiscence or dream would diffuse itself over his face, and then wane away only anew to return.

The Chaplain coming to see him and finding him thus, and perceiving no sign that he was conscious of his presence, attentively regarded him for a space, then slipping aside, withdrew for the time, peradventure feeling that even he the minister of Christ though receiving his stipend from Mars had no consolation to proffer which could result in a peace transcending that which he beheld. But in the small hours he came again. And the prisoner now awake to his surroundings noticed his approach and civilly, all but cheerfully, welcomed him. But it was to little purpose that in the interview following the good man sought to bring Billy Budd to some godly understanding that he must die, and at dawn. True, Billy himself freely referred to his death as a thing close at hand; but it was something in the way that children will refer to death in general, who yet among their other sports will play a funeral with hearse and mourners.

Not that like children Billy was incapable of conceiving what death really is. No, but he was wholly without irrational fear of it, a fear more prevalent in highly civilized communities than those so-called barbarous ones which in all respects stand nearer to unadulterate Nature. And, as elsewhere said, a barbarian Billy radically was; as much so, for all the costume, as his countrymen the British captives, living trophies, made to march in the Roman triumph of Germanicus.[32] Quite as much so as those later barbarians, young men probably, and picked specimens among the earlier British converts to Christianity, at least nominally such and taken to Rome (as today converts from lesser isles of the sea may be taken to London) of whom the Pope of that time, admiring the strangeness of their personal beauty so unlike the Italian stamp, their clear ruddy complexion and curled flaxen locks, exclaimed, "Angles" (meaning *English* the modern derivative) "Angles do you call them? And is it because they look so like angels?" Had it been later in time one would think that the Pope had in mind Fra Angelico's [33] seraphs some of whom, plucking apples in gardens of the Hesperides have the faint rose-bud complexion of the more beautiful English girls.

If in vain the good Chaplain sought to impress the young barbarian with ideas of death akin to those conveyed in the skull, dial, and cross-bones on old tombstones; equally futile to all appearance were his efforts to bring home to him the thought of salvation and a Saviour. Billy listened, but less out of awe or reverence perhaps than from a certain natural politeness; doubtless at bottom regarding all that in much the same way that most mariners of his class take any discourse abstract or out of the common tone of the work-a-day world. And this sailor-way of taking clerical discourse is not wholly unlike the way in which the pioneer of Christianity full of transcendent miracles was received long ago on tropic isles by any superior *savage* so called—a Tahitian say of Captain Cook's time or shortly after that time. Out of natural courtesy he received, but did not appropriate. It was like a gift placed in the palm of an outreached hand upon which the fingers do not close.

But the *Indomitable's* Chaplain was a discreet man possessing the good sense of a good heart. So he insisted not in his vocation here. At the instance of Captain Vere, a lieutenant had apprised him of pretty much everything as to Billy; and since he felt that innocence was even a better thing than religion wherewith to go to Judgement, he reluctantly withdrew; but in his emotion not without first performing an act strange enough in an Englishman, and under the circumstances yet more so in any regular priest. Stooping over, he kissed on the fair cheek his fellow-man, a felon in martial law, one who though on the confines of death he felt he could never convert to a dogma; nor for all that did he fear for his future.

Marvel not that having been made acquainted with the young sailor's essential innocence (an irruption of heretic thought hard to suppress) the worthy man lifted not a finger to avert the doom of such a martyr to martial discipline. So to do would not only have been as idle as invoking the desert, but would also have been an audacious transgression of the bounds of his function, one as exactly prescribed to him by military law as that of the boatswain or any other naval officer. Bluntly put, a chaplain is the minister of the Prince of Peace serving in the host of the God of War—Mars. As such, he is as incongruous as that musket of Blücher etc. at Christmas. Why then is he there? Because he indirectly subserves the purpose attested by the cannon; because too he lends the sanction of the religion of the meek to that which practically is the abrogation of everything but brute Force.

32. Roman . . . Germanicus: in 17 A.D. Nero Claudius Germanicus, nephew of Tiberius, was famous for his campaigns against the German tribes. (When he was adopted by his uncle he took the name of Germanicus Julius Caesar.) **33. Fra Angelico:** Italian painter (1387–1455).

26

THE NIGHT so luminous on the spar-deck but otherwise on the cavernous ones below, levels so like the tiered galleries in a coal-mine—the luminous night passed away. But, like the prophet in the chariot disappearing in heaven and dropping his mantle to Elisha, the withdrawing night transferred its pale robe to the breaking day. A meek shy light appeared in the East, where stretched a diaphanous fleece of white furrowed vapor. That light slowly waxed. Suddenly *eight bells* was struck aft, responded to by one louder metallic stroke from forward. It was four o'clock in the morning. Instantly the silver whistles were heard summoning all hands to witness punishment. Up through the great hatchways rimmed with racks of heavy shot, the watch below came pouring, overspreading with the watch already on deck the space between the mainmast and foremast including that occupied by the capacious *launch* and the black booms tiered on either side of it, boat and booms making a summit of observation for the powder-boys and younger tars. A different group comprising one watch of topmen leaned over the rail of that sea-balcony, no small one in a seventy-four, looking down on the crowd below. Man or boy none spake but in whisper, and few spake at all. Captain Vere—as before, the central figure among the assembled commissioned officers—stood nigh the break of the poop-deck facing forward. Just below him on the quarter-deck the marines in full equipment were drawn up much as at the scene of the promulgated sentence.

At sea in the old time, the execution by halter of a military sailor was generally from the fore-yard. In the present instance, for special reasons the main-yard was assigned. Under an arm of that weather or lee yard the prisoner was presently brought up, the Chaplain attending him. It was noted at the time and remarked upon afterwards, that in this final scene the good man evinced little or nothing of the perfunctory. Brief speech indeed he had with the condemned one, but the genuine Gospel was less on his tongue than in his aspect and manner towards him. The final preparations personal to the latter being speedily brought to an end by two boatswain's-mates, the consummation impended. Billy stood facing aft. At the penultimate moment, his words, his only ones, words wholly unobstructed in the utterance were these—"God bless Captain Vere!" Syllables so unanticipated coming from one with the ignominious hemp about his neck—a conventional felon's benediction directed aft towards the quarters of honor; syllables too delivered in the clear melody of a singing-bird on the point of launching from the twig, had a phenomenal effect, not unenhanced by the rare personal beauty of the young sailor spiritualized now through late experiences so poignantly profound.

Without volition as it were, as if indeed the ship's populace were but the vehicles of some vocal current electric, with one voice from alow and aloft came a resonant sympathetic echo—"God bless Captain Vere!" And yet at that instant Billy alone must have been in their hearts, even as he was in their eyes.

At the pronounced words and the spontaneous echo that voluminously rebounded them, Captain Vere, either through stoic self-control or a sort of momentary paralysis induced by emotional shock, stood erectly rigid as a musket in the ship-armorer's rack.

The hull deliberately recovering from the periodic roll to leeward was just regaining an even keel, when the last signal a preconcerted dumb one was given. At the same moment it chanced that the vapory fleece hanging low in the East, was shot through with a soft glory as of the fleece of the Lamb of God seen in mystical vision and simultaneously therewith, watched by the wedged mass of upturned faces, Billy ascended; and, ascending, took the full rose of the dawn.

In the pinioned figure, arrived at the yard-end, to the wonder of all no motion was apparent, none save that created by the ship's motion, in moderate weather so majestic in a great ship ponderously cannoned.

27

A Digression

WHEN some days afterward in reference to the singularity just mentioned, the Purser a rather ruddy rotund person more accurate as an accountant than profound as a philosopher, said at mess to the Surgeon, "What testimony to the force lodged in will-power" the latter, saturnine, spare and tall, one in whom a discreet causticity went along with a manner less genial than polite, replied, "Your pardon, Mr. Purser. In a hanging scientifically conducted—and under special orders I myself directed how Budd's was to be effected—any movement following the completed suspension and originating in the body suspended, such movement indicates mechanical spasm in the muscular system. Hence the absence of that is no more attributable to will-power as you call it than to horse-power—begging your pardon."

"But this muscular spasm you speak of, is not that in a degree more or less invariable in these cases?"

"Assuredly so, Mr. Purser."

"How then, my good sir, do you account for its absence in this instance?"

"Mr. Purser, it is clear that your sense of the singularity in this matter equals not mine. You account for it by what you call will-power a term not yet included in the lexicon of science. For me I do not, with my present knowledge pretend to account for it at all. Even should we assume the hypothesis that at the first touch of the halyards the action of Budd's heart, intensified by extraordinary emotion at its climax, abruptly stopt—much like a watch when in carelessly winding it up you strain at the finish, thus snapping the chain—even under that hypothesis how account for the phenomenon that followed?"

"You admit then that the absence of spasmodic movement was phenomenal."

"It was phenomenal, Mr. Purser, in the sense that it was an appearance the cause of which is not immediately to be assigned."

"But tell me, my dear sir," pertinaciously continued the other, "was the man's death effected by the halter, or was it a species of euthanasia?"

"*Euthanasia,* Mr. Purser, is something like your *will-power:* I doubt its authenticity as a scientific term—begging your pardon again. It is at once imaginative and metaphysical,—in short, Greek. But" abruptly changing his tone "there is a case in the sick-bay that I do not care to leave to my assistants. Beg your pardon, but excuse me." And rising from the mess he formally withdrew.

28

THE SILENCE at the moment of execution and for a moment or two continuing thereafter, a silence but emphasized by the regular wash of the sea against the hull or the flutter of a sail caused by the helmsman's eyes being tempted astray, this emphasized silence was gradually disturbed by a sound not easily to be verbally rendered. Whoever has heard the freshet-wave of a torrent suddenly swelled by pouring showers in tropical mountains, showers not shared by the plain; whoever has heard the first muffled murmur of its sloping advance through precipitous woods, may form some conception of the sound now heard. The seeming remoteness of its source was because of its murmurous indistinctness since it came from close-by, even from the men massed on the ship's open deck. Being inarticulate, it was dubious in significance further than it seemed to indicate some capricious revulsion of thought or feeling such as mobs ashore are liable to, in the present instance possibly implying a sullen revocation on the men's part of their involuntary echoing of Billy's benediction. But ere the murmur had time to wax into clamor it was met by a strategic command, the more telling that it came with abrupt unexpectedness.

"Pipe down the starboard watch Boatswain, and see that they go."

Shrill as the shriek of the sea-hawk, the whistles of the Boatswain and his Mates pierced that ominous low sound, dissipating it; and yielding to the mechanism of discipline the throng was thinned by one half. For the remainder most of them were set to temporary employments connected with trimming the yards and so forth, business readily to be got up to serve occasion by any officer-of-the-deck.

Now each proceeding that follows a mortal sentence pronounced at sea by a drum-head court is characterised by promptitude not perceptibly merging into hurry, though bordering that. The hammock, the one which had been Billy's bed when alive, having already been ballasted with shot and otherwise prepared to serve for his canvas coffin, the last offices of the sea-undertakers, the Sail-Maker's Mates, were now speedily completed. When everything was in readiness a second call for all hands made necessary by the strategic movement before mentioned was sounded and now to witness burial.

The details of this closing formality it needs not to give. But when the tilted plank let slide its freight into the sea, a second strange human murmur was heard, blended now with another inarticulate sound proceeding from certain larger sea-fowl whose attention having been attracted by the peculiar commotion in the water resulting from the heavy sloped dive of the shotted hammock into the sea, flew screaming to the spot. So near the hull did they come, that the stridor or bony creak of their gaunt double-jointed pinions was audible. As the ship under light airs passed on, leaving the burial-spot astern, they still kept circling it low down with the moving shadow of their outstretched wings and the croaked requiem of their cries.

Upon sailors as superstitious as those of the age preceding ours, men-of-war's men too who had just beheld the prodigy of repose in the form suspended in air and now foundering in the deeps; to such mariners the action of the sea-fowl though dictated by mere animal greed for prey, was big with no prosaic significance. An uncertain movement began among them, in which some encroachment was made. It was tolerated but for a moment. For suddenly the drum beat to quarters, which familiar sound happening at least twice every day, had upon the present occasion a signal peremptoriness in it. True martial discipline long continued superinduces in average man a sort of impulse of docility whose operation at the official sound of command much resembles in its promptitude the effect of an instinct.

The drum-beat dissolved the multitude, distributing most of them along the batteries of the two covered gun-decks. There, as wont, the guns' crews stood by their respective cannon erect and silent. In due course the First Officer, sword under arm and standing in his place on the quarter-deck formally received the successive reports of the sworded Lieutenants commanding the sections of batteries below; the last of which reports being made the summed report he delivered with the customary salute to the Commander. All this occupied time, which in the present case, was the object of beating to quarters at an hour prior to the customary one. That such variance from usage was authorized by an officer like Captain Vere, a martinet as some deemed him, was evidence of the necessity for unusual action implied in what he deemed to be temporarily the mood of his men. "With mankind" he would say "forms, measured forms are everything; and that is the import couched in the story of Orpheus with his lyre spell-binding the wild denizens of the wood." And this he once applied to the disruption of forms going on across the Channel and the consequences thereof.

At this unwonted muster at quarters, all proceeded as at the regular hour. The band on the quarter-deck played a sacred air. After which the Chaplain went through the customary morning service. That done, the drum beat the retreat, and toned by music and religious rites subserving the discipline and purpose of war, the men in their wonted orderly manner, dispersed to the places allotted them when not at the guns.

And now it was full day. The fleece of low-hanging vapor had vanished, licked up by the sun that late had so glorified it. And the circumambient air in the clearness of its serenity was like smooth white marble in the polished block not yet removed from the marble-dealer's yard.

29

THE SYMMETRY of form attainable in pure fiction can not so readily be achieved in a narration essentially having less to do with fable than with fact. Truth uncompromisingly told will always have its ragged edges; hence the conclusion of such a narration is apt to be less finished than an architectural finial.

How it fared with the Handsome Sailor during the year of the Great Mutiny has been faithfully given. But though properly the story ends with his life, something in way of sequel will not be amiss. Three brief chapters will suffice.

In the general re-christening under the Directory of the craft originally forming the navy of the French monarchy, the *St. Louis* line-of-battle ship was named the *Athéiste*. Such a name, like some other substituted ones in the Revolutionary fleet while proclaiming the infidel audacity of the ruling power was yet, though not so intended to be, the aptest name, if one consider it, ever given to a war-ship; far more so indeed than the *Devastation,* the *Erebus* (the *Hell*) and similar names bestowed upon fighting-ships.

On the return-passage to the English fleet from the detached cruise during which occurred the events already recorded, the *Indomitable* fell in with the *Athéiste*. An engagement ensued; during which Captain Vere in the act of putting his ship alongside the enemy with a view of throwing his boarders across her bulwarks, was hit by a musket-ball from a port-hole of the enemy's main cabin. More than disabled he dropped to the deck and was carried below to the same cock-pit where some of his men already lay. The senior Lieutenant took command. Under him the enemy was finally captured and though much crippled was by rare good fortune successfully taken into Gibraltar, an English port not very distant from the scene of the fight. There, Captain Vere with the rest of the wounded was put ashore. He lingered for some days, but the end came. Unhappily he was cut off too early for the Nile and Trafalgar. The spirit that spite its philosophic austerity may yet have indulged in the most secret of all passions, ambition, never attained to the fulness of fame.

Not long before death while lying under the influence of that magical drug which soothing the physical frame mysteriously operates on the subtler element in man, he was heard to murmur words inexplicable to his attendant—"Billy Budd, Billy Budd." That these were not the accents of remorse, would seem clear from what the attendant said to the *Indomitable's* senior officer of marines who as the most reluctant to condemn of the members of the drum-head court, too well knew though here he kept the knowledge to himself, who Billy Budd was.

30

SOME few weeks after the execution, among other matters under the head of *News from the Mediterranean,* there appeared in a naval chronicle of the time, an authorized weekly publication, an account of the affair. It was doubtless for the most part written in good faith, though the medium, partly rumor, through which the facts must have reached the writer, served to deflect and in part falsify them. The account was as follows—

"On the tenth of the last month a deplorable occurrence took place on board H.M.S. *Indomitable*. John Claggart, the ship's master-at-arms, discovering that some sort of plot was incipient among an inferior section of the ship's company, and that the ringleader was one William Budd; he, Claggart in the act of arraigning the man before the Captain was vindictively stabbed to the heart by the suddenly drawn sheath-knife of Budd.

"The deed and the implement employed, sufficiently suggest that though mustered into the service under an English name the assassin was no Englishman, but one of those aliens adopting English cognomens whom the present extraordinary necessities of the Service have caused to be admitted into it in considerable numbers.

"The enormity of the crime and the extreme depravity of the criminal, appear the greater in view of the character of the victim, a middle-aged man respectable and discreet, belonging to that minor official grade, the petty-officers, upon whom, as none know better than the commissioned gentlemen, the efficiency of His Majesty's navy so largely depends. His function was a responsible one; at once onerous and thankless and his fidelity in it the greater because of his strong patriotic impulse. In this instance as in so many other instances in these days, the character of this unfortunate man signally refutes, if refutation were needed, that peevish saying attributed to the late Dr. Johnson, that patriotism is the last refuge of a scoundrel.

"The criminal paid the penalty of his crime. The promptitude of the punishment has proved salutary. Nothing amiss is now apprehended aboard H.M.S. *Indomitable*."

The above appearing in a publication now long ago superannuated and forgotten is all that hitherto has stood in human record to attest what manner of men respectively were John Claggart and Billy Budd.

31

EVERYTHING is for a term remarkable in navies. Any tangible object associated with some striking incident of the service is converted into a monument. The spar from which the foretopman was suspended, was for some few years kept trace of by the blue-jackets. Their knowledge followed it from ship to dock-yard and again from dock-yard to ship, till pursuing it even when at last reduced to a mere dock-yard boom. To them a chip of it was as a piece of the Cross. Ignorant though they were of the secret facts of the tragedy, and not thinking but that the penalty was somehow unavoidably inflicted from the naval point of view, for all that they instinctively felt that Billy was a sort of man as incapable of mutiny as of wilful murder. They recalled the fresh young image of the Handsome Sailor, that face never deformed by a sneer or subtler vile freak of the heart within. Their impression of him was doubtless deepened by the fact that he was gone, and in a measure mysteriously gone. On the gun-decks of the *Indomitable* the general estimate of his nature and its unconscious simplicity eventually found rude utterance from another foretopman one of his own watch gifted, as some sailors are, with an artless poetic temperament. The tarry hands made some lines which after circulating among the shipboard crew for a while, finally got rudely printed at Portsmouth as a ballad. The title given to it was the sailor's.

BILLY IN THE DARBIES [34]

Good of the Chaplain to enter Lone Bay
And down on his marrow-bones here and pray
For the like just o' me, Billy Budd.—But look:
Through the port comes the moon-shine astray!
It tips the guard's cutlas and silvers this nook;
But 'twill die in the dawning of Billy's last day.
A jewel-block they'll make of me tomorrow,
Pendant pearl from the yard-arm-end
Like the ear-drop I gave to Bristol Molly—
O, 'tis me, not the sentence they'll suspend.
Ay, Ay, all is up; and I must up too
Early in the morning, aloft from alow.
On an empty stomach, now, never it would do.
They'll give me a nibble—bit o' biscuit ere I go.
Sure, a messmate will reach me the last parting cup;
But, turning heads away from the hoist and the belay,
Heaven knows who will have the running of me up!
No pipe to those halyards.—But aren't it all sham?
A blur's in my eyes; it is dreaming that I am.
A hatchet to my hawser? all adrift to go?
The drum roll to grog, and Billy never know?
But Donald he has promised to stand by the plank;
So I'll shake a friendly hand ere I sink.
But—no! It is dead then I'll be, come to think.—
I remember Taff the Welshman when he sank.
And his cheek it was like the budding pink.
But me they'll lash me in hammock, drop me deep.
Fathoms down, fathoms down, how I'll dream fast asleep.
I feel it stealing now. Sentry, are you there?
Just ease this darbies at the wrist,
And roll me over fair,
I am sleepy, and the oozy weeds about me twist.

END OF BOOK

April 19th
1891

34. **Darbies:** handcuffs.

R. W. B. LEWIS
Editor

Walt Whitman

1819–1892

WALT WHITMAN is the most blurred, even contradictory figure in the classical or mid-nineteenth-century period of American literature. Recent scholarship and criticism have been clearing things up a good deal; but both the poet and his work remain something of a jumble. For a number of decades, Whitman was the most misrepresented of our major poets: and the misrepresentation began with Whitman himself, in the last twenty-five years of his life. It was during those years, from 1867 onwards, that Whitman—initially a very self-exposed and self-absorbed poet—became willfully self-concealing, while at the same time he asserted in various ways an entity, a being, a persona radically other than the being that lay at the heart of his best poetry.

The chief mode of such concealment and assertion was not creative; it was editorial. Whitman wrote little poetry of lasting value after "Passage to India" (1871); what he did do in those later years was constantly to reshuffle the contents of his expanding book: to disperse the poems out of their original and effective order, to arrange them in new and fundamentally misleading groups, to suppress some of the more telling and suggestive of the items, and to revise or delete a series of key passages. The result of this process was a serious shift of emphasis whereby the authentic Whitman was gradually dismembered and replaced by a synthetic entity that was more posture than poet, more mere representative than sovereign person. It, or he, was the representative—in nearly the conventional political sense—of a rather shallowly and narrowly conceived democratic culture: a hearty voice at the center of a bustling and progressive republic, a voice that saluted the pioneers, echoed the sound of America singing, itself sang songs of joy that foretold the future union of the nation and the world and the cosmos, chanted the square deific, and wept over the country's captain lying cold and dead on the deck of the ship of state. Other and truer aspects of Whitman continued to exert an appeal, especially in certain lively corners of Europe. But in the English-speaking world, it was primarily the bombastic, or, as his disciples sometimes said, the "cosmic" Whitman that was better known; and it was this Whitman that was either revered or—in most literary circles after the advent of T. S. Eliot—dismissed or simply disregarded.

So much needs to be said: for our first task, and the task this Introduction confronts, is to disentangle Whitman, to separate the real from the unpersuasive, to separate the poet from the posture. To do that, we have, first of all, to put Whitman's poems back into their original and chronological order. It might be argued that we have no right to tamper with the poet's own editorial judgment; that *Leaves of Grass* is, after all, Whitman's book and that we are bound to take it in the order and the form he eventually decided on. The answer to this proposition is that there is no satisfactory way around the critical necessity of discriminating among Whitman's successive revisions of his own work, of appealing from the Whitman of 1867 and 1871 and later to the earlier Whitman of 1855 and 1856 and 1860. The dates just named are all dates of various editions of *Leaves of Grass;* and the latter three, the ones we appeal *to,* are those of the editions in which most (not all) of the real Whitman is to be found. This Whitman is a great and unique figure who is also the recognizable ancestor of many significant poetic developments since his creative prime—from *symboliste* poetry to imagism to more recent neoromantic and, less interestingly, "beat" writing; a chief, though by no means the only, American begetter of Wallace Stevens and Hart Crane, to some extent of Ezra Pound (as he once reluctantly confessed), and to an obscure but genuine degree of T. S. Eliot.

The importance of chronology, in Whitman's case, cannot be exaggerated. Without it, we can have no clear sense of Whitman's development as a consciousness and as a craftsman: an affair of far graver concern with Whitman than with many other poets of his stature. For, as I shall propose, the development of his consciousness and his craft, from moment to moment and year to year, is the very root of his poetic subject matter. It is what his best poems are mainly about, or what they re-enact: the thrust and withdrawal, the heightening and declining, the flowing and ebbing of his psychic and creative energy. Whitman's poetry has to do with the drama of the psyche or "self" in its mobile and complex relation *to* itself, to the world of natural and human objects, and to the creative act. What is attempted here, consequently, is a sort of chart of Whitman's development—in the belief that such a chart is not simply a required preliminary for getting at Whitman, but rather that it is the proper way to identify the poetic achievement, and to evaluate it. The poems selected have been grouped chronologically, according to the edition of *Leaves of Grass* in which they first appeared; though not always in the precise *version* in which they were first written (see Reading Suggestions: Holloway). And in a case like Whitman's, the chart of the development is not finally separable from the graph of the life, or biography; the biographical material, therefore, has likewise been distributed among the successive commentaries on the editions of Whitman's single lifelong book.

I: 1855

WHEN *Leaves of Grass* was published on July 4, 1855, Walt Whitman, now thirty-six years old, was living in Brooklyn with his parents and brothers, earning an occasional dollar by carpentering. Both his family and his carpentry served as sources of allusion and metaphor in the poetry; but neither—that is, neither his heredity nor his temporary employment—help much to explain how a relatively indolent odd-jobber and sometime journalist named Walter Whitman developed into Walt Whitman the poet. His mother, whom he salutes in "There Was a Child Went Forth" for having "conceiv'd him in her womb and birth'd him" (the birthday being the last day in May, 1819; the place, rural Long Island), was of Dutch and Quaker descent, not especially cultivated, and remembered by her son, in the same poem of 1855, as quiet and mild and clean. His father was a farmer of deteriorating fortunes, temper, and health: "manly, mean, anger'd, unjust" in his son's account; and it is a psychological curiosity that the father died within a week of the son's first public appearance, or birth, as a poet. Other members of the family were sources of that compassionate intimacy with the wretched and the depraved reflected, for example, in "Song of Myself":

The lunatic is carried at last to the asylum a confirm'd case . . . .
The prostitute draggles her shawl, her bonnet bobs on her tipsy and pimpled neck . . . .
Voices of the diseas'd and despairing and of thieves and dwarfs . . . .

Two of Whitman's brothers were diseased, one of them dying eventually in an insane asylum and the other (who was also a drunkard) married to a woman who became a prostitute. Yet another brother was a congenital idiot; and one of Whitman's sisters suffered from severe nervous melancholy. From these surroundings emerged the figure who, in the carpentering imagery of "Song of Myself" felt "sure as the most certain sure, plumb in the uprights, well entretied, braced in the beams"; a figure who not only felt like that but could write like that.

So remarkable and indeed so sudden has the appearance of Whitman the poet seemed, and out of so unlikely and artistically inhospitable a background, that literary historians have been driven to making spectacular guesses about the miraculous cause of it: an intense love affair, for instance, with a Creole lady of high degree; an intense love affair with an unidentified young man; a mystical seizure; the explosive impact of Emerson or of Carlyle or of George Sand. The literary influences can be documented, though they can scarcely be measured; with the other guesses, evidence is inadequate either to support or altogether to discount them. But perhaps the problem itself has not been quite properly shaped. Whitman's poetic emergence was remarkable enough; but it was not, in fact, particularly sudden. Nor was the career, seen retrospectively, as haphazard and aimless as one might suppose. Looked at from a sufficient distance, Whitman's life shows the same pattern of thrust and withdrawal, advance and retreat, that pulsates so regularly in the very metrics as well as the emotional attitudes of his verses; and to much the same effect. Up to about 1850, when he was thirty-one, Whitman—like the child in the autobiographical poem already quoted—was always going forth, always brushing up against the numberless persons and things of his world, and always *becoming* the elements he touched, as they became part of him. After 1850, he withdrew for a while into the privacies not only of his family but, more importantly, of his own imagination, in touch now with what he called the "Me myself"—his genius, or muse. It was this latter union between man and muse that, by 1855, produced the most extraordinary first volume of poems this country has so far seen.

One of the things Whitman did not become was a scholar, or even a college graduate. His school days, all spent in the Brooklyn to which his family moved in 1823, ended when he was eleven. Thereafter he was apprenticed as a typesetter for a Long Island newspaper; and characteristically, the boy not only worked at the job, he *became* a typesetter, and typesetting became a part of his imagination. The look of a printed page and the rhetoric of punctuation were integral elements in his poetry—the printing of which he actually set with his own hands or carefully supervised. Between 1831 and 1836, Whitman occasionally wrote articles as well as set type for the paper; and he continued to compose fugitive little pieces from time to time during the five years following, from 1836 to 1841, while he was teaching in a variety of schools in a variety of Long Island villages. Writing, too, became part of him; and Whitman became a writer—at least by intention, announcing very firmly in a newspaper article of 1840, that he "would compose a wonderful and ponderous book . . . . [treating] the nature and peculiarities of men, the diversities of their characters . . . . Yes: I *would* write a book! And who shall say that it might not be a very pretty book?"

In 1841, Whitman moved into New York City, where he was absorbed especially by what he called "the fascinating chaos" of lower Broadway, and by the life of saloons and theaters, of opera and art museums.[1] Operatic techniques and museum lore went into his later verses; but what Whitman became at this stage was that elegant stroller, or *boulevardier*, known as a dandy. This role persisted during the five years passed as reporter for a number of New York newspapers; and even after he returned to Brooklyn in 1846 and became editor of the *Eagle*, he came back by ferry to stroll Manhattan on most afternoons. But he was a dandy much caught up in public and political affairs. Among the personae he took on was that of the political activist, an ardent Free-soiler in fact, arguing the exclusion of Negro

[1] Of special importance to Whitman were the Brooklyn Art Union, established by a group of Brooklyn painters about 1850, and the Egyptian Museum at 659 Broadway, in Manhattan. Whitman wrote an article about the former for the New York *Evening Post* in February, 1851; he was personally acquainted with several of the younger painters involved, and he was particularly observant of their techniques for handling light and color. Through visits to the Egyptian Museum, meanwhile, and through considerable study under the supervision of his friend, the Museum's proprietor, Dr. Abbot, Whitman became remarkably well versed in Egyptology—allusions drawn from which are frequent and suggestive in *Leaves of Grass*.

slavery from the territories with such editorial vehemence that its owner fired him in February, 1848. Within a matter of days, however, Whitman left for what turned out to be a three-month stay in New Orleans, where he served as assistant editor to that city's *Crescent*. It was there that rumor once assigned him the affair with the Creole lady, that soul-turning initiation into love that is said to have made a poet of him. The legend is almost certainly baseless; but something did happen to Whitman nonetheless. During the long weeks of travel, passing over the vast stretches of land and along the great rivers and the lakes (all that "geography and natural life" he catalogues so lavishly in the 1855 Preface), Whitman had his first encounter with the national landscape, and became (it may be hazarded) another of the personalities announced in *Leaves of Grass:* an American.

Back in Brooklyn, Whitman accepted the post of editor-in-chief on the liberal *Freeman*, and stayed with it till he resigned in political outrage the following year. He had clearly "become" a journalist, an uncommonly able and effective one; his best poetry sprang in good part from a journalistic imagination—"I witness the corpse with its dabbled hair, I note where the pistol has fallen." At the same time, the forth-going impulse was nearly—for the moment—exhausted. After expressing his sense of both national and personal betrayal by the Fugitive Slave Law in 1850, Whitman withdrew from the political arena; withdrew from active or regular journalism, and from the life of the city. He moved back to his family and commenced a leisurely existence in which, according to his brother George, "he would lie abed late, and after getting up would write a few hours if he took the notion"—or work at "house-building" for a bit, with his father and brothers, if he took that notion. Now he became a workman; and it was in the role of working-class artisan that he presented himself both in the verses of the 1855 *Leaves of Grass* and in the portrait which appeared as substitute for the author's name in the front of the volume.

For Whitman, I am suggesting, the act of becoming a poet was not a sudden or an unpredictable one. He had always been in process of becoming a poet, and the figures he successively became, from his school days onward, were not false starts or diversions, but moments in the major process. Typesetter, reporter, dandy, stroller in the city, political activist, surveyor of the national scenery, skilled editor, representative American workman: none of these was ever fully replaced by any other, nor were all at last replaced by the poet. They were absorbed into the poet; and if they do not explain the appearance of genius (nothing can explain that), they explain to some real degree the kind of writing—observant, ambulatory, varied, politically aware, job-conscious—in which *this* particular genius expressed itself.

Signs and symptoms of the poet proper, however, can also be isolated over a good many years. The determination to write a "wonderful" book, in 1840, has already been mentioned; but that was presumably to be a philosophical disquisition in prose. In the early 1840's, the writer-in-general became a writer of fiction, and Whitman contributed a number of moralistic short stories to different New York periodicals, all signed by "Walter Whitman" and none worth remembering. Not much later than that, certainly not later than 1847, Whitman's aspiration turned towards poetry. He began to carry a pocket-size notebook about with him; in this he would jot down topics for poems as they occurred, experimental lines, and trial workings of new metrical techniques. The process was stepped up from 1850 onwards. In June, 1850, the New York *Tribune* published two free-verse poems by Whitman, the second—later called *Europe: The 72d and 73d Year of These States*, on the uprisings of 1848—to be included as the eighth item in the 1855 *Leaves of Grass*. It was probably in 1852 that he composed, though he did not publish, a fairly long poem called "Pictures" which had everything characteristic of his genuine poetry except its maritime movement. And in 1854, the repeal of the Missouri Compromise, and the arrest in Boston of a runaway slave named Anthony Burns, drew from Whitman a forty-line satiric exclamation that would comprise the ninth poem in the first edition—later called "A Boston Ballad."

These creative forays were increasingly stimulated by Whitman's reading, which was not only wide but, as evidence shows, surprisingly careful. He had reviewed works by Carlyle, George Sand, Emerson, Goethe, and others for the Brooklyn *Eagle*. He had known Greek and Roman literature, in translation, for years. "I have wonder'd since," he remarked in *A Backward Glance* (1888), "why I was not overwhelm'd by these mighty masters. Likely because I read them . . . . in the full presence of Nature, under the sun . . . . [with] the sea rolling in." (The comment suggests much of the quality of Whitman's poetry, wherein a natural atmosphere and sea-rhythms help provide fresh versions of ancient and traditional archetypes.) It should be stressed that Whitman's literary education at this time, though it was by no means skimpy, was fairly conventional. It included the major English poets, Shakespeare and Milton especially; but it did not include Oriental writing nor the literature of the mystical tradition nor that of German idealism —except as those sources reached him faintly through his occasional readings in the essays of Emerson. This is probably to be reckoned fortunate: Whitman's mystical instinct, during his best creative years, was held effectively in check by a passion for the concrete, a commitment to the actual; and discussion of his "mysticism" is well advised to follow his example. Whitman became acquainted, too, with such American writers as Longfellow and Bryant, both of whom he came later to know personally. In addition, he took to making extensive notes and summaries of a long list of periodical essays, mostly dealing with art and artists.

"Art and Artists," in fact, was the title of an essay which Whitman himself read to the Brooklyn Art Union in 1851. And it was here that he first developed his large notion of the artist as hero—of the artist, indeed, as savior or redeemer of the community to which he offers his whole being as champion (sacrificial, if necessary) of freedom and humanity and spiritual health. "Read well the death of Socrates," he said portentously, "and of greater than Socrates." The image of the modern poet as godlike —even Christlike ("greater than Socrates")— was to run through and beneath Whitman's poetry from "Song of Myself" to "Passage to India"; and often, as here, it drew added intensity from Whitman's disillusion with other possible sources for that miraculous national transformation scene he seems to have waited for during most of his life. It was an extravagant notion; but it was one that anticipated several not much less extravagant images, in the twentieth century, of the artist as hero. It was this image, anyhow, that Whitman sought to bring into play in the whole body of the 1855 *Leaves of Grass* and particularly in "Song of Myself."

The first edition contained a long Preface introducing the poet-hero who is then imaginatively created in the poems that follow. There were twelve of the latter, unnumbered and untitled and of varying length, with unconventional but effective typography—for example:

The atmosphere is not a perfume . . . . it has no
 taste of the distillation . . . . it is odorless,
It is for my mouth forever. . . . I am in love with
 it.

The first and by far the longest entry was, of course, the poem that in 1881 was labeled "Song of Myself." It is in part genuine though highly original autobiography; in part, it is a form of wish projection. We may think of it, among many other things, as a free-flowing recapitulation of the two processes I have been describing—the process by which a man of many roles becomes a poet, and the process by which the poet becomes a sort of god. There are as many significant aspects to "Song of Myself" as there are critical discussions and analyses of it; if the comment here is mainly limited to the enlargement of its central figure—that is to the question of its structure—it is because the structure tends to confirm one's sense of Whitman's characteristic movement both in life and in poetry. For if, again, this strange, sometimes baffling, stream-of-consciousness poem does have a discernible structure, an "action" with a beginning, middle, and end, it is almost certainly one that involves the two events or processes just named.

More than one astute reader, while acknowledging a typical pulse or rhythm in the poem, a tidal ebb and flow, has nonetheless denied to it any sustained and completed design. But it may be ventured, perhaps, that "Song of Myself" has not so much a single structure as a number of provisional structures—partly because Whitman, like Melville, believed in a deliberate absence of finish in a work of art; more importantly because of what we may call Whitman's democratic aesthetic. Just as the political activist was absorbed into the poet at some time after 1850, so, and at the same moment, a practical concern with the workings of a democratic society was carried over into the aesthetic realm and applied to the workings of poetry, to the writing and the reading of it. The shape of "Song of Myself" depended, in Whitman's view, on the creative participation of each reader—"I round and finish little," he remarked in A *Backward Glance*, "the reader will always have his or her part to do, just as much as I have had mine." In a real sense, the poem was intended to have as many structures as there were readers; and the reason was this, that Whitman aimed not simply to create a poet and then a god, but to assist at the creation of the poetic and godlike in every reader.

Like Emerson, Whitman was here giving a democratic twist to the European Romantic notion of the poet as mankind's loftiest figure. By both Emerson and Whitman that notion got democratized—the poet's superiority, for them, lay exactly in his representativeness. "The poet is representative," Emerson had said, in his essay "The Poet." "He stands among partial men for the complete man, and apprises us not of his wealth, but of the common wealth." This is what Whitman meant when he spoke of "the great poet" as "the equable man"; and it is what he asserted in the opening lines of "Song of Myself":

> I celebrate myself and sing myself
> And what I assume you shall assume.

As one or two commentators—notably Roy Harvey Pearce—have rightly suggested, "Song of Myself" is the first recognizable American epic; but if so, it is an epic of this peculiar and modern sort. It does not celebrate a hero and an action of ancient days; it creates (and its action *is* creative) a hero of future days—trusting thereby to summon the heroism implicit in each individual.

Considered in these terms, as the epic consequence of a democratic aesthetic, "Song of Myself" shows a variable number of structural parts. This reader discovers but does not insist upon the following. The invocation leads, in Sections 1 and 2, into a transition from the artificial to the natural—from perfume in houses to the atmosphere of the woods; uncontaminated nature is the scene of the drama. Next comes the recollection of the union—mystical in kind, sexual in idiom—between the two dimensions of the poet's being: the limited, conditioned Whitman and the "Me, myself," his creative genius, what Emerson might have called the Over-Soul. This was the union that was consummated somehow and sometime in the early 1850's, and out of which there issued the poem in which the union was itself re-enacted.

There follows a long portion, continuing at least through Section 17, where—as a result of union—the *man* becomes a *poet*, and by the very act of creation. What is created is a world, an abundant world of persons and places and things—all sprung into existence by the action of seeing and naming:

> The little one sleeps in its cradle,
> I lift the gauze and look a long time . . . .
> The suicide sprawls on the bloody floor of the bedroom,
> I witness the corpse with its dabbled hair . . . .
> Where are you off to, lady? for I see you . . . .

The democratic aesthetic is most palpably at work here. What we take at first to be sheer disorder, what some early reviewers regarded as simple slovenliness and lack of form, is in fact something rather different. It is the representation of moral and spiritual and aesthetic equality; of a world carefully devoid of rank or hierarchy. In "Song of Myself," this principle of moral equivalence is not so much stated as "suggested" (one of Whitman's favorite words), and suggested by "indirection" (another favorite word)—by the artfully casual juxtaposition of normally unrelated and unrelatable elements, a controlled flow of associations. Thus:

> The prostitute draggles her shawl, her bonnet bobs on her tipsy and pimpled neck . . . .
> The President holding a cabinet council is surrounded by the great Secretaries,
> On the piazza walk three matrons stately and friendly with twined arms,
> The crew of the fish-smack pack repeated layers of halibut in the hold,
> The Missourian crosses the plains toting his wares and his cattle

and so on. In the 1855 Preface, Whitman was willing to make the case explicit: "Each precise object or condition or combination or process exhibits a beauty." And he there illustrated the idea in a succession of still more surprising incongruities: "the multiplication table . . . . old age . . . . the carpenter's trade . . . . the grand-opera."

When, therefore, towards the end of this phase of the poem, the speaker begins to claim for himself the gradually achieved role of poet, it is as the poet of every mode of equality that he particularly wishes to be acknowledged. The announcement runs through Section 25:

I play not marches for accepted victors only, I play
marches for conquer'd and slain persons . . .
I am the poet of the Body, and I am the poet of the Soul . . . .
I am the poet of the woman the same as the man . . . .
I am not the poet of goodness only, I do not decline to be the poet of wickedness also . . . .

The *poet* now makes ready for the second great adventure, the long journey, as we may say, towards *godhood.* By way of preparation, he undergoes a second ecstatic experience in Sections 26 and following: an experience of an almost overpoweringly sensuous kind, with the sense of touch so keen as to endanger his health or his sanity: "You villain touch! . . . . you are too much for me." The poet survives, and in Section 33 he is "afoot with [his] vision." In the visionary flight across the universe that is then recounted, the poet enlarges into a divine being by *becoming* each and every element within the totality that he experiences; while the universe in turn is drawn together into a single and harmonious whole since each element in it is invested in common with a portion of the poet's emergent divinity. It is no longer the prostitute who draggles her shawl, the President who holds a cabinet council, the Missourian who crosses the plain: it is "I" who does all that:

I anchor my ship for a little while only . . . .
I go hunting polar furs and the seal . . . .
I am the man, I suffer'd, I was there . . . .
I am the hounded slave, I wince at the bite of dogs . . . .

And the "I" is itself no longer the individual man-poet; it is the very force or *élan vital* of all humanity.

The journey lasts through Section 33; and in its later moments, as it will be noticed, the traveler associates especially with the defeated, the wretched, the wicked, the slaughtered. Whitman's poetic pores were oddly open, as were Melville's, to the grand or archetypal patterns common to the human imagination—so psychologists like Carl Jung tell us—in all times and places; and the journey of "Song of Myself" requires, at this point, the familiar descent into darkness and hell—until (Section 33) "corpses rise, gashes heal, fastenings roll from me," and an enormous resurrection is accomplished. But what gets reborn, what "troop[s] forth" from the grave is not the poet simply; it is the poet "replenish'd with supreme power," the poet become a divine figure. Just as, by the poetic act of creating a world, the man had been previously grown into a poet; so now, by experiencing and so to speak melting into the world's totality to its furthest width and darkest depth, the poet expands into a divinity. He has approximated at last that "greater than Socrates" invoked by Whitman in 1851; he has become that saving force which Whitman had proposed was to be the true role of the American poet. It is the divinity who speaks through Sections 39 to 51, proclaiming his divine inheritance ("Taking to myself the exact dimensions of Jehovah," etc.), performing as healer and comforter ("Let the physician and the priest go home"), exhorting every man to his supreme and unique effort. For it is a divinity who insists at every turn that he speaks but for the divine potential of all men. And, having done so, in Section 52 he departs.

Wallace Stevens, the most sophisticated among Whitman's direct poetic descendants, once specified his ancestor's recurrent and dual subject matter in the course of a resonant salute to him: "Walt Whitman walking along a ruddy shore / . . . . singing and chanting the things that are part of him / The worlds that were and will be, death and day"—from "Like Decorations in a Nigger Cemetery." "Death and day," with its corollary "life and night," is as apt a phrase as one can think of for the extremes between which Whitman's poetry habitually alternates. "Song of Myself" is Whitman's masterpiece, and perhaps America's, in the poetry of "day"—"the song of me rising from bed and meeting the sun"; while "To Think of Time"—or "Burial Poem," as Whitman once called it—belongs initially to the poetry of "death," and "The Sleepers" to the poetry of "night." But although both the latter, in their very different ways, explore in depth the dark undergrounds of experience, both return—as "Song of Myself" does—with the conviction of a sort of absolute life. "I swear I think there is nothing but immortality": so ends the meditation in "To Think of Time." And such is the determining sense everywhere in the 1855 edition; we shall shortly have occasion to contrast it with the sense of things in the edition of 1860. It may be helpful, meanwhile, to glance at the 1855 poem "There Was a Child Went Forth," to see how Whitman's characteristic psychological movement was reflected in his poetic technique—how the shifting play of his consciousness was reflected in the shifting play of his craft.

"There Was a Child Went Forth" is Whitman's most unequivocal account of the thrust towards being. It is a poem about growth, about burgeoning and sprouting; and it grows itself, quite literally, in size and thickness. The difference in the sheer physical or typographical look of the first and last stanzas is an immediate clue to the poem's thematic development. Yet what the poet enacts, on the technical side, is not an altogether uninterrupted increase in substance and vitality. The process is rather one of alternation, of enlarging and retracting, of stretching and shrinking—in which, however, the impulse towards growth is *always* dominant. The quantitatively shrunken fourth stanza, for example, is flanked by the longer eight-line stanza that precedes it, and the longest or eighteen-line stanza that follows it and completes the poem's swelling motion: giving us a process in fact of stretching-shrinking-stretching. The same process is present more artfully still within the first stanza, with its rhythmic shift from short line to longer line to still longer and back to shorter once again; but where the line that contains the quantitative shrink is nonetheless a line accentuated by the word "stretching"—"Or for many years or stretching cycles of years." The psychic stretching is thus quietly affirmed at the instant of technical shrinking; and it is the stretching impulse that triumphs and defines the poem.

The same effect is accomplished metrically. "There Was a Child Went Forth" is what is now called free verse; and no doubt the word "free" in this context would have had, had Whitman known the whole term, a political aura, and become a part of his democratic aesthetic. Whitman was the first American poet to break free from the convention of iambic pentameter as the principal and most decorous meter for poetry in English; in so doing he added to the declaration of literary independence—from England, chiefly—that had been triumphantly proclaimed for his generation in Emerson's "The American Scholar" and was the predictable artistic consequence of the political fact. Whitman's was a major gesture of technical liberation, for which every American poet after him has reason to be grateful; every such poet, as William Carlos Williams (a manifest heir of Whitman) has said, must show cause why iambic pentameter is proper for him. But it was not an act of purely negative liberation; it was emancipation with a purpose. It freed Whitman to attempt a closer approximation of metrics and the kind of experience he naturally aimed to express; and it made possible an eventual and occasional return to older and more orderly metrics—to possess them, to use them freshly, to turn them to the poet's established poetic intentions. The long uneven alternations I have been describing could hardly have been conveyed by a recurring five-stress line, or iambic pentameter, or by a fixed and even alternation, let us say, of five-stress line and four-stress line. Whitman instinctively depended not on the regular alternating current of the iambic, but on an irregular alternation of *rising* and of *falling* rhythms—something that corresponded happily with the rise and fall of the felt life, with the flowing and ebbing: and the rising rhythm, once again, is always in command.

"There wăs ă child wĕnt forth."

And in the poem's conclusion—when a world and a child have been brought fully to interdependent life—the rhythm settles back in a line that neither rises nor falls; a line that rests in a sort of permanent stillness; a subdued iambic of almost perfectly even stress—a convention repossessed in the last long slow series of monosyllables broken only and rightly by the key words "became," "always," and "every."

It is not possible to invoke the imagery of stretching and shrinking without being reminded of sexual analogies, and thereby of the sexual element so prevalent in Whitman's poetry. That element was notably, even blatantly more central to the 1856 edition—it was about several poems in this edition that Thoreau, otherwise much taken with Whitman, said that "It is as if the beasts spoke"—and it operated most tellingly in 1860. Still, it was evident enough in 1855 to startle sensibilities. "Song of Myself" exhibits a degree of sexual bravado mixed with a trace of sexual nostalgia. But the sexual aspect is more apparent in the poem that inhabits the world where Freud and Jung would look for signs of the sexual impulse—the world of dreams. "The Sleepers"—or "Sleep-Chasings" according to its 1860 title—is not only a poem of night and death—"I wander all night in my visions . . . . the white features of corpses"—it is a poem of profound psychic disturbance, as the speaker makes clear at once in a superb line that gained force from the 1855 typography: "Wandering and confused . . . . lost to myself . . . . ill-assorted . . . . contradictory." A portion of sexual shame contributes to the uncertainty and deepens the sense of terror—the terror, as Richard Chase has usefully hazarded, of the ego, or conscious self, confronting the id, or the unconscious, and being threatened by extinction. But in the manner typical of the first *Leaves of Grass*, the poem moves to the discovery of solace amidst fear, of pattern amidst the random. Descending through the planes of night, "The Sleepers" encounters in its own heart of darkness sources of maternal comfort and spiritual revelation. Guilt is transcended and harmony restored. The adjectives of the opening stanza—"wandering, confused, lost to myself, ill-assorted, contradictory"—are matched and overcome by the adjectives of the poem's close: "sane, relieved, resumed, free, supple, awake." There has occurred what Jung would call the reintegration of the personality; the ill-assorted psyche has become whole again after passing through what Jung would also call the "night journey." In "The Sleepers," Whitman displayed once more his remarkable talent for arriving by intuition at the great archetypes. And the night journey concludes in that confident recovery of day, that perfect reconciliation with night, that is the distinctive mark of the edition of 1855.

II: 1856

THE SECOND edition of *Leaves of Grass* appeared in June, 1856, less than a year after the first. There had been several more *printings* of the latter; and indeed, during the intervening months Whitman was mainly occupied with the new printings and with reading—and writing—reviews of his work. He still lived with his family in Brooklyn, but he had virtually given up any practical employment. He had no "business," as his mother told a visitor from Concord (Bronson Alcott)—"no business but going out and coming in to eat, drink, write and sleep." The same visitor quoted Whitman himself as saying that he only "lived to make pomes." Over the months he had made twenty new ones, and included them all in the considerably expanded second edition.

Conventional norms of printing crept back a little into this edition. All the poems, old and new, were now numbered and given titles, the new poems always including the word "poem"—a word that obviously had a charismatic power for Whitman at the time. Among the poems added were: "Poem of Wonder at the Resurrection of Wheat"—to be known more tamely as "This Compost"; "Bunch Poem"—later "Spontaneous Me"; and "Sundown Poem"—later "Crossing Brooklyn Ferry." The physical appearance of the poems had also become a trifle more conventional, as the eccentric but effective use of multiple dots was abandoned in favor of semicolons and commas. The poetry lost thereby its vivid impression of sistole and diastole, of speech and silence, of utterance and pause, always so close to Whitman's psychic and artistic intention: for example, "I am the man . . . . I suffered . . . . I was there" gets crowded together by punctuation and contraction into "I am the man, I suffer'd, I was there." But the earlier mode of punctuation might well have become exceedingly tiresome; and Whitman, in any event, had arrived at that necessary combination of originality and convention by which the most vigorous of talents always perpetuates itself.

For the rest, the new poems dilate upon the determining theme and emotion of the first edition. There is still the awareness of evil, both general and personal: "I am he who knew what it was to be evil / . . . . Had guile, anger, lust, hot wishes I dared not speak / . . . . the wolf, the snake, the hog, not wanting in me" (an unmistakable and highly suggestive borrowing from *King Lear*, III.iv.87 ff.—Whitman drew more on literary sources than he or his critics have normally admitted). There is even a fleeting doubt of his own abilities: "The best I had done seem'd to me blank and suspicious," a note that would become primary in the 1860 edition. But by and large, the compelling emotion is one of unimpeded creative fertility, of irresistible forward-thrusting energy. It registers the enormous excitement of the discovered vocation and of its miracle-making nature: Whitman's response to the experience of having published his first volume and to the headiest of the reviews of the book. Contrary to some reports, including Whitman's forgetful old-age account, the first edition had a reasonably good sale; and among the many reviews in America and England, some were admiring, some were acutely perceptive, and one or two were downright reverential and spoke of Whitman as almost that "greater than Socrates" he had been hoping to become. Much the most stirring for Whitman, of course, was the famous letter from Emerson, which found *Leaves of Grass* "the most extraordinary piece of wit and wisdom that America has yet contributed," with "incomparable things said incomparably well in it." One sentence from this letter—and without Emerson's permission—adorned the back cover of the 1856 edition: "I greet you at the beginning of a great career."

The tone of the new poems, consequently, was one of achieved and boundless fertility. This is the poetry of day and the poetry of unending flow. The feeling, indeed, is so large and intense as to produce a sense of profound awe: a sense, almost, of terror. That sense arises from Whitman's convinced and total association of his own fecundity ("Spontaneous Me") with the fecundity of nature-at-large ("This Compost"), an association itself enough to intoxicate one. It arises, too, from Whitman's startling view that the creative accomplishment —of the man-poet and of nature—issues from something superficially ugly or shameful or diseased or dead. "Spontaneous Me" mingles two kinds of poems: those that result from the artistic act and those that are involved with the physical act. The act of love, the expression of sexual energy, however, whether metaphorical or physical, whether heterosexual or homosexual, carries with it a sweeping sensation of shame ("the young man all color'd, red, ashamed, angry"). But the experience fulfills itself in triumph and pride, just as Whitman had deliberately expanded the erotic dimension of the new volume in triumph and pride; it leads to a great "oath of procreation," procreation in every sort; it ends in a full consciousness of wholesome abundance. In much the same way, nature, in "This Compost," reproduces life each spring out of the rotting earth. "Every spear of grass rises out of what was once a catching disease." The conduct of nature—creating life out of death, health out of sickness, beauty out of foulness, "sweet things out of such corruption" —provided Whitman with an example, an analogy to his own creative experience, so immense as to terrify him.

But the terror, needless to say, did not disempower but electrified him. The most far-ranging and beautiful of the new poems, "Crossing Brooklyn Ferry," shows Whitman writing under the full force of his assurance—of his assured identification with the *élan vital* of all things. The interplay of the self and the large world it thrusts forward into is on a scale not unlike that of "Song of Myself"; the flow of the consciousness merges with the flow of reality. Every item encountered is a "dumb beautiful minister" to Whitman's responsive spirit; all the items in the universe are "glories strung like beads on my smallest sights and hearings." The complex of natural and human and created objects now forms a sort of glowing totality that is always in movement, always frolicking on. "Crossing Brooklyn Ferry" presents a vision of an entirety moving forward: a vision that is mystical in its sense of oneness but that is rendered in the most palpable and concrete language—the actual picture of the harbor is astonishingly alive and visible. And the poem goes beyond its jubilant cry of the soul—"Flow on river!"—to reach a peace that really does pass any normal understanding. Whitman was to write poetry no less consummate; but he was never again to attain so final a peak of creative and visionary intoxication.

III: 1860

WHITMAN, as we have heard his mother saying, was always "going out and coming in." She meant quite literally that her son would go out of the house in the morning, often to travel the ferry to Manhattan and to absorb the spectacle of life, and would come back into the household to eat and sleep, perhaps to write. But she unwittingly gave a nice maternal formula to the larger, recurring pattern in Whitman's career—the foray into the world and the retreat back into himself and into a creative communion with his genius. The poetry he came in to write—though the 1856 edition just examined—reflected that pattern in content and rhythm, and in a way to celebrate the commanding power of the outward and forward movement. The early poetry bore witness as well, to be sure, of the darker mode of withdrawal, the descent into the abysses of doubt, self-distrust, and the death-consciousness; but it was invariably overcome in a burst of visionary renewal. The poetry of 1855 and 1856 is the poetry of day, of flood tide.

The 1860 *Leaves of Grass*, however, gives voice to genuine desolation. In it, betimes, the self appears as shrunken, indeed as fragmented; the psyche as dying; the creative vigor as dissipated. The most striking of the new poems belong to the poetry not of day but of death. A suggestive and immediate verbal sign of the new atmosphere may be found in the difference of title between so characteristic a poem of 1855 as "There Was a Child *Went Forth*" and perhaps the key 1860 poem, "As I *Ebb'd* with the Ocean of Life." Yet the case must be put delicately and by appeal to paradox. For in a sense, the new death-poetry represents in fact Whitman's most remarkable triumph over his strongest feelings of personal and artistic defeat. There has been a scholarly debate over the precise degree of melancholy in the 1860 edition, one scholar emphasizing the note of dejection and another the occasional note of cheerfulness; but that debate is really beside the point. What we have is poetry that expresses the sense of loss so sharply and vividly that substantive loss is converted into artistic gain.

During the almost four years since June, 1856, Whitman had once again gone out and come back in; but this time the withdrawal was compelled by suffering and self-distrust. Whitman's foray into the open world, beginning in the fall of 1856, took the form, first, of a brief new interest in the political scene; and second, of a return to journalism, as editor-in-chief of the Brooklyn *Daily Times* from May, 1857 until June, 1859. In the morning, he busied himself writing editorials and articles for the newspaper; in the afternoon, he traveled into New York, to saunter along lower Broadway and to sit watchful and silent near or amidst the literati who gathered in Pfaff's popular Swiss restaurant in the same neighborhood. In the evening, he continued to write—prolifically: seventy poems, more or less, in the first year after the 1856 edition and probably a few more in the months immediately following. Then there occurred a hiatus: a blank in our knowledge of Whitman's life, and apparently a blank in his creative activity. We cannot say just when the hiatus began—sometime in 1858, one judges. It ended, anyhow, at some time before the publication in the December, 1859 issue of the New York *Saturday Press* of a poem called "A Child's Reminiscence"—its familiar title being "Out of the Cradle Endlessly Rocking."

On the political side, Whitman's disenchantment was even swifter than usual. The choices offered the American public in the election of 1856—Buchanan, Frémont, and Fillmore—seemed to him false, debased, and meaningless; and he called—in an unpublished pamphlet—for a president who might play the part of "Redeemer." His disappointment with the actual, in short, led as before to an appeal for some "greater than Socrates" to arise in America; and, also as before, Whitman soon turned from the political figure to the *poet*, in fact to himself, to perform the sacred function, asserting in his journal that *Leaves of Grass* was to be "the New Bible." (Not until 1866 would the two aspirations fuse in a poem—"When Lilacs Last in the Dooryard Bloom'd"—that found a new idiom of almost Biblical sonority to celebrate death in the person of a Redeemer President, Abraham Lincoln.) Meanwhile, however, Whitman's private and inner life was causing him far more grief and dismay than the public life he had been observing.

A chief cause for Whitman's season of despair, according to most Whitman biographers, was a homosexual love affair during the silent months: an affair that undoubtedly took place, that was the source at once of profound joy and profound guilt, and that, when it ended, left Whitman with a desolating sense of loss. Poems like "A Hand-Mirror" and "Hours Continuing Long, Sore and Heavy-Hearted" testify with painful clarity both to the guilt and to the subsequent misery of loneliness. At the same time, poems like "As I Ebb'd with the Ocean of Life" and "So Long!" strike a different and perhaps deeper note of loss: a note, that is, of poetic decline, of the loss not so much of a human loved one but of creative energy—accompanied by a loss of confidence in everything that energy had previously brought into being. There had been a hint of this in "Crossing Brooklyn Ferry" in 1856—"The best I had done seem'd to me blank and suspicious"—but there self-doubt had been washed away in a flood of assurance. Now it had become central and almost resistant to hope. It may be that the fear of artistic sterility was caused by the moral guilt; but it seems no less likely that the artistic apprehension was itself at the root of the despair variously echoed in 1860. If so, the apprehension was probably due to a certain climacteric in Whitman's psychic career—what is called *la crise de quarantaine*, the psychological crisis some men pass through when they reach the age of forty. Whitman was forty in May, 1859; and it was in the month after his birthday that he wrote two aggressive and, one cannot but feel, disturbed articles for the Brooklyn *Daily Times*—on prostitution and the right to unmarried sexual love—that resulted in his dismissal from the paper. Characteristically dismissed, Whitman characteristically withdrew. But no doubt the safest guess is that it was a conjunction of these factors—*la quarantaine*, the temporary but fearful exhaustion of talent after so long a period of fertility, the unhappy love affair—that begot the new poems which, in the 1860 edition, gave "death and night" their prominence.

The edition of 1860 contained 154 poems: which is to say that 122 had been composed since 1856, and of these, as has been said, seventy by the summer of 1857. Most of the other fifty, it can be hazarded, were written late in 1859 and in the first six months of 1860. It can also be hazarded that among those latter fifty poems were nearly all the best of the new ones—those grouped under the title "Calamus," the name Whitman gave to his poetry of masculine love (including, from our selection, "Scented Herbage," "Hours Continuing," "Whoever You Are," "City of Orgies," "A Glimpse," and "I Saw in Louisiana"); as well as "Out of the Cradle," "As I Ebb'd" (published in the April, 1860, issue of the *Atlantic Monthly* as "Bardic Symbols"), and "So Long!"

"A Hand-Mirror" records a feeling of self-loathing almost unequaled in English or American poetry. And it is representative of the entire volume in its emphatic reversal of an earlier work and an earlier course of feeling. In "This Compost," in 1856, Whitman was seized with a wonder verging on terror at the capacity of nature and of man to produce the beautiful out of the foul or shameful; here, in 1860, he is smitten with the dreadful conviction of having, in his own being, produced the foul and the shameful out of the potentially beautiful. "Hours Continuing Long, Sore and Heavy-Hearted" is a statement of pain so severe, so unmitigated, that Whitman deleted the poem from all subsequent editions of *Leaves of Grass*. These poems of pain are uncommonly painful to read; and yet, in the other major new poems of 1860, we find Whitman executing what might be called the grand Romantic strategy—the strategy of converting private devastation into artistic achievement; of composing poetry of high distinction out of a feeling of personal, spiritual, and almost metaphysical extinction. Keats's "Ode on a Grecian Urn" offers an example of the same, at one chronological extreme; as, at another, does Hart Crane's "The Broken Tower."

That strategy is, indeed, what the 1860 edition may be said to be about; for more than the other versions of *Leaves of Grass*, that of 1860 has a sort of plot buried in it. The plot—in a very reduced summary—consists in the discovery that "death" is the source and beginning of "poetry"; with "death" here understood to involve several kinds and sensations of loss, of suffering, of disempowering guilt, of psychic fragmentation; and "poetry" as the awakening of the power to catch and to order reality in language. What had so fundamentally changed since 1855 and 1856 was Whitman's concept of reality. In 1855, as we have seen, the thought of death led to a flat denial of it: "I swear I think there is nothing but immortality." But in "Scented Herbage" of 1860 he arrives at an opposite conclusion: "For now," as he says, "it is convey'd to me that you [death] are . . . . the real reality." If Whitman's poetic faculty had formerly been quickened by his sense of the absolute life, it now finds its inspiration in the adventure of death. In "So Long!" Whitman confesses to the death of his talent: "It appears to me that I am dying . . . . My songs cease, I abandon them." Yet in "Scented Herbage" poetry is identified as the very herbage and flower of death, as Baudelaire had a few years earlier identified poetry as the flower of evil; his new poems, for Whitman, are "growing up above me above death." By 1860 Whitman had reached the perception of Wallace Stevens—in "Sunday Morning" (1923)—that "death is the mother of beauty."

Stevens' phrase might serve as motto for the 1860 edition; as it might also serve for another of the several titles for the poem that was first called "A Child's Reminiscence," then "A Word Out of the Sea," and finally (in 1871) "Out of the Cradle Endlessly Rocking." Whatever else occurs in this in every sense brilliant poem, there unmistakably occurs the discovery of poetic power, the magical power of the word, through the experience—here presented as vicarious—of the departure and loss, perhaps the death, of the loved one. It is one of the most handsomely *made* of Whitman's poems; the craft is relaxed, firm, and sure. Only an artist in virtuoso control of his technical resources would attempt a poem with such effortless alternation of narrative (or recitatif) and impassioned aria, such dazzling metrical shifts, such hypnotic exactitude of language, not to mention a narrative "point of view" of almost Jamesian complexity: the man of forty recalling the child of, say, twelve observing the calamitous love affair of two other beings, and the same man of forty projecting, one assumes, his own recent and adult bereavement into the experience of an empathic child. Whitman, by 1860, was very impressively the poet in that word's original meaning of "maker," in addition to being still the poet as inspired singer; and "Out of the Cradle Endlessly Rocking"—for all its supple play of shadows and glancing light—will bear the utmost weight of analysis. But it has perhaps been sufficiently probed elsewhere (see Reading Suggestions), and this Introduction will instead take a longer look at "As I Ebb'd with the Ocean of Life."

We will not be far wrong, and in any case it will illuminate the pattern of Whitman's career, if we take this poem as an almost systematic inversion of the 1855 poem "There Was a Child Went Forth," as well as an inversion of a key moment—Sections 4 and 5—in the 1855 "Song of Myself." As against that younger Whitman of morning and of spring, of the early lilacs and the red morning-glories, here is the Whitman of the decline of the day and of the year—a poet now found "musing late in the autumn day" (the phrase should be read slowly, as though the chief words were, in the older fashion, divided by dots). All the sprouts and blossoms and fruit of "There Was a Child Went Forth" are here replaced, in the poetically stunning second stanza by:

> Chaff, straw, splinters of wood, weeds, and the sea-gluten,
> Scum, scales from shining rocks, leaves of salt-lettuce, left by the tide;

to which are added, later, "A few sands and dead leaves," "a trail of drift and debris," and finally:

> loose windrows, little corpses,
> Froth snowy white, and bubbles,
> (See from my dead lips the ooze exuding at last . . . .)

The poem's rhythm, instead of pulsating outwards in constantly larger spirals (though it seems to try to do that occasionally), tends to fall back on itself, to fall away, almost to disintegrate—no poem of Whitman's shows a more cunning fusion of technique and content. It is here, quite properly, the falling rather than the rising rhythm that catches the ear. As against

> "There was a child went forth,"

we now hear:

> "Where the fierce old mother endlessly cries
> for her castaways"

—a dying fall that conveys the shrinking away, the psychological slide towards death, the slope into oblivion that the poem is otherwise concerned with.

The major turn in the action appears in the grammatical shift from the past tense of Section 1 ("As I ebb'd," etc.) to the present tense of Section 2 ("As I wend," and so on). It is a shift from the known to the unknown, a shift indeed not so much from one moment of time to another as from the temporal to the timeless, and a shift not so much accomplished as desired. For what produces in the poet his feeling of near-death is just his conviction that neither he nor his poetry has ever known or ever touched upon the true and timeless realm of reality. The essential reality from which he now feels he has forever been cut off is rendered as "the real Me." To get the full force of the despondent confession of failure, one should place the lines about "the real Me" next to those Sections 4 and 5 in "Song of Myself" where Whitman had exultantly recalled the exact opposite. There he had celebrated a perfect union between the actual Me and the real Me: between the here-and-now Whitman and that timeless being, that Over-Soul or genius that he addressed as the Me myself. *That*, I suggest, was Whitman's real love affair; that was the union that was consummated in 1855 and that ended—so Whitman temporarily felt—in disunion three or fours years later; "the real Me" was the loved one that departed. And now, divorced and disjoined from the real Me, the actual Me threatens to come apart, to collapse into a trail of drift and debris, with ooze exuding from dead lips. (So, by analogy, a Puritan might have felt when cut off, through sin, from the God that created him.)

Still, as Richard Chase has insisted, this poem is saved from any suggestion of whimpering self-pity by the astonishing and courageous tone of self-mockery—in the image of the real Me ridiculing the collapsing Me:

> . . . . before all my arrogant poems the real Me stands yet untouch'd, untold, altogether unreach'd,
> Withdrawn far, mocking me with mock-congratulatory signs and bows,
> With peals of distant ironical laughter at every word I have written,
> Pointing in silence to these songs, and then to the sand beneath.

It is an image of immeasurable effect. And it is, so to speak, a triumph over its own content. Anyone who could construct an image of the higher power—the one he aspires toward—standing far off and mocking him with little satiric bows and gestures, comparing and consigning his verses to the sandy debris under his feet: such a person has already conquered his sense of sterility, mastered his fear of spiritual and artistic death, rediscovered his genius, and returned to the fullest poetic authority. Within the poem, Whitman identifies the land as his father and the fierce old sea as his mother; he sees himself as alienated no less from them than from the real Me, and he prays to both symbolic parents for a rejuvenation of his poetic force, a resumption of "the secret of the murmuring I love." But the prayer is already answered in the very language in which it is uttered; Whitman never murmured more beautifully; and this is why, at the depth of his ebbing, Whitman can say, parenthetically, that the flow will return.

IV: 1867

IF WHITMAN, by the spring of 1860, had not been "rescued" by his own internal capacity for resurgence, he would, more than likely, have been rescued anyhow by the enormous public event that began the following April with the outbreak of a national civil war. During the war years, Whitman "went forth" more strenuously than in any other period of his life, and he immersed himself more thoroughly in the activities and sufferings of his fellows. The immediate poetic fruit of the experience was a small, separately published volume of fifty-three new poems, in 1865, called *Drum-Taps,* with a *Sequal to Drum-Taps*—containing "When Lilacs Last in the Dooryard Bloom'd"—tacked on to the original in 1866. Both titles were added as an Appendix to the fourth edition of *Leaves of Grass* in 1867, which otherwise contained only a handful of new poems. Several of Whitman's war poems have a certain lyric strength, either of compassion or of sheer imagistic precision; and the meditation occasioned by the death of Lincoln is among his finest artistic achievements. Nonetheless—and however remarkable and admirable his human performance was during the war—it was in this same period that Whitman the poet began to yield to Whitman the prophet, and what had been most compelling in his poetry to give way to the misrepresentation and concealment that disfigured *Leaves of Grass* over the decades to follow.

Until the last days of 1862, Whitman remained in Brooklyn, formally unemployed, making what he could out of earnings from *Leaves of Grass* and—once the fighting had started—following the course of the war with the liveliest concern. He was initially very much on the side of the North, which he regarded as the side of freedom, justice, and human dignity. But as time went on, he came to be increasingly on the side of the nation as a whole, more anxious to heal wounds than to inflict them—and this, of course, is what he literally turned to doing in 1863. In December of the previous year, he learned that his younger brother Jeff had been wounded. Whitman journeyed south at once, found his brother recuperating satisfactorily near Falmouth, Virginia, and stayed for eight memorable days among the forward troops in the battle area. It was only eight days, but the spectacle of horror and gallantry of which he was the closest eye-witness had an enduring, almost a conversionary effect upon him. He came back north only as far as Washington; and from that moment until 1867, he spent every free moment in the military hospitals, ministering to the needs of the wounded. He became, in fact, a "wound-dresser," though a dresser primarily of spiritual wounds, bearing gifts, writing letters, comforting, sustaining, exhorting; he became, indeed the physician-priest with whom, in "Song of Myself," he had associated the figure of the poet.

He made a living in Washington through a series of governmental jobs: as assistant to the deputy paymaster for a while; as clerk in the Indian Bureau—a position from which he was summarily dismissed when the bureau chief read *Leaves of Grass* and pronounced it unpardonably obscene; finally in the office of the Department of Interior. Here he stayed, relatively prosperous and content, until he suffered a partly paralysing stroke in 1873. It was in the same year that, traveling north, ill and exhausted, he settled almost by accident in Camden, New Jersey, where he lived until his death in 1892.

In short, when Whitman went forth this time, or was drawn forth, into the American world of war, he was drawn not merely into New York City but into the center of the country's national life: to the actual battlefields, to the seat of the nation's political power, to the offices of government, to the hospitals, and into the presence of the men who carried on their bodies the burden of the nation's tragedy. It is not surprising that the outer and public life of the country absorbed most of his energy; it is only regrettable that, as a result, and in the course of time, the solitary singer disappeared into the public bard, into the singer of democracy, of companionship, the singer not of "this compost" but of "these States." This was the figure celebrated by William Douglas O'Connor in a book written as an angry and rhapsodic defense of Whitman at the time of his dismissal from the Indian Bureau; a book which, in its title, provided the phrase which all but smothered the genuine Whitman for almost a century: *The Good Gray Poet* (1866).

There had been a faint but ominous foreshadowing of the good gray poet in the 1860 edition: in the frontispiece, where Whitman appeared for the first time as the brooding, far-gazing prophetic figure; in the first tinkerings with and slight revisions of the earlier poems; and in the group of poems called "Chants Democratic," the volume's major blemish. The 1867 edition had no frontispiece at all; but now the process of revising, deleting, and rearranging was fully at work. A number of the "Calamus" poems on manly love, for example, were removed from *Leaves of Grass* once and for all: those which acknowledged or deplored his erotic attraction to another man—including "Hours Continuing." The sexuality of "Song of Myself" and "The Sleepers" was toned down by deleting in particular the orgasmic imagery in both of them. Much of the bizarre and the frantic was taken out of the 1856 and 1860 poetry, in the interest, as Roger Asselineau has put it, of placing "the accent on the poet-prophet rather than on the lover." In a general way, it was the intense and personal *self* of Whitman that got shaded over by the new editing—that self, in its always rhythmic and sometimes wild oscillations, that was the true source and subject of the true poetry. The private self was reshaped into the public person, and the public stage on which this person chanted and intoned became the major subject of the would-be national bard. Whitman became less and less the original artist singing by indirection of his own psychic advances and retreats; he was becoming and wanted to become the Poet of Democracy. No longer the watchful solitary, he was changing into the Poet of Comradeship.

It should not be assumed that, because these were postures, they were necesssarily false or worthless; they were simply uncongenial to Whitman's kind of poetry. In the same year, 1867, that *Leaves of Grass* unveiled the prophet of the democratic culture, Whitman also published in the New York *Galaxy* a prose essay called "Democracy," where he set forth much of the evidence that, a few years later, went into the longer essay "Democratic Vistas"—as cogent and searching an account of the conditions of democracy in America, and of their relation to the life of letters, as any American has ever written. But what Whitman could do with this material in prose, he could not do effectively in verse. The democratic element in the early poems was, as has been suggested, an aesthetic element. It was part of the very stress and rhythm of the verse, implicit in the poet's way of looking at persons and things, in the principle of equality in his catalogues and the freedom of his meters, in the dynamic of his relation to his readers. Tackling democracy head on in poetry, Whitman became unpersuasive, even boring.

In the same way, Whitman's poems about the actual war were least striking when they were least personal. There is critical disagreement on this point, but in one reader's opinion, Melville wrote far more authentic war-poetry. Melville could do so because he had what Whitman did not—a powerful sense of history as allegory, so that, in "The Conflict of Convictions" (see p. 921) for example, he could suggest the thrust and scale of the struggle in a frame of grand tragedy and in a somberly prophetic mode that the aspiring prophet, Whitman, could never approach. Whitman, the man, had entered the public arena, but his muse did not follow him there; and the enduring poems culled from the war are rather of the intimate and lyrical variety—tender reminiscences or crisp little vignettes like "Cavalry Crossing a Ford," where the image is everything.

There appears among these poems, however, like an unexpected giant out of an earlier age, the work that is widely regarded as Whitman's supreme accomplishment: "When Lilacs Last in the Dooryard Bloom'd." This poem does not, in fact, have quite the artistic finality of "As I Ebb'd" or "Out of the Cradle"; or rather, its finality is more on the surface, where it is asserted, than in the interior and self-completing pulse of the verses. But like the other two poems just named, "When Lilacs Last in the Dooryard Bloom'd"—a string of words, D. H. Lawrence once said, that mysteriously makes the ear tingle—has to do with the relation between death and poetry. The death of Lincoln provided the occasion, and the emergent grief of an entire nation served as large but distant background. What is enacted in the foreground, however, is what so often summoned up Whitman's most genuine power: the effort to come to terms with profound sorrow by converting that sorrow into poetry. By finding the language of mourning, Whitman found the answer to the challenge of death. By focusing not on the public event but rather on the vibrations *of* that event—vibrations converted into symbols—within his private self, Whitman produced one of his masterpieces and perhaps his last unmistakable one.

V: 1871 and Later

THE transformation that both Whitman's figure and his work had slowly undergone was acknowledged by Whitman himself in his Preface to the fifth edition of *Leaves of Grass*, which had two identical printings in 1871 and 1872, while Whitman was still in Washington. The earlier editions, he said, had dealt with the "*Democratic Individual*" (the italics are his); in the new edition, he is concerned instead with the "vast, composite, electric *Democratic Nationality*." It was never clear just what the latter entity amounted to; and any case, Whitman was not able to make it susceptible to satisfactory poetic expression. It became the subject not of poetry but of oratory and rant—elements that had always been present in Whitman's work but that, for the most part, had hitherto been sweetened by music and, as it were, liquified by verbal sea-drift.

Oratory and rant were unhappily notable even in the most interesting of the new poems added to the 1871 edition, "Passage to India." But the case of "Passage to India" is peculiar. It was stimulated by several public events (including, for one, the opening of the Suez Canal), stimuli usually dangerous for Whitman unless he could instantly personalise them, as here he could not. The poem bespeaks not only the ultimate union of all times and places and peoples, but finds in that condition a universal reality; and as Richard Chase has remarked, "Whenever [Whitman] headed for the universal he was headed for trouble." The poem moves swiftly away from the tough entanglements of the concrete that were the vital strength of works as different as "Song of Myself" or "Crossing Brooklyn Ferry" or "As I Ebb'd"; and, arriving at a realm of bodiless vapor, Whitman can only utter such bodiless lines as: "the past—the infinite greatness of the past!"—which is an exclamation without content. Yet "Passage to India" is included in the selections that follow, because, while providing an example of Whitman's bombast, it also seems to this editor technically most accomplished. It completes a kind of parabola of Whitman's craftsmanship: from 1855, where consciousness and craft were discovering each other; through 1856 and 1860, where power and technique were very closely fused; to the later sixties, where technique almost superseded content. The technique in question is primarily a manipulation of sound-patterns, something too involved to be analysed here in detail: an extremely skillful distribution of sheer sounds, without any regard for substance. "Passage to India" is interesting too, by way of historical footnote, for the obsessive effect it was to have more than fifty years later on Hart Crane. It virtually supplied the initiating force for *The Bridge*, especially for the "Atlantis" section, the first portion of his symbolist epic that Crane composed.

Whitman spent the last nineteen years of his life in Camden, New Jersey. He made a partial recovery from the stroke of 1873, but then suffered further seizures from time to time until the one that carried him off. In between these bouts, he continued to "go out" as much as he could: to nearby Philadelphia frequently, to Baltimore and Washington, to New York, and once—in 1879—to Kansas, Colorado, and Canada. Otherwise he remained in Camden, writing short and generally trivial poems, a great amount of prose, and countless letters to friends and admirers all over the world. His old age was punctuated by a series of controversies about him in the public press: in 1876, for example, when a clamor from England to raise a subscription for Whitman was countered by a verbal assault upon him in the New York *Tribune* by Bayard Taylor. The charge was almost always obscenity; in the instance mentioned, the charge only aroused the English to greater efforts, and Whitman was so encouraged as to feel, in his own word, "saved" by the contributions—then and later—of Rossetti, Tennyson, Ruskin, Gosse, Saintsbury, and others. Longfellow and Oscar Wilde, old Dr. Holmes and Henry James, Sr., were among the visitors to his Camden home. He became the genius of the city; and his birthday became an annual celebration. It was amid such flurries of support and defamation, idolatry and contempt, that the old man—cheerful and garrulous to the end—succumbed at last to a horde of diseases that would have killed most men many years sooner.

Whitman *was*, as M. Asselineau says of him, a "heroic invalid." But it may be that his physical and psychological heroism as a man was what produced, by overcompensating for the terrible discomforts he felt, the relentless optimism of so much of his writing in the last two decades—optimism not only about himself and his condition, but about America and about history: for which and in which every disaster, every betrayal was seen by Whitman as a moment in the irresistible progress of things toward the better. The "word signs" of his poetry after 1867 became, as Whitman himself remarked in *A Backward Glance O'er Travel'd Roads* (1888), "Good Cheer, Content and Hope," along with "Comradeship for all lands." Those were also the words that fixed and froze the popular understanding of the poet.

Mention of *A Backward Glance*, however, reminds one that Whitman's most valuable work after 1867 tended to be in prose rather than in verse. The sixth edition of *Leaves of Grass*, printed in 1876 and called the "Centennial Edition" (America's centennial—America now being Whitman's subject), added almost no significant new poetry; but it did include the remarkable essay "Democratic Vistas." The latter poises a noble emphasis upon individual integrity against the moral squalor of a society that was already an impossible mixture of chaos and conformity; and in its plea for "national original archetypes in literature" that will truly "put the nation in form," it presents one of the great statements about the relation between art and culture. The next or seventh edition, that of 1881–82, contained the fine little image of the copulative collision of two eagles: an image based on a written description of such an event by Whitman's friend John Burroughs; and a poem that, with two others, gave cause for the suppression of the entire volume, following a complaint by the Society for the Prevention of Vice. But this edition was also characterised by endless revisions and expurgations, and now, especially, of regroupings of earlier poems: the process whereby the old man steadily buried his youth. In the same year, though, Whitman also published a separate volume of prose: *Specimen Days and Collect*. In it, along with *Specimen Days* and the several indispensable prefaces to *Leaves of Grass*, were "Democratic Vistas," Civil War reminiscences, and Whitman's annual lecture on Lincoln. *A Backward Glance* first appeared in 1888; the following year it served as the Preface to, and was the one memorable new piece of writing in, the *Leaves of Grass* of 1889.

Though it is indeed memorable and even beguiling, *A Backward Glance* is also somewhat misleading. In it, the real motivations and the actual achievement of *Leaves of Grass* lay half-forgotten behind the comradeship, good cheer, and democratic enthusiasm of the ailing elderly bard. Like F. Scott Fitzgerald, Whitman could have said, though one cannot imagine him doing so, that he had found his proper form at a certain moment in his career, but that he had then been diverted into other forms, other endeavors less appropriate to his talent. The fact that it was in these other forms that Whitman's reputation got established make the development more lamentable. At his best, Whitman was not really the bard of the democratic society at all; nor was he the prophet of the country's and the world's glorious future. He was, perhaps, the poet of an aesthetic and moral democracy. But he was above all the poet of the self and of the self's swaying motion—outward into a teeming world where objects were "strung like beads of glory" on his sight; backwards into private communion with the "real Me." He was the poet of the self's motion downwards into the abysses of darkness and guilt and pain and isolation, and upwards to the creative act in which darkness was transmuted into beauty. When the self became lost to the world, Whitman was lost for poetry. But before that happened, Whitman had, in his own example, made poetry possible in America.

READING SUGGESTIONS

BIOGRAPHICAL AND CRITICAL

GAY WILSON ALLEN, *The Solitary Singer* (1955). The definitive biography, detailed and absorbing.

GAY WILSON ALLEN, *Walt Whitman Handbook* (1957). Valuable survey of Whitman's main concerns and methods of writing.

ROGER ASSELINEAU, *The Evolution of Walt Whitman* (1960). The most satisfying account, edition by edition, of the evolution both of *Leaves of Grass* and of Whitman as a man and a poet; the most useful, in this regard, for the Introduction in the present volume.

RICHARD CHASE, *Walt Whitman Reconsidered* (1955). The most dependable critical study of Whitman's poetry, steadily illuminating and thoroughly sensible.

F. O. MATTHIESSEN, *American Renaissance* (1941). Of the several general studies of mid-nineteenth-century American literature, this volume remains the most searching and authoritative; and the author's examination of Whitman's style is especially distinguished.

JAMES E. MILLER, JR., *A Critical Guide to Leaves of Grass* (1957). Close analysis, sometimes dogged but often most rewarding, of a number of the key poems; followed by a speculative discussion of the over-all structure of *Leaves of Grass*.

The section on Whitman and especially "Song of Myself" in Roy Harvey Pearce, *The Continuity of American Poetry* (1961), has some extremely fresh and important things to say about Whitman as an "epic poet."

Four interrelated studies of "Out of the Cradle Endlessly Rocking" will be included in a volume of English Institute essays, all relating to Whitman, to be published in 1962 by the Columbia University Press.

EDITIONS

Further study of Whitman, even if it is to be purely critical, ought to begin by a consideration of the actual texts of the early editions, something recent scholarship has made possible for every reader.

MALCOLM COWLEY, editor, *Walt Whitman's Leaves of Grass: The First (1855) Edition* (1959; paperback 1961). The exact text of the first edition is here preceded by a most valuable Introduction.

ROY HARVEY PEARCE, editor, *The 1860 Edition of Leaves of Grass* (1961). An extremely welcome publication of what many critics regard as the most significant of the editions of *Leaves of Grass*.

EMORY HOLLOWAY, editor, *Leaves of Grass by Walt Whitman* (1926). Includes the indispensable list of "variorum readings"—showing the various revisions and deletions from edition to edition—compiled by Oscar Lovell Triggs.

GAY WILSON ALLEN AND SCULLEY BRADLEY, general editors, *The Collected Writings of Walt Whitman*. A projected edition in fourteen volumes of everything Whitman ever wrote, including his correspondence (two volumes already in print, 1961), his essays, journalistic articles, fiction, diaries and notebooks, his early poems; and a complete two-volume variorum edition of *Leaves of Grass*.

Probably the best easily available edition of the standard *Leaves of Grass* based on Whitman's final grouping of the poems and old-age versions (plus suppressed poems and selected prose) is James E. Miller, Jr., editor, *Walt Whitman: Complete Poetry and Selected Prose* (1959).

POEMS

I: 1855

◇

THE FOLLOWING poems appeared untitled—and their individual stanzas and sections unnumbered—as the first, third, fourth, and tenth of the twelve items that made up the first edition of *Leaves of Grass*. The book was published simultaneously in New York and Brooklyn, on or about July 4, 1855. The name of the author did not appear on the cover or title page, but facing the title page was a portrait of Whitman in canvas trousers and open shirt and with his hat on. On the following page, in small print, the work was copyrighted by "Walter Whitman." The four poems selected are intended to represent, among other things, the profound and characteristic alternation in Whitman's poetry between the sense of burgeoning life, of the psyche's forward thrust—"Song of Myself" and "There Was a Child Went Forth"—and the sense of death and dying, of the night-side of experience—"The Sleepers" and "To Think of Time." In the 1855 edition, the force of life is always absolutely victorious, and death, finally, is denied any reality. "Song of Myself," in addition, is Whitman's longest and most comprehensive poem, and it remains, perhaps, America's most authentic verse epic, though an epic of a very modern and indeed peculiar kind.

◇

SONG OF MYSELF

1

I celebrate myself, and sing myself,
And what I assume you shall assume,
For every atom belonging to me as good belongs to you.

I loafe and invite my soul,
I lean and loafe at my ease observing a spear of summer grass.

My tongue, every atom of my blood, form'd from this soil, this air,
Born here of parents born here from parents the same, and their parents the same,
I, now thirty-seven years old in perfect health begin,
Hoping to cease not till death.

Creeds and schools in abeyance,
Retiring back a while sufficed at what they are, but never forgotten,
I harbor for good or bad, I permit to speak at every hazard,
Nature without check with original energy.

2

Houses and rooms are full of perfumes, the shelves are crowded with perfumes,
I breathe the fragrance myself and know it and like it,
The distillation would intoxicate me also, but I shall not let it.

The atmosphere is not a perfume, it has no taste of the distillation, it is odorless,
It is for my mouth forever, I am in love with it,

SONG OF MYSELF. Untitled in 1855; "A Poem of Walt Whitman, an American," 1856; "Walt Whitman" in 1860 and 1867; not "Song of Myself" until 1881. **1. 8.** (Numbered references are to stanza and line.) **thirty-seven years old:** Whitman in fact was at most barely thirty-six, probably only thirty-five, when he "began" this poem. Lines 6–13 were written in 1860 as part of "Starting from Paumanok" and were transferred to "Song of Myself" in 1881.

I will go to the bank by the wood and become undisguised and naked,
I am mad for it to be in contact with me.

The smoke of my own breath,
Echoes, ripples, buzz'd whispers, love-root, silk-thread, crotch and vine,
My respiration and inspiration, the beating of my heart, the passing of blood and air through my lungs,
The sniff of green leaves and dry leaves, and of the shore and dark-color'd sea-rocks, and of hay in the barn,
The sound of the belch'd words of my voice loos'd to the eddies of the wind,
A few light kisses, a few embraces, a reaching around of arms,
The play of shine and shade on the trees as the supple boughs wag,
The delight alone or in the rush of the streets, or along the fields and hill-sides,
The feeling of health, the full-noon trill, the song of me rising from bed and meeting the sun.

Have you reckon'd a thousand acres much? have you reckon'd the earth much?
Have you practis'd so long to learn to read?
Have you felt so proud to get at the meaning of poems?

Stop this day and night with me and you shall possess the origin of all poems,
You shall possess the good of the earth and sun, (there are millions of suns left,)
You shall no longer take things at second or third hand, nor look through the eyes of the dead, nor feed on the spectres in books,
You shall not look through my eyes either, nor take things from me,
You shall listen to all sides and filter them from your self.

3

I have heard what the talkers were talking, the talk of the beginning and the end,
But I do not talk of the beginning or the end.

There was never any more inception than there is now,
Nor any more youth or age than there is now,
And will never be any more perfection than there is now,
Nor any more heaven or hell than there is now.

Urge and urge and urge,
Always the procreant urge of the world.
Out of the dimness opposite equals advance, always substance and increase, always sex,
Always a knit of identity, always distinction, always a breed of life.

To elaborate is no avail, learn'd and unlearn'd feel that it is so.

Sure as the most certain sure, plumb in the uprights, well entretied, braced in the beams,
Stout as a horse, affectionate, haughty, electrical,
I and this mystery here we stand.

Clear and sweet is my soul, and clear and sweet is all that is not my soul.

Lack one lacks both, and the unseen is proved by the seen,
Till that becomes unseen and receives proof in its turn.

Showing the best and dividing it from the worst age vexes age,
Knowing the perfect fitness and equanimity of things, while they discuss I am silent, and go bathe and admire myself.

Welcome is every organ and attribute of me, and of any man hearty and clean,
Not an inch nor a particle of an inch is vile, and none shall be less familiar than the rest.

I am satisfied—I see, dance, laugh, sing;
As the hugging and loving bed-fellow sleeps at my side through the night, and withdraws at the peep of the day with stealthy tread,
Leaving me baskets cover'd with white towels swelling the house with their plenty,
Shall I postpone my acceptation and realization and scream at my eyes,
That they turn from gazing after and down the road,
And forthwith cipher and show me to a cent,
Exactly the value of one and exactly the value of two, and which is ahead?

4

Trippers and askers surround me,
People I meet, the effect upon me of my early life or the ward and city I live in, or the nation,
The latest dates, discoveries, inventions, societies, authors old and new,
My dinner, dress, associates, looks, compliments, dues,
The real or fancied indifference of some man or woman I love,
The sickness of one of my folks or of myself, or ill-doing or loss or lack of money, or depressions or exaltations,
Battles, the horrors of fratricidal war, the fever of doubtful news, the fitful events;
These come to me days and nights and go from me again,
But they are not the Me myself.

Apart from the pulling and hauling stands what I am,
Stands amused, complacent, compassionating, idle, unitary,
Looks down, is erect, or bends an arm on an impalpable certain rest,
Looking with side-curved head curious what will come next,
Both in and out of the game and watching and wondering at it.

Backward I see in my own days where I sweated through fog with linguists and contenders,
I have no mockings or arguments, I witness and wait.

5

I believe in you my soul, the other I am must not abase itself to you,
And you must not be abased to the other.

Loafe with me on the grass, loose the stop from your throat,
Not words, not music or rhyme I want, not custom or lecture, not even the best,
Only the lull I like, the hum of your valvèd voice.

I mind how once we lay such a transparent summer morning,
How you settled your head athwart my hips and gently turn'd over upon me,
And parted the shirt from my bosom-bone, and plunged your tongue to my bare-stript heart,
And reach'd till you felt my beard, and reach'd till you held my feet.

Swiftly arose and spread around me the peace and knowledge that pass all the argument of the earth,

3. 23. **hugging and loving bed-fellow:** In 1855, the "bed-fellow" is identified as God, the source of the poet's spiritual abundance ("baskets cover'd with white towels").

And I know that the hand of God is the promise of my own,
And I know that the spirit of God is the brother of my own,
And that all the men ever born are also my brothers, and the women my sisters and lovers,
And that a kelson of the creation is love,
And limitless are leaves stiff or drooping in the fields,
And brown ants in the little wells beneath them,
And mossy scabs of the worm fence, heap'd stones, elder, mullein and poke-weed.

6

A child said *What is the grass?* fetching it to me with full hands,
How could I answer the child? I do not know what it is any more than he.

I guess it must be the flag of my disposition, out of hopeful green stuff woven.

Or I guess it is the handkerchief of the Lord,
A scented gift and remembrancer designedly dropt,
Bearing the owner's name someway in the corners, that we may see and remark, and say *Whose?*

Or I guess the grass is itself a child, the produced babe of the vegetation.

Or I guess it is a uniform hieroglyphic,
And it means, Sprouting alike in broad zones and narrow zones,
Growing among black folks as among white,
Kanuck, Tuckahoe, Congressman, Cuff, I give them the same, I receive them the same.

And now it seems to me the beautiful uncut hair of graves.

Tenderly will I use you curling grass,
It may be you transpire from the breasts of young men,
It may be if I had known them I would have loved them,
It may be you are from old people, or from offspring taken soon out of their mothers' laps,
And here you are the mothers' laps.

This grass is very dark to be from the white heads of old mothers,
Darker than the colorless beards of old men,
Dark to come from under the faint red roofs of mouths.
O I perceive after all so many uttering tongues,
And I perceive they do not come from the roofs of mouths for nothing.

I wish I could translate the hints about the dead young men and women,
And the hints about old men and mothers, and the offspring taken soon out of their laps.

What do you think has become of the young and old men?
And what do you think has become of the women and children?

They are alive and well somewhere,
The smallest sprout shows there is really no death,
And if ever there was it led forward life, and does not wait at the end to arrest it,
And ceas'd the moment life appear'd.

5. 14. **kelson:** a line of joined timbers, fastened by bolts.

All goes onward and outward, nothing collapses,
And to die is different from what any one supposed, and luckier.

7

Has any one supposed it lucky to be born?
I hasten to inform him or her it is just as lucky to die, and I know it.

I pass death with the dying and birth with the new-wash'd babe, and am not contain'd between my hat and boots,
And peruse manifold objects, no two alike and every one good,
The earth good and the stars good, and their adjuncts all good.

I am not an earth nor an adjunct of an earth,
I am the mate and companion of people, all just as immortal and fathomless as myself,
(They do not know how immortal, but I know.)

Every kind for itself and its own, for me mine male and female,
For me those that have been boys and that love women,
For me the man that is proud and feels how it stings to be slighted,
For me the sweet-heart and the old maid, for me mothers and the mothers of mothers,
For me lips that have smiled, eyes that have shed tears,
For me children and the begetters of children.

Undrape! you are not guilty to me, nor stale nor discarded,
I see through the broadcloth and gingham whether or no,
And am around, tenacious, acquisitive, tireless, and cannot be shaken away.

8

The little one sleeps in its cradle,
I lift the gauze and look a long time, and silently brush away flies with my hand.

The youngster and the red-faced girl turn aside up the bushy hill,
I peeringly view them from the top.

The suicide sprawls on the bloody floor of the bedroom,
I witness the corpse with its dabbled hair, I note where the pistol has fallen.

The blab of the pave, tires of carts, sluff of boot-soles, talk of the promenaders,
The heavy omnibus, the driver with his interrogating thumb, the clank of the shod horses on the granite floor,
The snow-sleighs, clinking, shouted jokes, pelts of snow-balls,
The hurrahs for popular favorites, the fury of rous'd mobs,
The flap of the curtain'd litter, a sick man inside borne to the hospital,
The meeting of enemies, the sudden oath, the blows and fall,
The excited crowd, the policeman with his star quickly working his passage to the centre of the crowd,
The impassive stones that receive and return so many echoes,
What groans of over-fed or half-starv'd who fall sunstruck or in fits,
What exclamations of women taken suddenly who hurry home and give birth to babes,
What living and buried speech is always vibrating here, what howls restrain'd by decorum,
Arrests of criminals, slights, adulterous offers made, acceptances, rejections with convex lips,
I mind them or the show or resonance of them—I come and I depart.

9

The big doors of the country barn stand open and ready,
The dried grass of the harvest-time loads the slow-drawn wagon,
The clear light plays on the brown gray and green intertinged,
The armfuls are pack'd to the sagging mow.

I am there, I help, I came stretch'd atop of the load,
I felt its soft jolts, one leg reclined on the other,
I jump from the cross-beams and seize the clover and timothy,
And roll head over heels and tangle my hair full of wisps.

10

Alone far in the wilds and mountains I hunt,
Wandering amazed at my own lightness and glee,
In the late afternoon choosing a safe spot to pass the night,
Kindling a fire and broiling the fresh-kill'd game,
Falling asleep on the gather'd leaves with my dog and gun by my side.

The Yankee clipper is under her sky-sails, she cuts the sparkle and scud,
My eyes settle the land, I bend at her prow or shout joyously from the deck.

The boatmen and clam-diggers arose early and stopt for me,
I tuck'd my trowser-ends in my boots and went and had a good time;
You should have been with us that day round the chowder-kettle.

I saw the marriage of the trapper in the open air in the far west, the bride was a red girl,
Her father and his friends sat near cross-legged and dumbly smoking, they had moccasins to their feet and large thick blankets hanging from their shoulders,
On a bank lounged the trapper, he was drest mostly in skins, his luxuriant beard and curls protected his neck, he held his bride by the hand,
She had long eyelashes, her head was bare, her coarse straight locks descended upon her voluptuous limbs and reach'd to her feet.

The runaway slave came to my house and stopt outside,
I heard his motions crackling the twigs of the woodpile,
Through the swung half-door of the kitchen I saw him limpsy and weak,
And went where he sat on a log and led him in and assured him,
And brought water and fill'd a tub for his sweated body and bruis'd feet,
And gave him a room that enter'd from my own, and gave him some coarse clean clothes,
And remember perfectly well his revolving eyes and his awkwardness,
And remember putting plasters on the galls of his neck and ankles;
He staid with me a week before he was recuperated and pass'd north,
I had him sit next me at table, my fire-lock lean'd in the corner.

11

Twenty-eight young men bathe by the shore,
Twenty-eight young men and all so friendly;
Twenty-eight years of womanly life and all so lonesome.

She owns the fine house by the rise of the bank,
She hides handsome and richly drest aft the blinds of the window.

Which of the young men does she like the best?
Ah the homeliest of them is beautiful to her.

Where are you off to, lady? for I see you,
You splash in the water there, yet stay stock still in your room.

Dancing and laughing along the beach came the twenty-ninth bather,
The rest did not see her, but she saw them and loved them.

The beards of the young men glisten'd with wet, it ran from their long hair,
Little streams pass'd all over their bodies.

An unseen hand also pass'd over their bodies,
It descended tremblingly from their temples and ribs.

The young men float on their backs, their white bellies bulge to the sun, they do not ask who seizes fast to them,
They do not know who puffs and declines with pendant and bending arch,
They do not think whom they souse with spray.

12

The butcher-boy puts off his killing-clothes, or sharpens his knife at the stall in the market,
I loiter enjoying his repartee and his shuffle and break-down.

Blacksmiths with grimed and hairy chests environ the anvil,
Each has his main-sledge, they are all out, there is a great heat in the fire.

From the cinder-strew'd threshold I follow their movements,
The lithe sheer of their waists plays even with their massive arms,
Overhand the hammers swing, overhand so slow, overhand so sure,
They do not hasten, each man hits in his place.

13

The negro holds firmly the reins of his four horses, the block swags underneath on its tied-over chain,
The negro that drives the long dray of the stone-yard, steady and tall he stands pois'd on one leg on the string-piece,
His blue shirt exposes his ample neck and breast and loosens over his hip-band,
His glance is calm and commanding, he tosses the slouch of his hat away from his forehead,
The sun falls on his crispy hair and mustache, falls on the black of his polish'd and perfect limbs.

I behold the picturesque giant and love him, and I do not stop there,
I go with the team also.

In me the caresser of life wherever moving, backward as well as forward sluing,
To niches aside and junior bending, not a person or object missing,
Absorbing all to myself and for this song.

Oxen that rattle the yoke and chain or halt in the leafy shade, what is that you express in your eyes?
It seems to me more than all the print I have read in my life.

My tread scares the wood-drake and wood-duck on my distant and day-long ramble,
They rise together, they slowly circle around.

I believe in those wing'd purposes,
And acknowledge red, yellow, white, playing within me,
And consider green and violet and the tufted crown intentional,
And do not call the tortoise unworthy because she is not something else,
And the jay in the woods never studied the gamut, yet trills pretty well to me,
And the look of the bay mare shames silliness out of me.

14

The wild gander leads his flock through the cool night,
Ya-honk he says, and sounds it down to me like an invitation,
The pert may suppose it meaningless, but I listening close,
Find its purpose and place up there toward the wintry sky.

The sharp-hoof'd moose of the north, the cat on the house-sill, the chickadee, the prairie-dog,
The litter of the grunting sow as they tug at her teats,
The brood of the turkey-hen and she with her half-spread wings,
I see in them and myself the same old law.

The press of my foot to the earth springs a hundred affections,
They scorn the best I can do to relate them.

I am enamour'd of growing out-doors,
Of men that live among cattle or taste of the ocean or woods,
Of the builders and steerers of ships and the wielders of axes and mauls, and the drivers of horses,
I can eat and sleep with them week in and week out.

What is commonest, cheapest, nearest, easiest, is Me,
Me going in for my chances, spending for vast returns,
Adorning myself to bestow myself on the first that will take me,
Not asking the sky to come down to my good will,
Scattering it freely forever.

15

The pure contralto sings in the organ loft,
The carpenter dresses his plank, the tongue of his foreplane whistles its wild ascending lisp,
The married and unmarried children ride home to their Thanksgiving dinner,
The pilot seizes the king-pin, he heaves down with a strong arm,
The mate stands braced in the whale-boat, lance and harpoon are ready,
The duck-shooter walks by silent and cautious stretches,
The deacons are ordain'd with cross'd hands at the altar,
The spinning-girl retreats and advances to the hum of the big wheel,
The farmer stops by the bars as he walks on a First-day loafe and looks at the oats and rye,
The lunatic is carried at last to the asylum a confirm'd case,
(He will never sleep any more as he did in the cot in his mother's bedroom;)
The jour printer with gray head and gaunt jaws works at his case,
He turns his quid of tobacco while his eyes blurr with the manuscript;

13. 19. **gamut:** the whole musical scale. 15. 12. **jour:** a person who works for wages, not himself.

The malform'd limbs are tied to the surgeon's table,
What is removed drops horribly in a pail;
The quadroon girl is sold at the auction-stand, the drunkard nods by the bar-room stove,
The machinist rolls up his sleeves, the policeman travels his beat, the gate-keeper marks who pass,
The young fellow drives the express-wagon, (I love him, though I do not know him;)
The half-breed straps on his light boots to compete in the race,
The western turkey-shooting draws old and young, some lean on their rifles, some sit on logs,
Out from the crowd steps the marksman, takes his position, levels his piece;
The groups of newly-come immigrants cover the wharf or levee,
As the woolly-pates hoe in the sugar-field, the overseer views them from his saddle,
The bugle calls in the ball-room, the gentlemen run for their partners, the dancers bow to each other,
The youth lies awake in the cedar-roof'd garret and harks to the musical rain,
The Wolverine sets traps on the creek that helps fill the Huron,
The squaw wrapt in her yellow-hemm'd cloth is offering moccasins and bead-bags for sale,
The connoisseur peers along the exhibition-gallery with half-shut eyes bent sideways,
As the deck-hands make fast the steamboat the plank is thrown for the shore-going passengers,
The young sister holds out the skein while the elder sister winds it off in a ball, and stops now and then for the knots,
The one-year wife is recovering and happy having a week ago borne her first child.
The clean-hair'd Yankee girl works with her sewing-machine or in the factory or mill,
The paving-man leans on his two-handed rammer, the reporter's lead flies swiftly over the note-book, the sign-painter is lettering with blue and gold,
The canal boy trots on the tow-path, the book-keeper counts at his desk, the shoemaker waxes his thread,
The conductor beats time for the band and all the performers follow him,
The child is baptized, the convert is making his first professions,
The regatta is spread on the bay, the race is begun, (how the white sails sparkle!)
The drover watching his drove sings out to them that would stray,
The pedler sweats with his pack on his back, (the purchaser higgling about the odd cent;)
The bride unrumples her white dress, the minute-hand of the clock moves slowly,
The opium-eater reclines with rigid head and just-open'd lips,
The prostitute draggles her shawl, her bonnet bobs on her tipsy and pimpled neck,
The crowd laugh at her blackguard oaths, the men jeer and wink to each other,
(Miserable! I do not laugh at your oaths nor jeer you;)
The President holding a cabinet council is surrounded by the great Secretaries,
On the piazza walk three matrons stately and friendly with twined arms,
The crew of the fish-smack pack repeated layers of halibut in the hold,
The Missourian crosses the plains toting his wares and his cattle,
As the fare-collector goes through the train he gives notice by the jingling of loose change,
The floor-men are laying the floor, the tinners are tinning the roof, the masons are calling for mortar,
In single file each shouldering his hod pass onward the laborers;
Seasons pursuing each other the indescribable crowd is gather'd, it is the fourth of Seventh-month, (what salutes of cannon and small arms!)
Seasons pursuing each other the plougher ploughs, the mower mows, and the winter-grain falls in the ground;
Off on the lakes the pike-fisher watches and waits by the hole in the frozen surface,
The stumps stand thick round the clearing, the squatter strikes deep with his axe,

15. 52. **Seventh-month:** in 1855, "July"; Whitman began to affect the Quaker habit of referring to months by numbers in 1860.

Flatboatmen make fast towards dusk near the cotton-wood or pecan-trees,
Coon-seekers go through the regions of the Red river or through those drain'd by the Tennessee, or through those of the Arkansas,
Torches shine in the dark that hangs on the Chattahooche or Altamahaw,
Patriarchs sit at supper with sons and grandsons and great-grandsons around them,
In walls of adobie, in canvas tents, rest hunters and trappers after their day's sport,
The city sleeps and the country sleeps,
The living sleep for their time, the dead sleep for their time,
The old husband sleeps by his wife and the young husband sleeps by his wife;
And these tend inward to me, and I tend outward to them,
And such as it is to be of these more or less I am,
And of these one and all I weave the song of myself.

16

I am of old and young, of the foolish as much as the wise,
Regardless of others, ever regardful of others,
Maternal as well as paternal, a child as well as a man,
Stuff'd with the stuff that is coarse and stuff'd with the stuff that is fine,
One of the Nation of many nations, the smallest the same and the largest the same,
A Southerner soon as a Northerner, a planter nonchalant and hospitable down by the Oconee I live,
A Yankee bound my own way ready for trade, my joints the limberest joints on earth and the sternest joints on earth,
A Kentuckian walking the vale of the Elkhorn in my deer-skin leggings, a Louisianian or Georgian,
A boatman over lakes or bays or along coasts, a Hoosier, Badger, Buckeye;
At home on Kanadian snow-shoes or up in the bush, or with fishermen off Newfoundland,
At home in the fleet of ice-boats, sailing with the rest and tacking,
At home on the hills of Vermont or in the woods of Maine, or the Texan ranch,
Comrade of Californians, comrade of free North-Westerners, (loving their big proportions,)
Comrade of raftsmen and coalmen, comrade of all who shake hands and welcome to drink and meat,
A learner with the simplest, a teacher of the thoughtfullest,
A novice beginning yet experient of myriads of seasons,
Of every hue and caste am I, of every rank and religion,
A farmer, mechanic, artist, gentleman, sailor, quaker,
Prisoner, fancy-man, rowdy, lawyer, physician, priest.

I resist any thing better than my own diversity,
Breathe the air but leave plenty after me,
And am not stuck up, and am in my place.

(The moth and the fish-eggs are in their place,
The bright suns I see and the dark suns I cannot see are in their place,
The palpable is in its place and the impalpable is in its place.)

17

These are really the thoughts of all men in all ages and lands, they are not original with me,
If they are not yours as much as mine they are nothing, or next to nothing,
If they are not the riddle and the untying of the riddle they are nothing,
If they are not just as close as they are distant they are nothing.

This is the grass that grows wherever the land is and the water is,
This is the common air that bathes the globe.

18

With music strong I come, with my cornets and my drums,
I play not marches for accepted victors only, I play marches for conquer'd and slain persons.

Have you heard that it was good to gain the day?
I also say it is good to fall, battles are lost in the same spirit in which they are won.

I beat and pound for the dead,
I blow through my embouchures my loudest and gayest for them.

Vivas to those who have fail'd!
And to those whose war-vessels sank in the sea!
And to those themselves who sank in the sea!
And to all generals that lost engagements, and all overcome heroes!
And the numberless unknown heroes equal to the greatest heroes known!

19

This is the meal equally set, this the meat for natural hunger,
It is for the wicked just the same as the righteous, I make appointments with all,
I will not have a single person slighted or left away,
The kept-woman, sponger, thief, are hereby invited,
The heavy-lipp'd slave is invited, the venerealee is invited;
There shall be no difference between them and the rest.

This is the press of a bashful hand, this the float and odor of hair,
This the touch of my lips to yours, this the murmur of yearning,
This the far-off depth and height reflecting my own face,
This the thoughtful merge of myself, and the outlet again.

Do you guess I have some intricate purpose?
Well I have, for the Fourth-month showers have, and the mica on the side of a rock has.

Do you take it I would astonish?
Does the daylight astonish? does the early redstart twittering through the woods?
Do I astonish more than they?

This hour I tell things in confidence,
I might not tell everybody, but I will tell you.

20

Who goes there? hankering, gross, mystical, nude;
How is it I extract strength from the beef I eat?

What is a man anyhow? what am I? what are you?
All I mark as my own you shall offset it with your own,
Else it were time lost listening to me.

I do not snivel that snivel the world over,
That months are vacuums and the ground but wallow and filth.

18. 6. **embouchures:** one of Whitman's Gallicisms, in this case meaning the mouthpiece of a musical instrument.

Whimpering and truckling fold with powders for invalids, conformity goes to the fourth-remov'd,
I wear my hat as I please indoors or out.

Why should I pray? why should I venerate and be ceremonious?

Having pried through the strata, analyzed to a hair, counsel'd with doctors and calculated close,
I find no sweeter fat than sticks to my own bones.

In all people I see myself, none more and not one a barley-corn less,
And the good or bad I say of myself I say of them.

I know I am solid and sound,
To me the converging objects of the universe perpetually flow,
All are written to me, and I must get what the writing means.

I know I am deathless,
I know this orbit of mine cannot be swept by a carpenter's compass,
I know I shall not pass like a child's carlacue cut with a burnt stick at night.

I know I am august,
I do not trouble my spirit to vindicate itself or be understood,
I see that the elementary laws never apologize,
(I reckon I behave no prouder than the level I plant my house by, after all.)

I exist as I am, that is enough,
If no other in the world be aware I sit content,
And if each and all be aware I sit content.

One world is aware and by far the largest to me, and that is myself,
And whether I come to my own to-day or in ten thousand or ten million years,
I can cheerfully take it now, or with equal cheerfulness I can wait.
My foothold is tenon'd and mortis'd in granite,
I laugh at what you call dissolution,
And I know the amplitude of time.

21

I am the poet of the Body and I am the poet of the Soul,
The pleasures of heaven are with me and the pains of hell are with me,
The first I graft and increase upon myself, the latter I translate into a new tongue.

I am the poet of the woman the same as the man,
And I say it is as great to be a woman as to be a man,
And I say there is nothing greater than the mother of men.

I chant the chant of dilation or pride,
We have had ducking and deprecating about enough,
I show that size is only development.

Have you outstript the rest? are you the President?
It is a trifle, they will more than arrive there every one, and still pass on.

20. 20. carlacue: curlicue.

I am he that walks with the tender and growing night,
I call to the earth and sea half-held by the night.

Press close bare-bosom'd night—press close magnetic nourishing night!
Night of south winds—night of the large few stars!
Still nodding night—mad naked summer night.

Smile O voluptuous cool-breath'd earth!
Earth of the slumbering and liquid trees!
Earth of departed sunset—earth of the mountains misty-topt!
Earth of the vitreous pour of the full moon just tinged with blue!
Earth of shine and dark mottling the tide of the river!
Earth of the limpid gray of clouds brighter and clearer for my sake!
Far-swooping elbow'd earth—rich apple-blossom'd earth!
Smile, for your lover comes.

Prodigal, you have given me love—therefore I to you give love!
O unspeakable passionate love.

22

You sea! I resign myself to you also—I guess what you mean,
I behold from the beach your crooked inviting fingers,
I believe you refuse to go back without feeling of me,
We must have a turn together, I undress, hurry me out of sight of the land,
Cushion me soft, rock me in billowy drowse,
Dash me with amorous wet, I can repay you.

Sea of stretch'd ground-swells,
Sea breathing broad and convulsive breaths,
Sea of the brine of life and of unshovell'd yet always-ready graves,
Howler and scooper of storms, capricious and dainty sea,
I am integral with you, I too am of one phase and of all phases.

Partaker of influx and efflux I, extoller of hate and conciliation,
Extoller of amies and those that sleep in each others' arms,

I am he attesting sympathy,
(Shall I make my list of things in the house and skip the house that supports them?)

I am not the poet of goodness only, I do not decline to be the poet of wickedness also.

What blurt is this about virtue and about vice?
Evil propels me and reform of evil propels me, I stand indifferent,
My gait is no fault-finder's or rejecter's gait;
I moisten the roots of all that has grown.

Did you fear some scrofula out of the unflagging pregnancy?
Did you guess the celestial laws are yet to be work'd over and rectified?

I find one side a balance and the antipodal side a balance,
Soft doctrine as steady help as stable doctrine,
Thoughts and deeds of the present our rouse and early start.

This minute that comes to me over the past decillions,
There is no better than it and now.

What behaved well in the past or behaves well to-day is not such a wonder,
The wonder is always and always how there can be a mean man or an infidel.

23

Endless unfolding of words of ages!
And mine a word of the modern, the word En-Masse.

A word of the faith that never balks,
Here or henceforward it is all the same to me, I accept Time absolutely.

It alone is without flaw, it alone rounds and completes all,
That mystic baffling wonder alone completes all.

I accept Reality and dare not question it,
Materialism first and last imbuing.

Hurrah for positive science! long live exact demonstration!
Fetch stonecrop mixt with cedar and branches of lilac,
This is the lexicographer, this the chemist, this made a grammar of the old cartouches,
These mariners put the ship through dangerous unknown seas,
This is the geologist, this works with the scalpel, and this is a mathematician.

Gentlemen, to you the first honors always!
Your facts are useful, and yet they are not my dwelling,
I but enter by them to an area of my dwelling.

Less the reminders of properties told my words,
And more the reminders they of life untold, and of freedom and extrication,
And make short account of neuters and geldings, and favor men and women fully equipt.
And beat the gong of revolt, and stop with fugitives and them that plot and conspire.

24

Walt Whitman, a kosmos, of Manhattan the son,
Turbulent, fleshy, sensual, eating, drinking and breeding,
No sentimentalist, no stander above men and women or apart from them,
No more modest than immodest.

Unscrew the locks from the doors!
Unscrew the doors themselves from their jambs!

Whoever degrades another degrades me,
And whatever is done or said returns at last to me.

Through me the afflatus surging and surging, through me the current and index.

I speak the pass-word primeval, I give the sign of democracy,
By God! I will accept nothing which all cannot have their counterpart of on the same terms.

23. 2. En-Masse: a favorite Whitman Gallicism, meaning "humanity-as-a-whole." **24. 1. kosmos:** Whitman's spelling for his concept of the individual as containing the universe within himself.

Through me many long dumb voices,
Voices of the interminable generations of prisoners and slaves,
Voices of the diseas'd and despairing and of thieves and dwarfs,
Voices of cycles of preparation and accretion,
And of the threads that connect the stars, and of wombs and of the father-stuff,
And of the rights of them the others are down upon,
Of the deform'd, trivial, flat, foolish, despised,
Fog in the air, beetles rolling balls of dung.

Through me forbidden voices,
Voices of sexes and lusts, voices veil'd and I remove the veil,
Voices indecent by me clarified and transfigur'd.

I do not press my fingers across my mouth,
I keep as delicate around the bowels as around the head and heart,
Copulation is no more rank to me than death is.
I believe in the flesh and the appetites,
Seeing, hearing, feeling, are miracles, and each part and tag of me is a miracle.

Divine am I inside and out, and I make holy whatever I touch or am touch'd from,
The scent of these arm-pits aroma finer than prayer,
This head more than churches, bibles, and all the creeds.

If I worship one thing more than another it shall be the spread of my own body, or
any part of it,
Translucent mould of me it shall be you!
Shaded ledges and rests it shall be you!
Firm masculine colter it shall be you!
Whatever goes to the tilth of me it shall be you!
You my rich blood! your milky stream pale strippings of my life!
Breast that presses against other breasts it shall be you!
My brain it shall be your occult convolutions!
Root of wash'd sweet-flag! timorous pond-snipe! nest of guarded duplicate eggs! it shall
be you!
Mix'd tussled hay of head, beard, brawn, it shall be you!
Trickling sap of maple, fibre of manly wheat, it shall be you!
Sun so generous it shall be you!
Vapors lighting and shading my face it shall be you!
You sweaty brooks and dews it shall be you!
Winds whose soft-tickling genitals rub against me it shall be you!
Broad muscular fields, branches of live oak, loving lounger in my winding paths, it shall
be you!
Hands I have taken, face I have kiss'd, mortal I have ever touch'd, it shall be you.

I dote on myself, there is that lot of me and all so luscious,
Each moment and whatever happens thrills me with joy,
I cannot tell how my ankles bend, nor whence the cause of my faintest wish,
Nor the cause of the friendship I emit, nor the cause of the friendship I take again.

That I walk up my stoop, I pause to consider if it really be,
A morning-glory at my window satisfies me more than the metaphysics of books.

To behold the day-break!
The little light fades the immense and diaphanous shadows,
The air tastes good to my palate.

Hefts of the moving world at innocent gambols silently rising, freshly exuding,
Scooting obliquely high and low.

Something I cannot see puts upward libidinous prongs,
Seas of bright juice suffuse heaven.

The earth by the sky staid with, the daily close of their junction,
The heav'd challenge from the east that moment over my head,
The mocking taunt, See then whether you shall be master!

25

Dazzling and tremendous how quick the sun-rise would kill me,
If I could not now and always send sun-rise out of me.

We also ascend dazzling and tremendous as the sun,
We found our own O my soul in the calm and cool of the daybreak.

My voice goes after what my eyes cannot reach,
With the twirl of my tongue I encompass worlds and volumes of worlds.

Speech is the twin of my vision, it is unequal to measure itself,
It provokes me forever, it says sarcastically,
Walt you contain enough, why don't you let it out then?

Come now I will not be tantalized, you conceive too much of articulation,
Do you not know O speech how the buds beneath you are folded?
Waiting in gloom, protected by frost,
The dirt receding before my prophetical screams,
I underlying causes to balance them at last,
My knowledge my live parts, it keeping tally with the meaning of all things,
Happiness, (which whoever hears me let him or her set out in search of this day.)

My final merit I refuse you, I refuse putting from me what I really am,
Encompass worlds, but never try to encompass me,
I crowd your sleekest and best by simply looking toward you.

Writing and talk do not prove me,
I carry the plenum of proof and every thing else in my face,
With the hush of my lips I wholly confound the skeptic.

26

Now I will do nothing but listen,
To accrue what I hear into this song, to let sounds contribute toward it.

I hear bravuras of birds, bustle of growing wheat, gossip of flames, clack of sticks cooking my meals,
I hear the sound I love, the sound of the human voice,
I hear all sounds running together, combined, fused or following,
Sounds of the city and sounds out of the city, sounds of the day and night,
Talkative young ones to those that like them, the loud laugh of work-people at their meals,
The angry base of disjointed friendship, the faint tones of the sick,
The judge with hands tight to the desk, his pallid lips pronouncing a death-sentence,
The heave'e'yo of stevedores unlading ships by the wharves, the refrain of the anchor-lifters,

The ring of alarm-bells, the cry of fire, the whirr of swift-streaking engines and hose-carts with premonitory tinkles and color'd lights,
The steam-whistle, the solid roll of the train of approaching cars,
The slow march play'd at the head of the association marching two and two,
(They go to guard some corpse, the flag-tops are draped with black muslin.)
I hear the violoncello, ('tis the young man's heart's complaint,)
I hear the key'd cornet, it glides quickly in through my ears,
It shakes mad-sweet pangs through my belly and breast.

I hear the chorus, it is a grand opera,
Ah this indeed is music—this suits me.

A tenor large and fresh as the creation fills me,
The orbic flex of his mouth is pouring and filling me full.

I hear the train'd soprano (what work with hers is this?)
The orchestra whirls me wider than Uranus flies,
It wrenches such ardors from me I did not know I possess'd them,
It sails me, I dab with bare feet, they are lick'd by the indolent waves,
I am cut by bitter and angry hail, I lose my breath,
Steep'd amid honey'd morphine, my windpipe throttled in fakes of death,
At length let up again to feel the puzzle of puzzles,
And that we call Being.

27

To be in any form, what is that?
(Round and round we go, all of us, and ever come back thither,)
If nothing lay more develop'd the quahaug in its callous shell were enough.

Mine is no callous shell,
I have instant conductors all over me whether I pass or stop,
They seize every object and lead it harmlessly through me.

I merely stir, press, feel with my fingers, and am happy,
To touch my person to some one else's is about as much as I can stand.

28

Is this then a touch? quivering me to a new identity,
Flames and ether making a rush for my veins,
Treacherous tip of me reaching and crowding to help them,
My flesh and blood playing out lightning to strike what is hardly different from myself,
On all sides prurient provokers stiffening my limbs,
Straining the udder of my heart for its withheld drip,
Behaving licentious toward me, taking no denial,
Depriving me of my best as for a purpose,
Unbuttoning my clothes, holding me by the bare waist,
Deluding my confusion with the calm of the sunlight and pasture-fields,
Immodestly sliding the fellow-senses away,
They bribed to swap off with touch and go and graze at the edges of me,
No consideration, no regard for my draining strength or my anger,
Fetching the rest of the herd around to enjoy them a while,
Then all uniting to stand on a headland and worry me.
The sentries desert every other part of me,
They have left me helpless to a red marauder,
They all come to the headland to witness and assist against me.

I am given up by traitors,
I talk wildly, I have lost my wits, I and nobody else am the greatest traitor,
I went myself first to the headland, my own hands carried me there.

You villain touch! what are you doing? my breath is tight in its throat,
Unclench your floodgates, you are too much for me.

29

Blind loving wrestling touch, sheath'd hooded sharp-tooth'd touch!
Did it make you ache so, leaving me?

Parting track'd by arriving, perpetual payment of perpetual loan,
Rich showering rain, and recompense richer afterward.

Sprouts take and accumulate, stand by the curb prolific and vital,
Landscapes projected masculine, full-sized and golden.

30

All truths wait in all things,
They neither hasten their own delivery nor resist it,
They do not need the obstetric forceps of the surgeon,
The insignificant is as big to me as any,
(What is less or more than a touch?)
Logic and sermons never convince,
The damp of the night drives deeper into my soul.

(Only what proves itself to every man and woman is so,
Only what nobody denies is so.)

A minute and a drop of me settle my brain,
I believe the soggy clods shall become lovers and lamps,
And a compend of compends is the meat of a man or woman,
And a summit and flower there is the feeling they have for each other,
And they are to branch boundlessly out of that lesson until it becomes omnific,
And until one and all shall delight us, and we them.

31

I believe a leaf of grass is no less than the journey-work of the stars,
And the pismire is equally perfect, and a grain of sand, and the egg of the wren,
And the tree-toad is a chef-d'œuvre for the highest,
And the running blackberry would adorn the parlors of heaven,
And the narrowest hinge in my hand puts to scorn all machinery,
And the cow crunching with depress'd head surpasses any statue,
And a mouse is miracle enough to stagger sextillions of infidels.

I find I incorporate gneiss, coal, long-threaded moss, fruits, grains, esculent roots,
And am stucco'd with quadrupeds and birds all over,
And have distanced what is behind me for good reasons,
But call any thing back again when I desire it.

In vain the speeding or shyness,
In vain the plutonic rocks send their old heat against my approach,
In vain the mastodon retreats beneath its own powder'd bones,

30. 14. omnific: all-creating.

In vain objects stand leagues off and assume manifold shapes,
In vain the ocean settling in hollows and the great monsters lying low,
In vain the buzzard houses herself with the sky,
In vain the snake slides through the creepers and logs,
In vain the elk takes to the inner passes of the woods,
In vain the razor-bill'd auk sails far north to Labrador,
I follow quickly, I ascend to the nest in the fissure of the cliff.

32

I think I could turn and live with animals, they are so placid and self-contain'd,
I stand and look at them long and long.

They do not sweat and whine about their condition,
They do not lie awake in the dark and weep for their sins,
They do not make me sick discussing their duty to God,
Not one is dissatisfied, not one is demented with the mania of owning things,
Not one kneels to another, nor to his kind that lived thousands of years ago,
Not one is respectable or unhappy over the whole earth.
So they show their relations to me and I accept them,
They bring me tokens of myself, they evince them plainly in their possession.

I wonder where they get those tokens,
Did I pass that way huge times ago and negligently drop them?

Myself moving forward then and now and forever,
Gathering and showing more always and with velocity,
Infinite and omnigenous, and the like of these among them,
Not too exclusive toward the reachers of my remembrancers,
Picking out here one that I love, and now go with him on brotherly terms.

A gigantic beauty of a stallion, fresh and responsive to my caresses,
Head high in the forehead, wide between the ears,
Limbs glossy and supple, tail dusting the ground,
Eyes full of sparkling wickedness, ears finely cut, flexibly moving.

His nostrils dilate as my heels embrace him,
His well-built limbs tremble with pleasure as we race around and return.
I but use you a minute, then I resign you, stallion,
Why do I need your paces when I myself out-gallop them?
Even as I stand or sit passing faster than you.

33

Space and Time! now I see it is true, what I guess'd at,
What I guess'd when I loaf'd on the grass,
What I guess'd while I lay alone in my bed,
And again as I walk'd the beach under the paling stars of the morning.

My ties and ballasts leave me, my elbows rest in sea-gaps,
I skirt sierras, my palms cover continents,
I am afoot with my vision.

By the city's quadrangular houses—in log huts, camping with lumber-men,
Along the ruts of the turnpike, along the dry gulch and rivulet bed,
Weeding my onion-patch or hoeing rows of carrots and parsnips, crossing savannas, trailing in forests,

Prospecting, gold-digging, girdling the trees of a new purchase,
Scorch'd ankle-deep by the hot sand, hauling my boat down the shallow river,
Where the panther walks to and fro on a limb overhead, where the buck turns furiously at the hunter,
Where the rattlesnake suns his flabby length on a rock, where the otter is feeding on fish,
Where the alligator in his tough pimples sleeps by the bayou,
Where the black bear is searching for roots or honey, where the beaver pats the mud with his paddle-shaped tail;
Over the growing sugar, over the yellow-flower'd cotton plant, over the rice in its low moist field,
Over the sharp-peak'd farmhouse, with its scallop'd scum and slender shoots from the gutters,
Over the western persimmon, over the long-leav'd corn, over the delicate blue-flower flax,
Over the white and brown buckwheat, a hummer and buzzer there with the rest,
Over the dusky green of the rye as it ripples and shades in the breeze;
Scaling mountains, pulling myself cautiously up, holding on by low scragged limbs,
Walking the path worn in the grass and beat through the leaves of the brush,
Where the quail is whistling betwixt the woods and the wheat-lot,
Where the bat flies in the Seventh-month eve, where the great gold-bug drops through the dark,
Where the brook puts out of the roots of the old tree and flows to the meadow,
Where cattle stand and shake away flies with the tremulous shuddering of their hides,
Where the cheese-cloth hangs in the kitchen, where andirons straddle the hearth-slab, where cobwebs fall in festoons from the rafters;
Where trip-hammers crash, where the press is whirling its cylinders,
Where the human heart beats with terrible throes under its ribs,
Where the pear-shaped balloon is floating aloft, (floating in it myself and looking composedly down,)
Where the life-car is drawn on the slip-noose, where the heat hatches pale-green eggs in the dented sand,
Where the she-whale swims with her calf and never forsakes it,
Where the steam-ship trails hind-ways its long pennant of smoke,
Where the fin of the shark cuts like a black chip out of the water,
Where the half-burn'd brig is riding on unknown currents,
Where shells grow to her slimy deck, where the dead are corrupting below;
Where the dense-starr'd flag is borne at the head of the regiments,
Approaching Manhattan up by the long-stretching island,
Under Niagara, the cataract falling like a veil over my countenance,
Upon a door-step, upon the horse-block of hard wood outside,
Upon the race-course, or enjoying picnics or jigs or a good game of base-ball,
At he-festivals, with blackguard gibes, ironical license, bull-dances, drinking, laughter,
At the cider-mill tasting the sweets of the brown mash, sucking the juice through a straw,
At apple-peelings wanting kisses for all the red fruit I find,
At musters, beach-parties, friendly bees, huskings, house-raisings;
Where the mocking-bird sounds his delicious gurgles, cackles, screams, weeps,
Where the hay-rick stands in the barn-yard, where the dry-stalks are scatter'd, where the brood-cow waits in the hovel,
Where the bull advances to do his masculine work, where the stud to the mare, where the cock is treading the hen,
Where the heifers browse, where geese nip their food with short jerks,
Where sun-down shadows lengthen over the limitless and lonesome prairie,
Where herds of buffalo make a crawling spread of the square miles far and near,
Where the humming-bird shimmers, where the neck of the long-lived swan is curving and winding,

Where the laughing-gull scoots by the shore, where she laughs her near-human laugh,
Where bee-hives range on a gray bench in the garden half hid by the high weeds,
Where band-neck'd partridges roost in a ring on the ground with their heads out,
Where burial coaches enter the arch'd gates of a cemetery,
Where winter wolves bark amid wastes of snow and icicled trees,
Where the yellow-crown'd heron comes to the edge of the marsh at night and feeds upon small crabs,
Where the splash of swimmers and divers cools the warm noon,
Where the katy-did works her chromatic reed on the walnut-tree over the well,
Through patches of citrons and cucumbers with silver-wired leaves,
Through the salt-lick or orange glade, or under conical firs,
Through the gymnasium, through the curtain'd saloon, through the office or public hall;
Pleas'd with the native and pleas'd with the foreign, pleas'd with the new and old,
Pleas'd with the homely woman as well as the handsome,
Pleas'd with the quakeress as she puts off her bonnet and talks melodiously,
Pleas'd with the tune of the choir of the whitewash'd church,
Pleas'd with the earnest words of the sweating Methodist preacher, impress'd seriously at the camp-meeting;
Looking in at the shop-windows of Broadway the whole forenoon, flatting the flesh of my nose on the thick plate glass,
Wandering the same afternoon with my face turn'd up to the clouds, or down a lane or along the beach,
My right and left arms round the sides of two friends, and I in the middle;
Coming home with the silent and dark-cheek'd bush-boy, (behind me he rides at the drape of the day,)
Far from the settlements studying the print of animals' feet, or the moccasin print,
By the cot in the hospital reaching lemonade to a feverish patient,
Nigh the coffin'd corpse when all is still, examining with a candle;
Voyaging to every port to dicker and adventure,
Hurrying with the modern crowd as eager and fickle as any,
Hot toward one I hate, ready in my madness to knife him,
Solitary at midnight in my back yard, my thoughts gone from me a long while,
Walking the old hills of Judæa with the beautiful gentle God by my side,
Speeding through space, speeding through heaven and the stars,
Speeding amid the seven satellites and the broad ring, and the diameter of eighty thousand miles,
Speeding with tail'd meteors, throwing fire-balls like the rest,
Carrying the crescent child that carries its own full mother in its belly,
Storming, enjoying, planning, loving, cautioning,
Backing and filling, appearing and disappearing,
I tread day and night such roads.

I visit the orchards of spheres and look at the product,
And look at quintillions ripen'd and look at quintillions green.

I fly those flights of a fluid and swallowing soul,
My course runs below the soundings of plummets.

I help myself to material and immaterial,
No guard can shut me off, no law prevent me.

I anchor my ship for a little while only,
My messengers continually cruise away or bring their returns to me.

I go hunting polar furs and the seal, leaping chasms with a pike-pointed staff, clinging to topples of brittle and blue.

I ascend to the foretruck,
I take my place late at night in the crow's-nest,
We sail the arctic sea, it is plenty light enough,
Through the clear atmosphere I stretch around on the wonderful beauty,
The enormous masses of ice pass me and I pass them, the scenery is plain in all directions,
The white-topt mountains show in the distance, I fling out my fancies toward them,
We are approaching some great battle-field in which we are soon to be engaged,
We pass the colossal outposts of the encampment, we pass with still feet and caution,
Or we are entering by the suburbs some vast and ruin'd city,
The blocks and fallen architecture more than all the living cities of the globe.

I am a free companion, I bivouac by invading watchfires,
I turn the bridegroom out of bed and stay with the bride myself,
I tighten her all night to my thighs and lips.

My voice is the wife's voice, the screech by the rail of the stairs,
They fetch my man's body up dripping and drown'd.

I understand the large hearts of heroes,
The courage of present times and all times,
How the skipper saw the crowded and rudderless wreck of the steam-ship, and Death chasing it up and down the storm,
How he knuckled tight and gave not back an inch, and was faithful of days and faithful of nights,
And chalk'd in large letters on a board, *Be of good cheer, we will not desert you;*
How he follow'd with them and tack'd with them three days and would not give it up.
How he saved the drifting company at last,
How the lank loose-gown'd women look'd when boated from the side of their prepared graves,
How the silent old-faced infants and the lifted sick, and the sharp-lipp'd unshaved men;
All this I swallow, it tastes good, I like it well, it becomes mine,
I am the man, I suffer'd, I was there.

The disdain and calmness of martyrs,
The mother of old, condemn'd for a witch, burnt with dry wood, her children gazing on,
The hounded slave that flags in the race, leans by the fence, blowing, cover'd with sweat,
The twinges that sting like needles his legs and neck, the murderous buckshot and the bullets,
All these I feel or am.

I am the hounded slave, I wince at the bite of the dogs,
Hell and despair are upon me, crack and again crack the marksmen,
I clutch the rails of the fence, my gore dribs, thinn'd with the ooze of my skin,
I fall on the weeds and stones,
The riders spur their unwilling horses, haul close,
Taunt my dizzy ears and beat me violently over the head with whip-stocks.

Agonies are one of my changes of garments.
I do not ask the wounded person how he feels, I myself become the wounded person,
My hurts turn livid upon me as I lean on a cane and observe.

33. 131. **dribs:** i.e., dribbles.

I am the mash'd fireman with breast-bone broken,
Tumbling walls buried me in their debris,
Heat and smoke I inspired, I heard the yelling shouts of my comrades,
I heard the distant click of their picks and shovels,
They have clear'd the beams away, they tenderly lift me forth.

I lie in the night air in my red shirt, the pervading hush is for my sake,
Painless after all I lie exhausted but not so unhappy,
White and beautiful are the faces around me, the heads are bared of their fire-caps,
The kneeling crowd fades with the light of the torches.

Distant and dead resuscitate,
They show as the dial or move as the hands of me, I am the clock myself.

I am an old artillerist, I tell of my fort's bombardment,
I am there again.

Again the long roll of the drummers,
Again the attacking cannon, mortars,
Again to my listening ears the cannon responsive.

I take part, I see and hear the whole,
The cries, curses, roar, the plaudits for well-aim'd shots,
The ambulanza slowly passing trailing its red drip,
Workmen searching after damages, making indispensable repairs,
The fall of grenades through the rent roof, the fan-shaped explosion,
The whizz of limbs, heads, stone, wood, iron, high in the air.

Again gurgles the mouth of my dying general, he furiously waves with his hand,
He gasps through the clot *Mind not me—mind—the entrenchments.*

34

Now I tell what I know in Texas in my early youth,
(I tell not the fall of Alamo,
Not one escaped to tell the fall of Alamo,
The hundred and fifty are dumb yet at Alamo,)
'Tis the tale of the murder in cold blood of four hundred and twelve young men.

Retreating they had form'd in a hollow square with their baggage for breastworks,
Nine hundred lives out of the surrounding enemy's, nine times their number, was the price they took in advance,
Their colonel was wounded and their ammunition gone,
They treated for an honorable capitulation, receiv'd writing and seal, gave up their arms and march'd back prisoners of war.

They were the glory of the race of rangers,
Matchless with horse, rifle, song, supper, courtship,
Large, turbulent, generous, handsome, proud, and affectionate,
Bearded, sunburnt, drest in the free costume of hunters,
Not a single one over thirty years of age.

The second First-day morning they were brought out in squads and massacred, it was beautiful early summer,

34. 5. **the tale of the murder:** the shooting of several hundred American prisoners of war by order of the Mexican general Santa Anna, at Goliad, Texas, in March, 1836.

The work commenced about five o'clock and was over by eight.

None obey'd the command to kneel,
Some made a mad and helpless rush, some stood stark and straight,
A few fell at once, shot in the temple or heart, the living and dead lay together,
The maim'd and mangled dug in the dirt, the new-comers saw them there,
Some half-kill'd attempted to crawl away,
These were despatch'd with bayonets or batter'd with the blunts of muskets.
A youth not seventeen years old seiz'd his assassin till two more came to release him,
The three were all torn and cover'd with the boy's blood.

At eleven o'clock began the burning of the bodies;
That is the tale of the murder of the four hundred and twelve young men.

35

Would you hear of an old-time sea-fight?
Would you learn who won by the light of the moon and stars?
List to the yarn, as my grandmother's father the sailor told it to me.

Our foe was no skulk in his ship I tell you, (said he,)
His was the surly English pluck, and there is no tougher or truer, and never was, and never will be;
Along the lower'd eve he came horribly raking us.

We closed with him, the yards entangled, the cannon touch'd,
My captain lash'd fast with his own hands.

We had receiv'd some eighteen pound shots under the water,
On our lower-gun-deck two large pieces had burst at the first fire, killing all around and blowing up overhead.

Fighting at sun-down, fighting at dark,
Ten o'clock at night, the full moon well up, our leaks on the gain, and five feet of water reported,
The master-at-arms loosing the prisoners confined in the after-hold to give them a chance for themselves.

The transit to and from the magazine is now stopt by the sentinels,
They see so many strange faces they do not know whom to trust.

Our frigate takes fire,
The other asks if we demand quarter?
If our colors are struck and the fighting done?

Now I laugh content, for I hear the voice of my little captain,
We have not struck, he composedly cries, *we have just begun our part of the fighting.*

Only three guns are in use,
One is directed by the captain himself against the enemy's main-mast,
Two well serv'd with grape and canister silence his musketry and clear his decks.

The tops alone second the fire of this little battery, especially the main-top,
They hold out bravely during the whole of the action.

Not a moment's cease,
The leaks gain fast on the pumps, the fire eats toward the powder-magazine.
One of the pumps has been shot away, it is generally thought we are sinking.

Serene stands the little captain,
He is not hurried, his voice is neither high nor low,
His eyes give more light to us than our battle-lanterns.

Toward twelve there in the beams of the moon they surrender to us.

36

Stretch'd and still lies the midnight,
Two great hulls motionless on the breast of the darkness,
Our vessel riddled and slowly sinking, preparations to pass to the one we have conquer'd,
The captain on the quarter-deck coldly giving his orders through a countenance white as a sheet,
Near by the corpse of the child that serv'd in the cabin,
The dead face of an old salt with long white hair and carefully curl'd whiskers,
The flames spite of all that can be done flickering aloft and below,
The husky voices of the two or three officers yet fit for duty,
Formless stacks of bodies and bodies by themselves, dabs of flesh upon the masts and spars,
Cut of cordage, dangle of rigging, slight shock of the soothe of waves,
Black and impassive guns, litter of powder-parcels, strong scent,
A few large stars overhead, silent and mournful shining,
Delicate sniffs of sea-breeze, smells of sedgy grass and fields by the shore, death-messages given in charge to survivors,
The hiss of the surgeon's knife, the gnawing teeth of his saw,
Wheeze, cluck, swash of falling blood, short wild scream, and long, dull, tapering groan,
These so, these irretrievable.

37

You laggards there on guard! look to your arms!
In at the conquer'd doors they crowd! I am possess'd!
Embody all presences outlaw'd or suffering,
See myself in prison shaped like another man.
And feel the dull unintermitted pain,
For me the keepers of convicts shoulder their carbines and keep watch.
It is I let out in the morning and barr'd at night.

Not a mutineer walks handcuff'd to jail but I am handcuff'd to him and walk by his side,
(I am less the jolly one there, and more the silent one with sweat on my twitching lips.)

Not a youngster is taken for larceny but I go up too, and am tried and sentenced.

Not a cholera patient lies at the last gasp but I also lie at the last gasp,
My face is ash-color'd, my sinews gnarl, away from me people retreat.

Askers embody themselves in me and I am embodied in them,
I project my hat, sit shame-faced, and beg.

38

Enough! enough! enough!
Somehow I have been stunn'd. Stand back!
Give me a little time beyond my cuff'd head, slumbers, dreams, gaping,
I discover myself on the verge of a usual mistake.

That I could forget the mockers and insults!
That I could forget the trickling tears and the blows of the bludgeons and hammers!
That I could look with a separate look on my own crucifixion and bloody crowning!

I remember now,
I resume the overstaid fraction,
The grave of rock multiplies what has been confided to it, or to any graves,
Corpses rise, gashes heal, fastenings roll from me.

I troop forth replenish'd with supreme power, one of an average unending procession,
Inland and sea-coast we go, and pass all boundary lines,
Our swift ordinances on their way over the whole earth,
The blossoms we wear in our hats the growth of thousands of years.

Eleves, I salute you! come forward!
Continue your annotations, continue your questionings.

39

The friendly and flowing savage, who is he?
Is he waiting for civilization, or past it and mastering it?

Is he some Southwesterner rais'd out-doors? is he Kanadian?
Is he from the Mississippi country? Iowa, Oregon, California?
The mountains? prairie-life, bush-life? or sailor from the sea?

Wherever he goes men and women accept and desire him,
They desire he should like them, touch them, speak to them, stay with them.

Behavior lawless as snow-flakes, words simple as grass, uncomb'd head, laughter, and naivetè,
Slow-stepping feet, common features, common modes and emanations,
They descend in new forms from the tips of his fingers,
They are wafted with the odor of his body or breath, they fly out of the glance of his eyes.

40

Flaunt of the sunshine I need not your bask—lie over!
You light surfaces only, I force surfaces and depths also.

Earth! you seem to look for something at my hands,
Say, old top-knot, what do you want?

Man or woman, I might tell how I like you, but cannot,
And might tell what it is in me and what it is in you, but cannot,
And might tell that pining I have, that pulse of my nights and days.

Behold, I do not give lectures or a little charity,
When I give I give myself.

38. 16. Eleves: a French word meaning "students," here probably "disciples."

You there, impotent, loose in the knees,
Open your scarf'd chops till I blow grit within you,
Spread your palms and lift the flaps of your pockets,
I am not to be denied, I compel, I have stores plenty and to spare,
And any thing I have I bestow.

I do not ask who you are, that is not important to me,
You can do nothing and be nothing but what I will infold you.

To cotton-field drudge or cleaner of privies I lean,
On his right cheek I put the family kiss,
And in my soul I swear I never will deny him.

On women fit for conception I start bigger and nimbler babes,
(This day I am jetting the stuff of far more arrogant republics.)

To any one dying, thither I speed and twist the knob of the door,
Turn the bed-clothes toward the foot of the bed,
Let the physician and the priest go home.

I seize the descending man and raise him with resistless will,
O despairer, here is my neck,
By God, you shall not go down! hang your whole weight upon me.

I dilate you with tremendous breath, I buoy you up,
Every room of the house do I fill with an arm'd force,
Lovers of me, bafflers of graves.

Sleep—I and they keep guard all night,
Not doubt, not disease shall dare to lay finger upon you,
I have embraced you, and henceforth possess you to myself,
And when you rise in the morning you will find what I tell you is so.

41

I am he bringing help for the sick as they pant on their backs,
And for strong upright men I bring yet more needed help.

I heard what was said of the universe,
Heard it and heard it of several thousand years;
It is middling well as far as it goes—but is that all?

Magnifying and applying come I,
Outbidding at the start the old cautious hucksters,
Taking myself the exact dimensions of Jehovah,
Lithographing Kronos, Zeus his son, and Hercules his grandson,
Buying drafts of Osiris, Isis, Belus, Brahma, Buddha,
In my portfolio placing Manito loose, Allah on a leaf, the crucifix engraved,
With Odin and the hideous-faced Mexitli and every idol and image,
Taking them all for what they are worth and not a cent more,
Admitting they were alive and did the work of their days,
(They bore mites as for unfledg'd birds who have now to rise and fly and sing for themselves,)
Accepting the rough deific sketches to fill out better in myself, bestowing them freely on each man and woman I see,
Discovering as much or more in a framer framing a house,

Putting higher claims for him there with his roll'd-up sleeves driving the mallet and chisel,
Not objecting to special revelations, considering a curl of smoke or a hair on the back of my hand just as curious as any revelation,
Lads ahold of fire-engines and hook-and-ladder ropes no less to me than the gods of the antique wars,
Minding their voices peal through the crash of destruction,
Their brawny limbs passing safe over charr'd laths, their white foreheads whole and unhurt out of the flames;
By the mechanic's wife with her babe at her nipple interceding for every person born,
Three scythes at harvest whizzing in a row from three lusty angels with shirts bagg'd out at their waists,
The snag-tooth'd hostler with red hair redeeming sins past and to come,
Selling all he possesses, traveling on foot to fee lawyers for his brother and sit by him while he is tried for forgery;
What was strewn in the amplest strewing the square rod about me, and not filling the square rod then,
The bull and the bug never worshipp'd half enough,
Dung and dirt more admirable than was dream'd,
The supernatural of no account, myself waiting my time to be one of the supremes,
The day getting ready for me when I shall do as much good as the best, and be as prodigious;
By my life-lumps! becoming already a creator,
Putting myself here and now to the ambush'd womb of the shadows.

42

A call in the midst of the crowd,
My own voice, orotund sweeping and final.

Come my children,
Come my boys and girls, my women, household and intimates,
Now the performer launches his nerve, he has pass'd his prelude on the reeds within.

Easily written loose-finger'd chords—I feel the thrum of your climax and close.

My head slues round on my neck,
Music rolls, but not from the organ,
Folks are around me, but they are no household of mine.

Ever the hard unsunk ground,
Ever the eaters and drinkers, ever the upward and downward sun, ever the air and the ceaseless tides,
Ever myself and my neighbors, refreshing, wicked, real,
Ever the old inexplicable query, ever that thorn'd thumb, that breath of itches and thirsts,
Ever the vexer's *hoot! hoot!* till we find where the sly one hides and bring him forth,
Ever love, ever the sobbing liquid of life,
Ever the bandage under the chin, ever the trestles of death.

Here and there with dimes on the eyes walking,
To feed the greed of the belly the brains liberally spooning,
Tickets buying, taking, selling, but in to the feast never once going,
Many sweating, ploughing, thrashing, and then the chaff for payment receiving,
A few idly owning, and they the wheat continually claiming.

This is the city and I am one of the citizens,
Whatever interests the rest interests me, politics, wars, markets, newspapers, schools,
The mayor and councils, banks, tariffs, steamships, factories, stocks, stores, real estate and personal estate.

The little plentiful manikins skipping around in collars and tail'd coats,
I am aware who they are, (they are positively not worms or fleas,)
I acknowledge the duplicates of myself, the weakest and shallowest is deathless with me,
What I do and say the same waits for them,
Every thought that flounders in me the same flounders in them.

I know perfectly well my own egotism,
Know my omnivorous lines and must not write any less,
And would fetch you whoever you are flush with myself.

Not words of routine this song of mine,
But abruptly to question, to leap beyond yet nearer bring;
This printed and bound book—but the printer and the printing-office boy?
The well-taken photographs—but your wife or friend close and solid in your arms?
The black ship mail'd with iron, her mighty guns in her turrets—but the pluck of the captain and engineers?
In the houses the dishes and fare and furniture—but the host and hostess, and the look out of their eyes?
The sky up there—yet here or next door, or across the way?
The saints and sages in history—but you yourself?
Sermons, creeds, theology—but the fathomless human brain,
And what is reason? and what is love? and what is life?

43

I do not despise you priests, all time, the world over,
My faith is the greatest of faiths and the least of faiths,
Enclosing worship ancient and modern and all between ancient and modern,
Believing I shall come again upon the earth after five thousand years,
Waiting responses from oracles, honoring the gods, saluting the sun,
Making a fetich of the first rock or stump, powowing with sticks in the circle of obis,
Helping the llama or brahmin as he trims the lamps of the idols,
Dancing yet through the streets in a phallic procession, rapt and austere in the woods a gymnosophist,
Drinking mead from the skull-cup, to Shastas and Vedas admirant, minding the Koran,
Walking the teokallis, spotted with gore from the stone and knife, beating the serpent-skin drum,
Accepting the Gospels, accepting him that was crucified, knowing assuredly that he is divine,
To the mass kneeling or the puritan's prayer rising, or sitting patiently in a pew,
Ranting and frothing in my insane crisis, or waiting dead-like till my spirit arouses me.
Looking forth on pavement and land, or outside of pavement and land,
Belonging to the winders of the circuit of circuits.

One of that centripetal and centrifugal gang I turn and talk like a man leaving charges before a journey.
Down-hearted doubters, dull and excluded,
Frivolous, sullen, moping, angry, affected, dishearten'd, atheistical,
I know every one of you, I know the sea of torment, doubt, despair and unbelief.

43. 6. **obis:** amulets with magical powers. 43. 8. **gymnosophist:** ancient Hindu philosopher, member of sect that went nearly naked and devoted itself to mystical contemplation. 43. 10. **teokallis:** Mexican temples.

How the flukes splash!
How they contort rapid as lightning, with spasms and spouts of blood!

Be at peace bloody flukes of doubters and sullen mopers,
I take my place among you as much as among any,
The past is the push of you, me, all, precisely the same,
And what is yet untried and afterward is for you, me, all precisely the same.

I do not know what is untried and afterward,
But I know it will in its turn prove sufficient, and cannot fail.

Each who passes is consider'd, each who stops is consider'd, not a single one can it fail.

It cannot fail the young man who died and was buried,
Nor the young woman who died and was put by his side,
Nor the little child that peep'd in at the door, and then drew back and was never seen again,
Nor the old man who has lived without purpose, and feels it with bitterness worse than gall,
Nor him in the poor house tubercled by rum and the bad disorder,
Nor the numberless slaughter'd and wreck'd, nor the brutish koboo call'd the ordure of humanity,
Nor the sacs merely floating with open mouths for food to slip in,
Nor any thing in the earth, or down in the oldest graves of the earth,
Nor any thing in the myriads of spheres, nor the myriads of myriads that inhabit them,
Nor the present, nor the least wisp that is known.

44

It is time to explain myself—let us stand up.

What is known I strip away,
I launch all men and women forward with me into the Unknown.

The clock indicates the moment—but what does eternity indicate?

We have thus far exhausted trillions of winters and summers,
There are trillions ahead, and trillions ahead of them.

Births have brought us richness and variety,
And other births will bring us richness and variety.

I do not call one greater and one smaller,
That which fills its period and place is equal to any.

Were mankind murderous or jealous upon you, my brother, my sister?
I am sorry for you, they are not murderous or jealous upon me,
All has been gentle with me, I keep no account with lamentation,
(What have I to do with lamentation?)

I am an acme of things accomplish'd, and I an encloser of things to be.

My feet strike an apex of the apices of the stairs,
On every step bunches of ages, and larger bunches between the steps,
All below duly travel'd, and still I mount and mount.

43. 34. **koboo:** wild men; brutish forms of humanity.

Rise after rise bow the phantoms behind me,
Afar down I see the huge first Nothing, I know I was even there,
I waited unseen and always, and slept through the lethargic mist,
And took my time, and took no hurt from the fetid carbon.

Long I was hugg'd close—long and long.

Immense have been the preparations for me,
Faithful and friendly the arms that have help'd me.

Cycles ferried my cradle, rowing and rowing like cheerful boatmen,
For room to me stars kept aside in their own rings,
They sent influences to look after what was to hold me.

Before I was born out of my mother generations guided me,
My embryo has never been torpid, nothing could overlay it.

For it the nebula cohered to an orb,
The long slow strata piled to rest it on,
Vast vegetables gave it sustenance,
Monstrous sauroids transported it in their mouths and deposited it with care.

All forces have been steadily employ'd to complete and delight me,
Now on this spot I stand with my robust soul.

45

O span of youth! ever-push'd elasticity.
O manhood, balanced, florid and full.

My lovers suffocate me,
Crowding my lips, thick in the pores of my skin,
Jostling me through streets and public halls, coming naked to me at night,
Crying by day *Ahoy!* from the rocks of the river, swinging and chirping over my head,
Calling my name from flower-beds, vines, tangled underbrush,
Lighting on every moment of my life,
Bussing my body with soft balsamic busses,
Noiselessly passing handfuls out of their hearts and giving them to be mine.

Old age superbly rising! O welcome, ineffable grace of dying days!

Every condition promulges not only itself, it promulges what grows after and out of itself,
And the dark hush promulges as much as any.

I open my scuttle at night and see the far-sprinkled systems,
And all I see multiplied as high as I can cipher edge but the rim of the farther systems.
Wider and wider they spread, expanding, always expanding,
Outward and outward and forever outward.

My sun has his sun and round him obediently wheels,
He joins with his partners a group of superior circuit,
And greater sets follow, making specks of the greatest inside them.

44. 34. **sauroids:** large fish with lizard-like jaws, now extinct.

There is no stoppage and never can be stoppage,
If I, you, and the worlds, and all beneath or upon their surfaces, were this moment reduced back to a pallid float, it would not avail in the long run,
We should surely bring up again where we now stand,
And surely go as much farther, and then farther and farther.

A few quadrillions of eras, a few octillions of cubic leagues, do not hazard the span or make it impatient,
They are but parts, any thing is but a part.

See ever so far, there is limitless space outside of that,
Count ever so much, there is limitless time around that.

My rendezvous is appointed, it is certain,
The Lord will be there and wait till I come on perfect terms,
The great Camerado, the lover true for whom I pine will be there.

46

I know I have the best of time and space, and was never measured and never will be measured.

I tramp a perpetual journey, (come listen all!)
My signs are a rain-proof coat, good shoes, and a staff cut from the woods,
No friend of mine takes his ease in my chair,
I have no chair, no church, no philosophy,
I lead no man to a dinner-table, library, exchange,
But each man and each woman of you I lead upon a knoll,
My left hand hooking you round the waist,
My right hand pointing to landscapes of continents and the public road.

Not I, not any one else can travel that road for you,
You must travel it for yourself.

It is not far, it is within reach,
Perhaps you have been on it since you were born and did not know,
Perhaps it is everywhere on water and on land.

Shoulder your duds dear son, and I will mine, and let us hasten forth,
Wonderful cities and free nations we shall fetch as we go.

If you tire, give me both burdens, and rest the chuff of your hand on my hip,
And in due time you shall repay the same service to me,
For after we start we never lie by again.

This day before dawn I ascended a hill and look'd at the crowded heaven,
And I said to my spirit *When we become the enfolders of those orbs, and the pleasure and knowledge of every thing in them, shall we be fill'd and satisfied then?*
And my spirit said *No, we but level that lift to pass and continue beyond.*

You are also asking me questions and I hear you,
I answer that I cannot answer, you must find out for yourself.

Sit a while dear son,
Here are biscuits to eat and here is milk to drink,

46. 16. fetch: fetch up at, reach.

But as soon as you sleep and renew yourself in sweet clothes, I kiss you with a good-by kiss and open the gate for your egress hence.

Long enough have you dream'd contemptible dreams,
Now I wash the gum from your eyes,
You must habit yourself to the dazzle of the light and of every moment of your life.

Long have you timidly waded holding a plank by the shore,
Now I will you to be a bold swimmer,
To jump off in the midst of the sea, rise again, nod to me, shout, and laughingly dash with your hair.

47

I am the teacher of athletes,
He that by me spreads a wider breast than my own proves the width of my own,
He most honors my style who learns under it to destroy the teacher.

The boy I love, the same becomes a man not through derived power, but in his own right,
Wicked rather than virtuous out of conformity or fear,
Fond of his sweetheart, relishing well his steak,
Unrequited love or a slight cutting him worse than sharp steel cuts,
First-rate to ride, to fight, to hit the bull's eye, to sail a skiff, to sing a song or play on the banjo.
Preferring scars and the beard and faces pitted with small-pox over all latherers,
And those well-tann'd to those that keep out of the sun.

I teach straying from me, yet who can stray from me?
I follow you whoever you are from the present hour,
My words itch at your ears till you understand them.

I do not say these things for a dollar or to fill up the time while I wait for a boat,
(It is you talking just as much as myself, I act as the tongue of you,
Tied in your mouth, in mine it begins to be loosen'd.)

I swear I will never again mention love or death inside a house,
And I swear I will never translate myself at all, only to him or her who privately stays with me in the open air.

If you would understand me go to the heights or water-shore,
The nearest gnat is an explanation, and a drop or motion of waves a key,
The maul, the oar, the hand-saw, second my words.

No shutter'd room or school can commune with me,
But roughs and little children better than they.

The young mechanic is closest to me, he knows me well,
The woodman that takes his axe and jug with him shall take me with him all day,
The farm-boy ploughing in the field feels good at the sound of my voice,
In vessels that sail my words sail, I go with fishermen and seamen and love them.

The soldier camp'd or upon the march is mine,
On the night ere the pending battle many seek me, and I do not fail them,
On that solemn night (it may be their last) those that know me seek me.

My face rubs to the hunter's face when he lies down alone in his blanket,
The driver thinking of me does not mind the jolt of his wagon,
The young mother and old mother comprehend me,
The girl and the wife rest the needle a moment and forget where they are,
They and all would resume what I have told them.

48

I have said that the soul is not more than the body,
And I have said that the body is not more than the soul,
And nothing, not God, is greater to one than one's self is,
And whoever walks a furlong without sympathy walks to his own funeral drest in his shroud,
And I or you pocketless of a dime may purchase the pick of the earth,
And to glance with an eye or show a bean in its pod confounds the learning of all times,
And there is no trade or employment but the young man following it may become a hero,
And there is no object so soft but it makes a hub for the wheel'd universe,
And I say to any man or woman, Let your soul stand cool and composed before a million universes.

And I say to mankind, Be not curious about God,
For I who am curious about each am not curious about God,
(No array of terms can say how much I am at peace about God and about death.)

I hear and behold God in every object, yet understand God not in the least,
Nor do I understand who there can be more wonderful than myself.

Why should I wish to see God better than this day?
I see something of God each hour of the twenty-four, and each moment then,
In the faces of men and women I see God, and in my own face in the glass,
I find letters from God dropt in the street, and every one is sign'd by God's name,
And I leave them where they are, for I know that wheresoe'er I go
Others will punctually come for ever and ever.

49

And as to you Death, and you bitter hug of mortality, it is idle to try to alarm me.

To his work without flinching the accoucheur comes,
I see the elder-hand pressing receiving supporting,
I recline by the sills of the exquisite flexible doors,
And mark the outlet, and mark the relief and escape.

And as to you Corpse I think you are good manure, but that does not offend me,
I smell the white roses sweet-scented and growing,
I reach to the leafy lips, I reach to the polish'd breasts of melons.

And as to you Life I reckon you are the leavings of many deaths,
(No doubt I have died myself ten thousand times before.)

I hear you whispering there O stars of heaven,
O suns—O grass of graves—O perpetual transfers and promotions,
If you do not say any thing how can I say any thing?

Of the turbid pool that lies in the autumn forest,
Of the moon that descends the steeps of the soughing twilight,
Toss, sparkles of day and dusk—toss on the black stems that decay in the muck,
Toss to the moaning gibberish of the dry limbs.

I ascend from the moon, I ascend from the night,
I perceive that the ghastly glimmer is noonday sunbeams reflected,
And debouch to the steady and central from the offspring great or small.

50

There is that in me—I do not know what it is—but I know it is in me.

Wrench'd and sweaty—calm and cool then my body becomes,
I sleep—I sleep long.

I do not know it—it is without name—it is a word unsaid,
It is not in any dictionary, utterance, symbol.

Something it swings on more than the earth I swing on,
To it the creation is the friend whose embracing awakes me.

Perhaps I might tell more. Outlines! I plead for my brothers and sisters.

Do you see O my brothers and sisters?
It is not chaos or death—it is form, union, plan—it is eternal life—it is Happiness.

51

The past and present wilt—I have fill'd them, emptied them,
And proceed to fill my next fold of the future.

Listener up there! what have you to confide to me?
Look in my face while I snuff the sidle of evening,
(Talk honestly, no one else hears you, and I stay only a minute longer.)

Do I contradict myself?
Very well then I contradict myself,
(I am large, I contain multitudes.)

I concentrate toward them that are nigh, I wait on the door-slab.

Who has done his day's work? who will soonest be through with his supper?
Who wishes to walk with me?

Will you speak before I am gone? will you prove already too late?

52

The spotted hawk swoops by and accuses me, he complains of my gab and my loitering.

I too am not a bit tamed, I too am untranslatable,
I sound my barbaric yawp over the roofs of the world.

49. 20. **debouch:** military term, here slightly misused, meaning to march out of a confined place. 51. 4. **sidle:** edging-along movement (here the slipping-in of evening).

The last scud of day holds back for me,
It flings my likeness after the rest and true as any on the shadow'd wilds,
It coaxes me to the vapor and the dusk.

I depart as air, I shake my white locks at the runaway sun,
I effuse my flesh in eddies, and drift it in lacy jags.

I bequeath myself to the dirt to grow from the grass I love,
If you want me again look for me under your boot-soles.

You will hardly know who I am or what I mean,
But I shall be good health to you nevertheless,
And filter and fibre your blood.

Failing to fetch me at first keep encouraged,
Missing me one place search another,
I stop somewhere waiting for you.

TO THINK OF TIME

1

To think of time—of all that retrospection,
To think of to-day, and the ages continued henceforward.

Have you guess'd you yourself would not continue?
Have you dreaded these earth-beetles?
Have you fear'd the future would be nothing to you?

Is to-day nothing? is the beginningless past nothing?
If the future is nothing they are just as surely nothing.

To think that the sun rose in the east—that men and women were flexible, real, alive—that every thing was alive,
To think that you and I did not see, feel, think, nor bear our part,
To think that we are now here and bear our part.

2

Not a day passes, not a minute or second without an accouchement,
Not a day passes, not a minute or second without a corpse.

The dull nights go over and the dull days also,
The soreness of lying so much in bed goes over,
The physician after long putting off gives the silent and terrible look for an answer,
The children come hurried and weeping, and the brothers and sisters are sent for,
Medicines stand unused on the shelf, (the camphor-smell has long pervaded the rooms,)
The faithful hand of the living does not desert the hand of the dying,
The twitching lips press lightly on the forehead of the dying,
The breath ceases and the pulse of the heart ceases,
The corpse stretches on the bed and the living look upon it,
It is palpable as the living are palpable.

TO THINK OF TIME. Untitled in 1855, "Burial Poem" in 1856; "To Think of Time" in 1871. **2. 1. accouchement:** childbirth.

The living look upon the corpse with their eyesight,
But without eyesight lingers a different living and looks curiously on the corpse.

3

To think the thought of death merged in the thought of materials,
To think of all these wonders of city and country, and others taking great interest in them, and we taking no interest in them.

To think how eager we are in building our houses,
To think others shall be just as eager, and we quite indifferent.

(I see one building the house that serves him a few years, or seventy or eighty years at most,
I see one building the house that serves him longer than that.)

Slow-moving and black lines creep over the whole earth—they never cease—they are the burial lines,
He that was President was buried, and he that is now President shall surely be buried.

4

A reminiscence of the vulgar fate,
A frequent sample of the life and death of workmen,
Each after his kind.

Cold dash of waves at the ferry-wharf, posh and ice in the river, half-frozen mud in the streets,
A gray discouraged sky overhead, the short last daylight of December,
A hearse and stages, the funeral of an old Broadway stage-driver, the cortege mostly drivers.

Steady the trot to the cemetery, duly rattles the death-bell,
The gate is pass'd, the new-dug grave is halted at, the living alight, the hearse uncloses,
The coffin is pass'd out, lower'd and settled, the whip it laid on the coffin, the earth is swiftly shovel'd in,
The mound above is flatted with the spades—silence,
A minute—no one moves or speaks—it is done,
He is decently put away—is there any thing more?

He was a good fellow, free-mouth'd, quick-temper'd, not bad-looking,
Ready with life or death for a friend, fond of women, gambled, ate hearty, drank hearty,
Had known what it was to be flush, grew low-spirited toward the last, sicken'd, was help'd by a contribution,
Died, aged forty-one years—and that was his funeral.

Thumb extended, finger uplifted, apron, cape, gloves, strap, wet-weather clothes, whip carefully chosen,
Boss, spotter, starter, hostler, somebody loafing on you, you loafing on somebody, headway, man before and man behind,
Good day's work, bad day's work, pet stock, mean stock, first out, last out, turning-in at night,

4. 4. **posh**: slush.

To think that these are so much and so nigh to other drivers, and he there takes no interest in them.

5

The markets, the government, the working-man's wages, to think what account they are through our nights and days,
To think that other working-men will make just as great account of them, yet we make little or no account.

The vulgar and the refined, what you call sin and what you call goodness, to think how wide a difference,
To think the difference will still continue to others, yet we lie beyond the difference.

To think how much pleasure there is,
Do you enjoy yourself in the city? or engaged in business? or planning a nomination and election? or with your wife and family?
Or with your mother and sisters? or in womanly housework? or the beautiful maternal cares?
These also flow onward to others, you and I flow onward,
But in due time you and I shall take less interest in them.

Your farm, profits, crops—to think how engross'd you are,
To think there will still be farms, profits, crops, yet for you of what avail?

6

What will be will be well, for what is is well,
To take interest is well, and not to take interest shall be well.

The domestic joys, the daily housework or business, the building of houses, are not phantasms, they have weight, form, location,
Farms, profits, crops, markets, wages, government, are none of them phantasms,
The difference between sin and goodness is no delusion,
The earth is not an echo, man and his life and all the things of his life are well-consider'd.

You are not thrown to the winds, you gather certainly and safely around yourself,
Yourself! yourself! yourself, for ever and ever!

7

It is not to diffuse you that you were born of your mother and father, it is to identify you,
It is not that you should be undecided, but that you should be decided,
Something long preparing and formless is arrived and form'd in you,
You are henceforth secure, whatever comes or goes.

The threads that were spun are gather'd, the weft crosses the warp, the pattern is systematic.

The preparations have every one been justified,
The orchestra have sufficiently tuned their instruments, the baton has given the signal.

The guest that was coming, he waited long, he is now housed,
He is one of those who are beautiful and happy, he is one of those that to look upon and be with is enough.

The law of the past cannot be eluded,
The law of the present and future cannot be eluded,
The law of the living cannot be eluded, it is eternal,
The law of promotion and transformation cannot be eluded,
The law of heroes and good-doers cannot be eluded,
The law of drunkards, informers, mean persons, not one iota thereof can be eluded.

8

Slow moving and black lines go ceaselessly over the earth,
Northerner goes carried and Southerner goes carried, and they on the Atlantic side and they on the Pacific,
And they between, and all through the Mississippi country, and all over the earth.

The great masters and kosmos are well as they go, the heroes and good-doers are well,
The known leaders and inventors and the rich owners and pious and distinguish'd may be well,
But there is more account than that, there is strict account of all.

The interminable hordes of the ignorant and wicked are not nothing,
The barbarians of Africa and Asia are not nothing,
The perpetual successions of shallow people are not nothing as they go.

Of and in all these things,
I have dream'd that we are not to be changed so much, nor the law of us changed,
I have dream'd that heroes and good-doers shall be under the present and past law,
And that murderers, drunkards, liars, shall be under the present and past law,
For I have dream'd that the law they are under now is enough.

And I have dream'd that the purpose and essence of the known life, the transient,
Is to form and decide identity for the unknown life, the permanent.

If all came but to ashes of dung,
If maggots and rats ended us, then Alarum! for we are betray'd,
Then indeed suspicion of death.

Do you suspect death? if I were to suspect death I should die now,
Do you think I could walk pleasantly and well-suited toward annihilation?

Pleasantly and well-suited I walk,
Whither I walk I cannot define, but I know it is good,
The whole universe indicates that it is good,
The past and the present indicate that it is good.

How beautiful and perfect are the animals!
How perfect the earth, and the minutest thing upon it!
What is called good is perfect, and what is called bad is just as perfect,
The vegetables and minerals are all perfect, and the imponderable fluids perfect;
Slowly and surely they have pass'd on to this, and slowly and surely they yet pass on.

9

I swear I think now that every thing without exception has an eternal soul!
The trees have, rooted in the ground! the weeds of the sea have! the animals!

I swear I think there is nothing but immortality!

That the exquisite scheme is for it, and the nebulous float is for it, and the cohering is for it!
And all preparation is for it—and identity is for it—and life and materials are altogether for it!

THE SLEEPERS

I

I wander all night in my vision,
Stepping with light feet, swiftly and noiselessly stepping and stopping,
Bending with open eyes over the shut eyes of sleepers,
Wandering and confused, lost to myself, ill-assorted, contradictory,
Pausing, gazing, bending, and stopping.

How solemn they look there, stretch'd and still,
How quiet they breathe, the little children in their cradles.
The wretched features of ennuyés, the white features of corpses, the livid faces of drunkards, the sick-gray faces of onanists,
The gash'd bodies on battle-fields, the insane in their strong-door'd rooms, the sacred idiots, the new-born emerging from gates, and the dying emerging from gates,
The night pervades them and infolds them.

The married couple sleep calmly in their bed, he with his palm on the hip of the wife, and she with her palm on the hip of the husband,
The sisters sleep lovingly side by side in their bed,
The men sleep lovingly side by side in theirs,
And the mother sleeps with her little child carefully wrapt.

The blind sleep, and the deaf and dumb sleep,
The prisoner sleeps well in the prison, the runaway son sleeps,
The murderer that is to be hung next day, how does he sleep?
And the murder'd person, how does he sleep?

The female that loves unrequited sleeps,
And the male that loves unrequited sleeps,
The head of the money-maker that plotted all day sleeps,
And the enraged and treacherous dispositions, all, all sleep.

I stand in the dark with drooping eyes by the worst-suffering and the most restless,
I pass my hands soothingly to and fro a few inches from them,
The restless sink in their beds, they fitfully sleep.

Now I pierce the darkness, new beings appear,
The earth recedes from me into the night,
I saw that it was beautiful, and I see that what is not the earth is beautiful.

I go from bedside to bedside, I sleep close with the other sleepers each in turn,
I dream in my dream all the dreams of the other dreamers,
And I become the other dreamers.

I am a dance—play up there! the fit is whirling me fast!

THE SLEEPERS. Untitled in 1855; "Night Poem" in 1856; "Sleep-Chasings" in 1860; "The Sleepers" in 1871.

I am the ever-laughing—it is new moon and twilight,
I see the hiding of douceurs, I see nimble ghosts whichever way I look,
Cache and cache again deep in the ground and sea, and where it is neither ground nor sea.

Well do they do their jobs those journeymen divine,
Only from me can they hide nothing, and would not if they could,
I reckon I am their boss and they make me a pet besides,
And surround me and lead me and run ahead when I walk,
To lift their cunning covers to signify me with stretch'd arms, and resume the way;
Onward we move, a gay gang of blackguards! with mirth-shouting music and wild-flapping pennants of joy!

I am the actor, the actress, the voter, the politician,
The emigrant and the exile, the criminal that stood in the box,
He who has been famous and he who shall be famous after to-day,
The stammerer, the well-formed person, the wasted or feeble person.

I am she who adorn'd herself and folded her hair expectantly,
My truant lover has come, and it is dark.

Double yourself and receive me darkness,
Receive me and my lover too, he will not let me go without him.

I roll myself upon you as upon a bed, I resign myself to the dusk.

He whom I call answers me and takes the place of my lover,
He rises with me silently from the bed.

Darkness, you are gentler than my lover, his flesh was sweaty and panting,
I feel the hot moisture yet that he left me.

My hands are spread forth, I pass them in all directions,
I would sound up the shadowy shore to which you are journeying.

Be careful darkness! already what was it touch'd me?
I thought my lover had gone, else darkness and he are one,
I hear the heart-beat, I follow, I fade away.

l. 34. douceurs: gifts or bribes, derived from a French word originally meaning "sweetnesses." **l. 59. I . . . away:** Following this line, the original poem contained three stanzas that were deleted in 1881:

O hotcheeked and blushing! O foolish hectic!
O for pity's sake, no one must see me now! . . . . my clothes were stolen while I was abed,
Now I am thrust forth, where shall I run?

Pier that I saw dimly last night when I looked from the windows,
Pier out from the main, let me catch myself with you and stay . . . . I will not chafe you;
I feel ashamed to go naked about the world,
And am curious to know where my feet stand . . . . and what is this flooding me, childhood or manhood . . . . and the hunger that crosses the bridge between.

The cloth laps a first sweet eating and drinking,
Laps life-swelling yolks . . . . laps ear of rose-corn, milky and just ripened:
The white teeth stay, and the boss-tooth advances in darkness,
And the liquor is spilled on lips and bosoms by touching glasses, and the best liquor afterwards.

2

I descend my western course, my sinews are flaccid,
Perfume and youth course through me and I am their wake.

It is my face yellow and wrinkled instead of the old woman's,
I sit low in a straw-bottom chair and carefully darn my grandson's stockings.

It is I too, the sleepless widow looking out on the winter midnight,
I see the sparkles of starshine on the icy and pallid earth.

A shroud I see and I am the shroud, I wrap a body and lie in the coffin,
It is dark here under ground, it is not evil or pain here, it is blank here, for reasons.

(It seems to me that everything in the light and air ought to be happy,
Whoever is not in his coffin and the dark grave let him know he has enough.)

3

I see a beautiful gigantic swimmer swimming naked through the eddies of the sea,
His brown hair lies close and even to his head, he strikes out with courageous arms, he urges himself with his legs,
I see his white body, I see his undaunted eyes,
I hate the swift-running eddies that would dash him head-foremost on the rocks.

What are you doing unruffianly red-trickled waves?
Will you kill the courageous giant? will you kill him in the prime of his middle age?

Steady and long he struggles,
He is baffled, bang'd, bruis'd, he holds out while his strength holds out,
The slapping eddies are spotted with his blood, they bear him away, they roll him, swing him, turn him,
His beautiful body is borne in the circling eddies, it is continually bruis'd on rocks,
Swiftly and out of sight is borne the brave corpse.

4

I turn but do not extricate myself,
Confused, a past-reading, another, but with darkness yet.

The beach is cut by the razory ice-wind, the wreck-guns sound,
The tempest lulls, the moon comes floundering through the drifts.

I look where the ship helplessly heads end on, I hear the burst as she strikes, I hear the howls of dismay, they grow fainter and fainter.

I cannot aid with my wringing fingers,
I can but rush to the surf and let it drench me and freeze upon me.

I search with the crowd, not one of the company is wash'd to us alive,
In the morning I help pick up the dead and lay them in rows in a barn.

5

Now of the older war-days, the defeat at Brooklyn,
Washington stands inside the lines, he stands on the intrench'd hills amid a crowd of officers,
His face is cold and damp, he cannot repress the weeping drops,

He lifts the glass perpetually to his eyes, the color is blanch'd from his cheeks,
He sees the slaughter of the southern braves confided to him by their parents.

The same at last and at last when peace is declared,
He stands in the room of the old tavern, the well-belov'd soldiers all pass through,
The officers speechless and slow draw near in their turns,
The chief encircles their necks with his arm and kisses them on the cheek,
He kisses lightly the wet cheeks one after another, he shakes hands and bids good-by to the army.

6

Now what my mother told me one day as we sat at dinner together,
Of when she was a nearly grown girl living home with her parents on the old homestead.

A red squaw came one breakfast-time to the old homestead,
On her back she carried a bundle of rushes for rush-bottoming chairs,
Her hair, straight, shiny, coarse, black, profuse, half-envelop'd her face,
Her step was free and elastic, and her voice sounded exquisitely as she spoke.

My mother look'd in delight and amazement at the stranger,
She look'd at the freshness of her tall-borne face and full and pliant limbs,
The more she look'd upon her she loved her,
Never before had she seen such wonderful beauty and purity,
She made her sit on a bench by the jamb of the fireplace, she cook'd food for her,
She had no work to give her, but she gave her remembrance and fondness.

The red squaw staid all the forenoon, and toward the middle of the afternoon she went away,
O my mother was loth to have her go away,
All the week she thought of her, she watch'd for her many a month,
She remember'd her many a winter and many a summer,
But the red squaw never came nor was heard of there again.

7

A show of the summer softness—a contact of something unseen—an amour of the light and air,
I am jealous and overwhelm'd with friendliness,
And will go gallivant with the light and air myself.

O love and summer, you are in the dreams and in me,
Autumn and winter are in the dreams, the farmer goes with his thrift,
The droves and crops increase, the barns are well-fill'd.

Elements merge in the night, ships make tacks in the dreams,
The sailor sails, the exile returns home,
The fugitive returns unharm'd, the immigrant is back beyond months and years,
The poor Irishman lives in the simple house of his childhood with the well-known neighbors and faces,
They warmly welcome him, he is barefoot again, he forgets he is well off,
The Dutchman voyages home, and the Scotchman and Welshman voyage home, and the native of the Mediterranean voyages home,
To every port of England, France, Spain, enter well-fill'd ships,
The Swiss foots it toward his hills, the Prussian goes his way, the Hungarian his way, and the Pole his way,
The Swede returns, and the Dane and Norwegian return.

The homeward bound and the outward bound,
The beautiful lost swimmer, the ennuyé, the onanist, the female that loves unrequited, the money-maker,
The actor and actress, those through with their parts and those waiting to commence,
The affectionate boy, the husband and wife, the voter, the nominee that is chosen and the nominee that has fail'd,
The great already known and the great any time after to-day,
The stammerer, the sick, the perfect-form'd, the homely,
The criminal that stood in the box, the judge that sat and sentenced him, the fluent lawyers, the jury, the audience,
The laughter and weeper, the dancer, the midnight widow, the red squaw,
The consumptive, the erysipalite, the idiot, he that is wrong'd,
The antipodes, and every one between this and them in the dark,
I swear they are averaged now—one is no better than the other,
The night and sleep have liken'd them and restored them.

I swear they are all beautiful,
Every one that sleeps is beautiful, every thing in the dim light is beautiful,
The wildest and bloodiest is over, and all is peace.

Peace is always beautiful,
The myth of heaven indicates peace and night.
The myth of heaven indicates the soul,
The soul is always beautiful, it appears more or it appears less, it comes or it lags behind,
It comes from its embower'd garden and looks pleasantly on itself and encloses the world,
Perfect and clean the genitals previously jetting, and perfect and clean the womb cohering,
The head well-grown proportion'd and plumb, and the bowels and joints proportion'd and plumb.

The soul is always beatuiful,
The universe is duly in order, every thing is in its place,
What has arrived is in its place and what waits shall be in its place,
The twisted skull waits, the watery or rotten blood waits,
The child of the glutton or venerealee waits long, and the child of the drunkard waits long, and the drunkard himself waits long,
The sleepers that lived and died wait, the far advanced are to go on in their turns, and the far behind are to come on in their turns,
The diverse shall be no less diverse, but they shall flow and unite—they unite now.

8

The sleepers are very beautiful as they lie unclothed,
They flow hand in hand over the whole earth from east to west as they lie unclothed,
The Asiatic and African are hand in hand, the European and American are hand in hand,
Learn'd and unlearn'd are hand in hand, and male and female are hand in hand,
The bare arm of the girl crosses the bare breast of her lover, they press close without lust, his lips press her neck,
The father holds his grown or ungrown son in his arms with measureless love, and the son holds the father in his arms with measureless love,
The white hair of the mother shines on the white wrist of the daughter,
The breath of the boy goes with the breath of the man, friend is inarm'd by friend,
The scholar kisses the teacher and the teacher kisses the scholar, the wrong'd is made right,

The call of the slave is one with the master's call, and the master salutes the slave,
The felon steps forth from the prison, the insane becomes sane, the suffering of sick persons is reliev'd,
The sweatings and fevers stop, the throat that was unsound is sound, the lungs of the consumptive are resumed, the poor distress'd head is free,
The joints of the rheumatic move as smoothly as ever, and smoother than ever,
Stiflings and passages open, the paralyzed become supple,
The swell'd and convuls'd and congested awake to themselves in condition,
They pass the invigoration of the night and the chemistry of the night, and awake.

I too pass from the night,
I stay a while away O night, but I return to you again and love you.

Why should I be afraid to trust myself to you?
I am not afraid, I have been well brought forward by you,
I love the rich running day, but I do not desert her in whom I lay so long,
I know not how I came of you and I know not where I go with you, but I know I came well and shall go well.

I will stop only a time with the night, and rise betimes,
I will duly pass the day O my mother, and duly return to you.

THERE WAS A CHILD WENT FORTH

There was a child went forth every day,
And the first object he look'd upon, that object he became,
And that object became part of him for the day or a certain part of the day,
Or for many years or stretching cycles of years.

The early lilacs became part of this child,
And grass and white and red morning-glories, and white and red clover, and the song of the phœbe-bird,
And the Third-month lambs and the sow's pink-faint litter, and the mare's foal and the cow's calf,
And the noisy brood of the barnyard or by the mire of the pond-side,
And the fish suspending themselves so curiously below there, and the beautiful curious liquid,
And the water-plants with their graceful flat heads, all became part of him.

The field-sprouts of Fourth-month and Fifth-month became part of him,
Winter-grain sprouts and those of the light-yellow corn, and the esculent roots of the garden,
And the apple-trees cover'd with blossoms and the fruit afterward, and wood-berries, and the commonest weeds by the road,
And the old drunkard staggering home from the outhouse of the tavern whence he had lately risen,
And the schoolmistress that pass'd on her way to the school,
And the friendly boys that pass'd, and the quarrelsome boys,
And the tidy and fresh-cheek'd girls, and the barefoot negro boy and girl,
And all the changes of city and country wherever he went.

THERE WAS A CHILD WENT FORTH. Untitled in 1855; "Poem of the Child That Went Forth, and Always Goes Forth, Forever and Forever" in 1856; present title in 1867.

His own parents, he that had father'd him and she that had conceiv'd him in her womb and birth'd him,
They gave this child more of themselves than that,
They gave him afterward every day, they became part of him.

The mother at home quietly placing the dishes on the supper-table,
The mother with mild words, clean her cap and gown, a wholesome odor falling off her person and clothes as she walks by,
The father, strong, self-sufficient, manly, mean, anger'd, unjust,
The blow, the quick loud word, the tight bargain, the crafty lure,
The family usages, the language, the company, the furniture, the yearning and swelling heart,
Affection that will not be gainsay'd, the sense of what is real, the thought if after all it should prove unreal,
The doubts of day-time and the doubts of night-time, the curious whether and how,
Whether that which appears so is so, or is it all flashes and specks?
Men and women crowding fast in the streets, if they are not flashes and specks what are they?
The streets themselves and the façades of houses, and goods in the windows,
Vehicles, teams, the heavy-plank'd wharves, the huge crossing at the ferries,
The village on the highland seen from afar at sunset, the river between,
Shadows, aureola and mist, the light falling on roofs and gables of white or brown two miles off,
The schooner near by sleepily dropping down the tide, the little boat slack-tow'd astern,
The hurrying tumbling waves, quick-broken crests, slapping,
The strata of color'd clouds, the long bar of maroon-tint away solitary by itself, the spread of purity it lies motionless in,
The horizon's edge, the flying sea-crow, the fragrance of salt marsh and shore mud,
These became part of that child who went forth every day, and who now goes, and will always go forth every day.

II: 1856

◇

THESE poems, along with sixteen others, were added to the second, or 1856, edition of *Leaves of Grass*. All thirty-two poems in this edition were titled, numbered, and classified. Earlier eccentricities of punctuation and spacing were much restrained. On the back cover of the edition, there was quoted—without permission—a line from the letter Emerson had written to Whitman on receipt of the first edition: "I greet you at the beginning of a great career." Many of the new poems reflect an excitement verging on intoxication: an emotion generated in part by responses like that of Emerson, and by Whitman's conviction that he had found his true vocation and that the vocation was a great one. The excitement takes the form of an identification of Whitman's own artistic and physical fecundity and the mysterious and paradoxical fecundity of nature. "Crossing Brooklyn Ferry" is perhaps Whitman's most satisfying and accomplished "visionary" poem.

◇

SPONTANEOUS ME

Spontaneous me, Nature,
The loving day, the mounting sun, the friend I am happy with,
The arm of my friend hanging idly over my shoulder,
The hillside whiten'd with blossoms of the mountain ash,

SPONTANEOUS ME. "Bunch Poem" in 1856; present title in 1867.

The same late in autumn, the hues of red, yellow, drab, purple, and light and dark green,
The rich coverlet of the grass, animals and birds, the private untrimm'd bank, the primitive apples, the pebble-stones,
Beautiful dripping fragments, the negligent list of one after another as I happen to call them to me or think of them,
The real poems, (what we call poems being merely pictures,)
The poems of the privacy of the night, and of men like me,
This poem drooping shy and unseen that I always carry, and that all men carry,
(Know once for all, avow'd on purpose, wherever are men like me, are our lusty lurking masculine poems,)
Love-thoughts, love-juice, love-odor, love-yielding, love-climbers, and the climbing sap,
Arms and hands of love, lips of love, phallic thumb of love, breasts of love, bellies press'd and glued together with love,
Earth of chaste love, life that is only life after love,
The body of my love, the body of the woman I love, the body of the man, the body of the earth,
Soft forenoon airs that blow from the south-west,
The hairy wild-bee that murmurs and hankers up and down, that gripes the full-grown lady-flower, curves upon her with amorous firm legs, takes his will of her, and holds himself tremulous and tight till he is satisfied;
The wet of woods through the early hours,
Two sleepers at night lying close together as they sleep, one with an arm slanting down across and below the waist of the other,
The smell of apples, aromas from crush'd sage-plant, mint, birch-bark,
The boy's longings, the glow and pressure as he confides to me what he was dreaming,
The dead leaf whirling its spiral whirl and falling still and content to the ground,
The no-form'd stings that sights, people, objects, sting me with,
The hubb'd sting of myself, stinging me as much as it ever can any one,
The sensitive, orbic, underlapp'd brothers, that only privileged feelers may be intimate where they are,
The curious roamer the hand roaming all over the body, the bashful withdrawing of flesh where the fingers soothingly pause and edge themselves,
The limpid liquid within the young man,
The vex'd corrosion so pensive and so painful,
The torment, the irritable tide that will not be at rest,
The like of the same I feel, the like of the same in others,
The young man that flushes and flushes, and the young woman that flushes and flushes,
The young man that wakes deep at night, the hot hand seeking to repress what would master him,
The mystic amorous night, the strange half-welcome pangs, visions, sweats,
The pulse pounding through palms and trembling encircling fingers, the young man all color'd, red, ashamed, angry;
The souse upon me of my lover the sea, as I lie willing and naked,
The merriment of the twin babes that crawl over the grass in the sun, the mother never turning her vigilant eyes from them,
The walnut-trunk, the walnut-husks, and the ripening or ripen'd long-round walnuts,
The continence of vegetables, birds, animals,
The consequent meanness of me should I skulk or find myself indecent, while birds and animals never once skulk or find themselves indecent,
The great chastity of paternity to match the great chastity of maternity,
The oath of procreation I have sworn, my Adamic and fresh daughters,
The greed that eats me day and night with hungry gnaw, till I saturate what shall produce boys to fill my place when I am through,
The wholesome relief, repose, content,
And this bunch pluck'd at random from myself,
It has done its work—I toss it carelessly to fall where it may.

THIS COMPOST

1

Something startles me where I thought I was safest,
I withdraw from the still woods I loved,
I will not go now on the pastures to walk,
I will not strip the clothes from my body to meet my lover the sea,
I will not touch my flesh to the earth as to other flesh to renew me.

O how can it be that the ground itself does not sicken?
How can you be alive you growths of spring?
How can you furnish health you blood of herbs, roots, orchards, grain?
Are they not continually putting distemper'd corpses within you?
Is not every continent work'd over and over with sour dead?

Where have you disposed of their carcasses?
Those drunkards and gluttons of so many generations?
Where have you drawn off all the foul liquid and meat?
I do not see any of it upon you to-day, or perhaps I am deceiv'd,
I will run a furrow with my plough, I will press my spade through the sod and turn it up underneath,
I am sure I shall expose some of the foul meat.

2

Behold this compost! behold it well!
Perhaps every mite has once form'd part of a sick person—yet behold!
The grass of spring covers the prairies,
The bean bursts noiselessly through the mould in the garden,
The delicate spear of the onion pierces upward,
The apple-buds cluster together on the apple-branches,
The resurrection of the wheat appears with pale visage out of its graves,
The tinge awakes over the willow-tree and the mulberry-tree,
The he-birds carol mornings and evenings while the she-birds sit on their nests,
The young of poultry break through the hatch'd eggs,
The new-born of animals appear, the calf is dropt from the cow, the colt from the mare,
Out of its little hill faithfully rise the potato's dark green leaves,
Out of its hill rises the yellow maize-stalk, the lilacs bloom in the dooryards,
The summer growth is innocent and disdainful above all those strata of sour dead.

What chemistry!
That the winds are really not infectious,
That this is no cheat, this transparent green-wash of the sea which is so amorous after me,
That it is safe to allow it to lick my naked body all over with its tongues,
That it will not endanger me with the fevers that have deposited themselves in it,
That all is clean forever and forever,
That the cool drink from the well tastes so good,
That blackberries are so flavorous and juicy,
That the fruits of the apple-orchard and the orange-orchard, that melons, grapes, peaches, plums, will none of them poison me,
That when I recline on the grass I do not catch any disease,
Though probably every spear of grass rises out of what was once a catching disease.

THIS COMPOST. "Poem of Wonder at the Resurrection of Wheat" in 1856; present title in 1867. **2. 13. the lilacs . . . dooryards:** This line was added in 1871, some years after the composition of "When Lilacs Last in the Dooryard Bloom'd."

Now I am terrified at the Earth, it is that calm and patient,
It grows such sweet things out of such corruptions,
It turns harmless and stainless on its axis, with such endless successions of diseas'd corpses,
It distills such exquisite winds out of such infused fetor,
It renews with such unwitting looks its prodigal, annual, sumptuous crops,
It gives such divine materials to men, and accepts such leavings from them at last.

CROSSING BROOKLYN FERRY

1

Flood-tide below me! I see you face to face!
Clouds of the west—sun there half an hour high—I see you also face to face.

Crowds of men and women attired in the usual costumes, how curious you are to me!
On the ferry-boats the hundreds and hundreds that cross, returning home, are more curious to me than you suppose,
And you that shall cross from shore to shore years hence are more to me, and more in my meditations, than you might suppose.

2

The impalpable sustenance of me from all things at all hours of the day,
The simple, compact, well-join'd scheme, myself disintegrated, every one disintegrated yet part of the scheme,
The similitudes of the past and those of the future,
The glories strung like beads on my smallest sights and hearings, on the walk in the street and the passage over the river,
The current rushing so swiftly and swimming with me far away,
The others that are to follow me, the ties between me and them,
The certainty of others, the life, love, sight, hearing of others.

Others will enter the gates of the ferry and cross from shore to shore,
Others will watch the run of the flood-tide,
Others will see the shipping of Manhattan north and west, and the heights of Brooklyn to the south and east,
Others will see the islands large and small;
Fifty years hence, others will see them as they cross, the sun half an hour high,
A hundred years hence, or ever so many hundred years hence, other will see them,
Will enjoy the sunset, the pouring-in of the flood-tide, the falling-back to the sea of the ebb-tide.

3

It avails not, time nor place—distance avails not,
I am with you, you men and women of a generation, or ever so many generations hence,
Just as you feel when you look on the river and sky, so I felt,
Just as any of you is one of a living crowd, I was one of a crowd,
Just as you are refresh'd by the gladness of the river and the bright flow, I was refresh'd,
Just as you stand and lean on the rail, yet hurry with the swift current, I stood yet was hurried,
Just as you look on the numberless masts of ships and the thick-stemm'd pipes of steamboats, I look'd.

CROSSING BROOKLYN FERRY. "Sun-down Poem" in 1856; present title in 1860.

I too many and many a time cross'd the river of old,
Watched the Twelfth-month sea-gulls, saw them high in the air floating with motionless wings, oscillating their bodies,
Saw how the glistening yellow lit up parts of their bodies and left the rest in strong shadow,
Saw the slow-wheeling circles and the gradual edging toward the south,
Saw the reflection of the summer sky in the water,
Had my eyes dazzled by the shimmering track of beams,
Look'd at the fine centrifugal spokes of light round the shape of my head in the sun-lit water,
Look'd on the haze on the hills southward and south-westward,
Look'd on the vapor as it flew in fleeces tinged with violet,
Look'd toward the lower bay to notice the vessels arriving,
Saw their approach, saw aboard those that were near me,
Saw the white sails of schooners and sloops, saw the ships at anchor,
The sailors at work in the rigging or out astride the spars,
The round masts, the swinging motion of the hulls, the slender serpentine pennants,
The large and small steamers in motion, the pilots in their pilot-houses,
The white wake left by the passage, the quick tremulous whirl of the wheels,
The flags of all nations, the falling of them at sunset,
The scallop-edged waves in the twilight, the ladled cups, the frolicsome crests and glistening,
The stretch afar growing dimmer and dimmer, the gray walls of the granite storehouses by the docks,
On the river the shadowy group, the big steam-tug closely flank'd on each side by the barges, the hay-boat, the belated lighter,
On the neighboring shore the fires from the foundry chimneys burning high and glaringly into the night,
Casting their flicker of black contrasted with wild red and yellow light over the tops of houses, and down into the clefts of streets.

4

These and all else were to me the same as they are to you,
I loved well those cities, loved well the stately and rapid river,
The men and women I saw were all near to me,
Others the same—others who look back on me because I look'd forward to them,
(The time will come, though I stop here to-day and to-night.)

5

What is it then between us?
What is the count of the scores or hundreds of years between us?

Whatever it is, it avails not—distance avails not, and place avails not,
I too lived, Brooklyn of ample hills was mine,
I too walk'd the streets of Manhattan island, and bathed in the waters around it,
I too felt the curious abrupt questionings stir within me.
In the day among crowds of people sometimes they came upon me,
In my walks home late at night or as I lay in my bed they came upon me,
I too had been struck from the float forever held in solution,
I too had receiv'd identity by my body,
That I was I knew was of my body, and what I should be I knew I should be of my body.

5. 9. **float:** Both the word and the line are elusive, but "float" is probably used here in its obsolete sense of flux or flood.

6

It is not upon you alone the dark patches fall,
The dark threw its patches down upon me also,
The best I had done seem'd to me blank and suspicious,
My great thoughts as I supposed them, were they not in reality meagre?
Nor is it you alone who know what it is to be evil,
I am he who knew what it was to be evil,
I too knitted the old knot of contrariety,
Blabb'd, blush'd, resented, lied, stole, grudg'd,
Had guile, anger, lust, hot wishes I dared not speak,
Was wayward, vain, greedy, shallow, sly, cowardly, malignant,
The wolf, the snake, the hog, not wanting in me,
The cheating look, the frivolous word, the adulterous wish, not wanting,
Refusals, hates, postponements, meanness, laziness, none of these wanting,
Was one with the rest, the days and haps of the rest,
Was call'd by my nighest name by clear loud voices of young men as they saw me approaching or passing,
Felt their arms on my neck as I stood, or the negligent leaning of their flesh against me as I sat,
Saw many I loved in the street or ferry-boat or public assembly, yet never told them a word,
Lived the same life with the rest, the same old laughing, gnawing, sleeping,
Play'd the part that still looks back on the actor or actress,
The same old role, the role that is what we make it, as great as we like,
Or as small as we like, or both great and small.

7

Closer yet I approach you,
What thought you have of me now, I had as much of you—I laid in my stores in advance,
I consider'd long and seriously of you before you were born.

Who was to know what should come home to me?
Who knows but I am enjoying this?
Who knows, for all the distance, but I am as good as looking at you now, for all you cannot see me?

8

Ah, what can ever be more stately and admirable to me than masthemm'd Manhattan?
River and sunset and scallop-edg'd waves of flood-tide?
The sea-gulls oscillating their bodies, the hay-boat in the twilight, and the belated lighter?
What gods can exceed these that clasp me by the hand, and with voices I love call me promptly and loudly by my nighest name as I approach?

What is more subtle than this which ties me to the woman or man that looks in my face?
Which fuses me into you now, and pours my meaning into you?

We understand then do we not?
What I promis'd without mentioning it, have you not accepted?
What the study could not teach—what the preaching could not accomplish is accomplish'd, is it not?

9

Flow on, river! flow with the flood-tide, and ebb with the ebb-tide!
Frolic on, crested and scallop-edg'd waves!
Gorgeous clouds of the sunset! drench with your splendor me, or the men and women generations after me!
Cross from shore to shore, countless crowds of passengers!
Stand up, tall masts of Mannahatta! stand up, beautiful hills of Brooklyn!
Throb, baffled and curious brain! throw out questions and answers!
Suspend here and everywhere, eternal float of solution!
Gaze, loving and thirsting eyes, in the house or street or public assembly!
Sound out, voices of young men! loudly and musically call me by my nighest name!
Live, old life! play the part that looks back on the actor or actress!
Play the old role, the role that is great or small according as one makes it!
Consider, you who peruse me, whether I may not in unknown ways be looking upon you;
Be firm, rail over the river, to support those who lean idly, yet haste with the hasting current;
Fly on, sea-birds! fly sideways, or wheel in large circles high in the air;
Receive the summer sky, you water, and faithfully hold it till all downcast eyes have time to take it from you!
Diverge, fine spokes of light, from the shape of my head, or any one's head, in the sunlit water!
Come on, ships from the lower bay! pass up or down, white-sail'd schooners, sloops, lighters!
Flaunt away, flags of all nations! be duly lower'd at sunset!
Burn high your fires, foundry chimneys! cast black shadows at nightfall! cast red and yellow light over the tops of the houses!
Appearances, now or henceforth, indicate what you are,
You necessary film, continue to envelop the soul,
About my body for me, and your body for you, be hung our divinest aromas,
Thrive, cities—bring your freight, bring your shows, ample and sufficient rivers,
Expand, being than which none else is perhaps more spiritual,
Keep your places, objects than which none else is more lasting.

You have waited, you always wait, you dumb, beautiful ministers,
We receive you with free sense at last, and are insatiate henceforward,
Not you any more shall be able to foil us, or withhold yourselves from us,
We use you, and do not cast you aside—we plant you permanently within us,
We fathom you not—we love you—there is perfection in you also,
You furnish your parts toward eternity,
Great or small, you furnish your parts toward the soul.

TO YOU

Whoever you are, I fear you are walking the walks of dreams,
I fear these supposed realities are to melt from under your feet and hands,
Even now your features, joys, speech, house, trade, manners, troubles, follies, costume, crimes, dissipate away from you,
Your true soul and body appear before me,
They stand forth out of affairs, out of commerce, shops, work, farms, clothes, the house, buying, selling, eating, drinking, suffering, dying.

TO YOU. "Poem of You, Whoever you Are" in 1856; present title in 1860.

Whoever you are, now I place my hand upon you, that you be my poem,
I whisper with my lips close to your ear,
I have loved many women and men, but I love none better than you.

O I have been dilatory and dumb,
I should have made my way straight to you long ago,
I should have blabb'd nothing but you, I should have chanted nothing but you.

I will leave all and come and make the hymns of you,
None has understood you, but I understand you,
None has done justice to you, you have not done justice to yourself,
None but has found you imperfect, I only find no imperfection in you,
None but would subordinate you, I only am he who will never consent to subordinate you,
I only am he who places over you no master, owner, better, God, beyond what waits intrinsically in yourself.

Painters have painted their swarming groups and the centre-figure of all,
From the head of the centre-figure spreading a nimbus of gold-color'd light,
But I paint myriads of heads, but paint no head without its nimbus of gold-color'd light,
From my hand from the brain of every man and woman it streams, effulgently flowing forever.

O I could sing such grandeurs and glories about you!
You have not known what you are, you have slumber'd upon yourself all your life,
Your eyelids have been the same as closed most of the time,
What you have done returns already in mockeries,
(Your thrift, knowledge, prayers, if they do not return in mockeries, what is their return?)

The mockeries are not you,
Underneath them and within them I see you lurk,
I pursue you where none else has pursued you,
Silence, the desk, the flippant expression, the night, the accustom'd routine, if these conceal you from others or from yourself, they do not conceal you from me,
The shaved face, the unsteady eye, the impure complexion, if these balk others they do not balk me,
The pert apparel, the deform'd attitude, drunkenness, greed, premature death, all these I part aside.

There is no endowment in man or woman that is not tallied in you,
There is no virtue, no beauty in man or woman, but as good is in you,
No pluck, no endurance in others, but as good is in you,
No pleasure waiting for others, but an equal pleasure waits for you.

As for me, I give nothing to any one except I give the like carefully to you,
I sing the songs of the glory of none, not God, sooner than I sing the songs of the glory of you.

Whoever you are! claim your own at any hazard!
These shows of the East and West are tame compared to you,
These immense meadows, these interminable rivers, you are immense and interminable as they,

These furies, elements, storms, motions of Nature, throes of apparent dissolution, you are he or she who is master or mistress over them,
Master or mistress in your own right over Nature, elements, pain, passion, dissolution.

The hopples fall from your ankles, you find an unfailing sufficiency,
Old or young, male or female, rude, low, rejected by the rest, whatever you are promulges itself,
Through birth, life, death, burial, the means are provided, nothing is scanted,
Through angers, losses, ambition, ignorance, ennui, what you are picks its way.

III: 1860

THE 1860 edition of *Leaves of Grass* contained the following new poems, along with 113 others. This was the most carefully and meaningfully organized of all the versions of *Leaves of Grass* (see Reading Suggestions). The arrangement is so artful as to suggest a story or plot being unfolded in it—the story, perhaps, of the poet discovering his creative powers through the experience of moral and psychological death. The note of suffering, of a sense of loss so intense as to approximate death, is what characterizes the best of the new poems. But in poems like "As I Ebb'd with the Ocean of Life" and "Out of the Cradle Endlessly Rocking"—two of Whitman's masterpieces—the private loss is transformed into immense artistic gain.

A HAND-MIRROR

Hold it up sternly—see this it sends back, (who is it? is it you?)
Outside fair costume, within ashes and filth,
No more a flashing eye, no more a sonorous voice or springy step,
Now some slave's eye, voice, hands, step,
A drunkard's breath, unwholesome eater's face, venerealee's flesh,
Lungs rotting away piecemeal, stomach sour and cankerous,
Joints rheumatic, bowels clogged with abomination,
Blood circulating dark and poisonous streams,
Words babble, hearing and touch callous,
No brain, no heart left, no magnetism of sex;
Such from one look in this looking-glass ere you go hence,
Such a result so soon—and from such a beginning!

HOURS CONTINUING LONG, SORE AND HEAVY-HEARTED

Hours continuing long, sore and heavy-hearted,
Hours of the dusk, when I withdraw to a lonesome and unfrequented spot, seating myself, leaning my face in my hands;
Hours sleepless, deep in the night, when I go forth, speeding swiftly the country roads, or through the city streets, or pacing miles and miles, stifling plaintive cries;
Hours discouraged, distracted—for the one I cannot content myself without, soon I saw him content himself without me;
Hours when I am forgotten, (O weeks and months are passing, but I believe I am never to forget!)

44. **hopples:** fetters for legs of animals. HOURS CONTINUING LONG, SORE AND HEAVY-HEARTED. "Calamus, No. 9" in 1860; rejected in 1867.

Sullen and suffering hours! (I am ashamed—but it is useless—I am what I am;)
Hours of my torment—I wonder if other men ever have the like, out of the like feelings?
Is there even one other like me—distracted—his friend, his lover, lost to him?
Is he too as I am now? Does he still rise in the morning, dejected, thinking who is lost to him? and at night, awaking, think who is lost?
Does he too harbor his friendship silent and endless? harbor his anguish and passion?
Does some stray reminder, or the casual mention of a name, bring the fit back upon him, taciturn and deprest?
Does he see himself reflected in me? In these hours, does he see the face of his hours reflected?

I SAW IN LOUISIANA A LIVE-OAK GROWING

I saw in Louisiana a live-oak growing,
All alone stood it and the moss hung down from the branches,
Without any companion it grew there uttering joyous leaves of dark green.
And its look, rude, unbending, lusty, made me think of myself,
But I wonder'd how it could utter joyous leaves standing alone there without its friend near, for I knew I could not,
And I broke off a twig with a certain number of leaves upon it, and twined around it a little moss,
And brought it away, and I have placed it in sight in my room,
It is not needed to remind me as of my own dear friends,
(For I believe lately I think of little else than of them,)
Yet it remains to me a curious token, it makes me think of manly love;
For all that, and though the live-oak glistens there in Louisiana solitary in a wide flat space,
Uttering joyous leaves all its life without a friend a lover near,
I know very well I could not.

CITY OF ORGIES

City of orgies, walks and joys,
City whom that I have lived and sung in your midst will one day make you illustrious,
Not the pageants of you, not your shifting tableaus, your spectacles, repay me,
Not the interminable rows of your houses, nor the ships at the wharves,
Nor the processions in the streets, nor the bright windows with goods in them,
Nor to converse with learn'd persons, or bear my share in the soiree or feast;
Not those, but as I pass O Manhattan, your frequent and swift flash of eyes offering me love,
Offering response to my own—these repay me,
Lovers, continual lovers, only repay me.

A GLIMPSE

A glimpse through an interstice caught,
Of a crowd of workmen and drivers in a bar-room around the stove late of a winter night, and I unremark'd seated in a corner,

I SAW IN LOUISIANA A LIVE-OAK GROWING. "Calamus, No. 20" in 1860; present title in 1867. 1. **live-oak:** evergreen oak of southern U.S. CITY OF ORGIES. "Calamus, No. 18" in 1860; present title in 1867. A GLIMPSE. "Calamus, No. 29" in 1860; present title in 1867. 1. **interstice:** chink.

Of a youth who loves me and whom I love, silently approaching and seating himself near, that he may hold me by the hand,
A long while amid the noises of coming and going, of drinking and oath and smutty jest,
There we two, content, happy in being together, speaking little, perhaps not a word.

WHOEVER YOU ARE HOLDING ME NOW IN HAND

Whoever you are holding me now in hand;
Without one thing all will be useless,
I give you fair warning before you attempt me further,
I am not what you supposed, but far different.

Who is he that would become my follower?
Who would sign himself a candidate for my affections?

The way is suspicious, the result uncertain, perhaps destructive,
You would have to give up all else, I alone would expect to be your sole and exclusive standard,
Your novitiate would even then be long and exhausting,
The whole past theory of your life and all conformity to the lives around you would have to be abandon'd,
Therefore release me now before troubling yourself any further, let go your hand from my shoulders,
Put me down and depart on your way.

Or else by stealth in some wood for trial,
Or back of a rock in the open air,
(For in any roof'd room of a house I emerge not, nor in company,
And in libraries I lie as one dumb, a gawk, or unborn, or dead,)
But just possibly with you on a high hill, first watching lest any person for miles around approach unawares,
Or possibly with you sailing at sea, or on the beach of the sea or some quiet island,
Here to put your lips upon mine I permit you,
With the comrade's long-dwelling kiss or the new husband's kiss,
For I am the new husband and I am the comrade.

Or if you will, thrusting me beneath your clothing,
Where I may feel the throbs of your heart or rest upon your hip,
Carry me when you go forth over land or sea;
For thus merely touching you is enough, is best,
And thus touching you would I silently sleep and be carried eternally.

But these leaves conning you con at peril,
For these leaves and me you will not understand,
They will elude you at first and still more afterward, I will certainly elude you,
Even while you should think you had unquestionably caught me, behold!
Already you see I have escaped from you.

For it is not for what I have put into it that I have written this book,
Nor is it by reading it you will acquire it,
Nor do those know me best who admire me and vauntingly praise me,
Nor will the candidates for my love (unless at most a very few) prove victorious,

WHOEVER YOU ARE HOLDING ME NOW IN HAND. "Calamus, No. 3" in 1860; present title in 1867.

Nor will my poems do good only, they will do just as much evil, perhaps more,
For all is useless without that which you may guess at many times and not hit, that which I hinted at;
Therefore release me and depart on your way.

SO LONG!

To conclude, I announce what comes after me.

I remember I said before my leaves sprang at all,
I would raise my voice jocund and strong with reference to consummations.

When America does what was promis'd,
When through these States walk a hundred millions of superb persons,
When the rest part away for superb persons and contribute to them,
When breeds of the most perfect mothers denote America,
Then to me and mine our due fruition.

I have press'd through in my own right,
I have sung the body and the soul, war and peace have I sung, and the songs of life and death,
And the songs of birth, and shown that there are many births.

I have offer'd my style to every one, I have journey'd with confident step;
While my pleasure is yet at the full I whisper *So long!*
And take the young woman's hand and the young man's hand for the last time.

I announce natural persons to arise,
I announce justice triumphant,
I announce uncompromising liberty and equality,
I announce the justification of candor and the justification of pride.

I announce that the identity of these States is a single identity only,
I announce the Union more and more compact, indissoluble,
I announce splendors and majesties to make all the previous politics of the earth insignificant.

I announce adhesiveness, I say it shall be limitless, unloosen'd,
I say you shall yet find the friend you were looking for.

I announce a man or woman coming, perhaps you are the one, (*So long!*)
I announce the great individual, fluid as Nature, chaste, affectionate, compassionate, fully arm'd.

I announce a life that shall be copious, vehement, spiritual, bold,
I announce an end that shall lightly and joyfully meet its translation.

I announce myriads of youths, beautiful, gigantic, sweet-blooded,
I announce a race of splendid and savage old men.

O thicker and faster—(*So long!*)
O crowding too close upon me,
I foresee too much, it means more than I thought,
It appears to me I am dying.

Hasten throat and sound your last,
Salute me—salute the days once more. Peal the old cry once more.

Screaming electric, the atmosphere using,
At random glancing, each as I notice absorbing,
Swiftly on, but a little while alighting,
Curious envelop'd messages delivering,
Sparkles hot, seed ethereal down in the dirt dropping,
Myself unknowing, my commission obeying, to question it never daring,
To ages and ages yet the growth of the seed leaving,
To troops out of the war arising, they the task I have set promulging,
To women certain whispers of myself bequeathing, their affection me more clearly explaining,
To young men my problems offering—no dallier I—I the muscle of their brains crying,
So I pass, a little time vocal, visible, contrary,
Afterward a melodious echo, passionately bent for, (death making me really undying,)
The best of me then when no longer visible, for toward that I have been incessantly preparing.

What is there more, that I lag and pause and crouch extended with unshut mouth?
Is there a single final farewell?

My songs cease, I abandon them,
From behind the screen where I hid I advance personally solely to you.

Camerado, this is no book,
Who touches this touches a man,
(Is it night? are we here together alone?)
It is I you hold and who holds you,
I spring from the pages into your arms—decease calls me forth.

O how your fingers drowse me,
Your breath falls around me like dew, your pulse lulls the tympans of my ears,
I feel immerged from head to foot,
Delicious, enough.

Enough O deed impromptu and secret,
Enough O gliding present—enough O summ'd-up past.

Dear friend whoever you are take this kiss,
I give it especially to you, do not forget me,
I feel like one who has done work for the day to retire awhile,
I receive now again of my many translations, from my avataras ascending, while others doubtless await me,
An unknown sphere more real than I dream'd, more direct, darts awakening rays about me, *So long!*
Remember my words, I may again return,
I love you, I depart from materials,
I am as one disembodied, triumphant, dead.

SCENTED HERBAGE OF MY BREAST

Scented herbage of my breast,
Leaves from you I glean, I write, to be perused best afterwards,

SCENTED HERBAGE OF MY BREAST. "Calamus, No. 2" in 1860; present title in 1867. Some of the allusions in the poem are evidently drawn from a picture Whitman had seen of the burial of Osiris, the Egyptian god of the dead and of rebirth.

Tomb-leaves, body-leaves growing up above me above death,
Perennial roots, tall leaves, O the winter shall not freeze you delicate leaves,
Every year shall you bloom again, out from where you retired you shall emerge again;
O I do not know whether many passing by will discover you or inhale your faint odor, but I believe a few will;
O slender leaves! O blossoms of my blood! I permit you to tell in your own way of the heart that is under you,
O I do not know what you mean there underneath yourselves, you are not happiness,
You are often more bitter than I can bear, you burn and sting me,
Yet you are beautiful to me you faint-tinged roots, you make me think of death,
Death is beautiful from you, (what indeed is finally beautiful except death and love?)
O I think it is not for life I am chanting here my chant of lovers, I think it must be for death,
For how calm, how solemn it grows to ascend to the atmosphere of lovers,
Death or life I am then indifferent, my soul declines to prefer,
(I am not sure but the high soul of lovers welcomes death most,)
Indeed O death, I think now these leaves mean precisely the same as you mean,
Grow up taller sweet leaves that I may see! grow up out of my breast!
Spring away from the conceal'd heart there!
Do not fold yourself so in your pink-tinged roots timid leaves!
Do not remain down there so ashamed, herbage of my breast!
Come I am determin'd to unbare this broad breast of mine, I have long enough stifled and choked;
Emblematic and capricious blades I leave you, now you serve me not,
I will say what I have to say by itself,
I will sound myself and comrades only, I will never again utter a call only their call,
I will raise with it immortal reverberations through the States,
I will give an example to lovers to take permanent shape and will through the States,
Through me shall the words be said to make death exhilarating.
Give me your tone therefore O death, that I may accord with it,
Give me yourself, for I see that you belong to me now above all, and are folded inseparably together, you love and death are,
Nor will I allow you to balk me any more with what I was calling life,
For now it is convey'd to me that you are the purports essential,
That you hide in these shifting forms of life, for reasons, and that they are mainly for you,
That you beyond them come forth to remain, the real reality,
That behind the mask of materials you patiently wait, no matter how long,
That you will one day perhaps take control of all,
That you will perhaps dissipate this entire show of appearance,
That may-be you are what it is all for, but it does not last so very long,
But you will last very long.

AS I EBB'D WITH THE OCEAN OF LIFE

1

As I ebb'd with the ocean of life,
As I wended the shores I know,
As I walk'd where the ripples continually wash you Paumanok,
Where they rustle up hoarse and sibilant,
Where the fierce old mother endlessly cries for her castaways,

AS I EBB'D WITH THE OCEAN OF LIFE. Published as "Bardic Symbols" in the April, 1860, *Atlantic Monthly;* "Leaves of Grass, No. 1" in the 1860 edition; "Elemental Drifts" in 1867; present title in 1881. 1. 3. **Paumanok:** Indian name for Long Island.

I musing late in the autumn day, gazing off southward,
Held by this electric self out of the pride of which I utter poems,
Was seiz'd by the spirit that trails in the lines underfoot,
The rim, the sediment that stands for all the water and all the land of the globe.

Fascinated, my eyes reverting from the south, dropt, to follow those slender windrows,
Chaff, straw, splinters of wood, weeds, and the sea-gluten,
Scum, scales from shining rocks, leaves of salt-lettuce, left by the tide,
Miles walking, the sound of breaking waves the other side of me,
Paumanok there and then as I thought the old thought of likenesses,
These you presented to me you fish-shaped island,
As I wended the shores I know,
As I walk'd with that electric self seeking types.

2

As I wend to the shores I know not,
As I list to the dirge, the voices of men and women wreck'd,
As I inhale the impalpable breezes that set in upon me,
As the ocean so mysterious rolls toward me closer and closer,
I too but signify at the utmost a little wash'd-up drift,
A few sands and dead leaves to gather,
Gather, and merge myself as part of the sands and drift.

O baffled, balk'd, bent to the very earth,
Oppress'd with myself that I have dared to open my mouth,
Aware now that amid all that blab whose echoes recoil upon me I have not once had the least idea who or what I am,
But that before all my arrogant poems the real Me stands yet untouch'd, untold, altogether unreach'd,
Withdrawn far, mocking me with mock-congratulatory signs and bows,
With peals of distant ironical laughter at every word I have written,
Pointing in silence to these songs, and then to the sand beneath.
I perceive I have not really understood any thing, not a single object, and that no man ever can,
Nature here in sight of the sea taking advantage of me to dart upon me and sting me,
Because I have dared to open my mouth to sing at all.

3

You oceans both, I close with you,
We murmur alike reproachfully rolling sands and drift, knowing not why,
These little shreds indeed standing for you and me and all.

You friable shore with trails of debris,
You fish-shaped island, I take what is underfoot,
What is yours is mine my father.

I too Paumanok,
I too have bubbled up, floated the measureless float, and been wash'd on your shores,
I too am but a trail of drift and debris,
I too leave little wrecks upon you, you fish-shaped island.

I throw myself upon your breast my father,
I cling to you so that you cannot unloose me,
I hold you so firm till you answer me something.

3. 4. friable: easily crumbled.

Kiss me my father,
Touch me with your lips as I touch those I love,
Breathe to me while I hold you close the secret of the murmuring I envy.

4

Ebb, ocean of life, (the flow will return,)
Cease not your moaning you fierce old mother,
Endlessly cry for your castaways, but fear not, deny not me,
Rustle not up so hoarse and angry against my feet as I touch you or gather from you.

I mean tenderly by you and all,
I gather for myself and for this phantom looking down where we lead, and following me and mine.

Me and mine, loose windrows, little corpses,
Froth, snowy white, and bubbles,
(See, from my dead lips the ooze exuding at last,
See, the prismatic colors glistening and rolling,)
Tufts of straw, sands, fragments,
Buoy'd hither from many moods, one contradicting another,
From the storm, the long calm, the darkness, the swell,
Musing, pondering, a breath, a briny tear, a dab of liquid or soil,
Up just as much out of fathomless workings fermented and thrown,
A limp blossom or two, torn, just as much over waves floating, drifted at random,
Just as much for us that sobbing dirge of Nature,
Just as much whence we come that blare of the cloud-trumpets,
We, capricious, brought hither we know not whence, spread out before you,
You up there walking or sitting,
Whoever you are, we too lie in drifts at your feet.

OUT OF THE CRADLE ENDLESSLY ROCKING

Out of the cradle endlessly rocking,
Out of the mocking-bird's throat, the musical shuttle,
Out of the Ninth-month midnight,
Over the sterile sands and the fields beyond, where the child leaving his bed wander'd alone, bareheaded, barefoot,
Down from the shower'd halo,
Up from the mystic play of shadows twining and twisting as if they were alive,
Out from the patches of briers and blackberries,
From the memories of the bird that chanted to me,
From your memories sad brother, from the fitful risings and fallings I heard,
From under that yellow half-moon late-risen and swollen as if with tears,
From those beginning notes of yearning and love there in the mist,
From the thousand responses of my heart never to cease,
From the myriad thence-arous'd words,
From the word stronger and more delicious than any,

3. 16. **Breathe . . . envy:** This line, in the 1860 edition, was followed by:

> For I fear I shall become crazed, if I cannot emulate it, and utter myself as well as it.
> Sea-raff! Crook-tongued waves!
> O, I will yet sing, some day, what you have said to me.

Those lines were dropped in 1867. OUT OF THE CRADLE ENDLESSLY ROCKING. Published as "A Child's Reminiscence" in the December, 1859, New York *Saturday Press;* "A Word Out of the Sea" in the 1860 edition; present title in 1871. **1. Out . . . rocking:** This line read: "Out of the rocked cradle" in 1860; present version is that of 1871. **2. Out . . . shuttle:** In 1860, this line was followed by: "Out of the boy's mother's womb, and from the nipples of her breasts"—dropped in 1867.

From such as now they start the scene revisiting,
As a flock, twittering, rising, or overhead passing,
Borne hither, ere all eludes me, hurriedly,
A man, yet by these tears a little boy again,
Throwing myself on the sand, confronting the waves,
I, chanter of pains and joys, uniter of here and hereafter,
Taking all hints to use them, but swiftly leaping beyond them,
A reminiscence sing.

Once Paumanok,
When the lilac-scent was in the air and Fifth-month grass was growing,
Up this seashore in some briers,
Two feather'd guests from Alabama, two together,
And their nest, and four light-green eggs spotted with brown,
And every day the he-bird to and fro near at hand,
And every day the she-bird crouch'd on her nest, silent, with bright eyes,
And every day I, a curious boy, never too close, never disturbing them,
Cautiously peering, absorbing, translating.

Shine! shine! shine!
Pour down your warmth, great sun!
While we bask, we two together.

Two together!
Winds blow south, or winds blow north,
Day come white, or night come black,
Home, or rivers and mountains from home,
Singing all time, minding no time,
While we two keep together.

Till of a sudden,
May-be kill'd, unknown to her mate,
One forenoon the she-bird crouch'd not on the nest,
Nor return'd that afternoon, nor the next,
Nor ever appear'd again.

And thenceforward all summer in the sound of the sea,
And at night under the full of the moon in calmer weather,
Over the hoarse surging of the sea,
Or flitting from brier to brier by day,
I saw, I heard at intervals the remaining one, the he-bird,
The solitary guest from Alabama.

Blow! blow! blow!
Blow up sea-winds along Paumanok's shore;
I wait and I wait till you blow my mate to me.

Yes, when the stars glisten'd,
All night long on the prong of a moss-scallop'd stake,
Down almost amid the slapping waves,
Sat the lone singer wonderful causing tears.

He call'd on his mate,
He pour'd forth the meanings which I of all men know.

Yes my brother I know,
The rest might not, but I have treasur'd every note,
For more than once dimly down to the beach gliding,
Silent, avoiding the moonbeams, blending myself with the shadows,
Recalling now the obscure shapes, the echoes, the sounds and sights after their sorts,
The white arms out in the breakers tirelessly tossing,
I, with bare feet, a child, the wind wafting my hair,
Listen'd long and long.

Listen'd to keep, to sing, now translating the notes,
Following you my brother.

Soothe! soothe! soothe!
Close on its wave soothes the wave behind,
And again another behind embracing and lapping, every one close,
But my love soothes not me, not me.

Low hangs the moon, it rose late,
It is lagging—O I think it is heavy with love, with love.

O madly the sea pushes upon the land,
With love, with love.

O night! do I not see my love fluttering out among the breakers?
What is that little black thing I see there in the white?

Loud! loud! loud!
Loud I call to you, my love!
High and clear I shoot my voice over the waves,
Surely you must know who is here, is here,
You must know who I am, my love.

Low-hanging moon!
What is that dusky spot in your brown yellow?
O it is the shape, the shape of my mate!
O moon do not keep her from me any longer.

Land! land! O land!
Whichever way I turn, O I think you could give me my mate back again if you only would,
For I am almost sure I see her dimly whichever way I look.

O rising stars!
Perhaps the one I want so much will rise, will rise with some of you.

O throat! O trembling throat!
Sound clearer through the atmosphere!
Pierce the woods, the earth,
Somewhere listening to catch you must be the one I want.

Shake out carols!
Solitary here, the night's carols!
Carols of lonesome love! death's carols!
Carols under that lagging, yellow, waning moon!
O under that moon where she droops almost down into the sea!
O reckless despairing carols.

But soft! sink low!
Soft! let me just murmur,
And do you wait a moment you husky-nois'd sea,
For somewhere I believe I heard my mate responding to me,
So faint, I must be still, be still to listen,
But not altogether still, for then she might not come immediately to me.

Hither my love!
Here I am! here!
With this just-sustain'd note I announce myself to you,
This gentle call is for you my love, for you.

Do not be decoy'd elsewhere,
That is the whistle of the wind, it is not my voice,
That is the fluttering, the fluttering of the spray,
Those are the shadows of leaves.

O darkness! O in vain!
O I am very sick and sorrowful.

O brown halo in the sky near the moon, drooping upon the sea!
O troubled reflection in the sea!
O throat! O throbbing heart!
And I singing uselessly, uselessly all the night.

O past! O happy life! O songs of joy!
In the air, in the woods, over fields,
Loved! loved! loved! loved! loved!
But my mate no more, no more with me!
We two together no more.

The aria sinking,
All else continuing, the stars shining,
The winds blowing, the notes of the bird continuous echoing,
With angry moans the fierce old mother incessantly moaning,
On the sands of Paumanok's shore gray and rustling,
The yellow half-moon enlarged, sagging down, drooping, the face of the sea almost touching,
The boy ecstatic, with his bare feet the waves, with his hair the atmosphere dallying,
The love in the heart long pent, now loose, now at last tumultuously bursting,
The aria's meaning, the ears, the soul, swiftly depositing,
The strange tears down the cheeks coursing,
The colloquy there, the trio, each uttering,
The undertone, the savage old mother incessantly crying,
To the boy's soul's questions sullenly timing, some drown'd secret hissing,
To the outsetting bard.

Demon or bird! (said the boy's soul,)
Is it indeed toward your mate you sing? or is it really to me?
For I, that was a child, my tongue's use sleeping, now I have heard you,
Now in a moment I know what I am for, I awake,
And already a thousand singers, a thousand songs, clearer, louder and more sorrowful than yours,
A thousand warbling echoes have started to life within me, never to die.

O you singer solitary, singing by yourself, projecting me,
O solitary me listening, never more shall I cease perpetuating you,
Never more shall I escape, never more the reverberations,
Never more the cries of unsatisfied love be absent from me,
Never again leave me to be the peaceful child I was before what there in the night,
By the sea under the yellow and sagging moon,
The messenger there arous'd, the fire, the sweet hell within,
The unknown want, the destiny of me.

O give me the clew! (it lurks in the night here somewhere,)
O if I am to have so much, let me have more!

A word then, (for I will conquer it,)
The word final, superior to all,
Subtle, sent up—what is it?—I listen;
Are you whispering it, and have been all the time, you sea waves?
Is that it from your liquid rims and wet sands?

Whereto answering, the sea,
Delaying not, hurrying not,
Whisper'd me through the night, and very plainly before daybreak,
Lisp'd to me the low and delicious word death,
And again death, death, death, death,
Hissing melodious, neither like the bird nor like my arous'd child's heart,
But edging near as privately for me rustling at my feet,
Creeping thence steadily up to my ears and laving me softly all over,
Death, death, death, death, death.

Which I do not forget,
But fuse the song of my dusky demon and brother,
That he sang to me in the moonlight on Paumanok's gray beach,
With the thousand responsive songs at random,
My own songs awaked from that hour,
And with them the key, the word up from the waves,
The word of the sweetest song and all songs,
That strong and delicious word which, creeping to my feet,
(Or like some old crone rocking the cradle, swathed in sweet garments, bending aside,)
The sea whisper'd me.

IV: 1867

◇

¶ IN 1865, Whitman published a separate little volume of war poems called *Drum-Taps,* to which, in the following year, he added a *Sequel to Drum-Taps,* including "When Lilacs Last in the Dooryard Bloom'd" and others. The poems contained were then attached as an Appendix to the fourth, or 1867, edition of *Leaves of Grass* and later still were incorporated into the main text. It was in the 1867 edition, too, that Whitman made the first of the extensive revisions, deletions, and rearrangements of the sequence of poems that so greatly changed—in fact, distorted—the character of *Leaves of Grass.* In the poem occasioned by the death of Lincoln, however, Whitman arrived at what many readers take to be his supreme accomplishment.

◇

CAVALRY CROSSING A FORD

A line in long array where they wind betwixt green islands,
They take a serpentine course, their arms flash in the sun—hark to the musical clank,
Behold the silvery river, in it the splashing horses loitering stop to drink.
Behold the brown-faced men, each group, each person a picture, the negligent rest on the saddles,
Some emerge on the opposite bank, others are just entering the ford—while,
Scarlet and blue and snowy white,
The guidon flags flutter gayly in the wind.

BIVOUAC ON A MOUNTAIN SIDE

I see before me now a traveling army halting,
Below a fertile valley spread, with barns and the orchards of summer,
Behind, the terraced sides of a mountain, abrupt, in places rising high,
Broken, with rocks, with clinging cedars, with tall shapes dingily seen,
The numerous camp-fires scatter'd near and far, some away up on the mountain,
The shadowy forms of men and horses, looming, large-sized, flickering,
And over all the sky—the sky! far, far out of reach, studded, breaking out, the eternal stars.

THE WOUND-DRESSER

I

An old man bending I come among new faces,
Years looking backward resuming in answer to children,
Come tell us old man, as from young men and maidens that love me,
(Arous'd and angry, I'd thought to beat the alarum, and urge relentless war,
But soon my fingers fail'd me, my face droop'd and I resign'd myself,
To sit by the wounded and soothe them, or silently watch the dead;)
Years hence of these scenes, of these furious passions, these chances,
Of unsurpass'd heroes, (was one side so brave? the other was equally brave;)
Now be witness again, paint the mightiest armies of earth,
Of those armies so rapid so wondrous what saw you to tell us?
What stays with you latest and deepest? of curious panics,
Of hard-fought engagements or sieges tremendous what deepest remains?

2

O maidens and young men I love and that love me,
What you ask of my days those the strangest and sudden your talking recalls,
Soldier alert I arrive after a long march cover'd with sweat and dust,
In the nick of time I come, plunge in the fight, loudly shout in the rush of successful charge,
Enter the captur'd works—yet lo, like a swift-running river they fade,
Pass and are gone they fade—I dwell not on soldiers' perils or soldiers' joys,
(Both I remember well—many of the hardships, few the joys, yet I was content.)

But in silence, in dreams' projections,
While the world of gain and appearance and mirth goes on,

THE WOUND-DRESSER. "The Dresser" in 1867; present title in 1881.

So soon what is over forgotten, and waves wash the imprints off the sand,
With hinged knees returning I enter the doors, (while for you up there,
Whoever you are, follow without noise and be of strong heart.)

Bearing the bandages, water and sponge,
Straight and swift to my wounded I go,
Where they lie on the ground after the battle brought in,
Where their priceless blood reddens the grass the ground,
Or to the rows of the hospital tent, or under the roof'd hospital,
To the long rows of cots up and down each side I return,
To each and all one after another I draw near, not one do I miss,
An attendant follows holding a tray, he carries a refuse pail,
Soon to be fill'd with clotted rags and blood, emptied, and fill'd again.

I onward go, I stop,
With hinged knees and steady hand to dress wounds,
I am firm with each, the pangs are sharp yet unavoidable,
One turns to me his appealing eyes—poor boy! I never knew you,
Yet I think I could not refuse this moment to die for you, if that would save you.

3

On, on I go, (open doors of time! open hospital doors!)
The crush'd head I dress, (poor crazed hand tear not the bandage away,)
The neck of the cavalry-man with the bullet through and through I examine,
Hard the breathing rattles, quite glazed already the eye, yet life struggles hard,
(Come sweet death! be persuaded O beautiful death!
In mercy come quickly.)

From the stump of the arm, the amputated hand,
I undo the clotted lint, remove the slough, wash off the matter and blood,
Back on his pillow the soldier bends with curv'd neck and side falling head,
His eyes are closed, his face is pale, he dares not look on the bloody stump,
And has not yet look'd on it.

I dress a wound in the side, deep, deep,
But a day or two more, for see the frame all wasted and sinking,
And the yellow-blue countenance see.

I dress the perforated shoulder, the foot with the bullet-wound,
Cleanse the one with a gnawing and putrid gangrene, so sickening, so offensive,
While the attendant stands behind aside me holding the tray and pail.

I am faithful, I do not give out,
The fractur'd thigh, the knee, the wound in the abdomen,
These and more I dress with impassive hand, (yet deep in my breast a fire, a burning flame.)

4

Thus in silence in dreams' projections,
Returning, resuming, I thread my way through the hospitals,
The hurt and wounded I pacify with soothing hand,
I sit by the restless all the dark night, some are so young,
Some suffer so much, I recall the experience sweet and sad,
(Many a soldier's loving arms about this neck have cross'd and rested,
Many a soldier's kiss dwells on these bearded lips.)

RECONCILIATION

Word over all, beautiful as the sky,
Beautiful that war and all its deeds of carnage must in time be utterly lost,
That the hands of the sisters Death and Night incessantly softly wash again, and ever again, this soil'd world;
For my enemy is dead, a man divine as myself is dead,
I look where he lies white-faced and still in the coffin—I draw near,
Bend down and touch lightly with my lips the white face in the coffin.

WHEN LILACS LAST IN THE DOORYARD BLOOM'D

1

When lilacs last in the dooryard bloom'd,
And the great star early droop'd in the western sky in the night,
I mourn'd, and yet shall mourn with ever-returning spring.

Ever-returning spring, trinity sure to me you bring,
Lilac blooming perennial and drooping star in the west,
And thought of him I love.

2

O powerful western fallen star!
O shades of night—O moody, tearful night!
O great star disappear'd—O the black murk that hides the star!
O cruel hands that hold me powerless—O helpless soul of me!
O harsh surrounding cloud that will not free my soul.

3

In the dooryard fronting an old farm-house near the white-wash'd palings,
Stands the lilac-bush tall-growing with heart-shaped leaves of rich green,
With many a pointed blossom rising delicate, with the perfume strong I love,
With every leaf a miracle—and from this bush in the dooryard,
With delicate-color'd blossoms and heart-shaped leaves of rich green,
A sprig with its flower I break.

4

In the swamp in secluded recesses,
A shy and hidden bird is warbling a song.

Solitary the thrush,
The hermit withdrawn to himself, avoiding the settlements,
Sings by himself a song.

Song of the bleeding throat,
Death's outlet song of life, (for well dear brother I know,
If thou wast not granted to sing thou would'st surely die.)

5

Over the breast of the spring, the land, amid cities,
Amid lanes and through old woods, where lately the violets peep'd from the ground, spotting the gray debris,
Amid the grass in the fields each side of the lanes, passing the endless grass,

Passing the yellow-spear'd wheat, every grain from its shroud in the dark-brown fields uprisen,
Passing the apple-tree blows of white and pink in the orchards,
Carrying a corpse to where it shall rest in the grave,
Night and day journeys a coffin.

6

Coffin that passes through lanes and streets,
Through day and night with the great cloud darkening the land,
With the pomp of the inloop'd flags with the cities draped in black,
With the show of the States themselves as of crape-veil'd women standing,
With processions long and winding and the flambeaus of the night,
With the countless torches lit, with the silent sea of faces and the unbared heads,
With the waiting depot, the arriving coffin, and the sombre faces,
With dirges through the night, with the thousand voices rising strong and solemn,
With all the mournful voices of the dirges pour'd around the coffin,
The dim-lit churches and the shuddering organs—where amid these you journey,
With the tolling tolling bells' perpetual clang,
Here, coffin that slowly passes,
I give you my sprig of lilac.

7

(Nor for you, for one alone,
Blossoms and branches green to coffins all I bring,
For fresh as the morning, thus would I chant a song for you O sane and sacred death.

All over bouquets of roses,
O death, I cover you over with roses and early lilies,
But mostly and now the lilac that blooms the first,
Copious I break, I break the sprigs from the bushes,
With loaded arms I come, pouring for you,
For you and the coffins all of you O death.)

8

O western orb sailing the heaven,
Now I know what you must have meant as a month since I walk'd,
As I walk'd in silence the transparent shadowy night,
As I saw you had something to tell as you bent to me night after night,
As you droop'd from the sky low down as if to my side, (while the other stars all look'd on,)
As we wander'd together the solemn night, (for something I know not what kept me from sleep,)
As the night advanced, and I saw on the rim of the west how full you were of woe,
As I stood on the rising ground in the breeze in the cool transparent night,
As I watch'd where you pass'd and was lost in the netherward black of the night,
As my soul in its trouble dissatisfied sank, as where you sad orb,
Concluded, dropt in the night, and was gone.

9

Sing on there in the swamp,
O singer bashful and tender, I hear your notes, I hear your call,
I hear, I come presently, I understand you,
But a moment I linger, for the lustrous star has detain'd me,
The star my departing comrade holds and detains me.

10

O how shall I warble myself for the dead one there I loved?
And how shall I deck my song for the large sweet soul that has gone?
And what shall my perfume be for the grave of him I love?

Sea-winds blown from east and west,
Blown from the Eastern sea and blown from the Western sea, till there on the prairies meeting,
These and with these and the breath of my chant,
I'll perfume the grave of him I love.

11

O what shall I hang on the chamber walls?
And what shall the pictures be that I hang on the walls,
To adorn the burial-house of him I love?

Pictures of growing spring and farms and homes,
With the Fourth-month eve at sundown, and the gray smoke lucid and bright,
With floods of the yellow gold of the gorgeous, indolent, sinking sun, burning, expanding the air,
With the fresh sweet herbage under foot, and the pale green leaves of the trees prolific,
In the distance the flowing glaze, the breast of the river, with a wind-dapple here and there,
With ranging hills on the banks, with many a line against the sky, and shadows,
And the city at hand with dwellings so dense, and stacks of chimneys,
And all the scenes of life and the workshops, and the workmen homeward returning.

12

Lo, body and soul—this land,
My own Manhattan with spires, and the sparkling and hurrying tides, and the ships,
The varied and ample land, the South and the North in the light, Ohio's shores and flashing Missouri,
And ever the far-spreading prairies cover'd with grass and corn.

Lo, the most excellent sun so calm and haughty,
The violet and purple morn with just-felt breezes,
The gentle soft-born measureless light,
The miracle spreading bathing all, the fulfill'd noon,
The coming eve delicious, the welcome night and the stars,
Over my cities shining all, enveloping man and land.

13

Sing on, sing on you gray-brown bird,
Sing from the swamps, the recesses, pour your chant from the bushes,
Limitless out of the dusk, out of the cedars and pines.

Sing on dearest brother, warble your reedy song,
Loud human song, with voice of uttermost woe.

O liquid and free and tender!
O wild and loose to my soul—O wondrous singer!
You only I hear—yet the star holds me, (but will soon depart,)
Yet the lilac with mastering odor holds me.

14

Now while I sat in the day and look'd forth,
In the close of the day with its light and the fields of spring, and the farmers preparing their crops,
In the large unconscious scenery of my land with its lakes and forests,
In the heavenly aerial beauty, (after the perturb'd winds and the storms,)
Under the arching heavens of the afternoon swift passing, and the voices of children and women,
The many-moving sea-tides, and I saw the ships how they sail'd,
And the summer approaching with richness, and the fields all busy with labor,
And the infinite separate houses, how they all went on, each with its meals and minutia of daily usages,
And the streets how their throbbings throbb'd, and the cities pent—lo, then and there,
Falling upon them all and among them all, enveloping me with the rest,
Appear'd the cloud, appear'd the long black trail,
And I knew death, its thought, and the sacred knowledge of death.

Then with the knowledge of death as walking one side of me,
And the thought of death close-walking the other side of me,
And I in the middle as with companions, and as holding the hands of companions,
I fled forth to the hiding receiving night that talks not,
Down to the shores of the water, the path by the swamp in the dimness,
To the solemn shadowy cedars and ghostly pines so still.

And the singer so shy to the rest receiv'd me,
The gray-brown bird I know receiv'd us comrades three,
And he sang the carol of death, and a verse for him I love.

From deep secluded recesses,
From the fragrant cedars and the ghostly pines so still,
Came the carol of the bird.

And the charm of the carol rapt me,
As I held as if by their hands my comrades in the night,
And the voice of my spirit tallied the song of the bird.

Come lovely and soothing death,
Undulate round the world, serenely arriving, arriving,
In the day, in the night, to all, to each,
Sooner or later delicate death.

Prais'd be the fathomless universe,
For life and joy, and for objects and knowledge curious,
And for love, sweet love—but praise! praise! praise!
For the sure-enwinding arms of cool-enfolding death.

Dark mother always gliding near with soft feet,
Have none chanted for thee a chant of fullest welcome?
Then I chant it for thee, I glorify thee above all,
I bring thee a song that when thou must indeed come, come unfalteringly.

Approach strong deliveress,
When it is so, when thou hast taken them I joyously sing the dead,
Lost in the loving floating ocean of thee,
Laved in the flood of thy bliss O death.

WHEN LILACS LAST IN THE DOORYARD BLOOM'D. 14. 27. The italicized song bore a title, "Death Carol," in the 1871 edition.

From me to thee glad serenades,
Dances for thee I propose saluting thee, adornments and feastings for thee,
And the sights of the open landscape and the high-spread sky are fitting,
And life and the fields, and the huge and thoughtful night.

The night in silence under many a star,
The ocean shore and the husky whispering wave whose voice I know,
And the soul turning to thee O vast and well-veil'd death,
And the body gratefully nestling close to thee.

Over the tree-tops I float thee a song,
Over the rising and sinking waves, over the myriad fields and the prairies wide,
Over the dense-pack'd cities all and the teeming wharves and ways,
I float this carol with joy, with joy to thee O Death.

15

To the tally of my soul,
Loud and strong kept up the gray-brown bird,
With pure deliberate notes spreading filling the night.

Loud in the pines and cedars dim,
Clear in the freshness moist and the swamp-perfume,
And I with my comrades there in the night.

While my sight that was bound in my eyes unclosed,
As to long panoramas of visions.

And I saw askant the armies,
I saw as in noiseless dreams hundreds of battle-flags,
Borne through the smoke of the battles and pierc'd with missiles I saw them,
And carried hither and yon through the smoke, and torn and bloody,
And at last but a few shreds left on the staffs, (and all in silence,)
And the staffs all splinter'd and broken.

I saw battle-corpses, myriads of them,
And the white skeletons of young men, I saw them,
I saw the debris and debris of all the slain soldiers of the war,
But I saw they were not as was thought,
They themselves were fully at rest, they suffer'd not,
The living remain'd and suffer'd, the mother suffer'd,
And the wife and the child and the musing comrade suffer'd,
And the armies that remain'd suffer'd.

16

Passing the visions, passing the night,
Passing, unloosing the hold of my comrades' hands,
Passing the song of the hermit bird and the tallying song of my soul,
Victorious song, death's outlet song, yet varying ever-altering song,
As low and wailing, yet clear the notes, rising and falling, flooding the night,
Sadly sinking and fainting, as warning and warning, and yet again bursting with joy,
Covering the earth and filling the spread of the heaven,
As that powerful psalm in the night I heard from recesses,
Passing, I leave thee lilac with heart-shaped leaves,
I leave thee there in the door-yard, blooming, returning with spring.

I cease from my song for thee,
From my gaze on thee in the west, fronting the west, communing with thee,
O comrade lustrous with silver face in the night.

Yet each to keep and all, retrievements out of the night,
The song, the wondrous chant of the gray-brown bird,
And the tallying chant, the echo arous'd in my soul,
With the lustrous and drooping star with the countenance full of woe,
With the holders holding my hand nearing the call of the bird,
Comrades mine and I in the midst, and their memory ever to keep, for the dead I loved so well,
For the sweetest, wisest soul of all my days and lands—and this for his dear sake,
Lilac and star and bird twined with the chant of my soul,
There in the fragrant pines and the cedars dusk and dim.

V: 1871 AND LATER

THERE were further editions of *Leaves of Grass* in 1871, 1876, 1881, 1889, and 1891. Neither the quality nor the number of the new poems added to these editions was very impressive; though "Passage to India" (1871) is technically fascinating, and "Good-Bye My Fancy" (1891) is a suitable and touching farewell by Whitman to his imagination and to the life it had sustained. Whitman suffered a stroke in 1873 and was semi-invalided during his latter years. At the same time, he had become a public figure and a spokesman to the nation. These roles were not congenial to his poetic talent, but in them he did compose a good deal of interesting and sometimes powerful prose: some of it polemic about the national culture—like "Democratic Vistas" in 1871—some of it personal reminiscence—like "A Backward Glance O'er Travel'd Roads" in 1888.

SPARKLES FROM THE WHEEL

Where the city's ceaseless crowd moves on the livelong day,
Withdrawn I join a group of children watching, I pause aside with them.

By the curb toward the edge of the flagging,
A knife-grinder works at his wheel sharpening a great knife,
Bending over he carefully holds it to the stone, by foot and knee,
With measur'd tread he turns rapidly, as he presses with light but firm hand,
Forth issue then in copious golden jets,
Sparkles from the wheel.

The scene and all its belongings, how they seize and affect me,
The sad sharp-chinn'd old man with worn clothes and broad shoulder-band of leather,
Myself effusing and fluid, a phantom curiously floating, now here absorb'd and arrested,
The group, (an unminded point set in a vast surrounding,)
The attentive, quiet children, the loud, proud, restive base of the streets,
The low hoarse purr of the whirling stone, the light-press'd blade,
Diffusing, dropping, sideways-darting, in tiny showers of gold,
Sparkles from the wheel.

A NOISELESS PATIENT SPIDER

A noiseless patient spider,
I mark'd where on a little promontory it stood isolated,

Mark'd how to explore the vacant vast surrounding,
It launch'd forth filament, filament, filament, out of itself,
Ever unreeling them, ever tirelessly speeding them.

And you O my soul where you stand,
Surrounded, detached, in measureless oceans of space,
Ceaselessly musing, venturing, throwing, seeking the spheres to connect them,
Till the bridge you will need be form'd, till the ductile anchor hold,
Till the gossamer thread you fling catch somewhere, O my soul.

PASSAGE TO INDIA

1

Singing my days,
Singing the great achievements of the present,
Singing the strong light works of engineers,
Our modern wonders, (the antique ponderous Seven outvied,)
In the Old World the east the Suez canal,
The New by its mighty railroad spann'd,
The seas inlaid with eloquent gentle wires;
Yet first to sound, and ever sound, the cry with thee O soul,
The Past! the Past! the Past!

The Past—the dark unfathom'd retrospect!
The teeming gulf—the sleepers and the shadows!
The past—the infinite greatness of the past!
For what is the present after all but a growth out of the past?
(As a projectile form'd, impell'd, passing a certain line, still keeps on,
So the present, utterly form'd, impell'd by the past.)

2

Passage O soul to India!
Eclaircise the myths Asiatic, the primitive fables.

Not you alone proud truths of the world,
Nor you alone ye facts of modern science,
But myths and fables of eld, Asia's, Africa's fables,
The far-darting beams of the spirit, the unloos'd dreams,
The deep diving bibles and legends,
The daring plots of the poets, the elder religions;
O you temples fairer than lilies pour'd over by the rising sun!
O you fables spurning the known, eluding the hold of the known, mounting to heaven!
You lofty and dazzling towers, pinnacled, red as roses, burnish'd with gold!
Towers of fables immortal fashion'd from mortal dreams!
You too I welcome and fully the same as the rest!
You too with joy I sing.

Passage to India!
Lo, soul, seest thou not God's purpose from the first?
The earth to be spann'd, connected by network,
The races, neighbors, to marry and be given in marriage,

PASSAGE TO INDIA. This poem was occasioned by the completion of the North American railroad, the laying of the first Atlantic cable, and the opening of the Suez Canal. 2. 2. **Eclaircise:** a Gallicism, here meaning "explain" or "clear up."

The oceans to be cross'd, the distant brought near,
The lands to be welded together.

A worship new I sing,
You captains, voyagers, explorers, yours,
You engineers, you architects, machinists, yours,
You, not for trade or transportation only,
But in God's name, and for thy sake O soul.

3

Passage to India!
Lo soul for thee of tableaus twain.
I see in one the Suez canal initiated, open'd,
I see the procession of steamships, the Empress Eugenie's leading the van,
I mark from on deck the strange landscape, the pure sky, the level sand in the distance,
I pass swiftly the picturesque groups, the workmen gather'd,
The gigantic dredging machines.

In one again, different, (yet thine, all thine, O soul, the same,)
I see over my own continent the Pacific railroad surmounting every barrier,
I see continual trains of cars winding along the Platte carrying freight and passengers,
I hear the locomotives rushing and roaring, and the shrill steam-whistle,
I hear the echoes reverberate through the grandest scenery in the world,
I cross the Laramie plains, I note the rocks in grotesque shapes, the buttes,
I see the plentiful larkspur and wild onions, the barren, colorless, sage-deserts,
I see in glimpses afar or towering immediately above me the great mountains, I see the Wind river and the Wahsatch mountains,
I see the Monument mountain and the Eagle's Nest, I pass the Promontory, I ascend the Nevadas,
I scan the noble Elk mountain and wind around its base,
I see the Humboldt range, I thread the valley and cross the river,
I see the clear waters of lake Tahoe, I see forests of majestic pines,
Or crossing the great desert, the alkaline plains, I behold enchanting mirages of waters and meadows,
Marking through these and after all, in duplicate slender lines,
Bridging the three or four thousand miles of land travel,
Tying the Eastern to the Western sea,
The road between Europe and Asia.

(Ah Genoese thy dream! thy dream!
Centuries after thou art laid in thy grave,
The shore thou foundest verifies thy dream.)

4

Passage to India!
Struggles of many a captain, tales of many a sailor dead,
Over my mood stealing and spreading they come,
Like clouds and cloudlets in the unreach'd sky.

Along all history, down the slopes,
As a rivulet running, sinking now, and now again to the surface rising,
A ceaseless thought, a varied train—lo, soul, to thee, thy sight, they rise,
The plans, the voyages again, the expeditions;
Again Vasco de Gama sails forth,
Again the knowledge gain'd, the mariner's compass,

Lands found and nations born, thou born America,
For purpose vast, man's long probation fill'd,
Thou rondure of the world at last accomplish'd.

5

O vast Rondure, swimming in space,
Cover'd all over with visible power and beauty,
Alternate light and day and the teeming spiritual darkness,
Unspeakable high processions of sun and moon and countless stars above,
Below, the manifold grass and waters, animals, mountains, trees,
With inscrutable purpose, some hidden prophetic intention,
Now first it seems my thought begins to span thee.

Down from the gardens of Asia descending radiating,
Adam and Eve appear, then their myriad progeny after them,
Wandering, yearning, curious, with restless explorations,
With questionings, baffled, formless, feverish, with never-happy hearts,
With that sad incessant refrain, *Wherefore unsatisfied soul?* and *Whither O mocking life?*

Ah who shall soothe these feverish children?
Who justify these restless explorations?
Who speak the secret of impassive earth?
Who bind it to us? what is this separate Nature so unnatural?
What is this earth to our affections? (unloving earth, without a throb to answer ours,
Cold earth, the place of graves.)

Yet soul be sure the first intent remains, and shall be carried out,
Perhaps even now the time has arrived.

After the seas are all cross'd, (as they seem already cross'd,)
After the great captains and engineers have accomplish'd their work,
After the noble inventors, after the scientists, the chemist, the geologist, ethnologist,
Finally shall come the poet worthy of that name,
The true son of God shall come singing his songs.

Then not your deeds only O voyagers, O scientists and inventors, shall be justified,
All these hearts as of fretted children shall be sooth'd,
All affection shall be fully responded to, the secret shall be told,
All these separations and gaps shall be taken up and hook'd and link'd together,
The whole earth, this cold, impassive, voiceless earth, shall be completely justified,
Trinitas divine shall be gloriously accomplish'd and compacted by the true son of God, the poet,
(He shall indeed pass the straits and conquer the mountains,
He shall double the cape of Good Hope to some purpose,)
Nature and Man shall be disjoin'd and diffused no more,
The true son of God shall absolutely fuse them.

6

Year at whose wide-flung door I sing!
Year of the purpose accomplish'd!
Year of the marriage of continents, climates and oceans!
(No mere doge of Venice now wedding the Adriatic,)
I see O year in you the vast terraqueous globe given and giving all,
Europe to Asia, Africa join'd, and they to the New World,
The lands, geographies, dancing before you, holding a festival garland,
As brides and bridegrooms hand in hand.

Passage to India!
Cooling airs from Caucasus, far, soothing cradle of man,
The river Euphrates flowing, the past lit up again.

Lo soul, the retrospect brought forward,
The old, most populous, wealthiest of earth's lands,
The streams of the Indus and the Ganges and their many affluents,
(I my shores of America walking to-day behold, resuming all,)
The tale of Alexander on his warlike marches suddenly dying,
On one side China and on the other Persia and Arabia,
To the south the great seas and the bay of Bengal,
The flowing literatures, tremendous epics, religions, castes,
Old occult Brahma interminably far back, the tender and junior Buddha,
Central and southern empires and all their belongings, possessors,
The wars of Tamerlane, the reign of Aurungzebe,
The traders, rulers, explorers, Moslems, Venetians, Byzantium, the Arabs, Portuguese,
The first traveler famous yet, Marco Polo, Batouta, the Moor,
Doubts to be solv'd, the map incognita, blanks to be fill'd,
The foot of man unstay'd, the hands never at rest,
Thyself O soul that will not brook a challenge.

The mediæval navigators rise before me,
The world of 1492, with its awaken'd enterprise,
Something swelling in humanity now like the sap of the earth in spring,
The sunset splendor of chivalry declining.

And who art thou sad shade?
Gigantic, visionary, thyself a visionary,
With majestic limbs and pious beaming eyes,
Spreading around with every look of thine a golden world,
Enhuing it with gorgeous hues.

As the chief histrion,
Down to the footlights walks in some great scena,
Dominating the rest I see the Admiral himself,
(History's type of courage, action, faith,)
Behold him sail from Palos leading his little fleet,
His voyage behold, his return, his great fame,
His misfortunes, calumniators, behold him a prisoner, chain'd,
Behold his dejection, poverty, death.

(Curious in time I stand, noting the efforts of heroes,
Is the deferment long? bitter the slander, poverty, death?
Lies the seed unreck'd for centuries in the ground? lo, to God's due occasion,
Uprising in the night, it sprouts, blooms,
And fills the earth with use and beauty.)

7

Passage indeed O soul to primal thought,
Not lands and seas alone, thy own clear freshness,
The young maturity of brood and bloom,
To realms of budding bibles.

6. 37. **histrion:** actor (from "histrionic").

O soul, repressless, I with thee and thou with me,
Thy circumnavigation of the world begin,
Of man, the voyage of his mind's return.
To reason's early paradise,
Back, back to wisdom's birth, to innocent intuitions,
Again with fair creation.

8

O we can wait no longer,
We too take ship O soul,
Joyous we too launch out on trackless seas,
Fearless for unknown shores on waves of ecstasy to sail,
Amid the wafting winds, (thou pressing me to thee, I thee to me, O soul,)
Caroling free, singing our song of God,
Chanting our chant of pleasant exploration.

With laugh and many a kiss,
(Let others deprecate, let others weep for sin, remorse, humiliation,)
O soul thou pleasest me, I thee.

Ah more than any priest O soul we too believe in God,
But with the mystery of God we dare not dally.

O soul thou pleasest me, I thee,
Sailing these seas or on the hills, or waking in the night,
Thoughts, silent thoughts, of Time and Space and Death, like waters flowing,
Bear me indeed as through the regions infinite,
Whose air I breathe, whose ripples hear, lave me all over,
Bathe me O God in thee, mounting to thee,
I and my soul to range in range of thee.

O Thou transcendent,
Nameless, the fibre and the breath,
Light of the light, shedding forth universes, thou centre of them,
Thou mightier centre of the true, the good, the loving,
Thou moral, spiritual fountain—affection's source—thou reservoir,
(O pensive soul of me—O thirst unsatisfied—waitest not there?
Waitest not haply for us somewhere there the Comrade perfect?)
Thou pulse—thou motive of the stars, suns, systems,
That, circling, move in order, safe, harmonious,
Athwart the shapeless vastnesses of space,
How should I think, how breathe a single breath, how speak, if out of myself,
I could not launch, to those, superior universes?

Swiftly I shrivel at the thought of God,
At Nature and its wonders, Time and Space and Death,
But that I, turning, call to thee O soul, thou actual Me,
And lo, thou gently masterest the orbs,
Thou matest Time, smilest content at Death,
And fillest, swellest full the vastnesses of Space.

Greater than stars or suns,
Bounding O soul thou journeyest forth;
What love than thine and ours could wider amplify?
What aspirations, wishes, outvie thine and ours O soul?
What dreams of the ideal? what plans of purity, perfection, strength,

What cheerful willingness for others' sake to give up all?
For others' sake to suffer all?

Reckoning ahead O soul, when thou, the time achiev'd,
The seas all cross'd, weather'd the capes, the voyage done,
Surrounded, copest, frontest God, yieldest, the aim attain'd,
As fill'd with friendship, love complete, the Elder Brother found,
The Younger melts in fondness in his arms.

9

Passage to more than India!
Are thy wings plumed indeed for such far flights?
O soul, voyagest thou indeed on voyages like those?
Disportest thou on waters such as those?
Soundest below the Sanscrit and the Vedas?
Then have thy bent unleash'd.

Passage to you, your shores, ye aged fierce enigmas!
Passage to you, to mastership of you, ye strangling problems!
You, strew'd with the wrecks of skeletons, that, living, never reach'd you.

Passage to more than India!
O secret of the earth and sky!
Of you O waters of the sea! O winding creeks and rivers!
Of you O woods and fields! of you strong mountains of my land!
Of you O prairies! of you gray rocks!
O morning red! O clouds! O rain and snows!
O day and night, passage to you!

O sun and moon and all you stars! Sirius and Jupiter!
Passage to you!

Passage, immediate passage! the blood burns in my veins!
Away O Soul! hoist instantly the anchor!
Cut the hawsers—haul out—shake out every sail!
Have we not stood here like trees in the ground long enough?
Have we not grovel'd here long enough, eating and drinking like mere brutes?
Have we not darken'd and dazed ourselves with books long enough?

Sail forth—steer for the deep waters only,
Reckless O soul, exploring, I with thee, and thou with me,
For we are bound where mariner has not yet dared to go,
And we will risk the ship, ourselves and all.

O my brave soul!
O farther farther sail!
O daring joy, but safe! are they not all the seas of God?
O farther, farther, farther sail!

THE DALLIANCE OF THE EAGLES

Skirting the river road, (my forenoon walk, my rest,)
Skyward in air a sudden muffled sound, the dalliance of the eagles,
The rushing amorous contact high in space together,

The clinching interlocking claws, a living, fierce, gyrating wheel,
Four beating wings, two beaks, a swirling mass tight grappling,
In tumbling turning clustering loops, straight downward falling,
Till o'er the river pois'd, the twain yet one, a moment's lull,
A motionless still balance in the air, then parting, talons loosing,
Upward again on slow-firm pinions slanting, their separate diverse flight,
She hers, he his, pursuing.

GOOD-BYE MY FANCY!

Good-bye my Fancy!
Farewell dear mate, dear love!
I'm going away, I know not where,
Or to what fortune, or whether I may ever see you again,
So Good-bye my Fancy.

Now for my last—let me look back a moment;
The slower fainter ticking of the clock is in me,
Exit, nightfall, and soon the heart-thud stopping.

Long have we lived, joy'd, caress'd together;
Delightful!—now separation—Good-bye my Fancy.

Yet let me not be too hasty,
Long indeed have we lived, slept, filter'd, become really blended into one;
Then if we die we die together, (yes, we'll remain one,)
If we go anywhere we'll go together to meet what happens,
May-be we'll be better off and blither, and learn something,
May-be it is yourself now really ushering me to the true songs, (who knows?)
May-be it is you the mortal knob really undoing, turning—so now finally,
Good-bye—and hail! my Fancy.

PROSE

PREFACE TO THE 1855 EDITION OF LEAVES OF GRASS

AMERICA does not repel the past or what it has produced under its forms or amid other politics or the idea of castes or the old religions . . . accepts the lesson with calmness . . . is not so impatient as has been supposed that the slough still sticks to opinions and manners and literature while the life which served its requirements as passed into the new life of the new forms . . . perceives that the corpse is slowly borne from the eating and sleeping rooms of the house . . . perceives that it waits a little while in the door . . . that it was fittest for its days . . . that its action has descended to the stalwart and wellshaped heir who approaches . . . and that he shall be fittest for his days.

The Americans of all nations at any time upon the earth have probably the fullest poetical nature. The United States themselves are essentially the greatest poem. In the history of the earth hitherto the largest and most stirring appear tame and orderly to their ampler largeness and stir. Here at last is something in the doings of man that corresponds with the broadcast doings of the day and night. Here is not merely a nation but a teeming nation of nations. Here is action untied from strings necessarily blind to particulars and details magnificently moving in vast masses. Here is the hospitality which forever indicates heroes. . . . Here are the roughs and beards and space and ruggedness and nonchalance that the soul loves. Here the performance disdaining the trivial unapproached in the tremendous audacity of its crowds and groupings and the push of its perspective spreads with crampless and flowing breadth and showers its prolific and splendid extravagance. One sees it must indeed own the riches of the summer and winter, and need never be bankrupt while corn grows from the ground or the orchards drop apples or the bays contain fish or men beget children upon women.

Other states indicate themselves in their deputies . . . but the genius of the United States is not best or most in its executives or legislatures, nor in its ambassadors or authors or colleges or churches or parlors, nor even in its newspapers or inventors . . . but always most in the common people. Their manners speech dress friendships—the freshness and candor of their physiognomy—the picturesque looseness of their carriage . . . their deathless attachment to freedom—their aversion to anything indecorous or soft or mean—the practical acknowledgment of the citizens of one state by the citizens of all other states—the fierceness of their roused resentment—their curiosity and welcome of novelty—their self-esteem and wonderful sympathy—their susceptibility to a slight—the air they have of persons who never knew how it felt to stand in the presence of superiors—the fluency of their speech—their delight in music, the sure symptom of manly tenderness and native elegance of soul . . . their good temper and openhandedness—the terrible significance of their elections—the President's taking off his hat to them not they to him—these too are unrhymed poetry. It awaits the gigantic and generous treatment worthy of it.

The largeness of nature or the nation were monstrous without a corresponding largeness and generosity of the spirit of the citizen. Not nature nor swarming states nor streets and steamships nor prosperous business nor farms nor capital nor learning may suffice for the ideal of man . . . nor suffice the poet. No reminiscences may suffice either. A live nation can always cut a deep mark and can have the best authority the cheapest . . . namely from its own soul. This is the sum of the profitable uses of individuals or states and of present action and grandeur and of the subjects of poets.—As if it were necessary to trot back generation after generation to the eastern records! As if the beauty and sacredness of the demonstrable must fall behind that of the mythical! As if men do not make their mark out of any times! As if the opening of the western continent by discovery and what has transpired since in North and South America were less than the small theatre of the antique or the aimless sleepwalking of the middle ages! The pride of the United States leaves the wealth and finesse of the cities and all returns of commerce and agriculture and all the magnitude of geography or shows of exterior victory to enjoy the breed of fullsized men or one fullsized man unconquerable and simple.

The American poets are to enclose old and new for America is the race of races. Of them a bard is to be commensurate with a people. To him the other continents arrive as contributions . . . he gives them reception for their sake and his own sake. His spirit responds to his country's spirit . . . he incarnates its geography and natural life and rivers and lakes. Mississippi with annual freshets and changing chutes, Missouri and Columbia and Ohio and Saint Lawrence with the falls and beautiful masculine Hudson, do not embouchure where they spend themselves more than they embouchure into him. The blue breadth over the inland sea of Virginia and Maryland and the sea off Massachusetts and Maine and over Manhattan bay and over Champlain and Erie and over Ontario and Huron and Michigan and Superior, and over the Texan and Mexican and Floridian and Cuban seas and over the seas of California and Oregon, is not tallied by the blue breadth of the waters below more than the breadth of above and below is tallied by him. When the long Atlantic coast stretches longer and the Pacific coast stretches longer he easily stretches with them north or south. He spans between them also from east to west and reflects what is between them. On him rise solid growths that offset the growths of pine and cedar and hemlock and liveoak and locust and chestnut and cypress and hickory and limetree and cottonwood and tuliptree and cactus and wildvine and tamarind and persimmon . . . and tangles as tangled as any canebreak or swamp . . . and forests coated with transparent ice and icicles hanging from the boughs and crackling in the wind . . . and sides and peaks of mountains . . . and pasturage sweet and free as savannah or upland or prairie . . . with flights and songs and screams that answer those of the wildpigeon and highhold and orchard-oriole and coot and surf-duck and redshouldered-hawk and fish-hawk and white-ibis and indian-hen and cat-owl and water-pheasant and qua-bird and pied-sheldrake and blackbird and mockingbird and buzzard and condor and night-heron and eagle. To him the hereditary countenance descends both mother's and father's. To him enter the essences of the real things and past and present events—of the enormous diversity of temperature and agriculture and mines—the tribes of red aborigines—the weather-beaten vessels entering new ports or making landings on rocky coasts—the first settlements north or south—the rapid stature and muscle—the haughty defiance of '76, and the war and peace and formation of the constitution . . . the union always surrounded by blatherers and always calm and impregnable—the perpetual coming of immigrants—the wharfhem'd cities and superior marine—the unsurveyed interior—the loghouses and clearings and wild animals and hunters and trappers . . . the free commerce—the fisheries and whaling and gold-digging—the endless gestation of new states—the convening of Congress every December, the members duly coming up from all climates and the uttermost parts . . . the noble character of the young mechanics and of all free American workmen and workwomen . . . the general ardor and friendliness and enterprise—the perfect equality of the female with the male . . . the large amativeness—the fluid movement of the population—the factories and mercantile life and laborsaving machinery—the Yankee swap—the New-York firemen and the target excursion—the southern plantation life—the character of the northeast and of the northwest and southwest—slavery and the tremulous spreading of hands to protect it, and the stern opposition to it which shall never cease till it ceases or the speaking of tongues and the moving of lips cease. For such the expression of the American poet is to be transcendant and new. It is to be indirect and not direct or descriptive or epic. Its quality goes through these to much more. Let the age and wars of other nations be chanted and their eras and characters be illustrated and that finish the verse. Not so the great psalm of the republic. Here the theme is creative and has vista. Here comes one among the wellbeloved stonecutters and plans with decision and science and sees the solid and beautiful forms of the future where there are now no solid forms.

Of all nations the United States with veins full of poetical stuff most need poets and will doubtless have the greatest and use them the greatest. Their Presidents shall not be their common referee so much as their poets shall. Of all mankind the great poet is the equable man. Not in him but off from him things are grotesque or eccentric or fail of their sanity. Nothing out of its place is good and nothing in its place is bad. He bestows on every object or quality its fit proportions neither more nor less. He is the arbiter of the diverse and he is the key. He is the equalizer of his age and land . . . he supplies what wants supplying and checks what wants checking. If peace is the routine out of him speaks the spirit of peace, large, rich, thrifty, building vast and populous cities, encouraging agriculture and the arts and commerce—lighting the study of man, the soul, immortality—federal, state or municipal government, marriage, health, freetrade, intertravel by land and sea . . . nothing too close, nothing too far off . . . the stars not too far off. In war he is the most deadly force of the war. Who recruits him recruits horse and foot . . . he fetches parks of artillery the best that engineer ever knew. If the time becomes slothful and heavy he knows how to arouse it . . . he can make every word he speaks draw blood. Whatever stagnates in the flat of custom or obedience or legislation he never stagnates. Obedience does not master him, he masters it. High up out of reach he stands turning a concentrated light . . . he turns the pivot with his finger . . . he baffles the swiftest runners as he stands and easily overtakes and envelops them. The time straying toward infidelity and confections and persiflage he withholds by his steady faith . . . he spreads out his dishes . . . he offers the sweet firmfibred meat that grows men and women. His brain is the ultimate brain. He is no arguer . . . he is judgment. He judges not as the judge judges but as the sun falling around a helpless thing. As he sees the farthest he has the most faith. His thoughts are the hymns of the praise of things. In the talk on the soul and eternity and God off of his equal plane he is silent. He sees eternity less like a play with a prologue and denouement . . . he sees eternity in men and women . . . he does not see men and women as dreams or dots. Faith is the antiseptic of the soul . . . it pervades the common people and preserves them . . . they never give up believing and expecting and trusting. There is that indescribable freshness and unconsciousness about an illiterate person that humbles and mocks the power of the noblest expressive genius. The poet sees for a certainty how one not a great artist may be just as sacred as the greatest artist. . . . The power to destroy or remould is freely used by him but never the power of attack. What is past is past. If he does not expose superior models and prove himself by every step he takes he is not what is wanted. The presence of the greatest poet conquers . . . not parleying or struggling or any prepared attempts. Now he has passed that way see after him! there is not left any vestige of despair or misanthropy or cunning or exclusiveness or the ignominy of a nativity or color or delusion of hell or the necessity of hell . . . and no man thenceforward shall be degraded for ignorance or weakness or sin.

The greatest poet hardly knows pettiness or triviality. If he breathes into any thing that was before thought small it dilates with the grandeur and life of the universe. He is a seer . . . he is individual . . . he is complete in himself . . . the others are as good as he, only he sees it and they do not. He is not one of the chorus . . . he does not stop for any regulations . . . he is the president of regulation. What the eyesight does to the rest he does to the rest. Who knows the curious mystery of the eyesight? The other senses corroborate themselves, but this is removed from any proof but its own and foreruns the identities of the spiritual world. A single glance of it mocks all the investigations of man and all the instruments and books of the earth and all reasoning. What is marvelous? what is unlikely? what is impossible or baseless or vague? after you have once just opened the space of a peachpit and given audience to far and near and to the sunset and had all things enter with electric swiftness softly and duly without confusion or jostling or jam.

The land and sea, the animals, fishes and birds, the sky of heaven and the orbs, the forests mountains and rivers, are not small themes . . . but folks expect of the poet to indicate more than the beauty and dignity which always attach to dumb real objects . . . they expect him to indicate the path between reality and their souls. Men and women perceive the beauty well enough . . . probably as well as he. The passionate tenacity of hunters, woodmen, early risers, cultivators of gardens and orchards and fields, the love of healthy women for the manly form, seafaring persons, drivers of horses, the passion for light and the open air, all is an old varied sign of the unfailing perception of beauty and of a residence of the poetic in outdoor people. They can never be assisted by poets to perceive . . . some may but they never can. The poetic quality is not marshalled in rhyme or uniformity or abstract addresses to things nor in melancholy complaints or good precepts, but is the life of these and much else and is in the soul. The profit of rhyme is that it drops seeds of a sweeter and more luxuriant rhyme, and of uniformity that it conveys itself into its own roots in the ground out of sight. The rhyme and uniformity of perfect poems show the free growth of metrical laws and bud from them as unerringly and loosely as lilacs or roses on a bush, and take shapes as compact as the shapes of chestnuts and oranges and melons and pears, and shed the perfume impalpable to form. The fluency and ornaments of the finest poems or music or orations or recitations are not independent but dependent. All beauty comes from beautiful blood and a beautiful brain. If the greatnesses are in conjunction in a man or woman it is enough . . . the fact will prevail through the universe . . . but the gaggery and gilt of a million years will not prevail. Who troubles himself about his ornaments or fluency is lost. This is what you shall do: Love the earth and sun and the animals, despise riches, give alms to every one that asks, stand up for the stupid and crazy, devote your income and labor to others, hate tyrants, argue not concerning God, have patience and indulgence toward the people, take off your hat to nothing known or unknown or to any man or number of men, go freely with powerful uneducated persons and with the young and with the mothers of families, read these leaves in the open air every season of every year of your life, re-examine all you have been told at school or church or in any book, dismiss whatever insults your own soul, and your very flesh shall be a great poem and have the richest fluency not only in its words but in the silent lines of its lips and face and between the lashes of your eyes and in every motion and joint of your body. . . . The poet shall not spend his time in unneeded work. He shall know that the ground is always ready plowed and manured . . . others may not know it but he shall. He shall go directly to the creation. His trust shall master the trust of everything he touches . . . and shall master all attachment.

The known universe has one complete lover and that is the greatest poet. He consumes an eternal passion and is indifferent which chance happens and which possible contingency of fortune or misfortune and persuades daily and hourly his delicious pay. What balks or breaks others is fuel for his burning progress to contact and amorous joy. Other proportions of the reception of pleasure dwindle to nothing to his proportions. All expected from heaven or from the highest he is rapport with in the sight of the daybreak or a scene of the winter-woods or the presence of children playing or with his arm round the neck of a man or woman. His love above all love has leisure and expanse . . . he leaves room ahead of himself. He is no irresolute or suspicious lover . . . he is sure . . . he scorns intervals. His experience and the showers and thrills are not for nothing. Nothing can jar him . . . suffering and darkness cannot—death and fear cannot. To him complaint and jealousy and envy are corpses buried and rotten in the earth . . . he saw them buried. The sea is not surer of the shore or the shore of the sea than he is of the fruition of his love and of all perfection and beauty.

The fruition of beauty is no chance of hit or miss . . . it is inevitable as life . . . it is exact and plumb as gravitation. From the eyesight proceeds another eyesight and from the hearing proceeds another hearing and from the voice proceeds another voice eternally curious of the harmony of things with man. To these respond perfections not only in the committees that were supposed to stand for the rest but in the rest themselves just the same. These understand the law of perfection in masses and floods . . . that its finish is to each for itself and onward from itself . . . that it is profuse and impartial . . . that there is not a minute of the light or dark nor an acre of the earth or sea without it—nor any direction of the sky nor any trade or employment nor any turn of events. This is the reason that about the proper expression of beauty there is precision and balance . . . one part does not need to be thrust above another. The best singer is not the one who has the most lithe and powerful organ . . . the pleasure of poems is not in them that take the handsomest measure and similes and sound.

Without effort and without exposing in the least how it is done the greatest poet brings the spirit of any or all events and passions and scenes and persons some more and some less to bear on your individual character as you hear or read. To do this well is to compete with the laws that pursue and follow time. What is the purpose must surely be there and the clue of it must be there . . . and the faintest indication is the indication of the best and then becomes the clearest indication. Past and present and future are not disjoined but joined. The greatest poet forms the consistence of what is to be from what has been and is. He drags the dead out of their coffins and stands them again on their feet . . . he says to the past, Rise and walk before me that I may realize you. He learns the lesson . . . he places himself where the future becomes present. The greatest poet does not only dazzle his rays over character and scenes and passions . . . he finally ascends and finishes all . . . he exhibits the pinnacles that no man can tell what they are for or what is beyond . . . he glows a moment on the extremest verge. He is most wonderful in his last half-hidden smile or frown . . . by that flash of the moment of parting the one that sees it shall be encouraged or terrified afterwards for many years. The greatest poet does not moralize or make applications of morals . . . he knows the soul. The soul has that measureless pride which consists in never acknowledging any lessons but its own. But it has sympathy as measureless as its pride and the one balances the other and neither can stretch too far while it stretches in company with the other. The inmost secrets of art sleep with the twain. The greatest poet has lain close betwixt both and they are vital in his style and thoughts.

The art of art, the glory of expression and the sunshine of the light of letters is simplicity. Nothing is better than simplicity . . . nothing can make up for excess or for the lack of definiteness. To carry on the heave of impulse and pierce intellectual depths and give all subjects their articulations are powers neither common nor very uncommon. But to speak in literature with the perfect rectitude and insouciance of the movements of animals and the unimpeachableness of the sentiment of trees in the woods and grass by the roadside is the flawless triumph of art. If you have looked on him who has achieved it you have looked on one of the masters of the artists of all nations and times. You shall not contemplate the flight of the graygull over the bay or the mettlesome action of the blood horse or the tall leaning of sunflowers on their stalk or the appearance of the sun journeying through heaven or the appearance of the moon afterward with any more satisfaction than you shall contemplate him. The greatest poet has less a marked style and is more the channel of thoughts and things without increase or diminution, and is the free channel of himself. He swears to his art, I will not be meddlesome, I will not have in my writing any elegance or effect or originality to hang in the way between me and the rest like curtains. I will have nothing hang in the way, not the richest curtains. What I tell I tell for precisely what it is. Let who may exalt or startle or fascinate or sooth I will have purposes as health or heat or snow has and be as regardless of observation. What I experience or portray shall go from my composition without a shred of my composition. You shall stand by my side and look in the mirror with me.

The old red blood and stainless gentility of great poets will be proved by their unconstraint. A heroic person walks at his ease through and out of that custom or precedent or authority that suits him not. Of the traits of the brotherhood of writers savans musicians inventors and artists nothing is finer than silent defiance advancing from new free forms. In the need of poems philosophy politics mechanism science behaviour, the craft of art, an appropriate native grand-opera, shipcraft, or any craft, he is greatest forever and forever who contributes the greatest original practical example. The cleanest expression is that which finds no sphere worthy of itself and makes one.

The messages of great poets to each man and woman are, Come to us on equal terms, Only then can you understand us, We are no better than you, What we enclose you enclose, What we enjoy you may enjoy. Did you suppose there could be only one Supreme? We affirm there can be unnumbered Supremes, and that one does not countervail another any more than one eyesight countervails another . . . and that men can be good or grand only of the consciousness of their supremacy within them. What do you think is the grandeur of storms and dismemberments and the deadliest battles and wrecks and the wildest fury of the elements and the power of the sea and the motion of nature and of the throes of human desires and dignity and hate and love? It is that something in the soul which says, Rage on, Whirl on, I tread master here and everywhere, Master of the spasms of the sky and of the shatter of the sea, Master of nature and passion and death, And of all terror and all pain.

The American bards shall be marked for generosity and affection and for encouraging competitors. . . . They shall be kosmos . . . without monopoly or secrecy . . . glad to pass any thing to any one . . . hungry for equals night and day. They shall not be careful of riches and privilege . . . they shall be riches and privilege . . . they shall perceive who the most affluent man is. The most affluent man is he that confronts all the shows he sees by equivalents out of the stronger wealth of himself. The American bard shall delineate no class of persons nor one or two out of the strata of interests nor love most nor truth most nor the soul most nor the body most . . . and not be for the eastern states more than the western or the northern states more than the southern.

Exact science and its practical movements are no checks on the greatest poet but always his encouragement and support. The outset and remembrance are there . . . there are the arms that lifted him first and brace him best . . . there he returns after all his goings and comings. The sailor and traveler . . . the atomist chemist astronomer geologist phrenologist spiritualist mathematician historian and lexicographer are not poets, but they are the lawgivers of poets and their construction underlies the structure of every perfect poem. No matter what rises or is uttered they sent the seed of the conception of it . . . of them and by them stand the visible proofs of souls . . . always of their fatherstuff must be begotten the sinewy races of bards. If there shall be love and content between the father and the son and if the greatness of the son is the exuding of the greatness of the father there shall be love between the poet and the man of demonstrable science. In the beauty of poems are the tuft and final applause of science.

Great is the faith of the flush of knowledge and of the investigation of the depths of qualities and things. Cleaving and circling here swells the soul of the poet yet is president of itself always. The depths are fathomless and therefore calm. The innocence and nakedness are resumed . . . they are neither modest nor immodest. The whole theory of the special and supernatural and all that was twined with it or educed out of it departs as a dream. What has ever happened . . . what happens and whatever may or shall happen, the vital laws enclose all . . . they are sufficient for any case and for all cases . . . none to be hurried or retarded . . . any miracle of affairs or persons inadmissible in the vast clear scheme where every motion and every spear of grass and the frames and spirits of men and women and all that concerns them are unspeakably perfect miracles all referring to all and each distinct and in its place. It is also not consistent with the reality of the soul to admit that there is anything in the known universe more divine than men and women.

Men and women and the earth and all upon it are simply to be taken as they are, and the investigation of their past and present and future shall be unintermitted and shall be done with perfect candor. Upon this basis philosophy speculates ever looking toward the poet, ever regarding the eternal tendencies of all toward happiness never inconsistent with what is clear to the senses and to the soul. For the eternal tendencies of all toward happiness make the only point of sane philosophy. Whatever comprehends less than that . . . whatever is less than the laws of light and of astronomical motion . . . or less than the laws that follow the thief the liar the glutton and the drunkard through this life and doubtless afterward . . . or less than vast stretches of time or the slow formation of density or the patient unheaving of strata—is of no account. Whatever would put God in a poem or system of philosophy as contending against some being or influence, is also of no account. Sanity and ensemble characterise the great master . . . spoilt in one principle all is spoilt. The great master has nothing to do with miracles. He sees health for himself in being one of the mass . . . he sees the hiatus in singular eminence. To the perfect shape comes common ground. To be under the general law is great for that is to correspond with it. The master knows that he is unspeakably great and that all are unspeakably great . . . that nothing for instance is greater than to conceive children and bring them up well . . . that to be is just as great as to perceive or tell.

In the make of the great masters the idea of political liberty is indispensable. Liberty takes the adherence of heroes wherever men and women exist . . . but never takes any adherence or welcome from the rest more than from poets. They are the voice and exposition of liberty. They out of ages are worthy the grand idea . . . to them it is confided and they must sustain it. Nothing has precedence of it and nothing can warp or degrade it. The attitude of great poets is to cheer up slaves and horrify despots. The turn of their necks, the sound of their feet, the motions of their wrists, are full of hazard to the one and hope to the other. Come nigh them awhile and though they neither speak or advise you shall learn the faithful American lesson. Liberty is poorly served by men whose good intent is quelled from one failure or two failures or any number of failures, or from the casual indifference or ingratitude of the people, or from the sharp show of the tushes of power, or the bringing to bear soldiers and cannon or any penal statutes. Liberty relies upon itself, invites no one, promises nothing, sits in calmness and light, is positive and composed, and knows no discouragement. The battle rages with many a loud alarm and frequent advance and retreat . . . the enemy triumphs . . . the prison, the handcuffs, the iron necklace and anklet, the scaffold, garrote and leadballs do their work . . . the cause is asleep . . . the strong throats are choked with their own blood . . . the young men drop their eyelashes toward the ground when they pass each other . . . and is liberty gone out of that place? No never. When liberty goes it is not the first to go nor the second nor third to go . . . it waits for all the rest to go . . . it is the last. . . . When the memories of the old martyrs are faded utterly away . . . when the large names of patriots are laughed at in the public halls from the lips of the orators . . . when the boys are no more christened after the same but christened after tyrants and traitors instead . . . when the laws of the free are grudgingly permitted and laws for informers and bloodmoney are sweet to the taste of the people . . . when I and you walk abroad upon the earth stung with compassion at the sight of numberless brothers answering our equal friendship and calling no man master—and when we are elated with noble joy at the sight of slaves . . . when the soul retires in the cool communion of the night and surveys its experience and has much extasy over the word and deed that put back a helpless innocent person into the gripe of the gripers or into any cruel inferiority . . . when those in all parts of these states who could easier realize the true American character but do not yet—when the swarms of cringers, suckers, doughfaces, lice of politics, planners of sly involutions for their own preferment to city offices or state legislatures or the judiciary or congress or the presidency, obtain a response of love and natural deference from the people whether they get the offices or no . . . when it is better to be a bound booby and rogue in office at a high salary than the poorest free mechanic or farmer with his hat unmoved from his head and firm eyes and a candid and generous heart . . . and when servility by town or state or the federal government or any oppression on a large scale or small scale can be tried on without its own punishment following duly after in exact proportion against the smallest chance of escape . . . or rather when all life and all the souls of men and women are discharged from any part of the earth —then only shall the instinct of liberty be discharged from that part of the earth.

As the attributes of the poets of the kosmos concentre in the real body and soul and in the pleasure of things they possess the superiority of genuineness over all fiction and romance. As they emit themselves facts are showered over with light . . . the daylight is lit with more volatile light . . . also the deep between the setting and rising sun goes deeper many fold. Each precise object or condition or combination or process exhibits a beauty . . . the multiplication table its—old age its—the carpenter's trade its—the grand-opera its . . . the hugehulled cleanshaped New-York clipper at sea under steam or full sail gleams with unmatched beauty . . . the American circles and large harmonies of government gleam with theirs . . . and the commonest definite intentions and actions with theirs. The poets of the kosmos advance through all interpositions and coverings and turmoils and stratagems to first principles. They are of use . . . they dissolve poverty from its need and riches from its conceit. You large proprietor they say shall not realize or perceive more than any one else. The owner of the library is not he who holds a legal title to it having bought and paid for it. Any one and every one is owner of the library who can read the same through all the varieties of tongues and subjects and styles, and in whom they enter with ease and take residence and force toward paternity and maternity, and make supple and powerful and rich and large. . . . These American states strong and healthy and accomplished shall receive no pleasure from violations of natural models and must not permit them. In paintings or mouldings or carvings in mineral or wood, or in the illustrations of books or newspapers, or in any comic or tragic prints, or in the patterns of woven stuffs or anything to beautify rooms or furniture or costumes, or to put upon cornices or monuments or on the prows or sterns of ships, or to put anywhere before the human eye indoors or out, that which distorts honest shapes or which creates unearthly beings or places or contingencies is a nuisance and revolt. Of the human form especially it is so great it must never be made ridiculous. Of ornaments to a work nothing outre can be allowed . . . but those ornaments can be allowed that conform to the perfect facts of the open air and that flow out of the nature of the work and come irrepressibly from it and are necessary to the completion of the work. Most works are most beautiful without ornament. . . . Exaggerations will be revenged in human physiology. Clean and vigorous children are jetted and conceived only in those communities where the models of natural forms are public every day. . . . Great genius and the people of these states must never be demeaned to romances. As soon as histories are properly told there is no more need of romances.

The great poets are also to be known by the absence in them of tricks and by the justification of perfect personal candor. Then folks echo a new cheap joy and a divine voice leaping from their brains: How beautiful is candor! All faults may be forgiven of him who has perfect candor. Henceforth let no man of us lie, for we have seen that openness wins the inner and outer world and that there is no single exception, and that never since our earth gathered itself in a mass have deceit or subterfuge or prevarication attracted its smallest particle or the faintest tinge of a shade—and that through the enveloping wealth and rank of a state or the whole republic of states a sneak or sly person shall be discovered and despised . . . and that the soul has never been once fooled and never can be fooled . . . and thrift without the loving nod of the soul is only a fœtid puff . . . and there never grew up in any of the continents of the globe nor upon any planet or satellite or star, nor upon the asteroids, nor in any part of ethereal space, nor in the midst of density, nor under the fluid wet of the sea, nor in that condition which precedes the birth of babes, nor at any time during the changes of life, nor in that condition that follows what we term death, nor in any stretch of abeyance or action afterward of vitality, nor in any process of formation or reformation anywhere, a being whose instinct hated the truth.

Extreme caution or prudence, the soundest organic health, large hope and comparison and fondness for women and children, large alimentiveness and destructiveness and causality, with a perfect sense of the oneness of nature and the propriety of the same spirit applied to human affairs . . . these are called up of the float of the brain of the world to be parts of the greatest poet from his birth out of his mother's womb and from her birth out of her mother's. Caution seldom goes far enough. It has been thought that the prudent citizen was the citizen who applied himself to solid gains and did well for himself and his family and completed a lawful life without debt or crime. The greatest poet sees and admits these economies as he sees the economies of food and sleep, but has higher notions of prudence than to think he gives much when he gives a few slight attentions at the latch of the gate. The premises of the prudence of life are not the hospitality of it or the ripeness and harvest of it. Beyond the independence of a little sum laid aside for burial-money, and of a few clapboards around and shingles overhead on a lot of American soil owned, and the easy dollars that supply the year's plain clothing and meals, the melancholy prudence of the abandonment of such a great being as a man is to the toss and pallor of years of moneymaking with all their scorching days and icy nights and all their stifling deceits and underhanded dodgings, or infinitesimals of parlors, or shameless stuffing while others starve . . . and all the loss of the bloom and odor of the earth and of the flowers and atmosphere and of the sea and of the true taste of the women and men you pass or have to do with in youth or middle age, and the issuing sickness and desperate revolt at the close of a life without elevation or naivete, and the ghastly chatter of a death without serenity or majesty, is the great fraud upon modern civilization and forethought, blotching the surface and system which civilization undeniably drafts, and moistening with tears the immense features it spreads and spreads with such velocity before the reached kisses of the soul. . . . Still the right explanation remains to be made about prudence. The prudence of the mere wealth and respectability of the most esteemed life appears too faint for the eye to observe at all when little and large alike drop quietly aside at the thought of the prudence suitable for immortality. What is wisdom that fills the thinness of a year or seventy or eighty years to wisdom spaced out by ages and coming back at a certain time with strong reinforcements and rich presents and the clear faces of wedding-guests as far as you can look in every direction running gaily toward you? Only the soul is of itself . . . all else has reference to what ensues. All that a person does or thinks is of consequence. Not a move can a man or woman make that affects him or her in a day or a month or any part of the direct lifetime or the hour of death but the same affects him or her onward afterward through the indirect lifetime. The indirect is always as great and real as the direct. The spirit receives from the body just as much as it gives to the body. Not one name of word or deed . . . not of venereal sores or discolorations . . . not the privacy of the onanist . . . not of the putrid veins of gluttons or rum-drinkers . . . not peculation or cunning or betrayal or murder . . . no serpentine poison of those that seduce women . . . not the foolish yielding of women . . . not prostitution . . . not of any depravity of young men . . . not of the attainment of gain by discreditable means . . . not any nastiness of appetite . . . not any harshness of officers to men or judges to prisoners or fathers to sons or sons to fathers or of husbands to wives or bosses to their boys . . . not of greedy looks or malignant wishes . . . nor any of the wiles practised by people upon themselves . . . ever is or ever can be stamped on the programme but it is duly realized and returned, and that returned in further performances . . . and they returned again. Nor can the push of charity or personal force ever be any thing else than the profoundest reason, whether it bring arguments to hand or no. No specification is necessary . . . to add or substract or divide is in vain. Little or big, learned or unlearned, white or black, legal or illegal, sick or well, from the first inspiration down the windpipe to the last expiration out of it, all that a male or female does that is vigorous and benevolent and clean is so much sure profit to him or her in the unshakable order of the universe and through the whole scope of it forever. If the savage or felon is wise it is well . . . if the greatest poet or savan is wise it is simply the same . . . if the President or chief justice is wise it is the same . . . if the young mechanic or farmer is wise it is no more or less . . . if the prostitute is wise it is no more nor less. The interest will come round . . . all will come round. All the best actions of war and peace . . . all help given to relatives and strangers and the poor and old and sorrowful and young children and widows and the sick, and to all shunned persons . . . all furtherance of fugitives and of the escape of slaves . . . all the self-denial that stood steady and aloof on wrecks and saw others take the seats of the boats . . . all offering of substance or life for the good old cause, or for a friend's sake or opinion's sake . . . all pains of enthusiasts scoffed at by their neighbors . . . all the vast sweet love and precious suffering of mothers . . . all honest men baffled in strifes recorded or unrecorded . . . all the grandeur and good of the few ancient nations whose fragments of annals we inherit . . . and all the good of the hundreds of far mightier and more ancient nations unknown to us by name or date or location . . . all that was ever manfully begun, whether it succeeded or not . . . all that has at any time been well suggested out of the divine heart of man or by the divinity of his mouth or by the shaping of his great hands . . . and all that is well thought or done this day on any part of the surface of the globe . . . or on any of the wandering stars or fixed stars by those there as we are here . . . or that is henceforth to be well thought or done by you whoever you are, or by any one—these singly and wholly inured at their time and inure now and will inure always to the identities from which they sprung or shall spring. . . . Did you guess any of them lived only its moment? The world does not so exist . . . no parts palpable or impalpable so exist . . . no result exists now without being from its long antecedent result, and that from its antecedent, and so backward without the farthest mentionable spot coming a bit nearer to the beginning than any other spot. . . . Whatever satisfies the soul is truth. The prudence of the greatest poet answers at last the craving and glut of the soul, is not contemptuous of less ways of prudence if they conform to its ways, puts off nothing, permits no let-up for its own case or any case, has no particular sabbath or judgment-day, divides not the living from the dead or the righteous from the unrighteous, is satisfied with the present, matches every thought or act by its correlative, knows no possible forgiveness or deputed atonement . . . knows that the young man who composedly periled his life and lost it has done exceeding well for himself, while the man who has not periled his life and retains it to old age in riches and ease has perhaps achieved nothing for himself worth mentioning . . . and that only that person has no great prudence to learn who has learnt to prefer real longlived things, and favors body and soul the same, and perceives the indirect assuredly following the direct, and what evil or good he does leaping onward and waiting to meet him again—and who in his spirit in any emergency whatever neither hurries or avoids death.

The direct trial of him who would be the greatest poet is today. If he does not flood himself with the immediate age as with vast oceanic tides . . .

and if he does not attract his own land body and soul to himself and hang on its neck with incomparable love and plunge his semitic muscle into its merits and demerits . . . and if he be not himself the age transfigured . . . and if to him is not opened the eternity which gives similitude to all periods and locations and processes and animate and inanimate forms, and which is the bond of time, and rises up from its inconceivable vagueness and infiniteness in the swimming shape of today, and is held by the ductile anchors of life, and makes the present spot the passage from what was to what shall be, and commits itself to the representation of this wave of an hour and this one of the sixty beautiful children of the wave—let him merge in the general run and wait his development. . . . Still the final test of poems or any character or work remains. The prescient poet projects himself centuries ahead and judges performer or performance after the changes of time. Does it live through them? Does it still hold on untired? Will the same style and the direction of genius to similar points be satisfactory now? Has no new discovery in science or arrival at superior planes of thought and judgment and behaviour fixed him or his so that either can be looked down upon? Have the marches of tens and hundreds and thousands of years made willing detours to the right hand and the left hand for his sake? Is he beloved long and long after he is buried? Does the young man think often of him? and the young woman think often of him? and do the middle-aged and the old think of him?

A great poem is for ages and ages in common and for all degrees and complexions and all departments and sects and for a woman as much as a man and a man as much as a woman. A great poem is no finish to a man or woman but rather a beginning. Has any one fancied he could sit at last under some due authority and rest satisfied with explanations and realize and be content and full? To no such terminus does the greatest poet bring . . . he brings neither cessation or sheltered fatness and ease. The touch of him tells in action. Whom he takes he takes with firm sure grasp into live regions previously unattained . . . thenceforward is no rest . . . they see the space and ineffable sheen that turn the old spots and lights into dead vacuums. The companion of him beholds the birth and progress of stars and learns one of the meanings. Now there shall be a man cohered out of tumult and chaos . . . the elder encourages the younger and shows him how . . . they too shall launch off fearlessly together till the new world fits an orbit for itself and looks unabashed on the lesser orbits of the stars and sweeps through the ceaseless rings and shall never be quiet again.

There will soon be no more priests. Their work is done. They may wait awhile . . . perhaps a generation or two . . . dropping off by degrees. A superior breed shall take their place . . . the gangs of kosmos and prophets en masse shall take their place. A new order shall arise and they shall be the priests of man, and every man shall be his own priest. The churches built under their umbrage shall be the churches of men and women. Through the divinity of themselves shall the kosmos and the new breed of poets be interpreters of men and women and of all events and things. They shall find their inspiration in real objects today, symptoms of the past and future . . . They shall not deign to defend immortality or God or the perfection of things or liberty or the exquisite beauty and reality of the soul. They shall arise in America and be responded to from the remainder of the earth.

The English language befriends the grand American expression . . . it is brawny enough and limber and full enough. On the tough stock of a race who through all change of circumstances was never without the idea of political liberty, which is the animus of all liberty, it has attracted the terms of daintier and gayer and subtler and more elegant tongues. It is the powerful language of resistance . . . it is the dialect of common sense. It is the speech of the proud and melancholy races and of all who aspire. It is the chosen tongue to express growth faith self-esteem freedom justice equality friendliness amplitude prudence decision and courage. It is the medium that shall well nigh express the inexpressible.

No great literature nor any like style of behaviour or oratory or social intercourse or household arrangements or public institutions or the treatment by bosses of employed people, nor executive detail or detail of the army or navy, nor spirit of legislation or courts or police or tuition or architecture or songs or amusements or the costumes of young men, can long elude the jealous and passionate instinct of American standards. Whether or no the sign appears from the mouths of the people, it throbs a live interrogation in every freeman's and freewoman's heart after that which passes by or this built to remain. Is it uniform with my country? Are its disposals without ignominious distinctions? Is it for the evergrowing communes of brothers and lovers, large, well-united, proud beyond the old models, generous beyond all models? Is it something grown fresh out of the fields or drawn from the sea for use to me today here? I know that what answers for me an American must answer for any individual or nation that serves for a part of my materials. Does this answer? or is it without reference to universal needs? or sprung of the needs of the less developed society of special ranks? or old needs of pleasure overlaid by modern science and forms? Does this acknowledge liberty with audible and absolute acknowledgment, and set slavery at naught for life and death? Will it help breed one goodshaped and wellhung man, and a woman to be his perfect and independent mate? Does it improve manners? Is it for the nursing of the young of the republic? Does it solve readily with the sweet milk of the nipples of the breasts of the mother of many children? Has it too the old everfresh forbearance and impartiality? Does it look with the same love on the last born and those hardening toward stature, and on the errant, and on those who disdain all strength of assault outside of their own?

The poems distilled from other poems will probably pass away. The coward will surely pass away. The expectation of the vital and great can only be satisfied by the demeanor of the vital and great. The swarms of the polished deprecating and reflectors and the polite float off and leave no remembrance. America prepares with composure and goodwill for the visitors that have sent word. It is not intellect that is to be their warrant and welcome. The talented, the artist, the ingenious, the editor, the statesman, the erudite . . . they are not unappreciated . . . they fall in their place and do their work. The soul of the nation also does it work. No disguise can pass on it . . . no disguise can conceal from it. It rejects none, it permits all. Only toward as good as itself and toward the like of itself will it advance half-way. An individual is as superb as a nation when he has the qualities which make a superb nation. The soul of the largest and wealthiest and proudest nation may well go half-way to meet that of its poets. The signs are effectual. There is no fear of mistake. If the one is true the other is true. The proof of a poet is that his country absorbs him as affectionately as he has absorbed it.

DEMOCRATIC VISTAS

As THE greatest lessons of Nature through the universe are perhaps the lessons of variety and freedom, the same present the greatest lessons also in New World politics and progress. If a man were ask'd, for instance, the distinctive points contrasting modern European and American political and other life with the old Asiatic cultus, as lingering-bequeath'd yet in China and Turkey, he might find the amount of them in John Stuart Mill's profound essay on Liberty in the future, where he demands two main constituents, or sub-strata, for a truly grand nationality—1st, a large variety of character—and 2nd, full play for human nature to expand itself in numberless and even conflicting directions—(seems to be for general humanity much like the influences that make up, in their limitless field, that perennial health-action of the air we call the weather—an infinite number of currents and forces, and contributions, and temperatures, and cross purposes, whose ceaseless play of counterpart upon counterpart brings constant restoration and vitality). With this thought—and not for itself alone, but all it necessitates, and draws after it—let me begin my speculations.

America, filling the present with greatest deeds and problems, cheerfully accepting the past, including feudalism (as, indeed, the present is but the legitimate birth of the past, including feudalism), counts, as I reckon, for her justification and success (for who, as yet, dare claim success?) almost entirely on the future. Nor is that hope unwarranted. Today, ahead, though dimly yet, we see, in vistas, a copious, sane, gigantic offspring. For our New World I consider far less important for what it has done, or what it is, than for results to come. Sole among nationalities, these States have assumed the task to put in forms of lasting power and practicality, on areas of amplitude rivaling the operations of the physical kosmos, the moral political speculations of ages, long, long deferr'd, the democratic republican principle, and the theory of development and perfection by voluntary standards, and self-reliance. Who else, indeed, except the United States, in history, so far, have accepted in unwitting faith, and, as we now see, stand, act upon, and go security for, these things?

But preluding no longer, let me strike the keynote of the following strain. First premising that, though the passages of it have been written at widely different times (it is, in fact, a collection of memoranda, perhaps for future designers, comprehenders), and though it may be open to the charge of one part contradicting another—for there are opposite sides to the great question of democracy, as to every great question—I feel the parts harmoniously blended in my own realization and convictions, and present them to be read only in such oneness, each page and each claim and assertion modified and temper'd by the others. Bear in mind, too, that they are not the result of studying up in political economy, but of the ordinary sense, observing, wandering among men, these States, these stirring years of war and peace. I will not gloss over the appalling dangers of universal suffrage in the United States. In fact, it is to admit and face these dangers I am writing. To him or her within whose thought rages the battle, advancing, retreating, between democracy's convictions, aspirations, and the people's crudeness, vice, caprices, I mainly write this essay. I shall use the words America and democracy as convertible terms. Not an ordinary one is the issue. The United States are destined either to surmount the gorgeous history of feudalism, or else prove the most tremendous failure of time. Not the least doubtful am I on any prospects of their material success. The triumphant future of their business, geographic and productive departments, on larger scales and in more varieties than ever, is certain. In those respects the republic must soon (if she does not already) outstrip all examples hitherto afforded, and dominate the world.[1]

Admitting all this, with the priceless value of our political institutions, general suffrage (and fully acknowledging the latest, widest opening of the doors), I say that, far deeper than these, what finally and only is to make of our Western world a nationality superior to any hitherto known, and outtopping the past, must be vigorous, yet unsuspected Literatures, perfect personalities and sociologies, original, transcendental, and expressing (what, in highest sense, are not yet express'd at all) democracy and the modern. With these, and out of these, I promulgate new races of Teachers, and of perfect Women, indispensable to endow the birth-stock of a New World For feudalism, caste, the ecclesiastic traditions, though palpably retreating from political institutions, still hold essentially, by their spirit, even in this country, entire possession of the more important fields, indeed the very subsoil, of education, and of social standards and literature.

I say that democracy can never prove itself beyond cavil, until it founds and luxuriantly grows its own forms of art, poems, schools, theology, displacing all that exists, or that has been produced anywhere in the past, under opposite influences. It is curious to me that while so many voices, pens, minds, in the press, lecture rooms, in our Congress, etc., are discussing intellectual topics, pecuniary dangers, legislative problems, the suffrage, tariff and labor questions, and the various business and benevolent needs of America, with propositions, remedies, often worth deep attention, there is one need, a hiatus the profoundest, that no eye seems to perceive, no voice to state. Our fundamental want today in the United States, with closest, amplest reference to present conditions, and to the future, is of a class, and the clear idea of a class, of native authors, literatuses, far different, far higher in grade, than any yet known, sacerdotal, modern, fit to cope with our occasions, lands, permeating the whole mass of American mentality, taste, belief, breathing into it a new breath of life, giving it decision, affecting politics far more than the popular superficial suffrage, with results inside and underneath the elections of Presidents or Congresses—radiating, begetting appropriate teachers, schools, manners, and, as its grandest result, accomplishing (what neither the schools nor the churches and their clergy have hitherto accomplish'd, and without which this nation will no more stand, permanently, soundly, than a house will stand without a sub-stratum), a religious and moral character beneath the political and productive and intellectual bases of the States. For know you not, dear, earnest reader, that the people of our land may all read and write, and may all pos-

DEMOCRATIC VISTAS. 1. " 'From a territorial area of less than nine hundred thousand square miles, the Union has expanded into over four millions and a half—fifteen times larger than that of Great Britain and France combined—with a shore line, including Alaska, equal to the entire circumference of the earth, and with a domain within these lines far wider than that of the Romans in their proudest days of conquest and renown. With a river, lake, and coastwise commerce estimated at over two thousand millions of dollars per year; with a railway traffic of four to six thousand millions per year, and the annual domestic exchanges of the country running up to nearly ten thousand millions per year; with over two thousand millions of dollars invested in manufacturing, mechanical, and mining industry; with over five hundred millions of acres of land in actual occupancy, valued, with their appurtenances, at over seven thousand millions of dollars, and producing annually crops valued at over three thousand millions of dollars; with a realm which, if the density of Belgium's population were possible, would be vast enough to include all the present inhabitants of the world; and with equal rights guaranteed to even the poorest and humblest of our forty millions of people—we can, with a manly pride akin to that which distinguish'd the palmiest days of Rome, claim,' etc., etc., etc.,—*Vice-President Colfax's Speech*, July 4, 1870.

"Later—*London 'Times (Weekly), June 23, '82.*

" 'The wonderful wealth-producing power of the United States defies and sets at naught the grave drawbacks of a mischievous protective tariff, and has already obliterated, almost wholly, the traces of the greatest of modern civil wars. What is especially remarkable in the present development of American energy and success is its wide and equable distribution. North and south, east and west, on the shores of the Atlantic and the Pacific, along the chain of the great lakes, in the valley of the Mississippi, and on the coasts of the Gulf of Mexico, the creation of wealth and the increase of population are signally exhibited. It is quite true, as has been shown by the recent apportionment of population in the House of Representatives, that some sections of the Union have advanced, relatively to the rest, in an extraordinary and unexpected degree. But this does not imply that the States which have gained no additional representatives or have actually lost some have been stationary or have receded. The fact is that the present tide of prosperity has risen so high that it has overflowed all barriers, and has fill'd up the backwaters, and established something like an approach to uniform success' " [Whitman's note].

sess the right to vote—and yet the main things may be entirely lacking?—(and this to suggest them).

View'd, today, from a point of view sufficiently over-arching, the problem of humanity all over the civilized world is social and religious, and is to be finally met and treated by literature. The priest departs, the divine literatus comes. Never was anything more wanted than, today, and here in the States, the poet of the modern is wanted, or the great literatus of the modern. At all times, perhaps, the central point in any nation, and that whence it is itself really sway'd the most, and whence it sways others, is its national literature, especially its archetypal poems. Above all previous lands, a great original literature is surely to become the justification and reliance (in some respects the sole reliance of American democracy).

Few are aware how the great literature penetrates all, gives hue to all, shapes aggregates and individuals, and, after subtle ways, with irresistible power, constructs, sustains, demolishes at will. Why tower, in reminiscence, above all the nations of the earth, two special lands, petty in themselves, yet inexpressibly gigantic, beautiful, columnar? Immortal Judah lives, and Greece immortal lives, in a couple of poems.

Nearer than this. It is not generally realized, but it is true, as the genius of Greece, and all the sociology, personality, politics, and religion of those wonderful states, resided in their literature or æsthetics, that what was afterwards the main support of European chivalry, the feudal, ecclesiastical, dynastic world over there—forming its osseous structure, holding it together for hundreds, thousands of years, preserving its flesh and bloom, giving it form, decision, rounding it out, and so saturating it in the conscious and unconscious blood, breed, belief, and intuitions of men, that it still prevails powerful to this day, in defiance of the mighty changes of time—was its literature, permeating to the very marrow, especially that major part, its enchanting songs, ballads, and poems.[2]

2. "See, for hereditaments, specimens, Walter Scott's *Border Minstrelsy*, Percy's collection, Ellis's early *English Metrical Romances*, the European continental poems of Walter of Aquitania, and the Nibelungen, of pagan stock, but monkish-feudal redaction; the history of the Troubadours, by Fauriel; even the far-back cumbrous old Hindu epics, as indicating the Asian eggs out of which European chivalry was hatch'd; Ticknor's chapters on the Cid, and on the Spanish poems and poets of Calderon's time. Then always, and, of course, as the superbest poetic culmination-expression of feudalism, the Shaksperean dramas, in the attitudes, dialogue, characters, etc., of the princes, lords, and gentlemen, the pervading atmosphere, the implied and express'd standard of manners, the high port and proud stomach, the regal embroidery of style, etc." [W].

To the ostent of the senses and eyes, I know, the influences which stamp the world's history are wars, uprisings or downfalls of dynasties, changeful movement of trade, important inventions, navigation, military or civil governments, advent of powerful personalities, conquerors, etc. These of course play their part; yet, it may be, a single new thought, imagination, abstract principle, even literary style, fit for the time, put in shape by some great literatus, and projected among mankind, may duly cause changes, growths, removals, greater than the longest and bloodiest war, or the most stupendous merely political, dynastic, or commercial overturn.

In short, as, though it may not be realized, it is strictly true, that a few first-class poets, philosophs, and authors have substantially settled and given status to the entire religion, education, law, sociology, etc., of the hitherto civilized world, by tingeing and often creating the atmospheres out of which they have arisen, such also must stamp, and more than ever stamp, the interior and real democratic construction of this American continent, today, and days to come. Remember also this fact of difference, that, while through the antique and through the mediæval ages, highest thoughts and ideals realized themselves, and their expression made its way by other arts, as much as, or even more than by, technical literature (not open to the mass of persons, or even to the majority of eminent persons), such literature in our day and for current purposes is not only more eligible than all the other arts put together, but has become the only general means of morally influencing the world. Painting, sculpture, and the dramatic theatre, it would seem, no longer play an indispensable or even important part in the workings and mediumship of intellect, utility, or even high æsthetics. Architecture remains, doubtless with capacities, and a real future. Then music, the combiner, nothing more spiritual, nothing more sensuous, a god, yet completely human, advances, prevails, holds highest place; supplying in certain wants and quarters what nothing else could supply. Yet in the civilization of today it is undeniable that, over all the arts, literature dominates, serves beyond all—shapes the character of church and school—or, in any rate, is capable of doing so. Including the literature of science, its scope is indeed unparallel'd.

Before proceeding further, it were perhaps well to discriminate on certain points. Literature tills its crops in many fields, and some may flourish, while others lag. What I say in these Vistas has its main bearing on imaginative literature, especially poetry, the stock of all. In the department of science, and the specialty of journalism, there appear, in these States, promises, perhaps fulfillments, of highest earnestness, reality and life. These, of course, are modern. But in the region of imaginative, spinal and essential attributes, something equivalent to creation is, for our age and lands, imperatively demanded. For not only is it not enough that the new blood, new frame of democracy shall be vivified and held together merely by political means, superficial suffrage, legislation, etc., but it is clear to me that, unless it goes deeper, gets at least as firm and as warm a hold in men's hearts, emotions and belief, as, in their days, feudalism or ecclesiasticism, and inaugurates its own perennial sources, welling from the center forever, its strength will be defective, its growth doubtful, and its main charm wanting. I suggest, therefore, the possibility, should some two or three really original American poets (perhaps artists or lecturers) arise, mounting the horizon like planets, stars of the first magnitude, that, from their eminence, fusing contributions, races, far localities, etc., together, they would give more compaction and more moral identity (the quality today most needed) to these States, than all its Constitutions, legislative and judicial ties, and all its hitherto political, warlike, or materialistic experiences. As, for instance, there could hardly happen anything that would more serve the States, with all their variety of origins, their diverse climes, cities, standards, etc., than possessing an aggregate of heroes, characters, exploits, sufferings, prosperity or misfortune, glory or disgrace, common to all, typical of it all—no less, but even greater would it be to possess the aggregation of a cluster of mighty poets, artists, teachers, fit for us, national expressers, comprehending and effusing for the men and women of the States, what is universal, native, common to all, inland and seaboard, northern and southern. The historians say of ancient Greece, with her ever-jealous autonomies, cities and states, that the only positive unity she ever own'd or receiv'd, was the sad unity of a common subjection, at the last, to foreign conquerors. Subjection, aggregation of that sort, is impossible to America; but the fear of conflicting and irreconcilable interiors, and the lack of a common skeleton, knitting all close, continually haunts me. Or, if it does not, nothing is plainer than the need, a long period to come, of a fusion of the States into the only reliable identity, the moral and artistic one. For, I say, the true nationality of the States, the genuine union, when we come to a mortal crisis, is, and is to be, after all, neither the written law, nor (as is generally supposed) either self-interest, or common pecuniary or material objects—but the fervid and tremendous IDEA, melting everything else with resistless heat, and solving all lesser and definite distinctions in vast, indefinite, spiritual, emotional power.

It may be claim'd (and I admit the weight of the claim) that common and general worldly prosperity, and a populace well-to-do, and with all life's material comforts, is the main thing, and is enough. It may be argued that our republic is, in performance, really enacting today the grandest arts, poems, etc., by beating up the wilderness into fertile farms, and in her railroads, ships, machinery, etc. And it may be ask'd, Are these not better, indeed, for America, than any utterances even of greatest rhapsode, artist, or literatus?

I too hail those achievements with pride and joy: then answer that the soul of man will not with such only—nay, not with such at all—be finally satisfied; but needs what, (standing on these and on all things, as the feet stand on the ground), is addressed to the loftiest, to itself alone.

Out of such considerations, such truths, arises for treatment in these Vistas the important question of character, of an American stock-personality, with literatures and arts for outlets and return-expressions, and, of course, to correspond, within outlines common to all. To these, the main affair, the thinkers of the United States, in general so acute, have either given feeblest attention, or have remain'd, and remain, in a state of somnolence.

For my part, I would alarm and caution even the political and business reader, and to the utmost extent, against the prevailing delusion that the establishment of free political institutions, and plentiful intellectual smartness, with general good order, physical plenty, industry, etc. (desirable and precious advantages as they all are), do, of themselves, determine and yield to our experiment of democracy the fruitage of success. With such advantages at present fully, or almost fully, possess'd—the Union just issued, victorious, from the struggle with the only foes it need ever fear (namely, those within itself, the interior ones), and with unprecedented materialistic advancement—society, in these States, is canker'd, crude, superstitious and rotten. Political, or law-made society is, and private, or voluntary society, is also. In any vigor, the element of the moral conscience, the most important, the verteber to State or man, seems to me either entirely lacking, or seriously enfeebled or ungrown.

I say we had best look our times and lands searchingly in the face, like a physician diagnosing some deep disease. Never was there, perhaps, more hollowness at heart than at present, and here in the United States. Genuine belief seems to have left us. The underlying principles of the States are not honestly believ'd in (for all this hectic glow, and these melodramatic screamings), nor is humanity itself believ'd in. What penetrating eye does not everywhere see through the mask? The spectacle is appalling. We live in an atmosphere of hypocrisy throughout. The men believe not in the women, nor the women in the men. A scornful superciliousness rules in literature. The aim of all the *littérateurs* is to find something to make fun of. A lot of churches, sects, etc., the most dismal phantasms I know, usurp the name of religion. Conversation is a mass of badinage. From deceit in the spirit, the mother of all false deeds, the offspring is already incalculable. An acute and candid person, in the revenue department in Washington, who is led by the course of his employment to regularly visit the cities, north, south, and west, to investigate frauds, has talked much with me about his discoveries. The depravity of the business classes of our country is not less than has been supposed, but infinitely greater. The official services of America, national, state, and municipal, in all their branches and departments, except the judiciary, are saturated in corruption, bribery, falsehood, maladministration; and the judiciary is tainted. The great cities reek with respectable as much as non-respectable robbery and scoundrelism. In fashionable life, flippancy, tepid amours, weak infidelism, small aims, or no aims at all, only to kill time. In business (this all-devouring modern word, business), the one sole object is, by any means, pecuniary gain. The magician's serpent in the fable ate up all the other serpents; and moneymaking is our magician's serpent, remaining today sole master of the field. The best class we show, is but a mob of fashionably dress'd speculators and vulgarians. True, indeed, behind this fantastic farce, enacted on the visible stage of society, solid things and stupendous labors are to be discover'd, existing crudely and going on in the background, to advance and tell themselves in time. Yet the truths are none the less terrible. I say that our New World democracy, however great a success in uplifting the masses out of their sloughs, in materialistic development, products, and in a certain highly deceptive superficial popular intellectuality, is, so far, an almost complete failure in its social aspects, and in really grand religious, moral, literary, and æsthetic results. In vain do we march with unprecedented strides to empire so colossal, outvying the antique, beyond Alexander's, beyond the proudest sway of Rome. In vain have we annex'd Texas, California, Alaska, and reach north for Canada and south for Cuba. It is as if we were somehow being endow'd with a vast and more and more thoroughly appointed body, and then left with little or no soul.

Let me illustrate further, as I write, with current observations, localities, etc. The subject is important, and will bear repetition. After an absence, I am now again (September 1870) in New York City and Brooklyn, on a few weeks' vacation. The splendor, picturesqueness, and oceanic amplitude and rush of these great cities, the unsurpassed situation, rivers and bay, sparkling sea-tides, costly and lofty new buildings, façades of marble and iron, of original grandeur and elegance of design, with the masses of gay color, the preponderance of white and blue, the flags flying, the endless ships, the tumultuous streets, Broadway, the heavy, low, musical roar, hardly ever intermitted, even at night; the jobbers' houses, the rich shops, the wharves, the great Central Park, and the Brooklyn Park of hills (as I wander among them this beautiful fall weather, musing, watching, absorbing)—the assemblages of the citizens in their groups, conversations, trades, evening amusements, or along the by-quarters—these, I say, and the like of these, completely satisfy my senses of power, fullness, motion, etc., and give me, through such senses and appetites, and through my æsthetic conscience, a continued exaltation and absolute fulfillment. Always and more and more, as I cross the East and North rivers, the ferries, or with the pilots in their pilot-houses, or pass an hour in Wall Street, or the Gold Exchange, I realize (if we must admit such partialisms) that not Nature alone is great in her fields of freedom and the open air, in her storms, the shows of night and day, the mountains, forests, sea—but in the artificial, the work of man too is equally great—in this profusion of teeming humanity—in these ingenuities, streets, goods, houses, ships—these hurrying, feverish, electric crowds of men, their complicated business genius (not least among the geniuses), and all this mighty, many-threaded wealth and industry concentrated here.

But sternly discarding, shutting our eyes to the glow and grandeur of the general superficial effect, coming down to what is of the only real importance, Personalities, and examining minutely, we question, we ask, Are there, indeed, *men* here worthy the name? Are there athletes? Are there perfect women, to match the generous material luxuriance? Is there a pervading atmosphere of beautiful manners? Are there crops of fine youths, and majestic old persons? Are there arts worthy freedom and a rich people? Is there a great moral and religious civilization—the only justification of a great material one? Confess that to severe eyes, using the moral microscope upon humanity, a sort of dry and flat Sahara appears, these cities, crowded with petty grotesques, malformations, phantoms, playing meaningless antics. Confess that everywhere, in shop, street, church, theatre, barroom, official chair, are pervading flippancy and vulgarity, low cunning, infidelity—everywhere the youth puny, impudent, foppish, prematurely ripe—everywhere an abnormal libidinousness, unhealthy forms, male, female, painted, padded, dyed, chignon'd, muddy complexions, bad blood, the capacity for good motherhood decreasing or decreas'd, shallow notions of beauty, with a range of manners, or rather lack of manners (considering the advantages enjoy'd), probably the meanest to be seen in the world.[3]

Of all this, and these lamentable conditions, to breathe into them the breath recuperative of sane and heroic life, I say a new-founded literature, not merely to copy and reflect existing surfaces, or pander to what is called taste—not only to amuse, pass away time, celebrate the beautiful, the refined, the past, or exhibit technical, rhythmic, or grammatical dexterity—but a literature underlying life, religious, consistent with science, handling the elements and forces with competent power, teaching and training men—and, as perhaps the most precious of its results, achieving the entire redemption of woman out of these incredible holds and webs of silliness, millinery, and every kind of dyspeptic depletion—and thus insuring to the States a strong and sweet Female Race, a race of perfect Mothers—is what is needed.

And now, in the full conception of these facts and points, and all that they infer, pro and con—with yet unshaken faith in the elements of the American masses, the composites, of both sexes, and even consider'd as individuals—and ever recognizing in them the broadest bases of the best literary and æsthetic appreciation—I proceed with my speculations, Vistas.

First, let us see what we can make out of a brief, general, sentimental consideration of political democracy, and whence it has arisen, with regard to some of its current features, as an aggregate, and as the basic structure of our future literature and authorship. We shall, it is true, quickly and continually find the origin-idea of the singleness of man, individualism, asserting itself, and cropping forth, even from the opposite ideas. But the mass, or lump character, for imperative reasons, is to be ever carefully weigh'd, borne in mind, and provided for. Only from it, and from its proper regulation and potency, comes the other, comes the chance of individualism. The two are contradictory, but our task is to reconcile them.[4]

The political history of the past may be summ'd up as having grown out of what underlies the words, order, safety, caste, and especially out of the need of some prompt deciding authority, and of cohesion at all cost. Leaping time, we come to the period within the memory of people now living, when, as from some lair where they had slumber'd long, accumulating wrath, sprang up and are yet active (1790, and on even to the present, 1870) those noisy eructations, destructive iconoclasms, a fierce sense of wrongs, amid which moves the form, well known in modern history, in the Old World, stain'd with much blood, and mark'd by savage reactionary clamors and demands. These bear, mostly, as on one inclosing point of need.

For after the rest is said—after the many time-honor'd and really true things for subordination, experience, rights of property, etc., have been listen'd to and acquiesced in—after the valuable and well-settled statement of our duties and relations in society is thoroughly conn'd over and exhausted—it remains to bring forward and modify everything else with the idea of that Something a man is (last precious consolation of the drudging poor), standing apart from all else, divine in his own right, and a woman in hers, sole and untouchable by any canons of authority, or any rule derived from precedent, state-safety, the acts of legislatures, or even from what is called religion, modesty, or art. The radiation of this truth is the key of the most significant doing of our immediately preceding three centuries, and has been the political genesis and life of America. Advancing

3. "Of these rapidly sketch'd hiatuses, the two which seem to be most serious are, for one, the condition, absence, or perhaps the singular abeyance, of moral conscientious fiber all through American society; and, for another, the appaling depletion of women in their powers of sane athletic maternity, their crowning attribute, and ever making the woman, in loftiest spheres, superior to the man.

I have sometimes thought, indeed, that the sole avenue and means of a reconstructed sociology depended, primarily, on a new birth, elevation, expansion, invigoration of woman, affording, for races to come (as the conditions that antedate birth are indispensable), a perfect motherhood. Great, great, indeed, far greater than they know, is the sphere of women. But doubtless the question of such new sociology all goes together, includes many vaired and complex influences and premises, and the man as well as the woman, and the woman as well as the man" [W].

4. "The question hinted here is one which time only can answer. Must not the virtue of modern Individualism, continually enlarging, usurping all, seriously affect, perhaps keep down entirely, in America, the like of the ancient virtue of Patriotism, the fervid and absorbing love of general country? I have no doubt myself that the two will merge, and will mutually profit and brace each other, and that from them a greater product, a third, will arise. But I feel that at present they and their oppositions form a serious problem and paradox in the United States" [W].

visibly, it still more advances invisibly. Underneath the fluctuations of the expressions of society, as well as the movements of the politics of the leading nations of the world, we see steadily pressing ahead and strengthening itself, even in the midst of immense tendencies toward aggregation, this image of completeness in separation, of individual personal dignity, of a single person, either male or female, characterized in the main, not from extrinsic acquirements or position, but in the pride of himself or herself alone; and, as an eventual conclusion and summing up (or else the entire scheme of things is aimless, a cheat, a crash), the simple idea that the last, best dependence is to be upon humanity itself, and its own inherent, normal, full-grown qualities without any superstitious support whatever. This idea of perfect individualism it is indeed that deepest tinges and gives character to the idea of the aggregate. For it is mainly or altogether to serve independent separatism that we favor a strong generalization, consolidation. As it is to give the best vitality and freedom to the rights of the States (every bit as important as the right of nationality, the union), that we insist on the identity of the Union at all hazards.

The purpose of democracy—supplanting old belief in the necessary absoluteness of establish'd dynastic rulership, temporal, ecclesiastical, and scholastic, as furnishing the only security against chaos, crime, and ignorance—is, through many transmigrations and amid endless ridicules, arguments, and ostensible failures, to illustrate, at all hazards, this doctrine or theory that man, properly train'd in sanest, highest freedom, may and must become a law, and series of laws, unto himself, surrounding and providing for, not only his own personal control, but all his relations to other individuals, and to the State; and that, while other theories, as in the past histories of nations, have proved wise enough, and indispensable perhaps for their conditions, *this,* as matters now stand in our civilized world, is the only scheme worth working from, as warranting results like those of Nature's laws, reliable, when once establish'd to carry on themselves.

The argument of the matter is extensive, and, we admit, by no means all on one side. What we shall offer will be far, far from sufficient. But while leaving unsaid much that should properly even prepare the way for the treatment of this many-sided question of political liberty, equality, or republicanism—leaving the whole history and consideration of the feudal plan and its products, embodying humanity, its politics and civilization, through the retrospect of past time (which plan and products, indeed, make up all of the past, and a large part of the present) —leaving unanswer'd, at least by any specific and local answer, many a well-wrought argument and instance, and many a conscientious declamatory cry and warning—as, very lately, from an eminent and venerable person abroad [5] —things, problems, full of doubt, dread, suspense (not new to me, but old occupiers of many an anxious hour in city's din, or night's silence), we still may give a page or so, whose drift is opportune. Time alone can finally answer these things. But as a substitute in passing, let us, even if fragmentarily, throw forth a short direct or indirect suggestion of the premises of that other plan, in the new spirit, under the new forms, started here in our America.

As to the political section of Democracy, which introduces and breaks ground for further and vaster sections, few probably are the minds, even in these republican States, that fully comprehend the aptness of that phrase, "the government of the people, by the people, for the people," which we inherit from the lips of Abraham Lincoln; a formula whose verbal shape is homely wit, but whose scope includes both the totality and all minutiæ of the lesson.

The People! Like our huge earth itself, which, to ordinary scansion, is full of vulgar contradictions and offense, man, viewed in the lump, displeases, and is a constant puzzle and affront to the merely educated classes. The rare, cosmical, artist-mind, lit with the Infinite, alone confronts his manifold and oceanic qualities—but taste, intelligence and culture (so-called), have been against the masses, and remain so. There is plenty of glamour about the most damnable crimes and hoggish meannesses, special and general, of the feudal and dynastic world over there, with its *personnel* of lords and queens and courts, so well dress'd and so handsome. But the People are ungrammatical, untidy, and their sins gaunt and ill bred.

Literature, strictly consider'd, has never recog-

5. " 'Shooting Niagara'—I was at first roused to much anger and abuse by this essay from Mr. Carlyle, so insulting to the theory of America—but happening to think afterwards how I had more than once been in the like mood, during which his essay was evidently cast, and seen persons and things in the same light (indeed, some might say there are signs of the same feeling in these Vistas)—I have since read it again, not only as a study, expressing as it does certain judgments from the highest feudal point of view, but have read it with respect as coming from an earnest soul, and as contributing certain sharp-cutting metallic grains, which, if not gold or silver, may be good, hard, honest iron" [W].

nized the People, and, whatever may be said, does not today. Speaking generally, the tendencies of literature, as hitherto pursued, have been to make mostly critical and querulous men. It seems as if, so far, there were some natural repugnance between a literary and professional life, and the rude rank spirit of the democracies. There is, in later literature, a treatment of benevolence, a charity business, rife enough it is true; but I know nothing more rare, even in this country, than a fit scientific estimate and reverent appreciation of the People —of their measureless wealth of latent power and capacity, their vast, artistic contrasts of lights and shades—with, in America, their entire reliability in emergencies, and a certain breadth of historic grandeur, of peace or war, far surpassing all the vaunted samples of book-heroes, or any *haut ton* coteries, in all the records of the world.

The movements of the late Secession War, and their results, to any sense that studies well and comprehends them, show that popular democracy, whatever its faults and dangers, practically justifies itself beyond the proudest claims and wildest hopes of its enthusiasts. Probably no future age can know, but I well know, how the gist of this fiercest and most resolute of the world's warlike contentions resided exclusively in the unnamed, unknown rank and file; and how the brunt of its labor of death was, to all essential purposes, volunteered. The People, of their own choice, fighting, dying for their own idea, insolently attack'd by the secession-slave-power, and its very existence imperil'd. Descending to detail, entering any of the armies, and mixing with the private soldiers, we see and have seen august spectacles. We have seen the alacrity with which the American-born populace, the peaceablest and most good-natured race in the world, and the most personally independent and intelligent, and the least fitted to submit to the irksomeness and exasperation of regimental discipline, sprang, at the first tap of the drum, to arms—not for gain, nor even glory, nor to repel invasion—but for an emblem, a mere abstraction—for the life, *the safety of the flag*. We have seen the unequal'd docility and obedience of these soldiers. We have seen them tried long and long by hopelessness, mismanagement, and by defeat; have seen the incredible slaughter toward or through which the armies (as at first Fredericksburg, and afterward at the Wilderness), still unhesitatingly obey'd orders to advance. We have seen them in trench, or crouching behind breastwork, or tramping in deep mud, or amid pouring rain or thick-falling snow, or under forced marches in hottest summer (as on the road to get to Gettysburg—vast suffocating swarms, divisions, corps, with every single man so grimed and black with sweat and dust, his own mother would not have known him—his clothes all dirty, stain'd and torn, with sour, accumulated sweat for perfume—many a comrade, perhaps a brother, sunstruck, staggering out, dying, by the roadside, of exhaustion—yet the great bulk bearing steadily on, cheery enough, hollow-bellied from hunger, but sinewy with unconquerable resolution.

We have seen this race proved by wholesale, by drearier, yet more fearful tests—the wound, the amputation, the shatter'd face or limb, the slow hot fever, long impatient anchorage in bed, and all the forms of maiming, operation, and disease. Alas! America have we seen, though only in her early youth, already to hospital brought. There have we watch'd these soldiers, many of them only boys in years—mark'd their decorum, their religious nature and fortitude, and their sweet affection. Wholesale, truly. For at the front, and through the camps, in countless tents, stood the regimental, brigade, and division hospitals; while everywhere amid the land, in or near cities, rose clusters of huge, whitewash'd, crowded, one-story wooden barracks; and there ruled agony with bitter scourge, yet seldom brought a cry; and there stalk'd death by day and night along the narrow aisles between the rows of cots, or by the blankets on the ground, and touch'd lightly many a poor sufferer, often with blessed, welcome touch.

I know not whether I shall be understood, but I realize that it is finally from what I learn'd personally mixing in such scenes that I am now penning these pages. One night in the gloomiest period of the war, in the Patent Office hospital in Washington city, as I stood by the bedside of a Pennsylvania soldier, who lay, conscious of quick approaching death, yet perfectly calm, and with noble, spiritual manner, the veteran surgeon, turning aside, said to me, that though he had witness'd many, many deaths of soldiers, and had been a worker at Bull Run, Antietam, Fredericksburg, etc., he had not seen yet the first case of man or boy that met the approach of dissolution with cowardly qualms or terror. My own observation fully bears out the remark.

What have we here, if not, towering above all talk and argument, the plentifully supplied, last-needed proof of democracy, in its personalities? Curiously enough, too, the proof on this point comes, I should say, every bit as much from the south, as from the north. Although I have spoken only of the latter, yet I deliberately include all. Grand, common stock! to me the accomplish'd and convincing growth, prophetic of the future; proof undeniable to sharpest sense, of perfect beauty, tenderness and pluck, that never feudal lord, nor Greek, nor Roman breed, yet rival'd. Let no tongue ever speak in disparagement of the American races, north or south, to one who has been through the war in the great army hospitals.

Meantime, general humanity (for to that we return, as, for our purposes, what it really is, to bear in mind), has always, in every department, been full of perverse maleficence, and is so yet. In downcast hours the soul thinks it always will be—but soon recovers from such sickly moods. I myself see clearly enough the crude, defective streaks in all the strata of the common people; the specimens and vast collections of the ignorant, the credulous, the unfit and uncouth, the incapable, and the very low and poor. The eminent person just mention'd sneeringly asks whether we expect to elevate and improve a nation's politics by absorbing such morbid collections and qualities therein. The point is a formidable one, and there will doubtless always be numbers of solid and reflective citizens who will never get over it. Our answer is general, and is involved in the scope and letter of this essay. We believe the ulterior object of political and all other government (having, of course, provided for the police, the safety of life, property, and for the basic statute and common law, and their administration, always first in order), to be among the rest, not merely to rule, to repress disorder, etc., but to develop, to open up to cultivation, to encourage the possibilities of all beneficent and manly outcroppage, and of that aspiration for independence, and the pride and self-respect latent in all characters. (Or, if there be exceptions, we cannot, fixing our eyes on them alone, make theirs the rule for all.)

I say the mission of government, henceforth, in civilized lands, is not repression alone, and not authority alone, not even of law, nor by that favorite standard of the eminent writer, the rule of the best men, the born heroes and captains of the race (as if such ever, or one time out of a hundred, get into the big places, elective or dynastic)—but higher than the highest arbitrary rule, to train communities through all their grades, beginning with individuals and ending there again, to rule themselves. What Christ appear'd for in the moral-spiritual field for human-kind, namely, that in respect to the absolute soul, there is in the possession of such by each single individual, something so transcendent, so incapable of gradations (like life), that, to that extent, it places all beings on a common level, utterly regardless of the distinctions of intellect, virtue, station, or any height or lowliness whatever—is tallied in like manner, in this other field, by democracy's rule that men, the nation, as a common aggregate of living identities, affording in each a separate and complete subject for freedom, worldly thrift and happiness, and for a fair chance for growth, and for protection in citizenship, etc., must, to the political extent of the suffrage or vote, if no further, be placed, in each and in the whole, on one broad, primary, universal, common platform.

The purpose is not altogether direct; perhaps it is more indirect. For it is not that democracy is of exhaustive account in itself. Perhaps, indeed, it is (like Nature), of no account in itself. It is that, as we see, it is the best, perhaps only, fit and full means, formulater, general caller-forth, trainer, for the million, not for grand material personalities only, but for immortal souls. To be a voter with the rest is not so much; and this, like every institute, will have its imperfections. But to become an enfranchised man, and now, impediments removed, to stand and start without humiliation, and equal with the rest; to commence, or have the road clear'd to commence, the grand experiment of development, whose end (perhaps requiring several generations), may be the forming of a full-grown man or woman—that *is* something. To ballast the State is also secured, and in our times is to be secured, in no other way.

We do not (at any rate I do not), put it either on the ground that the People, the masses, even the best of them, are, in their latent or exhibited qualities, essentially sensible and good—nor on the ground of their rights; but that good or bad, rights or no rights, the democratic formula is the only safe and preservative one for coming times. We endow the masses with the suffrage for their own sake, no doubt; then, perhaps still more, from another point of view, for community's sake. Leaving the rest to the sentimentalists, we present freedom as sufficient in its scientific aspect, cold as ice, reasoning, deductive, clear and passionless as crystal.

Democracy too is law, and of the strictest, amplest kind. Many suppose (and often in its own ranks the error), that it means a throwing aside of law, and running riot. But, briefly, it is the superior law, not alone that of physical force, the body, which, adding to, it supersedes with that of the spirit. Law is the unshakable order of the universe forever; and the law over all, and law of laws, is the law of successions; that of the superior law, in time, gradually supplanting and overwhelming the inferior one. (While, for myself, I would cheerfully agree—first covenanting that the formative tendencies shall be administered in favor, or at least not against it, and that this reservation be closely construed—that until the individual or community show due signs, or be so minor and fractional as not to endanger the State, the condition of authoritative tutelage may continue, and self-government must abide its time.) Nor is the æsthetic point, always an important one, without fascination for highest aiming souls. The common ambition strains for elevations, to become some privileged exclusive. The master sees greatness and health in being part of the mass; nothing will do as well as common ground. Would you have in yourself the divine, vast, general law? Then merge yourself in it.

And, topping democracy, this most alluring record, that it alone can bind, and ever seeks to bind, all nations, all men, of however various and distant lands, into a brotherhood, a family. It is the old, yet ever-modern dream of earth, out of her eldest and her youngest, her fond philosophers and poets. Not that half only, individualism, which isolates. There is another half, which is adhesiveness or love, that fuses, ties, and aggregates, making the races comrades, and fraternizing all. Both are to be vitalized by religion (sole worthiest elevator of man or State), breathing into the proud, material tissues, the breath of life. For I say at the core of democracy, finally, is the religious element. All the religions, old and new, are there. Nor may the scheme step forth, clothed in resplendent beauty and command, till these, bearing the best, the latest fruit, the spiritual, shall fully appear.

A portion of our pages we might indite with reference toward Europe, especially the British part of it, more than our own land, perhaps not absolutely needed for the home reader. But the whole question hangs together, and fastens and links all peoples. The liberalist of today has this advantage over antique or medieval times, that his doctrine seeks not only to individualize but to universalize. The great word Solidarity has arisen. Of all dangers to a nation, as things exist in our day, there can be no greater one than having certain portions of the people set off from the rest by a line drawn—they not privileged as others, but degraded, humiliated, made of no account. Much quackery teems, of course, even on democracy's side, yet does not really affect the orbic quality of the matter. To work in, if we may so term it, and justify God, His divine aggregate, the People (or, the veritable horned and sharp-tailed Devil, *His* aggregate, if there be who convulsively insist upon it)—this, I say, is what democracy is for; and this is what our America means, and is doing—may I not say, has done? If not, she means nothing more, and does nothing more, than any other land. And, as by virtue of its cosmical, antiseptic power, Nature's stomach is fully strong enough not only to digest the morbific matter always presented, not to be turn'd aside, and perhaps, indeed, intuitively gravitating thither—but even to change such contributions into nutriment for highest use and life—so American democracy's. That is the lesson we, these days, send over to European lands by every western breeze.

And truly, whatever may be said, in the way of abstract argument, for or against the theory of a wider democratizing of institutions in any civilized country, much trouble might well be saved to all European lands by recognizing this palpable fact (for a palpable fact it is), that some form of such democratizing is about the only resource now left. *That,* or chronic dissatisfaction continued, mutterings which grow annually louder and louder, till, in due course, and pretty swiftly in most cases, the inevitable crisis, dynastic ruin. Anything worthy to be call'd statesmanship in the Old World, I should say, among the advanced students, adepts, or men of any brains, does not debate today whether to hold on, attempting to lean back and monarchize, or to look forward and democratize—but *how,* and in what degree and part, most prudently to democratize.

The eager and often inconsiderate appeals of reformers and revolutionists are indispensable, to counterbalance the inertness and fossilism making so large a part of human institutions. The latter will always take care of themselves—the danger being that they rapidly tend to ossify us. The former is to be treated with indulgence, and even with respect. As circulation to air, so is agitation and a plentiful degree of speculative license to political and moral sanity. Indirectly, but surely, goodness, virtue, law (of the very best), follow freedom. These, to democracy, are what the keel is to the ship, or saltness to the ocean.

The true gravitation-hold of liberalism in the United States will be a more universal ownership of property, general homesteads, general comfort—a vast, intertwining reticulation of wealth. As the human frame, or, indeed, any object in this manifold universe, is best kept together by the simple miracle of its own cohesion, and the necessity, exercise, and profit thereof, so a great and varied nationality, occupying millions of square miles, were firmest held and knit by the principle of the safety and endurance of the aggregate of its middling property owners. So that, from another point of view, ungracious as it may sound, and a paradox after what we have been saying, democracy looks with suspicious, ill-satisfied eye upon the very poor, the ignorant, and on those out of business. She asks for men and women with occupations, well-off, owners of houses and acres, and with cash in the bank—and with some cravings for literature, too; and must have them, and hastens to make them. Luckily, the seed is already well sown, and has taken ineradicable root.[6]

Huge and mighty are our days, our republican lands—and most in their rapid shiftings, their changes, all in the interest of the cause. As I write this particular passage (November 1868), the din of disputation rages around me. Acrid the temper of the parties, vital the pending questions. Congress convenes; the President sends his message; reconstruction is still in abeyance; the nomination and the contest for the twenty-first Presidentiad draw close, with loudest threat and bustle. Of these, and all the like of these, the eventuations I know not; but well I know that behind them, and whatever their eventuations, the vital things remain safe and certain, and all the needed work goes on. Time, with soon or later superciliousness, disposes of Presidents, Congressmen, party platforms, and such. Anon, it clears the stage of each and any mortal shred that thinks itself so potent to its day; and at and after which (with precious, golden exceptions once or twice in a century), all that relates to sir potency is flung to molder in a burial-vault, and no one bothers himself the least bit about it afterwards. But the People ever remain, tendencies continue, and all the idiocratic transfers in unbroken chain go on.

In a few years the dominion-heart of America will be far inland, toward the West. Our future national capital may not be where the present one is. It is possible, nay likely, that in less than fifty years, it will migrate a thousand or two miles, will be refounded, and everything belonging to it made on a different plan, original, far more superb. The main social, political, spine-character of the States will probably run along the Ohio, Missouri and Mississippi rivers, and west and north of them, including Canada. Those regions, with the group of powerful brothers toward the Pacific (destined to the mastership of that sea and its countless paradises of islands), will compact and settle the traits of America, with all the old retain'd, but more expanded, grafted on newer, hardier, purely native stock. A giant growth, composite from the rest, getting their contribution, absorbing it, to make it more illustrious. From the north, intellect, the sun of things, also the idea of unswayable justice, anchor amid the last, the wildest tempests. From the south the living soul, the animus of good and bad, haughtily admitting no demonstration but its own. While from the west itself comes solid personality, with blood and brawn, and the deep quality of all-accepting fusion.

Political democracy, as it exists and practically works in America, with all its threatening evils, supplies a training school for making first-class men. It is life's gymnasium, not of good only, but of all. We try often, though we fall back often. A brave delight, fit for freedom's athletes, fills these arenas, and fully satisfies, out of the action in them, irrespective of success. Whatever we do not attain, we at any rate attain the experiences of the fight, the hardening of the strong campaign, and throb with currents of attempt at least. Time is ample. Let the victors come after us. Not for nothing does evil play its part among us. Judging from the main portions of the history of the world, so far, justice is always in jeopardy, peace walks amid hourly pitfalls, and of slavery, misery, meanness, the craft of tyrants and the credulity of the populace, in some of the protean forms, no voice can at any time say, They are not. The clouds break a little, and the sun shines out—but soon and certain the lowering darkness falls again, as if to last forever. Yet is there an immortal courage and prophecy in every sane soul that cannot, must not, under any circumstances, capitulate. *Vive,* the attack—the perennial assault! *Vive,* the unpopular cause—the spirit that audaciously aims —the never-abandon'd efforts, pursued the same amid opposing proofs and precedents.

Once, before the war (alas! I dare not say how many times the mood has come!) I, too, was fill'd with doubt and gloom. A foreigner, an acute and good man, had impressively said to me, that day—putting in form, indeed, my own observations: "I have travel'd much in the United States, and watch'd their politicians, and listen'd to the speeches of the candidates, and read the journals, and gone into the public-houses, and heard the unguarded talk of men. And I have found your vaunted America honeycomb'd from top to toe with infidelism, even to itself and its own programme. I have mark'd the brazen hell-faces of secession and slavery gazing defiantly from all the

6. "For fear of mistake, I may as well distinctly specify, as cheerfully included in the model and standard of these Vistas, a practical, stirring, wordly, money-making, even materialistic character. It is undeniable that our farms, stores, offices, dry goods, coal and groceries, enginery, cash accounts, trades, earnings, markets, etc., should be attended to in earnest, and actively pursued, just as if they had a real and permanent existence. I perceive clearly that the extreme business energy, and this almost maniacal appetite for wealth prevalent in the United States, are parts of amelioration and progress, indispensably needed to prepare the very results I demand. My theory includes riches, and the getting of riches, and the amplest products, power, activity, inventions, movements, etc. Upon them, as upon substrata, I raise the edifice design'd in these Vistas" [W].

windows and doorways. I have everywhere found, primarily, thieves and scalliwags arranging the nominations to offices, and sometimes filling the offices themselves. I have found the north just as full of bad stuff as the south. Of the holders of public office in the Nation or the States or their municipalities, I have found that not one in a hundred has been chosen by any spontaneous selection of the outsiders, the people, but all have been nominated and put through by little or large caucuses of the politicians, and have got in by corrupt rings and electioneering, not capacity or desert. I have noticed how the millions of sturdy farmers and mechanics are thus the helpless supple-jacks of comparatively few politicians. And I have noticed more and more, the alarming spectacle of parties usurping the government, and openly and shamelessly wielding it for party purposes."

Sad, serious, deep truths. Yet are there other, still deeper, amply confronting, dominating truths. Over those politicians and great and little rings, and over all their insolence and wiles, and over the powerfullest parties, looms a power, too sluggish maybe, but ever holding decisions and decrees in hand, ready, with stern process, to execute them as soon as plainly needed—and at times, indeed, summarily crushing to atoms the mightiest parties, even in the hour of their pride.

In saner hours far different are the amounts of these things from what, at first sight, they appear. Though it is no doubt important who is elected governor, mayor, or legislator (and full of dismay when incompetent or vile ones get elected, as they sometimes do), there are other, quieter contingencies, infinitely more important. Shams, etc., will always be the show, like ocean's scum; enough, if waters deep and clear make up the rest. Enough, that while the piled embroider'd shoddy gaud and fraud spreads to the superficial eye, the hidden warp and weft are genuine, and will wear forever. Enough, in short, that the race, the land which could raise such as the late rebellion, could also put it down.

The average man of a land at last only is important. He, in these States, remains immortal owner and boss, deriving good uses, somehow, out of any sort of servant in office, even the basest (certain universal requisities, and their settled regularity and protection, being first secured); a nation like ours, in a sort of geological formation state, trying continually new experiments, choosing new delegations, is not served by the best men only, but sometimes more by those that provoke it—by the combats they arouse. Thus national rage, fury, discussion, etc., better than content. Thus, also, the warning signals, invaluable for after times.

What is more dramatic than the spectacle we have seen repeated, and doubtless long shall see—the popular judgment taking the successful candidates on trial in the offices—standing off, as it were, and observing them and their doings for a while, and always giving, finally, the fit, exactly due reward? I think, after all, the sublimest part of political history, and its culmination, is currently issuing from the American people. I know nothing grander, better exercise, better digestion, more positive proof of the past, the triumphant result of faith in human-kind, than a well-contested American national election.

Then still the thought returns (like the thread-passage in overtures), giving the key and echo to these pages. When I pass to and fro, different latitudes, different seasons, beholding the crowds of the great cities, New York, Boston, Philadelphia, Cincinnati, Chicago, St. Louis, San Francisco, New Orleans, Baltimore—when I mix with these interminable swarms of alert, turbulent, good-natured, independent citizens, mechanics, clerks, young persons—at the idea of this mass of men, so fresh and free, so loving and so proud, a singular awe falls upon me. I feel, with dejection and amazement, that among our geniuses and talented writers or speakers, few or none have yet really spoken to this people, created a single image-making work for them, or absorb'd the central spirit and the idiosyncrasies which are theirs—and which, thus, in highest ranges, so far remain entirely uncelebrated, unexpress'd.

Dominion strong is the body's; dominion stronger is the mind's. What has fill'd, and fills today our intellect, our fancy, furnishing the standards therein, is yet foreign. The great poems, Shakspere included, are poisonous to the idea of the pride and dignity of the common people, the life-blood of democracy. The models of our literature, as we get it from other lands, ultramarine, have had their birth in courts, and bask'd and grown in castle sunshine; all smells of princes' favors. Of workers of a certain sort, we have, indeed, plenty, contributing after their kind; many elegant, many learn'd, all complacent. But touch'd by the national test, or tried by the standards of democratic personality, they wither to ashes. I say I have not seen a single writer, artist, lecturer, or what not, that has confronted the voiceless but ever erect and active, pervading, underlying will and typic aspiration of the land, in a spirit kindred to itself. Do you call those genteel little creatures American poets? Do you term that perpetual, pistareen, paste-pot work, American art, American drama, taste, verse? I think I hear, echoed as from some mountaintop afar in the west, the scornful laugh of the Genius of these States.

Democracy, in silence, biding its time, ponders its own ideals, not of literature and art only—not of men only, but of women. The idea of the women of America (extricated from this daze, this fossil and unhealthy air which hangs about the word *lady*) develop'd, raised to become the robust equals, workers, and, it may be, even practical and political deciders with the men—greater than man, we may admit, through their divine maternity, always their towering, emblematical attribute—but great, at any rate, as man, in all departments; or, rather, capable of being so, soon as they realize it, and can bring themselves to give up toys and fictions, and launch forth, as men do, amid real, independent, stormy life.

Then, as toward our thought's finalè (and, in that, over-arching the true scholar's lesson), we have to say there can be no complete or epical presentation of democracy in the aggregate, or anything like it, at this day, because its doctrines will only be effectually incarnated in any one branch, when, in all, their spirit is at the root and center. Far, far, indeed, stretch, in distance, our Vistas! How much is still to be disentangled, freed! How long it takes to make this American world see that it is, in itself, the final authority and reliance!

Did you, too, O friend, suppose democracy was only for elections, for politics, and for a party name? I say democracy is only of use there that it may pass on and come to its flower and fruits in manners, in the highest forms of interaction between men, and their beliefs—in religion, literature, colleges, and schools—democracy in all public and private life, and in the army and navy.[7] I have intimated that, as a paramount scheme, it has yet few or no full realizers and believers. I do not see, either, that it owes any serious thanks to noted propagandists or champions, or has been essentially help'd, though often harm'd, by them. It has been and is carried on by all the moral forces, and by trade, finance, machinery, intercommunications, and, in fact, by all the developments of history, and can no more be stopp'd than the tides, or the earth in its orbit. Doubtless, also, it resides, crude and latent, well down in the hearts of the fair average of the American-born people, mainly in the agricultural regions. But it is not yet, there or anywhere, the fully receiv'd, the fervid, the absolute faith.

I submit, therefore, that the fruition of democracy, on aught like a grand scale, resides altogether in the future. As, under any profound and comprehensive view of the gorgeous-composite feudal world, we see in it, through the long ages and cycles of ages, the results of a deep, integral, human and divine principle, or fountain, from which issued laws, ecclesia, manners, institutes, costumes, personalities, poems (hitherto unequal'd), faithfully partaking of their source, and indeed only arising either to betoken it, or to furnish parts of that varied-flowing display, whose center was one and absolute—so, long ages hence, shall the due historian or critic make at least an equal retrospect, an equal history for the democratic principle. It too must be adorn'd, credited with its results—then, when it, with imperial power, through amplest time, has dominated mankind—has been the source and test of all the moral, æsthetic, social, political, and religious expressions and institutes of the civilized world—has begotten them in spirit and in form, and has carried them to its own unprecedented heights—has had (it is possible) monastics and ascetics, more numerous, more devout than the monks and priests of all previous creeds—has sway'd the ages with a breadth and rectitude tallying Nature's own—has fashion'd, systematized, and triumphantly finish'd and carried out, in its own interest, and with unparallel'd success, a new earth and a new man.

Thus we presume to write, as it were, upon things that exist not, and travel by maps yet unmade, and a blank. But the throes of birth are upon us; and we have something of this advantage in seasons of strong formations, doubts, suspense—for then the afflatus of such themes haply may fall upon us, more or less; and then, hot from surrounding war and revolution, our speech, though without polish'd coherence, and a failure by the standard called criticism, comes forth, real at least as the lightnings.

And maybe we, these days, have, too, our own reward—(for there are yet some, in all lands, worthy to be so encouraged). Through not for us the joy of entering at the last the conquered city—not ours the chance ever to see with our own eyes the peerless power and splendid *éclat* of the democratic principle, arriv'd at meridian, filling the world with effulgence and majesty far beyond those of past history's kings, or all dynastic sway—there is yet, to whoever is eligible among us, the

7. "The whole present system of the officering and personnel of the army and navy of these States, and the spirit and letter of their trebly-aristocratic rules and regulations, is a monstrous exotic, a nuisance and revolt, and belong here just as much as orders of nobility, or the Pope's council of cardinals. I say if the present theory of our army and navy is sensible and true, then the rest of America is an unmitigated fraud" [W].

prophetic vision, the joy of being toss'd in the brave turmoil of these times—the promulgation and the path, obedient, lowly reverent to the voice, the gesture of the god, or holy ghost, which others see not, hear not—with the proud consciousness that amid whatever clouds, seductions, or heart-wearying postponements, we have never deserted, never despair'd, never abandon'd the faith.

So much contributed, to be conn'd well, to help prepare and brace our edifice, our plann'd Idea—we still proceed to give it in another of its aspects—perhaps the main, the high façade of all. For to democracy, the leveler, the unyielding principle of the average, surely join'd another principle, equally unyielding, closely tracking the first, indispensable to it, opposite (as the sexes are opposite), and whose existence, confronting and ever modifying the other, often clashing, paradoxical, yet neither of highest avail without the other, plainly supplies to these grand cosmic politics of ours, and to the launch'd forth mortal dangers of republicanism, today, or any day, the counterpart and offset whereby Nature restrains the deadly original relentlessness of all her first-class laws. This second principle is individuality, the pride and centripetal isolation of a human being in himself—identity—personalism. Whatever the name, its acceptance and thorough infusions through the organizations of political commonalty now shooting Aurora-like about the world, are of utmost importance, as the principle itself is needed for very life's sake. It forms, in a sort, or is to form, the compensating balance-wheel of the successful working machinery of aggregate America.

And, if we think of it, what does civilization itself rest upon—and what object has it, what its religions, arts, schools, etc., but rich, luxuriant, varied personalism? To that, all bends; and it is because toward such result democracy alone, on anything like Nature's scale, breaks up the limitless fallows of human-kind, and plants the seed, and gives fair play, that its claims now precede the rest. The literature, songs, æsthetics, etc., of a country are of importance principally because they furnish the materials and suggestions of personality for the women and men of that country, and enforce them in a thousand effective ways.[8]

As the topmost claim of a strong consolidating of the nationality of these States is, that only by such powerful compaction can the separate States secure that full and free swing within their spheres, which is becoming to them, each after its kind, so will individuality, and unimpeded branchings, flourish best under imperial republican forms.

Assuming Democracy to be at present in its embryo condition, and that the only large and satisfactory justification of it resides in the future, mainly through the copious production of perfect characters among the people, and through the advent of a sane and pervading religiousness, it is with regard to the atmosphere and spaciousness fit for such characters, and of certain nutriment and cartoon-draftings proper for them, and indicating them for New World purposes, that I continue the present statement—an exploration, as of new ground, wherein, like other primitive surveyors, I must do the best I can, leaving it to those who come after me to do much better. (The service, in fact, if any, must be to break a sort of first path or track, no matter how rude and ungeometrical.)

We have frequently printed the word Democracy. Yet I cannot too often repeat that it is a word the real gist of which still sleeps, quite unawaken'd, notwithstanding the resonance and the many angry tempests out of which its syllables have come, from pen or tongue. It is a great word, whose history, I suppose, remains unwritten, because that history has yet to be enacted. It is, in some sort, younger brother of another great and often-used word, Nature, whose history also waits unwritten. As I perceive, the tendencies of our day, in the States (and I entirely respect them), are toward those vast and sweeping movements, influences, moral and physical, of humanity, now and always current over the planet, on the scale

8. "After the rest is satiated, all interest culminates in the field of persons, and never flags there. Accordingly in this field have the great poets and literatuses signally toiled. They too, in all ages, all lands, have been creators, fashioning, making types of men and women, as Adam and Eve are made in the divine fable. Behold, shaped, bred by orientalism, feudalism, through their long growth and culmination, and breeding back in return—(when shall we have an equal series, typical of democracy?)—behold, commencing in primal Asia (apparently formulated, in what beginning we know, in the gods of the mythologies, and coming down thence), a few samples out of the countless product, bequeath'd to the moderns, bequeath'd to America as studies. For the men, Yudishtura, Rama, Arjuna, Solomon, most of the Old and New Testament characters; Achilles, Ulysses, Theseus, Prometheus, Hercules, Aeneas, Plutarch's heroes; the Merlin of Celtic bards; the Cid, Arthur and his knights, Siegfried and Hagen in the Nibelungen; Roland and Oliver: Roustam in the Shah-Nemah; and so on to Milton's Satan, Cervantes' Don Quixote, Shakspere's Hamlet, Richard II. Lear, Marc Antony, etc., and the modern Faust. These, I say, are models, combined, adjusted to other standards than America's, but of priceless value to her and hers.

"Among women, the goddesses of the Egyptian, Indian, and Greek mythologies, certain Bible characters, especially the Holy Mother; Cleopatra, Penelope; the portraits of Brunhelde and Chriemhilde in the Nibelungen; Oriana, Una, etc.; the modern Consuelo, Walter Scott's Jeanie and Effie Deans, etc., etc. (Yet women portrayed or outlin'd at her best, or as perfect human mother, does not hitherto, it seems to me, fully appear in literature)" [W].

of the impulses of the elements. Then it is also good to reduce the whole matter to the consideration of a single self, a man, a woman, on permanent grounds. Even for the treatment of the universal, in politics, metaphysics, or anything, sooner or later we come down to one single, solitary soul.

There is, in sanest hours, a consciousness, a thought that rises, independent, lifted out from all else, calm, like the stars, shining eternal. This is the thought of identity—yours for you, whoever you are, as mine for me. Miracle of miracles, beyond statement, most spiritual and vaguest of earth's dreams, yet hardest basic fact, and only entrance to all facts. In such devout hours, in the midst of the significant wonders of heaven and earth (significant only because of the Me in the center), creeds, conventions, fall away and become of no account before this simple idea. Under the luminousness of real vision, it alone takes possession, takes value. Like the shadowy dwarf in the fable, once liberated and look'd upon, it expands over the whole earth, and spreads to the roof of heaven.

The quality of BEING, in the object's self, according to its own central idea and purpose, and of growing therefrom and thereto—not criticism by other standards, and adjustments thereto—is the lesson of Nature. True, the full man wisely gathers, culls, absorbs; but if, engaged disproportionately in that, he slights or overlays the precious idiocrasy and special nativity and intention that he is, the man's self, the main thing, is a failure, however wide his general cultivation. Thus, in our times, refinement and delicatesse are not only attended to sufficiently, but threaten to eat us up, like a cancer. Already, the democratic genius watches, ill-pleased, these tendencies. Provision for a little healthy rudeness, savage virtue, justification of what one has in one's self, whatever it is, is demanded. Negative qualities, even deficiencies, would be a relief. Singleness and normal simplicity and separation, amid this more and more complex, more and more artificialized state of society—how pensively we yearn for them! how we would welcome their return!

In some such direction, then—at any rate enough to preserve the balance—we feel called upon to throw what weight we can, not for absolute reasons, but current ones. To prune, gather, trim, conform, and ever cram and stuff, and be genteel and proper, is the pressure of our days. While aware that much can be said even in behalf of all this, we perceive that we have not now to consider the question of what is demanded to serve a half-starved and barbarous nation, or set of nations, but what is most applicable, most pertinent, for numerous congeries of conventional, over-corpulent societies, already becoming stifled and rotten with flatulent, infidelistic literature, and polite conformity and art. In addition to establish'd sciences, we suggest a science as it were of healthy average personalism, on original-universal grounds, the object of which should be to raise up and supply through the States a copious race of superb American men and women, cheerful, religious, ahead of any yet known.

America has yet morally and artistically originated nothing. She seems singularly unaware that the models of persons, books, manners, etc., appropriate for former conditions and for European lands, are but exiles and exotics here. No current of her life, as shown on the surfaces of what is authoritatively called her society, accepts or runs into social or æsthetic democracy; but all the currents set squarely against it. Never, in the Old World, was thoroughly upholster'd exterior appearance and show, mental and other, built entirely on the idea of caste, and on the sufficiency of mere outside acquisition—never were glibness, verbal intellect more the test, the emulation—more loftily elevated as head and sample—than they are on the surface of our republican States this day. The writers of a time hint the mottoes of its gods. The word of the modern, say these voices, is the word Culture.

We find ourselves abruptly in close quarters with the enemy. This word Culture, or what it has come to represent, involves, by contrast, our whole theme, and has been, indeed, the spur, urging us to engagement. Certain questions arise. As now taught, accepted and carried out, are not the processes of culture rapidly creating a class of supercilious infidels, who believe in nothing? Shall a man lose himself in countless masses of adjustments, and be so shaped with reference to this, that, and the other, that the simply good and healthy and brave parts of him are reduced and clipp'd away, like the bordering of box in a garden? You can cultivate corn and roses and orchards—but who shall cultivate the mountain peaks, the ocean, and the tumbling gorgeousness of the clouds? Lastly—is the readily given reply that culture only seeks to help, systematize, and put in attitude, the elements of fertility and power, a conclusive reply?

I do not so much object to the name, or word, but I should certainly insist, for the purposes of these States, on a radical change of category, in the distribution of precedence. I should demand a programme of culture, drawn out, not for a single class alone, or for the parlors or lecture rooms, but with an eye to practical life, the west, the workingmen, the facts of farms and jackplanes and engineers, and of the broad range of the women also of the middle and working strata, and with reference to the perfect equality of women, and of a grand and powerful motherhood. I should demand of this programme or theory a scope generous enough to include the widest human area. It must have for its spinal meaning the formation or a typical personality of character, eligible to the uses of the high average of men—and *not* restricted by conditions ineligible to the masses. The best culture will always be that of the manly and courageous instincts, and loving perceptions, and of self-respect—aiming to form, over this continent, an idiocrasy of universalism, which, true child of America, will bring joy to its mother, returning to her in her own spirit, recruiting myriads of offspring, able, natural, perceptive, tolerant, devout believers in her, America, and with some definite instinct why and for what she has arisen, most vast, most formidable of historic births, and is, now and here, with wonderful step, journeying through Time.

The problem, as it seems to me, presented to the New World, is, under permanent law and order, and after preserving cohesion (ensemble-Individuality), at all hazards, to vitalize man's free play of special Personalism, recognizing in it something that calls ever more to be consider'd, fed, and adopted as the sub-stratum for the best that belongs to us (government indeed is for it), including the new æsthetics of our future.

To formulate beyond this present vagueness—to help line and put before us the species, or a specimen of the species, of the democratic ethnology of the future, is a work toward which the genius of our land, with peculiar encouragement, invites her well-wishers. Already certain limnings, more or less grotesque, more or less fading and watery, have appear'd. We too (repressing doubts and qualms) will try our hand.

Attempting, then, however crudely, a basic model or portrait of personality for general use for the manliness of the State (and doubtless that is most useful which is most simple and comprehensive for all, and toned low enough), we should prepare the canvas well beforehand. Parentage must consider itself in advance. (Will the time hasten when fatherhood and motherhood shall become a science—and the noblest science?) To our model, a clear-blooded, strong-fibered physique is indispensable; the questions of food, drink, air, exercise, assimilation, digestion, can never be intermitted. Out of these we descry a well-begotten selfhood—in youth, fresh, ardent, emotional, aspiring, full of adventure; a maturity, brave, perceptive, under control, neither too talkative nor too reticent, neither flippant nor somber; of the bodily figure, the movements easy, the complexion showing the best blood, somewhat flush'd, breast expanded, and erect attitude, a voice whose sound outvies music, eyes of calm and steady gaze, yet capable also of flashing—and a general presence that holds its own in the company of the highest. (For it is native personality, and that alone, that endows a man to stand before presidents or generals, or in any distinguished collection, with *aplomb*—and *not* culture, or any knowledge or intellect whatever.)

With regard to the mental-educational part of our model, enlargement of intellect, stores of cephalic knowledge, etc., the concentration thitherward of all the customs of our age, especially in America, is so overweening, and provides so fully for that part, that, important and necessary as it is, it really needs nothing from us here—except, indeed, a phrase of warning and restraint. Manners, costumes, too, though important, we need not dwell upon here. Like beauty, grace of motion, etc., they are results. Causes, original things, being attended to, the right manners unerringly follow. Much is said, among artists, of "the grand style," as if it were a thing by itself. When a man, artist or whoever, has health, pride, acuteness, noble aspirations, he has the motive-elements of the grandest style. The rest is by manipulation (yet that is no small matter).

Leaving still unspecified several sterling parts of any model fit for the future personality of America, I must not fail, again and ever, to pronounce myself on one, probably the least attended to in modern times—a hiatus, indeed, threatening its gloomiest consequences after us. I mean the simple, unsophisticated Conscience, the primary moral element. If I were asked to specify in what quarter lie the grounds of darkest dread, respecting the America of our hopes, I should have to point to this particular. I should demand the invariable application to individuality, this day and any day, of that old, ever-true plumb-rule of persons, eras, nations. Our triumphant modern civilizee, with his all-schooling and his wondrous appliances, will still show himself but an amputation while this deficiency remains. Beyond (assuming a more hopeful tone), the vertebration of the manly and womanly personalism of our Western world, can only be, and is, indeed, to be (I hope), its all penetrating Religiousness.

The ripeness of Religion is doubtless to be looked for in this field of individuality, and is a result that no organization or church can ever achieve. As history is poorly retain'd by what the technists call history, and is not given out from their pages, except the learner has in himself the sense of the well-wrapt, never yet written, perhaps impossible to be written, history—so Religion, although casually arrested, and, after a fashion, preserv'd in the churches and creeds, does not depend at all upon them, but is a part of the identified soul, which, when greatest, knows not bibles in the old way, but in new ways—the identified soul, which can really confront Religion when it extricates itself entirely from the churches, and not before.

Personalism fuses this, and favors it. I should say, indeed, that only in the perfect uncontamination and solitariness of individuality may the spirituality of religion positively come forth at all. Only here, and on such terms, the meditation, the devout ecstasy, the soaring flight. Only here, communion with the mysteries, the eternal problems, whence? whither? Alone, and identity, and the mood—and the soul emerges, and all statements, churches, sermons, melt away like vapors. Alone, and silent thought and awe, and aspiration—and then the interior consciousness, like a hitherto unseen inscription, in magic ink, beams out its wondrous lines to the sense. Bibles may convey, and priests expound, but it is exclusively for the noiseless operation of one's isolated Self, to enter the pure ether of veneration, reach the divine levels, and commune with the unutterable.

To practically enter into politics is an important part of American personalism. To every young man, north and south, earnestly studying these things, I should here, as an offset to what I have said in former pages, now also say, that maybe to views of very large scope, after all, perhaps the political (perhaps the literary and sociological) America goes best about its development its own way—sometimes, to temporary sight, appalling enough. It is the fashion among dillettants and fops (perhaps I myself am not guiltless), to decry the whole formulation of the active politics of America, as beyond redemption, and to be carefully kept away from. See you that you do not fall into this error. America, it may be, is doing very well upon the whole, notwithstanding these antics of the parties and their leaders, these half-brain'd nominees, and many ignorant ballots, and many elected failures and blatherers. It is the dillettants, and all who shirk their duty, who are not doing well. As for you, I advise you to enter more strongly yet into politics. I advise every young man to do so. Always inform yourself; always do the best you can; always vote. Disengage yourself from parties. They have been useful, and to some extent remain so; but the floating, uncommitted electors, farmers, clerks, mechanics, the masters of parties—watching aloof, inclining victory this side or that side—such are the ones most needed, present and future. For America, if eligible at all to downfall and ruin, is eligible within herself, not without; for I see clearly that the combined foreign world could not beat her down. But these savage, wolfish parties alarm me. Owning no law but their own will, more and more combative, less and less tolerant of the idea of ensemble and of equal brotherhood, the perfect equality of the States, the ever-overarching American ideas, it behooves you to convey yourself implicitly to no party, nor submit blindly to their dictators, but steadily hold yourself judge and master over all of them.

So much (hastily toss'd together, and leaving far more unsaid), for an ideal, or intimations of an ideal, toward American manhood. But the other sex, in our land, requires at least a basis of suggestion.

I have seen a young American woman, one of a large family of daughters, who, some years since, migrated from her meager country home to one of the northern cities, to gain her own support. She soon became an expert seamstress, but finding the employment too confining for health and comfort, she went boldly to work for others, to housekeep, cook, clean, etc. After trying several places, she fell upon one where she was suited. She has told me that she finds nothing degrading in her position; it is not inconsistent with personal dignity, self-respect, and the respect of others. She confers benefits and receives them. She has good health; her presence itself is healthy and bracing; her character is unstain'd; she has made herself understood, and preserves her independence, and has been able to help her parents, and educate and get places for her sisters; and her course of life is not without opportunities for mental improvement, and of much quiet, uncosting happiness and love.

I have seen another woman who, from taste and necessity conjoin'd, has gone into practical affairs, carries on a mechanical business, partly works at it herself, dashes out more and more into real hardy life, is not abash'd by the coarseness of the contact, knows how to be firm and silent at the same time, holds her own with unvarying coolness and decorum, and will compare, any day, with superior carpenters, farmers, and even boatmen and drivers. For all that, she has not lost the charm of the womanly nature, but preserves and bears it fully, though through such rugged presentation.

Then there is the wife of a mechanic, mother of two children, a woman of merely passable English education, but of fine wit, with all her sex's grace and intutitions, who exhibits, indeed, such a noble female personality, that I am fain to record it here. Never abnegating her own proper independence, but always genially preserving it, and what belongs to it—cooking, washing, child-nursing, house-tending—she beams sunshine out of all these duties, and makes them illustrious. Physiologically sweet and sound, loving work, practical, she yet knows that there are intervals, however few, devoted to recreation, music, leisure, hospitality—and affords such intervals. Whatever she does and wherever she is, that charm, that indescribable perfume of genuine womanhood attends her, goes with her, exhales from her, which belongs of right to all the sex, and is, or ought to be, the invariable atmosphere and common aureola of old as well as young.

My dear mother once described to me a resplendent person, down on Long Island, whom she knew in early days. She was known by the name of the Peacemaker. She was well toward eighty years old, of happy and sunny temperament, had always lived on a farm, and was very neighborly, sensible and discreet, an invariable and welcom'd favorite, especially with young married women. She had numerous children and grandchildren. She was uneducated, but possess'd a native dignity. She had come to be a tacitly agreed upon domestic regulator, judge, settler of difficulties, shepherdess, the reconciler in the land. She was a sight to draw near and look upon, with her large figure, her profuse snow-white hair (uncoif'd by any headdress or cap), dark eyes, clear complexion, sweet breath, and peculiar personal magnetism.

The foregoing portraits, I admit, are frightfully out of line from these imported models of womanly personality—the stock feminine characters of the current novelists, or of the foreign court poems (Ophelias, Enids, princesses, or ladies of one thing or another), which fill the envying dreams of so many poor girls, and are accepted by our men, too, as supreme ideals of feminine excellence to be sought after. But I present mine just for a change.

Then there are mutterings (we will not now stop to heed them here, but they must be heeded), of something more revolutionary. The day is coming when the deep questions of woman's entrance amid the arenas of practical life, politics, the suffrage, etc., will not only be argued all around us, but may be put to decision, and real experiment.

Of course, in these States, for both man and woman, we must entirely recast the types of highest personality from what the oriental, feudal, ecclesiastical worlds bequeath us, and which yet possess the imaginative and æsthetic fields of the United States, pictorial and melodramatic, not without use as studies, but making sad work, and forming a strange anachronism upon the scenes and exigencies around us. Of course, the old undying elements remain. The task is, to successfully adjust them to new combinations, our own days. Nor is this so incredible. I can conceive a community, today and here, in which, on a sufficient scale, the perfect personalities, without noise meet; say in some pleasant western settlement or town, where a couple of hundred best men and women, of ordinary worldly status, have by luck been drawn together, with nothing extra of genius or wealth, but virtuous, chaste, industrious, cheerful, resolute, friendly and devout. I can conceive such a community organized in running order, powers judiciously delegated—farming, building, trade, courts, mails, schools, elections, all attended to; and then the rest of life, the main thing, freely branching and blossoming in each individual, and bearing golden fruit. I can see there, in every young and old man, after his kind, and in every woman after hers, a true personality, develop'd, exercised proportionately in body, mind, and spirit. I can imagine this case as one not necessarily rare or difficult, but in buoyant accordance with the municipal and general requirements of our times. And I can realize it in the culmination of something better than any stereotyped *éclat* of history or poems. Perhaps unsung, undramatized, unput in essays or biographies—perhaps even some such community already exists, in Ohio, Illinois, Missouri, or somewhere, practically fulfilling itself, and thus outvying, in cheapest vulgar life, all that has been hitherto shown in best ideal pictures.

In short, and to sum up, America, betaking herself to formative action (as it is about time for more solid achievement, and less windy promise), must, for her purposes, cease to recognize a theory of character grown of feudal aristocracies, or form'd by merely literary standards, or from any ultramarine full-dress formulas of culture, polish, caste, etc., and must sternly promulgate her own new standard, yet old enough, and accepting the old, the perennial elements, and combining them into groups, unities, appropriate to the modern, the democratic, the west, and to the practical occasions and needs of our own cities, and of the agricultural regions. Ever the most precious in the common. Ever the fresh breeze of field, or hill or lake, is more than any palpitation of fans, though of ivory, and redolent with perfume; and the air is more than the costliest perfumes.

And now, for fear of mistake, we may not intermit to beg our absolution from all that genuinely is, or goes along with, even Culture. Pardon us, venerable shade! if we have seem'd to speak lightly of your office. The whole civilization of the earth, we know, is yours, with all the glory and the light thereof. It is, indeed, in your own spirit, and seeking to tally the loftiest teachings of it, that we aim these poor utterances. For you, too, mighty minister! know that there is something greater than you, namely, the fresh, eternal qualities of Being. From them, and by them, as you, at your best, we too evoke the last, the needed help, to vitalize our country and our days. Thus we pronounce not so much against the principle of culture; we only supervise it, and promulgate along with it, as deep, perhaps a deeper, principle. As we have shown the New World including in itself the all-leveling aggregate of democracy, we show it also including the all-varied, all-permitting, all-free theorem of individuality, and erecting therefor a lofty and hitherto unoccupied framework or platform, broad enough for all, eligible to every farmer and mechanic—to the female equally with the male—a towering selfhood, not physically perfect only—not satisfied with the mere mind's and learning's stores, but religious, possessing the idea of the infinite (rudder and compass sure amid this troublous voyage, o'er darkest, wildest wave, through stormiest wind, of man's or nation's progress)—realizing, above the rest, that known humanity, in deepest sense, is fair adhesion to itself, for purposes beyond—and that, finally, the personality of mortal life is most important with reference to the immortal, the unknown, the spiritual, the only permanently real, which as the ocean waits for and receives the rivers, waits for us each and all.

Much is there, yet, demanding line and outline in our Vistas, not only on these topics, but others quite unwritten. Indeed, we could talk the matter, and expand it, through lifetime. But it is necessary to return to our original premises. In view of them, we have again pointedly to confess that all the objective grandeurs of the world, for highest purposes, yield themselves up, and depend on mentality alone. Here, and here only, all balances, all rests. For the mind, which alone builds the permanent edifice, haughtily builds it to itself. By it, with what follows it, are convey'd to mortal sense the culminations of the materialistic, the known, and a prophecy of the unknown. To take expression, to incarnate, to endow a literature with grand and archetypal models—to fill with pride and love the utmost capacity, and to achieve spiritual meanings, and suggest the future—these, and these only, satisfy the soul. We must not say one word against real materials; but the wise know that they do not become real till touched by emotions, the mind. Did we call the latter imponderable? Ah, let us rather proclaim that the slightest song-tune, the countless ephemera of passions aroused by orators and tale-tellers, are more dense, more weighty than the engines there in the great factories, or the granite blocks in their foundations.

Approaching thus the momentous spaces, and considering with reference to a new and greater personalism, the needs and possibilities of American imaginative literature, through the medium-light of what we have already broach'd, it will at once be appreciated that a vast gulf of difference separates the present accepted condition of these spaces, inclusive of what is floating in them, from any condition adjusted to, or fit for, the world, the America, there ought to be indicated, and the copious races of complete men and women, along these Vistas crudely outlined. It is, in some sort, no less a difference than lies between that long-continued nebular state and vagueness of the astronomical worlds, compared with the subsequent state, the definitely-form'd worlds themselves, duly compacted, clustering in systems, hung up there, chandeliers of the universe, beholding and mutually lit by each other's lights, serving for ground of all substantial foothold, all vulgar uses—yet serving still more as an undying chain and echelon of spiritual proofs and shows. A boundless field to fill! A new creation, with needed orbic works launch'd forth, to revolve in free and lawful circuits—to move, self-poised, through the ether, and shine like heaven's own suns! With such, and nothing less, we suggest that New World literature, fit to rise upon, cohere, and signalize in time, these States.

What, however, do we more definitely mean by New World literature? Are we not doing well enough here already? Are not the United States this day busily using, working, more printer's type, more presses, than any other country? uttering and absorbing more publications than any other? Do not our publishers fatten quicker and deeper? (helping themselves, under shelter of a delusive and sneaking law, or rather absence of law, to most of their forage, poetical, pictorial, historical, romantic, even comic, without money and without price—and fiercely resisting the timidest proposal to pay for it). Many will come under this delusion—but my purpose is to dispel it. I say that a nation may hold and circulate rivers and oceans of very readable print, journals, magazines, novels, library books, "poetry," etc.—such as the States today possess and circulate—of unquestionable aid and value—hundreds of new volumes annually composed and brought out here, respectable enough, indeed unsurpass'd in smartness and erudition—with further hundreds, or rather millions (as by free forage or theft aforementioned), also thrown into the market—and yet, all the while, the said nation, land, strictly speaking, may possess no literature at all.

Repeating our inquiry, what, then, do we mean by real literature? especially the democratic literature of the future? Hard questions to meet. The clues are inferential, and turn us to the past. At best, we can only offer suggestions, comparisons, circuits.

It must still be reiterated, as, for the purpose of these memoranda, the deep lesson of history and time, that all else in the contributions of a nation or age, through its politics, materials, heroic personalities, military *éclat,* etc., remains crude, and defers, in any close and thoroughgoing estimate, until vitalized by national, original archetypes in literature. They only put the nation in form, finally tell anything—prove, complete anything—perpetuate anything. Without doubt, some of the richest and most powerful and populous communities of the antique world, and some of the grandest personalities and events, have, to after and present times, left themselves entirely unbequeath'd. Doubtless, greater than any that have come down to us, were among those lands, heroisms, persons, that have not come down to us at all, even by name, date, or location. Others have arrived safely, as from voyages over wide, century-stretching seas. The little ships, the miracles that have buoy'd them, and by incredible chances safely convey'd them (or the best of them, their meaning and essence) over long wastes, darkness, lethargy, ignorance, etc., have been a few inscriptions—a few immortal compositions, small in size, yet compassing what measureless values of reminiscence, contemporary portraitures, manners, idioms and beliefs, with deepest inference, hint, thought, to tie and touch forever the old, new body, and the old, new soul! These! and still these! bearing the freight so dear—dearer than pride—dearer than love. All the best experience of humanity, folded, saved, freighted to us here. Some of these tiny ships we call Old and New Testament, Homer, Aeschylus, Plato, Juvenal, etc. Precious minims! I think, if we were forced to choose, rather than have you, and the likes of you, and what belongs to, and has grown of you, blotted out and gone, we could better afford, appalling as that would be, to lose all actual ships, this day fasten'd by wharf, or floating on wave, and see them, with all their cargoes, scuttled and sent to the bottom.

Gathered by geniuses of city, race or age, and put by them in highest of art's forms, namely, the literary form, the peculiar combinations and the outshows of that city, age, or race, its particular modes of the universal attributes and passions, its faiths, heroes, lovers and gods, wars, traditions, struggles, crimes, emotions, joys (for the subtle spirit of these), having been pass'd on to us to illumine our own selfhood, and its experiences—what they supply, indispensable and highest, if taken away, nothing else in all the world's boundless storehouses could make up to us, or ever again return.

For us, along the great highways of time, those monuments stand—those forms of majesty and beauty. For us those beacons burn through all the nights. Unknown Egyptians, graving hieroglyphs; Hindus, with hymn and apothegm and endless epic; Hebrew prophet, with spirituality, as in flashes of lightning, conscience like red-hot iron, plaintive songs and screams of vengeance for tyrannies and enslavement; Christ, with bent head, brooding love and peace, like a dove; Greek, creating eternal shapes of physical and æsthetic proportion; Roman, lord of satire, the sword, and the codex;—of the figures, some far off and veil'd, others nearer and visible; Dante, stalking with lean form, nothing but fiber, not a grain of superfluous flesh; Angelo, and the great painters, architects, musicians; rich Shakspere, luxuriant as the sun, artist and singer of feudalism in its sunset, with all the gorgeous colors, owner thereof, and using them at will; and so to such as German Kant and Hegel, where they, though near us, leaping over the ages, sit again, impassive, imperturbable, like the Egyptian gods. Of these, and the like of these, is it too much, indeed, to return to our favorite figure, and view them as orbs and systems of orbs, moving in free paths in the spaces of that other heaven, the kosmic intellect, the soul?

Ye powerful and resplendent ones! ye were, in your atmospheres, grown not for America, but rather for her foes, the feudal and the old—while our genius is democratic and modern. Yet could ye, indeed, but breathe your breath of life into our New World's nostrils—not to enslave us, as now, but, for our needs, to breed a spirit like your own—perhaps (dare we to say it?) to dominate, even destroy, what you yourselves have left! On your plane, and no less, but even higher and wider, must we mete and measure for today and here.

I demand races of orbic bards, with unconditional, uncompromising sway. Come forth, sweet democratic despots of the west!

By points like these we, in reflection, token what we mean by any land's or people's genuine literature. And thus compared and tested, judging amid the influence of loftiest products only, what do our current copious fields of print, covering in manifold forms, the United States, better, for an analogy, present, than, as in certain regions of the sea, those spreading, undulating masses of squid, through which the whale swimming, with head half out, feeds?

Not but that doubtless our current so-called literature (like an endless supply of small coin) performs a certain service, and maybe too, the service needed for the time, (the preparation-service, as children learn to spell). Everybody reads, and truly nearly everybody writes, either books, or for the magazines or journals. The matter has magnitude, too, after a sort. But is it really advancing? or, has it advanced for a long while? There is something impressive about the huge editions of the dailies and weeklies, the mountain-stacks of white paper piled in the press-vaults, and the proud, crashing, ten-cylinder presses, which I can stand and watch any time by the half hour. Then (though the States in the field of imagination present not a single first-class work, not a single great literatus), the main objects, to amuse, to titillate, to pass away time, to circulate the news, and rumors of news, to rhyme, and read rhyme, are yet attain'd, and on a scale of infinity. Today, in books, in the rivalry of writers, especially novelists, success (so-called) is for him or her who strikes the mean flat average, the sensational appetite for stimulus, incident, persiflage, etc., and depicts, to the common caliber, sensual, exterior life. To such, or the luckiest of them, as we see, the audiences are limitless and profitable; but they cease presently. While this day, or any day, to workmen portraying interior or spiritual life, the audiences were limited, and often laggard—but they last forever.

Compared with the past, our modern science soars, and our journals serve—but ideal and even ordinary romantic literature, does not, I think, substantially advance. Behold the prolific brood of the contemporary novel, magazine tale, theatre play, etc. The same endless thread of tangled and and superlative love story, inherited, apparently from the Amadises and Palmerins of the 13th, 14th, and 15th centuries over there in Europe. The costumes and associations brought down to date, the seasoning hotter and more varied, the dragons and ogres left out—but the *thing,* I should say, has not advanced—is just as sensational, just as strain'd—remains about the same, nor more, nor less.

What is the reason our time, our lands, that we see no fresh local courage, sanity, of our own—the Mississippi, stalwart Western men, real mental and physical facts, Southerners, etc., in the body of our literature? especially the poetic part of it. But always, instead, a parcel of dandies and ennuyees, dapper little gentlemen from abroad, who flood us with their thin sentiment of parlors, parasols, piano songs, tinkling rhymes, the five-hundredth importation—or whimpering and crying about something, chasing one aborted conceit after another, and forever occupied in dyspeptic amours with dyspeptic women. While, current and novel, the grandest events and revolutions, and stormiest passions of history, are crossing today with unparalleled rapidity and magnificence over the stages of our own and all the continents, offering new materials, opening new vistas, with largest needs, inviting the daring launching forth of conceptions in literature, inspired by them, soaring in highest regions, serving art in its highest (which is only the other name for serving God, and serving humanity), where is the man of letters, where is the book, with any nobler aim than to follow in the old track, repeat what has been said before—and, as its utmost triumph, sell well, and be erudite or elegant?

Mark the roads, the processes, through which these States have arrived, standing easy, henceforth ever-equal, ever-compact, in their range today. European adventures? the most antique? Asiatic or African? old history—miracles—romances? Rather, our own unquestion'd facts. They hasten, incredible, blazing bright as fire. From the deeds and days of Columbus down to the present, and including the present—and especially the late Secession War—when I con them, I feel, every leaf, like stopping to see if I have not made a mistake, and fall'n on the splendid figments of some dream. But it is no dream. We stand, live, move, in the huge flow of our age's materialism—in its spirituality. We have founded for us the most positive of lands. The founders have pass'd to other spheres—but what are these terrible duties they have left us?

Their politics the United States have, in my opinion, with all their faults, already substantially establish'd, for good, on their own native, sound, long-vista'd principles, never to be overturn'd, offering a sure basis for all the rest. With that, their future religious forms, sociology, literature, teachers, schools, costumes, etc., are of course to make a compact whole, uniform, on tallying principles. For how can we remain, divided, contradicting ourselves, this way? [9] I say we can only attain harmony and stability by consulting ensemble and the ethic purports, and faithfully building upon them. For the New World, indeed, after two grand stages of preparation-strata, I perceive that now a third stage, being ready for (and without which the other two were useless), with unmistakable signs appears. The First stage was the planning and putting on record the political foundation rights of immense masses of people—indeed all people—in the organization or republican National, State, and municipal governments, all constructed with reference to each, and each to all. This is the American programme, not for classes, but for universal man, and is embodied in the compacts of the Declaration of Independence, and, as it began and has now grown, with its amendments, the Federal Constitution—and in the State governments, with all their interiors, and with general suffrage; those having the sense not only of what is in themselves, but that their certain several things started, planted, hundreds of others in the same direction duly arise and follow. The Second stage relates to material prosperity, wealth, produce, laborsaving machines, iron, cotton, local, State, and continental railways, intercommunication and trade with all lands, steamships, mining, general employment, organization of great cities, cheap appliances for comfort, numberless technical schools, books, newspapers, a currency for money circulation, etc. The Third stage, rising out of the previous ones, to make them and all illustrious, I, now, for one, promulge, announcing a native expression-spirit, getting into form, adult, and through mentality, for these States, self-contain'd, different from others, more expansive, more rich and free, to be evidenced by original authors and poets to come, by American personalities, plenty of them, male and female, traversing the States, none excepted —and by native superber tableaux and growths of language, songs, operas, orations, lectures, architecture—and by a sublime and serious Religious Democracy sternly taking command, dissolving the old, sloughing off surfaces, and from its own interior and vital principles, reconstructing, democratizing society.

For America, type of progress, and of essential faith in man, above all his errors and wickedness —few suspect how deep, how deep it really strikes. The world evidently supposes, and we have evidently supposed so too, that the States are merely to achieve the equal franchise, an elective government—to inaugurate the respectability of labor, and become a nation of practical operatives, law-abiding, orderly, and well-off. Yes, those are indeed parts of the task of America; but they not only do not exhaust the progressive conception, but rather arise, teeming with it, as the mediums of deeper, higher progress. Daughter of a physical revolution—mother of the true revolutions, which are of the interior life, and of the arts. For so long as the spirit is not changed, any change of appearance is of no avail.

The old men, I remember as a boy, were always talking of American independence. What is independence? Freedom from all laws or bonds except those of one's own being, control'd by the universal ones. To lands, to man, to woman, what is there at last to each, but the inherent soul, nativity, idiosyncrasy, free, highest poised, soaring its own flight, following out itself?

At present, these States, in their theology and social standards (of greater importance than their political institutions) are entirely held possession of by foreign lands. We see the sons and daughters of the New World, ignorant of its genius, not yet inaugurating the native, the universal, and the near still importing the distant, the partial, and the dead. We see London, Paris, Italy—not original, superb, as where they belong—but second-hand here, where they do not belong. We see the shreds of Hebrews, Romans, Greeks; but where, on her own soil, do we see, in any faithful, highest, proud expression, America herself? I sometimes question whether she has a corner in her own house.

Not but that in one sense, and a very grand one, good theology, good art, or good literature, has certain features shared in common. The combination fraternizes, ties the races—is, in many particulars, under laws applicable indifferently to all, irrespective of climate or date, and, from whatever source, appeals to emotions, pride, love, spirituality, common to human-kind. Nevertheless, they touch a man closest (perhaps only actually touch him), even in these, in their expression through autochthonic lights and shades, flavors, fondnesses, aversions, specific incidents, illustrations, out of his own nationality, geography, surroundings, antecedents, etc. The spirit and the form are one, and depend far more on associa-

9. "Note, today, an instructive, curious spectacle and conflict. Science (twin, in its fields, of Democracy in its)—Science, testing absolutely all thoughts, all works, has already burst well upon the world—a sun, mounting, most illuminating, most glorious—surely never again to set. But against it, deeply entrench'd, holding possession, yet remains (not only through the churches and schools, but by imaginative literature, and unregenerate poetry), the fossil theology of the mythic-materialistic, superstitious, untaught and credulous, fable-loving, primitive ages of humanity" [W].

tion, identity, and place, than is supposed. Subtly interwoven with the materiality and personality of a land, a race—Teuton, Turk, Californian, or what not—there is always something—I can hardly tell what it is—history but describes the results of it—it is the same as the untellable look of some human faces. Nature, too, in her stolid forms, is full of it—but to most it is there a secret. This something is rooted in the invisible roots, the profoundest meanings of that place, race, or nationality; and to absorb and again effuse it, uttering words and products as from its midst, and carrying it into highest regions, is the work, or a main part of the work, of any country's true author, poet, historian, lecturer, and perhaps even priest and philosoph. Here, and here only, are the foundations for our really valuable and permanent verse, drama, etc.

But at present (judged by any higher scale than that which finds the chief ends of existence to be to feverishly make money during one half of it, and by some "amusement," or perhaps foreign travel, flippantly kill time, the other half), and considered with reference to purposes of patriotism, health, a noble personality, religion, and the democratic adjustments, all these swarms of poems, literary magazines, dramatic plays, resultant so far from American intellect, and the formation of our best ideas, are useless and a mockery. They strengthen and nourish no one, express nothing characteristic, give decision and purpose to no one, and suffice only the lowest level of vacant minds.

Of what is called the drama, or dramatic presentation in the United States, as now put forth at the theatres, I should say it deserves to be treated with the same gravity, and on a par with the questions of ornamental confectionery at public dinners, or the arrangement of curtains and hangings in a ballroom—nor more, nor less. Of the other, I will not insult the reader's intelligence (once really entering into the atmosphere of these Vistas), by supposing it necessary to show, in detail, why the copious dribble, either of our little or well-known rhymesters, does not fulfill, in any respect, the needs and august occasions of this land. America demands a poetry that is bold, modern, and all-surrounding and kosmical, as she is herself. It must in no respect ignore science or the modern, but inspire itself with science and the modern. It must bend its vision toward the future, more than the past. Like America, it must extricate itself from even the greatest models of the past, and, while courteous to them, must have entire faith in itself, and the products of its own democratic spirit only. Like her, it must place in the van, and hold up at all hazards, the banner of the divine pride of man in himself (the radical foundation of of the new religion). Long enough have the People been listening to poems in which common humanity, deferential, bends low, humiliated, acknowledging superiors. But America listens to no such poems. Erect, inflated, and fully self-esteeming be the chant; and then America will listen with pleased ears.

Nor may the genuine gold, the gems, when brought to light at last, be probably usher'd forth from any of the quarters currently counted on. Today, doubtless, the infant genius of American poetic expression (eluding those highly refined imported and gilt-edged themes, and sentimental and butterfly flights, pleasant to orthodox publishers —causing tender spasms in the coteries, and warranted not to chafe the sensitive cuticle of the most exquisitely artificial gossamer delicacy), lies sleeping far away, happily unrecognized and uninjur'd by the coteries, the art-writers, the talkers and critics of the saloons, or the lecturers in the colleges—lies sleeping, aside, unrecking itself, in some western idiom, or native Michigan or Tennessee repartee, or stump speech—or in Kentucky or Georgia, or the Carolinas—or in some slang or local song or allusion of the Manhattan, Boston, Philadelphia, or Baltimore mechanic—or up in the Maine woods—or off in the hut of the California miner, or crossing the Rocky Mountains, or along the Pacific railroad—or on the breasts of the young farmers of the northwest, or Canada, or boatmen of the lakes. Rude and coarse nursing beds, these; but only from such beginnings and stocks, indigenous here, may haply arrive, be grafted, and sprout in time, flowers of genuine American aroma, and fruits truly and fully our own.

I say it were a standing disgrace to these States —I say it were a disgrace to any nation, distinguish'd above others by the variety and vastness of its territories, its materials, its inventive activity, and the splendid practicality of its people, not to rise and soar above others, also in its original styles in literature and art, and its own supply of intellectual and æsthetic masterpieces, archetypal, and consistent with itself. I know not a land except ours that has not, to some extent, however small, made its title clear. The Scotch have their born ballads, subtly expressing their past and present, and expressing character. The Irish have theirs. England, Italy, France, Spain, theirs. What has America? With exhaustless mines of the richest ore of epic, lyric, tale, tune, picture, etc., in the Four Years' War; with, indeed, I sometimes think, the richest masses of material ever afforded a nation, more variegated, and on a larger scale—the first sign of proportionate, native, imaginative Soul, and first-class works to match, is (I cannot too often repeat), so far wanting.

Long ere the second centennial arrives, there will be some forty to fifty great States, among them Canada and Cuba. When the present century closes, our population will be sixty or seventy millions. The Pacific will be ours, and the Atlantic mainly ours. There will be daily electric communication with every part of the globe. What an age! What a land! Where, elsewhere, one so great? The individuality of one nation must then, as always, lead the world. Can there be any doubt who the leader ought to be? Bear in mind, though, that nothing less than the mightiest original non-subordinated SOUL has ever really, gloriously led, or ever can lead. (This Soul—its other name, in these Vistas, is LITERATURE.)

In fond fancy leaping those hundred years ahead let us survey America's works, poems, philosophies, fulfilling prophecies, and giving form and decision to best ideals. Much that is now undream'd of, we might then perhaps see establish'd, luxuriantly cropping forth, richness, vigor of letters and of artistic expression, in whose products character will be a main requirement, and not merely erudition or elegance.

Intense and loving comradeship, the personal and passionate attachment of man to man—which, hard to define, underlies the lessons and ideals of the profound saviors of every land and age, and which seems to promise, when thoroughly develop'd, cultivated, and recognized in manners and literature, the most substantial hope and safety of the future of these States, will then be fully express'd.[10]

A strong-fibered joyousness and faith, and the sense of health *al fresco,* may well enter into the preparation of future noble American authorship. Part of the test of a great literatus shall be the absence in him of the idea of the covert, the lurid, the maleficent, the devil, the grim estimates inherited from the Puritans, hell, natural depravity, and the like. The great literatus will be known, among the rest, by his cheerful simplicity, his adherence to natural standards, his limitless faith in God, his reverence, and by the absence in him of doubt, ennui, burlesque, persiflage, or any strained and temporary fashion.

Nor must I fail, again and yet again, to clinch, reiterate more plainly still (O that indeed such survey as we fancy may show in time this part completed also!) the lofty aim, surely the proudest and the purest, in whose service the future literatus, of whatever field, may gladly labor. As we have intimated, offsetting the material civilization of our race, our nationality, its wealth, territories, factories, population, products, trade, and military and naval strength, and breathing breath of life into all these, and more, must be its moral civilization—the formulation, expression, aidancy whereof, is the very highest height of literature. The climax of this loftiest range of civilization, rising above all the gorgeous shows and results of wealth, intellect, power, and art, as such—above even theology and religious fervor—is to be its development, from the eternal bases, and the fit expression, of absolute Conscience, moral soundness, Justice. Even in religious fervor there is a touch of animal heat. But moral conscientiousness, crystalline, without flaw, not Godlike only, entirely human, awes and enchants forever. Great is emotional love, even in the order of the rational universe. But, if we must make gradations, I am clear there is something greater. Power, love, veneration, products, genius, æsthetics, tried by subtlest comparisons, analyses, and in serenest moods, somewhere fail, somehow become vain. Then noiseless, with flowing steps, the lord, the sun, the last ideal comes. By the names right, justice, truth, we suggest, but do not describe it. To the world of men it remains a dream, an idea as they call it. But no dream is it to the wise—but the proudest, almost only solid lasting thing of all. Its analogy in the material universe is what holds together this world, and every object upon it, and carries its dynamics on forever sure and safe. Its lack, and the persistent shirking of it, as in life, sociology, literature, politics, business, and even sermonizing, these times, or any times, still leaves the abysm, the mortal flaw and smutch, mocking civilization today, with all its unquestion'd triumphs, and all the civilization so far known.[11]

10. "It is to the development, identification, and general prevalence of that fervid comradship (the adhesive love, at least rivaling the amative love hitherto possessing imaginative literature, if not going beyond it), that I look for the counterbalance and offset of our materialistic and vulgar American democracy, and for the spiritualization thereof. Many will say it is a dream, and will not follow my inferences; but I confidently expect a time when there will be seen, running like a half-hid warp through all the myriad audible and visible worldly interests of America, threads of manly friendship, fond and loving, pure and sweet, strong and life-long, carried to degrees hitherto unknown—not only giving tone to individual character, and making it unprecedently emotional, muscular, heroic, and refined, but having the deepest relations to general politics. I say democracy infers such loving comradship, as its most inevitable twin or counterpart, without which it will be incomplete, in vain, and incapable of perpetuating itself" [W].

11. "I am reminded as I write that out of this very conscience, or idea of conscience, of intense moral right, and in its name and strain'd construction, the worst fanaticisms, wars, persecutions,

Present literature, while magnificently fulfilling certain popular demands, with plenteous knowledge and verbal smartness, is profoundly sophisticated, insane, and its very joy is morbid. It needs tally and express Nature, and the spirit of Nature, and to know and obey the standards. I say the question of Nature, largely considered, involves the questions of the æsthetic, the emotional, and the religious—and involves happiness. A fitly born and bred race, growing up in right conditions of outdoor as much as indoor harmony, activity and development, would probably, from and in those conditions, find it enough merely *to live*—and would, in their relations to the sky, air, water, trees, etc., and to the countless common shows, and in the fact of life itself, discover and achieve happiness—with Being suffused night and day by wholesome extasy, surpassing all the pleasures that wealth, amusement, and even gratified intellect, erudition, or the sense of art, can give.

In the prophetic literature of these States (the reader of my speculations will miss their principal stress unless he allows well for the point that a new Literature, perhaps a new Metaphysics, certainly a new Poetry, are to be, in my opinion, the only sure and worthy supports and expressions of the American Democracy), Nature, true Nature, and the true idea of Nature, long absent, must, above all, become fully restored, enlarged, and must furnish the pervading atmosphere to poems, and the test of all high literary and æsthetic compositions. I do not mean the smooth walks, trimm'd hedges, poseys and nightingales of the English poets, but the whole orb, with its geologic history, the kosmos, carrying fire and snow, that rolls through the illimitable areas, light as a feather, though weighing billions of tons. Furthermore, as by what we now partially call Nature is intended, at most, only what is entertainable by the physical conscience, the sense of matter, and of good animal health—on these it must be distinctly accumulated, incorporated, that man, comprehending these, has, in towering superaddition, the moral and spiritual consciences, indicating his destination beyond the ostensible, the mortal.

To the heights of such estimate of Nature indeed ascending, we proceed to make observations for our Vistas, breathing rarest air. What is I believe called Idealism seems to me to suggest (guarding against extravagance, and ever modified even by its opposite) the course of inquiry and desert of favor for our New World metaphysics, their foundation of and in literature, giving hue to all.[12]

murders, etc., have yet, in all lands, in the past, been broach'd, and have come to their devilish fruition. Much is to be said, but I may say here, and in response, that side by side with the unflagging stimulation of the elements of religion and conscience must henceforth move with equal sway, science, absolute reason, and the general proportionate development of the whole man. These scientific facts, deductions, are divine too—precious counted parts of moral civilization, and with physical health, indispensable to it, to prevent fanaticism. For abstract religion, I perceive, is easily led astray, ever credulous, and is capable of devouring, remorseless, like fire and flame. Conscience, too, isolated from all else, and from the emotional nature, may but attain the beauty and purity of glacial, snowy ice. We want, for these States, for the general character, a cheerful, religious fervor, endured with the ever-present modifications of the human emotions, friendship, benevolence, with a fair field for scientific inquiry, the right of individual judgment, and always the cooling influences of material Nature" [W].

12. "The culmination and fruit of literary artistic expression, and its final fields of pleasure for the human soul, are in metaphysics, including the mysteries of the spiritual world, the soul itself, and the question of the immortal continuation of our identity. In all ages, the mind of man has brought up here—and always will. Here, at least, of whatever race or era, we stand on common ground. Applause, too, is unanimous, antique or modern. Those authors who work well in this field—though their reward, instead of a handsome percentage, or royalty, may be but simply the laurel crown of the victors in the great Olympic games—will be dearest to humanity, and their works, however aesthetically defective, will be treasur'd forever. The altitude of literature and poetry has always been religion—and always will be. The Indian Vedas, the Nackas of Zoroaster, the Talmud of the Jews, the Old Testament, the Gospel of Christ and His disciples, Plato's works, the Koran of Mohammed, the Edda of Snorro, and so on toward our own day, to Swedenborg, and to the invaluable contributions of Leibnitz, Kant, and Hegel—these, with such poems only in which (while singing well of persons and events, of the passions of man, and the shows of the material universe), the religious tone, the consciousness of mystery, the recognition of the future, of the unknown, of Deity over and under all, and of the divine purpose, are never absent, but indirectly give tone to all—exhibit literature's real heights and elevations, towering up like the great mountains of the earth.

"Standing on this ground—the last, the highest, only permanent ground—and sternly criticizing, from it, all works, either of the literary, or any art, we have peremptorily to dismiss every pretensive production, however fine its aesthetic or intellectual points, which violates or ignores, or even does not celebrate, the central divine idea of All, suffusing universe, of eternal trains of purpose, in the development, by however slow degrees, of the physical, moral, and spiritual kosmos. I say he has studied, meditated to no profit, whatever may be his mere erudition, who has not absorb'd this simple consciousness and faith. It is not entirely new—but it is for Democracy to elaborate it, and look to build upon and expand from it, with uncompromising reliance. Above the doors of teaching the inscription is to appear, Though little or nothing can be absolutely known, perceived, except from a point of view which is evanescent, yet we know at least one permanency, that Time and Space, in the will of God, furnish successive claims, completions of material births and beginnings, solve all discrepancies, fears and doubts, and eventually fulfill happiness—and that the prophecy of those births, namely spiritual results, throws the true arch over all teaching, all science. The local considerations of sin, disease, deformity, ignorance, death, etc., and their measurement by the superficial mind, and ordinary legislation and theology, are to be met by science, boldly accepting, promulging this faith, and planting the seeds of superber laws—of the explication of the physical universe through the spiritual—and clearing the way for a religion, sweet and unimpugnable alike to little child or great savan" [W].

The elevating and etherealizing ideas of the unknown and of unreality must be brought forward with authority, as they are the legitimate heirs of the known, and of reality, and at least as great as their parents. Fearless of scoffing, and of the ostent, let us take our stand, our ground, and never desert it, to confront the growing excess and arrogance of realism. To the cry, now victorious—the cry of sense, science, flesh, incomes, farms, merchandise, logic, intellect, demonstrations, solid perpetuities, buildings of brick and iron, or even the facts of the shows of trees, earth, rocks, etc., fear not, my brethren, my sisters, to sound out with equally determin'd voice, that conviction brooding within the recesses of every envision'd soul—illusions! apparitions! figments all! True, we must not condemn the show, neither absolutely deny it, for the indispensability of its meanings; but how clearly we see that, migrate in soul to what we can already conceive of superior and spiritual points of view, and palpable as it seems under present relations, it all and several might, nay certainly would, fall apart and vanish.

I hail with joy the oceanic, variegated, intense practical energy, the demand for facts, even the business materialism of the current age, our States. But woe to the age and land in which these things, movements, stopping at themselves, do not tend to ideas. As fuel to flame, and flame to the heavens, so must wealth, science, materialism—even this democracy of which we make so much—unerringly feed the highest mind, the soul. Infinitude the flight: fathomless the mystery. Man, so diminutive, dilates beyond the sensible universe, competes with, outcopes space and time, meditating even one great idea. Thus, and thus only, does a human being, his spirit, ascend above, and justify, objective Nature, which, probably nothing in itself, is incredibly and divinely serviceable, indispensable, real, here. And as the purport of objective Nature is doubtless folded, hidden, somewhere here—as somewhere here is what this globe and its manifold forms, and the light of day, and night's darkness, and life itself, with all its experiences, are for—it is here the great literature, especially verse, must get its inspiration and throbbing blood. Then may we attain to a poetry worthy the immortal soul of man, and which, while absorbing materials, and, in their own sense, the shows of Nature, will, above all, have, both directly and indirectly, a freeing, fluidizing, expanding, religious character, exulting with science, fructifying the moral elements, and stimulating aspirations, and meditations on the unknown.

The process, so far, is indirect and peculiar, and though it may be suggested, cannot be defined. Observing, rapport, and with intuition, the shows and forms presented by Nature, the sensuous luxuriance, the beautiful in living men and women, the actual play of passions, in history and life—and, above all, from those developments either in Nature or human personality in which power (dearest of all to the sense of the artist) transacts itself—out of these, and seizing what is in them, the poet, the æsthetic worker in any field, by the divine magic of his genius, projects them, their analogies, by curious removes, indirections, in literature and art. (No useless attempt to repeat the material creation, by daguerreotyping the exact likeness by mortal mental means.) This is the image-making faculty, coping with material creation, and rivaling, almost triumphing over it. This alone, when all the other parts of a specimen of literature or art are ready and waiting, can breathe into it the breath of life, and endow it with identity.

"The true question to ask," says the Librarian of Congress in a paper read before the Social Science Convention at New York, October 1869, "The true question to ask respecting a book, is, *has it help'd any human soul?*" This is the hint, statement, not only of the great literatus, his book, but of every great artist. It may be that all works of art are to be first tried by their art qualities, their image-forming talent, and their dramatic, pictorial, plot-constructing, euphonious and other talents. Then, whenever claiming to be first-class works, they are to be strictly and sternly tried by their foundation in, and radiation, in the highest sense and always indirectly, of, the ethic principles, and eligibility to free, arouse, dilate.

As, within the purposes of the kosmos, and vivifying all meterology, and all the congeries of the mineral, vegetable and animal worlds—all the physical growth and development of man, and all the history of the race of politics, religions, wars, etc., there is a moral purpose, a visible or invisible intention, certainly underlying all—its results and proof needing to be patiently waited for—needing intuition, faith, idiosyncrasy, to its realization, which many, and especially the intellectual, do not have—so in the product, or congeries of the product, of the greatest literatus. This is the last, profoundest measure and test of a first-class literary or æsthetic achievement, and when understood and put in force must fain, I say, lead to works, books, nobler than any hitherto known. Lo! Nature (the only complete, actual poem), existing calmly in the divine scheme, containing all, content, careless of the criticisms of a day, or these

endless and wordy chatterers. And lo! to the consciousness of the soul, the permanent identity, the thought, the something, before which the magnitude even of democracy, art, literature, etc., dwindles, becomes partial, measurable—something that fully satisfies (which those do not). That something is the All, and the idea of All, with the accompanying idea of eternity, and of itself, the soul, buoyant, indestructible, sailing space forever, visiting every region, as a ship the sea. And again lo! the pulsations in all matter, all spirit, throbbing forever—the eternal beats, eternal systole and diastole of life in things—wherefrom I feel and know that death is not the ending, as was thought, but rather the real beginning—and that nothing ever is or can be lost, nor ever die, nor soul, nor matter.

In the future of these States must arise poets immenser far, and make great poems of death. The poems of life are great, but there must be the poems of the purports of life, not only in itself, but beyond itself. I have eulogized Homer, the sacred bards of Jewry, Aeschylus, Juvenal, Shakspere, etc., and acknowledged their inestimable value. But (with perhaps the exception in some, not all respects, of the second-mention'd) I say there must, for future and democratic purposes, appear poets (dare I to say so?) of higher class even than any of those—poets not only possess'd of the religious fire and abandon of Isaiah, luxuriant in the epic talent of Homer, or for proud characters as in Shakspere, but consistent with the Hegelian formulas, and consistent with modern science. America needs, and the world needs, a class of bards who will, now and ever, so link and tally the rational physical being of man, with the ensembles of time and space, and with this vast and multiform show, Nature, surrounding him, ever tantalizing him, equally a part, and yet not a part of him, as to essentially harmonize, satisfy, and put at rest. Faith, very old, now scared away by science, must be restored, brought back by the same power that caused her departure—restored with new sway, deeper, wider, higher than ever. Surely, this universal ennui, this coward fear, this shuddering at death, these low, degrading views, are not always to rule the spirit pervading future society, as it has the past, and does the present. What the Roman Lucretius sought most nobly, yet all too blindly, negatively to do for his age and and its successors, must be done positively by some great coming literatus, especially poet, who, while remaining fully poet, will absorb whatever science indicates, with spiritualism, and out of them, and out of his own genius, will compose the great poem of death. Then will man indeed confront Nature, and confront time and space, both with science, and *con amore,* and take his right place, prepared for life, master of fortune and misfortune. And then that which was long wanted will be supplied, and the ship that had it not before in all her voyages, will have an anchor.

There are still other standards, suggestions, for products of high literatuses. That which really balances and conserves the social and political world is not so much legislation, police, treaties, and dread of punishment, as the latent eternal intuitional sense, in humanity, of fairness, manliness, decorum, etc. Indeed, this perennial regulation, control, and oversight, by self-suppliance, is *sine qua non* to democracy; and a highest, widest aim of democratic literature may well be to bring forth, cultivate, brace, and strengthen this sense, in individuals and society. A strong mastership of the general inferior self by the superior self, is to be aided, secured, indirectly, but surely, by the literatus, in his works, shaping, for individual or aggregate democracy, a great passionate body, in and along with which goes a great masterful spirit.

And still, providing for contingencies, I fain confront the fact, the need of powerful native philosophs and orators and bards, these States, as rallying points to come, in times of danger, and to fend off ruin and defection. For history is long, long, long. Shift and turn the combinations of the statement as we may, the problem of the future of America is in certain respects as dark as it is vast. Pride, competition, segregation, vicious wilfulness, and license beyond example, brood already upon us. Unwieldly and immense, who shall hold in behemoth? who bridle leviathan? Flaunt it as we choose, athwart and over the roads of our progress loom huge uncertainty, and dreadful, threatening gloom. It is useless to deny it: Democracy grows rankly up the thickest, noxious, deadliest plants and fruits of all—brings worse and worse invaders—needs newer, larger, stronger, keener compensations and compellers.

Our lands, embracing so much (embracing indeed the whole, rejecting none), hold in their breast that flame also, capable of consuming themselves, consuming us all. Short as the span of our national life has been, already have death and downfall crowded close upon us—and will again crowd close, no doubt, even if warded off. Ages to come may never know, but I know, how narrowly during the late Secession War—and more than once, and more than twice or thrice—our Nationality (wherein bound up, as in a ship in a storm, depended, and yet depend, all our best life, all hope, all value), just grazed, just by a hair escaped destruction. Alas! to think of them! the agony and bloody sweat of certain of those hours! those cruel, sharp, suspended crises!

Even today, amid these whirls, incredible flippancy, and blind fury of parties, infidelity, entire lack of first-class captains and leaders, added to the plentiful meanness and vulgarity of the ostensible masses—that problem, the labor question, beginning to open like a yawning gulf, rapidly widening every year—what prospect have we? We sail a dangerous sea of seething currents, cross and undercurrents, vortices—all so dark, untried—and whither shall we turn? It seems as if the Almighty had spread before this nation charts of imperial destinies, dazzling as the sun, yet with many a deep intestine difficulty, and human aggregate of cankerous imperfection—saying, lo! the roads, the only plans of development, long and varied with all terrible balks and ebullitions. You said in your soul, I will be empire of empires, overshadowing all else, past and present, putting the history of Old-World dynasties, conquests behind me, as of no account—making a new history, a history of democracy, making old history a dwarf—I alone inaugurating largeness, culminating time. If these, O lands of America, are indeed the prizes, the determinations of your soul, be it so. But behold the cost, and already specimens of the cost. Thought you greatness was to ripen for you like a pear? If you would have greatness, know that you must conquer it through ages, centuries—must pay for it with a proportionate price. For you too, as for all lands, the struggle, the traitor, the wily person in office, scrofulous wealth, the surfeit of prosperity, the demonism of greed, the hell of passion, the decay of faith, the long postponement, the fossil-like lethargy, the ceaseless need of revolutions, prophets, thunderstorms, deaths, births, new projections and invigorations of ideas and men.

Yet I have dream'd, merged in that hidden-tangled problem of our fate, whose long unraveling stretches mysteriously through time—dream'd out, portray'd, hinted already—a little or a larger band—a band of brave and true, unprecedented yet—arm'd and equipt at every point—the members separated, it may be, by different dates and States, or south, or north, or east, or west—Pacific, Atlantic, Southern, Canadian—a year, a century here, and other centuries there—but always one, compact in soul, conscience-conserving, God-inculcating, inspired achievers, not only in literature, the greatest art, but achievers in all art—a new, undying order, dynasty, from age to age transmitted—a band, a class, at least as fit to cope with current years, our dangers, needs, as those who, for their times, so long, so well, in armor or in cowl, upheld and made illustrious, that far-back feudal, priestly world. To offset chivalry, indeed, those vanish'd countless knights, old altars, abbeys, priests, ages and strings of ages, a knightlier and more sacred cause today demands, and shall supply, in a New World, to larger, grander work, more than the counterpart and tally of them.

Arrived now, definitely, at an apex for these Vistas, I confess that the promulgation and belief in such a class or institution—a new and greater literatus order—its possibility (nay certainty), underlies these entire speculations—and that the rest, the other parts, as superstructures, are all founded upon it. It really seems to me the condition, not only of our future national and democratic development, but of our perpetuation. In the highly artificial and materialistic bases of modern civilization, with the corresponding arrangements and methods of living, the force-infusion of intellect alone, the depraving influences of riches just as much as poverty, the absence of all high ideals in character—with the long series of tendencies, shapings, which few are strong enough to resist, and which now seem, with steam-engine speed, to be everywhere turning out the generations of humanity like uniform iron castings—all of which, as compared with the feudal ages, we can yet do nothing better than accept, make the best of, and even welcome, upon the whole, for their oceanic practical grandeur, and their restless wholesale kneading of the masses—I say of all this tremendous and dominant play of solely materialistic bearings upon current life in the United States, with the results as already seen, accumulating, and reaching far into the future, that they must either be confronted and met by at least an equally subtle and tremendous force-infusion for purposes of spiritualization, for the pure conscience, for genuine æsthetics, and for absolute and primal manliness and womanliness—or else our modern civilization, with all its improvements, is in vain, and we are on the road to a destiny, a status, equivalent, in its real world, to that of the fabled damned.

Prospecting thus the coming unsped days, and that new order in them—marking the endless train of exercise, development, unwind, in nation as in man, which life is for—we see, fore-indicated, amid these prospects and hopes, new law-forces of spoken and written language—not merely the pedagogue-forms, correct, regular, familiar with precedents, made for matters of outside propriety, fine words, thoughts definitely told out—but a language fann'd by the breath of Nature, which leaps overhead, cares mostly for impetus and effects, and for what it plants and invigorates to grow—tallies life and character, and seldomer tells a thing than suggests or necessitates it. In fact, a new theory of literary composition for imaginative works of the very first class, and especially for highest poems, is the sole course open to these States. Books are to be call'd for, and supplied, on the assumption that the process of reading is not a half-sleep, but, in highest sense, an exercise, a gymnast's struggle; that the reader is to do something for himself, must be on the alert, must himself or herself construct indeed the poem, argument, history, metaphysical essay—the text furnishing the hints, the clue, the start or framework. Not the book needs so much to be the complete thing, but the reader of the book does. That were to make a nation of supple and athletic minds, fell-train'd, intuitive, used to depend on themselves, and not on a few coteries of writers.

Investigating here, we see, not that it is a little thing we have, in having the bequeath'd libraries, countless shelves of volumes, records, etc.; yet how serious the danger, depending entirely on them, of the bloodless vein, the nerveless arm, the false application, at second or third hand. We see that the real interest of this people of ours in the theology, history, poetry, politics, and personal models of the past (the British islands, for instance, and indeed all the past), is not necessarily to mold ourselves or our literature upon them, but to attain fuller, more definite comparisons, warnings, and the insight to ourselves, our own present, and our own far grander, different, future history, religion, social customs, etc. We see that almost everything that has been written, sung, or stated, of old, with reference to humanity under the feudal and oriental institutes, religions, and for other lands, needs to be rewritten, resung, restated, in terms consistent with the institution of these States, and to come in range and obedient uniformity with them.

We see, as in the universes of the material kosmos, after meteorological, vegetable, and animal cycles, man at last arises, born through them, to prove them, concentrate them, to turn upon them with wonder and love—to command them, adorn them, and carry them upward into superior realms—so, out of the series of the preceding social and political universes, now arise these States. We see that while many were supposing things established and completed, really the grandest things always remain; and discover that the work of the New World is not ended, but only fairly begun.

We see our land, America, her literature, æsthetics, etc., as, substantially, the getting in form, or effusement and statement, of deepest basic elements and loftiest final meanings, of history and man—and the portrayal (under the eternal laws and conditions of beauty) of our own physiognomy, the subjective tie and expression of the objective, as from our own combination, continuation, and points of view—and the deposit and record of the national mentality, character, appeals, heroism, wars, and even liberties—where these, and all, culminate in native literary and artistic formulation, to be perpetuated; and not having which native, first-class formulation, she will flounder about, and her other, however imposing, eminent greatness, prove merely a passing gleam; but truly having which, she will understand herself, live nobly, nobly contribute, emanate, and, swinging, poised safely on herself, illumin'd and illuming, become a full-form'd world, and divine Mother not only of material but spiritual worlds, in ceaseless succession through time—the main thing being the average, the bodily, the concrete, the democratic, the popular, on which all the superstructures of the future are to permanently rest.

1871

A BACKWARD GLANCE O'ER TRAVEL'D ROADS

PERHAPS the best of songs heard, or of any and all true love, or life's fairest episodes, or sailors', soldiers' trying scenes on land or sea, is the *résumé* of them, or any of them, long afterwards, looking at the actualities away back past, with all their practical excitations gone. How the soul loves to float amid such reminiscences!

So here I sit gossiping in the early candle-light of old age—I and my book—casting backward glances over our travel'd road. After completing, as it were, the journey—(a varied jaunt of years, with many halts and gaps of intervals—or some lengthen'd ship-voyage, wherein more than once the last hour had apparently arrived, and we seem'd certainly going down—yet reaching port in a sufficient way through all discomfitures at last)—After completing my poems, I am curious to review them in the light of their own (at the time unconscious, or mostly unconscious) intentions, with certain unfoldings of the thirty years they seek to embody. These lines, therefore, will probably blend the weft of first purposes and speculations, with the warp of that experience afterwards, always bringing strange developments.

Result of seven or eight stages and struggles extending through nearly thirty years, (as I nigh my three-score-and-ten I live largely on memory,) I look upon "Leaves of Grass," now finish'd to the end of its opportunities and powers, as my definitive *carte visite* to the coming generations of the New World,[1] if I may assume to say so. That I have not gain'd the acceptance of my own time, but have fallen back on fond dreams of the future —anticipations—("still lives the song, though Regnar dies")—That from a worldly and business point of view "Leaves of Grass" has been worse than a failure—that public criticism on the book and myself as author of it yet shows mark'd anger and contempt more than anything else—("I find a solid line of enemies to you everywhere,"—letter from W. S. K., Boston, May 28, 1884)—And that solely for publishing it I have been the object of two or three pretty serious special official buffetings—is all probably no more than I ought to have expected. I had my choice when I commenc'd. I bid neither for soft eulogies, big money returns, nor the approbation of existing schools and conventions. As fulfill'd, or partially fulfill'd, the best comfort of the whole business (after a small band of the dearest friends and upholders ever vouchsafed to man or cause—doubtless all the more faithful and uncompromising—this little phalanx!—for being so few) is that, unstopp'd and unwarp'd by any influence outside the soul within me, I have had my say entirely my own way, and put it unerringly on record—the value thereof to be decided by time.

In calculating that decision, William O'Connor and Dr. Bucke are far more peremptory than I am. Behind all else that can be said, I consider "Leaves of Grass" and its theory experimental—as, in the deepest sense, I consider our American republic itself to be, with its theory. (I think I have at least enough philosophy not to be too absolutely certain of any thing, or any results.) In the second place, the volume is a *sortie*—whether to prove triumphant, and conquer its field of aim and escape and construction, nothing less than a hundred years from now can fully answer. I consider the point that I have positively gain'd a hearing, to far more than make up for any and all other lacks and withholdings. Essentially, *that* was from the first, and has remain'd throughout, the main object. Now it seems to be achiev'd, I am certainly contented to waive any otherwise momentous drawbacks, as of little account. Candidly and dispassionately reviewing all my intentions, I feel that they were creditable—and I accept the result, whatever it may be.

After continued personal ambition and effort, as a young fellow, to enter with the rest into competition for the usual rewards, business, political, literary, &c.—to take part in the great *mêlée,* both for victory's prize itself and to do some good —After years of those aims and pursuits, I found myself remaining possess'd, at the age of thirty-one to thirty-three, with a special desire and conviction. Or rather, to be quite exact, a desire that had been flitting through my previous life, or hovering on the flanks, mostly indefinite hitherto, had steadily advanced to the front, defined itself, and finally dominated everything else. This was a feeling or ambition to articulate and faithfully express in literary or poetic form, and uncompromisingly, my own physical, emotional, moral, intellectual, and æsthetic Personality, in the midst of, and tallying, the momentous spirit and facts of its immediate days, and of current America—and to exploit that Personality, identified with place and date, in a far more candid and comprehensive sense than any hitherto poem or book.

Perhaps this is in brief, or suggests, all I have sought to do. Given the Nineteenth Century, with the United States, and what they furnish as area and points of view, "Leaves of Grass" is, or seeks to be, simply a faithful and doubtless self-will'd record. In the midst of all, it gives one man's—the author's—identity, ardors, observations, faiths, and thoughts, color'd hardly at all with any decided coloring from other faiths or other identities. Plenty of songs had been sung—beautiful, matchless songs—adjusted to other lands than these—another spirit and stage of evolution; but I would sing, and leave out or put in, quite solely with reference to America and to-day. Modern science and democracy seem'd to be throwing out their challenge to poetry to put them in its statements in contradistinction to the songs and myths of the past. As I see it now (perhaps too late,) I have unwittingly taken up that challenge and made an attempt at such statements—which I certainly would not assume to do now, knowing more clearly what it means.

For grounds for "Leaves of Grass," as a poem, I abandon'd the conventional themes, which do not appear in it: none of the stock ornamentation, or choice plots of love or war, or high, exceptional personages of Old-World song; nothing, as I may say, for beauty's sake—no legend, or myth, or romance, nor euphemism, nor rhyme. But the broadest average of humanity and its identities in the now ripening Nineteenth Century, and especially

A BACKWARD GLANCE O'ER TRAVEL'D ROADS. 1. "When Champollion, on his death-bed, handed to the printer the revised proof of his *Egyptian Grammar*, he said gayly, 'Be careful of this—it is my *carte de visite* to posterity' " [W].

in each of their countless examples and practical occupations in the United States to-day.

One main contrast of the ideas behind every page of my verses, compared with establish'd poems, is their different relative attitude towards God, towards the objective universe, and still more (by reflection, confession, assumption, &c.) the quite changed attitude of the ego, the one chanting or talking, towards himself and towards his fellow-humanity. It is certainly time for America, above all, to begin this readjustment in the scope and basic point of view of verse; for everything else has changed. As I write, I see in an article on Wordsworth, in one of the current English magazines, the lines, "A few weeks ago an eminent French critic said that, owing to the special tendency to science and to its all-devouring force, poetry would cease to be read in fifty years." But I anticipate the very contrary. Only a firmer, vastly broader, new area begins to exist—nay, is already form'd—to which the poetic genius must emigrate. Whatever may have been the case in years gone by, the true use for the imaginative faculty of modern times is to give ultimate vivification to facts, to science, and to common lives, endowing them with the glows and glories and final illustriousness which belong to every real thing, and to real things only. Without that ultimate vivification—which the poet or other artist alone can give—reality would seem incomplete, and science, democracy, and life itself, finally in vain.

Few appreciate the moral revolutions, our age, which have been profounder far than the material or inventive or war-produced ones. The Nineteenth Century, now well towards its close (and ripening into fruit the seeds of the two preceding centuries [2])—the uprisings of national masses and shiftings of boundary-lines—the historical and other prominent facts of the United States—the war of attempted Secession—the stormy rush and haste of nebulous forces—never can future years witness more excitement and din of action—never completer change of army front along the whole line, the whole civilized world. For all these new and evolutionary facts, meanings, purposes, new poetic messages, new forms and expressions, are inevitable.

My Book and I—what a period we have presumed to span! those thirty years from 1850 to '80—and America in them! Proud, proud indeed may we be, if we have cull'd enough of that period in its own spirit to worthily waft a few live breaths of it to the future!

Let me not dare, here or anywhere, for my own purposes, or any purposes, to attempt the definition of Poetry, nor answer the question what it is. Like Religion, Love, Nature, while those terms are indispensable, and we all give a sufficiently accurate meaning to them, in my opinion no definition that has ever been made sufficiently encloses the name Poetry; nor can any rule or convention ever so absolutely obtain but some great exception may arise and disregard and overturn it.

Also it must be carefully remember'd that first-class literature does not shine by any luminosity of its own; nor do its poems. They grow of circumstances, and are evolutionary. The actual living light is always curiously from elsewhere—follows unaccountable sources, and is lunar and relative at the best. There are, I know, certain controling themes that seem endlessly appropriated to the poets—as war, in the past—in the Bible, religious rapture and adoration—always love, beauty, some fine plot, or pensive or other emotion. But, strange as it may sound at first, I will say there is something striking far deeper and towering far higher than those themes for the best elements of modern song.

Just as all the old imaginative works rest, after their kind, on long trains of presuppositions, often entirely unmention'd by themselves, yet supplying the most important bases of them, and without which they could have had no reason for being, so "Leaves of Grass," before a line was written, presupposed something different from any other, and, as it stands, is the result of such presupposition. I should say, indeed, it were useless to attempt reading the book without first carefully tallying that preparatory background and quality in the mind. Think of the United States to-day—the fact of these thirty-eight or forty empires solder'd in one—sixty or seventy millions of equals, with their lives, their passions, their future—these incalculable, modern, American, seething multitudes around us, of which we are inseparable parts! Think, in comparison, of the petty environage and limited area of the poets of past or present Europe, no matter how great their genius. Think of the absence and ignorance, in all cases hitherto, of the multitudinousness, vitality, and the unprecedented stimulants of to-day and here. It almost seems as if a poetry with cosmic and dynamic features of magnitude and limitlessness suitable to the human soul, were never possible

2. "The ferment and germination even of the United States to-day, dating back to, and in my opinion mainly founded on, the Elizabethan age in English history, the age of Francis Bacon and Skakspere. Indeed, when we pursue it, what growth or advent is there that does not date back, until lost—perhaps its most tantalizing clues lost—in the receded horizons of the past?" [W].

before. It is certain that a poetry of absolute faith and equality for the use of the democratic masses never was.

In estimating first-class song, a sufficient Nationality, or, on the other hand, what may be call'd the negative and lack of it, (as in Goethe's case, it sometimes seems to me,) is often, if not always, the first element. One needs only a little penetration to see, at more or less removes, the material facts of their country and radius, with the coloring of the moods of humanity at the time, and its gloomy or hopeful prospects, behind all poets and each poet, and forming their birthmarks. I know very well that my "Leaves" could not possibly have emerged or been fashion'd or completed, from any other era than the latter half of the Nineteenth Century, nor any other land than democratic America, and from the absolute triumph of the National Union arms.

And whether my friends claim it for me or not, I know well enough, too, that in respect to pictorial talent, dramatic situations, and especially in verbal melody and all the conventional technique of poetry, not only the divine works that to-day stand ahead in the world's reading, but dozens more, transcend (some of them immeasurably transcend) all I have done, or could do. But it seem'd to me, as the objects in Nature, the themes of æstheticism, and all special exploitations of the mind and soul, involve not only their own inherent quality, but the quality, just as inherent and important, of *their point of view,*[3] the time had come to reflect all themes and things, old and new, in the lights thrown on them by the advent of America and democracy—to chant those themes through the utterance of one, not only the grateful and reverent legatee of the past, but the born child of the New World—to illustrate all through the genesis and ensemble of to-day; and that such illustration and ensemble are the chief demands of America's prospective imaginative literature. Not to carry out, in the approved style, some choice plot of fortune or misfortune, or fancy, or fine thoughts, or incidents, or courtesies—all of which has been done overwhelmingly and well, probably never to be excell'd—but that while in such æsthetic presentation of objects, passions, plots, thoughts, &c., our lands and days do not want, and probably will never have, anything better than they already possess from the bequests of the past, it still remains to be said that there is even towards all those a subjective and contemporary point of view appropriate to ourselves alone, and to our new genius and environments, different from anything hitherto; and that such conception of current or gone-by life and art is for us the only means of their assimilation consistent with the Western world.

Indeed, and anyhow, to put it specifically, has not the time arrived when, (if it must be plainly said, for democratic America's sake, if for no other) there must imperatively come a readjustment of the whole theory and nature of Poetry? The question is important, and I may turn the argument over and repeat it: Does not the best thought of our day and Republic conceive of a birth and spirit of song superior to anything past or present? To the effectual and moral consolidation of our lands (already, as materially establish'd, the greatest factors in known history, and far, far greater through what they prelude and necessitate, and are to be in future)—to conform with and build on the concrete realities and theories of the universe furnish'd by science, and henceforth the only irrefragable basis for anything, verse included—to root both influences in the emotional and imaginative action of the modern time, and dominate all that precedes or opposes them—is not either a radical advance and step forward, or a new verteber of the best song indispensable?

The New World receives with joy the poems of the antique, with European feudalism's rich fund of epics, plays, ballads—seeks not in the least to deaden or displace those voices from our ear and area—holds them indeed as indispensable studies, influences, records, comparisons. But though the dawn-dazzle of the sun of literature is in those poems for us of to-day—though perhaps the best parts of current character in nations, social groups, or any man's or woman's individuality, Old World or New, are from them—and though if I were ask'd to name the most precious bequest to current American civilization from all the hitherto ages, I am not sure but I would name those old and less old songs ferried hither from east and west—some serious words and debits remain; some acrid considerations demand a hearing. Of the great poems receiv'd from abroad and from the ages, and to-day enveloping and penetrating America, is there one that is consistent with these United States, or essentially applicable to them as they are and are to be? Is there one whose underlying basis is not a denial and insult to democracy? What a comment it forms, anyhow, on this era of literary fulfilment, with the splendid day-rise of science and resuscitation of history, that our chief religious and poetical works are not our own, nor adapted to our light, but have been

3. "According to Immanuel Kant, the last essential reality, giving shape and significance to all the rest" [W].

furnish'd by far-back ages out of their arriere and darkness, or, at most, twilight dimness! What is there in those works that so imperiously and scornfully dominates all our advanced civilization, and culture?

Even Shakspere, who so suffuses current letters and art (which indeed have in most degrees grown out of him,) belongs essentially to the buried past. Only he holds the proud distinction for certain important phases of that past, of being the loftiest of the singers life has yet given voice to. All, however, relate to and rest upon conditions, standards, politics, sociologies, ranges of belief, that have been quite eliminated from the Eastern hemisphere, and never existed at all in the Western. As authoritative types of song they belong in America just about as much as the persons and institutes they depict. True, it may be said, the emotional, moral, and æsthetic natures of humanity have not radically changed—that in these the old poems apply to our times and all times, irrespective of date; and that they are of incalculable value as pictures of the past. I willingly make those admissions, and to their fullest extent; then advance the points herewith as of serious, even paramount importance.

I have indeed put on record elsewhere my reverence and eulogy for those never-to-be-excell'd poetic bequests, and their indescribable preciousness as heirlooms for America. Another and separate point must now be candidly stated. If I had not stood before those poems with uncover'd head, fully aware of their colossal grandeur and beauty of form and spirit, I could not have written "Leaves of Grass." My verdict and conclusions as illustrated in its pages are arrived at through the temper and inculcation of the old works as much as through anything else—perhaps more than through anything else. As America fully and fairly construed is the legitimate result and evolutionary outcome of the past, so I would dare to claim for my verse. Without stopping to qualify the averment, the Old World has had the poems of myths, fictions, feudalism, conquest, caste, dynastic wars, and splendid exceptional characters and affairs, which have been great; but the New World needs the poems of realities and science and of the democratic average and basic equality, which shall be greater. In the centre of all, and object of all, stands the Human Being, towards whose heroic and spiritual evolution poems and everything directly or indirectly tend, Old World or New.

Continuing the subject, my friends have more than once suggested—or may be the garrulity of advancing age is possessing me—some further embryonic facts of "Leaves of Grass," and especially how I enter'd upon them. Dr. Bucke has, in his volume, already fully and fairly described the preparation of my poetic field, with the particular and general plowing, planting, seeding, and occupation of the ground, till everything was fertilized, rooted, and ready to start its own way for good or bad. Not till after all this, did I attempt any serious acquaintance with poetic literature. Along in my sixteenth year I had become possessor of a stout, well-cramm'd one thousand page octavo volume (I have it yet,) containing Walter Scott's poetry entire—an inexhaustible mine and treasury of poetic forage (especially the endless forests and jungles of notes)—has been so to me for fifty years, and remains so to this day.[4]

Later, at intervals, summers and falls, I used to go off, sometimes for a week at a stretch, down in the country, or to Long Island's seashores—there, in the presence of outdoor influences, I went over thoroughly the Old and New Testaments, and absorb'd (probably to better advantage for me than in any library or indoor room—it makes such difference *where* you read,) Shakspere, Ossian, the best translated versions I could get of Homer, Eschylus, Sophocles, the old German Nibelungen, the ancient Hindoo poems, and one or two other masterpieces, Dante's among them. As it happen'd, I read the latter mostly in an old wood. The Iliad (Buckley's prose version,) I read first thoroughly on the peninsula of Orient, northeast end of Long Island, in a shelter'd hollow of rocks and sand, with the sea on each side. (I have wonder'd since why I was not overwhelm'd by those mighty masters. Likely because I read them, as described, in the full presence of Nature, under the sun, with the far-spreading landscape and vistas, or the sea rolling in.)

Toward the last I had among much else look'd over Edgar Poe's poems—of which I was not an admirer, tho' I always saw that beyond their limited range of melody (like perpetual chimes of music bells, ringing from lower *b* flat up to *g*) they were melodious expressions, and perhaps never excell'd ones, of certain pronounc'd phases of human morbidity. (The Poetic area is very spacious

4. "Sir Walter Scott's *Complete Poems;* especially including *Border Minstrelsy;* then *Sir Tristrem; Lay of the Last Minstrel; Ballads from the German; Marmion; Lady of the Lake; Vision of Don Roderick; Lord of the Isles; Rokeby; Bridal of Triermain; Field of Waterloo; Harold the Dauntless;* all the Dramas; various Introductions, endless interesting Notes, and Essays on Poetry, Romance, &c.

"Lockhart's 1833 (or '34) edition with Scott's latest and copious revisions and annotations. (All the poems were thoroughly read by me, but the ballads of the *Border Minstrelsy* over and over again)" [W].

—has room for all—has so many mansions!) But I was repaid in Poe's prose by the idea that (at any rate for our occasions, our day) there can be no such thing as a long poem. The same thought had been haunting my mind before, but Poe's argument, though short, work'd the sum out and proved it to me.

Another point had an early settlement, clearing the ground greatly. I saw, from the time my enterprise and questionings positively shaped themselves (how best can I express my own distinctive era and surroundings, America, Democracy?) that the trunk and centre whence the answer was to radiate, and to which all should return from straying however far a distance, must be an identical body and soul, a personality—which personality, after many considerations and ponderings I deliberately settled should be myself—indeed could not be any other. I also felt strongly (whether I have shown it or not) that to the true and full estimate of the Present both the Past and the Future are main considerations.

These, however, and much more might have gone on and come to naught (almost positively would have come to naught,) if a sudden, vast, terrible, direct and indirect stimulus for new and national declamatory expression had not been given to me. It is certain, I say, that, although I had made a start before, only from the occurrence of the Secession War, and what it show'd me as by flashes of lightning, with the emotional depths it sounded and arous'd (of course, I don't mean in my own heart only, I saw it just as plainly in others, in millions)—that only from the strong flare and provocation of that war's sights and scenes the final reasons-for-being of an autochthonic and passionate song definitely came forth.

I went down to the war fields in Virginia (end of 1862), lived thenceforward in camp—saw great battles and the days and nights afterward—partook of all the fluctuations, gloom, despair, hopes again arous'd, courage evoked—death readily risk'd—*the cause,* too—along and filling those agonistic and lurid following years, 1863–'64–'65 —the real parturition years (more than 1776–'83) of this henceforth homogeneous Union. Without those three or four years and the experiences they gave, "Leaves of Grass" would not now be existing.

But I set out with the intention also of indicating or hinting some point-characteristics which I since see (though I did not then, at least not definitely) were bases and object-urgings toward those "Leaves" from the first. The word I myself put primarily for the description of them as they stand at last, is the word Suggestiveness. I round and finish little, if anything; and could not, consistently with my scheme. The reader will always have his or her part to do, just as much as I have had mine. I seek less to state or display any theme or thought, and more to bring you, reader, into the atmosphere of the theme or thought—there to pursue your own flight. Another impetus-word is Comradeship as for all lands, and in a more commanding and acknowledg'd sense than hitherto. Other word-signs would be Good Cheer, Content, and Hope.

The chief trait of any given poet is always the spirit he brings to the observation of Humanity and Nature—the mood out of which he contemplates his subjects. What kind of temper and what amount of faith report these things? Up to how recent a date is the song carried? What the equipment, and special raciness of the singer—what his tinge of coloring? The last value of artistic expressers, past and present—Greek æsthetes, Shakspere —or in our own day Tennyson, Victor Hugo, Carlyle, Emerson—is certainly involv'd in such questions. I say the profoundest service that poems or any other writings can do for their reader is not merely to satisfy the intellect, or supply something polish'd and interesting, nor even to depict great passions, or persons or events, but to fill him with vigorous and clean manliness, religiousness, and give him *good heart* as a radical possession and habit. The educated world seems to have been growing more and more ennuyed for ages, leaving to our time the inheritance of it all. Fortunately there is the original inexhaustible fund of buoyancy, normally resident in the race, forever eligible to be appeal'd to and relied on.

As for native American individuality, though certain to come, and on a large scale, the distinctive and ideal type of Western character (as consistent with the operative political and even money-making features of United States' humanity in the Nineteenth Century as chosen knights, gentlemen and warriors were the ideals of the centuries of European feudalism) it has not yet appear'd. I have allow'd the stress of my poems from beginning to end to bear upon American individuality and to assist it—not only because that is a great lesson in Nature, amid all her generalizing laws, but as counterpoise to the leveling tendencies of Democracy—and for other reasons. Defiant of ostensible literary and other conventions, I avowedly chant "the great pride of man in himself," and permit it to be more or less a *motif* of nearly all my verse. I think this pride indispensable to an American. I think it not inconsistent with obedience, humility, deference, and self-questioning.

Democracy has been so retarded and jeopardized by powerful personalities, that its first instincts are fain to clip, conform, bring in stragglers, and reduce everything to a dead level. While the ambitious thought of my song is to help the forming of a great aggregate Nation, it is, perhaps, altogether through the forming of myriads of fully develop'd and enclosing individuals. Welcome as are equality's and fraternity's doctrines and popular education, a certain liability accompanies them all, as we see. That primal and interior something in man, in his soul's abysms, coloring all, and, by exceptional fruitions, giving the last majesty to him—something continually touch'd upon and attain'd by the old poems and ballads of feudalism, and often the principal foundation of them—modern science and democracy appear to be endangering, perhaps eliminating. But that forms an appearance only; the reality is quite different. The new influences, upon the whole, are surely preparing the way for grander individualities than ever. To-day and here personal force is behind everything, just the same. The times and depictions from the Iliad to Shakspere inclusive can happily never again be realized—but the elements of courageous and lofty manhood are unchanged.

Without yielding an inch the working-man and working-woman were to be in my pages from first to last. The ranges of heroism and loftiness with which Greek and feudal poets endow'd their god-like or lordly born characters—indeed prouder and better based and with fuller ranges than those—I was to endow the democratic averages of America. I was to show that we, here and to-day, are eligible to the grandest and the best—more eligible now than any times of old were. I will also want my utterances (I said to myself before beginning) to be in spirit the poems of the morning. (They have been founded and mainly written in the sunny forenoon and early midday of my life.) I will want them to be the poems of women entirely as much as men. I have wish'd to put the complete Union of the States in my songs without any preference or partiality whatever. Henceforth, if they live and are read, it must be just as much South as North—just as much along the Pacific as Atlantic—in the valley of the Mississippi, in Canada, up in Maine, down in Texas, and on the shores of Puget Sound.

From another point of view "Leaves of Grass" is avowedly the song of Sex and Amativeness, and even Animality—though meanings that do not usually go along with those words are behind all, and will duly emerge; and all are sought to be lifted into a different light and atmosphere. Of this feature, intentionally palpable in a few lines, I shall only say the espousing principle of those lines so gives breath of life to my whole scheme that the bulk of the pieces might as well have been left unwritten were those lines omitted. Difficult as it will be, it has become, in my opinion, imperative to achieve a shifted attitude from superior men and women towards the thought and fact of sexuality, as an element in character, personality, the emotions, and a theme in literature. I am not going to argue the question by itself; it does not stand by itself. The vitality of it is altogether in its relations, bearings, significance—like the clef of a symphony. At last analogy the lines I allude to, and the spirit in which they are spoken, permeate all "Leaves of Grass," and the work must stand or fall with them, as the human body and soul must remain as an entirety.

Universal as are certain facts and symptoms of communities or individuals all times, there is nothing so rare in modern conventions and poetry as their normal recognizance. Literature is always calling in the doctor for consultation and confession, and always giving evasions and swathing suppressions in place of that "heroic nudity" [5] on which only a genuine diagnosis of serious cases can be built. And in respect to editions of "Leaves of Grass" in time to come (if there should be such) I take occasion now to confirm those lines with the settled convictions and deliberate renewals of thirty years, and to hereby prohibit, as far as word of mine can do so, any elision of them.

Then still a purpose enclosing all, and over and beneath all. Ever since what might be call'd thought, or the budding of thought, fairly began in my youthful mind, I had had a desire to attempt some worthy record of that entire faith and acceptance ("to justify the ways of God to man" is Milton's well-known and ambitious phrase) which is the foundation of moral America. I felt it all as positively then in my young days as I do now in my old ones; to formulate a poem whose every thought or fact should directly or indirectly be or connive at an implicit belief in the wisdom, health, mystery, beauty of every process, every concrete object, every human or other existence, not only consider'd from the point of view of all, but of each.

While I can not understand it or argue it out, I fully believe in a clue and purpose in Nature, entire and several; and that invisible spiritual results, just as real and definite as the visible, eventuate all concrete life and all materialism, through Time. My book ought to emanate buoyancy and gladness legitimately enough, for it was grown out of those

5. "*Nineteenth Century*, July, 1883" [W].

elements, and has been the comfort of my life since it was originally commenced.

One main genesis-motive of the "Leaves" was my conviction (just as strong to-day as ever) that the crowning growth of the United States is to be spiritual and heroic. To help start and favor that growth—or even to call attention to it, or the need of it—is the beginning, middle and final purpose of the poems. (In fact, when really cipher'd out and summ'd to the last, plowing up in earnest the interminable average fallows of humanity—not "good government" merely, in the common sense—is the justification and main purpose of these United States.)

Isolated advantages in any rank or grace or fortune—the direct or indirect threads of all the poetry of the past—are in my opinion distasteful to the republican genius, and offer no foundation for its fitting verse. Establish'd poems, I know, have the very great advantage of chanting the already perform'd, so full of glories, reminiscences dear to the minds of men. But my volume is a candidate for the future. "All original art," says Taine, anyhow, "is self-regulated, and no original art can be regulated from without; it carries its own counterpoise, and does not receive it from elsewhere—lives on its own blood"—a solace to my frequent bruises and sulky vanity.

As the present is perhaps mainly an attempt at personal statement or illustration, I will allow myself as further help to extract the following anecdote from a book, *Annals of Old Painters,* conn'd by me in youth. Rubens, the Flemish painter, in one of his wanderings through the galleries of old convents, came across a singular work. After looking at it thoughtfully for a good while, and listening to the criticisms of his suite of students, he said to the latter, in answer to their questions (as to what school the work implied or belong'd,) "I do not believe the artist, unknown and perhaps no longer living, who has given the world this legacy, ever belong'd to any school, or ever painted anything but this one picture, which is a personal affair—a piece out of a man's life."

"Leaves of Grass" indeed (I cannot too often reiterate) has mainly been the outcropping of my own emotional and other personal nature—an attempt, from first to last, to put *a Person,* a human being (myself, in the latter half of the Nineteenth Century, in America,) freely, fully and truly on record. I could not find any similar personal record in current literature that satisfied me. But it is not on "Leaves of Grass" distinctively *as literature*, or a specimen thereof, that I feel to dwell, or advance claims. No one will get at my verses who insists upon viewing them as a literary performance, or attempt at such performance, or as aiming mainly toward art or æstheticism.

I say no land or people or circumstances ever existed so needing a race of singers and poems differing from all others, rigidly their own, as the land and people and circumstances of our United States need such singers and poems to-day, and for the future. Still further, as long as the States continue to absorb and be dominated by the poetry of the Old World, and remain unsupplied with autochthonous song, to express, vitalize and give color to and define their material and political success, and minister to them distinctively, so long will they stop short of first-class Nationality and remain defective.

In the free evening of my day I give to you, reader, the foregoing garrulous talk, thoughts, reminiscences,

As idly drifting down the ebb,
Such ripples, half-caught voices, echo from the shore.

Concluding with two items for the imaginative genius of the West, when it worthily rises—First, what Herder taught to the young Goethe, that really great poetry is always (like the Homeric or Biblical canticles) the result of a national spirit, and not the privilege of a polish'd and select few; Second, that the strongest and sweetest songs yet remain to be sung.

1888

FROM

SPECIMEN DAYS

¶ *Specimen Days* (1882), from which the following items are taken, is Whitman's kind of autobiography: random and lyrical reminiscences of his early years in Manhattan, literary encounters and opinions, diary-jottings on his day-to-day activities and predilections. One passage can be read as an illuminating, belated footnote to the poem "Crossing Brooklyn Ferry," another to "As I Ebb'd" and "Out of the Cradle," and still a third (the conversation with Emerson) to "Spontaneous Me." Included in *Specimen Days,* as well, was the body of Whitman's prose writing about the Civil War and Lincoln, previously published (1875) as *Memoranda During the War*. There is a good deal of literary interest in comparing Whitman's report on the Battle of Chancellorsville with Stephen Crane's wholly imaginative recreation of the same battle in *The Red Badge of Courage* (1895).

MY PASSION FOR FERRIES

LIVING in Brooklyn or New York city from this time forward, my life, then, and still more the following years, was curiously identified with Fulton ferry, already becoming the greatest of its sort in the world for general importance, volume, variety, rapidity, and picturesqueness. Almost daily, later, ('50 to '60,) I cross'd on the boats, often up in the pilot-houses where I could get a full sweep, absorbing shows, accompaniments, surroundings. What oceanic currents, eddies, underneath—the great tides of humanity also, with ever-shifting movements. Indeed, I have always had a passion for ferries; to me they afford inimitable, streaming, never-failing, living poems. The river and bay scenery, all about New York island, any time of a fine day—the hurrying, splashing sea-tides—the changing panorama of steamers, all sizes, often a string of big ones outward bound to distant ports—the myriads of white-sail'd schooners, sloops, skiffs, and the marvellously beautiful yachts—the majestic sound boats as they rounded the Battery and came along towards 5, afternoon, eastward bound—the prospect off towards Staten island, or down the Narrows, or the other way up the Hudson—what refreshment of spirit such sights and experiences gave me years ago (and many a time since.) My old pilot friends, the Balsirs, Johnny Cole, Ira Smith, William White, and my young ferry friend, Tom Gere—how well I remember them all.

BROADWAY SIGHTS

BESIDES Fulton ferry, off and on for years, I knew and frequented Broadway—that noted avenue of New York's crowded and mixed humanity, and of so many notables. Here I saw, during those times, Andrew Jackson, Webster, Clay, Seward, Martin Van Buren, filibuster Walker, Kossuth, Fitz Greene Halleck, Bryant, the Prince of Wales, Charles Dickens, the first Japanese ambassadors, and lots of other celebrities of the time. Always something novel or inspiriting; yet mostly to me the hurrying and vast amplitude of those never-ending human currents. I remember seeing James Fenimore Cooper in a court-room in Chambers street, back of the city hall, where he was carrying on a law case—(I think it was a charge of libel he had brought against some one.) I also remember seeing Edgar A. Poe, and having a short interview with him, (it must have been in 1845 or '6,) in his office, second story of a corner building, (Duane or Pearl street.) He was editor and owner or part owner of "the Broadway Journal." The visit was about a piece of mine he had publish'd. Poe was very cordial, in a quiet way, appear'd well in person, dress, &c. I have a distinct and pleasing remembrance of his looks, voice, manner and matter; very kindly and human, but subdued, perhaps a little jaded. For another of my reminiscences, here on the west side, just below Houston street, I once saw (it must have been about 1832, of a sharp, bright January day) a bent, feeble but stout-built very old man, bearded, swathed in rich furs, with a great ermine cap on his head, led and assisted, almost carried, down the steps of his high front stoop (a dozen friends and servants, emulous, carefully holding, guiding him) and then lifted and tuck'd in a gorgeous sleigh, envelop'd in other furs, for a ride. The sleigh was drawn by as fine a team of horses as I ever saw. (You needn't think all the best animals are brought up nowadays; never was such horseflesh as fifty years ago on Long Island, or south, or in New York city; folks look'd for spirit and mettle in a nag, not tame speed merely.) Well, I, a boy of perhaps thirteen or fourteen, stopp'd and gazed long at the spectacle of that fur-swathed old man, surrounded by friends and servants, and the careful seating of him in the sleigh. I remember the spirited, champing horses, the driver with his whip, and a fellow-driver by his side, for extra prudence. The old man, the subject of so much attention, I can almost see now. It was John Jacob Astor.

The years 1846, '47, and there along, see me still in New York city, working as writer and printer, having my usual good health, and a good time generally.

OMNIBUS JAUNTS AND DRIVERS

ONE PHASE of those days must by no means go unrecorded—namely, the Broadway omnibuses, with their drivers. The vehicles still (I write this paragraph in 1881) give a portion of the character of Broadway—the Fifth avenue, Madison avenue, and Twenty-third street lines yet running. But the flush days of the old Broadway stages, characteristic and copious, are over. The Yellow-birds, the Red-birds, the original Broadway, the Fourth avenue, the Knickerbocker, and a dozen others of twenty or thirty years ago, are all gone. And the men specially identified with them, and giving vitality and meaning to them—the drivers—a strange, natural, quick-eyed and wondrous race—(not only Rabelais and Cervantes would have gloated upon them, but Homer and Shakspere would)—how well I remember them, and must here give a word about them. How many hours, forenoons and afternoons—how many exhilarating night-times I have had—perhaps June or July, in cooler air—riding the whole length of Broadway, listening to some yarn, (and the most vivid yarns ever spun, and the rarest mimicry)—or perhaps I declaiming some stormy passage from Julius Cæsar or Richard, (you could roar as loudly as you chose in that heavy, dense, uninterrupted street-bass.) Yes, I knew all the drivers then, Broadway Jack, Dressmaker, Balky Bill, George Storms, Old Elephant, his brother Young Elephant (who came afterward,) Tippy, Pop Rice, Big Frank, Yellow Joe, Pete Callahan, Patsy Dee, and dozens more; for there were hundreds. They had immense qualities, largely animal—eating, drinking, women—great personal pride, in their way—perhaps a few slouches here and there, but I should have trusted the general run of them, in their simple good-will and honor, under all circumstances. Not only for comradeship, and sometimes affection—great studies I found them also. (I suppose the critics will laugh heartily, but the influence of those Broadway omnibus jaunts and drivers and declamations and escapades undoubtedly enter'd into the gestation of "Leaves of Grass.")

A NIGHT BATTLE, OVER A WEEK SINCE

MAY 12.—There was part of the late battle at Chancellorsville, (second Fredericksburgh,) a little over a week ago, Saturday, Saturday night and Sunday, under Gen. Joe Hooker, I would like to give just a glimpse of—(a moment's look in a terrible storm at sea—of which a few suggestions are enough, and full details impossible.) The fighting had been very hot during the day, and after an intermission the latter part, was resumed at night, and kept up with furious energy till 3 o'clock in the morning. That afternoon (Saturday) an attack sudden and strong by Stonewall Jackson had gain'd a great advantage to the southern army, and broken our lines, entering us like a wedge, and leaving things in that position at dark. But Hooker at 11 at night made a desperate push, drove the secesh forces back, restored his original lines, and resumed his plans. This night scrimmage was very exciting, and afforded countless strange and fearful pictures. The fighting had been general both at Chancellorsville and northeast at Fredericksburgh. (We hear of some poor fighting, episodes, skedaddling on our part. I think not of it. I think of the fierce bravery, the general rule.) One corps, the 6th, Sedgwick's, fights four dashing and bloody battles in thirty-six hours, retreating in great jeopardy, losing largely but maintaining itself, fighting with the sternest desperation under all circumstances, getting over the Rappahannock only by the skin of its teeth, yet getting over. It lost many, many brave men, yet it took vengeance, ample vengeance.

But it was the tug of Saturday evening, and through the night and Sunday morning, I wanted to make a special note of. It was largely in the woods, and quite a general engagement. The night was very pleasant, at times the moon shining out full and clear, all Nature so calm in itself, the early summer grass so rich, and foliage of the trees—yet there the battle raging, and many good fellows lying helpless, with new accessions to them, and every minute amid the rattle of muskets and crash of cannon, (for there was an artillery contest too,) the red life-blood oozing out from heads or trunks or limbs upon that green and dew-cool grass. Patches of the woods take fire, and several of the wounded, unable to move, are consumed—quite large spaces are swept over, burning the dead also—some of the men have their hair and beards singed—some, burns on their faces and hands—others holes burnt in their clothing. The flashes of fire from the cannon, the quick flaring flames and smoke, and the immense roar—the musketry so general, the light nearly bright enough for each side to see the other—the crashing, tramping of men—the yelling—close quarters—we hear the secesh yells—our men cheer loudly back, especially if Hooker is in sight—hand to hand conflicts, each side stands up to it, brave, determin'd as demons, they often charge upon us—a thousand deeds are done worth to write newer greater poems on—and still the woods on fire—still many are not only scorch'd—too many, unable to move, are burn'd to death.

Then the camps of the wounded—O heavens, what scene is this?—is this indeed *humanity*—these butchers' shambles? There are several of them. There they lie, in the largest, in an open space in the woods, from 200 to 300 poor fellows—the groans and screams—the odor of blood, mixed with the fresh scent of the night, the grass, the trees—that slaughter-house! O well is it their mothers, their sisters cannot see them—cannot conceive, and never conceiv'd, these things. One man is shot by a shell, both in the arm and leg—both are amputated—there lie the rejected members. Some have their legs blown off—some bullets through the breast—some indescribably horrid wounds in the face or head, all mutilated, sickening, torn, gouged out—some in the abdomen—some mere boys—many rebels, badly hurt—they take their regular turns with the rest, just the same as any—the surgeons use them just the same. Such is the camp of the wounded—such a fragment, a reflection afar off of the bloody scene

—while over all the clear, large moon comes out at times softly, quietly shining. Amid the woods, that scene of flitting souls—amid the crack and crash and yelling sounds—the impalpable perfume of the woods—and yet the pungent, stifling smoke—the radiance of the moon, looking from heaven at intervals so placid—the sky so heavenly—the clear-obscure up there, those buoyant upper oceans—a few large placid stars beyond, coming silently and languidly out, and then disappearing—the melancholy, draperied night above, around. And there, upon the roads, the fields, and in those woods, that contest, never one more desperate in any age or land—both parties now in force—masses—no fancy battle, no semi-play, but fierce and savage demons fighting there—courage and scorn of death the rule, exceptions almost none.

What history, I say, can ever give—for who can know—the mad, determin'd tussle of the armies, in all their separate large and little squads—as this—each stepp'd from crown to toe in desperate, mortal purports? Who know the conflict, hand-to-hand—the many conflicts in the dark, those shadowy-tangled, flashing-moonbeam'd woods—the writhing groups and squads—the cries, the din, the cracking guns and pistols—the distant cannon—the cheers and calls and threats and awful music of the oaths—the indescribable mix—the officers' orders, persuasions, encouragements—the devils fully rous'd in human hearts—the strong shout, *Charge, men, charge*—the flash of the naked sword, and rolling flame and smoke? And still the broken, clear and clouded heaven—and still again the moonlight pouring silvery soft its radiant patches over all. Who paint the scene, the sudden partial panic of the afternoon, at dusk? Who paint the irrepressible advance of the second division of the Third corps, under Hooker himself, suddenly order'd up—those rapid-filing phantoms through the woods? Who show what moves there in the shadows, fluid and firm—to save, (and it did save,) the army's name, perhaps the nation? as there the veterans hold the field. (Brave Berry falls not yet—but death has mark'd him—soon he falls.)

A CAVALRY CAMP

I AM writing this, nearly sundown, watching a cavalry company (acting Signal service,) just come in through a shower, making their night's camp ready on some broad, vacant ground, a sort of hill, in full view opposite my window. There are the men in their yellow-striped jackets. All are dismounted; the freed horses stand with drooping heads and wet sides; they are to be led off presently in groups, to water. The little wall-tents and shelter tents spring up quickly. I see the fires already blazing, and pots and kettles over them. Some among the men are driving in tent-poles, wielding their axes with strong, slow blows. I see great huddles of horses, bundles of hay, groups of men (some with unbuckled sabres yet on their sides,) a few officers, piles of wood, the flames of the fires, saddles, harness, &c. The smoke streams upward, additional men arrive and dismount—some drive in stakes, and tie their horses to them; some go with buckets for water, some are chopping wood, and so on.

July 6th.—A steady rain, dark and thick and warm. A train of six-mule wagons has just pass'd bearing pontoons, great square-end flat-boats, and the heavy planking for overlaying them. We hear that the Potomac above here is flooded, and are wondering whether Lee will be able to get back across again, or whether Meade will indeed break him to pieces. The cavalry camp on the hill is a ceaseless field of observation for me. This forenoon there stand the horses, tether'd together, dripping, steaming, chewing their hay. The men emerge from their tents, dripping also. The fires are half quench'd.

July 10th.—Still the camp opposite—perhaps fifty or sixty tents. Some of the men are cleaning their sabres (pleasant to-day,) some brushing boots, some laying off, reading, writing—some cooking, some sleeping. On long temporary cross-sticks back of the tents are cavalry accoutrements—blankets and overcoats are hung out to air—there are the squads of horses tether'd, feeding, continually stamping and whisking their tails to keep off flies. I sit long in my third story window and look at the scene—a hundred little things going on—peculiar objects connected with the camp that could not be described, any one of them justly, without much minute drawing and coloring in words.

A NEW YORK SOLDIER

THIS afternoon, July 22d, I have spent a long time with Oscar F. Wilber, company G, 154th New York, low with chronic diarrhœa, and a bad wound also. He asked me to read him a chapter in the New Testament. I complied, and ask'd him what I should read. He said, "Make your own choice." I open'd at the close of one of the first books of the evangelists, and read the chapters describing the latter hours of Christ, and the scenes at the crucifixion. The poor, wasted young man ask'd me to read the following chapter also, how Christ rose again. I read very slowly, for Oscar was feeble. It pleased him very much, yet the tears were in his eyes. He ask'd me if I enjoy'd religion. I said, "Perhaps not, my dear, in the way you mean, and yet, may-be, it is the same thing." He said, "It is my chief reliance." He talk'd of death, and said he did not fear it. I said, "Why, Oscar, don't you think you will get well?" He said, "I may, but it is not probable." He spoke calmly of his condition. The wound was very bad, it discharg'd much. Then the diarrhœa had prostrated him, and I felt that he was even then the same as dying. He behaved very manly and affectionate. The kiss I gave him as I was about leaving he return'd fourfold. He gave me his mother's address, Mrs. Sally D. Wilber, Alleghany post-office, Cattaraugus county, N.Y. I had several such interviews with him. He died a few days after the one just described.

HOSPITALS ENSEMBLE

AUG., SEP., AND OCT., '63.—I am in the habit of going to all, and to Fairfax seminary, Alexandria, and over Long bridge to the great Convalescent camp. The journals publish a regular directory of them—a long list. As a specimen of almost any one of the larger of these hospitals, fancy to yourself a space of three to twenty acres of ground, on which are group'd ten or twelve very large wooden barracks, with, perhaps, a dozen or twenty, and sometimes more than that number, small buildings, capable altogether of accommodating from five hundred to a thousand or fifteen hundred persons. Sometimes these wooden barracks or wards, each of them perhaps from a hundred to a hundred and fifty feet long, are rang'd in a straight row, evenly fronting the street; others are plann'd so as to form an immense V; and others again are ranged around a hollow square. They make altogether a huge cluster, with the additional tents, extra wards for contagious diseases, guard-houses, sutler's stores, chaplain's house; in the middle will probably be an edifice devoted to the offices of the surgeon in charge and the ward surgeons, principal attachés, clerks, &c. The wards are either letter'd alphabetically, ward G, ward K, or else numerically, 1, 2, 3, &c. Each has its ward surgeon and corps of nurses. Of course, there is, in the aggregate, quite a muster of employés, and over all the surgeon in charge. Here in Washington, when these army hospitals are all fill'd, (as they have been already several times,) they contain a population more numerous in itself than the whole of the Washington of ten or fifteen years ago. Within sight of the capitol, as I write, are some thirty or forty such collections, at times holding from fifty to seventy thousand men. Looking from any eminence and studying the topography in my rambles, I use them as landmarks. Through the rich August verdure of the trees, see that white group of buildings off yonder in the outskirts; then another cluster half a mile to the left of the first; then another a mile to the right, and another a mile beyond, and still another between us and the first. Indeed, we can hardly look in any direction but these clusters are dotting the landscape and environs. That little town, as you might suppose it, off there on the brow of a hill, is indeed a town, but of wounds, sickness, and death. It is Finley hospital, northeast of the city, on Kendall green, as it used to be call'd. That other is Campbell hospital. Both are large establishments. I have known these two alone to have from two thousand to twenty-five hundred inmates. Then there is Carver hospital, larger still, a wall'd and military city regularly laid out, and guarded by squads of sentries. Again, off east, Lincoln hospital, a still larger one; and half a mile further Emory hospital. Still sweeping the eye around down the river toward Alexandria, we see, to the right, the locality where the Convalescent camp stands, with its five, eight, or sometimes ten thousand inmates. Even all these are but a portion. The Harewood, Mount Pleasant, Armory-square, Judiciary hospitals, are some of the rest, and all large collections.

THE INAUGURATION

MARCH 4.[1]—The President very quietly rode down to the capitol in his own carriage, by himself, on a sharp trot, about noon, either because he wish'd to be on hand to sign bills, or to get rid of marching in line with the absurd procession, the muslin temple of liberty, and pasteboard monitor. I saw him on his return, at three o'clock, after the performance was over. He was in his plain two-horse barouche, and look'd very much worn and tired; the lines, indeed, of vast responsibilities, intricate questions, and demands of life and death, cut deeper than ever upon his dark brown face; yet all the old goodness, tenderness, sadness, and canny shrewdness, underneath the furrows. (I never see that man without feeling that he is one to become personally attach'd to, for his combination of purest, heartiest tenderness, and native western form of manliness.) By his side sat his little boy, of ten years. There were no soldiers, only a lot of civilians on horseback, with huge yellow scarfs over their shoulders, riding around the carriage. (At the inauguration four years ago, he rode down and back again sur-

THE INAUGURATION. 1. **March 4:** March 4, 1865.

rounded by a dense mass of arm'd cavalrymen eight deep, with drawn sabres; and there were sharpshooters station'd at every corner on the route.) I ought to make mention of the closing levee of Saturday night last. Never before was such a compact jam in front of the White House —all the grounds fill'd, and away out to the spacious sidewalks. I was there, as I took a notion to go—was in the rush inside with the crowd—surged along the passage-ways, the blue and other rooms, and through the great east room. Crowds of country people, some very funny. Fine music from the Marine band, off in a side place. I saw Mr. Lincoln, drest all in black, with white kid gloves and a claw-hammer coat, receiving, as in duty bound, shaking hands, looking very disconsolate, and as if he would give anything to be somewhere else.

THE REAL WAR WILL NEVER GET IN THE BOOKS

AND SO good-bye to the war. I know not how it may have been, or may be, to others—to me the main interest I found, (and still, on recollection, find,) in the rank and file of the armies, both sides, and in those specimens amid the hospitals, and even the dead on the field. To me the points illustrating the latent personal character and eligibilities of these States, in the two or three millions of American young and middle-aged men, North and South, embodied in those armies —and especially the one-third or one-fourth of their number, stricken by wounds or disease at some time in the course of the contest—were of more significance even than the political interests involved. (As so much of a race depends on how it faces death, and how it stands personal anguish and sickness. As, in the glints of emotions under emergencies, and the indirect traits and asides in Plutarch, we get far profounder clues to the antique world than all its more formal history.)

Future years will never know the seething hell and the black infernal background of countless minor scenes and interiors, (not the official surface-courteousness of the Generals, not the few great battles) of the Secession war; and it is best they should not—the real war will never get in the books. In the mushy influences of current times, too, the fervid atmosphere and typical events of those years are in danger of being totally forgotten. I have at night watch'd by the side of a sick man in the hospital, one who could not live many hours. I have seen his eyes flash and burn as he raised himself and recurr'd to the cruelties on his surrender'd brother, and mutilations of the corpse afterward. (See, in the preceding pages, the incident at Upperville—the seventeen kill'd as in the description, were left there on the ground. After they dropt dead, no one touch'd them—all were made sure of, however. The carcasses were left for the citizens to bury or not, as they chose.)

Such was the war. It was not a quadrille in a ball-room. Its interior history will not only never be written—its practicality, minutiæ of deeds and passions, will never be even suggested. The actual soldier of 1862–'65, North and South, with all his ways, his incredible dauntlessness, habits, practices, tastes, language, his fierce friendship, his appetite, rankness, his superb strength and animality, lawless gait, and a hundred unnamed lights and shades of camp, I say, will never be written—perhaps must not and should not be.

The preceding notes may furnish a few stray glimpses into that life, and into those lurid interiors, never to be fully convey'd to the future. The hospital part of the drama from '61 to '65, deserves indeed to be recorded. Of that many-threaded drama, with its sudden and strange surprises, its confounding of prophecies, its moments of despair, the dread of foreign interference, the interminable campaigns, the bloody battles, the mighty and cumbrous and green armies, the drafts and bounties—the immense money expenditure, like a heavy-pouring constant rain—with, over the whole land, the last three years of the struggle, an unending, universal mourning-wail of women, parents, orphans—the marrow of the tragedy concentrated in those Army Hospitals—(it seem'd sometimes as if the whole interest of the land, North and South, was one vast central hospital, and all the rest of the affair but flanges) —those forming the untold and unwritten history of the war—infinitely greater (like life's) than the few scraps and distortions that are ever told or written. Think how much, and of importance, will be—how much, civic and military, has already been—buried in the grave, in eternal darkness.

SEA-SHORE FANCIES

EVEN as a boy, I had the fancy, the wish, to write a piece, perhaps a poem, about the sea-shore—that suggesting, dividing line, contact, junction, the solid marrying the liquid—that curious, lurking something, (as doubtless every objective form finally becomes to the subjective spirit,) which means far more than its mere first sight, grand as that is—blending the real and ideal, and each made portion of the other.[1] Hours, days, in my Long Island youth and early man-

SEA-SHORE FANCIES. 1. December, 1876.

hood, I haunted the shores of Rockaway or Coney island, or away east to the Hamptons or Montauk. Once, at the latter place, (by the old lighthouse, nothing but sea-tossings in sight in every direction as far as the eye could reach,) I remember well, I felt that I must one day write a book expressing this liquid, mystic theme. Afterward, I recollect, how it came to me that instead of any special lyrical or epical or literary attempt, the sea-shore should be an invisible *influence,* a pervading gauge and tally for me, in my composition. (Let me give a hint here to young writers. I am not sure but I have unwittingly follow'd out the same rule with other powers besides sea and shores—avoiding them, in the way of any dead set at poetizing them, as too big for formal handling—quite satisfied if I could indirectly show that we have met and fused, even if only once, but enough—that we have really absorb'd each other and understand each other.)

There is a dream, a picture, that for years at intervals, (sometimes quite long ones, but surely again, in time,) has come noiselessly up before me, and I really believe, fiction as it is, has enter'd largely into my practical life—certainly into my writings, and shaped and color'd them. It is nothing more or less than a stretch of interminable white-brown sand, hard and smooth and broad, with the ocean perpetually, grandly, rolling in upon it, with slow-measured sweep, with rustle and hiss and foam, and many a thump as of low bass drums. This scene, this picture, I say, has risen before me at times for years. Sometimes I wake at night and can hear and see it plainly.

MY TRIBUTE TO FOUR POETS

APRIL 16.[1]—A short but pleasant visit to Longfellow. I am not one of the calling kind, but as the author of "Evangeline" kindly took the trouble to come and see me three years ago in Camden, where I was ill, I felt not only the impulse of my own pleasure on that occasion, but a duty. He was the only particular eminence I called on in Boston, and I shall not soon forget his lit-up face and glowing warmth and courtesy, in the modes of what is called the old school.

And now just here I feel the impulse to interpolate something about the mighty four who stamp this first American century with its birthmarks of poetic literature. In a late magazine one of my reviewers, who ought to know better, speaks of my "attitude of contempt and scorn and intolerance" toward the leading poets—of my "deriding" them, and preaching their "uselessness." If anybody cares to know what I think—and have long thought and avow'd—about them, I am entirely willing to propound. I can't imagine any better luck befalling these States for a poetical beginning and initiation than has come from Emerson, Longfellow, Bryant, and Whittier. Emerson, to me, stands unmistakably at the head, but for the others I am at a loss where to give any precedence. Each illustrious, each rounded, each distinctive. Emerson for his sweet, vital-tasting melody, rhym'd philosophy, and poems as amber-clear as the honey of the wild bee he loves to sing. Longfellow for rich color, graceful forms and incidents—all that makes life beautiful and love refined—competing with the singers of Europe on their own ground, and, with one exception, better and finer work than that of any of them. Bryant pulsing the first interior verse-throbs of a mighty world—bard of the river and the wood, ever conveying a taste of open air, with scents as from hayfields, grapes, birch-borders—always lurkingly fond of threnodies—beginning and ending his long career with chants of death, with here and there through all, poems, or passages of poems, touching the highest universal truths, enthusiasms, duties—morals as grim and eternal, if not as stormy and fateful, as anything in Eschylus. While in Whittier, with his special themes—(his outcropping love of heroism and war, for all his Quakerdom, his verses at times like the measur'd step of Cromwell's old veterans)—in Whittier lives the zeal, the moral energy, that founded New England—the splendid rectitude and ardor of Luther, Milton, George Fox—I must not, dare not, say the wilfulness and narrowness—though doubtless the world needs now, and always will need, almost above all, just such narrowness and wilfulness.

MY TRIBUTE TO FOUR POETS. **1. April 16:** April 16, 1881.

BOSTON COMMON—MORE OF EMERSON

OCT. 10–13.[1]—I spend a good deal of time on the Common, these delicious days and nights—every mid-day from 11.30 to about 1—and almost every sunset another hour. I know all the big trees, especially the old elms along Tremont and Beacon streets, and have come to a sociable-silent understanding with most of them, in the sunlit air, (yet crispy-cool enough,) as I saunter along the wide unpaved walks. Up and down this breadth by Beacon street, between these same old elms, I walk'd for two hours, of a bright sharp February mid-day twenty-one years ago,[2]

BOSTON COMMON. **1. Oct. 10–13:** October 10–13, 1881. **2. bright . . . ago:** This meeting, in fact, took place in late *March,* 1860.

with Emerson, then in his prime, keen, physically and morally magnetic, arm'd at every point, and when he chose, wielding the emotional just as well as the intellectual. During those two hours he was the talker and I the listener. It was an argument-statement, reconnoitring, review, attack, and pressing home, (like an army corps in order, artillery, cavalry, infantry,) of all that could be said against that part (and a main part) in the construction of my poems, "Children of Adam." More precious than gold to me that dissertation—it afforded me, ever after, this strange and paradoxical lesson; each point of E.'s statement was unanswerable, no judge's charge ever more complete or convincing, I could never hear the points better put—and then I felt down in my soul the clear and unmistakable conviction to disobey all, and pursue my own way. "What have you to say then to such things?" said E., pausing in conclusion. "Only that while I can't answer them at all, I feel more settled than ever to adhere to my own theory, and exemplify it," was my candid response. Whereupon we went and had a good dinner at the American House. And thenceforward I never waver'd or was touch'd with qualms, (as I confess I had been two or three times before).

AUTHOR-TITLE INDEX

THIS is a combined index for both volumes of *Major Writers of America*. The appropriate volume number is indicated by a roman numeral after each entry. Authors' names are in **boldface type**, and the page numbers of the introductions to their writings are in *italics*.

INDEX OF FIRST LINES BY VOLUME

VOLUME I

VOLUME II